THE OFFICIAL® PRICE GUIDE TO

Records

ELEVENTH EDITION

JERRY OSBORNE

HOUSE OF COLLECTIBLES • NEW YORK

Important Notice. All of the information, including valuations, in this book has been compiled from the most reliable sources, and every effort has been made to eliminate errors and questionable data. Nevertheless, the possibility of error, in a work of such immense scope, always exists. The publisher will not be held responsible for losses which may occur in the purchase, sale, or other transaction of items because of information contained herein. Readers who feel they have discovered errors are invited to *write* and inform us, so they may be corrected in subsequent editions. Those seeking further information on the topics covered in this book are advised to refer to the complete line of *Official Price Guides* published by the House of Collectibles.

Published by: House of Collectibles
201 East 50th Street
New York, New York 10022

Distributed by Ballantine Books, a division of Random House, Inc., New York, and simultaneously in Canada by Random House of Canada Limited, Toronto.

Cover photo by George Kerrigan

Manufactured in the United States of America

ISSN: 0747-7392

ISBN: 0-876-37963-3

Eleventh Edition: March 1995

10 9 8 7 6 5 4 3 2 1

CONTENTS

ACKNOWLEDGMENTS

The single most important element in updating and revising a price and reference guide is reader input. From dealers and collectors scattered throughout the country we receive suggestions, additions and corrections. Every single piece of data we receive is carefully reviewed, with all appropriate and usable information utilized in the next edition of this guide.

As enthusiastically as we encourage your contribution, let us equally encourage that when you write, you will either type or print your name clearly on both the envelope and contents. It's as frustrating for us to receive a mailing of useful information, and not be able to credit the sender, as it probably is for the sender to not see his or her name in the Acknowledgments section.

In compiling this edition, information supplied by the people whose names appear below was of great importance. To these good folks, our deepest gratitude is extended. The amount of data and investment of time, of course, varied, but without each and every one of them this book would have been something less than it is.

Here then, alphabetically listed, are the contributors to this edition:

Bob Alaniz
Moo Avvento
Loren Ayresman
Chris Bagley
Gary R. Baird
Don Baker
Howard F. Banney
William S. Barr
Russ Bell
Richard L. Benjamin
Jack Berkus
George Bigelow
George Biggans
Jean Blankenship
Dale Blount
Keith O. Briggs
Denise Brown
Charlie Browne
Rich Brumtrap
John Bruno
Gary Cafara
B. Caffaro
Billy Cagle
Thomas Calcaine
Dave Cameron
Tim Carbaugh
Bruce B. Carson
Marty Childress
Bob Ciofalo
Bob Clere
Morris Coffey Jr.
Gary Conley
Dan Crawford
Nicky D'Andrea
Lori DeCapua
Dan Dailey
Robert Del Prete
James M. Doidge
Doug Dornbos
Edward C. Drietz
Dan Dubry
Jarrod Ebner
Kirt Edblom
Bruce C. Elrod
Michael S. English
Glenn Fausel
Frank Fazio
Richard D. Fickau
Doug Fields
Sven Forsberg
Zeke Foster
Cher Frazier
John Froidl
Arnie Ganem
Jean-Marc Gargiulo
Rich C. Gesner
Tom Giacoponello
Franklin E. Goodale
Ray Gora
Janice Gordon
Charles T. Gray
Steve Griffin
James O. Guthrie
Buck Hafeman
André Helling
Hey Joe
Horace W. Hodges
Bill Hoover
Todd Hutchinson
Mark M. Johnston
Don Kirsch
Stanton Klose
David Kopache
Harvey Kragt
Bruce Laytham

Allan Lemieux
Paul Levy
Viktor Linder
Dominic Lobue
Frank H. Magyar
Harold D. Mathews
Joe McDonald
Stephanie McVeigh
David B. Mescon
Chris Messner
Lester Miller
John Mlachnik
Craig Moore
Drew Murray
Mike Murray
Charles Neu
Jayne Neu
Carl Nys
Mike Ohr
Linda Ann Osborne
Victor Pearlin
Alex Peavey
Wesley L. Peterson
Jim Philbrook
Donald F. Powell
Linda K. Prater
Chester Prudhomme
Lynn Pulsipher
Wayne Ranzer
Maxine Rix
Robert A. Rogers
Eileen Rowe
Ron Rowe
Eric Rubin
Larry Sanford
Trish Scarmuzzi
Tom Schoeck
Leland Scott
Michael Sharritt
David Sherman
Rick Siebler
Louie Silvani
Walt Stempek
Wayne Stierle
Paul Studstill
John Susco
Stanley Tarence
Ed Tataryn
Jeff Thames
Tom Thomas
Weldon T. Toms
Jim Ulmer
Wm. Van Orden
Bernie Vogel
Sally V. Voort
Alex Wallach
Jim Weaver
Harold W. Wentz
Joel Whitburn
Danny A. White
B.A. Wilson
Reggie Wilson
Morgan Wright
Dick Yandell
Robert E. Zimmermann
John W. Zurzolo

Records

INTRODUCTION

In determining what should be included in *The Official Price Guide to Records,* we have considered many factors. Our goal is to make the guide helpful, convenient, and applicable; for avid record connoisseurs as well as for those who are simply curious about the value of old records.

As an author-publisher team, we have put together 50 record guides and reference books over the past 20 years. As a result of this considerable experience, we have developed some basic criteria that serve as the foundation for the guide.

First, we had to establish which records most people would own—the answer being those records made by *charted* artists. Thus, we began with the national pop or pop and rock charts published by *Billboard, Cash Box*, and other trade publications. Then, because there has been so much chart crossover since the development of rock and roll—particularly between the black (rhythm and blues, soul, dance, etc.) music surveys and the top pop hits—we have included those charts as well.

Whether a song charted as a *single*, an *extended play* (EP), or a *long-playing* (LP) record, and regardless of whether it charted as "Race," "Rhythm and Blues," "Soul," "Disco," "Dance music," or "Sepia," you'll find that record priced here.

Performers who regularly appear on other charts—such as "Jazz," "Adult Contemporary," "Country," "Gospel," and "Classical"—do occasionally cross over to the pop/rock and black charts, and all who have are also included in this edition. However, these music forms are intrinsically diverse enough to require separate publications for truly comprehensive coverage.

Why Certain Records Are Not Listed

It is very important to keep in mind the aforementioned guidelines. Much of the mail we receive is from folks who, failing to read the introductory material, cannot comprehend why certain, often obscure, records are not in this edition. A country music fan, for example, might not understand why Eddy Arnold is listed in this book while Floyd Tillman is not. Similarly, the jazz buff might be bewildered when finding Dave Brubeck here but not Art Farmer. While both Tillman and Farmer had numerous hits on their respective charts, they have never appeared on the pop charts. Eddy Arnold and Dave Brubeck, on the other hand, placed both singles and albums on the pop charts.

Surprisingly, of the top 25 artists of each decade of Billboard's country and western charts, from the forties through the eighties, there are only four artists who are not represented in this edition. All of the others managed at least one appearance on the pop charts.

Just because we're listing all of the aforementioned charted artists, however, does not mean we are listing *only* charted records by those artists. Once an artist is included in the guide, we list and price *every known release* by that performer. Using country singer Hank Thompson as an example, let's show how comprehensive the coverage in this guide really is:

Despite his prominence in country and western music, Hank Thompson had only one song on the Billboard Hot 100; a single that remained on the chart for just one week and only managed to reach #99 (*She's Just a Whole Lot Like You*). Having qualified for this guide with that one charted appearance, every known single (45 and 78rpm), extended play, and long-playing album by Hank Thompson, from 1946 to present, is documented and priced in this edition. The reason behind the extensiveness of this coverage is if people like a performer well enough to put even one record on the charts, they may own other records by that artist,without regard to chart success.

In summary, everyone who made the pop/rock (1950-1988) or black music charts (1942-1988) are included here, with not only their charted records, but their *entire* recorded output. This often includes 78rpm issues made 20 or 30 years before the '50s and should effectively cover most of the records to be found in the library of the average person.

One can now price tens of thousands of 78s with this book; records originally issued as far back as the 1920s and as recently as 1962. Also, we now provide a separate section and pricing data for simultaneously released 45s and 78s, a common practice for most labels in the '50s.

This is but one of many price and reference books available. If you need information on recordings not found in this edition, please write to the author (address on next page). We will gladly provide you with information on our other titles in print, as well as those in various stages of production.

How the Prices Are Determined

Record values shown in *The Official Price Guide to Records* are averaged using information derived from a number of traditional sources. Most influential in arriving at current values is our established "marked copy" review program. Dozens of the world's most active dealers and collectors receive a copy of the most recent edition in which, throughout the year, they mark changing prices. When it's time to prepare a revised edition, all marked copies are returned to us for analysis and processing.

Besides the annotated copies, we receive hundreds of letters each year, from folks like yourself, suggesting corrections and/or additions to the guide.

Another extremely important source of pricing information are publications such as *DISCoveries*, magazines where hobbyists buy, sell, and trade music collectibles. We painstakingly review these issues, as well as other industry publications, carefully comparing prices being asked to those shown in the most recent edition of *The Official Price Guide to Records*. If marketplace trading indicates prices in the guide need to be increased or decreased, the changes are made. With our frequent publishing schedule, it is never long before the corrected prices appear in print.

What makes this step in the pricing process so vital is that nothing more verifiably illustrates the out-of-print record marketplace than everyday sales lists placed by dealers from around the country and around the globe.

Record prices, as with most collectibles, can vary drastically from one area of the country to another. Having reviewers and annotators in every state, as well as in Europe, Asia, and beyond, enables us to present a realistic average of the highest and lowest current asking prices for an identically graded copy of each record.

Other sources of consequential information include: set sales and auction lists that are private mailings, trading activity at record conventions, personal visits with collectors and to retail locations around the country, and hundreds of hours on the telephone with key advisors.

Although the record marketplace information in this edition was believed accurate at press time, it is ever subject to market changes. At any time, major bulk discoveries, quantity dumps, sudden increases wrought by an artist's death, overnight stardom that creates a greater demand for earlier material, and other such events and trends can easily affect scarcity and demand. Through diurnal research, keeping track of the day-to-day changes and discoveries taking place in the fascinating world of record collecting is a relatively simple and ongoing procedure.

To ensure the greatest possible accuracy, *The Official Price Guide to Records* prices are averaged from data culled from all of the aforementioned sources.

How You Can Help

Obviously, we can never get too much input or too many reviewers. We wholeheartedly encourage you to submit whatever information you feel would be useful in building a better record guide. The quantity of data is not a factor. No amount is too little or too much. The extensive list of names in the Acknowledgments chapter clearly indicate the magnitude of our team of advisors.

When preparing additions for this guide, please try to list records in generally the same format as is used in the guide: artist's name, label, catalog number, title, year of release (if known), and price range. Since our data base is computer stored alphabetically by artist, there's no need to note *The Official Price Guide to Records* page number.

Wax Fax

One frequently used method of forwarding data to us is by fax. For your convenience, we now have a dedicated fax line (360 / 385-6572). Use this service to quickly and easily transmit additions, corrections, price updates, and suggestions. Be sure to include your name, address, and phone number so we can acknowledge your contribution and, if necessary, contact you. Whether it's a marked copy of the guide, a letter, or a fax, type or clearly print your name so we may accurately credit you in the next edition.

Please submit all additions, corrections, suggestions to:

Jerry Osborne
P.O. Box 255
Port Townsend, WA 98368
Fax: (360) 385-6572

About the Format

Our arrangement of listings is the most logical way to present so much information in such a convenient, easy-to-carry package. It is a format—the *only* format—with unlimited potential for continued expansion.

The structure of *The Official Price Guide to Records* allows us to include all of the following formats in one multi-purpose guidebook: 7-inch singles, both 33rpm and 45rpm; 78rpm singles, both 7-inch and 10-inch; 12-inch singles, both 33rpm and 45rpm; extended play 33rpm and 45rpm EPs; long play 10, and 12-inch LPs; picture sleeves; promotional issues, and more.

Once you locate an artist's section, their records are listed alphabetically by LABEL. Individual listings for each label appear in numerical order. In many instances, listings that are numerical by selection number are also chronological in sequence of release, but there are also times where this is not the case. This format is especially helpful when using the guide along with an artist or label discography. Since the year of release is also provided for each listing, the reader knows immediately the pattern being followed by the label at the time.

Once familiar with the format, you'll find it easy and functional. However, do take time to familiarize yourself with the array. Reading all of the introductory pages and reviewing the sample listing should answer most reader questions. Having exhausted the supplied introductory material, please feel free to write or call if you have a question about the guide.

The documenting and pricing of so many recordings is made possible by selectively economizing on space; listing individual titles when necessary but not when it's possible to group a number of equally valuable releases together on one line. Again, any time it is necessary to have a separate listing on a record in order to clearly and accurately present the information, we will do it. Also, whenever a specific selection number is noted, whether listed as an exception or not, the title will also be given for easy identification.

One facet of our approach of great concern is the artist who had one or more records of a value indicated for a particular label or series, but who also had one release (or more) that is a notable exception. Every effort has been made to separately document such exceptions; however, due to the sheer bulk of information herein, some may be missed. If you know of any, let us know about them.

You will find that the expansion of an artist's section, moving more toward individual rather than grouped listings, will be as commonplace in subsequent volumes of this series, as with this edition. There are hundreds of artists with revised sections in this volume, listing many more individual titles and catalog numbers than ever before. With some performers, it is, or perhaps soon will be, necessary to list every single record separately.

The decision to expand a section is partly based on reader input. Many examples of individual pricing in this edition can be directly attributed to a letter or call suggesting the need to do so. We're always listening and would love to hear from *you*.

Grading and the Price Range

The pricing shown in this edition represents the price *range* for near mint condition copies. The value range allows for the countless variables that affect record pricing. Often, the range will widen as the dollar amount increases, making a $750 to $1000 range as logical as a $3 to $5 range.

The standardized system of record grading, used and endorsed by Osborne Enterprises, the House of Collectibles, and buyers and sellers worldwide, is as follows:

MINT: A *mint* item must be absolutely perfect. Nothing less can be honestly described as mint. Even brand new purchases can easily be flawed in some manner and not qualify as mint. To allow for tiny blemishes, the highest grade used in our record guide series is *near mint*. An absolutely pristine mint, or still sealed, item may carry a slight premium above the near-mint range shown in this guide.

VERY GOOD: Records in *very good* condition should have a minimum of visual or audible imperfections, which should not detract much from your enjoyment of owning them. This grade is halfway between good and near mint.

GOOD: Practically speaking, the grade of *good* means that the item is good enough to fill a gap in your collection until a better copy becomes available. Good condition merchandise will show definite signs of wear and tear, probably evidencing that no protective care was given the item. Even so, records in good condition should play all the way through without skipping.

Most older records are going to be in something less than near mint, or *excellent* condition. It is very important to use the near-mint price range in this guide only as a starting point in record appraising. Be honest about actual condition. Apply the same standards to the records you trade or sell as you would want one from whom you were buying to observe. Visual grading may be unreliable. Accurate grading may require playing the record (play-grading).

Use the following formula to determine values on lesser condition copies:

For *very good* condition, figure about 60% to 80% of the near mint price range given in this guide.

Some dealers now report that a VG+ record priced at $4 or $40 will sell ahead of a mint item priced at $5 or $50. Also, with many of the older pieces that cannot be found in near-mint, VG or VG+ may be the highest grade available. This significantly narrows the gap between VG and the near-mint range.

For *good* condition, figure about 20% to 40% of the near-mint price range given in this guide.

The 10 Point Grading System

Quickly gaining in popularity is a grading system based on the often-used 10 point scale. Supporters feel that grading with the 10 point system allows for a more precise description of records that are in less than mint condition. Instead of vague terms like VG++ (very good plus plus)—which may merely be a duplication of M-- (mint minus minus)—assigning a specific number provides a far more accurate classification of condition.

Most of the records you are likely to buy or sell will no doubt be graded somewhere between 5 and 10.

After using this system ourselves for a few years, we are inclined to agree that it is more precise. Customers who have purchased records from us have, without exception, been pleased with this way of grading.

The following table shows how the 10 point system equates with the more established terms:

10: MINT
9: NEAR-MINT
8: Better than VG but below NM
7: VERY GOOD
6: Better than G but below VG
5: GOOD
4: Better than POOR but below G
3: POOR

The Bottom Line

All the price guides and reporting of previous sales in the world won't change the fundamental fact that true value is nothing more than what one person is willing to accept and what another is prepared to pay. Actual value is based on scarcity and demand. It's always been that way and always will.

A recording—or anything for that matter—can be 50 or 100 years old, but if no one wants it, the actual value will certainly be minimal. **Just because something is old does not necessarily make it valuable.** Someone has to want it!

On the other hand, a recent release can have exceptionally high value if it has already become scarce and is by an artist whose following has created a demand. A record does not have to be old to be valuable.

Record Types Defined

With the inconsistent language used by the record companies in describing an EP or an LP, we've determined that a language guideline of some sort was needed in order to compile a useful record guide.

Some labels call a 10-inch LP an "EP" if it has something less than the prescribed number of tracks found on their LPs. Others call an EP a "Little LP." A few companies have even created special names, associated only with their own label, for the basic record formats.

Having carefully analyzed all of this, we have adopted the following classifications of record configurations, which consistently categorize all types, sizes, and speeds in one section or another:

Singles: 78rpm are those that play at 78rpm! Though 78s are almost always 10-inch discs, a few 7-inch 78rpm singles have been made.

Albums: 78rpm are multi-disc sets, with heavy cardboard covers and individual, bound-in jackets to hold each record. Most sets contained eight songs on four 78rpms, although some albums have either more than or fewer than four discs.

Singles: 7-Inch can be either 45rpm or 33 1/3 (always referred to simply as "33") speed singles. If a 7-inch single has more than one track on either side, then it's an EP.

Singles are priced strictly as a disc, with a separate section devoted to picture sleeves (which are often traded separately). If we know that picture sleeves exist for a given artist, a separate grouping will appear for the label, price, and applicable year of release. Should you know of picture sleeves not documented in this edition, please advise us accordingly.

There have been a few 5-inch discs manufactured, but for the sake of keeping singles with singles (and since we don't want to establish a "Singles: 5-Inch" category), such curios will be included with the 7-inch singles.

EPs: 7-Inch 33/45rpm are 7-inch discs that have more than one track on one or both sides. Even if labeled an "EP" by the manufacturer, if it's pressed on a 10, or 12-inch disc it's an LP in our book. Unless so noted, all EPs are presumed to be accompanied by their original covers, in a condition about equal to the disc. An appropriate adjustment in value should be made to compensate for any differences in this area. Exceptions, such as EPs with paper sleeves or no sleeve at all, are designated as such when known.

LPs: 10/12-Inch 33rpm is self explanatory. The only possible confusion that might exist here is with 12-inch singles. If it's 10 or 12 inches in diameter, and labeled, priced, and marketed as a 12-inch single (Maxi-Single, etc.), then that's where you'll find it in this guide, regardless of its speed. Often, 12-inch singles will have a 12-inch die-cut cardboard sleeve or jacket; but many have covers that are exactly like LP jackets, with photos of the artist, etc. Unless so noted, all LPs are presumed to be accompanied by their original covers, in a condition about equal to the disc. An appropriate adjustment in value should be made to compensate for any differences in this area.

Other record type headings used in this edition, such as **Picture Sleeves, Promotional Singles,** etc., should be crystal-clear.

Cross-referencing and Multiple Artists' Recordings

The cross-referencing in this edition should provide the easiest possible method of discovering other sections of the book where a particular artist is featured or appears in any capacity.

We've tried to hold to a minimum unexplained cross-references, opting to concentrate more on those cross-references for which the reader can effortlessly understand the rationalization. Minimized is the unnecessary duplication of cross-references. For example, it is not necessary to list every group in which Eric Clapton played, under each and every one of those sections. What we've done is simply indicate "Also see Eric Clapton," where you will find a complete cross-referencing to all other sections where he appears.

Some artists have several sections, one right after the other, because they were involved in different duets and/or compilation releases. In such instances, the primary artist (whose section begins first) is not cross-referenced after each and every subsequent section, but only after the last section wherein that artist is involved. This, in effect, blocks the beginning and the end of releases pertaining to that performer. If you don't find the listing you're searching for right away, remember to check the sections that follow, as the artist may have been joined by someone else on that recording causing it to appear in a separate section.

Artist headings and resultant cross-referencing appear in two different formats in this guide. For example:

LEWIS, Jerry Lee, Carl Perkins & Johnny Cash

Listings under this type heading are those wherein the artists perform *together*. Often these releases will also include solo tracks by one or all of the performers in addition to those on which they collaborate.

LEWIS, Jerry Lee / Carl Perkins / Johnny Cash

This heading, with names separated by a slash, indicates there are selections on *separate* tracks by each of the named artists, but they do not perform together.

The parameter set for these compilation releases is four different performers or less. Compilations containing five or more individual performers are, for purposes of compiling this edition, classified as **Various Artists** issues, which are documented in another price guide.

Whenever more than one act is featured on a record, cross-references appear under all of the other artists on the disc, who have a section of their own in this edition, directing the reader to the location of the listing in question. If you're looking up a record with a different artist on each side, and you don't find it under one artist, be sure to try looking for the flip-side artist.

Not all releases containing more than one artist are given separate sections. In some cases it makes more sense to include such records in the primary section for the most important artist. We will rarely create separate sections for multiple artist discs when the other performers on the issue do not have a section of their own in this edition.

To illustrate this point, Hank Williams Jr. had several duet issues with Lois Johnson; Gene Ammons shared an LP with Sonny Stitt. Even though Johnson and Stitt do not have individual sections in this book (they didn't make the pop singles or LPs charts), such recordings may be important to collectors of Williams and Ammons. For that reason, they are included in their respective artist's section.

On the other hand, a duet by Brenda Lee and Willie Nelson requires a separate section, since either or both may be of interest to the researcher. Also, both are individually pop-charted artists. There are a few isolated exceptions to this policy, simply because every section in this edition was separately prepared and customized in whatever manner necessary to provide the user with the most usable information.

Promotional Issues

Separate documenting and pricing of promotional issues is, in most cases, unnecessary. Because most of the records issued during the primary period covered in this guide were simultaneously pressed for promotional purposes, a separate listing of them would theoretically double the size of an already large book.

Rather, we've chosen to list promotional copies separately when we have the knowledge that an alternate price (either higher or lower) consistently is asked for them. For the most part, promos of everyday releases will fall into the same range—usually toward the high end—given for store stock copies. Some may stretch the range slightly, but not enough to warrant separate pricing. Premiums may be paid for promos that have different (longer, shorter, differently mixed, etc.) versions of tunes, even though the artist may not be particularly hot in the collecting marketplace.

When identified as a "Promotional issue," we are usually describing a record with a special promotional ("Not For Sale," "Dee Jay Copy," etc.) label or sleeve, and not a *designate* promo. Designate promos are identical to commercial releases, except they have been rubber or mechanically stamped, stickered, written on by hand, or in some way altered to accommodate their use for promotional purposes. There are very few designate promos listed in this edition, and those that are (such as in the Elvis Presley section) are clearly identified as such.

Colored Vinyl Pressings

Records known to exist on both black vinyl and colored vinyl (vinyl is the term used regardless of whether it's polystyrene or vinyl) are listed separately since there is usually a value difference. However, some colored vinyl releases were never pressed on black vinyl, and since there is no way to have the record other than on colored vinyl, it may or may not be specifically noted as being on colored vinyl.

Because the true color of some colored vinyl pressings may be a judgment call (is it red or is it dark pink . . . is it dark blue or is it purple?), we're using "colored vinyl" to indicate any pressings that are not standard black vinyl. Likewise for multi-color and clear vinyl issues.

Foreign Releases

This edition by design lists only U.S. releases. There is, however, an occasional exception. A handful of records that were widely distributed in the United States or sold via widespread U.S. advertising, even though manufactured outside the country, are included. Such anomalies would appear only in the more sophisticated sections of the guide.

There are also a few significant Canadian releases in this edition. The collectors' market for out-of-print Canadian records is mostly a U.S. market. The trading of rare Canadian discs between Canadian collectors is not nearly as widespread as those instances that involve a U.S. buyer or seller.

The millions of overseas releases certainly have collector value to fans in those countries as well as to stateside collectors. Unfortunately, the tremendous volume of material and the variances in pricing make it impossible to comprehensively document and price imports.

Bootlegs and Counterfeits

Bootleg and counterfeit records are not priced in this guide, though a few are cited, along with information on how to distinguish them from an original.

For the record, a bootleg recording is one illegally manufactured, usually containing material not previously available in a legitimate form. Often, with the serious collector in mind, a boot will package previously issued tracks that have achieved some degree of value or scarcity. If the material is easily available, legally, then there would be no gain for the bootlegger.

The counterfeit record is one manufactured as close as possible in sound and appearance to the source disc from which it was inspired. Not all counterfeits were created to fool an unsuspecting buyer into thinking he or she was buying an authentic issue, but some were. Many were designated in some way, such as a slight marking or variance, so as not to allow them to be confused with originals. Such a fake record primarily exists to fill a gap in the collector's file until the real thing comes along.

With both bootleg and with counterfeit records, the appropriate and deserving recipients of royalties are, of course, denied remuneration for their works.

Since most of the world's valuable records have been counterfeited, it is always a good idea to consult with an expert when there is any doubt. The trained eye can usually spot a fake.

This is not to say *unauthorized* releases are excluded from the book. There are many legitimate releases that are unauthorized by one entity or another; records that are neither bootleg or counterfeit. Unauthorized does not necessarily mean illegal.

Group Names and Personnel

One problem that we'll never completely solve involves the many instances where groups using the exact same name are lumped together with other groups who are completely different. Whenever known to be different, these groups are given separate sections; however, there are times when we simply do not know. If you can shed any light in this area, we'd love to hear from you. Thanks to readers, many such groups have been sorted since our last edition.

The listing sequence for artists using the same name is chronological. Thus, the ABC group, Silk, who had a release in 1969, is listed ahead of the Philadelphia International group, Silk, that first recorded in 1979.

As often as not, there will have been group members that have come and gone over the years. Reflecting this turnover in our listing of members' names may cause some confusion, when the reader sees 12 different members shown for a group named the Five Satins. We've tried, whenever possible, to list the original line-up first, followed by later members. Also, the lead singer is usually listed first. We welcome additional information on group members from readers. One of the most reliable sources of this data is the LP covers, which often list members. If you can fill in the members' names on any groups where we don't list that information, we'll see that it gets into our next edition. Hundreds of group members have been added since the ninth edition of this guide.

When group members' names are given, there is a likelihood that not all of the members named appear on all of the releases documented. It is also possible that not all of the members named ever recorded with all of the other members shown at the same time.

When the names of key session personnel are known, they will appear in the same area where "Members" are shown. Especially important in the "Session" section are musicians and background vocalists who also have their own listings in the guide.

As more and more group members are named in future editions, there will be added cross-referencing to reflect the constant shuffle of performers from one group to another.

Parenthetical Notes

Some of the information that may be found in parentheses following the artist heading has already been covered. However, other uses of this space include:

- Complete artist and group or artist and band names. Some artists were shown as being with one group on a few releases and with another on other issues. We've tried to present the information the way, or many ways, that it was shown on the actual record label.

- Variations of spelling or names for the same artist. With some artists, it's convenient to have everything in one section; however, when it is illogical to combine listings, perhaps because the performer was popular under more than one name (such as Johnny Cymbal and Derek), you'll find individual sections for each name. Cross-references will be used to help you locate things easily. Having "Kenneth Rogers" in parentheses is not intended to mean that Kenneth is Kenny's real name. Rather, we're letting you know that some releases credit him as Kenneth Rogers instead of Kenny Rogers.

- Names of guest performers who may or may not be credited on the actual label, but who we feel you should know were involved in some of the records listed in that section.
- Real names of artists, but only when we feel they need to be given. We have no desire to give the real names of everyone who has recorded under a pseudonym, but there are times when you do need this information, particularly when they have also recorded under their real name or when more than one person has recorded under the same pseudonym. To help sort things out, we will, when known, give you the real name of someone who has recorded under a nom de guerre, such as Guitar Slim (a.k.a. Johnny Winter).

A few of the more prolific labels with lengthy names are abbreviated in this guide. They are: ABC-PAR (ABC-Paramount); MFSL (Mobile Fidelity Sound Lab); RCA (RCA Victor); 20TH FOX (20th Century-Fox); U.A. (United Artists); W.B. (Warner Brothers).

Oldies Labels and Reissues

An effort has been made to include many "oldies" or reissue records in the guide. Though many reissues of this type are of no value beyond their current retail cost, some are. Look at some of the early RCA Victor Gold Standard Series Elvis Presley releases, for example.

- The main reason we've included these reissues is to eliminate confusion, especially among younger collectors. Often, they'll discover a hit tune on a label, like Lana or Lost-Nite, and think it's an original release predating the label that had the hit single.
- If there are reissues numbered as part of a label's standard release series, and not documented in this edition, please tell us about them.

Using This Guide: Additional Points

The alphabetization used makes finding any artist or label easy, but a few guidelines may speed the process along for you:

- New in this edition is a designation—positioned flush right, on a separate line beneath the artist heading—indicating the year the artist *first* appeared on one or more of the Billboard record charts. The applicable charts (using Joel Whitburn's Record Research series) and their codes are as follows:

Pop and Rock (shown as P&R)

This is a catch-all category that represents the nation's best sellers. It includes the pop charts of the pre-rock era as well as the mainstream rock and roll hits of the mid-'50s to present. Obviously, when we show "P&R '42," the intention is not that there was a "rock" chart in 1942 as "P&R" can mean either pop or rock—or both.

Blues / Rhythm & Blues / Soul (shown as R&B)

Though there have been many different descriptions used to categorize black music, we have chosen the familiar "R&B" to indicate an appearance on these charts.

Country & Western (shown as C&W)

Even though every country performer in the guide made the pop chart at one time or another, the year shown indicates the year they made their first chart appearance—regardless of which chart. If their chart debut is shown only as C&W, you can be sure they eventually made the pop charts or they wouldn't be in this edition.

Long Playing Albums (shown as LP)

Indicates the artist's appearance on Billboard's best-selling albums chart, which includes music of many different styles. Separate charts do exist for both country albums and black music albums; however these were not available at press time. It is likely that, in future editions, we will incorporate information from those charts into our listings.

• Names that are simply letters (and are not intended to be pronounced as a word) are found at the beginning of the listings under each letter of the alphabet (i.e., ABC, AC-DC, GQ, SSQ, etc.). The same rule applies to acronyms and to initials (i.e., G.T.O, MFSB, etc.). When known, we'll parenthetically tell you what the abbreviation represents.

• Names are listed in the alphabetical order of the first word. This means you'll find Rock Squad before Rocket. Most hyphenated names are looked upon as whole words—Mello-Kings and Re-Flex are treated the same as Mellokings and Reflex. There are exceptions; names like A-Ha and T-Bones which do not resemble whole words. These are found near the beginning of the alphabet and not as though they are Aha or Tbones.

• Divided names (i.e., De Vorzon, El Dorados, etc.) are alphabetically listed as though they were a one-word name.

• Possessive names precede similarly spelled names that are not possessive. For example, KNIGHT'S would be found before KNIGHTS, regardless of what follows the comma.

• The articles "A" or "The" have been dropped from group names in this guide even though they may appear on the records as part of the name.

• With record labels, the listings appear in alphabetical/numeric/chronological order. Prefixes are generally not used (they make it more difficult to scan the numbers) unless they are necessary for identification. With some artists (Beatles, Elvis, etc.) it is essential at times because of constant reissues.

• Some sections make use of the label prefixes to sort things out, but most use a number series. If the numbers are duplicated by the label, or if any of a variety of confusing similarities exist, we may resort to the prefixes for clarity.

• Anytime we find that the monaural or the stereo issue of a particular record is in need of a separate listing (because there is a price difference for one that is outside the boundaries of the price range of the other), we will gladly provide same. If there is but one listing, this indicates that we have no reason to believe there is much difference in the two forms. A little application of the known variables will help in this area. For example, if the range is $20 to $30 for a 1960 LP and you know that the stereo issue is in true stereo, it's safe to place the mono at the low end of the range ($20 to $25) and the stereo at the high end ($25 to $30). The calculation may be reversed for late '60s and for most electronically reprocessed issues.

• We believe the year or years of release given in the far-right column to be accurate. If we don't know the correct year, the column is left blank. In some cases the record may have been released in one year and debuted on the nation's music charts the following year. This is common for year-end issues and explains why you may remember a hit as being from 1966, although we list it as a 1965 release.

• When multiple years are indicated, such as "64-66," it means the records described on that line spanned the years 1964 through 1966. They may have had one issue in 1964 and another in 1966, or may have had eight releases during those years. It does not mean that we believe the release came out sometime between 1964 and 1966.

- Unusual though it may be, a few records have been issued with no artist or label given. You will find this on both singles and albums. These items are filed here by title.
- There are hundreds of double albums (two discs in one package) priced in the guide, but they are not necessarily identified as double LPs. They are, nevertheless, included in the price range.

Guidelines for Pricing Records Not in This Edition

Since it is impossible for us to include *every* record ever produced, a few guidelines may assist you in evaluating records not found in this edition:

Pop Singles on 45rpm: Most pop (i.e. non-rock) vocal and instrumental 45s from the '50s are available for under $10. From many rock-oriented dealers, pop singles can often be bought for less than $5. The few exceptions are likely to be folks with charted hits, and those will be found in the guide.

Pop music singles from the '60s to present are seldom going to sell for over $5; usually around $3.

Pop Singles on 78rpm: Most pop 78s are available for under $5. Until the late '40s or early '50s, an *album* was a gatefold binder with a number of 78s, usually in individual paper sleeves. Prices on these pop albums will vary, but most will fall in the $20 to 50 range.

Pop Long Play Albums: From the '50s, 12-inch pop LPs generally are found for under $30 to $40. Ten-inch LPs may go for $25 to $50. Pop vocalists with jazz releases (such as the first Johnny Mathis LP) are an exception, but those should be found in this book.

Most pop LPs from the '60s to present can be found for $5 to $15.

Pop Extended Play Albums: Pop EPs are scarce, as are all EPs, but many are still very reasonable. Most can be found for under $10 to 25.

Easy Listening Music: The average easy listening record will be worth about half of the price ranges shown for Pop Music.

Country Music on 45rpm: Most country music vocal and instrumental 45s from the '50s are available for under $15; many for less than $10. Obvious exceptions are any that border on rockabilly or country rock. Don't take any country record for granted! Play both sides of every disc, as it is always possible you'll discover a great country rocker.

Country music singles from the '60s to present are seldom going to sell for over $5.

Country Music on 78rpm: Most of the country 78s should fall into the $10 to $40 range. There are, however, many older 78s with prices well into three figures; some even higher.

Country Music Long Play Albums: From the '50s, 12-inch LPs generally are found for under $30 to $60. Ten-inch LPs may go for $50 to $100. As always, the range will vary widely depending on the following and collectibility of the artist.

Most country LPs from the '60s to present can be found for $10 to $25. Again, there are exceptions.

Country Music Extended Play Albums: Very, very few country music EPs were big sellers, which means nearly all are rare. You may find they are in the same price range as the '50s LPs above; some will bring even more than LPs from the same time period.

Jazz Singles on 45rpm: Most jazz 45s from the '50s are available for under $10; perhaps less than $5. The few exceptions are likely to be artists with charted hits, which will be found in the guide.

Jazz singles from the '60s to present are seldom going to sell for over $5.

Jazz Singles on 78rpm: Most jazz 78s are available for under $20. Until the late '40s or early '50s, an *album* was a gatefold binder with a number of 78s, usually in individual paper sleeves. Prices on these jazz albums will vary, but most will fall in the $25 to $75 range.

Jazz Long Play Albums: From the '50s, 12-inch jazz LPs generally are found for under $50 to $100. Ten-inch LPs may go for $75 to $200.

Most jazz LPs from the '60s to present can still be found for $15 to $30.

Jazz Extended Play Albums: As with country, very few jazz EPs were big sellers. All are rare. You may find they are in the same price range as the '50s jazz LPs above; some will bring even more than LPs from the same time period.

Comedy and Personality Long Play Albums: From the '50s and '60s, 12-inch comedy and personality (not soundtrack or original cast) LPs generally are found for under $15 to $40.

Most comedy and personality LPs from the '70s to present can be had for $5 to $15.

In summary, there is no way these few paragraphs can constitute a complete price guide for the millions of non-rock records that exist. If such generic generalizations were possible, while guaranteeing unerring accuracy, the entire price guide would be about ten pages. It is the exceptions that make record pricing so complicated and difficult to document.

Our goal here is simply to provide a rough idea of the value of recordings that are outside the parameters of the guide.

What to Expect When Selling Records to a Dealer

As nearly everyone in the hobby knows, there is a noteworthy difference between the prices reported in this guide and the prices that one can expect a dealer to pay when buying records for resale. Unless a dealer is buying for a personal collection and without thoughts of resale, he or she is simply not in a position to pay full price. Dealers work on a percentage basis, largely determined by the total dollar investment, quality, and quantity of material offered as well as the general financial condition and inventory of the dealer at the time.

Another very important consideration is the length of time it will take the dealer to recover at least the amount of the original investment. The greater the demand for the stock and the better the condition, the quicker the return and therefore the greater the percentage that can be paid. Our experience has shown that, day-in and day-out, most dealers will pay from 25% to 50% of *guide* or *book* prices. And that's assuming they are planning to resell at guide prices. If they traditionally sell below guide, that will be reflected in what they can pay for stock.

If you have records to sell, it would be wise to check with several shops. In doing so you'll begin to get a good idea of the value of your collection to a dealer.

Also, consult the Directory of Buyers and Sellers in this guide for the names of many dealers who not only might be interested in buying, but from whom many collectible records are available for purchase.

Whether you wish to sell the records you have, or add out-of-print discs to your collection, check out *DISCoveries* magazine. Each issue is packed with ads, features, discographies, collecting tips and more. If getting into the record marketplace is important to you, *DISCoveries* is recommended. (Trader Publications, Box 1050, Dubuque, Iowa 52003. Sample issue available upon request).

Concluding Thoughts

The purpose of this guide is to report as accurately as possible the most recent prices asked and paid for records within the area of its coverage. There are two key words here that deserve emphasis: **Guide** and **Report.**

We cannot stress enough that this book is only a guide. There always have and always will be instances of records selling well above and below the prices shown within these pages. These extremes are recognized in the final averaging process; but it's still important to understand that just because we've reported a 30-year-old record as having a $25 to $50 near-mint value, doesn't mean that a collector of that material should be hesitant to pay $75 for it. How badly he or she wants it and how often it's possible to purchase it at any price should be the prime factors considered, not the fact that we last reported it at a lower price. Of course, we'd like to know about sales of this sort so that the next edition can reflect the new pricing information.

Our objective is to report and reflect record marketplace activity; not to *establish* prices. For that reason, and if given the choice, we'd prefer to be a bit behind the times rather than ahead. With this guide being regularly revised, it will never be long before the necessary changes are reported within these pages.

We encourage record companies, artist management organizations, talent agencies, publicists, and performers to make certain that we are on the active mailing list for new release information, press releases, bios, publicity photos, and anything pertaining to recordings.

There is an avalanche of helpful information in this guide to aid the collector in determining what is valuable and what may not be worth fooling with, but the wise fan will also keep abreast of current trends and news through the pages of the fanzines and publications devoted to his/her favorite forms of music.

SAMPLE LISTING

(Excerpted from the Supremes section)

Artist's primary heading

SUPREMES

May also be shown on some releases as . . .

(Diana Ross & the Supremes)

P&R/R&B '62

The chart or charts and year artist *first* appeared on Billboard. For this group, it's both Pop & Rock and Rhythm & Blues — i n 1962

Singles: 7–inch

Label names, selection numbers and titles

AMERICAN INT'L PICTURES ("Dr. Goldfoot and the Bikini Machine") 30-40 66
(Single-sided promotional disc, used to promote the film of the same name.)

GEORGE ALEXANDER INC. (1079 "The Only Time I'm Happy") 30-40 65
(Special premium record. Has a Supremes interview on the flip side.)

Near-mint price range

MOTOWN (1008 "I Want a Guy") 500-1000 61

MOTOWN (1027 "Your Heart Belongs to Me") 15-25 62

MOTOWN (1034 "Let Me Go the Right Way") 15-20 62

Years of release

MOTOWN (1040 "My Heart Can't Take It No More") 25-35 63

MOTOWN (1044 "A Breath Taking, First Sight Soul Shaking, One Night Love Making, Next Day Heart Breaking Guy") 50-75 63

MOTOWN (1044 "A Breath Taking Guy") 15-25 63
(Reissue, with shorter title.)

Category or type of items listed in this section

Picture Sleeves

MOTOWN (1027 "Your Heart Belongs to Me") 50-100 62

LPs: 10/12–inch 33rpm

MOTOWN (606 "Meet the Supremes") 400-600 63
(Front cover pictures each member sitting on a chair.)

Helpful explanatory notes

MOTOWN (606 "Meet the Supremes") 50-75 63
(Front cover pictures the head of each group member.)

Group members or session personnel

Members: Diana Ross; Mary Wilson; Florence Ballard; Cindy Birdsong.

References to other, related sections

Also see BALLARD, Florence
Also see DIAMOND, Neil / Diana Ross & Supremes
Also see PRIMETTES
Also see ROSS, Diana
Also see WILSON, Mary

A's

LP '81

Singles: 7-inch

ARISTA 3-5 79

LPs: 10/12-inch 33rpm

ARISTA 5-10 79-81

Members: Richard Bush; Rick DiFonzo; Michael Snyder; Terry Bortman; Rocco Nolte.

A.B. SKHY

P&R '69

Singles: 7-inch

MGM 3-5 69-70

LPs: 10/12-inch 33rpm

MGM 10-12 69-70

Member: Dennis Geyer

ABC

P&R/LP '82

Singles: 12-inch 33/45rpm

MERCURY 4-6 83-87

Singles: 7-inch

MERCURY 3-4 82-87

Picture Sleeves

MERCURY 3-4 82-87

LPs: 10/12-inch 33rpm

MERCURY 5-10 82-87

Members: Martin Fry; Steve Singleton; Mark White.

AC/DC

LP '77

Singles: 12-inch 33/45rpm

ATLANTIC 5-10 79

(Promotional issue only.)

Singles: 7-inch

ATCO 3-5 77

ATLANTIC 3-5 77-85

Picture Sleeves

ATLANTIC 3-5 81-83

LPs: 10/12-inch 33rpm

ATCO 5-15 76-90

ATLANTIC 5-10 77-86

Members: Bonn Scott; Angus Young; Mark Evans; Malcomb Young; Phil Rudd; Cliff Williams; Brian Johnson; Chris Slade; Simon Wright.

Also see DIO, Ronnie

Also see FIRM

ADC BAND

R&B/LP '78

Singles: 7-inch

COTILLION 3-5 78-82

LPs: 10/12-inch 33rpm

COTILLION 5-10 78-82

Members: Michael Judkins; Arwell Mathew Jr; Audrey Mathew; Mark Patterson.

A-HA

P&R/D&D/LP '85

Singles: 7-inch

REPRISE 3-4 85-86

W.B. 3-4 85-87

Picture Sleeves

W.B. 3-4 85-87

LPs: 10/12-inch 33rpm

REPRISE 5-10 85-86

W.B. 5-10 85-88

Members: Morten Harket; Mags Furuholem; Pal Waaktaar.

AM-FM

R&B '82

Singles: 7-inch

DAKAR 3-5 82

Also see MASON, Vaughn

APB

D&D '83

Singles: 12-inch 33/45rpm

IMPORT 4-6 83

SLEEPING BAG 4-6 84

Singles: 7-inch

IMPORT 3-4 83

LPs: 10/12-inch 33rpm

MCA 5-10 83

AWB: see AVERAGE WHITE BAND

AALON

R&B '77

Singles: 7-inch

ARISTA 3-5 77

LPs: 10/12-inch 33rpm

ARISTA 5-10 77

Members: Aalon Butler; Ronnie Hammond.

Also see WAR

ABACO DREAM

P&R/R&B '69

Singles: 7-inch

A&M 4-6 69-70

Members: Paul Douglas; Dave Williams; Dennis Williams; Frank Maid; Mike Sassano.

ABBA

P&R/LP '74

Singles: 12-inch 33/45rpm

ATLANTIC 4-8 77-79

Singles: 7-inch

ATLANTIC 3-6 75-82

Picture Sleeves

ATLANTIC 3-6 77-82

LPs: 10/12-inch 33rpm

ATLANTIC (Except 300) 10-20 74-84

ATLANTIC (300 "Abba") 15-25 78

(Promotional issue only.)

CBS INT'L 8-12 80

EPIC 5-8 79

K-TEL 8-10 80

NAUTILUS (20 "Arrival") 15-25 82

(Half-speed mastered.)

SILVER EAGLE 8-10 84

Members: Anni-frid Lyngstad; Bjorn Ulvaeus; Benny Andersson; Agnetha Faltskog.

Also see BJORN & BENNY
Also see FALTSKOG, Agnetha
Also see FRIDA

ABBA / Spinners / Firefall / England Dan & John Ford Coley

EPs: 7-inch 33/45rpm

W.B. SPECIAL PRODUCTS 5-10 78
(Coca-Cola/Burger King promotional issue. Issued with paper sleeve.)

Also see ABBA
Also see ENGLAND DAN & John Ford Coley
Also see FIREFALL
Also see SPINNERS

ABBEY TAVERN SINGERS

P&R '66

Singles: 7-inch

HBR.. 4-8 66

EPs: 7-inch 33/45rpm

V.I.P. (60402 "Off to Dublin in the Green")................................. 15-25 66

LP: 10/12-inch 33rpm

V.I.P. (402 "Off to Dublin in the Green")................................. 30-60 66

ABBOTT, Billy, & Jewels

P&R '63

Singles: 7-inch

PARKWAY 5-10 63-64

ABBOTT, Gregory

P&R/R&B/LP '86

Singles: 12-inch 33/45rpm

COLUMBIA 4-6 86-88

Singles: 7-inch

COLUMBIA 3-4 86-88

Picture Sleeves

COLUMBIA 3-4 86-88

LPs: 10/12-inch 33rpm

COLUMBIA 5-10 87

ABDUL, Paula

P&R/R&B/LP '88

(With Wild Pair)

Singles: 7-inch

VIRGIN.. 3-4 88-91

Picture Sleeves

VIRGIN.. 3-4 88-89

LPs: 10/12-inch 33rpm

VIRGIN.. 5-8 88-89

ABRAMS, Colonel

R&B/D&D '84

Singles: 12-inch 33/45rpm

MCA 4-6 85-87
STREETWISE.................................. 4-6 84

Singles: 7-inch

MCA 3-4 85-87
STREETWISE.................................. 3-4 84

LPs: 10/12-inch 33rpm

MCA... 5-8 86

ABRAMS, Miss, & Strawberry Point School Third Grade Class

P&R '70

Singles: 7-inch

A&M 3-5 71
REPRISE 3-5 70

Picture Sleeves

REPRISE 3-5 70

LPs: 10/12-inch 33rpm

REPRISE 8-12 72

ACCENTS

P&R '58

(Featuring Robert Draper Jr.)

Singles: 7-inch

BRUNSWICK (55100 "Wiggle Wiggle") 8-15 58
BRUNSWICK (55123 "Ching a Ling").................................. 10-15 58-59
CORAL.. 10-15 59
JUBILEE 5-10 59

Members: Robert Draper Jr.; Robert Armstrong; James Jackson; Billy Hood; Arvid Garrett; Israel Goudeau Jr.

ACCENTS (With David Gates): see GATES, David

ACCEPT

LP '84

Singles: 7-inch

PORTRAIT....................................... 3-4 84-89

Picture Sleeves

PORTRAIT....................................... 3-4 84-86

LPs: 10/12-inch 33rpm

PVC.. 5-10 83
PASSPORT 5-10 81
PORTRAIT...................................... 5-10 84-89

ACE

P&R/LP '75

Singles: 7-inch

ABC.. 3-5 76-78
ANCHOR 3-5 75-77

LPs: 10/12-inch 33rpm

ANCHOR 8-12 74-77

Members: Paul Carrack; Fran Byrne; Tex Comer; Phil Harris; Alan "Bam" King; Jon Woodhead.

Also see CARRACK, Paul

ACE, Buddy

R&B '66

Singles: 78rpm

DUKE 5-10 56-57
PEACOCK 8-12 55

Singles: 7-inch

DUKE (100 series) 10-20 56-58
DUKE (300 & 400 series)............... 4-8 60-69
FIDELITY 6-12 59
PAULA 3-5 70-72

PEACOCK (1659 "I Told You So") 15-25 55
SPECIALTY 10-15 59

ACE, Johnny

R&B '52

(With the Beale Streeters)

Singles: 78rpm

DUKE 10-15 52-55

Singles: 7-inch

ABC 3-4 73
DUKE 15-25 52-55
MCA 3-4 84

EPs: 7-inch 33/45rpm

DUKE (71 "Memorial Album") ... 15-25 63
(Jukebox issue only.)
DUKE (80 "Memorial Album") 150-200 55
DUKE (81 "Tribute Album")... 150-200 55

LPs: 10/12-inch 33rpm

DUKE (70 "Memorial Album") 500-600 55
(10-inch LP.)
DUKE (71 "Memorial Album") 150-250 57
(No playing card shown on cover.)
DUKE (71 "Memorial Album") ... 60-80 61
(Playing card shown on cover.)
DUKE (X-71 "Memorial Album").. 8-10 74
MCA 4-6 83
Also see BLAND, Bobby
Also see OTIS, Johnny

ACE, Johnny / Earl Forrest

Singles: 78rpm

FLAIR 20-35 53

Singles: 7-inch

FLAIR (1015 "Midnight Hours Journey") 50-75 53
Also see ACE, Johnny
Also see FORREST, Earl

ACE SPECTRUM

P&R '74

Singles: 7-inch

ATLANTIC 3-5 74-76

LPs: 10/12-inch 33rpm

ATLANTIC 8-10 74-76
Members: Henry Zant; Troy Johnson; Rudy Gay; Elliot Isaac.

ACKLES, David

LP '72

Singles: 7-inch

ELEKTRA 3-6 68-72

LPs: 10/12-inch 33rpm

COLUMBIA 5-10 73
ELEKTRA 8-12 69-72

ACKLIN, Barbara

P&R/R&B/LP '68

Singles: 7-inch

BRUNSWICK 4-8 67-73
CAPITOL 3-5 74-75
ERIC 3-4 83
SPECIAL AGENT (203 "I'm Not Mad Anymore") 25-50

Picture Sleeves

BRUNSWICK 5-10 68

LPs: 10/12-inch 33rpm

BRUNSWICK 10-15 68-71
CAPITOL 5-10 75
Also see CHANDLER, Gene, and Barbara Acklin

ACT I

R&B '73

Singles: 7-inch

SPRING 3-5 73-74

LPs: 10/12-inch 33rpm

SPRING 5-10 74

ACTUALS: see VOCAL AIRES / Actuals

ACUFF, Roy

(With the Smoky Mountain Boys; with Crazy Tennesseeans)

P&R '38

Singles: 78rpm

BANNER 10-20
CAPITOL 4-8 53-55
COLUMBIA 5-10 45-49
CONQUEROR 10-20
DECCA 4-8 55
MGM 5-10 51
MELOTONE 10-20
OKEH 5-10 40-45
ORIOLE 10-20
PERFECT 10-20
ROMEO 10-20
VOCALION 8-12 38-40

Singles: 7-inch

CAPITOL (2385 thru 3209) 5-10 53-55
COLUMBIA (20000 series) 10-20 52
DECCA 5-10 55
HICKORY (314 thru 362) 3-6 73-75
HICKORY (1073 thru 1664) 4-8 58-72
MGM 10-20 51
Also see NITTY GRITTY DIRT BAND & Roy Acuff

ACUFF, Roy, & Kitty Wells

C&W '56

Singles: 7-inch

DECCA 4-8 56

Singles: 7-inch

DECCA 5-10 56
Also see ACUFF, Roy
Also see WELLS, Kitty

AD LIBS

P&R/R&B '65

Singles: 7-inch

A.G.P.(100 "New York in the Dark") 100-150 66
BLUE CAT 5-10 65
CAPITOL 3-6 70
ESKEE ("New York in the Dark") 200-300 66
(Number not known.)

KAREN (1527 "Think of Me") 15-20 66
PHILIPS 4-8 67
SHARE 3-6 69

Members: Mary Ann Thomas; Danny Austin; Hugh Harris; J.T. Taylor; Norm Donegan; Dave Watts.

ADAM & ANTS

P&R '82

Singles: 12-inch 33/45rpm

EPIC 4-8 81

Singles: 7-inch

EPIC 3-5 81

LPs: 10/12-inch 33rpm

EDITIONS EG 5-10 82
EPIC 8-10 81-82

Members: Adam Ant; Johnny Bivouac; Andy Watson; Dave Barb.
Also see ANT, Adam
Also see BOW WOW WOW

ADAMS, Bobby

R&B '70

Singles: 7-inch

BATTLE 4-8 63
BIG B. (778"The Kind of Man") 100-200
COLPIX 5-10 61
HOMETOWN 3-6 70
PET (803 "I Want My Lovin'") 15-25 58
PURDY (102 "Don't You Feel It") 10-20 64

ADAMS, Bobby, & Norma Jean Carpenter

Singles: 7-inch

KINGSTAR 3-5 71

Also see ADAMS, Bobby

ADAMS, Bryan

(B.G. Adams)

P&R/LP '82

Singles: 12-inch 33/45rpm

A&M 4-6 82-87
(Black vinyl.)
A&M 5-10 84
(Colored vinyl.)

Singles: 7-inch

A&M (Except 474) 3-5 80-87
(Black vinyl.)
A&M (474 "Let Me Take You Dancing") 8-12 79
A&M (Colored vinyl) 4-6

Picture Sleeves

A&M (Except 474) 3-5 80-87
A&M (474 "Let Me Take You Dancing") 10-15 79

LPs: 10/12-inch 33rpm

A&M 5-10 80-87

Also see DION
Also see SWEENY TODD

ADAMS, Bryan, & Tina Turner

Singles: 7-inch

A&M 3-4 85

Picture Sleeves

A&M 3-4 85

Also see ADAMS, Bryan
Also see TURNER, Tina

ADAMS, Faye

R&B '53

Singles: 78rpm

ATLANTIC 10-15 52-53
HERALD 10-15 53-57
IMPERIAL 8-12 55-57

Singles: 7-inch

ABC 3-4 73
ATLANTIC 20-35 52-53
COLLECTABLES 3-4 82
HERALD (Black vinyl) 10-20 53-57
HERALD (Colored vinyl) 25-50 53
IMPERIAL 10-20 55-57
LIDO 5-10 59-60
SAVOY 5-10 61
WARWICK 5-10 61

LPs: 10/12-inch 33rpm

COLLECTABLES 6-8 88
SAVOY 5-10 76
WARWICK (2031 "Shake a Hand") 50-75 61

ADAMS, Faye / Little Esther / Maxine Brown

LPs: 10/12-inch 33rpm

MUSICTONE (7001 "Great Female R&B Package") 20-30 65

Also see BROWN, Maxine

ADAMS, Faye / Little Esther / Shirley & Lee

LPs: 10/12-inch 33rpm

ALMOR (103 "Golden Souvenirs") 10-20

Also see ADAMS, Faye
Also see LITTLE ESTHER
Also see SHIRLEY & LEE

ADAMS, Gayle

R&B '80

Singles: 7-inch

PRELUDE 3-4 80-81

LPs: 10/12-inch 33rpm

PRELUDE 5-10 82

ADAMS, Johnny

R&B '62

Singles: 7-inch

ARIOLA AMERICAN 3-4 78
ATLANTIC 3-5 71-72
HELP ME 3-5 74-76
J.B. 3-5 76
MODERN 4-8 67
PACEMAKER (255 "Let Them Talk") 10-15
PAID 3-4 84
RIC 5-10 59-62
RON 4-8 64-65

SSS INT'L 3-5 68-74
(Black vinyl.)
SSS INT'L (809 "I Won't Cry") 5-10 69
(Colored vinyl.)
WATCH 4-8 63

LPs: 10/12-inch 33rpm

ARIOLA AMERICAN 5-10 78
CHELSEA 10-20 77
HELP ME 8-10 74-76
SSS INT'L 10-15 70

ADAMS, Johnny, & Gondoliers

Singles: 7-inch

RIC (957 "Knocked Out") 10-20 59
Also see ADAMS, Johnny

ADAMS, Marie

(With Bill Harvey's Band; with Three Tons of Joy)

R&B '52

Singles: 78rpm

PEACOCK 5-10 51-54

Singles: 7-inch

CAPITOL 5-10 58
PEACOCK 10-20 51-54
VANTAGE 3-5 73
Also see OTIS, Johnny

ADAMS, Oleta

LP '90

LPs: 10/12-inch 33rpm

FONTANA 5-8 90

ADDEO, Leo, & His Orchestra

LP '61

LPs: 10/12-inch 33rpm

CAMDEN 5-10 61

ADDERLEY, Julian Cannonball"

(Cannonball Adderley Orchestra; Quintet; Sextet)

P&R/R&B '61

Singles: 7-Inch

BLUE NOTE 4-8 59
CAPITOL 3-8 61-73
RIVERSIDE 4-6 61-64

EPs: 7-Inch 33/45rpm

EMARCY 10-20 55

LPs: 10/12-Inch 33rpm

BLUE NOTE 20-30 58
(Label reads "Blue Note Records Inc. - New York, U.S.A.")
BLUE NOTE 15-25 66
(Label reads "Blue Note Records - A Division Of Liberty Records Inc.")
CAPITOL (Except 2200 and 2300 series) 8-15 66-80
CAPITOL (2200 and 2300 series) 12-25 64-65
DOBRE 5-8 77
EMARCY (400 series) 8-12 76
EMARCY (36000 series) 30-40 55-58
EVEREST 8-12 71
FANTASY 8-12 73-75
LIMELIGHT 10-20 66
MERCURY (1000 series) 5-10 81
MERCURY (20000 and 60000 series) 15-30 61-62
MILESTONE 6-12 73-82
PACIFIC JAZZ 15-25 62
RIVERSIDE (032 thru 142) 5-8 82-85
RIVERSIDE (200 thru 400 series) 15-30 58-63
RIVERSIDE (1100 series) 20-30 59-60
RIVERSIDE (3000 series) 10-15 68
RIVERSIDE (9000 series) 15-25 60-63
SAVOY (2200 series) 8-12 76
SAVOY (12018 "Presenting Cannonball") 50-75 55
TRIP 5-10 75
VSP 10-20 65
WING 8-12 68
Also see WILSON, Nancy, & Cannonball Adderley

ADDERLEY, Julian "Cannonball," & John Coltrane

LPs: 10/12-Inch 33rpm

LIMELIGHT 10-20 65
MERCURY 15-25 61
Also see COLTRANE, John

ADDERLEY, Julian "Cannonball," & Sergio Mendes

LPs: 10/12-Inch 33rpm

CAPITOL 10-15 68-71
EVEREST 5-10 73
Also see ADDERLEY, Julian "Cannonball"
Also see MENDES, Sergio

ADDRISI BROTHERS

P&R '59

Singles: 7-inch

BELL 3-5 74
BRAD 10-20 58
BUDDAH 3-5 77
COLUMBIA 3-5 72-73
DEL-FI 8-15 59
ELEKTRA 3-4 81
IMPERIAL 5-10 60
POM POM 5-10 62
PRIVATE STOCK 3-5 75
SCOTTI BROTHERS 3-4 79
VALIANT 4-8 64-65
W.B. 3-8 62-68

Picture Sleeves

SCOTTI BROTHERS 3-4 79

LPs: 10/12-inch 33rpm

BUDDAH 5-10 77
COLUMBIA 5-10 72
Members: Dick Addrisi; Don Addrisi.

ADE, King Sunny
(With His African Beats)

LP '83

Singles: 12-inch 33/45rpm

MANGO 4-6 83

Singles: 7-inch

MANGO 3-4 83

LPs: 10/12-inch 33rpm

MANGO 5-10 83

ADVANCE

D&D '83

Singles: 12-inch 33/45rpm

POLYDOR 4-6 83

Singles: 7-inch

POLYDOR 3-4 83

ADVENTURES

P&R/LP '88

Singles: 12-inch 33/45rpm

ELEKTRA 4-8 88-90

Singles: 7-inch

ELEKTRA 3-4 88-90

Picture Sleeves

ELEKTRA 3-4 88

LPs: 10/12-inch 33rpm

ELEKTRA 5-8 88

Member: Terry Sharpe.

ADVENTURES of STEVIE V.

P&R '90

Singles: 7-inch

MERCURY 3-4 90

Members: Steve Vincent; Melodie Washington; Mick Walsh.

AEROSMITH

P&R/LP '73

Singles: 7-inch

COLUMBIA 3-5 73-80
GEFFEN 3-4 85-90

Picture Sleeves

GEFFEN 3-4 85-89

LPs: 10/12-inch 33rpm

COLUMBIA (Except KC-32005) .. 5-15 73-86
COLUMBIA (KC-32005 Aerosmith") 20-25 73
(Orange cover. Incorrectly shows *Walking the Dog* as *Walking the Dig.*)
COLUMBIA (KC-32005 Aerosmith") 10-12 73
(Correctly lists *Walking the Dog.*)
GEFFEN 5-10 85-87

Promotional LPs

COLUMBIA (187 "Pure Gold") .. 50-55 76
(Boxed set of the group's first three LPs.)

Members: Steve Tyler; Tom Hamilton; Joey Kramer; Joe Perry; Brad Whitford; Rick Dufay; Jimmy Crespo.
Also see PERRY, Joe, Project
Also see RUN-D.M.C.

AFRIKA BAMBAATAA: see BAMBAATAA, Afrika

AFRIQUE

P&R/R&B/LP '73

Singles: 7-inch

MAINSTREAM 3-5 73

LPs: 10/12-inch 33rpm

MAINSTREAM 8-12 73

Members: David T. Walker; Chuck Rainey.

AFRO CUBAN BAND

R&B '78

Singles: 7-inch

ARISTA 3-4 78

LPs: 10/12-inch 33rpm

ARISTA 5-10 78

AFTER the FIRE

P&R/D&D/LP '83

Singles: 12-inch 33/45rpm

EPIC 4-8 83

Singles: 7-inch

EPIC 3-4 83-84

LPs: 10/12-inch 33rpm

EPIC 5-10 82

Members: Peter Banks; Andy Piercy; Ivor Twidell; Tim Haywell; Nick Battle.
Also see BANKS, Peter

AFTERBACH

R&B '81

Singles: 7-inch

COLUMBIA/ARC 3-4 81

LPs: 10/12-inch 33rpm

COLUMBIA/ARC 5-10 81

Members: Robert Brooken; Mike Brooken.

AFTERNOON DELIGHTS

P&R/R&B '81

Singles: 12-inch 33/45rpm

MCA 4-8 81

Singles: 7-inch

MCA 3-4 81

LPs: 10/12-inch 33rpm

MCA 5-10 81

AIDA

D&D '84

Singles: 12-inch 33/45rpm

VANGUARD 4-6 84

Singles: 7-inch

VANGUARD 3-4 84

LPs: 10/12-inch 33rpm

VANGUARD 5-8 84

AIR SUPPLY

P&R/LP '80

Singles: 7-inch

ARISTA 3-4 80-86
FLASHBACK 3-4 82

Picture Sleeves

ARISTA 3-4 80-86

LPs: 10/12-inch 33rpm

ARISTA 5-10 80-86
COLUMBIA 10-15 77

MFSL (113 "The One That You Love") 20-25 84
NAUTULIS (31 "Lost in Love") .. 15-25 82
Members: Graham Russell; Russell Hitchcock; David Moyse; Criston Barker; Ralph Cooper; David Green; Frank Esler-Smith; Rex Goh.

AIRWAVES

P&R '78

Singles: 7-inch

A&M 3-4 78-79

LPs: 10/12-inch 33rpm

A&M 5-10 78-79
Members: John David; Dave Charles; Ray Martinez.

AKENS, Jewel

P&R/R&B '65

Singles: 7-inch

AMERICAN INT'L ARTISTS 3-4 75
CAPEHART 5-10 61
COLGEMS 4-8 67
CREST 4-8 62
ERA 4-8 65
MINASA 4-8 65
RTV 3-5 72
WEST-ONE 3-5

LPs: 10/12-inch 33rpm

ERA 20-30 65

AKKERMAN, Jan
(With Kaz Lux)

LP '73

Singles: 7-inch

ATLANTIC 3-4 77-79

LPs: 10/12-inch 33rpm

ATCO 10-12 73
ATLANTIC 5-10 76-79
SIRE 10-15 73

AL B. SURE!

P&R/R&B/LP '88

Singles: 7-inch

W.B. 3-4 88-90

Picture Sleeves

W.B. 3-4 88-90

LPs: 10/12-inch 33rpm

W.B. 5-8 88-90
Also see JONES, Quincy, James Ingram, Al B. Sure, El DeBarge & Barry White

ALABAMA
(Alabama Band)

C&W '77

Singles: 7-inch

GRT 4-8 77
MDJ 3-5 79-80
RCA 3-5 80-93
RCA GOLD STANDARD 3-4 82
SUN (Colored vinyl) 4-8 81

Picture Sleeves

GRT 10-20 77
RCA 3-4 80-90

LPs: 10/12-inch 33rpm

ABC/WATERMARK ("American Country Countdown Presents Alabama") 8-12 88
(No selection number used. Promotional issue only.)
ALABAMA RECORDS (78 9-01 "The Alabama Band") 200-400 78
PLANTATION 40-60 81
RCA 5-10 80-90
SONNY 30-50 79
Members: Randy Owen; Jeff Cook; Teddy Gentry; R. Scott; Mark Herndon.
Also see RICHIE, Lionel, & Alabama
Also see WILD COUNTRY

ALAIMO, Steve
(With the Redcoats)

P&R '62

Singles: 7-inch

ABC 3-6 66-67
ABC-PAR 4-8 64-66
ATCO 3-6 67-71
CHECKER 6-12 61-63
DADE 8-12 59
DICKSON 8-12 60
ENTRANCE 3-5 71-72
ERIC 3-4 83
IMPERIAL 5-10 60-63
LIFETIME 20-30 58
MARLIN (Except 6064) 10-20 59
MARLIN (6064 "I Want You to Love Me") 10-20 59

EPs: 7-inch 33/45rpm

ABC-PAR (531 "Where the Action Is") 8-15 65
(Jukebox issue only.)

LPs: 10/12-inch 33rpm

ABC-PAR 15-25 65-66
CHECKER 20-30 61-63
CROWN 10-15 63
Also see RIVERS, Johnny / Steve Alaimo

ALAIMO, Steve, & Betty Wright

Singles: 7-inch

ATCO 3-6 69
Also see ALAIMO, Steve
Also see WRIGHT, Betty

ALARM

LP '83

Singles: 7-inch

I.R.S. 3-4 83-90

Picture Sleeves

I.R.S. 3-4 83-89

LPs: 10/12-inch 33rpm

I.R.S. 5-10 83-91
Members: Mike Peters; Nigel Twist; Dave Sharp; Eddie MacDonald.

ALBERT, Eddie

Singles: 78rpm

KAPP 4-8 54-56

Singles: 7-inch

COLUMBIA 3-5 68
HICKORY.................................... 3-6 64-65
KAPP....................................... 5-10 54-56

Picture Sleeves

KAPP (134 "Little Child")........... 10-15 56

LPs: 10/12-inch 33rpm

COLUMBIA 8-12 68
HAMILTON.................................. 10-15 59

ALBERT, Eddie, & Sondra Lee

P&R '56

Singles: 78rpm

KAPP....................................... 4-8 56

Singles: 7-inch

KAPP....................................... 5-10 56

Also see ALBERT, Eddie

ALBERT, Morris

P&R/LP '75

Singles: 7-inch

RCA.. 3-5 75-76

LPs: 10/12-inch 33rpm

RCA.. 5-10 75-76

ALBERTI, Willy

P&R '59

Singles: 7-inch

EPIC 3-6 59
LONDON.................................... 3-6 59

LPs: 10/12-inch 33rpm

LONDON.................................... 5-15 59

ALBRIGHT, Gerald

R&B '87

Singles: 7-inch

ATLANTIC.................................. 3-4 87-88

LPs: 10/12-inch 33rpm

ATLANTIC.................................. 5-8 88

ALCATRAZZ

LP '84

Singles: 7-inch

ROCSHIRE 4-8 83

Picture Sleeves

ROCSHIRE 8-15 83

LPs: 10/12-inch 33rpm

CAPITOL................................... 15-25 85
ROCSHIRE 15-25 83-84

Members: Graham Bonnet; Steve Vai; Yngwie Malmsteen.
Also see RAINBOW
Also see MALMSTEEN, Yngwie J.
Also see SCHENKER, Michael, Group

ALDO NOVA: see NOVA, Aldo

ALDRICH, Renee

R&B '87

Singles: 7-inch

JAM PACKED 3-4 87

ALDRICH, Ronnie

LP '61

LPs: 10/12-inch 33rpm

LONDON PHASE 4 ....5-15 61-71

ALEEM

(Featuring Leroy Burgess; Aleems)

R&B/D&D '84

Singles: 12-inch 33/45rpm

ATLANTIC.................................4-6 87
NIA 5-8 85

Singles: 7-inch

ATLANTIC.................................3-4 86-87
NIA 3-5 84-85

LPs: 10/12-inch 33rpm

ATLANTIC.................................5-10 87

Members: Leroy Burgess; Taharqa Aleem; Tunde-Ra Aleem.
Also see BLACK IVORY

ALEEMS: see ALEEM

ALESSI

P&R '82

Singles: 7-inch

A&M 3-4 77-79
QWEST......................................3-4 82

Picture Sleeves

A&M 3-4 77-79

LPs: 10/12-inch 33rpm

A&M 5-10 76-79
QWEST......................................5-10 82

Members: Bill Alessi; Bob Alessi.

ALEXANDER, Arthur

P&R/R&B '62

Singles: 7-inch

AT YOU......................................3-6
BUDDAH.....................................3-6 75-76
DOT 5-10 62-64
GORDA.......................................4-8
MONUMENT................................4-8 68
MUSIC MILL 4-8 77
SOUND STAGE 7.........................4-8 65-71
W.B. 3-6 72-73

EPs: 7-inch 33/45rpm

DOT ("You Better Move On").....25-35 62
(Number not known.)

LPs: 10/12-inch 33rpm

DOT (3434 "You Better Move On").......................................35-45 62
(Monaural.)
DOT (25434 "You Better Move On").......................................40-55 62
(Stereo.)
W.B. 8-15 72

Also see ALEXANDER, June

ALEXANDER, David

R&B '87

Singles: 7-inch

SOUND TOWN 3-4 87

ALEXANDER, Goldie

R&B '82

Singles: 7–inch

ARISTA 3-4 82

ALEXANDER, Joe, & Cubans

Singles: 78rpm

BALLAD (1008 "Oh Maria")... 300-500 55

Singles: 7–inch

BALLAD (1008 "Oh Maria"). 800-1200 55

Members: Joe Alexander; Chuck Berry; Faith Douglas; Freddy Golden.

Also see BERRY, Chuck

ALEXANDER, June

(Arthur Alexander)

Singles: 7–inch

JUDD (1020 "Sally Sue Brown") 25-35 60

Also see ALEXANDER, Arthur

ALEXANDER, Margie

R&B '74

Singles: 12–inch 33/45rpm

CHI-SOUND 4-8 77

Singles: 7–inch

ATLANTIC 3-5 71

CHI-SOUND 3-4 76-77

FUTURE STARS 3-5 74

ALFI & HARRY

P&R '56

(David Seville)

Singles: 78rpm

LIBERTY 4-8 55-57

Singles: 7–inch

LIBERTY 5-10 55-57

Also see SEVILLE, David

ALFIE: see SILAS, Alfie

ALFONZO

R&B '82

(Alfonzo Jones)

Singles: 12–inch 33/45rpm

JOE-WES 4-6 83

Singles: 7–inch

JOE-WES 3-4 82

LARC 3-4 82

LPs: 10/12–inch 33rpm

LARC 5-10 83

ALI, Muhammad, & Frank Sinatra

LPs: 10/12–inch 33rpm

ST. JOHN'S (1 "Ali and His Gang Fight Tooth Decay") 20-40
(Promotional issue only.)

Also see CLAY, Cassius

Also see SINATRA, Frank

ALIAS

LP '90

Singles: 7–inch

MERCURY 3-5 79-80

LPs: 10/12–inch 33rpm

EMI 5-8 90

MERCURY 5-10 79

Members: Fred Curci; Steve DeMarchi; Dorman Cogburn; Jimmy Dougherty; Jo Jo Billingsley; Leon Wilkeson; Billy Powell; Barry Harwood; Ricky Powell; Artimus Pyle.

Also see COLLINS, Allen, Band

Also see LYNYRD SKYNYRD

Also see SHERIFF

ALICE COOPER: see COOPER, Alice

ALICE WONDER LAND

P&R '63

Singles: 7–inch

BARDELL (774 "He's Mine")...... 10-20 63

UNITED INTERNATIONAL 10-15

ALISHA

R&B/D&D '84

Singles: 12–inch 33/45rpm

VANGUARD 4-6 84-86

Singles: 7–inch

MCA 3-4 90

RCA 3-4 87

VANGUARD 3-4 84-86

Picture Sleeves

RCA 3-4 87

LPs: 10/12–inch 33rpm

MCA 5-8 90

ALIVE 'N KICKING

(Alive 'N Kickin')

P&R/LP '70

Singles: 7–inch

ROULETTE 4-8 70-71

LPs: 10/12–inch 33rpm

ROULETTE (42052 "Alive 'N Kickin'") 20-30 70

ROULETTE (42052 "Alive 'N Kickin'") 40-60 70
(Promotional issue.)

ALL POINTS BULLETIN BAND

R&B '76

Singles: 7–inch

LITTLE CITY 3-5 75-79

ALL SPORTS BAND

P&R '81

Singles: 7–inch

RADIO 3-4 81-82

LPs: 10/12–inch 33rpm

RADIO 5-10 81

ALLAN, Davie

(With the Arrows)

P&R '65

Singles: 7–inch

A.O.A. 3-6 76

CUDE (101 "War Path") 30-40 63

MARC (3223 "War Path") 20-30 63

MGM 3-6 71-73

MRC 3-5 84

PRIVATE STOCK 3-5 74

SIDEWALK 10-15 64

TOWER 5-10 65-68
WHAT 3-5 82

LPs: 10/12-inch 33rpm

ALKOR 5-10 84
ARROW DYNAMICS 8-12 85
TOWER 15-25 65-68
WHAT 5-10 83

Members: Davie Allan; Steve Pugh; Larry Brown; Paul Johnson; Don Manning; Tony Allwine.
Also see ANNETTE
Also see CURB, Mike
Also see DALE, Dick
Also see HONDELLS
Also see NAYLOR, Jerry
Also see PARIS SISTERS
Also see RONSTADT, Linda
Also see STAFFORD, Terry

ALLAN, Davie / Eternity's Children / Main Attraction / Sunrays

EPs: 7-inch 33/45rpm

TOWER (4557 "Selections from April Albums") 25-50 68
(Promotional issue only.)
Also see ALLAN, Davie
Also see ETERNITY'S CHILDREN
Also see MAIN ATTRACTION
Also see SUNRAYS

ALLEN, Annisteen

(With Her Home Town Boys)

R&B '53

Singles: 78rpm

CAPITOL 10-15 55
DECCA 10-15 56-57
FEDERAL 10-15 51-52
KING 10-15 46-54

Singles: 7-inch

CAPITOL 10-20 55
DECCA 10-20 56-57
KING 15-25 53-54
TRUE SOUND 5-8
WIG 5-10 59

Also see ALLEN, Ernestine
Also see GREER, John

ALLEN, Annisteen, & Melvin Moore

Singles: 7-inch

TODD 5-10 59

Also see ALLEN, Annisteen

ALLEN, Dayton

LP '60

LPs: 10/12-inch 33rpm

GRAND AWARD 10-15 60

ALLEN, Donna

R&B '86

Singles: 7-inch

OCEANA 3-4 88
TWENTY-ONE 3-4 86-87

LPs: 10/12-inch 33rpm

OCEANA 5-8 88
TWENTY-ONE 5-10 86-87

ALLEN, Ernestine

(Annisteen Allen)

Singles: 7-inch

TRU-SOUND 5-10 62

LPs: 10/12-inch 33rpm

TRU-SOUND 20-35 62

Also see ALLEN, Annisteen

ALLEN, Jonelle

R&B '78

Singles: 7-inch

ALEXANDER STREET 3-4 78

ALLEN, Lee

P&R '58

Singles: 78rpm

ALADDIN 8-15 56
EMBER 10-15 58

Singles: 7-inch

ALADDIN 10-20 56
COLLECTABLES 3-4 82
EMBER 8-12 58-59
WAND 4-8 60s

EPs: 7-inch 33/45rpm

EMBER (103 "Walkin' with Mr. Lee") 40-60 58

LPs: 10/12-inch 33rpm

EMBER (200 "Walkin' with Mr. Lee") 75-125 58
(Red label.)
EMBER (200 "Walkin' with Mr Lee") 60-80 58
("Logs" label. Ember logo is formed with logs.)
EMBER (Black label) 25-35 60

Also see DOMINO, Fats
Also see BLASTERS
Also see LITTLE RICHARD
Also see SMITH, Huey
Also see STRAY CATS

ALLEN, Peter

LP '79

Singles: 12-inch 33/45rpm

A&M 4-8 79

Singles: 7-inch

A&M 3-5 74-82
ARISTA 3-4 83-84
METROMEDIA 3-5 71-73

LPs: 10/12-inch 33rpm

A&M 5-10 74-82
ARISTA 5-10 83-84
METROMEDIA 10-15 71-72

Also see ALLEN, Chris & Peter

ALLEN, R. Justice

R&B '86

Singles: 7-inch

CATAWBA 3-4 86

ALLEN, Rance, Group

R&B '73

Singles: 7-inch

CAPITOL 3-5 77-79
GOSPEL TRUTH 3-5 72-73
STAX 3-4 78-81
TRUTH 3-5 74-75

LPs: 10/12-inch 33rpm

CAPITOL 5-10 77-79
GOSPEL TRUTH 8-12 72-74
MYRRH 5-10 84
STAX 5-10 78-81
TRUTH 8-10 75

Members: Rance Allen; Thomas Allen; Steven Allen; Esau Allen; Linda Mendez; Annie Mendez; Judy Mendez.

ALLEN, Rex

(With the Arizona Wranglers & Jerry Byrd)

C&W '49

Singles: 78rpm

DECCA (Except 30651) 4-8 52-57
DECCA (30651 "Knock Knock, Rattle") 8-15 56
MERCURY 5-10 49-55

Singles: 7-inch

BUENA VISTA 4-8 59
DECCA (Except 28000 thru 30000 series) 3-8 56-72
DECCA (28000 & 29000 series) . 5-10 52-56
DECCA (30000 series except 30651) 5-10 56
DECCA (30651 "Knock Knock, Rattle") 15-20 56
JMI 3-5 73
MERCURY 5-10 53-62
WILDCAT 4-6

Picture Sleeves

MERCURY 5-10 63

EPs: 7-inch 33/45rpm

DECCA 10-20 56
MERCURY 10-20 53-56

LPs: 10/12-inch 33rpm

BUENA VISTA 20-25 61
COLLECTOR'S CLASSICS 5-10
CORAL 5-10 73
DECCA (5000 series) 10-15 68-70
(Decca LP numbers in this series preceded by a "7" or a "DL-7" are stereo issues.)
DECCA (8000 series) 20-30 56-58
DESIGN 10-15 62
DISNEYLAND 6-10 70
HACIENDA 20-25
JMI 5-10
MCA 5-10
MERCURY 10-20 62
PICKWICK/HILLTOP 10-15 65
VOCALION 6-10 70
WING 10-15 64-66

Session: Jud Conlon Singers.
Also see PAGE, Patti, & Rex Allen

ALLEN, Richie

(With the Pacific Surfers)

P&R '60

Singles: 7-inch

ERA 5-10 61
IMPERIAL 8-15 60-63
TOWER 4-8 66

LPs: 10/12-inch 33rpm

IMPERIAL 40-60 63

Member: Richie Podolor.

ALLEN, Ricky

R&B '63

Singles: 7-inch

AGE 4-8 63-64
APOGEE 4-8 64
BRIGHT STAR 4-8 66-67
FOUR BROTHERS (401 "I Can't Stand Signifying") 8-12
U.S.A. 4-8 65

ALLEN, Steve

P&R/LP '55

Singles: 78rpm

BRUNSWICK 4-8 53
CORAL 4-8 55-56

Singles: 7-inch

BRUNSWICK 5-10 53
CORAL 5-10 55-56
DOT 4-8 59-66
DUNHILL (Except 4097) 3-5 67-68
DUNHILL (4097 "Here Comes Sgt. Pepper") 4-8 67
SIGNATURE 3-6 59-60

Picture Sleeves

DOT 5-10 65

EPs: 7-inch 33/45rpm

BRUNSWICK 10-20 53
CORAL 10-20 55-56
DECCA 15-20 55
WOODBURY'S 10-20

LPs: 10/12-inch 33rpm

COLUMBIA (2554 "Steve Allen") 20-30 56
(10-inch LP.)
CORAL (100 "Jazz Story") 25-35 59
(Narration by Steve Allen, music by various artists.)
CORAL (57000 series, except 57099) 15-20 55-56
CORAL (57099 "The James Dean Story") 35-50 56
(With Bill Randle.)
CORAL (57400 series) 10-20 63
(Monaural.)
CORAL (7-57400 series) 10-20 63
(Stereo.)
DECCA 20-25 55
DOT (Except 3472 & 3517) 10-20 59-66

DOT (3472 "Steve Allen's Funny Fone Calls") 15-20 63
DOT (3517 "More Funny Fone Calls") 15-20 63
DUNHILL 8-10 67
EMARCY 15-20 58
HAMILTON 10-15 59-64
MERCURY 10-15 61
PETE 5-10 69
ROULETTE 15-20 59
SIGNATURE (Except 1004) 15-20 59
SIGNATURE (1004 "Man on the Street") 30-40 59
(With Louis Nye, Tom Poston and Don Knotts.)
Also see PRESLEY, Elvis

ALLEN, Steve, & Jayne Meadows

Singles: 78rpm

CORAL 4-8 55

Singles: 7-inch

CORAL 5-10 55
Also see ALLEN, Steve

ALLEN, Vee

R&B '73

Singles: 7-inch

LION 3-5 73
MCA 3-4 83

LPs: 10/12-inch 33rpm

MCA 5-10 83

ALLEN, Woody

LP '64

Singles: 7-inch

U.A. 3-5 72

Picture Sleeves

U.A. 4-6 72

LPs: 10/12-inch 33rpm

BELL 10-15 67
CAPITOL 8-12 68
CASABLANCA 8-12 79
COLPIX 20-30 64-65
U.A. (800 series) 6-10 77
U.A. (9900 series) 8-12 72

ALLENS, Arvee
(Ritchie Valens)

Singles: 7-inch

DEL-FI (4114 "Fast Freight") 20-30 59
Also see VALENS, Ritchie

ALLEY CATS

P&R/R&B '63

Singles: 7-inch

EPIC 5-10 65
PHILLES (108 "Puddin n' Tain") 15-20 62
WHIPPETT 10-20 56-57
Members: Chester Pipkin; Gary Pipkin; Bobby Sheen; Sheridan Spencer; Brice Coefield; James Barker.
Also see PIPKINS
Also see SHEEN, Bobby

ALLISON, Gene

P&R/R&B '57

Singles: 78rpm

CALVERT 10-15 56
DECCA 5-10 57
VEE JAY 5-10 57

Singles: 7-inch

CALVERT 15-25 56
CHAMPION 5-10 59
CHEROKEE 5-10 59
DECCA 10-15 57
MONUMENT 4-8 65
REF-O-REE 4-8
VALDOT 4-8 62
VEE JAY 8-15 57-60

LPs: 10/12-inch 33rpm

VEE JAY (1009 "Gene Allison") 100-125 59
(Maroon label.)
VEE JAY (1009 "Gene Allison") .25-40 59
(Black label.)

ALLISONS

P&R '63

Singles: 7-inch

COLUMBIA 4-8 61
SMASH 4-8 62
TIP (1011 "Surfer Street") 15-20 63

ALLMAN, Duane

LP '72

LPs: 10/12-inch 33rpm

CAPRICORN 8-12 72-74
Also see DEREK & DOMINOS

ALLMAN, Duane & Gregg

LP '72

Singles: 7-inch

BOLD 5-8 73

LPs: 10/12-inch 33rpm

BOLD (301 "Duane & Gregg Allman") 20-25 72
(Gatefold cover.)
BOLD (301 "Duane & Gregg Allman") 8-10 73
(Standard cover.)
SPRINGBOARD 8-10 75
Also see ALLMAN, Duane
Also see ALLMAN, Gregg
Also see ALLMAN BROTHERS BAND
Also see ALLMAN JOYS

ALLMAN, Gregg
(Gregg Allman Band)

P&R/LP '73

Singles: 7-inch

CAPRICORN 3-5 73-77
EPIC 3-4 87-89

LPs: 10/12-inch 33rpm

CAPRICORN 8-12 73-77
EPIC 5-10 87-89

ROBERT KLEIN ("Interview") ... 40-60 81
(Promotional issue only.)
Also see ALLMAN, Duane & Gregg
Also see ALLMAN & WOMAN
Also see ALLMAN BROTHERS BAND
Also see ALLMAN JOYS

ALLMAN & WOMAN

Singles: 7-inch

W.B. 3-5 77

LPs: 10/12-inch 33rpm

W.B. 8-10 77
Members: Gregg Allman; Cher.
Also see ALLMAN, Gregg
Also see CHER

ALLMAN BROTHERS BAND

LP '70

Singles: 7-inch

ARISTA 3-4 80-81
CAPRICORN (Except 036) 3-5 71-79
CAPRICORN (036 "Jessica").... 30-50 73

Picture Sleeves

ARISTA 3-5 81

EPs: 7-inch 33/45rpm

ATLANTIC.............................. 10-20 73
(Jukebox issue only.)
CAPRICORN.......................... 10-20 73
(Jukebox issue only.)

LPs: 10/12-inch 33rpm

ARISTA 5-10 80-81
ATCO 15-20 69-73
CAPRICORN (Except 802) 8-15 72-79
CAPRICORN (802 "The Allman Brothers Band at the Fillmore East")..... 15-20 71
EPIC.. 5-8 90
K-TEL 5-10
MFSL (157 "Eat a Peach")........ 20-25 85
POLYDOR (6339 "Best of the Allman Brothers Band")............. 5-10 89
POLYDOR (839-417 "The Allman Brothers Band")...................... 25-35 89
(Six-LP boxed set, with booklet.)
Members: Duane Allman; Gregg Allman; Dicky Betts; Berry Oakley; Butch Trucks; Johnny Johanson; Les Dudek; Chuck Leavell; David Goldflies; Paul Hornsby; Dan Toler.
Also see ALLMAN, Duane & Gregg
Also see BETTS, Richard
Also see DUDEK, Les
Also see HOUR GLASS
Also see SEA LEVEL
Also see 31ST of FEBRUARY

ALLMAN JOYS

Singles: 7-inch

DIAL (4046 "Spoonful") 25-35 66

LPs: 10/12-inch 33rpm

DIAL 10-15 73
Members: Duane Allman; Gregg Allman; Bob Keller; Maynard Portwood; Ralph Balinger; Ronnie Wilkin; Tommy Amato; Jack Jackson; Bobby Dennis; Bill Connell.
Also see ALLMAN, Duane & Gregg

ALMEIDA, Laurindo

(With the Modern Jazz Quartet; with Bossa Nova All Stars)

LP '62

Singles: 7-inch

ATLANTIC.......................................4-6 64
CAPITOL...3-8 55-65
PACIFIC JAZZ 5-8 55

EPs: 7-inch 33/45rpm

CAPITOL.......................................5-15 56-59
CORAL...5-10 54-56
PACIFIC JAZZ 10-15 54

LPs: 10/12-inch 33rpm

ATLANTIC.....................................10-20 64
CAPITOL (Except 8000 series) .15-25 59-65
CAPITOL (8000 series) 20-35 56-58
CORAL..25-45 54-56
CRYSTAL CLEAR 5-8 80
DAYBREAK 5-10 73
DOBRE 5-10 76-77
INNER CITY...................................5-8 79
PACIFIC JAZZ (7 "Laurindo Almeida Quartet") 50-75 54
(10-inch LP.)
PACIFIC JAZZ (13 "Laurindo Almeida Quartet, Vol. 2") 50-75 54
(10-inch LP.)
SURREY 10-20 65
WORLD PACIFIC 25-40 56-62
Also see BYRD, Charlie
Also see DAVIS, Sammy, Jr., & Laurindo Almeida
Also see GETZ, Stan, & Laurindo Almeida
Also see SOMMERS, Joanie, & Laurindo Almeida

ALMEIDA, Laurindo / Chico Hamilton

LPs: 10/12-inch 33rpm

JAZZTONE 10-20 64
Also see ALMEIDA, Laurindo
Also see HAMILTON, Chico

ALMOND, Marc

P&R/LP '89

Singles: 7-inch

CAPITOL...3-4 89

Picture Sleeves

CAPITOL...3-4 89

LPs: 10/12-inch 33rpm

CAPITOL...5-8 89
Also see MARK - ALMOND BAND
Also see SOFT CELL

ALPACA PHASE III

R&B '74

Singles: 7-inch

ATLANTIC.......................................3-5 74

ALPERT, Herb

(With Tijuana Brass; Herbie Alpert)

P&R/LP '62

Singles: 12-inch 33/45rpm

A&M 4-6 79-84
(Black vinyl.)

A&M 5-8 84
(Colored vinyl.)

Singles: 7–inch

A&M (Except 700 series) 3-5 66-87
A&M (700 series) 3-8 62-66
ANDEX 4-6 59
CAROL 4-6 59
ROWE/AMI 4-8 66
("Play Me" Sales Stimulator promotional issue.)

Picture Sleeves

A&M (Except 700 series) 3-5 66-87
A&M (700 series) 3-6 65-66

EPs: 7–inch 33/45rpm

A&M 4-8 65-66
(Jukebox issues only.)

LPs: 10/12–inch 33rpm

A&M (Except 100 series) 5-10 66-87
A&M (100 series) 8-15 62-66
MFSL (053 "Rise") 25-50 81
Also see HALL, Lani, & Herb Alpert

ALPERT, Herb, & Hugh Masekela

LP '78

Singles: 7–inch

A&M/HORIZON 3-4 78

Picture Sleeves

A&M/HORIZON 3-5 78

LPs: 10/12–inch 33rpm

A&M/HORIZON 5-10 78
Also see ALPERT, Herb
Also see MASEKELA, Hugh

ALPHAVILLE

P&R/D&D/LP '84

Singles: 12–inch 33/45rpm

ATLANTIC 4-6 84-86

Singles: 7–inch

ATLANTIC 3-4 84-88

Picture Sleeves

ATLANTIC 3-4 84-88

LPs: 10/12–inch 33rpm

ATLANTIC 5-10 84-86
Members: Marian Gold; Bernie Lloyd; Frank Mertens.

ALTON & JOHNNY

R&B '80

Singles: 7–inch

POLYDOR 3-4 80
Members: Johnny Bristol; Alton McClain.
Also see BRISTOL, Johnny
Also see McCLAIN, Alton, & Destiny

ALVIN, Dave
(With the Red Devils)

LP '87

Singles: 7–inch

ENIGMA 5-8 87

LPs: 10/12–inch 33rpm

EPIC 5-10 87
Also see BLASTERS
Also see X

ALVIN LEE: see LEE, Alvin

ALWAYS, Billy

R&B '82

Singles: 7–inch

EPIC 3-4 88
WAYLO 3-4 82

AMAZING RHYTHM ACES

C&W/P&R/LP '75

Singles: 7–inch

ABC 3-5 75-79
COLUMBIA 3-4 79
W.B. 3-4 80

LPs: 10/12–inch 33rpm

ABC 10-20 75-78
COLUMBIA 10-15 79
W.B. 8-10 80
Members: Russell Smith; James Brown Jr; Byrd Burton; Stick Davis; Billy Earhart III; James Hooker; Butch McDade.

AMAZULU

P&R '87

Singles: 7–inch

MANGO 3-4 87
Members: Ann Marie Ruddock; Sharon Bailey; Lesley Beach.

AMBASSADORS

R&B '69

Singles: 7–inch

ARCTIC 3-6 68-69
ATLANTIC 4-8 67-68
SOUND STAGE 7 .... 4-8 67-68
TIME 4-8

LPs: 10/12–inch 33rpm

ARCTIC 10-15 69
Members: Bobby Todd; Herley Johnson; Orlando Oliphant.
Also see CREME D' COCOA

AMBOY DUKES

P&R/LP '68

Singles: 7–inch

MAINSTREAM 6-12 67-69

LPs: 10/12–inch 33rpm

AUDIOFIDELITY (1005 "Journey to the Center of the Mind") 8- 12 83
(Picture disc.)
MAINSTREAM (801 "Journeys and Migrations") 15-20 74
MAINSTREAM (6104 "Amboy Dukes") 35-55 68
MAINSTREAM (6112 "Journey to the Center of the Mind") 35-55 68
MAINSTREAM (6118 Migration") 30-40 68
MAINSTREAM (6125 "Best of the Original Amboy Dukes") 25-35 69
POLYDOR 10-20 70
Members: Ted Nugent; Greg Arama; Rusty Day; John Drake; Steve Farmer; Dave Palmer; Andy Solomon; Rod Grange; K.J. Knight; John Angelos.

Also see NUGENT, Ted

AMBROSIA

P&R/LP '75

Singles: 7–inch

20TH FOX 3-5 74-78
W.B. 3-4 78-82

LPs: 10/12–inch 33rpm

NAUTILUS 10-15 81
(Half-speed mastered.)
20TH FOX 8-10 74-78
W.B. 5-10 78-82

Members: David Pack; Burleigh Drummond; Joe Puerta; Christopher North.
Also see PACK, David
Also see PARSONS, Alan, Project

AMECHE, Don, & Frances Langford

LP '62

EPs: 7–inch 33/45rpm

COLUMBIA 8-15 61
(Promotional only.)

LPs: 10/12–inch 33rpm

COLUMBIA (1000 & 8000 series) 15-20 61-62
COLUMBIA (30000 series) 8-12 71

AMERICA

P&R/LP '72

Singles: 7–inch

AMERICAN INT'L......................... 3-5 79
CAPITOL.................................... 3-4 79-85
W.B. 3-5 72-77

Picture Sleeves

AMERICAN INT'L......................... 3-6 79
CAPITOL.................................... 3-4 82-83
W.B. 3-5 72-74

LPs: 10/12–inch 33rpm

CAPITOL.................................... 5-10 79-85
W.B. (Except 2576)..................... 8-12 72-77
W.B. (2576 "America") 15-25 71
(Does NOT include *A Horse with No Name.*)
W.B. (2576 "America") 8-12 72
(Has *A Horse with No Name.*)

Members: Gerry Beckley; Dan Peek; Dewey Bunnell.
Also see PEEK, Dan

AMERICAN BREED

P&R '67

Singles: 7–inch

ABC.. 3-5 75
ACTA.. 4-8 67-69
MCA 3-4 84
PARAMOUNT 3-5 70

Picture Sleeves

ACTA.. 8-10 68

LPs: 10/12–inch 33rpm

ACTA.. 15-20 67-68

Members: Gary Loizzo; Al Ciner; Chuck Colbert; Lee Graziano; Kevin Murphy.
Also see RUFUS

AMERICAN COMEDY NETWORK

P&R '84

Singles: 7–inch

CRITIQUE.................................. 3-4 84

LPs: 10/12–inch 33rpm

CRITIQUE.................................. 5-10 84

AMERICAN DREAM

LP '70

Singles: 7–inch

AMPEX 3-5 70
DEMIK....................................... 4-8 68

Picture Sleeves

AMPEX 3-5 70

LPs: 10/12–inch 33rpm

AMPEX 15-20 70

Members: Nick Jameson; Dooley Van Winkle; Nicky Indelicato; Don Ferris; Mickey Brook.

AMERICAN FLYER

P&R/LP '76

Singles: 7–inch

U.A. 3-5 76-77

Picture Sleeves

U.A. 3-5 76-77

LPs: 10/12–inch 33rpm

U.A. 8-10 76-77

Members: Eric Kaz; Steve Katz; Craig Fuller; Doug Yule.
Also see PURE PRAIRIE LEAGUE
Also see VELVET UNDERGROUND

AMES, Ed

P&R '65

Singles: 7–inch

RCA 3-8 63-73

Picture Sleeves

RCA 3-8 67

LPs: 10/12–inch 33rpm

CAMDEN 4-8 72-73
RCA 5-15 64-77

Also see AMES BROTHERS

AMES, Nancy

P&R '64

Singles: 7–inch

ABC.. 3-5 68
EPIC (Except 10056) 3-5 66-68
EPIC (10056 "I Don't Want to Talk About It") 8-12 66
LIBERTY 3-6 61-65
SC 3-5 68

Picture Sleeves

EPIC... 4-6 66

LPs: 10/12–inch 33rpm

EPIC... 5-12 66-68
LIBERTY 8-18 61-65

Also see LOPEZ, Trini, with the Ventures & Nancy Ames

AMES BROTHERS

P&R '49

Singles: 78rpm

CORAL 4-8 50-53
RCA 3-8 53-57

Singles: 7-inch

CORAL 8-15 50-53
EPIC 3-6 62-63
RCA 5-15 53-62

Picture Sleeves

EPIC 4-8 62
RCA 10-15 60

EPs: 7-inch 33/45rpm

CORAL 10-20 50-53
RCA 10-20 53-61

LPs: 10/12-inch 33rpm

CORAL 15-30 53-62
EPIC 10-15 63
RCA (1000 series) 5-10 75
RCA (1200 thru 2200 series) 15-30 55-61
RCA (2800 series) 8-15 64
RCA (6000 series) 5-10 72
VOCALION 5-10 68

Members: Ed Ames; Joe Ames; Gene Ames; Vic Ames.

Also see AMES, Ed

Also see COMO, Perry / Ames Brothers / Harry Belafonte / Radio City Music Hall Orch.

Also see MOONEY, Art, & His Orchestra

AMESBURY, Bill

P&R '74

Singles: 7-inch

CASABLANCA 3-5 74-75

LPs: 10/12-inch 33rpm

CAPITOL 5-10 76
CASABLANCA 8-10 74

AMMONS, Gene

R&B '47

Singles: 78rpm

CHESS 4-8 50
DECCA 3-6 54
MERCURY 5-10 47-53
PRESTIGE 3-8 51-57

Singles: 7-inch

ARGO 4-8 62
DECCA 5-10 54
MERCURY 5-10 50-53
PRESTIGE (100 thru 400 series).. 3-8 60-68
PRESTIGE (700 series) 3-5 69-73

(This "700" series can easily be distinguished from the early fifties "700" series that follows. The company address is shown as in New Jersey. In the '50s the company was in New York.)

PRESTIGE (713 thru 921) 5-10 51-57
(Black vinyl.)
PRESTIGE (713 thru 921) 10-20 51-57
(Colored vinyl.)
RAY BRA 4-6
SAVOY 4-8 60
UNITED 5-10 53-54

EPs: 7-inch 33/45rpm

EMARCY 20-30 54
PRESTIGE 25-50 51

LPs: 10/12-inch 33rpm

ARGO 15-20 62
CHESS 15-25 59
EMARCY (400 series) 8-12 76
EMARCY (26000 series) 40-60 54
(10-inch LPs.)
ENJA 5-10 81
MERCURY 15-20 60-63
OLYMPIC 5-10 74
PRESTIGE (014 thru 192) 5-10 82-85
PRESTIGE (7010 thru 7132) 20-30 55-58

(Each of the following LPs in this series was reissued using the original selection number but a different title: Prestige 7050, *All Star Jam Session,* was reissued as *Woofin' & Tweetin;* Prestige 7039, *Hi-Fi Jam Session,* was reissued as *Happy Blues,* and Prestige 7060, *Jammin' with Gene,* was reissued as *Not Really the Blues.* These three 1960 reissues are valued in the $15 to $25 range.)

PRESTIGE (7146 thru 7287) 15-25 58-64
PRESTIGE (7300 & 7400 series) 10-20 65-68
PRESTIGE (7500 thru 7800 series) 8-15 68-70
PRESTIGE (10000 series) 5-10 71-74
PRESTIGE (24000 series) 8-12 73-81
ROOTS 5-10 76
SAVOY 15-25 61
TRIP 5-10 73-75
VEE JAY 15-25 60
WING 10-20 60-63

Also see McDUFF, Brother Jack, & Gene Ammons

AMMONS, Gene, & Richard "Groove" Holmes

LPs: 10/12-inch 33rpm

PACIFIC JAZZ (32 "Groovin' with Jug") 15-25 61

Also see HOLMES, Richard "Groove"

AMMONS, Gene, & Sonny Stitt

Singles: 78rpm

PRESTIGE 4-8 50-51

Singles: 7-inch

PRESTIGE (700 series) 5-10 50-51
(Black vinyl.)
PRESTIGE (700 series) 10-20 50-51
(Colored vinyl.)

EPs: 7-inch 33/45rpm

PRESTIGE 25-50 51

LPs: 10/12-inch 33rpm

ARGO 15-25 63
CADET 10-20 67
CHESS 15-25 60

PRESTIGE (107 "Gene Ammons") 60-100 51
(10–inch LP.)
PRESTIGE (112 "Gene Ammons with Sonny Stitt") 60-100 51
(10–inch LP.)
PRESTIGE (127 "The Gene Ammons Band") 60-100 52
(10–inch LP.)
PRESTIGE (149 "The Gene Ammons Quartet") 50-100 51
(10–inch LP.)
PRESTIGE (7600 series) 6-10 69
PRESTIGE (10000 series) 5-10 76
VERVE (8400 series) 15-20 61-62
(Reads "MGM Records - a Division of Metro-Goldwyn-Mayer, Inc." at bottom of label.)
VERVE (8800 series) 8-12 72
(Reads "Manufactured By MGM Record Corp.," or mentions either Polydor or Polygram at bottom of label.)
Also see AMMONS, Gene

AMOS & ANDY

P&R '29

Singles: 78rpm

VICTOR 20-30 29

AMUZEMENT PARK
(Amusement Park Band)

R&B '82

Singles: 7–inch

ATLANTIC 3-4 84-85
OUR GANG 3-4 82-83

LPs: 10/12–inch 33rpm

ATLANTIC 5-10 84
Members: Paul Richmond; Darryl Ellis; Aaron Jamal; Norval Hodges; Fred Entesari; Reuben Locke Jr.; Rico McFarland.

ANA

P&R '87

Singles: 7–inch

PARC 3-4 87-90

Picture Sleeves

PARC 3-4 87

ANACOSTIA

R&B '72

Singles: 7–inch

COLUMBIA 3-5 72-75
MCA 3-4 77
ROULETTE 3-4 84
TABU 3-4 78-79

LPs: 10/12–inch 33rpm

MCA 5-10 77
TABU 5-10 78

ANDERSEN, Eric

LP '72

Singles: 7–inch

ARISTA 3-4 75-77
COLUMBIA 3-4 72
W.B. 3-4 68-71

LPs: 10/12–inch 33rpm

ARISTA 5-10 75-77
COLUMBIA 8-10 72
VANGUARD 15-20 65-70
W.B. 10-15 68-70

ANDERSON, Bill
(With the Po' Folks; with Jordanaires; Whispering Bill Anderson)

C&W '58

Singles: 12–inch 33/45rpm

MCA 4-8 78

Singles: 7–inch

DECCA (30000 series) 5-10 58-59
DECCA (31000 series) 4-8 60-66
DECCA (32000 & 33000 series) 3-6 67-72
MCA 3-4 73-81
SOUTHERN TRACKS 3-4 82-87
SWANEE 3-4 85
TNT 4-6 59

Picture Sleeves

DECCA 4-8 63-69

EPs: 7–inch 33/45rpm

DECCA 5-10 63-65

LPs: 10/12–inch 33rpm

CORAL 4-6 73
DECCA (4192 thru 4686) 15-20 62-65
DECCA (4771 thru 5344) 10-15 66-72
(Decca LP numbers in this series preceded by a "7" or a "DL-7" are stereo issues.)
DECCA (7100 series) 15-20 69
DECCA (7200 series) 10-12 72
EPIC 5-10 82-85
MCA 5-10 73-80
SOUTHERN TRACKS 5-10 84
VOCALION 8-12 68-71
Session: Jordanaires.
Also see COE, David Allan, & Bill Anderson
Also see KERR, Anita

ANDERSON, Bill, & Jan Howard

C&W '66

Singles: 7–inch

DECCA 3-5 66-71
Also see HOWARD, Jan

ANDERSON, Bill, & Mary Lou Turner

C&W '78

Singles: 7–inch

MCA 3-5 78
Also see ANDERSON, Bill

ANDERSON, Carl

R&B '84

Singles: 12–inch 33/45rpm

EPIC 4-6 82-86

Singles: 7–inch

EPIC 3-4 82-86

LPs: 10/12–inch 33rpm

EPIC 5-10 82-86
Also see LORING, Gloria, & Carl Anderson

ANDERSON, Elton

P&R/R&B '60

Singles: 7-inch

CAPITOL 4-8 62
LANOR 4-8 63
MERCURY 8-12 59-61
VIN 10-20 58

ANDERSON, Ernestine

LP '58

Singles: 7-inch

MERCURY 3-4 60-62
SUE 3-4 63-64

EPs: 7-inch 33/45rpm

MERCURY 5-10 59

LPs: 10/12-inch 33rpm

MERCURY 15-25 58-60
OMEGA DISK 10-15 59
SUE 10-15 63
WING 10-15 64

ANDERSON, Jesse

P&R/R&B '70

Singles: 7-inch

CADET 4-6 67-68
JEWEL 3-5 72
OUTTA CYTE (100 "Oh Wow Man") 8-12
THOMAS 3-5 70

ANDERSON, John

C&W '77

Singles: 7-inch

ACE of HEARTS 4-6 74
MCA 3-4 87
W.B. 3-5 77-87

LPs: 10/12-inch 33rpm

W.B. 5-8 77-87

Session: Waylon Jennings.
Also see HAGGARD, Merle
Also see HARRIS, Emmylou
Also see JENNINGS, Waylon

ANDERSON, Jon

LP '76

Singles: 12-inch 33/45rpm

ATLANTIC 4-6 82

Singles: 7-inch

ATLANTIC 3-5 76-82
COLUMBIA 3-4 88
ELEKTRA (Except 69580) 3-4 84-85
ELEKTRA (69580 "Save All Your Love) 3-4 85
(Black vinyl.)
ELEKTRA (69580 "Save All Your Love) 4-8 85
(Colored vinyl, special Christmas edition.)

LPs: 10/12-inch 33rpm

ATLANTIC 5-10 76-82
COLUMBIA 5-10 88
ELEKTRA 5-10 85

Promotional LPs

ATLANTIC ("An Evening with Jon Anderson") 20-30 76
(Jon Anderson interviews, and music from his *Olias of Sunhillow* LP, as well as selections by Yes.Number not known.)
Also see JON & VANGELIS
Also see TANGERINE DREAM / Jon Anderson / Bryan Ferry
Also see YES

ANDERSON, Lale

P&R '61

Singles: 7-inch

KING 3-6 61-62

LPs: 10/12-inch 33rpm

UNIVERSE 5-15 61

ANDERSON, Laurie

LP '82

Singles: 12-inch 33/45rpm

W.B. 4-6 81

Singles: 7-inch

W.B. 3-4 81-89

EPs: 7-inch 33/45rpm

W.B. 3-5 81

LPs: 10/12-inch 33rpm

W.B. (Except 25192) 5-10 82-89
W.B. (25192 "United States Live") 35-45 85
(Five-LP set.)
Also see GLASS, Philip

ANDERSON, Leroy
(With His Pops Concert Orchestra)

P&R '51

Singles: 78rpm

DECCA 3-5 51-57

Singles: 7-inch

DECCA 3-6 51-62

EPs: 7-inch 33/45rpm

DECCA 5-10 51-58

LPs: 10/12-inch 33rpm

DECCA 12-25 51-63
MGM 10-20 62

ANDERSON, Liz & Lynn

C&W '68

Singles: 7-inch

RCA 3-6 68

Also see ANDERSON, Lynn

ANDERSON, Lynn

C&W '66

Singles: 7-inch

CHART 3-5 66-71
COLUMBIA 3-4 70-80
MERCURY 3-4 86-89
PERMIAN 3-4 83
RCA 3-5 68

Picture Sleeves

COLUMBIA 3-6 70-72

EPs: 7–inch 33/45rpm

COLUMBIA 4-8 72
(Promotional only.)

LPs: 10/12–inch 33rpm

ALBUM GLOBE 5-10 76
CHART (Except 1050) 8-15 67-71
CHART (1050 "Lynn Anderson")10-20 72
COLUMBIA 6-10 70-80
HARMONY................................ 5-10 71-73
MOUNTAIN DEW........................ 5-10
PERMIAN.................................. 5-10 83
PICKWICK 5-10
TIME-LIFE................................ 5-10 81
Session: Jordanaires.
Also see ANDERSON, Liz, & Lynn

ANDERSON, Lynn, & Jerry Lane

C&W '67

Singles: 7–inch

CHART...................................... 3-5 67

ANDERSON, Lynn, & Gary Morris

C&W '83

Singles: 7–inch

PERMIAN.................................. 3-4 83
Also see ANDERSON, Lynn
Also see MORRIS, Gary

ANDERSON, Michael

LP '88

Singles: 7–inch

A&M 3-4 88

LPs: 10/12–inch 33rpm

A&M 5-8 88

ANDERSON, Roshell

R&B '73

Singles: 7–inch

EXCELLO.................................. 3-5 71
SUNBURST 3-5 73-74

ANDERSON, Vicki
(Vikki Anderson; Vickie Anderson)

Singles: 7–inch

BROWNSTONE......................... 3-5 71-72
DELUXE.................................... 4-8 66
FONTANA.................................. 4-8 64
KING 3-6 66-70
SMASH 4-8 65
TUFF 3-6 67
Also see BROWN, James, & Vickie Anderson

ANDREA TRUE CONNECTION: see TRUE, Andrea

ANDREWS, Chris

P&R '66

Singles: 7–inch

ATCO 4-8 66
RCA.. 3-6 69

ANDREWS, Inez
(With the Andrewettes)

R&B '73

Singles: 7–inch

MCA...3-4 84
SONG BIRD.................................3-4 64-73

LPs: 10/12–inch 33rpm

MCA...5-10 84
SAVOY.......................................5-10 80-81

ANDREWS, Julie

P&R '62

Singles: 7–inch

BUENA VISTA 3-6 65
COLUMBIA..................................3-5 67
DECCA 3-5 67
LONDON.....................................3-6 60
RCA 3-4 70

Picture Sleeves

BUENA VISTA 4-8 65

EPs: 7–inch 33/45rpm

RCA 10-20 56

LPs: 10/12–inch 33rpm

ANGEL......................................15-25 58
COLUMBIA (1700 & 8500
series)......................................15-25 62
COLUMBIA (31000 series).........8-12 72
HARMONY..................................8-10 70-72
RCA (1000 series) 8-12 70
RCA (1400 thru 1600 series).....20-30 56-58
RCA (3800 series) 8-15 67
20TH FOX...................................8-15 68

ANDREWS, Julie, & Carol Burnett

LP '62

LPs: 10/12–inch 33rpm

COLUMBIA (2200 & 5800
series)......................................15-25 62
COLUMBIA (31000 series) 8-15 72
Also see BURNETT, Carol

ANDREWS, Julie, & Andre Previn / Vic Damone / Jack Jones / Marian Anderson

EPs: 7–inch 33/45rpm

RCA (277 "We Wish You a Merry
Christmas") 3-5 69
(Radio Shack Special Collector's Edition.)
Also see ANDREWS, Julie
Also see DAMONE, Vic
Also see JONES, Jack
Also see PREVIN, Andre

ANDREWS, Lee
(With the Hearts; with Pancho Villa Orchestra)

P&R/R&B '57

Singles: 78rpm

ARGO 10-20 57
CHESS......................................10-20 57
GOTHAM 25-50 56
MAIN LINE 30-60 57
RAINBOW.............................100-200 54

Singles: 7-inch

ARGO....................................... 20-35 57

CASINO (110 "Baby, Come Back")................................... 20-30 58

CASINO (452 "Try the Impossible") 400-500 58
(Red and white label, with playing cards at top.)

CASINO (452 "Try the Impossible") 100-150 58
(Black label.)

CHESS (1665 "Long Lonely Nights") 15-20 57
(Silver top label with chess pieces.)

CHESS (1665 "Long Lonely Nights") 5-10
(Blue label.)

CHESS (1675 "Teardrops") 15-20 57
(Silver top label with chess pieces.)

CHESS (1675 "Teardrops") 5-10
(Blue label.)

CHESS (9000 series).................. 3-5

COLLECTABLES 3-4 82

CRIMSON 4-8 67-68

GOTHAM (318 "Bluebird of Happiness")........................ 100-125 56

GOTHAM (320 "Lonely Room") 100-125 56

GOTHAM (321 "Just Suppose") 100-125 56

GOWEN 5-10 61

GRAND 5-8 62

JORDAN 15-25 60

LANA... 3-6 64

LOST-NITE 3-5 65

MAIN LINE (102 "Long Lonely Nights") 150-200 57
(Green label.)

MAIN LINE (102 "Long Lonely Nights") 100-150 57
(Black label, with Philadelphia address shown.)

MAIN LINE (102 "Long Lonely Nights") 15-25 62
(Black label, no address shown.)

MAIN LINE (105 "Teardrops")..... 8-10 62

PARKWAY 5-8 62-63

RAINBOW (252 "Maybe You'll Be There") 250-350 54
(Black vinyl.)

RAINBOW (252 "Maybe You'll Be There") 500-750 54
(Colored vinyl. Print is small, with the title line being about 1 1/2" long.)

RAINBOW (252 "Maybe You'll Be There") 8-12 62
(Colored vinyl. Print is noticeably larger than on 1954 issue.)

RAINBOW (256 "White Cliffs of Dover")...............................500-750 54
(Yellow label.)

RAINBOW (256 "White Cliffs of Dover")....................................8-12 62
(Blue label.)

RAINBOW (259 "The Bells of St. Mary's")...............................250-300 54
(Yellow label.)

RAINBOW (259 "The Bells of St. Mary's")...................................8-12 62
(Blue label.)

RCA 5-10 66

SWAN (4065 "I Miss You So") .75-125 60

SWAN (4076 "A Night Like This")..............................100-150 61

SWAN (4076 "P.S. I Love You")..................................150-200 61

U.A. (100 series).......................10-20 58-59

U.A. (500 series)..........................5-10 63

LPs: 10/12-inch 33rpm

COLLECTABLES...........................6-8 82-85

LOST-NITE (1 "Lee Andrews and the Hearts")..............................8-10 81
(Colored vinyl 10-inch LP.)

LOST-NITE (2 "Lee Andrews and the Hearts")..............................8-10 81
(Colored vinyl 10-inch LP.)

LOST-NITE (100 series) 10-20 65

POST 10-15 70s

Members: Lee Andrews; Arthur Thompson; Roy Calhoun; Wendell Calhoun; Butch Curry; Ted Weems.

ANDREWS, Patty

P&R '49

Singles: 78rpm

CAPITOL......................................3-5 55-56

DECCA 4-8 50-54

Singles: 7-inch

CAPITOL......................................4-8 55-56

DECCA 5-10 50-54

Also see ANDREWS SISTERS

ANDREWS, Ruby

P&R/R&B '67

Singles: 7-inch

ABC...3-5 76-77

ZODIAC 4-6 67-71

LPs: 10/12-inch 33rpm

ABC...8-10 77

ZODIAC 10-15 72

Also see STACKHOUSE, Ruby

ANDREWS SISTERS

P&R '38

Singles: 78rpm

CAPITOL......................................3-5 56

DECCA 5-10 38-57

Singles: 7-inch

ABC...3-4 74

CAPITOL.. 4-8 56
DECCA.. 5-10 50-57
DOT.. 3-5 64
KAPP.. 3-6 59
PARAMOUNT 3-4 73-74

Picture Sleeves

DECCA.. 5-10 57

EPs: 7–inch 33/45rpm

DECCA.. 5-15 51-58

LPs: 10/12–inch 33rpm

ABC.. 5-10 74
CAPITOL.. 5-10 64
DECCA (4000 series)................. 8-12 67
(Decca LP numbers in this series preceded by a "7" or a "DL-7" are stereo issues.)
DECCA (5000 series)............... 20-40 49-54
(10–inch LPs.)
DECCA (8000 series)............... 15-25 55-58
DOT.. 6-12 61-67
HAMILTON.. 5-10 64-65
MCA 8-12 73
PARAMOUNT 5-10 73-74

Members: Patty Andrews; Maxene Andrews; Laverne Andrews.
Also see ANDREWS, Patty
Also see CROSBY, Bing
Also see FOLEY, Red, & Andrews Sisters
Also see MIRANDA, Carmen, & Andrews Sisters
Also see PAUL, Les

ANDREWS SISTERS & Ernest Tubb
(With the Texas Troubadors)

C&W '49

Singles: 78rpm

DECCA.. 5-8 49

Also see ANDREWS SISTERS
Also see TUBB, Ernest

ANGEL

LP '75

Singles: 7–inch

CASABLANCA.. 3-4 75-80

LPs: 10/12–inch 33rpm

CASABLANCA.. 5-10 75-80

Members: Barry Brandt; Frank DiMino; Greg Giuffria; Mickey Jones; Punky Meadows; Felix Robinson.
Also see CHERRY PEOPLE
Also see GIUFFRIA
Also see WILSON, Carl

ANGEL, Johnny T: see JOHNNY T. ANGEL

ANGEL CITY

LP '80

Singles: 7–inch

EPIC.. 3-4 80-82

LPs: 10/12–inch 33rpm

EPIC.. 5-10 80-82
MCA 5-10 85

Members: Doc Neeson; Rick Brewster; John Brewster.

ANGELA

D&D '85

Singles: 12–inch 33/45rpm

SUTRA.. 4-6 85

ANGELIC GOSPEL SINGERS

R&B '49

Singles: 78rpm

GOTHAM 5-10 49

ANGELS

P&R '61

Singles: 7–inch

ASCOT.. 5-8 63
CAPRICE 5-10 61-62
COLLECTABLES.. 3-4 82
ERIC 3-4 74
POLYDOR 3-5 74
RCA 5-8 67-68
SMASH 4-8 63-64

Picture Sleeves

SMASH (1854 "I Adore Him") 10-15 63

LPs: 10/12–inch 33rpm

ASCOT (13009 "The Angels Sing 12 of Their Greatest Hits").......20-30 64
(Monaural.)
ASCOT (16009 "The Angels Sing 12 of Their Greatest Hits").......30-40 64
(Stereo.)
CAPRICE (LP-1001 "And the Angels Sing") 40-50 62
(Monaural.)
CAPRICE (SLP-1001 "And the Angels Sing") 50-75 62
(Stereo.)
COLLECTABLES..........................5-8 80s
SMASH (27039 "My Boyfriend's Back") 30-40 63
(Monaural.)
SMASH (67039 "My Boyfriend's Back") 50-75 63
(Stereo.)
SMASH (27048 "A Halo to You")......................................30-40 63
(Monaural.)
SMASH (67048 "A Halo to You")......................................40-60 63
(Stereo.)

Members: Linda Jansen; Barbara Allbut; Phyllis "Jiggs" Allbut; Peggy Santaglia.
Also see DUSK
Also see SEDAKA, Neil, & Tokens / Angels / Jimmy Gilmer & Fireballs
Also see STARLETS

ANIMAL LOGIC

LP '89

LPs: 10/12–inch 33rpm

I.R.S. 5-8 89

ANIMALS

(Eric Burdon & the Animals; Original Animals)

P&R '64

Singles: 7–inch

ABKCO ... 3-4 75
COLLECTABLES ... 3-4 82
I.R.S. ... 3-4 83
JET ... 3-4 77
MGM ... 5-10 64-71
MGM CELEBRITY SCENE ("The Animals") ... 35-45 66
(Boxed set of five singles with bio insert and title strips.)

Picture Sleeves

MGM (13264 "House of the Rising Sun") ... 10-20 64
MGM (13274 "I'm Crying") ... 10-15 64
MGM (13298 "Boom Boom") ... 10-15 64
MGM (13339 "Bring It on Home to Me") ... 8-12 65
MGM (13769 "San Franciscan Nights") ... 5-10 67
MGM (13868 "Monterey") ... 5-10 67

LPs: 10/12–inch 33rpm

ABKCO ... 8-12 73-76
ACCORD ... 5-10 82
I.R.S. ... 5-10 83-85
MGM ... 15-30 64-69
PICKWICK ... 5-10 71
SCEPTER/CITATION ... 5-10 76
SPRINGBOARD ... 5-10 72
U.A. ... 5-10 77
WAND ... 8-12 70

Members: Eric Burdon; Alan Price; Hilton Valentine; Chas Chandler; John Steel; John Weider.

Also see BURDON, Eric
Also see PRICE, Alan
Also see WEIDER, John

ANIMOTION

D&D '84

Singles: 12–inch 33/45rpm

MERCURY ... 4-6 84-85

Singles: 7–inch

CASABLANCA ... 3-4 86
MERCURY ... 3-4 84-85
POLYDOR ... 3-4 89

Picture Sleeves

CASABLANCA ... 3-4 86
MERCURY ... 3-4 84-85
POLYDOR ... 3-4 89

LPs: 10/12–inch 33rpm

CASABLANCA ... 5-10 86
MERCURY ... 5-10 84-85
POLYDOR ... 5-8 89

Members: Astrid Plane; Bill Wadhams; Paul Engemann; Cynthia Rhodes; Charles Ottavio.

Also see DEVICE

ANITA & So-And-So's

(Anita Kerr Singers)

P&R '62

Singles: 7–inch

RCA ... 5-8 62

Also see KERR, Anita

ANKA, Paul

(With the Don Costa Orchestra)

P&R/R&B '57

Singles: 78rpm

ABC-PAR ... 10-20 57
RPM ... 10-20 56

Singles: 12–inch 33/45rpm

COLUMBIA ... 4-6 83

Singles: 7–inch

ABC-PAR (104 "Share Your Love") ... 15-25 58
(Promotional, fan club issue.)
ABC-PAR (296-1 "My Heart Sings") ... 25-35 58
(Stereo Compact 33 Single.)
ABC-PAR (9831 thru 9956) ... 10-15 57-58
ABC-PAR (9987 "My Heart Sings") ... 8-12 58
(Monaural.)
ABC-PAR (9987 "My Heart Sings") ... 20-30 58
(Stereo.)
ABC-PAR (10011 "I Miss You So") ... 8-12 59
(Monaural.)
ABC-PAR (S-10011 "I Miss You So") ... 20-30 59
(Stereo.)
ABC-PAR (10022 "Lonely Boy") ... 8-12 59
(Monaural.)
ABC-PAR (S-10022 "Lonely Boy") ... 20-30 59
(Stereo.)
ABC-PAR (10040 "Put Your Head on My Shoulder") ... 8-12 59
(Monaural.)
ABC-PAR (S-10040 "Put Your Head on My Shoulder") ... 20-30 59
ABC-PAR (10064 "Time to Cry") ... 8-12 59
(Monaural.)
ABC-PAR (S-10064 "Time to Cry") ... 20-30 59
(Stereo.)
ABC-PAR (10082 "Puppy Love") ... 5-10 60
(Monaural.)
ABC-PAR (S-10082 "Puppy Love") ... 20-30 60
(Stereo.)
ABC-PAR (10106 "My Home Town") ... 5-10 60
(Monaural.)

ABC-PAR (S-10106 "My Home Town") 20-30 60
(Stereo.)
ABC-PAR (10132 "Hello Young Lovers") 5-10 60
(Monaural.)
ABC-PAR (10132 "Hello Young Lovers") 20-30 60
(Stereo.)
ABC-PAR (10147 "Summer's Gone") 5-10 60
(Monaural.)
ABC-PAR (S-10147 "Summer's Gone") 20-30 60
(Stereo.)
ABC-PAR (10168 "The Story of My Love") 5-10 61
(Monaural.)
ABC-PAR (S-10168 "The Story of My Love") 20-30 61
(Stereo.)
ABC-PAR (10194 thru 10338)..... 5-10 61-62
BARNABY 3-5 71
BUDDAH 3-5 72-78
COLUMBIA 3-4 83-85
ERIC.. 3-5 74
FAME 3-5 73
RCA (Except 2000, 8000, 9000 and 10000 series) 3-8 67-79
RCA (2000 series)..................... 10-20 62
(With "VLP" or "VP" prefix. Stereo Compact 33 series.)
RCA (37-7977 "Love Me Warm and Tender") 15-25 62
(Compact 33 Single.)
RCA (47-7977 "Love Me Warm and Tender") 5-10 62
RCA (8000 series, except 8893). 5-10 62-66
RCA (8893 "I Can't Help Lovin' You") 15-25 66
RCA (9000 series)...................... 5-10 67-69
RCA (10000 series)..................... 3-4 78-81
RPM (472 "I Confess")............. 25-35 56
RPM (499 "I Confess")............. 20-35 56
U.A. 3-4 75-77

Picture Sleeves

ABC-PAR (Except 9956)........... 12-25 58-61
ABC-PAR (9956 "Just Young") . 50-75 58
COLUMBIA 3-4 83
ERIC.. 3-4 74
RCA (Except 11000 series)......... 5-10 62-65
RCA (11000 series)..................... 3-4 78
U.A. 3-5 75

EPs: 7–inch 33/45rpm

ABC.. 12-15 60s
(Jukebox issue only.)
ABC-PAR 25-35 59
SIRE.. 10-12 74
(Jukebox issue only.)

LPs: 10/12–inch 33rpm

ABC-PAR (ABC-240 "Paul Anka") 25-35 58
(Monaural.)
ABC-PAR (ABCS-240 "Paul Anka") 35-50 58
(Stereo.)
ABC-PAR (ABC-296 "My Heart Sings") 25-35 59
(Monaural.)
ABC-PAR (ABCS-296 "My Heart Sings") 35-45 59
(Stereo.)
ABC-PAR (ABC-323 "Big 15") ...25-35 60
(Monaural.)
ABC-PAR (ABCS-323 "Big 15") .35-45 60
(Stereo.)
ABC-PAR (ABC-347 "For Young Lovers") 25-30 60
(Monaural.)
ABC-PAR (ABCS 347 "For Young Lovers") 30-35 60
(Stereo.)
ABC-PAR (ABC-353 "Anka at the Copa")..............................25-30 60
(Monaural.)
ABC-PAR (ABCS-353 "Anka at the Copa")..............................30-35 60
(Stereo.)
ABC-PAR (ABC-360 "It's Christmas Everywhere") 25-30 60
(Monaural.)
ABC-PAR (ABCS-360 "It's Christmas Everywhere") 30-35 60
(Stereo.)
ABC-PAR (ABC-371 "Strictly Instrumental")..........................20-30 61
(Monaural.)
ABC-PAR (ABCS-371 "Strictly Instrumental")..........................25-35 61
(Stereo.)
ABC-PAR (ABC-390 "His Big 15 Vol. 2") 20-30 61
(Monaural.)
ABC-PAR (ABCS-390 "His Big 15, Vol. 2") 25-35 61
(Stereo.)
ABC-PAR (ABC-409 "His Big 15, Vol. 3") 20-30 62
(Monaural.)
ABC-PAR (ABCS-409 "His Big 15, Vol. 3") 25-35 62
(Stereo.)
ABC-PAR (ABC-420 "Diana")....20-30 62
(Monaural.)
ABC-PAR (ABCS-420 "Diana")..25-30 62
(Stereo.)
ACCORD 5-10 81
BUDDAH....................................5-10 71-76

CAMDEN 5-10 74
COLUMBIA 5-10 83-85
LIBERTY 5-10 81-83
PICKWICK 5-10 75
RCA (Except "LPM" & "LSP" series) 5-10 75-81
RCA (2000 thru 4000" series) ... 10-25 62-70
(With "LPM" prefix. Monaural.)
RCA (2000 thru 4000" series) ... 15-30 62-70
(With "LSP" prefix. Stereo.)
RANWOOD 5-10 81
RIVERA (0047 "Paul Anka and Others") 25-40 63
(Has two tracks by Paul Anka.)
RHINO 5-10 86
SIRE 10-12 74-78
U.A. 5-10 74-78

Also see ANN-MARGRET
Also see COSTA, Don, Orchestra
Also see MARLO, Micki

ANKA, Paul, & Odia Coates

P&R '74

Singles: 12–inch 33/45rpm

EPIC 4-6 77

Singles: 7–inch

EPIC 3-4 76
U.A. 3-4 74-75

Also see COATES, Odia

ANKA, Paul / Sam Cooke / Neil Sedaka

LPs: 10/12–inch 33rpm

RCA 15-20 64

Also see COOKE, Sam
Also see SEDAKA, Neil

ANKA, Paul, & Karla DeVito

Singles: 12–inch 33/45rpm

COLUMBIA 4-6 83

Singles: 7–inch

COLUMBIA 3-4 83

ANKA, Paul, George Hamilton IV & Johnny Nash

P&R '58

Singles: 7–inch

ABC-PAR 5-10 58

Also see ANKA, Paul
Also see HAMILTON, George
Also see NASH, Johnny

ANNETTE

(Annette Funicello; with the Afterbeats; with Upbeats)

P&R '59

Singles: 78rpm

DISNEYLAND (102 "How Will I Know") 15-25 58

Singles: 7–inch

BUENA VISTA (336, "Jo-Jo the Dog Faced Boy"/"Lonely Guitar") 10-15 59
BUENA VISTA (336, "Jo-Jo the Dog Faced Boy"/"Love Me Forever").......... 8-15 59
(Note different flip side.)
BUENA VISTA (339 thru 354)...... 8-15 59-60
BUENA VISTA (359 thru 407).... 15-25 60-62
BUENA VISTA (414 "Teenage Wedding") 20-30 63
BUENA VISTA (427 thru 436).... 15-25 63-64
BUENA VISTA (337 "The Wah Watusi") 10-15 64
BUENA VISTA (438 "Something Borrowed") 15-25 65
BUENA VISTA (440 "The Monkey's Uncle") 10-20 65
(With the Beach Boys.)
BUENA VISTA (442 thru 475).... 10-15 65-66
DISNEYLAND 8-10 57-58
JUGGY 8-10
STARVIEW 5-10 83
TOWER (326 "What's a Girl to Do") 20-25 67
(Name misspelled, shown as "Annettte.")

Picture Sleeves

BUENA VISTA (339 thru 354).... 10-20 59-60
BUENA VISTA (359 thru 407, except 384) 20-30 60-62
BUENA VISTA (384 "Blue Muu Muu") 40-60 62
BUENA VISTA (414 "Teenage Wedding") 50-100 63
BUENA VISTA (427 "Promise Me Anything") 40-60 63
BUENA VISTA (431 thru 436).... 15-30 64
BUENA VISTA (437 "The Wah Watusi") 10-15 64
BUENA VISTA (438 "Something Borrowed") 20-30 65
BUENA VISTA (440 "The Monkey's Uncle") 15-25 65
BUENA VISTA (442 thru 475).... 10-15 65-66
DISNEYLAND 25-35 58

EPs: 7–inch 33/45rpm

BUENA VISTA (3301 "Annette") 40-60 59
DISNEYLAND (04 "Tall Paul") ... 30-40 58
DISNEYLAND (69 "Mickey Mouse Club Featuring Annette") 35-45 58

LPs: 10/12–inch 33rpm

BUENA VISTA (3301 "Annette") 35-50 59
BUENA VISTA (3302 "Annette Sings Anka") 35-50 60
(With bonus color photo.)
BUENA VISTA (3302 "Annette Sings Anka") 30-35 60
(Without bonus photo.)
BUENA VISTA (3303 thru 3508) 25-40 60-64
BUENA VISTA (4037 "Annette Funicello") 15-25 72

DISNEYLAND (Except 3906).... 15-30 62-75
(Includes numerous Mouseketeer cast albums that involve or feature Annette.)
DISNEYLAND (3906 "Snow White—As Told By Annette") 20-40
MICKEY MOUSE (12 thru 24)... 35-50 57-58
(Includes numerous Mouseketeer cast albums that involve or feature Annette.)
RHINO (Except 702) 8-10 84
RHINO (702 "Best of Annette"). 12-15 84
(Picture disc.)
SILHOUETTE.......................... 10-15 81
STARVIEW (4001 "Country Album") 8-12 84
(Standard issue.)
STARVIEW (4001 "Country Album") 15-20 84
(Limited edition series.)
Session: Davie Allan.
Also see ALLAN, Davie
Also see AVALON, Frankie, & Annette
Also see BEACH BOYS

ANNETTE / Jimmy Dodd

Singles: 78rpm

DISNEYLAND (758 "How Will I Know"/"Annette")................... 15-25 58
(10–inch single.)
DISNEYLAND (758 "How Will I Know"/"Annette")................... 20-30 58
(Five–inch single.)

Picture Sleeves

DISNEYLAND (758 "How Will I Know"/"Annette")................... 20-40 58

ANNETTE / Hayley Mills

LPs: 10/12–inch 33rpm

BUENA VISTA/DISNEYLAND (3508 "Annette & Hayley Mills") 300-400 64
(Cover reads Buena Vista but label is Disneyland. Issued with paper cover. TV mail order offer. One side by each artist.)
Also see MILLS, Hayley

ANNETTE & Tommy Sands

Singles: 7–inch

BUENA VISTA (802 "The Parent Trap") 10-20 61
(45 single.)
BUENA VISTA (802 "The Parent Trap") 25-35 61
(Compact 33 Single.)

Picture Sleeves

BUENA VISTA (802 "The Parent Trap") 20-30 61
Also see ANNETTE
Also see SANDS, Tommy

ANNIE G.

D&D '84

Singles: 12–inch 33/45rpm

MCA 4-6 84

Singles: 7–inch

MCA 3-4 84

ANN-MARGRET

P&R '61

Singles: 12–inch 33/45rpm

AVCO EMBASSY (4547 Today") 10-15 70
FIRST AMERICAN (1207 "Everybody Needs Somebody Sometime")............. 5-10 81
MCA (1867 "Midnight Message"). 5-10 80
(Promotional issue only.)
MCA (1867 "What I Do to Men").. 5-10 80
OCEAN/ARIOLA AMERICA........... 4-8 79-80
RAM (1001 "Everybody Needs Somebody Sometime") 5-10 81
RAM 4-8 81

Singles: 7–inch

FIRST AMERICAN........................ 3-5 81
MCA 3-5 79-80
OCEAN/ARIOLA AMERICA........... 3-5 79-80
RCA (VLP-2251 "Vivacious One").................................... 30-50 62
(Five-disc, jukebox set. With title strips.)
RCA (37-7857 "Lost Love")........ 15-25 61
(Compact 33 Single.)
RCA (47-7857 "Lost Love").......... 5-10 61
RCA (37-7894 "I Just Don't Understand")................... 15-25 61
(Compact 33 Single.)
RCA (47-7894 "I Just Don't Understand") 5-10 61
RCA (37-7952 "It Do Me So Good") 15-25 61
(Compact 33 Single.)
RCA (47-7952 "It Do Me So Good").. 5-10 61
RCA (7986 thru 9109)................. 5-10 61-66

Picture Sleeves

RCA (7894 "I Just Don't Understand") 10-15 61
RCA (7952 "It Do Me So Good") 10-15 61
RCA (7986 "What Am I Supposed to Do")..................... 10-20 61
RCA (8061 "Jim Dandy") 15-20 62
RCA (8168 "Bye Bye Birdie")..... 15-25 63

EPs: 7–inch 33/45rpm

RCA (2251 "The Vivacious One")... 15-25 62
RCA (2659 "Mr. Wonderful")...... 15-25 63
RCA (4358 "On the Way Up").... 15-25 62
RCA (9058 "On the Way Up").... 15-25 62

LPs: 10/12–inch 33rpm

LHI 12-15 68-69
LAGNIAPPE 1959 ("Be My Guest")................................ 100-200 59
(Cast LP produced by the Boys Tri-Ship

Club of New Trier High School. Includes *Tropical Heat Wave* by Ann-Margret Olson.)
MCA 5-10 80
NORTHWESTERN UNIVERSITY/RCA (5760 "Among Friends")........ 50-100 60
(Cast LP for the *Waa-Mu Show of 1960* from Northwestern University. Lists Ann-Margret Olson as a dancer.)
RCA (LPM-2399 "And Here She Is") 10-20 61
(Monaural.)
RCA (LSP-2399 "And Here She Is") 15-25 61
(Stereo.)
RCA (LPM-2453 "On the Way Up") 10-20 62
(Monaural.)
RCA (LSP-2453 "On the Way Up") 15-25 62
(Stereo.)
RCA (LPM-2251 "Vivacious One") 10-20 62
(Monaural.)
RCA (LSP-2251 "Vivacious One") 15-25 62
(Stereo.)
RCA (LPM-2659 "Bachelor's Paradise") 10-20 63
(Monaural.)
RCA (LSP-2659 "Bachelor's Paradise") 15-25 63
(Stereo.)
RCA/NARM ("Tenth Anniversary Convention") 40-60 68
(Has *Bye Bye Birdie* by Ann-Margret, plus tracks by the Limeliters, Al Hirt, Paul Anka, Homer & Jethro, Peter Nero, Eddy Arnold, John Gary, Chet Atkins, Floyd Cramer, Anita Kerr Singers, Boots Randolph, Myron Cohen, Barry Sadler, Henry Mancini, Jack Jones, and Harry Belafonte. Promotional, souvenir issue only.)
Also see ANKA, Paul
Also see ARNOLD, Eddy
Also see ATKINS, Chet
Also see BELAFONTE, Harry
Also see COHEN, Myron
Also see CRAMER, Floyd
Also see HOMER & JETHRO
Also see JONES, Jack
Also see KERR, Anita
Also see LIMELITERS
Also see MANCINI, Henry
Also see NERO, Peter
Also see RANDOLPH, Boots
Also see SADLER, Barry

ANN-MARGRET & John Gary

LP '64

LPs: 10/12-inch 33rpm

RCA (LPM-2947 "Broadway Hits") 10-20 64
(Monaural.)
RCA (LSP-2947 "Broadway Hits") 15-25 64
(Stereo.)
Also see GARY, John

ANN-MARGRET & Lee Hazlewood

Singles: 7-inch

LHI 4-6 68-69

LPs: 10/12-inch 33rpm

LHI (12007 "The Cowboy and the Lady") 15-20 69
Also see HAZLEWOOD, Lee

ANN-MARGRET & Al Hirt

Singles: 7-inch

RCA (VLP-2690 "Beauty and the Beard") 25-50 64
(Five-disc, jukebox set. With title strips.)
RCA (9524 "Slowly") 5-10 68

EPs: 7-inch 33/45rpm

RCA (LSP-2690 "Beauty and the Beard") 15-25 64

LPs: 10/12-inch 33rpm

RCA (LPM-2690 "Beauty and the Beard") 10-20 64
(Monaural.)
RCA (LSP-2690 "Beauty and the Beard") 15-25 64
(Stereo.)
Also see HIRT, Al

ANN-MARGRET / Kitty Kalen / Della Reese

LPs: 10/12-inch 33rpm

RCA (2724 "3 Great Girls") 15-20 63
Also see ANN-MARGRET
Also see KALEN, Kitty
Also see REESE, Della

ANOTHER BAD CREATION

LP '91

LPs: 10/12-inch 33rpm

MOTOWN 5-8 91

ANT, Adam

LP '82

Singles: 12-inch 33/45rpm

EPIC 4-6 82-85

Singles: 7-inch

EPIC 3-4 82-85

Picture Sleeves

EPIC 3-4 84

LPs: 10/12-inch 33rpm

EPIC 5-10 82-85
MCA 5-8 90
Also see ADAM & ANTS

ANTELL, Peter
(Pete Antell)

P&R '62

Singles: 7-inch

BOUNTY (103 "The Times They Are a-Changin'" 15-25 65
CAMEO 5-10 62-63

ANTHONY, Alan

R&B '82

Singles: 7-inch

CHALET 3-4 82

ANTHONY, Markus

R&B '86

Singles: 7-inch

ROCK & ROLL 3-4 86

ANTHONY, Ray, & His Orchestra

P&R '49

Singles: 78rpm

CAPITOL 3-5 49-57

Singles: 7-inch

CAPITOL 3-6 50-62

EPs: 7-inch 33/45rpm

CAPITOL 5-10 52-59

LPs: 10/12-inch 33rpm

CAPITOL 5-15 52-62

Also see BEACH BOYS
Also see SINATRA, Frank

ANTHONY & CAMP

R&B '86

Singles: 12-inch 33/45rpm

W.B. 4-6 86

Singles: 7-inch

W.B. 3-4 86

Picture Sleeves

W.B. 3-4 86

LPs: 10/12-inch 33rpm

W.B. 5-10 86

Member: Anthony Malloy.
Also see TEMPER

ANTHONY & IMPERIALS: see LITTLE ANTHONY & IMPERIALS

ANTHRAX

LP '85

LPs: 10/12-inch 33rpm

ISLAND 5-10 85-90
MEGAFORCE 5-10 87-91

Members: Joey Belladonna; Greg D'Angelo; Frank Bello.
Also see WHITE LION

AORTA

LP '69

Singles: 7-inch

ATLANTIC (2545 "Strange") 10-20 68
COLUMBIA (44870 "Strange") 5-10 69
HAPPY TIGER (567 "Sandcastles") 10-15 70

LPs: 10/12-inch 33rpm

COLUMBIA (9785 "Aorta") 15-25 69
COLUMBIA (38000 series) 5-10
HAPPY TIGER (1010 "Aorta 2") 35-55 70

Members: Bill Herman; Billy Jones; Jim Donlinger; Jim Nyeholt.

APOLLO 100

P&R/LP '72

Singles: 7-inch

MEGA 3-4 71-72

LPs: 10/12-inch 33rpm

MEGA 5-10 72

Member: Tom Parker.

APOLLONIA 6

P&R/R&B/D&D/LP '84

Singles: 12-inch 33/45rpm

W.B. 4-6 84-85

Singles: 7-inch

W.B. 3-4 84-85

Picture Sleeves

W.B. 3-4 84-85

LPs: 10/12-inch 33rpm

W.B. 5-10 84-85

Members: Patty Kotero; Brenda Bennett; Susan Moonsie.
Also see VANITY 6

APPALACHIANS

P&R '63

Singles: 7-inch

ABC-PAR 4-8 62-63
GOLDIE 8-10

APPALOOSA

LP '69

LPs: 10/12-inch 33rpm

COLUMBIA 10-15 69
WHITE GOLD 5-10 82

Members: Robin Batteaux; Al Kooper.
Also see KOOPER, Al

APPLEJACKS

P&R '58

Singles: 78rpm

CAMEO 5-10 57-58
DECCA 5-10 54
PRESIDENT 5-10 56
TONE-CRAFT 5-10 55

Singles: 7-inch

CAMEO (100 series) 10-15 57-60
CAMEO (200 & 300 series) 5-10 61-64
DECCA 8-12 54
PRESIDENT 8-12 56
TONE-CRAFT 8-12 55

Member: Dave Appell.

APRIL
(April Stevens)

Singles: 7-inch

A&M 3-5 74

Also see STEVENS, April

APRIL & NINO: see TEMPO, Nino, & April Stevens

APRIL WINE

P&R '72

Singles: 7–inch

BIG TREE 3-5 72-75
CAPITOL.................................... 3-4 78-85
LONDON.................................... 3-4 76-78

Picture Sleeves

CAPITOL (Except 4975) 3-4 81-84
CAPITOL (4975 "Just Between You and Me").................................. 3-4 81
(Sleeve opens to a 22"x15" poster.)
CAPITOL (4975 "Just Between You and Me").................................. 3-4 81
(Standard sleeve—no poster.)

LPs: 10/12–inch 33rpm

AQUARIUS 5-10
ATLANTIC................................. 5-10 81
BIG TREE 10-15 72-75
CAPITOL.................................. 5-10 78-85
LONDON................................. 10-12 76-77

Members: Steve Lang; Jerry Mercer; Myles Goodwyn; Brian Greenway; Gary Moffet.

AQUARIAN DREAM

LP '76

Singles: 7–inch

BUDDAH 3-5 76-77
ELEKTRA.................................... 3-4 78

LPs: 10/12–inch 33rpm

BUDDAH 8-10 76
ELEKTRA.................................. 5-10 78-79

Members: Claude Bartee; Pete Bartee; Jacques Burvick; Mike Fowler; Valerie Horn; Gloria Jones; Pat Shannon.

Also see CONNORS, Norman

AQUARIANS

LP '69

Singles: 7–inch

UNI 3-6 69

LPs: 10/12–inch 33rpm

UNI 12-15 69

AQUATONES

P&R/R&B '58

Singles: 78rpm

FARGO (1001 "You") 20-30 58

Singles: 7–inch

FARGO 10-20 58-61

LPs: 10/12–inch 33rpm

FARGO (3001 "The Aquatones Sing for You").................... 125-175 64
RELIC/FARGO (5033 "The Aquatones Sing for You")........................... 8-10

Members: Barbara Lee; Larry Vannata; Vic Castro; Russ Nagy; Mike Roma; Tom Vivona.

ARBORS

P&R '66

Singles: 7–inch

CARNEY (1011 "A Symphony for Susan") 10-20 66
COLUMBIA 3-5 73
(Black vinyl.)
COLUMBIA 5-10 73
(Colored vinyl. Promotional issue only.)
COLUMBIA HALL of FAME 3-4
DATE 4-6 66-70
(Black vinyl.)
DATE 5-10 66-70
(Colored vinyl. Promotional issue only.)
MERCURY 3-5 65

LPs: 10/12–inch 33rpm

ARBORS MUSIC 8-10
DATE 12-15 67-68
VANGUARD.............................15-20 62

Members: Ed Farran; Fred Farran; Scott Herrick; Tom Herrick.

ARCADIA

P&R/D&D/LP '85

Singles: 12–inch 33/45rpm

CAPITOL......................................4-6 85-86

Singles: 7–inch

CAPITOL......................................3-4 85-86

Picture Sleeves

CAPITOL......................................3-4 85-86

LPs: 10/12–inch 33rpm

CAPITOL....................................5-10 85-86

Members: Roger Taylor; Simon LeBon; Nick Rhodes.

Also see DURAN DURAN
Also see TAYLOR, Roger

ARCHIBALD

(With Dave Bartholomew's Band)

R&B '50

Singles: 78rpm

COLONY (105 "Little Miss Muffett") 25-50 51
IMPERIAL 15-35 50-57

Singles: 7–inch

IMPERIAL (Except 5212)...........20-50 52-57
IMPERIAL (5212 "Early Morning Blues") 50-75 52

ARCHIES

P&R/LP '68

Singles: 7–inch

CALENDAR 4-8 68-69
ERIC 3-4 81
KIRSHNER 3-8 69-72
(Includes 5 1/2–inch flexi-discs.)
RCA 3-8 72

Picture Sleeves

CALENDAR 8-15 68
KIRSHNER 8-10 69-71

LPs: 10/12–inch 33rpm

ACCORD (7149 "Straight A's")....8-10 81
BACK-TRAC 5-10 85
BRYLEN (4415 "Archies")..........10-20 82
CALENDAR (101 "Archies") 15-25 68
CALENDAR (103 "Everything's Archie") 15-25 69

CALENDAR (103 "Sugar Sugar") 10-15 70
51 WEST (16002 "Archies") 5-10 79
KIRSHNER (105 "Jingle Jangle") 15-25 69
KIRSHNER (107 "Sunshine") 15-25 70
KIRSHNER (109 "Greatest Hits") 15-25 70
KIRSHNER (110 "This Is Love") 15-25 71
RCA (0221 "The Archies") 15-25 70
(Promotional issue only.)
Members: Ron Dante, Jeff Barry; Toni Wine, plus assorted guests.
Also see BLOOM, Bobby
Also see GREENWICH, Ellie
Also see KIM, Andy
Also see STEVENS, Ray
Also see TEMPO, Nino

ARCHIES / Johnny Thunder

Singles: 7-inch

COLLECTABLES 3-4 80s
Also see THUNDER, Johnny

ARDEN, Toni

P&R '49

Singles: 78rpm

COLUMBIA 3-6 49-54
DECCA 3-6 57-57
RCA 3-6 55-56

Singles: 7-inch

COLUMBIA 5-10 50-54
DECCA 5-10 57-59
MISHAWAKA 3-5
RCA 5-10 55-56

EPs: 7-inch 33/45rpm

DECCA 8-15 58
COLUMBIA 10-15 56

LPs: 10/12-inch 33rpm

DECCA 12-25 57-59

AREA CODE 615

LP '69

Singles: 7-inch

POLYDOR 3-5 69-70

LPs: 10/12-inch 33rpm

POLYDOR 8-12 69-70
Members: Charlie McCoy; Norbert Putnam.
Also see McCOY, Charlie

ARENA BRASS

LP '63

LPs: 10/12-inch 33rpm

EPIC 10-15 62

ARGENT

P&R/LP '72

Singles: 7-inch

DATE 3-6 70
EPIC 4-8 69-74

LPs: 10/12-inch 33rpm

EPIC 10-20 69-75
U.A. 5-10 76
Members: Rod Argent; Russ Ballard; Robert Henrit; Jim Rodford; John Verity.
Also see BALLARD, Russ
Also see WINTER, Johnny / Argent / Chambers Brothers / John Hammond
Also see ZOMBIES

ARKADE

P&R '70

Singles: 7-inch

DUNHILL 4-6 70-71

Picture Sleeves

DUNHILL 4-6 71

ARLEN, Harold, & "Friend"

LP: 10/12-inch 33rpm

COLUMBIA (OL-6520 "Harold Sings Arlen") 25-35 66
(Monaural.)
COLUMBIA (OS-2920 "Harold Sings Arlen") 20-40 66
(Stereo.)
COLUMBIA (CSP-2920 "Harold Sings Arlen") 5-10
Members: Harold Arlen; Barbra Streisand.
Also see STREISAND, Barbra

ARMADA ORCHESTRA

LP '76

LPs: 10/12-inch 33rpm

SCEPTER 4-8 75

ARMAGEDDON

LP '75

Singles: 7-inch

CAPITOL 3-6 71-72
CREATIVE SOUND 4-6 71

LPs: 10/12-inch 33rpm

A&M 8-12 75
AMOS 15-20 70
Members: Keith Relf; Louis Cennamo; Martin Pugh.
Also see RENAISSANCE
Also see YARDBIRDS

ARMATRADING, Joan

LP '76

Singles: 12-inch 33/45rpm

A&M 4-6 83

Singles: 7-inch

A&M 3-5 74-86
CUBE 4-8 71

Picture Sleeves

A&M 3-5 83

EPs: 7-inch 33/45rpm

A&M (2391 "Me, Myself + 6 More") 5-10 83
(Promotional issue only.)

LPs: 10/12-inch 33rpm

A&M (Except 12) 8-12 73-90
A&M (12 "Talk Under Ladders") .15-25 81
(Promotional issue only.)

ARMEN, Kay

P&R '43

Singles: 78rpm

DECCA 4-8 42-58

Singles: 7-inch

DECCA 5-12 55-59

EPs: 7-inch 33/45rpm

MGM 10-20 54-55

LPs: 10/12-inch 33rpm

DECCA (5000 series) 20-40 54
(10-inch LP)
DECCA (8000 series) 10-20 59
MGM (200 series) 20-40 54
MGM (3000 series) 15-30 55

ARMENTA

D&D '83

Singles: 12-inch 33/45rpm

SAVOIR FAIRE 4-6 83

ARMORED SAINT

LP '84

Singles: 12-inch 33/45rpm

CHRYSALIS 4-6 86

Singles: 7-inch

CHRYSALIS 3-4 84-86

LPs: 10/12-inch 33rpm

CHRYSALIS 5-10 84-87

ARMS, Russell

P&R '57

Singles: 78rpm

EPIC 3-6 54-56
ERA 3-6 56-57

Singles: 7-inch

EPIC 5-10 54-56
ERA 5-10 56-57

LPs: 10/12-inch 33rpm

ERA 10-20 57

ARMSTRONG, Chuck

R&B '76

Singles: 7-inch

R&R 3-5 76

ARMSTRONG, Louis

(With His All Stars)

P&R '26

Singles: 78rpm

CAPITOL 4-8 56
COLUMBIA (2500 thru 2700 series) 15-25 32
COLUMBIA (40000 series) 4-8 56-66
DECCA 5-15 35-58
OKEH 20-30 26-31
RCA 4-8 56
VICTOR 10-20 33
VOCALION 10-20 36

Singles: 7-inch

A&M 3-4 88
ABC 3-5 67-73
AMSTERDAM 3-5 71
AUDIO FIDELITY 3-5 71
AVCO EMBASSY 3-5 71
BRUNSWICK 4-6 67-68
BUENA VISTA 3-6 68
CAPITOL 5-10 56
COLUMBIA 5-10 56-66
CONTINENTAL 3-5 71
DECCA (25000 series) 4-6 61-64
DECCA (27000 thru 29000 series) 8-10 50-56
DECCA (30000 thru 31000 series) 5-10 56-59
DOT 4-8 59
EPIC 3-6 69
KAPP 4-6 64-69
MGM 4-8 59-60
MERCURY 4-6 64-66
RCA 5-10 56
U.A. 3-6 68-69
VERVE 4-8 59-60

Picture Sleeves

A&M 3-4 88
BUENA VISTA 5-8 68
CONTINENTAL 3-6 71
KAPP 5-10 64
MGM 8-12 59
MERCURY 5-10 64

Note: Multi-disc, 1950s boxed sets are in the $15 to $25 range. At this time we do not have specific numbers and titles.

EPs: 7-inch 33/45rpm

COLUMBIA 5-15 55-59
DECCA 8-15 55-57
RCA 10-20 53-59

LPs: 10/12-inch 33rpm

ABC 5-10 68-76
AMSTERDAM 5-10 70
AUDIO FIDELITY 15-25 60-64
BIOGRAPH 5-10 73
BRUNSWICK (58004 "Jazz Classics") 50-100 50
(10-inch LP.)
BRUNSWICK (75000 series) 8-15 68-71
BUENA VISTA 8-12 68
CHIAROSCURO 5-10 77
COLUMBIA (500 thru 900 series) 25-50 54-57
COLUMBIA (2600 series) 8-15 67
COLUMBIA (9400 series) 8-15 67
COLUMBIA (30000 series) 5-12 71-80
CORAL 5-10 73
DECCA (155 "Satchmo") 50-100 65
(Boxed 4-LP set. Includes booklet.)
DECCA (195 "Satchmo at Symphony Hall") 30-50 66
(Boxed 2-LP set.)
DECCA (4000 series) 10-20 61-63
DECCA (5000 series) 25-50 51-54
(10-inch LPs.)
DECCA (8000 series) 15-25 55-59

DECCA (9000 series)................. 8-15 67
(Decca LP numbers in this series preceded by a "7" or a "DL-7" are stereo issues.)
EVEREST 5-10 71-76
GNP 8-12 77
GUEST STAR 5-10 64
HARMONY................................. 5-10 69
JAZZ HERITAGE 5-10 80
JAZZ PANORAMA (1204 "Fireworks")............................ 15-20
JEMI 5-10
KAPP... 10-15 64
MCA 6-10 73-82
MERCURY 10-15 66
METRO 10-15 65
MILESTONE 5-10 74-75
OLYMPIC 5-10 74
PAUSA 5-10 83
RCA (1300 & 1400 series)........ 25-50 53-56
RCA (2300 thru 2900 series) 10-20 61-64
(With "LPM" or "LSP" prefix.)
RCA (2600 series)...................... 5-10 77
(With "CPL1" prefix.)
RCA (5500 series)...................... 8-12 77
RCA (6000 series)...................... 8-12 71
SAGA 5-10 72
STORYVILLE 5-10 80
TRIP 5-10 72
U.A. 8-15 68-69
VANGUARD............................... 8-12 76
VERVE 15-20 60-64
VOCALION................................. 5-10 68-69
Also see BARRY, John
Also see BRUBECK, Dave
Also see CROSBY, Bing, Louis Armstrong, Rosemary Clooney & Hi-Los
Also see FITZGERALD, Ella, & Louis Armstrong
Also see KAYE, Danny, & Louis Armstrong
Also see JENKINS, Gordon
Also see MILLS BROTHERS, & Louis Armstrong

ARMSTRONG, Louis, & Duke Ellington

Singles: 7-inch

ROULETTE 4-6 63

LPs: 10/12-inch 33rpm

MFSL (155 "Recording for the First Time")........................ 15-25 85
ROULETTE (100 series)............ 8-12 71
ROULETTE (52000 series)....... 15-25 63
Also see ELLINGTON, Duke

ARMSTRONG, Louis, & Guy Lombardo

Singles: 7-inch

CAPITOL..................................... 3-6 66
Also see LOMBARDO, Guy

ARMSTRONG, Louis, & Oscar Peterson

Singles: 7-inch

VERVE 4-6 59

LPs: 10/12-inch 33rpm

VERVE 15-25 59
Also see ARMSTRONG, Louis
Also see PETERSON, Oscar

ARNELL, Ginny

P&R '63

Singles: 7-inch

DECCA 5-10 60
MGM 4-8 63-65
WARWICK 5-10 61

LPs: 10/12-inch 33rpm

MGM 15-25 64
Also see JAMIE & JANE

ARNIE'S LOVE

R&B '86

Singles: 12-inch 33/45rpm

PROFILE.......................................4-6 85-86

ARNO, Audrey

(With the Hazy Osterwald Sextet)

P&R '61

Singles: 7-inch

DECCA 4-8 61

ARNOLD, Calvin

P&R/R&B '68

Singles: 7-inch

IX CHAINS 3-5 75
VENTURE.......................................4-8 67-69

ARNOLD, Eddy

("The Tennessee Plowboy"; with His Tennessee Plowboys)

C&W '45

Singles: 78rpm

BLUEBIRD (0527 "Each Minute Seems Like a Million Years")..........................25-50 45
RCA (Except 1800 thru 3100 series)...10-20 46-49
RCA (1800 thru 3100 series).....15-30 46-49

Singles: 7-inch

DIAMOND P (1009 "If the Whole World Stopped Lovin") 5-10 73
(Promotional issue only.)
MGM 3-5 73-76
RCA (0001 thru 0476)...............10-20 50-51
(Black vinyl. Black or turquoise labels.)
RCA (0001 thru 0476)...............25-50 50-51
(Colored vinyl. Price for any in this series on colored vinyl.)
RCA (0100 thru 0700 series).........3-5 69-72
(Orange labels.)
RCA (2000 series) 5-10 62
(Compact 33 stereo single.)
RCA (3000 thru 6000 series).....10-20 50-57
RCA (7000 series) 5-12 57-62
RCA (8000 & 9000 series).............3-8 62-71
RCA (10000 thru 13000 series).....3-5 76-83

Picture Sleeves

RCA 8-15 56-66

EPs: 7-inch 33/45rpm

RCA (100 series) 10-12 61
(With "LPC" prefix. Compact 33 Double.)

RCA (280 "Best Wishes")......... 10-20
(Promotional issue only.)
RCA (200 thru 900 series) 10-15 52-56
(With "EPA" prefix.)
RCA (1100 & 1200 series) 15-20 55-56
(With "EPB" prefix.)
RCA (1400 & 1500 series) 8-12 57
(With "EPA" prefix.)
RCA (3000 series)..................... 20-40 52-54
(With "EPB" prefix.)
RCA (4000 & 5000 series) 8-15 57-59
(With "EPA" prefix.)

LPs: 10/12-inch 33rpm

CAMDEN (Except "ACL1 series) 8-18 60-72
CAMDEN ("ACL1" series) 5-10 72-74
GREEN VALLEY 8-10 76
K-TEL....................................... 8-10 74
MGM 8-12 74-76
RCA (AHL1, ANL1, APL1,
& AYL1 series)......................... 5-10 73-81
RCA (CPL1 series)..................... 8-12 83
RCA (209 "Eddy Arnold") 15-20 66
(Promotional issue only.)
RCA (1100 thru 2200 series) 20-30 55-60
(Monaural. with "LPM" prefix.)
RCA (2300 thru 2900 series) 12-20 60-64
(Monaural. with "LPM" prefix.)
RCA (3000 series)..................... 45-55 52-54
(10-inch LPs. with "LPM" prefix.)
RCA (3000 series)..................... 8-12 64-68
(12-inch LPs. with "LPM" prefix.)
RCA (1900 thru 3400 series) 15-25 60-65
(Stereo. with "LSP" prefix. "LSP" numbers below 1900 were reprocessed stereo issues of '50s LPs. They were issued in the '60s and are in the $10-$15 range.)
RCA (3500 thru 4800 series) 10-20 66-73
RCA (6000 series)..................... 8-12 70
SUNRISE 5-10 79
TIME-LIFE................................ 5-10 81

Also see ANN-MARGRET
Also see PRESLEY, Elvis / Hank Snow / Eddy Arnold / Jim Reeves

ARPEGGIO

P&R/R&B/LP '79

Singles: 7-inch

POLYDOR................................. 3-4 78-80

LPs: 10/12-inch 33rpm

POLYDOR................................. 5-10 78-80

ARRINGTON, Steve
(Steve Arrington's Hall of Fame)

R&B '82

Singles: 12-inch 33/45rpm

ATLANTIC................................. 4-6 83-86

Singles: 7-inch

ATLANTIC................................. 3-4 83-86
KONGLATHER 3-4 82
MANHATTAN.............................. 3-4 87

LPs: 10/12-inch 33rpm

ATLANTIC.................................5-10 83-86

Also see SLAVE

ARROWS (With Davie Allan): see ALLAN, Davie

ART ATTACK

D&D '83

Singles: 12-inch 33/45rpm

B.M.O...4-6 83

Singles: 7-inch

B.M.O...3-4 83

LPs: 10/12-inch 33rpm

B.M.O...5-10 83

ART in AMERICA

LP '83

Singles: 7-inch

PAVILLION 3-4 83

LPs: 10/12-inch 33rpm

PAVILLION 5-10 83

ART of NOISE

D&D '83

Singles: 12-inch 33/45rpm

CHINA...4-6 86
ISLAND 4-6 83-84

Singles: 7-inch

CHINA...3-4 86-88
ISLAND 3-4 83-84

Picture Sleeves

CHINA...3-4 86-88

LPs: 10/12-inch 33rpm

CHINA...5-10 86-88
CHRYSALIS.................................5-10 86-87
ISLAND 5-10 84-85

Members: Anne Dudley; Gary Langan; J.J. Jeczalik.
Also see ELECTRONIC
Also see HORN, Trevor, Paul Morley, & Art of Noise

ART of NOISE & Duane Eddy

P&R '86

Singles: 7-inch

CHINA...3-4 86

Picture Sleeves

CHINA...3-4 86

Also see EDDY, Duane

ART of NOISE & Max Headroom

P&R '86

Singles: 7-inch

CHINA...3-4 86

Picture Sleeves

CHINA...3-4 86

ART of NOISE & Tom Jones

P&R '88

Singles: 7-inch

CHINA...3-4 88

Picture Sleeves

CHINA...3-4 88

Also see ART of NOISE
Also see JONES, Tom

ARTISTICS

R&B '65

Singles: 7-inch

BRUNSWICK 3-8 66-73
OKEH 4-8 63-66

LPs: 10/12-inch 33rpm

BRUNSWICK 10-20 67-73
OKEH 15-25 67

Members: Marvin Smith; Bernard Reed; Larry Johnson; Tommy Green; Aaron Floyd; Morris Williams.
Also see DUKAYS

ARTISTS UNITED AGAINST APARTHEID

P&R/R&B/D&D/LP '85

Singles: 12-inch 33/45rpm

MANHATTAN 4-6 85

Singles: 7-inch

MANHATTAN 3-4 85

Picture Sleeves

MANHATTAN 3-4 85

LPs: 10/12-inch 33rpm

MANHATTAN 5-10 85

ARVON, Bobby

P&R '77

Singles: 7-inch

ARIOLA AMERICAN 3-4 76
FIRST ARTISTS 3-4 77-78

LPs: 10/12-inch 33rpm

FIRST ARTISTS 5-10 78
MTA 5-10

ASH, Daniel

LP '91

LPs: 10/12-inch 33rpm

BEGGAR'S BANQUET 5-8 91

ASHE, Clarence

P&R/R&B '64

Singles: 7-inch

ABC-PAR 4-8 65
CHESS 4-8 64
J&S 4-8 64
MASTER 4-8 65

ASHE, Clarence, & Hartsy Maye

Singles: 7-inch

J&S 4-8 65

Also see ASHE, Clarence

ASHFORD & SIMPSON

R&B/LP '73

Singles: 12-inch 33/45rpm

CAPITOL 4-6 82-86
W.B. 4-6 79

Singles: 7-inch

CAPITOL 3-4 82-89
EMI AMERICA 3-4 84-85
W.B. 3-4 73-81

Picture Sleeves

CAPITOL 3-4 80-86

LPs: 10/12-inch 33rpm

CAPITOL 5-10 82-89
W.B. (Except HS series) 5-10 73-81
W.B. ("HS" series) 12-18 79-80
(Half-speed mastered.)

Members: Nick Ashford; Valerie Simpson.
Also see JONES, Quincy
Also see SIMPSON, Valerie
Also see VALERIE & NICK

ASHLEY, Del
(David Gates)

Singles: 7-inch

MANCHESTER (101 "There's a Heaven") 30-40 60s
PLANETARY (103 "Little Miss Stuck-Up") 10-20 65

Also see GATES, David

ASHLEY, Tyrone
(With the Funky Music Machine)

R&B '70

Singles: 7-inch

PHIL-L.A. of SOUL 3-5 70-71
U.A. 3-4 78

LPs: 10/12-inch 33rpm

U.A. 5-10 78

ASHTON, GARDNER & DYKE

P&R/LP '71

Singles: 7-inch

CAPITOL 3-5 70-72

LPs: 10/12-inch 33rpm

CAPITOL 8-12 70-72

Members: Tony Ashton; Kim Gardner; Roy Dyke.
Also see ASHTON, Tony, & Jon Lord
Also see BADGER

ASIA

P&R/LP '82

Singles: 12-inch 33/45rpm

GEFFEN 4-6 82-85

Singles: 7-inch

GEFFEN 3-4 82-85

Picture Sleeves

GEFFEN 3-4 81-85

LPs: 10/12-inch 33rpm

GEFFEN 5-10 82-90

Members: Steve Howe; Carl Palmer; John Wetton; Geoff Downes; Mandy Mayer.
Also see BUGGLES
Also see EMERSON, LAKE & PALMER
Also see HOWE, Steve, Band

ASLEEP at the WHEEL

C&W '74

Singles: 7-inch

ARISTA 3-4 90-91
CAPITOL 3-4 75-79
EPIC (06671 thru 08087) 3-4 87-88
EPIC (50000 series) 4-6 74

LPs: 10/12-inch 33rpm

CAPITOL 10-15 75-79
EPIC (BG-33000 series) 15-25 75
EPIC (EG-33000 series) 10-15

EPIC (KE-33000 series)............ 10-15 74
EPIC (PE-33000 series).............. 5-10
MCA 5-10 80-84
U.A. 15-25 73

Members: Ray Benson; Chris O'Connell; Danny Levin; Reuben Gosfield.

ASPHALT JUNGLE

R&B '80

Singles: 7–inch

TEC 3-4 80

ASSEMBLED MULTITUDE

P&R '70

Singles: 7–inch

ATLANTIC.................................. 3-5 70-72
ERIC.. 3-4 81

LPs: 10/12–inch 33rpm

ATLANTIC.................................. 8-10 70

ASSOCIATION

P&R/LP '66

Singles: 7–inch

COLUMBIA 3-5 72
ELEKTRA.................................... 3-4 81
JUBILEE...................................... 4-8 65
MUMS 3-5 73
RCA... 3-5 75
VALIANT 4-8 66
W.B. 3-6 67-71

Picture Sleeves

VALIANT 5-10 66

LPs: 10/12–inch 33rpm

COLUMBIA 8-10 72
VALIANT 12-20 66
W.B. 8-12 67-71

Members: Gary Alexander; Ted Bluechel Jr; Brian Cole; Russ Giguere; Terry Kirkman; Cliff Nivison; Larry Ramos; Richard Thompson; Jim Yester; Larry Ramos.

Also see MAMAS & PAPAS / Association / Fifth Dimension
Also see MIKE & DEAN
Also see NEW CHRISTY MINSTRELS
Also see PEDESTRIANS / Association / Five Americans / Soulblenders

ASSOCIATION / Bobby Vee / Mike Love / Mary MacGregor

LPs: 10/12–inch 33rpm

HITBOUND (1005 "New Memories")............................ 10-15 83

Also see LOVE, Mike
Also see MacGREGOR, Mary
Also see VEE, Bobby

ASTAIRE, Fred

P&R '29

Singles: 78rpm

BRUNSWICK 10-20 35-38
COLUMBIA 15-25 29-34
DECCA... 5-10 43
MGM 4-8 51-53
MERCURY 3-6 53
RCA... 3-5 55
VERVE.. 3-5 56
VICTOR 15-20 31-33

Singles: 7–inch

AVA.. 4-6 63
CHOREO 4-6 62
CLEF.. 5-10 57
KAPP 4-8 59
MGM 5-10 51-52
MERCURY.................................. 5-10 53
RCA 5-10 55
VERVE....................................... 5-10 56

EPs: 7–inch 33/45rpm

CLEF... 10-15 57
EPIC... 10-15 57
MGM 10-20 51-53
VERVE..................................... 10-15 59

LPs: 10/12–inch 33rpm

CAMDEN 10-20 59-60
CHOREO 10-20 61
CLEF.. 15-30 57
EPIC (3000 series).................... 15-30 57
EPIC (13000 & 15000 series) 8-15 66
KAPP 15-25 59
LION... 10-20 59
MGM (100 series) 25-50 52
MGM (3000 series) 15-30 52-55
MONMOUTH EVERGREEN...... 10-20 71
VERVE..................................... 15-30 56-59
VOCALION 8-15 64
X.. 20-25 57

Also see CROSBY, Bing, & Fred Astaire

ASTAIRE, Fred, & Jane Powell

P&R '51

Singles: 78rpm

MGM 4-8 51

Singles: 7–inch

MGM 5-10 51

Also see POWELL, Jane

ASTAIRE, Fred, & Red Skelton / Helen Kane

(With Andre Previn)

EPs: 7–inch 33/45rpm

MGM 8-10 50

(Not issued with cover, actually a three-track single.)

Also see ASTAIRE, Fred
Also see PREVIN, Andre
Also see SKELTON, Red

ASTLEY, Jon

P&R/LP '87

Singles: 7–inch

ATLANTIC.................................... 3-4 87-88

Picture Sleeves

ATLANTIC.................................... 3-4 87-88

LPs: 10/12–inch 33rpm

ATLANTIC.................................. 5-10 87

ASTLEY, Rick

P&R '87

Singles: 7-inch

RCA.. 3-4 87-91

Picture Sleeves

RCA.. 3-4 87-89

LPs: 10/12-inch 33rpm

RCA.. 5-8 87-89

ASTORS

P&R/R&B '65

Singles: 7-inch

STAX....................................... 10-20 63-67

Members: Curtis Johnson; Richard Harris; Eddie Stanbeck; Sam Byrnes.

ASTRONAUTS

P&R/LP '63

Singles: 7-inch

PALLADIUM (610 "Come Along Baby") 75-125 61

RCA.. 5-10 63-65

Picture Sleeves

RCA.. 20-30 63

EPs: 7-inch 33/45rpm

RCA.. 25-40 63

RCA WURLITZER DISCOTHEQUE (100 "Discotheque Music")............. 30-40 64
(Promotional issue only.)

LPs: 10/12-inch 33rpm

RCA.. 20-30 63-67

Members: Stormy Patterson; Robert Demmon; Dennis Lindsey; James Gallagher; Richard Fifield.

ASTRONAUTS / Liverpool Five

LPs: 10/12-inch 33rpm

RCA (251 "Stereo Festival")...... 25-45 67
(Promotional issue only.)

Also see ASTRONAUTS
Also see LIVERPOOL FIVE

ASWAD

LP '88

LPs: 10/12-inch 33rpm

ISLAND 5-10 84

MANGO....................................... 5-10 84-88

Members: Candy McKenzie; Brinsley Forde; Donald Griffiths; Courtney Hemmings; George Oban; Angus Gaye; Bunny McKenzie; Trevor Bow.

ASYLUM CHOIR

Singles: 7-inch

SHELTER.................................... 3-5 71

SMASH 4-6 69

LPs: 10/12-inch 33rpm

SHELTER (2000 series)............. 8-10 74

SHELTER (8000 series)........... 10-15 71

SHELTER (52000 series)........... 5-10 75

SMASH (67107 "Look Inside").. 25-30 68
(With toilet tissue cover.)

SMASH (67107 "Look Inside").. 10-15 68
(With photo cover.)

Members: Leon Russell; Marc Benno.

Also see BENNO, Marc
Also see RUSSELL, Leon

ATKINS

R&B '82

Singles: 7-inch

W.B. 3-4 82

LPs: 10/12-inch 33rpm

W.B. 5-10 82

ATKINS, Chet

C&W '55

Singles: 78rpm

BLUEBIRD (0072 "I Know When I'm Blue") 10-20 50

BULLET (617 "Guitar Blues")...50-100 46

RCA 5-15 47-57

Singles: 7-inch

RCA (0100 thru 0400 series).....12-25 50-51
(Black or turquoise labels.)

RCA (0100 thru 0700 series).........3-5 71-74
(Orange labels.)

RCA (4000 & 5000 series).........10-20 51-55

RCA (6000 & 7000 series)...........5-15 55-62

RCA (8000 & 9000 series)............3-8 62-71

RCA (10000 thru 13000 series).....3-5 75-83

Picture Sleeves

RCA 5-10 61-67

EPs: 7-inch 33/45rpm

RCA (100 series) 8-12 61
(With "LPC" prefix. Compact 33 Double.)

RCA (500 thru 900 series)...........8-15 55-56
(With "EPA" prefix.)

RCA (1100 & 1200 series).........10-20 55-56
(With "EPB" prefix.)

RCA (1300 thru 1500 series).......8-15 56-57
(With "EPA" prefix.)

RCA (3000 series) 15-25 52-54
(With "EPB" prefix.)

RCA (4000 & 5000 series)...........5-10 58-60

SESAC (13 "Mr. Atkins, If You Please")..........................20-30 59
(Promotional issue only.)

LPs: 10/12-inch 33rpm

CAMDEN 8-12 61-72

CANDLELITE.............................10-15

COLUMBIA 5-10 83-85

DOLTON....................................15-20 67

PICKWICK/CAMDEN..................8-10 75

RCA (AHL1, ANL1, APL1, & AYL1 series)...........................5-10 73-83

RCA (CPL1 series) 8-12 77

RCA (1000 series) 25-35 54
(With "LPM" prefix.)

RCA (1100 thru 2200 series, except 1236)..........................15-25 55-60
(With "LPM" prefix.)

RCA (1236 "Stringin' Along with Chet Atkins")....................30-40 55
(With "LPM" prefix.)

RCA (2300 thru 2900 series) 10-15 60-64
(With "LPM" prefix.)
RCA (3000 series)..................... 45-55 53
(10–inch LPs. With "LPM" prefix.)
RCA (3000 series)...................... 8-12 64-68
(12–inch LPs. With "LPM" prefix.)
RCA (2000 & 3000 series) 10-15 66-69
(With "LSC" prefix.)
RCA (1900 thru 3500 series) 10-20 60-66
(Stereo. With "LSP" prefix. LSP numbers below 1900 were reprocessed stereo issues of '50s LPs. They were issued in the '60s are in the $10 to $15 range.)
RCA (3500 thru 4800 series) 8-15 68-73
RCA (6000 series)...................... 8-12 70-72
TIME-LIFE 5-10 81
Also see ANN-MARGRET
Also see ATKINS STRING COMPANY
Also see CHARLES, Ray, George Jones, & Chet Atkins
Also see COUNTRY HAMS
Also see GIBSON, Don
Also see KERR, Anita
Also see NELSON, Willie
Also see PRESLEY, Elvis
Also see PURE PRAIRIE LEAGUE
Also see REED, Jerry, & Chet Atkins
Also see SNOW, Hank, & Chet Atkins

ATKINS, Chet, & Boston Pops

LP: 10/12–inch 33rpm

RCA.. 10-20 66-69
Also see BOSTON POPS ORCHESTRA

ATKINS, Chet, Floyd Cramer & Danny Davis

Singles: 7–inch

RCA.. 3-5 77

LPs: 10/12–inch 33rpm

RCA.. 5-8 77
Also see DAVIS, Danny

ATKINS, Chet, Floyd Cramer & Boots Randolph

LPs: 10/12–inch 33rpm

PICKWICK 5-8 71
Also see CRAMER, Floyd
Also see RANDOLPH, Boots

ATKINS, Chet, & Mark Knopfler

LPs: 10/12–inch 33rpm

COLUMBIA 5-8 90

ATKINS, Chet, & Les Paul

Singles: 7–inch

RCA.. 3-4 78

LPs: 10/12–inch 33rpm

RCA.. 5-10 78
Also see PAUL, Les

ATKINS, Chet / Faron Young

EPs: 7–inch 33/45rpm

SESAC (48 "No Greater Love") 20-30 59
(Promotional issue only.)
Also see ATKINS, Chet
Also see YOUNG, Faron

ATKINS, Christopher

P&R '82

Singles: 7–inch

POLYDOR 3-4 82

Picture Sleeves

POLYDOR 3-4 82

ATKINS STRING COMPANY

C&W '75

Singles: 7–inch

RCA 3-4 75
Member: Chet Atkins.
Also see ATKINS, Chet

ATLANTA

C&W '83

Singles: 7–inch

MCA...3-4 84-85
MDJ..3-5 83
SOUTHERN TRACKS 3-4 87-88

Picture Sleeves

MDJ..3-4 83

LPs: 10/12–inch 33rpm

MCA...5-10 84
Members: Dick Stevens; Brad Griffis; Tony Ingram; Allen David; John Holder; Jeff Baker; Al Collay; Bill Packard.
Also see VOGUES

ATLANTA DISCO BAND

R&B '75

Singles: 7–inch

ARIOLA AMERICA 3-4 76

LPs: 10/12–inch 33rpm

ARIOLA AMERICA 5-10 76

ATLANTA RHYTHM SECTION

P&R/LP '74

Singles: 7–inch

COLUMBIA 3-4 81
DECCA 3-5 72
MCA...3-4 73
POLYDOR 3-4 74-80

LPs: 10/12–inch 33rpm

COLUMBIA 5-10 81
DECCA 12-20 72
MCA...5-10 77
MFSL (038 "Champagne Jam") .25-50 79
POLYDOR 5-10 74-80
Members: Ronnie Hammond; Rodney Justo; Robert Nix; Barry Bailey; J.R. Cobb; Dean Daughtry; Paul Goddard.
Also see CANDYMEN
Also see CLASSICS IV
Also see MANILOW, Barry / Atlanta Rhythm Section

ATLANTIC STARR

R&B '78

Singles: 12–inch 33/45rpm

A&M 4-6 79-85

Singles: 7–inch

A&M 3-4 78-86
MANHATTAN.................................3-4 86
W.B. 3-4 87-89

Picture Sleeves

A&M 3-4 78-86
W.B. 3-4 87

LPs: 10/12-inch 33rpm

A&M 5-10 78-85
W.B. 5-10 87-89

Members: Sharon Bryant; David Lewis; Wayne Lewis; Jonathan Lewis; William Sudderth; Damon Rentie; Clifford Archer; Joe Phillips; Porter Carroll; Koran Daniels; Barbara Weathers.

Also see BRYANT, Sharon

ATOMIC ROOSTER

LP '71

Singles: 7-inch

ELEKTRA.................................... 3-5 71-72

LPs: 10/12-inch 33rpm

ELEKTRA.................................. 10-20 71-73
PVC.. 5-10 83

Members: Chris Farlowe; Pete French; Steve Bolton; John Cann; Vincent Crane; Paul Hammond; Carl Palmer; Johnny Mandala; Rick Parnell.

Also see BROWN, Arthur
Also see FARLOWE, Chris

ATTACK, Art: see ART ATTACK

ATTILA

LPs: 10/12-inch 33rpm

BACK-TRAC 5-10 85
D&J 5-8 80
EPIC (30030 "Attila")................. 40-50 70

Members: Billy Joel; Jon Small.

Also see JOEL, Billy

ATTITUDE

R&B/D&D '83

Singles: 12-inch 33/45rpm

ATLANTIC.................................. 4-6 83

Singles: 7-inch

ATLANTIC.................................. 3-4 83

LPs: 10/12-inch 33rpm

ATLANTIC.................................. 5-10 83

ATTITUDES

P&R/R&B '76

Singles: 7-inch

DARK HORSE 3-5 75-76

Picture Sleeves

DARK HORSE 3-5 75

LPs: 10/12-inch 33rpm

DARK HORSE 5-10 76-77

Members: Danny Kortchmar; David Foster; Jim Keltner; Paul Stallworth.

AU GO-GO SINGERS

Singles: 7-inch

ROULETTE (4577 "Pink Polemoniums")....................... 10-15 64

LPs: 10/12-inch 33rpm

ROULETTE (R-25280 "They Call Us Au Go-Go Singers") 30-40 64
(Monaural.)

ROULETTE (SR-25280 "They Call Us Au Go-Go Singers") 40-50 64
(Stereo.)

Members: Steven (Stephen) Stills; Richie Furay.

Also see FURAY, Richie
Also see STILLS, Stephen

AUDIENCE

P&R '71

Singles: 7-inch

ELEKTRA....................................3-5 71-72

LPs: 10/12-inch 33rpm

AUDIENCE 10-15 71-72
ELEKTRA...................................8-12 72

Members: Trevor Williams; Howard Werth; Pat Neubergh; Nick Judd; Tony Connor; Keith Gemmell.

AUDIO TWO

LP '88

LPs: 10/12-inch 33rpm

FIRST PRIORITY..........................5-8 88

AUDREY

P&R '56

Singles: 78rpm

PLUS (104 "Dear Elvis") 10-20 56

Singles: 7-inch

PLUS (104 "Dear Elvis") 20-25 56
(Break-in novelty with excerpts of several Elvis Sun tracks.)

Also see PRESLEY, Elvis

AUGER, Brian

(With Trinity; Brian Auger's Oblivion Express)

P&R/LP '70

Singles: 7-inch

ATCO 4-6 68-69
RCA 3-5 70-74

EPs: 7-inch 33/45rpm

ATCO (4536 "Red Beans & Rice").5-8 69
(Labeled an EP by Atco, though only has one track on each side. Not issued with cover.)

LPs: 10/12-inch 33rpm

ATCO 12-15 69
CAPITOL...................................10-12 69
POLYDOR 5-10 74
RCA 6-10 70-77
W.B. 5-10 77

Also see DRISCOLL, Julie, & Brian Auger

AUGIE: see MEYERS, Augie

AUGUST, Jan

P&R '46

Singles: 78rpm

MERCURY...................................3-6 46-57

Singles: 7-inch

MERCURY...................................4-10 50-62

EPs: 7-inch 33/45rpm

MERCURY...................................5-15 50-56

LPs: 10/12-inch 33rpm

MERCURY.................................10-25 50-62

WING 6-12 59
Also see HAYMAN, Richard, Orchestra

AURRA

R&B '80

Singles: 12-inch 33/45rpm

SALSOUL.. 4-6 82

Singles: 7-inch

DREAM 3-4 80
SALSOUL.. 3-4 81-83

LPs: 10/12-inch 33rpm

DREAM 5-10 80
SALSOUL.. 5-10 81-83
Members: Curt Jones; Starleana Young; Steve Washington; Tom Lockett Jr.; Phillip Fields.
Also see DEJA
Also see SLAVE

AUSTIN, Gene

P&R '25

Singles: 78rpm

COLUMBIA 3-5 54-56
DECCA.. 3-5 56
VICTOR.. 4-8 25-35

Singles: 7-inch

COLUMBIA 4-8 54-56
DECCA.. 4-6 56
RCA.. 4-8 57

Picture Sleeves

RCA.. 5-10 57

EPs: 7-inch 33/45rpm

RCA.. 5-10 53

LPs: 10/12-inch 33rpm

DOT.. 8-15 60s
RCA.. 10-20 53-57
X.. 10-20 54

AUSTIN, Patti

R&B '69

Singles: 12-inch 33/45rpm

QWEST 4-6 84-86

Singles: 7-inch

ABC.. 5-10 68
CTI 3-4 76-80
COLUMBIA 4-8 71-73
CORAL (62455 "He's Good Enough for Me") 10-20 65
CORAL (62471 "I Wanna Be Loved").. 10-20 65
CORAL (62478 "Someone's Gonna Cry").. 50-100 66
CORAL (62491 "Take Away the Pain Stain") 10-20 66
CORAL (62500 "Leave a Little Love").. 10-20 66
CORAL (62511 "What a Difference a Day Made") 10-20 67
CORAL (62518 "Only All the Time").. 10-20 67
CORAL (62541 "You're Too Much a Part of Me").. 10-20 67
CORAL (62548 "All My Love")... 10-20 68
QWEST.. 3-4 81-86
U.A. 3-4 69-70

LPs: 10/12-inch 33rpm

CTI 5-10 77-80
GRP 5-8 90
QWEST.. 5-10 81-86
Also see JONES, Quincy
Also see WALDEN, Narada Michael, & Patti Austin
Also see YUTAKA

AUSTIN, Patti, & Jerry Butler

Singles: 7-inch

CTI 3-4 83
Also see BUTLER, Jerry

AUSTIN, Patti, & James Ingram

P&R '82

Singles: 7-inch

QWEST.. 3-4 82-84
Also see AUSTIN, Patti
Also see INGRAM, James

AUSTIN, Sil
(With the Allstars)

P&R/R&B '56

Singles: 78rpm

JUBILEE 4-6 54-55
MERCURY.. 3-5 56-65

Singles: 7-inch

JUBILEE 5-10 54-55
MERCURY 5-15 56-65
SSS INT'L 3-4 70
SEW CITY.. 4-6 66

EPs: 7-inch 33/45rpm

MERCURY.. 10-15 56-57

LPs: 10/12-inch 33rpm

MERCURY.. 10-25 59-67
SSS INT'L 8-10 70-82
WING 10-12 63-68

AUSTIN, Sil, & Red Prysock

Singles: 7-inch

MERCURY 4-6 61

LPs: 10/12-inch 33rpm

MERCURY (20434 "Battle Royal") 15-25 61
(Monaural.)
MERCURY (60106 "Battle Royal") 20-30 61
(Stereo.)
SSS INT'L 8-10 69
WING 10-12 63-68
Also see AUSTIN, Sil

AUTOGRAPH

P&R '84

Singles: 7-inch

RCA 3-4 84-85

Picture Sleeves

RCA 3-4 84-85

LPs: 10/12-inch 33rpm

RCA 5-10 84-87

Member: Steve Plunkett.

AUTOMATIC MAN

LP '76

Singles: 7–inch

ISLAND 3-4 76-77

LPs: 10/12–inch 33rpm

ISLAND 5-10 76-77

Members: Michael Schrieve; Todd Cochran; Doni Harvey; Pat Thrall.

AUTRY, Gene

(With the Cass County Boys & the Pinafores)

P&R '33

Singles: 78rpm

CHAMPION 50-75
CLARION 50-75
CONQUEROR 25-75
COLUMBIA 5-10 45-56
DECCA 50-75
DIVA 50-75
HARMONY 20-30
OKEH 10-20 40-45
PERFECT 30-60
QRS (1044 "Living in the Mountains") 3500-4500 29
ROMEO (5109 "Silver Haired Daddy of Mine") 300-500 32
ROMEO (5110 "Jailhouse Blues") 300-500 32
VELVET TONE 50-75
VOCALION 25-50 35-40

Singles: 7–Inch

COLUMBIA (06189 "Statue in the Bay") 3-4 86
COLUMBIA (20700 thru 21500 series) 5-10 50-56
COLUMBIA (38700 thru 40500 series) 5-10 50-55
COLUMBIA (44000 series) 3-5 68
MISTLETOE 3-5 74
REPUBLIC 3-8 59-76

Picture Sleeves

COLUMBIA HALL of FAME (33165 "Rudolph the Red-Nosed Reindeer") 4-6 69
REPUBLIC (2002 "Santa's Comin' in a Whirlybird") 5-10 59

EPs: 7–inch 33/45rpm

COLUMBIA 40-50 51-56

LPs: 10/12–inch 33rpm

BIRCHMONT 8-12
CHALLENGE 25-30 58
COLUMBIA (55 thru 154) 80-100 51-55
(10–inch LPs.)
COLUMBIA (600 series) 80-100 55
COLUMBIA (1000 series) 8-10 70-82
COLUMBIA (1500 series) 20-25 61
COLUMBIA (2500 series) 80-100 56
(10–inch LPs.)
COLUMBIA (0137 "Merry Christmas") 40-60 50
(10–inch LP.)
COLUMBIA (8000 series) 80-100
COLUMBIA (9001 "Western Classics") 40-60 51
(10–inch LPs.)
COLUMBIA (9002 "Western Classics, Vol. 2") 40-60 51
(10–inch LPs.)
COLUMBIA (15000 series) 8-10 81
COLUMBIA (37000 series) 5-10 82
DESIGN 8-10
ENCORE 6-10 80
GRT 10-15 77
GRAND PRIX 8-10
HALLMARK 8-12
HARMONY (7100 thru 7300 series) 20-30 56-65
HARMONY (9500 series) 15-25 59-64
HARMONY (11000 series) 10-15 64-66
HURRAH 5-10
MELODY RANCH 20-25 65
MISTLETOE 8-12 74
MURRAY HILL (897296;"Melody Ranch Radio Show") 45-55
(Four-LP set.)
RCA (2600 series) 25-30 62
RADIOLA 5-10 75
REPUBLIC (1900 series) 5-10
REPUBLIC (6000 series) 5-15 76-78
STARDAY 6-10 78

AVALON, Frankie

P&R/R&B '58

Singles: 78rpm

CHANCELLOR 10-20 57-58
X 10-15 54

Singles: 7–inch

ABC 3-5 74
AMOS 3-4 69
BOBCAT 3-4 83
CHANCELLOR (1 "Shy Guy") 15-20
(Acnecare promotional special products issue.)
CHANCELLOR (1004 "Cupid") 15-20 57
CHANCELLOR (1011 thru 1026) 8-12 57-58
CHANCELLOR (1031 "Venus") 10-20 58
(Monaural)
CHANCELLOR (1031 "Venus") 20-30 58
(Stereo.)
CHANCELLOR (1036 "Bobby Sox to Stockings") 8-12 59
(Monaural.)
CHANCELLOR (1036 "Bobby Sox to Stockings") 15-25 59
(Stereo.)

CHANCELLOR (1040 "Just Ask Your Heart") 8-12 59
(Monaural.)
CHANCELLOR (1040 "Just Ask Your Heart") 15-25 59
(Stereo.)
CHANCELLOR (1045 "Why") 8-12 59
(Monaural.)
CHANCELLOR (1045 "Why") ... 15-25 59
(Stereo.)
CHANCELLOR (1048 thru 1131) 5-10 60-63
CHANCELLOR (1134 "Come Fly with Me") 15-25 63
CHANCELLOR (1135 Cleopatra") 10-15 63
CHANCELLOR (1139 "Beach Party") 10-15 64
COLLECTABLES 3-4 81
DE LITE 3-4 76-78
ERIC 3-4 73
MCA 3-4 84
METROMEDIA 3-5 70
REGALIA 3-5 72
REPRISE 4-6 68-69
U.A. 4-8 64-65
X 10-20 54

Picture Sleeves

CHANCELLOR (1026 thru 1045) 10-25 58-59
CHANCELLOR (1048 thru 1125) 8-15 60-63
DE LITE 3-4 78
U.A. 4-8 64

EPs: 7–inch 33/45rpm

CHANCELLOR 20-30 58-60
X 20-30 55

Promotional EPs

CHANCELLOR (303 "Ballad of the Alamo") 50-75 60
(With complete publicity kit.)
CHANCELLOR (303 "Ballad of the Alamo") 20-30 60
(Without publicity kit.)
CHANCELLOR (5004 "Swingin' on a Rainbow") 20-30 59
(White label. Includes paper sleeve with note from Frankie, thanking dee jays for their support.)

LPs: 10/12–inch 33rpm

ABC 5-10 73
CHANCELLOR (5001 "Frankie Avalon") 35-50 58
CHANCELLOR (5002 "Young Frankie Avalon") 35-45 59
(Black vinyl.)
CHANCELLOR (5002 "Young Frankie Avalon") 75-100 59
(Colore vinyl.)
CHANCELLOR (5004 "Swingin' on a Rainbow") 35-45 59
(With bound-in photo page.)
CHANCELLOR (CHL-5011 "Summer Scene") 25-35 60
(Monaural.)
CHANCELLOR (CHLS-5011 "Summer Scene") 30-40 60
(Stereo.)
CHANCELLOR (CHL-5018 "A Whole Lot of Frankie") 25-35 61
CHANCELLOR (CHL-5022 "About Mr. Avalon") 20-30 61
(Monaural.)
CHANCELLOR (CHLS-5022 "About Mr. Avalon") 25-35 61
(Stereo.)
CHANCELLOR (CHL-5025 "Italiano") 20-25 62
(Monaural.)
CHANCELLOR (CHLS-5025 "Italiano") 20-30 62
CHANCELLOR (CHL-5027 "You Are Mine") 20-25 62
(Monaural.)
CHANCELLOR (CHLS-5027 "You Are Mine") 20-30 62
(Stereo.)
CHANCELLOR (CHL-5031 "Christmas Album") 20-25 62
(Monaural.)
CHANCELLOR (CHLS-5031 "Christmas Album") 20-30 62
(Stereo.)
CHANCELLOR (CHL-5032 "Cleopatra") 20-25 62
(Monaural.)
CHANCELLOR (CHLS-5032 "Cleopatra") 20-30 62
(Stereo.)
CHANCELLOR (69801 "Young and in Love") 50-75 60
(LP with felt cover and 3-D portrait, suitable for hanging, in a special box.)
CHANCELLOR (69801 "Young and in Love") 25-40 60
(LP without the box.)
DE-LITE 5-10 76-78
EVEREST 5-10 82
51 WEST 5-10
LIBERTY 5-10 82
MCA 5-10 85
METROMEDIA 5-10 70
SUNSET 8-10 69
TRIP 5-10 77
U.A. 15-20 64
(With "UAL" or "UAS" prefix.)
U.A. 5-10 75
(With "UA-LA" prefix.)

Also see FABIAN / Frankie Avalon

AVALON, Frankie, & Annette

Singles: 12-inch 33/45rpm

PACIFIC STAR (5698 "Merry Christmas") ... 15-25 81
(Picture disc.)

Singles: 7-inch

PACIFIC STAR (569 "Merry Christmas") ... 3-6 81
(Black vinyl.)
PACIFIC STAR (569 "Merry Christmas") ... 15-20 81
(Colored vinyl.)

Picture Sleeves

PACIFIC STAR (569 "Merry Christmas") ... 4-8 81
Also see ANNETTE
Also see AVALON, Frankie

AVANT-GARDE

P&R '68

Singles: 7-inch

COLUMBIA ... 4-6 67-68

AVERAGE, Johnny, Band: see JOHNNY AVERAGE BAND

AVERAGE WHITE BAND
(AWB)

P&R/R&B/LP '74

Singles: 7-inch

ARISTA ... 3-4 80
ATLANTIC ... 3-4 74-80
MCA ... 3-5 73-74

LPs: 10/12-inch 33rpm

ARISTA ... 5-8 80
ATLANTIC (Except 19000 series) 8-12 74-76
ATLANTIC (19000 series) ... 5-10 77-80
MCA (Except 345) ... 8-10 73-75
MCA (345 "Show Your Hand") .. 15-20 73
(With "Jack-in-the-box" cover.)
MCA (345 "Show Your Hand") ... 8-10 73
(With standard cover.)
Members: Roger Ball; Malcolm Duncan; Steve Ferrone; Alan Gorrie; Robbie McIntosh; Onnie McIntyre; Hamish Stuart.
Also see FOREVER MORE
Also see KING, Ben E., & Average White Band
Also see STONE the CROWS

AXE

P&R/LP '82

Singles: 7-inch

ATCO ... 3-4 82-84
MCA ... 3-4 79-80

LPs: 10/12-inch 33rpm

ATCO ... 5-10 82-84
MCA ... 5-10 79-80
Member: Bobby Barth.
Also see BABYFACE

AXTON, Hoyt
(With the Sherwood Singers)

C&W/P&R '74

Singles: 7-inch

A&M ... 3-5 73-76
BRIAR ... 4-8 61
CAPITOL ... 3-5 71-72
COLGEMS ... 3-6 67
COLUMBIA ... 3-5 69
ELEKTRA ... 3-4 81
HORIZON ... 4-6 62-63
JEREMIAH ... 3-4 79-83
MCA ... 3-4 77-78
20TH FOX ... 4-6 66
VEE JAY ... 4-6 64-65

Picture Sleeves

A&M ... 3-5 73-74

LPs: 10/12-inch 33rpm

A&M ... 5-10 73-77
ACCORD ... 5-10 82
ALLEGIANCE ... 5-10 84
BRYLEN ... 5-10 82
CAPITOL ... 8-10 71
COLUMBIA ... 8-10 69
EXODUS ... 10-15 66
HORIZON ... 15-20 62-63
JEREMIAH ... 8-10 79-82
LAKE SHORE ... 5-10 81
MCA ... 5-10 77-78
SURREY ... 15-18 65
VEE JAY ... 10-15 64-65
VEE JAY INT'L (Except 1000 series) ... 5-10 74-77
VEE JAY INT'L (1000 series) ... 10-12 74

AXTON, Hoyt, & Chambers Brothers

Singles: 7-inch

HORIZON ... 4-8 62

LPs: 10/12-inch 33rpm

HORIZON ... 15-20 63
Also see AXTON, Hoyt
Also see CHAMBERS BROTHERS

AYERS, Roy
(Roy Ayers' Ubiquity)

LP '74

Singles: 12-inch 33/45rpm

COLUMBIA ... 4-6 84-85
POLYDOR ... 4-6 79

Singles: 7-inch

COLUMBIA ... 3-4 84-86
POLYDOR ... 3-4 77

LPs: 10/12-inch 33rpm

ATLANTIC ... 8-12 68-76
COLUMBIA ... 5-10 84-86
ELEKTRA ... 5-10 78
POLYDOR ... 6-10 70-82
Also see DUNLAP, Gene
Also see MANN, Herbie
Also see UBIQUITY

AYERS, Roy, and Wayne Henderson

Singles: 7–inch

POLYDOR.................................... 3-4 79-80

LPs: 10/12–inch 33rpm

POLYDOR.................................. 5-10 80

Also see AYERS, Roy
Also see HENDERSON, Wayne

AZTEC CAMERA

LP '83

Singles: 12–inch 33/45rpm

SIRE... 5-10 84

Singles: 7–inch

SIRE... 3-6 83-88

Picture Sleeves

SIRE... 3-6 84-88

LPs: 10/12–inch 33rpm

SIRE... 8-15 83-87

AZTECA

LP '73

Singles: 7–inch

COLUMBIA 3-5 72-73

LPs: 10/12–inch 33rpm

COLUMBIA 10-12 72-73

Members: Coke Escovedo; Tony Smith.
Also see ESCOVEDO, Coke
Also see MALO
Also see SANTANA

B

B ANGIE B

LP '91

LPs: 10/12-inch 33rpm

CAPITOL..................................... 5-8 91

B.B.C.S. & A.

R&B '82

Singles: 7-inch

SAM 3-4 82

B.B. & Q. Band

(Brooklyn, Bronx & Queens Band)

LP '81

Singles: 12-inch 33/45rpm

CAPITOL..................................... 4-8 81-83

Singles: 7-inch

CAPITOL..................................... 3-5 81-83
IN YOUR FACE.............................. 3-4 86

LPs: 10/12-inch 33rpm

CAPITOL..................................... 5-10 81-83

B. BEAT GIRLS

D&D '83

Singles: 12-inch 33/45rpm

25 WEST 4-6 83

Singles: 7-inch

25 WEST 3-4 83

B. BUMBLE & STINGERS

P&R '61

Singles: 7-inch

DYMO 4-8
MERCURY 4-8 66
RENDEZVOUS 5-10 61-63
TRIAD 4-6

Members: Billy Brumble; Ron Brady; Fred Richard; Ernie Freeman.
Also see FREEMAN, Ernie

B.C.G.: see CREWE, Bob

B-52s

LP '79

Singles: 12-inch 33/45rpm

W.B. 4-6 86

Singles: 7-inch

B-52s (52 "Rock Lobster")......... 15-20 78
REPRISE 3-4 89-91
W.B. (Except 927) 3-4 79-86
W.B. (927 "Give Me Back My Man").. 3-5 81
(Promotional issue only.)

Picture Sleeves

B-52s (52 "Rock Lobster")......... 25-50 78
REPRISE 3-4 89
W.B. 3-5 80-83

LPs: 10/12-inch 33rpm

REPRISE 5-8 89-91
W.B. 5-10 79-86

Members: Cindy Wilson; Keith Strickland; Fred Schneider III; Ricky Wilson; Kate Pierson.

B-H-Y

(Baker-Harris-Young)

R&B '79

Singles: 7-inch

SALSOUL 3-5 79

LPs: 10/12-inch 33rpm

SALSOUL 5-10 79

Members: Ron Baker; Norman Harris; Earl Young.
Also see MFSB
Also see TRAMMPS

B.T. EXPRESS

P&R/R&B/LP '74

Singles: 12-inch 33/45rpm

COAST to COAST 4-6 81
COLUMBIA 4-6 81

Singles: 7-inch

COAST to COAST 3-4 82
COLUMBIA 3-5 76-80
EARTHTONE 3-4 84
ROADSHOW 3-5 74-75
SCEPTER 3-6 74

LPs: 10/12-inch 33rpm

COAST to COAST 5-10 82
COLUMBIA 5-10 76-80
ROADSHOW 10-12 74-76
SCEPTER 8-10 74

Members: Carlos Ward; Bill Risbrook; Richard Thompson; Michael Jones; Dennis Rowe; Leslie Ming; Barbara Joyce Lomas.

BTO: see BACHMAN - TURNER OVERDRIVE

BABE RUTH

LP '73

Singles: 7-inch

CAPITOL...................................... 3-4 76
HARVEST 3-5 73-76

LPs: 10/12-inch 33rpm

HARVEST 5-10 73-76

Members: Ellie Hope; Steve Gurl; Jenny Haan; Dave Hewitt; Ray Knott; Bernie Marsden; Alan Shacklock; Ed Spevock.

BABY JANE & ROCK-A-BYES

P&R '63

Singles: 7-inch

SPOKANE..................................... 8-10 63
U.A. 5-10 62

BABY RAY

(Ray Eddlemon)

P&R '66

Singles: 7-inch

IMPERIAL 8-15 66-67

LPs: 10/12-inch 33rpm

IMPERIAL 15-20 67

BABY RAY & FERNS

Singles: 7-inch

DONNA... 25-35 63

Member: Frank Zappa.
Also see ZAPPA, Frank

BABYFACE

P&R '89

Singles: 7–inch

ASI 3-5 76-77

LPs: 10/12–inch 33rpm

ASI 10-12 77

Also see AXE

BABYFACE

R&B '87

Singles: 7–inch

SOLAR 3-4 87-89

LPs: 10/12–inch 33rpm

SOLAR 5-8 89

Members: Kenny "Babyface" Edmonds; Antonio "L.A." Reid.
Also see DEELE

BABYLON A.D.

LP '89

LPs: 10/12–inch 33rpm

ARISTA 5-8 89

BABYS

P&R/LP '77

Singles: 7–inch

CHRYSALIS 3-5 77-81

Picture Sleeves

CHRYSALIS 3-5 80

LPs: 10/12–inch 33rpm

CHRYSALIS 5-10 77-81

Members: Mike Corby; John Waite; Tony Brock; Wally Stocker; Johnthan Cain.
Also see BAD ENGLISH
Also see JOURNEY

BACHARACH, Burt

P&R '63

Singles: 7–inch

A&M 3-5 68-74
CABOT 3-5
KAPP 3-6 63-65
LIBERTY 3-5 66
U.A. 3-5 67

Picture Sleeves

A&M 3-5 71

EPs: 7–inch 33/45rpm

A&M 4-8 68-73

LPs: 10/12–inch 33rpm

A&M (Except 1) 5-10 67-74
A&M (1 "Radio Interview") 8-15 74
(Promotional issue only.)
KAPP 8-15 65
MCA 5-10 73

BACHARACH, Burt / Glen Campbell / Dionne Warwick

LPs: 10/12–inch 33rpm

CHEVROLET (6658 "On the Move") 10-20 70
(Chevrolet promotional issue.)
Also see CAMPBELL, Glen
Also see WARWICK, Dionne

BACHELORS

P&R/LP '64

Singles: 7–inch

LONDON 5-10 63-72

Picture Sleeves

LONDON 10-15 64-65

LPs: 10/12–inch 33rpm

LONDON 10-25 64-72

Members: Con Cluskey; Declan Stokes; John Stokes.

BACHMAN, Randy

Singles: 7–inch

POLYDOR 3-4 78

LPs: 10/12–inch 33rpm

POLYDOR 5-10 78
RCA (1100 series) 5-10 75
RCA (4300 series) 10-15 70

Also see BACHMAN - TURNER - BACHMAN
Also see BACHMAN - TURNER OVERDRIVE
Also see GUESS WHO
Also see IRONHORSE

BACHMAN - TURNER - BACHMAN

LPs: 10/12–inch 33rpm

REPRISE 8-10 75

Members: Randy Bachman; C.F. Turner; Robin Bachman.
Also see BACHMAN-TURNER OVERDRIVE

BACHMAN - TURNER OVERDRIVE

P&R/LP '73

Singles: 7–inch

COMPLEAT 3-4 84-85
MERCURY 3-5 73-79

Picture Sleeves

MERCURY 3-5 74-75

LPs: 10/12–inch 33rpm

COMPLEAT 5-10 84-85
CURB 5-8 86
MERCURY 6-12 73-79

Members: Randy Bachman; C.F. Turner; Robin Bachman; Tim Bachman; Jim Clench; Norman Durkee; Blair Thornton.
Also see BACHMAN, Randy

BACK STREET CRAWLER (Crawler)

LP '75

Singles: 7–inch

EPIC 3-4 77-78

LPs: 10/12–inch 33rpm

ATCO 10-12 75-76
EPIC (Except PAL-349001) 5-10 77-78
EPIC (PAL-349001 "Crawler") ... 25-30 78
(Picture disc.)

Members: Tony Braunagel; John Bundrick; Paul Kossoff; Mike Montgomery; Geoff Whitehorn; Terry Wilson Slesser.
Also see CUMMINGS, Burton / Cheap Trick / Crawler
Also see FREE
Also see KOSSOFF, Paul

BACKUS, Jim

(With Friend; Jim Bakus; Mr. McGoo & Dennis Farnon Orchestra)

P&R '58

Singles: 7-inch

JUBILEE.. 6-12 58-59

EPs: 7-inch 33/45rpm

RCA (1362 "McGoo in Hi-Fi").... 25-30 56

LPs: 10/12-inch 33rpm

DORE.. 8-10 74

RCA (1362 "McGoo in Hi-Fi").... 30-50 56

Also see HOPE, Bob

BAD BOYS FEATURING K LOVE

R&B/D&D '85

Singles: 12-inch 33/45rpm

STARLITE.. 4-6 85

Singles: 7-inch

STARLITE.. 3-4 85

BAD COMPANY

P&R/LP '74

Singles: 12-inch 33/45rpm

ATLANTIC.. 4-8 88

(Promotional only.)

Singles: 7-inch

ATLANTIC.. 3-4 86-89

SWAN SONG.. 3-5 74-84

Picture Sleeves

ATLANTIC.. 3-4 86-89

SWAN SONG.. 3-5 79-82

LPs: 10/12-inch 33rpm

ATCO.. 5-8 90

ATLANTIC.. 5-10 86-88

SWAN SONG.. 5-10 74-84

Members: Paul Rodgers; Brian Howe; Boz Burrell; Simon Kirke; Mick Ralphs; Mick Jones.

Also see FIRM

Also see FOREIGNER

Also see FREE

Also see KING CRIMSON

Also see NUGENT, Ted

Also see RODGERS, Paul

BAD ENGLISH

P&R/LP '89

LPs: 10/12-inch 33rpm

EPIC.. 5-8 89

Members: John Waithe; Jonathan Cain; Neal Schon; Ricky Phillips; Dean Castronovo.

Also see BABYS

Also see JOURNEY

BAD GIRLS

R&B '81

Singles: 7-inch

BC.. 3-4 81

BAD HABITS

Singles: 7-inch

PAULA.. 5-10 70-72

Members: Delaney Bramlett; Bonnie Bramlett.

Also see DELANEY & BONNIE

BADAROU, Wally

R&B '86

Singles: 7-inch

ISLAND.. 3-4 86

LPs: 10/12-inch 33rpm

ISLAND.. 5-10 86

BADFINGER

P&R '69

Singles: 7-inch

AMERICOM (301 "Maybe Tomorrow")........................ 100-200 69

(Plastic "Pocket Disc" soundsheet.)

APPLE (1815 "Come and Get It") 8-15 70

APPLE (1822 "No Matter What") . 8-15 70

APPLE (1841 "Day After Day").... 8-15 71

APPLE (1844 "Baby Blue")......... 8-15 72

APPLE (1864 "Apple of My Eye")........................ 15-25 73

ATLANTIC.. 3-4 81

ELEKTRA.. 3-5 79

RADIO.. 3-4 81

W.B. 3-6 74

Promotional Singles

APPLE (1841 "Day After Day") .. 50-75 71

White label.)

APPLE (1844 "Baby Blue")........ 30-50 72

(White label.)

APPLE (1864 "Apple of My Eye")........................ 15-25 73

Picture Sleeves

APPLE (1844 "Baby Blue")........... 5-8 72

LPs: 10/12-inch 33rpm

APPLE (3364 "Magic Christian Music")........................ 15-25 70

APPLE (3367 "No Dice")............ 25-35 70

APPLE (3387 "Straight Up") 75-100 71

APPLE (3411 "Ass") 15-20 73

ELEKTRA (175 "Airwaves")....... 10-15 79

RADIO (16030 "Say No More").... 5-10 81

RYKODISC (0189 "Day After Day")........................ 15-25 90

(Clear vinyl.)

W.B. (2762 "Badfinger")............ 15-20 74

W.B (2827 "Wish You Were Here")........................ 20-30 74

Members: Tom Evans; Mike Gibbons; Pete Ham; Joey Molland; Peter Clarke; Tony Kaye.

Also see IVEYS

BADGER

LP '73

LPs: 10/12-inch 33rpm

ATCO.. 10-12 73

EPIC.. 8-10 74

Members: Roy Dyke; Kim Gardner; Dave Foster; Tony Kaye; Jackie Lomax; Brian Parrish; Paul Pilnick.

Also see ASHTON, GARDNER & DYKE

Also see LOMAX, Jackie

BADLANDS
LP '89

LPs: 10/12-inch 33rpm

ATLANTIC 5-8 89-91

BAERWALD, David
LP '90

LPs: 10/12-inch 33rpm

A&M 5-8 90

BAEZ, Joan
LP '61

Singles: 7-inch

A&M 3-5 72-77
DECCA 3-5 72
PORTRAIT 3-5 77-79
RCA 3-5 72
VANGUARD (6 "Maria Dolores") 5-10
(Stereo. Jukebox issue.)
VANGUARD (35000 series).......... 4-8 63-69
VANGUARD (35100 series).......... 3-5 70-71

Picture Sleeves

A&M 4-6 72
PORTRAIT 3-5 79
RCA 4-6 72
VANGUARD (6 "Deportee") 5-10 60s
(Promotional issue only.)
VANGUARD (35031 "There But for Fortune") 15-25 65

LPs: 10/12-inch 33rpm

A&M (Except 8375) 6-10 72-77
A&M (8375 "Joan Baez - Radio Airplay Album") 10-15 76
(Promotional issue only.)
EMUS 5-10 79
FANTASY 10-15
NAUTILUS 25-35 81
(Half-speed mastered.)
PICKWICK 5-10 73
PORTRAIT 5-10 77-79
SQUIRE 10-20 63
VANGUARD (41/42 "Ballad Book") 10-12 72
VANGUARD (105/106 "Country Music Album") 10-20 79
VANGUARD (077 thru 123) 20-30 60-63
VANGUARD (160 thru 306) 12-25 64-69
VANGUARD (308 thru 332) 6-10 69-73
VANGUARD (400 series)........... 5-10
(Vanguard numbers 077 through 446 may be preceded by a "2," indicating stereo, or a "9" or "79" for mono issues.)
VANGUARD (6500 series).......... 8-12 71
VANGUARD (6500 series)........ 10-12 70-71
Also see WILSON, Dennis / Ram Jam / Joan Baez

BAEZ, Joan, Bill Wood & Ted Alevizos

LP: 10/12-inch 33rpm

VERITAS (62202 "Folksingers 'Round Harvard Square") 100-200 60
(Without text in upper right corner reading: "This is the historic album featuring the original first recordings of America's Most Exciting Folk Singer — The Best of Joan Baez." A limited, numbered edition.)
VERITAS (62202 "Folksingers 'Round Harvard Square") 50-100 61
(Cover has "This is the historic album featuring the original first recordings of America's Most Exciting Folk Singer — The Best of Joan Baez.")
Also see BAEZ, Joan

BAGBY, Doc
P&R '57

Singles: 78rpm

OKEH 5-10 57

Singles: 7-inch

END 5-10 60
KAISER 5-10 59
OKEH 5-10 57
RED TOP 15-20 59
TALLY HO 5-10 61
VIM 5-10 57

EPs: 10/12-inch 33rpm

EPIC (7190 "Dumplins") 50-75 57

LPs: 10/12-inch 33rpm

KING 25-35 59
Also see TERRY, Sonny

BAGBY, Doc / Luis Rivera

LPs: 10/12-inch 33rpm

KING 25-35 59
Also see BAGBY, Doc

BAGDASARIAN, Ross

Singles: 7-inch

IMPERIAL 3-5 69
LIBERTY (55000 thru 55200 series) 5-10 56-60
LIBERTY (55300 thru 56000 series) 3-8 61-70
MERCURY 5-10 54

LPs: 10/12-inch 33rpm

LIBERTY 20-30 66
Also see SEVILLE, David

BAILEY, Arthur
D&D '84

Singles: 12-inch 33/45rpm

ATLANTIC 4-6 84

Singles: 7-inch

ATLANTIC 3-4 84

BAILEY, J.R.
R&B '68

Singles: 7-inch

CALLA 4-6 68
MALA 5-8
MAM 3-5 74
MIDLAND INT'L 3-5 75
RCA 3-5 76
SPRING 3-4 84
TOY 3-5 72-73

U.A. 3-4 78
VIRGO 3-5

LPs: 10/12-inch 33rpm

MAM 8-10 74
U.A. 5-10 78

Also see CADILLACS
Also see CRICKETS

BAILEY, Pearl

R&B '46

Singles: 78rpm

COLUMBIA 4-8 46-50
CORAL 3-6 52-55
MERCURY 3-6 56
ROULETTE 3-6 57
SUNSET 3-6 56
VERVE 3-6 56

Singles: 7-inch

COLUMBIA (38000 series) 5-10 50
COLUMBIA (43000 series) 3-6 66
CORAL 5-10 52-55
DECCA 3-6 64
MERCURY 5-10 56
PROJECT 3 .... 3-5 68-70
RCA (500 series) 3-5 71
RCA (9400 series) 3-6 67
ROULETTE 4-8 59-68
SUNSET 5-10 56
VERVE 5-10 56

EPs: 7-inch 33/45rpm

COLUMBIA 10-20 52-56
CORAL 10-20 54
ROULETTE 10-15 57

LPs: 10/12-inch 33rpm

ACCORD 5-10 83
COLUMBIA (900 series) 20-35 57
COLUMBIA (2600 series) 25-40 56
(10-inch LPs.)
COLUMBIA (6000 series) 25-40 50
(10-inch LPs.)
CORAL (56000 series) 25-40 54
(10-inch LPs.)
CORAL (57000 series) 20-30 57
CO-STAR 15-20 58
MERCURY (Except 100 series) 20-30 56-58
MERCURY (100 series) 8-12 69
PROJECT 3 .... 5-10 70
RCA (4500 series) 5-10 71
ROULETTE (100 series) 8-12 71
ROULETTE (25000 & 25100 series) 15-25 57-63
ROULETTE (25200 & 25300 series) 10-15 64-65
VOCALION 15-25 58
WING 15-25 59-63

BAILEY, Pearl, & Mike Douglas

Singles: 7-inch

PROJECT 3 .... 3-6 68

Also see DOUGLAS, Mike

BAILEY, Pearl / Rose Murphy / Ivie Anderson

LP: 10/12-inch 33rpm

GRAND PRIX 10-15 60s

Also see BAILEY, Pearl
Also see MURPHY, Rose

BAILEY, Philip

R&B/LP '83

Singles: 12-inch 33/45rpm

COLUMBIA 4-6 83-86

Singles: 7-inch

COLUMBIA 3-4 83-86

Picture Sleeves

COLUMBIA 3-4 85

LPs: 10/12-inch 33rpm

COLUMBIA 5-10 83-86

Also see EARTH, WIND & FIRE

BAILEY, Philip, & Phil Collins

P&R/R&B '84

Singles: 12-inch 33/45rpm

COLUMBIA 4-6 84

Singles: 7-inch

COLUMBIA 3-4 84

Picture Sleeves

COLUMBIA 3-4 84

Also see BAILEY, Philip
Also see COLLINS, Phil

BAILEY, Philip, & Little Richard

Singles: 7-inch

WTG (08492 "Twins") 3-4 88

Also see BAILEY, Phil
Also see LITTLE RICHARD

BAILEY, Razzy
(Razzie Bailey; Razzy)

P&R '74

Singles: 7-inch

ABC-PAR 4-6 67
B&K 8-12 59
CAPRICORN 3-5 75
ERASTUS 3-5 76
MCA 3-4 84-86
MGM 3-5 74
1-3-4 .... 3-5 69
PEACH 5-10 66
RCA 3-4 77-84
SOUNDS of AMERICA 3-4 86-89

Picture Sleeves

RCA 3-4 80-81

LPs: 10/12-inch 33rpm

MCA 5-10 85-86
PLANTATION 5-8 81
RCA 5-10 79-84

BAIO, Scott

LP '82

Singles: 7-inch

RCA 3-4 82-83

LPs: 10/12-inch 33rpm

RCA 5-10 82-83

BAJA MARIMBA BAND

P&R '63

Singles: 7–inch

A&M 3-5 66-67
ALMO 3-6 63-66
BELL 3-5 73
SHOUT 3-4 81

Picture Sleeves

A&M 3-8 66-68

EPs: 7–inch 33/45rpm

A&M 4-8 68

LPs: 10/12–inch 33rpm

A&M 5-10 64-70
BELL 5-10 73

Member: Julius Wechter.
Also see DENNY, Martin
Also see MONTEZ, Chris

BAKER, Anita

R&B/LP '83

Singles: 7–inch

BEVERLY GLEN 3-4 83-84
ELEKTRA 3-4 86-90

Picture Sleeves

ELEKTRA 3-4 86-89

LPs: 10/12–inch 33rpm

BEVERLY GLEN 5-10 83
ELEKTRA 5-10 86-90

Also see CHAPTER 8
Also see WINANS & Anita Baker

BAKER, Arthur

D&D '84

Singles: 12–inch 33/45rpm

ATLANTIC 4-6 84

BAKER, George
(George Baker Selection)

P&R/LP '70

Singles: 7–inch

COLOSSUS 4-6 70
W.B. 3-5 75-76

Picture Sleeves

COLOSSUS 5-8 70

LPs: 10/12–inch 33rpm

COLOSSUS 15-20 70
W.B. 10-15 76

BAKER, Ginger
(Ginger Baker's Air Force)

P&R/LP '70

Singles: 7–inch

ATCO 3-5 70

LPs: 10/12–inch 33rpm

ATCO 12-15 70-72
AXIOM 8-12 90
SIRE 5-10 77
POLYDOR 8-10 72-79

Also see BAKER - GURVITZ ARMY
Also see BLIND FAITH
Also see CREAM
Also see WINWOOD, Steve

BAKER, Lavern
(With the Gliders)

R&B '55

Singles: 78rpm

ATLANTIC 10-15 53-57

Singles: 7–inch

ATLANTIC (1000 series, except 1004) 10-25 54-58
ATLANTIC (1004 "Soul on Fire") 30-40 53
ATLANTIC (2000 series, except 2001) 10-20 59-65
ATLANTIC (2001 "It's So Fine") 20-30 58
BRUNSWICK (55291 "Baby" 10-20 66
BRUNSWICK (55297 "Call Me Darling") 10-20 66
BRUNSWICK (55311 "Wrapped, Tied and Tangled") 25-35 67

EPs: 7–inch 33/45rpm

ATLANTIC (566 "Lavern Baker - Tweedle Dee" 50-75 56
ATLANTIC (588 "Lavern Baker - Jim Dandy" 50-75 57
ATLANTIC (617 "Lavern Baker - I Cried a Tear" 40-60 58

LPs: 10/12–inch 33rpm

ATCO 8-10 71
ATLANTIC (Except 8002, 8007 & 8030) 15-20 59-63
ATLANTIC (8002 "Lavern") 50-75 57
(Black label.)
ATLANTIC (8002 "Lavern") 20-30 59
(Red label.)
ATLANTIC (8007 "Lavern Baker") 40-60 57
ATLANTIC (8030 "Blues Ballads") 35-45 59
(Black label.)
ATLANTIC (8030 "Blues Ballads") 35-45 59
(White label.)
ATLANTIC (8030 "Blues Ballads") 20-30 59
(Red label.)
BRUNSWICK 10-15 70

Session: King Curtis.
Also see KING CURTIS
Also see RHODES, Todd
Also see WILSON, Jackie, & LaVern Baker

BAKER, Lavern, & Ben E. King

Singles: 7–inch

ATLANTIC 5-10 60

Also see KING, Ben E.

BAKER, Lavern, & Jimmy Ricks

Singles: 7–inch

ATLANTIC 5-10 61

Also see BAKER, Lavern

BAKER - GURVITZ ARMY

LP '75

Singles: 7–inch

ATCO 3-5 74-76
JANUS 3-5 75

LPs: 10/12–inch 33rpm

ATCO 8-10 75-76
JANUS 10-12 75

Members: Ginger Baker; Adrian Gurvitz; Paul Gurvitz; Peter Lemer; John Norman; Snips.
Also see BAKER, Ginger
Also see GURVITZ, Adrian

BALAAM & ANGEL

LP '88

LPs: 10/12–inch 33rpm

VIRGIN 5-10 87-89

Members: Mark Morris; Jim Morris; Des Morris; Ian McKean.

BALANCE

P&R/LP '81

Singles: 7–inch

PORTRAIT 3-4 81-82

LPs: 10/12–inch 33rpm

PORTRAIT 5-10 81-82

Also see BLUES MAGOOS

BALDRY, Long John
(With the Hootchie Cootchie Men)

P&R '68

Singles: 7–inch

A&M 4-6 68
ASCOT 4-8 66-67
EMI AMERICA 3-4 79
W.B. 3-6 68-72

LPs: 10/12–inch 33rpm

ASCOT 15-25 65
CASABLANCA 5-10 75-76
EMI AMERICA 5-10 79-80
JANUS 10-15
MUSICLINE 5-8 86
U.A. 8-10 71
W.B. 8-10 71-72

BALDRY, Long John, & Kathi McDonald

Singles: 7–inch

EMI AMERICA 3-4 79

Picture Sleeves

EMI AMERICA 3-4 79

Also see BALDRY, Long John
Also see McDONALD, Kathi

BALIN, Marty

P&R/LP '81

Singles: 7–inch

CHALLENGE 20-25 62
EMI AMERICA 3-4 81-84

Picture Sleeves

EMI AMERICA 3-4 81

LPs: 10/12–inch 33rpm

EMI AMERICA 8-10 81-83

Also see JEFFERSON AIRPLANE
Also see JEFFERSON STARSHIP

BALL, Kenny
(With His Jazzmen)

P&R/LP '62

Singles: 7–inch

DECCA 3-5 67
GUYDEN 3-5 61
KAPP 3-5 62-64

Picture Sleeves

KAPP 4-8 62

LPs: 10/12–inch 33rpm

JAZZOLOGY 5-10 79
KAPP 10-25 62-64

Members: Kenny Ball; Johnny Bennett; Dave Jones; Colin Bates; Vic Pitts; Ron Bowden; Diz Disley.

BALLADS

P&R/R&B '68

Singles: 7–inch

VENTURE 4-8 68

BALLARD, Hank
(With the Midnight Lighters; with Dapps)

R&B '68

Singles: 7–inch

KING 4-8 68
PEOPLE 3-5 72
POLYDOR 3-5 72
SILVER FOX 3-6 70
STANG 3-5 75

LPs: 10/12–inch 33rpm

KING (1000 series) 10-15 69

BALLARD, Hank, & Midnighters

R&B '59

Singles: 7–inch

GUSTO 3-4 78
KING (5171 "The Twist") 10-15 59
KING (5195 "Kansas City") 8-12 59
KING (5215 "Sugaree") 8-12 59
(Monaural.)
KING (S-5215 "Sugaree") 20-25 59
(Stereo.)
KING (5245 thru 6131) 5-10 59-67
LE JOINT 3-5 79

Picture Sleeves

KING (5491 "The Continental Walk") 10-15 61

EPs: 7–inch 33/45rpm

FEDERAL (333 "Their Greatest Hits") 75-125 54
KING (333 "Their Greatest Hits") 25-35 58
KING (435 "Singin' & Swingin, Vol. 1") 25-35 59
KING (435 "Singin' & Swingin, Vol. 2") 25-35 59
KING (793 "Jumpin' Hank Ballard") 25-35 62

KING (7815 "1963 Sound of Hank Ballard & Midnighters") 15-25 59

LPs: 10/12–inch 33rpm

FEDERAL (90 "Their Greatest Hits") 1500-2500 54
(10–inch LP.)
FEDERAL (541 "Their Greatest Hits") 500-600 57
(White cover.)
FEDERAL (541 "Their Greatest Hits") 400-500 57
(Tan or red cover.)
KING (541 "Their Greatest Hits") 50-100 58
KING (581 "Midnighters, Vol. 2") 50-100 58
KING (600 thru 800 series, except KS-740) 25-40 59-64
KING (KS-740 "Spotlight on Hank Ballard") 75-100 61
(Stereo.)
KING (900 series) 15-20 65-68
KING (5000 series) 8-10 77

Also see BALLARD, Hank
Also see MIDNIGHTERS
Also see ROYALS

BALLARD, Hank, & Midnighters / Viceroys

Singles: 7–inch

KING/BETHLEHEM (5719 "That Low Down Move") 10-15 63
(The Viceroys side has a Bethlehem label. Promotional issue only.)

Also see BALLARD, Hank, & Midnighters

BALLARD, Russ

P&R/LP '80

Singles: 7–inch

EMI AMERICA 3-4 84-85
EPIC 3-5 74-80

LPs: 10/12–inch 33rpm

EMI AMERICA 5-8 84-85
EPIC 8-10 74-80

Also see ARGENT
Also see UNIT 4+2

BALLIN' JACK

P&R/LP '71

Singles: 7–inch

COLUMBIA 3-5 71
MERCURY 3-5 73

LPs: 10/12–inch 33rpm

COLUMBIA 10-12 70-72
MERCURY 8-10 73-74

BALLOON FARM

P&R '68

Singles: 7–inch

LAURIE 4-8 68

BALTIMORA

P&R '85

Singles: 12–inch 33/45rpm

MANHATTAN 4-6 86

Singles: 7–inch

MANHATTAN 3-4 85-86

Picture Sleeves

MANHATTAN 3-4 85

LPs: 10/12–inch 33rpm

MANHATTAN (53020 "Living in the Background") 5-10 85

BALTIMORE & OHIO Marching Band

P&R '67

Singles: 7–inch

JUBILEE 3-6 67

LPs: 10/12–inch 33rpm

JUBILEE 10-15 67

BAMA

P&R '79

Singles: 7–inch

FREE FLIGHT (Black vinyl) 3-5 79
FREE FLIGHT (Colored vinyl) 4-6 79
(Promotional issues only.)

LPs: 10/12–inch 33rpm

FREE FLIGHT 5-10 79

BAMBAATAA, Afrika

(With James Brown; with Soul Sonic Force; with Family)

P&R/R&B '82

Singles: 12–inch 33/45rpm

TOMMY BOY 4-6 83-86

Singles: 7–inch

TOMMY BOY 3-4 82-86

LPs: 10/12–inch 33rpm

TOMMY BOY 5-10 83-86

Also see BROWN, James
Also see SHANGO

BANANA SPLITS

P&R '69

Singles: 7–inch

DECCA 4-8 68-69

Picture Sleeves

DECCA 8-10 69-70

EPs: 7–inch 33/45rpm

KELLOGG 8-12 69

LPs: 10/12–inch 33rpm

DECCA 10-15 69

BANANARAMA

P&R/D&D/LP '83

Singles: 12–inch 33/45rpm

LONDON 4-6 83-88

Singles: 7–inch

LONDON 3-4 82-88

Picture Sleeves

LONDON 3-4 82-88

LPs: 10/12–inch 33rpm

LONDON 5-10 83-88

Members: Sarah Dallin; Keren Woodward; Siobhan Fahey.
Also see BAND AID

BAND, The

P&R/LP '68

Singles: 7-inch

CAPITOL (Except 2000 series)..... 3-5 71-77
CAPITOL (2000 series)................ 4-8 67-70
W.B. 3-4 78

Picture Sleeves

CAPITOL (2705 "Rag Mama Rag") 4-8 70

LPs: 10/12-inch 33rpm

CAPITOL (Except 2955) 10-15 69-85
CAPITOL (2955 "Music from Big Pink") 15-20 68
MFSL (039 "Music from Big Pink")..................................... 25-50 80
W.B. (737 "The Last Waltz") 20-30 78
(Promotional issue only.)
W.B. (3146 "The Last Waltz") ... 15-20 78
(Three-LP set.)

Members: Levon Helm; Rick Danko; Garth Hudson; Richard Manuel; Robbie Robertson.
Also see DANKO, Rick
Also see DYLAN, Bob
Also see HAWKINS, Ronnie
Also see HELM, Levon
Also see LEVON & HAWKS
Also see MILLER, Steve / Band / Quicksilver Messinger Service
Also see ROBERTSON, Robbie

BAND AID

P&R '84

Singles: 7-inch

COLUMBIA (04749 "Do They Know It's Christmas") 3-4 84

Picture Sleeves

COLUMBIA (04749 "Do They Know It's Christmas") 3-5 84

Members: Bananarama; Paul McCartney; Boomtown Rats; Boy George; Phil Collins; Duran Duran; Bob Geldof; Heaven 17; Kool & Gang; George Michael; John Moss; Spandau Ballet; Status Quo; Sting; U2; Ultravox; Paul Weller; Paul Young.
Also see BANANARAMA
Also see BOOMTOWN RATS
Also see COLLINS, Phil
Also see CULTURE CLUB
Also see DURAN DURAN
Also see GELDORF, Bob
Also see HEAVEN 17
Also see KOOL & GANG
Also see SPANDAU BALLET
Also see STATUS QUO
Also see STING
Also see STYLE COUNCIL
Also see U2
Also see ULTRAVOX
Also see WHAM
Also see YOUNG, Paul

BAND of GOLD

P&R/R&B '84

Singles: 7-inch

RCA 3-4 85

BAND of the Black Watch

P&R/LP '76

Singles: 7-inch

PRIVATE STOCK..........................3-5 75-76

LPs: 10/12-inch 33rpm

PRIVATE STOCK..........................5-10 76

BANDIT

P&R '79

Singles: 7-inch

ARIOLA AMERICA.......................3-4 79
POLYDOR 3-4 79

LPs: 10/12-inch 33rpm

ARIOLA AMERICA.......................5-10 78-79

Members: Joey Newman; Kevin Barnhill; Tommy Eaton; Danny Gorman; David Rossa.

BANDOLERO

D&D '84

Singles: 12-inch 33/45rpm

SIRE...4-6 84

Singles: 7-inch

SIRE...3-4 84

LPs: 10/12-inch 33rpm

ECLIPSE.......................................8-10 75

BANDWAGON

R&B '68

Singles: 7-inch

EPIC...4-6 68

BANG

P&R//LP '72

Singles: 7-inch

CAPITOL.......................................3-5 72-74

LPs: 10/12-inch 33rpm

CAPITOL.......................................8-12 72-73

BANG TANGO

LP '89

LPs: 10/12-inch 33rpm

MECHANIC...................................5-8 89-91

BANGLES

LP '84

Singles: 12-inch 33/45rpm

COLUMBIA...................................4-6 85-88

Singles: 7-inch

COLUMBIA...................................3-4 84-88
DEF JAM.......................................3-4 87
DOWNKIDDIE (001 "Getting Out of Hand")...................................5-10 81

Picture Sleeves

COLUMBIA...................................3-4 84-88
DEF JAM.......................................3-4 87
DOWNKIDDIE (001 "Getting Out of Hand")...................................10-20 81

(Back of sleeve shows Downkiddie Records as being in Los Angeles, California.)
DOWNKIDDIE (001 "Getting Out of Hand") 8-15 81
(Back of sleeve shows Downkiddie Records as being in Torrance, California.)

LPs: 10/12-inch 33rpm

COLUMBIA 5-10 84-90
I.R.S. 6-10 83

Members: Vicki Peterson; Debbi Peterson; Susanna Hoffs; Annette Zilinskas; Michael Steele.
Also see BANGS
Also see HOFFS, Susanna

BANGOR FLYING CIRCUS

LP '69

Singles: 7-inch

DUNHILL 3-5 70

LPs: 10/12-inch 33rpm

DUNHILL 12-15 69

Members: Michael Tegza; David Wolinski; Alan DeCarlo.

BANGS

Singles: 7-inch

DOWNKIDDIE (001 "Getting Out of Hand") 20-30 81

Picture Sleeves

DOWNKIDDIE (001 "Getting Out of Hand") 30-50 81

Members: Vicki Peterson; Debbi Peterson; Susanna Hoffs.
Also see BANGLES

BANKS, Bunny, Trio

R&B '43

Singles: 78rpm

SAVOY 5-10 43

Members: Ernie Ransom; Henry Padgett; Clem Moorman.

BANKS, Darrell

P&R/R&B '66

Singles: 7-inch

ATCO (6484 "Angel Baby") 15-25 67
COTILLION 5-10 68
REVILOT 10-20 66
SOULTOWN 5-10 66
VOLT 4-8 69

LPs: 10/12-inch 33rpm

ATCO (216 "Darrell Banks Is Here") 15-25 67
(Monaural.)
ATCO (216 "Darrell Banks Is Here") 25-30 67
(Stereo.)
VOLT 10-15 69

BANKS, Peter

LP '73

Singles: 7-inch

CAPITOL 3-5 73

LPs: 10/12-inch 33rpm

CAPITOL 10-12 73

Also see AFTER the FIRE
Also see BLODWYN PIG
Also see FLASH
Also see YES

BANKS, Ron

R&B '83

Singles: 12-inch 33/45rpm

CBS ASSOCIATED 4-6 83

Singles: 7-inch

ABC 3-5 75
CBS ASSOCIATED 3-4 83

LPs: 10/12-inch 33rpm

CBS ASSOCIATED 5-10 83

Also see DRAMATICS

BANKS, Rose

R&B '76

Singles: 7-inch

MOTOWN 3-5 76
SOURCE 3-4 80

LPs: 10/12-inch 33rpm

MOTOWN 8-10 76

Also see SLY & Family Stone

BANKS, Tony

LP '79

Singles: 7-inch

ATLANTIC 3-4 83
CHARISMA 3-4 79

LPs: 10/12-inch 33rpm

ATLANTIC 5-10 83
CHARISMA 5-10 79

Also see GENESIS

BANKS & HAMPTON

R&B '77

Singles: 7-inch

W.B. 3-5 76-77

LPs: 10/12-inch 33rpm

W.B. 5-10 77

Members: Homer Banks; Carl Hampton.

BANZAII

P&R/R&B '75

Singles: 7-inch

SCEPTER 3-5 75

BARBARA & BROWNS

P&R/R&B '64

Singles: 7-inch

CADET 4-8 66
SOUND of MEMPHIS 3-5 72
STAX 5-10 64

Member: Barbara Brown.

BARBARA & UNIQUES

R&B '70

Singles: 7-inch

ABBOTT 3-5 72
ARDEN 3-5 70
NEW CHICAGO SOUND 3-5 70
20TH FOX 3-5 74

Members: Barbara Livsey; Gwen Livsey; Doris Lindsey.

BARBARA LYNN: see LYNN, Barbara

BARBARIANS

P&R '65

Singles: 7-inch

JOY (290 "Hey Little Bird") 20-30 65
LAURIE (3308 "Are You a Boy or Are You a Girl") 10-15 65
LAURIE (3321 "What the New Breed Say") 10-20 65
LAURIE (3326 "Moulty") 10-20 66

LPs: 10/12-inch 33rpm

LAURIE (2033 "Barbarians") 50-70 66
RHINO 5-10 79

Also see ELEGANTS

BARBER, Chris
(Chris Barber's Jazz Band)

P&R/R&B '59

Singles: 7-inch

ATLANTIC 4-8 59
LAURIE 4-8 58-63
LONDON 4-6 62

Picture Sleeves

LAURIE 5-10 59

LPs: 10/12-inch 33rpm

ARCHIVE of FOLK MUSIC 8-12 68
ATLANTIC 15-25 59
COLPIX 15-25 59
LAURIE 15-25 59-62

Also see DR. JOHN & Chris Barber

BARBER, Frank, Orchestra

P&R/LP '82

Singles: 7-inch

VICTORY 3-4 82

LPs: 10/12-inch 33rpm

VICTORY 5-10 82

BARBIERI, Gato

LP '73

Singles: 7-inch

A&M 3-5 76-79
U.A. 3-5 73

LPs: 10/12-inch 33rpm

A&M 5-10 76-79
ARISTA 8-10 75
FLYING DUTCHMAN 5-10 70-80
IMPULSE 8-10 73-75
U.A. 5-10 73

BARBOUR, Dave

P&R '50

Singles: 78rpm

CAPITOL 5-10 50-51

Singles: 7-inch

ARWIN 4-8 59
CAPITOL 5-10 50-51

EPs: 7-inch 33/45rpm

CAPITOL 5-15 54
DECCA 5-15 53

LPs: 10/12-inch 33rpm

DECCA 15-25 53

BARBOUR, Keith

P&R/LP '69

Singles: 7-inch

BARNABY 3-5 71
EPIC 3-6 69-70

LPs: 10/12-inch 33rpm

EPIC 15-20 69

BARBUSTERS

P&R '87

Singles: 7-inch

CBS ASSOCIATED 3-4 87

Also see JETT, Joan

BARCLAY, Eddie

P&R '55

Singles: 78rpm

RAMA 5-10 55
TICO 5-10 55

Singles: 7-inch

RAMA 5-10 55
TICO 5-10 55

LP: 10/12-inch 33rpm

MONUMENT 10-20 66

BARCLAY JAMES HARVEST

LP '77

Singles: 7-inch

HARVEST 3-5 73
MCA 3-5 76-77
POLYDOR 3-5 75-79

LPs: 10/12-inch 33rpm

HARVEST 8-12 73
MCA 8-10 77
POLYDOR 8-10 74-80
SIRE 10-15 70-71

Members: Les Holroyd; John Lees; John Pritchard; Stewart "Wolly" Wolstenholme.

BARD, Annette

Singles: 7-inch

IMPERIAL 20-25 60

Also see CONNORS, Carol

BARDENS, Peter
(Pete Bardens)

LP '87

LPs: 10/12-inch 33rpm

CAPITOL 5-10 87
VERVE/FORECAST 10-12 71

Also see CAMEL
Also see THEM

BARDEUX

P&R/LP '88

Singles: 7-inch

ENIGMA 3-4 89
SYNTHICIDE 3-4 88

Picture Sleeves

SYNTHICIDE 3-4 88

LPs: 10/12-inch 33rpm

ENIGMA 5-8 89
SYNTHICIDE 5-8 88
Members: Stacy Smith; Jazz; Melanie Taylor.

BARE, Bobby
(With the All American Boys; with Hillsiders; with Bobby Bare Jr; with Family; with Jeannie Bare)

C&W/P&R '62

Singles: 78rpm

CAPITOL.................................. 5-10 57

Singles: 7-inch

CAPITOL.................................. 10-15 57
COLUMBIA 3-5 78-85
EMI AMERICA 3-4 85-86
FRATERNITY............................... 8-15 58-61
MERCURY 3-5 70-72
RCA (Except 8000 & 9000 series) 3-5 69-77
RCA (8000 & 9000 series) 4-8 62-68
RICE..................................... 3-5 73-74

Picture Sleeves

RCA...................................... 5-10 62-65

LPs: 10/12-inch 33rpm

CAMDEN................................... 8-12 68-73
COLUMBIA 5-10 78-85
LITTLE DARLIN 8-12
MERCURY 10-15 70-72
PICKWICK 5-10 75-80
PICKWICK/HILLTOP 10-15 65
RCA (ANL1 & APL1 series) 8-12 73-77
RCA (AYL1 series)........................ 5-10 81
RCA (LPM-2776 thru
LPM-3994)................................ 10-20 63-68
(Monaural.)
RCA (LSP-2776 thru
LSP-3994)................................ 15-25 63-68
(Stereo.)
RCA (4000 series)........................ 10-15 69-71
RCA (6000 series) 8-15 73
SEARS 10-15
SUN (136 "Bobby Bare's Greatest
Hits") 15-25 74
U.A. 8-12 75-76
Session: Anita Kerr Singers.
Also see BOWMAN, Don
Also see CASH, Rosanne, & Bobby Bare
Also see KERR, Anita
Also see ORBISON, Roy / Bobby Bare / Joey Powers
Also see PARSONS, Bill

BARE, Bobby, Liz Anderson & Norma Jean

C&W '66

Singles: 7-inch

RCA...................................... 4-6 66

LPs: 10/12-inch 33rpm

BARE TRACKS 8-12
RCA...................................... 12-20 66

BARE, Bobby, & Skeeter Davis
(Skeeter Davis & Bobby Bare)

C&W '65

Singles: 7-inch

RCA (8000 & 9000 series)............3-6 65-70

LPs: 10/12-inch 33rpm

RCA 10-15 65-70
Also see DAVIS, Skeeter

BARE, Bobby, / Donna Fargo / Jerry Wallace

LPs: 10/12-inch 33rpm

OUT of TOWN DIST 5-10 82
Also see BARE, Bobby
Also see FARGO, Donna
Also see WALLACE, Jerry

BAR-KAYS

P&R/R&B '67

Singles: 12-inch 33/45rpm

MERCURY..................................4-6 79-85

Singles: 7-inch

MERCURY..................................3-5 76-84
STAX.....................................3-4 78-81
VOLT.....................................3-6 67-74

LPs: 10/12-inch 33rpm

MERCURY..................................5-10 76-87
STAX.....................................5-10 78-81
VOLT.....................................10-15 67-74
Members: Jimmy King; Phalon Jones; Carl Cunningham; Ron Caldwell; Larry Dodson; James Alexander; Charles Allen; Vernon Burch; Ben Cauley; Donnelle Hagan; Harvey Henderson; Winston Stewart.
Also see REDDING, Otis
Also see NEWCOMERS

BARKER, Blue Lu

R&B '48

Singles: 78rpm

APOLLO...................................5-10 46-48
CAPITOL..................................6-12 48-50
DECCA 10-20 39-40

Singles: 7-inch

CAPITOL..................................20-30 50

BARKLEY, Tyrone

R&B '79

Singles: 7-inch

MIDSONG INT'L 3-4 79

BARLOW, Dean, & Crickets

Singles: 78rpm

JAY-DEE..................................10-20 54

Singles: 7-inch

BEACON (555 "Be Faithful"/"I'm
Not the One You Love")...........10-15 63
JAY-DEE (785 "Your Love") 50-75 54
JAY-DEE (786 "Just You").........50-75 54
JAY-DEE (795 "I'm Going to
Live My Life Alone")..............75-100 54
Also see CRICKETS

BARLOW, Dean, & Crickets / Deep River Boys

Singles: 78rpm

BEACON 10-20 54

Singles: 7–inch

BEACON (104 "Be Faithful"/"Sleepy Little Cowboy") 40-60 54

Also see BARLOW, Dean, & Crickets
Also see DEEP RIVER BOYS

BARNES, Cheryl

P&R '79

Singles: 7–inch

MILLENNIUM 3-4 77
POLYDOR 3-4 80
RCA 3-4 79

BARNES, J.J.

(With the Del Fi's)

P&R/R&B '66

Singles: 7–inch

BUDDAH 4-8 69
GROOVESVILLE 10-15 67
INVASION 4-6 70
KABLE (437 "Won't You Let Me Know") 75-125 60
MAGIC TOUCH 4-6 70
MICKAY'S (3004 "Just One More Time") 50-75 62
MICKAY'S (4472 "Get a Hold of Yourself") 50-75 62
PERCEPTION 4-6 74
REVILOT (Except 222) 10-15 68
REVILOT (222 "Out Love Is in the Pocket") 50-75 68
RICH (1005 "Won't You Let Me Know") 50-100 60
RIC-TIC 10-15 65-66
RING (101 "She Ain't Ready")... 20-30 64
SCEPTER (1266 "Just One More Time") 20-30 64
VOLT 10-15 69

LPs: 10/12–inch 33rpm

PERCEPTION 10-15 74

BARNES, J.J., & Steve Mancha

LPs: 10/12–inch 33rpm

VOLT (6001 "Rare Stamps") 10-15 69

Also see BARNES, J.J.
Also see HOLIDAYS
Also see MANCHA, Steve

BARNES, Jimmy

P&R/LP '86

Singles: 7–inch

GEFFEN 3-4 86-88

Picture Sleeves

GEFFEN 3-4 88

LPs: 10/12–inch 33rpm

GEFFEN 5-10 86

Also see COLD CHISEL
Also see INXS & Jimmy Barnes

BARNET, Charlie, & Orchestra

R&B '42

Singles: 78rpm

APOLLO 4-8 48
BANNER 4-8 34
BLUEBIRD 5-10 35-41
CONQUEROR 4-8 34
DECCA 4-8 42-43
MELOTONE 4-8 34
ORIOLE 4-8 34
PERFECT 4-8 33
ROMEO 4-8 33

BARNUM, H.B.

P&R '61

Singles: 7–inch

CAPITOL (Except 5932) 5-10 65-68
CAPITOL (5932 "Heartbreaker") 20-40 67
DECCA 3-5 71
ELDO 5-10 60-61
IMPERIAL 5-10 64
MUN RAB 5-10 59
RCA (Except 8112) 5-10 61-63
RCA (8112 "It Hurts Too Much to Cry") 40-60 62
ULTRA SONIC 5-10 60
U.A. 3-5 73

Picture Sleeves

RCA (8112 "It Hurts Too Much to Cry") 50-75 62

LPs: 10/12–inch 33rpm

CAPITOL 12-20 65
RCA 15-20 62
TROPIC ISLE 15-25 59

Also see ROBINS

BARONS

R&B '56

Singles: 78rpm

IMPERIAL 15-25 55-56

Singles: 7–inch

IMPERIAL (5343 "Eternally Yours") 50-100 55
(Black vinyl.)
IMPERIAL (5343 "Eternally Yours") 200-300 55
(Colored vinyl. Promotional issue.)
IMPERIAL (5359 "My Dream My Love") 40-60 55
IMPERIAL (5370 "Cold Kisses") 35-55 55
IMPERIAL (5383 "So Long My Darling") 35-55 56
IMPERIAL (5397 "Don't Walk Out") 25-35 56
IMPERIAL (66000 series) 8-12 64

BARRABAS

LP '75

Singles: 7–inch

ATCO 3-5 75-76

LPs: 10/12-inch 33rpm

ATCO 5-10 75-76
RCA 8-10 72-73

Members: Jo Tejada; Ricky Morales; Miquel Morales; Juan Videl; Daniel Louis; Ernest Duarte.

BARRACUDA

D&D '83

Singles: 12-inch 33/45rpm

EPIC 4-6 83

Singles: 7-inch

EPIC 3-4 83

BARRETT, Richard
(With the Chantels; with Sevilles)

P&R '58

Singles: 7-inch

ATLANTIC 5-10 62
CRACKERJACK 10-15 63
GONE 15-25 59
MGM 15-25 58
METRO 10-15 58
SEVILLE 10-15 60
20TH FOX 8-12 59

Also see CHANTELS

BARRETT, Syd

LP '74

Singles: 12-inch 33/45rpm

CAPITOL 8-12 88
(Promotional only. With special cover.)

LPs: 10/12-inch 33rpm

CAPITOL 5-10 74-88
HARVEST (Except 11314) 10-20 70-74
HARVEST (11314 "Madcap Laughs") 20-30 70

Members: Syd Barrett; Dave Gilmour; Roger Waters; Vic Seywell; Mike Ratledge.
Also see PINK FLOYD

BARRETTO, Ray

P&R/R&B '63

Singles: 7-inch

ASCOT 5-10 66
ATLANTIC 3-6 77-78
FANIA 5-15 68-72
RIVERSIDE 5-10 61
ROULETTE 3-4
TICO 5-10 63
U.A. 5-10 65-67

LPs: 10/12-inch 33rpm

ATLANTIC 5-10 76-78
CTI 5-10 81
FANIA 5-10 68-73
FANTASY 8-10 73
RIVERSIDE 10-15 61-66
TICO 10-15 62-63
U.A. 8-15 65-67

Also see LYTLE, Johnny, & Ray Barretto

BARRON KNIGHTS

P&R '79

Singles: 7-inch

DECCA 5-10 67
EPIC (Except 9835) 3-4 79
EPIC (9835 "Pop Go the Workers") 5-10 65
MERCURY 3-5 72

Members: Barron Anthony; Peanut Langford; Butch Baker; Dave Ballinger; Duke D'mond.

BARROW, Keith

R&B '78

Singles: 12-inch 33/45rpm

COLUMBIA 4-6 79

Singles: 7-inch

CAPITOL 3-4 80
COLUMBIA 3-4 76-79
JEWEL 3-5 73

LPs: 10/12-inch 33rpm

CAPITOL 5-10 80
UMBIA 5-10 77
JEWEL 8-10 73

BARRY, Claudja

P&R/LP '78

Singles: 12-inch 33/45rpm

CHRYSALIS 4-6 79
EPIC 4-6 86-87
PERSONAL 4-6 83
TSR 4-6 85

Singles: 7-inch

CHRYSALIS 3-4 79-84
EPIC 3-4 86-87
MIRAGE 3-4 82
PERSONAL 3-4 83
SALSOUL 3-4 77-78

LPs: 10/12-inch 33rpm

CHRYSALIS 5-10 79-84
HANDSHAKE 5-10 82
SALSOUL 5-10 77-78

BARRY, Claudja, & Ronnie Jones

LPs: 10/12-inch 33rpm

HANDSHAKE 5-10 82

Also see BARRY, Claudja

BARRY, Jan: see BERRY, Jan

BARRY, Joe

P&R/R&B '61

Singles: 7-inch

ABC/DOT 3-4 77
JIN 10-15 60-62
NUGGET 4-8
SMASH 4-8 61-62

Picture Sleeves

SMASH 10-15 61

LPs: 10/12-inch 33rpm

ABC/DOT 5-10 77

BARRY, John, Orchestra

P&R '65

Singles: 12–inch 33/45rpm

CASABLANCA (20146 "The Chase") 10-12 78

Singles: 7–inch

A&M 3-4 83
CAPITOL (4200 series) 4-6 59
CAPITOL (5400 series) 3-4 86
COLUMBIA 3-5 65-70
EPIC 3-4 72
KING 3-6 61
MCA 3-4 85
MGM 3-5 66
MERCURY 3-6 64
20TH FOX 3-5 64
U.A. 3-6 63-65
W.B. 3-5 68

Picture Sleeves

U.A. 5-10 65

LPs: 10/12–inch 33rpm

CAPITOL (2500 series) 10-15 66
COLUMBIA (1003 "Ready When You Are Mr. J.B.") 8-12 70
COLUMBIA (2493 "Great Movie Themes") 10-15 66
COLUMBIA (2708 "You Only Live Twice") 8-12 67
(Stereo.)
COLUMBIA (9293 "Great Movie Themes") 10-15 66
COLUMBIA (9508 "You Only Live Twice") 8-12 67
(Monaural.)
U.A. (91 "James Bond Tenth Anniversary") 8-12 72
U.A. (3424 "Goldfinger and Other Favorites") 8-12 65
U.A. (6424 "Goldfinger and Other Favorites") 10-12 65

You'll find many more listings by this artist in *The Official Price Guide to Movie/TV Soundtracks and Original Cast Albums,* containing over 8,000 listings.

Also see ARMSTRONG, Louis
Also see BASIE, Count
Also see BASSEY, Shirley
Also see JONES, Tom
Also see MONRO, Matt
Also see SINATRA, Nancy

BARRY, Len

P&R/R&B/LP '65

Singles: 7–inch

AMY 4-6 68-69
BUDDAH 3-5 72
CAMEO 4-8 64
DECCA 4-8 65-66
MCA 3-4 83
MERCURY 4-8 64
PARAMOUNT 3-5 73
PARKWAY 4-8 65
RCA 4-6 67-68
SCEPTER 3-6 69-70

EPs: 7–inch 33/45rpm

DECCA (74720 "1-2-3") 8-15 65
(Jukebox issue only.)

LPs: 10/12–inch 33rpm

BUDDAH 10-15 72
CAMEO 20-25 64
DECCA 20-25 65
RCA 15-20 67

Also see DOVELLS

BARRY & TAMERLANES

P&R/R&B '63

Singles: 7–inch

VALIANT 5-10 63-65

LPs: 10/12–inch 33rpm

VALIANT (406 "I Wonder What She's Doing Tonight") 50-75 63

Members: Barry DeVorzon; Terry Smith; Bodie Chandler.
Also see DE VORZON, Barry

BARTHOLOMEW, Dave

R&B '50

Singles: 78rpm

BAYOU 10-20 53
DECCA 10-20 51
DELUXE 10-20 47-50
IMPERIAL 10-20 50-57
JAX 10-20 50
KING 20-40 51-52

Singles: 7–inch

DECCA (48216 "Tra-La-La") 75-100 51
IMPERIAL (5210 "Who Drank the Beer While I Was in the Rear") 75-100 52
IMPERIAL (5249 "No More Black Nights") 75-100 51
IMPERIAL (5273 "Texas Hop") 75-125 53
IMPERIAL (5322 "Another Mule") 20-40 54
IMPERIAL (5350 "Every Night Every Day") 20-40 55
IMPERIAL (5373 "Shrimp and Gumbo") 20-30 56
IMPERIAL (5390 "Would You") 20-30 56
IMPERIAL (5408 "Lovin' You") 15-25 56
IMPERIAL (5500 thru 5800 series) 10-20 56-61
KING (4482 "Sweet Home Blues") 100-150 51
KING (4508 "In the Alley") 100-200 52
KING (4523 "Lawdy, Lawdy Lard") 100-150 52
(Black vinyl.)
KING (4523 "Lawdy, Lawdy Lard") 200-300 52
(Colored vinyl.)

KING (4544 "My Ding-A-Ling") ... 100-200 52
KING (4559 "The Golden Rule") ... 50-100 52
KING (4585 "High Flying Woman") ... 50-100 53

LPs: 10/12–inch 33rpm

IMPERIAL (9162/12076 "Fats Domino Presents Dave Bartholomew & His Great Big Band") ... 40-50 61
IMPERIAL (9217/12217 "New Orleans House Party") ... 40-50 63
Imperial 9000 numbers are mono, 12000 are stereo.
Also see ARCHIBALD
Also see DOMINO, Fats
Also see KING, Jewel
Also see RHODES, Todd
Also see LEWIS, Smiley

BARTLEY, Chris

P&R/R&B '67

Singles: 7–inch

BUDDAH ... 3-5 71
MUSICOR ... 3-5 72
VANDO ... 4-8 67-68

LPs: 10/12–inch 33rpm

VANDO ... 15-20 67

BARTON, Eileen

P&R '50

Singles: 78rpm

CORAL ... 4-8 51-56
MERCURY ... 4-8 53
NATIONAL ... 5-10 50

Singles: 7–inch

CORAL ... 5-10 51-56
CREST ... 4-8 62
MGM ... 5-8 59
MERCURY ... 5-10 53
20TH FOX ... 3-6 63
U.A. (Except 206) ... 4-8 59
U.A. (206 "The Joke") ... 15-25 60

EPs: 7–inch 33/45rpm

CORAL ... 5-10 54

LPs: 10/12–inch 33rpm

CORAL ... 15-25 54
Also see DESMOND, Johnny, Eileen Barton & McGuire Sisters

BARTON, Lou Ann

LP '82

Singles: 7–inch

ASYLUM ... 3-4 82

LPs: 10/12–inch 33rpm

ANTONE'S ... 5-10 89
ASYLUM ... 8-12 82

BARTZ, Gary
(Gary Bartz Nu Troop)

R&B '77

Singles: 7–inch

ARISTA ... 3-4 80
CAPITOL ... 3-4 77-78

LPs: 10/12–inch 33rpm

ARISTA ... 5-10 80
CAPITOL ... 5-10 77-78
CATALYST ... 5-10 76
MILESTONE ... 10-15 68-69
PRESTIGE ... 6-10 73-75
VEE JAY ... 5-10 78

BASIA
(Basia Trzetrzelewska)

P&R/LP '88

Singles: 7–inch

EPIC ... 3-4 88-90

LPs: 10/12–inch 33rpm

EPIC ... 5-8 88-90

BASIC BLACK

LP '90

LPs: 10/12–inch 33rpm

MOTOWN ... 5-8 90

BASIE, Count

P&R '37

Singles: 78rpm

COLUMBIA ... 5-10 43-51
CLEF ... 4-8 52-56
DECCA (Except 1300 thru 3000 series) ... 5-10 41-53
DECCA (1300 thru 3000 series) ... 8-15 37-40
MERCURY ... 4-8 52-53
OKEH ... 4-8 52

Singles: 7–inch

ABC-PAR ... 3-5 66
BRUNSWICK ... 3-5 67
CLEF ... 5-10 52-56
COLUMBIA (33000 series) ... 3-4 76
COLUMBIA (38000 & 39000 series) ... 5-10 50-51
COMMAND ... 3-5 67
DECCA ... 5-10 53
HAPPY TIGER ... 3-5 70
MERCURY ... 5-10 52-53
OKEH ... 5-10 52
REPRISE ... 3-6 63
ROULETTE (Except "SSR" series) 4-8 58-63
ROULETTE ("SSR" series) ... 8-15 59
(Stereo.)
U.A. ... 3-5 66
VERVE ... 3-5 60-67

EPs: 7–inch 33/45rpm

BRUNSWICK ... 10-15 54
CAMDEN ... 8-15 58
CLEF ... 10-20 52-55
COLUMBIA ... 10-20 50
CORAL ... 10-20
DECCA ... 10-20 53
EPIC ... 10-20 55
RCA (Except 5000 series) ... 10-20 54
RCA (5000 series) ... 8-12 59
ROULETTE ... 8-12 58-60

VERVE 10-15 56

LPs: 10/12-inch 33rpm

ABC 5-10 76
ABC-PAR 10-15 66
ACCORD 5-10 82-83
AMERICAN 15-25 57
BRIGHT ORANGE 5-10 73
BRUNSWICK (54000 series) 10-20 63-67
BRUNSWICK (58000 series) 25-35 54
(10-inch LPs.)
CAMDEN 10-20 58-60
CIRCLE 40-50 54
CLEF (120 "Count Basie & His Orchestra") 100-200 52
(10-inch LP.)
CLEF (148 "The Count Basie Big Band") 100-200 52
(10-inch LP.)
CLEF (164 "The Count Basie Sextet") 100-200 52
(10-inch LP.)
CLEF (626 "Dance Session") 50-100 53
CLEF (647 "Dance Session, Volume 2") 50-100 53
CLEF (633 "Basieana") 50-100 53
CLEF (666 "Basie") 50-100 54
CLEF (678 "Basie Swings - Joe Williams Sings") 50-100 55
CLEF (685 "Count Basie") 50-80 56
CLEF (700 series) 20-30 56
COLISEUM 8-12 67
COLUMBIA (700 & 900 series) 20-30 56-57
COLUMBIA (6079 "Dance Parade") 25-35 49
(10-inch LPs)
COLUMBIA (31000 series) 10-12 72
COMMAND 10-15 66-71
DAYBREAK 6-10 71
DECCA (100 series) 15-25 64
DECCA (5000 series) 25-35 50-53
(10-inch LPs.)
DECCA (8000 series) 10-15 65
DOCTOR JAZZ 5-10 85-86
DOT 8-12 68
EMARCY (26000 series) 30-45 54
(10-inch LPs.)
EMUS 5-10 79
EPIC (1000 & 1100 series) 25-35 54
(10-inch LPs.)
EPIC 25-35 55
FLYING DUTCHMAN 6-10 71
HAPPY TIGER 8-12 70
HARMONY (7000 series) 10-20 60
HARMONY (11000 series) 5-10 67-69
IMPULSE 10-20 62
JAZZ PANORAMA 50-75 52
MCA 8-12 77-82
MGM 6-10 70
MFSL (129 "Basie Plays Hefti") 15-25 85
MPS 10-12 72
MERCURY (25000 series) 25-35 50-51
(10-inch LPs.)
METRO 6-10 65-66
OLYMPIC 5-10 74
PABLO 5-10 74-83
PAUSA 5-10 83
PRESTIGE 5-10 82
RCA (500 series) 10-15 65
RCA (1100 series) 25-35 54
REPRISE 10-15 63-65
ROULETTE (100 series) 12-18 71
ROULETTE (52003 thru 52106) 15-20 58-64
ROULETTE (52111/12/13 "The World of Count Basie") 30-40 64
(3-LP set.)
SCEPTER 5-10 74
SOLID STATE 8-12 68
TRIP 5-10 75
U.A. 10-15 66
VSP 10-15 66
VANGUARD 15-25 57
VERVE 5-10 73-84
(Reads "Manufactured By MGM Record Corp.," or mentions either Polydor or Polygram at bottom of label.)
VERVE (2000 series) 20-30 56
(Reads "Verve Records, Inc." at bottom of label.)
VERVE (2500 series) 8-12 77-82
VERVE (2600 series) 5-10 82
VERVE (6000 series) 20-30 56
(Reads "Verve Records, Inc." at bottom of label.)
VERVE (8000 & 8100 series) 15-25 56-57
(Reads "Verve Records, Inc." at bottom of label.)
VERVE (8200 thru 8400) 15-20 58-61
(Reads "Verve Records, Inc." at bottom of label.)
VERVE (8500 thru 8600 series) 10-15 62-67
(Reads "MGM Records - a Division of Metro-Goldwyn-Mayer, Inc." at bottom of label.)
VERVE (8700 series) 6-10 69
(Reads "MGM Records - a Division of Metro-Goldwyn-Mayer, Inc." at bottom of label.)
VERVE (68000 series) 10-20 63-65
(Reads "MGM Records - a Division of Metro-Goldwyn-Mayer, Inc." at bottom of label.)

Also see BARRY, John
Also see BENNETT, Tony, & Count Basie
Also see BREWER, Teresa, & Count Basie
Also see CROSBY, Bing, & Count Basie
Also see DAVIS, Sammy, Jr., & Count Basie
Also see FITZGERALD, Ella, & Count Basie
Also see JACQUET, Illinois, & Count Basie
Also see MILLS BROTHERS, & Count Basie
Also see PRYSOCK, Arthur, & Count Basie
Also see SINATRA, Frank, & Count Basie
Also see STARR, Kay, & Count Basie
Also see WILLIAMS, Joe

Also see WILSON, Jackie, & Count Basie

BASIE, Count, & Tony Bennett

EPs: 7–inch 33/45rpm

ROULETTE 6-10 59

LPs: 10/12–inch 33rpm

ROULETTE 10-20 59-63

Also see BENNETT, Tony

BASIE, Count, & Billy Eckstine

Singles: 7–inch

ROULETTE (Except "SSR" series) 4-8 59

ROULETTE ("SSR" series) 8-15 59

LPs: 10/12–inch 33rpm

ROULETTE 15-20 59

Also see ECKSTINE, Billy

BASIE, Count, & Duke Ellington

Singles: 7–inch

COLUMBIA 4-6 62

LPs: 10/12–inch 33rpm

ACCORD 5-10 82

COLUMBIA 15-20 62

Also see ELINGTON, Duke

BASIE, Count, & Maynard Ferguson

LPs: 10/12–inch 33rpm

ROULETTE 10-20 65

Also see FERGUSON, Maynard

BASIE, Count, & Benny Goodman

LPs: 10/12–inch 33rpm

ABC 8-12 73

VANGUARD 15-25 59

Also see GOODMAN, Benny

BASIE, Count, & Oscar Peterson

LPs: 10/12–inch 33rpm

PABLO 5-10 75-83

VERVE 15-20 59

Also see PETERSON, Oscar

BASIE, Count, & Sarah Vaughan

LPs: 10/12–inch 33rpm

ROULETTE 15-20 61

BASIE, Count, Sarah Vaughan & Joe Williams

Singles: 7–inch

ROULETTE 4-8 60

LPs: 10/12–inch 33rpm

ROULETTE 15-20 60

Joe Williams is also a featured vocalist on many of the recordings included in the section of listings for Count Basie.

Also see BASIE, Count

Also see VAUGHAN, Sarah

BASIL, Toni

P&R/LP '82

Singles: 12–inch 33/45rpm

CHRYSALIS 4-6 82-85

Singles: 7–inch

A&M (791 "Breakaway") 100-200 66

CHRYSALIS 3-4 82-85

CHRYSALIS/VIRGIN (2638 Mickey") 4-6 81

(With Radialchoice logo.)

Picture Sleeves

CHRYSALIS 3-4 82-84

LPs: 10/12–inch 33rpm

CHRYSALIS 5-10 82-84

BASKERVILLE HOUNDS

P&R '69

Singles: 7–inch

AVCO EMBASSY (4504 "Hold Me") 3-5 69

BUDDAH 5-10 67

DOT 5-10 67

TEMA ("Hold Me") 5-10 68

(No selection number used.)

TEMA (125 "Debbie") 8-12 66

TEMA (128 "Space Rock") 5-10 67

TEMA (131 "Christmas Is Here") . 5-10 67

LPs: 10/12–inch 33rpm

DOT 15-20 67

BASS, Fontella

P&R/R&B '65

Singles: 7–inch

ABC 3-4 74

BOBBIN 5-10 61

CHECKER 5-10 65-66

CHESS 3-5 75-85

ERIC 3-5 73

GUSTO 3-4

MCA 3-4 83

PAULA 3-5 74

PRANN (5005 "My Good Lovin") . 5-10

SONJA 4-8 60s

LPs: 10/12–inch 33rpm

CHECKER 15-20 66

PAULA 5-10 71

BASS, Fontella, & Bobby McClure

Singles: 7–inch

CHECKER 3-5 65-66

Also see McCLURE, Bobby

BASS, Fontella, & Tina Turner

Singles: 7–inch

SONJA (2006 "Poor Little Fool") .. 5-10 62

(Shown only as by Fontella Bass.)

VESUVIUS (1002 "Poor Little Fool") 10-15 60s

Also see BASS, Fontella

Also see TURNER, Tina

BASSEY, Shirley

P&R/LP '65

Singles: 78rpm

COLUMBIA 5-10 57

Singles: 12–inch 33/45rpm

U.A. 4-6 79

Singles: 7–inch

COLUMBIA 5-10 57

EPIC 4-8 59
MGM 3-6 60
U.A. 3-5 61-79

LPs: 10/12-inch 33rpm

EPIC 10-20 62
LIBERTY 4-6 81-82
MGM 12-20 60
PHILIPS 10-15 65
SPRINGBORAD 5-10 75
U.A. 4-6 80
(With "LM" prefix.)
U.A. 10-15 62-72
(With "UAL" or "UAS" prefix.)
U.A. 5-10 73-79
(With "UA-LA" prefix.)

Also see BARRY, John
Also see NELSON, Willie / Nat "King" Cole / Johnny Mathis / Shirley Bassey

BATAAN, Joe
(With the Mestizo Band)

R&B '69

Singles: 7-inch

FANIA 5-15
SALSOUL 3-4 80
UPTITE 3-5 69

LPs: 10/12-inch 33rpm

SALSOUL 5-10 80-81

BATDORF & RODNEY

LP '72

Singles: 7-inch

ARISTA 3-5 75
ASYLUM 3-5 72
ATLANTIC 3-5 71-72

LPs: 10/12-inch 33rpm

ATLANTIC 8-12 71
ARISTA 6-10 75
ASYLUM 8-10 72

Members: John Batdorf: Mark Rodney.

BAUHAUS

LP '89

Singles: 7-inch

A&M 3-4 83

LPs: 10/12-inch 33rpm

A&M 5-10 83
BEGGARS BANQUET 8-12 89

Members: Daniel; Ash; David Jor; Kevin Haskins.
Also see LOVE & ROCKETS

BAUMANN, Peter

D&D '83

Singles: 12-inch 33/45rpm

PORTRAIT 4-6 82-83

Singles: 7-inch

PORTRAIT 3-4 83

LPs: 10/12-inch 33rpm

PORTRAIT 5-10 82-83
VIRGIN 8-10 77

Also see TANGERINE DREAM

BAXTER, Duke

P&R '69

Singles: 7-inch

MERCURY 3-5 70
VMC 5-10 69

LPs: 10/12-inch 33rpm

VMC 15-20 69

BAXTER, Les
(With His Orchestra & Chorus; Les Baxter Balladeers)

P&R '51

Singles: 78rpm

CAPITOL 3-6 50-57

Singles: 7-inch

A/S 3-4 70
CAPITOL 4-8 50-61
GNP 3-5 64-69
LINK 3-5 64
REPRISE 3-5 62-63

Picture Sleeves

REPRISE (20120 "Theme from *The Manchurian Candidate*" 40-60 62
(A Frank Sinatra collectible, as his name is shown on this cover.)

EPs: 7-inch 33/45rpm

CAPITOL 5-10 51-56
GNP 5-10 67-69
RCA 5-10 52
REPRISE 4-8 64

LPs: 10/12-inch 33rpm

ALSHIRE 5-10 70-85
AMERICAN INT'L (1028 "Dunwich Horror") 20-25 70
(Soundtrack.)
CAPITOL (200 thru 900 series) 10-20 51-58
CAPITOL (1000 thru 1800 series) 5-15 58-63
CAPITOL (11000 series) 4-6 77-79
GNP 5-10 69
RCA 15-25 52
REPRISE 10-15 62-63
VARESE SARABANDE (81103 "Dunwich Horror") 8-10 79

Also see CROSBY, Bing, & Bob Hope
Also see WAKELY, Jimmy

BAY CITY ROLLERS

P&R/LP '75

Singles: 7-inch

ARISTA 3-4 75-78
BELL 3-5 72-76
FLASHBACK 3-4 80

Picture Sleeves

ARISTA 3-4 75-77

LPs: 10/12-inch 33rpm

ARISTA 5-10 75-79
BELL 6-12 74

Members: Les McKeowen; Eric Faulkner; Stuart Wood; Alan Longmuir; Derek Longmuir; Billy Lyall; Pat McGlynn; Ian Mitchell.

Also see ROLLERS

BAYER, Carole: see SAGER, Carole Bayer

BAZUKA

(Tony Camillo's Bazuka)

P&R/R&B '75

Singles: 7–inch

A&M 3-5 75
VENTURE 3-4 79

LPs: 10/12–inch 33rpm

A&M 5-10 75

BEACH BOYS

P&R/LP '62

Singles: 12–inch 33/45rpm

CAPITOL (9711 "Rock & Roll to the Rescue") 10-15 86
(Promotional issue only.)
CAPITOL (9796 "California Dreamin") 10-15 86
(Promotional issue only.)
CAPITOL (15234 "Rock & Roll to the Rescue") 5-10 86
CARIBOU (2080 "Getcha Back") 10-15 86
(Promotional issue only.)
CARIBOU (9028 "Here Comes the Night") 5-10 79
CARIBOU (9028 "Here Comes the Night") 20-25 79
(Promotional issue only.)

Singles: 7–inch

BROTHER 5-10 67
CANDIX (301 "Surfin") 150-250 61
(Label reads "Distributed by Era Record Sales Inc.")
CANDIX (301 "Surfin") 200-250 61
(Label does NOT say "Distributed by Era Record Sales Inc.")
CANDIX (331 "Surfin") 125-175 62
CAPITOL (2000 series except 2765) 5-10 67-69
CAPITOL (2765 "Cottonfields") 15-20 70
CAPITOL (3924 "Surfin' USA") 3-5 74
CAPITOL (4000 series except 4880) 8-12 62-63
CAPITOL (4880 "Ten Little Indians") 15-20 62
CAPITOL (5000 series, except 5096 & 5312) 5-10 63-66
(Orange/yellow labels.)
CAPITOL (5096 "Little Saint Nick") 12-18 63
CAPITOL (5312 "The Man with All the Toys") 12-18 63
CAPITOL (5000 series) 3-4 81-86
(Black labels.)
CAPITOL (6000 series) 5-10 67-68
CAPITOL (44000 series) 3-4 89
CARIBOU 3-5 79-86
ELEKTRA 3-4 88
ODE '70 .... 12-15 71
REPRISE (0101 thru 0107") 4-6 73
("Back to Back" reissue series.)
REPRISE (0894 "Add Some Music to Your Day") 5-10 70
REPRISE (0929 "Slip On Through") 5-10 70
REPRISE (0957 "Tears in the Morning") 12-15 70
REPRISE (0998 "Cool, Cool Water") 60-75 71
REPRISE (1015 "Long Promised Road") 20-25 71
REPRISE (1047 "Long Promised Road") 20-25 71
REPRISE (1058 "Surf's Up") 45-50 71
REPRISE (1091 "Cuddle Up") 25-30 72
REPRISE (1101 "Marcella") 25-30 72
REPRISE (1138 "Sail on Sailor") 8-12 73
REPRISE (1156 "California Saga") 10-15 73
REPRISE (1310 "I Can Hear Music") 3-5 74
REPRISE (1321 "Child of Winter") 20-30 74
REPRISE (1325 "Sail on Sailor") 5-10 75
REPRISE (1336 "Wouldn't It be Nice") 5-10 75
REPRISE (1354 thru 1394) 3-5 76-78
X (301 "Surfin") 200-300 61

Promotional Singles

CAPITOL (2360 "Bluebirds Over the Mountain") 15-20 69
CAPITOL (2936/7 "Salt Lake City") 175-200 65
CAPITOL (4093 "Little Honda") 15-20 75
CAPITOL CUSTOM ("Spirit of America") 125-150 63
CARIBOU (557 "Here Comes the Night") 10-12 79
(Blue vinyl.)
CARIBOU (557 "Here Comes the Night") 50-60 79
(Special Edition autographed copies. Blue vinyl.)
CARIBOU (9026 "Here Comes the Night") 10-15 79
EVA-TONE (0300 "Living Doll") 3-4 87
(Barbie Doll promotional issue.)
ODE '70 (66016 "Wouldn't It Be Nice-Live Version") 35-40 71
REPRISE (557-2 "Sail On Sailor") 75-100 73
REPRISE (0998 "Cool, Cool Water") 45-50 71
REPRISE (1310 "I Can Hear Music") 30-50 74

WHAT'S IT ALL ABOUT (449/450 & 507/508)................................ 20-25
(Public service radio station issues. Program disc 449/450 has the Beach Boys on one side and Dr. Hook on the flip. 507/508 features the Beach Boys on one side and the Rolling Stones on the other.)
Note: Promo singles not listed separately are presumed to fall into the same price range as commercial issues.

Picture Sleeves

BROTHER (1001 "Heroes and Villains") 50-100 67
CAPITOL (2068 "Darlin") 10-20 67
CAPITOL (4777 "Surfin' Safari") 20-30 62
CAPITOL (4880 "Ten Little Indians") 75-100 62
CAPITOL (5118 "Fun, Fun, Fun") 10-20 63
CAPITOL (5174 "I Get Around") 10-20 64
CAPITOL (5245 "When I Grow Up").. 10-20 64
CAPITOL (5306 "Dance, Dance, Dance") 10-20 64
CAPITOL (5372 "Do You Wanna Dance") 10-20 65
CAPITOL (5395 "Help Me Rhonda") 10-20 65
CAPITOL (5464 "California Girls") 10-20 65
CAPITOL (5540 "The Little Girl I Once Knew") 10-20 65
CAPITOL (5561 "Barbara Ann") 100-125 65
CAPITOL (5602 "Sloop John B.") 10-20 66
CAPITOL (5676 "Good Vibrations") 10-20 66
CARIBOU.................................... 3-6 79-86

EPs: 7–inch 33/45rpm

BROTHER (1 "Radio Spot Backing Tracks") 225-250 73
(Promotional issue only.)
CAPITOL (189 "Best of the Beach Boys") 15-20 66
(With "LLP" prefix. Jukebox issue only.)
CAPITOL (1981 "Surfer Girl") ... 45-55 63
CAPITOL (2186 "10 Little Indians") 300-325 64
(One side of this EP contains selections by Ray Anthony.)
CAPITOL (2027 "Shut Down, Vol. 2") 45-55 64
CAPITOL (2269 "The Beach Boys Today") 50-75 65
(Jukebox issue only.)
CAPITOL (2293/94 "Beach Boys' Party") 125-150 65
(Jukebox issue only.)
CAPITOL (2545 "Best of the Beach Boys") 50-75 66
(With "DU" prefix. Jukebox issue only.)
CAPITOL (2545 "Best of the Beach Boys") 15-20 66
CAPITOL (2754/55 "Brian Wilson Introduces Selections").........................350-375 64
(Promotional issue only. Includes selections from *Beach Boys Concert* and *Beach Boys Songbook*.)
CAPITOL (5267 "4 By the Beach Boys") 35-45 66
REPRISE (2118 "Mount Vernon and Fairway")..................................8-10 73
(Originally packaged with Reprise LP 2118, "Holland.")
ROCK SHOPPE ("The Beach Years")...................................75-100 75
(Demo disc for "A Six Hour Radio Special." Also contains excerpts by Jan & Dean, Dick Dale, and the Surfaris. Narrated by Roger Christian. Promotional issue, pressed in a quantity of 200 copies.)
W.B. (422 "Sunflower Promotional Spots") 100-125 70
W.B. (534 "Vote '72") 35-45 72
(Promotional issue only.)
WHAT'S IT ALL ABOUT 20-25 70s
(Promotional issue only.)

LPs: 10/12–inch 33rpm

ACCORD 5-10 83
BROTHER (9001 "Smiley Smile") 15-20 67
BROTHER/SUNKIST (9431 "25 Years of Good Vibrations")....................10-20 86
(Includes tour booklet. Sold at Beach Boys concerts.)
CAPITOL (133 "20/20")............10-20 69
CAPITOL (133 "20/20")............30-35 69
(With "SKAO-8" prefix. Capitol Record Club issue.)
CAPITOL (253 "Close Up")........35-40 69
CAPITOL (442 "Good Vibrations") 20-25 70
CAPITOL (500 "All Summer Long/ California Girls").........................8-12 70
CAPITOL (701 "Dance, Dance, Dance/ Fun, Fun, Fun")..........................8-12 71
CAPITOL (1808 thru 1998)........15-25 63-67
(With "DT" prefix.)
CAPITOL (1808 thru 1998)..........5-10 75-78
(With "SM" prefix.)
CAPITOL (1808 thru 1998)........20-35 62-63
(With "T" or "ST" prefix.)
CAPITOL (2027 "Shut Down Vol. 2") 8-15 63
(With "DT" prefix.)

BEACH BOYS

CAPITOL (2027 "Shut Down Vol. 2") 5-10 75
(With "SM" prefix.)

CAPITOL (2027 "Shut Down Vol. 2") 15-20 63
(With "T" or "ST" prefix.)

CAPITOL (2110 "All Summer Long").................... 25-30 64
(With *Don't Break Down*. On this pressing, *Don't Back Down* was incorrectly shown as *Don't Break Down*.)

CAPITOL (2110 "All Summer Long").................... 15-20 64
(With "Don't Back Down" shown correctly.)

CAPITOL (2164 "Beach Boys' Christmas Album") 5-10 75
(With "SM" prefix.)

CAPITOL (2164 "Beach Boys' Christmas Album") 20-35 64
(With "T" or "ST" prefix.)

CAPITOL (2198 "Beach Boys Concert").................... 10-15 64
(With "T" or "ST" prefix.)

CAPITOL (2198 "Beach Boys Concert").................... 5-10
(With "SM" prefix.)

CAPITOL (2269 "The Beach Boys Today").................... 15-20 65
(With "T" or "DT" prefix.)

CAPITOL (2354 "Summer Days and Summer Nights").................... 20-35 65
(With "T" or DT" prefix.)

CAPITOL (2398 "Beach Boys Party") 30-35 65
(With "SMAS" prefix. Price includes 15 bonus photos. Deduct $8-12 if these photos are missing.)

CAPITOL (2398 "Beach Boys Party") 20-30 65
(With "MAS" prefix. Price includes 15 bonus photos. Deduct $8 to $12 if these photos are missing.)

CAPITOL (2458 "Pet Sounds") 15-20 66
(With "T" or DT" prefix.)

CAPITOL (2545 "Best of the Beach Boys").................... 10-15 66
(With "T" or DT" prefix.)

CAPITOL (2706 "Best of the Beach Boys, Volume 2") 10-15 67
(With "T" or "DT" prefix.)

CAPITOL (2813 "Beach Boys Deluxe Set").................... 100-125 67
(With "TCL" prefix.)

CAPITOL (2813 "Beach Boys Deluxe Set") 35-40 67
(With "DTCL" prefix.)

CAPITOL (2859 "Wild Honey") . 10-15 67
(With "T" or "ST" prefix.)

CAPITOL (ST-8-2891 "Smiley Smile") 60-75 69
(With "ST-8" prefix. Capitol Record Club issue.)

CAPITOL (2893 "Stack-o-Tracks") 100-150 68
(With music-lyrics booklet.)

CAPITOL (2893 "Stack-o-Tracks") 50-75 68
(Without music-lyrics booklet.)

CAPITOL (2893 "Stack-o-Tracks") 100-125 69
(With "ST-8" prefix. Capitol Record Club issue.)

CAPITOL (2895 "Friends")........10-15 68

CAPITOL (2945 "Best of the Beach Boys, Volume, 3") 35-40 68

CAPITOL (3352 "Sunflower").....30-35 70
(With "SKAO-9" prefix. Capitol Record Club issue.)

CAPITOL (6994 "Golden Years of the Beach Boys")....................25-30 75
(TV mail-order offer.)

CAPITOL (48421 "Pet Sounds")....5-8 90

CAPITOL (11000 thru 16000 except 11384)....................5-15 74-86

CAPITOL (11384 Spirit of America") 15-20 75

CAPITOL (92639 "Still Cruisin")...5-10 89

CAPITOL (123946 "Best of the Beach Boys, Vol. 1")........20-25 74
(RCA Record Club issue.)

CAPITOL (153477 "Rarities") 20-25 75
(RCA Record Club issue.)

CAPITOL (233559 "Endless Summer")....................20-25 74
(RCA Record Club issue.)

CAPITOL (233593 "American Summer")....................20-25 75
(RCA Record Club issue.)

CARIBOU....................5-10 78-85

ERA....................12-18 69

EVEREST 5-10 81

MFSL (116 "Surfer Girl")..........15-25 84

PAIR....................10-12 84

PICKWICK 8-12 72-75

REPRISE (2118 "Holland")........15-20 73
(With *Mount Vernon & Fairway* EP.)

REPRISE (2118 "Holland") 8-12 73
(Without *Mount Vernon & Fairway* EP.)

REPRISE (2166 "Wild Honey/ 20-20") 8-10 74

REPRISE (2166 "Friends/ Smiley Smile")....................8-10 74

REPRISE (2223 "Good Vibrations/Best of the Beach Boys") 8-10 75

REPRISE (2251 "15 Big Ones") ..8-10 76

REPRISE (2258 "Love You") 8-10 77

REPRISE (2268 "M.I.U. Album") .8-10 78

REPRISE (6382 "Sunflower")...... 8-12 70
REPRISE (6453 "Surf's Up")..... 20-25 71
(Capitol Record Club issue.)
REPRISE (6484 "The Beach Boys in Concert") 8-10 73
RONCO..................................... 8-10 78
SEARS (608 "Summertime Blues")................................ 100-125 70
(Sold only at Sears retail stores.)
SESSIONS............................. 15-20 80
SPRINGBOARD (4021 "Greatest Hits: 1961-1963") 8-12 72
WAND (688 "Greatest Hits")..... 10-15 72

Promotional LPs

BROTHER (9431 "Good Vibrations from the Beach Boys") 10-15 86
(Sunkist promotional issue.)
CAPITOL (1 "Open House").. 175-200 78
CAPITOL (2754/5 "Beach Boys' Concert") 300-350 64
CAPITOL (3123 "Silver Platter Service")............................... 75-100 64
(With selections by the Hollyridge Strings.)
CAPITOL (3133 "Silver Platter Service")............................ 125-150 64
("Beach Boys Christmas Special.")
CAPITOL (3266 "Silver Platter Service")............................... 75-100 67
CARIBOU (1024 "Keepin' the Summer Alive")................................ 45-50 80
CRAWDADDY ("Brian Wilson Interview") 90-100 77
(Issued to radio stations only.)
MORE MUSIC (03-179-72 "Good Vibrations from London") 50-60
MUTUAL RADIO ("Dick Clark Presents the Beach Boys") 150-175 81
(Three-LP boxed set.)
REPRISE ("Radio Spot Backing Tracks for Beach Boys in Concert")..... 225-250 73

Members: Brian Wilson; Carl Wilson; Dennis Wilson; Mike Love; Al Jardine; Bruce Johnston; Ricky Fataar; Blondie Chaplin.

Note: Promos NOT listed separately are priced in the same range as commercial issues.

Also see ANNETTE
Also see ANTHONY, Ray
Also see BEATLES / Beach Boys / Buddy Holly
Also see CAMPBELL, Glen
Also see CAPTAIN & TENNILLE
Also see CHICAGO
Also see CLAYTON, Merry
Also see DALE, Dick / Surfaris / Surf Kings
Also see DR. HOOK
Also see EVERLY BROTHERS & Beach Boys
Also see FAT BOYS & Beach Boys
Also see JAN & DEAN / Beach Boys
Also see JETT, Joan
Also see KENNY & CADETS
Also see PETERSEN, Paul
Also see ROLLING STONES
Also see ROTH, David Lee
Also see SURVIVORS
Also see WILSON, Brian
Also see WILSON, Brian, and Mike Love
Also see WILSON, Carl
Also see WILSON, Dennis

BEACH BOYS / Jan & Dean

LPs: 10/12-inch 33rpm

CAPITOL (8149 "The Beach Boys/ Jan & Dean").........................10-20 81
(Sold only at Radio Shack stores. Realistic #S1-7010.)
EXACT...5-8 81

Also see JAN & DEAN

BEACH BOYS & Little Richard

Singles: 7-inch

CRITIQUE..................................3-5 87

Picture Sleeves

CRITIQUE..................................3-5 87

Also see LITTLE RICHARD

BEACH BOYS / Tony & Joe

Singles: 7-inch

ERA..3-5 70

Also see TONY & JOE

BEACH BOYS with Frankie Valli & 4 Seasons

Singles: 7-inch

FBI 3-5 84

Also see 4 SEASONS

BEACH BOYS / Carl Wilson

LPs: 10/12-inch 33rpm

BROTHER (2083 "Pet Sounds"/ "So Tough") 10-20 72

Also see BEACH BOYS

BEACH BUMS

Singles: 7-inch

ARE YOU KIDDING ME?..........20-30 66

Member: Bob Seger.

Also see SEGER, Bob

BEACON STREET UNION

LP '68

Singles: 7-inch

MGM 5-10 67-69
RTP 5-10 69

LPs: 10/12-inch 33rpm

MGM (4517 "The Eyes of the Beacon Street Union")..................................15-25 68
MGM (4568 "The Clown Died in Marvin Gardens") 15-25 68

Members: John Lincoln Wright; Robert Rhodes; Paul Tartachny; Wayne Ulaky; Richard Weisberg.

BEAR, Edward: see EDWARD BEAR

BEAR ESSENCE STARRING MARIANNA

D&D '84

Singles: 12-inch 33/45rpm

MOBY DICK..................................4-6 84

BEARS

LP '88

LPs: 10/12-inch 33rpm

I.R.S. 8-10 87-88

BEASLEY, Walter

R&B '87

Singles: 12-inch 33/45rpm

POLYDOR.................................. 4-6 88

Singles: 7-inch

POLYDOR.................................. 3-4 87-88

LPs: 10/12-inch 33rpm

POLYDOR.................................. 5-10 87-88

BEAST

LP '69

LPs: 10/12-inch 33rpm

COTILLION 10-12 69

EVOLUTION 8-10 70

BEASTIE BOYS

P&R/R&B/LP '86

Singles: 12-inch 33/45rpm

DEF JAM.................................... 4-6 86-87

Singles: 7-inch

DEF JAM.................................... 3-4 86-87

LPs: 10/12-inch 33rpm

CAPITOL..................................... 5-8 89

DEF JAM.................................. 5-10 86-87

Members: Adam Horovitz; Adam Yaunch; Michael Diamond.

BEASTMASTER

R&B '84

Singles: 12-inch 33/45rpm

TOMMY BOY 4-6 84

BEAT, B: see B. BEAT GIRLS

BEAT FARMERS

LP '85

Singles: 7-inch

RHINO... 3-4 85

LPs: 10/12-inch 33rpm

MCA/CURB 5-10 86-87

RHINO...................................... 5-10 85

BEATLES

P&R '64

Singles: 12-inch 33/45rpm

ULTIMIX (120 "Twist & Shout"). 40-60 88
(Promotional issue only.)

Singles: 7-inch

AMERICOM ("Yellow Submarine") 400-600 69
(Plastic "Pocket Disc" soundsheet. Number not known.)

AMERICOM (221 "Hey Jude")............................... 200-400 69
(Plastic "Pocket Disc" soundsheet.)

AMERICOM (335 "Get Back")................................ 200-400 69
(Plastic "Pocket Disc" soundsheet.)

AMERICOM (382 "Ballad of John & Yoko")....................200-400 69
(Plastic "Pocket Disc" soundsheet.)

APPLE 4-6 71-75

ATCO (6302 "Sweet Georgia Brown") 25-35 64
(Shown as by "The Beatles with Tony Sheridan.")

ATCO (6308 "Ain't She Sweet")...8-12 64
(Shown as by "The Beatles - Vocal By John Lennon.")

ATLANTIC....................................3-4 83-86

CAPITOL (Orange, black or purple label) 3-4 75-86
(Includes reissues of 1964-1975 material and original pressings of 1975-1986 releases.)

CAPITOL (2056 "Hello Goodbye").4-6 67
(Orange/yellow "swirl" label.)

CAPITOL (2056 "Hello Goodbye")................................8-10 68
(Red/orange "target" label.)

CAPITOL (2138 "Lady Madonna").4-6 68
(Orange/yellow "swirl" label.)

CAPITOL (2138 "Lady Madonna") 8-10 68
(Red/orange "target" label.)

CAPITOL (B-5100 "Movie Medley"/"Fab Four on Film") 60-70 81
(First issued with *Movie Medley* backed with *Fab Four on Film,* which was the Beatles talking about the film *A Hard Day's Night.*)

CAPITOL (B-5100 "Movie Medley"/"I'm Happy Just to Dance with You")..3-4 81

CAPITOL (B-5107 "Movie Medley")......................................3-4 82

CAPITOL (B-5189 "Love Me Do")..3-4 82
(Black vinyl.)

CAPITOL (B-5189 "Love Me Do")....................................15-25 82
(Colored vinyl. The Capitol 5000 series of the '80s differs from the 5000 series of 1964 by use of the "B" prefix.)

CAPITOL (5112 thru 5964)..........8-15 64-67
(Price range here is for orange/yellow swirl label issues.)

CAPITOL (5112 "I Want to Hold Your Hand") 3-4 84
(*I Want to Hold Your Hand* was reissued as a STEREO single in 1984. Even though the reissue is on the orange/yellow label, it has black print around the border of the label. 1964 issues have this print in white letters.)

CAPITOL (5112 thru 5964)........12-15 68
(Red/orange target label issues.)

CAPITOL (5555 "We Can Work It Out")..................................450-500 68
(Red and white "Starline" label. Issued in error.)

CAPITOL (6061 thru 6066)....... 25-35 65
(Green label "Starline" series.)
CAPITOL (6061 thru 6066)....... 10-15 69
(Red & orange label.)
CAPITOL (6278 thru 6300)........... 3-4 81
(Blue label "Starline" series.)
CAPITOL (17488 "Birthday")......... 3-5 94
(Colored vinyl, 30th Anniversary jukebox issue.)
CAPITOL (17688 "She Loves You")3-5 94
(Colored vinyl, 30th Anniversary jukebox issue.)
CAPITOL (17689 "I Want to Hold Your Hand").. 3-5 94
(Colored vinyl, 30th Anniversary jukebox issue.)
CAPITOL (17690 "Can't Buy Me Love").. 3-5 94
(Colored vinyl, 30th Anniversary jukebox issue.)
CAPITOL (17691 "Help") 3-5 94
(Colored vinyl, 30th Anniversary jukebox issue.)
CAPITOL (17692 "A Hard Day's Night").. 3-5 94
(Colored vinyl, 30th Anniversary jukebox issue.)
CAPITOL (17693 "All You Need Is Love").. 3-5 94
(Colored vinyl, 30th Anniversary jukebox issue.)
CAPITOL (17694 "Hey Jude")....... 3-5 94
(Colored vinyl, 30th Anniversary jukebox issue.)
CAPITOL (17695 "Let It Be") 3-5 94
(Colored vinyl, 30th Anniversary jukebox issue.)
CAPITOL (17696 "Eleanor Rigby") 3-5 94
(Colored vinyl, 30th Anniversary jukebox issue.)
CAPITOL (17697 "Penny Lane")... 3-5 94
(Colored vinyl, 30th Anniversary jukebox issue.)
CAPITOL (17698 "Something")..... 3-5 94
(Colored vinyl, 30th Anniversary jukebox issue.)
CAPITOL (17699 "Twist & Shout") 3-5 94
(Colored vinyl, 30th Anniversary jukebox issue.)
CAPITOL (56785 "Love Me Do")... 40-50 92
(Intended to be black vinyl but issued on red vinyl by mistake. Reportedly 1,500 made. 30th Anniversary jukebox issue.)
CAPITOL (56785 "Love Me Do")... 3-5 93
(Black vinyl. 30th Anniversary jukebox issue.)
CAPITOL (72144 "All My Loving")..................................80-100 71
(An error in production created a U.S. pressing of the Canadian release, *All My Loving/This Boy.*)
CICADELIC/BIODISC...................3-5 90
COLLECTABLES..........................3-4 82
DECCA (31382 "My Bonnie")..........................4000-5000 62
(Shown as by Tony Sheridan & Beat Brothers. Note: Price is for a *COMMERCIAL*, not promotional, issue. Commercial copies are on Decca's black label with silver print and a multi-color stripe across the center of the label. Black and silver Decca labels without the other colors are bootlegs.)
IBC (0082 "Murray the 'K' and the Beatles As It Happened").............4-6 76
MGM (13213 "My Bonnie")........15-20 64
(Shown as by the Beatles with Tony Sheridan.)
MGM (13227 "Why").................15-20 64
(Shown as by the Beatles with Tony Sheridan.)
MURRAY the "K" & BEATLES (33 Single) 20-25 64
(Reissued in 1976 as IBC 0082.)
OLDIES 45.................................5-10 64
SWAN (4152 "She Loves You")..................................200-250 63
(White label, with red print. Titles are in quotes. Does NOT have "Don't Drop Out" on label.)
SWAN (4152 "She Loves You")..................................175-225 63
(White label, with red print. No quotes on titles. Does NOT have "Don't Drop Out" on label.)
SWAN (4152 "She Loves You")..................................150-200 63
(White label, with red print. No quotes on titles. Says "Don't Drop Out" on label.)
SWAN (4152 "She Loves You")..................................150-200 63
(White label, with blue print. No quotes on titles. Says "Don't Drop Out" on label.)
SWAN (4152 "She Loves You"). 10-20 64
(Black label.)
SWAN (4182 "Sie Liebt Dich")...35-45 64
(With "She Loves You" following "Sie Liebt Dich" on the same line. White label with red print.)
SWAN (4182 "Sie Liebt Dich")...30-60 64
(With "She Loves You" under "Sie Liebt Dich" on a separate line. White label with orange print.)
SWAN (4182 "Sie Liebt Dich")...25-35 64
(With "She Loves You" under "Sie Liebt

Dich" on a separate line. White label with red print.)
TOLLIE (9001 "Twist and Shout") 20-30 64
(Black label.)
TOLLIE (9001 "Twist and Shout") 25-35 64
(Yellow label with blue print.)
TOLLIE (9001 "Twist and Shout") 35-45 64
(Yellow label with black print. Label name in brackets.)
TOLLIE (9001 "Twist and Shout") 15-20 64
(Yellow label with black print. Label name is either in a box or is by itself, with no lines, box or brackets.)
TOLLIE (9001 "Twist and Shout") 20-30 64
(Yellow label with green print. Label name is all in uppercase letters.)
TOLLIE (9001 "Twist and Shout") 15-25 64
(Yellow label with green print. Label name is all in lowercase letters.)
TOLLIE (9008 "Love Me Do") ... 30-35 64
(Black label.)
TOLLIE (9008 "Love Me Do") ... 25-30 64
(Yellow label.)
TOPAZ (1353 "Seattle Press Conference") 4-6 89
VEE JAY (498 "Please Please Me").................................... 500-700 63
(Credits "BEATTLES." Black label with rainbow circle. Has thin lettering and oval logo.)
VEE JAY (498 "Please Please Me").................................... 450-550 63
(Credits "BEATTLES." Black label with rainbow circle. Has bold lettering and oval logo.)
VEE JAY (498 "Please Please Me").................................... 500-600 63
(Credits "BEATTLES." Black label with rainbow circle. Has brackets logo.)
VEE JAY (498 "Please Please Me").................................... 600-700 63
(Credits "BEATLES." Black label with rainbow circle. Has thin lettering and oval label logo.)
VEE JAY (498 "Please Please Me").................................... 700-900 63
(Credits "BEATLES." Black label with rainbow circle. Has brackets logo.)
VEE JAY (498 "Please Please Me").................................... 700-800 63
(Credits "BEATLES." Black label with rainbow circle. Has thin lettering and oval logo.)
VEE JAY (522 "From Me to You")...................................125-150 63
(Black label with horizontal silver lines.)
VEE JAY (522 "From Me to You")...................................75-100 63
(Black label. With rainbow circle.)
VEE JAY (581 "Please Please Me") 100-150 64
(Purple label.)
VEE JAY (581 "Please Please Me") 75-100 64
(White label.)
VEE JAY (581 "Please Please Me") 30-40 64
(Yellow label.)
VEE JAY (581 "Please Please Me") 15-25 64
(Black label with horizontal silver lines.)
VEE JAY (581 "Please Please Me") 30-40 64
(Black label. No rainbow circle.)
VEE JAY (581 "Please Please Me") 20-25 64
(Black label with rainbow circle.)
VEE JAY (587 "Do You Want to Know a Secret")................................30-40 64
(Yellow label.)
VEE JAY (587 "Do You Want to Know a Secret")................................15-25 64
(Black label with horizontal silver lines.)
VEE JAY (587 "Do You Want to Know a Secret")................................15-25 64
(Black label. No horizontal lines. With either "Vee Jay" or "VJ" logo.)
VEE JAY (587 "Do You Want to Know a Secret")................................30-40 64
(Black label. No rainbow circle.)
VEE JAY (587 "Do You Want to Know a Secret")................................20-25 64
(Black label with rainbow circle.)

Picture Sleeves

APPLE (Except 2531)................12-18 68-70
APPLE (2531 "Ballad of John & Yoko") 15-20 69
ATCO (6308 "Ain't She Sweet") 100-125 64
CAPITOL/HOLIDAY INN........800-900 64
(Promotional sleeve, pictures the four Beatles on front and their first three Capitol LPs on the back. Not known to have been issued containing any particular single.)
CAPITOL (2056 "Hello Goodbye")................................18-20 67
CAPITOL (2138 "Lady Madonna") 12-18 68
CAPITOL (4000 series except 4506)...4-6 76
CAPITOL (4506 "Girl")..............10-15 78

CAPITOL (5100 "Movie Medley"/ "Fab Four on Film") 10-15 81
(With "B" prefix.)
CAPITOL (5107 "Movie Medley"/"I'm Happy Just to Dance with You") . 3-4 81
(With "B" prefix.)
CAPITOL (B-5189 "Love Me Do"). 3-4 82
(With "B" prefix. This recent Capitol 5000 series differs from the 5000 series of 1964 by its use of the "B" prefix.)
CAPITOL (5112 "I Want to Hold Your Hand") 20-30 64
CAPITOL (5112 WMCA Radio Promotional Sleeve)............................. 650-750 64
(Back side of this sleeve pictures WMCA dee jays. Front side is identical to standard commercial issue.)
CAPITOL (5112 "I Want to Hold Your Hand") 3-4 84
(This reissue sleeve is clearly dated "1984" in lower left corner.)
CAPITOL (5150 "Can't Buy Me Love")............................... 300-500 64
CAPITOL CUSTOM ("Music City KFWBeatles").................... 550-600 64
(Promotional sleeve for the "Souvenir Record" from KFWB and Wallichs Music City.)
CAPITOL (5222 "A Hard Day's Night")................................. 20-25 64
CAPITOL (5234 "I'll Cry Instead")................................ 35-45 64
CAPITOL (5235 "And I Love Her")...................................... 30-35 64
CAPITOL (5255 "Slow Down").. 35-40 64
CAPITOL (5327 "I Feel Fine")... 12-15 64
CAPITOL (5371 "Eight Days a Week") 10-12 65
CAPITOL (5407 "Ticket to Ride") 35-50 65
CAPITOL (5439 "Leave My Kitten Alone") 450-500 85
CAPITOL (5476 "Help") 15-20 65
CAPITOL (5498 "Yesterday").... 12-18 65
CAPITOL (5555 "We Can Work It Out")...................................... 15-20 65
CAPITOL (5587 "Nowhere Man").................................... 12-18 66
CAPITOL (5651 "Paperback Writer")................................. 12-18 66
CAPITOL (5715 "Yellow Submarine") 12-18 66
CAPITOL (5810 "Penny Lane"). 25-30 67
CAPITOL (5964 "All You Need Is Love")...................................... 8-12 67
CARROL JAMES (3301 "The Carroll James Interview with the Beatles")..... 10-15 84
CICADELIC/BIODISC 3-5 90
COLLECTABLES......................... 3-4 82
IBC (0082 "Murray the 'K' and the Beatles As It Happened")...............................4-6 76
MGM (13213 "My Bonnie") 35-40 64
MGM (13227 "Why")...............75-100 64
MURRAY the "K" and the BEATLES.................................60-75 64
(Reissued in 1976 as IBC 0082.)
SWAN 30-35 63
TOLLIE.....................................35-40 64
VEE JAY SPECIAL CHRISTMAS SLEEVE................................30-40 64
(Standard center-cut paper sleeve printed with the Beatles' faces and "We Wish You a Merry Christmas and a Happy New Year." Issued with assorted Vee Jay singles during the holiday season.)
VEE JAY (581 "Please Please Me") 100-125 64
(Pictures the four Beatles.)
VEE JAY (581 "Please Please Me") 500-600 64
(Reads "The Record That Started Beatlemania" across the top. Does not picture the group.)
VEE JAY (587 "Do You Want to Know a Secret") 35-40 64

Promotional Singles

APPLE ("Let It Be")...................20-25 70
(Identified as "Beatles Promo 1970." Single-sided promo issue.)
ATCO (6302 "Sweet Georgia Brown" 75-125 64
ATCO (6308 "Ain't She Sweet") 90-100 64
BACKSTAGE (1100 series, except 1112 & 1122)................8-10 82-83
(Picture discs.)
BACKSTAGE (1112 "Oui Presents the Silver Beatles") 5-10 82
(*Oui* magazine promotional giveaway. Features a *Like Dreamers Do/Love of the Loved* montage. Mailing also included *Oui* News Release and subscription form. This is not a picture disc single, as the other Backstage 1100 series singles are.)
BACKSTAGE (1122 "Like Dreamers Do")........................25-35 82
(Picture disc, with photo of *Penthouse* "Pet.")
CAPITOL (2056 "Hello Goodbye")..............................60-80 67
CAPITOL (2138 "Lady Madonna") 50-75 68
CAPITOL (4274 "Got to Get You Into My Life")..........................20-25 76
CAPITOL (4347 "Helter Skelter") 20-25 76
CAPITOL (4347 "Ob-La-Di, Ob-La-Da") 20-25 76
CAPITOL (4506 "Girl") 75-90 78

CAPITOL (4612 "Sgt. Pepper's Lonely Hearts Club Band"-"With a Little Help From My Friends") 12-15 78
CAPITOL (5100 "Movie Medley"/ "Fab Four on Film") 15-20 81
(First issued with *Movie Medley* backed with *Fab Four on Film,* which was the Beatles talking about the film *A Hard Day's Night.* Later issues had *I'm Happy Just to Dance with You* on the flip side.)
CAPITOL (5112 "I Want to Hold Your Hand") 8-10 84
(Though the promo of this single is actually numbered 9076, we have it listed both ways for your convenience.)
CAPITOL (PB-5189 "Love Me Do") 10-12 82
(With "PB" prefix. Promo copies of this issue were on commercial stock labels, but are quickly identified by the printing of an "Intro" time of :13 on the right side of the label. Also, store stock copies were B-5189, not PB-5189.)
CAPITOL (5624 "Twist & Shout") 8-10 86
CAPITOL (5810 "Penny Lane") 90-100 67
CAPITOL (5964 "All You Need Is Love") 70-85 67
(This promo, as well as many Capitol issues by other artists, was shipped in a "Rush" paper sleeve. It's possible a slight premium may be placed on these sleeves, although they were NOT identified in any way as a Beatles item.)
CAPITOL (9076 "I Want to Hold Your Hand") 8-10 84
CAPITOL (9758 "Movie Medley") 30-35 81
(With "SPRO" prefix.)
CAPITOL CUSTOM (2637 "Music City KFWBeatles") 200-250 64
(Radio KFWB and Wallichs Music City promo disc, "The Beatles Talking"/"You Can't Do That.")
CARROL JAMES (3301 "The Carroll James Interview with the Beatles") 8- 12 84
CREATIVE RADIO (B-1 "The Beatle Invasion") 10-20
(Radio show demo. Flip side is "Inside Paul McCartney.")
DECCA (31382 "My Bonnie") 500-600 62
(Shown as by Tony Sheridan & Beat Brothers. Pink label with black lettering.)
MBRF (55551 "Decade") 100-150 72
(Contains radio spots for the "Beatles 1962-1966" and "Beatles 1967-1970.")
MGM (13213 "My Bonnie") 90-100 64
(Shown as by the Beatles with Tony Sheridan.)
MGM (13227 "Why") 75-125 64
(Shown as by the Beatles with Tony Sheridan.)
STRAWBERRY FIELDS FOREVER (21 "How Do You Do It") 5-10 76
(Beatles convention souvenir issue. Colored vinyl. With insert.)
SWAN (4152 "She Loves You") 150-200 63
SWAN (4152 "I'll Get You") 175-225 64
(Single-sided pressing. Flip side has blank grooves.)
SWAN (4182 "Sie Liebt Dich") 125-150 64
TOLLIE (9001 "Twist and Shout") 100-125 64
TOLLIE (9008 "Love Me Do") 100-125 64
TOPAZ (1353 "Seattle Press Conference") 4-8 89
U.A. (2357 "A Hard Day's Night") 800-1200 64
U.A. (42370 "Let It Be") 400-700 70
(Has three radio advertisements for the film.)
VEE JAY (8 "Anna"/"Ask Me Why") 10000-12000 64
VEE JAY (498 "Please Please Me") 500-700 63
VEE JAY (522 "From Me to You") 250-350 63
VEE JAY (581 "Please Please Me," Purple label) 125-150 64
VEE JAY (581 "Please Please Me," White label) 100-125 64
VEE JAY (587 "Do You Want to Know a Secret") 150-200 64
WHAT'S IT ALL ABOUT 15-20

Plastic Soundsheets/Flexi-Discs

AMERICOM 350-450 69
(Four–inch "Pocket Discs.")
EVA-TONE (8464 "All My Loving") 5-10 82
(Back side reads either "Compliments of Musicland" or "Compliments of Discount.")
EVA-TONE (8464 "All My Loving") 15-20 82
(Back side reads "Compliments of Sam Goody.")
EVA-TONE (830771 "Till There Was You") 3-5 83
EVA-TONE (420826 "All My Loving") 5-10 82
(Back side reads either "Compliments of Musicland" or "Compliments of Discount.")
EVA-TONE (420826 "All My Loving") 15-20 82
(Back side reads "Compliments of Sam Goody.")
EVA-TONE (420827 "Magical Mystery Tour") 5-10 82

(Back side reads either "Compliments of Musicland" or "Compliments of Discount ")
EVA-TONE (420827 "Magical Mystery Tour") 15-20 82
(Back side reads "Compliments of Sam Goody.")
EVA-TONE (420828 "Rocky Raccoon") 5-10 82
(Back side reads either "Compliments of Musicland" or "Compliments of Discount.")
EVA-TONE (420828 "Rocky Raccoon") 15-20 82
(Back side reads "Compliments of Sam Goody.")
EVA-TONE (1214825 "The Beatles German Medley) 30-40 83
OFFICIAL BEATLES FAN CLUB ("1964 Season's Greetings from the Beatles")............................. 175-200 64
OFFICIAL BEATLES FAN CLUB ("1965 Beatles Christmas Record") 100-125 65
OFFICIAL BEATLES FAN CLUB ("1966 Season's Greetings from the Beatles")............................ 100-125 66
OFFICIAL BEATLES FAN CLUB ("1967 Christmas Time Is Here Again") 100-125 67
OFFICIAL BEATLES FAN CLUB ("1968 Beatles Christmas Record").... 50-75 68
OFFICIAL BEATLES FAN CLUB ("1969 Happy Christmas")................. 40-50 69
SILHOUETTE............................... 6-10 86

EPs: 7–inch 33/45rpm

CAPITOL (EAP 1-2121 "Four By the Beatles").......................... 100-150 64
CAPITOL (R-5365 "4-By the Beatles")............................ 100-125 65
VEE JAY (VJEP 1-903 "Souvenir of Their Visit to America") 75-85 64
(Solid black label with either oval or block style Vee Jay logo.)
VEE JAY (VJEP 1-903 "Souvenir of Their Visit to America") 90-110 64
(Solid black label with brackets Vee Jay logo.)
VEE JAY (VJEP 1-903 "Souvenir of Their Visit to America") 45-55 64
(Black label with rainbow color-band. All four song titles in same size type.)
VEE JAY (VJEP 1-903 "Souvenir of Their Visit to America") 60-80 64
(Black label with rainbow color-band. Has "Ask Me Why" in much larger type size than other titles.)

Promotional EPs

CAPITOL 33 COMPACT (2047 "Meet the Beatles")....................... 200-225 64
(Jukebox issue only.)
CAPITOL 33 COMPACT (2080 "Beatles Second Album").................. 200-225 64
(Jukebox issue only.)
CAPITOL 33 COMPACT (2108 "Something New") 250-300 64
(Jukebox issue only.)
CAPITOL 33 COMPACT (2548/49 "Open-End Interview")..........................550-600 64
(Issued with a paper sleeve and script, which represents about $300-400 of the value.)
CAPITOL 33 COMPACT (2598/99 "Second Open-End Interview") 500-600 64
(Issued with a paper sleeve and script, which represents about $300-400 of the value.)
CAPITOL (2720/21 "The Beatles Introduce New Songs")........500-600 64
(45rpm EP with John Lennon about Cilla Black's *It's for You,* and Paul talking about Peter & Gordon's *I Don't Want to See You Again.*)
CAPITOL 33 COMPACT (2905/06 "The Capitol Souvenir Record") ...250-300 64
(Issued with a paper sleeve and script, which represents about $100-125 of the value. Contains excerpts of 15 different songs by 15 artists, including the Beatles.)
VEE JAY (903 "Souvenir of Their Visit to America") 100-150 64
(White label with blue print. Price is for disc only.)
VEE JAY (903 "Souvenir of Their Visit to America") 1500-2000 64
(Special sleeve in which some copies of the EP were supplied to radio stations.)

LPs: 10/12–inch 33rpm

ALBUM GLOBE (8146 "Happy Michaelmas") 8-12 81
APPLE (101 "The Beatles") 25-30 68
(With Capitol logo at bottom of label.)
APPLE (101 "The Beatles") 20-25 71
(Without Capitol logo at bottom of label.)
APPLE (153 "Yellow Submarine")...........................12-18 69
(With Capitol logo at bottom of label.)
APPLE (153 "Yellow Submarine") 10-12 71
(Without Capitol logo at bottom of label.)
APPLE (383 "Abbey Road").......12-18 69
(With Capitol logo at bottom of label.)
APPLE (383 "Abbey Road").......10-12 71
(Without Capitol logo at bottom of label.)
APPLE (385 "Hey Jude") 15-25 70
(With Capitol logo at bottom of label.)
APPLE (385 "Hey Jude") 10-12 71
(Without Capitol logo at bottom of label.)

APPLE (ST-2047 "Meet the Beatles")................................ 12-18 71
(With Capitol logo at bottom of label.)
APPLE (ST-2047 "Meet the Beatles")................................ 10-12 71
(Without Capitol logo at bottom of label.)
APPLE (ST-2080 "The Beatles' Second Album") 12-18 71
(With Capitol logo at bottom of label.)
APPLE (ST-2080 "The Beatles' Second Album") 10-12 71
(Without Capitol logo at bottom of label.)
APPLE (ST-2108 "Something New") 12-18 71
(With Capitol logo at bottom of label.)
APPLE (ST-2108 "Something New") 10-12 71
(Without Capitol logo at bottom of label.)
APPLE (ST-2222 "The Beatles' Story") 12-18 71
(With Capitol logo at bottom of label.)
APPLE (ST-2228 "The Beatles' Story") 10-12 71
(Without Capitol logo at bottom of label.)
APPLE (ST-2228 "Beatles '65") 12-18 71
(With Capitol logo at bottom of label.)
APPLE (ST-2228 "Beatles '65") 10-12 71
(Without Capitol logo at bottom of label.)
APPLE (ST-2309 "Early Beatles")................................ 12-18 71
(With Capitol logo at bottom of label.)
APPLE (ST-2309 "Early Beatles")................................ 10-12 71
(Without Capitol logo at bottom of label.)
APPLE (ST-2358 "Beatles VI").. 12-18 71
(With Capitol logo at bottom of label.)
APPLE (ST-2358 "Beatles VI").. 10-12 71
(Without Capitol logo at bottom of label.)
APPLE (ST-2386 "Help")........... 12-18 71
(With Capitol logo at bottom of label.)
APPLE (ST-2386 "Help").......... 10-12 71
(Without Capitol logo at bottom of label.)
APPLE (ST-2442 "Rubber Soul") 12-18 71
(With Capitol logo at bottom of label.)
APPLE (ST-2442 "Rubber Soul") 10-12 71
(Without Capitol logo at bottom of label.)
APPLE (ST-2576 "Revolver").... 12-18 71
(With Capitol logo at bottom of label.)
APPLE (ST-2576 "Revolver").... 10-12 71
(Without Capitol logo at bottom of label.)
APPLE (SMAS-2653 "Sgt. Pepper's Lonely Hearts Club Band")...... 12-18 71
(With Capitol logo at bottom of label.)
APPLE (SMAS-2653 "Sgt. Pepper's Lonely Hearts Club Band")...... 10-12 71
(Without Capitol logo at bottom of label.)
APPLE (SMAL-2835 "Magical Mystery Tour").....................................12-18 71
(With Capitol logo at bottom of label.)
APPLE (SMAL-2835 "Magical Mystery Tour").....................................10-12 71
(Without Capitol logo at bottom of label.)
APPLE (3403 "1962-1966") 15-20 73
APPLE (3404 "1967-1970") 15-20 73
APPLE (34001 "Let It Be").........10-15 70
ATCO (169 "Ain't She Sweet").75-100 64
(Monaural. Also contains selections by the Swallows.)
ATCO (169 "Ain't She Sweet") 100-150 64-69
(Stereo. Also contains selections by the Swallows.)
AUDIO FIDELITY (339 "First Movement," Picture disc)..............................8-12 82
AUDIO RARITIES (2452 "The Complete Silver Beatles)..........................6-10 82
AUDIO RARITIES (30003 "The Silver Beatles)..................................15-20 82
(Picture disc.)
BACKSTAGE (Except 1111)......10-15 82-83
BACKSTAGE (1111 "Like Dreamers Do")..20-25 82
(Three-LP set. Contains two picture discs and a white vinyl LP.)
BACKSTAGE (1111 "Like Dreamers Do")..30-45 82
(Three-LP set. Contains two picture discs and a GRAY vinyl LP.)
BACKSTAGE (1111 "Like Dreamers Do")..30-40 82
(Three-LP set. Includes any of the custom issues, which had various logos printed on the reverse side of the picture discs.)
BACKSTAGE (1111 "Like Dreamers Do")..15-20 82
(Three-LP set. No custom artwork on picture disc. With gatefold cover.)
BACKSTAGE (1111 "Like Dreamers Do")..12-15 82
(Two-LP set. With standard cover.)
BACKSTAGE (1111 "Like Dreamers Do")..20-25 82
CAPITOL (101 "The Beatles") ...10-12 76
(Orange label.)
CAPITOL (101 "The Beatles") 8-12 78
(Purple label.)
CAPITOL (101 "The Beatles") 6-10 84
(Black label.)
CAPITOL (153 "Yellow Submarine")..............................8-10 76
(Orange label.)
CAPITOL (153 "Yellow Submarine")..............................6-10 78
(Purple label.)

CAPITOL (153 "Yellow Submarine") 5-10 84
(Black label.)
CAPITOL (383 "Abbey Road") 8-10 76
(Orange label.)
CAPITOL (383 "Abbey Road") 6-10 78
(Purple label.)
CAPITOL (383 "Abbey Road") 5-10 84
(Black label.)
CAPITOL (385 "Hey Jude") 8-10 76
(Orange label.)
CAPITOL (385 "Hey Jude") 6-10 78
(Purple label.)
CAPITOL (385 "Hey Jude") 5-10 84
(Black label.)
CAPITOL (T-2047 "Meet the Beatles") 30-45 64
(Monaural.)
CAPITOL (ST 2047 "Meet the Beatles") 20-25 64
(Stereo. Black label with white print around border.)
CAPITOL (ST-2047 "Meet the Beatles") 20-30 69
(Green label.)
CAPITOL (ST-2047 "Meet the Beatles") 8-12 76
(Orange label.)
CAPITOL (ST-2047 "Meet the Beatles") 6-10 78
(Purple label.)
CAPITOL (ST-2047 "Meet the Beatles") 5-10 84
(Black label with black print around border.)
CAPITOL (ST-8-2047 "Meet the Beatles") 25-30 64-69
(Capitol Record Club issue.)
CAPITOL (T-2080 "The Beatles' Second Album") 30-40 64
(Monaural.)
CAPITOL (ST-2080 "The Beatles' Second Album") 20-25 64
(Stereo. Black label with white print around border.)
CAPITOL (ST-2080 "The Beatles' Second Album") 20-30 69
(Green label.)
CAPITOL (ST-2080 "The Beatles' Second Album") 8-12 76
(Orange label.)
CAPITOL (ST-2080 "The Beatles' Second Album") 6-10 78
(Purple label.)
CAPITOL (ST-2080 "The Beatles' Second Album") 5-10 84
(Black label with black print around border.)
CAPITOL (ST-8-2080 "The Beatles' Second Album") 25-30 64-69
(Capitol Record Club issue.)
CAPITOL (T-2108 "Something New") 30-40 64
(Monaural.)
CAPITOL (ST-2108 "Something New") 20-25 64
(Stereo. Black label with white print around border.)
CAPITOL (ST-2108 "Something New") 20-30 69
(Green label.)
CAPITOL (ST-2108 "Something New") 8-12 76
(Orange label.)
CAPITOL (ST-2108 "Something New") 6-10 78
(Purple label.)
CAPITOL (ST-2108 "Something New") 5-10 84
(Black label with black print around border.)
CAPITOL (ST-8-2108 "Something New") 25-35 64-69
(Capitol Record Club issue.)
CAPITOL (TBO-2222 "The Beatles' Story") 30-35 64
(Monaural.)
CAPITOL (STBO-2222 "The Beatles' Story") 30-35 64
(Stereo. Black label with white print around border.)
CAPITOL (STBO-2222 "The Beatles' Story") 20-25 69
(Green label.)
CAPITOL (STBO-2222 "The Beatles' Story") 8-12 76
(Orange label.)
CAPITOL (STBO-2222 "The Beatles' Story") 8-10 78
(Purple label.)
CAPITOL (STBO-2222 "The Beatles' Story") 6-10 84
(Black label with black print around border.)
CAPITOL (T-2228 "Beatles '65") 30-40 65
(Monaural.)
CAPITOL (ST-2228 "Beatles '65") 20-25 65
(Stereo. Black label with white print around border.)
CAPITOL (ST-2228 "Beatles '65") 20-25 69
(Green label.)
CAPITOL (ST-2228 "Beatles '65") 8-12 76
(Orange label.)
CAPITOL (ST-2228 "Beatles '65") 6-10 78
(Purple label.)

CAPITOL (ST-2228 "Beatles '65").. 5-10 84
(Black label with black print around border.)
CAPITOL (T-2309 "The Early Beatles")................................ 30-40 65
(Monaural.)
CAPITOL (ST-2309 "The Early Beatles")................................ 20-25 65
(Stereo. Black label with white print around border.)
CAPITOL (ST-2309 "The Early Beatles")................................ 20-25 69
(Green label.)
CAPITOL (ST-2309 "The Early Beatles")................................. 8-12 76
(Orange label.)
CAPITOL (ST-2309 "The Early Beatles")................................. 6-10 78
(Purple label.)
CAPITOL (ST-2309 "The Early Beatles")................................. 5-10 84
(Black label with black print around border.)
CAPITOL (T-2358 "Beatles VI") 30-40 65
(Monaural.)
CAPITOL (ST-2358 "Beatles VI").. 20-25 65
(Stereo. Black label with white print around border.)
CAPITOL (ST-2358 "Beatles VI").. 20-25 69
(Green label.)
CAPITOL (ST-2358 "Beatles VI") 8-12 76
(Orange label.)
CAPITOL (ST-2358 "Beatles VI") 6-10 78
(Purple label.)
CAPITOL (ST-2358 "Beatles VI") 5-10 84
(Black label with black print around border.)
CAPITOL (MAS-2386 "Help") ... 30-40 65
(Monaural.)
CAPITOL (SMAS-2386 "Help"). 20-25 65
(Stereo. Black label with white print around border.)
CAPITOL (SMAS-2386 "Help"). 20-25 69
(Green label.)
CAPITOL (SMAS-2386 "Help")... 8-12 76
(Orange label.)
CAPITOL (SMAS-2386 "Help")... 6-10 78
(Purple label.)
CAPITOL (SMAS-2386 "Help")... 5-10 84
(Black label with black print around border.)
CAPITOL (SMAS-8-2386 "Help")................................ 25-30 65-69
(Capitol Record Club issue.)
CAPITOL (T-2442 "Rubber Soul") 30-40 65
(Monaural.)
CAPITOL (ST-2442 "Rubber Soul") 20-25 65
(Stereo. Black label with white print around border.)
CAPITOL (ST-2442 "Rubber Soul") 20-25 69
(Green label.)
CAPITOL (ST-2442 "Rubber Soul") 8-12 76
(Orange label.)
CAPITOL (ST-2442 "Rubber Soul") 6-10 78
(Purple label.)
CAPITOL (ST-2442 "Rubber Soul") 5-10 84
(Black label with black print around border.)
CAPITOL (SW-2442 "Rubber Soul") 5-10
CAPITOL (ST-8-2442 "Rubber Soul") 25-35 65
(Capitol Record Club issue.)
CAPITOL (T-2553 "Yesterday and Today") 1500-2500 66
(Monaural. FIRST STATE "Butcher cover" issues.)
CAPITOL (ST-2553 "Yesterday and Today") 5000-10000 66
(Stereo. FIRST STATE "Butcher Cover" issues.)
CAPITOL (T-2553 "Yesterday and Today") 300-600 66
(Monaural. PASTE OVER or PEELED "Butcher cover" copies.)
CAPITOL (ST-2553 "Yesterday and Today") 400-700 66
(Stereo. PASTE OVER or PEELED "Butcher cover" copies.)
Note: the wide range of values exists here due to varied opinions on the practice of peeling the "Trunk cover" from the "Butcher cover." The expertise used in the peeling is also a major factor affecting the value of these LPs.
CAPITOL (T-2553 "Yesterday and Today") 30-40 66
(Monaural. "Trunk cover.")
CAPITOL (ST-2553 "Yesterday and Today") 20-25 66
(Stereo. Black label with white print around border. "Trunk cover.")
CAPITOL (ST-2553 "Yesterday and Today") 20-25 69
(Green label.)
CAPITOL (ST-2553 "Yesterday and Today") 8-12 76
(Orange label.)
CAPITOL (ST-2553 "Yesterday and Today") 6-10 78
(Purple label.)

CAPITOL (ST-2553 "Yesterday and Today").. 5-10 84
(Black label with black print around border.)
CAPITOL (ST-8-2553 "Yesterday and Today")................................... 25-35 66-69
(Capitol Record Club issue.)
CAPITOL (T-2576 "Revolver").. 30-40 66
(Monaural.)
CAPITOL (ST-2576 "Revolver") 20-25 66
(Stereo. Black label with white print around border.)
CAPITOL (ST-2576 "Revolver") 20-25 69
(Green label.)
CAPITOL (ST-2576 "Revolver").. 8-12 76
(Orange label.)
CAPITOL (ST-2576 "Revolver").. 6-10 78
(Purple label.)
CAPITOL (ST-2576 "Revolver").. 5-10 84
(Black label with black print around border.)
CAPITOL (ST-8-2576 "Revolver")................................ 25-35 66-69
(Capitol Record Club issue.)
CAPITOL (MAS-2653 "Sgt. Pepper's Lonely Hearts Club Band")............... 50-100 67
(Monaural.)
CAPITOL (SMAS-2653 "Sgt. Pepper's Lonely Hearts Club Band")................ 30-40 67
(Stereo. Black label with white print around border.)
CAPITOL (SMAS-2653 "Sgt. Pepper's Lonely Hearts Club Band")................ 18-22 69
(Green label.)
CAPITOL (SMAS-2653 "Sgt. Pepper's Lonely Hearts Club Band").................. 8-12 76
(Orange label.)
CAPITOL (SMAS-2653 "Sgt. Pepper's Lonely Hearts Club Band").................. 6-10 78
(Purple label.)
CAPITOL (SMAS-2653 "Sgt. Pepper's Lonely Hearts Club Band").................. 5-10 84
(Black label with black print around border.)
CAPITOL (MAL-2835 "Magical Mystery Tour")................................. 75-150 67
(Monaural.)
CAPITOL (SMAL-2835 "Magical Mystery Tour")..................................... 30-40 67
(Stereo. Black label with white print around border.)
CAPITOL (SMAL-2835 "Magical Mystery Tour")..................................... 18-22 69
(Green label.)
CAPITOL (SMAL-2835 "Magical Mystery Tour").. 8-12 76
(Orange label.)
CAPITOL (SMAL-2835 "Magical Mystery Tour").. 6-10 78
(Purple label.)
CAPITOL (SMAL-2835 "Magical Mystery Tour")..5-10 84
(Black label with black print around border.)
CAPITOL (3403 "The Beatles/ 1962-1966")...............................8-12 78
CAPITOL (3404 "The Beatles/ 1967-1970")...............................8-12 78
CAPITOL (11537 "Rock 'N' Roll Music")...................................12-18 76
CAPITOL (11638 "Beatles at the Hollywood Bowl").......................8-10 77
CAPITOL (11711 "Love Songs")..6-10 77
CAPITOL (11840 "Sgt. Pepper's Lonely Hearts Club Band")..................15-20 78
(Picture disc.)
CAPITOL (11841 "The Beatles")20-30 78
(Colored vinyl.)
CAPITOL (11842 "The Beatles/ 1962-1966")..............................20-25 78
CAPITOL (11843 "The Beatles/ 1967-1970")..............................20-25 78
CAPITOL (11900 "Abbey Road," Picture disc)..........................50-100 78
CAPITOL (11921 "A Hard Day's Night").......................................8-10 79
(Purple label.)
CAPITOL (11921 "A Hard Day's Night").......................................5-10 84
(Black label with black print around border.)
CAPITOL (11922 "Let It Be").......8-10 79
(Purple label.)
CAPITOL (11922 "Let It Be").......5-10 84
(Black label with black print around border.)
CAPITOL (12009 "Rarities")......40-60 78
CAPITOL (12060 "The Beatles Rarities")...................................6-10 80
CAPITOL (12199 "Reel Music")...6-10 82
CAPITOL (12245 "The Beatles 20 Greatest Hits")...........................8-12 82
(Purple label.)
CAPITOL (12245 "The Beatles 20 Greatest Hits")...........................5-10 84
(Black label.)
CAPITOL (16020 "Rock 'N' Roll Music, Volume I").......................5-10 80
CAPITOL (16021 "Rock 'N' Roll Music, Volume II")......................5-10 80
CAPITOL (48062 "Magical Mystery Tour")..8-10 87
CAPITOL (90043 "Past Masters, Vol. 1")..6-10 88
CAPITOL (90044 "Past Masters, Vol. 2")..6-10 88
CAPITOL/APPLE......................10-12 68-75
(A "Capitol/Apple" label is simply the Apple label with the Capitol logo near the bottom of the label.)
CAPITOL RECORD CLUB (Except ST-8-2553)..............................25-35 60s

(Includes Record Club issues on the Capitol label only. Releases on other labels, available through the club, are listed by their label name.)
CAPITOL RECORD CLUB (ST-8-2553 "Yesterday and Today") 40-45 66
CICADELIC 5-10 85-87
CLARION (601 "The Amazing Beatles & Other Great English Sounds"). 60-75 66
(Stereo. Back cover lists song titles. Also contains selections by the Swallows.)
CLARION (601 "The Amazing Beatles & Other Great English Sounds")75-100 66
(Stereo. Back cover does NOT list song titles. Also contains selections by the Swallows.)
CLARION (601 "The Amazing Beatles & Other Great English Sounds"). 50-75 66
(Monaural. Also contains selections by the Swallows.)
CREATIVE RADIO ("The Beatle Invasion") 35-45
(Three-LP set, includes 12x19 poster.)
GREAT NORTHWEST MUSIC... 5-10 78
H.S.R.D. 8-12 82
HALL of MUSIC........................ 12-18 81
HERITAGE SOUND.................. 8-10 82
I-N-S RADIO NEWS ("American Tour with Ed Rudy #2") 12-18 80
LINGASONG............................ 10-12 77
LLOYDS ("The Great American Tour-1965 Live Beatlemania Concert") 125-175 65
(With selections by the Liverpool Lads.)
MFSL (1 "The Beatles, the Collection")......................... 400-500 82
(14-LP boxed set. Includes booklet and alignment tool.)
MFSL (023 "Abbey Road")........ 25-50 79
MFSL (047 "Magical Mystery Tour") 25-50 81
MFSL (072 "The Beatles") 25-50 82
MFSL/UHQR (100 "Sgt. Pepper's Lonely Hearts Club Band") 200-400 82
(Boxed set. Silver label, with "UHQR" near top.)
MFSL (100 "Sgt. Pepper's Lonely Hearts Club Band") 15-25 84
(White label. No "UHQR" on label.)
MFSL (101 "Please Please Me")...................................... 25-50 84
MFSL (102 "With the Beatles") 50-100 84
MFSL (103 "A Hard Day's Night") 25-50 84
MFSL (104 "Beatles for Sale") .. 25-50 84
MFSL (105 "Help") 25-50 84
MFSL (106 "Rubber Soul")........ 25-50 84
MFSL (107 "Revolver").............. 25-50 84
MFSL (108 "Yellow Submarine")25-50 84
MFSL (109 "Let It Be") 25-50 84
MGM (E-4215 "The Beatles with Tony Sheridan and Guests") ...45-55 64
(Monaural. With selections by Tony Sheridan and by the Titans.)
MGM (SE-4215 "The Beatles with Tony Sheridan and Guests") .75-100 64
(Stereo. With selections by Tony Sheridan and by the Titans.)
METRO (M-563 "This Is Where It Started")................................40-50 66
(Also contains selections by Tony Sheridan and by the Titans.)
METRO (MS-563 "This Is Where It Started")................................50-75 66
(Also contains selections by Tony Sheridan and by the Titans.)
MUSIC INTERNATIONAL............5-10 85
PAC..15-20 81
PBR INT'L 20-30 78
PHOENIX 10 ....5-10 82
PHOENIX 20 ....5-10 83
PICKWICK (Except 90071)..........8-12 78-79
PICKWICK (90071 "Recorded Live In Hamburg, 1962, Volume 3") 15-20 78
POLYDOR (4504 "In the Beginning, Circa 1960")...........................12-15 70
(With gatefold cover.)
POLYDOR (4504 "In the Beginning, Circa 1960")..............................5-10 81-84
(With standard cover.)
POLYDOR (93199 "In the Beginning, Circa 1960")............................15-18 70
(Capitol Record Club issue.)
RPN (RADIO PULSEBEAT NEWS) "American Tour with Ed Rudy #2")...........40-50 64
(This LP was occasionally issued with a "Teen Talk" booklet. The value of the booklet is approximately the same as for the LP. This edition has NO pictures of the Beatles on the LP cover.)
RPN (RADIO PULSEBEAT NEWS) ("1965 Talk Album, Ed Rudy with New U.S. Tour") 50-75 65
RAVEN.......................................5-10 81
SAVAGE (69 "The Savage Young Beatles") 75-100 68
(Label is yellow. Cover is orange.)
SAVAGE (69 "The Savage Young Beatles") 40-50 68
(Label is orange. Cover is yellow.)
SILHOUETTE 8-12 81-84
STERLING PRODUCTIONS (6481 "I Apologize") 70-80 66
(Price includes bonus 8x10 photo, which represents $5-15 of the value.)
U.A. (UAL-3366 "A Hard Day's Night") 25-30 64
(Monaural.)

U.A. (UAS-6366 "A Hard Day's Night") 30-40 64
(Stereo. Black label.)
U.A. (UAS-6366 "A Hard Day's Night") 20-25 68-70
(Stereo. Pink and orange or black and orange label.)
U.A. (UAS-6366 "A Hard Day's Night") 10-15 71
(Stereo. Tan label.)
U.A. (UAS-6366 "A Hard Day's Night") 8-12 77
(Stereo. Orange and yellow label.)
U.A. (90828 "A Hard Day's Night") 75-100 65
(Capitol Record Club issue.)
VEE JAY (202 "Hear the Beatles Tell All") 50-60 64
(Monaural. Black label with rainbow color-band.)
VEE JAY (202 "Hear the Beatles Tell All") 5-10 79
(Stereo.)
VEE JAY (202 "Hear the Beatles Tell All") 5-10 87
(Picture disc.)
VEE JAY (1062 "Introducing the Beatles") 325-375 63
(Monaural. With *Love Me Do* and *P.S. I Love You.* Back cover pictures 25 other Vee Jay albums.)
VEE JAY (1062 "Introducing the Beatles") 800-1200 63
(Stereo. With *Love Me Do* and *P.S. I Love You.* Back cover pictures 25 other Vee Jay albums.)
VEE JAY (1062 "Introducing the Beatles") 250-400 63-64
(Monaural. With *Love Me Do* and *P.S. I Love You.* Back cover is blank. May be regarded as a promotional issue, however nothing on the LP supports that theory.)
VEE JAY (1062 "Introducing the Beatles") 600-800 63-64
(Stereo. With *Love Me Do* and *P.S. I Love You.* Back cover is blank. Regarded by some as a promo; however, nothing on the LP supports that theory.)
VEE JAY (1062 "Introducing the Beatles") 100-150 64
(Monaural. With *Love Me Do* and *P.S. I Love You.* Back cover lists contents. Has brackets style label logo.)
VEE JAY (1062 "Introducing the Beatles") 150-250 64
(Stereo. With *Love Me Do* and *P.S. I Love You.* Back cover lists contents. Has brackets style label logo.)
VEE JAY (1062 "Introducing the Beatles") 60-75 64
(Monaural. With *Love Me Do* and *P.S. I Love You.* Back cover lists contents. Oval style label logo.)
VEE JAY (1062 "Introducing the Beatles") 150-200 64
(Stereo. With *Love Me Do* and *P.S. I Love You* listed on cover and disc, but actually plays *Ask Me Why* and *Please Please Me.*)
VEE JAY (1062 "Introducing the Beatles") 150-200 64
(Stereo. With *Ask Me Why* and *Please Please Me.* For any of the label styles or logo designs.)
VEE JAY (1062 "Introducing the Beatles") 40-60 64
(Monaural, rainbow color-band label. With *Ask Me Why* and *Please Please Me.*)
VEE JAY (1062 "Introducing the Beatles") 65-80 64
(Monaural, black label, no color-band. With *Ask Me Why* and *Please Please Me.* With brackets or oval style logo.)
VEE JAY (1062 "Introducing the Beatles") 35-45 64
(Monaural, black label, no color-band. With *Ask Me Why* and *Please Please Me.* Label logo has neither oval nor brackets.)
VEE JAY (1092 "Songs, Pictures and Stories") 50-75 64
(Monaural.)
VEE JAY (1092 "Songs, Pictures and Stories") 150-200 64
(Stereo.)
VEE JAY (1092 "Songs and Pictures).................................8-10
(Reissue.)

Promotional LPs

ABC/WATERMARK ("Ringo's Yellow Submarine") 700-800 84
(Set of 24 LPs in eight boxed sets, featuring Ringo Starr telling the story of the Beatles. Issued to radio stations only.)
APPLE (SBC-100 "The Beatles' Christmas Album") 90-100 70
(Special issue for Beatles fan club members.)
APPLE FILMS (004 "The Yellow Submarine") 400-450 69
(Contains the advertisements used on radio stations to promote the film.)
ATCO (33-169 "Ain't She Sweet") 300-350 64
(Also contains selections by the Swallows.)
BACKSTAGE (Colored vinyl).....20-30 82
CAPITOL ("Help, Open-End Interview") 550-650 65
(Issued with programmer's script.)

CAPITOL ("The Platinum Beatles Collection") 475-500 84
(18-LP boxed set.)
CAPITOL (SPRO-8969 "Rarities") 35-40 78
CAPITOL (SMAS-11638 "Beatles at the Hollywood Bowl") 90-100 77
CAPITOL (12199 "Reel Music") 45-55 82
(Colored vinyl.)
CAPITOL/EMI (BC-13 "The Beatles Collection") 250-300 78
(14-LP boxed set.)
I-N-S RADIO NEWS (1 "Beatlemania Tour Coverage") 150-200 64
(An open-end interview. Includes a script.)
LINGASONG (7001 "Live! At the Star-Club") 90-100 77
(Blue vinyl.)
LINGASONG (7001 "Live! At the Star-Club") 75-90 77
(Red vinyl.)
LINGASONG (7001 "Live! At the Star-Club") 30-40 77
(Black vinyl.)
ORANGE (12880 "The Silver Beatles") 35-45 85
RAVEN 15-20 81
U.A. (UA-HELP "United Artists Presents `Help!") 400-450 65
(Contains the advertisements used on radio stations to promote the film.)
U.A. (UA-HELP INT "Special Open-End Interview") 500-550 65
(Price includes script and programming information, which represents about $50-75 of the value.)
U.A. (2359/60 "Special Beatles Half Hour Open End Interview") 500-550 64
(Price includes 12-pages of script and programming information, which represents about $50-75 of the value.)
U.A. (2362/63 "United Artists Presents *A Hard Day's Night*") 400-450 64
(Contains the advertisements used on radio stations to promote the film.)
U.A. (UAL-6366 "A Hard Day's Night") 300-350 64
(White label.)

Members: John Lennon; Paul McCartney; George Harrison; Pete Best; Ringo Starr.

Also see BEST, Pete
Also see CLAY, Tom
Also see HARRISON, George
Also see LENNON, John
Also see MARTIN, George
Also see McCARTNEY, Paul
Also see PRESLEY, Elvis / Beatles
Also see PRESTON, Billy
Also see SHANKAR, Ravi
Also see SILKIE
Also see STARR, Ringo

BEATLES / Beach Boys / Buddy Holly

LPs: 10/12–inch 33rpm

CREATIVE RADIO SHOWS (Demo of "Specials") 75-100 79
(Promotional issue only.)
Also see HOLLY, Buddy

BEATLES / Beach Boys / Kingston Trio

Plastic Soundsheets/Flexi-Discs:

EVA-TONE (8464 "Surprise Gift from the Beatles, Beach Boys & Kingston Trio") 300-350 64
(Plastic soundsheet.)
EVA-TONE (8464 "Surprise Gift from the Beatles, Beach Boys & Kingston Trio") 200-250 64
(Five–inch edition of the above plastic soundsheet.)
Also see BEACH BOYS
Also see KINGSTON TRIO

BEATLES / Jerry Blabber

Singles: 7–inch

QUEST.......................................5-10 65

BEATLES / 4 Seasons

LPs: 10/12–inch 33rpm

VEE JAY (DX-30 "Beatles Vs. the Four Seasons") 300-400 64
(Monaural.)
VEE JAY (DXS-30 "Beatles Vs. the Four Seasons") 500-750 64
(Stereo.)
Price includes a bonus Beatles poster, which represents $80 to $100 of the value.
Also see 4 SEASONS

BEATLES / Frank Ifield

LPs: 10/12–inch 33rpm

VEE JAY (1085 "The Beatles & Frank Ifield") 750-1000 64
(Monaural. Pictures the Beatles on cover.)
VEE JAY (1085 "The Beatles & Frank Ifield") 2000-3000 64
(Stereo. Pictures the Beatles on cover.)
VEE JAY (1085 "Jolly What! the Beatles & Frank Ifield") 75-90 64
(Monaural. Pictures an Englishman on cover.)
VEE JAY (1085 "Jolly What! the Beatles & Frank Ifield") .. 150-200 64
(Stereo. Pictures an Englishman on cover.)
Also see IFIELD, Frank

BEATLES / Loretta Lynn

Singles: 7–inch

VEE JAY (581 "Please Please Me"/"Before I'm over You") 50-100 64
(This pairing is the result of a production error.)
Also see BEATLES
Also see LYNN, Loretta

BEATLES BLAST at STADIUM (Described by Erupting Fans)

LPs: 10/12-inch 33rpm

AUDIO JOURNAL.................... 10-20 66
(*Beatles Blast,* etc." is the title of the LP. Featuring only noise, made by fans at a Shea Stadium concert. No artists are credited.

BEATS INTERNATIONAL

P&R/LP '90

LPs: 10/12-inch 33rpm

ELEKTRA.................................. 5-8 90
Members: Norman Cook; Lester Noel; Lindy Layton; Andy Boucher; Luke Cresswell.
Also see HOUSEMARTINS

BEATTY, E.C.

P&R '59

Singles: 7-inch

CAMPBELL................................ 5-10 64
COLONIAL................................ 8-15 59-61

BEAU, Toby: see TOBY BEAU

BEAU BRUMMELS

P&R/LP '65

Singles: 7-inch

AUTUMN (8 "Laugh Laugh")....... 8-12 64
(White label.)
AUTUMN (8 "Laugh Laugh")....... 5-10 64
(Orange label. Different edit than on white label.)
AUTUMN (10 thru 24)................ 5-10 65
PEP.. 3-4
RHINO...................................... 3-4 82
VAULT...................................... 4-6 67
W.B. 4-8 66-75

Picture Sleeves

PEP.. 3-4
RHINO...................................... 3-4 82

LPs: 10/12-inch 33rpm

ACCORD.................................... 5-10 82
AUTUMN (103 "Introducing the Beau Brummels").................... 40-50 65
AUTUMN (104 "Beau Brummels, Vol. 2")................. 40-50 65
JAS.. 8-10
POST 8-10
RHINO...................................... 5-10 81-82
VAULT (114 "Best of the Beau Brummels")........................... 25-30 67
VAULT (121 "Beau Brummels, Vol. 44")................................ 15-20 68
W.B. (Except 1644).................. 20-25 67-75
W.B. (1644 "Beau Brummels '66").. 30-35 66
Members: Sal Valentino; Ron Elliott; Ron Meagher; Declan Mulligan; John Petersen.

BEAU COUP

P&R '87

Singles: 7-inch

AMHERST 3-4 87
ROCK & ROLL..............................3-4 84-85

BEAU-MARKS

P&R '60

Singles: 7-inch

MAINSTREAM..............................4-6 68
PORT 5-10 62
RUST 5-10 61
SHAD 10-15 60
TIME (1032 "Rockin' Blues")......20-30 61

BEAUMONT, Jimmy (With the Skyliners; Jimmie Beaumont)

P&R '61

Singles: 7-inch

BANG (525 "You Got Too Much Going for You")......................15-20 66
CAPITOL......................................3-5 74
COLPIX......................................5-10 61
DRIVE 3-5 76
GALLANT....................................5-10
MAY 8-10 61-63
Also see SKYLINERS

BEAUVOIR, Jean

P&R/LP '86

Singles: 12-inch 33/45rpm

COLUMBIA 4-6 86

Singles: 7-inch

COLUMBIA 3-4 86

Picture Sleeves

COLUMBIA 3-4 86

LPs: 10/12-inch 33rpm

COLUMBIA 5-10 86
Also see LITTLE STEVEN & Disciples of Soul
Also see PLASMATICS

BE-BOP DELUXE

LP '76

Singles: 7-inch

HARVEST 3-5 75-78

LPs: 10/12-inch 33rpm

HARVEST (Black vinyl)................5-10 76-78
HARVEST (Colored vinyl)..........15-20 77-78

Promotional LPs

HARVEST (8531 "Be Bop's Biggest") 25-35 75
Members: Richard Brown; Robert Bryan; Nicholas Chatterton-Dew; Andrew Clarke; Simon Fox; Paul Jeffreys; Milton R. James; Bill Nelson; Ian Parkin; Charles Tumahai.

BECK, Jeff (Jeff Beck Group; with Terry Bozzio & Tony Hymas)

P&R/LP '68

Singles: 7-inch

EPIC (10000 series)......................4-8 67-69
EPIC (50000 series)......................3-6 75-76

LPs: 10/12-inch 33rpm

ACCORD.................................... 5-10 81
EPIC (Except 43000 series)........ 8-12 68-89
EPIC (43000 series)................. 15-20 80-82
(Half-speed mastered.)
MFP.. 8-10
SPRINGBOARD......................... 5-10 75

Promotional LPs

EPIC (151 "Everything You Always Wanted to Hear") 15-25 76
EPIC (850 "Then and Now") 25-30 80

Also see BECK, BOGERT & APPICE
Also see CLAPTON, Eric, Jeff Beck & Jimmy Page
Also see DONOVAN & Jeff Beck Group
Also see HALL, Jimmy
Also see HAMMER, Jan
Also see HARRISON, George / Jeff Beck / Dave Edmunds
Also see HONEYDRIPPERS
Also see LORD SUTCH
Also see POWELL, Cozy
Also see YARDBIRDS

BECK, Jeff, & Rod Stewart

P&R '85

Singles: 7-inch

EPIC.. 3-4 85

Picture Sleeves

EPIC.. 3-4 85

BECK, Jeff, Ronnie Wood & Rod Stewart

LPs: 10/12-inch 33rpm

EPIC (33779 "Truth") 10-15 75

Also see BECK, Jeff
Also see STEWART, Rod
Also see WOOD, Ron

BECK, Jimmy

P&R '59

Singles: 7-inch

ASTRA 5-10
CHAMPION............................. 10-20 59

BECK, Joe

LP '75

Singles: 7-inch

POLYDOR................................ 3-4 77

LPs: 10/12-inch 33rpm

KUDU 8-10 75
POLYDOR................................. 5-10 77
VERVE/FORECAST 10-15 69

Also see PHILLIPS, Esther, & Joe Beck

BECK, BOGERT & APPICE

Singles: 7-inch

EPIC.. 3-5 73

LPs: 10/12-inch 33rpm

EPIC.. 10-12 73

Members: Jeff Beck; Tim Bogert; Carmine Appice.
Also see BECK, Jeff
Also see CACTUS
Also see SCOTT, Neal
Also see VANILLA FUDGE

BECK FAMILY

R&B '79

Singles: 7-inch

LE JOINT 3-5 79

Members: Tony Beck; Tyrone Beck; Mendy Beck; Joanna Beck; Donnie Wilson; Nick Mundy.

BECKHAM, Bob

P&R '59

Singles: 7-inch

DECCA 4-8 59-63
MONUMENT................................3-5 67
SMASH 3-6 65

Picture Sleeves

DECCA 5-10 59

LPs: 10/12-inch 33rpm

DECCA 15-20 59

BECKMEIER BROTHERS

P&R '79

Singles: 7-inch

CASABLANCA.............................3-4 79

LPs: 10/12-inch 33rpm

CASABLANCA...........................5-10 79

Members: Fred Beckmeier; Steve Beckmeier.

BEE, Celi: CELI BEE

BEE, Jimmy
(With Ernie Fields Jr.'s Orchestra)

R&B '76

Singles: 7-inch

ALA 3-5 73
CALLA...3-5 76
KENT 3-5 70
KIMBERLY.................................5-10
HAMILTON 5-10 59
20TH FOX....................................5-8 66-67
U.A. 3-5 71

LPs: 10/12-inch 33rpm

ALA (1975 "Live")......................10-15 73

BEE, Molly

P&R '53

Singles: 78rpm

CAPITOL......................................3-8 53-58
CORAL...3-6 55
DOT 3-6 56

Singles: 7-inch

CAPITOL....................................5-10 53-58
CORAL.......................................5-10 55
DOT 5-10 56
GRANITE......................................3-5 74-75
LIBERTY.......................................4-8 63-64
MGM 3-6 65-67

Picture Sleeves

MGM 5-10 65

EPs: 7-inch 33/45rpm

CAPITOL....................................5-10 58

LPs: 10/12-inch 33rpm

ACCORD 5-10 82
ALBUM GLOBE 5-10

CAPITOL 15-25 58
GRANITE 5-10 74
MGM 10-15 65-67

BEE GEES

P&R/LP '67

Singles: 7–inch

ATCO 4-10 67-72
ATLANTIC 3-5
RSO 3-5 73-84
W.B. 3-4 87-89

Picture Sleeves

RSO 3-5 83
W.B. 3-4 87-89

EPs: 7–inch 33/45rpm

ATCO (4523 Horizontal") 15-25 68
(Promotional issue only. Tracks are from *Horizontal,* though shown only as "Atco LP 33-233" on this label.)
ATCO (4535 Odessa") 10-20 69
(Promotional issue only.)
ATCO (37264 "Rare, Precious and Beautiful") 8-15 69
(Promotional issue only.)
RSO (200 "Greatest Hits") 5-10 79
(Promotional issue only.)

LPs: 10/12–inch 33rpm

ATCO (Except TL-ST-142) 12-25 67-72
ATCO (TL-ST-142 "Odessa").... 30-50 69
(Promotional issue only.)
RSO (Except 1) 5-10 73-84
RSO (1 "Words and Music")...... 40-60
(Promotional issue only.)
W.B. 5-10 87-89
Members: Barry Gibb; Maurice Gibb; Robin Gibb; Vince Melouney; Colin Petersen.
Also see GIBB, Andy
Also see GIBB, Barry
Also see GIBB, Maurice
Also see GIBB, Robin
Also see SANG, Samantha

BEECHER, Johnny, & His Buckingham Road Quintet

P&R '63

Singles: 7–inch

ASTRA 3-6
CHARTER 4-8 63
OMEGA 5-8 58
W.B. 3-5 63

LPs: 10/12–inch 33rpm

CHARTER 15-20 63

BEEFEATERS

Singles: 7–inch

ELEKTRA (45013 "Please Let Me Love You") 50-75 64
Members: David Crosby; Gene Clark; Jim McGuinn.
Also see BYRDS

BEEFHEART, Captain: see CAPTAIN BEEFHEART

BEGINNING of the END

P&R/R&B '71

Singles: 7–inch

ALSTON 3-5 71-72

LPs: 10/12–inch 33rpm

ALSTON 10-12 71-76

BELAFONTE, Harry

P&R '52

Singles: 78rpm

JUBILEE 6-12 54
RCA 4-8 57
ROOST (501 "Lean on Me") 10-15 49

Singles: 7–inch

COLUMBIA 3-4 81
JUBILEE 10-20 54
RCA (0300 series) 5-8 57
RCA (0400 thru 0600 series) 3-5 71-72
RCA (4000 & 5000 series) 5-10 52-55
RCA (6000 & 7000 series) 4-8 55-62
RCA (8000 & 9000 series) 3-6 62-67

Picture Sleeves

RCA (Except 9200 series) 6-12 55-59
RCA (9200 series) 3-6 69

EPs: 7–inch 33/45rpm

CAPITOL 15-20 55
JUBILEE 20-30 54
RCA (Except 24) 10-20 54-61
RCA (SPD-24 "Best of Belafonte") 30-60 56
(Ten-EP boxed set, with inserts.)

LPs: 10/12–inch 33rpm

BOOK of the MONTH RECORDS 15-20 83
CAMDEN 5-10 73-74
COLUMBIA 5-10 81
CORONET 8-15
RCA (0000 thru 0900 series) 5-10 73
RCA (1000 thru 1900 series) 15-25 54-59
(With "LOP," "LPM" or "LSP" prefix.)
RCA (2400 series) 5-10 78-81
(With "AYL1 or "CPL1" prefix.)
RCA (2000 & 3000 series, except 2449) 10-20 60-67
(With "LPM" or "LSP" prefix.)
RCA (2449 "Midnight Special") .. 20-40 62
(With Bob Dylan playing harmonica on the title track—his first appearance on record.)
RCA (3800 series) 5-10 75
RCA (4000 series) 10-15 68-71
RCA (6000 series) 15-25 59-72
Also see ANN-MARGRET
Also see COMO, Perry / Ames Brothers / Harry Belafonte / Radio City Music Hall Orch.
Also see DYLAN, Bob
Also see ROBINSON, Sugar "Chile" / Harry Belafonte

BELAFONTE, Harry, & Lena Horne

LP '59

LPs: 10/12–inch 33rpm

RCA 15-25 59
Also see HORNE, Lena

BELAFONTE, Harry, & Miriam Makeba

LP '65

LPs: 10/12-inch 33rpm

RCA.. 10-15 65

Also see MAKEBA, Miriam

BELAFONTE, Harry, & Nana Mouskouri

LP '66

LPs: 10/12-inch 33rpm

RCA.. 10-15 66

Also see BELAFONTE, Harry
Also see MOUSKOURI, Nana

BELEW, Adrian

LP '82

Singles: 7-inch

ATLANTIC.................................. 3-4 89-90

Picture Sleeves

ATLANTIC.................................. 3-4 89

LPs: 10/12-inch 33rpm

ATLANTIC.................................. 5-8 89-90
ISLAND 5-10 82-83

Also see KING CRIMSON

BELL, Archie
(With the Drells)

P&R/R&B/LP '68

Singles: 12-inch 33/45rpm

PHILADELPHIA INT'L.................. 4-6 79
PLAYHOUSE 4-6 84

Singles: 7-inch

ATLANTIC.................................. 4-8 68-72
BECKETT................................... 3-4 81-84
EAST-WEST 3-4
GLADES.................................... 3-5 73
OVIDE (228 "Tighten Up") 15-25 67
PHILADELPHIA INT'L.................. 3-6 76-79
TSOP 3-6 75-76

LPs: 10/12-inch 33rpm

ATLANTIC.................................. 10-15 68-69
BECKETT................................... 5-10 81-84
PHILADELPHIA INT'L.................. 8-10 75-79
TSOP 5-8 75

Members: Archie Bell; Huey Butler; James Wise; Joe Cross; Lee Bell; Willie Parnell.
Also see PHILADELPHIA INTERNATIONAL ALL STARS

BELL, Benny
(Featuring Paul Wynn)

P&R '75

Singles: 78rpm

COCKTAIL PARTY SONGS (202 "Shaving Cream")................................ 15-25 46

Singles: 7-inch

ENTERPRISE 4-8 62
VANGUARD............................... 3-5 75

LPs: 10/12-inch 33rpm

BELL ENTERPRISES 10-20
VANGUARD............................... 10-15 75
ZION.. 10-20

BELL, Biv DeVoe

LP '90

LP: 10/12-inch 33rpm

MCA...5-8 90

BELL, Jerry

R&B '81

Singles: 7-inch

MCA...3-4 80-81

BELL, Madeline

P&R/R&B '68

Singles: 7-inch

ASCOT.......................................5-8 64-65
BRUT 3-5 73
MOD..4-6 67
PHILIPS 4-6 67-68
PYE...3-5 76

LPs: 10/12-inch 33rpm

PHILIPS 15-20 68
PYE...8-10 76

Also see BLUE MINK
Also see MANN, Manfred
Also see SPACE
Also see WATERS, Roger

BELL, Maggie

P&R/LP '74

Singles: 7-inch

ATLANTIC..................................3-5 73-74
SWAN SONG..............................3-5 76

LPs: 10/12-inch 33rpm

ATLANTIC................................10-12 74
SWAN SONG..............................8-10 75

Also see STONE the CROWS

BELL, Maggie, & Bobby Whitlock

Singles: 7-inch

SWAN SONG..............................3-4 83-84

Also see BELL, Maggie
Also see WHITLOCK, Bobby

BELL, Randy

P&R '84

Singles: 7-inch

EPIC..3-4 84

Picture Sleeves

EPIC..3-4 84

BELL, Rueben

R&B '72

Singles: 7-inch

ALARM......................................3-5 75-77
DELUXE.....................................3-5 72-73
MURCO (1035 "It's Not That Easy") 5-10 68
MURCO (1046 "You're Gonna Miss Me") 25-50 68
SILVER FOX...............................4-6 69

BELL, Vincent
(With the Bell Men)

P&R/LP '70

Singles: 7–inch

DECCA.. 4-6 67-70
INDEPENDENT (102 "Quicksand") 20-30 60
MUSICOR.. 4-6 64
VERVE.. 4-8 63

LPs: 10/12–inch 33rpm

DECCA.. 8-15 67-70
INDEPENDENT 20-30 60
MUSICOR.............................. 10-15 64
VERVE.............................. 10-15 64

Also see FERRENTE & TEICHER
Also see RAMRODS

BELL, William

P&R '62

Singles: 7–inch

KAT FAMILY 3-4 83-84
MERCURY 3-5 76-77
STAX (Except 100 series)............ 3-6 67-74
STAX (100 series)..................... 10-15 61-67
WILBE 3-4 86

LPs: 10/12–inch 33rpm

KAT FAMILY 5-10 83-84
MERCURY 8-10 77
STAX.. 10-12 67-74

Also see CLAY, Judy, & William Bell

BELL, William, & Janice Bullock

R&B '86

Singles: 7–inch

WILBE 3-4 86

Also see BULLOCK, Janice

BELL, William, & Mavis Staples

Singles: 7–inch

STAX.. 4-6 69

Also see STAPLES, Mavis

BELL, William, & Carla Thomas

Singles: 7–inch

STAX.. 4-6 69-70

Also see BELL, William
Also see THOMAS, Carla

BELL & JAMES

R&B '78

Singles: 12–inch 33/45rpm

A&M 4-6 79
LORIMAR.. 4-6 80

Singles: 7–inch

A&M 3-4 78-84
LORIMAR.. 3-4 80

Picture Sleeves

A&M 3-5 78-81

LPs: 10/12–inch 33rpm

A&M 5-10 79-84

Members: Leroy Bell; Casey James.

BELL BIV DeVOE

P&R '90

Singles: 7–inch

MCA.. 3-4 90

LPs: 10/12–inch 33rpm

MCA.. 5-8 90

Members: Ricky Bell; Michael Bivins; Ronnie DeVoe.
Also see NEW EDITION

BELL NOTES

P&R/R&B '59

Singles: 7–inch

AUTOGRAPH 10-20 60
ERIC.. 3-5 73
MADISON.................................. 5-10 60
TIME (Blue label) 15-20 59
TIME (Red label)......................... 5-10 59-60

EPs: 7–inch 33/45rpm

TIME (100 "I've Had It") 60-100 59

Members: Carl Bonura; Ray Ceroni, Lenny Giambalvo; Pete Kane; John Casey.

BELL SISTERS
(With Phil Harris)

P&R '52

Singles: 78rpm

BERMUDA.................................. 4-8 53
RCA 4-8 50-53

Singles: 7–inch

BERMUDA.................................. 5-10 53
RCA.. 5-10 50-53

Members: Kay Bell; Cynthia Bell.
Also see HARRIS, Phil
Also see RENE, Henri, & His Orchestra

BELLAMY, David

P&R '75

Singles: 7–inch

W.B.. 3-5 75

Also see BELLAMY BROTHERS

BELLAMY BROTHERS
(With Forester Sisters)

C&W/P&R/LP '76

Singles: 7–inch

CURB.. 3-4 84-87
CURB/MCA.................................. 3-4 88-89
ELEKTRA/CURB 3-4 82
MCA.. 3-4 87
W.B./CURB.................................. 3-4 76-83

LPs: 10/12–inch 33rpm

ELEKTRA.................................. 5-10 83
MCA/CURB.................................. 5-10 84-90
W.B.. 8-10 76-83

Members: David Bellamy; Howard Bellamy.
Also see BELLAMY, David

BELLAMY BROTHERS & Forester Sisters

C&W '86

Singles: 7–inch

CURB.. 3-4 86
W.B.. 3-4 90

Also see BELLAMY BROTHERS
Also see FORESTER SISTERS

BELLE, Regina

P&R/R&B/LP '87

Singles: 7–inch

COLUMBIA 3-4 87-88
ELEKTRA.................................... 3-4 87-88

LPs: 10/12–inch 33rpm

COLUMBIA 5-10 87-88

Also see BRYSON, Peabo, & Regina Belle

BELLE EPOQUE

P&R/R&B '78

Singles: 7–inch

BIG TREE 3-4 78

BELLE STARS

P&R/D&D/LP '83

Singles: 12–inch 33/45rpm

W.B. 4-6 83-84

Singles: 7–inch

CAPITOL..................................... 3-4 89
W.B. 3-4 83-84

Picture Sleeves

W.B. 3-4 83

LPs: 10/12–inch 33rpm

W.B. 5-10 83-84

BELLS

P&R/LP '71

Singles: 7–inch

MGM 3-5 73
POLYDOR.................................... 3-5 70-73

LPs: 10/12–inch 33rpm

POLYDOR................................ 10-15 71-72

Members: Jacki Ralph; Cliff Edwards; Frank Mills.
Also see MILLS, Frank

BELLUS, Tony

P&R '59

Singles: 7–inch

ABC.. 3-4 73
COLLECTABLES.......................... 3-4 81
KING 4-8 65
NRC 8-15 59-60

Picture Sleeves

NRC (035 "Hey Little Darlin'") ... 25-40 59
NRC (051 "The Echo of an Old Song")......................... 20-30 60

LPs: 10/12–inch 33rpm

NRC (8 "Robbin' the Cradle with Tony Bellus")......................... 50-100 60
SHI-FI (11 "Gems of Tony Bellus").................................. 20-40

BELMONTS

(Belmonts with Dion)

P&R '61

Singles: 12–inch 33/45rpm

STRAWBERRY (1107 "I'll Never Fall in Love Again") 5-10 76

Singles: 7–inch

COLLECTABLES.......................... 3-4 81
CRYSTAL BALL............................ 4-6 79
DOT 10-15 68-69
LAURIE (Except 3080).................. 3-5 75-78
LAURIE (3080 "Such a Long Way") 10-15 61
MOHAWK (106 "Teenage Clementine") 25-50 57
ROULETTE.................................... 3-4
SABINA (Except 521) 10-20 61-64
SABINA (521 "Nothing in Return")................................... 20-30 64
SABRINA (500 "Tell Me Why") .. 15-25 61

SABRINA (501 "Don't Get Around Much Anymore")............................... 15-25 61
(In 1961, after #502, Sabrina changed its name to Sabina.)
STRAWBERRY.............................. 3-5 76-77
SURPRISE (1000 "Tell Me Why") 40-60 61
U.A. (809 thru 966) 10-15 65
U.A. (50007 "Come with Me") 15-20 66

LPs: 10/12–inch 33rpm

BUDDAH (5123 "Cigars, Acappella, Candy")................................... 25-50 72
CRYSTAL BALL............................ 8-12 80
DOT (25949 "Summer Love") 25-30 69
SABINA (5001 "Carnival of Hits") 75-125 62
STRAWBERRY............................ 10-15 78
UPTOWN..................................... 5-10 88

Members: Carlo Mastrangelo; Fred Milano; Angelo D'Aleo; Frank Lyndon.
Also see DION & BELMONTS
Also see SOUL, Jimmy / Belmonts

BELMONTS, Freddy Cannon & Bo Diddley

Singles: 12–inch 33/45rpm

ROCK & ROLL TRAVELLING SHOW.. 4-6

LPs: 10/12–inch 33rpm

DOWNTOWN................................ 5-10

Also see BELMONTS
Also see CANNON, Freddy
Also see DIDDLEY, Bo

BELOUIS SOME

P&R/D&D '85

Singles: 12–inch 33/45rpm

CAPITOL...................................... 4-6 85

Singles: 7–inch

CAPITOL...................................... 3-4 85

LP: 10/12–inch 33rpm

CAPITOL...................................... 5-8 85

BELOVED, The

LP '90

LPs: 10/12–inch 33rpm

ATLANTIC.................................... 5-8 90

BELOYD

R&B '77

Singles: 7-inch

20TH FOX 3-4 77

BELUSHI, John

P&R '78

Singles: 7-inch

MCA 3-4 78

Also see BLUES BROTHERS
Also see NATIONAL LAMPOON

BELVIN, Jesse
(With the Sharptones)

R&B '56

Singles: 78rpm

CASH 15-25 56
HOLLYWOOD......................... 20-40 53-56
MODERN 10-20 56-57
SPECIALTY (435 "Confusin' Blues").............................. 25-35 52
SPECIALTY (500 series) 15-25 55

Singles: 7-inch

ALADDIN (3431 "Let Me Dream")................................. 25-30 58
CASH (1056 "Beware") 60-100 56
(Reissued in 1959 as by the Capris.)
CLASS 8-12 60
COLLECTABLES 3-4 81
CUSTOM...................................... 4-8
ERIC.. 3-4 73
HOLLYWOOD (412 "Love Comes Tumbling Down"................. 150-250 53
HOLLYWOOD (1059 "Betty My Darling"........................ 100-200 56
IMPACT....................................... 4-8 62
JAMIE.. 8-15 59
KENT.. 8-15 59
KNIGHT.................................... 10-15 59
MODERN 12-25 56-57
RCA (7387 "Funny")................ 15-25 58
RCA (47-7469 "Guess Who").... 15-25 59
(Monaural.)
RCA (61-7469 "Guess Who").... 25-45 59
(Stereo.)
RCA (7543 "Here's a Heart")..... 15-25 59
RCA (7596 "Give Me Love") 15-25 59
RCA (7675 "Something Happens to Me").. 15-25 60
RCA (8040 "Guess Who")........... 5-10 62
SPECIALTY (435 "Confusin' Blues")................................ 75-100 52
SPECIALTY (550 "Gone")......... 25-35 55
TENDER (518 "Beware") 25-30 59

EPs: 7-inch 33/45rpm

RCA (2089 "Just Jesse Belvin") 25-40 59
RCA (2105 "Mr. Easy") 25-40 60

LPs: 10/12-inch 33rpm

CAMDEN................................ 15-20 66
CORONET 8-12 60s
CROWN 20-25 60-63
RCA (0900 series) 8-10 75
RCA (LPM-2089 "Just Jesse Belvin")..................................30-40 59
(Monaural.)
RCA (LSP-2089 "Just Jesse Belvin")..................................30-40 59
(Stereo.)
RCA (LPM-2105 "Mr. Easy")......30-40 60
(Monaural.)
RCA (LSP-2105 "Mr. Easy") 30-40 60
(Stereo.)
UNITED....................................10-15

Also see BENTON, Brook / Jesse Belvin
Also see CHARGERS
Also see CLIQUES
Also see JESSE & MARVIN
Also see SHIELDS

BELVIN, Jesse, & Five Keys / Feathers

Singles: 7-inch

CANDLELITE (427 "Love Song")10-15 63

Also see FIVE KEYS

BELVIN, Jesse, & Three Dots and a Dash

Singles: 78rpm

IMPERIAL (5115 "All That Wine Is Gone")..................................50-75 51
IMPERIAL (5164 "I'll Never Love Again") 50-75 51

Singles: 7-inch

IMPERIAL (5115 "All That Wine Is Gone")...............................400-500 51
IMPERIAL (5164 "I'll Never Love Again") 400-500 51

Also see BELVIN, Jesse

BENATAR, Pat

P&R/LP '79

Singles: 12-inch 33/45rpm

CHRYSALIS...............................4-8 79-86
COLUMBIA ("Le Bel Age").........10-15
(No selection number used. Promotional issue only.)

Singles: 7-inch

CHRYSALIS...............................3-5 79-89
SUNSHINE 8-12 78
TRACE (5293 "Day Gig")...........20-30 74

Picture Sleeves

CHRYSALIS...............................3-5 79-89

LPs: 10/12-inch 33rpm

CHRYSALIS...............................5-10 79-91
MFSL (057 "In the Heat of the Night")..........................20-40 81

Also see COXON'S ARMY

BENNETT, Boyd
(With the Rockets; with Southlanders)

P&R/R&B '55

Singles: 78rpm

KING 8-15 54-57

Singles: 7-inch

KING (1400 series) 20-30 54-55
(Maroon labels.)
KING (1400 series) 10-20 56
(Blue labels.)
KING (4000 series) 10-15 56-58
KING (5000 series) 5-10 58-63
MERCURY 5-10 59-61

EPs: 7-inch 33/45rpm

KING (377 "Boyd Bennett")... 100-200 56
KING (383 "Rock & Roll with Boyd Bennett & His Rockets")...... 100-200 56

LPs: 10/12-inch 33rpm

KING (594 "Boyd Bennett") 1500-2000 58

BENNETT, Joe, & Sparkletones

P&R/R&B '57

Singles: 78rpm

ABC-PAR 10-15 57-58

Singles: 7-inch

ABC 3-4 73
ABC-PAR 15-20 57-58
PARIS 10-15 59-60

LPs: 10/12-inch 33rpm

MCA 5-10 83

BENNETT, Tony

P&R '51

Singles: 78rpm

COLUMBIA 4-8 50-57

Singles: 7-inch

COLUMBIA (1600 series) 5-10
(Colored vinyl. Promotional issue only.)
COLUMBIA (06000 series) 3-4 86
COLUMBIA (38000 thru 41000 series) 5-10 50-61
COLUMBIA (42000 thru 45000 series) 3-8 61-70
IMPROV 3-4 75-77
MGM 3-5 73
VERVE 3-5 72-73

Picture Sleeves

COLUMBIA (1600 series) 5-10
(Promotional issue only.)
COLUMBIA (40000 & 41000 series) 5-10 53-61
COLUMBIA (42000 thru 44000 series) 3-6 61-67
IMPROV 3-4 75

EPs: 7-inch 33/45rpm

COLUMBIA 5-15 55-59

LPs: 10/12-inch 33rpm

COLUMBIA (Except 600 thru 1200 series) 6-12 59-86
COLUMBIA (600 thru 1200 series) 10-25 55-59
FANTASY 8-12
HARMONY 5-10 69-73
IMPROV 5-10 75-78
MGM 6-10 73
MGM/VERVE 6-10 72
MFSL 20-30 84
Also see GETZ, Stan

BENNETT, Tony, & Count Basie

EPs: 7-inch 33/45rpm

COLUMBIA 6-10 59

LPs: 10/12-inch 33rpm

COLUMBIA 10-20 59
Also see BASIE, Count

BENNETT, Tony / Al Tornello

LPs: 10/12-inch 33rpm

GUEST STAR 5-10 64
Also see BENNETT, Tony

BENNO, Marc

LP '72

Singles: 7-inch

A&M 3-5 71-79

LPs: 10/12-inch 33rpm

A&M 8-12 70-79
MCA 5-10

BENSON, George

(George "Bad" Benson)

LP '69

Singles: 78rpm

GROOVE 5-10 54

Singles: 12-inch 33/45rpm

W.B. 4-6 80-83

Singles: 7-inch

A&M 3-6 68-70
ARISTA 3-5 77
CTI 3-5 75-78
COLUMBIA 4-8 66-67
GROOVE (0024 "It Should Have Been Me #2") 20-40 54
PRESTIGE 4-8 64
W.B. 3-4 76-89

Picture Sleeves

ARISTA 3-5 77
W.B. 3-4 78-86

LPs: 10/12-inch 33rpm

A&M 8-12 68-76
CTI 8-10 71-78
COLUMBIA 8-10 66-67
(With "CL" or "CS" prefix.)
COLUMBIA 5-10 76
(With "CG" or "PC" prefix.)
MFSL (011 "Breezin") 25-50 78
POLYDOR 5-10 76
VERVE 10-12 69
W.B. 5-10 75-89
Also see FRANKLIN, Aretha, & George Benson
Also see McDUFF, Brother Jack

BENSON, George, & Earl Klugh

LP '87

LP: 10/12-inch 33rpm

W.B. 5-8 87
Also see BENSON, George
Also see KLUGH, Earl

BENT FABRIC: see FABRIC, Bent

BENTLEY, Erlene

D&D '83

Singles: 12–inch 33/45rpm

MEGATONE.................................4-6 83
TVI..4-6 84

Singles: 7–inch

MEGATONE.................................3-4 83

BENTON, Brook

(With the Dixie Flyers)

P&R '58

Singles: 78rpm

EPIC..5-10 56
OKEH...5-10 55

Singles: 7–inch

ALL PLATINUM...........................3-5 76
BRUT...3-5 73
COTILLION.................................5-10 68-72
EPIC..10-20 56
MGM..3-5 72
MERCURY (10000 series)..........5-15 59-65
(Monaural.)
MERCURY (70000 series)........10-20 60-61
(Stereo.)
MUSICOR...................................3-5 77
OKEH...10-20 55
OLDE WORLD............................3-4 77-78
RCA...4-8 65-67
REPRISE...................................4-6 67-68
STAX...3-5 74
VIK..8-15 57-58

Picture Sleeves

MERCURY..................................5-10 60-64
RCA...4-8 65

EPs: 7–inch 33/45rpm

MERCURY..................................10-20 59-61

LPs: 10/12–inch 33rpm

ALL PLATINUM...........................8-10 76
CAMDEN (Except 564)..............8-10 70
CAMDEN (564 "Brook Benton") 15-20 60
COTILLION.................................8-10 69-72
EPIC (3573 "Brook Benton at His Best")...................................15-25 59
HARMONY..................................8-12 65
MGM..8-10 73
MERCURY (20000 series)........15-30 59-65
(Monaural.)
MERCURY (60000 series)........20-35 59-65
(Stereo.)
MERCURY (822321 "Greatest Hits")..5-8 84
MUSICOR...................................8-10 77
OLDE WORLD............................5-10 77
RCA (APL1 series)....................8-10 75
(With "APL1" prefix.)
RCA (LPM/LSP series).............10-12 66
(With "LPM" or "LSP" prefix.)
REPRISE...................................8-12 67-68
WING...8-10 66

Session: King Curtis.
Also see KING CURTIS
Also see TROGGS / Brook Benton

BENTON, Brook / Jesse Belvin

LPs: 10/12–inch 33rpm

CROWN......................................12-15 63

Also see BELVIN, Jesse

BENTON, Brook, & Damita Jo

Singles: 7–inch

MERCURY..................................5-10 63

Also see DAMITA JO

BENTON, Brook / Chuck Jackson / Jimmy Soul

LPs: 10/12–inch 33rpm

ALMOR (106 "Stargazing")........10-20 60s

Also see JACKSON, Chuck
Also see SOUL, Jimmy

BENTON, Brook / Jackie Jocko

LPs: 10/12–inch 33rpm

STRAND (1121 "The Dynamic Brook Benton Sings")..............10-20 63

BENTON, Brook, & Dinah Washington

P&R '60

Singles: 7–inch

MERCURY (10032 "A Rockin' Good Way")..........................10-20 60
(Stereo.)
MERCURY (71565 "Baby")..........5-10 60
MERCURY (71629 "A Rockin' Good Way")..............................5-10 60
(Monaural.)

Picture Sleeves

MERCURY..................................5-10 60

EPs: 7–inch 33/45rpm

MERCURY..................................10-15 60

LPs: 10/12–inch 33rpm

MERCURY..................................15-25 60

Also see BENTON, Brook
Also see WASHINGTON, Dinah

BERG, Gertrude

LP '65

LPs: 10/12–inch 33rpm

AMY..8-15 65

BERGEN, Polly

LP '57

Singles: 78rpm

COLUMBIA.................................3-6 57
JUBILEE....................................4-6 56
RCA...4-8 50-51

Singles: 7–inch

COLUMBIA.................................5-10 57-61
JUBILEE....................................5-10 56
RCA...5-10 50-51

EPs: 7–inch 33/45rpm

COLUMBIA.................................5-15 57
JUBILEE....................................5-15 56

LPs: 10/12-inch 33rpm

CAMDEN.................................. 15-20 56
COLUMBIA.................................. 15-25 57-61
HARMONY.................................. 10-20 60
JUBILEE.................................. 15-25 56
PHILIPS.................................. 10-20 63

BERGEN, Polly / Fran Warren / Lynn Roberts

LPs: 10/12-inch 33rpm

RKO.................................. 10-20 59

Also see BERGEN, Polly

BERLIN

P&R/D&D/LP '83

Singles: 12-inch 33/45rpm

GEFFEN.................................. 4-6 83-84

Singles: 7-inch

COLUMBIA.................................. 3-4 86
GEFFEN.................................. 3-4 82-86
I.R.S.................................. 3-4 80

Picture Sleeves

COLUMBIA.................................. 3-4 86
GEFFEN.................................. 3-4 83-86

LPs: 10/12-inch 33rpm

ENIGMA ("Pleasure Victim")... 50-100 82
GEFFEN.................................. 5-10 82-86

Members: Terri Nunn; John Crawford; Rob Brill.

BERLIN PHILHARMONIC

P&R '70

Singles: 7-inch

POLYDOR.................................. 3-6 69

Member: Karl Boehm.

BERMAN, Shelley

LP '59

LPs: 10/12-inch 33rpm

METRO.................................. 8-12 65
VERVE (15000 series).................. 10-20 59-64

BERMUDAS

P&R '64

Singles: 7-inch

ERA.................................. 5-10 64

Member: Rickie Page.

BERNARD, Chuck
(Chuck Benard)

R&B '66

Singles: 7-inch

MAVERICK.................................. 5-8
MI BOUTE.................................. 8-10
ST. LAWRENCE.................................. 4-8 67
SATELLITE.................................. 5-8 65-66
ZODIAC.................................. 3-5 70-71

BERNARD, Rod
(With the Twisters)

P&R/R&B '59

Singles: 7-inch

ABC.................................. 3-4 74
ARBEE.................................. 4-8 65-66
ARGO.................................. 8-10 59
CARL.................................. 10-20 57
COLLECTABLES.................................. 3-4 81
COPYRIGHT.................................. 4-6 68
CRAZY CAJUN.................................. 3-4 78
HALL.................................. 5-10 61-64
HALLWAY.................................. 5-10 61-64
JIN (105 "This Should Go On Forever").................. 25-40 59
JIN (200 series).................................. 3-5 74-76
MERCURY.................................. 5-10 59-61
TEARDROP.................................. 5-10 64-65

LPs: 10/12-inch 33rpm

JIN (4007 "Rod Bernard").......... 50-75 60s

Also see SHONDELLS / Rod Bernard / Warren Storm / Skip Stewart

BERNSTEIN, Elmer, & Orchestra

P&R '56

Singles: 78rpm

DECCA.................................. 3-6 56

Singles: 7-inch

AVA.................................. 3-8 62-65
CAPITOL.................................. 4-8 59-60
CHOREO.................................. 3-5 62
COLUMBIA.................................. 3-5 65
DECCA.................................. 4-8 56
DOT.................................. 3-5 66
U.A.................................. 3-5 65-68

EPs: 7-inch 33/45rpm

CAPITOL.................................. 3-8 59

LPs: 10/12-inch 33rpm

CAPITOL.................................. 4-8 59-60
COLUMBIA.................................. 5-15 60
DOT 10-15.................................. 59
HAMILTON.................................. 4-8 59

Also see CARR, Vikki

You'll find many more listings by this artist in *The Official Price Guide to Movie/TV Soundtracks and Original Cast Albums,* containing over 8,000 listings.

BERNSTEIN, Leonard, & His Orchestra

LP '60

LPs: 10/12-inch 33rpm

CAMDEN.................................. 8-15 55-56
COLUMBIA (919 "What Is Jazz").................. 20-40 56

You'll find many more listings by this artist in *The Official Price Guide to Movie/TV Soundtracks and Original Cast Albums,* containing over 8,000 listings.

COLUMBIA (31000 series).......... 5-10 71
COLUMBIA MASTERWORKS... 10-20

BERNSTEIN, Leonard, & Dave Brubeck

LPs: 10/12-inch 33rpm

COLUMBIA.................................. 12-25 60

Also see BERNSTEIN, Leonard, & His Orchestra
Also see BRUBECK, Dave

BERRY, Chuck

P&R/R&B '55

Singles: 78rpm

CHESS (1600 series)............... 30-60 55-58
CHESS (1700 thru 1729)......... 50-100 58-59
CHESS (1737 "My Childhood Sweetheart") 75-125 59
CHESS (1747 "Too Pooped to Pop") 100-200 60

Singles: 7-inch

ATCO 3-4 79
CHESS (1604 thru 1615)......... 15-25 55-56
CHESS (1626 thru 1645)......... 10-20 56
CHESS (1653 thru 1729)......... 10-15 57-59
CHESS (1737 thru 1963)......... 5-10 59-69
CHESS (2000 & 9000 series)....... 3-5 70-73
ERIC... 3-4 73
MERCURY 4-8 66-72
PHILO 8-15 66
("Hip Pocket" Record.)

Picture Sleeves

CHESS (1898 "No Particular Place to Go")................................. 10-20 64
CHESS (1906 "You Never Can Tell")....................................... 10-20 64
CHESS (1912 "Little Marie")..... 10-20 64
CHESS (1916 "Promised Land")10-20 64

EPs: 7-inch 33/45rpm

CHESS (5118 "After School Session")............................... 40-60 57
CHESS (5118 "Head over Heels") 75-100 57
CHESS (5119 "Rock & Roll Music")........................... 40-60 58
CHESS (5121 "Sweet Little 16") 40-60 58
CHESS (5124 "Pickin' Berries") 40-60 58
CHESS (5126 "Sweet Little Rock & Roller")...................... 40-60 58

LPs: 10/12-inch 33rpm

ACCORD....................................... 5-10 82
ATCO 5-10 79
BROOKVILLE 12-15 73
CHESS (Except 1400 & 9000 series) 10-20 66-76
CHESS (1426 "After School Session")................................ 50-75 57
CHESS (1432 "One Dozen Berrys")..................................... 50-75 58
CHESS (1435 "Chuck Berry's on Top") 50-75 59
CHESS (1448 "Rockin' at the Hops") 50-75 59
CHESS (1456 "Chuck Berry's New Jukebox Hits")........................ 25-40 61
CHESS (1465 "More Chuck Berry").................................... 30-40 62
CHESS (1465 "Chuck Berry Twist")....................................20-25 62
(Reissue with title change.)
CHESS (1480 "Chuck Berry on Stage")....................................20-25 63
CHESS (1485 "Chuck Berry's Greatest Hits") 25-30 64
CHESS (1488 "St. Louis to Liverpool")..................................20-25 64
CHESS (1495 "Chuck Berry in London") 25-30 65
CHESS (1498 "Fresh Berrys")...20-25 65
CHESS (9000 series)..................5-10 85
CHESS/MCA...................................5-8 89
EVEREST 8-10 76
GUSTO 5-10 78
MCA..8-12 86-87
MAGNUM.....................................10-12 69
MERCURY...................................15-25 67-72
PICKWICK.....................................8-10 72
TRIP 8-10 78
UPFRONT.......................................5-10 79

Also see ALEXANDER, Joe, & Cubans
Also see DIDDLEY, Bo, & Chuck Berry
Also see MILLER, Steve

BERRY, Chuck, & Howlin' Wolf

LPs: 10/12-inch 33rpm

CHESS...15-20 69

Also see BERRY, Chuck
Also see HOWLIN' WOLF

BERRY, Jan

(Jan; Jan Barry)

Singles: 7-inch

A&M 5-10 77-78
LIBERTY (55845 "The Universal Coward")...................................10-15 66
ODE '70 (Except 66023 & 66034)..15-20 72-77
ODE '70 (66023 "Mother Earth")25-40 72
(With insert note from Jan. Promotional issue only.)
ODE '70 (66023 "Mother Earth")20-30 72
(Without insert note from Jan.)
ODE '70 (66034 "Don't You Just Know It") 30-40 73
(With Brian Wilson.)
RIPPLE (6101 "Tomorrow's Teardrops")..............................30-45 61

Picture Sleeves

LIBERTY (55845 "The Universal Coward")............................100-125 66

Also see JAN & ARNIE
Also see JAN & DEAN
Also see WILSON, Brian

BERTEI, Adele

D&D '83

Singles: 12-inch 33/45rpm

GEFFEN 4-6 83

Singles: 7–inch

GEFFEN 3-4 83

BEST, Peter

Singles: 7–inch

CAMEO (391 "Boys") 20-35 66
(Shown as by "Peter Best, formerly of the Beatles.")
CAPITOL (2092 "Carousel of Love") 20-35 67
HAPPENING (117 "If You Can't Get Her") 40-50 66
HAPPENING (405 "Don't Play with Me Little Girl") 40-50 66
MR. MAESTRO (711 "I Can't Do Without You Now") 40-50 65
(Shown as by "Best of the Beatles, Peter Best.")
MR. MAESTRO (712 "Casting My Spell") 40-50 65
(Shown as by "Best of the Beatles, Peter Best.")
ORIGINAL BEATLES DRUMMER (800 "I'll Try Anyway") 40-50 64

Picture Sleeves

CAMEO (391 "Boys") 50-75 66

LPs: 10/12–inch 33rpm

BEST FAN CLUB 25-30 66
PHOENIX 10 .... 10-15 82
SAVAGE (71 "Best of the Beatles") 100-125 65

Also see BEATLES

BETHEA, Harmon

(Bethea; with Maskman & the Agents)

R&B '73

Singles: 7–inch

DYNAMO 4-6 69-71
MUSICOR 3-5 70-74

Also see MASKMAN & AGENTS

BETTERS, Harold

P&R/R&B '64

Singles: 7–inch

GATEWAY 4-6 63-65
REPRISE 4-6 66-67

LPs: 10/12–inch 33rpm

GATEWAY 12-15 64-66
REPRISE 12-15 65-67

BETTS, Dickey: see BETTS, Richard

BETTS, Richard

(Dickey Betts & Great Southern; Dickey Betts Band)

LP '74

Singles: 7–inch

ARISTA 3-5 77-78
CAPRICORN 3-5 74-76

LPs: 10/12–inch 33rpm

ARISTA 5-10 77-78
CAPRICORN 8-10 74
EPIC 5-8 88

Also see ALLMAN BROTHERS BAND

BEVEL, Charles

(Charles "Mississippi" Bevel)

R&B '74

Singles: 7–inch

A&M 3-5 73-74

LPs: 10/12–inch 33rpm

A&M 8-10 73-74

BEVERLY & DUANE

R&B '78

Singles: 7–inch

ARIOLA AMERICA 3-5 78-79

Members: Beverly Wheeler; Duane Williams.

BEVERLY SISTERS

(Beverley Sisters)

P&R '56

Singles: 78rpm

LONDON 4-6 56

Singles: 7–inch

LONDON 5-10 56
MERCURY 5-10 60

LPs: 10/12–inch 33rpm

CAPITOL 10-20 61

BICKERSONS: see AMECHE, Don, & Frances Langford

BIDDU

(Biddu Orchestra)

P&R/R&B '75

Singles: 7–inch

COLOSSUS 3-5 70
EPIC 3-5 75-77

LPs: 10/12–inch 33rpm

EPIC 5-10 76-77

BIG AUDIO DYNAMITE

LP '85

Singles: 12–inch 33/45rpm

COLUMBIA (1739 "James Brown") 6-10 89
(Promotional issue only.)
COLUMBIA (1899 "Contact") 5-8 89
(Promotional issue only.)
COLUMBIA (2302 "Medicine Show") 5-8 86
(Promotional issue only.)
COLUMBIA (2520 "C'mon Every Beatbox") 5-8 86
(Promotional issue only.)
COLUMBIA (2697 "Hollywood Boulevard") 5-8 86
(Promotional issue only.)
COLUMBIA (8133 "Other 99") 5-8 88
(Promotional issue only.)
COLUMBIA (5000 thru 8000 series) 4-6 85-90

Singles: 7–inch

COLUMBIA (5000 series except 5841) 3-5 85

COLUMBIA (5841 "Medicine Show") 4-6 85
(White label. Promotional issue only.)
COLUMBIA (6000 series, except 6053) 3-5 86
COLUMBIA (6053 "E = MC^2 ") 4-6 85
(White label. Promotional issue only.)
COLUMBIA (6364 "C'mon Every Beatbox") 4-6 86
(White label. Promotional issue only.)
COLUMBIA (6708 "Badrock City") 4-6 86
(White label. Promotional issue only.)
COLUMBIA (8000 series) 3-5 88

Picture Sleeves

COLUMBIA (5841 "Medicine Show") 5-8 85
(Promotional issue only.)
COLUMBIA (6053 "E = MC^2 ") 5-8 85
(Promotional issue only.)
COLUMBIA (07955 "Just Play Music") 4-6
COLUMBIA (8094 "Other 99") 4-6 88

LPs: 10/12-inch 33rpm

COLUMBIA 5-10 85-89
Members: Mick Jones; Don Letts; Leo Williams; Greg Roberts; Dan Donovan; Flea.
Also see BIG AUDIO DYNAMITE II
Also see CLASH

BIG AUDIO DYNAMITE II

Singles: 12-inch 33/45rpm

COLUMBIA (4044 "Rush Dance"). 5-8 91
COLUMBIA (657640 "Rush") 5-10 91
(Promotional issue only.)

LPs: 10/12-inch 33rpm

COLUMBIA 8-10 91
Members: Mick Jones; Gary Stonadge; Chris Kavanagh; Nick Hawkins.
Also see BIG AUDIO DYNAMITE

BIG BOPPER

(Jape Richardson; Jiles Perry Richardson Jr.)

P&R/R&B '58

Singles: 7-inch

D (1008 "Chantilly Lace") 100-150 58
MERCURY (30000 series) 5-10 60
MERCURY (70000 series) 8-15 58-59

LPs: 10/12-inch 33rpm

MERCURY (20402 "Chantilly Lace") 250-300 59
(Black label.)
MERCURY (20402 "Chantilly Lace") 250-300 59
(Pink label. Promotional issue only.)
MERCURY (20402 "Chantilly Lace") 75-100 64
(Red label.)
MERCURY (20402 "Chantilly Lace") 10-15 81
(Chicago "skyline" label.)
PICKWICK 20-30 73
RHINO 5-8 89
Also see DEL-VIKINGS / Diamonds / Big Bopper / Gaylords
Also see RICHARDSON, Jape

BIG BROTHER & Holding Co.

(Big Brother)

LP '67

Singles: 7-inch

COLUMBIA 5-10 68-71
MAINSTREAM 5-10 67-68

Picture Sleeves

COLUMBIA (44626 "Piece of My Heart") 10-20 68

LPs: 10/12-inch 33rpm

COLUMBIA 15-25 68-71
MADE to LAST 5-10 84
MAINSTREAM (6099 "Big Brother and the Holding Company") 20-35 67
Members: Janis Joplin; David Getz; Sam Andrew; Peter Albin, Jim Gurley; David Schallock; Nick Gravenites; Kathi McDonald.
Also see JOPLIN, Janis
Also see McDONALD, Kathi

BIG COUNTRY

P&R/D&D/LP '83

Singles: 12-inch 33/45rpm

MERCURY 4-6 83-86

Singles: 7-inch

MERCURY 3-4 83-86
REPRISE 3-4 88

Picture Sleeves

MERCURY 3-4 83-84

LPs: 10/12-inch 33rpm

MERCURY 5-10 83-86
REPRISE 5-8 88
Members: Stuart Adamson; Bruce Watson; Mark Brzezicki; Tony Butler.

BIG MAYBELLE

(Mable Smith)

R&B '53

Singles: 78rpm

KING 8-12 48-49
OKEH 5-15 53-56
SAVOY 5-10 56-58

Singles: 7-inch

BRUNSWICK 4-8 63
CHESS 4-8 66
OKEH 15-30 53-56
PARAMOUNT 3-5 73
PORT 4-8 65
ROJAC 4-8 64-69
SAVOY 5-15 56-61
SCEPTER 4-8 64

EPs: 7-inch 33/45rpm

EPIC (7071 "Big Maybelle Sings the Blues") 25-50 57

LPs: 10/12-inch 33rpm

BRUNSWICK 15-25 62-68
ENCORE 10-15 67
EPIC 8-10 83

BIG PIG

PARAMOUNT ... 8-10 73
ROJAC ... 10-12 67-69
SAVOY (14005 "Big Maybelle Sings") ... 40-50 57
SAVOY (14011 "Blues, Candy and Big Maybelle") ... 40-50 57
SCEPTER ... 15-20 64
UPFRONT ... 8-10 73

BIG PIG

P&R/LP '88

Singles: 7-inch

A&M ... 3-4 88

Picture Sleeves

A&M ... 3-4 88

BIG RIC

P&R '83

Singles: 7-inch

ROCK & ROLL ... 3-4 83
SCOTTI BROTHERS ... 3-4 83

LPs: 10/12-inch 33rpm

SCOTTI BROTHERS ... 5-10 83-84

Member: Joel Porter.

BIG SAMBO
(With the House Wreckers)

P&R '62

Singles: 7-inch

ERIC ... 4-8 62

BIG THREE

Singles: 7-inch

FM ... 5-10 63
ROULETTE ... 4-8 66
TOLLIE ... 4-8 64

LPs: 10/12-inch 33rpm

ACCORD ... 5-10 82
FM ... 15-25 63-64
ROULETTE ... 15-20 68

Members: Cass Elliott; Tim Rose; Denny Dougherty.
Also see ELLIOTT, Cass
Also see MAMAS & PAPAS

BIG THREE TRIO

R&B '48

Singles: 78rpm

BULLET ... 15-25 47
COLUMBIA ... 15-25 47-51
DELTA ... 15-25 49
DOT ... 10-15 52
OKEH ... 10-15 51-53

Singles: 7-inch

COLUMBIA (30239 "Blip Blip") .. 50-75 51
OKEH ... 25-50 51-53

Members: Willie Dixon; Leonard "Baby Doo" Caston; Bernard Dennis.
Also see DIXON, Willie
Also see HOWARD, Rosetta

BILK, Mr. Acker
(With His Paramount Jazz Band; with Leon Young String Chorale)

P&R/R&B/LP '62

Singles: 7-inch

ATCO ... 4-6 61-66
REPRISE ... 3-5 62

LPs: 10/12-inch 33rpm

ASCOT ... 8-15 62
ATCO ... 10-20 62-66

BILK, Mr. Acker, & Bent Fabric

LPs: 10/12-inch 33rpm

ATCO ... 8-12 65

Also see BILK, Mr. Acker
Also see FABRIC, Bent

BILL BLACK'S COMBO: see BLACK, Bill

BILLION DOLLAR BABIES

LP '77

Singles: 7-inch

POLYDOR (Except 14406) ... 4-6 77
POLYDOR (14406 "Too Young") . 8-12 77
(Promotional issue only.)

LPs: 10/12-inch 33rpm

POLYDOR (Except 022) ... 12-15 77
POLYDOR (022 "Battle Axe") ... 20-25 77
(Promotional issue only.)

Also see COOPER, Alice

BILLY ALWAYS: see ALWAYS, Billy

BILLY & Baby Gap

R&B '85

Singles: 7-inch

TOTAL EXPERIENCE ... 3-4 85

Members: Billy Young; Anthony Walker
Also see GAP BAND

BILLY & BEATERS

LP '81

Singles: 7-inch

ALFA ... 3-4 81

Picture Sleeves

ALFA ... 3-4 81

LPs: 10/12-inch 33rpm

ALFA ... 5-10 81

Member: Billy Vera.
Also see VERA, Bill

BILLY & LILLIE
(Billy Ford & the Thunderbirds; vocal by Freddie Pinkard)

P&R/R&B '58

Singles: 78rpm

SWAN ... 5-10 57

Singles: 7-inch

ABC ... 3-5 73
ABC-PAR (10421 "Love Me Sincerely") ... 15-25 63
CAMEO ... 4-8 66
COLLECTABLES ... 3-4 81
SWAN ... 6-12 57-61

Members: Billy Ford; Lillie Bryant.

BILLY & SUE

Singles: 7–inch

CREW 3-5 70

Members: William Oliver Swofford; Lesley Gore.
Also see GORE, Lesley
Also see OLIVER

BILLY JOE & CHECKMATES
(Billy Joe Hunter)

P&R '62

Singles: 7–inch

DORE 4-8 61-66

BILLY SATELLITE

P&R/LP '84

Singles: 7–inch

CAPITOL 3-4 84

Picture Sleeves

CAPITOL 3-4 84

LPs: 10/12–inch 33rpm

CAPITOL 5-10 84

Member: Monty Bryom.

BIMBO JET

P&R '75

Singles: 7–inch

SCEPTER 3-5 75

BIONIC BOOGIE

R&B/LP '78

Singles: 12–inch 33/45rpm

RP 4-8

Singles: 7–inch

POLYDOR 3-4 77-78

LPs: 10/12–inch 33rpm

POLYDOR 5-10 78

Member: Gregg Diamond.

BIRD, J.

D&D '84

Singles: 12–inch 33/45rpm

WARRIOR 4-6 84

BIRDLEGS & PAULINE and Their Versatility Birds

P&R/R&B '63

Singles: 7–inch

CUCA (1125 "Spring") 20-35 63
(Credits "Birdlegs & His Versatility Birds.")
VEE JAY (510 "Spring") 5-10 63

LPs: 10/12–inch 33rpm

CUCA (4000 "Birdlegs & Pauline") 50-100 63

Members: Sidney Banks; Pauline Banks.
Also see LITTLE BEAVER

BIRDSONG, Edwin

R&B '81

Singles: 12–inch 33/45rpm

PHILADELPHIA INT'L 4-6 78-79
SALSOUL 4-6 81-84

Singles: 7–inch

BAMBOO 3-6
PHILADELPHIA INT'L 3-4 78
POLYDOR 3-5 71-72
SALSOUL 3-4 81-84

LPs: 10/12–inch 33rpm

PHILADELPHIA INT'L 5-10 78
POLYDOR 8-10 71-73

BIRKIN, Jane, & Serge Gainsbourg

P&R '69

Singles: 7–inch

FONTANA 3-6 69

LPs: 10/12–inch 33rpm

FONTANA 6-12 70

BISHOP, Elvin
(Elvin Bishop Group; with Crabshaw Rising)

P&R/LP '74

Singles: 7–inch

CAPRICORN 3-5 74-79
EPIC 3-5 72-75
FILLMORE 3-5 70-71
W.B. 3-5 72

LPs: 10/12–inch 33rpm

ALLIGATOR 5-8 91
CAPRICORN 8-12 74-78
EPIC 8-12 72-75
FILLMORE 10-15 69-72

Also see BUTTERFIELD, Paul
Also see GRATEFUL DEAD / Elvin Bishop Group

BISHOP, Stephen

P&R '76

Singles: 7–inch

ABC 3-5 76-78
W.B. 3-4 80-83

Picture Sleeves

ABC (12435 "Animal House") 4-8 78

LPs: 10/12–inch 33rpm

ABC 6-12 76-78
MCA 5-10 80
W.B. 5-10 80

Also see GRUSIN, Dave
Also see NEWMAN, Randy

BISHOP, Stephen, & Yvonne Elliman

Singles: 7–inch

W.B. 3-4 80

Also see BISHOP, Stephen
Also see ELLIMAN, Yvonne

BITS & PIECES

R&B '81

Singles: 7–inch

MANGO 3-4 81
NASCO 3-5 73-74
PARAMOUNT 3-5 74

BIZ MARKIE
(Marcel Hall)

R&B '86

Singles: 7–inch

COLD CHILL 3-4 88-90
PRISM 3-4 86

Picture Sleeves

COLD CHILL 3-4 90

LPs: 10/12-inch 33rpm

COLD CHILL 5-8 88-90

BJORN & BENNY

Singles: 7-inch

PLAYBOY 8-10 72-74
(With Anna and Freida.)

Members: Bjorn Ulvaeus; Benny Anderson.
Also see ABBA

BLACK, Bill
(Bill Black's Combo)

P&R/R&B '59

Singles: 7-inch

COLUMBIA 3-5 70
ECHO 3-5 72
GUSTO 3-4 83
HI (Except 2000 series) 3-6 67-78
HI (2000 series) 5-10 59-66
LONDON 3-4 84
MEGA 3-5 71-74
MOTOWN 3-4 83

Picture Sleeves

HI 5-10 60-62

EPs: 7-inch 33/45rpm

MEGA (192 "Jukebox Favorites") 5-10 72
(Jukebox issue.)

LPs: 10/12-inch 33rpm

COLUMBIA 8-10 69-70
51 WEST 5-10 84
HI (6000 & 8000 series) 5-10 77-78
HI (12001 thru 12005) 15-30 60-62
HI (12006 thru 12041) 10-20 62-68
HI (32000 thru 32010) 15-30 61-63
HI (32011 thru 32110) 10-20 63-77
MEGA 5-10 71-74
ZODIAC 5-10 77

Also see CANNON, Ace
Also see PRESLEY, Elvis

BLACK, Cilla

P&R '64

Singles: 7-inch

BELL 3-4 68
CAPITOL 5-10 64-66
DJM 3-6 68-70
EMI AMERICA 3-5 74
PRIVATE STOCK 3-5 75-76

LPs: 10/12-inch 33rpm

CAPITOL (T-2308 "Is It Love").. 20-30 65
(Monaural.)
CAPITOL (ST-2308 "Is It Love") 25-35 65
(Stereo.)

BLACK, Clint

C&W/LP '89

Singles: 7-inch

RCA 3-4 89-92

LPs: 10/12-inch 33rpm

RCA 5-8 89-90

Also see ROGERS, Roy, & Clint Black

BLACK, Jay

P&R '80

Singles: 12-inch 33/45rpm

MILLENIUM (20614 "Love Is in the Air") 15-20 78
(Single-sided disc. Promotional issue only.)
MILLENIUM (20614 "Love Is in the Air"/"Please Stay") 8-12 78

Singles: 7-inch

ATLANTIC/MIGRATION 3-5 75
K-TEL (562 "This Magic Moment") 30-40 82
(Canadian. Credited to "Jay Black of Jay and the Americans.")
MIDSONG 3-4 80
MILLENNIUM 3-5 78
PRIVATE STOCK 3-5 76
ROULETTE (7198 "One Night Affair") 10-15 76
(Same track on both sides. Promotional issue only.)
U.A. 4-8 67

Picture Sleeves

U.A. 5-10 67

Also see JAY & AMERICANS

BLACK, Jay / Caress

Singles: 12-inch 33/45rpm

ROULETTE (2005 "One Night Affair") 10-15 76
(For the promotional issue, with Jay Black on both sides, see his section above.)

Also see BLACK, Jay

BLACK, Jeanne

C&W/P&R/R&B '60

Singles: 7-inch

CAPITOL 3-6 60-62

LPs: 10/12-inch 33rpm

CAPITOL 15-20 60

BLACK, Marion

R&B '71

Singles: 7-inch

AVCO EMBASSY 3-5 71
SHAKAT 3-5 74

BLACK, Oscar

P&R '61

Singles: 78rpm

ATLANTIC 15-20 51
GROOVE 5-10 54-55

Singles: 7-inch

ATLANTIC (956 "Troubled Mind Blues") 50-100 51
GROOVE 25-50 54-55
SAVOY 5-10 61

BLACK, Oscar, & Sue Allen

Singles: 78rpm

GROOVE 5-10 54-55

Singles: 7-inch

GROOVE 25-50 54-55

Also see BLACK, Oscar

BLACK, Shelly

R&B '76

Singles: 7-inch

VIGOR 3-5 76-77

BLACK, Stanley, & His Orchestra

LP '62

LPs: 10/12-inch 33rpm

LONDON PHASE 4 .... 5-15 62-65

BLACK, Terry

P&R '64

Singles: 7-inch

DUNHILL 4-8 65-66

TOLLIE 5-10 64-65

Picture Sleeves

TOLLIE 5-10 65

BLACK, Terry, & Laurel Ward

P&R '72

Singles: 7-inch

KAMA SUTRA 3-5 72

Also see BLACK, Terry

BLACK BLOOD

R&B '75

Singles: 7-inch

CHRYSALIS 3-5 77

MAINSTREAM 3-5 75

LPs: 10/12-inch 33rpm

CHRYSALIS 5-10 77

MAINSTREAM 8-10 75

BLACK BOX

P&R/LP '90

Singles: 7-inch

RCA 3-4 90

LPs: 10/12-inch 33rpm

RCA 5-8 90

Member: Martha Wash.

Also see WEATHER GIRLS

BLACK FLAMES

R&B '87

Singles: 7-inch

DEF JAM 3-4 87

BLACK HEAT

R&B '73

Singles: 7-inch

ATLANTIC 3-5 72-74

LPs: 10/12-inch 33rpm

ATLANTIC 8-10 72-75

BLACK ICE

R&B '77

Singles: 7-inch

AMHERST 3-5 76

HDM 3-5 77

MONTAGE 3-4 81-84

LPs: 10/12-inch 33rpm

AMHERST 8-10 76

MONTAGE 5-10 82

BLACK IVORY

R&B '71

Singles: 7-inch

BUDDAH 3-5 75-84

KWANZA 3-5 74

PANORAMIC 3-4 85

PERCEPTION 3-5 72

TODAY 3-5 71-73

LPs: 10/12-inch 33rpm

BUDDAH 5-10 75-84

TODAY 10-12 72-73

Member: Leroy Burgess.

Also see ALEEM

BLACK MAMBA

D&D '84

Singles: 12-inch 33/45rpm

GARAGE 4-6 84

BLACK 'N BLUE

LP '84

Singles: 7-inch

GEFFEN 3-4 84-88

LPs: 10/12-inch 33rpm

GEFFEN 5-10 84-88

BLACK OAK ARKANSAS
(Black Oak)

LP '71

Singles: 7-inch

ATCO 3-5 71-75

CAPRICORN 3-5 77-78

ENTERPRISE 3-5 70

MCA 3-5 75-77

LPs: 10/12-inch 33rpm

ATCO 8-15 71-84

CAPRICORN 8-10 77-78

MCA 8-12 75-77

STAX 10-15 74

Members: Jim Mangrum; Ruby Starr; Rickie Reynolds; Stanley Knight; Harvey Jett; Jimmy Henderson; Pat Daugherty; Tom Aldridge.

BLACK OAK ARKANSAS / Cooper Brothers

LPs: 10/12-inch 33rpm

CAPRICORN (0005 "I'd Rather Be Sailing") 10-15 78

(Promotional issue only.)

Also see BLACK OAK ARKANSAS

Also see COOPER BROTHERS

BLACK PEARL

LP '69

Singles: 7-inch

ATLANTIC 3-6 69

PROPHESY 3-6 70

LPs: 10/12-inch 33rpm

ATLANTIC 12-15 69

PROPHESY 15-20 70

BLACK SABBATH

P&R/LP '70

Singles: 7-inch

I.R.S. 3-4 89
W.B. 3-5 70-76

LPs: 10/12-inch 33rpm

I.R.S. 5-8 89
W.B. (Except 1000 & 2000 series) 5-10 76-84
W.B. (1000 & 2000 series) 8-15 70-76
W.B. 5-10 87

Members: Ozzy Osbourne; Tony Iommi; Kip Treavor; Bill Ward; Ronnie Dio; Terry "Geezer" Butler.
Also see DIO, Ronnie
Also see OSBOURNE, Ozzy

BLACK SATIN
(Featuring Fred Parris)

R&B '75

Singles: 7-inch

BUDDAH 3-5 75

LPs: 10/12-inch 33rpm

BUDDAH (5654 "Black Satin") 8-10 76
BUDDAH (5654 "Black Satin") .. 25-35 76
(Promotional issue.)

Members: Fred Parris; Rich Freeman; Jimmy Curtis; Nate Marshall.
Also see FIVE SATINS

BLACK UHURU

LP '82

Singles: 7-inch

ISLAND 3-4 84

LPs: 10/12-inch 33rpm

ISLAND 5-10 84
MANGO 5-10 80-85
MESA 5-8 90

BLACKBYRDS

P&R/R&B/LP '74

Singles: 7-inch

FANTASY 3-5 74-84

LPs: 10/12-inch 33rpm

FPM 10-12 75
FANTASY 10-15 74-84

Members: Gary Hart; Joe Hall III; Stephe Johnson; Keith Killgo; Orville Saunders; Kevin Toney.
Also see BYRD, Donald

BLACKFOOT

P&R/LP '79

Singles: 7-inch

ATCO 3-4 79-84

LPs: 10/12-inch 33rpm

ANTILLES 5-10 78
ATCO 5-10 79-84
EPIC 8-10 76
ISLAND 10-12 75

Members: Rick Medlocke; Jackson Spires; Charlie Hargrett; Greg Walker.
Also see LYNYRD SKYNYRD

BLACKFOOT, J.D.
(With Ann Hines; J. Blackfoot)

R&B '83

Singles: 7-inch

EDGE 3-4 86-87
FANTASY 4-8 74
PHILIPS 8-12 69-70
SOUND TOWN 3-5 83-86

LPs: 10/12-inch 33rpm

FANTASY (9468 "Song of Crazy Horse") 15-25 74
FANTASY (9487 "Southbound & Gone") 15-25 75
MERCURY (61288 "The Ultimate Prophecy") 40-60 70
SOUND TOWN 5-10 84-85

Also see SOUL CHILDREN

BLACKJACK

P&R/LP '79

Singles: 7-inch

POLYDOR 3-5 79-84
20TH FOX 4-8 76

LPs: 10/12-inch 33rpm

POLYDOR 5-10 79-80

Members: Michael Bolotin; Tony Battaglia; Bruce Kulick; Chuck Kirkpatrick; Jan Mullaney.
Also see BOLTON, Michael

BLACKMORE, Ritchie
(Ritchie Blackmore's Rainbow)

Singles: 7-inch

POLYDOR 3-5 75

LPs: 10/12-inch 33rpm

POLYDOR (6049 "Ritchie Blackmore's Rainbow") 8-10 75

Also see BLACKMORE'S RAINBOW
Also see LORD SUTCH

BLACKMORE'S RAINBOW

LP '75

Singles: 7-inch

OYSTER 3-5 76
POLYDOR 3-5 75-79

LPs: 10/12-inch 33rpm

OYSTER 8-12 75-76

Members: Ritchie Blackmore; Roger Glover; Ronnie Dio.
Also see BLACKMORE, Ritchie
Also see DEEP PURPLE
Also see DIO, Ronnie
Also see RAINBOW

BLACKSMOKE

R&B '76

Singles: 7-inch

CHOCOLATE CITY 3-5 76

BLACKWELL

P&R '69

Singles: 7-inch

ASTRO 3-6 69-70
BUTTERFLY 3-4 78

LPs: 10/12-inch 33rpm

ASTRO 8-10 69
BUTTERFLY 5-10 78

BLACKWELL, Charlie

P&R '59

Singles: 7-inch

W.B. 4-8 59

BLADES, Ruben

LP '88

Singles: 7-inch

ATLANTIC 3-5
ELEKTRA 3-4 88

BLADES of GRASS

P&R '67

Singles: 7-inch

FINE (57027 "It Isn't Easy") 20-30 67
JUBILEE 4-8 67-68

LPs: 10/12-inch 33rpm

JUBILEE 12-20 67

Members: Bruce Ames; Marc Black; Frank DiChiara; Dave Gordon.

BLAKE & HINES

R&B '87

Singles: 7-inch

MOTOWN 3-4 87

Members: Cory Blake; Andra Hines.

BLANC, Mel
(With the Sportsmen & Billy May)

P&R '48

Singles: 78rpm

CAPITOL (5221 "Seasons Greetings from Capitol") 10-20 49
(Promotional issue only. Also contains greetings from other Capitol artists.)
CAPITOL 10-20 48-54

Singles: 7-inch

CAPITOL (Except PRO-15) 15-30 50-54
CAPITOL (PRO-15 "I Taut I Taw a Record Dealer") 30-50 51
(Mel Blanc provides the voice of assorted cartoon characters, though he is not credited on label. Promotional issue only.)
W.B. 5-10 60

EPs: 7-inch 33/45rpm

CAPITOL (436 "Party Panic") 35-50 53

LPs: 10/12-inch 33rpm

CAPITOL (436 "Party Panic") 50-75 53
(10-inch LP.)
CAPITOL (3200 series) 15-30 61-63
GOLDEN 10-20 61

Also see HUNT, Pee Wee

BLANCHARD, Jack, & Misty Morgan

C&W '69

Singles: 7-inch

EPIC 3-4 73-75
MEGA 3-5 71-73
WAYSIDE 3-5 69-70

LPs: 10/12-inch 33rpm

MEGA 8-12 72
WAYSIDE 10-15 70

BLANCMANGE

D&D '83

Singles: 12-inch 33/45rpm

ISLAND 4-6 83-84
SIRE 4-6 84-85

Singles: 7-inch

ISLAND 3-4 83-84
SIRE 3-4 84-85

LPs: 10/12-inch 33rpm

ISLAND 5-10 82-84
SIRE 5-10 84-85

BLAND, Billy

P&R/R&B '60

Singles: 78rpm

OLD TOWN 5-10 55-57

Singles: 7-inch

ATLANTIC 3-4 84
COLLECTABLES 3-4 81
TIP TOP 10-15 58
OLD TOWN (1016 thru 1035) 10-20 55-57
OLD TOWN (1076 thru 1143) 6-12 60-63
ST. LAWRENCE 4-8

BLAND, Bobby
(Bobby "Blue" Bland)

R&B '57

Singles: 78rpm

CHESS 10-20 54
MODERN 15-25 52

Singles: 7-inch

ABC 3-4 73-78
DUKE (105 "I.O.U. Blues") 75-100 54
DUKE (115 "No Blow, No Show") 50-100 54
DUKE (141 "It's My Life, Baby") 30-60 56
DUKE (146 thru 196) 15-30 57-58
DUKE (300 series) 5-10 60-66
DUKE (400 series) 4-8 66-72
DUNHILL 3-4 74
FAIRWAY 8-10 79
KENT 5-10
MCA 3-4 79-84
MALACO 3-4
ST. LAWRENCE 4-8

LPs: 10/12-inch 33rpm

ABC 5-10 75-78
ABC/DUKE 5-10 73
BLUESWAY 5-10 73
DUKE (74 "Two Steps from the Blues") 50-75 61
DUKE (75 "Here's the Man") 45-55 62
DUKE (77 "Call On Me") 35-50 63
DUKE (78 "Ain't Nothing You Can Do") 35-50 64
DUKE (79 "Soul of the Man") 25-45 66

DUKE (84 "Best of Bobby Bland") 25-40 67
DUKE (86 "Best of Bobby Bland, Vol. 2") 25-40 68
DUKE (88 "Touch of the Blues") 25-40 68
DUKE (89 "Spotlighting the Man").................................. 20-40 69
DUKE (90 "If Loving You Is Wrong") 15-25 70
DUKE (92 "Introspective")......... 20-25 74
DUNHILL.................................. 8-15 73-74
MCA 5-10 79-84

Also see ACE, Johnny

BLAND, Bobby, & B.B. King

R&B '76

Singles: 7-inch

ABC.................................. 3-4 78
IMPULSE 3-5 76

LPs: 10/12-inch 33rpm

DUNHILL.................................. 10-12 74
IMPULSE 8-10 76
MCA 5-10 82

Also see KING, B.B.

BLAND, Bobby / Little Junior Parker

LPs: 10/12-inch 33rpm

DUKE (DLP-72 "Barefoot Rock") 100-150 58
DUKE (X-72 "Barefoot Rock")... 10-12 74

Also see PARKER, Little Junior

BLAND, Bobby, & Ike Turner

Singles: 7-inch

KENT.................................. 5-10 62

Also see TURNER, Ike

BLAND, Bobby / Johnny Guitar Watson

LPs: 10/12-inch 33rpm

CROWN (5358 "2 in Blues") 20-30 63

Also see BLAND, Bobby
Also see WATSON, Johnny

BLANE, Marcie

P&R/R&B '62

Singles: 7-inch

LONDON.................................. 3-4 84
SEVILLE.................................. 5-10 62-65

BLAST, C.L.

R&B '80

Singles: 7-inch

ATLANTIC.................................. 3-6 69
COTILLION 3-4 80
PARK PLACE.................................. 3-4 85
STAX.................................. 4-8 67
UNITED.................................. 3-5 70-71

LPs: 10/12-inch 33rpm

COTILLION 5-10 80

BLASTERS

LP '82

Singles: 7-inch

MCA.................................. 3-4 84
SLASH 3-5 81-85

Picture Sleeves

SLASH 3-4 81-85

LPs: 10/12-inch 33rpm

ROLLIN' ROCK (021 "American Music").................................. 50-75 80
SLASH 8-12 81-85

Members: David Alvin; Phil Alvin; John Bazz; Gene Taylor; Bill Bateman; Steve Berlin; Lee Allen.
Also see ALLEN, Lee
Also see ALVIN, Dave
Also see HARTMAN, Dan / Blasters
Also see X

BLAZE

P&R '76

Singles: 7-inch

EPIC.................................. 3-5 76-77
FRATERNITY 3-5 76

BLEND

P&R '78

Singles: 7-inch

MCA.................................. 3-4 78-79

LPs: 10/12-inch 33rpm

MCA.................................. 5-10 78-79

Member: Jim Drown.

BLENDELLS

P&R '64

Singles: 7-inch

COLLECTABLES.................................. 3-4 81
COTILLION.................................. 4-8 68
ERA.................................. 3-5 73
RAMPART 8-10 64
REPRISE 4-8 64-65

Also see SONNY & CHER / Bill Medley / Lettermen / Blendells

BLENDERS

P&R '63

Singles: 7-inch

CORTLAND 5-10 62
MAR-V-LUS ("Your Love Has Got Me Down") 100-200 66
(No selection number used.)
VISION (1000 "I Asked for Your Hand") 40-50 62
WITCH 10-15 63

BLEYER, Archie
(With Maria Alba)

P&R '54

Singles: 78rpm

ARC 8-15 35
CADENCE 5-10 54-57
VOCALION 8-15 34

Singles: 7-inch

CADENCE 8-15 54-57

LPs: 10/12-inch 33rpm

CADENCE (3044 "Moonlight Serenade") 15-25 62
(Monaural.)

CADENCE (25044 "Moonlight Serenade") 20-30 62
(Stereo.)

Also see CHORDETTES
Also see GODFREY, Arthur, with Archie Bleyer
Also see HAYES, Bill

BLIND FAITH

LP '69

Singles: 7-inch

RSO 3-6 77

LPs: 10/12-inch 33rpm

ATCO (304A "Blind Faith") 20-30 69
(Front cover pictures a nude girl.)

ATCO (304B "Blind Faith") 10-12 69
(Front cover pictures the group.)

MFSL (186 "Blind Faith") 25-35 69
(Half-speed mastered.)

RSO 5-10 76
(Reissue. Pictures nude girl.)

Members: Eric Clapton; Ginger Baker; Steve Winwood; Rick Grech.
Also see BAKER, Ginger
Also see CLAPTON, Eric
Also see FAMILY
Also see WINWOOD, Steve

BLOCH, Ray, & Orchestra

P&R '46

Singles: 78rpm

CORAL 4-8 52-57
SIGNATURE 4-8 47

Singles: 7-inch

CORAL 5-12 53

Picture Sleeves

CORAL (9-1327 "From Here to Eternity") 300-500 53
(Pictures Frank Sinatra, Burt Lancaster, Montgomery Clift, Donna Reed, and Deborah Kerr.)

LPs: 10/12-inch 33rpm

AMBASSADOR 8-12
CORAL 10-25 52-57

Also see SINATRA, Frank

BLODWYN PIG

LP '69

Singles: 7-inch

A&M 3-6 69-70

LPs: 10/12-inch 33rpm

A&M (3000 series) 5-10 82
A&M (4000 series) 10-15 69-70

Members: Blodwyn; Mick Abrahams; Peter Banks; Ron Berg; Clive Bunker; Jack Lancaster; Andy Pyle.
Also see ABRAHAMS, Mick, Band
Also see BANKS, Peter

BLONDIE

LP '78

Singles: 12-inch 33/45rpm

CHRYSALIS 5-10 78-84

Singles: 7-inch

CHRYSALIS 3-5 77-84
PRIVATE STOCK 6-10 76-77

Picture Sleeves

CHRYSALIS 3-8 79-82

LPs: 10/12-inch 33rpm

CHRYSALIS (Except 5001) 5-10 76-84
CHRYSALIS (5001 "Parallel Lines") 15-25 78
(Picture disc.)
MFSL (050 "Parallel Lines") 20-40 81
PRIVATE STOCK 15-20 75

Members: Deborah Harry; Clem Burke; Jimmy Destri; Chris Stein; Gary Valontine; Fred Smith; Nigel Harrison.
Also see HARRY, Debbie

BLOOD, SWEAT & TEARS

LP '68

Singles: 7-inch

ABC 3-4 78
COLUMBIA 3-5 69-77

Picture Sleeves

COLUMBIA 3-5 70-72

LPs: 10/12-inch 33rpm

ABC 5-10 77
COLUMBIA (Except 9619 & 49619) 10-15 69-76
COLUMBIA (9619 "Child Is Father to the Man") 20-30 68
COLUMBIA (49619 "Child Is Father to the Man") 25-35 68
(Half-speed mastered.)
LAX (1865 "Nuclear Blues") 5-10 80
(Black vinyl.)
LAX (1865 "Nuclear Blues") 10-12 80
(Colored vinyl. Promotional issue only.)

Members: David Clayton-Thomas; Al Kooper; Jerry Hyman; Fred Lipsius; Dick Halligan; Bobby Colomby; Lew Soloff; Chuck Winfield; Steve Katz; James Thomas Fielder; Dave Bargeron; Georg Wadenius; Lou Matini Jr.; Bobby Doyle.
Also see CLAYTON-THOMAS, David
Also see FRANKLIN, Aretha / Union Gap / Blood, Sweat & Tears / Moby Grape
Also see KOOPER, Al
Also see STREISAND, Barbra

BLOODROCK

P&R '71

Singles: 7-inch

CAPITOL 3-6 69-75

Promotional Singles

CAPITOL (3451 "Bloodrock Interview By Sol Smaizys") 4-8 72

LPs: 10/12-inch 33rpm

CAPITOL 15-35 69-75

Members: Jim Rutledge; Eddie Grundy; Steve Hill; Lee Pickens; Nick Taylor; Warren Ham.

BLOODSTONE

P&R/R&B/LP '73

Singles: 12-inch 33/45rpm

MOTOWN 4-6 79
T-NECK 4-6 82-85

Singles: 7-inch

EPIC 3-4 82
LONDON 3-5 73-76
MOTOWN 3-4 79
T-NECK 3-4 82-85

Picture Sleeves

LONDON 3-5 74-76

LPs: 10/12-inch 33rpm

LONDON 8-10 73-74
MOTOWN 5-10 78
T-NECK 5-10 82

Members: Harry Williams; Charles McCormick; Charles Love; Steve Ferrone; Roger Lee Durham; Willis Draffen.

BLOOM, Bobby

P&R/LP '70

Singles: 7-inch

EARTH 4-8 69
KAMA SUTRA 5-10 67
L&R 4-8 70
MGM 5-10 70-73
ROULETTE 3-5 70
WHITE WHALE 4-8 69

LPs: 10/12-inch 33rpm

BUDDAH 8-12 71
L&R 10-15 70

Also see ARCHIES
Also see MUSIC EXPLOSION

BLOOMFIELD, Mike

LP '69

LPs: 10/12-inch 33rpm

CLOUDS 5-10 78
COLUMBIA (9000 series) 12-15 69
COLUMBIA (37000 series) 6-10 81-83
GUITAR PLAYER 8-10 77
HARMONY 8-10 71
TAKOMA 5-10 77-81
W.B. (7674 "Steelyard Blues") 4-8 73
WATERHOUSE 5-10 81

Also see DYLAN, Bob
Also see KGB

BLOOMFIELD, Mike, Dr. John & John Paul Hammond

LP '73

LPs: 10/12-inch 33rpm

COLUMBIA 8-10 73

Also see DR. JOHN
Also see HAMMOND, John

BLOOMFIELD, Mike, & Nick Graventes

LPs: 10/12-inch 33rpm

COLUMBIA 10-12 69

Also see ELECTRIC FLAG

BLOOMFIELD, Mike, & Al Kooper

LP '69

LPs: 10/12-inch 33rpm

COLUMBIA 12-20 68
MFSL (178 "Super Session") 15-25 85

Also see KOOPER, Al
Also see MOBY GRAPE

BLOOMFIELD, Mike, Al Kooper & Steve Stills

LP '68

Singles: 7-inch

COLUMBIA 3-6 68

LPs: 10/12-inch 33rpm

COLUMBIA 10-15 68
MFSL 15-20 85

Also see BLOOMFIELD, Mike
Also see STILLS, Stephen

BLOSSOMS

P&R '61

Singles: 7-inch

BELL 4-8 69-70
CAPITOL 8-12 57-58
CHALLENGE 10-15 61-62
CLASSIC ARTISTS 3-5 89
EEOC (8172 "Things Are Changing") 75-100 65
(Equal Employment Opportunity Center promotional issue.)
EPIC 3-5 77
LION 3-5 72
MGM 8-12 68
ODE 5-10 67-69
OKEH 5-10 62-63
REPRISE 4-8 65-67

Picture Sleeves

EEOC (8172 "Things Are Changing") 75-100 65
(Promotional issue only.)

LPs: 10/12-inch 33rpm

LION 8-12 72

Members: Darlene "Love" Wright; Gloria Jones; Fanita James-Barrett; Annette Williams; Nanette Williams-Jackson; Grazia Nitzsche; Jean King.

Also see BOB B. SOXX & Blue Jeans
Also see EDDY, Duane
Also see FABARES, Shelley
Also see LOVE, Darlene
Also see PRESLEY, Elvis
Also see WILSON, Brian

BLOW, Kurtis

P&R/R&B/LP '80

Singles: 12-inch 33/45rpm

MERCURY 4-6 80-86

Singles: 7-inch

MERCURY 3-4 80-86
POLYDOR 3-4 85

LPs: 10/12-inch 33rpm

MERCURY 5-10 80-86

Also see KING DREAM CHORUS & Holiday Crew
Also see KRUSH GROVE ALL STARS

BLOW MONKEYS

P&R/LP '86

Singles: 12-inch 33/45rpm

RCA.. 4-6 85-87

Singles: 7-inch

RCA.. 3-4 85-87

LPs: 10/12-inch 33rpm

RCA.. 5-10 85-87

Members: Robert Howard; Tony Kiley; Neville Henry; Mick Anker.

BLOWFLY

LP '80

Singles: 7-inch

WEIRD WORLD.......................... 3-4 80

LPs: 10/12-inch 33rpm

WEIRD WORLD.......................... 8-10 80

BLU, Peggi

R&B '87

Singles: 7-inch

CAPITOL.................................. 3-4 87

BLU, Peggi, & Bert Robinson

R&B '87

Singles: 7-inch

CAPITOL.................................. 3-4 87

Also see BLU, Peggi
Also see ROBINSON, Bert

BLUE

P&R '77

Singles: 7-inch

IRIS.. 3-4

MCA/PIG (Colored vinyl).............. 4-6 77
(Promotional issue only.)

RSO.. 3-5 73-75

ROCKET.................................. 3-5 77

LPs: 10/12-inch 33rpm

RSO.. 8-10 73

ROCKET.................................. 5-10 77

Members: Tim Donald; Ian MacMillan; Jimmy McCullough; Hugh Nicholson.
Also see MARMALADE

BLUE, David
(David Cohen)

P&R '73

Singles: 7-inch

ASYLUM.................................. 3-5 73

REPRISE.................................. 3-6 69

LPs: 10/12-inch 33rpm

ASYLUM.................................. 8-10 73-76

ELEKTRA.................................. 12-15 66

REPRISE.................................. 12-15 68

Also see COUNTRY JOE & FISH

BLUE BARRON & His Orchestra

P&R '38

Singles: 78rpm

BLUEBIRD.................................. 4-6 38-41

MGM.. 3-6 47-55

Singles: 7-inch

MGM.. 4-6 50-55

EPs: 7-inch 33/45rpm

MGM.. 4-8 54-55

LPs: 10/12-inch 33rpm

MGM.. 10-20 54

BLUE BELLES
(Starlets)

R&B '62

Singles: 7-inch

NEWTOWN.................................. 8-10 62

PEAK.. 5-10 62

Picture Sleeves

PEAK.. 15-25 62

Also see LABELLE, Patti

BLUE CHEER

P&R/LP '68

Singles: 7-inch

MERCURY.................................. 3-5 76

PHILIPS.................................. 8-12 68-70

Picture Sleeves

PHILIPS (40516 "Summertime Blues")................................ 10-15 68

LPs: 10/12-inch 33rpm

MEGAFORCE.............................. 5-10 85

PHILIPS (9001 "Vincebus Eruption")................................ 5-10 80

PHILIPS (600264 "Vincebus Eruption")................................ 30-50 68

PHILIPS (600278 "Outside Inside")................................ 40-60 68

PHILIPS (600305 "New! Improved!")................................ 30-50 69

PHILIPS (600333 "Blue Cheer") 30-50 70

PHILIPS (600347 "Original Human Being")................................ 30-50 70

PHILIPS (600350 "Oh Pleasant Hope")................................ 40-60 71

Members: Leigh Stephens; Paul Whaley; Dick Peterson; Randy Holden; Tony Rainer; Bruce Stephens; Ralph Kellogg; Gary Yoder.

BLUE DIAMONDS

P&R '60

Singles: 7-inch

LONDON.................................. 4-8 62-63

Members: Riem de Wolf; Rudy de Wolf.

BLUE HAZE

P&R '72

Singles: 7-inch

A&M.. 3-5 72-74

BLUE JAYS
(Leon Peels & Bluejays)

P&R '61

Singles: 7-inch

CLASSIC ARTISTS...................... 3-5 89

COLLECTABLES.......................... 3-4 81

ERA.. 3-4 72

MILESTONE (2008 "Lover's Island")................................ 15-30 61
(Blue label. Opinions differ as to which came

first—the dark blue, or light blue and white label.)
MILESTONE (2008 "Lover's Island") 10-15 61
(Green label.)
MILESTONE (2009 "Tears Are Falling") 25-35 61
MILESTONE (2010 "Let's Make Love") 15-25 61
MILESTONE (2012 "The Right to Love") 15-25 62
MILESTONE (2014 "Venus My Love") 50-75 62
Member: Leon Peels.

BLUE JAYS / Little Caesar & Romans

LPs: 10/12-inch 33rpm

MILESTONE (1001 "Blue Jays Meet Little Caesar & Romans") 50-100 62
(Black vinyl.)
MILESTONE (1001 "Blue Jays Meet Little Caesar & Romans") 150-200 62
(Colored vinyl.)
Also see BLUE JAYS
Also see LITTLE CAESAR & ROMANS

BLUE MAGIC

R&B '73

Singles: 12-inch 33/45rpm

MIRAGE 4-6 83

Singles: 7-inch

ATCO 3-5 73-76
CAPITOL 3-4 81
LIBERTY 3-6 69
MIRAGE 3-4 83
WMOT 3-5

LPs: 10/12-inch 33rpm

ATCO 8-10 74-77
ATLANTIC 5-10 83
CAPITOL 5-10 81
COLLECTABLES 6-8 86
MIRAGE 5-10 83
Members: Ted Mills; Margie Joseph; Vernon Sawyer; Wendell Sawyer; Richard Pratt; Keath Beaton.
Also see JOSEPH, Margie

BLUE MERCEDES

P&R/LP '88

Singles: 7-inch

MCA 3-4 88

Picture Sleeves

MCA 3-4 88

LPs: 10/12-inch 33rpm

MCA 5-8 88
Members: David Titlow; Duncan Millar.

BLUE MINK

P&R '70

Singles: 7-inch

BELL 3-5 71-72
MCA 3-5 73-74
PHILIPS 3-6 69-70

Picture Sleeves

PHILIPS 4-8 70

LPs: 10/12-inch 33rpm

MCA 8-10 73
PHILIPS 12-15 69-70
Members: Madeline Bell; Roger Cook; Barry Morgan; Herbie Flowers; Alan Parker; Ann Odell; Roger Coulan; Ray Cooper.
Also see BELL, Madeline

BLUE MURDER

LP '89

Singles: 7-inch

GEFFEN 3-4 89

LPs: 10/12-inch 33rpm

GEFFEN 5-8 89
Member: Tony Franklin.
Also see FIRM

BLUE NILE

LP '90

LPs: 10/12-inch 33rpm

A&M 5-8 90

BLUE NOTES

P&R '60

Singles: 78rpm

JOSIE 20-30 56-57

Singles: 7-inch

COLLECTABLES 3-4 81
JALYNNE 15-25 60
JOSIE (800 "If You Love Me") .75-100 56
JOSIE (814 "Letters") 50-75 57
JOSIE (823 "Retribution Blues") 40-60 57
RED TOP 5-8 63
3 SONS 10-20 62
UNI 4-8 69
VAL-UE 15-20 60

LPs: 10/12-inch 33rpm

COLLECTABLES 5-10 82
Members: Harold Melvin; Jesse Gillis Jr.; Roosevelt Brodie; Frank Peaker; Bernard Williams; John Atkins; Lawrence Brown.
Also see BLUENOTES
Also see MELVIN, Harold, & Blue Notes

BLUE OYSTER CULT

LP '72

Singles: 12-inch 33/45rpm

COLUMBIA 4-6 80

Singles: 7-inch

COLUMBIA 3-4 72-84
WHAT'S IT ALL ABOUT 8-12
(Promotional issue only.)

Picture Sleeves

COLUMBIA (02000 & 04000 series) 3-4 81-84
COLUMBIA (45000 series) 4-8 72

EPs: 7-inch 33/45rpm

COLUMBIA (40 "Bootleg EP") ... 20-25 72

LPs: 10/12-inch 33rpm

ABC RADIO ("A Night on the Road") 35-50 81
(Promotional issue only.)
COLUMBIA (Except 31000 thru 33000 series) 5-10 76-84
COLUMBIA (31000 thru 33000 series) 6-12 72-75

Members: Al Bouchard; Joe Bouchard; Eric Bloom; Alan Lanier; Donald "Buck Dharma" Roeser.

BLUE PRINT

D&D '83

Singles: 12-inch 33/45rpm

FANTASY 4-6 83

BLUE RIDGE RANGERS
(John Fogerty)

C&W/P&R '73

Singles: 7-inch

FANTASY 3-5 72-73

LPs: 10/12-inch 33rpm

FANTASY 10-12 73

Also see FOGERTY, John

BLUE STARS

P&R '55

Singles: 78rpm

MERCURY 3-6 55-56

Singles: 7-inch

MERCURY 5-10 55-56

Member: Blossom Dearie.

BLUE SWEDE

P&R/LP '74

Singles: 7-inch

EMI AMERICA 3-5 73-75

Picture Sleeves

EMI AMERICA 3-5 73-74

LPs: 10/12-inch 33rpm

EMI AMERICA 8-10 74-75

Members: Bjorn Skifs; Jan Guldback; Bosse Liljedahl; Michael Areklew; Ladislau Balaz; Tommy Berglund; Hinke Ekestubble.

BLUE ZONE U.K.

P&R '88

Singles: 7-inch

ARISTA 3-4 88

Picture Sleeves

ARISTA 3-4 88

Members: Lisa Stansfield; Andy Morris; Ian Devaney.

BLUENOTES

P&R '59

Singles: 7-inch

BROOKE 8-12 59-60

Picture Sleeves

BROOKE 15-25 60

Also see BLUE NOTES
Also see HAMILTON, George, IV

BLUENOTES / Five Echoes / Five Chances

LPs: 10/12-inch 33rpm

CONSTELLATION (5 "Collectors Showcase, Groups Three") 20-25 64

Also see BLUENOTES

BLUES BROTHERS

P&R/LP '78

Singles: 7-inch

ATLANTIC 3-5 78-81
(Black vinyl.)
ATLANTIC 5-10
(Colored vinyl. Promotional issue only.)

Picture Sleeves

ATLANTIC 3-6 78-80

LPs: 10/12-inch 33rpm

ATLANTIC 10-15 78-81

Members: Dan Aykroyd; John Belushi.
Also see BELUSHI, John

BLUES IMAGE

LP '69

Singles: 7-inch

ATCO 4-8 69-71

LPs: 10/12-inch 33rpm

ATCO 10-20 69-70

Members: Mike Pinera; Joe Lala; Frank Konte; Malcolm Jones; Manuel Bertematti.
Also see PINERA, Mike

BLUES MAGOOS

P&R/LP '66

Singles: 7-inch

ABC 4-8 68-70
GANIM (1000 "Who Do You Love") 20-40 69
MERCURY (30000 series) 3-5 76
MERCURY (70000 series) 8-12 66-68
VERVE/FOLKWAYS (5006 "So I'm Wrong") 20-30 66
VERVE/FOLKWAYS (5044 "So I'm Wrong") 15-25 67

Picture Sleeves

MERCURY (72660 "Pipe Dream") 10-20 67
MERCURY (72692 "One By One") 10-20 67

LPs: 10/12-inch 33rpm

ABC 8-10 69-70
MERCURY (21096 "Psychedelic Lollipop") 40-50 66
(Monaural.)
MERCURY (21104 "Electric Comic Book") 30-40 67
(Monaural. Add $5 to $10 if accompanied by comic book insert.)
MERCURY (61096 "Psychedelic Lollipop") 25-40 66
(Red label. Stereo.)

MERCURY (61096 "Psychedelic Lollipop") 8-10
(Chicago "skyline" label.)
MERCURY (61104 "Electric Comic Book") 30-45 67
(Stereo. Add $5 to $10 if accompanied by comic book insert.)
MERCURY (61167 "Basic Blues Magoos") 20-30 68
Members: Geoff Daking; Mike Esposito; Ron Gilbert; Ralph Scala; Emil Thielhelm.
Also see BALANCE

BLUES PROJECT

LP '66

Singles: 7-inch

CAPITOL 5-8 72
MCA 3-5 73
VERVE/FOLKWAYS 10-15 66-67

LPs: 10/12-inch 33rpm

CAPITOL 10-15 72
ELEKTRA 5-10 80
MCA 8-10 73
MGM 8-12 70-74
VERVE/FOLKWAYS 15-25 66
VERVE/FORECAST 12-20 66-70
Members: Al Kooper; Roy Blumenfeld; David Cohen; Tommy Flanders; Richard Green; John Gregory; Don Gretmar; Danny Kalb; Steve Katz; Andy Kulbert; Bill Lussenden; Chicken Hirsch.
Also see KOOPER, Al
Also see SEATRAIN

BLUES TRAVELER

LP '91

LPs: 10/12-inch 33rpm

A&M 5-8 91

BLUES WOMAN
(Marion Abernathy)

R&B '46

Singles: 78rpm

JUKE BOX 8-12 46

BO, Eddie

P&R/R&B '69

Singles: 78rpm

ACE 5-10 56-57
APOLLO 10-20 55-56

Singles: 7-inch

ACE 10-15 56-59
APOLLO (Except 509) 15-25 55-56
APOLLO (509 "Dearest One") .. 30-50 57
AT LAST 4-8 63
BLUE JAY 4-8 64
BO-SOUND 3-5 71
CAPITOL 5-10 61
CHECKER 10-15 58
CHESS (Except 1600 series) 4-8 62
CHESS (1600 series) 10-15 58
CINDERELLA 4-8 63
RIC 5-10 59-62
SEVEN B 4-8 66-68
SCRAM 4-6 69
SWAN 5-10 62
Also see BO, Little
Also see PARKER, Robert

BO, Eddie, & Inez Cheatham

Singles: 7-inch

SEVEN B 4-8 68
Also see BO, Eddie

BO, Little
(Eddie Bo)

Singles: 78rpm

ACE (501 "Baby") 15-25 55

Singles: 7-inch

ACE (501 "Baby") 50-75 55
Also see BO, Eddie

BO DIDDLEY: see DIDDLEY, Bo

BO PETE
(Harry Nilsson)

Singles: 7-inch

CRUSADER (103 "Baa Baa Black Sheep") 20-30 64
TRY (501 "Groovy Little Suzy")..20-40 64
Also see NILSSON

BOB & EARL

P&R '62

Singles: 7-inch

ABC 3-4 73
CHENE 4-8 64
COLLECTABLES 3-4 81
CRESTVIEW 3-6 69
ISLAND 3-5
LOMA 4-8 64
MARC 6-12 63-64
MIRWOOD 5-8 66
TEMPE (104 "Oh Baby Doll") 10-20 62
TIP (1013 "As We Dance") 8-12 64
UNI 4-6 70
WHITE WHALE 10-15 69

LPs: 10/12-inch 33rpm

CRESTVIEW 15-20 69
TIP (9011 "Harlem Shuffle") 20-30 64
UPFRONT 10-15
Members: Earl Nelson; Bobby Relf.
Also see WHITE, Barry

BOB B. SOXX & Blue Jeans

P&R/R&B '62

Singles: 7-inch

PHILLES (107 "Zip-a-Dee Doo-Dah") 10-15 62
PHILLES (110 "Why Do Lovers Break Each Other's Heart") 10-15 63
PHILLES (113 "Not Too Young to Get Married") 10-15 63

LPs: 10/12-inch 33rpm

PHILLES (4002 "Zip-a-Dee Doo-Dah") 75-125 63
Members: Bobby Sheen; Darlene Love; Carolyn Willis; Fanita James-Barrett.
Also see BLOSSOMS

Also see HONEY CONE
Also see LOVE, Darlene
Also see RONETTES / Crystals / Darlene Love / Bob B. Soxx & Blue Jeans
Also see SHEEN, Bobby

BOBBETTES

P&R/R&B '57

Singles: 78rpm

ATLANTIC 8-10 57

Singles: 7-inch

ATLANTIC 10-20 57-60
DIAMOND 5-8 62-65
END 5-10 61
GALLIANT 10-15 60
GONE 10-15 61
JUBILEE 5-8 62
KING 5-10 61-62
MAYHEW 3-5 72-74
RCA 10-20 66
TRIPLE-X 10-20 60

Members: Emma Pought; Jannie Pought; Heather Dixon; Laura Webb; Helen Gathers.
Session: King Curtis.
Also see KING, Ben E.
Also see KING CURTIS

BOBBY & MIDNITES

LP '81

Singles: 7-inch

ARISTA 3-4 81
COLUMBIA 3-4 84

LPs: 10/12-inch 33rpm

ARISTA 5-10 81
COLUMBIA 5-10 84

Members: Bob Weir; David Garland.
Also see WEIR, Bob

BOBBY LEE: see LEE, Bobby

BOBO, Willie
(With the Bo-Gents)

LP '66

Singles: 7-inch

BLUE NOTE 3-5 77
CAPITOL 3-5 76
JUPITER JAZZ 3-5 75
TICO 8-12 59
VERVE 4-8 65-69

LPs: 10/12-inch 33rpm

BLUE NOTE 5-10 77
COLUMBIA 8-10 78-79
MGM 5-10
ROULETTE 15-25 63-64
SUSSEX 8-10
TICO 10-20
TRIP 5-10
VERVE 10-20 65-69

Also see DIXIE HUMMINGBIRDS
Also see HANCOCK, Herbie, & Willie Bobo

BOCEPHUS
(Hank Williams Jr.)

Singles: 7-inch

VERVE (10540 "Meter Reader Maid") 20-30 67

Also see WILLIAMS, Hank, Jr.

BoDEANS

LP '86

Singles: 7-inch

SLASH 3-4 86-89

LPs: 10/12-inch 33rpm

SLASH 5-10 86-89
SLASH/REPRISE 5-8 91

Members: Sammy Llanas; Kurt Neumann; Guy Hoffman; Bob Griffin.

BOFILL, Angela

R&B/LP '79

Singles: 12-inch 33/45rpm

ARISTA 4-6 81-85

Singles: 7-inch

ARISTA 3-4 81-85
GRP 3-5 79

LPs: 10/12-inch 33rpm

ARISTA 5-10 81-85
GRP 8-10 78-79

BOHANNON
(Hamilton Bohannon)

R&B '74

Singles: 12-inch 33/45rpm

COMPLEAT 4-6 84-85
MERCURY 5-8 77-80
MCA 4-6 84
PHASE II 4-6 80-83

Singles: 7-inch

DAKAR 3-5 73-75
MERCURY 3-4 77-80
PHASE 2 .... 3-4 80-83

LPs: 10/12-inch 33rpm

DAKAR 10-12 73-75
MERCURY 8-10 77-80
PHASE 2 .... 5-10 80-83

BOHANNON, Hamilton, & Dr. Perri Johnson *R&B '81*

Singles: 12-inch 33/45rpm

PHASE 2 .... 4-6 81

Singles: 7-inch

PHASE 2 .... 3-4 81

Also see BOHANNON

BOHN, Rudi, & His Band

LP '61

LPs: 10/12-inch 33rpm

LONDON PHASE 4 .... 5-12 61

BOILING POINT

R&B '78

Singles: 7-inch

BULLET 3-5 78

BOLIN, Tommy

LP '75

Singles: 7-inch

NEMPEROR 3-5 76

LPs: 10/12-inch 33rpm

COLUMBIA 8-10 76
NEMPEROR (400 series) 10-12 75
NEMPEROR (37000 series) 5-10 81

Also see JAMES GANG
Also see ZEPHYR

BOLTON, Michael

(Michael Boloton)

P&R/LP '83

Singles: 12-inch 33/45rpm

COLUMBIA 4-8 85
(Promotional issue only.)

Singles: 7-inch

COLUMBIA 3-4 83-91
RCA.. 3-5 75-76

Picture Sleeves

COLUMBIA 3-4 88

LPs: 10/12-inch 33rpm

COLUMBIA 5-10 83-91
RCA.. 8-10 75-76

Also see BLACKJACK

BOMBERS

R&B '79

Singles: 7-inch

WEST END 3-5 79

LPs: 10/12-inch 33rpm

WEST END 8-12 79

BON JOVI, Jon

(Bon Jovi)

P&R/LP '84

Singles: 7-inch

MERCURY 3-4 84-90

Picture Sleeves

MERCURY 3-4 84-89

LPs: 10/12-inch 33rpm

MERCURY 5-10 84-90

Members: Jon Bon Jovi; Richie Sambora; David Bryan; Alec John Such; Tico Torres.

BON ROCK

D&D '84

Singles: 12-inch 33/45rpm

EARTHTONE 4-6 84

LPs: 10/12-inch 33rpm

EARTHTONE 5-10 84

Member: Keith Rogers.

BOND, Angelo

R&B/LP '75

Singles: 7-inch

ABC 3-5 75-76

LPs: 10/12-inch 33rpm

ABC 8-10 75-77

BOND, Bobby

C&W '72

Singles: 7-inch

DANCELAND..............................5-10 61
HICKORY....................................3-5 72
MGM 3-5 68
PARROT 4-8 66
WAND 4-8 65
W.B. 3-5 69

BOND, Johnny

(With the Red River Valley Boys)

C&W '47

Singles: 78rpm

COLUMBIA (Except 21521).........5-15 45-56
(Columbia 20545 through 20787 were also issued on 7-inch 33 singles, any of which may be in the $15 to $25 range.)
COLUMBIA (21521 "The Little Rock Roll") 8-12 56

Singles: 7-inch

COLUMBIA (Except 21521).......10-20 51-56
COLUMBIA (21521 "The Little Rock Roll") 30-45 56
CONQUEROR 10-25
DITTO 5-10 59
GILLETTE 3-4
KING 3-4
LAMB & LION 3-5 74
LONDON.......................................3-5
MGM 3-5 73
OKEH...8-15 41-45
REPUBLIC (2000 series)............5-10 60
SMASH 4-6 62
STARDAY (618 thru 951) 4-8 63-72
STARDAY (7021 thru 9292) 3-4 72-74
20TH FOX.....................................4-8 60

EPs: 7-inch 33/45rpm

COLUMBIA 10-20 58
REPUBLIC 10-20 60
STARDAY 10-15 63

LPs: 10/12-inch 33rpm

CMH..5-10 77
CAPITOL......................................8-12 69
CATTLE 5-10
DANNY 5-10
HARMONY...................................10-20 64-65
LAMB & LION 5-10 74
NASHVILLE 5-10 71
SHASTA.......................................10-15
STARDAY (147 thru 298) 20-30 61-64
STARDAY (333 "Ten Little Bottles") 15-20 65-66
STARDAY (354 "Famous Hot Rodders I Have Known") 25-30 65
STARDAY (368 thru 472) 10-20 66-71
STARDAY (900 series)...............6-10 74

Also see HANK & FRANK

BOND, Johnny, & Lefty Frizzell

Singles: 78rpm

COLUMBIA 5-10 56-57

Singles: 7-inch

COLUMBIA 10-15 56-57

Also see BOND, Johnny
Also see FRIZZELL, Lefty

BONDS, Gary "U.S."
(U.S. Bonds)

P&R/R&B '60

Singles: 12-inch 33/45rpm

EMI (9666 "Gary U.S. Bonds").. 25-30 81
(Promotional issue only.)

Singles: 7-inch

ABC 3-4 73
ATCO 3-6 69
BLUFF CITY.............................. 3-5 74
BOTANIC 4-6 68
COLLECTABLES 3-4 81
EMI AMERICA 3-4 81-82
LEGRAND (1003 thru 1012)..... 10-15 60-61
(Purple label.)
LEGRAND (1003 thru 1012)...... 5-10 62-63
(Multi-color label.)
LEGRAND (1015 thru 1020)...... 8-12 62
LEGRAND (1022 thru 1041)..... 10-20 62-66
LEGRAND (1043 thru 1046)..... 10-15 66-67
MCA 3-4 84
PRODIGAL................................ 3-5 75
SUE.. 3-6 70

Picture Sleeves

EMI AMERICA 4-8 81-82
LEGRAND (1008 "Quarter to Three").......................... 10-15 61
LEGRAND (1009 "School Is Out")................................ 10-15 61

LPs: 10/12-inch 33rpm

EMI AMERICA 5-10 81-82
LEGRAND (1000 series)............ 5-10 86
LEGRAND (3001 "Dance 'Till Quarter to Three").................. 40-60 61
LEGRAND (3002 "Twist Up Calypso").............................. 40-60 62
LEGRAND (3003 "Greatest Hits") 40-60 62
MCA 5-10 84
PHOENIX.................................. 5-10 84
RHINO...................................... 5-10 84

Session: Bruce Springsteen.
Also see CHECKER, Chubby / Gary U.S. Bonds
Also see GREENWICH, Ellie
Also see JACKSON, Chuck
Also see KING, Ben E.
Also see SPRINGSTEEN, Bruce

BONE SYMPHONY

D&D '83

Singles: 12-inch 33/45rpm

CAPITOL.................................... 4-6 83

Singles: 7-inch

CAPITOL.......................................3-4 83

LPs: 10/12-inch 33rpm

CAPITOL.....................................5-10 83

BONES

P&R '72

Singles: 7-inch

MCA...3-5 73
SIGNPOST 4-6 72

LPs: 10/12-inch 33rpm

MCA 8-10 73
SIGNPOST 10-12 72

Members: Dan Faragher; Jimmy Faragher.
Also see FARAGHER BROTHERS

BONES, Elbow: see ELBOW BONES

BONES, Mr. Goon, & Mr. Ford: see MR. GOON BONES & MR. FORD

BONEY M

P&R '77

Singles: 12-inch 33/45rpm

CARRERE 4-6 85
SIRE...4-6 79

Singles: 7-inch

ATCO 3-5 76-77
ATLANTIC...................................3-5 77
SIRE...3-4 78-79

Picture Sleeves

SIRE...3-4 79

LPs: 10/12-inch 33rpm

ATCO 10-12 76
ATLANTIC...................................8-10 77
SIRE...5-10 77-79

Members: Marcia Barrett; Bobby Farrell; Liz Mitchell; Maizie Williams.

BONHAM

P&R/LP '89

Singles: 7-inch

WTG...3-4 89

LPs: 10/12-inch 33rpm

WTG...5-8 89

Members: Daniel MacMaster; Jason Bonham; Ian Hatton; John Smithson.

BONNIE & TREASURES
(Featuring Charlott O'Hara)

P&R '65

Singles: 7-inch

PHI DAN (5505 "Home of the Brave")..............................30-40 65

Also see MID AMERICANS / Bonnie & Treasures

BONNIE LOU
(Bonnie Lou Kath)

C&W '53

Singles: 78rpm

KING 4-6 53-55

Singles: 7-inch

FRATERNITY 5-10 58
KING 5-10 53-55

BONNIE SISTERS
(With Mickey "Guitar" Baker Orch; with Randy Carlos Cha Cha Rhythms)

P&R '56

Singles: 78rpm

RAINBOW 5-10 56

Singles: 7-inch

RAINBOW 10-20 56

Members: Jean Bonnie; Pat Bonnie; Sylvia Bonnie. Session: Mickey Baker.

Also see BAKER, Mickey

BONO, Sonny: see SONNY

BONOFF, Karla

LP '77

Singles: 7-inch

COLUMBIA 3-4 77-84

Picture Sleeves

COLUMBIA 3-4 77-84

LPs: 10/12-inch 33rpm

COLUMBIA 5-10 77-82

BONZO DOG BAND
(Bonzo Dog Doo-Dah Band)

LP '72

Singles: 7-inch

IMPERIAL 3-6 69
LIBERTY 4-8 68
U.A. 3-5 71-72

LPs: 10/12-inch 33rpm

IMPERIAL 15-20 68-70
LIBERTY 5-10 83
U.A. 10-15 71-74

Members: Vivian Stanshall; Neil Innes; Roger Ruskin Spear; Hughie Flint; Tony Kaye; Dave Richards; Andy Roberts.

Also see RUTLES

BONZO GOES to WASHINGTON

D&D '84

Singles: 12-inch 33/45rpm

SLEEPING BAG 4-6 84

BOOGALOO
(With the Gallant Crew; Kent Harris)

R&B '56

Singles: 78rpm

CREST 10-15 56

Singles: 7-inch

CREST (1030 "Cops and Robbers") 15-25 56
(Black vinyl.)
CREST (1030 "Cops and Robbers") 35-55 56
(Colored vinyl.)

BOOGIE BOYS

R&B/D&D/LP '85

Singles: 12-inch 33/45rpm

CAPITOL 4-6 84-88

Singles: 7-inch

CAPITOL 3-4 84-88

LPs: 10/12-inch 33rpm

CAPITOL 5-10 85-88

Member: William Stroman.

BOOGIE DOWN PRODUCTIONS

LP '88

LPs: 10/12-inch 33rpm

JIVE 5-8 88-91

BOOGIE MAN
(John Lee Hooker)

Singles: 78rpm

ACORN (308 "Morning Blues") .. 20-30 50

Also see HOOKER, John Lee

BOOGIE MAN ORCHESTRA

R&B '75

Singles: 7-inch

BOOGIE MAN 3-5 75

BOOK of LOVE

D&D '85

Singles: 12-inch 33/45rpm

SIRE 4-6 84-85

Singles: 7-inch

SIRE 3-4 84-90

Picture Sleeves

SIRE 3-4 88

LPs: 10/12-inch 33rpm

SIRE 5-10 86-91

BOOKER, Chuckii

P&R/LP '89

LPs: 10/12-inch 33rpm

ATLANTIC 5-8 89

BOOKER, James

P&R/R&B '60

Singles: 7-inch

PEACOCK 3-5 60-64

LPs: 10/12-inch 33rpm

ROUNDER 5-10 84

Also see LITTLE BOOKER

BOOKER, John Lee
(John L. Booker; John Lee Hooker)

Singles: 78rpm

CHANCE 25-75 51
CHESS 20-40 51
DELUXE 15-25 53
GONE (60 "Mad Man Blues") 100-200 51
MODERN 10-20 51
ROCKIN' 15-25 53

Singles: 7-inch

CHANCE (1108 "Miss Lorraine") 300-500 51
CHANCE (1110 "Graveyard Blues") 300-500 51
CHANCE (1122 "609 Boogie") 300-500 51
DELUXE (6004 "Blue Monday") 75-100 53
DELUXE (6032 "Pouring Down Rain") 50-100 53

DELUXE (6004 "Blue Monday") 50-100 53
DELUXE (6046 "My Baby Don't Love Me") 50-100 53
MODERN (852 "Ground Hog Blues") 50-75 51
ROCKIN' (525 "Pouring Down Rain") 75-100 53
Also see HOOKER, John Lee

BOOKER T. & PRISCILLA

LP '71

Singles: 7–inch

A&M 3-5 71-73

LPs: 10/12–inch 33rpm

A&M 8-10 71-73
Members: Booker T. Jones; Priscilla Coolidge-Jones.
Also see COOLIDGE-JONES, Priscilla

BOOKER T. & MGs

P&R/R&B/LP '62

Singles: 12–inch 33/45rpm

A&M 4-8 82-84

Singles: 7–inch

A&M 3-4 81-82
ASYLUM 3-5 77
EPIC 3-5 75
STAX (Except 100 series) 3-6 67-71
STAX (100 series) 4-8 62-66

LPs: 10/12–inch 33rpm

A&M 8-10 72-81
ASYLUM 5-10 77
ATLANTIC 10-12 68
ATLANTIC/ATCO (133 "Excerpts from *In the Christmas Spirit*) 15-20 66
(Promotional issue only. One side is excerpts from *Soul Christmas*, a various artists LP.)
EPIC 8-10 74
PICKWICK 5-10
STAX (700 series, except 701 & 713) 20-30 65-68
STAX (701 "Green Onions") 25-40 62
STAX (713 "In the Spirit of Chirstmas") 25-35 66
(Hands and keyboard drawing on front cover. Back has 1966 copyright date.)
STAX (713 "In the Spirit of Chirstmas") 15-25 67
(Christmas ornament cover. Back has 1967 copyright date.)
STAX (2000 series) 10-20 68-71
STAX (8000 series) 5-10 81-84
Members: Booker T. Jones; Steve Cropper; Al Jackson; Louis Steinberg; Willie Hall.
Also see BOOKER T. & PRISCILLA
Also see CROPPER, Steve
Also see MGs
Also see MAR-KEYS / Booker T. & MGs
Also see RANDLE, Del
Also see REDDING, Otis
Also see SANTANA
Also see SIMON, PAUL

BOOM, Taka

P&R/R&B/LP '79

Singles: 7–inch

ARIOLA 3-4 79
MIRAGE 3-4 85

LPs: 10/12–inch 33rpm

ARIOLA 5-10 79
Also see UNDISPUTED TRUTH

BOOMTOWN RATS

LP '79

Singles: 7–inch

COLUMBIA 3-4 79-80

LPs: 10/12–inch 33rpm

COLUMBIA 5-10 79-85
MERCURY 8-12 77
Members: Bob Geldof; Pete Briquette; Gerry Cott; Simon Crowe; Johnny Fingers; Garry Roberts.
Also see BAND AID
Also see GELDOF, Bob

BOONE, Daniel

P&R/LP '72

Singles: 7–inch

EPIC 3-5 72
MERCURY 3-5 72-74
PYE 3-4 75

LPs: 10/12–inch 33rpm

MERCURY 10-12 72

BOONE, Debby

P&R/C&W/LP '77

Singles: 7–inch

LAMB & LION 3-4 80-84
W.B./CURB 3-4 77-81

Picture Sleeves

W.B./CURB 3-4 78

LPs: 10/12–inch 33rpm

LAMB & LION 5-10 80-84
W.B./CURB 5-10 77-80
Also see BOONE, Pat, & Boone Girls
Also see BOONE GIRLS

BOONE, Pat

P&R/R&B '55

Singles: 78rpm

DOT 4-8 55-58
REPUBLIC 5-10 54

Singles: 7–inch

ABC 3-4 74-75
BUENA VISTA 3-5 73
CAPITOL 3-5 70
CHEVROLET/RCA (4988 "June Is Bustin' Out All Over") 10-15 58
(Promotional issue for Chevrolet dealers. Narration by Bob Lund.)
DOT (200 series) 8-12 59-60
(Stereo.)
DOT (15000 series) 5-10 55-57
(Maroon label.)

DOT (15000 & 16000 series, except 16658) 4-8 57-66
(Black label.)
DOT (16658 "Beach Girl") 5-10 64
(With Bruce Johnston and Terry Melcher.)
DOT (17000 series) 3-6 66-75
HITSVILLE 3-5 76-77
LION 3-4 72
MC 3-4 77
MCA 3-4 84
MGM 3-5 71-73
MELODYLAND 3-5 74-76
ORCHID 3-4 89
REPUBLIC 10-15 54
SRG 3-4 88
TETRAGRAMMATON 3-5 69
W.B. 3-4 80-81

Picture Sleeves

DOT 8-15 57-62

EPs: 7-inch 33/45rpm

DOT 8-12 57-60

LPs: 10/12-inch 33rpm

ABC 5-10 74
BIBLE VOICE 5-10 70
CANDLELITE 6-10
(Mail-order offer.)
DOT (3000 series) 20-35 55-56
(Maroon label.)
DOT (3000 series, except 3501) 10-20 57-67
(Black label. Monaural series.)
DOT (3501 "Pat Boone Sings Guess Who") 25-35 63
DOT (9000 "April Love") 30-40 57
(Soundtrack.)
DOT (25000 series, except 25270 & 25501) 10-20 58-68
(Stereo series.)
DOT (25270 "Moonglow") 10-20 60
(Black vinyl.)
DOT (25270 "Moonglow") 30-50 60
(Colored vinyl.)
DOT (25501 "Pat Boone Sings Guess Who") 25-40 63
FAMOUS TWINSET 5-8 74
HAMILTON 10-12 65
HITSVILLE 8-10 76
LAMB & LION 5-10 73-81
MC 5-10 77
MCA 5-10 82
MGM 5-10 73
PARAMOUNT 5-10 74
PICKWICK 5-10 79
SUPREME 6-10 70
TETRAGRAMMATON 10-12 69
WORD 5-10 75-84

Also see BRUCE & TERRY
Also see FONTANE SISTERS
Also see HUSKY, Ferlin / Pat Boone
Also see JENKINS, Gordon, & His Orchestra
Also see WARD, Robin

BOONE, Pat & Shirley

(Pat Boone Family)

Singles: 7-inch

DOT 4-6 62-64
MGM 3-5 72
MELODYLAND 3-5 75
MOTOWN 3-5 74
W.B. 3-4 79

EPs: 7-inch 33/45rpm

DOT 5-10 59

LPs: 10/12-inch 33rpm

DOT 10-20 62
LION 5-10 72
WORD 5-10 71

BOONE, Pat, & Boone Girls

Singles: 7-inch

LION 3-4 72

Also see BOONE, Pat & Shirley
Also see BOONE GIRLS

BOONE FAMILY: see BOONE, Pat & Shirley

BOONE GIRLS

(Boones)

Singles: 7-inch

LAMB & LION 3-4 77
LION 3-4 72
MGM 3-5 71-73
MOTOWN 3-5 75
W.B. 3-4 77

LPs: 10/12-inch 33rpm

LAMB & LION 5-10 77-83

Also see BOONE, Debbie
Also see BOONE, Pat, & Boone Girls

BOONE'S JUMPIN' JACKS

R&B '43

Singles: 78rpm

DECCA 10-15 43

Members: Chester Boone; George Johnson; Chauncey Graham; Vernon King; Lloyd Phillips; Buster Smith.

BOOTEE, Duke

R&B '82

Singles: 7-inch

MERCURY 3-4 84

Also see MELLE MEL & Duke Bootee

BOOTSY'S RUBBER BAND

(William "Bootsy" Collins; Bootsy)

R&B/LP '76

Singles: 12-inch 33/45rpm

W.B. 5-10 79-82

Singles: 7-inch

W.B. 3-4 75-82

Picture Sleeves

W.B. 3-4 75-82

LPs: 10/12-inch 33rpm

W.B. 5-15 76-82

Members: William "Bootsy" Collins; Phelp Collins; Frankie Waddy; Gary Cooper; Fred Wesley; Rick Gardner; Robert Johnson; Maceo Parker; Gary Shider; Mike Hampton; Bennie Worrell.
Also see PARLIAMENT
Also see SWEAT BAND
Also see ZAPP

BOOTY PEOPLE

R&B '76

Singles: 7–inch

CALLA 3-5 76

LPs: 10/12–inch 33rpm

ABC 5-10 77

BOO-YAA T.R.I.B.E.

LP '90

LPs: 10/12–inch 33rpm

4TH & BROADWAY 5-8 90

BOOZE, Bea
(Muriel Nichols)

R&B '42

Singles: 78rpm

APOLLO 15-25 50
DECCA 20-35 42-44

BOPPERS

R&B '79

Singles: 7–inch

FANTASY 3-4 78

BOSTIC, Earl

R&B '48

Singles: 78rpm

GOTHAM 5-10 46-48
KING 5-10 47-58
MAJESTIC 5-10 46

Singles: 7–inch

KING (500 series) 3-5 77
KING (4000 series, except 4491) 10-15 50-57
(Black vinyl.)
KING (4491 "I Got Loaded") 25-35 52
KING (4000 series) 20-30 52-56
(Colored vinyl.)
KING (5000 series) 5-10 57-65
KING (6000 series) 4-8 65-69
KING (15000 series) 3-5 72

EPs: 7–inch 33/45rpm

KING 10-25 52-62

LPs: 10/12–inch 33rpm

KING (64 "Earl Bostic & His Alto Sax") 50-100 51
(Black vinyl. 10–inch LP.)
KING (64 "Earl Bostic & His Alto Sax") 100-200 51
(Colored vinyl. 10–inch LP.)
KING (72 "Earl Bostic & His Alto Sax") 50-100 52
(10–inch LP.)
KING (76 "Earl Bostic & His Alto Sax") 50-100 52
(10–inch LP.)
KING (77 "Earl Bostic & His Alto Sax") 50-100 52
(10–inch LP.)
KING (78 "Earl Bostic & His Alto Sax") 50-100 52
(10–inch LP.)
KING (79 "Earl Bostic & His Alto Sax") 50-100 52
(10–inch LP.)
KING (95 "Earl Bostic Plays Old Standards") 50-100 54
(10–inch LP.)
KING (103 "Earl Bostic & His Alto Sax") 50-100 54
(10–inch LP.)
KING (119 "Earl Bostic & His Alto Sax") 50-100 54
(10–inch LP.)
KING (500 series) 20-50 55-58
KING (600 thru 1000 series) 8-18 59-70
PHILLIPS 8-12 68
KING (5000 series) 8-15 77
Also see PAGE, Hot Lips

BOSTIC, Earl, & Bill Doggett

Singles: 78rpm

KING 5-10 56

Singles: 7–inch

KING 10-15 56
Also see BOSTIC, Earl
Also see DOGGETT, Bill

BOSTIC, Sam

R&B '85

Singles: 7–inch

ATLANTIC 3-4 85

BOSTON

P&R/LP '76

Singles: 12–inch 33/45rpm

EPIC (491 "Don't Look Back") 5-8 78
(Promotional issue only.)

Singles: 7–inch

EPIC 3-5 76-79
MCA 3-4 85-87

Picture Sleeves

MCA 3-4 85-87

LPs: 10/12–inch 33rpm

EPIC (E99-34188 "Boston") 15-25 78
(Picture disc.)
EPIC (HE-34188 "Boston") 12-15 80
(Half-speed mastered.)
EPIC (34188 "Boston") 15-25 76
(With "JE" or "PE" prefix.)
EPIC (35000 series) 10-12 78
EPIC (HE-45000 series) 12-15 81
(Half-speed mastered.)
MCA 5-10 85-87

Members: Brad Delp; Tom Scholz; Barry Goudreau; Sib Hashian; Fran Sheehan.
Also see GOUDREAU, Barry
Also see ORION the HUNTER

BOSTON POPS ORCHESTRA (Conducted by Arthur Fiedler)

P&R '38

Singles: 78rpm

RCA 3-5 49-57
VICTOR 3-6 38

Singles: 7-inch

POLYDOR 3-4 70
RCA 3-8 50-65

Picture Sleeves

RCA (8378 "I Want to Hold Your Hand") 10-15 64

EPs: 7-inch 33/45rpm

RCA 4-8 50-61

LPs: 10/12-inch 33rpm

DEUTSCHE GRAMMOPHON 4-8 78
MIDSONG INT'L 4-8 79
POLYDOR 5-10 71-72
RCA 5-20 50-69

Also see ATKINS, Chet, & Boston Pops
Also see ELLINGTON, Duke, & Boston Pops
Also see HIRT, Al, & Boston Pops
Also see NERO, Peter
Also see SHERMAN, Allan

BOSTON POPS ORCHESTRA (Conducted by John Williams)

LP '80

LPs: 10/12-inch 33rpm

PHILIPS 5-10 80-86

Also see WILLIAMS, John

BOSWELL, Connee

P&R '32

Singles: 78rpm

BRUNSWICK 5-10 32-44
DECCA 5-10 35-56

Singles: 7-inch

CHARLES 4-8 62
DECCA 5-10 50-56

EPs: 7-inch 33/45rpm

DECCA 5-15 56
RCA 5-10 57

LPs: 10/12-inch 33rpm

DECCA 15-25 56
RCA 10-20 57

Also see BOSWELL SISTERS
Also see CROSBY, Bing, & Connee Boswell

BOSWELL SISTERS

P&R '31

Singles: 78rpm

BRUNSWICK 5-15 31-35
DECCA 5-10 35-37

Members: Connie Boswell; Martha Boswell; Vet Boswell.
Also see BOSWELL, Connie

BOTTOM & COMPANY

R&B '74

Singles: 7-inch

MOTOWN 3-5 74-75

LPs: 10/12-inch 33rpm

GORDY 8-10 76

BOTTOM LINE

R&B '76

Singles: 7-inch

GREEDY 3-5 76

LPs: 10/12-inch 33rpm

GREEDY 8-10 76

BOURGEOIS - TAGG

P&R/LP '86

Singles: 7-inch

ISLAND 3-4 86-87

LPs: 10/12-inch 33rpm

ISLAND 5-10 86-87

Members: Brent Bourgeois; Larry Tagg.

BOW WOW WOW

LP '81

Singles: 12-inch 33/45rpm

RCA 4-6 83

Singles: 7-inch

RCA 3-4 81-84

Picture Sleeves

RCA 3-4 82

LPs: 10/12-inch 33rpm

HARVEST 5-10 82
RCA 5-10 81-84

Promotional LPs

RCA ("Special Radio Series") 10-15 81

Members: Annabella Lu Win; Matt Ashman; Dave Barbarossa; Leroy Gorman.
Also see ADAM & ANTS

BOWEN, Jimmy

P&R/R&B '57

Singles: 78rpm

ROULETTE 5-10 57

Singles: 7-inch

CAPEHART 5-10 61-62
CREST 5-10 61
REPRISE 5-10 64-66
ROULETTE (Except 4002) 10-20 57-60
ROULETTE (4002 "Party Doll") 30-40 57
(Credited to "Jimmy Bowen with the Rhythm Orchids" though actually by Buddy Knox.)

Picture Sleeves

CAPEHART (5005 "Teenage Dreamworld") 30-40 61

EPs: 7-inch 33/45rpm

ROULETTE (302 "Jimmy Bowen") 40-50 57

LPs: 10/12-inch 33rpm

REPRISE (6210 "Sunday Morning with the Comics") 20-25 66

ROULETTE (25004 "Jimmy Bowen")............................ 75-100 57
(Black label.)
ROULETTE (25004 "Jimmy Bowen")............................ 100-150 57
(White label. Promotional issue only.)
ROULETTE (25004 "Jimmy Bowen")................................ 5-10
(Reissue for the Outlet Book Co. and Publishers Central Bureau, and labeled as such.)
Also see KNOX, Buddy / Jimmy Bowen

BOWIE, David

P&R/LP '72

Singles: 12–inch 33/45rpm

EMI AMERICA 5-10 82-87
RCA.. 10-15 79-80

Promotional 12–inch Singles

EMI AMERICA 8-15 82-87
RCA.. 15-25 79-80

Singles: 7–inch

BACKSTREET 3-5 82
DERAM (85009 "Rubber Band") 20-40 67
EMI AMERICA 3-5 83-87
(Black vinyl.)
EMI AMERICA (8231 "Blue Jean") 5-8 84
(Colored vinyl.)
LONDON (20079 "The Laughing Gnome").............................. 15-25 73
MERCURY (72949 "Space Oddity") 30-40 69
MERCURY (73075 "Memory of a Free Festival")........................ 35-50 70
RCA.. 3-6 71-84
W.B. (5815 "Can't Help Thinking About Me") 50-75 66

Picture Sleeves

BACKSTREET (1767 "Cat People") 4-8 82
EMI AMERICA 3-5 83-87
RCA (0001 "Time")............... 200-400 73
RCA (0719 "Starman")............. 15-20 72
RCA (0876 "Space Oddity")...... 10-15 73
RCA (12078 "Ashes to Ashes"). 10-15 80
RCA (12134 "Fashion").............. 5-10 80
RCA (13660 "White Light White Heat") 3-5 83
RCA (13769 "1984").................... 3-5 80

Promotional Singles

BACKSTREET 5-10 82
DERAM (85009 "Rubber Band") 30-40 67
EMI AMERICA (8158 thru 8190)... 4-8 83-84
EMI AMERICA (8231 "Blue Jean") 4-8 84
EMI AMERICA (8246 thru 8308)... 4-8 83-86
EMI AMERICA (8380 "Day in Day Out") 4-8 87
EMI AMERICA (8380 "Day in Day Out")..............................15-20 87
(Colored vinyl. Boxed edition.)
EMI AMERICA (43000 series).......4-8 87
LONDON (20079 "The Laughing Gnome")..................15-25 73
MERCURY (311 "All the Madmen") 40-60 70
MERCURY (72949 "Space Oddity")...................................30-50 69
MERCURY (73075 "Memory of a Free Festival") 40-60 70
RCA 5-12 71-84
W.B. (5815 "Can't Help Thinking About Me")..............................50-75 66
WHAT'S IT ALL ABOUT 10-20 70s

EPs: 7–inch 33/45rpm

RCA 20-25 70s
(Promotional issues only.)

LPs: 10/12–inch 33rpm

DERAM (16003 "David Bowie")................................100-125 67
(Monaural.)
DERAM (18003 "David Bowie")................................100-150 67
(Stereo.)
EMI AMERICA 5-10 83-87
LONDON..10-20 73-85
MFSL (064 "Rise and Fall of Ziggy Stardust" 20-40 82
MFSL (083 "Let's Dance") 15-25 82
MERCURY (61246 "Man of Words/ Man of Music").......................75-100 69
MERCURY (61246 "Space Oddity") 10-15 72
MERCURY (61325 "The Man Who Sold the World")...............................25-40 71
PRECISION (1 "Don't Be Fooled By the Name").........................20-25 81
(10–inch LP.)
RCA (0291 "Bowie Pin Ups").....10-15 73
RCA (0576 "Diamond Dogs")..............................1500-2000 74
(With "Dog Genitals" cover.)
RCA (0576 "Diamond Dogs").....10-15 74
(With dog's genitals covered.)
RCA (0700 thru 1300 series).....10-15 74-76
RCA (1732 "Changesone Bowie")...............................100-125 76
(With alternate take of *John, I'm Only Dancing.*)
RCA (1732 "Changesone Bowie")....................................10-20 76
(With the commonly issued take of *John, I'm Only Dancing.*)
RCA (2000 thru 2500)................10-15 77
RCA (2743 "Peter and the Wolf") 10-15 78

(Black vinyl. With Eugene Ormandy & Philadelphia Orchestra.)
RCA (2743 "Peter and the Wolf") 35-55 78
(Colored vinyl. With Eugene Ormandy & Philadelphia Orchestra.)
RCA (2900 thru 4200 series) 5-10 79-82
RCA (4600 thru 4800 series) 10-15 71-73
(With "LSP" prefix.)
RCA (4700 thru 4900 series, except 4862)................. 5-10 83-84
(With "AFL," "AYL" or "CPL" prefix.)
RCA 4862 "Ziggy Stardust")........ 5-10 83
(Black vinyl.)
RCA 4862 "Ziggy Stardust")...... 40-80 83
(Clear vinyl.)
RYKODISC (Except 0120/2)....... 8-12 87-90
RYKODISC (0120/2 "Sound and Vision").................................. 50-75 89
(Boxed, 6-LP set.)

Promotional LPs

DERAM (18003 "David Bowie").............................. 200-300 67
EMI AMERICA (9960 "Let's Talk").................................... 40-70 83
MERCURY (61246 "Man of Words/ Man of Music") 75-125 69
MERCURY (61325 "The Man Who Sold the World") 75-125 71
RCA (0200 thru 4800 series) 20-40 71-73
(With programmer's strip on front cover.)
RCA (2697 "Bowie Now").......... 30-50 78
RCA (3016 "An Evening with David Bowie")..................... 100-200 78
RCA (3545 "Bowie 1980")......... 50-75 80
RCA (3829 "RCA Special Radio Series")........................ 30-50 80
RCA (3840 "Interview") 35-50 80
RCA (11306 "Peter and the Wolf") 30-40 78
Also see HOUSTON, Cissy
Also see KHAN, Chaka
Also see QUEEN & David Bowie
Also see SPIDERS from MARS
Also see TURNER, Tina
Also see VANDROSS, Luther

BOWIE, David / Joe Cocker / Youngbloods

LPs: 10/12-inch 33rpm

MERCURY (SRD-2-29 "Zig Zag Festival") 40-60 70
(Promotional issue only.)
Also see COCKER, Joe
Also see YOUNGBLOODS

BOWIE, David, & Bing Crosby

Singles: 7-inch

RCA.. 3-6 83

Picture Sleeves

RCA.. 4-8 83
Also see CROSBY, Bing

BOWIE, David, & Mick Jagger

P&R/D&D '85

Singles: 12-inch 33/45rpm

EMI AMERICA (19200 "Dancing in the Streets")..................................8-12 85

Singles: 7-inch

EMI AMERICA (8288 "Dancing in the Streets")....................................3-4 85

Picture Sleeves

EMI AMERICA (8288 "Dancing in the Streets")....................................3-5 85
Also see JAGGER, Mick

BOWIE, David, & Pat Metheny Group

P&R/D&D '85

Singles: 12-inch 33/45rpm

EMI AMERICA 4-8 85

Singles: 7-inch

EMI AMERICA 3-4 85

Picture Sleeves

EMI AMERICA 3-4 85

LPs: 10/12-inch 33rpm

EMI AMERICA 5-10 85
Also see METHENY, Pat

BOWIE, David / Iggy Pop

Singles: 12-inch 33/45rpm

RCA (10956 "Sound & Vision")..30-50 77
(Promotional issue only.)
Also see BOWIE, David
Also see POP, Iggy

BOWLES, Rick

P&R '82

Singles: 7-inch

POLYDOR 3-4 82

LPs: 10/12-inch 33rpm

POLYDOR 5-10 82

BOX of FROGS

LP '84

Singles: 7-inch

EPIC..3-4 84-86

LPs: 10/12-inch 33rpm

EPIC..5-10 84-86
Members: Chris Dreja; Jim McCarty; Jeff Beck.
Also see YARDBIRDS

BOX TOPS

P&R/R&B/LP '67

Singles: 7-inch

BELL 3-5 70-71
GUSTO 3-4 84
HI 3-5 72-73
MALA 4-8 67-69
SPEHRE SOUND 4-8 67
STAX...3-5 74

LPs: 10/12-inch 33rpm

BELL 10-20 67-69
COTILLION 10-15 71
KORY...5-10 77
RHINO 5-10 82

Members: Alex Chilton; Rick Allen; Tom Boggs; Harold Cloud; Bill Cunningham; John Evans; Swain Scharfar; Gary Talley; Danny Smythe; Rick Stevens.

BOY GEORGE
(George O'Dowd)

P&R/R&B/LP '87

Singles: 7–inch

VIRGIN.. 3-4 87-89

LPs: 10/12–inch 33rpm

VIRGIN.. 5-10 87-89

Also see CULTURE CLUB

BOY MEETS GIRL

P&R/LP '85

Singles: 7–inch

A&M 3-4 85
RCA.. 3-4 88-89

Picture Sleeves

A&M 3-4 85
RCA.. 3-4 88-89

LPs: 10/12–inch 33rpm

A&M 5-10 85
RCA.. 5-8 88

Members: George Merrill; Shannon Rubicam.

BOYCE, Tommy

P&R '62

Singles: 7–inch

A&M (Except 826)........................ 4-8 66
A&M (826 "In Case the Wind Should Blow")........................ 10-12 66
CAPITOL.. 3-5 71
COLPIX 8-10 66
DOT.. 10-15 60
MGM 8-10 65
RCA (7000 series)........................ 10-15 61
RCA (8000 series)........................ 8-12 62-63
R-DELL 15-20 58
WOW.. 8-12 61

LPs: 10/12–inch 33rpm

CAMDEN.. 15-20 68

Also see CLOUD, Christopher

BOYCE, Tommy, & Bobby Hart
(Boyce & Hart)

P&R/LP '67

Singles: 7–inch

A&M 4-8 67-69
AQUARIAN 3-6 68

Picture Sleeves

A&M 5-10 67-69
AQUARIAN 5-8 68

LPs: 10/12–inch 33rpm

A&M 10-20 67-69

Also see ATTORNEYS
Also see BOYCE, Tommy
Also see DOLENZ, JONES, BOYCE & HART

BOYD, Eddie
(With His Chess Men; Eddie Boyd Blues Combo; Little Eddie Boyd & His Boogie Band)

R&B '52

Singles: 78rpm

CHESS.. 10-20 50-56
HERALD 40-60 52
J.O.B. 20-25 52-58
RCA 10-20 47-50

Singles: 7–inch

ART TONE.. 5-10 62
BEA & BABY 5-10 59
CHESS (1523 "Cool Kind Treatment")........................ 25-50 52
CHESS (1533 "24 Hours") 25-50 53
CHESS (1541 "Third Degree") .. 25-50 53
CHESS (1552 "That's When I Miss You") 25-50 53
CHESS (1561 "Picture in the Frame") 20-40 54
CHESS (1573 "Hush Baby, Don't You Cry") 20-40 54
CHESS (1576 "Driftin") 20-40 54
CHESS (1582 "Story of Bill") 15-30 55
CHESS (1595 "Real Good Feeling") 15-30 55
CHESS (1606 "I'm a Prisoner") . 15-30 55
CHESS (1634 "Just a Fool") 15-25 56
CHESS (1660 "I Got a Woman") 15-25 56
CHESS (Colored vinyl) 75-125 54

(We are unable at this time to specify exactly which Chess numbers were pressed on colored vinyl.)

HERALD (406 "I'm Goin' Downtown")........................ 75-125 52
J.O.B. (1007 "Five Long Years")........................ 40-60 52
(Black vinyl.)
J.O.B. (1007 "Five Long Years")........................ 75-125 52
(Colored vinyl.)
J.O.B. (1009 "It's Miserable to Be Alone")........................ 40-60 53
J.O.B. (1114 "I Love You")......... 30-50 57
LA SALLE 5-10 61
MOJO.. 5-10
ORIOLE (1316 "Five Long Years")........................ 20-30 58
PALOS 4-8 63-64
PUSH.. 5-10 62
RCA (50-0006 "What Makes These Things Happen to Me")............ 35-50 50
(Colored vinyl.)

EPs: 7–inch 33/45rpm

ESQUIRE.. 15-20 60

LPs: 10/12–inch 33rpm

EPIC.. 20-25 69
LONDON.. 15-20 69

Also see DIXON, Willie
Also see GREEN, Peter

BOYD, Jimmy
(Little Jimmy Boyd)

P&R/C&W '52

Singles: 78rpm

COLUMBIA (Except 21571) 4-8 52-56
COLUMBIA (21571 "Rockin' Down the Mississippi") 10-15 56

Singles: 7-inch

CAPITOL 4-8 63
COLUMBIA (152 "I Saw Mommy Kissing Santa Claus") 10-20 52
COLUMBIA (21571 "Rockin' Down the Mississippi") 30-40 56
COLUMBIA (39000 & 40000 series) 10-20 52-56
IMPERIAL 3-6 66-67
MGM (12788 "Cream Puff") 40-50 59
TAKE TEN 4-8 63
VEE JAY 4-8 65

Picture Sleeves

COLUMBIA (152 "I Saw Mommy Kissing Santa Claus") 15-25 52
(With die-cut center hole.)

EPs: 7-inch 33/45rpm

COLUMBIA (1913 "Jimmy Boyd") 10-15 50s

Also see LAINE, Frankie, & Jimmy Boyd

BOYD, Jimmy, & Rosemary Clooney

P&R '53

Singles: 78rpm

COLUMBIA 4-8 53

Singles: 7-inch

COLUMBIA (39000 series) 8-12 53
COLUMBIA (41000 series) 4-8 60

Also see BOYD, Jimmy
Also see CLOONEY, Rosemary

BOYD, Little Eddie: see BOYD, Eddie

BOYER, Bonnie

P&R '79

Singles: 12-inch 33/45rpm

COLUMBIA 4-6 79

Singles: 7-inch

COLUMBIA 3-4 79

LPs: 10/12-inch 33rpm

COLUMBIA 5-10 79

BOYER, Charles

LP '66

Singles: 7-inch

VALIANT 3-6 65

LPs: 10/12-inch 33rpm

VALIANT 10-20 65

BOYLAN, Terence

LP '77

Singles: 7-inch

ASYLUM 3-4 77-80

LPs: 10/12-inch 33rpm

ASYLUM 5-10 77-80
VERVE/FORECAST 12-15 69

Session: Darius Davenport.

BOYS

P&R/LP '88

Singles: 7-inch

MOTOWN 3-4 88-90

Picture Sleeves

MOTOWN 3-4 88

LPs: 10/12-inch 33rpm

MOTOWN 5-8 88-90

BOYS BAND

P&R '82

Singles: 7-inch

ELEKTRA 3-4 82

Picture Sleeves

ELEKTRA 3-4 82

LPs: 10/12-inch 33rpm

ASYLUM 5-10 82

Members: Rusty Golden; Chris Golden; Greg Gordon; B.J. Lowry.

BOYS CLUB

P&R/LP '88

Singles: 7-inch

MCA 3-4 88

Picture Sleeves

MCA 3-4 88

LPs: 10/12-inch 33rpm

MCA 5-8 88

Members: Joe Pasquale; Gene Hunt.
Also see JETS

BOYS DON'T CRY

P&R/LP '86

Singles: 12-inch 33/45rpm

PROFILE 4-6 86

Singles: 7-inch

PROFILE 3-4 86

LPs: 10/12-inch 33rpm

PROFILE 5-10 86

Member: Nick Richards.

BOYS in the Band

P&R/R&B '70

Singles: 7-inch

SPRING 3-5 70

BOYS on the Block

R&B '87

Singles: 7-inch

FANTASY 3-4 87

BOYZ II MEN

P&R/R&B/LP '91

Singles: 7-inch

MOTOWN 3-4 91

LPs: 10/12-inch 33rpm

MOTOWN 5-8 91

BOZE, Calvin

R&B '50

Singles: 78rpm

ALADDIN.................................. 10-20 50-52
G&G (1029 "Safronia B.") 30-50 46
SCORE 10-15 48

Singles: 7-inch

ALADDIN (3045 "Waitin' and Drinkin") 50-100 50
ALADDIN (3055 "Safronia B.") 50-100 50
ALADDIN (3065 "Lizzie Lou") ... 50-75 50
ALADDIN (3072 "Stinkin' from Drinkin") 40-60 50
ALADDIN (3079 "Beale Street on Saturday Night")................ 40-50 51
ALADDIN (3086 "Slippin' and Slidin").................................. 40-50 51
ALADDIN (3100 "I've Got News for You")........................ 40-50 51
ALADDIN (3110 "I'm Gonna Steam off the Stamp") 40-50 52
ALADDIN (3160 "Shamrock") ... 40-50 52
ALADDIN (3122 "My Friend Told Me")............................... 40-50 52
ALADDIN (3132 "Good Time Sue") 40-50 52
ALADDIN (3147 "Looped")........ 40-50 52
ASTRA 5-10
IMPERIAL 5-10 62

Also see JOHNSON, Marvin

BRADLEY, James
(With the Bill Smith Combo)

R&B '79

Singles: 7-inch

CHESS..................................... 5-10 60
MALACO 3-4 79-84
MANCO..................................... 5-10 61

LPs: 10/12-inch 33rpm

MALACO 5-10 84

BRADLEY, Jan

P&R/R&B '63

Singles: 7-inch

ADANTI 4-8 65
CHESS...................................... 4-8 62-68
DOYLEN 4-8 70
ERIC... 3-4 73
FORMAL (Except 1044)............. 5-10 62-63
FORMAL (1044 "Mama Didn't Lie").. 15-25 62
HOOTENANNY........................... 5-8 62
NIGHT OWL............................... 5-8 63
SOUND SPECTRUM 4-8 65

BRADLEY, Owen
(Owen Bradley Quintet)

C&W/P&R '49

Singles: 78rpm

CORAL 4-8 49-50
DECCA...................................... 3-8 54-57

Singles: 7-inch

CORAL 5-10 50
DECCA 5-10 54-61

EPs: 7-inch 33/45rpm

CORAL......................................10-20 54
DECCA 10-20 58

LPs: 10/12-inch 33rpm

CORAL......................................15-25 53-55
DECCA 15-25 58-60

Also see PLEIS, Jack, & Owen Bradley

BRADSHAW, Terry

C&W/P&R '76

Singles: 7-inch

BENSON.......................................3-4 80
MERCURY 3-5 76

Picture Sleeves

BENSON.......................................3-4 80

LPs: 10/12-inch 33rpm

BENSON.......................................5-10 80
HEARTWARMING 5-10 82
MERCURY....................................6-12 76

BRADSHAW, Tiny

R&B '50

Singles: 78rpm

KING 5-15 50-55

Singles: 7-inch

GUSTO 3-4 80-83
KING (4357 "I Hate You") 25-50 50
KING (4397 "Butterfly")..............25-50 50
KING (4457 "Bradshaw Boogie") 25-50 50
KING (4487 "T-99")...................75-150 52
KING (4497 "The Train Kept A-Rollin")................................75-150 52
KING (4547 "Rippin' & Runnin")..................................75-150 52
KING (4577 thru 4787)...............20-40 52-55

(For King 4000 series colored vinyl singles, the price range will double or triple.)

EPs: 7-inch 33/45rpm

KING (208 thru 360)...................25-50 52-56

LPs: 10/12-inch 33rpm

KING (74 "Off and On")..........100-200 52
(10-inch LP.)
KING (501 "Tiny Bradshaw") ...75-125 55
KING (653 "Great Composer")...30-50 59
KING (953 "24 Great Songs")....20-30 66

BRAGG, Billy

LP '88

Singles: 7-inch

ELEKTRA.......................................3-4 88

LPs: 10/12-inch 33rpm

ELEKTRA.......................................5-8 88

BRAINSTORM

P&R/R&B/LP '77

Singles: 12-inch 33/45rpm

TABU 4-6 77-79

Singles: 7-inch

RCA.......... 3-4 82
TABU.......... 3-4 76-79

LPs: 10/12-inch 33rpm

RCA.......... 5-10 82
TABU.......... 5-10 77-79

Members: Belita Woods; Charles Overton; Jeryl Bright; Larry Sims; Jerry Kent; Renell Gousalves; Willie Wooten; Lamont Johnson; Trenita Womack.

BRAM TCHAIKOVSKY: see TCHAIKOVSKY, Bram

BRAMLETT, Bonnie

LP '75

Singles: 7-inch

CAPRICORN.......... 3-5 75-78
COLUMBIA.......... 3-5 72-73
REFUGE.......... 3-4 81

LPs: 10/12-inch 33rpm

CAPRICORN.......... 8-10 75-78
COLUMBIA.......... 10-12 72-73

Also see DELANEY & BONNIE
Also see LITTLE FEAT

BRAMLETT, Delaney
(With Bekka Bramlett; with Blue Diamond)

Singles: 7-inch

COLUMBIA (45950 "Are You a Beatle Or a Rolling Stone").......... 5-10 73
CREAM.......... 3-4 81
GNP.......... 4-8 64-66
INDEPENDENCE.......... 4-8 67

LPs: 10/12-inch 33rpm

COLUMBIA.......... 8-10 72-73
MGM.......... 8-10 75
PRODIGAL.......... 8-10 77

Also see DELANEY & BONNIE
Also see RIO, Chuck, & Delaney

BRAND X

LP '76

Singles: 7-inch

PASSPORT.......... 3-4 78

LPs: 10/12-inch 33rpm

PASSPORT.......... 5-10 76-84

Members: Phil Collins; John Goodsall; Percy Jones; Robin Lumley; Morris Pert.
Also see COLLINS, Phil

BRAND NUBIAN

LP '91

LPs: 10/12-inch 33rpm

ATLANTIC.......... 4-8 91

BRANDON, Bill

R&B '72

Singles: 7-inch

BELL (733 "Rainbow Road").......... 5-10
MOONSONG.......... 10-20 72-73
PIEDMONT.......... 3-6 76
PRELUDE.......... 3-5 77-78
QUINVY (7007 "Strange Feeling").......... 50-75
SOUTH CAMP.......... 4-8 67
TOWER (430 "Rainbow Road").......... 20-30 68

BRANDOS

LP '87

LPs: 10/12-inch 33rpm

RELATIVITY.......... 5-10 87

BRANIGAN, Laura

P&R/LP '82

Singles: 12-inch 33/45rpm

ATLANTIC.......... 4-8 82-87

Singles: 7-inch

ATLANTIC.......... 3-4 80-90
EMI AMERICA.......... 3-4 84

Picture Sleeves

ATLANTIC.......... 3-4 80-87

LPs: 10/12-inch 33rpm

ATLANTIC.......... 5-10 82-90
EMI AMERICA.......... 5-10 84

Also see COHEN, Leonard
Also see MEADOW

BRANNEN, John

LP '88

LPs: 10/12-inch 33rpm

APACHE.......... 5-8 88

BRASS CONSTRUCTION

P&R/R&B/LP '76

Singles: 12-inch 33/45rpm

CAPITOL.......... 4-6 83
LIBERTY.......... 4-6 82

Singles: 7-inch

CAPITOL.......... 3-4 83
DOCC.......... 3-5
LIBERTY.......... 3-4 82
U.A.......... 3-5 75-80

LPs: 10/12-inch 33rpm

CAPITOL.......... 5-10 83
U.A.......... 5-10 75-80
LIBERTY.......... 5-10 82

Members: Randy Muller; Wade Williamston; Joe Wong; Wayne Parris; Mickey Grudge; Morris Price; Jesse Ward; Sandy Billups; Larry Payton.

BRASS FEVER

R&B '77

Singles: 7-inch

IMPULSE.......... 3-5 76-77

LPs: 10/12-inch 33rpm

IMPULSE.......... 8-10 76

BRASS RING

P&R/LP '66

Singles: 7-inch

ABC.......... 3-5 70
DUNHILL (Except 4090).......... 4-6 66-69
DUNHILL (4090 "Love in the Open Air").......... 10-20 67
ITCO.......... 3-5 69

Picture Sleeves

DUNHILL (4090 "Love in the Open Air").......... 15-25 67

(Billed on sleeve as "Paul McCartney's First NON Beatle Song.")

LPs: 10/12-inch 33rpm

DUNHILL.......................................8-12 66-73
ITCO...6-10 70
PROJECT 3 ....6-10 72

Members: Phil Bodner.
Also see BODNER, Phil, Sextet
Also see McCARTNEY, Paul

BRAT PACK

P&R '90

Singles: 7-inch

VENDETTA....................................3-4 90

BRAUN, Bob
(With the Fun Bunch)

P&R/LP '62

Singles: 7-inch

AUDIO FIDELITY............................3-6 65
DECCA...4-8 62
FRATERNITY...................................3-6 64-66
KING 4-8 59
QCA 3-5 73
U.A. 3-5 67
WRAYCO 3-5 71

Picture Sleeves

DECCA...5-8 62
QCA 3-5 73

EPs: 7-inch 33/45rpm

DECCA...5-10 63

LPs: 10/12-inch 33rpm

AUDIO FIDELITY............................8-12 65
DECCA...10-20 62
U.A. 8-12 67
WRAYCO 5-10 71

BRAVOS, Los: see LOS BRAVOS

BRAXTON, Dhar
(With Chocolette)

R&B '86

Singles: 12-inch 33/45rpm

SLEEPING BAG..............................4-6 86

Singles: 7-inch

SLEEPING BAG..............................3-4 86

BREAD
(David Gates & Bread)

LP '69

Singles: 7-inch

ASYLUM (45054 "Make It with You") 4-6 70s
(Label misprint; Asylum should be Elektra.)
ELEKTRA (Except 45666 & 45668)...3-5 70-77
ELEKTRA (45666 "Dismal Day") .. 5-8 69
ELEKTRA (45668 "Could I")..........4-6 69

Picture Sleeves

ELEKTRA...4-8 70-72

LPs: 10/12-inch 33rpm

ELEKTRA (100 & 1000 series) ... 8-12 73-77
ELEKTRA (5000 series).............15-25 72-73
(Quadrophonic series.)
ELEKTRA (74000 & 75000 series, except 75015 & 75056) 10-15 69-73
ELEKTRA (75015 "Baby I'm a Want You")...........................15-25 72
(With die-cut cover.)
ELEKTRA (75015 "Baby I'm a Want You")...........................10-15 72
(Standard cover.)
ELEKTRA (75056 "Best of Bread")......................................25-35 73
K-TEL..5-10 82

Members: David Gates; James Griffin; Mike Botts; Larry Knechtel; Robb Royer.
Also see GATES, David
Also see GRIFFIN, James

BREAK MACHINE

R&B/D&D '84

Singles: 12-inch 33/45rpm

SIRE..4-6 84

Singles: 7-inch

BLACK SCORPIO...........................3-5
SIRE..3-4 84

Members: Lindell Blake; Lindsay Blake; Cortez Jordan.

BREAKFAST CLUB

P&R/R&B/LP '87

Singles: 7-inch

MCA 3-4 87

Picture Sleeves

MCA 3-4 87

LPs: 10/12-inch 33rpm

MCA 5-10 87

BREAKWATER

R&B/LP '79

Singles: 7-inch

ARISTA...3-5 79-80

LPs: 10/12-inch 33rpm

ARISTA...5-10 79-80

Members: Kae Williams; Lincoln Gilmore; James Jones; Gene Robinson Jr.; Vince Garnell; Greg Scott; John Braddock; Steve Green.
Also see BLACK MAGIC

BREATHE

P&R/LP '88

Singles: 12-inch 33/45rpm

A&M 4-8 87

Singles: 7-inch

A&M 3-4 87-90

Picture Sleeves

A&M 3-4 88-89

LPs: 10/12-inch 33rpm

A&M 5-8 87-90

Members: David Glasper; Ian Spice; Michael Delahunty; Marcus Lillington.

BREATHLESS

P&R '80

Singles: 7-inch

EMI AMERICA 3-4 79

LPs: 10/12-inch 33rpm

EMI AMERICA 5-10 79-80

BRECKER BROTHERS

P&R/R&B/LP '75

Singles: 7-inch

ARISTA 3-5 75-80

LPs: 10/12-inch 33rpm

ARISTA 5-10 75-81

Members: Mike Brecker; Randy Brecker; Dave Sanborn.

Also see DREAMS

BREMERS, Beverly

P&R '71

Singles: 7-inch

COLUMBIA 3-5 75-77

ERIC 3-4 83

SCEPTER 3-5 71-75

Picture Sleeves

SCEPTER 4-6 72

LPs: 10/12-inch 33rpm

SCEPTER 8-10 72

BRENDA & HERB

R&B '78

Singles: 7-inch

H&L 3-5 78

Members: Brenda Reid; Herb Rooney.

Also see EXCITERS

BRENDA & PETE: see LEE, Brenda, & Pete Fountain

BRENDA & Big Dudes

R&B '86

Singles: 12-inch 33/45rpm

CAPITOL 4-6 86

Singles: 7-inch

CAPITOL 3-4 86

LPs: 10/12-inch 33rpm

CAPITOL 5-10 86

BRENDA & TABULATIONS

P&R/R&B/LP '67

Singles: 12-inch 33/45rpm

CHOCOLATE CITY 4-6 77

Singles: 7-inch

CHOCOLATE CITY 3-5 76-77

DIONN 5-10 67-69

EPIC 3-5 72-75

TOP & BOTTOM 4-6 69-71

LPs: 10/12-inch 33rpm

CHOCOLATE CITY 5-10 77

DIONN (2000 "Dry Your Eyes") 20-30 67

TOP & BOTTOM 15-20 70

Members: Brenda Payton; Jerry Joures; Eddie Jackson; Maurice Coates; Dennis Dozier; Donald Ford; Deborah Martin; Lee Smith; Kenneth Wright; Pat Mercer.

BRENDA LEE: see LEE, Brenda

BRENNAN, Walter

(With Billy Vaughn's Orchestra & Chorus)

P&R '60

Singles: 7-inch

DOT 5-10 60

KAPP 3-5 71

LIBERTY 4-8 62-64

RPC 8-10 61

Picture Sleeves

DOT 10-15 60

LIBERTY 8-12 62-63

LPs: 10/12-inch 33rpm

DOT 15-25 60

EVEREST 15-20 60

HAMILTON 8-10 65

LIBERTY 15-25 62

LONDON 6-10 70

RPC 15-25 62

SUNSET 8-10 66

U.A. 5-10 75

Also see VAUGHN, Billy

BRENSTON, Jackie

(With His Delta Cats)

R&B '51

Singles: 78rpm

CHESS (Except 1458) 10-20 51-53

CHESS (1458 "Rocket 88") 30-50 51

(See note below regarding 45 rpms.)

FEDERAL 5-10 56-57

Singles: 7-inch

CHESS (1458 "Rocket 88") ... 300-500 51

(With Ike Turner on guitar. Original 45s from 1951 are not known to exist. There are legit reissue 45s, made circa 1954. These have a delta symbol [Δ] and the number stamped in the trail-off. Fakes, without the delta mark, also exist.)

CHESS (1469 "In My Real Gone Rocket") 150-250 51

CHESS (1496 "Leo the Louse") 100-150 52

CHESS (1532 "The Blues Got Me Again") 50-100 53

FEDERAL 20-35 56-57

SUE 5-10 61

Also see TURNER, Ike

BRENSTON, Jackie / Muddy Waters

Singles: 7-inch

CHESS (113 "Rocket 88") 3-5

Also see BRENSTON, Jackie

Also see WATERS, Muddy

BREWER, Teresa

(With the Lancers; with Dixieland Band; with Mickey Mantle; with Bobby Wayne)

P&R '50

Singles: 78rpm

CORAL 5-10 52-57

LONDON.................................... 5-10 50-52

Singles: 7-inch

ABC.................................... 3-5 67
AMSTERDAM.................................... 3-5 72-73
CORAL (60000 & 61000 series) 10-20 52-58
CORAL (62000 & 65000 series) . 5-10 58-64
DOCTOR JAZZ.................................... 3-4 83
FLYING DUTCHMAN.................................... 3-5 72
LONDON.................................... 8-12 50-52
PHILIPS.................................... 4-8 63-67
PROJECT 3.................................... 3-4 82
RCA (11882 "Merry Christmas")... 4-6 79
(With picture label. Special products issue.)
SSS INT'L.................................... 3-5 68
SIGNATURE.................................... 3-4 74-83

Picture Sleeves

CORAL.................................... 5-10 58-60
SIGNATURE.................................... 3-4 80

EPs: 7-inch 33/45rpm

CORAL.................................... 8-15 55-60
LONDON.................................... 10-20 51

LPs: 10/12-inch 33rpm

AMSTERDAM.................................... 6-10 73-74
COLUMBIA.................................... 5-10 81
CORAL (7 "Best of Teresa Brewer").................................... 10-20 65
CORAL (56072 "A Bouquet of Hits from Teresa Brewer").................................... 25-40 52
(10-inch LP.)
CORAL (56093 "Till I Waltz Again with You").................................... 25-40 53
(10-inch LP.)
CORAL (57027 thru 57297)...... 15-25 55-59
CORAL (57315 thru 57351)...... 10-20 60-65
DOCTOR JAZZ.................................... 5-10 79-83
FLYING DUTCHMAN.................................... 6-10 73-74
IMAGE.................................... 5-10 78
LONDON (1006 "Teresa Brewer").................................... 50-75 51
(10-inch LP.)
MCA.................................... 5-10 83
PHILIPS.................................... 10-15 63-67
PROJECT 3.................................... 5-10 82
RCA.................................... 5-10 75
SIGNATURE.................................... 5-10 74-75
VOCALION.................................... 8-12 69
WING.................................... 8-10 66

BREWER, Teresa, & Count Basie

LPs: 10/12-inch 33rpm

DOCTOR JAZZ.................................... 5-10 84
Also see BASIE, Count

BREWER, Teresa, & Duke Ellington

LPs: 10/12-inch 33rpm

COLUMBIA.................................... 5-10 81
FLYING DUTCHMAN.................................... 6-10 74
Also see BREWER, Teresa
Also see ELLINGTON, Duke

BREWER & SHIPLEY

P&R/LP '71

Singles: 7-inch

A&M.................................... 4-8 68-69
BUDDAH.................................... 3-5 70
CAPITOL.................................... 3-5 74-75
KAMA SUTRA.................................... 3-5 70-73

Picture Sleeves

KAMA SUTRA.................................... 3-6 72

LPs: 10/12-inch 33rpm

A&M.................................... 12-15 68
ACCORD.................................... 5-10 83
CAPITOL.................................... 8-10 74-75
KAMA SUTRA.................................... 10-12 70-76
Members: Mike Brewer; Tom Shipley.

BRIAN & BRENDA

R&B '78

Singles: 7-inch

ROCKET.................................... 3-5 76-78
Members: Brian Russell; Brenda Russell.

BRICK

P&R/R&B/LP '76

Singles: 12-inch 33/45rpm

BANG.................................... 4-6 79-82

Singles: 7-inch

BANG.................................... 3-4 76-82
MAINSTREET.................................... 3-5 76
STREET.................................... 3-5 76

LPs: 10/12-inch 33rpm

BANG.................................... 5-10 76-82
Members: Jimmy Brown; Regi Hargis; Eddie Irons; Ray Ransom; Don Nevins.

BRICKELL, Edie
(With the New Bohemians)

P&R/LP '88

Singles: 7-inch

GEFFEN.................................... 3-4 88-90

Picture Sleeves

GEFFEN.................................... 3-4 88-89

LPs: 10/12-inch 33rpm

GEFFEN.................................... 5-8 88-90

BRIDES of FUNKENSTEIN

R&B/LP '78

Singles: 7-inch

ATLANTIC.................................... 3-4 78-80

LPs: 10/12-inch 33rpm

ATLANTIC.................................... 5-10 78-80
Members: Lynn Mabry; Dawn Silva.
Also see PARLIAMENT

BRIDGES, Alicia

P&R/R&B/LP '78

Singles: 12-inch 33/45rpm

SECOND WAVE.................................... 4-6 84
POLYDOR.................................... 4-6 78-79

Singles: 7-inch

A.V.I..................................... 3-4 82
MEGA.................................... 3-5 72
POLYDOR.................................... 3-4 78-79

SECOND WAVE 3-4 84
ZODIAC.. 3-5 73

LPs: 10/12–inch 33rpm

POLYDOR................................. 5-10 78-79

BRIDGEWATER, Dee Dee

R&B/LP '78

Singles: 12–inch 33/45rpm

ELEKTRA..................................... 4-6 79-80

Singles: 7–inch

ELEKTRA..................................... 3-5 78-79

LPs: 10/12–inch 33rpm

ATLANTIC................................. 8-10 76
ELEKTRA.................................. 5-10 78-80

BRIEF ENCOUNTER

R&B '76

Singles: 7–inch

CAPITOL...................................... 3-5 76-77
SEVENTY SEVEN 3-5 72-73

Members: Maurice Whittington; Gary Bailey; Larry Bailey; Belmont Bailey; Monte Bailey.

BRIGGS, Lillian

P&R '55

Singles: 78rpm

EPIC.. 4-8 56

Singles: 7–inch

ABC-PAR 4-8 61
CORAL....................................... 5-10 59-60
EPIC.. 10-20 56
SUNBEAM 5-10 58

EPs: 7–inch 33/45rpm

EPIC (7163 "High Priestess of Rock 'N' Roll") 20-30 56

Also see HAWKINS, Screamin' Jay / Lillian Briggs

BRIGHT, Larry
(Pete Roberts)

P&R '60

Singles: 7–inch

BRIGHT... 4-8 65
DEL-FI (Except 4204) 5-10 63-64
DEL-FI (4204 "Surfin' Queen").. 10-20 63
DONNA 4-8 64
DOT... 4-8 66
EDIT 8-12 62
HIGHLAND................................ 8-12 61
JOJO 3-5 76
ORIGINAL SOUND 3-5 71
RENDEZVOUS (124 "Hold Me"). 8-10 60
(Reissued as by Pete Roberts.)
TIDE (006 thru 1083) 10-20 60-62

Also see ROBERTS, Pete

BRIGHT, Larry / Humdingers

Singles: 7–inch

JAYE JOSEPH 4-8 64

Also see BRIGHT, Larry

BRIGHTER SIDE of DARKNESS

P&R/R&B '72

Singles: 7–inch

STAR VUE 5-10

20TH FOX....................................3-5 72-75

LPs: 10/12–inch 33rpm

20TH FOX..................................8-10 73

Members: Darryl Lamont; Ralph Eskridge; Larry Washington; Randolph Murph.

BRILEY, Martin

P&R '83

Singles: 7–inch

EMI AMERICA 3-4 84
MERCURY.....................................3-4 81-84

LPs: 10/12–inch 33rpm

MERCURY..................................5-10 81-85

Also see GREENSLADE

BRIMMER, Charles

R&B '75

Singles: 7–inch

CHELSEA 3-5 75-76

LPs: 10/12–inch 33rpm

CHELSEA 8-10 76-77

BRINKLEY & PARKER

R&B '74

Singles: 7–inch

DARNEL 3-5 74

BRISCOE, Jimmy, & Little Beavers

R&B '73

Singles: 7–inch

ATLANTIC.....................................3-5 71
J-CITY 3-5 72
PHI-KAPPA...................................3-5 73-75
SALSOUL 3-4 79
WANDERICK.................................3-5 77

LPs: 10/12–inch 33rpm

PHI-KAPPA................................10-12 74
WANDERICK...............................8-10 77

Members: Jimmy Briscoel; Stanford Stansbury; Robert Makins; Kevin Brown; Maurice Pully.

BRISTOL, Johnny

P&R/R&B/LP '74

Singles: 7–inch

ATLANTIC.....................................3-5 76-78
HANDSHAKE.................................3-4 80-81
MGM 3-5 74-75

LPs: 10/12–inch 33rpm

ATLANTIC...................................5-10 76-78
HANDSHAKE...............................5-10 81
MGM 8-12 74-75

Also see ALTON & JOHNNY
Also see STEWART, Amii, & Johnny Bristol

BRISTOL, Johnny, & Spyder Turner

Singles: 7–inch

POLYDOR 3-4 83

Also see BRISTOL, Johnny
Also see TURNER, Spyder

BRITISH LIONS

P&R/LP '78

Singles: 7–inch

RSO 3-5 78

LPs: 10/12-inch 33rpm

RSO 5-10 78

Members: John Fiddler; Dale Griffin; Overend Watts; Ray Major; Morgan Fisher.

Also see MOTT the HOOPLE

BRITNY FOX

P&R/LP '88

Singles: 7-inch

COLUMBIA 3-4 88-89

LPs: 10/12-inch 33rpm

COLUMBIA 5-8 88-89

Member: Dean Davidson.

BRITTEN, Benjamin

LP '63

LPs: 10/12-inch 33rpm

LONDON 10-20 63

BROADWAY

P&R/R&B '76

Singles: 7-inch

GRANITE 3-5 76

HILLTAK 3-4 78

LPs: 10/12-inch 33rpm

HILLTAK 8-10 79

BROMBERG, David

LP '72

Singles: 7-inch

COLUMBIA 3-5 72-73

FANTASY 3-4 77-79

LPs: 10/12-inch 33rpm

ATLANTIC 5-10 80

COLUMBIA 8-12 72-77

FANTASY 8-12 76-80

Also see GRATEFUL DEAD

Also see HARRISON, George

Also see LOGGINS & MESSINA / David Bromberg

Also see SAHM, Doug

BRONNER BROTHERS

R&B '84

Singles: 7-inch

NEIGHBOR 3-4 84

BRONSKI BEAT

P&R/D&D '84

Singles: 12-inch 33/45rpm

MCA 4-6 84-86

Singles: 7-inch

MCA 3-4 84-86

Picture Sleeves

MCA 3-4 84

LPs: 10/12-inch 33rpm

MCA 5-10 85-86

Members: Jimmy Somerville; Steve Bronski; Larry Steinbachek.

Also see COMMUNARDS

Also see SOMERVILLE, Jimmy

BROOD, Herman

(With Wild Romance)

P&R/LP '79

Singles: 7-inch

ARIOLA AMERICA 3-4 79

LPs: 10/12-inch 33rpm

ARIOLA AMERICA 8-10 79-80

TOWNHOUSE 5-10 82

BROOKINS, Robert

R&B '86

Singles: 12-inch 33/45rpm

MCA 4-6 86

Singles: 7-inch

MCA 3-4 86

BROOKLYN BRIDGE

(Johnny Maestro & Brooklyn Bridge)

P&R '68

Singles: 7-inch

BROOKLYN BRIDGE (881 "Christmas Is") 10-15 88

BUDDAH 4-8 68-72

COLLECTABLES 3-4 84

ERIC 3-5 78

FLASHBACK 3-4 70s

HARVEY (500 "Worst That Could Happen") 5-10 81

(Colored vinyl.)

RADIO ACTIVE GOLD 3-4

LPs: 10/12-inch 33rpm

BUDDAH (5000 series) 20-25 69-72

BUDDAH (69000 series) 5-10 84

COLLECTABLES 5-10 80s

Members: Johnny Maestro; Fred Ferrara; Les Cauchi; Mike Gregorio; Tom Sullivan; Carolyn Wood; Jimmy Rosica; Richie Macioce; Artie Cantanzarita; Shelly Davis; Joe Ruvio.

Also see ISLEY BROTHERS / Brooklyn Bridge

Also see MAESTRO, Johnny

BROOKLYN DREAMS

P&R '77

Singles: 12-inch 33/45rpm

CASABLANCA 4-6 79

MILLENNIUM 4-6 78

Singles: 7-inch

CASABLANCA 3-4 79-80

MILLENNIUM 3-5 77-78

LPs: 10/12-inch 33rpm

CASABLANCA 5-10 79-80

MILLENNIUM 8-10 77

Members: Joe Esposito; Eddie Hokenson; Bruce Sudano.

Also see ESPOSITO, Joe "Bean"

Also see SUMMER, Donna

BROOKS, Donnie

P&R '60

Singles: 7-inch

CHALLENGE 4-8 66

COLLECTABLES 3-4 81

DJ 4-8 65

ERA (3000 series) 5-10 59-62

ERA (3100 series) 4-6 68

HAPPY TIGER 3-5 70-71

MIDSONG 3-5 79

OAK 3-5 71

REPRISE 3-5 64-65
YARDBIRD.................................. 3-6 68-69

Picture Sleeves

ERA.. 8-12 60-61

Promotional Singles

ERA ("Mission Bell"/"Doll House") 50-75 60
(Distributed during a personal appearance.)

LPs: 10/12-inch 33rpm

ERA (105 "The Happiest") 30-40 61
OAK... 8-10 71
WISHBONE................................. 5-10 75
Also see BUSH, Dick
Also see FAIRE, Johnny
Also see JORDAN, Johnny

BROOKS, Ella

R&B '87

Singles: 7-inch

QMI 3-4 87

BROOKS, Eloise, & Dreamers

Singles: 78rpm

ALADDIN (3303 "My Plea")....... 20-30 55

Singles: 7-inch

ALADDIN (3303 "My Plea")... 100-150 55

BROOKS, Garth

C&W '89

Singles: 7-inch

CAPITOL..................................... 3-4 89-92

LPs: 10/12-inch 33rpm

CAPITOL..................................... 5-8 90-92

BROOKS, Hadda

(Hadda Brooks Trio)

R&B '47

Singles: 78rpm

LONDON................................ 10-15 50
MODERN 10-20 45-52
MODERN MUSIC..................... 10-20 47
OKEH 5-10 54

Singles: 7-inch

ALWIN.. 3-5 69
ARWIN 5-10 59
LONDON (684 "I Hadn't Anyone Till You")................................. 25-50 50
MODERN (100 series) 15-25 52
MODERN (804 "Let's Be Sweethearts Again") 50-75 51
MODERN (825 "When a Woman Cries") 50-75 51
MODERN (841 "I Feel So Good")..................................... 50-75 51
MODERN (861 "Romance in the Dark")............................. 40-60 52
MODERN (1008 "Close Your Eyes").................................... 10-15 56
MODERN MUSIC (Colored vinyl) . 4-6 86
OKEH 15-25 54

EPs: 7-inch 33/45rpm

LONDON (6149 "Presenting Hadda Brooks") 25-40 54
MODERN (114 "Boogie")...........30-50 52

LPs: 10/12-inch 33rpm

CROWN (5010 "Femme Fatale") 25-50 57
CROWN (5374 "Hadda Brooks Sings & Swings") 15-25 63
MODERN (1210 "Femme Fatale") 50-100 56
Members: Hadda Brooks; Basie Day; Al Wichard; Jim Black.

BROOKS, Hadda / Pete Johnson

LPs: 10/12-inch 33rpm

CROWN (5058 "Boogie")...........20-35 58
Also see BROOKS, Hadda
Also see JOHNSON, Pete

BROOKS, Louis

(With His Hi-Toppers)

R&B '55

Singles: 78rpm

EXCELLO 8-15 52-57

Singles: 7-inch

EXCELLO (2000 series) 25-50 52-53
EXCELLO (2100 series) 15-25 57-59

BROOKS, Mel

R&B '82

Singles: 7-inch

WMOT...3-4 82
Also see REINER, Carl, & Mel Brooks

BROOKS, Nancy

P&R '79

Singles: 7-inch

ARISTA...3-4 79

BROOKS, Ramona

R&B '77

Singles: 7-inch

MANHATTAN.................................3-5 77
U.A. 3-5 77

LPs: 10/12-inch 33rpm

MANHATTAN...............................8-10 78

BROOM, Bobby

R&B '81

Singles: 7-inch

ARISTA...3-4 81-84
GRP 3-4 81

LPs: 10/12-inch 33rpm

GRP 5-10 81

BROS

P&R/LP '88

Singles: 7-inch

EPIC..3-4 88

Picture Sleeves

EPIC..3-4 88

LPs: 10/12-inch 33rpm

EPIC..5-8 88

BROTHER BLUES & Back Room Boys
(Champion Jack Dupree)

Singles: 78rpm

ABBEY 20-30 50

Also see DUPREE, Champion Jack

BROTHER BONES
(With His Shadows)

R&B '49

Singles: 78rpm

TEMPO (652 "Sweet Georgia Brown") 15-25 48

Member: Joe Darensbourg.
Also see DARENSBOURG, Joe

BROTHER to BROTHER

P&R/R&B '74

Singles: 7-inch

SUGAR HILL................................ 3-4 81
TURBO...................................... 3-5 74-77
WIN OR LOSE 3-5

LPs: 10/12-inch 33rpm

SUGAR HILL............................... 5-10 81
TURBO...................................... 10-12 74-77

Members: Michael Burton; Bill Jones; Frankie Prescott; Yogi Horton.

BROTHERHOOD

R&B '76

Singles: 7-inch

COLUMBIA 3-5 70
DIAL 3-6 69
MCA 3-4 78
RCA.. 3-6 69

Picture Sleeves

RCA.. 4-8 69

LPs: 10/12-inch 33rpm

MCA 5-10 78
RCA... 12-15 69

Members: Drake Levin; Michael Smith; Phil Volk; Ron Collins.
Also see REVERE, Paul, & Raiders
Also see WOMACK, Bobby

BROTHERHOOD of MAN

P&R/LP '70

Singles: 7-inch

BELL 3-5 74
DERAM 3-5 70-72
LONDON.................................... 5-8
PRIVATE STOCK 3-5 77
PYE 3-5 75-76

LPs: 10/12-inch 33rpm

DERAM 10-12 70
PYE.. 8-10 76

Member: Tony Burrows.
Also see BURROWS, Tony

BROTHERLY LOVE

R&B '72

Singles: 7-inch

MUSIC MERCHANT 5-10 72

LPs: 10/12-inch 33rpm

MUSIC MERCHANT (104 "Brotherly Love")....................................25-50 72

BROTHERS by CHOICE

R&B '78

Singles: 7-inch

ALA 3-4 78-80
FRETONE....................................3-5 75

BROTHERS FOUR

P&R/LP '60

Singles: 7-inch

COLUMBIA (Except 43547)...........4-8 59-69
COLUMBIA (43547 "Ratman & Bobbin in the Clipper Caper") 5-10 69
FANTASY 3-5 70

Picture Sleeves

COLUMBIA 5-10 60-63

LPs: 10/12-inch 33rpm

COLUMBIA 10-20 59-69
FANTASY 8-12 70
FIRST AMERICAN........................5-10 81
GRT 10-12 77
HARMONY..................................6-10 69-72

Members: Bob Flick; Dick Foley; John Paine; Mike Kirkland.

BROTHERS GUIDING LIGHT
(Featuring David)

R&B '73

Singles: 7-inch

MERCURY....................................3-5 73

BROTHERS JOHNSON

P&R '75

Singles: 12-inch 33/45rpm

A&M (Black vinyl)...........................4-6 78-85
A&M (Colored vinyl).....................5-10 78-85

Singles: 7-inch

A&M 3-4 76-88

Picture Sleeves

A&M 3-5 76-85

LPs: 10/12-inch 33rpm

A&M (Except PR-4714)................5-10 76-85
A&M (PR-4714 "Blam").............15-25 79
(Picture disc.)

Members: Louis Johnson; George Johnson.
Also see JONES, Quincy, & Brothers Johnson

BROTHERS of SOUL

R&B '68

Singles: 7-inch

BOO (112 "Love Is Fever")........15-25 70
BOO (1004 "Hurry Don't Linger") 15-25 68
BOO (1005 "Come on Back") 15-25 68
BOO (1006 "I'd Be Grateful")...50-100 69
SHOCK 5-10

Members: Richard Knight; Robert Eaton; Fred Bridges.

BROWN, Al, and His Tunetoppers
(Featuring Cookie Brown)

P&R/R&B '60

Singles: 7–inch

AMY 5-10 60-61

EPs: 7–inch 33/45rpm

AMY (1 "Madison Dance Party") 35-45 60

LPs: 10/12–inch 33rpm

AMY (1 "Madison Dance Party") 45-50 60

BROWN, Alex

P&R/D&D '85

Singles: 12–inch 33/45rpm

MERCURY 4-6 85

Singles: 7–inch

MERCURY 3-4 85
ROXBURY 3-5 76

BROWN, Arthur
(Crazy World of Arthur Brown; Arthur Brown's Kingdom Come)

P&R/LP '68

Singles: 7–inch

ATLANTIC 4-8 68
TRACK 4-6 68-69

LPs: 10/12–inch 33rpm

ATLANTIC 15-20 68
GULL 8-10 75
PASSPORT 10-12 74
RECKLESS 5-10 88
TRACK 10-15 68

Also see ATOMIC ROOSTER
Also see PARSONS, Alan, Project

BROWN, Bobby

P&R/R&B/LP '86

Singles: 12–inch 33/45rpm

MCA 4-6 86

Singles: 7–inch

MCA 3-4 86-89

Picture Sleeves

MCA 3-4 86-89

LPs: 10/12–inch 33rpm

MCA 5-10 86-89

Also see MEDEIROS, Glenn, & Bobby Brown
Also see NEW EDITION

BROWN, Boots
(With Blockbusters; with Pelugelpipers; with Dan Drew; Shorty Rogers)

P&R '58

Singles: 78rpm

RCA 3-5 53-57

Singles: 7–inch

DOT 3-6 68
RCA 5-10 53-60

EPs: 7–inch 33/45rpm

GROOVE (1000 "Rock That Beat") 20-35 55

LPs: 10/12–inch 33rpm

GROOVE (1000 "Rock That Beat") 50-100 55

BROWN, Buster

P&R/R&B '60

Singles: 78rpm

FIRE (1008 "Fannie Mae") 300-400 59

Singles: 7–inch

ABC 3-4 73
CHECKER 5-10 63
FIRE 10-15 59-62
GWENN 5-10 62
NOCTURN 5-10
OLDIES 45 3-5
RCA 3-5 74
ROULETTE 3-4 72
SEROCK 4-8 63

LPs: 10/12–inch 33rpm

COLLECTABLES 6-8 88
FIRE (102 "The New King of the Blues") 100-200 60
(Blue cover. Track listing includes *Blueberry Hill* and *When Things Go Wrong.*)
FIRE (102 "The New King of the Blues") 75-125 60
(White cover. With *Blueberry Hill* and *When Things Go Wrong* replaced by *Going on a Picnic* and *Corena.*)
SOUFFLE 10-15 73

BROWN, Charles
(With Johnny Moore's Three Blazers)

R&B '49

Singles: 78rpm

ALADDIN 10-20 49-57
CASH 5-10 57
HOLLYWOOD 8-12 54
SWING TIME 15-25 52

Singles: 7–inch

ACE 5-10 59
ALADDIN (3076 "Black Night") 50-100 51
ALADDIN (3091 "I'll Always Be in Love with You") 25-50 51
ALADDIN (3092 "Seven Long Days") 25-50 52
ALADDIN (3116 "Hard Times") .. 25-50 52
ALADDIN (3120 "My Last Affair") 25-50 52
ALADDIN (3138 "Without Your Love") 25-50 52
ALADDIN (3157 "Rollin' Like a Pebble in the Sand") 50-75 52
ALADDIN (3163 "Evening Shadows") 25-50 53
ALADDIN (3176 "Take Me") 25-50 53
ALADDIN (3191 "Lonesome Feeling") 25-50 53
ALADDIN (3200 & 3300 series). 15-30 53-58
CASH 15-25 57
EAST-WEST 10-20 58
GALAXY 5-8 66

HOLLYWOOD (1006 "Pleading for Your Love") 20-30 54
IMPERIAL 5-10 62-63
JEWEL 3-5 71-74
KING 5-10 60-64
LIBERTY 3-4 84
LILLY 5-10 62
MAINSTREAM 4-8 65
NOLA 5-10 63
STARDAY 3-6 69
SWING TIME (253 "I'll Miss You") 50-100 52
SWING TIME (259 "Be Fair with Me") 50-100 52

LPs: 10/12–inch 33rpm

ALADDIN (702 "Mood Music") 200-300 52
(10–inch LP. Black vinyl.)
ALADDIN (702 "Mood Music") 450-550 52
(10–inch LP. Colored vinyl.)
ALADDIN (809 "Mood Music") 100-200 57
BIG TOWN 8-10 77-78
BLUESWAY 8-10 70
IMPERIAL (9178 "Million Sellers") 50-75 62
JEWEL 8-15 72
KING (775 "Christmas Songs"). 30-50 61
KING (878 "The Great Charles Brown") 30-50 63
KING (5000 series) 5-10
MAINSTREAM (300 series) 8-12 72
MAINSTREAM (6000/56000 series) 10-20 65
SCORE (4011 "Driftin' Blues") 100-150 57
Also see BROWN, Floyd
Also see CHARLES, Ray / Charles Brown
Also see McCRACKLIN, Jimmy / T-Bone Walker / Charles Brown
Also see MOORE, Johnny
Also see SCOTT, Mabel

BROWN, Charles / Basin Street Boys

Singles: 78rpm

CASH 5-10 57

Singles: 7–inch

CASH (1052 "Lost in the Night") 10-20 57
Also see BASIN STREET BOYS

BROWN, Charles / Lloyd Glenn

Singles: 78rpm

HOLLYWOOD 5-10 54

Singles: 7–inch

HOLLYWOOD (1021 "Merry Christmas Baby") 20-30 54
Also see GLENN, Lloyd

BROWN, Charles, & Jimmy McCracklin

LPs: 10/12–inch 33rpm

IMPERIAL (9257 "Best of the Blues") 25-50 64
Also see McCRACKLIN, Jimmy

BROWN, Charles, & Amos Milburn
(Charles Brown / Amos Milburn)

Singles: 7–inch

ACE 5-10 59
KING (5000 series) 5-10 61
KING (6000 series) 3-5 75

LPs: 10/12–inch 33rpm

GRAND PRIX (421 "Original Blues Sound") 10-15 64
(With Jackie Shane and Bob Marshall & Crystals.)
Also see BROWN, Charles
Also see MILBURN, Amos

BROWN, Chuck, & Soul Searchers

R&B '78

Singles: 12–inch 33/45rpm

SOURCE 4-8 78-79

Singles: 7–inch

SOUL SEARCHERS 3-4 84
SOURCE 3-5 78-80
T.T.E.D. 3-4 84

LPs: 10/12–inch 33rpm

SOURCE 5-10 79

BROWN, Clarence "Gatemouth"

R&B '49

Singles: 78rpm

ALADDIN 10-20 47
PEACOCK 10-20 49-57

Singles: 7–inch

CUE 4-8 64
PEACOCK (1600 "Just Got Lucky") 50-100 52
PEACOCK (1607 thru 1619) 20-40 52-53
PEACOCK (1633 thru 1696) 10-25 54-60

LPs: 10/12–inch 33rpm

MUSIC IS MEDICINE 8-10 78
ROUNDER 5-10 82
Also see McVEA, Jack

BROWN, Cleo

R&B '49

Singles: 78rpm

BLUE 5-10 51
CAPITOL 5-10 49

BROWN, Clyde

R&B '73

Singles: 7–inch

ATLANTIC 3-5 73-74

BROWN, Danny Joe, & Danny Joe Brown Band

LP '81

Singles: 7–inch

EPIC 3-4 81

LPs: 10/12–inch 33rpm

EPIC 5-10 81

Also see MOLLY HATCHET

BROWN, Dee, & Lola Grant

R&B '66

Singles: 7–inch

SHURFINE.................................... 4-8 66

BROWN, Dennis

R&B '82

Singles: 12–inch 33/45rpm

A&M 4-6 82

Singles: 7–inch

A&M 3-4 81-82

STUDIO ONE................................. 3-5 72

LPs: 10/12–inch 33rpm

A&M 5-10 81-82

BROWN, Don

P&R '78

Singles: 7–inch

FIRST AMERICAN........................ 3-5 77-78

BROWN, Gloria D.

R&B '86

Singles: 7–inch

KRYSTAL..................................... 3-4 86

BROWN, James

(With His Famous Flames; with J.B.s)

R&B '56

Singles: 12–inch 33/45rpm

CHURCHILL.................................. 4-6 83

POLYDOR..................................... 4-6 78

Singles: 78rpm

FEDERAL (Except 12348) 10-15 56-58

FEDERAL (12348 "I Want You So Bad") 20-40 59

Singles: 7–inch

AUGUSTA.................................... 3-4 83

BACKSTREET 3-4 83

BETHLEHEM 8-15 69

CHURCHILL.................................. 3-4 83

FEDERAL (12000 series)............ 8-15 56-60

(Monaural.)

FEDERAL (S-12352 "I've Got to Change") 20-30 59

(Stereo.)

FEDERAL (S-12361 "Good, Good Lovin").................................. 20-30 59

(Stereo.)

KING (5000 series) 8-15 60-65

KING (6000 series) 5-10 65-71

PEOPLE....................................... 3-6 71-76

POLYDOR.................................... 3-5 71-84

SCOTTI BROTHERS 3-4 86-88

SMASH 5-10 64-66

T.K.. 3-5 80-81

Picture Sleeves

KING (5842 "Oh Baby Don't You Weep") 5-10 64

POLYDOR 3-5 72-84

SCOTTI BROTHERS.....................3-4 85-86

SMASH 5-10 64

EPs: 7–inch 33/45rpm

KING 15-30 59-63

SMASH 10-20 65-66

(Jukebox issues only.)

LPs: 10/12–inch 33rpm

AGUSTA SOUND 5-8

AUDIO FIDELITY (326 "James Brown") 8-12 83

CHURCHILL 5-10 83

HRB 8-10 73

KING (610 "Please, Please, Please") 100-150 59

(Cover pictures a woman's legs.)

KING (635 "Try Me") 100-150 59

(Cover pictures a woman with a smoking gun.)

KING (683 "James Brown & His Famous Flames *Think*").......100-150 60

(Cover pictures a baby.)

KING (683 "James Brown & His Famous Flames *Think*")...........25-40 61

(Cover has pictures of James Brown.)

KING (743 "The Always Amazing James Brown and the Famous Flames") 50-75 61

(Cover is pink and blue.)

KING (771 "Jump Around")........50-75 62

KING (780 "The Exciting James Brown") 50-75 62

KING (804 "James Brown and the Famous Flames Tour the U.S.A." 50-75 62

KING (826 "Apollo Theatre Presents the James Brown Show") 40-60 63

KING (851 "Prisoner of Love")...30-50 63

KING (883 "Pure Dynamite") 25-50 64

KING (900 series) 15-25 65-66

KING (1000 & 1100 series, except 1038) 10-15 67-71

KING (1038 "Thinking About Little Willie John") 30-35 68

POLYDOR 5-10 71-84

SCOTTI BROTHERS....................5-8 86-88

SMASH 10-20 64-68

SOLID SMOKE 5-10 80-81

T.K. 5-10 80

Also see BAMBAATAA, Afrika, James Brown
Also see BYRD, Bobby, & James Brown
Also see J.B.s
Also see POETS

BROWN, James, & Vicki Anderson

P&R '67

Singles: 7–inch

KING 4-6 67-70

Also see ANDERSON, Vicki

BROWN, James, Band

Singles: 7-inch

KING 4-8 61

Also see WESLEY, Fred, & Horny Horns

BROWN, James, & Lyn Collins

P&R/R&B '72

Singles: 7-inch

POLYDOR.................................... 3-5 72

Also see COLLINS, Lyn

BROWN, James, & Marva Whitney

Singles: 7-inch

KING 3-6 69

Also see BROWN, James
Also see WHITNEY, Marva

BROWN, Jim Ed
(Jim Edward Brown)

C&W '65

Singles: 7-inch

RCA (Except 8000 & 9000 series) 3-5 69-81
RCA (8000 & 9000 series) 3-8 65-68

LPs: 10/12-inch 33rpm

RCA (Except 3000 & 4000 series) 5-10 73-81
RCA (3000 & 4000 series) 8-12 66-72
(With "LPM" or "LSP" prefix.)

Session: Mary Cates; Margie Cates.
Also see BROWNS
Also see CATES SISTERS
Also see SOME of CHET'S FRIENDS

BROWN, Jim Ed, & Helen Cornelius

C&W '76

Singles: 7-inch

RCA.. 3-5 76-81

Also see BROWN, Jim Edward
Also see CORNELIUS, Helen

BROWN, Jim Edward & Maxine: see BROWNS

BROWN, Jim Edward, Maxine & Bonnie: see BROWNS

BROWN, Jocelyn

P&R/R&B/D&D '84

Singles: 12-inch 33/45rpm

JELLYBEAN................................. 4-6 86
VINYL DREAMS 4-6 84

Singles: 7-inch

JELLYBEAN................................. 3-4 86
VINYL DREAMS 3-4 84
W.B. 3-4 86-87

LPs: 10/12-inch 33rpm

JELLYBEAN............................ 5-10 86
VINYL DREAMS 5-10 84

Also see INNER LIFE
Also see SALSOUL ORCHESTRA

BROWN, Julie

LP '85

Singles: 7-inch

BULLETZ 3-5 83
RHINO.. 3-4 84
SIRE.. 3-4 87

Picture Sleeves

BULLETZ 3-5 83

LPs: 10/12-inch 33rpm

RHINO 5-10 85

BROWN, Julius

D&D '83

Singles: 12-inch 33/45rpm

WEST END 4-6 83-84

BROWN, Les, & His Orchestra
(With His Band of Renown; with His Duke University Blue Devils)

P&R '39

Singles: 78rpm

BLUEBIRD 5-10 38-40
CAPITOL....................................3-5 56-57
COLUMBIA 5-10 42-57
CONQUEROR 5-10 41
CORAL......................................3-6 53-57
DECCA 5-10 36-40
OKEH.......................................5-10 41-42

Singles: 7-inch

CAPITOL....................................3-8 56-59
COLUMBIA 5-10 50-60
CORAL......................................3-6 53-59
SIGNATURE 3-6 60

EPs: 7-inch 33/45rpm

CAPITOL...................................5-10 56-58
COLUMBIA 5-10 54-56
CORAL......................................5-10 53-56

LPs: 10/12-inch 33rpm

CAPITOL..................................10-20 56-59
COLUMBIA 10-25 50-61
CORAL.....................................15-30 55-60
HARMONY..................................8-15 59
KAPP 8-15 59
MEDALLION 8-15 61

Also see DAY, Doris

BROWN, Louise

P&R '61

Singles: 7-inch

WITCH 5-10 61

BROWN, Maxine

P&R '60

Singles: 7-inch

ABC..3-4 75
ABC-PAR.................................5-10 61-62
AVCO EMBASSY 3-5 71
COLLECTABLES..........................3-4 81
COMMONWEALTH UNITED.........4-6 69-70
ERIC 3-4 83
NOMAR.....................................5-10 61
WAND 5-10 63-67
WHAM...4-8

Picture Sleeves

WAND (135 "Ask Me") 10-15 63
WHAM (7036 "All in My Mind") ..10-15

EPs: 7–inch 33/45rpm

COMMONWEALTH UNITED (1001 "Maxine Brown") 5-10 69
(Promotional issue only.)

LPs: 10/12–inch 33rpm

COLLECTABLES 6-8 88
COMMONWEALTH UNITED 10-12 69
GUEST STAR 10-12 64
WAND 15-25 63-67

Also see ADAMS, Faye / Little Esther / Maxine Brown
Also see JACKSON, Chuck, & Maxine Brown

BROWN, Maxine / Irma Thomas

LPs: 10/12–inch 33rpm

GRAND PRIX 12-15 64

Also see BROWN, Maxine
Also see THOMAS, Irma

BROWN, Miquel

D&D '83

Singles: 12–inch 33/45rpm

TSR 4-6 83

Singles: 7–inch

POLYDOR................................. 3-4 79
TSR 3-4 83

LPs: 10/12–inch 33rpm

POLYDOR................................. 5-10 78
TSR 5-10 85

BROWN, Nappy

(With the Gibralters; with Southern Sisters)

P&R/R&B '55

Singles: 78rpm

SAVOY 5-10 55-57

Singles: 7–inch

SAVOY (1100 series)............... 10-20 55
SAVOY (1500 series)............... 10-15 57-60
SAVOY (1600 series)................. 5-10 61-63

LPs: 10/12–inch 33rpm

SAVOY (14002 "Nappy Brown Sings")................................ 50-100 57
SAVOY (14025 "The Right Time")................................... 40-60 60
SAVOY (14427 "Nappy Brown") . 8-15 77

BROWN, O'chi

R&B '86

Singles: 12–inch 33/45rpm

MERCURY 4-6 86

Singles: 7–inch

MERCURY 3-4 86

LPs: 10/12–inch 33rpm

MERCURY 5-10 86

BROWN, Odell

(With the Organ-izers)

LP '67

Singles: 7–inch

CADET 3-6 67-68

LPs: 10/12–inch 33rpm

CADET 10-15 67-69
PAULA 8-10 74

BROWN, Oscar, Jr.

P&R/R&B '74

Singles: 7–inch

ATLANTIC....................................3-5 74
COLUMBIA 5-10 60-62
FONTANA....................................4-8 65-66
MAD 8-12 59

LPs: 10/12–inch 33rpm

ATLANTIC....................................5-10
COLUMBIA 15-25 61-63
FONTANA..................................10-15 66

BROWN, Peter

P&R/R&B '77

Singles: 12–inch 33/45rpm

COLUMBIA 4-6 84
RCA 4-6 83

Singles: 7–inch

COLUMBIA 3-4 84
DRIVE...3-5 77-80
RCA 3-4 83

LPs: 10/12–inch 33rpm

COLUMBIA 5-10 84
DRIVE...5-10 78
RCA 5-10 82-83

BROWN, Peter, & Betty Wright

P&R/R&B '78

Singles: 7–inch

DRIVE...3-5 78

Also see BROWN, Peter
Also see WRIGHT, Betty

BROWN, Polly

P&R/R&B '75

Singles: 7–inch

ARIOLA AMERICA 3-5 75-76
BEL 3-5 73
GTO 3-5 74

Also see PICKETTYWITCH
Also see SWEET DREAMS

BROWN, Randy

(Randy Brown & Company)

R&B '78

Singles: 12–inch 33/45rpm

MILLENNIUM.................................4-6 78

Singles: 7–inch

CHOCOLATE CITY 3-4 80-81
IX CHAINS 3-5 75
PARACHUTE..................................3-5 78-79
STAX...3-4 80
TRUTH..3-5 74-75

LPs: 10/12–inch 33rpm

CHOCOLATE CITY 5-10 80-81
PARACHUTE..................................5-10 78-79
STAX...5-10 80-81

BROWN, Roy

(With His Mighty-Mighty Men)

R&B/C&W '48

Singles: 78rpm

DELUXE (1000 series)...............15-25 47-48

DELUXE (3300 thru 3318) 10-20 49-51
GOLD STAR 15-25 48
IMPERIAL 15-20 57
KING 10-20 52-57

Singles: 7–inch

BLUESWAY 4-8 67
DELUXE (3319 "Bar Room Blues")............................... 150-200 51
(Black vinyl.)
DELUXE (3319 "Bar Room Blues")............................... 200-400 51
(Colored vinyl.)
DELUXE (3323 "I've Got the Last Laugh Now") 75-100 51
(Black vinyl.)
DELUXE (3323 "I've Got the Last Laugh Now") 150-250 51
(Colored vinyl.)
FRIENDSHIP 5-10
GUSTO 3-4 83
HOME of the BLUES................ 15-25 60-61
IMPERIAL (5510 "Hip Shakin' Baby") 20-30 57
KING (4000 series) 25-50 52-56
KING (5000 series) 8-12 59-60
MERCURY 3-5 71
MOBILE FIDELITY...................... 3-5 72
TRU-LOVE 4-6

EPs: 7–inch 33/45rpm

KING (254 "Roy Brown")......... 50-100 53

LPs: 10/12–inch 33rpm

BLUESWAY 10-20 68-73
EPIC.. 10-15 71
INTERMEDIA 5-10 84
KING (956 "24 Hits") 35-45 66
KING (1100 series) 10-15 71
KING (5000 series) 8-10 79

Also see HARRIS, Wynonie / Roy Brown
Also see VINSON, Eddie / Roy Brown / Wynonie Harris

BROWN, Ruth
(With the Rhythmakers)

R&B '49

Singles: 78rpm

ATLANTIC (Except 800 series)... 8-12 51-57
ATLANTIC (800 series)............ 10-20 49-50

Singles: 7–inch

ATLANTIC (919 "Teardrops from My Eyes")............................ 200-250 50
ATLANTIC (948 "Shine On")..... 25-50 51
ATLANTIC (962 thru 993) 20-30 52-53
ATLANTIC (1005 thru 1091) 10-20 53-56
ATLANTIC (1100 series)........... 10-15 57-58
ATLANTIC (2000 series)............ 5-10 59-60
DECCA...................................... 4-8 64
MAINSTREAM 5-8
NOSLEN 4-8 64
PHILIPS 5-10 62
SYKE... 4-8 69

EPs: 7–inch 33/45rpm

ATLANTIC (505 "Ruth Brown Sings") 50-75 53
ATLANTIC (535 "Ruth Brown Sings") 50-75 53
ATLANTIC (585 "Ruth Brown Sings") 35-60 57
PHILIPS 10-15 62

LPs: 10/12–inch 33rpm

ATLANTIC (1308 "Last Date with Ruth Brown")............................50-70 59
ATLANTIC (SD-1308 "Last Date with Ruth Brown")..........................75-100 59
(Stereo.)
ATLANTIC (8004 "Ruth Brown") 50-75 57
(Black label.)
ATLANTIC (8004 "Ruth Brown") 30-40 60
(Red label.)
ATLANTIC (8026 "Miss Rhythm")..................................35-50 59
(Black label.)
ATLANTIC (8026 "Miss Rhythm")..................................35-50 59
(White label.)
ATLANTIC (8026 "Miss Rhythm")..................................15-25 60
(Red label.)
ATLANTIC (8080 "Best of Ruth Brown") 15-25 63
COBBLESTONE 8-10 72
DOBRE 5-10 78
MAINSTREAM (300 series).........8-10 72
MAINSTREAM (6000 series).....12-15 65
PHILIPS 12-15 62
SKYE 10-12 70

Also see BRADLEY, Will, & Ray McKinley
Also see JACKSON, Willis
Also see JOHNSON, Buddy

BROWN, Ruth, & Clyde McPhatter

R&B '55

Singles: 78rpm

ATLANTIC.................................8-12 55

Singles: 7–inch

ATLANTIC................................10-20 55

Also see BROWN, Ruth
Also see McPHATTER, Clyde

BROWN, Sam

P&R '89

Singles: 7–inch

A&M 3-4 89

Picture Sleeves

A&M 3-4 89

BROWN, Savoy: see SAVOY BROWN

BROWN, Sawyer: see SAWYER BROWN

BROWN, Sharon

R&B '82

Singles: 12–inch 33/45rpm

PROFILE.....................................4-6 83

Singles: 7–inch
PROFILE.................................... 3-4 82-83

BROWN, Shawn

R&B/D&D '85

Singles: 12–inch 33/45rpm
JWP... 4-6 85

Singles: 7–inch
JWP... 3-4 85

BROWN, Veda

R&B '73

Singles: 7–inch
RAKEN....................................... 3-5 75
STAX... 3-5 73-74

BROWN, Wini
(With the Boyfriends)

R&B '52

Singles: 78rpm
COLUMBIA 4-8 51
MERCURY 15-25 52

Singles: 7–inch
COLUMBIA (872 "A Good Man Is Hard to Find")..................... 10-20 51
JARO.................................... 10-15 60
MERCURY (5870 "Here in My Heart")........................... 75-125 52
MERCURY (8270 "Be Anything")........................... 75-125 52
Members: Wini Brown; Joe Van Loan; Percy Green; Fred Francis; Warren Suttles.
Also see DOGGETT, Bill
Also see HAMPTON, Lionel

BROWN SUGAR

P&R '76

Singles: 7–inch
ABKCO...................................... 3-5 72
CAPITOL.................................... 3-5 76
CHELSEA 3-5 73-74
Member: Clydie King.
Also see KING, Clydie

BROWNE, Duncan

LP '79

Singles: 7–inch
IMMEDIATE 3-6 69
RAK.. 3-5 72
SIRE... 3-4 79

LPs: 10/12–inch 33rpm
IMMEDIATE 10-15 68
SIRE... 5-10 79

BROWNE, Jackson

P&R/LP '72

Singles: 12–inch 33/45rpm
ASYLUM 4-6 81-82
ELEKTRA.................................. 4-8 89
(Promotional only.)

Singles: 7–inch
ASYLUM 3-4 72-86
COLUMBIA 3-4 86
ELEKTRA.................................. 3-4 80-89

Picture Sleeves
ASYLUM 3-5 80-86
ELEKTRA.....................................4-8 80

LPs: 10/12–inch 33rpm
ASYLUM (Except 5051)..............8-10 72-86
ASYLUM (5051 "Jackson Browne")...............................10-15 72
(With burlap cover.)
ASYLUM (5051 "Jackson Browne")..................................8-10 72
(Without burlap.)
ELEKTRA ("Jackson Browne's First Album")..................................25-35 67
(Promotional issue only.)
ELEKTRA (60830 "World in Motion")...................................5-8 89
MFSL (055 "Pretender")............20-40 81
Also see CLEMONS, Clarence, & Jackson Browne
Also see LINDLEY, David
Also see SPRINGSTEEN, Bruce / Jackson Browne

BROWNE, Reno, & Her Buckaroos: see HALEY, Bill

BROWNE, Tom

LP '79

Singles: 12–inch 33/45rpm
ARISTA.......................................4-6 83

Singles: 7–inch
ARISTA.......................................3-4 83-84
GRP 3-4 79-82

LPs: 10/12–inch 33rpm
ARISTA.....................................5-10 83-84
GRP 5-10 79-82

BROWNMARK

R&B '88

Singles: 7–inch
MOTOWN 3-4 88
Also see MAZARATI
Also see PRINCE

BROWNS
(Jim Edward & Maxine Brown; Jim Edward, Maxine & Bonnie Brown; with the Louisiana Hayride Band; Browns featuring Jim Edward Brown)

C&W '54

Singles: 78rpm
FABOR.......................................5-10 54-55
RCA 4-8 56-57

Singles: 7–inch
COLUMBIA 4-8 62
FABOR.....................................10-20 54-55
RCA (6480 thru 7427)...............10-15 56-58
RCA (47-7555 "The Three Bells")......................................5-10 59
(Monaural.)
RCA (61-7555 "The Three Bells").....................................10-15 59
(Stereo.)

RCA (47-7614 "Scarlet Ribbons") ... 5-10 59
(Monaural.)
RCA (61-7614 "Scarlet Ribbons") ... 10-15 59
(Stereo.)
RCA (47-7700 "Old Lampligher") 5-10 60
(Monaural.)
RCA (61-7700 "Old Lampligher") ... 10-15 60
(Stereo.)
RCA (47-7755 "Lonely Little Robin") ... 5-10 60
(Monaural.)
RCA (61-7755 "Lonely Little Robin") ... 10-15 60
(Stereo.)
RCA (47-7780 "Wiffenpoof Song") ... 5-10 60
(Monaural.)
RCA (61-7780 "Wiffenpoof Song") ... 10-15 60
(Stereo.)
RCA (47-7820 "Send Me the Pillow You Dream On") ... 5-10 60
(Monaural.)
RCA (61-7820 "Send Me the Pillow You Dream On") ... 10-15 60
(Monaural.)
RCA (7820 "Blue Christmas") ... 5-10 60
RCA (37-7866 "Angel's Dolly") .. 10-15 61
(Compact 33 single.)
RCA (47-7866 "Angel's Dolly") ... 4-8 61
RCA (37-7917 "My Baby's Gone") ... 10-15 61
(Compact 33 single.)
RCA (47-7917 "My Baby's Gone") 4-8 61
RCA (37-7969 "Foolish Pride") . 10-15 61
(Compact 33 single.)
RCA (47-7969 "Foolish Pride") ... 4-8 61
RCA (37-7997 "Remember Me") ... 10-15 62
(Compact 33 single.)
RCA (47-7997 "Remember Me") ... 4-8 62
RCA (8066 thru 9364) ... 4-8 62-67

Picture Sleeves

RCA (7700 "The Old Lampligher") ... 10-15 60
RCA (7755 "Lonely Little Robin") ... 10-15 60
RCA (7780 "Wiffenpoof Song") . 10-15 60

EPs: 7-inch 33/45rpm

RCA ... 10-20 57-60

LPs: 10/12-inch 33rpm

CAMDEN ... 8-12 65-68
RCA (1000 thru 3000 series) ... 5-10 75-81
(With "ANL1" or "AYL1" prefix.)
RCA (1438 Jim Edward, Maxine & Bonnie Brown") ... 35-55 57
(With "LPM" prefix.)
RCA (2000 series) ... 15-30 59-65
(With "LPM" or "LSP" prefix.)
RCA (3000 series) ... 12-20 65-67
(With "LPM" or "LSP" prefix.)
Members: Jim Edward Brown; Maxine Brown; Bonnie Brown.
Also see BROWN, Jim Ed
Also see BROWN, Maxine
Also see COOKE, Sam / Rod Lauren / Neil Sedaka / Browns

BROWNSVILLE

Singles: 7-inch

EPIC ... 3-4 79

LPs: 10/12-inch 33rpm

EPIC (Black vinyl) ... 8-10 79
EPIC (Colored vinyl) ... 12-15 79
Also see BROWNSVILLE STATION

BROWNSVILLE STATION

P&R/LP '72

Singles: 7-inch

BIG TREE ... 3-5 72-74
EPIC ... 3-5 79
HIDEOUT (1957 "Rock & Roll Holiday") ... 8-12 69
PALLADIUM ... 4-8 70
POLYDOR ... 3-5 70
PRIVATE STOCK ... 3-5 77
W.B. (7501 "That's Fine") ... 4-8 71

LPs: 10/12-inch 33rpm

BIG TREE ... 10-12 72-75
EPIC (Black vinyl) ... 8-10 78
EPIC (Colored vinyl) ... 10-20 78
(Promotional issue only.)
PALLADIUM (1004 "Brownsville Station") ... 20-25 70
PRIVATE STOCK ... 8-10 77
W.B. ... 12-15 70
Members: Tony Driggins; Cub Koda; Michael Lutz; Henry Weck; Bruce Nazarian.
Also see BROWNSVILLE
Also see SEGER, Bob

BRUBECK, Dave, Quartet

(Dave Brubeck Trio; Octet; with Paul Desmond)

LP '55

Singles: 78rpm

COLUMBIA ... 4-8 55-57
FANTASY ... 4-8 52-55

Singles: 7-inch

COLUMBIA (Except 40000 & 41000 series) ... 3-6 62-65
COLUMBIA (40000 & 41000 series) ... 5-10 55-61
FANTASY (500 series) ... 5-10 52-55

Picture Sleeves

COLUMBIA ... 5-10 61-63

EPs: 7–inch 33/45rpm

COLUMBIA 10-25 55-59
FANTASY................................ 15-30 51-57

LPs: 10/12–inch 33rpm

ATLANTIC (79 "Fantasy Years"). 8-12 74
COLUMBIA (566 "Jazz Goes to College") 50-75 54
COLUMBIA (590 "Dave Brubeck at Storyville") 50-75 54
COLUMBIA (622 "Brubeck Time")................................... 40-60 55
COLUMBIA (699 "Jazz: Red Hot and Cool") 40-60 55
COLUMBIA (826 "Dave Brubeck Quintet at Carnegie Hall 20-30 63
COLUMBIA (878 "Brubeck Plays Brubeck") 30-50 56
COLUMBIA (932 "Brubeck, Jay & Kai at Newport") 30-50 57
COLUMBIA (984 "Jazz Impressions of the U.S.A.") 30-50 57
COLUMBIA (1000 thru 1200 series) 20-35 57-59
COLUMBIA (1300 thru 2300 series) 12-25 59-65
COLUMBIA (6321 "Jazz Goes to College") 50-100 54
(10–inch LP.)
COLUMBIA (6322 "Jazz Goes to College") 50-75 54
(10–inch LP.)
COLUMBIA (6330 "Dave Brubeck at Storyville") 50-75 54
(10–inch LP.)
COLUMBIA (6331 "Dave Brubeck at Storyville") 50-75 54
(10–inch LP.)
COLUMBIA (8000 series) 20-45 57-59
(Stereo series.)
COLUMBIA (8100 thru 9300 series) 15-30 59-66
(Stereo series.)
CROWN 10-15 62-64
FANTASY (1 "Dave Brubeck Trio") 100-150 51
(10–inch LP. Colored vinyl.)
FANTASY (2 "Dave Brubeck Trio") 100-150 51
(10–inch LP. Colored vinyl.)
FANTASY (3 "Dave Brubeck Octet") 100-150 52
(10–inch LP. Colored vinyl.)
FANTASY (5 "Dave Brubeck Quartet with Paul Desmond") 100-150 52
(10–inch LP. Colored vinyl.)
FANTASY (7 "Dave Brubeck Quartet with Paul Desmond") 100-150 53
(10–inch LP. Colored vinyl.)
FANTASY (8 "At Storyville") .. 100-150 53
(10–inch LP. Colored vinyl.)
FANTASY (10 "Jazz at the Black Hawk") 100-150 53
(10–inch LP. Colored vinyl.)
FANTASY (11 "Jazz at Oberlin")............................ 100-150 53
(10–inch LP. Colored vinyl.)
FANTASY (13 "Jazz at the College of the Pacific")........ 100-150 54
(10–inch LP. Colored vinyl.)
FANTASY (16 "Old Sounds from San Francisco") 100-150 55
(10–inch LP. Colored vinyl.)
FANTASY (204 "Dave Brubeck Trio") 75-125 56
(Colored vinyl.)
FANTASY (205 "Dave Brubeck Trio") 50-100 56
FANTASY (210 "Jazz at the Black Hawk") 50-100 56
FANTASY (223 "Jazz at the College of the Pacific")...........50-100 56
FANTASY (229 "Dave Brubeck Quartet with Paul Desmond") 50-100 56
FANTASY (230 "Dave Brubeck Quartet with Paul Desmond") 50-100 56
FANTASY (239 "Dave Brubeck Octet")...................................50-100 56
FANTASY (240 "At Storyville") 50-100 57
FANTASY (245 "Jazz at Oberlin")...............................50-100 57
FANTASY (3300 series) 15-25 62
HORIZON 5-10 76
JAZZTONE (1272 "Dave Brubeck") 25-50 57

Members: Dave Brubeck; Paul Desmond; Cal Tjader; Dick Collins; David Van Kriedt; Joe Morello; Eugene Wright.

Also see ARMSTRONG, Louis
Also see BERNSTEIN, Leonard, & Dave Brubeck
Also see RUSHING, Jimmy
Also see TJADER, Cal

BRUBECK, Dave, & Paul Desmond

LP '76

Singles: 7–inch

A&M 3-5 76
HORIZON 3-5 75

LPs: 10/12–inch 33rpm

HORIZON 6-10 74-75

As a member of Dave Brubeck's group, Paul Desmond was often credited prominently on releases which, for consistency, appear in the Brubeck section.

Also see DESMOND, Paul

BRUBECK, Dave, & Gerry Mulligan

Singles: 7–inch

COLUMBIA 3-4 68

LPs: 10/12–inch 33rpm

COLUMBIA 8-15 68-73
VERVE 8-12 73

Also see BRUBECK, Dave
Also see MULLIGAN, Gerry

BRUCE, Jack

(Jack Bruce Band; with Friends)

LP '69,

Singles: 7–inch

RSO 3-5 74-75

LPs: 10/12–inch 33rpm

ATCO 10-15 69-71
EPIC 5-10 80
POLYDOR 8-12 72
RSO 5-10 74-77

Also see CREAM
Also see MAYALL, John
Also see ROCKET 88
Also see WEST, BRUCE & LAING

BRUCE, Jack, & Robin Trower

LP '82

LPs: 10/12–inch 33rpm

CHRYSALIS (1352 "Truce")........ 5-10 82

BRUCE, Jack, Bill Lordan & Robin Trower

LP '81

LPs: 10/12–inch 33rpm

CHRYSALIS (1324 "B.L.T.") 5-10 81

Also see BRUCE, Jack
Also see TROWER, Robin

BRUCE, Lenny

LP '75

Singles: 7–inch

FANTASY (Black vinyl) 5-10
FANTASY (Colored vinyl) 10-15

Picture Sleeves

W.B. (598 "The Law, Language and Lenny Bruce") 20-30 74

EPs: 7–inch 33/45rpm

FANTASY (2 "Curran Theater Concert")................... 10-20
(Promotional issue only.)

LPs: 10/12–inch 33rpm

CAPITOL (2630 "Why Did Lenny Bruce Die")............................ 15-20 66
DOUGLAS................................... 15-25 68-71
FANTASY (1 "Lenny Bruce") 50-75
(Promotional issue only.)
FANTASY (7001 "Lenny Bruce's Interviews of Our Times") 30-40 58
(THICK red vinyl.)
FANTASY (7001 "Lenny Bruce's Interviews of Our Times") 15-20
(Black vinyl.)
FANTASY (7001 "Lenny Bruce's Interviews of Our Times") 8-12
(THIN red vinyl.)
FANTASY (7003 "The Sick Humor of Lenny Bruce") 30-40 58
(THICK red vinyl.)
FANTASY (7003 "The Sick Humor of Lenny Bruce") 15-20
(Black vinyl.)
FANTASY (7003 "The Sick Humor of Lenny Bruce") 8-12
(THIN red vinyl.)
FANTASY (7007 "I Am Not a Nut, Elect Me") 30-40 59
(THICK red vinyl.)
FANTASY (7007 "I Am Not a Nut, Elect Me") 15-20
(Black vinyl.)
FANTASY (7007 "I Am Not a Nut, Elect Me") 8-12
(THIN red vinyl.)
FANTASY (7011 "Lenny Bruce, American") 30-40 62
(THICK red vinyl.)
FANTASY (7011 "Lenny Bruce, American") 15-20
(Black vinyl.)
FANTASY (7011 "Lenny Bruce, American") 8-12
(THIN red vinyl.)
FANTASY (7012 "The Best of Lenny Bruce") 25-30 63
(THICK red vinyl.)
FANTASY (7012 "The Best of Lenny Bruce") 15-20
(Black vinyl.)
FANTASY (7012 "The Best of Lenny Bruce") 8-12
(THIN red vinyl.)
FANTASY (7017 "Thank You Masked Man").........................10-15 72
FANTASY (34201 "Lenny Bruce Live at the Curran Theatre")...........10-15 72
FANTASY (79003 "The Real Lenny Bruce")...................................8-12 75
LENNY BRUCE RECORDS ("Recordings Submitted As Evidence in the San Francisco Obscenity Trial in March, 1962") 75-100 62
PHILLES (4010 "Lenny Bruce Is Out Again") 50-75 66
REPRISE (6329 "The Berkeley Concert")...............................15-20 69
U.A. (3580 "Midnight Concert").. 15-20 67
U.A. (9800 "At Carnegie Hall")... 15-20 71
W.B. (9101 "The Law, Language and Lenny Bruce") 10-20 74
(Promotional issue only.)

BRUCE & TERRY

P&R '64

Singles: 7-inch

COLUMBIA 5-10 64-66

Members: Bruce Johnston; Terry Melcher.
Also see BOONE, Pat
Also see HONDELLS
Also see JOHNSTON, Bruce
Also see MELCHER, Terry, & Bruce Johnston
Also see NEWTON, Wayne
Also see RIP CHORDS
Also see SAGITTARIUS

BRUFORD, Bill

LP '79

Singles: 7-inch

POLYDOR.............................. 3-5 78-80

LPs: 10/12-inch 33rpm

POLYDOR.............................. 5-10 79-80

Also see YES

BRUNSON, Tyrone "Tystick"

R&B '82

Singles: 12-inch 33/45rpm

BELIEVE in a DREAM................ 4-6 82-84

Singles: 7-inch

BELIEVE in a DREAM................ 3-4 82-84

LPs: 10/12-inch 33rpm

BELIEVE in a DREAM................ 5-10 82-84

Also see SPECIAL DELIVERY

BRYANT, Anita

P&R '59

Singles: 7-inch

CARLTON.............................. 4-8 58-61
COLUMBIA 4-8 61-67
DISNEYLAND 3-4
TRIP 3-5

Picture Sleeves

COLUMBIA 4-8 61-67
DISNEYLAND 3-5

EPs: 7-inch 33/45rpm

ACSP (1779 "See America
with AC") 5-10
(Promotional issue for AC Spark Plugs.)

LPs: 10/12-inch 33rpm

CARLTON.............................. 10-20 59-61
COLUMBIA 8-15 62-67
HARMONY 6-12

BRYANT, Anita / Jo Stafford & Gordon MacRae

Singles: 7-inch

COLUMBIA 5-10 60

Also see MacRAE, Gordon, & Jo Stafford

BRYANT, Leon

R&B '81

Singles: 7-inch

DE-LITE 3-4 81-84

LPs: 10/12-inch 33rpm

DE-LITE 5-10 84

BRYANT, Ray, Combo

P&R/R&B '60

Singles: 7-inch

ATLANTIC.............................. 4-8
CADET 3-6 66-67
COLUMBIA 4-8 60-64
SIGNATURE 4-8 60

Picture Sleeves

CADET 4-6 67
COLUMBIA 8-12 60

LPs: 10/12-inch 33rpm

CADET.............................. 10-20 66-67
COLUMBIA 15-30 60-62
EPIC (3279 "Ray Bryant Trio")...40-60 56
PRESTIGE/NEW JAZZ............ 15-25 62
SIGNATURE 15-25 60
SUE.............................. 15-30 60-64

Also see CARTER, Betty, & Ray Bryant

BRYANT, Sharon

P&R/LP '89

Singles: 7-inch

WING 3-4 89

Picture Sleeves

WING 3-4 89

LPs: 10/12-inch 33rpm

WING 5-8 89

Also see ATLANTIC STARR

BRYSON, Peabo

R&B '76

Singles: 7-inch

BULLET 3-5 76-77
CAPITOL.............................. 3-4 77-83
COLUMBIA 3-4 91
ELEKTRA.............................. 3-4 84-88
MCA 3-4 84
SHOUT 3-5 75

Picture Sleeves

CAPITOL.............................. 3-4 81-83
ELEKTRA.............................. 3-4 85-88

LPs: 10/12-inch 33rpm

BULLET 8-10 76
CAPITOL.............................. 5-10 78-84
COLUMBIA 5-8 91
ELEKTRA.............................. 5-10 84-86

Also see COLE, Natalie, & Peabo Bryson
Also see MANCHESTER, Melissa, & Peabo Bryson
Also see ZAGER, Michael, Moon Band, & Peabo Bryson

BRYSON, Peabo, & Regina Belle

R&B '87

Singles: 7-inch

ELEKTRA.............................. 3-4 88

Also see BELLE, Regina
Also see COLE, Natalie, & Peabo Bryson
Also see FLACK, Roberta, & Peabo Bryson

BUBBLE PUPPY

P&R/LP '69

Singles: 7–inch

INT'L ARTISTS (128 "Hot Smoke and Sasafrass") 15-20 69
INT'L ARTISTS (133 "Beginning") 15-25 69
INT'L ARTISTS (136 "Days of Our Time") 15-25 70
INT'L ARTISTS (138 "Hurry Sundown") 15-25 69

Promotional Singles

INT'L ARTISTS (Black vinyl) 20-30 69-70
INT'L ARTISTS (Colored vinyl) . 25-50 70

LPs: 10/12–inch 33rpm

INT'L ARTISTS (10 "A Gathering of Promises") 100-125 69
(Green label)
INT'L ARTISTS (10 "A Gathering of Promises") 150-200 69
(White label. Promotional issue only.)
Members: Rod Prince; Todd Potter; Roy Cox; M. Taylor; Dave Fore.
Also see MUSIC MACHINE / Bubble Puppy

BUCHANAN, Bill

Singles: 7–inch

GONE (5032 "The Thing") 15-25 58
U.A. 8-12 62
Also see BUCHANAN & ANCELL
Also see BUCHANAN & CELLA
Also see BUCHANAN & GOODMAN
Also see BUCHANAN & GREENFIELD

BUCHANAN, Roy

LP '72

Singles: 7–inch

ALLIGATOR 3-4 85-86
ATLANTIC 3-4 76-78
BOMARC 10-15 61
POLYDOR 3-5 72-75
SWAN 4-8 61

LPs: 10/12–inch 33rpm

ALLIGATOR 5-10 85
ATLANTIC 5-10 76-77
BIOYA 30-40 71
POLYDOR 8-15 72-75
WATERHOUSE 5-10 81
Also see CANNON, Freddy
Also see GREGG, Bobby
Also see HAWKINS, Dale

BUCHANAN & ANCELL

P&R '57

Singles: 78rpm

FLYING SAUCER 10-20 57

Singles: 7–inch

FLYING SAUCER 20-25 57
Members: Bill Buchanan; Bob Ancell.
Also see BUCHANAN, Bill

BUCHANAN & CELLA

Singles: 7–inch

ABC-PAR 10-20 59
Member: Bill Buchanan.
Also see BUCHANAN, Bill

BUCHANAN & GOODMAN

P&R/R&B '56

Singles: 78rpm

LUNIVERSE (Except 101) 15-25 56-58
LUNIVERSE (101 "Flying Saucer") 25-30 56
(Label is printed "Universe," with a handwritten "L," making "Luniverse.")
LUNIVERSE (101 "Flying Saucer") 15-25 56
(Label is "Luniverse.")
LUNIVERSE (101X "Back to Earth") 25-50 56
RADIO-ACTIVE 10-15

Singles: 7–inch

COMIC 10-15 59
LUNIVERSE (Except 101) 15-30 56-58
LUNIVERSE (101 "Flying Saucer") 30-40 56
(Label is printed "Universe," with a handwritten "L," making "Luniverse.")
LUNIVERSE (101 "Flying Saucer") 15-25 56
(Label is "Luniverse.")
LUNIVERSE (101X "Back to Earth") 100-125 56
NOVELTY 10-15 59
RADIO-ACTIVE (101 "Flying Saucer") 50-75 56
(No artist credit shown. Unauthorized issue.)
Members: Bill Buchanan; Dickie Goodman.
Also see BUCHANAN, Bill
Also see GOODMAN, Dickie

BUCHANAN & GREENFIELD

Singles: 7–inch

NOVEL (711 "The Invasion") 15-20 64
(Red label.)
NOVEL (711 "The Invasion") 3-5 72
(Red and white label.)
Members: Bill Buchanan; Howard Greenfield.
Also see BUCHANAN, Bill

BUCHANAN BROTHERS

C&W '46

Singles: 78rpm

VICTOR 5-10 46

BUCHANAN BROTHERS

P&R '69

Singles: 7–inch

EVENT 3-6 69-71

LPs: 10/12–inch 33rpm

EVENT (101 "Medicine Man") 20-25 69
Members: Terry Cashman; Gene Pistilli; Tommy West.
Also see CASHMAN, PISTILLI & WEST

BUCK

R&B '75

Singles: 7-inch

PLAYBOY 3-5 75

BUCKEYE

P&R '79

Singles: 7-inch

POLYDOR.................................... 3-4 79

LPs: 10/12-inch 33rpm

POLYDOR.................................. 5-10 79

Member: Ronn Price.

BUCKINGHAM, Lindsey

P&R/LP '81

Singles: 7-inch

ASYLUM 3-4 81
ELEKTRA................................... 3-4 84
W.B. 3-4 83

Picture Sleeves

ASYLUM 3-4 81

LPs: 10/12-inch 33rpm

ASYLUM 5-10 81
ELEKTRA................................. 5-10 84

Also see BUCKINGHAM NICKS
Also see EGAN, Walter
Also see FLEETWOOD MAC
Also see STEWART, John

BUCKINGHAM NICKS

Singles: 7-inch

POLYDOR.................................. 3-5 73-79

Picture Sleeves

POLYDOR.................................. 3-5 73

LPs: 10/12-inch 33rpm

POLYDOR (5058 "Buckingham Nicks")................................. 30-40 73

Members: Lindsey Buckingham; Stevie Nicks.
Also see BUCKINGHAM, Lindsey
Also see NICKS, Stevie

BUCKINGHAMS

P&R '66

Singles: 7-inch

COLUMBIA 4-8 67-70
RED LABEL 3-4 85
ROWE/AMI.............................. 10-20 66
("Play Me" Sales Stimulator promotional issue.)
SPECTRA-SOUND 10-20 67
U.S.A. 10-15 66-67

Picture Sleeves

COLUMBIA 8-15 67-68

LPs: 10/12-inch 33rpm

COLUMBIA 15-25 67-75
RED LABEL 5-10 85
U.S.A. (107 "Kind of a Drag").... 50-75 67
(With 13 tracks.)
U.S.A. (107 "Kind of a Drag").... 30-40 67
(With 12 tracks.)

Members: Dennis Tufano; Carl Giammerse; Nick Fortune; Marty Grebb; Dennis Miccoli; Jon-Jon Poulos.
Also see TUFANO & GIAMMERSE

BUCKLEY, Tim

LP '67

Singles: 7-inch

DISC REET.................................. 3-5 73-74
ELEKTRA.................................... 4-8 66-67

LPs: 10/12-inch 33rpm

DISC REET................................ 8-10 73-74
ELEKTRA (Except 74004) 15-20 67-70
ELEKTRA (74004 "Tim Buckley")............................... 25-35 66
RHINO 5-10 83
STRAIGHT (Except 1060) 15-25 70
STRAIGHT (1060 "Blue Afternoon")............................ 25-35 69
W.B. 10-15 70-72

BUCKNER & GARCIA

P&R '80

Singles: 12-inch 33/45rpm

COLUMBIA 4-6 82

Singles: 7-inch

BGO 4-6 81
COLUMBIA 3-4 81

Picture Sleeves

COLUMBIA 3-4 81

LPs: 10/12-inch 33rpm

COLUMBIA 5-10 82

Members: Jerry Buckner; Gary Garcia.
Also see WILLIS "The Guard" & Vigorish

BUCKWHEAT

P&R/LP '72

Singles: 7-inch

LONDON...................................... 3-5 71-73

LPs: 10/12-inch 33rpm

LONDON................................. 10-12 71-73

BUCKWHEAT ZYDECO

LP '87

LPs: 10/12-inch 33rpm

ISLAND 5-10 87-90

BUD & TRAVIS

P&R '60

Singles: 7-inch

LIBERTY 4-8 59-65
WORLD PACIFIC 5-8 59

LPs: 10/12-inch 33rpm

LIBERTY 10-20 59-65
SUNSET 8-15 67

Members: Bud Dashiel; Travis Edmonson.
Also see DASHIEL, Bud, & Kinsmen
Also see EDMONSON, Travis

BUDD, Julie

(Julie)

Singles: 7-inch

A&M 3-4 81
ALSTON...................................... 3-4 77
BELL 3-5 70
MGM 3-6 68
RCA 3-5 72-73

TOM CAT 3-5 76-77

LPs: 10/12-inch 33rpm

MGM 12-20 68
RCA.. 10-15 71

Also see JULIE

BUDDY & CLAUDIA

R&B '55

Singles: 78rpm

CHESS...................................... 8-10 55

Singles: 7-inch

CHESS...................................... 10-15 55

Members: Buddy Griffin; Claudia Swann.

BUENA VISTAS

P&R '66

Singles: 7-inch

BB 4-6
MARQUEE................................. 5-10 68
SWAN 10-15 66

BUFFALO SPRINGFIELD

P&R/LP '67

Singles: 7-inch

ATCO 5-10 67-68

LPs: 10/12-inch 33rpm

ATCO (105 "Retrospective") 8-10 75
ATCO (200 "Buffalo Springfield")............................ 30-50 66
(Contains *Baby Don't Scold Me*.)
ATCO (200 "Buffalo Springfield")............................ 15-25 67
(*Baby Don't Scold Me* replaced by *For What It's Worth*.)
ATCO (226 thru 283)................ 20-30 67-69
ATCO (806 "Buffalo Springfield")............................ 15-20 73

Members: Stephen Stills; Neil Young; Jim Messina; Richie Furay; Jim Fielder; Doug Hastings; Dewey Martin; Bruce Palmer.
Also see FURAY, Richie
Also see MARTIN, Dewey, & Medicine Ball
Also see MESSINA, Jim
Also see PALMER, Bruce
Also see POCO
Also see STILLS, Stephen
Also see YOUNG, Neil

BUFFETT, Jimmy

C&W '73

Singles: 7-inch

ABC.. 3-5 75-78
ASYLUM 3-4 80
BARNABY 3-5 70-72
DUNHILL.................................. 3-5 73-75
FULL MOON 3-4 80
MCA (Black vinyl)...................... 3-4 79-86
MCA (Colored vinyl) 3-6 85

LPs: 10/12-inch 33rpm

ABC.. 8-10 76-78
BARNABY 10-15 70-77
DUNHILL.................................. 10-15 73-74
MCA 5-10 79-90
U.A. 8-10 75

BUFFETT, Mary

D&D '84

Singles: 12-inch 33/45rpm

MOBY DICK..................................4-6 84

Singles: 7-inch

MOBY DICK..................................3-4 84

BUGGLES

P&R/LP 79

Singles: 7-inch

CARRERE 3-4 82
ISLAND 3-4 79-83

Promotional Singles

CARRERE ("Fade Away") 3-4 82
(Soundsheet. Originally included in a magazine.)

LPs: 10/12-inch 33rpm

CARRERE 5-10 82
ISLAND 5-10 80

Members: Trevor Horn; Geoff Downes.
Also see ASIA
Also see YES

BUGNON, Alex

LP '89

LP: 10/12-inch 33rpm

ORPHEUS 5-8 89-90

BULL & MATADORS

P&R/R&B '68

Singles: 7-inch

TODDLIN' TOWN 5-10 68-69

BULLDOG

P&R/LP '72

Singles: 7-inch

BUDDAH......................................3-5 72-74
DECCA 3-5 72
GUYDEN......................................3-5 71
MCA 3-5 73

LPs: 10/12-inch 33rpm

BUDDAH......................................8-12 74
DECCA 12-20 72

Members: Gene Cornish; Dino Danelli; Billy Hocher; Eric Thorngren; John Turi.
Also see RASCALS

BULLENS, Cindy

P&R '79

Singles: 7-inch

CASABLANCA..............................3-4 79-80
U.A. 3-4 78-79

LPs: 10/12-inch 33rpm

CASABLANCA..............................5-10 79
U.A. 5-10 78

Also see ALPHA BAND

BULLET

P&R '71

Singles: 7-inch

BIG TREE 3-5 71-72

BULLETBOYS

LP '88

Singles: 7–inch

W.B. 3-4 89

Picture Sleeves

W.B. 3-4 89

LPs: 10/12–inch 33rpm

W.B. 5-8 89

BULLOCK, Janice

R&B '87

Singles: 7–inch

WRC.. 3-4 87

Also see BELL, William, & Janice Bullock

BUMBLE, B: see B. BUMBLE & STINGERS

BUMBLE BEE UNLIMITED

P&R/R&B '76

Singles: 7–inch

MERCURY 3-5 76-77
RCA.. 3-4 79

LPs: 10/12–inch 33rpm

RCA.. 5-10 79

BUONO, Victor

LP '71

Singles: 7–inch

DORE.. 3-5 71
FAMILY 3-5 71

LPs: 10/12–inch 33rpm

DORE.. 5-10 71

BUOYS

P&R '71

Singles: 7–inch

POLYDOR.................................. 3-5 73
RANSOM 5-10
SCEPTER 3-6 69-71

Picture Sleeves

SCEPTER 4-6 70

LPs: 10/12–inch 33rpm

SCEPTER 10-15 71

Members: Jerry Hludzik; Bill Kelly; Chris Hanlon; Fran Brozena; Carl Siracuse.
Also see DAKOTA
Also see JERRY KELLY

BURBANK, Gary, & Band McNally

C&W/P&R '80

Singles: 7–inch

OVATION 3-5 80

BURCH, Vernon

R&B '75

Singles: 12–inch 33/45rpm

CHOCOLATE CITY...................... 4-6 79-80
SPECTOR.................................. 4-6 81

Singles: 7–inch

CHOCOLATE CITY...................... 3-4 78-80
COLUMBIA 3-4 77-78
SPECTOR.................................. 3-4 81-84
U.A. 3-5 75

LPs: 10/12–inch 33rpm

CHOCOLATE CITY 5-10 79-80
COLUMBIA 8-10 77-78
SPECTOR..................................5-10 81-84
U.A. 8-10 74-76

BURDON, Eric

(Eric Burdon Band)

LP '74

Singles: 7–inch

CAPITOL....................................3-5 74

LPs: 10/12–inch 33rpm

CAPITOL....................................8-10 74-75
LAX 5-10 81-84
VERVE......................................10-12 72

Also see ANIMALS

BURDON, Eric, & War

(With Sharon Scott)

P&R/LP '70

Singles: 7–inch

ABC..3-5 76
CAPITOL....................................5-10 74-75
LIBERTY 3-5
MGM 5-10 70

Picture Sleeves

MGM 4-6 70

LPs: 10/12–inch 33rpm

ABC..8-10 77
MGM (Except 4710)..................10-15 70
MGM (4710 "Black Man's Burdon")..................................20-30 70
(Promotional issue only.)

Also see WAR

BURDON, Eric, & Jimmy Witherspoon

Singles: 7–inch

MGM 3-5 71

LPs: 10/12–inch 33rpm

MGM 10-15 71

Also see BURDON, Eric
Also see WITHERSPOON, Jimmy

BURGESS, Richard James

D&D '84

Singles: 12–inch 33/45rpm

CAPITOL....................................4-6 84

Singles: 7–inch

CAPITOL....................................3-4 84

LPs: 10/12–inch 33rpm

CAPITOL....................................5-10 84

BURKE, Ceele

R&B '43

Singles: 78rpm

CAPITOL....................................5-10

BURKE, Keni

R&B '81

Singles: 7–inch

DARK HORSE 3-5 77-78
RCA 3-4 81-82

LPs: 10/12-inch 33rpm

DARK HORSE 8-10 77
RCA 5-10 81-82
Also see FIVE STAIRSTEPS

BURKE, Solomon

P&R/R&B '61

Singles: 12-inch 33/45rpm

SAVOY 4-6 84

Singles: 78rpm

APOLLO 5-10 56-57

Singles: 7-inch

ABC/DUNHILL 3-5 74
AMHERST 3-5 78
APOLLO 15-25 56-58
ATLANTIC 4-8 61-68
BELL 3-6 69-70
CHESS 3-5 75-77
DUNHILL 3-5 74
INFINITY 3-5 79
MGM 3-5 70-73
ODEON 4-6
PRIDE 3-5 72-73
SINGULAR 5-10 60

LPs: 10/12-inch 33rpm

ABC/DUNHILL 10-12 74
APOLLO (498 "Solomon Burke") 60-100 62
ATLANTIC (8000 series) 25-45 62-64
ATLANTIC (8100 series) 15-30 65-68
BELL 12-20 69
CHESS 8-10 75-76
CLARION 12-20 64
INFINITY 5-10 79
KENWOOD 12-20 64
MGM 10-15 71-72
PRIDE 8-12 73
ROUNDER 5-10 84
SAVOY 5-10 81-83
Also see CHARLES, Ray / Somomon Burke
Also see SOUL CLAN

BURKE, Solomon, & Lady Lee

Singles: 7-inch

PRIDE 3-5 73
Also see BURKE, Solomon

BURNETT, Carol

LP '72

LPs: 10/12-inch 33rpm

DECCA 15-25 61-64
COLUMBIA 8-12 71
RCA 10-15 67
TETRAGRAMMATON 8-12 69
VOCALION 8-12 68
Also see ANDREWS, Julie, & Carol Burnett

BURNETT, J. Henry

Singles: 7-inch

UNI 4-6 72

LPs: 10/12-inch 33rpm

UNI 10-15 72
Also see BURNETT, T-Bone

BURNETT, T-Bone
(J. Henry Burnett)

LP '83

Singles: 7-inch

W.B. 3-4 83

LPs: 10/12-inch 33rpm

TAKOMA 5-10 80
W.B. 5-10 82-83
Also see BLACK TIE
Also see BURNETT, J. Henry
Also see LEGENDARY STARDUST COWBOY

BURNETTE, Billy
(With Jawbone)

C&W '79

Singles: 7-inch

A&M 3-5 76
COLUMBIA 3-4 80-81
CURB 3-4 86
POLYDOR 3-5 79
W.B. (7300 series) 4-6 69

LPs: 10/12-inch 33rpm

COLUMBIA 5-10 80-81
ENTRANCE 10-12 72
MCA/CURB 5-10 86
POLYDOR 5-10 79
Also see FLEETWOOD MAC

BURNETTE, Billy, & Christine McVie

Singles: 12-inch 33/45rpm

MCA/CURB (17040 "It Ain't Over") 5-8 85
(Promotional issue only.)
Also see BURNETTE, Billy
Also see McVIE, Christine

BURNETTE, Billy Joe
(Billy Burnette)

C&W '90

Singles: 7-inch

BADGER 3-4 90
DEVILLE (134 "Blue Misery") 8-12 65
GOLD STANDARD 3-5
GUSTO-STARDAY (167 "Welcome Home Elvis") 4-8 77
GUSTO-STARDAY (9009 "The Colonel and the King") 8-12 78
(Promotional issue only.)
K-ARK 3-5 70
MAGIC LAMP (613 "Miss Ping Pong") 10-15 65
PD 3-5
PALOMINO 3-5
TEDDY BEAR 4-6 77
TELEMEDIA 3-4 81
W.B. 4-8 69

LPs: 10/12-inch 33rpm

GUSTO 10-20 77
Also see BARNETT, Billy
Also see LEGENDS

BURNETTE, Dorsey

P&R '60

Singles: 78rpm

ABBOTT.................................. 10-20 56

Singles: 7-inch

ABBOTT (188 "Devil's Queen"). 25-35 56
ABBOTT (190 "At a Distance") . 25-35 56
CALLIOPE.................................. 3-5 77
CAPITOL.................................. 3-5 71-74
CEE-JAM (16 "Bertha-Lou")...... 50-75 57
COLLECTABLES........................ 3-4 81
CONDOR.................................. 4-6 70
DOT.. 8-12 61
ELEKTRA.................................. 3-5 79-80
ERA.. 5-10 60-69
HAPPY TIGER.......................... 4-6 70
HICKORY.................................. 4-8 67
IMPERIAL (5561 "Try").............. 10-20 59
IMPERIAL (5597 "Misery")........ 10-20 59
IMPERIAL (5668 "Your Love").. 10-20 60
IMPERIAL (5987 "Circle Rock").. 8-10 63
LIBERTY.................................. 4-8 69
MC.. 3-5 77
MEL-O-DY.............................. 10-15 64
MELODYLAND.......................... 3-5 75-76
MERRI (206 "Lucy Darling")........ 8-12 60
MOVIE STAR............................ 4-8
MUSIC FACTORY...................... 4-8 68
REPRISE.................................. 5-10 62-63
SMASH.................................... 5-10 66
SURF (5019 "Bertha Lou").... 150-200 57
U.S. NAVY ("Be a Navy Man").. 10-20 60s
(U.S. Navy recruiting promotional issue.)

Picture Sleeves

ERA (3033 "The River and the Mountain")........................ 15-25 61
REPRISE (246 "Four for Texas")................................ 20-30 63
U.S. NAVY ("Be a Navy Man").. 15-25 60s
(U.S. Navy recruiting promotional issue.)

LPs: 10/12-inch 33rpm

CALLIOPE.............................. 8-10 77
CAPITOL.............................. 10-12 72-73
DOT (3456 "Dorsey Burnette Sings").................................. 20-40 63
(Monaural.)
DOT (25456 "Dorsey Burnette Sings").................................. 25-50 63
(Stereo.)
ERA (EL-102 "Tall Oak Tree") .. 40-80 60
(Monaural.)
ERA (ES-102 "Tall Oak Tree")................................ 100-150 60
(Stereo.)
ERA (800 series).................... 15-20 69
GUSTO.................................. 5-10
TRIP...................................... 8-12 74

Also see BURNETTE, Johnny & Dorsey

BURNETTE, Johnny

(With the Rock'n Roll Trio)

P&R '60

Singles: 78rpm

CORAL.....................................15-25 56-57
VON (106 "Go Mule Go")...........50-75 54

Singles: 7-inch

CAPITOL....................................8-12 63-64
CHANCELLOR (1116 "I Wanna Thank You Folks")......................................10-15 62
CHANCELLOR (1129 "Remember Me")......................................10-15 62
CORAL (61651 "Tear It Up")......60-80 56
CORAL (61651 "Tear It Up")....75-100 56
(Promotional issue only.)
CORAL (61675 "Midnight Train")......................................60-80 56
CORAL (61675 "Midnight Train")....................................75-100 56
(Promotional issue only.)
CORAL (61719 "Honey Hush")..60-80 56
CORAL (61719 "Honey Hush")....................................75-100 56
(Promotional issue only.)
CORAL (61758 "Lonesome Train")......................................60-80 56
CORAL (61758 "Lonesome Train")....................................75-100 56
(Promotional issue only.)
CORAL (61829 "Eager Beaver Baby")......................................40-60 57
CORAL (61829 "Eager Beaver Baby")......................................60-80 57
(Promotional issue only.)
CORAL (61869 "Drinkin' Wine Spo-Dee-O-Dee")......................40-60 57
CORAL (61869 "Drinkin' Wine Spo-Dee-O-Dee")......................60-80 57
(Promotional issue only.)
CORAL (61918 "Rock Billy Boogie")....................................40-60 57
CORAL (61918 "Rock Billy Boogie")....................................60-80 57
(Promotional issue only.)
FREEDOM (44001 "I'm Restless")..................................30-40 58
FREEDOM (44011 "Gumbo") 30-40 59
FREEDOM (44017 "Sweet Baby Doll")...............................20-40 59
LIBERTY....................................10-20 60
(Green and silver label.)
LIBERTY......................................8-15 60-62
(Multi-color label.)
LIBERTY ALL-TIME HITS..............3-5
MAGIC LAMP (515 "Bigger Man")......................................20-30 64
SAHARA......................................5-10 64
U.A...3-4 84
VON (106 "Go Mule Go").......200-400 54

Picture Sleeves

LIBERTY (55285 "You're Sixteen")............................ 15-20 60
LIBERTY (55298 "Little Boy Sad")............................ 15-20 61
LIBERTY (55318 "Big, Big World")............................ 15-20 61
MAGIC LAMP (515 "Bigger Man")............................ 75-100 64

EPs: 7–inch 33/45rpm

LIBERTY (1004 "Dreamin")....... 40-60 60
LIBERTY (1011 "Johnny Burnette's Hits")............................ 50-75 61

LPs: 10/12–inch 33rpm

CORAL (57080 "Johnny Burnette and the Rock'n Roll Trio")........... 1000-1500 56
(Counterfeits can be identified by their lack of printing on the spine and hand-etched identification numbers in the trail-off. Originals have the numbers mechanically stamped. Canadian issues are worth at least as much as U.S. issues.)
LIBERTY (3179 "Dreamin")....... 30-40 60
(Monaural.)
LIBERTY (7179 "Dreamin")....... 40-60 60
(Stereo.)
LIBERTY (3183 "Johnny Burnette")............................ 30-40 61
(Monaural.)
LIBERTY (7183 "Johnny Burnette")............................ 40-50 61
(Stereo.)
LIBERTY (3190 "Johnny Burnette Sings")............................ 30-40 61
(Monaural.)
LIBERTY (7190 "Johnny Burnette Sings")............................ 40-50 61
(Stereo.)
LIBERTY (3206 "Johnny Burnette's Hits and Other Favorites").................. 30-40 62
(Monaural.)
LIBERTY (7206 "Johnny Burnette's Hits and Other Favorites").................. 40-50 62
(Stereo.)
LIBERTY (3255 "Roses Are Red")............................ 30-40 62
(Monaural.)
LIBERTY (7255 "Roses Are Red")............................ 40-50 62
(Stereo.)
LIBERTY (3389 "The Johnny Burnette Story").................. 30-40 64
(Monaural.)
LIBERTY (7389 "The Johnny Burnette Story").................. 40-50 64
(Stereo.)
LIBERTY (7300 series)............ 25-30 63
LIBERTY (10000 series)............ 5-10 81
MCA............................ 5-10 82
SOLID SMOKE (Black vinyl)........5-10 78-80
SOLID SMOKE (Colored vinyl)..10-15 78
SUNSET............................15-25 67
U.A............................10-15 75

Members (Trio): Johnny Burnette; Dorsey Burnette; Paul Burlison.
Also see BURLISON, Paul
Also see BURNETTE, Dorsey
Also see BURNETTE, Johnny
Also see VEE, Bobby / Johnny Burnette / Ventures / Fleetwoods

BURNETTE, Johnny & Dorsey
(Burnette Brothers)

Singles: 7–inch

CORAL (62190 "Blues Stay Away from Me")..................25-35 60
IMPERIAL............................15-20 58
REPRISE............................5-10 63

Also see BURNETTE, Dorsey
Also see BURNETTE, Johnny
Also see TEXANS

BURNETTE, Rocky
(With the Rock 'N Roll Trio)

P&R/LP '80

Singles: 7–inch

EMI AMERICA............................3-4 80

LPs: 10/12–inch 33rpm

EMI AMERICA............................5-10 80-82
GOODS............................5-10 82
KYD............................5-10 83

Also see BURNETTE, Randy, & Rocky Burnette

BURNING SENSATIONS

LP '83

Singles: 7–inch

CAPITOL............................3-4 83

LPs: 10/12–inch 33rpm

CAPITOL............................5-10 83

BURNS, George

P&R/C&W/LP '80

Singles: 7–inch

MERCURY............................3-4 80-81

Picture Sleeves

MERCURY............................3-4 80

EPs: 7–inch 33/45rpm

COLPIX............................5-10 60s

LPs: 10/12–inch 33rpm

BUDDAH............................6-10 72
MERCURY............................5-10 80
PRIDE............................5-10

Also see MARTIN, Dean

BURNS, George, & Gracie Allen

P&R '33

Singles: 78rpm

COLUMBIA............................10-15 33

LPs: 10/12–inch 33rpm

MARK '56............................8-15

Also see BURNS, George

BURRAGE, Harold
(Harold Barrage)

R&B '65

Singles: 78rpm

ALADDIN ... 10-15 52
COBRA ... 10-15 56-57
DECCA ... 10-15 50
STATES ... 10-20 54

Singles: 7-inch

ALADDIN (3194 "Sweet Brown Gal") ... 25-40 52
COBRA ... 15-25 56-58
DECCA (48175 "Hi-Yo") ... 25-50 50
FOXY ... 4-8 62
M-PAC ... 4-8 62-65
PASO ... 5-10 61
STATES (144 "Feel So Fine") . 50-100 54
(Black vinyl.)
STATES (144 "Feel So Fine") 100-200 50
(Colored vinyl.)
VEE JAY ... 5-10 60
VIVID ... 4-8 64

BURRELL

R&B '88

Singles: 7-inch

VIRGIN ... 3-4 88

BURRELL, Kenny

LP '63

Singles: 7-inch

CADET ... 4-8 66

LPs: 10/12-inch 33rpm

CADET ... 10-20 66
VERVE ... 10-15 68

BURRELL, Kenny, & Jimmy Smith

LP '63

LPs: 10/12-inch 33rpm

VERVE ... 10-20 66-68

Also see BURRELL, Kenny
Also see SMITH, Jimmy

BURRITO BROTHERS

C&W '81

Singles: 7-inch

CURB ... 3-4 81-84
EPIC ... 3-4 81

LPs: 10/12-inch 33rpm

A&M ... 8-10 80
CURB ... 5-10 81-82

Members: Pete Battin; Pete Kleinow; Greg Harris; Ed Ponder; Gib Guilbeau; John Beland.
Also see BATTIN, Pete
Also see FLYING BURRITO BROTHERS
Also see SWAMPWATER

BURROWS, Tony

P&R '70

Singles: 7-inch

BELL ... 3-5 70-72

Also see BROTHERHOOD of MAN
Also see EDISON LIGHTHOUSE
Also see FIRST CLASS

BURTNICK, Glen

P&R/LP '87

Singles: 7-inch

A&M ... 3-4 87

Picture Sleeves

A&M ... 3-4 87

LPs: 10/12-inch 33rpm

A&M ... 5-10 87

BURTON, Jenny

R&B/D&D '83

Singles: 12-inch 33/45rpm

ATLANTIC ... 4-6 83-85

Singles: 7-inch

ATLANTIC ... 3-4 83-86

LPs: 10/12-inch 33rpm

ATLANTIC ... 5-10 83-85

Also see C-BANK

BURTON, Jenny, & Patrick Jude

P&R '84

Singles: 7-inch

ATLANTIC ... 3-4 84

Picture Sleeves

ATLANTIC ... 3-4 84

Also see BURTON, Jenny

BURTON, Richard

P&R '65

Singles: 7-inch

MGM ... 4-6 65

BUS BOYS

LP '80

Singles: 7-inch

ARISTA ... 3-4 80-84

LPs: 10/12-inch 33rpm

ARISTA ... 5-10 80-82

Members: Gus Loundermon; Brian O'Neal; Kevin O'Neal; Michael Jones; Victor Johnson; Steve Felix.

BUSCH, Lou, Orchestra

P&R '55

Singles: 78rpm

CAPITOL ... 3-5 55-56

Singles: 7-inch

CAPITOL ... 4-8 55-56

Also see CARR, Joe "Fingers"

BUSH, Kate

P&R '79

Singles: 12-inch 33/45rpm

EMI AMERICA ... 4-6 85-86

Singles: 7-inch

COLUMBIA ... 3-4 89
EMI AMERICA (8000 series) ... 3-8 78-86
EMI AMERICA (9605 "Hounds of Love") ... 8-10 85
(Long version/Short version. Promotional issue only.)
GEFFEN ... 3-4 87
HARVEST ... 5-8 78-79

Picture Sleeves

EMI AMERICA (8285 "Running Up That Hill") 4-6 85
EMI AMERICA (8302 "Hounds of Love") 4-6 85
GEFFEN 3-4 87
HARVEST 10-15 78

LPs: 10/12-inch 33rpm

COLUMBIA 5-10 89
EMI AMERICA 6-12 78-86
HARVEST 10-15 78

Also see GABRIEL, Peter, & Kate Bush

BUSH, Little David
(David Ruffin)

Singles: 7-inch

VEGA (1002 "You and I") 150-200 59

Also see RUFFIN, David

BUSHKIN, Joe

LP '56

LPs: 10/12-inch 33rpm

CAPITOL 15-25 56

Singles: 7-inch

ARLEN 10-20 63-64

Members: Jack Baker; Fran Parda; Rick LaFrenier; Richard Eriksen; Tink Hermanson.
Also see BOLD
Also see COLE, Fred E.
Also see TROPHIES

BUTANES

P&R '61

Singles: 7-inch

ENRICA 10-20 61

BUTCHER, Jon
(John Butcher Axis)

P&R '83

Singles: 7-inch

CAPITOL 3-4 85-89
POLYDOR 3-4 83-84

Picture Sleeves

CAPITOL 3-4 85-87

LPs: 10/12-inch 33rpm

CAPITOL 5-10 85-89
POLYDOR 5-10 83-84

Members: Jon Butcher; Thom Gimbell; Derek Blevins; Bob Jefferies.

BUTLER, Billy
(With the Chanters; with Infinity; with Enchanters)

P&R/R&B '65

Singles: 7-inch

BRUNSWICK 4-8 66-68
CURTOM 3-5 76
OKEH 4-8 63-66
MEMPHIS 3-5 71
PRIDE 3-5 72-73

LPs: 10/12-inch 33rpm

EDSEL 5-10 86
OKEH 15-20 66
PRESTIGE 10-15 69-70
PRIDE 10-12 73

Members: Billy Butler; Earl Batts; Jess Tillman; Larry Wade; Phyllis Know.
Also see CHANTERS
Also see INFINITY

BUTLER, Carl

C&W '61

Singles: 78rpm

CAPITOL 5-10 51-52
OKEH 4-8 54-55

Singles: 7-inch

CAPITOL 8-12 51-52
COLUMBIA 4-8 59-63
OKEH 6-10 54-55

LPs: 10/12-inch 33rpm

COLUMBIA 10-20 63
HARMONY 8-15 66-71

BUTLER, Carl & Pearl

C&W '62

Singles: 7-inch

COLUMBIA 4-8 62-69

LPs: 10/12-inch 33rpm

CMH 5-10 80
CHART 3-5 71
COLUMBIA 10-20 64-70
HARMONY 8-12 72
PEDACA 5-10

Also see BUTLER, Carl
Also see BUTLER, Pearl

BUTLER, Champ

P&R '51

Singles: 78rpm

COLUMBIA 3-8 50-54
CORAL 3-8 55-56

Singles: 7-inch

COLUMBIA 5-10 50-54
CORAL 5-10 55-56
GILLETTE 4-6 62

EPs: 7-inch 33/45rpm

COLUMBIA 8-15 53

LPs: 10/12-inch 33rpm

GILLETTE 10-20 62

BUTLER, Champ, & George Cates

Singles: 78rpm

CORAL 3-5 55

Singles: 7-inch

CORAL 4-8 55

Also see BUTLER, Champ
Also see CATES, George

BUTLER, Jerry
(With the Impressions)

P&R/R&B '58

Singles: 78rpm

ABNER (1013 "For Your Precious Love") 10-20 58
(Issued on 45 as FALCON 1013. The Abner 78 uses the Falcon 1013 number.)

Singles: 7-inch

ABNER 10-15 58-60
COLLECTABLES 3-4 81
ERIC 3-4 73
FALCON (1013 "For Your Precious Love") 15-25 58
FOUNTAIN 3-4 82
MCA 3-4 83
MERCURY 3-8 67-74
MISTLETOE 3-5 75
MOTOWN 3-5 76-77
OLDIES 45 3-5
PHILADELPHIA INT'L 3-4 78-81
TRIP 3-5
VEE JAY (280 "For Your Precious Love") 500-600 58
VEE JAY (354 thru 715) 5-10 60-66
VEE JAY (1971 "Aware of Love") 15-25 63
(Stereo compact 33 single.)

Picture Sleeves

VEE JAY 8-12 61-64

LPs: 10/12-inch 33rpm

ABNER (2001 "Jerry Butler Esquire") 75-125 59
BUDDAH 12-20 69
EXODUS 5-10
FOUNTAIN 5-10 82
DYNASTY 12-18
KENT 10-15 68
LOST-NITE 8-10 81
MERCURY 8-15 67-84
MOTOWN 5-10 76-77
PHILADELPHIA INT'L 5-10 78-81
POST 5-10
PRIDE 8-10 72
UPFRONT 8-10
SCEPTER 8-10
SIRE 8-12 77
SUNSET 10-12 68
TRIP 10-12 71-78
U.A. 8-10 75
VEE JAY (1000 series) 25-45 60-64
VEE JAY (1100 series) 20-30 64-65

Members (Impressions): Jerry Butler; Sam Gooden; Richard Brooks; Arthur Brooks; Curtis Mayfield.

Also see AUSTIN, Patti, & Jerry Butler
Also see CHANDLER, Gene, & Jerry Butler
Also see IMPRESSIONS
Also see McPHATTER, Clyde / Little Richard / Jerry Butler
Also see RIVERS, Johnny / 4 Seasons / Jerry Butler / Jimmy Soul

BUTLER, Jerry, & Brenda Lee Eager

P&R/R&B '72

Singles: 7-inch

MERCURY 3-4 71-73

LPs: 10/12-inch 33rpm

MERCURY 8-10 73

Also see EAGER, Brenda Lee

BUTLER, Jerry, & Betty Everett

LP '64

Singles: 7-inch

ABC 3-4 73
VEE JAY 3-5 64

LPs: 10/12-inch 33rpm

BUDDAH 10-15 69
TRADITION 5-10 82
VEE JAY 20-30 64

Also see DELLS
Also see EVERETT, Betty

BUTLER, Jerry, & Debra Henry

R&B '82

Singles: 7-inch

PHILADELPHIA INT'L 3-4 80

Also see SILK

BUTLER, Jerry, & Stix Hooper

Singles: 7-inch

MCA 3-4 83

Also see HOOPER, Stix

BUTLER, Jerry, & Thelma Houston

LP '77

Singles: 7-inch

MOTOWN 3-5 77

LPs: 10/12-inch 33rpm

MOTOWN 5-10 77

Also see BUTLER, Jerry
Also see HOUSTON, Thelma

BUTLER, Jonathan

LP '86

Singles: 7-inch

JIVE 3-4 86-88

Picture Sleeves

JIVE 3-4 87

LPs: 10/12-inch 33rpm

JIVE 5-10 86-88

Also see TURNER, Ruby

BUTTERFIELD, Paul

(Butterfield Blues Band; Paul Butterfield's Better Days)

LP '65

Singles: 7-inch

BEARSVILLE 3-5 73-81
ELEKTRA 4-8 67-69

Picture Sleeves

ELEKTRA 4-8 67

LPs: 10/12-inch 33rpm

AMHERST 5-8 86
BEARSVILLE 8-10 73-81
ELEKTRA 10-20 65-76
RED LIGHTNIN' ("An Offer You Can't Refuse") 30-40 72
(Single sided promotional LP.)

Also see BISHOP, Elvin

BUTTERFLYS
(Ellie Greenwich)

P&R '64

Singles: 7-inch

RED BIRD 10-20 64
Also see GREENWICH, Ellie

BUZZCOCKS

LP '80

Singles: 7-inch

I.R.S. 3-4 79-80

LPs: 10/12-inch 33rpm

I.R.S. 5-10 79
Members: Pete Shelley; Steve Diggle; Howard Devoto; Steve Garvey; John Maher.
Also see SHELLEY, Pete

BY ALL MEANS

R&B '88

Singles: 7-inch

ISLAND 3-4 88-89

LPs: 10/12-inch 33rpm

ISLAND 5-8 89
Members: James Vorner; Lynn Roderick; Billy Sheppard.

BYAS, Don

R&B '48

Singles: 78rpm

SAVOY 8-12

BYRD, Bobby
(With the Byrds; with James Brown Band)

R&B '65

Singles: 7-inch

BROWNSTONE 3-5 71-72
FEDERAL 5-10 63
INTERNATIONAL BROTHERS 3-5 75
KING 3-6 67-71
KWANZA 3-5 73
SMASH 8-15 64-65
ZEPHYR 8-12

LPs: 10/12-inch 33rpm

KING 10-15 70
Also see KING, Anna, & Bobby Byrd

BYRD, Bobby, & James Brown

R&B '68

Singles: 7-inch

KING 4-6 68
Also see BROWN, James
Also see BYRD, Bobby

BYRD, Charlie

P&R '62

Singles: 7-inch

RIVERSIDE 3-6 62-63

LPs: 10/12-inch 33rpm

COLUMBIA 15-25 65-69
OFFBEAT 25-35 59-60
RIVERSIDE 15-25 62-82
SAVOY 30-45 58
Also see ALMEIDA, Laurindo
Also see GETZ, Stan, & Charlie Byrd

BYRD, Charlie, & Woody Herman

LPs: 10/12-inch 33rpm

EVEREST 10-20 63
PICKWICK 6-12 66
Also see BYRD, Charlie
Also see HERMAN, Woody

BYRD, Donald

LP '64

Singles: 7-inch

BLUE NOTE 3-5 75-77
ELEKTRA 3-4 78-82

LPs: 10/12-inch 33rpm

BETHLEHEM 15-25 60
BLUE NOTE 15-25 59-65
(Label reads "Blue Note Records Inc. - New York, U.S.A.")
BLUE NOTE 10-20 66-77
(Label reads "Blue Note Records - a Division of Liberty Records Inc.")
COLUMBIA (998 "Jazz Lab") 40-60 57
(With Gigi Gryce.)
COLUMBIA (1058 "Jazz Lab, Vol. 2, Modern Jazz Perspective") 40-60 57
(With Gigi Gryce.)
ELEKTRA 5-10 78-82
JAZZLAND (6 "Hard Bop") 30-40
JUBILEE (1059 "Jazz Lab") 40-60 57
(With Gigi Gryce.)
PRESTIGE (7062 "Two Trumpets") 75-100 56
(Yellow label. With Art Farmer.)
PRESTIGE (7080 "Youngbloods") 60-80 57
(Yellow label. With Phil Woods.)
PRESTIGE (7092 "Three Trumpets") 60-80 57
(Yellow label. With Art Farmer & Idrees Sulieman.)
REGENT (6056 "Jazz Eyes") 40-60 57
SAVOY (12032 "Byrd's Word") 40-60 56
(With Frank Foster.)
TRANSITION (4 "Byrd's Eye View") 50-80 55
(With Hank Mobley.)
TRANSITION (5 "Byrd Jazz") 50-80 55
(With Yusef Lateef.)
TRANSITION (17 "Byrd Blows on Beacon Hill") 50-80 56
VERVE 20-30 58
Also see BLACKBYRDS

BYRD, Gary
(With G.B. Experience)

R&B '83

Singles: 12-inch 33/45rpm

WONDIRECTION 4-6 83

Singles: 7-inch

RCA 3-5 73
REAL THING 3-5

BYRD, Jerry

P&R '50

Singles: 78rpm

MERCURY 3-6 53-55

Singles: 7–inch

MERCURY 4-8 53-55
MONUMENT 4-6 60-62

EPs: 7–inch 33/45rpm

DECCA...................................... 8-12 58
MERCURY 10-20 53-55

LPs: 10/12–inch 33rpm

DECCA..................................... 15-30 58
LEHUA 8-10
MERCURY (Except 25000 series) 10-20 58-64
MERCURY (25000 series)........ 20-40 53-54
(10–inch LPs.)
MONUMENT 12-25 61-63
WING 10-15 60-66
Also see ALLEN, Rex
Also see KIRK, Red

BYRD, Roy

(With His Blues Jumpers; Roy "Bald Head" Byrd; with His New Orleans Rhythm; Roland Byrd)

R&B '50

Singles: 78rpm

ATLANTIC (947 "Hey Little Girl") 50-75 50
FEDERAL (12061 "K.C. Blues") 50-75 52
(All Federal 45s known to exist are bootlegs.)
FEDERAL (12073 "Rockin' with Fess").................................... 50-75 52
MERCURY (8175 "Bald Head") 30-40 50
MERCURY (8184 "Her Mind Is Gone")..................................... 30-50 50
Also see PROFESSOR LONGHAIR

BYRD, Russell

P&R '61

Singles: 7–inch

SYMBOL 5-10 62
WAND 5-10 61

BYRDS

P&R/LP '65

Singles: 7–inch

ASYLUM 3-5 73
COLUMBIA (1600 series) 4-6 73
COLUMBIA (43271 "Mr. Tambourine Man")...................................... 5-10 65
(Black vinyl.)
COLUMBIA (43271 "Mr. Tambourine Man").................................... 50-75 65
(Colored vinyl. Promotional issue only.)
COLUMBIA (43332 "I'll Feel a Whole Lot Better") 5-10 65
(Black vinyl.)
COLUMBIA (43332 "I'll Feel a Whole Lot Better")..................................50-75 65
(Colored vinyl. Promotional issue only.)
COLUMBIA (43332 "All I Really Want to Do").......................................5-10 65
(Black vinyl.)
COLUMBIA (43332 "All I Really Want to Do")....................................50-75 65
(Colored vinyl. Promotional issue only.)
COLUMBIA (43424 "Turn Turn Turn")...5-10 65
(Black vinyl.)
COLUMBIA (43424 "Turn Turn Turn")......................................50-75 65
(Colored vinyl. Promotional issue only.)
COLUMBIA (43501 thru 45761).....4-8 66-72
SCHOLASTIC 5-10 66

Picture Sleeves

COLUMBIA (Except 43271).......12-25 65-71
COLUMBIA (43271 "Mr. Tambourine Man") 100-150 65
(Promotional issue only.)
COLUMBIA (43578 "Eight Miles High").......................................15-25 65
COLUMBIA (44157 "Have You Seen Her Face").....................15-25 65

EPs: 7–inch 33/45rpm

COLUMBIA (10287 "The Byrds")..................................40-60 66
(Columbia Special Products issue for the Scholastic Book Services.)
COLUMBIA (116003/4 "Fifth Dimension Open-End Interview") 50-75 66
(Promotional issue only.)

LPs: 10/12–inch 33rpm

ASYLUM 8-10 73
COLUMBIA (2000 series)..........20-25 65-67
COLUMBIA (9000 series)..........15-25 65-69
COLUMBIA (30000 thru 33000 series).......................................8-12 70-75
COLUMBIA (34000 thru 37000 series).......................................5-10 75-81
COLUMBIA (46773 "The Byrds") 30-40 90
(Four-LP set. Includes booklet.)
TOGETHER 15-20 69

Promotional LPs

BROADCAST ("Byrds Live")......35-45 81
COLUMBIA (2000 series)..........40-50 65-67
(White label.)
COLUMBIA (9000 series)..........35-45 65-69
(White label.)
COLUMBIA (116003/4 "Fifth Dimension" Interview Album).................100-125 66
MURRAY HILL............................5-10 87
PAIR...10-12 83
REALM......................................8-12 76
RHINO 5-10 88

Members: Jim (Roger) McGuinn; Gene Clark; David Crosby; Chris Hillman; Michael Clark; Gram Parsons; Clarence White; Gene Parsons; John York; Skip Battin. Session: Jay Dee Maness.

Also see BEEFEATERS
Also see CLARK, Gene
Also see CROSBY, David
Also see HILLMAN, Chris
Also see McGUINN, Roger
Also see PACIFIC STEEL CO.
Also see PARSONS, Gram

BYRNE, David

LP '81

Singles: 12-inch 33/45rpm

SIRE.. 4-6 82

LPs: 10/12-inch 33rpm

ECM.. 5-8 85
LUAKA BOP................................ 5-8 89
SIRE.. 5-10 81

Also see ENO, Brian
Also see TALKING HEADS

BYRNES, Edd "Kookie," with Joanie Sommers & Mary Kaye Trio

Singles: 7-inch

W.B. 5-10 59

Picture Sleeves

W.B. 8-12 59

Also see KAYE, Mary
Also see SOMMERS, Joanie

BYRNES, Edward

(Edd "Kookie" Byrnes; with Connie Stevens & Don Ralke's Orchestra; with Friend; with Mary Kaye Trio.)

P&R '59

Singles: 7-inch

W.B. (5047 "Kookie Kookie")....... 5-10 59
W.B. (S-5047 "Kookie Kookie"). 10-20 59
(Stereo.)
W.B. (5087 thru 5121)................ 5-10 59

Picture Sleeves

W.B. 15-20 59

EPs: 7-inch 33/45rpm

W.B. (1309 "Edd "Kookie" Byrnes") 15-25 59

LPs: 10/12-inch 33rpm

W.B. (1309 "Kookie")................ 25-35 59

Also see BYRNES, Edd "Kookie," with Joanie Sommers & Mary Kaye Trio
Also see RALKE, Don
Also see STEVENS, Connie

BYRON, D.L.

LP '80

Singles: 7-inch

ARISTA 3-4 80

LPs: 10/12-inch 33rpm

ARISTA 5-10 80

BYRON, Junior

D&D '83

Singles: 12-inch 33/45rpm

VANGUARD................................ 4-6 83

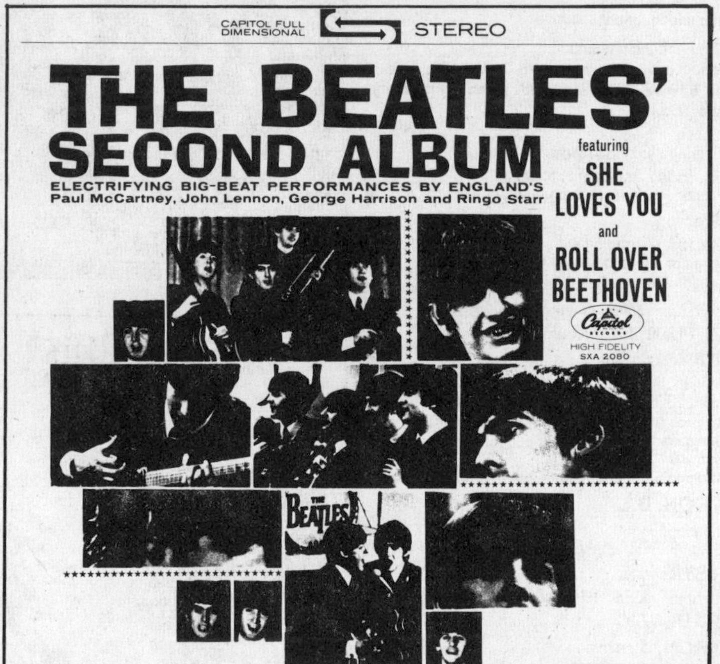

Capitol ST-2080—Seeburg Part No. 641

C

C & C Music Factory
(Clivilles & Cole)

LP '91

LPs: 10/12-inch 33rpm

COLUMBIA 5-8 91

C & SHELLS

R&B '69

Singles: 7-inch

COTILLION 3-4 69
ZANZEE 3-5 72

Members: Calvin White; Andrea Bolden; Lonzine Wright.
Also see SANDPEBBLES

C-BANK
(Featuring Jenny Burton)

R&B/D&D '83

Singles: 7-inch

NEXT PLATEAU 3-4 83

Also see BURTON, Jenny

C.C. & COMPANY

P&R '76

Singles: 7-inch

SUSSEX 3-5 75
20TH CENTURY/WESTBOUND... 3-5 75

Also see C.J. & CO.

C.C.S.
(Collective Consciousness Society)

P&R/LP '71

Singles: 7-inch

BELL 3-5 73
RAK 4-8 71

LPs: 10/12-inch 33rpm

RAK 15-20 71-72

Member: Alexis Korner.

C.J. & CO.
(C.C. & COMPANY)

P&R '77

Singles: 7-inch

WESTBOUND 3-5 77-78

LPs: 10/12-inch 33rpm

WESTBOUND 5-10 77-78

Members: Dennis Coffey; Cornelius Brown; Joni Tolbert; Charles Clark; Connie Durden; Curtis Durden.
Also see C.C. & COMPANY
Also see COFFEY, Dennis

C.L. BLAST: see BLAST, C.L.

C.O.D.s

P&R '65

Singles: 7-inch

KELLMAC (1003 "Michael") 5-10 65
KELLMAC (1005 "Pretty Baby") 10-20 66
KELLMAC (1012 "Coming Back Girl") 50-100 66

Members: Larry Brownlee; Robert Lewis; Carl Washington.
Also see LOST GENERATION
Also see MYSTIQUE

C.Q.D.

D&D '83

Singles: 12-inch 33/45rpm

EMERGENCY 4-6 83

CABOOSE

P&R '70

Singles: 7-inch

ENTERPRISE 3-5 70

LPs: 10/12-inch 33rpm

ENTERPRISE 10-15 71

CACTUS

LP '70

Singles: 7-inch

ATCO 5-8 70-72

LPs: 10/12-inch 33rpm

ATCO 20-25 70-72

Members: Carmine Appice; Tim Bogert; Pete French; Werner Fritzschings; Duane Hitchings; Jerry Norris; Mike Pinera; Roland Robinson; Rusty Day; Jim McCarty.
Also see BECK, BOGERT & APPICE
Also see DAY, Rusty
Also see NEW CACTUS BAND
Also see PINERA, Mike
Also see THEE IMAGE

CACTUS WORLD NEWS

LP '86

Singles: 7-inch

MCA 3-4 86

LPs: 10/12-inch 33rpm

MCA 5-10 86

CADETS

P&R/R&B '56

Singles: 78rpm

MODERN (Except 971) 15-25 55-57
MODERN (971 "If It Is Wrong")..20-40 55

Singles: 7-inch

COLLECTABLES 3-4 81
MODERN (Except 971) 20-40 55-57
MODERN (971 "If It Is Wrong")75-100 55

LPs: 10/12-inch 33rpm

CROWN (370 "The Cadets") 25-40 63
CROWN (5015 "Rockin' 'n Reelin") 75-100 57
RELIC 10-15

Members: Ted Taylor; Aaron Collins; Will "Dub" Jones; Willie Davis; Lloyd McGraw; Prentice Moreland; Tom Fox; Randolph Jones.
Also see FLARES
Also see JACKS
Also see TAYLOR, Ted

CADILLAC, Flash: see FLASH CADILLAC

CADILLACS

(With the Jesse Powell Orchestra)

P&R '55

Singles: 78rpm

JOSIE (765 "Gloria") 25-50 54
JOSIE (769 "Wishing Well") 25-50 54
JOSIE (773 thru 820) 15-30 55-57
REO (8002 "No Chance") 15-25 55
(Canadian.)
REO (8071 "Speedoo") 15-25 55
(Canadian.)

Singles: 7-inch

ABC 3-4 73
ARCTIC (101 "Fool") 50-100 64
CAPITOL 8-12 62
JOSIE (765 "Gloria") 300-400 54
JOSIE (769 "Wishing Well") .. 350-450 54
JOSIE (773 "No Chance") 40-60 55
JOSIE (778 "Down the Road") .. 40-60 55
JOSIE (785 "Speedoo") 25-50 55
JOSIE (792 "Zoom") 25-50 56
JOSIE (798 "Betty My Love") 25-50 56
JOSIE (800 series, except 820) 10-20 56-60
JOSIE (820 "My Girl Friend") 25-50 57
JOSIE (900 series) 5-10 63
JUBILEE (9010 "Romeo") 30-50 62
(Stereo.)
LANA 3-6 64
MERCURY 15-25 61
REO (8002 "No Chance") 30-40 55
(Canadian.)
REO (8071 "Speedoo") 25-35 55
(Canadian.)
SMASH 5-10 61
VIRGO 3-5 72-73

LPs: 10/12-inch 33rpm

CADAVER 5-10
HARLEM HITPARADE 10-15 70s
JUBILEE (1045 "The Fabulous
Cadillacs") 300-400 57
(Blue label.)
JUBILEE (1045 "The Fabulous
Cadillacs") 200-250 59
(Flat black label.)
JUBILEE (1045 "The Fabulous
Cadillacs") 50-100 60
(Glossy black label.)
JUBILEE (1089 "The Crazy
Cadillacs") 150-250 58
(Flat black label.)
JUBILEE (1089 "The Crazy
Cadillacs") 75-125 60
(Glossy black label.)
JUBILEE (5009 "Twistin' with
the Cadillacs") 50-75 62
(Monaural.)
JUBILEE (5009 "Twistin' with
the Cadillacs") 75-125 62
(Stereo.)
MURRAY HILL (1195 "The Very Best
of the Cadillacs") 5-10 88
MURRAY HILL (1285 "The
Cadillacs") 30-35
(Five-LP boxed set.)

Members: Earl "Speedoo" Carroll; Jim "Papa" Clark; Gus Willingham; Bobby Phillips; Laverne Drake; Charles Brooks; James Bailey; Earl Wade.

Also see BAILEY, J.R.
Also see BREWSTER, Ray, & Cadillacs
Also see CARROL, Earl, & Original Cadillacs
Also see CRICKETS
Also see CRYSTALS
Also see FIVE CROWNS
Also see HOWARD, Gregory
Also see MISSLES
Also see NEW YORK CITY
Also see OPALS
Also see ORIGINAL CADILLACS
Also see PEARLS
Also see POWELL, Jesse
Also see RAY, Bobby, & Cadillacs
Also see SCHOOLBOYS
Also see SOLITAIRES
Also see SPEEDO & CADILLACS

CADILLACS / Orioles

LPs: 10/12-inch 33rpm

JUBILEE (1117 "The Cadillacs Meet
the Orioles") 75-100 61
Also see CADILLACS
Also see ORIOLES

CAESAR, Shirley

(With the Caesar Singers)

P&R/R&B '75

Singles: 7-inch

HOB/SCEPTER 3-5 73-75
ROADSHOW 3-5 77-78

LPs: 10/12-inch 33rpm

HOB 8-12 70-75
ROADSHOW 5-10 77
TRIP 5-10 77

CAESAR & CLEO

P&R '65

Singles: 7-inch

REPRISE 10-15 64-65
VAULT 15-25 63

Picture Sleeves

REPRISE (0419 "Let the Good
Times Roll") 25-50 65

Members: Salvatore "Sonny" Bono; Cher LaPiere.

Also see SONNY & CHER

CAESAR & ROMANS: see LITTLE CAESAR & ROMANS

CAESARS

R&B '67

Singles: 7-inch

LANIE (2001 "Lala I Love
You") 75-125 67
LANIE (2002 "Girl I Miss You") .. 25-35 67

CAFE
(With the Hearns Sisters)
D&D '84
Singles: 12–inch 33/45rpm
MONTAGE.................................4-6 84

CAFFERTY, John
(With the Beaver Brown Band)
LP '83
Singles: 7–inch
SCOTTI BROTHERS...................3-4 84-86
Picture Sleeves
SCOTTI BROTHERS...................3-4 84-86
LPs: 10/12–inch 33rpm
SCOTTI BROTHERS.................5-10 84-89
Also see EDDIE & CRUISERS

CAIN, Joe, & Red Parrot Orchestra
R&B '83
Singles: 7–inch
ZOO YORK.................................3-4 83

CAIN, Jonathan
(Jonathan Cain Band)
P&R '76
Singles: 7–inch
BEARSVILLE..............................3-5 76
OCTOBER..................................3-5 75-76
LPs: 10/12–inch 33rpm
BEARSVILLE............................5-10 77
Also see BABYS
Also see CAIN, Tane
Also see JOURNEY

CAIN, Tane
P&R/LP '82
Singles: 7–inch
RCA...3-4 82-83
LPs: 10/12–inch 33rpm
RCA.......................................5-10 82
Also see CAIN, Jonathan

CAIN, Tasso: see TASSO-CAIN

CAINE, General
R&B '82
Singles: 12–inch 33/45rpm
CAPITOL...................................4-6 84
TABU.......................................4-6 82-84
Singles: 7–inch
CAPITOL...................................3-4 84
TABU.......................................3-4 82-84
LPs: 10/12–inch 33rpm
TABU.....................................5-10 82-84

CAIOLA, Al
(Al Caiola & His Orchestra)
P&R '60
Singles: 78rpm
RCA...4-8 53-55
REGENCY..................................4-8 56
Singles: 7–inch
AVLANCHE................................3-4 73
PREFERRED...............................3-6 59-60
RCA...4-8 53-55
REGENCY..................................4-8 56
U.A..3-6 60-68
EPs: 7–inch 33/45rpm
RCA.......................................5-10 53
LPs: 10/12–inch 33rpm
ATCO....................................10-15 60
BAINBRIDGE..............................5-8 80
CAMDEN..................................8-12 62
CHANCELLOR.........................10-15 60
RCA......................................10-15 59
ROULETTE.............................10-15 60
SAVOY...................................15-25 56
TIME.....................................10-20 60-61
TWO WORLDS...........................8-10 72
UNART.....................................8-12 67
U.A..10-15 60-69
Also see TONES

CALDERA
R&B/LP '77
Singles: 7–inch
CAPITOL...................................3-5 76
LPs: 10/12–inch 33rpm
CAPITOL.................................8-10 76-79

CALDWELL, Bobby
P&R/R&B/LP '78
Singles: 12–inch 33/45rpm
MCA...4-6 84-85
Singles: 7–inch
CLOUDS....................................3-4 78-80
PBR INT'L.................................3-4 76
POLYDOR..................................3-4 82-83
MCA...3-4 84-85
LPs: 10/12–inch 33rpm
CLOUDS..................................5-10 78-80
MCA.......................................5-10 84
POLYDOR................................5-10 82
Also see CAPTAIN BEYOND

CALDWELL, Rue
R&B/D&D '83
Singles: 12–inch 33/45rpm
CRITIQUE..................................4-6 83
Singles: 7–inch
CRITIQUE..................................3-4 83

CALE, J.J.
P&R/LP '72
Singles: 7–inch
LIBERTY (55840 "Dick Tracy")....5-10 66
MERCURY..................................3-4 83-84
SHELTER...................................3-5 71-81
LPs: 10/12–inch 33rpm
MCA.......................................5-10 81
MERCURY................................5-10 82-85
SHELTER...............................10-15 71-79
SILVERTONE.............................5-8 80
Also see LEATHERCOATED MINDS

CALE, John

LP '81

Singles: 7-inch

A&M 3-4 81
COLUMBIA 3-5 70
I.R.S. 3-4 79-80
REPRISE 3-5 72

Picture Sleeves

I.R.S. 3-4 79-80

LPs: 10/12-inch 33rpm

A&M 5-10 81
COLUMBIA 12-15 70-71
I.R.S. 5-10 79
ISLAND 8-10 75-77
PASSPORT 5-10 84
REPRISE 10-12 72-73
ZE 5-10 83

Also see AYERS, Kevin
Also see EARTH OPERA
Also see PRIMATIVES
Also see REED, Lou, & John Cale
Also see VELVET UNDERGROUND

CALEN, Frankie

P&R '61

Singles: 7-inch

BEAR 4-8 62
EPIC 4-8 63-64
KIP (1517 "Pretty Dimple") 8-12
NRC (029 "Angel Face") 5-10 59
NRC (5008 "Angel Face") 5-10 59
SPARK 15-20 61
U.A. 4-8 62

CALHOON

R&B '75

Singles: 12-inch 33/45rpm

W.B./SPECTOR 4-8 75

Singles: 7-inch

W.B./SPECTOR 3-5 75-76

CALIFORNIA RAISINS

LP '87

Singles: 7-inch

ATLANTIC 3-4 88
PRIORITY (Black vinyl) 3-4 87-88
PRIORITY (7915 "What Does It Take to Win Your Love") 4-6 88
(Colored vinyl.)

Picture Sleeves

PRIORITY 3-5 87-88

LPs: 10/12-inch 33rpm

PRIORITY 5-10 87-88

Member: Buddy Miles.
Also see MILES, Buddy

CALL, The

P&R/LP '83

Singles: 12-inch 33/45rpm

ELEKTRA 4-6 86

Singles: 7-inch

ELEKTRA 3-4 86
MCA 3-4 89
MERCURY 3-4 83

Picture Sleeves

MCA 3-4 89

LPs: 10/12-inch 33rpm

ELEKTRA 5-10 86-87
MCA 5-8 89
MERCURY 5-10 82-83

CALLENDER, Bobby

P&R '63

Singles: 7-inch

CORAL 5-10 67
ROULETTE (4471 "Little Star") 8-12 63

LPs: 10/12-inch 33rpm

MGM (4557 "Rainbow") 75-125 68
(Includes lyrics insert.)

CALLIER, Terry

R&B '79

Singles: 12-inch 33/45rpm

ERECT 4-6 82

Singles: 7-inch

CADET (Except 5623) 50-75 68
CADET (5623 "Look at Me Now") 5-10 69-73
ELEKTRA 3-5 78-79

LPs: 10/12-inch 33rpm

CADET 10-12 72-73
CHESS 10-15 71
ELEKTRA 8-10 78-79

CALLOWAY

P&R/LP '90

Singles: 7-inch

SOLAR 3-4 90

Picture Sleeves

SOLAR 3-4 90

LPs: 10/12-inch 33rpm

SOLAR 5-8 90

Members: Cino-Vincent Calloway; Reggie Calloway.
Also see MIDNIGHT STAR

CALLOWAY, Cab

(With Cab Jivers; with Caballiers)

P&R '30

Singles: 78rpm

ABC-PAR 4-8 56
BANNER 8-12 31-32
BELL 4-8 53-55
BLUEBIRD 5-10 49
BRUNSWICK 5-15 30-36
COLUMBIA 5-10 42-49
CONQUEROR 8-12 38-41
DOMINO 10-15 30
HI-TONE 5-8 49
JEWEL 8-12 31
MEL-O-DEE 10-20 31
MELOTONE 8-12 32-33
OKEH 5-10 40-42
ORIOLE 8-12 32-33

PERFECT 8-12 32
RCA.. 4-8 49
REGAL 5-12 31-51
ROMEO... 8-12 32-33
SIGNATURE 5-8 49
VARIETY....................................... 8-12 33-37
VICTOR.. 5-15 33-34
VOCALION.................................... 5-10 38-40

Singles: 7–inch

ABC-PAR 10-15 56
BELL 10-15 53-55
BOOM 4-6 65
CORAL.. 4-8 61-62
GONE... 5-10 58
OKEH (6896 "Willow Weep for Me")............................... 20-30 52
RCA (007 "Rooming House Boogie")...................... 50-75 49
RCA (8000 series)........................ 4-6 62
RCA (11000 series)...................... 3-5 78

EPs: 7–inch 33/45rpm

EPIC (7000 series).................. 10-20 53

LPs: 10/12–inch 33rpm

BRUNSWICK (58010 "Cab Calloway") 40-60 52
CORAL (57408 "Blues Make Me Happy") 15-20 62
(Monaural.)
CORAL (757408 "Blues Make Me Happy") 20-30 62
(Stereo.)
EPIC (3265 "Cab Calloway")....... 30-50 57
GONE (101 "Cotton Club Revue") 30-50 58
GUEST STAR 10-15 60s
RCA (LPM-2021 "Hi De Hi De Ho")....................................... 15-25 60
(Monaural.)
RCA (LSP-2021 "Hi De Hi De Ho")....................................... 25-35 60
(Stereo.)

CALVERT, Eddie

P&R '53

Singles: 78rpm

CAPITOL...................................... 3-5 56
ESSEX 3-5 53-54

Singles: 7–inch

ABC-PAR 4-6 60-61
CAPITOL...................................... 4-8 56
ESSEX 4-8 53-54

LPs: 10/12–inch 33rpm

ABC-PAR 10-15 60-62

CAMBRIDGE, Godfrey

LP '64

LPs: 10/12–inch 33rpm

EPIC..................................... 10-20 64-68

CAMBRIDGE STRINGS & SINGERS

P&R '61

Singles: 7–inch

LONDON......................................3-5 61
Also see KNIGHTSBRIDGE STRINGS

CAMEL

LP '74

Singles: 7–inch

JANUS 3-5 74-77

LPs: 10/12–inch 33rpm

ARISTA.......................................5-10 79
JANUS 8-10 74-77
PASSPORT 5-10 81
Members: Peter Bardens; Doug Ferguson; Andy Latimer; Andy Ward.
Also see BARDENS, Peter
Also see STRANGE BREW

CAMEO

R&B/LP '77

Singles: 12–inch 33/45rpm

ATLANTA ARTISTS.........................4-6 83-86
CHOCOLATE CITY 4-6 78-80

Singles: 7–inch

ATLANTA ARTISTS..........................3-4 83-88
CHOCOLATE CITY 3-5 75-82

Picture Sleeves

ATLANTA ARTISTS..........................3-4 86-88

LPs: 10/12–inch 33rpm

ATLANTA ARTISTS.......................5-10 83-90
CHOCOLATE CITY 5-10 77-82
Members: Tomi Jenkins; Larry Blackmon; Nathan Leftenant.
Also see EAST COAST
Also see SINGLETON, Charlie

CAMERON
(Rafael Cameron)

R&B/LP '80

Singles: 7–inch

SALSOUL 3-4 80-82

LPs: 10/12–inch 33rpm

SALSOUL.......................................5-10 80-82

CAMERON, G.C.

R&B '71

Singles: 7–inch

MALACO 3-4 83
MOTOWN 3-5 73-77
MOWEST 3-5 71-73

LPs: 10/12–inch 33rpm

MOTOWN 5-10 74-77
Also see SPINNERS

CAMERON, Rafael: see CAMERON

CAMOUFLAGE

P&R '88

Singles: 12–inch 33/45rpm

ROULETTE...4-6 79

Singles: 7–inch

ATLANTIC..3-4 88
ROULETTE...3-5 76

Picture Sleeves

ATLANTIC 3-4 88

LPs: 10/12–inch 33rpm

ATLANTIC 5-8 88

CAMP, Hamilton

(Hamid Hamilton Camp & Skymonters; Bob Camp)

P&R '68

Singles: 7–inch

AMERICAN INT'L 3-5 71

W.B. 4-8 68

LPs: 10/12–inch 33rpm

ELEKTRA (200 series) 12-15 64

ELEKTRA (75000 series) 8-10 73

MOUNTAIN RAILROAD 5-10

W.B. 10-15 67-69

Also see GIBSON, Bob, & Bob Camp

CAMPBELL, Debbie

P&R '75

Singles: 7–inch

PLAYBOY 3-5 75

CAMPBELL, Glen

(With the Glen-Aires; with Green River Boys)

P&R '61

Singles: 7–inch

ATLANTIC AMERICA 3-4 82-86

CAPEHART 10-20 61

CAPITOL (2000 & 3000 series) 3-6 68-74

CAPITOL (4000 series) 3-5 75-81

(Orange or purple labels.)

CAPITOL (4783 thru 5360) 5-10 61-65

(Orange/yellow swirl labels.)

CAPITOL (5441 "Guess I'm Dumb") 30-40 65

(With Brian Wilson.)

CAPITOL (5504 thru 5939) 4-8 65-67

CAPITOL STARLINE 3-5

CENECO 10-15

CREST 10-15 61-62

(Mistakenly shown as "Glen Cambpbell" on some Crest labels.)

EVEREST 3-6 69

STARDAY 3-6 68

MCA 3-4 84-89

MIRAGE 3-4 81

UNIVERSAL 3-4 89

W.B. 3-4 80

Picture Sleeves

CAPITOL (Except 4856 & 5279) ... 3-6 68-74

CAPITOL (4856 "Long Black Limousine") 10-15 62

CAPITOL (5279 "Summer, Winter, Spring and Fall") 8-12 64

EPs: 7–inch 33/45rpm

CAPITOL 5-10 68-69

(Jukebox issues.)

CAPITOL/CHEVROLET (55 "The Glen Campbell Good Time Hour") 5-10 60s

CAPITOL CREATIVE PROD. 5-10 60s

LPs: 10/12–inch 33rpm

ATLANTIC AMERICA 5-10 82-86

BUCKBOARD 8-10

CAPITOL (103 thru 752) 8-15 68-71

CAPITOL (1810 "Big Bluegrass Special") 75-100 62

(Shown as by the Green River Boys Featuring Glen Campbell.)

CAPITOL (1881 thru 2392) 20-40 63-65

(With "T" or "ST" prefix.)

CAPITOL (2809 thru 2978) 8-15 67-69

(With "T" or "ST" prefix.)

CAPITOL (SM-2000 series) 5-10 78

CAPITOL (11000 thru 16000 series) 5-10 72-82

CAPITOL (94000 series) 8-15 72

(Capitol Record Club issues.)

CAPITOL (120000 series) 5-10

(Capitol Record Club issues.)

CAPITOL CREATIVE PROD. 8-12

CUSTOM TONE 15-20

LONGINES ("Glen Campbell's Golden Favorites") 20-30 72

(Six-LP, boxed set.)

PICKWICK 8-10 64-73

STARDAY 15-20 68-69

Session: Jerry Puckett.

Also see BACHARACH, Burt / Glen Campbell / Dionne Warwick

Also see BEACH BOYS

Also see CAPEHART, Jerry

Also see CHAMPS

Also see FABARES, Shelley

Also see FANN BAND

Also see FLEAS

Also see FOLKSWINGERS

Also see FORD, Tennessee Ernie, & Glen Campbell

Also see GEE CEES

Also see HONDELLS

Also see IN-GROUP

Also see LEGENDARY MASKED SURFERS

Also see MARTIN, Dean / Glen Campbell

Also see NELSON, Willie

Also see PUCKETT, Jerry

Also see RIP CHORDS

Also see ROGERS, Weldon

Also see SAGITTARIUS

Also see SWEET SOULS

Also see TILLIS, Mel, & Glen Campbell

Also see TUCKER, Tanya, & Glen Campbell

Also see WILSON, Brian

CAMPBELL, Glen, & Rita Coolidge

C&W/P&R '80

Singles: 7–inch

CAPITOL 3-4 80

Also see COOLIDGE, Rita

CAMPBELL, Glen, & Bobbie Gentry

C&W/LP '68

Singles: 7–inch

CAPITOL 3-5 68-70

EPs: 7-inch 33/45rpm

CAPITOL 8 10 68
(Jukebox issue only.)

LPs: 10/12-inch 33rpm

CAPITOL 8-10 68
Also see GENTRY, Bobbie

CAMPBELL, Glen / Lettermen / Ella Fitzgerald / Sandler & Young

LPs: 10/12-inch 33rpm

CAPITOL (56 "B.F. Goodrich Presents Christmas 1969") 10-15 69
(Promotional, special products issue.)
Also see FITZGERALD, Ella
Also see LETTERMEN
Also see SANDLER & YOUNG

CAMPBELL, Glen, & Anne Murray

C&W/P&R/LP '71

Singles: 7-inch

CAPITOL 3-5 71-72

LPs: 10/12-inch 33rpm

CAPITOL 5-10 71-80

CAMPBELL, Glen / Anne Murray / Kenny Rogers / Crystal Gayle

LP: 10/12-inch 33rpm

CAPITOL/U.A. (11743-F-19 "Glen/Anne/Kenny/Crystal") 300-500 78
(Four framed picture disc set. Promotional issue only.)
Also see GAYLE, Crystal
Also see MURRAY, Anne
Also see ROGERS, Kenny

CAMPBELL, Glen, & Billy Strange

LPs: 10/12-inch 33rpm

SURREY 12-20 65
Also see STRANGE, Billy

CAMPBELL, Glen, & Steve Wariner

C&W '87

Singles: 7-inch

MCA 3-4 87
Also see CAMPBELL, Glen
Also see WARINER, Steve

CAMPBELL, Jim

P&R '70

Singles: 7-inch

LAURIE 3-6 69-70

CAMPBELL, Jo Ann

P&R '60

Singles: 78rpm

ELDORADO 10-20 57
POINT 10-20 56

Singles: 7-inch

ABC-PAR 10-20 60-62
(Monaural.)
ABC-PAR (10134 "Kookie Little Paradise") 20-40 60
(Stereo.)
CAMEO 5-10 62-63
ELDORADO 15-20 57
GONE 10-20 59
POINT 15-25 56
RORI 4-8

LPs: 10/12-inch 33rpm

ABC-PAR (393 "Twistin' and Listenin") 40-50 62
(Monaural.)
ABC-PAR (393 "Twistin' and Listenin" 50-60 62
(Stereo.)
CAMEO (1026 "All the Hits of Jo Ann Campbell") 25-30 62
CORONET (199 "Starring Jo Ann Campbell") 25-30 62
END (306 "I'm Nobody's Baby") .40-60 59
Also see JO ANN & TROY

CAMPER VAN BEETHOVEN

LP '88

LPs: 10/12-inch 33rpm

VIRGIN 5-8 88-89

CANDELA

R&B '82

Singles: 12-inch 33/45rpm

ARISTA 4-6 83

Singles: 7-inch

ARISTA 3-4 82-83

CANDI

P&R '88

Singles: 7-inch

I.R.S. 3-4 88

Picture Sleeves

I.R.S. 3-4 88

CANDLEMASS

LP '89

LPs: 10/12-inch 33rpm

METAL BLADE 5-8 89

CANDY & KISSES

P&R/R&B '64

Singles: 7-inch

CAMEO 10-15 64
COLLECTABLES 3-4 81
DECCA 4-8 68
R&L 10-15 63
SCEPTER 8-12 65-66
Members: Candy Nelson; Suzanne Nelson; Jeanette Johnson.

CANDYMAN

P&R/LP '90

Singles: 7-inch

EPIC 3-4 90

LPs: 10/12-inch 33rpm

EPIC 5-8 90

CANDYMEN

P&R/LP '67

Singles: 7-inch

ABC 4-8 67-69
LIBERTY 3-6 70

LPs: 10/12–inch 33rpm

ABC 15-25 67-68

Members: Rodney Justo; Barry Bailey; Dean Daughtry; Billy Gilmore; Paul Goddard; John Adkins; Bob Nix.

Also see ATLANTA RHYTHM SECTION
Also see BEAVERTEETH
Also see CLASSICS IV
Also see ORBISON, Roy

CANE, Gary
(With His Friends)

P&R '60

Singles: 7–inch

SHELL 8-12 60-61

CANNED HEAT
(Heat Brothers)

LP '67

Singles: 7–inch

ALA 3-4 84
ATLANTIC 3-5 74
LIBERTY 4-6 68-71
U.A. 3-5 71-73

Picture Sleeves

LIBERTY 4-8 67-69

LPs: 10/12–inch 33rpm

ACCORD 5-10 81
ALA 8-10 84
ATLANTIC 10-12 73-74
JANUS 12-15 69
LIBERTY (1000 series) 5-10 80
LIBERTY (7000 series) 15-20 67-69
LIBERTY (10000 series) 5-10 81
LIBERTY (11000 series) 10-15 69-70
PICKWICK 5-10 70s
SCEPTER 10-15
SUNSET 10-15 71
U.A. 10-15 71-75
WAND 15-20 70

Members: Bob Hite; Joel Scott Hill; Harvey Mandel; Mark Andes; Ed Bayer; Frank Cook; Richard Hite; Chris Morgan; James Shane; Gene Taylor; Larry Taylor; Henry Vestine; Alan Wilson; Adolfo "Fito" de la Parra.

Also see GAMBLERS
Also see HILL, Joel
Also see HOOKER, John Lee, & Canned Heat
Also see LITTLE RICHARD
Also see MANDEL, Harvey
Also see SMOKE

CANNED HEAT & CHIPMUNKS

Singles: 7–inch

LIBERTY 15-25 68-70

Also see CANNED HEAT
Also see CHIPMUNKS

CANNIBAL & HEADHUNTERS

P&R/LP '65

Singles: 7–inch

AIRES 4-8 68
CAPITOL 3-6 69
COLLECTABLES 3-4 81
DATE 4-8 66
ERA 3-5 73
RAMPART 5-10 65-66

LPs: 10/12–inch 33rpm

DATE (3001 "Land of 1000 Dances") 20-25 66
RAMPART (3302 "Land of 1000 Dances") 40-50 65

Members: Frankie "Cannibal" Garcia; Robert Jaramillo; Joe Jaramillo; Richard Lopez.

CANNON, Ace
(Johnny "Ace" Cannon)

P&R '61

Singles: 7–inch

FERNWOOD (135 "Hoe Down Rock") 5-10 63
FERNWOOD (137 "Big Shot") 5-10 64
HI (2000 series) 5-10 61-66
HI (2100 thru 2300 series) 3-8 66-76
LOUIS (2001 "Tuff") 15-25 61
MOTOWN 3-4 82
SANTO 4-8 62

Picture Sleeves

HI 5-10 62-63

EPs: 7–inch 33/45rpm

HI (1133 "In the Spotlight") 5-10 68
(Jukebox issue.)

LPs: 10/12–inch 33rpm

ALLEGIANCE 5-10 84
GUSTO 5-10 80
HI (007 thru 040) 10-20 62-67
(Numbers in this series are preceeded by a "12" for mono or a "32" for stereo issues.)
HI (043 thru 090) 6-10 68-75
(Numbers in this series are preceded by a "32," indicating stereo.)
HI (6000 & 8000 series) 8-10 77-79
MOTOWN 5-10 83

Also see BLACK, Bill
Also see CANNON, Johnny

CANNON, Freddy
(Freddie Cannon)

P&R/R&B '59

Singles: 7–inch

AMHERST 3-5
BUDDAH 3-5 71
CLARIDGE 3-5 74-76
ERIC 3-4 78
HQ ("Kennywood Park") 4-6 87
(KDKA promotional issue only. No selection number used.)
MCA 3-5 74
METROMEDIA 3-5 72
ROYAL AMERICAN 3-6 69-70
SIRE 4-6 69
SWAN 5-10 59-64
W.B. 4-8 64-67
WE MAKE ROCK & ROLL RECORDS 4-6 68

Picture Sleeves

HQ ("Kennywood Park")............... 5-8 87
(KDKA promotional issue only. No selection number used.)
SWAN 15-25 59-62
W.B. 10-20 64-65

LPs: 10/12-inch 33rpm

RHINO....................................... 5-10 82
SWAN (502 "The Explosive Freddy Cannon"..................... 50-75 60
(Monaural.)
SWAN (502 "The Explosive Freddy Cannon"..................... 65-90 60
(Stereo.)
SWAN (504 "Happy Shades of Blue") 50-75 62
SWAN (505 "Solid Gold Hits")... 50-75 61
SWAN (507 "Palisades Park") .. 50-75 62
SWAN (511 "Freddy Cannon Steps Out")............................ 50-75 62
W.B. (1544 "Freddie Cannon").. 30-40 64
W.B. (1612 "Action")................ 30-40 64
W.B. (1628 "Greatest Hits") 30-40 64

Also see BUCHANAN, Roy
Also see DANNY & JUNIORS
Also see G-CLEFS
Also see SLAY, Frank

CANNON, Freddy, & Belmonts

Singles: 7-inch

MIA SOUND................................ 4-6 81

Also see BELMONTS, Freddy Cannon & Bo Diddley
Also see CANNON, Freddy

CANO, Eddie

LP '62

Singles: 7-inch

DUNHILL.................................... 3-6 66-67
GNP 4-6 62
REPRISE 4-8 62-65

LPs: 10/12-inch 33rpm

DUNHILL.................................. 10-15 67
GNP 8-15 61-62
RCA.. 8-15 62
REPRISE 8-15 62-65

CANTINA BAND

P&R '81

Singles: 7-inch

MILLENNIUM.............................. 5-8 81

Member: Lou Christie.
Also see CHRISTIE, Lou

CANTRELL, Lana

LP '68

Singles: 7-inch

EAST COAST 3-4 74
POLYDOR.................................. 3-4 74-75
RCA.. 3-6 66-69

LPs: 10/12-inch 33rpm

RCA.. 8-15 67-69

CANYON

P&R '75

Singles: 7-inch

MAGNA-GLIDE............................3-5 75

CAPALDI, Jim

P&R/LP '72

Singles: 12-inch 33/45rpm

ISLAND......................................4-8 88
(Promotional only.)
RSO 4-6 79

Singles: 7-inch

ATLANTIC..................................3-4 83
ISLAND......................................3-5 72-88
RSO 3-4 78

Picture Sleeves

ATLANTIC..................................3-4 83

LPs: 10/12-inch 33rpm

ATLANTIC................................5-10 83
CAPITOL..................................8-10 72
ISLAND....................................6-12 73-88
RSO 5-10 78-79

Also see TRAFFIC

CAPITOL'S MYSTERY ARTIST
(Nancy Wilson)

Singles: 7-inch

CAPITOL (1667 "Something Wonderful Happens")...............5-10 60
(Promotional issue only. Nancy's name is not shown on label.)

Also see WILSON, Nancy

CAPITOLS

P&R/R&B/LP '66

Singles: 7-inch

COLLECTABLES.........................3-4 81
KAREN.......................................4-8 66-68

LPs: 10/12-inch 33rpm

ATCO.......................................15-20 66
COLLECTABLES.........................6-8 88
SOLID SMOKE 5-10 85

Members: Sam George; Don Storball; Richard McDougall.

CAPRELLS

R&B '77

Singles: 7-inch

ARIOLA AMERICA 3-5 76
BANO (100 "Walk On By")..........8-10
CRS (008 "Which One Will It Be") .5-8

CAPRIS

P&R '60

Singles: 7-inch

AMBIENT SOUND........................3-6 82
COLLECTABLES.........................3-4 81
LOST NITE (101 "There's a Moon Out Tonight").........................20-30 60
(Pink label.)
LOST NITE (101 "There's a Moon Out Tonight")..............................5-10 60s
(Yellow label.)

MR. PEEKE (118 "Limbo") 8-12 63
OLD TOWN (1094 "There's a Moon Out Tonight") 10-20 60
OLD TOWN (1099 "Where I Fell in Love") 25-35 60
OLD TOWN (1103 "Why Do I Cry") 20-30 60
OLD TOWN (1107 "Girl in My Dreams") 30-50 61
PLANET (1010 "There's a Moon Out Tonight") 150-250 60
TROMMERS (101 "There's a Moon Out Tonight") 25-35 60

LPs: 10/12-inch 33rpm

AMBIENT SOUND 5-10 82
COLLECTABLES 6-8 84

Members: Nick "Santos" Santamaria; Mike Mitchell; Vince Narcardo; John Apostol; Frank Reina.

CAPTAIN & TENNILLE

P&R/LP '75

Singles: 7-inch

A&M 3-5 75-78
BUTTERSCOTCH CASTLE (001 "The Way I Want to Touch You") 50-75 73
JOYCE (101 "The Way I Want to Touch You") 20-40 74
CASABLANCA 3-5 79-80

Picture Sleeves

A&M 4-6 75-78

LPs: 10/12-inch 33rpm

A&M 8-10 75-79
CASABLANCA 5-10 79

Members: Daryl Dragon; Toni Tennille.
Also see BEACH BOYS
Also see DRAGONS
Also see TENNILLE, Toni
Also see YELLOW BALLOON

CAPTAIN BEEFHEART
(With His Magic Band)

LP '72

Singles: 7-inch

A&M (794 "Diddy Wah Diddy").. 50-75 66
A&M (818 "Moonchild") 40-60 66
BUDDAH 4-8 67-69
EPIC 3-5 82
MERCURY 3-5 74
REPRISE 3-6 72
VIRGIN 3-5 82

Promotional Singles

REPRISE (434 "Lick My Decals Off, Baby") 40-50 70
REPRISE (447 "Talking About") 40-50 71
REPRISE (514 "Click Clack").... 25-40 71
REPRISE (547 "Low Yo Yo Stuff") 40-50 72
(Issued with gatefold, EP-like, cover.)

LPs: 10/12-inch 33rpm

A&M 5-10 84
ACCORD 5-10 83
BIZARRE 10-12 72
BLUE THUMB (1 "Strictly Personal") 20-30 68
(Black label.)
BLUE THUMB (1 "Strictly Personal") 10-15 69
(Tan label.)
BUDDAH (1001 "Safe As Milk").25-35 67
(Monaural. Add $10 to $15 if accompanied by 4" x 15" "Safe As Milk" bumper sticker.)
BUDDAH (5001 "Safe As Milk").25-30 67
(Stereo. Add $10 to $15 if accompanied by 4" x 15" "Safe As Milk" bumper sticker.)
BUDDAH (5077 "Mirror Man") ...10-15 71
BUDDAH (5063 "Safe As Milk")...8-12 70
D.I.R. (57 "Direct News, Week of 12-18-78") 35-45 78
(Five, 5-minute radio programs, one of which has an interview with Don Van Vliet. Promotional issue only.)
EPIC 5-10 82
MERCURY (709 "Unconditionally Guaranteed") 8-12 74
MERCURY (1018 "Bluejeans and Moonbeams") 8-12 74
REPRISE (2027 "Trout Mask Replica") 8-12 77
REPRISE (2050 "Spotlight Kid") 10-15 72
REPRISE (2115 "Clear Spot") ... 10-20 72
(With embossed "Clear Spot" plastic bag.)
REPRISE (2115 "Clear Spot") ... 15-20 72
(White label. Has printed inserts instead of standard cover. Promotional issue only.)
STRAIGHT (1053 "Trout Mask Replica") 30-40 68
(With lyrics sleeve.)
STRAIGHT (1053 "Trout Mask Replica") 20-25 68
(Without lyrics sleeve.)
STRAIGHT (6420 "Lick My Decals Off, Baby") 10-15 70
VIRGIN 5-10 80-82
W.B. 5-10 78

Members: Don "Captain Beefheart" Van Vliet; Doug Moon; Paul Blakely; Alex St. Claire; Jerry Handley; Ry Cooder; Jeff Cotton; John French; Bill "Zoot Horn Rollo" Harkleroad; Rockette Morton; Jimmy Semens; Jerry Handsley; Ty Grimes.
Also see COODER, Ry
Also see MALLARD
Also see MOTHERS of INVENTION
Also see MU
Also see TRIANGLE

CAPTAIN BEYOND

LP '72

Singles: 7-inch

CAPRICORN 3-5 73

LPs: 10/12-inch 33rpm

CAPRICORN (Except 0105) 8-12 72-73

CAPRICORN (0105 "Captain Beyond") 45-55 72
(With 3-D cover.)
CAPRICORN (0105 "Captain Beyond") 15-25 72
(With standard cover.)
W.B. 8-10 77

Members: Bobby Caldwell; Rod Evans; Willie Daffern; Lee Dorman; Larry Reinhardt.
Also see CALDWELL, Bobby
Also see DEEP PURPLE
Also see IRON BUTTERFLY

CAPTAIN RAPP

D&D '83

Singles: 12–inch 33/45rpm

BECKET 4-6 83

Singles: 7–inch

BECKET 3-4 83

CAPTAIN SKY

(Daryl Cameron)

R&B '78

Singles: 12–inch 33/45rpm

WMOT 4-6 81

Singles: 7–inch

A.V.I. 3-5 79-82
TEC 3-4 80
TRIPLE 3-4 86
WMOT 3-4 81

LPs: 10/12–inch 33rpm

A.V.I. 5-10 78-82
TEC 5-10 80

CARA, Irene

P&R '80

Singles: 12–inch 33/45rpm

CASABLANCA 4-6 83
GEFFEN 4-6 83

Singles: 7–inch

CASABLANCA 3-4 83
GEFFEN 3-4 83-85
RSO 3-4 80
NETWORK 3-4 81

Picture Sleeves

GEFFEN 3-4 83

LPs: 10/12–inch 33rpm

GEFFEN 5-10 83-85
NETWORK 5-10 82
RSO 5-10 80

CARAVAN

LP '75

Singles: 7–inch

BTM 3-5 75
DK 3-4 83
LONDON 3-5 71

LPs: 10/12–inch 33rpm

ARISTA 5-10 76
BTM 5-10 75
LONDON 12-15 71-75
VERVE/FORECAST 15-20 69

Members: Steve Miller; Richard Coughlan; Pye Hastings; John Perry; Geoff Richards; Jan Schelhaas; Dave Sinclair; Richard Sinclair; Mike Wedgewood.
Also see HATFIELD & NORTH

CARAVELLES

P&R '63

Singles: 7–inch

SMASH 4-8 63-65

LPs: 10/12–inch 33rpm

SMASH (27044 "You Don't Have to Be a Baby to Cry") 20-30 63
(Monaural.)
SMASH (67044 "You Don't Have to Be a Baby to Cry") 20-30 63
(Stereo.)

Members: Lois Wilkinson; Andrea Simpson.

CARDENAS, Luis

P&R '86

Singles: 7–inch

ALLIED ARTISTS 3-4 86

Picture Sleeves

ALLIED ARTISTS 3-4 86

LPs: 10/12–inch 33rpm

ALLIED ARTISTS 5-10 86

Also see RENEGADE

CARDINALS

R&B '51

Singles: 78rpm

ATLANTIC 15-25 51-57

Singles: 7–inch

ATLANTIC (952 "I'll Always Love You") 75-100 51
ATLANTIC (958 "Wheel of Fortune") 75-100 52
ATLANTIC (972 "The Bump") .. 50-100 52
ATLANTIC (995 "You Are My Only Love") 75-100 53
ATLANTIC (1025 "Under a Blanket of Blue") 50-75 54
ATLANTIC (1054 "The Door Is Still Open") 40-60 55
ATLANTIC (1067 "Two Things I Love") 20-40 55
ATLANTIC (1079 "There Goes My Heart to You") 20-40 55
ATLANTIC (1090 "Off Shore") ... 20-40 56
ATLANTIC (1100 series) 15-25 56-57

EPs: 7–inch 33/45rpm

BIM BAM BOOM (1000 "The Cardinals") 6-12 70s

Members: Ernie Warren; Meredith Brothers; Leon Hardy; Donald Johnson; Jack "Sam" Aydelotte; Luther MacArthur; James Brown; Lee Tarver.

CAREFREES

P&R '64

Singles: 7–inch

LONDON INT'L (10614 "We Love You Beatles") 8-12 64

LONDON INT'L (10615 "Paddy Wack") ... 5-8 64

Picture Sleeves

LONDON INT'L (10614 "We Love You Beatles") ... 10-20 64

LPs: 10/12-inch 33rpm

LONDON (379 "We Love You All") ... 35-45 64

Members: Lyn Cornell; Betty Prescott; Barbara Kay.
Also see BREAKAWAYS
Also see VERNON'S GIRLS

CAREY, Mariah

P&R/LP '90

Singles: 7-inch

COLUMBIA ... 3-4 90

LPs: 10/12-inch 33rpm

COLUMBIA ... 5-8 90

CAREY, Tony

P&R/LP '83

Singles: 7-inch

MCA ... 3-4 84
ROCSHIRE ... 3-4 83

Picture Sleeves

MCA ... 3-4 84
ROCSHIRE ... 3-4 83

LPs: 10/12-inch 33rpm

MCA ... 5-10 84
ROCSHIRE ... 5-10 83

Also see PLANET P PROJECT
Also see RAINBOW

CARGILL, Henson

P&R/C&W '67

Singles: 7-inch

ARCO ... 4-6 67
ATLANTIC ... 3-5 73-74
COPPER MOUNTAIN ... 3-4 79-80
ELEKTRA ... 3-5 75
MEGA ... 3-5 71-73
MONUMENT ... 4-6 67-70
RUFF ... 4-6
TOWER ... 3-6 68

LPs: 10/12-inch 33rpm

ATLANTIC ... 6-10 73
HARMONY ... 6-10 72
MEGA ... 6-10 72
MONUMENT ... 8-12 68-70

CARLA & RUFUS: see RUFUS & CARLA

CARLIN, George

LP '72

Singles: 7-inch

LITTLE DAVID ... 3-5 72-75
RCA ... 4-8 67

Picture Sleeves

LITTLE DAVID ... 5-10 72

LPs: 10/12-inch 33rpm

ATLANTIC ... 5-10 81
CAMDEN ... 8-10 72
EARDRUM ... 5-10 84
ERA ... 8-12 72
LITTLE DAVID ... 5-10 72-85
RCA ... 10-15 67

CARLISLE, Belinda

P&R/LP '86

Singles: 12-inch 33/45rpm

I.R.S. ... 4-6 86

Singles: 7-inch

I.R.S. ... 3-4 86-87
MCA ... 3-4 87-90

Picture Sleeves

I.R.S. ... 3-4 86-87
MCA ... 3-4 87-88

LPs: 10/12-inch 33rpm

I.R.S. ... 5-10 86-87
MCA ... 5-10 87-90

Also see GO-GOs

CARLISLE, Steve

P&R '81

Singles: 7-inch

MCA ... 3-4 81-82

LPs: 10/12-inch 33rpm

MCA ... 5-10 82

CARLOS, Walter

LP '69

LPs: 10/12-inch 33rpm

COLUMBIA ... 8-12 69-72

CARLTON, Carl
(Little Carl Carlton)

P&R/R&B '68

Singles: 12-inch 33/45rpm

20TH FOX ... 4-6 80

Singles: 7-inch

ABC ... 3-5 73-76
BACK BEAT ... 3-6 68-75
CASABLANCA ... 3-4 86
GOLDEN WORLD (23 "Nothin' No Sweeter Than Love") ... 10-20 65
LANDO (8527 "So What") ... 30-40 65
MCA ... 3-4 84
MERCURY ... 3-5 77
RCA ... 3-4 82
20TH FOX ... 3-4 81-82

LPs: 10/12-inch 33rpm

ABC ... 10-12 74
BACK BEAT ... 10-15 73
CASABLANCA ... 5-10 86
RCA ... 5-10 82
20TH FOX ... 5-10 81

CARLTON, Larry

LP '78

Singles: 7-inch

GRP ... 3-4 90
MCA ... 3-4 85-86
UNI ... 4-6 68-69
W.B. ... 3-5 78-83

LPs: 10/12-inch 33rpm

ATLANTIC 5-10 84
BLUE THUMB 10-12 73
GRP 5-8 90
MCA 5-10 85-87
UNI 12-18 68
W.B. 5-10 78-83
Also see CRUSADERS
Also see POST, Mike

CARMAN, Pauli

R&B '86

Singles: 12-inch 33/45rpm

COLUMBIA 4-6 86

Singles: 7-inch

COLUMBIA 3-4 86-87

LPs: 10/12-inch 33rpm

COLUMBIA 5-10 86

CARMEN, Eric

P&R/LP '75

Singles: 12-inch 33/45rpm

GEFFEN 4-6 85

Singles: 7-inch

ARISTA (Except 9000 series) 3-5 75-80
ARISTA (9000 series) 3-4 88
COOL 3-4 86
EPIC 3-6 70
GEFFEN 3-4 84-85
RCA 3-4 87

Picture Sleeves

ARISTA (0266 "She Did It") 3-5 77
ARISTA (0295 "Boats Against the Current") 4-6 77
(Promotional issue only.)
ARISTA (9000 series) 3-4 88
GEFFEN 3-4 85

LPs: 10/12-inch 33rpm

ARISTA (Except 4057) 5-10 77-88
ARISTA (AL-4057 "Eric Carmen") 8-10 75
ARISTA (AQ-4057 "Eric Carmen") 15-20 75
(Quadraphonic.)
GEFFEN 5-10 85
Also see CYRUS ERIE
Also see MANDRELL, Louise, & Eric Carmen
Also see QUICK
Also see RASPBERRIES

CARN, Jean: see CARNE, Jean

CARNE, Jean
(Jean Carn)

R&B/LP '77

Singles: 7-inch

ATLANTIC 3-4 88
MOTOWN 3-4 82
OMNI 3-4 86
PHILADELPHIA INT'L 3-4 77-80
TSOP 3-4 81

LPs: 10/12-inch 33rpm

OMNI 5-10 86
PHILADELPHIA INT'L 5-10 76-80
MOTOWN 5-10 82
TSOP 5-10 81
Also see JOHNSON, Al, & Jean Carn
Also see MILITELLO, Bobby, & Jean Carn

CARNES, Kim

P&R '79

Singles: 12-inch 33/45rpm

EMI AMERICA 4-6 80-85

Singles: 7-inch

A&M 3-5 75-82
AMOS 3-6 71-72
EMI AMERICA 3-4 79-86
ELEKTRA 3-4 84

Picture Sleeves

EMI AMERICA 3-4 80-86

LPs: 10/12-inch 33rpm

A&M (3000 series) 5-10 82
A&M (4000 series) 8-10 75-77
AMOS 12-18 71
EMI AMERICA 5-10 79-86
MCA 5-10 84
MFSL (073 "Mistaken Identity") 20-30 82
Session: Lyle Lovett.
Also see COTTON, Gene, & Kim Carnes
Also see LOVETT, Lyle
Also see ROGERS, Kenny, & Kim Carnes
Also see STRIESAND, Barbra, & Kim Carnes
Also see SUGAR BEARS
Also see U.S.A. for AFRICA

CARNES, Kim, & Dave Ellington

Singles: 7-inch

AMOS 3-5 72
Also see CARNES, Kim

CARNIVAL

LP '69

Singles: 7-inch

U.A. 3-5 71
WORLD PACIFIC 3-6 69

LPs: 10/12-inch 33rpm

WORLD PACIFIC 10-15 69
Member: Terry Fisher.
Also see FISHER, Terry

CAROSONE, Renato

P&R '58

Singles: 7-inch

CAPITOL 4-8 58

CARPENTER, Carleton, & Debbie Reynolds

P&R '51

Singles: 78rpm

MGM 4-8 51

Singles: 7-inch

MGM 5-10 51

EPs: 7-inch 33/45rpm

MGM 5-15 51
Also see REYNOLDS, Debbie

CARPENTER, Mary Chapin

C&W/LP '89

Singles: 7-inch

COLUMBIA 3-4 89-92

LPs: 10/12-inch 33rpm

COLUMBIA 5-8 89-90

CARPENTER, Thelma

P&R '60

Singles: 78rpm

COLUMBIA 4-8 50
MAJESTIC 5-10 45-46

Singles: 7-inch

COLUMBIA 10-15 50
CORAL (Except 62272) 5-10 60-62
CORAL (62272 "Heartaches") .. 20-30 61

LPs: 10/12-inch 33rpm

CORAL (57433 "Thinking of You Tonight") 15-25 63
(Monaural.)
CORAL (7-57433 "Thinking of You Tonight") 25-35 63
(Stereo.)

CARPENTERS

P&R/LP '70

Singles: 7-inch

A&M (Except 2735) 3-6 69-82
A&M (2735) 10-15
(Promotional issue only. Title not known.)

Picture Sleeves

A&M (Except 2735) 3-6 70-81
A&M (2735 "Yesterday Once More") 10-15
(Promotional issue only. With paper sleeve.)

EPs: 7-inch 33/45rpm

A&M 10-15 72-85

LPs: 10/12-inch 33rpm

A&M (3000 series) 8-15 71-85
A&M (4000 series, except 4205). 8-15 70-83
A&M (4205 "Offering") 20-35 69
A&M (4205 "Ticket to Ride") 10-15 71
A&M (5100 series") 5-8 90
A&M (50000 series) 15-25 74-75
(Quadrophonic series.)
A&M (6000 series) 8-12 85
MFP (50431 "Ticket to Ride").... 10-15 70

Members: Karen Carpenter; Richard Carpenter; Tony Peluso.
Also see CARPENTER, Karen
Also see CARPENTER, Richard

CARR, Cathy

P&R '56

Singles: 78rpm

CORAL 5-8 53-56
FRATERNITY 5-8 55-56

Singles: 7-inch

ABC 3-4 73
COLLECTABLES 3-4 81
CORAL 8-10 53-56
FRATERNITY 8-10 55-56
LAURIE 5-10 62-63
ROULETTE (Except 4152) 5-10 59-61
ROULETTE (4152 "I'm Gonna Change Him") 5-10 59
(Monaural.)
ROULETTE (SSR-4152 "I'm Gonna Change Him") 10-15 59
(Stereo.)
SMASH 4-8 61

EPs: 7-inch 33/45rpm

BRUNSWICK 10-20 57

LPs: 10/12-inch 33rpm

DOT 15-25 66
FRATERNITY (1005 "Ivory Tower") 40-50 57
RCA 10-20 64
ROULETTE (R-25077 "Shy")..... 25-40 59
(Monaural.)
ROULETTE (SR-25077 "Shy") .. 30-50 59
(Stereo.)

CARR, James

P&R/R&B '66

Singles: 7-inch

ATLANTIC 3-5 71
GOLDWAX 4-8 65-69

LPs: 10/12-inch 33rpm

GOLDWAX 12-20 67-68

Also see SOUL STIRRERS

CARR, Jerry

R&B '81

Singles: 7-inch

CHERIE 3-4 81

CARR, Joe "Fingers"

P&R '50

(Lou Busch)

Singles: 78rpm

CAPITOL 3-6 50-57

Singles: 7-inch

CAPITOL 5-10 50-59
CORAL 4-6 63
DOT 3-6 66
W.B. 4-8 60-62

EPs: 7-inch 33/45rpm

CAPITOL 5-15 51-57

LPs: 10/12-inch 33rpm

CAPITOL (Except 2000 series) . 15-30 51-61
CAPITOL (2000 series) 10-15 64
CORAL 10-15 63
DOT 10-15 66
W.B. 10-20 60-62

Also see BUSCH, Lou
Also see FORD, Tennessee Ernie, & Joe "Fingers" Carr
Also see FRAZIER, Dallas, & Joe "Fingers" Carr
Also see PROVINE, Dorothy, & Joe "Fingers" Carr
Also see YOUNG, Vicki, & Joe Carr

CARR, Valerie

P&R '58

Singles: 7-inch

ATLAS 4-8 64
ROULETTE 5-10 58-61

LPs: 10/12-inch 33rpm

ROULETTE (25094 "Ev'ry Hour, Ev'ry Day") 25-35 59

CARR, Vikki

LP '64

Singles: 7-inch

COLUMBIA 3-5 71-75
LIBERTY 4-8 62-69

Picture Sleeves

COLUMBIA 3-5 74
LIBERTY 4-8 67

LPs: 10/12-inch 33rpm

COLUMBIA 8-10 71-75
LIBERTY (Except 10000 series) 10-20 63-70
LIBERTY (10000 series) 5-10 81
SUNSET 8-12
U.A. 5-10 71-80

Also see BERNSTEIN, Elmer

CARR, Wynona

(Sister Wynona Carr)

R&B '57

Singles: 7-inch

REPRISE 5-10 61-63
SPECIALTY 5-10 59-60

LPs: 10/12-inch 33rpm

REPRISE 10-20 62
SPECIALTY 8-10 88

CARRACK, Paul

P&R/LP '82

Singles: 12-inch 33/45rpm

CHRYSALIS 4-8 87
(Promotional only.)

Singles: 7-inch

CHRYSALIS 3-4 87
EPIC 3-4 82

Picture Sleeves

CHRYSALIS 3-4 87-88

LPs: 10/12-inch 33rpm

CHRYSALIS 5-10 87-89
EPIC 5-10 82

Also see ACE
Also see MIKE + the MECHANICS
Also see ROXY MUSIC
Also see SQUEEZE

CARRADINE, Keith

P&R/LP '76

Singles: 7-inch

ABC 3-5 75
ASYLUM 3-5 78
VALA 3-4 83

LPs: 10/12-inch 33rpm

ASYLUM 8-10 76

CARRINGTON, Terri Lyne

LP '89

LPs: 10/12-inch 33rpm

FORECAST 5-8 89

CARROLL, Andrea

P&R '63

Singles: 7-inch

BIG TOP (515 "The Doolang")...30-40 64
BIG TOP (3156 "It Hurts to Be Sixteen") 8-12 63
EPIC (9438 "Young & Lonely") 50-100 61
(Yellow label.)
EPIC (9438 "Young & Lonely") ..50-75 61
(White label. Promotional issue.)
EPIC (9450 "Please Don't Talk to the Lifeguard") 10-15 61
EPIC (9471 "Gee Dad") 15-20 61
EPIC (9523 "Fifteen Shades of Pink") 15-20 62

Picture Sleeves

EPIC (9471 "Gee Dad") 25-35 61
RCA (8618 "Sally Fool") 8-12 65
U.A. (982 "The World Isn't Big Enough") 8-15 66
U.A. (50039 "Hey Beach Boy") 8-15 66

LPs: 10/12-inch 33rpm

B.T. PUPPY (1017 "Side by Side") 20-30 60s
(With Beverly Warren.)

CARROLL, Andrea / Beverly Warren

LPs: 10/12-inch 33rpm

B.T. PUPPY (1017 "Andrea Carroll and Beverly Warren") 50-75 69

Also see CARROLL, Andrea
Also see WARREN, Beverly

CARROLL, Bernadette

P&R '64

Singles: 7-inch

COLLECTABLES 3-4 81
JULIA 4-8 62
LAURIE 5-10 63-64

CARROLL, Bob

P&R '53

Singles: 78rpm

BALLY 4-8 56-57
DERBY 4-8 53
MGM 4-8 55

Singles: 7-inch

BALLY 5-10 56-57
DERBY 5-10 53
DOT 3-6 66
MGM 5-10 55
MURBO 3-6 67
UNART 4-8 59
U.A. 4-8 59-59

Picture Sleeves

U.A. 5-10 58

Also see JENKINS, Gordon, & His Orchestra

CARROLL, Cathy

P&R '62

Singles: 7-inch

CHEER.................................... 10-15 63-64
DOT.. 4-8 66
MUSICOR.................................. 4-8 65
PHILIPS.................................... 4-8 63
TRIODEX.................................. 10-15 61
W.B. 5-10 62-63

CARROLL, David, Orchestra

P&R '54

Singles: 78rpm

MERCURY.................................. 3-5 53-57

Singles: 7-inch

MERCURY.................................. 4-8 53-62

EPs: 7-inch 33/45rpm

MERCURY.................................. 5-10 54-59

LPs: 10/12-inch 33rpm

MERCURY.................................. 8-18 53-62
WING....................................... 5-10 59

Also see CONTINO, Dick

CARROLL, Jim

(Jim Carroll Band)

LP '80

Singles: 12-inch 33/45rpm

ATLANTIC.................................. 4-8 83
(Promotional only.)

Singles: 7-inch

A&M... 3-5 72
ATCO....................................... 3-4 80-81
ATLANTIC.................................. 3-4 83

LPs: 10/12-inch 33rpm

A&M... 10-15 71
ATCO....................................... 5-10 80-82
ATLANTIC.................................. 5-10 83

CARROLL, Ronnie

P&R '63

Singles: 7-inch

PHILIPS.................................... 4-8 63-66

CARROLL BROTHERS

P&R '62

Singles: 7-inch

CAMEO (140 "Red Hot")........... 50-75 58
CAMEO (200 series)................. 5-10 62
FELSTED................................... 5-10 59

LPs: 10/12-inch 33rpm

CAMEO (1015 "College Twist
Party")...................................... 25-35 62

Members: Pete Carroll; Dick Noble; Bill McGraw; Jimmy Chick; Kenneth Dorn.
Also see CARROLL, Pete

CARS

P&R/LP '78

Singles: 12-inch 33/45rpm

ELEKTRA.................................. 5-10 86
(Promotional issues only.)

Singles: 7-inch

ELEKTRA.................................. 3-5 78-88

Picture Sleeves

ELEKTRA.................................. 3-5 78-88

LPs: 10/12-inch 33rpm

ELEKTRA (Except 5E-567)......... 5-10 78-87
ELEKTRA (5E-567 "Shake It
Up")... 50-100 81
(Picture disc. Promotional issue only.)
NAUTILUS................................ 15-20 82
(Half-speed mastered.)

Members: Ric Ocasek; Elliot Easton; Benjamin Orr; Greg Hawkes; Dave Robinson.
Also see EASTON, Elliot
Also see MILKWOOD
Also see MODERN LOVERS
Also see OCASEK, Ric
Also see ORR, Benjamin

CARSON, Kit

P&R '55

Singles: 78rpm

CAPITOL.................................. 4-8 55

Singles: 7-inch

CAPITOL.................................. 8-10 55

CARSON, Mindy

P&R '46

Singles: 78rpm

COLUMBIA................................ 4-8 52-56

Singles: 7-inch

COLUMBIA................................ 8-12 52-56
JOY.. 4-8 60
RCA... 8-12 50-52

Also see MITCHELL, Guy, & Mindy Carson

CARTER, Benny, & His Orchestra

R&B/C&W '44

(Featuring Savannah Churchill)

Singles: 78rpm

BLUEBIRD................................ 4-8 41
BRUNSWICK............................. 4-8 46
CAPITOL.................................. 4-8 42-44
COLUMBIA (2898 "Devil's
Holiday")................................. 10-20 33
(Colored plastic.)
DECCA..................................... 4-8 40
OKEH...................................... 4-8 40
VOCALION............................... 4-8 35-40

Also see CHURCHILL, Savannah

CARTER, Carlene

(With Rockpile)

C&W '79

Singles: 7-inch

EPIC.. 3-4 83
REPRISE.................................. 3-4 90-91
W.B. 3-4 78-82

LPs: 10/12-inch 33rpm

EPIC.. 5-10 83
W.B. 5-10 78-82

Also see CARTER FAMILY
Also see EDMUNDS, Dave, & Carlene Carter
Also see ORRALL, Robert Ellis
Also see ROCKPILE
Also see SOUTHERN PACIFIC & Carlene Carter

CARTER, Carlene, & Dave Edmunds

C&W '80

Singles: 7-inch

W.B. 3-4 80

Also see CARTER, Carlene
Also see EDMUNDS, Dave

CARTER, Clarence

P&R/R&B '67

Singles: 12-inch 33/45rpm

ICHIBAN.................... 4-6 88

Singles: 7-inch

ABC.................... 3-5 75-76
ATLANTIC (2000 series).................... 4-8 68-72
ATLANTIC (13000 series).................... 3-4
FAME (Except 1000 series).................... 3-5 72-73
FAME (1000 series).................... 4-8 67
FUTURE STARS.................... 3-5
ICHIBAN.................... 3-4 88
RONN.................... 3-5 77
VENTURE.................... 3-4 80-81

LPs: 10/12-inch 33rpm

ABC.................... 8-10 74-76
ATLANTIC.................... 10-20 68-71
BIG C.................... 5-10 83
BRYLEN.................... 5-10 84
FAME.................... 10-12 73
ICHIBAN.................... 5-10 86-88
VENTURE.................... 5-10 80-81

CARTER, Clarence & Candi

Singles: 7-inch

ATLANTIC.................... 3-5 72

Also see CARTER, Clarence

CARTER, Mel

P&R/R&B '63

Singles: 7-inch

ABKCO.................... 3-4 84
AMOS.................... 3-5 69-70
ARWIN.................... 5-10 60
BELL.................... 3-6 68-69
CREAM.................... 3-4 81
DERBY.................... 5-10 63
IMPERIAL.................... 4-8 64-66
LIBERTY.................... 4-6 67-68
MERCURY.................... 4-8 62
PHILLIPS.................... 4-8 62
ROMAR.................... 3-5 73-74
TRI-STATE.................... 10-15 59

LPs: 10/12-inch 33rpm

AMOS.................... 10-12 70
DERBY (702 "When a Boy Falls in Love").................... 50-100 63
IMPERIAL.................... 15-20 65-66
LIBERTY.................... 12-20 67
SUNSET.................... 10-12 68-70

CARTER, Mel / Vic Dana

EPs: 7-inch 33/45rpm

ROWE/AMI.................... 5-10 60s

(Colored vinyl. Jukebox issue.)

Also see DANA, Vic

CARTER, Mel, & Clydie King

Singles: 7-inch

PHILIPS.................... 4-8 62

Also see CARTER, Mel
Also see KING, Clydie, & Sweet Things

CARTER, Ralph

P&R/R&B '75

Singles: 7-inch

MERCURY.................... 3-5 75-76

CARTER, Ron

LP '77

LPs: 10/12-inch 33rpm

MILESTONE.................... 5-10 77-78
MOTOWN.................... 5-8 84

CARTER, Valerie

LP '77

Singles: 7-inch

COLUMBIA.................... 3-4 77-79

LPs: 10/12-inch 33rpm

COLUMBIA.................... 8-10 77-78

Also see LITTLE FEAT
Also see MONEY, Eddie, & Valerie Carter

CARTER, Valerie, & Henry Paul

Singles: 7-inch

ATLANTIC.................... 3-4 82

Also see CARTER, Valerie

CARTER BROTHERS

R&B '65

Singles: 7-inch

COLEMAN.................... 8-10 64
JEWEL.................... 4-8 65-67
MISTY.................... 5-10 60s
TALENT SCOUT.................... 5-10 60s

Members: Jerry Carter; Al Carter; Roman Carter.

CARTER FAMILY

P&R 28

Singles: 78rpm

BANNER.................... 35
BLUEBIRD.................... 15-25 30s
DECCA.................... 10-20 30s
MONTEGOMERY WARD.................... 15-25 30s
VICTOR (20000 series).................... 50-150 28
VICTOR (40000 series).................... 25-75 28
VOCALION.................... 25-35

Members: A.P. Carter; Sara Carter; Maybelle Carter; Anita Carter; June Carter; Helen Carter; Joe Carter; Janette Carter; Carlene Carter.

Also see CARTER, Anita
Also see CARTER, June
Also see CARTER SISTERS
Also see CASH, Johnny, & Carter Family

CARTRELL, Delia

R&B '71

Singles: 7-inch

RIGHT ON.................... 3-5 71-72

CARTRIDGE, Flip

P&R '66

Singles: 7–inch

PARROT 4-8 66-67

CASCADES

P&R/R&B/LP '63

Singles: 7–inch

ABC 3-4 73
ARWIN 4-8 66
CANBASE 3-5 72
CHARTER 10-15 64
COLLECTABLES 3-4 81
GOLDIES 3-5 73
LIBERTY 4-8 65
PROBE 3-6 68
RCA 5-10 63-64
RENEE 10-20
SMASH 4-8 67
UNI 3-6 69-70
VALIANT 5-10 62-63
W.B. 3-4

Picture Sleeves

PROBE 4-8 68
RCA 8-12 63

LPs: 10/12–inch 33rpm

BLOSSOM 10-15
CASCADES (6820 "What Goes On Inside the Cascades") 20-35
UNI 15-20 69
VALIANT (W-405 "Rhythm of the Rain") 40-60 63
(Monaural.)
VALIANT (WS-405 "Rhythm of the Rain") 50-100 63
(Stereo.)

Members: Bill Preston; Dick Snyder; Danny Mark; Tommy Larson; Dave Zaibel; Larry Prater; John Gummoe; David Stevens; David Wilson;

CASCADES / Sir Douglas Quintet

Singles: 7–inch

TRIP 3-5 70s

Also see CASCADES
Also see SIR DOUGLAS QUINTET

CASEY, Al

(Al Casey Combo; with the K-C Ettes)

P&R/R&B '62

Singles: 78rpm

DOT 5-10 56-57
MCI 8-12 55

Singles: 7–inch

BLUE HORIZON (925 "Cookin") 15-25 62
CHALLENGE 5-10 60
DOT (15524 "A Fool's Blues") ... 10-20 56
DOT (15563 "Guitar Man") 15-25 57
GREGMARK (5 "Caravan") 5-10 61
(Shown as by Duane Eddy, but actually by Al Casey.)
HIGHLAND (1002 "Got the Teenage Blues") 25-40 59
HIGHLAND (1004 "Night Beat"). 15-25 60
LIBERTY 10-20 58
MCI 10-20 55
RAMCO 8-10 61
STACY (Except 962) 10-15 62-64
STACY (962 "Surfin' Hootenany") 10-15 63
(Black vinyl.)
STACY (962 "Surfin' Hootenany") 25-40 63
(Colored vinyl.)
U.A. (158 "Stinger") 10-20 59

LPs: 10/12–inch 33rpm

STACY (100 "Surfin' Hootenany") 30-50 63
(Black vinyl.)
STACY (100 "Surfin' Hootenany") 100-125 63
(Colored vinyl.)

Also see CLARK, Sanford
Also see EDDY, Duane
Also see EXOTIC GUITARS
Also see HONEYS
Also see JONES, Art
Also see RAINTREE COUNTY SINGERS
Also see REYNOLDS, Jody
Also see ROGERS, Frantic Johnny
Also see SHARPE, Ray
Also see STORMS

CASH, Alvin

(With Crawlers; with Registers)

P&R '65

Singles: 7–inch

CHESS 3-5 70
COLLECTABLES 3-4 81
DAKAR 3-5 76
ERIC 3-4 73
MAR-V-LUS 4-8 65-67
SEVENTY SEVEN 3-5 72
TODDLIN' TOWN 3-5 68-69
TRIP 4-6
WESTBOUND 3-6
XL ("Twine Time") 15-25 65
(Number not known.)

LPs: 10/12–inch 33rpm

MAR-V-LUS 15-20 65
SOUND STAGE "7" 10-15 73

CASH, Johnny

(With the Tennessee Two; with Tennessee Three)

C&W '55

Singles: 78rpm

SUN 8-15 55-57

Singles: 7–inch

CACHET 3-5 80
COLUMBIA (Except 41000 thru 43000 series) 3-8 67-85

COLUMBIA (41000 & 42000 series) 10-20 60-62
(With "3" prefix. Compact 33 singles)
COLUMBIA (41000 & 42000 series) 6-12 58-64
(With "4" prefix.)
COLUMBIA BOOK & RECORD LIBRARY ("The Bug That Tried to Crawl Around the World") 4-8 60s
COLUMBIA (43000 series) 4-8 64-66
SSS/SUN (Black vinyl) 3-5 69-70
SSS/SUN (Colored vinyl) 5-10 69-70
(Promotional issues only.)
SCOTTI BROS 3-4 82
SUN (200 series) 10-20 55-58
SUN (300 series) 8-12 58-62

EPs: 7–inch 33/45rpm

COLUMBIA (Except juke EPs) .. 10-20 58-60
COLUMBIA (Jukebox EPs) 20-30 69
SUN 15-20 58

Picture Sleeves

COLUMBIA (Except 41000 & 42000 series) 3-5 67-85
COLUMBIA (41000 series) 10-15 58-61
COLUMBIA (42000 series) 5-10 61-64
COLUMBIA (44000 series) .... -36 68
SUN (295 "Guess Things Happen That Way") 10-15 58

LPs: 10/12–inch 33rpm

BUCKBOARD 5-10
CACHET 5-10
COLUMBIA (29 "The World of Johnny Cash") 8-12 70
COLUMBIA (363 "Legends and Love Songs") 10-15 68
(Columbia Record Club issue.)
COLUMBIA (1200 thru 1799) 15-30 58-61
(With "CL" prefix. Monaural.)
COLUMBIA (8100 thru 8599) 20-40 58-61
(With "CS" prefix. Stereo.)
COLUMBIA (1800 thru 2650) 10-20 62-68
(With "CL" prefix. Monaural.)
COLUMBIA (2004 "The Heart of Johnny Cash") 15-25 60s
(Columbia Star Series.)
COLUMBIA (8600 thru 9478) 10-20 62-68
(With "CS" prefix. Stereo.)
COLUMBIA (9600 thru 9943) 8-12 69-70
(With "CS" prefix.)
COLUMBIA (10000 series) 5-10 73
COLUMBIA (30000 thru 38000 series) 5-15 70-82
COLUMBIA/SUFFOLK 8-10 79
DESIGN 5-8
DORAL 20-40
(Promotional mail-order LP from Doral cigarettes.)
HARMONY 8-12 69
LONGINES SYMPHONETTE 5-8
OUT of TOWN DIST 5-10 82
PICKWICK 5-10 70s
POWER PAK 5-10
PRIORITY 5-10 81-82
SSS/SUN 5-10 69-84
SHARE 5-10
STACK-O-HITS 5-8
SUN (1220 "Johnny Cash and His Hot and Blue Guitar") 40-50 56
SUN (1235 "Songs That Made Him Famous") 35-45 58
SUN (1240 "Greatest") 25-40 59
SUN (1245 "Johnny Cash Sings Hank Williams and Other Favorties") 20-35 60
SUN (1255 "Now Here's Johnny Cash") 20-30 61
SUN (1270 "All Aboard the Blue Train") 20-30 63
SUN (1275 "Original Sun Sound of Johnny Cash") 20-30 64
TRIP 8-10 74
U.A. 10-12 68

Session: George Jones; Marty Robbins; Waylon Jennings.

Also see BROOKS, Karen, & Johnny Cash
Also see DEL RAY, Martin
Also see JONES, George
Also see KILGORE, Merle
Also see RICH, Charlie
Also see ROBBINS, Marty / Johnny Cash / Ray Price
Also see STATLER BROTHERS

CASH, Johnny, & June Carter

(Johnny Cash & June Carter Cash)

C&W '64

Singles: 7–inch

COLUMBIA 3-5 67-83

LPs: 10/12–inch 33rpm

COLUMBIA (9500 series) 10-20 64-67
COLUMBIA (32000 series) 5-10 73
HARMONY 6-10 72

Also see CARTER, June
Also see JENNINGS, Waylon, Willie Nelson, Johnny Cash, & Kris Kristofferson

CASH, Johnny, & Carter Family

(Carter Family with Johnny Cash)

C&W '63

Singles: 7–inch

COLUMBIA 3-8 63-72

CASH, Johnny, Carter Family & Oak Ridge Boys

C&W '73

Singles: 7–inch

COLUMBIA 3-5 73

Also see CARTER FAMILY
Also see OAK RIDGE BOYS

CASH, Johnny, & Mother Maybelle Carter

C&W '73

Singles: 7–inch

COLUMBIA 3-5 73

Also see CARTER FAMILY

CASH, Johnny, Rosanne Cash & Everly Brothers

C&W '89

Singles: 7–inch

MERCURY (872 420-7 "Ballad of a Teenage Queen")........................ 3-4 89

Also see CASH, Rosanne
Also see EVERLY BROTHERS

CASH, Johnny / Roy Clark / Linda Ronstadt

LPs: 10/12–inch 33rpm

POINTED STAR (10178 "Concert Behind Prison Walls") 10-15 78

(NAPA special products TV soundtrack.)

Also see CASH, Rosanne
Also see CLARK, Roy
Also see RONSTADT, Linda

CASH, Johnny / Billy Grammer / Wilburn Brothers

LPs: 10/12–inch 33rpm

PICKWICK/HILLTOP 10-15 65

Also see GRAMMER, Billy

CASH, Johnny, & Levon Helm

Singles: 7–inch

A&M 3-4 80

Also see HELM, Levon

CASH, Johnny, & Waylon Jennings

C&W '86

Singles: 7–inch

COLUMBIA 3-4 78-86
EPIC.. 3-4 80

Also see JENNINGS, Waylon

CASH, Johnny, Carl Perkins & Jerry Lee Lewis

LPs: 10/12–inch 33rpm

COLUMBIA 5-10 82

Also see PERKINS, Carl, Jerry Lee Lewis, Roy Orbison & Johnny Cash

CASH, Johnny, & Hank Williams Jr.

C&W '88

Singles: 7–inch

MERCURY 3-4 88

Also see WILLIAMS, Hank, Jr.

CASH, Johnny / Tammy Wynette

LPs: 10/12–inch 33rpm

COLUMBIA (5418 "King & Queen").................................. 10-15

(Columbia Musical Treasury issue.)

Also see CASH, Johnny
Also see WYNETTE, Tammy

CASH, Rosanne

C&W '80

Singles: 7–inch

COLUMBIA 3-4 80-90

Picture Sleeves

COLUMBIA 3-4 81

EPs: 7–inch 33/45rpm

COLUMBIA 4-8 85

LPs: 10/12–inch 33rpm

COLUMBIA 6-10 79-90

Also see CASH, Johnny, Rosanne Cash & Everly Brothers
Also see CROWELL, Rodney, & Rosanne Cash
Also see NITTY GRITTY DIRT BAND, Rosanne Cash & John Hiatt

CASH, Rosanne, & Bobby Bare

C&W '79

Singles: 7–inch

COLUMBIA 3-4 79

Also see BARE, Bobby
Also see CASH, Rosanne

CASH, Tommy

C&W '68

Singles: 7–inch

AUDIOGRAPH..............................3-4 83
ELEKTRA.....................................3-5 75
EPIC...3-6 68-73
MONUMENT.................................3-4 77-79
MUSICOR....................................4-8 65
20TH FOX....................................3-4 76
U.A. 4-6 66-68

LPs: 10/12–inch 33rpm

ELEKTRA...................................5-10 75
EPIC..8-12 69-72
MONUMENT...............................5-10 78
U.A. 10-12 68

CA$HFLOW

R&B/LP '86

Singles: 12–inch 33/45rpm

ATLANTA ARTISTS......................4-6 86

Singles: 7–inch

ATLANTA ARTISTS......................3-4 86
MERCURY....................................3-4 86

LPs: 10/12–inch 33rpm

ATLANTA ARTISTS....................5-10 86

CASHMAN, Terry

(With the Men)

P&R '76

Singles: 7–inch

BOOM (005 "Try Me")..................8-10 66
LIFESONG (Except 45096 thru 45115).......................................3-5 76-82
LIFESONG (45096 thru 45115 "Talkin' Baseball")....................................3-5 76

(Price is for any individual disc. Complete set of 20 versions may be valued at $50 to $125.)

Picture Sleeves

LIFESONG (45096 thru 45115 "Talkin' Baseball") 3-5 76
(Price is for any individual sleeve. Complete set of 20 may be valued at $50 to $125.)

LPs: 10/12-inch 33rpm

LIFESONG 5-10 76-77

CASHMAN & WEST

P&R/LP '72

Singles: 7-inch

ABC 3-4 74
DUNHILL 3-5 72-74
LIFESONG 3-5 75

Picture Sleeves

DUNHILL 3-5 72

LPs: 10/12-inch 33rpm

ABC 8-10 74
DUNHILL 8-12 72-74

Members: Terry Cashman; Tommy West.
Also see CROCE, Jim
Also see GENE & TOMMY
Also see MORNING MIST

CASHMAN & WEST / Gordon Jenkins & His Orchestra

LPs: 10/12-inch 33rpm

DUNHILL (SPDJ-17 "Manhattan Tower") 10-15 72
(10-inch LP.)
Also see CASHMAN & WEST
Also see JENKINS, Gordon, & His Orchestra

CASHMAN, PISTILLI & WEST

Singles: 7-inch

ABC 4-6 68
CAPITOL 3-5 69-71

LPs: 10/12-inch 33rpm

ABC 12-15 68
CAPITOL 10-15 69-71

Members: Terry Cashman; Gene Pistilli; Tommy West.
Also see BUCHANAN BROTHERS
Also see CASHMAN, Terry
Also see PISTILLI, Gene
Also see WEST, Tommy

CASHMAN, PISTILLI & WEST / Steve Karmen

Singles: 7-inch

PONTIAC ("GTO Rock") 10-15 70
(Promotional issue of "1970 Pontiac Theme Music.")
Also see CASHMAN, PISTILLI & WEST

CASHMERE

R&B/D&D '83

Singles: 12-inch 33/45rpm

PHILLY WORLD 4-6 83
TNT 4-6 84

Singles: 7-inch

PHILLY WORLD 3-4 83-85

LPs: 10/12-inch 33rpm

PHILLY WORLD 5-10 83-85

CASINOS

(Gene Hughes & Casinos; with Saturns)

P&R/LP '67

Singles: 7-inch

ABC 3-5 73
AIRTOWN (002 "That's the Way") 10-15 67
CERTRON 5-8 70
COLLECTABLES 3-4 81
FRATERNITY 5-10 65-71
ITZY (2 "Do You Recall") 20-30 63
MILLION 5-8 72
NAME (001 "Do You Recall") 200-300 62
OLIMPIC (251 "Do You Recall") 75-125 63
TERRY (115 "Gee Whiz") 25-50 64
TERRY (116 "That's the Way") 12-25 64
TRIP 3-5
U.A. 4-6 68

LPs: 10/12-inch 33rpm

FRATERNITY (1019 "Then You Can Tell Me Goodbye") 20-30 67
Member: Gene Hughes.

CASINOS / Fireflies

Singles: 7-inch

ERA 3-5 70s
Also see CASINOS
Also see FIREFLIES

CASLONS

P&R '61

Singles: 7-inch

AMY 10-20 61-62
SEECO 10-20 61

CASON, Rich, & Galactic Orchestra

R&B '83

Singles: 12-inch 33/45rpm

PRIVATE I 4-6 84

Singles: 7-inch

LARC 3-4 83
PRIVATE I 3-4 84

CASPER

R&B '80

Singles: 7-inch

A.V.I. 3-4 84
ATLANTIC 3-4 83-84

LPs: 10/12-inch 33rpm

A.V.I. 5-10 84
ATLANTIC 5-10 83

CASS, Mama: see ELLIOTT, Cass

CASSIDY, David

P&R '71

Singles: 7-inch

BELL 3-5 71-73
FLASHBACK 3-4 73
MCA 3-4 79
RCA 3-5 75-77

Picture Sleeves

BELL 3-5 71-73

LPs: 10/12-inch 33rpm

BELL 10-15 72-74
RCA 8-12 74-76

Also see PARTRIDGE FAMILY
Also see WILSON, Carl

CASSIDY, Shaun

P&R/LP '77

Singles: 7-inch

W.B. 3-4 77-80

Picture Sleeves

W.B. 3-4 77-78

LPs: 10/12-inch 33rpm

W.B. 8-10 77-80

CASSIDY, Shaun, and Todd Rundgren's Utopia

Singles: 7-inch

W.B. 3-4 80

Also see CASSIDY, Shaun
Also see UTOPIA

CASTAWAYS

P&R '65

Singles: 7-inch

BEAR (2000 "Feel So Fine") 25-35 67
COLLECTABLES 3-4 81
ERA 3-4 72
ERIC 3-4 78
FONTANA 4-8 68
LANA 3-6 64
SOMA 5-12 65

Members: Richard Robey; Robert Folschon; Ron Hensley; James Donna; Dennis Craswell.
Also see CROW

CASTAWAYS / Gestures

Singles: 7-inch

TERRIFIC 4-6 60s

Also see CASTAWAYS
Also see GESTURES

CASTELLS

P&R '61

Singles: 7-inch

COLLECTABLES 3-4 80
DECCA 4-8 65-66
ERA 5-10 61-63
LAURIE 15-20 68
U.A. 4-8 68
W.B. (Except 5421) 4-8 64
W.B. (5421 "I Do") 50-60 64
(With Brian Wilson.)

LPs: 10/12-inch 33rpm

ERA (EL-109 "So This Is Love") 40-60 62
(Monaural.)
ERA (ES-109 "So This Is Love") 60-80 62
(Stereo.)

Members: Chuck Girard; Bob Ussery; Tom Hicks; Joe Kelly.
Also see GIRARD, Chuck
Also see WILSON, Brian

CASTER, Jimmy: see CASTOR, Jimmy

CASTLE, David

P&R '77

Singles: 7-inch

PARACHUTE 3-5 77-79

LPs: 10/12-inch 33rpm

PARACHUTE 8-10 77-79

CASTLE SISTERS

P&R '62

Singles: 7-inch

ROULETTE 5-10 59-60
TERRACE 5-10 62-63
TRIODEX 5-10 61

Picture Sleeves

TERRACE 10-15 62

CASTLEMAN, Boomer

(Boomer Clarke)

P&R '75

Singles: 7-inch

CREME 3-4 86
MUMS 3-5 75
SRO (218 "Summertime Blues") 4-6 86
(Promotional issue only.)

Also see LEWIS & CLARKE

CASTOR, Jimmy

(Jimmy Castor Bunch; Jimmy Caster Quintet)

P&R/R&B '66

Singles: 12-inch 33/45rpm

SALSOUL 4-6 83

Singles: 7-inch

ATLANTIC 3-5 74-77
CAPITOL 4-6 68-69
CLOWN 5-10 62
COMPASS 4-6 68
COTILLION 3-4 79
DECCA 4-8 66
DREAM 3-4 84-85
DRIVE 3-4 78
JET SET 4-8 65
KINETIC 3-6 70
LM 5-8
LONG DISTANCE 3-4 81
RCA 3-5 71-73
SALSOUL 3-4 82
SLEEPING BAG 3-4 88
SMASH 4-8 66-67

LPs: 10/12-inch 33rpm

ATLANTIC 8-10 74-77
COTILLION 5-10 79
CRYSTAL BALL 8-10 81
DREAM 5-10 83
DRIVE 5-10 78
LONG DISTANCE 5-10 80
PAUL WINLEY 5-15
RCA 10-15 72-75
SMASH 15-20 67

Members: Jimmy Castor; Gerry Thomas; Doug Gibson; Lenny Fridie Jr.; Harry Jonson; Bobby Manigault.
Also see CLINTONIAN CUBS
Also see JOEY & TEENAGERS
Also see LYMON, Lewis

CASTOR, Jimmy, & Juniors

Singles: 78rpm

ATOMIC (100 "This Girl of Mine") 40-60 57
WING (90078 "I Promise") 25-35 56

Singles: 7-inch

ATOMIC (100 "This Girl of Mine") 100-200 57
WING (90078 "I Promise") 75-125 56
Also see CASTOR, Jimmy

CASWELL, Johnny

P&R '63

Singles: 7-inch

DECCA (32017 "I.O.U.") 50-75 66
LUV (250 "Faces") 8-12 67
SMASH 5-10 63-64
Also see CRYSTAL MANSION

CAT MOTHER
(With the All Night News Boys)

P&R/LP '69

Singles: 7-inch

POLYDOR 3-6 69-72

LPs: 10/12-inch 33rpm

POLYDOR 20-30 69-73

CATCH

R&B '84

Singles: 12-inch 33/45rpm

COLUMBIA 4-6 84-85

Singles: 7-inch

COLUMBIA 3-4 84-85

CATE BROTHERS
(Cates Gang)

P&R/R&B/LP '76

Singles: 7-inch

ASYLUM 3-5 76-78
ELEKTRA 3-4 77
METROMEDIA 3-5 70

LPs: 10/12-inch 33rpm

ASYLUM 5-10 75-77
ATLANTIC 5-10 79
METROMEDIA 10-12 70-73
Members: Earl Cate; Ernie Cate.

CATES, George

P&R '55

Singles: 78rpm

CORAL 3-6 51-57

Singles: 7-inch

CORAL 5-10 51-57
DOT 3-6 62
SIGNATURE 3-6 59-60

EPs: 7-inch 33/45rpm

CORAL 5-10 54-57

LPs: 10/12-inch 33rpm

CORAL 10-20 54-57
Also see BUTLER, Champ, & George Cates

CATHY & JOE

P&R '64

Singles: 7-inch

SMASH 4-8 64-65
Members: Cathy Bunn; Joe Wegman.

CATHY JEAN
(With the Roomates)

P&R '61

Singles: 7-inch

ERIC 3-4 73
PHILIPS (Except 40014) 8-12 63
PHILIPS (40014 "Believe Me") 10-20 62
VALMOR 10-15 61-62

LPs: 10/12-inch 33rpm

VALMOR (78 "At the Hop") 400-500 62
(Reissue. Has titles printed on cover. Does not picture the group.)
VALMOR (789 "At the Hop") 350-450 61
(Pictures Cathy Jean & Roomates. Note different number.)
Also see ROOMATES

CAVALIERE, Felix

P&R '80

Singles: 7-inch

BEARSVILLE 3-5 74-75
EPIC 3-4 80

LPs: 10/12-inch 33rpm

BEARSVILLE 10-12 74-75
EPIC (705 "Castles in the Air") 15-20 79
(Interview and music. Promotional issue only.)
EPIC (35990 "Castles in the Air") 5-10 79
Also see RASCALS

CAVALLARO, Carmen

P&R '45

Singles: 78rpm

DECCA 3-6 45-57

Singles: 7-Inch

DECCA 3-8 50-61

EPs: 7-Inch 33/45rpm

DECCA (Except 844) 5-10 50-59
DECCA (844 "The Eddy Duchin Story") 20-30 56
(Boxed three-EP set.)

LPs: 10/12-Inch 33rpm

DECCA (Except "The Eddy Duchin Story") 10-20 50-61
DECCA (DL-8289 "Eddy Duchin Story") 25-35 56
(Soundtrack. Monaural.)
DECCA (DL7-8289 "The Eddy Duchin Story") 25-30 59
(Soundtrack. Stereo.)
DECCA (8396 "The Eddy Duchin Story") 60-75 56

(Soundtrack. Also has music from three other shows.)
DECCA (DL-9121 "The Eddy Duchin Story") 10-15 65
(Soundtrack. Monaural.)
DECCA (DL7-9121 "The Eddy Duchin Story") 10-15 65
(Soundtrack. Stereo.)
VOCALION.............................. 10-15 59

CAVALLARO, Carmen, Featuring Al Cernick

Singles: 78rpm

DECCA (24330 "Dream Girl") ... 15-25 48
DECCA (24410 "Evelyn")......... 15-25 48
DECCA (24488 "Ah, But It Happens") 15-25 48
Also see CAVALLARO, Carmen
Also see MITCHELL, Guy

CAZZ

(Robert Lewis)

P&R '78

Singles: 7–inch

NUMBER.................................... 3-4 78

CELEBRATION

(Featuring Mike Love)

P&R '78

Singles: 7–inch

MCA 3-4 78
PACIFIC ARTS 5-10 79

Promotional Singles

MCA (1982 "Almost Summer, KRTH 101 Version")............... 10-12 78

LPs: 10/12–inch 33rpm

MCA (3037 "Almost Summer").... 8-10 78
(Soundtrack.)
PACIFIC ARTS 8-12 79
Members: Mike Love; Charles Lloyd; Steve Leach; Ron Altbach; Linda Mallah; Suzanne Wallach; Irene Cathaway; Al Perkins; Tim Weston.
Also see LOVE, Mike

CELI BEE & Buzzy Bunch

P&R/R&B/LP '77

Singles: 7–inch

APA 3-5 77-78

LPs: 10/12–inch 33rpm

APA 5-10 77-79

CELLARFUL OF NOISE

P&R '88

Singles: 7–inch

CBS 3-4 88

CELLOS

P&R '57

Singles: 78rpm

APOLLO 10-20 57

Singles: 7–inch

APOLLO (510 "Rang Tang Ding Dong") 30-40 57
(No subtitle used.)
APOLLO (510 "Rang Tang Ding Dong").................................15-25 57
(With "I Am the Japanese Sandman" subtitle.)
APOLLO (515 "Under Your Spell")25-50 57
APOLLO (516 "The Be-Bop Mouse").................................25-50 57
APOLLO (524 "I Beg for Your Love")............................40-60 58
Members: Cliff Williams; Ken Levinson; Alvin Campbell; Bill Montgomery; Alton Thomas.

CENTERFOLD

R&B '88

Singles: 7–inch

COLUMBIA 3-4 88

CENTRAL LINE

P&R/R&B '81

Singles: 12–inch 33/45rpm

MERCURY 4-6 84-85

Singles: 7–inch

MERCURY 3-4 81-85

LPs: 10/12–inch 33rpm

MERCURY 5-10 82-85
Members: Linton Beckles; Lipson Francis; Henry Defoe; Camelle Hinds.

CERRONE

(Jean-Marc Cerrone)

P&R/R&B/LP '77

Singles: 12–inch 33/45rpm

PAVILLION 4-6 82
PERSONAL 4-6 84

Singles: 7–inch

ATLANTIC....................................3-4 79
COTILLION..................................3-5 77-78
PAVILLION 3-4 82
PERSONAL..................................3-4 84

LPs: 10/12–inch 33rpm

ATLANTIC..................................5-10 79
COTILLION.................................5-10 77-79
PAVILLION 5-10 82

CERRONE & La Toya Jackson

R&B '86

Singles: 12–inch 33/45rpm

PALASS.......................................4-6 86
Also see CERRONE
Also see JACKSON, La Toya

CETERA, Peter

LP '82

Singles: 7–inch

FULL MOON.................................3-4 82-88

Picture Sleeves

FULL MOON.................................3-4 82-88

LPs: 10/12–inch 33rpm

FULL MOON..............................5-10 81-88
W.B. 5-8 86
Also see CHER & Peter Cetera
Also see CHICAGO
Also see FALTSKOG, Agnetha, & Peter Cetera

CETERA, Peter, & Amy Grant

P&R '87

Singles: 7–inch

FULL MOON 3-4 86

Picture Sleeves

FULL MOON 3-4 86

Also see CETERA, Peter
Also see GRANT, Amy

CHABUKOS

R&B '73

Singles: 7–inch

MAINSTREAM 3-5 73

CHACKSFIELD, Frank, Orchestra

P&R '53

Singles: 78rpm

LONDON.................................... 3-6 53-57

Singles: 7-Inch

LONDON.................................... 4-8 53-61

EPs: 7-Inch 33/45rpm

LONDON.................................... 5-10 53-61

LPs: 10/12-Inch 33rpm

LONDON.................................... 5-15 53-61
RICHMOND 5-12 59-62

CHAD

R&B '87

Singles: 7–inch

RCA.. 3-4 87-88

CHAD & JEREMY

P&R/LP '64

Singles: 7–inch

COLLECTABLES......................... 3-4 81
COLUMBIA (Except 43277).......... 4-8 65-68
COLUMBIA (43277 "Before and After")...................................... 4-8 65
(Black vinyl.)
COLUMBIA (43277 "Before and After")................................... 10-15 65
(Colored vinyl. Promotional issues only.)
ERIC.. 3-4 73
LANA... 3-6 60s
ROCSHIRE 3-4 84
TRIP 3-5 70s
WORLD ARTISTS...................... 5-10 64-65

Picture Sleeves

COLUMBIA 5-10 65-66
WORLD ARTISTS....................... 8-12 64-65

LPs: 10/12–inch 33rpm

CAPITOL (2000 series)............ 15-20 66
CAPITOL (12000 & 16000 series) 5-10 80
COLUMBIA 20-25 65-68
FIDU 10-12
HARMONY 12-15 69
MDA (6000 "Olde English Gold")................................... 10-20
ROCSHIRE 5-10 84
SIDEWALK............................... 12-20 69
TRADITION REST 10-12
WORLD ARTISTS (2002 "Yesterday's Gone")...................................20-40 64
(Monaural.)
WORLD ARTISTS (2005 "Chad & Jeremy Sing for You")..........................20-40 65
(Monaural.)
WORLD ARTISTS (3002 "Yesterday's Gone")...................................30-50 64
(Stereo.)
WORLD ARTISTS (3005 "Chad & Jeremy Sing for You")..........................30-50 65
(Stereo.)

Members: Chad Stuart; Jeremy Clyde.
Also see STUART, Chad

CHAIN REACTION

R&B '77

Singles: 7–inch

ARIOLA AMERICA 3-5 76
DELICKS....................................5-10 69
DIAL 5-10 68
GRT 4-6 70
OSHOWLEO (1 "Lady in Red")..10-15
VERVE.....................................10-20 68

Member: Norris Harris.
Also see CHOCOLATE SYRUP
Also see MOMENT of TRUTH

CHAIRMEN of the Board

(Chairmen; Chairman of the Board)

P&R/R&B/LP '70

Singles: 7–inch

INVICTUS 3-6 70-76
SURFSIDE....................................3-5 82

Picture Sleeves

INVICTUS 3-5 70-72

LPs: 10/12–inch 33rpm

INVICTUS 12-20 70-74

Members: General Norman Johnson; Eddie Curtis; Harrison Kennedy; Danny Woods.
Also see JOHNSON, General

CHAKA KHAN: see KHAN, Chaka

CHAKACHAS

P&R/R&B/LP '72

Singles: 7–inch

AVCO EMBASSY 3-5 72
JANUS 3-5 74
POLYDOR 3-5 71-75

LPs: 10/12–inch 33rpm

AVCO EMBASSY 8-10 72
POLYDOR 8-12 72

CHAKIRIS, George

LP '62

Singles: 7–inch

CAPITOL.......................................3-6 62-65
HORIZON 4-6 62

Picture Sleeves

CAPITOL.....................................5-10 63

LPs: 10/12–inch 33rpm

CAPITOL...................................10-20 62-65

HORIZON ... 15-20 62

CHAMBERLAIN, Richard

P&R '62

Singles: 7-inch

MCA ... 3-4 77
MGM ... 4-6 62-65

Picture Sleeves

MGM ... 5-10 62-65

LPs: 10/12-inch 33rpm

MGM ... 15-20 63-65
METRO ... 8-12 66

CHAMBERS BROTHERS

P&R/LP '68

Singles: 7-inch

AVCO ... 3-6 74-75
COLUMBIA ... 5-10 66-73
PROVERB (1021 "I Trust in God") ... 10-20 60s
ROXBURY ... 3-6 76
TEAR DROP ... 3-6 74
VAULT ... 8-15 65-69

Picture Sleeves

COLUMBIA ... 4-8 68-69

LPs: 10/12-inch 33rpm

AVCO ... 8-12 74-75
CHELSEA ... 8-10 77
COLUMBIA (20 "Love, Peace and Happiness") ... 20-30 69
(Two LPs, the second being *The Chambers Brothers Live at Bill Graham's Fillmor East.*)
COLUMBIA (2000 & 9000 series) 15-20 67-68
COLUMBIA (30000 series, except 31158) ... 10-20 71-75
COLUMBIA (31158 "Oh My God") ... 40-60 72
FANTASY ... 10-15 74
RIVERSIDE ... 10-15 68
ROXBURY ... 8-10 76
VAULT (100 series) ... 15-20 67-70
VAULT (9003 "People Get Ready") ... 20-30 65

Members: Joe Chambers; Willie Chambers; Lester Chambers; George Chambers; Brian Keenan.

Also see AXTON, Hoyt, & Chambers Brothers
Also see DANE, Barbara, & Chambers Brothers
Also see PEANUT BUTTER CONSPIRACY / Ashes / Chambers Brothers
Also see WINTER, Johnny / Argent / Chambers Brothers / John Hammond

CHAMBLEE, Eddie

R&B '49

Singles: 78rpm

CORAL ... 5-10 52
FEDERAL ... 5-10 52
MERCURY ... 5-10 57
UNITED ... 10-20 54
MIRACLE ... 10-15 47-51
UNITED ... 5-10 53

Singles: 7-inch

CORAL ... 20-35 52
FEDERAL ... 20-35 52
MERCURY ... 10-20 57
UNITED ... 15-25 54

LPs: 10/12-inch 33rpm

EMARCY ... 25-45 58-60
PRESTIGE ... 20-30 64

Also see WASHINGTON, Dinah

CHAMPAGNE

P&R '77

Singles: 7-inch

ARIOLA AMERICA ... 3-5 77-78

Picture Sleeves

ARIOLA AMERICA ... 3-5 77

CHAMPAIGN

P&R/R&B/LP '81

Singles: 12-inch 33/45rpm

COLUMBIA ... 4-6 83

Singles: 7-inch

COLUMBIA ... 3-4 81-85

LPs: 10/12-inch 33rpm

COLUMBIA ... 5-10 81-85

Members: Rena Jones; Pauli Carman; Michael Day; Dana Walden; Michael Reed; Howard Reeder; Rocky Maffit.

CHAMPLIN, Bill

P&R '81

Singles: 7-inch

ELEKTRA ... 3-4 81-82
EPIC ... 3-5 78

LPs: 10/12-inch 33rpm

ELEKTRA ... 5-10 82
EPIC ... 5-10 78

Also see CHICAGO
Also see SONS of CHAMPLIN

CHAMPS

P&R/R&B '58

Singles: 78rpm

CHALLENGE ... 10-20 58

Singles: 7-inch

CHALLENGE ... 5-15 58-65
ERIC ... 3-4 78
LANA ... 3-6 64
REPUBLIC ... 3-5 76

EPs: 7-inch 33/45rpm

CHALLENGE (7100 "Tequila") ... 25-50 58
CHALLENGE (7101 "Caramba") ... 25-50 58

LPs: 10/12-inch 33rpm

CHALLENGE (601 "Go Champs Go!") ... 50-100 58
(Black vinyl.)
CHALLENGE (601 "Go Champs Go!") ... 250-350 58
(Colored vinyl.)
CHALLENGE (605 "Everybody's Rockin' with the Champs") ... 50-75 58

CHALLENGE (613 "Go Champs Go!") 40-60 62
CHALLENGE (614 "The Champs Play *All American*") 40-60 62
(Monaural.)
CHALLENGE (2514 "The Champs Play *All American*") 50-75 62
(Stereo.)
DESIGN SPOTLIGHT SERIES. 10-15 60s
INTERNATIONAL AWARD 10-20 60s
POINT 10-20 60s
SPECTRUM 10-20 60s

Members: Dave Burgess; Danny "Chuck Rio" Flores; Gene Alden; Dale Norris; Joe Burness; Van Norman; Jim Seals; Dash Crofts; Dean Beard; Bobby Morris; Glen Campbell; Jerry Cole; Keith MacKendrick; Chuch Downs; Rich Grissom; Keith MacKendrick; Mo Marshall; Dean McDaniel; Johnny Meeks; Gary Nieland; Curtis Paul; Jerry Puckett; Leon Sanders; Dave Smith; John Trombatore.

Also see APOLLOS
Also see BEARD, Dean
Also see BURGESS, Dave
Also see CAMPBELL, Glen
Also see COLE, Jerry
Also see DEMONS
Also see RIO, Chuck
Also see ROXSTERS
Also see SEALS & CROFTS
Also see SHADOWS FIVE
Also see THINK
Also see VINCENT, Gene

CHAMPS / Cyclones

LPs: 10/12-inch 33rpm

DESIGN SPOTLIGHT SERIES. 10-20 60s

Also see CHAMPS

CHAMPS' BOYS ORCHESTRA

P&R/R&B '76

Singles: 7-inch

JANUS 3-5 76

CHANDLER, Gene
(Eugene Dixon)

P&R/R&B/LP '62

Singles: 12-inch 33/45rpm

20TH FOX 4-8 79

Singles: 7-inch

BRUNSWICK 4-8 67-68
CHECKER 4-8 66-69
CHI-SOUND 3-5 79-82
COLLECTABLES 3-4 81
CONSTELLATION 4-8 63-66
CURTOM 3-5 72-73
ERIC 3-4 73
FASTFIRE 3-4 86
MCA 3-4 84
MARSEL 3-5 76
MERCURY 3-5 70
SOLID SMOKE 3-4 84
20TH FOX 3-4 78-79
VEE JAY 5-10 61-63

LPs: 10/12-inch 33rpm

BRUNSWICK 12-15 67-69
CHECKER 15-20 67
CHI-SOUND/20TH-FOX 5-10 78-79
CONSTELLATION 15-25 64-66
KENT 5-10 86
MERCURY 10-15 70
SOLID SMOKE 5-10 84
20TH FOX 5-10 78-81
UPFRONT 8-10
VEE JAY (1040 "The Duke of Earl") 50-100 62
(Monaural.)
VEE JAY (1040 "The Duke of Earl") 100-150 62
(Stereo.)

At least six early Vee Jay tracks, including *Duke of Earl,* were actually by the Dukays, not just Gene Chandler.

Also see CARTER, Calvin
Also see DUKAYS
Also see DUKE of EARL

CHANDLER, Gene, & Barbara Acklin

P&R/R&B '68

Singles: 7-inch

BRUNSWICK 4-8 68-69

Also see ACKLIN, Barbara

CHANDLER, Gene, & Jerry Butler
(Gene & Jerry)

P&R/R&B/LP '71

Singles: 7-inch

MERCURY 3-6 70

Also see BUTLER, Jerry

CHANDLER, Gene, & Jamie Lynn

R&B '83

Singles: 7-inch

SALSOUL 3-4 83

Also see CHANDLER, Gene

CHANDLER, Karen
(Eve Young)

P&R '52

Singles: 78rpm

CORAL 4-8 52-55
DECCA 4-6 56

Singles: 7-inch

CARLTON 4-8 60
CORAL 5-10 52-55
DECCA 5-10 56
DOT 3-5 67-68
MOHAWK 4-8 62
STRAND 4-8 61
SUNBEAM 4-8 59
TIVOLI 3-6 65

EPs: 7-inch 33/45rpm

CORAL 8-15 52

LPs: 10/12-inch 33rpm

STRAND 10-20 61

Also see FONTAINE, Eddie, & Karen Chandler

CHANDLER, Karen, & Jimmy Wakely

Singles: 78rpm

DECCA.......................... 4-8 56

Singles: 7-inch

DECCA.......................... 5-10 56

Also see CHANDLER, Karen
Also see WAKELY, Jimmy

CHANDLER, Kenny

P&R '63

Singles: 7-inch

AMY.......................... 4-8 63
COLLECTABLES.......................... 3-4 81
CORAL.......................... 4-8 62
EPIC.......................... 4-8 65-66
LAURIE.......................... 5-10 62-63
TOWER.......................... 4-8 67-68
U.A... 8-10 61

CHANGE

P&R/R&B/LP '80

Singles: 12-inch 33/45rpm

ATLANTIC.......................... 4-6 84
RFC.......................... 4-6 83

Singles: 7-inch

ATLANTIC.......................... 3-4 81-85
RFC.......................... 3-4 80
W.B... 3-4 80

LPs: 10/12-inch 33rpm

ATLANTIC.......................... 5-10 81-85
RFC.......................... 5-10 80
W.B... 5-10 80

Members: Paolo Granolio; David Romani; James Robinson; Deborah Cooper.
Also see VANDROSS, Luther

CHANGIN' TIMES

P&R '65

Singles: 7-inch

PHILIPS.......................... 10-20 65-66

CHANNEL, Bruce

P&R/R&B/LP '62

Singles: 7-inch

CHARAY.......................... 4-6 68
COLLECTABLES.......................... 3-4 81
ELEKTRA.......................... 3-4 80
KING.......................... 5-10 59-60
LE CAM (100 series).......................... 5-10 64
LE CAM (953 "Hey Baby").......................... 10-20 62
LE CAM (1100 & 7200 series).......................... 3-5 77
MALA.......................... 4-8 67-68
MANCO (1035 "Run Romance, Run").......................... 8-12 62
MEL-O-DY (112 "Satisfied Mind").......................... 10-15 64
MEL-O-DY (114 "You Never Looked Better").......................... 10-15 64
NAP.......................... 3-5
SHAH.......................... 4-8 64
SMASH.......................... 4-8 62-63
SOFT.......................... 4-8 60s
TEEN AGER (601 "Run Romance, Run").......................... 20-30 59
ZUMA.......................... 3-5 77

Picture Sleeves

SMASH.......................... 8-12 62-63

LPs: 10/12-inch 33rpm

SMASH (27008 "Hey! Baby").......................... 30-50 62
(Monaural.)
SMASH (67008 "Hey! Baby").......................... 25-40 62
(Stereo.)

CHANNEL, Bruce / Paul & Paula

Singles: 7-inch

ERA.......................... 3-4

Also see CHANNEL, Bruce
Also see PAUL & PAULA

CHANSON

P&R/LP '78

Singles: 7-inch

ARIOLA AMERICA.......................... 3-4 78-79

LPs: 10/12-inch 33rpm

ARIOLA AMERICA.......................... 5-10 78

Also see EVANS, Linda

CHANTAYS

P&R/R&B/LP '63

Singles: 7-inch

ABC.......................... 3-4 74
COLLECTABLES.......................... 3-4 81
DOT.......................... 4-8 63
DOWNEY (104 "Pipeline").......................... 20-30 63
DOWNEY (108 "Monsoon").......................... 15-25 63
DOWNEY (116 thru 130).......................... 10-20 63-65
MCA.......................... 3-4 84

LPs: 10/12-inch 33rpm

DOT (3516 "Pipeline").......................... 25-30 63
(Monaural.)
DOT (25516 "Pipeline").......................... 30-40 63
(Stereo.)
DOT (3771 "Two Sides of the Chantays").......................... 25-30 63
(Monaural.)
DOT (25771 "Two Sides of the Chantays").......................... 30-40 63
(Stereo.)
DOWNEY (1002 "Pipeline").......................... 100-175 63

Members: Bob Marshall; Bob Welch; Bob Spickard; Brian Carman; Steve Cahn; Warren Waters

CHANTELS

P&R '57

Singles: 78rpm

END.......................... 15-25 57

Singles: 7-inch

ABC.......................... 3-4 73
CARLTON.......................... 5-10 61
END (1001 "He's Gone").......................... 35-60 57
(Black label.)
END (1005 "Maybe").......................... 30-50 57
(Black label.)

END (White or gray label) 10-20 58-59
END (Multi-color label) 8-15 58-61
ERIC 3-4 73
LANA 3-6 64
LUDIX 5-10 63
RCA 3-6 70
ROULETTE 3-6 69-71
TCF 4-8 65
VERVE 4-8 66

EPs: 7-inch 33/45rpm

END (201 "I Love You So") ... 100-125 58
END (202 "I Love You So") 75-100 58

LPs: 10/12-inch 33rpm

CARLTON (LP-144 "The Chantels on Tour/ Look in My Eyes") 50-100 62
(Monaural.)
CARLTON (STLP-144 "The Chantels on Tour/ Look in My Eyes") 75-150 62
(Stereo.)
END (301 "We're the Chantels") 500-600 58
(Pictures the group on front cover.)
END (301 "The Chantels") 100-150 59
(Pictures a juke box on front cover.)
END (312 "There's Our Song Again") 50-75 62
FORUM (9104 "The Chantels Sing Their Favorites") 25-40 64
ROULETTE 5-10

Members: Arlene Smith; Lois Harris; Renee Minus; Sonia Gorring; Jackie Landry.
Also see BARRETT, Richard

CHANTERS

P&R/R&B '61

Singles: 7-inch

DE LUXE (6162 "My My Darling") 30-40 58
DE LUXE (6166 "Row Your Boat") 25-35 58
(Black label.)
DE LUXE (6166 "Row Your Boat") 10-15
(Yellow label.)
DE LUXE (6172 "Five Little Kisses") 30-40 58
DE LUXE (6191 "No, No, No").. 20-30 61
DE LUXE (6194 "My My Darling") 20-30 61
DE LUXE (6200 "Row Your Boat") 10-15 63
GUSTO 3-4 77
SSP (1001 "Heavenly You")...... 15-20

Members: Bud Johnson Jr; Larry Pendegrass; Fred Paige; Bobby Thompson; Elliot Green.
Also see JOHNSON, Bud, Orchestra
Also see VOICES FIVE

CHAPIN, Harry

P&R/LP '72

Singles: 7-inch

BOARDWALK 3-4 80-81
DUNHILL 3-4 88
ELEKTRA 3-5 72-79

LPs: 10/12-inch 33rpm

BOARDWALK 5-10 80
DUNHILL 5-10 88
ELEKTRA 8-12 72-79

CHAPLAIN, Paul
(With His Emeralds; Paul Chaplin)

P&R '60

Singles: 7-inch

ELGIN 5-10
HARPER 10-20 60-61

CHAPLIN, Angelica

R&B '87

Singles: 7-inch

MERCURY 3-4 87

CHAPLIN, Paul: see CHAPLAIN, Paul

CHAPMAN, Tracy

P&R/LP '88

Singles: 7-inch

ELEKTRA 3-4 88-89

Picture Sleeves

ELEKTRA 3-4 88-89

LPs: 10/12-inch 33rpm

ELEKTRA 5-8 88-89

CHAPTER 8

R&B '79

Singles: 12-inch 33/45rpm

ARIOLA AMERICA 4-8 79
BEVERLY GLEN 4-6 85

Singles: 7-inch

ARIOLA AMERICA 3-5 79-80
BEVERLY GLEN 3-4 85

Members: Anita Baker; Michael Powell; David Washington; Carolyn Crawford; Valerie Pinkston.

LPs: 10/12-inch 33rpm

ARIOLA AMERICA 5-10 79

Also see BAKER, Anita
Also see DETROIT EMERALDS

CHARADE
(Featuring Jessica)

D&D '83

Singles: 12-inch 33/45rpm

PROFILE 4-6 83

CHARGERS

P&R '58

Singles: 7-inch

RCA (7301 "Old MacDonald").... 15-25 58
RCA (7417 "Here in My Heart") . 15-25 58

Members: Jesse Belvin; James Scott; Ben Easley; Dunbar White; Johnny White; Mitchell Alexander; Jimmy Norman.
Also see BELVIN, Jesse
Also see NORMAN, Jimmy

CHARIOTEERS

P&R '40

Singles: 78rpm

BRUNSWICK	15-25	38-39
COLUMBIA	15-25	39-49
DECCA	15-25	35
JOSIE	10-20	55
KEYSTONE	10-20	52
LANG-WORTH	10-20	40s
(16-inch transcriptions.)		
MGM	20-30	57
OKEH	15-25	40-42
TUXEDO	10-20	55
VOCALION	15-25	38-39

Singles: 7-inch

COLUMBIA (168 "A Kiss and a Rose")	400-600	50
(Microgroove 33 single.)		
COLUMBIA (363 "This Side of Heaven")	400-600	50
(Microgroove 33 single.)		
JOSIE (787 "I've Got My Heart on My Sleeve")	50-75	55
MGM (12569 "The Candles")	50-75	57
TUXEDO (891 "Thanks for Yesterday")	50-75	55

LPs: 10/12-inch 33rpm

COLUMBIA (6014 "Sweet and Low")	150-200	49
(10-inch LP.)		
HARMONY (7089 "The Charioteers & Billy Williams")	50-100	57

Members: Billy Williams; Eddie Jackson; Ira Williams; Howard Daniel; James Sherman.
Also see SINATRA, Frank, & Charioteers
Also see WILLIAMS, Billy

CHARLENE
(Charlene Duncan)

P&R '77

Singles: 7-inch

MOTOWN	3-5	76-85
PRODIGAL	3-5	76-77

Picture Sleeves

PRODIGAL	3-5	77

LPs: 10/12-inch 33rpm

MOTOWN	5-10	82-85
PRODIGAL	8-10	76

CHARLENE & Stevie Wonder

P&R '82

Singles: 7-inch

MOTOWN	3-4	82

Picture Sleeves

MOTOWN	3-4	82

Also see CHARLENE
Also see WONDER, Stevie

CHARLES, Bobby

R&B '56

Singles: 78rpm

CHESS	10-15	55-57

Singles: 7-inch

BEARSVILLE	3-5	73
CHESS	20-30	55-58
HUB CITY	5-10	63
IMPERIAL	8-15	58-60
JEWEL	5-10	64
PAULA	4-8	65
RICE & GRAVY	3-4	86-90

LPs: 10/12-inch 33rpm

BEARSVILLE	10-15	72
CHESS	8-12	76

CHARLES, Jimmy
(With the Revelletts)

P&R/R&B '60

Singles: 7-inch

ABC	3-4	73
COLLECTABLES	3-4	81
ERIC	3-4	79
MCA	3-4	84
PROMO	10-15	60
ROULETTE	3-4	71

Picture Sleeves

PROMO	15-25	60-61

CHARLES, Lee

R&B '68

Singles: 7-inch

BAMBOO	3-5	70-71
BRUNSWICK	3-6	69
HOT WAX	3-5	73
INVICTUS	3-5	74
REVUE	4-8	68

CHARLES, Ray
(With the Raelettes)

R&B '51

Singles: 78rpm

ATLANTIC	5-10	52-58
JAX	10-20	52
ROCKIN'	5-10	53
SWING BEAT	15-25	49
SWING TIME	10-20	50-53
ATLANTIC	10-15	52-58

Singles: 7-inch

ABC	3-8	66-73
ABC-PAR (Monaural)	4-8	60-66
ABC-PAR (Stereo)	10-15	61-62
ABC/TRC	3-6	
ATLANTIC (976 "Roll with Me Baby")	50-75	52
ATLANTIC (984 "The Sun's Gonna Shine Again")	30-60	53
ATLANTIC (999 "Mess Around")	30-60	53
ATLANTIC (1000 series)	12-25	53-57
ATLANTIC (2000 series)	5-10	58-68
ATLANTIC (3000 series)	3-5	77-79
BARONET	4-8	62
COLUMBIA	3-4	82-87
CROSSOVER	3-5	73-78

DUNHILL GOLDIES 3-4 73
HURRAH 8-12
IMPULSE 5-10 61
MAYFAIR (121 "Pony Boy") 4-8
(With "Uncle Stu.")
RCA 3-5 76
ROCKIN' (504 "Walkin' and
Talkin") 100-200 53
SITTIN' in WITH (641 "Baby Let me Hear You
Call My Name") 75-150 52
SWING TIME (250 "Baby Let Me Hold Your
Hand") 75-100 51
SWING TIME (274 "Kiss Me
Baby") 75-100 52
SWING TIME (300 "Baby Let Me Hear You
Call My Name") 75-100 52
SWING TIME (326 "The Snow Is
Falling") 50-100 53
TANGERINE 3-4 71
TIME 3-5 62

Picture Sleeves

ABC 3-6 68-70

EPs: 7–inch 33/45rpm

ABC-PAR 10-20 60-62
ATLANTIC 20-30 56-59

LPs: 10/12–inch 33rpm

ABC (Except 590) 10-12 66-73
ABC (590 "A Man & His Soul") .. 20-25 67
ABC-PAR (300 series) 15-25 60-61
ABC-PAR (400 & 500 series) 10-20 62-66
AHED 8-12
(TV mail-order offer.)
ATLANTIC (500 series) 10-15 73
ATLANTIC (900 "The Ray Charles Story,
Vols. 1 & 2") 30-40 62
(Combines Atlantic 8063 and 8064.)
ATLANTIC (1259 "The Great
Ray Charles") 45-60 57
ATLANTIC (1279 "Soul
Brothers") 40-50 58
(With Milt Jackson.)
ATLANTIC (1289 "Ray Charles
at Newport") 40-50 58
ATLANTIC (1312 "Genius of
Ray Charles") 30-45 59
ATLANTIC (1360 "Soul
Meeting") 20-35 62
(With Milt Jackson. Number indicates a '61 release, but not actually issued until 1962.)
ATLANTIC (1369 "Genius
After Hours") 20-35 61
ATLANTIC (1500 series) 8-10 70
ATLANTIC (3700 series) 20-22 82
ATLANTIC (7000 series) 12-15 64
ATLANTIC (8006 "Ray
Charles") 45-60 57
(Black label.)
ATLANTIC (8006 "Ray
Charles") 25-35 59
(Red label.)
ATLANTIC (8025 "Yes Indeed") 30-40 59
(Black label.)
ATLANTIC (8025 "Yes Indeed") 25-35 60
(Red label.)
ATLANTIC (8029 "What'd I
Say") 30-40 59
(Black label.)
ATLANTIC (8029 "What'd I
Say") 25-35 60
(Red label.)
ATLANTIC (8039 "Ray Charles
in Person") 30-40 60
(Black label.)
ATLANTIC (8039 "Ray Charles
in Person") 25-35 60
(Red label.)
ATLANTIC (8052 "The Genius
Sings the Blues") 20-30 61
ATLANTIC (8054 "Dot the
Twist") 20-30 61
ATLANTIC (8063 "The Ray Charles Story,
Vol. 1") 20-25 62
ATLANTIC (8064 "The Ray Charles Story,
Vol. 2") 20-25 62
ATLANTIC (8083 "The Ray Charles Story,
Vol. 3") 20-25 63
ATLANTIC (8094 "The Ray Charles Story,
Vol. 4") 20-25 64
ATLANTIC (19000 series) 5-10 77-80
BARONET 15-20 62
BLUESWAY 8-10 73
BULLDOG 5-10 84
COLUMBIA 5-10 83-86
CORONET 8-10
CROSSOVER 8-15 73-76
DESIGN 10-15 62
EVEREST 8-10 70-82
GUEST STAR 10-20 64
HOLLYWOOD (504 "The Original Ray
Charles") 100-150 59
HOLLYWOOD 505: see CHARLES, Ray / Charles Brown)
HURRAH 5-10
IMPULSE 20-30 61
INTERMEDIA 5-10 84
KING 8-10 77
PALACE 5-10
PREMIER 8-10
SCEPTER 8-12
STRAND 10-15 60s
TANGERINE 10-12 70-73
UPFRONT 8-10 70s

Also see COOKIES
Also see GUITAR SLIM
Also see FULSON, Lowell
Also see JOEL, Billy, & Ray Charles
Also see JONES, Quincy, Ray Charles & Chaka Khan

Also see MAXIM TRIO
Also see RAELETTES
Also see U.S.A. for AFRICA

CHARLES, Ray / Charles Brown

LPs: 10/12-inch 33rpm

HOLLYWOOD (505 "The Fabulous Artistry of Ray Charles")................. 100-150 59
(Brown, barely credited, provides four tracks.)

CHARLES, Ray / Solomon Burke

LPs: 10/12-inch 33rpm

GRAND PRIX............................ 10-20 64
Also see BURKE, Solomon

CHARLES, Ray, & Betty Carter

LP '61

Singles: 7-inch

ABC-PAR 5-10 61-62

LPs: 10/12-inch 33rpm

ABC-PAR (ABC-385 "Ray Charles & Betty Carter")...................... 50-75 61
(Monaural.)
ABC-PAR (ABCS-385 "Ray Charles & Betty Carter")................... 75-100 61
(Stereo.)
Also see CARTER, Betty

CHARLES, Ray, & Clint Eastwood

C&W '80

Singles: 7-inch

W.B. 3-4 80

CHARLES, Ray, & Mickey Gilley

C&W '85

Singles: 7-inch

COLUMBIA 3-4 85
Also see GILLEY, Mickey

CHARLES, Ray / Ivory Joe Hunter / Jimmy Rushing

LPs: 10/12-inch 33rpm

DESIGN (909 "Three of a Kind") 15-20 60s
(Black label, silver print.)
DESIGN (909 "Three of a Kind") 10-15 60s
(Black, red, blue and yellow label.)
Also see HUNTER, Ivory Joe

CHARLES, Ray, George Jones & Chet Atkins

C&W '83

Singles: 7-inch

COLUMBIA 3-4 83
Also see ATKINS, Chet
Also see JONES, George

CHARLES, Ray, & Cleo Laine

LP '76

LPs: 10/12-inch 33rpm

RCA... 10-12 76
Also see LAINE, Cleo

CHARLES, Ray & Jimmy Lewis

P&R/R&B '69

Singles: 7-inch

ABC...3-4 69
TANGERINE.................................3-6 68

CHARLES, Ray / Little Richard / Sam Cooke

LPs: 10/12-inch 33rpm

ALMOR (102 "Soul Blues")........10-20
Also see COOKE, Sam
Also see LITTLE RICHARD

CHARLES, Ray, & Willie Nelson

C&W '84

Singles: 7-inch

COLUMBIA 3-4 84
Also see NELSON, Willie

CHARLES, Ray / Arbee Stidham / Li'l Son Jackson / James Wayne.

LPs: 10/12-inch 33rpm

MAINSTREAM.............................8-12 71
Also see JACKSON, Li'l Son
Also see WAYNE, James

CHARLES, Ray, & B.J. Thomas

C&W '84

Singles: 7-inch

COLUMBIA 3-4 85
Also see THOMAS, B.J.

CHARLES, Ray, & Hank Williams Jr.

C&W '85

Singles: 7-inch

COLUMBIA 3-4 85
Also see CHARLES, Ray
Also see WILLIAMS, Hank, Jr.

CHARLES, Ray, Singers

P&R '55

Singles: 78rpm

JUBILEE 3-5 54
MGM 3-6 51-56

Singles: 7-inch

COMMAND 3-5 64-70
DECCA 3-6 58-59
JUBILEE 4-8 54
MGM 4-8 51-56

EPs: 7-inch 33/45rpm

CADENCE 5-10 50s
DECCA 5-10 59
ESSEX 5-10 50s
JAMESTOWN..............................8-15 57
MGM 5-15 55-57

LPs: 10/12-inch 33rpm

ABC...5-10 73
ALSHIRE....................................5-10 70
ATCO 8-12 68
CAMDEN 6-10 67
COMMAND.................................8-12 62-71
DECCA 10-15 58-60
MCA..4-6 82
MGM (100 series)........................5-10 71

MGM (3000 series) 10-20 55-60
MGM (4000 series) 8-15 63-66
METRO 6-10 65
SOMERSET 5-10 64
VOCALION................................ 8-10 66

CHARLES, Sonny
(With Checkmates Ltd.)

P&R/R&B '69

Singles: 7–inch

A&M 4-8 68-73
CAPITOL.................................... 4-8 66-67
FRATERNITY.............................. 4-8 64
HIGHRISE.................................. 3-4 82
RCA.. 3-5 72

LPs: 10/12–inch 33rpm

HIGHRISE................................ 5-10 82
A&M 15-25 69

Also see CHECKMATES LTD.

CHARLES, Tommy *P&R '56*

Singles: 78rpm

DECCA...................................... 5-10 56
WILLETT (111 "Hey There Baby") 15-25 57

Singles: 7–inch

DECCA.................................... 10-15 56
WILLETT (111 "Hey There Baby") 40-60 57

Session: Anita Kerr Singers.
Also see KERR, Anita

CHARLESTON CITY ALL STARS

LP '57

LPs: 10/12-Inch 33rpm

GRAND AWARD........................ 5-15 57-59

CHARLESTON EXPRESS with Jesse Wales

C&W '84

Singles: 7–inch

SOUNDWAVES 3-4 84-85

CHARLIE

P&R/LP '77

Singles: 7–inch

ARISTA 3-5 79
JANUS 3-4 77-78
MIRAGE...................................... 3-4 83
RCA.. 3-4 81

Picture Sleeves

ARISTA 3-5 79
MIRAGE...................................... 3-4 83

LPs: 10/12–inch 33rpm

ARISTA 5-10 79
COLUMBIA 8-10 76
JANUS 8-10 77-78
MIRAGE.................................... 5-10 83
RCA.. 5-10 81

Member: Terry Thomas.

CHARME

R&B '84

Singles: 7–inch

ATLANTIC.....................................3-4 84
RCA 3-4 79-85

LPs: 10/12–inch 33rpm

RCA 5-10 79-85

CHARMETTES
(Charmetts)

P&R/R&B '63

Singles: 7–inch

FEDERAL 5-10 59
HI 5-10 59
KAPP 10-15 63-64
MALA 5-10 64
MARLIN 10-20 62
MELOMEGA 5-10 62
MONA 5-10 60
TRI DISC.....................................5-10 62
WORLD ARTISTS 5-10 65

CHARMS
(Otis Williams & the Charms)

P&R/R&B '54

Singles: 78rpm

CHART..5-15 55-56
DELUXE.....................................10-15 54-57
ROCKIN' 20-40 53

Singles: 7–inch

CHART (608 "Love's Our Inspiration")...............................15-25 55
CHART (613 "Heart of a Rose") 15-25 56
CHART (623 "I'll Be True").........15-25 56
DELUXE (6000 "Heaven Only Knows")..................................75-125 53
DELUXE (6014 "Happy Are We")...75-100 53
DELUXE (6034 "Bye-Bye Baby") 75-100 54
DELUXE (6050 "Quiet Please") 50-100 54
DELUXE (6056 "My Baby Dearest Darling")................................50-100 54
DELUXE (6062 thru 6098).........15-30 54-56
DELUXE (6100 series)..............12-25 57-59
(Monaural)
DELUXE (6185 "Tears of Happiness") 25-45 59
(Stereo.)
GUSTO 3-4 77
KING 5-10 60-63
OKEH 4-8 65-66
ROCKIN' (516 "Heaven Only Knows")................................200-350 53
STOP 5-8

EPs: 7–inch 33/45rpm

DELUXE (357 "Hits By the Charms")............................150-200 55

DELUXE (364 "Hits By the Charms") 150-200 55
DELUXE (385 "Otis Williams and the Charms") 100-200 56
KING (357 "Hits By the Charms") 50-75 58
KING (364 "Hits By the Charms, Vol. 2") 50-75 58
KING (385 "Otis Williams & His Charms") 50-75 58

LPs: 10/12-inch 33rpm

DELUXE (570 "All Their Hits") 300-400 58
(With color photo of the group on cover.)
KING (614 "This Is Otis Williams and the Charms") 100-125 59

Members: Otis Williams; Ron Bradley; Don Peark; Joe Renn; Richard Parker.
Also see WILLIAMS, Otis

CHARO
(With the Salsoul Orchestra)

LP '77

Singles: 7-inch

CAPITOL 3-5 76
SALSOUL 3-5 77-78

LPs: 10/12-inch 33rpm

SALSOUL 5-10 77-78

Also see SALSOUL ORCHESTRA

CHARTBUSTERS

P&R '64

Singles: 7-inch

BELL 4-8 67
CRUSADER 8-12 65
MUTUAL 5-10 64-65

CHARTS

P&R '57

Singles: 7-inch

ABC 3-4 73
COLLECTABLES 3-4 80s
ENJOY (1002 "Deserie") 10-20 62
EVERLAST (5001 "Deserie") 25-50 57
EVERLAST (5002 "Dance Girl") 20-40 57
EVERLAST (5006 "You're the Reason") 20-40 58
EVERLAST (5008 "All Because of Love") 20-40 58
EVERLAST (5010 "My Diane") . 20-40 58
EVERLAST (5026 "Deserie") 10-20 63
GUYDEN 5-10 59
VELVTONE 10-20
WAND (1112 "Deserie") 10-20 66
WAND (1124 "Livin' the Nightlife") 25-50 66

LPs: 10/12-inch 33rpm

COLLECTABLES 8-10 86
LOST-NITE 8-12 81

Members: Joe Grier; Steve Brown; Ross Buford; Glen Jackson; Leroy Binns.
Also see COOPER, Les

CHASE

P&R/LP '71

Singles: 7-inch

EPIC 3-5 71-76

LPs: 10/12-inch 33rpm

EPIC 10-12 71-76

Members: Bill Chase; Jerry Van Blair; Jay Burrid; Dennis Johnson; Ted Piercefield: Phil Porter; Terry Richards; Angel South; Alan Ware.

CHASE, Ellison

P&R '76

Singles: 7-inch

BIG TREE 3-5 76-77
COLUMBIA 3-4 82
MAGNA-GLIDE 3-5 75

LPs: 10/12-inch 33rpm

COLUMBIA/ARC 5-10 82

CHATER, Kerry

P&R '77

Singles: 7-inch

W.B. 3-5 76-78

LPs: 10/12-inch 33rpm

W.B. 5-10 77-78

Also see PUCKETT, Gary

CHAZ

R&B '82

Singles: 7-inch

PROMISE 3-4 82

CHEAP TRICK

LP '77

Singles: 12-inch 33/45rpm

EPIC 4-6 83

Singles: 7-inch

ASYLUM 3-4 81
EPIC 3-5 77-90
PASHA 3-4 84

Picture Sleeves

EPIC (Except 50814) 3-5 79-88
EPIC (50814 "Voices") 4-8 79
(Promotional issue only.)

EPs: 7-inch 33/45rpm

CSP 4-8 81
(Nestles candy promotional issue.)

LPs: 10/12-inch 33rpm

EPIC 5-10 76-90
EPIC/NU-DISC 10-15 80
(Includes bonus single.)
PASHA 5-10 84

Members: Robin Zander; Tom Petersson; Rick Nielson; Bun E. Carlos; Jon Briant.
Also see CUMMINGS, Burton / Cheap Trick / Crawler
Also see FUSE
Also see GRIM REAPERS
Also see NAZZ

CHEATHAM, Oliver

R&B '83

Singles: 7-inch

CRITIQUE 3-4 86-87
MCA 3-4 83

LPs: 10/12-inch 33rpm

MCA 5-10 83

CHECKER, Chubby
(With Dee Dee Sharp)

P&R '59

Singles: 7-inch

ABKCO 3-4 72
AMHERST 3-5 76
BUDDAH 4-6 69
MCA 3-4 82
PARKWAY (006 "The Jet") 10-15 62
PARKWAY (100 series) 5-10 66
PARKWAY (804 thru 810) 10-20 59-60
PARKWAY (811 "The Twist"/ "Toot") 15-25 60
(White label.)
PARKWAY (811 "The Twist"/ "Toot") 10-15 60
(Orange label.)
PARKWAY (811 "The Twist"/ "Twistin' U.S.A.") 5-10 61
(Yellow/orange or orange label.)
PARKWAY (811 "The Twist").... 20-30 61
(Colored vinyl.)
PARKWAY (813 thru 959).......... 5-10 60-66
PARKWAY (965 "You Just Don't Know") 100-200 66
PARKWAY (989 "Hey You! Little Boo-Ga-Loo") 5-10 66
20TH FOX 4-6 73-74

Picture Sleeves

PARKWAY 8-15 61-65

EPs: 7-inch 33/45rpm

PARKWAY 15-20 61
(Includes Compact 33 Doubles.)

LPs: 10/12-inch 33rpm

ABKCO 8-10 72
D.C.M. 4-6
EVEREST 5-10 81
51 WEST 5-10 84
MCA 8-10 82
PARKWAY 15-30 60-66
Also see DREAMLOVERS
Also see FAT BOYS & Chubby Checker

CHECKER, Chubby / Gary U.S. Bonds

LPs: 10/12-inch 33rpm

EXACT 5-10 80
Also see BONDS, Gary "U.S."

CHECKER, Chubby, & Bobby Rydell

LP '61

Singles: 7-inch

CAMEO (12 "Your Hits & Mine") 10-20 61
(Promotional issue only.)
CAMEO (200 series) 5-10 61-62

Picture Sleeves

CAMEO 5-10 61

LPs: 10/12-inch 33rpm

CAMEO 20-30 61-63
Also see RYDELL, Bobby

CHECKER, Chubby, & Dee Dee Sharp

LP '62

LPs: 10/12-inch 33rpm

CAMEO 20-30 62
Also see CHECKER, Chubby
Also see SHARP, Dee Dee

CHECKMATES LTD.
(Featuring Sonny Charles)

P&R/LP '69

Singles: 7-inch

A&M 4-6 69
CAPITOL (5603 "Do the Walk") . 10-20 66
CAPITOL (5753 "Kissin' Her and Cryin' for You") 20-30 68
CAPITOL (5814 "Please Don't Take My World Away") 10-20 67
CAPITOL (5922 "A&I") 10-20 67
FANTASY 3-5 77-78
GREEDY 3-5 77
RUSTIC 3-5 74

LPs: 10/12-inch 33rpm

A&M (4183 "Love Is All We Have to Give") 15-25 69
CAPITOL (2840 "Live") 25-35 67
FANTASY 8-10 77
IKON 5-10
POLYDOR 8-10 76
RUSTIC 8-10 74
Members: Sonny Charles; Bill Van Buskirk; Marvin Smith; Bobby Stevens; Harvey Trees.
Also see CHARLES, Sonny

CHEECH & CHONG

LP '71

Singles: 7-inch

A&M 3-4
EPIC/ODE 3-5 77
MCA 3-4 85
ODE 3-5 71-77
W.B. 3-4 78

Picture Sleeves

A&M 3-4
MCA 3-4 85
ODE 8-12 73-77
W.B. 3-4 78

EPs: 7-inch 33/45rpm

ODE (8 "Cheech & Chong") 5-8 71

LPs: 10/12-inch 33rpm

EPIC/ODE 8-10 77
MCA 5-8 85
ODE 8-12 71-76
W.B. 8-10 78-80
Members: Richard Marin; Thomas Chong.
Also see TAYLOR, Bobby

CHEE-CHEE & PEPPY

P&R/R&B '71

Singles: 7-inch

BUDDAH 3-5 71

LPs: 10/12-inch 33rpm

BUDDAH ... 10-15 72

Members: Dorothy Moore; Keith Bolling.
Also see MOORE, Dorothy

CHEEKS, Judy

P&R/R&B '78

Singles: 7-inch

DREAM ... 3-4 80
SALSOUL ... 3-4 78
U.A. ... 3-5 73

LPs: 10/12-inch 33rpm

SALSOUL ... 5-10 78
U.A. ... 8-10 73

CHEERS

P&R '54

Singles: 78rpm

CAPITOL ... 5-10 54-56
MERCURY ... 5-10 57

Singles: 7-inch

CAPITOL ... 10-20 54-56
MERCURY ... 8-15 57

EPs: 7-inch 33/45rpm

CAPITOL (584 "Bazoom") ... 50-75 55

Members: Bert Convy; Gil Garfield; Susan Allen.

CHEMAY, Joe
(Joe Chemay Band)

P&R '81

Singles: 7-inch

UNICORN ... 3-4 81

LPs: 10/12-inch 33rpm

UNICORN ... 5-10 81

CHEQUERED PAST

LP '84

Singles: 7-inch

EMI AMERICA ... 3-4 84

LPs: 10/12-inch 33rpm

EMI AMERICA ... 5-10 84

Members: Clem Burke; Nigel Harrison.

CHER
(Cher Bono; Cher Allman)

P&R/LP '65

Singles: 12-inch 33/45rpm

CASABLANCA ... 8-10 79-82

Singles: 7-inch

ATCO ... 3-6 69-72
ATLANTIC ... 4-6 69
CASABLANCA ... 3-5 79
COLUMBIA ... 3-5 82
GEFFEN ... 3-4 87-90
IMPERIAL ... 5-10 64-68
KAPP ... 3-5 71-72
LIBERTY ... 3-4 82
MCA ... 3-5 73-75
U.A. ... 3-5 71-72
W.B. ... 3-5 75-77
W.B./SPECTOR ... 3-5 74

Picture Sleeves

COLUMBIA ... 3-5 82
GEFFEN ... 3-4 87-89

LPs: 10/12-inch 33rpm

ATCO ... 15-20 69
CASABLANCA (Except NBPIX-7133) ... 8-12 79
CASABLANCA (NBPIX-7133 "Take Me Home") ... 30-40 79
(Picture disc.)
COLUMBIA ... 5-10 82
GEFFEN ... 5-10 87-91
IMPERIAL ... 15-25 65-68
KAPP ... 12-15 71-72
LIBERTY ... 5-10 81
MCA ... 10-15 73-74
SPRINGBOARD ... 8-10 72
SUNSET ... 8-10 70
U.A. ... 8-10 71-75
W.B. ... 8-15 75-77

Also see ALLMAN & WOMAN
Also see CHERILYN / Cherilyn's Group
Also see MASON, Bonnie Jo
Also see SONNY & CHER

CHER & Peter Cetera

P&R '89

Singles: 7-inch

GEFFEN ... 3-4 89

Picture Sleeves

GEFFEN ... 3-4 89

Also see CETERA, Peter

CHER & NILSSON

Singles: 7-inch

SPECTOR ... 3-5 75

Members: Cher; Harry Nilsson.
Also see CHER
Also see NILSSON

CHERI

P&R/R&B '82

Singles: 12-inch 33/45rpm

21 ... 4-6 83

Singles: 7-inch

21 ... 3-4 83
VENTURE ... 3-4 82

Members: Rosalind Hunt; Amy Roslyn.

CHERILYN / Cherilyn's Group
(Cher Bono)

Singles: 7-inch

IMPERIAL (66081 "Dream Baby") ... 20-30 64

Also see CHER

CHERRELLE

P&R/R&B/D&D/LP '84

Singles: 12-inch 33/45rpm

TABU ... 4-6 84-86

Singles: 7-inch

TABU ... 3-4 84-88

Picture Sleeves

TABU ... 3-4 88

LPs: 10/12-inch 33rpm

TABU ... 5-10 84-88

Also see O'NEAL, Alexander, & Cherrelle

CHERRY, Ava

R&B '80

Singles: 12–inch 33/45rpm

CAPITOL.. 4-6 82

Singles: 7–inch

CAPITOL.. 3-4 82
CURTOM 3-4 80
RSO 3-4 80

LPs: 10/12–inch 33rpm

RSO 5-10 80

CHERRY, Don

P&R '54

Singles: 78rpm

COLUMBIA 4-8 55-59
DECCA.. 5-10 50-56

Singles: 7–inch

COLUMBIA 5-10 55-59
DECCA.. 8-12 50-56
MONUMENT.................................... 3-5 65-78
STRAND 4-8 59
VERVE 4-8 62
WARWICK 4-8 60

EPs: 7–inch 33/45rpm

COLUMBIA 8-15 56

LPs: 10/12–inch 33rpm

COLUMBIA 15-25 56
HARMONY...................................... 10-15 59
MONUMENT.................................... 8-12 66-73

Also see DAY, Doris, & Don Cherry

CHERRY, Neneh

P&R/LP '89

Singles: 7–inch

VIRGIN.. 3-4 89

Picture Sleeves

VIRGIN.. 3-4 89

LPs: 10/12–inch 33rpm

VIRGIN.. 5-8 89

CHERRY PEOPLE

P&R '68

Singles: 7–inch

HERITAGE....................................... 4-8 68-69

Picture Sleeves

HERITAGE....................................... 6-10 68

LPs: 10/12–inch 33rpm

HERITAGE....................................... 15-20 68

Members: Punky Meadows; Doug Grimes; Chris Grimes; Rocky Isaac.
Also see ANGEL

CHERYL LYNN: see LYNN, Cheryl

CHESNUTT, Mark

C&W/LP '90

Singles: 7–inch

MCA 3-4 90-91

LPs: 10/12–inch 33rpm

MCA 5-8 90-91

CHET, FLOYD & DANNY: see ATKINS, Chet, Floyd Cramer & Danny Davis

CHEYNE

R&B/D&D '85

Singles: 12–inch 33/45rpm

MCA 4-6 85

CHIC

P&R/R&B/LP '77

Singles: 12–inch 33/45

ATLANTIC.. 4-8 78-83

Singles: 7–inch

ATLANTIC.. 3-5 77-83
MIRAGE... 3-4 82

Picture Sleeves

ATLANTIC.. 3-5 78-80

LPs: 10/12–inch 33rpm

ATLANTIC.. 5-10 77-82

Also see HONEYDRIPPERS
Also see NORMA JEAN
Also see RODGERS, Nile
Also see ROUNDTREE

CHIC / Leif Garrett / Roberta Flack / Genesis

EPs: 7–inch 33/45rpm

W.B. SPECIAL PRODUCTS........8-12 78

(Coca-Cola/Burger King promotional issue. Issued with paper sleeve.)

Also see CHIC
Also see FLACK, Roberta
Also see GARRETT, Leif
Also see GENESIS

CHICAGO

P&R/LP '69

Singles: 12–inch 33/45rpm

COLUMBIA 4-8 80

Singles: 7–inch

COLUMBIA 3-6 69-80
FULL MOON..................................... 3-4 82-86
REPRISE 3-4 88-91
W.B. 3-4 87

Picture Sleeves

COLUMBIA 3-6 69-77
FULL MOON..................................... 3-4 84-86
REPRISE 3-4 88-89
W.B. 3-4 87

EPs: 7–inch 33/45rpm

COLUMBIA 10-15 70-73

(Jukebox issues only.)

LPs: 10/12–inch 33rpm

ACCORD 5-10 81
COLUMBIA ("Chicago") 200-250 76

(No selection number used. Boxed set of first 10 LPs [17 discs]. Promotional issue only.)

COLUMBIA (8 "Chicago Transit Authority") 25-35 69
COLUMBIA (24 "Chicago II")..... 20-30 70
COLUMBIA (C2-30110 "Chicago III").......................... 10-20 70

COLUMBIA (C2Q-30110 "Chicago III") 20-25 74
(Quadrophonic.)
COLUMBIA (30863 "Chicago IV") 15-20 71
COLUMBIA (CAX-30865 "Chicago IV") 20-30 71
(Four-LP boxed edition. Includes three posters, booklet and card.)
COLUMBIA (CQ-30865 "Chicago IV") 20-30 74
(Quadrophonic.)
COLUMBIA (31102 thru 38590).. 8-15 72-82
(With "C2," "FC," "HC," "KC," "JC," or "PC" prefix.)
COLUMBIA (31102 thru 34200) 15-25 74-76
(Quadrophonic. With "CQ," "C2Q," "GQ," or "PCQ" prefix.)
COLUMBIA (43000 & 44000 series) 15-25 82
(Half-speed mastered.)
FULL MOON 5-10 82-86
MFSL (128 "Chicago Transit Authority") 15-25 85
REPRISE 5-8 88-89
MAGNUM 10-12 78
W.B. 5-8 86

Members: Peter Cetera; Terry Kath; Robert Lamm; James Pankow; Lee Loughnane; Daniel Seraphine; Walter Parazaider; Bill Champlin; Donnie Dacus; Jason Scheff.
Also see BEACH BOYS
Also see CETERA, Peter
Also see CHAMPLIN, Bill
Also see LAMM, Robert

CHICAGO BEARS SHUFFLIN' CREW

P&R/R&B '86

Singles: 12-inch 33/45rpm

RED LABEL 4-8 85

Singles: 7-inch

RED LABEL 3-4 85

Picture Sleeves

RED LABEL 3-4 85

Members: Walter Payton; Willie Gault; Mike Singletary; Jim McMahon; Otis Wilson; Steve Fuller; Mike Richardson; Richard Dent; Gary Fencik; William Perry.

CHICAGO GANGSTERS

R&B '75

Singles: 7-inch

GOLD PLATE.................................. 3-5 75-76
RCA.. 3-5 78
RED COACH.................................. 3-5 74-75

LPs: 10/12-inch 33rpm

GOLD PLATE.......................... 10-12 75-76

Members: Sam McCant; James McCant; Larry McCant; Chris McCant.

CHICAGO LOOP

P&R '66

Singles: 7-inch

DYNO VOICE 4-8 66-67
MERCURY.......................................4-8 67-68

CHICAGO TRANSIT AUTHORITY: see CHICAGO

CHICANO, El: see EL CHICANO

CHICORY

(Chicory Tip)

P&R '72

Singles: 7-inch

EPIC..3-5 72-73

LPs: 10/12-inch 33rpm

EPIC...10-12 72

CHIEFTAINS

LP '76

Singles: 7-inch

ISLAND...3-5 76

LPs: 10/12-inch 33rpm

COLUMBIA....................................5-10 78-80
ISLAND...5-10 75-78

Also see MORRISON, Van, & Chieftains

CHIFFONS

P&R '60

Singles: 7-inch

B.T. PUPPY 3-5 70
BIG DEAL (6003 "Tonight's the Night")....................................35-50 60
BUDDAH...4-8 71
LAURIE...5-10 63-76
REPRISE 10-15 62
WILDCAT (601 "Never Never").. 10-20 61

LPs: 10/12-inch 33rpm

B.T. PUPPY (1011 "My Secret Love")....................................35-45 70
COLLECTABLES...........................5-10 87
LAURIE (2018 "He's So Fine")...35-50 63
LAURIE (2020 "One Fine Day").35-50 63
LAURIE (LLP-2036 "Sweet Talkin' Guy").......................................35-45 66
(Monaural.)
LAURIE (SLP-2036 "Sweet Talkin' Guy").......................................40-50 66
(Stereo.)
LAURIE (4001 "Everything You Always Wanted to Hear") 10-20 75

Members: Judy Craig; Barbara Lee; Patricia Bennett; Sylvia Peterson.
Also see CHRISTIE, Lou, & Classics / Isley Brothers / Chiffons
Also see COASTERS / Crew-Cuts / Chiffons
Also see FOUR PENNIES

CHILD, Desmond, & Rouge

P&R/R&B/LP '79

Singles: 12-inch 33/45rpm

CAPITOL...4-8 79

Singles: 7–inch

CAPITOL (Black vinyl) 3-4 79-82
CAPITOL (Colored vinyl).............. 4-6 79

LPs: 10/12–inch 33rpm

CAPITOL (Black vinyl) 5-10 79
CAPITOL (Colored vinyl)........... 15-20 79

Also see VIDAL, Maria

CHILD, Jane

P&R/LP '90

Singles: 7–inch

W.B. 3-4 90

LPs: 10/12–inch 33rpm

W.B. 3-4 90

CHILDS, Toni

P&R/LP '88

Singles: 7–inch

A&M 3-4 88-90

Picture Sleeves

A&M 3-4 88

LPs: 10/12–inch 33rpm

A&M 5-8 88-91

CHI-LITES

P&R/R&B/LP '69

Singles: 12–inch 33/45rpm

LARC.. 4-8 83
PRIVATE 1 .... 4-6 84

Singles: 7–inch

BLUE ROCK (4007 "I'm So Jealous") 15-25 65
BLUE ROCK (4020 "The Monkey") 15-25 65
BLUE ROCK (4037 "She's Mine") 25-50 65
BRUNSWICK 3-8 69-78
CHI-SOUND................................. 3-4 80-82
EPIC... 3-4 83
INPHASION 3-5 79
LARC.. 3-4 83
MERCURY 3-5 76-77
O'RETTA...................................... 4-8 70
PRIVATE I 3-4 84
REVUE 5-10 67-68
20TH FOX 3-4 81

LPs: 10/12–inch 33rpm

BRUNSWICK 10-15 69-74
CHI-SOUND................................. 5-8 80-82
EPIC.. 5-10 83-84
LARC... 5-10 83
MERCURY 5-10 77
PICKWICK 5-10 70s
20TH FOX 5-10 80-81

Members: Eugene Record; Creadel Jones; Robert Lester; Marshall Thompson; Danny Johnson.

Also see JOHNSON, Danny
Also see PITMAN, Donnell
Also see RECORD, Eugene
Also see WILSON, Jackie, & Chi-Lites

CHILL FACTOR

R&B '87

Singles: 7–inch

W.B. 3-4 87

CHILL TOWN

D&D '83

Singles: 12–inch 33/45rpm

A&M 4-6 83

CHILLIWACK

P&R '72

Singles: 12–inch 33/45rpm

MUSHROOM (0611 "Dreams, Dreams, Dreams") 10-15 78
(Clear vinyl. Promotional issue only.)

Singles: 7–inch

A&M 3-5 72
MILLENNIUM................................ 3-4 81-83
MUSHROOM 3-5 76-80
PARROT 3-5 71
SIRE... 3-5 74-76

LPs: 10/12–inch 33rpm

A&M 10-15 71-73
MILLENNIUM................................ 5-10 81-82
MUSHROOM 8-12 77-80
PARROT 15-20 70
SIRE... 10-15 75

Members: Bill Henderson; Howard Froese; Claire Lawrence; Glen Miller; Ross Turney.

CHIMES

P&R '60

Singles: 7–inch

ABC... 3-4 75
COLLECTABLES.......................... 3-4 81
ERIC 3-4 70s
LAURIE 10-15 60
LOST-NITE 3-4 70s
METRO INT'L 5-10 63
MUSIC NOTE (1101 "Once in Awhile") 10-20 61
RESERVE (120 "When School Starts Again") 30-40 57
TAG (444 "Once in Awhile"/"Summer Night") 10-20 60
(Maroon label.)
TAG (444 "Once in Awhile"/"Summer Night") 5-10 60
(Green label.)
TAG (444 "Once in Awhile"/"Oh How I Love You So") 10-20 60
(Though shown as by the Chimes, *Oh How I Love You So* is by the BiTones.)
TAG (445 "I'm in the Mood for Love") 8-12 61
TAG (447 "Let's Fall in Love").... 10-15 61
TAG (450 "My Love") 10-20 62
TRIP 3-5 70s

LPs: 10/12–inch 33rpm

CHIMES 8-12

Member: Lenny Cocco.

CHIMES / Huey "Piano" Smith

Singles: 7–inch

OLDIES 45 3-5

Also see CHIMES
Also see SMITH, Huey

CHIMES

P&R/LP '90

LPs: 10/12–inch 33rpm

COLUMBIA 5-8 90

Member: Pauline Henry.

CHINA CRISIS

D&D '84

Singles: 12–inch 33/45rpm

VIRGIN....................................... 4-6 82
W.B. 4-6 83-84

Singles: 7–inch

VIRGIN....................................... 3-4 82
W.B. 3-4 84

LPs: 10/12–inch 33rpm

A&M 5-10 87
W.B. 5-10 84-85

CHIP E. INC. Featuring K. Joy

D&D '85

Singles: 12–inch 33/45rpm

D.J. INT'L 4-6 85

CHIPMUNKS

(Starring Alvin, Theodore, & Simon; Featuring David Seville)

P&R/R&B '58

Singles: 7–inch

AMERICAN TELECARD........... 10-15 64
(Cardboard flexi-disc.)
DOT.. 4-6 67
LIBERTY (Except 77000 series). 5-10 58-74
LIBERTY (77000 series).......... 10-20 59
(Stereo.)
MISTLETOE................................ 3-5 75
SUNSET...................................... 3-6 68
U.A. 3-5 74

Picture Sleeves

LIBERTY 5-10 59-65

EPs: 7–inch 33/45rpm

LIBERTY 10-20 59-64

LPs: 10/12–inch 33rpm

LIBERTY (3132 "Let's All Sing with the Chipmunks")......................... 20-30 59
(Monaural. Black vinyl. Cover shows Chipmunks as animals. If Chipmunks are drawn as cartoon characters, deduct 50%.)
LIBERTY (3132 "Let's All Sing with the Chipmunks")......................... 25-40 59
(Monaural. Colored vinyl. Cover shows Chipmunks as animals. If Chipmunks are drawn as cartoon characters, deduct 50%.)
LIBERTY (3159 "Sing Again with the Chipmunks")......................... 20-30 60
(Monaural. Cover shows Chipmunks as animals. If Chipmunks are drawn as cartoon characters, deduct 50%.)
LIBERTY (3170 "Around the World with the Chipmunks") 20-30 60
(Monaural. Cover shows Chipmunks as animals. If Chipmunks are drawn as cartoon characters, deduct 50%.)
LIBERTY (3200 thru 3400 series)...................................10-20 61-65
(Monaural.)
LIBERTY (7132 "Let's All Sing with the Chipmunks") 20-35 59
(Stereo. Black vinyl. Cover shows Chipmunks as animals. If Chipmunks are drawn as cartoon characters, deduct 50%.)
LIBERTY (7132 "Let's All Sing with the Chipmunks") 25-45 59
(Stereo. Colored vinyl. Cover shows Chipmunks as animals. If Chipmunks are drawn as cartoon characters, deduct 50%.)
LIBERTY (7159 "Sing Again with the Chipmunks") 20-35 60
(Stereo. Cover shows Chipmunks as animals. If Chipmunks are drawn as cartoon characters, deduct 50%.)
LIBERTY (7170 "Around the World with the Chipmunks") 20-35 60
(Stereo. Cover shows Chipmunks as animals. If Chipmunks are drawn as cartoon characters, deduct 50%.)
LIBERTY (7200 thru 7400 series)...................................10-20 61-65
(Stereo.)
LIBERTY (10000 series).............5-10 82
PICKWICK 5-10 80
SUNSET 8-15 68-69
U.A. 5-10 74-76

Also see CANNED HEAT & CHIPMUNKS
Also see SEVILLE, David

CHIPMUNKS

(Starring Alvin, Theodore, & Simon; Featuring David Seville Jr.)

LP '80

Singles: 7–inch

EXCELSIOR 3-4 80
RCA 3-4 81-82

Picture Sleeves

EXCELSIOR 3-4 80
RCA 3-4 81

LPs: 10/12–inch 33rpm

EXCELSIOR 5-10 80
PICKWICK INT'L.........................5-10 80
RCA 5-10 81-82

CHIYO & CRESCENTS: see CRESCENTS

CHOCOLATE MILK

R&B/LP '75

Singles: 12–inch 33/45rpm

RCA 4-6 83

Singles: 7-inch

RCA 3-5 75-83

LPs: 10/12-inch 33rpm

RCA 5-10 77-82

Members: Frank Richard; Amadee Castanell; Robert Doban, Joe Foxx; Mario Tio; Dwight Richards.

CHOCOLATE SYRUP

R&B '71

Singles: 7-inch

AVCO EMBASSY 3-5 71
BROWN DOG 3-5 74
LAW TON 3-5

Members: L.J. Reynolds; Lenny Wolfe; Jimmy Holiday; Norris Harris.
Also see CHAIN REACTION
Also see MOMENT of TRUTH
Also see REYNOLDS, L.J.

CHOCOLETE

D&D '85

Singles: 12-inch 33/45rpm

SUPERTRONICS 4-6 85

CHOICE FOUR

R&B '74

Singles: 7-inch

RCA 3-5 74-76

LPs: 10/12-inch 33rpm

RCA 8-10 74-75

Members: Bobby Hamilton; Pete Marshall; Ted Maduro; Charles Blagmore.

CHOICE MCs Featuring Fresh Gordon

R&B/D&D '85

Singles: 12-inch 33/45rpm

TOMMY BOY 4-6 85

Singles: 7-inch

TOMMY BOY 3-4 85

CHOIR

P&R '67

Singles: 7-inch

CANADIAN AMERICAN (203 "It's Cold Outside") 25-35 67
INTREPID 4-6 70
ROULETTE 10-15 67-68

EPs: 7-inch 33/45rpm

BOMP 8-10 76

Members: Wally Bryson; David Smalley; Jim Bonfanti.
Also see RASPBERRIES

CHOIRBOYS

P&R '89

Singles: 7-inch

WTG 3-4 89

Member: Mark Gable.

CHOPS

R&B '84

Singles: 12-inch 33/45rpm

ATLANTIC 4-6 84

Singles: 7-inch

ATLANTIC 3-4 84

LPs: 10/12-inch 33rpm

ATLANTIC 5-10 84

CHORDCATS

Singles: 78rpm

CAT 10-15 54

Singles: 7-inch

CAT (112 "Hold Me, Baby") 20-40 54

Members: Carl Feaster; Claude Feaster; Jimmy Keys; Floyd McRae; William Edwards.
Also see CHORDS

CHORDETTES
(With Archie Bleyer; with Jeff Kron & Jackie Ertel)

P&R '54

Singles: 78rpm

CADENCE 5-10 54-57
COLUMBIA 5-10 50-54

Singles: 7-inch

BARNABY 3-5 70-76
CADENCE 8-15 54-63
COLUMBIA 10-15 50-54
ERIC 3-4 78

Picture Sleeves

CADENCE (Except 1366) 10-20 58-61
CADENCE (1366 "No Wheels") 15-25 59
(Promotional issue only. Pictures Jeff and Jackie. Sleeve and disc has *No Wheels* on both sides.)
CADENCE (1366 "A Girl's Work Is Never Done") 10-15 59
(Pictures only Jackie.)

EPs: 7-inch 33/45rpm

CADENCE 10-20 57-61
COLUMBIA (Except 201 thru 401) 10-25 54-57
COLUMBIA (201 "Harmony Time") 30-40 50
(Four-disc boxed set.)
COLUMBIA (241 "Harmony Time, Vol. 2") 30-40 51
(Four-disc boxed set.)
COLUMBIA (309 "Harmony Encores") 30-40 52
(Four-disc boxed set.)
COLUMBIA (401 "Your Requests) 30-40 53
(Four-disc boxed set.)

LPs: 10/12-inch 33rpm

BACK-TRAC 5-10
BARNABY 8-10 76
CADENCE (1002 "Close Harmony") 20-30 55
CADENCE (3001 "Chordettes") 20-35 57
CADENCE (3020 "Barbershop Harmonies") 20-30 58
CADENCE (3062 "Never on Sunday") 20-30 62
CADENCE (25062 "Never on Sunday") 25-35 62

COLUMBIA (956 "Listen")......... 20-35 57
COLUMBIA (2519 "Chordettes")......................... 25-35 56
(10–inch LP.)
COLUMBIA (6111 "Harmony Time")................................... 30-40 50
(10–inch LP.)
COLUMBIA (6170 "Harmony Time, Vol. 2") 30-40 51
(10–inch LP.)
COLUMBIA (6218 "Harmony Encores") 30-40 52
(10–inch LP.)
COLUMBIA (6285 "Your Requests)............................... 30-40 53
(10–inch LP.)
EVEREST 5-10 82
HARMONY 12-15 59

Members: Margie Needham; Janet Ertel; Carol Bushman; Lynn Evans.
Also see BLEYER, Archie

CHORDS

P&R/R&B '54

Singles: 78rpm

CAT (104 "Sh-Boom"/"Cross over the Bridge") 15-25 54
CAT (104 "Sh-Boom"/"Little Maiden")................................ 10-20 54
CAT (109 "Zippety Zum")........... 5-10 54
QUALITY (1268 "Sh-Boom")..... 25-50 54
(Canadian.)
QUALITY (1293 "Zippety Zum") 10-20 54
(Canadian.)

Singles: 7–inch

CAT (104 "Sh-Boom"/"Cross over the Bridge") 50-75 54
CAT (104 "Sh-Boom"/"Little Maiden")................................ 25-40 54
CAT (109 "Zippety Zum").......... 20-30 54
QUALITY (1268 "Sh-Boom"). 150-200 54
(Canadian.)
QUALITY (1293 "Zippety Zum") 15-20 54
(Canadian.)

Members: Carl Feaster; Claude Feaster; Jimmy Keys; Floyd McRae; William Edwards.
Also see CHORDCATS
Also see SH-BOOMS

CHRIS & KATHY

Singles: 7–inch

MONOGRAM 10-15 64

Members: Chris Montez; Kathy Young.
Also see MONTEZ, Chris
Also see YOUNG, Kathy

CHRISTIAN, Chris
(With Amy Holland)

P&R '81

Singles: 7–inch

BOARDWALK 3-4 81-82

Picture Sleeves

BOARDWALK 3-4 81

LPs: 10/12–inch 33rpm

BORADWALK 5-10 81
HOME SWEET HOME................5-10 81
MYRRH......................................5-10 83-84

Also see COTTON, LLOYD & CHRISTIAN
Also see HOLLAND, Amy

CHRISTIANS

LP '88

LPs: 10/12–inch 33rpm

ISLAND 5-8 88

CHRISTIE

P&R/LP '70

Singles: 7–inch

EPIC...3-5 70-71

LPs: 10/12–inch 33rpm

EPIC...10-15 70

Members: Jeff Christie; Mike Blakely; Vic Elmes.

CHRISTIE, Dean
(Dean Christy)

P&R '62

Singles: 7–inch

MERCURY 4-8 63-64
SWL 5-10 62
SELECT (715 "Heart Breaker")..10-15 62
SELECT (718 "Teenage Jezebel") 15-25 62
TOP FLIGHT (113 "So Much")...20-30 60s

CHRISTIE, Janice

D&D '85

Singles: 12–inch 33/45rpm

SUPERTRONICS 4-6 85-86

Singles: 7–inch

SUPERTRONICS 3-4 85-86

Also see FATBACK

CHRISTIE, Lou
(With the Classics; Lou Christy)

P&R/R&B/LP '63

Singles: 12–inch 33/45rpm

PLATEAU (4551 "Guardian Angels") 40-50 81

Singles: 7–inch

ABC...3-5 73
ALCAR (207 "Close Your Eyes") 15-20 63
ALCAR (208 "You're with It") 20-25 63
AMERICAN MUSIC MAKERS (006 "The Jury") 25-30
BUDDAH.......................................5-15 68-72
C&C (102 "The Gypsy Cried") .75-100 62
CO & CE (235 "Outside the Gates of Heaven")......................................5-10 66
COLPIX..6-12 64-66
COLUMBIA 10-15 67
EPIC..10-15 76
MGM (Except 13473)...................5-10 65-66
MGM (13473 "Rhapsody in the Rain")................................10-15 66
(With "making out in the rain" lyrics.)

MGM (13473 "Rhapsody in the Rain") 5-10 66
(With "fell in love in the rain" lyrics.)
MIDLAND INT'L.......... 10-15 76-77
MIDSONG.......... 10-12 77
PLATEAU (4551 "Guardian Angels").......... 40-50 81
ROULETTE (4457 "The Gypsy Cried").......... 15-20 62
(White label with color spokes.)
ROULETTE (4457 "The Gypsy Cried").......... 5-10 63
(Pink label.)
ROULETTE (4481 "Two Faces Have I").......... 15-25 63
(White label with color spokes.)
ROULETTE (4481 "Two Faces Have I").......... 5-10 63
(Pink label.)
ROULETTE (4457 thru 4527) 5-10 62-63
ROULETTE (4545 "Stay")......... 10-15 64
ROULETTE (4554 "When You Dance").......... 20-25 64
SLIPPED DISC.......... 10-15 76
THREE BROTHERS.......... 5-15 73-75
WORLD (1002 "The Jury")........ 25-30

Picture Sleeves

COLPIX (799 "Big Time").......... 10-20 66
MGM (13473 "Rhapsody in the Rain").......... 8-12 66
MGM (13533 "Painter").......... 8-12 66
MGM (13576 "If My Car Could Only Talk").......... 20-25 66

LPs: 10/12–inch 33rpm

BUDDAH (5052 "I'm Gonna Make You Mine").......... 10-15 69
BUDDAH (5073 "Paint America Love").......... 15-20 69
CO & CE (1231 "Lou Christie Strikes Back").......... 30-50 66
COLPIX (4001 "Lou Christie Strikes Again").......... 20-25 66
(Gold label.)
COLPIX (4001 "Lou Christie Strikes Again").......... 10-20 66
(Blue label.)
CSP (18260 "Lou Christie Does Detroit").......... 5-8
51 WEST ("Lou Christie Does Detroit").......... 10-15 83
MGM (4360 "Lightnin' Strikes") . 12-18 66
MGM (4394 "Painter of Hits").... 15-20 66
RHINO.......... 5-8 88
ROULETTE (25208 "Lou Christie").......... 50-60 63
(Cover has a blue background.)
ROULETTE (25208 "Lou Christie").......... 30-40 63
(Cover has white wall background.)
ROULETTE (25332 "Lou Christie Strikes Again").......... 20-30 63
(Repackage of Co & Ce 1231, *Lou Christie Strikes Back.*)
UNDERGROUND (50002 "Self Expression").......... 8-10 83
(Canadian.)
THREE BROTHERS (2000 "Lou Christie").......... 15-20 74

Also see CHRISTY, Chic
Also see CLASSICS
Also see CRITTERS / Young Rascals / Lou Christie
Also see GORE, Leslie, & Lou Christie
Also see LUGEE & LIONS
Also see MARCY JOE
Also see SACCO
Also see ZADORA, Pia, & Lou Christie

CHRISTIE, Lou / Len Barry & Dovells / Bobby Rydell / Tokens

LPs: 10/12–inch 33rpm

WYNCOTE.......... 10-20

Also see DOVELLS
Also see RYDELL, Bobby
Also see TOKENS

CHRISTIE, Lou, & Classics / Isley Brothers / Chiffons

LPs: 10/12–inch 33rpm

SPIN-O-RAMA (173 "Lou Christie and the Classics").......... 20-30 66

Also see CHIFFONS
Also see ISLEY BROTHERS

CHRISTIE, Lynn, & Deckers

Singles: 7–inch

NAR.......... 8-12 57

CHRISTIE, Susan

P&R '66

Singles: 7–inch

COLUMBIA.......... 4-8 66-67

CHRISTMAS SPIRIT

Singles: 7–inch

WHITE WHALE (290 "Christmas Is My Time of Year").......... 50-75 69

Members: Mark Volman; Howard Kaylan; Linda Ronstadt.
Also see RONSTADT, Linda
Also see TURTLES

CHRISTOPHER, Gavin

R&B '79

Singles: 7–inch

E.M.I.......... 3-4 88
ISLAND.......... 3-5 76
MANHATTAN.......... 3-4 86
RSO.......... 3-4 79

Picture Sleeves

MANHATTAN.......... 3-4 86

LPs: 10/12–inch 33rpm

ISLAND.......... 8-10 76
MANHATTAN.......... 5-10 86
RSO.......... 5-10 79

CHRISTOPHER, Paul & Shawn

P&R '75

Singles: 7–inch

CASABLANCA 3-5 75

Also see CHRISTOPHER, Shawn

CHRISTY, Chic

Singles: 7–inch

HAC.. 15-25 62

Members: Lou Christie; Kay Chick; Susan Christie.

Also see CHRISTIE, Lou

CHRISTY, Dean: see CHRISTIE, Dean

CHRISTY, Don
(Sonny Bono)

Singles: 7–inch

FIDELITY 10-15 60
GO.. 10-15 60
NAME.. 10-15 60
SPECIALTY 10-15 59

Also see SONNY

CHRISTY, June

P&R '53

Singles: 78rpm

CAPITOL.................................... 3-8 51-57

Singles: 7–inch

CAPITOL (1800 thru 3900 series) 5-10 51-58
CAPITOL (4000 thru 4800 series) 3-8 59-62

EPs: 7–inch 33/4rpm

CAPITOL.................................... 5-15 53-55

LPs: 10/12–inch 33rpm

CAPITOL (516 "Something Cool") 25-40 54
(With "H" prefix. 10–inch LP.)
CAPITOL (516 "Something Cool") 15-25 55
(Green label. With "T" prefix.)
CAPITOL (516 "Something Cool") 10-20 60
(Black label. With "T" or "ST" prefix.)
CAPITOL (516 "Something Cool") 5-10 75
(With "SM" prefix.)
CAPITOL (600 thru 900 series). 15-25 55-57
(Green label.)
CAPITOL (600 thru 900 series). 10-15 60
(Black label.)
CAPITOL (1000 thru 2400 series) 10-20 60-65
CAPITOL (11000 series)............ 5-10 79
DISCOVERY 5-10 82
SEABREEZE............................. 5-10 80

CHRISTY, June, with Stan Kenton

EPs: 7–inch 33/45rpm

CAPITOL.................................... 5-10 56

LPs: 10/12–inch 33rpm

CAPITOL (656 "Duet")..............20-35 56
(10–inch LP.)

Also see CHRISTY, June
Also see JONES, Jonah
Also see KENTON, Stan, & His Orchestra

CHRISTY, Lou: see CHRISTIE, Lou

CHUBB ROCK

LP '91

LPs: 10/12–inch 33rpm

SELECT 5-8 91

CHUCKLES
(Featuring Teddy Randazzo)

Singles: 7–inch

ABC-PAR 5-10 61

Also see RANDAZZO, Teddy
Also see THREE CHUCKLES

CHUNG, Wang: see WANG CHUNG

CHUNKY A
(Arsenio Hall)

P&R/LP '89

Singles: 7–inch

MCA 3-4 89

Picture Sleeves

MCA 3-4 89

LPs: 10/12–inch 33rpm

MCA 5-8 89

CHURCH, Eugene
(With the Fellows)

P&R/R&B '58

Singles: 7–inch

CLASS 5-10 58-60
COLLECTABLES.........................3-4 81
KING 5-10 61-63
RENDEZVOUS 5-10 60
SPECIALTY 10-20 57
WORLD PACIFIC (77866 "Dollar Bill")..10-15 67

Also see CLIQUES

CHURCHILL, Savannah
(With the Five Kings; with Striders; with Four Tunes)

R&B '45

Singles: 78rpm

ARGO 4-8 56
DECCA 4-8 53-55
KAY-RON....................................5-10 56
MANOR.......................................5-10 45-48
RCA 5-10 51-52
REGAL (3309 "Once There Lived a Fool") 25-50 50
REGAL (3313 "Wedding Bells")...5-10 50

Singles: 7–inch

ARGO 10-20 56
DECCA 8-15 53-55
JAMIE 8-15 60
KAY-RON..................................10-15 56
RCA 10-20 51-52

REGAL (3309 "Once There Lived a Fool") 100-150 50

EPs: 7-inch 33/45rpm

CAMDEN (270 "Love and Sin"). 35-50 55
CAMDEN (282 "Savannah Churchill Sings") 35-50 55

Also see CARTER, Benny, & Orchestra
Also see FOUR TUNES

CI CI

R&B '85

Singles: 7-inch

CREATIVE FUNK 3-4 85

CINDERELLA

P&R/LP '86

Singles: 12-inch 33/45rpm

MERCURY 4-8 88
(Promotional only.)

Singles: 7-inch

MERCURY 3-4 86-90

Picture Sleeves

MERCURY 3-4 86-89

LPs: 10/12-inch 33rpm

MERCURY 5-10 86-90

Members: Tom Keifer; Fred Coury; Eric Brittingham; Jeff LaBar.

CINDY & ROY

R&B '79

Singles: 12-inch 33/45rpm

CASABLANCA 4-8 79

Singles: 7-inch

CASABLANCA 3-4 79

LPs: 10/12-inch 33rpm

CASABLANCA 5-10 79

Member: Cynthia Biggs.

CINEMA

D&D '84

Singles: 12-inch 33/45rpm

PROFILE 4-6 84

CIRCUS

P&R '73

Singles: 7-inch

METROMEDIA 3-6 72-73

LPs: 10/12-inch 33rpm

HEMISPHERE 10-15 74
METROMEDIA 15-25 73

Members: Tom Dobeck; Frank Salle; Craig Balzer; Phil Alexander; Mick Sabol; Bruce Balzer.
Also see STANLEY, Michael, Band

CIRCUT

D&D '84

Singles: 12-inch 33/45rpm

4TH & BROADWAY 4-6 84-85

CISSEL, Chuck

R&B '79

Singles: 7-inch

ARISTA 3-5 79-80

LPs: 10/12-inch 33rpm

ARISTA 5-10 80

CISSEL, Chuck, & Marva King

R&B '82

Singles: 7-inch

ARISTA 3-4 82

Also see CISSEL, Chuck

CISYK, Kacey
(Original Cast of You Light Up My Life)

P&R '77

Singles: 7-inch

ABC 3-5 78
ARISTA 3-5 78

CITISPEAK

R&B/D&D/ '84

Singles: 7-inch

STREETWISE 3-4 84

CITY BOY

LP '76

Singles: 7-inch

AIRBOY 3-5 77
ATLANTIC 3-4 79-81
MERCURY 3-5 76-78

Picture Sleeves

MERCURY 3-5 78

LPs: 10/12-inch 33rpm

ATLANTIC 5-10 80
MERCURY 8-10 76-78

Members: Steve Broughton; Lol Mason; Mike Slamer; Max Thomas; Roy Ward; Chris Dunn; Roger Kent.

CLANCY BROTHERS
(With Lou Killen; with Robbie O'Connell)

LPs: 10/12-inch 33rpm

AUDIO FIDELITY 8-12 71-73
COLUMBIA 8-15 70
VANGUARD 5-12 74-83

CLANCY BROTHERS & Tommy Makem

LP '63

Singles: 7-inch

COLUMBIA 3-6 62-69

LPs: 10/12-inch 33rpm

COLUMBIA 10-20 62-69
HARMONY 6-10 71-72
SHANACHIE 5-10
TRADITION 10-15 67-69

Also see CLANCY BROTHERS

CLANDESTINE

D&D '84

Singles: 12-inch 33/45rpm

SLEEPING BAG 4-6 84

CLANNAD

LP '86

LPs: 10/12-inch 33rpm

RCA 5-10 84-88

CLANTON, Ike

P&R '60

Singles: 7-inch

ACE 5-10 59-60
MERCURY 5-10 62-63
Also see DEL-VIKINGS / Ike Clanton
Also see EDDY, Duane

CLANTON, Jimmy
(With His Rockets; Jimmie Clanton)

P&R/R&B '58

Singles: 78rpm

ACE 10-15 57

Singles: 7-inch

ABC 3-4 73
ACE (Except 567) 5-10 57-63
ACE (567 "My Own True Love") . 5-10 59
(Monaural.)
ACE (567 "My Own True Love") 15-25 59
(Stereo.)
COLLECTABLES 3-4 81
ERIC 3-4 73
IMPERIAL 4-8 67-68
LAURIE 4-6 69
MALA 4-8 65
OLDIES 45 3-5
PHILIPS 4-8 63-64
SPIRAL 3-5 71
STARCREST 3-5 76
STARFIRE 3-5 78
VIN 4-8 62

Promotional Singles

ACE (644 "Venus in Blue Jeans") 10-20 62
ACE (51860 "The Slave") 8-15 60
(Promotional, bonus disc with the *Jimmy's Happy/Jimmy's Blue* LP.)
U.A. ("Teenage Millionaire") 5-10 62
(Cardboard 5-inch flexi-disc.)

Picture Sleeves

ACE (Except 51860) 8-15 59-63
ACE (51860 "The Slave") 15-25 60
(Promotional only, mail-order bonus offer to buyers of the *Jimmy's Happy/Jimmy's Blue* LP. All copies of this sleeve were autographed by Clanton.)
PHILIPS 5-10 64
STARCREST 4-6 76

EPs: 7-inch 33/45rpm

ACE (Black vinyl) 20-35 59-61
ACE (Colored vinyl) 35-50 60

LPs: 10/12-inch 33rpm

ACE (100 "Jimmy's Happy/ Jimmy's Blue") 60-80 60
(Black vinyl.)
ACE (100 "Jimmy's Happy/ Jimmy's Blue") 75-125 60
(Colored vinyl.)
ACE (1001 "Just a Dream") 50-75 59
ACE (1007 "Jimmy's Happy") 40-50 60
ACE (1008 "Jimmy's Blue") 40-50 60
ACE (1011 "My Best to You") 50-75 61
ACE (1014 "Teenage Millionaire") 50-75 61
ACE (1026 "Venus in Blue Jeans") 40-60 61
MONTAGNE 10-15 81
PHILLIPS 15-25 64
Also see DALE, Jimmy

CLANTON, Jimmy / Frankie Ford / Jerry Lee Lewis / Patsy Cline

EPs: 7-inch 33/45rpm

MEMORY LANE 3-5 92
(Promotional issue only.)
Also see CLINE, Patsy
Also see FORD, Frankie
Also see LEWIS, Jerry Lee

CLANTON, Jimmy / Bristow Hopper

LPs: 10/12-inch 33rpm

DESIGN 15-20

CLANTON, Jimmy, & Mary Ann Mobley

Singles: 7-inch

ACE 5-10 61

Picture Sleeves

ACE 10-15 61
Also see CLANTON, Jimmy

CLAPTON, Eric

P&R/LP '70

Singles: 12-inch 33/45rpm

W.B. (2248 "Forever Man") 5-10 85
(Promotional issue only.)
W.B. (2683 "Miss You") 5-10 85
(Promotional issue only.)

Singles: 7-inch

ATCO 4-6 70-71
DUCK 3-4 83-86
POLYDOR 3-5 72-73
RSO 3-5 74-82
W.B. 3-4 86

Picture Sleeves

DUCK 3-4 85-89
RSO 3-5 80-81
W.B. 3-4 86

LPs: 10/12-inch 33rpm

ATCO (329 "Eric Clapton") 20-30 70
ATCO (803 "History of Eric Clapton") 20-30 72
DUCK 5-10 83-89
MFSL (030 "Slowhand") 25-50 79
MFSL (183 "Bluesbreakers") 15-20 87
POLYDOR (Except 835261) 8-15 72-73
POLYDOR (835261 "Crossroads") 30-40 88
(Boxed 6-LP set.)
RSO (Except 035, 1009 & 4801) . 8-20 73-82
RSO (035 "Slowhand") 20-25 77
(Colored vinyl. Promotional issue only.)

RSO (1009 "Limited Backless").. 40-50 78
(Colored vinyl. Promotional issue only.)
RSO (4801 "461 Ocean Blvd.")... 8-12 74
(With *Give Me Strength.*)
Also see BLIND FAITH
RSO (4801 "461 Ocean Blvd.")... 5-10 74
(*Give Me Strength* is replaced with *Better Make It Through the Day.*)
Also see BLIND FAITH
Also see COOLIDGE, Rita
Also see CREAM
Also see CURTIS, Sonny
Also see DELANEY & BONNIE
Also see DEREK & DOMINOES
Also see GUY, Buddy, with Dr. John & Eric Clapton / Buddy Guy & J. Geils Band
Also see HARRISON, George
Also see LOMAX, Jackie
Also see MAYALL, John
Also see RUSSELL, Leon
Also see SPANN, Otis
Also see STARR, Ringo
Also see TOWNSHEND, Pete, & Ronnie Lane
Also see WATERS, Roger
Also see YARDBIRDS

CLAPTON, Eric, Jeff Beck & Jimmy Page

LPs: 10/12-inch 33rpm

RCA (4624 "Guitar Boogie")...... 10-15 71
Also see BECK, Jeff
Also see PAGE, Jimmy

CLAPTON, Eric, & Tina Turner

Singles: 7-inch

DUCK 3-4 87

Picture Sleeves

DUCK 3-4 87
Also see CLAPTON, Eric
Also see TURNER, Tina

CLARK, Chris

R&B '66

Singles: 7-inch

MOTOWN 10-15 67-68
V.I.P. (25031 "Do Right Baby Do Right")............................. 10-15 65
V.I.P. (25038 "Love's Gone Mad")................................... 50-60 66
(Title incorrect on label.)
V.I.P. (25038 "Love's Gone Bad") 10-20 66
(Title corrected.)
V.I.P. (25041 " I Love You") 10-15 67

LPs: 10/12-inch 33rpm

MOTOWN (664 "Soul Sounds") 40-60 67
WEED (801 "CC Rides Again"). 50-75

CLARK, Chuck

Singles: 7-inch

RELIABLE 4-8 62
SHERATON 4-8 62
U.A. 4-8 62

CLARK, Claudine
(With the Spinners)

P&R/R&B '62

Singles: 7-inch

CHANCELLOR 5-10 62-63
COLLECTABLES..........................3-4 81
ERIC 3-4 73
HERALD (521 "Teenage Blues") 20-30 58
JAMIE 4-8 64
TCF 4-8 64

LPs: 10/12-inch 33rpm

CHANCELLOR (5029 "Party Lights")...................................40-60 62

CLARK, Dave, Five
(With Friends)

P&R/LP '64

Singles: 7-inch

CONGRESS (212 "I Knew It All the Time") 10-15 64
EPIC (2000 series).........................4-6 72
EPIC (9656 thru 10894)..............5-15 64-72
HOLLYWOOD...............................3-4 93
JUBILEE (5476 "Chaquita").......10-20 64
LAURIE (3188 "I Walk the Line")..25-35 63
RUST (5078 "I Walk the Line") ..20-30 64

Promotional Singles

EPIC (9656 thru 9833)..............10-20 64-65
EPIC (9863 "Over and Over")....10-20 65
(Black vinyl.)
EPIC (9863 "Over and Over")....25-35 65
(Colored vinyl.)
EPIC (9882 thru 10894)............10-20 65-72

Picture Sleeves

CONGRESS (212 "I Knew It All the Time") 15-25 64
EPIC (2000 series).........................5-8 72
EPIC (9656 thru 10265)............10-20 64-67
EPIC (10375 thru 10684)...........15-25 68-72
HOLLYWOOD (65909 "Over and Over") 4-6 93
HOLLYWOOD (65912 "Do You Love Me") 4-6 93

EPs: 7-inch 33/45rpm

COLUMBIA/AURAVISION ("Catch Us If You Can")..20-40 65
(Promotional issue made for Ponds. Single-sided, square, cardboard disc.)
EPIC..15-25 66
(Jukebox issues only.)

LPs: 10/12-inch 33rpm

CUSTOM (1098 "It's Happening")..............................15-20 60s
EPIC (24093 "Glad All Over") ..75-125 64
(Instruments are not pictured on cover.)
EPIC (24093 "Glad All Over") 20-30 64
(Instruments are pictured on cover.)

EPIC (24104 "The Dave Clark Five Return") 20-30 64
EPIC (24117 "American Tour") . 20-30 64
EPIC (24128 "Coast to Coast") . 20-30 64
EPIC (24139 "A Weekend in London") 20-30 65
EPIC (24162 "Having a Wild Weekend") 20-30 65
EPIC (24178 "I Like It Like That") 20-30 65
EPIC (24185 "Greatest Hits") 20-30 66
EPIC (24198 "Try Too Hard") 20-30 66
EPIC (24212 "Satisfied with You") 20-30 66
EPIC (24221 "More Greatest Hits") 20-30 66
EPIC (24236 "5 By 5") 20-30 67
EPIC (24312 "You Got What It Takes") 20-30 67
EPIC (24354 "Everybody Knows") 20-30 68
EPIC (26000 series) 15-25 64-68
(Reprocessed stereo issues.)
EPIC (30434 "Dave Clark Five") 35-50 71
EPIC (33459 "Glad All Over Again") 20-25 75

Promotional LPs

EPIC (77238 "The Dave Clark Interviews") 40-45 65
I-N-S RADIO NEWS (1006 "It's Here Luv") 75-100 64
Members: Dave Clark; Mike Smith; Lenny Davidson; Denny Payton; Rick Huxley.

CLARK, Dave, Five / Rick Astor & Switchers

LPs: 10/12–inch 33rpm

CORTLEIGH (1073 "Dave Clark Five") 15-25 66
(Has only two Dave Clark Five tracks.)

CLARK, Dave, Five / Lulu

Singles: 7–inch

EPIC (10260/65 "Everybody Knows"/ "Best of Both Worlds") 10-20 67
(Promotional issue only.)
Also see LULU

CLARK, Dave, Five / Playbacks

LPs: 10/12–inch 33rpm

CROWN (400 "Playbacks") 20-25 64
(Stereo.)
CROWN (5400 "Playbacks") 20-25 64
(Monaural.)
CROWN (473 "Chaquita - In Your Heart") 20-25 65
(Stereo.)
CROWN (5473 "Chaquita - In Your Heart") 20-25 65
(Monaural.)
(The Crown LPs have only two Dave Clark Five tracks on each.)
Also see CLARK, Dave, Five

CLARK, Dee

P&R/R&B '58

Singles: 7–inch

ABC 3-4 73
ABNER (Monaural) 8-15 58-60
ABNER (Stereo) 20-25 59-60
CHELSEA 3-5 75
COLLECTABLES 3-4 83
ERIC 3-4 73
COLUMBIA 4-8 67
CONSTELLATION 8-15 63-65
FALCON 15-25 58
LIBERTY 8-15 70
MCA 3-4 84
ROCKY 3-5 73
VEE JAY (Monaural) 5-10 60-63
VEE JAY (Stereo) 15-25 60-63
U.A. 3-5 71
WAND 4-8 68
W.B. 3-5 73

Picture Sleeves

ABNER (1029 "Hey Little Girl") .. 15-25 59

EPs: 7–inch 33/45rpm

ABNER (900 "Dee Clark") 40-60 61
VEE JAY (900 "Dee Clark") 25-50 61

LPs: 10/12–inch 33rpm

ABNER (LP-2000 "Dee Clark") .. 40-60 59
(Monaural.)
ABNER (SR-2000 "Dee Clark") . 50-75 59
(Stereo.)
ABNER (LP-2002 "How About That") 40-60 59
(Monaural.)
ABNER (SR-2002 "How About That") 50-75 59
(Stereo.)
SOLID SMOKE 5-10 84
SUNSET (5217 "Wondering") 10-15 68
VEE JAY (1019 "You're Looking Good") 20-30 60
VEE JAY (1028 "Dee Clark") 20-30 61
VEE JAY (1037 "Hold On, It's Dee Clark") 20-30 61
VEE JAY (1047 "The Best of Dee Clark") 20-30 64
Also see DELLS
Also see UPCHURCH, Phil

CLARK, Gene

(With the Gosdin Brothers)

LP '74

Singles: 7–inch

ASYLUM 3-5 74
COLUMBIA (43000 series) 5-8 66
RSO 3-4 77

LPs: 10/12–inch 33rpm

A&M 10-15 71

ASYLUM	8-10	74
COLUMBIA (2618 "Gene Clark")	20-30	67
(Monaural.)		
COLUMBIA (9418 "Gene Clark")	25-35	67
(Stereo.)		
COLUMBIA (31123 "Early L.A. Sessions")	10-15	72
RSO	5-10	77
TAKOMA	5-10	84

Also see BYRDS
Also see DILLARD & CLARK
Also see NEW CHRISTY MINSTRELS

CLARK, Petula
(Pet Clark)

P&R '64

Singles: 78rpm

CORAL	5-10	53-54
KING	5-10	54
MGM	5-10	55

Singles: 7-inch

CORAL	10-20	53-54
DUNHILL	3-5	74
ERIC	3-4	83
IMPERIAL	5-10	59-60
JANUS	3-5	76
KING	10-20	54
LAURIE	4-8	62-63
LONDON	4-8	62
MGM (12000 series)	10-20	55
MGM (14000 series)	3-6	72-74
ROWE/AMI	5-10	66
("Play Me" Sales Stimulator promotional issue.)		
SCOTTI BROTHERS	3-4	82
W.B.	3-8	64-69
WARWICK	5-10	61

EPs: 7-inch 33/45rpm

W.B.	5-10	65-66
(Jukebox issues only.)		

LPs: 10/12-inch 33rpm

GNP	8-10	73
IMPERIAL (9079 "Pet Clark")	15-25	65
(Monaural.)		
IMPERIAL (12027 "Pet Clark")	20-30	65
(Stereo.)		
LAURIE (2032 "In Love")	20-25	65
(Monaural.)		
LAURIE (S-2032 "In Love")	25-35	65
(Stereo.)		
LAURIE (2043 "Petula Clark Sings for Everybody")	15-20	65
(Monaural.)		
LAURIE (2043 "Petula Clark Sings for Everybody")	20-25	65
(Stereo.)		
MGM	8-12	72
PREMIER	15-25	64
SUNSET	10-20	66
W.B.	10-20	65-71

Also see FELICIANO, Jose / Petula Clark

CLARK, Roy

C&W/P&R '63

Singles: 7-inch

ABC	3-5	74-79
ABC/DOT	3-5	75-77
CAPITOL	4-8	61-66
CHURCHILL	3-4	82-84
DOT	3-6	68-74
HALLMARK	3-4	89
MCA	3-4	79-84
SILVER DOLLAR	3-4	86
SONGBIRD	3-4	81
TOWER	3-6	67

LPs: 10/12-inch 33rpm

ABC	5-10	77-79
ABC/DOT	6-10	74-77
CAPITOL (300 series)	10-12	69
CAPITOL (1700 thru 2500 series)	10-20	62-66
(With "T" or "ST" prefix.)		
CAPITOL (2400 series)	5-10	81
(With "SM" prefix.)		
CAPITOL (11000 series)	8-12	74-75
CAPITOL (12000 thru 16000 series)	5-10	80-81
CHURCHILL	5-10	82
DOT	8-12	68-74
MCA	5-8	79-84
PICKWICK/HILLTOP	10-15	66
SONGBIRD	5-10	81
TOWER	10-15	67-68
WORD	5-10	75

Also see CASH, Johnny / Roy Clark / Linda Ronstadt

CLARK, Sanford

P&R/R&B/C&W '56

Singles: 78rpm

DOT	10-15	56
MCI (1003 "The Fool")	25-40	55

Singles: 7-inch

ABC	3-4	74
DOT (15000 series)	20-30	56
(Maroon label.)		
DOT (15000 series, except 15738)	10-20	56-58
(Black label.)		
DOT (15738 "Modern Romance")	75-100	58
JAMIE	10-15	58-60
LHI	4-8	67-68
MCI (1003 "The Fool")	50-75	55
RAMCO	4-8	66
TREY	5-8	61
W.B.	4-8	64-65

Also see CASEY, Al
Also see REYNOLDS, Jody

CLARK, Sanford, & Duane Eddy

Singles: 7–inch

JAMIE (1107 "Sing 'Em Some Blues") 15-25 58

Also see CLARK, Sanford
Also see EDDY, Duane

CLARK, Steve

C&W '84

Singles: 7–inch

MERCURY 3-4 84

CLARK SISTERS

R&B/D&D '83

Singles: 12–inch 33/45rpm

ELEKTRA 4-6 83

Singles: 7–inch

ELEKTRA 3-4 83

CLARKE, Allan

P&R '78

Singles: 7–inch

ASYLUM 3-5 76
ATLANTIC 3-5 78
ELEKTRA 3-4 80
EPIC 3-5 72

LPs: 10/12–inch 33rpm

ASYLUM 8-10 76
ATLANTIC 5-10 78
ELEKTRA 5-10 80
EPIC 10-15 72

Also see HOLLIES
Also see PARSONS, Alan, Project

CLARKE, Stanley
(Stan Clarke)

LP '75

Singles: 12–inch 33/45rpm

EPIC 4-6 83-85
NEMPEROR 4-8 79

Singles: 7–inch

EPIC 3-4 80-85
NEMPEROR 3-5 75-79

LPs: 10/12–inch 33rpm

EPIC 5-10 80-85
NEMPEROR 8-12 74-79
POLYDOR 10-12 73

Also see RETURN to FOREVER

CLARKE, Stanley, & George Duke

P&R/R&B '81

Singles: 12–inch 33/45rpm

EPIC 4-6 83

Singles: 7–inch

EPIC 3-4 81-84

LPs: 10/12–inch 33rpm

EPIC 5-10 81-83

Also see CLARKE, Stanley
Also see DUKE, George

CLARKE, Tony

P&R/R&B '64

Singles: 7–inch

CHESS 6-12 64-65
CHICKORY 4-6 70
ERIC 3-5 78
M-S (206 "A Wrong Man") 50-100 68

CLASH

LP '79

Singles: 12–inch 33/45rpm

EPIC (617 "Gates of the West") 15-20 79
(Promotional issue only.)
EPIC (723 "Clampdown") 15-20 79
(Promotional issue only.)
EPIC (905 "Magnificent Seven") 15-20 80
(Promotional issue only.)
EPIC (2036 "Call Up") 8-12 81
(Blue label. Promotional issue only.)
EPIC (2036 "Call Up") 8-12 81
(Roulette wheel label. Promotional issue only.)
EPIC (2230 "This Is England") 8-12 85
(Promotional issue only.)
EPIC (2277 "Fingerpoppin") 8-12 85
(Blue label. Promotional issue only.)
EPIC (2662 "This Is Radio Clash") 15-20 81
(Promotional issue only.)
EPIC (3144 "Rock the Casbah") 8-12 82
EPIC (6899 "Radio Clash") 5-10 87
EPIC (7829 "Rock the Casbah") 5-10 89
(Mixed masters issue.)

Singles: 7–inch

EPIC (1178 "Gates of the West") 4-6 79
(Promotional issue only. Issued with promo edition of *The Clash*.)
EPIC (3006 "Should I Stay") 8-10 82
(Promotional issue only.)
EPIC (3088 "London Calling") 5-8 80
(Hall of Fame series.)
EPIC (3245 "Rock the Casbah") 8-10 82
(Promotional issue only.)
EPIC (3547 "Should I Stay") 3-5 82
EPIC (3571 "Should I Stay") 15-20 82
(Single sided disc. Promotional issue only.)
EPIC (5749 "Train in Vain") 15-20 79
(10–inch single. Promotional issue only.)
EPIC (5788 "Clampdown") 15-20 79
(10–inch single. Promotional issue only.)
EPIC (8470 "Should I Stay") 5-8 82
(Hall of Fame series.)
EPIC (20000 series) 3-5 82
EPIC (30000 series) 3-5 82
EPIC (50000 series, except 50738, 50851 & 51013) 3-5 79-81
EPIC (50738 "White Man in Hammersmith Palais") 5-10 79
EPIC (50851 "Train in Vain") 10-15 79
(Promotional issue only.)
EPIC (51013 "Hitsville UK") 10-15 80
(Promotional issue only.)

Picture Sleeves

EPIC (3061 "Should I Stay")...... 10-15 82
(Shown as "Special Limited Edition.")
EPIC (3547 "Should I Stay")........ 5-10 82
(Lists B-side, *Cool Confusion.*)
EPIC (3547 "Should I Stay")...... 10-15 82
(No B-side shown. Promotional issue only.)

LPs: 10/12-inch 33rpm

EPIC (913 "Sandinista Now").... 15-20 80
(Promotional issue only.)
EPIC (952 "If Music Could Talk").. 15-20 81
(Promotional issue only.)
EPIC (1574 "World According to Clash") 30-35 82
(Black cover, with printing.)
EPIC (1574 "World According to Clash") 25-30 82
(Black cover, with no printing)
EPIC (1592 "Combat Rock")..... 40-50 82
(Logo picture disc, with "Face the Future" sticker. Promotional issue only.)
EPIC (35543 "Give 'Em Enough Rope")........................ 5-10 78
(Blue label.)
EPIC (35543 "Give 'Em Enough Rope")....................... 10-15 78
(White label. Promotional issue only. With insert.)
EPIC (36060 "The Clash") 5-10 79
EPIC (36060 "The Clash") 15-20 79
(White label. Promotional issue only. With lyric insert and bonus single, #1178 *Gates of the West*)
EPIC (36328 "London Calling"). 10-15 79
EPIC (36328 "London Calling"). 15-20 79
(White label. Promotional issue only. With lyric sleeve.)
EPIC (37037 "Sandinista") 15-20 80
(Promotional issue only. With *Armagideon Times #3*)
EPIC (37037 "Sandinista") 10-15 80
(With *Armagideon Times #3.*)
EPIC (37689 "Combat Rock") 8-10 82
(Black label.)
EPIC (37689 "Combat Rock") 5-8 82
(Blue label.)
EPIC (37689 "Combat Rock")... 10-15 82
(Promotional issue only. With lyric sleeve.)
EPIC (37689 "Combat Rock")... 40-50 82
(Limited edition, camouflage vinyl. Promotional issue only. With "Face the Future" sticker.)
EPIC (38540 "Black Market Clash") 5-10 80
EPIC (40017 "Cut the Crap") 5-10 85
EPIC (40017 "Cut the Crap") 10-15 85
(Promotional issue only.)
EPIC (44035 "Story of the Clash")...............................10-15 88
EPIC (53191 "Super Black Market Clash")..................................30-40 93
(Limited edition, three 10-inch LPs.)
EPIC/NU-DISC (36846 "Black Market Clash")........................10-15 80
(10–inch LP.)

Members: Joe Strummer; Mick Jones; Nick Sheppard; Pete Howard; Paul Simonon; Topper Headon; Terry Chimes; Vince White.
Also see BIG AUDIO DYNAMITE

CLASS ACTION

D&D '83

Singles: 12–inch 33/45rpm

SLEEPING BAG 4-6 83

CLASSIC IV: see CLASSICS IV

CLASSIC SULLIVANS

R&B '73

Singles: 7–inch

KWANZA.......................................4-6 73
MASTER KEY (03 "Shame, Shame, Shame")..................................15-25

Members: Eddie Sullivan; Lorraine; Barbara Sullivan.

CLASSICS

Singles: 7–inch

STARR (508 "Close Your Eyes") 100-125 60
(Reissued on Alcar 207, credited to Lou Christie & Classics.)

Members: Lou Christie; Kay Chick; Shirley Herbert; Ken Krease.
Also see CHRISTIE, Lou
Also see LUGEE & LIONS

CLASSICS

R&B '61

Singles: 7–inch

BED-STUY 4-6
COLLECTABLES (1275 "P.S. I Love You")..3-4 83
(Colored vinyl.)
DART (1015 "Cinderella")..........20-25 60
DART (1024 "Life Is But a Dream")..................................60-80 61
DART (1032 "Angel Angela")....20-25 61
ERIC 3-4 82
MERCURY 15-20 61
MUSICNOTE (118 "P.S. I Love You")..10-20 63
MUSICNOTE (1116 "Till Then"). 10-20 63
(Black vinyl.)
MUSICNOTE (1116 "Till Then")...................................50-100 63
(Colored vinyl.)
PICCOLO 10-15 65
STORK (2 "You'll Never Know") 15-25 64
STREAM LINE 10-15 61
TRIP 3-5

LPs: 10/12–inch 33rpm

CRYSTAL BALL......................... 8-10 84

Members: Emil Stuccio; Tony Victor; John Gamble; Jamie Troy.

CLASSICS IV

(Dennis Yost & Classics IV; Classics)

P&R '67

Singles: 7–inch

AMERICAN PIE 3-4 90s
CAPITOL................................. 10-15 66-67
GUSTO 3-4
IMPERIAL (Except 66328)........... 4-8 67-70
IMPERIAL (66328 "Stormy"/"Ladies Man").................................... 10-20 68
IMPERIAL (66328 "Stormy"/"24 Hours of Loneliness") 4-8 68
(Note different flip.)
LIBERTY (Except SP-36)............. 3-5 70
LIBERTY (SP-36 "Song").......... 15-25 70
(Radio spots. Promotional issue only.)
MGM 3-5 75
MGM/SOUTH.............................. 3-5 72-73
PLAYBACK 3-4 90
SILVER SPOTLIGHT SERIES...... 3-5
U.A. 3-5 71

LPs: 10/12–inch 33rpm

ACCORD.................................... 5-10 81
IMPERIAL 12-20 68-69
KOALA (14258 "Greatest Hits of the Classic IV").............................. 8-10 79
(Mistakenly credits group as the "Classic IV.")
LIBERTY (10000 series) 5-10 82-85
LIBERTY (11000 series) 10-12 70
MGM/SOUNDS of the SOUTH ... 8-10 73
SUNSET................................. 10-12 70
U.A. 8-10 75

Members: Dennis Yost; James Cobb; Dean Daughtry; Wally Eaton; Auburn Burrell; Kim Venable; Joe Wilson; Mike Sharpe.

Also see ATLANTA RHYTHM SECTION
Also see CANDYMEN
Also see YOST, Dennis

CLASSICS IV / Mac Davis

LPs: 10/12–inch 33rpm

VINTAGE 10-15

Also see CLASSICS IV
Also see DAVIS, Mac

CLAY, Andrew Dice

LP '89

LPs: 10/12–inch 33rpm

DEF AMERICAN 5-8 89-91

CLAY, Cassius

(Cassius Marcellus Clay Jr; Muhammed Ali)

LP '63

Singles: 7–inch

COLUMBIA (43007 "Stand by Me")..................................... 10-20 64
COLUMBIA (75717 "Will the Real Sonny Liston Please Fall Down")........25-40 64
(Promotional issue only.)

Picture Sleeves

COLUMBIA (43007 "Stand by Me") 25-35 64

LPs: 10/12–inch 33rpm

COLUMBIA (2093 "I Am the Greatest") 30-40 63
(Monaural.)
COLUMBIA (8893 "I Am the Greatest") 35-45 63
(Stereo.)

Also see ALI, Muhammad, & Frank Sinatra

CLAY, Judy

R&B '70

Singles: 7–inch

ATLANTIC......................................3-5 69-70
EMBER 5-10 61-62
LA VETTE (1004 "Let It Be Me")..5-10
SCEPTER 4-8 64-66
STAX...4-6 68-69

Also see VERA, Billy, & Judy Clay

CLAY, Judy, & William Bell

P&R/R&B '68

Singles: 7–inch

STAX...4-6 68

Also see BELL, William
Also see CLAY, Judy

CLAY, Otis

R&B '67

Singles: 12–inch 33/45rpm

PAULA 4-8 85

Singles: 7–inch

COTILLION 3-6 68-71
DAKAR...3-6 69
ECHO (2002 "Check It Out")........5-10
ELKA..3-5 75
GLADES (1736 "All I Need Is You")...5-10
HI 3-5 72-73
KAYVETTE 3-5 77
ONE-DERFUL..................................4-8 65-67

LPs: 10/12–inch 33rpm

HI 8-12 73-77

CLAY, Tom

(With the Blackberries; with Raybor Voices)

P&R/R&B/LP '71

Singles: 7–inch

BIG TOP 10-15 60
CHANT (103 "Marry Me") 50-100 59
MOTOWN 3-4 81
MOWEST 3-5 71
OFFICIAL IBBB INTERVIEW ("Remember, We Don't Like Them, We Love Them") 15- 25 64
(Tom Clay interviews the Beatles. Promotional issue only.)

LPs: 10/12–inch 33rpm

MOWEST 10-15 71

Also see BEATLES

CLAYDERMAN, Richard

LP '84

LPs: 10/12-Inch 33rpm

COLUMBIA 5-8 84

CLAYTON, Merry

P&R '70

Singles: 7–inch

CAPITOL 4-8 63-65
MCA 3-4 80-88
ODE '70 .... 3-5 70-76

LPs: 10/12–inch 33rpm

MCA 5-10 80
ODE (34000 series) 5-10 77
ODE (77000 series) 10-12 71-75

Also see BEACH BOYS
Also see SCOTT, Tom
Also see WYCOFF, Michael

CLAYTON, Willie

R&B '84

Singles: 7–inch

COMPLEAT 3-4 85

CLAYTON-THOMAS, David

LP '69

Singles: 7–inch

COLUMBIA 3-5 72
DECCA 4-6 69
RCA 3-5 73

LPs: 10/12–inch 33rpm

ABC 5-10 78
COLUMBIA 10-15 72
DECCA 15-20 69
RCA 8-12 73-74

Also see BLOOD, SWEAT & TEARS

CLEAN LIVING

P&R '72

Singles: 7–inch

VANGUARD 3-5 72

LPs: 10/12–inch 33rpm

VANGUARD 8-10 72-73

CLEAR LIGHT

LP '67

Singles: 7–inch

ELEKTRA 5-10 67

LPs: 10/12–inch 33rpm

ELEKTRA (4011 "Clear Light").. 15-25 67

Members: Cliff DeYoung; Douglas Lubahn; Michael Ney; Ralph Schuckett; Bob Seal; Dallas Taylor.

CLEFS of Lavender Hill

P&R '66

Singles: 7–inch

DATE 10-20 66-67
THAMES ("Stop! Get a Ticket") 25-35 66
(Number not known.)

CLEFTONES
(Herb Cox & Cleftones)

P&R/R&B '56

Singles: 78rpm

GEE 15-25 56-57

Singles: 7–inch

ABC 3-4 73
CLASSIC ARTISTS 3-5 90
GEE (Red label) 15-25 56-58
GEE (Gray label) 5-10 61-63
ROULETTE (4000 series) 8-12 58-60
ROULETTE GOLDEN GOODIES..3-5 70s
WARE 5-10 64

LPs: 10/12–inch 33rpm

EMUS 5-10 79
GEE (GLP-705 "Heart and Soul") 100-150 61
(Monaural.)
GEE (SGLP-705 "Heart and Soul") 150-200 61
(Stereo.)
GEE (GLP-707 "For Sentimental Reasons") 150-200 62
(Monaural.)
GEE (SGLP-707 "For Sentimental Reasons") 200-250 62
(Stereo.)

Members: Herbie Cox; Berman Patterson; Bill McClain; Charles James; Warren Corbin; Pat Span; Eugene Pearson.

Also see DRIFTERS
Also see HARPTONES / Cleftones

CLEGG, Johnny, & Savuka

LP '88

LPs: 10/12–inch 33rpm

CAPITOL 5-8 88-90

CLEMMONS, Angela

R&B '80

Singles: 12–inch 33/45rpm

PORTRAIT 4-6 82

Singles: 7–inch

EPIC 3-4 80
PORTRAIT 3-4 82-87

LPs: 10/12–inch 33rpm

PORTRAIT 5-10 82

CLEMONS, Clarence
(With the Red Bank Rockers)

LP '83

Singles: 7–inch

COLUMBIA 3-4 83-85

LPs: 10/12–inch 33rpm

COLUMBIA 5-10 83-85

Also see FRANKLIN, Aretha
Also see SPRINGSTEEN, Bruce

CLEMONS, Clarence, & Jackson Browne

P&R '85

Singles: 7–inch

COLUMBIA 3-4 85

Also see BROWNE, Jackson

CLIFF, Jimmy

P&R '69

Singles: 12-inch 33/45rpm

COLUMBIA 4-6 83-84

Singles: 7-inch

A&M 3-6 69-70
COLUMBIA 3-4 82-84
MANGO..................................... 3-5 73-75
MCA 3-5 81
REPRISE 3-5 74-77
VEEP....................................... 4-8 67-68

Picture Sleeves

A&M 3-6 69

LPs: 10/12-inch 33rpm

A&M 10-20 70
COLUMBIA 5-10 82
ISLAND 8-10 74
MCA 5-10 80-81
MANGO................................... 8-10 75
REPRISE 8-10 73-76
VEEP.................................... 15-20 69
W.B. 5-10 78

CLIFF, Jimmy, Elvis Costello & Attractions

Singles: 12-inch 33/45rpm

COLUMBIA 5-10 86
(Promotional issue only.)

Singles: 7-inch

COLUMBIA 3-4 86

Picture Sleeves

COLUMBIA 3-4 86
Also see CLIFF, Jimmy
Also see COSTELLO, Elvis

CLIFFORD, Buzz

P&R/C&W/R&B '61

Singles: 7-inch

BOW ("14 Karet") 20-30 59
(Number not known.)
CAPITOL................................... 4-8 67
COLUMBIA (41876 "Baby Sittin' Boogie") 30-50 60
(With "3" prefix. Compact 33 Single.)
COLUMBIA (41979 "Simply Because")............................... 30-50 61
(With "3" prefix. Compact 33 Single.)
COLUMBIA (42019 "I'll Never Forget") 30-50 61
(With "3" prefix. Compact 33 Single.)
COLUMBIA (42290 "Forever").. 30-50 62
(With "3" prefix. Compact 33 Single.)
COLUMBIA (41774 "Hello Mr. Moonlight") 10-15 60
(With "4" prefix.)
COLUMBIA (41876 "Baby Sitter Boogie") 20-30 60
(Note slightly different title. With "4" prefix.)
COLUMBIA (41876 "Baby Sittin' Boogie") 5-10 61
(With "4" prefix.)
COLUMBIA (41979 "Simply Because") 15-25 61
(With "4" prefix.)
COLUMBIA (42019 "I'll Never Forget")................................ 15-25 61
(With "4" prefix.)
COLUMBIA (42177 "Moving Day") 5-10 61
(With "4" prefix.)
COLUMBIA (42290 "Forever")... 15-25 62
(With "4" prefix.)
DOT 4-6 69-70
ERIC 3-4 83
RCA 4-8 66
ROULETTE 4-8 62-63

Picture Sleeves

COLUMBIA 15-20 61-62

LPs: 10/12-inch 33rpm

COLUMBIA (1616 "Baby Sittin' Boogie") 40-60 61
(Monaural.)
COLUMBIA (8416 "Baby Sittin' Boogie") 50-75 61
(Monaural.)
DOT 15-20 69

CLIFFORD, Linda

R&B '74

Singles: 12-inch 33/45rpm

CAPITOL................................... 4-6 82
RSO 4-8 79
RED LABEL 4-6 85

Singles: 7-inch

CAPITOL................................... 3-4 80-82
CURTOM 3-4 77-78
GEMIGO 3-5 75
PARAMOUNT 3-5 74
POLYDOR 3-5 73
RSO 3-4 79-80
RED LABEL 3-4 84-85

LPs: 10/12-inch 33rpm

CAPITOL.................................. 5-10 80-82
CURTOM 8-10 77-80
RSO 5-10 79-80
Also see MAYFIELD, Curtis, & Linda Clifford

CLIFFORD, Mike

P&R '62

Singles: 7-inch

AIR 3-5 71
AMERICAN INT'L 3-5 70
CAMEO 4-8 65-66
COLUMBIA 4-8 61-62
LIBERTY 5-10 59
SIDEWALK 4-8 67-68
U.A. 4-8 62-65

Picture Sleeves

COLUMBIA 5-10 61

LPs: 10/12-inch 33rpm

U.A. 15-25 65

CLIFFORD, Mike, with Patience & Prudence

Singles: 7-inch

LIBERTY 5-10 59

Also see CLIFFORD, Mike
Also see PATIENCE & PRUDENCE

CLIMAX

(Sonny Geraci & Climax)

P&R/LP '72

Singles: 7-inch

ARISTA 3-4 81
BELL 3-5 71
CAROUSEL 3-5 70-71
FLASHBACK 3-4 73
PARAMOUNT 3-5 70
PATTI PLATTERS 4-8 67
ROCKY ROAD 3-5 72-73

LPs: 10/12-inch 33rpm

ROCKY ROAD 12-15 72

Members: Sonny Geraci; John Bahler; Tom Bahler; Jon Jon Gultman; Walt Nims.
Also see LOVE GENERATION
Also see OUTSIDERS

CLIMAX BLUES BAND

LP '70

Singles: 7-inch

SIRE 3-5 71-79
W.B. 3-4 79-82

LPs: 10/12-inch 33rpm

SIRE (Except 6000 series) 10-15 69-76
SIRE (6000 series) 8-10 77-79
VIRGIN 5-10 83
W.B. 5-10 79-81

Members: Climax Chicago Blues Band; Colin Cooper; John Cuffley; Peter Haycock; Derek Holt; Richard Jones; Arthur Wood.

CLIMIE FISHER

P&R/LP '88

Singles: 7-inch

CAPITOL 3-4 88

Picture Sleeves

CAPITOL 3-4 88

LPs: 10/12-inch 33rpm

CAPITOL 5-8 88

Members: Simon Clime; Rob Fisher.
Also see NAKED EYES

CLINE, Patsy

C&W/P&R '57

Singles: 78rpm

CORAL 5-10 55-56
DECCA 5-10 57

Singles: 7-inch

CORAL 10-20 55-56
DECCA (25000 series) 3-8 65-69
DECCA (29963 thru 30846) 8-12 57-59
DECCA (30929 "Gotta Lot of Rhythm in My Soul") 10-15 59
DECCA (31000 series) 4-8 59-64
EVEREST (2000 series) 4-8 62-64
EVEREST (20005 "I Don't Wanta") 10-15 62
4 STAR (11 "Hidin' Out") 5-10 56
4 STAR (1033 "Life's Railway to Heaven") 3-5 78
KAPP 4-8 65
MCA 3-5 73-80
STARDAY (7000 series) 4-8 65
STARDAY (8000 series) 3-5 71

Picture Sleeves

DECCA (Except 30221) 5-10 62-63
DECCA (30221 "Walkin After Midnight") 15-20 62-63

EPs: 7-inch 33/45rpm

CORAL (81159 "Songs by Patsy Cline") 35-50 58
DECCA (Except 2542) 15-25 61-65
DECCA (2542 "Patsy Cline") 35-50 57
4 STAR ("Patsy Cline") 25-35 57
(Reissue of *Patsy Cline* [Decca 2542]. Issued with paper sleeve. Number not known. Promotional issue only.)
PATSY CLINE 25-35 57

LPs: 10/12-inch 33rpm

ACCORD 5-10 81
ALBUM GLOBE 5-10
ALLEGIANCE 5-10 84
COLUMBIA 12-15 69
(Columbia Musical Treasury issue.)
COUNTRY FIDELITY 5-10 82
DECCA (176 "Patsy Cline Story") 25-40 63
(Includes booklet.)
DECCA (4200 series) 20-30 61-62
DECCA (4500 series) 15-25 64
DECCA (4800 series) 10-15 67
DECCA (8611 "Patsy Cline") 30-45 57
EVEREST (300 series) 5-10 75
EVEREST (1200 series) 15-20 62-64
51 WEST 5-10 82
H.S.R.D. 8-10 84
LONGINES 8-12
MCA 5-10 80-89
METRO 10-20 65
PICKWICK/HILLTOP 10-12 65-68
SEARS 10-15
VOCALION 10-15 65-69

Session: Jordanaires; Anita Kerr Singers.
Also see HAGGARD, Merle / Patsy Cline
Also see KERR, Anita
Also see REEVES, Jim, & Patsy Cline

CLINE, Patsy / Cowboy Copas / Hawkshaw Hawkins

LPs: 10/12-inch 33rpm

STARDAY 15-20 65

Also see COPAS, Cowboy
Also see HAWKINS, Hawkshaw

CLINE, Patsy / Hank Locklin / Miller Brothers / Eddie Marvin

EPs: 7–inch 33/45rpm

4 STAR (136 Hidin' Out") 25-50 56
(Promotional 10–inch, 45rpm. Not issued with cover.)
Also see LOCKLIN, Hank

CLINE, Patsy / Pete Pike / Jack Bradshaw / Miller Brothers

EPs: 7–inch 33/45rpm

4 STAR (137 "Come On In") 25-50 56
(Promotional 10–inch, 45rpm. Not issued with cover.)
Also see CLINE, Patsy
Also see CLINE, Patsy / Hank Locklin / Miller Brothers / Eddie Marvin

CLINTON, George
(George Clinton Band)

R&B/LP '82

Singles: 12–inch 33/45rpm

CAPITOL 4-8 82-86

Singles: 7–inch

ABC 3-5 74
CAPITOL 3-4 83-86
PAISLEY PARK 3-4 89

Picture Sleeves

CAPITOL 3-4 80s

LPs: 10/12–inch 33rpm

ABC 8-10 74
CAPITOL 5-10 82-86
INVICTUS 10-12 73
PAISLEY PARK 5-8 89
Also see PARLIAMENTS

CLIQUE

P&R '69

Singles: 7–inch

ABC 3-5 73
CINEMA (001 "Splash") 25-35 67
SCEPTER 10-20 67
WHITE WHALE 8-15 69-71

LPs: 10/12–inch 33rpm

WHITE WHALE (7126 "The Clique") 10-20 69

CLIQUES

P&R '56

Singles: 78rpm

MODERN 10-15 56

Singles: 7–inch

MODERN (987 "The Girl in My Dreams") 20-30 56
Members: Jesse Belvin; Eugene Church.
Also see BELVIN, Jesse
Also see CHURCH, Eugene

CLOCKS

P&R '82

Singles: 7–inch

BOULEVARD 3-4 82

LPs: 10/12–inch 33rpm

BOULEVARD 5-10 82

CLOCKWORK

R&B/D&D '84

Singles: 12–inch 33/45rpm

PRIVATE I 4-6 84

Singles: 7–inch

PRIVATE I 3-4 84

CLOONEY, Rosemary

P&R '51

Singles: 78rpm

COLUMBIA 4-6 50-57

Singles: 7–inch

APCO 3-5 75
COLUMBIA 5-10 50-57
CORAL 4-8 59
DOT 3-6 68
GIBSON/COLUMBIA 10-15 55
("Musicards," with fold-out covers.)
MGM 3-8 59-65
RCA 3-6 60-61
REPRISE 3-6 63-64
SATURDAY EVENING POST (1055 "Hollywood's Favorite Songbird") 15-20 54
(Promotional issue only. Includes interview script.)

Picture Sleeves

RCA 5-10 60

EPs: 7–inch 33/45rpm

COLUMBIA 10-20 51-56
EPIC (7139/7140/7141 "Clooney Sisters") 10-15 56
(Price is for any of three volumes.)
MGM 5-10 58-60

LPs: 10/12–inch 33rpm

COLUMBIA (500 thru 1200 series, except 6297) 15-25 54-58
COLUMBIA (6297 "While We're Young") 25-35 51
(10–inch LP.)
CONCORD JAZZ 5-10 78-83
CORAL 10-15 59
EPIC (3160 "Clooney Sisters") .. 20-30 56
HARMONY 8-15 59-68
MGM (Except 1000 series) 10-15 59-62
MGM (1000 series) 8-12 67
RCA 10-15 60-63
REPRISE 8-15 63-64
Also see BOYD, Jimmy, & Rosemary Clooney
Also see CROSBY, Bing, Louis Armstrong, Rosemary Clooney & Hi-Los
Also see GOODMAN, Benny, Trio, & Rosemary Clooney
Also see HERMAN, Woody

Also see HOPE, Bob, & Rosemary Clooney

CLOONEY, Rosemary, & Bing Crosby

Singles: 7–inch

RCA.. 4-8 59

LPs: 10/12–inch 33rpm

CAMDEN.................................... 6-10 69
CAPITOL (2300 series).............. 8-12 65
CAPITOL (11000 series)............ 5-10 77

Also see CROSBY, Bing

CLOONEY, Rosemary, & Marlene Dietrich

Singles: 78rpm

COLUMBIA 4-6 52

Singles: 7–inch

COLUMBIA 5-10 52

EPs: 7–inch 33/45rpm

COLUMBIA (1699 "Rosie & Marlene")................................ 15-20 52

Also see DIETRICH, Marlene

CLOONEY, Rosemary, & Jose Ferrer

Singles: 78rpm

COLUMBIA 4-6 54

EPs: 7–inch 33/45rpm

MGM 10-20 58

Also see FERRER Jose

CLOONEY, Rosemary, & Hi-Los

LP '57

EPs: 7–inch 33/45rpm

COLUMBIA 5-10 57

LPs: 10/12–inch 33rpm

COLUMBIA (1006 "Ring Around Rosie")....................... 20-25 57

Also see HI-LOs

CLOONEY, Rosemary, & Dick Haymes

LPs: 10/12–inch 33rpm

EXACT 5-10 80

Also see HAYMES, Dick

CLOONEY, Rosemary, & Guy Mitchell
(With Joanne Gilbert)

P&R '51

EPs: 7–inch 33/45rpm

COLUMBIA (377 "Red Garters")................................ 15-20 54
(Soundtrack.)

LPs: 10/12–inch 33rpm

COLUMBIA (6282 "Red Garters")................................ 40-50 54
(10–inch LP. Soundtrack.)

Also see MITCHELL, Guy

CLOONEY, Rosemary, & Perez Prado

Singles: 7–inch

RCA.. 4-8 60

LPs: 10/12–inch 33rpm

RCA.. 10-12 60

Also see CLOONEY, Rosemary
Also see PRADO, Perez

CLOUD, Christopher
(Tommy Boyce)

Singles: 7–inch

CHELSEA 3-5 72-73

LPs: 10/12–inch 33rpm

CHELSEA 10-15 73

Also see BOYCE, Tommy

CLOUT

P&R '78

Singles: 7–inch

EPIC...3-4 78-79

LPs: 10/12–inch 33rpm

EPIC...5-10 79-80

CLOVERS

R&B '51

Singles: 78rpm

ATLANTIC (900 series) 20-40 51-53
ATLANTIC (1000 series) 5-15 53-56
RAINBOW.............................100-150 51

Singles: 7–inch

ATLANTIC (934 "Don't You Know I Love You") 100-150 51
ATLANTIC (944 "Fool, Fool, Fool") 75-100 51
ATLANTIC (963 "One Mint Julep")...................................50-75 52
ATLANTIC (969 "Ting-A-Ling")..50-75 52
ATLANTIC (977 "I Played the Fool") 50-75 52
ATLANTIC (989 "Yes It's You") .50-75 53
ATLANTIC (1000 "Good Lovin") 40-60 53
ATLANTIC (1010 "Comin' On")..30-50 53
ATLANTIC (1022 "Lovey Dovey") 30-50 54
ATLANTIC (1035 "Your Cash Ain't Nothin' But Trash") 30-50 54
ATLANTIC (1046 "I Confess") ...30-50 54
ATLANTIC (1052 "Blue Velvet") 25-50 54
ATLANTIC (1060 "Love Bug") ...25-50 55
ATLANTIC (1073 "Nip Sip").......25-50 55
ATLANTIC (1083 "Devil Or Angel") 25-50 56
ATLANTIC (1094 "Your Tender Lips")..25-50 56
ATLANTIC (1100 series) 15-25 56-58
ATLANTIC (2000 series) 5-10 61
BRUNSWICK...............................5-10 63
JOSIE...4-8 68
POPLAR 15-25 58
PORT 5-10 65
PORWIN 5-10 63
RIPETE 3-4 88
U.A. 10-15 59-61
WINLEY (255 "Wrapped Up in a Dream")................................20-30 61
WINLEY (655 "I Need You Now") 20-30 62

EPs: 7-inch 33/45rpm

ATLANTIC (504 "The Clovers Sing") 75-100 56
ATLANTIC (537 "The Clovers Sing") 75-100 56
ATLANTIC (590 "The Clovers Sing") 60-85 57

LPs: 10/12-inch 33rpm

ATCO 10-12 71
ATLANTIC (1248 "The Clovers") 150-250 56
ATLANTIC (8009 "Clovers").. 100-175 57
(Black label.)
ATLANTIC (8009 "The Clovers") 40-60 59
(Red label.)
ATLANTIC (8034 "The Clovers' Dance Party")......................... 50-80 59
GRAND PRIX.......................... 10-15 64
POPLAR (1001 "The Clovers in Clover") 75-100 58
TRIP 8-10 72
U.A. (3033 "Clovers in Clover"). 50-75 59
(Monaural.)
U.A. (6033 "Clovers in Clover"). 50-75 59
(Stereo.)
U.A. (3099 "Love Potion Number Nine") 50-75 60
(Monaural.)
U.A. (6099 "Love Potion Number Nine") 75-100 60
(Stereo.)

Members: John "Buddy" Bailey; Harold Winley; Hal Lucas; Bill Harris; Matthew McQuater; Charlie White; Billy Mitchell. Session: King Curtis.

Also see HARPTONES / Paragons / Jesters / Clovers
Also see JACKSON, Willis
Also see KING CURTIS
Also see MITCHELL, Billy

CLUB HOUSE

P&R/R&B '83

Singles: 12-inch 33/45rpm

ATLANTIC.................................. 4-6 83

Singles: 7-inch

ATLANTIC.................................. 3-4 83

CLUB NOUVEAU

R&B/LP '86

Singles: 12-inch 33/45rpm

W.B. 4-6 86

Singles: 7-inch

TOMMY BOY 3-4 88
W.B. 3-4 86-88

LPs: 10/12-inch 33rpm

W.B. 5-10 86-88

COASTERS

P&R/R&B '56

Singles: 78rpm

ATCO 10-20 56-57

Singles: 7-inch

ATCO (6064 "Down in Mexico").25-50 56
(Maroon label.)
ATCO (6073 "One Kiss Led to Another")............................25-35 56
(Maroon label.)
ATCO (6087 "Searchin")...........20-30 57
(Maroon label.)
ATCO (6087 "Searchin")...........15-20 57
(Yellow and white label.)
ATCO (6098 thru 6178) 10-20 57-60
ATCO (6186 thru 6356) 8-15 61-65
ATCO (6379 "Crazy Baby") 20-30 65
ATCO (6407 "She's a Yum Yum")..8-10 66
DATE 5-10 67-68
KING 3-6 71-73
KING/GUSTO 3-5 79
TURNTABLE....................................4-8 69

EPs: 7-inch 33/45rpm

ATCO (4501 "Rock & Roll with the Coasters") 50-70 58
ATCO (4503 "Keep Rockin")......50-70 58
ATCO (4506 "The Coasters") 30-50 59
ATCO (4507 "Top Hits")............30-50 59

LPs: 10/12-inch 33rpm

ATCO (101 "The Coasters") 75-100 58
(Yellow label.)
ATCO (101 "The Coasters") 25-50 59
(Yellow and white label.)
ATCO (111 "Greatest Hits").......50-75 59
ATCO (123 "One By One") 40-50 60
(Monaural.)
ATCO (SD-123 "One By One")..50-60 60
(Stereo.)
ATCO (135 "Coast Along") 30-40 59
(Monaural.)
ATCO (SD-135 "Coast Along") ..40-50 59
(Stereo.)
ATCO (371 "Their Greatest Recordings") 10-20 71
ATLANTIC.................................10-12 82
CLARION 12-15 64
KING 10-12 71
POWER PAK 5-10 83
TRIP..8-10 72-76

Members: Bobby Nunn; Leon Hughes; Carl Gardner; Billy Guy; Adolph Jacobs; Cornel Gunter; Will Jones; Earl Carroll; Ronnie Bright; Jimmy Norman. Session: King Curtis.

Also see CARROLL, Earl, & Original Cadillacs
Also see HENDRICKS, Bobby
Also see KING, Ben E.
Also see KING CURTIS
Also see NORMAN, Jimmy
Also see ROBINS

COASTERS / Crew-Cuts / Chiffons

LPs: 10/12-inch 33rpm

EXACT 5-10 80

Also see CHIFFONS
Also see CREW-CUTS

COASTERS / Drifters

LPs: 10/12-inch 33rpm

TVP 10-15
(TV mail-order offer.)
Also see DRIFTERS

COATES, Odia

P&R '75

Singles: 12-inch 33/45rpm

EPIC 4-6 77

Singles: 7-inch

BUDDAH 3-5 73
EPIC 3-4 78
U.A. 3-4 74-75

LPs: 10/12-inch 33rpm

U.A. 8-10 75
Also see ANKA, Paul, & Odia Coates

COBB, Joyce

P&R '79

Singles: 7-inch

CREAM 3-4 79-80
TRUTH 3-5 75

COBHAM, Billy

(Billy Cobham's Glass Menagerie; with George Duke Band)

LP '73

Singles: 12-inch 33/45rpm

COLUMBIA 4-6 80

Singles: 7-inch

ATLANTIC 3-5 75-77
COLUMBIA 3-4 78-80

LPs: 10/12-inch 33rpm

ATLANTIC 5-10 73-79
COLUMBIA 5-10 77-80
ELEKTRA 5-10 82-83
Also see DUKE, George

COCCIANTE, Richard

P&R '76

Singles: 7-inch

20TH FOX 3-5 76

LPs: 10/12-inch 33rpm

20TH FOX 5-10 76

COCHISE

P&R '71

Singles: 7-inch

U.A. 3-5 71

EPs: 7-inch 33/45rpm

U.A. 10-12 71

LPs: 10/12-inch 33rpm

U.A. 10-12 71
Member: Mick Grabham.

COCHRAN, Eddie

P&R/R&B '57

Singles: 78rpm

CREST (1026 "Skinny Jim")........ 50-100 56
LIBERTY 10-15 57

Singles: 7-inch

CAPEHART (5003 "Rough Stuff") 10-20 60
CREST (1026 "Skinny Jim") .. 150-200 56
LIBERTY (54000 series) 5-10 62
LIBERTY (55056 "Sittin' in the Balcony") 15-25 57
LIBERTY (55070 "Mean When I'm Mad") 15-25 58
LIBERTY (55087 "Drive In Show") 15-25 57
LIBERTY (55112 "Twenty Flight Rock") 20-30 58
LIBERTY (55123 "Jeannie Jeannie Jeannie") 20-30 58
LIBERTY (55138 "Pretty Girl") ... 15-25 58
LIBERTY (55144 "Summertime Blues") 15-25 58
LIBERTY (55166 "C'mon Everybody") 15-25 58
(Green label.)
LIBERTY (55166 "C'mon Everybody") 10-20 58
(Black label.)
LIBERTY (55177 "Teenage Heaven") 15-25 59
LIBERTY (55203 "Somethin' Else") 15-25 59
(With horizontal silver lines.)
LIBERTY (55203 "Somethin' Else") 10-20 59
(Without horizontal silver lines.)
LIBERTY (55217 "Hallelujah, I Love Her So") 10-20 59
LIBERTY (55242 "Cut Across Shorty") 15-25 60
(Green label.)
LIBERTY (55242 "Cut Across Shorty") 10-20 61
(Black label.)
LIBERTY (55278 "Sweetie Pie") 10-20 60
LIBERTY (55389 "Weekend") 20-30 61

Picture Sleeves

CAPEHART (5003 "Rough Stuff") 35-50 60
LIBERTY (55070 "Mean When I'm Mad") 750-1000 58

EPs: 7-inch 33/45rpm

LIBERTY (3061-1/2/3 "Singin' to My Baby") 100-150 58
(Price is for any of three volumes.)

LPs: 10/12-inch 33rpm

LIBERTY (3061 "Singin' to My Baby") 200-300 58
(Green label.)
LIBERTY (3061 "Singin' to My Baby") 40-60 60
(Black label.)

LIBERTY (3172 "Memorial Album") 50-100 60
LIBERTY (3220 "Never to Be Forgotten") 50-100 62
(Black label.)
LIBERTY (3220 "Never to Be Forgotten") 75-90 62
(Yellow label. Promotional issue only.)
LIBERTY (10000 series) 5-10 81-83
SUNSET (1123 "Summertime Blues") 15-25 66
U.A. (428 "Very Best of Eddie Cochran") 10-15 75
U.A. (9959 "Legendary Masters") 15-20 71
Also see COCHRAN BROTHERS

COCHRAN, Hank

C&W '62

Singles: 7-inch

CAPITOL 3-4 78
DOT 3-5 70
ELEKTRA 3-4 80
GAYLORD 4-8 62-63
LIBERTY 4-8 62-63
MONUMENT 3-6 67-68
RCA 4-8 64-66

LPs: 10/12-inch 33rpm

CAPITOL 5-10 78
ELEKTRA 5-10 80
MONUMENT 10-15 68
RCA 10-20 65
Session: Merle Haggard; Willie Nelson.
Also see COCHRAN BROTHERS
Also see HAGGARD, Merle

COCHRAN, Hank, & Willie Nelson

Singles: 7-inch

CAPITOL 3-5 78
Also see COCHRAN, Hank
Also see NELSON, Willie

COCHRAN, Wayne
(With the C.C. Riders)

LP '68

Singles: 7-inch

BETHLEHEM 3-5 70
CHESS 4-8 67-68
DECK 3-5
EPIC 3-5 72
GALA (117 "Last Kiss") 10-15 64
GALICO (106 "Last Kiss") 10-20 64
KING (5000 series) 5-10 63-65
KING (6000 series) 4-8 65-71
MERCURY 4-8 65-67
SCOTTIE 10-15 59
SOFT 4-8 65

Picture Sleeves

CHESS 4-8 67
MERCURY 5-10 65

LPs: 10/12-inch 33rpm

BETHLEHEM 12-15 70
CHESS 20-30 68
EPIC 8-10 72
KING 15-25 70
Also see REDDING, Otis

COCHRAN BROTHERS

Singles: 78rpm

EKKO (1000 series) 30-45 56
EKKO (3001 "Tired and Sleepy") 50-100 56

Singles: 7-inch

EKKO (1003 "Two Blue Singing Stars") 75-125 56
EKKO (1005 "Guilty Conscience") 75-125 56
EKKO (3001 "Tired and Sleepy") 100-150 56
Members: Eddie Cochran; Hank Cochran. (Eddie and Hank were not really brothers).
Also see COCHRAN, Eddie
Also see COCHRAN, Hank

COCHRANE, Tom
(With Red Rider)

LP '86

Singles: 7-inch

CAPITOL 3-4 86
RCA 3-4 88

LPs: 10/12-inch 33rpm

CAPITOL 5-10 86
RCA 5-8 88
Also see RED RIDER

COCK ROBIN

P&R/D&D '85

Singles: 12-inch 33/45rpm

COLUMBIA 4-6 85

Singles: 7-inch

COLUMBIA 3-4 85

LPs: 10/12-inch 33rpm

COLUMBIA 5-10 85-87
Members: Peter Kingsbery Anna LaCazio.

COCKBURN, Bruce

P&R/LP '80

Singles: 7-inch

GOLD MOUNTAIN 3-4 84
MCA 3-4 86
MILLENNIUM 3-4 80

LPs: 10/12-inch 33rpm

EPIC 10-15 71-72
GOLD CASTLE 5-8 89
GOLD MOUNTAIN 5-10 84
ISLAND 8-10 77-78
MCA 5-10 86
MILLENNIUM 5-10 80-81
TRUE NORTH 8-10 77-78

COCKER, Joe
(With the Chris Stainton Band)

P&R '68

Singles: 7-inch

A&M 3-6 68-78

ASYLUM 3-4 78-79
CAPITOL 3-4 84-88
ISLAND 3-4 82-83
PHILIPS 10-15 65

Picture Sleeves

A&M 3-5 69-74
CAPITOL 3-4 84

LPs: 10/12–inch 33rpm

A&M (Except 3100 series) 8-15 69-77
A&M (3100 series) 5-10 82
ASYLUM (Except 145) 5-10 78-79
ASYLUM (145 "Luxury You Can Afford") 5-10 79
ASYLUM (145 "Luxury You Can Afford") 10-20 79
(Picture disc. Promotional issue only.)
CAPITOL 5-10 84-90
ISLAND 5-8 82

Also see ARNOLD, Vance, & Avengers
Also see BOWIE, David / Joe Cocker / Youngbloods
Also see CRUSADERS
Also see GREASE BAND
Also see RUSSELL, Leon

COCKER, Joe, & Jennifer Warnes

P&R '82

Singles: 7–inch

ISLAND 3-4 82

Picture Sleeves

ISLAND 3-4 82

Also see COCKER, Joe
Also see WARNES, Jennifer

COCO, El: see EL COCO

COCTEAU TWINS

LP '88

LPs: 10/12–inch 33rpm

CAPITOL 5-8 88
4AD 5-8 90

CODAY, Bill

R&B '71

Singles: 7–inch

CRAJON (48203 "Right On Baby") 50-75 70
CRAJON (48204 "Get Your Lie Straight") 4-8 71
(At least one source shows this label as "Crayon." We're not yet sure who's right.)
EPIC 3-6 73-75
GALAXY (777 "Get Your Lie Straight") 4-6 71
GALAXY (779 "When You Find a Fool, Bump His Head") 4-8 71
GALAXY (781 "I Got a Thing") 4-8 71

CODY, Commander: see COMMANDER CODY

COE, David Allan

C&W '74

Singles: 7–inch

COLUMBIA 3-5 74-87
SSS INT'L (Black vinyl) 3-5 71-72
SSS INT'L (Colored vinyl) 5-10 71-72
(Promotional issues only.)

LPs: 10/12–inch 33rpm

COLUMBIA 5-10 72-86
SSS INT'L (9 "Penitentiary Blues") 25-40 70

Also see JONES, George, & David Allan Coe

COE, David Allan, & Bill Anderson

Singles: 7–inch

COLUMBIA 3-5 80

Also see ANDERSON, Bill

COE, David Allan, & Willie Nelson

C&W '86

Singles: 7–inch

COLUMBIA 3-4 86

Also see COE, David Allan
Also see NELSON, Willie
Also see NELSON, Willie / Jerry Lee Lewis / Carl Perkins / David Allan Coe

COFFEE

R&B '82

Singles: 7–inch

DELITE 3-4 80-82

COFFEY, Dennis

(With the Detroit Guitar Band; with Lyman Woodward Trio)

P&R/LP '71

Singles: 7–inch

MAVERICK 3-6 69
SUSSEX 3-5 70-74
W.B. 3-5 74
20TH CENTURY/WESTBOUND 3-5 75-76
WESTBOUND 3-4 77-78

LPs: 10/12–inch 33rpm

SUSSEX 10-12 70-75
20TH CENTURY/WESTBOUND 8-10 75-76
WESTBOUND 5-10 77

Also see C.C. & COMPANY
Also see C.J. & CO.

COHEN, Leonard

LP '68

Singles: 7–inch

COLUMBIA 3-6 68-73

LPs: 10/12–inch 33rpm

COLUMBIA 10-12 68-85
W.B. 8-12 77

Also see BRANIGAN, Laura

COHEN, Myron

LP '66

LPs: 10/12–inch 33rpm

RCA 10-15 66

Also see ANN-MARGRET

COHN, Marc

C&W/LP '91

Singles: 7–inch

ATLANTIC 3-4 91

LPs: 10/12-inch 33rpm

ATLANTIC 5-8 91

COLD BLOOD

LP '69

Singles: 7-inch

ABC 3-5 75
REPRISE 3-5 72-73
SAN FRANCISCO 3-6 70

EPs: 7-inch 33/45rpm

SAN FRANCISCO (3309 "Cold Blood") 5-10 70
(Promotional issue only.)

LPs: 10/12-inch 33rpm

ABC 8-10 76
REPRISE 10-12 72-73
SAN FRANCISCO 12-15 69-70
W.B. 8-10 74

Members: Lydia Pense; Michael Andreas; Rod Ellicott; Frank Davis; Jerry Jonutz; Danny Hull; Larry Field.

Also see PENSE, Lydia, & New Invaders

COLD CHISEL

LP '81

Singles: 7-inch

ELEKTRA 3-4 81

LPs: 10/12-inch 33rpm

ELEKTRA 5-10 80-82

Members: Jimmy Barnes; Don Walker; Steve Prestwich; Phil Small; Ian Moss.

Also see BARNES, Jimmy

COLDER, Ben

(Sheb Wooley)

C&W/P&R '62

Singles: 7-inch

MGM 4-8 62-73
PORTLAND 3-6 78
SCORPION 3-5 79-80
SUNBIRD 3-4 80
TPL 3-5 87

LPs: 10/12-inch 33rpm

LAKESHORE (621 "Ben Colder & Sheb Wooley") 10-20
(Mail order offer.)
LAKESHORE/GUSTO (110 "Greatest Hits of Sheb Wooley & Ben Colder") 8-12 79
(Mail order offer.)
MGM (139 "Ben Colder") 8-12 70
MGM (4421 thru 4876) 10-20 66-73
MGM (4173 "Spoofing the Big Ones") 15-25 63

Also see WOOLEY, Sheb

COLE, Ann

(With the Suburbans)

R&B '56

Singles: 78rpm

BATON 4-8 56-57
TIMELY 4-8 54

Singles: 7-inch

BATON 10-20 56-57
MGM 5-10 60
ROULETTE 10-20 62
SIR 5-10 59-60
TIMELY 10-20 54

COLE, Bobby

P&R '68

Singles: 7-inch

DATE 3-6 68-69

COLE, Cozy

(With His All Stars; with Gary Chester; with Pete Johnson; with Red Norvo; Cozy Cole Septet)

R&B '44

Singles: 78rpm

MGM 3-6 54

Singles: 7-inch

ARTISTIQUE 4-8 61
BETHLEHEM 4-8 63
CHARLIE PARKER 4-8 62
CORAL 4-8 62-67
FELSTED 5-10 58
GRAND AWARD 5-8 58
KING 4-8 59-60
LOVE 10-15 58-59
MGM 5-10 54
MERCURY 5-8 58
RANDOM 4-8 60

Picture Sleeves

RANDOM 5-10 60

EPs: 7-inch 33/45rpm

AFTER HOURS 15-20 55
MGM 15-20 54
WALDORF 5-8

LPs: 10/12-inch 33rpm

AFTER HOURS 25-30 55
CHARLIE PARKER 15-20 62
COLUMBIA 10-15 66
CORAL 15-20 62-64
EVEREST 8-10 74
FELSTED 15-20 59
KING 20-25 59-60
LOVE 20-25 59
PARIS 20-25 58
SAVOY 8-12 72-77
TRIP 8-10 74

Also see HAMPTON, Lionel
Also see SHEARING, George, Quintet

COLE, Cozy, & Illnois Jacquet

LPs: 10/12-inch 33rpm

AUDITION 25-35 55

Also see COLE, Cozy
Also see JACQUET, Illnois

COLE, Gardner

P&R '88

Singles: 7-inch

W.B. 3-4 88

Picture Sleeves

W.B. 3-4 88

COLE, Jude

P&R/LP '90

Singles: 7–inch

REPRISE 3-4 90

LPs: 10/12–inch 33rpm

REPRISE 5-8 90

Also see MARTIN, Moon

COLE, King, Trio: see COLE, Nat King

COLE, Nat "King"

(King Cole Trio; Quintet; Quartet)

R&B '42

Singles: 78rpm

AMMOR 15-25 42
ATLAS 10-20 43-45
CAPITOL (100 thru 700 series)... 5-10 43-49
CAPITOL (800 thru 4600 series)... 4-8 50-58
CAPITOL (15000 series)............... 3-8 47-49
DAVIS & SCHWEGLER........... 20-40 39-40
DECCA.................................... 10-20 42-47
DISC....................................... 15-25 42
EXCELSIOR 10-20 42-45
SAVOY 10-15 46
VARSITY 15-25 40

Singles: 7–inch

CAPITOL (Except 800 thru 4200 series) 4-8 61-69
CAPITOL (889 thru 4623) 5-15 50-61
(Purple label.)
TAMPA (134 "Vom-Vim Veedle") 8-12 57

Picture Sleeves

CAPITOL.................................. 5-10 59-66
TAMPA (134 "Vom-Vim-Veedle") 10-20 57

EPs: 7–inch 33/45rpm

CAPITOL................................. 10-20 50-60
DECCA.................................... 10-20 56

LPs: 10/12–inch 33rpm

CAMAY 8-12
CAPITOL (Except 100 thru 2900 series) 5-15 61-82
CAPITOL (H-156 "Nat King Cole At the Piano")...................... 50-100 49
(10–inch LP.)
CAPITOL (H-177 "Nat King Cole Trio") 50-75 49
(10–inch LP.)
CAPITOL (H-220 "Nat King Cole Trio") 50-75 50
(10–inch LP.)
CAPITOL (H-332 "Penthouse Serenade") 50-75 52
(10–inch LP.)
CAPITOL (H-357 "Unforgetable")...................... 50-75 52
(10–inch LP.)
CAPITOL (100 thru 900 series). 20-35 55-58
(With "T" prefix.)
CAPITOL (1000 thru 2900 series).................................10-20 58-68
(With "T" or "ST" prefix.)
CAPITOL.................................5-10
(With "SM" prefix.)
CROWN 8-12 64
DECCA (8260 "In the Beginning") 35-50 56
DYNAMIC HOUSE.....................5-10 72
MCA 5-10 73
MARK '56 ....5-10 76
MONARCH ("Nat King Cole") ..75-100 53
(Colored vinyl.)
PICKWICK 5-10 70s
SCORE (4019 "King Cole Trio") 20-40 58
SPINORAMA 10-15 60s
VSP 10-15 66
WYNCOTE..............................10-15 63

Also see FOUR KNIGHTS
Also see KENTON, Stan
Also see LUTCHER, Nellie, & Nat "King" Cole
Also see MARTIN, Dean, & Nat "King" Cole
Also see NELSON, Willie / Nat "King" Cole / Johnny Mathis / Shirley Bassey
Also see PRESLEY, Elvis
Also see PRESLEY, Elvis / Frank Sinatra / Nat "King" Cole
Also see SINATRA, Frank / Nat King Cole

COLE, Nat "King" / Phil Flowers

LPs: 10/12–inch 33rpm

EXCELSIOR 5-10

COLE, Nat "King," & Stubby Kaye

Singles: 7–inch

CAPITOL..................................3-6 65

Picture Sleeves

CAPITOL..................................4-8 65

COLE, Nat "King," & His Trio / George Kingston

LPs: 10/12–inch 33rpm

WYNCOTE..............................10-15 60s

Also see COLE, Nat "King"

COLE, Nat "King," & George Shearing

LPs: 10/12–inch 33rpm

CAPITOL................................20-30 61

Also see SHEARING, George, Quintet

COLE, Natalie

(With George Shearing)

P&R/R&B/LP '75

Singles: 12–inch 33/45rpm

EPIC.......................................4-6 83
MODERN 4-6 85

Singles: 7–inch

CAPITOL..................................3-4 75-80
EMI...3-4 88-89
EPIC.......................................3-4 83
MANHATTAN...........................3-4 87
MODERN 3-4 85

Picture Sleeves

EMI...3-4 88-89

MANHATTAN 3-4 87

MODERN 3-4 85

LPs: 10/12-inch 33rpm

CAPITOL 8-12 75-82

EMI 5-8 89

ELEKTRA 5-8 91

EPIC 5-10 83

MANHATTAN 5-10 87

MFSL (032 "Thankful") 25-50 79

MFSL (081 "Natalie Cole Sings George Shearing Plays") 20-30 82

MODERN 5-10 85

Also see PARKER, Ray, Jr., & Natalie Cole

Also see SHEARING, George, Quintet

COLE, Natalie, & Peabo Bryson

R&B/LP '79

Singles: 7-inch

CAPITOL 3-4 79

LPs: 10/12-inch 33rpm

CAPITOL 5-10 79

Also see BRYSON, Peabo

Also see COLE, Natalie

COLE, Sami Jo

(Sami Jo & Friends; Sami Jo Cole)

C&W/P&R '74

Singles: 7-inch

ELEKTRA 3-4 81

FAME 3-5 71-72

MGM 3-5 74-75

POLYDOR 3-5 76

LPs: 10/12-inch 33rpm

MGM 5-10 74-75

COLE, Tony

P&R '72

Singles: 7-inch

20TH FOX 3-4 73-74

LPs: 10/12-inch 33rpm

20TH FOX 8-10 73

COLEMAN, Durell

R&B/LP '85

Singles: 7-inch

ISLAND 3-4 85

LPs: 10/12-inch 33rpm

ISLAND 5-10 85

COLLAGE

R&B '83

Singles: 12-inch 33/45rpm

CONSTELLATION 4-6 86

MCA 4-6 85

SOLAR 4-6 83

Singles: 7-inch

CONSTELLATION 3-4 86

MCA 3-4 85

SOLAR 3-4 82-83

LPs: 10/12-inch 33rpm

CONSTELLATION 5-10 86

SOLAR 5-10 81-83

COLLAY & SATELLITES

P&R '60

Singles: 7-inch

SHO-BIZ (1002 "Last Chance") 15-25 60

COLLEY, Keith

P&R '63

Singles: 7-inch

CHALLENGE 4-6 66-70

COLUMBIA 4-6 68

ERA 5-10 61-62

JAF 4-8

UNICAL 5-10 63-64

VEE JAY 4-8 65

COLLIER, Mitty

R&B '63

Singles: 7-inch

CHESS 5-10 61-68

ENTRANCE 3-5 72

ERIC 3-4 78

PEACHTREE 3-6 69-70

LPs: 10/12-inch 33rpm

CHESS 15-25 65-66

GOSPEL ROOTS 5-10 79

COLLINS, Al

(Al "Jazzbo" Collins)

P&R '53

Singles: 78rpm

ACE (500 "I Got the Blues for You") 15-25 55

BRUNSWICK 4-8 53

Singles: 7-inch

ACE (500 "Shuckin' Stuff") 75-100 55

BRUNSWICK (86001 "Little Red Riding Hood") 10-15 53

IDONGOTOSHOWYOUNOSTINKINBADGES (1225 "Hip Nite B-4 Xmas") 10-15

(Label name is correct—read: "I Don't Got to Show You No Stinkin' Badges"—and is not the result of a typist gone berserk.)

"SINCERELY YOURS" 5-8

(No label name used.)

Picture Sleeves

BRUNSWICK (86001 "Little Red Riding Hood") 20-30 53

LPs: 10/12-inch 33rpm

CORAL (57035 "East Coast Jazz Scene") 50-75 56

Also see FREED, Alan, Steve Allen, Al "Jazzbo" Collins & Modernaires

COLLINS, Al "Jazzbo," & Lou Stein

Singles: 78rpm

BRUNSWICK (80226 "Three Little Pigs") 5-10 53

Singles: 7-inch

BRUNSWICK (80226 "Three Little Pigs") 10-15 53

Also see COLLINS, Al

Also see STEIN, Lou

COLLINS, Albert
(With the Ice Breakers)

R&B/LP '72

Singles: 12–inch 33/45rpm

ALLIGATOR (5 "Cold Snap") 5-10 86
(Promotional issue only.)

Singles: 7–inch

GREAT SCOTT (007 "Albert's Alley") 15-25
HALL 5-10 64
HALL WAY 8-12 63
IMPERIAL 4-6 69
KANGAROO (104 "Collins Shuffle") 25-50 58
LIBERTY 3-5 70
TCF HALL 4-8 65-66
TUMBLEWEED 3-5 72-73
20TH FOX 4-6 68

LPs: 10/12–inch 33rpm

ALLIGATOR 5-10 79-87
BLUE THUMB 10-15 69
BRYLEN 5-10 84
IMPERIAL 10-15 69-70
TCF HALL (8002 "Cool Sound of Albert Collins") 30-35 65
TUMBLEWEED 10-15 71

COLLINS, Albert, Robert Cray & Johnny Copeland

LP '86

Singles: 12–inch 33/45rpm

ALLIGATOR (5 "T-Bone Shuffle") 5-10 86
(Promotional issue only.)

LPs: 10/12–inch 33rpm

ALLIGATOR 5-10 86
Also see COLLINS, Albert
Also see CRAY, Robert

COLLINS, Dave & Ansell

P&R '71

Singles: 7–inch

BIG TREE 3-5 71-72

LPs: 10/12–inch 33rpm

BIG TREE 10-12 71

COLLINS, Dorothy

P&R '55

Singles: 78rpm

AUDIOVOX 4-8 54-55
CORAL 4-8 55-56
DECCA 4-8 52
MGM 4-8 50-51

Singles: 7–inch

AUDIOVOX 5-10 54-55
CORAL 5-10 55-56
DECCA 5-10 52
GOLD EAGLE 4-8 61
MGM 5-10 50-51
ROULETTE 4-6 63
TOP RANK 5-10 59-60

EPs: 7–inch 33/45rpm

CORAL 5-10 55-56
MGM 5-10 55

LPs: 10/12–inch 33rpm

CORAL 15-25 55-57
MOTIVATION 10-15 62
TOP RANK 10-15 60
VOCALION 5-10 65

COLLINS, Judy

LP '64

Singles: 7–inch

ELEKTRA (Except 45253 & 45008 thru 45680) 3-5 70-84
ELEKTRA (45253 "Send in the Clowns") 3-5 75
ELEKTRA (45008 thru 45680) 4-8 64-69

Picture Sleeves

ELEKTRA (Except "The Hostage") 3-5 69-84
ELEKTRA ("The Hostage") 4-8 73
(Promotional issue only.)

LPs: 10/12–inch 33rpm

ELEKTRA (Except 200 & 300 series) 10-15 67-84
ELEKTRA (209 "Maid of Constant Sorrow") 30-40 61
ELEKTRA (222 "Golden Apples of the Sun") 25-35 62
ELEKTRA (243 "Judy Collins No. 3") 20-30 63
(Monaural.)
ELEKTRA (7-243 "Judy Collins No. 3") 25-35 63
(Stereo.)
ELEKTRA (253 "Running for My Life") 5-8 80
ELEKTRA (300 series) 15-20 65-68
(Monaural.)
ELEKTRA (7-300 series) 15-20 65-72
(Stereo.)
ELEKTRA (60001 "Times of Our Lives") 5-8 82

COLLINS, Judy, & T.G. Sheppard

Singles: 7–inch

ELEKTRA 3-4 84
Also see COLLINS, Judy
Also see SHEPPARD, T.G.

COLLINS, Keanya
(Kenya Collins)

R&B '69

Singles: 7–inch

BLUE ROCK 3-6 69
ITCO 3-6 69
KEANYA (1 "Love Bandit") 15-25
PM 3-5

COLLINS, Lyn
(With the Famous Flames)

P&R/R&B '72

Singles: 7–inch

PEOPLE 3-5 72-76

LPs: 10/12–inch 33rpm

PEOPLE 10-12 72-75

Also see BROWN, James & Lyn Collins

COLLINS, Phil

P&R/LP '81

Singles: 12–inch 33/45rpm

ATLANTIC 4-6 84-86

Singles: 7–inch

ATLANTIC 3-4 81-90

Picture Sleeves

ATLANTIC 3-4 81-90

LPs: 10/12–inch 33rpm

ATLANTIC 5-10 81-90

Also see BAILEY, Philip, & Phil Collins
Also see BAND AID
Also see BRAND X
Also see FLAMING YOUTH
Also see GENESIS

COLLINS, Phil, & Marilyn Martin

P&R '85

Singles: 7–inch

ATLANTIC 3-4 85

Picture Sleeves

ATLANTIC 3-4 85

Also see COLLINS, Phil
Also see MARTIN, Marilyn

COLLINS, Rodger
(Roger Collins)

R&B '67

Singles: 7–inch

FANTASY 3-5 73
GALAXY 3-8 66-73
POMPEII 3-6 69

COLLINS, William: see BOOTSY'S RUBBER BAND

COLLINS, Willie

R&B '86

Singles: 7–inch

CAPITOL 3-4 86

COLLINS & COLLINS

R&B '80

Singles: 7–inch

A&M 3-4 80

LPs: 10/12–inch 33rpm

A&M 5-10 80

Members: Bill Collins; Tonee Collins.

COLOMBO, Chris: see COLUMBO, Chris

COLONEL ABRAMS: see ABRAMS, Colonel

COLORS

D&D '83

Singles: 12–inch 33/45rpm

FIRST TAKE 4-6 83

Singles: 7–inch

BECKET 3-4 82

COLOSSEUM

LP '71

Singles: 7–inch

DUNHILL 3-6 69-71

LPs: 10/12–inch 33rpm

DUNHILL 10-15 69-70
W.B. 10-15 71

Members: Jon Heisman; Dick Heckstall-Smith; David Greenslade; Dave Clempson; Mark Clarke; Chris Farlowe; Barbara Thompson; Louis Gennamo.
Also see FARLOWE, Chris

COLTER, Jessi
(Mirriam Johnson; Mirriam Eddy)

C&W/P&R '75

Singles: 7–inch

CAPITOL 3-5 75-82
RCA 3-6 69-72

LPs: 10/12–inch 33rpm

CAPITOL 5-10 75-81
RCA 8-12 70

Also see EDDY, Duane & Mirriam
Also see JENNINGS, Waylon, & Jessi Colter

COLTRANE, Alice

LP '71

LPs: 10/12–inch 33rpm

IMPULSE 8-10 71-74
W.B. 5-10 77-78

COLTRANE, Alice, & Carlos Santana

LP '74

LPs: 10/12–inch 33rpm

COLUMBIA 6-10 74

Also see COLTRANE, Alice
Also see SANTANA

COLTRANE, Chi

P&R/LP '72

Singles: 7–inch

CLOUDS 3-5 78
COLUMBIA 3-5 72-73

LPs: 10/12–inch 33rpm

CLOUDS 5-10 77
COLUMBIA 8-12 72-73

COLTRANE, John

LP '67

Singles: 78rpm

PRESTIGE 5-10 57

Singles: 7–inch

ATLANTIC 4-8 60-61
PRESTIGE 5-10 57-64

LPs: 10/12–inch 33rpm

ATLANTIC (1300 & 1400 series) 20-40 59-66
BLUE NOTE (1577 "Blue Train") 100-150 51
(Label gives New York street address for Blue Note Records.)

BLUE NOTE (1577 "Blue Train") 35-55 59
(Label reads "Blue Note Records Inc. - New York, U.S.A.")
COLTRANE (4950 "Cosmic Music") 150-200 66
COLTRANE (5000 "Cosmic Music") 150-200 66
IMPULSE (Except 6 thru 77)..... 10-25 66-71
IMPULSE (6 thru 77)................ 25-45 61-65
JAZZLAND 20-40 61
PRESTIGE (7043 "Two Tenors") 50-100 56
(Yellow label.)
PRESTIGE (7043 "Two Tenors") 25-35 64
(Blue label.)
PRESTIGE (7105 "Coltrane") . 50-100 57
(Yellow label.)
PRESTIGE (7105 "Coltrane") ... 25-35 57
(Blue label.)
PRESTIGE (7123 "John Coltrane & Red Garland Trio").................. 50-75 57
(Yellow label.)
PRESTIGE (7123 "Traneing In").................. 25-35 64
(Blue label, logo on right. Reissue of *John Coltrane & Red Garland Trio.*)
PRESTIGE (7123 "Traneing In").................. 15-25 69
(Blue label, logo at top.)
PRESTIGE (7142 "Soultrane").. 40-70 58
(Yellow label.)
PRESTIGE (7158 "Cattin")........ 40-70 59
(Yellow label.)
PRESTIGE (7158 "Cattin")........ 25-35 64
(Blue label.)
PRESTIGE (7131 "Wheelin' and Dealin") 40-70 59
(Yellow label.)
PRESTIGE (7188 "Lush Life") .. 40-70 60
(Yellow label.)
PRESTIGE (7188 "Lush Life") .. 25-35 64
(Blue label.)
PRESTIGE (7200 series).......... 20-40 61-64
(Yellow label.)
PRESTIGE (7200 series).......... 15-25 64
(Blue label.)
PRESTIGE (7300 series).......... 15-25 65
U.A. 25-35 62
Also see ADDERLEY, Julian "Cannonball," & John Coltrane
Also see ELLINGTON, Duke, & John Coltrane

COLTRANE, John, & Miles Davis

LPs: 10/12-inch 33rpm

PRESTIGE 10-20 64
Also see DAVIS, Miles

COLTRANE, John, & Thelonious Monk

LPs: 10/12-inch 33rpm

JAZZLAND.................. 20-30 61
MILESTONE 8-12 73
RIVERSIDE (Except 039) 10-20 65-68
RIVERSIDE (039 "Thelonious Monk & John Coltrane").................. 5-10 82
Also see COLTRANE, John
Also see MONK, Thelonious

COLTS

R&B '55

Singles: 78rpm

MAMBO (112 "Adorable")......... 35-50 55
VITA.................. 10-20 55-56

Singles: 7-inch

ANTLER (4003 "Never No More") 20-40 57
ANTLER (4007 "Guiding Angel") 20-40 57
MAMBO (112 "Adorable") 200-300 55
PLAZA (505 "Sweet Sixteen").... 10-15 62
VITA (112 "Adorable")........... 100-150 55
VITA (121 "Sweet Sixteen") 50-75 56
VITA (130 "Never No More")...... 50-75 56
Members: Joe Crunby; Rubin Grunby; Leroy Smith; Carl Moland; Don Wyatt.

COLTS / Red Coats

Singles: 7-inch

DEL-CO 15-25 59
Also see COLTS

COLUMBO, Chris
(Chris Colombo Quintet)

P&R '63

Singles: 7-inch

BATTLE 4-8 62
MAXX.................. 3-6 64
STRAND 4-8 63

LPs: 10/12-inch 33rpm

MERCURY.................. 5-10 75
STRAND 10-15 63

COLVIN, Shawn

LP '89

LPs: 10/12-inch 33rpm

COLUMBIA 5-8 89

COMATEENS

D&D '83

Singles: 12-inch 33/45rpm

MERCURY.................. 4-6 83-84

Singles: 7-inch

MERCURY.................. 3-4 83-84

LPs: 10/12-inch 33rpm

CACHALOT 5-10 81
MERCURY.................. 5-10 83

COMER, Tony & Crosswinds

R&B '84

Singles: 7-inch

VIDCOM.................. 3-4 84

COMMANDER CODY

(With His Lost Planet Airmen)

LP '71

Singles: 7-inch

ABC 3-5 75
ARISTA 3-5 77
DOT 3-5 73-74
MCA 3-4 83
PARAMOUNT 3-5 71-74
W.B. 3-5 75

Picture Sleeves

PARAMOUNT 3-5 72-73

LPs: 10/12-inch 33rpm

ARISTA 5-10 77
PARAMOUNT 10-12 71-74
W.B. 8-10 75-76

COMMODORES

P&R/R&B/LP '74

Singles: 12-inch 33/45rpm

MOTOWN 4-8 79-85
POLYDOR 4-6 86

Singles: 7-inch

ATLANTIC 5-10 69
MOTOWN 3-5 74-85
(Black vinyl.)
MOTOWN (1307 "Machine Gun") . 4-6 74
(Colored vinyl. Promotional issue only.)
MOWEST 3-5 72
POLYDOR 3-4 86

Picture Sleeves

MOTOWN 3-5 85
POLYDOR 3-4 86

LPs: 10/12-inch 33rpm

MOTOWN (Except 39) 8-10 74-87
MOTOWN (39 "1978 Platinum Tour") 15-20 78
(Promotional issue only.)
POLYDOR 5-10 86

Members: Lionel Ritchie; William King; Ronald LaPread; Tommy McClary; Walter Orange; Milan Williams.

Also see McCLARY, Thomas
Also see RICHIE, Lionel

COMMON SENSE

R&B '81

Singles: 7-inch

BC 3-4 81

COMMUNARDS

P&R/LP '86

Singles: 12-inch 33/45rpm

MCA 4-6 86

Singles: 7-inch

MCA 3-4 86-88

LPs: 10/12-inch 33rpm

MCA 5-10 86-88

Members: Jimmy Sommerville; Sara Jane Morris; Richard Coles.

Also see BRONSKI BEAT
Also see SOMERVILLE, Jimmy

COMO, Perry

(With Hugo Winterhalter's Orchestra; with Ramblers)

P&R '43

Singles: 78rpm

BLUEBIRD 5-10 50
RCA 5-10 43-58

Singles: 7-inch

BLUEBIRD 10-20 50
RCA (237 "Supper Club Favorites") 15-25 49
(Three disc set.)
RCA (0071 "Ave Maria") 10-15 49
(Black vinyl.)
RCA (0071 "Ave Maria") 15-25 49
(Colored vinyl.)
RCA (0100 thru 0900 series) 3-6 69-73
RCA (VP-2000 series) 8-12 59
(Stereo.)
RCA (2700 thru 7400 series) 8-20 48-59
RCA (61-7000 series) 8-12 58-60
(Stereo.)
RCA (7500 thru 9700 series) 4-10 59-69
RCA (10000 thru 13000 series) 3-5 74-83

Picture Sleeves

RCA (3800 thru 7100 series) 10-20 53-58
RCA (7200 thru 9700 series) 5-15 58-69

EPs: 7-inch 33/45rpm

CAMDEN 5-10 50s
RCA (Except SPD series) 10-25 52-70
RCA (SPD-27 "Perry Como") 40-60 56
(Boxed 10-EP set. Includes inserts and biography booklet.)
RCA (SPD-28 "Perry Como Highlighter") 20-30 56
(Sampler from Kleenex Tissue. Includes picture cover.)

LPs: 10/12-inch 33rpm

CAMDEN 5-15 57-74
RCA (0100 thru 4000 series) 5-15 73-83
(With "AFL1," "ANL1," "APL1," "AQL1," "AYL1," "CPL1," or "DVL2" prefix.)
RCA (1004 "Saturday Night with Mr. C") 20-30 58
RCA (1007 "Golden Records") 20-30 58
RCA (LPM-1085 "So Smooth") 20-40 55
RCA (LPM-1172 "I Believe") 20-40 56
RCA (LPM-1176 "Relaxing with Perry Como") 20-40 56
RCA (LPM-1177 "Sentimental Date with Perry Como") 20-40 56
RCA (LPM-1191 "Perry Como Sings Hits from Broadway Shows") 20-40 56
RCA (LPM-1243 Perry Sings Christmas Music") 20-40 56
RCA (LPM-1463 We Get Letters") 20-30 57
RCA (LPM-1800 thru LPM-2900 series) 15-25 58-63

RCA (LSP-1085 thru LSP-1463) 10-20 62 68
(Electronic stereo reissues.)
RCA (LSP-1800 thru LSP-2900 series) 15-30 58-63
(Stereo.)
RCA (3013 "TV Favorites") 25-50 52
(10–inch LP.)
RCA (3044 "Supper Club Favorites") 25-50 52
(10–inch LP.)
RCA (3124 "Broadway") 25-50 53
(10–inch LP.)
RCA (3133 "Christmas") 25-50 53
(10–inch LP.)
RCA (3188 "I Believe") 25-50 53
(10–inch LP.)
RCA (3224 "Golden Records") .. 25-50 54
(10–inch LP.)
RCA (3300 thru 4500 series) 8-15 64-71
(With "LPM" or "LSP" prefix.)
READER'S DIGEST 8-15 75

COMO, Perry / Ames Brothers / Harry Belafonte / Radio City Music Hall Orchestra

EPs: 7–inch 33/45rpm

RCA (SP-35 "Merry Christmas") 10-20 56
(Record dealer giveaway. Issued with paper sleeve.)
Also see AMES BROTHERS
Also see BELAFONTE, Harry
Also see WINTERHALTER, Hugo, & His Orchestra

COMO, Perry, & Eddie Fisher

P&R '52

Singles: 78rpm

RCA 4-8 52

Singles: 7–inch

RCA 5-10 52
Also see FISHER, Eddie

COMO, Perry, & Fontane Sisters

P&R '50

Singles: 78rpm

RCA 4-8 50-51

Singles: 7–inch

RCA 8-15 50-51
Also see FONTANE SISTERS

COMO, Perry, & Betty Hutton

P&R '50

Singles: 78rpm

RCA 4-8 50

Singles: 7–inch

RCA 8-15 50
Also see HUTTON, Betty

COMO, Perry, & Jaye P. Morgan

Singles: 78rpm

RCA 4-8 55

Singles: 7–inch

RCA 5-10 55
Also see COMO, Perry
Also see MORGAN, Jaye P.

COMPAGNONS DE LA CHANSON: see LES COMPAGNONS DE LA CHANSON

COMPANY B

P&R/LP '87

Singles: 7–inch

ATLANTIC 3-4 87-89

LPs: 10/12–inch 33rpm

ATLANTIC 5-10 87-89
Members: Donna Huntley; Julie Marie; Susan Johnson; Lori L.

COMPANY of WOLVES

LP '90

LPs: 10/12–inch 33rpm

MERCURY 5-8 90

COMPTON'S MOST WANTED

LP '90

LPs: 10/12–inch 33rpm

ORPHEUS 5-8 90-91

COMSTOCK, Bobby
(With the Counts)

P&R '59

Singles: 7–inch

ASCOT 8-15 64-66
ATLANTIC 10-15 60
BLAZE (349 "Tennessee Waltz") 10-20 59
ERIC 3-4 73
FESTIVAL 10-15 61
JUBILEE 5-10 60-63
LAWN 8-12 62-64
MOHAWK 10-15 61
TRIUMPH 10-15 59

LPs: 10/12–inch 33rpm

ASCOT (16026 "Out of Sight") ... 30-45 66
BLAZE ("Tennessee Waltz") .. 100-150
Session: King Curtis.
Also see KING CURTIS

CON FUNK SHUN

P&R/R&B/LP '77

Singles: 12–inch 33/45rpm

MERCURY 4-6 83-86

Singles: 7–inch

FRETONE 3-5 74
MERCURY 3-4 77-86

LPs: 10/12–inch 33rpm

51 WEST 5-10 83
MERCURY 5-10 76-86
Members: Michael Cooper; Louis McCall; Karl Fuller; Paul Harrell; Danny Thomas; Felton Pilate II.
Also see COOPER, Michael

CONCEPT

R&B '85

Singles: 7–inch

TUCKWOOD 3-4 85

CONCRETE BLONDE

LP '87

Singles: 7-inch

I.R.S. 3-4 87-90

LPs: 10/12-inch 33rpm

I.R.S. 5-10 87-90

Members: Johnette Napolitano; James Mankey.

CONDUCTOR

P&R '82

Singles: 7-inch

JAMIE 5-10 61
MONTAGE 3-4 82

LPs: 10/12-inch 33rpm

MONTAGE 5-10 82

CONEY HATCH

LP '83

LPs: 10/12-inch 33rpm

MERCURY 5-10 83-85

CONLEE, John

C&W '78

Singles: 7-inch

ABC 3-4 78
ABC/DOT 3-4 76-77
COLUMBIA 3-4 86-87
MCA 3-4 79-85
16TH AVE. 3-4 89-90

LPs: 10/12-inch 33rpm

ABC 8-10 78
COLUMBIA 5-10 86-87
MCA 5-10 79-86

CONLEY, Arthur

P&R/R&B/LP '67

Singles: 7-inch

ATCO 3-5 67-70
CAPRICORN 3-4 71-74
FAME 3-5 66
JOTIS 3-5 66

LPs: 10/12-inch 33rpm

ATCO 15-25 67-69

Also see ARTHUR & CORVETS
Also see SOUL CLAN

CONNICK, Harry, Jr.

(Harry Connick Jr. Trio)

LP '89

LPs: 10/12-inch 33rpm

COLUMBIA 5-8 90-91

CONNIE

R&B/D&D '85

Singles: 12-inch 33/45rpm

SUNNYVIEW 4-6 85-86

Singles: 7-inch

SUNNYVIEW 3-4 85-86

CONNIFF, Ray

(With the Rockin' Rhythm Boys; Ray Conniff Orchestra & Chorus)

P&R/LP '57

Singles: 78rpm

BRUNSWICK 4-8 57
COLUMBIA 3-5 56-57
CORAL 4-8 55

Singles: 7-inch

BRUNSWICK 5-10 57
COLUMBIA 3-8 56-82
CORAL 5-10 55

Picture Sleeves

COLUMBIA 3-8 60-64

EPs: 7-inch 33/45rpm

COLUMBIA (Except 10041/2/3) ... 5-10 56-59
COLUMBIA (10041/2/3 "Dance the Bop") 8-12 57
(Price is for either volume.)

LPs: 10/12-inch 33rpm

COLUMBIA (Except 925 & 1004) 5-15 58-82
COLUMBIA (925 "S'Wonderful") 10-20 56
COLUMBIA (1004 "Dance the Bop") 15-25 57
HARMONY 4-8 69

Also see MATHIS, Johnny
Also see ROBBINS, Marty

CONNOR, Chris

P&R '56

Singles: 78rpm

ATLANTIC 3-5 56-57
BETHLEHEM 4-6 54-55

Singles: 7-inch

ATLANTIC 4-8 56-62
BETHLEHEM (1200 & 1300 series) 5-10 54-55
BETHLEHEM (3000 series) 3-4 64
FM 3-6 63

EPs: 7-inch 33/45rpm

ATLANTIC 15-25 56-57
BETHLEHEM 20-40 54-56

LPs: 10/12-inch 33rpm

ABC-PAR 10-20 65-66
ATLANTIC (601 "George Gershwin Almanac") 40-60 57
ATLANTIC (1240 "He Loves Me He Loves Me Not") 40-50 57
ATLANTIC (1228 "Chris Connor") 40-50 57
ATLANTIC (1286 "Jazz Date") ... 40-50 58
ATLANTIC (1290 "Chris Craft") . 40-50 58
ATLANTIC (1307 "Sad Cafe") 30-40 59
(Monaural.)
ATLANTIC (SD-1307 "Sad Cafe") 35-45 59
(Stereo.)
ATLANTIC (8014 "I Miss You So") 40-50 58

ATLANTIC (8032 "Witchcraft").. 30-40 59
(Monaural.)
ATLANTIC (SD-8032 "Witchcraft") 35-45 59
(Stereo.)
ATLANTIC (8040 "In Person") .. 30-40 59
(Monaural.)
ATLANTIC (SD-8040 "In Person") 35-45 59
(Stereo.)
ATLANTIC (8046 "Portrait") 25-35 60
(Monaural.)
ATLANTIC (SD-8046 "Portrait") 35-45 60
(Stereo.)
ATLANTIC (8061 "Free Spirits") 20-30 62
(Monaural.)
ATLANTIC (SD-8061 "Free Spirits") 25-35 62
(Stereo.)
BETHLEHEM (20 "This Is Chris") 40-50 55
(Maroon label.)
BETHLEHEM (56 "Chris") 40-50 56
(Maroon label.)
BETHLEHEM (1001 Lullabys of Birdland") 75-100 54
(10–inch LP.)
BETHLEHEM (1002 Lullabys for Lovers, Vol. 2") 75-100 54
(10–inch LP.)
BETHLEHEM (6000 series) 10-12 78
(Gray label.)
BETHLEHEM (6004 "Lullabys of Birdland") 40-50 56
(Maroon label.)
BETHLEHEM (6005 "Lullabys for Lovers") 40-50 56
(Maroon label.)
BETHLEHEM (6006 "Bethlehem Girls") 40-50 56
(Maroon label.)
FM 10-15 63

Also see BON BONS
Also see FERGUSON, Maynard, & Chris Connor
Also see SIMONE, Nina, Chris Connor & Carmen McRae

CONNORS, Norman

R&B/LP '75

Singles: 7–inch

ARISTA 3-4 78-81
BUDDAH 3-5 74-77
CAPITOL 3-4 88

LPs: 10/12–inch 33rpm

ARISTA 5-10 78-81
BUDDAH 10-12 75-78
NOVUS 5-10 81

Session: Michael Henderson; Pharoah Sanders; Jean Cain; Phyllis Hyman; Prince Phillip Mitchell.
Also see AQUARIAN DREAM
Also see HENDERSON, Michael
Also see HYMAN, Phyllis

CONSUMER RAPPORT

P&R/R&B '75

Singles: 7–inch

WING and a PRAYER 3-5 75-76

Member: Frank Floyd.

CONTI, Bill

P&R '77

Singles: 7–inch

ARISTA 3-4 82
U.A. 3-5 77-78

LPs: 10/12–inch 33rpm

MCA 5-10 79
U.A. 8-12 78-79

CONTINENTAL 4
(Continental Four)

P&R/R&B '71

Singles: 7–inch

JAY WALKING 3-5 71-72

LPs: 10/12–inch 33rpm

JAY WALKING 10-15 71

Members: Fred Kelly; Anthony Burke; Ronnie McGregor; Larry McGregor.

CONTINENTAL MINIATURES

P&R '78

Singles: 7–inch

LONDON 3-5 78

Picture Sleeves

LONDON 3-5 78

CONTINO, Dick

P&R '54

Singles: 78rpm

MERCURY 3-5 54-57

Singles: 7–inch

DOT 3-6 66-67
MERCURY 4-8 54-64

EPs: 7–inch 33/45rpm

MERCURY 5-10 55-59

LPs: 10/12–inch 33rpm

DOT 5-15 64-66
HAMILTON 5-10 64-66
MERCURY 8-15 56-63
WING 5-10 63

Also see CARROLL, David

CONTOURS
(With Jack Surrell)

P&R/R&B '62

Singles: 12–inch 33/45rpm

MOTOWN 4-8 88

Singles: 7–inch

GORDY 8-15 62-67
HOB (116 "I'm So Glad") 75-100 61
MOTOWN (400 series) 3-4 82-88
MOTOWN (1008 "Whole Lotta Woman") 350-450 61
MOTOWN (1012 "Funny") 450-650 61
TAMLA (7012 "Shake Sherry") 75-125 62
(Tamla label with Gordy selection number.)

ROCKET 3-4 80

Picture Sleeves

MOTOWN 3-4 88

EPs: 7-inch 33/45rpm

MOTOWN (2002 " Contours")... 15-25 60s

LPs: 10/12-inch 33rpm

GORDY (901 "Do You Love Me")................................... 50-100 62

MOTOWN 5-10 82

Members: Dennis Edwards; Bill Gordon; Sylvester Potts; Billy Hoggs; Joe Billingslea; Joe Stubbs; Hubert Johnson; Huey Davis.

Also see EDWARDS, Dennis

CONTRABAND

LP '91

LPs: 10/12-inch 33rpm

IMPACT................................... 5-8 91

CONTROLLERS

(With Valerie DeMece)

R&B '76

Singles: 12-inch 33/45rpm

MCA 4-6 85-86

Singles: 7-inch

JUANA 3-4 76-82

MCA 3-4 85-88

LPs: 10/12-inch 33rpm

JUANA 8-10 77-79

MCA 5-10 86

WINDHAM HILL 5-10 85

Members: Larry McArthur; Regie McArthur; Ricky Lewis; Leonard Brown.

CONVERTION

R&B '81

Singles: 7-inch

SAM 3-4 81

VANGUARD................................... 3-4 83

LPs: 10/12-inch 33rpm

VANGUARD................................... 5-10 83

CONWAY BROTHERS

R&B '85

Singles: 7-inch

ICHIBAN................................... 3-4 87

PBT 3-4 86

PAULA 3-4 85

Members: Huston Conway; Jim Conway; Fredrick Conway; Hiawatha Conway.

CONWELL, Tommy, & Young Rumblers

P&R/LP '88

Singles: 12-inch 33/45rpm

COLUMBIA 4-8 88

(Promotional only.)

Singles: 7-inch

COLUMBIA 3-4 88

Picture Sleeves

COLUMBIA 3-4 88

LPs: 10/12-inch 33rpm

ANTENNA................................... 10-15 86

COLUMBIA 5-8 88

Members: Tommy Conwell; Rob Miller; Paul Slivka; Jim Hannum; Chris Day.

Also see HOOTERS

COODER, Ry

LP '72

Singles: 7-inch

MUSICOR 4-8 66

REPRISE 3-6 69-72

W.B. 3-5 77-82

LPs: 10/12-inch 33rpm

MFSL (085 "Jazz")................................... 25-50 82

REPRISE 8-12 72-76

W.B. 5-10 77-87

Also see CAPTAIN BEEFHEART

Also see HOPKINS, Nicky

Also see LITTLE FEAT

COOK, Tony

D&D '84

Singles: 12-inch 33/45rpm

HALFMOON................................... 4-6 84

COOKE, Dale

(Sam Cooke)

Singles: 78rpm

SPECIALTY 5-10 57

Singles: 7-inch

SPECIALTY 15-25 57

Also see COOKE, Sam

COOKE, SAM

(With the Soul Stirrers)

P&R/R&B '57

Singles: 78rpm

KEEN 10-15 57

SPECIALTY 8-12 57

Singles: 7-inch

CHERIE 3-5 71

COLLECTABLES................................... 3-4 81

KEEN (Black/silver label)........... 10-15 57

KEEN (Multi-color label).............. 8-12 57-60

(Monaural.)

KEEN (Multi-color label).............20-30 58-60

(Stereo.)

KEEN (Black/multi-color label)..... 8-12 59-61

(Monaural.)

KEEN (Black/multi-color label)... 15-25 60

(Stereo.)

RCA (7000 & 8000 series)........... 5-10 60-66

(With "47" prefix.)

RCA (7000 series) 15-25 60-61

(Stereo. With "61" prefix.)

SPECIALTY (SPBX series)........ 12-15 87

(Boxed set of six colored vinyl singles.)

SPECIALTY (500 & 600 series)... 8-12 57-59

SPECIALTY (900 series) 3-5 70-72

Picture Sleeves

RCA 10-20 60-65

EPs: 7-inch 33/45rpm

KEEN (2001/2002/2003 "Songs By Sam Cooke") 30-40 57
(Price is for any of three volumes.)
KEEN (2012/2013/2014 "Tribute to the Lady") 20-30 59
(Price is for any of three volumes.)
KEEN (2006 "Encore") 20-40 58
KEEN (2008 "Encore, Vol. 2") ... 20-40 58
RCA (126 "Sam Cooke Sings"). 10-20 61
(Compact 33.)
RCA (3373 "Sam Cooke") 15-20 64
(Jukebox issue.)
RCA (4375 "Another Saturday Night") 15-25 63

LPs: 10/12-inch 33rpm

CAMDEN 8-10 68-74
CANDLELITE 15-20 74
(Mail-order offer.)
CHERIE 8-10 71
FAMOUS 10-20 69
KEEN (2001 "Sam Cooke") 35-45 58
KEEN (2003 "Encore") 35-45 58
KEEN (2004 "Tribute to the Lady") 30-40 59
KEEN (86101 "Hit Kit") 35-45 59
KEEN (86103 "I Thank God") 30-40 60
KEEN (86106 "Wonderful World") 30-40 60
PHOENIX 10 .... 5-10 81
PICKWICK 5-10 76
RCA (2000 & 3000 series) 15-35 60-68
(With "LPM" or "LSP" prefix.)
RCA (2000 thru 5000 series) 5-10 78-85
(With "AFL1," "ANL1" or "AYL1" prefix.)
RCA (7000 series) 8-12 86
SAR 3-5 61
SOUFFLE 5-10
SPECIALTY 8-12 69-89
TRIP 8-10 72-76
UPFRONT 8-10 73

Also see ANKA, Paul / Sam Cooke / Neil Sedaka
Also see CHARLES, Ray / Little Richard / Sam Cooke
Also see COOKE, Dale
Also see RAWLS, Lou
Also see SOUL STIRRERS

COOKE, Sam / Rod Lauren / Neil Sedaka / Browns

EPs: 7-inch 33/45rpm

RCA (33-99 "Compact 33 Double") 15-20 60
(With the same four songs on each side, mono on one side, stereo on the reverse.)

Also see BROWNS
Also see LAUREN, Rod
Also see SEDAKA, Neil

COOKE, Sam / Lloyd Price / Larry Williams / Little Richard

LPs: 10/12-inch 33rpm

SPECIALTY (2112 "Our Significant Hits") 25-35 60
(Black and gold label.)

Also see COOKE, Sam
Also see LITTLE RICHARD
Also see PRICE, Lloyd
Also see WILLIAMS, Larry

COOKER
(Norman Des Rosiers)

P&R '74

Singles: 7-inch

SCEPTER 3-5 73-74

LPs: 10/12-inch 33rpm

SCEPTER 8-10 74

COOKER, John Lee
(John Lee Hooker)

Singles: 7-inch

KING (4504 "Stomp Boogie") 50-75 52

Also see HOOKER, John Lee

COOKIE & His Cupcakes
(Cookie & His Berry Cups)

P&R '59

Singles: 7-inch

CHESS 5-10 63
JUDD 10-20 59
KHOURY'S (703 "Matilda") 20-30 59
LYRIC 10-15 63-64
MERCURY 5-10 61
PAULA 4-8 65-68

Members: Terry "Cookie" Clinton; Shelton Dunaway; Lil' Alfred.

COOKIE & His Cupcakes / Little Alfred

Singles: 7-inch

LYRIC 8-12 64

Also see COOKIE & His Cupcakes

COOKIES

R&B '56

Singles: 78rpm

ATLANTIC 5-10 55-57
JOSIE 5-10 57
LAMP (8008 "Don't Let Go") 10-20 54

Singles: 7-inch

ATLANTIC 15-25 55-60
JOSIE 15-25 57
LAMP (8008 "Don't Let Go") 20-30 54

Members: Earl-Jean McCree; Margie Hendrix; Pat Lyles.

Also see CHARLES, Ray
Also see COOKIES (Group that follows)
Also see DILLARD, Varetta
Also see WILLIS, Chuck

COOKIES

P&R/R&B '62

Singles: 7-inch

ABC 3-4 74
DIMENSION 10-20 62-64

ERIC... 3-4 73
MCA... 3-4 83

Member: Earl-Jean McCree.
Also see EARL-JEAN

COOKIES / Little Eva / Carole King

LPs: 10/12-inch 33rpm

DIMENSION (6001 "The Dimension Dolls, Vol. 1")........................ 50-75 63

Also see COOKIES
Also see KING, Carole
Also see LITTLE EVA

COOL HEAT

P&R '70

Singles: 7-inch

FORWARD (152 "Are You Nuts")...................................... 5-10 70

Also see WIND

COOLEY, Eddie

(With the Dimples)

P&R '56

Singles: 78rpm

ROYAL ROOST........................ 10-15 56-57

Singles: 7-inch

ABC... 3-4 73
ROULETTE................................. 5-10 60
ROYAL ROOST........................ 10-20 56-57
TRIUMPH.................................... 8-12 59

COOLIDGE, Rita

P&R '69

Singles: 7-inch

A&M... 3-5 71-83
PEPPER..................................... 4-8 68-69

Picture Sleeves

A&M... 3-6 72-83

LPs: 10/12-inch 33rpm

A&M... 5-10 71-83

Promotional LPs

A&M ("In-Store Sampler - Rita Coolidge").............................. 10-15

Also see CAMPBELL, Glen, & Rita Coolidge
Also see CLAPTON, Eric
Also see KRISTOFFERSON, Kris, & Rita Coolidge

COOPER, Alice

(Alice Cooper Group)

LP '69

Promotional Singles: 12-inch 33/45rpm

EPIC (1347 "I Got a Line on You") 5-8
EPIC (1663 "Poison").................. 5-8 89
EPIC (1686 "Trash")................... 5-8 89
EPIC (1890 "I'm Your Gun").......... 5-8 89
MCA (17177 "He's Back")............ 5-8 86
MCA (17205 "Give It Up")............ 5-8 86
W.B. (864 "Clones")................. 10-15 80
W.B. (1059 "I Like Girls")............. 5-8

Singles: 7-inch

ATLANTIC.................................... 3-5 75
EPIC... 3-4 89-90
MCA... 3-4 86-87
STRAIGHT (101 "Reflected").... 15-25 69
STRAIGHT (7398 "Shoe Salesman").............................15-20 70
W.B. 3-5 70-82

Promotional Singles

ATLANTIC...................................5-10 75
MCA...3-6 86-87
W.B. 8-12 70-80

Picture Sleeves

MCA...3-4 87
W.B. 4-8 72-80

EPs: 7-inch 33/45rpm

W.B. 15-25 73
(Jukebox issues only.)

LPs: 10/12-inch 33rpm

ATLANTIC...................................5-10 75-78
EPIC...5-8 89
MFSL (063 "Welcome to My Nightmare").........................25-50 82
MCA...5-10 86-87
STRAIGHT (1051 "Pretties for You")......................................30-40 69
(Cover has a drawing of a woman raising her dress, with a yellow sticker covering her crotch area. Price is for cover with sticker still intact.)
STRAIGHT (1051 "Pretties for You")......................................20-30 69
(Cover shows the woman with the sticker removed and panties showing.)
W.B. (Except 1883, 2567 & 2623)..8-12 73-84
W.B. (1883 "Love It to Death")...25-30 71
(Black cover has Cooper's right thumb showing through his wrap. Does NOT have white block reading "Including Their Hit *I'm Eighteen.*")
W.B. (1883 "Love It to Death")...15-20 71
(Black cover has Cooper's right thumb showing through his wrap. Has white block reading "Including Their Hit *I'm Eighteen.*" Also includes issue with huge white stripes at top and bottom of cover.)
W.B. (1883 "Love It to Death").....5-10 71
(Black cover does NOT have Cooper's right thumb showing through his wrap. Has the white block reading "Including Their Hit *I'm Eighteen.*")
W.B. (2567 "Killer")...................15-18 71
(With poster and 1972 calendar.)
W.B. (2567 "Killer")......................5-10 72
(Without poster and calendar.)
W.B. (2623 "School's Out")........30-40 72
(With panties attached. Panties came in four different colors: pink, white, yellow, and blue. Back cover does not list titles.)
W.B. (2623 "School's Out")........15-20 72
(With panties attached. Back cover lists titles.)

W.B. (2623 "School's Out") 5-10 72
(With no paper panties. Back cover lists titles.)
W.B. (2685 "Billion Dollar Babies") 5-10 73
W.B. (BS4-2685 "Billion Dollar Babies") 20-25 73
(Quad issue.)
W.B. (2748 "Muscle of Love") 5-10 73
W.B. (BBS4-2748 "Muscle of Love") 20-25 73
(Quad issue.)
W.B. (2803 thru 3581) 5-10 74-81
W.B./STRAIGHT (1051 "Pretties for You") 15-18 69
W.B./STRAIGHT (1845 "Easy Action") 30-35 70
(With the name "Alice Cooper" in black letters on front cover.)
W.B./STRAIGHT (1845 "Easy Action") 5-10 70
(With "Alice Cooper" in white letters on front.)

Promotional LPs

CHELSEA PROD ("Allison's Tea House") 25-30 74
STRAIGHT (1051 "Pretties for You") 45-55 69
(Cover has drawing of a woman raising her dress, with a yellow sticker covering her crotch area. Price is for cover with sticker still intact.)
STRAIGHT (1051 "Pretties for You") 30-40 69
(Cover shows the woman with the sticker removed and panties showing.)
STRAIGHT (1845 "Easy Action")25-30 70
STRAIGHT (1883 "Love It to Death") 20-25 71
W.B. 20-40 71-78
(Includes all white label promo labels.)
W.B./STRAIGHT ("Pretties for You") 25-30 69

Members: Alice Cooper; Dennis Dunaway; Glen Buxton; Michael Bruce; Neal Smith; Kane Roberts; Ken K. Mary.
Also see BILLION DOLLAR BABIES
Also see FROST
Also see NAZZ
Also see SPIDERS

COOPER, Les, & Soul Rockers

P&R/R&B '62

Singles: 7–inch

ABC 3-4 73
ARRAWAK 4-8 65
ATCO 3-6 69
DIMENSION (1023 "Motor City") 10-15 64
ENJOY 4-8 65
EVERLAST 5-10 62
SAMAR 4-8 66

LPs: 10/12–inch 33rpm

EVERLAST (202 "Wiggle Wobble") 40-60 63

Members: Les Cooper; Joe Grier.
Also see CHARTS

COOPER, Michael

R&B '87

Singles: 7–inch

W.B. 3-4 87-88

LPs: 10/12–inch 33rpm

W.B. 5-8 88

Also see CON FUNK SHUN

COOPER, Pat

LP '66

LPs: 10/12–inch 33rpm

U.A. 10-15 66-69

COOPER BROTHERS

P&R '78

Singles: 7–inch

CAPRICORN 3-4 78-79

LPs: 10/12–inch 33rpm

CAPRICORN 5-10 78-79

Members: Richard Cooper; Brian Cooper.
Also see BLACK OAK ARKANSAS / Cooper Brothers

COPAS, Cowboy

(Cowboy "Poppy" Copas; Lloyd Copas; with Kathy Copas)

C&W '46

Singles: 78rpm

KING 5-15 44-57

Singles: 7–inch

DOT 10-20 57-58
KING (951 thru 1507) 10-20 50-55
KING (4865 thru 5270) 5-10 55-59
KING (5392 thru 5734) 4-8 60-63
STARDAY (476 thru 750) 4-8 60-66
STARDAY (7000 series) 3-6 64
STARDAY (8000 series) 3-4 71

EPs: 7–inch 33/45rpm

KING 15-25 52-53
STARDAY 10-20 60

LPs: 10/12–inch 33rpm

GUEST STAR 10-15
KING (553 "All-Time Hits") 45-55 57
KING (556 "Favorite Sacred Songs") 40-50 57
KING (619 thru 835) 25-35 59-64
KING (894 thru 1049) 8-12 64-69
NASHVILLE 8-12 68-70
PICKWICK/HILLTOP 10-12 66
STARDAY (113 "All Time Country Music Great") 20-30 60
STARDAY (133 "Inspirational Songs") 20-30 61
STARDAY (144 "Songs That Made Him Famous") 20-30 62

STARDAY (157 "Opry Star Spotlight") 20-30 63
STARDAY (175 "Mr. Country Music") 20-30 64
STARDAY (200 series) 12-25 64-67
STARDAY (300 series) 10-20 65-67
STARDAY (400 series) 8-12 68-70
Also see COPAS, Lloyd

COPAS, Cowboy / Hawkshaw Hawkins

LPs: 10/12-inch 33rpm

KING 12-25 63-66
Also see CLINE, Patsy / Cowboy Copas / Hawkshaw Hawkins
Also see COPAS, Cowboy
Also see HAWKINS, Hawkshaw

COPAS, Lloyd

Singles: 7-inch

DOT (15735 "Circle Rock") 60-80 58
Also see COPAS, Cowboy

COPE, Julian

P&R/LP '87

Singles: 7-inch

ISLAND 3-4 87-88

Picture Sleeves

ISLAND 3-4 87

LPs: 10/12-inch 33rpm

ISLAND 5-10 87-88
Also see TEARDROP EXPLODES

COPELAND, Ken

Singles: 78rpm

IMPERIAL 4-8 57
LIN (5007 "Fanny Brown") 10-15 58

Singles: 7-inch

DOT 8-12 58
IMPERIAL 10-15 57
LIN (5007 "Fanny Brown") 20-30 58

COPELAND, Ken / Mints

P&R '57

Singles: 78rpm

IMPERIAL 8-12 57
LIN 10-15 56-57

Singles: 7-inch

IMPERIAL 10-15 57
LIN (5007 "Pledge of Love") 15-25 56
LIN (5017 "Fanny Brown") 20-30 57
Also see COPELAND, Ken

COPELAND, Stewart
(Stuart Copeland)

LP '83

LPs: 10/12-inch 33rpm

A&M 5-10 83-85
Also see POLICE

COPELAND, Stewart, & Stan Ridgway

Singles: 7-inch

A&M 3-4 83
Also see COPELAND, Stewart
Also see WALL of VOODOO

COPELAND, Vivian

R&B '69

Singles: 7-inch

D'ORO 3-6 69
MALA 4-8 67

COREA, Chick

LP '76

Singles: 7-Inch

POLYDOR 3-4 79

LPs: 10/12-Inch 33rpm

BLUE NOTE 8-12 75-78
ECM 5-10 75-80
ELEKTRA 5-8 83
PACIFIC JAZZ 5-8 81
POLYDOR 6-12 76-78
VERVE 8-10 76
W.B. 5-8 80-81
Also see HANCOCK, Herbie, & Chick Corea
Also see RETURN to FOREVER

COREY, Jill

P&R '54

Singles: 78rpm

COLUMBIA 3-6 54-57

Singles: 7-inch

COLUMBIA 5-10 54-60
MERCURY 4-8 62

EPs: 7-inch 33/45rpm

COLUMBIA 8-12 55-57

LPs: 10/12-inch 33rpm

COLUMBIA 15-25 56-57

CORLEY, Al

P&R '85

Singles: 7-inch

MERCURY 3-4 85

Picture Sleeves

MERCURY 3-4 85

CORLEY, Bob

P&R '55

Singles: 78rpm

RCA 3-5 56
STARS 10-15 55

Singles: 7-inch

RCA 5-10 56
STARS 20-25 55

CORNBREAD & BISCUITS

P&R/R&B '60

Singles: 7-inch

MASKE 5-10 60

CORNELIUS BROTHERS & Sister Rose

P&R/R&B '71

Singles: 7-inch

PLATINUM 8-12 70
U.A. 3-5 70-74

LPs: 10/12-inch 33rpm

PICKWICK 5-10 76
U.A. 10-15 72-76

Members: Ed Cornelius; Carter Cornelius; Rose Cornelius.

CORNELL, Don

P&R '50

Singles: 78rpm

CORAL 3-6 52-57

Singles: 7-inch

ABC-PAR 3-6 65
CORAL 5-10 52-57
DOT 4-8 59-60
JAYBEE 3-5 69
JUBILEE 3-6 62
SIGNATURE 4-8 59-60
20TH FOX 3-6 64

EPs: 7-inch 33/45rpm

CORAL 5-10 54-56

LPs: 10/12-inch 33rpm

ABC-PAR 8-12 66
CORAL 15-25 54-57
DOT 10-15 59
MOVIETONE 5-10 66
SIGNATURE 10-15 59
VOCALION 8-15 59

Also see KAYE, Sammy

CORNELL, Don, Johnny Desmond & Alan Dale

P&R '53

Singles: 78rpm

CORAL 3-6 53

Singles: 7-inch

CORAL 5-10 53

EPs: 7-inch 33/45rpm

CORAL 5-10 54

Also see CORNELL, Don
Also see DALE, Alan
Also see DESMOND, Johnny

CORNER BOYS

R&B '69

Singles: 7-inch

NEPTUNE 4-6 69

Members: Victor Drayton; Jerry Akines, Reginald Turner; Ernie Brooks; Johnny Bellman.

CORONETS

R&B '53

Singles: 78rpm

CHESS 40-60 53
GROOVE 25-50 55

Singles: 7-inch

CHESS (1549 "Nadine") 150-200 53
(Silver top label with chess pieces.)
CHESS (1549 "Nadine") 5-10
(Blue label.)
CHESS (1553 "It Would Be Heavenly") 250-350 53
(Black vinyl.)
CHESS (1553 "It Would Be Heavenly") 500-750 53
(Colored vinyl.)
GROOVE (0114 "I Love You More") 75-125 55
GROOVE (0116 "Hush") 100-150 55

Members: Charles Carothers; Lester Russaw; George Lewis; William Griggs; Sam Griggs; Babby Ward.

CORPORATION

LP '69

Singles: 7-inch

CAPITOL (2467 "Highway") 10-15 69
CUCA (1496 "You Make Me Feel Good") 10-15 68

LPs: 10/12-inch 33rpm

AGE of AQUARIUS (4150 "Hassels in My Mind") 30-50 68
AGE of AQUARIUS (4250 "Get on Our Swing") 20-30 69
CAPITOL (175 "The Corporation") 20-30 69

Members: Danny Peil; Ken Berdoll; John Kondos; Nicholas Kondos; Pat McCarthy; Gerald Smith.

CORSAIRS
(Featuring Jay "Bird" Uzzell)

P&R '61

Singles: 7-inch

CHESS 5-10 62
ERIC 3-4 78
SMASH 5-10 61
TUFF 5-10 61-64

CORTEZ, Dave "Baby"
(With the Moon People; Baby Cortez)

P&R/R&B '59

Singles: 7-inch

ABC 3-4 74
ALL PLATINUM 3-5 72
ARGO 4-8 64
CHESS 4-8 63
CLOCK 5-10 59-62
COLLECTABLES 3-4 81
EMIT 4-8 62
ERIC 3-4 73
FIRE 5-10 60
JULIA 15-25 62
OKEH (7100 series) 10-20 58
OKEH (7200 series) 4-8 64
ROULETTE 4-8 65-68
SOUND 3-5 71
SPEED 3-5
T-NECK 3-6 69
WINLEY 4-8 62

EPs: 7-inch 33/45rpm

CLOCK 20-30 59-61
RCA (EPA-4342 "Dave 'Baby' Cortez & His Happy Organ") 15-25 59
(Monaural.)
RCA (ESP-4342 "Dave 'Baby' Cortez & His Happy Organ") 35-50 59
(Stereo.)

LPs: 10/12–inch 33rpm

CHESS 25-30 62
CLOCK.................................... 25-35 60-63
CORONET 10-15 60s
CROWN 15-20 63
DESIGN 10-15 60s
METRO 10-20 65
RCA (LPM-2099 "Dave 'Baby' Cortez & His Happy Organ") 25-35 59
(Monaural.)
RCA (LSP-2099 "Dave 'Baby' Cortez & His Happy Organ") 35-50 59
(Stereo.)
ROULETTE 15-20 65-66
Also see ISLEY BROTHERS & Dave "Baby" Cortez
Also see VALENTINES

CORTEZ, Dave "Baby" / Jerry's House Rockers

LPs: 10/12–inch 33rpm

CROWN 10-20 63
Also see CORTEZ, Dave "Baby"

CORYELL, Larry

LP '69

LPs: 10/12–inch 33rpm

ARISTA 5-10 76
VANGUARD............................ 10-15 69
Also see ELEVENTH HOUR / ELVENTH HOUSE
Also see MOUZON, Alphonse, & Larry Croyell

COSBY, Bill

LP '64

Singles: 12–inch 33/45rpm

MOTOWN (110 "Super Special for Radio") 5-10 82
(Promotional issue only.)

Singles: 7–inch

CAPITOL.................................... 3-5 76-78
UNI 3-6 69-70
W.B. 3-5 65-67

EPs: 7–inch 33/45rpm

W.B. (274 "A Taste of Cosby").... 5-10
(Promotional issue only.)

LPs: 10/12–inch 33rpm

CAPITOL.................................... 5-10 76-78
COLUMBIA (40270 "Music from the Bill Cosby Show")............... 5-10 86
(Featuring Grover Washington Jr.)
GEFFEN.................................... 5-10 86
MCA 5-10 73
MOTOWN 5-10 82
PARTEE..................................... 5-10
TETRAGRAMMATON................ 6-10 69
UNI 5-10 69-72
W.B. (Except 249)................... 10-15 64-70
W.B. (249 "Best of Bill Cosby") . 15-20 69
(Promotional issue only.)
Also see ROSS, Diana, & Bill Cosby / Diana Ross & Jackson Five
Also see WASHINGTON, Grover, Jr.

COSBY, Bill, & Ozzie Davis

LPs: 10/12–inch 33rpm

BLACK FORUM 8-12 72
Also see COSBY, Bill

COSTA, Don, Orchestra

P&R '59

Singles: 78rpm

ABC-PAR 4-8 56-57
ESSEX..4-8 55

Singles: 7–inch

ABC-PAR 5-10 56-57
COLUMBIA 3-5 62-63
DCP 3-5 64-65
ESSEX.......................................5-10 55
JAMIE 4-8 59
MGM 3-5 66-72
MERCURY 3-5 68
U.A. 4-8 59-62
VERVE...3-5 67

Picture Sleeves

U.A. 5-10 60
VERVE...4-8 67

LPs: 10/12–inch 33rpm

ABC-PAR 15-30 56-61
COLUMBIA 10-20 62-63
DCP 5-10 64-65
HARMONY.................................5-10 65
MERCURY 5-10 68-69
U.A. 10-20 59-62
VERVE.......................................5-10 67
Also see ANKA, Paul
Also see DE CASTRO SISTERS
Also see MANN, Gloria

COSTANDINOS, Alec R.

(With the Syncophonic Orchestra)

LP '78

Singles: 7–inch

CASABLANCA.............................3-4 79

LPs: 10/12–inch 33rpm

CASABLANCA...........................5-10 78-79

COSTELLO, Elvis

(With the Attractions; Costello Show)

LP '77

Singles: 12–inch 33/45rpm

COLUMBIA 5-15 83-85

Singles: 7–inch

CBS (Black vinyl) 3-5 79
CBS (Colored vinyl) 10-20 79
COLUMBIA 3-5 77-86
W.B. 3-4 89

Promotional Singles

COLUMBIA 5-10 77-86

Picture Sleeves

COLUMBIA (Except 10919)...........3-6 81-85
COLUMBIA (10919 "Accidents Will Happen")...............................15-20 78
(Promotional issue only.)
W.B. 3-4 89

EPs: 7–inch 33/45rpm

COLUMBIA (529 "Live at Hollywood High")..................... 10-20 78
(Bonus EP. Included with the LP *Armed Forces.*)
COLUMBIA (11251 "I Can't Stand Up for Falling Down")............. 10-20 80
COLUMBIA (11251 "I Can't Stand Up for Falling Down")............. 20-30 80
(White label. Promotional issue only.)

LPs: 10/12–inch 33rpm

COLUMBIA (30000 series, except 35709) 8-12 77-86
COLUMBIA (35709 "Armed Forces")................................ 15-25 79
(Includes the bonus EP *Live At Hollywood High.*)
COLUMBIA (35709 "Armed Forces")................................ 8-12 79
(Without *Live At Hollywood High* EP.)
COLUMBIA (35709 "Armed Forces")................................ 30-40 79
(Colored vinyl.)
COLUMBIA/COSTELLO (35331 "This Year's Model")......................... 20-30 78
COLUMBIA (40000 series, except 48157).. 5-8 85-86
COLUMBIA (48157 "Imperial Bedroom")............................. 30-40 82
(Half-speed mastered.)
W.B. 5-10 89-91

Promotional LPs

COLUMBIA ("My Aim Is True"/ "This Year's Model")............. 75-125 79
(Picture disc. No number given.)
COLUMBIA (529 "Live at Hollywood High") 30-45 79
COLUMBIA (958 "Tom Snyder Interview")................................ 25-35 81
COLUMBIA (1318 "Almost Blue") 25-35 81
COLUMBIA (35709 "Armed Forces")................................ 20-25 79
(With programming sticker on cover.)
COLUMBIA/COSTELLO (847 "Taking Liberties")............................ 30-35 80
KING BISCUIT FLOWER HOUR (For July 13, 1980)................................. 75-125
WESTWOOD ONE ("Off the Record")................................ 40-60

Also see CLIFF, Jimmy, Elvis Costello & Attractions
Also see HIATT, John
Also see NICK & ELVIS
Also see WHEELER, Caron

COTTON, Gene

P&R '74

Singles: 7–inch

ABC.. 3-5 75-77
ARIOLA AMERICA....................... 3-5 77-79
GENE COTTON ("Child of Peace").......................................4-6 81
(No actual label name or number. A gift to radio stations. With explanatory insert.)
KNOLL 3-4 81-82
MYRRH.......................................3-5 74

LPs: 10/12–inch 33rpm

ABC..8-10 76-77
ACCORD 5-10 83
ARIOLA AMERICA 5-10 78-79
BUDDAH.....................................8-10 74-75
CAPITOL.....................................8-10 71
IMPACT 15-20
KNOLL 5-10 81-82
MYRRH.......................................8-10 73

COTTON, Gene, & Kim Carnes

P&R '78

Singles: 7–inch

ARIOLA AMERICA 3-4 78

Also see CARNES, Kim
Also see COTTON, Gene

COTTON, James

(James Cotton Blues Band; with Matt "Guitar" Murphy & Luther Tucker)

LP '67

Singles: 12–inch 33/45rpm

ERECT...4-6 82

Singles: 78rpm

SUN (199 "My Baby") 75-100 54
SUN (206 "Cotton Crop Blues").50-75 54

Singles: 7–inch

BUDDAH.....................................3-5 75
LOMA....................................10-15 66
SUN (199 "My Baby") 300-400 54
SUN (206 "Cotton Crop Blues")..........................250-350 54
VERVE/FOLKWAYS......................4-8 67
VERVE/FORECAST 4-8 67-69

LPs: 10/12–inch 33rpm

ACCORD 5-10 83
ALLIGATOR..................................5-10 84
ANTONE'S..................................5-10 88
BUDDAH..................................10-12 74-76
CAPITOL..................................10-12 71
ERECT.......................................5-10 82
INTERMEDIA.............................5-10 84
VANGUARD..............................10-15 68
VERVE/FOLKWAYS.................10-20 67
VERVE/FORECAST 10-15 66-69

Also see WATERS, Muddy

COTTON, James, Carey Bell, Junior Wells, & Billy Branch

LPs: 10/12–inch 33rpm

ALLIGATOR (4790 "Harp Attack") 5-10 90

Also see BELL, Carey
Also see WELLS, Junior

COTTON, Josie

P&R/LP '82

Singles: 12-inch 33/45rpm

BOMP.................................... 5-10 80
ELEKTRA (11538 "Johnny Are You Queer") 5-10 82

Singles: 7-inch

ELEKTRA (Black vinyl) 3-4 82-84
ELEKTRA (Colored vinyl)........... 5-10 82
WEA (79292 "Johnny Are You Queer")...................................... 3-5 82

Picture Sleeves

ELEKTRA...................................... 3-4 82-84
WEA (79292 "Johnny Are You Queer") 3-5 82

LPs: 10/12-inch 33rpm

ELEKTRA.................................. 5-10 82

COTTON, LLOYD & CHRISTIAN

P&R '75

Singles: 7-inch

20TH FOX.................................. 3-5 75-76

LPs: 10/12-inch 33rpm

20TH FOX................................ 8-12 75-76

Members: Darryl Cotton; Michael Lloyd; Chris Christian.

Also see CHRISTIAN, Chris

COUCHOIS

LP '79

Singles: 7-inch

W.B. 3-4 79-80

LPs: 10/12-inch 33rpm

W.B. 5-10 79-80

COUGAR, John: see MELLENCAMP, John Cougar

COULTER, Clifford

R&B '80

Singles: 7-inch

COLUMBIA 3-4 80

LPs: 10/12-inch 33rpm

COLUMBIA 5-10 80

COUNT BASIE: see BASIE, Count

COUNT FIVE

P&R/LP '66

Singles: 7-inch

DOUBLE-SHOT (104 "Psychotic Reaction") 8-12 66
(Label name at top.)
DOUBLE-SHOT (104 "Psychotic Reaction") 4-6 66
(Label name on left side.)
DOUBLE-SHOT (106 thru 141)... 5-10 66-69

LPs: 10/12-inch 33rpm

DOUBLE-SHOT (1001 "Psychotic Reaction") 25-35 66
(Monaural.)
DOUBLE-SHOT (5001 "Psychotic Reaction")..............................30-40 66
(Stereo.)

COUNTRY BOYS & City Girls

R&B '76

Singles: 7-inch

HAPPY FOX 3-5 76

Member: Lee Maye.

COUNTRY COALITION

P&R '70

Singles: 7-inch

ABC...3-5 70-73
ABC/BLUESWAY..........................3-5 70

LPs: 10/12-inch 33rpm

ABC/BLUESWAY......................10-12 70

COUNTRY HAMS

Singles: 7-inch

EMI (3977 "Walking in the Park with Eloise")....................10-20 74

Picture Sleeves

EMI (3977 "Walking in the Park with Eloise")....................50-60 74

Promotional Singles

EMI (3977 "Walking in the Park with Eloise")....................25-35 74

Members: Paul McCartney & Wings; Chet Atkins; Floyd Cramer.

Also see ATKINS, Chet
Also see CRAMER, Floyd
Also see McCARTNEY, Paul

COUNTRY JOE & FISH

P&R/LP '67

Singles: 7-inch

VANGUARD...............................5-10 67-69

Picture Sleeves

VANGUARD...............................8-15 68

EPs: 7-inch 33/45rpm

RAG BABY (1001 "Rag Baby")..30-40 66
RAG BABY (1002 "Rag Baby")..30-40 66
RAG BABY (1003 "Rag Baby")..30-40 66

LPs: 10/12-inch 33rpm

FANTASY 8-10 75-77
VANGUARD (Except 9266).......10-20 67-71
VANGUARD (9266 "I Feel Like I'm Fixin' to Die")......................20-30 67
(With cut-out pictures and poster game.)
VANGUARD (9266 "I Feel Like I'm Fixin' to Die") 10-20 67
(Without pictures and poster.)

Members: Country Joe McDonald; David Cohen; Mark Kapner; Barry Melton; Bob Steele; Richard Saunders; Mark Ryan.

Also see BLUE, David
Also see McDONALD, Country Joe

COUNTS

R&B '54

Singles: 78rpm

DOT 10-20 53-56
NOTE (20000 "Sweet Names")..20-40 56

Singles: 7-inch

DOT (1199 "Hot Tamales") 20-40 51
DOT (1188 "Darling Dear") 30-40 53
DOT (1210 "My Dear, My Darling") 30-40 54
DOT (1226 "Baby, I Want You") 30-40 54
DOT (1235 "Let Me Go Lover"). 20-30 54
DOT (1243 "From This Day On") 20-30 55
DOT (1265 "Sally Walker")....... 15-25 55
DOT (1275 "Heartbreaker")....... 15-25 56
DOT (16105 "Darling Dear") 10-15 60
NOTE (20000 "Sweet Names") 100-150 56

COUNTS

LP '72

Singles: 7-inch

AWARE 3-5 74
WESTBOUND 3-5 72
YES (103 "Ask the Lonely") 8-10

LPs: 10/12-inch 33rpm

AWARE 8-10 75
AWARE/GRC 8-10 73
GRC 8-10 73
TCB 4-8
WESTBOUND 8-10 72

COURTNEY, David

LP '75

LPs: 10/12-inch 33rpm

U.A. 8-10 75

COURTNEY, Lou

(Lew Courtney)

P&R/R&B '67

Singles: 7-inch

BUDDAH 10-15 69
EPIC 3-5 73-75
HURDY GURDY 3-5
IMPERIAL 5-10 63-64
PHILIPS (40287 "I Watched You Slowly Slip Away") 50-100 65
POP SIDE 5-10 67
RAGS 4-8 73
RIVERSIDE 5-10 66-67
VERVE 5-10 68

LPs: 10/12-inch 33rpm

EPIC 8-10 74
RCA 8-10 76
RIVERSIDE 15-20 67

COURTSHIP

P&R '72

Singles: 7-inch

CAPITOL 3-5 70
GLADES 3-5 72
TAMLA 3-5 72

COUSIN ICE

D&D '85

Singles: 12-inch 33/45rpm

URBAN ROCK 4-6 85

COVAY, Don

(With the Goodtimers; with Jefferson Lemon Blues Band; Don "Pretty Boy" Covay)

P&R '62

Singles: 7-inch

ARNOLD (1002 "Pony Time") 10-15 61
ATLANTIC 5-10 65-70
BIG TOP 8-12 60
BLAZE (350 "Standing in the Doorway") 20-30 58
CAMEO 8-15 62-63
COLUMBIA (42197 "Now That I Need You") 75-100 61
LANDA 5-10 64
MERCURY 3-6 72-75
NEWMAN 3-4 80
PARKWAY 5-10 63-64
PHILADELPHIA INT'L 3-6 76
ROSEMART 5-10 64
SUE (709 "Believe It Or Not") 20-30 58
U-VON 3-6 77

LPs: 10/12-inch 33rpm

ATLANTIC 15-25 65-69
JANUS 8-12 72
MERCURY 8-10 74
PHILADELPHIA INT'L 8-10 76
VERSATILE 8-10 78

Also see GOODTIMERS
Also see PRETTY BOY
Also see SOUL CLAN

COVEN

P&R '71

Singles: 7-inch

BUDDAH 3-5 74
LION 3-5 71
MGM 3-5 71-73
MERCURY 3-6 69
SGC 5-8 68
W.B. 3-5 71-73

LPs: 10/12-inch 33rpm

BUDDAH 8-10 74
MGM 10-12 71-72
MERCURY 12-15 69

Members: Jinx Dawson; Teresa Kelly.

COVER GIRLS

P&R/R&B/LP '87

Singles: 7-inch

FEVER 3-4 87-88

Picture Sleeves

FEVER 3-4 87-88

LPs: 10/12-inch 33rpm

CAPITOL 5-8 89-90
FEVER 5-10 87

COWARD, Noel

LP '56

LPs: 10/12–inch 33rpm

COLUMBIA (5063 "Noel Coward at Las Vegas") 20-30 55

COWBOY COPAS: see COPAS, Cowboy

COWBOY CHURCH SUNDAY SCHOOL

P&R '55

Singles: 78rpm

DECCA 3-5 54-55
VOSS 3-5 54

Singles: 7–inch

DECCA 5-10 54-55
VOSS 5-10 54

Picture Sleeves

DECCA 10-20 54

EPs: 7–inch 33/45rpm

DECCA 8-12 55

COWBOY JUNKIES

LP '89

LPs: 10/12–inch 33rpm

RCA 5-8 89-90

COWSILLS

P&R/LP '67

Singles: 7–inch

JODA (103 "All I Really Want to Be Is Me") 10-20 65
LONDON 3-4 71-72
MGM 3-5 67-71
PHILIPS 4-8 66-67

Picture Sleeves

MGM 4-8 67-69
PHILIPS 5-10 66

EPs: 7–inch 33/45rpm

MGM (1 "The Cowsills") 15-25 68
(Promotional issue from the American Dairy Assocaition.)

LPs: 10/12–inch 33rpm

LONDON 8-10 71
MGM 10-12 67-71
WING 10-12 68

Members: Bill Cowsill; Barry Cowsill; John Cowsill; Susan Cowsill; Bob Cowsill; Paul Cowsill; Barbara Cowsill.

Also see COWSILL, Bill
Also see COWSILL, John
Also see COWSILL, Susan

COX, Wally

P&R '53

Singles: 78rpm

RCA 3-5 53

Singles: 7–inch

ARVEE 4-8 60
GEORGE 4-8 61
RCA (5278 "What a Crazy Guy") 5-10 53
WAND 3-5 70

Picture Sleeves

RCA (5278 "What a Crazy Guy") 10-20 53

COXON'S ARMY

LPs: 10/12–inch 33rpm

TRACE ("Coxson's Army") 100-200 75
(No selection number used.)

Members: Phil Coxson; Pat Benatar.
Also see BENATAR, Pat

COYOTE SISTERS

P&R '84

Singles: 7–inch

MOROCCO 3-4 84

Picture Sleeves

MOROCCO 3-4 84

LPs: 10/12–inch 33rpm

MOROCCO 5-10 84

Members: Leah Kunkel; Marty Gwinn; Renee Armand.

CRABBY APPLETON

P&R/LP '70

Singles: 7–inch

ELEKTRA 3-5 70-72

LPs: 10/12–inch 33rpm

ELEKTRA 8-10 70-71

Member: Michael Fennelly.

CRACK the SKY

LP '76

Singles: 12–inch 33/45rpm

GRUDGE 4-8 88
(Promotional only.)

Singles: 7–inch

GRUDGE 3-4 88-90
LIFESONG 3-5 76-79

LPs: 10/12–inch 33rpm

GRUDGE 5-8 88-90
LIFESONG (Except 8000 series) 10-15 75-78
LIFESONG (8000 series) 5-10 81

Members: Rick Withowski; Joe Macre; Joe D'Amico.

CRADDOCK, Billy "Crash

(Billy Craddock "Crash" Craddock; Billy Graddock)

P&R '59

Singles: 7–inch

ABC 3-5 72-78
ABC/DOT 3-5 75-77
ATLANTIC 3-4 89
CAPITOL 3-5 78-82
CARTWHEEL 3-5 71-72
CEE CEE 3-4 83
CHART 3-6 67-73
COLONIAL 10-15 58
COLUMBIA 5-10 59-60
DATE 8-12 58
KING (Except 5912) 5-10 64-65
KING (5912 "Betty Betty") 15-25 64

MERCURY 5-10 61-62
SKY CASTLE ("Smacky Mouth")........................... 20-30
(No selection number used. Shows Columbia identification numbers, 26671/26672.)

Picture Sleeves

COLUMBIA (41470 "Don't Destroy Me") 15-25 59
COLUMBIA (41619 "All I Want Is You") 15-25 60

EPs: 7–inch 33/45rpm

ABC... 4-8 74
(Jukebox issue only.)

LPs: 10/12–inch 33rpm

ABC... 6-10 72-78
ABC/AT EASE.......................... 10-12 78
(Special issue for the Armed Forces.)
ABC/DOT 8-10 76-77
CAPITOL.. 5-10 78-83
CARTWHEEL.............................. 10-12 71-72
CHART 8-12 73
HARMONY.............................. 10-12 73
KING (912 "I'm Tore Up").......... 45-55 64
STARDAY 8-10
MCA 5-10 82

CRAMER, Floyd

(With the Louisiana Hayride Band; with Keyboard Kick Band)

P&R '54

Singles: 78rpm

ABBOTT.. 3-5 53-54
MGM 3-5 55-57

Singles: 7–inch

ABBOTT 5-10 53-54
MGM 5-8 55-57
RCA (Except 7000 & 8000 series) 3-5 67-81
RCA (7000 & 8000 series) 4-8 61-66

Picture Sleeves

RCA.. 6-12 61-63

EPs: 7–inch 33/45rpm

MGM 8-12 57
RCA.. 5-10 61-63

LPs: 10/12–inch 33rpm

ALSHIRE 8-12 68
CAMDEN....................................... 6-12 65-74
MGM (3500 series) 15-20 57
MGM (4200 series) 10-15 64
MGM (4600 series) 8-12 70
RCA (0100 thru 4000 series) 5-10 73-81
(With "AHL1," ANL1," "APD1," "APL1," or "AYL1" prefix.)
RCA (2000 thru 4000 series) 10-20 60-73
(With "LPM" or "LSP" prefix.)
Also see ANN-MARGRET
Also see ATKINS, Chet, Floyd Cramer & Danny Davis
Also see ATKINS, Chet, Floyd Cramer & Boots Randolph
Also see COUNTRY HAMS
Also see FRANCIS, Connie
Also see KERR, Anita
Also see PRESLEY, Elvis
Also see REEVES, Jim
Also see SOME of CHET'S FRIENDS

CRAMER, Floyd / Peter Nero / Frankie Carle

LPs: 10/12–inch 33rpm

RCA 10-15 63
Also see CRAMER, Floyd
Also see NERO, Peter

CRAMPTON SISTERS

P&R '64

Singles: 7–inch

ABC...4-8 66
DCP 5-10 64

CRANE, Les

P&R/LP '71

Singles: 7–inch

W.B. 3-5 71

Picture Sleeves

W.B. 4-8 71

LPs: 10/12–inch 33rpm

W.B. 5-10 71

CRAWFORD, Carolyn

R&B '65

Singles: 7–inch

MERCURY 3-4 79
MOTOWN (1050 "Forget About Me") 20-30 63
MOTOWN (1064 "My Smile Is Just a Frown Turned Upside Down") 25-35 64
MOTOWN (1064 "My Smile Is Just a Frown [Turned Upside Down]") 15-20 64
(Repressing—note title variation.)
MOTOWN (1070 "My Heart").....30-40 64
PHILADELPHIA INT'L....................3-5 74-75
Also see CHAPTER 8

CRAWFORD, Hank

LP '64

Singles: 7–inch

ATLANTIC......................................3-8 61-70
KUDU 3-5 72

LPs: 10/12–inch 33rpms

ATLANTIC...................................10-20 61-73
KUDU..10-12 72-76

CRAWFORD, Johnny

P&R '61

Singles: 7–inch

ABC...3-4 73
CINDY 4-6
COLLECTABLES..............................3-4 81
DEL-FI...5-10 61-64
SIDEWALK 4-8 67-68
WYNNE (124 "Ask")...................10-15 60

Picture Sleeves

DEL-FI.......................................10-15 61-63
SIDEWALK 5-8 68

EPs: 7–inch 33/45rpm

GRASON (6515 "The Restless Ones") 10-15 66

LPs: 10/12–inch 33rpm

DEL-FI (1220 "The Captivating Johnny Crawford") 20-30 62
DEL-FI (1223 "A Young Man's Fancy") 20-30 62
DEL-FI (1224 "Rumors") 20-30 63
DEL-FI (1229 "Greatest Hits")... 20-30 63
DEL-FI (1248 "Greatest Hits, Vol. 2") 20-30 63
GUEST STAR 15-20 63
RHINO 5-10 82
SUPREME (110 "Songs from *The Restless Ones*) 15-20 66
(Soundtrack. Monaural.)
SUPREME (210 "Songs from *The Restless Ones*) 20-30 66
(Soundtrack. Stereo.)

CRAWFORD, Michael

LP '88

LPs: 10/12–inch 33rpm

COLUMBIA 5-8 88

CRAWFORD, Randy

R&B '79

Singles: 12–inch 33/45rpm

W.B. 4-6 83

Singles: 7–inch

COLUMBIA 3-5 72-73
MCA 3-4 81
W.B. 3-5 77-86

Picture Sleeves

COLUMBIA 3-5 72

LPs: 10/12–inch 33rpm

RCA 5-10 84
W.B. 8-10 76-89
Also see CRUSADERS
Also see JARREAU, Al, & Randy Crawford
Also see SPRINGFIELD, Rick, & Randy Crawford

CRAWLER: see BACK STREET CRAWLER

CRAY, Robert
(Robert Cray Band)

LP '86

Singles: 12–inch 33/45rpm

MERCURY 4-8 88
(Promotional only.)

Singles: 7–inch

MERCURY 3-4 87-88

Picture Sleeves

MERCURY 3-4 87-88

LPs: 10/12–inch 33rpm

HIGHTONE 5-10 83-87
MERCURY 5-10 86
TOMATO 10-20 80
Also see COLLINS, Albert, Robert Cray & Johnny Copeland

CRAY, Robert, Band, & Memphis Horns

LP '90

LPs: 10/12–inch 33rpm

MERCURY 5-8 90
Also see CRAY, Robert
Also see MEMPHIS HORNS

CRAYTON, Pee Wee

R&B '48

Singles: 78rpm

ALADDIN 10-20 51
FLAIR 10-15 55
4 STAR 10-20 47
IMPERIAL 10-15 54-55
MODERN 8-12 49-51
POST 8-12 55
RECORDED in HOLLYWOOD .. 10-20 54
VEE JAY 8-12 56-57

Singles: 7–inch

ALADDIN (3112 "When It Rains It Pours") 50-100 51
EDCO (1009 "Ev'ry Night 'Bout This Time") 20-30
EDCO (1010 "Money Tree") 20-30
FLAIR (1061 "Central Avenue Blues") 10-20 55
(By Pee Wee Crayton even though shown as by the Carroll County Boys. The flip, *Dizzy*, is by the Carroll County Boys.)
FOX (10069 "Give Me One More Chance") 15-25
GUYDEN 5-10 61
IMPERIAL (5288 "Do Unto Others") 25-40 54
IMPERIAL (5297 "Win-o") 25-40 54
IMPERIAL (5321 "I Need Your Love") 25-40 54
IMPERIAL (5338 "My Idea About You") 25-40 55
IMPERIAL (5345 "Eyes Full of Tears") 25-40 55
IMPERIAL (5353 "Yours Truly"). 25-40 55
JAMIE 3-5 61
MODERN 20-30 51
POST (2007 "I Must Go On")..... 20-30 55
RECORDED in HOLLYWOOD (408 "Pappy's Blues") 50-75 54
RECORDED in HOLLYWOOD (426 "Baby Pat the Floor") 50-75 54
SMASH 4-8 62
VEE JAY (214 "Frosty Night").... 25-35 56
VEE JAY (252 "I Found Peace of Mind") 25-35 57
VEE JAY (266 "Fiddle De Dee") 25-35 57

LPs: 10/12–inch 33rpm

CROWN (5175 "Pee Wee Crayton") 40-50 59
MURRAY BROTHERS 5-10 83

VANGUARD........................... 8-12 71

CRAZY ELEPHANT

P&R '69

Singles: 7–inch

BELL 4-8 69-70
SPHERE SOUND 4-6 69

LPs: 10/12–inch 33rpm

BELL 15-20 69
Member: Robert Spencer.

CRAZY HORSE

LP '71

Singles: 7–inch

EPIC........................... 3-5 72
M.O.C........................... 4-8
REPRISE 3-5 71-72

LPs: 10/12–inch 33rpm

EPIC........................... 8-12 72-76
RCA........................... 5-10 78
REPRISE 10-15 71-72
Members: Ralph Molina; Billy Talbot; Leon Whitsell; George Whitsell; Ry Cooder; Mike Curtis; Greg Leroy; Bob Notkoff; Neil Young.
Also see YOUNG, Neil

CRAZY OTTO

P&R/LP '55

Singles: 78rpm

DECCA........................... 3-5 55-57

Singles: 7–inch

DECCA........................... 4-8 55-61
MGM 3-5 62

EPs: 7–inch 33/45rpm

DECCA........................... 5-10 55-58

LPs: 10/12–inch 33rpm

DECCA........................... 8-18 55-61
MGM 6-12 63
VOCALION........................... 8-10 59

CRAZY WORLD of ARTHUR BROWN: see BROWN, Arthur

CREACH, Papa John

LP '72

Singles: 7–inch

BUDDAH........................... 3-5 76
DJM........................... 3-4 79
GRUNT 3-5 71-72

LPs: 10/12–inch 33rpm

BUDDAH........................... 8-12 75-77
DJM........................... 6-10 77-78
GRUNT 10-15 71-74
Also see HOT TUNA
Also see JEFFERSON STARSHIP

CREAM

LP '67

Singles: 7–inch

ATCO 4-8 67-70

EPs: 7–inch 33/45rpm

ATCO ("Goodbye Cream")........ 10-15 69
(Promotional issue only.)

LPs: 10/12–inch 33rpm

ATCO (206 "Fresh Cream").......25-35 67
(With *I Feel Free*. On RSO reissues, this track is replaced with *Spoonful*.)
ATCO (206 "Fresh Cream").......10-20 67
(Without *I Feel Free*.)
ATCO (232 "Disraeli Gears") 20-30 67
ATCO (291 "Best of Cream").....20-30 69
ATCO (328 "Live Cream")..........20-30 70
ATCO (700 "Wheels of Fire").....20-30 68
ATCO (7001 "Goodbye") 20-30 69
ATCO (7005 "Live Cream, Vol. 2") 20-30 72
MFSL (066 "Wheels of Fire") 30-40 82
POLYDOR 10-12 72-73
RSO (Except 015)...........................5-10 72-83
RSO (015 "Classic Cuts") 35-45 75
(Promotional issue only.)
SPRINGBOARD 10-12
Members: Eric Clapton; Jack Bruce; Ginger Baker.
Also see BAKER, Ginger
Also see BRUCE, Jack
Also see CLAPTON, Eric

CREATIVE SOURCE

R&B '73

Singles: 7–inch

POLYDOR 3-5 75
SUSSEX 3-5 73-74

LPs: 10/12–inch 33rpm

POLYDOR 8-10 75-76
SUSSEX 10-12 74
Members: Don Wyatt; Celeste Rhodes; Steve Flanagan; Barbara Berryman; Barbara Lewis.
Also see COLTS

CREATURES

LP '90

LPs: 10/12–inch 33rpm

GEFFEN 5-8 90

CREEDENCE CLEARWATER REVIVAL

P&R/LP '68

Singles: 12–inch 33/45rpm

FANTASY (238 "Creedence Medley")...........................10-15 85
FANTASY (759 "I Heard It Through the Grapevine")...........................15-20 76
(Promotional issue only.)

Singles: 7–inch

FANTASY (Except 2832)..............3-6 69-85
FANTASY (2832 "45 Revolutions Per Minute")...........................40-60 70
LIBERTY 3-5
SCORPIO (412 "Porterville") 15-25 68

Picture Sleeves

FANTASY (Except 2832)............5-10 69-76
FANTASY (2832 "45 Revolutions Per Minute")...........................20-25 70

LPs: 10/12-inch 33rpm

BEVERLY ("Willie and the Poor Boys") 75-100
(Half-speed mastered. Number not known.)
FANTASY (1 thru 70) 8-15 73-78
FANTASY (4500 series) 5-10 80-85
(Includes reissues of 8382 through 9404.)
FANTASY (8382 thru 9404) 8-15 68-72
FANTASY (9418 thru 9621) 5-10 72-82
K-TEL 8-12 78
MFSL (037 "Cosmo's Factory"). 30-50 79
SWEET THUNDER (13 "Green River") 75-100 75
(Half-speed mastered.)
W.B. SPECIAL PRODUCTS (3514 "Greatest Hits") 10-15 85
(TV mail-order offer.)

Members: John Fogerty; Tom Fogerty; Doug Clifford; Stuart Cook.
Also see FOGERTY, John
Also see FOGERTY, Tom
Also see GOLLIWOGS
Also see HARRISON, Don, Band

CREME, Lol, & Kevin Godley: see GODLEY, Kevin, & Lol Creme

CREME D'COCOA

R&B '78

Singles: 7-inch

VENTURE 3-5 78-80

LPs: 10/12-inch 33rpm

VENTURE 8-10 79
Also see AMBASSADORS
Also see EBONYS

CRENSHAW, Marshall

P&R/LP '82

Singles: 12-inch 33/45rpm

SHAKE (104 "Marshall Crenshaw") 20-25 81
W.B. 5-10 82

Singles: 7-inch

W.B. 3-4 82-85

LPs: 10/12-inch 33rpm

W.B. 5-10 82-85

CREOLE, Kid: see KID CREOLE

CRESCENDOS

P&R/R&B '58

Singles: 78rpm

NASCO 5-10 57

Singles: 7-inch

ABC 3-4 73
MCA 3-4 84
NASCO (6005 "Oh Julie") 10-20 57
NASCO (6009 "School Girl") 10-20 58
NASCO (6021 "Young and in Love") 10-20 58
SCARLET 10-15 60-61
TAP (7027 "Oh Julie") 10-15 57

Picture Sleeves

NASCO (6009 "School Girl") 20-30 58
NASCO (6021 "Young and in Love") 20-30 58
TAP (7027 "Oh Julie") 15-25 57

LPs: 10/12-inch 33rpm

GUEST STAR (1453 "Oh Julie") 20-30 62

Members: George Lanuis; Ken Brigham; James Hall; Tommy Fortner.
Also see 4 SEASONS

CRESCENTS

(Chiyo & Crescents)

P&R '63

Singles: 7-inch

BREAK OUT (4 "Pink Dominos") 15-25 63
(With straight horizontal lines.)
BREAK OUT (4 "Pink Dominos") 15-20 63
(With jagged horizontal lines.)
ERA (3116 "Pink Dominos") 5-10 63

CRESTS

(Original Crests; with Al Browne & His Orchestra)

P&R '57

Singles: 78rpm

JOYCE 103 ("Sweetest One") .50-100 57
JOYCE 105 ("No One to Love") 75-125 57

Singles: 7-inch

ABC 3-4 73
APT 5-10 65
CAMEO 5-10 63-64
COED (Except 501) 10-20 58-62
COED (501 "Pretty Little Angel") 50-75 58
COLLECTABLES 3-4 81-83
CORAL (62403 "You Blew Out the Candles") 15-25 64
ERIC 3-4 73
GOLDIES 45 3-4
HARVEY (501 "16 Candles") 5-10 81
(Colored vinyl.)
JOYCE 103 ("Sweetest One") 100-150 57
(With the oversize letter "Y" in the Joyce logo.)
JOYCE 103"(Sweetest One") 15-25
(With all of the letters the same size in the Joyce logo.)
JOYCE 105"(No One to Love") 100-125 57
KING TUT 4-8
LANA 3-6 64
LOST-NITE 3-5
MCA 3-4 73
MUSICTONE 5-10 62
ORIGINAL SOUND 3-4 87
SELMA (311 "Guilty") 10-20 62
SELMA (4000 "Did I Remember") 20-30 63

TIMES SQUARE (2 "No One to Love") 15-20 62
(Colored vinyl.)
TIMES SQUARE (6 "Baby") 12-15 64
(Selection number on both sides is 6.)
TIMES SQUARE (97 "Baby") 15-20 64
(Selection number on B-side is 6.)
TRANS ATLAS 10-20 62
TRIP 3-5 70s

EPs: 7–inch 33/45rpm

COED (101 "The Angels Listened In") 300-350 59

LPs: 10/12–inch 33rpm

COED (901 "The Crests Sing All Biggies") 200-250 60
COED (904 "Best of the Crests") 150-200 60
COLLECTABLES (5009 "Greatest Hits") 8-10 82
COLLECTABLES (5009 "Greatest Hits") 10-15 82
(Picture disc.)
POST 8-12 70s
RHINO 5-10 90

Members: Johnny Maestro; Tom Gough; Harold Torres; Jay Carter; James Ancrum.
Also see MAESTRO, Johnny

CRESTS / Skyliners

Singles: 7–inch

ORIGINAL SOUND 3-4 84

Also see SKYLINERS

CRESTS / Cal York & Roamers

Singles: 7–inch

HIT 5-15 60s

Also see CRESTS

CRETONES

P&R/LP '80

Singles: 7–inch

PLANET 3-4 80-81

Picture Sleeves

PLANET 3-4 80

LPs: 10/12–inch 33rpm

PLANET 5-10 80-81

CREW-CUTS

P&R '54

Singles: 78rpm

MERCURY 4-6 54-57

Singles: 7–inch

ABC-PAR 4-6 63
CHESS 4-6 64
FIREBIRD 3-5 70
MERCURY 5-10 54-57
RCA 4-8 58-60
VEE JAY 4-6 63
WARWICK 4-8 60-61
WHALE 4-6 62

EPs: 7–inch 33/45rpm

MERCURY 10-20 54-57

LPs: 10/12–inch 33rpm

CAMAY 10-15
MERCURY 25-50 55-56
PICCADILLY 8-10 80
RCA 20-30 59-60
WING 15-25 59-60

Members: Ray Perkins; John Perkins; Rudi Maugeri; Pat Barrett.
Also see COASTERS / Crew-Cuts / Chiffons

CREW-CUTS / Junior Powell & Charlotte Grubic

LPs: 10/12–inch 33rpm

RCA CUSTOM ("The Crew-Cuts Have a Ball") 20-30 59
(Special products issue for Ebonite Co. One side has "Bowling Tips By Top Stars")

Also see CREW-CUTS

CREWE, Bob

(Bob Crewe Generation; B.C.G.; with Rays)

P&R '60

Singles: 78rpm

CORAL 3-6 56

Singles: 7–inch

ABC-PAR 5-10 61
DYNO VOICE 3-6 66-68
CORAL 8-10 56
CREWE 3-5 71
ELEKTRA 3-5 76-77
ERIC 3-4 73
JUBILEE 8-12 54
MELBA 8-12 57
METROMEDIA 3-5 72
SPOTLIGHT 15-25 56
20TH FOX 3-5 76
U.T. 8-12 59
VIK 5-10 57
WARWICK 5-10 59-61

Picture Sleeves

DYNO VOICE 3-6 67

LPs: 10/12–inch 33rpm

CGC 10-12 70
CREWE 10-15
DYNO VOICE 10-12 67-68
ELEKTRA 8-10 76-77
GAMBLE 3-4 69
PHILLIPS (200150 "All the Song Hits of the 4 Seasons") 15-20 64
(Monaural. Includes lyrics sheet.)
PHILLIPS (200238 "The 4 Seasons Hits") 10-15 67
(Monaural.)
PHILLIPS (600150 "All the Song Hits of the 4 Seasons") 15-20 64
(Stereo. Includes lyrics sheet.)
PHILLIPS (600238 "The 4 Seasons Hits") 10-15 67
(Stereo.)
WARWICK 15-25 60-61

Also see LA ROSA, Julius, & Bob Crew Generation

CRICKETS

R&B '53

Singles: 78rpm

JAY-DEE 25-35 53
MGM 20-30 53

Singles: 7–inch

DAVIS (459 "I'm Going to Live My Life Alone") 40-60 58
JAY-DEE (777 "Dreams and Wishes") 100-150 53
JAY-DEE (781 "I'm Not the One You Love") 100-150 53
MGM (11428 "You're Mine") ... 75-125 53
MGM (11507 "For You I Have Eyes") 75-125 53

LPs: 10/12–inch 33rpm

RELIC 8-12

Members: Harold Johnson; Leon Carter; Eugene Stapleton; Rodney Jackson; Grover "Dean" Barlow; J.R. Bailey; Robert Spencer; Freddy Barksdale; Robert Bynum; William Lindsay; Joe Dias.

Also see BARLOW, Dean, & Crickets
Also see CADILLACS

CRICKETS

Singles: 7–inch

BARNABY 15-25 72
BRUNSWICK (55124 "Love's Made a Fool of You") 15-25 59
BRUNSWICK (55153 "When You Ask About Love") 15-25 59
CORAL (62198 "More Than I Can Say") 15-25 60
EPIC (08028 "T-Shirt") 3-4 88
LIBERTY 10-20 61-65
(Black, commercial labels)
LIBERTY 15-25 61-65
(Cream or white labels. Promotional issues only.)
MGM 10-15 73
MUSIC FACTORY 15-20 68

Note: Records by Buddy Holly & Crickets, even if credited only to the Crickets, are listed in the BUDDY HOLLY section.

Promotional Singles

BRUNSWICK (55124 "Love's Made a Fool of You") 20-30 59
BRUNSWICK (55153 "When You Ask About Love") 20-30 59
CORAL (62198 "More Than I Can Say") 20-30 60
EPIC (08028 "T-Shirt") 3-4 88

EPs: 7–inch 33/45rpm

B.H.M.S. 3-6 78
CORAL (81192 "Crickets") 75-100 63
(With Buddy Holly on one track, *It's Too Late.*)

LPs: 10/12–inch 33rpm

BARNABY (30268 "Rockin' '50s Rock & Roll") 15-25 70
CORAL (57320 "In Style") 40-60 60
KOALA 8-10
LIBERTY (3272 "Something Old, Something New, Something Blue, Somethin' Else") 30-40 64
(Monaural.)
LIBERTY (3351 "California Sun") 30-40 64
(Monaural.)
LIBERTY (7272 "Something Old, Something New, Something Blue, Somethin' Else") 40-50 64
(Stereo.)
LIBERTY (7351 "California Sun") 40-50 64
(Stereo.)
VERTIGO 10-20 73

Note: Records by Buddy Holly & Crickets, even if credited only to the Crickets, are listed in the BUDDY HOLLY section.

Members: Sonny Curtis; Jerry Naylor; Glen D. Hardin; Jerry Allison; Joe Mauldin; Earl Sinks; David Box.

Also see HOLLY, Buddy
Also see IVAN
Also see JENNINGS, Waylon
Also see NAYLOR, Jerry
Also see PRESLEY, Elvis
Also see VEE, Bobby, & Crickets

CRIMSON, King: see KING CRIMSON

CRISS, Peter

LP '78

Singles: 7–inch

CASABLANCA 3-5 79-80

LPs: 10/12–inch 33rpm

CASABLANCA (7122 "Peter Criss") 12-20 78
(With poster order form.)
CASABLANCA (7122 "Peter Criss") 8-12 78
(Without poster order form.)
CASABLANCA (7240 "Out of Control") 25-50 80

Also see KISS

CRITTERS

P&R/LP '66

Singles: 7–inch

KAPP 5-10 65-69
MCA 3-4 84
MUSICOR (1044 "Georgianna") 10-20 65
PRANCER 4-8 68
PROJECT 3 .... 4-8 67-69

Picture Sleeves

KAPP (769 "Mr. Dieingly Sad") 8-12 66
PROJECT 3 .... 4-8 67-69

LPs: 10/12–inch 33rpm

BACK-TRAC 5-10 85

KAPP (1485 "Younger Girl")...... 20-30 66
(Monaural.)
KAPP (3485 "Younger Girl")...... 25-35 66
(Stereo.)
PROJECT 3 .... 15-20 68

CRITTERS / Young Rascals / Lou Christie

LPs: 10/12–inch 33rpm

BOTIQUE.............................. 10-20 66
(Tracks shown as by the Young Rascals are actually by Felix & Escorts.)
Also see CHRISTIE, Lou
Also see CRITTERS

CROCE, Jim

P&R/LP '72

Singles: 7–inch

ABC.. 3-5 72-74
LIFESONG 3-5 75-76

Picture Sleeves

ABC.. 4-6 73

EPs: 7–inch 33/45rpm

ABC.. 10-12 73
(Jukebox issue only.)

LPs: 10/12–inch 33rpm

ABC.. 10-12 72-74
BURNS MEDIA (1-2 "The Faces I've Been")............................ 40-60 75
(Two-LP set. Promotional issue only.)
CASHWEST 8-10 77
COMMAND 12-15 74-75
LIFESONG 10-15 75-78
MFSL (079 "You Don't Mess Around with Jim")................... 25-50 82
Session: Maury Muehleisen; Tommy West; Gary Chester; Marty Nelson; Joe Macho; Terry Cashman; Ellie Greenwich; David Spinozza.
Also see CASHMAN & WEST
Also see GREENWICH, Ellie

CROCE, Jim & Ingrid

(Jim & Ingrid)

Singles: 7–inch

CAPITOL................................ 10-15 69

LPs: 10/12–inch 33rpm

CAPITOL (315 "Croce") 30-35 69
PICKWICK 5-10 70s
Also see CROCE, Jim

CROCHET, Cleveland

(With the Sugar Bees; with His Hillbilly Ramblers)

P&R '60

Singles: 7–inch

GOLDBAND 5-10 60-61
LYRIC...................................... 5-10

LPs: 10/12–inch 33rpm

GOLDBAND (7749 "Cleveland Crochet and All the Sugar Bees")............... 35-50 61

CROCKETT, G.L.

(G. Davy Crockett)

P&R/R&B '65

Singles: 78rpm

CHIEF 10-20 57

Singles: 7–inch

CHECKER (1121 "Look Out Mabel")...................................20-30 65
CHIEF (7010 "Look Out Mabel")...................................50-75 57
4 BROTHERS 5-10 65

CROOK, General

R&B '70

Singles: 7–inch

CAPITOL....................................3-6 69
DOWN to EARTH 3-6 70-71
WAND 3-5 74

LPs: 10/12–inch 33rpm

CAPITOL...................................10-15 70
WAND 10-12 74

CROSBY, Beverly

R&B '77

Singles: 7–inch

BAREBACK 3-5 77

CROSBY, Bing

(With the Andrews Sisters; with Gary Crosby; with Victor Young Orchestra; with Grady Martin & His Slew Foot Five)

P&R '31

Singles: 78rpm

BRUNSWICK...........................10-20 32-34
DECCA 5-15 34-57
KAPP 3-5 57
VICTOR 10-20 31

Singles: 7–inch

AMOS 3-5 69
CAPITOL.....................................4-6 63
COLUMBIA 4-6 59
CROWLEY'S/CROSBY ("How Lovely Is Christmas") 10-20
(Promotional issue made for Crowley's Milk Co.)
DAYBREAK 3-5 71
DECCA (23281 thru 30828).........5-10 51-59
DECCA (31000 series) 4-8 61-65
KAPP 4-6 57
LONDON......................................3-4 77
MGM 4-6 60
POLYDOR 3-4 78
RCA 4-6 60
REPRISE 4-6 64-67
U.A. 3-5 75
VERVE 4-6

Picture Sleeves

DECCA 5-10 53-63
DAYBREAK 3-5 71
KAPP 4-8 57

EPs: 7–inch 33/45rpm

BRUNSWICK 5-15 50-55
COLUMBIA 8-12 50-57
DECCA ("Old Masters") 20-30
(Boxed EP set. No number shown.)
DECCA (Except 1700) 6-15 50-59
DECCA (1700 "Deluxe Box Set") 75-100 54
(17-EP set.)
RCA 5-10 57
THREE on ONE (407 "Bing Crosby Sings 2 New Christmas Songs") 5-10 50s
(Though labeled "45 Extended Play," actually has only one song on each side. May not have been issued with cover.)
VERVE (5022 "Bing Sings While Bregman Swings") 10-15 59
(With envelope/sleeve.)

LPs: 10/12–inch 33rpm

AMOS 8-10 69
ARGO 10-15 76
BIOGRAPH 5-10 73
BRUNSWICK (54000 series) 15-25 55
BRUNSWICK (58000 series) 25-40 52
(10–inch LPs.)
CAPITOL (2300 series) 8-12 65
CAPITOL (11000 series) 5-10 77-78
CITADEL 5-10 78
COLUMBIA (43 "Bing in Hollywood") 10-15 67
COLUMBIA (2502 "Der Bingle") 20-30 56
(10–inch LP.)
COLUMBIA (6027 "Classics") ... 20-40 49
(10–inch LP.)
COLUMBIA (6105 "Classics, Vol. 2") 20-40 50
(10–inch LP.)
COLUMBIA (35000 series) 5-10 78-79
COLUMBIA SPECIAL PROD. 5-8 77
DECCA (151 "Bing Crosby, a Musical Autobiography") 50-75 65
(Boxed set. Includes booklet.)
DECCA (4000 series) 20-50 61-64
DECCA (5000 series) 15-25 49-55
(10–inch LPs.)
DECCA (6000 series) 25-50 55-56
(10–inch LPs.)
DECCA (8000 series) 15-25 54-59
(Black label with silver print.)
DECCA (8000 series) 8-15 60-72
(Black label with horizontal rainbow stripe.)
DECCA (8700 series) 8-12 64
DECCA (9000 series) 10-20 61-62
(Decca LP numbers in this series preceded by a "7" or a "DL-7" are stereo issues.)
DECCA CUSTOM (34461 "Bing Crosby") 10-20
(Promotional issue, made for La-Z-Boy.)
ENCORE 8-10 68
GOLDEN 10-15 57-59
HARMONY (7000 series) 10-15 57
HARMONY (11000 series) 5-10 69
LONDON 5-10 77
MCA 5-10 73-82
MGM 10-15 61-64
METRO 5-10 65
P.I.P. 5-10 71
POLYDOR 5-10 77
RCA (500 series) 6-10 72
RCA (1400 thru 2000 series) 10-20 57-59
(With "LPM" or "LSP" prefix.)
RCA (2000 series) 5-10 77
(With "CPL1" prefix.)
REPRISE 8-12 64
20TH FOX 5-10 79
U.A. 5-10 76
VERVE/MGM (2030 "Bing Sings While Bregman Swings") 25-50 56
VOCALION (3600 series) 10-15 57
VOCALION (3700 series) 5-10 66
W.B. 10-15 60-62
X 15-25 54

Also see ANDREWS SISTERS
Also see BOWIE, David, & Bing Crosby
Also see CROSBY, Gary, Phillip, Dennis, Lindsay & Bing
Also see DORSEY, Jimmy
Also see MARTIN, Grady, & His Slew Foot Five
Also see SINATRA, Frank, Bing Crosby & Dean Martin
Also see YOUNG, Victor

CROSBY, Bing & Gary

P&R '50

Singles: 78rpm

DECCA 3-5 50-51

Singles: 7–inch

DECCA 4-8 50-51

CROSBY, Bing, & Louis Armstrong

P&R '51

Singles: 78rpm

CAPITOL 3-5 56
DECCA 3-5 51

Singles: 7–inch

CAPITOL 4-8 56
DECCA 4-8 51
MGM 3-5 60

LPs: 10/12–inch 33rpm

MGM (100 series) 5-10 70
MGM (3800 series) 10-20 60
SOUNDS RARE 5-10 83

CROSBY, Bing, Louis Armstrong, Rosemary Clooney & Hi-Los

Singles: 7–inch

COLUMBIA (6277 "Music to Shave By") 5-10 50s
(Special products flexi-disc from Remington.)

Also see ARMSTRONG, Louis
Also see CLOONEY, Rosemary
Also see CROSBY, Bing, & Louis Armstrong

CROSBY, Bing, & Fred Astaire

LPs: 10/12-inch 33rpm

U.A. 5-8 77

Also see ASTAIRE, Fred

CROSBY, Bing, & Count Basie

LPs: 10/12-inch 33rpm

DAYBREAK.......... 8-12 72

Also see BASIE, Count

CROSBY, Bing, & Connee Boswell

P&R '37

Singles: 78rpm

DECCA.......... 4-8 37-40

LPs: 10/12-inch 33rpm

DECCA.......... 15-25 52

Also see BOSWELL, Connee

CROSBY, Bing, & Judy Garland

P&R '45

Singles: 78rpm

DECCA.......... 5-10 45

Also see GARLAND, Judy

CROSBY, Bing, Dick Haymes & Andrews Sisters

P&R '47

Singles: 78rpm

DECCA.......... 5-10 47

Also see HAYMES, Dick

CROSBY, Bing, & Bob Hope

P&R '45

Singles: 78rpm

DECCA.......... 5-10 45

EPs: 7-inch 33/45rpm

CAPITOL CUSTOM (2263 "Vacation Road to Minnesota").......... 5-10
(Issued to promote Minnesota tourism.)

Also see BAXTER, Les
Also see HOPE, Bob

CROSBY, Bing, & Louis Jordan

P&R '45

Singles: 78rpm

DECCA.......... 5-10 45

Also see JORDAN, Louis

CROSBY, Bing, & Grace Kelly

P&R '56

Singles: 78rpm

CAPITOL.......... 3-5 56

Singles: 7-inch

CAPITOL.......... 5-10 56

CROSBY, Bing / Grace Kelly / Frank Sinatra / Celeste Holm

Singles: 7-inch

CAPITOL (281 "Interviews for use with Capitol Soundtrack LP, *High Society*").......... 50-100 56
(Promotional issue only.)

CROSBY, Bing, & Peggy Lee

Singles: 78rpm

DECCA.......... 3-5 52

Singles: 7-inch

DECCA.......... 5-10 52

Also see LEE, Peggy

CROSBY, Bing, & Johnny Mercer

P&R '38

Singles: 78rpm

DECCA.......... 5-8 38-40

Also see MERCER, Johnny

CROSBY, Bing, & Mills Brothers
(With Connee Boswell)

P&R '31

Singles: 78rpm

BRUNSWICK.......... 5-10 31-32

Also see MILLS BROTHERS

CROSBY, Bing, & Frank Sinatra

Singles: 78rpm

CAPITOL.......... 3-5 56

Singles: 7-inch

CAPITOL.......... 5-10 56

Also see SINATRA, Frank

CROSBY, Bing, & Mel Torme
(With the Mel-Tones)

P&R '46

Singles: 78rpm

DECCA.......... 4-8 46

Also see TORME, Mel

CROSBY, Bing, & Orson Welles

LPs: 10/12-inch 33rpm

DECCA (6000 "The Small One, the Happy Prince").......... 10-25 50
(10-inch LP.)

Also see CROSBY, Bing
Also see WELLES, Orson

CROSBY, Chris

P&R '64

Singles: 7-inch

ATLANTIC.......... 4-8 67
CHALLENGE.......... 4-8 64-65
COLUMBIA.......... 3-6 69
DORE.......... 4-8 61
MGM.......... 4-8 64
W.B. 3-5 63

Picture Sleeves

MGM.......... 5-10 64

LPs: 10/12-inch 33rpm

MGM.......... 15-20 64

CROSBY, David

LP '71

Singles: 7-inch

ATLANTIC.......... 3-5 71

LPs: 10/12-inch 33rpm

A&M.......... 5-8 89
ATLANTIC.......... 10-15 71

Also see BYRDS
Also see GRATEFUL DEAD
Also see JEFFERSON AIRPLANE
Also see SLICK, Grace

CROSBY, David, & Graham Nash

P&R '71

Singles: 7-inch

ABC 3-5 75-77
ATLANTIC 3-5 72

LPs: 10/12-inch 33rpm

ABC 8-10 75-78
ATLANTIC 10-15 72

Also see CROSBY, David
Also see NASH, Graham

CROSBY, Eddie

C&W '49

Singles: 78rpm

DECCA 4-8 49

CROSBY, Gary

Singles: 7-inch

DECCA 5-10 55
GREGMARK (11 "That's Alright Baby") 10-15 62
HICKORY (1448 "Town Girl") 5-10 66

CROSBY, Gary, Phillip, Dennis, Lindsay & Bing

P&R '50

Singles: 78rpm

DECCA 5-8 50

Singles: 7-inch

DECCA (40181 "A Crosby Christmas") 10-15 50

Picture Sleeves

DECCA (1-134 "A Crosby Christmas") 20-40 50
(Sleeve for 45)
DECCA (796 "A Crosby Christmas") 10-20 50
(Sleeve for 78.)

Also see CROSBY, Bing
Also see CROSBY, Gary

CROSBY, STILLS & NASH

P&R/LP '69

Singles: 7-inch

ATLANTIC 3-6 69-89

Picture Sleeves

ATLANTIC 3-8 70-89

LPs: 10/12-inch 33rpm

ATLANTIC (Except 8229) 8-10 77-83
ATLANTIC (8229 "Crosby, Stills & Nash") 15-20 69

Members: David Crosby; Stephen Stills; Graham Nash.

CROSBY, STILLS, NASH & YOUNG

P&R/LP '70

Singles: 7-inch

ATLANTIC 3-5 70

Picture Sleeves

ATLANTIC 3-6 70

EPs: 7-inch 33/45rpm

ATLANTIC 10-15 70
(Jukebox issue only.)

LPs: 10/12-inch 33rpm

ATLANTIC (165 "Celebration Copy") 25-35 70s
(Promotional issue only.)
ATLANTIC (902 "4-Way Street") 12-20 71
(With photo applied to cover.)
ATLANTIC (7200 "Deja Vu") 15-20 70
(With photo applied to cover.)
ATLANTIC (7200 "Deja Vu") 8-12
(With photo printed on cover.)
ATLANTIC (16000 thru 19000 series) 5-10 74-82
ATLANTIC (8000 series) 5-10 83
MFSL (088 "Deja Vu") 25-50 82

Promotional LPs

Members: David Crosby; Stephen Stills; Graham Nash; Neil Young.

Also see CROSBY, David
Also see CROSBY, STILLS & NASH
Also see NASH, Graham
Also see STILLS, Stephen
Also see YOUNG, Neil

CROSS, Christopher

P&R/LP '80

Singles: 7-inch

COLUMBIA 3-4 85
REPRISE 3-4 88
W.B. 3-4 79-85

Picture Sleeves

REPRISE 3-4 88
W.B. 3-4 80-85

LPs: 10/12-inch 33rpm

COLUMBIA 5-10 85
REPRISE 5-8 88
W.B. 5-10 79-85

Also see McDONALD, Michael

CROSS, Jimmy

P&R '65

Singles: 7-inch

CHICKEN 4-8 65
RECORDO 5-10 61
RED BIRD 5-10 65
TOLLIE 5-10 64

CROSS COUNTRY

(Tokens)

P&R/LP '73

Singles: 7-inch

ATCO 3-6 73-74

LPs: 10/12-inch 33rpm

ATCO 10-15 73

Members: Jay Siegel; Phil Margo; Mitch Margo.

Also see TOKENS

CROUCH, Andrae

(With His Disciples)

R&B '80

Singles: 7-inch

LIGHT 3-4 76-80
W.B. 3-4 81

LPs: 10/12-inch 33rpm

ACCORD....................................82 5-8
LIGHT.. 5-8 68-82
W.B. 5-8 81

Also see JACKSON, Michael

CROW
(David Wagner)

P&R/LP '69

Singles: 7-inch

AMARET 3-6 69-72
INNER EAR (427 "Autumn of Tomorrow") 25-50

LPs: 10/12-inch 33rpm

AMARET 10-15 69-73

Members: David Wagner; Dennis Craswell.
Also see CASTAWAYS

Singles: 7-inch

WESTBOUND.................................. 3-4 79

LPs: 10/12-inch 33rpm

WESTBOUND............................... 5-10 79

CROWDED HOUSE

LP '86

Singles: 12-inch 33/45rpm

CAPITOL.. 4-6 86

Singles: 7-inch

CAPITOL.. 3-4 86-88

Picture Sleeves

CAPITOL.. 3-4 87-88

LPs: 10/12-inch 33rpm

CAPITOL...................................... 5-10 86-88

Members: Neil Finn; Paul Hester; Nick Seymour; Tim Finn.
Also see SPLIT ENZ

CROWELL, Rodney

C&W '78

Singles: 7-inch

COLUMBIA 3-4 86-90
W.B. 3-4 78-82

LPs: 10/12-inch 33rpm

COLUMBIA 5-8 86-90
W.B. 5-10 78-81

Session: Karen Brooks.
Also see HARRIS, Emmylou

CROWELL, Rodney, & Rosanne Cash

C&W '88

Singles: 7-inch

COLUMBIA 3-4 88

Also see CASH, Rosanne
Also see CROWELL, Rodney

CROWN HEIGHTS AFFAIR

R&B '74

Singles: 12-inch 33/45rpm

SBK.. 4-6 89

Singles: 7-inch

DELITE.. 3-5 75-82
RCA.. 3-5 73-74

LPs: 10/12-inch 33rpm

DELITE.. 5-10 75-82
RCA... 10-12 74-78

Members: Phil Thomas; Ray Rock; Bert Reid; James Baynard; Ray Reid; William Anderson; Howard Young; Muki Wilson.

CROWS

P&R/R&B '54

Singles: 78rpm

RAMA (3 "Seven Lonely Days").25-50 53
RAMA (5 "Gee")........................25-50 53
RAMA (10 "Heartbreaker").......50-100 53
RAMA (29 "Baby") 40-60 54
RAMA (30 "Miss You")............50-100 54
RAMA (50 "Baby Doll") 40-60 54
TICO (1082 "Mambo Shevitz")...40-60 51

Singles: 7-inch

RAMA (3 "Seven Lonely Days")..............................250-350 53
RAMA (5 "Gee")........................50-75 53
(Black vinyl. Blue label. No clouds or lines around "Rama" logo.)
RAMA (5 "Gee")........................35-50 53
(Black vinyl. Blue label. With clouds and lines around "Rama" logo.)
RAMA (5 "Gee")....................200-300 53
(Colored vinyl.)
RAMA (5 "Gee")........................15-25 56
(Red label.)
RAMA (10 "Heartbreaker").....250-350 53
(Black vinyl.)
RAMA (10 "Heartbreaker").....500-700 53
(Colored vinyl.)
RAMA (29 "Baby") 100-150 54
RAMA (30 "Miss You")..........250-350 54
(Black vinyl.)
RAMA (30 "Miss You")..........500-700 54
(Colored vinyl.)
RAMA (50 "Baby Doll") 250-350 54
TICO (1082 "Mambo Shevitz")..............................100-150 51
(Black vinyl.)
TICO (1082 "Mambo Shevitz")..............................200-300 51
(Colored vinyl.)

LPs: 10/12-inch 33rpm

MURRAY HILL.................................5-8 88

Members: Daniel "Sonny" Norton; Harold Major; Jerry Hamilton; Mark Jackson; Bill Davis.
Also see HARPTONES / Crows

CRUDUP, Big Boy
(Arthur "Big Boy" Crudup)

R&B '45

Singles: 78rpm

ACE (503 "I Wonder")...........175-225 53
BLUEBIRD 8-12 41-46
CHAMPION (108 "I Wonder") 200-250 52
GROOVE 10-15 53-54
RCA 5-10 47-53

Singles: 7-inch

FIRE..5-10 62

GROOVE (0011 "I Love My Baby") 30-40 53
GROOVE (0026 "She's Got No Hair") 30-40 54
GROOVE (5005 "Mean Ol' Frisco")................................ 30-40 54
RCA (0000 "That's All Right") 200-225 49
(Colored vinyl.)
RCA (0001 "Boy Friend Blues")................................ 50-100 49
(Colored vinyl.)
RCA (0013 "Shout Sister, Shout") 50-100 49
(Colored vinyl.)
RCA (0032 "Hoodoo Lady Blues")................................ 50-100 50
(Colored vinyl.)
RCA (0046 "Come Back Baby") 50-100 49
(Colored vinyl.)
RCA (0074 "Dust My Broom"). 50-100 50
(Colored vinyl.)
RCA (0092 "Mean Old Santa Fe") 50-100 50
(Colored vinyl.)
RCA (0100 "Lonesome World to Me") 50-100 50
(Colored vinyl.)
RCA (0105 "She's Just Like Caldonia")..................... 50-100 50
(Colored vinyl.)
RCA (0117 "Nobody Wants Me").................................... 50-100 50
(Colored vinyl.)
RCA (0126 "Roberta Blues")... 50-100 50
(Colored vinyl.)
RCA (0141 "Too Much Competition") 50-100 50
(Colored vinyl.)
RCA (4367 "Love Me Mama"). 50-100 51
RCA (4572 "Goin' Back to Georgia").............................. 50-75 52
RCA (4753 "Worried About You Baby") 50-75 52
RCA (4933 "Second Man Blues").................................. 50-75 52
RCA (5070 "Pearly Lee") 50-75 52
RCA (5167 "Keep on Drinkin'") . 50-75 53
RCA (5563 "My Wife and Women") 50-75 53

EPs: 7-inch 33/45rpm

CAMDEN (415 "Arthur 'Big Boy' Crudup")............................ 100-125 57

LPs: 10/12-inch 33rpm

COLLECTABLES......................... 6-8 88
DELMARK.............................. 15-25 69
FIRE (103 "Mean Ol' Frisco") 125-175 62
RCA.. 10-20 71
TRIP (7501 "Mean Ol' Frisco").... 8-12 75

Also see CRUDUP, Percy Lee
Also see CRUMP, Arthur
Also see JAMES, Elmore

CRUDUP, Percy Lee

(Arthur Crudup)

Singles: 78rpm

CHECKER (754 "Open Your Book")..................................20-30 52

Also see CRUDUP, Big Boy

CRUISE, Pablo: see PABLO CRUISE

CRUM, Simon

(Ferlin Husky)

C&W '55

Singles: 78rpm

CAPITOL..5-10 55-57

Singles: 7-inch

ABC..3-5 74
CAPITOL..5-15 55-63

LPs: 10/12-inch 33rpm

CAPITOL (1880 "The Unpredictable Simon Crum").................................75-100 63

Also see HUSKY, Ferlin

CRUMP, Arthur

(Arthur Crudup)

Singles: 78rpm

CHAMPION ("I Wonder")..........60-75

Also see CRUDUP, Big Boy

CRUSADERS

LP '71

Singles: 7-inch

ABC...3-4 78
BLUE THUMB................................3-5 72-77
CHISA...3-5 71
MCA...3-4 79-86
MOWEST.......................................3-5

LPs: 10/12-inch 33rpm

BLUE THUMB...........................10-12 73-77
GRP 5-8 91
MCA...8-10 79-86
MFSL (010 "Chain Reaction")....25-50 78
(Half-speed mastered.)
MOTOWN 10-12 73
MOWEST....................................10-12 72

Members: Larry Carlton; Pops Popwell.
Also see CARLTON, Larry
Also see COCKER, Joe
Also see CRAWFORD, Randy
Also see HOOPER, Stix
Also see JAZZ CRUSADERS
Also see SAMPLE, Joe

CRUSADERS & B.B. King

Singles: 7-inch

MCA...3-4 82

LPs: 10/12-inch 33rpm

MCA...8-10 82

Also see CRUSADERS
Also see KING, B.B.

CRUZADOS

LP '85

Singles: 7–inch

ARISTA 3-4 85

LPs: 10/12–inch 33rpm

ARISTA 5-10 85-87

Members: Tito Larriva; Chalo Quintana; Steve Hufsteter; Tony Marsico; Marshall Rohner.

CRYAN' SHAMES

P&R '66

Singles: 7–inch

COLUMBIA 4-8 66-70
DESTINATION 5-10 66

Picture Sleeves

COLUMBIA 8-12 67

LPs: 10/12–inch 33rpm

BACK-TRAC 5-10 85
COLUMBIA (2589 "Sugar and Spice")................................. 20-25 66
(Monaural.)
COLUMBIA (2786 "A Scratch in the Sky")............................. 20-25 67
(Monaural.)
COLUMBIA (9389 "Sugar and Spice")................................... 15-20 66
(Stereo.)
COLUMBIA (9586 "A Scratch in the Sky")............................. 15-20 67
(Stereo.)
COLUMBIA (9719 "Synthesis"). 15-20 69

CRYSTAL, Billy

P&R/D&D/LP '85

Singles: 12–inch 33/45rpm

A&M 4-6 85

Singles: 7–inch

A&M 3-4 85

Picture Sleeves

A&M 3-5 85

LPs: 10/12–inch 33rpm

A&M 5-10 85

CRYSTAL GAYLE: see GAYLE, Crystal

CRYSTAL GRASS

R&B '75

Singles: 7–inch

POLYDOR.................................... 3-5 75
PRIVATE STOCK 3-5 76

LPs: 10/12–inch 33rpm

MERCURY 5-10 78
POLYDOR.................................. 8-10 75

CRYSTAL MANSION

P&R '68

Singles: 7–inch

CAPITOL...................................... 3-6 68-70
COLOSSUS 3-5 70-71
RARE EARTH 3-5 72
20TH FOX.................................... 3-4 79

LPs: 10/12–inch 33rpm

CAPITOL....................................12-15 69
RARE EARTH 10-12 72
20TH FOX.....................................5-10 79

Also see CASWELL, Johnny

CRYSTALS

P&R/R&B '61

Singles: 7–inch

MICHELLE.......................................4-8 67
PAVILLION 3-4 82
PHILLES (100 "There's No Other") 8-12 61
PHILLES (102 "Uptown") 8-12 62
PHILLES (105 "He Hit Me") 15-20 62
PHILLES (106 "He's a Rebel").....8-12 62
PHILLES (109 "He's Sure the Boy I Love") 8-12 62
PHILLES (111 "Let's Dance the Screw") 300-400 63
(White label. Promotional Issue Only.)
PHILLES (111 "Let's Dance the Screw") 400-600 63
(Blue label. Has "Let's Dance" in smaller print and in parenthesis. Also has identification numbers *stamped* in vinyl. Blue label copies with "Let's Dance" in the same size print as "The Screw - Part 1" and with identification numbers hand etched are counterfeits.)
PHILLES (112 "Da Do Ron Ron") 8-12 63
PHILLES (115 "Then He Kissed Me") 8-12 63
PHILLES (119 "Little Boy") 10-12 63
PHILLES (122 "All Grown Up")..10-12 64
U.A. 4-8 65-66

LPs: 10/12–inch 33rpm

PHILLES (4000 "The Crystals Twist Uptown") 200-300 62
(Monaural. Blue label.)
PHILLES (4000 "The Crystals Twist Uptown") 500-750 62
(Monaural. White label. Promotional issue only.)
PHILLES (4000 "The Crystals Twist Uptown") 400-600 62
(Stereo.)
PHILLES (4001 "He's a Rebel") 200-300 63
(Monaural. Blue label.)
PHILLES (4001 "He's a Rebel") 500-750 63
(White label. Promotional issue only.)
PHILLES (4003 "Crystals") 150-250 63
(Monaural. Blue label.)
PHILLES (4003 "Crystals") 500-750 63
(White label. Promotional issue only.)

PHILLES (90722 "The Crystals Twist Uptown") 750-1000 62
(Capitol Record Club issue.)
Members: Barbara Alston; Lala Brooks; Dee Dee Kennibrew; Patricia Wright; Mary Thomas.
Also see LOVE, Darlene
Also see RONETTES / Crystals / Darlene Love / Bob B. Soxx & Blue Jeans

CUBA, Joe
(Joe Cuba Sextet)

P&R/R&B/LP '66

Singles: 7–inch

ROULETTE 3-5 71
TICO 4-6 66

LPs: 10/12–inch 33rpm

TICO 10-15 66-67

CUCA

R&B '88

Singles: 7–inch

ALPHA INT 3-4 88

CUES

P&R '55

Singles: 78rpm

CAPITOL 5-10 55-56
JUBILEE 5-10 55
LAMP 5-10 54
PREP 8-10 57

Singles: 7–inch

CAPITOL 10-20 55-56
JUBILEE 15-20 55
LAMP 10-20 54
PREP 10-15 57
Members: Ollie Jones; Jimmy Breedlove; Abe DeCosta; Robey Kirk; Eddie Barnes.
Also see RAVENS

CUFF LINKS

P&R/LP '69

Singles: 7–inch

ATCO 3-5 72
DECCA 3-6 69-71
MCA 3-4 84

Picture Sleeves

DECCA (32533 "Tracy") 5-10 69
(Gatefold sleeve. Promotional issue only.)

LPs: 10/12–inch 33rpm

DECCA 15-25 69-70
Members: Ron Dante; Rupert Holmes.
Also see HOLMES, Rupert

CUGAT, Xavier

P&R '35

Singles: 78rpm

COLUMBIA 4-8 41-55
RCA 3-6 50-57
VICTOR 4-8 35-41

Singles: 7–inch

COLUMBIA 5-10 50-55
DECCA 3-5 65
MERCURY 4-6 62-64
RCA 5-10 50-62

EPs: 7–inch 33/45rpm

COLUMBIA 5-15 55-59
MERCURY 5-15 53-54

LPs: 10/12–inch 33rpm

CAMDEN 10-15 59
COLUMBIA 10-20 62
DECCA 10-20 65-69
HARMONY 10-15 60
MERCURY 10-30 53-67
RCA (Except 3021) 15-25 58-60
RCA (3021 "Siboney") 25-40 53
(10–inch LP.)

CUGAT, Xavier, & Dinah Shore

LPs: 10/12–inch 33rpm

RCA (3022 "Tangos") 25-40 53

CUGINI
(Donald Cugini)

P&R '79

Singles: 7–inch

SCOTTI BROTHERS 3-4 79

CULLEY, Frank
(Frank "Floorshow" Culley; with the Buddy Tate Orchestra)

R&B '49

Singles: 78rpm

ATLANTIC 10-20 49-51
BATON 5-10 56
LENOX 15-25 49

Singles: 7–inch

BATON 10-20 56

EPs: 7–inch 33/45rpm

BATON (7001/2 "Rock & Roll") 50-100 56
(Price is for either volume.)

LPs: 10/12–inch 33rpm

BATON (1201 "Rock & Roll"). 150-250 56

CULT
(Southern Death Cult; Death Cult)

LP '85

Singles: 12–inch 33/45rpm

SIRE 4-6 85-86

Singles: 7–inch

SIRE 3-4 85-89

Picture Sleeves

SIRE 3-4 85-89

LPs: 10/12–inch 33rpm

SIRE 5-10 85-89
Members: Ian Astbury; Billy Duffy; Jamie Stewart; Les Warner; Matt Sorum.
Also see GUNS `N' ROSES

CULTURE CLUB
(Featuring Boy George)

P&R '82

Singles: 12–inch 33/45rpm

EPIC/VIRGIN 4-6 82-86

Singles: 7–inch

EPIC/VIRGIN 3-4 82-86

Picture Sleeves

EPIC/VIRGIN 3-4 83-86

LPs: 10/12-inch 33rpm

EPIC/VIRGIN 5-10 82-86

Members: Boy George; Jon Moss; Roy Hay; Michael Craig.

Also see BAND AID

Also see BOY GEORGE

Also see STEWART, Jermaine

CUMMINGS, Burton

P&R/LP '76

Singles: 7-inch

ALFA 3-4 81

PORTRAIT 3-5 76-78

Picture Sleeves

ALFA 3-4 81

PORTRAIT 3-5 78

EPs: 7-inch 33/45rpm

PORTRAIT 4-8 77

(Issued with a paper sleeve.)

LPs: 10/12-inch 33rpm

ALFA 5-10 81

PORTRAIT 8-10 76-78

Also see GUESS WHO

Also see ROGERS, Dann

CUMMINGS, Burton / Cheap Trick / Crawler

EPs: 7-inch 33/45rpm

COLUMBIA (1129 "Music for Every Ear") 15-25 77

(Promotional issue only.)

Also see CHEAP TRICK

Also see BACK STREET CRAWLER

Also see WILSON, Dennis / Ram Jam / Joan Baez

CUNHA, Rick

P&R/C&W '74

Singles: 7-inch

COLUMBIA 3-5 75

GRC 3-5 74

LPs: 10/12-inch 33rpm

COLUMBIA 8-10 75

GRC 10-12 74

Also see JENNINGS, Waylon

CUPIDS

P&R '63

Singles: 7-inch

AANKO (1002 "Brenda") 75-100 63

KC (115 "Brenda") 10-15 63

CURB, Mike

(Mike Curb Congregation; with Sidewalk Sounds; with Curbstones; with Rebalairs; with Waterfall)

P&R/LP '70

Singles: 7-inch

BUENA VISTA 3-5 75

FORWARD 3-6 69

MGM 3-4 70

REPRISE (0287 "Hot Dawg") 10-20 64

SMASH (1938 "The Rebel") 10-15 64

TOWER 10-15 66

W.B. 3-5 77

Picture Sleeves

BUENA VISTA 5-10 75

FORWARD 4-8 69

LPs: 10/12-inch 33rpm

BUENA VISTA 8-12

COBURT 8-12 70

FORWARD 5-10

MGM 5-10 71

Also see ALLAN, Davie

Also see DAVIS, Sammy, Jr.

Also see OSMONDS

Also see WILLIAMS, Hank, Jr.

CURE

D&D/LP '83

Singles: 12-inch 33/45rpm

ELEKTRA 4-6 85-86

SIRE 4-6 83-85

Singles: 7-inch

ELEKTRA 3-4 85-89

SIRE 3-4 83-85

Picture Sleeves

ELEKTRA 3-4 86-89

LPs: 10/12-inch 33rpm

A&M 8-10 81

ELEKTRA 5-10 85-89

PVC 8-10 80

SIRE 5-10 83-85

Members: Robert Smith; Laurence Tolhurst.

CURIOSITY KILLED the CAT

P&R/LP '87

Singles: 7-inch

MERCURY 3-4 87

Picture Sleeves

MERCURY 3-4 87

LPs: 10/12-inch 33rpm

MERCURY 5-8 87

CURRENT

P&R '77

Singles: 7-inch

PLAYBOY 3-4 77

CURRIE, Cherie & Marie

P&R '79

Singles: 7-inch

CAPITOL 3-5 79-80

Picture Sleeves

CAPITOL 3-5 79

LPs: 10/12-inch 33rpm

CAPITOL 5-10 79-81

Also see RUNAWAYS

CURRY, Clifford

(Cliff Curry)

P&R/R&B '67

Singles: 7-inch

ABBOTT 3-5 72

C.C. 4-6

CAPRICE 3-5 72

ELF.................................... 4-8 67-69
RIDGECREST (1202 "Kiss Kiss Kiss")........................ 15-25 59
SSS INT'L.................................... 3-5
Also see NOTATIONS

CURRY, Louis

R&B '68

Singles: 7-inch

M-S.................................... 5-10 68
REEL.................................... 10-20

CURRY, Mini

R&B '87

Singles: 7-inch

TOTAL EMP.................................... 3-4 87

CURRY, Tim
(With Original Roxy Cast)

P&R/LP '79

Singles: 7-inch

A&M.................................... 3-4 78-81
ODE.................................... 3-5 76
ODE '70.................................... 3-4 74

Picture Sleeves

A&M.................................... 3-4 79

LPs: 10/12-inch 33rpm

A&M.................................... 5-10 78-89
Also see WILSON, Brian

CURTIE & BOOMBOX

P&R/D&D '85

Singles: 12-inch 33/45rpm

RCA.................................... 4-6 85

Singles: 7-inch

RCA.................................... 3-4 85
Member: Curtie Fortune.

CURTIS, Chantal

R&B '79

Singles: 7-inch

KEYLOCK.................................... 3-5 79

CURTIS, T.C.

D&D '85

Singles: 12-inch 33/45rpm

SIRE.................................... 4-6 85

CURTOLA, Bobby
(With the Martells)

P&R '62

Singles: 7-inch

DEL-FI.................................... 5-10 61-63
KING.................................... 4-8 67
TARTAN.................................... 4-8 63-66

Picture Sleeves

DEL-FI.................................... 10-15 61-62

CUT

R&B '86

Singles: 7-inch

SUPERTRONICS.................................... 3-4 86

CUTTING CREW

P&R/LP '87

Singles: 7-inch

VIRGIN.................................... 3-4 87-89

Picture Sleeves

VIRGIN.................................... 3-4 87-89

LPs: 10/12-inch 33rpm

VIRGIN.................................... 5-10 87-89

CYBOTRON

R&B '83

Singles: 12-inch 33/45rpm

FANTASY.................................... 4-6 82-84

Singles: 7-inch

FANTASY.................................... 3-4 83-84

LPs: 10/12-inch 33rpm

FANTASY.................................... 5-10 83-84

CYCLONES

P&R '58

Singles: 7-inch

TROPHY (500 "Bullwhip Rock") 15-25 58
TROPHY (503 "Aftermath")....... 15-25 58
Member: Bill Taylor.

CYMANDE

P&R/R&B/LP '73

Singles: 7-inch

JANUS.................................... 3-5 72-73

LPs: 10/12-inch 33rpm

JANUS.................................... 10-12 72-74

CYMARRON

P&R/LP '71

Singles: 7-inch

ENTRANCE.................................... 3-5 71-72

LPs: 10/12-inch 33rpm

ENTRANCE.................................... 10-12 71
Members: Rick Yancey; Richard Mainegra; Sherrill Parks.

CYMBAL, Johnny

P&R '63

Singles: 7-inch

AMARET.................................... 3-6 69
COLUMBIA.................................... 4-8 66
DCP (1135 "Go VW, Go")......... 10-15 65
KAPP.................................... 5-15 63-64
KEDLEN.................................... 10-15 63
MCA.................................... 3-4 84
MGM.................................... 8-15 60-61
MUSICOR.................................... 4-8 67
VEE JAY.................................... 4-8 63

Picture Sleeves

DCP (1135 "Go VW, Go")......... 15-25 65

LPs: 10/12-inch 33rpm

KAPP (1324 "Mr. Bass Man") 25-35 63
(Monaural.)
KAPP (3324 "Mr. Bass Man") 30-40 63
(Stereo.)
Also see DEREK

CYMONE, Andre

R&B '82

Singles: 12–inch 33/45rpm

COLUMBIA 4-6 82-86

Singles: 7–inch

COLUMBIA 3-4 82-86

LPs: 10/12–inch 33rpm

COLUMBIA 5-10 82-86

Also see PRINCE
Also see WATLEY, Jody

CYNTHIA & JOHNNY O

P&R '90

LPs: 10/12–inch 33rpm

MICMAC.................................... 5-8 90

CYRÉ

R&B '87

Singles: 7–inch

FRESH 3-4 87

CYRKLE

P&R/LP '66

Singles: 7–inch

COLUMBIA (Except 43589)........ 5-10 65-68

COLUMBIA (43589 "Red Rubber Ball")................................. 5-10 65
(Black vinyl.)

COLUMBIA (43589 "Red Rubber Ball")................................ 10-15 65
(Colored vinyl Promotional issue only.)

Picture Sleeves

COLUMBIA 20-30 66-68

LPs: 10/12–inch 33rpm

COLUMBIA (2544 "Red Rubber Ball")................................ 20-25 66

COLUMBIA (9344 "Red Rubber Ball")................................ 25-30 66

COLUMBIA (2632 "Neon")........ 20-25 67
(Monaural.)

COLUMBIA (9432 "Neon")........ 20-30 67
(Stereo.)

FLYING DUTCHMAN/AMSTERDAM (12007 "The Minx") 20-25 70
(Soundtrack.)

CYRKLE / Paul Revere & Raiders

Singles: 7–inch

COLUMBIA (466 "Camaro")...... 10-15 66
(Special Products Chevrolet promotional issue only.)

Picture Sleeves

COLUMBIA (466 "Camaro")...... 15-25 66
(Special Products Chevrolet promotional issue only.)

COLUMBIA (43000 series) 5-10 66-67

Members: Don Danneman; Marty Fried; Tom Dawes; John Simon; Michael Losekamp.

Also see CYRKLE
Also see REVERE, Paul, & Raiders
Also see SIMON, Paul

THE DAVE CLARK FIVE
CONGRESS
"I KNEW IT ALL THE TIME"
B/W "THAT'S WHAT I SAID"
CG 212

CHRISTMAS
IS MY TIME OF YEAR
(H. Kaylan and C. Douglas)
WW 290
WHITE WHALE
Engineer: Eddie Brackett
Studio: Harmony Recorders
THE CHRISTMAS SPIRIT
Produced and Arranged by Chip Douglas and Howie Kaylan
For the Douglas F. Hatfield Foundation
WHITE WHALE RECORDS • 8961 SUNSET BOULEVARD • LOS ANGELES, CALIF.

THE CRESCENDOS
OH! JULIE · ANGEL FACE
98c
SPECIAL VALUE
39c
7027
Top
RECORDS
45 RPM

TAG
RECORDS
Miller Music
ASCAP 2:30
G-102
Vocal By
THE CHIMES
ONCE IN AWHILE
THE CHIMES
dir. A. LEONETTI

Freddy Cannon
"PALISADES PARK"

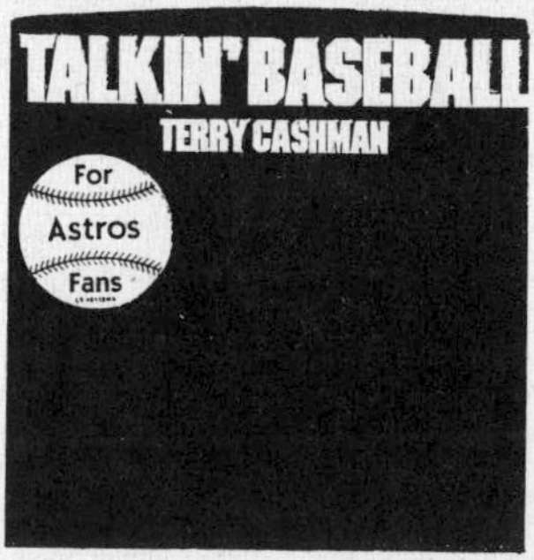
TALKIN' BASEBALL
TERRY CASHMAN
For
Astros
Fans

D

D MOB
(Featuring Cathy Dennis)
P&R '89
Singles: 7-inch
FFRR.. 3-4 89-90
LPs: 10/12-inch 33rpm
FFRR.. 3-4 89

D - NICE
LP '90
LPs: 10/12-inch 33rpm
JIVE.. 5-8 90

"D" TRAIN
LP '82
Singles: 12-inch 33/45rpm
PRELUDE 4-6 81-85
Singles: 7-inch
PRELUDE 3-4 81-85
LPs: 10/12-inch 33rpm
PRELUDE 5-10 82-85
Members: James "D Train" Williams; Hubert Eaves III.
Also see WILLIAMS, James "D Train"

D., Eddie: see EDDIE D.

DB's
LP '87
LPs: 10/12-inch 33rpm
I.R.S. 5-10 87

DFX2
LP '83
Singles: 7-inch
MCA 3-4 83
LPs: 10/12-inch 33rpm
MCA 5-10 83

D.J. JAZZY JEFF & Fresh Prince
R&B '86
Singles: 7-inch
JIVE.. 3-4 87-89
WORD-UP.................................. 3-4 86
Picture Sleeves
JIVE.. 3-4 88-89
LPs: 10/12-inch 33rpm
JIVE.. 5-10 87-89
Also see SIMPSONS

D.J. MAGIC MIKE
LP '90
LPs: 10/12-inch 33rpm
CHEETAH 5-8 90
Also see VICIOUS BASE Featuring D.J. Magic Mike

DMX, Davy: see DAVY DMX

DNA Featuring Suzanne Vega
P&R '90
Singles: 7-inch
A&M 3-4 90
Also see VEGA, Suzanne

D.O.A.
LP '90
LPs: 10/12-inch 33rpm
RESTLESS 5-8 90

D.O.C.
LP '89
LPs: 10/12-inch 33rpm
RUTHLESS.................................. 5-8 89

D.R.I.
LP '88
LPs: 10/12-inch 33rpm
METAL BLADE 5-8 88-89

DADDY DEWDROP
P&R '71
Singles: 7-inch
CAPITOL...................................... 3-5 75
INPHASION 3-4 78-79
SUNFLOWER 3-6 70-72
SUNFLOWER/MGM 3-5 73
LPs: 10/12-inch 33rpm
SUNFLOWER 12-15 71

DADDY O's
P&R '58
Singles: 7-inch
CABOT.. 8-10 58

DAFFAN, Ted
(With His Texans)
P&R '43
Singles: 78rpm
COLUMBIA 4-8 46-55
OKEH.. 4-8 43-45
Singles: 7-inch
COLUMBIA 5-10 55
Members: George Strange; Chuck Keeshan; Leon Seago.

DAHL, Steve, & Teenage Radiation
P&R '79
Singles: 7-inch
COHO 3-5 79
OVATION...................................... 3-5 79
Picture Sleeves
OVATION...................................... 3-5 79

DAILY, E.G.
(Elizabeth G. Daily)
P&R/R&B '86
Singles: 12-inch 33/45rpm
A&M 4-6 86
Singles: 7-inch
A&M 3-4 86
Picture Sleeves
A&M 3-4 86

LPs: 10/12–inch 33rpm

A&M 5-10 86

DAISY DILLMAN BAND: see DILLMAN BAND

DA'KRASH

R&B/LP '88

Singles: 7–inch

CAPITOL.. 3-4 88

LPs: 10/12–inch 33rpm

CAPITOL.. 5-8 88

DALBELLO

D&D '84

Singles: 12–inch 33/45rpm

CAPITOL.. 4-6 84

Singles: 7–inch

CAPITOL.. 3-4 84

DALE, Alan

(With Connie Haines)

P&R '48

Singles: 78rpm

COLUMBIA 4-6 50-51
CORAL.. 3-6 52-56
DECCA.. 3-5 52

Singles: 7–inch

ABC-PAR 3-6 64
ADVANCE.. 3-6
COLUMBIA 5-10 50-51
CORAL (60000 & 61000 series) . 5-10 52-56
CORAL (62000 series)................ 3-6 63
DECCA.. 4-8 52
EMKAY.. 3-6 62
FTP 3-6 61
MGM 4-8 59
SINCLAIR (1003 "A Teenage Girl").. 15-25 61

EPs: 7–inch 33/45rpm

CORAL.. 5-15 52-56

LPs: 10/12–inch 33rpm

CORAL.. 15-25 55-56
FORD 10-15 63
U.A. 10-15 60

Also see CORNELL, Don, Johnny Desmond & Alan Dale

DALE, Dick

(With His Del-tones)

P&R '61

Singles: 7–inch

CAPITOL.. 8-12 63-64
COLUMBIA 3-5 87
CONCERT ROOM 4-8 63
COUGAR 4-8 67
CUPID 10-20 60
DELTONE (4939 "Misirlou")...... 40-60 58
DELTONE (4940 "Peppermint Man").. 40-60 58
DELTONE (5012 "Oh Wee Marie").. 35-50 58
DELTONE (5013 "Stop Teasing").. 25-35 59
DELTONE (5014 "Jessie Pearl").. 35-50 60
DELTONE (5017 "Let's Go Trippin") 10-15 61
(No mention of Rendezvous Records.)
DELTONE (5017 "Let's Go Trippin") 8-10 61
(Reads "Distributed by Rendezvous Records.")
DELTONE (5018 "Shake and Stomp").. 10-15 62
DELTONE (5019 "Miserlou") 10-15 62
(Reissue of 4939. Note spelling change.)
DELTONE (5020 "Peppermint Man") 10-15 62
DELTONE (5028 "Run for Life") 10-15 63
GNP 3-5 75
RENDEZVOUS (204 "Reincarnation Parts 1 & 2").. 8-12 62
SATURN 10-15 63
YES.. 10-20

Promotional Singles

CAPITOL ("Thunder Wave"/ "Spanish Kiss") 8-10 64
(Bonus single, packaged with the *Surf Age* LP by Jerry Cole and His Spacemen.)
CAPITOL (2320 "Peppermint Man")25-35 63
(Compact 33 Single)

Picture Sleeves

CAPITOL (Except 2320) 12-25 63
CAPITOL (2320 "Peppermint Man") 35-45 63
(Promotional Compact 33 Single sleeve.)
COLUMBIA 4-6 87
YES.. 4-8

LPs: 10/12–inch 33rpm

BALBOA.. 5-10 83
CAPITOL (T-1930 "King of the Surf Guitar").. 30-40 63
(Monaural.)
CAPITOL (ST-1930 "King of the Surf Guitar").. 40-50 63
(Stereo.)
CAPITOL (T-2002 "Checkered Flag") 25-35 63
(Monaural.)
CAPITOL (ST-2002 "Checkered Flag") 30-40 63
(Stereo.)
CAPITOL (T-2053 "Mr. Eliminator") 30-35 64
(Monaural.)
CAPITOL (ST-2053 "Mr. Eliminator").. 35-40 64
CAPITOL (T-2111 "Summer Surf").. 40-50 64

(Monaural. With *Movin' Surf,* a bonus single by Jerry Cole & His Spacemen.)
CAPITOL (T-2111 "Summer Surf") 35-45 64
(Monaural. Without bonus single.)
CAPITOL (ST-2111 "Summer Surf") 45-55 64
(Stereo. With *Movin' Surf,* a bonus single by Jerry Cole & His Spacemen.)
CAPITOL (ST-2111 "Summer Surf") 40-50 64
(Stereo. Without bonus single.)
CAPITOL (T-2293 "Rock Out with Dick Dale Live at Ciro's") 30-35 65
(Monaural.)
CAPITOL (2293 "Rock Out with Dick Dale Live at Ciro's") 35-40 65
(Stereo.)
DELTONE (1001 "Surfer's Choice") 30-40 61
DELTONE (1886 "Surfer's Choice") 40-60 63
(Distributed by Capitol.)
DUBTONE 15-20 63
GNP 8-12 75
Also see ALLAN, Davie
Also see BEACH BOYS / Dick Dale / Surfaris / Surf Kings
Also see VAUGHAN, Stevie Ray, & Dick Dale

DALE, Dick / Jerry Cole / Super Stocks / Mr. Gasser & Weirdos

EPs: 7-inch 33/45rpm

CAPITOL (2663 "The Big Surfing Sounds") 35-50 64
(Promotional issue only.)

DALE, Dick / Surfaris / Fireballs

LPs: 10/12-inch 33rpm

ALMOR (108 "World of Surfin"). 10-20 60s
ALMOR (109 "Hot Rod Drag City") 10-20 60s
Also see FIREBALLS

DALE, Dick / Surfaris / Surf Kings (Beach Boys)

LPs: 10/12-inch 33rpm

GUEST STAR (1433 "Surf Kings") 20-30 63
(Credits the Beach Boys, though there are no tracks by the Beach Boys. Also, tracks credited to the Surfaris are by the Original Surfaris.)
GUEST STAR (1433 "Surf Kings") 15-20 63
(Does not credit the Beach Boys.)
Also see ORIGINAL SURFARIS

DALE, Dick / Francine York

Singles: 7-inch

UNITED STATES ARMY (1301 "Enlistment Twist") 10-15 62
(Promotional issue only.)
Also see DALE, Dick

DALE, Jimmy
(Jimmy Clanton)

Singles: 7-inch

DREW-BLAN (1003 "My Pride and Joy") 15-25 61
Also see CLANTON, Jimmy

DALE & GRACE

P&R/R&B '63

Singles: 7-inch

COLLECTABLES 3-4 70s
ERIC 3-4 70s
GUYDEN 3-5 72
HBR 4-8 66
MICHELLE 5-10 63-64
MONTEL 4-8 63-67
MONTEL MICHELLE (942 "What Am I Living For") 4-8 64
(Shows both label names.)
TRIP 3-4 70s

LPs: 10/12-inch 33rpm

MONTEL (100 "I'm Leaving It Up to You") 35-50 64
Members: Dale Houston; Grace Broussard

DALHART, Vernon
(With Gladys Rice; with Al Bernard)

P&R '17

Singles: 78rpm

BANNER 15-25 20s
BLACK PATTI 75-125
BRUNSWICK 10-20 20s
BUDDY 50-100
CAMEO 15-25 20s
CHAMPION 15-25 20s
CLARION 10-20
COLUMBIA 5-15 22-30s
DOMINO 15-25 20s
EDISON 20-50 17-20s
EDISON AMBEROL 15-25 20s
GENNETT 15-25 20s
HARMONY 15-25 20s
HERSCHEL 25-50
HERWIN 25-50
OKEH 10-20 24
PATH 15-25 20s
PERFECT 15-25 20s
RCA 5-10 49
REGAL 15-25 20s
VICTOR 10-20 21-30s
VOCALION 15-25 20s

Singles: 7-inch

RCA (0016 "Prisoner's Song") ... 15-25 49

DALHART, Vernon, & Carson Robison

P&R '28

Singles: 78rpm

VICTOR 10-20 27-28

Also see DALHART, Vernon

DALLARA, Tony

P&R '58

Singles: 7-inch

MERCURY 5-10 58-60
VESUVIUS 4-8 61-62

LPs: 10/12-inch 33rpm

VESUVIUS 8-10 62

DALTON, Kathy

P&R/LP '74

Singles: 7-inch

DISC REET 3-5 74

LPs: 10/12-inch 33rpm

DISC REET 8-12 73-74

DALTON & DUBARRI

R&B '79

Singles: 7-inch

ABC 3-5 76
COLUMBIA 3-5 73-74
HILLTAK 3-4 79

LPs: 10/12-inch 33rpm

ABC 8-10 76
COLUMBIA 10-12 73-74
HILLTAK 5-10 79

Members: Gary Dalton; Kent Dubarri.

DALTREY, Roger

P&R/LP '73

Singles: 7-inch

A&M 3-5 75-76
ATLANTIC 3-4 84-87
MCA 3-5 73-82
MCA/GOLDHAWKE 3-5 75-77
ODE 3-5 72-73
POLYDOR 3-4 80-81
TRACK 3-5 73

Picture Sleeves

ATLANTIC 3-4 84-85
POLYDOR 3-5 80

LPs: 10/12-inch 33rpm

ATLANTIC 5-10 84-87
MCA 10-15 71-82
POLYDOR 5-8 80
TRACK 10-12 73

Also see WHO

DALTREY, Roger, & Steve Gibbons

Singles: 12-inch 33/45rpm

MCA 5-10
(Promotional issue only.)

Also see GIBBONS, Steve, Band

DALTREY, Roger, & Rick Wakeman

Singles: 7-inch

A&M 3-5 75

LPs: 10/12-inch 33rpm

A&M 8-10 75

Also see DALTREY, Roger
Also see WAKEMAN, Rick

DAMARIS

R&B '84

Singles: 7-inch

COLUMBIA 3-4 84

DAMIAN, Michael

P&R '81

Singles: 7-inch

CYPRESS 3-4 89
LEG 3-4 81

Picture Sleeves

CYPRESS 3-4 89
LEG 3-4 81

LPs: 10/12-inch 33rpm

CYPRESS 5-8 89

DAMIANO, Joe
(Josef Damiano)

P&R '59

Singles: 7-inch

CHANCELLOR 5-10 59-60

DAMITA JO
(Damita Joe)

P&R '53

Singles: 78rpm

RCA 4-6 53

Singles: 7-inch

EPIC (Black vinyl) 3-5 65-67
EPIC (Colored vinyl) 4-8 66
MELIC 3-6 64
MERCURY 4-8 60-64
RCA 5-10 53
RANWOOD 3-5 68-71
VEE JAY 3-6 65

Picture Sleeves

EPIC 4-8 65
MERCURY 5-10 61-63

EPs: 7-inch 33/45rpm

MERCURY 5-10 60-61

LPs: 10/12-inch 33rpm

CAMDEN 6-10 65
EPIC 8-15 65-67
MERCURY 12-25 61-63
RANWOOD 5-10 68
VEE JAY 10-15 65

Also see BENTON, Brook, & Damita Jo

DAMITA JO & Billy Eckstine

Singles: 7-inch

MERCURY 3-6 63

Also see ECKSTINE, Billy

DAMITA JO with Steve Gibson & Red Caps

Singles: 78rpm

RCA (6281 "Always") 5-10 55

Singles: 7-inch

ABC-PAR 5-10 61
RCA (6281 "Always") 10-15 55

LPs: 10/12-inch 33rpm

ABC-PAR (378 "Big 15") 40-50 61

Also see DAMITA JO
Also see GIBSON, Steve

DAMN YANKEES

P&R/LP '90

Singles: 7-inch

W.B. 3-4 90

LPs: 10/12-inch 33rpm

W.B. 5-8 90

Members: Ted Nugent; Jack Blades; Tommy Shaw; Michael Cartellone.
Also see NIGHT RANGER
Also see NUGENT, Ted
Also see STYX

DAMNATION
(Featuring Adam Blessing)

LP '70

Singles: 7-inch

U.A. 3-5 71-72

LPs: 10/12-inch 33rpm

U.A. 10-15 69-71

DAMON, Liz
(Liz Damon's Orient Express)

P&R '70

Singles: 7-inch

ABC 3-5 73
ANTHEM 5-10 71-72
DONCY 5-8 78
MAKAHA 5-10 70
WHITE WHALE 3-5 70

LPs: 10/12-inch 33rpm

ANTHEM ("Liz Damon and the Orient Express") 15-25 71
DELILAH 8-12
MAKAHA 10-20 70
WHITE WHALE 8-12 71

DAMONE, Vic

P&R '47

Singles: 78rpm

COLUMBIA 3-6 56-57
MERCURY 3-6 48-55
MERCURY/SAV-WAY (5053 "Ivy") 100-150 47
(Picture disc. Promotional issue only.)
MERCURY/SAV-WAY (5056 "You Do") 100-150 47
(Picture disc. Promotional issue only.)

Singles: 7-inch

CAPITOL 4-6 61-64
COLUMBIA 5-10 56-61
DOLTON 4-6 62
MGM 3-5 72-73
MERCURY 5-10 50-55
RCA 3-6 66-69
REBECCA 3-5 77
UNITED TALENT 3-5 70
W.B. 4-6 65-66

EPs: 7-inch 33/45rpm

CAPITOL CUSTOM ("Vic Damone Swings with A&W) 10-15 62
(Special products issue for A&W Root Beer.)
COLUMBIA 5-10 56-58
MERCURY 8-12 50-56

LPs: 10/12-inch 33rpm

CAPITOL 10-20 61-64
COLUMBIA (900 thru 1500 series) 15-25 56-61
COLUMBIA (1900 series) 10-20 62
COLUMBIA (8000 thru 8300 series) 20-30 58-61
COLUMBIA (8700 series) 10-15 62
DOLTON 10-15 64
HARMONY 5-10 66-67
HOLLYWOOD 5-10
MERCURY (Except 25000 series) 8-12 69
MERCURY (25000 series) 15-30 50-56
RCA 8-12 66-68
UNITED TALENT 5-10
W.B. 10-15 65
WING 10-15 59-63

Also see ANDREWS, Julie & Andre Previn / Vic Damone / Jack Jones / Marian Anderson
Also see FISHER, Eddie / Vic Damone / Dick Haymes
Also see PAGE, Patti, & Vic Damone

Singles: 7-inch

KIRSHNER 4-8

Also see TOKENS

DANA, Bill
(Jose Jimenez)

LP '60

Singles: 7-inch

A&M 4-8 65-66
KAPP 5-15 61-63
SIGNATURE 5-10 60

Picture Sleeves

KAPP 10-20 61-62

EPs: 7-inch 33/45rpm

KAPP 10-20 61

LPs: 10/12-inch 33rpm

A&M 8-12 68
CAPITOL 6-10 70
HBR 8-10 66
KAPP 12-25 60-64
ROULETTE 12-25 61
SIGNATURE 20-25 60

DANA, Vic

P&R '61

Singles: 7-inch

CASINO 3-5 76
COLUMBIA 3-5 71
DOLTON 4-8 61-65
LIBERTY 3-6 68-70
MGM 3-5 75

Picture Sleeves

DOLTON 5-10 62-66

LPs: 10/12-inch 33rpm

DOLTON (Except 2013/8013)... 15-25 62-65

DOLTON (2013).......... 15-25 61
(Monaural.)

DOLTON (8013).......... 20-30 61
(Stereo.)

LIBERTY 8-15 67-70

SUNSET.......... 8-10 67

Also see CARTER, Mel / Vic Dana

DANCER, Terri

R&B '86

Singles: 7-inch

REFLECTION 3-4 86

DANCER, PRANCER & NERVOUS

P&R '59

Singles: 7-inch

CAPITOL.......... 5-10 59

Picture Sleeves

CAPITOL.......... 8-10 59

Member: Russ Regan.

DANDLEERS: see DANLEERS

DANE, Dana

R&B '85

Singles: 12-inch 33/45rpm

PROFILE.......... 4-6 85

Singles: 7-inch

PROFILE.......... 3-4 85-90

LPs: 10/12-inch 33rpm

PROFILE.......... 5-10 86-90

DANGERFIELD, Rodney

LP '80

Singles: 12-inch 33/45rpm

RCA.......... 4-6 83

Singles: 7-inch

RCA.......... 3-4 83

Picture Sleeves

RCA.......... 3-4 83

LPs: 10/12-inch 33rpm

DECCA.......... 15-20 66

CASABLANCA 5-10 80

RCA.......... 5-10 83

RHINO.......... 5-10 80

DANGEROUS TOYS

LP '89

Singles: 7-inch

COLUMBIA 5-8 89-90

LPs: 10/12-inch 33rpm

COLUMBIA 5-8 89-91

DANIELS, Charlie

(Charlie Daniels Band; with the Jaguars)

C&W/P&R/LP '73

Singles: 7-inch

EPIC.......... 3-5 76-86

HANOVER (4541 "Robot
Romp").......... 10-20 59

KAMA SUTRA.......... 3-6 73-76

PAULA (200 series) 5-10 66

PAULA (400 series) 3-5 76

EPs: 7-inch 33/45rpm

KAMA SUTRA (10 "Volunteer
Jam").......... 5-8 74
(Bonus EP packaged with *Fire on the Mountain* LP.)

LPs: 10/12-inch 33rpm

CAPITOL (11000 series) 8-10 75

CAPITOL (16000 series) 5-10 80

EPIC (Except 273) 5-10 76-91

EPIC (273 "Everything You Always
Wanted to Hear") 10-15 77
(Promotional issue only.)

KAMA SUTRA.......... 10-15 73-76

MFSL (176 "Million Mile
Reflections").......... 15-20 85

Also see LEE, Johnny, Michael Martin Murphey, & Charlie Daniels

DANKO, Rick

LP '77

Singles: 7-inch

ARISTA.......... 3-4 78

LPs: 10/12-inch 33rpm

ARISTA.......... 8-10 77

Also see BAND

DANKWORTH, Johnny

(Johnnie Dankworth)

P&R '56

Singles: 78rpm

CAPITOL.......... 3-5 55-56

Singles: 7-inch

CAPITOL.......... 4-8 55-56

FONTANA.......... 3-5 63-66

20TH FOX.......... 3-5 66

LPs: 10/12-inch 33rpm

FONTANA (Except 7559) 6-12 64-69

FONTANA (27559 "The Idol").... 15-20 66
(Soundtrack. Monaural.)

FONTANA (67559 "The Idol")....20-25 66
(Soundtrack. Stereo.)

ROULETTE.......... 10-15 60-61

TOP RANK.......... 10-15 60

DANLEERS

(Dandleers)

P&R/R&B '58

Singles: 7-inch

ABC.......... 3-4 75

AMP 3 (1005 " One Summer
Night").......... 5-8

AMP 3 (2115 " One Summer
Night").......... 25-35 58

COLLECTABLES.......... 3-4 80s

EPIC (9367 "Half a Block
from an Angel").......... 15-25 60

EPIC (9421 "Little Lover").......... 15-25 60

EVEREST (19412 "Foolish")......20-30 61

LE MANS 4-8 64
MERCURY 10-20 58-59
SMASH 4-8 64

Members: Jimmy Weston; Johnny Lee; Nat McCune; Willie Ephriam; Roosevelt Mays; Doug Ebron; Louis Williams; Terry Wilson; Frank Clemens; Bill Carey.

Also see FOUR FELLOWS

DANNY & JUNIORS
(With Joe Terry)

P&R/R&B '57

Singles: 78rpm

ABC-PAR 10-20 57-58

Singles: 7-inch

ABC 3-5 73
ABC-PAR 10-30 57-59
CRUNCH 4-6 73
DOWNTOWN 3-4 93
GOLDIES 45 .... 3-5 73
GUSTO 3-5 79
GUYDEN 8-10 62
LUV 5-10 68
MCA 3-4 70s
MERCURY 5-10 64
ROULETTE 3-5 70s
SINGULAR (711 "At the Hop") 75-100 57
(Blue label.)
SINGULAR (711 "At the Hop").... 5-10
(Black label.)
SWAN 8-12 60-62
TOPAZ 3-6 87

EPs: 7-inch 33/45rpm

ABC-PAR (11 "At the Hop") .. 250-350 58
SWAN (4084 "Just Because"). 75-125 62
(Not issued with cover. Promotional issue only.)

Picture Sleeves

SWAN (4064 "Candy Cane Sugar Plum") 50-75 60

LPs: 10/12-inch 33rpm

MCA 5-10 83

Members: Danny Rapp; Frank Maffei; Joe Terry; Dave White.

Also see CANNON, Freddy

DANNY WILSON

P&R/LP '87

Singles: 7-inch

VIRGIN 3-4 87

Picture Sleeves

VIRGIN 3-4 87

LPs: 10/12-inch 33rpm

VIRGIN 5-10 87

Members: Gary Clark; Kit Clark; Ged Grimes.

DANSE SOCIETY

D&D '84

Singles: 12-inch 33/45rpm

ARISTA 4-6 84

Singles: 7-inch

ARISTA 3-4 84

DANTE
(With the Evergreens; with His Friends)

P&R '60

Singles: 7-inch

A&M 5-10 66
IMPERIAL 15-25 61-62
MADISON 8-12 60-61

LPs: 10/12-inch 33rpm

MADISON (1002 "Dante and the Evergreens") 150-200 61

Members: Don "Dante" Drowty; Bill Young; Frank Rosenthal; Tony Moon.

DANTE & His Friends: see DANTE

DANTE & EVERGREENS: see DANTE

DANZIG

LP '88

Singles: 7-inch

DEF AMERICAN 3-4 88-90

LPs: 10/12-inch 33rpm

DEF AMERICAN 5-8 88-90

D'ARBY, Terence Trent

P&R/R&B/LP '87

Singles: 7-inch

COLUMBIA 3-4 87-89

Picture Sleeves

COLUMBIA 3-4 87-89

LPs: 10/12-inch 33rpm

COLUMBIA 5-10 87-89

DARENSBOURG, Joe, & His Dixie Flyers

P&R '58

Singles: 7-inch

LARK 4-8 58-59

LPs: 10/12-inch 33rpm

DIXIELAND JUBILEE 5-10 75
GHB 5-10 77

DARIAN, Fred
(Freddy Darian)

P&R '61

Singles: 7-inch

DEL-FI 5-10 60
GARDENA 5-10 61
JAF 4-8 61-63
MAHALO 4-8 63
OKEH 5-10 59
RCA 5-10 59
U.A. 4-8 63

DARIN, Bobby
(With the Jaybirds; with Rinky Dinks; Bob Darin)

P&R/R&B/C&W '58

Singles: 78rpm

ATCO 10-15 57-58
DECCA 8-15 56-57

Singles: 7–inch

ATCO ("She's Tanfastic")... 15-20
(Promotional issue only. No selection number used.)
ATCO (6103 thru 6127)... 10-20 57-58
ATCO (6133 "Plain Jane")... 10-20 59
(Monaural.)
ATCO (SD-45-6133 "Plain Jane")... 20-30 59
(Stereo.)
ATCO (6140 thru 6334)... 6-12 59-65
ATLANTIC... 4-8 65-67
CAPITOL... 5-8 62-65
DECCA (29883 "Rock Island Line")... 20-30 56
DECCA (29922 "Blue Eyed Mermaid")... 30-50 56
DECCA (30031 "The Greatest Builder")... 20-30 56
DECCA (30225 "Dealer in Dreams")... 25-40 57
DECCA (30737 "Dealer in Dreams")... 10-15 59
DIMENSION... 3-6 70
DIRECTION... 3-6 68-70
MOTOWN... 3-5 71-72

Picture Sleeves

ATCO (Except 6211)... 8-18 59-62
ATCO (6211 "Ave Maria")... 75-100 61
CAPITOL... 5-10 62-65

EPs: 7–inch 33/45rpm

ATCO (1001 "For Teenagers Only")... 40-60 60
(Promotional issue only. Issued with paper sleeve.)
ATCO (4502 "Bobby Darin")... 35-45 58
ATCO (4504 "That's All")... 25-35 59
ATCO (4505 "Bobby Darin")... 30-45 59
ATCO (4508 "This Is Darin")... 20-30 59
ATCO (4512 "At the Copa")... 20-30 60
ATCO (4513 "For Teenagers Only")... 30-50 60
CAPITOL CUSTOM/ARTISTIC ("Bobby Darin")... 20-30 63
(Promotional issue only. Issued with paper sleeve.)
DECCA (2676 "Bobby Darin")... 50-75 60

LPs: 10/12–inch 33rpm

ATCO (Except 102 & 131)... 20-35 59-67
ATCO (102 "Bobby Darin")... 40-60 58
ATCO (131 "The Bobby Darin Story")... 35-40 61
(White cover.)
ATCO (131 "The Bobby Darin Story")... 10-15 72
(Black cover.)
ATLANTIC... 15-25 66-67
BAINBRIDGE... 5-10 81
CANDLELITE... 15-20 76
CAPITOL... 20-25 62-66
CLARION... 15-20 64
DIRECTION... 12-20 68-70
IMPERIAL HOUSE... 12-15 76
MOTOWN (100 series)... 5-10 82
MOTOWN (738 "Finally")... 150-250 72
(Promotional issue only.)
MOTOWN (753 "Bobby Darin")... 10-20 72
MOTOWN (813 "Darin: 1936-1973")... 10-15 74
W.B. (3501 "Original Bobby Darin")... 20-30 76
(Three-LP mail-order offer.)
Session: King Curtis.
Also see DING DONGS
Also see KING CURTIS
Also see RINKY DINKS

DARLIN, Florraine

P&R '62

Singles: 7–inch

EPIC... 8-10 62-63
RIC... 4-8 64

DARLING CRUEL

LP '89

LPs: 10/12–inch 33rpm

MIKA... 5-8 89

DARNELL, Larry
(With the Fortunes)

R&B '49

Singles: 78rpm

DELUXE... 5-10 57
OKEH... 5-10 51-53
REGAL... 10-15 49-51
SAVOY... 5-10 55

Singles: 7–inch

ANNA (1109 (With Tears in My Eyes")... 200-300 60
ARGO (5364 "Look at Me")... 20-30 60
ARGO (5372 "With Tears in My Eyes")... 15-25 60
DELUXE... 10-20 57
MISTY... 4-6
OKEH... 10-20 51-53
REGAL... 10-20 51
SAVOY (1151 "That's All I Want from You")... 15-25 55
WARWICK... 8-12 59

EPs: 7–inch 33/45rpm

EPIC (7072 "For You My Love") 30-40 61
Session: Mickey Baker.

DARRELL, Johnny

C&W '65

Singles: 7–inch

CAPRICORN... 3-5 74-75
CARTWHEEL... 3-5 71-72
GUSTO... 3-4 78
MONUMENT... 3-5 73
U.A.... 4-6 65-70

Picture Sleeves

U.A. 3-6 67

LPs: 10/12-inch 33rpm

CAPRICORN 6-10 75
GUSTO 5-10
SUNSET 6-10 68-70
U.A. 8-12 66-70

DARRELL, Johnny / George Jones / Willie Nelson

LPs: 10/12-inch 33rpm

SUNSET 8-10 69
Also see DARRELL, Johnny
Also see JONES, George
Also see NELSON, Willie

DARREN, James
(Jimmy Darren)

P&R '59

Singles: 7-inch

ABC 3-4 74
BUDDAH 3-5 70
COLPIX (102 "There's No Such Thing") 5-10 58
COLPIX (113 "Gidget") 5-10 59
COLPIX (119 "Angel Face") 5-10 59
(Monaural.)
COLPIX (SCP-119 "Angel Face") 10-20 59
(Stereo.)
COLPIX (128 thru 708) 5-10 59-63
COLPIX (758 "Punch & Judy") 10-20 64
COLPIX (765 "Married Man") 5-10 64
ERIC 3-4
KIRSHNER 3-5 71-72
MCA 3-4
MGM 3-5 73
PRIVATE STOCK 3-5 75-77
RCA 3-5 78
W.B. 4-8 65-68

Picture Sleeves

COLPIX 8-15 58-61

LPs: 10/12-inch 33rpm

COLPIX (406 "Album No. 1") 20-30 60
COLPIX (418 "Gidget Goes Hawaiian") 20-30 61
COLPIX (424 "For All Sizes") 20-30 62
COLPIX (428 "Love Among the Young") 20-30 62
KIRSHNER 10-20 71-72
W.B. 15-20 67

DARREN, James / Shelley Fabares / Paul Petersen

LP '63

LPs: 10/12-inch 33rpm

COLPIX (444 "Teenage Triangle") 25-35 63
COLPIX (468 "More Teenage Triangle") 25-35 63
Also see DARREN, James
Also see FABARES, Shelley
Also see PETERSEN, Paul

DARTELLS

P&R/R&B/LP '63

Singles: 7-inch

ARLEN (509 "Hot Pastrami") 8-12 63
(Black vinyl.)
ARLEN (509 "Hot Pastrami") 20-30 63
(Colored vinyl.)
ARLEN (513 "Dance Everybody, Dance") 10-15 63
DOT 4-8 63-64
HBR 4-8 66

LPs: 10/12-inch 33rpm

DOT (3522 "Hot Pastrami") 25-30 63
(Monaural.)
DOT (25522 "Hot Pastrami") 25-30 63
(Stereo.)
Member: Doug Phillips.

DASH, Sarah

P&R/R&B/LP '79

Singles: 12-inch 33/45rpm

MEGATONE 4-6 83

Singles: 7-inch

KIRSHNER 3-4 79-81

LPs: 10/12-inch 33rpm

KIRSHNER 5-10 78-81
Also see LABELLE, Patti

DATE with SOUL

Singles: 7-inch

YORK (408 "Yes Sir That's My Baby") 15-25 67
(Previously issued as by Hale and the Hushabyes. See that listing for members.)
Also see HALE & HUSHABYES

DAVE & SUGAR
(Dave Rowland & Sugar)

C&W '75

Singles: 7-inch

ELEKTRA 3-4 81
RCA 3-5 75-82

LPs: 10/12-inch 33rpm

ELEKTRA 5-10 81
RCA 5-10 76-82
Members: Dave Rowland; Vicki Hackeman-Baker; Jackie Frantz; Sue Powell; Melissa Dean; Jamie Kaye.
Also see PRIDE, Charley

DAVID, F.R.

P&R '83

Singles: 7-inch

CARRERE AMERICA 3-4 83

LPs: 10/12-inch 33rpm

CARRERE AMERICA 5-10 83

DAVID & DAVID

P&R/LP '86

Singles: 7-inch

A&M 3-4 86-87

Picture Sleeves

A&M 3-4 86-87

LPs: 10/12-inch 33rpm

A&M 5-10 86

Members: David Baerwald; David Rickets.

DAVID & JONATHAN

P&R '66

Singles: 7-inch

AMY 4-8 68
CAPITOL 4-8 66-67
20TH FOX 4-6 66

Picture Sleeves

CAPITOL 5-10 66

LPs: 10/12-inch 33rpm

CAPITOL (2473 "Michelle") 20-30 66

Members: Roger Greenaway; Roger Cook.

DAVID & LEE

Singles: 7-inch

G.S.P. (1 "Sad September") 20-30 62

Members: David Gates; Leon Russell.
Also see GATES, David
Also see RUSSELL, Leon

DAVIDSON, John

LP '66

Singles: 7-inch

COLUMBIA 3-6 66-71
MERCURY 3-5 73
20TH FOX 3-5 73-77

Picture Sleeves

COLUMBIA 4-6 66-69

LPs: 10/12-inch 33rpm

COLPIX 10-15 65
COLUMBIA 5-10 66-80
HARMONY 4-6 72
MERCURY 5-10 73
20TH FOX 5-10 74-76

DAVIE, Hutch
(With His Honky-Tonkers)

P&R '58

Singles: 7-inch

ATCO 5-10 58-59
CANADIAN AMERICAN 4-8 61
CLARIDGE 4-8 66
CONGRESS 4-8 62
DYNO VOICE 3-6 68

LPs: 10/12-inch 33rpm

ATCO (105 "Much Hutch") 20-30 59

Also see RAY, James

DAVIES, Dave

LP '80

Singles: 7-inch

RCA 3-5 80
REPRISE 15-20 67-68
W.B. 3-4 83

Picture Sleeves

RCA (12089 "Wild Man") 10-15 80

LPs: 10/12-inch 33rpm

RCA 8-12 80-81
W.B. 5-10 83

Also see KINKS

DAVIS, Betty

R&B '73

Singles: 7-inch

ISLAND 3-5 75-76
JUST SUNSHINE 3-5 73-74

LPs: 10/12-inch 33rpm

ISLAND 5-10 75
JUST SUNSHINE 6-10 73-74

DAVIS, Billy, Jr.
(Billy Davis)

R&B '75

Singles: 7-inch

ABC 3-5 75
COBBLESTONE 4-6 69
EPSOM 4-8 61
HI 4-8 68

LPs: 10/12-inch 33rpm

SAVOY 5-10 82

Also see FIFTH DIMENSION

DAVIS, Carl, & Chi-Sound Orchestra

R&B '77

Singles: 7-inch

CHI-SOUND 3-5 77

DAVIS, Danny
(With the Nashville Brass; with Arlene Baird; with Titans; with Nashville Strings; Danny Davis Orchestra;)

LP '69

Singles: 78rpm

BLUE JAY 3-5 54
HICKORY 3-5 54
MGM 3-6 51-53

Singles: 7-inch

BLUE JAY 4-8 54
CABOT 3-6 59
HICKORY 4-8 54
LIBERTY 3-6 59
MGM (11000 series) 5-10 51-53
MGM (13000 series) 3-5 62-65
RCA 3-4 69-84
THUNDER 3-6 59
VERVE 3-5 61

LPs: 10/12-inch 33rpm

MGM 8-18 61-65
RCA SPECIAL PRODUCTS (0176 "America 200 Years Young") 10-15 76
(Special Products issue for the Amana Corp.)
RCA 5-10 69-84

Also see ATKINS, Chet, Floyd Cramer & Danny Davis
Also see LOCKLIN, Hank, with Danny Davis & Nashville Brass

DAVIS, Danny, & Byron Lee

Singles: 7-inch

MGM 4-6 64

DAVIS, Danny, Nashville Brass & Dona Mason

C&W '87

Singles: 7–inch

JAROCO 3-4 87

DAVIS, Danny, Willie Nelson, & Nashville Brass

LP '80

Singles: 7–inch

RCA 3-4 80

LPs: 10/12–inch 33rpm

RCA 5-10 80

Also see DAVIS, Danny
Also see LOCKLIN, Hank
Also see NEWMAN, Jimmy C., Danny Davis & Nashville Brass

DAVIS, Geater

R&B '70

Singles: 7–inch

HOUSE of ORANGE 3-5 70
SEVENTY 3-5 73

DAVIS, Jimmy & Junction

P&R/LP '87

Singles: 7–inch

QMI MUSIC 3-4 87

Picture Sleeves

QMI MUSIC 3-4 87

LPs: 10/12–inch 33rpm

MCA 5-10 87

DAVIS, John, & Monster Orchestra

R&B '76

Singles: 12–inch 33/45rpm

COLUMBIA 4-8 79

Singles: 7–inch

COLUMBIA 3-5 78-79
SAM 3-5 76-78

LPs: 10/12–inch 33rpm

COLUMBIA 5-10 79

DAVIS, Krystal

D&D '85

Singles: 12–inch 33/45rpm

URBAN ROCK 4-6 85

DAVIS, Mac

C&W/P&R '70

Singles: 7–inch

CAPITOL 4-8 65
COLUMBIA 3-5 70-78
CASABLANCA 3-4 80-84
JAMIE 5-10 62
MCA 3-4 85-86
VEE JAY 5-10 63

Picture Sleeves

COLUMBIA 3-5 70-75

LPs: 10/12–inch 33rpm

ACCORD 5-10 82
CASABLANCA 5-10 81-85
COLUMBIA 8-10 70-83
MCA 5-10 80
SPRINGBOARD 6-10
TRIP 8-10 73

Also see CLASSICS IV / Mac Davis

DAVIS, Martha

R&B '48

Singles: 78rpm

CORAL 4-8 51-52
DECCA 4-8 48
JEWEL 4-8 48
URBAN 5-10 46

Singles: 7–inch

CORAL 10-20 51-52

LPs: 10/12–inch 33rpm

ABC-PAR (213 "Tribute to Fats Waller") 40-50 57

Also see JORDAN, Louis

DAVIS, Martha

P&R/LP '87

Singles: 7–inch

CAPITOL 3-4 87

Picture Sleeves

CAPITOL 3-4 87

LPs: 10/12–inch 33rpm

CAPITOL 5-10 87

Also see MOTELS

DAVIS, Mary

R&B '87

Singles: 7–inch

TABU 3-4 87

DAVIS, Miles
(Miles Davis Sextet)

LP '61

Singles: 78rpm

BLUE NOTE 3-6 54-56
PRESTIGE 3-6 52-57

Singles: 7-Inch

BLUE NOTE (1600 series) 5-10 54-56
COLUMBIA (02000 thru 03000 series) 3-4 81-83
COLUMBIA (10000 series) 3-6 75
COLUMBIA (41000 thru 46000 series) 3-8 61-74
PRESTIGE (100 thru 400 series) .. 4-8 57-66
PRESTIGE (700 thru 900 series) 5-10 52-55

EPs: 7-Inch 33/45rpm

BLUE NOTE 15-25 52
CAPITOL (459 "Jeru") 50-100 53
COLUMBIA 6-10 59
PRESTIGE 12-20 52-53

LPs: 10/12-Inch 33rpm

BLUE NOTE (100 series) 8-12 73
BLUE NOTE (1500 series) 25-50 56-58
(Label gives New York street address for Blue Note Records.)
BLUE NOTE (1500 series) 15-25 58
(Label reads "Blue Note Records Inc. - New York, U.S.A.")

BLUE NOTE (1500 series)........ 10-20 66
(Label shows Blue Note Records as a division of either Liberty or United Artists.)
BLUE NOTE (5013 "Miles Davis")100-150 52
(10-Inch LP.)
BLUE NOTE (5022 "Tempus Fugit")................................ 100-150 53
(10-Inch LP.)
BLUE NOTE (5044 "Miles Davis")................................ 100-150 54
(10-Inch LP.)
CAPITOL (H-459 "Jeru")....... 100-150 53
(10-Inch LP.)
CAPITOL (T-459 "Jeru") 35-50 53
CAPITOL (762 "Birth of Cool") .. 50-75 56
CAPITOL (1900 series)............ 10-20 63
CAPITOL (11000 series)............ 8-12 72
CAPITOL (16000 series)............ 5-10 81
COLUMBIA (20 "Friday and Saturday Nights in Person") 25-30 61
(Monaural.)
COLUMBIA (26 "Bitches Brew") . 8-12 70
COLUMBIA (820 "Friday and Saturday Nights in Person") 30-40 61
(Stereo.)
COLUMBIA (900 thru 1600 series) 20-35 57-61
(With six black Columbia "eye" logos on red label.)
COLUMBIA (1800 thru 2300 series) 15-25 61-65
COLUMBIA (8000 thru 8400 series) 20-35 58-62
(With six black Columbia "eye" logos on red label.)
COLUMBIA (8600 thru 9800 series) 10-20 61-69
COLUMBIA (10000 series) 6-10 73
COLUMBIA (30000 series, except 36976) 6-12 70-85
COLUMBIA (36976 "The Miles Davis Collection").................. 30-40 80
(Six-LP set.)
COLUMBIA (40000 series) 8-12 81-85
DEBUT (043 "Blue Moods").......... 5-8 83
DEBUT (120 "Blue Moods")..... 50-100 55
FANTASY................................ 15-20 62
FONTANA............................... 10-15 65
MFSL (177 "Someday My Prince Will Come")................ 15-25 85
MOODSVILLE......................... 15-20 63
NEW JAZZ 10-15 64
PRESTIGE (004 thru 093) 5-8 80-85
PRESTIGE (100 series).......... 50-100 52-54
(10-Inch LPs.)
PRESTIGE (7007 thru 7166) 40-60 55-59
(Yellow label.)
PRESTIGE (7168 thru 7281) 20-30 60-64
(Yellow label.)
PRESTIGE (7000 thru 7600 series)......................................6-12 64-69
(Blue label.)
PRESTIGE (7700 thru 7800 series)......................................6-12 70-71
PRESTIGE (24000 series)...........8-12 72-78
SAVOY.......................................12-20 61
TRIP...5-10 73
U.A. 8-10 71
W.B. 5-10 86-89
Also see COLTRANE, John, & Miles Davis
Also see FORREST, Jimmy

DAVIS, Miles, & Thelonious Monk

LPs: 10/12-Inch 33rpm

COLUMBIA 10-20 64
Also see DAVIS, Miles
Also see JACQUET, Illinois, & Miles Davis
Also see MONK, Thelonious

DAVIS, Miz

R&B '76

Singles: 7-inch

NEW..3-5 76

DAVIS, Paul

(With Susan Collins)

P&R '70

Singles: 7-inch

ARISTA.......................................3-4 81-82
BANG (Except 500 series).............3-5 73-80
BANG (500 series).........................3-6 68-72
CAPITOL/CURB 3-4 86
FLASHBACK.................................3-4 82
SOLID GOLD 3-5 73

LPs: 10/12-inch 33rpm

ARISTA.......................................5-10 81
BANG...10-12 72-82
Also see OSMOND, Marie, & Paul Davis
Also see TUCKER, Tanya, Paul Davis & Paul Overstreet

DAVIS, Rainy

R&B '86

Singles: 12-inch 33/45rpm

SUPERTRONICS 4-6 86

Singles: 7-inch

COLUMBIA 3-4 87-88
SUPERTRONICS 3-4 86

DAVIS, Ruth

R&B '78

Singles: 7-inch

CLARIDGE...................................3-4 78
Also see KIRKLAND, Bo, & Ruth Davis

DAVIS, Sammy, Jr.

(Sammy Davis)

P&R '54

Singles: 7-inch

A.L.B.B. (38032 "The House I Live In").......................................3-5
(Promotional issue only.)
APPLAUSE 3-4 82

DECCA (25500 series)................ 3-6 62
DECCA (29000 thru 31000 series) 5-10 54-60
DECCA (32000 series)................ 3-5 69
ECOLOGY 3-4 71
MGM 3-5 71-79
VERVE 4-6 60
REPRISE 3-6 61-71
20TH FOX.................................. 3-5 75-76
W.B. 3-4 77

Picture Sleeves

A.L.B.B. (38032 "The House I Live In") 5-10
(Promotional issue only.)

EPs: 7–inch 33/45rpm

CAPITOL 5-15 54
DECCA...................................... 8-12 54-55

LPs: 10/12–inch 33rpm

DECCA (100 series)............... 10-20 66
DECCA (4000 series)............... 10-20 61-65
DECCA (8100 thru 8700 series) 20-30 54-58
DECCA (8900 series)............... 10-20 59
DECCA (9032 "Mr. Wonderful") 60-70 56
(Soundtrack.)
HARMONY 5-10 69-71
MCA 5-10 77
MGM 5-10 72-73
MOTOWN 6-10 70
RCA (1086 "Three Penny Opera")................................. 15-25 64
REPRISE 10-20 61-69
20TH FOX (Except 5014)........... 5-10 76
20TH FOX (FXG-5014 "Of Love and Desire") 25-30 64
(Soundtrack. Monaural.)
20TH FOX (SXG-5014 "Of Love and Desire") 35-40 64
(Soundtrack. Stereo.)
W.B. 5-10 77
U.A. (5187 "Salt and Pepper")... 15-20 68
(Soundtrack.)
VOCALION................................ 5-10 68

Also see CURB, Mike
Also see SINATRA, Frank, Sammy Davis Jr. & Dean Martin

DAVIS, Sammy, Jr., & Laurindo Almeida

LPs: 10/12–inch 33rpm

REPRISE 10-15 67

Also see ALMEIDA, Laurindo

DAVIS, Sammy, Jr., & Count Basie

LP '65

Singles: 7–inch

VERVE 3-5 65

LPs: 10/12–inch 33rpm

MGM 6-10 73
VERVE 10-15 65

Also see BASIE, Count

DAVIS, Sammy, Jr., & Carmen McRae

Singles: 7–inch

DECCA 5-10 55

EPs: 7–inch 33/45rpm

DECCA 5-10 59

LPs: 10/12–inch 33rpm

DECCA 10-20 59

Also see McRAE, Carmen

DAVIS, Sammy, Jr., & Buddy Rich

LPs: 10/12–inch 33rpm

REPRISE 10-20 66

Also see RICH, Buddy

DAVIS, Sammy, Jr. / Joya Sherril

LPs: 10/12–inch 33rpm

DESIGN 5-10 60s

Also see DAVIS, Sammy, Jr.

DAVIS, Sherry
(With Buddy Holly)

Singles: 7–inch

FASHION (1001 "Humble Heart")50-75 57

Also see HOLLY, Buddy

DAVIS, Skeeter

C&W '58

Singles: 7–inch

MERCURY 3-5 76-77
PART TWO 3-4 80
RCA (Except 7000 thru 9600 series) 3-5 69-74
RCA (7000 thru 8300 series) 5-10 58-64
RCA (8400 thru 9600 series) 4-8 64-68

Picture Sleeves

RCA 5-8 63

EPs: 7–inch 33/45rpm

RCA 5-10 63

LPs: 10/12–inch 33rpm

CAMDEN 5-10 65-74
GUSTO 5-10 78
RCA (2000 & 3000 series, except 3790)............................ 10-15 60-68
RCA (3790 "Skeeter Davis Sings Buddy Holly") 20-30 67
TUDOR 5-10 84

Also see BARE, Bobby, & Skeeter Davis
Also see DAVIS SISTERS
Also see HAMILTON, George, IV, & Skeeter Davis
Also see JENNINGS, Waylon
Also see POSEY, Sandy / Skeeter Davis
Also see WAGONER, Porter, & Skeeter Davis

DAVIS, Skeeter, & Don Bowman

C&W '68

Singles: 7–inch

RCA 4-8 68

DAVIS, Skeeter, & George Hamilton IV

C&W '70

Singles: 7–inch

RCA 3-5 70

LPs: 10/12–inch 33rpm

RCA 10-12 70

Also see HAMILTON, George, IV

DAVIS, Skeeter, & NRBQ

Singles: 7-inch

ROUNDER 3-5 85

Also see DAVIS, Skeeter
Also see NRBQ

DAVIS, Spencer

(Spencer Davis Group; with Peter Jameson)

P&R '66

Singles: 7-inch

ALLEGIANCE 3-4 84
ATCO 5-10 66
FONTANA 8-12 64
U.A. 4-8 66-72
VERTIGO 3-4 73-74

Picture Sleeves

U.A. 8-12 66-67

LPs: 10/12-inch 33rpm

ALLEGIANCE 5-10 84
DATE 10-12 70
FONTANA 20-30 66
ISLAND 5-10 83
MEDIARTS 10-12 71
RHINO 5-10 84
U.A. 15-30 67-75
VERTIGO 10-12 73-74
WING 10-15

Members: Spencer Davis; Steve Winwood; Pete York; Brian Dexter; Ray Fenwick; Ken Salmon; Muff Winwood.
Also see WINWOOD, Steve

DAVIS, Tim

P&R '72

Singles: 7-inch

METROMEDIA 3-5 72-73

LPs: 10/12-inch 33rpm

METROMEDIA 8-10 72-74

Also see MILLER, Steve

DAVIS, Tyrone

P&R/R&B '68

Singles: 7-inch

ABC 4-6 68
COLUMBIA 3-5 76-81
DAKAR 3-6 68-77
EPIC 3-4 83
FUTURE 3-4 87-88
HIGHRISE 3-4 82-83
OCEAN FRONT 3-4 83-84

LPs: 10/12-inch 33rpm

COLUMBIA 8-10 76-81
DAKAR 10-15 69-76
EPIC 5-10 83
HIGHRISE 5-10 82

DAVIS SISTERS

C&W '53

Singles: 78rpm

FORTUNE 8-12 53
RCA 5-10 53-56

Singles: 7-inch

FORTUNE (174 "Kaw-Liga") 10-20 52
FORTUNE (175 "Heartbreak Ahead") 10-20 52
RCA (5000 & 6000 series) 10-15 53-56

Members: Skeeter Davis; Betty J. "Bee Jay" Davis.
Also see DAVIS, Skeeter

DAVIS SISTERS / Roy Hall

Singles: 78rpm

FORTUNE (170 "Jealous Love") 10-15 53

Singles: 7-inch

FORTUNE (170 "Jealous Love") 20-30 53

Also see DAVIS SISTERS
Also see HALL, Roy

DAVY DMX

(Davy D; David Reeves)

R&B/D&D '84

Singles: 12-inch 33/45rpm

CBS ASSOCIATED 4-6 84

Singles: 7-inch

CBS ASSOCIATED 3-4 84
DEF JAM 3-4 87

DAWN

(With Tony Orlando)

P&R/LP '70

Singles: 7-inch

BELL 3-5 70-72
FLASHBACK 3-5 70s

LPs: 10/12-inch 33rpm

BELL 10-12 70-71

Members: Tony Orlando; Joyce Wilson; Telma Hopkins.
Also see ORLANDO, Tony, & Dawn

DAWN

Singles: 7-inch

ARISTA 3-5 75
ELEKTRA 3-5 76-77

Members: Joyce Wilson; Telma Hopkins.
Also see DAWN (With Tony Orlando)

DAWSON, Cliff

R&B '82

Singles: 7-inch

BOARDWALK 3-4 82

DAWSON, Cliff, & Renee Diggs

R&B '83

Singles: 7-inch

BOARDWALK 3-4 83

Also see DAWSON, Cliff
Also see STARPOINT

DAY, Arlan

P&R '81

Singles: 7-inch

PASHA 3-4 81

DAY, Bobby

(With the Satellites; with Blossoms; Bobby Byrd)

P&R '57

Singles: 78rpm

CLASS 5-10 57

Singles: 7–inch

CLASS 8-12 57-59
RCA 5-8 63-64
RENDEZVOUS 5-10 60-62
SURE SHOT 4-8 67

LPs: 10/12–inch 33rpm

CLASS (5002 "Rockin' with Robin") 75-100 59
RHINO 5-10 84

DAY, Dennis

(With Jack Benny)

P&R '47

Singles: 78rpm

CAPITOL 3-5 56
RCA 3-5 47-54

Singles: 7–inch

CAPITOL 4-8 56
RCA 4-8 50-54
REPRISE 3-6 62
SHAMROCK 3-6 59

EPs: 7–inch 33/45rpm

CAPITOL 5-10 56
RCA 5-10 50-59

LPs: 10/12–inch 33rpm

BLUEBIRD 5-10 60
CAMDEN 5-10 64-66
CAPITOL 10-20 56
DESIGN 5-10
MASTERSEAL 10-20
RCA (3036 "My Wild Irish Rose") 15-25 52
REPRISE 5-10 63
ROULETTE 10-15 63

DAY, Doris

(With the Mellomen; with Norman Luboff Choir; with Buddy Clark)

P&R '47

Singles: 78rpm

COLUMBIA 4-8 47-57

Singles: 7–inch

ARWIN (250 "Everlasting Arms") 5-10 50s
COLUMBIA (38000 & 39000 series) 5-10 50-53
COLUMBIA (40000 thru 44000 series) 4-8 54-67

Picture Sleeves

COLUMBIA 10-20 57-61

EPs: 7–inch 33/45rpm

COLUMBIA 10-30 50-59

LPs: 10/12–inch 33rpm

COLUMBIA (1 "Listen to Day") . 20-30 60
COLUMBIA (600 thru 1300 series) 15-30 55-59
COLUMBIA (1400 thru 2100 series) 10-20 60-64
COLUMBIA (2500 series) 20-35 56
(10–inch LPs.)
COLUMBIA (6000 series) 25-50 49-55
(10–inch LPs.)
COLUMBIA (8000 thru 8900 series) 15-30 58-64
COLUMBIA (2200 thru 2300 series) 10-25 64-65
(Monaural.)
COLUMBIA (9000 thru 9100 series) 15-35 64-65
(Stereo.)
HARMONY 8-12 66-72

Also see BROWN, Les, & His Orchestra
Also see STREISAND, Barbra / Doris Day / Jim Nabors / Andre Kostelanetz

DAY, Doris, & Don Cherry

EPs: 7–inch 33/45rpm

COLUMBIA 10-20 56

Also see CHERRY, Don

DAY, Doris, & Frankie Laine

P&R '52

Singles: 78rpm

COLUMBIA 3-6 52

Singles: 7–inch

COLUMBIA 5-10 52

Also see LAINE, Frankie

DAY, Doris, & Andre Previn

LPs: 10/12–inch 33rpm

COLUMBIA 10-20 62

Also see PREVIN, Andre

DAY, Doris, & Johnnie Ray

P&R '53

Singles: 78rpm

COLUMBIA 3-6 52-53

Singles: 7–inch

COLUMBIA 5-10 52-53

Also see RAY, Johnnie

DAY, Doris, & Frank Sinatra

P&R '49

Singles: 78rpm

COLUMBIA 3-6 49

Singles: 7–inch

COLUMBIA 5-10 49

DAY, Doris / Frank Sinatra

LP '55

EPs: 7–inch 33/45rpm

COLUMBIA (571 "Young at Heart") 10-15 55
COLUMBIA (34178 "Young at Heart") 30-50 54
(Promotional issue only.)

LPs: 10/12–inch 33rpm

COLUMBIA (6339 "Young at Heart") 40-60 55
(Soundtrack. 10–inch LP.)

Also see DAY, Doris
Also see DAY, Doris, & Frank Sinatra
Also see SINATRA, Frank

DAY, Margie

R&B '50

Singles: 78rpm

CAT (118 "Ho-Ho")........ 5-10 55
DECCA........ 4-8 54
DOT........ 4-8 54

Singles: 7-inch

CAT (118 "Ho-Ho")........ 20-25 55
COED........ 4-8 61
DECCA........ 15-25 54
DOT........ 15-20 54
LEGRAND........ 10-20 62
MARTHAY........ 10-20 60s

Also see GRIFFIN BROTHERS

DAY, Morris

P&R/R&B/D&D/LP '85

Singles: 12-inch 33/45rpm

W.B. 4-6 85-86

Singles: 7-inch

W.B. 3-4 85-88

Picture Sleeves

W.B. 3-4 85-88

LPs: 10/12-inch 33rpm

W.B. 5-10 85-88

Also see TIME

DAYBREAK

P&R '70

Singles: 7-inch

PRELUDE........ 3-4 80
UNI........ 3-4 70

DAYE, Cory

P&R/LP '79

Singles: 7-inch

N.Y.I. 3-4 79

LPs: 10/12-inch 33rpm

N.Y.I. 5-10 79

Also see DR. BUZZARD'S ORIGINAL SAVANNAH BAND

DAYE, Johnny

R&B '65

Singles: 7-inch

JOMADA........ 4-8 65-66
PARKWAY........ 4-8 66
STAX........ 4-6 68

DAYNE, Taylor

P&R '87

Singles: 7-inch

ARISTA........ 3-4 87-90

Picture Sleeves

ARISTA........ 3-4 87-89

LPs: 10/12-inch 33rpm

ARISTA........ 5-8 87-90

DAYTON

R&B '81

Singles: 7-inch

CAPITOL........ 3-4 82-85
LIBERTY........ 3-4 81-82
U.A. 3-4 80

LPs: 10/12-inch 33rpm

CAPITOL........ 5-10 83
LIBERTY........ 5-10 81-82
U.A. 5-10 80

DAZZ BAND

R&B '80

Singles: 12-inch 33/45rpm

GEFFEN........ 4-6 86
MOTOWN........ 4-8 80-85

Singles: 7-inch

GEFFEN........ 3-4 86
MOTOWN........ 3-4 80-85
RCA........ 3-4 88

LPs: 10/12-inch 33rpm

GEFFEN........ 5-10 86
MOTOWN........ 5-10 80-85

Also see KINSMAN DAZZ

DE LA SOUL

LP '89

Singles: 7-inch

TOMMY B........ 3-4 89

D'COCOA, Creme: see CREME D'COCOA

DEACONS

R&B '68

Singles: 7-inch

CAMELOT........ 8-10
SHAMA........ 10-20 68

DEAD BOYS

LP '77

Singles: 7-inch

SIRE........ 3-5 77-78
SIRE........ 5-10 77-78
(Promotional issues only.)

LPs: 10/12-inch 33rpm

BOMP........ 8-10 80
SIRE........ 15-25 77-78

Members: Stiv Bators; Jimmy Zero, John Blitz; Cheetah Chrome; Jeff Jizz.
Also see BATORS, Stiv

DEAD MILKMEN

LP '87

Singles: 7-inch

ENIGMA........ 3-4 87-90

LPs: 10/12-inch 33rpm

ENIGMA........ 5-10 87-90

DEAD OR ALIVE

D&D '84

Singles: 12-inch 33/45rpm

EPIC........ 4-6 84-86

Singles: 7-inch

EPIC........ 3-4 84-89

Picture Sleeves

EPIC........ 3-4 84-89

LPs: 10/12-inch 33rpm

EPIC........ 5-10 84-89

Members: Pete Burns; Wayne Hussey.

Also see MISSION
Also see SISTERS of MERCY

DEADLY NIGHTSHADE

P&R '76

Singles: 7–inch

PHANTOM 3-5 76

LPs: 10/12–inch 33rpm

PHANTOM 8-10 76

DEAL, Bill
(With the Rhondels)

P&R '69

Singles: 7–inch

BUDDAH 3-5 71-72
CHESLICK 4-6
COLLECTABLES 3-4 80s
ERIC.. 3-4 70s
HERITAGE................................ 4-8 68-70
POLYDOR................................. 3-5 70-73
RED LION 3-4 79

Picture Sleeves

HERITAGE................................ 8-10 69

LPs: 10/12–inch 33rpm

HERITAGE.............................. 15-20 69
RHINO..................................... 5-10 86

DEAN, Alan

P&R '52

Singles: 78rpm

LONDON.................................. 3-5 51
MGM 3-5 51-56
RAMA...................................... 4-6 56-57

Singles: 7–inch

LONDON.................................. 5-10 51
MGM 4-8 51-56
RAMA...................................... 5-10 56-57

DEAN, Debbie
(With the Petites; with Paulette Singers)

P&R '61

Singles: 7–inch

MOTOWN (1007 "Don't Let Him Shop Around")........................ 25-35 61
MOTOWN (1014 "Itsy Bity Pity Love")................................ 15-25 62
MOTOWN (1025 "Everybody's Talking About My Baby") 20-30 62
TREVA (223 "Take My Hand").. 10-15 66
V.I.P. (25044 "Why Am I Lovin' You") 100-200 68

Picture Sleeves

MOTOWN (1025 "Everybody's Talking About My Baby") 50-100 62

DEAN, Hazell
(Hazel Dean)

D&D '83

Singles: 12–inch 33/45rpm

QUALITY.................................. 4-6 84
TSR 4-6 83

Singles: 7–inch

LONDON.................................. 3-5 76

DEAN, Jimmy
(Jimmie Dean)

P&R '57

Singles: 78rpm

COLUMBIA 4-8 57
4 STAR 5-10 54
MERCURY 4-8 56

Singles: 7–inch

CASINO 3-5 76
CHURCHILL 3-4 83
COLUMBIA (40000 thru 43000 series, except 42175)........................ 5-10 57-66
COLUMBIA (42175 "Big Bad John")................................... 10-12 61
(Dean says: "At the bottom of this mine lies one hell of a man.")
COLUMBIA (42175 "Big Bad John")..................................... 4-8 61
(Dean says: "At the bottom of this mine lies a big, big man.")
COLUMBIA (45000 & 46000 series) 3-5 74
4 STAR (1600 series) 10-15 54
4 STAR (1700 series) 5-8 59
KING 4-6 64
MERCURY................................. 5-10 56
RCA 3-6 66-71

Picture Sleeves

COLUMBIA (Except 41025)......... 5-10 59-66
COLUMBIA (41025 "Little Sandy Sleighfoot") 10-20 57

EPs: 7–inch 33/45rpm

COLUMBIA 8-12 57

LPs: 10/12–inch 33rpm

ACCORD 5-10 82
BRYLEN.................................... 5-10
CASINO 5-10 76
COLUMBIA (1025; Jimmy Dean's Hour of Prayer")....................... 20-30 57
COLUMBIA (1500 thru 2500 series)................................... 10-25 61-66
(Monaural.)
COLUMBIA (8000 & 9000 series)................................... 10-25 61-68
(Stereo. With "CS" prefix.)
COLUMBIA (9200 series) 5-10
(With "PC" prefix.)
COLUMBIA (10000 series) 6-10 73
COLUMBIA SPECIAL PROD....... 5-10
CROWN 10-15 60s
GRT 5-10 77
GUEST STAR 8-10 60s
HARMONY................................ 8-12 60-69
KING 12-18 61
LA BREA (8014 "Bummin' Around with Jimmy Dean")................................... 20-30

MERCURY (20319 "Jimmy Dean Sings His Television Favorites")............. 20-30 57
PICKWICK/HILLTOP 10-12 65
RCA.. 8-12 67-71
SPIN-O-RAMA 8-10 60s
WING 8-12 64
WYNCOTE................................ 8-10 60s

DEAN, Jimmy / Luke Gordon

LP: 10/12-inch 33rpm

PREMIER................................ 10-15 60s

DEAN, Jimmy / Johnny Horton

LPs: 10/12-inch 33rpm

STARDAY 15-20 65

Also see HORTON, Johnny

DEAN, Jimmy / Marvin Rainwater

LPs: 10/12-inch 33rpm

PREMIER (9054 "Showtime")... 10-15

DEAN, Jimmy / Marvin Rainwater / Rusty Evans

LPs: 10/12-inch 33rpm

ALMOR 10-15 60s

Also see RAINWATER, Marvin

DEAN, Jimmy, & Dottie West

Singles: 7-inch

RCA... 3-5 71

LPs: 10/12-inch 33rpm

RCA.. 8-10 70

Also see DEAN, Jimmy
Also see WEST, Dottie

DEAN, Paul

LP '89

LPs: 10/12-inch 33rpm

COLUMBIA 5-8 89

DEAN & JEAN

P&R '63

Singles: 78rpm

EMBER (1048 "We're Gonna Get Married") 15-25 58

Singles: 7-inch

EMBER 5-10 58-62
RUST 4-8 63-65

Members: Welton Young; Brenda Lee Jones.
Also see JONES, Brenda

DEAN & MARC

P&R '59

Singles: 7-inch

BULLSEYE (1025 "Tell Him No").. 10-20 59
BULLSEYE (1026 "Beginning of Love").................................... 10-20 59
CHECK MATE (1008 "Boogie-Woogie Twist") 15-25 61
HICKORY.................................... 4-8 63-65
MAY 5-10 63

Members: Dean Mathis; Marc Mathis.
Also see NEWBEATS

DEANE, Debbie: see DEAN, Debbie

DEANE, Shelbra

R&B '76

Singles: 7-inch

CASINO 3-5 76-77

DEAUVILLE, Ronnie

LP '57

Singles: 7-inch

ERA (1056 "Laura") 10-15 58

Picture Sleeves

ERA (1056 "Laura") 20-40 58

LPs: 10/12-inch 33rpm

ERA (20002 "Smoke Dreams")..20-40 57

DE BARGE
(DeBarges)

R&B/LP '82

Singles: 12-inch 33/45rpm

GORDY...4-6 85-86

Singles: 7-inch

GORDY...3-4 81-86
STRIPED H....................................3-4 87

Picture Sleeves

GORDY...3-4 85-86

LPs: 10/12-inch 33rpm

GORDY.......................................5-10 81-86
MOTOWN 5-8 80s

Members: Eldra BeBarge; Marty DeBarge; James DeBarge; Bunny De Barge.
Also see DE BARGE, Bunny
Also see DE BARGE, EL
Also see JONES, Quincy, James Ingram, Al B. Sure, El DeBarge & Barry White
Also see KING DREAM CHORUS & Holiday Crew
Also see SWITCH

DE BARGE, Bunny

R&B/LP '87

Singles: 12-inch 33/45rpm

GORDY...4-6 87

Singles: 7-inch

GORDY...3-4 87

LPs: 10/12-inch 33rpm

MOTOWN 5-8 87

Also see DE BARGE

DE BARGE, Chico

P&R/R&B/LP '86

Singles: 12-inch 33/45rpm

MOTOWN 4-6 86-87

Singles: 7-inch

MOTOWN 3-4 86-88

Picture Sleeves

MOTOWN 3-4 86

LPs: 10/12-inch 33rpm

MOTOWN 5-10 86-87

DE BARGE, El
(With DeBarge)

R&B/D&D '85

Singles: 12-inch 33/45rpm

GORDY...4-6 86-87

Singles: 7-inch

GORDY...3-4 81-87

LPs: 10/12-inch 33rpm

GORDY 5-10 81-87

Also see DE BARGE

DEBBIE DEB

R&B/D&D '84

Singles: 12-inch 33/45rpm

JAMPACKED 4-6 85
SUNNYVIEW 4-6 84

Singles: 7-inch

JAMPACKED 3-4 87

Also see TRINERE / Freestyle / Debbie Deb

DEBLANC

R&B '76

Singles: 7-inch

ARISTA 3-5 75-76

Members: Ralph DeBlano; Linda Carriere.
Also see DYNASTY
Also see STARFIRE

DE BURGH, Chris

P&R '83

Singles: 7-inch

A&M 3-5 75-87

Picture Sleeves

A&M 3-4 86

LPs: 10/12-inch 33rpm

A&M 8-10 76-86

DE CARO, Nick

P&R/LP '69

Singles: 7-inch

A&M 3-5 67-69

LPs: 10/12-inch 33rpm

A&M 5-10 69
BLUE THUMB 5-10 77

DE CASTRO, Peggy

Singles: 7-inch

SPOTLITE 5-15 62

Also see DE CASTRO SISTERS

DE CASTRO SISTERS
(With Don Costa's Orchestra)

P&R '54

Singles: 78rpm

ABBOTT 3-5 54-56
RCA 3-5 56
TICO 3-5 52

Singles: 7-inch

ABC-PAR 4-8 58
ABBOTT 5-10 54-56
CAPITOL 4-8 60-61
RCA 5-10 56
TICO 5-10 52
ZODIAC 3-4 77

LPs: 10/12-inch 33rpm

ABBOTT (5002 "DeCastro
Sisters") 35-45 56
CAPITOL 15-25 60-61
20TH FOX 8-15 65

Members: Peggy DeCastro; Babette DeCastro; Cherie DeCastro.
Also see COSTA, Don, Orchestra
Also see DE CASTRO, Peggy

DECO

R&B '83

Singles: 12-inch 33/45rpm

QWEST 4-6 84-85

Singles: 7-inch

QWEST 3-4 84-85

LPs: 10/12-inch 33rpm

QWEST 5-10 84

Members: Philip Ingram; Zane Giles.
Also see PAYNE, Scherrie
Also see SWITCH

DEE, Dave, Dozy, Beaky, Mick & Tich

LP '67

Singles: 7-inc

ATLANTIC 3-4 83
FONTANA 5-10 66-67
IMPERIAL 4-8 67-68

LPs: 10/12-inch 33rpm

FONTANA (27567 "Greatest
Hits") 20-30 67
(Monaural.)
FONTANA (67567 "Greatest
Hits") 25-30 67
(Stereo.)
IMPERIAL (12402 "Time to
Take Off") 20-25 68

Also see DOZY, BEAKY, MICK & TICH

DEE, Jackie
(Jackie DeShannon)

Singles: 78rpm

GONE 30-35 57

Singles: 7-inch

GONE (5008 "I'll Be True") 30-45 57
LIBERTY (55148 "Buddy") 25-40 58

Also see DE SHANNON, Jackie

DEE, Jay
(Earl Nelson)

R&B '74

Singles: 7-inch

W.B. 3-5 74

DEE, Jimmy
(With the Offbeats)

P&R '58

Singles: 7-inch

CUTIE 4-8 63
DOT (15664 "Henrietta") 15-20 57
DOT (15721 "You're Late
Miss Kate") 20-30 58
HEAR ME 4-8
INNER-GLO (105 "Guitar
Pickin' Man") 75-100
SCOPE (103 "I Ain't Givin'
Up Nothin") 15-25 59
TNT (148 "Henrietta") 25-50 57

TNT (152 "You're Late Miss Kate") 40-60 58
TNT (161 "I Feel Like Rockin'") . 40-60 59
TAPER (101 "I Ain't Givin' Up Nothin") 30-50 59

DEE, Joey

(With the Starliters; with New Starliters; with the Hawk)

P&R/R&B/LP '61

Singles: 7–inch

ABC 3-4 73
BONUS (7009 "Lorraine") 15-25 63
CANEIL 3-5
JUBILEE 4-8 66-67
LITTLE (813 "Lorraine") 100-150
ROULETTE 5-10 61-63
ROULETTE GOLDEN GOODIES . 3-4
SCEPTER 5-10 60
SUNBURST 3-5 73
TONSIL RECORDS 3-6 70
VASELINE HAIR TONIC (12 "Learn to Dance the Peppermint Twist") 10-20 62
(Special products issue from Chesebrough-Ponds.)

Picture Sleeves

BONUS (7009 "Lorraine") 25-35 63
ROULETTE 8-12 62

EPs: 7–inch 33/45rpm

DIPLOMAT 10-12 62

LPs: 10/12–inch 33rpm

ACCORD 5-10 82
ROULETTE 15-25 61-63
SCEPTER 15-25 62
Also see RASCALS

DEE, Joey, & Starliters / Dion

Singles: 7–inch

MONUMENT 5-10 61
Also see DION

DEE, Joey, & Starliters / Randy Andy & Candymen

EPs: 7–inch 33/45rpm

DIPLOMAT (66-2 "Come Twist with Me") 15-20 62
Also see DEE, Joey

DEE, Johnny

(John D. Loudermilk; Featuring Joe Tanner on Guitar)

P&R '57

Singles: 78rpm

COLONIAL (430 "Sittin' in the Balcony") 10-15 57

Singles: 7–inch

BULLET 8-12 53
COLONIAL (430 "Sittin' in the Balcony") 15-20 57
(Has "45 RPM" on left side of label.)
COLONIAL (430 "Sittin' in the Balcony") 10-15 57
(Has "45 RPM" on right side of label.)
COLONIAL (430 "Sittin in the Balcony") 8-12 57
(No "45 RPM" on label. Reads "Dist. by AM-PAR Record Corp.")
COLONIAL (435 "1000 Concrete Blocks") 15-20 57
DOT 5-10 58

Picture Sleeves

COLONIAL (430 "Sittin in the Balcony") 30-40 57
Also see LOUDERMILK, John D.

DEE, Kiki

(Kiki Dee Band)

P&R '71

Singles: 7–inch

LIBERTY 4-6 68
MCA 3-5 73-77
POSSE 3-4 81
RCA 3-4 81
RARE EARTH 3-5 71
ROCKET 3-5 73-79
TAMLA 3-6 70
WORLD PACIFIC 4-8 66

LPs: 10/12–inch 33rpm

LIBERTY (7600 series) 15-20 69
LIBERTY (10000 series) 5-10 81
MCA/ROCKET 8-12 73-74
RCA 5-10 81
ROCKET 8-10 77-78
TAMLA 15-20 70
Also see JOHN, Elton, & Kiki Dee

DEE, Lenny

P&R/LP '55

Singles: 78rpm

DECCA 3-4 56-61

Singles: 7–inch

DECCA 3-5 56-61

EPs: 7–inch 33/45rpm

DECCA 4-8 59

LPs: 10/12–inch 33rpm

DECCA 5-15 55-70

DEE, Lola

(With Stubby & the Buccaneers)

P&R '54

Singles: 78rpm

BALLY 3-6 57
MERCURY 3-5 54-56
WING 5-10 55-56

Singles: 7–inch

BALLY 5-10 57
MERCURY 5-10 54-56
WING 10-20 55-56

DEE, Lola, & Rusty Draper

Singles: 78rpm

MERCURY 3-6 56

Singles: 7-inch

MERCURY 5-10 56

Also see DEE, Lola

Also see DRAPER,Rusty

DEE, Neecy

D&D '85

Singles: 12-inch 33/45rpm

TNT 4-6 85

DEE, Tommy

P&R '59

Singles: 7-inch

CHALLENGE 8-10 60
CREST (1067 "Angel of Love") ... 8-12 59
PIKE 5-10 61
SIMS 10-15 66

DEE, Tommy, with Teen Tones & Orchestra / Teen Tones

P&R '59

Singles: 7-inch

CREST (1057 "Three Stars") 15-20 59
(Flip, *I'll Never Change,* is also credited to Teen Tones here and to Carol Kay and the Teen-Aires on copies below. The track is exactly the same on both discs.)

DEE, Tommy, with Carol Kay & Teen-Aires / Carol Kay & Teen-Aires

P&R '59

Singles: 7-inch

CREST (1057 "Three Stars") 10-15 59
(Monaural.)
CREST (1057 "Three Stars") 25-35 59
(Stereo.)

Also see DEE, Tommy

DEE JAY & RUNAWAYS

P&R '66

Singles: 7-inch

COULEE (109 "Love Bug Crawl") 20-35 60s
IGL (100 "Jenny Jenny") 100-150 65
IGL (103 "Peter Rabbit") 20-40 66
SMASH 4-8 66
SONIC 4-8 68
STONE (45 "Don't You Ever")... 20-30 66

Members: Denny Storey; John Senn; Gary Lind; Terry Klein; Bob; Tom.

DEEE-LITE

P&R/LP '90

LPs: 10/12-inch 33rpm

ELEKTRA 5-8 90

DEELE

R&B '83

Singles: 7-inch

SOLAR 3-4 83-88

LPs: 10/12-inch 33rpm

SOLAR 5-10 84-88

Members: Kenny "Babyface" Edmonds; Antonio "L.A." Reid; Darnell Bristol; Kevin Roberson; Carlos Green.

Also see BABYFACE

Also see MANCHILD

DEEP PURPLE

P&R/LP '68

Singles: 12-inch 33/45rpm

MERCURY 4-8 87

Singles: 7-inch

GRP 3-5 73
MERCURY 3-4 84-87
TETRAGRAMMATON 5-10 68-69
W.B. 3-6 70-73
W.B./PURPLE 3-4 74-75

Picture Sleeves

MERCURY 3-5 85
TETRAGRAMMATON 8-15 68
W.B./PURPLE 3-5 74-75

EPs: 7-inch 33/45rpm

W.B./PURPLE 10-20 74
(Jukebox issue.)

LPs: 10/12-inch 33rpm

MERCURY 6-12 84-88
PASSPORT 5-10 88
PORTRAIT 5-10 82
RCA 5-8 90
SCEPTER/CITATION 8-10 72
TETRAGRAMMATON (102 "Shades of Deep Purple") 20-30 68
TETRAGRAMMATON (107 "Book of Taliesyn") 20-30 69
TETRAGRAMMATON (119 "Deep Purple") 20-30 69
W.B. (Except 3000 series) 15-25 70-74
W.B. (3000 series) 5-10 77
W.B./PURPLE 10-15 74-80

Members: Ritchie Blackmore; Jon Lord; Ian Paice; Rod Evans; Nick Simper; Roger Glover; Ian Gillan; David Coverdale.

Also see BLACKMORE'S RAINBOW
Also see CAPTAIN BEYOND
Also see COVERDALE, David
Also see GILLAN, Ian
Also see GLOVER, Roger
Also see LORD, Jon
Also see PAICE, ASHTON & LORD
Also see TRAPEZE
Also see WHITESNAKE

DEEP RIVER BOYS

P&R '48

Singles: 78rpm

BEACON 10-15 52-54
BLUEBIRD (10676 "I Was a Fool to Let You Go") 15-25 40
BLUEBIRD (10847 "Bird in the Hand") 15-25 40
BLUEBIRD (11178 "My Heart at Thy Sweet Voice") 15-25 41
BLUEBIRD (11217 "I Wish I Had Died in My Cradle") 15-25 41
JAY-DEE 10-15 54
LANG-WORTH 10-20
(16-inch transcriptions, made in the '40s.)

PILOTONE 10-20 46
RCA 10-20 40-53
VICTOR 15-25 40
VIK 5-10 56

Singles: 7–inch

BEACON (104 "Sleepy Little Cowboy") 40-60 54
BEACON (9143 "Truthfully") 40-60 52
BEACON (9146 "All I Need Is You") 40-60 52
GALLANT 10-15 59
JAY-DEE (788 "No One Else Will Do") 25-35 54
MICHELLE 4-8 65
RCA (0078 "Free Grace") 30-50 50
(Colored vinyl.)
RCA (5268 "Biggest Fool") 20-30 53
SEECO 10-15 60
VIK (0205 "All My Love Belongs to You") 15-20 56
VIK (0224 "You're Not to Old") .. 15-20 56
WAND 5-10 61

Picture Sleeves

GALLANT (2001 "I Don't Know Why") 15-25 59

EPs: 7–inch 33/45rpm

CAMDEN (341 "Presenting the Deep River Boys") 20-30 56
WALDORF MUSIC HALL (113 "Songs of Jubilee") 50-75 56
(May also be shown as *Spirituals and Jubilees.*)
WALDORF MUSIC HALL (114 "Songs of Jubilee") 50-75 56
(Black vinyl. Has picture of group on cover.
WALDORF MUSIC HALL (114 "Spirituals and Jubilees") 75-100 56
(Colored vinyl. No picture of group on cover.)

LPs: 10/12–inch 33rpm

CAMDEN (303 "Presenting the Deep River Boys") 40-60 56
CAPITOL (6050 "Presenting Harry Douglas and the Deep River Boys") 20-40
(Canadian.)
QUE (104 "Midnight Magic") ... 50-75 57
WALDORF MUSIC HALL (108" Songs of Jubilee") 75-125 56
(10–inch LP. Label gives title as *Spirtuals and Jubilees.*)
X (1019 "Deep River Boys") 60-80 56

Members: Harry Douglas; Vernon Gardner; George Lawson; Ed Ware; Carter Wilson.
Also see BARLOW, Dean, & Crickets / Deep River Boys

DEEP VELVET

R&B '73

Singles: 7–inch

AWARE 3-5 73

DEES, Rick

(With His Cast of Idiots; Rick & Cast of Idiots)

P&R/R&B '76

Singles: 12–inch 33/45rpm

RSO 4-8 78
STAX 4-8 78

Singles: 7–inch

ATLANTIC (89481 "I Wanna Be Elvis") 4-8 85
FRETONE (040 "Disco Duck") 5-10 76
RSO (Except 860) 3-5 76-77
RSO (860 "He Ate Too Many Jelly Donuts") 8-10 77
RSO/POLYDOR 3-5 76-77
STAX 3-5 78

Picture Sleeves

ATLANTIC 3-4 86
STAX 3-5 78

LPs: 10/12–inch 33rpm

ATLANTIC 5-10 85
RSO 8-10 77

DEES, Sam

R&B '73

Singles: 7–inch

ATLANTIC 3-5 73-75
CHESS 3-5 71
LOLO 4-6 69
POLYDOR 3-4 78
SSS INT'L (732 "I Need You Girl") 15-25 68

LPs: 10/12–inch 33rpm

ATLANTIC 5-10 75

DEES, Sam, & Bettye Swann

Singles: 7–inch

BIG TREE 3-5 76

Also see DEES, Sam
Also see SWANN, Bettye

DEF LEPPARD

LP '80

Singles: 12–inch 33/45rpm

MERCURY 4-8 80-87
(Promotional only.)

Singles: 7–inch

MERCURY 3-4 80-89

EPs: 7–inch 33/45rpm

BLUDGEON RIFFOLA 10-15 78

Picture Sleeves

MERCURY (Except 811 215 7) 3-4 80-89
MERCURY (811 215 7 "Photograph") 3-6 83

LPs: 10/12–inch 33rpm

MERCURY 5-10 80-88

Members: Joe Elliott; Pete Willis; Rick Allen; Steve Clark; Phil Collen; Rick Savage; Vivian Campbell
Also see DIO, Ronnie

DE FRANCO FAMILY
(Featuring Tony DeFranco)

P&R/LP '73

Singles: 7–inch

20TH FOX (Except 2214)............. 3-5 73-74
20TH FOX (2214 "We Belong Together")............ 4-8 75

Picture Sleeves

20TH FOX.............. 3-5 73-74

LPs: 10/12–inch 33rpm

20TH FOX.............. 8-12 73-74

Members: Tony DeFranco; Benny DeFranco; Merlina DeFranco; Marisa DeFranco; Nino DeFranco.

DEJA

P&R/R&B/LP '87

Singles: 7–inch

VIRGIN.............. 3-4 87-88

Picture Sleeves

VIRGIN.............. 3-4 87

LPs: 10/12–inch 33rpm

VIRGIN.............. 5-10 87-88

Members: Curt Jones; Starleana Young.
Also see AURRA
Also see SLAVE

DE JOHN SISTERS

P&R '54

Singles: 78rpm

COLUMBIA.............. 3-6 57
EPIC.............. 4-6 54-56
OKEH.............. 4-8 53

Singles: 7–inch

COLUMBIA.............. 10-15 57
EPIC.............. 8-12 54-56
OKEH.............. 10-15 53
SUNBEAM.............. 8-12 59
U.A. 4-8 60

LPs: 10/12–inch 33rpm

U.A. 15-25 60

Members: Julie DeGiovanni; Dux DeGiovanni.

DEJONAY, Zena

D&D '84

Singles: 12–inch 33/45rpm

TVI.............. 4-6 84

DEKKER, Desmond, & Aces

P&R/LP '69

Singles: 7–inch

UNI.............. 3-6 69-70

LPs: 10/12–inch 33rpm

UNI.............. 20-25 69

DEL AMITRI

LP '90

LPs: 10/12–inch 33rpm

A&M.............. 5-8 90

DELACARDOS

P&R '61

Singles: 7–inch

ELGEY (1001 "Letter to a School Girl").............. 30-40 59
IMPERIAL.............. 5-10 63
SHELL (308 "Dream Girl").............. 15-25 61
SHELL (311 "Love Is the Greatest Thing").............. 15-25 62
U.A. 10-15 61

DELANEY & BONNIE
(Delaney & Bonnie and Friends)

LP '69

Singles: 7–inch

ATCO.............. 3-6 70-72
COLUMBIA.............. 3-5 72-73
ELEKTRA.............. 3-5 69
INDEPENDENCE.............. 4-8 67
STAX.............. 4-8 68-69

LPs: 10/12–inch 33rpm

ATCO.............. 15-25 70-72
COLUMBIA.............. 15-25 72
ELEKTRA.............. 15-25 69
GNP.............. 15-25 70
STAX.............. 15-25 69

Members: Delaney Bramlett; Bonnie Bramlett.
Also see BAD HABITS
Also see BRAMLETT, Bonnie
Also see BRAMLETT, Delaney
Also see CLAPTON, Eric
Also see LANI & BONI
Also see ROGERS, Dann
Also see SHINDOGS
Also see WHITLOCK, Bobby

DELBERT & GLEN

P&R '72

Singles: 7–inch

CLEAN.............. 3-5 72-73

LPs: 10/12–inch 33rpm

CLEAN.............. 12-20 72-73

Members: Delbert McClinton; Glen Clark.
Also see McCLINTON, Delbert
Also see PRINE, John / Daryl Hall & John Oates / Barnaby Bye / Delbert & Glen

DELEGATES

P&R '72

Singles: 7–inch

MAINSTREAM.............. 5-10 72

LPs: 10/12–inch 33rpm

MAINSTREAM.............. 10-15 73

DELEGATION

P&R/R&B/LP '79

Singles: 12–inch 33/45rpm

SHADYBROOK.............. 4-8 77

Singles: 7–inch

MCA.............. 3-5 76
MERCURY.............. 3-4 80-81
SHADYBROOK.............. 3-4 77-79

LPs: 10/12–inch 33rpm

MERCURY.............. 5-10 80-81
SHADYBROOK.............. 5-10 79

Members: Ray Patterson; Ricky Bailey; Bruce Dunbar.

DELFONICS

P&R/R&B '68

Singles: 7–inch

CAMEO 4-8 67
COLLECTABLES 3-4 80s
FLASHBACK 3-5 70s
MOON SHOT 4-8 68
PHILLY GROOVE 3-6 68-73
ROULETTE 3-5 73

LPs: 10/12–inch 33rpm

KORY 8-10 77
PHILLY GROOVE 10-20 68-74
POOGIE 5-10 81
COLLECTABLES 6-8 88

Members: Major Harris; William Hart; Wilbert Hart; Randy Cain; Richie Daniels.
Also see HARRIS, Major

DEL FUEGOS

LP '85

Singles: 7–inch

SLASH 3-4 85-87

Picture Sleeves

SLASH 3-4 86

LPs: 10/12–inch 33rpm

RCA 5-8 89
SLASH 5-10 85-87

DELIVERANCE

P&R '80

Singles: 7–inch

COLUMBIA 3-4 80

DELLS

R&B '56

Singles: 78rpm

VEE JAY (166 "Dreams of Contentment") 50-75 55
VEE JAY (200 series) 15-25 56-57

Singles: 12–inch 33/45rpm

ABC 4-6 79

Singles: 7–inch

ABC 3-5 73-78
ARGO 5-10 62
CADET 3-6 67-75
CHESS 3-4 73
COLLECTABLES 3-4 80s
MCA 3-4 79
MERCURY 3-5 75-77
PRIVATE I 3-4 84
20TH FOX 3-4 80-82
VEE JAY (166 "Dreams of Contentment") 100-150 55

Note: Vee Jay 134, *Tell the World*, is listed in the following section for DELLS / Count Morris.

VEE JAY (204 "Oh, What a Night") 50-75 56
VEE JAY (230 "Movin' On") 20-40 56
VEE JAY (236 "Why Do You Have to Go?") 20-40 57
VEE JAY (251 "Distant Love") ... 20-40 57
VEE JAY (258 "Pain in My Heart") 20-40 57
VEE JAY (274 "The Springer") .. 15-25 58
VEE JAY (292 "I'm Calling") 15-25 58
VEE JAY (300 "Wedding Day") .. 50-75 58
VEE JAY (324 "Dry Your Eyes") 20-40 58
VEE JAY (338 thru 712) 5-15 59-65

LPs: 10/12–inch 33rpm

ABC 8-10 78
BUDDAH 10-15 69
CADET 10-20 68-75
LOST-NITE 8-10 81
MERCURY 10-15 75-77
PRIVATE I 5-10 84
TRIP 10-12 73
20TH FOX 5-10 80-81
UPFRONT 10-15 68
VEE JAY (1010 "Oh What a Night") 400-500 59
(Maroon label, with thin circular ring.)
VEE JAY (1010 "Oh What a Night") 300-400 59
(Maroon label, with thick circular ring.)
VEE JAY (1010 "Oh What a Night") 100-200 61
(Black label. Monaural.)
VEE JAY (1010 "Oh What a Night") 100-200 61
(Black label. Stereo.)
VEE JAY (1141 "It's Not Unusual") 100-200 65

Members: Johnny Funches; Mike McGill; Marvin Junior; Vern Allison; Johnny Carter.
Also see BUTLER, Jerry, & Betty Everett
Also see CLARK, Dee
Also see LEWIS, Barbara
Also see SOUTH, Joe / Dells

DELLS / Count Morris

Singles: 78rpm

VEE JAY (134 "Tell the World") 75-150 55

Singles: 7–inch

VEE JAY (134 "Tell the World") 400-500 55
(Black vinyl.)
VEE JAY (134 "Tell the World") 700-900 55
(Colored vinyl.)
Also see DELLS

DELLS & DRAMATICS

R&B '75

Singles: 7–inch

CADET 3-5 75
Also see DELLS
Also see DRAMATICS

DE LORY, Al

P&R '70

Singles: 7–inch

CAPITOL.................................... 3-6 68-71
CHAAT (1001 "Hot Saki") 5-10
EUREKA 4-8 61
PHI DAN.................................... 4-8 65

LPs: 10/12–inch 33rpm

CAPITOL.................................... 5-15 69-70

DEL-PHIS

(Martha & the Vandellas)

Singles: 7–inch

CHECK MATE (1005 "It Takes Two")................................ 100-200 61
Also see MARTHA & VANDELLAS
Also see VELLS

DELPHS, Jimmy

P&R/R&B '68

Singles: 7–inch

CARLA (1904 "Dancing a Hold in the World") 100-200 68
CARLA (2535 "Almost") 10-20 67
KAREN.................................... 5-10 68

DELTA RHYTHM BOYS

P&R/R&B '46

Singles: 78rpm

ATLANTIC (889 "The Laugh's on Me").................................. 25-50 49
ATLANTIC (900 "Nobody Knows")................................ 25-40 50
DECCA.................................... 10-20 42-55
MUSICRAFT 10-20 49
RCA.. 10-20 47-48

Singles: 7–inch

DECCA (29000 series)............. 20-35 54-55
DECCA (48140 "You Are Closer to My Heart")........................... 50-75 50
DECCA (48148 "It's All in Your Mind")............................ 50-75 50
LONDON (1145 "Blow Out the Candle")........................... 15-25 52
MERCURY (1407 "I've Got You Under My Skin")...................... 20-30 52
MERCURY (1408 "They Didn't Believe Me")........................... 20-30 52
MERCURY (1409 "All the Things You Are").................... 10-20 52
PHILIPS 4-8 62
RCA (5094 "I'll Never Get Out of This World Alive")............... 25-35 53
RCA (5217 "Long Gone Baby"). 20-25 53

EPs: 7–inch 33/45rpm

RCA (3085 "Dry Bones")......... 75-100 50
(Double EP.)

LPs: 10/12–inch 33rpm

CAMDEN (313 "The Delta Rhythm Boys")....................... 40-50 56
CORAL (57358 "Swingin' Spirituals")..............................20-30 60
ELEKTRA (138 "The Delta Rhythm Boys").........................25-35 57
JUBILEE (1022 "Delta Rhythm Boys in Sweden")............................25-50 57
(Black vinyl.)
JUBILEE (1022 "Delta Rhythm Boys in Sweden")..........................75-100 57
(Colored vinyl.)
MERCURY (25153 "The Delta Rhythm Boys")......................75-100 53
(10–inch LP.)
RCA (3085 "Dry Bones")........100-150 50
(10–inch LP.)
Members: Traverse Crawford, Karl Jones; Kell Pharr; Lee Gaines.
Also see LUNCEFORD, Jimmie, & Orchestra

DEL-VIKINGS

(Featuring Krips Johnson; with Joey Biscoe)

P&R/R&B '57

Singles: 78rpm

DOT 10-15 57
FEE BEE 20-40 56-57
MERCURY..................................5-10 57

Singles: 7–inch

ABC..3-5 75
ABC-PAR (10208 "I'll Never Stop Crying").........................10-15 61
ABC-PAR (10248 "I Hear Bells")..20-30 61
ABC-PAR (10278 "Kiss Me") 8-12 62
ABC-PAR (10304 "One More River to Cross") 10-15 62
ABC-PAR (10341 "Confession of Love")..................................8-12 62
ABC-PAR (10385 "An Angel Up in Heaven").........................25-35 63
ABC-PAR (10425 "Too Many Miles") 8-12 63
ALPINE (66 "The Sun")............25-35 60
BVM 3-5 90
BIM BAM BOOM..........................3-5 72
BLUE SKY 3-4
BROADCAST..............................3-4
COLLECTABLES..........................3-4 80
CRUISIN' 3-4
DRC (101 "Can't You See") 20-30
DOT (15000 series) 10-15 57
DOT (16000 series) 8-12 60-61
FEE BEE (173 "Welfare Blues") 3-5 77
FEE BEE (205 "Come Go with Me")..................................50-80 56
(Has "45 RPM" on each side at top of label. With two sets of thin, horizontal, double parallel lines.)
FEE BEE (205 "Come Go with Me")..................................10-20 61

(Does not have "45 RPM." With one set of lines, one thick, one thin.)
FEE BEE (206 "Down in Bermuda") 40-60 57
FEE BEE (210 "What Made Maggie Run/Down By the Stream") 40-60 57
FEE BEE (210 "What Made Maggie Run/Uh Uh Baby") 40-60 57
FEE BEE (210 "What Made Maggie Run/When I Come Home") 50-75 57
FEE BEE (214 "Whispering Bells") 50-75 57
FEE BEE (218 "I'm Spinning") .. 50-75 57
FEE BEE (221 "Willette") 40-60 57
FEE BEE (227 "Tell Me") 15-25 59
FEE BEE (902 "True Love") 20-30 61
GATEWAY (743 "We Three") ... 15-25 64
GOLDIES 3-4
JOJO 3-6 76
LIGHTNING 3-4
LUNIVERSE (106 "Somewhere over the Rainbow") 35-50 57
LUNIVERSE (110 "Heaven in Paradise") 35-50 58
LUNIVERSE (113 "White Cliffs of Dover") 35-50 58
LUNIVERSE (114 "There I Go") 35-50 58
MCA 3-4 70s
MERCURY (30000 series) 4-6 61
MERCURY (70000 series) 8-15 57-63
SCEPTER 4-6 72
SHIP 3-4

Picture Sleeves

ALPINE (66 "The Sun") 40-60 60

EPs: 7–inch 33/45rpm

DOT (1058 "Come Go with Us") 200-300 57
MERCURY (3359 "They Sing, They Swing") 50-100 57
MERCURY (3362 "They Sing, They Swing") 75-100 57
MERCURY (3363 "They Sing, They Swing") 75-100 57

LPs: 10/12–inch 33rpm

BVM 5-8 91
COLLECTABLES 6-8 80-83
DOT (3695 "Come Go with Me") 200-400 66
JANGO (778 "Greatest Hits") 12-18
LUNIVERSE (1000 "Come Go with the Del Vikings") 300-400 57
MERCURY (20314 "They Sing, They Swing") 75-125 57
MERCURY (20353 "Del Vikings' Record Session") 75-125 58

Members: Kripp Johnson; Norman Wright; Clarence Quick; Don Jackson; Gus Backus; Joey Briscoe; David Lerchey; Bill Blakely; Ritzi Lee; Billy Woodruff.

Also see KING, Ben E.

DEL-VIKINGS / Ike Clanton

Singles: 7–inch

ERA 3-5

Also see CLANTON, Ike

DEL-VIKINGS / Diamonds / Big Bopper / Gaylords

Singles: 7–inch

MERCURY (53 "60 Second Spots") 20-40 58
(Promotional issue only.)

Also see BIG BOPPER
Also see DIAMONDS
Also see GAYLORDS

DEL-VIKINGS / Sonnets

LPs: 10/12–inch 33rpm

CROWN (5368 "The Del-Vikings and the Sonnets") 20-30 63
(Tracks shown by the Sonnets are actually by either the Meadowlarks or the Sounds.)

Also see DEL-VIKINGS

DE MARCO, Ralph

P&R '59

Singles: 7–inch

GUARANTEED 5-10 59
SHELLEY (1011 "Donna") 20-30 60
20TH FOX 4-8 62

Picture Sleeves

GUARANTEED 10-15 59

DE MATTEO, Nicky

(With the Sorrows)

P&R '60

Singles: 7–inch

ABC-PAR 5-10 61
ACE (110 "Please Don't Go Away") 10-20 57
CAMEO 5-10 65-66
DIAMOND 5-15 63
END (1021 "School House Rock") 15-25 58
GUYDEN 5-10 60
PARIS 8-12 59
TORE 8-12 59

DEMENSIONS

(Dimensions)

P&R '60

Singles: 7–inch

COLLECTABLES 3-4 80s
CORAL (Except 65611) 10-20 61-63
CORAL (65611 "As Time Goes By") 5-8 67
MOHAWK (116 "Over the Rainbow") 20-30 60
(Maroon label.)
MOHAWK (116 "Over the Rainbow") 15-20 60
(Brown label.)

MOHAWK (116 "Over the Rainbow")............................ 10-15 61
(Red label.)
MOHAWK (120 "Zing Went the Strings of My Heart").................................. 10-15 60
MOHAWK (121 "God's Christmas") 20-30 60
MOHAWK (123 "A Tear Fell")... 25-35 60
OLD HIT 3-5

Picture Sleeves

CORAL (62344 "My Foolish Heart")................................. 15-25 63

LPs: 10/12-inch 33rpm

CORAL (57430 "My Foolish Heart")............................. 75-125 63
(Monaural.)
CORAL (7-57430 "My Foolish Heart")............................... 85-125 63
(Stereo.)
CRYSTAL BALL......................... 8-10
MCA 5-10

Members: Lenny Dell; Phil Del Giudice; Howard Margolin; Marisa Martelli.

DEMIAN, Max
(Max Demian Band)

LP '79

Singles: 7-inch

RCA.. 3-4 79

LPs: 10/12-inch 33rpm

RCA.. 8-10 79-80

DENNIS, Cathy

LP '90

LPs: 10/12-inch 33rpm

POLYDOR.................................. 5-8 90

DENNY, Martin
(Exotic Sounds of Martin Denny)

P&R/R&B/LP '59

Singles: 7-inch

LIBERTY (55000 series)............... 3-6 59-67
LIBERTY (56000 series)............... 3-4 69
LIBERTY (77000 series)............ 5-10 59-60
(Stereo.)

Picture Sleeves

LIBERTY 5-10 59-63

EPs: 7-inch 33/45rpm

LIBERTY 5-10 59

LPs: 10/12-inch 33rpm

FIRST AMERICAN...................... 5-10 81
LIBERTY 10-20 59-69
SUNSET................................... 5-10 66-68
U.A. 5-10 74-80

Also see BAJA MARIMBA BAND
Also see ZENTER, Si

DENNY, Sandy

LP '74

Singles: 7-inch

A&M 3-5 72-73

LPs: 10/12-inch 33rpm

A&M 8-12 71-72
ISLAND 8-10 74-76

Also see FAIRPORT CONVENTION
Also see LED ZEPPELIN

DENNY, Sandy, & Strawbs

LPs: 10/12-inch 33rpm

PICKWICK..................................10-15 73

Also see DENNY, Sandy
Also see STRAWBS

DENVER, John

LP '69

Singles: 12-inch 33/45rpm

RCA (11189 "Bet on the Blues")..5-10 77
(Promotional issue only.)

Singles: 7-inch

ALLEGIANCE 3-4
CHERRY MOUNTAIN (02 "Flying Or Me") 3-5 86
RCA (Except 0067 thru 0955)........3-5 74-86
RCA (0067 thru 0955)...................4-8 70-74

Promotional Singles

EVA-TONE (106026 "Trees for America")...............................3-5 86
RCA (2008 "Rocky Mountain High").......................................5-10 72

Picture Sleeves

ALLEGIANCE 3-4
CHERRY MOUNTAIN (02 "Flying Or Me") 3-5 86
RCA (Except 2008)........................3-5 74-86
RCA (2008 "Rocky Mountain High").......................................5-10 72
(Promotional issue only.)

LPs: 10/12-inch 33rpm

HJD (66 "John Denver Sings") 200-300 66
(Promotional issue only. Less than 300 copies made as Christmas gifts for friends.)
MOS ("Something to sing About")..................................50-100 66
(Promotional issue only. No actual label name is used. Has three Denver tracks not available elsewhere.)
MERCURY (704 "Beginnings")..10-15 72
(With illustration on cover.)
MERCURY (704 "Beginnings")....8-10 74
(With mountain scene photo on cover.)
RCA (0101 thru 3449)...................5-10 73-80
RCA (0075 "The John Denver Radio Show")..........................20-30 74
(Single-sided LP. Promotional issue only.)
RCA (0683 "The Second John Denver Radio Show") 20-30 74
RCA (4000 series) 10-15 69-72
(Orange labels.)
RCA (4000 & 5000 series)...........5-10 81-85
(Black labels.)

RCA (5398 "The John Denver Holiday Radio Show") 10-20 84
(Promotional issue only.)
WINDSTAR 5-8 90
Also see BURTON, James
Also see DENVER, BOISE & JOHNSON
Also see MITCHELL, Chad, Trio
Also see MURPHEY, Michael
Also see TRAVERS, Mary
Also see WONDER, Stevie / John Denver

DENVER, John, & Placido Domingo

P&R '82

Singles: 7–inch

COLUMBIA 3-4 82
Also see DOMINGO, Placido

DENVER, John, & Emmylou Harris

C&W '83

Singles: 7–inch

RCA.. 3-4 83
Also see HARRIS, Emmylou

DENVER, John, & Muppets

LP '79

Singles: 7–inch

RCA.. 3-4 79

LPs: 10/12–inch 33rpm

RCA.. 5-10 79-83

DENVER, John, & Olivia Newton-John

P&R '75

Singles: 7–inch

RCA.. 3-5 75
Also see NEWTON-JOHN, Olivia

DENVER, John, & Nitty Gritty Dirt Band

C&W '89

Singles: 7–inch

UNIVERSAL.................................. 3-4 89
Also see NITTY GRITTY DIRT BAND

DENVER, John / Diana Ross

Singles: 7–inch

WHAT'S IT ALL ABOUT.............. 4-8 81
(Public service, radio station issue.)
Also see ROSS, Diana

DENVER, John, & Sylvie Vartan

Singles: 7–inch

RCA.. 3-4 84

DENVER, BOISE & JOHNSON

Singles: 7–inch

REPRISE (0695 "Take Me to Tomorrow") 5-10 68
Member: John Denver; Michael Johnson.
Also see DENVER, John
Also see JOHNSON, Michael

DEODATO

(Eumir Deodato)

P&R/R&B/LP '73

Singles: 12–inch 33/45rpm

W.B. 4-6 84

Singles: 7–inch

CTI 3-4 73-77
MCA..3-4 74-76
W.B. 3-4 78-84

Picture Sleeves

CTI 3-4 73

LPs: 10/12–inch 33rpm

CTI 8-10 73-74
MCA..6-10 76
MUSE..8-10 73-76
W.B. 5-10 78-82
Also see TROPEA

DEPECHE MODE

LP '81

Singles: 12–inch 33/45rpm

SIRE...4-6 81-87

Singles: 7–inch

SIRE...3-4 81-90

Picture Sleeves

SIRE...3-4 85-88

LPs: 10/12–inch 33rpm

SIRE...5-10 81-90

DEREK

(Johnny Cymbal)

P&R '68

Singles: 7–inch

BANG...4-8 68-69
SOLID GOLD 3-5 73
Also see CYMBAL, Johnny

DEREK B

R&B '88

Singles: 7–inch

PROFILE......................................3-4 88

DEREK & CYNDI

R&B '74

Singles: 7–inch

THUNDER 3-5 74

Picture Sleeves

THUNDER 3-5 74

DEREK & DOMINOS

LP '70

Singles: 7–inch

ATCO...3-5 70-72
RSO 3-4 73

LPs: 10/12–inch 33rpm

ATCO (704 "Layla") 20-30 70
POLYDOR 8-10 74
RSO 5-10 77
Members: Eric Clapton; Jim Gordon; Carl Radle; Bobby Whitlock; Duane Allman.
Also see ALLMAN, Duane
Also see CLAPTON, Eric
Also see WHITLOCK, Bobby

DERRINGER, Rick

(Derringer; with the McCoys)

LP '73

Singles: 7–inch

BLUE SKY 3-5 74-80

EPIC... 3-4 83

LPs: 10/12-inch 33rpm

BLUE SKY................................ 8-18 73-81
MERCURY........................... 10-20 74
PASSPORT............................. 5-10 83

Also see McCOYS

DERRINGER, Rick, & Edgar Winter Group

LPs: 10/12-inch 33rpm

BLUE SKY................................ 8-10 75

Also see DERRINGER, Rick
Also see WINTER, Edgar

DE SANTO, Sugar Pie
(Umpeylia Balinton)

R&B '60

Singles: 7-inch

BRUNSWICK.............................. 4-8 67-68
CADET....................................... 4-8 66
CHECK..................................... 8-12 60
CHECKER.................................. 4-8 63-66
GEDINSON................................ 4-8 62
JASMAN..................................... 4-6 74
SOUL CLOCK............................ 3-6 69
VELTONE............................. 10-20 60
WAX.. 4-8 64

EPs: 7-inch 33/45rpm

CHECKER (2979 "Sugar Pie").. 30-40 61

LPs: 10/12-inch 33rpm

CHECKER (2979 "Sugar Pie").. 40-50 61

Also see HANK & Sugar Pie
Also see JAMES, Etta, & Sugar Pie DeSanto

DE SARIO, Teri

P&R '78

Singles: 7-inch

CASABLANCA............................ 3-5 78

LPs: 10/12-inch 33rpm

CASABLANCA.......................... 5-10 80

DE SARIO, Teri, & K.C.

R&B '80

Singles: 7-inch

CASABLANCA............................ 3-5 79-80

Also see DE SARIO, Teri
Also see K.C. & Sunshine Band

DE SHANNON, Jackie

P&R '63

Singles: 7-inch

AMHERST................................ 6-12 78
ATLANTIC................................ 5-10 72-74
CAPITOL.................................. 5-10 71
COLUMBIA (Except 10221)....... 5-10 75
COLUMBIA (10221 "Boat to Sail")...................................... 10-15 76
(With Brian Wilson.)
EDISON INT'L (416 "I Wanna Go Home")........................ 50-100 60
EDISON INT'L (418 "Put My Baby Down")....................... 50-100 60
IMPERIAL................................... 4-8 65-70
LIBERTY (55000 series, except 55602)........................ 15-25 60-64
LIBERTY (55602 "Little Yellow Roses").......................... 8-10 63
(Black vinyl.)
LIBERTY (55602 "Little Yellow Roses")........................ 15-25 63
(Colored vinyl. Promotional issue only.)
LIBERTY (56000 series)............. 5-10 70
MGM... 4-8 65
RCA... 3-4 80

Picture Sleeves

LIBERTY (55526 "Faded Love")75-100 63

LPs: 10/12-inch 33rpm

AMHERST (1010 "You're the Only Dancer")......................... 15-25 77
ATLANTIC................................ 10-15 72-74
CAPITOL.................................. 15-20 71
COLUMBIA................................ 10-15 75
IMPERIAL (9286 "This Is Jackie De Shannon")........................ 25-50 65
(Monaural.)
IMPERIAL (9294 "You Won't Forget Me")............................ 25-50 65
(Monaural.)
IMPERIAL (9296 "In the Wind") .25-50 65
(Monaural.)
IMPERIAL (9328 "Are You Ready for This")...................... 25-50 66
(Monaural.)
IMPERIAL (9344 "New Image") .25-50 67
(Monaural.)
IMPERIAL (9352 "For You") 25-50 67
(Monaural.)
IMPERIAL (12286 "This Is Jackie De Shannon")............... 25-50 65
(Stereo.)
IMPERIAL (12294 "You Won't Forget Me")............................ 25-50 65
(Stereo.)
IMPERIAL (12296 "In the Wind").................................... 25-50 65
(Stereo.)
IMPERIAL (12328 "Are You Ready for This")...................... 25-50 66
(Stereo.)
IMPERIAL (12344 "New Image").................................. 25-50 67
(Stereo.)
IMPERIAL (12352 "For You") 25-50 67
(Stereo.)
IMPERIAL (12386 "Me About You").................................... 25-50 68
IMPERIAL (12404 "What the World Needs Now Is Love")......................... 25-50 68
IMPERIAL (12415 "Laurel Canyon")................................ 25-50 68
IMPERIAL (12442 "Put a Little Love in Your Heart").................................. 25-50 69

IMPERIAL (12453 "To Be Free") 25-50 70
LIBERTY (3320 "Jackie De Shannon") 50-100 63
(Monaural.)
LIBERTY (3390 "Breakin' It Up On the Beatles Tour") 50-100 64
(Monaural.)
LIBERTY (7320 "Jackie De Shannon") 75-100 63
(Stereo.)
LIBERTY (7390 "Breakin' It Up on the Beatles Tour") 75-100 64
(Stereo.)
LIBERTY (10000 series) 5-10 82
SUNSET 10-15 68-71
U.A. 8-10 75
Also see DEE, Jackie
Also see HALE & HUSHABYES
Also see SHANNON, Jackie
Also see WILSON, Brian

DE SHANNON, Jackie / Bobby Vee / Eddie Hodges

LPs: 10/12-inch 33rpm

LIBERTY (3430 "C'mon Let's Live a Little") 15-20 66
(Monaural. Soundtrack)
LIBERTY (7430 "C'mon Let's Live a Little") 20-25 66
(Stereo. Soundtrack)
Also see DE SHANNON, Jackie
Also see HODGES, Eddie
Also see VEE, Bobby

DESHAWN, Tony

R&B '87

Singles: 7-inch

AMAZON 3-4 87

DESMOND, Johnny

P&R '46

Singles: 78rpm

CORAL 3-5 52-56
MGM 3-6 50-51

Singles: 7-inch

COLUMBIA 4-8 59-60
CORAL 5-10 52-56
DIAMOND 3-6 62
EDGEWOOD 3-6 62
MGM 5-10 50-51
MUSICANZA 3-4
RCA 3-6 63
RED LITE 5-8
20TH FOX 3-6 64
VIGOR 3-4 73

Picture Sleeves

CORAL 5-10 55

EPs: 7-inch 33/45rpm

CORAL 8-15 54-56
MGM 10-20 52
P.R.I. (11 "So Nice") 5-10

LPs: 10/12-inch 33rpm

CAMDEN 10-20 53-54
COLUMBIA 5-10 59-60
CORAL 15-25 55-56
LION 10-15 56
MGM 10-20 55
MAYFAIR 10-15 58
MOVIETONE 5-10 66
P.R.I. (98 "90th Anniversary Album") 10-20
(Colored vinyl. Promotional issue for Montgomery Ward stores.)
VOCALION 5-10 66
Also see CORNELL, Don, Johnny Desmond & Alan Dale

DESMOND, Johnny, Eileen Barton & McGuire Sisters

P&R '54

Singles: 78rpm

CORAL 4-8 54
Also see BARTON, Eileen
Also see McGUIRE SISTERS

DESMOND, Johnny / John Gary / Gordon MacRae

LP: 10/12-inch 33rpm

INT'L AWARD 8-15 60s
Also see DESMOND, Johnny
Also see GARY, John
Also see MacRAE, Gordon

DESMOND, Paul
(Paul Desmond Quartet)

LP '63

Singles: 7-Inch

A&M 3-5 69-70
RCA VICTOR 3-8 62-63

LPs: 10/12-Inch 33rpm

A&M 5-15 69-76
CTI 8-12 75
CAMDEN 8-12 73
DISCOVERY 5-8 81
FANTASY (21 "Paul Desmond") 40-60 54
(10-inch LP.)
FANTASY (220 "Paul Desmond") 20-40 56
RCA (2400 & 2500 series) 15-25 62-63
RCA (2800 series) 5-10 78
RCA (3300 & 3400 series) 10-20 65-66
W.B. 20-30 60
Also see BRUBECK, Dave, & Paul Desmond
Also see MULLIGAN, Gerry, & Paul Desmond

DESTINATION

R&B '77

Singles: 12-inch 33/45rpm

BUTTERFLY 4-6 79

Singles: 7-inch

A.V.I. 3-5 77
BUTTERFLY 3-4 79

LPs: 10/12-inch 33rpm

A V I 8-10 77
BUTTERFLY 5-10 79

DET REIRRUC & Club Rappers

D&D '85

Singles: 12-inch 33/45rpm

CLUB 4-6 85

DETECTIVE

LP '77

Singles: 7-inch

SWAN SONG 3-5 77-78

LPs: 10/12-inch 33rpm

SWAN SONG 10-12 77-78

Member: Michael Des Barres.

DETERGENTS

P&R '64

Singles: 7-inch

KAPP 5-10 66
ROULETTE 5-10 64-65

Picture Sleeves

ROULETTE (4590 "Leader of the Laundromat") 15-25 64

LPs: 10/12-inch 33rpm

ROULETTE (25308 "The Many Faces of the Detergents") 25-35 65

Members: Ron Dante; Tommy Wynn; Danny Jordan.

DETROIT

LP '72

Singles: 7-inch

PARAMOUNT 3-5 70-71

LPs: 10/12-inch 33rpm

PARAMOUNT 10-15 71-72

Also see ROCKETS
Also see RYDER, Mitch, & Detroit Wheels

DETROIT EMERALDS

P&R/R&B '68

Singles: 7-inch

RIC-TIC 10-15 68
WESTBOUND 3-6 70-78

LPs: 10/12-inch 33rpm

WESTBOUND 10-15 71-78

Members: Abrim Tilmon; Ivory Tilmon; Cleophus Tilmon; Raymond Tilmon; James Mitchell; Paul Riser; Maurice King; Johnny Allen.
Also see CHAPTER 8

DETROYT

R&B '84

Singles: 7-inch

TABU 3-4 84

DE VAUGHN, William

P&R/R&B/LP '74

Singles: 7-inch

ROXBURY 3-5 74
TEC 3-4 80

LPs: 10/12-inch 33rpm

ROXBURY 8-10 74
TEC 5-10 80

Also see MEGD

DEVICE

P&R/LP '86

Singles: 12-inch 33/45rpm

CHRYSALIS 4-8 86
(Promotional issue only.)

Singles: 7-inch

CHRYSALIS 3-4 86

Picture Sleeves

CHRYSALIS 3-4 86

LPs: 10/12-inch 33rpm

CHRYSALIS 5-8 86

Members: Paul Engemann; Holly Knight; Gene Black.
Also see ANIMOTION
Also see KNIGHT, Holly

DEVO

LP '78

Singles: 12-inch 33/45rpm

ENIGMA 4-6 88
W.B. 4-8 80-85

Singles: 7-inch

ASYLUM 3-4 81
BOOJI BOY 3-5 78
ENIGMA 3-4 88
FULL MOON 3-4 81
W.B. 3-5 78-85

Promotional Singles

W.B. (49826 "Beautiful World") 8-12 81
(Space helmet shaped disc. With helmet photo.)
W.B. (49826 Beautiful World") ... 50-75 81
(Colored vinyl, space helmet shaped disc. No photo. Experimental pressing only.)

Picture Sleeves

FULL MOON 3-4 81
W.B. 3-5 79-85

LPs: 10/12-inch 33rpm

ENIGMA 5-10 88
W.B. 5-10 78-88

Members: Mark Mothersbaugh; Bob Mothersbaugh; David Kendrick; Bob Casale; Gerald Casale.
Also see JACKSON, Jermaine

DE VOL, Frank, Orchestra (With the Rainbow Strings)

P&R '50

Singles: 78rpm

CAPITOL 3-5 50-56
KEM 3-5 55

Singles: 7-inch

ABC-PAR 3-5 64-65
CAPITOL 3-6 50-56
COLGEMS 3-5 68
COLUMBIA 3-5 59-62
KEM 3-6 55

Picture Sleeves

COLGEMS 3-5 68

LPs: 10/12-inch 33rpm

ABC-PAR 5-10 65-66
COLGEMS (COM-108 "Guess Who's Coming to Dinner") 20-25 68
(Soundtrack. Monaural.)
COLGEMS (COS-108 "Guess Who's Coming to Dinner") 25-30 68
(Soundtrack. Stereo.)
COLGEMS (COMO-5006 "The Happening") 15-20 67
(Soundtrack. Monaural.)
COLGEMS (COSO-5006 "The Happening") 20-25 67
(Soundtrack. Stereo.)
COLUMBIA 8-10 59-63
HARMONY 5-10 65

DEVONS

R&B '69

Singles: 7-inch

KING 3-6 69

DE VORZON, Barry

LP '76

Singles: 7-inch

COLUMBIA 8-12 59-61
RCA 10-20 57-59
W.B. 3-4 81

LPs: 10/12-inch 33rpm

A&M 5-10 76
ARISTA 5-10 76

Also see BARRY & TAMERLANES

DE VORZON, Barry, & Perry Botkin Jr.

P&R '76

Singles: 7-inch

A&M 3-5 76-77

Picture Sleeves

A&M 3-5 76

LPs: 10/12-inch 33rpm

A&M 5-10 76

Also see DE VORZON, Barry

DEVOTIONS

P&R '64

Singles: 7-inch

DELTA (1001 "Rip Van Winkle") 50-75 61
KAPE 5-10
ROULETTE (4406 "Rip Van Winkle") 25-30 61
(White label.)
ROULETTE (4541 "Rip Van Winkle") 8-10 64
(Orange label.)
ROULETTE (4556 "Sunday Kind of Love") 15-20 64
ROULETTE (4580 "Snow White") 10-20 64

Members: Joe Pardo; Frank Pardo; Bob Weisbrod; Ray Sanchez; Bob Havorka; Louis DeCarlo; Larry Frank

DEVOTIONS

R&B '70

Singles: 7-inch

COLOSSUS 3-6 70

DEXTER, Al, & Troopers

P&R/R&B '43

Singles: 7-inch

COLUMBIA 4-8 46
EKKO 4-6 55
OKEH 5-10 43-44
VOCALION 10-20

Singles: 7-inch

EKKO 5-10 55

LPs: 10/12-inch 33rpm

CAPITOL (1701 "Greatest Hits") 20-30 62
COLUMBIA (9005 "Songs of the Southwest") 30-40
(10-inch LP.)

DEXY'S MIDNIGHT RUNNERS

P&R/LP '83

Singles: 7-inch

EMI AMERICA 3-4 81
MERCURY 3-4 82-83

Picture Sleeves

MERCURY 5-10 82-83

LPs: 10/12-inch 33rpm

EMI AMERICA 5-10 81
MERCURY 5-10 82-83

DEY, Tracey

P&R '63

Singles: 7-inch

AMY 8-12 63-65
COLUMBIA 5-10 66
LIBERTY 10-20 63
VEE JAY 10-20 62

DE YOUNG, Cliff

P&R '74

Singles: 7-inch

MCA 3-5 73-75

Picture Sleeves

MCA 3-5 74

LPs: 10/12-inch 33rpm

MCA 10-12 73-75

DE YOUNG, Dennis

P&R/LP '84

Singles: 12-inch 33/45rpm

MCA 4-8 88
(Promotional only.)

Singles: 7-inch

A&M 3-4 83-86

Picture Sleeves

A&M 3-4 84-86

LPs: 10/12-inch 33rpm

A&M 5-10 84-86
MCA 5-8 88

Also see STYX

DIABLOS

(Featuring Nolan Strong; with Maurice King Orchestra)

R&B '56

Singles: 78rpm

FORTUNE.................................. 8-15 54-57

Singles: 7-inch

FORTUNE (509 thru 522)......... 15-25 54-56
FORTUNE (525 thru 563)......... 10-20 57-64
FORTUNE (574 "The Way You Dog Me Around")................................ 10-15 80
(Colored vinyl.)

Picture Sleeves

FORTUNE.................................. 15-25 64

LPs: 10/12-inch 33rpm

FORTUNE (8010 "Fortune of Hits")................................ 50-75 61
FORTUNE (8012 "Fortune of Hits, Vol. 2")........................ 40-60 62
FORTUNE (8015 "Mind over Matter")........................... 40-60 63
FORTUNE (80810 "Fortune of Hits")................................ 10-15

Members: Nolan Strong; Bob "Chico" Edwards; Juan Guiterriec; Willie Hunter, Quentin Eubanks; Jim Strong; George Scott; J.W. Johnson.

DIAMOND, Gregg

(Gregg Diamond's Starcruiser; Gregg Diamond's Bionic Boogie)

R&B '78

Singles: 12-inch 33/45rpm

POLYDOR.................................. 4-6 79

Singles: 7-inch

MARLIN.................................. 3-5 78
POLYDOR.................................. 3-4 79-80

LPs: 10/12-inch 33rpm

MARLIN.................................. 5-10 78
MERCURY.................................. 5-10 79
POLYDOR.................................. 5-10 77-78

DIAMOND, Joel

(Joel Diamond Experience)

P&R '81

Singles: 12-inch 33/45rpm

CASABLANCA.................................. 4-6 79

Singles: 7-inch

ATLANTIC.................................. 3-4 82
CASABLANCA.................................. 3-4 79-84
MOTOWN.................................. 3-4 81

LPs: 10/12-inch 33rpm

CASABLANCA.................................. 8-10 79

DIAMOND, Leo

P&R '53

Singles: 78rpm

AMBASSADOR.................................. 3-5 51-53
RCA.................................. 3-5 55

Singles: 7-inch

AMBASSADOR.................................. 4-8 53
RCA.................................. 3-6 55

DIAMOND, Neil

P&R/LP '66

Singles: 12-inch 33/45rpm

COLUMBIA (1586 "Heartlight")....6-10 82

Singles: 7-inch

BANG (100 series)........................3-4
("Best Hits" reissue series.)
BANG (500 & 700 series)..............3-8 66-73
CAPITOL...3-4 80-81
COLUMBIA (02600 thru 06100 series)..3-4 81-86
COLUMBIA (10000 & 11000 series)..3-5 74-80
COLUMBIA (33000 series)...........3-4
("Hall of Fame" series.)
COLUMBIA (42809 "Clown Town")...............................150-200 63
COLUMBIA (45000 series)...........3-5 73-74
MCA (40000 series).......................3-5 73
MCA (60000 series).......................3-4 73
PHILCO.....................................10-20 66-67
("Hip-Pocket" flexi-disc.)
SOLID ROCK.....................................3-4
UNI...3-6 68-72

Promotional Singles

BANG (Except 55075)................5-10 66-73
UNI (55075 "Two-Bit Manchild") 15-20 68
(Colored vinyl.)
CAPITOL...3-5 80-81
COLUMBIA (1115 "Song Sung Blue")..3-6 77
COLUMBIA (1193 "September Morn")..3-6 79
(An alternate version.)
COLUMBIA (02600 thru 11000).....3-5 74-86
COLUMBIA (42809 "Clown Town")...............................100-200 63
COLUMBIA (45000 series)...........4-8 73-74
MCA...3-5 73
UNI...5-10 68-72
WHAT'S IT ALL ABOUT..............8-15 70s

Picture Sleeves

CAPITOL...3-5 80-81
COLUMBIA.......................................3-6 73-86
UNI...4-8 68-70

EPs: 7-inch 33/45rpm

COLUMBIA (32919 "Serenade") 10-20 74
MCA (34989 "12 Greatest Hits") 10-20 74
UNI (34818 "Neil Diamond Gold")..10-20 71
UNI (34871 "Stones")................10-20 71

Note: all EPs listed were made for jukebox use.

LPs: 10/12-inch 33rpm

BANG (214 "The Feel of Neil Diamond")..............................50-100 66
BANG (217 "Just For You").......20-40 67
BANG (219 "Greatest Hits").......20-40 68

BANG (221 "Shilo") 40-50 70
BANG (224 "Do It") 30-40 71
BANG (227 "Double Gold") 20-35 73
CAPITOL 5-10 80
COLUMBIA (30000 series) 8-12 73-86
COLUMBIA (40000 series) 5-10 86-89
COLUMBIA (42550 "Jonathan Livingston Seagull") 15-25 81
(Half-speed mastered.)
COLUMBIA (45025 "Best Years of Our Lives") 5-8 89
COLUMBIA (46525 "You Don't Bring Me Flowers") 15-25 80
(Half-speed mastered.)
COLUMBIA (47628 "On the Way to the Sky") 15-25 82
(Half-speed mastered.)
DIRECT-to-DISK 10-20
FROG KING (1 "Early Classics") 25-50 78
(Includes music and lyrics songbook. Columbia Record Club issue.)
HARMONY (30023 "Chartbusters") 15-25 70
(A compilation, containing the 1963 Columbia tracks, and the otherwise unavailable *I've Never Been the Same.*)
MCA 6-15 72-81
MFSL (024 "Hot August Night") 25-50 79
MFSL (071 "Jazz Singer") 20-30 82
UNI (11 Neil Diamond D.J. Sampler") 25-50 71
(Promotional souvenir issue only.)
UNI (1913 "Open-End Interview with Neil Diamond") 25-50 72
(Promotional issue only.)
UNI (73030 "Velvet Gloves and Spit") 20-35 68
(Does not contain *Shilo*)
UNI (73030 "Velvet Gloves and Spit") 15-25 70
(With *Shilo.*)
UNI (73047 "Brother Love's Traveling Salvation Show") 20-35 69
UNI (73047 "Sweet Caroline/Brother Love's Traveling Salvation Show") 15-25 69
UNI (73071 "Touching You, Touching Me") 15-25 69
UNI (73084 "Gold") 15-25 70
UNI (73092 "Tap Root Manuscript") 15-25 70
(Some 70000 series LPs were reissued in the 90000 series, with the only change being the first digit.)
UNI (93106 "Stones") 15-25 71
UNI (93136 "Moods") 15-25 72
UNI (93501 "Tap Root Manuscript") 15-25 70
(Capitol Record Club issue.)

Also see NEIL & JACK
Also see STREISAND, Barbra, & Neil Diamond
Also see TEN BROKEN HEARTS

DIAMOND, Neil / Diana Ross & Supremes

LPs: 10/12–inch 33rpm

MCA (734727 "It's Happening") .30-40 72
(One side of LP devoted to each artist.)
Also see DIAMOND, Neil
Also see SUPREMES

DIAMOND REO

P&R '75

Singles: 7–inch

BIG TREE 3-5 75
BUDDAH...3-5 77

LPs: 10/12–inch 33rpm

BIG TREE 8-10 75
KAMA SUTRA...............................8-10 76
PICCADILLY 5-10 79
Members: Frank Czuri; Bob McKeag.
Also see SILENCERS

DIAMOND RIO

C&W/LP '91

Singles: 7–inch

ARISTA 3-4 91

LPs: 10/12–inch 33rpm

ARISTA 5-8 91
Members: Marty Roe; Dan Truman; Brian Prout; Jim Olander; Dana Williams; Gene Johnson.

DIAMONDS

P&R/R&B '56

Singles: 78rpm

CORAL...4-8 55-56
MERCURY 4-8 56-57

Singles: 7–inch

CHURCHILL 3-4 87
CORAL...5-10 55-56
MERCURY 5-10 56-62

Picture Sleeves

MERCURY (71291 "High Sign") 10-20 58

EPs: 7–inch 33/45rpm

BRUNSWICK.............................15-20 57
MERCURY 10-20 56-61

LPs: 10/12–inch 33rpm

MERCURY 20-40 57-60
WING 15-25 59
Members: David Somerville; Phil Leavitt; Bill Reed; Ted Kowalski; Bob Duncan.
Also see DEL-VIKINGS / Diamonds / Big Bopper / Gaylords
Also see VEE, Bobby / Diamonds / Drifters

DIAMONDS / Georgia Gibbs / Sarah Vaughan / Florian Zabach

EPs: 7–inch 33/45rpm

MERCURY (4026 "Tops in Pops") 15-20 50s
Also see GIBBS, Georgia
Also see VAUGHAN, Sarah
Also see ZABACH, Florian

DIAMONDS & Pete Rugolo

LPs: 10/12-inch 33rpm

MERCURY (60076 "The Diamonds Meet Pete Rugolo") 45-55 59

Also see DIAMONDS

DIANE RAY: see RAY, Diane

DIBANGO, Manu

P&R/R&B/LP '73

Singles: 7-inch

ATLANTIC 3-5 73

LPs: 10/12-inch 33rpm

ATLANTIC 8-10 73

DICK & DEEDEE

P&R '61

Singles: 7-inch

DOT 4-8 68-69
LAMA 15-20 61
LIBERTY 5-10 61-62
U.A. 3-4
W.B. 4-8 62-69

Picture Sleeves

W.B. 12-25 63-64

LPs: 10/12-inch 33rpm

LIBERTY (3236 "Tell Me"/"The Mountain's High") 40-50 62
(Monaural.)
LIBERTY (7236 "Tell Me"/"The Mountain's High") 40-50 62
W.B. (1500 "Young and in Love") 20-30 63
W.B. (1538 "Turn Around") 20-30 64
W.B. (1586 "Thou Shalt Not Steal") 20-30 65
W.B. (1623 "Songs We've Sung on Shindig") 20-30 65

Members: Dick St. John; Dee Dee Sperling.

DICK & DON: see ADDRISI BROTHERS

DICK LEE: see LEE, Dick

DICKENS, Jimmy

(Little Jimmy Dickens; Jimmie Dickens)

C&W '49

Singles: 78rpm

COLUMBIA 5-10 49-57

Singles: 7-inch

COLUMBIA (10000 series) 3-5 76
COLUMBIA (20000 & 21000 series) 10-20 50-56
COLUMBIA (40000 series) 8-12 56
COLUMBIA (41000 series, except 41173) 8-12 57-60
COLUMBIA (41173 "I Got a Hole in My Pocket") 30-45 57
COLUMBIA (42000 thru 44000 series) 4-8 60-67
DECCA 3-6 67-69
LITTLE GEM 3-5 75
PARTRIDGE 3-4 80
STARDAY 3-5 73
U.A. 3-5 70-72

EPs: 7-inch 33/45rpm

COLUMBIA (Except 2800 series) 15-20 52-57
COLUMBIA (2800 series) 10-15 57-58

LPs: 10/12-inch 33rpm

COLUMBIA (1047 "Raisin' the Dickens") 40-50 57
COLUMBIA (1500 thru 2500 series) 10-20 60-66
(Monaural.)
COLUMBIA (8300 thru 9600 series) 15-25 60-68
(Stereo.)
COLUMBIA (10000 & 11000 series) 6-10 70-73
COLUMBIA (38000 series) 5-10 84
DECCA 10-12 68-69
GUSTO 5-10
HARMONY (7000 series) 10-15 64-65
HARMONY (9000 series) 20-30 54
HARMONY (11000 series) 8-12 67
QCA 6-10 75

DICKY DOO & DONT'S

P&R/R&B '58

Singles: 7-inch

ASCOT 4-8 65
CASINO 3-5
COLLECTABLES 3-4 80s
DANNA 4-8 67
ITZY 4-8
SWAN 8-12 58-59
U.A. 8-10 60-61

LPs: 10/12-inch 33rpm

DANNA (1566 "Live at Eagle Rock") 40-60
U.A. (3094 "Madison and Other Dances") 25-30 60
(Monaural.)
U.A. (3097 "Teen Scene") 25-30 60
U.A. (6094 "Madison and Other Dances") 30-40 60
(Stereo.)
U.A. (6097 "Teen Scene") 30-40 60
(Stereo.)

Members: Gerry Granahan; Harvey Davis; Jerry Grant; Ray Gangi; Joey Paige.

Also see GRANAHAN, Gerry

DICKIE LEE: see LEE, Dickie

DICKINSON, Bruce

LP '90

LPs: 10/12-inch 33rpm

COLUMBIA 5-8 90

DICTATORS

LP '77

Singles: 7-inch

ASYLUM 3-4 77

LPs: 10/12–inch 33rpm

ASYLUM 8-12 77-78
EPIC 10-12 75

DIDDLEY, Bo

R&B '55

Singles: 78rpm

CHECKER 15-30 55-57

Singles: 7–inch

ABC 3-5 74
CHECKER (814 thru 850) 15-25 55-56
CHECKER (860 thru 896) 10-20 57-58
CHECKER (907 "Bo Meets the Monster") 20-30 58
CHECKER (914 thru 997) 5-10 59-62
CHECKER (1019 thru 1200) 5-10 62-69
CHESS 3-5 71-72
RCA 3-5 76

EPs: 7–inch 33/45rpm

CHESS (5125 "Bo Diddley") 40-60 58
(With cardboard cover.)
CHESS (5125 "Bo Diddley") 30-40 58
(With paper cover.)

LPs: 10/12–inch 33rpm

ACCORD 5-10 82
CHECKER (1436 "Go Bo Diddley") 75-100 57
CHECKER (2974 "Have Guitar Will Travel") 50-75 59
CHECKER (2976 "Bo Diddley in the Spotlight") 50-75 60
CHECKER (2977 "Bo Diddley Is a Gunslinger") 65-75 61
CHECKER (2980 "Bo Diddley in a Lover") 40-60 61
CHECKER (2982 "Bo Diddley's a Twister") 40-50 62
CHECKER (2984 "Bo Diddley") 35-45 62
CHECKER (2985 "Bo Diddley and Company") 40-60 63
CHECKER (2987 "Surfin' with Bo Diddley") 35-45 63
(Most of the tracks on this LP are by the Megatons.)
CHECKER (2988 "Bo Diddley's Beach Party") 35-45 63
CHECKER (2989 "Bo Diddley's 16 All-Time Greatest Hits") 25-35 63
CHECKER (2992 "Hey Good Lookin'") 25-35 64
CHECKER (2996 "500% More Man") 25-35 64
CHECKER (3001 "The Originator") 25-35 66
CHECKER (3006 "Go Bo Diddley") 25-35 67
CHECKER (3007 "Boss Man").. 40-60 67
CHECKER (3013 "The Black Gladiator") 25-35 69
CHESS (1431 "Bo Diddley") 75-100 58
CHESS (8000 series) 5-10 83
CHESS (50000 series) 10-20 71-74
CHESS (60000 series) 15-25 74
MCA/CHESS 5-8 88
RCA (1229 "20th Anniversary of Rock 'N Roll") 10-20 76
(With numerous guest stars.)

Members: Jody Williams; Cliff James; Frank Kirkland; Jerome Green. Session: Willie Dixon; Otis Spann; Moonglows.

Also see BELMONTS, Freddy Cannon & Bo Diddley
Also see DIXON, Willie
Also see MOONGLOWS
Also see SPANN, Otis

DIDDLEY, Bo, & Chuck Berry

Singles: 7–inch

CHECKER (13370 "Bo's Beat") 4-8 64

LPs: 10/12–inch 33rpm

CHECKER (2991 "Two Great Guitars") 20-25 64

Also see BERRY, Chuck

DIDDLEY, Bo, Howlin' Wolf & Muddy Waters

LPs: 10/12–inch 33rpm

CHECKER (3010 "Super Super Blues Band") 15-20 68

Also see DIDDLEY, Bo
Also see HOWLIN' WOLF
Also see WATERS, Muddy

DIESEL

P&R/LP '81

Singles: 7–inch

REGENCY 3-4 81

LPs: 10/12–inch 33rpm

REGENCY 8-10 81

DIETRICH, Marlene

P&R '52

Singles: 78rpm

COLUMBIA 4-8 55

Singles: 7–inch

COLUMBIA 5-10 55

LPs: 10/12–inch 33rpm

COLUMBIA (105 "Marlena Dietrich Overseas") 40-60 52
(10–inch LP.)
COLUMBIA (316 "Dietrich in Rio") 25-35 59
COLUMBIA (2615 "Marlena Dietrich Overseas") 30-50 56
(10–inch LP.)
COLUMBIA (4975 "At the Cafe de Paris") 30-50 55
DECCA (5100 "Souvenir Album") 40-60 49
(10–inch LP.)
DECCA (7021 "Curtain Call") 30-40 51
DECCA (8465 "Marlene Dietrich") 25-35 57

MCA (1501 "Her Complete Recordings") 5-10 70s
VOX (3040 "Dietrich Sings") 50-75
Also see CLOONEY, Rosemary, & Marlene Dietrich

DIFFORD & TILBROOK

LP '84

Singles: 7-inch

A&M 3-4 84

LPs: 10/12-inch 33rpm

A&M 5-10 84
Members: Chris Difford; Glenn Tilbrook.
Also see SQUEEZE

DIFOSCO
(Difosco Erwin)

R&B '76

Singles: 7-inch

EARTHQUAKE 3-5 71
ROXBURY 3-5 76
20TH FOX 3-5 78
Also see IRWIN, Big D.

DIGITAL UNDERGROUND

P&R/LP '90

LPs: 10/12-inch 33rpm

TOMMY BOY 5-8 90-91

DILLARD, Varetta
(With the Roamers; with Four Students)

R&B '52

Singles: 78rpm

GROOVE 5-10 55-56
SAVOY 5-10 53-55

Singles: 7-inch

CUB 4-8 60-61
GROOVE (0139 "Darling, Listen to the Words of This Song") 20-30 56
GROOVE (0152 thru 0177) 12-25 56-57
RCA 10-15 57
SAVOY 10-20 53-55
TRIUMPH 8-12 59
Also see COOKIES

DILLARD & CLARK

LP: 10/12-inch 33rpm

A&M 10-15 68-69
Members: Doug Dillard; Gene Clark.
Also see CLARK, Gene
Also see DILLARDS

DILLARDS

P&R '71

Singles: 7-inch

ANTHEM 3-5 71-72
CAPITOL 4-6 65
ELEKTRA 4-8 63-69
POPPY 3-5 74
U.A. 3-5 75
WHITE WHALE 3-5 70

LPs: 10/12-inch 33rpm

ANTHEM 6-10 72
ELEKTRA (200 series) 20-30 63-65
(Gold label.)
ELEKTRA (7-200 series) 20-30 63-65
(Gold label.)
ELEKTRA (7-200 series) 10-15
(Brown label.)
ELEKTRA (74000 series) 8-12 68
FLYING FISH 5-10 77-81
POPPY 8-12 73
20TH FOX 8-12 73
Members: Doug Dillard; Rodney Dillard; Dean Webb; Mitch Jayne; Joe Osborn.
Also see DILLARD & CLARK
Also see NELSON, Rick

DILLARDS & John Hartford

LPs: 10/12-inch 33rpm

FLYING FISH 5-10 80s
Also see DILLARDS
Also see HARTFORD, John

DILLMAN BAND
(Daisy Dillman Band)

LP '78

Singles: 7-inch

RCA 3-4 81
U.A. 3-5 77-78

LPs: 10/12-inch 33rpm

RCA 5-10 81
U.A. 5-10 78
Members: Steve Seamans; Steve Solmonson; Tom Eckhoff.

DI MEOLA, Al
(Al Di Meola Project)

LP '76

Singles: 12-inch 33/45rpm

COLUMBIA 4-6 84

Singles: 7-inch

COLUMBIA 3-4 76-84

LPs: 10/12-inch 33rpm

COLUMBIA 5-10 76-83
EMI 5-10 88
Also see RETURN to FOREVER

DING DONGS
(Bobby Darin)

Singles: 7-inch

BRUNSWICK (55073 "Early in the Morning") 75-100 58
Also see DARIN, Bobby

DINNING, Mark

P&R '59

Singles: 78rpm

MGM 4-8 57

Singles: 7-inch

CAMEO 4-8 64
HICKORY 4-8 65-66
MGM (Except 12775 & 12980) 5-10 57-63
MGM (12775 "Cutie Cutie") 10-15 59
MGM (12980 "Top 40, News, Weather and Sports") 15-20 61
(With mention of Patrice Lumumba in lyrics.)
MGM (12980 "Top 40, News, Weather and Sports") 5-10 61

(With no mention of Patrice Lumumba in lyrics.)
MGM GOLDEN CIRCLE 3-5
U.A. 3-5 67-68

Picture Sleeves

MGM 10-15 60

LPs: 10/12–inch 33rpm

MGM (E-3828 "Teen Angel") 40-60 60
(Monaural.)
MGM (SE-3828 "Teen Angel") .. 50-75 60
(Stereo.)
MGM (E-3855 "Wanderin'")....... 40-60 60
(Monaural.)
MGM (SE-3855 "Wanderin'") 50-75 60
(Stereo.)

DINO

P&R '88

Singles: 7–inch

4TH & BROADWAY 3-4 88-89
ISLAND 3-4 90

Picture Sleeves

4TH & BROADWAY 3-4 89

LPs: 10/12–inch 33rpm

4TH & BROADWAY 5-8 89
ISLAND 5-8 90

DINO, Kenny

P&R '61

Singles: 12–inch 33/45rpm

KDK PRODUCTIONS ("Love Songs for Seka") 15-25 80
(Picture disc with photo of adult-film star, Seka.)

Singles: 7–inch

COLUMBIA (43062 "Betty Jean") 5-10 64
DOT.. 4-8 61
MUSICOR 5-10 61-62
RADNOR.. 4-6 60s
SMASH 4-8 63-64

DINO, Paul

P&R '61

Singles: 7–inch

ENTRE 4-8 63
PROMO...................................... 5-10 60-61

DINO, DESI & BILLY

P&R/LP '65

Singles: 7–inch

COLUMBIA 3-6 69
UNI.. 3-6 69
REPRISE (Except 0965) 4-8 64-69
REPRISE (0965 "Lady Love")... 10-15 70

Picture Sleeves

REPRISE 5-10 65-68

LPs: 10/12–inch 33rpm

REPRISE 15-25 65-66
UNI 12-20 69
Members: Dino Martin; Desi Arnaz Jr; Billy Hinsche.

DIO: see DIO, Ronnie

DIO, Ronnie

(With the Redcaps; with Prophets; Dio)

LP '83

Singles: 7–inch

ATLANTIC (2145 "Love Pains"). 15-20 62
JOVE..10-20 63
KAPP 5-10 65
LAWN (218 "Gonna Make It Alone")..................................10-15 63
PARKWAY 4-8 67
SENCA.....................................15-25 61
SWAN (4165 "Mr. Misery") 8-12 63
W.B. 3-4 83-86

LPs: 10/12–inch 33rpm

JOVE ("Dio At Domino's")..........40-60 63
W.B. 5-10 83-87
Members: Ronnie James Dio; Vinny Appice; Jimmy Bain; Vivian Campbell; Claude Schell; Craig Goldie;Rowan Robertson; Jen Johansson; Simon Wright; Terry Cook.
Also see AC/DC
Also see BLACKMORE'S RAINBOW
Also see HEAR 'N AID
Also see MALMSTEEN, Yngwie J.

DION

(Dion DiMucci)

P&R '60

Singles: 7–inch

ARISTA 3-4 89
BIG TREE/SPECTOR.....................3-5 76
COLUMBIA (3-42662 "Ruby Baby") 25-35 62
(Compact 33 single.)
COLUMBIA (4-42662 "Ruby Baby") 5-10 62
COLUMBIA (42776 "This Little Girl")..5-10 63
COLUMBIA (42810 "Be Careful of Stones You Throw") 5-10 63
(Black vinyl.)
COLUMBIA (42810 "Be Careful of Stones You Throw") 20-30 63
(Colored vinyl. Promotional issue only.)
COLUMBIA (42852 "Donna the Prima Donna") 5-10 63
(Black vinyl.)
COLUMBIA (42852 "Donna the Prima Donna") 20-30 63
(Colored vinyl. Promotional issue only.)
COLUMBIA (42917 thru 44719)...5-10 63-68
LAURIE (100 series).......................3-4
LAURIE (3000 & 3100 series)......5-10 60-63
LAURIE (3400 series) 4-6 68-69
LIFESONG.......................................3-5 78-79
MYRRH..3-5 85
SPECTOR...3-5 75
W.B. (Except 814)............................3-6 69-79
W.B. (814 "The Wanderer") 5-10 79
(Promotional issue only.)

W.B./SPECTOR 3-5 75

Picture Sleeves

ARISTA 3-4 89
COLUMBIA (Except 42662)...... 10-20 64-66
COLUMBIA (42662 "Ruby Baby") 30-40 62
(Promotional sleeve for *Ruby Baby,* but does not show title or number. Simply reads, "Dion Is Now on Columbia Records.")
COLUMBIA (42662 "Ruby Baby") 10-15 62
(Commercially issued sleeve.)
LAURIE 10-15 60-62

LPs: 10/12-inch 33rpm

ABEL 8-10
ARISTA 6-12 77-89
COLLECTABLES 6-8 85-87
COLUMBIA 15-25 63-73
DAYSPRING............................. 5-10 80-86
LAURIE (2004 "Alone with Dion") 20-30 61
LAURIE (2009 "Runaround Sue") 20-30 61
(Black vinyl.)
LAURIE (2009 "Runaround Sue") 75-100 61
(Colored vinyl.)
LAURIE (2012 "Lovers Who Wander")......................... 20-30 62
LAURIE (2015 "Love Came to Me").. 20-30 63
LAURIE (2017 "Dion Sings to Sandy and All Other Girls") 20-30 63
LAURIE (2019 "15 Million Sellers")................................ 20-30 63
LAURIE (2022 "More of Dion's Greatest Hits")....................... 20-30 63
LAURIE (2047 "Dion").............. 15-20 68
LAURIE (4000 series) 8-15
LIFESONG 5-10 78
PAIR... 10-12 86
REALM 5-10
W.B. 10-15 69-76

Also see ADAMS, Bryan
Also see DEE, Joey, & Starliters / Dion
Also see EDMUNDS, Dave
Also see LANG, K.D.
Also see REED, Lou
Also see SIMON, Paul
Also see SMYTH, Patty

DION / Glen Stuart Chorus

LPs: 10/12-inch 33rpm

ABEL 8-10

DION, Celine

LP '91

LPs: 10/12-inch 33rpm

EPIC.. 5-8 88

DION & BELMONTS
(Featuring Dion DiMucci)

P&R/R&B '58

Singles: 7-inch

ABC...4-8 66-67
COLLECTABLES..........................3-4 80s
LAURIE (3013 "I Wonder Why").......................................25-30 58
(Gary label.)
LAURIE (3013 "I Wonder Why").......................................15-20 58
(Blue label.)
LAURIE (3013 "I Wonder Why")..5-10 59
(Red and white label.)
LAURIE (3015 "No One Knows")..................................15-20 58
(Blue label.)
LAURIE (3015 "No One Knows")...5-8 58
(Red and white label.)
LAURIE (3021 "Don't Pity Me")..10-15 58
LAURIE (3027 "Teenager in Love")...8-12 59
(Monaural.)
LAURIE (S-3027 "Teenager in Love")..................................20-30 59
(Stereo.)
LAURIE (3035 thru 3059) 8-15 59-60
LAURIE DOUBLE GOLD 3-5 78
MOHAWK (107 "Tag Along").....30-40 57
ROCK"N MANIA 3-5

Picture Sleeves

LAURIE 10-20 59-60

EPs: 7-inch 33/45rpm

LAURIE (301 "Their Hits")..........50-75 59
LAURIE (302 "Where Or When")......................................40-60 59

LPs: 10/12-inch 33rpm

ABC (599 "Together Again")......15-25 67
ARISTA.......................................8-12 84
COLLECTABLES..........................6-8 85
GRT 8-10 75
JUKE BOX (95140 "A Teenager in Love")......................................20-30
(Four-LP boxed set. Also includes Dion solo tracks.)
LAURIE (1002 "Presenting Dion and the Belmonts") 75-100 59
LAURIE (2002 "Presenting Dion and the Belmonts")...............50-80 60
LAURIE (2006 "Wish Upon a Star")..30-40 60
LAURIE (2013 "Dion Sings His Greatest Hits–with the Belmonts")..........20-30 62
LAURIE (2016 "By Special Request")................................30-40 62
LAURIE (4001 "Everything You Always Wanted to Hear") 8-12 76

LAURIE (6000 "60 Greatest") ... 15-20
(Standard cover.)
LAURIE (6000 "60 Greatest") ... 20-30
(Boxed edition.)
PICKWICK 8-10 75
RHINO.................................... 5-10 87
W.B. 10-15 73
Also see BELMONTS

DION & BELMONTS / Belmonts

LPs: 10/12-inch 33rpm

MIASOUND (001 "Half & Half"). 15-20 81
(One side by Dion & the Belmonts, the other by the Belmonts.)

DION & TIMBERLANES

(Featuring Dion DiMuci)

Singles: 7-inch

JUBILEE (5294 "Chosen Few") 15-25 57
MOHAWK (105 "Chosen Few") 30-35 57
VIRGO...................................... 3-5 73
Also see DION

DIONNE & FRIENDS

P&R/R&B '85

Singles: 7-inch

ARISTA 3-4 85

Picture Sleeves

ARISTA 3-4 85
Members: Dionne Warwick; Elton John; Stevie Wonder; Gladys Knight.
Also see JOHN, Elton
Also see KNIGHT, Gladys
Also see WONDER, Stevie

DIONNE & KASHIF

P&R/R&B '87

Singles: 7-inch

ARISTA 3-4 87
Members: Dionne Warwick; Kashif.
Also see KASHIF
Also see WARWICK, Dionne

DIPLOMATS

P&R/R&B '64

Singles: 7-inch

AROCK (1004 "Here's a Heart") 10-20 64
DYNAMO 5-10 68-69
MAY 8-12 61
MINIT 5-10 66
WAND 5-10 65

DIRECT CURRENT

R&B '79

Singles: 7-inch

T.E.C. 3-5 79

DIRE STRAITS

P&R/LP '79

Singles: 12-inch 33/45rpm

W.B. 4-6 83

Singles: 7-inch

W.B. 3-4 79-88

Picture Sleeves

W.B. 3-4 79-86

LPs: 10/12-inch 33rpm

W.B. 5-10 78-88
Member: Mark Knopfler.

DIRKSEN, Senator Everett McKinley

P&R '66

Singles: 7-inch

CAPITOL.................................. 3-6 66

Picture Sleeves

CAPITOL.................................. 4-8 66

LPs: 10/12-inch 33rpm

BELL 5-10 70
CAPITOL.................................. 10-15 66-67

DIRT BAND: see NITTY GRITTY DIRT BAND

DIRTY LOOKS

LP '88

LPs: 10/12-inch 33rpm

ATLANTIC................................ 5-8 88-89
STIFF 5-10 80

DISCO FOUR

R&B '82

Singles: 12-inch 33/45rpm

PROFILE.................................. 4-6 83

Singles: 7-inch

PROFILE.................................. 3-4 82-83

DISCO 3

R&B '84

Singles: 12-inch 33/45rpm

SUTRA..................................... 4-6 83

Singles: 7-inch

SUTRA..................................... 3-4 84
Members: Darren Robinson; Mark Morales; Damon Wimbley.
Also see FAT BOYS

DISCOTAYS / Guess Who: see GUESS WHO / Discotays

DISCO-TEX & His Sex-O-Lettes

P&R/R&B '74

Singles: 7-inch

CHELSEA 3-5 74-76

LPs: 10/12-inch 33rpm

CHELSEA 8-10 75-76
MUSICOR 5-10 79

DIVINE

D&D '83

LPs: 10/12-inch 33rpm

O 5-10 83

DIVINE SOUNDS

R&B/D&D '84

Singles: 7-inch

SPECIFIC 3-4 84

DIVING for PEARLS

P&R '89

Singles: 7-inch

EPIC....................................... 3-4 89

DIVINYLS

LP '85

Singles: 12-inch 33/45rpm

CHRYSALIS.................................4-6 85

Singles: 7-inch

CHRYSALIS.................................3-4 83-86
VIRGIN.................................3-4 91

Picture Sleeves

CHRYSALIS.................................3-4 85

LPs: 10/12-inch 33rpm

CHRYSALIS.................................5-10 83-86
VIRGIN.................................5-8 91

Members: Christina Amphlett; Mark McEntee; Rick Grossman.
Also see HOODOO GURUS

DIXIE CUPS

P&R/R&B/LP '64

Singles: 7-inch

ABC-PAR.................................4-8 65-66
ANTILLES.................................3-4 87
LANA.................................3-6 60s
RED BIRD.................................5-10 64-65
TRIP.................................3-5 70s

Picture Sleeves

ANTILLES.................................3-4 87

EPs: 7-inch 33/45rpm

ABC-PAR.................................15-25 65

LPs: 10/12-inch 33rpm

ABC-PAR (ABC-525 "Riding High").................................25-30 65
(Monaural.)
ABC-PAR (ABCS-525 "Riding High").................................30-40 65
(Stereo.)
RED BIRD (RB-100 "Chapel of Love").................................35-45 64
(Monaural.)
RED BIRD (RBS-100 "Chapel of Love").................................50-75 64
(Stereo.)
RED BIRD (RB-103 "Iko Iko") ... 35-45 64
(Monaural.)
RED BIRD (RBS-103 "Iko Iko"). 40-60 64
(Stereo.)

Members: Barbara Hawkins; Rosa Hawkins; Joan Johnson.

DIXIE DREGS

(Dregs)

LP '78

Singles: 7-inch

ARISTA.................................3-4 80-82
CAPRICORN.................................3-4 77-79

LPs: 10/12-inch 33rpm

ARISTA.................................5-10 80-82
CAPRICORN.................................5-10 78-79

Members: Steve Morse; Rog Morganstein; T. Lavitz; Andy West; Alan Sloan.
Also see MORSE, Steve, Band

DIXIE DRIFTER

(Enoch Gregory)

P&R/R&B '65

Singles: 7-inch

AMY.................................4-6 68
IX CHAINS.................................3-5 74
ROULETTE.................................4-8 65

DIXIE HUMMINGBIRDS

R&B '73

Singles: 78rpm

OKEH.................................3-5 53

Singles: 7-inch

ABC.................................3-5 73-74
OKEH.................................5-10 53
PEACOCK.................................3-6 59-74

LPs: 10/12-inch 33rpm

CONSTELLATION.................................5-10 64
GOSPEL ROOTS.................................5-10 80
PEACOCK.................................5-10 59-78

Members: Ira Tucker; James Walker; James Davis; Willie Bobo; Beechie Thompson; Howard Carroll.
Also see BOBO, Willie
Also see SIMON, Paul

DIXIEAIRES

(Dixie-Aires)

R&B '48

Singles: 78rpm

EXCLUSIVE.................................5-10 48-49
GOTHAM.................................5-10 48
HARLEM.................................10-20 55
LENOX.................................5-10 49
SITTIN' in WITH.................................5-10 50

Singles: 7-inch

HARLEM (2326 "Traveling All Alone").................................100-150 55

Members: Joe Van Loan; Clyde Reddick; Henry Owens; Conrad Frederick; Arlandus Wilson; Willie Ray; Joe Floyd; John Hines; Bob Kornegay; J.C. Giuyard.
Also see DU DROPPERS

DIXIEBELLES

P&R/R&B '63

Singles: 7-inch

MONUMENT.................................3-5 72
SOUND STAGE 7.................................4-8 63-64

EPs: 7-inch 33/45rpm

SOUND STAGE 7.................................15-20 63

LPs: 10/12-inch 33rpm

SOUND STAGE 7.................................20-30 63
MONUMENT.................................15-20 65

Also see SMITH, Jerry

DIXON, Don

LP '87

LPs: 10/12-inch 33rpm

ENIGMA.................................5-10 87

DIXON, Floyd

R&B '49

Singles: 78rpm

ALADDIN 10-20 50-52
CASH 10-15 54
CAT 10-15 54
MODERN 8-12 49-50
PEACOCK 8-12 50
SUPREME 10-15 47
SWING TIME 10-15 47

Singles: 7–inch

ALADDIN (3135 "Wine Wine Wine") 75-150 52
ALADDIN (3144 "Red Cherries") 75-100 52
(Black vinyl.)
ALADDIN (3144 "Red Cherries") 150-250 52
(Colored vinyl.)
ALADDIN (3151 "Tired, Broke and Busted") 75-100 52
CASH (1057 "Oh Baby") 25-50 54
CAT (106 "Moonshine") 25-50 54
CAT (114 "Hey Bartender") 20-40 54
CHATTAHOOCHEE 4-8 64
CHECKER 10-20 58
DODGE 8-12 61
EBB 15-20 57
JELLO 10-15 60
KENT 8-12 58
SPECIALTY (468 "Hard Living Alone") 25-50 53
(Black vinyl.)
SPECIALTY (468 "Hard Living Alone") 75-125 53
(Colored vinyl.)
SPECIALTY (477 "Hole in the Wall") 25-50 53
(Black vinyl.)
SPECIALTY (477 "Hole in the Wall") 75-125 53
(Colored vinyl.)
SPECIALTY (486 "Ooh-Eee Ooh-Eee") 25-50 53
(Black vinyl.)
SPECIALTY (486 "Ooh-Eee Ooh-Eee") 75-125 53
(Colored vinyl.)
SWINGIN' 8-10 60

LPs: 10/12–inch 33rpm

INCULCATION 8-10

DIXON, Floyd, & Johnny Moore's Three Blazers

Singles: 78rpm

ALADDIN 15-25 50

Singles: 7–inch

ALADDIN (3101 "Do I Love You") 40-60 50
ALADDIN (3166 "Broken Hearted Traveller") 40-60 50
ALADDIN (3196 "Married Woman") 40-60 50
ALADDIN (3221 "Bad Neighborhood") 40-60 50
ALADDIN (3230 "You Need Me Now") 40-60 50
Also see MOORE, Johnny

DIXON, Willie
(With the Big Wheels)

R&B '55

Singles: 78rpm

CHECKER 10-20 55-56

Singles: 7–inch

CHECKER (822 "Walkin the Blues") 20-30 55
CHECKER (828 "Crazy for My Baby") 20-30 55
CHECKER (851 "Twenty-Nine Ways") 20-30 56
CHECKER (1100 series) 4-8 67

LPs: 10/12–inch 33rpm

BLUE HORIZON 10-12 70
COLUMBIA 10-15 70
OVATION 8-10 74-76
ROOTS N' BLUES 5-8 90
SPIVEY 8-10
YAMBO 8-10
Also see BOYD, Eddie
Also see DIDDLEY, Bo
Also see REED, Jimmy
Also see TAYLOR, Koko
Also see WELLS, Junior
Also see WILLIAMSON, Sonny Boy
Also see WITHERSPOON, Jimmy

DIXON, Willie, & Memphis Slim

Singles: 7–inch

PRESTIGE BLUESVILLE 4-8 62

LPs: 10/12–inch 33rpm

BATTLE 15-25 63
FOLKWAYS 8-12
PRESTIGE BLUESVILLE (1003 "Willie's Blues") 25-35 60
VERVE (3007 "Blues Every Which Way") 25-35 61
Also see BIG THREE TRIO
Also see DIXON, Willie
Also see MEMPHIS SLIM

DOBKINS, Carl, Jr.

P&R/R&B '59

Singles: 7–inch

ATCO 4-8 64
CHALET 3-6 69
COLPIX 4-8 65
DECCA 5-10 59-62
FRATERNITY 5-10 58
MCA 3-4 70s

Picture Sleeves

DECCA 5-10 59-60

EPs: 7–inch 33/45rpm

DECCA (2664 "My Heart Is an Open Book")............ 50-75 59

LPs: 10/12–inch 33rpm

DECCA (8938 "Carl Dobkins Jr.")............ 40-50 59
(Monaural.)
DECCA (7-8938 "Carl Dobkins Jr.")............ 50-65 59
(Stereo.)
Also see LEE, Brenda / Carl Dobkins Jr.

DOC BOX & B. Fresh

P&R '90

Singles: 7–inch

MOTOWN 3-4 90

DOC SAUSAGE & His Mad Lads

R&B '50

Singles: 78rpm

REGAL............ 5-8 50

DOCKETT, Jimmy

R&B '73

Singles: 7–inch

FLO FEEL 3-5 73
HULL............ 4-8 64-65

DR. AMERICA

R&B '82

Singles: 7–inch

ELEKTRA............ 3-4 82

DOCTOR & MEDICS

P&R/LP '86

Singles: 7–inch

I.R.S. 3-4 86

Picture Sleeves

I.R.S. 3-4 86

LPs: 10/12–inch 33rpm

I.R.S. 5-8 86

DR. BUZZARD'S ORIGINAL SAVANNAH BAND

P&R/R&B/LP '76

Singles: 7–inch

RCA............ 3-5 76-80

LPs: 10/12–inch 33rpm

ELEKTRA............ 5-10 79
PASSPORT............ 5-10
RCA............ 8-10 76-80
Members: August Darnell; Stony Browder Jr.; Cora Daye; Mickey Sezilla; Andy Hernandez.
Also see DAYE, Cory
Also see KID CREOLE & COCONUTS

DOCTOR FEELGOOD

(Doctor Feelgood & Interns)

P&R '62

Singles: 7–inch

COLUMBIA 4-8 65-66
EPIC............ 3-5 70s
MASTER SOUND 4-8 67
OKEH 5-10 62-63
1-3-4............ 4-8 68

LPs: 10/12–inch 33rpm

OKEH (12101 "Doctor Feelgood") 25-35 62
(Monaural.)
OKEH (14101 "Doctor Feelgood") 35-45 62
(Stereo.)
NUMBER ONE............ 15-20
Also see PIANO RED

DR. HOOK

(With the Medicine Show)

P&R/LP '72

Singles: 7–inch

CAPITOL (4000 series) 3-5 75-80
CAPITOL (8220 "The Stimu") 4-8 75
(Promotional issue only.)
CASABLANCA............ 3-4 80-82
COLUMBIA 3-5 71-74

Picture Sleeves

CAPITOL (4000 series) 3-5 75-80
CAPITOL (8220 "The Stimu") 8-10 75
(Promotional issue only.)
CASABLANCA............ 3-4 82
COLUMBIA 3-5 71-72

LPs: 10/12–inch 33rpm

CAPITOL............ 8-10 75-81
CASABLANCA............ 5-10 80-82
COLUMBIA (Except 34147)............ 15-20 72-74
COLUMBIA (34147 "Best of Dr. Hook") 5-10 76
Also see BEACH BOYS
Also see SAWYER, Ray

DOCTOR J.R. KOOL & Other Roxannes

LP '85

Singles: 12–inch 33/45rpm

COMPLEAT 4-6 85

Singles: 7–inch

COMPLEAT 3-4 85

LPs: 10/12–inch 33rpm

COMPLEAT 5-10 85

DR. JECKYLL & Mr. Hyde

R&B '82

Singles: 12–inch 33/45rpm

PROFILE............ 4-6 83-86

Singles: 7–inch

PROFILE............ 3-4 83-86

LPs: 10/12–inch 33rpm

PROFILE............ 5-10 84-86

DR. JOHN

(Mac Rebennack)

LP '71

Singles: 7–inch

ATCO 3-5 72-74
COLUMBIA 3-4 82
HORIZON 3-4 79
RCA 3-4 78

STREETWISE 3-4 84
W.B. 3-4 81

EPs: 7-inch 33/45rpm

ATCO (4521 "Dr. John")............. 5-10 72
(Promotional issue only.)

LPs: 10/12-inch 33rpm

A&M 8-10 79
ACCORD...................................... 5-10 81
ACE 10-12
ATCO (Except 200 & 300 series) 8-12 72-74
ATCO (200 & 300 series).......... 12-15 68-71
BAROMETER 10-12 74
CLEANCUTS 5-10 82-84
HORIZON.................................... 5-10 79
KARATE...................................... 8-10 78
SPRINGBOARD....................... 10-12 72
TRIP 8-10 75-76
U.A. 8-10 75
W.B. 5-10 89

Also see BLOOMFIELD, Mike, Dr. John & John Paul Hammond
Also see GUY, Buddy, Dr. John & Eric Clapton / Buddy Guy & J. Geils Band
Also see REBENNACK, Mac
Also see SAHM, Doug
Also see SIMPSONS

DR. JOHN & Chris Barber's Jazz & Blues Band

LPs: 10/12-inch 33rpm

GREAT SOUTHERN.................. 8-10 90

Also see BARBER, Chris

DR. JOHN & Libby Titus

Singles: 7-inch

W.B. 3-4 81

Also see DR. JOHN

DR. WEST'S MEDICINE SHOW & Junk Band

P&R '66

Singles: 7-inch

GO GO (100 "The Eggplant That Ate Chicago") 5-10 66
GO GO (102 "Playboys and Bums") 5-10 67
GO GO (104 "You Can Fly") 5-10 67
GREGAR.. 4-8 68
ROWE/AMI.................................... 4-8 66
("Play Me" Sales Stimulator promotional issue.)

Picture Sleeves

GO GO (102 "Playboys and Bums") 10-20 67

LPs: 10/12-inch 33rpm

GO GO (002 "The Eggplant That Ate Chicago")......................... 20-30 67
GREGAR.................................. 15-20 60s

Also see GREENBAUM, Norman

DODDS, Nella

P&R/R&B '64

Singles: 7-inch

WAND (167 "Come See About Me") 8-12 64
WAND (171 thru 187) 5-10 64
WAND (1111 "Gee Whiz") 10-15 65
WAND (1136 "Honey Boy") 50-75 65

DOE, John

LP '90

LPs: 10/12-inch 33rpm

DGC 5-8 90

Also see X

DOGGETT, Bill

P&R/R&B '56

Singles: 78rpm

KING 3-6 53-57

Singles: 7-inch

ABC-PAR 3-6 64
CHUMLEY 3-4 74
COLUMBIA...4-8 62-63
GUSTO 3-4 80s
KING (4000 series) 10-20 53-56
KING (5000 series) 5-15 56-65
KING (6000 series) 3-8 66-71
ROULETTE...3-6 67
SUE..4-6 64
W.B. 4-8 61

Picture Sleeves

COLUMBIA 5-10 62

EPs: 7-inch 33/45

KING 8-15 53-59

LPs: 10/12-inch 33rpm

ABC-PAR 10-15 65
COLUMBIA 10-20 62-63
HARMONY...................................10-15 67
KING (82 thru 118)......................20-40 52-55
(10-inch LPs.)
KING (500 thru 900 series)........12-25 56-66
ROULETTE...................................10-15 66
STARDAY 5-10
W.B. 12-20 61-62

Session: Howard Tate; Bill Butler; Clifford Scott.
Also see BOSTIC, Earl, & Bill Doggett
Also see BROWN, Wini
Also see FITZGERALD, Ella, & Bill Doggett
Also see HUMES, Helen
Also see JACQUET, Illinois
Also see TATE, Howard

DOKKEN
(Don Dokken)

LP '83

Singles: 7-inch

ELEKTRA..3-4 83-88

Picture Sleeves

ELEKTRA..3-4 87

LPs: 10/12-inch 33rpm

ELEKTRA.......................................5-10 83-88
GEFFEN 5-8 90

Also see HEAR 'N AID

DOLBY, Thomas

P&R/R&B/D&D/LP '83

Singles: 12–inch 33/45rpm

CAPITOL 4-6 83-84

Singles: 7–inch

CAPITOL 3-4 83-84
HARVEST 3-4 82

Picture Sleeves

CAPITOL 3-4 83-84

LPs: 10/12–inch 33rpm

CAPITOL 5-10 83-84
EMI 5-8 88
HARVEST 5-10 83

Also see DOLBY'S CUBE

DOLBY'S CUBE

(Thomas Dolby)

Singles: 12–inch 33/45rpm

CAPITOL 4-6 84

Singles: 7–inch

CAPITOL 3-4 84

Also see DOLBY, Thomas

DOLCE, Joe

P&R/LP '81

Singles: 7–inch

MCA 3-5 81
METROMEDIA 3-4 81

LPs: 10/12–inch 33rpm

MCA 5-8 81

DOLENZ, Micky

(Mickey Dolenz)

P&R '67

Singles: 7–inch

CHALLENGE (59353 "Don't Do It") 10-20 66
CHALLENGE (59372 "Huff Puff") 10-20 67
MGM 8-12 71-72
ROMAR 8-10 73-74

Picture Sleeves

CHALLENGE (59353 "Don't Do It") 10-20 66
CHALLENGE (59372 "Huff Puff") 20-30 67

LPs: 10/12–inch 33rpm

CHRYSALIS 8-10 79

Also see MONKEES
Also see NILSSON

DOLENZ, Micky, Davy Jones & Peter Tork

Singles: 7–inch

CHRISTMAS RECORDS 8-12 76
(Fan club, mail-order issue. Issued with special poster.)

Members: Micky Dolenz; David Jones; Peter Tork.
Also see MONKEES

DOLENZ, JONES, BOYCE & HART

Singles: 7–inch

CAPITOL (4180 "I Remember the Feeling") 10-15 75
CAPITOL (4271 "I Love You") ... 10-15 75

LPs: 10/12–inch 33rpm

CAPITOL 10-15 76

Members: Micky Dolenz; David Jones; Tommy Boyce; Bobby Hart.
Also see BOYCE, Tommy, & Bobby Hart
Also see DOLENZ, Micky
Also see JONES, Davy, & Micky Dolenz

DOLLAR

P&R '79

Singles: 7–inch

CARRERE 3-5 79

DOLPHINS

P&R '64

Singles: 7–inch

EMPRESS 5-10 61
FRATERNITY 4-8 64-65
GEMINI 4-8 62
LAURIE 5-10 63
SHAD (5020 "Tell-Tale Kisses") 20-30 60

DOMINGO, Placido

P&R/LP '81

Singles: 7–inch

CBS 3-4 81-84

LPs: 10/12–inch 33rpm

CBS 5-10 81-84
EMI 5-8 91
RCA 5-10 82

Also see DENVER, John, & Placido Domingo

DOMINO, Fats

R&B '50

Singles: 78rpm

IMPERIAL 10-30 50-57

Singles: 7–inch

ABC 3-5 73
ABC-PAR (455 "I Got a Right to Cry") 10-20 63
(Stereo Compact 33.)
ABC-PAR (10000 series) 5-10 63-64
BROADMOOR 4-8 67
IMPERIAL (5099 "Korea Blues") 200-225 52
IMPERIAL (5167 "You Know I Miss You") 150-200 52
IMPERIAL (5180 "Goin' Home") 100-150 52
IMPERIAL (5197 "Poor Poor Me") 50-100 52
IMPERIAL (5209 "How Long") . 50-100 52
(Black vinyl.)
IMPERIAL (5209 "How Long") 150-250 52
(Colored vinyl.)

IMPERIAL (5220 "Nobody Loves Me") 50-100 53
(Black vinyl.)
IMPERIAL (5220 "Nobody Loves Me") 150-250 53
(Colored vinyl.)
IMPERIAL (5231 "Going to the River") 50-100 53
(Black vinyl.)
IMPERIAL (5231 "Going to the River") 150-250 53
(Colored vinyl.)
IMPERIAL (5240 "Please Don't Leave Me") 40-80 53
(Black vinyl.)
IMPERIAL (5240 "Please Don't Leave Me") 150-250 53
(Colored vinyl.)
IMPERIAL (5251 "You Said You Love Me") 40-80 53
IMPERIAL (5262 "Something's Wrong") 25-50 53
(Black vinyl.)
IMPERIAL (5262 "Something's Wrong") 100-200 53
(Colored vinyl.)
IMPERIAL (5272 "Little School Girl") 20-40 54
IMPERIAL (5283 "Baby, Please") 20-40 54
IMPERIAL (5301 "You Can Pack Your Suitcase") 20-40 54
IMPERIAL (5313 "Love Me") 20-40 54
IMPERIAL (5323 "I Know") 20-40 54
IMPERIAL (5340 "Don't You Know") 20-30 55
IMPERIAL (5348 thru 5396) 10-20 55-56
IMPERIAL (5407 "Blueberry Hill") 10-15 56
(Black vinyl.)
IMPERIAL (5407 "Blueberry Hill") 75-125 56
(Colored vinyl.)
IMPERIAL (5417 thru 5477) 10-15 56-57
IMPERIAL (5492 "Yes My Darling") 8-12 58
(Black vinyl.)
IMPERIAL (5492 "Yes My Darling") 75-125 58
(Colored vinyl.)
IMPERIAL (5515 thru 5980) 5-10 58-63
IMPERIAL (66000 series) 4-6 64
IMPERIAL GOLDEN SERIES 3-5 70s
MERCURY 4-8 65
REPRISE 4-6 68-70
TOOT TOOT (001 "My Toot Toot") 3-5 85
(With Doug Kershaw.)
U.A. 3-5 74
W.B. 3-5 80

Picture Sleeves

IMPERIAL (5428 "I'm Walkin'") 15-25 57
IMPERIAL (5477 "The Big Beat") 15-20 57
IMPERIAL (5606 "I Want to Walk You Home") 10-20 59
IMPERIAL (5629 "Be My Guest") 10-20 59
MERCURY (72485 "It's Never Too Late") 20-30 65

EPs: 7-inch 33/45rpm

ABC-PAR 15-25 64-65
IMPERIAL (Except 127) 25-50 56-57
IMPERIAL (127 "Fats Domino–America's Outstanding Piano Stylist") 50-100 53
(Red, script logo label.)
IMPERIAL (127 "Fats Domino–America's Outstanding Piano Stylist") 25-50 56
(Maroon label.)
MERCURY 15-25 65
(Jukebox issues only.)

LPs: 10/12-inch 33rpm

ABC-PAR 15-20 63-65
CANDLELITE 12-15 76
EVEREST 8-10 74-77
GRAND AWARD 10-15 60s
HARLEM HITPARADE 8-10 75
HARMONY 10-15 69
IMPERIAL (Except 9004 thru 9040) 20-40 58-63
IMPERIAL (9004 "Rock 'n Rollin'") 60-100 56
IMPERIAL (9009 "Fats Domino Rock 'n Rollin'") 60-100 56
IMPERIAL (9028 "This Is Fats Domino") 60-100 57
IMPERIAL (9038 "Here Stands Fats Domino") 60-100 57
IMPERIAL (9040 "This Is Fats") 60-100 57
LIBERTY 5-10 80-81
MERCURY (21039 "Fats Domino '65") 15-20 65
(Monaural.)
MERCURY (61039 "Fats Domino '65") 15-20 65
(Stereo.)
PICKWICK 8-12 70s
REPRISE (6304 "Fats Is Back") 20-30 68
REPRISE (6439 "Fats") 300-400 71
SUNSET 12-15 66-71
TOMATO 10-20 89
U.A. 8-10 71-80

Also see ALLEN, Lee
Also see BARTHOLOMEW, Dave
Also see PRICE, Lloyd
Also see ROE, Tommy / Impressions / Fats Domino

DOMINATRIX

D&D '84

Singles: 12-inch 33/45rpm

STREETWISE 4-6 84

DOMINOES

R&B/P&R '51

Singles: 78rpm

DELUXE (309 "Sixty Minute Man"/ "Chicken Blues") 300-500 51
(Canadian. Note different flip than on U.S. issue.)
FEDERAL (12001 "Do Something for Me") 20-40 50
FEDERAL (12010 "Harbor Lights") 100-200 50
FEDERAL (12022 "Sixty Minute Man") 20-30 51
FEDERAL (12039 "I Am with You") 20-30 51
FEDERAL (12059 "That's What You're Doing to Me") 20-30 52
FEDERAL (12068 "Have Mercy Baby") 20-30 52
FEDERAL (12072 "Love, Love, Love") 20-30 52

Singles: 7-inch

FEDERAL (12001 "Do Something for Me") 350-400 50
FEDERAL (12022 "Sixty Minute Man") 150-200 51
FEDERAL (12039 "I Am with You") 200-300 51
FEDERAL (12059 "That's What You're Doing to Me") 250-300 52
FEDERAL (12068 "Have Mercy Baby") 100-175 52
FEDERAL (12072 "Love, Love, Love") 100-125 52
For later Federal numbers, EPs, and LPs, see the Billy Ward & Dominoes section.
GUSTO 3-5 80s

Members: Billy Ward; Clyde McPhatter; Charlie White; William Lamont; Bill Brown.
Also see GREENWOOD, Lil, & Dominoes
Also see LITTLE ESTHER & DOMINOES
Also see McPHATTER, Clyde
Also see WARD, Billy, & Dominoes

DON & GOODTIMES

(Don Gallucci)

P&R/LP '67

Singles: 7-inch

BURDETTE (3 "Colors of Life"). 10-20 66
DUNHILL 5-10 65
EPIC 5-10 67-68
JERDEN 8-12 66
PICCADILLY 5-10 60s
WAND 5-10 64

Picture Sleeves

EPIC (10199 "Happy & Me") 10-20 67

LPs: 10/12-inch 33rpm

BURDETTE (300 "Greatest Hits") 40-50 66
EPIC (24311 "So Good") 15-20 67
(Monaural.)
EPIC (26311 "So Good") 15-20 67
(Stereo.)
PANORAMA (104 "Harpo") 30-40
PICCADILLY (3394 "Goodtime Music") 5-10 82
WAND (679 "Where the Action Is") 25-35 67

Members: Don Gallucci; Jeff Hawks; Joe Newman.
Also see KINGSMEN
Also see TOUCH

DON & JUAN

P&R '62

Singles: 7-inch

BIG TOP (3079 "What's Your Name") 8-12 62
BIG TOP (3106 "Two Fools Are We") 10-15 62
BIG TOP (3121 "Magic Wand") .20-30 62
BIG TOP (3145 "True Love Never Runs Smooth") 10-20 63
ERIC 3-4 70s
MALA (469 "Lonely Man") 8-12 63
MALA (484 "Sincerely") 8-12 63
MALA (509 "Heartbreaking Truth") 15-25 65
TERRIFIC 3-5 70s
TWIRL (2021 "Because I Love You") 15-25 66

Members: Roland Trone: Claude Johnson.

DON, DICK N' JIMMY

P&R '54

Singles: 78rpm

CROWN 4-8 54-55
DOT 4-8 54

Singles: 7-inch

CROWN 8-12 54-55
DOT 8-12 54

LPs: 10/12-inch 33rpm

CROWN (5005 "Spring Fever") .25-35 57
DOT 15-25 59
MODERN (1205 "Spring Fever") 35-50 56
VERVE 15-25 59

Members: Don Sutton; Dick Rock; Jimmy Cook.

DONALDSON, Bo, & Heywoods

(Heywoods)

P&R '72

Singles: 7-inch

ABC 3-5 73-75
CAPITOL 3-5 76
FAMILY 3-5 72-74
PLAYBOY 3-5 77

Picture Sleeves

ABC 3-5 74

LPs: 10/12–inch 33rpm

ABC 5-10 74
CAPITOL 5-8 76
FAMILY 8-12 72

DONALDSON, Lou

(Lou Donaldson Quintet)

LP '63

Singles: 78rpm

BLUE NOTE 3-5 52-57

Singles: 7–inch

ARGO 4-6 63-65
BLUE NOTE (100 thru 300 series) 3-5 73-74
BLUE NOTE (1500 & 1600 series) 5-10 52-58
BLUE NOTE (1700 thru 1900 series) 4-8 58-72

LPs: 10/12–inch 33rpm

ARGO 10-20 63-65
BLUE NOTE 8-15 64-80
(Label shows Blue Note Records as a division of either Liberty or United Artists.)
BLUE NOTE (1500 series) 25-50 57-58
(Label gives New York street address for Blue Note Records.)
BLUE NOTE (1500 series) 15-25 58
(Label reads "Blue Note Records Inc. - New York, USA.")
BLUE NOTE (1500 series) 10-20 66
(Label shows Blue Note Records as a division of either Liberty or United Artists.)
BLUE NOTE (4000 & 84000 series) 15-25 58-63
(Label reads "Blue Note Records Inc. - New York, U.S.A.")
BLUE NOTE (5000 series) 50-75 52-54
(10–inch LPs.)
BLUE NOTE (5000 series) 50-75 52-54
(10–inch LPs.)
CADET 8-12 65-71
COTILLION 5-10 76-77
SUNSET 5-10 69-71
TRIP 5-10 79

DONEGAN, Lonnie

(With His Skiffle Group)

P&R '56

Singles: 78rpm

LONDON 3-6 56
MERCURY 3-6 56

Singles: 7–inch

ABC 3-4 76
APT 4-8 62
ATLANTIC 4-8 60-61
DOT 4-8 61
FELSTED 4-8 61
HICKORY 4-6 64-65
LONDON 8-12 56
MCA 3-4
MERCURY 5-10 56

LPs: 10/12–inch 33rpm

ABC-PAR 15-20 63
ATLANTIC 20-30 60
DOT (3159 "Lonnie Donegan") .. 25-35 59
DOT (3394 "Lonnie Donegan") .. 20-30 61
U.A. 10-12 77

DONNA LYNN: see LYNN, Donna

DONNER, Ral

(With the Starfires; with Scotty Moore, D.J. Fontana & Jordanaires)

P&R '61

Singles: 7–inch

ABC 3-5 73
CHICAGO FIRE 8-10 74
END (19 "You Don't Know What You've Got") 10-20 63
FONTANA (1502 "Poison Ivy League") 10-20 64
FONTANA (1515 "Good Lovin'") 10-20 65
GONE (5102 "Girl of My Best Friend") 30-40 60
(Black label.)
GONE (5100 series, except 5108 & 5119) 10-15 61-62
(Multi-color labels.)
GONE (5108 "To Love"/"And Then") 15-25 61
(Shortly after this release, *You Don't Know What You've Got* was issued using the same selection number.)
GONE (5108 "You Don't Know What You've Got") 10-15 61
GONE (5114 "Please Don't Go") . 8-12 61
GONE (5119 "School of Heartbreakers") 30-40 61
GONE (5121 "She's Everything"/ "Because We're Young") 10-20 61
GONE (5121 "She's Everything"/ "Will You Love Me in Heaven") 15-25 61
(*Will You Love Me in Heaven* is by an unknown girl group, though credited on the label to Ral Donner.)
GONE (5125 "To Love Someone"/"Will You Love Me in Heaven") 10-15 61
(*Will You Love Me in Heaven* is sung by Ral Donner.)
GONE (5129 "Loveless Life") 10-15 62
GONE (5133 "To Love") 10-15 61
MJ (222 "My Heart Sings") 4-8 70
MID-EAGLE 4-8 68-76
RED BIRD (057 "Love Isn't Like That") 100-150 66
REPRISE (20135 "Christmas Day") 20-30 62
REPRISE (20141 "I Got Burned") 20-30 63

RISING SONS 5-10 68
ROULETTE 3-5 71
SCOTTIE (1310 "Tell Me Why") 150-250 59
SMASH (34774 "Good Lovin'") . 25-35 65
(Promotional issue only.)
STARFIRE (100 "Wait a Minute Now") 5-10 78
STARFIRE (103 "Christmas Day") 5-10 78
STARFIRE (114 "Rip It Up") 5-10 79
(Black vinyl.)
STARFIRE (114 "Rip It Up") 10-25 79
(Picture disc.)
SUNLIGHT 8-10 72
TAU (105 "Lonliness of a Star") 35-50 63
(Blue label. First issue—1,000 made.)
TAU (105 "Lonliness of a Star") 20-30 63
(Yellow label. 2,000 made.)
THUNDER (7801 "The Day the Beat Stopped") 4-6 78
(Clear vinyl.)

Picture Sleeves

MJ (222 "My Heart Sings") 5-10 70
REPRISE (20141 "I Got Burned") 50-75 63
STARFIRE 5-10 78-79

LPs: 10/12–inch 33rpm

AUDIO RESEARCH 12-15 80
GONE (5012 "Takin' Care of Business") 75-100 61
GONE (5033 "Elvis Scrapbook") 10-15
GYPSY 8-12 79
MURRAY HILL 5-10 88
STARFIRE (1004 "An Evening with Ral Donner") 10-15 82
(Multi-color vinyl.)
Session: Scotty Moore; Jordanaires.
Also see PRESLEY, Elvis

DONNER, Ral / Ray Smith / Bobby Dale

LPs: 10/12–inch 33rpm

CROWN 15-20 63
Also see SMITH, Ray

DONNER, Ral / Zantees

Singles: 7–inch

EVA-TONE/GOLDMINE 3-4 79
(Soundsheet.)
Also see DONNER, Ral

DONNIE & DREAMERS

P&R '61

Singles: 7–inch

DECCA (31312 "Carole") 30-40 61
WHALE (500 "Count Every Star") 15-25 61
WHALE (505 "My Memories of You") 25-35 61

DONOVAN

(Donovan P. Leitch)

P&R/LP '65

Singles: 12–inch 33/45rpm

ALLEGIANCE (1437 "Donovan") . 5-10 83

Singles: 7–inch

ALLEGIANCE 3-4 83
ARISTA 3-5 77
EPIC 4-8 66-76
(Black vinyl.)
EPIC (10045 "Sunshine Superman") 10-15 66
(Colored vinyl. Promotional issue only.)
EPIC MEMORY LANE 3-5
HICKORY 8-15 65-68

Picture Sleeves

EPIC 5-10 66-71

LPs: 10/12–inch 33rpm

ALLEGIANCE 5-10 83
ARISTA 8-10 77
BELL 10-12 73
COLUMBIA 5-10 73
EPIC (Except 26439) 10-20 66-76
EPIC (BXN-26439 "Greatest Hits") 15-20 69
(Gatefold cover. Includes booklet.)
EPIC (PE-26439 "Greatest Hits") 5-10 77
HICKORY (123 "Catch the Wind") 20-40 65
HICKORY (127 "Fairy Tale") 20-40 65
HICKORY (135 "The Real Donovan") 20-40 66
HICKORY (143 "Like It Is") 20-40 68
HICKORY (149 "The Best of Donovan") 20-40 69
JANUS 10-12 70-71
KORY 5-10 77
PYE 8-10 76

DONOVAN & Jeff Beck Group

P&R '69

Singles: 7–inch

EPIC 4-8 69
Also see BECK, Jeff
Also see DONOVAN

DOO, Dickey: see DICKEY DOO & DON'TS

DOOBIE BROTHERS

P&R/LP '72

Singles: 12–inch 33/45rpm

W.B. 4-8 79

Singles: 7–inch

ASYLUM 3-4 80
CAPITOL 3-4 89
SESAME STREET 3-4 81
W.B. 3-5 71-83

Picture Sleeves

CAPITOL 3-4 89
SESAME STREET 3-4 81

W.B. 3-5 79-83

EPs: 7-inch 33/45rpm

W.B. 10-20 74
(Jukebox issue.)

LPs: 10/12-inch 33rpm

CAPITOL 5-8 89-91
MFSL (122 "Takin' It to the Streets") 10-15 84
NAUTILUS (5 "Captain & Me").. 25-35 80
(Half-speed mastered.)
NAUTILUS (18 "Minute by Minute") 15-20 81
(Half-speed mastered.)
PICKWICK 6-10 80
W.B. 6-12 71-83

Members: Tom Johnston; Patrick Simmons; John Hartman; Tiran Porter; Jeff "Skunk" Baxter; Michael McDonald; John McFee; Chet McCracken.

Also see McDONALD, Michael
Also see SIMMONS, Patrick

DOOBIE BROTHERS, James Hall & James Taylor

Singles: 7-inch

ASYLUM 3-4 80

Also see TAYLOR, James

DOOBIE BROTHERS, & Nicolette Larson

Singles: 7-inch

W.B. 3-5 79

Also see LARSON, Nicolette

DOOBIE BROTHERS / Kate Taylor & Simon-Taylor Family

Singles: 7-inch

W.B. 3-4 80

Picture Sleeves

W.B. 3-4 80

Also see DOOBIE BROTHERS
Also see SIMON SISTERS
Also see TAYLOR, James
Also see TAYLOR, Kate
Also see TAYLOR, Livingston

DOOLITTLE BAND

(Dandy & Doolittle Band)

P&R '80

Singles: 7-inch

COLUMBIA 3-4 80

DOORS

P&R/LP '67

Singles: 7-inch

ELEKTRA (Except 45000 series).. 3-4 79-83
ELEKTRA (45000 series) 4-8 67-72

Promotional Singles

ELEKTRA (45000 series) 8-15 67-72

Picture Sleeves

ELEKTRA (45000 series) 10-15 67-69

LPs: 10/12-inch 33rpm

ELEKTRA (500 series) 5-10 78-80
ELEKTRA (4007 "The Doors")...20-35 67
(Monaural.)
ELEKTRA (4014 "Strange Days") 15-25 67
(Monaural.)
ELEKTRA (5035 "Best of the Doors") 15-20 73
ELEKTRA (EKS-6001 "Weird Scenes Inside the Gold Mine") 12-15 72
ELEKTRA (8E-6001 "Weird Scenes Inside the Gold Mine") 8-12 73
ELEKTRA (9002 "Absolutely Live") 15-20 70
ELEKTRA (60000 series)............ 5-10 83-91
ELEKTRA (74007 "The Doors").20-25 67
ELEKTRA (74014 "Strange Days") 15-25 67
ELEKTRA (74024 "Waiting for the Sun") 15-20 68
ELEKTRA (75005 "The Soft Parade") 10-20 69
ELEKTRA (75007 "Morrison Hotel/Hard Rock Cafe") 12-15 70
ELEKTRA (74079 "Doors 13")...12-15 70
ELEKTRA (75011 "L.A. Woman") 25-35 71
(With die-cut cover.)
ELEKTRA (75011 "L.A. Woman") 5-10
(With standard cover.)
ELEKTRA (75017 "Other Voices") 8-12 71
ELEKTRA (75038 "Full Circle")....8-12 72
MFSL (051 "The Doors")........... 15-20 76

Members: Jim Morrison; Robbie Krieger; Ray Manzarek; John Densmore.

Also see MANZAREK, Ray

DORADOS, El: see EL DORADOS

DO-RAY-ME TRIO

(Do-Re-Mi-Trio Featuring Buddy Hawkins; Do Ray & Me)

R&B '48

Singles: 78rpm

BRUNSWICK 5-10 53
COMMODORE 10-15 47-48
CORAL 5-10 54
IVORY 8-15 49-50
RAINBOW 5-10 52
VARIETY 5-10 57

Singles: 7-inch

BRUNSWICK 15-25 53
CORAL 15-25 54
IVORY (001 "Let's Go Down Town") 20-30 50
RAINBOW (181 "She Would Not Yield") 20-30 52
REET 5-10 50s
STEREO CRAFT 5-10 59
VARIETY 8-10 57

LPs: 10/12–inch 33rpm

STEREO CRAFT (508 "That Wonderfully Musically Do Ray Mi Trio")...... 30-45 59

DORE, Charlie

P&R/LP '80

Singles: 7–inch

CHRYSALIS.................................. 3-4 81
ISLAND 3-4 80-81

LPs: 10/12–inch 33rpm

ISLAND 5-10 80-81

DORMAN, Harold

P&R/R&B '60

Singles: 7–inch

ABC.. 3-5 73
COLLECTABLES......................... 3-4
RITA... 8-10 60
SANTO...................................... 4-8 62
SUN.. 5-10 61-62
TINCE 5-10 60

DORSEY, Gerry

Singles: 7–inch

HICKORY (1337 "Baby, Turn Around")................................ 8-12 65

Also see HUMPERDINCK, Engelbert

DORSEY, Jimmy, Orchestra & Chorus

(With Bob Eberly)

P&R '35

Singles: 78rpm

BELL 3-5 54
COLUMBIA 3-5 50-52
DECCA...................................... 2-6 35-57
FRATERNITY............................ 3-5 57
MGM 3-5 54
OKEH 10-15 29

Singles: 7–inch

ABC.. 3-4 73
BELL 3-5 54
COLUMBIA 3-6 50-52
CORAL ("60M" Series)............. 10-15 50
(Boxed, 4-disc sets.)
DECCA...................................... 3-6 51-67
DOT.. 3-4 63
EPIC... 3-4 59
FRATERNITY............................ 3-5 57-60
MGM 3-4 54

EPs: 7–inch 33/45rpm

COLUMBIA 4-8 52-56

LPs: 10/12–inch 33rpm

COLUMBIA 10-20 55-56
CORAL.................................... 10-20 54
DECCA.................................... 10-20 57-66
EPIC... 8-12 59
FRATERNITY.......................... 10-20 57
HINDSIGHT 5-10 81
LION....................................... 10-20 56
MCA 5-10 75

Also see CROSBY, Bing, & Jimmy Dorsey
Also see MARTIN, Dean / Bob Eberly / Gordon MacRae

DORSEY, Lee

P&R/R&B '61

Singles: 7–inch

ABC..3-4 78
ABC-PAR (10192 "Lotti Mo") 5-10 61
ACE..8-10 61
AMY 4-8 65-69
CONSTELLATION....................10-20 64
FLASHBACK...............................3-5 65
FURY 5-10 61-63
GUSTO 3-4 80s
POLYDOR 3-5 70-72
REX (1005 "Rock") 15-20 58
ROULETTE..................................3-5 70s
SANSU...4-8 67
SMASH 4-8 63
SPRING 3-5 71
VALIANT (1001 "Lotti Mo") 20-30 58

LPs: 10/12–inch 33rpm

AMY (8010 "Ride Your Pony")...20-25 66
AMY (8011 "New Lee Dorsey")..20-25 66
ARISTA..5-10 85
FURY (1002 "Ya Ya") 35-45 62
POLYDOR 10-12 70
SPHERE SOUND (7003 "Ya Ya")..15-25 67

DORSEY, Tommy, Orchestra

(Starring Warren Covington)

P&R '35

Singles: 78rpm

BELL 4-8 54
(7–inch disc.)
BLUEBIRD 3-6 40
DECCA 3-5 52-64
OKEH..10-15 29
RCA 3-5 49-57
VICTOR 3-6 35-48

Singles: 7–inch

DECCA 3-4 52-64
MCA...3-4 73
RCA 3-4 50-57

EPs: 7–inch 33/45rpm

COLUMBIA 4-8 52-56
DECCA 4-8 52-63
RCA 4-6 51-61
WALDORF 4-8 50s

LPs: 10/12–inch 33rpm

ACCORD 5-10 82
BRIGHT ORANGE.......................5-10 73
CAMDEN (Except 200 series) 5-10 61-73
CAMDEN (200 series) 10-20 53-55
COLPIX.....................................10-20 58-63
COLUMBIA 10-20 58
CORAL..5-10 73
CORONET...................................5-10 60s
DECCA 10-20 52-60
GOLDEN MUSIC SOCIETY 15-20 56

HARMONY 5-10 65-72
MCA 5-10 75-81
MOVIETOWN 8-10 67
RCA 10-20 51-82
SPRINGBORAD 6-10 77
20TH FOX 10-15 59-73

Also see GARLAND, Judy / Tommy Dorsey
Also see SINATRA, Frank

DOSS, Kenny

R&B '80

Singles: 7-inch

BEARSVILLE 3-5 80

LPs: 10/12-inch 33rpm

BEARSVILLE 5-10 80

DOTTIE & RAY

R&B '65

Singles: 7-inch

LE SAGE 4-8 65

DOUBLE

P&R/LP '86

Singles: 12-inch 33/45rpm

A&M 4-8 86

Singles: 7-inch

A&M 3-4 86

Picture Sleeves

A&M 3-4 86

LPs: 10/12-inch 33rpm

A&M 5-10 86

Members: Kurt Maloo; Felix Haug.

DOUBLE ENTENTE

D&D '84

Singles: 12-inch 33/45rpm

COLUMBIA 4-6 84

Singles: 7-inch

COLUMBIA 3-4 84

DOUBLE EXPOSURE

P&R/R&B/LP '76

Singles: 12-inch 33/45rpm

GOLD COAST 4-6 81

Singles: 7-inch

SALSOUL 3-4 76-79

LPs: 10/12-inch 33rpm

SALSOUL 8-10 76-79

Members: James Williams; Joseph Harris; Leonard Davis; Charles Whittington.

DOUBLE IMAGE

P&R '83

Singles: 7-inch

CBS ASSOCIATED 3-4 83
CURB 3-4 83

LPs: 10/12-inch 33rpm

ECM 5-10 79

DOUBLE VISION

D&D '84

Singles: 12-inch 33/45rpm

PROFILE 4-6 84

DOUCETTE

(Jerry Doucette)

P&R/LP '78

Singles: 7-inch

MUSHROOM 3-4 77-79

LPs: 10/12-inch 33rpm

MUSHROOM 5-10 78-79

DOUG E. FRESH & Get Fresh Crew

R&B/D&D '85

Singles: 12-inch 33/45rpm

REALITY 4-6 85

Singles: 7-inch

REALITY 3-4 85-88

LPs: 10/12-inch 33rpm

REALITY 5-8 88

DOUGLAS, Carl

(With the Big Stampede)

P&R/R&B/LP '74

Singles: 7-inch

ERIC 3-4 70s
OKEH 5-10 66-67
20TH FOX 4-6 74-75

LPs: 10/12-inch 33rpm

20TH FOX 10-15 74

DOUGLAS, Carol

P&R/R&B '74

Singles: 12-inch 33/45rpm

MIDSONG INT'L 4-6 78

Singles: 7-inch

MIDLAND INT'L 3-5 74-79
RCA 3-5 76
20TH FOX 3-4 81

Picture Sleeves

MIDLAND INT'L 3-5 77-88

LPs: 10/12-inch 33rpm

MIDLAND INT'L 8-10 75-80

DOUGLAS, Mike

P&R '65

Singles: 7-inch

BANANA 5-10
BLUE RIVER 4-6 66
DECCA 3-6 69
EPIC 4-6 65-67
IMAGE 3-5 77
MGM 3-4 71-73
PROJECT 3 3-5 68
STAX 3-5 74

Picture Sleeves

EPIC 4-8 65-66

LPs: 10/12-inch 33rpm

ATLANTIC 5-10 76
EPIC 10-15 65-67
HARMONY 8-12 68

Also see BAILEY, Pearl, & Mike Douglas

DOUGLAS, Ronny

P&R '61

Singles: 7-inch

DECCA.. 4-8 63
EPIC.. 4-8 65
EVEREST 5-10 61

DOVALE, Debbie

P&R '63

Singles: 7-inch

ROULETTE............................ 10-15 63-64

DOVE, Ronnie

(With the Beltones)

P&R '64

Singles: 7-inch

ABC... 3-4 74
DECCA (31288 "Party Doll") 8-10 61
DECCA (32000 & 33000 series) ... 3-5 71-73
DIAMOND (100 & 200 series)....... 4-6 64-70
DIAMOND (300 series) 3-4 87
ERIC.. 3-4 70s
HITSVILLE 3-5 76
JALO (1406 "Saddest Song").... 15-20 62
MC.. 3-4 78
MCA 3-4 73
MELODYLAND 3-5 75-76
MOTION...................................... 3-4 81
MOON SHINE.............................. 3-4 83
SWAN 4-6 63
WRAYCO..................................... 3-5 71

Picture Sleeves

DIAMOND 4-8 66

LPs: 10/12-inch 33rpm

CERTRON 10-12 70
DIAMOND 15-25 65-70
DESIGN (186 "Swingin' Teen
Sounds") 10-15 64
(Four tracks by Dove; six by Terry Phillips.)
MCA 8-10 73
POWER PAK 8-12 75

DOVELLS

P&R/R&B '61

Singles: 7-inch

ABKCO.. 3-4 83
COLLECTABLES.......................... 3-4 80s
DECCA.. 3-6 70
EVENT 3-6 70-74
MGM 4-6 66-73
PARKWAY (Except 819 & 827) .. 5-10 62-63
PARKWAY (819 "No No No").... 10-15 61
PARKWAY (827 "Bristol Stomp"/"Out in the
Cold") 10-15 61
PARKWAY (827 "Bristol Stomp"/"Letters of
Love").. 5-8 61
(Note different flip.)
SWAN 4-8 65
VERVE 3-5 73

Picture Sleeves

PARKWAY 5-10 62-63

LPs: 10/12-inch 33rpm

DOVCO.......................................5-10 76
PARKWAY (7006 "The Bristol
Stomp")...................................30-50 61
PARKWAY (7010 "All the Hits
of the Teen Groups") 25-40 62
PARKWAY (7021 "For Your
Hully Gully Party")...................25-40 63
PARKWAY (7025 "You Can't
Sit Down")...............................25-40 63
WYNCOTE.................................10-20 65

Members: Len Barry; Arnie Satin; Jerry Summers; Danny Brooks; Mike Dennis.

Also see BARRY, Len

Also see CHRISTIE, Lou / Len Barry & Dovells / Bobby Rydell / Tokens

Also see ORLONS / Dovells

DOWELL, Joe

P&R '61

Singles: 7-inch

JOURNEY.....................................3-5 73
MONUMENT.................................4-6 66
SMASH 4-8 61-63

Picture Sleeves

JOURNEY.....................................3-5 73
SMASH 5-10 61-62

LPs: 10/12-inch 33rpm

SMASH 15-25 61-62
WING 10-15 66

DOWNING, Al

(Big Al Downing)

P&R '63

Singles: 7-inch

CARLTON (489 "Miss Lucy").....20-30 58
CHALLENGE (59006 "Down on
the Farm")...............................20-30 58
CHESS (1000 series)..................5-10 62
CHESS (2000 series)....................3-5 75
COLUMBIA....................................4-8 64
DOOR KNOB.................................3-4 89
HOUSE of the FOX........................3-5 71
JANUS 3-5 74
KANSOMA.....................................4-8 62
LENOX...4-8 63
POLYDOR 3-5 76
SILVER FOX...................................3-4
TEAM 3-4 82-84
V-TONE 5-10 61
VINE ST. 3-4 87
W.B. 3-4 78-80
WHITE ROCK (1111 "Down on
the Farm")..............................50-100 58
WHITE ROCK (1113 "Miss
Lucy")....................................50-100 58

LPs: 10/12-inch 33rpm

TEAM 5-10 83-85

Also see LITTLE ESTHER & Big Al Downing

DOWNING, Don

R&B '73

Singles: 7–inch

ABNER.. 4-8 62
CHAN 4-8
ROADSHOW................................ 3-5 73
SCEPTER 3-5 74

LPs: 10/12–inch 33rpm

ROADSHOW............................. 5-10 79

DOWNING, Will

R&B '88

Singles: 7–inch

ISLAND 3-4 88

DOZIER, Gene, & Brotherhood

R&B '67

Singles: 7–inch

MINIT 4-8 67-68

LPs: 10/12–inch 33rpm

MINIT 10-15 67

DOZIER, Lamont

P&R/R&B '72

Singles: 12–inch 33/45rpm

M&M.. 4-6 82
W.B. 4-8 79

Singles: 7–inch

ABC.. 3-5 73-76
COLUMBIA 3-4 81
INVICTUS 3-5 72-73
M&M... 3-4 82
MEL-O-DY (102 "Dearest One")75-100 62

LPs: 10/12–inch 33rpm

ABC 8-10 73-74
COLUMBIA 5-10 81
INVICTUS 8-12 74
M&M.. 5-10 82
W.B. 8-10 76-79

Also see ANTHONY, Lamont
Also see HOLLAND, Eddie, & Lamont Dozier
Also see VOICE MASTERS

DRAFI

(Drafi Deutscher)

P&R '66

Singles: 7–inch

LONDON.................................. 4-8 66-67

DRAGON

P&R/D&D '84

Singles: 12–inch 33/45rpm

POLYDOR................................. 4-6 84

Singles: 7–inch

POLYDOR.................................. 3-4 83-84
PORTRAIT 3-5 78-79

LPs: 10/12–inch 33rpm

POLYDOR.............................. 5-10 83
PORTRAIT 5-10 78

DRAGON, Carmen

LP '62

LPs: 10/12–inch 33rpm

CAPITOL................................10-20 62

DRAKE, Charlie

P&R '62

Singles: 7–inch

U.A. (Except 398)..........................4-8 61-62
U.A. (398 "My Boomerang
Won't Come Back")................15-20 61
(With "Practiced till I was BLACK in the face" lyrics.)
U.A. (398 "My Boomerang
Won't Come Back")....................4-8 61
(With "Practiced till I was BLUE in the face" lyrics.)

DRAKE, Guy

C&W/P&R '70

Singles: 7–inch

MALLARD 3-5 71
ROYAL AMERICAN.....................3-5 70

LPs: 10/12–inch 33rpm

OVATION.....................................5-10 74
ROYAL AMERICAN.................15-20 70
TRIP...8-12 70s

DRAKE, Pete

(With His Talking Steel Guitar)

P&R/LP '64

Singles: 7–inch

SMASH 3-6 64-65
STARDAY 3-5 66
STOP 3-5 68-70

LPs: 10/12–inch 33rpm

CANAAN 8-12 68
CUMBERLAND...........................12-20 63
PICKWICK/HILLTOP 8-12 67
MOUNTAIN DEW 8-10
SMASH 10-15 64-65
STARDAY 15-25 62-65
STOP 6-10 70

DRAMATICS

(Ron Banks & Dramatics)

R&B '67

Singles: 7–inch

ABC...3-6 75-77
CADET 3-6 74
CAPITOL.......................................3-4 82
CRACKERJACK (4015 "Toy
Soldier") 40-60 63
FANTASY 3-4 86
MAINSTREAM 3-6 75
MCA 3-4 79-80
SPORT (101 "All Because of
You")..35-50 67
VOLT...4-8 71-73
WINGATE (22 "Baby I Need
You")..25-35 67

LPs: 10/12-inch 33rpm

ABC 8-10 75-78
CADET 8-12 74
CAPITOL 5-10 82
FANTASY 5-10 86
MCA 5-10 80
STAX 8-10 77-78
VOLT 10-15 72-74

Members: Ron Banks; Elbert Wilkins; L.J. Reynolds; William Howard; Larry Demps; Lenny Mayes; Carl Smalls; Willie Ford.
Also see BANKS, Ron
Also see DELLS & DRAMATICS
Also see DYNAMICS
Also see REYNOLDS, L.J.
Also see UNDISPUTED TRUTH

DRAPER, Rusty

C&W/P&R '53

Singles: 78rpm

MERCURY 3-5 52-57

Singles: 7-inch

KL 3-5 80
MERCURY 4-8 52-62
MONUMENT 3-5 63-70

EPs: 7-inch 33/45rpm

MERCURY 10-15 54-56

LPs: 10/12-inch 33rpm

GOLDEN CREST 5-10 73
HARMONY 5-10 72
MERCURY 10-20 54-62
MONUMENT 8-12 65-75
WING 8-12 63-64

Also see DEE, Lola, & Rusty Draper

DREAD ZEPPELIN

LP '90

LPs: 10/12-inch 33rpm

I.R.S. 5-8 90

DREAM ACADEMY

P&R/LP '85

Singles: 7-inch

MCA 3-4 79
W.B. 3-4 85-86

Picture Sleeves

W.B. 3-4 85-86

LPs: 10/12-inch 33rpm

REPRISE 5-10 87
W.B. 5-10 85

DREAM SYNDICATE

LP '84

LPs: 10/12-inch 33rpm

A&M 5-10 84
SLASH 5-10

Also see TEXTONES

DREAM WEAVERS
(Featuring Wade Buff)

P&R '55

Singles: 78rpm

DECCA 3-5 55-56

Singles: 7-inch

DECCA 5-10 55-56

EPs: 7-inch 33/45rpm

DECCA 10-20 56

Member: Wade Buff.

DREAMBOY

R&B/LP '84

Singles: 7-inch

QWEST 3-4 83-84

LPs: 10/12-inch 33rpm

QWEST 5-10 83-84

DREAMLOVERS

P&R '61

Singles: 7-inch

CAMEO 8-12 64
CASINO (1308 "Amazons and Coyotes") 10-15 64
COLLECTABLES 3-4 82
COLUMBIA (42698 "Sad Sad Boy") 10-15 63
COLUMBIA (42752 "Sad Sad Boy") 5-8 63
COLUMBIA (42842 "Pretty Little Girl") 20-40 63
DOWN ("If I Should Lose You") 40-60 60s
(Number not known.)
END (1114 "If I Should Lose You") 8-12 62
HERITAGE 10-15 61-62
LEN (1006 "Take It from a Fool") 100-200 60
MERCURY 5-10 66-67
SWAN (4167 "Amazons and Coyotes") 15-20 63
(White label.)
SWAN (4167 "Amazons and Coyotes") 8-12 63
(Black label.)
V-TONE 10-15 60-61
W.B. (5619 "You Gave Me Somebody to Love") 10-20 65

LPs: 10/12-inch 33rpm

COLLECTABLES 6-8 82
COLUMBIA (2020 "The Bird") 30-40 63
(Monaural.)
COLUMBIA (8820 "The Bird") 35-45 63
(Stereo.)
HERITAGE 8-12 79

Members: Tommy Ricks; Cleveland Hammock; Cliff Dunn; Morris Gardner; Ray Dunn.
Also see CHECKER, Chubby

DREAMS

LP '70

Singles: 7-inch

COLUMBIA 3-5 71-72
D.C. 4-6 69

LPs: 10/12-inch 33rpm

COLUMBIA 10-15 70-71

Also see BRECKER BROTHERS

DREAMS SO REAL

LP '88

LPs: 10/12–inch 33rpm

ARISTA 5-8 88
FATHER'S HOUSE 8-10 86
I.R.S. 5-10 87

Members: Barry Marler; Drew Worsham; Trent Allen.

DRENNON, Eddie, & B.B.S. Unlimited

R&B '75

Singles: 7–inch

FRIENDS & CO. 3-5 75

DRESSLAR, Len

(Len Dresslar Singers)

P&R '56

Singles: 78rpm

MERCURY 4-8 56

Singles: 7–inch

CAPITOL 3-6 63
MERCURY 5-15 56
UNIVERSAL (76936 "Cubs Song") 5-10

DREW, Patti

(With the Drew-Vels)

P&R/R&B '67

Singles: 7–inch

CAPITOL 4-8 67-69
INNOVATION 3-5 75
QUILL 4-8 65

LPs: 10/12–inch 33rpm

CAPITOL 10-20 69-70

DREW-VELS

(Featuring Patti Drew)

P&R '63

Singles: 7–inch

CAPITOL 8-12 63-64

LPs: 10/12–inch 33rpm

CAPITOL (2804 "Tell Him") 20-30 67

Members: Patti Drew; Erma Drew; Lorraine Drew; Carlton Black.

Also see DREW, Patti

DREWS, J.D.

P&R '80

Singles: 7–inch

UNICORN 3-4 80

DRIFTER, Dixie: see DIXIE DRIFTER,

DRIFTERS

(Clyde McPhatter & the Drifters)

R&B '53

Singles: 78rpm

ATLANTIC 10-20 53-57
CROWN 30-40 54

Singles: 7–inch

ATLANTIC (1006 "Money Honey") 35-55 53
ATLANTIC (1019 "Such a Night") 30-40 54
ATLANTIC (1029 "Honey Love") 30-40 54
ATLANTIC (1043 "Bip Bam") 20-30 54
ATLANTIC (1048 "White Christmas") 20-30 54
ATLANTIC (1055 "Whatcha Gonna Do") 10-20 55
ATLANTIC (1078 "Adorable") 10-20 55
ATLANTIC (1089 thru 2127) 10-20 56-62
ATLANTIC (2134 thru 2786) 5-15 62-71
ATLANTIC OLDIES SERIES 3-5 70s
BELL 3-5 73-74
CROWN (108 "The World Is Changing") 100-150 54

Picture Sleeves

ATLANTIC (2260 "Saturday Night at the Movies") 10-15 64
ATLANTIC (2261 "The Christmas Song") 15-25 64

EPs: 7–inch 33/45rpm

ATLANTIC 30-40 55-58

LPs: 10/12–inch 33rpm

ARISTA 8-12 76
ATCO 10-12 71
ATLANTIC (8003 "Clyde McPhatter and the Drifters") 100-200 57
(Black label.)
ATLANTIC (8003 "Clyde McPhatter and the Drifters") 30-40 59
(Red label.)
ATLANTIC (8022 "Rockin' and Driftin") 100-150 59
(Black label.)
ATLANTIC (8022 "Rockin' and Driftin") 100-150 59
(White label.)
ATLANTIC (8022 "Rockin' and Driftin") 25-35 59
(Red label.)
ATLANTIC (8041 "The Drifters' Greatest Hits") 40-60 60
ATLANTIC (8059 "Save the Last Dance for Me") 40-60 62
(Monaural.)
ATLANTIC (SD-8059 "Save the Last Dance for Me") 50-70 62
(Stereo.)
ATLANTIC (8073 "Up on the Roof") 30-40 63
(Monaural.)
ATLANTIC (SD-8073 "Up on the Roof") 40-50 63
(Stereo.)
ATLANTIC (8093 "Biggest Hits") 30-40 64
(Monaural.)

ATLANTIC (SD-8093 "Biggest Hits") 40-50 64
(Stereo.)
ATLANTIC (8099 "Under the Boardwalk") 40-60 64
(Monaural. With black and white group photo.)
ATLANTIC (8099 "Under the Boardwalk") 20-30 64
(Monaural. With color group photo.)
ATLANTIC (SD-8099 "Under the Boardwalk") 50-70 64
(Stereo. With black and white group photo.)
ATLANTIC (SD-8099 "Under the Boardwalk") 25-35 64
(Stereo. With color group photo.)
ATLANTIC (8100 series) 20-30 65-68
CANDLELITE 10-15 70s
CLARION 15-20 64
GUSTO 5-10 80
MUSICOR 5-10 74
TRIP 5-10 76

Members: Clyde McPhatter; Bill Pinckney; Johnny Moore; Ben E. King; Rudy Lewis; Elsbeary Hobbs; Charlie Hughes; Jim Millender; Charlie Thomas; Andrew Thrasher; Gerhart Thrasher; Willie Ferbie; Jimmy Oliver; David Baughn; Bobby Lee Hollis; Bobby Hendricks; Tommy Evans; Johnny Williams; Eugene Pearson; Abdul Samad; Tommy Evans; Dock Green; Freddie Houston.

Also see CLEFTONES
Also see COASTERS / Drifters
Also see HENDRICKS, Bobby
Also see JOHN, Little Willie / Drifters
Also see KING, Ben E.
Also see McPHATTER, Clyde
Also see MOONGLOWS
Also see VEE, Bobby / Diamonds / Drifters

DRIFTERS / Lesley Gore / Roy Orbison / Los Bravos

EPs: 7-inch 33/45rpm

SWINGERS for COKE 50-75 66
(Promotional issue only. Each artist sings a song about Coca Cola. Has paper cover.)

Also see GORE, Lesley
Also see LOS BRAVOS
Also see ORBISON, Roy

DRIFTERS / Little Joey & Flips

Singles: 7-inch

GRAY'S FERRY 3-5

Also see DRIFTERS
Also see LITTLE JOEY & FLIPS

DRIVIN' 'N' CRYIN'

LP '88

LPs: 10/12-inch 33rpm

ISLAND 5-8 88-91
688 RECORDS 5-10 86

Members: Kevin Kinney; Tim Nielsen; Paul Lenz.

DRUPI

P&R '73

Singles: 7-inch

A&M 3-5 73

DRUSKY, Roy

C&W '60

Singles: 78rpm

COLUMBIA 5-8 55-56
STARDAY 5-8 55

Singles: 7-inch

CAPITOL.......................................3-5 74-76
COLUMBIA 8-12 55-56
DECCA 5-10 60-64
MERCURY.....................................3-8 63-73
PLANTATION 3-4 79-80
SCORPION.....................................3-5 77
STARDAY (185 "Such a Fool")..10-15 55

EPs: 7-inch 33/45rpm

DECCA 4-8 61-63

LPs: 10/12-inch 33rpm

CAPITOL......................................5-10 76
DECCA 12-20 61-62
HARMONY....................................10-12 65
MCA 5-8 80s
MERCURY.....................................10-20 64-72
PICKWICK/HILLTOP 8-12 70s
PLANTATION 5-10 79-80
SCORPION.....................................5-10 76
VOCALION 8-12 70
WING 10-15 64-66

Also see WELLS, Kitty, & Roy Drusky

DRUSKY, Roy, & Priscilla Mitchell

C&W '67

Singles: 7-inch

MERCURY......................................4-6 67

Also see DRUSKY, Roy

DUALS

P&R '61

Singles: 7-inch

COLLECTABLES 3-4 80s
INFINITY (032 "Big Race") 20-30 64
STAR REVUE (1031 "Stick Shift") 50-75 61
SUE (745 "Stick Shift")..............10-15 61

LPs: 10/12-inch 33rpm

SUE (2002 "Stick Shift")............50-80 61

Members: John Lagemann; Henry Bellinger.

DUBS
(Richard Blandon & Dubs)

P&R '57

Singles: 78rpm

GONE 10-15 57
JOHNSON (102 "Don't Ask Me to Be Lonely") 100-200 57

Singles: 7-inch

ABC-PAR (10056 "Early in the Morning") 10-20 59

ABC-PAR (10100 "Don't Laugh at Me")........ 30-40 60
ABC-PAR (10150 "For the First Time")........ 10-20 60
ABC-PAR (10198 "If I Only Had Magic")........ 15-25 61
ABC-PAR (10269 "Lullaby")...... 15-25 61
CLASSIC ARTISTS........ 3-5 90
CLIFTON........ 3-5 73
END (1108 "This to Me Is Love")........ 30-40 62
GONE (5002 "Don't Ask Me to Be Lonely")........ 50-75 57
(With double image, shadow-like lettering.)
GONE (5002 "Don't Ask Me to Be Lonely")........ 25-45 57
(With normal lettering.)
GONE (5011 "Could This Be Magic")........ 25-45 57
GONE (5020 "Beside My Love")........ 25-45 58
GONE (5034 "Be Sure My Love")........ 25-45 58
GONE (5046 "Chapel of Dreams")........ 25-45 58
(Black label.)
GONE (5046 "Chapel of Dreams")........ 15-25 60
(Multi-color label.)
GONE (5138 "Is There a Love for Me")........ 25-45 62
(Black label.)
JOHNSON (97 "Connie")........ 4-6 73
JOHNSON (98 "Somebody Goofed")........ 4-6 73
JOHNSON (102 "Don't Ask Me to Be Lonely")........ 750-1000 57
JOSIE........ 10-15 63
LANA........ 3-6 64
MARK-X........ 10-15 60
OLDIES 45........ 3-6 64
ROULETTE........ 3-4 70s
VICKI........ 10-15 62
WILSHIRE (201 "Just You")...... 20-30 63
ZIRKON (5002 "Chapel of Dreams")........ 5-10

LPs: 10/12-inch 33rpm

CANDLELITE........ 10-15 73
MURRAY HILL........ 5-10 88

Members: Richard Blandon; Billy Carlisle; Cleveland Still; James Miller; Tom Gardner; Tom Grate; Cordell Brown; Dave Shelley.

DUBS / Actuals

Singles: 78rpm

CANDLELITE (438 "We Three"). 5-10 72

DUBS / Shells

LPs: 10/12-inch 33rpm

CANDLELITE........ 8-10 70s
JOSIE (4001 "The Dubs Meet the Shells")........ 75-150 62

Also see DUBS
Also see SHELLS

DUBSET

D&D '84

Singles: 12-inch 33/45rpm

ELEKTRA........ 4-6 84

DUCES of RHYTHM & Tempo Toppers

(Featuring Little Richard)

Singles: 78rpm

PEACOCK........ 15-25 53-54

Singles: 7-inch

PEACOCK (1616 "Fool at the Wheel")........ 50-75 53
PEACOCK (1628 "Always")........ 50-75 54

Also see LITTLE RICHARD
Also see TEMPO TOPPERS

DUCHIEN, Armand

D&D '84

Singles: 12-inch 33/45rpm

A&M........ 4-6 84

DUDEK, Les

LP '77

Singles: 7-inch

COLUMBIA........ 3-5 77-78

LPs: 10/12-inch 33rpm

COLUMBIA........ 8-12 75-81

Also see ALLMAN BROTHERS BAND

DUDLEY, Dave

P&R '63

Singles: 78rpm

KING........ 4-8 55-56

Singles: 7-inch

COLUMBIA........ 3-4 78
CURIO........ 4-8
GOLDEN RING........ 4-8 63
GOLDEN WING (3020 "Six Days on the Road")........ 5-8 63
(Black vinyl.)
GOLDEN WING (3020 "Six Days on the Road")........ 10-20 63
(Colored vinyl.)
JUBILEE........ 5-10 62
KING (4000 series)........ 8-12 55-56
KING (5000 series)........ 4-6 63
MERCURY........ 3-8 63-73
NRC........ 5-10 59
NEW STAR........ 4-8 62
RICE........ 3-5 73-78
STARDAY........ 5-10 60
SUN (Black vinyl)........ 3-4 79-80
SUN (Colored vinyl)........ 4-6 79-80
U.A........ 3-5 75-76
VEE (7003 "Maybe I Do")........ 8-12 61

LPs: 10/12-inch 33rpm

GOLDEN RING (110 "Six Days on the Road")........ 25-30 63

MERCURY 10-15 64-73
MOUNTAIN DEW........................ 8-12 69
NASHVILLE 8-12 68
PLANTATION........................... 5-10 81
RICE.. 3-4 78
SUN... 5-10 80
U.A. 8-12 75-76
WING 8-12 68
Also see JAMES, Sonny / Dave Dudley / Sunny Williams

DUDLEY, Dave, & Tom T. Hall

C&W '70

Singles: 7–inch

MERCURY 3-5 70
Also see HALL, Tom T.

DUDLEY, Dave, & Karen O'Donnal

C&W '72

Singles: 7–inch

MERCURY 3-5 72

DUDLEY, Dave / Link Wray

LPs: 10/12–inch 33rpm

GUEST STAR 10-20 63
Also see DUDLEY, Dave
Also see WRAY, Link

DU DROPPERS

R&B '53

Singles: 78rpm

GROOVE 15-25 53-55
RCA... 10-20 53
RED ROBIN 20-40 52-53

Singles: 7–inch

GROOVE (0001 "Dead Broke") 40-60 54
GROOVE (0013 "Just Whisper") 50-75 54
GROOVE (0036 "Let Nature Take It's Course") 30-40 54
GROOVE (0104 "Talk That Talk").. 20-40 55
GROOVE (0120 "You're Mine Already")........................ 20-40 55
RCA (5229 "I Wanna Know") 25-35 53
RCA (5321 "I Found Out")......... 25-30 53
RCA (5425 "Whatever You're Doin'") 25-30 53
RCA (5504 "Don't Pass Me By") 25-30 53
RED ROBIN (108 "Can't Do Sixty No More").................. 100-125 52
(Black vinyl.)
RED ROBIN (108 "Can't Do Sixty No More").................. 200-300 52
(Colored vinyl.)
RED ROBIN (116 "Come On and Love Me Baby").................. 100-125 53

EPs: 7–inch 33/45rpm

GROOVE (2 "Talk That Talk")................................ 100-200 55
GROOVE (5 "Tops in Rhythm & Blues") 100-200 55
Members: Julius Ginyard; Willie Ray; Eddie Hashaw; Harvey Ray; Bob Kornegay; Prentice Moreland; Joe Van Loan; Charlie Hughes.
Also see DIXIEAIRES
Also see GALE, Sunny, & Du Droppers

DUKAYS

P&R '61

Singles: 7–inch

JERRY-O 5-10 64
NAT...8-12 61-62
OLDIES 45.................................4-6 60s
VEE JAY 5-8 62
Members: Eugene "Gene Chandler" Dixon; James Lowe; Earl Edwards; Ben Broyles, Shirley Jones; Charles Davis; Claude McRae.
Also see ARTISTICS
Also see CHANDLER, Gene

DUKE, Doris

P&R/R&B '70

Singles: 7–inch

CANYON....................................3-5 70

DUKE, George

LP '75

Singles: 12–inch 33/45rpm

ELEKTRA...................................4-6 85-86
EPIC...4-6 83

Singles: 7–inch

ELEKTRA...................................3-4 85-86
EPIC...3-4 77-83

LPs: 10/12–inch 33rpm

ELEKTRA.................................5-10 85-86
EPIC.......................................5-10 77-83
MPS/BASF 8-10 74-76
Also see CLARKE, Stanley, & George Duke
Also see COBHAM, Billy
Also see MOTHERS of INVENTION

DUKE, Patty

P&R/LP '65

Singles: 7–inch

U.A. 4-8 65-68

Picture Sleeves

U.A. 8-10 65

LPs: 10/12–inch 33rpm

U.A. 15-20 65-68

DUKE & DRIVERS

P&R '75

Singles: 7–inch

ABC..3-5 75

LPs: 10/12–inch 33rpm

ABC..8-10 76

DUKE BAYOU

(Champion Jack Dupree)

Singles: 78rpm

APOLLO 15-25 50
Also see DUPREE, Champion Jack

DUKE JUPITER

P&R '82

Singles: 7–inch

COAST to COAST 3-4 82
MOROCCO 3-4 84-85

LPs: 10/12–inch 33rpm

COAST TO COAST 5-10 82-83
MERCURY 5-10 80
MOROCCO 5-10 84

DUKE of EARL

(Gene Chandler)

P&R '62

Singles: 7–inch

VEE JAY 5-8 62
Also see CHANDLER, Gene

DUKES OF DIXIELAND

LP '57

LPs: 10/12-Inch 33rpm

AUDIO FIDELITY 5-15 55-61
COLUMBIA 5-10 62
EPIC 5-15 56
RCA VICTOR 5-10 59

DULFER, Candy

LP '91

LPs: 10/12–inch 33rpm

ARISTA 5-8 91

DUNCAN, Darryl

R&B '88

Singles: 7–inch

MOTOWN 3-4 88

DUNCAN SISTERS

R&B '79

Singles: 12–inch 33/45rpm

EAR MARC 4-6 79

Singles: 7–inch

EAR MARC 3-4 79-80
HI 3-5 75

DUNDAS, David

P&R '76

Singles: 7–inch

CHRYSALIS 3-5 76-77

LPs: 10/12–inch 33rpm

CHRYSALIS 8-10 77

DUNLAP, Gene

(With the Ridgeways)

R&B '81

Singles: 12–inch 33/45rpm

CAPITOL 4-6 82

Singles: 7–inch

CAPITOL 3-4 81-83

LPs: 10/12–inch 33rpm

CAPITOL 5-10 81-83
Also see AYERS, Roy
Also see WYNNE, Philippe

DUNN & Bruce Street

R&B '82

Singles: 7–inch

DEVAKI 3-4 81-82
Members: Dunn Pearson; Bruce Gray

DUNN & McCASHEN

P&R '70

Singles: 7–inch

CAPITOL 3-6 69-70

LPs: 10/12–inch 33rpm

CAPITOL 10-12 69-70
COLUMBIA 12-15 71
Members: Don Dunn; Tony McCashen.

DUPREE, Champion Jack

R&B '55

Singles: 78rpm

ALERT 10-15 46
APOLLO 10-15 49-50
CELEBRITY 10-15 46
CONTINENTAL 10-20 45
JOE DAVIS 10-15 46
KING 8-12 53-55
RED ROBIN 25-40 53-54
VIK 5-10 57

Singles: 7–inch

ATLANTIC 5-10 61
EVERLAST 4-8 64
FEDERAL 5-10 61
GUSTO 3-4 80s
KING (4695 "Walkin' Upside Your Head") 10-20 53
KING (4706 "Rub a Little Boogie") 10-20 53
RED ROBIN (109 "Stumblin' Block Blues") 150-200 53
RED ROBIN (112 "Highway Blues") 150-200 53
RED ROBIN (130 "Drunk Again") 150-200 54
VIK (260 "Dirty Woman") 20-30 57
VIK (279 "Old Time Rock & Roll") 20-30 57

LPs: 10/12–inch 33rpm

ARCHIVE of FOLK MUSIC 10-15 68
ATLANTIC (8019 "Blues from the Gutter") 75-100 59
(Green label.)
ATLANTIC (8019 "Blues from the Gutter") 40-60 59
(Black label.)
ATLANTIC (8019 "Blues from the Gutter") 40-60 59
(White label.)
ATLANTIC (8019 "Blues from the Gutter") 20-30 59
(Red label.)

ATLANTIC (8045 "Natural and Soulful Blues")........................30-40 61
(Monaural.)
ATLANTIC (SD-8045 "Natural and Soulful Blues")........................40-50 61
(Stereo.)
ATLANTIC (8056 "Champion of the Blues")..............................30-40 61
(Monaural.)
ATLANTIC (SD-8056 "Champion of the Blues")..............................40-50 61
(Stereo.)
ATLANTIC (8255 "Blues from the Gutter")..............................8-10 70
BLUE HORIZON......................10-15 69
EVEREST..............................8-12
FOLKWAYS (3825 "Women Blues of Champion Jack Dupree")........20-30 61
GNP..............................8-12 74
JAZZMAN..............................5-10 82
KING (735 "Champion Jack Dupree Sings the Blues")..............................50-60 61
KING (1084 "Walking the Blues")..............................10-15 70
LONDON..............................10-15 69
OKEH (12103 "Cabbage Greens")..............................25-35 63
STORYVILLE..............................5-10 82

Members: Jack Dupree; Larry Dale; Al Lucas; Gene Moore; Stick McGhee; Willie Jones; Pete Brown.
Also see McGHEE, Brownie
Also see McGHEE, Stick

DUPREE, Champion Jack, & Mickey Baker

LPs: 10/12-inch 33rpm

SIRE..............................10-15 69

DUPREE, Jack, & Mr. Bear

Singles: 78rpm

GROOVE..............................5-10 56
KING..............................5-10 55

Singles: 7-inch

GROOVE (0171 "Lonely Road Blues")..........................15-25 56
KING (4812 "Walking the Blues")..............................15-25 55

Members: Jack Dupree; Teddy "Mr. Bear" McRae; Larry Dale; Al Lucas; Gene Moore.
Also see DUPREE, Champion Jack

DUPREE, Robbie

P&R/R&B/LP '80

Singles: 7-inch

ELEKTRA..............................3-4 80-81

Picture Sleeves

ELEKTRA..............................3-4 80

LPs: 10/12-inch 33rpm

ELEKTRA..............................5-10 80-81

DUPREES

P&R/LP '62

Singles: 7-inch

COED (569 thru 580)..................5-10 62-63
COED (584 "Why Don't You Believe Me"/"The Things I Love")........................15-25 63
COED (584 "Why Don't You Believe Me"/"My Dearest One")..........................5-10 63
(Note different flip.)
COED (585 thru 596)..................5-10 63-65
COLLECTABLES..........................3-4 80
COLUMBIA..............................8-12 65-67
ERIC..............................3-4 70s
1ST CHOICE..............................3-5 89
HERITAGE..............................4-8 68-70
LOST-NITE..............................3-5 70s
(Black vinyl.)
LOST-NITE..............................10-15
(Colored vinyl.)
RCA..............................3-6 75

Picture Sleeves

COLUMBIA..............................10-20 66
HERITAGE..............................4-8 68

LPs: 10/12-inch 33rpm

COED (905 "You Belong to Me")..............................50-100 62
COED (906 "Have You Heard")..............................50-100 63
COLLECTABLES..............................6-8 80
1ST CHOICE..............................10-15 87
HERITAGE (35002 "Total Recall")..............................20-30 68
PICCADILLY..............................8-12 80
POST (1000 "The Duprees Sing")..............................15-25
POST (1000 "The Duprees Sing, Vol. 2")..............................15-20

Members: Joey "Vann" Canzano; Mike Arnone; Tom Bialaglow; John Salvato; Joe Santollo; Richie Rosato.
Also see ITALIAN ASPHALT & Pavement Company

DUPREES / RIVIERAS

LPs: 10/12-inch 33rpm

LOST NITE (Jerry Blavat Presents Drive-In Sounds")..............................10-15 70s

Also see DUPREES
Also see RIVIERAS

DURAN DURAN

(Duranduran)

P&R/LP '82

Singles: 12-inch 33/45rpm

CAPITOL..............................4-8 82-87

Singles: 7-inch

CAPITOL (Black vinyl)....................3-4 82-90
CAPITOL (Colored vinyl)..............5-10 86-87
(Promotional issues only.)
HARVEST..............................3-4 81-82

Picture Sleeves

CAPITOL..............................3-4 83-89

HARVEST 3-4 82

EPs: 7-inch 33/45rpm

HARVEST 15-20 82

LPs: 10/12-inch 33rpm

CAPITOL 5-10 82-90
HARVEST (12158 "Duran Duran") 8-12 82
MFSL (182 "Seven and the Ragged Tiger") 15-25 87

Members: Nick Rhodes; Roger Taylor; John Taylor, Andy Taylor; Simon LeBon; Warren Cuccurullo.

Also see ARCADIA
Also see BAND AID
Also see MISSING PERSONS
Also see POWER STATION
Also see TAYLOR, Andy
Also see TAYLOR, John

DURANTE, Jimmy

P&R '34

Singles: 78rpm

BRUNSWICK 5-10 34
DECCA 4-8 44-57

Singles: 7-inch

DECCA 4-8 51-59
W.B. 3-4 63-70

EPs: 7-inch 33/45rpm

DECCA 5-10 54-56
MGM 5-10 53-55
VARSITY 5-10 55

LPs: 10/12-inch 33rpm

DECCA (9000 series) 15-25 54-56
DECCA (78000 series) 8-12 70
HARMONY 8-12 68
LIGHT 5-10 71
LION 15-20 56
MGM (3200 series) 15-25 55
MGM (4200 series) 10-15 64
ROULETTE 15-20 61
W.B. 10-15 63-67

Also see GOLDSBORO, Bobby / Jimmy Durante
Also see KAYE, Danny, Jimmy Durante, Jane Wyman & Groucho Marx
Also see MARTIN, Dean
Also see PRESLEY, Elvis

DURY, Ian, & Blockheads

LP '78

Singles: 7-inch

STIFF (Except 23 & 1179) 3-5 79-81
STIFF/COLUMBIA (23 "Sweet Gene Vincent") 5-10 78
(Yellow vinyl. Promotional issue only.)
STIFF (1179 "Hit Me with Your Rhythm Stick") 4-8 79
(Bonus issued with the *Do It Yourself* LP. Promotional issue only.)

Picture Sleeves

STIFF/EPIC (Except 1179) 3-5 79-81
STIFF/COLUMBIA (23 "Sweet Gene Vincent") 4-8
(Yellow vinyl.)
STIFF/EPIC (1179 "Hit Me with Your Rhythm Stick") 4-8 78
(Bonus issue with the *Do It Yourself* LP. Promotional issue only.)

LPs: 10/12-inch 33rpm

POLYDOR 5-10 81
STIFF/EPIC (Except 36104) 5-10 78-82
STIFF/EPIC (36104 "Do It Yourself") 10-15 79
(Includes bonus single *Hit Me with Your Rhythm Stick.*)

Also see JANKEL, Chas

DUSK

P&R '71

Singles: 7-inch

BELL 4-6 71-72

Member: Peggy Santiglia.

Also see ANGELS

DUVALL, Huelyn

P&R '59

Singles: 78rpm

CHALLENGE 10-15 58

Singles: 7-inch

CHALLENGE (1012 "Comin' Or Goin'") 25-35 58
(Blue label.)
CHALLENGE (1012 "Comin' Or Goin'") 10-20 58
(Maroon label.)
CHALLENGE (59002 "Humdinger") 10-20 58
CHALLENGE (59014 "Little Boy Blue") 15-25 58
CHALLENGE (59025 "Juliette"). 10-20 58
CHALLENGE (59069 "Pucker Paint") 15-25 59
STARFIRE (600 "It's No Wonder") 30-35 59
TWINKLE (506 "Beautiful Dreamer") 40-60 50s

DYER, Ada

R&B '88

Singles: 7-inch

MOTOWN 3-4 88

DYKE & BLAZERS

P&R/R&B/LP '67

Singles: 7-inch

ARTCO 8-10 67
ORIGINAL SOUND 4-8 67-70

LPs: 10/12-inch 33rpm

ORIGINAL SOUND (8876 "Funky Broadway") 30-35 67
ORIGINAL SOUND (8877 "Dyke's Greatest Hits") 20-30 67

Member: Arlester "Dyke" Christian.

DYLAN, Bob
(With the Band)

LP '63

Singles: 7-inch

ASYLUM ... 3-6 74
COLUMBIA (10106 "Tangled Up in Blue") ... 8-12 75
COLUMBIA (10217 "Million Dollar Bash") ... 8-12 75
COLUMBIA (10245 "Hurricane")... 3-5 75
COLUMBIA (10298 "Mozambique")... 3-5 75
COLUMBIA (10454 "Rita Mae") .. 8-12 77
COLUMBIA (10805 "Baby Stop Crying") ... 4-8 78
COLUMBIA (10851 "Changing of the Guards")... 8-12 78
COLUMBIA (11000 series) ... 3-5 79-80
COLUMBIA (13-0000 series) ... 3-4
COLUMBIA (18-0000 series) ... 3-4 81
COLUMBIA (38-0000 thru 0400)... 3-4 84-86
COLUMBIA (42656 "Mixed Up Confusion") ... 275-325 63
COLUMBIA (42856 "Blowin' in the Wind") ... 150-200 63
COLUMBIA (43242 "Subterranean Homesick Blues")... 10-20 65
(Gray label.)
COLUMBIA (43242 "Subterranean Homesick Blues")... 4-8 65
(Red label.)
COLUMBIA (43346 "Like a Rolling Stone") ... 4-8 65
COLUMBIA (43389 "Positively 4th Street")... 10-20 65
(Gray label.)
COLUMBIA (43389 "Positively 4th Street")... 4-8 65
(Red label.)
COLUMBIA (43477 "Can You Please Crawl Out Your Window")... 10-12 65
COLUMBIA (43683 "I Want You"). 4-8 66
COLUMBIA (43541 "One of Us Must Know")... 8-12 66
COLUMBIA (43592 "Rainy Day Women #12 and 35) ... 4-8 66
COLUMBIA (43792 "Just Like a Woman") ... 4-8 66
COLUMBIA (44069 "Leopard-Skin Pill-Box Hat")... 8-12 67
COLUMBIA (44826 "I Threw It All Away")... 8-10 69
COLUMBIA (44926 "Lay Lady, Lay")... 4-8 69
COLUMBIA (45004 "Tonight I'll Be Staying Here with You) ... 8-10 69
COLUMBIA (45199 "Wigwam")... 5-10 69
COLUMBIA (45409 "Watching the River Flow")... 5-10 71
COLUMBIA (45516 "George Jackson")... 8-10 71
COLUMBIA (45913 "Knockin' on Heaven's Door")... 3-5 73
COLUMBIA (45982 "A Fool Such As I") ... 3-5 73

Picture Sleeves

COLUMBIA (02510 "Heart of Mine")... 4-8 81
COLUMBIA (10245 "Hurricane") ... 25-50 75
COLUMBIA (11235 "Slow Train") 5-10 80
COLUMBIA (43242 "Subterranean Homesick Blues") ... 300-500 65
(Promotional issue only.)
COLUMBIA (43242 "Subterranean Homesick Blues") ... 40-60 65
(Columbia "Hit Pack" picture sleeve.)
COLUMBIA (43389 "Positively 4th Street")... 25-35 65
COLUMBIA (43683 "I Want You") ... 20-25 66

Promotional Singles

ASYLUM ... 8-12 74
COLUMBIA (25 "All the Tired Horses")... 30-40 70
COLUMBIA (1039 "If Not for You")... 30-40 71
COLUMBIA (10106 "Tangled Up in Blue") ... 10-20 75
COLUMBIA (10245 "Hurricane") 15-20 75
COLUMBIA (10245 Hurricane")... 20-30 75
(Compact 33 Single.)
COLUMBIA (10298 "Mozambique") ... 8-10 75
COLUMBIA (10454 "Rita Mae"). 10-20 77
COLUMBIA (10805 "Baby Stop Crying") ... 10-20 78
COLUMBIA (11000 series) ... 4-8 79-80
COLUMBIA (18-0000 series)... 3-6 81
COLUMBIA (38-0000 thru 0400)... 3-5 84-86
COLUMBIA (42856 "Blowin' in the Wind") ... 200-300 63
(Add $100 to $200 if accompanied by "Rebel with a Cause" letter-insert, which introduces Bob Dylan.)
COLUMBIA (43242 "Subterranean Homesick Blues") ... 40-60 65
(Black vinyl.)
COLUMBIA (43242 "Subterranean Homesick Blues") ... 50-100 65
(Colored vinyl.)
COLUMBIA (43346 "Like a Rolling Stone") ... 40-60 65
(Black vinyl. Labels may show identification numbers "JZSP-110939/110940," but not selection number, 43346.)

COLUMBIA (43346 "Like a Rolling Stone") 50-100 65
(Colored vinyl.)
COLUMBIA (43389 "Positively 4th Street") 30-40 65
(Black vinyl.)
COLUMBIA (43389 "Positively 4th Street") 50-100 65
(Colored vinyl.)
COLUMBIA (43389 "Positively 4th Street") 75-100 65
(Outtake promo. Has an alternate take of *Can You Please Crawl Out Your Window.*)
COLUMBIA (43477 "Can You Please Crawl Out Your Window") 40-60 65
COLUMBIA (43683 "I Want You") 30-45 66
(Black vinyl.)
COLUMBIA (43683 "I Want You") 50-100 66
(Colored vinyl.)
COLUMBIA (43541 "One of Us Must Know") 40-55 66
COLUMBIA (43592 "Rainy Day Women #12 and 35") 30-40 66
COLUMBIA (43792 "Just Like a Woman") 30-40 66
(Black vinyl.)
COLUMBIA (43792 "Just Like a Woman") 50-100 66
(Colored vinyl.)
COLUMBIA (44069 "Leopard-Skin Pill-Box Hat") 30-40 67
COLUMBIA (44826 "I Threw It All Away") 15-25 69
COLUMBIA (44926 "Lay Lady, Lay") 15-25 69
COLUMBIA (45004 "Tonight I'll Be Staying Here with You") 15-25 69
COLUMBIA (45199 "Wigwam"). 15-25 69
COLUMBIA (45409 "Watching the River Flow") 15-25 71
COLUMBIA (45516 "George Jackson") 15-25 71
COLUMBIA (45913 "Knockin' on Heaven's Door") 10-20 73
COLUMBIA (45982 "A Fool Such As I") 10-20 73
COLUMBIA (75606 "Blowin' in the Wind") 250-400 63
("Special Album Excerpt.")

EPs: 7–inch 33/45rpm

COLUMBIA (319 "Step Lively") 100-150 65
COLUMBIA (9128 "Bringing It All Back Home") 125-175 65
(Jukebox issue only.)
COLUMBIA/PLAYBACK 75-100 73
(Promotional issue only. Contains four tracks by four different artists.)

LPs: 10/12–inch 33rpm

ASYLUM (201 "Before the Flood") 10-15 74
ASYLUM (1003 "Planet Waves") 15-20 74
(Without cut corner.)
ASYLUM (1003 "Planet Waves") . 8-10 74
(With cut corner.)
ASYLUM (EQ-1003 "Planet Waves") 15-20 74
(Quadrophonic.)
COLUMBIA (C2L-41 "Blonde on Blonde") 40-60 66
(Monaural. With "female photos" on inside of jacket.)
COLUMBIA (C2L-41 "Blonde on Blonde") 15-25 66
(Monaural. With Dylan photo replacing female photos.)
COLUMBIA (C2S-841 "Blonde on Blonde") 40-60 66
(Stereo. With "female photos" on inside of jacket.)
COLUMBIA (C2S-841 "Blonde on Blonde") 15-25 66
(Stereo. With Dylan photo replacing female photos.)
COLUMBIA (CL-1779 "Bob Dylan") 125-175 62
(Monaural. Red and black label with six Columbia "eye" boxes.)
COLUMBIA (CL-1779 "Bob Dylan") 20-30 62
(Monaural. Red label, without six Columbia "eye" boxes.)
COLUMBIA (CL-1986 "The Freewheelin' Bob Dylan") 2500-3000 63
(Monaural. With *Let Me Die in My Footsteps, Talkin' John Birch Society Blues, Gamblin' Willie's Dead Man's Hand,* and *Rocks and Gravel,* which may also be shown as *Solid Gravel.* We suggest verification of the above tracks by listening to the LP, rather than accepting the information printed on the label. In fact, some copies of the rare pressing have reissue labels. Identification numbers of this press are XLP-58717-1A and XLP-58718-1A.)
COLUMBIA (CL-1986 "The Freewheelin' Bob Dylan") 20-30 63
(Monaural. With the above tracks replaced by four others.)
COLUMBIA (CL-2105 "The Times They Are A-Changin") 20-30 64
(Monaural.)

COLUMBIA (CL-2193 "Another Side of Bob Dylan") 15-20 64
(Monaural.)
COLUMBIA (CL-2328 "Bringin' It All Back Home") 15-25 65
(Monaural.)
COLUMBIA (CL-2389 "Highway 61 Revisited")..................... 100-125 65
(Monaural. With alternate take of *From a Buick 6.* The alternate take begins with a harmonica riff. This pressing has a "-1" at the end of the identification number, stamped in the vinyl trailoff.)
COLUMBIA (CL-2389 "Highway 61 Revisited").............................. 10-15 65
(Monaural.)
COLUMBIA (KCL-2663 "Bob Dylan's Greatest Hits") 15-25 67
(Monaural.)
COLUMBIA (CL-2804 "John Wesley Harding")............................. 60-100 68
(Monaural.)
COLUMBIA (CS-8579 "Bob Dylan") 150-200 62
(Stereo. Red and black label with six Columbia "eye" boxes.)
COLUMBIA (CS-8579 "Bob Dylan") 25-40 62
(Stereo. Red label, without six Columbia "eye" boxes.)
COLUMBIA (PC-8579 "Bob Dylan") 5-10
COLUMBIA (CS-8786 "The Freewheelin' Bob Dylan") 20-30 63
(Stereo.)
COLUMBIA (PC-8786 "The Freewheelin' Bob Dylan") 5-10
COLUMBIA (CS-8905 "The Times They Are A-Changin").................... 20-30 64
(Stereo.)
COLUMBIA (CS-8993 "Another Side of Bob Dylan") 15-25 64
(Stereo.)
COLUMBIA (CS-9128 "Bringin' It All Back Home") 15-25 65
(Stereo.)
COLUMBIA (CS-9189 "Highway 61 Revisited")..................... 100-150 65
(Stereo. With alternate take of *From a Buick 6.* The alternate take begins with a harmonica riff. This pressing has a "-1" at the end of the identification number, stamped in the vinyl trailoff.)
COLUMBIA (CS-9189 "Highway 61 Revisited")........................ 10-20 65
(Stereo.)
COLUMBIA (KCS-9463 "Bob Dylan's Greatest Hits") 15-25 67
(Stereo.)
COLUMBIA (CS-9604 "John Wesley Harding")................................20-30 68
(Stereo.)
COLUMBIA (KCS-9825 "Nashville Skyline")..................................8-12 69
COLUMBIA (C2X-30050 "Self Portrait")................................50-60 70
(With "360-Degree Stereo" at bottom of label.)
COLUMBIA (C2X-30050 "Self Portrait")................................10-15 70
(Without "360-Degree Stereo" at bottom of label.)
COLUMBIA (KC-30290 "New Morning") 8-10 70
COLUMBIA (KC-31120 "Greatest Hits Vol. 2") 10-12 71
COLUMBIA (KC-32460 "Pat Garrett and Billy the Kid")......................8-10 73
(Soundtrack.)
COLUMBIA (KC-32747 "Dylan")..8-10 73
COLUMBIA (CQ-32872 "Nashville Skyline")................................25-35 74
(Quadrophonic.)
COLUMBIA (PC-33235 "Blood on the Tracks") 25-35 75
(With mural pictured on the back cover.)
COLUMBIA (PC-33235 "Blood on the Tracks") 8-12 75
(With liner notes on the back cover.)
COLUMBIA (PC2-33682 "The Basement Tapes")..................10-12 75
COLUMBIA (PC-33893 "Desire").8-10 76
COLUMBIA (PCQ-33893 "Desire")..............................25-35 76
(Quadrophonic.)
COLUMBIA (PC-34349 "Hard Rain")..8-10 76
COLUMBIA (JC-35453 "Street Legal")..8-10 78
COLUMBIA (PC2-36067 "Bob Dylan at Budokan") 8-10 79
COLUMBIA (FC-36120 "Slow Train Comin")..............................8-10 79
COLUMBIA (FC-36553 "Saved").8-10 80
COLUMBIA (FC-37496 "Shot of Love")..8-10 81
COLUMBIA (PC-38819 "Infidels")8-10 83
COLUMBIA (C5X-38830 Biograph")..............................20-30 85
(Boxed set of five LPs, includes 36-page booklet.)
COLUMBIA (FC-39944 "Real Live")..5-10 84
COLUMBIA (FC-40110 "Empire Burlesque") 5-10 85
COLUMBIA (OC-40439 "Knocked Out Loaded") 5-10 86

COLUMBIA (OC-40957 "Down in the Groove")............................ 5-10 88
COLUMBIA (HC-43235 "Blood on the Tracks")........................... 20-30 83
(Half-speed mastered.)
COLUMBIA (45281 "Oh Mercy"). 5-10 89
COLUMBIA (46794 "Under the Red Sky")................................ 5-10 90
COLUMBIA (47382 "The Bootleg Series Volumes 1 - 3") 15-20 89
COLUMBIA (HC-49825 "Nashville Skyline")............................... 20-30 81
(Half-speed mastered.)
FOLKWAYS (5322 "Bob Dylan Vs. A.J. Weberman").......... 100-175
ISLAND (1 "Before the Flood").. 25-30 74
MFSL (114 "The Times They Are a-Changing") 10-15

Promotional LPs

ASYLUM (201 "Before the Flood")................................... 25-40 74
ASYLUM (1003 "Planet Waves")................................ 25-40 74
COLUMBIA (422 "Renaldo and Clara")................................ 25-35 76
(Soundtrack.)
COLUMBIA (798 "Saved") 25-35 80
COLUMBIA (1259 "Dylan London Interview") 25-35 80
COLUMBIA (1263 "Shot of Love")................................... 25-35 81
COLUMBIA (1471 "Electric Lunch")................................. 15-25 83
COLUMBIA (1770 "Infidels")..... 10-20 83
COLUMBIA (C2L-41 "Blonde on Blonde") 60-75 66
(Monaural. With "female photos" on inside of jacket.)
COLUMBIA (C2S-841 "Blonde on Blonde") 60-75 66
(Stereo. With "female photos" on inside of jacket.)
COLUMBIA (CL-1779 "Bob Dylan") 200-300 62
(Monaural.)
COLUMBIA (CL-1986 "The Freewheelin' Bob Dylan") 2500-3000 63
(Monaural. With *Let Me Die in My Footsteps, Talkin' John Birch Society Blues, Gamblin' Willie's Dead Man's Hand,* and *Rocks and Gravel,* which may also be shown as *Solid Gravel.* We suggest verification of the above tracks by listening to the LP, rather than accepting the information printed on the label. In fact, some copies of the rare pressing have reissue labels. Identification numbers of this press are XLP-58717-1A and XLP-58718-1A.)
COLUMBIA (CL-1986 "The Freewheelin' Bob Dylan") 75-100 63
(Monaural. With the above tracks replaced by four others.)
COLUMBIA (CL-2105 "The Times They Are A-Changin")............75-100 64
COLUMBIA (CL-2193 "Another Side of Bob Dylan") 60-75 64
(Monaural.)
COLUMBIA (CL-2328 "Bringin' It All Back Home").................................60-75 65
(Monaural.)
COLUMBIA (CL-2389 "Highway 61 Revisited")..........................60-75 65
(Monaural.)
COLUMBIA (KCL-2663 "Bob Dylan's Greatest Hits") 60-75 67
(Monaural.)
COLUMBIA (CL-2804 "John Wesley Harding")................................50-60 68
(Monaural.)
COLUMBIA (CS-8579 "Bob Dylan") 200-300 62
(Stereo.)
COLUMBIA (CS-8786 "The Freewheelin' Bob Dylan") 75-100 63
(Stereo.)
COLUMBIA (CS-8905 "The Times They Are A-Changin") 75-100 64
(Stereo.)
COLUMBIA (CS-8993 "Another Side of Bob Dylan") 60-75 64
(Stereo.)
COLUMBIA (CS-9128 "Bringin' It All Back Home")..................................60-75 65
(Stereo.)
COLUMBIA (CS-9189 "Highway 61 Revisited")..........................60-75 65
(Stereo.)
COLUMBIA (KCS-9463 "Bob Dylan's Greatest Hits")....................................60-75 67
(Stereo.)
COLUMBIA (KCS-9825 "Nashville Skyline")................................50-60 69
COLUMBIA (30050 "Self Portrait")..................................50-60 70
COLUMBIA (31120 "Greatest Hits Vol. 2") 10-20 71
COLUMBIA (32460 "Pat Garrett and Billy the Kid").....................15-25 73
(Soundtrack.)
COLUMBIA (32747 "Dylan")......10-15 73
COLUMBIA (33235 "Blood on the Tracks") 20-25 75
COLUMBIA (33682 "The Basement Tapes") 10-15 75
COLUMBIA (33893 "Desire").....10-15 76
COLUMBIA (34349 "Hard Rain")....................................10-15 76

COLUMBIA (35453 "Street Legal") 10-15 78
COLUMBIA (36067 "Bob Dylan at Budokan") 10-20 79
COLUMBIA (36120 "Slow Train Comin") 10-15 79
COLUMBIA (36553 "Saved") 10-15 80
COLUMBIA (37496 "Shot of Love") 10-15 81
COLUMBIA (38819 "Infidels") ... 10-15 83
COLUMBIA (39944 "Real Live") 10-15 84
COLUMBIA (40110 "Empire Burlesque") 10-15 85
COLUMBIA (40439 "Knocked Out Loaded") 10-15 86
COLUMBIA (43235 "Blood on the Tracks") 25-35 83
(Half-speed mastered.)
COLUMBIA (49825 "Nashville Skyline") 25-35 81
(Half-speed mastered.)
FOLKWAYS (5322 "Bob Dylan Vs. A.J. Weberman") 75-100
ISLAND (1 "Before the Flood").. 25-35 74
MFSL (114 "The Times They Are A-Changin") 20-25 80s
WESTWOOD ONE ("Dylan on Dylan") 150-200 84
(Five-LP set. Issued for radio broadcast only.)
WESTWOOD ONE ("Dylan on Dylan") 100-150 84
(Three-LP set. Shorter version of the above show.)

Session: Michael Bloomfield; Al Kooper; Paul Griffin; Bobby Gregg; Charlie McCoy; Frank Owens; Russ Savakus; Harvey Goldstein.

Also see BAND
Also see BELAFONTE, Harry
Also see BLOOMFIELD, Mike
Also see GREGG, Bobby
Also see HARRISON, George
Also see KOOPER, Al
Also see McCOY, Charlie
Also see SAHM, Doug
Also see TRAVELING WILBURYS
Also see U.S.A. for AFRICA

DYLAN, Bob, & Grateful Dead

LP '89

LPs: 10/12–inch 33rpm

COLUMBIA (45056 "Dylan and the Dead") 5-10 89

Also see GRATEFUL DEAD

DYLAN, Bob, & Heartbreakers / Michael Rubini

Singles: 7–inch

MCA 3-4 86

Also see DYLAN, Bob
Also see PETTY, Tom, & Heartbreakers

DYNAMIC BREAKERS

R&B '85

Singles: 12–inch 33/45rpm

SUNNYVIEW 4-6 85

Singles: 7–inch

SUNNYVIEW 3-4 85

DYNAMIC CORVETTES

R&B '75

Singles: 7–inch

ABET 3-5 75

DYNAMIC SUPERIORS

P&R/R&B '74

Singles: 12–inch 33/45rpm

MOTOWN 4-6 77

Singles: 7–inch

MOTOWN 3-5 74-77

LPs: 10/12–inch 33rpm

MOTOWN 8-10 74-77

Members: Tony Washington; Maurice Washington; Michael McCalpin; George Spann; George Peterback.

DYNAMICS

P&R/R&B '63

Singles: 7–inch

BIG TOP 5-10 63-64
BLACK GOLD 3-5 73-74
COTILLION 4-6 68-69

LPs: 10/12–inch 33rpm

BLACK GOLD 8-10 73
COTILLION 12-15 69

DYNA-SORES

P&R '60

Singles: 7–inch

RENDEZVOUS 8-12 60

Member: Jimmy Norman.
Also see NORMAN, Jimmy

DYNASTY

R&B '79

Singles: 7–inch

SOLAR 3-4 79-88

LPs: 10/12–inch 33rpm

SOLAR 5-10 79-82

Members: Kevin Spencer; Nidra Beard; Linda Carriere; Leon Sylvers.
Also see DE BLANK
Also see STARFIRE
Also see SYLVERS

DYNATONES

P&R/R&B '66

Singles: 7–inch

HBR 4-8 66
ST. CLAIR 8-10 66

LPs: 10/12–inch 33rpm

HBR 20-25 66

DYNELL, Johnny, & New York 88

D&D '83

Singles: 12–inch 33/45rpm

ACME 4-6 83-84

DYSON, Clifton

R&B '82

Singles: 12–inch 33/45rpm

MOTOWN	4-8	79

Singles: 7–inch

MOTOWN	3-4	79
NETWORK	3-4	82

LPs: 10/12–inch 33rpm

AFTER HOURS	5-10	82
NETWORK	5-10	82

DYSON, Ronnie

P&R/R&B/LP '70

Singles: 12–inch 33/45rpm

COTILLION	4-6	83

Singles: 7–inch

COLUMBIA	3-5	69-78
COTILLION	3-4	82-83

Picture Sleeves

COLUMBIA	3-5	73-75

LPs: 10/12–inch 33rpm

COLUMBIA	8-10	70-79
COTILLION	5-10	82-83

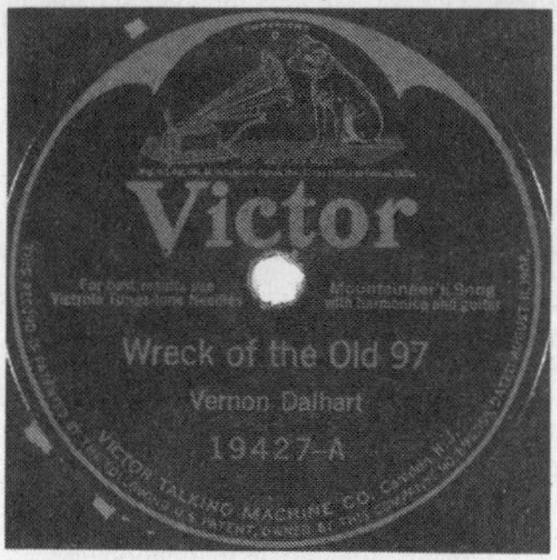

HULLY GULLY BABY

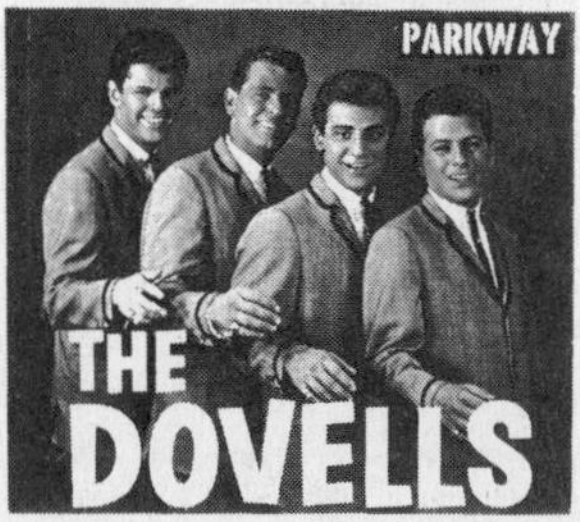

E

E., Sheila: see SHEILA E.

EBN/OZN
(EBN-OZN)

D&D '83

Singles: 12–inch 33/45rpm

ELEKTRA.................................... 4-6 83-84

Singles: 7–inch

ELEKTRA.................................... 3-4 84

LPs: 10/12–inch 33rpm

ELEKTRA.................................... 5-10 84

Members: Ebn; Ozn.

EBO

R&B '85

Singles: 12–inch 33/45rpm

DOMINO 4-6 85

Singles: 7–inch

DOMINO 3-4 85

ELO: see ELECTRIC LIGHT ORCHESTRA

EMF

LP '91

LPs: 10/12–inch 33rpm

EMI.................................... 5-8 91

EPMD

R&B/LP '88

LPs: 10/12–inch 33rpm

FRESH.................................... 5-8 88-89
RAL/COLUMBIA.................................... 5-8 91

Members: Erick Sermon; Parrish Smith.

EQ

D&D '86

Singles: 12–inch 33/45rpm

ATLANTIC.................................... 4-6 86

E.U.
(Experience Unlimited)

R&B '88

Singles: 7–inch

ISLAND 3-4 86
MANHATTAN.................................... 3-4 88

Picture Sleeves

MANHATTAN.................................... 3-4 88

LPs: 10/12–inch 33rpm

ISLAND 5-10 86
VIRGIN.................................... 5-8 89

EAGER, Brenda Lee
(With the Peaches)

R&B '73

Singles: 12–inch 33/45rpm

PRIVATE I.................................... 4-6 84

Singles: 7–inch

MERCURY 3-5 72-74
PLAYBOY 3-5 75
PRIVATE I.................................... 3-4 84

Also see BUTLER, Jerry, & Brenda Lee Eager

EAGLES

P&R/LP '72

Singles: 7–inch

ASYLUM.................................... 3-5 72-80
FULL MOON.................................... 3-4 81

Picture Sleeves

ASYLUM.................................... 3-5 78

LPs: 10/12–inch 33rpm

ASYLUM.................................... 8-12 72-82
MFSL (126 "Hotel California")....25-35 84

Members: Don Felder; Glenn Frey; Don Henley; Randy Meisner; Timothy B. Schmit; Joe Walsh; Bernie Leadon.

Also see FELDER, Don
Also see FREY, Glenn
Also see HENLEY, Don
Also see LEADON, Bernie
Also see LEE, Johnny / Eagles
Also see MEISNER, Randy
Also see NEWMAN, Randy
Also see POCO
Also see RONSTADT, Linda
Also see SCHMIT, Timothy B.
Also see SIMMONS, Patrick
Also see VITALE, Joe
Also see WALSH, Joe

EARLAND, Charles
(Charles Earland's Odyssey; Charlie Earland Jr.)

LP '70

Singles: 7–inch

COLUMBIA.................................... 3-4 81-82
MERCURY.................................... 3-5 76
PRESTIGE.................................... 3-5 70-74
QUAKER TOWN.................................... 4-8 64

LPs: 10/12–inch 33rpm

COLUMBIA.................................... 5-10 80
MERCURY.................................... 5-10 76-78
MUSE.................................... 5-10 80
PRESTIGE.................................... 5-10 70-75
RARE BIRD.................................... 5-10 71
TRIP.................................... 5-10 73

EARLE, Steve
(With the Dukes)

C&W '83

Singles: 12–inch 33/45rpm

MCA.................................... 4-6 86

Singles: 7–inch

EPIC.................................... 3-4 83-85
MCA.................................... 3-4 86-90
UNI.................................... 3-4 88

Picture Sleeves

EPIC.................................... 3-4 84

EPs: 7–inch 33/45rpm

LSI.................................... 5-10 82

LPs: 10/12–inch 33rpm

MCA.................................... 5-10 86-90
UNI.................................... 5-8 88

EARL-JEAN

(Earl Jean McCree)

P&R '64

Singles: 7–inch

COLPIX 4-8 64

Also see COOKIES
Also see KING, Ben E.

EARLS

(Larry Chance & the Earls)

P&R '62

Singles: 12–inch 33/45rpm

WOODBURY 6-10 76-77

Singles: 7–inch

ABC 5-10 68
ATLANTIC 3-5
BARRY 4-8 63
CLIFTON 3-5 74
COLLECTABLES 3-4 80s
COLUMBIA 3-5 75
HARVEY 4-8 75
MEMORIES 3-5
MR. "G" 5-10 67
OLD TOWN (1130 "Remember Then") 20-25 62
(Blue label.)
OLD TOWN (1130 "Remember Then") 8-12 63
(Multi-color label.)
OLD TOWN (1133 "Never") 10-15 63
(Blue label.)
OLD TOWN (1133 "Never") 8-12 63
(Multi-color label.)
OLD TOWN (1141 "Look My Way") 8-12 63
OLD TOWN (1145 "Kissin") 8-12 63
OLD TOWN (1149 "I Believe") .. 15-25 63
(Blue label.)
OLD TOWN (1149 "I Believe") .. 10-15 63
(Multi-color label.)
OLD TOWN (1169 "Ask Anybody") 10-15 64
OLD TOWN (1181 "Remember Me Baby") 20-30 65
(Promotional issue only.)
OLD TOWN (1182 "Remember Me Baby") 8-12 65
ROADHOUSE (1021 "I'm All Alone") 4-6
(Colored vinyl.)
ROME (101 "Life Is But a Dream"/ "It's You") 25-50 61
ROME (101 "Life Is But a Dream"/ "Without You") 15-20 61
ROME (102 "Lookin' for My Baby") 20-25 61
ROME (112 "Little Boy and Girl") .. 3-5 76
ROME (114 "All Through Our Teens") 5-8 76
(Black vinyl.)
ROME (114 "All Through Our Teens") 5-10 76
(Colored vinyl.)
ROME (5117 "My Heart's Desire") 20-30 62
(Black vinyl.)
ROME (5117 "My Heart's Desire") 15-25 62
(Colored vinyl.)
WOODBURY 3-5 77

EPs: 7–inch 33/45rpm

CRYSTAL BALL 5-10

LPs: 10/12–inch 33rpm

CHANCE (1001 "Today") 8-12 83
CRYSTAL BALL 8-10
OLD TOWN (104 "Remember Me Baby") 200-250 63
(Counterfeits exist but can be identified by their 1/2–inch vinyl trail-off and poor fidelity. Originals have a 3/4–inch trail-off and excellent fidelity.)
RAINBOW (1001 "Live") 8-12 87
WOODBURY (104 "Remember Me Baby") 10-15 76

Members: Larry Chance; Robert Del Din; Jack Wray; Ed Harder.

EARLS / Pretenders

Singles: 7–inch

ROME/POWER MARTIN 3-5 76

Also see EARLS

EARONS

R&B '83

Singles: 12–inch 33/45rpm

ISLAND 4-6 84

Singles: 7–inch

BOARDWALK 3-4 83
ISLAND 3-4 84

Members: Earon .28; Earon .18; Earon .22; Earon 33; Earon .69.

EARTH OPERA

P&R/LP '69

Singles: 7–inch

ELEKTRA 4-8 67-69

LPs: 10/12–inch 33rpm

ELEKTRA 10-15 68-69

Members: Peter Rowan; Paul Dillon; Dave Grishman; Bill Stevenson; John Nagy; Billy Mundi; John Cale.
Also see CALE, John
Also see RHINOCEROS

EARTH QUAKE: see EARTHQUAKE

EARTH, WIND & FIRE

P&R/R&B/LP '71

Singles: 12–inch 33/45rpm

COLUMBIA 4-8 75-83

Singles: 7–inch

ARC 3-4 78-82
COLUMBIA 3-5 73-90
W.B. 3-5 71

Picture Sleeves

ARC 3-4 80
COLUMBIA 3-5 74-88

LPs: 10/12-inch 33rpm

COLUMBIA (Except 47000 series) 8-15 72-90
COLUMBIA (47000 series) 15-20 81-82
(Half-speed mastered.)
COLUMBIA/ARC (Except 35647) 8-15 75-81
COLUMBIA/ARC (35647 "Best of Earth, Wind & Fire") 8-10 79
COLUMBIA/ARC (35647 "Best of Earth, Wind & Fire") 15-20 79
(Picture disc. Promotional issue only.)
MFSL (159 "That's the Way of the World") 15-25 85
W.B. 10-15 71-74

Members: Philip Bailey; Maurice White; Verdine White; Ronnie Laws; Fred White; Andy Woolfolk, Larry Dunn; Ralph Johnson; Al McKay; Johnny Graham; Wade Flemons.

Also see BAILEY, Philip
Also see FLEMONS, Wade
Also see LAWS, Ronnie
Also see LEWIS, Ramsey

EARTH, WIND & FIRE with the Emotions

P&R/R&B '79

Singles: 12-inch 33/45rpm

ARC 4-8 79

Singles: 7-inch

ARC 3-4 79-80

LPs: 10/12-inch 33rpm

ARC 5-10 79

Also see EMOTIONS

EARTH, WIND & FIRE & Ramsey Lewis

R&B '74

Singles: 7-inch

COLUMBIA 3-5 74-75

Also see EARTH, WIND & FIRE
Also see LEWIS, Ramsey

EARTHQUAKE
(Earth Quake)

LP '69

Singles: 7-inch

A&M 3-5 72
BESERKLEY 3-5 76-77

LPs: 10/12-inch 33rpm

A&M 10-12 71-78
BESERKLEY 8-10 76-80

Also see KIHN, Greg, Band / Earthquake / Modern Lovers / Rubinoos
Also see KIHN, Greg, Band / Earthquake / Rubinoos / Jonathan Richman

EAST, Thomas
(With the Fabulous Playboys)

R&B '69

Singles: 7-inch

LION 3-5 73
MGM 3-5 73
TODDLIN' TOWN 4-8 68-69

EAST COAST

R&B '79

Singles: 7-inch

RSO 3-5 79

Members: Gregory Johnson; Larry Blackmon; Gary Dow; Eric Rurham; Anthony Lockett; Arnett Leftenant; Nathan Leftenant.

Also see CAMEO

EAST L.A. CAR POOL

P&R '75

Singles: 7-inch

GRC 3-5 75

EASTBOUND EXPRESSWAY

R&B '79

Singles: 7-inch

AVI 3-5 78-79

EASTERHOUSE

P&R '89

Singles: 7-inch

COLUMBIA 3-4 89

Members: Andy Perry; Ivor Perry.

EASTON, Elliot

LP '85

Singles: 7-inch

ELEKTRA 3-4 85

LPs: 10/12-inch 33rpm

ELEKTRA 5-10 85

Also see CARS

EASTON, Sheena

P&R/LP '81

Singles: 12-inch 33/45rpm

EMI AMERICA 4-6 81-86

Singles: 7-inch

EMI AMERICA 3-4 81-86
LIBERTY 3-4 81
MCA 3-4 88-91
RCA 3-4 89

Picture Sleeves

EMI AMERICA 3-6 81-86
RCA 3-4 89

LPs: 10/12-inch 33rpm

EMI AMERICA 5-10 81-86
MCA 5-8 88-91

Also see PRINCE & Sheena Easton
Also see ROGERS, Kenny, & Sheena Easton

EASTWOOD, Clint

Singles: 7-inch

CAMEO (240 "Rowdy") 10-20 63
CERTRON 4-6 70
GNP (177 "Get Yourself Another Fool") 15-25 65
GOTHIC (005 "Unknown Girl") .. 10-20 61
PARAMOUNT 4-8 69
W.B. 3-4 81

Picture Sleeves

CAMEO (240 "Rowdy") 30-50 63
CERTRON 5-8 70

GNP (177 "Get Yourself Another Fool") 50-75 65
GOTHIC (005 "Unknown Girl").. 10-20 61

LPs: 10/12-inch 33rpm

CAMEO (1056 "Cowboy Favorites") 75-125 63

Also see CHARLES, Ray, & Clint Eastwood
Also see HAGGARD, Merle, & Clint Eastwood
Also see SHEPPARD, T.G., & Clint Eastwood

EASY RIDERS
(With Terry Gilkyson)

Singles: 78rpm

COLUMBIA 3-5 57

Singles: 7-inch

COLUMBIA 5-10 57

LPs: 10/12-inch 33rpm

EPIC 10-15 63

Also see GILKYSON, Terry

EASY STREET
P&R '76

Singles: 7-inch

CAPRICORN 3-5 76

LPs: 10/12-inch 33rpm

CAPRICORN 8-10 76-77

EASYBEATS
P&R/LP '67

Singles: 7-inch

ASCOT 8-12 66
RARE EARTH 4-8 69
U.A. 5-8 67-69

Picture Sleeves

ASCOT 10-20 66

LPs: 10/12-inch 33rpm

RARE EARTH (517 "Easy Ridin'") 10-20 70
RHINO 5-10 85
U.A. (3588 "Friday on My Mind") 30-40 67
(Monaural.)
U.A. (6588 "Friday on My Mind") 30-40 67
(Stereo.)
U.A. (6667 "Falling off the Edge of the World") 30-40 68

Members: Steve Wright; Harry Vanda; George Young; Dick Diamonde.
Also see FLASH & PAN

EAZY-E
LP '88

LPs: 10/12-inch 33rpm

RUTHLESS 5-8 88

EBB TIDE
(Ebb K. Harrison, Sr.)

R&B '75

Singles: 7-inch

SOUND GEMS 3-5 75-76

EBONEE WEBB
(Ebony Web)

R&B/LP '81

Singles: 7-inch

CAPITOL 3-4 81-84
HI 3-5 70-73

LPs: 10/12-inch 33rpm

CAPITOL 5-10 81-84

EBONY
D&D '83

Singles: 12-inch 33/45rpm

QUALITY/RFC 4-6 83-84

EBONY, IVORY & JADE
R&B '75

Singles: 7-inch

COLUMBIA 3-5 75

EBONY RHYTHM FUNK CAMPAIGN
R&B '75

Singles: 7-inch

INNOVATION 3-5 75
MCA 3-5 72

LPs: 10/12-inch 33rpm

UNI 5-10 72

EBONY WEB: see EBONEE WEBB

EBONYS
P&R/R&B '71

Singles: 7-inch

BUDDAH 3-5 76
PHILADELPHIA INT'L 3-5 71-74
SOUL CLICK 3-5 70s

LPs: 10/12-inch 33rpm

PHILADELPHIA INT'L 8-10 73

Members: Jenny Holmes; David Beasley; James Tuten; Clarence Vaughn.
Also see CREME D'COCOA

ECHO & BUNNYMEN
LP '81

Singles: 12-inch 33/45rpm

SIRE 5-10 81-86

Singles: 7-inch

SIRE 3-4 81-87

Picture Sleeves

SIRE 3-4 87

LPs: 10/12-inch 33rpm

SIRE 5-10 81-87

ECHOES
P&R '61

Singles: 7-inch

ASCOT 15-20 65
COLUMBIA 5-10 60
FELSTED (8614 "Angel of Love") 30-40 61
SRG (101 "Baby Blue") 25-40 60
SEG-WAY (103 "Baby Blue") 8-12 61
SEG-WAY (106 "Sad Eyes") 8-12 61
SEG-WAY (1002 "Angel of My Heart") 15-20 62

EPs: 7–inch 33/45rpm

CRYSTAL BALL 4-6

LPs: 10/12–inch 33rpm

CRYSTAL BALL 5-10

Members: Harry Doyle; Tom Morrissey; Tom Duffy.

ECHOES / Four Esquires

Singles: 7–inch

ROULETTE GOLDEN GOODIES. 3-5 70s

Also see ECHOES
Also see FOUR ESQUIRES

ECKSTINE, Billy

R&B '44

Singles: 78rpm

DELUXE 10-15 45
MGM 5-10 47-56
NATIONAL 5-10 45-48
RCA 4-8 56

Singles: 7–inch

A&M 3-5 76
ENTERPRISE 3-5 70-74
MGM 8-15 50-56
MERCURY 4-8 59-64
MOTOWN 8-15 65-68
RCA 8-12 56
ROULETTE 5-10 59-60

Picture Sleeves

MERCURY 5-10 62

EPs: 7–inch 33/45rpm

EMARCY 10-20 54-55
KING 10-20 53
MGM 10-20 50-56
MOTOWN (60632 "Prime of My Life") 15-25 65
RENDITION 15-25 50

LPs: 10/12–inch 33rpm

AUDIO LAB (1549 "Mr. B") 30-40 60
EMARCY (26025 "Blues for Sale") 50-100 54
(10–inch LP.)
EMARCY (26027 "Love Songs of Mr. B") 50-100 54
EMARCY (36010 "I Surrender Dear") 30-60 55
EMARCY (36029 "Blues for Sale") 25-50 55
EMARCY (36030 "Love Songs of Mr. B") 50-100 55
EMARCY (36129 "Eckstine's Imagination") 25-50 55
ENTERPRISE 5-10 71-74
KING (12 "The Great Mr. B")... 75-125 52
(10–inch LP.)
MGM (219 "Tenderly") 30-50 53
(10 Inch LP.)
MGM (257 "I Let a Song Go Out of My Heart") 40-60 55
(10 Inch LP.)
MGM (3176 "Mr. B with a Beat") 15-25 55
MGM (3209 "Rendezvous") 15-25 56
MGM (3275 "That Old Feeling"). 15-25 55
MERCURY 15-25 57-64
METRO 10-15 65
MOTOWN (632 "Prime of My Life") 15-25 65
MOTOWN (646 "My Way") 15-25 66
MOTOWN (677 "For Love of Ivy") 10-20 69
NATIONAL (2001 "Billy Eckstine Sings") 75-125 50
(10–inch LP.)
REGENT 20-40 56-57
ROULETTE 15-25 60
SAVOY 8-10 76-79
TRIP 5-10 75
WING 8-12 67

Also see BASIE, Count, & Billy Eckstine
Also see DAMITA JO & Billy Eckstine

ECKSTINE, Billy, & Woody Herman

Singles: 78rpm

MGM 4-8 51

Singles: 7–inch

MGM 5-10 51

Also see HERMAN, Woody, & Orch.

ECKSTINE, Billy, & Quincy Jones

Singles: 7–inch

MERCURY 3-6 62

LPs: 10/12–inch 33rpm

MERCURY 15-25 62

Also see JONES, Quincy

ECKSTINE, Billy /Arthur Prysock

LPs: 10/12–inch 33rpm

GUEST STAR 5-10 64

Also see PRYSOCK, Arthur

ECKSTINE, Billy, & Sarah Vaughan

Singles: 78rpm

MGM 4-8 52

Singles: 7–inch

MGM 5-10 52
MERCURY 5-10 57-59

LPs: 10/12–inch 33rpm

GUEST STAR 5-10 64
LION 15-25 59
MERCURY (20316 "Best of Irving Berlin") 20-30 57

Also see ECKSTINE, Billy
Also see VAUGHAN, Sarah

ECSTASY, PASSION & PAIN

P&R/R&B '74

Singles: 12–inch

ROULETTE 4-6 84

Singles: 7–inch

ROULETTE 3-4 74-76

LPs: 10/12–inch 33rpm

ROULETTE 8-10 74

Members: Barbara Roy; Bill Gardner; Joseph Williams Jr.; Althea Smith; Alan Tizer.
Also see ROY, Barbara

EDDIE, John

P&R/LP '86

Singles: 7–inch

COLUMBIA 3-4 86

Picture Sleeves

COLUMBIA 3-4 86

LPs: 10/12–inch 33rpm

COLUMBIA 5-10 86

EDDIE & BETTY

P&R '59

Singles: 7–inch

LARK 5-10 59
SIX THOUSAND 10-15 57
W.B. 5-10 59

LPs: 10/12–inch 33rpm

W.B. 15-20 59

Members: Eddie Cole; Betty Cole.

EDDIE & CRUISERS

(John Cafferty & Beaver Brown Band)

P&R '83

Singles: 7–inch

SCOTTI BROTHERS 3-4 83

Also see CAFFERTY, John

EDDIE & DUTCH

P&R '70

Singles: 7–inch

IVANHOE 3-5 70

EDDIE & ERNIE

R&B '65

Singles: 7–inch

CHECKER 5-10 63
CHESS 4-8 66
EASTERN 4-8 65-66
REVUE 3-5 69

Members: Eddie Campbell; Ernie Johnson.

EDDIE & FREDDIE

R&B '77

Singles: 7–inch

OCTOBER 3-5 77

EDDIE & TIDE

(Eddie Rice)

P&R '85

Singles: 12–inch 33/45rpm

SPIN 4-8 88
(Promotional only.)

Singles: 7–inch

ATCO 3-4 85

EDDIE D.

(Eddie Drummond)

R&B '85

Singles: 12–inch 33/45rpm

PHILLY WORLD 4-6 85

Singles: 7–inch

PHILLY WORLD 3-4 85

EDDY, Duane

(With the Rebels; with Rebelettes; with His Rock-a-billies; with His Twangy Guitar)

P&R/C&W/R&B '58

Singles: 78rpm

FORD (500 "Ramrod") 50-75 57
JAMIE 10-20 58

Singles: 7–inch

BIG TREE 5-10 72
CAPITOL 3-4 87
COLPIX 5-10 65-66
CONGRESS 3-5 70
ELEKTRA 3-5 77
FORD (500 "Ramrod") 75-125 57
(Credited to Duane Eddy, but is by Al Casey.)
GREGMARK (5 "Caravan") 5-10 61
(Credited to Duane Eddy, but is by Al Casey.)
JAMIE (73 "Peter Gunn") 25-50 61
(Compact 33 single.)
JAMIE (1100 series) 8-15 58-61
(Monaural.)
JAMIE (1100 series) 15-25 59-60
(Stereo.)
JAMIE (1200 series) 5-10 61-62
RCA 5-10 61-65
REPRISE 5-15 66-68
UNI 4-6 70

Picture Sleeves

CAPITOL 3-4 87
COLPIX (788 "House of the Rising Sun") 25-40 66
JAMIE 15-25 59-61
RCA 10-15 62-64

EPs: 7–inch 33/45rpm

JAMIE 20-40 59-60
RCA/WURLITZER DISCOTHEQUE MUSIC 15-25 64

LPs: 10/12–inch 33rpm

CAMDEN 8-15
CAPITOL 8-10 87
COLPIX (490 "Duane A-Go-Go") 25-30 65
COLPIX (494 "Duane Eddy Does Bob Dylan") 25-30 65
JAMIE (Except 3000, 3011 & 3026) 15-30 59-63
JAMIE (3000 "Have Twangy Guitar Will Travel") 20-40 58
(White cover.)
JAMIE (3000 "Have Twangy Guitar Will Travel") 15-30 58
(Red cover.)
JAMIE (3011 "Songs of Our Heritage") 50-75 60
(Colored vinyl.)

JAMIE (3011 "Songs of Our Heritage") 20-30 60
(Gatefold cover. Black vinyl.)
JAMIE (3011 "Songs of Our Heritage") 15-20 61
(Standard cover. Black vinyl.)
JAMIE (3026 "16 Greatest Hits") 15-20 64
RCA ("LPM"/"LSP" series) 20-30 62-66
RCA ("ANL1" series) 5-10 78
REPRISE 15-20 66-67
SIRE 10-15 75
Session: Duane Eddy; Al Casey; Corki Casey; Donnie Owens; Plas Johnson; Steve Douglas; Ike Clanton; Mike Bermani; Waylon Jennings; Willie Nelson; Kin Vassy.
Also see ART of NOISE
Also see BLOSSOMS
Also see CASEY, Al
Also see CLANTON, Ike
Also see CLARK, Sanford, & Duane Eddy
Also see DOUGLAS, Steve
Also see FOGERTY, John
Also see JENNINGS, Waylon
Also see JIMMY & DUANE
Also see JOHNSON, Plas
Also see NELSON, Willie
Also see OWENS, Donnie
Also see SHARPE, Ray
Also see THOMAS, B.J.

EDDY, Duane & Mirriam

Singles: 7-inch

REPRISE (0622 "Guitar on My Mind") 10-15 67
Also see EDDY, Duane

EDELMAN, Randy

P&R '75

Singles: 7-inch

ARISTA 3-5 77-79
LION 3-5 73
MGM 3-5 73
SUNFLOWER 3-5 71-72
20TH FOX 3-5 74-76

LPs: 10/12-inch 33rpm

ARISTA 5-10 77-79
LION 8-10 72
MGM 8-10 72
SUNFLOWER 8-12 71
20TH FOX 8-10 74-78

EDEN'S CHILDREN

LP '68

Singles: 7-inch

ABC 11053 "Goodbye Girl") 5-10 68

LPs: 10/12-inch 33rpm

ABC (624 "Eden's Children") 20-30 68
ABC (652 "Sure Looks Real") ... 15-25 68

EDGE, Graeme

(Graeme Edge Band; with Adrian Gurvitz)

LP '75

Singles: 7-inch

LONDON 3-5 77
THRESHOLD 3-5 74

LPs: 10/12-inch 33rpm

LONDON (686 "Paradise Ballroom") 8-12 77
THRESHOLD (15 "Kick off Your Muddy Boots") 10-15 75
Also see GURVITZ, Adrian
Also see MOODY BLUES

EDISON LIGHTHOUSE

P&R '70

Singles: 7-inch

BELL 3-6 70-71
FLASHBACK 3-5 70s
Member: Tony Burrows.
Also see BURROWS, Tony

EDMUNDS, Dave

P&R '70

Singles: 12-inch 33/45rpm

COLUMBIA (Except 1725) 4-8 85-87
(Promotional issue only.)
COLUMBIA (1725 "Information") . 8-12 84
(Picture disc. Promotional issue only.)

Singles: 7-inch

COLUMBIA 3-4 80-85
MAM (3601 "I Hear You Knocking") 5-8 70
(Black label.)
MAM (3601 "I Hear You Knocking") 3-6 70
(Blue label.)
MAM (3608 "I'm Coming Home") ... 3-6 71
RCA 3-6 73-74
SWAN SONG 3-5 77-81

Promotional Singles

COLUMBIA (1576 "Run Rudolph Run") 4-6 82
(Compact 33 single.)
COLUMBIA (03428 "Run Rudolph Run") 3-5 82

Picture Sleeves

COLUMBIA 3-4 85
SWAN SONG 3-5 81

LPs: 10/12-inch 33rpm

ATLANTIC (320 "College Network") 35-45
(Promotional issue only.)
CAPITOL 5-8 90
COLUMBIA (Except 1725) 5-10 80-87
COLUMBIA (1725 Information") 15-25 83
(Picture disc. Promotional issue only.)
MAM (3 "Rockpile") 30-40 72
RCA (4238 "Subtle As a Flying Mallet") 5-10 82
RCA (5003 "Subtle As a Flying Mallet") 10-12
SWAN SONG 8-10 77-81
Also see CARTER, Carlene, & Dave Edmunds
Also see DION

Also see EDMUNDS, Dave
Also see HARRISON, George / Jeff Beck / Dave Edmunds
Also see LEWIS, Huey, & News
Also see LOVE SCULPTURE
Also see LOWE, Nick, & Dave Edmunds

EDSELS

P&R '61

Singles: 7-inch

ABC 3-4 75
CAPITOL 10-20 61-62
DOT (16311 "My Whispering Heart") 15-20 62
DUB (2843 "Lama Rama Ding Dong") 30-50 58
DUB (2843 "Rama Lama Ding Dong") 10-20 58
(Note variation of title.)
EMBER 10-15 61
LOST-NITE 4-6 70s
MUSICTONE 5-10 64
ROULETTE (4151 "Do You Love Me") 15-20 59
TAMMY (1010 "What Brought Us Together") 20-30 60
TAMMY (1014 "Three Precious Words") 20-30 61
TAMMY (1023 "The Girl I Love") 15-25 61
TWIN 10-12 61

Members: George Jones Jr; Larry Green; James Reynolds; Marshall Sewell; Harry Green.

EDWARD BEAR

P&R '70

Singles: 7-inch

CAPITOL 3-5 70-74

Picture Sleeves

CAPITOL 3-5 72-73

LPs: 10/12-inch 33rpm

CAPITOL 8-10 70-73

EDWARDS, Alton

R&B '82

Singles: 12-inch 33/45rpm

COLUMBIA 4-6 82

Singles: 7-inch

COLUMBIA 3-4 82

EDWARDS, Bobby

P&R/C&W '61

Singles: 7-inch

BLUEBONNET 5-10 59
CAPITOL 4-8 61-63
CHART 4-6 68
CREST 5-10 61
MANCO 4-8 62
MUSICOR 4-8 65
POLARIS 3-5

EDWARDS, Dee

R&B '79

Singles: 12-inch 33/45rpm

COTILLION 4-6 79

Singles: 7-inch

COTILLION 3-6 78-80
D TOWN (1024 "He Told Me Lies") 20-40 65
D TOWN (1031 "What a Party") 10-20 66
D TOWN (1048 "His Majesty My Love") 15-25 66
D TOWN (1063 "All the Way Home") 20-40 66
RCA 5-10 72
TUBA 10-20 62

LPs: 10/12-inch 33rpm

COTILLION 5-10 80

EDWARDS, Dennis

P&R/R&B/LP '84

Singles: 12-inch 33/45rpm

GORDY 4-6 84

Singles: 7-inch

GORDY 3-4 84-85
INT'L SOULVILLE (100 "I Didn't Have to But I Did") 400-600
MOTOWN 3-4

LPs: 10/12-inch 33rpm

GORDY 5-10 84-85

Also see CONTOURS
Also see TEMPTATIONS

EDWARDS, Jayne

D&D '83

Singles: 12-inch 33/45rpm

PROFILE 4-6 83-84

Singles: 7-inch

PROFILE 3-4 83-84

LPs: 10/12-inch 33rpm

PROFILE 5-10 84

EDWARDS, Jimmy

(Jimmie Edwards)

C&W '57

Singles: 78rpm

MERCURY 5-10 57

Singles: 7-inch

MERCURY 10-15 57-58
RCA 5-10 59-60

EDWARDS, John

R&B '73

Singles: 7-inch

AWARE 4-8 73-74
BELL (45205 "Look on Your Face") 25-50 72
COTILLION 3-6 76-77

LPs: 10/12-inch 33rpm

AWARE 5-10 74
CREED 5-10 75
GENERAL/GRC 5-10 74

EDWARDS, Jonathan

P&R/LP '71

Singles: 7–inch

ATCO 3-5 72-73
CAPRICORN 3-5 71
W.B. 3-4 77

LPs: 10/12–inch 33rpm

AMERICAN MELODY 5-8
ATCO 8-10 72-74
CAPRICORN 10-12 71
REPRISE 8-10 74
W.B. 8-10 77

EDWARDS, Jonathan & Darlene

(Paul Weston & Jo Stafford)

LPs: 10/12–inch 33rpm

COLUMBIA (1024 "Piano Artistry") 25-40 57
CORINTHIAN 5-10

Also see STAFFORD, Jo
Also see WESTON, Paul, Orchestra

EDWARDS, Tom

P&R '57

Singles: 78rpm

CORAL 4-8 57

Singles: 7–inch

CORAL 5-10 57

EDWARDS, Tommy

P&R/R&B '51

Singles: 78rpm

MGM 4-8 51-58
TOP 10-20 49-50

Singles: 7–inch

MGM (10000 & 11000 series) 5-10 51-55
MGM (12000 & 13000 series) 4-8 55-65
MGM (50000 series) 10-15 59
(Stereo.)

Picture Sleeves

MGM 8-12 60

EPs: 7–inch 33/45rpm

MGM (1003 "It's All In the Game") 20-30 52
MGM (1614 "It's All In the Game") 10-15 58
MGM (1666/1667/1668 "For Young Lovers") 10-15 59
(Monaural. Price is for any volume.)
MGM (SX-1666/1667/1668 "For Young Lovers") 10-20 59
(Stereo. Price is for any volume.)

LPs: 10/12–inch 33rpm

LION 10-15 59
MGM 15-25 58-63
METRO 8-12 65
REGENT (6096 "Tommy Edwards Sings") 20-30 58

EDWARDS, Vincent

(Vince Edwards)

P&R/LP '62

Singles: 7–inch

CAPITOL 4-8 62
COLPIX 4-8 65
DECCA (31000 series) 4-8 62-63
DECCA (34039 "Open End Interview") 8-12 62
(Promotional issue only.)
DECCA (34074 "Unchained Melody") 5-10 62
(Stereo 33.)
KAMA SUTRA 4-6 67
RUSS-FI (1 "Oh Babe") 5-10 59
RUSS-FI (7001 "Why Did You Leave Me") 4-8 62

Picture Sleeves

COLPIX 4-8 65
DECCA (4311 "Vincent Edwards Sings") 10-20 62
(Monaural.)
DECCA (7-4311 "Vincent Edwards Sings") 15-25 62
(Stereo.)
KAMA SUTRA 4-8 67

EPs: 7–inch 33/45rpm

DECCA 8-10 62

LPs: 10/12–inch 33rpm

DECCA 10-20 62-63

EGAN, Walter

P&R/LP '77

Singles: 7–inch

BACKSTREET 3-4 83
COLUMBIA 3-4 77-79

Picture Sleeves

BACKSTREET 3-4 83

LPs: 10/12–inch 33rpm

BACKSTREET 5-8 83
COLUMBIA 5-10 77-80

Also see BUCKINGHAM, Lindsey
Also see NICKS, Stevie

EGG CREAM Featuring Andy Adams

LP '77

Singles: 7–inch

PYRAMID 3-5 77

LPs: 10/12–inch 33rpm

PYRAMID 5-10 77

Member: Andy Adams.

EGYPTIAN LOVER

R&B '84

Singles: 12–inch 33/45rpm

EGYPTIAN 4-6 84-86

Singles: 7–inch

EGYPTIAN 3-4 84-86
FREAK BEAT 3-4 84

LPs: 10/12–inch 33rpm

EGYPTIAN 5-10 85

EIGHT SECONDS

P&R '87

Singles: 7–inch

POLYDOR.................................... 3-4 87

Picture Sleeves

POLYDOR.................................... 3-4 87

8TH DAY

(Eighth Day)

P&R/R&B/LP '71

Singles: 7–inch

A&M 3-4 83
INVICTUS 3-5 71-72
KAPP... 4-8 67-69

Picture Sleeves

KAPP... 5-8 68

LPs: 10/12–inch 33rpm

A&M 5-10 83
INVICTUS 8-10 71-73
KAPP...................................... 10-15 68

Members: Melvin Davis; Tony Newton; Bruce Nazarion; Michael Anthony; Anita Sherman; Carole Stallings; Lynn Harter.

EIGHTH WONDER

P&R '88

Singles: 7–inch

WTG.. 3-4 88-89

Picture Sleeves

WTG.. 3-4 88

Members: Patsy Kensit; Jamie Kensit.

EL CHICANO

P&R/R&B/LP '70

Singles: 7–inch

GORDO..................................... 3-6 70
KAPP/GORDO 3-5 70-72
MCA 3-5 73-75
RFR.. 3-4 82
SHADYBROOK........................... 3-4 77-78

LPs: 10/12–inch 33rpm

KAPP..................................... 10-12 70-72
MCA 8-10 73-74

Members: Jerry Salas; Mickey Lespron; Fred Sanchez; Bob Espinosa; Andre Baeza.
Also see TIERRA

EL COCO

(Coco)

P&R/R&B '76

Singles: 12–inch 33/45rpm

A.V.I. 4-8 76-85

Singles: 7–inch

A.V.I. 3-5 75-85

LPs: 10/12–inch 33rpm

A.V.I. 5-10 75-85

EL DEBARGE: see DE BARGE, El

EL DORADOS

P&R/R&B '55

Singles: 78rpm

VEE JAY (115 "Baby I Need You") 10-20 54
VEE JAY (118 "Annie's Answer") 20-40 54
(With Hazel McCollum.)
VEE JAY (127: "One More Chance")...............................35-60 54
VEE JAY (147 "At My Front Door").....................................10-20 55
VEE JAY (165 "I'll Be Forever Lovin' You")..............................10-20 55
VEE JAY (180 thru 302)............10-20 56-57

Singles: 7–inch

COLLECTABLES..........................3-4
VEE JAY (115 "Baby I Need You")..50-75 54
(Black vinyl.)
VEE JAY (115 "Baby I Need You")...................................250-400 54
(Colored vinyl.)
VEE JAY (118 "Annie's Answer") 50-75 54
(Black vinyl. With Hazel McCollum.)
VEE JAY (118 "Annie's Answer") 150-225 54
(Colored vinyl.)
VEE JAY (127: "One More Chance")............................125-175 54
VEE JAY (147 "At My Front Door")......................................20-30 55
VEE JAY (165 "I'll Be Forever Lovin' You")..............................20-30 55
VEE JAY (180 "Now That You've Gone")....................................20-30 56
VEE JAY (197 "A Fallen Tear")..30-40 56
VEE JAY (211 "Bim Bam Boom")....................................30-40 56
VEE JAY (250 "Tears on My Pillow")..................................20-30 57
VEE JAY (263 "Three Reasons Why") 75-100 58
VEE JAY (302 "Lights Are Low")..50-100 58

LPs: 10/12–inch 33rpm

COLLECTABLES (20 "Best of the El Dorados").........................8-10 80s
(10–inch LP.)
LOST-NITE 5-10 81
SOLID SMOKE 5-10 82
VEE JAY (1001 "Crazy Little Mama") 300-400 58
(Maroon label.)
VEE JAY (1001 "Crazy Little Mama") 150-250 58
(Black label.)
Note: Vee Jay 1001 also contains two tracks by the Magnificants.

Members: Pirkle Lee Moses Jr; Arthur Bassett; Louis Bradley; James Maddox; Jewel Jones; Richard Nickens; Johnny Carter; Ted Long; John McCall; Douglas Brown.
Also see MAGNIFICENTS

ELAINE & ELLEN

R&B '80

Singles: 7-inch

OVATION 3-4 80

ELBERT, Donnie

P&R/R&B '57

Singles: 78rpm

DELUXE 5-10 57

Singles: 7-inch

ALL PLATINUM 3-5 72
AVCO 3-5 72
COMMAND PERFORMANCE 3-5
CUB 4-8 63
DELUXE 10-20 57-58
GATEWAY 4-8 64-65
GUSTO 3-4 80s
JALYNNE (107 "Mommie's Gone") 15-25 60
JALYNNE (110 "Lucille") 5-10 62
RARE BULLET 3-5 70
RED TOP 15-20
TRIP 3-5
VEE JAY 5-15 60

LPs: 10/12-inch 33rpm

ALL PLATINUM 10-15 71
DELUXE 10-15 71
KING (629 "The Sensational Donnie Elbert Sings") 50-100 59
SUGARHILL 5-10 81
TRIP 8-10 72

ELBOW BONES & RACKETEERS

D&D '83

Singles: 12-inch 33/45rpm

EMI AMERICA 4-6 83

Singles: 7-inch

EMI AMERICA 3-4 84

Members: Ginchy Dan; Stephanie Fuller.

ELECTRIC BOYS

P&R/LP '90

Singles: 7-inch

ATCO 3-4 90

LPs: 10/12-inch 33rpm

ATCO 5-8 90

ELECTRIC EXPRESS

P&R/R&B '71

Singles: 7-inch

KEY-VAC (2930 "Hearsay......... 25-50
LINCO 4-8 71

ELECTRIC FLAG
(Electric Flag Music Band)

LP '68

Singles: 7-inch

ATLANTIC 3-5 74-75
COLUMBIA 4-8 67
SIDEWALK 8-12 67

Picture Sleeves

COLUMBIA 5-10 67

LPs: 10/12-inch 33rpm

ATLANTIC 8-10 74
COLUMBIA 10-15 68-71

Also see BLOOMFIELD, Mike, & Nick Gravenites
Also see GRAVENTES, Nick
Also see MILES, Buddy, Express

ELECTRIC INDIAN

P&R/R&B/LP '69

Singles: 7-inch

MARMADUKE 5-10 69
U.A. 3-6 69

LPs: 10/12-inch 33rpm

U.A. 10-15 69

Also see MFSB

ELECTRIC LIGHT ORCHESTRA

LP '72

(ELO)

Singles: 12-inch 33/45rpm

JET 10-15 78

Singles: 7-inch

JET/CBS 3-5 77-86
JET/U.A. (Except 1000) 3-5 77
JET/U.A. (1000 "Telephone Line") . 4-8 77
(Colored vinyl. Promotional issue only.)
MCA 3-4 80
U.A. 3-4 72-77

Picture Sleeves

JET 3-5 78-79
JET/CBS 3-4 86
JET/U.A. 3-5 77
MCA 3-4 80
U.A. 3-6 74-77

LPs: 10/12-inch 33rpm

CBS 8-10 86
JET/CBS (Except 36966 & 40000 series) 5-10 78-86
JET/CBS (36966 "Box of Their Best") 20-25 80
(Boxed set of two LPs, *Out of the Blue* and *Discovery*, and the bonus single, *Doin' That Crazy Thing*.)
JET/CBS (40000 series) 20-25 80-83
(Half-speed mastered.)
U.A. (Except 546) 10-15 72-76
U.A. (546 "Face the Music") 25-30 75
(Banded for airplay.Promotional issue only.)
U.A./JET (Except 123 & 823) 8-12 76-77
U.A./JET (123 "Olé ELO") 25-35 76
(Colored vinyl. Promotional issue only.)
U.A./JET (823 "Out of the Blue") 10-15 76
(Black vinyl.)
U.A./JET (823 "Out of the Blue") 30-40 76
(Colored vinyl. Promotional issue only.)

Also see LYNNE, Jeff
Also see NEWTON-JOHN, Olivia, & Electric Light Orchestra
Also see WOOD, Roy

ELECTRIC MIND

D&D '83

Singles: 12–inch 33/45rpm

EMERGENCY 4-6 83

ELECTRIC PRUNES

P&R '66

Singles: 7–inch

REPRISE (PRO-277 "Sanctus") 35-45 67
(Promotional issue only.)
REPRISE (PRO-0305 "Help Us") 25-35 68
(Promotional issue only.)
REPRISE (0473 "Little Olive")... 25-35 66
REPRISE (0532 "I Had Too Much to Dream") 10-15 66
REPRISE (0564 "Get Me to the World on Time") 10-20 67
REPRISE (0594 "Dr. Do Good") 10-20 67
REPRISE (0607 "The Great Banana Hoax") 10-20 67
REPRISE (0652 "You Never Had It Better") 20-30 68
REPRISE (0805 "Hey Mr. President") 10-20 69
REPRISE (0833 "Violet Rose"). 25-35 69
REPRISE (0858 "Love Grows") 15-20 69

LPs: 10/12–inch 33rpm

REPRISE (6248 "I Had Too Much to Dream") 20-30 67
REPRISE (6262 "Underground") 30-40 67
REPRISE (6257 "Mass in F Minor") 20-30 67
REPRISE (6262 "Release of an Oath") 15-25 68
REPRISE (6342 "Just Good Rock 'N' Roll") 15-25 69

ELECTRONIC

P&R '90

Singles: 7–inch

W.B. 3-4 90

LPs: 10/12–inch 33rpm

W.B. 5-8 91

Members: Bernard Sumner; John Marr; Neil Tennant; David Palmer; Anne Dudley.
Also see ART of NOISE
Also see NEW ORDER
Also see PET SHOP BOYS

ELECTRONIC CONCEPT ORCHESTRA

LP '69

LPs: 10/12–inch 33rpm

LIMELIGHT 5-10 69
MERCURY 5-10 70

Member: Eddie Higgins.

ELEGANTS

(Vito & Elegants)

P&R/R&B '58

Singles: 7–inch

ABC..3-5 73
ABC-PAR (10219 "Tiny Cloud").15-20 61
APT (25005 "Little Star")............25-35 58
(Silver print on black label.)
APT (25005 "Little Star")............15-25 58
(White or multi-color label.)
APT (25017 "Goodnight") 25-35 58
APT (25029 "Payday") 15-25 59
BIM BAM BOOM.........................5-10 74
(Black vinyl.)
BIM BAM BOOM..........................3-4 74
(Colored vinyl.)
CRYSTAL BALL...........................3-5
HULL (732 "Little Boy Blue")......35-40 60
LAURIE (3283 "Barbara Beware") 15-25 65
LAURIE (3298 "Wake Up") 20-30 65
LAURIE (3324 "Belinda") 10-15 65
MCA 3-4
PHOTO (2662 "A Dream Can Come True") 15-20 63
PLANET (2727 "Human Angel") 3-5
(Colored vinyl.)
ROULETTE..................................3-4 71
U.A. 10-15 60-61

Picture Sleeves

CRYSTAL BALL...........................3-5
PHOTO (2662 "A Dream Can Come True") 25-35 63
(Add $10 to $20 if accompanied by printed insert.)

LPs: 10/12–inch 33rpm

CRYSTAL BALL...........................8-10 90
MURRAY HILL (210 "Little Star").8-10 86

Members: Vito Picone; Frank Tardagno; Carman Romano; Jimmy Moschella; Artie Venosa.
Also see BARBARIANS

ELEGANTS / Poni-Tails

Singles: 7–inch

ROULETTE..................................3-5 73

Also see ELEGANTS
Also see PONI-TAILS

ELEKTRIK DRED

R&B '83

Singles: 7–inch

SOUNDS of FLORIDA..................3-4 83

ELEKTRO, Eve

D&D '84

Singles: 12–inch 33/45rpm

BLACK SUIT 4-6 84

ELEPHANTS MEMORY

LP '69

Singles: 7–inch

APPLE (1854 "Liberation Special") 4-8 72
BUDDAH 4-8 69
METROMEDIA 3-6 70-71
RCA 3-5 74

Promotional Singles

APPLE (1854 "Liberation Special") 15-25 72

Picture Sleeves

APPLE (1854 "Liberation Special") 5-10 72
METROMEDIA 4-8 70

LPs: 10/12–inch 33rpm

APPLE 10-15 72
BUDDAH 10-15 69-74
METROMEDIA 10-12 70
MUSE 8-10 70s
RCA 8-10 74

Also see LENNON, John

ELEVENTH HOUR

P&R '74

Singles: 7–inch

BELL 3-5 71
20TH FOX 3-5 74-76

LPs: 10/12–inch 33rpm

ARISTA 6-10 75
20TH FOX 8-10 74-76

ELEVENTH HOUSE

(With Larry Coryell)

LP '74

Singles: 7–inch

VANGUARD 3-5 74

LPs: 10/12–inch 33rpm

ARISTA 5-10 75
VANGUARD (40036 "Introducing the Eleventh House with Larry Coryell") 10-20 74
(Quadrophonic.)
VANGUARD (79342 "Introducing the Eleventh House with Larry Coryell") 8-12 74

Members: Larry Coryell; Kenny Nolan.
Also see CORYELL, Larry
Also see MOUZON, Alphonse, & Larry Croyell

ELGART, Larry

(With His Manhattan Swing Orchestra)

P&R/LP '82

Singles: 78rpm

DECCA 3-4 54-55

Singles: 7–inch

DECCA 3-6 54-55
MGM 3-5 61-62
RCA 3-5 59-83

EPs: 7–inch 33/45rpm

BRUNSWICK 5-10 54
DECCA 5-10 54-55

LPs: 10/12–inch 33rpm

BRUNSWICK 15-25 54
(10–inch LPs.)
CAMDEN 5-10 60-73
DECCA 10-20 54-55
MGM 8-12 60-62
RCA 5-10 59-83

ELGART, Les, Orchestra

P&R/LP '56

Singles: 78rpm

COLUMBIA 3-5 53-57

Singles: 7–inch

COLUMBIA (40000 series, except 40180) 3-6 53-62
COLUMBIA (40180 "Bandstand Boogie") 15-20 54
COLUMBIA (56767 "Bandstand Twist") 5-10 62
(Promotional issue only.)
GOLD-MOR 3-4 73

EPs: 7–inch 33/45rpm

COLUMBIA 5-10 53-59

LPs: 10/12–inch 33rpm

COLUMBIA 10-20 53-62
HARMONY 5-10 66

ELGART, Les & Larry

LP '64

Singles: 7–inch

COLUMBIA 3-4 64-68
SWAMPFIRE 3-4 69

Picture Sleeves

COLUMBIA 3-5 65

LPs: 10/12–inch 33rpm

COLUMBIA (Except 38000 series) 8-15 57-68
COLUMBIA (38000 series) 5-10 82
HARMONY 5-10 68-73
SWAMPFIRE 5-10 70

Also see ELGART, Larry
Also see ELGART, Les

ELGINS

P&R/R&B '66

Singles: 7–inch

V.I.P. 10-20 66-71

LPs: 10/12–inch 33rpm

V.I.P. (400 "Darling Baby") 50-100 66

Members: Saundra Mallet; Cleo Miller; Robert Flemming; John Dawson; Norbert McClean.

ELI'S SECOND COMING

R&B '76

Singles: 7–inch

SILVER BLUE 3-5 76-78

Members: Bobby Eli.
Also see MFSB

ELLEDGE, Jimmy

P&R '61

Singles: 7-inch

4 STAR.......... 3-5 75
HICKORY.......... 3-5 65-67
LITTLE DARLIN'.......... 3-5 68
RCA (Except 8012).......... 4-8 61-64
RCA (8012 "Can't You See It in My Eyes").......... 10-20 62
SIMS.......... 3-6 64

Picture Sleeves

RCA.......... 5-10 62-63

ELLIMAN, Yvonne

P&R '71

Singles: 7-inch

DECCA.......... 3-5 71-72
MCA.......... 3-4
RSO.......... 3-5 74-79

Picture Sleeves

RSO.......... 3-5 78

LPs: 10/12-inch 33rpm

DECCA.......... 10-15 72
MCA.......... 8-12 73
RSO.......... 6-10 77-79

Also see BISHOP, Stephen, & Yvonne Elliman

ELLINGTON, Duke

P&R '27

Singles: 78rpm

CAPITOL.......... 3-5 53-56
COLUMBIA.......... 3-5 50-53
RCA.......... 3-5 51-55

Singles: 7-inch

BELL.......... 3-4 73
BETHLEHEM.......... 3-6 58-60
CAPITOL (2000 series).......... 4-8 53-56
COLUMBIA (33000 series).......... 3-4 76
COLUMBIA (39000 series).......... 5-10 50-53
COLUMBIA (40000 thru 42000 series).......... 3-6 58-61
COLUMBIA PRICELESS EDITION.......... 5-10
RCA (0300 series).......... 3-4 74
RCA (4000 thru 6000 series).......... 4-8 51-55
REPRISE.......... 3-5 67

EPs: 7-inch 33/45rpm

BRUNSWICK.......... 10-20 54
CAPITOL.......... 10-20 53-56
COLUMBIA.......... 10-20 50-56
RCA.......... 10-20 52-60
ROYALE.......... 10-20 50s

LPs: 10/12-inch 33rpm

ALLEGIANCE.......... 5-8 84
ALLEGRO.......... 25-50 54
(10-inch LPs.)
ATLANTIC.......... 5-10 71-82
BASF.......... 5-10 73
BETHLEHEM.......... 15-30 56-57
BRIGHT ORANGE.......... 5-10 73
BRUNSWICK (54000 series).......... 15-30 56
BRUNSWICK (58000 series).......... 30-50 54
(10-inch LPs.)
CAMDEN (400 series).......... 15-25 58
CAPITOL (400 series).......... 25-50 53
(With "H" prefix. 10-inch LPs.)
CAPITOL (400 thru 600 series).......... 25-40 55-57
CAPITOL (1600 series).......... 10-20 61
(With "T" prefix.)
CAPITOL (11000 series).......... 5-10 72-77
CAPITOL (16000 series).......... 4-6 81
COLUMBIA (27 "The Ellington Era, Volume 1).......... 25-40 63
COLUMBIA (39 "The Ellington Era, Volume 2, 1927-1940).......... 25-40 66
COLUMBIA (500 thru 900 series).......... 20-30 54-57
COLUMBIA (1085 thru 2029 except 1360).......... 15-30 57-63
(Monaural.)
COLUMBIA (1360 "Anatomy of a Murder").......... 35-50 59
(Soundtrack. Monaural.)
COLUMBIA (4000 series).......... 25-50 55
COLUMBIA (6000 series).......... 30-60 50
(10-inch LPs.)
COLUMBIA (8053 thru 9600, except 8166).......... 10-20 57-68
(Stereo.)
COLUMBIA (8166 "Anatomy of a Murder").......... 45-60 59
(Soundtrack. Stereo.)
COLUMBIA (14000 series).......... 5-10 79
(Columbia Special Products series.)
COLUMBIA (32000 thru 38000 series).......... 5-10 73-82
COLUMBIA SPECIAL PROD.......... 8-10 82
DECCA.......... 8-15 67-70
DOCTOR JAZZ.......... 5-8 84
EVEREST.......... 5-10 70-73
FANTASY.......... 6-12 71-75
FLYING DUTCHMAN.......... 5-10 69
HARMONY.......... 5-10 67-71
IMPULSE (Except 9200 series).......... 15-20 62
IMPULSE (9200 series).......... 8-12 73
ODYSSEY.......... 8-12 68
PABLO.......... 5-10 76-80
PRESTIGE.......... 6-12 73-77
RCA (500 series).......... 10-20 64-69
RCA (0700 thru 2000 series).......... 5-8 75-78
(With "ANL1" or "APL1" prefix.)
RCA (1000 series).......... 25-40 54
(With "LJM" or "LPT" prefix.)
RCA (1300 thru 2800 series).......... 10-30 57-66
(With "LPM" or "LSP" prefix.)
RCA (3000 series).......... 25-50 52-53
(10-inch LPs.)
RCA (3500 thru 3900 series).......... 8-15 66-68
RCA (4000 series).......... 8-10 81

RCA (6009 "The Indispensible Duke Ellington") 20-30 61
RCA (6042 "This Is Duke Ellington") 10-15 71
REPRISE 10-20 63-68
RIVERSIDE (Except 100 series) 10-20 62-64
RIVERSIDE (100 series) 15-30 56-59
RON-LETTE 15-30 58
SOLID STATE 5-10 70
SUNSET 5-10 69
TRIP 5-10 75-76
U.A. (Except 14000 & 15000 series) 5-10 72
U.A. (14000 & 15000 series) 15-25 62
VERVE 10-15 67
X (3037 "Duke Ellington") 25-50 55
(10-inch LP.)

Also see ARMSTRONG, Louis, & Duke Ellington
Also see BASIE, Count, & Duke Ellington
Also see BREWER, Teresa, & Duke Ellington
Also see CARROLL, Diahann, & Duke Ellington Orchestra
Also see FITZGERALD, Ella, & Duke Ellington
Also see HIBBLER, Al, & Duke Ellington
Also see JACKSON, Mahalia, & Duke Ellington
Also see SINATRA, Frank, & Duke Ellington

ELLINGTON, Duke, & Boston Pops Orchestra

LP '66

LP: 10/12-inch 33rpm

RCA 10-15 66

Also see BOSTON POPS ORCHESTRA

ELLINGTON, Duke, & John Coltrane

LPs: 10/12-inch 33rpm

IMPULSE 15-25 63

Also see COLTRANE, John

ELLINGTON, Duke, & Johnny Hodges

LPs: 10/12-inch 33rpm

PRESTIGE 8-10 81
VERVE (Except 8800 series) 15-30 59-60
VERVE (8800 series) 8-12 73

Also see ELLINGTON, Duke
Also see HODGES, Johnny

ELLIOT, Cass
(Mama Cass)

P&R/LP '68

Singles: 7-inch

DUNHILL 3-6 68-70
RCA 3-5 71-73

LPs: 10/12-inch 33rpm

DUNHILL 10-20 68-72
PICKWICK 8-12
RCA 10-15 72-73

Also see BIG THREE
Also see MAMAS & PAPAS
Also see MASON, Dave, & Mama Cass
Also see MUGWUMPS

ELLIS, Ray, Orchestra

P&R '60

Singles: 78rpm

COLUMBIA 3-8 57

Singles: 7-inch

COLUMBIA 3-8 57
MGM 3-5 59-60
RCA 3-5 61

EPs: 7-inch 33/45rpm

COLUMBIA 5-10 57

LPs: 10/12-inch 33rpm

COLUMBIA 10-20 57
HARMONY 10-15 59
MGM 10-15 59-60
RCA 10-15 61

ELLIS, Shirley

P&R/R&B '63

Singles: 7-inch

COLUMBIA 4-8 67
CONGRESS 4-8 63-65

Picture Sleeves

CONGRESS 5-10 64-65

LPs: 10/12-inch 33rpm

COLUMBIA 15-20 67
CONGRESS 20-25 64-65

Also see SHIRLEE MAY

ELLISON, Lorraine

R&B '65

Singles: 7-inch

LOMA 3-5 67-68
MERCURY 4-8 65-66
SHARP 4-8 63
W.B. 3-6 66-69

LPs: 10/12-inch 33rpm

W.B. (1000 series) 15-20 67-69
W.B. (2000 series) 8-10 74

ELMO & ALMO

P&R '67

Singles: 7-inch

DADDY BEST 4-6 67

ELMO 'N' PATSY

C&W '84

Singles: 7-inch

ELMO 'N' PATSY 3-5 79
EPIC 3-4 84
OINK 3-4 80
SOUNDWAVES 3-4 81

LPs: 10/12-inch 33rpm

OINK 5-10 80

Members: Elmo Shropshire; Patsy Trigg.

ELUSION

R&B '81

Singles: 7-inch

COTILLION 3-4 81

LPs: 10/12-inch 33rpm

COTILLION 5-10 81

ELY, Joe

C&W '77

Singles: 7–inch

MCA 3-4 77-81
SOUTHCOAST 3-4 81

LPs: 10/12–inch 33rpm

MCA 5-10 77-81
SOUTHCOAST 5-10 81

EMERSON, Keith

LP '81

LPs: 10/12–inch 33rpm

BACKSTREET 5-10 81

EMERSON, Keith, & Nice

Singles: 7–inch

MERCURY 3-5 72

LPs: 10/12–inch 33rpm

MERCURY 12-15 72

Also see EMERSON, Keith
Also see EMERSON, LAKE & PALMER
Also see NICE

EMERSON, LAKE & PALMER

P&R/LP '71

Singles: 7–inch

ATLANTIC 3-5 77-80
COTILLION 3-5 71-72
MANTICORE 3-5 74
POLYDOR 3-4 86

Promotional Singles

ATLANTIC ("Brain Salad Surgery") 4-6 78
(Number not known.)

LPs: 10/12–inch 33rpm

ATLANTIC (Except 281) 8-10 77-80
ATLANTIC (281 "Emerson, Lake & Palmer") 12-15 77
(With the London Philharmonic Orchestra. Also contains interviews with the three members. Promotional issue only.)
COTILLION 12-15 71-72
MFSL (031 "Pictures at an Exhibition") 15-25 80
MFSL (203 "Tarkus") 10-20 94
MANTICORE 10-12 73-74

Members: Keith Emerson; Greg Lake; Carl Palmer.
Also see ASIA
Also see EMERSON, LAKE & POWELL
Also see 3

EMERSON, LAKE & POWELL

P&R/LP '86

—Singles: 7–inch

POLYDOR 3-4 86

Picture Sleeves

POLYDOR 3-4 86

LPs: 10/12–inch 33rpm

POLYDOR 5-10 86

Members: Keith Emerson; Greg Lake; Cozy Powell.
Also see EMERSON, Keith
Also see EMERSON, LAKE & PALMER
Also see LAKE, Greg
Also see POWELL, Cozy

EMMERSON, Les

P&R '73

Singles: 7–inch

LION 3-5 73

Also see FIVE MAN ELECTRICAL BAND

EMOTIONS

P&R '62

Singles: 7–inch

BRAINSTORM 4-6 68
CALLA 4-8 65
CRYSTAL BALL 3-5 90
JASON SCOTT 4-8
KAPP 5-10 62-63
KARATE 4-8 64
LAURIE (3167 "Starlit Night") 10-15 63
20TH FOX 10-15 63-64
VARDAN 4-8 65

LPs: 10/12–inch 33rpm

CRYSTAL BALL 5-8 90
MAGIC CARPET 5-10

Members: Joe Favale; Tony Maltese; Don Colluri; Larry Cusamanno; Joe Nigro; Sal Covais.

EMOTIONS

P&R/R&B '69

Singles: 12–inch 33/45rpm

RED LABEL 4-6 84

Singles: 7–inch

ARC 3-4 80-81
COLUMBIA 3-5 76-81
STAX 3-4 77-79
MOTOWN 3-4 85
RED LABEL 3-4 84
TWIN STACKS 4-8 68
VOLT 3-6 69-74

LPs: 10/12–inch 33rpm

ARC 5-8 79-81
COLUMBIA 5-10 76-81
MOTOWN 5-10 85
RED LABEL 5-10 84
STAX 5-10 77-79
VOLT 10-20 69-74

Members: Sheila Hutchinson; Wanda Hutchinson; Jeanette Hutchinson.
Also see EARTH, WIND & FIRE with the EMOTIONS

EMPERORS

P&R/R&B '66

Singles: 7–inch

BRUNSWICK 4-8 67
MALA 5-10 66-67

ENCHANTERS

P&R '61

Singles: 7–inch

BALD EAGLE (3001 "Come on Baby, Let's Do the Stroll") 15-25 58
BAMBOO 10-15 61

CANDELITE (432 "Oh Rose Marie") 8-10 64
EP-SOM (103 "I Need Your Love") 100-150 62
J.J.&M. (1562 "Oh Rose Marie") 100-150 62
MUSITRON (1072 "I Lied to My Heart") 30-40 61
ORBIT (532 "Touch of Love") ... 15-20 59
SHARP (105 "We Make Mistakes") 10-20 60
STARDUST (102 "Raindrops") 300-500
TOM TOM (301 "Surf Blast") 25-35 63

ENCHANTERS

P&R/R&B '64

Singles: 7-inch

LOMA 4-8 65-66
W.B. 5-10 64

Members: Samuel Bell; Charles Boyer; Zola Pearnell.
Also see MIMMS, Garnet, & Enchanters

ENCHANTMENT

R&B '76

Singles: 7-inch

COLUMBIA 3-4 82-84
DESERT MOON 3-5 76
RCA 3-4 80
ROADSHOW 3-5 77-78
U.A. 3-5 76-77

LPs: 10/12-inch 33rpm

COLUMBIA 5-10 82
RCA 5-10 80
ROADSHOW 8-10 77-79
U.A. 8-10 77

Members: Bobby Green; Mickey Clanton; Joe Thomas; Davis Banks; Emanuel Johnson.

ENDGAMES

D&D '83

Singles: 12-inch 33/45rpm

FLIP 4-6 83
MCA 4-6 83

Singles: 7-inch

MCA 3-4 84

LPs: 10/12-inch 33rpm

MCA 5-10 84

ENERGETICS

R&B '79

Singles: 7-inch

ATLANTIC 3-5 79
TIP TOP 4-6

LPs: 10/12-inch 33rpm

ATLANTIC 5-10 79

ENGLAND DAN & John Ford Coley

P&R/LP '76

Singles: 7-inch

A&M 3-5 71-77
BIG TREE 3-5 76-80
MCA 3-4 80

LPs: 10/12-inch 33rpm

A&M 10-12 71-73
BIG TREE 8-10 76-79
MCA 5-10 80

Members: Dan Seals; John Ford Coley.
Also see ABBA / Spinners / Firefall / England Dan & John Ford Coley
Also see COLEY, John Ford
Also see SEALS, Dan
Also see SOUTHWEST F.O.B.

ENGLISH, Barbara

(Barbara Jean English)

R&B '73

Singles: 7-inch

ALITHIA 4-6 73-74
AURORA (155 "Sittin' in the Corner") 50-75 65
MALA (488 "Easy Come Easy Go") 10-20 64
REPRISE (290 "I've Got a Date") 10-20 65
REPRISE (349 "Small Town Girl") 10-20 65
ROULETTE (4428 "We Need Them") 20-30 62
W.B. (5685 "All Because I Love Somebody") 10-15 65

LPs: 10/12-inch 33rpm

ALITHIA 8-10 73

ENGLISH, Jackie

P&R '80

Singles: 7-inch

VENTURE 3-4 80

ENGLISH, Scott

(With the Accents; with Dedications)

P&R '64

Singles: 7-inch

DOT (16099 "White Cliffs of Dover") 10-15 60
JANUS (171 "Brandy") 8-10 71
JANUS (192 "Woman in My Life") .3-5 72
JOKER (777 "Ugly Pills") 15-25 62
SPOKANE (4003 "High on a Hill") 8-15 64
SPOKANE (4007 "Here Comes the Pain") 10-20 64
SULTAN (4003 "High on a Hill") 15-25 63
SULTAN (5500 "Rags to Riches") 20-30 61

ENGLISH BEAT

LP '80

Singles: 12-inch 33/45rpm

I.R.S. 4-6 83-85

Singles: 7-inch

I.R.S. 3-4 83-85

LPs: 10/12-inch 33rpm

I.R.S. 5-10 82-85
SIRE 5-10 80-81

Members: Andy Cox; David Steele; Roger Charley; Dave Wakeling.
Also see FINE YOUNG CANNIBALS
Also see GENERAL PUBLIC

ENGLISH CONGREGATION

P&R '72

Singles: 7-inch

ATCO 3-5 72
SIGNPOST................................ 3-5 73

LPs: 10/12-inch 33rpm

SIGNPOST................................ 8-10 73

ENIGMA

LP '91

LPs: 10/12-inch 33rpm

CHARISMA 5-8 91

ENNIS, Ethel

LP '64

Singles: 78rpm

JUBILEE.................................... 4-8 56

Singles: 7-inch

JUBILEE.................................... 5-10 56
RCA.. 5-10 64

LPs: 10/12-inch 33rpm

CAPITOL................................. 15-25 58
JUBILEE.................................. 20-40 56-63
RCA... 15-25 64

ENO, Brian

(Eno)

LP '74

Singles: 7-inch

ISLAND 3-5 72

LPs: 10/12-inch 33rpm

ANTILLES 8-10 73-78
EDITIONS E.G. 5-10 81-82
ISLAND 8-10 73-78
PVC.. 5-10 79
SIRE... 5-10 81
Also see BYRNE, David
Also see ROXY MUSIC

ENTERTAINERS IV

R&B '66

Singles: 7-inch

DORE....................................... 4-8 66

ENTOUCH

(Featuring Keith Sweat)

P&R/LP '90

Singles: 7-inch

VINTERTAINMENT...................... 3-4 90

LPs: 10/12-inch 33rpm

VINTERTAINMENT...................... 5-8 90
Members: Eric McCaine; Free.
Also see SWEAT, Keith
Also see TOUCH

ENUFF Z'NUFF

P&R '89

Singles: 7-inch

ATCO 3-4 89-90

Picture Sleeves

ATCO 3-4 89

ENTWISTLE, John

(John Entwistle's Rigor Mortis; John Entwistle's Ox)

LP '71

Singles: 7-inch

DECCA 3-5 72
TRACK..................................... 3-5 73

LPs: 10/12-inch 33rpm

ATCO 5-10 81
DECCA 10-15 71-72
MCA/TRACK.............................. 8-10 72-75
Also see TOWNSHEND, Pete, & Ronnie Lane
Also see WHO

ENUFF Z'NUFF

LP '89

LPs: 10/12-inch 33rpm

ATCO 5-8 89-91

EN VOGUE

P&R/LP '90

LPs: 10/12-inch 33rpm

ATLANTIC................................. 5-8 90

ENYA

P&R/LP '89

Singles: 7-inch

GEFFEN 3-4 89

Picture Sleeves

GEFFEN 3-4 89

LPs: 10/12-inch 33rpm

GEFFEN 5-8 89

EON

R&B '78

Singles: 7-inch

ARIOLA AMERICA 3-4 78

LPs: 10/12-inch 33rpm

ARIOLA AMERICA 5-10 78
SCEPTER.................................. 8-10 73

EPIC SPLENDOR

P&R '67

Singles: 7-inch

HOT BISCUIT 4-8 67-68

Picture Sleeves

HOT BISCUIT (1452 "It Could Be Wonderful") 8-10 68

EPOQUE, Belle: see BELLE EPOQUE

EPPS, Preston

P&R '59

Singles: 7-inch

ADMIRAL.................................. 4-8 65
EMBASSY................................. 5-10 62
JO JO 3-6 69
MAJESTY 4-8
ORIGINAL SOUND (4 "Bongo Rock") 8-15 60
(Monaural.)

ORIGINAL SOUND (4 "Bongo Rock") 15-25 60
(Stereo.)
ORIGINAL SOUND (9 thru 17) ... 6-12 60-61
POLO (218 "Bongo Rock 1965")... 4-8 65
TOP RANK.................................. 5-10 59

EPs: 7-inch 33/45rpm

ORIGINAL SOUND (1001 "Bongo Rock") 15-25 60

LPs: 10/12-inch 33rpm

ORIGINAL SOUND (5002 "Bongo Bongo Bongo").......................... 30-40 60
(Monaural.)
ORIGINAL SOUND (8851 "Bongo Bongo Bongo").......................... 30-50 60
(Stereo.)
ORIGINAL SOUND (5009 "Surfin' Bongos") 25-40 63
(Monaural.)
ORIGINAL SOUND (8872 "Surfin' Bongos") 25-50 63
(Stereo.)
TOP RANK (349 "Bongola")...... 30-50 61
Also see SKYLINERS / Preston Epps

EQUALS

P&R '68

Singles: 7-inch

BANG 5-10 70
PRESIDENT.................................. 5-10 67-68
RCA.. 4-8 68

LPs: 10/12-inch 33rpm

LAURIE (2045 "Unequalled") 20-25 67
PRESIDENT............................ 15-25 68-69
RCA.. 10-15 68
Members: Eddy Grant; Derv Gordon.
Also see GRANT, Eddy

ERAMUS HALL

R&B '84

Singles: 12-inch 33/45rpm

CAPITOL.. 4-6 84

Singles: 7-inch

CAPITOL.. 3-4 84

LPs: 10/12-inch 33rpm

CAPITOL.. 5-10 84

ERASURE

LP '87

Singles: 7-inch

SIRE.. 3-4 82-89

Picture Sleeves

SIRE.. 3-4 88

LPs: 10/12-inch 33rpm

SIRE.. 5-10 82-89

ERIC

D&D '84

Singles: 12-inch 33/45rpm

MEMO 4-6 84

ERIC B. & RAKIM

R&B '86

Singles: 7-inch

4TH & BROADWAY........................3-4 87-88
ZAKIA..3-4 86

LPs: 10/12-inch 33rpm

4TH & BROADWAY........................5-10 87
MCA..5-8 90
UNI...5-8 88

ERNIE / Sesame Street Kids
(Jim Henson as "Ernie")

P&R '79

Singles: 7-inch

COLUMBIA 3-5 70
Also see HENSON, Jim

ERUPTION

P&R/R&B/LP '78

Singles: 12-inch 33/45rpm

ARIOLA AMERICA 4-8 78
HANSA..4-8 70s

Singles: 7-inch

ARIOLA AMERICA 3-4 78

LPs: 10/12-inch 33rpm

ARIOLA AMERICA 5-10 78
Member: Precious Wilson.
Also see WILSON, Precious

ESCAPE CLUB

P&R/LP '88

Singles: 7-inch

ATLANTIC.......................................3-4 88-91

Picture Sleeves

ATLANTIC.......................................3-4 88-89

LPs: 10/12-inch 33rpm

ATLANTIC.......................................5-8 88-91

ESCORTS

R&B '73

Singles: 7-inch

ALITHIA 3-5 73-74

LPs: 10/12-inch 33rpm

ALITHIA 8-10 73-74
Members: Reginald Hayes; Robert Arrington; Laurence Franklin; Stephen Carter; William Dugger; Frank Heard; Marion Murphy.

ESCOVEDO, Coke

P&R/LP '76

Singles: 7-inch

MERCURY 3-5 76-77

LPs: 10/12-inch 33rpm

MERCURY 5-10 76-77
Also see AZTECA
Also see SANTANA

ESMERALDA, Santa: see SANTA ESMERALDA

ESPOSITO, Joe "Bean"

P&R '83

Singles: 7-inch

CASABLANCA..................................3-4 83
Also see BROOKS, Pattie, & Joe Esposito

Also see BROOKLYN DREAMS
Also see RUSSELL, Brenda

ESQUIRE

LP '87

LPs: 10/12-inch 33rpm

GEFFEN.................................... 5-10 87

ESQUIRE BOYS

P&R '53

Singles: 78rpm

DOT.. 5-10 55
GUYDEN.. 5-10 54
NICKELODEON............................ 5-10 53
RAINBOW..................................... 5-10 52-53

Singles: 7-inch

DOT.. 10-15 55
FRANSIL...................................... 5-10 61
GUYDEN...................................... 8-12 54
NICKELODEON (102 "Guitar Boogie Shuffle")...................... 10-15 53
RAINBOW (100 & 200 series)... 10-20 52-53
(Black vinyl.)
RAINBOW (100 & 200 series)... 20-35 52-53
(Colored vinyl.)

ESQUIRES

P&R/R&B '67

Singles: 7-inch

B&G.. 4-8
BUNKY... 4-8 67-68
CAPITOL...................................... 3-6 69
JU-PAR.. 3-5 76
LAMARR...................................... 3-5 71
SALEM....................................... 5-10 65
TOWER...................................... 5-10 65
WAND.. 4-8 68-69

LPs: 10/12-inch 33rpm

BUNKY (300 "Get on Up and Get Away")................................ 20-25 68
Members: Millard Edwards; Gilbert Alvis; Betty Moorer; Sam Pace; Harvey Scales; Shawn Taylor.
Also see SCALES, Harvey

ESSENCE

R&B '75

Singles: 7-inch

EPIC... 3-5 75-77

LPs: 10/12-inch 33rpm

SAVOY.. 5-10 78
Members: Marzette Griffith; Anthony Redmond.

ESSEX

P&R/R&B/LP '63

Singles: 7-inch

BANG... 4-8 66
ROULETTE.................................. 5-8 63-64

LPs: 10/12-inch 33rpm

ROULETTE (25234 "Easier Said Than Done")............................... 25-35 63
ROULETTE (25235 "A Walkin' Miracle")................................. 20-35 63
ROULETTE (25246 "Young and Lively")...................................20-30 64
Members: Anita Humes; Walter Vickers; Rodney Taylor; Billie Hill; Rudolph Johnson.

ESSEX, David

P&R '73

Singles: 7-inch

COLUMBIA.................................3-5 73-76
RSO..3-4 79
UNI..4-8 67

Picture Sleeves

COLUMBIA.................................3-5 73-74
UNI..5-10 67

LPs: 10/12-inch 33rpm

COLUMBIA (CQ-32560 "Rock On")..15-25 74
(Quadrophonic)
COLUMBIA (KC-32560 "Rock On")..15-20 73
COLUMBIA (33289 "David Essex")..8-15 74
COLUMBIA (33813 "All the Fun of the Fair")..................................8-15 75
MERCURY..................................5-10 83

ESTEFAN, Gloria

P&R/LP '89

Singles: 7-inch

EPIC..3-4 89-91

LPs: 10/12-inch 33rpm

EPIC..5-8 89-91
Also see MIAMI SOUND MACHINE

ESTUS, Deon

LP '89

Singles: 7-inch

MIKA..3-4 89

LPs: 10/12-inch 33rpm

MIKA..5-8 89

ESTUS, Deon, & George Michael

P&R '89

Singles: 7-inch

MIKA..3-4 89

Picture Sleeves

MIKA..3-4 89
Also see ESTUS, Deon
Also see MICHAEL, George

ETERNALS

P&R '59

Singles: 7-inch

COLLECTABLES..........................3-4
HOLLYWOOD (68 "Rockin' in the Jungle")..............................10-20 59
(White or blue label.)
HOLLYWOOD (68 "Rockin' in the Jungle")................................8-10 59
(Yellow label.)
HOLLYWOOD (70 "Babalu's Wedding Day").........................15-20 59
(Red label.)

HOLLYWOOD (70 "Babalu's Wedding Day") 8-12 59
(Blue label.)
WARWICK (611 "Blind Date") ... 10-15 60
Members: Charles Girona; Alex Miranda; Fred Hodge; Ernie Sierra; Arnold Torres; George Villanueva.

ETERNITY'S CHILDREN

P&R '68

Singles: 7-inch

A&M 5-8 67
LIBERTY 4-6 70
TOWER 4-6 68-69

Picture Sleeves

TOWER 5-10 68

LPs: 10/12-inch 33rpm

TOWER (5123 "Eternity's Children") 20-25 68
TOWER (5144 "Timeless") 20-25 68
Member: Bruce Blackman.
Also see ALLAN, Davie / Eternity's Children / Main Attraction / Sunrays
Also see KORONA
Also see STARBUCK

ETHERIDGE, Melissa

LP '88

Singles: 7-inch

ISLAND 3-4 89

Picture Sleeves

ISLAND 3-4 89

LPs: 10/12-inch 33rpm

ISLAND 5-8 89

ETHICS

R&B '69

Singles: 7-inch

GOLDEN FLEECE 4-8 74
PHALANX 10-20
VENT 8-12 68-69
Member: Ronald Tyson.
Also see LOVE COMMITTEE

ETTA & HARVEY

P&R/R&B '60

Singles: 7-inch

CHESS (1760 "If I Can't Have You") 10-20 60
CHESS (1771 "Spoonful") 10-20 60
Members: Etta James; Harvey Fuqua.
Also see HARVEY
Also see JAMES, Etta

ETZEL, Roy
(With the Jupiter Serenaders)

LP '65

Singles: 7-inch

HICKORY 4-8 63
MGM 4-6 65-67
PRESIDENT 4-8 61
TIME 4-8 61

LPs: 10/12-inch 33rpm

MGM 8-12 65

EUBANKS, Jack

P&R '61

Singles: 7-inch

MONUMENT 4-8 61-64

LPs: 10/12-inch 33rpm

MONUMENT 10-20 66

EUCLID BEACH BAND

P&R '79

Singles: 7-inch

EPIC/CLEVELAND INT'L 3-4 78-79
SCENE 4-6 78

LPs: 10/12-inch 33rpm

EPIC 5-10 79

EUROGLIDERS

P&R/LP '84

Singles: 7-inch

COLUMBIA 3-4 84

LPs: 10/12-inch 33rpm

COLUMBIA 5-10 84
Member: Grace Knight.

EUROPE

LP '86

Singles: 12-inch 33/45rpm

EPIC 4-8 86
(Promotional only.)

Singles: 7-inch

EPIC 3-4 86-88

Picture Sleeves

EPIC 3-4 87-88

LPs: 10/12-inch 33rpm

EPIC 5-10 86-88
Members: Joey Tempest; John Leven; Mic Michaeli; Kee Marcello; Ian Haughland.

EURYTHMICS

P&R/D&D/LP '83

Singles: 12-inch 33/45rpm

RCA 4-6 83-86

Singles: 7-inch

ARISTA 3-4 89-91
RCA 3-4 83-88

Picture Sleeves

ARISTA 3-4 89
RCA 3-4 83-88

LPs: 10/12-inch 33rpm

ARISTA 5-8 89-91
RCA 5-10 83-88
Members: Annie Lennox; Dave Stewart.
Also see LENNOX, Annie, & Al Green
Also see TOURISTS

EURYTHMICS & Aretha Franklin

P&R/D&D '85

Singles: 12-inch 33/45rpm

RCA 4-6 85

Singles: 7-inch

RCA 3-4 85
Also see EURYTHMICS
Also see FRANKLIN, Aretha

EVANS, Linda

R&B '79

Singles: 7-inch

ARIOLA 3-5 79
WATTSOUND 3-5 73
Also see CHANSON

EVANS, Margie

R&B '73

Singles: 7-inch

ICA 3-5 77
U.A. 3-5 73

EVANS, Paul
(With the Curls)

P&R '59

Singles: 7-inch

ATCO 5-10 59-60
BIG TREE 3-5 75
CARLTON 5-10 61-62
CINNAMON INT'L 3-4 80
COLLECTABLES 3-4 80s
COLUMBIA 3-6 68
DECCA 5-10 58
DOT 3-5 73
EPIC 4-8 64-65
GUARANTEED 5-10 59-60
KAPP 4-8 62-63
LAURIE 3-5 71
MERCURY 3-5 74-75
MUSICOR 3-5 77
RCA 8-10 57
RANWOOD 3-5 72
SPRING 3-4 78-79

LPs: 10/12-inch 33rpm

CARLTON (129 "Hear Paul Evans in Your Home Tonight") 25-35 61
(Monaural.)
CARLTON (129 "Hear Paul Evans in Your Home Tonight") 35-50 61
(Stereo.)
CARLTON (130 "Folk Songs of Many Lands") 20-25 61
(Monaural.)
CARLTON (130 "Folk Songs of Many Lands") 20-30 61
(Stereo.)
GUARANTEED (1000 "Fabulous Teens") 30-45 60
(Monaural.)
GUARANTEED (1000 "Fabulous Teens") 40-50 60
(Stereo.)
KAPP (1346 "21 Years in a Tennessee Jail") 20-25 64
(Monaural.)
KAPP (1475 "Another Town, Another Jail") 20-30 66
(Monaural.)
KAPP (3346 "21 Years in a Tennessee Jail") 20-45 64
(Stereo.)
KAPP (3475 "Another Town, Another Jail") 20-30 66

EVANS, Paul & Mimi

Singles: 7-inch

EPIC 4-8 64
Also see EVANS, Paul

EVANS, Warren

R&B '45

Singles: 78rpm

NATIONAL 5-8 45
Also see JOHNSON, Buddy

EVASIONS

R&B '81

Singles: 7-inch

SAM 3-4 81

EVE ELEKTRO: see ELEKTRO, Eve

EVERETT, Betty
(With the Daylighters)

P&R/R&B '63

Singles: 7-inch

ABC 4-6 66-67
C.J. 10-20 61-64
COBRA 15-25 57-58
COLLECTABLES 3-4 80s
DOTTIE (1126 "Tell Me Darling") 15-25
ERIC 3-4 70s
FANTASY 3-5 70-74
OLDIES 45 .... 3-5 60s
ONE-DERFUL 5-10 62
UNI 4-6 68-69
VEE JAY 5-10 63-65

LPs: 10/12-inch 33rpm

FANTASY 8-10 75
SUNSET 10-15 68
UNI 10-15 69
VEE JAY (1077 "It's in His Kiss") 25-50 64
VEE JAY (1122 "The Very Best of Betty Everett") 25-35 65
Also see BUTLER, Jerry, & Betty Everett

EVERETT, Betty / Ketty Lester

LPs: 10/12-inch 33rpm

GRAND PRIX 10-15 64
Also see LESTER, Ketty

EVERETT, Betty / Impressions

LPs: 10/12-inch 33rpm

CUSTOM 10-15 64
Also see EVERETT, Betty
Also see IMPRESSIONS

EVERLY, Don

C&W '76

Singles: 7-inch

ABC/HICKORY 3-5 75-77

HICKORY/MGM 3-5 76
ODE 3-5 70-74

LPs: 10/12–Inch 33rpm

ABC/HICKORY 8-10 76-77
ODE 8-12 70-74

Also see HARRIS, Emmylou
Also see KIMBERLY, Adrian

EVERLY, Phil

C&W '80

Singles: 7–inch

CAPITOL.................................... 3-4 83
CURB.. 3-4 80-81
ELEKTRA.................................... 3-4 79
PYE 3-5 73-76
RCA.. 3-5 73

LPs: 10/12–inch 33rpm

ELECTRA.................................. 5-10 79
PYE 8-10 75-76
RCA.. 8-10 73

EVERLY BROTHERS

P&R/R&B '57

Singles: 78rpm

CADENCE.................................. 20-30 57-58
COLUMBIA (21496 "The Sun Keeps Shining")................................ 50-75 56

Singles: 7–inch

BARNABY 3-4 70-76
CADENCE.............................. 10-15 57-61
(Silver and maroon, or blue labels)
CADENCE.................................. 5-10 61-62
(Red label.)
COLUMBIA (21496 "The Sun Keeps Shining")............................ 75-100 56
ERIC.. 3-4 70s
MERCURY 3-4 84-86
RCA.. 3-6 72-73
W.B. (5151 "Cathy's Clown")....... 8-10 60
(Monaural.)
W.B. (S-5151 "Cathy's Clown"). 20-30 60
(Stereo.)
W.B. (5163 thru 5833)................ 5-10 60-69
W.B. (5857 "Fifi the Flea")......... 15-25 67
(Credits "Don Everly Brother" on one side, and "Phil Everly Brother" on the flip.)
W.B. (5901 thru 7425).................. 4-8 67-70

Promotional Singles

BARNABY 3-6 70-76
CADENCE.............................. 15-25 57-62
(Black vinyl.)
CADENCE (1348 "All I Have to Do Is Dream") 25-50
(Colored vinyl.)
COLUMBIA (21496 "The Sun Keeps Shining").......................... 150-250 56
MERCURY 3-5 84-86
RCA.. 4-8 72-73
W.B. (5151 "Cathy's Clown")..... 35-45 60
(Colored vinyl.)
W.B. (5163 "So Sad") 35-45 60
(Colored vinyl.)
W.B. (5199 "Ebony Eyes")........35-45 61
(Colored vinyl.)

Picture Sleeves

CADENCE (1337 "Wake Up Little Susie")..........................50-100 57
CADENCE (1355 "Problems")...20-40 58
CADENCE (1369 "Till I Kissed You")....................................20-40 59
CADENCE (1376 "Let It Be Me") 20-40 60
W.B. (5151 "Cathy's Clown") 15-25 60
W.B. (5163 "So Sad") 15-20 60
W.B. (5199 "Ebony Eyes").........15-20 61
W.B. (5220 "Temptation") 15-20 61
W.B. (5250 "Crying in the Rain") 10-20 62
W.B. (5273 "That's Old Fashioned")..............................10-20 62
W.B. (5297 "Don't Ask Me to Be Friends") 10-20 62
MERCURY 3-5 84

EPs: 7–inch 33/45rpm

CADENCE (4 "Dream with the Everly Brothers")......................25-35 61
CADENCE (104 "The Everly Brothers")...............................30-50 57
CADENCE (105 "The Everly Brothers")...............................30-50 57
CADENCE (107 "The Everly Brothers")...............................30-50 58
CADENCE (108/109/110 "Songs Our Daddy Taught Us") 25-45 58
(Price is for any of three volumes.)
CADENCE (111 "The Everly Brothers")...............................25-45 59
CADENCE (118 "The Everly Brothers")...............................25-35 59
CADENCE (121 "Very Best of The Everly Brothers") 25-35 60
CADENCE (333 "Rockin' with the Everly Brothers")...............25-35 61
W.B. (1381-1 "Foreverly Yours") 15-25 60
(Black vinyl.)
W.B. (1381-1 "Foreverly Yours")25-50 60
(Colored vinyl. Promotional issue only.)
W.B. (1381-2 "Especially for You")......................................15-25 60
W.B. (5501 "The Everly Brothers Plus Two Oldies") 15-25 61

LPs: 10/12–inch 33rpm

ARISTA.......................................8-12 84
BARNABY (350 "Original Greatest Hits") 10-15 70
BARNABY (30260 "End of an Era")..10-15 71
BARNABY (4000 series).............6-10 77
BARNABY (6006 "Greatest Hits") 8-12

CADENCE (3003 "The Everly Brothers") 75-125 58
CADENCE (3016 "Songs Our Daddy Taught Us") 50-75 58
CADENCE (3025 "The Everly Brothers' Best") 75-100 59
(Blue cover.)
CADENCE (3040 "The Fabulous Style of the Everly Brothers") 50-75 60
CADENCE (3059 "Folk Songs") 35-40 63
CADENCE (3062 "15 Everly Hits") 45-65 63
CADENCE (25040 "The Fabulous Style of the Everly Brothers") 75-100 60
(Stereo.)
CADENCE (25059 "Folk Songs") 35-40 63
(Stereo.)
CADENCE (25062 "15 Everly Hits") 45-65 63
(Stereo.)
CANDLELITE 10-15 76
HARMONY 10-12 68-70
MERCURY 5-10 84-86
PAIR 8-12 84
PASSPORT 5-10 84-86
RCA 8-12 72
RHINO (214 "All They Had to Do Was Dream") 5-10 85
RHINO (258 "Heartache and Memories") 8-10 85
(Picture disc.)
RONCO 8-10
W.B. (1381 "It's Everly Time") ... 25-40 60
W.B. (1395 "A Date with the Everly Brothers") 30-40 60
(With gatefold cover and eight "wallet pix" cut-out photos.)
W.B. (1395 "A Date with the Everly Brothers") 15-20 61
(With standard cover.)
W.B. (1418 "Songs for Both Sides of an Evening") 25-30 61
W.B. (1430 "Instant Party") 20-30 62
W.B. (1471 "Golden Hits") 20-30 62
W.B. (1483 "Christmas with the Everly Brothers") 20-25 61
W.B. (1513 "Great Country Hits") 20-25 63
W.B. (1554 "Very Best of the Everly Brothers") 15-20 64
(Yellow cover. Green label.)
W.B. (1554 "Very Best of the Everly Brothers") 10-15 70
(Blue cover. Green label.)
W.B. (1554 "Very Best of the Everly Brothers") 8-12 72
(Blue cover. "Skyline" label.)
W.B. (1578 "Rock 'N' Soul") 20-25 65
W.B. (1585 "Gone Gone Gone") 20-25 65
W.B. (1605 "Beat and Soul") 15-25 65
W.B. (1620 "In Our Image") 15-25 66
W.B. (1646 "Two Yanks in London") 15-25 66
(With the Hollies.)
W.B. (1676 "The Hit Sound of the Everly Brothers") 15-20 67
W.B. (1708 "Everly Brothers Sing") 15-25 67
W.B. (1752 "Roots") 15-25 68
W.B. (1858 "The Everly Brothers Show") 12-15 70

Promotional LPs

W.B. (134 "The Everly Brothers") 75-100 61
(One sided, 10–inch LP with five tracks from *The Everly Brothers - Both Sides of an Evening* [WB 1418]. Promotional issue only.)
W.B. (135 "Souvenir Sampler") .. 50-80 61
(Don and Phil discussing *The Everly Brothers - Both Sides of an Evening.* Has an LP discount coupon on sleeve. Promotional issue only.)
W.B. (1381 "It's Everly Time") .. 50-100 60
W.B. (1395 "A Date with the Everly Brothers") 75-100 60
(With gatefold cover and eight "wallet pix" cut-out photos.)
W.B. (1418 "Both Sides of an Evening") 50-75 61
W.B. (1430 "Instant Party") 50-75 62
W.B. (1471 "Golden Hits") 50-75 62
W.B. (1483 "Christmas with the Everly Brothers") 50-75 61
W.B. (1513 "Great Country Hits") 30-60 63
W.B. (1554 "Very Best of the Everly Brothers") 30-60 64
(Yellow cover.)
W.B. (1578 "Rock'N' Soul") 30-60 65
W.B. (1585 "Gone Gone Gone") 30-60 65
W.B. (1605 "Beat 'N' Soul") 25-50 65
W.B. (1620 "In Our Image") 25-50 66
W.B. (1646 "Two Yanks in London") 25-50 66
W.B. (1676 "The Hit Sound of the Everly Brothers") 25-50 67
W.B. (1708 "The Everly Brothers Sing") 25-50 67
W.B. (1752 "Roots") 20-40 68
W.B. (1858 "The Everly Brothers Show") 20-30 70

Members: Don Everly; Phil Everly.
Also see CASH, Johnny, Rosanne Cash & Everly Brothers
Also see EVERLY, Don
Also see EVERLY, Phil
Also see HOLLIES

EVERLY BROTHERS & Beach Boys

Singles: 7-inch

CAPITOL (44297 "Don't Worry Baby") 3-5 88

Picture Sleeves

CAPITOL (44297 "Don't Worry Baby") 3-5 88

Also see BEACH BOYS

EVERY FATHER'S TEENAGE SON

P&R '67

Singles: 7-inch

BUDDAH 4-8 67

EVERY MOTHER'S NIGHTMARE

LP '70

LPs: 10/12-inch 33rpm

ARISTA 5-8 90

EVERY MOTHER'S SON

P&R/LP '67

Singles: 7-inch

MGM 4-8 67-68

POLYDOR 3-4

Picture Sleeves

MGM 4-8 67

LPs: 10/12-inch 33rpm

MGM 10-20 67

EVERYTHING BUT the GIRL

LP '90

LPs: 10/12-inch 33rpm

ATLANTIC 5-8 90

EVERYTHING is EVERYTHING

P&R '69

Singles: 7-inch

VANGUARD APOSTOLIC 4-6 69

LPs: 10/12-inch 33rpm

VANGUARD 15-20 69

EXCELLENTS

P&R '62

Singles: 7-inch

BLAST (205 "Coney Island Baby") 15-25 62
(Red label.)

BLAST (205 "Coney Island Baby") 10-15 62
(Red and white label.)

BLAST (205 "Coney Island Baby") 40-60 62
(White label.)
(Promotional issue only.)

BLAST (205 "Coney Island Baby") 10-15 65
(Purple label.)

BLAST (207 "I Hear a Rhapsody") 20-30 63
(Some question whether or not this is the same group as on the other Blast issues.)

COLLECTABLES 3-4

MERMAID (106 "Love No One But You") 75-100 64
(Label pictures a mermaid.)

MERMAID (106 "Love No One But You") 25-50
(Mermaid not pictured.)

OLD TIMER 4-8 64

EXCELS

P&R '61

Singles: 7-inch

GONE (5094 "My Foolish Heart") 15-25 60

RSVP (111 "Can't Help Lovin' That Girl of Mine") 20-30 61

EXCITERS

P&R/R&B '62

Singles: 7-inch

BANG (515 "A Little Bit of Soap") 5-10 66

BANG (518 "Weddings Make Me Cry") 15-25 66

LIBERTY 3-4

ROULETTE 5-10 64

RCA (9633 "If You Want My Love") 15-25 68

RCA (9723 "Blowing Up My Mind") 15-25 68

SHOUT 5-10 66-67

TODAY 4-8 70

U.A. 5-10 62-63

Picture Sleeves

ROULETTE 10-20 64

LPs: 10/12-inch 33rpm

RCA (4211 "Caviar & Chitlins") .. 20-30 69

ROULETTE 15-20 66

SUNSET 10-12 70

TODAY 8-10 71

U.A. (3264 "Tell Him") 30-40 63
(Monaural.)

U.A. (6264 "Tell Him") 40-50 63
(Stereo.)

Members: Brenda Reid; Herb Rooney; Carol Johnson; Lillian Walker.

Also see BRENDA & HERB

EXECUTIVE

R&B '81

Singles: 7-inch

20TH FOX 3-4 81

EXECUTIVE SUITE

R&B '73

Singles: 7-inch

BABYLON 3-5 73-74

JUBILEE 4-6 69

U.A. 3-5 75

EXILE

P&R '77

Singles: 7-inch

ARISTA 3-4 89-91

EXITS

ATCO ... 3-5 77
COLUMBIA ... 3-6 69-70
EPIC ... 3-4 83-88
MCA/CURB ... 3-4 85-86
W.B./CURB ... 3-4 78-81
WOODEN NICKEL ... 3-5 72-73

LPs: 10/12–inch 33rpm

EPIC ... 5-10 83-88
MCA/CURB ... 5-8 85-86
RCA ... 5-10 78
W.B. ... 5-10 78-81
WOODEN NICKEL ... 8-10 73

Members: J.P. Pennington; Les Taylor; Sonny LeMaire; Marlon Hargis; Steve Goetzman.

EXITS

R&B '67

Singles: 7–inch

GEMINI ... 5-10 67
KAPP (2028 "Another Sundown in Watts") ... 15-25 69

EXODUS

LP '87

LPs: 10/12–inch 33rpm

ARISTA ... 5-10 87
CAPITOL ... 5-8 90
COMBAT ... 5-8 87-89

EXOTIC GUITARS

LP '68

Singles: 7–inch

RANWOOD ... 3-5 68-70

LPs: 10/12–inch 33rpm

RANWOOD ... 5-10 68-70

Member: Al Casey.
Also see CASEY, Al
Also see PLATTERS / Exotic Guitars

EXPOSE

D&D '85

Singles: 12–inch 33/45rpm

ARISTA ... 4-6 85-89

Singles: 7–inch

ARISTA ... 3-4 85-90

Picture Sleeves

ARISTA ... 3-4 87-89

LPs: 10/12–inch 33rpm

ARISTA ... 5-10 86-89

Members: Jeanette Jurado; Gioia Bruno; Ann Curless.

EXPRESS, B.T: see B.T. EXPRESS

EXTRA Ts

R&B '82

Singles: 7–inch

SUNNYVIEW ... 3-4 82

EXTREME

LP '89

LPs: 10/12–inch 33rpm

A&M ... 5-8 89-90

EYE to EYE

P&R/LP '82

Singles: 7–inch

W.B. ... 3-4 82-83

LPs: 10/12–inch 33rpm

W.B. ... 5-10 82-83

Also see MARSHALL-HAIN

EZO

LP '87

LPs: 10/12–inch 33rpm

GEFFEN ... 5-10 87

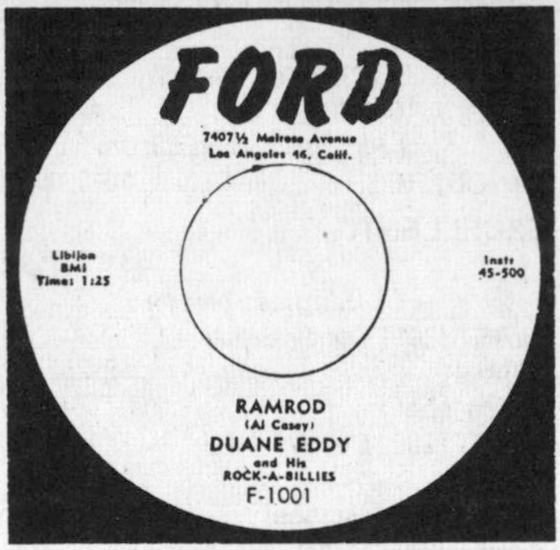

F

F., Simon
P&R '87

(Simon Fellowes)

Singles: 7–inch

REPRISE 3-4 87

FCC

(Funky Communication Committee)

P&R/LP '79

Singles: 7–inch

FREE FLIGHT (Black vinyl) 3-4 79
FREE FLIGHT (Colored vinyl)........ 3-5 79
(Promotional issue only.)

LPs: 10/12–inch 33rpm

FREE FLIGHT 5-8 79
RCA........ 5-10 80

FLB: see FAT LARRY'S BAND

FABARES, Shelley

P&R/LP '62

Singles: 7–inch

COLPIX (Except 721)........ 5-10 62-64
COLPIX (721 "Football Season's Over")........ 50-100 64
DUNHILL (4001 "My Prayer") ... 15-25 65
DUNHILL (4041 "See Ya 'Round on the Rebound")........ 15-25 65
ERIC........ 3-4
VEE JAY (632 "Lost Summer Love")........ 15-25 64

Picture Sleeves

COLPIX (621 "Johnny Angel") 50-100 62
COLPIX (636 "Johnny Loves Me")........ 40-60 62

LPs: 10/12–inch 33rpm

COLPIX (426 "Shelley") 35-45 62
(Monaural.)
COLPIX (426 "Shelley") 45-55 62
(Stereo.)
COLPIX (431 "The Things We Did Last Summer")........ 35-45 62
(Monaural.)
COLPIX (431 "The Things We Did Last Summer")........ 45-55 62
(Stereo.)

Also see BLOSSOMS
Also see DARREN, James / Shelley Fabares / Paul Petersen
Also see PETERSEN, Paul, & Shelley Fabares

FABIAN

(With the Fabulous Four)

P&R/R&B/LP '59

Singles: 7–inch

ABC........ 3-5 74
CHANCELLOR (1020 "I'm in Love")........ 15-20 58
CHANCELLOR (1024 "Be My Steady Date")........ 15-20 58
CHANCELLOR (1029 "I'm a Man") 10-15 58
(Monaural.)
CHANCELLOR (1029 "I'm a Man") 15-25 58
(Stereo.)
CHANCELLOR (1033 "Turn Me Loose")........ 10-15 59
(Monaural.)
CHANCELLOR (1033 "Turn Me Loose")........ 15-25 59
(Stereo.)
CHANCELLOR (1037 "Tiger") ... 10-15 59
(Monaural.)
CHANCELLOR (1037 "Tiger") ... 15-25 59
(Stereo.)
CHANCELLOR (1041 "Come on and Get Me")........ 8-12 59
(Monaural.)
CHANCELLOR (1041 "Come on and Get Me")........ 15-25 59
(Stereo.)
CHANCELLOR (1044 "Hound Dog Man")........ 8-12 59
(Monaural.)
CHANCELLOR (1044 "Hound Dog Man")........ 15-25 59
(Stereo.)
CHANCELLOR (1047 "String Along") 8-12 60
(Monaural.)
CHANCELLOR (1047 "String Along") 15-25 60
(Stereo.)
CHANCELLOR (1061 thru 1092). 8-15 60-61
COLLECTABLES........ 3-4 80s
CREAM 3-5 77
DOT 5-10 62
ERIC 3-4 70s

Picture Sleeves

CHANCELLOR (1029 "I'm a Man") 10-20 58
CHANCELLOR (1033 "Turn Me Loose")........ 10-20 59
CHANCELLOR (1037 "Tiger") ... 10-20 59
CHANCELLOR (1041 "Come On and Get Me")........ 10-20 59
CHANCELLOR (1044 "Hound Dog Man")........ 10-20 59
CHANCELLOR (1047 "String Along") 10-20 60
CHANCELLOR (1051 "Strollin' in the Springtime") 10-20 60
CHANCELLOR (1055 "King of Love")........ 10-20 60
CHANCELLOR (1061 "Kissin' and Twistin'") 10-20 60

CHANCELLOR (1067 "Hold On") 10-20 61
CHANCELLOR (1079 "You're Only Young Once") 10-20 61
CHANCELLOR (1084 "A Girl Like You") 15-25 61
CHANCELLOR (1092 "Wild Party") 15-25 61
CREAM 3-5 77

EPs: 7–inch 33/45rpm

CHANCELLOR (301 "Hound Dog Man") 15-25 60
CHANCELLOR (5003 "Hold That Tiger!") 15-25 59
(Black label. Price for any of three volumes.)
CHANCELLOR (5003 "Excerpts from *Hold That Tiger!*") 25-40 59
(With paper sleeve. White label. Promotional issue only.)
CHANCELLOR (5005 "The Fabulous Fabian") 20-30 60
CHANCELLOR (9802 "Young and Wonderful") 20-30 60

LPs: 10/12–inch 33rpm

ABC 10-12 73
CHANCELLOR (5003 "Hold That Tiger") 25-35 59
(Monaural.)
CHANCELLOR (5003 "Hold That Tiger") 35-45 59
(Stereo.)
CHANCELLOR (5005 "The Fabulous Fabian") 25-35 59
(Monaural.)
CHANCELLOR (5005 "The Fabulous Fabian") 35-45 59
(Stereo.)
CHANCELLOR (5012 "The Good Old Summertime") 25-35 60
(Monaural.)
CHANCELLOR (5012 "The Good Old Summertime") 35-45 60
(Stereo.)
CHANCELLOR (5019 "Rockin' Hot") 40-50 61
CHANCELLOR (5024 "16 Fabulous Hits") 40-50 62
CHANCELLOR (69802 "Young and Wonderful") 25-35 60
EVEREST 5-10 83
MCA 5-10 85
TRIP 8-10 77
U.A. 10-12 75
Also see FABULOUS FOUR

FABIAN / Frankie Avalon

Singles: 7–inch

CHANCELLOR/WIBG 99 ("When the Saints Go Marchin' In") 25-50 61
(Colored vinyl. Radio station special products issue. No selection number used. Flip is by the Live Five, who were the WIBG dee jays.)

LPs: 10/12–inch 33rpm

CHANCELLOR (5009 "The Hit Makers") 40-50 60
MCA 5-10 85
Also see AVALON, Frankie
Also see FABIAN

FABRIC, Bent

P&R/LP '62

Singles: 7–inch

ATCO 4-6 62-65

Picture Sleeves

ATCO (6226 "Alley Cat") 10-15 62

LPs: 10/12–inch 33rpm

ATCO 8-15 62-63
Also see BILK, Mr. Acker, & Bent Fabric

FABRIQUE, Tina

D&D '84

Singles: 12–inch 33/45rpm

PRISM 4-6 84

FABULOUS COUNTS

R&B '69

Singles: 7–inch

HIGHLAND (1171 "So Far Away") 25-50 60s
KIM (811 "Money") 5-10 60s
MOIRA 3-6 68-70

LPs: 10/12–inch 33rpm

COTILLION 10-12 69

FABULOUS FARQUAHR
(Farquahr)

LP '70

Singles: 7–inch

ELEKTRA 3-5 71
VERVE/FORECAST 4-8 68-69
W.B. 3-6 70

LPs: 10/12–inch 33rpm

ELEKTRA 8-10 70
VERVE/FORECAST 10-15 69

FABULOUS POODLES

P&R/LP '79

Singles: 7–inch

EPIC 3-5 79

LPs: 10/12–inch 33rpm

EPIC 5-10 76-79

FABULOUS RHINESTONES

P&R/LP '72

Singles: 7–inch

JUST SUNSHINE 3-5 72

Picture Sleeves

JUST SUNSHINE 3-5 72

LPs: 10/12–inch 33rpm

JUST SUNSHINE 8-10 72-73

FABULOUS THUNDERBIRDS

LP '81

Singles: 7–inch

CBS ASSOCIATED........................ 3-4 86-89
CHRYSALIS........................ 3-4 79-81
ELEKTRA........................ 3-4 88

Picture Sleeves

CBS ASSOCIATED........................ 3-4 86-87

LPs: 10/12–inch 33rpm

CBS ASSOCIATED........................ 5-10 86-89
CHRYSALIS........................ 5-10 79-81
TAKOMA........................ 10-15 79

Members: Kim Wilson; Jimmie Vaughan; Preston Hubbard; Fran Christina.
Also see SANTANA
Also see VAUGHAN BROTHERS

FACE to FACE

P&R/D&D/LP '84

Singles: 12–inch 33/45rpm

EPIC........................ 4-6 84
PORTRAIT........................ 4-6 84

Singles: 7–inch

EPIC........................ 3-4 84
MERCURY........................ 3-4 88
PORTRAIT........................ 3-4 84

Picture Sleeves

EPIC........................ 3-4 84

LPs: 10/12–inch 33rpm

EPIC........................ 5-10 84
MERCURY........................ 5-8 88

FACENDA, Tommy

P&R/R&B '59

Singles: 7–inch

ATLANTIC (2051 thru 2078 "High School U.S.A.")........................ 15-20 59
(Price is for any of the 28 different, custom versions, each of which names high schools in a specific geographic area of the country.)
LEGRANDE (1001 "High School U.S.A.")........................ 8-15 59
(We've yet to learn how to positively identify original pressings, as many reissues exist.)
NASCO........................ 8-12 58

Session: King Curtis.
Also see KING CURTIS
Also see VINCENT, Gene

FACES

LP '70

Singles: 7–inch

W.B. 3-6 71-75

Picture Sleeves

W.B. 3-6 73

LPs: 10/12–inch 33rpm

MERCURY........................ 8-12 73
W.B. 10-20 70-76

Members: Rod Stewart; Ron Wood; Ronnie Lane.
Also see McLAGAN, Ian
Also see SMALL FACES
Also see STEWART, Rod
Also see WOOD, Ron

FACHIN, Eria

P&R '88

Singles: 7–inch

CRITIQUE........................3-4 88

Picture Sleeves

CRITIQUE........................3-4 88

FACTS of LIFE

R&B '76

Singles: 7–inch

KAYVETTE........................3-5 76-77

LPs: 10/12–inch 33rpm

KAYVETTE........................8-10 77

Members: Jean Davis; Keith William; Chuck Carter.

FAGEN, Donald

P&R/R&B/LP '82

Singles: 7–inch

W.B. 3-4 82-88

Picture Sleeves

W.B. 3-4 82-88

LPs: 10/12–inch 33rpm

MFSL (120 "Nightfly")........................15-25 84
W.B. 5-10 82-88

Also see JAY & AMERICANS
Also see STEELY DAN

FAGEN, Donald, & Walter Becker

LPs: 10/12–inch 33rpm

PVC........................5-10 85

Also see FAGEN, Donald

FAGIN, Joe

P&R '82

Singles: 7–inch

MILLENNIUM........................3-4 82

FAIR, Yvonne

R&B '74

Singles: 7–inch

DADE........................4-8 63
KING........................4-8 62
MOTOWN........................3-5 74-76
SMASH........................4-8 66
SOUL........................3-6 70

LPs: 10/12–inch 33rpm

MOTOWN........................5-10 76

FAIRCHILD, Barbara

C&W '69

Singles: 7–inch

CAPITOL........................3-4 86
COLUMBIA........................3-4 69-78
DOWN HOME........................3-4 80
KAPP........................3-5 68

LPs: 10/12–inch 33rpm

AUDIOGRAPH........................5-10 82
COLUMBIA........................8-12 70-78
PAID........................5-10 81

Session: Jordanaires.
Also see WALKER, Billy, & Barbara Fairchild

FAIRE, Johnny
(Donnie Brooks)

Singles: 7-inch

FABLE (601 "If I'm a Fool"/"You Gotta Walk That Line") 40-50 57
FABLE (601 "If I'm a Fool"/"Make Up Your Mind Baby") 40-50 57
(Note different flip.)
SURF (5019 "Bertha Lou") 40-50 58
SURF (5024 "Betcha I Getcha") 20-30 58
Also see BROOKS, Donnie

FAIRGROUND ATTRACTION
P&R '88

Singles: 7-inch

RCA 3-4 88-89

Picture Sleeves

RCA 3-4 88

LPs: 10/12-inch 33rpm

RCA 5-8 88
Members: Eddi Reader; Mark Nevin.

FAIRPORT CONVENTION
LP '71

Singles: 7-inch

A&M 3-5 71-72

LPs: 10/12-inch 33rpm

A&M 10-12 69-74
COTILLION 10-15 70
VARRICK/ROUNDER 5-10 86
ISLAND 8-10 74-75
Also see DENNY, Sandy
Also see MATTHEWS, Ian
Also see THOMPSON, Richard

FAIRWEATHER
(Andy Fairweather-Low)

LPs: 10/12-inch 33rpm

NEON 8-10 71
Also see FAIRWEATHER-LOW, Andy

FAIRWEATHER-LOW, Andy
P&R '75

Singles: 7-inch

A&M 3-5 75-77

LPs: 10/12-inch 33rpm

A&M 8-10 74-76
W.B. 5-10 80
Also see FAIRWEATHER
Also see WILLIE & Poor Boys

FAITH, Adam
P&R '65

Singles: 7-inch

AMY 4-8 64-65
CAPITOL 4-8 65-66
CUB 5-10 59
DOT 4-8 62

LPs: 10/12-inch 33rpm

AMY (8005 "Adam Faith") 20-30 65
MGM (3951 "England's Top Singer") 25-30 61
W.B. 8-12 74

FAITH, Gene
R&B '70

Singles: 7-inch

VIRTUE 3-6 69-70

FAITH, Percy, Orchestra
P&R '50

Singles: 78rpm

COLUMBIA 3-4 50-57

Singles: 7-inch

COLUMBIA 3-10 50-76

Picture Sleeves

COLUMBIA 5-10 60

EPs: 7-inch 33/45rpm

COLUMBIA 5-10 50-59
ROYALE 5-10 50s

LPs: 10/12-inch 33rpm

COLUMBIA 5-15 51-82
HARMONY 5-10 68-72
Also see SANDERS, Felicia

FAITH, Percy, Orchestra / Johnny Mathis

Singles: 7-inch

COLUMBIA 5-10
Also see FAITH, Percy, Orchestra
Also see MATHIS, Johnny

FAITH BAND
P&R '78

Singles: 7-inch

MERCURY 3-5 78-79
VILLAGE 3-6 78

LPs: 10/12-inch 33rpm

BROWN BAG 10-12 73
MERCURY 5-10 78-79
VILLAGE 6-12 77

FAITH, HOPE & CHARITY
P&R/R&B '70

Singles: 7-inch

MAXWELL 3-5 70
RCA 3-5 75-77
SUSSEX 3-5 72
20TH FOX 3-4 78-80

LPs: 10/12-inch 33rpm

RCA 8-10 75
SUSSEX 8-10 72
20TH FOX 5-10 80
Members: Brenda Hilliard; Albert Bailey; Zulema Crusseaux; Daine Destry.
Also see ZULEMA

FAITH NO MORE
P&R/LP '90

Singles: 7-inch

SLASH 3-4 90

LPs: 10/12-inch 33rpm

SLASH 5-8 90
Members: Chuck Moseley; Roddy Bottum; Bill Gould; Mike Bordin; Jim Martin; Mike Patton.

FAITHFULL, Marianne

P&R '64

Singles: 12–inch 33/45rpm

ISLAND 4-6 83

Singles: 7–inch

ISLAND 3-4 79
LONDON (Except 1022) 4-8 64-72
LONDON (1022 "Sister Morphine")............................ 75-100 69
(With the Rolling Stones.)

Picture Sleeves

LONDON.................................... 5-10 65

LPs: 10/12–inch 33rpm

ISLAND 5-10 79-90
LONDON.................................. 15-25 65-69
Also see ROLLING STONES

FALANA, Lola

R&B '75

Singles: 7–inch

AMOS.. 3-5
RCA... 3-4 75
REPRISE 5-10 67

FALCO

D&D/LP '83

Singles: 12–inch 33/45rpm

A&M 4-6 82-86

Singles: 7–inch

A&M 3-4 82-86

Picture Sleeves

A&M 3-4 86

LPs: 10/12–inch 33rpm

A&M 5-10 83-86

FALCONS

P&R/R&B '59

Singles: 78rpm

SILHOUETTE.......................... 30-40 57

Singles: 7–inch

ANNA (1110 "Just for Your Love")................................ 50-100 60
ATLANTIC.................................. 5-10 62-63
BIG WHEEL 4-8 66
CHESS (1743 "Just for Your Love")................................... 15-20 59
FALCON (1006 "Now That It's Over") 75-100 57
FLICK (001 "You're So Fine") 125-150 59
FLICK (008 "You Must Know I Love You") 50-75 60
KUDO (661 "This Heart of Mine")................................ 200-400 58
LIBERTY 3-4
LU PINE (103 "I Found a Love") 30-50 62
LU PINE (124 "Lonely Nights") 50-100 62
LU PINE (1003 "I Found a Love")...................................... 10-20 62
LU PINE (1024 "Lonely Nights") 20-40 62
MERCURY (70940 "Baby That's It") 15-25 56
SILHOUETTE (522 "Can This Be Christmas")...................200-300 57
(Flip, *Sent Up*, is Silhouette 521, a number also used for a Charmers release.)
UNART (2013 "You're So Fine") 10-20 59
UNART (2013-S "You're So Fine") 50-75 59
(Stereo—albeit reprocessed.)
UNART (2022 "Country Shack")..8-12 59
U.A. 12-25 59-60

EPs: 7–inch 33/45rpm

U.A. (10010 "The Falcons") 50-75 59
Members: Wilson Pickett; Joe Stubbs; Eddie Floyd; Arnet Robinson; Ben Rice; Lance Finnie; Sonny Monroe.
Also see FLOYD, Eddie
Also see PICKETT, Wilson

FALTERMEYER, Harold

P&R/R&B '85

Singles: 7–inch

MCA 3-4 85

Picture Sleeves

MCA...3-4 85
Also see LABELLE, Patti, & Harold Faltermeyer

FALTERMEYER, Harold, & Steve Stevens

Singles: 12–inch 33/45rpm

COLUMBIA 4-8 86
(Promotional issue only.)

Singles: 7–inch

COLUMBIA 3-4 86
Also see FALTERMEYER, Harold

FALTSKOG, Agnetha

P&R/LP '83

Singles: 7–inch

POLYDOR 3-4 83

Picture Sleeves

POLYDOR 3-5 83

LPs: 10/12–inch 33rpm

POLYDOR 5-10 83
Also see ABBA

FALTSKOG, Agnetha, & Peter Cetera

P&R '88

Singles: 7–inch

ATLANTIC....................................3-4 88

Picture Sleeves

ATLANTIC....................................3-4 88
Also see CETERA, Peter
Also see FALTSKOG, Agnetha

FAME: see KIDS from "FAME"

FAME, Georgie

(With the Blue Flames)

P&R/LP '65

Singles: 7–inch

EPIC...3-6 68-70
IMPERIAL 4-8 65-67
ISLAND 3-5 75

EPs: 7–inch 33/45rpm

EPIC.. 5-10 68
(Jukebox issues only.)

LPs: 10/12–inch 33rpm

EPIC.. 10-20 68-70
IMPERIAL 15-20 65-66
ISLAND...................................... 8-10 75
Also see FAME & PRICE – Price & Fame Together

FAME & PRICE - Price & Fame Together

Singles: 7–inch

REPRISE 3-5 71
Members: Georgie Fame; Alan Price.
Also see FAME, Georgie
Also see PRICE, Alan

FAMILY

LP '72

Singles: 7–inch

LITTLE CITY 3-5 77
U.A. 3-5 71-73

LPs: 10/12–inch 33rpm

REPRISE 15-20 68-70
U.A. 10-12 71-73
Members; Rick Grech; John Weider.
Also see BLIND FAITH
Also see WEIDER, John

FAMILY

P&R/R&B/D&D/LP '85

Singles: 12–inch 33/45rpm

PAISLEY PARK........................... 4-6 85

Singles: 7–inch

PAISLEY PARK........................... 3-4 85

Picture Sleeves

PAISLEY PARK........................... 3-4 85

LPs: 10/12–inch 33rpm

PAISLEY PARK......................... 5-10 85
Members: Paul Peterson; Jerome Benton; Susannah Melvoin; Jellybean Johnson.
Also see TIME

FAMILY DREAM

R&B '87

Singles: 7–inch

MOTOWN 3-4 87

FAMILY PLANN

R&B '75

Singles: 7–inch

DRIVE 3-5 75

FANCY

P&R '74

Singles: 7–inch

BIG TREE 3-5 74
POISON RING 3-6 71

LPs: 10/12–inch 33rpm

BIG TREE 8-10 74
POISON RING 12-20 71
RCA... 5-10 79
Members: Al Ranaudo; Billy Durso.

FANCY

D&D '85

Singles: 12–inch 33/45rpm

PERSONAL 4-6 85

FANNY

P&R/LP '71

Singles: 7–inch

CASABLANCA..............................3-5 74-75
REPRISE 3-5 70-73

LPs: 10/12–inch 33rpm

CASABLANCA............................8-10 74
REPRISE 10-12 70-73
Members: Jean Millington; June Millington; Alice de Buhr; Nickey Barclay; Patti Quatro; Wendy Haas; Brie Howard.

FANTASTIC FIVE KEYS

Singles: 7–inch

CAPITOL..................................5-10 62
Also see FIVE KEYS

FANTASTIC FOUR

P&R/R&B '67

Singles: 7–inch

EASTBOUND...............................3-5 73-74
RIC-TIC (Except 113 & 121)......10-18 66-68
RIC-TIC (113 "Can't Stop Looking for My Baby").......................100-200 66
RIC-TIC (121 "Can't Stop Looking for My Baby")............................50-75 66
SOUL 8-15 68-70
WESTBOUND..............................3-5 75-79

LPs: 10/12–inch 33rpm

SOUL (717 "Best of the Fantastic Four")..................................25-40 69
20TH FOX/WESTBOUND 8-10 76
WESTBOUND............................8-10 75-78
Members: Joe Pruitt; James Epps; Robert Pruitt; Toby Childs; Ernest Newsome; Cleveland Horn.

FANTASTIC JOHNNY C.
(Johnny Corley)

P&R/R&B '67

Singles: 7–inch

KAMA SUTRA...............................3-5 70
PHIL L.A. of SOUL.......................4-8 67-73

LPs: 10/12–inch 33rpm

PHIL L.A. of SOUL.................15-20 68

FANTASTICS

P&R '72

Singles: 7–inch

BELL 10-20 71-72
DERAM 5-10 69
Members: Jerome Ramos; Don Haywoode; John Cheatdom; Rich Pitts.
Also see VELOURS

FANTASY

P&R/LP '70

Singles: 7–inch

IMPERIAL 3-6 69
LIBERTY 3-5 70

LPs: 10/12–inch 33rpm

LIBERTY 10-15 70

FANTASY

R&B '81

Singles: 12–inch 33/45rpm

QUALITY.................................... 4-6 83

Singles: 7–inch

PAVILLION.................................. 3-4 81

LPs: 10/12–inch 33rpm

PAVILLION.................................. 5-10 81-82

FANTAYZEE, Haysi: see HAYSI FANTAYZEE

FAR CORPORATION

P&R '86

Singles: 7–inch

ATCO 3-4 86

Picture Sleeves

ATCO 3-4 86

LPs: 10/12–inch 33rpm

ATCO 5-10 86

Members: Robin McAuley; Bobby Kimball; Steve Lukather; Dave Paich.

Also see TOTO

FARAGHER BROTHERS

P&R '79

Singles: 7–inch

ABC.. 3-5 76-77

POLYDOR.................................... 3-4 79

LPs: 10/12–inch 33rpm

ABC.. 5-10 79

POLYDOR.................................... 5-10 78-79

Members: Jimmy Faragher; Dan Faragher; Tom Faragher; Dave Faragher.

Also see BONES

FARDON, Don

P&R '68

Singles: 7–inch

CHELSEA 3-5 73

GNP 4-8 68

LPs: 10/12–inch 33rpm

DECCA...................................... 10-12 70

GNP 15-20 68

FARGO, Donna

C&W/P&R/LP '72

Singles: 7–inch

ABC.. 3-4 78

ABC/DOT 3-5 74-77

CHALLENGE 5-8 68

CLEVELAND INT'L 3-4 84-91

COLUMBIA 3-4 83

DECCA...................................... 3-5 72

DOT.. 3-5 72-74

MCA.. 3-4 81

MERCURY 3-4 86-87

RCA.. 3-4 82

RAMCO...................................... 8-10 67

SONGBIRD................................... 3-4 81

W.B. 3-5 76-81

Picture Sleeves

DOT 3-6 72-74

W.B. 3-5 76-80

LPs: 10/12–inch 33rpm

ABC/DOT.................................... 5-10 74-77

DOT 8-12 72-73

MCA.. 5-8 80s

MERCURY.................................... 5-10 86

PICKWICK/HILLTOP 5-10 70s

RCA 5-10 83

SONGBIRD................................... 4-8 81

W.B. 5-10 76-80

Session: Jordanaires.

Also see BARE, Bobby / Donna Fargo / Jerry Wallace

FARGO, Donna, & Billy Joe Royal

C&W '87

Singles: 7–inch

MERCURY.................................... 3-4 87

Also see FARGO, Donna

Also see ROYAL, Billy Joe

FARNHAM, John

(Johnny Farnham)

P&R '90

Singles: 7–inch

RCA 3-4 90

Also see LITTLE RIVER BAND

FARQUAHR: see FABULOUS FARQUAHR

FARRELL, Billy

(Bill Farrell)

R&B '49

Singles: 78rpm

EPIC....................................... 5-10 57

IMPERIAL 5-10 54

MGM 5-10 49

MERCURY 5-10 56

Singles: 7–inch

DATE 10-15 58

EPIC....................................... 10-15 57

IMPERIAL 15-25 54

MERCURY.................................... 10-15 56

TEL (1000 "You Were Only Fooling").......... 10-20 58

FARRELL, Eileen

LP '61

Singles: 7–inch

LONDON..................................... 3-5 65

LPs: 10/12–inch 33rpm

COLUMBIA 10-20 60-63

HARMONY.................................... 5-10 68

FARRENHEIT

LP '87

Singles: 12–inch 33/45rpm

W.B. 4-8 87

(Promotional only.)

Singles: 7–inch

W.B. 3-4 87

LPs: 10/12–inch 33rpm

W.B. 5-10 87

FARROW, Cee

P&R/R&B '83

Singles: 7-inch

ROCSHIRE 3-4 83

Picture Sleeves

ROCSHIRE 3-4 83

FASCINATIONS

R&B '66

Singles: 7-inch

A&G.. 15-25 65
MAYFIELD 4-8 66-67
Members: Bernadine Boswell Smith; Shirley Walker; Fern Bledsoe; Joanne Levell.
Also see FASINATIONS

FASINATIONS

Singles: 7-inch

ABC-PAR 5-10 62-63
Also see FASCINATIONS

FAST RADIO

D&D '83

Singles: 12-inch 33/45rpm

RADAR...................................... 4-6 83

FASTER PUSSYCAT

LP '87

Singles: 7-inch

ELEKTRA.................................... 3-4 87-90

LPs: 10/12-inch 33rpm

ELEKTRA.................................... 5-10 87-90
Members: Taime Downe; Brent Muscat; Greg Steele; Mark Michals; Eric Stacy; Brett Bradshaw.

FASTWAY

LP '83

Singles: 7-inch

COLUMBIA 3-4 83-86

LPs: 10/12-inch 33rpm

COLUMBIA 5-10 83-86
GWR 5-8 89

FAT BOYS

R&B '84

Singles: 12-inch 33/45rpm

EMPEROR.................................... 4-6 92
SUTRA...................................... 4-6 84-86

Singles: 7-inch

SUTRA...................................... 3-4 84-86
TIN PAN APPLE 3-4 87-89

Picture Sleeves

TIN PAN APPLE 3-5 88

LPs: 10/12-inch 33rpm

SUTRA...................................... 5-10 84-87
TIN PAN APPLE 5-10 87-89
Members: Darren Robinson; Mark Morales; Damon Wimbley.
Also see DISCO 3
Also see KING DREAM CHORUS & Holiday Crew
Also see KRUSH GROVE ALL STARS

FAT BOYS & Beach Boys

P&R/R&B '87

Singles: 7-inch

TIN PAN APPLE (885960 "Wipeout")........................4-6 87
(Shown only as by the "Fat Boys.")
TIN PAN APPLE (885960 "Wipeout")........................3-4 87
(Shown as by "Fat Boys and the Beach Boys.")

Picture Sleeves

TIN PAN APPLE (885960 "Wipeout")........................3-5 87
Also see BEACH BOYS

FAT BOYS & Chubby Checker

P&R/R&B '88

Singles: 7-inch

TIN PAN APPLE 3-4 88

Picture Sleeves

TIN PAN APPLE 3-4 88
Also see CHECKER, Chubby
Also see FAT BOYS

FAT LARRY'S BAND
(FLB)

R&B '78

Singles: 12-inch 33/45rpm

WMOT....................................... 4-6 78-79

Singles: 7-inch

FANTASY 3-4 79-82
OMMI 3-4 86
STAX....................................... 3-5 77
WMOT....................................... 3-4 78-82

LPs: 10/12-inch 33rpm

FANTASY 5-10 80
OMMI 5-10 86
STAX....................................... 8-10 77
WMOT....................................... 5-10 78-82
Members: Larry James; Art Capehart; Doug Jones; Jimmy Lee; Erskine Williams; Ted Cohen; Darryl Grant; Larry Labes.

FAT MATTRESS

LP '69

LPs: 10/12-inch 33rpm

ATCO 10-20 69-70

FATBACK
(Fatback Band)

R&B '73

Singles: 12-inch 33/45rpm

SPRING 4-6 83-84

Singles: 7-inch

COTILLION 3-4 83-85
EVENT 3-5 74-76
PERCEPTION................................. 3-5 72-74
POLYDOR 3-4 79
SPRING 3-5 76-85

LPs: 10/12-inch 33rpm

COTILLION 5-10 83-85
EVENT 8-10 74-76

PERCEPTION 8-10 72
POLYDOR 5-10 79
SPRING 5-10 76-84

Members: Bill Curtis; Johnny King; George Williams; Johnny Flippin; Earl Shelton; George Adam; Fred Demerey; George Victory; Gerry Thomas.

Also see CHRISTIE, Janice

FATES WARNING

LP '87

LPs: 10/12-inch 33rpm

ENIGMA 5-10 87
METAL BLADE 5-8 88-89

FAX, Tony

R&B '68

Singles: 7-inch

CALLA 4-6 68

FAYE, Alma

R&B '79

Singles: 12-inch 33/45rpm

CASABLANCA 4-6 79

Singles: 7-inch

CASABLANCA 3-4 79

FAZE-O

R&B/LP '78

Singles: 7-inch

SHE 3-5 77-79

LPs: 10/12-inch 33rpm

SHE 5-10 77-79

Members: Keith Harrison; Ralph Aikens; Roger Parker; Tyrone Crum; Robert Neal Jr.

FEARON, Phil

R&B '86

Singles: 7-inch

COOLTEMPO 3-4 86
ISLAND 3-4 86

FEATHER

P&R '70

Singles: 7-inch

WHITE WHALE 3-5 70

LPs: 10/12-inch 33rpm

COLUMBIA 10-12 70

FEATHERBED

(Barry Manilow)

Singles: 7-inch

BELL (133 "Could It Be Magic") 15-25 71
BELL (971 "Amy") 15-25 71

Also see MANILOW, Barry

FEE WAYBILL: see WAYBILL, Fee

FEEL

R&B '82

Singles: 12-inch 33/45rpm

SUTRA 4-6 82-83

Singles: 7-inch

SUTRA 3-4 82-83

FEELGOOD, DR: see DR. FEELGOOD

FEELIES

LP '88

LP: 10/12-inch 33rpm

A&M 5-8 88

FELDER, Don

P&R '81

Singles: 7-inch

ASYLUM 3-4 83
FULL MOON/ASYLUM 3-4 81
MCA 3-4

Picture Sleeves

FULL MOON/ASYLUM 3-4 81

LPs: 10/12-inch 33rpm

ASYLUM 5-10 83
ELEKTRA 5-8 83

Also see EAGLES
Also see PURE PRAIRIE LEAGUE

FELDER, Wilton

R&B/LP '78

Singles: 7-inch

ABC 3-4 78
MCA 3-4 79-85

LPs: 10/12-inch 33rpm

ABC 5-10 78
MCA 5-10 80-85
PACIFIC JAZZ 8-12 69

Also see JAZZ CRUSADERS
Also see TASTE of HONEY

FELDER, Wilton, & Bobby Womack

R&B '85

Singles: 7-inch

MCA 3-4 80-85

Picture Sleeves

MCA 3-4 80-85

Also see FELDER, Wilton
Also see WOMACK, Bobby

FELDMAN, Victor

(Victor Feldman All Stars; Trio; Quartet; Vic Feldman)

P&R '62

Singles: 7-inch

AVA 3-5 63
INFINITY 3-5 62
PACIFIC JAZZ 3-5 66
VEE JAY 3-5 64

LPs: 10/12-inch 33rpm

AVA 10-20 63
CONTEMPORARY 15-25 58-60
INTERLUDE 15-20 59
MODE 20-30 58
NAUTILUS 10-20 82
(Half-speed mastered.)
PACIFIC JAZZ 10-15 67-68
PALTO ALTO 5-10 83-84
RIVERSIDE 15-20 61
VEE JAY 15-25 59-65
WORLD PACIFIC 15-25 62

FELICIANO, Jose

P&R/R&B/LP '68

Singles: 7–inch

ALA 3-4 80
MOTOWN 3-4 81-83
PRIVATE STOCK 3-5 76-77
RCA... 3-6 64-75

LPs: 10/12–inch 33rpm

CAMDEN.................................... 8-10 72
MOTOWN 5-10 81
PRIVATE STOCK 6-10 76-77
RCA.. 8-15 65-76
Also see SCHUUR, Diane

FELICIANO, Jose / Petula Clark

EPs: 7–inch 33/45rpm

TK (334 "Mackenna's Gold")..... 10-20 69
Also see CLARK, Petula

FELICIANO, Jose, & Quincy Jones

LPs: 10/12–inch 33rpm

RCA (4096 "Mackenna's Gold") 15-25 69
(Soundtrack.)
Also see FELICIANO, Jose
Also see JONES, Quincy

FELIX & JARVIS

R&B '82

Singles: 7–inch

RFC/QUALITY 3-4 82-83

FELLINI, Suzanne

P&R '80

Singles: 7–inch

CASABLANCA 3-4 80

LPs: 10/12–inch 33rpm

CASABLANCA 5-10 80

FELONY

P&R/LP '83

Singles: 7–inch

ROCK & ROLL 3-4 83-84

LPs: 10/12–inch 33rpm

ROCK & ROLL 5-10 83

FELTS, Narvel

P&R '60

Singles: 78rpm

MERCURY 5-10 57

Singles: 7–inch

ABC 3-4 76
ACTION..................................... 4-8 70
ARA.. 4-8 64-65
CELEBRITY CIRCLE 4-8 65
CINNAMON................................ 3-5 73-74
COLLAGE 3-4 79
COMPLEAT 3-4 82-83
CONE.. 3-4 92
DOT.. 3-5 75-77
EVERGREEN............................. 3-4 82-91
GMC... 3-4 81
GROOVE 4-8 63
HI (2100 series)......................... 4-8 67
HI (2300 series) 3-5 76
HI COUNTRY (8000 series) 4-6 72-73
KARI...3-4 80
LOBO 3-4 82
MCA..3-4 79
MERCURY 8-12 57
PINK...10-15 59-60
RENAY..4-8 62-65
RENEGADE.................................2-4 91
STARLINE 5-10 62

Picture Sleeves

CONE..3-4 92

LPs: 10/12–inch 33rpm

ABC 5-10 78
ABC/DOT 8-10 75-77
CINNAMON 8-10 73-74
HI 8-10 76

FELTS, Narvel / Red Sovine / Mel Tillis

LPs: 10/12–inch 33rpm

POWER PAK 5-10 80s
Also see SOVINE, Red

FELTS, Narvel, & Sharon Vaughn

C&W '74

Singles: 7–inch

CINNAMON 3-5 74
Also see FELTS, Narvel

FEMME FATALE

LP '89

LPs: 10/12–inch 33rpm

MCA 5-8 89

FENDER, Freddy
(Baldemar Huerta)

C&W/P&R/LP '75

Singles: 7–inch

ABC..3-4 76-79
ABC/DOT 4-6 75-77
ARV INT'L 3-5 75
ARGO 10-15 60
DISCOS DOMINANTE................5-10
DUNCAN...................................10-20 59
GRT 4-8 75-76
GOLDBAND.................................4-8 60s
IMPERIAL 8-12 60
MCA..3-4 82
NORCO..4-8 63-65
STARFLITE..................................3-4 79-80
W.B. 3-4 83

LPs: 10/12–inch 33rpm

ABC..5-10 78-79
ABC/DOT 8-10 75-77
ACCORD 5-10 81
GRT 8-10 75
STARFLITE..................................5-10 80
Also see HUERTA, Baldemar

FENDERMEN

P&R/C&W '60

Singles: 7–inch

COLLECTABLES 3-4 80s
CUCA (1003 "Mule Skinner Blues") 50-75 60
DAB 4-8
ERA 3-5 72
ERIC 3-4 70s
KOALA 3-4
SOMA 6-10 60-61

LPs: 10/12–inch 33rpm

SOMA (1240 "Mule Skinner Blues") 800-1200 60

Members: Phil Humphrey; Jimmy Sundquist; John Howard.

FERGUSON, Helena

P&R/R&B '67

Singles: 7–inch

COMPASS 4-8 67-68

FERGUSON, Jay

P&R '77

Singles: 7–inch

ASYLUM 3-5 77-79
CAPITOL 3-4 82

LPs: 10/12–inch 33rpm

ASYLUM 8-10 76-79
CAPITOL 5-10 80-82

Also see JO JO GUNNE
Also see SPIRIT

FERGUSON, Johnny

P&R '60

Singles: 7–inch

MGM 5-10 59-60

FERGUSON, Maynard
(Maynard Ferguson Sextet)

LP '73

Singles: 78rpm

CAPITOL 3-5 50-51
EMARCY 3-5 54
MERCURY 3-4 55

Singles: 12–inch 33/45rpm

COLUMBIA 4-6 79

Singles: 7–inch

CAMEO 3-5 63
CAPITOL 5-10 50-51
COLUMBIA 3-4 71-82
EMARCY 5-10 54
MAINSTREAM 3-5 71-72
MERCURY 5-10 55
ROULETTE 4-8 59-62

EPs: 7–inch 33/45rpm

EMARCY 5-15 54-57

LPs: 10/12–inch 33rpm

BETHLEHEM 5-10 78
CAMEO 15-20 63
COLUMBIA 5-10 71-82
EMARCY (400 series) 5-10 76
EMARCY (1000 series) 5-10 81
EMARCY (26017 "Hollywood Party") 50-100 54
(10–inch LP.)
EMARCY (26024 "Dimensions") 50-100 54
(10–inch LP.)
EMARCY (36000 series) 20-40 55-57
ENTERPRISE 8-12 68
MAINSTREAM (300 series) 6-10 71-72
MAINSTREAM (6000 series) 15-20 64
(Stereo.)
MAINSTREAM (56000 series) 10-20 64
(Monaural.)
MERCURY 12-20 60
PALTO ALTO 5-10 83
PRESTIGE 8-12 69
ROULETTE 12-25 58-72
SKYLARK (17 "Great Jazz Solos") 25-50 53
TRIP 5-10 74
WYNCOTE 5-10 60s

Also see BASIE, Count, & Maynard Ferguson
Also see KENTON, Stan
Also see MANN, Herbie / Maynard Ferguson

FERGUSON, Maynard, & Chris Connor

Singles: 7–inch

ATLANTIC 4-6 61

LPs: 10/12–inch 33rpm

ATLANTIC (8049 "Double Exposure") 25-35 61
(Monaural.)
ATLANTIC (SD-8049 "Double Exposure") 35-45 61
(Stereo.)
ROULETTE (52068 "Two's Company") 40-60 58

Also see CONNOR, Chris
Also see FERGUSON, Maynard

FERKO STRING BAND

P&R '48

Singles: 78rpm

MEDIA 3-5 55
PALDA 4-6 48
SAVOY 3-5 55

Singles: 7–inch

ARGO 3-5 63
FERKO 4-8 50s
MEDIA 4-8 55
SAVOY 4-8 55

LPs: 10/12–inch 33rpm

ABC-PAR 10-15 63
ALSHIRE 4-6 76
REGENT 12-20 56-59
SURE 6-12 65-73

FERRANTE & TEICHER

P&R/R&B '60

Singles: 78rpm

COLUMBIA 3-5 53
ENTRE 3-6 53

Singles: 7-inch

ABC-PAR 3-6 58-62
COLUMBIA 4-8 53
ENTRE 5-10 53
U.A. 3-5 59-79

Picture Sleeves

U.A. (Except 231 to 300).............. 4-8 63-69
U.A. (231 to 300)......................... 5-10 60-61

EPs: 7-inch 33/45rpm

ABC-PAR 4-8 58-60
MGM 10-20 54
U.A. 4-8 69

LPs: 10/12-inch 33rpm

ABC... 5-10 73-76
ABC-PAR 8-15 58-66
AVANT GARDE 5-10
COLUMBIA 8-15 55-73
DORAL..................................... 10-20
(Promotional mail-order issue, from Doral cigarettes.)
GUEST STAR 4-8 64
HARMONY................................ 5-10 64-70
LIBERTY 5-10 81-84
MGM 20-40 54
METRO 5-10 66
MISTLETOE.............................. 4-6 75
SUNSET.................................... 5-10 70-71
WESTMINSTER....................... 12-20 55-58
UNART..................................... 5-10 67
U.A. 5-15 60-80
URANIA.................................... 4-8

Members: Arthur Ferrante; Louis Teicher.
Also see BELL, Vincent

FERRARI

R&B '82

Singles: 12-inch 33/45rpm

SUGAR HILL............................. 4-6 82

Singles: 7-inch

SUGAR HILL............................. 3-4 82

FERRER, Jose

(With the Ferrers)

P&R '54

Singles: 78rpm

COLUMBIA 3-5 54-55

Singles: 7-inch

COLUMBIA 4-8 54-55
EPIC.. 3-5 68
RCA... 4-6 60

Picture Sleeves

RCA... 4-6 60

LPs: 10/12-inch 33rpm

MGM 8-12 62-65

Also see CLOONEY, Rosemary, & Jose Ferrer

FERRY, Bryan

P&R/LP '76

Singles: 12-inch 33/45rpm

W.B. 4-6 85

Singles: 7-inch

ATLANTIC.................................. 3-4 74-79
REPRISE 3-4 88
W.B. 3-4 85

Picture Sleeves

REPRISE 3-4 88

LPs: 10/12-inch 33rpm

ATLANTIC................................ 10-12 72-78
REPRISE 5-10 87
W.B. 5-10 85

Also see TANGERINE DREAM / Jon Anderson / Bryan Ferry

FERRY, Bryan, & Roxy Music

LP '89

LPs: 10/12-inch 33rpm

REPRISE 5-10 89

Also see FERRY, Bryan
Also see ROXY MUSIC

FESTIVAL

P&R/LP '80

Singles: 7-inch

RSO 3-4 79

LPs: 10/12-inch

RSO 5-10 79

FESTIVALS

R&B '70

Singles: 7-inch

BLUE ROCK 3-6 69
COLOSSUS................................ 3-5 70-71
GORDY....................................... 3-5 72
SMASH 4-8 66-68

FETCHIN' BONES

LP '89

LPs: 10/12-inch 33rpm

CAPITOL.................................... 5-8 89

FEVA, Sandra

R&B '79

Singles: 7-inch

CATAWBA 3-4 87
KRISMA 3-4 86
VENTURE................................... 3-5 79-81

LPs: 10/12-inch 33rpm

VENTURE................................. 5-10 81

FEVER

R&B '79

Singles: 12-inch 33/45rpm

FANTASY 4-6 79-82
JDC 4-6 85

Singles: 7-inch

FANTASY 3-4 79-82

LPs: 10/12-inch 33rpm

FANTASY 5-10 79-80

Member: Clydene Jackson.

FEVER TREE

P&R/LP '68

Singles: 7-inch

AMPEX.................................... 10-20 70
MAINSTREAM 5-10 67
UNI (Except 55060).................. 10-20 68-69
UNI (55060 "San Francisco Girls") 8-12 68
(Black vinyl.)
UNI (55060 "San Francisco Girls") 20-40 68
(Colored vinyl. Promotional issue only.)

LPs: 10/12-inch 33rpm

AMPEX.................................... 12-20 70
MCA 8-10 76
UNI (73024 "Fever Tree") 20-30 68
UNI (73040 "Another Time, Another Place") 15-25 68
UNI (73067 "Creation") 15-25 70
Members: Dennis Keller; Rob Landes; E.E. Wolfe; John Tuttle. Session: Frank Davis.

FIDELITYS

P&R '58

Singles: 7-inch

BATON 10-15 58
SIR 10-20 59-60
Members: Buddy Miles.
Also see MILES, Buddy

FIEDLER, Arthur: see BOSTON POPS ORCHESTRA

FIELD, Sally

P&R/LP '67

Singles: 7-inch

COLGEMS 4-6 67-68

Picture Sleeves

COLGEMS 4-8 67

LPs: 10/12-inch 33rpm

COLGEMS 10-20 67

FIELDS, Ernie

P&R/R&B '59

Singles: 7-inch

CAPITOL.................................. 4-6 64
RENDEZVOUS 4-8 59-62

LPs: 10/12-inch 33rpm

RENDEZVOUS (1309 "In the Mood")................................... 30-40 60

FIELDS, Kim

R&B '84

Singles: 12-inch 33/45rpm

CRITIQUE 4-6 84

Singles: 7-inch

CRITIQUE 3-4 84

FIELDS, Lee

R&B '86

Singles: 7-inch

BDA....................................... 3-4 86

FIELDS, Richard "Dimples" (Dimples)

R&B/LP '81

Singles: 12-inch 33/45rpm

RCA 4-6 84-85

Singles: 7-inch

BOARDWALK.............................3-4 81-83
COLUMBIA 3-4 87
RCA 3-4 84-85

LPs: 10/12-inch 33rpm

BOARDWALK...........................5-10 81-82
RCA 5-10 84

FIELDS, W.C.

LP '69

LPs: 10/12-inch 33rpm

AMERICAN 5-10 75
COLUMBIA 6-10 69-77
DECCA 8-12 68
HARMONY...............................6-10 70
HUDSON 15-25 60
MARK '56 (571 "Original Radio Broadcasts") 30-50 78
(Picture disc.)

FIELDS, W.C., & Mae West

LPs: 10/12-inch 33rpm

HARMONY...............................6-10 70
PROSCENIUM.........................15-20 60
Also see FIELDS, W.C.
Also see WEST, Mae

FIESTA

R&B '78

Singles: 7-inch

ARISTA.......................................3-5 78

FIESTAS

P&R/R&B '59

Singles: 7-inch

COLLECTABLES.........................3-4 80s
OLD TOWN (1062 "So Fine") 25-35 59
(With piano intro. Identification number is "ZTSP 29364.")
OLD TOWN (1062 "So Fine") 10-20 59
(No piano intro. Identification number is "920.")
OLD TOWN (1069 thru 1104)....10-20 59-60
OLD TOWN (1111 "Hobo's Prayer")................................25-35 59-60
OLD TOWN (1122 thru 1166)....10-20 62-64
OLD TOWN (1178 "Think Smart")................................50-75 65
OLD TOWN (1189 "Ain't She Sweet") 10-15 65
RESPECT 3-5 75
STRAND (25046 "Julie")...........20-30 61
VIGOR 3-5 74
Members: Tom Bullock; Eddie Morris; Sam Ingalls; Preston Love.
Also see ROBERT & JOHNNY / Fiestas

FIFTH ANGEL

LP '88

LPs: 10/12-inch 33rpm

EPIC 5-8 88

FIFTH AVE.

R&B '87

Singles: 7-inch

PARADISE 3-4 87

FIFTH DIMENSION
(5th Dimension)

P&R/LP '67

Singles: 7-inch

ABC 3-5 75-76
ARISTA 3-5 75
BELL 3-5 70-74
MOTOWN 3-4 78-79
SOUL CITY 4-8 66-70
SUTRA 3-4 83

Picture Sleeves

SOUL CITY 4-8 67-69

LPs: 10/12-inch 33rpm

ABC 8-10 75
ARISTA 8-10 75
BELL 8-12 70-74
KORY 8-10 77
MOTOWN 5-10 78-79
RHINO 5-10 86
SOUL CITY 10-15 67-70

Members: Marilyn McCoo; Billy Davis Jr; Lamonte McLemore; Florence LaRue; Ron Townson.
Also see DAVIS, Billy, Jr.
Also see MAMAS & PAPAS / Association / Fifth Dimension
Also see McCOO, Marilyn, & Billy Davis Jr.

FIFTH ESTATE

P&R '67

Singles: 7-inch

JUBILEE 5-10 67-69
RED BIRD (064 "Love Is All a Game") 10-15 66

LPs: 10/12-inch 33rpm

JUBILEE (JGM-8005 "Ding Dong the Witch Is Dead") 20-30 67
(Monaural.)
JUBILEE (JGS-8005 "Ding Dong the Witch Is Dead") 25-35 67
(Stereo.)

Members: Wayne Wadhams; Rick Engler; Doug Ferrara; Bill Shute; Ken Evans.

50 GUITARS of TOMMY GARRETT

LP '61

Singles: 7-Inch

LIBERTY 3-5 66-68

LPs: 10/12-Inch 33rpm

LIBERTY 5-15 61-71
MUSICOR 5-10 76-78
U.A. 5-8 73

Also see GARRETT, Tommy

52ND STREET

D&D '83

Singles: 12-inch 33/45rpm

A&M 4-6 83
MCA 4-6 85-87
PROFILE 4-6 84

Singles: 7-inch

MCA 3-4 85-86

LPs: 10/12-inch 33rpm

MCA 5-10 86

FIGURES on the BEACH

D&D '84

Singles: 12-inch 33/45rpm

METRO AMERICAN 4-6 84

Singles: 7-inch

SIRE 3-4 89

Picture Sleeves

SIRE 3-4 89

FILE 13

D&D '84

Singles: 12-inch 33/45rpm

PROFILE 4-6 84

FINE YOUNG CANNIBALS

P&R/LP '86

Singles: 12-inch 33/45rpm

I.R.S. 4-6 86-89

Singles: 7-inch

I.R.S. 3-4 86-90

Picture Sleeves

I.R.S. 3-4 86-89

LPs: 10/12-inch 33rpm

I.R.S. 5-10 86-90

Members: Roland Gift; Danny Cox; David Steele.
Also see ENGLISH BEAT

FINISHED TOUCH

R&B '78

Singles: 7-inch

MOTOWN 3-5 78

LPs: 10/12-inch 33rpm

MOTOWN 5-10 78

FINN, Tim

LP '83

Singles: 7-inch

A&M 3-4 83

LPs: 10/12-inch 33rpm

A&M 5-10 83

Also see SPLIT ENZ

FINNEGAN, Larry

P&R '62

Singles: 7-inch

CORAL 4-8 62
OLD TOWN 5-10 62-63
RIC 8-10 64

FINNEY, Albert

LP '77

Singles: 7-inch

MOTOWN 3-4 77

LPs: 10/12-inch 33rpm

MOTOWN 5-10 77

FIONA

(Fiona Flanagan; with Kip Winger)

P&R/LP '85

Singles: 7-inch

ATLANTIC.................................. 3-4 84-89

Picture Sleeves

ATLANTIC.................................. 3-4 89

LPs: 10/12-inch 33rpm

ATLANTIC.................................. 5-10 84-89

FIORILLO, Elisa

P&R/LP '88

Singles: 7-inch

CHRYSALIS................................ 3-4 88-90

Picture Sleeves

CHRYSALIS................................ 3-4 88

LPs: 10/12-inch 33rpm

CHRYSALIS................................ 5-8 88

Also see JELLYBEAN & Elisa Fiorillo

FIRE & RAIN

P&R '73

Singles: 7-inch

MERCURY 3-5 73

LPs: 10/12-inch 33rpm

MERCURY 8-10 73

FIRE INC.

P&R '84

Singles: 7-inch

MCA 3-4 84

Picture Sleeves

MCA 3-4 84

FIREBALLET

LP '75

Singles: 7-inch

PASSPORT................................ 3-5 75-76

LPs: 10/12-inch 33rpm

PASSPORT................................ 8-10 75-76

FIREBALLS

P&R '59

Singles: 7-inch

ASTRA (1021 "Sweet Talk") 4-8 66

ATCO 4-8 67-70

DOT.. 4-8 63-67

KAPP (248 "Fireball") 75-100 59

TOP RANK (2008 "Torquay")...... 8-12 59

TOP RANK (2026 "Bulldog")....... 8-12 59

(Monaural.)

TOP RANK (2026-ST "Bulldog") 15-25 59

(Stereo.)

TOP RANK (2038 "Foot Patter"). 8-12 60

(Monaural.)

TOP RANK (2038-ST "Foot Patter").................................. 15-25 60

(Stereo.)

TOP RANK (2054 "Vaquero") 8-12 61

TOP RANK (2081 "Sweet Talk"). 8-12 61

TOP RANK (3003 "Rik-A-Tik")..... 8-12 61

WARWICK 5-10 61

EPs: 7-inch 33/45rpm

TOP RANK (1000 "Fireballs") 50-75 60

LPs: 10/12-inch 33rpm

ATCO 10-14 68-69

TOP RANK (324 "Fireballs") 45-55 60

TOP RANK (343 "Vaquero") 45-60 60

(Monaural.)

TOP RANK (643 "Vaquero") 50-75 60

(Stereo.)

WARWICK (2042 "Here Are the Fireballs")............................ 45-60 61

Members: Chuck Tharp; George Tomsco; Dan Trammell; Eric Budd; Stan Lark; Doug Roberts; Jimmy Gilmer; Keith McCormick.

Also see DALE, Dick / Surfaris / Fireballs

Also see GILMER, Jimmy

Also see STRING-A-LONGS

FIREFALL

P&R/LP '76

Singles: 7-inch

ATLANTIC................................. 3-5 76-82

Picture Sleeves

ATLANTIC................................. 3-5 78-79

LPs: 10/12-inch 33rpm

ATLANTIC................................. 5-10 76-83

Members: Rick Roberts; Jack Bartley; Larry Burnette; Mike Clarke; Scott Kirkpatrick; Dave Muse; Mark Andes; Peter Graves.

Also see ABBA / Spinners / Firefall / England Dan & John Ford Coley

Also see FLYING BURRITO BROTHERS

Also see MANILOW, Barry / Firefall

Also see ROBERTS, Rick

Also see SPIRIT

FIREFLIES

P&R '59

Singles: 7-inch

CANADIAN AMERICAN 8-12 60

ERIC 3-4 70s

HAMILTON 4-8 63

RIBBON 8-12 59-60

TAURUS (355 "You Were Mine") 8-12 62

TAURUS (366 "My Prayer for You")...................................... 10-15 62

LPs: 10/12-inch 33rpm

TAURUS (1002 "You Were Mine")................................. 75-125 61

(Monaural.)

TAURUS (1002 "You Were Mine")................................. 250-350 61

(Stereo.)

Members: Ritchie Adams; Lee Reynolds; John Viscelli; Paul Giacolone.

Also see CASINOS / Fireflies

FIREFLY

P&R/R&B '75

Singles: 7-inch

A&M 3-5 75

FIREFLY

R&B '81

Singles: 7-inch

EMERGENCY 3-4 81

FIREHOUSE

LP '91

LPs: 10/12-inch 33rpm

EPIC 5-8 91

FIRESIGN THEATRE

LP '69

Singles: 7-inch

COLUMBIA (Except 34) 3-6 69
COLUMBIA (34 "This Side") 4-8 70
(Single-sided, promotional disc.)

Picture Sleeves

COLUMBIA (34 "This Side") 5-10 70

LPs: 10/12-inch 33rpm

BUTTERFLY 5-10 77
COLUMBIA 8-15 69-74
EPIC 5-10 74
MORWAY 5-8 85
RHINO 5-10 79-82

Members: Phil Proctor; John Fresno; Philip Austin; David Ossman; Cy Faryar.

FIRM, The

P&R/LP '85

Singles: 7-inch

ATLANTIC 3-4 85-86

Picture Sleeves

ATLANTIC 3-4 85-86

LPs: 10/12-inch 33rpm

ATLANTIC 5-10 85-86

Members: Jimmy Page; Paul Rodgers; Tony Franklin; Chris Slade.

Also see AC/DC
Also see BAD COMPANY
Also see BLUE MURDER
Also see MANN, Manfred
Also see PAGE, Jimmy
Also see RODGERS, Paul

FIRST CHOICE

P&R/R&B/LP '73

Singles: 12-inch 33/45rpm

FIRST CHOICE 4-6 83
SALSOUL 4-6 84

Singles: 7-inch

GOLD MINE 3-5 77-79
PHILLY GROOVE 3-5 73-74
WAND 3-5 72
W.B. 3-5 76

LPs: 10/12-inch 33rpm

GOLD MINE 5-10 77-80
KORY 8-10 77
PHILLY GROOVE 8-10 73-74

Members: Rochelle Fleming; Annette Guest; Joyce Jones; Wardell Piper.

Also see PIPER, Wardell

FIRST CIRCLE

R&B '87

Singles: 7-inch

EMI AMERICA 3-4 87

FIRST CLASS

R&B '74

Singles: 7-inch

ALL PLATINUM 3-5 76-77
EBONY SOUNDS 3-5 75
TODAY 3-5 74
UK 3-5 74-75

LPs: 10/12-inch 33rpm

ALL PLATINUM 5-10 76
PARK-WAY 5-10 80
SUGARHILL 5-10 81

Members: Harold Bell; Fred Marshall; Sylvester Redditt.

FIRST CLASS

P&R '74

Singles: 7-inch

PRIVATE STOCK/UK 3-5 76
UK 3-5 74-75

LPs: 10/12-inch 33rpm

UK 8-10 74

Members: Tony Burrows; John Carter; Charles Mills; Del John; Spencer James; Eddie Richards; Robin Shaw; Clive Barrett.

Also see BROTHERHOOD of MAN
Also see BURROWS, Tony
Also see EDISON LIGHTHOUSE
Also see PIPKINS

FIRST EDITION

P&RLP '68

Singles: 7-inch

REPRISE 4-8 67-68

LPs: 10/12-inch 33rpm

REPRISE 12-20 67-68

Members: Kenny Rogers; Mike Settle; Thelma Lou Camacho; Terry Williams; Mickey Jones.

Also see CAMACHO, Thelma
Also see NEW CHRISTY MINSTRELS
Also see ROGERS, Kenny, & First Edition

FIRST FAMILY........

h

POLYDOR 3-5 74

FIRST LOVE

R&B '80

Singles: 12-inch 33/45rpm

CHYCAGO INT'L 4-6 82

Singles: 7-inch

CHYCAGO INT'L 3-4 82
CIM 3-4 83
DAKAR 3-4 80

LPs: 10/12-inch 33rpm

CHYCAGO INT'L 5-10 82

Members: Yvonne Gage.

Also see GAGE, Yvonne

FISCHER, Lisa

LP '91

LPs: 10/12–inch 33rpm

ELEKTRA 5-8 91

FISCHER, Wild Man

LPs: 10/12–inch 33rpm

BIZARRE (6332 "An Evening with Wild Man Fischer") 20-30 69
(With Frank Zappa & Mothers of Invention.)
RHINO 5-10 81
Also see MOTHERS of INVENTION

FISCHOFF, George

(George Fischoff Keyboard Komplex; with the Peppers; with Luv Ens)

P&R '74

Singles: 7–inch

COLUMBIA 3-5 77
DRIVE 3-5 79
HERITAGE 3-4 81
P.I.P. 3-5 75
RANWOOD 3-5 76
REWARD 3-4 84
U.A. 3-5 72-74

FISHBONE

LP '88

LPs: 10/12–inch 33rpm

COLUMBIA 5-8 88-91

FISHER, Eddie *P&R '50*

Singles: 78rp

RCA 3-5 50-57

Singles: 7–inch

ABC-PAR 4-6 61
DOT 3-5 65-66
MUSICOR 3-5 69
RCA (3000 thru 6000 series) 5-10 50-57
RCA (7000 thru 9000 series) 4-8 57-68
RAMROD 4-6 60-63
7 ARTS 4-6 61
TRANS ATLAS 4-6 62

Picture Sleeves

RCA (5000 series) 15-25 53-55
RCA (6000 series) 10-15 55-57
RAMROD 4-8 60

EPs: 7–inch 33/45rpm

RCA 10-20 51-58

LPs: 10/12–inch 33rpm

CAMDEN 6-10 63
DOT 10-15 65-67
FAMOUS TWINSETS 8-12 74
HAMILTON 6-10 66
RCA (1024 thru 2504) 15-30 55-62
RCA (3025 thru 3231) 20-35 52-54
(10–inch LPs.)
RCA (3375 "Best of Eddie Fisher") 10-15 65
RCA (3700 & 3800 series) 10-20 66-67
RAMROD (1 "At the Winter Garden") 10-20 63
RAMROD (6001 "Scent of Mystery") 50-60 60
(Soundtrack. Monaural.)
RAMROD (6001 "Scent of Mystery") 75-85 60
(Soundtrack Stereo.)
Also see COMO, Perry, & Eddie Fisher

FISHER, Eddie / Vic Damone / Dick Haymes

LPs: 10/12–inch 33rpm

ALMOR 10-15
Also see DAMONE, Vic
Also see HAYMES, Dick

FISHER, Eddie, & Debbie Reynolds

EPs: 7–inch 33/45rpm

RCA (4018 "Bundle of Joy") 15-25 56
(Soundtrack.)

LPs: 10/12–inch 33rpm

RCA (1399 "Bundle of Joy") 40-50 56
(Soundtrack.)
Also see FISHER, Eddie
Also see REYNOLDS, Debbie

FISHER, Herb, Trio

R&B '50

Singles: 78rpm

MODERN 5-10 50

FISHER, Mary Ann

P&R '61

Singles: 7–inch

FIRE 5-10 59-60
IMPERIAL 4-8 62
SEG-WAY 4-8 61

FISHER, Miss Toni: see FISHER, Toni

FISHER, Toni

(Miss Toni Fisher)

P&R '59

Singles: 7–inch

BIG TOP 5-10 62
CAPITOL 4-8 67
COLLECTABLES 3-4 80s
COLUMBIA 5-10 61
ERA 3-5 72
SIGNET 5-10 59-64
SMASH 4-8 63

LPs: 10/12–inch 33rpm

SIGNET (509 "The Big Hurt") 30-40 60

FISHER, Tricia Leigh *P&R '90*

Singles: 7–inc

ATCO 3-4 90

FISHER, Willie

R&B '77

Singles: 7–inch

TIGRESS 3-5 77

FIT

R&B '88

Singles: 7–inch

A&M 3-4 88

Members: Vince Ebo; Chuck Gentry.
Also see SWEET INSPIRATIONS

FITZGERALD, Ella

P&R '36

Singles: 78rpm

DECCA (800 thru 3000 series) . 10-15 36-41
DECCA (18000 thru 29000 series) 5-10 42-54
VERVE 3-5 54-57

Singles: 7–inch

CAPITOL 3-5 67-68
DECCA (27000 & 28000 series) 10-20 50-53
DECCA (29000 series).......... 8-15 54-56
DECCA (30000 series except 30405).......... 5-10 56-67
DECCA (30405 "Goody Goody") 15-25 57
PABLO 3-4 75
PRESTIGE 3-5 69
REPRISE 3-5 69-71
SALLE 4-6 68
VERVE (10000 series).......... 5-10 56-59
VERVE (10100 thru 10300 series, except 10340) 4-6 60-65
VERVE (10340 "Ringo Beat") 8-12 64

Picture Sleeves

VERVE 5-10 59-60

EPs: 7–inch 33/45rpm

DECCA.......... 15-30 50-58
VERVE 10-25 56-61

LPs: 10/12–inch 33rpm

ATLANTIC.......... 5-10 72
BAINBRIDGE 5-10 81
CAPITOL (2000 series).......... 8-15 67-68
CAPITOL (11000 series).......... 5-10 78
CAPITOL (16000 series).......... 4-6 82
COLUMBIA 5-10 73
CORAL.......... 4-8 73
DECCA (156 "The Best of Ella Fitzgerald").......... 25-35 58
(Black label with silver print.)
DECCA (156 "The Best of Ella Fitzgerald").......... 15-20 65
(Black label with horizontal rainbow band.)
DECCA (4000 series).......... 10-20 61-67
DECCA (5084 "Souvenir Album") 75-125 49
(10–inch LP.)
DECCA (5300 "Gershwin Songs") 75-125 51
(10–inch LP.)
DECCA (8000 series).......... 20-40 55-59
EVEREST 5-10 73
MCA 5-10 76-82
MGM 5-10 70
MPS 5-10 72
METRO.......... 10-15 65-66
OLYMPIC.......... 5-10 74
PABLO 5-10 75-83
REPRISE 8-12 69-71
VERVE (29 "Ella Fitzgerald Sings the George & Ira Gershwin Songbook") 30-40 64
(Five-LP reissue of Verve 4029.)
VERVE (2500 & 2600 series) 5-10 76-82
(Reads "Manufactured By MGM Record Corp.," or mentions either Polydor or Polygram at bottom of label.)
VERVE (4001 thru 4009) 25-50 56
(Reads "Verve Records, Inc." at bottom of label.)
VERVE (4010 "Ella Fitzgerald Sings the Duke Ellington Song Book")..........75-125 56
(Four-LP set.)
VERVE (4013 thru 4015) 20-40 57
(Reads "Verve Records, Inc." at bottom of label.)
VERVE (4019 "Ella Fitzgerald Sings the Irving Berlin Songbook")..........20-40 58
VERVE (4020 thru 4028) 20-40 58-59
(Reads "Verve Records, Inc." at bottom of label.)
VERVE (4029 "Ella Fitzgerald Sings the George & Ira Gershwin Songbook") 40-60 59
(Five-LP set, containing individual LPs 4024 thru 4028.)
VERVE (4036 thru 4071) 10-20 59-66
VERVE (6000 series)..........20-35 57-59
(Reads "Verve Records, Inc." at bottom of label.)
VERVE (6100 series)..........15-20 60
(Reads "Verve Records, Inc." at bottom of label.)
VERVE (8200 series)..........20-30 58
(Reads "Verve Records, Inc." at bottom of label.)
VERVE (64036 thru 64071) 10-20 59-66
VERVE (67000 & 68000 series) ..8-15 67-73
VERVE (2610000 series)..........20-30 83
VOCALION 6-10 67

Also see CAMPBELL, Glen / Lettermen / Ella Fitzgerald / Sandler & Young
Also see RIDDLE, Nelson

FITZGERALD, Ella, & Louis Armstrong

R&B '46

Singles: 78rpm

DECCA 3-6 53

EPs: 7–inch 33/45rpm

VERVE..........15-30 56

LPs: 10/12–inch 33rpm

METRO 5-10 67
VERVE (4003 "Ella & Louis").....40-60 56

VERVE (4006 "Ella & Louis Again") 50-100 56
VERVE (4011 "Porgy & Bess") . 25-50 57
(Monaural.)
VERVE (6040 "Porgy & Bess") . 40-65 57
(Stereo.)
VERVE (8811 "Ella & Louis")...... 5-10 72
Also see ARMSTRONG, Louis

FITZGERALD, Ella, & Count Basie
LP '63

LPs: 10/12-inch 33rpm
PABLO 5-10 79
VERVE 15-20 63
Also see BASIE, Count

FITZGERALD, Ella / Bill Doggett

Singles: 78rpm
DECCA....................................... 3-5 53

Singles: 7-inch
DECCA....................................... 5-10 53

LPs: 10/12-inch 33rpm
VERVE 10-20 62
Also see DOGGETT, Bill

FITZGERALD, Ella, & Duke Ellington

Singles: 7-inch
VERVE 4-6 66

LPs: 10/12-inch 33rpm
VERVE 10-20 65-67
Also see ELLINGTON, Duke

FITZGERALD, Ella / Billie Holiday

LPs: 10/12-inch 33rpm
MCA 5-10 76
VERVE (6022 "At Newport")..... 40-50 58
(Stereo.)
VERVE (8234 "At Newport")..... 30-40 58
(Monaural.)

FITZGERALD, Ella / Billie Holiday / Lena Horne

EPs: 7-inch 33/45rpm
COLUMBIA (2531 "Ella, Lena & Billie").................................. 25-45 56

LPs: 10/12-inch 33rpm
COLUMBIA (2531 "Ella, Lena & Billie")................................ 75-100 56
(10-inch LP.)
Also see HOLIDAY, Billie
Also see HORNE, Lena

FITZGERALD, Ella, & Ink Spots

Singles: 78rpm
DECCA (18000 series)................ 4-8 44-45

EPs: 7-inch 33/45rpm
DECCA....................................... 5-10 53
Also see INK SPOTS

FITZGERALD, Ella, & Antonio Carlos Jobim

LPs: 10/12-inch 33rpm
PABLO 5-10 81
Also see JOBIM, Antonio Carlos

FITZGERALD, Ella, & Louis Jordan
R&B '46

Singles: 78rpm
DECCA (23000 series) 4-8 46
Also see JORDAN, Louis

FITZGERALD, Ella, & Peggy Lee
LP '55

LPs: 10/12-inch 33rpm
DECCA (8166 "Pete Kelly's Blues") 40-60 55
Also see LEE, Peggy

FITZGERALD, Ella, & Mills Brothers
P&R '37

Singles: 78rpm
DECCA 4-8 37
Also see MILLS BROTHERS

FITZGERALD, Ella, & Oscar Peterson

LPs: 10/12-inch 33rpm
PABLO 5-10 76
Also see FITZGERALD, Ella
Also see PETERSON, Oscar

FIVE AMERICANS
P&R/LP '66

Singles: 7-inch
ABC-PAR (10686 "Love Love Love").......................................5-10 65
ABNAK (Except 109) 10-15 67-69
(Black vinyl.)
ABNAK (Except 109) 15-25 67-69
(Colored vinyl.)
ABNAK (109 "I See the Light")... 15-25 65
(Black vinyl.)
ABNAK (109 "I See the Light")... 15-25 65
(Colored vinyl.)
HBR 5-10 65-66
JETSTAR (104 "It's You Girl") ... 10-15 65
JETSTAR (105 "Slippin' & Slidin")................................15-20 65
PHILCO/FORD (10 "Western Union")................................10-20 67
("Hip-Pocket" flexi-disc.)

Picture Sleeves
ABNAK (125 "Stop Light").......... 10-15 67
ABNAK (126 "Guided Tour")...... 10-15 68
HBR (468 "Evol-Not Love") 10-20 66

LPs: 10/12-inch 33rpm
ABNAK..20-30 67-68
HBR (8503 "I See the Light") 30-35 66
(Monaural.)
HBR (9503 "I See the Light") 35-40 66
(Stereo.)
Members: Michael Rabon; Jimmy Wright; John Durrill.
Also see PEDESTRIANS / Association / Five Americans / Soulblenders

FIVE BY FIVE

P&R '68

Singles: 7–inch

PAULA 5-15 67-70

LPs: 10/12–inch 33rpm

PAULA 15-20 69

5 CHANELS

(Chanels)

P&R '58

Singles: 7–inch

DEB (500 "The Reason") 15-25 58

Also see CHANELS

FIVE DU-TONES

P&R/R&B '63

Singles: 7–inch

ONE-DERFUL............................ 5-10 63-65

Members: Andrew Butler; Frank McCurrey; Willie Guest; LeRoy Joyce; Andy Butler.

FIVE EMPREES

(Five Empressions)

P&R '65

Singles: 7–inch

FREEPORT................................ 5-10 65-66

GOLD STANDARD 4-8
(Colored vinyl.)

SMASH 4-8 66

LPs: 10/12–inch 33rpm

FREEPORT (3001 "The Five Emprees [Little Miss Sad]") 35-45 65
(Monaural.)

FREEPORT (3001 "Little Miss Sad") 20-30 66
(Reissue.)

FREEPORT (4001 "The Five Emprees [Little Miss Sad]") 30-40 65
(Stereo.)

FREEPORT (4001 "Little Miss Sad") 25-35 66
(Reissue.)

Also see FIVE EMPRESSIONS

FIVE EMPRESSIONS

(Five Emprees)

Singles: 7–inch

FREEPORT................................ 8-12 65

Also see FIVE EMPREES

FIVE FLIGHTS UP

P&R '70

Singles: 7–inch

T.A... 3-5 70-71

FIVE KEYS

(Rudy West & the Five Keys; 5 Keys)

R&B '51

Singles: 78rpm

ALADDIN (3085 "With a Broken Heart") 100-200 51

ALADDIN (3099 "The Glory of Love") 100-200 51

ALADDIN (3113 "It's Christmas Time") 150-250 51

ALADDIN (3118 "Yes Sir, That's My Baby") 50-100 52

ALADDIN (3119 "Darlin") 50-100 52

ALADDIN (3127 "Red Sails in the Sunset") 75-125 52

ALADDIN (3131 "Mistakes") .. 200-350 52

ALADDIN (3136 "I Hadn't Anyone Til You") 75-125 52

ALADDIN (3158 "I Cried for You") 200-300 52

ALADDIN (3167 "Can't Keep from Crying") 150-250 53

ALADDIN (3175 "There Ought to Be a Law") 75-125 53

ALADDIN (3190 "These Foolish Things") 50-100 53

ALADDIN (3204 "Teardrops in Your Eyes") 50-100 53

ALADDIN (3214 "My Saddest Hour") 50-100 53

ALADDIN (3228 "Someday Sweetheart") 50-100 54

ALADDIN (3245 "Deep in My Heart") 50-100 54

ALADDIN (3263 "My Love") ... 100-150 55

ALADDIN (3312 "Story of Love") 40-60 56

CAPITOL................................. 10-20 54-57

GROOVE (0031 "I'll Follow You") 400-600 51

Singles: 7–inch

ALADDIN (3099 "The Glory of Love") 350-500 51

ALADDIN (3113 "It's Christmas Time") 500-750 51

ALADDIN (3118 "Yes Sir, That's My Baby") 400-600 52

ALADDIN (3119 "Darlin") 500-600 52

ALADDIN (3127 "Red Sails in the Sunset") 750-850 52

ALADDIN (3131 "Mistakes") .. 500-750 52

ALADDIN (3136 "I Hadn't Anyone Til You") 500-750 52

ALADDIN (3158 "I Cried for You") 300-600 52

ALADDIN (3167 "Can't Keep from Crying") 300-500 53

ALADDIN (3175 "There Ought to Be a Law") 250-500 53

ALADDIN (3190 "These Foolish Things") 750-1000 53

ALADDIN (3204 "Teardrops in Your Eyes") 250-500 53

ALADDIN (3214 "My Saddest Hour") 300-500 53
(Flat blue label.)

ALADDIN (3214 "My Saddest Hour")................................ 250-350 53
(Glossy blue label.)
ALADDIN (3228 "Someday Sweetheart") 300-500 54
ALADDIN (3245 "Deep in My Heart")................................ 300-500 54
ALADDIN (3263 "My Love").. 150-250 55
ALADDIN (3312 "Story of Love")................................ 150-250 56
CAPITOL (2945 "Ling Ting Tong") 15-25 54
CAPITOL (3032 "Close Your Eyes")................................... 15-25 55
CAPITOL (3127 "The Verdict") . 15-25 55
CAPITOL (3185 "I Wish I'd Never Learned to Read").................. 15-25 55
CAPITOL (3267 "Gee Whittakers")............................. 15-25 55
CAPITOL (3318 "What Goes On")...................................... 15-25 56
CAPITOL (3392 "I Dreamt I Dwelt in Heaven") 15-25 56
(Standard 45rpm hole.)
CAPITOL (3392 "I Dreamt I Dwelt in Heaven") 20-25 56
(LP-size, 1/4-inch hole. Purple label.)
CAPITOL (3392 "I Dreamt I Dwelt in Heaven") 25-30 56
(LP-size, 1/4-inch hole. White label. Promotional issue only.)
CAPITOL (3455 "Peace and Love")...................................... 15-25 56
CAPITOL (3502 "Out of Sight, Out of Mind")......................... 15-25 56
CAPITOL (3597 "Wisdom of a Fool").................................... 15-25 56
CAPITOL (3660 "Let There Be You") 15-25 57
CAPITOL (3710 "Four Walls")... 10-20 57
CAPITOL (3738 "This I Promise You") 10-20 57
CAPITOL (3786 "Face of an Angel") 10-20 57
CAPITOL (3830 "Do Anything") 10-20 57
CAPITOL (3861 "From Me to You") 8-12 58
CAPITOL (3948 "With All My Heart")..................................... 8-12 58
CAPITOL (4009 "Handy Andy") .. 8-12 58
CAPITOL (4092 "Our Great Love")...................................... 8-12 58
CAPITOL (6000 series)................. 5-8 64
CLASSIC ARTISTS...................... 3-5 89
GROOVE (0031 "I'll Follow You") 2500-3000 51
GUSTO 3-4
IMPERIAL 3-5 62
KING (5221 "I Took Your Love for a Toy") 15-25 59
KING (5273 thru 5877)................8-15 59-64
LANDMARK...................................3-5 73
OWL..3-5 73
SEG-WAY (1008 "Out of Sight Out of Mind").............................8-12 62

EPs: 7–inch 33/45rpm

CAPITOL (572 "Five Keys").....75-125 55
CAPITOL (828 "The Five Keys on Stage")...........................100-150 57
(Pictures one group member's thumb in a phallic-like position.)
CAPITOL (828 "The Five Keys on Stage")............................50-100 57
(Reworked cover, with thumb removed from picture.)
CRYSTAL (101 "Five Keys")...... 10-15

LPs: 10/12–inch 33rpm

ALADDIN (806 "Best of the 5 Keys") 1000-1200 56
(Maroon label. Bootlegs have the Score reissue cover art but using the Aladdin name and number. There is no original Aladdin LPs titled *On the Town.*)
CAPITOL (828 "The Five Keys on Stage")...........................150-200 57
(In cover photo, group member on left is holding his right hand in in a phallic-like position.)
CAPITOL (828 "The Five Keys on Stage")............................75-125 57
(Reworked cover, with offending hand removed from the picture.)
CAPITOL (1769 "The Fantastic Five Keys") 75-125 62
(With "T" prefix.)
CAPITOL (1769 "The Fantastic Five Keys") 8-10 77
(With "M" prefix.)
GREAT GROUP CLASSICS........8-12 70s
HARLEM HITPARADE 10-15 72
KING (688 "The Five Keys") ..200-300 60
KING (692 "Rhythm & Blues Hits: Past and Present")..............200-300 60
SCORE (4003 "On the Town")...............................350-450 57
(Repackage of *Best of the 5 Keys,* Aladdin 806. See that listing for bootleg information.)

Members: Rudy West; Ripley Ingram; Maryland Pierce; Dickie Smith; Ray Loper; Bernie West; Ulysses Hicks; Thomas Threat.

Also see BELVIN, Jesse, & Five Keys / Feathers
Also see FANTASTIC FIVE KEYS

FIVE KEYS / Ferlin Husky

EPs: 7–inch 33/45rpm

CAPITOL (503 "Five Keys/ Ferlin Husky") 60-80 57

Also see FIVE KEYS
Also see HUSKY, Ferlin

FIVE MAN ELECTRICAL BAND

P&R/LP '71

Singles: 7-inch

CAPITOL 4-8 68-69
LION 3-5 72-73
LIONEL 3-5 71
MGM 4-8 70
POLYDOR 3-5 74

LPs: 10/12-inch 33rpm

CAPITOL 15-20 69
LION 10-12 73
LIONEL 10-15 70-71
MGM 10-15 70
PICKWICK 5-10 70s

Member: Les Emmerson.
Also see EMMERSON, Les

FIVE RED CAPS

(5 Red Caps)

P&R/R&B/C&W '44

Singles: 78rpm

BEACON 10-20 43-45
GANNETT 10-20 43-45
JOE DAVIS 10-20 43-45
DAVIS 10-15 46
MGM 10-15 48

Members: Steve Gibson; Jim Springs; Romaine Brown; Dave Patillo; Emmett Matthews.
Also see GIBSON, Steve

FIVE ROYALES

(5 Royales)

R&B '53

Singles: 78rpm

APOLLO 10-25 51-55
KING 8-15 54-56

Singles: 7-inch

ABC-PAR 5-10 62
APOLLO (441 "Courage to Love") 50-75 52
(Black vinyl.)
APOLLO (441 "Courage to Love") 100-150 52
(Colored vinyl.)
APOLLO (443 "Baby, Don't Do It") 50-75 52
APOLLO (446 "Help Me, Somebody") 50-75 53
APOLLO (448 "Laundromat Blues") 50-75 53
APOLLO (449 "I Want to Thank You") 40-60 53
APOLLO (452 "I Do") 35-45 54
APOLLO (454 "Cry Some More") 35-45 54
APOLLO (458 "What's That") 30-40 54
APOLLO (467 "With All Your Heart") 30-40 55
GUSTO 3-5 80s
HOME of the BLUES 5-10 60-62
KING (4740 thru 4785) 30-40 54-55
KING (4806 thru 4973) 20-30 55-56
KING (5000 series) 10-20 57-64
SMASH 5-8 64-65
TODD 5-10 63
VEE JAY 5-10 61-62

LPs: 10/12-inch 33rpm

APOLLO (488 "The Rockin' 5 Royales") 800-1100 59
(Green cover.)
APOLLO (488 "The Rockin' 5 Royales") 500-1000 59
(Yellow cover.)
KING (580 "Dedicated to You") 250-400 58
KING (616 "The 5 Royales Sing for You") 150-250 59
KING (678 "The 5 Royales") 150-250 60
KING (955 "24 All Time Hits") 30-60 66

Members: Johnny Tanner; Eugene Tanner; Lowman Pauling; Clarence Pauling; Jim Moore; Otto Jeffries; Obadiah "Scoop" Carter.
Also see JOHN, Little Willie / 5 Royales / Earl (Connelly) King / Midnighters
Also see ROYAL SONS QUINTET

FIVE SATANS

Singles: 7-inch

JCP (1014 "Here's to You") 10-20 60s

FIVE SATINS

(5 Satins)

P&R/R&B '56

Singles: 78rpm

EMBER 10-20 56-57
STANDORD (100 "All Mine") 50-100 56
STANDORD (200 "In the Still of the Nite") 75-125 56

Singles: 7-inch

ABC 3-4 73
CANDLELITE 3-6 70s
CHANCELLOR 10-15 62
COLLECTABLES 3-4 80s
CUB 15-20 60-61
EMBER (1005 "In the Still of the Nite") 100-200 56
(Has Ember label pasted over Standord label. Can be identified by the identification number 6106 in the vinyl trail-off.)
EMBER (1005 "In the Still of the Nite") 15-25 56
EMBER (1005 "[I'll Remember] in the Still of the Nite") 50-100 56
(White label. Promotional issue.)
EMBER (1005 "[I'll Remember] in the Still of the Nite") 25-40 59
(Red label. Reads "Special Demand Release.")
EMBER (1005 "[I'll Remember] in the Still of the Nite") 15-25 60
(Multi-color "logs" label.)

EMBER (1005 "[I'll Remember] In the Still of the Nite") 10-15 60s
(Black label. Some pressings read *In the Still of the Night,* instead of "Nite.")
EMBER (1008 "Wonderful Girl") 15-25 56
EMBER (1014 "Oh, Happy Day") 15-25 57
EMBER (1019 "To the Aisle").... 15-25 57
EMBER (1025 "Our Anniversary").......................... 15-25 57
(Red label.)
EMBER (1025 "Our Anniversary").......................... 10-15 57
(Black label.)
EMBER (1028 "Million to One"). 15-25 58
EMBER (1038 "A Night to Remember")....................... 15-25 58
EMBER (1056 thru 1070).......... 10-20 59-61
ELEKTRA (47411 "Memories of Days Gone By").............................. 15-25 82
FIRST (104 "When Your Lover Comes Along")...................... 30-40 59
(Orange label.)
FIRST (104 "When Your Lover Comes Along")...................... 15-25 59
(Green label.)
FLASHBACK.............................. 3-6 65
KIRSHNER................................. 3-5 73-74
KLIK 5-10 73
LANA.. 3-6 64
NIGHTRAIN 4-6 70
RCA.. 3-6 71
ROULETTE................................ 5-8 64
SAMMY (103 "No One Knows") 20-30
S.G. 3-5 90
STANDORD (100 "All Mine") 300-450 56
(Red label. Copies on a maroon-brown label are unauthorized reissues.)
STANDORD (200 "In the Still of the Nite") 800-1200 56
(Red label. Reads "Produced By Martin Kuegull.")
STANDORD (200 "In the Still of the Nite") 400-500 56
(Red label.)
STANDORD (5051 "All Mine") .. 25-40
TIME MACHINE.......................... 4-8 62
TIMES SQUARE...................... 10-15 63
(Colored vinyl.)
U.A. 10-20 61
W.B. 5-10 63

EPs: 7–inch 33/45rpm

EMBER (100 "The Five Satins Sing") 50-75 60
(Red label.)
EMBER (100 "The Five Satins Sing") 25-35 61
(Black or multi-color label.)
EMBER (101 "The Five Satins Sing, Vol. 2")...............50-75 60
(Red label.)
EMBER (101 "The Five Satins Sing, Vol. 2")................25-35 61
(Black or multi-color label.)
EMBER (102 "The Five Satins Sing, Vol. 3")................50-75 60
(Red label.)
EMBER (102 "The Five Satins Sing, Vol. 3")................25-35 61
(Black or multi-color label.)
EMBER (104 "In the Still of the Night")......................150-250 61

LPs: 10/12–inch 33rpm

CELEBRITY SHOWCASE.........10-12 70
COLLECTABLES........................5-10 84
EMBER (100 "The Five Satins Sing") 200-300 57
(Red label. Group is pictured on front cover.)
EMBER (100 "The Five Satins Sing") 50-100 58
(Multi-color label. Black vinyl.)
EMBER (100 "The Five Satins Sing") 500-750 58
(Multi-color label. Colored vinyl.)
EMBER (100 "The Five Satins Sing") 35-50 60
(Black label.)
EMBER (401 "The Five Satins Encore").................................50-75 60
(Black label.)
EMBER (401 "The Five Satins Encore")...................................35-50 61
(Multi-color label.)
LOST-NITE 6-10 81
MT. VERNON (108 "The Five Satins Sing") 20-30
RELIC 8-10

Members: Fred Parris; Louis Peebles; Stan Dortch; Jim Freeman; Nate Moseley; Bill Baker; Jimmy Curtis; Nate Marshall; Ed Martin; John Brown; Tom Killebrew; Al Denby; Jess Murphy; Wes Forbes; Richard Freeman.

Also see BLACK SATIN
Also see CARYL, Naomi
Also see GRANAHAN, Gerry
Also see NEW YORK CITY
Also see NEW YORKERS
Also see PARRIS, Fred
Also see SOUTHSIDE JOHNNY & Asbury Dukes

FIVE SATINS / Pharotones

Singles: 7–inch

TIMES SQUARE.........................5-10 63

FIVE SATINS / Youngtones / Youngsters / Shells

EPs: 7–inch 33/45rpm

NEW YORK CITY (1002 "Gus Gossert Presents")................................10-15 71

Also see FIVE SATINS
Also see SHELLS

FIVE SPECIAL

P&R/R&B/LP '79

Singles: 7–inch

ELEKTRA.................................... 3-4 79-80

LPs: 10/12–inch 33rpm

ELEKTRA.................................... 5-10 79

Member: Byran Banks.

FIVE STAIRSTEPS

(Stairsteps; with Cubie)

P&R/R&B '66

Singles: 7–inch

BUDDAH 4-6 67-68
COLLECTABLES 3-4 80s
CURTOM 4-6 68-69
GOLD 4-6
WINDY C.................................... 4-8 66-67

Picture Sleeves

BUDDAH 4-8 67-68

LPs: 10/12–inch 33rpm

BUDDAH 10-12 68-70
COLLECTABLES 6-8 85
CURTOM 8-10 69
WINDY C.............................. 10-15 67

Members: Clarence Burke Jr.; James Burke; Keni Burke; Dennis Burke; Cubie Burke; Aloha Burke.

Also see BURKE, Keni
Also see INVISIBLE MAN'S BAND
Also see ISLEY BROTHERS / Brooklyn Bridge
Also see STAIRSTEPS

FIVE STAR

P&R/R&B/D&D/LP '85

Singles: 12–inch 33/45rpm

RCA... 4-6 85-86

Singles: 7–inch

RCA... 3-4 85-87

Picture Sleeves

RCA... 3-4 86

LPs: 10/12–inch 33rpm

RCA... 5-10 85-86

5000 VOLTS

P&R '75

Singles: 7–inch

PHILIPS 3-5 75
PRIVATE STOCK 3-5 76

FIXX

P&R/LP '82

Singles: 12–inch 33/45rpm

MCA 4-6 82-86

Singles: 7–inch

MCA 3-5 82-90
RCA... 3-4 89

Picture Sleeves

MCA 3-5 83-84
RCA... 3-4 89

LPs: 10/12–inch 33rpm

MCA (Except 8642)..................... 5-10 82-91
MCA (8642 "Talkabout") 8-12 80s
(Interviews with Fixx. Promotional issue only.)
RCA 5-8 89

Members: Cy Curnin; Adam Woods; Danny Brown; Alfi Agies; Jamie West; Rupert Greenall.

FIZZY QWICK

R&B '86

Singles: 7–inch

MOTOWN 3-4 86

FLACK, Roberta

LP '70

Singles: 7–inch

ATLANTIC...................................3-5 69-88
MCA 3-4 81
VIVA...3-4 83

Picture Sleeves

ATLANTIC...................................3-4 78-82

LPs: 10/12–inch 33rpm

ATLANTIC.................................5-10 69-88
VIVA...5-10 83

Also see CHIC / Leif Garrett / Roberta Flack / Genesis
Also see McCANN, Les
Also see WATANABE, Sadao, & Roberta Flack

FLACK, Roberta, & Peabo Bryson

R&B/LP '80

Singles: 7–inch

ATLANTIC...................................3-4 80
CAPITOL.....................................3-4 83

Picture Sleeves

CAPITOL.....................................3-4 83

LPs: 10/12–inch 33rpm

ATLANTIC.................................5-10 80
CAPITOL...................................5-10 83

Also see BRYSON, Peabo
Also see FLACK, Roberta

FLACK, Roberta, & Donny Hathaway

R&B/LP '72

Singles: 7–inch

ATLANTIC...................................3-5 71-80

LPs: 10/12–inch 33rpm

ATLANTIC.................................5-10 72-80

Also see HATHAWAY, Donny

FLACK, Roberta, & Eric Mercury

R&B '83

Singles: 7–inch

ATLANTIC...................................3-4 83

Also see FLACK, Roberta

FLAGG, Fannie

LP '67

LPs: 10/12–inch 33rpm

RCA 10-15 66

FLAME

P&R '70

Singles: 7–inch

BROTHER 10-15 70-71

LPs: 10/12–inch 33rpm

BROTHER (2500 "The Flame") .20-30 70
(Includes bonus poster.)

Members: Rick Fataar; Terry "Blondie" Chaplin; Steve Fataar; Brother Fataar.

Also see RUTLES

FLAME

LP '77

Singles: 7–inch

RCA... 3-4 78

LPs: 10/12–inch 33rpm

RCA... 5-10 77-78

Members: Marge Raymond; Jim Crespo; Frank Ruby.

FLAMIN' GROOVIES

LP '76

Singles: 7–inch

BOMP... 3-5 74
EPIC... 4-6 69-70
KAMA SUTRA... 3-5 71
SIRE... 4-6 76-79

Picture Sleeves

BOMP... 4-8 74

EPs: 7–inch 33/45rpm

SKYDOG... 5-10

LPs: 10/12–inch 33rpm

BUDDAH... 10-12 77
EPIC (26487 "Supernazz")........ 35-45 69
KAMA SUTRA (2021 "Flamingo")........................... 15-25 70
(Pink label.)
KAMA SUTRA (2021 "Flamingo")........................... 10-15 70s
(Blue label.)
KAMA SUTRA (2031 "Teenage Head")................................ 15-25 71
(Pink label.)
KAMA SUTRA (2031 "Teenage Head")................................ 10-15 70s
(Blue label.)
SIRE... 10-12 76-79
SNAZZ (2371 "Sneakers") 60-80 68
(10–inch LP.)
VOXX... 5-10

Members: Roy Loney; Cyril Jordan; George Alexander; Tim Lynch; Danny Mihm; Chris Wilson; James Farrell; David Wright.

FLAMING EMBER

P&R '69

Singles: 7–inch

HOT WAX... 3-6 69-70

LPs: 10/12–inch 33rpm

HOT WAX... 10-15 70-71

Members: Joe Sladich; Jerry Plunk; Bill Ellis; Jim Bugnel.
Also see FLAMING EMBERS

FLAMINGOS
(With Red Holloway's Orchestra)

R&B '56

Singles: 78rpm

CHANCE (1133 "Someday, Someway")........................... 50-100 53
CHANCE (1140 "That's My Desire")................................ 50-100 53
CHANCE (1145 "Golden Teardrops")............................ 50-100 53
CHANCE (1149 "Plan for Love").. 50-100 53
CHANCE (1154 "Cross over the Bridge")............................ 50-100 54
CHANCE (1162 "Blues in the Letter")................................ 50-100 54
CHECKER (815 "When")........... 15-25 55
CHECKER (821 "Please Come Back Home")........................... 15-30 55
CHECKER (830 "I'll Be Home") . 15-30 56
CHECKER (837 thru 915)........... 8-15 56-57
DECCA... 5-10 57
PARROT (808 "Dream of a Lifetime")................................ 50-100 54
PARROT (812 "I'm Yours")...... 75-150 55

Singles: 7–inch

ABC... 3-5 73
CHANCE (1133 "If I Can't Have You")........................... 300-400 53
(Black vinyl.)
CHANCE (1133 "If I Can't Have You")........................... 500-750 53
(Colored vinyl.)
CHANCE (1140 "That's My Desire")................................ 300-400 53
(Black vinyl.)
CHANCE (1140 "That's My Desire")................................ 500-750 53
(Colored vinyl.)
CHANCE (1145 "Golden Teardrops")............................ 500-750 53
(Black vinyl.)
CHANCE (1145 "Golden Teardrops")........................ 1500-2500 53
(Colored vinyl.)
CHANCE (1149 "Plan for Love").. 400-500 53
(Yellow and black label.)
CHANCE (1149 "Plan for Love").. 300-400 53
(Blue and silver label.)
CHANCE (1154 "Cross over the Bridge")............................ 400-600 54
CHANCE (1162 "Blues in the Letter")................................ 250-350 54
CHECKER (815 "When")........... 25-50 55
CHECKER (821 "Please Come Back Home")........................... 25-50 55
CHECKER (830 "I'll Be Home") . 25-50 56
CHECKER (837 "Kiss from Your Lips")............................ 20-30 56
CHECKER (846 "The Vow")...... 20-30 56
CHECKER (853 "Would I Be Crying")........................... 20-30 56
CHECKER (915 "Dream of a Lifetime")............................ 10-20 59

CHECKER (1084 "Lover Come Back to Me")............................ 5-10 64
CHECKER (1091 "Goodnight Sweetheart") 5-10 64
CHESS.. 3-4 73
COLLECTABLES 3-4 80s
DECCA..................................... 8-15 57-59
END (1035 "Please Wait for Me").................................... 30-40 58
(Title later changed to *Lovers Never Say Goodbye.*)
END (1035 "Lovers Never Say Goodbye")....................... 10-20 58
END (1040 "But Not for Me") 10-15 58
END (1044 "At the Prom")......... 10-15 58
END (1046 "I Only Have Eyes For You"/"At the Prom") 10-15 59
END (1046 "I Only Have Eyes for You"/ "Goodnight Sweetheart")......... 15-25 59
(Note different flip.)
END (1046 "I Only Have Eyes for You")....................... 40-50 59
(Stereo.)
END (1055 "Love Walked In")..... 8-12 59
(Monaural.)
END (1055 "Love Walked In")... 35-45 59
(Stereo.)
END (1062 thru 1124)................ 6-12 59-62
JULMAR....................................... 4-6 69
OLDIES 45 .... 4-8 64
PARROT (808 "Dream of a Lifetime")........................... 250-300 54
(Black vinyl.)
PARROT (808 "Dream of a Lifetime")......................... 750-1000 54
(Colored vinyl.)
PARROT (811 "I Really Don't Want to Know") 500-750 55
(Black vinyl.)
PARROT (811 "I Really Don't Want to Know") 3000-4000 55
(Colored vinyl.)
PARROT (812 "I'm Yours")... 250-300 55
(Black vinyl.)
PARROT (812 "I'm Yours"). 750-1000 55
(Colored vinyl.)
PHILIPS 4-8 66
POLYDOR.................................... 3-5 70
RONZE... 3-5 71-76
ROULETTE.................................. 5-8 63
TIMES SQUARE 8-12 64
VEE JAY 5-10 61
WORLDS 3-5 75

EPs: 7–inch 33/45rpm

END (205 "Goodnight Sweetheart") 40-60 59
(Monaural.)
END (205 "Goodnight Sweetheart") 50-85 59
(Stereo.)

LPs: 10/12–inch 33rpm

CHECKER (1433 "Flamingos") 75-125 59
(Monaural.)
CHECKER (3005 "Flamingos")..25-50 66
(Stereo.)
CHESS...6-12 76-84
CONSTELLATION 15-20 64
EMUS..5-10 79
END (304 "Flamingo Serenade")..............................30-50 59
(Monaural.)
END (304 "Flamingo Serenade")..............................50-75 59
(Stereo.)
END (307 "Flamingo Favorites") 20-35 60
(Monaural.)
END (307 "Flamingo Favorites") 25-40 60
(Stereo.)
END (308 "Requestfully Yours")..................................20-35 60
(Monaural.)
END (308 "Requestfully Yours") 25-40 60
(Stereo.)
END (316 "The Sound of the Flamingos")............................20-35 62
(Monaural.)
END (316 "The Sound of the Flamingos")..................25-40 62
(Stereo.)
LOST-NITE 5-10 81
MEKA...10-15
PHILLIPS 15-25 66
RONZE 10-15 72-73
ROULETTE.....................................8-10 81-84
SOLID SMOKE 5-10 82

Members: Sollie McElroy; John Carter; Zeke Carey; Jake Carey; Paul Wilson; Nate Nelson; Tommy Hunt; Terry Johnson.
Also see HUNT, Tommy

FLAMINGOS / Moonglows

Singles: 7–inch

TRIP..3-5

LPs: 10/12–inch 33rpm

VEE JAY (1052 "The Flamingos Meet the Moonglows") 30-40 62
Also see FLAMINGOS
Also see MOONGLOWS

FLANAGAN, Ralph

P&R '49

Singles: 78rpm

BLUEBIRD 3-6 49
RCA 3-5 50-57

Singles: 7–inch

CORAL..3-6 61

IMPERIAL 3-8 59
RCA... 4-8 50-57

EPs: 7-inch 33/45rpm

CAMDEN....................................... 4-8 54
RCA... 5-10 51-57

LPs: 10/12-inch 33rpm

CAMDEN.................................. 10-20 54
GOLDEN ERA.............................. 4-8 76
IMPERIAL 8-15 58-59
RCA.. 10-20 51-57

FLARES
(Flairs)

P&R/R&B '61

Singles: 7-inch

COLLECTABLES.......................... 3-4 80s
FELSTED (8604 "Loving You")... 8-12 60
FELSTED (8607 "Jump and Bump") 8-12 60
PRESS 4-8 62-63

Picture Sleeves

FELSTED (8607 "Jump and Bump") 20-30 60

LPs: 10/12-inch 33rpm

PRESS (73001 "Encore of Foot Stompin' Hits") 25-35 61
(Monaural.)
PRESS (83001 "Encore of Foot Stompin' Hits") 30-40 61
(Stereo.)
Members: Aaron Collins; Willie Davis; Tom Miller; Randy Jones.
Also see CADETS
Also see PEPPERS

FLARES / Ramrocks

Singles: 7-inch

FELSTED (8624 "Foot Stompin") 6-10 61
Also see FLARES

FLASH

P&R/LP '72

Singles: 7-inch

CAPITOL.. 3-5 72

LPs: 10/12-inch 33rpm

CAPITOL (11000 series)............ 5-10 77
(With "SM" prefix.)
CAPITOL (11000 series)............ 8-10 72-73
(With "SMAS" or "ST" prefix.)
Also see BANKS, Peter

FLASH & PAN

P&R/LP '79

Singles: 12-inch 33/45rpm

EPIC.. 4-6 81-83

Singles: 7-inch

EPIC.. 3-4 79-83

LPs: 10/12-inch 33rpm

EPIC.. 5-10 79-82
Members: Harry Vanda; George Young.
Also see EASYBEATS

FLASH CADILLAC & Continental Kids

P&R '74

Singles: 7-inch

EPIC..4-8 72-74
PRIVATE STOCK 4-6 74-77

LPs: 10/12-inch 33rpm

EPIC...10-12 72-74
PRIVATE STOCK 8-10 75
Also see WOLFMAN JACK

FLATT, Lester, & Earl Scruggs
(With the Foggy Mountain Boys; Flatt & Scruggs)

C&W '52

Singles: 78rpm

COLUMBIA 4-8 51-57
MERCURY 5-10 49-53

Singles: 7-inch

COLUMBIA (20000 & 21000 series)..8-15 51-56
COLUMBIA (40000 thru 42000 series)..5-10 56-63
COLUMBIA (43000 thru 45000 series) 4-8 64-67
MERCURY 10-15 50-53

Picture Sleeves

COLUMBIA 4-8 62-68
MERCURY 4-6 68

EPs: 7-inch 33/45rpm

COLUMBIA 10-20 57-60

LPs: 10/12-inch 33rpm

COLUMBIA (30 "Flatt & Scruggs") 8-12 75
COLUMBIA (400 series) 10-15 69
COLUMBIA (1000 & 2000 series, except 1019)............................10-25 60-68
COLUMBIA (1019 "Foggy Mountain Jamboree") 30-50 57
COLUMBIA (8000 & 9000 series)......................................10-25 60-70
(With "CS" prefix.)
COLUMBIA (8000 & 9000 series) 5-10
(With "PC" prefix.)
COLUMBIA (10000 series) 6-12 73
COLUMBIA (30000 thru 37000 series) 5-12 70-82
COPPER CREEK 5-10
COUNTY.......................................5-10
EVEREST 5-10 71-82
51 WEST.......................................5-10 80s
HARMONY...................................8-15 60-71
MERCURY (20000 series).........20-40 58-63
(Monaural.)
MERCURY (60000 series).........20-30 63
(Stereo.)
MERCURY (61000 series).........10-15 68
NASHVILLE 8-10 70
PICKWICK/HILLTOP 8-12 68

POWER PAK 5-10
ROUNDER
WING 8-12 68
Members: Lester Flatt; Earl Scruggs; Mac Wiseman; Jim Shoemate; Cedric Rainwater.
Also see SCRUGGS, Earl

FLATT, Lester, Earl Scruggs, & Doc Watson

LPs: 10/12-inch 33rpm

COLUMBIA 10-15 67
Also see FLATT, Lester, & Earl Scruggs
Also see WATSON, Doc

FLAVOR

P&R '68

Singles: 7-inch

COLUMBIA 4-6 68

Picture Sleeves

COLUMBIA 4-6 68

LPs: 10/12-inch 33rpm

JU-PAR 8-10 77

FLAVOUR, La: see LA FLAVOUR

FLEAS

Singles: 7-inch

CHALLENGE (9115 "Scratchin") 20-30 61
Members: Dave Burgess; Glen Campbell; Jerry Fuller; Ricky Nelson.
Also see CLAMPBELL, Glen
Also see FULLER, Jerry
Also see NELSON, Rick

FLEETWOOD, Mick

LP '81

LPs: 10/12-inch 33rpm

RCA.. 5-10 81
Also see FLEETWOOD MAC

FLEETWOOD MAC

LP '68

Singles: 12-inch 33/45rpm

W.B. (652 "Go Your Own Way") 15-25 76
(Promotional issue only.)
W.B. (2688 "Big Love").............. 15-25 87
(Promotional issue only.)

Singles: 7-inch

BLUE HORIZON 4-8 70
DJM.. 4-8 73
EPIC (10351 "Black Magic Woman") 5-10 68
EPIC (10368 "Stop Messin' Around") 5-10 68
EPIC (10436 "Albatross").............. 3-5 69
EPIC (11029 "Albatross").............. 3-5 73
EPIC (139609 "Albatross")............ 4-8
(Promotional issue only.)
REPRISE 3-6 69-76
W.B. (Except 8304)...................... 3-4 77-90
W.B. (8304 "Go Your Own Way") 8-12 76

Picture Sleeves

EPIC (139609 "Albatross")......... 8-10 69
(Promotional issue only.)
W.B. 3-6 77-88

LPs: 10/12-inch 33rpm

BLUE HORIZON (3801 "Fleetwood Mac in Chicago") 20-25 70
BLUE HORIZON (4803 "Blues Jam in Chicago, Vol. 1") 20-25 70
BLUE HORIZON (4805 "Blues Jam in Chicago, Vol. 2") 20-25 70
BLUE HORIZON (66227 "Blues Jam at Chess") 20-25 69
BLUE HORIZON (83110 "Mr. Wonderful") 20-25
COLUMBIA SPECIAL PROD.......8-12 73
EPIC (26402 "Peter Green's Fleetwood Mac")....................................20-30 68
EPIC (26446 "English Rose") 20-25 69
EPIC (30632 "Black Magic Woman") 15-25 71
(Repackage of *Fleetwood Mac* and *English Rose.*)
EPIC (33740 "English Rose") 10-15 73
EPIC (33740 "Fleetwood Mac/ English Rose") 10-15 74
(Repackage of *Black Magic Woman.*)
MFSL (012 "Fleetwood Mac")....30-60 78
MFSL (119 "Mirage") 20-30 84
NAUTILUS (8 "Rumours")..........20-30 80
(Half-speed mastered.)
REPRISE (Except 6368).............8-15 70-77
REPRISE (6368 "Then Play On")..15-25 69
(Without *Oh Well.*)
REPRISE (6368 "Then Play On")..10-15 69
(With *Oh Well.*)
SIRE...8-10 75-77
VARRICK 5-10 85
W.B. 8-12 77-90
Members: Mick Fleetwood; John McVie; Peter Green; Jeremy Spencer; Danny Kirwin; Christine McVie; Bob Welch; Bob Weston; Dave Walker; Lindsay Buckingham; Stevie Nicks; Rick Vito; Billy Burnette.
Also see BUCKINGHAM, Lindsay
Also see BURNETTE, Billy
Also see FLEETWOOD, Mick
Also see GREEN, Peter
Also see MAYALL, John
Also see McVIE, Christine
Also see NICKS, Stevie
Also see WELCH, Bob

FLEETWOOD MAC / Danny Kirwan

Singles: 7-inch

DJM..4-8 73
Also see FLEETWOOD MAC

FLEETWOODS

P&R/R&B '59

Singles: 7-inch

DOLPHIN (1 "Come Softly to Me") 15-25 59
(No mention of distribution by Liberty.)

DOLPHIN (1 "Come Softly to Me") 10-20 59
(Reads: "Distributed by Liberty Record Sales Co.")
DOLTON (3 "Graduation's Here") 5-10 59
(Monaural.)
DOLTON (S-3 "Graduation's Here") 15-25 59
(Stereo.)
DOLTON (5 thru 315) 5-15 59-66
LIBERTY (55188 "Come Softly to Me") 8-12 59
(Monaural.)
LIBERTY (77188 "Come Softly to Me") 10-20 59
(Stereo.)
U.A. 3-5 74

Picture Sleeves

DOLTON (22 "Runaround") 10-15 60

EPs: 7-inch 33/45rpm

DOLTON (502 "Fleetwoods") 20-30 60

LPs: 10/12-inch 33rpm

DOLTON (2001 "Mr. Blue") 25-35 59
(Monaural.)
DOLTON (8001 "Mr. Blue") 30-40 59
(Stereo.)
DOLTON (2002 thru 2039) 20-30 60-65
(Monaural.)
DOLTON (8002 thru 8039) 20-35 60-65
(Stereo.)
LIBERTY 5-10 82-83
SUNSET 10-15 66
U.A. 8-10 75

Members: Gary Troxel; Barbara Ellis; Gretchen Christopher.
Also see VEE, Bobby / Johnny Burnette / Ventures / Fleetwoods

FLEMONS, Wade
(With the Newcomers)

P&R/R&B '58

Singles: 7-inch

VEE JAY (Maroon label) 15-25 58-59
VEE JAY (Black label) 10-20 61-63

LPs: 10/12-inch 33rpm

VEE JAY (1011 "Wade Flemons") 40-50 59
(Maroon label.)
VEE JAY (1011 "Wade Flemons") 15-25 61
(Black label.)

Also see EARTH, WIND & FIRE
Also see SKYLINERS / Wade Flemons

FLENOY, Julian

R&B '86

Singles: 7-inch

KMA 3-4 86

FLESH for LULU

LP '87

Singles: 12-inch 33/45rpm

MCA 4-6 85

Singles: 7-inch

MCA 3-4 85

LPs: 10/12-inch 33rpm

CAPITOL 5-10 87
MCA 5-10 85

Members: Nick Marsh; James Mitchell; Rocco Barker; Kevin Mills; Derek Grenning.

FLESHTONES

LP '82

Singles: 7-inch

I.R.S. 3-4 81-82

LPs: 10/12-inch 33rpm

I.R.S. 5-10 81-82

Members: Jonithan Weiss; Marek Pakulski; Keith Streng; Bill Milhiser; Peter Zaromba.

FLETCHER, Darrow

P&R/R&B '66

Singles: 7-inch

CONGRESS 3-5 70
CROSSOVER 3-4 75-79
GROOVY 4-8 66
REVUE 4-6 68
UNI 3-5 70-71

FLETCHER, Dusty

R&B '47

Singles: 78rpm

NATIONAL 8-12 47

FLETCHER, Lois

P&R '74

Singles: 7-inch

PLAYBOY 3-5 74

FLEX, M.C., & FBI Crew

D&D '84

Singles: 12-inch 33/45rpm

POSSE 3-4 84

FLINT, Shelby

P&R '60

Singles: 7-inch

CADENCE 5-10 58
QUANTUM 4-6
VALIANT 4-8 60-66

LPs: 10/12-inch 33rpm

VALIANT (401 "Shelby Flint") 25-40 61
VALIANT (403 "Shelby Flint Sings Folk") 25-35 61
(Monaural.)
VALIANT (WS-403 "Shelby Flint Sings Folk") 35-50 61
(Stereo.)
VALIANT (5003 "Cast Your Fate to the Wind") 15-25 66
(Monaural.)

VALIANT (25003 "Cast Your Fate to the Wind") 20-30 66
(Stereo.)

FLIP CARTRIDGE: see CARTRIDGE, Flip

FLIRTATIONS

P&R '69

Singles: 7-inch

DERAM 4-6 69
PARROT 4-8 68

LPs: 10/12-inch 33rpm

DERAM 15-20 69
Members: Ernestine Pearce; Shirley Pearce; Viola Billups.
Also see GYPSIES

FLIRTATIONS

D&D '83

Singles: 12-inch 33/45rpm

D&D 4-6 83

FLIRTS

D&D '84

Singles: 12-inch 33/45rpm

CBS ASSOCIATES 4-6 86
TELEFON.................................... 4-6 84

Singles: 7-inch

CBS ASSOCIATES 3-4 86
O RECORDS 3-4 82

LPs: 10/12-inch 33rpm

CBS ASSOCIATES 5-10 86
O RECORDS 5-10 82

FLOATERS

P&R/R&B/LP '77

Singles: 7-inch

ABC 3-4 77-79

Picture Sleeves

ABC 3-4 77

LPs: 10/12-inch 33rpm

ABC 5-10 77-79
Members: Charles Clark; Paul Mitchell; Ralph Mitchell; Larry Cunningham; Jonathan Murray.

FLOCK, The

LP '69

Singles: 7-inch

COLUMBIA 4-6 69-70
DESTINATION 5-10 66-67
U.S.A... 4-8 68

LPs: 10/12-inch 33rpm

COLUMBIA 10-15 69-71
MERCURY 8-10 75

FLOCK of SEAGULLS, A

P&R/LP '82

Singles: 12-inch 33/45rpm

JIVE... 4-6 82-83

Singles: 7-inch

JIVE... 3-4 82-86

Picture Sleeves

JIVE... 3-4 82-84

LPs: 10/12-inch 33rpm

JIVE 5-10 82-86

FLOOD, Dick

(With the Pathfinders)

P&R '59

Singles: 7-inch

EPIC...4-6 61-62
KAPP 3-6 65
MONUMENT.................................4-8 59-60
NASCO 3-5 71-72
NUGGET......................................3-6 68
TOTEM 3-6 67

FLOS

R&B '87

Singles: 7-inch

SUPERSTAR I. 3-4 87

FLOTSAM & JETSAM

LP '88

Singles: 12-inch 33/45rpm

ELEKTRA.....................................4-8 88
(Promotional only.)

Singles: 7-inch

ELEKTRA.....................................3-4 88

LPs: 10/12-inch 33rpm

ELEKTRA.....................................5-8 88
MCA 5-8 90

FLOYD, Eddie

P&R/R&B '66

Singles: 7-inch

ATLANTIC..................................5-10 65
LU-PINE......................................8-12 63
MALACO 3-6 77
MERCURY 3-6 78
SAFICE 5-10 64
STAX...3-8 66-75

LPs: 10/12-inch 33rpm

ATCO 8-10 74
MALACO 5-10 77
STAX...10-20 67-79
Also see FALCONS
Also see MOORE, Dorothy, & Eddie Floyd
Also see REDDING, Otis / Carla Thomas / Sam & Dave / Eddie Floyd

FLOYD, Eddie, & Mavis Staples

Singles: 7-inch

STAX...3-6 69
Also see FLOYD, Eddie
Also see STAPLES, Mavis

FLOYD, King: see KING FLOYD

FLYING BURRITO BROTHERS

LP '69

Singles: 7-inch

A&M 3-6 69-70
COLUMBIA 3-5 76
REGENCY 3-4 80

LPs: 10/12-inch 33rpm

A&M 10-15 69-76

COLUMBIA 8-10 75-76
REGENCY 5-10 80
SHILO ("Sneaky Pete") 20-30 79
(Number not known.)

Members: Gram Parsons; Chris Hillman; Bernie Leadon; Al Perkins; Rick Roberts; Mike Clarke; Pete Battin; Pete Kleinow; Greg Harris; Ed Ponder; Gib Guilbeau; John Beland

Also see BURRITO BROTHERS
Also see FIREFALL
Also see HILLMAN, Chris
Also see PARSONS, Gram

FLYING LIZARDS

P&R '79

Singles: 7-inch

VIRGIN 3-4 79

Picture Sleeves

VIRGIN 3-4 79

LPs: 10/12-inch 33rpm

VIRGIN 5-10 80

FLYING MACHINE

P&R/LP '69

Singles: 7-inch

CONGRESS 4-8 69-70
JANUS 4-8 69

LPs: 10/12-inch 33rpm

JANUS 10-15 69

Members: Tony Newman; Stuart Coleman; Steve Jones; Paul Wilkinson.

Also see TAYLOR, James

FOCUS

P&R/LP '73

Singles: 7-inch

ATCO 3-5 75
SIRE 3-5 73

LPs: 10/12-inch 33rpm

ATCO 8-10 74-75
SIRE 8-10 72-77

Also see AKKERMAN, Jan

FOCUS

R&B '87

Singles: 7-inch

EMI AMERICA 3-4 87

FOCUS & P.J. Proby

LPs: 10/12-inch 33rpm

HARVEST 5-10 78

Also see FOCUS
Also see PROBY, P.J.

FOGELBERG, Dan

LP '74

Singles: 7-inch

COLUMBIA 4-6 73
EPIC 3-5 74-75
FULL MOON/EPIC 3-5 75-82
FULL MOON 3-4 82-87

Picture Sleeves

FULL MOON/EPIC 3-4 80-87

LPs: 10/12-inch 33rpm

COLUMBIA 10-15 72
EPIC 8-10 74-78
EPIC/FULL MOON 8-10 75-82
FULL MOON 5-10 82-90

Also see FOOLS GOLD

FOGELBERG, Dan, & Tim Weisberg

LP '78

Singles: 7-inch

FULL MOON/EPIC 3-4 78-80

LPs: 10/12-inch 33rpm

FULL MOON/EPIC 5-10 78

Also see FOGELBERG, Dan
Also see WEISBERG, Tim

FOGERTY, John

P&R '72

Promotional Singles: 12-inch 33/45rpm

W.B. (2234 "Old Man Down the Road") 5-10 84
W.B. (2267 "Rock & Roll Girls") ... 5-10 85
W.B. (2337 "I Can't Help Myself") 5-10 85
W.B. (2362 "Vanz Kant Danz) 5-10 85
W.B. (2363 "Vanz Kant Danz-Edit") 5-10 85
W.B. (2514 "Eye of the Zombie") . 5-10 86

Singles: 7-inch

ASYLUM 3-5 75-76
FANTASY 3-6 73
W.B. 3-4 84-86

Picture Sleeves

W.B. 3-5 84-87

LPs: 10/12-inch 33rpm

ASYLUM (1046 "John Fogerty") .. 5-10 75
W.B. (25203 "Centerfield") 10-15 84
(Last track is mistitled, *Zanz Kant Danz.*)
W.B. (25203 "Centerfield") 5-8 85
(Last track is *Vanz Kant Danz.*)
W.B. (25449 "Eye of the Zombie") . 5-8 85

Also see BLUE RIDGE RANGERS
Also see CREEDENCE CLEARWATER REVIVAL
Also see EDDY, Duane

FOGERTY, Tom
(With the Blue Velvets)

LP '72

Singles: 7-inch

FANTASY 3-5 71-82
ORCHESTRA ("Now You're Not Mine") 35-50 62
(Number not known.)
ORCHESTRA (1010 "Have You Ever Been Lonely") 35-50 61
ORCHESTRA (6177 "Come On Baby") 35-50 61
(Despite the higher number, this was the first Orchestra single.)

Picture Sleeves

FANTASY 3-5 71

LPs: 10/12-inch 33rpm

FANTASY 8-10 72-81

Members: Tom Fogerty; John Fogerty; Doug Clifford; Stuart Cook.

Also see CREEDENCE CLEARWATER REVIVAL
Also see SAUNDERS, Merl

FOGHAT

P&R/LP '72

Singles: 7-inch

BEARSVILLE 3-5 72-80
MARK-O HILDENEN ("Goin' Home for Christmas '86") 3-4 86

Picture Sleeves

BEARSVILLE 3-5 79
MARK-O HILDENEN ("Goin' Home for Christmas '86") 3-4 86

LPs: 10/12-inch 33rpm

BEARSVILLE 5-10 72-83

Members: Dave Peverett; Roger Earl; Rod Price; Tony Stevens; Erik Cartwright; Nick Jameson.
Also see JAMESON, Nick
Also see SAVOY BROWN
Also see WISHBONE ASH

FOLEY, Ellen

P&R/LP '79

Singles: 7-inch

EPIC/CLEVELAND INT'L............. 3-4 79-83

Picture Sleeves

EPIC/CLEVELAND INT'L............. 3-5 80

LPs: 10/12-inch 33rpm

EPIC/CLEVELAND INT'L........... 5-10 79-83

Also see MEAT LOAF

FOLEY, Red

(With the Cumberland Valley Boys; with His Log Cabin Quartet; with Betty Foley; with Anita Kerr Singers; with Grady Martin & His Slew Foot Five)

C&W '44

Singles: 78rpm

BANNER 10-15
DECCA (Except 30067 & 30674).. 4-10 42-57
DECCA (30067 "Rock 'N' Reelin") 10-20 56
DECCA (30674 "Crazy Little Guitar Man")........................... 10-20 58
MELOTONE 10-15
ORIOLE.................................... 10-15

Singles: 7-inch

DECCA (25000 series)................. 4-8 61-67
DECCA (27000 thru 29000 series) 8-15 50-56
DECCA (30000 series, except 30067 & 30674)... 5-10 56-59
DECCA (30067 "Rock 'N Reelin") 20-30 56
DECCA (30674 "Crazy Little Guitar Man")........................... 20-30 58
DECCA (31000 thru 32000 series) 4-8 60-67
DECCA (46000 series)................. 4-6 68
MCA 3-5 73

EPs: 7-inch 33/45rpm

DECCA...................................... 10-20 53-59

LPs: 10/12-inch 33rpm

CORAL...5-8 73
COUNTRY MUSIC.......................6-10 76
DECCA (100 series) 15-25 64
DECCA (4000 series, except 4140)..10-25 61-67
DECCA (4140 "Company's Comin'") 25-30 61
DECCA (5303 "Red Foley Souvenir Album")....................40-60 51
(10-inch LP.)
DECCA (5338 "Lift Up Your Voice") 40-60 51
(10-inch LP.)
DECCA (7100 series) 15-25 64
DECCA (8294 "Red Foley Souvenir Album")....................25-50 56
DECCA (8296 "Beyond the Sunset") 25-50 56
DECCA (8767 "He Walks with Thee")..............................20-40 58
DECCA (8806 "My Keepsake Album") 20-40 58
DECCA (8847 "Let's All Sing with Red Foley").....................20-30 59
DECCA (8903 "Let's All Sing to Him")......................................25-35 59
DECCA (75000 series) 8-12 68-69
DECCA/DICKIES ("Red Foley's Dickies Souvenir Album")..................50-100 58
(Special Products issue for the Dickies company.)
MCA...5-8 80s
PICKWICK/HILLTOP 8-12 66
VOCALION 6-12 65-71

Also see KERR, Anita
Also see WELK, Lawrence, & His Orchestra
Also see WELLS, Kitty, & Red Foley

FOLEY, Red, & Andrews Sisters

Singles: 78rpm

DECCA 4-8 54

Also see ANDREWS SISTERS

FOLEY, Red, & Little Foleys

Singles: 78rpm

DECCA 4-8 50

Singles: 7-inch

DECCA 10-15 50

Picture Sleeves

DECCA 20-30 50

Members: Red Foley; Shirley Foley, Julie Foley; Jenny Foley.
Also see FOLEY, Red

FOLKSWINGERS

LP '63

Singles: 7-inch

WORLD PACIFIC 4-6 66

LPs: 10/12-inch 33rpm

WORLD PACIFIC 10-20 63-66

Members: Glen Campbell; Tut Taylor; Harihar Rao.
Also see CAMPBELL, Glen
Also see SHANK, Bud

FONTAINE, Eddie
(Eddie Reardon)

P&R '58

Singles: 78rpm

ARGO.. 5-10 58-59
DECCA....................................... 5-10 56-57
JALO 25-35 56
VIK 5-10 56
X... 5-10 54-56

Singles: 7-inch

ARGO.. 10-15 58-59
CHANCELLOR.............................. 15-25 58
DECCA....................................... 10-20 56-57
JALO (102 "Where Is Da Woman") 50-75 56
LIBERTY 4-8 65
SUNBEAM (105 "Nothing Shakin'")................................ 30-50 58
VIK 10-15 56
W.B. 4-8 62-63
X... 10-15 54

Also see REARDON, Eddie

FONTAINE, Eddie, & Karen Chandler

Singles: 78rpm

DECCA....................................... 4-8 57

Singles: 7-inch

DECCA....................................... 5-10 57

Also see CHANDLER, Karen

FONTAINE, Eddie, & Gerry Granahan

Singles: 7-inch

SUNBEAM 10-15 58

Also see FONTAINE, Eddie
Also see GRANAHAN, Gerry

FONTAINE, Frankie
(Frank Fontaine)

LP '63

Singles: 7-inch

ABC-PAR 3-6 62-65
CAPITOL...................................... 3-6 63

Picture Sleeves

ABC-PAR 5-8 62
CAPITOL...................................... 5-8 63

LPs: 10/12-inch 33rpm

ABC-PAR 10-20 62-66
MGM 6-10 67

FONTANA, Wayne

Singles: 7-inch

BRUT 3-5 73
MGM 4-8 66-67
METROMEDIA.............................. 4-6 69

LPs: 10/12-inch 33rpm

MGM (4459 "Wayne Fontana"). 15-25 67

FONTANA, Wayne, & Mindbenders

P&R/LP '65

Singles: 7-inch

FONTANA.................................... 5-10 65

LPs: 10/12-inch 33rpm

FONTANA (27542 "The Game of Love")..................................... 30-35 65
(Monaural.)
FONTANA (67542 "The Game of Love")..................................... 35-40 65
(Stereo.)

Members: Wayne Fontana; Graham Gouldman; Bob Land; Paul Hancox; Eric Stewart; Rick Rothwell; James O'Neil.
Also see FONTANA, Wayne
Also see MINDBENDERS

FONTANE SISTERS

P&R '51

Singles: 78rpm

DOT 3-6 54-60
RCA 4-8 51-54

Singles: 7-inch

DOT 5-10 54-60
RCA 8-12 51-54

Picture Sleeves

RCA (5524 "Kissing Bridge") 10-15 54

EPs: 7-inch 33/45rpm

DOT 10-15 56-57

LPs: 10/12-inch 33rpm

DOT (Except 108)....................... 15-25 56-63
DOT (108 "Fontane Sisters") 25-40 55
(10-inch LP.)

Members: Bea Fontane; Marge Fontane; Geri Fontane.
Also see BOONE, Pat
Also see COMO, Perry, & Fontane Sisters

FOOLS, The

P&R/LP '80

Singles: 12-inch 33/45rpm

PVC... 4-6

Singles: 7-inch

EMI AMERICA 3-4 80-81

Picture Sleeves

EMI AMERICA 3-5 80

LPs: 10/12-inch 33rpm

EMI AMERICA (Except 9393)...... 5-10 80-81
EMI AMERICA (9393 "April Fools Day")... 10-15 80
(Promotional issue only.)

FOOLS GOLD

P&R/LP '76

Singles: 7-inch

COLUMBIA 3-5 77
MORNING SKY 3-5 76

LPs: 10/12-inch 33rpm

COLUMBIA 8-10 77
MORNING SKY 8-10 76

Also see FOGELBERG, Dan

FORBERT, Steve

P&R/LP '79

Singles: 7–inch

NEMPEROR 3-4 79-82

LPs: 10/12–inch 33rpm

NEMPEROR 5-10 79-82

FORCE M.D.s

R&B/LP '84

Singles: 12–inch 33/45rpm

TOMMY BOY 4-6 84-86

Singles: 7–inch

TOMMY BOY 3-4 84-88
W.B. 3-4 86

Picture Sleeves

TOMMY BOY 3-4 86-88
W.B. 3-4 86

LPs: 10/12–inch 33rpm

TOMMY BOY 5-10 84-87

FORD, Ernie: see FORD, Tennessee Ernie

FORD, Frankie

P&R/R&B '59

Singles: 78rpm

ACE (549 "Cheatin' Woman") ... 25-50 58
ACE (554 "Sea Cruise") 200-300 59

Singles: 7–inch

ABC 3-4 73-74
ACE 8-15 58-60
BRIARMEADE 3-5
CINNAMON 3-5
COLLECTABLES 3-4 81
CONSTELLATION 4-8 63
DOUBLOON 4-8 67
IMPERIAL 5-10 60-62
PAULA 3-5 71
SYC 3-4 82
20TH FOX 4-8 60s

Picture Sleeves

ACE (592 "Chinatown") 15-25 60

EPs: 7–inch 33/45rpm

ACE (105 "Best of Frankie Ford") 50-75 59

LPs: 10/12–inch 33rpm

ACE (1005 "Let's Take a Sea Crusie") 75-125 59
BRIARMEADE 8-10 76

Also see CLANTON, Jimmy / Frankie Ford / Jerry Lee Lewis / Patsy Cline
Also see SMITH, Huey

FORD, Lita

LP '84

Singles: 7–inch

MERCURY 3-5 84
RCA 3-4 88-90

Picture Sleeves

RCA 3-4 88-90

LPs: 10/12–inch 33rpm

MERCURY 5-10 84
RCA 5-8 88-90

Also see RUNAWAYS

FORD, Lita, & Ozzy Osbourne

Singles: 7–inch

RCA 3-4 89

Picture Sleeves

RCA 3-4 89

Also see FORD, Lita
Also see OSBOURNE, Ozzy

FORD, Mary: see PAUL, Les, & Mary Ford

FORD, Pennye

R&B '84

Singles: 12–inch 33/45rpm

TOTAL EXPERIENCE 4-6 84-85

Singles: 7–inch

TOTAL EXPERIENCE 3-4 84-85

LPs: 10/12–inch 33rpm

TOTAL EXPERIENCE 5-10 85

FORD, Robben

LP '88

LPs: 10/12–inch 33rpm

W.B. 5-8 88

FORD, Tennessee Ernie

(With the Green Valley Singers & Orchestra; Tennessee Ernie)

C&W/P&R '49

Singles: 78rpm

CAPITOL (1 "Sixteen Tons") 4-6 69
(Promotional "Special Commemorative Pressing" for Ford's 20th year on Capitol.)
CAPITOL (1200 thru 2900 series) . 3-6 50-57
CAPITOL (40000 series) 3-8 49-50

Singles: 7–inch

CAPITOL (1275 thru 2900 series) 5-15 50-54
(Purple labels. Ford's many "Boogie" titles represent the higher end of this price range.)
CAPITOL (2000 thru 4100 series) . 3-4 70-75
(Orange labels.)
CAPITOL (3000 thru 4400 series) . 4-8 54-60
CAPITOL (4500 thru 5700 series) . 3-5 61-67

Picture Sleeves

CAPITOL 5-10 55-60

EPs: 7–inch 33/45rpm

CAPITOL (Except 413) 5-10 55-61
CAPITOL (413 "Backwoods Boogie and Blues") 20-30 53
GREEN GIANT (2566 "When Pea-Pickers Get Together") 10-15
(Mail order offer. Add $3 to $5 if with special mailer/sleeve. Promotional issue made for the Green Giant Co.)

LPs: 10/12–inch 33rpm

CAPITOL (Except 888) 5-15 56-80
CAPITOL (888 "Ol' Rockin' Ern") 35-50 57
EVEREST 5-10 70s
PICKWICK 5-10 70s

READER'S DIGEST (241 "Tennessee Ernie Ford") 20-40
(Boxed, eight-LP set. With booklet.)
Session: Jordanaires.
Also see HUTTON, Betty, & Tennessee Ernie Ford
Also see LAWRENCE, Steve / Tennessee Ernie Ford
Also see LEE, Brenda / Tennessee Ernie Ford
Also see STARR, Kay, & Tennessee Ernie Ford

FORD, Tennessee Ernie, & Glen Campbell

LPs: 10/12-inch 33rpm

CAPITOL.................................. 10-12 75
Also see CAMPBELL, Glen

FORD, Tennessee Ernie, & Joe "Fingers" Carr

C&W '51

Singles: 78rpm

CAPITOL.................................. 4-8 51

Singles: 7-inch

CAPITOL.................................. 5-10 51
Also see CARR, Joe "Fingers"

FORD, Tennessee Ernie, & Dinning Sisters

Singles: 78rpm

CAPITOL.................................. 4-8 50s

Singles: 7-inch

CAPITOL.................................. 5-10 50s

FORD, Tennessee Ernie, & Andra Willis

C&W '75

Singles: 7-inch

CAPITOL.................................. 3-5 75
Also see FORD, Tennessee Ernie

FORDHAM, Julia

LP '88

LPs: 10/12-inch 33rpm

VIRGIN.................................. 5-8 88-90

FORECAST

R&B '80

Singles: 12-inch 33/45rpm

RCA.................................. 4-6 83

Singles: 7-inch

ARIOLA.................................. 3-4 80
RCA.................................. 3-4 83

LPs: 10/12-inch 33rpm

RCA.................................. 5-10 83

FOREIGNER

P&R/LP '77

Singles: 7-inch

ATLANTIC.................................. 3-4 77-90
ATLANTIC/W.B. 3-4 79

Picture Sleeves

ATLANTIC.................................. 3-4 78-88

LPs: 10/12-inch 33rpm

ATLANTIC.................................. 5-10 77-91
GEFFEN.................................. 5-10 85
MFSL (052 "Double Vision")...... 25-50 81
Members: Lou Gramm; Rick Wills; Mick Jones; Dennis Elliott; Ian McDonald; Al Greenwood.
Also see BAD COMPANY
Also see FRASER, Andy
Also see NEW JERSEY MASS CHOIR
Also see SPYS
Also see WALKER, Junior

FOREST, Earl: see FORREST, Earl

FOREST, Jimmy
(Jimmy Forrest)

R&B '52

Singles: 78rpm

UNITED.................................. 5-10 52-55

Singles: 7-inch

PRESTIGE.................................. 4-6 61-62
TRIUMPH.................................. 4-8 59
UNITED (Except 113) 5-10 52-55
UNITED (110 "Night Train")....... 10-20 52
(Black vinyl.)
UNITED (110 "Night Train")....... 25-35 52
(Colored vinyl.)

LPs: 10/12-inch 33rpm

NEW JAZZ (8250 "Forrest Fire") 25-50 60
NEW JAZZ (8293 "Soul Street") 25-50 62
PRESTIGE.................................. 20-30 61-62
(Yellow label.)
PRESTIGE.................................. 10-20 64
(Blue label.)
UNITED 002 "Night Train") 75-100 57
(10-inch LP.)
Also see DAVIS, Miles

FORESTER SISTERS

C&W '85

Singles: 7-inch

W.B. 3-4 84-91

LPs: 10/12-inch 33rpm

W.B. 5-8 85-91
Members: Kathy Forester; Kim Forester; June Forester; Christy Forester.
Also see BELLAMY BROTHERS & Forester Sisters

FOREVER MORE

LP '70

Singles: 7-inch

RCA 3-5 69-70

LPs: 10/12-inch 33rpm

RCA 10-15 69-70
Also see AVERAGE WHITE BAND

FORMATIONS

P&R '68

Singles: 7-inch

BANK (1007 "At the Top of the Stairs") 20-30 67
MGM (13899 "At the Top of the Stairs") 5-8 68
MGM (13963 "Love's Not Only for the Heart").................................. 10-20 68
MGM (14009 "Don't Get Close")..8-12 68
Members: Victor Drayton; Jerry Akines; Reginald Turner; Ernie Brooks; Johnny Bellman.

Also see CORNER BOYS

FORREST

D&D '83

Singles: 12-inch 33/45rpm

PROFILE 4-6 83

FORREST, Earl

(Earl Forest)

R&B '53

Singles: 78rpm

DUKE (Except 103) 5-10 52
DUKE (103 "Rock the Bottle") ... 10-20 52
METEOR 25-45 53

Singles: 7-inch

DUKE (108 "Whoopin' and Hollerin") 25-35 52
DUKE (113 "Last Night's Dream") 20-30 53
DUKE (121 "Out on a Party") .. 120-30 54
DUKE (130 "Your Kind of Love") 20-30 54
DUKE (300 series) 4-8 62-63
METEOR (5005 "I Wronged a Woman") 50-100 53

Also see ACE, Johnny / Earl Forrest

FORREST, Jimmy: see FOREST, Jimmy

FORTUNE

P&R '85

Singles: 7-inch

MCA/CAMEL 3-4 85

Picture Sleeves

MCA/CAMEL 3-4 85

LPs: 10/12-inch 33rpm

MCA/CAMEL 5-10 86

FORTUNES

P&R '65

Singles: 7-inch

CAPITOL 3-5 71-74
COLLECTABLES 3-4 80s
LONDON 3-4
PRESS (9773 "You've Got Your Troubles") 10-15 65
(White label, commercial issue.)
PRESS (9773 "You've Got Your Troubles") 5-10 65
(Color label.)
PRESS (9798 "Here It Comes Again") 10-15 65
(White label, commercial issue.)
PRESS (9798 "Here It Comes Again") 10-15 65
(Red or orange labels.)
PRESS (9811 "This Golden Ring") 5-10 66
U.A. 4-8 67-68
WORLD PACIFIC 3-5 70

LPs: 10/12-inch 33rpm

CAPITOL 8-10 71-73
COCA-COLA ("It's the Real Thing") 30-40 60s
(Special products issue.)
PRESS (73002 "The Fortunes") 20-25 65
(Monaural.)
PRESS (83002 "The Fortunes") 25-30 65
(Stereo.)
WORLD PACIFIC 8-10 70

Members: Glen Dale; Barry Pritchard; Shel MacRae.

FORUM

P&R '67

Singles: 7-inch

MIRA 10-15 67
PENTHOUSE 10-20 66

LPs: 10/12-inch 33rpm

MIRA 15-20 67

Members: Phil Campos; Rene Nole; Riselle Vaine.

FOSTER, Bruce

P&R '77

Singles: 7-inch

MILLENIUM 3-5 77

Picture Sleeves

MILLENIUM 5-10 77

LPs: 10/12-inch 33rpm

MILLENIUM 8-15 77

FOSTER, David

P&R '85

Singles: 7-inch

ATLANTIC 3-4 85-88

Picture Sleeves

ATLANTIC 3-4 85-88

LPs: 10/12-inch 33rpm

ATLANTIC 5-10 86-88
MFSL (123 "The Best of Me") 15-25 84

FOSTER, David, & Olivia Newton-John

P&R '86

Singles: 7-inch

ATLANTIC 3-4 86

Also see FOSTER, David
Also see NEWTON-JOHN, Olivia

FOSTER, Ian

R&B '87

Singles: 7-inch

MCA 3-4 87

FOSTER & LLOYD

C&W '87

Singles: 7-inch

RCA 3-4 87-90

LPs: 10/12-inch 33rpm

RCA 5-10 86-90

Members: Radney Foster; Bill Lloyd.

FOTOMAKER

P&R/LP '78

Singles: 7-inch

ATLANTIC 3-5 78-79

LPs: 10/12-inch 33rpm

ATLANTIC.................................5-10 78-79

Members: Gene Cornish; Dino Dannelli; Wally Bryson.

Also see RASCALS

Also see RASPBERRIES

FOUNDATIONS

P&R '67

Singles: 7-inch

ERIC (912 "Build Me Up Buttercup")................................3-4 70s

(True stereo.)

UNI...3-6 67-71

LPs: 10/12-inch 33rpm

UNI...15-20 68-69

Members: Clem Curtis; Colin Young.

FOUNTAIN, Pete

P&R/LP '60

Singles: 7-inch

CORAL.......................................3-5 58-62

LPs: 10/12-inch 33rpm

CORAL.......................................5-15 59-69

FIRST AMERICAN........................4-8 78

GUEST STAR.............................5-10 64

SOUTHLAND (215 "New Orleans to L.A.")................................15-25 56

Also see HIRT, Al, & Pete Fountain

Also see LEE, Brenda, & Pete Fountain

FOUNTAIN, Roosevelt, & Pens of Rhythm

P&R '63

Singles: 7-inch

PRINCE-ADAMS.......................10-20 62-63

FOUR ACES

P&R '51

Singles: 78rpm

DECCA.......................................5-10 51-57

FLASH (103 "Who's to Blame"). 10-20 50

MERION (104 "Wanted").........10-20 52

VICTORIA (Black vinyl)..............8-12 51

VICTORIA (101 "Sin")..............10-20 51

(Colored vinyl.)

Singles: 7-inch

ABC-PAR....................................4-8 60

DECCA (25000 series).................4-8 61-64

DECCA (27000 & 28000 series). 8-15 51-53

DECCA (29000 thru 31000 series)....................................5-10 54-60

FLASH (103 "Who's to Blame"). 10-20 50

MERION (104 "Wanted")..........10-15 52

VICTORIA (101 "Sin")..............15-25 51

(Black vinyl.)

VICTORIA (101 "Sin")..............35-50 51

(Colored vinyl.)

VICTORIA (102 "There's a Christmas Tree in Heaven")....................10-20 51

Picture Sleeves

ABC-PAR..................................5-10 60

EPs: 7-inch 33/45rpm

DECCA.....................................10-20 52-59

LPs: 10/12-inch 33rpm

ACCORD....................................5-10 81-82

CRANE NOTTIS..........................8-10 77

DECCA (4013 "Golden Hits").....15-25 60

DECCA (5429 "Four Aces").......20-40 52

(10-inch LP.)

DECCA (8122 thru 8693)...........15-30 55-58

DECCA (8766 "Swingin' Aces").15-25 58

(Monaural.)

DECCA (8766 "Swingin' Aces") 20-30 58

(Stereo. With "DL-7" prefix.)

DECCA (8855 "Hits from Broadway")..............................15-25 59

(Monaural.)

DECCA (8855 "Hits from Broadway")..............................20-30 59

(Stereo. With "DL-7" prefix.)

DECCA (8944 "Beyond the Blue Horizon").........................10-20 59

(Monaural.)

DECCA (8944 "Beyond the Blue Horizon").........................15-25 59

(Stereo.)

MCA..5-10 74

U.A...10-15 61

VOCALION.................................5-10 69

WESTOWN..................................5-8

Members: Al Alberts; Louis Silvestri; Dave Mahoney; Sol Vocarro.

Also see LEE, Brenda / Bill Haley & Comets / Kalin Twins / Four Aces

FOUR ACES / Four Lads / Four Preps

LPs: 10/12-inch 33rpm

EXACT.......................................5-10 80

Also see FOUR ACES

Also see FOUR LADS

Also see FOUR PREPS

FOUR BLAZES

R&B '52

Singles: 7-inch

UNITED (114 "Mary Jo")...........30-50 52

(Black vinyl.)

UNITED (114 "Mary Jo").........75-100 52

(Colored vinyl.)

UNITED (125 "Night Train").......15-25 52

UNITED (127 "Stop Boogie Woogie")................................15-25 52

UNITED (146 "Not Any More Tears")....................................15-25 53

UNITED (158 "Ella Louise").......15-25 53

UNITED (168 "My Great Love Affair")....................................15-25 54

UNITED (177 "Do the Do").......15-25 54

UNITED (191 "She Needs to Be Loved")..........................15-25 55

(Reissued as by the Blasers.)

Member: Tommy Braden.

FOUR BUDDIES

(With Lefty Bates Orchestra)

R&B '51

Singles: 78rpm

SAVOY 20-40 50-53

Singles: 7–inch

IMPERIAL (66018 "I Want to Be the Boy You Love") 25-50 64
SAVOY (769 "I Will Wait") 250-350 50
SAVOY (779 "Don't Leave Me Now") 200-300 51
SAVOY (789 "My Summer's Gone") 100-200 51
SAVOY (817 "Heart & Soul"). 100-200 51
SAVOY (845 "You're Part of Me") 100-150 52
SAVOY (866 "What's the Matter with Me") 100-150 52
SAVOY (888 "My Mother's Eyes") 100-150 53
SAVOY (891 "I'd Climb the Highest Mountain") 100-150 53

Members: Leon Harrison; Greg Carroll; Bert Palmer; Tommy Smith.
Also see FOUR BUDS

FOUR BUDS

Singles: 78rpm

SAVOY 20-40 50

Singles: 7–inch

SAVOY (769 "I Will Wait") 250-350 50
(Second pressings shown as by the Four Buddies.)
Also see FOUR BUDDIES

4 BY FOUR

P&R/R&B/LP '87

Singles: 7–inch

CAPITOL 3-4 87

Picture Sleeves

CAPITOL 3-4 87

LPs: 10/12–inch 33rpm

CAPITOL 5-10 87

FOUR COINS

P&R '54

Singles: 78rpm

EPIC 3-6 54-59

Singles: 7–inch

COLUMBIA 3-6 67
EPIC 5-10 54-59
JOY 3-6 64
JUBILEE 3-6 61-62
MGM 4-8 60-61
VEE JAY 4-8 62-63

Picture Sleeves

EPIC 5-10 57

EPs: 7–inch 33/45rpm

EPIC 5-10 55-58

LPs: 10/12–inch 33rpm

EPIC 10-20 55-58
MGM 10-15 61
ROULETTE 10-15 65

FOUR DATES

P&R '58

Singles: 7–inch

CHANCELLOR 8-12 58
Also see FABIAN

FOUR ESQUIRES

P&R '56

Singles: 78rpm

CADENCE 4-8 55
PARIS 4-8 57
PILGRIM 4-8 56

Singles: 7–inch

CADENCE 5-10 55
PARIS 8-15 57
PILGRIM 5-10 56
TERRACE 4-8 63
Also see ECHOES / Four Esquires

FOUR FELLOWS

R&B '55

Singles: 78rpm

DERBY 30-50 54
GLORY 10-20 55-57

Singles: 7–inch

DERBY (862 "I Tried") 200-300 54
GLORY (231 "I Wish I Didn't Know You") 30-40 55
GLORY (234 "Soldier Boy") 20-30 55
GLORY (236 "Angels Say") 20-30 55
GLORY (238 "Fallen Angel") 20-30 56
GLORY (241 "Petticoat Baby") ..30-40 56
GLORY (242 "Darling You") 50-75 56
GLORY (244 "I Sit in My Window") 20-30 56
GLORY (248 "You Don't Know Me") 20-30 56
GLORY (250 "Give Me Back My Broken Heart") 25-35 57
GLORY (263 "You're Still in My Heart") 20-30 57
NESTOR (27 "Remember") ... 100-200 58

Members: David Jones; Ted Williams; Larry Banks; Jim McGowan.
Also see McLAURIN, Bette

450 SL

R&B '85

Singles: 7–inch

GOLDEN BOY 3-4 85

FOUR FRESHMEN

P&R '52

Singles: 78rpm

CAPITOL 3-5 50-57

Singles: 7–inch

CAPITOL 3-8 50-65
DECCA 3-5 67
LIBERTY 3-5 68

Picture Sleeves

CAPITOL.................................... 3-8 63

EPs: 7–inch 33/45rpm

CAPITOL.................................. 5-10 54-59

LPs: 10/12–inch 33rpm

CAPITOL (With "SM" prefix) 5-10 75-79
CAPITOL (522 thru 992).......... 15-30 54-58
(With "T" prefix.)
CAPITOL (1000 & 2000 series) 10-20 58-64
(With "T" or "ST" prefix.)
CREATIVE WORLD.................. 5-10 72
LIBERTY 5-10 68-82
PHONORAMA............................. 5-8 82
SUNSET.................................. 5-10 70

Members: Don Barbour; Ross Barbour; Ken Errair; Bob Flanagan; Hal Kratzsch; Bill Comstock.

FOUR JACKS and a Jill

P&R/LP '68

Singles: 7–inch

RCA... 4-8 68

LPs: 10/12–inch 33rpm

RCA.. 10-15 68

FOUR KNIGHTS

P&R '51

Singles: 78rpm

CAPITOL.................................. 5-10 51-57
CORAL...................................... 8-12 49
DECCA.................................. 10-15 46-47
LANG-WORTH........................ 10-20 40s
(16-inch transcriptions.)

Singles: 7–inch

CAPITOL (346 "Spotlight Songs") 30-50 52
(Boxed set of three singles.)
CAPITOL (1587 thru 1914) 15-30 51-52
CAPITOL (1930 thru 2517) 10-20 52-53
CAPITOL (2654 "Oh Baby Mine")................................. 20-30 53
CAPITOL (2654 "I Get So Lonely").................................. 8-12 53
(Note title change.)
CAPITOL (2782 thru 3730) 8-12 54-57
CORAL (61936 thru 62110) 5-10 58-59
DECCA (48018 "He'll Understand and Say Well Done")..................... 50-75 52
SOUVENIR 4-8 62

EPs: 7–inch 33/45rpm

CAPITOL (346 "Spotlight Songs") 50-75 52
(Two-EP set.)
CAPITOL (414 "The Four Knights Sing") 40-60 53
CAPITOL (506 "I Get So Lonely")............................... 40-60 54

LPs: 10/12–inch 33rpm

CAPITOL (H-346 "Spotlight Songs") 100-200 52
(10–inch LP.)
CAPITOL (T-346 "Spotlight Songs") 100-200 55
CORAL (57221 "Four Knights") 50-100 58
CORAL (57309 "Million Dollar Baby") 30-60 60
(Monaural.)
CORAL (757309 "Million Dollar Baby") 50-75 60
(Stereo.)

Members: Gene Alford; John Wallace; Clarence Dixon; Oscar Broadway.

Also see COLE, Nat "King"
Also see HUNT, Pee Wee

FOUR LADS

P&R '52

Singles: 78rpm

COLUMBIA 3-5 52-58
OKEH...4-6 52

Singles: 7–inch

COLUMBIA 4-8 52-60
DOT 3-5 62
FONA..3-4 77-78
KAPP 3-6 60-61
OKEH...5-10 52
U.A. 3-5 63-69

Picture Sleeves

COLUMBIA 10-15 56-59
KAPP 4-8 60

EPs: 7–inch 33/45rpm

COLUMBIA 5-15 55-59

LPs: 10/12–inch 33rpm

AC 8-10
COLUMBIA (912 "On the Sunny Side")...........................20-30 56
COLUMBIA (1045 "The Four Lads Sing Frank Loesser") 20-30 57
COLUMBIA (1111 "Four on the Aisle")...............................15-25 58
(Monaural.)
COLUMBIA (1223 "Breezin' Along") 15-25 58
(Monaural.)
COLUMBIA (1235 "Greatest Hits") 15-25 58
COLUMBIA (1299 thru 1550).....10-20 59-60
(Monaural.)
COLUMBIA (2576 "Stage Show") 20-30 56
(10–inch LP.)
COLUMBIA (6329 "Stage Show") 25-40 54
(10–inch LP.)
COLUMBIA (8035 "Breezin' Along") 20-30 58
(Stereo.)
COLUMBIA (8047 "Four on the Aisle")...............................20-30 58
(Stereo.)

COLUMBIA (8106 thru 8350).... 15-25 59-60
(Stereo.)
DOT.. 10-15 62-63
ENCORE.. 5-8 86
FONA.. 8-12 76-77
KAPP.. 10-15 61
HARMONY.. 5-10 69
U.A. 8-12 64
VIKING.. 5-10
Members: Frankie Busseri; Jimmy Arnold; Connie Coderini; Bernie Toorish.
Also see FOUR ACES / Four Lads / Four Preps
Also see LAINE, Frankie, & Four Lads
Also see RAY, Johnnie

FOUR LOVERS

P&R '56

Singles: 78rpm

EPIC (9255 "My Life for Your Love") 50-100 57
RCA.. 10-15 56-57

Singles: 7-inch

EPIC (9255 "My Life for Your Love") 250-300 57
MAGIC CARPET.......................... 3-5
RCA (6518 "You're the Apple of My Eye") 20-30 56
RCA (6519 "Honey Love") 20-30 56
RCA (6646 "Jambalaya") 15-25 56
RCA (6768 "Happy Am I") 15-25 57
RCA (6812 "Shake a Hand")..... 20-30 57
RCA (6819 "Night Train") 15-25 57

EPs: 7-inch 33/45rpm

RCA (869 "The Four Lovers") 150-200 56
RCA (871 "Joyride")............. 400-500 56

LPs: 10/12-inch 33rpm

RCA (1317 "Joyride")........... 500-750 56
Members: Frankie Valli; Tom Devito; Nick Devito; Hank Majewski.
Also see 4 SEASONS
Also see VALLI, Frankie

FOUR LOVERS / Homer & Jethro

EPs: 7-inch 33/45rpm

RCA (47 "The Four Lovers/ Homer & Jethro") 30-50 56
(Promotional only. Not issued with cover.)
Also see HOMER & JETHRO

FOUR LOVERS / Teddi King

EPs: 7-inch 33/45rpm

RCA (64 "The Four Lovers/ Teddi King") 30-50 56
(Promotional only. Not issued with cover.)

FOUR MINTS

R&B '73

Singles: 7-inch

CAPSOUL................................ 8-15 73
HOLIDAY 10-20 73

LPs: 10/12-inch 33rpm

CAPSOUL................................ 10-20 73

FOUR PENNIES

P&R '63

Singles: 7-inch

LAURIE..3-5
RUST (5070 "When the Boy's Happy") 15-25 63
RUST (5071 "My Block")...........15-25 63
Members: Judy Craig; Barbara Lee; Patricia Bennett; Sylvia Peterson.
Also see CHIFFONS

FOUR PREPS

P&R '56

Singles: 78rpm

CAPITOL..3-6 56-57

Singles: 7-inch

CAPITOL (3576 thru 5074, except 4568)..............................5-10 56-63
CAPITOL (4568 "Dream Boy, Dream") 20-30 61
CAPITOL (5143 "A Letter to the Beatles") 15-25 64
CAPITOL (5178 thru 5921)............4-8 64-67

Picture Sleeves

CAPITOL..8-12 61-62

EPs: 7-inch 33/45rpm

CAPITOL..8-15 56-58

LPs: 10/12-inch 33rpm

CAPITOL..15-25 58-67
Members: Bruce Belland; Glen Larson; Marv Ingraham; Ed Cobb; Don Clarke.
Also see FOUR ACES / Four Lads / Four Preps
Also see KINGSTON TRIO / Four Preps

4 SEASONS

(Four Seasons; Frankie Valli & 4 Seasons)

P&R/R&B/LP '62

Singles: 7-inch

BOB CREWE PRESENTS.........10-15 70
(Promotional issue only.)
COLLECTABLES (Except 9) 3-4 81
COLLECTABLES (9 "Greatest Hits")..30-40 81
(Boxed 6 disc set. Colored vinyl.)
COLUMBIA (6675 "Big Man's World")..25-35 64
(Promotional soundsheet.)
CREWE (333 "And That Reminds Me") 4-8 69
GONE (5122 "Bermuda")...........20-40 61
MCA/CURB..................................3-5 85-86
MOTOWN 5-10 73
MOWEST..................................5-10 72
OLDIES 45..................................4-8 62-63
PHILIPS (40166 thru 40662)..........4-8 64-69
PHILIPS (40688 "Lay Me Down") 15-25 70
PHILIPS (40694 "Where Are My Dreams")..........................20-25 70
PHILIPS DOUBLE-HIT 4-8
RAINBOW..................................4-8 62

SEASONS 4-EVER (Black vinyl) .. 4-6 71
SEASONS 4 EVER (Colored vinyl).. 10-12 71
VEE JAY (456 thru 562)............ 5-10 62-63
VEE JAY (576 "Stay"/ "Peanuts") 40-50 63
VEE JAY (582 "Stay"/"Goodnight My Love").. 5-10 64
VEE JAY (597 "Alone") 10-15 64
(Yellow label.)
VEE JAY (597 "Alone") 8-10 64
(Black label.)
VEE JAY (597 "Alone") 5-8 64
(Multi-color label.)
VEE JAY (608 thru 719)........... 10-15 64-66
VEE JAY (901 "Peanuts") 75-100 63
(Single-sided. Promotional issue only.)
WABC RADIO (77 "Cousin Brucie Go Go") 75-100 64
(Special products custom pressing. Colored vinyl.)
WXYZ-DETROIT (121003 "Jody Reynolds' Theme")................ 50-75 65
(Special products custom pressing.)
W.B. 3-5 75-80
WIBBAGE (WIBG "Jody Reynolds' Theme")................ 50-75 65
(Special products custom pressing.)

Picture Sleeves

CREWE (333 "And That Reminds Me") 10-15 69
PHILIPS (Except 40542).......... 10-20 64-70
PHILIPS (40542 "Saturday's Father")................................... 20-30 68
(Fold-out sleeve.)
PHILIPS (40542 "Saturday's Father") 5-10 68
(Standard sleeve.)
VEE JAY (539 "Candy Girl") 30-40 64
VEE JAY (626 "I Saw Mommy Kissing Santa Claus")......................... 15-20 64

EPs: 7-inch 33/45rpm

MAGIC CARPET 4-8
PHILIPS (2705 "Edizone D'Oro") 20-30 68
(Jukebox issue.)
VEE JAY (901 "Peanuts + 3") ... 20-35 64
VEE JAY (902 "Alone + 3") 20-35 64

LPs: 10/12-inch 33rpm

ARISTA 8-12 84
CANDLELITE (151 "Complete Musical Treasury") 35-45 82
(Boxed 5-LP set.)
CANDLELITE (151B "Souvenirs in Gold") 10-15 82
(Bonus LP, offered to buyers of the above set.)
ERA.. 5-10 82
FBI... 10-15 84
GUEST STAR (1481 "Bermuda & Spanish Lace")......................................15-20 64
(Also has tracks by the Barrons, a.k.a. the Crescendos.)
KOALA..5-10 80
K-TEL.......................................15-20 77
LONGINES (95833 "Greatest Hits of Frankie Valli & 4 Seasons") 25-35
(Boxed 4-LP set. TV mail-order offer.)
LONGINES (95833 "Greatest Hits of Frankie Valli & 4 Seasons") 20-30
(Gatefold 4-LP set. TV mail-order offer.)
MCA..5-10 85
MCA/CURB.................................5-10 88
MOTOWN 5-10 80
MOWEST 10-12 72
PHILIPS (200124 "Dawn and 11 Other Great Hits") 15-20 64
(Monaural.)
PHILIPS (200129 "Born to Wander")...................................15-20 64
(Monaural.)
PHILIPS (200146 "Rag Doll") 15-20 64
(Monaural.)
PHILIPS (200164 "The 4 Seasons Entertain You")..........................15-20 65
(Monaural.)
PHILIPS (200193 "Big Hits By Burt Bacharach, Hal David & Bob Dylan") 50-65 65
(Photos of group on front and back cover. Monaural.)
PHILIPS (200193 "Big Hits By Burt Bacharach, Hal David & Bob Dylan") 15-20 65
(No group photos on cover. Monaural.)
PHILIPS (200196 "Gold Vault of Hits") 15-20 65
(Monaural.)
PHILIPS (200201 "Working My Way Back to You")...........................15-20 66
(Monaural.)
PHILIPS (200221 "2nd Gold Vault of Hits") 15-20 66
(Monaural.)
PHILIPS (200222 "Lookin' Back") 15-20 66
(Monaural.)
PHILIPS (200223 "Christmas Album")......................................15-25 66
(Stereo.)
PHILIPS (200243 "New Gold Hits")..15-20 67
(Monaural.)
PHILIPS (600124 "Dawn and 11 Other Great Hits") 15-20 64
(Stereo.)

PHILIPS (600129 "Born to Wander") 15-20 64
(Stereo.)
PHILIPS (600146 "Rag Doll").... 15-20 64
(Stereo.)
PHILIPS (600164 "The 4 Seasons Entertain You") 15-20 65
(Stereo.)
PHILIPS (600193 "Big Hits By Burt Bacharach, Hal David & Bob Dylan") 50-65 65
(Photos of group on front and back cover. Stereo.)
PHILIPS (600193 "Big Hits By Burt Bacharach, Hal David & Bob Dylan") 15-20 65
(No group photos on cover. Stereo.)
PHILIPS (600196 "Gold Vault of Hits") 15-20 65
(Stereo.)
PHILIPS (600201 "Working My Way Back to You") 15-20 66
(Stereo.)
PHILIPS (600221 "2nd Gold Vault of Hits") 15-20 66
(Stereo.)
PHILIPS (600222 "Lookin' Back") 15-20 66
(Stereo.)
PHILIPS (600223 "Christmas Album") 15-25 66
(Stereo.)
PHILIPS (600243 "New Gold Hits") 15-20 67
(Stereo.)
PHILIPS (600290 "Genuine Imitation Life Gazette") 35-45 69
(Yellow cover.)
PHILIPS (600290 "Genuine Imitation Life Gazette") 10-15 69
(White cover.)
PHILIPS (341 "Half and Half"). 110-15 70
PHILIPS (2-6501 "Edizone D'Oro") 20-25 68
(With either red or blue cover.)
PICKWICK 8-10 70
PRIORITY 8-10 86
PRIVATE STOCK 10-12 75
RHINO (Except 72998) 6-12
RHINO (72998 "25th Anniversary") 15-25 87
(4-LP set.)
SEARS (609 "Brotherhood of Man") 20-30 70
TIME-LIFE (15 "Rock & Roll Era") 15-20 87
VEE JAY (1053 "Sherry") 30-40 62
(Monaural.)
VEE JAY (1053 "Sherry") 50-75 62
(Stereo.)
VEE JAY (1055 "Four Seasons Greetings") 30-40 62
VEE JAY (1056 "Big Girls Don't Cry") 30-40 63
VEE JAY (1059 "Ain't That a Shame") 30-40 63
VEE JAY (1065 "Golden Hits") .. 30-40 63
VEE JAY (1082 "Folk-Nanny")... 40-50 64
VEE JAY (1082 "Stay and Other Great Hits") 20-30 64
(Repackage of *Folk-Nanny.*)
VEE JAY (1088 "More Golden Hits") 25-35 64
VEE JAY (1121 "We Love Girls") 25-35 64
VEE JAY (1154 "Recorded Live on Stage") 25-35 65
WCI (502 "Silver Anniversary") .. 15-25 85
(3-LP set.)
W.B. 8-10 75-81

Members: Frankie Valli; Tom Devito; Nick Devito; Hank Majewski; Bob Gaudio; Charlie Calello; Nick Massi; Joe Long; Don Ciccione; Bill Deloach; Paul Wilson; Jerry Corbetta.

Also see BEACH BOYS with Frankie Valli & 4 Seasons
Also see BEATLES / 4 Seasons
Also see CRESCENDOS
Also see CREWE, Bob
Also see FOUR LOVERS
Also see JAN & DEAN / Roy Orbison / 4 Seasons / Shirelles
Also see RASCALS / Buggs / Four Seasons / Johnny Rivers
Also see RIVERS, Johnny / 4 Seasons / Jerry Butler / Jimmy Soul
Also see ROYAL TEENS
Also see SANTOS, Larry
Also see SIMON, Paul
Also see VALLI, Frankie
Also see WONDER WHO

4 SEASONS / Connie Francis / Barbara Brown & Buggs

LPs: 10/12-inch 33rpm

CORONET (244 "At the Hop")... 15-25 64

Also see FRANCIS, Connie

4 SEASONS / Little Royal

Singles: 7-inch

GORDA 4-8 65

4 SEASONS / Scarlets

Singles: 7-inch

OLDIES 45 .... 5-10 63

4 SEASONS / Ray Stevens

Singles: 7-inch

OLDIES 45 .... 5-10 63

Also see 4 SEASONS
Also see STEVENS, Ray

FOUR SONICS

P&R/R&B '68

Singles: 7-inch

SPORT.. 4-8 68

Members: Eddy Daniels; James Johnson; Steve Gaston; Willie Frazier.

FOUR SPORTSMEN

P&R '61

Singles: 7-inch

SUNNYBROOK (1 "Surrender") 25-35 60
SUNNYBROOK (2 thru 6).......... 8-12 61-62

FOUR TOPS

P&R/R&B '64

Singles: 12-inch 33/45rpm

ABC.. 4-8 77-78
MOTOWN 4-8 80

Singles: 78rpm

CHESS (1623 "Could It be You") 50-75 56

Singles: 7-inch

ABC/DUNHILL 3-5 75-79
ARISTA 3-4 88
CASABLANCA............................. 3-4 81-82
CHESS (1623 "Could It be You") 100-200 56
COLUMBIA (41755 "Lonely Summer")............................. 50-75 60
COLUMBIA (43356 "Lonely Summer") 15-25 65
DUNHILL....................................... 3-5 72-74
MOTOWN (400 series) 3-4
MOTOWN (1062 thru 1254).......... 3-8 64-72
MOTOWN (1706 thru 1854).......... 3-4 83-86
MOTOWN/TOPPS (5 "I Can't Help Myself")............................ 50-75 67
MOTOWN/TOPPS (9 "Baby I Need Your Loving") 50-75 67
(Topps Chewing Gum promotional item. Single-sided, cardboard flexi, picture disc.)
RSO 3-4 82
RIVERSIDE (4534 "Pennies from Heaven") 50-75 62

Picture Sleeves

ARISTA 3-4 88
MOTOWN (1073 "Ask the Lonely")....................................... 50-75 64
MOTOWN (1098 "Reach Out I'll Be There")............................ 20-40 66
MOTOWN (1164 "It's All in the Game").. 8-10 70
MOTOWN (1175 "Just Seven Numbers")............................... 8-10 71
RSO 3-5 82

EPs: 7-inch 33/45rpm

MOTOWN (60647 "On Top") 25-50 66
CASABLANCA........................... 5-10 81-82
COMMAND 10-12 74
DUNHILL..................................... 8-10 72-74
GORDY...................................... 5-10 85
MOTOWN (100 & 200 series)....... 5-10 82-84
MOTOWN (622 "Four Tops").....20-30 64
MOTOWN (634 "Second Album") 15-25 65
MOTOWN (647 "On Top") 15-20 66
MOTOWN (654 "Live")..............15-25 66
MOTOWN (662 "Greatest Hits") 12-20 67
MOTOWN (704 thru 748) 10-20 70-72
MOTOWN (764 "Best of the Four Tops") 10-15 73
MOTOWN (6000 series)..............5-8 83-86
MOTOWN (9809 "Anthology") ... 15-20 74
MOTOWN (M9809 "Anthology") 10-15 86
PICKWICK 5-8 74
NATURAL RESOURCES 8-10 78
WORKSHOP (217 "Jazz Impressions")........................500-750 62

Members: Levi Stubbs; Lawrence Payton; Abdul "Duke" Fakir; Obie Benson.
Also see HOLLAND - DOZIER
Also see PAYTON, Lawrence
Also see SUPREMES & Four Tops

FOUR TOPS / Temptations

LPs: 10/12-inch 33rpm

SILVER EAGLE 6-10 87

Also see FOUR TOPS
Also see TEMPTATIONS

FOUR TUNES

P&R/R&B '53

Singles: 78rpm

ARCO...5-10 50
COLUMBIA 5-10 48
JUBILEE 5-10 53-57
MANOR...5-10 46-49
RCA 5-15 49-53

Singles: 7-inch

JUBILEE (5128 "Marie") 20-30 53
JUBILEE (5132 thru 5276)......... 12-25 53-57
JUBILEE (6000 "Marie") 5-10 59
KAY-RON (1000 "I Want to Be Loved") 20-30 54
KAY-RON (1005 "I Understand")..................................20-30 54
RCA (0008 "You're Heartless") 100-150 49
(Colored vinyl.)
RCA (0016 "My Last Affair") ..100-150 49
(Colored vinyl.)
RCA (0042 "I'm Just a Fool in Love").......................100-150 49
(Colored vinyl.)
RCA (0072 "Am I Blue")..........75-125 50
(Colored vinyl.)
RCA (0085 "Old Fashioned Love")...................................75-125 50
(Colored vinyl.)
RCA (0131 "May That Day Never Come")........................75-125 51

RCA (3881 "Do I Worry") 30-40 50
RCA (3967 "Cool Water").......... 25-35 50
RCA (4102 "Wishing You Were Here Tonight") 25-35 51
RCA (4241 "I Married an Angel") 15-25 51
RCA (4280 "It's No Sin") 20-30 51
RCA (4305 "Early in the Morning").............................. 15-25 51
RCA (4427 "I'll See You in My Dreams") 20-30 51
RCA (4489 "Come What May"). 10-20 52
RCA (4663 "I Wonder") 10-20 52
RCA (4828 "They Don't Understand") 10-20 52
RCA (4968 "I Don't Want to Set the World on Fire") 20-30 52
RCA (5532 "Don't Get Around Much Anymore") 15-25 53
VIRGO.. 3-4 72

EPs: 7-inch 33/45rpm

RCA (586 "Four Tunes") 50-75 54

LPs: 10/12-inch 33rpm

JUBILEE (1039 "12 x 4").......... 50-75 57

Members: Jim Nabbie; Danny Owens; William "Pat" Best; Jimmy Gordon; Deek Watson.
Also see CHURCHILL, Savannah

FOUR TUNES / Shadows

LPs: 10/12-inch 33rpm

CHICAGO 8-10 88

Also see FOUR TUNES

FOUR VAGABONDS

P&R/R&B '43

Singles: 78rpm

APOLLO.................................. 10-20 46-47
ATLAS.................................... 10-20 46
BLUEBIRD 15-30 42-43
LLOYDS (102 "P.S. I Love You") 25-40 53
MERCURY 15-25 46
MIRACLE 10-15 49

Singles: 7-inch

LLOYDS (102 "P.S. I Love You") 200-300 53

EPs: 7-inch 33/45rpm

LLOYDS (706 "Four Vagabonds") 200-300 54

Members: Johnny Jordan; Robert O'Neal; Ray Grant; Norval Taborn.
Also see VAGABONDS

FOUR VOICES

P&R '56

Singles: 78rpm

COLUMBIA 4-8 55-57

Singles: 7-inch

ABC-PAR 4-8 61
COLUMBIA 5-10 55-60
PEACOCK................................. 4-8 62

FOUR WINDS

(4 Winds; Tokens)

Singles: 7-inch

B.T. PUPPY 5-8 69
CRYSTAL BALL..............................3-5 77
SWING...10-20 64

Also see TOKENS

FOUR-EVERS

(Four Evers)

P&R '64

Singles: 7-inch

CHATTAHOOCHEE 4-8 64
COLUMBIA (42303 "You Belong to Me") 30-50 62
COLUMBIA (42303 "You Belong to Me") 75-100 62
(With "3" prefix. Compact 33 Single.)
COLUMBIA (43886 "A Lovely Way to Spend an Evening") 5-10 66
CONSTELLATION.....................10-15 65
CRYSTAL BALL..............................3-6
JAMIE 5-10 63
JASON SCOTT...............................3-5
RED BIRD.....................................10-15 66
SMASH (1853 "It's Love")..........10-15 63
SMASH (1887 "Please Be Mine")..10-20 63
SMASH (1887 "Be My Girl") 10-20 64
(Same selection number used on both issues above.)
SMASH (1921 "Doo Be Dum")...10-15 63

LPs: 10/12-inch 33rpm

MAGIC CARPET..........................8-10

FOURPLAY

LP '91

LP: 10/12-inch 33rpm

W.B. 5-8 91

Members: Bob James; Lee Ritenour; Harvey Mason; Nathan East.
Also see JAMES, Bob
Also see RITENOUR, Lee

FOWLEY, Kim

LP '69

Singles: 7-inch

CAPITOL...4-6 72-73
CREATIVE FAMILY 15-25
IMPERIAL 5-10 68-69
LIVING LEGEND 10-15 65-66
LOMA...5-10 66
ORIGINAL SOUND.........................4-8 60s
REPRISE 5-10 67
TOWER..5-10 67

LPs: 10/12-inch 33rpm

CAPITOL (11075 "I'm Bad").......15-25 72
CAPITOL (11159 "International Heroes")...................................10-20 73
CAPITOL (11248 "Automatic")...10-20 74
IMPERIAL (12413 "Born to Be Wild") 15-25 68

IMPERIAL (12423 "Outrageous") 15-25 69
IMPERIAL (12443 "Good Clean Fun") 15-20 69
PVC (7906 "Sunset Boulevard") . 8-12 79
TOWER (5080 "Love Is Alive and Well") 25-30 67
Also see KING LIZARD
Also see PAUL & VICTORS / Kim Fowley

FOX
(Noosha Fox)
P&R '75

Singles: 7–inch

ARIOLA/GTO 3-5 75
GTO 3-5 74

LPs: 10/12–inch 33rpm

ARIOLA AMERICA 8-10 75

FOX, Charles
P&R '81

Singles: 7–inch

HANDSHAKE 3-4 81

FOX, Samantha
P&R/LP '86

Singles: 12–inch 33/45rpm

JIVE 4-6 86

Singles: 7–inch

JIVE 3-4 86-89

Picture Sleeves

JIVE 3-4 86-89

LPs: 10/12–inch 33rpm

JIVE 5-10 86-88

FOX, Virgil
LP '71

LPs: 10/12–inch 33rpm

DECCA 10-12 71

FOXX, Inez
(With Charlie Foxx)
P&R/R&B '63

Singles: 7–inch

DYNAMO 4-6 67-70
LANA 3-6 60s
MUSICOR 4-8 66-68
SUE 4-8 65
SYMBOL 5-10 63-64
VOLT 3-5 72-73
U.A. 3-5 74

LPs: 10/12–inch 33rpm

DYNAMO 10-15 67
SUE (1037 "Inez & Charlie Fox") 20-25 65
(Monaural.)
SUE (1037 "Inez & Charlie Fox") 25-30 65
(Stereo.)
SYMBOL (4400 "Mockingbird"). 35-45 63
VOLT 8-10 73
Also see PLATTERS / Inez & Charlie Foxx / Jive Five / Tommy Hunt

FOXX, Redd
(With Hattie Noel)
LP '72

Singles: 78rpm

DOOTO (Except 416) 3-5 57-61
DOOTO (416 "Real Pretty Mama") 10-15 57
DOOTONE 3-5 56-57
SAVOY 5-10 46

Singles: 7–inch

DOOTO (Except 416) 5-10 57-61
DOOTO (416 "Real Pretty Mama") 15-25 57
DOOTONE 8-12 56-57

EPs: 7–inch 33/45rpm

DOOTO 5-10 57-61
DOOTONE 5-10 56-57

LPs: 10/12–Inch 33rpm

ATLANTIC 5-10 75
AUTHENTIC 15-25 55-56
DOOTO 5-15 60-74
DOOTONE 10-20 57
KING 5-10 69-71
LAFF 5-10 79
LOMA 8-12 66-68
MF 5-8
RCA 5-10 72
W.B. 8-10 69

FOZZIE BEAR: see KERMIT / Fozzie Bear

FRAMPTON, Peter
LP '72

Singles: 7–inch

A&M (Except 1988) 3-5 74-81
A&M (1988 "Tried to Love") 3-6 77
(With Mick Jagger.)
A&M (1988 "Tried to Love") 10-15 77
(White label, promotional issue.)
ATLANTIC 3-4 86

Picture Sleeves

A&M (Except 1988) 3-5 74-81
A&M (1988 "Tried to Love") 4-6 77
ATLANTIC 3-4 86

LPs: 10/12–inch 33rpm

A&M (3000 & 4000 series) 6-12 72-82
ATLANTIC 5-10 86-89

Promotional LPs

A&M (3703 "Frampton Comes Alive") 10-15 79
(Picture disc.)
A&M (4704 "I'm in You") 15-25 77
(Picture disc.)
ATLANTIC (848 "Frampton Is Alive") 8-15 86
Also see FRAMPTON'S CAMEL
Also see JAGGER, Mick
Also see STARR, Ringo

FRAMPTON'S CAMEL

(Peter Frampton)

Singles: 7–inch

A&M 5-10 72-73

LPs: 10/12–inch 33rpm

A&M 10-20 73

Also see FRAMPTON, Peter
Also see HUMBLE PIE

FRANCE JOLI: see JOLI, France

FRANCHI, Sergio

(With Anna Moffo)

LP '62

Singles: 7–inch

LAX 3-4 79
METROMEDIA 3-4 71-72
RCA 3-6 62-67
U.A. 3-5 69-70

LPs: 10/12–inch 33rpm

FOUR CORNERS 6-10 66
RCA 5-15 62-77
U.A. 5-10 70

FRANCIS, Connie

P&R/R&B '58

Singles: 78rpm

MGM 4-8 55-58

Singles: 7–inch

GSF 3-5 73
IVANHOE 3-5 70s
MGM CELEBRITY SCENE (CS6-5 "Connie Francis") 30-40 66
(Boxed set of five singles with bio insert and title strips.)
MGM (9 "Rock-a-Bye Your Baby with a Dixie Melody") 20-30 60
(Stereo.)
MGM (10 "I Almost Lost My Mind") 20-30 60
(Stereo.)
MGM (3000 series) 3-5 71
MGM (12015 "Freddy") 25-50 55
MGM (12056 "Oh, Please Make Him Jealous") 25-50 55
MGM (12122 thru 12555) 15-25 55-57
MGM (12588 thru 13116) 5-15 58-63
MGM (13127 thru 14091 except 13550) 5-10 64-69
MGM (13550 "A Nurse in the U.S. Army Corp") 20-25 66
(Promotional issue only.)
MGM (14500 series) 3-5 81
MGM (50117 "My Happiness") .. 20-30 58
(Stereo.)
MGM (50129 "You're Gonna Miss Me") 20-30 59
(Stereo.)
MGM (50133 "Among My Souvenirs") 20-30 59
(Stereo.)
POLYDOR 3-4 83

Picture Sleeves

MGM (12000 series except 12738) 5-15 58-61
MGM (12738 "My Happiness") .. 10-15 58
(Pink sleeve.)
MGM (12738 "My Happiness") .. 15-25 58
(Black and white sleeve.)
MGM (13000 series, except 13505 & 13773) 5-10 61-68
MGM (13505 "Empty Chapel") ... 10-20 66
MGM (13773 "My Heart Cries for You") 10-20 67
MGM (14000 series, except 14058 & 14091) 3-6 68-69
MGM (14058 "Gone Like the Wind") 10-20 69
MGM (14091 "Mr. Love") 10-20 69

EPs: 7–inch 33/45

MGM 10-20 58-62

LPs: 10/12–inch 33rpm

LEO 12-15 60s
LION 12-15 60s
MGM (100 series) 10-15 70
MGM (E-3686 "Who's Sorry Now") 30-40 58
(Yellow label. Monaural.)
MGM (SE-3686 "Who's Sorry Now") 15-25 60
(Reprocessed stereo.)
MGM (E-3761 "Exciting Connie Francis") 25-35 58
(Yellow label. Monaural.)
MGM (SE-3761 "Exciting Connie Francis") 30-40 58
(Yellow label. Stereo.)
MGM (E-3776 & E-3969) 20-30 60-61
(Monaural.)
MGM (SE-3776 & SE-3969) 20-35 60-61
(Monaural.)
MGM (E-4000 series) 15-25 62-68
(Monaural.)
MGM (SE-4000 series) 15-25 62-69
(Monaural.)
MGM (5400 series) 5-10
MGM (10000 series) 8-12 71
MGM (91000 series) 10-15 60s
(Capitol Record Club series.)
MATI-MOR (8002 "Brylcreem Presents Sing Along with Connie Francis") 15-25 61
(Promotional issue, made for Brylcreem.)
METRO 10-15 65-66
MGM/SESSIONS 10-12 75
POLYDOR 5-10 83

Session: Jordanaires; Boots Randolph.
Also see CRAMER, Floyd
Also see 4 SEASONS / Connie Francis / Barbara Brown & Buggs
Also see RANDOLPH, Boots

FRANCIS, Connie, & Marvin Rainwater

Singles: 78rpm

MGM 5-10 57

Singles: 7-inch

MGM 10-15 57

Also see FRANCIS, Connie
Also see RAINWATER, Marvin

FRANCIS, Connie, & Hank Williams Jr.

LPs: 10/12-inch 33rpm

MGM 15-25 64

Also see FRANCIS, Connie
Also see WILLIAMS, Hank, Jr.

FRANKE & KNOCKOUTS

P&R/LP '81

Singles: 7-inch

MCA 3-4 84
MILLENNIUM 3-4 81-82

LPs: 10/12-inch 33rpm

MCA 5-10 84
MILLENNIUM 5-10 81-82

FRANKIE & SPINDELS

R&B '68

Singles: 7-inch

ROC-KER 4-8 68

FRANKIE GOES to HOLLYWOOD

P&R/D&D/LP '84

Singles: 12-inch 33/45rpm

ISLAND 4-6 84-86

Singles: 7-inch

ISLAND 3-4 84-86

Picture Sleeves

ISLAND 3-4 84-85

LPs: 10/12-inch 33rpm

ISLAND 5-10 84-86

Members: Holly Johnson; Paul Rutherford.
Also see JOHNSON, Holly

FRANKLIN, Aretha

R&B '60

Singles: 12-inch 33/45rpm

ARISTA 4-8 84-86

Singles: 7-inch

ARISTA 3-5 80-91
ATLANTIC (2000 series) 3-6 67-74
ATLANTIC (3000 series) 3-4 74-79
ATLANTIC (13000 series) 3-4
CHECKER 5-10 60
COLUMBIA (Except 44000 series) 4-8 60-67
COLUMBIA (44000 series) 3-6 67-68
CHESS 3-5 73

Picture Sleeves

ARISTA 3-4 85-87
COLUMBIA 5-10 62-63

EPs: 7-inch 33/45rpm

ATLANTIC (33093 "Let It Be") .. 10-15 70
(Promotional issue only.)
COLUMBIA 10-15 64
(Jukebox issues.)

LPs: 10/12-inch 33rpm

ARISTA 5-10 80-89
ATLANTIC (Except "QD" series) .8-15 67-79
ATLANTIC ("QD" series) 15-20 73
(Quadrophonic.)
BATTLE 5-15
CANDLELITE 8-10 77
CHECKER 15-20 65
COLUMBIA (12 "Aretha Franklin") 10-15 68
COLUMBIA (1612 thru 2281) 12-25 61-64
(Monaural.)
COLUMBIA (2300 thru 2700 series) 10-20 65-67
(Monaural.)
COLUMBIA (8402 thru 9081) 15-30 61-64
(With "CS" prefix. Stereo.)
COLUMBIA (9100 thru 9700 series) 10-15 65-69
(With "CS" prefix. Stereo.)
COLUMBIA (10000 series) 5-10 73
COLUMBIA (30000 series) 5-10 72-82
HARMONY 10-12 68-71
UPFRONT 5-10 79

Also see CLEMONS, Clarence
Also see EURYTHMICS & Aretha Franklin
Also see SANTANA
Also see SIMON, Paul
Also see SWEET INSPIRATIONS
Also see WOLF, Peter

FRANKLIN, Aretha, & George Benson

P&R/R&B '81

Singles: 7-inch

ARISTA 3-4 81

Picture Sleeves

ARISTA 3-4 81

Also see BENSON, George

FRANKLIN, Aretha, with James Cleveland & Southern California Community Choir

EPs: 7-inch 33/45rpm

ATLANTIC (1025 "Amazing Grace") 4-8 72
(Promotional issue only.)

LPs: 10/12-inch 33rpm

ATLANTIC 6-10 72

FRANKLIN, Aretha, & Larry Graham

Singles: 7-inch

ARISTA 3-4 87

Also see GRAHAM, Larry

FRANKLIN, Aretha, & Whitney Houston

P&R '89

Singles: 7-inch

ARISTA 3-4 89

Picture Sleeves

ARISTA 3-4 89

Also see HOUSTON, Whitney

FRANKLIN, Aretha, & Elton John

P&R '89

Singles: 7–inch

ARISTA 3-4 89

Picture Sleeves

ARISTA 3-4 89

Also see JOHN, Elton

FRANKLIN, Aretha, & George Michael

P&R/R&B '87

Singles: 7–inch

ARISTA 3-4 87

Picture Sleeves

ARISTA 3-4 87

Also see MICHAEL, George

FRANKLIN, Aretha / Union Gap / Blood, Sweat & Tears / Moby Grape

EPs: 7–inch 33/45rpm

COLUMBIA (791 "The Tipalet Experience").......................... 15-25 68

(Columbia Special Products issue for Tipalet cigars.)

Also see BLOOD, SWEAT & TEARS
Also see FRANKLIN, Aretha
Also see MOBY GRAPE
Also see PUCKETT, Gary

FRANKLIN, Bobby
(With Insanity; with Friends)

R&B '75

Singles: 7–inch

BABY... 3-5 75
COLUMBIA 3-5 76
LAKESIDE..................................... 3-5 72
THOMAS....................................... 4-8 69

FRANKLIN, Carolyn

R&B '69

Singles: 7–inch

RCA... 3-5 69-73

LPs: 10/12–inch 33rpm

RCA.. 10-12 69-73

FRANKLIN, Doug
(With the Bluenotes)

P&R '58

Singles: 7–inch

COLONIAL................................. 5-10 58-59

FRANKLIN, Erma

P&R/R&B '67

Singles: 7–inch

BRUNSWICK 4-8 69
EPIC... 10-20 61-63
SHOUT....................................... 5-10 67-68

LPs: 10/12–inch 33rpm

BRUNSWICK 10-15 69
EPIC (619 "Her Name Is Erma") 30-40 62
(Stereo.)
EPIC (3824 "Her Name Is Erma") 20-30 62
(Monaural.)

FRANKLIN, Rodney

R&B/LP '80

Singles: 7–inch

COLUMBIA 3-4 80-86

LPs: 10/12–inch 33rpm

COLUMBIA 5-10 80-86

FRANTICS

P&R '59

Singles: 7–inch

BOLO 5-10 62
DOLTON 10-15 59-61
SEAFAIR.......................................4-8 64

Members: Ron Petersen; Dick Goodman; Jim Manolides; Chuck Schoning; Bob Hosko.

Also see MOBY GRAPE

FRASER, Andy

P&R '84

Singles: 7–inch

ISLAND 3-4 84

Picture Sleeves

ISLAND 3-4 84

Also see FREE

FRAZIER, Dallas

P&R '66

Singles: 78rpm

CAPITOL.......................................4-8 54

Singles: 7–inch

CAPITOL (2000 thru 2400 series) .3-6 67-69
CAPITOL (2800 & 2900 series) ...8-12 54
CAPITOL (5500 series) 4-8 65
JAMIE 5-10 59
MERCURY 4-6 64
MUSIKRON...................................4-8 61
RCA 3-5 71-73
20TH FOX......................................3-5 75

LPs: 10/12–inch 33rpm

CAPITOL...................................10-20 66-67
RCA 8-12 70-71

FRAZIER, Dallas, & Joe "Fingers" Carr

Singles: 78rpm

CAPITOL.......................................3-5 54

Singles: 7–inch

CAPITOL.....................................5-10 54

EPs: 7–inch 33/45rpm

CAPITOL.....................................8-12 54

Also see CARR, Joe "Fingers"
Also see FRAZIER, Dallas

FREBERG, Stan
(Stan Freberg Show; with Billy May's Orch.)

P&R '51

Singles: 78rpm

CAPITOL.....................................5-15 50-57

Singles: 7–inch

BELFAST SPARKLING WATER (1515 "Invisible Bubbles") 50-75
(Product commercials for radio use.)

BIG SOUND (2 "Jockey's Little Helper") 35-50
(Product commercials for radio use.)
BUBBLE UP (2227 "Music to Bubble Up By")....................... 20-30 60s
(Product commercials for radio use.
BUTTERNUT COFFEE (2000 "Instant Sales for Instant Butternut by Instant Freberg") 40-50 60s
(Product commercials for radio use.
BUTTERNUT COFFEE (2237 "Amazing Butternut Coffee") 25-35 60s
(Product commercials for radio use.)
CAPITOL (303 "The Do-It-Yourself Dragnet") 50-100 53
(Capitol in-house, record sales promotional issue only.)
CAPITOL (1200 thru 3100 series, except 2125)............... 15-25 50-54
CAPITOL (2125 "Abe Snake for President") 30-40 52
CAPITOL (3200 thru 5700 series)10-20 54-66
COCA COLA BOTTLING CO. (2227 Music to Bubble-Up By")......... 30-50 60s
(Product commercials for radio use.)
CONTADINA (4476 "The Whole Peeled Bounce") 35-50
(Product commercials for radio use. With the Hi Lo's.)
MILKY WAY (23300 "Tom Sweet & His Milky Way Machine") 35-50
PITTSBURGH PAINT (1/2 "Four Pittsburgh Paint Commercials") 20-30
(Product commercials for radio use.)
RADIO (2225 "Who Listens to Radio") 25-40
(Promotional spots for advertising with radio.)
SOUTHERN BAPTIST CHURCH (101578 "Southern Baptist Radio and TV Commission") 15-20
(Product commercials for radio use.)
STAINLESS STEEL (1369 "Stainless Steel") 35-50
(Product commercials for radio use.)
STAN FREBERG on COMMERCIALS ("Rubblemeyer Farms") 40-60 70s
(Promotional issue only. Commercial parodies, comparing right and wrong production of radio spots.)
TERMINIX (3540 "Floor Show, Now Going on at Your House")...................... 30-40
(Product commercials for radio use.)
UNITED PRESBYTERIAN CHURCH (101578 "The Presbyterian Church") 15-20
(Product commercials for radio use.)
ZEE (2020 "Zee with Freberg - Hey You Up There").......................35-50
(Product commercials for radio use.)
ZEE (24005 "Zee Spot Commercials") 35-50
(Product commercials for radio use.)

Picture Sleeves

BUBBLE UP (2227 "Music to Bubble Up By") 85-100 60s
(Gatefold sleeve.)
CAPITOL (415 "Wun'erful Wun'erful") 15-20 57
(Promotional issue only.)
CAPITOL (4097 "Green Christmas") 8-12 58
CAPITOL (4329 "The Old Payola Roll Blues") 15-20 60
CAPITOL (5726 "Flackman and Reagan")...............................10-15 66
H.I.S. (122667 "Funny Record by Stan Freberg for H.I.S.")..........35-50
(Product commercials for radio use.)
PITTSBURGH PAINT (1/2 "Four Pittsburgh Paint Commercials") 20-30
(Reads: "The Stations Representatives Assn. presents: Some Exciting New Commercials for Radio!")
RADIO (2225 "Who Listens to Radio")...............................25-40
(Promotional spots for using radio advertising.)
SOUTHERN BAPTIST CHURCH (101578 "Southern Baptist Radio & TV Commission").................15-20
(Product commercials for radio use.)
TERMINIX (3540 "Floor Show"). 10-20
(Product commercials for radio use.)
ZEE (2020 "Zee Here, Mr. Freberg")...............................35-50
(Product commercials for radio use.)

EPs: 7–inch 33/45rpm

CAPITOL (415 "Wun'erful Wun'erful") 15-25 57
(Single-sided, two track promotional issue. Add $10 to $20 if accompanied by "Two Sides of Bubbling Hilarity" insert. Issued with generic Capitol paper sleeve.)
CAPITOL (496 "Any Requests") 20-30 54
CAPITOL (628 "Real St. George") 15-25 55
CAPITOL (731 "Elderly Man River") 40-50 58
(Promotional issue only.)
CAPITOL (1101 "Omaha")........15-25 59
CAPITOL (1589 "Stan Freberg")...............................25-40 61
(Compact 33.)
CAPITOL (3192 "Ugly Duckling")...............................15-25

SWIMSUITSMANSHIP (2080 "Swimsuitsmanship")........... 100-125
(Promotional issue only. Cover reads: "Fit Facts and Figures, You and Rose Marie Reid.")
UNITED PRESBYTERIAN CHURCH (1400 "Is God Dead?")........... 30-45
(Product commercials for radio use.)

LPs: 10/12–inch 33rpm

BEKINS (27713 "Bekins Presents the Sound of Moving")............ 35-50
(Product commercials for radio use.)
BUTTERNUT COFFEE (2000 "Instant Butternut Coffee") 40-60 60s
(Product commercials for radio use.)
CAPITOL (777 "A Child's Garden of Freberg") 20-40 57
CAPITOL (1035 "The Best of the Stan Freberg Shows")............ 40-60 58
CAPITOL (1242 "Stan Freberg with the Original Cast") 20-35 59
(With "T" prefix.)
CAPITOL (1242 "Stan Freberg with the Original Cast") 12-20 69
(With "DT" prefix.)
CAPITOL (1242 "Stan Freberg with the Original Cast") 5-10 75
(With "SM" prefix.)
CAPITOL (1573 "Stan Freberg Presents the United States of America, Volume 1 - the Early Years")............... 25-25 61
(With "W" or "SW" prefix.)
CAPITOL (1694 "Face the Funnies")................................25-35 62
CAPITOL (1816 "Madison Avenue Werewolf")............................. 25-35 62
CAPITOL (2020 "Best of Stan Freberg")............................... 15-25 64
CAPITOL (2551 "Freberg Underground")........................ 15-25 66
(With "T" or "ST" prefix.)
CAPITOL (2551 "Freberg Underground").......................... 5-10 75
(With "SM" prefix.)
CAPITOL (3264 "Mickey Mouse's Birthday Party")...................... 15-25 63
CAPITOL (11000 series)............ 5-10 78
CAPITOL (80700 "Uncle Stan Wants You")........................... 60-80 61
(Promotional issue for the LP series, *Stan Freberg Presents the United States of America.*)
COCA COLA (2468 "The Freedle Family Singers") 175-200
COLUMBIA (105948 "Hey, Look Us Over") 60-75
(Promotional issue only. With booklet.)
FREBERG LTD. (2343 "Woburn-Salada Tea") 35-50
(Product commercials for radio use.)
KAISER FOIL (22077 "A Kaiser Foil Salesman Faces Life").........125-175
(10-inch LP. Product commercials for radio use.)
MEADOWGOLD (2152 "Meadowgold Dairies") 85-100
(Product commercials for radio use.)
OREGON (2039 "Oregon Soundtrack") 125-150
(Product commercials for radio use. Includes press kit.)
RADIO (3 "Radio Briefings") 35-50
(Promotional spots for using radio advertising.)
RADIO (1499 "More Here Than Meets the Ear") 30-45
(Promotional spots for using radio advertising.)
RADIO (2226 "Who Listens to Radio") 35-50
(Promotional spots for using radio advertising.)
TV GUIDE (2889 "TV Guide Spots") 60-75
(Product commercials for radio use.)
Note: Advertising agency discs containing commercials for radio station use are listed by product name, since there are no other label names used.
Members: Stan Freberg; Daws Butler; June Foray; George Burns; Jesse White; Peter Leeds; Paul Frees; Billy May.

FRED, John
(With His Playboy Band)

P&R '59

Singles: 7–inch

JEWEL 5-10 64-65
MONTEL....................................10-15 59-62
N-JOY 8-12
PAULA 4-8 65-69
UNI..3-6 69-70

LPs: 10/12–inch 33rpm

PAULA 15-25 66-68
UNI..10-15 70

FRED & New J.B.s
(Fred Wesley)

Singles: 7–inch

PEOPLE.......................................3-5 75

LPs: 10/12–inch 33rpm

PEOPLE.....................................5-10 75
Also see WESLEY, Fred

FREDDIE & DREAMERS

P&R/LP '65

Singles: 7–inch

CAPITOL (5053 "I'm Telling You Now") 15-20 63
CAPITOL (5137 "You Were Made for Me") 15-20 63
ERIC 3-4 70s
MERCURY 4-8 64-65
SUPER K 3-6 70
TOWER (125 "I'm Telling You Now") 5-10 65

Picture Sleeves

MERCURY 5-10 65

EPs: 7–inch 33/45rpm

MERCURY (74 "Interview with the Dreamers") 20-30 65
(Promotional issue only.)
MERCURY (661 "Fun Loving Freddie and the Dreamers") 20-30 65
(Jukebox issue only.)

LPs: 10/12–inch 33rpm

CAPITOL 8-10 76-79
MERCURY 20-30 65-66
TOWER (5003 "I'm Telling You Now") 15-25 65
(Also includes tracks by: Linda Laine and the Sinners; Four Just Men; Mike Rabin and the Toggery Five; and Heinz.)
Also see JONES, Tom / Freddie & Dreamers / Johnny Rivers

FREDDIE & DREAMERS / Beat Merchants

P&R '65

Singles: 7–inch

TOWER (127 "You Were Made for Me") 5-10 65
Also see FREDDIE & DREAMERS

FREDDIE & DREAMERS / Just Four Men

Singles: 7–inch

TOWER (163 "Send a Letter to Me") 5-10 65
Also see FREDDIE & DREAMERS

FREDERICK

R&B/D&D '85

Singles: 12–inch 33/45rpm

HEAT 4-6 85

Singles: 7–inch

HEAT 3-4 85

FREDERICK II

R&B '71

Singles: 7–inch

VULTURE 3-5 71

FREE

LP '69

Singles: 7–inch

A&M 3-6 70-71
ISLAND 3-5 72

Picture Sleeves

A&M 4-6 70

LPs: 10/12–inch 33rpm

A&M 8-15 69-75
ISLAND (Except 7) 8-10 73
ISLAND (7 "The Free Story") 25-30 73
(Includes booklet. Promotional issue only.)
Members: Andy Fraser; Paul Rodgers; Simon Kirke; Paul Kossoff.
Also see BACK STREET CRAWLER
Also see BAD COMPANY
Also see FRASER, Andy
Also see KOSSOFF, Paul
Also see RODGERS, Paul
Also see WILLIE & Poor Boys

FREE EXPRESSION

R&B '81

Singles: 7–inch

VANGUARD 3-4 81

FREE LIFE

R&B '79

Singles: 7–inch

EPIC 3-5 78

LPs: 10/12–inch 33rpm

EPIC 5-10 78

FREE MOVEMENT

P&R/R&B '71

Singles: 7–inch

COLUMBIA 3-5 71
DECCA 3-5 71

LPs: 10/12–inch 33rpm

COLUMBIA 8-10 72

FREED, Alan

(With His Rock 'N Roll Band)

Singles: 78rpm

CORAL 5-10 56-58

Singles: 7–inch

CORAL 8-15 56-58

EPs: 7–inch 33/45rpm

CORAL (81136 "Rock 'N Roll Dance Party") 30-50 56

LPs: 10/12–inch 33rpm

BRUNSWICK (54043 "The Alan Freed Rock 'N Roll Show") 75-100 59
(With "Guests" Buddy Holly & Crickets, Jackie Wilson & Terry Noland.)
CORAL (57063 "Rock 'N Roll Dance Party, Vol. 1") 40-60 56
(With the Modernaires.)
CORAL (57115 "Rock 'N Roll Dance Party, Vol. 2") 40-60 56
(With Jimmy Cavello & His House Rockers.)
CORAL (57177 "TV Record Hop") 40-60 57
CORAL (57213 "Rock Around the Block") 40-60 58

CORAL (57216 "Alan Freed Presents the King's Henchmen") 40-60 58
(With King Curtis, Sam "The Man" Taylor, Count Hastings, Kenny Burrell, Everett Barksdale, Ernie Hayes.)
Also see KING CURTIS
Also see HOLLY, Buddy
Also see WILSON, Jackie

FREED, Alan, Steve Allen, Al "Jazzbo" Collins & Modernaires

Singles: 78rpm

CORAL 4-8 56

Singles: 7-inch

CORAL 8-12 56
Also see COLLINS, Al
Also see FREED, Alan

FREEDOM

R&B '79

Singles: 7-inch

ABC 3-5 70
MALACO 3-4 79

LPs: 10/12-inch 33rpm

ABC 10-12 70
COTILLION 10-12 71

FREEEZ

R&B/D&D '83

Singles: 12-inch 33/45rpm

STREETWISE 4-6 83

Singles: 7-inch

STREETWISE 3-4 83

LPs: 10/12-inch 33rpm

STREETWISE 5-10 83
Also see ROCCA, John

FREEMAN, Bobby

P&R/R&B '58

Singles: 7-inch

ABC 3-4 73
AUTUMN 4-8 63-64
DOUBLE SHOT 3-6 69-70
GUSTO 3-4 80s
JOSIE 10-15 58-62
KING 5-10 60-65
LOMA 4-8 67
RNOR 3-4
VIRGO 3-5 72

Picture Sleeves

RNOR 5-10

LPs: 10/12-inch 33rpm

AUTUMN (102 "C'mon and Swim") 20-30 64
JOSIE (4007 "Get in the Swim") 15-25 65
JUBILEE (1086 "Do You Wanna Dance") 35-50 59
(Monaural.)
JUBILEE (1086 "Do You Wanna Dance") 50-75 59
(Stereo.)
JUBILEE (5010 "Twist with Bobby Freeman") 20-30 62
KING (930 "The Lovable Style of Bobby Freeman") 30-35 65

FREEMAN, Bobby, & Chuck Jackson

LPs: 10/12-inch 33rpm

GRAND PRIX 15-20 64
Also see FREEMAN, Bobby
Also see JACKSON, Chuck

FREEMAN, Ernie

(Ernie Freeman Combo)

R&B '56

Singles: 78rpm

CASH 3-6 56

Singles: 7-inch

AVA 4-8 64
CASH 8-12 56
IMPERIAL (Except 5752) 5-10 57-62
IMPERIAL (5752 "Theme from Igor") 8-12 61
KING 5-10 60
LIBERTY 4-8 62

EPs: 7-inch 33/45rpm

DOOTONE (209 "Jazz Organ") . 10-15 56

LPs: 10/12-inch 33rpm

DUNHILL 10-15 67
IMPERIAL 15-25 57-62
LIBERTY 10-20 62-63
Members: Ernie Freeman; Irvin Ashby; Joe Comfort; R. Martinez.
Also see B. BUMBLE & STINGERS
Also see NELSON, Willie
Also see OTIS, Johnny
Also see SIR CHAUNCEY
Also see WITHERSPOON, Jimmy

FREEMAN, John

R&B '77

Singles: 7-inch

DAKAR 3-5 77

FREESTYLE

(Freestyle Express)

R&B '84

Singles: 7-inch

MUSIC SPECIALISTS 3-4 84-86
Member: Tony Butler.
Also see TRINERE / Freestyle / Debbie Deb

FREHLEY, Ace

P&R/LP '78

Singles: 7-inch

CASABLANCA 3-5 78

LPs: 10/12-inch 33rpm

CASABLANCA (7121 "Ace Frehley") 12-20 78
(With poster order form.)
CASABLANCA (7121 "Ace Frehley") 8-12 78
(Without poster order form.)

CASABLANCA (PIX-7121 "Ace Frehley")................................ 40-50 79
(Picture disc.)
MEGAFORCE............................ 5-10 87-89
Also see FREHLEY'S COMET
Also see KISS

FREHLEY'S COMET

LP '88

LPs: 10/12-inch 33rpm

MEGAFORCE............................ 5-8 88
Also see FREHLEY, Ace

FRENCH, Don

P&R '59

Singles: 7-inch

LANCER.................................. 5-10 59

FRESH, Doug, E.: see DOUG E. FRESH & Get Fresh Crew

FRESH BAND

D&D '84

Singles: 12-inch 33/45rpm

ARE 'N BE.................................. 4-6 84

FRESH 3 MCs

R&B '84

Singles: 12-inch 33/45rpm

PROFILE.................................... 4-6 84

Singles: 7-inch

PROFILE.................................... 3-4 84

LPs: 10/12-inch 33rpm

PROFILE.................................... 5-10 84
Also see PUMPKIN & Profile All-Stars

FREY, Glenn

P&R/LP '82

Singles: 12-inch 33/45rpm

MCA 4-6 84-85

Singles: 7-inch

ASYLUM 3-4 82
MCA 3-4 84-89

Picture Sleeves

ASYLUM 3-4 82
MCA 3-4 84-88

LPs: 10/12-inch 33rpm

ASYLUM 5-10 82
MCA 5-10 84-89
Also see EAGLES

FRIDA
(Anni-Frid Lyngstad)

P&R/LP '82

Singles: 7-inch

ATLANTIC................................. 3-5 82

LPs: 10/12-inch 33rpm

ATLANTIC................................. 5-10 82
Also see ABBA

FRIEDMAN, Dean

P&R/LP '77

Singles: 7-inch

LIFESONG................................. 3-4 77-78

LPs: 10/12-inch 33rpm

LIFESONG................................. 5-10 77-78
RECORD CO-OP 5-10 82

FRIEDMAN, Kinky

C&W '73

Singles: 7-inch

ABC.. 3-5 75
EPIC... 3-4 76-85
SOUND FACTORY...................... 3-4 81
SUNRISE 3-4 83

LPs: 10/12-inch 33rpm

ABC.. 5-10 74
EPIC... 5-10 76
VANGUARD............................... 5-10 73

FRIEND & LOVER

P&R '68

Singles: 7-inch

ABC.. 4-8 67
CADET CONCEPT 3-5
VERVE/FORECAST 4-8 68

LPs: 10/12-inch 33rpm

VERVE/FORECAST 12-15 68
Members: James Post; Cathy Post.

FRIENDS of DISTINCTION

P&R/R&B/LP '69

Singles: 7-inch

RCA 3-5 69-73

LPs: 10/12-inch 33rpm

COLLECTABLES........................ 5-10 88
RCA 10-15 69-73
Members: Floyd Butler; Jessica Cleaves; Harry Elston; Charlene Gibson; Barbara Jean Love.

FRIJID PINK

P&R/LP '70

Singles: 7-inch

LION.. 4-8 72
LONDON.................................... 3-5
PARROT 5-10 69-71

LPs: 10/12-inch 33rpm

FANTASY (9464 "All Pink Inside")................................ 10-15 74
LIONEL (1004 "Earth Omen").... 10-20 72
PARROT (71033 "Frijid Pink") ... 15-25 70
PARROT (71041 "Defrosted") ... 15-25 70

FRIPP, Robert

LP '79

LPs: 10/12-inch 33rpm

EDITIONS E.G. 5-10 79-81
POLYDOR 5-10 79-81
Also see KING CRIMSON

FRIPP, Robert, & Andy Summers

LP '82

LPs: 10/12-inch 33rpm

A&M 5-10 82-84
Also see FRIPP, Robert
Also see POLICE

FRIPP & ENO

LPs: 10/12–inch 33rpm

ANTILLES 8-10 73

Members: Robert Fripp; Brian Eno.
Also see ENO, Brian
Also see FRIPP, Robert

FRITZ, Joe

(Joe "Papoose" Fritz)

R&B '50

Singles: 78rpm

MODERN 5-10 50
PEACOCK.................................. 5-10 51-54
SITTIN' in WITH 5-10 50-51

Singles: 7–inch

JET STREAM 4-8 66
PEACOCK (1627 "Honey, Honey") 15-30 54
PEACOCK (1640 "Cerelle") 15-30 51
SITTIN' in WITH (559 "Please Get off My Mind") 50-75 50

FRIZZELL, David

C&W '70

Singles: 7–inch

CAPITOL.................................... 3-5 73-74
CARTWHEEL................................ 3-5 71
COLUMBIA 3-5 70
COMPLEAT 3-4 87
NASHVILLE AMERICA 3-4 86
RSO 3-5 76
VIVA... 3-4 83-85
W.B. 3-4 81-82

Also see HAGGARD, Merle

FRIZZELL, David, & Shelly West

C&W '81

(Frizzell & West)

Singles: 7–inch

VIVA.. 3-4 83-85
W.B. 3-4 81-83

FRIZZELL, Lefty

C&W '50

Singles: 78rpm

COLUMBIA 5-15 50-57

Singles: 7–inch

ABC... 3-5 73-76
COLUMBIA (20000 & 21000 series) 10-20 50-56
COLUMBIA (40000 & 41000 series) 5-15 56-61
COLUMBIA (42000 thru 45000 series, except 42924) 3-8 61-72
COLUMBIA (42924 "Saginaw, Michigan") 4-6 64
(Black vinyl.)
COLUMBIA (42924 "Saginaw, Michigan") 10-15 64
(Colored vinyl. Promotional issue only.)

EPs: 7–inch 33/45rpm

COLUMBIA 12-25 51-59

LPs: 10/12–inch 33rpm

ABC..8-12 73-77
COLUMBIA (1342 "The One and Only Lefty Frizzell").................30-40 59
COLUMBIA (2169 "Saginaw, Michigan")............................20-30 64
COLUMBIA (2386 "The Sad Side of Life")...................................15-25 65
COLUMBIA (2488 "Lefty Frizzell's Greatest Hits") 15-25 66
(Monaural.)
COLUMBIA (2772 "Puttin' On")..15-25 67
COLUMBIA (8969 "Saginaw, Michigan")..............................25-35 64
COLUMBIA (9019 "Songs of Jimmie Rodgers") 75-100 51
(10–inch LP.)
HARMONY (9021 "Listen to Lefty")..................................75-100 52
(10–inch LP.)
COLUMBIA (9186 "The Sad Side of Life")...................................20-25 65
COLUMBIA (9288 "Lefty Frizzell's Greatest Hits") 20-25 66
(Stereo. With "CS" prefix.)
COLUMBIA (9288 "Lefty Frizzell's Greatest Hits") 5-10
(With "PC" prefix.)
COLUMBIA (9572 "Puttin' On")..20-25 67
COLUMBIA (10000 series).........5-12 73-83
COLUMBIA (30000 series).........5-12 75-82
HARMONY (7241 "Songs of Jimmie Rodgers") 30-40 60
HARMONY (11000 series) 8-15 66-68
MCA...8-12 82
ROUNDER...................................5-10 80-83

Also see BOND, Johnny, & Lefty Frizzell
Also see PRICE, Ray / Lefty Frizzell / Carl Smith
Also see SMITH, Carl / Lefty Frizzell / Marty Robbins

FROGMEN

P&R '61

Singles: 7–inch

ASTRA (1009 "Underwater") 25-35 61
ASTRA (1010 "Beware Below") .25-35 61
CANDIX (314 "Underwater")......15-25 61
CANDIX (326 "Beware Below") .15-25 61
SCOTT (101 "Tioga")................10-20 64
SCOTT (102 "Underwater").......10-20 64
TEE JAY (131 "Sea Haunt") 15-25 64
(Black vinyl.)
TEE JAY (131 "Sea Haunt") 25-50 64
(Colored vinyl.)

FROMAN, Jane

P&R '34

Singles: 78rpm

CAPITOL.......................................3-5 52-56
DECCA 4-6 34

Singles: 7-inch

CAPITOL.................................... 3-6 52-56

EPs: 7-inch 33/45rpm

CAPITOL.................................... 5-15 52-56

LPs: 10/12-inch 33rpm

CAPITOL.................................... 15-25 52-56
STAR-TONE.................................... 10-15

Also see MARTIN, Dean / Jane Froman

FRONT, The

LP '90

LPs: 10/12-inch 33rpm

COLUMBIA.................................... 5-8 90

FROST
(Dick Wagner & Frost)

LP '69

Singles: 7-inch

DATE.................................... 5-10 68
VANGUARD.................................... 4-8 69-70

LPs: 10/12-inch 33rpm

VANGUARD.................................... 10-20 69-70

Also see COOPER, Alice

FROST, Frank
(With the Night Hawks)

R&B '66

Singles: 7-inch

JEWEL.................................... 4-8 66-67
PHILLIPS INT'L.................................... 8-12 61

LPs: 10/12-inch 33rpm

JEWEL.................................... 8-10 74
PHILLIPS INT'L. (1975 "Hey Boss Man!").................... 800-1200 61

FROST, Max, & Troopers

P&R '68

Singles: 7-inch

SIDEWALK.................................... 8-12 68
TOWER.................................... 5-10 68-69

Picture Sleeves

TOWER (478 "Paxton Quigley's Had the Course").................... 8-12 68

LPs: 10/12-inch 33rpm

TOWER (5147 "Shape of Things to Come").................... 25-35 68

Member: Davie Allan.
Also see ALLAN, Davie

FROST, Thomas & Richard

P&R '69

Singles: 7-inch

IMPERIAL.................................... 3-6 69
UNI.................................... 3-6 72

LPs: 10/12-inch 33rpm

UNI.................................... 8-10 72

FROZEN GHOST

P&R/LP '87

Singles: 7-inch

ATLANTIC.................................... 3-4 87

LPs: 10/12-inch 33rpm

ATLANTIC.................................... 5-10 87

Members: Wolf Hassel; Arnold Lanni.

Also see SHERIFF

FRYE, David

LP '69

LPs: 10/12-inch 33rpm

BUDDAH.................................... 5-10 71-72
ELEKTRA.................................... 8-12 69-71

FUGS
(Village Fugs)

LP '66

Singles: 7-inch

ESP.................................... 5-10 66

LPs: 10/12-inch 33rpm

BROADSIDE (304 "Ballads of Contemporary Protest, Point of Views, and General Dissatisfaction").................... 300-400 66
ESP (1018 "Fugs First Album")..30-50 66
(Reissue of Broadside 304.)
ESP (1028 "The Fugs").................... 25-40 66
ESP (1038 "Virgin Fugs").................... 25-40 67
ESP (2018 "Fugs Four").................... 20-25 67
PVC.................................... 5-10 82
REPRISE (6280 "Tenderness Junction").................... 15-25 67
REPRISE (6305 "It Crawled Into My Hand, Honest").................... 15-25 67
REPRISE (6359 "A Belle of Avenue").................... 10-20 69
REPRISE (6396 "Golden Filth").10-20 70

Members: Ed Saunders; John Anderson; Lee Crabtree; Pete Kearney; Tuli Kupferberg; Vinny Leary; Ken Weaver; Pete Stampfel; Steve Weber.
Also see HOLY MODAL ROUNDERS

FULL FORCE

R&B/D&D '85

Singles: 12-inch 33/45rpm

COLUMBIA.................................... 4-6 85-86

Singles: 7-inch

COLUMBIA.................................... 3-4 85-87

LPs: 10/12-inch 33rpm

COLUMBIA.................................... 5-10 85-87

Also see LISA LISA

FULLER, Bobby
(Bobby Fuller Four; with Jim Reese & Embers; with Fanatics)

P&R/LP '66

Singles: 7-inch

ABC.................................... 3-4 73
HI-TONE.................................... 4-8
DONNA (1403 "Those Memories of You").................... 25-35 65
EASTWOOD (0345 "Not Fade Away").................... 15-25 62
ERIC.................................... 3-4 70s
EXETER (122 "Wine, Wine, Wine").................... 50-100 64
EXETER (124 "I Fought the Law").................... 75-125 64
EXETER (126 "Fool of Love")..50-100 64
LIBERTY.................................... 10-15 65

MUSTANG 5-10 65-66
TODD (1090 "Saturday Night") . 15-25 60s
YUCCA (141 "You're in Love").. 25-35 62
YUCCA (144 "My Heart Jumped")............................ 25-35 62

LPs: 10/12-inch 33rpm

MUSTANG (900 "KRLA King of the Wheels")........................ 60-75 66
(Monaural.)
MUSTANG (900 "KRLA King of the Wheels")...................... 75-100 66
(Stereo.)
MUSTANG (901 "I Fought the Law") 35-45 66
(Monaural.)
MUSTANG (901 "I Fought the Law") 45-55 66
(Stereo.)
RHINO...................................... 5-10 81
VOXX 5-10 84

Members: Bobby Fuller; Randy Fuller; Duane Quirico; Jim Reese; Dalton Powell; Johnny Barbata.
Also see SHINDIGS

FULLER, Bobby / Seeds

Singles: 7-inch

TRIP 3-6 70s

Also see FULLER, Bobby
Also see SEEDS

FULLER, Jerry

P&R '59

Singles: 7-inch

ABC 3-5 78
BELL 4-6 72
CHALLENGE (59052 "Betty My Angel") 15-25 59
CHALLENGE (59085 thru 59269)..................................... 10-20 60-65
CHALLENGE (59279 "I Got Carried Away")................................ 20-30 65
CHALLENGE (59307 "Don't Look at Me Like That")............................ 5-10 65
CHALLENGE (59329 "Double Life")... 15-25 66
COLUMBIA 3-5 70
LIN (5011 "Blue Memories")...... 15-25 58
LIN (5012 "Teenage Love")....... 15-25 58
LIN (5015 "Angel from Above") . 15-25 58
LIN (5017 "Fanny Brown") 15-25 58
LIN (5019 "Lipstick & Rouge")... 15-25 59
MCA 3-5 79

LPs: 10/12-inch 33rpm

LIN (100 "Teenage Love")......... 25-35 60
MCA 5-10 79

FULLER, Jerry, & Diane Maxwell

Singles: 7-inch

CHALLENGE (59074 "Above and Beyond") 10-15 60

Also see FULLER, Jerry
Also see MAXWELL, Diane

FULSON, Lowell

(Lowell Folsom; Lowel Fulsom)

R&B '48

Singles: 78rpm

ALADDIN 25-35 51
BIG TOWN.................................8-12 46-47
CASH 5-10 57
CHECKER 5-10 54-57
DOWN TOWN.............................5-10 49
GILT EDGE................................5-10 51
HOLLYWOOD.............................5-10 55
PARROT 20-30 53
RPM 5-10 50
SCOTTY'S RADIO 8-12 46
SWING TIME 5-10 46-53
TRILON.......................................8-12 47-48

Singles: 7-inch

ALADDIN (3088 "Double Trouble Blues") 50-75 53
ALADDIN (3104 "Night & Day") .50-75 51
ALADDIN (3104 "Stormin' and Rainin'") 40-60 53
(Black vinyl.)
ALADDIN (3104 "Stormin' and Rainin'") 75-125 53
(Colored vinyl.)
ALADDIN (3217 "Don't Leave Me, Baby") 25-50 53
ALADDIN (3233 "Blues Never Fail")..25-50 53
CASH 15-25 57
CHECKER (804 "Reconsider Baby") 15-25 54
CHECKER (812 "Check Yourself")......................................15-25 55
CHECKER (820 thru 937)..........10-20 55-59
CHECKER (952 thru 1046)..........8-12 60-62
GRANITE 3-4 76
HOLLYWOOD (1029 "Rocking After Midnight")...............................20-30 55
HOLLYWOOD (1103 "Guitar Shuffle") 8-10 62
JEWEL 3-6 69-73
KENT 3-8 64-70
MOVIN' 4-8 64
PARROT (787 "I've Been Mistreated")..............................50-75 53
(Black vinyl.)
PARROT (787 "I've Been Mistreated")............................75-125 53
(Colored vinyl.)
SWING TIME (289 "Let's Live Right") 20-30 51
SWING TIME (295 "Guitar Shuffle") 20-30 51
SWING TIME (301 "The Highway Is My Home") 20-30 51

SWING TIME (308 "Black Widow Spider") 20-30 51
SWING TIME (315 "Raggedy Daddy Blues") 20-30 52
SWING TIME (320 "Ride Until the Sun Goes Down") 20-30 52
SWING TIME (325 "Upstairs") .. 20-30 52
SWING TIME (330 "I Love My Baby") 20-30 52
SWING TIME (335 "Cash Box Boogie") 20-30 53
SWING TIME (338 "I've Been Mistreated") 20-30 52

Picture Sleeves

KENT 5-8 67

LPs: 10/12-Inch 33rpm

ARHOOLIE 10-12 62
BIG TOWN 5-10 78
CHESS (408 "Hung Down Head") 15-20
JEWEL 8-10 70-73
KENT 10-15 65-71
UNITED 8-12

Members: Lowell Fulson; Lloyd Glenn; Earl Brown; Bob Harvey; Bill Hadnott.

Also see CHARLES, Ray
Also see GLENN, Lloyd
Also see JAMES, Ulysses / Lowell Fulson
Also see MEMPHIS SLIM & Lowell Fulson
Also see TURRENTINE, Stanley

FUN & GAMES

P&R '69

Singles: 7-inch

UNI 5-10 68

LPs: 10/12-inch 33rpm

UNI (73042 "Elephant Candy") . 15-25 68

Members: Paul Guille; Joe Romano; Rick Romano; Sam Irwin; Joe Dugan; Carson Graham.

FUN BOY THREE

LP '83

Singles: 7-inch

CHRYSALIS 3-4 82-83

LPs: 10/12-inch 33rpm

CHRYSALIS 5-10 82-83

Also see SPECIALS

FUN FUN

D&D '84

Singles: 12-inch 33/45rpm

TSR 4-6 84-85

FUNICELLO, Annette: see ANNETTE

FUNK, Professor: see PROFESSOR FUNK

FUNK DELUXE

R&B/D&D '84

Singles: 7-Inch

SALSOUL 3-4 83-84

LPs: 10/12-inch 33rpm

SALSOUL 5-10 83

FUNKADELIC
(Featuring George Clinton)

P&R/R&B '69

Singles: 7-inch

W.B. 3-4 78-79
WESTBOUND 3-6 69-76

Picture Sleeves

W.B. 3-4 78-81

LPs: 10/12-inch 33rpm

20TH CENTURY/WESTBOUND . 8-15 75
W.B. 5-10 76-81
WESTBOUND (215 "Let's Take It to the Stage") 30-50 75
WESTBOUND (227 "Tales of Kidd Funkadelic") 30-50 76
WESTBOUND (1001 "Standing on the Verge") 30-50 74
WESTBOUND (1004 "Greatest Hits") 25-35 75
WESTBOUND (2000 "Funkadelic") 40-50 70
WESTBOUND (2001 "Free Your Mind") 30-50 70
WESTBOUND (2007 "Maggot Brain") 40-60 71
WESTBOUND (2020 "America Eats Its Young") 30-50 72
WESTBOUND (2022 "Cosmic Slop") 30-50 73

Also see PARLIAMENTS

FUNKADELIC

R&B/LP '81

Singles: 7-inch

LAX 3-4 81

LPs: 10/12-inch 33rpm

LAX 5-10 81

Note: This group was formed by three former members of the preceding Westbound/Warner Bros. band.

Also see FUNKADELIC (Featuring George Clinton)
Also see JUNIE

FUNKY COMMUNICATION COMMITTEE: see FCC

FUNKY KINGS

P&R '76

Singles: 7-inch

ARISTA 3-5 76

LPs: 10/12-inch 33rpm

ARISTA 5-10 76

FUNN

R&B '81

Singles: 7-inch

MAGIC 3-5 81

FURAY, Richie

LP '76

Singles: 7-inch

ASYLUM 3-4 77-79

LPs: 10/12–inch 33rpm

ASYLUM 5-10 76-82

Also see BUFFALO SPRINGFIELD
Also see POCO
Also see SOUTHER-HILLMAN-FURAY

FURIOUS FIVE

R&B '84

Singles: 12–inch 33/45rpm

SUGAR HILL................................ 4-6 84-85

Singles: 7–inch

SUGAR HILL................................ 3-4 84-85

FURIOUS FIVE & Sugarhill Gang

R&B '81

Singles: 12–inch 33/45rpm

SUGAR HILL................................ 4-6 81

Singles: 7–inch

SUGAR HILL................................ 3-4 81

Also see FURIOUS FIVE
Also see SUGARHILL GANG

FURYS

P&R '63

Singles: 7–inch

MACK IV 8-10 63

FUSE ONE

LP '82

LPs: 10/12–inch 33rpm

CTI 5-10 82

FUTURE

R&B '88

Singles: 7–inch

HOUSTON INT'L.......................... 3-4 87

FUTURES

R&B '73

Singles: 7–inch

AVALANCHE 3-4
GAMBLE 3-5 73
PHILADELPHIA INT'L.................. 3-4 81

LPs: 10/12–inch 33rpm

PHILADELPHIA INT'L................ 5-10 81

Members: James King; Kenny Crew; Harry McGilkerry; Frank Washington; John King.
Also see MASON, Barbara

FUZZ

P&R/R&B/LP '71

Singles: 7–inch

CALLA... 3-5 71
ROULETTE 3-5 70s

LPs: 10/12–inch 33rpm

CALLA..................................... 10-12 71

Members: Sheila Young; Barbara Gilliam; Val Williams.

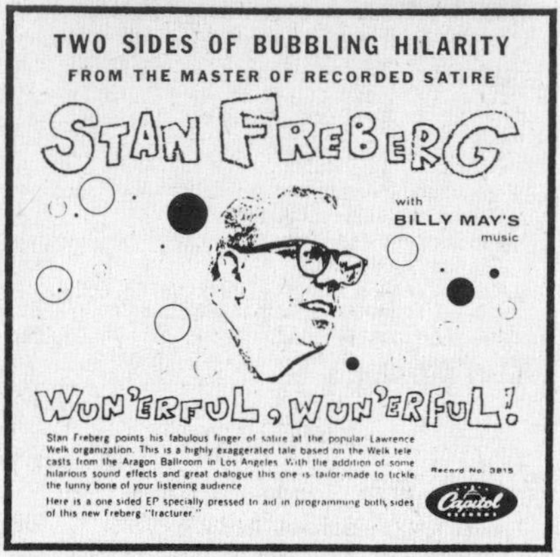

TWO SIDES OF BUBBLING HILARITY
FROM THE MASTER OF RECORDED SATIRE
STAN FREBERG
with
BILLY MAY'S
music
WUN'ERFUL, WUN'ERFUL!
Stan Freberg points his fabulous finger of satire at the popular Lawrence Welk organization. This is a highly exaggerated tale based on the Welk telecasts from the Aragon Ballroom in Los Angeles. With the addition of some hilarious sound effects and great dialogue this one is tailor-made to tickle the funny bone of your listening audience.
Here is a one sided EP specially pressed to aid in programming both sides of this new Freberg "fracturer."
Record No. 3815
Capitol

G

G., Kenny: see KENNY G.

G.L.O.B.E. & Whiz Kid

R&B '83

Singles: 12-inch 33/45rpm

TOMMY BOY 4-6 83

Singles: 7-inch

TOMMY BOY 3-4 83

G-CLEFS

P&R/R&B '56

Singles: 78rpm

PARIS 4-8 57
PILGRIM 4-8 56

Singles: 7-inch

LOMA 4-8 66
PARIS (502 "Symbol of Love").. 15-25 57
PARIS (502 "Symbol of Love").. 10-20 57
PILGRIM (715 "Ka Ding Dong") 15-25 56
(Purple label, no pilgrims.)
PILGRIM (715 "Ka Ding Dong").. 8-12 56
(Red label with pilgrims.)
PILGRIM (720 "Cause You're Mine") 10-20 56
REGINA 10-15 64
ROULETTE 3-5 70s
TERRACE 5-10 61-63
VEEP 4-8 65-66

Also see CANNON, Freddy

P&R/R&B/LP '79

Singles: 7-inch

ARISTA 3-5 79-82

LPs: 10/12-inch 33rpm

ARISTA 5-10 79-81

G.T.
(Gary Taylor)

R&B '83

Singles: 12-inch 33/45rpm

A&M 4-6 83

Singles: 7-inch

A&M 3-4 83

LPs: 10/12-inch 33rpm

A&M 5-8 83

GABOR SZABO: see SZABO, Gabor

GABRIEL

P&R '78

Singles: 7-inch

ABC 3-5 76-77
EPIC 3-4 78-79

LPs: 10/12-inch 33rpm

ABC 8-10 75-76
EPIC 5-10 78

Members: Terry Lauber; Frank Butorac.

GABRIEL, Peter

P&R/LP '77

Singles: 12-inch 33/45rpm

GEFFEN 4-6 82-86

Singles: 7-inch

ATCO 3-5 77
ATLANTIC 3-5 78
GEFFEN 3-4 82-90
MERCURY 3-4 80
WTG 3-4 89
W.B. 3-4 86

Picture Sleeves

GEFFEN 3-4 86
MERCURY 3-4 80

LPs: 10/12-inch 33rpm

ATCO 10-12 77
ATLANTIC 8-10 78
GEFFEN 5-10 82-90
MERCURY 5-10 80

Also see GENESIS

GABRIEL, Peter, & Kate Bush

P&R '87

Singles: 7-inch

GEFFEN 3-4 87

Picture Sleeves

GEFFEN 3-4 87

Also see BUSH, Kate

GABRIEL & ANGELS

P&R '62

Singles: 7-inch

AMY (823 "Zing Went the Strings of My Heart") 25-35 61
AMY (35802 "Chumba") 10-20 60
NORMAN 8-12 61-62
SWAN 5-10 62-63

GADABOUTS

P&R '56

Singles: 78rpm

MERCURY 4-8 54-56
WING 4-8 55

Singles: 7-inch

JARO 5-10 60
MERCURY 8-12 54-56
WING 5-10 55

GADSON, James

R&B '72

Singles: 7-inch

CREAM 3-5 72

Also see SOUL RUNNERS

GADSON, Mel

P&R '60

Singles: 7-inch

BIG TOP (3034 "Comin' Down with Love") 10-20 60

GAGE, Yvonne

R&B '84

Singles: 7–inch

ATLANTIC 3-5 81
CIM 3-4 84

Also see FIRST LOVE

GAGNON, Andre

P&R '76

Singles: 7–inch

LONDON 3-5 76

GAIL, Sunny: see GALE, Sunny

GAILLARD, Slim

(Slim Gaillard Trio)

P&R/R&B '46

Singles: 78rpm

BEL-TONE 10-15 45
CADET 10-15 46
COLUMBIA 5-10 40s
OKEH 5-15 40-42
VOCALION 10-20 38-40

Singles: 7–inch

DOT 10-15 59
EPIC 4-8 68

EPs: 7–inch 33/45rpm

CLEF 10-20 53
KING 10-20 54
NORGRAN 10-20 54
ROYALE 10-20 50s

LPs: 10/12–inch 33rpm

CLEF (126 "Mish Mash") 25-50 53
CLEF (138 "Slim Cavorts") 25-50 53
DOT (3190 "Slim Gaillard Rides Again") 20-30 59
(Monaural.)
DOT (25190 "Slim Gaillard Rides Again") 25-40 59
(Stereo.)
KING (80 "Boogie") 50-75 50s
(10–inch LP.)
NORGRAN (13 "Slim Gaillard") 25-40 54
VERVE (2013 "Smorgasbord") . 20-40 56

Also see GILLESPIE, Dizzy, & Slim Gaillard

GAINES, Earl

(Earl Gains)

R&B '66

Singles: 7–inch

CHAMPION 5-10 58-60
DELUXE 4-6 68-69
HBR 4-8 66
HOLLYWOOD 4-8 67
SEVENTY SEVEN 3-5 73

LPs: 10/12–inch 33rpm

DELUXE 10-15 69
EXCELLO 3-5 62
HBR 10-15 66

GAINES, Rosie

R&B '85

Singles: 7–inch

EPIC 3-4 85

GALE, Eric

LP '77

Singles: 7–inch

COLUMBIA 3-4 78-80

LPs: 10/12–inch 33rpm

COLUMBIA 5-10 77-80
ELEKTRA 5-10 83
KUDU 8-10 73

Also see GRUSIN, Dave

GALE, Sunny

(With the Saints & Sinners Dixieland Band; with Ralph Burns Orchestra; Sunny Gail)

P&R '52

Singles: 78rpm

DECCA 3-6 56-57
DERBY 3-6 52
RCA 3-5 52-56

Singles: 7–inch

BLAINE 3-5 65
CANADIAN AMERICAN 3-6 63-64
DECCA 5-10 56-59
DERBY 8-12 52
RCA (4000 thru 6000 series) 6-12 52-56
RCA (9000 series) 3-5 68
RIVERSIDE 3-5 63
STAGE 4-8 62
TERRACE 3-6 62
THIMBLE 3-4 74
WARWICK 4-8 60-61

EPs: 7–inch 33/45rpm

KING 5-10
RCA 5-10 56

LPs: 10/12–inch 33rpm

CANADIAN AMERICAN 10-20 64
RCA (1277 "Sunny and Blue") ... 20-30 56
WARWICK (2018 "Sunny") 15-25 60

Also see WILCOX, Eddie, Orchestra

GALE, Sunny, & Du Droppers

Singles: 78rpm

RCA 5-10 53

Singles: 7–inch

RCA (5543 "The Note in the Bottle") 10-20 53

Also see DU DROPPERS
Also see GALE, Sunny

GALENS

P&R '63

Singles: 7–inch

CHALLENGE 5-8 63-65

GALLAGHER, Rory

LP '72

LPs: 10/12–inch 33rpm

ATCO 10-12 71-72
CHRYSALIS 5-10 75-80

MERCURY 5-10 82
POLYDOR.................................. 8-10 72-75
SPRINGBOARD........................ 8-12 76
Also see TASTE

GALLAGHER & LYLE

P&R '76

Singles: 7-inch

A&M 3-4 73-78

LPs: 10/12-inch 33rpm

A&M 8-10 73-78
CAPITOL (SM-10000 series) 5-10 77
CAPITOL (ST-11000 series)....... 8-12 72
Members: Ben Gallagher; Graham Lyle.
Also see McGUINNESS FLINT

GALLAHADS

P&R '56

Singles: 78rpm

CAPITOL.................................... 3-5 55
JUBILEE.................................... 3-5 56
VIK 3-5 57

Singles: 7-inch

CAPITOL.................................. 5-10 55
JUBILEE.................................. 5-10 56
VIK 5-10 57

GALLERY

P&R/LP '72

Singles: 7-inch

SUSSEX..................................... 3-5 72

Picture Sleeves

SUSSEX (239 "I Believe in Music") 4-6 72

LPs: 10/12-inch 33rpm

SUSSEX................................. 10-12 72-73
Member: Jim Gold.

GALLOP, Frank

P&R '58

Singles: 7-inch

ABC-PAR 5-10 58
KAPP.. 4-6 66
MUSICOR 4-6 66

Picture Sleeves

MUSICOR 4-8 66

LPs: 10/12-inch 33rpm

MUSICOR 10-15 66

GALLOWAY, Leata

R&B '88

Singles: 7-inch

COLUMBIA 3-4 88

GALWAY, James

LP '79

Singles: 7-inch

RCA.. 3-4 81

LPs: 10/12-inch 33rpm

RCA.. 5-8 79-80
Also see LAINE, Cleo, & James Galway

GALWAY, James, & Sylvia

C&W '83

Singles: 7-inch

RCA 3-4 83
Also see GALWAY, James
Also see SYLVIA

GAMBLE, Dee Dee Sharp: see SHARP, Dee Dee

GAMMA

LP '79

Singles: 7-inch

ELEKTRA.....................................3-4 79-82

LPs: 10/12-inch 33rpm

ELEKTRA...................................5-10 79-82
Members: Dave Pattison; Ronnie Montrose; Denny Carmassi.
Also see HEART
Also see MONTROSE

GANG of FOUR

LP '81

Singles: 12-inch 33/45rpm

W.B. 4-6 80-84

Singles: 7-inch

W.B. 3-4 80-84

LPs: 10/12-inch 33rpm

W.B. 5-10 80-83
Also see SHRIEKBACK

GANG STARR

LP '91

LPs: 10/12-inch 33rpm

CHRYSALIS.................................5-8 91

GANG'S BACK

R&B '82

Singles: 7-inch

HANDSHAKE................................3-4 82

GANGSTERS

R&B '79

Singles: 7-inch

HEAT 3-4 79-81
MONTAGE....................................3-4 82

LPs: 10/12-inch 33rpm

MONTAGE..................................5-10 82

GANT, Cecil
(Pvt. Cecil Gant "The G.I. Sing-Sation"; with His Trio)

R&B '44

Singles: 78rpm

BRONZE.....................................5-10 44
BULLET 5-10 46
DOT (1000 series) 4-8 50-51
DOWN BEAT 5-8 49
4 STAR 5-10 47
GILT-EDGE (Except 500) 5-10 44-47
GILT-EDGE (500 "I Wonder")..75-100 45
(Cardboard picture disc.)
IMPERIAL 5-10 50-51
KING 10-12 47
NATIONAL..................................5-10 44

SWING TIME 5-8 49

Singles: 7-inch

DECCA (30320 "I Wonder") 10-20 57
DECCA (48171 "Someday You'll Be Sorry") 20-30 50
DECCA (48185 "It's Christmas Time Again") 20-30 50
DECCA (48191 "Train Time Blues No. 2") 20-30 50
DECCA (48200 "Shot Gun Boogie") 25-40 51
DECCA (48212 "My Little Baby") 20-30 51
DECCA (48231 "Owl Stew") 20-30 50
DECCA (48249 "God Bless My Daddy") 20-30 50
DOT (1121 "Train Time Blues") 20-30 52
GILT-EDGE (5090 "I Wonder") . 20-30 55

LPs: 10/12-inch 33rpm

KING (671 "The Incomprable Cecil Gant") 40-50 60
RED MILL ("Piano and Voice") 50-100
(No selection number used. Colored vinyl.)
SOUND (601 "The Incomprable Cecil Gant") 75-100 57

GANTS

P&R '65

Singles: 7-inch

LIBERTY 10-15 65-67

LPs: 10/12-inch 33rpm

LIBERTY 15-25 65-66

GAP, Billy & Baby: see BILLY & Baby Gap

GAP BAND

R&B '77

Singles: 12-inch 33/45rpm

PASSPORT 4-6 83
TOTAL EXPERIENCE 4-6 82-86

Singles: 7-inch

A&M 3-5 75
CAPITOL 3-4 89
MEGA 3-4 84
MERCURY 3-4 79-84
PASSPORT 3-4 83
RCA 3-4 87
SHELTER 3-5 74
TATTOO 3-5 77
TOTAL EXPERIENCE 3-4 82-87

Picture Sleeves

TOTAL EXPERIENCE 3-4 82

LPs: 10/12-inch 33rpm

CAPITOL 5-8 89
MERCURY 5-10 79-80
PASSPORT 5-10 83
SHELTER 8-10 74
TATTOO 8-10 77
TOTAL EXPERIENCE 5-10 82-86

Members: Charles Wilson; Ronnie Wilson; Robert Wilson.
Also see BILLY & Baby Gap

GARCIA, Jerry

(Jerry Garcia Band)

P&R/LP '72

Singles: 7-inch

DOUGLAS 3-6 73
ROUND 4-6 72-74
W.B. 4-6 72

LPs: 10/12-inch 33rpm

ARISTA 5-10 78-82
ROUND 8-10 74-75
U.A. 8-10 76
W.B. (2582 "Garcia") 35-45 72

Also see DYLAN, Bob, & Grateful Dean
Also see GRATEFUL DEAD
Also see HART, Mickey
Also see IT'S a BEAUTIFUL DAY
Also see JAMES & Good Brothers
Also see JEFFERSON AIRPLANE
Also see LAMB
Also see OLD and in the WAY
Also see ROWANS
Also see WALES, Howard, & Jerry Garcia

GARCIA, Jerry, & Robert Hunter

Singles: 7-inch

ROUND (102 "Sampler for Dead Heads") 50-75 74
(Includes letter about the Grateful Dead LP, *The Mars Hotel,* and some miniature LP covers. Promotional fan club issue.)
ROUND (102 "Sampler for Dead Heads") 25-35 74
(Price for disc without inserts.)

Also see GARCIA, Jerry
Also see GRATEFUL DEAD

GARDNER, Dave

(Brother Dave Gardner)

P&R '57

Singles: 7-inch

DECCA (30627 "Slick Slacks") ..15-30 58
OJ 5-10 57
RCA 3-8 59-61

LPs: 10/12-inch 33rpm

CAMDEN 5-10 73
CAPITOL 15-25 63
RCA 15-25 60-64
TOWER 10-20 67

GARDNER, Don, & Dee Dee Ford

P&R/R&B '62

Singles: 7-inch

FIRE 5-10 62
FLASHBACK 3-5 65
KC 5-10 62
LUDIX 4-8 63
RED TOP 4-8 63
TRU-GLO-TOWN 4-8 66

LPs: 10/12-inch 33rpm

FIRE (105 "Need Your Lovin'") 50-100 62
SUE (1044 "Don Gardner & Dee Dee Ford in Sweden") 20-30 66

Also see WASHINGTON, Baby, & Don Gardner

GARDNER, Joanna

R&B '85

Singles: 7–inch

PHILLY WORLD 3-4 85

GARDNER, Reggie

R&B '71

Singles: 7–inch

CAPITOL.................................... 3-5 71

GARDNER, Taana

R&B '81

Singles: 7–inch

WEST END 3-4 81

GARFUNKEL, Art

P&R/LP '73

Singles: 7–inch

COLUMBIA 3-4 73-81

Picture Sleeves

COLUMBIA 3-4 81

LPs: 10/12–inch 33rpm

COLUMBIA (30000 series) 8-12 73-81
(With "FC," "JC," "KC" or "PC" prefix.
COLUMBIA (30000 series) 10-20 73-75
(With "CQ" or "PCQ" prefix. Quad issues.)
COLUMBIA (40000 series) 5-8 88
COLUMBIA (47000 series) 10-20 78
(Half-speed mastered.)
Also see GARR, Artle
Also see SIMON & GARFUNKEL

GARFUNKEL, Art / Amy Grant

LPs: 10/12–inch 33rpm

COLUMBIA (40212 "Animals' Christmas") 8-10 86
(Includes booklet.)
Also see GRANT, Amy

GARFUNKEL, Art, James Taylor & Paul Simon

P&R '78

Singles: 7–inch

COLUMBIA.................................. 3-5 78
Also see GARFUNKEL, Art
Also see SIMON, Paul
Also see TAYLOR, James

GARI, Frank

P&R '60

Singles: 7–inch

ATLANTIC.................................. 5-8 62
CAPITOL.................................... 4-6 68
CRUSADE................................. 6-12 60-62
RIBBON 6-12 59

Picture Sleeves

CRUSADE.............................. 10-20 61-62

GARLAND, Judy

P&R '39

Singles: 78rpm

CAPITOL.................................... 3-5 56-57
COLUMBIA 3-5 53-54
DECCA (Except 2000 through 4000 series)..............................5-10 42-55
DECCA (2000 thru 4000 series) 10-15 39-42

Singles: 7–inch

ABC..3-5 67
CAPITOL.....................................5-10 56-63
COLUMBIA (40000 series)..........8-15 53-54
DECCA (25000 series) 4-8 65
DECCA (29000 series) 8-10 55
MGM GOLDEN CIRCLE...............3-5 69
W.B. 3-5 63

Promotional Singles

CAPITOL ("After You've Gone"/ "When You're Smiling")............10-20 59

Picture Sleeves

CAPITOL ("After You've Gone"/ "When You're Smiling")............15-25 59
(Sleeve reads "Two of the Top Tunes from *Garland at the Grove*.")

EPs: 7–inch 33/45rpm

CAPITOL (676 "Miss Show Business")...............................10-20 55
CAPITOL (734 "Judy")..............10-20 56
CAPITOL (835 "Alone") 10-20 57
CAPITOL (1569 "Judy at Carnegie Hall")........................10-15 62
COLUMBIA (1201 "A Star Is Born")......................................15-20 54
(Soundtrack.)
COLUMBIA (2598 "Judy Garland")................................20-30 57
COLUMBIA (7621 "Born in a Trunk") 25-50 56
DECCA (620 "Judy Garland at the Palace/ Greatest Performances")........10-20 55
DECCA (661 "The Wizard of Oz")...15-25 51
DECCA (2050 "Judy Garland, Volume 2") 12-20 53
MGM (40 "Easter Parade") 30-50 50
(Gatefold cover.)
MGM (268 "If You Feel Like Singing, Sing") 10-20 54
MGM (1038 "Get Happy")..........10-20 55
MGM (1116 "Look for the Silver Lining")...................................10-20 55
MGM (1122 "Judy Garland")......10-20 55

LPs: 10/12–inch 33rpm

ABC (620 Judy Garland at Home at the Palace") 10-15 67
ABC (30007 "Judy Garland the ABC Collection") 5-10 76
AEI (3101 "Meet Me in St. Louis"/ "The Harvey Girls")................10-15
(Soundtrack. Reissue.)
ACCESSOR...............................8-15
AUDIOFIDELITY (311 "Judy Garland")..................................8-10 83
(Picture disc.)

C.I.T. 8-12
CAPITOL (676 "Miss Show Business")............................. 30-40 55
(With "W" prefix.)
CAPITOL (676 "Miss Show Business")............................. 10-20 63
(With "SW" prefix.)
CAPITOL (734 "Judy")............. 25-35 56
(With "T" prefix.)
CAPITOL (734 "Judy")............. 10-20 63
(With "DT" prefix.)
CAPITOL (835 "Alone")............ 25-35 57
(With "T" prefix.)
CAPITOL (835 "Alone")............ 10-20 63
(With "DT" prefix.)
CAPITOL (1036 "Judy in Love") 20-35 58
CAPITOL (1118 "Garland at the Grove")................................. 40-60 59
CAPITOL (1188 "The Letter") ... 25-35 59
(With John Ireland.)
CAPITOL (1467 "Judy - That's Entertainment") 20-35 60
CAPITOL (1569 "Judy at Carnegie Hall") 20-35 61
CAPITOL (1710 "The Garland Touch").................................. 20-30 62
CAPITOL (1861 "I Could Go On Singing")............................... 25-30 63
(Soundtrack. With "W" prefix.)
CAPITOL (1861 "I Could Go On Singing")...............................35-40 63
(Soundtrack. With "SW" prefix.)
CAPITOL (1941 "Our Love Letter") 15-20 63
(With John Ireland.)
CAPITOL (1999 "The Hits of Judy Garland") 20-30 64
(With "T" or "ST" prefix.)
CAPITOL (1999 "The Hits of Judy Garland") 5-10 75
(With "SM" prefix.)
CAPITOL (2062 "Just for Openers")............................... 15-25 64
CAPITOL (2988 "Judy Garland Deluxe Set") 20-35 68
CAPITOL (11763 "Alone").......... 5-10 78
CAPITOL (11876 "Judy - That's Entertainment") 5-10 79
CAPITOL (12034 "Just for Openers")................................. 5-10 80
CAPITOL (16175 "The Hits of Judy Garland") 4-6 81
COLUMBIA (762 "Born in a Trunk") 50-100 56
(10–inch LP.)
COLUMBIA (1101 "A Star Is Born") 20-25 58
(Soundtrack.)
COLUMBIA (1201 "A Star Is Born")....................................35-45 54
(Soundtrack. Deluxe boxed edition.)
COLUMBIA (8740 "A Star Is Born")....................................20-30 63
(Soundtrack.)
COLUMBIA (10011 "A Star Is Born")..5-12 73
(Soundtrack.)
COLUMBIA/CSP (8740 "A Star Is Born")..5-10
(Soundtrack.)
COMPUNSONIC..........................8-12
DRG...10-20
DECCA (5 "Collector's Items: 1936-1945") 15-25 70
DECCA (172 "The Best of Judy Garland")................................15-20 63
(Monaural.)
DECCA (7-172 "The Best of Judy Garland")................................15-20 63
(Stereo.)
DECCA (4199 "The Magic of Judy Garland")................................15-20 61
DECCA (5152 "Wizard of Oz")...25-50 52
(Soundtrack. 10–inch LP.)
DECCA (6020 "Judy Garland at the Palace") 35-45 55
DECCA (8190 "Judy Garland - Greatest Performances").......................35-45 55
DECCA (8387 "The Wizard of Oz")...20-35 56
(Soundtrack. One side, *The Song Hits from Pinocchio,* does not feature Judy.)
DECCA (8498 "Meet Me in St. Louis"/ "The Harvey Girls").................60-70 57
(Soundtrack. Different show on each side.)
DECCA (75150 "Judy Garland's Greatest Hits") 8-12 69
DECCA (78387 "Wizard of Oz").10-15 67
(Soundtrack.)
51 WEST......................................5-10
HARMONY (11366 "A Star Is Born").......................................10-15 69
(Soundtrack.)
JUNO (1000 "Judy–London 1969") 6-12 69
MCA (4003 "The Best of Judy Garland")...................................10-15 73
MGM (1 "Golden Years at MGM")....................................15-25 69
MGM (21 "The Pirate")..............50-75 51
(Soundtrack. With Gene Kelly. 10–inch LP.)
MGM (82 "Judy Garland Sings") 50-100 51
MGM (113 "Judy Garland")..........8-12 70
MGM (3149 "Judy Garland")......35-45 54

MGM (3234 "The Pirate") 25-30 55
(Soundtrack. With Gene Kelly.)
MGM (3464 "The Wizard of Oz") 35-45 61
(Soundtrack.)
MGM (3771 "Words and Music") 15-25 60
MGM (3989 "The Judy Garland Story, Volume 1") 15-20 61
MGM (3996 "The Wizard of Oz") 15-20 61
(Soundtrack.)
MGM (4005 "The Judy Garland Story, Volume 2") 15-20 61
MGM (4204 "The Very Best of Judy Garland") 12-20 64
MARK '56 (632 "Live in San Francisco") 50-75 79
(Picture disc.)
METRO (505 "Judy Garland") 10-15 65
METRO (581 "Judy Garland in Song") 10-15 66
PARAGON 5-10
PHOENIX 10 8-12
PICKWICK 5-10 70s
RADIANT 6-12
RADIOLA 5-10
SPRINGBOARD 5-10
STANYAN 5-10 74
STAR TONE 5-10
TRIP (9 "16 Greatest Hits") 5-10 76
TROPHY 5-10

Also see CROSBY, Bing, & Judy Garland
Also see HAYMES, Dick, & Judy Garland
Also see MARTIN, Dean
Also see YOUNG, Victor

GARLAND, Judy / Tommy Dorsey

Singles: 78rpm

VOGUE ("The Trolley Song") 750-1000 46
(Picture disc.)

Also see DORSEY, Tommy

GARLAND, Judy, & Liza Minnelli

LP '65

Singles: 7–inch

CAPITOL 4-6 65

LPs: 10/12–inch 33rpm

CAPITOL (2295 "Live at the London Palladium") 15-20 65
CAPITOL (11191 "Live at the London Palladium") 5-10 73
MFSL (048 "Live at the London Palladium") 20-35 81
TROLLEY CAR 5-10

Also see GARLAND, Judy
Also see MINNELLI, Liza

GARLOW, Clarence

R&B '50

Singles: 78rpm

ALADDIN 8-15 52
FEATURE 10-15 51-54
FOLK STAR 5-10 54
FLAIR 10-20 54
GOLDBAND 5-10 56-57
LYRIC 10-15 51
MACY'S 5-10 49

Singles: 7–inch

ALADDIN (3179 "New Bon Ton Roula") 50-75 52
ALADDIN (3225 "You Got Me Crying") 50-75 52
FEATURE (3005 "If I Keep on Worrying") 40-60 54
FLAIR (1021 "Crawfishin'") 50-75 54
FOLK STAR (1130 "Za Belle") 25-40 54
FOLK STAR (1199 "No No Baby") 25-40 54
GOLDBAND 10-20 56-57

GARNER, Erroll

(Erroll Garner Trio)

R&B '49

Singles: 78rpm

COLUMBIA 3-8 50-57
MERCURY 4-8 54

Singles: 7-Inch

ABC-PAR 3-6 61-62
COLUMBIA 3-8 50-70
MGM 3-5 66-69
MERCURY (70000 series) 4-8 54
MERCURY (72000 & 73000 series) 3-6 63-71
REPRISE 3-6 63

EPs: 7-Inch 33/45rpm

ATLANTIC 5-15 56
BRUNSWICK 5-15 53
COLUMBIA 5-15 50-59
EMARCY 5-15 56
KING 5-15 54
MERCURY 5-15 54-56
SAVOY 5-15 51-55

LPs: 10/12-Inch 33rpm

ABC-PAR 15-25 61
ATLANTIC (109 "Rhapsody") 50-100 49
(10–inch LP.)
ATLANTIC (112 "Piano Solos") 50-100 50
(10–inch LP.)
ATLANTIC (128 "Passport to Fame") 50-100 51
(10–inch LP.)
ATLANTIC (138 "Piano Solos") 50-100 52
(10–inch LP.)
ATLANTIC (1227 "Greatest Garner") 30-40 56
BARONET 15-25 61
BLUE NOTE (5000 series) 20-40 52-53
(10–inch LP.)

COLUMBIA (535 "At the Piano") 45-65 53
(Red and gold label.)
COLUMBIA (535 "At the Piano") 30-50 56
(Red and black label.)
COLUMBIA (583 "Gems") 40-60 54
(Red and gold label.)
COLUMBIA (583 "Gems") 30-50 56
(Red and black label.)
COLUMBIA (617 "Gonest") 40-60 55
(Red and gold label.)
COLUMBIA (617 "Gonest") 30-50 56
(Red and black label.)
COLUMBIA (651 "Music for Tired Lovers") 25-50 55
(Red and gold label.)
COLUMBIA (883 "Concert by the Sea") 25-50 56
COLUMBIA (939 thru 1587) 15-35 57-61
COLUMBIA (2540 "Garnerland") 30-50 56
(10–inch LP.)
COLUMBIA (6139 "Piano Moods") 50-75 50
COLUMBIA (6173 "Gems") 50-75 51
COLUMBIA (8000 series) 15-25 60
COLUMBIA (9000 series) 6-12 70
COLUMBIA SPECIAL PROD. 5-8 79
DIAL (205 "Garner Trio") 75-100 50
(10–inch LP.)
DIAL (902 "Gaslight Session") .. 60-80 50
(10–inch LP.)
EMARCY (26000 series) 20-40 54
(10–inch LP.)
EMARCY (36000 series) 20-30 55-56
ENRICA 15-25 59
EVEREST 5-10 70
GRAND AWARD 20-35 56
HARMONY 8-12 68
JAZZTONE 20-35 57
KING (265-17 "Erroll Garner") ... 50-75 54
(10–inch LP.)
KING (540 "Erroll Garner") 25-35 58
LONDON 8-12 72-73
MGM 10-20 65-68
MERCURY (20009 "At the Piano") 50-75 50
MERCURY (20055 "Mambo") ... 40-60 54
MERCURY (20063 "Solitaire") .. 40-60 54
MERCURY (20090 "Afternoon of an Elf") 40-60 55
MERCURY (20662 thru 20859) 15-25 62-63
(Monaural.)
MERCURY (25117 "At the Piano") 50-75 51
(10–inch LP.)
MERCURY (25157 "Gone with Garner") 50-75 51
(10–inch LP.)
MERCURY (60662 thru 60859) . 20-30 62-63
(Stereo.)
MERCURY (61000 series) 8-12 70
REPRISE 12-25 63
RONDO-LETTE 15-25 58
ROOST (10 "Piano Magic") 30-60 52
(10–inch LP.)
ROOST (2213 "Giants") 25-40 56
SAVOY (1100 series) 5-10 78
SAVOY (2000 series) 5-10 76
SAVOY (12002 "Erroll Garner") . 30-50 55
SAVOY (12003 "Erroll Garner, Vol. 2") 30-50 55
SAVOY (12008 "Erroll Garner") . 30-50 55
SAVOY (15000 "At the Piano") 75-125 49
(10–inch LP.)
SAVOY (15001 "At the Piano, Vol. 2") 75-125 50
(10–inch LP.)
SAVOY (15002 "At the Piano, Vol. 3") 75-125 50
(10–inch LP.)
SAVOY (15004 "At the Piano, Vol. 4") 75-125 50
(10–inch LP.)
SAVOY (15026 "At the Piano, Vol. 5") 75-125 50
(10–inch LP.)
TRIP 5-10 74
WING 10-20 62
Also see STARR, Kay / Erroll Garner

GARNETT, Gale

P&R/C&W/LP '64

Singles: 7–inch

RCA 4-8 64-67

Picture Sleeves

RCA 4-8 64

LPs: 10/12–inch 33rpm

RCA 10-15 64-66

GARNETT, Gale, & Gentle Reign

Singles: 7–inch

COLUMBIA 4-6 68

LPs: 10/12–inch 33rpm

COLUMBIA 8-12 68-69
Also see GARNETT, Gale

GARR, Artie

(Art Garfunkel)

Singles: 7–inch

OCTAVIA (8002 "Private Love") 20-30 61
WARWICK (515 "Beat Love") 20-30 59
Also see GARFUNKEL, Art

GARRAFFA, Donna

D&D '85

Singles: 12–inch 33/45rpm

ARTIST INT'L 4-6 85

GARRETT, Lee

P&R/R&B '76

Singles: 7-inch

CHRYSALIS 3-5 76

GARRETT, Leif

P&R/LP '77

Singles: 7-inch

ATLANTIC 3-5 77-78
SCOTTI BROS 3-4 78-81

Picture Sleeves

ATLANTIC 3-5 77-78
SCOTTI BROS 3-4 78-81

LPs: 10/12-inch 33rpm

ATLANTIC 5-10 77
SCOTTI BROS 5-10 78-81

Also see CHIC / Roberta Flack / Leif Garrett / Genesis

GARRETT, Scott
(Scott Garret)

P&R '59

Singles: 7-inch

LAURIE (Except 3029) 5-10 59
LAURIE (3029 "Love Story") 20-30 59
(With the Mystics.)
OKEH 5-10 60

Also see MYSTICS

GARRETT, Siedah

R&B/D&D '85

Singles: 12-inch 33/45rpm

QWEST 4-6 85

Singles: 7-inch

QWEST 3-4 85-88

Picture Sleeves

QWEST 3-4 85-88

Also see JACKSON, Michael

GARRETT, Tommy
(Tommy Garrett & 25 Pianos)

LPs: 10/12-Inch 33rpm

LIBERTY 8-15 62

Also see 50 GUITARS of TOMMY GARRETT

GARRETT, Vernon

R&B '69

Singles: 78rpm

MODERN 5-10 57

Singles: 7-inch

ICA 3-5 77
KAPP 3-5 70
MODERN 10-15 57
VENTURE 4-8 69

GARRETT, Vernon, & Marie Franklin

Singles: 7-inch

VENTURE 3-5 76

GARRETT'S CREW

R&B '83

Singles: 7-inch

CLOCKWORK 3-4 83

GARY, John

LP '63

Singles: 7-inch

ACE 3-5 62
BIG B 3-5 64
FRATERNITY 3-6 59-66
RCA 3-5 63-71
ST. JAMES 3-5 63

EPs: 7-inch 33/45rpm

RCA (2804 "John Gary") 4-8 63
(Stereo Compact 33.)

LPs: 10/12-inch 33rpm

CAMDEN 5-10 68
CHURCHILL 4-8 77
METRO 5-10 65
RCA 5-15 63-78
SPIN-O-RAMA 5-10 60s

Also see ANN-MARGRET & John Gary
Also see DESMOND, Johnny / John Gary / Gordon MacRae

GARY & CLYDE

Singles: 7-inch

REV (3523 "Why Not Confess") 15-25 59

Members: Gary Paxton; Clyde Batton.
Also see SKIP & FLIP

GARY & DAVE

P&R '73

Singles: 7-inch

LONDON 3-5 73

Members: Gary Weeks; Dave Beckett.

GARY O'
(Gary O'Connor)

P&R '81

Singles: 7-inch

RCA 3-4 85

Picture Sleeves

RCA 3-4 85

LPs: 10/12-inch 33rpm

CAPITOL 5-10 81

GARY'S GANG

P&R/R&B/LP '79

Singles: 12-inch 33/45rpm

COLUMBIA 4-8 79
RADAR 4-6 83

Singles: 7-inch

COLUMBIA 3-5 79
RADAR 3-4 83

LPs: 10/12-inch 33rpm

COLUMBIA 5-10 79

Members: Gary Turnier; Eric Matthew.

GASCA, Luis

LP '72

LPs: 10/12-inch 33rpm

BLUE THUMB 8-10 72

GATES, David
(With the Accents)

P&R/LP '73

Singles: 7-inch

ARISTA 3-4 81
DEL-FI (4206 "No One Really Loves a Clown") 10-20 63
EAST WEST (123 "Walkin' and Talkin'") 75-100 59
ELEKTRA.................................. 3-5 73-80
MALA (413 "You'll Be My Baby") 40-50 60
MALA (418 "Happiest Man Alive")................................... 40-50 61
MALA (427 "Jo-Baby") 40-50 61
PERSPECTIVE ("Jo-Baby").... 50-100 58
(No selection number used. 1200 made.)
PLANETARY (108 "Once Upon a Time")................................. 10-15 65
ROBBINS (1008 "Jo-Baby")...... 35-45 61

Picture Sleeves

ELEKTRA.................................. 3-5 77

LPs: 10/12-inch 33rpm

ARISTA 5-10 81
ELEKTRA.................................. 8-15 73-80

Also see ASHLEY, Del
Also see BREAD

GATES, Ed "Great"
(Edward White)

R&B '49

Singles: 78rpm

ALADDIN.................................... 4-8 55
SELECTIVE 5-10 49

Singles: 7-inch

ALADDIN................................. 10-15 55
SPECIALTY 5-10 59

GATLIN, Larry
(With the Gatlin Brothers Band; with Family & Friends; Gatlin Quartet)

P&R '74

Singles: 7-inch

CAPITOL.................................... 3-4 90
COLUMBIA 3-5 79-88
MONUMENT 3-5 73-78
UNIVERSAL................................ 3-4 89

LPs: 10/12-inch 33rpm

COLUMBIA 5-10 79-86
MONUMENT............................. 5-10 74-78
SWORD & SHIELD (9009 "The Old Country Church") 25-50 61
(By the Gatlin Quartet, which included sister Donna.)

Members: Larry Gatlin; Steve Gatlin; Rudy Gatlin.

GATLIN, Larry, & Janie Frickie
(With the Gatlin Brothers)

C&W '87

Singles: 7-inch

COLUMBIA 3-4 87

GATTON, Danny
(Danny Gatton Band; with Billy Windsor)

LP '91

Singles: 7-inch

NRG...3-4 87-90

Picture Sleeves

NRG...3-4 90

LPs: 10/12-inch 33rpm

ELEKTRA.....................................5-8 91
NRG..5-10 87

Members: Danny Gatton; Billy Windsor; John Previti; Dave Elliot; Jim Cavanaugh; Randy Hart.

GAYE, Marvin
(With the Love Tones)

P&R/R&B '62

Singles: 12-inch 33/45rpm

COLUMBIA 4-6 83-85

Singles: 7-inch

COLUMBIA 3-4 82-85
DETROIT FREE PRESS ("The Teen Beat Song")...........................50-100 66
(Promotional issue only.)
MOTOWN 3-4
MOTOWN/TOPPS (6 "How Sweet It Is to Be Loved By You")..............50-75 67
(Topps Chewing Gum promotional item. Single-sided, cardboard flexi, picture disc. Issued with generic paper sleeve.)
TAMLA ("Witchcraft")............300-500 61
(Promotional issue only. No selection number used. Credited to "Marvin Gay.")
TAMLA ("My Way")...................30-50 65
(Promotional issue only. No selection number used.)
TAMLA (1800 series)....................3-4 86
TAMLA (54041 "Let Your Conscience Be Your Guide").......................50-75 61
TAMLA (54055 "Sandman").......45-55 62
TAMLA (54063 "Soldier's Plea") 25-30 62
(Credits only Marvin Gaye.)
TAMLA (54063 "Soldier's Plea") 15-25 62
(Credits Marvin Gaye and "Love Tones.")
TAMLA (54068 "Stubborn Kind of Fellow")...............................15-25 62
TAMLA (54075 thru 54185) 5-15 63-69
TAMLA (54190 "Gonna Give Her All the Love I've Got") 4-8 69
(Black vinyl.)
TAMLA (54190 "Gonna Give Her All the Love I've Got")...............................10-15 69
(Colored vinyl. Promotional issue only.)
TAMLA (54195 thru 54280) 3-6 70-77

Picture Sleeves

TAMLA (1800 series)....................3-4 86
TAMLA (54095 "Try It Baby").....20-40 64
TAMLA (54101 "Baby, Don't You Do It") 20-40 64
TAMLA (54138 "Little Darlin' I Need You") 30-50 66

TAMLA (54280 "Got to Give It Up") 4-8 77

EPs: 7-inch 33/45rpm

MOTOWN (2016 "Marvin Gaye") 15-25 60s
TAMLA (60252 "Greatest Hits") 20-30 66

LPs: 10/12-inch 33rpm

COLUMBIA 5-10 82-85
KORY 8-10 76-77
MOTOWN 8-12 64-83
NATURAL RESOURCES 5-10 78
TAMLA (221 "Soulful Moods") 400-600 61
TAMLA (239 "That Stubborn Kind of Fella") 75-125 63
TAMLA (242 "On Stage") 25-50 63
TAMLA (251 "When I'm Alone I Cry") 25-50 64
TAMLA (252 "Greatest Hits") 15-25 64
TAMLA (258 "How Sweet It Is") 15-25 65
TAMLA (266 "Moods") 40-60 66
TAMLA (278 thru 299) 10-20 67-69
TAMLA (300 series) 8-15 70-81
TAMLA (6100 series) 5-10 86
Also see MARTHA & VANDELLAS
Also see MARVELETTES / Mary Wells / Miracles / Marvin Gaye
Also see MOONGLOWS

GAYE, Marvin / Gladys Knight & Pips

Singles: 7-inch

MOTOWN 4-8 68
Also see KNIGHT, Gladys

GAYE, Marvin, & Diana Ross

LP '73

Singles: 7-inch

MOTOWN 3-5 73-74

LPs: 10/12-inch 33rpm

MOTOWN 8-12 73
Also see ROSS, Diana

GAYE, Marvin, & Tammi Terrell

P&R '67

Singles: 7-inch

TAMLA 4-8 67-70

LPs: 10/12-inch 33rpm

MOTOWN 5-10 80-82
TAMLA 10-15 67-70
Also see TERRELL, Tammi

GAYE, Marvin, & Mary Wells

P&R/R&B/LP '64

Singles: 7-inch

MOTOWN 5-10 64

Picture Sleeves

MOTOWN (1057 "What's the Matter with You Baby") 20-40 64

LPs: 10/12-inch 33rpm

MOTOWN (613 "Together") 25-50 64
Also see WELLS, Mary

GAYE, Marvin, & Kim Weston

P&R/R&B '64

Singles: 7-inch

TAMLA 5-10 64-67

LPs: 10/12-inch 33rpm

TAMLA (270 "Marvin Gaye & Kim Weston") 20-25 66
Also see GAYE, Marvin
Also see WESTON, Kim

GAYLE, Crystal

C&W '70

Singles: 7-inch

COLUMBIA 3-5 79-82
DECCA 4-6 70-72
ELEKTRA 3-4 82
MCA 3-4 77
U.A. 3-5 74-80
W.B. 3-4 83-90

Picture Sleeves

COLUMBIA 3-5 79-82
U.A. 4-8 77

LPs: 10/12-inch 33rpm

COLUMBIA 5-10 79-83
ELEKTRA 5-10 82
LIBERTY 5-10 80-82
MCA 5-10 78
MFSL (043 "We Must Believe in Magic") 20-40 80
U.A. (Except "Somebody Loves You picture disc") 5-10 75-80
U.A. ("Somebody Loves You") .75-100 78
(Picture disc. Promotional issue only. One of a four-artist, four-LP set.)
W.B. 5-10 83-90
Also see CAMPBELL, Glen / Anne Murray / Kenny Rogers / Crystal Gayle
Also see RABBITT, Eddie, & Crystal Gayle

GAYLE, Crystal, & Gary Morris

C&W '88

Singles: 7-inch

W.B. 3-4 85-88
Also see MORRIS, Gary

GAYLE, Crystal, & Tom Waits

LPs: 10/12-inch 33rpm

COLUMBIA 5-10 82
Also see GAYLE, Crystal
Also see WAITS, Tom

GAYLORD, Ronnie

P&R '54

Singles: 78rpm

MERCURY 3-5 54-55
WING 3-5 55-56

Singles: 7-inch

MERCURY 4-8 54-55
WING 4-8 55-56

EPs: 7-inch 33/45rpm

MERCURY 5-10 55
Also see GAYLORD & HOLIDAY

GAYLORD & HOLIDAY

LP '76

Singles: 7-inch

NATURAL RESOURCES	3-4	77
PALMER	3-6	67
PRODIGAL	3-4	76
VERVE	4-8	66

LPs: 10/12-inch 33rpm

NATURAL RESOURCES	5-10	76
PRODIGAL	5-10	75
VMI	5-10	72

Members: Ronnie Gaylord; Burt Holiday.
Also see GAYLORD, Ronnie
Also see GAYLORDS

GAYLORDS

P&R '52

Singles: 78rpm

MERCURY	4-6	52-57

Singles: 7-inch

MERCURY	5-15	52-62
TIME	4-8	64

EPs: 7-inch 33/45rpm

MERCURY	5-15	54-56

LPs: 10/12-inch 33rpm

MERCURY (Except 25198)	12-25	55-63
MERCURY (25198 "By Request") (10-inch LP.)	20-30	55
TIME	10-15	64
WING	10-20	59-64

Members: Ronnie Gaylord; Don Rea; Burt (Holiday) Bonaldi; Billy Christ.
Also see GAYLORD & HOLIDAY
Also see DEL-VIKINGS / Diamonds / Big Bopper / Gaylords

GAYNOR, Gloria

P&R '74

Singles: 12-inch 33/45rpm

POLYDOR	4-6	78
SILVER BLUE	4-6	83

Singles: 7-inch

COLUMBIA	3-5	73
JOCIDA	4-8	65
MGM	3-5	74-75
POLYDOR	3-5	76-81
SILVER BLUE	3-4	83

LPs: 10/12-inch 33rpm

ATLANTIC	5-10	82
MGM	8-10	75
POLYDOR	5-10	76-80

GAYNOR, Mel

R&B '55

Singles: 78rpm

MODERN	4-8	55

Singles: 7-inch

MODERN	10-15	55

GAYTEN, Paul

R&B '47

Singles: 78rpm

ARGO	5-10	57
CHECKER	5-10	55-56
DELUXE	5-10	47-49
OKEH	5-10	52-55
REGAL	5-10	49-51

Singles: 7-inch

ANNA	10-20	59-60
ARGO	12-25	57-58
CHECKER (801 thru 836)	10-20	55-58
OKEH	10-20	52-55

Also see HENRY, Clarence
Also see NEWSOM, Chubby, & Her Hip Shakers

GEDDES, David

P&R '75

Singles: 7-inch

ATCO	3-5	75
BIG TREE	3-5	75
H&L	3-5	77
ZODIAC	3-5	77

LPs: 10/12-inch 33rpm

BIG TREE	8-10	75

GEE, Spoonie: see SPOONIE GEE

GEILS, J., Band

(Geils)

P&R/LP '71

Singles: 12-inch 33/45rpm

EMI AMERICA	4-8	82-84

Singles: 7-inch

ATLANTIC	3-5	71-78
EMI AMERICA (Black vinyl)	3-4	78-84
EMI AMERICA (Colored vinyl) (Promotional issue only.)	5-8	78
PRIVATE I	3-4	85

Picture Sleeves

ATLANTIC	3-5	73-78
EMI AMERICA	3-4	78-84
PRIVATE I	3-4	85

LPs: 10/12-inch 33rpm

ATLANTIC (Black vinyl)	8-12	70-80
ATLANTIC (Colored vinyl)	15-20	73
EMI AMERICA	5-10	78-84
NAUTILUS (25 "Love Stinks") (Half-speed mastered.)	15-20	82

Also see GUY, Buddy, with Dr. John & Eric Clapton / Buddy Guy with the J. Geils Band
Also see WOLF, Peter

GELDOF, Bob

P&R '86

Singles: 7-inch

ATLANTIC	3-4	86

Picture Sleeves

ATLANTIC	3-4	86

LPs: 10/12-inch 33rpm

ATLANTIC	5-10	86

Also see BAND AID
Also see BOOMTOWN RATS

GEM

D&D '84

Singles: 12-inch 33/45rpm

STREETKING ... 4-6 84

Singles: 7-inch

STREETKING ... 3-4 84

GENE & DEBBE

P&R '67

Singles: 7-inch

HICKORY ... 3-5 70
TRX ... 4-6 67-69

LPs: 10/12-inch 33rpm

TRX (1001 "Here and Now") ... 15-25 68
Members: Gene Thomas; Debbe Nevills.
Also see THOMAS, Gene

GENE & EUNICE

R&B '55

Singles: 78rpm

ALADDIN ... 4-8 55
COMBO ... 4-8 55

Singles: 7-inch

ALADDIN ... 10-20 55
CASE ... 5-10 59
COLLECTABLES ... 3-4
COMBO ... 10-20 55
ERA ... 3-5 72
LILLY ... 4-8 62
U.A. ... 3-4

EPs: 7-inch 33/45rpm

CASE (100 "Gene & Eunice") ... 25-35 59
(Issued with paper sleeve.)
Members: Gene Forrest; Eunice Levy.

GENE (Chandler) & JERRY (Butler): see CHANDLER, Gene, & Jerry Butler

GENE & TOMMY

Singles: 7-inch

ABC ... 4-8 67
Members: Terry Cashman; Tommy West.
Also see CASHMAN & WEST

GENE & WENDELL (With the Sweethearts)

R&B '61

Singles: 7-inch

PHILIPS ... 4-8 62-63
RAY STARR ... 5-10 61-62

GENE LOVES JEZEBEL

LP '86

Singles: 12-inch 33/45rpm

GEFFEN ... 4-6 86

Singles: 7-inch

GEFFEN ... 3-4 86-90

Picture Sleeves

GEFFEN ... 3-4 88

LPs: 10/12-inch 33rpm

GEFFEN ... 5-10 86-90
Members: Michael Aston; Jay Aston; James Stevenson; Chris Bell; Peter Rizzo.
Also see THOMPSON TWINS

GENERAL CAINE: see CAINE, General

GENERAL KANE

R&B '86

Singles: 12-inch 33/45rpm

MOTOWN ... 5-10 86

Singles: 7-inch

MOTOWN ... 3-4 86-87

LPs: 10/12-inch 33rpm

MOTOWN ... 5-10 86

GENERAL PUBLIC

P&R/D&D/LP '84

Singles: 12-inch 33/45rpm

I.R.S. ... 4-6 84-86

Singles: 7-inch

I.R.S. ... 3-4 84-86

Picture Sleeves

I.R.S. ... 3-4 84

LPs: 10/12-inch 33rpm

I.R.S. ... 5-10 84-86
Members: Roger Charley; Dave Wakeling.
Also see ENGLISH BEAT

GENESIS

LP '73

Singles: 12-inch 33/45rpm

ATLANTIC ... 4-6 86

Singles: 7-inch

ATCO ... 3-5 76-77
ATLANTIC ... 3-4 78-87
CHARISMA ... 4-6 73
PARROT (3018 "Silent Sun") ... 10-15 68
(Promotional issue only.)

Promotional Singles

ATCO ... 3-5 76-77
ATLANTIC ... 3-4 78-86
CHARISMA ... 4-8 73
PARROT ... 10-15 68

Picture Sleeves

ATLANTIC ... 3-5 80-87

EPs: 7-inch 33/45rpm

ATLANTIC (1800 "Spot the Pigeon") ... 5-10 77
(Promotional issue only.)

LPs: 10/12-inch 33rpm

ABC ... 8-10 74
ATCO ... 8-15 74-77
ATLANTIC ... 5-10 78-86
BUDDAH (5659 "Best of Genesis") ... 10-15 76
CHARISMA ... 8-12 72-79
IMPULSE ... 15-25 70
LONDON (600 series) ... 10-15 74
LONDON (50000 series) ... 5-10 77
MCA ... 5-10 78
MFSL (062 "Trick of the Tail") ... 25-50 82
Members: Phil Collins; Peter Gabriel; Tony Banks; Steve Hackett; Anthony Phillips; Mike Rutherford.
Also see BANKS, Tony
Also see CHIC / Roberta Flack / Leif Garrett / Genesis
Also see COLLINS, Phil

Also see GABRIEL, Peter
Also see HACKETT, Steve
Also see PHILLIPS, Anthony
Also see RUTHERFORD, Mike

GENTLE GIANT

LP '72

Singles: 7-inch

CAPITOL 3-5 74-78
COLUMBIA 3-5 72-73

LPs: 10/12-inch 33rpm

CAPITOL 5-10 74-80
COLUMBIA 8-10 72-73
VERTIGO 10-15 71

Members: Derek Shulman; Ray Shulman; Phil Shulman; Gary Green; Kerry Minnear; Tony Visconti; John Weathers; Martin Smith.

GENTLE PERSUASION

P&R '83

Singles: 7-inch

CAPITOL 3-4 83
W.B. 5-10 78

GENTRY, Bobbie

P&R/C&W/R&B/LP '67

Singles: 7-inch

BRUNSWICK 3-5 75
CAPITOL 3-6 67-76
W.B. 3-5 76-78

Picture Sleeves

CAPITOL 3-6 67-72
W.B. 3-5 76

LPs: 10/12-inch 33rpm

CAPITOL (Except "SM" series)... 8-15 67-71
CAPITOL ("SM" series) 5-10 81
W.B. ("*Ode to Billie Joe:* Radio Salute to Bobbie Gentry") 15-20 76
(Promotional issue only.)

Also see CAMPBELL, Glen, & Bobbie Gentry
Also see REYNOLDS, Jody, & Bobbie Gentry

GENTRYS

P&R/LP '65

Singles: 7-inch

BELL 4-8 68
CAPITOL 3-5 72
MGM (Except 13690) 4-8 65-67
MGM (13690 "There's a Love")... 8-10 67
STAX 3-5 74
SUN (1108 thru 1122) 3-6 70-71
(Black vinyl.)
SUN (1108 thru 1122) 10-15 70-71
(Colored vinyl. Promotional issues only.)
SUN (1126 "God Save Our Country") 10-20 71
YOUNGSTOWN (600 "Little Drops of Water") 15-25 65
YOUNGSTOWN (601 "Keep On Dancing") 15-25 65

Picture Sleeves

MGM 5-10 65

LPs: 10/12-inch 33rpm

MGM 20-30 65-70
SUN 20-30 70

Members: Larry Raspberry; Jimmy Johnson; Bruce Bowles; Pat Neal; Jimmy Hart.

GENTY

R&B '80

Singles: 7-inch

VENTURE 3-5 80

GEORGE, Barbara

P&R/R&B '61

Singles: 7-inch

AFO 5-10 61-62
SUE 4-8 62-63
U.A. 3-5 74

LPs: 10/12-inch 33rpm

AFO (5001 "I Know") 50-75 62

GEORGE, Lowell

LP '79

Singles: 7-inch

W.B. 3-5 78-79

LPs: 10/12-inch 33rpm

W.B. 5-10 78-79

Also see LITTLE FEAT
Also see MOTHERS of INVENTION

GEORGE, Robin

P&R '85

Singles: 7-inch

BRONZE 3-4 85

Picture Sleeves

BRONZE 3-4 85

GEORGE & GENE (Jones & Pitney): see JONES, George, & Gene Pitney

GEORGIA SATELLITES

P&R/LP '86

Singles: 12-inch 33/45rpm

ELEKTRA 4-8 89
(Promotional only.)

Singles: 7-inch

ELEKTRA 3-4 86-89

Picture Sleeves

ELEKTRA 3-4 86-87

LPs: 10/12-inch 33rpm

ELEKTRA 5-10 86-89

Members: Dan Baird; Rick Richards; Rich Price.

GEORGIO

P&R/R&B/LP '87

Singles: 7-inch

MACOLO 3-4 87
MOTOWN 3-4 87

Picture Sleeves

MOTOWN 3-4 87

LPs: 10/12-inch 33rpm

MOTOWN 5-10 87

GERARD, Danyel

P&R '72

Singles: 7-inch

COLUMBIA 4-6 72
MGM/VERVE 3-5 72

LPs: 10/12-inch 33rpm

VERVE 8-12 71

GERARDO

LP '91

LPs: 10/12-inch 33rpm

INTERSCOPE 5-8 91

GERRARD, Donny

P&R '76

Singles: 7-inch

GREEDY 3-5 76-77
ROCKET 3-5 76

LPs: 10/12-inch 33rpm

GREEDY 8-10

Also see SKYLARK

GERRY & PACEMAKERS

P&R/LP '64

Singles: 7-inch

ERIC 3-4 70s
LAURIE (3196 "I Like It") 10-15 63
LAURIE (3233 "How Do You Do It") 8-12 64
LAURIE (3251 thru 3370) 5-10 64-67

LPs: 10/12-inch 33rpm

ACCORD 5-10 81
CAPITOL 5-10 79
LAURIE 15-25 64-66
LAURIE/CAPITOL 8-10 81
(Label reads "Mfd. by Capitol Records." Record club issue.)
U.A. 20-25 65

Member: Gerry Marsden.
Also see MARTIN, George, & His Orchestra

GESTURES

P&R '64

Singles: 7-inch

SOMA 5-10 64-65

Member: Dale Menton.
Also see CASTAWAYS / Gestures

GET WET

P&R '81

Singles: 7-inch

BOARDWALK 3-4 81

Picture Sleeves

BOARDWALK 3-4 81

LPs: 10/12-inch 33rpm

BOARDWALK 5-10 81

GETO BOYS

LP '90

(Ghetto Boys)

LPs: 10/12-inch 33rpm

DEF AMERICAN 5-8 90
RAP-A-LOT 5-8 90

GETZ, Stan

(Stan Getz Quintet)

LP '92

Singles: 78rpm

CLEF 3-5 53-54
DAWN 3-5 54
MERCURY 3-5 53
NORGRAN 3-5 54-55
PRESTIGE 3-5 50-53
ROOST 3-5 50-53

Singles: 7-inch

CLEF 4-8 53-54
COLUMBIA 3-4 75-80
DAWN 4-8 54
MGM 3-5 65
MERCURY 4-8 53
NORGRAN 4-8 54-55
PRESTIGE 4-8 50-53
ROOST 4-8 50-53
VERVE 3-6 60-72

EPs: 7-inch 33/45rpm

CLEF 10-20 53
DALE 15-25 51
NORGRAN (11 thru 155) 20-30 53-55
NORGRAN (2000-6 "At the Shrine") 50-100 55
(Six-EP boxed set.)
PRESTIGE (1309 "Stan Getz") .. 20-40 52
ROOST 15-25 50-53

LPs: 10/12-inch 33rpm

A&M 5-8 90
AMERICAN RECORDING SOCIETY 20-30 57
BARONET 10-20 62
BLUE RIBBON 10-20 61
CLEF (137 "Stan Getz Plays") . 75-100 53
(10-inch LP.)
CLEF (143 "Artistry of Stan Getz") 75-100 53
(10-inch LP.)
COLUMBIA 5-10 74-82
CONCORD JAZZ 5-10 81
CROWN (5002 "Groovin' High") 20-35 57
DALE (21 "Retrospect") 100-150 51
(10-inch LP.)
INNER CITY 5-10 78
JAZZ MAN 5-10 82
JAZZTONE 20-30 57
MGM (Except 4312) 5-10 70
MGM (4312 "Mickey One") 12-20 65
(Soundtrack.)
METRO 10-15 65
MODERN (1202 "Groovin' High") 35-50 56
NEW JAZZ 15-25 59
NORGRAN (4 "Stan Getz") 100-150 53
(10-inch LP.)

NORGRAN (1000 Interpretations")........ 50-100 54
NORGRAN (1008 "Interpretations, Vol. 2") 50-100 54
NORGRAN (1029 "Interpretations, Vol. 3") 50-100 55
NORGRAN (1032 "West Coast Jazz") 40-60 55
NORGRAN (1087 "Stan Getz '57") 40-60 57
NORGRAN (2000-2 "At the Shrine") 100-200 55
(With booklet.)
PRESTIGE (102 "Stan Getz") 100-200 52
(10–inch LPs)
PRESTIGE (7002 thru 7022) 25-50 56
(Yellow label.)
PRESTIGE (7252 thru 7256) 25-50 56
(Yellow label.)
PRESTIGE (7000 series)........ 8-18 64-68
(Blue label.)
PRESTIGE (24000 series)........ 8-12 72-79
ROOST (103 "Stan Getz Years") 30-40 64
ROOST (402 "Stan Getz") 100-150 50
(10–inch LPs)
ROOST (404 "Stan Getz and the Swedish All Stars")........ 100-125 51
(10–inch LPs)
ROOST (407 "Jazz at Storyville") 75-100 53
(10–inch LPs)
ROOST (411 "Jazz at Storyville, Vol. 2") 75-100 54
(10–inch LP.)
ROOST (420 "Jazz at Storyville, Vol. 3") 75-100 54
(10–inch LP.)
ROOST (417 "Chamber Music") 75-100 54
(10–inch LP.)
ROOST (2207 "Sounds of Stan Getz") 25-40 56
ROOST (2249 thru 2258)........ 20-30 63
ROULETTE 8-12 71-72
SAVOY (1100 series)........ 5-10 77
SAVOY (9004 "All Star Series") 100-150 51
(10–inch LPs)
SEECO (7 "Highlights in Modern Jazz") 75-125 54
(10–inch LP.)
VSP 8-12 66-67
VERVE 25-50 57-60
(Reads "Verve Records, Inc." at bottom of label.)
VERVE 15-30 61-72
(Reads "MGM Records - a Division of Metro-Goldwyn-Mayer, Inc." at bottom of label.)
VERVE 5-10 73-84
(Reads "Manufactured By MGM Record Corp.," or mentions either Polydor or Polygram at bottom of label.)

Also see BENNETT, Tony
Also see GILLESPIE, Dizzy, & Stan Getz
Also see HAMPTON, Lionel, & Stan Getz
Also see HOLIDAY, Billie, & Stan Getz
Also see TJADER, Cal, & Stan Getz

GETZ, Stan, & Laurindo Almeida

Singles: 7–inch

VERVE 4-6 66

LPs: 10/12–inch 33rpm

VERVE 10-15 66

Also see ALMEIDA, Laurindo

GETZ, Stan, & Charlie Byrd

P&R/LP '62

Singles: 7–inch

MGM 3-4 78
VERVE 3-5 62

LPs: 10/12–inch 33rpm

VERVE 15-25 62

Also see BYRD, Charlie

GETZ, Stan, & Astrud Gilberto

P&R/LP '64

Singles: 7–inch

MGM 3-4 78
VERVE 4-6 64-65

LPs: 10/12–inch 33rpm

VERVE 15-25 64

Also see GILBERTO, Astrud

GETZ, Stan, & Oscar Peterson

LPs: 10/12–inch 33rpm

VERVE 20-40 57-60
(Reads "Verve Records, Inc." at bottom of label.)
VERVE 10-20 61-72
(Reads "MGM Records - a Division of Metro-Goldwyn-Mayer, Inc." at bottom of label.)

Also see GETZ, Stan
Also see PETERSON, Oscar

GIANT

P&R/LP '89

Singles: 7–inch

A&M 3-4 89-90

LPs: 10/12–inch 33rpm

A&M 5-8 89
MERCURY 8-10 70

Members: Dann Huff; David Huff.

GIANT STEPS

P&R/LP '88

Singles: 7–inch

A&M 3-4 88-89

LPs: 10/12–inch 33rpm

A&M 5-8 88

GIBB, Andy

P&R/R&B/LP '77

Singles: 7-inch

RSO 3-4 77-81

Picture Sleeves

RSO 3-4 77-78

LPs: 10/12-inch 33rpm

RSO 5-10 77-80

Also see BEE GEES
Also see NEWTON-JOHN, Olivia, & Andy Gibb

GIBB, Andy, & Victoria Principal

P&R '81

Singles: 7-inch

RSO 3-5 81

Picture Sleeves

RSO 5-10 81

Also see GIBB, Andy

GIBB, Barry

P&R '80

Singles: 12-inch 33/45rpm

MCA 4-6 84

Singles: 7-inch

ATCO 3-5 77
MCA 3-4 84

Picture Sleeves

MCA 3-4 84

LPs: 10/12-inch 33rpm

MCA 5-10 84

Also see BEE GEES
Also see STREISAND, Barbra, & Barry Gibb
Also see WARWICK, Dionne

GIBB, Maurice

Singles: 7-inch

ATCO 3-5 70

Also see BEE GEES

GIBB, Robin

P&R '78

Singles: 12-inch 33/45rpm

MIRAGE 4-6 84

Singles: 7-inch

ATCO 3-5 69-71
EMI AMERICA 3-4 85
MIRAGE 3-4 84
POLYDOR 3-4 83
RSO 3-5 78
SESAME STREET 3-5 78

Picture Sleeves

EMI AMERICA 3-4 85
MIRAGE 3-4 84
POLYDOR 3-4 83
SESAME STREET 3-5 78

LPs: 10/12-inch 33rpm

ATCO 8-10 70
MIRAGE 5-10 84
POLYDOR 5-10 83

Also see BEE GEES
Also see LEVY, Marcy, & Robin Gibb

GIBBONS, Steve, Band

P&R '76

Singles: 7-inch

MCA/GOLD HAWKE 3-5 76-78
POLYDOR 3-5 78

LPs: 10/12-inch 33rpm

MCA 8-10 76-77
POLYDOR 5-10 78-80

Also see DALTREY, Roger, & Steve Gibbons

GIBBS, Doug

R&B '72

Singles: 7-inch

OAK 3-5 72

GIBBS, Georgia

P&R '50

Singles: 78rpm

CORAL 4-8 50-51
MERCURY 4-8 51-57

Singles: 7-Inch

BELL 4-6 64-66
CORAL 8-12 50-51
EPIC (Except 9606) 4-8 63-64
EPIC (9606 "Tater Poon") 8-15 63
IMPERIAL 4-8 60
KAPP 5-8 59
MERCURY 5-15 51-57
RCA 4-8 57-67
ROULETTE 5-8 58-59

EPs: 7-Inch 33/45rpm

MERCURY 10-20 54-56
ROYALE (239 "Georgia Gibbs Sings") 10-20 50s
(Colored vinyl.)

LPs: 10/12-inch 33rpm

BELL 10-15 66
CORAL (56037 "Ballin' the Jack") 30-40 51
(10-inch LP.)
CORAL (57183 "Her Nibs") 20-25 57
EMARCY (36103 "Swingin' with Gibbs") 15-25 57
EPIC 10-20 63
IMPERIAL 10-20 60
MERCURY (20071 "Music and Memories") 20-25 55
MERCURY (20114 "Song Favorites of Georgia Gibbs") 20-25 56
MERCURY (20170 "Swingin' with Her Nibs") 20-25 56
MERCURY (25175 "Georgia Gibbs Sings Oldies") 25-35 53
(10-inch LP.)
MERCURY (25199 "The Man That Got Away") 20-35 55
(10-inch LP.)
SUNSET 8-12 66
TOPPS 10-20

Also see DIAMONDS / Georgia Gibbs / Sarah Vaughan

GIBBS, Terri

C&W '80

Singles: 7–inch

HORIZON.................................... 3-4 87
MCA.. 3-4 80-83
TEM.. 3-4 82
W.B. 3-4 85

LPs: 10/12–inch 33rpm

HORIZON.................................... 5-8 87
MCA.. 5-10 81-83
PHONORAMA.............................. 5-10 84
W.B. 5-8 85

Also see MATTEA, Kathy

GIBSON, Beverly Ann

R&B '59

Singles: 7–inch

DEB.. 5-10 59
JUBILEE..................................... 4-8 63
LANDA.. 4-8 61

GIBSON, Debbie

P&R/LP '87

Singles: 7–inch

ATLANTIC.................................. 3-4 87-90

Picture Sleeves

ATLANTIC.................................. 3-4 87-90

LPs: 10/12–inch 33rpm

ATLANTIC.................................. 5-10 87-89

GIBSON, Don

C&W '56

Singles: 78rpm

COLUMBIA.................................. 5-10 52-54
MGM.. 10-15 55-56
RCA... 5-10 51

Singles: 7–inch

ABC/HICKORY............................ 3-5 75-78
COLUMBIA (20000 series).......... 8-15 52-54
HICKORY.................................... 3-5 70-72
MCA.. 3-5 79
MGM (12109 "Run Boy")........... 15-25 55
MGM (12194 "Sweet Dreams"). 15-25 56
MGM (12290 "I Ain't Gonna
Waste My Time")..................... 20-30 56
MGM (12331 "I Believed in
You").. 15-25 56
MGM (12393 "I'm Gonna Fool
Everybody")............................. 20-30 57
MGM (12494 "I Ain't a-Studing
You Baby")............................... 25-35 57
RCA (0400 series)..................... 10-20 51
RCA (4300 & 4400 series)........ 10-20 51-52
RCA (7000 series, except 7762). 8-15 58-61
RCA (47-7762 "Legend in My
Time")...................................... 6-10 60
(Monaural.)
RCA (61-7762 "Legend in My
Time")...................................... 15-20 60
(Stereo.)
RCA (8000 & 9000 series)........... 4-8 62-70
W.B./CURB................................ 3-4 80

Picture Sleeves

RCA... 5-10 63

EPs: 7–inch 33/45rpm

COLUMBIA.................................. 15-20 57
RCA... 10-20 58-59

LPs: 10/12–inch 33rpm

ABC/HICKORY............................ 6-10 75-78
CAMDEN..................................... 10-15 65-74
HARMONY (7300 series).......... 15-20 65
HARMONY (31000 series)......... 5-10 72
HICKORY.................................... 8-12 70-72
HICKORY/MGM........................... 6-10 73-75
LION (70069 "Songs By
Don Gibson")............................ 50-75 58
MGM.. 8-12 70
METRO....................................... 12-18 65
RCA (1743 thru 2878)............... 20-30 58-63
(With "LPM" prefix. Monaural.)
RCA (1743 thru 2878)............... 25-40 58-63
(With "LSP" prefix. Stereo.)
RCA (3376 thru 4378)............... 10-20 63-70
(With "LPM" or "LSP" prefix.)

Session: Jordanaires.

Also see WEST, Dottie, & Don Gibson

GIBSON, Don, & Sue Thompson

C&W '71

Singles: 7–inch

HICKORY.................................... 3-5 71-76

LPs: 10/12–inch 33rpm

HICKORY.................................... 8-12 73
HICKORY/MGM........................... 5-10 75

Also see GIBSON, Don
Also see THOMPSON, Sue

GIBSON, Ginny

P&R '53

Singles: 78rpm

ABC-PAR.................................... 3-5 56
DERBY.. 3-5 52
MGM.. 3-5 51-55

Singles: 7–inch

ABC-PAR.................................... 4-8 56
DERBY.. 5-10 52
MGM.. 5-10 51-55

EPs: 7–inch 33/45rpm

JD.. 8-12

GIBSON, Johnny

(Johnny Gibson Trio)

P&R '62

Singles: 7–inch

BIG TOP..................................... 4-8 61-63
LAURIE...................................... 4-8 64
TWIRL.. 4-8

Also see JOHNNY & HURRICANES

GIBSON, Steve
(With the Red Caps; with Original Red Caps)
P&R '48

Singles: 78rpm

ABC-PAR 8-12 56-57
BEACON 10-20 44
MERCURY 8-15 47-54
RCA 8-15 51-55

Singles: 7-inch

ABC-PAR 8-15 56-60
BAND BOX 4-8 62
HI LO 15-20 58
HUNT 10-15 59
JAY DEE (796 "It Hurts Me But I Like It") 20-30 54
MERCURY (1253 "I Don't Want to Set the World on Fire") 75-125 49
MERCURY (1255 "Blueberry Hill") 75-125 49
MERCURY (5380 "I'll Never Love Anyone Else") 75-125 50
MERCURY (8038 "San Antonio Rose") 40-60 51
MERCURY (8069 "Wedding Bells") 40-60 51
MERCURY (8146 "Blueberry Hill") 40-60 51
MERCURY (70389 "Wedding Bells") 30-40 54
RCA (0127 "I'm to Blame") 30-45 51
RCA (0138 "Would I Mind") 30-45 51
RCA (3986 "The Thing") 40-50 50
RCA (4076 "Three Dollars and Ninety-Eight Cents") 30-40 51
RCA (4294 "Shame") 30-40 51
RCA (4670 "Two Little Kisses"). 20-30 52
RCA (5103 "Truthfully") 20-30 52
RCA (5130 "Big Game Hunter") 20-30 53
RCA (6096 thru 6345) 10-15 55
ROSE 8-12 59-60
STAGE (3001 "Blueberry Hill").. 15-25

EPs: 7-inch 33/45rpm

MERCURY (3215 "Blueberry Hill") 100-200 52

LPs: 10/12-inch 33rpm

MERCURY (25115 "You're Driving Me Crazy") 200-300 52
(10-inch LP. Title on label is *Harmony Time.*)
MERCURY (25116 "Blueberry Hill") 200-300 52
(10-inch LP. Title on label is *Singing & Swinging.*)

Also see DAMITA JO with Steve Gibson & Red Caps
Also see FIVE RED CAPS
Also see GIBSON, Steve
Also see GREGG, Bobby

GIBSON, Steve, & His Red Caps / Damita Jo with Steve Gibson & the Red Caps

Singles: 78rpm

RCA (5987 "My Tzatskele") 8-15 55

Singles: 7-inch

RCA (5987 "My Tzatskele") 30-40 55

Also see DAMITA JO with Steve Gibson & Red Caps
Also see GIBSON, Steve

GIBSON BROTHERS
P&R/R&B/LP '79

Singles: 12-inch 33/45rpm

ISLAND 4-6 79

Singles: 7-inch

ISLAND 3-4 79

LPs: 10/12-inch 33rpm

HOMESTEAD 5-8 90
ISLAND 5-8 79

GIDEA PARK
(Featuring Adrian Baker)
P&R '82

Singles: 7-inch

PROFILE 3-4 82

GILBERTO, Astrud
LP '64

Singles: 7-inch

CTI 3-5 71
VERVE 3-5 67-70

LPs: 10/12-inch 33rpm

IMAGE 5-10 78
PERCEPTION 5-10 72
VERVE 8-15 65-70

Also see GETZ, Stan, & Astrud Gilberto
Also see JOBIM, Antonio Carlos
Also see JONES, Quincy
Also see WANDERLEY, Walter

GILBERTO, Astrud, & Stanley Turrentine

LPs: 10/12-inch 33rpm

CTI 5-10 71

Also see GILBERTO, Astrud
Also see TURRENTINE, Stanley

GILDER, Nick
P&R/LP '78

Singles: 7-inch

CHRYSALIS 3-5 76-79

Picture Sleeves

CHRYSALIS 3-5 78

LPs: 10/12-inch 33rpm

CASABLANCA 5-10 80
CHRYSALIS 5-10 77-79

Also see SWEENY TODD

GILKYSON, Terry
(With the Easy Riders; with South Coasters)
P&R '57

Singles: 78rpm

COLUMBIA 3-5 54-57
DECCA 4-6 51-52

Singles: 7-inch

COLUMBIA ... 5-10 54-57
DECCA ... 5-10 51-52

Picture Sleeves

COLUMBIA (40817 "Marianne") 10-15 57

EPs: 7-inch 33/45rpm

COLUMBIA ... 5-15 57
DECCA ... 5-15 53

LPs: 10/12-inch 33rpm

DECCA (5263 "Folk Songs By a Solitary Singer") ... 20-40 50
DECCA (5305 "Solitary Singer") 20-40 51
(10-inch LP.)
DECCA (5457 "Golden Minutes of Folk Music") ... 20-30 53
(10-inch LP.)
KAPP ... 10-20 60-63

Members: Terry Gilkyson; Rich Dehr.
Also see EASY RIDERS
Also see LAINE, Frankie, & Easy Riders
Also see MARTIN, Dean
Also see WEAVERS & Terry Gilkyson

GILL, Johnny

R&B '83

Singles: 7-inch

COTILLION ... 3-4 83-85
MOTOWN ... 3-4 90

Picture Sleeves

MOTOWN ... 3-4 90

LPs: 10/12-inch 33rpm

COTILLION ... 5-10 83-85
MOTOWN ... 5-8 90

Also see LATTISAW, Stacy, & Johnny Gill
Also see NEW EDITION

GILL, Vince

C&W '84

Singles: 7-inch

MCA ... 3-4 89-91
RCA ... 3-4 84-89

LPs: 10/12-inch 33rpm

MCA ... 5-8 90-91
RCA ... 5-8 84-89

Also see PURE PRAIRIE LEAGUE

GILLAN, Ian

(Gillan)

LP '80

Singles: 7-inch

OYSTER ... 3-5 76

LPs: 10/12-inch 33rpm

ISLAND ... 5-10 77-78
OYSTER ... 8-10 76
VIRGIN ... 5-10 80

Also see DEEP PURPLE

GILLESPIE, Dizzy

(With His All Star Quintet)

P&R '45

Singles: 7-inch

ATLANTIC ... 4-8 52-53
CONTEMPORARY ... 4-6 53
GUILD ... 5-10 45
NORGRAN ... 4-6 54-56
PRESTIGE ... 4-6 51
RCA ... 4-6 48-49

Singles: 7-inch

ATLANTIC ... 8-12 52-53
CONTEMPORARY ... 5-10 53
LIMELIGHT ... 3-5 65-67
NORGRAN ... 5-10 54-56
PERCEPTION ... 3-5 69
PHILIPS ... 3-6 64
SOLID STATE ... 3-5 69
VERVE ... 3-8 57-62

EPs: 7-inch 33/45rpm

ATLANTIC (514/521 "Dizzy Gillespie") ... 25-50 52
CLEF (153 "Dizzy with Strings") 25-50 53
CLEF (291/292/293/294 "Roy & Diz") ... 20-40 55
(Price is for any volume.)
DEE GEE (4000/4003/4004 "Dizzy Gillespie") ... 40-60 51
(Price is for any volume.)
DISCOVERY (13 "Dizzy Plays") 25-50 50
GNP (1/2/3 "Dizzy Gillespie") ... 25-50 50
(Price is for any volume.)
NORGRAN (114/115 "Big Band") ... 25-50 55
(Price is for either volume.)
RCA (432 "Dizzier & Dizzier") ... 20-40 54

LPs: 10/12-inch 33rpm

ALLEGRO (3017 "Dizzy Gillespie Plays") ... 40-60 52
(10-inch LP.)
ALLEGRO (3083 "Dizzy Gillespie") ... 40-60 52
(10-inch LP.)
ALLEGRO (4023 "Dizzy Gillespie") ... 40-60 53
(10-inch LP.)
AMERICAN RECORDING SOCIETY (405 "Big Band Jazz") ... 60-80 55
AMERICAN RECORDING SOCIETY (423 "Big Band Jazz") ... 60-80 55
ATLANTIC (138 "Dizzy Gillespie") ... 200-300 52
(10-inch LP.)
ATLANTIC (142 "Dizzy Gillespie, Vol. 2") ... 200-300 52
ATLANTIC (1257 "Dizzy at Home and Abroad") ... 75-100 57
(Black label, silver print.)
BARONET (105 "A Handful of Modern Jazz") ... 20-40 61
BLUE NOTE (5017 "Horn of Plenty") ... 150-200 52
(10-inch LP.)

CLEF (136 "Dizzy with Strings") 125-150 53
(10–inch LP.)
CLEF (641 "Roy & Diz") 75-100 55
(With Roy Eldridge.)
CLEF (671 "Roy & Diz, Vol. 2") 75-100 55
CLEF (730 "Trumpet Kings")... 75-100 56
CLEF (731 "Trumpet Battle") .. 75-100 56
CONTEMPORARY (2504 "Dizzy in Paris") 100-150 53
(10–inch LP.)
DEE GEE (1000 "Dizzy Gillespie") 200-250 51
(10–inch LP.)
DIAL (212 "Modern Trumpets") 75-125 52
(10–inch LP.)
DISCOVERY (3013 "Dizzy Plays") 150-200 50
(10–inch LP.)
GNP (4 "Dizzy Gillespie") 100-200 50
(10–inch LP.)
GNP (23 "Dizzy Gillespie") 50-75 57
IMPULSE 10-20 67
LIMELIGHT 15-25 64-67
MERCURY 15-25 66
NORGRAN (1003 "Afro Dizzy") 75-100 54
NORGRAN (1023 "Big Band") 75-100 55
NORGRAN (1083 "Jazz Recital") 75-100 56
NORGRAN (1084 "World Statesman") 75-100 56
NORGRAN (1090 "Big Band") .. 60-80 56
PHILIPS 20-30 62-65
RCA (530 "Dizzy Gillespie") 15-25 66
RCA (1009 "Dizzier & Dizzier") . 50-75 54
RCA (2398 "The Greatest") 30-50 61
REGENT (6043 "School Days") 50-75 57
RON-LETTE (11 "Dizzy Gillespie") 25-50 58
ROOST (106 "Diz & Bird") 75-100 59
(Boxed 2-LP set.)
ROOST (414 "Dizzy over Paris") 150-200 53
ROOST (2214 "Concert in Paris") 50-75 57
ROOST (2234 "Diz & Bird in Concert") 50-75 59
SAVOY (12000 series) 25-50 55-57
SOLID STATE 10-20 68-69
TRIBUTE 10-15 69
VSP 15-25 66
VERVE (6047 "Have Trumpet, Will Excite") 50-75 59
(Stereo.)
VERVE (6068 "Ebullient") 50-75 59
(Stereo.)
VERVE (6117 "Greatest Trumpet") 50-75 60
(Stereo.)
VERVE (8000 series) 15-30 62-67
(With "MGM Records - a Division of Metro-Goldwyn-Mayer, Inc." at bottom of label.)
VERVE (8015 "Jazz from Paris") 50-75 57
(Reads "Verve Records, Inc." at bottom of label.)
VERVE (8017 "Dizzy in Greece") 50-75 57
(Reads "Verve Records, Inc." at bottom of label.)
VERVE (8109 "Trumpet Kings") 50-75 57
(Reads "Verve Records, Inc." at bottom of label.)
VERVE (8110 "Trumpet Battle") 50-75 57
(Reads "Verve Records, Inc." at bottom of label.)
VERVE (8173 "Jazz Recital") 50-75 57
(Reads "Verve Records, Inc." at bottom of label.)
VERVE (8174 "World Statesman") 50-75 57
(Reads "Verve Records, Inc." at bottom of label.)
VERVE (8178 "Big Band") 50-75 57
(Reads "Verve Records, Inc." at bottom of label.)
VERVE (8191 "Afro Dizzy") 50-75 57
(Reads "Verve Records, Inc." at bottom of label.)
VERVE (8198 "For Musicians Only") 50-75 58
(Reads "Verve Records, Inc." at bottom of label.)
VERVE (8208 "Mantecia") 50-75 58
(Reads "Verve Records, Inc." at bottom of label.)
VERVE (8214 "Dizzy & Stuff") ... 40-60 58
(Reads "Verve Records, Inc." at bottom of label.)
VERVE (8260 "Duets") 50-75 58
(Reads "Verve Records, Inc." at bottom of label.)
VERVE (8262 "Sunny Side Up") 50-75 58
(Reads "Verve Records, Inc." at bottom of label.)
VERVE (8313 "Have Trumpet, Will Excite") 50-75 59
(Monaural. Reads "Verve Records, Inc." at bottom of label.)
VERVE (8328 "Ebullient") 50-75 59
(Monaural. Reads "Verve Records, Inc." at bottom of label.)
VERVE (8352 "Greatest Trumpet") 50-75 60

(Monaural. Reads "Verve Records, Inc." at bottom of label.)
VERVE (8386 "Portrait")........... 50-75 60
(Monaural. Reads "Verve Records, Inc." at bottom of label.)
VERVE (8394 "Gillespiana") 50-75 61
(Monaural. Reads "Verve Records, Inc." at bottom of label.)
VERVE (68386 "Portrait").......... 50-75 60
(Stereo. Reads "Verve Records, Inc." at bottom of label.)
VERVE (68394 "Gillespiana") ... 50-75 61
(Stereo. Reads "Verve Records, Inc." at bottom of label.)

GILLESPIE, Dizzy, & Slim Gaillard

LPs: 10/12–inch 33rpm

ULTRAPHONIC (50273 "Gaillard & Gillespie") 30-50 58
Also see GAILLARD, Slim

GILLESPIE, Dizzy, & Stan Getz

EPs: 7–inch 33/45rpm

NORGRAN (3/4 "Dizzy Gillespie & Stan Getz Sextet") 40-60 53
(Price is for either volume.)
NORGRAN (32 "Dizzy Gillespie & Stan Getz Sextet [Vol. 2]") 40-60 53

LPs: 10/12–inch 33rpm

NORGRAN (2 "Dizzy Gillespie & Stan Getz Sextet") 150-250 53
(10–inch LP.)
NORGRAN (18 "Dizzy Gillespie & Stan Getz Sextet [Vol. 2]") 150-250 53
NORGRAN (1050 "Dizzy Gillespie & Stan Getz Sextet") 75-125 56
VERVE (8141 "Dizzy Gillespie & Stan Getz Sextet") 50-75 57
VERVE (68141 "Diz & Getz").... 15-25 66
Also see GETZ, Stan
Also see GILLESPIE, Dizzy

GILLEY, Mickey

(With the Urban Cowboy Band)

P&R '74

Singles: 7–inch

ACT 1 .... 4-8 66
ASYLUM 3-4 80
ASTRO (Except 100 series).......... 3-5 71-73
ASTRO (100 series)................. 10-20 63-65
DARYL 4-8 63
DOT (15706 "Call Me Shorty").. 50-75 58
EPIC... 3-4 78-86
ERIC... 4-6 64
GOLDBAND 4-8 64
GRT.. 3-5 70
KHOURY'S (712 "Drive-In Movie") 15-20 59
LYNN.. 10-20 60-61
MINOR (106 "Ooh Wee").......... 60-80 57
PAULA (Except 400 series) 4-6 66-68
PAULA (400 series) 3-5 74-84
PLAYBOY 3-5 74-77
POTOMAC.................................10-15 60
PRINCESS.....................................8-12 62
RESCO 3-5 74
REX (1007 "Grapevine")...........20-25 58
SABRA.......................................10-15 61
SAN..10-15 63
SUPREME 8-12 62
TCF HALL 4-8 65

LPs: 10/12–inch 33rpm

ASTRO (Except 101)..................8-10 73-78
ASTRO (101 "Lonely Wine")....75-150 64
EPIC..5-10 79-86
PAULA (Except 2000 series).......5-10 81
PAULA (2195 "Down the Line") .20-25 67
PAULA (2224 "Mickey Gilley At His Best")..............................10-12 74
PAULA (2234 "Mickey Gilley").....8-10 78
PLAYBOY 8-12 74-78
Also see CHARLES, Ray, & Mickey Gilley
Also see HAGGARD, Merle / Mickey Gilley / Willie Knight

GILLEY, Mickey, & Barbi Benton

C&W '75

Singles: 7–inch

PLAYBOY 3-5 75

Picture Sleeves

PLAYBOY 3-5 75

GILLEY, Mickey, & Johnny Lee

Singles: 7–inch

EPIC...3-4 81
Also see LEE, Johnny
Also see NELSON, Willie / Johnny Lee / Mickey Gilley

GILLEY, Mickey, & Charly McClain

(Charly McClain & Mickey Gilley)

C&W '84

Singles: 7–inch

EPIC...3-4 83-84
Also see GILLEY, Mickey

GILMER, Jimmy

(With the Fireballs)

P&R/R&B/LP '63

Singles: 7–inch

ABC..3-4 74
ATCO 4-8 68
DECCA 10-15 59
DOT 4-8 63-66
HAMILTON 4-8 63
WARWICK (547 "True Love Ways") 10-20 60

LPs: 10/12–inch 33rpm

ATCO 10-12 68-69
CROWN 15-20 63
DOT (3512 "Torquay") 15-25 63
(Monaural.)
DOT (3545 "Sugar Shack")........15-25 63
(Monaural.)

DOT (3577 "Buddy's Buddy").... 40-50 64
(Monaural.)
DOT (3643 "Lucky 'Leven")....... 15-25 63
(Monaural.)
DOT (3668 "Folkbeat")............. 15-25 63
(Monaural.)
DOT (3709 "Campusology")...... 15-25 63
(Monaural.)
DOT (25512 "Torquay") 20-30 63
(Stereo.)
DOT (25545 "Sugar Shack")..... 20-30 63
(Stereo.)
DOT (25577 "Buddy's Buddy") 75-100 64
(Stereo.)
DOT (25643 "Lucky 'Leven")..... 20-30 63
(Stereo.)
DOT (25668 "Folkbeat")........... 20-30 63
(Stereo.)
DOT (25709 "Campusology").... 20-30 63
(Stereo.)
DOT (25856 "Firewater").......... 20-30 63

Also see FIREBALLS
Also see JIM & MONICA
Also see SEDAKA, Neil, & Tokens / Angels / Jimmy Gilmer and the Fireballs

GILMOUR, David

LP '78

Singles: 12–inch 33/45rpm

COLUMBIA 4-6 84-86

Singles: 7–inch

COLUMBIA 3-4 84-86

Picture Sleeves

COLUMBIA 3-4 84

LPs: 10/12–inch 33rpm

COLUMBIA 5-10 78-85

Also see PINK FLOYD

GILREATH, James

P&R/R&B '63

Singles: 7–inch

JOY 4-8 63-64

GILSTRAP, Jim

P&R/R&B/LP '75

Singles: 7–inch

BELL 3-5 74
ROXBURY 3-5 75-76

LPs: 10/12–inch 33rpm

ROXBURY 5-10 75-76

GINA GO-GO

P&R '89

Singles: 7–inch

CAPITOL..................................... 3-4 89

GINIE LYNN: see LYNN, Ginie

GIORGIO: see MORODER, Giorgio

GIOVANNI, Nikki, & New York Community Choir

LP '71

LPs: 10/12–inch 33rpm

RIGHT-ON 4-8 71

GIPSY KINGS

LP '88

LPs: 10/12–inch 33rpm

MUSICIAN 5-8 88-89

GIRLFRIENDS

P&R '63

Singles: 7–inch

COLPIX....................................10-15 63-64
MELIC 5-10 63
PIONEER..................................10-15 60

Members: Carolyn Willis; Gloria Goodson; Nannette Jackson.
Also see HONEY CONE

GIRLS CAN'T HELP IT

D&D '83

LPs: 10/12–inch 33rpm

SIRE...5-10 83-84

GIRLSCHOOL

LP '82

Singles: 7–inch

MERCURY 3-4 82

LPs: 10/12–inch 33rpm

MERCURY.................................5-10 82
STIFF AMERICA.......................5-10 82

GIRLTALK

D&D '84

Singles: 7–inch

GEFFEN 3-4 84

GIUFFRIA

P&R/LP '84

Singles: 12–inch 33/45rpm

MCA 4-8 84
(Promotional only.)

Singles: 7–inch

MCA...3-4 84-85
MCA/CAMEL..............................3-4 85-86

Picture Sleeves

MCA 3-4 84-85

LPs: 10/12–inch 33rpm

MCA 5-10 84-85
MCA/CAMEL.............................5-10 85-86

Members: Gregg Giuffria; David Glen Eisley; Craig Goldy; Chuck Wright; Lanny Cordola; David Sikes; Alan Krigger.
Also see ANGEL
Also see HEAR 'N AID
Also see HOUSE of LORDS

GIVENS FAMILY

R&B '85

Singles: 7–inch

PJ..3-4 86
SUGAR HILL...............................3-4 85

GLADIOLAS

P&R/R&B '57

Singles: 78rpm

EXCELLO.................................. 15-25 57

Singles: 7-inch

EXCELLO (2101 "Little Darlin"). 25-50 57
EXCELLO (2110 "Run, Run Little Joe") 25-50 57
EXCELLO (2120 "I Wanta Know")................................ 25-50 57
EXCELLO (2136 "Say You'll Be Mine") 20-40 58

Members: Maurice Williams; Norman Wade; Bill Massey; Willie Jones; Earl Gainey; Bobby Robinson.
Also see WILLIAMS, Maurice, & Zodiacs

GLADSTONE

P&R '72

Singles: 7-inch

ABC... 3-5 72

LPs: 10/12-inch 33rpm

ABC... 8-10 72-73

Members: H.L. Voelker; Michael Rabon; Doug Rhone.

GLAHE, Will, & His Orchestra

P&R '39

Singles: 78rpm

LONDON.................................... 3-4 55-57
RCA.. 3-5 48
VICTOR..................................... 3-5 39-40

Singles: 7-inch

LONDON.................................... 4-8 55-60

LPs: 10/12-inch 33rpm

LONDON.................................. 10-15 55-60

GLASS, Philip

LP '82

LPs: 10/12-inch 33rpm

CBS... 5-10 82-86

Also see ANDERSON, Laurie
Also see RONSTADT, Linda

GLASS BOTTLE

P&R '71

Singles: 7-inch

AVCO....................................... 3-5 71
AVCO EMBASSY......................... 3-5 70

LPs: 10/12-inch 33rpm

AVCO....................................... 8-12 71

Member: Gary Criss.

GLASS FAMILY

R&B '78

Singles: 7-inch

SIDEWALK (920 "Teenage Rebellion")............................ 10-20 67
W.B. (309 "Guess I'll Let You Go")...................................... 10-15 69
(Promotional issue only.)
W.B. (7262 "Guess I'll Let You Go") 5-10 69

LPs: 10/12-inch 33rpm

W.B. (1776 "Electric Band").......15-25 69

Members: Ralph Parrett; Gary Green.

GLASS HARP

LP '71

Singles: 7-inch

DECCA 4-8 71-72
UNITED AUDIO 8-12

LPs: 10/12-inch 33rpm

DECCA 10-20 71-72
MCA..5-10

Members: Phil Keaggy; Dan Pecchio; John Ferra.

GLASS HOUSE

P&R/R&B '69

Singles: 7-inch

INVICTUS 3-6 69-72

LPs: 10/12-inch 33rpm

INVICTUS 8-10 71-72
KIRSHNER 8-10 71

Members: Scherrie Payne; Ty Hunter; Larry Mitchell; Pearl Jones; Eric Dunham.
Also see HUNTER, Ty
Also see PAYNE, Scherrie

GLASS MOON

LP '80

Singles: 7-inch

RADIO...3-4 82

LPs: 10/12-inch 33rpm

RADIO...5-10 80-82

GLASS TIGER

P&R/LP '86

Singles: 12-inch 33/45rpm

MANHATTAN...............................4-6 86

Singles: 7-inch

EMI/MANHATTAN 3-4 88
MANHATTAN...............................3-4 86-87

Picture Sleeves

EMI/MANHATTAN 3-4 88
MANHATTAN...............................3-4 86-87

LPs: 10/12-inch 33rpm

EMI/MANHATTAN 5-8 88
MANHATTAN...............................5-10 86

GLAZER, Tom

(With the Children's Do-Re-Mi Chorus; with Dotty Evans & Robin Morgan)

P&R/LP '63

Singles: 78rpm

COLUMBIA 5-10 53-55
CORAL..5-10 56

Singles: 7-inch

COLUMBIA 5-10 53-55
CORAL..5-10 56
KAPP 4-8 63-64
U.A. 4-8 66-67

Picture Sleeves

KAPP 5-10 63

LPs: 10/12–inch 33rpm

CAMDEN 5-10 64-65
KAPP 10-15 63-64
COLUMBIA 20-30 55
HARMONY 10-15 59
MERCURY 15-25 55
MOTIVATION 5-10 62
RIVERSIDE 10-15 61
U.A. 10-15 66
WASHINGTON 10-15 59
WONDERLAND 10-15 63

GLEASON, Jackie
(Jackie Gleason's Orchestra)

P&R '53

Singles: 78rpm

CAPITOL 3-5 52-57
DECCA (27000 series) 3-5 51

Singles: 7–inch

CAPITOL 5-10 52-62
DECCA (27000 series) 4-8 51

EPs: 7–inch 33/45rpm

CAPITOL (Except 511) 5-15 53-60
CAPITOL (511 "And Awa-a-ay We Go") 50-75 54
(Double EP set.)
CAPITOL (511 "And Awa-a-ay We Go") 75-100 54
(With "EBF" prefix. Boxed two-EP set.)

LPs: 10/12–inch 33rpm

CAPITOL (Except 511) 5-15 53-69
CAPITOL (511 "And Awa-a-y We Go") 75-100 54
(10–inch LP. Has songs by Jackie, sung in character by: Joe the Bartender; The Loud Mouth; Ralph Kramden; Fenwick Babbitt; Reggie Van Gleason III, & Poor Soul.)
Also see MARTIN, Dean / Jackie Gleason

GLENCOVES

P&R '63

Singles: 7–inch

SELECT 5-8 63-64

GLENN, Darrell

C&W/P&R '53

Singles: 78rpm

DOT 3-6 56
RCA 3-6 54
VALLEY 4-8 53

Singles: 7–inch

COLUMBIA 3-6 66-67
DOT 10-15 56
FASHION 5-10 60
LONGHORN 4-8 65
NRC 8-12 58
POMPEII 3-6 68-69
RCA 5-10 54
ROBBIE 3-6 64
TWINKLE (505 "That's Right") .. 30-50
VALLEY 8-12 53

LPs: 10/12–inch 33rpm

NRC 12-20 59

GLENN, Garry

R&B '87

Singles: 7–inch

MOTOWN 3-4 87

GLENN, Lloyd

R&B '50

Singles: 78rpm

ALADDIN 3-6 56-57
HOLLYWOOD 4-8 54
SWING TIME 5-10 52-54

Singles: 7–inch

ALADDIN 8-12 56-59
HOLLYWOOD 10-15 54
IMPERIAL 4-8 62
SWING TIME 20-30 52-54

LPs: 10/12–inch 33rpm

ALADDIN (808 "Chica-Boo") 50-75 56
(Black vinyl.)
ALADDIN (808 "Chica-Boo") .. 150-200 56
(Colored vinyl.)
BLACK & BLUE 8-10 77
IMPERIAL (9174 "Chica-Boo") .. 30-40 62
(Monaural.)
IMPERIAL (12174 "Chica-Boo") 30-40 62
(Stereo.)
SCORE (4006 "Piano Stylings") 50-100 56
SCORE (4020 "After Hours") ... 50-100 57
SWING TIME (1901 "Lloyd Glenn") 125-150 54
(10–inch LP.)
Also see BROWN, Charles / Lloyd Glenn
Also see FULSON, Lowell
Also see MILLER, Red, Trio
Also see WALKER, T-Bone

GLITTER, Gary
(With the Glitter Band)

P&R/LP '72

Singles: 7–inch

ARISTA 3-5 75
BELL 3-5 72-74

LPs: 10/12–inch 33rpm

BELL 8-10 72
EPIC 6-10 81
Also see GLITTER BAND

GLITTER BAND

P&R/R&B '76

Singles: 7–inch

ARISTA 3-5 75-76

LPs: 10/12–inch 33rpm

ARISTA 8-10 76
Member: Pete Gill.
Also see GLITTER, Gary
Also see MOTORHEAD

GLORIES

P&R/R&B '67

Singles: 7-inch

DATE (1553 "I Stand Accused") . 5-10 67
DATE (1559 "Sing Me a Love Song") 10-20 67
DATE (1593 "Stand By") 10-20 68
DATE (1615 "I Worship You Baby") 20-40 67
DATE (1622 "No News") 10-20 67

Members: Yvonne Gearing; Betty Stokes; Mildred Vaney.
Also see QUIET ELEGANCE

GLOVER, Roger

LP '76

Singles: 7-inch

21 .... 3-4 84
UK 8-10 75

LPs: 10/12-inch 33rpm

POLYDOR 5-10 78
21 .... 5-10 84
U.K. 8-10 75

Also see DEEP PURPLE
Also see RAINBOW

GO WEST

P&R/R&B/D&D/LP '85

Singles: 7-inch

CHRYSALIS 3-4 85-87

Picture Sleeves

CHRYSALIS 3-4 85-87

LPs: 10/12-inch 33rpm

CHRYSALIS 5-10 85-87

Members: Peter Cox; Richard Drummie.

GOANNA

P&R/LP '83

Singles: 7-inch

ATCO 3-4 83

Picture Sleeves

ATCO 3-4 83

LPs; 10/12-inch 33rpm

ATCO 5-10 83

GODFATHERS

LP '88

LPs: 10/12-inch 33rpm

EPIC 5-8 88-89

GODFREY, Arthur

P&R '47

Singles: 78rpm

COLUMBIA 3-5 50-56
DECCA (29000 series) 3-4 55

Singles: 7-inch

COLUMBIA 5-10 50-56
CONTEMPO 3-6 63-64
DECCA (29000 series) 5-8 55
MGM 3-6 66
MTA 3-5 69
SIGNATURE 4-8 60
VEE JAY 3-6 65

Picture Sleeves

MGM 5-10 66

EPs: 7-inch 33/45rpm

COLUMBIA 8-15 52-56

LPs: 10/12-inch 33rpm

ADMIRAL 8-12 67
CAMDEN 8-12 66-67
CAPITOL 8-15 62
COLUMBIA 10-20 53-61
CONTEMPO 8-15
HARMONY 10-15 59
RCA 5-10 73
SIGNATURE 8-15 60

Also see MARINERS

GODFREY, Arthur, with Archie Bleyer

EPs: 7-inch 33/45rpm

CADENCE 10-20 54

LPs: 10/12-inch 33rpm

CADENCE (540 "Christmas with Godfrey and the Little Godfreys") 30-40 54
(10-inch LP.)

Also see BLEYER, Archie

GODFREY, Arthur /Carmel Quinn / Frank Parker / Janette Davis

(With Will Rowland & His Orchestra)

EPs: 7-inch 33/45rpm

COLUMBIA ("Arthur Godfrey & His Friends") 8-10 50s
(No selection number used.)

Also see GODFREY, Arthur
Also see QUINN, Carmel

GODFREY, John, Trio

R&B '51

Singles: 78rpm

CHESS 4-8 51
HILLTOP 5-10 51

GODLEY, Kevin, & Lol Creme

(Godley & Creme)

P&R/D&D/LP '85

Singles: 12-inch 33/45rpm

POLYDOR 4-8 85

Singles: 7-inch

MERCURY 3-5 77
MIRAGE 3-4 82
POLYDOR 3-4 85

Picture Sleeves

POLYDOR 3-4 85

LPs: 10/12-inch 33rpm

MERCURY 10-15 77
MIRAGE 5-10 82
POLYDOR 5-10 85

Also see SCAFFOLD
Also see 10CC

GODSPELL

(Robin Lamont & Original "Godspell" Cast)

P&R '72

Singles: 7-inch

BELL 3-5 72

GODWIN, Peter

D&D '83

Singles: 12-inch 33/45rpm

POLYDOR 4-6 83

GODZ

LP '78

Singles: 7-inch

MILLENIUM................................ 3-5 78

LPs: 10/12-inch 33rpm

CASABLANCA........................... 5-10 78
MILLENIUM/CASABLANCA 5-10 78

GOFFIN, Louise

P&R/LP '79

Singles: 7-inch

ASYLUM 3-5 79
ELEKTRA................................... 3-5 79

LPs: 10/12-inch 33rpm

ASYLUM 5-10 79-81

GO-GOs

P&R/LP '81

Singles: 12-inch 33/45

I.R.S 4-8 82-84

Singles: 7-inch

I.R.S. (Except 8001)..................... 3-5 81-85
I.R.S. (8001 "We Got the Beat").... 4-8 82
(Picture disc.)

Picture Sleeves

I.R.S. 3-5 81-85

LPs: 10/12-inch 33rpm

I.R.S. 5-10 81-90
Members: Belinda Carlisle; Charlotte Caffey; Jane Wiedlin; Margot Olaverria; Elissa Bello; Gina Schook; Kathy Valentine.
Also see CARLISLE, Belinda
Also see GRACES
Also see TEXTONES
Also see VENTURES
Also see WIEDLIN, Jane

GOLD, Angie

D&D '85

Singles: 12-inch 33/45rpm

PASSION 4-6 85

GOLD, Marty, & His Orchestra

LP '63

Singles: 7-inch

KAPP 3-5 58-59
RCA.. 3-5 60-61

EPs: 7-inch 33/45rpm

KAPP 4-8 59
VIK 5-10 56-57

LPs: 10/12-inch 33rpm

KAPP....................................... 8-12 59
RCA... 8-12 59-63
VIK 10-20 56-57

GOLDDIGGERS

LP '69

Singles: 7-inch

METROMEDIA........................... 3-5 69
RCA 3-5 72

LPs: 10/12-Inch 33rpm

METROMEDIA.............................8-12 69
RCA 5-10 71
Member: Jimmi Cannon.
Also see MARTIN, Dean

GOLDE, Frannie

P&R '79

Singles: 7-inch

ATLANTIC...................................3-5 76-77
BIG TREE 3-5 76
PORTRAIT...................................3-5 79

LPs: 10/12-inch 33rpm

ATLANTIC...................................8-10 76
PORTRAIT...................................5-10 79

GOLDEN EARRING

P&R/LP '74

Singles: 7-inch

ATLANTIC...................................3-5 70
MCA 3-5 76-78
POLYDOR (2000 series) 3-4 79
POLYDOR (14000 series) 3-6 69
TRACK...3-5 74-75
21 ....3-4 82-86

Picture Sleeves

21 ....3-5 84

LPs: 10/12-inch 33rpm

ATLANTIC.................................15-20 69
CAPITOL (164 "Miracle Mirror").30-35 69
CAPITOL (2823 "Winter Harvest")...................................30-35 67
CAPITOL (11315 "Golden Earring")................................10-12 74
DWARF 10-20
MCA...6-10 75-81
POLYDOR 5-10 79-80
TRACK (396 "Moontan")............20-25 73
(With nude showgirl on cover.)
TRACK (396 "Moontan")............10-12 73
(Showgirl not nude on cover.)
TRACK (2139 "Switch") 8-12 75
21 ....5-10 82-86

GOLDEN GATE STRINGS
(With Stu Phillips)

LP '67

LPs: 10/12-inch 33rpm

EPIC...5-10 67
Also see HOLLYRIDGE STRINGS

GOLDSBORO, Bobby

P&R '62

Singles: 7-inch

CURB..3-4 80-82
EPIC...3-5 77
LAURIE 5-8 62-63
U.A. (Except 672 thru 980) 4-6 66-73
U.A. (672 thru 980) 5-8 63-66
VISTA..3-5 74

Picture Sleeves

U.A. (Except 710)........................ 4-8 66-74
U.A. (710 "Whenever He Holds You")........................ 8-12 64

LPs: 10/12-inch 33rpm

CURB........................ 5-10 80-82
DORAL........................ 15-25
(Promotional mail-order issue, from Doral cigarettes.)
EPIC........................ 8-10 77
K-TEL........................ 5-10
LIBERTY........................ 5-10 81
SUNSET........................ 8-12 60s
U.A........................ 10-20 64-76

Also see ORBISON, Roy
Also see REEVES, Del, & Bobby Goldsboro

GOLDSBORO, Bobby / Jimmy Durante

Singles: 7-inch

LIGHT (608 "We Gotta Start Lovin'")........................ 4-8 71

Also see DURANTE, Jimmy

GOLLIWOGS

Singles: 7-inch

FANTASY (590 "Don't Tell Me No Lies")........................ 40-60 64
FANTASY (597 "You Came Walking")........................ 40-60 65
FANTASY (599 "You got Nothing on Me")........................ 30-50 65
SCORPIO (404 "Brown Eyed Girl")........................ 30-50 65
SCORPIO (405 "Fragile Child") 30-50 66
SCORPIO (408 "Walking on the Water")........................ 30-50 66
SCORPIO (412 "Porterville")..... 40-60 67

LPs: 10/12-inch 33rpm

FANTASY (9474 "Pre-Creedence")........................ 10-15 75

Members: John Fogerty; Tom Fogerty; Doug Clifford; Stuart Cook.
Also see CREEDENCE CLEARWATER REVIVAL

GOMM, Ian

P&R/LP '79

Singles: 7-inch

STIFF........................ 3-5 79

LPs: 10/12-inch 33rpm

STIFF........................ 5-10 79-80

GONE ALL STARS

P&R '58

Singles: 7-inch

GONE........................ 10-15 58
ROULETTE........................ 3-5 71

EPs: 7-inch 33/45rpm

GONE (101 "Dancin' Bandstand")........................ 35-55 58

Member: Buddy Lucas.

GONZALES, Terri

R&B '82

Singles: 7-inch

BECKET........................ 3-4 82

GONZALEZ

P&R/R&B/LP '79

Singles: 12-inch 33/45rpm

CAPITOL........................ 4-6 79

Singles: 7-inch

CAPITOL........................ 3-5 78-79

LPs: 10/12-inch 33rpm

CAPITOL........................ 5-10 78-80

GOOD QUESTION

P&R '88

Singles: 7-inch

PAISLEY PARK........................ 3-4 88

Picture Sleeves

PAISLEY PARK........................ 3-4 88

GOODIE

R&B '82

Singles: 12-inch 33/45rpm

TOTAL EXPERIENCE........................ 4-6 82-84

Singles: 7-inch

TOTAL EXPERIENCE........................ 3-4 82-84

LPs: 10/12-inch 33rpm

TOTAL EXPERIENCE........................ 5-10 83

GOODIES

P&R '75

Singles: 7-inch

20TH FOX........................ 3-5 75

GOODING, Cuba

R&B/D&D '83

Singles: 12-inch 33/45rpm

STREETWISE........................ 4-6 83

Singles: 7-inch

MOTOWN........................ 3-5 78-79
STREETWISE........................ 3-4 83

LPs: 10/12-inch 33rpm

MOTOWN........................ 5-10 78-79

Also see MAIN INGREDIENT

GOODMAN, Benny, Orchestra
(Benny Goodman Sextet)

P&R '31

Singles: 78rpm

CAPITOL........................ 3-6 40s
COLUMBIA (Except 2856)........... 5-15 33-56
COLUMBIA (2856 "Your Mother's Son-In-Law")........................ 30-50 34
(Colored plastic. Vocal by Billie Holiday.)
MELOTONE........................ 10-20 31
VICTOR (Except 25808)........... 5-15 36-58
VICTOR (25808 "Popcorn Man")........................ 750-1000 39

Singles: 7-inch

CAPITOL........................ 4-8 50s
CHESS........................ 4-6 59
COLUMBIA (Except 250)........... 4-8 50-56

COLUMBIA (250 "1938 Carnegie Hall Concert") 25-45 50s
(Boxed, two LP set.)
COMMAND 3-5 67
DECCA 3-5 62
RCA 4-8 50-59

EPs: 7-inch 33/45rpm

BRUNSWICK 5-10 54
CAPITOL 5-10 55-56
COLUMBIA 5-10 50-58
DECCA (798 "The Benny Goodman Story") 10-15 56
MGM 4-8 59
RCA 5-10 50-59

LPs: 10/12-inch 33rpm

ABC 6 10 76
BRIGHT ORANGE 5-10 73
BRUNSWICK 10-20 54
CAMDEN 5-10 63-65
CAPITOL 5-15 55-78
CENTURY 5-10 79
CHESS 5-15 59
COLPIX 8-12 62
COLUMBIA (Except 160) 5-15 50-82
COLUMBIA (160 "The Famous 1938 Carnegie Hall Concert") 25-40
(Boxed, two-LP set. Includes cardboard inner sleeves.)
COMMAND 5-10 67
DECCA (188 "The Benny Goodman Story, Volumes 1 & 2") 25-35
DECCA (8252 "The Benny Goodman Story, Volume 1") 20-30 56
DECCA (8253 "The Benny Goodman Story, Volume 2") 20-30 56
DECCA (7-8252 "The Benny Goodman Story, Volume 1") 15-20 59
(Reprocessed stereo.)
DECCA (7-8253 "The Benny Goodman Story, Volume 2") 15-20 59
(Reprocessed stereo.)
EVEREST 5-10 73
HARMONY 5-10 59-60
LONDON 5-10 72-78
LONDON/PHASE 4 .... 5-10 71-72
MCA 5-10 80
MGM 5-15 59
MARK '56 .... 5-10 77
MEGA 5-10 72-74
MUSICMASTERS 5-10
PAUSA 5-10 83
PRESTIGE 5-10 69
QUINTESSENCE 4-8 79
RCA (Except 6703) 5-15 50-78
RCA (6703 "The Golden Age of Swing") 15-20 55
SUNBEAM 5-10 73
TIME-LIFE (354 "Into the '70s" .. 10-20 72
(Boxed, three-LP set. Includes booklet.)
WESTINGHOUSE ("World Favorites") 20-30 58
((No selection number used.)
X 10-15 54

Also see BASIE, Count, & Benny Goodman
Also see HOLIDAY, Billie
Also see LEE, Peggy

GOODMAN, Benny, Trio, with Rosemary Clooney

Singles: 78rpm

COLUMBIA 3-5 50-56

Singles: 7-inch

COLUMBIA 5-10 56

LPs: 10/12-inch 33rpm

COLUMBIA 15-25 56

Also see CLOONEY, Rosemary
Also see GOODMAN, Benny, Orchestra

GOODMAN, Dickie

P&R '61

Singles: 7-inch

AUDIO SPECTRUM 10-20 64
CASH 4-6 75
COTIQUE 4-8 69
DIAMOND 10-15 62
EXTRAN 5-8 82
GOODNAME 3-5 88
HOTLINE 4-6 79
J.M.D. 15-20 62
JANUS 3-6 77
M.D 10-20 61
MARK-X 10-20 61
MONTAGE 3-5 82
PRELUDE 3-5 80
RAINY WEDNESDAY 4-8 73-75
RAMGO 8-12 70
RED BIRD 10-15 66
RHINO 3-5 84
RORI 10-15 61
SHARK 4-6 79
SHELL 3-5 84
SHOCK 4-6 77
20TH FOX 10-15 63
TWIRL 10-15 66
WACKO 3-5 81
Z-100 .... 3-5 84

LPs: 10/12-inch 33rpm

CASH (6000 "Mr. Jaws") 25-30 75
COMET (69 "My Son the Joke") 20-30 64
IX CHAINS 12-15 73
RHINO 5-10 83
RORI (3301 "Many Heads of Dickie Goodman") 50-75 62

Also see BUCHANAN & GOODMAN

GOODMAN, Steve

LP '75

Singles: 7-inch

ASYLUM 3-5 75-81
BUDDAH 3-5 72-73

LPs: 10/12-inch 33rpm
ASYLUM 5-10 75-80
BUDDAH 8-12 71-76
RED PAJAMAS 5-10 83-87

GOODMAN, Steve, & Phoebe Snow

Singles: 7-inch
ASYLUM 3-4 80
Also see GOODMAN, Steve
Also see SNOW, Phoebe

GOODTIMERS

P&R '61

Singles: 7-inch
ARNOLD 5-10 61
EPIC 4-8 61
Member: Don Covay.
Also see COVAY, Don

GOODWIN, Don

P&R '73

Singles: 7-inch
SILVER BLUE 3-5 73

GOODWIN, Ron

P&R '57

Singles: 78rpm
CAPITOL 3-5 56-57

Singles: 7-inch
CAPITOL 4-10 56-59
KING 4-6 61

LPs: 10/12-inch 33rpm
CAPITOL 8-15 57-60
Also see VINCENT, Gene / Frank Sinatra / Sonny James / Ron Goodwin

GOODY GOODY

P&R/R&B '78

Singles: 7-inch
ATLANTIC 3-5 78

LPs: 10/12-inch 33rpm
ATLANTIC 5-10 78

GOON SQUAD

R&B/D&D '85

Singles: 12-inch 33/45rpm
EPIC 4-6 85

Singles: 7-inch
EPIC 3-4 85

GOOSE CREEK SYMPHONY
(Goose Creek)

P&R/LP '72

Singles: 7-inch
CAPITOL 3-6 70-72

LPs: 10/12-inch 33rpm
CAPITOL 10-15 70-72
COLUMBIA 8-12 74
RLO 8-12
Members: Mike McFadden; Ed Black.

GORDON, Barry
(With Art Mooney & His Orchestra)

P&R '55

Singles: 78rpm
MGM 4-8 55-56

Singles: 7-inch
ABC 4-6 68
CAPITOL 3-5 71
CADENCE 4-8 62
DUNHILL 4-6 68
ERA 4-8 59
MGM 5-10 55-56
MERCURY 4-8 61
U.A. 4-6 64-66

Picture Sleeves
MGM (12092 "Nuttin' for Christmas") 10-20 56

LPs: 10/12-inch 33rpm
U.A. 8-15 66
Also see MOONEY, Art, & His Orchestra

GORDON, Robert
(With Link Wray)

P&R/LP '77

Singles: 12-inch 33/45rpm
PRIVATE STOCK 10-15 78
RCA 8-12 81
(Promotional issue only.)

Singles: 7-inch
PRIVATE STOCK 4-6 77-78
RCA (Black vinyl) 3-5 79-81
RCA (Colored vinyl) 8-12 79-81
(Promotional issue only.)

Picture Sleeves
PRIVATE STOCK (45203 "Fire") . 5-10 79
RCA (11471 "It's Only Make Believe") 5-10 79

LPs: 10/12-inch 33rpm
PRIVATE STOCK 8-10 77-78
RCA (Black vinyl) 5-10 79-82
RCA (Colored vinyl) 20-30 79

Promotional LPs
RCA (3411 "Robert Gordon"/"Live From Paradise in Boston") 35-45 79
Also see WRAY, Link

GORDON, Roscoe

R&B '51

Singles: 78rpm
CHESS (1487 "Booted") 30-50 52
DUKE (101 "Tell Daddy") 30-50 52
DUKE (106 thru 129) 10-20 53-54
FLIP (227 "Just Love Me Baby") 50-100 55
RPM (322 "Roscoe's Boogie") ... 35-50 50
RPM (336 "A Dime a Dozen") 25-35 50
RPM (344 thru 384) 20-30 51-53
SUN (Except 227 & 237) 30-40 56-58
SUN (227 "Just Love Me Baby") 75-100 55

SUN (237 "The Chicken") 50-75 56

Singles: 7-inch

ABC-PAR 5-10 62-63
CHESS (1487 "Booted")........ 200-300 52
COLLECTABLES 3-4 81
DUKE (106 "T-Model Boogie").. 40-60 53
DUKE (109 "Too Many Women") 25-50 53
DUKE (114 "Ain't No Use") 25-50 53
DUKE (129 "Three Cent Love") 25-50 54
DUKE (300 series) 5-10 60
FLIP (227 "Just Love Me Baby") 200-300 55
FLIP (237 "The Chicken") 20-30 56
OLD TOWN 4-6 64
RPM (324 "Saddle the Cow") 250-350 50
RPM (336 "Dime a Dozen") .. 100-200 50
RPM (344 "Booted") 50-100 51
RPM (350 "No More Doggin'") .. 50-75 51
RPM (358 "New Orleans Wimmen") 50-75 51
RPM (365 "What You Got on Your Mind") 50-75 51
RPM (369 "Trying") 40-60 52
RPM (373 "Lucille") 40-60 52
RPM (379 "Just in from Texas") 40-60 52
RPM (384 "We're All Loaded").. 40-60 52
SUN (Except 227 & 237).......... 25-50 56-58
SUN (227 "Just Love Me Baby") 400-500 55
SUN (237 "The Chicken") 100-200 56
VEE JAY 5-10 59-61

Also see ROSCOE & BARBARA

GORE, Lesley

P&R/R&B/LP '63

Singles: 7-inch

A&M 3-6 75-76
CREWE 3-6 70-71
MERCURY (72119 thru 72206) .. 5-10 63
MERCURY (72245 "Je Ne Sais Plus") 10-20 64
MERCURY (72259 thru 72726) .. 5-10 64-67
MERCURY (72842 thru 72969) 10-15 68-69
MOWEST 3-6 72

Picture Sleeves

A&M 5-10 75-76
MERCURY 10-15 63-67

LPs: 10/12-inch 33rpm

A&M 8-10 75
MERCURY (8000 series)........... 5-10 80
MERCURY (20000 & 60000 series) 20-30 63-68
MOWEST 8-10 72
POLYDOR 5-10 85
WING 10-20 67-69

Also see BILLY & SUE
Also see DRIFTERS / Leslie Gore / Roy Orbison / Los Bravos

GORE, Leslie, & Lou Christie

Singles: 7-inch

MANHATTAN (50039 "Since I Don't Have You") 5-8 86

Also see CHRISTIE, Lou
Also see GORE, Leslie

GORE, Martin L.

LP '89

LPs: 10/12-inch 33rpm

SIRE...5-8 89

GORE, Michael

P&R '84

Singles: 7-inch

CAPITOL.......................................3-4 84

GORKY PARK

LP '89

Singles: 7-inch

MERCURY 3-4 90

LPs: 10/12-inch 33rpm

MERCURY 5-8 89

GORL, Robert

D&D '84

Singles: 12-inch 33/45rpm

ELEKTRA.......................................4-6 84

Singles: 7-inch

ELEKTRA.......................................3-4 84

GORME, Eydie

P&R '54

Singles: 78rpm

ABC-PAR 3-5 55-62

Singles: 7-inch

ABC-PAR 4-8 55-62
CALENDAR 3-6 67
COLUMBIA 3-8 62-68
(Black vinyl.)
COLUMBIA (43082 "I Want You to Be My Baby")........................5-10 64
(Colored vinyl.)
CORAL...5-10 53-55
GALA 3-5 76
MGM 3-5 71-73
RCA 3-5 69-70
U.A. 3-6 60-76

Picture Sleeves

COLUMBIA 4-8 62-63

LPs: 10/12-inch 33rpm

ABC-PAR 15-25 57-65
APPLAUSE 4-6 81
COLUMBIA 10-20 63-73
GALA 5-8 76
HARMONY 5-10 68-71
MGM 5-10 71
RCA 5-10 68-70
U.A. 10-20 61-62
VOCALION 8-15 63

Also see LAWRENCE, Steve, & Eydie Gorme

GOUDREAU, Barry

LP '80

Singles: 7-inch

PORTRAIT 3-4 79

LPs: 10/12-inch 33rpm

PORTRAIT 5-10 79

Also see BOSTON

GOULET, Robert

P&R/LP '62

Singles: 7-inch

ABC 3-5 74
ARTISTS of AMERICA 3-5 75
COLUMBIA (Black vinyl) 3-6 61-70
COLUMBIA (Colored vinyl) 5-10 63
MGM 3-5 73
MERLIN 3-5 71
PARAMOUNT 3-5 74

Picture Sleeves

ABC 3-6 74
COLUMBIA (Except 59227) 3-6 62-65
COLUMBIA (59227 "The Moon Was Yellow") 5-10 63
(Promotional issue only.)

EPs: 7-inch 33/45rpm

COLUMBIA (9096 "Robert Goulet") 4-8 65
(Jukebox issue.)

LPs: 10/12-inch 33rpm

ARTISTS of AMERICA 5-10 76
COLUMBIA 5-15 61-73
HARMONY 5-10 71-72
MERLIN 5-10 71
ORINDA 5-10 78

GRACE, Fredi, & Rhinestone

R&B '82

Singles: 7-inch

RCA 3-4 82

GRACE, Leda

R&B '81

Singles: 7-inch

POLYDOR 3-4 81

GRACES

P&R/LP '89

LPs: 10/12-inch 33rpm

A&M 5-8 89

Members: Charlotte Caffey; Meredith Brooks; Gia Ciambotti.
Also see GO-GOs

GRACIE, Charlie

P&R/R&B '57

Singles: 78rpm

CADILLAC 15-25 53-54
CAMEO 10-15 57
20TH CENTURY 10-20 55

Singles: 7-inch

ABKCO 3-5 75
CADILLAC (141 "Boogie Woogie Blues") 75-125 53
CADILLAC (144 "Rockin' & Rollin") 75-125 54
CAMEO 10-20 57-59
CORAL 5-10 59
DIAMOND 10-20 65
FELSTED 5-10 61
PRESIDENT 5-10 62
SOCK & SOUL 4-6 70
ROULETTE 5-10 59-61
20TH CENTURY (5035 "Honey Honey") 35-55 55

GRADDOCK, Billy: see CRADDOCK, Billy

GRADUATES

P&R '59

Singles: 7-inch

CORSICAN 10-20 59
SHAN-TODD 10-20 59

Picture Sleeves

CORSICAN 20-30 59

GRAHAM, Jaki

R&B '85

Singles: 12-inch 33/45rpm

CAPITOL 4-6 86

Singles: 7-inch

CAPITOL 3-4 86

LPs: 10/12-inch 33rpm

CAPITOL 5-10 86

GRAHAM, Jaki, & David Grant

R&B '86

Singles: 12-inch 33/45rpm

CAPITOL 4-6 86

Singles: 7-inch

CAPITOL 3-4 86

Also see GRAHAM, Jaki
Also see GRANT, David

GRAHAM, Larry

(Graham Central Station; with Graham Central Station)

P&R/LP '74

Singles: 7-inch

ARISTA 3-4 87
W.B. 3-5 74-83

Picture Sleeves

W.B. 3-5 80

LPs: 10/12-inch 33rpm

W.B. 5-10 73-83

Also see FRANKLIN, Aretha, & Larry Graham
Also see SLY & Family Stone

GRAINGERS

R&B '81

Singles: 7-inch

BC 3-4 81

GRAMM, Lou

P&R/LP '87

Singles: 7-inch

ATLANTIC....3-4 87-90

Picture Sleeves

ATLANTIC....3-4 87

LPs: 10/12-inch 33rpm

ATLANTIC....5-10 87-89

Also see FOREIGNER

GRAMMER, Billy

P&R/R&B '58

Singles: 7-inch

DECCA....4-8 61-66
EPIC....4-6 66-67
EVEREST....5-8 60
MERCURY....3-6 68-69
MONUMENT (Except 400 series)....3-5 75-76
MONUMENT (400 series)....5-10 59-63
RICE....4-6 67
STOP....3-5 69

EPs: 7-inch 33/45rpm

DECCA....5-10 64

LPs: 10/12-inch 33rpm

CLASSIC CHRISTMAS....5-10 77
DECCA....10-15 62-64
EPIC....8-12 67
MONUMENT (4000 "Travelin' On")....15-20 59
(With *Lost in a Small Cafe.*)
MONUMENT (8039 "Travelin' On")....8-12 66
(*Lost in a Small Cafe* is replaced with *Gotta Travel On.*)
STONEWAY....5-10 75
VOCALION....6-12 68

Also see CASH, Johnny / Billy Grammer / Wilburn Brothers

GRANAHAN, Gerry

(Granahan-Quintal Band)

P&R '58

Singles: 12-inch 33/45rpm

DOWNTOWN....5-8 87

Singles: 7-inch

CANADIAN AMERICAN....5-10 60
CAPRICE (Except 108)....5-10 61
CAPRICE (108 "Dance Girl, Dance")....50-75 61
(With the Wildwoods, a.k.a. the Five Satins.)
COLLECTABLES....3-4
GONE....8-12 59-60
SUNBEAM....15-20 58-59
20TH FOX....5-10 63
VEEP....4-8 65

Picture Sleeves

GONE (5081 "Look for Me")....15-25 60

Also see DICKY DOO & DON'TS
Also see FIVE SATINS
Also see FONTAINE, Eddie, & Gerry Granahan
Also see GRANT, Jerry, & Rockabilly Bandits

GRANATA, Rocca, & International Quintet

P&R '59

Singles: 7-inch

LAURIE....3-6 59

Picture Sleeves

LAURIE....5-8 59

GRAND CANYON

P&R '74

Singles: 7-inch

BANG....4-6 74
FAITHFUL VIRTUE....3-5 70

GRAND FUNK RAILROAD

(Grand Funk)

P&R/LP '69

Singles: 7-inch

CAPITOL (Black vinyl)....3-6 69-76
CAPITOL (Colored vinyl)....5-8 73
(Promotional issue only.)
FULL MOON....3-4 81
MCA....3-5 76-77

Picture Sleeves

CAPITOL....3-6 71-76
FULL MOON....3-4 81
MCA....3-5 76

LPs: 10/12-inch 33rpm

CAPITOL (307 thru 853)....8-15 69-71
CAPITOL (11000 series, except 11207)....6-12 72-76
CAPITOL (11207 "We're an American Band")....6-10 73
(Black vinyl.)
CAPITOL (11207 "We're an American Band")....20-30 73
(Colored vinyl. Promotional issue only.)
CAPITOL (12000 & 16000 series)....5-10 80-81
FULL MOON....5-10 81-83
MCA....8-10 76

Members: Mark Farner; Don Brewer; Mel Schacher; Craig Frost.
Also see FARNER, Mark, & Don Brewer
Also see KNIGHT, Terry, & Pack

GRANDMASTER FLASH & Furious Five

(With the Furious Five; with Melle Mel; Grandmaster Flash)

R&B '80

Singles: 12-inch 33/45

ATLANTIC....4-6 84
ELEKTRA....4-6 85-86
SUGAR HILL....4-6 80-85

Singles: 7-inch

ATLANTIC....3-4 84
ELEKTRA....3-4 85-87
MCA....3-4 85
SUGAR HILL....3-5 80-85

Picture Sleeves
ATLANTIC.................................... 3-4 84
LPs: 10/12-inch 33rpm
ELEKTRA.................................. 5-10 86-88
SUGAR HILL.............................. 5-10 82-85
Also see JACKSON, Rebbie
Also see KHAN, Chaka
Also see KING DREAM CHORUS & Holiday Crew
Also see MELLE MEL & Duke Bootee

GRANDMIXER D. ST.

R&B/D&D '83
Singles: 12-inch 33/45rpm
ISLAND 4-6 83
Singles: 7-inch
ISLAND 3-4 83

GRANT, Al
(Al Cernick)
Singles: 78rpm
KING (15004 thru 15045).......... 10-20 49-50
Also see MITCHELL, Guy

GRANT, Amy

P&R/LP '85
Singles: 7-inch
A&M 3-4 85-90
MYRRH 3-5 80-85
Picture Sleeves
A&M 3-4 85-88
LPs: 10/12-inch 33rpm
A&M 5-10 85-91
MYRRH 5-10 80-85
Also see CETERA, Peter, & Amy Grant
Also see GARFUNKEL, Art / Amy Grant

GRANT, David

R&B/D&D '83
Singles: 12-inch 33/45rpm
CHRYSALIS................................ 4-6 83
Singles: 7-inch
CAPITOL.................................... 3-4 86
CHRYSALIS................................ 3-4 83
Also see GRAHAM, Jaki, & David Grant
Also see LINX

GRANT, Earl

P&R/R&B '58
Singles: 78rpm
PRINCE...................................... 4-8 56
Singles: 7-inch
DECCA....................................... 3-8 58-70
PRINCE (1201 "One-Way
Street").................................. 5-10 56
(Black vinyl.)
PRINCE (1201 "One-Way
Street")................................ 10-20 56
(Colored vinyl.)
EPs: 7-inch 33/45rpm
DECCA..................................... 5-10 59-62
LPs: 10/12-inch 33rpm
DECCA..................................... 8-18 59-70
MCA 5-10 76
VOCALION............................... 5-10 69-70

GRANT, Eddy

R&B '79
Singles: 12-inch 33/45rpm
EPIC...4-6 80-82
PORTRAIT..................................4-6 83-85
Singles: 7-inch
EPIC...3-4 79-80
PORTRAIT..................................3-4 83-85
Picture Sleeves
PORTRAIT..................................3-4 84
LPs: 10/12-inch 33rpm
EPIC...5-10 79-80
PORTRAIT................................5-10 83-85
Also see EQUALS

GRANT, Eleanor

R&B '76
Singles: 7-inch
CBS ASSOCIATED 3-4 84-85
CATAWBA 3-4 83
COLUMBIA..................................3-4 76

GRANT, Gogi

P&R '55
Singles: 78rpm
ERA...3-5 55-56
RCA 3-5 52-57
Singles: 7-inch
CHARTER...................................4-6 63
ERA...5-10 55-56
LIBERTY 4-8 60-61
MONUMENT...............................3-6 66-67
PETE..3-6 68-69
RCA 5-10 52-58
20TH FOX...................................4-6 61-62
Picture Sleeves
20TH FOX.................................5-10 61
EPs: 7-inch 33/45rpm
ERA...10-20 56
RCA (Except 1030).....................5-10 57-58
RCA (4112 "Helen Morgan
Story")....................................15-25 57
(Soundtrack.)
LPs: 10/12-inch 33rpm
CHARTER..................................8-12 64
ERA (106 "The Wayward Wind") .8-12
ERA (20001 "Suddenly There's
Gogi Grant")............................15-25 56
(Black vinyl.)
ERA (20001 "Suddenly There's
Gogi Grant")............................30-50 56
(Colored vinyl.)
LIBERTY 8-15 60
PETE...6-10 68-70
RCA (Except 1030)...................10-20 57-59
RCA (1030 "Helen Morgan
Story")....................................60-70 57
(Soundtrack.)

GRANT, Janie

P&R '61

Singles: 7-inch

CAPRICE 10-15 61-62
PARKWAY (982 "My Heart, Your Heart") 15-25 66
U.A. 5-10 63-65
Also see RAY, James

GRANT, Jerry, & Rockabilly Bandits

(Gerry Granahan)

Singles: 7-inch

ATCO (6100 "Talkin' About Love") 20-30 57
Also see GRANAHAN, Gerry

GRANT, Tom

R&B '81

Singles: 7-inch

WMOT 3-5 81

GRAPEFRUIT

P&R '68

Singles: 7-inch

EQUINOX 4-8 68

LPs: 10/12-inch 33rpm

DUNHILL 10-12 68
RCA 10-12 69

GRASS ROOTS

(Rob Grill & the Grass Roots)

P&R '66

Singles: 7-inch

ABC 3-5 70
DUNHILL (Except 4013) 4-8 66-74
DUNHILL (4013 "Mr. Jones") 8-12 65
DUNHILL OLDIES 3-5 70s
HAVEN 3-5 75-76
MCA 3-4 82
OAK 4-6
ROULETTE 3-5 70s

Picture Sleeves

DUNHILL 5-8 67-70

EPs: 7-inch 33/45rpm

DUNHILL (165 "Grass Roots").... 8-12 71
(Promotional issue only.)

LPs: 10/12-inch 33rpm

ABC 8-10 76
COMMAND 8-10 74
DUNHILL 10-20 66-73
GUSTO 5-8 78
HAVEN 8-10 75
MCA 5-10 82
PICKWICK 5-8 78
Members: Rob Grill; Warren Entner; Creed Bratton; Erik Coonce. Session: Denny Provisor; Joel Larson; Joe Osborn; P.F. Sloan.
Also see MERRY-GO-ROUND
Also see SLOAN, P.F.

GRATEFUL DEAD

LP '67

Singles: 12-inch 33/45rpm

ARISTA 5-10 88

Singles: 7-inch

ARISTA (Black vinyl) 3-5 77-88
ARISTA (Colored vinyl) 4-6 87
FLASHBACK 3-4 80
GRATEFUL DEAD 8-15 73-76
SCORPIO (201 "Don't Ease Me In") 75-150 66
W.B. 10-15 67-73

Promotional Singles

ARISTA 4-6 77-87
GRATEFUL DEAD 12-20 73-76
W.B. 10-20 67-73

Picture Sleeves

ARISTA (0519 "Alabama Getaway") 4-6 80
ARISTA (9606 "Touch of Grey") 3-5 87
GRATEFUL DEAD (03 "U.S. Blues") 15-20 74
W.B. (7186 "Dark Star") 35-55 68

EPs: 7-inch 33/45rpm

W.B. (226 "American Beauty")... 20-30 70
(Jukebox issue only.)
W.B. (544 "Europe 72") 20-30 72
(Jukebox issue only.)

LPs: 10/12-inch 33rpm

ARISTA 5-10 77-90
DIRECT-DISK 10-15 79
GRATEFUL DEAD (01 "Wake of the Flood") 15-25 73
(No mention on cover of distribution by United Artists.)
GRATEFUL DEAD (01 "Wake of the Flood") 10-15 70s
(Reads "Distribution by United Artists" on cover.)
GRATEFUL DEAD (102 "Mars Hotel") 20-25 74
(No mention on cover of distribution by United Artists.)
GRATEFUL DEAD (102 "Mars Hotel") 10-15 70s
(Reads "Distribution by United Artists" on cover.)
GRATEFUL DEAD (494 "Blues for Allah") 20-25 75
GRATEFUL DEAD (620 "Steal Your Face") 25-30 76
GRATEFUL DEAD (40132 "One from the Vault") 5-10 91
MFSL (014 "American Beauty") . 40-80 78
MFSL (172 "From the Mars Hotel") 15-25 85
PAIR 6-12 84
PRIDE 12-20 73

SUNFLOWER (5001 "Vintage Dead") 25-35 70
SUNFLOWER (5004 "Historic Dead") 25-35 71
W.B. (W-1689 "Grateful Dead") 40-60 67
(Monaural. Gold label.)
W.B. (WS-1689 "Grateful Dead") 25-35 67
(Stereo. Gold label.)
W.B. (1689 "Grateful Dead") 20-30 67
(With Warner Bros. - Seven Arts "W7" label.)
W.B. (1689 "Grateful Dead") 10-20 71
(With Warner Bros. "Arrowhead" label. Cover has copyright date on back.)
W.B. (1749 "Anthem of the Sun") 20-30 68
(Background cover color is purple. With Warner Bros. - Seven Arts "W7" label.)
W.B. (1749 "Anthem of the Sun") 10-20 71
(Background cover color is white. With Warner Bros. "Arrowhead" logo on label.)
W.B. (1790 "Aoxomoxoa") 20-30 69
(With Warner Bros. - Seven Arts "W7" label.)
W.B. (1790 "Aoxomoxoa") 10-20 71
(With Warner Bros. "Arrowhead" label. Cover has copyright date on back.)
W.B. (1830 "Live Dead") 25-35 69
(With Warner Bros. - Seven Arts "W7" label. Issued with bonus pamphlet.)
W.B. (1830 "Live Dead") 15-20 71
(With Warner Bros. "Arrowhead" label. Cover has copyright date on back.)
W.B. (1869 "Workingman's Dead") 20-30 70
(With Warner Bros. - Seven Arts "W7" label.)
W.B. (1869 "Workingman's Dead") 10-15 71
(With Warner Bros. "Arrowhead" label. Cover has copyright date on back.)
W.B. (1893 "American Beauty") 15-25 70
(With Warner Bros. - Seven Arts "W7" label.)
W.B. (1893 "American Beauty") 10-15 71
(With Warner Bros. "Arrowhead" label. Cover has copyright date on back.)
W.B. (1893 "American Beauty") .. 5-10 75
(With Warner Blvd./street and trees label.)
W.B. (1935 "Skull & Roses") 15-25 71
(Title shown is commonly used to describe what is actually an untitled LP. Includes bonus sticker picturing cover art.)
W.B. (2668 "Europe '72") 15-25 72
W.B. (2721 "History of the Grateful Dead, Vol. 1") 10-15 73
W.B. (2764 "Skeletons from the Closet") 8-12 74
W.B. (3091 "What a Strange Trip It's Been") 8-10 77

Promotional LPs

ARISTA (35 "Grateful Dead Sampler") 40-50 78
ARISTA (7001 "Terrapin Station") 20-25 77
(The lengthy *Terrapin Station* track is banded for radio station airplay.)
Members: Jerry Garcia; Ron McKernan; Bob Weir; Bill Kreutzman; Phil Lesh; Mickey Hart; Tom Constanten; Ned Lagin; Robert Hunter; Keith Godchaux; Donna Godchaux; Brent Mydland.
Also see CROSBY, David
Also see GARCIA, Jerry
Also see GARCIA, Jerry, & Robert Hunter
Also see HART, Mickey
Also see KANTER, Paul, & Grace Slick
Also see NEW RIDERS of the Purple Sage
Also see SILVER
Also see WEIR, Bob

GRATEFUL DEAD / Elvin Bishop Group

Singles: 7–inch

W.B. (7627 "Johnny B. Goode") 10-20 72
Also see BISHOP, Elvin
Also see GRATEFUL DEAD

GRAVES, Billy

P&R '59

Singles: 7–inch

MONUMENT (Except 401) 4-8 59-66
MONUMENT (401 "The Shag") ... 8-12 59

GRAVES, Carl

P&R/R&B '74

Singles: 7–inch

A&M 3-5 74
ARIOLA AMERICA 3-5 75-77
Also see SKYLARK

GRAY, Claude

C&W '60

Singles: 7–inch

COLUMBIA 4-6 64-66
COUNTRY INT'L 3-4 81-86
D 5-10 59-60
DECCA 3-6 66-71
GRANNY WHITE 3-5 76-82
MERCURY 4-8 60-64
MILLION 3-5 72-73

LPs: 10/12–inch 33rpm

DECCA 8-12 67-68
MERCURY 15-20 62
MILLION 5-10 72
PICKWICK/HILLTOP 8-12 67

GRAY, Claude, & Norma Jean

C&W '82

Singles: 7–inch

GRANNY WHITE 3-4 82
Also see GRAY, Claude

GRAY, Diva, & Oyster

R&B '80

Singles: 7–inch

COLUMBIA 3-4 79-80

LPs: 10/12-inch 33rpm

COLUMBIA 5-10 79

Also see ROUNDTREE

GRAY, Dobie

P&R '63

Singles: 12-inch 33/45rpm

INFINITY 5-8 79

Singles: 7-inch

ARISTA 3-4 83
CAPITOL (Except 5853) 3-4 86
CAPITOL (5853 "River Deep, Mountain High") 5-8 67
CAPRICORN................................ 3-5 76-77
CHARGER 4-8 64-66
COLLECTABLES 3-4 81
CORDAK................................ 5-10 62-64
DECCA................................ 3-5 73
ERIC................................ 3-4 70s
GUSTO 3-4 85
INFINITY 3-5 78-79
JAF................................ 4-8 63
MCA 3-4 73-75
REAL FINE................................ 8-12 62
ROBOX 3-4 81
STRIPE 8-12 60-61
WHITE WHALE (300 "Rose Garden")................................ 4-8 69
WHITE WHALE (330 "What a Way to Go")................................ 100-200 69
WHITE WHALE (342 "Honey, You Can't Take It Back")................................ 25-50 70

LPs: 10/12-inch 33rpm

CAPITOL................................ 5-10 86
CAPRICORN................................ 8-10 76
CHARGER 15-20 65
DECCA................................ 8-10 73
INFINITY 6-10 79
MCA 8-10 73-74
ROBOX 5-10 81
STRIPE 10-12

GRAY, Glen, & Casa Loma Orchestra

P&R '31

Singles: 78rpm

CAPITOL................................ 3-5 56-57
DECCA................................ 3-5 55
MERCURY 3-5 47

Singles: 7-inch

CAPITOL................................ 4-8 56-58
DECCA................................ 4-8 55

EPs: 7-inch 33/45rpm

CAPITOL 5-10 56-58

LPs: 10/12-inch 33rpm

CAPITOL................................ 5-15 56-63

GRAY, Maureen

P&R '62

Singles: 7-inch

CHANCELLOR................................ 15-25 61-62
LANDA 8-12 62

MERCURY................................ 5-10 63-64

GREAN, Charles

(Charles Randolph Grean Sounde)

P&R/LP '69

Singles: 7-inch

DOT 3-6 67
RANWOOD................................ 3-5 69-79

LPs: 10/12-inch 33rpm

RANWOOD................................ 6-12 69-70

GREASE BAND

LP '71

Singles: 7-inch

SHELTER 3-5 71

LPs: 10/12-inch 33rpm

SHELTER 8-10 71

Member: Henry McCullough.
Also see COCKER, Joe
Also see McCARTNEY, Paul

GREAT!! SOCIETY!!

Singles: 7-inch

COLUMBIA (44583 "Sally Go 'Round the Roses") 10-15 68
NORTHBEACH (1001 "Someone to Love")................................ 75-150 66

Member: Grace Slick.
Also see JEFFERSON AIRPLANE
Also see SLICK, Grace

GREAT WHITE

LP '84

Singles: 7-inch

CAPITOL................................ 3-4 86-90
EMI AMERICA 3-4 84

Picture Sleeves

CAPITOL................................ 3-4 86-89

LPs: 10/12-inch 33rpm

CAPITOL................................ 5-10 86-91
EMI AMERICA 5-10 84
ENIGMA................................ 5-8 88
GREENWORLD................................ 5-10 85

Members: Jack Russell; Mark Kendall; Michael Ardie; Audie Desbrow; Tony Montana.

GREAVES, R.B.

P&R/R&B '69

Singles: 7-inch

ATCO 3-5 69-70
BAREBACK 3-5 77
MGM 3-5 73
MIDSONG................................ 3-4 80
SUNFLOWER 3-5 72
20TH FOX................................ 3-5 74

LPs: 10/12-inch 33rpm

ATCO 15-20 69

GREBENSHIKOV, Boris

LP '89

LPs: 10/12-inch 33rpm

COLUMBIA 5-8 89

GRECCO, Cyndi

P&R '76

Singles: 7-inch

PRIVATE STOCK 3-5 76-77

LPs: 10/12-inch 33rpm

PRIVATE STOCK 5-8 76

GRECH, Rick

LP '73

Singles: 7-inch

RSO 3-5 73

LPs: 10/12-inch 33rpm

RSO 5-10 73

GRECO, Buddy
(Buddy Greco Trio)

P&R '47

Singles: 78rpm

CORAL 3-6 51-55
KAPP 3-5 56

Singles: 7-inch

CORAL 5-10 51-55
EPIC 4-8 58-67
HERALD 5-8 59
KAPP 5-8 56
MGM 3-5 71-72
REPRISE 3-6 66-68
SCEPTER 3-5 69

Picture Sleeves

EPIC 4-8 64-65

EPs: 7-inch 33/45rpm

CORAL 5-10 55

LPs: 10/12-inch 33rpm

CORAL 15-25 55
EPIC 10-15 60-66
HARMONY 8-12 68
KAPP 10-15 61
MVM 10-15 60s
REPRISE 8-12 67
SCEPTER 5-10 69-73
VOCALION 8-12 64

GREELEY, George

LP '61

Singles: 7-inch

W.B. 3-5 59-62

Picture Sleeves

W.B. 3-5 62

EPs: 7-inch 33/45rpm

CAPITOL 5-10 56

LPs: 10/12-inch 33rpm

CAPITOL 5-15 56
RAVE 10-20 56
W.B. 5-10 59-61

GREEN, Al
(With the Soul Mates)

P&R/R&B '67

Singles: 7-inch

A&M 3-4 87
BELL 3-5 72-73
FLASHBACK 3-5 70s
HI 3-5 70-78
HOT LINE 8-12 67
MOTOWN 3-4 82-85

Picture Sleeves

HI 3-5 77

LPs: 10/12-inch 33rpm

A&M 5-10 87
BELL 8-10 72
HI 10-12 69-78
HOT LINE (1500 "Back Up Train") 20-30 67
KORY 8-10 77
MELODY 5-10
MOTOWN 5-10 82-85
MYRRH 5-10 80-83

Also see LENNOX, Annie, & Al Green

GREEN, Darren

R&B '73

Singles: 7-inch

RCA 3-5 73-74

GREEN, Garland

P&R/R&B '69

Singles: 7-inch

CASINO 3-5 76
COTILLION 3-6 71
GAMMA 20-40 67
OCEAN FRONT 3-4 83
RCA 3-6 77
REVUE 5-10 67-68
SPRING 3-5 74-75
UNI 4-8 69

LPs: 10/12-inch 33rpm

OCEAN FRONT 5-10 83
RCA 8-10 74-78
UNI 10-12 70

GREEN, Grant

LP '71

LPs: 10/12-inch 33rpm

BLUE NOTE 15-25 61-65
(Label reads "Blue Note Records Inc. - New York, U.S.A.")
BLUE NOTE 10-15 66-71
(Label reads "Blue Note Records - a Division of Liberty Records Inc.")
VERVE 10-18 65
VERSATILE 5-10 78

GREEN, Jack

LP '80

Singles: 7-inch

RCA 3-4 80

LPs: 10/12-inch 33rpm

RCA 5-10 80

Also see PRETTY THINGS
Also see T. REX

GREEN, Lil: see GREENE, Lil

GREEN, Lorne: see GREENE, Lorne

GREEN, Peter

LP '80

LPs: 10/12-inch 33rpm

REPRISE 8-10 71
SAIL 5-10 79-80

Also see BOYD, Eddie
Also see FLEETWOOD MAC

GREEN, Sonny

R&B '73

Singles: 7-inch

HILL 3-5 73

GREEN BERETS

R&B '70

Singles: 7-inch

UNI 3-5 70

GREEN on RED

LP '86

LPs: 10/12-inch 33rpm

ENIGMA 5-10 85
MERCURY 5-10 86

GREEN RIVER BOYS: see CAMPBELL, Glen

GREENBAUM, Norman

P&R/LP '70

Singles: 7-inch

GREGAR 4-6 69-70
REPRISE 3-5 70-71

Picture Sleeves

REPRISE 5-8 69

LPs: 10/12-inch 33rpm

GREGAR 15-20 70
REPRISE 12-15 69-72

Also see DR. WEST'S MEDICINE SHOW & Junk Band

GREENBERG, Steve

P&R '69

Singles: 7-inch

TRIP 4-6 69

GREENE, Al: see GREEN, Al

GREENE, Barbara

P&R/R&B '68

Singles: 7-inch

ATCO (6250 "Long Tall Sally").. 25-30 62
RENEE 8-10 68
VIVID 4-8 64

Also see DELLS

GREENE, Jack
(With the Jolly Green Giants)

C&W '65

Singles: 7-inch

DECCA 3-8 65-72
EMH 3-4 83-84
FRONTLINE 3-5 80
MCA 3-5 73-74

LPs: 10/12-inch 33rpm

CORAL 4-8 73
DECCA 8-18 66-71
51 WEST 5-10 84
FRONTLINE 5-10 80
MCA 5-10 73

GREENE, Jack, & Jeannie Seely

C&W '72

Singles: 7-inch

DECCA 3-5 69-72

LPs: 10/12-inch 33rpm

DECCA 8-12 70-72
MCA 4-6 73
PINNACLE 5-10 78
RDS 5-10 79

Also see GREENE, Jack
Also see SEELY, Jeannie

GREENE, Laura

R&B '80

Singles: 7-inch

RCA 10-20 67
SOUND TREK 3-5 80

GREENE, Lil

P&R '40

Singles: 78rpm

ALADDIN 5-10 50
ATLANTIC (951 "Every Time") .. 10-15 51
BLUEBIRD 10-15 39-46
GROOVE 5-8 56
RCA 8-12 46-48

Singles: 7-inch

ATLANTIC (951 "Every Time") .. 50-75 51
GROOVE (5004 "Why Don't You Do Right") 10-15 56

LPs: 10/12-inch 33rpm

ROSETTA 5-10 86

GREENE, Lorne

P&R/C&W/LP '64

Singles: 7-inch

COLUMBIA 3-6 69
GRT 3-5 70-71
RCA 4-8 62-66

Picture Sleeves

RCA 5-10 63-65

LPs: 10/12-inch 33rpm

CAMDEN 5-10 70
MGM 5-10 71
RCA 10-20 63-66

GREENWICH, Ellie
(Ellie Gaye)

P&R '67

Singles: 7-inch

BELL 4-8 69
RED BIRD (034 "Baby") 20-30 65
RCA ("Silly Isn't It") 15-25 50s
(Credited to Ellie Gaye. Number not known.)
U.A. 8-12 67
VERVE 4-6 70-73

LPs: 10/12-inch 33rpm

U.A. (6648 "Ellie Greenwich Composes, Producers and Sings") 30-40 68
VERVE 10-15 73
Also see ARCHIES
Also see BONDS, Gary "U.S."
Also see BUTTERFLYS
Also see CROCE, Jim
Also see RAINDROPS

GREENWOOD, Lee

(Lee Greenwood Affair)

C&W '81

Singles: 7-inch

DOT.. 3-6 69
MCA 3-4 81-88
PARAMOUNT 3-5 71

Picture Sleeves

MCA 3-4 83

LPs: 10/12-inch 33rpm

MCA 5-10 82-88
Also see MANDRELL, Barbara, & Lee Greenwood

GREENWOOD COUNTY SINGERS

(Greenwoods)

P&R '64

Singles: 7-inch

DECCA.. 4-6 64-66
KAPP... 4-6 64-66

Picture Sleeves

KAPP... 4-6 64

LPs: 10/12-inch 33rpm

DECCA.................................... 10-15 64
KAPP....................................... 10-15 64-66
RCA.. 8-12 70

GREENWOODS: see GREENWOOD COUNTY SINGERS

GREER, Big John, & Four Students

Singles: 78rpm

GROOVE 5-10 55

Singles: 7-inch

GROOVE (0131 "A Man and a Woman") 10-20 55
Also see GREER, John

GREER, John

(Big John Greer; with Rhythm Rockers)

R&B '52

Singles: 78rpm

RCA.. 10-20 49-53

Singles: 7-inch

RCA (0007 "Drinkin' Wine Spoo-Dee-O-Dee")................ 35-50 49
(Colored vinyl.)
RCA (0029 "If I Told You Once")................................ 35-50 49
(Colored vinyl)
RCA (0051 "Rocking Jenny Jones")................................ 35-50 50
(Colored vinyl)
RCA (0076 "I'll Never Do That Again").........................35-50 50
(Colored vinyl.)
RCA (0096 "Cheatin'") 35-50 50
(Colored vinyl.)
RCA (0104 "Red Juice") 35-50 50
(Colored vinyl.)
RCA (0108 "Once There Lived a Fool")..........................15-25 51
RCA (0113 "Why Did You Go")..15-25 51
RCA (0125 "Clambake Boogie") 15-25 51
RCA (0137 "Rockin' with Big John")..................................15-25 51
RCA (4293 "Have Another Drink")..................................15-25 51
RCA (4348 "Got You on My Mind")..................................15-25 51
RCA (4484 "Strong Red Whiskey")................................15-25 52
RCA (5037 "I'm the Fat Man")....15-25 52
RCA (5170 "You Played on My Piano") 15-25 53
RCA (5259 "Ride Pretty Baby") .15-25 53
RCA (5531 "Drinkin' Fool").........15-25 53
Also see ALLEN, Annisteen
Also see GREER, Big John, & Four Students

GREGG, Bobby

(With His Friends; Bobby Grego)

P&R/R&B '62

Singles: 7-inch

COTTON...................................8-12 62
EPIC..4-8 62-66

LPs: 10/12-inch 33rpm

EPIC (24051 "Let's Stomp and Wild Weekend") 20-25 63
(Monaural.)
EPIC (26051 "Let's Stomp and Wild Weekend") 25-30 63
(Stereo.)
Also see BUCHANAN, Roy
Also see DYLAN, Bob
Also see GIBSON, Steve

GREGORY, Dick

LP '61

Singles: 7-inch

VEE JAY 4-8 62

LPs: 10/12-inch 33rpm

COLPIX...................................10-20 61-64
POPPY...8-15 69-73
VEE JAY 10-20 62-64

GREY & HANKS

R&B '78

Singles: 7-inch

RCA 3-5 78-80

LPs: 10/12-inch 33rpm

RCA 5-10 79-80
Members: Zane Grey; Len Hanks

GRIFFIN, Billy

R&B '83

Singles: 7-inch

ATLANTIC 3-4 86
COLUMBIA 3-4 83-86

LPs: 10/12-inch 33rpm

COLUMBIA 5-10 84-86

Also see MIRACLES

GRIFFIN, Merv

(With the Griffin Family Singers)

P&R '51

Singles: 78rpm

COLUMBIA 3-5 53
RCA 3-5 51-52

Singles: 7-inch

CAMEO 3-5 63-64
CARLTON 4-8 61
COLUMBIA 5-10 53
CORAL 3-6 66
DOT 3-5 68
GRIFFIN 3-5 73
MGM 4-6 65-67
MERCURY 4-6 62
METROMEDIA 3-5 70
RCA 5-10 51-52

EPs: 7-inch 33/45rpm

RCA (3000 series) 5-10 52

LPs: 10/12-inch 33rpm

CAMEO 8-15 64
CARLTON 10-20 61
MGM 8-15 65-66
METROMEDIA 5-10 69
RCA (3000 series) 15-25 52
(10-inch LPs.)

Also see MARTIN, Freddy, & His Orchestra

GRIFFIN, Reggie, & Technofunk

R&B '82

Singles: 7-inch

SWEET MOUNTAIN 3-4 82

Also see MANCHILD
Also see WEST STREET MOB

GRIFFIN BROTHERS

(Featuring Tommy Brown; featuring Margie Day)

R&B '50

Singles: 78rpm

DOT 5-10 50-52

Singles: 7-inch

DOT (1071 "Weeping and Crying") 25-40 51
DOT (1094 "It'd Surprise You") . 20-30 51
DOT (1095 "The Teaser") 20-30 51
DOT (1104 "I'm Gonna Jump in the River") 20-30 52
DOT (1105 "Coming Home") 20-30 52
DOT (1108 "Ace in the Hole") ... 35-45 52
DOT (1114 "My Story") 15-25 53
DOT (1117 "I Wanna Go Back") 15-25 53
DOT (1144 "My Story") 15-25 53
DOT (1145 "Black Bread") 15-25 53
DOT (16000 series) 5-10 60

Members: Jimmy Griffin; Edward "Buddy" Griffin.
Also see DAY, Margie

GRIFFITH, Andy

(Deacon Andy Griffith)

P&R '54

Singles: 78rpm

CAPITOL 5-10 53-57

Singles: 7-inch

CAPITOL (2500 series) 4-6 69
CAPITOL (2600 thru 3600 series) 10-20 53-57
CAPITOL (4000 & 5000 series) 4-8 59-63
(Purple or orange/yellow swirl labels.)
CAPITOL (4000 series) 3-5 76
(Orange labels.)
COLONIAL ("What It Was—Was Football") 15-25 53
(Number not known.)
COLUMBIA 5-10 72

EPs: 7-inch 33/45rpm

CAPITOL 20-30 54-61

LPs: 10/12-inch 33rpm

CAPITOL (872 "A Face in the Crowd") 35-50 57
(Soundtrack.)
CAPITOL (962 "Just for Laughs") 35-45 58
CAPITOL (1100 thru 1600 series) 30-40 59-61
CAPITOL (2000 series) 15-25 64-67
COLUMBIA 5-10 72

GRIFFITH, Johnny, Inc.

R&B '73

Singles: 7-inch

RCA 3-5 73

GRIFFITHS, Marcia

P&R '89

Singles: 7-inch

MANGO 3-4 89

GRIM REAPER

LP '84

Singles: 7-inch

RCA/EBONY 3-4 80s
RCA/EBONY/EVA-TONE 5-10 85
(Soundsheet. Promotional issue only.)
RCA 3-4 85

Picture Sleeves

RCA/EBONY 3-4

LPs: 10/12-inch 33rpm

RCA 5-10 84-87

GRIMES, Tiny
(Tiny Grimes Quintet; Swingtet)

R&B '48

Singles: 78rpm

APOLLO	4-8	53
ATLANTIC	5-10	48-52
BLUE NOTE	5-10	47
GOTHAM	4-8	50
RED ROBIN	4-8	52
SAVOY	5-10	46-48

Singles: 7-inch

APOLLO	8-15	53
ATLANTIC (990 "Begin the Beguine")	20-30	52
B&F	4-8	59
GOTHAM	10-20	50
RED ROBIN (123 "Juicy Fruit")	15-25	52
UNITED	10-20	55

LPs: 10/12-inch 33rpm

PRESTIGE SWINGSVILLE	15-20	60
U.A.	12-15	62

GRIN

LP '71

Singles: 7-inch

A&M	3-5	74
SPINDIZZY	3-5	71-72
THUNDER	3-5	

LPs: 10/12-inch 33rpm

A&M	8-10	73
COLUMBIA	5-10	
SPINDIZZY	8-10	71-73

Member: Nils Lofgren.
Also see LOFGREN, Nils

GRINDERSWITCH

LP '77

Singles: 7-inch

ATCO	3-5	77-78

LPs: 10/12-inch 33rpm

ATCO	8-10	77
CAPRICORN	8-10	74-76

GRISMAN, David

LP '80

LPs: 10/12-inch 33rpm

ROUNDER	5-8	83
W.B.	5-10	80-81

GRISSOM, Jimmy
(With the Red Callender Sextet)

R&B '51

Singles: 78rpm

HOLLYWOOD	4-8	51

Singles: 7-inch

ARGO	4-6	64

LPs: 10/12-inch 33rpm

ARGO	10-15	64

GROCE, Larry

P&R/C&W/LP '76

Singles: 7-inch

PEACEABLE	3-5	75
W.B.	3-5	75

LPs: 10/12-inch 33rpm

DAYBREAK	8-10	71-72
W.B.	8-10	76

GROSS, Felix

R&B '49

Singles: 78rpm

DOWN BEAT	5-10	54-49
SAVOY	5-10	49

GROSS, Henry

P&R/LP '75

Singles: 7-inch

A&M	3-5	74-75
LIFESONG	3-5	76-78

LPs: 10/12-inch 33rpm

ABC-PAR	8-10	71
A&M	8-10	73-75
CAPITOL	5-10	81
LIFESONG	8-10	76-78

Also see SHA NA NA

GROUND HOG
(Joe Richardson)

R&B '74

Singles: 7-inch

GEMIGO	3-5	74

Also see TENDER SLIM

GRUSIN, Dave
(Dave Grusin Quintet; Dave Grusin & NY/LA Dream Band)

LP '80

Singles: 7-inch

DECCA	3-6	68-69
EPIC	4-8	63
W.B.	3-4	83

LPs: 10/12-inch 33rpm

COLUMBIA	10-20	65
EPIC	15-25	62
GRP	5-10	80-89
POLYDOR	5-10	77
SHEFFIELD LAB	8-15	77-82
VERSATILE	5-10	78

Also see BISHOP, Stephen
Also see GALE, Eric

GRUSIN, Dave, & Lee Ritenour

LP '85

LP: 10/12-inch 33rpm

GRP	5-10	85

Also see GRUSIN, Dave
Also see RITENOUR, Lee

GUADALCANAL DIARY

LP '88

LPs: 10/12-inch 33rpm

ELEKTRA	5-10	86-89

Members: Rhett Crowe; Murray Attaway; John Poe; Jeff Walls.

GUARALDI, Vince
(Vince Guaraldi Trio)

P&R '62

Singles: 7-inch

FANTASY 4-6 62-66

LPs: 10/12-inch 33rpm

FANTASY (3200 series) 20-30 56-58
FANTASY (3300 series) 15-25 62-66
FANTASY (8000 series) 15-25 62
FANTASY (8300 series) 10-20 63-66
MFSL (112 "Jazz Impressions of Black Orpheus") 20-40 84
W.B. 8-12 68-69

GUARD, Dave, & Whiskeyhill Singers

Singles: 7-inch

CAPITOL 4-8 62

LPs: 10/12-inch 33rpm

CAPITOL 15-20 62

Members: Dave Guard; Cyrus Faryar; Judy Hensky; David "Buck" Wheat.
Also see KINGSTON TRIO

GUCCI CREW II

LP '89

LPs: 10/12-inch 33rpm

GUCCI 5-8 89

GUESS WHO

P&R '65

Singles: 7-inch

AMY 10-20 67
FONTANA 10-15 69
HILLTAK 3-5 78-79
QUALITY 10-20 65-68
(Cnadian.)
RCA 3-6 69-76
RCA RECORDING SERVICES (55829 "Two Wheel Freedom") 4-8
SCEPTER (1295 "Shakin' All Over") 8-12 65
SCEPTER (12000 series) 10-20 65-66

Picture Sleeves

RCA 8-12 70

LPs: 10/12-inch 33rpm

HILLTAK 5-10 79
MGM 12-15 69
PICKWICK 8-10 72
PIP 8-10 71
PRIDE 8-10 73
RCA (Except "AYL1" & LSP-4000 series) 8-12 73-80
RCA ("AYL1" series) 5-10 80
RCA (1000 "Best of the Guess Who") 10-20 71
(With bonus, black light poster.)
RCA (1000 "Best of the Guess Who") 8-12 71
(Without poster.)
RCA (4141 thru 4830) 12-25 69-72
(With "LSP" prefix.)
SCEPTER 8-10 73
SPRINGBOARD 8-10 72
WAND 12-15 69

Members: Chad Allen; Burton Cummings; Randy Bachman; Domenic Troiano.
Also see BACHMAN, Randy
Also see CUMMINGS, Burton
Also see TROIANO, Domenic
Also see WOLFMAN JACK

GUESS WHO / Discotays

Singles: 7-inch

SCEPTER (1295 "Shakin' All Over") 15-20 65

Also see GUESS WHO

GUIDRY, Greg

P&R/LP '82

Singles: 7-inch

COLUMBIA 3-4 82

LPs: 10/12-inch 33rpm

COLUMBIA/BADLAND 5-10 82

GUITAR, Bonnie

C&W/P&R '57

Singles: 78rpm

DOT 5-10 57
FABOR (Except 4018) 5-10 55-56
FABOR (4018 "Dark Moon") 10-15 57
4 STAR 5-10 56

Singles: 7-inch

ABC 3-5 74
CHARTER 4-6
COLUMBIA 3-5 72
DOLTON 5-10 59
DOT (15000 series) 8-12 57-59
DOT (16000 & 17000 series) 4-6 66-69
FABOR (138 "Ra Ta Ta Ta") 4-8 64
FABOR (4013 "If You See My Love Dancing") 10-20 55
FABOR (4017 "Clinging Vine") 10-20 56
FABOR (4018 "Dark Moon") 20-30 57
4 STAR (1003 "Honey on the Moon") 3-5 80
4 STAR (1006 "I Want to Spend My Life with You") 10-20 56
JERDEN 5-10 63
MCA 3-5 74
PARAMOUNT 3-5 70
PLAYBACK 3-4 89
RCA 10-20 61-62
RADIO 5-10 58

LPs: 10/12-inch 33rpm

CAMDEN 6-12 69
DOT (Except 3069) 10-15 59-68
DOT (3069 "Moonlight and Shadows") 15-20 57
HAMILTON 8-12 65
PARAMOUNT 8-12 70
PICKWICK 6-12 70

GUITAR SLIM
(Eddie Jones)

P&R/R&B '54

Singles: 78rpm

ATCO 5-10 56
IMPERIAL 8-12 54
SPECIALTY 5-10 55

Singles: 7-inch

ATCO (6072 "Oh Yeah")........... 20-30 56
IMPERIAL (5278 "Woman Troubles")............................... 40-50 54
IMPERIAL (5310 "New Arrival") 40-50 54
SPECIALTY (482 "The Things That I Used to Do")......................... 20-30 55
SPECIALTY (490 "The Story of My Life") 20-30 54
SPECIALTY (527 "Later for You, Baby") 15-25 56
SPECIALTY (536 "Sufferin' Mind")..................................... 15-25 55
SPECIALTY (542 "Our Only Child") 15-25 55
SPECIALTY (551 "I Got Sumpin' for You") 15-25 55
SPECIALTY (557 "Quicksand") 15-25 56
SPECIALTY (569 "Sum'thin' to Remember You By") 15-25 56

LPs: 10/12-inch 33rpm

SPECIALTY 8-10 70-88

Also see CHARLES, Ray

GUITAR SLIM
(Johnny Winter)

Singles: 7-inch

DIAMOND JIM (204 "Crying in My Heart")............................ 75-100 62
(Reissued as by Texas "Guitar" Slim.)

Also see TEXAS "GUITAR" SLIM
Also see WINTER, Johnny

GUN

LP '90

LPs: 10/12-inch 33rpm

A&M 5-8 90

Members: Mark Rankin; Giuliano Gizzi; Dante Gizzi; Scott Shields; Baby Stafford.

GUNHILL ROAD

P&R '73

Singles: 7-inch

KAMA SUTRA.............................. 3-5 73
MERCURY 3-5 72

LPs: 10/12-inch 33rpm

KAMA SUTRA............................ 8-10 72
MERCURY 8-10 71

GUNS 'N' ROSES

LP '87

Singles: 12-inch 33/45rpm

GEFFEN....................................... 4-8 89

Singles: 7-inch

GEFFEN....................................... 3-4 88-92

Picture Sleeves

GEFFEN 3-4 88-89

EPs: 7-inch 33/45rpm

UZI SUICIDE ("Live Like a Suicide")................................50-100 86

LPs: 10/12-inch 33rpm

GEFFEN (Except 24148 & 24617).......................................5-10 88-89
GEFFEN (24148 "Appetite for Destruction")..................100-150 87
(With robot/rape painting on cover.)
GEFFEN (24148 "Appetite for Destruction")..........................5-8 87
(With skulls and cross cover.)
GEFFEN (24617 "Spaghetti Incident")..................................10-15 93
(Colored vinyl.)

Members: Axl Rose; Slash; Duff McKagan; Saul Hudson; Steve Adler; Izzy Stradlin; Matt Sorum; Dizzy Reed; Gilby Clarke.

Also see CULT

GUNTER, Arthur

R&B '55

Singles: 78rpm

EXCELLO 5-15 55-58

Singles: 7-inch

EXCELLO (2047 "Baby Let's Play House")............................10-20 55
EXCELLO (2053 "She's Mine, All Mine")...................................10-20 55
EXCELLO (2058 "Honey Babe")10-20 55
EXCELLO (2073 thru 2204).........5-10 56-61

LPs: 10/12-inch 33rpm

EXCELLO 10-15 71

GUNTER, Shirley
(With the Flairs; with Queens)

R&B '54

Singles: 78rpm

FLAIR (Except 1076) 8-15 54-55
FLAIR (1076 "How Can I Tell You") 10-20 55
MODERN....................................5-10 56

Singles: 7-inch

FLAIR (Except 1076) 10-20
FLAIR (1076 "How Can I Tell You") 30-60 55
MODERN..................................10-20 56
TANGERINE 4-8 65

Members: Shirley Gunter; Lula Bea Kinney; Lula Mae Suggs; Zola Taylor.

GUTHRIE, Arlo

LP '67

Singles: 7-inch

REPRISE 3-6 67-77

LPs: 10/12-inch 33rpm

REPRISE....................................8-10 67-76
U.A. 10-15 69
W.B. 5-10 77-81

Also see SEEGER, Pete, & Arlo Guthrie

GUTHRIE, Gwen

R&B '82

Singles: 12-inch 33/45rpm

GARAGE 4-6 85
ISLAND 4-6 83-85

Singles: 7-inch

GARAGE 3-4 85
ISLAND 3-4 82-85
POLYDOR 3-4 86-87
W.B. 3-4 88

Picture Sleeves

POLYDOR 3-4 86

LPs: 10/12-inch 33rpm

GARAGE 5-10 85
ISLAND 5-10 85
POLYDOR 5-8 86

Also see HOWARD, George
Also see LIMIT

GUY

R&B/LP '88

LPs: 10/12-inch 33rpm

MCA 5-8 90
UPTOWN 5-8 88

GUY, Bob
(Frank Zappa)

Singles: 7-inch

DONNA (1380 "Letter from Jeepers") 50-75 61

Also see ZAPPA, Frank

GUY, Buddy

R&B '62

Singles: 7-inch

ARTISTIC 10-15 58-59
CHESS 5-10 60-65

LPs: 10/12-inch 33rpm

BLUE THUMB 8-10 70
CHESS 10-12 69
VANGUARD 12-15 68

Also see WELLS, Junior, & Buddy Guy

GUY, Buddy, with Dr. John & Eric Clapton / Buddy Guy with the J. Geils Band

Singles: 7-inch

ATCO (6890 "Man of Many Words") 4-8 72

Also see CLAPTON, Eric
Also see DR. JOHN
Also see GEILS, J., Band

GYPSIES

R&B '65

Singles: 7-inch

CAPRICE 5-10 66
OLD TOWN (1168 "Blue Bird") . 10-20 64
OLD TOWN (1180 "Jerk It") 10-20 65
OLD TOWN (1184 "It's a Woman's World") 40-60 65
OLD TOWN (1193 "Oh I Wonder Why") 10-20 66

Members: Betty Pearce; Ernestine Pearce; Shirley Pearce; Loctine Johnson.
Also see FLIRTATIONS

GYPSY

P&R/LP '70

Singles: 7-inch

METROMEDIA 3-5 70
RCA 3-5 72

LPs: 10/12-inch 33rpm

METROMEDIA 8-10 70-71
RCA 8-10 72-73

LORNE
GREENE
AN OL'
TIN CUP
SAND
LORNE'S NEW SINGLE AS FEATURED ON HIS NBC-TV
SPECIAL MAY3rd "LORNE GREENE'S AMERICAN WEST"

IT'S MY
PARTY
Lesley Gore
72119

PERSPECTIVE
SOUND
121057500
SIDE
1
45 RPM
JO-BABY
(D. Gates)
the ACCENTS
Vocal By DAVID GATES
A PRODUCT OF PERSPECTIVE STUDIOS · TULSA, OKLAHOMA, U.S.A.

MARIANNE
GOODBYE
CHIQUITA
4-40817
COLUMBIA
TERRY
GILKYSON
AND THE
EASY RIDERS

Swing Time
LOS ANGELES
CALIFORNIA
ST 311A
ASCAP
Time 2:35
LLOYD GLENN
Plays
BOOGIE WOOGIE ON
ST. LOUIS BLUES
(Handy)
With
ORCHESTRA

Scorpio
Cireco-BMI
TIME: 2:14
408
Produced by
Paul Rose
WALKING ON THE WATER
THE GOLLIWOGS

MICKEY GILLEY
THE
LINE

H

HACKETT, Buddy

P&R '53

Singles: 78rpm

CORAL 3-5 53-56

Singles: 7-inch

CORAL 5-10 53-56
LAUREL 4-8 60

LPs: 10/12-inch 33rpm

CORAL 8-15 65
DOT 10-15 59

HACKETT, Steve

LP '76

Singles: 7-inch

CHARISMA 3-4 80
CHRYSALIS 3-5 76-79
EPIC 3-4 81

LPs: 10/12-inch 33rpm

CHARISMA 5-10 80
CHRYSALIS 5-10 76-79
EPIC 5-10 81

Also see GTR
Also see GENESIS

HAGAR, Sammy

P&R/LP '77

Singles: 7-inch

CAPITOL 3-5 76-79
COLUMBIA 3-4 87
GEFFEN (Except 29246) 3-4 82-87
GEFFEN (29246 "Two Sides of Love") 3-4 84
(Black vinyl.)
GEFFEN (29246 "Two Sides of Love") 4-8 84
(Colored vinyl.)

Picture Sleeves

CAPITOL 3-5 79
COLUMBIA 3-4 87
GEFFEN 3-4 82-87

LPs: 10/12-inch 33rpm

CAPITOL 5-10 77-82
GEFFEN 5-10 82-87

Also see HAGAR, SCHON, AARONSON, SHRIEVE
Also see MONTROSE
Also see VAN HALEN

HAGAR, SCHON, AARONSON, SHRIEVE

P&R/LP '84

Singles: 7-inch

GEFFEN 3-4 84

Picture Sleeves

GEFFEN 3-4 84

LPs: 10/12-inch 33rpm

GEFFEN 5-10 84

Members: Sammy Hagar; Neal Schon; Ken Aaronson; Michael Shrieve.
Also see HAGAR, Sammy
Also see SCHON, Neal, & Jan Hammer
Also see SANTANA

HAGEN, Nina
(Nina Hagen Band)

LP '82

Singles: 12-inch 33/45rpm

COLUMBIA 4-6 84-85

Singles: 7-inch

COLUMBIA 3-4 80-85

LPs: 10/12-inch 33rpm

COLUMBIA 5-10 80-83

HAGGARD, Merle
(With the Strangers)

C&W '63

Singles: 7-inch

CAPITOL 3-8 65-77
COLUMBIA 3-4 83
CURB 3-4 90
EPIC 3-4 81-89
MCA 3-5 77-85
MERCURY 3-4 83
TALLY 10-20 63-65

Picture Sleeves

CAPITOL 4-8 67-71
MCA 3-5 77-80

EPs: 7-inch 33/45rpm

CAPITOL 8-15 71
(Jukebox issues only.)

LPs: 10/12-inch 33rpm

ALBUM GLOBE 5-10 80s
CAPITOL (168 thru 735) 8-15 69-71
(With "T," "ST," "STBB" or "SWBB" prefix.)
CAPITOL (168 thru 735) 4-8 69-71
(With "SKA0" or SM" prefix.)
CAPITOL (796 "Merle Haggard's Strangers and Friends Honky Tonkin'") 20-30 71
CAPITOL (803 "Land of Many Churches") 50-75 71
CAPITOL (823 "Truly the Best of Merle Haggard") 40-60 71
CAPITOL (835 "Someday We'll Look Back") 8-12 71
CAPITOL (882 "Let Me Tell You About a Song") 8-12 72
CAPITOL (2300 thru 2900 series) 15-25 65-68
(With "T," "ST" or "SKAO" prefix.)
CAPITOL (2700 thru 2900 series) 5-10 80s
(With "SM" prefix.)
CAPITOL (11000 thru 16000 series) 5-10 72-82
EPIC 5-10 81-86
MCA 4-8 77-84
MERCURY 5-10 83
PICKWICK/HILLTOP 8-12 60s

SONGBIRD 5-10 81

Session: Jordanaires; James Burton; Marty Haggard; Johnny Gimble; Ronnie Reno; Bobby Wayne.

Also see ANDERSON, John
Also see COCHRAN, Hank
Also see HAGGARD, Marty
Also see PAYCHECK & HAGGARD

HAGGARD, Merle / Patsy Cline

LPs: 10/12-inch 33rpm

OUT of TOWN DIST 5-10 82

Also see CLINE, Patsy

HAGGARD, Merle, & Clint Eastwood

C&W '80

Singles: 7-inch

ELEKTRA.................................... 3-4 80

Picture Sleeves

ELEKTRA.................................... 3-4 80

HAGGARD, Merle, & Janie Fricke

C&W '84

Singles: 7-inch

EPIC 3-4 84

HAGGARD, Merle / Mickey Gilley / Willie Knight

LPs: 10/12-inch 33rpm

OUT of TOWN DIST 5-10 82

Also see GILLEY, Mickey

HAGGARD, Merle / Sonny James

LPs: 10/12-inch 33rpm

CAPITOL.................................. 10-15 60s

Also see JAMES, Sonny

HAGGARD, Merle, & George Jones

(George Jones & Merle Haggard)

C&W/LP '82

Singles: 7-inch

EPIC (03405 "C.C. Waterback") ... 3-4 82
EPIC (03405 "C.C. Waterback") ... 4-8 82
(Picture disc.)

LPs: 10/12-inch 33rpm

EPIC.. 5-10 82

Also see JONES, George

HAGGARD, Merle, & Willie Nelson

(Willie Nelson & Merle Haggard)

C&W/LP '83

Singles: 7-inch

EPIC.. 3-4 83-87

LPs: 10/12-inch 33rpm

EPIC.. 5-10 83

Also see NELSON, Willie

HAGGARD, Merle, & Bonnie Owens

C&W '64

Singles: 7-inch

TALLY 10-20 64

HAGGARD, Merle, & Leona Williams

C&W '78

Singles: 7-inch

CAPITOL...................................... 3-5 78
MERCURY 3-4 83

HAHN, Carol

D&D '83

Singles: 12-inch 33/45rpm

NICKLE..4-6 83

HAHN, Joyce

P&R '57

Singles: 78rpm

CADENCE 3-5 57

Singles: 7-inch

CADENCE 4-8 57

HAIRCUT ONE HUNDRED

P&R/LP '82

Singles: 7-inch

ARISTA..3-4 82

LPs: 10/12-inch 33rpm

ARISTA......................................5-10 82

Member: Nick Heyward.

Also see HEYWARD, Nick

HAIRSTON, Curtis

D&D '83

Singles: 12-inch 33/45rpm

PRETTY PEARL...........................4-6 83

Singles: 7-inch

ATLANTIC....................................3-4 87
PRETTY PEARL...........................3-4 84-85

HALE & HUSHABYES

Singles: 7-inch

APOGEE (104 "Yes Sir, That's My Baby") 50-100 65
REPRISE (0299 "Yes Sir, That's My Baby") 20-40 64
(Reissued in 1967 as by a Date with Soul.)

Members: Brian Wilson; Sonny & Cher; Blossoms; Jack Nitzsche; Jackie DeShannon; Darlene Love; Edna Wright; Albert Stone.

Also see BLOSSOMS
Also see DATE with SOUL
Also see DE SHANNON, Jackie
Also see HONEY CONE
Also see LOVE, Darlene
Also see NITZSCHE, Jack
Also see SONNY & CHER
Also see WILSON, Brian

HALEY, Bill

(With His Comets; with Saddlemen; with Saddle Men; with Four Aces of Western Swing; with Reno Browne & Her Buckaroos)

P&R '53

Singles: 78rpm

ATLANTIC (727 "I'm Gonna Dry Ev'ry Tear with a Kiss")........250-350 50
COWBOY (1201 "Too Many Parties Too Many Pals") 300-500 48
COWBOY (1202 "Candy Kisses")...................................300-500 49
COWBOY (1203 "The Covered Wagon Rolled Right Along").............250-300 49
COWBOY (1204 "Behind the Eight Ball") 250-300 50

COWBOY (1205 "Candy Kisses") 250-350 50
COWBOY (1701 "Candy Kisses") 250-350 49
COWBOY (1701 "My Palomino and I") 250-350 49
(By Reno Browne & Her Buckaroos featuring Bill Haley. The Cowboy 1701 number is used twice.)
DECCA (29124 "Rock Around the Clock") 50-100 54
(Black label with gold print.)
DECCA (29124 "Rock Around the Clock") 25-50 54
(Black label with silver print. Decca multi-color labels are $4 to $8 reissues.)
DECCA (29204 "Shake, Rattle & Roll") 50-80 54
(Black label with gold print.)
DECCA (29204 "Shake, Rattle & Roll") 25-50 54
(Black label with silver print.)
DECCA (29317 thru 30530) 15-30 54-57
DECCA (30592 thru 30781) 20-40 58
DECCA (30844 "I Got a Woman") 25-50 59
DECCA (30873 "A Fool Such As I") 40-60 59
DECCA (30926 "Caldonia") 50-75 59
DECCA (30956 "Ooh, Look-a-There Ain't She Pretty") 50-100 59
ESSEX 15-25 52-55
HOLIDAY (105 "Rocket 88") . 100-150 51
HOLIDAY (108 "Green Tree Boogie") 100-150 51
HOLIDAY (111 "A Year Ago This Christmas") 100-150 51
HOLIDAY (113 "Jukebox Cannonball") 100-150 51
KEYSTONE (5101 "Deal Me a Hand") 500-750 50
KEYSTONE (5102 "Susan Van Dusan") 500-1000 50

Singles: 7–inch

APT (25081 "Burn That Candle") 15-20 65
APT (25087 "Haley A-Go-Go").. 15-20 65
ARZEE 8-12 77
DECCA (29000 series) 20-35 54-56
(With silver lines on both sides of the name Decca.)
DECCA (29000 series) 10-20 54-56
(With a star and silver lines under the name Decca.)
DECCA (30000 series) 10-20 56-59
DECCA (31000 series) 5-10 60-64
DECCA (72000 series) 4-6 69
ESSEX (102 "Rock Around the Clock") 10-20 60s
(Though long considered by many to be a bootleg, this 45 was reportedly made by Essex owner Dave Miller. We are therefore treating it as a reissue.)
ESSEX (303 "Rock the Joint") 500-750 52
(Colored vinyl.)
ESSEX (303 "Rock the Joint") ...65-75 52
(Black vinyl. Block style logo.)
ESSEX (303 "Rock the Joint") ...55-65 52
(Black vinyl. Script style logo.)
ESSEX (305 "Rocking Chair on the Moon") 50-100 52
ESSEX (310 "Real Rock Drive") 50-100 52
ESSEX (321 "Crazy Man Crazy") 30-50 53
ESSEX (327 "Fractured") 30-40 53
ESSEX (332 "Live It Up") 25-35 53
ESSEX (340 "Ten Little Indians") 25-35 53
ESSEX (348 "Chattanooga Choo-Choo") 20-30 54
ESSEX (374 "Jukebox Cannonball") 40-60 54
ESSEX (381 "Rocket 88") 100-125 55
ESSEX (399 "Rock the Joint") ... 35-50 55
GONE (5111 "Spanish Twist") ... 15-25 61
GONE (5116 "Riviera") 15-25 61
HOLIDAY (113 "Jukebox Cannonball") 300-400 51
JANUS 8-12 71
JUKEBOX 3-4 90
KAMA SUTRA 5-10 70
MCA 3-5 74-80
NEWTOWN (5013 "Tenor Man") 10-15 63
NEWTOWN (5014 "Midnight in Washington") 10-15 63
NEWTOWN (5024 "Dance Around the Clock") 10-15 63
NEWTOWN (5025 "Tandy") 10-15 63
OLD GOLD 3-5 82
RADIO ACTIVE 4-8 70
TRANSWORLD (200 & 300 series) 60-75 54
TRANSWORLD (718 "Real Rock Drive") 50-75 53
U.A. 5-10 69
W.B. (5145 "Candy Kisses") 15-25 60
W.B. (5154 "Chick Safari") 15-25 60
W.B. (5171 "So Right Tonight") . 15-25 60
W.B. (5228 "Flip, Flop & Fly") 15-25 60
W.B. (7124 "Rock Around the Clock") 10-15 68

Picture Sleeves

ARZEE 8-12 77
DECCA (30314 "Billy Goat") 40-60 57

DECCA (30530 "Mary, Mary Lou")....................................... 25-35 58

EPs: 7–inch 33/45rpm

ARZEE (137 "Bill Haley Sings") 20-30 77
CLAIRE (4779 "Bill Haley and the Comets")............................. 15-20 78
DECCA (2168 "Shake, Rattle & Roll")....................................... 40-60 54
DECCA (2209 "Dim, Dim the Lights")...................................... 40-60 55
DECCA (2322 "Razzle Dazzle") 40-60 56
DECCA (2398/2399/2400 "He Digs Rock & Roll")....................................... 40-60 56
(Price is for any of three volumes.)
DECCA (2416/2417/2418 "Rock'n Roll Stage Show")....................................... 40-50 56
(Price is for any of three volumes.)
DECCA (2532 "Rockin' the Oldies")....................................... 30-40 57
DECCA (2533 "Rock 'N' Roll Party")....................................... 30-40 57
DECCA (2534 "Rockin' & Rollin'")....................................... 30-40 57
DECCA (2564 "Rockin' Around the World")....................................... 30-40 57
DECCA (2576 "Rockin' Around Europe")....................................... 30-40 57
DECCA (2577 "Rockin' Around the Americas")............................. 30-40 57
DECCA (2615/2616 "Rockin' the Joint")....................................... 30-40 58
(Price is for either of two volumes.)
DECCA (2638 "Bill Haley's Chicks")....................................... 30-40 58
DECCA (2670 "Bill Haley and His Comets")............................. 30-40 59
DECCA (2671 "Strictly Instrumental")............................. 30-40 59
DECCA (72638 "Bill Haley's Chicks")....................................... 50-75 59
(Stereo.)
DECCA (72670 "Bill Haley and His Comets")............................. 50-75 59
(Stereo.)
DECCA (72671 "Strictly Instrumental")............................. 50-75 59
(Stereo.)
ESSEX (102 "Dance Party") ... 50-100 54
ESSEX (117/118/119 "Rock with Bill Haley and the Comets")................. 50-100 54
(Price is for any of three volumes.)
SOMERSET (460 "Rock with Bill Haley and the Comets")............................. 40-60 55
TRANSWORLD (117/118/119 "Rock with Bill Haley & Comets")................ 50-100 54
(Price is for any of three volumes. May be titled *For Your Dance Party.*)

LPs: 10/12–inch 33rpm

ACCORD....................................... 5-10 81-82
ALSHIRE....................................... 8-10 79
AMBASSADOR............................. 8-15 70-87
BUDDAH....................................... 5-10 84
CORAL....................................... 8-10 73
DECCA (5560 "Shake, Rattle & Roll")....................................... 250-350 54
(10–inch LP.)
DECCA (7211 "Golden Hits")..... 12-18 72
DECCA (8225 "Rock Around the Clock")............................. 75-125 55
(All black label with silver print.)
DECCA (8225 "Rock Around the Clock")............................. 20-40 60
(Black label with rainbow color stripe. Reads "M'F'D by Decca Records Inc. New York, U.S.A.")
DECCA (8225 "Rock Around the Clock")............................. 15-20 68
(Black label with rainbow color stripe. Reads "Mfr'd by Decca Records, a Div. of MCA Inc. New York, U.S.A.")
DECCA (8315 "He Digs Rock & Roll")....................................... 50-100 56
DECCA (8345 "Rock'n Roll Stage Show")............................. 50-100 56
DECCA (8569 "Rockin' the Oldies")....................................... 50-100 57
DECCA (8692 "Rockin' Around the World")............................. 50-75 58
DECCA (8775 "Rockin' the Joint")....................................... 50-75 58
DECCA (8821 "Bill Haley's Chicks")....................................... 40-60 58
DECCA (8964 "Strictly Instrumental")............................. 35-50 60
DECCA (75027 "Greatest Hits") 12-20 68
DECCA (78225 "Rock Around the Clock")............................. 50-75 59
(All black label with silver print.)
DECCA (78225 "Rock Around the Clock")............................. 50-75 59
(Black label with rainbow color stripe.)
DECCA (78692 "Rockin' Around the World")............................. 20-30 62
DECCA (78821 "Bill Haley's Chicks")....................................... 50-80 58
DECCA (78964 "Strictly Instrumental")............................. 40-65 60
ESSEX (202 "Rock with Bill Haley and the Comets")............................. 200-300 54
EXACT....................................... 5-10 80
51 WEST....................................... 5-10 83
GNP....................................... 8-12 74-76
GREAT NORTHWEST 8-12 81
GUEST STAR............................. 12-20 65
JANUS....................................... 8-12 72
JOKER....................................... 5-10 81
KAMA SUTRA (2014 "Bill Haley's Scrapbook")............................. 20-30 70

KAMA SUTRA (2014 "Bill Haley's Scrapbook") 20-30 70
KOALA 8-10 79
MCA 6-10 73-88
PAIR 5-8 86
PHOENIX 5-10 81
PICKWICK 8-10 71-74
ROULETTE 15-20 62
SILHOUETTE 5-10 81
SOMERSET (1300 "Rock and Roll Dance Party") 200-400 58
(Monaural.)
SOMERSET (1600 "Rock and Roll Dance Party") 200-400 58
(Stereo [Reprocessed]. Also includes tracks by: the Dinning Sisters; Bunny Paul; Ken Carson; Escorts; Aristocrats; Swingers; and the House Rockers.)
SOMERSET (4600 "Rock with Bill Haley and the Comets") 75-125 58
SPRINGBOARD 8-10 77
SUN 10-15 80
TRANSWORLD (202 "Rock with Bill Haley and the Comets") 200-300 56
VOCALION 15-25 63
W.B. (W-1378 "Bill Haley & His Comets") 25-35 60
(Monaural.)
W.B. (WS-1378 "Bill Haley & His Comets") 35-45 60
(Stereo.)
W.B. (W-1391 "Haley's Jukebox") 25-35 60
(Monaural.)
WARNER (WS-1391 "Haley's Jukebox") 35-45 60
(Stereo.)
W.B. (1831 "Rock & Roll Revival") 8-12 70
Also see BROWNE, Reno, & Her Buckaroos
Also see DOWNHOMERS
Also see KINGSMEN
Also see LEE, Brenda / Bill Haley & Comets / Kalin Twins / Four Aces
Also see LOPEZ, Trini / Scott Gregory

HALEY, Bill / Phil Flowers

Singles: 7-inch

KASEY (7006 "ABC Boogie") 10-15 61

Picture Sleeves

KASEY (7006 "ABC Boogie") 25-35 61

HALEY, Bill / Bunny Paul / Dinning Sisters

EPs: 7-inch 33/45rpm

SOMERSET (460 "Rock and Roll Dance Party") 30-40 55
Also see PAUL, Bunny, & Harptones

HALEY, Bill / Boots Randolph

Singles: 7-inch

LOGO (7005 "Yakety Sax") 8-12 61
Also see HALEY, Bill
Also see RANDOLPH, Boots

HALL, Daryl

(With Gulliver)

LP '80

Singles: 7-inch

AMY 4-8 69
CHELSEA 3-6 76
RCA 3-4 80-87

Picture Sleeves

RCA 3-4 80-87

LPs: 10/12-inch 33rpm

RCA 5-10 80-86
Also see KNIGHT, Holly
Also see U.S.A. for AFRICA

HALL, Daryl, & Ruth Copeland

Singles: 7-inch

RCA 3-4 76
Also see HALL, Daryl

HALL, Daryl, & John Oates

(Hall & Oates)

P&R/LP '74

Singles: 12-inch 33/45rpm

RCA 4-8 78-85

Singles: 7-inch

ARISTA 3-4 88-90
ATLANTIC 3-5 72-77
CHELSEA 3-5 76
RCA 3-5 76-84
RCA GOLD STANDARD 3-4 83-84

Picture Sleeves

ARISTA 3-4 88
RCA 3-5 77-85

Promotional Singles

RCA (Colored vinyl) 5-8 85
(One side by Daryl Hall and one side by John Oates.)

LPs: 10/12-inch 33rpm

ARISTA 5-8 88-90
ATLANTIC 8-12 72-77
CHELSEA 10-12 76
MFSL (069 "Abandoned Luncheonette") 20-30 82
RCA (Black vinyl) 5-10 75-84
RCA (Colored vinyl) 10-12 78

Promotional LPs

RCA ("Special Radio Series") 15-25 81
Also see PRINE, John / Daryl Hall & John Oates / Barnaby Bye / Delbert & Glen

HALL, Daryl, John Oates, David Ruffin & Eddie Kendrick

P&R/R&B/LP '85

Singles: 7-inch

RCA 3-4 85

Picture Sleeves

RCA 3-4 85

LPs: 10/12-inch 33rpm

RCA 5-8 85
Also see KENDRICK, David

Also see RUFFIN, David

HALL, Ellis, Jr.

R&B '83

Singles: 7-inch

H.C.R.C. 3-4 83

HALL, Jimmy

P&R/LP '80

Singles: 7-inch

EPIC 3-5 80-82

LPs: 10/12-inch 33rpm

EPIC 5-10 80

Also see BECK, Jeff
Also see WET WILLIE

HALL, John
(John Hall Band)

P&R/LP '81

Singles: 7-inch

ASYLUM 3-5 78
COLUMBIA 3-5 79
EMI AMERICA 3-4 81-83

LPs: 10/12-inch 33rpm

ASYLUM 5-10 78
COLUMBIA 8-10 70
EMI AMERICA 5-10 81-82

Also see ORLEANS

HALL, Lani

P&R '81

Singles: 7-inch

A&M 3-5 71-85

Picture Sleeves

A&M 3-5 72-85

LPs: 10/12-inch 33rpm

A&M 5-10 72-85

Also see MENDES, Sergio

HALL, Lani, & Herb Alpert

Singles: 7-inch

A&M 3-4 81

Also see ALPERT, Herb
Also see HALL, Lani

HALL, Larry

P&R '59

Singles: 7-inch

EVER GREEN (1001 "Sandy") . 25-35 59
GOLD LEAF 4-8 62
HOT (1 "Sandy") 15-25 59
STRAND 5-10 59-62

LPs: 10/12-inch 33rpm

STRAND (1005 "Sandy") 40-50 60

HALL, Randy

R&B '84

Singles: 7-inch

MCA 3-4 84-88

LPs: 10/12-inch 33rpm

MCA 5-10 84

HALL, Tom T.
(With the Storytellers)

C&W '67

Singles: 7-inch

MERCURY (Except 70000 series). 3-5 77-86
MERCURY (70000 series) 3-8 67-77
RCA 3-5 77-81

LPs: 10/12-inch 33rpm

MERCURY (500 thru 1100 series) 5-10 73-77
MERCURY (5000 thru 8000 series) 5-10 78-84
MERCURY (61000 series) 8-15 69-71
MERCURY (80000 series) 5-10 83-86
OUT of TOWN DIST 5-10 82
RCA 5-10 78-81

Session: Johnny Rodriguez; Gary Sargeants.
Also see DUDLEY, Dave, & Tom T. Hall
Also see PAGE, Patti, & Tom T. Hall
Also see RODRIGUEZ, Johnny

HALL, Tom T., & Earl Scruggs

C&W '82

Singles: 7-inch

COLUMBIA 3-4 82

LPs: 10/12-inch 33rpm

COLUMBIA 5-10 82

Also see FLATT, Lester, & Earl Scruggs
Also see HALL, Tom T.

HALL & OATES: see HALL, Daryl, & John Oates

HALLORAN, Jack, Singers

P&R '62

Singles: 7-inch

DOT 3-5 63

HALLYDAY, David

P&R '87

Singles: 7-inch

SCOTTI BROS. 3-4 87

Picture Sleeves

SCOTTI BROS. 3-4 87

HALOS

P&R '61

Singles: 7-inch

7 ARTS 10-15 61
TRANS ATLAS 5-8 62

LPs: 10/12-inch 33rpm

WARWICK (2046 "The Halos") 50-100 62

Member: Arthur Crier.
Also see KING, Ben E.
Also see LEE, Curtis
Also see MANN, Barry

HAMBLEN, Stuart

C&W '49

Singles: 78rpm

COLUMBIA 4-8 49-57

Singles: 7-inch

BLUEBIRD 5-10 59
COLUMBIA 5-10 50-62
CORAL 4-8 59

KAPP.......... 4-8 66
LAMB & LION.......... 3-5 74
RCA (0500 series).......... 3-5 71
RCA (5000 & 6000 series).......... 5-15 54-56

EPs: 7–inch 33/45rpm

COLUMBIA.......... 5-10 58-59
RCA.......... 5-15 54-60

LPs: 10/12–inch 33rpm

CAMDEN.......... 5-15 59-66
COLUMBIA.......... 5-15 61-62
CORAL.......... 10-20 60
KAPP.......... 5-10 66
LAMB & LION.......... 5-8 74
RCA.......... 15-30 54-57
SACRED.......... 5-8
WORD.......... 5-8

HAMILTON, Bobby

P&R '58

Singles: 7–inch

APT.......... 8-12 58-59
DECCA.......... 5-10 59
DIANA.......... 5-10 59

HAMILTON, Chico

(Chico Hamilton Trio; Quartet; Quintet; with Players)

LP '64

Singles: 7-Inch

COLUMBIA.......... 4-6 61
CORAL.......... 4-6 62
ENTERPRISE.......... 3-5 74
IMPULSE.......... 4-6 64-67
PACIFIC JAZZ (600 series).......... 5-10 54-55
PACIFIC JAZZ (88000 series).......... 4-6 66

EPs: 7-Inch 33/45rpm

DECCA.......... 15-25 57
PACIFIC JAZZ.......... 20-40 55-56

LPs: 10/12-Inch 33rpm

BLUE NOTE.......... 5-10 75
COLUMBIA.......... 15-25 60-62
CROWN.......... 10-20 63
DECCA (8614 "Jazz from Sweet Smell of Success").......... 25-40 57
DISCOVERY.......... 5-8 81
ELEKTRA.......... 5-8 80
EVEREST.......... 5-8 79
FLYING DUTCHMAN.......... 8-10 71
IMPULSE.......... 10-20 63-71
INSTANT.......... 10-20 64
MERCURY.......... 5-10 77
ODYSSEY.......... 10-20 68
PACIFIC JAZZ (17 "The Chico Hamilton Trio").......... 75-100 55
(10–inch LP.)
PACIFIC JAZZ (39 "Spectacular Chico Hamilton").......... 15-25 62
PACIFIC JAZZ (1209 "Chico Hamilton Quintet").......... 50-75 55
PACIFIC JAZZ (1216 "In Hi Fi") 50-75 56
PACIFIC JAZZ (1220 "Chico Hamilton Trio").......... 50-75 57
PACIFIC JAZZ (1225 "Chico Hamilton Quintet").......... 50-75 57
PACIFIC JAZZ (20000 series).......... 10-20 68
REPRISE.......... 15-25 63
SESAC.......... 35-55 59
(Promotional issue only.)
SOLID STATE.......... 10-15 68-69
SUNSET.......... 8-15 68
W.B. (1245 "With Strings Attached").......... 50-75 58
W.B. (1271 "Goings East").......... 50-75 58
W.B. (1344 "Three Faces of Chico").......... 40-60 59
WORLD PACIFIC (1000 & 1200 series).......... 25-40 58-60

Also see ALMEIDA, Laurindo / Chico Hamilton

HAMILTON, Chico, & Charles Lloyd

LPs: 10/12-Inch 33rpm

COLUMBIA.......... 10-15 68

Also see HAMILTON, Chico
Also see LLOYD, Charles, Quartet

HAMILTON, George, IV

(With the Country Gentlemen)

P&R '56

Singles: 78rpm

ABC-PAR.......... 3-6 56-57
COLONIAL.......... 10-15 56

Singles: 7–inch

ABC.......... 3-5 78
ABC/DOT.......... 3-5 77
ABC-PAR (9000 series).......... 10-20 56-59
ABC-PAR (10000 series).......... 5-15 59-65
COLONIAL (420 "A Rose and a Baby Ruth").......... 50-75 56
COLONIAL (451 "Sam").......... 25-35 56
GRT.......... 3-5 76
MCA.......... 3-5 79-80
RCA.......... 3-8 61-74

EPs: 7–inch 33/45rpm

ABC-PAR.......... 10-20 58

LPs: 10/12–inch 33rpm

ABC.......... 8-10 72-77
ABC-PAR.......... 25-50 58-63
CAMDEN.......... 8-10 68-73
HARMONY.......... 8-10 70
LAMB & LION.......... 8-10 74
MCA.......... 5-10 80
RCA ("APL1" series).......... 8-10 74-76
RCA ("LPM" & "LSP" series).......... 10-20 61-73

Also see ANKA, Paul, George Hamilton IV & Johnny Nash
Also see BLUENOTES
Also see DAVIS, Skeeter, & George Hamilton IV

HAMILTON, George, V

C&W '88

Singles: 7–inch

MTM 3-4 88

HAMILTON, Roy

P&R/R&B '54

Singles: 78rpm

EPIC 5-8 54-57

Singles: 7–inch

AGP 4-8 69
CAPITOL 4-8 67
EPIC 5-15 54-67
MGM (13138 thru 13175) 5-10 63
MGM (13217 "The Panic Is On") 25-35 64
MGM (13247 "Unchained Melody") 5-10 64
MGM (13291 "You Can Count On Me") 25-35 64
MGM (13315 "Sweet Violet") 5-10 65
RCA (8641 thru 8813) 5-10 65-66
RCA (8960 "Crackin' Up Over You") 15-25 66
RCA (9061 "I Taught Her Everything She Knows") 5-10 67
RCA (9171 "So High My Love") 25-45 67

Picture Sleeves

EPIC 10-20 60-62

EPs: 7–inch 33/45rpm

EPIC 10-20 54-59

LPs: 10/12–inch 33rpm

CBS 5-8
EPIC (518 "With All My Love") .. 25-35 58
(Stereo.)
EPIC (525 "Why Fight the Feeling") 20-30 59
(Stereo.)
EPIC (530 "Come Out Swingin'") 20-30 59
(Stereo.)
EPIC (535 "Have Blues Must Travel") 20-30 59
(Stereo.)
EPIC (551 "Spirituals") 20-25 60
(Stereo.)
EPIC (578 "Soft 'N' Warm") 20-25 60
(Stereo.)
EPIC (595 "You Can Have Her") 20-25 61
(Stereo.)
EPIC (610 "Only You") 20-25 61
(Stereo.)
EPIC (632 "You'll Never Walk Alone") 10-20 65
(Stereo.)
EPIC (1023 "You'll Never Walk Alone") 50-100 54
(10–inch LP.)
EPIC (1103 "The Voice of Roy Hamilton") 50-100 55
(10–inch LP.)
EPIC (3176 "Roy Hamilton") 25-50 57
EPIC (3294 "You'll Never Walk Alone") 50-75 54
EPIC (3364 "Golden Boy") 30-40 57
EPIC (3519 "With All My Love") . 15-25 58
(Monaural.)
EPIC (3545 "Why Fight the Feeling") 15-25 59
(Monaural.)
EPIC (3561 "Come Out Swingin") 15-25 59
(Monaural.)
EPIC (3580 "Have Blues Must Travel") 15-25 59
(Monaural.)
EPIC (3628 "At His Best") 15-25 60
(Monaural.)
EPIC (3654 "Spirituals") 15-25 60
(Monaural.)
EPIC (3717 "Soft 'N' Warm") 15-25 60
(Monaural.)
EPIC (3775 "You Can Have Her") 15-25 61
(Monaural.)
EPIC (3807 "Only You") 15-25 61
(Monaural.)
EPIC (24000 "Mr. Rock & Soul") 15-25 62
(Monaural.)
EPIC (24009 "Greatest Hits") 15-25 63
(Monaural.)
EPIC (24316 "Greatest Hits, Vol. 2") 10-20 67
(Monaural.)
EPIC (26000 "Mr. Rock and Soul") 20-25 62
(Stereo.)
EPIC (26009 "Greatest Hits") 15-25 63
(Stereo.)
EPIC (26316 "Greatest Hits, Vol. 2") 10-20 67
(Stereo.)
MGM (4139 "Warm Soul") 15-25 63
MGM (4233 "Sentimental, Lonely and Blue") 15-25 64
RCA (3532 "Impossible Dream") 15-25 66

HAMILTON, Russ

P&R/R&B '57

Singles: 78

pm

KAPP 4-8 57

Singles: 7–inch

KAPP 5-10 57-64
MGM 4-8 60

LPs: 10/12-inch 33rpm

KAPP (1076 "Rainbow") ... 45-55 57

HAMILTON, JOE FRANK & DENNISON

P&R '76

Singles: 7-inch

PLAYBOY ... 3-5 76-77

Picture Sleeves

PLAYBOY ... 3-5 76

LPs: 10/12-inch 33rpm

PLAYBOY ... 8-10 76-77

Members: Dan Hamilton; Joe Frank Carollo; Alan Dennison.

HAMILTON, JOE FRANK & REYNOLDS

P&R/LP '71

Singles: 7-inch

ABC ... 3-5 72
DUNHILL ... 3-5 71
PLAYBOY ... 3-5 75-76

Picture Sleeves

PLAYBOY ... 3-5 76

LPs: 10/12-inch 33rpm

DUNHILL ... 8-10 71-72
PICKWICK ... 5-8 70s
PLAYBOY ... 8-10 75-77

Members: Dan Hamilton; Joe Frank Carollo; Tom Reynolds.

Also see HAMILTON, JOE FRANK & DENNISON
Also see T-BONES

HAMLISCH, Marvin

P&R/LP '74

Singles: 12-inch 33/45rpm

U.A. ... 4-6 77

Singles: 7-inch

A&M ... 3-5 74-76
ARISTA ... 3-4 79
MCA ... 3-5 74-83
PLANET ... 3-4 80
U.A. ... 3-4 71-77

LPs: 10/12-inch 33rpm

MCA ... 5-10 74
SOUTHERN CROSS ... 5-10 83

HAMMEL, Karl, Jr.

(Carl Hammel)

P&R '61

Singles: 7-inch

ARLISS (1007 "Summer Souvenirs") ... 10-20 61
ARLISS (1011 "Sittin' Alphabetically") ... 30-40 61
GONE (5059 "My Broken Heart") ... 10-15 59
LAURIE ... 5-10 63
20TH FOX ... 4-8 66

HAMMER, Jan

(Jan Hammer Group)

P&R/R&B/D&D '85

Singles: 12-inch 33/45rpm

MCA ... 4-6 85

Singles: 7-inch

ASYLUM ... 3-4 79
MCA ... 3-4 85
NEMPEROR ... 3-5 76-78

Picture Sleeves

MCA ... 3-4 85

LPs: 10/12-inch 33rpm

ECM ... 5-10
MPS ... 5-10 76
NEMPEROR ... 5-10 74-86
VANGAURD ... 5-10 77

Also see BECK, Jeff
Also see GOODMAN, Jerry, & Jan Hammer
Also see SCHON, Neal, & Jan Hammer

HAMMER, M.C.

(Hammer; Stanley Burrell)

LP '88

Singles: 7-inch

CAPITOL ... 3-4 88-90

LPs: 10/12-inch 33rpm

CAPITOL ... 5-8 88-90

Also see OAKTOWN'S 3-5-7

HAMMOND, Albert

P&R/LP '72

Singles: 7-inch

EPIC ... 3-5 76
MUMS ... 3-5 72-75

LPs: 10/12-inch 33rpm

COLUMBIA ... 5-10 81-82
EPIC ... 8-10 77
MUMS ... 8-10 72-74

Also see MAGIC LANTERNS
Also see SPRINGSTEEN, Bruce / Albert Hammond / Loudon Wainwright, III / Taj Mahal

HAMMOND, Johnny

(John Hammond)

LP '71

Singles: 7-inch

MILESTONE ... 4-8 75

LPs: 10/12-inch 33rpm

KUDU ... 8-12 71-72

HAMPSHIRE, Keith

(With the Ladys)

P&R '72

Singles: 7-inch

A&M ... 3-5 72-74
RCA ... 3-5 71

HAMPTON, Lionel

P&R '37

Singles: 7-inch

CLEF ... 4-8 55
BRUNSWICK ... 3-5 74
COLUMBIA ... 3-4 76
DECCA (Except 140 & 154) ... 5-10 50-53
DECCA (140 "Moonglow") ... 15-25 51
(Four disc boxed set)
DECCA (154 "Just Jazz") ... 15-25 53
(Four disc boxed set)

GLAD HAMP 4-6 60-67
IMPULSE 3-6 65
MGM 4-8 51-61
NORGREN 4-6 56

EPs: 7–inch 33/45rpm

CAMDEN 4-8 50s
CLEF 10-30 53-56
COLUMBIA 8-15 56
DECCA 8-15 51-53
EMARCY 8-12 56
EPIC 8-12 56
GLAD HAMP 5-10 62
MGM 10-20 56
MERCURY 8-15 55
NORGREN 10-30 55
RCA 8-15 54-57

LPs: 10/12–inch 33rpm

AMERICAN RECORDING SOCIETY (403 "Swinging Jazz") 75-100 56
(Includes booklet.)
AUDIO FIDELITY 15-25 57-59
BLUENOTE (5046 "Rockin' and Groovin") 75-100 53
(10–inch LP.)
BRUNSWICK 5-10 74
CAMDEN (400 & 500 series) 15-25 58-59
CLEF (142 "Lionel Hampton Quartet") 50-75 53
(10–inch LP.)
CLEF (611 "Lionel Hampton Quartet") 40-60 53
CLEF (628 "Lionel Hampton Quintet") 40-60 54
CLEF (642 "Lionel Hampton Quintet") 40-60 54
CLEF (667 "Quartet/Quintet") 40-60 55
CLEF (670 "Big Band") 40-60 55
CLEF (673 "Big Band") 40-60 55
CLEF (735 "Flying Home") 40-60 56
CLEF (736 "Swingin' with Hamp") 40-60 56
CLEF (744 "Hamp's Big Four") 40-60 56
CLEF (709 "Lionel Hampton Trio") 40-60 56
COLUMBIA (711 "Wailin' at the Trianon") 35-45 56
COLUMBIA (1304 thru 1661) 15-25 59-61
(Monaural.)
COLUMBIA (8110 thru 8461) 20-30 59-61
(Stereo.)
CONTEMPORARY (3502 "Lionel Hampton Swings in Paris") 40-60 55
CORAL 15-25 63
DECCA (4000 series) 20-30 61-63
(Monaural.)
DECCA (7-4000 series) 20-30 61-63
(Stereo.)
DECCA (5320 "Boogie Woogie") 40-60 51
(10–inch LP.)
DECCA (7013 "Just Jazz") 30-50 53
(10–inch LP.)
DECCA (8200 series) 25-35 56
DECCA (9000 series) 20-30 58
DECCA (79000 series) 10-15 69
EMARCY (26037 "In Paris") 40-60 53
(10–inch LP.)
EMARCY (26038 "Crazy Hamp") 40-60 53
(10–inch LP.)
EMARCY (36032 "In Paris") 30-40 53
EMARCY (36034 "Crazy Hamp") 30-40 56
EPIC (3190 "Lionel Hampton Apollo Hall Concert 1954") 40-50 56
EPIC (16027 "Many Splendored Vibes") 20-30 62
(Monaural.)
EPIC (17027 "Many Splendored Vibes") 25-35 62
(Stereo.)
GNP (15 "Lionel Hampton with the Jazz All Stars") 40-60 57
GLAD HAMP (1001 thru 1009) 10-20 61-65
GLAD HAMP (1020 & 1021) 5-10 80
GLAD HAMP (3000 series) 10-20 62
HARMONY (7000 series) 15-25 58-61
HARMONY (32000 series) 5-10 73
IMPULSE 15-25 65
LAURIE 5-10 78
MCA 5-8 75-82
MGM (285 "Oh Rock") 50-75 51
(10–inch LP.)
MGM (3386 "Oh Rock") 25-35 56
MUSE 5-8 79
NORGREN (1080 "Lionel Hampton & His Giants") 50-75 55
PERFECT (12002 "Hampton Swings") 30-50 59
RCA (1000 "Hot Mallets") 40-60 54
RCA (1422 "Jazz Flamenco") 30-40 57
RCA (LPM-2318 "Swing Classics") 25-30 61
(Monaural.)
RCA (LSP-2318 "Swing Classics") 30-35 61
(Stereo.)
RCA (3900 series) 10-15 68
RCA (5536 "The Complete Lionel Hampton") 50-60 76
(Six LP boxed set.)
SUTRA 5-10 81
VERVE (2018 "Lionel Hampton Plays Love Songs") 40-50 56
VERVE (2500 series) 5-10 82
VERVE (8019 thru 8228) 20-35 57-58

WHO'S WHO in JAZZ................ 5-10 78-81
Also see BROWN, Wini
Also see CARTER, Betty
Also see COLE, Cozy

HAMPTON, Lionel & Stan Getz

LPs: 10/12-inch 33rpm

NORGREN (1037 "Hamp and Getz")................................. 75-100 55
VERVE (8128 "Hamp & Getz") . 40-60 57
Also see GETZ, Stan

HAMPTON, Lionel & Dinah Washington

R&B '44

Singles: 78rpm

DECCA.................................. 5-10 44-47

LPs: 10/12-inch 33rpm

DECCA (8088 "All American Award Concert")..................... 40-60 54
Also see HAMPTON, Lionel
Also see WASHINGTON, Dinah

HANCOCK, Herbie

LP '67

Singles: 12-inch 33/45rpm

COLUMBIA 4-6 79-85

Singles: 7-inch

BLUE NOTE................................ 3-6 62-65
COLUMBIA 3-5 74-88
W.B. 3-5 69-72

LPs: 10/12-inch 33rpm

BLUE NOTE............................ 15-25 62-65
(Label reads "Blue Note Records Inc. - New York, U.S.A.")
BLUE NOTE.............................. 8-15 66-71
(Label shows Blue Note Records as a division of either Liberty or United Artists.)
COLUMBIA 6-12 67-85
W.B. 8-15 70-74
Also see SANTANA
Also see SUMMERS, Bill

HANCOCK, Herbie, & Willie Bobo

LPs: 10/12-inch 33rpm

BLUE NOTE.............................. 5-10 73
Also see BOBO, Willie
Also see HANCOCK, Herbie

HANCOCK, Herbie, & Chick Corea

LP '79

LPs: 10/12-inch 33rpm

COLUMBIA 5-10 79
POLYDOR................................. 8-10 79
Also see COREA, Chick
Also see HANCOCK, Herbie

HANDY, John
(John Handy Quartet; Quintet)

P&R/R&B/LP '76

Singles: 7-inch

IMPULSE 3-5 76-77
COLUMBIA 4-6 66-69

LPs: 10/12-inch 33rpm

IMPULSE 5-10 76-77

COLUMBIA 10-15 66-68
RCA 10-15 67
ROULETTE (52000 series)........15-25 60
ROULETTE (52100 series)........10-15 66-67
W.B. 5-10 78

HANK & Sugar Pie

Singles: 78rpm

FEDERAL 5-8 55

Singles: 7-inch

FEDERAL (12217 "I'm So Lonely")...............................20-25 55
Member: Hank Huston; Umpeylia Balinton.
Also see DE SANTO, Sugar Pie

HANSON & DAVIS

D&D '85

Singles: 12-inch 33/45rpm

FRESH...4-6 85-86

Singles: 7-inch

FRESH...3-4 86

HANSSON, Bo

LP '73

Singles: 7-inch

CHARISMA..................................3-5 73
SIRE..3-5 76-77

LPs: 10/12-inch 33rpm

FAMOUS CHARISMA................8-10 72-73
PVC...5-10 79
SIRE..8-10 76-77

HAPPENINGS

P&R/LP '66

Singles: 7-inch

ABC...3-4 73
B.T. PUPPY (Except 181).............4-8 66-69
B.T. PUPPY (181 "Have Yourself a Merry Little Christmas").....................20-30 67
(Promotional issue only.)
BIG TREE 3-5 72
ERIC 3-4
JUBILEE 3-6 69-71
MIDLAND INT'L 3-5 77
MUSICORE...................................3-5 72
TRIP 3-5
VIRGO 3-4 72

Picture Sleeves

B.T. PUPPY 5-15 67-69

LPs: 10/12-inch 33rpm

B.T. PUPPY (1001 "The Happenings") 15-25 66
B.T. PUPPY (1003 "Psycle")......15-25 67
B.T. PUPPY (1004 "Golden Hits")......................................25-35 68
JUBILEE (8028 "Piece of Mind") 15-20 69
JUBILEE (8030 "Greatest Hits") 15-20 69
POST 8-12
Member: Bob Miranda; Tom Guliano; Ralph DeVito; Dave Libert; Bernie Laporte; Mike LaNeue.
Also see TOKENS / Happenings

HAPPY MONDAYS

LP '91

LPs: 10/12-inch 33rpm

ELEKTRA 5-8 91

HARBOR, Pearl: see PEARL HARBOR

HARDCASTLE, Paul

R&B/D&D '84

Singles: 12-inch 33/45rpm

CHRYSALIS 4-6 85-86
PROFILE 4-6 84

Singles: 7-inch

CHRYSALIS 3-4 85-86
PROFILE 3-4 84-85

Picture Sleeves

CHRYSALIS 3-4 85

LPs: 10/12-inch 33rpm

CHRYSALIS 5-10 86
PROFILE 5-10 85

HARDEN TRIO

P&R/LP '66

Singles: 7-inch

COLUMBIA 3-4 65-68
PAPA JOE 3-4 72

LPs: 10/12-inch 33rpm

COLUMBIA 10-15 66-68
HARMONY 8-12 70

Members: Arlene Harden; Bobby Harden; Robbie Harden. Session: Karen Wheeler.

HARDIN, Tim

P&R/LP '69

Singles: 7-inch

COLUMBIA 3-5 69-72
VERVE/FOLKWAYS 3-5 66-70
VERVE/FORECAST 3-5 67-71

LPs: 10/12-inch 33rpm

ATCO 8-15 67
COLUMBIA (9787 "Suite for Susan Moore and Damian") 20-30 69
COLUMBIA (30551 "Bird on a Wire") 15-20 70
COLUMBIA (37164 "Shock of Grace") 5-10 81
MGM 6-10 70-74
POLYDOR 5-10 81
VERVE/FORECAST 10-20 66-69

HARDLY WORTHIT PLAYERS

(Featuring Senator Bobby & Senator McKinley)

P&R '67

Singles: 7-inch

PARKWAY 4-8 67

LPs: 10/12-inch 33rpm

PARKWAY 10-20 66-67

Also see SENATOR BOBBY

HARDTIMES

P&R '66

Singles: 7-inch

WORLD PACIFIC 5-10 66-68

LPs: 10/12-inch 33rpm

WORLD PACIFIC 15-25 66-68

Members: Lee Kiefer; Rudy Romero; Bob Morris; Bill Richardson.
Also see STEPPENWOLF
Also see T.I.M.E.

HARDY, Hagood

P&R '75

Singles: 7-inch

CAPITOL 3-5 75-78
HERITAGE 3-5 71

LPs: 10/12-inch 33rpm

CAPITOL 4-8 75-76

HARDY BOYS

LP '69

Singles: 7-inch

RCA 4-6 69-70

LPs: 10/12-inch 33rpm

RCA 10-15 69-70

HARLEM RIVER DRIVE

(Featuring Eddie Palmieri)

R&B '75

Singles: 7-inch

ARISTA 3-5 75
ROULETTE 3-5 70-72

LPs: 10/12-inch 33rpm

ROULETTE 8-10 71
TICO 5-10 72

Members: Eddie Palmieri; Jimmy Norman.
Also see NORMAN, Jimmy

HARLEY, Steve

(With Cockney Rebel)

P&R '76

Singles: 7-inch

CAPITOL 3-5 78
EMI 3-5 75-77

LPs: 10/12-inch 33rpm

CAPITOL 5-10 78
EMI 5-10 75-77

HARMONICATS

(Jerry Murad's Harmonicats)

P&R '47

Singles: 78rpm

MERCURY 3-5 50-57
UNIVERSAL 3-6 48
VITACOUSTIC 4-8 47

Singles: 7-inch

COLUMBIA 3-5 61-67
MERCURY 4-8 50-60

Picture Sleeves

COLUMBIA 5-10 60

EPs: 7-inch 33/45rpm

MERCURY 5-10 50-61

LPs: 10/12-inch 33rpm

COLUMBIA 8-15 61-67
HARMONY 5-10 66
MERCURY 5-15 50-69
WING 5-10 59-64

Members: Jerry Murad; Al Fiore; Don Les.

HARNELL, Joe, His Orchestra
(With His Trio)

P&R '62

Singles: 7–inch

COLUMBIA 3-5 66-68
EPIC.. 3-6 59-60
KAPP... 3-5 61-65
MCA 3-4 78
MEDALLION 3-5 61-62
MOTOWN 3-5 69-70

Picture Sleeves

KAPP... 4-8 63

LPs: 10/12–inch 33rpm

CAPITOL..................................... 5-8 77
COLUMBIA 5-10 66
EPIC... 5-15 59-63
KAPP.. 5-15 63-66
MEDALLION 5-15 61
MOTOWN 5-10 70

HARNEY, Ben, & Sheryl Lee Ralph

R&B '83

Singles: 7–inch

GEFFEN...................................... 3-4 83

Also see RALPH, Sheryl Lee

HAROLD, Prince: see PRINCE HAROLD

HARPER, Janice

P&R '57

Singles: 7–inch

CAPITOL.................................. 5-10 58-60
PREP 5-10 57
RCA... 4-6 66

LPs: 10/12–inch 33rpm

CAPITOL............................... 15-20 58-60

HARPER, Toni
(With the Eddie Beale Sextet)

R&B '48

Singles: 78rpm

COLUMBIA 5-10 48

Singles: 7–inch

RCA... 5-10 60-61

LPs: 10/12–inch 33rpm

RCA....................................... 15-20 60

Also see LIMELITERS

HARPERS BIZARRE

P&R/LP '67

Singles: 7–inch

FOREST BAY CO 3-5 76
W.B. 3-6 67-72

EPs: 7–inch 33/45rpm

W.B. 4-8 68
(Jukebox issues only.)

LPs: 10/12–inch 33rpm

FOREST BAY CO 8-10 76
W.B. 10-20 67-68

Members: Ted Templeman; John Petersen; Dick Yount; Dick Scoppettone; John Peterson.

HARPO, Slim

P&R/R&B '61

Singles: 78rpm

EXCELLO 10-20 57

Singles: 7–inch

ABC...3-5 73
EXCELLO (2113 "I'm a King Bee")...25-50 57
(Orange label.)
EXCELLO (2113 "I'm a King Bee")...40-60 57
(White label. Promotional issue only.)
EXCELLO (2138 "Wondering and Worrying")..............................15-25 58
(Orange label.)
EXCELLO (2138 "Wondering and Worrying")..............................15-25 58
(White label. Promotional issue only.)
EXCELLO (2162 "One More Day")......................................15-25 59
(Orange label.)
EXCELLO (2162 "One More Day")......................................15-25 59
(White label. Promotional issue only.)
EXCELLO (2184 "Blues Hang Over") 15-25 60
EXCELLO (2194 "Rainin' in My Heart")....................................10-15 61
EXCELLO (2200 series) 5-15 62-68
EXCELLO (2300 series) 4-8 69-71

LPs: 10/12–inch 33rpm

EXCELLO (Except 8003 & 8005)......................................10-20 68-70
EXCELLO (8003 "Raining in My Heart")...............................30-50 61
EXCELLO (8005 "Baby, Scratch My Back") 20-30 66

HARPTONES
(Harp-Tones; featuring Willie Winfield)

P&R '61

Singles: 78rpm

ANDREA...................................10-20 56
BRUCE 15-25 53-55
GEE 10-20 57
PARADISE.................................20-30 56
RAMA.......................................10-20 56-57
TIP TOP 10-20 56

Singles: 7–inch

AMBIENT SOUND.........................4-6 82
ANDREA (100 "What Is Your Decision")...............................20-30 56
(With chain-like horizontal lines.)
ANDREA (100 "What Is Your Decision")...............................15-25 56
(With straight horizontal lines.)
BRUCE (101 "A Sunday Kind of Love")............................300-500 53
("Bruce" in script lettering.)

BRUCE (101 "A Sunday Kind of Love")................................ 25-50 53
("Bruce" in block lettering.)
BRUCE (102 "My Memories of You")...................................... 25-50 54
(With straight horizontal lines.)
BRUCE (102 "My Memories of You")...................................... 10-15
(With jagged horizontal lines.)
BRUCE (104 "I Depended on You")...................................... 40-60 54
BRUCE (109 "Forever Mine") ... 30-60 54
(With the Shytans.)
BRUCE (113 "Since I Fell for You")...................................... 30-50 54
BRUCE (128 "I Almost Lost My Mind")................................ 30-50 55
COED (540 "Answer Me My Love")...................................... 10-15 60
COMPANION (102 "All in Your Mind")............................ 20-25 61
COMPANION (103 "What Will I Tell My Heart")............................ 50-70 61
CUB (9097 "Devil in Velvet")..... 10-15 61
GEE (1045 "Cry Like I Cried")... 15-25 57
KT (201 "Sunset")..................... 40-50 63
OLDIES 45.................................... 4-8 60s
PARADISE (101 "Life Is But a Dream")........................ 50-75 56
(Maroon label.)
PARADISE (101 "Life Is But a Dream")........................ 20-30 56
(Purple label.)
PARADISE (103 "My Success") 50-75 56
PARADISE (103 "It All Depends on You")................................ 50-75 56
(Maroon label.)
PARADISE (103 "It All Depends on You")................................ 20-30 56
(Purple label.)
RAMA (203 "Three Wishes")..... 20-30 56
RAMA (214 "The Masquerade Is Over")................................ 20-30 56
RAMA (221 "The Shrine of Saint Cecilia")......................... 20-30 57
RAVEN (8001 "Sunday Kind of Love")................................ 10-15 62
ROULETTE.................................. 3-5 71
TIP TOP (401 "My Memories of You")................................ 25-35 56
WARWICK (512 "Love Me Completely")........................... 15-25 59
WARWICK (551 "No Greater Miracle")................................ 15-25 59

EPs: 7-inch 33/45rpm

BRUCE (201 "The Sensational Harptones").................. 5000-10000 54

LPs: 10/12-inch 33rpm

AMBIENT SOUND (37718 "Love Needs")....................................8-12 82
HARLEM HITPARADE (5006 "The Harptones")...............................10-15 70s
MURRAY HILL.................................5-8 88
RARE BIRD 8-10
RELIC 8-10 70s

Members: Willie Winfield; Nicky Clark; Bill Brown; Bill Dempsey; Bill Galloway; Raoul Cita; Jimmy Beckum; Lynn Daniels; Vicki Burgess; Margaret Moore; Fred Taylor.
Also see PAUL, Bunny, & Harptones

HARPTONES / Cleftones

Singles: 7-inch

ROULETTE.......................................3-5 71
Also see CLEFTONES

HARPTONES / Crows

LPs: 10/12-inch 33rpm

ROULETTE................................15-20 72
Also see CROWS

HARPTONES / Paragons

LPs: 10/12-inch 33rpm

MUSICNOTE 20-30 64

HARPTONES / Paragons / Jesters / Clovers

LPs: 10/12-inch 33rpm

GRAND PRIX.............................10-20 60s
Also see CLOVERS
Also see HARPTONES
Also see JESTERS
Also see PARAGONS

HARRELL, Grady

R&B '85

Singles: 7-inch

MCA...3-5 85

HARRIS, Betty

P&R/R&B '63

Singles: 7-inch

JUBILEE 8-10 63-69
PROM 3-4
SSS INT'L.....................................3-6 69
SANSU..4-8 66-68

HARRIS, Bobby

R&B '65

Singles: 7-inch

ATLANTIC.....................................4-8 65
Also see LUNDY, Pat, & Bobby Harris

HARRIS, Brenda Jo

R&B '68

Singles: 7-inch

ROULETTE.....................................4-6 68

HARRIS, Damon

R&B '79

Singles: 12-inch 33/45rpm

WMOT..4-6 78-79

Singles: 7-inch

WMOT..3-5 78-79

LPs: 10/12-inch 33rpm

WMOT.. 5-10 78

Also see IMPACT
Also see TEMPTATIONS

HARRIS, David

R&B '74

Singles: 7-inch

PLEASURE.................................. 3-5 74

HARRIS, Eddie

P&R/R&B/LP '61

Singles: 7-inch

ABC.. 3-5 73
ATLANTIC.................................... 3-6 65-77
COLUMBIA.................................. 4-6 64
VEE JAY...................................... 5-8 61-63
W.B.. 3-4 81

LPs: 10/12-inch 33rpm

ANGELACO.................................. 5-10 81
ATLANTIC.................................... 6-12 65-81
BUDDAH...................................... 8-12 69
COLUMBIA.................................. 10-20 64-68
CRUSADERS................................ 5-10 82
GNP.. 5-10 73
HARMONY.................................. 5-10 72
RCA... 5-10 78
SUNSET....................................... 5-10 69
TRIP.. 5-10 73
VEE JAY (3016 thru 3028)........ 20-35 61-62
VEE JAY (3031 thru 3034)........ 15-25 63

Also see McCANN, Les, & Eddie Harris
Also see MOORE, Shelly, & Eddie Harris

HARRIS, Eddie, & John Klemmer

LPs: 10/12-Inch 33rpm

CRUSADERS................................ 5-8 82

Also see HARRIS, Eddie
Also see KLEMMER, John

HARRIS, Emmylou

(With Her Hot Band; with Cheryl White & Sharon White)

C&W/P&R '75

Singles: 7-inch

JUBILEE...................................... 5-10 69-70
REPRISE (Except 1341)............... 3-5 75-77
REPRISE (1341 "Light of the
Stable")...................................... 4-6 75
W.B.. 3-5 77-86

Picture Sleeves

REPRISE..................................... 3-5 75-77
WARNER..................................... 3-4 80-86

LPs: 10/12-inch 33rpm

EMUS... 5-10 79
JUBILEE (8031 "Gliding Bird").. 60-80 69
MFSL (015 "Quarter Moon
in a Ten-Cent Town").............. 30-40 78
REPRISE..................................... 8-10 75
W.B.. 5-10 77-87

Members: James Burton; Glen D. Hardin; Emory Gordy; Ronnie Tutt.
Also see ANDERSON, John
Also see CONLEY, Earl Thomas, & Emmylou Harris
Also see CRICKETS
Also see CROWELL, Rodney
Also see DENVER, John, & Emmylou Harris
Also see EVERLY, Don
Also see LITTLE FEAT
Also see ORBISON, Roy, & Emmylou Harris / Craig Hundley
Also see OWENS, Buck, & Emmylou Harris
Also see PARSONS, Gram
Also see PARTON, Dolly
Also see PARTON, Dolly, Linda Ronstadt, & Emmylou Harris
Also see PRESLEY, Elvis
Also see RONSTADT, Linda, & Emmylou Harris
Also see TUCKER, Tanya
Also see WINCHESTER, Jesse
Also see YOUNG, Neil

HARRIS, Emmylou, & Don Williams

C&W '81

Singles: 7-inch

W.B.. 3-4 81

Also see WILLIAMS, Don

HARRIS, Gene

(With the Three Sounds)

R&B '74

Singles: 7-inch

BLUE NOTE................................. 3-5 71-77

LPs: 10/12-inch 33rpm

BLUE NOTE................................. 5-10 71-77

HARRIS, Huey "Baby"

R&B '85

Singles: 7-inch

PROFILE...................................... 3-4 85

HARRIS, Major

(Major Harris Boogie Blues Band)

P&R/R&B/LP '75

Singles: 7-inch

ATLANTIC.................................... 4-6 75-76
OKEH (7314 "Just Love Me") ... 15-25 68
OKEH (7327 "Like a Rolling
Stone")...................................... 30-60 69
POP ART..................................... 3-4 83
WMOT... 3-5 76-81

LPs: 10/12-inch 33rpm

ATLANTIC.................................... 8-10 75
RCA... 5-10 78
WMOT... 8-10 76

Also see DELFONICS

HARRIS, Peppermint: see PEPPERMINT HARRIS

HARRIS, Phil

P&R '33

Singles: 78rpm

ARA... 4-8 46
COLUMBIA.................................. 4-8 33
DECCA.. 4-6 35
RCA... 3-6 47-54

Singles: 7-inch

COLISEUM.................................. 3-5 68
MEGA.. 3-4 73

MONTCLARE	3-4	76
RCA	5-10	50-54
REPRISE	3-5	62
VISTA	3-5	67-70

Picture Sleeves

MONTCLARE	3-5	76

EPs: 7–inch 33/45rpm

RCA	5-10	53-60

LPs: 10/12–inch 33rpm

CAMDEN	8-12	63
MEGA	5-10	72-74
RCA (1900 series)	10-20	59
RCA (3000 series)	20-30	53-54
ZODIAC	5-10	77

Also see BELL SISTERS
Also see SHORE, Dinah, Tony Martin, Betty Hutton & Phil Harris

HARRIS, Richard

P&R/LP '68

Singles: 7–inch

ATLANTIC	3-5	74-75
DUNHILL	3-6	68-75

Picture Sleeves

DUNHILL (Except 4134)	4-8	70-72
DUNHILL (4134 "MacArthur Park")	3-6	68
DUNHILL (4134 "MacArthur Park")	8-12	68

(Special promotional sleeve, labeled as such.)

EPs: 7–inch 33/45rpm

DUNHILL	4-6	68

(Jukebox issues only.)

LPs: 10/12–inch 33rpm

ATLANTIC	6-10	74-75
DUNHILL	8-15	68-74
PICKWICK	5-8	78

HARRIS, Rolf

P&R/R&B/LP '63

Singles: 7–inch

EPIC (Except 9721)	4-8	63-66
EPIC (9721 "Ringo for President")	10-15	64
MGM	3-5	70
20TH FOX	8-12	60-61

Picture Sleeves

EPIC	8-12	63-64

LPs: 10/12–inch 33rpm

EPIC	20-30	63-64

HARRIS, Sam

P&R/D&D/LP '84

Singles: 12–inh 33/45rpm

MOTOWN	4-6	84-86

Singles: 7–inch

MOTOWN	3-4	84-86

Picture Sleeves

MOTOWN	3-4	84-86

LPs: 10/12–inch 33rpm

MOTOWN	5-10	84-86

HARRIS, Thurston
(With the Sharps)

P&R/R&B '57

Singles: 78rpm

ALADDIN	4-6	57

Singles: 7–inch

ALADDIN	10-15	57-61
CUB	4-8	62
DOT	4-8	62-63
IMPERIAL	4-8	63
REPRISE	4-8	64

HARRIS, Tony

P&R '57

Singles: 78rpm

EBB	5-10	56-57

Singles: 7–inch

EBB	10-15	56-57

HARRIS, Wynonie
(With Lucky Millinder)

R&B '46

Singles: 78rpm

ALADDIN	10-20	47
APOLLO	10-20	45-46
ATCO	8-12	56
BULLET	10-20	46
HAMP-TONE	10-20	45
KING	10-20	47-57
PHILO	10-20	45

Singles: 7–inch

ATCO (6081 "Destination Love")	15-25	56
KING (4210 "Good Rockin' Tonight")	50-100	52
KING (4461 "Bloodshot Eyes")	50-100	51
KING (4468 "I'll Never Give Up")	50-100	51
KING (4485 "Lovin' Machine") (Black vinyl.)	50-100	51
KING (4485 "Lovin' Machine") (Colored vinyl.)	200-300	51
KING (4507 "My Playful Baby's Gone")	50-100	51
KING (4526 "Keep on Churnin'")	50-100	52
KING (4555 "Night Train")	50-100	52
KING (4565 "Adam Come and Get Your Rib")	50-100	52
KING (4592 "Greyhound")	50-100	52
KING (4593 "Bad News, Baby")	50-100	52
KING (4620 "Wasn't That Good")	50-100	53

KING (4635 "The Deacon Don't Like It") 50-100 53
KING (4662 "Tremblin'") 50-75 53
KING (4668 "Please, Louise") ... 50-75 53
KING (4685 "Quiet Whiskey") ... 50-75 53
KING (4716 "Shake That Thing") 50-75 54
KING (4724 "Don't Take My Whiskey Away from Me") 50-75 54
KING (4763 "Christina") 25-50 54
KING (4774 "Good Mambo Tonight") 25-50 54
KING (4789 "Mr. Dollar") 25-50 54
KING (4814 "Drinkin' Sherry Wine") 25-50 54
KING (4826 "Wine, Wine, Sweet Wine") 25-40 54
KING (4839 "Shotgun Wedding") 25-40 54
KING (4900 & 5000 series) 15-25 56-57
KING (5050 "Big Old Country Fool") 10-20 57
KING (5073 "There's No Substitute for Love") 10-20 57
KING (5100 thru 5400 series) 5-10 58-60
ROULETTE 4-8 60

EPs: 7–inch 33/45rpm

KING (260 "Wynonie Harris") 300-400 54

LPs: 10/12–inch 33rpm

KING (1086 "Good Rockin' Blues") 10-15 72

Also see MILBURN, Amos / Wynonie Harris / Crown Prince Waterford
Also see MILLINDER, Lucky, & His Orchestra

HARRIS, Wynonie / Roy Brown

LPs: 10/12–inch 33rpm

KING (607 "Battle of the Blues") 100-200 58
KING (627 "Battle of the Blues, Vol. 2") 100-200 58

HARRIS, Wynonie / Roy Brown / Eddie Vinson

LPs: 10/12–inch 33rpm

KING (668 "Battle of the Blues, Vol. 4") 200-300 60

Also see BROWN, Roy
Also see HARRIS, Wynonie
Also see VINSON, Eddie

HARRISON, Don, Band

P&R/LP '76

Singles: 7–inch

ATLANTIC 4-8 76
MERCURY 4-8 77

LPs: 10/12–inch 33rpm

ATLANTIC 8-10 76
MERCURY 8-10 77

Members: Don Harrison; Doug Clifford; Stu Cook.
Also see CREEDENCE CLEARWATER REVIVAL

HARRISON, George

LP '69

Singles: 12–inch 33/45rpm

DARK HORSE (949 "All Those Years Ago") 25-30 81
(Promotional issue only. Includes title sleeve.)
DARK HORSE (1075 "Wake Up My Love") 20-25 82
(Promotional issue only. Includes title sleeve.)
DARK HORSE (2845 "Got My Mind Set on You") 15-20 87
(Promotional issue only. Includes picture cover.)
DARK HORSE (2885 "When We Was Fab") 15-20 88
(Promotional issue only.)
DARK HORSE (2889 "Devil's Radio") 15-20 87
(Promotional issue only. Includes picture cover.)

Singles: 7–inch

APPLE (1828 "What Is Life") 4-6 71
APPLE (1836 "Bangla Desh") 4-6 71
APPLE (1862 "Give Me Love") 4-6 73
APPLE (1877 "Dark Horse") 4-6 74
APPLE (1879 "Ding Dong Ding Dong") 4-6 74
APPLE (1884 "You") 3-5 75
APPLE (1885 "This Guitar") 4-6 75
APPLE (2995 "My Sweet Lord") 4-6 70
CAPITOL (Orange label) 5-15 76
CAPITOL (Purple label) 3-5 78
CAPITOL (Black label) 3-6 83-87
CAPITOL STARLINE 3-5 77-87
DARK HORSE (0410 "All Those Years Ago") 3-5 81
DARK HORSE (8294 "This Song") 4-6 76
DARK HORSE (8313 "Crackerbox Palace") 3-4 77
DARK HORSE (8763 "Blow Away") 3-4 79
DARK HORSE (8844 "Love Comes to Everyone") 3-5 79
DARK HORSE (27913 "This Is Love") 3-5 88
DARK HORSE (28131 "When We Was Fab") 3-4 88
DARK HORSE (28178 "Got My Mind Set on You") 3-4 87
DARK HORSE (29744 "I Really Love You") 15-20 83
DARK HORSE (29864 "Wake Up My Love") 3-5 82
DARK HORSE (49725 "All Those Years Ago") 3-4 81

DARK HORSE (49785 "Teardrops") 3-5 81
W.B. (22807 "Cheer Down") 3-4 89

Picture Sleeves

APPLE (1828 "What Is Life") 20-30 71
APPLE (1836 "Bangla Desh") ... 10-15 71
APPLE (1877 "Dark Horse") 40-60 74
APPLE (1879 "Ding Dong Ding Dong") 10-15 74
APPLE (1884 "You") 10-15 75
APPLE (2995 "My Sweet Lord") 15-25 70
DARK HORSE (8294 "This Song") 15-20 76
DARK HORSE (8294 "This Song") 40-50 76
(Special promotional sleeve issued with promo single. Price includes insert flyer with "The Story Behind *This Song,*" which represents about $15 to $20 of the value.)
DARK HORSE (8763 "Blow Away") 4-6 79
DARK HORSE (8844 "Love Comes to Everyone") 250-350 79
DARK HORSE (27913 "This Is Love") 3-5 88
DARK HORSE (28131 "When We Was Fab") 3-4 88
DARK HORSE (28178 "Got My Mind Set on You") 3-4 87
DARK HORSE (49725 "All Those Years Ago") 3-4 81
W.B. (22807 "Cheer Down") 3-4 89

Promotional Singles

APPLE (1862 "Give Me Love") . 25-35 73
APPLE (1879 "Ding Dong Ding Dong") 25-30 74
APPLE (1877 "Dark Horse") 30-40 74
APPLE (1879 "Ding Dong Ding Dong") 20-30 74
APPLE (1884 "You") 25-35 75
APPLE (1885 "This Guitar") 25-35 75
APPLE/20TH FOX (791 "Concert for Bangla Desh") 400-500 71
(Four radio spots. Issued only to radio stations.)
DARK HORSE (8294 "This Song") 10-15 76
DARK HORSE (8313 "Crackerbox Palace") 10-15 77
DARK HORSE (8763 "Blow Away") 10-12 79
DARK HORSE (8844 "Love Comes to Everyone") 10-15 79
DARK HORSE (27913 "This Is Love") 10-12 88
DARK HORSE (28131 "When We Was Fab") 10-12 88
DARK HORSE (28178 "Got My Mind Set on You") 10-15 87
DARK HORSE (29744 "I Really Love You") 10-12 83
DARK HORSE (29864 "Wake Up My Love") 10-12 82
DARK HORSE (49725 "All Those Years Ago") 8-10 81
DARK HORSE (49725 "All Those Years Ago") 10-12 81
DARK HORSE (49785 "Teardrops") 10-12 81
W.B. (22807 "Cheer Down") 8-12 89

LPs: 10/12–inch 33rpm

APPLE (639 "All Things Must Pass") 30-40 70
(Three-LP boxed set. Includes bonus poster.)
APPLE (3350 "Wonderwall Music") 15-25 68
APPLE (3385 "Concert for Bangla Desh") 30-40 71
(Three-LP boxed set. Includes 64-page booklet. Also has Eric Clapton, Bob Dylan, Ringo Starr, Leon Russell, Ravi Shankar, and others.)
APPLE (3410 "Living in the Material World") 10-12 73
APPLE (3418 "Dark Horse") 10-15 73
APPLE (3420 "Extra Texture") ... 10-12 75
CAPITOL (639 "All Things Must Pass") 15-25 76-78
(Orange or purple labels. Three-LP boxed set. Includes bonus poster.)
CAPITOL (639 "All Things Must Pass") 25-35 83
(Black label. 3-LP boxed set. Includes bonus poster.)
CAPITOL (11578 "The Best of George Harrison") 8-12 76
(Custom label with six photos of Harrison. Also contains tracks by the Beatles that feature George.)
CAPITOL (11578 "The Best of George Harrison") 30-40 77
(Orange label.)
CAPITOL (11578 "The Best of George Harrison") 8-10 78-83
(Purple or black labels.)
CAPITOL (12248 "Concert For Bangla Desh") 250-300 82
(2-LP set.)
CAPITOL (16000 series) 10-20 81
DARK HORSE (3005 "Thirty-Three and 1/3") 8-10 76
DARK HORSE (3255 "George Harrison") 8-10 79
DARK HORSE (3492 "Somewhere in England") 5-10 81
DARK HORSE (23734 "Gone Troppo") 8-12 82

DARK HORSE (25643 "Cloud Nine") 8-10 87
DARK HORSE (25726 "Best of Dark Horse") 8-10 89
ZAPPLE (3358 "Electronic Music") 15-25 69

Promotional LPs

DARK HORSE ("Dark Horse Radio Special") 175-225 74
DARK HORSE (649 "A Personal Music Dialogue with George Harrison at 33⅓") 30-40 76
DARK HORSE (23734 "Gone Troppo") 20-25 82
(An audiophile Quiex II vinyl pressing.)

Also see BEATLES
Also see BROMBERG, David
Also see CLAPTON, Eric
Also see DYLAN, Bob
Also see HODGE, Chris
Also see RUSSELL, Leon
Also see SCOTT, Tom
Also see SHANKAR, Ravi
Also see SPLINTER
Also see TRAVELING WILBURYS

HARRISON, George / Jeff Beck / Dave Edmunds

Singles: 12-inch 33/45rpm

COLUMBIA (2034 "I Don't Want to Do It") 10-20 85
(Has one song by each artist.)
COLUMBIA (2085 "I Don't Want to Do It") 10-20 85
(Promotional issue only. Has the Harrison song on both sides.)

Singles: 7-inch

COLUMBIA (04887 "I Don't Want to Do It") 3-4 85

Promotional Singles

COLUMBIA (04887 "I Don't Want to Do It") 8-12 85
(Has the Harrison song on both sides.)

HARRISON, George / Dave Edmunds / Jeff Beck

Singles: 12-inch 33/45rpm

COLUMBIA (2034 "I Don't Want to Do It") 10-20 85
(Promotional issue only.)

Also see BECK, Jeff
Also see EDMUNDS, Dave
Also see HARRISON, George

HARRISON, Jerry
(With the Casual Gods)

LP '88

LPs: 10/12-inch 33rpm

FLY/SIRE 5-8 90
SIRE 5-8 88

HARRISON, Reggie: see HIPPIES / Reggie Harrison

HARRISON, Wes

LP '63

Singles: 7-inch

PHILIPS 8-12 63

LPs: 10/12-inch 33rpm

PHILIPS 15-25 63

HARRISON, Wilbert
(With the Roamers; with His Kansas City Playboys; Wilburt Harrison; Wilbur Harrison)

P&R/R&B '59

Singles: 78rpm

DELUXE 10-20 52-53

Singles: 7-inch

ABC 3-4 73
BRUNSWICK 3-5 74
CONSTELLATION 4-8 64
DELUXE (6002 "This Woman of Mine") 40-50 52
DELUXE (6031 "Gin and Coconut Milk") 40-50 53
DOC 5-10 62
FURY 5-10 59-62
GLADES 8-12 59
HOUSE of SOUND 4-6
NEPTUNE 4-8 61
PORT 4-8 65
ROCKIN' (526 "This Woman of Mine") 75-100 52
ROULETTE 3-5 67
SSS INT'L 3-5 71
SAVOY (1100 series) 10-20 54
SAVOY (1500 series) 5-10 59
SEA HORN 4-8 63
SUE (11 "Let's Work Together") 5-8 69
(Company address at bottom of label.)
SUE (11 "Let's Work Together") 4-6 69
(Company address at top.)
SUE (11 "Let's Work Together") 3-5 69
(Company address on left side.)

LPs: 10/12-inch 33rpm

BUDDAH 8-12 71
CHELSEA 8-10 77
JUGGERNAUT 8-12 71
RELIC 5-10 90
SPHERE SOUND 25-40 65
SUE 15-25 70
WET SOUL 10-15 70

HARRY, Debbie
(Deborah Harry)

P&R/R&B/LP '81

Singles: 12-inch 33/45rpm

CHRYSALIS 4-6 81-83
GEFFEN 4-6 85-86

Singles: 7-inch

CHRYSALIS 3-5 81-83
GEFFEN 3-4 85-87

Picture Sleeves

CHRYSALIS 3-5 81

GEFFEN.. 3-4 86-87

LPs: 10/12-inch 33rpm

CHRYSALIS.............................. 5-10 81
GEFFEN.................................... 5-10 86
SIRE.. 5-8 89

Also see BLONDIE
Also see WIND in the WILLOWS

HART, Corey

P&R/D&D/LP '84

Singles: 7-inch

EMI AMERICA 3-4 84-87
EMI MANHATTAN 3-4 88

Picture Sleeves

EMI AMERICA 3-4 84-86
EMI MANHATTAN 3-4 88

LPs: 10/12-inch 33rpm

EMI AMERICA 5-10 84-86
EMI MANHATTAN 5-8 89

HART, Freddie
(With the Heartbeats)

C&W '59

Singles: 78rpm

CAPITOL...................................... 4-8 53-55
COLUMBIA (Except 21512).......... 4-8 56-57
COLUMBIA (21512 "Dig Boy, Dig") 10-15 56

Singles: 7-inch

CAPITOL (2500 thru 3000 series) 5-10 53-55
(Purple labels.)
CAPITOL (2600 thru 4600 series) 3-5 70-79
(Orange labels.)
COLUMBIA (Except 21512)........ 5-10 56-63
COLUMBIA (21512 "Dig Boy, Dig") 25-35 56
KAPP.. 3-8 65-72
MCA 3-5 73
MONUMENT................................ 4-6 63-64
SUNBIRD.................................... 3-4 80-81

Picture Sleeves

KAPP... 4-6 68
SUNBIRD..................................... 3-5 80

LPs: 10/12-inch 33rpm

BRYLEN................................... 5-10 84
CAPITOL................................... 5-10 70-79
COLUMBIA (1700 series) 20-25 62
COLUMBIA (13000 series) 10-12 72
CORAL.. 5-8 73
HARMONY................................ 8-12 67-73
KAPP... 8-15 65-69
MCA 8-12 75
PICKWICK/HILLTOP 8-12 70s
SUNBIRD.................................. 5-10 80
VOCALION................................ 8-10 72

HART, Freddie / Sammi Smith / Jerry Reed

LPs: 10/12-inch 33rpm

HARMONY.................................6-10 72

Also see HART, Freddie
Also see REED, Jerry
Also see SMITH, Sammi

HART, Mickey

LP '72

Singles: 7-inch

W.B. 4-8 71-72

LPs: 10/12-inch 33rpm

RELIX...5-10 85
W.B. 10-20 72

Also see GRATEFUL DEAD

HART, Mickey, Airto & Flora Purim

LPs: 10/12-inch 33rpm

REFERENCE...............................8-10 83

Also see HART, Mickey
Also see MOREIRA, Airto
Also see PURIM, Flora

HART, Rita

D&D '84

Singles: 12-inch 33/45rpm

ENVELOPE...................................4-6 84

HART, Rod

C&W/P&R '76

Singles: 7-inch

IBC 3-4 80
PHOENIX SUN 3-6 68
PLANTATION 3-5 76-77

LPs: 10/12-inch 33rpm

PLANTATION 5-10 76

HARTFORD, John

C&W '67

Singles: 7-inch

AMPEX 3-5 71
FLYING FISH.................................3-4 84
RCA 4-8 66-70

LPs: 10/12-inch 33rpm

FLYING FISH..............................5-10 76-84
RCA 8-12 67-70
W.B. 8-10 71-72

Also see DILLARDS & John Hartford

HARTLEY, Keef, Band

LP '70

Singles: 7-inch

DERAM 3-5 70-73

LPs: 10/12-inch 33rpm

DERAM 10-12 69-73

Also see MAYALL, John

HARTMAN, Dan

P&R/R&B/LP '78

Singles: 12-inch 33/45rpm

BLUE SKY 4-6 78-81
MCA..4-6 84-85

Singles: 7-inch

BLUE SKY 3-5 76-81

MCA 3-4 84-85
PORTRAIT 3-4 81

Picture Sleeves

MCA 3-4 84-85

LPs: 10/12-inch 33rpm

BLUE SKY (Except 246) 5-10 76-81
BLUE SKY (246 "Who Is Dan Hartman")................................ 8-15 75
(Promotional issue only.)
MCA 5-10 84-85
Also see WINTER, Edgar

HARTMAN, Dan / Blasters

Singles: 7-inch

MCA 3-4 84

Picture Sleeves

MCA 3-4 84
Also see BLASTERS
Also see HARTMAN, Dan

HARVEST, Barclay James: see BARCLAY JAMES HARVEST

HARVEST, King: see KING HARVEST

HARVEY
(Harvey "Formerly of the Moonglows"; Harvey Fuqua)

Singles: 7-inch

CHESS (1725 "Twelve Months of the Year")................................ 20-30 59
CHESS (1749 "Blue Skies")...... 10-20 60
TRI-PHI (1017 "She Loves Me So") 20-30 62
TRI-PHI (1024 "Come On and Answer Me")........................... 25-40 63
Also see ETTA & HARVEY
Also see HARVEY & ANN
Also see HARVEY & MOONGLOWS
Also see NEW BIRTH

HARVEY, Alex
(Sensational Alex Harvey Band)

LP '75

Singles: 7-inch

ATLANTIC.................................... 3-5 75
CAPITOL...................................... 3-5 72
VERTIGO 3-5 73-75

LPs: 10/12-inch 33rpm

CAPITOL.................................... 8-12 72
ATLANTIC.................................. 8-10 75
VERTIGO 8-10 73-75

HARVEY, Phil
(Phil Spector)

Singles: 7-inch

IMPERIAL (5583 "Bumbershoot")...................... 50-75 59
Also see HARVEY with Doc & Dwellers
Also see RONETTES / Crystals / Darlene Love / Bob B. Soxx & Blue Jeans
Also see TEDDY BEARS

HARVEY, Steve

D&D '84

Singles: 12-inch 33/45rpm

LONDON.......................................4-6 84

Singles: 7-inch

LONDON.......................................3-4 84

HARVEY with Doc & Dwellers
(Phil Spector)

Singles: 7-inch

ANNETTE (1002 "Oh Baby") 10-20
Also see HARVEY, Phil

HARVEY & ANN

Singles: 7-inch

HARVEY (121 "What Can You Do")..20-30 63
Members: Harvey Fuqua; Ann Bogan.
Also see HARVEY
Also see LOVE, PEACE & HAPPINESS

HARVEY & MOONGLOWS
(Harvey Fuqua)

Singles: 7-inch

CHESS (1705 "Ten Commandments of Love")..................................15-25 58
CHESS (1738 "Mama Loocie")..10-20 59
Also see HARVEY
Also see MOONGLOWS

HARVEY & Seven Sounds
(Harvey Scales)

Singles: 7-inch

CUCA (1155 "New York City").......4-8 63
Also see SCALES, Harvey

HARVEY BOYS

P&R '57

Singles: 78rpm

CADENCE 4-6 57

Singles: 7-inch

CADENCE 5-10 57

HASHIM

D&D '84

Singles: 12-inch 33/45rpm

CUTTING EDGE...........................4-6 84

HASLAM, Annie

LP '77

Singles: 7-inch

SIRE...3-5 78

LPs: 10/12-inch 33rpm

SIRE...8-12 77
Also see RENAISSANCE

HASSAN & 7-11

R&B/D&D '84

Singles: 7-inch

EASY STREET 3-4 84

HASSLES

Singles: 7-inch

U.A. 8-12 67-69

Picture Sleeves

U.A. 10-12 67-69

LPs: 10/12–inch 33rpm

LIBERTY 8-10 81
U.A. (6631 "The Hassles") 20-30 68
U.A. (6699 "Hour of the Wolf") .. 20-30 68
Members: William (Billy) Joel; Howard Blauvelt; Johathan Small; Richard McKenner; John Dizek.
Also see JOEL, Billy

HATCHER, Roger
(Little Roger Hatcher)

R&B '76

Singles: 7–inch

BROWN DOG 3-5 76
DOTTY'S.................................... 5-10 64
EXCELLO (2297 "Sweetest Girl in the World") 15-25 68

HATFIELD, Bobby

P&R '69

Singles: 7–inch

MOONGLOW............................. 5-10 63
VERVE 4-8 68-69
W.B. 3-5 72

LPs: 10/12–inch 33rpm

MGM 10-12 71
Also see RIGHTEOUS BROTHERS

HATHAWAY, Donny

P&R/R&B '70

Singles: 7–inch

ATCO 3-6 69-78

LPs: 10/12–inch 33rpm

ATCO 8-10 70-78
ATLANTIC................................. 5-10 80
Also see FLACK, Roberta, & Donny Hathaway

HATHAWAY, Donny, & June Conquest

P&R '72

Singles: 7–inch

CURTOM (1971 "I Thank You").... 3-5 72
(Previously issued as by June & Donnie.)
Members: Donny Hathaway; June Conquest.
Also see CONQUEST, June
Also see JUNE & DONNIE

HATHAWAY, Donny, & Margie Joseph

Singles: 7–inch

ATCO 3-5 72
Also see HATHAWAY, Donny
Also see JOSEPH, Margie

HATHAWAY, Lalah

LP '90

LPs: 10/12–inch 33rpm

VIRGIN...................................... 5-8 90

HAVENS, Richie

LP '68

Singles: 7–inch

A&M 3-5 77
DOUGLAS.................................. 4-8 68
ELEKTRA................................... 3-4 80
MGM 3-5 70
ODE '70..................................... 3-5 72
STORMY FOREST 3-5 70-74
VERVE/FOLKWAYS..................... 4-8 66-68
VERVE/FORECAST 4-8 68-69

LPs: 10/12–inch 33rpm

A&M 8-10 76
DOUGLAS 12-15 68
ELEKTRA................................... 5-10 80
MGM 8-10 70
ODE '70 .... 8-10 73
RBI 5-10 87
STORMY FOREST 10-12 69-74
VERVE/FOLKWAYS................... 12-15 67-68
VERVE/FORECAST 12-15 67-69

HAWK, The
(Jerry Lee Lewis)

Singles: 7–inch

PHILLIPS INT'L......................... 15-20 60
Also see LEWIS, Jerry Lee

HAWKINS, Dale
(With the Escapades)

P&R/R&B '57

Singles: 78rpm

CHECKER 10-20 56-57

Singles: 7–inch

ABC-PAR 4-8 65
ATLANTIC.................................. 5-10 61-62
BELL 4-8 69
CHECKER (800 series) 20-25 56-57
(Maroon label with checkerboard design at top.)
CHECKER (800 series) 8-12 57-58
(Maroon label with Checker name on side.)
CHECKER (800 series) 4-6
(Blue label.)
CHECKER (900 series) 5-10 58-61
LINCOLN 4-8
TILT... 5-10 61
ZONK.. 8-12 62

Picture Sleeves

CHECKER (944 "Poor Little Rhode Island") 40-60 60

LPs: 10/12–inch 33rpm

BELL (6036 "L.A., Memphis and Tyler, Texas") 20-30 69
CHESS (1429 "Suzy-Q")........ 250-300 58
ROULETTE (R-25175 "Let's All Twist at Miami Beach Peppermint Lounge") 40- 60 62
(Monaural.)
ROULETTE (SR-25175 "Let's All Twist at Miami Beach Peppermint Lounge") 50- 80 62
(Stereo.)
Also see BUCHANAN, Roy

HAWKINS, Edwin, Singers

P&R/R&B/LP '69

Singles: 7–inch

BUDDAH...................................... 3-5 71-72
PAVILION 3-6 69

LPs: 10/12-inch 33rpm

BUDDAH 8-12 71-72
PAVILION 10-12 69

Members: Edwin Hawkins; Walter Hawkins; Tramaine Hawkins; Daniel Hawkins; Elaine Kelley; Norma King; Dorothy Morrison; Barbara Gill; Shirley Miller; Edwin Miller; Donald Henderson.

Also see ISLEY BROTHERS / Brooklyn Bridge
Also see MELANIE
Also see MORRISON, Dorothy

HAWKINS, Erskine *P&R '36*

Singles: 78rpm

BLUEBIRD 5-15 39-44
BRUNSWICK 4-8 53
DECCA 4-6 56
CORAL 4-8 50-54
KING 5-10 51-52
VICTOR/RCA 5-10 45-52
VOCALION 5-15 36-37

Singles: 7-inch

BRUNSWICK 5-10 53
DECCA 5-10 56
CORAL 5-10 52-54
KING (4514 "Steel Guitar Rag") 15-20 52
(Black vinyl.)
KING (4514 "Steel Guitar Rag") 30-40 52
(Colored vinyl.)
KING (4522 "Down Home Jump") 15-20 52
(Black vinyl.)
KING (4522 "Down Home Jump") 30-40 52
(Colored vinyl.)
KING (4574 "New Gin Mill Special") 15-20 52
KING (4597 "The Way You Look Tonight") 15-20 52
KING (4686 "Double Shot") 15-20 53

EPs: 7-inch 33/45rpm

RCA 10-20 59

LPs: 10/12-inch 33rpm

CORAL 30-50 54
DECCA 20-30 61
IMPERIAL 20-30 62
RCA 25-40 60

HAWKINS, Erskine, & Four Hawks

Singles: 78rpm

KING 10-20 53

Singles: 7-inch

KING (4671 "My Baby, Please") 50-75 53
KING (4686 "Double Shot") 25-50 53

Also see HAWKINS, Erskine

HAWKINS, Hawkshaw *C&W '48*

Singles: 78rpm

KING 4-8 46-53
RCA 3-6 55-57

Singles: 7-inch

COLUMBIA 4-8 59-62
KING (900 thru 1100 series) 5-10 50-53
KING (5000 series) 4-8 60-64
RCA 5-10 55-59
STARDAY 3-5 71

EPs: 7-inch 33/45rpm

KING 8-12 53

LPs: 10/12-inch 33rpm

CAMDEN 10-15 64-66
GLADWYNNE (2006 "Country & Western Cavalcade") 60-80
HARMONY 10-15 63
KING (500 series) 20-35 58-59
KING (800 series) 15-25 63-64
KING (1000 series) 8-12 69
LA BREA (8020 "Hawkshaw Hawkins") 60-80
NASHVILLE 8-12 69
STARDAY 5-10

Also see CLINE, Patsy / Cowboy Copas / Hawkshaw Hawkins
Also see COPAS, Cowboy / Hawkshaw Hawkins

HAWKINS, Jalacy
(Jay Hawkins)

Singles: 7-inch

MERCURY (70549 "This Is All") 50-75 55
TIMELY (1004 "Baptize Me in Wine") 50-75 54
TIMELY (1005 "Please Try to Understand") 50-75 54
WING (90005 "Well, I Tried") 20-30 55
WING (90055 "Even Though") 20-30 56

Also see HAWKINS, Screamin' Jay

HAWKINS, Jennell *R&B '61*

Singles: 7-inch

AMAZON 4-8 61-63
DYNAMIC 4-8 61
DYNAMITE 4-8 61
OLDIES 45 3-5

LPs: 10/12-inch 33rpm

AMAZON (AM-1001 "Many Moods of Jenny") 20-30 61
(Monaural.)
AMAZON (AS-1001 "Many Moods of Jenny") 25-40 61
(Stereo.)
AMAZON (AM-1002 "Moments to Remember") 20-30 62
(Monaural.)
AMAZON (AS-1002 "Moments to Remember") 25-40 62

HAWKINS, Ronnie
(With the Hawks) *P&R/R&B '59*

Singles: 7-inch

COTILLION 3-5 70-71
HAWK 5-10
MONUMENT 3-5 72-73

ROULETTE (4154 "Forty Days") 10-15 59
ROULETTE (SSR-4154 "Forty Days") 20-30 59
(Stereo.)
ROULETTE (4177 "Mary Lou") 10-15 59
ROULETTE (SSR-4177 "Mary Lou") 20-30 59
(Stereo.)
ROULETTE (4209 thru 4502) 5-10 59-63

LPs: 10/12-inch 33rpm

ACCORD 5-10 83
COTILLION 10-15 70-71
MONUMENT 8-12 72-75
ROULETTE (25078 "Ronnie Hawkins") 50-75 59
(Black vinyl. Monaural.)
ROULETTE (SR-25078 "Ronnie Hawkins") 75-100 59
(Black vinyl. Stereo.)
ROULETTE (25078 "Ronnie Hawkins") 175-225 59
(Colored vinyl.)
ROULETTE (25102 "Mr. Dynamo") 50-75 60
(Black vinyl. Monaural.)
ROULETTE (SR-25102 "Mr. Dynamo") 75-100 60
(Black vinyl. Stereo.)
ROULETTE (25102 "Mr. Dynamo") 175-225 60
(Colored vinyl.)
ROULETTE (25120 "Folk Ballads") 50-75 60
(Monaural.)
ROULETTE (SR-25120 "Folk Ballads") 75-100 60
(Stereo.)
ROULETTE (25137 "Songs of Hank Williams") 50-75 60
(Monaural.)
ROULETTE (SR-25137 "Songs of Hank Williams") 75-100 60
(Stereo.)
ROULETTE (42045 "Best of Ronnie Hawkins") 25-35 70
U.A. 5-10 79

Also see BAND
Also see LENNON, John
Also see LEVON & HAWKS

HAWKINS, Roy

R&B '50

Singles: 78rpm

DOWN TOWN (2018 "Christmas Blues") 10-20 48
DOWN TOWN (2020 "It's Too Late to Change") 10-20 48
DOWN TOWN (2024 "Forty Jim") 10-20 48
DOWN TOWN (2025 "Quarter to One") 10-20 48
MODERN 8-15 48-54
RPM 10-15 54

Singles: 7-inch

KENT 5-10 62
MODERN (826 "The Thrill Is Gone") 35-55 51
MODERN (852 "Gloom and Misery All Around") 35-55 51
MODERN (853 "I Don't Know Just What to Do") 35-55 51
MODERN (859 "Highway 59") 20-30 52
MODERN (869 "Doin' All Right") 20-30 52
MODERN (898 "Bad Luck Is Falling") 20-30 54
RPM (440 "Is It Too Late") 15-25 54
RHYTHM (120 "I Hate to Be Alone") 30-40 58

HAWKINS, Sam

(With the Crystals)

R&B '65

Singles: 7-inch

ARNOLD 3-5 63
BLUE CAT 5-8 65
DECCA 5-10 59-61
GONE 10-15 59
SHELL 4-8

HAWKINS, Screamin' Jay

(Jalacy Hawkins)

Singles: 78rpm

APOLLO 4-8 56-57
GRAND 4-8 57
OKEH 4-8 56-57

Singles: 7-inch

APOLLO 10-20 56-58
DECCA (32100 "I Put a Spell on You") 25-35 67
ENRICA 4-8 62
EPIC 4-8 63
GRAND 10-20 57
OKEH 10-20 56-57
PHILLIPS 3-5 70
PROVIDENCE 4-6
QUEEN BEE 3-5 73
RCA 3-5 74

LPs: 10/12-inch 33rpm

EPIC (3448 "At Home with Screamin' Jay Hawkins") 150-250 56
EPIC (3457 "I Put a Spell on You") 100-150 57
EPIC (26457 "I Put a Spell on You") 15-25 69
HOT LINE (10024 "Portrait of a Man and His Woman") 15-25
MIDNIGHT 5-10 88

PHILLIPS (600319 "What That Is") 15-25 69
PHILLIPS (600336 "Screamin' Jay Hawkins") 15-25 70
SOUNDS of HAWAII (5015 "A Night at Forbidden City") 20-30
VERSATILE 8-10 78

Also see HAWKINS, Jalacy

HAWKINS, Screamin' Jay / Lillian Briggs

LPs: 10/12-inch 33rpm

CORONET 10-15

Also see BRIGGS, Lillian

HAWKINS, Screamin' Jay, & Pat Newborn

Singles: 7-inch

CHANCELLOR 4-8 62

Also see HAWKINS, Screamin' Jay

HAWKINS, Screamin' Jay, & Fuzztones

LPs: 10/12-inch 33rpm

MIDNIGHT 5-10

HAWKS

P&R '81

Singles: 7-inch

COLUMBIA 3-4 81

LPs: 10/12-inch 33rpm

COLUMBIA 5-10 81

HAWKWIND

LP '73

Singles: 7-inch

ATCO 3-5 75
U.A. 3-5 71-73

LPs: 10/12-inch 33rpm

ATCO 8-10 75
SIRE 5-10 78
U.A. 10-15 71-74

Also see MOTORHEAD

HAWLEY, Deane
(With the Crystals)

P&R '60

Singles: 7-inch

DORE 8-12 59-61
LIBERTY 8-12 61-62
SUNDOWN 4-8
VALOR (2003 "Don't Keep Me Guessin") 25-35 59
W.B. 4-8 64

HAY, Colin James
(Colin Hay Band)

P&R/LP '87

Singles: 7-inch

COLUMBIA 3-4 87

Picture Sleeves

COLUMBIA 3-4 87

LPs: 10/12-inch 33rpm

COLUMBIA 5-10 87
MCA 5-10 90

Also see MEN AT WORK

HAYES, Bill
(With the Archie Bleyer's Orchestra)

P&R '55

Singles: 78rpm

ABC-PAR 5-10 57
ABC-PAR (9895 "Bop Boy") 10-20 58
CADENCE 4-6 55-56
MGM 3-5 55

Singles: 7-inch

ABC-PAR (Except 9895) 8-12 57
ABC-PAR (9895 "Bop Boy") 35-50 58
ABLE 4-8
BARNABY 3-5 76
CADENCE 5-10 55-56
DAYBREAK 3-5 74
KAPP 5-8 59
MGM 5-10 55
SHAW 4-6 65

Picture Sleeves

ABC-PAR 8-12 57
CADENCE 10-20 55

EPs: 7-inch 33/45rpm

MGM 10-20 55

LPs: 10/12-inch 33rpm

ABC-PAR 20-30 57
DAYBREAK 5-10 74
KAPP 10-15 60

Also see BLEYER, Archie

HAYES, Isaac
(Isaac Hayes Movement)

P&R/R&B/LP '69

Singles: 12-inch 33/45rpm

COLUMBIA 4-6 85-86

Singles: 7-inch

ABC 3-5 77
BRUNSWICK 4-8 64
COLUMBIA 3-4 85-87
ENTERPRISE 3-6 69-74
HBS 3-5 75-76
POLYDOR 3-4 78-80
SAN AMERICAN 3-5 70
STAX 3-5 78

LPs: 10/12-inch 33rpm

ABC-PAR 8-10 75-77
ATLANTIC 8-10 72
COLUMBIA 5-10 86
ENTERPRISE 10-12 68-75
HBS 8-12 75-77
POLYDOR 5-10 77-81
STAX 5-10 77-82

Also see REDDING, Otis

HAYES, Isaac, & Millie Jackson

R&B/LP '79

Singles: 7-inch

POLYDOR 3-4 79-80

LPs: 10/12-inch 33rpm

POLYDOR 5-10 79

Also see JACKSON, Millie

HAYES, Isaac, & David Porter

R&B '72

Singles: 7–inch

ENTERPRISE ... 3-5 72

Also see PORTER, David

HAYES, Isaac, & Dionne Warwick

R&B/LP '77

Singles: 7–inch

ABC ... 3-5 77

LPs: 10/12–inch 33rpm

ABC ... 10-15 77

Also see HAYES, Isaac
Also see WARWICK, Dionne

HAYES, Linda

(With the Platters; with Tony Williams; with Flairs)

R&B '53

Singles: 78rpm

ANTLER ... 5-10 56
DECCA ... 5-10 55
HOLLYWOOD (Except 1032) ... 5-10 53-55
HOLLYWOOD (1032 "Our Love Is Forever Blessed") ... 10-15 55
KING ... 5-10 55
RECORDED in HOLLYWOOD ... 5-10 53

Singles: 7–inch

ANTLER ... 10-20 56
DECCA ... 10-20 55
HOLLYWOOD (Except 1032) ... 15-25 53-55
HOLLYWOOD (1032 "Our Love Is Forever Blessed") ... 30-40 55
KING (4752 "My Name Ain't Annie") ... 30-40 54
KING (4773 "Please Have Mercy") ... 20-30 55

Also see MOORE, Johnny, & Linda Hayes
Also see PLATTERS

HAYES, Peter Lind

P&R '49

Singles: 78rpm

DECCA ... 4-6 49

Singles: 7–inch

DOT ... 4-8 59

HAYES, Peter Lind, & Mary Healy

Singles: 7–inch

COLUMBIA ... 4-8 55
ESSEX ... 4-8 53
KAPP ... 4-8 56

Also see HAYES, Peter Lind

HAYES, Richard

P&R '49

Singles: 78rpm

MERCURY ... 3-6 49-55

Singles: 7–inch

ABC-PAR ... 8-15 56
COLUMBIA ... 4-8 60-61
CONTEMPO ... 4-6 64
DECCA ... 4-6 61
MERCURY ... 5-10 50-55

EPs: 7–inch 33/45rpm

MERCURY ... 8-15 54

LPs: 10/12–inch 33rpm

MERCURY ... 10-20 55

HAYES, Richard, & Kitty Kallen

P&R '51

Singles: 7–inch

MERCURY ... 5-10 50-51

Also see HAYES, Richard
Also see KALLEN, Kitty

HAYMAN, Richard, Orchestra

(With Jan August)

P&R '53

Singles: 78rpm

MERCURY ... 3-6 50-57

Singles: 7–inch

COMMAND ... 3-5 69
MGM ... 3-6 65
MERCURY ... 3-8 50-62
MUSICOR ... 3-5 73

EPs: 7–inch 33/45rpm

MERCURY ... 4-8 51-59

LPs: 10/12–inch 33rpm

ASCOT ... 5-10 64
COMMAND ... 5-10 69
MAINSTREAM ... 5-10 67
MERCURY ... 10-20 51-64
TIME ... 5-10 63-64
WING ... 5-10 62-64

Also see AUGUST, Jan

HAYMES, Dick

P&R/R&B '43

Singles: 78rpm

CAPITOL ... 3-5 56
DECCA ... 4-8 43-54

Singles: 7–inch

CAPITOL ... 5-10 56
GNP ... 3-5 75
DECCA ... 5-10 50-54
WARWICK ... 3-6 60

EPs: 7–inch 33/45rpm

CAPITOL ... 5-10 56
DECCA ... 5-10 50-54

LPs: 10/12–inch 33rpm

AUDIOPHILE ... 5-10 78
CAPITOL ... 10-20 56
CORAL ... 4-6 73
DAYBREAK ... 5-10 74
DECCA ... 10-20 50-54
GLENDALE ... 5-10 84
MCA ... 5-10 76-83
WARWICK ... 8-15 60

Also see CLOONEY, Rosemary, & Dick Haymes
Also see CROSBY, Bing, Dick Haymes & Andrews Sisters
Also see FISHER, Eddie / Vic Damone / Dick Haymes
Also see JAMES, Harry, & Dick Haymes

Also see MERMAN, Ethel, Dick Haymes

HAYMES, Dick, & Andrews Sisters

P&R '48

Singles: 78rpm

DECCA ... 4-6 48

Also see ANDREWS SISTERS

HAYMES, Dick, & Judy Garland

P&R '47

Singles: 78rpm

DECCA ... 4-6 47

Also see GARLAND, Judy
Also see HAYMES, Dick

HAYWARD, Justin

P&R '75

Singles: 7–inch

COLUMBIA ... 3-5 78
DERAM ... 3-5 77
RED BIRD ... 10-15 66

LPs: 10/12–inch 33rpm

DERAM (4801 "Night Flight") ... 8-12 80
DERAM (18073 "Songwriter") ... 10-20 77

HAYWARD, Justin, & John Lodge

P&R/LP '75

Singles: 7–inch

THRESHOLD ... 3-5 75

Picture Sleeves

THRESHOLD ... 3-5 75

LPs: 10/12–inch 33rpm

THRESHOLD (14 "Blue Jays") . 10-15 75
THRESHOLD (101 "Blue Jays") 15-25 75
(Promotional issue only. Interview with script.)

Also see HAYWARD, Justin
Also see LODGE, John
Also see MOODY BLUES

HAYWARD, Leon: see HAYWOOD, Leon

HAYWOOD, Leon
(Leon Hayward)

P&R/R&B '65

Singles: 12–inch 33/45rpm

CASABLANCA ... 4-6 83
MCA ... 4-8 79
20TH FOX ... 4-6 80

Singles: 7–inch

ATLANTIC ... 3-5 71-72
CAPITOL ... 10-15 69-70
CASABLANCA ... 3-4 83
COLUMBIA ... 3-5 76-77
DECCA ... 4-6 67-68
EPIC ... 3-4 80-81
EVEJIM ... 4-8
FAT FISH (8005 "Soul Cargo") . 15-25 66
GALAXY ... 4-6 67
IMPERIAL ... 5-15 65-66
MCA ... 3-5 77-79
MODERN ... 3-4 84
20TH FOX ... 3-5 74-80

LPs: 10/12–inch 33rpm

CASABLANCA ... 5-10 83
DECCA ... 8-12 67
GALAXY ... 8-12 67
MCA ... 5-10 78-79
20TH FOX ... 5-10 73-80

HAZARD, Robert

P&R/LP '83

Singles: 7–inch

RCA ... 3-4 83

LPs: 10/12–inch 33rpm

RCA ... 5-10 83

HAZE

R&B '75

Singles: 7–inch

ASI ... 3-5 75
MOONSPELL ... 5-8 78

LPs: 10/12–inch 33rpm

ASI ... 8-10 74

HAZLEWOOD, Lee

Singles: 7–inch

CAPITOL ... 3-5 72
JAMIE ... 5-10 60
LHI ... 4-6 68
MCA ... 3-4 79-80
MGM ... 4-6 66-67
REPRISE ... 4-6 65-68
SMASH ... 5-8 61

LPs: 10/12–inch 33rpm

CAPITOL ... 8-10 72
HARMONY ... 8-12 67
MGM ... 10-15 66-67
MERCURY ... 10-15 63
REPRISE ... 10-15 64-65

Also see ANN-MARGRET & Lee Hazlewood
Also see SHACKLEFORDS
Also see SINATRA, Nancy, & Lee Hazlewood

HEAD, Murray
(With the Trinidad Singers; Murry Head)

P&R '70

Singles: 12–inch 33/45rpm

CHESS ... 4-6 85

Singles: 7–inch

A&M ... 3-5 76
CAPITOL ... 4-6 67
CHESS ... 3-4 84-85
DECCA ... 3-6 69-71
RCA ... 3-4 85

Picture Sleeves

CHESS ... 3-4 85
DECCA ... 3-5 70-71
RCA ... 3-4 85

LPs: 10/12–inch 33rpm

A&M ... 8-10 76
COLUMBIA ... 5-10 72

HEAD, Roy
(With the Traits)

P&R/R&B/LP '65

Singles: 7–inch

ABC 3-5 73-79
ABC/DOT 3-5 76-77
AVION 3-4 83
BACK BEAT 4-8 65-67
CHURCHILL 3-4 81
DUNHILL 3-5 70
ELEKTRA 3-4 79-80
MEGA 3-5 74
MERCURY 4-6 68
NSD 3-4 82
SCEPTER 4-8 65-66
SHANNON 3-5 75
TMI 3-5 71-73
TNT 8-10 65
TEXAS CRUDE 3-4 85

LPs: 10/12–inch 33rpm

ABC 8-10 73-78
DUNHILL 10-12 70
ELEKTRA 5-10 79-80
SCEPTER (532 "Treat Me Right") 15-25 65
(Monaural.)
SCEPTER (532 "Treat Me Right") 20-30 65
(Stereo. With an "SS" prefix.)
TMI 8-10 72
TNT (101 "Roy Head and the Traits") 100-150 65
(Counterfeits can be identified by their content. They include *Treat Her Right,* as well as other later Head tracks on side two. Originals do not have these.)

HEAD EAST

P&R/LP '75

Singles: 7–inch

A&M 3-5 75-79

Picture Sleeves

A&M 3-5 78

LPs: 10/12–inch 33rpm

A&M 5-10 75-80
ALLEGIANCE 5-10 83
Members: John Schlitt; Mike Sommerville; Roger Boyd; Steve Huston.

HEADBOYS

P&R/LP '79

Singles: 7–inch

RSO 3-5 79

LPs: 10/12–inch 33rpm

RSO 5-10 79

HEADHUNTERS

LP '75

LPs: 10/12–inch 33rpm

ARISTA 5-10 75-78

HEADPINS

P&R '83

Singles: 7–inch

ATCO 3-5 82
SOLID GOLD 3-5 83

Picture Sleeves

SOLID GOLD 3-5 83

LPs: 10/12–inch 33rpm

ATCO 5-10 82
SOLID GOLD 5-8 83
Member: Darby Mills.

HEALEY, Jeff
(Jeff Healey Band)

LP '88

Singles: 7–inch

ARISTA 3-4 89-90

Picture Sleeves

ARISTA 3-4 89

LPs: 10/12–inch 33rpm

ARISTA 5-8 89-90
Members: Jeff Healey; Joe Rockman; Tom Stephen.

HEAP, Jimmy
(With the Melody Masters & Perk Williams)

P&R/C&W '56

Singles: 78rpm

CAPITOL 4-6 53-55

Singles: 7–inch

CAPITOL 10-15 53-55
D 8-10 59
DART 5-10 60
FAME (502 "Little Jewel") 200-250 58
FAME (509 "Night Cap") 8-15 61
FAME (510 "Go Get Em") 8-15 61
FAME (511 "Flint Rock") 8-15 61
IMPERIAL 4-8 60

HEAR 'N AID

LP '86

LPs: 10/12–inch 33rpm

MERCURY/POLYGRAM 5-8 85
Members: Tommy Aldridge; Dave Alford; Carmine Appice; Vinny Appice; Jimmy Bain; Frankie Banali; Eric Bloom; Mick Brown; Vivian Campbell; Carlos Cavazo; Amir Derakh; Ronnie James Dio; Don Dokken; Kevin Dubrow; Brad Gillis; Craig Goldy; Chris Hager; Rob Halford; Chris Holmes; Blackie Lawless; Geroge Lynch; Yngwie Malmsteed; Mick Mars; Dave Meniketti; Dave Murray; Vince Neil; Ted Nugent; Eddie Ojeda; Jeff Pilson; Donald Roeser; Rudy Sarzo; Chaude Schnell; Neal Schon; Paul Shortino; Adrian Smith; Spinal Tap; Mark Stein; Geoff Tate Matt Thor.

Also see DIO, Ronnie
Also see DOKKEN
Also see GIUFFRIA
Also see MALMSTEEN, Yngwie J.
Also see NUGENT, Ted
Also see QUIET RIOT
Also see SPINAL TAP

HEART

P&R/LP '76

Singles: 12-Inch 33/45rpm

CAPITOL.. 4-6 85
MUSHROOM 4-8 76
PORTRAIT 4-8 77-79

Promotional 12-inch Singles

MUSHROOM (7023 "Dreamboat Annie).. 8-10 76
PORTRAIT (16445 "Straight On").. 8-10 78

Singles: 7-inch

CAPITOL.. 3-4 85-90
EPIC... 3-5 81-83
MUSHROOM 3-6 76-79
PORTRAIT 3-5 77-79

Picture Sleeves

CAPITOL.. 3-4 85-90
EPIC (Except 04047) 3-5 82-83
EPIC (04047 "How Can I Refuse") 3-5 83
EPIC (04047 "How Can I Refuse") 8-10 83
(Promotional sleeve. Labeled: Demonstration Only—Not for Sale.)

LPs: 10/12-inch 33rpm

CAPITOL.. 5-10 85-90
CAPITOL RADIO STAR ("Audio Cue Card") 10-15 87
(Radio interview. Promotional issue only.)
EPIC... 5-10 80-83
MUSHROOM (MRS-5005 "Dreamboat Annie") 8-12 76
MUSHROOM (MRS-5008 "Magazine")........................... 50-75 77
(First issue. Last track on Side One is *Magazine.*)
MUSHROOM (MRS-5008 "Magazine")............................. 5-10 77
(Second issue. First track on Side Two is *Magazine.* There are also other differences in song order.)
MUSHROOM (MRS-1-SP "Magazine")............................. 8-12 78
(Picture Disc.)
MUSHROOM (MRS-2-SP "Dreamboat Annie") 10-15 79
(Picture Disc.)
NAUTILUS 20-25 80
(Half-speed mastered.)
PORTRAIT (30000 series).......... 5-10 77-81
PORTRAIT (40000 series)........ 12-15 81
(Half-speed mastered.)

Members: Nancy Wilson; Ann Wilson; Howard Leese; Steve Fossen; Roger Fisher; Mike Derosier; Mark Andes; Denny Carmassi.

Also see BORDERSONG
Also see GAMMA
Also see SPIRIT
Also see WILSON, Ann & Daybreaks
Also see WILSON, Nancy

HEART & SOUL

(Heart & Soul Orchestra)

P&R/R&B '77

Singles: 7-inch

CASABLANCA..............................3-5 77

HEART BEATS QUINTET

(With Russell Jacquet & His Orchestra)

Singles: 10-inch

CANDLELITE (437 "Tormented")............................10-20 72
(Colored vinyl 45 rpm.)
CANDLELITE (437 "Tormented")..............................8-15 72
(Black vinyl 45 rpm.)

Singles: 7-inch

CANDLELITE (1135 "Tormented") 3-5 76
NETWORK (71200 "Tormented")..........................50-100 55
(Black vinyl. Pastel yellow label.)
NETWORK (71200 "Tormented")............................25-50
(Black vinyl. Bright yellow label.)
NETWORK (71200 "Tormented")............................10-15
(Colored vinyl.)

Members: James Sheppard; Albert Crump; Vernon Walker; Wally Roker; Rob Adams.

Also see HEARTBEATS
Also see JACQUET, Russell

HEARTBEATS

P&R/R&B '56

Singles: 78rpm

GEE 8-12 57
HULL...10-20 55-56
RAMA...8-12 56-57

Singles: 7-inch

COLLECTABLES..........................3-4
GEE (1043 "When I Found You")......................................15-20 57
GEE (1047 "After New Year's Eve") 15-20 57
(Red label.)
GEE (1047 "After New Year's Eve") 5-10 57
(Gray label.)
GEE (1061 "People Are Talking") 5-10 60
GEE (1062 "Darling, How Long").5-10 60
GUYDEN (2011 "One Million Years")....................................15-20 59
(Yellow label.)
GUYDEN (2011 "One Million Years")....................................10-15 59
(Purple label.)
HULL (711 "Crazy for You")...100-150 55
(White label. Promotional issue only.)
HULL (711 "Crazy for You").....50-100 55
(Pink label.)
HULL (711 "Crazy for You").......20-40 55
(Black label.)

HULL (713 "Darling How Long")................................ 50-100 56
HULL (716 "People Are Talking")................................ 50-100 56
HULL (720 "A Thousand Miles Away")................................ 100-150 56
(Black label.)
HULL (720 "A Thousand Miles Away")................................ 20-30 56
(Red label.)
RAMA (216 "A Thousand Miles Away")................................ 15-20 56
RAMA (222 "I Won't Be the Fool Anymore")................................ 25-35 57
RAMA (231 "Everybody's Somebody's Fool")................................ 15-25 57
ROULETTE (4000 series)........... 5-10 58-59

LPs: 10/12-inch 33rpm

EMUS................................ 5-10 79
ROULETTE (25107 "A Thousand Miles Away")................................ 75-125 60
ROULETTE (59019 "A Thousand Miles Away")................................ 5-8 81

Members: James Sheppard; Albert Crump; Vernon Walker; Wally Roker; Rob Adams.
Also see HEART BEATS QUINTET

HEARTBEATS / Shep & Limelights

LPs: 10/12-inch 33rpm

ROULETTE (115 "Echoes of a Rock Era")................................ 35-45 72

Also see HEARTBEATS
Also see SHEP & LIMELIGHTS

HEARTS

R&B '55

Singles: 78rpm

BATON................................ 5-10 55-56

Singles: 7-inch

BATON................................ 10-20 55-56
J&S................................ 15-25 57-58
LAVENDER................................ 5-10 62
TUFF................................ 5-10 63
ZELLS................................ 5-10 63

LPs: 10/12-inch 33rpm

ZELLS (337 "I Feel Good") ... 100-200 63

Members: Justine "Baby" Washington; Rex Garvin; Pat Ford; Joyce Peterson; Zell Sanders.
Also see JAYNETTS
Also see WASHINGTON, Baby

HEARTSFIELD

P&R '74

Singles: 7-inch

MERCURY................................ 3-5 74

LPs: 10/12-inch 33rpm

COLUMBIA................................ 5-10 77
MERCURY................................ 8-10 73-75

HEARTSMAN, Johnny

R&B '57

Singles: 7-inch

MUSIC CITY................................ 8-12 57

HEAT

R&B '80

Singles: 7-inch

MCA................................ 3-5 79-81

LPs: 10/12-inch 33rpm

MCA................................ 5-10 79-81

HEATH, Ted

P&R '56

Singles: 78rpm

LONDON................................ 3-4 50-61

Singles: 7-inch

LONDON................................ 3-6 50-61

EPs: 7-inch 33/45rpm

LONDON................................ 4-8 51-56

LPs: 10/12-inch 33rpm

LONDON................................ 5-15 50-62
RICHMOND................................ 5-10 62

HEATH, Walter

R&B '74

Singles: 7-inch

BUDDAH................................ 3-5 74

HEATH BROTHERS

R&B '81

Singles: 7-inch

COLUMBIA................................ 3-5 79-81

LPs: 10/12-inch 33rpm

COLUMBIA................................ 5-10 79-81

HEATHERTON, Joey

P&R/LP '72

Singles: 7-inch

CORAL (62422 "That's How It Goes")................................ 10-20 64
CORAL (62451 "Hullabaloo")..... 10-20 65
CORAL (62459 "But He's Not Mine")................................ 10-20 65
DECCA (31962 "When You Call Me Baby")................................ 25-50 66
MGM................................ 5-10 72-73

Picture Sleeves

CORAL (62422 "That's How It Goes")................................ 15-25 64
MGM................................ 5-10 72

LPs: 10/12-inch 33rpm

MGM................................ 10-15 72

HEATWAVE

P&R/R&B/LP '77

Singles: 12-inch 33/45rpm

EPIC................................ 4-8 77-82

Singles: 7-inch

EPIC................................ 3-5 77-82

LPs: 10/12-inch 33rpm

EPIC................................ 5-10 77-82

Member: Keith Wilder; Rod Temperton; Ernie Berger; John Wilder; Eric Johns.

HEAVEN & EARTH

R&B '76

Singles: 7–inch

OVATION 3-5 72-73

LPs: 10/12–inch 33rpm

OVATION 8-10 73

HEAVEN BOUND

(With Tony Scotti)

P&R '71

Singles: 7–inch

MGM 3-5 71

LPs: 10/12–inch 33rpm

MGM 8-12 72

Members: Joan Medora; Eddie Medora; Michael Lloyd; Tom Oliver.

HEAVEN'S EDGE

LP '90

LPs: 10/12–inch 33rpm

COLUMBIA 5-8 90

HEAVEN 17

P&R/D&D/LP '83

Singles: 12–inch 33/45rpm

ARISTA 4-6 83-84

Singles: 7–inch

ARISTA 3-4 83-84

LPs: 10/12–inch 33rpm

ARISTA 8-10 83

VIRGIN 5-10 87

Members: Glenn Gregory; Craig Marsh; Martyn Ware.

Also see BAND AID

Also see HUMAN LEAGUE

HEAVENER, David

C&W '81

Singles: 7–inch

BRENT 3-4 81-82

HEAVY D. & BOYZ

R&B '86

Singles: 12–inch 33/45rpm

MCA 4-6 86

Singles: 7–inch

MCA 3-4 86-88

LPs: 10/12–inch 33rpm

MCA 5-10 86-87

UPTOWN 5-8 89

HEBB, Bobby

P&R/R&B/LP '66

Singles: 7–inch

BOOM 4-8 66

CADET 3-6 72

FM 5-10 61

LAURIE 3-5 75

PHILIPS 5-10 66-67

RICH 10-15 60

SCEPTER 4-8 66

Picture Sleeves

PHILIPS 5-10 66

LPs: 10/12–inch 33rpm

EPIC 10-12 70

PHILLIPS 15-20 66

HEBB, Bobby / Billy Sha-Rae

Singles: 7–inch

LAURIE 3-4

Also see HEBB, Bobby

HEDGEHOPPERS ANONYMOUS

P&R '65

Singles: 7–inch

PARROT 5-8 65-66

Also see KING, Jonathan

HEFTI, Neal

(With His Orchestra; Neal Hefti Quintet; with Mello-Larks)

LP '55

Singles: 78rpm

CORAL 3-5 51-57

EPIC 3-5 55-56

Singles: 7–inch

COLUMBIA 3-5 65

CORAL 4-6 51-59

DOT 3-5 67-68

EPIC 4-6 55-56

RCA 3-5 66

REPRISE 3-5 62

U.A. 3-5 65-66

Picture Sleeves

RCA 4-8 66-67

RCA GOLD STANDARD SERIES 3-4 89

EPs: 7–inch 33/45rpm

CORAL 4-8 52-56

X 4-8 55

LPs: 10/12–inch 33rpm

COLUMBIA 8-15 60

CORAL 10-20 52-60

EPIC 10-15 56

RCA (3621 "Hefti in Gotham City") 10-20 66

REPRISE 8-15 62

20TH FOX 8-12 64

U.A. (573 "Definitely Hefti") 8-15 67

X 10-15 55

You'll find many more listings by this artist in *The Official Price Guide to Movie/TV Soundtracks and Original Cast Albums*, containing over 8,000 listings.

HEIGHT, Donald

R&B '66

Singles: 7–inch

DAKAR 3-5 76

JUBILEE 5-10 63-69

KING 10-20 60

OLD TOWN 10-20 64-65

RCA 5-10 65

ROULETTE 5-10 65

SHOUT 5-10 66-68

SOOZEE 8-12 62

Also see HOLLYWOOD FLAMES

HEIGHT, Ronnie

P&R '59

Singles: 7–inch

BAMBOO 5-10 61
DORE....................................... 5-10 59
ERA.. 5-10 59-61

HEINTJE

LP '70

Singles: 7–inch

MGM 3-6 70

LPs: 10/12–inch 33rpm

MGM 8-10 70

HELIX

LP '83

LPs: 10/12–inch 33rpm

CAPITOL.................................. 5-10 83-87
GRUDGE 5-8 90

HELLO PEOPLE

LP '74

Singles: 7–inch

ABC/DUNHILL 3-5 75-76
PHILIPS 4-6 68

Picture Sleeves

PHILIPS 5-8 68

LPs: 10/12–inch 33rpm

ABC/DUNHILL 8-10 74
ABC-PAR.................................. 8-10 75
MEDIARTS................................ 12-15 70
PHILLIPS 15-20 68

HELLOWEEN

LP '87

LPs: 10/12–inch 33rpm

MX... 10-15 86
RCA... 5-10 87-89

HELM, Levon
(With the RCO All-Stars)

LP '77

Singles: 7–inch

A&M 3-4 80
ABC 3-5 78
CAPITOL.................................. 3-4 82
MCA 3-4 80

LPs: 10/12–inch 33rpm

ABC-PAR 5-10 77-78
A&M 5-10 80
CAPITOL.................................. 5-10 82
MCA 5-10 80

Also see BAND
Also see CASH, Johnny, & Levon Helm
Also see HAMMOND, John
Also see LEVON & HAWKS

HELMS, Bobby

C&W/P&R/R&B '57

Singles: 78rpm

DECCA..................................... 5-10 56-57

Singles: 7–inch

BLACK ROSE 3-4 83-84
CAPITOL...................................3-5 70
CERTRON 3-5 70
COLUMBIA 4-8 64
DECCA (Except 29947)..............5-10 57-62
DECCA (29947 "Tennessee Rock and Roll") 20-30 56
GUSTO 3-5 74
KAPP 4-6 65-67
LARRICK 3-5 75
LITTLE DARLIN' 3-6 67-79
MCA...3-4
MILLION...................................3-5 72
MISTLETOE...............................3-5 74
PLAYBACK 3-4

Picture Sleeves

CERTRON 4-6 70
DECCA ("New Singing Sensation") 10-20 57
(Pictures Helms, but no number or title shown. With die-cut center hole.)
DECCA (30194 "Fraulein") 15-20 57
DECCA (30513 "Jingle Bell Rock") 8-15 57

EPs: 7–inch 33/45rpm

DECCA 10-20 57-59

LPs: 10/12–inch 33rpm

CERTRON 8-10 70
COLUMBIA 12-15 63
DECCA (8638 "Bobby Helms Sings to My Special Angel")..................30-40 57
HARMONY................................10-12 67
KAPP 10-15 66
LITTLE DARLIN' 10-12 68
MCA...5-10 83
MISTLETOE...............................5-10 74
VOCALION 10-12 65

Also see KERR, Anita

HELMS, Jimmy

R&B '73

Singles: 78rpm

CAPITOL...................................5-10 55

Singles: 7–inch

CAPITOL...................................10-15 55
DATE 4-8 67
MGM 3-5 73

HENDERSON, Finis

R&B '83

Singles: 7–inch

MOTOWN 3-4 83

LPs: 10/12–inch 33rpm

MOTOWN 5-10 83

Also see WEAPONS of PEACE

HENDERSON, Joe

P&R/R&B/LP '62

Singles: 7–inch

ABC..3-5 73

KAPP 4-6 64
RIC 4-6 64
TODD 4-8 62-63
VIRGO 3-5 72

LPs: 10/12–inch 33rpm

TODD 20-25 62

HENDERSON, Michael

R&B/LP '76

Singles: 12–inch 33/45rpm

EMI AMERICA 4-6 86

Singles: 7–inch

BUDDAH 3-5 76-83
EMI AMERICA 3-4 86

LPs: 10/12–inch 33rpm

ACCORD 5-10
BUDDAH 8-12 76-83
EMI AMERICA 5-10 86

Also see CONNORS, Norman
Also see HYMAN, Phyllis, & Michael Henderson

HENDERSON, Ron, & Choice of Colour

R&B '77

Singles: 7–inch

CHELSEA 3-5 77

HENDERSON, Skitch

LP '65

EPs: 7–inch 33/45rpm

CAPITOL 10-20 50-54
DECCA 5-15 56
RCA 5-10 57-58

LPs: 10/12–inch 33rpm

CAPITOL (H-110 "Keyboard Sketches) 25-45 50
(10–inch LP.)
CAPITOL (502 "A Man and His Music") 15-25 54
COLUMBIA 5-15 65
DECCA (8000 series) 15-25 56
RCA 15-25 57-58
SEECO (62 "Skitch Henderson") 25-45
SEECO (401 "Latin Favorites") . 20-35 56

HENDERSON, Wayne
(With the Freedom Sounds)

R&B '78

Singles: 7–inch

POLYDOR 3-5 78-79

LPs: 10/12–inch 33rpm

ABC 5-10 77
ATLANTIC 8-12 67-68
POLYDOR 5-10 78-79

Also see AYERS, Roy, & Wayne Henderson

HENDERSON, Willie
(With the Soul Explosions)

P&R/R&B '70

Singles: 7–inch

BRUNSWICK 3-6 70
PLAYBOY 3-5 74

LPs: 10/12–inch 33rpm

BRUNSWICK 10-12 69-74

HENDRICKS, Bobby

P&R/R&B '58

Singles: 7–inch

MGM 10-20 63
MERCURY 5-10 61
SUE 10-20 58-60

Also see COASTERS
Also see DRIFTERS

HENDRIX, Jimi

P&R/LP '67

Singles: 7–inch

AUDIO FIDELITY (167 "No Such Animal") 10-15
REPRISE (Except 0572 & 0665) . 5-10 67-72
REPRISE (0572 "Hey Joe") 20-30 67
REPRISE (0665 "Up from the Skies") 10-15 68
TRIP 3-4 72

Promotional Singles

REPRISE (Except 0572 & 0665) . 6-10 67-72
REPRISE (0572 "Hey Joe") 25-30 67
REPRISE (0665 "Up from the Skies") 10-20 68

Picture Sleeves

AUDIO FIDELITY (167 "No Such Animal") 15-25
REPRISE (0572 "Hey Joe") 60-80 67

EPs: 7–inch 33/45rpm

REPRISE (595 "And a Happy New Year") 75-100 74
(Promotional issue only. Issued with paper sleeve.)

LPs: 10/12–inch 33rpm

ABC (82-41 "Jimi Hendrix: a Tribute") 150-200 82
(Five LPs plus cue sheets. Promotional issue only.)
ACCORD 5-10 81
BBC ROCK HOUR/LONDON WAVELENGTH ("Jimi Hendrix Special") 50-75 81
CAPITOL (12000 series) 5-10 86
CAPITOL (15000 series) 4-8 86
(Mini LP.)
CRAWDADDY 200-250 75
PHOENIX 10 (320 "Rare Hendrix") 8-10 80s
PICKWICK 8-10 75
WESTWOOD ONE ("Psychedelic Psnack [Psalute to Jimi Hendrix]") 20-25 89
(Promotional issue only.)
NUTMEG (1001 "High, Live 'N' Dirty") 15-20 78
(Colored vinyl.)
REPRISE (840 "Jimi Hendrix - Christmas Medley") 40-50 79
(Promotional issue only.)

REPRISE (2025 "Smash Hits") . 25-35 69
(Orange and brown label. Price includes bonus poster, which represents about $15-$20 of the value.)
REPRISE (2025 "Smash Hits")... 8-10 71
(Brown label.)
REPRISE (2029 "Historic Performances") 8-10 70
REPRISE (2034 "Cry of Love")... 8-10 70
REPRISE (2040 "Rainbow Bridge") 10-15 71
REPRISE (2049 "In the West") . 10-15 72
REPRISE (2103 "War Heroes") 10-15 72
REPRISE (2204 "Crash Landing") 10-15 75
REPRISE (2229 "Midnight Lightning") 10-15 75
REPRISE (2245 "Essential Jimi Hendrix") 8-12 78
REPRISE (2276 "Smash Hits")... 5-10 77
REPRISE (2293 "Essential Jimi Hendrix, Vol. 2") 200-300 79
(Includes the bonus single, *Gloria*, extended version.)
REPRISE (2293 "Essential Jimi Hendrix, Vol. 2") 10-15 79
(Without the bonus single.)
REPRISE (2299 "Nine to the Universe") 5-10 80
REPRISE (R-6261 "Are You Experienced") 45-65 67
(Monaural. Green, pink and yellow label.)
REPRISE (RS-6261 "Are You Experienced") 45-65 67
(Stereo. Green, pink and yellow label.)
REPRISE (6261 "Are You Experienced") 12-20 68
(Orange and brown label.)
REPRISE (6261 "Are You Experienced") 5-10 71
(Brown label.)
REPRISE (R-6281 "Axis: Bold As Love") 175-225 68
(Monaural. Orange and brown label.)
REPRISE (RS-6281 "Axis: Bold As Love") 15-20 68
(Stereo. Green, pink and yellow label.)
REPRISE (RS-6281 "Axis: Bold As Love") 5-10 71
(Brown label.)
REPRISE (6307 "Electric Ladyland") 12-15 68
(Orange and brown label.)
REPRISE (6307 "Electric Ladyland") 8-10 71
(Brown label.)
REPRISE (6481 "From the film *Jimi Hendrix*") 15-20 73
(Soundtrack.)
REPRISE (22306 "Jimi Hendrix Concerts") 8-10 82
REPRISE (25119 "Kiss the Sky") 5-10 84
REPRISE (25358 "Jimi Plays Monterey") 5-10 86
RHINO 5-10 82
ROLLING STONE PROD. (82-24 "The Jimi Hendrix Profile") 50-100 82
(Two LPs plus cue sheets. Promotional issue only.)
RYKO 10-15 87-88
SHOUT 10-15 72
(White label with red and blue printing.)
SHOUT 8-10
(Yellow label.)
SPRINGBOARD 8-10 72
TRIP (9500 "Rare Hendrix") 15-25 72
(Gatefold cover with Hendrix poster inside.)
TRIP (9500 "Rare Hendrix") 10-15 72
(Standard cover.)
TRIP (9501 "Roots of Hendrix") . 10-15 72
TRIP (9523 "Genius of Jimi Hendrix") 10-15 74
U.A. 8-10 75
WESTWOOD ONE ("Rock & Roll Never Forgets—Jimi Hendrix") 150-200 83
(Five LPs plus cue sheets. Promotional issue only.)
WESTWOOD ONE ("Jimi Hendrix, Live and Unreleased") 400-500 88
(Eight LPs plus cue sheets. Promotional issue only.)
Also see REDDING, Otis / Jimi Hendrix

HENDRIX, Jimi, & Isley Brothers

LPs: 10/12–inch 33rpm

T-NECK 10-15 71
Also see ISLEY BROTHERS

HENDRIX, Jimi, & Curtis Knight

LPs: 10/12–inch 33rpm

CAPITOL (659 "Flashing") 8-10 70
CAPITOL (2856 "Get That Feeling") 10-15 67
CAPITOL (2894 "Flashing") 10-15 68
51 WEST 5-10 82

HENDRIX, Jimi, & Little Richard

Singles: 7–inch

ALANNA 3-6 72

LPs: 10/12–inch 33rpm

ALANNA 10-12 72
EVEREST 6-10 74
PICKWICK 6-10 73
Also see LITTLE RICHARD

HENDRIX, Jimi, & Buddy Miles

LPs: 10/12–inch 33rpm

CAPITOL (472 "Band of Gypsies") 10-12 70
Also see MILES, Buddy

HENDRIX, Jimi, & Lonnie Youngblood

LP '71

LPs: 10/12-inch 33rpm

MAPLE (6004 "Two Great Experiences Together") 20-25 71

Also see HENDRIX, Jimi
Also see YOUNGBLOOD, Lonnie

HENDRIX, Patti

R&B '78

Singles: 7-inch

HILLTAK.. 3-5 78
20TH FOX... 3-5 74

HENDRYX, Nona

P&R/R&B/D&D/LP '83

Singles: 12-inch 33/45rpm

RCA.. 4-6 83-86

Singles: 7-inch

EMI AMERICA 3-4 87
EPIC... 3-5 77
RCA.. 3-4 83-87

Picture Sleeves

EMI AMERICA 3-4 87

LPs: 10/12-inch 33rpm

EMI AMERICA 5-8 87
EPIC... 5-10 77
RCA.. 5-10 83-87

Also see LABELLE, Patti

HENHOUSE FIVE PLUS TOO

P&R '77

Singles: 7-inch

W.B./AHAB.. 3-5 76-77

Member: Ray Stevens.
Also see STEVENS, Ray

HENLEY, Don

P&R/LP '82

Singles: 12-inch 33/45rpm

GEFFEN... 4-6 85

Singles: 7-inch

ASYLUM 3-4 82-83
GEFFEN... 3-4 84-89

Picture Sleeves

ASYLUM 3-4 82
GEFFEN... 3-4 84-89

LPs: 10/12-inch 33rpm

ASYLUM 5-10 82-83
GEFFEN... 5-10 84-89

Also see EAGLES
Also see HORNSBY, Bruce
Also see NICKS, Stevie, & Don Henley

HENRY, Clarence
(Clarence "Frogman" Henry)

P&R/R&B '56

Singles: 78rpm

ARGO... 10-15 56-57

Singles: 7-inch

ARGO (5200 series)................. 10-15 56-58
ARGO (5300 & 5400 series) 5-10 59-63
CADET 4-8 66
DIAL... 4-6 67
PARROT... 4-8 64-66
CHESS.. 3-5 73
ERIC 3-5 73
MAISON DE SOUL 3-5 77

LPs: 10/12-inch 33rpm

ARGO (4009 "You Always Hurt the One You Love") 50-75 61
CADET (4009 "You Always Hurt the One You Love") 20-30 65
(Cadet 4009 LPs can be found in Argo 4009 covers.)
ROULETTE.......................................15-20 69

Also see GAYTEN, Paul

HENSLEY, Ken

LP '73

Singles: 7-inch

MERCURY..3-5 73

LPs: 10/12-inch 33rpm

MERCURY..8-10 73
W.B. 8-10 75

Also see URIAH HEEP

HENSON, Jim
(Jim Henson's Muppets)

P&R '70

Singles: 7-inch

COLUMBIA...3-5 72
SIGNATURE..5-8 60

Singles: 12-inch 33/45rpm

COLUMBIA...5-10 71

Also see ERNIE
Also see KERMIT / Fozzie Bear

HERB the "K"

R&B '85

Singles: 7-inch

PRIVATE I...3-4 85

HERMAN, Keith

P&R '79

Singles: 7-inch

RADIO...3-5 79

HERMAN, Woody, & Orchestra

P&R '37

Singles: 78rpm

CAPITOL...3-5 54-56
COLUMBIA..3-6 45-48
DECCA 4-6 37-45
MARS..3-5 52-53

Singles: 7-inch

CADET...3-5 69
CAPITOL...4-8 54-56
CENTURY...3-4 79
CHURCHILL 3-4 79
COLUMBIA 3-5 65-76
FANTASY 3-5 73-74
MCA...3-5 73
MARS..4-8 52-53
PHILIPS 3-5 62

EPs: 7–inch 33/45rpm

CAPITOL 5-10 55-56
COLUMBIA 8-12 52-54
DECCA 5-10 56
MGM 5-10 55

LPs: 10/12–inch 33rpm

ACCORD 5-10 82
ATLANTIC (1300 series) 10-20 60
ATLANTIC (90000 series) 5-10 82
BRIGHT ORANGE 5-10 73
CADET 8-12 69-71
CAPITOL 5-10 72-75
(With "M" or "SM" prefix.)
CAPITOL 10-25 55-62
(With "T" or "ST" prefix.)
CENTURY 5-10 78
CHESS 5-10 76
COLUMBIA (500 series) 15-25 55
COLUMBIA (2300 & 2400 series) 5-15 65-66
COLUMBIA (2500 series) 15-25 52-54
(10–inch LPs.)
COLUMBIA (6000 series) 15-25 49-55
COLUMBIA (9000 series) 5-15 65-67
COLUMBIA (32000 series) 5-10 74
CONCORD JAZZ 5-10 81-83
CROWN 10-15 59
DECCA (4000 series) 8-15 64
DECCA (8000 series) 10-25 56
EVEREST (Except 200 & 300 series) 10-20 59-63
EVEREST (200 & 300 series) 5-10 74-78
FPM 5-10 75
FANTASY 5-10 71-81
HARMONY 5-10 72
JAZZLAND 10-20 60
MGM 10-25 55
METRO 5-12 65
PHILIPS 10-15 62-65
ROULETTE 10-20 59
SURREY 8-12 66
TREND 5-10 81
TRIP 5-10 75
VSP 8-12 66-67
VERVE 8-15 63-68
WHO'S WHO in JAZZ 5-10 78
WING 5-10

Also see BYRD, Charlie, & Woody Herman
Also see CLOONEY, Rosemary
Also see ECKSTINE, Billy, & Woody Herman

HERMAN'S HERMITS

P&R '64

Singles: 7–inch

ABKCO 3-4
BUDDAH 3-5 74-76
MGM 4-6 64-69
PRIVATE STOCK 3-5 75

Picture Sleeves

MGM 5-12 65-67

LPs: 10/12–inch 33rpm

ABKCO 5-10 73-76
MGM (Except 4478) 10-20 65-68
MGM (E-4478 "Blaze") 35-45 67
(Monaural.)
MGM (SE-4478 "Blaze") 10-20 67
(Stereo.)

Members: Peter Noone; Derek Leckenby; Karl Green; Keith Hopwood; Barry Whitwham.
Also see PAGE, Jimmy

HERNANDEZ, Patrick

P&R/LP '79

Singles: 12–inch 33/45rpm

COLUMBIA 4-6 79

Singles: 7–inch

COLUMBIA 3-4 79

LPs: 10/12–inch 33rpm

COLUMBIA 5-10 79

HESITATIONS

R&B '67

Singles: 7–inch

B.T. PUPPY 4-8 68
GWP 4-8 69
KAPP 5-10 66-68

LPs: 10/12–inch 33rpm

KAPP 10-15 67-68

Members: George Scott; Fred Deal; Leonard Veal.

HEWETT, Howard

R&B '85

Singles: 7–inch

ARISTA 3-4 88
ELEKTRA 3-4 85-90

Picture Sleeves

ELEKTRA 3-4 86

LPs: 10/12–inch 33rpm

ELEKTRA 5-8 85-90

Also see SHALAMAR
Also see WARWICK, Dionne, & Howard Hewett

HEYETTES

P&R '76

Singles: 7–inch

LONDON 3-5 76

Picture Sleeves

LONDON 5-10 76

LPs: 10/12–inch 33rpm

LONDON 5-10 76

HEYWARD, Nick

LP '84

Singles: 7–inch

ARISTA 3-4 83-84

LPs: 10/12–inch 33rpm

ARISTA 5-10 83

Also see HAIRCUT ONE HUNDRED

HEYWOOD, Eddie

P&R '45

Singles: 78rpm

DECCA 3-5 45-53
MERCURY 3-5 55-57

Singles: 7-inch

DECCA ... 4-6 51-53
LIBERTY ... 3-5 61-63
MERCURY ... 3-6 55-61
20TH FOX ... 3-5 63

EPs: 7-inch 33/45rpm

COLUMBIA ... 4-8 52
DECCA ... 4-8 56
MERCURY ... 4-8 55-56

LPs: 10/12-inch 33rpm

BRUNSWICK ... 10-15 55
CAPITOL ... 5-10 67-69
COLUMBIA ... 10-20 52
CORAL ... 10-15 55
DECCA ... 10-15 56
EPIC ... 10-15 56
LIBERTY ... 8-12 62-63
MERCURY ... 10-15 55-60
RCA ... 10-12 59
SUNSET ... 5-10 66
VOCALION ... 5-10 66
WING ... 8-12 59-64

Also see HOLIDAY, Billie, & Eddie Heywood
Also see WINTERHALTER, Hugo, & His Orchestra

HEYWOODS: see DONALDSON, Bo, & Heywoods

HI TEX 3 Featuring Ya Kid K

P&R '90

Singles: 7-inch

SBK ... 3-4 90

HIATT, John

LP '87

Singles: 12-inch 33/45rpm

A&M ... 4-8 87
(Promotional only.)
GEFFEN ... 4-8 85
(Promotional only.)

Singles: 7-inch

A&M ... 3-4 87-90
GEFFEN ... 3-4 85
MCA ... 3-4 79-90

LPs: 10/12-inch 33rpm

A&M ... 5-10 87-90
GEFFEN ("Riot with Hiatt") ... 25-35
(Promotional issue only.)

Also see COSTELLO, Elvis

HIBBLER, Al

R&B '48

Singles: 78rpm

ALADDIN ... 4-6 56
ATLANTIC ... 5-10 50
CHESS ... 5-10 51
CLEF ... 4-6 54
COLUMBIA ... 4-6 50
DECCA ... 4-6 55-57
MERCURY ... 4-6 52-56
MIRACLE ... 5-10 48
NORGRAN ... 4-6 54-55
ORIGINAL ... 4-8 55

Singles: 7-inch

ALADDIN ... 5-10 56
ATLANTIC (925 "The Blues Came Tumbling Down") ... 30-40 51
ATLANTIC (932 "Travelin' Light") ... 30-40 51
ATLANTIC (945 "This Is Always") ... 30-40 51
ATLANTIC (1071 "Danny Boy") ... 15-25 55
CLEF ... 4-8 54
COLUMBIA ... 5-10 50
DECCA ... 4-8 55-59
MCA ... 3-4 74
MERCURY ... 4-8 52-56
NORGRAN ... 4-8 54-55
ORIGINAL ... 5-10 55
REPRISE ... 4-6 61-62
SATIN ... 3-6 66
TOP RANK ... 4-6 60
VEGAS ... 3-6 67

EPs: 7-inch 33/45rpm

CLEF ... 10-15 51
DECCA ... 5-10 55-57
NORGRAN ... 10-15 53
RCA ... 5-10 55

LPs: 10/12-inch 33rpm

ATLANTIC ... 10-20 56
CLEF ... 15-25 54
DECCA (8000 series) ... 10-20 56-59
DECCA (75000 series) ... 5-10 69
LMI ... 8-12 65
MCA ... 5-10 76
NORGRAN (4 "Favorites") ... 30-40 53
REPRISE ... 8-15 61
TRIP ... 4-8 77
VERVE ... 10-20 55

Also see HOLIDAY, Billie, & Al Hibbler
Also see McSHANN, Jay

HIBBLER, Al, & Duke Ellington

Singles: 7-inch

COLUMBIA (33000 series) ... 3-4 76

LPs: 10/12-inch 33rpm

COLUMBIA ... 15-25 56

Also see ELLINGTON, Duke
Also see HIBBLER, Al

HICKEY, Ersel

P&R '58

Singles: 7-inch

APOLLO (761 "Upside Down Love") ... 15-25 62
BLACK CIRCLE ... 3-5 72
EPIC ... 10-15 58-60
JANUS ... 3-5 71
KAPP ... 8-12 61
LAURIE ... 8-12 63
MAGNUM ... 3-4 84
RAMESES ... 3-5 76
TOOT ... 8-12

UNIFAX 3-5 74

EPs: 7–inch 33/45rpm

EPIC (7206 "Ersel Hickey in Lover's Land") 75-100 58

HICKS, Clair, & Love Exchange

D&D '84

Singles: 12–inch 33/45rpm

KN 4-6 84

HICKS, Dan, & His Hot Licks

LP '71

Singles: 7–inch

BLUE THUMB 3-5 73-74

LPs: 10/12–inch 33rpm

BLUE THUMB 8-10 71-73
EPIC 10-12 69
W.B. 5-10 78

HIDDEN STRENGTH

R&B '76

Singles: 7–inch

U.A. 3-5 76

HI-FI FOUR

P&R '56

Singles: 78rpm

KING 4-6 56

Singles: 7–inch

KING 10-15 56

HI-FIVE

LP '90

LPs: 10/12–inch 33rpm

JIVE 5-8 90

HIGGINS, Bertie

P&R '81

Singles: 7–inch

CBS ASSOCIATED 3-4 85
KAT FAMILY 3-4 81-82
SOUTHERN TRACKS 3-4 87-89

LPs: 10/12–inch 33rpm

KAT FAMILY 5-10 82

HIGGINS, Bertie, & Roy Orbison

Singles: 7–inch

SOUTHERN TRACKS (2010 Leah") 3-4 89
Also see HIGGINS, Bertie
Also see ORBISON, Roy

HIGGINS, Monk
(With the Specialties)

R&B '66

Singles: 7–inch

BUDDAH 3-5 74
CHESS 3-6 67
SOLID STATE 3-6 68
ST. LAWRENCE 4-6 66
U.A. 3-5 72-73

LPs: 10/12–inch 33rpm

BUDDAH 5-10 74
SOLID STATE 8-12 69

U.A. 8-10 72
Also see MASON, Barbara

HIGH INERGY

P&R/R&B/LP '77

Singles: 12–inch 33/45rpm

GORDY 4-6 83

Singles: 7–inch

GORDY (Black vinyl) 3-5 77-83
GORDY (Colored vinyl) 3-6
(Promotional only.)

LPs: 10/12–inch 33rpm

GORDY 5-10 77-83
Members: Barbara Mitchell; Vernessa Mitchell; Linda Howard; Michelle Rumph.
Also see ROBINSON, Smokey, & Barbara Mitchell

HIGH KEYES

P&R '63

Singles: 7–inch

ATCO 10-20 63-64
Members: Troy Keyes; Jim Williams; Bob Haggard; Cliff Rice.

HIGHLIGHTS
(Featuring Frank Pizani)

P&R '56

Singles: 78rpm

BALLY 4-8 56-57

Singles: 7–inch

BALLY 8-12 56-58

HIGHTOWER, Willie

R&B '69

Singles: 7–inch

CAPITOL 4-6 69
FAME 3-5 70

HIGHWAYMEN

P&R/LP '61

Singles: 7–inch

ABC-PAR 4-6 65-66
LIBERTY 3-4 81
U.A. 4-8 61-64

LPs: 10/12–inch 33rpm

ABC-PAR 8-15 66
LIBERTY 5-8 82
U.A. 15-20 61-65
Members: Steve Butts; Chan Daniels; Gil Robbins; Dave Fisher.

HILL, Bobby

R&B '69

Singles: 7–inch

LOLO (2305 "The Children") 5-8 69
LOLO (2307 "To the Bitter End") 25-50 70

HILL, Bunker

P&R/R&B '62

Singles: 7–inch

MALA (Except 464) 5-8 62
MALA (464 "The Girl Can't Dance") 8-12 63
Also see MIGHTY CLOUDS of JOY

HILL, Dan

LP '75

Singles: 7-inch

COLUMBIA 3-4 87
EPIC 3-4 80-81
20TH FOX 3-5 75-79

Picture Sleeves

20TH FOX 3-5 78

LPs: 10/12-inch 33rpm

EPIC 5-10 80-81
20TH FOX 5-10 75-80

HILL, Dan, & Vonda Sheppard

P&R '87

Singles: 7-inch

COLUMBIA 3-4 87

LPs: 10/12-inch 33rpm

COLUMBIA 5-10 87

Also see HILL, Dan

HILL, David

P&R '59

Singles: 78rpm

ALADDIN 3-6 57
RCA 3-6 57

Singles: 7-inch

ALADDIN 5-10 57
KAPP 5-10 59
RCA 5-10 57-58

HILL, Jessie

P&R/R&B '60

Singles: 7-inch

DOWNEY 5-10 64
MINIT 8-12 60-62
YOGI-MAN (607 "Hey Now Mama") 10-15

LPs: 10/12-inch 33rpm

BLUE THUMB 8-10 72

HILL, Lonnie

R&B '84

Singles: 7-inch

URBAN SOUND 3-4 84-85

LPs: 10/12-inch 33rpm

URBAN SOUND 5-10 85

HILL, Z.Z.

P&R/R&B '64

Singles: 7-inch

ATLANTIC 4-8 69-70
AUDREY 3-6 71-72
COLUMBIA 3-5 77-78
HILL 3-6 71-73
KENT 5-15 64-71
M.H. 5-10 63
M.H.R 3-6 75
MALACO 3-4 82-84
MAILBU 3-4
MESA 5-10 64
MANKIND 4-6 71-72
QUINCY 4-6 70
RARE BULLET 3-4 84
U.A. 3-6 73-75

LPs: 10/12-inch 33rpm

COLUMBIA 5-10 78-79
KENT 10-20 69-71
MALACO 5-10 82-84
MANKIND 8-12 71
U.A. 8-10 72-75

HILLAGE, Steve

LP '77

Singles: 7-inch

ATLANTIC 3-5 76-77

LPs: 10/12-inch 33rpm

ATLANTIC 8-10 76-77
VIRGIN 8-10 75

HILLMAN, Chris

LP '76

Singles: 7-inch

ASYLUM 3-5 76-77

LPs: 10/12-inch 33rpm

ASYLUM 5-10 76-77
SUGAR HILL 5-10 82-84

Also see BYRDS
Also see DESERT ROSE BAND
Also see FLYING BURRITO BROTHERS
Also see McGUINN,CLARK & HILLMAN
Also see SOUTHER - HILLMAN - FURAY BAND

HILLMAN, Chris, & Roger McGuinn

C&W '89

Singles: 7-inch

UNIVERSAL 3-4 89

Members: Roger McGuinn; Chris Hillman.
Also see HILLMAN, Chris
Also see McGUINN, Roger

HILLSIDE SINGERS

P&R '71

Singles: 7-inch

METROMEDIA 3-5 71-72

LPs: 10/12-inch 33rpm

METROMEDIA 8-12 71

HILLTOPPERS
(Hill Toppers)

P&R '52

Singles: 78rpm

DOT 3-5 52-57

Singles: 7-inch

ABC 3-4 74
DOT (15000 series) 5-10 52-60
DOT (16000 series) 4-6 63
3-J 3-6 66

EPs: 7-inch 33/45rpm

DOT 10-15 54-56

LPs: 10/12-inch 33rpm

DOT (105 "The Hilltoppers") 30-40 54
(10-inch LP.)
DOT (106 "The Hilltoppers") 30-40 54
(10-inch LP.)
DOT (3003 "Tops in Pops") 20-30 55

DOT (3029 "Towering Hilltoppers") 20-30 56
DOT (3073 "The Hilltoppers") 20-30 57
SOUVENIR 8-15 73

Members: Jimmy Sacca; Billy Vaughn; Don McGuire; Seymour Spiegelman.
Also see VAUGHN, Billy

HI-LOs

P&R '54

Singles: 78rpm

COLUMBIA 3-5 57
STARLITE 3-6 55-56
TREND 3-8 54

Singles: 7-inch

COLUMBIA 4-8 57-60
STARLITE 5-10 55-56
TREND 8-12 54

EPs: 7-inch 33/45rpm

COLUMBIA 5-10 57-58
KAPP 5-10 56
STARLITE 8-15 56

LPs: 10/12-inch 33rpm

COLUMBIA 15-25 57-60
KAPP 15-25 56-60
STARLITE 15-30 56

Members: Clark Burroughs; Don Shelton; Bob Morse; Gene Puerling.
Also see CLOONEY, Rosemary, & Hi-Los

HINDSIGHT

R&B '88

Singles: 7-inch

VIRGIN 3-4 88

HINDU LOVE GODS

LP '90

LPs: 10/12-inch 33rpm

GIANT 5-8 90

Members: Bill Berry Peter Buck; Mike Mills; Warren Zevon.
Also see R.E.M.
Also see ZEVON, Warren

HINES, Gregory

R&B '88

Singles: 7-inch

EPIC 3-4 87-88

Also see VANDROSS, Luther, & Gregory Hines

HINES, J., & Fellows

R&B '73

Singles: 7-inch

DELUXE 3-5 73

HINTON, Joe
(Little Joe Hinton)

P&R/R&B '63

Singles: 7-inch

ARVEE 4-8 61
BACKBEAT 5-10 59-65
HOTLANTA 8-10 74

Picture Sleeves

BACKBEAT 8-15 59-65

LPs: 10/12-inch 33rpm

BACKBEAT (60 "Funny") 20-25 65
DUKE 8-10 73

HIPPIES / Reggie Harrison

P&R '63

Singles: 7-inch

PARKWAY (863 "Memory Lane") 8-10 63

Also see STEREOS
Also see TAMS

HIPSWAY

P&R/LP '87

Singles: 7-inch

COLUMBIA 3-4 87

Picture Sleeves

COLUMBIA 3-4 87

LPs: 10/12-inch 33rpm

COLUMBIA 5-10 87

Member: John McElhone.
Also see TEXAS

HIROSHIMA

LP '79

Singles: 12-inch 33/45rpm

EPIC 4-6 85

Singles: 7-inch

ARISTA 3-4 80-84
EPIC 3-4 85

LPs: 10/12-inch 33rpm

ARISTA 5-10 79-84
EPIC 5-10 83-89

HIRT, Al

LP '61

Singles: 7-inch

CORAL 3-5 65
GWP 3-5 69-70
MONUMENT 3-4 74
RCA 3-6 61-68

Picture Sleeves

RCA 4-8 61-66

EPs: 7-inch 33/45rpm

RCA 4-8 62

LPs: 10/12-inch 33rpm

ACCORD 4-8 82
AUDIO FIDELITY 10-15 59-61
CAMDEN 5-10 67-71
CORAL 8-15 65
GWP 5-10 70-71
METRO 5-10 65
MONUMENT 5-8 74
RCA (Except 3309) 5-15 61-78
RCA (LPM-3309 "Best of Al Hirt") 10-15 65
(Monaural. Has Ann-Margret on one track.)
RCA (LSP-3309 "Best of Al Hirt") 15-20 65
(Stereo. Has Ann-Margret on one track.)
VOCALION 5-10 70

Also see ANN-MARGRET & Al Hirt

HIRT, Al, & Boston Pops Orchestra

LPs: 10/12–inch 33rpm

RCA.. 10-15 64

Also see BOSTON POPS ORCHESTRA

HIRT, Al, & Pete Fountain

LP '62

Singles: 7–inch

CORAL.. 3-6 61

EPs: 7–inch 33/45rpm

CORAL.. 4-8 62

LPs: 10/12–inch 33rpm

CORAL.. 8-15 61-62

MGM 8-15 64

MONUMENT 5-10 75

VERVE.. 10-20 61

Also see FOUNTAIN, Pete

HIRT, Al / Henry Mancini / Perez Prado

LPs: 10/12–inch 33rpm

RCA.. 8-15 63

Also see MANCINI, Henry

Also see PRADO, Perez

HIRT, Al, & Hugo Montenegro

LPs: 10/12–inch 33rpm

RCA (4275 "Viva Max")............ 15-20 70

(Soundtrack.)

Also see MONTENEGRO, Hugo

HIRT, Al, & Boots Randolph

Singles: 7–inch

MONUMENT 3-5 75

Also see HIRT, Al

Also see RANDOLPH, Boots

HITCHCOCK, Robyn

(With the Egyptians)

LP '88

Singles: 7–inch

A&M 3-4 88-90

LPs: 10/12–inch 33rpm

A&M 5-8 88-90

HO, Don

(With the Aliis)

P&R/LP '66

Singles: 7–inch

HEL 3-5 77

MEGA.. 3-5 74-75

REPRISE 3-6 65-71

LPs: 10/12–inch 33rpm

MEGA.. 4-8 74

REPRISE 5-15 65-70

HODGE, Chris

(With George Harrison)

P&R '72

Singles: 7–inch

APPLE.. 4-6 72-73

RCA.. 3-5 73-75

Picture Sleeves

APPLE.. 5-8 72

Also see HARRISON, George

HODGES, Charles

R&B '70

Singles: 7–inch

ALTO.. 10-15 65

CALLA.. 3-5 70

HODGES, Eddie

P&R '61

Singles: 7–inch

AURORA.. 4-6 65-66

BARNABY 3-5 76

CADENCE 8-15 61-62

COLUMBIA 4-8 62-63

DECCA 5-10 59

MGM 4-8 64

Picture Sleeves

CADENCE 10-15 61

COLUMBIA 5-10 63

EPs: 7–inch 33/45rpm

CADENCE (33-6 "Eddie Hodges")................................ 15-25 61

("Cadence Little LP." With cardboard insert in clear cover.)

Also see DE SHANNON, Jackie / Bobby Vee / Eddie Hodges

Also see MILLS, Hayley, & Eddie Hodges

HODGES, Johnny

P&R '37

Singles: 78rpm

BLUEBIRD.. 5-8 40-44

CLEF.. 4-6 53-56

COLUMBIA 4-6 51

GROOVE 4-6 56

MERCURY 4-6 51-53

NORGRAN.. 4-6 54-56

VARIETY.. 5-10 33

VOCALION 5-10 37

Singles: 7-Inch

CLEF.. 5-10 53-56

COLUMBIA 5-10 51

GROOVE 5-10 56

MERCURY.. 5-10 51-53

NORGRAN.. 5-10 54-56

VMC.. 3-6 68

VARIETY.. 5-10 33

VERVE.. 4-8 57-67

EPs: 7-Inch 33/45rpm

ATLANTIC.. 20-30 54

EPIC.. 15-25 55

NORGRAN.. 25-50 54

RCA (3000 "Alto Sax")............... 50-75 52

LPs: 10/12-Inch 33rpm

AMERICAN RECORDING (421 "Johnny Hodges & Ellington All Stars") .40-60 57

CLEF (111 "Johnny Hodges Collates") 100-200 52

(10–inch LP.)

CLEF (128 "Johnny Hodges Collates, Vol. 2") 100-200 52
(10–inch LP.)
ENCORE.................................. 10-15 68
EPIC (3105 "Hodge Podge")..... 50-75 55
EPIC (22000 series).................. 8-12 74
IMPULSE 10-20 65
INSTANT................................. 15-20 64
MCA 5-10 82
NORGRAN (1 "Swing with Johnny Hodges")................ 150-250 53
(10–inch LP.)
NORGRAN (1004 "Memories of Ellington")......................... 100-200 54
NORGRAN (1009 "More Johnny Hodges") 100-200 54
NORGRAN (1024 "Dance Bash") 100-200 55
NORGRAN (1045 "Creamy") 100-200 56
NORGRAN (1048 "Castle Rock") 100-200 56
NORGRAN (1055 "Ellingtonia")......................... 75-150 56
NORGRAN (1059 "In a Tender Mood") 75-150 56
NORGRAN (1060 "Used to Be Duke")............................ 75-150 56
NORGRAN (1061 "Blues")...... 75-150 56
PABLO 5-10 78
RCA (500 series)...................... 10-20 66
RCA (3000 "Alto Sax") 200-300 52
(10–inch LP.)
RCA (3800 series).................... 10-20 67
VSP 10-20 66-67
VERVE (8179 "Perdido")......... 50-100 57
VERVE (8180 "In a Mellow Tone") 50-100 57
VERVE (8203 "Duke's in Bed")50-100 57
VERVE (8271 "Big Sound")..... 50-100 58
(Reads "Verve Records, Inc." at bottom of label.)
VERVE (8271 "Big Sound")....... 15-25
(Reads "MGM Records - A Division Of Metro-Goldwyn-Mayer, Inc." at bottom of label.)
VERVE (8314 thru 8358) 25-45 59-60
(Reads "Verve Records, Inc." at bottom of label.)
VERVE (8314 thru 8358) 15-25 61-69
(Reads "MGM Records - A Division Of Metro-Goldwyn-Mayer, Inc." at bottom of label.)
VERVE 8-15 74-79
(Reads "Manufactured By MGM Record Corp.," or mentions either Polydor or Polygram at bottom of label.)
Also see ELLINGTON, Duke, & Johnny Hodges
Also see MULLIGAN, Gerry, & Johnny Hodges

HODGES, Johnny, & Lawrence Welk

LPs: 10/12-Inch 33rpm

DOT 10-20 66
Also see WELK, Lawrence

HODGES, Johnny, & Wild Bill Davis

LP '65

LPs: 10/12-Inch 33rpm

RCA 10-20 65-67
VERVE.......................................15-30 61-66
Also see HODGES, Johnny

HODGES, JAMES & SMITH

P&R/R&B '77

Singles: 12–inch 33/45rpm

LONDON......................................4-8 79

Singles: 7–inch

LONDON......................................3-5 76-79
PEOPLE.......................................3-5 70s
20TH FOX....................................3-5 75

LPs: 10/12–inch 33rpm

LONDON....................................5-10 78
Members: Pat Hodges; Denita James; Jessica Smith.

HODGSON, Roger

P&R/LP '84

Singles: 7–inch

A&M 3-4 84

LPs: 10/12–inch 33rpm

A&M 5-10 84-87
Also see SUPERTRAMP

HOFFS, Susanna

LP '91

LPs: 10/12–inch 33rpm

COLUMBIA 5-8 91
Also see BANGLES

HOG HEAVEN

P&R '71

Singles: 7–inch

ROULETTE....................................3-5 71

LPs: 10/12–inch 33rpm

ROULETTE...............................10-12 71
Members: Ron Rosman; Mike Vale; Peter Lucia; Eddie Gray.
Also see JAMES, Tommy, & Shondells

HOGG, Andrew

Singles: 78rpm

EXCLUSIVE (89 "He Knows How Much We Can Bear")..........................20-30 47
Also see HOGG, Smokey

HOGG, Smokey

(Andrew Hogg)

R&B '48

Singles: 78rpm

BULLET 15-25 48
COLONY 10-20 50
COMBO 10-20 52
CROWN 8-12 54
DECCA 15-25 37
EXCLUSIVE...............................15-25 47

FEDERAL 15-25 53
FIDELITY 10-20 52
IMPERIAL 5-10 50-53
INDEPENDENT 10-20 49
MACY'S 8-12 49
MERCURY 10-20 51
METEOR 20-30 54
MODERN 10-20 48-52
RAY'S RECORD 20-30 52
RECORDED in HOLLYWOOD ... 5-10 52
SHOW TIME 10-20 54
SITTIN' in WITH 5-10 51-52
SPECIALTY (300 series) 5-10 49
TOP HAT 10-20 52

Singles: 7–inch

COMBO (11 "Believe I'll Change Towns") 75-100 52
CROWN (122 "I Declare") 50-75 54
EBB 10-20 58
FEDERAL (12109 "Keep A-Walking") 50-75 53
FEDERAL (12117 "Your Little Wagon") 50-75 53
FEDERAL (12127 "Gone, Gone, Gone") 50-75 53
IMPERIAL (5269 "When I've Been Drinkin") 50-75 53
IMPERIAL (5290 "My Baby's Gone)" 50-75 53
MERCURY (8235 "Miss Georgia") 50-75 51
MERCURY (8228 "She's Always on My Mind") 50-75 51
METEOR (5021 "I Declare") 50-75 54
MODERN (884 "Baby Don't You Tear My Clothes") 50-75 51
MODERN (896 "Too Late, Old Man") 50-75 51
MODERN (924 "Can't Do Nothin'") 50-75 52
RAY'S RECORD (33 "Penitentiary Blues") 75-100 52
RAY'S RECORD (35 "I've Been Happy") 75-100 52
SHOW TIME (1101 "Ain't Gonna Play Second No Mo'") 50-75 54

LPs: 10/12–inch 33rpm

CROWN (5526 "Smokey Hogg Sings the Blues") 20-30 62
KENT 10-15
TIME (6 "Smokey Hogg") 40-50 62
UNITED 5-10

Also see HOGG, Andrew

HOLDEN, Ron

(With the Thunderbirds)

P&R/R&B '60

Singles: 7–inch

ABC 3-5 73
CHALLENGE (59360 "I Tried") .. 20-30 67
COLLECTABLES 3-4
DONNA (1315 "Love You So") .. 15-25 59
(Green label.)
DONNA (1315 "Love You So") .. 10-20 60
(Black label.)
DONNA (1324 thru 1335) 10-20 60-62
ELDO 10-20 61
LANA 3-6 60s
NITE OWL (10 "Love You So") . 50-75 60
NOW 3-6 74
RAMPART 5-10 65

LPs: 10/12–inch 33rpm

DONNA (DLP-2111 "Love You So") 40-60 60
(Monaural.)
DONNA (DLPS-2111 "Love You So") 50-75 60
(Stereo.)

Also see LITTLE CAESAR & ROMANS / Ron Holden

HOLIDAY, Billie

P&R '35

Singles: 78rpm

BRUNSWICK 10-20 35-38
CAPITOL 5-10 42
CLEF 5-8 53-55
COLUMBIA 5-8 51-52
COMMODORE 8-12 39
DECCA 5-15 45-52
MERCURY 5-8 52-53
OKEH 5-10 41
VOCALION 5-15 36-38

Singles: 7–inch

CLEF 5-10 53-55
COLUMBIA (30000 series) 5-10 51-52
DECCA (250 "Lover Man") 30-40 52
(Boxed set of four singles.)
DECCA (27000 series) 5-10 50-52
DECCA (48000 series) 5-10 51-52
KENT 3-5 73
MGM 4-6 59
MERCURY (89000 series) 5-10 52-53
U.A. 3-5 72
VERVE 4-8 59-62

Picture Sleeves

MGM 5-10 59

EPs: 7–inch 33/45rpm

CLEF 15-25 53-54
COLUMBIA 10-25 54-58
DECCA 5-15 56

LPs: 10/12–inch 33rpm

AJ 10-20
ALADDIN 40-60 56
AMERICAN RECORDING SOCIETY (409 "Velvet Moods") 50-75 56
AMERICAN RECORDING SOCIETY (431 "Lady Sings the Blues") 50-75 56
ATLANTIC 5-10 72

CLEF (118 "Favorites") 100-200 53
(10–inch LP.)
CLEF (144 "Evening with Billie") 100-200 54
(10–inch LP.)
CLEF (161 "Favorites") 100-200 54
(10–inch LP.)
CLEF (169 "Jazz at the Philharmonic") 100-150 55
CLEF (669 "Music for Torching") 30-50 55
CLEF (686 "A Recital") 75-125 56
CLEF (690 "Solitude") 75-125 56
CLEF (713 "Velvet Moods") 75-125 56
CLEF (718 "Jazz Recital") 75-125 56
CLEF (721 "Lady Sings the Blues") 75-125 56
COLUMBIA (21 "The Golden Years") 30-50 62
(Three-LP boxed set.)
COLUMBIA (40 "The Golden Years, Volume 2") 20-35 66
(Three-LP boxed set.)
COLUMBIA (637 "Lady Day") ... 50-75 54
(Red label with gold printing.)
COLUMBIA (637 "Lady Day") ... 30-40 56
(Red label with black and white printing.)
COLUMBIA (2600 series) 8-15 67
COLUMBIA (6129 "Billie Holiday Sings") 100-200 50
(10–inch LP.)
COLUMBIA (6163 "Billie Holiday Favorites") 100-200 51
(10–inch LP.)
COLUMBIA (1157 "Lady in Satin") 30-40 58
COLUMBIA (30000 series) 8-15 72-73
DECCA (100 series) 10-20 65-72
DECCA (5345 "Lover Man") .. 100-150 52
(10–inch LP.)
DECCA (8215 "The Lady Sings") 50-75 56
DECCA (8701 "Blues Are Brewin'") 50-75 58
DECCA (75000 series) 8-15 68
ESP 8-12 71-73
EVEREST 5-10 73-75
HARMONY 5-10 73
JAZZTONE (1209 "Billie Holiday Sings") 30-40 56
JOLLY ROGER (5020 "Billie Holiday") 75-100 54
KENT 5-10 73
MCA 5-10 73
MFSL (201 "In Rehearsal") 15-25 87
MGM (100 series) 6-10 70
MGM (3700 series) 20-40 59
MGM (4900 series) 5-10 74
MAINSTREAM 10-20 65
METRO 10-20 65
MONMOUTH-EVERGREEN 5-10 72
PARAMOUNT 5-10 73
PICKWICK 5-10
RIC 10-20 64
SCORE 25-50 57
SOLID STATE 8-12 69
TRIP 5-10 73
U.A. (5600 series) 5-10 72
U.A. (14000 & 15000 series) 20-30 62
VSP 8-15 66
VERVE 20-40 57-60
(Reads "Verve Records, Inc." at bottom of label.)
VERVE 10-25 61-72
(Reads "MGM Records - a Division of Metro-Goldwyn-Mayer, Inc." at bottom of label.)
VERVE 5-10 73-84
(Reads "Manufactured By MGM Record Corp.," or mentions either Polydor or Polygram at bottom of label.)
Also see FITZGERALD, Ella / Billie Holiday / Lena Horne

HOLIDAY, Billie, & Stan Getz

LPs: 10/12–inch 33rpm

DALE (25 "Billie & Stan") 150-200 51
(10–inch LP.)
Also see GETZ, Stan
Also see GOODMAN, Benny, Orchestra
Also see LYNNE, Gloria / Nina Simone / Billie Holiday

HOLIDAY, Billie, & Eddie Heywood

LPs: 10/12–inch 33rpm

COMMODORE (20005 "Billie Holiday, Volume 1") 100-150 50
(10–inch LP.)
COMMODORE (20006 "Billie Holiday, Volume 2") 100-150 50
(10–inch LP.)
COMMODORE (30008 "Billie Holiday, Volume 1") 40-60 59
COMMODORE (30011 "Billie Holiday, Volume 2") 40-60 59
Also see HEYWOOD, Eddie

HOLIDAY, Billie, & Al Hibbler

LPs: 10/12–inch 33rpm

IMPERIAL 20-30 62
SUNSET 8-15 67
Also see HIBBLER, Al
Also see HOLIDAY, Billie

HOLIDAY, Chico

P&R '59

Singles: 7–inch

CORAL 5-10 61-63
KARATE 5-10 65
NEW PHOENIX 8-12
RCA 5-10 59
SHAMLEY 4-8 69

HOLIDAY, Jimmy

P&R/R&B '63

Singles: 7-inch

DIPLOMACY 4-8 65
EVEREST 4-8 63-65
KENT 4-6 68
MINIT 4-8 66-68

LPs: 10/12-inch 33rpm

MINIT 15-25 66

HOLIDAY, Jimmy, & Clydie King

Singles: 7-inch

MINIT 4-8 67

Also see HOLIDAY, Jimmy
Also see KING, Clydie

HOLIDAYS

P&R/R&B '66

Singles: 7-inch

GOLDEN WORLD (36 "I Love You Forever") 10-20 66
GOLDEN WORLD (47 "No Greater Love") 10-20 66
GROOVE CITY (206 "Easy Living") 50-75 60s
REVILOT (210 "I Know She Cares") 15-25 67

Members: Edwin Starr; Steve Mancha; J.J. Barnes.
Also see BARNES, J.J., & Steve Mancha
Also see STARR, Edwin

HOLIEN, Danny

P&R '72

Singles: 7-inch

TUMBLEWEED 3-5 72

HOLLAND, Amy

P&R/LP '80

Singles: 7-inch

CAPITOL 3-4 80-83

Picture Sleeves

CAPITOL 3-4 80

LPs: 10/12-inch 33rpm

CAPITOL 5-10 80-83

Also see CHRISTIAN, Chris
Also see McDONALD, Michael

HOLLAND, Brian
(Briant Holland with the Band)

R&B '72

Singles: 7-inch

INVICTUS 4-6 72-73
KUDO (667 "In Nature Boy"). 300-500 58

Also see HOLLAND, Eddie
Also see HOLLAND - DOZIER

HOLLAND, Eddie
(With the Rayber Voices)

P&R/R&B '62

Singles: 7-inch

MERCURY (71290 "You")....... 75-100 58
MOTOWN (Except 1049).......... 15-25 61-64
MOTOWN (1049 "I'm on the Outside Looking In") 50-100 64
TAMLA (102 "Merry-Go-Round") 100-200 59
U.A. (172 "Merry-Go-Round") 15-25 59
U.A. (191 "Because I Love Her") 15-25 59
U.A. (207 "Magic Mirror") 15-25 60
U.A. (280 "Last Laugh") 15-25 61

Picture Sleeves

MOTOWN (1030 "If Cleopatra Took a Chance") 30-50 62

LPs: 10/12-inch 33rpm

MOTOWN (604 "Eddie Holland") 50-75 63

Members (Rayber Voices): Brian Holland; Raynoma Gordy; Robert Bateman; Sonny Sanders; Gwen Murray.
Also see HOLLAND, Brian
Also see JOHNSON, Marv
Also see STRONG, Barrett

HOLLAND, Eddie, & Lamont Dozier

Singles: 7-inch

MOTOWN 8-12 63

Also see DOZIER, Lamont
Also see HOLLAND, Eddie
Also see HOLLAND - DOZIER

HOLLAND – DOZIER
(With the Andantes & Four Tops; featuring Lamont Dozier)

P&R '72

Singles: 7-inch

INVICTUS 3-5 72-73
MOTOWN 15-20 63

Members: Brian Holland; Lamont Dozier
Also see FOUR TOPS
Also see HOLLAND, Brian
Also see HOLLAND, Eddie, & Lamont Dozier

HOLLIDAY, Jennifer

P&R/R&B '82

Singles: 12-inch 33/45rpm

GEFFEN 4-6 83-86

Singles: 7-inch

GEFFEN 3-4 82-87

Picture Sleeves

GEFFEN 3-4 85-86

LPs: 10/12-inch 33rpm

GEFFEN 5-10 82-86

HOLLIES

P&R '64

Singles: 12-inch 33/45rpm

EPIC 5-10 77

Singles: 7-inch

ATLANTIC 3-4 83
EPIC (2000 series) 3-5 71
(Reissue series.)
EPIC (10180 thru 10613) 4-8 67-70
EPIC (10677 "Dandelion Wine") ..5-10 70
EPIC (10716 "Survival of the Fittest") 8-12 71
EPIC (10754 "Row the Boat Together") 5-10 71

EPIC (10842 "The Baby") 5-10 72
EPIC (10871 thru 11100) 3-8 72-74
EPIC (50000 series)..................... 3-5 75-78
IMPERIAL (66026 thru 66070).. 10-15 64-65
IMPERIAL (66099 "Yes I Will").. 20-40 65
IMPERIAL (66119 thru 66258).... 5-10 66-68
IMPERIAL (66271 "If I Needed Someone") 20-40 65
LIBERTY (55674 "Stay") 25-40 64

Picture Sleeves

ATLANTIC.................................. 3-5 83
EPIC... 4-8 67
IMPERIAL 5-10 67

LPs: 10/12-inch 33rpm

ATLANTIC................................ 5-10 83
CAPITOL................................. 5-10 80
EPIC (24315 "Evolution") 15-25 67
(Monaural.)
EPIC (26315 "Evolution") 15-20 67
(Stereo.)
EPIC (26538 "He Ain't Heavy He's My Brother") 10-15 70
EPIC (30255 "Moving Finger") .. 10-15 71
EPIC (KE-30958 "Distant Light") 10-20 72
EPIC (AL-30958 "Distant Light") . 5-10 77
EPIC (31000 thru 35000 series).. 6-12 73-78
IMPERIAL 25-50 64-67
LIBERTY 5-10 84

Also see CLARKE, Allan
Also see EVERLY BROTHERS
Also see NASH, Graham
Also see PARSONS, Alan, Project
Also see SPRINGSTEEN, Bruce / Johnny Winter / Hollies
Also see TREMELOES / Hollies

HOLLIES / Peter Sellers

Singles: 7-inch

U.A. (50079 "After the Fox")...... 10-20 66

LPs: 10/12-inch 33rpm

U.A. (286 "After the Fox")........... 8-10 74
(Soundtrack.)
U.A. (4148 "After the Fox")........ 15-25 66
(Soundtrack. Monaural.)
U.A. (5148 "After the Fox")........ 25-35 66
(Soundtrack. Stereo.)

Also see HOLLIES

HOLLOWAY, Brenda

(With the Carrolls)

P&R/R&B '64

Singles: 7-inch

BREVIT 5-10 63
CATCH (109 You're My Only Love") 15-25 64
DONNA (1358 "Echo") 20-40 62
TAMLA ("Play It Cool, Stay in School") 300-500 60s
(No selection number used. Promotional issue only.)
TAMLA (54094 "Every Little Bit Hurts") 5-10 64
TAMLA (54099 "I'll Always Love You") 10-15 65
TAMLA (54099 "I'll Always Love You") 50-100 65
(Single-sided. Promotional issue only.)
TAMLA (54111 "When I'm Gone") 5-10 65
TAMLA (54115 thru 54137) 10-20 65-66
TAMLA (54144 "Til Johnny Comes") 100-200 67
TAMLA (54148 "Just Look What You've Done") 10-20 67
TAMLA (54155 "I Got to Find It") 10-20 67

Picture Sleeves

TAMLA (54111 "When I'm Gone") 20-40 65

LPs: 10/12-inch 33rpm

TAMLA (257 "Every Little Bit Hurts") 40-60 65

HOLLOWAY, Brenda, & Jess Harris

Singles: 7-inch

BREVIT ("Never Knew You Looked") 25-35 63
(Number not known.)

Also see HOLLOWAY, Brenda

HOLLOWAY, Loleatta

(With the Salsoul Orchestra)

R&B '73

Singles: 12-inch 33/45rpm

SALSOUL 4-8 83
STREETWISE...............................4-8 84

Singles: 7-inch

AWARE 3-5 73-75
GRC 3-5 73
GALAXY...3-5 71
GOLD MINE....................................3-5 76-77
SALSOUL 3-4 77-83

LPs: 10/12-inch 33rpm

GOLD MINE...............................5-10 77

Also see SALSOUL ORCHESTRA

HOLLOWAY, Loleatta, & Bunny Sigler

P&R/R&B '78

Singles: 7-inch

GOLD MINE.....................................3-5 78

Also see HOLLOWAY, Loleatta
Also see SIGLER, Bunny

HOLLY, Buddy

(With the Crickets; with Three Tunes; with Picks)

P&R/R&B '57

Singles: 12-inch 33/45rpm

SOLID SMOKE 5-10 79

Singles: 78rpm

BRUNSWICK (55009 "That'll Be the Day") 75-125 57
BRUNSWICK (55035 "Oh Boy") 75-125 58

BRUNSWICK (55053 "Maybe Baby") 75-125 58
BRUNSWICK (55072 "Think It Over").................................. 75-125 58
BRUNSWICK (55094 "It's So Easy").................................. 75-125 58
CORAL (61852 "Words of Love")................................ 100-150 57
CORAL (61885 "Peggy Sue") . 75-125 57
CORAL (61947 "Listen to Me") 75-125 58
CORAL (61985 "Rave On")..... 75-125 58
CORAL (62006 "Early in the Morning")............................ 75-125 58
CORAL (62051 "Heartbeat")... 75-125 58
DECCA (29854 "Blue Days - Black Nights") 75-125 56
DECCA (30166 "Modern Don Juan").................................. 75-125 56
DECCA (30434 "That'll Be the Day") 75-125 57
DECCA (30543 "Love Me")..... 75-125 58
DECCA (30650 "Ting-A-Ling") 75-125 58

Singles: 7–inch

BRUNSWICK (55009 "That'll Be the Day") 25-35 57
BRUNSWICK (55035 "Oh Boy") 25-35 58
BRUNSWICK (55053 "Maybe Baby") 20-30 58
BRUNSWICK (55072 "Think It Over")...................................... 20-30 58
BRUNSWICK (55094 "It's So Easy")...................................... 20-30 58
CORAL (61852 "Words of Love")................................ 150-200 57
CORAL (61885 "Peggy Sue") ... 20-30 57
CORAL (61947 "Listen to Me") . 20-30 58
CORAL (61985 "Rave On")....... 20-30 58
CORAL (62006 "Early in the Morning")................................ 20-30 58
CORAL (62051 "Heartbeat")..... 20-30 58
CORAL (62074 "It Doesn't Matter Anymore") 20-30 59
CORAL (62134 "Peggy Sue Got Married") 30-40 59
(Orange label.)
CORAL (62134 "Peggy Sue Got Married") 10-20 62
(Yellow label.)
CORAL (62210 "True Love Ways").................................... 30-40 60
CORAL (62329 "Reminiscing") . 20-30 62
CORAL (62352 "Bo Diddley") ... 25-35 63
CORAL (62369 "Brown Eyed Handsome Man") 25-35 63
CORAL (62390 "Rock Around with Ollie Vee")........................ 30-40 64
CORAL (62407 "Maybe Baby"). 30-40 64
CORAL (62448 "Slippin' and Slidin'") 50-75 65
CORAL (62554 "Rave On") 25-35 68
CORAL (62558 "Love Is Strange")..................................15-25 69
CORAL (65618 "That'll Be the Day")......................................15-25 69
DECCA (29854 "Blue Days - Black Nights") 100-150 56
(With silver lines on both sides of the name Decca.)
DECCA (29854 "Blue Days - Black Nights")..................................75-100 56
(With a star and silver lines under the name Decca.)
DECCA (30166 "Modern Don Juan")..................................100-150 56
(With silver lines on both sides of the name Decca.)
DECCA (30166 "Modern Don Juan")..75-100 56
(With a star and silver lines under the name Decca.)
DECCA (30434 "That'll Be the Day")..............................100-150 57
(With silver lines on both sides of the name Decca.)
DECCA (30434 "That'll Be the Day")...............................75-100 57
(With a star and silver lines under the name Decca.)
DECCA (30543 "Love Me")....100-150 58
(With silver lines on both sides of the name Decca.)
DECCA (30543 "Love Me")......75-100 58
(With a star and silver lines under the name Decca.)
DECCA (30650 "Ting-A-Ling")..................................100-150 58
(With silver lines on both sides of the name Decca.)
DECCA (30650 "Ting-A-Ling").75-100 58
(With a star and silver lines under the name Decca.)
MCA..3-6 73-78
MEMORY LANE 3-5

Promotional Singles

BRUNSWICK (55009 "That'll Be the Day")....................................50-75 57
BRUNSWICK (55035 "Oh Boy") 50-75 58
BRUNSWICK (55053 "Maybe Baby") 50-75 58
BRUNSWICK (55072 "Think It Over") 50-75 58
BRUNSWICK (55094 "It's So Easy") 50-75 58
CORAL (61852 "Words of Love")..................................100-200 57
CORAL (61885 "Peggy Sue")....50-75 57
CORAL (61947 "Listen to Me")..50-75 58
CORAL (61985 "Rave On") 50-75 58

CORAL (62006 "Early in the Morning")........................ 50-75 58
CORAL (62051 "Heartbeat")..... 50-75 58
CORAL (62074 "It Doesn't Matter Anymore")............................ 50-75 59
CORAL (62134 "Peggy Sue Got Married")............................ 50-75 59
CORAL (62210 "True Love Ways")................................ 50-75 60
CORAL (62329 "Reminiscing") . 50-75 62
CORAL (62352 "Bo Diddley") ... 50-75 63
CORAL (62369 "Brown Eyed Handsome Man")................. 50-75 63
CORAL (62390 "Rock Around with Ollie Vee")..................... 50-75 64
CORAL (62407 "Maybe Baby"). 50-75 64
CORAL (62448 "Slippin' and Slidin'") 50-75 65
CORAL (62554 "Rave On")...... 40-60 68
CORAL (62558 "Love Is Strange")............................ 40-60 69
(Price doubles if accompanied by dee jay insert sheet.)
CORAL (65618 "That'll Be the Day") 40-60 69
DECCA (29854 "Blue Days - Black Nights") 100-150 56
DECCA (30166 "Modern Don Juan")............................... 100-150 56
DECCA (30434 "That'll Be the Day") 100-150 57
DECCA (30543 "Love Me")... 100-150 58
DECCA (30650 "Ting-A-Ling")................................ 100-150 58

Picture Sleeves

CORAL (62558 "Love Is Strange")............................ 10-15 69
MCA 3-5 78

EPs: 7–inch 33/45rpm

BRUNSWICK (71036 "The Chirping Crickets")......................... 300-350 57
(With printed back cover.)
BRUNSWICK (71036 "The Chirping Crickets")......................... 350-450 57
(With blank back cover.)
BRUNSWICK (71038 "The Sound of the Crickets").................. 100-200 58
CORAL (81169 "Listen to Me").................................. 200-300 58
CORAL (81182 "The Buddy Holly Story") 150-250 59
CORAL (81191 "Buddy Holly")................................ 150-250 62
CORAL (81193 "Brown Eyed Handsome Man") 100-200 63
DECCA (2575 "That'll Be the Day")............................ 500-750 58
(With liner notes on the back cover.)
DECCA (2575 "That'll Be the Day")............................400-600 58
(With EP ads on the back cover.)

LPs: 10/12–inch 33rpm

BRUNSWICK (54038 "The Chirping Crickets") 200-300 57
CORAL (8 "Best of Buddy Holly") 75-125 66
CORAL (57210 "Buddy Holly") 100-150 58
(Maroon label.)
CORAL (57210 "Buddy Holly") ..25-50 63
(Black label.)
CORAL (57279 "The Buddy Holly Story")..........................75-100 59
(Maroon label. With red and black print on the back cover.)
CORAL (57279 "The Buddy Holly Story")............................50-75 59
(Maroon label. With black print on the back cover.)
CORAL (57279 "The Buddy Holly Story")............................30-40 63
(Black label. With pictures of other LPs, or black print, on the back cover.)
CORAL (57326 "The Buddy Holly Story Vol. II")..............100-125 60
(Maroon label.)
CORAL (57326 "The Buddy Holly Story Vol. II")....................25-50 63
(Black label.)
CORAL (57405 "Buddy Holly and the Crickets") 50-75 62
(Maroon label.)
CORAL (57405 "Buddy Holly and the Crickets") 25-45 63
(Black label.)
CORAL (57426 "Reminiscing") ..50-75 63
(Maroon label.)
CORAL (57426 "Reminiscing") ..20-40 63
(Black label.)
CORAL (57450 "Showcase").....40-50 64
CORAL (57463 "Holly in the Hills")..............................75-100 65
CORAL (57492 "Buddy Holly's Greatest Hits") 75-100 67
CORAL (757279 "The Buddy Holly Story")............................25-35 63
(Stereo.)
CORAL (757405 "Buddy Holly and the Crickets") 50-75 62
(Maroon label. Stereo.)
CORAL (757405 "Buddy Holly and the Crickets") 25-45 63
(Black label. Stereo.)
CORAL (757463 "Holly in the Hills")..................................40-60 65
(Stereo.)

CORAL (757504 "Giant") 40-80 69
(Stereo.)
CREATIVE RADIO ("The Day the Music Died")............................ 25-30
(Two-LP set, includes poster.)
DECCA (207 "A Rock & Roll Collection")............................ 15-20 72
DECCA (8707 "That'll Be the Day") 250-350 58
(Black label.)
DECCA (8707 "That'll Be the Day") 150-250 61
(Multi-color label.)
LIFE (8707 "That'll Be the Day") 150-250 61
(Multi-color Decca label, but with "Life" on label instead of Decca. Cover shows Decca, not Life.)
MCA (Except 6-80000)............... 8-12 75-85
MCA (6-80000 "The Complete Buddy Holly") 30-40 81
(Six-LP boxed set.)
VOCALION (3811 "The Great Buddy Holly") 90-110 67
(Monaural.)
VOCALION (73811 "The Great Buddy Holly") 20-30 67
(Reprocessed stereo.)
VOCALION (73923 "Good Rockin' Buddy Holly") 100-125 71
(Reprocessed stereo.)

Promotional LPs

BRUNSWICK (54038 "The Chirping Crickets")............................ 300-350 57
CORAL (Except 757504) 50-75 58-65
CORAL (757504 "Giant") 35-45 69
DECCA (8707 "That'll Be the Day") 350-450 58
(Pink label.)
PICK (1111 "Buddy Holly and the Picks")............................ 10-12 86
Also see BEATLES / Beach Boys / Buddy Holly
Also see CRICKETS
Also see FREED, Alan
Also see JENNINGS, Waylon
Also see KING, Ben E.
Also see PETTY, Norman, Trio
Also see PRESLEY, Elvis / Buddy Holly

HOLLY & ITALIANS
(Featuring Holly Beth Vincent)

LP '81

Singles: 7-inch

OVAL.. 3-5
VIRGIN.. 3-4 82

Picture Sleeves

OVAL.. 3-5

LPs: 10/12-inch 33rpm

VIRGIN.. 5-10 81-82

HOLLYRIDGE STRINGS
(Stu Phillips & Hollyridge Strings)

P&R/LP '64

Singles: 7-inch

CAPITOL.......................................3-6 61-68

EPs: 7-inch 33/45rpm

CAPITOL (2626 "Selections from *Beatles Songbook*") 5-10 64
(Promotional issue only.)

LPs: 10/12-inch 33rpm

CAPITOL.......................................5-15 64-78
Also see GOLDEN GATE STRINGS

HOLLYWOOD ARGYLES

P&R/R&B '60

Singles: 7-inch

ABC...3-4 74
CHATTAHOOCHEE 4-8 65
ERA...3-5 72
FELSTED.......................................4-8 63
FINER ARTS...................................4-8 61
LUTE...5-10 60
PAXLEY 5-10 61

LPs: 10/12-inch 33rpm

LUTE (9001 "Alley Oop") 250-350 60
Members: Gary Paxton; Gary Webb; Bobby Rey
Session: Gaynel Hodge.

HOLLYWOOD FLAMES
(Dave Ford & Hollywood Flames)

P&R/R&B '57

Singles: 78rpm

DECCA 15-30 54-55
EBB...5-10 57-59
LUCKY (001 "One Night with a Fool") 50-100 54
LUCKY (006 "Peggy")...............50-100 54
LUCKY (009 "Let's Talk It Over") 40-60 54
MONEY (202 "I'm Leaving").......25-50 54
SWING TIME (345 "Let's Talk It Over") 50-75 53
SWING TIME (346 "Go and Get Some More")...............................50-75 54

Singles: 7-inch

ATCO 5-10 59-60
CHESS..10-15 61
DECCA (29285 "Peggy") 50-60 54
DECCA (48331 "Let's Talk It Over") 50-60 55
EBB (119 "Buzz, Buzz, Buzz")....15-25 57
EBB (131 "Give Me Back My Heart")...10-20 58
EBB (144 "Strollin' on the Beach") 10-20 58
EBB (146 "Chains of Love").......10-20 58
EBB (149 "A Star Fell") 10-20 58
EBB (153 "Just for You")............15-25 58
EBB (158 "So Good")..................10-20 58
EBB (162 "Now That You've Gone") 10-20 59

EBB (163 "In the Dark") 10-20 59
GOLDIE.. 5-8 62
LUCKY (001 "One Night with a Fool")................................ 200-300 54
LUCKY (006 "Peggy") 200-300 54
LUCKY (009 "Let's Talk It Over")................................ 150-225 54
MONA-LEE (135 "Buzz, Buzz, Buzz")...................................... 10-20 59
MONEY (202 "I'm Leaving").. 200-300 54
SWING TIME (345 "Let's Talk It Over")............................ 300-400 53
SWING TIME (346 "Go and Get Some More")...................... 300-400 54
SYMBOL 5-10 65-66
VEE JAY 8-12 63

LPs: 10/12–inch 33rpm

SPECIALTY 6-10 88

Members: David Ford; Bobby Byrd; Gaynel Hodge; Clyde Tillis; Earl Nelson; Curtis Williams; Donald Height; Ray Brewster; John Berry; George Home.

HOLLYWOOD STARS

P&R '77

Singles: 7–inch

ARISTA 3-5 77

LPs: 10/12–inch 33rpm

ARISTA 8-10 77

Also see KINKS / Hollywood Stars

HOLLYWOOD STUDIO ORCHESTRA

LP '61

Singles: 7–inch

U.A. 4-8 59

LPs: 10/12–inch 33rpm

U.A. 10-15 61

HOLM, Michael

P&R '74

Singles: 7–inch

MERCURY 3-5 74

HOLMAN, Eddie

R&B '65

Singles: 7–inch

ABC.. 3-5 69-71
AGAPE... 3-4 82
ASCOT 5-10 63
BELL 10-20 68
DON-EL.................................... 10-20
GSF 3-6 73
PARKWAY 10-20 65-67
SALSOUL..................................... 3-5 77
SILVER BLUE 3-5 74

LPs: 10/12–inch 33rpm

ABC-PAR 10-12 70
SALSOUL.................................. 5-10 77

Also see HOLMAN, Eddie

HOLMAN, Eddie / Lamplighters

Singles: 7–inch

SCRIPT (12212 "Never Let Go")10-20
(Colored vinyl. Promotional issue only.)

HOLMES, Clint

P&R/LP '73

Singles: 7–inch

EPIC...3-5 73
PRIVATE STOCK 3-5 76-79

LPs: 10/12–inch 33rpm

EPIC..10-12 73

HOLMES, Jake

P&R/LP '70

Singles: 7–inch

COLUMBIA 3-5 71-72
POLYDOR 3-5 70
TOWER...4-6 67

Picture Sleeves

TOWER...4-6 67

LPs: 10/12–inch 33rpm

POLYDOR 8-12 70
TOWER......................................10-15 67

HOLMES, Jan

R&B '85

Singles: 7–inch

JAY JAY..3-4 85

HOLMES, Leroy, Orchestra

P&R '54

Singles: 78rpm

MGM 3-5 51-57

Singles: 7–inch

MGM 4-8 51-61
METRO 3-6 59
U.A. 3-5 67-68

Picture Sleeves

U.A. 4-8 67

EPs: 7–inch 33/45rpm

MGM 4-8 52-56
U.A. (10041 "Leroy Holmes & His Orchestra") 4-8 67
(Promotional issue only.)

LPs: 10/12–inch 33rpm

LION...5-10 59-60
MGM 5-15 52-62
U.A. 4-8 67-68

HOLMES, Richard "Groove"

P&R/R&B/LP '66

Singles: 7–inch

BLUE NOTE..................................3-5 71
FLYING DUTCHMAN 3-5 76
PACIFIC JAZZ 4-8 61-69
PRESTIGE.....................................3-6 66-69

LPs: 10/12–inch 33rpm

BLUE NOTE...............................5-10 71
FLYING DUTCHMAN 5-10 75-76
GROOVE MERCHANT...............5-10 72-75
LOMA..10-15 66
MUSE...5-10 78-80
PACIFIC JAZZ (Except 20000 series) 15-25 61-62

PACIFIC JAZZ (20000 series) 8-15 68-69
PRESTIGE 8-15 66-70
VERSATILE 5-10 78
W.B. 10-20 64
WORLD PACIFIC JAZZ 8-12 70
Also see AMMONS, Gene, & Richard "Groove" Holmes
Also see JONES, Brenda, & "Groove" Holmes
Also see McGRIFF, Jimmy
Also see WITHERSPOON, Jimmy

HOLMES, Richard "Groove," & Les McCann

LPs: 10/12-inch 33rpm

PACIFIC JAZZ 15-25 62
Also see HOLMES, Richard "Groove"
Also see McCANN, Les

HOLMES, Rupert

P&R '78

Singles: 7-inch

EPIC 3-6 74-76
INFINITY 3-5 79
MCA 3-4 80-81
PRIVATE STOCK 3-4 78

Picture Sleeves

EPIC 3-4 75

LPs: 10/12-inch 33rpm

ELEKTRA 5-10 81
EPIC 8-12 74-75
EXCELSIOR 5-8 80-81
INFINITY 5-10 79
MCA 5-10 80
PRIVATE STOCK 5-10 78
Also see CUFF LINKS
Also see STREET PEOPLE

HOMBRES

P&R/LP '67

Singles: 7-inch

SUN 4-8 69
VERVE/FORECAST (Except 5058) 4-8 67-68
VERVE/FORECAST (5058 "Let It All Hang Out") 5-10 67
VERVE/FORECAST (5058 "Let It Out") 4-8 67
(Note shortened title.)

LPs: 10/12-inch 33rpm

VERVE/FORECAST 15-20 67

HOMER & JETHRO

C&W/P&R '49

Singles: 78rpm

KING 5-15 46-53
FEDERAL 8-15 51
RCA 5-10 50-58

Singles: 7-inch

BLUEBIRD 4-8 59
KING 3-6 63
RCA (0100 series) 30-50 50
(Colored vinyl.)
RCA (0100 thru 0468) 15-30 50-51
(Black vinyl.)
RCA (0500 series) 3-5 71
RCA (4290 thru 7704) 10-20 51-59
RCA (47-7744 "Sink the Bismarck") 8-12 60
(Monaural.)
RCA (61-7744 "Sink the Bismarck") 15-25 60
(Stereo.)
RCA (7790 thru 9922) 4-8 60-70

Picture Sleeves

RCA (5000 series) 8-12 53
RCA (8000 series) 3-6 64

EPs: 7-inch 33/45rpm

AUDIO LAB 10-20 59
KING 15-25 53-54
RCA 15-25 53-57

LPs: 10/12-inch 33rpm

AUDIO LAB (1513 "Musical Madness") 25-50 58
CAMDEN 10-20 62-71
DIPLOMAT 8-12
GUEST STAR 10-15 63
KING (639 "They Sure Are Corny") 20-30 59
KING (800 series) 10-20 63
KING (1000 series) 8-12 67
NASHVILLE 8-12 69
RCA (1412 "Barefoot Ballads") .. 30-40 57
RCA (1516 "Worst of Homer & Jethro") 40-50 57
RCA (LPM-1880 "Life Can Be Miserable") 25-35 58
(Monaural.)
RCA (LSP-1880 "Life Can Be Miserable") 35-50 58
(Stereo.)
RCA (2100 thru 2900 series) 10-20 60-64
(Monaural. With "LPM" prefix.)
RCA (2100 thru 2900 series) 15-25 60-64
(Stereo. With "LSP" prefix.)
RCA (3112 "Homer & Jethro Fracture Frank Loesser") 50-100 53
(10–inch LP.)
RCA (3300 thru 4600 series) 8-15 65-72
Members: Henry "Homer" Haynes; Kenneth "Jethro" Burns.
Also see ANN-MARGRET
Also see FOUR LOVERS / Homer & Jethro

HOMER & JETHRO with June Carter

C&W '49

Singles: 78rpm

RCA 5-10 49
Also see HOMER & JETHRO

HONDELLS

P&R/LP '64

Singles: 7-inch

AMOS 4-8 69-70
COLUMBIA 5-10 67-68

MERCURY (72324 "Little Honda") 10-15 64
MERCURY (72366 "My Buddy Seat") 10-15 64
MERCURY (72405 "Little Sidewalk Surfer Girl") 8-12 65
MERCURY (72443 "Sea of Love") 8-12 65
MERCURY (72479 "Sea Cruise") 5-10 65
MERCURY (72523 "Follow Your Heart") 5-10 66
MERCURY (72563 "Younger Girl") 5-10 67
MERCURY (72605 "Kissin' My Life Away") 5-10 67

Promotional Singles

MERCURY (72324 "Hot Rod High") 20-25 64
(Shows *Hot Rod High* as the "A" side.)
MERCURY (72324 "Little Honda")15-20 64
(Shows *Little Honda* as the "A" side.)
MERCURY (72366 "My Buddy Seat") 15-20 64
MERCURY (72405 thru 72605) .. 8-12 65-67

Picture Sleeves

MERCURY (72366 "My Buddy Seat") 10-20 64
MERCURY (72479 "Sea Cruise") 10-20 65

LPs: 10/12-inch 33rpm

MERCURY (20940 "Go, Little Honda") 20-25 64
(Monaural.)
MERCURY (60940 "Go, Little Honda") 25-30 64
(Stereo.)
MERCURY (20982 "Hondells"). 20-25 64
(Monaural.)
MERCURY (20982 "Hondells"). 25-30 65
(Stereo.)

Members: Chuck Girard; Richard Burns; Brian Wilson; Wayne Edwards; Glen Campbell; Joe Kelly; Bruce Johnston; Terry Melcher; Jerry Naylor; Gary Usher. Session: Davie Allan.

Also see ALLEN, Davie
Also see BRUCE & TERRY
Also see CAMPBELL, Glen
Also see NAYLOR, Jerry
Also see WILSON, Brian

HONDELLS / Del Shannon / Martha & Vandellas

EPs: 7-inch 33/45rpm

PEPSI-COLA (8256 "Pepsi-Cola Ad Radio Youth Market, 1966") 15-20 66
(Promotional issue only.)

Also see MARTHA & VANDELLAS
Also see SHANNON, Del

HONDELLS / Dusty Springfield

Singles: 7-inch

COLLECTABLES 3-4 86

Also see HONDELLS
Also see SPRINGFIELD, Dusty

HONEY CONE

P&R/R&B '69

Singles: 7-inch

HOT WAX 3-6 69-76

LPs: 10/12-inch 33rpm

HOT WAX 8-10 70-72

Members: Edna Wright; Carolyn Willis; Shellie Clark; Sharon Cash.

Also see BOB B. SOXX & Blue Jeans
Also see GIRLFRIENDS

HONEYCOMBS

P&R '64

Singles: 7-inch

INTERPHON 5-10 64-65
W.B. 5-10 65-66

Picture Sleeves

INTERPHON (7713 "I Can't Stop") 10-20 64

LPs: 10/12-inch 33rpm

INTERPHON (88001 "Here Are the Honeycombs") 20-30 64
VEE JAY (88001 "Here Are the Honeycombs") 35-45 64

Members: Honey Lantree; John Lantree; Martin Murray; Denis D'Ell; Alan Ward.

HONEYCONES

P&R '58

Singles: 7-inch

EMBER 8-12 58-59

HONEYCUTT, Miki

R&B '77

Singles: 7-inch

PAULA 3-5 77

HONEYDRIPPERS

P&R/LP '84

Singles: 7-inch

ESPARANZA 3-4 84-85

Picture Sleeves

ESPARANZA 3-4 84-85

LPs: 10/12-inch 33rpm

ESPARANZA 5-10 84

Members: Jeff Beck; Jimmy Page; Robert Plant; Nile Rodgers.

Also see BECK, Jeff
Also see CHIC
Also see PAGE, Jimmy
Also see PLANT, Robert
Also see RODGERS, Nile

HONEYMOON SUITE

P&R/LP '84

Singles: 7-inch

W.B. 3-4 84-88

Picture Sleeves

W.B. 3-4 84-88

LPs: 10/12-inch 33rpm

W.B. 5-10 84-88

HOODOO GURUS

LP '86

Singles: 7-inch

A&M	3-4	85
RCA	3-4	89-90

LPs: 10/12-inch 33rpm

A&M	5-10	85
ELEKTRA	5-10	86-87
RCA	5-8	89-91

Members: David Faulkner; Rick Grossman.

Also see DIVINYLS

HOOK, Dr: see DR. HOOK

HOOKER, Frank, & Positive People

R&B '79

Singles: 7-inch

PANORAMA	3-4	79-80

HOOKER, John Lee

R&B '49

Singles: 78rpm

CHART	5-10	53
CHESS	20-40	52-54
JVB	15-30	53
MODERN	5-15	48-56
REGAL	8-12	50-51
SENSATION	8-12	49-50
SPECIALTY	5-10	54
VEE JAY	8-15	55-60

Singles: 7-inch

ABC	3-5	71-73
BATTLE	4-8	62
BLUESWAY	4-6	67-69
CHART	10-15	53
CHESS (1505 "High Priced Woman")	150-250	52
CHESS (1513 "Walkin' the Boogie")	40-80	52
CHESS (1562 "It's My Own Fault")	30-50	54
CHESS (1900 series)	4-8	66
ELMOR	5-8	
FEDERAL	5-10	60
FORTUNE	5-10	60
GALAXY	4-8	63
HI-Q	4-8	61
JVB (30 "Boogie Rambler")	50-75	53
JEWEL	3-5	70-77
KING	3-5	70
LAUREN	4-8	61
MODERN (835 "How Can You Do It")	30-60	51
MODERN (862 "Cold Chills All Over Me")	30-60	52
MODERN (886 "Bluebird Blues")	30-60	52
MODERN (893 "New Boogie Chillen")	30-60	52
MODERN (897 "Rock House Boogie")	30-60	53
MODERN (901 "It's a Stormin' and Rainin'")	25-50	53
MODERN (908 "Love Money Can't Buy")	25-50	53
MODERN (916 "Too Much Boogie")	25-50	53
MODERN (923 "Down Child")	25-50	54
MODERN (931 "I Wonder Little Darling")	25-50	54
MODERN (935 "I Tried Hard")	20-40	54
MODERN (942 "Cool Little Car")	20-40	54
MODERN (948 "Half a Stranger")	20-40	55
MODERN (958 "You Receive Me")	20-40	55
MODERN (966 "Hug & Squeeze")	20-40	55
MODERN (978 "Lookin' for a Woman")	20-40	56
SPECIALTY (528 "Everybody's Blues")	20-40	54
STARDAY	3-5	70
STAX	4-6	69
VEE JAY (164 "Mambo Chillen")	20-30	55
VEE JAY (188 "Every Night")	20-30	56
VEE JAY (205 "Baby Lee")	20-30	56
VEE JAY (233 "I'm So Worried, Baby")	15-25	57
VEE JAY (245 "I'm So Excited")	15-25	57
VEE JAY (255 "Little Wheel")	15-25	57
VEE JAY (265 "You Can Lead Me, Baby")	15-25	58
VEE JAY (293 "I Love You Honey")	15-25	58
VEE JAY (308 "Maudie")	15-25	59
VEE JAY (319 "Tennessee Blues")	15-25	59
VEE JAY (331 "Hobo Blues")	15-25	59
VEE JAY (349 "No Shoes")	15-25	60
VEE JAY (366 "Dusty Road")	15-25	60
VEE JAY (397 "Want Ad Blues")	15-25	60
VEE JAY (438 "Boom Boom")	10-15	62
VEE JAY (453 "She's Mine")	10-15	62
VEE JAY (493 "I Love Her")	25-50	63
VEE JAY (538 thru 708)	8-15	63-65

EPs: 7-inch 33/45rpm

IMPULSE	8-10	66

(Jukebox issues only.)

LPs: 10/12-inch 33rpm

ABC	8-12	71-74
ARCHIVE of FOLK MUSIC	10-12	68
ATCO (151 "Don't Turn Me from Your Door")	20-25	63

(Monaural.)

ATCO (SD-151 "Don't Turn Me from Your Door")	25-30	63

(Stereo.)

ATLANTIC 8-10 72
BATTLE 10-12
BLUESWAY 10-15 66-73
BRYLEN 5-10 84
BUDDAH 12-15 69
CHAMELEON 5-8 89
CHESS (1438 "House of the Blues") 25-35 61
CHESS (1454 "John Lee Hooker Plays and Sings the Blues") 25-35 61
CHESS (1500 series) 15-20 66
CROWN 10-20 62-63
CUSTOM 10-15
EVEREST 5-10 79-83
EXODUS 8-10
FANTASY 8-10 72-77
FORTUNE 8-12 69
GNP 8-10 74
GALAXY (201 "John Lee Hooker") 20-30 63
GREEN BOTTLE 10-12 72
IMPULSE 12-15 66
JEWEL 10-12 71
KENT 10-12 71
KING (727 "John Lee Hooker Sings Blues") 30-50 61
KING (1000 series) 10-12 70
MCA 5-10 83
MUSE 5-10 80
SPECIALTY 10-15 70
(Black and gold label.)
SPECIALTY 5-10 88
(Black and white label.)
STAX (2000 series) 10-12 69
STAX (4000 series) 8-10 77
TOMATO 5-10 78
TRADITION 10-12 69
TRIP 8-10 73-78
UNITED 10-12
U.A. 12-15 71-73
VEE JAY (1007 "I'm John Lee Hooker") 40-60 59
(Maroon label.)
VEE JAY (1007 "I'm John Lee Hooker") 20-30 61
(Black label.)
VEE JAY (1023 thru 1043) 25-40 60-62
VEE JAY (1049 thru 1078) 15-25 62-64
VERVE/FOLKWAYS 10-15 66
WAND 10-12 70

Also see BIRMINGHAM SAM & His Magic Guitar
Also see BOOGIE MAN
Also see BOOKER, John Lee
Also see COOKER, John Lee
Also see DELTA JOHN
Also see JOHN LEE
Also see JOHNNY LEE
Also see LITTLE PORK CHOPS
Also see MARTHA & VANDELLAS
Also see McGHEE, Sticks / John Lee Hooker
Also see MEMPHIS SLIM
Also see TEXAS SLIM
Also see WILLIAMS, Johnny

HOOKER, John Lee, & Canned Heat

LP '71

Singles: 7-inch

U.A. 3-5 71

LPs: 10/12-inch 33rpm

LIBERTY 10-15 71
RHINO 5-10 82

Also see CANNED HEAT

HOOKER, John Lee / Lightnin' Hopkins / J. Carroll

LPs: 10/12-inch 33rpm

GUEST STAR 15-20 64

Also see HOPKINS, Lightnin'

HOOKER, John Lee, & Little Eddie Kirkland

Singles: 78rpm

MODERN 5-10 52

Singles: 7-inch

MODERN (876 "It's Hurts Me So ") 30-60 52

HOOKER, John Lee / Eddie Kirkland / Eddie Burns / Sylvester Cotton

LPs: 10/12-inch 33rpm

UNITED (7783 "Detroit Blues") .. 10-20

Also see HOOKER, John Lee

HOOPER, Stix

LP '79

Singles: 7-inch

MCA 3-4 79-82

LPs: 10/12-inch 33rpm

MCA 5-10 79-82

Also see BUTLER, Jerry, & Stix Hooper
Also see CRUSADERS

HOOTERS

P&R/LP '85

Singles: 7-inch

ANTENNA (84 "Hanging on to a Heartbeat") 4-8 84
COLUMBIA 3-4 85-89
88 PERCENT (80 "Fightin' on the Same Side") 5-10 81
88 PERCENT (82 "All You Zombies") 5-10 82
MONTAGE 3-4 83

Picture Sleeves

COLUMBIA 3-4 85-87
88 PERCENT ("Fightin' on the Same Side") 5-10 81
88 PERCENT (82 "All You Zombies") 5-10 82

LPs: 10/12-inch 33rpm

COLUMBIA 5-10 85-89

Members: Rob Hyman; Eric Bazillian.
Also see CONWELL, Tommy, & Young Rumblers
Also see LAUPER, Cyndi

HOPE, Bob

LP '76

Singles: 78rpm

CAPITOL 3-5 52
RCA 3-5 56

Singles: 7-inch

CAPITOL 5-10 52
RCA 5-10 56

LPs: 10/12-inch 33rpm

CAPITOL 5-10 76
DECCA 10-20 63
RCA 15-25 60

Also see BACKUS, Jim
Also see CROSBY, Bing, & Bob Hope
Also see MARTIN, Dean

HOPE, Bob, & Eydie Adams

Singles: 7-inch

U.A. 4-6 63

Picture Sleeves

U.A. 4-8 63

HOPE, Bob, & Rosemary Clooney

Singles: 7-inch

RCA 4-8 59

Also see HOPE, Bob
Also see CLOONEY, Rosemary

HOPE, Ellie

D&D '83

Singles: 12-inch 33/45rpm

QUALITY 4-6 83

HOPE, Lynn

(Lynn Hope Quintet)

R&B '50

Singles: 78rpm

ALADDIN 4-6 54-56
PREMIUM 3-6 50

Singles: 7-inch

ALADDIN 10-20 54-56
KING 5-10 60

LPs: 10/12-inch 33rpm

ALADDIN (707 "Lynn Hope & His Tenor Sax") 100-150 55
(10-inch LP.)
ALADDIN (850 "Lynn Hope") .. 75-100 56
IMPERIAL 15-20 62
KING 15-25 61
SCORE (4015 "Tenderly") 25-50 57

HOPKIN, Mary

(Mary Hopkins)

P&R '68

Singles: 7-inch

APPLE/AMERICOM (238 "Those Were the Days") 150-250 69
(Four-inch flexi, "pocket disc.")
APPLE 4-8 68-72
ESKEE 4-8 66
RCA 3-5 76

Promotional Singles

APPLE 8-12 68-72
ESKEE 4-8 66
RCA 3-5 76

Picture Sleeves

APPLE 5-10 68-70

LPs: 10/12-inch 33rpm

AIR 8-10 72
APPLE 10-15 69-72

HOPKINS, Lightnin'

(Lightning Hopkins)

R&B '49

Singles: 78rpm

ACE 5-10 56
ALADDIN (3063 thru 3262) 25-50 50
CHART 4-8 55
DECCA 5-10 53
GOLD STAR (Except 671) 5-10 47-50
GOLD STAR (671 "Henny Penny Blues") 20-25 50
HARLEM 10-20 54-55
HERALD 5-10 54-55
LIGHTNING 20-30 55
MERCURY 5-10 52
MODERN 8-12 47-49
RPM 5-10 52-54
SITTIN' in WITH 5-10 51-53
TNT 20-30 53-54

Singles: 7-inch

ACE (516 "My Little Kewpie Doll") 20-30 56
ALADDIN (3063 "Shotgun") 75-100 50
ALADDIN (3077 "Moonrise Blues") 75-100 50
ALADDIN (3096 "Abilene") 75-100 51
ALADDIN (3117 "You Are Not Going to Worry My Life Anymore") 75-100 52
ALADDIN (3262 "My California") 50-75 54
ARHOOLIE 4-8 65
BLUESVILLE 5-15 60-63
CANDID 4-8 60-62
CHART 10-20 55
DART 5-10 60
DECCA (28841 "War Is Over") .. 15-25 53
DECCA (48306 "Merry Christmas") 15-25 53
DECCA (48312 "Highway Blues") 15-25 53
DECCA (48321 "I'm Wild About You, Baby") 15-25 53
FIRE 4-8 61
FLASHBACK 3-6 65
HARLEM (2321 "Contrary Mary") 100-150 54
HARLEM (2324 "Lightnin's Boogie") 100-150 54
HARLEM (2331 "Fast Life") ... 100-150 55
HARLEM (2336 "Old Woman Blues") 100-150 55

HERALD (425 "Lightnin's Boogie")	20-30	54
HERALD (428 "Lightnin's Special")	20-30	54
HERALD (436 "Sick Feeling Blues")	20-30	54
HERALD (443 "Nothin' But the Blues")	20-30	54
HERALD (449 "They Wonder Who I Am")	20-30	55
HERALD (500 series)	10-20	59-60
IMPERIAL	10-15	62
IVORY	8-12	61
JAX (315 "No Good Woman") (Colored vinyl.)	150-250	53
JAX (318 "Automobile") (Colored vinyl.)	150-250	53
JAX (321 "Contrary Mary") (Colored vinyl.)	150-250	54
JAX (635 "Coffee Blues") (Colored vinyl.)	100-200	54
JAX (642 "You Caused My Heart to Weep") (Colored vinyl.)	100-200	54
JEWEL	3-6	68-72
KENT	3-5	
KIMBERLEY	5-10	60
LIGHTNING (104 "Unsuccessful Blues")	250-350	55
MERCURY (70081 "Ain't It a Shame")	50-75	52
MERCURY (70191 "My Mama Told Me")	50-75	52
MERCURY (8274 "Sad News from Korea")	50-75	52
MERCURY (8293 "Gone with the Wind")	50-75	52
PRESTIGE	4-8	60-67
RPM (337 "Beggin' You to Stay")	25-40	51
RPM (346 "Jake Head")	50-75	52
RPM (351 "Don't Keep My Baby Long")	50-75	52
RPM (359 "Needed Time")	50-75	52
RPM (378 "Another Fool in Town")	50-75	53
RPM (388 "Black Cat")	50-75	53
RPM (398 "Sante Fe")	50-75	54
SHAD	5-10	59
SITTIN' in WITH (621 "New York Boogie") (Colored vinyl.)	150-250	51
SITTIN' in WITH (635 "Coffee Blues") (Colored vinyl.)	150-250	52
SITTIN' in WITH (642 "You Caused My Heart to Weep") (Colored vinyl.)	150-250	52
SITTIN' in WITH (644 "Jailhouse Blues") (Colored vinyl.)	150-250	52
SITTIN' in WITH (647 "Dirty House") (Colored vinyl.)	150-250	52
SITTIN' in WITH (652 "Papa Bones Boogie") (Colored vinyl.)	150-250	52
SITTIN' in WITH (658 "Broken Hearted Blues") (Colored vinyl.)	150-250	53
SITTIN' in WITH (660 "I've Been A Bad Man") (Colored vinyl.)	150-250	53
SITTIN' in WITH (661 "Down to the River") (Colored vinyl.)	150-250	53
TNT (8002 "Late in the Evening")	200-300	54
TNT (8003 "Leavin' Blues")	200-300	54
TNT (8010 "Moanin' Blues")	200-300	55
VAULT	3-5	70

Even among blues experts there is confusion over which of the Jax and Sittin' in With singles were pressed on colored plastic, which were on black, and which came both ways. Any additional information will appear in the first available edition of *Rockin' Records.*

LPs: 10/12–inch 33rpm

ARHOOLIE	10-15	68
BARNABY	8-10	71
BULLDOG	12-15	65
CANDID	20-30	61
COLLECTABLES	6-8	88
CROWN	20-25	61
DART	10-15	
EVEREST (241 "Lightnin' Hopkins")	10-15	69
EVEREST (342 "Autobiography in Blues")	5-10	79
FANTASY	8-10	72-81
FIRE (104 "Mojo Hand")	75-100	62
GUEST STAR	15-20	64
HARLEM HITPARADE	5-10	
HERALD (1012 "Lightnin' and the Blues")	100-200	60
IMPERIAL	20-30	62
INTERNATIONAL ARTISTS (6 "Free Form Patterns")	50-100	68
JAZZ MAN	5-10	82
JEWEL	10-12	67-70
MAINSTREAM	8-10	71-74
MOUNT VERNON	15-20	
OLYMPIC	8-10	73
PICKWICK	8-10	
POPPY	12-15	69
PRESTIGE	10-15	65-70

PRESTIGE/BLUESVILLE 20-25 61-64
RHINO 5-10 82
SCORE (4022 "Lightnin' Hopkins Strums the Blues") 50-75 59
SOUL PARADE 8-10
TIME 25-30 60-62
TOMATO 5-10 77
TRADITION (1035 thru 1040) ... 20-30 60
TRADITION (1056 thru 2000) ... 10-15 67-72
TRIP 5-10 71-78
UNITED 8-10
UPFRONT 8-12
VAULT 10-12 69
VEE JAY 20-30 62
VERVE 15-20 62
VERVE/FOLKWAYS 12-15 65-67

Also see HOOKER, John Lee / Lightnin' Hopkins / Johnny Carroll

HOPKINS, Lightnin,' & Sonny Terry

Singles: 7-inch

PRESTIGE BLUESVILLE 4-8 61

LPs: 10/12-inch 33rpm

PRESTIGE BLUESVILLE 15-20 61-63

Also see TERRY, Sonny

HOPKINS, Lightnin' / Brownie McGhee & Sonny Terry

LPs: 10/12-inch 33rpm

HORIZON (WP-1617 "Blues Hoot") 20-25 63
(Monaural.)
HORIZON (ST-1617 "Blues Hoot") 25-30 63
(Stereo.)

Also see McGHEE, Brownie, & Sonny Terry

HOPKINS, Lightnin,' & Thunder Smith

Singles: 78rpm

ALADDIN (165 "West Coast Blues") 50-100 47
ALADDIN (167 "Katie Mae Blues") 50-100 47
ALADDIN (168 "Feel So Bad") 50-100 47

Also see HOPKINS, Lightnin'

HOPKINS, Nicky

LP '72

Singles: 7-inch

COLUMBIA 3-5 72
DECCA (32139 "Mr. Pleasant") .. 5-10 67

LPs: 10/12-inch 33rpm

COLUMBIA 8-10 73
ROLLING STONE 10-15 72

Session: Mick Jagger; Bill Wyman; Charlie Watts; Ry Cooder.
Also see COODER, Ry
Also see JEFFERSON AIRPLANE
Also see LORD SUTCH
Also see NIGHT
Also see QUICKSILVER
Also see ROLLING STONES

HORAN, Eddie

R&B '78

Singles: 7-inch

HDM 3-5 78
MGM 3-5 74

HORN, Paul

R&B '78

Singles: 7-inch

MUSHROOM 3-5 78

HORN, Paul

R&B '78

Singles: 7-inch

MUSHROOM 3-5 78

LP: 10/12-inch 33rpm

COLUMBIA (36803 "Jingle Bell Jazz") 5-8 85
COLUMBIA (1677 thru 2050) 20-30 61-63
(Monaural.)
COLUMBIA (8477 thru 8850) 25-35 61-63
(Stereo.)
DOT (3091 "House of Horn") 40-60 57
DOT (9002 "Plenty of Horn") 40-60 58
EPIC 6-12 69-76
EVEREST 5-10 75
GPB 5-8 87
HI-FI JAZZ (615 "Something Blue") 30-50 60
IMPULSE 5-10 78
KUCKUCK 5-10 80-88
MUSHROOM 5-10 77-78
OVATION 8-12 70
RCA (3414 thru 3613) 15-25 65-66
(With "LPM" prefix. Monaural.)
RCA (3414 thru 3613) 15-30 65-66
(With "LSP" prefix. Stereo.)
SHELTER 8-12 71
WHO'S WHO in JAZZ 5-8 86-88
WORLD PACIFIC (Except 1266) 10-20 67-68
WORLD PACIFIC (1266 Impressions") 30-50 59

HORNE, Jimmy "Bo"

R&B '75

Singles: 12-inch 33/45rpm

SUNSHINE SOUND 4-8 79

Singles: 7-inch

ALSTON 3-5 75-77
DADE (2031 "I Can't Speak") 35-55
SUNSHINE SOUND 3-5 77-80

LPs: 10/12-inch 33rpm

SUNSHINE SOUND 5-10 78-80

HORNE, Lena

P&R '43

Singles: 78rpm

RCA 3-5 52-57

Singles: 7-inch

BUDDAH 3-5 71

CHARTER 4-6 63
DRG 3-4 86
GRYPHON 3-5 76
MCA 3-4 78
RCA (4000 thru 7000 series) 5-10 52-61
20TH FOX 4-6 63-64
U.A. 3-6 65-66

Picture Sleeves

RCA 4-8 62

EPs: 7–inch 33/45rpm

MGM 5-10 54-55
RCA 5-10 56-59

LPs: 10/12–inch 33rpm

BUDDAH 5-10 71
CAMDEN 10-20 56
CHARTER 10-15 63
CORONET 5-10
DRG 5-10 86
GOLDEN TONE 5-10
GRYPHON 5-10 75-76
LIBERTY 5-8 81
MFSL (094 "A Lady and Her Music") 20-40 82
MGM 15-30 54-55
POLYDOR 4-8
QWEST 5-10 81
RCA (Except 4300 series) 10-30 52-63
RCA (4300 series) 4-8 81
SPRINGBOARD 4-8 77
TOPS 15-30 56
20TH FOX 8-15 64
U.A. 8-15 65-66

Also see BELAFONTE, Harry, & Lena Horne
Also see FITZGERALD, Ella / Billie Holiday / Lena Horne

HORNE, Lena, & Michel Legrand

LPs: 10/12–inch 33rpm

GRYPHON 5-10 75

Also see LEGRAND, Michel

HORNE, Lena, & Gabor Szabo

LP '70

LPs: 10/12–inch 33rpm

SKYE 8-12 70

Also see HORNE, Lena
Also see SZABO, Gabor

HORNSBY, Bruce, & Range

P&R/LP '86

Singles: 7–inch

RCA 3-4 86-90

Picture Sleeves

RCA 3-4 87-88

LPs: 10/12–inch 33rpm

RCA 5-10 86-90

Also see HENLEY, Don

HORSLIPS

LP '78

Singles: 7–inch

DJM (Except 1036) 3-5 77-79
DJM (1036 "Sure the Boy Was Green") 4-8 77
(Colored vinyl.)
MERCURY 3-5 79
RCA 3-5 75

LPs: 10/12–inch 33rpm

ATCO 10-12 73-74
DJM 5-10 77-79
MERCURY 5-10 79-80
RCA 8-10 74

Members: Eamon Carr; John Fean; Jim Lockhart; Barry Devlin; Charles O'Connor.

HORTON, Jamie

P&R '60

Singles: 7–inch

ERIC 3-5 68
JOY 8-12 59-61

HORTON, Johnny

C&W '56

Singles: 78rpm

ABBOTT 10-15 51-52
COLUMBIA 5-15 56-57
CORMAC
MERCURY 5-15 54-55

Singles: 7–inch

ABBOTT (100 "Candy Jones") 20-30 51
ABBOTT (101 "Happy Millionaire") 20-30 51
ABBOTT (102 "Plaid and Calico") 20-30 51
ABBOTT (103 "Birds and Butterflies") 20-30 51
ABBOTT (104 "Go and Wash") 20-30 51
ABBOTT (105 "Shadows on the Old Bayou") 20-30 51
ABBOTT (106 "Words") 20-30 51
ABBOTT (107 "Long Rocky Road") 20-30 52
ABBOTT (108 "Somebody's Rockin' My Broken Heart") 20-30 52
ABBOTT (109 "Rhythm in My Baby's Walk") 20-30 52
ABBOTT (135 "Plaid & Calico") 15-20 53
CORMAC (1193 "Plaid and Calico") 75-100 51
CORMAC (1197 "Birds and Butterflies") 75-100 51
COLUMBIA (21504 "Honky Tonk Man") 15-25 56
COLUMBIA (21538 "I'm a One Woman Man") 10-20 56
COLUMBIA (40813 "I'm Coming Home") 15-25 57
COLUMBIA (40919 "She Knows Why") 10-15 57
COLUMBIA (40986 "I'll Do It Every Time") 10-15 57

COLUMBIA (41043 "Lover's Rock") 15-25 57
COLUMBIA (41110 "Honky Tonk Hardwood Floor") 30-50 58
COLUMBIA (41210 "All Grown Up") 10-15 58
COLUMBIA (41308 thru 44156).. 5-10 58-67
DOT (15996 "Plaid & Calico") 8-12 59
MERCURY (6412 "The Devil Sent Me You") 15-25 52
MERCURY (6418 "The Rest of Your Life") 15-25 52
MERCURY (70014 "I Won't Forget") 15-25 52
MERCURY (70100 "Tennessee Jive") 15-25 53
MERCURY (70156 "S.S. Lureline") 15-25 53
MERCURY (70198 "You You You") 15-25 53
MERCURY (70227 "All for the Love of a Girl") 15-25 53
MERCURY (70325 "Move Down the Line") 15-25 54
MERCURY (70399 "The Door of Your Mansion") 15-25 54
MERCURY (70462 "No True Love") 15-25 54
MERCURY (70636 "Ridin' the Sunshine Special") 15-25 55
MERCURY (70707 "Big Wheels Rollin") 15-25 55

Picture Sleeves

COLUMBIA (Except 41308) 8-12 59-64
COLUMBIA (41308 "When It's Springtime in Alaska") 10-20 59
(Blue and white sleeve. Promotional only.)
DOT 5-10 59

EPs: 7-inch 33/45rpm

COLUMBIA 15-25 57-60
MERCURY 15-25 55
SESAC (1201 "Free and Easy Songs") 30-40 59
(Promotional issues only.)

LPs: 10/12-inch 33rpm

BRIAR INT'L (104 "Done Rovin'") 100-150
COLUMBIA (CL-1300 thru CL-1700 series) 20-30 60-62
(Monaural.)
COLUMBIA (CL-2200 series).... 10-20 65
(Monaural.)
COLUMBIA (6418 "Johnny Horton") 10-15
(Record club offer.)
COLUMBIA (CS-8000 series) ... 25-30 60-63
(Stereo.)
COLUMBIA (PC-8000 series) 5-10
COLUMBIA (9000 series) 15-20 65-69
(Stereo. With "CS" prefix.)
COLUMBIA (30000 series) 10-15 71
CROWN 12-15 63
CUSTOM 10-15 60s
DOT (3221 "Johnny Horton") 25-40 59
(Monaural.)
DOT (25221 "Johnny Horton") ... 15-25 66
(Stereo.)
HARMONY 10-12 70-71
MERCURY (20478 "The Fantastic Johnny Horton") 25-40 59
PICKWICK/HILLTOP 10-15 65-68
SEARS 10-15 60s
(Promotional issue only.)
SESAC (1201 "Free and Easy Songs") 100-150 59
(Promotional issue only.)
Also see DEAN, Jimmy / Johnny Horton
Also see PRICE, Ray / Johnny Horton / Carl Smith / George Morgan

HORTON, Johnny / Sonny James

LPs: 10/12-inch 33rpm

CUSTOM 8-12
Also see JAMES, Sonny
Also see HORTON, Johnny

HOSANNA

R&B '76

Singles: 7-inch

CALLA 3-5 76

HOT

P&R/R&B/LP '77

Singles: 7-inch

BIG TREE 3-5 77-79

LPs: 10/12-inch 33rpm

BIG TREE 5-10 77-79
Members: Gwen Owens; Cathy Carson; Juanita Curiel.

HOT BUTTER

P&R/LP '72

Singles: 7-inch

MUSICOR 3-5 72

LPs: 10/12-inch 33rpm

MUSICOR 8-10 72-74
Members: Steve Jerome; Bill Jerome; Johnny Abbott; Stan Free; Dave Mullaney.

HOT CHOCOLATE

(Hot Chocolate Band)

P&R/R&B '75

Singles: 7-inch

APPLE 5-10 69
BELL 3-5 74
BIG TREE 3-5 75-77
EMI AMERICA 3-4 82
INFINITY 3-5 78-79
RAK 3-5 72-73

LPs: 10/12-inch 33rpm

BIG TREE 8-10 74-77
EMI AMERICA 5-10 82

INFINITY 5-10 78-79

Members: Errol Brown; Tony Wilson; Harvey Hinsley; Larry Ferguson; Tony Conner; Patrick Olive.

HOT CUISINE

R&B '81

Singles: 7–inch

PRELUDE 3-4 81

HOT LINE

R&B '74

Singles: 12–inch 33/45rpm

MEMO 4-6 84

Singles: 7–inch

RED COACH 3-5 74

HOT SAUCE

P&R/R&B '72

Singles: 7–inch

VOLT 3-5 72-74

HOT STREAK

D&D '83

Singles: 12–inch 33/45rpm

EASY STREET 4-6 83

HOT TUNA

LP '70

Singles: 7–inch

GRUNT 3-6 71-76

Picture Sleeves

GRUNT 4-8 72

LPs: 10/12–inch 33rpm

GRUNT 10-20 72-78
RCA (3000 series) 5-10 81
RCA (4000 series) 10-15 70-71
RELIX ("Acoustic Hot Tuna Splashdown") 10-15 84
(No selection number used.)

Members: Jack Casady; Jorma Kaukonen; Papa John Creach; Sammy Piazza.
Also see CREACH, Papa John
Also see JOPLIN, Janis / Hot Tuna
Also see KAUKONEN, Jorma

HOTBOX

R&B/D&D '84

Singles: 12–inch 33/45rpm

POLYDOR 4-6 84

Singles: 7–inch

POLYDOR 3-4 84

HOTEL

P&R '78

Singles: 7–inch

MCA 3-4 79-80
MERCURY 3-5 78

LPs: 10/12–inch 33rpm

MCA 5-10 79-80

HOTHOUSE FLOWERS

LP '88

Singles: 7–inch

LONDON 3-4 88-90

LPs: 10/12–inch 33rpm

LONDON 5-10 88-90

Members: Liam O'Maonlai; Fiachna O'Braonain; Peter O'Toole; Leo Barnes.

HOTLEGS

P&R '70

Singles: 7–inch

CAPITOL (Except 3043) 3-5 70-71
CAPITOL (3043 "Run Baby, Run") 10-15 71

LPs: 10/12–inch 33rpm

CAPITOL 15-20 71

Members: Eric Stewart; Kevin Godley; Lol Cream.
Also see 10CC

HOT-TODDYS

P&R '59

Singles: 7–inch

CORSICAN 10-20 59
SHAN-TODD 15-25 59
STRAND 8-12 60

Also see ROCKIN' REBELS

HOUR GLASS

(Greg Allman & Hour Glass)

Singles: 7–inch

LIBERTY (56002 "Nothing But Tears") 10-15 68

Picture Sleeves

LIBERTY (56002 "Nothing But Tears") 40-60 68

LPs: 10/12–inch 33rpm

LIBERTY 15-20 67-68
U.A. 10-15 73

Members: Duane Allman; Gregg Allman.
Also see ALLMAN BROTHERS BAND

HOUSE of FREAKS

LP '89

LPs: 10/12–inch 33rpm

RHINO 5-8 89

HOUSE of LORDS

LP '88

Singles: 7–inch

RCA/SIMMONS 3-4 89

Picture Sleeves

RCA/SIMMONS 3-4 89

LPs: 10/12–inch 33rpm

RCA/SIMMONS 5-8 88
SIMMONS 5-8 90

Members: James Christian; Gregg Giuffria; Chuck Wright; Lanny Cordola; Ken Mary.
Also see GIUFFRIA

HOUSE of LOVE

LP '88

LPs: 10/12–inch 33rpm

FONTANA 5-8 90
RELATIVITY 5-8 88

HOUSEMARTINS

LP '87

LPs: 10/12-inch 33rpm

ELEKTRA.................................. 5-10 87-88

Member: Norman Cook.
Also see BEATS INTERNATIONAL

HOUSTON, Cissy

(Sissie Houston; Cissie Houston)

R&B '70

Singles: 7-inch

COLUMBIA 3-4 79-80
COMMONWEALTH UNITED........ 3-5 70
CONGRESS (268 "Bring Him Back")................................ 30-50 66
JANUS 3-5 71
KAPP (814 "Don't Come Running to Me")................................ 15-25 67
PRIVATE STOCK 3-5 77-78

LPs: 10/12-inch 33rpm

COLUMBIA 5-10 79-80
JANUS 8-10 70
PRIVATE STOCK 5-10 77-78

Also see BOWIE, David
Also see MANN, Herbie, & Cissy Houston
Also see SWEET INSPIRATIONS

HOUSTON, David

(With Calvin Crawford)

C&W '63

Singles: 78rpm

RCA.. 5-10 56-57

Singles: 7-inch

BLACK ROSE 3-4 82
COLONIAL.................................. 3-5 78
COUNTRY INT'L........................... 3-4 80
DERRICK..................................... 3-4 79
ELEKTRA..................................... 3-5 78-79
EXCELSIOR.................................. 3-4 81
EPIC.. 3-8 63-76
NRC 8-12 59
PHILLIPS INTERNATIONAL....... 5-10 61
RCA (6611 "Sugar Sweet") 10-20 56
RCA (6696 "Blue Prelude") 10-15 56
RCA (6927 "One and Only") 30-40 57
RCA (7001 "Teenage Frankie and Johnny").......................... 15-25 57
SOUNDWAVES 3-4 83
STARDAY 3-5 77
SUN (400 series)......................... 5-10 66
SUN (1100 series)........................ 3-5 72

Picture Sleeves

EPIC.. 5-8 66-69

LPs: 10/12-inch 33rpm

CAMDEN...................................... 8-12 66
COLUMBIA 6-10 73
DELTA... 5-10 82
EPIC.. 5-15 64-76
EXACT 5-10 80
EXCELSIOR................................. 5-10 81
51 WEST..................................... 5-10 84
GUEST STAR.............................6-12 64
GUSTO 5-10 78
HARMONY..................................8-12 70-72
STARDAY 6-10 77

Also see JAMES, Sonny / David Houston
Also see JONES, George / Buck Owens / David Houston / Tommy Hill.

HOUSTON, David, & Barbara Mandrell

C&W '70

Singles: 7-inch

EPIC..3-5 70-74

LPs: 10/12-inch 33rpm

EPIC..8-15 72-75

Also see MANDRELL, Barbara

HOUSTON, David, & Tammy Wynette

C&W '68

Singles: 7-inch

EPIC..4-6 67

LPs: 10/12-inch 33rpm

EPIC..8-12 67
51 WEST......................................5-10 82

Also see HOUSTON, David
Also see WYNETTE, Tammy

HOUSTON, Joe

(With His Rockets; Mighty Joe Houston; Fabulous Joe Houston; Joe Houston Orchestra)

R&B '52

Singles: 78rpm

BAYOU 4-8 53
CASH 4-8 55
COMBO 4-8 54-57
CROWN 6-12 56
FREEDOM....................................5-10 49-50
IMPERIAL 4-8 52
LUCKY 4-8 54
MACY'S.......................................4-8 51
MERCURY...................................4-8 51
MODERN 4-8..............................52
MONEY..4-8 55
RPM 4-8 55
RECORDED in HOLLYWOOD......4-8 54
SPHINX.......................................4-8 51

Singles: 7-inch

BAYOU (004 "Moody")..............15-25 53
BAYOU (012 "Chittlin") 15-25 53
BAYOU (017 "Scramble") 15-25 53
CASH (1013 "Flying Home")......15-25 55
COMBO 10-15 54-59
CROWN 10-15 56
DOOTO 8-12 58
IMPERIAL (5201 "Earthquake").20-30 52
IMPERIAL (5213 "Atom Bomb") 20-30 53
KEM 5-10 61
LUCKY 15-25 54
MODERN (830 "Blow Joe, Blow")..30-50 51
MODERN (850 "Have a Ball")....20-30 52

MODERN (863 "Doin' the Lindy Hop") 20-30 52
MODERN (879 "Dig It") 20-30 52
MODERN (917 "Blowin' Crazy") 20-30 52
MONEY 10-20 55
RPM 10-20 55
RECORDED in HOLLYWOOD (423 "Jay's Boogie") 20-30 54

EPs: 7–inch 33/45rpm

COMBO (3 "Joe Houston") 40-60 54
COMBO (10 "Joe Houston") 40-60 55
MODERN/RPM (200 "The Fabulous Joe Houston") 50-75
(Cover shows Modern, but label shows RPM.)
TOPS (607 "Rock & Roll Party") 40-60 58

LPs: 10/12–inch 33rpm

BIG TOWN 5-10 78
COMBO (100 "Joe Houston") 150-200 55
(Cover has titles and color photo of Houston)
COMBO (100 "Joe Houston") . 50-100
(No photo or titles on cover. Has a saxophone as the "J" in Joe. No artist or title shown on label.)
COMBO (400 "Rockin' at the Drive-In") 50-100 55
CROWN 15-30 62-63
GOLD AWARD (8033 "Rock & Roll") 30-40
(Colored vinyl.)
MODERN (1206 "Joe Houston Blows All Night Long") 75-125 56
TOPS (1518 "Rock & Roll with Joe Houston") 50-80 58

HOUSTON, Thelma
(With Pressure Cooker)

P&R '70

Singles: 12–inch 33/45rpm

MCA 4-6 83

Singles: 7–inch

CAPITOL (5767 "Baby Mine")... 25-50 66
DUNHILL (Except 11) 4-8 70
DUNHILL (11 "Everybody Gets to Go to the Moon") 10-15 69
(Special Apollo 11 Mission promotional issue.)
MCA 3-4 83
MOTOWN 3-4 74-78
MOWEST 3-6 71-73
RCA 3-4 80-81
TAMLA 3-4 76-79

Picture Sleeves

DUNHILL (11 "Everybody Gets to Go to the Moon") 10-15 69
(Special Apollo 11 Mission promotional issue.)

LPs: 10/12–inch 33rpm

DUNHILL 10-15 69
MCA 5-10 83
MOTOWN 5-10 81-82
MOWEST 8-12 72
RCA 5-10 80-81
SHEFFIELD (2 "I've Got the Music in Me") 25-30 74
SHEFFIELD (200 "I've Got the Music in Me") 5-10 82
TAMLA 5-10 76-79
MYRRH 8-10 74
Also see BUTLER, Jerry, & Thelma Houston

HOUSTON, Whitney

P&R/R&B/LP '85

Singles: 12–inch 33/45rpm

ARISTA 4-6 85-89

Singles: 7–inch

ARISTA 3-4 85-91

Picture Sleeves

ARISTA 3-4 85-88

LPs: 10/12–inch 33rpm

ARISTA 5-10 85-91
Also see FRANKLIN, Aretha, & Whitney Houston
Also see KING DREAM CHORUS & Holiday Crew
Also see PENDERGRASS, Teddy, & Whitney Houston

HOWARD, Camille, Trio
(With Her Boy Friends)

R&B '48

Singles: 78rpm

FEDERAL 4-8 53
IMPERIAL 4-8 53
SPECIALTY 5-10 48-53
VEE JAY 4-8 56

Singles: 7–inch

FEDERAL (12125 "Excite Me, Daddy") 20-30 53
FEDERAL (12134 "Hurry Back, Baby") 20-30 53
FEDERAL (12147 "You're Lower Than a Mole") 20-30 53
IMPERIAL 15-25 53
SPECIALTY (443 "Old Baldy Boogie") 20-30 53
SPECIALTY (449 "Bacarolle Boogie") 20-30 53
VEE JAY 10-20 56
Members: Camille Howard; Roy Milton; Dallas Bartley.
Also see MILTON, Roy

HOWARD, Don

P&R '52

Singles: 78rpm

ESSEX 4-8 52
MERCURY 3-5 56
TRIPLE A (2503 "Oh Happy Day") 10-15 52

Singles: 7–inch

ESSEX 5-15 52
MERCURY 5-10 56

TRIPLE A (2503 "Oh Happy Day") 20-30 52

HOWARD, Eddy

P&R '40

Singles: 78rpm

MAJESTIC 4-8 46
MERCURY 3-5 50-57

Singles: 7–inch

MERCURY 5-10 50-61
MISHAWAKA 3-5 72

EPs: 7–inch 33/45rpm

MERCURY 5-10 50-59

LPs: 10/12–inch 33rpm

IMPERIAL 8-15 61
MERCURY 10-20 50-65
WING 5-10 60-63

HOWARD, George
(With Gwen Guthrie)

R&B '83

Singles: 12–inch 33/45rpm

MCA 4-6 86

Singles: 7–inch

MCA 3-4 86-90
PALO ALTO 3-4 83
TBA 3-4 84-86

LPs: 10/12–inch 33rpm

GRP 5-8 91
MCA 5-10 86-90
PALO ALTO 5-10 83
TBA 5-10 84-86
Also see GUTHRIE, Gwen

HOWARD, Gregory
(With the Cadillacs)

Singles: 7–inch

KAPP (536 "When in Love").. 100-150 63
(Black and red issue.)
KAPP (536 "When in Love")...... 50-75 63
(White label. Promotional issue only.)
Copies of *When in Love* on Gee, credited to the Gee-Tones, are boots from the mid-'70s.
Also see CADILLACS

HOWARD, Miki

R&B '86

Singles: 7–inch

ATLANTIC 3-4 86-90

LPs: 10/12–inch 33rpm

ATLANTIC 5-10 86-90
Also see SIDE EFFECT

HOWARD, Miki, & Gerald Levert

R&B '88

Singles: 7–inch

ATLANTIC 3-4 88
Also see HOWARD, Miki

HOWARD, Rosetta
(With the Big Three Trio)

R&B '48

Singles: 78rpm

COLUMBIA 5-10 48-55

Singles: 7–inch

COLUMBIA 15-25 51-55
Also see BIG THREE TRIO

HOWE, Steve, Band

LP '75

Singles: 7–inch

ATLANTIC 3-5 75-79

LPs: 10/12–inch 33rpm

ATLANTIC 5-10 75-79
Also see ASIA
Also see GTR
Also see YES

HOWLIN' WOLF
(Chester Burnett)

R&B '51

Singles: 78rpm

CHESS 15-25 51-57
RPM 25-50 51

Singles: 7–inch

CADET CONCEPT 4-8 60s
CHESS (1528 "My Last Affair") 75-100 53
CHESS (1557 "All Night Boogie") 40-60 53
CHESS (1566 "No Place to Go") 40-60 54
CHESS (1575 "Baby, How Long") 40-60 54
CHESS (1584 "I'll Be Around") .. 25-50 55
CHESS (1593 "Who Will Be Next") 25-50 55
CHESS (1600 series) 15-25 55-57
CHESS (1700 thru 1900 series) .. 5-10 58-66
CHESS (2000 series) 3-6 67-71

LPs: 10/12–inch 33rpm

CADET 10-12 69
CHESS (Except 1400 and 1500 series) 8-10 71-77
CHESS (1434 "Moaning in the Moonlight") 60-90 58
(Black label.)
CHESS (1469 "Howlin' Wolf") 50-70 62
(Black label.)
CHESS (1500 series, except 1502) 15-20 67-69
CHESS (1502 "Real Folk Blues") 25-35 66
CHESS/MCA (Except 9332) 5-8 89
CHESS/MCA (9332 "Howlin' Wolf") 35-45 91
(Five LP boxed set, with 32-page booklet.)
CROWN 15-20 62
CUSTOM 10-12
KENT 10-15 67
RPM (340 "Passing by Blues") 1000-2000 51
RPM (347 "My Baby Stole Off") 100-200 51
UNITED 8-10

Also see BERRY, Chuck, & Howlin' Wolf
Also see DIDDLEY, Bo, Howlin' Wolf & Muddy Waters
Also see ROBINSON, Freddy
Also see WATERS, Muddy, & Howlin' Wolf

HUANG CHUNG: see WANG CHUNG

HUBBARD, Freddie

LP '73

Singles: 12-Inch 33/45rpm

FANTASY....4-8 81

Singles: 7-Inch

ATLANTIC....3-5 69
BLUE NOTE....4-8 61-64
COLUMBIA....3-7 74-76

LPs: 10/12-Inch 33rpm

ATLANTIC....8-15 67-76
BLUE NOTE....15-25 60-65
(Label reads "Blue Note Records Inc. - New York, U.S.A.")
BLUE NOTE....8-15 66-76
(Label shows Blue Note Records as a division of either Liberty or United Artists.)
CTI....6-12 70-75
COLUMBIA....5-10 74-83
ELEKTRA....5-8 82
ENJA....5-8 81
FANTASY....5-8 81-83
IMPULSE....10-20 63-73
LIBERTY....5-8 81
PABLO....5-8 82-83
PAUSA....5-8 82

HUBBARD, Freddie, & Oscar Peterson

LPs: 10/12-Inch 33rpm

PABLO....5-10 80
Also see PETERSON, Oscar

HUBBARD, Freddie, & Stanley Turrentine

LPs: 10/12-Inch 33rpm

CTI....6-12 74
Also see HUBBARD, Freddie
Also see TURRENTINE, Stanley

HUDMON, R.B., Jr.

R&B '76

Singles: 7–inch

ATLANTIC....3-5 76-77
CAPITOL....3-5 71
COTILLION....3-5 78
1-2-3....3-6 68-70

LPs: 10/12–inch 33rpm

COTILLION....5-10 78

HUDSON

Singles: 7–inch

ELEKTRA....3-4 80
LIONEL....3-5 71
PLAYBOY....3-5 73
ROCKET....3-5 73

LPs: 10/12–inch 33rpm

ELEKTRA....5-10 80
Members: Bill Hudson; Brett Hudson; Mark Hudson.
Also see HUDSON BROTHERS

HUDSON, Al
(With the Soul Partners)

R&B '76

Singles: 12–inch 33/45rpm

ABC....4-8 77

Singles: 7–inch

ABC....3-5 76-79
ATCO....3-5 75-76

LPs: 10/12–inch 33rpm

ABC....8-10 77
Also see ONE WAY

HUDSON, David

P&R/R&B/LP '80

Singles: 7–inch

ALSTON....3-4 80

LPs: 10/12–inch 33rpm

ALSTON....5-10 80

HUDSON, Pookie
(With the Spaniels)

P&R '63

Singles: 7–inch

CHESS....5-10 66
DOUBLE-L....10-15 63
JAMIE (1319 "This Gets to Me") 25-50 66
NEPTUNE....10-15 61
PARKWAY....10-15 62
Also see SPANIELS

HUDSON & LANDRY

P&R/LP '71

Singles: 7–inch

DORE....3-5 71-74

LPs: 10/12–inch 33rpm

DORE....10-20 71-75
Members: Bob Hudson; Ron Landry.
Also see HUDSON, "Emperor" Bob, & Lawrence Welk

HUDSON BROTHERS

P&R/LP '74

Singles: 7–inch

ARISTA....3-5 76-78
CASABLANCA....3-5 74
MCA/ROCKET....3-5 74-76

Picture Sleeves

MCA/ROCKET....3-5 75

LPs: 10/12–inch 33rpm

CASABLANCA....8-10 74
PLAYBOY....8-10 72
MCA/ROCKET....8-10 74-75
Members: Bill Hudson; Brett Hudson; Mark Hudson.
Also see HUDSON

HUERTA, Baldemar
(El Bebop Kid)

Singles: 7–inch

FALCON (838 "Encaje De Chantilly" Chantilly Lace]")....15-25 58
Also see FENDER, Freddy

HUES CORPORATION

P&R '73

Singles: 7-inch

RCA.. 3-5 73-75
W.B. 3-5 77

LPs: 10/12-inch 33rpm

RCA.. 8-10 73-77
W.B. 5-10 77-78

Members: St. Clair Lee; H. Ann Kelly; Tommy Brown; Karl Russell; Fleming Williams.

HUFF, Leon

R&B '80

Singles: 7-inch

PHILLY INT'L 3-5 80-81

Also see MFSB
Also see ROMEOS

HUFF, Terry
(With Special Delivery)

R&B '76

Singles: 7-inch

MAINSTREAM 3-5 76
PHILADELPHIA INT'L..................... 3-4 80

LPs: 10/12-inch 33rpm

MAINSTREAM 5-10 76

Also see SPECIAL DELIVERY

HUGH, Grayson

LP '88

Singles: 7-inch

RCA.. 3-4 89-90

Picture Sleeves

RCA.. 3-4 89

LPs: 10/12-inch 33rpm

RCA.. 5-8 88

HUGH, Grayson, & Betty Wright

Singles: 7-inch

RCA.. 3-4 89

Also see HUGH, Grayson
Also see WRIGHT, Betty

HUGHES, Fred
(Freddie Hughes)

P&R/R&B '65

Singles: 7-inch

BRUNSWICK 3-6 69-71
CADET 4-6 68
COLLECTABLES 3-4 81
EXODUS 4-8 66
MINASA (709 "One Step Too Far") 15-25 65
VEE JAY 5-10 65
WAND 4-8 68-69
WEE 4-8

LPs: 10/12-inch 33rpm

BRUNSWICK 8-12 70
WAND 10-15 68

HUGHES, Jimmy

P&R/R&B '64

Singles: 7-inch

ATLANTIC.................................. 4-6 68
COLLECTABLES 3-4 81
FAME... 4-8 64-67
GUYDEN....................................... 4-8 62
VOLT.. 3-6 69-71

LPs: 10/12-inch 33rpm

ATCO.. 10-15 67
STAX... 5-10 85
VEE JAY 15-20 64
VOLT... 10-12 69

HUGHES, Rhetta

R&B '69

Singles: 12-inch 33/45rpm

ARIA... 4-6 83

Singles: 7-inch

ARIA... 3-4 83
COLUMBIA 4-6 67-68
SUTRA.. 3-4 80
TETRAGRAMMATON 4-6 68-69

LPs: 10/12-inch 33rpm

SUTRA.. 5-10 80
TETRAGRAMMATON 10-12 69

HUGHES, Rhetta, & Tennyson Stephens

LPs: 10/12-inch 33rpm

COLUMBIA 12-18 65

Also see HUGHES, Rhetta
Also see STEPHENS, Tennyson

HUGHES - THRALL

P&R '82

Singles: 7-inch

BOULEVARD................................ 3-4 82

Members: Glenn Hughes; Pat Thrall.

HUGO & LUIGI
(Hugo & Luigi Chorus)

P&R '55

Singles: 78rpm

MERCURY 3-5 55-56

Singles: 7-inch

MERCURY.................................... 5-10 55-56
RCA 4-8 59-60
ROULETTE................................... 4-8 58

Picture Sleeves

ROULETTE................................... 5-10 58

LPs: 10/12-inch 33rpm

FORUM... 5-10 60
MERCURY.................................... 5-15 56
RCA 5-10 60-63
ROULETTE................................... 5-12 59
WING 5-10 60

Members: Hugo Peretti; Luigi Creatore.

HULIN, T.K.

P&R '63

Singles: 7-inch

SMASH 4-8 63
L.K. (1001 "Little Bitty Boy")...100-200
L.K. (1119 "Baby, Be My Steady") 15-25 63

LPs: 10/12-inch 33rpm

STARLITE..................................... 10-12

HULLABALOOS

P&R '64

Singles: 7–inch

ROULETTE 4-8 64-65

Picture Sleeves

ROULETTE 10-20 64-65

LPs: 10/12–inch 33rpm

ROULETTE (25297 "England's Newest Singing Sensations") 25-30 65

ROULETTE (25310 "The Hullabaloos on Hullabaloo") 25-30 65

HUMAN BEINZ

(Human Beingz; with the Mammals)

P&R '67

Singles: 7–inch

CAPITOL 5-8 67-69

ELYSIAN (3376 "Hey Joe") 15-25 67

ELYSIAN (8687 "My Generation") 15-25 66

GATEWAY (828 "Gloria") 5-10 68

GATEWAY (838 "My Generation") 5-10 68

Picture Sleeves

CAPITOL (2119 "Turn on Your Lovelight") 10-15 68

LPs: 10/12–inch 33rpm

CAPITOL (2906 "Nobody But Me") 15-25 68

CAPITOL (2926 "Evolutions") ... 25-35 68

GATEWAY (3012 "Nobody But Me") 25-35 68

Members: Richard Belley; Mel Pachuta; Mike Tatman; Ting Markulin.

HUMAN BODY

R&B '84

Singles: 7–inch

BEARSVILLE 3-4 84

HUMAN LEAGUE

P&R/LP '82

Singles: 12–inch 33/45rpm

A&M 4-6 82-86

Singles: 7–inch

A&M 3-4 82-86

Picture Sleeves

A&M 3-4 82-85

LPs: 10/12–inch 33rpm

A&M 5-10 82-86

Members: Phil Oakey; Craig Marsh; Martyn Ware; Colin Thurston.

Also see HEAVEN 17

Also see LEAGUE UNLIMITED ORCHESTRA

Also see MORODER, Giorgio, & Phil Oakey

HUMBLE PIE

P&R/LP '71

Singles: 7–inch

A&M 3-5 71-75

ATCO 3-4 80

IMMEDIATE 4-8 69

Picture Sleeves

A&M 4-8 71-72

LPs: 10/12–inch 33rpm

A&M 8-12 70-82

ACCORD 5-10 82

ATCO 5-10 80-81

IMMEDIATE 10-15 68-72

Members: Steve Marriott; Peter Frampton; Greg Ridley; B.J. Cole; Jerry Shirley; Lyn Dobson.

Also see FRAMPTON, Peter

Also see SMALL FACES

HUMES, Helen

(With the Bill Doggett Octet)

R&B '45

Singles: 78rpm

ALADDIN 5-10 45

DECCA 4-8 52

MODERN (779 "I'm Gonna Let Him Ride") 20-30 50

Singles: 7–inch

DECCA (28113 "They Raided the Joint") 15-25 52

LPs: 10/12–inch 33rpm

COLUMBIA 8-10

Members (Octet): Bill Doggett; Johnny Brown; Bill Moore; Ernest Thompson; Ross Butler; Alfred Moore; Charles Harris; Elmer Warner.

Also see DOGGETT, Bill

Also see MILTON, Roy

HUMPERDINCK, Engelbert

(Gerry Dorsey)

P&R/LP '67

Singles: 7–inch

EH (1 "For My Friends") 10-15

(Promotional issue only.)

EPIC 3-5 76-83

PARROT 3-6 67-73

Picture Sleeves

PARROT 3-6 67-71

EPs: 7–inch 33/45rpm

PARROT 5-10 67-69

(Jukebox issues.)

LPs: 10/12–inch 33rpm

EPIC 5-10 76-83

LONDON 5-10 77

PARROT 5-15 67-77

TEE VEE 5-10

(TV mail order offer.)

Also see DORSEY, Gerry

HUMPHREY, Bobbi

R&B/LP '74

Singles: 12–inch 33/45rpm

EPIC 4-8 78-79

Singles: 7–inch

BLUE NOTE 3-5 71-76

EPIC 3-5 77-79

LPs: 10/12–inch 33rpm

BLUE NOTE 5-10 71-76

EPIC 5-10 78-79

HUMPHREY, Della

P&R/R&B '68

Singles: 7-inch

ARCTIC 4-6 68

HUMPHREY, Paul, & His Cool Aid Chemists

P&R/R&B/LP '71

Singles: 7-inch

LIZARD 3-6 70-71

LPs: 10/12-inch 33rpm

LIZARD 8-12 71

HUMPHRIES, Teddy

R&B '59

Singles: 7-inch

KING (5000 series) 5-10 59
KING (S-5000 series) 10-15 59
(Stereo.)
Session: Mickey Baker.

HUNT, Geraldine

R&B '70

Singles: 7-inch

ABC (10859 "Winner Take All"). 15-25 67
BOMBAY (4501 "He's for Real") 50-75 64
CHECKER (1028 "I Let Myself Go") 10-20 62
PRISM 3-4 80
ROULETTE 4-6 70-73
U.S.A. (732 "Sneak Around") 15-25 62
U.S.A. (737 "Sneak Around") 10-20 63

HUNT, Geraldine, & Charlie Hodges

Singles: 7-inch

CALLA 4-6 70
Also see HODGES, Charles
Also see HUNT, Geraldine

HUNT, Pee Wee

P&R '48

Singles: 78rpm

CAPITOL 3-5 48-57

Singles: 7-inch

CAPITOL 5-10 50-62
SAVOY 5-10 51

EPs: 7-inch 33/45rpm

CAPITOL 5-10 50-56
SAVOY 5-10 51

LPs: 10/12-inch 33rpm

CAPITOL 4-8 78
(With "SM" prefix.)
CAPITOL 15-30 50-63
(With "T" or "ST" prefix.)
GLENDALE 4-8 78
SAVOY (15042 "Dixieland") 25-35 54
(10-inch LP.)
TOPS 15-25 57
Also see BLANC, Mel
Also see FOUR KNIGHTS

HUNT, Tommy

P&R/R&B '61

Singles: 7-inch

ATLANTIC 4-8 65
CAPITOL 4-8 66
DYNAMO 4-8 67
SCEPTER 4-8 61-63

LPs: 10/12-inch 33rpm

DYNAMO (8001 "Greatest Hits") 15-25 67
SCEPTER (506 "I Just Don't Know What to Do with Myself") 25-35 62
Also see FLAMINGOS
Also see PLATTERS / Inez & Charlie Foxx / Jive Five / Tommy Hunt

HUNTER, Ian

LP '75

Singles: 7-inch

CHRYSALIS 3-4 79
COLUMBIA 3-5 75-83

LPs: 10/12-inch 33rpm

CHRYSALIS 5-10 79-81
COLUMBIA 8-10 75-79
Also see MOTT the HOOPLE

HUNTER, Ian, & Mick Ronson

LP '89

LPs: 10/12-inch 33rpm

MERCURY 5-8 89
Also see HUNTER, Ian
Also see RONSON, Mick

HUNTER, Ivory Joe
(With the Ivorytones)

R&B '45

Singles: 78rpm

ATLANTIC 5-10 55-58
EXCLUSIVE 10-15 45
4 STAR 8-12 48
KING 5-12 47-57
MGM 5-10 49-54
PACIFIC 10-15 45-47

Singles: 7-inch

ATLANTIC 8-12 55-58
CAPITOL 4-8 61-62
DOT 5-10 58-59
GOLDISC 5-10 60
KING (4424 "False Friend Blues") 25-35 51
KING (4443 "She's Gone Blues") 25-35 51
KING (4455 "Old Gal and New Gal Blues") 25-35 51
KING (5200 series) 5-10 59
MGM (500 series) 3-4 78
MGM (8011 "I Almost Lost My Mind") 25-35 49
MGM (10000 & 11000 series) 15-25 49-54
MGM (10578 "I Almost Lost My Mind") 20-30 49
PARAMOUNT 3-5 73

SMASH 4-8 63
SOUND STAGE 7 .... 4-6 68
STAX 5-8 64
VEE JAY 4-8 62
VEEP 4-8 67

EPs: 7-inch 33/45rpm

ATLANTIC (589 "Ivory Joe Hunter") 30-40 58
ATLANTIC (608 "Rock with Ivory Joe Hunter") 30-50 58
KING (265 "Ivory Joe Hunter") .. 30-50 54
MGM (1376/7/8 "I Get That Lonesome Feeling") 20-40 57
(Price is for any of three volumes.)

LPs: 10/12-inch 33rpm

ATLANTIC (8008 "Ivory Joe Hunter") 50-80 58
(Black Label.)
ATLANTIC (8008 "Ivory Joe Hunter") 40-60 59
(Red Label.)
ATLANTIC (8015 "Ivory Joe Hunter Sings the Old and the New") 50-80 58
(Black Label.)
ATLANTIC (8015 "Ivory Joe Hunter Sings the Old and the New") 40-60 59
(Red Label.)
DOT 15-25 64
EPIC 8-10 71
EVEREST 8-10 74
GOLDISC (403 "Fabulous Ivory Joe Hunter") 25-35 61
GRAND PRIX 10-15
HOME COOKING 5-10 89
KING (605 "16 Greatest Hits") .. 50-80 58
LION 15-20
MGM (3488 "I Get That Lonesome Feeling") 50-80 57
PARAMOUNT 8-10 74
SAGE (603 "Ivory Joe Hunter"). 25-35 59
SMASH 15-20 63
SOUND (603 "Ivory Joe Hunter") 50-80 57

Also see CHARLES, Ray / Ivory Joe Hunter / Jimmy Rushing
Also see TURNER, Sammy / Ivory Joe Hunter

HUNTER, Ivory Joe / Memphis Slim

LPs: 10/12-inch 33rpm

STRAND (1123 "The Artistry of Ivory Joe Hunter") 15-25

Also see MEMPHIS SLIM

HUNTER, John

P&R '84

Singles: 7-inch

PRIVATE I 3-4 84-85

LPs: 10/12-inch 33rpm

PRIVATE I 5-10 85

HUNTER, Tab

P&R/R&B '57

Singles: 78rpm

DOT 4-8 56-57
HEAR ("Tab Hunter") 20-30 56
(Seven-inch, cardboard disc, originally attached to front cover of *Hear* magazine. Double this price for magazine with record intact. Back cover has a similar disc by Jayne Mansfield.)

Singles: 7-inch

DOT 5-10 56-62
W.B. (Monaural) 5-10 58-59
W.B. (Stereo) 10-15 59
(With "S" prefix.)

Picture Sleeves

W.B. 10-20 58-60

EPs: 7-inch 33/45rpm

W.B. (EA-1221 "Tab Hunter") 15-25 58
(Monaural. Has one track not heard on stereo version.)
W.B. (ESB-1221 "Tab Hunter") .. 20-35 58
(Stereo. Has one track not heard on mono version.)

LPs: 10/12-inch 33rpm

DOT (3370 "Young Love") 25-30 61
(Monaural.)
DOT (25370 "Young Love") 20-30 61
(Stereo. Has some rerecorded tracks for stereo, that are the original recordings on the mono version.)
W.B. 25-35 58-60

HUNTER, Ty

(With the Voice Masters)

R&B '60

Singles: 7-inch

ANNA (1114 "Everything About You") 20-30 60
ANNA (1123 "Everytime") 20-30 60
CHECK MATE (1002 "Memories") 15-25 61
CHECK MATE (1015 "Lonely Baby") 15-25 61
CHESS 10-20 62-64
INVICTUS 10-15 72

Also see GLASS HOUSE
Also see ORIGINALS
Also see VOICE MASTERS

HUNTLEY, Chet, & David Brinkley

LP '64

LPs: 10/12-inch 33rpm

RCA 8-15 64-66

HURD, Debra

R&B '83

Singles: 7-inch

GEFFEN 3-4 83

HURRICANE

LP '88

LPs: 10/12-inch 33rpm

ENIGMA.................................... 5-10 85-90

Members: Robert Sarzo; Kelly Hansen; Jay Schellen; Tony Cavazo; Doug Aldrich.

HURT, Jim

P&R '80

Singles: 7-inch

SCOTTI BROTHERS.................. 3-4 80

HURT 'EM BAD & S.C. Band

R&B '82

Singles: 7-inch

PROFILE...................................... 3-4 82

HUSKER DU

LP '86

Singles: 12-inch 33/45rpm

W.B. 4-6 86

Singles: 7-inch

SST 3-4 85

W.B. 3-4 86

Picture Sleeves

SST 3-4 85

LPs: 10/12-inch 33rpm

SST 5-10 85

W.B. 5-10 86-87

Members: Bob Mould; Grant Hart; Greg Norton.

HUSKEY, Ferlin: see HUSKY, Ferlin

HUSKY, Ferlin

(With the Hush Puppies; with Hushpuppies; with Coon Creek Girls; with Bettie Husky; Ferlin Huskey)

C&W '55

Singles: 78rpm

CAPITOL..................................... 4-8 52-57

Singles: 7-inch

ABC... 3-5 73-75

ABC/DOT 3-5 75

CAPITOL (2000 thru 3400) 3-6 67-72

(Orange labels.)

CAPITOL (2300 thru 4300) 5-10 52-60

(Purple labels.)

CAPITOL (4400 thru 5900) 4-8 60-67

CACHET 3-4 80

FIRST GENERATION.................. 3-4 78

KING 4-8 60-61

EPs: 7-inch 33/45rpm

CAPITOL................................ 10-20 57-60

Picture Sleeves

CAPITOL..................................... 4-8 62-68

LPs: 10/12-inch 33rpm

ABC.. 5-10 73-75

AUDIOGRAPH ALIVE................ 5-10 82

CAPITOL (718 "Songs of the Home and Heart") 35-45 56

CAPITOL (880 "Boulevard of Broken Dreams").................... 30-40 57

CAPITOL (1200 thru 2800 series)......................................10-20 60-68

(With "T" or "ST" prefix.)

CAPITOL (1200 thru 2800 series).......................................5-10 68-75

(With "DT" or "SM" prefix.)

FIRST GENERATION...................5-8 78

KING (647 "Country Tunes Sung from the Heart") 25-35 59

KING (728 "Easy Livin'")...........25-35 60

PICKWICK 6-12

PICKWICK/HILLTOP 8-12 65

Also see FIVE KEYS / Ferlin Husky

Also see OWENS, Buck / Faron Young / Ferlin Husky

Also see SHEPARD, Jean, & Ferlin Husky

Also see VINCENT, Gene / Tommy Sands / Sonny James / Ferlin Husky

HUSKY, Ferlin / Pat Boone

Singles: 7-inch

U.S.A.F. 5-10 60

(Promotional issue only.)

Also see BOONE, Pat

Also see HUSKY, Ferlin

HUTCH, Willie

P&R/R&B/LP '73

Singles: 78rpm

MODERN 8-12 57

Singles: 7-inch

DUNHILL (4012 "The Duck") 25-50 65

MAVERICK 5-10 68

MODERN (1021 "I Can't Get Enough")................................20-30 57

MOTOWN 3-5 73-82

RCA 4-8 69

WHITFIELD..................................3-5 78-79

Picture Sleeves

MOTOWN 3-5 75

LPs: 10/12-inch 33rpm

MOTOWN 5-10 73-82

RCA 10-12 69

WHITFIELD.................................5-10 78-79

HUTSON, Leroy

(With the Free Spirit Symphony)

R&B '73

Singles: 7-inch

CURTOM 3-5 73-78

RSO 3-5 79

LPs: 10/12-inch 33rpm

CURTOM 8-10 73-78

Also see IMPRESSIONS

HUTTON, Betty

P&R '44

Singles: 78rpm

CAPITOL......................................4-8 44-56

RCA 4-6 50

VICTOR 4-8 46

Singles: 7-inch

CAPITOL....................................5-10 50-56

EPs: 7–inch 33/45rpm

CAPITOL 10-20 50-54

LPs: 10/12–inch 33rpm

CAPITOL (256 "Square in a Social Circle") 30-50 50
(10–inch LP.)
CAPITOL (547 "Satins & Spurs") 20-40 54
W.B. 15-25 59

Also see COMO, Perry, & Betty Hutton
Also see SHORE, Dinah, Tony Martin, Betty Hutton & Phil Harris

HUTTON, Betty, & Tennessee Ernie Ford

Singles: 78rpm

CAPITOL 4-8 54

Singles: 7–inch

CAPITOL 5-10 54

Also see FORD, Tennessee Ernie
Also see HUTTON, Betty

HUTTON, Danny

P&R '65

Singles: 7–inch

HBR 4-8 65
MGM 4-8 66

Picture Sleeves

HBR 10-15 65
MGM 8-12 66

LPs: 10/12–inch 33rpm

MGM 8-10 70

Also see THREE DOG NIGHT

HYDE, Paul, & Payolas

P&R/LP '85

Singles: 7–inch

A&M 3-4 85
I.R.S. 3-4

Picture Sleeves

A&M 3-4 85
I.R.S. 3-4

LPs: 10/12–inch 33rpm

A&M 5-10 85

HYLAND, Brian

P&R/R&B '60

Singles: 7–inch

ABC 3-5 73
ABC-PAR (Except 10400) 5-10 61-64
ABC-PAR (10400 "If Mary's There") 5-10 63
(Black vinyl.)
ABC-PAR (10400 "If Mary's There") 15-20 63
(Colored vinyl. Promotional issue only.)
DOT 4-6 67-69
KAPP 4-8 60-61
LEADER 10-15 60
MCA 3-4 73
PHILIPS 4-8 64-67
ROWE/AMI 5-10 66
("Play Me" Sales Stimulator promotional issue.)
ROULETTE 3-4
UNI 3-5 70-72

Picture Sleeves

ABC-PAR 8-15 61-63
KAPP (342 "Itsy Bitsy Teenie Weenie Yellow Polkadot Bikini") 15-20 60
KAPP (352 "Four Little Heels") .. 20-30 60
(Black and white sleeve. Promotional issue only.)
KAPP (352 "Four Little Heels") .. 10-20 60
(Color sleeve.)
KAPP (363 "I Gotta Go") 15-25 60
PHILIPS 4-8 64-67

LPs: 10/12–inch 33rpm

ABC-PAR 20-25 61-64
DOT 10-12 69
KAPP (1202 "Bashful Blonde") .. 25-30 60
(Monaural.)
KAPP (3202 "Bashful Blonde") .. 30-40 60
PHILIPS 15-20 64-66
PICKWICK 5-10
PRIVATE STOCK 5-10 77
RHINO 5-8
UNI 8-10 71
WING 10-12 67

HYMAN, Dick

(Dick Hyman Trio; with His Electric Eclectics)

P&R '54

Singles: 78rpm

MGM 3-4 54-57

Singles: 7–inch

COLUMBIA 3-5 74-75
COMMAND 3-6 61-70
EVEREST 4-6 60
MGM 4-8 54-62
RCA 3-4 62

Picture Sleeves

MGM (12149 "Mack the Knife") . 10-15 55

LPs: 10/12–inch 33rpm

ATLANTIC 5-10 75
COLUMBIA 5-10 74
COMMAND 5-15 60-73
EVEREST 5-10 60
FAMOUS DOOR 5-10 73
MCA 5-10 77
MGM 10-20 54-63
PROJECT 3 .... 5-10 71
RCA 4-8 80-83
SUNSET 5-10 66

HYMAN, Phyllis

R&B '76

Singles: 12–inch 33/45rpm

ARISTA 4-6 83

Singles: 7–inch

ARISTA 3-5 78-83

BUDDAH 3-5 77
DESERT MOON 3-5 76
PHILADELPHIA INT'L 3-4 86

LPs: 10/12-inch 33rpm

ARISTA 5-10 79-83
BUDDAH 5-10 77
PHILADELPHIA INT'L 5-10 86

HYMAN, Phyllis, & Michael Henderson

Singles: 7-inch

ARISTA 3-4 81

Also see CONNORS, Norman
Also see HENDERSON, Michael
Also see HYMAN, Phyllis

I

I LEVEL

D&D '83

Singles: 12-inch 33/45rpm

VIRGIN 4-6 82-84

Singles: 7-inch

VIRGIN 3-4 82-84

LPs: 10/12-inch 33rpm

VIRGIN 5-10 83

I.A.& P. CO: see ITALIAN ASPHALT & Pavement Co.

I.R.T.
(Interboro Rhythm Team)

D&D '84

Singles: 12-inch 33/45rpm

RCA 4-6 84

Singles: 7-inch

RCA 3-4 84

IAN, Janis

P&R/LP '67

Singles: 7-inch

CAPITOL 3-5 71
CASABLANCA 3-4 80
COLUMBIA 3-5 74-81
POLYDOR 3-5 78
VERVE 3-5
VERVE/FOLKWAYS 4-8 66-67
VERVE/FORECAST 4-6 68-69

Picture Sleeves

COLUMBIA 3-6 75

LPs: 10/12-inch 33rpm

CAPITOL 8-12 71-75
COLUMBIA 8-10 74-81
MGM 8-10 70
POLYDOR 8-10 75
VERVE/FOLKWAYS 10-15 67
VERVE/FORECAST 10-15 68-69

IAN & SYLVIA

LP '63

Singles: 7-inch

COLUMBIA 3-5 71-72
MGM 4-6 67-69
VANGUARD 4-8 63-68
VERVE/FOLKWAYS 3-6 67

Picture Sleeves

COLUMBIA 3-5 71

LPs: 10/12-inch 33rpm

AMPEX 8-10 70
COLUMBIA 6-10 71-73
MGM 8-12 67-70
VANGUARD 10-20 63-71
VERVE/FOLKWAYS 8-15 67

Members: Ian Tyson; Sylvia Fricker.

ICE CUBE

LP '90

LPs: 10/12-inch 33rpm

PRIORITY 5-8 90-91

ICE-T

LP '87

Singles: 7-inch

SIRE 3-4 88-90

Picture Sleeves

SIRE 3-4 88

LPs: 10/12-inch 33rpm

SIRE 5-10 87-91

ICEHOUSE

P&R/LP '81

Singles: 12-inch 33/45rpm

CHRYSALIS 4-6 81-86

Singles: 7-inch

CHRYSALIS 3-4 81-88

Picture Sleeves

CHRYSALIS 3-4 81-88

LPs: 10/12-inch 33rpm

CHRYSALIS 5-10 81-88

ICICLE WORKS

P&R/D&D/LP '84

Singles: 12-inch 33/45rpm

ARISTA 4-6 84

Singles: 7-inch

ARISTA 3-4 84

LPs: 10/12-inch 33rpm

ARISTA 5-10 84

ICON

LP '84

LPs: 10/12-inch 33rpm

CAPITOL 5-10 84

Members: Steve Clifford; Dan Wexler; Pat Dixon; John Aquilino; Tracy Wallach; Jerry Harrison.

IDEALS

R&B '66

Singles: 7-inch

CHECKER (920 "Knee Socks") . 15-25 59
CHECKER (979 "Knee Socks") . 10-15 61

PASO (6401 "Together")........... 30-50 61
PASO (6402 "Magic")................ 30-50 61
SATELLITE (2007 "Kissin'")........ 5-10 65
SATELLITE (2009 "You Hurt Me")... 10-15 66
SATELLITE (2011 "Kissing Won't Go Out of Style")........................... 15-25 66

Members: Major Lance; Sam Stewart; Reggie Jackson; Leonard Mitchell.
Also see LANCE, Major

IDES of MARCH

P&R '66

Singles: 7–inch

KAPP... 4-6 69
PARROT.. 5-10 66-67
RCA... 3-5 72-73
W.B. 3-6 69-71

LPs: 10/12–inch 33rpm

RCA.. 8-12 72-73
W.B. 10-15 70-71

Members: Jim Peterik; Mike Borch; Ray Herr; Bob Bergland; Chuck Soumar; John Larson; Larry Millas.

IDLE RACE

Singles: 7–inch

LIBERTY (55997 "Here We Go Round the Lemon Tree")........................... 10-15 67

LPs: 10/12–inch 33rpm

LIBERTY (7603 "Birthday Party")..................................... 25-30 69
SUNSET... 8-12 72

Members: Jeff Lynne; Greg Masters; Roger Spencer; Dave Pritchard.
Also see LYNNE, Jeff

IDOL, Billy

LP '81

Singles: 12–inch 33/45rpm

CHRYSALIS..................................... 4-6 81-86

Singles: 7–inch

CHRYSALIS..................................... 3-4 81-90

Picture Sleeves

CHRYSALIS..................................... 3-4 82-90

LPs: 10/12–inch 33rpm

CHRYSALIS (1377 "Billy Idol").. 10-20 82
(Promotional issue only.)
CHRYSALIS (4000 "Don't Stop") 8-10 81
CHRYSALIS (20000 series).......... 5-8 90
CHRYSALIS (40000 series)........ 5-10 82-87

IFIELD, Frank

P&R '62

Singles: 7–inch

CAPITOL.. 4-6 63-65
HICKORY... 3-6 66-71
MAM.. 3-5 71
VEE JAY 5-8 62-63
W.B. 3-5 79

LPs: 10/12–inch 33rpm

CAPITOL.. 10-20 63
HICKORY... 8-10 66-68
VEE JAY 10-20 62

Also see BEATLES / Frank Ifield

IGLESIAS, Julio

LP '83

Singles: 7–inch

ALAHAMBRA.................................. 3-6 72-75
COLUMBIA 3-4 83-89

LPs: 10/12–inch 33rpm

COLUMBIA 5-10 83-90

IGLESIAS, Julio, & Willie Nelson

(Willie Nelson & Julio Iglesias)

C&W/P&R '84

Singles: 7–inch

COLUMBIA (Except 04495)........... 3-4 84
COLUMBIA (04495 "As Time Goes By") 8-12 84

Picture Sleeves

COLUMBIA (Except 04495)........... 3-4 84
COLUMBIA (04495 "As Time Goes By") 10-15 84

Also see NELSON, Willie

IGLESIAS, Julio, & Diana Ross

P&R '84

Singles: 7–inch

COLUMBIA 3-4 84

Picture Sleeves

COLUMBIA 3-4 84

Also see ROSS, Diana

IGLESIAS, Julio, & Stevie Wonder

P&R '88

Singles: 7–inch

COLUMBIA 3-4 88

Picture Sleeves

COLUMBIA 3-4 88

Also see IGLESIAS, Julio
Also see WONDER, Stevie

IGGY & STOOGES: see POP, Iggy

IKETTES

P&R/R&B '62

Singles: 7–inch

ATCO 4-8 61-62
INNIS 4-8 64
MODERN 4-8 64-66
PHI-DAN 4-8
POMPEII 4-8 68
TEENA... 4-8 63
U.A. 3-6 71-72

LPs: 10/12–inch 33rpm

MODERN 15-20 65
U.A. 8-10 73-75

Members: Delores Johnson; Eloise Hester; Joshie Jo Armstead; Vanetta Fields; Jessie Smith; Robbie Montgomery.
Also see MAXAYN
Also see MIRETTES
Also see TURNER, Ike & Tina

ILLINOIS SPEED PRESS

LP '69

Singles: 7–inch

COLUMBIA 4-8 68-70

LPs: 10/12–inch 33rpm

COLUMBIA 10-15 69-70

Members: Paul Cotton; Rob Lewine; Fred Page; Kal David; Mike Anthony; Frank Bartoli.

Also see POCO

ILLUSION

(The Illusion)

P&R/LP '69

Singles: 7–inch

DYNO VOICE.................................. 4-8 68

STEED 4-6 69-71

LPs: 10/12–inch 33rpm

STEED 10-20 69-70

ILLUSION

LP '77

Singles: 7–inch

ISLAND 3-5 77-78

LPs: 10/12–inch 33rpm

ISLAND 5-10 77-78

ILLUSION

R&B '82

Singles: 7–inch

SUGAR HILL.................................. 3-4 82

ILLUSTRATED MAN

D&D '84

Singles: 7–inch

CAPITOL.................................. 3-4 84

IMAGINATION

R&B '82

Singles: 12–inch 33/45rpm

ELEKTRA.................................. 4-6 84

MCA 4-6 83

Singles: 7–inch

ELEKTRA.................................. 3-4 83

MCA 3-4 82-83

RCA.................................. 3-4 87

LPs: 10/12–inch 33rpm

MCA 5-10 82

IMPACT

P&R/R&B '76

Singles: 7–inch

ATCO 3-5 76

FANTASY.................................. 3-5 77-78

LPs: 10/12–inch 33rpm

ATCO 8-10 75

FANTASY 5-10 77

Members: Damon Harris; John Simms; Donald Tilghman; Charles Timmons.

Also see HARRIS, Damon

IMPALAS

(Featuring Joe "Speedo" Frazier)

P&R/R&B '59

Singles: 7–inch

CUB (Except 9022).................................. 8-10 59-60

CUB (9022 "I Ran All the Way Home").................................. 20-25 59

CUB (9022 "Sorry I Ran All the Way Home").................................. 8-10 59
(Note slightly different title.)

HAMILTON 10-15 59

MGM 3-5 64-78

U.G.H.A. (17 "My Hero").................................. 3-5 82

Picture Sleeves

U.G.H.A. (17 "My Hero").................................. 3-5 82

EPs: 7–inch 33/45rpm

CUB (5000 "Sorry, I Ran All the Way Home").................................. 100-150 59

LPs: 10/12–inch 33rpm

CUB (CUB-8003 "Sorry, I Ran All the Way Home").................................. 100-150 59
(Monaural.)

CUB (CUBS-8003 "Sorry, I Ran All the Way Home").................................. 150-250 59
(Stereo.)

Also see SPEEDO & IMPALAS

IMPALAS / Horst Jankowski & His Orchestra

Singles: 7–inch

COLLECTABLES.................................. 3-4 85

Also see IMPALAS

Also see JANKOWSKI, Horst, & His Orchestra

IMPELLITTERI

LP '88

LPs: 10/12–inch 33rpm

RELATIVITY 5-8 88

IMPERIALS

R&B/P&R '58

Singles: 7–inch

CAPITOL.................................. 8-12 63

CARLTON.................................. 10-15 61

END (1027 "Tears on My Pillow").................................. 15-20 58
(First pressing. Quickly repressed, crediting "Little Anthony & Imperials.")

LIBERTY 8-12 58

Also see LITTLE ANTHONY & IMPERIALS

IMPRESSIONS

(Featuring Jerry Butler)

R&B '58

Singles: 12–inch 33/45rpm

20TH FOX.................................. 4-8 79

Singles: 7–inch

ABC.................................. 4-8 66-68

ABC-PAR 5-10 61-66

ABNER.................................. 10-20 59-60

ADORE (901 "Popcorn Willie") ..25-45 64

BANDERA (2504 "Listen") 20-25 59

CHI-SOUND 3-5 81
COTILLION 3-5 76-77
CURTOM 3-6 68-76
MCA 3-4 87
PORT 5-10 62
SWIRL 10-15 62
20TH FOX 3-5 81
VEE JAY (424 thru 621)........... 10-15 61-64
(Vee Jay 280, *For Your Precious Love*, appears in the Jerry Butler section.)

Picture Sleeves

CURTOM 4-8 68

EPs: 7-inch 33/45rpm

CURTOM (20 "Do You Want to Win") 5-10 70
(Promotional issue only.)

LPs: 10/12-inch 33rpm

ABC 10-15 66-76
ABC-PAR 15-20 63-66
COTILLION 8-10 76
CURTOM 8-10 68-76
MCA 5-10 82
PICKWICK 8-10 75
SCEPTER/CITATION 8-10
SIRE 8-12 76
20TH FOX 5-10 79-81
UPFRONT 8-10

Members: Curtis Mayfield; Sam Gooden; Richard Brooks; Fred Cash; Leroy Hutson; Reggie Torlan; Ralph Johnson; Nate Evans.

Also see EVERETT, Betty / Impressions
Also see HUTSON, Leroy
Also see MAYFIELD, Curtis
Also see MYSTIQUE
Also see ROE, Tommy / Impressions / Fats Domino

IMPRESSIONS / Jerry Butler

LPs: 10/12-inch 33rpm

SIRE 5-10 77

Also see BUTLER, Jerry
Also see IMPRESSIONS

IMPRESSORS

Singles: 7-inch

CUB (9010 "Do You Love Her") 10-20 58
ONYX (514 "Is It Too Late")...... 30-40 57

IN CROWD

P&R '66

Singles: 7-inch

BRENT 5-10 65
HICKORY 10-15 65
MUSICOR (1111 "Do the Surfer Jerk") 10-20 65
RONN 10-20
SWAN 4-8 65
TOWER 5-8 65-66
VIVA 4-8 66-67

INCREDIBLE BONGO BAND

P&R/R&B '73

Singles: 7-inch

MGM 3-5 73
PRIDE 3-5 72-74

LPs: 10/12-inch 33rpm

PRIDE 8-10 73-74

INCREDIBLE STRING BAND

LP '68

LPs: 10/12-inch 33rpm

ELEKTRA 8-12 67-72
REPRISE 8-12 72-74

INCREDIBLES

R&B '66

Singles: 7-inch

AUDIO ARTS 4-8 66-68
CLASS 4-8 66
TETRAGRAMMATON 3-6 69

LPs: 10/12-inch 33rpm

AUDIO ARTS 10-12 70

INDECENT OBSESSION

P&R/LP '90

Singles: 7-inch

MCA 3-4 90

LPs: 10/12-inch 33rpm

MCA 5-8 90

INDEEP

R&B/D&D '83

Singles: 12-inch 33/45rpm

SOUND of NEW YORK 4-6 83-85

Singles: 7-inch

SOUND of NEW YORK 3-4 83-85

LPs: 10/12-inch 33rpm

SOUND of NEW YORK 5-10 83

INDEPENDENTS

P&R/R&B '72

Singles: 7-inch

WAND 3-6 72-74

LPs: 10/12-inch 33rpm

WAND 8-12 72-74

Members: Chuck Jackson; Maurice Jackson; Eric Thomas; Helen Curry.

INDIA

D&D '83

Singles: 12-inch 33/45rpm

WEST END 4-6 83

INDIGO GIRLS

P&R/LP '89

Singles: 7-inch

EPIC 3-4 89-90

LPs: 10/12-inch 33rpm

EPIC 5-8 89-90

INDIGOS

R&B '66

Singles: 7-inch

COR 5-10 65
CORNEL (515 "High School Social") 15-25 58
CORNEL (3001 "Servant of Love") 150-200 58

DATE.. 4-8 66
IMAGE..................................... 5-10 61
VERVE/FOLKWAYS 4-8 65

INDIOS TABAJARAS, Los: see LOS INDIOS TABAJARAS

INDIVIDUALS

R&B '75

Singles: 7–inch

P.I.P. 3-5 75
21 3-5

INDUSTRY

P&R '83

Singles: 7–inch

CAPITOL.................................... 3-4 83

INFINITY

(Featuring Billy Butler)

R&B '69

Singles: 7–inch

FOUNTAIN................................. 4-6 69
MERCURY 3-5 70
UNI 3-5 72

Members: Billy Butler; Earl Batts; Jess Tillman; Larry Wade; Phyllis Know.
Also see BUTLER, Billy

INFORMATION SOCIETY

P&R/LP '88

Singles: 7–inch

TOMMY BOY 3-4 88-90

Picture Sleeves

TOMMY BOY 3-4 88

LPs: 10/12–inch 33rpm

TOMMY BOY 5-8 88-90

INGMANN, Jorgen

P&R/R&B '61

Singles: 78rpm

MERCURY 4-8 56

Singles: 7–inch

ATCO 4-8 60-66
MERCURY 5-10 56
PARROT 4-8 64
U.A. INT'L.................................. 4-6 68

LPs: 10/12–inch 33rpm

ATCO 20-30 62
MERCURY 20-30 56
U.A. INT'L................................ 8-12 68

INGRAM

R&B '77

Singles: 7–inch

H&L 3-5 77

LPs: 10/12–inch 33rpm

H&L 8-10 77

INGRAM, James

R&B/D&D/LP '83

Singles: 12–inch 33/45rpm

QWEST 4-6 83

Singles: 7–inch

MCA 3-4 87
QWEST.......................................3-4 83-86
W.B. 3-4 90

Picture Sleeves

QWEST.......................................3-4 83-86

LPs: 10/12–inch 33rpm

QWEST.....................................5-10 83-86
W.B. 5-8 90

Also see AUSTIN, Patti, & James Ingram
Also see JONES, Quincy, & James Ingram
Also see ROGERS, Kenny, Kim Carnes & James Ingram
Also see RONSTADT, Linda, & James Ingram
Also see U.S.A. for AFRICA

INGRAM, James, & Michael McDonald

P&R/R&B '83

Singles: 7–inch

QWEST.......................................3-4 83

Also see INGRAM, James
Also see McDONALD, Michael

INGRAM, Luther

(With the G-Men)

R&B '69

Singles: 7–inch

DECCA (31794 "Ain't That Nice")..4-8 65
ERIC 3-4 70s
HIB (698 "If It's All the Same to You Babe")...................................50-75 67
KO KO.......................................5-10 67-78
PROFILE.....................................3-4 86-87
SMASH (2019 "Foxy Devil") 10-15 66

LPs: 10/12–inch 33rpm

KO KO.......................................8-10 71-76
(May also be shown as Koko—one word.)

INK SPOTS

(Charlie Fuqua's Ink Spots; Charlie Owens & Sensational Ink Spots)

P&R '39

Singles: 78rpm

BLUEBIRD...............................10-20 36
DECCA (800 series) 10-15 36
DECCA (1000 thru 4000 series)..5-10 36-42
DECCA (18000 thru 30000 series)..3-8 42-57

Singles: 7–inch

DECCA 5-15 50-61
GRAND AWARD..........................5-10 56
VERVE...4-8 60
X-TRA 4-8 60

EPs: 7–inch 33/45rpm

DECCA 5-15 54-56
GRAND AWARD..........................5-15 56
TOPS (606 "Ink Spots") 10-15 59
(Two-EP set.)
WALDORF MUSIC HALL 5-15 55

LPs: 10/12–inch 33rpm

AUDITION..................................10-20 56
COLORTONE 15-20 58
CORAL...4-6 73

CROWN (144 "Greatest Hits") .. 10-15 59
(Black vinyl.)
CROWN (144 "Greatest Hits") .. 20-40 59
(Colored vinyl.)
CROWN (448 "If I Didn't Care") 10-20 60s
CROWN (5197 "Sensational Ink Spots") 10-20 60s
DECCA (182 "Best of the Ink Spots") 10-20 65
(Monaural.)
DECCA (7-182 "Best of the Ink Spots") 10-20 65
(Stereo.)
DECCA (4297 "Our Golden Favorites") 10-20 63
(Monaural.)
DECCA (7-4297 "Our Golden Favorites") 10-20 63
(Stereo.)
DECCA (5000 series) 20-40 51-53
(10–inch LPs.)
DECCA (7000 & 8000 series) ... 15-30 54-59
DESIGN 5-10 60s
DIPLOMAT 5-10 64
EVEREST 5-10 82
EXACT 5-10 80
FORD (115 "Hawaiian Wedding Song") 15-25 62
GOLDEN TONE 5-10
GRAND AWARD 10-20 56-59
MCA 5-10 73
MAYFAIR 8-15
MODERN (7023 "Fabulous Ink Spots") 75-125
PAULA 5-10 72
PIROUETTE 10-20
SPIN-O-RAMA 5-10 60s
TOPS (1561 "The Ink Spots") ... 20-30 57
TOPS (1668 "The Ink Spots, Vol. 2") 15-20 59
VERVE 15-25 56-60
VOCALION 8-15 59-65
WALDORF MUSIC HALL (144 "Spirituals and Jubilees") 30-40 55
WALDORF MUSIC HALL (152 "Spirituals and Jubilees, Vol. 2") 30-40 55
WESCO ("Hawaiian Wedding Song") 25-35 62
(Number not known.)

Members: Bill Kenny; Orville Jones; Herb Kenny; Charlie Fuqua; Ivory "Deek" Watson; Bernie Mackey; Cliff Givens; Billy Bowen; Charlie Owens.
Also see FITZGERALD, Ella, & Ink Spots

INMAN, Autry

C&W '53

Singles: 78rpm

DECCA (Except 28629 & 29936).. 4-8 53-56
DECCA (28629 "That's All Right") 5-10 56
DECCA (29936 "Be Bop Baby") .. 5-10 56

Singles: 7–inch

DECCA (Except 28629 & 29936). 5-10 56
DECCA (28629 "That's All Right") 15-25 56
DECCA (29936 "Be Bop Baby") 25-50 56
EPIC 4-8 67-69
GLAD 5-10 60
JUBILEE 4-8 65-69
MERCURY 4-8 62
MILLION 3-5 72
RCA 5-10 58
RISQUE (103 "Niteclubbin'") 5-10
SIMS 4-8 63-64
U.A. 5-8 60

LPs: 10/12–inch 33rpm

ALSHIRE 8-12 69
EPIC 8-12 68
GUEST STAR 8-12
JUBILEE 10-20 64-69
MOUNTAIN DEW 15-25 63
SIMS 15-20 64

INMATES

P&R/LP '79

Singles: 7–inch

POLYDOR/RADAR 3-5 79

LPs: 10/12–inch 33rpm

POLYDOR 5-10 79-80

INNER CITY

P&R/LP '89

Singles: 7–inch

VIRGIN 3-4 89-90

Picture Sleeves

VIRGIN 3-4 89

LPs: 10/12–inch 33rpm

VIRGIN 5-8 89

INNER CITY JAM BAND

R&B '77

Singles: 7–inch

BAREBACK 3-5 77

INNER LIFE

R&B '79

Singles: 12–inch 33/45rpm

SALSOUL 4-6 83

Singles: 7–inch

PERSONAL 3-4 84
PRELUDE 3-5 79-80
SALSOUL 3-4 83

Member: Jocelyn Brown.
Also see BROWN, Jocelyn

INNERVISION

R&B '75

Singles: 7–inch

ARIOLA AMERICA 3-5 77
PRIVATE STOCK 3-5 75

INNOCENCE

P&R '66

Singles: 7–inch

KAMA SUTRA 4-8 66-67

LPs: 10/12–inch 33rpm

KAMA SUTRA 15-20 67

Members: Pete Anders; Vinnie Poncia.

INNOCENCE in DANGER

D&D '84

Singles: 12–inch 33/45rpm

EPIC 4-6 84

Singles: 7–inch

EPIC 3-4 84

INNOCENCE MISSION

LP '90

LPs: 10/12–inch 33rpm

A&M 5-8 90

INNOCENTS

P&R '60

Singles: 7–inch

DECCA 10-15 63
ERA 3-5 72
INDIGO 8-12 60-62
PORT 4-8
REPRISE (20112 "Oh How I Miss My Baby/Be Mine") 15-20 62
REPRISE (20125 "Oh How I Miss My Baby/You're Never Satisfied") 8-12 62
TRANS WORLD 10-15 60
W.B. (5450 "My Heart Stood Still") 15-25 64

LPs: 10/12–inch 33rpm

INDIGO (503 "Innocently Yours") 50-75 61

Members: Darron Stankey; Al Candaleria; Jim West.

Also see YOUNG, Kathy

INSIDERS

LP '87

Singles: 12–inch 33/45rpm

EPIC ("Ghost on the Beach") 4-8 87
(Promotional issue only.)

Singles: 7–inch

EPIC (07352 "Ghost on the Beach") 3-4 87
(Black vinyl.)
EPIC (07352 "Ghost on the Beach") 4-8 87
(Colored vinyl. Promotional issue only.)

Picture Sleeves

EPIC (07352 "Ghost on the Beach") 3-4 87

LPs: 10/12–inch 33rpm

EPIC (40630 "Ghost on the Beach") 5-10 87

INSTANT FUNK

P&R/R&B/LP '79

Singles: 12–inch 33/45rpm

SALSOUL 4-8 79-83

Singles: 7–inch

SALSOUL 3-5 78-83
TSOP 3-5 75-77

LPs: 10/12–inch 33rpm

SALSOUL 5-10 79-83
TSOP 5-10 76

INTERLUDE

R&B '80

Singles: 7–inch

STAR VISION INT'L 3-4 80

INTERNATIONAL ALL STARS

LP '61

LPs: 10/12–inch 33rpm

LONDON 5-10 61

INTRIGUES

P&R/R&B '69

Singles: 7–inch

TOOT 4-8 68
YEW 3-6 69-71

LPs: 10/12–inch 33rpm

YEW 10-15 70

INTRIQUE

R&B '87

Singles: 7–inch

COOLTEMPO 3-4 87

INTRUDERS

(Intruders Trio)

P&R '59

Singles: 7–inch

FAME 10-20 59

INTRUDERS

P&R/R&B '66

Singles: 7–inch

EXCEL 4-8
GAMBLE 4-6 66-73
GOWEN 5-10 62
PHILADELPHIA INT'L 3-5 72
RIPETE 3-5 85
TSOP 3-5 74-75

Picture Sleeves

GAMBLE 4-8 66

LPs: 10/12–inch 33rpm

GAMBLE 10-15 67-73
TSOP 8-10 75

Members: Sam Brown; Eugene Doughtry; Phil Terry; Robert Edwards; Bobby Starr.

INVINCIBLES

R&B '65

Singles: 7–inch

DOUBLE SHOT 5-10 66
INVINCIBLE 5-10 66
LOMA 5-10 66
RAMPART 5-10 69

W.B. 5-10 64-67

INVISIBLE MAN'S BAND

P&R/R&B/LP '80

Singles: 7-inch

BOARDWALK 3-4 81-82
MANGO................................... 3-4 80
MOVE'N GROOVE 3-4 83

LPs: 10/12-inch 33rpm

BOARDWALK 10-20 81
MANGO................................... 5-8 80

Members: Clarence Burke; Ken Burke; James Burke; Dennis Burke.
Also see FIVE STAIRSTEPS

INVITATIONS

R&B '73

Singles: 7-inch

SILVER BLUE 5-10 73

Members: Herman Colefield; Gary Grant; Bill Morris; Bobby Rivers.

INXS

P&R/LP '83

Singles: 12-inch 33/45rpm

ATCO 4-6 84
ATLANTIC.................................. 4-6 85-86

Singles: 7-inch

ATCO 3-4 83-85
ATLANTIC.................................. 3-4 85-90

Picture Sleeves

ATCO 3-4 83-84
ATLANTIC.................................. 3-4 85-90

LPs: 10/12-inch 33rpm

ATCO 5-10 83-85
ATLANTIC.................................. 5-10 85-90

Members: Micheal Hutchence; Tim Farriss; Andrew Farriss; Jon Farriss; Gary Beers; Kirk Pengilly.

INXS & Jimmy Barnes

P&R '87

Singles: 7-inch

ATLANTIC.................................. 3-4 87

Also see BARNES, Jimmy
Also see INXS

IRBY, Joyce "Fenderella"

P&R '90

Singles: 12-inch 33/45rpm

MOTOWN 4-8 90

Singles: 7-inch

MOTOWN 3-4 90

LPs: 10/12-inch 33rpm

MOTOWN 5-8 90

Also see KLYMAXX

IRIS, Donnie

P&R/LP '80

Singles: 7-inch

HME 3-4 85
MCA 3-4 80-83

Picture Sleeves

HME 3-4 85
MCA 3-4 82-83

LPs: 10/12-inch 33rpm

HME 5-10 85
MCA 5-10 80-83
MIDWEST 5-10 80

Also see JAGGERZ

IRISH ROVERS

P&R/LP '68

Singles: 7-inch

DECCA 3-6 68-70

LPs: 10/12-inch 33rpm

CLEVELAND INT'L 5-8 81
DECCA 8-15 68-72
MCA 5-10 73-77
SANDCASTLE 5-10 76

IRON BUTTERFLY

P&R/LP '68

Singles: 7-inch

ATCO 3-6 68-71
MCA 3-4 75

EPs: 7-inch 33/45rpm

ATCO (4524 "Iron Butterfly")......20-30 68
(Promotional issue only. Issued with paper sleeve.)

LPs: 10/12-inch 33rpm

ATCO (Except 227) 10-15 68-71
ATCO (227 "Heavy")..................15-20 68
MCA 8-10 75

Members: Doug Ingle; Mike Pinera; Larry Reinhardt; Ron Bushy; Lee Dorman; Erik Brann.
Also see CAPTAIN BEYOND
Also see PINERA, Mike

IRON MAIDEN

LP '81

Singles: 7-inch

CAPITOL (Except V-15375) 3-4 88
CAPITOL (V-15375 "Can I Play with Madness")..............................5-8 88
(Picture/shaped disc.)

LPs: 10/12-inch 33rpm

CAPITOL (Except "SEAX" series).......................................5-10 82-88
CAPITOL (SEAX-12215 "Number of the Beast") 15-25 82
(Picture disc.)
CAPITOL (SEAX-12306 "Piece of Mind")...................................20-30 83
(Picture disc.)
EPIC.. 5-8 90
HARVEST 5-10 80-82

Members: Bruce Dickinson; Dave Murray; Adrian Smith; Niko Mc Brian; Steve Harris.

IRONHORSE

P&R/LP '79

Singles: 7-inch

SCOTTI BROS............................ 3-4 79-80

LPs: 10/12-inch 33rpm

SCOTTI BROS............................ 5-10 79-80

Member: Randy Bachman.
Also see BACHMAN, Randy

IRWIN, Big Dee
(Difosco Erwin; Dee Irwin; with Little Eva)

P&R '63

Singles: 7–inch

BLISS 5-10
DIMENSION 5-10 63-64
FAIRMOUNT 8-12 66
IMPERIAL 5-10 68
ROTATE 10-20 65

Also see DIFOSCO
Also see ERWIN, Dee
Also see IRWIN, Dee, & Mamie Galore
Also see LITTLE EVA
Also see PASTELLS

IRWIN, Dee, & Mamie Galore

Singles: 7–inch

IMPERIAL 4-8 68-69

Also see IRWIN, Big Dee

ISAAK, Chris

LP '87

LPs: 10/12–inch 33rpm

REPRISE 5-8 89
W.B. 5-10 87

ISLANDERS
(Featuring Randy Starr)

P&R '59

Singles: 7–inch

MAYFLOWER 5-10 59-60

LPs: 10/12–inch 33rpm

MAYFLOWER 20-30 60

Members: Randy Starr; Frank Metis.
Also see STARR, Randy

ISLE of MAN

P&R/LP '86

Singles: 7–inch

PASHA 3-4 86

Picture Sleeves

PASHA 3-4 86

LPs: 10/12–inch 33rpm

PASHA 5-10 86

ISLEY, Ernie

LP '90

Singles: 7–inch

ELEKTRA 3-4 90

LPs: 10/12–inch 33rpm

ELEKTRA 5-8 90

Also see ISLEY BROTHERS

ISLEY, Ron

Singles: 7–inch

W.B. 3-4 89

LPs: 10/12–inch 33rpm

W.B. 5-8 89

Also see ISLEY BROTHERS
Also see STEWART, Rod, & Ronald Isley

ISLEY BROTHERS
(Featuring Ronald Isley)

P&R '59

Singles: 78rpm

TEENAGE (1004 "Angels Cried") 100-150 57

Singles: 12–inch 33/45rpm

T-NECK 4-8 79-83

Singles: 12–inch 33/45rpm

W.B. 4-6 87

Singles: 7–inch

ATLANTIC 5-10 61-65
CINDY (3009 "Don't Be Jealous") 50-100 58
GONE (5022 "Everybody's Gonna Rock and Roll") 25-50 58
GONE (5048 "My Love") 25-50 59
MARK-X (7003 "Rockin' MacDonald) 25-50 57
MARK-X (8000 "Rockin' MacDonald) 15-25 58
RCA (447-0500 series) 4-6 61
(Black label, RCA dog on top. Gold Standard.)
RCA (447-0500 series) 3-5 65
(Black label, RCA dog on left side. Gold Standard.)
RCA (47-7000 series) 10-20 59-60
RCA (61-7588 "Shout") 25-35 59
(Stereo.)
T-NECK (Except 501) 3-6 69-84
T-NECK (501 "Testify") 4-8 64
TAMLA 5-15 66-69
TEENAGE (1004 "Angels Cried") 200-400 57
U.A. 10-20 63-64
V.I.P. (25020 "I Hear a Symphony") 300-500 65
VEEP 4-8 66
WAND 8-12 62-63
W.B. 3-4 85-88

LPs: 10/12–inch 33rpm

BUDDAH 10-12 76
CAMDEN 8-10 73-75
COLLECTABLES 6-8 88
MOTOWN 5-10 80-82
PHILADELPHIA INT'L 5-10 78
PICKWICK 5-10 77
RCA (LPM-2156 "Shout!") 35-45 59
(Monaural.)
RCA (LSP-2156 "Shout!") 45-55 59
(Stereo.)
SCEPTER 10-20 66
SUNSET 8-10 69
T-NECK (Except 137 & 3004) 8-10 69-84
T-NECK (137 "Everything You Always Wanted to Hear") 10-15 76
(Promotional issue only.)

TAMLA (269 "This Old Heart of Mine") ... 25-50 66
TAMLA (275 "Soul on the Rocks") ... 15-25 67
TAMLA (287 "Doin' Their Thing") ... 15-20 69
TRIP ... 8-10 76
U.A. (500 series) ... 8-10 75
U.A. (6000 series) ... 20-25 63
WAND (WD-653 "Twist and Shout") ... 20-30 62
(Monaural.)
WAND (WDS-653 "Twist and Shout") ... 30-40 62
(Stereo.)
W.B. ... 5-10 85-87

Members: Ron Isley; Rudy Isley; O'Kelly Isley; Ernie Isley; Marvin Isley.
Also see CHRISTIE, Lou, & Classics / Isley Brothers / Chiffons
Also see HENDRIX, Jimi, & Isley Brothers
Also see ISLEY, Ernie
Also see ISLEY, Ron
Also see ISLEY - JASPER - ISLEY
Also see RASCALS / Isley Brothers

ISLEY BROTHERS & Dave "Baby" Cortez

LPs: 10/12-inch 33rpm

T-NECK ... 8-10 69

Also see CORTEZ, Dave "Baby"

ISLEY BROTHERS / Brooklyn Bridge

LP: 10/12-inch 33rpm

T-NECK (3004 "Live at Yankee Stadium") ... 20-30 69
(With guests, Edwin Hawkins Singers; Five Stairsteps, Sweet Cherries, and Judy White.)

Also see BROOKLYN BRIDGE
Also see FIVE STAIRSTEPS
Also see HAWKINS, Edwin, Singers

ISLEY BROTHERS / Go-Go's

EPs: 7-inch 33/45rpm

RCA/WURLITZER ... 10-15 64
(Promotional issue only.)

ISLEY BROTHERS / Marvin & Johnny

LPs: 10/12-inch 33rpm

CROWN ... 10-20 63

Also see MARVIN & JOHNNY

ISLEY - JASPER - ISLEY

R&B '84

Singles: 12-inch 33/45rpm

CBS ASSOCIATED ... 4-6 85-86

Singles: 7-inch

CBS ASSOCIATED ... 3-4 85-87

LPs: 10/12-inch 33rpm

CBS ASSOCIATED ... 5-10 85-86

Members: Marvin Isley; Chris Jasper; Ernie Isley.
Also see ISLEY BROTHERS
Also see JASPER, Chris

IT'S a BEAUTIFUL DAY
(Featuring David LaFlamme)

LP '69

Singles: 7-inch

COLUMBIA ... 4-8 69-73
SAN FRANCISCO SOUND ... 8-12 70

LPs: 10/12-inch 33rpm

COLUMBIA (1058 "Marrying Maiden") ... 15-20 70
COLUMBIA (9768 "It's a Beautiful Day") ... 20-30 69
COLUMBIA (30734 "Choice Quality Stuff/Anytime") ... 10-15 71
COLUMBIA (31338 "Live at Carnegie Hall") ... 10-15 72
COLUMBIA (32181 "It's a Beautiful Day . . . Today") ... 10-15 73
COLUMBIA (32660 "1001 Nights") ... 30-40 73
(Promotional issue only.)
SAN FRANCISCO SOUNDS (11790 "It's a Beautiful Day") ... 25-35 70

Also see GARCIA, Jerry
Also see LA FLAMME, David
Also see PABLO CRUISE

ITALIAN ASPHALT & Pavement Co.
(Duprees)

P&R '70

Singles: 7-inch

COLOSSUS ... 3-5 70

Picture Sleeves

COLOSSUS ... 4-6 70

LPs: 10/12-inch 33rpm

COLOSSUS ... 8-10 70

Also see DUPREES

IVAN
(Jerry Ivan Allison)

P&R '58

Singles: 7-inch

CORAL (62017 "Real Wild Child") ... 35-50 58
CORAL (62081 "Frankie Frankenstein") ... 50-75 59
CORAL (65607 "Real Wild Child") ... 20-25 67

Also see CRICKETS

IVAN / Johnny Tillotson

Singles: 7-inch

OLDIES 45 ... 5-8 64

Also see IVAN
Also see TILLOTSON, Johnny

IVES, Burl
(With the Trinidaddies)

P&R '48

Singles: 78rpm

COLUMBIA ... 3-8 50-51
DECCA ... 3-8 47-57

Singles: 7-inch

BELL ... 3-5 70

BIG TREE ... 3-5 71
BUENA VISTA ... 4-6 63
COLUMBIA (39000 series) ... 5-10 50-51
COLUMBIA (44000 series) ... 3-6 68-69
COLUMBIA (70000 series) ... 3-6 69
CYCLONE ... 3-5 70
DECCA (25000 series) ... 4-6 66-69
DECCA (27000 thru 30000 series) ... 5-10 50-59
DECCA (31000 thru 33000 series) ... 3-8 60-73
DISNEYLAND ... 4-6 64
MCA ... 3-5 73-74
MONKEY JOE ... 3-5 78

Picture Sleeves

BUENA VISTA ... 4-8 63
DECCA ... 4-8 62
U.A. ... 4-8 62

EPs: 7–inch 33/45rpm

COLUMBIA ... 5-15 51-55
DECCA ... 5-15 49-65

LPs: 10/12–inch 33rpm

BELL ... 5-10 71
CAEDMON ... 4-6 72
COLUMBIA (628 "Wayfaring Stranger") ... 20-35 55
COLUMBIA (1459 "Return of the Wayfaring Stranger") ... 15-25 60
COLUMBIA (2570 "Children's Favorites") ... 20-35 55
(10–inch LP.)
COLUMBIA (6058 "Wayfaring Stranger") ... 25-40 50
(10–inch LP.)
COLUMBIA (6109 "Wayfaring Stranger, Vol. 2") ... 25-40 51
(10–inch LP.)
COLUMBIA (6144 "Wayfaring Stranger, Vol. 3") ... 25-40 51
(10–inch LP.)
COLUMBIA (9000 series) ... 8-12 68-69
CORAL ... 4-8 73
DECCA (100 series) ... 15-25 61
DECCA (4000 series) ... 10-20 62-68
(Decca LP numbers in this series preceded by a "7" or a "DL-7" are stereo issues.)
DECCA (5013 "Ballads and Folk Songs") ... 20-40 49
(10–inch LP.)
DECCA (5080 "Ballads and Folk Songs, Vol. 2") ... 20-40 49
(10–inch LP.)
DECCA (5490 "Women—Songs of the Fair Sex") ... 20-30 53
(10–inch LPs)
DECCA (8000 series) ... 10-20 55-59
DISNEYLAND ... 8-12 63-64
EVEREST ... 5-10 78
HARMONY ... 8-15 59-70
MCA ... 5-10 73-75
SUNSET ... 5-10 70
UNART ... 6-12 67
U.A. ... 10-20 59-62
WORD ... 5-10 63-66

Session: Anita Kerr Singers.
Also see KERR, Anita
Also see MILLS, Hayley, & Burl Ives

IVES, Burl, with Grady Martin & His Slew Foot Five

C&W '52

Singles: 78rpm

DECCA ... 4-8 52

Singles: 7–inch

DECCA ... 8-12 49

IVES, Burl, with Captain Stubby & Buccaneers

C&W '49

Singles: 78rpm

DECCA ... 4-8 49

Also see IVES, Burl

IVEYS
(Badfinger)

P&R '69

Singles: 7–inch

APPLE (1803 "Maybe Tomorrow") ... 10-15 69
APPLE/AMERICOM (301 "Maybe Tomorrow") ... 150-250 69
(Four–inch flexi, "pocket disc.")
Also see BADFINGER

IVY

R&B '86

Singles: 7–inch

HEAT ... 3-4 86

IVY LEAGUE

P&R '65

Singles: 7–inch

CAMEO ... 5-10 65-66

LPs: 10/12–inch 33rpm

CAMEO (2000 "Tossing and Turning") ... 20-30 65

Members: John Carter; Ken Lewis; Perry Ford.

IVY THREE

P&R/R&B '60

Singles: 7–inch

SHELL ... 10-20 60-61

Brunswick
The "CHIRPING" CRICKETS

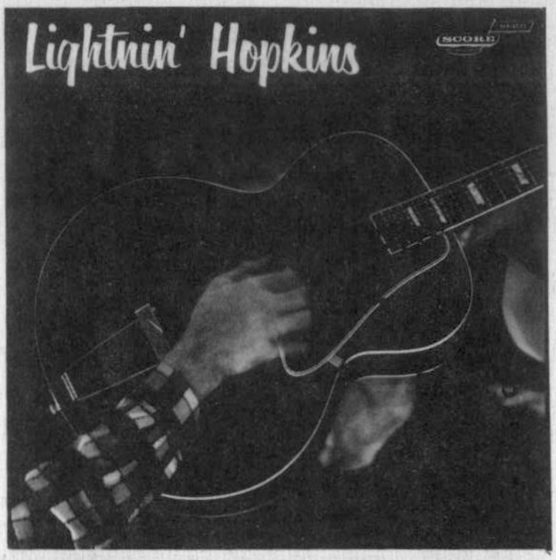
Lightnin' Hopkins
SCORE

DONNA
Maravilla Music BMI-2:58
1315
DO-1159-221
LOVE YOU SO
(Ron Holden)
RON HOLDEN
with
THE THUNDERBIRDS
A DIVISION OF STEREO-FI CORP., HOLLYWOOD 28, CALIF. U.S.A.

EH-1
Not For Sale
FOR MY FRIENDS
ENGELBERT HUMPERDINCK

clarence henry
you always hurt the one you love

Catch
RECORDS
REG U.S PAT. OFF.
PROMOTIONAL COPY
NOT FOR SALE
I AIN'T GONNA TAKE YOU BACK
By
BRENDA HOLLOWAY
109

J

J.B.s
(J.B.'s Internationals)

P&R '72

Singles: 7–inch

PEOPLE 3-5 72-76
POLYDOR 3-5 77-78

LPs: 10/12–inch 33rpm

PEOPLE 5-8 72-75

J.E. the P.C. from D.C.

R&B '87

Singles: 7–inch

PROFILE 3-4 87

J.J. FAD

P&R/R&B/LP '88

Singles: 7–inch

RUTHLESS 3-4 88

Picture Sleeves

RUTHLESS 3-4 88

LPs: 10/12–inch 33rpm

RUTHLESS 5-8 88
Members: Juana Burns; Dania Birks; Michelle Franklin.

JACK, Ballin': see BALLIN' JACK

JACKIE & STARLITES

R&B "62

Singles: 78rpm

FIRE/FURY (1000 "They Laughed at Me") 20-40 57

Singles: 7–inch

FIRE/FURY (1000 "They Laughed at Me") 75-125 57
FURY 10-15 62
HULL 15-20 63
MASCOT (128 "For All We Know") 15-20 62
MASCOT (130 "You Keep Telling Me") 20-25 63
MASCOT (131 "Walking from School") 15-20 63

LPs: 10/12–inch 33rpm

LOST-NITE 5-8 81
Member: Jackie Rue.

JACKIE LEE: see LEE, Jackie

JACKS

P&R/R&B '55

Singles: 78rpm

RPM (Except 428 & 433) 5-10 55-56
RPM (428 "Why Don't You Write Me"/ "Smack Dab in the Middle") 15-25 55
RPM (428 "Why Don't You Write Me"/ "My Darling") 10-20 55
(Note different flip side.)
RPM (433 "I'm Confessin'") 10-20 55

Singles: 7–inch

KENT 5-10 60
RPM (428 "Why Don't You Write Me"/ "Smack Dab in the Middle") ... 75-100 55
RPM (428 "Why Don't You Write Me"/ "My Darling") 25-40 55
(Note different flip side.)
RPM (433 "I'm Confessin'") 35-45 55
RPM (444 "This Empty Heart") .. 25-35 55
RPM (454 "How Soon") 20-30 56
RPM (458 "Why Did I Fall in Love") 25-35 56
RPM (467 "Let's Make Up") 25-35 56

LPs: 10/12–inch 33rpm

BEST 15-25
CROWN (372 "The Jacks") 30-50 62
(Stereo.)
CROWN (5021 "Jumpin' with the Jacks") 50-75 56
CROWN (5372 "The Jacks") 30-50 62
(Monaural.)
RPM (3006 "Jumpin' with the Jacks") 200-250 56
RELIC 10-15
UNITED 8-10 70s
Members: Willie Davis; Ted Taylor; Aaron Collins; Will Jones; Lloyd McCraw; Prentice Moreland.
Also see CADETS

JACKS, Susan

P&R '75

Singles: 7–inch

EPIC 3-4 80
MERCURY 3-5 75-76

LPs: 10/12–inch 33rpm

EPIC 5-8 80
Also see POPPY FAMILY

JACKS, Terry

P&R/LP '74

Singles: 7–inch

BELL 3-5 74
FLASHBACK 3-5 75
LONDON 3-5 73
PRIVATE STOCK 3-5 75-76

LPs: 10/12–inch 33rpm

BELL 8-10 74
Also see POPPY FAMILY

JACKSON, Bull Moose
(With His Buffalo Bearcats; with Flashcats; Moose Jackson)

R&B '46

Singles: 78rpm

ENCINO 10-20 57
KING 10-20 45-55
MGM 10-15 47
QUEEN 10-20 45-46

Singles: 7–inch

BOGUS 4-6 85

ENCINO (1004 "Understanding") 25-50 57
KING (4181 "I Love You, Yes I Do") 25-50 51
KING (4189 "I Want a Bowlegged Woman") 50-100 51
KING (4451 "Trust in Me") 25-50 51
KING (4462 "Unless") 25-50 51
KING (4472 "Cherokee Boogie") 25-50 51
KING (4493 "I'll Be Home for Xmas") 25-50 51
KING (4524 "Nosey Joe") 50-75 52
KING (4535 "Let Me Love You All Night") 25-50 52
KING (4551 "Bearcat Blues") 25-50 52
KING (4580 "Big Ten-Inch Record") 100-200 52
KING (4600 thru 4800 series) ... 15-25 53-55
SEVEN ARTS 5-10 61
WARWICK 5-10 60

Picture Sleeves

BOGUS 3-4 85

EPs: 7-inch 33/45rpm

KING (211 "Bull Moose Jackson Sings His All-Time Hits") 50-100 52
KING (261 "Bull Moose Jackson Sings His All-Time Hits, Vol. 2") 50-100 54

LPs: 10/12-inch 33rpm

AUDIO LAB (1524 "Bullmoose Jackson") 100-150 59
BOGUS 5-8 85

JACKSON, Chuck
(With the Vikings)

P&R/R&B '61

Singles: 7-inch

ABC 3-5 73-74
ALL PLATINUM 3-5 75-77
AMY 8-12 62
ATCO 5-8 61
BELTONE 5-10 61
DAKAR 3-5 72
EMI AMERICA 3-4 80
FEE BEE 10-20 60
MOTOWN (1118 thru 1152) 10-15 68-69
MOTOWN (1160 "The Day the World Stood Still") 150-250 70
SCEPTER 3-5 73
SUGAR HILL 3-4 81
VIBRATION 3-5 77
V.I.P. (25052 thru 25059) 10-15 69-71
V.I.P. (25067 "Who You Gonna Run To") 100-200 71
WAND 4-8 61-67

Picture Sleeves

WAND 5-10 63

LPs: 10/12-inch 33rpm

ABC 8-10 73
ALL PLATINUM 8-10 76
EMI-AMERICA 5-8 80
MOTOWN (667 "Chuck Jackson Arrives") 25-40 67
MOTOWN (687 "Goin' Back") 20-30 69
SCEPTER 8-10 72
SPINORAMA 10-15 60s
U.A. 8-10 75
V.I.P. (403 "Teardrops Keep Fallin") 20-40 70
WAND (Except 680) 15-25 61-67
WAND (680 "Dedicated to the King") 20-30 66

Also see BENTON, Brook / Chuck Jackson / Jimmy Soul
Also see BONDS, Gary "U.S."
Also see FREEMAN, Bobby, & Chuck Jackson
Also see JOHNSON, Kripp, & Chuck Jackson

JACKSON, Chuck, & Maxine Brown

P&R/R&B '65

Singles: 7-inch

WAND 4-8 65-67

LPs: 10/12-inch 33rpm

COLLECTABLES 6-8 88
WAND 15-25 65-66

Also see BROWN, Maxine

JACKSON, Chuck / Percy Sledge

Singles: 7-inch

TRIP 3-5

Also see SLEDGE, Percy

JACKSON, Chuck, & Tammi Terrell

LPs: 10/12-inch 33rpm

WAND 15-25 67

Also see TERRELL, Tammi

JACKSON, Chuck / Young Jesse

LPs: 10/12-inch 33rpm

GUEST STAR 8-12 64

Also see JACKSON, Chuck

JACKSON, Clarence

R&B '85

Singles: 7-inch

R&R 3-4 85

JACKSON, Deon

P&R/R&B '66

Singles: 7-inch

ABC 3-5 75
ATLANTIC 5-10 63-64
CARLA 4-8 66-69

LPs: 10/12-inch 33rpm

ATCO 15-20 66
COLLECTABLES 6-8 88

JACKSON, Earnest

P&R/R&B '73

Singles: 7-inch

STONE 3-5 73

JACKSON, Freddie

P&R/R&B/D&D/LP '85

Singles: 12-Inch 33/45rpm

CAPITOL....................................... 4-6 85-86

Singles: 7-inch

CAPITOL....................................... 3-4 85-90

Picture Sleeves

CAPITOL....................................... 3-4 85-88

LPs: 10/12-inch 33rpm

CAPITOL....................................... 5-8 85-90

Also see LAURENCE, Paul
Also see MOORE, Melba, & Freddie Jackson
Also see MYSTIC MERLIN

JACKSON, George

R&B '70

Singles: 7-inch

CHESS....................................... 3-6 75
CAMEO....................................... 5-10 66
DOT....................................... 5-10 65
DOUBLE R....................................... 5-10
ER MUSIC....................................... 3-5 70
FAME....................................... 4-8 69
HAPPY HOOKERS....................................... 3-4 85
HI (2100 series)....................................... 5-10 67
HI (2200 series)....................................... 3-6 72-73
MGM....................................... 3-6 73-74
MERCURY....................................... 10-15 67-68
MUSCLE SHOALS SOUNDS....... 3-6 79
PRANN....................................... 10-20 63
PUBLIC....................................... 10-15 68
VERVE (10658 "Love Highjacker")....................................... 15-25 70
WASHATAU....................................... 3-4 84

Also see OVATIONS

JACKSON, J.J.

(With the Jackels; with Jackals)

P&R/R&B '66

Singles: 7-inch

ABC....................................... 3-5 73
CALLA....................................... 4-8 66-67
EVEREST....................................... 4-8 62
LOMA....................................... 4-8 67-68
MAGNA....................................... 3-5 75
PRELUDE....................................... 10-20 59
STORM....................................... 10-15 59
W.B....................................... 4-6 69

LPs: 10/12-inch 33rpm

CALLA....................................... 15-25 67
CONGRESS....................................... 15-20 68
PERCEPTION....................................... 10-15 69-70
W.B....................................... 10-20 69

JACKSON, Jackie

Singles: 7-inch

MOTOWN....................................... 3-5 73

LPs: 10/12-inch 33rpm

MOTOWN....................................... 5-8 73

Also see JACKSONS

JACKSON, Janet

P&R/R&B/LP '82

Singles: 12-inch 33/45rpm

A&M....................................... 4-6 82-90

Singles: 7-inch

A&M....................................... 3-4 82-90

Picture Sleeves

A&M....................................... 3-4 83-87

LPs: 10/12-inch 33rpm

A&M....................................... 5-8 82-90

JACKSON, Jenny

R&B '76

Singles: 7-inch

FARR....................................... 3-5 76

JACKSON, Jermaine

P&R/R&B/LP '72

Singles: 12-inch 33/45rpm

ARISTA....................................... 4-6 84-89
MOTOWN....................................... 4-8 80-83

Singles: 7-inch

ARISTA....................................... 3-4 84-89
MOTOWN....................................... 3-5 72-83

Picture Sleeves

ARISTA....................................... 4-6 84-89
MOTOWN....................................... 3-5 81

LPs: 10/12-inch 33rpm

ARISTA....................................... 5-8 84-89
MOTOWN....................................... 5-8 72-82

Also see DEVO
Also see JACKSONS
Also see ORIGINALS & Jermaine Jackson

JACKSON, Jermaine, & Michael Jackson

Singles: 12-inch 33/45rpm

ARISTA....................................... 4-6 84

Also see JACKSON, Michael

JACKSON, Jermaine, & Pia Zadora

P&R/R&B '85

Singles: 7-inch

CURB....................................... 3-4 85

Also see JACKSON, Jermaine
Also see ZADORA, Pia

JACKSON, Joe

P&R/LP '79

Singles: 12-inch 33/45rpm

A&M....................................... 4-6 82-86

Singles: 7-inch

A&M (Except 18000)....................................... 3-5 79-86
A&M (18000 "I'm the Man")........ 10-15 79
(Boxed set of five 45s with sleeves and poster. Labeled "The 7-inch Album.")

Picture Sleeves

A&M....................................... 3-5 79-86

LPs: 10/12-inch 33rpm

A&M (3666 "Look Sharp")........ 10-20 79
(Double 10-inch LP set. Add $4 to $6 if "Look Sharp" button is included.)
A&M (3900 series)....................................... 5-8 87

A&M (4000 & 5000 series)	5-10	79-89
A&M (6000 series)	8-12	86-88
MFSL (080 "Night and Day")	20-30	82
VIRGIN	5-8	91

JACKSON, LaToya

R&B/LP '80

Singles: 12–inch 33/45rpm

LARC	4-6	83
PRIVATE I	4-6	84

Singles: 7–inch

LARC	3-4	83
POLYDOR	3-4	80-81
PRIVATE I	3-4	84-86

Picture Sleeves

PRIVATE I	3-4	84

LPs: 10/12–inch 33rpm

POLYDOR	5-8	80-81
PRIVATE I	5-8	84

Also see CERRONE & LaToya Jackson

JACKSON, Lil' Son

(With His Rockin' Rollers; Little Son Jackson)

R&B '48

Singles: 78rpm

GOLD STAR	5-10	48-50
IMPERIAL (5100 series)	4-8	51-52
MODERN	8-15	49

Singles: 7–inch

IMPERIAL (5204 "Journey Back Home")	50-100	52
IMPERIAL (5218 "Black and Brown")	50-100	52
IMPERIAL (5229 "Lonely Blues")	50-100	53
IMPERIAL (5237 "Spending Money Blues")	50-100	53
IMPERIAL (5248 "Movin' to the Country")	50-100	53
IMPERIAL (5259 "Dirty Work")	50-100	53
IMPERIAL (5267 "Thrill Me, Baby")	50-75	53
IMPERIAL (5276 "Big Rat")	50-75	53
IMPERIAL (5286 "Trouble Don't Last Always")	50-75	53
IMPERIAL (5300 "Get High Everybody")	50-75	53
IMPERIAL (5312 "How Long")	50-75	53
IMPERIAL (5319 "My Younger Days")	50-75	54
IMPERIAL (5339 "Sugar Mama")	50-75	54
IMPERIAL (5400 thru 5900 series)	15-25	56-63
POST (2014 "Lonely Blues")	20-30	53

LPs: 10/12–inch 33rpm

ARHOOLIE (1004 "Lil' Son Jackson")	25-35	60
IMPERIAL (9142 "Rockin' and Rollin'")	75-100	61

Also see CHARLES, Ray / Arbee Stidham / Li'l Son Jackson / James Wayne.

JACKSON, Mahalia

P&R '48

Singles: 78rpm

APOLLO	3-5	50-57
COLUMBIA	3-5	55-57

Singles: 7–inch

APOLLO (200 thru 500 series)	5-10	50-59
APOLLO (600 thru 700 series)	4-6	59-62
COLUMBIA	4-8	55-70
GRAND AWARD	4-8	58-59
KENWOOD	3-6	64-69

Picture Sleeves

APOLLO	4-8	62

EPs: 7–inch 33/45rpm

APOLLO	5-10	54-59
COLUMBIA	5-10	55-60

LPs: 10/12–inch 33rpm

APOLLO (201/2 "Spirituals")	15-20	54
APOLLO (482 "No Matter How You Pray")	10-15	59
APOLLO (499 "Mahalia Jackson")	10-15	62
APOLLO (1001 "Command Performance")	10-15	61
AUDIOFIDELITY	4-8	
(Reissue of Apollo 499.)		
CAEDMON	4-8	73
COLORTONE	5-8	
(Reissue of Grand Award 265.)		
COLUMBIA (CL-600 thru CL-2100 series)	10-20	55-64
COLUMBIA (CL-2400 thru CL-2600 series)	5-15	66-67
COLUMBIA (CS-8000 thru CS-8900 series)	10-20	59-64
(Stereo.)		
COLUMBIA (CS-9200 thru CS-9900 series)	5-15	66-69
(Stereo. Reissues, with a "CSP," "JCS" or "PC" prefix, are in the $5 to $10 range.)		
COLUMBIA (10000 series)	4-8	73
COLUMBIA (30000 series)	5-10	71-72
GRAND AWARD (265 "Spirtuals")	5-10	66
(Reissue of Grand Award 326.)		
GRAND AWARD (326 "Spirtuals")	15-25	55
HARMONY	5-10	68-72
KENWOOD	5-10	64-73
PRIORITY	4-6	82

JACKSON, Mahalia, & Duke Ellington

LPs: 10/12–inch 33rpm

COLUMBIA (CL-1162 "Black, Brown and Beige")	15-25	58
(Monaural.)		

COLUMBIA (CS-8015 "Black, Brown and Beige") 25-40 58
(Stereo.)
COLUMBIA (JCS-1162 "Black, Brown and Beige") 5-10
Also see ELLINGTON, Duke
Also see JACKSON, Mahalia

JACKSON, Marlon

R&B/LP '87

Singles: 7-inch

CAPITOL.................................... 3-4 87

LPs: 10/12-inch 33rpm

CAPITOL..................................... 5-8 87

JACKSON, Michael

P&R/R&B '71

Singles: 12-inch 33/45rpm

EPIC.. 4-8 79-87

Singles: 7-inch

EPIC (Except 07253) 3-5 79-88
EPIC (07253 "I Just Can't Stop Loving You").............................. 3-5 87
(Black vinyl.)
EPIC (07253 "I Just Can't Stop Loving You").............................. 5-8 87
(Colored vinyl. Promotional issue only.)
MCA (1786 "Someone in the Dark")................................... 25-50 83
(Promotional issue only.)
MOTOWN (Except 1914).............. 3-5 71-88
MOTOWN (1914 "Twenty Five Miles") 4-8 84
(Colored vinyl. Promotional issue only.)

Picture Sleeves

EPIC.. 3-5 83-88
MCA (1786 "Someone in the Dark")............................... 25-50 83
(Promotional issue only.)
MOTOWN (1202 "I Wanna Be Where You Are")................................. 3-5 72
MOTOWN (1914 "Twenty Five Miles") 4-8 84
(Promotional issue only.)

LPs: 10/12-inch 33rpm

EPIC (35000 thru 40000) 5-8 79-87
EPIC (45000 series)................. 10-15 80
(Half-speed mastered.)
MOTOWN 5-10 72-85
Also see CROUCH, Andrae
Also see GARRETT, Siedah
Also see JACKSON, Jermaine, & Michael Jackson
Also see JACKSONS
Also see JONES, Quincy
Also see McCARTNEY, Paul, & Michael Jackson
Also see ROCKWELL
Also see ROSS, Diana, & Michael Jackson
Also see U.S.A. for AFRICA
Also see VAN HALEN, Edward
Also see WINANS
Also see WONDER, Stevie, & Michael Jackson

JACKSON, Michael, & Mick Jagger / Jacksons

P&R '84

Singles: 12-inch 33/45rpm

EPIC (5022 "State of Shock") 8-12 84
(With special cover.)
EPIC (05022 "State of Shock") ..15-20 84
(Promotional issue with cover.)

Singles: 7-inch

EPIC (4503 "State of Shock") 3-5 84

Picture Sleeves

EPIC (4503 "State of Shock") 3-5 84
Also see JACKSON, Michael
Also see JACKSONS
Also see JAGGER, Mick

JACKSON, Mick

P&R '78

Singles: 7-inch

ATCO 3-5 78

JACKSON, Millie

R&B '71

Singles: 7-inch

GEFFEN 3-4 87
JIVE 3-4 86-88
MGM 3-6 69
SPRING 3-5 71-83

LPs: 10/12-inch 33rpm

JIVE 5-8 86
SPRING 5-8 73-83
POLYDOR 5-8 79
Also see HAYES, Isaac, & Millie Jackson
Also see JOHN, Elton, & Millie Jackson
Also see WHODINI & Millie Jackson

JACKSON, Moose: see JACKSON, Bull Moose

JACKSON, Paul, Jr.

R&B '88

Singles: 7-inch

ATLANTIC....................................3-4 88

JACKSON, Python Lee: see PYTHON LEE JACKSON

JACKSON, Randy

R&B '78

Singles: 7-inch

EPIC..3-5 78
Also see JACKSONS

JACKSON, Rebbie

P&R/R&B/D&D/LP '84

Singles: 12-inch 33/45rpm

COLUMBIA 4-6 84-86

Singles: 7-inch

COLUMBIA 3-4 84-86

Picture Sleeves

COLUMBIA 3-4 84

LPs: 10/12-inch 33rpm

COLUMBIA 5-8 84-86
Also see GRANDMASTER FLASH & Furious Five
Also see JACKSONS

JACKSON, Rebbie, & Robin Zander

R&B '86

Singles: 7-inch

COLUMBIA 3-4 86

Also see JACKSON, Rebbie

JACKSON, Shawne

R&B '74

Singles: 7-inch

PLAYBOY 3-5 74

JACKSON, Stonewall

C&W '58

Singles: 7-inch

COLUMBIA (Except 41000 series) 3-8 61-73
COLUMBIA (41000 series) 4-8 58-61
FIRST GENERATION 3-4 81
GRT 3-5 74
LITTLE DARLIN' 3-5 78-79
MGM 3-5 73
PHONORAMA 3-4 83

Picture Sleeves

COLUMBIA (41393 "Waterloo") .. 8-10 59

EPs: 7-inch 33/45rpm

COLUMBIA 5-10 59

LPs: 10/12-inch 33rpm

AUDIOGRAPH ALIVE 5-8 82
COLUMBIA (1391 "The Dynamic Stonewall Jackson") 20-30 59
(Monaural.)
COLUMBIA (1700 thru 2700 series) 8-15 62-67
(Monaural.)
COLUMBIA (8186 "The Dynamic Stonewall Jackson") 25-40 59
(Stereo.)
COLUMBIA (8500 thru 9900 series) 8-15 62-70
(Stereo.)
COLUMBIA (10000 series) 5-8 73
COLUMBIA (30000 series) 5-10 70-72
FIRST GENERATION 5-8 78
GRT 5-10 75-76
HARMONY 8-12 66-74
LITTLE DARLIN' 5-8 79
MYRRH 5-8 76
PHONORAMA 5-8
RURAL RHYTHM 5-10
SUNBIRD 5-8 80

Session: Jordanaires.

JACKSON, Walter

P&R/R&B '64

Singles: 7-inch

BRUNSWICK 3-6 73
CHI-SOUND 3-5 76-78
COLUMBIA (02000 series) 3-4 81
COLUMBIA (42000 series) 10-20 62-63
COTILLION 4-8 69
EPIC 5-10 66-68
KELLI-ARTS 3-4 83
OKEH 5-10 64-67
20TH FOX 3-6 79
USA 5-10 60s

Picture Sleeves

OKEH 8-12 66-67

LPs: 10/12-inch 33rpm

CHI-SOUND 8-10 76-78
COLUMBIA 5-8 81
EPIC 8-10 77
OKEH 10-20 65-69
20TH FOX 5-8 79

JACKSON, Wanda

(With the Party Timers)

P&R '60

Singles: 78rpm

CAPITOL 15-25 56-57
DECCA 10-20 54-55

Singles: 7-inch

ABC 3-5 75
CAPITOL (2000 thru 3000 series) . 3-8 67-72
(Orange or orange/yellow label.)
CAPITOL (3400 thru 4600 series) 10-25 56-61
(Purple label.)
CAPITOL (4700 thru 5900 series) . 4-8 61-67
DECCA (29267 "If You Don't Somebody Else Will") 20-40 54
DECCA (29253 "Right to Love") 20-40 54
DECCA (29514 "Tears at the Grand Ole Op'ry") 20-40 55
DECCA (29677 "It's the Same World") 10-20 55
DECCA (29803 "Wasted") 20-40 55
JIN 3-6
MYRRH 3-4 73-75

Picture Sleeves

CAPITOL 5-10 62-66

EPs: 7-inch 33/45rpm

CAPITOL (1041 "Wanda Jackson") 25-50 58

LPs: 10/12-inch 33rpm

CAPITOL (100 thru 600 series) ... 8-15 69-71
CAPITOL (1041 "Wanda Jackson") 50-100 58
CAPITOL (1384 "Rockin' with Wanda") 50-100 60
CAPITOL (1511 "There's a Party Goin' On") 75-100 61
(With "T" prefix. Monaural.)
CAPITOL (1511 "There's a Party Goin' On") 100-125 61
(With "ST" prefix. Stereo.)
CAPITOL (1596 "Right Or Wrong") 25-35 61
(With "T" prefix. Monaural.)
CAPITOL (1596 "Right Or Wrong") 35-45 61
(With "ST" prefix. Stereo.)

CAPITOL (1776 "Wonderful Wanda") 15-25 62
(With "T" prefix. Monaural.)
CAPITOL (1776 "Wonderful Wanda") 20-30 62
(With "ST" prefix. Stereo.)
CAPITOL (1911 "Love Me Forever") 15-25 63
(With "T" prefix. Monaural.)
CAPITOL (1911 "Love Me Forever") 20-30 63
(With "ST" prefix. Stereo.)
CAPITOL (2030 "Two Sides of Wanda Jackson") 35-40 64
(With "T" prefix. Monaural.)
CAPITOL (2030 "Two Sides of Wanda Jackson") 40-45 64
(With "ST" prefix. Stereo.)
CAPITOL (2300 thru 2900 series) 10-20 65-68
CAPITOL (11000 series) 5-8 72-73
DECCA (4224 "Lovin' Country Style") 40-50 62
GUSTO 5-8 80
MYRRH 5-8 73-76
PICKWICK/HILLTOP 8-12 65-68
VARRICK/ROUNDER 5-8 87
VOCALION 8-12 69
WORD 4-8 77

JACKSON, Wanda, & Billy Gray

C&W '54

Singles: 7-inch

DECCA (29140 "You Can't Have My Love") 10-20 54
Also see JACKSON, Wanda

JACKSON, Willis

(Willis "Gator Tail" Jackson & His Orch.; vocal By the 4'Gaters; with Jack McDuff)

LP '66

Singles: 78rpm

APOLLO 5-10 50
ATLANTIC 15-25 51-53
DELUXE 4-8 53

Singles: 7-inch

ATLANTIC (946 "Harlem Nocturne") 75-125 51
ATLANTIC (957 "Wine-O-Wine") 75-125 52
ATLANTIC (967 "Rock, Rock, Rock") 50-75 52
ATLANTIC (975 "Gator's Groove") 40-60 52
ATLANTIC (998 "Shake Dance") 40-60 53
CADET 4-8 66
DELUXE 10-15 53
FIRE 5-10 59
PRESTIGE 5-10 59-69
VERVE 4-8 64

LPs: 10/12-inch 33rpm

ATLANTIC 5-8 75
AUDIO-LAB 15-25 59
BIG CHANCE 5-10 75
CADET 10-20 66
COTILLION 5-8 76
MGM 10-20 64
MOODSVILLE 15-20 62
MUSE 5-8 76-81
PRESTIGE (2500 series) 5-8 82
PRESTIGE (7100 & 7200 series) 15-25 59-64
(Yellow label.)
PRESTIGE (7100 & 7200 series) 10-20 65
(Blue label.)
PRESTIGE (7300 thru 7800 series) 8-15 65-71
TRIP 5-10 73
VERVE 10-20 64-69
Also see BROWN, Ruth
Also see CLOVERS
Also see McDUFF, Brother Jack, & Willis Jackson

JACKSON SISTERS

R&B '73

Singles: 7-inch

PROPHESY 3-5 73

JACKSONS

(Jackson 5)

P&R/R&B '69

Singles: 12-inch 33/45rpm

EPIC 4-8 79-84
MOTOWN 5-10 83

Singles: 7-inch

DYNAMO (146 "You Don't Have to Be Over 21") 20-30 71
EPIC 3-5 76-81
MCA 3-4 87
MOTOWN ("ABC" Picture Disc) .20-30 70
(Single-sided cardboard cutout picture disc.)
MOTOWN (1157 "I Want You Back") 4-8 69
MOTOWN (1163 "ABC") 4-8 70
MOTOWN (1166 "The Love You Save") 4-6 70
(Black vinyl.)
MOTOWN (1166 "I Found That Girl") 10-20 70
(Colored vinyl. Same song on both sides. Promotional issue only.)
MOTOWN (1171 thru 1310) 3-6 70-75
MOTOWN (1356 "Forever Came Today") 3-5 75
(Black vinyl.)
MOTOWN (1356 "Forever Came Today") 10-15 75
(Colored vinyl. Promotional issue only.)
STEEL-TOWN (681 "Big Boy") ..30-40 68

STEEL-TOWN (682 "We Don't Have to Be Over 21") ... 25-35 71

Picture Sleeves

EPIC ... 3-5 76-84
MOTOWN ... 4-6 71-75

EPs: 7-inch 33/45rpm

MOTOWN ("Jackson Five") ... 25-50 70
(Five track flexi-disc.)
MOTOWN ("Sugar Daddy") ... 20-40 70s
(Three track, cardboard flexi-disc.)
MOTOWN (60718 "Jackson Five, Third Album") ... 15-25 70

LPs: 10/12-inch 33rpm

EPIC (30000 series, except picture discs) ... 5-8 76-84
EPIC (PAL-34835 "Goin' Places") ... 10-20 78
(Picture disc.)
EPIC (8E8-39576 "Victory") ... 10-15 84
(Picture disc.)
EPIC (40000 series) ... 5-8 89
EPIC (46000 series) ... 10-15 81
(Half-speed mastered.)
MCA ... 5-8 87
MOTOWN (100 series) ... 5-10 80
MOTOWN (700 series, except 713) ... 8-15 69-74
MOTOWN (713 "The Jackson 5 Christmas Album") ... 10-20 70
MOTOWN (800 series) ... 8-15 75-76
MOTOWN (5000 series) ... 5-8
MOTOWN (6000 series) ... 5-8 84
NATURAL RESOURCES ... 8-12 79
(Promotional issues only.)
PICKWICK ... 5-10 70s

Members: Michael Jackson; Jermaine Jackson; Jackie Jackson; Marlon Jackson; Tito Jackson; Randy Jackson; Rebbie Jackson.

Also see JACKSON, Jackie
Also see JACKSON, Jermaine
Also see JACKSON, Michael
Also see JACKSON, Randy
Also see JACKSON, Rebbie
Also see RIPPLES & WAVES Plus Michael
Also see ROSS, Diana, & Bill Cosby / Diana Ross & Jackson Five
Also see WONDER, Stevie

JACOBI, Lou

LP '66

LPs: 10/12-Inch 33rpm

CAPITOL ... 6-12 66
VERVE ... 5-10 67

JACOBS, Debbie

R&B/LP '79

Singles: 12-inch 33/45rpm

PERSONAL ... 4-6 84

Singles: 7-inch

MCA ... 3-4 79-80

LPs: 10/12-inch 33rpm

MCA ... 5-10 79-80

JACOBS, Dick, & His Orchestra

P&R '56

Singles: 7-inch

CORAL ... 3-5 54-62

EPs: 7-inch 33/45rpm

CORAL ... 5-15 56

LPs: 10/12-inch 33rpm

CORAL ... 10-20 56-60
VOCALION ... 5-10 60

JACOBS, Hank

P&R/R&B '64

Singles: 7-inch

CALL ME ... 4-6
IMPERIAL ... 5-10 62
SUE ... 4-8 63-64

LPs: 10/12-inch 33rpm

SUE (1023 "So Far Away") ... 20-30 64

JACQUET, Illinois

(With His All-Stars; Jacque Rabbit; with Russell Jacquet)

R&B '52

Singles: 78rpm

ARA ... 5-10 46
ALADDIN ... 5-10 45-54
APOLLO ... 5-10 46-47
MERCURY ... 4-8 52
PHILO ... 5-10 45
RCA ... 5-10 48-51
SAVOY ... 5-10 46

Singles: 7-inch

ALADDIN ... 10-20 53-54
ARGO ... 4-8 63-65
MERCURY ... 10-15 52
PRESTIGE ... 3-6 68-69
RCA (0011 "Black Velvet") ... 20-30 49
(Colored vinyl.)
RCA (0021 "Big Foot") ... 20-30 49
(Colored vinyl.)
RCA (0047 "Blue Satin") ... 20-30 49
(Colored vinyl.)
RCA (0087 "My Old Gal") ... 20-30 49
(Colored vinyl.)
RCA (0097 "Slow Down, Baby") 15-20 49
(Colored vinyl.)
VERVE ... 4-8 62

EPs: 7-inch 33/45rpm

APOLLO (602 "Jam Session") ... 50-75 50
CLEF (126 "Illinois Jacquet Collates") ... 25-40 51
CLEF (143 "Illinois Jacquet Collates") ... 25-40 51
CLEF (166 "Illinois Jacquet Collates, No. 2") ... 20-40 52
CLEF (167 "Illinois Jacquet Collates, No. 2") ... 20-40 52
CLEF (207 "Jazz Moods") ... 20-40 54
CLEF (374 "Illinois Jacquet and His Orchestra") ... 20-40 55

RCA (3236 "Black Velvet")........ 40-60 53
SAVOY.................................... 20-30 50-53

LPs: 10/12–inch 33rpm

ACCORD..................................... 5-8 82
ALADDIN (800 series)............... 50-60 56
APOLLO (104 "Jam Session")............................ 150-250 50
ARGO....................................... 15-25 63-65
CLEF (112 "Illinois Jacquet Collates")........................... 100-125 51
(10–inch LP. Has Mercury label with Clef logo and number.)
CLEF (129 "Illinois Jacquet Collates, No. 2")................. 100-125 52
(10–inch LP. Has Mercury label with Clef logo and number.)
CLEF (622 "Jazz Moods")....... 50-100 54
CLEF (676 "Illinois Jacquet and His Orchestra").............................. 50-75 55
CLEF (680 "The Kid & Brute")... 50-75 55
CLEF (700 "Jazz Moods")......... 40-60 56
CLEF (702 "Groovin'")............. 40-60 56
CLEF (750 "Swing's the Thing") 40-60 56
EPIC.. 15-25 63
GRAND AWARD (315 "Uptown Jazz")...................................... 20-35 56
IMPERIAL 15-25 62
JRC 5-8 79
PRESTIGE................................. 8-12 69-75
RCA (3236 "Black Velvet")........ 50-75 53
(10–inch LP.)
ROULETTE............................... 20-30 60
SAVOY (15024 "Tenor Sax") .. 50-100 53
(10–inch LP.)
TRIP 5-8 79
VERVE (2500 series).................. 5-10 82-87
VERVE (8000 series)............... 25-50 57-58
(Reads "Verve Records, Inc." at bottom of label.)
VERVE (8000 series)............... 10-20 61-65
(Reads "MGM Records - a Division of Metro-Goldwyn-Mayer, Inc." at bottom of label.)

Members: Illinois Jacquet; Johnny Otis; Russell Jacquet; Arthur Dennis; Henry Coker; Sir Charles; Ulysses Livingston; William Hadnott.

Also see COLE, Cozy, & Illinois Jacquet
Also see DOGGETT, Bill
Also see HEART BEATS QUINTET
Also see JAZZ at the Philharmonic
Also see OTIS, Johnny
Also see X-RAYS

JACQUET, Illinois, & Count Basie

LPs: 10/12–inch 33rpm

CLEF (701 "Port of Rico") 40-60 56

Also see BASIE, Count

JACQUET, Illinois, & Miles Davis

EPs: 7–inch 33/45rpm

ALADDIN (504 "Illinois Jacquet & His Tenor Sax")...................... 50-65 54
ALADDIN (511 "Illinois Jacquet & His Tenor Sax") 50-65 54

LPs: 10/12–inch 33rpm

ALADDIN (708 "Illinois Jacquet & His Tenor Sax") 100-150 54
(10–inch LP.)

Also see DAVIS, Miles

JACQUET, Illinois / Lester Young

EPs: 7–inch 33/45rpm

ALADDIN (501 "Battle of the Saxes") 50-65 54

LPs: 10/12–inch 33rpm

ALADDIN (701 "Battle of the Saxes") 100-150 54
(10–inch LP. Black vinyl.)
ALADDIN (701 "Battle of the Saxes") 200-250 54
(10–inch LP. Colored vinyl.)
ALADDIN (803 "Illinois Jacquet & His Tenor Sax") 60-80 56
(Has the eight tracks from *Battle of the Saxes,* plus four others.)

JADE WARRIOR

LP '72

Singles: 7–inch

VERTIGO....................................3-4 71-72

LPs: 10/12–inch 33rpm

ANTILLES....................................5-8 78
ISLAND......................................8-10 74-76
VERTIGO..................................10-12 71-72

JAGGER, Chris

LP '73

LPs: 10/12–inch 33rpm

ASYLUM......................................8-10 73-74

JAGGER, Mick

P&R/R&B/D&D/LP '85

Singles: 12–inch 33/45rpm

COLUMBIA (2060 "Lucky in Love")...4-8 85
(With special cover.)
COLUMBIA (2060 "Lucky in Love")....................................15-20 85
(Promotional issue with special cover.)
COLUMBIA (5181 "Just Another Night") 4-8 85
(With special cover.)
COLUMBIA (5181 "Just Another Night") 15-20 85
(Promotional issue with special cover.)
COLUMBIA (6926 "Let's Work") ..5-10 87
COLUMBIA (7492 "Throwaway").5-10 87
EPIC (5931 "Ruthless People") .10-15 86
(With special cover.)

Singles: 7–inch

COLUMBIA (04743 "Just Another Night") 3-5 85

COLUMBIA (04893 "Lucky in Love") 3-5 85
COLUMBIA (07306 "Let's Work") 3-5 87
COLUMBIA (07653 "Throwaway") 3-5 87
EPIC (06211 "Ruthless People") 3-5 86

Picture Sleeves

COLUMBIA (04743 "Just Another Night") 3-5 85
COLUMBIA (04893 "Lucky in Love") 3-5 85
COLUMBIA (07306 "Let's Work") 3-5 87
COLUMBIA (07653 "Throwaway") 3-5 87
EPIC (06211 "Ruthless People") 3-5 86

Promotional Singles

COLUMBIA (04743 "Just Another Night") 8-10 85
COLUMBIA (04893 "Lucky in Love") 8-10 85
COLUMBIA (07306 "Let's Work") 8-10 87
COLUMBIA (07653 "Throwaway") 8-10 87
EPIC (06211 "Ruthless People"). 5-10 86

LPs: 10/12–inch 33rpm

COLUMBIA (39940 "She's the Boss") 8-10 85
COLUMBIA (40919 "Primitive Cool") 8-10 87
EPIC 8-12 86
LONDON WAVELENGTH (006 "The Mick Jagger Special") 75-100 81
(Promotional issue only.)
ROLLING STONES (164 "Interview with Mick Jagger") 75-100 71
(Promotional issue only.)
U.A. (300 "Ned Kelly") 10-15 74
(Soundtrack.)
U.A. (5213 "Ned Kelly") 15-20 70
(Soundtrack.)

Also see BOWIE, David, & Mick Jagger
Also see FRAMPTON, Peter
Also see JACKSON, Michael, & Mick Jagger
Also see ROLLING STONES
Also see SIMON, Carly
Also see TOSH, Peter, & Mick Jagger
Also see WEST, Leslie
Also see WOLF, Peter, & Mick Jagger

JAGGERZ

P&R/LP '70

Singles: 7–inch

GAMBLE 4-8 68
JAGGERZ 3-5 74
KAMA SUTRA 3-6 70
WOODEN NICKEL 3-5 75

LPs: 10/12–inch 33rpm

GAMBLE 15-20 68
KAMA SUTRA 10-15 70
WOODEN NICKEL 8-10 75

Members: Dominic Ierace (a.k.a. Donnie Iris); Jim Pugliano; Jim Ross; Bill Maybray; Ben Faiella.
Also see IRIS, Donnie
Also see Q

JAGS

P&R '80

Singles: 7–inch

ISLAND 3-5 79-80

Picture Sleeves

ISLAND 3-5 79-80

LPs: 10/12–inch 33rpm

ISLAND 5-8 80-81

JAISUN

R&B '78

Singles: 7–inch

JETT SETT 3-5 78

JAK

R&B '85

Singles: 7–inch

EPIC 3-4 84-86

LPs: 10/12–inch 33rpm

EPIC 5-8 85

JA-KKI

P&R '76

Singles: 7–inch

PYRAMID 3-5 76
WEST END 3-5

JAM

LP '80

Singles: 7–inch

POLYDOR 3-5 78-83

Picture Sleeves

POLYDOR 3-5 80-83

LPs: 10/12–inch 33rpm

POLYDOR 5-8 77-83

Also see STYLE COUNCIL

JAMAICA BOYS

R&B '87

Singles: 7–inch

W.B. 3-4 87-88

JAMAICA GIRLS

D&D '83

Singles: 12–inch 33/45rpm

SLEEPING BAG 4-6 83

JAMAL, Ahmad

(Ahmad Jamal Trio; Quintet)

R&B/LP '58

Singles: 7-Inch

ARGO 4-8 57-65
CADET 3-6 66-68
CHESS 3-5 73
PARROTT 5-10 55
20TH FOX 3-5 73-80

EPs: 7-Inch 33/45rpm

ARGO 8-15 59-61

LPs: 10/12-Inch 33rpm

ABC 8-12 68
ARGO (610 thru 662) 20-40 56-60
ARGO (667 thru 758) 15-25 61-65
CADET 10-25 65-73

CATALYST.................................. 5-10 76
EPIC (600 series)..................... 15-30 63-65
EPIC (3212 "Ahmad Jamal
Trio")............................... 30-50 56
EPIC (3600 series)................... 20-30 59
IMPULSE 10-20 69-73
MOTOWN 5-10 80
PERSONAL CHOICE.................. 5-8 82
SHUBRA 5-8 83
20TH FOX................................ 5-10 73-80
WHO'S WHO in JAZZ................ 5-10 81

JAMES, Bob

(Bob James Trio)

P&R '74

Singles: 7-inch

CTI 3-5 74-77
COLUMBIA 3-5 79-83
TAPPAN ZEE/COLUMBIA........... 3-5 77-85

Picture Sleeves

COLUMBIA 3-5 79-80

LPs: 10/12-inch 33rpm

CTI 5-10 74-77
COLUMBIA 5-8 83
ESP 10-15 65
MERCURY 15-25 63
TAPPAN ZEE/COLUMBIA.......... 5-10 77-85

Also see FOURPLAY

JAMES, Bob, & Earl Klugh

LP '79

Singles: 7-inch

CAPITOL.................................... 3-4 82
TAPPAN ZEE/COLUMBIA........... 3-5 79

LPs: 10/12-inch 33rpm

CAPITOL.................................... 5-8 82
MFSL (124 "2 of a Kind")........... 20-30 84
TAPPAN ZEE/COLUMBIA.......... 5-10 79

Also see KLUGH, Earl

JAMES, Bob, & David Sanborn

LP '86

LPs: 10/12-inch 33rpm

W.B. 5-8 86-88

Also see JAMES, Bob
Also see SANBORN, David

JAMES, Elmore

(With His Broomdusters; Elmo James)

R&B '52

Singles: 78rpm

ACE 10-20 53
CHECKER.................................. 20-30 53
CHIEF 5-10 57
FLAIR 10-20 54-56
METEOR (5000 "I Believe")...... 20-30 53
METEOR (5003 "Sinful
Woman") 20-30 53
MODERN (983 "Wild About
You") 10-20 56
TRUMPET (146 "I Believe My Time
Ain't Long")............................ 15-25 52
VEE JAY 5-10 57

Singles: 7-inch

ACE (508 "My Time Ain't
Long") 100-200 53
CHECKER (777 "Country
Boogie") 200-400 53
CHESS..5-10 60
CHIEF (7001 "The Twelve
Year Old Boy")........................25-50 57
CHIEF (7004 "It Hurts Me Too") 25-50 57
CHIEF (7006 "Cry for Me
Baby") 25-50 57
ENJOY 10-15 65
FIRE..10-20 60-62
FLAIR (1011 "Early in the
Morning") 150-200 54
FLAIR (1014 "Can't Stop
Lovin'") 150-200 54
FLAIR (1022 "Strange Kinda
Feeling")..............................100-150 55
FLAIR (1031 "Make My Dreams
Come True") 100-200 55
FLAIR (1039 "Sho'nuff, I Do") 100-200 55
FLAIR (1048 "Dark and
Dreary") 100-200 56
FLAIR (1057 "Standing at
the Crossroads").................100-200 55
FLAIR (1062 "Late Hours
at Midnight").........................75-125 56
FLAIR (1069 "Happy Home")...75-125 56
FLAIR (1074 "Dust My Blues")100-150 56
FLAIR (1079 "Blues Before
Sunrise") 75-100 56
FLASHBACK.................................3-6 65
JEWEL (764 "Dust My Broom") 4-8 66
JEWEL (783 "Catfish Blues").........4-8 66
(Though credited to Elmo James, the flip sides of Jewel 764 and 783 are actually by Big Boy Crudup.)
KENT 4-8 60-67
METEOR (5000 "I Believe")...200-300 53
METEOR (5003 "Sinful
Woman") 200-300 53
MODERN (983 "Wild About
You") 150-250 56
M-PAC 4-8
S&M 4-8
SOUND 4-8
PHERE SOUND.............................4-8 65
VEE JAY 8-12 57

LPs: 10/12-inch 33rpm

BELL 10-12 68-69
BLUE HORIZON 10-12
CHESS..10-12 69
COLLECTABLES...........................6-8 88
CROWN (5168 "Blues After
Hours")....................................40-50 61
CUSTOM 8-12
INTERMEDIA.................................5-8 84

KENT (5022 "Original Folk Blues") ... 20-30 64
KENT (9000 series) ... 10-20 67-69
KENT TREASURE SERIES ... 5-8 86
RELIC ... 5-10 88
SPHERE SOUND (7002 "The Sky Is Crying") ... 25-35 60s
SPHERE SOUND (7008 "I Need You") ... 25-35 60s
TRIP ... 8-10 71-78
UNITED ... 10-12 60s
UPFRONT ... 8-10 70s

Also see CRUDUP, Big Boy

JAMES, Elmore, & John Brim

LPs: 10/12–inch 33rpm

CHESS ... 10-15 69

Also see JAMES, Elmore

JAMES, Etta

(Etta "Miss Peaches" James)

R&B '55

Singles: 78rpm

MODERN ... 10-15 55-56

Singles: 7–inch

ABC ... 3-5 74
ARGO ... 5-10 60-64
CADET ... 4-8 67-72
CHESS ... 3-5 73-76
KENT ... 10-15 58-60
MODERN (900 series) ... 15-25 55-56
MODERN (1000 series) ... 10-15 57-58
REGENCY ... 10-20
T-ELECTRIC ... 3-5 80
W.B. ... 3-5 78

LPs: 10/12–inch 33rpm

ARGO ... 20-30 61-65
ARRIVAL ... 5-10 83
CADET ... 10-15 67-71
CHESS ... 10-12 71-76
CROWN ... 20-30 61-63
INTERMEDIA ... 5-8 84
KENT (3002 "Miss Etta James") 15-25 61
(Black vinyl.)
KENT (3002 "Miss Etta James") 30-40 61
(Colored vinyl.)
T-ELECTRIC ... 5-8 80
UNITED ... 10-12
W.B. ... 5-8 78
WESTBOUND ... 8-10

Also see ETTA & HARVEY

JAMES, Etta, & Sugar Pie DeSanto

P&R '65

Singles: 7–inch

CADET ... 4-8 65-66

Also see DE SANTO, Sugar Pie
Also see JAMES, Etta

JAMES, Harry, & His Orchestra

P&R '38

Singles: 78rpm

BRUNSWICK ... 3-6 38
COLUMBIA ... 3-6 40-57
VARIETY ... 4-8 40

Singles: 7-Inch

COLUMBIA (33000 series) ... 3-5 76
COLUMBIA (38000 thru 40000 series) ... 5-8 50-56
DOT ... 3-6 65-66
GOLD-MOR ... 3-5 73
MGM ... 4-6 59-63

EPs: 7-Inch 33/45rpm

COLUMBIA ... 5-15 50-56

LPs: 10/12-Inch 33rpm

BAINBRIDGE ... 5-8 83
BRIGHT ORANGE ... 5-8 73
CAPITOL (600 thru 1500 series) ... 15-30 55-61
(With "T" or "ST" prefix.)
CAPITOL (1500 series) ... 10-20 62
(With "DT" prefix.)
CAPITOL (1500 series) ... 5-8 77
(With "M" prefix.)
COLUMBIA ... 10-30 50-67
COLUMBIA SPECIAL PROD. ... 5-8 79
DOT ... 8-15 66-67
HARMONY ... 10-20 59-72
LONDON ... 5-10 68
MGM ... 10-20 59-65
METRO ... 8-15 65-67
PICKWICK ... 5-10 70s
SHEFFIELD LAB ... 5-8 77-79

Also see KALLEN, Kitty
Also see SINATRA, Frank

JAMES, Harry, & Dick Haymes

LPs: 10/12-Inch 33rpm

CIRCLE ... 5-8 81

Also see HAYMES, Dick
Also see JAMES, Harry, & His Orchestra

JAMES, Jesse

P&R/R&B '67

Singles: 7–inch

T.T.E.D. ... 3-4 87
20TH FOX ... 3-8 67-75
UNI ... 4-6 69
ZEA (ZAY) ... 3-5 70-71

LPs: 10/12–inch 33rpm

20TH FOX ... 8-10 67

JAMES, Jimmy, & Vagabonds

P&R/R&B '68

Singles: 7–inch

ATCO ... 4-8 67-68
PYE ... 3-5 75-76

LPs: 10/12–inch 33rpm

ATCO ... 10-15 67
PYE ... 5-8 75

JAMES, Joni

P&R '52

Singles: 78rpm

MGM (222 "Let There Be Love") ... 100-200 53
(Four-disc boxed set.)
MGM (234 "Award Winning Album") ... 100-200 54
(Four disc boxed set.)
MGM (272 "Little Girl Blue") .. 100-200 54
(Four-disc boxed set.)
MGM (11000 & 12000 series)... 10-20 52-58
SHARP (46 "Let There Be Love") ... 25-50 52
SHARP (50 "You Belong to Me") ... 25-50 52

Singles: 7-inch

MGM (16 thru 19) ... 20-40 59-60
(Stereo compact 33 singles.)
MGM (11223 thru 12660) ... 15-25 52-58
MGM (12706 "There Goes My Heart") ... 10-15 58
(Monaural.)
MGM (12706 "There Goes My Heart") ... 20-30 58
(Stereo. Unusual numbering—most MGM stereo 45s are in the 50000 series. Billed as the industry's "First Single Stereo Disc.")
MGM (12746 thru 13304) ... 10-20 59-64
MGM (13288 "Sentimental Me") 50-75 64
(Promotional issue only.)
MGM (50111 "There Must be a Way") ... 15-25 59
(Stereo.)
MGM/GOLDEN CIRCLE (101 thru 104) ... 5-10 61
SHARP (46 "Let There Be Love") ... 150-250 52
SHARP (50 "You Belong to Me") ... 100-200 52

Picture Sleeves

MGM (12565 "Never Till Now"). 10-20 57
MGM (12706 "There Goes My Heart") ... 25-50 58
MGM (12779 "I Still Get a Thrill") ... 10-20 59
MGM (12895 "We Know") ... 10-20 60
MGM (12933 "My Last Date") ... 10-20 60
MGM (12948 "Be My Love") ... 10-20 61
MGM (13037 "You Were Wrong") ... 10-20 62

EPs: 7-inch 33/45rpm

MGM (222 "Let There Be Love") ... 50-75 53
MGM (234 "Award Winning Album") ... 50-75 54
MGM (272 "Little Girl Blue") ... 50-75 54
MGM (326 "When I Fall in Love") ... 20-40 55
(EPs 222 through 326 are two-disc sets.)
MGM (1160 "When I Fall in Love") ... 10-20 55
MGM (1172 "Have Yourself a Merry Little Christmas") ... 25-50 55
MGM (1211 thru 1617) ... 10-20 56-58
MGM (1652/3/4 "Songs of Hank Williams") ... 10-15 59
(Monaural. Price is for any of three volumes.)
MGM (1652/3/4 "Songs of Hank Williams") ... 30-40 59
(Stereo. Price is for any of three volumes.)
MGM (1656/7/8 "100 Strings and Joni") ... 10-15 59
(Monaural. Price is for any of three volumes.)
MGM (1656/7/8 "100 Strings and Joni") ... 30-40 59
(Stereo. Price is for any of three volumes.)
MGM (1672/3/4 "Joni Swings Sweet") ... 10-15 59
(Monaural. Price is for any of three volumes.)
MGM (1672/3/4 "Joni Swings Sweet") ... 30-40 59
(Stereo. Price is for any of three volumes.)
MGM (3328 "In the Still of the Night") ... 20-35 56
MGM (3533 "Songs By Jerome Kern & Harry Warren") ... 20-35 57

LPs: 10/12-inch 33rpm

MGM (222 "Let There Be Love") ... 75-125 53
(10-inch LP.)
MGM (234 "Award Winning Album") ... 75-125 54
(10-inch LP.)
MGM (272 "Little Girl Blue") ... 75-125 54
(10-inch LP.)
MGM (3240 "When I Fall in Love") ... 30-50 55
MGM (3328 "In the Still of the Night") ... 30-50 56
MGM (3346 "Award Winning Album, Vol. 1") ... 30-50 56
MGM (3347 "Little Girl Blue") ... 30-50 56
MGM (3348 "Let There Be Love") ... 30-50 56
MGM (3449 "Songs By Victor Young & Frank Losser") ... 30-50 56
MGM (3468 "Merry Christmas"). 30-50 56
MGM (3528 "Give Us This Day") ... 25-45 57
MGM (3533 "Songs By Jerome Kern & Harry Warren") ... 25-45 57

MGM (3602 "Among My Souvenirs")............................ 25-45 58
MGM (3623 "Ti Voglio Bene")... 25-45 58
MGM (3706 "Award Winning Album, Vol. 1") 25-45 58
MGM (E-3718 "Je T'Aime")....... 25-45 58
(Monaural.)
MGM (SE-3718 "Je T'Aime")..... 35-55 58
(Stereo.)
MGM (E-3729 "Songs By Hank Williams")....................... 25-45 59
(Monaural.)
MGM (SE-3729 "Songs By Hank Williams")....................... 35-55 59
(Stereo.)
MGM (E-3749 thru E-4286)....... 20-30 59-65
(Monaural.)
MGM (SE-3749 thru SE-4286).. 20-35 59-65
(Stereo.)

JAMES, Melvin

LP '87

LPs: 10/12-inch 33rpm

MCA 5-8 87

JAMES, Rick

(With the Stone City Band)

P&R/R&B/LP '78

Singles: 12-inch 33/45rpm

GORDY 4-6 79-85
MOTOWN 4-6 78-85

Singles: 7-inch

GORDY 3-5 78-85
MOTOWN 3-4 86
REPRISE 3-4 88

Picture Sleeves

GORDY 3-5 79-85

LPs: 10/12-inch 33rpm

GORDY 5-8 78-86
REPRISE 5-8 88

Also see TEMPTATIONS & Rick James

JAMES, Rick, & Friend

(With Smokey Robinson)

R&B '83

Singles: 7-inch

GORDY 3-5 83

JAMES, Rick, & Smokey Robinson

P&R '83

Singles: 7-inch

GORDY 3-5 83

Also see JAMES, Rick
Also see JAMES, Rick, & Friend
Also see ROBINSON, Smokey

JAMES, Rick, & Roxanne Shante

R&B '88

Singles: 7-inch

REPRISE 3-4 88

Also see SHANTE, Roxanne

JAMES, Sonny

(With the Southern Gentlemen; with Silver; with Tennessee State Prison Band; the Southern Gentleman)

C&W '53

Singles: 78rpm

CAPITOL..4-8 52-57

Singles: 7-inch

CAPITOL (2000 thru 3900)...........3-6 67-74
(Orange labels.)
CAPITOL (2200 thru 3800)..........8-15 52-57
(Purple labels.)
CAPITOL (3900 thru 5900)...........4-8 58-67
(Purple or orange/yellow swirl labels.)
CAPITOL (6000 series) 4-6 60s
CAPITOL CUSTOM ("Salute to KRAK")...................................15-20 67
(Promotional issue for a Sacramento radio station.)
COLUMBIA 3-5 72-78
DIMENSION..3-4 81-83
DOT 4-6 62
GROOVE 4-8 61
MONUMENT..3-5 79
NRC 5-8 60
RCA 4-8 61-62

Picture Sleeves

CAPITOL (Except 4268).............4-10 65-71
CAPITOL (4268 "Who's Next in Line")..6-10 59
COLUMBIA 3-5 72-75
DIMENSION..3-5 80s
NRC (050 "Jenny Lou").............10-15 60

EPs: 7-inch 33/45rpm

CAPITOL..8-15 57-58
CAPITOL CREATIVE PROD. 5-10 68

LPs: 10/12-inch 33rpm

ABC..5-8 77
BROOKVILLE 8-12 75
CAMDEN 8-12 60s
CAPITOL (100 thru 800).............8-12 68-71
CAPITOL (779 "The Southern Gentleman")............................25-35 57
CAPITOL (867 "Sonny") 20-30 57
CAPITOL (988 "Honey") 20-30 58
CAPITOL (1100 series) 15-25 59
CAPITOL (2000 thru 2800)..........8-15 64-68
CAPITOL (11000 series) 5-8 72-73
COLUMBIA 5-10 72-78
CROWN 8-12 60s
DIMENSION..5-8 82
DOT 15-20 62
GUEST STAR 10-15 64
HAMILTON 8-12 65
MONUMENT...5-8 79
PICKWICK 5-8 76
PICKWICK/HILLTOP 8-12 69
TVP 8-12 75

Also see HAGGARD, Merle / Sonny James

Also see HORTON, Johnny / Sonny James
Also see VINCENT, Gene / Tommy Sands / Sonny James / Ferlin Husky
Also see VINCENT, Gene / Frank Sinatra / Sonny James / Ron Goodwin

JAMES, Sonny / Dave Dudley / Sunny Williams

LPs: 10/12-inch 33rpm

DIPLOMAT.................................. 5-10 60s
Also see DUDLEY, Dave

JAMES, Sonny / David Houston

LPs: 10/12-inch 33rpm

PICKWICK/HILLTOP 8-12 67
Also see HOUSTON, David

JAMES, Sonny / Seekers

Singles: 7-inch

CAPITOL (5375 "I'll Keep Holding On"/ "I'll Never Find Another You") 4-8 65
(These two tracks were unintentionally pressed back-to-back.)
Also see JAMES, Sonny
Also see SEEKERS

JAMES, Tommy
(With the Shondells)

P&R/R&B/LP '66

Singles: 7-inch

ABC.. 3-5 73
FANTASY................................... 3-4 75-80
MCA 3-5 74
MILLENNIUM 3-5 79-81
ROULETTE................................ 4-8 66-73
TWENTY-ONE............................ 3-4 83

Picture Sleeves

FANTASY................................... 3-5 76
MILLENNIUM 3-5 71
ROULETTE................................ 5-10 66-67
TWENTY-ONE............................ 3-4 83

LPs: 10/12-inch 33rpm

FANTASY................................... 8-10 76-80
MILLENNIUM 5-8 80
RHINO....................................... 8-12 89
ROULETTE............................... 10-20 66-72
SCEPTER 8-10 73
SCEPTER/CITATION 5-8 82
TWENTY-ONE............................ 5-8 83
Members: Tommy James; Mike Vale; Ed Gray; Ron Rosman; Pete Lucia.
Also see HOG HEAVEN
Also see SHONDELLS

JAMES BOYS

P&R/R&B '68

Singles: 7-inch

PHIL L.A. of SOUL 4-6 68
Also see MFSB

JAMES GANG

LP '69

Singles: 7-inch

ABC... 3-5 70-72
ATCO 3-5 74-75
BLUESWAY 4-6 69

LPs: 10/12-inch 33rpm

ABC.......................................10-12 70-73
ATCO...8-10 74-76
BLUESWAY 10-15 69
COMMAND 8-10 74
MCA 5-8
Members: Joe Walsh; Tommy Bolin; Dominic Troiano.
Also see BOLIN, Tommy
Also see WALSH, Joe

JAMESON, Cody

C&W/P&R '77

Singles: 7-inch

ATCO 3-5 77

JAMESON, Nick

P&R '86

Singles: 7-inch

MOTOWN 3-4 86

LPs: 10/12-inch 33rpm

BEARSVILLE (6972 "Already Free")..8-12 77
MOTOWN 5-8 86
Also see FOGHAT

JAMESTOWN MASSACRE

P&R '72

Singles: 7-inch

W.B. 3-5 72

JAMIE & JANE

Singles: 7-inch

DECCA (30862 "Strolling") 15-20 59
DECCA (30934 "Faithful Our Love")......................................15-20 59
Members: Gene Pitney; Ginny Arnell.
Also see ARNELL, Ginny
Also see PITNEY, Gene

JAMIES

P&R '58

Singles: 7-inch

EPIC...5-10 58-63
EPIC (11000 series).....................3-4 74
U.A. 4-6 59

Picture Sleeves

EPIC (9281 "Summertime Summertime")........................15-20 58-63
Members: Tom Jamison; Serena Jamison.

JAMMERS

R&B '82

Singles: 7-inch

JUBILEE 4-8 66
LOMA..4-8 67

JAMUL

P&R '70

Singles: 7-inch

LIZARD 3-5 70

LPs: 10/12-inch 33rpm

LIZARD 10-12 70

JAN & ARNIE

(With Don Ralke's Orchestra)

P&R '58

Singles: 78rpm

ARWIN (108 "Jennie Lee").... 150-250 58

Singles: 7-inch

ARWIN (108 "Jennie Lee")........ 15-25 58
ARWIN (111 "Gas Money")....... 15-25 58
ARWIN (113 "I Love Linda")...... 15-25 58
DOT (16116 "Gas Money") 10-20 58
DORE (522 "Baby Talk")....... 150-200 59
(By Jan & Dean though shown on first pressings as by Jan & Arnie.)

EPs: 7-inch 33/45rpm

DOT (1097 "Jan & Arnie")..... 350-450 60
Members: Jan Berry; Arnie Ginsburg.
Also see BERRY, Jan
Also see JAN & DEAN
Also see RALKE, Don

JAN & DEAN

P&R/R&B '59

Singles: 7-inch

CAPITOL (89 "Jennie Lee")
(By Jan & Dean instead of Jan & Arnie.)
CHALLENGE (9120 "Wanted: One Girl") 10-20 61
CHALLENGE (9111 "Heart and Soul"/ "Those Words")...................... 25-35 61
CHALLENGE (9111 "Heart and Soul"/ "Midsummer Night's Dream").. 10-20 61
(Note different flip side.)
CHALLENGE (59111 "Heart and Soul") 10-20 61
COLUMBIA (44036 "Yellow Balloon")................................ 15-25 67
DORE.................................... 15-25 59-61
J&D (1 "Oh What a Beautiful Morning")........................... 150-200 87
(Private, limited, promotional, red vinyl pressing by Dean Torrence which he used as Christmas gifts. With Chris Farmer and Phil Bardowell.)
J&D (001 "California Lullabye"). 20-30 66
J&D (402 "Like a Summer Rain") 20-30 66
JAN & DEAN (10 "Hawaii") 45-60 66
JAN & DEAN (11 "Fan Tan")..... 50-75 66
LIBERTY (55397 "A Sunday Kind of Love")................................ 10-20 61
LIBERTY (55454 "Tennessee") 10-20 62
LIBERTY (55496 "Who Put the Bomp") 20-30 62
LIBERTY (55522 "She's Still Talkin' Baby Talk")........................... 50-75 62
LIBERTY (55531 "Linda")........... 8-12 63
LIBERTY (55580 thru 55727)...... 5-10 63-64
LIBERTY (55766 thru 55923)...... 8-12 63-66
MAGIC LAMP (401 "California Lullabye") 15-25 66
ODE (66111 "Fun City")............15-25 75
U.A. 10-20 72-76
W.B. (7151 "Only a Boy")...........25-35 67
W.B. (7219 "I Know My Mind")...25-35 68

Picture Sleeves

DORE (555 "We Go Together").35-50 60
DORE (576 "Gee")..................75-100 60
LIBERTY (Except 55766 & 55849).................................15-25 63-65
LIBERTY (55766 "From All Over the World") 80-125 65
LIBERTY (55849 "Folk City").....20-30 65
U.A. (50859 "Jenny Lee") 15-25 71

EPs: 7-inch 33/45rpm

ARTISTIC (227 "Original Golden Hits") 40-50 65
(Mail order offer.)

LPs: 10/12-inch 33rpm

ARTISTIC (227 "Original Golden Hits") 50-100 65
(Mail order offer. Also includes tracks by: Jerry Wallace; Champs; Ray Sharpe; Fireflies; Rosie and the Originals; and Gene & Eunice.)
AUDIO ENCORE 5-8 89
AXIS (45 "Very Best") 5-10
COLUMBIA (9461 "Save for a Rainy Day")....................1500-2000 67
(At least one sale of this LP has been confirmed. It DOES exist but is probably not a U.S. issue. Tracks are remixed from what is heard on the J&D LP of the same title. Does have one track, *Lullaby in the Rain*, which is not on the J&D LP.)
DEADMAN'S CURVE ("Live at Keystone Berkeley") 15-25 78
(With Papa Doo Ron Ron.)
DESIGN/STEREO SPEC..........10-20 64
DORE (101 "Jan & Dean").....150-250 60
(Price includes a 12"x12" Jan & Dean color photo, which represents $50 to $75 of the value.)
EMI..10-15 86
EMI/LIBERTY............................10-20 90
EXACT 5-8 80
EXCELSIOR 10-15 80
IMPERIAL HOUSE 5-8 80
INTERNATIONAL AWARD..........8-10
J&D (101 "Save for a Rainy Day")...................................200-250 67
K-TEL...5-10 70-89
LIBERTY (3248 thru 3403) 20-25 62-65
(Monaural.)
LIBERTY (3414 "Pop Symphony Number 1").............................40-45 65
(Monaural.)
LIBERTY (3417 thru 3460) 20-25 65-66
(Monaural.)

LIBERTY (7248 thru 7403)........ 20-30 62-65
(Stereo.)
LIBERTY (7414 "Pop Symphony Number 1")............................ 40-50 65
(Stereo.)
LIBERTY (7417 thru 7460)........ 20-30 65-66
(Stereo.)
LIBERTY (10000 series) 8-12 81-82
MAGIC CARPET........................ 10-12
PAIR (1071 "California Gold") ... 10-15
RHINO... 5-8 82
SILVER EAGLE (1039 "Silver Summer") 25-35 86
(Mail-order offer.)
SUNSET..................................... 10-15 67
U.A. 10-12 71-79

Members: Jan Berry; Dean Torrence.
Also see BEACH BOYS
Also see BEACH BOYS / Jan & Dean
Also see BERRY, Jan
Also see JAN & ARNIE
Also see LEGENDARY MASKED SURFERS

JAN & DEAN / Roy Orbison / Shirelles / 4 Seasons

EPs: 7-inch 33/45rpm

COKE ("Let's Swing the Jingle for Coca-Cola") 40-60 65
(Coca-Cola radio spots. Issued to radio stations only.)

Also see 4 SEASONS
Also see ORBISON, Roy
Also see SHIRELLES

JAN & DEAN with Randell Kirsch

Singles: 7-inch

JAN & DEAN (1 "Wa Ichi Nichi Shiow")................................. 5-10 87

Members: Jan Berry; Dean Torrence; Randell Kirsch; Gary Griffin; Chris Farmer; John Cowsil; Phil Bardowell; Mark Ward; Kevin Leonard; Bill Hollingshead; Dave Hoffman; Sue Nelson; Members of Shangahi audience.

JAN & DEAN / Soul Surfers

LPs: 10/12-inch 33rpm

L-J (101 "Jan & Dean with the Soul Surfers")......................... 35-45 63

Also see JAN & DEAN

JAN & KJELD

P&R '60

Singles: 7-inch

ALONCA 4-6 66
IMPERIAL 5-10 59
JARO INT'L................................ 5-10 60
KAPP... 5-10 60-61

Picture Sleeves

JARO INT'L................................ 5-10 60
KAPP... 5-10 60

LPs: 10/12-inch 33rpm

KAPP (1190 "Banjo Boy") 20-30 60

JANE, Baby: see BABY JANE

JANE'S ADDICTION

LP '88

LPs: 10/12-inch 33rpm

TRIPLE X.................................10-20
(Clear vinyl.)
W.B. 5-8 88-90

JANICE

R&B '86

Singles: 7-inch

BORN AGAIN 3-4 80
COTILLION...................................3-5 76
FANTASY 3-5 75-76

LPs: 10/12-inch 33rpm

FANTASY 6-10 75

JANIS, Johnny

P&R '57

Singles: 78rpm

ABC-PAR 4-8 57

Singles: 7-inch

ABC-PAR....................................5-10 57
BOMARC 5-10 59-60
COLUMBIA 5-10 60
CORAL..5-10 55
MONUMENT.................................4-6 66-68

LPs: 10/12-inch 33rpm

ABC-PAR (140 "For the First Time") 35-50 57
COLUMBIA 15-20 61
MONUMENT...............................10-15 65

JANKEL, Chas

R&B/LP '82

Singles: 12-inch 33/45rpm

A&M 4-6 83

Singles: 7-inch

A&M 3-4 82

LPs: 10/12-inch 33rpm

A&M 5-8 82

Also see DURY, Ian, & Blockheads

JANKOWSKI, Horst, Orchestra

P&R/LP '65

Singles: 7-inch

MERCURY....................................3-6 65-68

Picture Sleeves

MERCURY....................................3-6 65

LPs: 10/12-inch 33rpm

MERCURY..................................5-15 65-69

Also see IMPALAS / Horst Jankowski & His Orchestra

JARMELS

P&R/R&B '61

Singles: 7-inch

LAURIE 8-12 61-63

LPs: 10/12-inch 33rpm

COLLECTABLES.........................5-10 87

Members: Nate Ruff; Ray Smith; Tom Eldridge; Paul Burnett; Earl Christian; Major Harris.

JARRE, Jean-Michael

LP '77

Singles: 12–inch 33/45rpm

POLYDOR 4-6 86

Singles: 7–inch

POLYDOR 3-5 78-86

LPs: 10/12–inch 33rpm

DREYFUS 5-8 85-86
POLYDOR 5-8 77-86

Also see U.S.A. for AFRICA

JARREAU, Al
(Jarreau)

R&B/LP '76

Singles: 7–inch

MCA 3-4 87
RAYNARD (10022 "I'm Not Afraid") 50-100 60s
RAYNARD (10024 "Shake Up") 50-100 60s
REPRISE 3-5 76
W.B. 3-5 77-86

Picture Sleeves

MCA 3-4 87
W.B. 3-5 83-84

LPs: 10/12–inch 33rpm

MFSL (019 "All Fly Home") 25-50 78
REPRISE 5-10 76-88
W.B. 5-10 77-86

Also see U.S.A. for AFRICA

JARREAU, Al, & Randy Crawford

R&B '82

Singles: 7–inch

W.B. 3-4 82

Also see CRAWFORD, Randy
Also see JARREAU, Al

JARRETT, Keith

LP '75

LPs: 10/12–inch 33rpm

ATLANTIC 8-10 75
ECM 8-12 76-80
IMPULSE 8-10 75-77

JARVIS, Carol

P&R '57

Singles: 78rpm

BALLY 4-6 57
DOT 4-6 57

Singles: 7–inch

BALLY 5-10 57
DOT 5-10 57-59
ERA 5-10 60-61

JARVIS, Marion

R&B '74

Singles: 7–inch

ROXBURY 3-5 74

JASMIN

D&D '84

Singles: 12–inch 33/45rpm

TVI 4-6 84

JASON & SCORCHERS
(Jason & Nashville Scorchers)

LP '84

Singles: 7–inch

EMI AMERICA 3-4 84-86
PRAXIS 10-15 83-84

LPs: 10/12–inch 33rpm

EMI AMERICA 5-8 84-86

Member: Jason Ringenberg.

JASPER, Chris

R&B '87

Singles: 7–inch

CBS ASSOCIATED 3-4 87-88

LPs: 10/12–inch 33rpm

CBS ASSOCIATED 3-4 87

Also see ISLEY - JASPER - ISLEY

JAY, Dee: see DEE JAY

JAY, Jazzy: see JAZZY JAY

JAY, Morty
(With the Surfin' Cats)

P&R '63

Singles: 7–inch

LEGEND 8-12 63
20TH FOX 4-8 63

Picture Sleeves

LEGEND 10-15 63

JAY & AMERICANS

P&R '62

Singles: 7–inch

COLLECTABLES 3-5 92-93
EEOC (1140 "Things Are Changing") 50-100 65
(Equal Employment Opportunity Center promotional issue.)
FUTURA 3-5 72
U.A. (353 thru 992) 4-8 61-66
U.A. (50000 series) 3-6 66-71
U.A. (1600 series) 3-4
U.A. SILVER SPOTLIGHT 3-5

Picture Sleeves

EEOC (1140 "Things Are Changing") 50-100 65
(Equal Employment Opportunity Center promotional issue.)
U.A. 5-10 65-66

LPs: 10/12–inch 33rpm

PAIR 8-10 88
RHINO 5-8 86
SUNSET 10-12 69-70
UNART 8-12 68
U.A. (300 series) 5-8 75
U.A. (1000 series) 5-8 80

U.A. (3222 "She Cried") 20-25 62
(Monaural.)
U.A. (3300 "At the Cafe Wha") .. 20-25 63
(Monaural.)
U.A. (3407 "Come a Little Bit Closer") 15-25 64
(Monaural.)
U.A. (3417 thru 3562)............... 15-20 64-67
(Monaural.)
U.A. (6222 "She Cried") 20-30 62
(Stereo.)
U.A. (6300 "At the Cafe Wha") .. 20-30 63
(Stereo.)
U.A. (6407 "Come a Little Bit Closer") 20-25 64
(Stereo.)
U.A. (6417 thru 6762)............... 10-20 64-70
U.A. (90814 "Greatest Hits") 15-20 60s
(Record club issue.)

Members: Jay Traynor; Kenny Vance; Howard Kane; Jay Black.
Also see BLACK, Jay
Also see FAGEN, Donald

JAY & TECHNIQUES

P&R/R&B/LP '67

Singles: 7–inch

EVENT 3-5 76
GORDY 3-5 72
SMASH 4-8 67-69

Picture Sleeves

SMASH 4-8 67-68

LPs: 10/12–inch 33rpm

EVENT 8-10 75
SMASH 15-20 67-68

Members: Jay Proctor; John Walsh; Ron Goosly; Chuck Crowl; Dante Dancho; Karl Landis.

JAYA

P&R '89

Singles: 7–inch

LMR.. 3-4 89

Also see STEVIE B

JAYE, Jerry

P&R/LP '67

Singles: 7–inch

COLUMBIA 3-5 75
CONNIE (101)........................... 10-15 67
(Title not known.)
HI (2100 series)......................... 4-8 67-68
HI (2300 series)......................... 3-5 76-77
MEGA.. 3-5 71-74
RAINTREE 3-5 72

LPs: 10/12–inch 33rpm

HI (32000 series)...................... 15-20 67
HI (32100 series)....................... 5-8 76

JAYE, Miles

R&B/LP '87

Singles: 7–inch

ISLAND 3-4 87-89

LPs: 10/12–inch 33rpm

BEJAY (1370) 20-25 70
BEJAY (300 series)..................... 8-10 84
ISLAND 5-8 87-89
MCA 5-8 87

JAYHAWKS

P&R/R&B '56

Singles: 78rpm

ALADDIN 5-10 57
FLASH (Except 105).................... 5-10 56
FLASH (105 "Counting My Teardrops")............................... 20-40 56

Singles: 7–inch

ALADDIN (3393 "Everyone Should Know") 50-75 57
EASTMAN (792 "Start the Fire") 75-125 59
EASTMAN (798 "New Love")...75-125 59
FLASH (105 "Counting My Teardrops")......................... 100-150 56
FLASH (109 "Stranded in the Jungle")............................. 15-20 56
FLASH (111 "Love Train") 15-20 56
OLDIES 45.................................. 3-5

Members: James Johnson; Carl Fisher; Dave Govan; Carver Bunkern; Richard Owens.
Also see MARATHONS
Also see VIBRATIONS

JAYNETTS

P&R/R&B '63

Singles: 7–inch

J&S 4-8 65
TUFF 4-8 63-64

LPs: 10/12–inch 33rpm

TUFF (13 "Sally, Go 'Round the Roses") 50-75 63
(Includes *Dear Abby* by the Hearts.)

Members: Ethel Davis; Johnnie Louise; Mary Sue Wells; Ada Ray; Yvonne Bushnell.
Also see HEARTS
Also see JOHNNIE & JOE

JAZZ at the Philharmonic

R&B '49

Singles: 78rpm

MERCURY 3-6 49

Also see JACQUET, Illonis

JAZZ CRUSADERS

P&R '66

Singles: 7–inch

CHISA 3-5 70-71
PACIFIC JAZZ 4-8 62-68
WORLD PACIFIC 4-8 64-65

LPs: 10/12–inch 33rpm

BLUE NOTE................................ 5-10 75-80
CHISA 8-12 70
LIBERTY 8-12 70
PACIFIC JAZZ (27 thru 87) 20-35 61-64
PACIFIC JAZZ (10000 & 20000 series) 10-20 65-69

PAUSA 5-8 82
WORLD PACIFIC......................... 8-15 65

Members: Wilton Felder; Stix Hooper; Wayne Henderson; Joe Sample.

Also see CRUSADERS

Also see FELDER, Wilton

JAZZY JAY

R&B '84

Singles: 7–inch

ATLANTIC.................................... 3-4 84

JEAN, Cathy: see CATHY JEAN

JEAN, Earl: see EARL-JEAN

JEAN, Norma: see NORMA JEAN

JEAN & DARLINGS

P&R '67

Singles: 7–inch

VOLT.. 4-8 67-69

JECKYLL, Dr: see DR. JECKYLL

JEFF & ALETA

R&B '80

Singles: 7–inch

SRI 3-5 80

JEFFERSON

(Geoff Turton)

P&R '69

Singles: 7–inch

DECCA.. 4-6 69
JANUS 4-6 69

LPs: 10/12–inch 33rpm

JANUS 10-15 69

JEFFERSON, Morris

R&B '77

Singles: 7–inch

PARACHUTE 3-5 78

LPs: 10/12–inch 33rpm

PARACHUTE 5-8 78

JEFFERSON AIRPLANE

LP '66

Singles: 7–inch

ELEKTRA..................................... 3-4 88
GRUNT (0500 thru 0511).............. 3-5 71-72
GRUNT (10988 "White Rabbit") 10-20 77
(Colored vinyl. Promotional issue only.)
RCA (0150 thru 0343)................. 4-6 69-70
RCA (5156 "White Rabbit") 4-8 87
(Colored vinyl. Promotional issue only.)
RCA (8769 thru 9644)................ 5-10 66-68
(Dog on side of label.)
RCA (9000 series)......................... 3-4 89
(Dog near top of label.)

Picture Sleeves

GRUNT (0500 "Pretty As You Feel")... 5-10 71
GRUNT (0506 "Long John Silver")..................................... 10-15 72
RCA (Except 5156) 8-12 68-70
RCA (5156 "White Rabbit")............4-8 87
(Promotional issue only.)

LPs: 10/12–inch 33rpm

EPIC..5-8 89
GRUNT (0147 "Thirty Seconds over Winterland") 10-15 73
GRUNT (1001 "Bark")................30-60 71
GRUNT (1007 "Long John Silver") 30-60 72
GRUNT (0437 "Early Flight") 10-15 74
GRUNT (4386 "Bark")................10-15 82
PAIR..8-10 84
RCA (0320 ("Volunteers")..........15-20 73
(Quadrophonic.)
RCA (1511 "After Bathing at Baxter's") 20-30 67
(Black label. With "LPM" or "LSP" prefix.)
RCA (1511 "After Bathing at Baxter's") 10-12 71
(Orange label.)
RCA (3584 "Jefferson Airplane Takes Off")............................75-125 66
(Has 12 tracks. With "LPM" or "LSP" prefix.)
RCA (3584 "Jefferson Airplane Takes Off")..............................15-25 66
(Has 11 tracks. With "LPM" or "LSP" prefix.)
RCA (3584 "Jefferson Airplane Takes Off")..............................10-15 69
(Orange label.)
RCA (3661 "Worst of Jefferson Airplane")..................................5-10 80
RCA (3739 "Jefferson Airplane Takes Off")..................................5-10 80
RCA (3766 "Surrealistic Pillow") 20-30 67
(Black label. With "LPM" or "LSP" prefix.)
RCA (3766 "Surrealistic Pillow") 10-12 69
(Orange label.)
RCA (3766 "Surrealistic Pillow") 5-8 80s
(With "AYL" prefix.)
RCA (3797 "Crown of Creation") .5-10 80
RCA (3798 "Bless Its Pointed Little Head")..............................5-10 80
RCA (3867 "Volunteers") 5-10 81
RCA (4058 "Crown of Creation")10-15 68
RCA (4133 "Bless Its Pointed Little Head") 10-20 69
(Includes artwork insert.)
RCA (4238 "Volunteers") 10-15 69
RCA (4448 "Blows Against the Empire")............................10-15 70
(Black vinyl. Add $4 to $6 if accompanied by booklet.)
RCA (4448 "Blows Against the Empire")..........................75-100 70
(Clear vinyl. Promotional issue only.)
RCA (LSP-4459 "Worst of Jefferson Airplane") 10-15 70
RCA (AFL1-4459 "Worst of Jefferson Airplane") 5-10 80s

Members: Signe Anderson; Marty Balin; Paul Kantner; Jack Casady; Jorma Kaukonen; Skip Spence; Grace Slick; Craig Chaquico; Joey Covington; Papa John Creach; Spencer Dryden; Dave Freiberg.
Also see BALIN, Marty
Also see CREACH, Papa John
Also see CROSBY, David
Also see GARCIA, Jerry
Also see GREAT!! SOCIETY!!
Also see HAMMOND, John Paul
Also see HOPKINS, Nicky
Also see JEFFERSON STARSHIP
Also see KBC BAND
Also see KANTNER, Paul, & Grace Slick
Also see KAUKONEN, Jorma
Also see QUICKSILVER
Also see SLICK, Grace
Also see STILLS, Stephen

JEFFERSON STARSHIP

LP '74

Singles: 7-inch

GRUNT 3-5 74-84

Picture Sleeves

GRUNT 3-5 78-87
RCA.. 3-4 87-89

LPs: 10/12-inch 33rpm

GRUNT (0717 thru 1557).......... 10-15 74-76
GRUNT (1255 "Flight Log, 1966-1976") 15-20 77
(With simulated leather cover. Also has Jefferson Airplane, Hot Tuna, Grace Slick and Paul Kanter tracks.)
GRUNT (1255 "Flight Log, 1966-1976") 10-20 81
(With standard cover.)
GRUNT (2515 thru 3247).......... 10-15 78-79
GRUNT (3363 "Gold").............. 15-20 79
(Picture disc.)
GRUNT (3452 thru 6413)........... 6-12 79-87
RCA.. 5-8 81-89

Members: Grace Slick; Marty Balin; Paul Kantner; Aynsley Dunbar; Pete Sears; Mickey Thomas; John Barbata.
Note: Cross references that already appear under Jefferson Airplane are not duplicated below.
Also see HART, Mickey
Also see HOT TUNA
Also see JEFFERSON AIRPLANE
Also see KANTNER, Paul, & Jefferson Starship
Also see STARSHIP

JEFFREE

R&B '78

Singles: 7-inch

MCA 3-5 78-79

LPs: 10/12-inch 33rpm

MCA 5-8 79

JEFFREY, Joe
(Joe Jeffrey Group)

P&R '69

Singles: 7-inch

WAND 4-6 69

LPs: 10/12-inch 33rpm

WAND 10-15 69

JEFFREYS, Garland

LP '77

Singles: 7-inch

A&M 3-5 77-79
ARISTA...3-5 75
ATLANTIC.....................................3-5 73
EPIC...3-4 81-83

LPs: 10/12-inch 33rpm

A&M 5-8 77-79
ATLANTIC....................................8-10 73
EPIC...5-8 81-83

JEFFREYS, Garland, & Phoebe Snow

Singles: 7-inch

A&M 3-5 78

Picture Sleeves

A&M 3-5 78

Also see JEFFREYS, Garland
Also see SNOW, Phoebe

JELLY BEANS

P&R/R&B '64

Singles: 7-inch

ESKEE (001 "I'm Hip to You")....15-25 65
RED BIRD....................................5-10 64

Members: Diane Taylor; Maxine Herbert; Elyse Herbert; Alma Brewer.

JELLYBEAN
("Jellybean" Benitez; Featuring Steven Dante)

D&D '84

Singles: 12-inch 33/45rpm

EMI AMERICA 4-6 84-86

Singles: 7-inch

CHRYSALIS...................................3-4 87
EMI AMERICA...............................3-4 84-86

Picture Sleeves

CHRYSALIS...................................3-4 87
EMI AMERICA 3-4 85

LPs: 10/12-inch 33rpm

CHRYSALIS...................................5-8 87
EMI AMERICA 5-8 84-86

JELLYBEAN & Elisa Fiorillo

P&R '87

Singles: 7-inch

CHRYSALIS...................................3-4 87

Picture Sleeves

CHRYSALIS...................................3-4 87

Also see FIORILLO, Elisa
Also see JELLYBEAN

JENKINS, Donald
(With the Delighters)

P&R '63

Singles: 7-inch

CORTLAND (109 "Elephant Walk") 10-15 63
CORTLAND (112 "Somebody Help Me") 15-25 63

CORTLAND (116 "I've Settled Down") ... 15-25 64
DUCHESS (104 "Happy Days") 10-20 65

JENKINS, Gordon, & Orchestra

P&R '42

Singles: 78rpm

DECCA ... 3-6 50-56

Singles: 7-inch

COLUMBIA ... 4-6 64
DECCA ... 5-10 50-56
KAPP ... 4-8 60-64
TIME ... 4-6 62
X ... 4-8 55

EPs: 7-inch 33/45rpm

DECCA ... 5-15 51-56

LPs: 10/12-inch 33rpm

CAPITOL (700 series) ... 15-25 56
(With "T" prefix.)
CAPITOL (700 series) ... 10-15 61
(With "DT" prefix.)
CAPITOL (700 series) ... 4-8 75
(With "SM" prefix.)
COLUMBIA ... 10-20 62-63
CORAL ... 5-8 73
DECCA ... 15-30 51-63
(Decca LP numbers in this series preceded by a "7" or a "DL-7" are stereo issues.)
DOT ... 5-10 66
GWP ... 5-10 71
MCA ... 5-8 73-75
SUNSET ... 5-10 67
TIME ... 10-15 62-64

Also see ARMSTRONG, Louis
Also see BOONE, Pat
Also see CARROLL, Bob
Also see CASHMAN & WEST / Gordon Jenkins & His Orchestra
Also see LEE, Peggy
Also see WEAVERS

JENKINS, Gus

(Gus Jinkins)

P&R/R&B '56

Singles: 78rpm

COMBO ... 8-12 54
FLASH ... 5-10 56-57

Singles: 7-inch

CATALINA ... 4-8 63
COMBO (87 "I Been Working") . 30-50 54
FLASH ... 10-15 56-57
GENERAL ARTIST ... 4-8 64-69
PIONEER INT'L ... 5-10 59-62
SAR ... 4-8 64
TOWER ... 4-8 64-65

JENKINS, Kechia

R&B '88

Singles: 7-inch

PROFILE ... 3-4 88

JENKINS, Norma

R&B '76

Singles: 7-inch

CARNIVAL (528 "Need Someone to Love") ... 15-25
DESERT MOON ... 3-4 76

Also see KEYES, Troy, & Norma Jenkins

JENNIFER

(Jennifer Warnes)

Singles: 7-inch

PARROT ... 4-6 67-70

LPs: 10/12-inch 33rpm

PARROT ... 10-20 68-70

Also see WARNES, Jennifer

JENNINGS, Waylon

(With the Waylors; with Kimberlys; with Crickets; Waylon)

C&W '65

Singles: 7-inch

A&M (739 "Four Strong Winds") 10-15 64
A&M (722 "Rave On") ... 10-20 63
BAT (121636 "White Lightning") 30-50 62
BAT (121639 "Dream Baby") ... 25-35 62
BRUNSWICK (55130 "Jole Blon") ... 100-150 59
(Maroon label. With Buddy Holly & King Curtis.)
BRUNSWICK (55130 "Jole Blon") ... 75-100 59
(Yellow label. Promotional issue only.)
COLUMBIA ... 3-4 83
EPIC ... 3-4 91
RCA (Except 8572 thru 9642) ... 3-6 69-82
RCA (8572 thru 9642) ... 5-10 65-68
RAMCO ... 8-12 67
TREND '61 (102 "Another Blue Day") ... 20-30 61
TREND '63 (106 "The Stage") ... 50-75 63

Picture Sleeves

RCA ... 3-5 79-80

LPs: 10/12-inch 33rpm

A&M (4238 "Don't Think Twice") ... 25-30 69
BAT (1001 "Waylon Jennings at JD's") ... 200-300 64
(500 copies were pressed on Bat, then another 500 were done on Sounds Ltd.)
CAMDEN ... 8-15 67-76
EPIC ... 5-8 90
MCA ... 4-6
PICKWICK ... 5-10 75
RCA (0240 thru 3378) ... 5-10 73-79
RCA (3406 "Greatest Hits") ... 15-20 79
(Picture disc.)
RCA (3493 "What Goes Around Comes Around") ... 5-10 79
RCA (3523 "Folk Country") ... 15-25 66
RCA (3602 "Music Man") ... 5-10 80

RCA (3620 "Leavin' Town")....... 20-30 66
RCA (3660 "Waylon Sings Ol' Harlan")............................ 15-20 67
RCA (3663 "Are You Ready for the Country").................................... 5-8 80
RCA (3736 "Nashville Rebel")... 15-25 66
(Soundtrack.)
RCA (3737 "Good Hearted Woman").................................... 5-8 80
RCA (3825 "Love of the Common People").................. 15-25 67
RCA (3897 "Honky Tonk Heroes") 5-8 81
RCA (3918 "Hangin' On").......... 15-20 68
RCA (3942 "This Time")................ 5-8 81
RCA (4023 "Only the Greatest") 15-20 68
RCA (4072 "Dreaming My Dreams")............................. 5-8 81
RCA (4073 "The Ramblin' Man")... 5-8 81
RCA (4085 "Jewels")................ 15-20 68
RCA (4137 "Just to Satisfy You")...................................... 15-20 69
RCA (4163 "Waylon Live")........... 5-8 81
RCA (4164 "I've Always Been Crazy")...................................... 5-8 81
RCA (4180 "Country Folk")....... 15-25 69
RCA (4247 "Black on Black")........ 5-8 82
RCA (4250 "Music Man")............. 5-8 82
RCA (4260 "Waylon")............... 10-15 70
RCA (4341 "Best of Waylon Jennings")................................ 8-10 77
RCA (4418 "Singer of Sad Songs")................................ 10-15 70
RCA (4487 "The Taker/Tulsa") . 10-15 71
RCA (4567 "Cedartown Georgia")............................. 10-15 71
RCA (4647 "Good Hearted Woman")............................. 10-15 72
RCA (4673 "It's Only Rock & Roll")...................................... 5-8 83
RCA (4751 "Ladies Love Outlaws")............................. 10-15 72
RCA (4826 "Waylon & Co.")......... 5-8 83
RCA (4828 "Best of Waylon Jennings")................................ 5-8 83
RCA (4854 "Lonesome, On'ry and Mean")............................ 10-15 73
RCA (5400 series)...................... 5-10
SOUNDS (1001 "Waylon Jennings at JD's")............................ 200-250 64
(First issued on Bat.)
TIME-LIFE....................................... 5-8 81
VOCALION................................ 15-20 69

Session: Buddy Holly; King Curtis.
Also see ANDERSON, John
Also see BOWMAN, Don
Also see CRICKETS
Also see CUNHA, Rick
Also see DAVIS, Skeeter
Also see EDDY, Duane
Also see HOLLY, Buddy
Also see KIMBERLYS
Also see KING CURTIS
Also see MANDRELL, Barbara
Also see U.S.A. for AFRICA

JENNINGS, Waylon, & Anita Carter

C&W '68

Singles: 7-inch

RCA 4-8 68

JENNINGS, Waylon, & Jesse Colter
(Waylon & Jessi)

LP '81

Singles: 7-inch

RCA 3-5 69-71

LPs: 10/12-inch 33rpm

RCA (3931 "Leather and Lace") 5-8 81
Also see COLTER, Jesse

JENNINGS, Waylon, & Willie Nelson
(Waylon & Willie)

P&R '77

Singles: 7-inch

COLUMBIA 3-4 83
MCA 3-4 86
RCA 3-5 76-86

LPs: 10/12-inch 33rpm

AURA 5-8 83
COLUMBIA 5-8 83
RCA (2686 "Waylon & Willie")......5-10 78
RCA (2686 "Waylon & Willie")....20-25 78
(Colored vinyl. Promotional issue only.)
RCA (4455 "Waylon & Willie II").....5-8 82

JENNINGS, Waylon, Willie Nelson, Jessi Colter, & Tompall Glaser

LP '76

LPs: 10/12-inch 33rpm

RCA (1321 "The Outlaws") 5-10 76

JENNINGS, Waylon, Willie Nelson, Johnny Cash, & Kris Kristofferson

LP '85

Singles: 7-inch

COLUMBIA 3-4 85-90

LPs: 10/12-inch 33rpm

COLUMBIA 5-8 85-90
Also see CASH, Johnny
Also see KRISTOFFERSON, Kris
Also see NELSON, Willie

JENNINGS, Waylon / Johnny Paycheck

LPs: 10/12-inch 33rpm

OUT of TOWN DIST 5-8 82
Also see PAYCHECK, Johnny

JENNINGS, Waylon, & Jerry Reed

Singles: 7-inch

RCA 3-4 83
Also see REED, Jerry

JENNINGS, Waylon, & Hank Williams Jr.

Singles: 7-inch

RCA 3-4 83

Also see JENNINGS, Waylon
Also see WILLIAMS, Hank, Jr.

JENSEN, Kris

P&R '62

Singles: 7-inch

A&M ... 3-5 70
COLPIX ... 5-10 59
HICKORY ... 4-8 62-65
KAPP ... 4-8 61
LEADER ... 5-10 60-61

Picture Sleeves

HICKORY ... 10-15 62-64

LPs: 10/12-inch 33rpm

HICKORY (110 "Torture") ... 40-50 62

JEROME, Henry, & His Orchestra

LP '61

Singles: 7-inch

DECCA ... 3-5 60-64

EPs: 7-inch 33/45rpm

DECCA ... 4-6 61

LPs: 10/12-inch 33rpm

DECCA ... 5-12 60-64
ROULETTE ... 5-15 59

JERRY, Mungo: see MUNGO JERRY

JERRYO

(Jerry Murray)

P&R/R&B '67

Singles: 7-inch

SHOUT ... 4-8 67
WHITE WHALE ... 3-6 69

Also see TOM & JERRIO

JESSE & MARVIN

R&B '53

Singles: 78rpm

SPECIALTY ... 15-25 52

Singles: 7-inch

SPECIALTY (447 "Dream Girl") 50-75 52
(Black vinyl.)
SPECIALTY (447 "Dream Girl") ... 100-200 52
(Colored vinyl.)

Members: Jesse Belvin; Marvin Phillips.
Also see BELVIN, Jesse
Also see MARVIN & JOHNNY

JESTERS

P&R '57

Singles: 78rpm

WINLEY ... 10-15 57

Singles: 7-inch

ABC ... 3-4 73
AMY ... 3-5 62
COLLECTABLES ... 3-4 80s
CYCLONE (5011 "I Laughed") .. 25-45 58
LOST-NITE ... 4-6 63
WINLEY (218 "So Strange") ... 25-35 57
(With "Winley" in 3/16-inch letters.)
WINLEY (218 "So Strange") ... 8-12 61
(With "Winley" in 1/4-inch letters.)
WINLEY (221 "I'm Falling in Love") ... 35-45 57
(With "Winley" in 3/16-inch letters.)
WINLEY (221 "I'm Falling in Love") ... 10-15 61
(With "Winley" in 1/4-inch letters.)
WINLEY (225 "The Plea") ... 35-40 58
(With "Winley" in 3/16-inch letters.)
WINLEY (225 "The Plea") ... 10-15 61
(With "Winley" in 1/4-inch letters.)
WINLEY (242 "The Wind") ... 30-40 60
WINLEY (248 "That's How It Goes") ... 40-50 61
(Colored vinyl.)
WINLEY (248 "That's How It Goes") ... 20-30 61
(Black vinyl.)
WINLEY (252 "Come Let Me Show You") ... 20-30 61

LPs: 10/12-inch 33rpm

COLLECTABLES ... 6-8 86
LOST-NITE ... 5-8 81

Members: Len McKay; Adam Jackson; Jimmy Smith; Noel Grant; Leo Vincent; Melvin Lewis; Don Lewis.
Also see HARPTONES / Paragons / Jesters / Clovers

JESTERS / Paragons

LPs: 10/12-inch 33rpm

JOSIE ... 50-100 60s
JUBILEE (1098 "Jesters Meet the Paragons") ... 100-150 59
PAUL WINLEY PROD. (102 "Jesters Meet the Paragons") ... 20-25 65
WINLEY (6003 "War: Jesters Meet the Paragons") .50-100 60

Also see JESTERS
Also see PARAGONS

JESUS & MARY CHAIN

LP '86

Singles: 7-inch

W.B. ... 3-4 87-89

LPs: 10/12-inch 33rpm

REPRISE ... 5-8 86
W.B. ... 5-8 87-89

JESUS JONES

LP '91

LPs: 10/12-inch 33rpm

SBK ... 5-8 91

JETBOY

LP '88

LPs: 10/12-inch 33rpm

MCA ... 5-8 88

JETE, Le: see LE JETE

JETER, Genobia

R&B '86

Singles: 12-inch 33/45rpm

RCA ... 4-6 86

Singles: 7-inch

RCA... 3-4 86-87

LPs: 10/12-inch 33rpm

RCA... 5-8 86

JETER, Genobia, & Glenn Jones

R&B '87

Singles: 7-inch

RCA... 3-4 87

Also see JONES, Glenn

JETHRO TULL

LP '69

Singles: 12-inch 33/45rpm

CHRYSALIS.................................. 4-8 88-89
(Promotional only.)

Singles: 7-inch

CHRYSALIS.................................. 3-5 72-88
CHRYSALIS/REPRISE................ 4-8 69-72

Picture Sleeves

CHRYSALIS.................................. 3-5 74

EPs: 7-inch 33/45rpm

CHRYSALIS.................................. 8-12 71

LPs: 10/12-inch 33rpm

CHRYSALIS (Except CH4 & V5X series).. 6-12 73-89
CHRYSALIS (CH4 series)......... 10-12 73-74
(Quadrophonic issues.)
CHRYSALIS (V5X-41653 "Twenty Years of Jethro Tull")............. 50-75 88
(Boxed, five-LP set.)
MFSL (061 "Aqualung")............ 25-50 82
MFSL (092 "Broadsword and the Beast")............................. 20-30 82
MFSL (187 "Thick As a Brick").. 15-25 80s
REPRISE.................................. 10-15 69-72
REPRISE/CHRYSALIS (2106 "Living in the Past")............................ 15-20 72
(Price includes bonus, color booklet.)

Promotional LPs

CHRYSALIS (623 "Radio Show")10-20 76
(Music/interview with Ian Anderson about *Mu.*)

Members: Ian Anderson; Clive Bunker; Glen Cormick; John Evan; Barry Barlow; David Palmer; John Glascock; Jeff Hammond; Mick Abrahams.
Also see ABRAHAMS, Mick, Band
Also see WILD TURKEY

JETS

R&B/D&D '85

Singles: 12-inch 33/45rpm

MCA... 4-6 85-88

Singles: 7-inch

MCA... 3-4 85-89

Picture Sleeves

MCA... 3-4 86-88

LPs: 10/12-inch 33rpm

MCA... 5-8 85-89

Members: Elizabeth Wolfgram; Eugene Wolfgram (a.k.a. Gene Hunt).
Also see BOYS CLUB

JETT, Joan
(With the Blackhearts)

LP '81

Singles: 12-inch 33/45rpm

BLACKHEART/CBS...................... 4-8 88
(Promotional only.)
MCA... 4-8 83

Singles: 7-inch

BLACKHEART/CBS...................... 3-4 83-90
BOARDWALK............................... 3-5 81-82
MCA... 3-5 83

Picture Sleeves

BLACKHEART/CBS...................... 3-4 83-88
BOARDWALK............................... 3-5 81-82
MCA... 3-5 83

LPs: 10/12-inch 33rpm

BLACKHEART........................... 50-75 80
(Red label with black heart. No mention of CBS. Number not known.)
BLACKHEART/CBS...................... 5-8 83-90
BOARDWALK............................... 5-8 81-82
MCA... 5-8 83-84

Also see BARBUSTERS
Also see BEACH BOYS
Also see RUNAWAYS

JEWELS
(Crows)

Singles: 78rpm

RAMA (10 "Heartbreaker")..... 100-200 53

Singles: 7-inch

RAMA (10 "Heartbreaker")..... 300-500 53
(Black vinyl. May show *Heartbreaker* by the Crows and *Call a Doctor* by the Jewels on some labels.)
RAMA (10 "Heartbreaker")..... 500-750 53
(Colored vinyl.)

Also see CROWS

JEWELS

P&R/R&B '64

Singles: 7-inch

DIMENSION................................ 5-10 64-65

Members: Sandra Bears; Margie Clark; Martha Harvin; Grace Ruffin.

JIGSAW

P&R/LP '75

Singles: 7-inch

CHELSEA.................................... 3-5 75-76
20TH FOX................................... 3-5 77-78

LPs: 10/12-inch 33rpm

CHELSEA.................................... 8-10 75
ELEKTRA.................................... 5-8 82
20TH FOX................................... 5-8 77

JILL & RAY

Singles: 7-inch

LE CAM (979 "Hey Paula")........ 15-25 62

Members: Jill Jackson; Ray Hildebrand.
Also see PAUL & PAULA

JIM & INGRID: see CROCE, Jim & Ingrid

JIM & JEAN

P&R '68

Singles: 7–inch

VERVE/FOLKWAYS 4-8 68

LPs: 10/12–inch 33rpm

VERVE/FOLKWAYS 8-12 68

Members: Jim Glover; Jean Glover

JIM & MONICA

P&R '64

Singles: 7–inch

BETTY 8-12 64

Member: Jimmy Gilmer.
Also see GILMER, Jimmy

JIMENEZ, Jose: see DANA, Bill

JIMMY, Bobby, & Critters

R&B/LP '86

Singles: 12–inch 33/45rpm

MACOLA 4-6 86

LPs: 10/12–inch 33rpm

MACOLA 5-8 86

Member: Russ Parr.

JIMMY & DUANE

Singles: 7–inch

EB X. PRESTON (212 "Soda Fountain Girl") 100-200 55

Members: Jimmy Delbridge; Duane Eddy.
Also see EDDY, Duane

JIMMY G. & TACKHEADS

R&B '86

Singles: 7–inch

CAPITOL 3-4 85-86

LPs: 10/12–inch 33rpm

CAPITOL 5-8 86

JIMMY LEE & ARTIS: see LEE, Jimmy, & Artis

JINKINS, Gus: see JENKINS, Gus

JIVE BOMBERS

(Featuring Clarence "Bad Boy" Palmer; Clarence Palmer & Jive Bombers)

P&R/R&B '57

Single: 78rpm

CITATION 15-25 52
SAVOY 5-10 57-58

Singles: 7–inch

CITATION (1160 "It's Spring Again") 50-80 52
CITATION (1161 "Brown Boy"). 50-80 52
COLLECTABLES 3-4 85
MIDDLE TONE (20 "Anytime").. 15-25 64
SAVOY 10-20 57-59

LPs: 10/12–inch 33rpm

SAVOY 5-8 86

Members: Clarence Palmer; Earl Johnson; Allen Tinney; William Tinney.

JIVE BUNNY & MASTERMIXERS

P&R '89

Singles: 7–inch

MUSIC FACTORY 3-4 89-90

LPs: 10/12–inch 33rpm

MUSIC FACTORY 5-8 89

JIVE FIVE

(Featuring Eugene Pitt; Jive Fyve)

P&R/R&B '61

Singles: 7–inch

AMBIENT SOUND 3-5 82
BELTONE (1006 "My True Story") 10-20 61
BELTONE (1014 "Never Never") 15-25 61
BELTONE (2019 "No Not Again") 10-20 62
BELTONE (2024 "What Time Is It") 30-40 62
(White label. Vinyl is more brown than black.)
BELTONE (2024 "What Time Is It") 10-20 62
(Orange label.)
BELTONE (2029 "These Golden Rings") 30-40 62
(White label.)
BELTONE (2029 "These Golden Rings") 10-20 62
(Orange label.)
BELTONE (2030 "Lily Marlene") 10-20 62
BELTONE (2034 "Rain") 10-15 63
(Black vinyl.)
BELTONE (2034 "Rain") 20-30 63
(Vinyl color is more brown than black.)
BELTONE (3000 series) 10-15 62
DECCA 4-8 70
LANA 3-5
LOST-NITE 3-5 70s
MUSICOR 5-10 67-68
OLDIES 45 ....4-6 60s
RELIC 3-5 75-78
SKETCH (219 "United") 15-20 64
U.A. 10-20 64-66

LPs: 10/12–inch 33rpm

AMBIENT SOUND 5-8 82
AMBIENT SOUND/ROUNDER 5-8 84
COLLECTABLES 6-8 85
RELIC 8-10
U.A. (3455 "The Jive Five") 25-30 65
(Monaural.)
U.A. (6455 "The Jive Five") 30-35 65
(Stereo.)

Members: Eugene Pitt; Norm Johnson; Richard Harris; Jerry Hannah; Billy Prophet; Johnny Watson; Casey Spencer; Webster Harris.
Also see GENIES
Also see JYVE FYVE
Also see PLATTERS / Inez & Charlie Foxx / Jive Five / Tommy Hunt

JIVIN' GENE

(With the Jokers)

P&R '59

Singles: 7-inch

ABC 3-5 73
CHESS 4-8 64
HALL WAY 3-5 64
JIN (109 "Going Out with the Tide") 15-25 59
JIN (116 "Breakin' Up Is Hard to Do") 15-25 59
MERCURY 6-10 59-62
TFC/HALL 4-8 65

Member: Gene Bourgeois.

JO, Damita: see DAMITA Jo

JO, Marcy: see MARCY JOE

JO, Sami: see SAMI JO

JO ANN & TROY

P&R '64

Singles: 7-inch

ATLANTIC 8-12 64

Members: Jo Ann Campbell; Troy Seals.
Also see CAMPBELL, Jo Ann

JO JO GUNNE

P&R/LP '72

Singles: 7-inch

ASYLUM 3-5 72

LPs: 10/12-inch 33rpm

ASYLUM (Except 5071) 8-10 72-74
ASYLUM (5071 "Jumpin' the Gunne") 10-15 73
(With gatefold cover.)
ASYLUM (5071 "Jumpin' the Gunne") 8-10 73
(With standard cover.)

Member: Jay Ferguson.
Also see FERGUSON, Jay

JOBIM, Antonio Carlos

LP '65

Singles: 7-inch

A&M 4-6 67
CTI 3-5 70
MCA 3-5 74
VERVE 4-6 63-64

LPs: 10/12-inch 33rpm

A&M 8-12 67-70
CTI 8-12 70-71
CAPITOL 10-20 64
DISCOVERY 5-8 82
MCA 5-8 73
VERSATILE 5-8 78
VERVE (Except 3000 series) 10-20 63
VERVE (3000 series) 5-8 82
W.B. 8-15 65-80

Also see FITZGERALD, Ella, & Antonio Carlos Jobim
Also see GILBERTO, Astrud
Also see SINATRA, Frank, & Antonio Carlos Jobim

JOBOXERS

P&R/LP '83

Singles: 7-inch

RCA 3-4 83

LPs: 10/12-inch 33rpm

RCA 5-8 83

JOE, Billy: see BILLY JOE

JOE, Marcy: see MARCY JOE

JOE & ANN

R&B '60

Singles: 7-inch

ACE 5-10 60-62

JOE & EDDIE

LP '64

Singles: 7-inch

CAPITOL 4-8 59
GNP 4-8 62-65

LPs: 10/12-inch 33rpm

GNP 8-15 63-66

Members: Joe Gilbert; Eddie Brown.

JOEL, Billy

P&R/LP '74

Singles: 12-inch 33/45rpm

COLUMBIA 4-8 83

Singles: 7-inch

COLUMBIA (2628 "She's Got a Way") 4-6 81
(Promotional issue only.)
COLUMBIA (02518 thru 06526) 3-4 81-86
COLUMBIA (10000 & 11000 series) 3-5 74-80
COLUMBIA (40000 series) 3-5 73-74
COLUMBIA (70000 series) 3-4 89-94
EPIC 3-4 86
FAMILY (0900 "She's Got a Way") 10-20 73
FAMILY (0906 "Tomorrow Is Today") 10-20 73

Picture Sleeves

COLUMBIA (Except 02628) 3-5 79-87
COLUMBIA (02628 "She's Got a Way") 4-6 81
(Promotional issue only.)

LPs: 10/12-inch 33rpm

COLUMBIA (30000 & 40000 series) 5-10 73-89
(With "FC," "JC," "KC," "OC," "PC," "QC," or "TC" prefix.)
COLUMBIA (30000 series) 10-15 74-76
(With "CQ" or "PCQ" prefix. Quadraphonic.)
COLUMBIA (40000 series) 8-12
(With "C2X" prefix.)
COLUMBIA (HC-40000 series) 10-15 80-87
(Half-speed mastered.)
FAMILY PRODUCTIONS (2700 "Cold Spring Harbor") 35-45 71

Promotional LPs

COLUMBIA (326 "Souvenir") 25-35 75
COLUMBIA (402 "Interchords") 25-35 77
SKYCLAD (102 "A Tribute to Billy Joel") 6-8 91
(Clear vinyl. Intentionally has no music—by Billy Joel or anyone. Limited edition of 666 copies.)
Also see ATTILA
Also see HASSLES
Also see KHAN, Steve
Also see U.S.A. for AFRICA

JOEL, Billy, & Ray Charles

P&R '87

Singles: 7-inch

COLUMBIA 3-4 87

Picture Sleeves

COLUMBIA 3-4 87
Also see CHARLES, Ray

JOEL, Billy / Ricky Van Shelton

Singles: 7-inch

EPIC (74422 "All Shook Up") 3-4 92
Also see JOEL, Billy
Also see SHELTON, Ricky Van

JOESKI LOVE

R&B '86

Singles: 7-inch

VINTERTAINMENT 3-4 86

JOHANSEN, David

LP '79

Singles: 7-inch

BLUE SKY 3-5 78-82

LPs: 10/12-inch 33rpm

BLUE SKY 5-8 78-82
Also see NEW YORK DOLLS
Also see POINDEXTER, Buster, & His Banshees of Blue

JOHN, Dr: see DR. JOHN

JOHN, Elton

P&R/LP '70

Singles: 12-inch 33/45rpm

GEFFEN 4-8 83-85
(Promotional only.)
MCA 4-8 78-88
(Promotional only.)

Singles: 7-inch

CONGRESS (6017 "Lady Samatha") 20-30 69
CONGRESS (6022 "Border Song") 20-30 70
DJM (70008 "Lady Samatha") ... 40-60 69
EPIC 3-4 87
GEFFEN 3-5 81-86
MCA (40000 thru 40505) 3-6 72-76
MCA (40892 thru 40973) 3-5 78
MCA (40993 "Song for Guy") 4-6 78
(Promotional issue only.)
MCA (41042 thru 41293) 3-5 79-80
MCA (53196 thru 53000 series) 3-4 87-90
MCA/ROCKET 3-5 76-77
ROCKET 3-5 76-77
UNI 3-6 70-72
VIKING (1010 "From Denver to L.A.") 30-60 69
(Flip is by the Barbara Moore Singers.)

Picture Sleeves

GEFFEN 3-5 81-86
MCA (40344 thru 40505) 3-6 74-75
MCA (40892 thru 40973) 3-5 78
MCA (40993 "Song for Guy") 4-6 78
(Promotional issue only.)
MCA (41042 thru 41293) 3-5 79-80
MCA (53196 thru 53000 series) 3-4 87-88
MCA/ROCKET 3-5 76-77
ROCKET 3-5 76-77

EPs: 7-inch 33/45rpm

MCA (Except 40105) 8-10 73
(Jukebox issues.)
MCA (40105 "Saturday Night's Alright for Fighting") 3-5 73
(Single with two tracks on side two. Not issued with EP cover.)
UNI 10-12 70
(Jukebox issue only.)

LPs: 10/12-inch 33rpm

COLUMBIA SPECIAL PROD 5-8 81
D.D.L. (16614 "Goodbye Yellow Brick Road") 30-40 73
(Half-speed mastered.)
DJLP (403 "Empty Sky") 20-25 69
(U.K. issue, distributed in the U.S.A.)
GEFFEN 5-8 81-87
MCA (1995 "A Single Man") 35-45 79
(Promotional issue picture disc. "B" side pictures Elton from the rear.)
MCA (2015 thru 2130) 6-10 73-75
(Includes MCA reissues of UNI albums.)
MCA (2142 "Captain Fantastic and the Brown Dirt Cowboy") 10-12 75
(Includes poster, lyrics booklet, bio scrapbook and comic insert. Deduct $3 to $5 if these items are missing.)
MCA (2142 "Captain Fantastic") 50-100 79
(Colored vinyl. Promotional issue only.)
MCA (2163 thru 5121) 5-10 75-80
MCA (6000 series) 5-8 88-89
MCA (8000 series) 10-12 87
MCA (10003 "Goodbye Yellow Brick Road") 10-12 73
MCA (13921 "Thom Bell Sessions") 5-10 79
MCA (14591 "A Single Man") 8-12 79
(Picture disc.)
MCA (37000 series) 4-8 79
MCA/ROCKET (Except 1953) ... 10-12 76-77

MCA/ROCKET (1953 "Get Up and Dance") 20-25 77
(Promotional issue only.)
MFSL (160 "Goodbye Yellow Brick Road") 30-40 73
(Half-speed mastered.)
NAUTILUS (10003 "Goodbye Yellow Brick Road") 30-40 82
(Half-speed mastered.)
PARAMOUNT (6004 "Friends") 10-15 71
(Soundtrack.)
PICKWICK (3598 "Friends") 8-10 70s
(Soundtrack.)
SASSON/GEFFEN (2176 "Sasson Presents Elton John") 20-30 81
(Single-sided, four-track LP. Promotional issue only.)
UNI (73090 "Elton John") 15-20 70
(Includes booklet.)
UNI (73096 "Tumbleweed Connection") 15-20 71
(Includes booklet.)
UNI (93105 "11-17-70") 15-20 71
UNI (93120 "Madman Across the Water") 15-20 71
(Includes booklet.)
UNI (93135 "Honky Chateau") .. 15-20 72
VIKING (105 "The Games") .. 150-175 70
(Soundtrack. With Francis Lai & Barbara Moore Singers.)
Also see DIONNE & FRIENDS
Also see FRANKLIN, Aretha, & Elton John
Also see LAI, Francis, & His Orchestra
Also see MICHAEL, George
Also see OLSSON, Nigel
Also see RUSH, Jennifer, & Elton John
Also see SEDAKA, Neil
Also see STARR, Ringo
Also see WONDER, Stevie

JOHN, Elton, & Kiki Dee

Singles: 7-inch

ROCKET 3-5 76

Picture Sleeves

ROCKET 3-5 76
Also see DEE, Kiki

JOHN, Elton, & Lesley Duncan

Singles: 7-inch

MCA (1938 "Love Song") 15-20 76
(Promotional issue only.)

JOHN, Elton, & Millie Jackson

Singles: 7-inch

GEFFEN...................................... 3-4 85

Picture Sleeves

GEFFEN...................................... 3-4 85
Also see JACKSON, Millie

JOHN, Elton / John Lennon

Singles: 7-inch

MCA (40364 "Philadelphia Freedom") 3-5 75

Picture Sleeves

MCA (40364 "Philadelphia Freedom") 3-5 75
MCA (40364 WFIL radio "Philadelphia Freedom") 30-40 75
(Promotional issue only.)
Also see LENNON, John

JOHN, Elton / Tina Turner

Singles: 7-inch

POLYDOR (002 "Pinball Wizard") 25-35 75
(Promotional issue only.)
Also see JOHN, Elton
Also see TURNER, Tina

JOHN, Little Willie

R&B '55

Singles: 78rpm

KING 4-8 56-57

Singles: 7-inch

GUSTO 3-4 87
KING (4818 thru 5394)................8-15 56-60
KING (5428 thru 5949)..................4-8 61-64

EPs: 7-inch 33/45rpm

KING (423 "Talk to Me") 25-35 58

Picture Sleeves

GUSTO ("Fever") 3-4 87

LPs: 10/12-inch 33rpm

BLUESWAY 10-15 73
KING (564 "Fever") 70-90 56
(With brown cover.)
KING (564 "Fever") 20-40 59
(With blue cover.)
KING (596 "Talk to Me") 40-60 58
KING (603 "Mr. Little Willie John")....................................40-60 58
KING (691 "In Action") 100-125 60
KING (739 "Sure Things")..........20-40 61
KING (767 "The Sweet, the Hot, the Teenage Beat")..................20-40 61
KING (802 "Come On and Join Little Willie John") 20-30 62
KING (895 "These Are My Favorite Songs") 20-30 64
KING (949 "All Originals")..........20-30 66
KING (1081 "Free At Last")........20-30 70
Also see WILLIAMS, Paul

JOHN, Little Willie / Hank Ballard & the Midnighters

Singles: 7-inch

KING (5428 "Walk Slow"/"Hoochi Coochi Coo")....................................10-20 60

JOHN, Little Willie / Drifters

Singles: 7-inch

ATLANTIC (89189 "Fever") 3-4 89

Picture Sleeves

ATLANTIC (89189 "Fever") 3-4 89
Also see DRIFTERS

JOHN, Little Willie / 5 Royales / Earl King / Midnighters

EPs: 7-inch 33/45rpm

KING (387 "Rock & Roll Hit Parade")........................ 75-100 56

Also see 5 ROYALES
Also see JOHN, Little Willie
Also see MIDNIGHTERS

JOHN, Mable

P&R/R&B '66

Singles: 7-inch

MOTOWN (54081 "Who Wouldn't Love a Man Like That")............... 300-400 63
(May have been promotional only. Should have been on Tamla, as selection number indicates.)
STAX.. 10-20 66-68
TAMLA (54031 "Who Wouldn't Love a Man Like That")................. 75-100 60
TAMLA (54040 "No Love")...... 50-100 61
TAMLA (54050 "Take Me") 30-60 61
TAMLA (54081 "Who Wouldn't Love a Man Like That")................. 50-100 63

Also see RAELETTES

JOHN, Pope: see POPE JOHN

JOHN, Robert
(Bobby Pedrick Jr.)

P&R '68

Singles: 12-inch 33/45

CBS ASSOCIATED...................... 4-6 84

Singles: 7-inch

A&M 3-5 70-72
ARIOLA....................................... 3-5 78
ATLANTIC.................................. 3-5 71-73
COLUMBIA (Except 44697).......... 4-8 68-69
COLUMBIA (44697 "Can't Stop Loving You") 8-12 68
EMI AMERICA 3-4 79-80
MOTOWN 3-4 83

LPs: 10/12-inch 33rpm

COLUMBIA 10-20 68
EMI AMERICA 5-8 79-82
HARMONY.................................. 8-10 72

Also see PEDRICK, Bobby

JOHN & ERNEST

P&R/R&B '73

Singles: 7-inch

RAINY WEDNESDAY 4-8 73

Members: John Free; Ernest Smith.

JOHN LEE
(John Lee Hooker; John Lee's Groundhogs)

Singles: 78rpm

GOTHAM 10-15 53

Singles: 7-inch

PLANET 4-8 67

Also see HOOKER, John Lee

JOHNNIE & JOE
(Johnny & Joe; with Rex Garvin & His Orchestra)

P&R/R&B '57

Singles: 7-inch

ABC-PAR 8-15 60
AMBIENT SOUND.........................3-5 82
CHESS (1641 "I'll Be Spinning") 10-20 57
CHESS (1654 "Over the Mountain")..............................10-20 57
(Silver and blue label.)
CHESS (1654 "Over the Mountain").................................8-10 60
(Blue or multi-color label.)
CHESS (1769 "Across the Sea") .8-12 60
GONE (5024 "Who Do You Love").....................................15-25 61
J&S (Except 1664 & 4000 series)..................................15-25 57-59
J&S (1664 "Over the Mountain")..............................35-45 57
(With horizontal lines across label.)
J&S (1664 "Over the Mountain") 10-15 62
(Without horizontal lines across label.)
J&S (4000 series) 5-10 60s
TUFF 5-10 64

LPs: 10/12-inch 33rpm

AMBIENT SOUND 5-8 82

Members: Johnnie Louise Richardson; Joe Rivers.
Also see JAYNETTS

JOHNNY & DISTRACTIONS

LP '82

Singles: 7-inch

A&M 3-4 81-82

LPs: 10/12-inch 33rpm

A&M 5-8 81-82

JOHNNY & EXPRESSIONS

P&R/R&B '66

Singles: 7-inch

JOSIE..4-8 65-66

Member: Johnny Matthews.

JOHNNY & HURRICANES

P&R/R&B '59

Singles: 7-inch

ABC...3-5 73
ATILA 5-10 66-67
BIG TOP 5-10 60-63
JA-DA...8-12
JEFF 5-10 64
MALA 4-8 63
TWIRL (1001 "Crossfire") 30-40 59
WARWICK (502 "Crossfire")......15-20 59
("Warwick" in sans-serif, or block style print.)
WARWICK (502 "Crossfire")......10-15 59
("Warwick" in serif style print, but does not extend across entire label. "Crossfire" in quotes.)

WARWICK (502 "Crossfire") 8-10 59
("Warwick" in serif style print, extending across entire label. No quotes on Crossfire.)
WARWICK (509 "Red River Rock") 8-10 59
(Monaural.)
WARWICK (509-ST "Red River Rock") 20-30 59
(Stereo.)
WARWICK (513 "Reville Rock")... 5-10 59
(Monaural.)
WARWICK (513-ST "Reville Rock") 20-30 59
(Stereo.)
WARWICK (520 "Beatnik Fly").... 8-10 60
("Warwick" in serif style print.)
WARWICK (520 "Beatnik Fly")...... 5-8 60
(With Warwick horse and scroll logo.)

Picture Sleeves

BIG TOP (3036 "Down Yonder") 10-15 60
BIG TOP (3051 "Rocking Goose") 10-15 60
BIG TOP (3056 "You Are My Sunshine") 10-15 60
BIG TOP (3063 "Ja-Da") 10-15 61
BIG TOP (3076 "Old Smokie") .. 10-15 61
WARWICK (520 "Beatnik Fly").. 10-20 60

EPs: 7-inch 33/45rpm

WARWICK (700 "Johnny and the Hurricanes") 50-75 59

LPs: 10/12-inch 33rpm

ATILA (1030 "Live at the Star Club") 75-125 64
(Price includes fan club insert.)
BIG TOP (1302 "The Big Sound of Johnny and the Hurricanes") 45-55 60
(Monaural.)
BIG TOP (ST-1302 "The Big Sound of Johnny and the Hurricanes") 75-100 60
(Stereo.)
TWIRL (5002 "Beatnik Fly") 70-90 59
WARWICK (W-2007 "Johnny and the Hurricanes") 50-75 59
(Monaural.)
WARWICK (WST-2007 "Johnny and the Hurricanes") 75-100 59
(Stereo.)
WARWICK (W-2010 "Stormsville") 45-60 60
(Monaural.)
WARWICK (WST-2010 "Stormsville") 55-80 60
(Stereo.)

Members: Johnny Paris; Paul Tesluk; Dave Yorko; Lionel "Butch" Mattice; Bill Savitch; Eddie Fields.
Also see GIBSON, Johnny

JOHNNY & JAMMERS

Singles: 7-inch

DART (131 "School Day Blues") 200-250 59

Member: Johnny Winter.
Also see WINTER, Johnny

JOHNNY AVERAGE BAND

P/R '81

Singles: 7-inch

BEARSVILLE 3-5 81

LPs: 10/12-inch 33rpm

BEARSVILLE 5-8 81

Member: Nikki Wills.

JOHNNY HATES JAZZ

P&R/LP '88

Singles: 7-inch

VIRGIN 3-4 88

Picture Sleeves

VIRGIN 3-4 88

LPs: 10/12-inch 33rpm

VIRGIN 5-8 88

JOHNNY LEE

(John Lee Hooker)

Singles: 78rpm

DELUXE 10-15 52

Singles: 7-inch

DELUXE (6009 "I Came to See You Baby") 75-100 52

Also see HOOKER, John Lee

JOHNNY T. ANGEL

P&R '74

Singles: 7-inch

BELL 3-5 74

JOHNS, Sammy

C&W/P&R '74

Singles: 7-inch

ELEKTRA 3-4 81
GRC 3-5 73-75
MCA 3-4 88
REAL WORLD 3-5 80
W.B./CURB 3-5 76

LPs: 10/12-inch 33rpm

GRC 8-10 73
W.B. 5-10 77

JOHNSON, Al

R&B '80

Singles: 7-inch

COLUMBIA 3-5 80

LPs: 10/12-inch 33rpm

COLUMBIA 5-8 80

JOHNSON, Al, & Jean Carn

R&B '80

Singles: 7-inch

COLUMBIA 3-5 80

Also see CARNE, Jean
Also see JOHNSON, Al

JOHNSON, Benny

R&B '73

Singles: 7-inch

TODAY.... 3-5 73

JOHNSON, Betty

P&R '54

Singles: 78rpm

BALLY.... 4-6 56-57
BELL (1054 "This Is the Thanks I Get").... 5-10 54
(Seven-inch 78.)
NEW DISC.... 4-8 54
RCA.... 4-6 55

Singles: 7-inch

ATLANTIC.... 5-10 58-60
BALLY.... 5-10 56-57
BELL.... 3-5 71
COED.... 5-10 60
DOT.... 5-10 60
NEW DISC.... 10-20 54
RCA (6000 series).... 5-10 55
RCA (8000 series).... 4-8 63
REPUBLIC.... 5-10 60-61
WORLD ARTISTS.... 4-8 63

EPs: 7-inch 33/45rpm

RCA.... 8-12 57

LPs: 10/12-inch 33rpm

ATLANTIC (8017 "Betty Johnson").... 15-25 58
ATLANTIC (8027 "Songs You Heard When You Fell in Love").... 15-25 59
BALLY (12011 "The Touch").... 30-45 57

JOHNSON, Betty, with Three Beaus & a Peep / Anne Lloyd & Carillons

Singles: 7-inch

BELL (1031 "Cross over the Bridge").... 5-10 54
(Seven-inch 78.)

JOHNSON, Bill, & Musical Notes

(Bill Johnson Orchestra)

R&B '47

Singles: 78rpm

ALERT.... 10-15 46
HARLEM.... 5-10 46
KING.... 5-10 46-50
QUEEN.... 5-10 47
VICTOR.... 5-10 47-48

Singles: 7-inch

TRU-BLUE (414 "When Your Hair Has Turned to Silver").... 50-100 54
(Colored vinyl.)

JOHNSON, Blind Boy, & His Rhythms

(Champion Jack Dupree)

Singles: 78rpm

LENOX.... 10-15 46
Also see DUPREE, Champion Jack

JOHNSON, Bubber

(With the Dreamers)

P&R/R&B '55

Singles: 78rpm

KING.... 4-8 55-57
MERCURY.... 10-15 52

Singles: 7-inch

KING (4000 series).... 8-15 55-56
KING (5000 series).... 5-10 57-60
MERCURY (8285 "Forget if You Can").... 35-45 52

LPs: 10/12-inch 33rpm

KING (569 "Come Home").... 40-55 57
KING (624 "Sweet Love Songs").... 30-40 59

JOHNSON, Buddy

(Buddy Johnson & His Orchestra)

R&B '43

Singles: 78rpm

ATLANTIC.... 4-6 53
COLUMBIA.... 4-8 48
DECCA.... 4-8 42-54
MERCURY.... 4-6 53-56
RCA.... 4-6 56

Singles: 7-inch

ATLANTIC.... 5-10 53
DECCA (24996 "You Got to Walk That Chalk Line").... 15-25 50
DECCA (28907 "Talkin' About Another Man's Wife").... 10-20 53
DECCA (29058 "Handful of Stars").... 10-20 54
MERCURY.... 5-10 53-56
RCA.... 5-10 56
ROULETTE.... 4-8 59
WING.... 5-10 56

LPs: 10/12-inch 33rpm

FORUM.... 10-15
MERCURY (20072 "Buddy Johnson Wails").... 25-35 58
(Monaural.)
MERCURY (60072 "Buddy Johnson Wails").... 35-55 58
(Stereo.)
MERCURY (20209 "Rock 'N' Roll").... 30-40 58
MERCURY (20322 "Walkin").... 20-30 58
WING (1211 "Rock 'N' Roll").... 10-20 63
WING (12005 "Rock 'N' Roll").... 35-50 56
Also see BROWN, Ruth
Also see EVANS, Warren
Also see PRYSOCK, Arthur

JOHNSON, Buddy & Ella

P&R '60

Singles: 78rpm

MERCURY.... 4-6 56-57

Singles: 7-inch

MERCURY.... 5-10 56-61
ROULETTE.... 4-8 59

LPs: 10/12-inch 33rpm

MERCURY (20347 "Swing Me") 25-35 58
ROULETTE (R-25085 "Go Ahead and Rock & Roll")........ 20-30 59
(Monaural.)
ROULETTE (SR-25085 "Go Ahead and Rock & Roll")........ 30-40 59
Also see JOHNSON, Ella
Also see JOHNSON, Buddy

JOHNSON, Danny

R&B '79

Singles: 7-inch

FIRST AMERICAN........ 3-5 79

LPs: 10/12-inch 33rpm

FIRST AMERICAN........ 5-8 79
Also see CHI-LITES

JOHNSON, Don
(Don Johnson Band)

R&B '49

Singles: 7-inch

SPECIALTY........ 4-8 49

JOHNSON, Don

P&R/LP '86

Singles: 7-inch

EPIC........ 3-4 86

Picture Sleeves

EPIC........ 3-4 86

LPs: 10/12-inch 33rpm

EPIC........ 5-8 86
Also see STREISAND, Barbra, & Don Johnson

JOHNSON, Eric

LP '90

LPs: 10/12-inch 33rpm

CAPITOL........ 5-8 90

JOHNSON, General
(With the Chairmen; Norman Johnson)

R&B '76

Singles: 12-inch 33/45rpm

ARISTA........ 4-8 78

Singles: 7-inch

ARISTA........ 3-5 76-78
INVICTUS........ 3-5 71
SURFSIDE (Except "Down at the Boondocks")........ 3-5 80
SURFSIDE ("Down at the Boondocks")........ 5-10 80
(Colored vinyl. Promotional issue made for the Boondocks club. Number not known.)

LPs: 10/12-inch 33rpm

SURFSIDE (1001 "Success")..... 5-10 80
Also see CHAIRMEN of the BOARD
Also see SHOWMEN

JOHNSON, Holly

P&R '89

Singles: 7-inch

UNI........ 3-4 89
Also see FRANKIE GOES to HOLLYWOOD

JOHNSON, Howard

R&B/LP '82

Singles: 12-inch 33/45rpm

A&M........ 4-6 82-85

Singles: 7-inch

A&M........ 3-4 82-85

LPs: 10/12-inch 33rpm

A&M........ 5-8 82-85
Also see NITEFLYTE

JOHNSON, James Arthur

R&B '86

Singles: 7-inch

TUXEDO MUSIC........ 3-4 86

JOHNSON, Janice Marie

R&B '84

Singles: 7-inch

CAPITOL........ 3-4 84
Also see TASTE of HONEY

JOHNSON, Jesse
(Jesse Johnson's Revue)

P&R/R&B/D&D/LP '85

Singles: 12-inch 33/45rpm

A&M........ 4-6 85-88
(Black vinyl.)
A&M........ 5-8 85-88
(Colored vinyl.)

Singles: 7-inch

A&M........ 3-4 85-88
OLD TOWN........ 3-5 66

Picture Sleeves

A&M........ 3-4 85-88

LPs: 10/12-inch 33rpm

A&M........ 5-8 85-88
Also see TIME

JOHNSON, Jesse, & Sly Stone

P&R/R&B '86

Singles: 7-inch

A&M........ 3-4 86
Also see JOHNSON, Jesse
Also see STONE, Sly

JOHNSON, Jimmy
(With His Band featuring Hank Alexander)

R&B '65

Singles: 7-inch

MAGNUM........ 4-8 65

JOHNSON, Kevin

P&R '73

Singles: 7-inch

MAINSTREAM........ 3-5 73

JOHNSON, Kripp
(With the Dell Vikings; Krip Johnson)

Singles: 78rpm

DOT........ 5-8 57

Singles: 7-inch

DOT........ 8-12 57
MERCURY........ 10-15 59

JOHNSON, Kripp, and Chuck Jackson

Singles: 7-inch

DOT 8-12 58

Also see DEL-VIKINGS
Also see JACKSON, Chuck
Also see JOHNSON, Kripp

JOHNSON, L.V.

R&B '80

Singles: 7-inch

ICA 3-4 80-81

JOHNSON, Lonnie
(With Victoria Spivey)

P&R/R&B '48

Singles: 78rpm

ALADDIN 4-8 47
ARCO 4-8
BLUEBIRD 4-8 44
DISC 4-8 46-47
GROOVE 4-8 55
HOLIDAY 4-8 48
KING 4-8 47-57
PARADISE 4-8 52
RCA 4-8 46-50
RAMA 4-8 56
SCORE 4-8 49

Singles: 7-inch

FEDERAL 5-10 60
GROOVE (5003 "He's a Jelly-Roll Baker") 15-25 55
KING (4201 "Tomorrow Night"). 25-50 51
KING (4500 thru 4600 series) ... 30-60 51-53
KING (4700 thru 4900 series) ... 20-40 54-56
KING (5000 series) 5-10 57-65
KING (6000 series) 4-6 70
PRESTIGE 5-10 60-64
RAMA (9 "My Woman Is Gone") 20-40 53
(Black vinyl.)
RAMA (9 "My Woman Is Gone") 50-100 53
(Colored vinyl.)
RAMA (14 "Stick with Me Baby") 20-40 53
RAMA (19 "It's Been So Long"). 20-40 53
RAMA (20 "This Love of Mine") 20-40 53

EPs: 7-inch 33/45rpm

KING (267 "Lonnie Johnson") ... 25-50 54

LPs: 10/12-inch 33rpm

COLLECTOR'S CLASSICS 10-15
KING (520 "Lonesome Road") 1000-1500 56
KING (958 "12 Bar Blues") 15-20 66
KING (1083 "Tomorrow Night"). 10-15 70
PRESTIGE 10-15 69
PRESTIGE BLUESVILLE 20-30 60-63
ROOTS N' BLUES 5-8 90

JOHNSON, Lonnie, & Elmer Snowden

LPs: 10/12-inch 33rpm

PRESTIGE BLUESVILLE 20-30 61

JOHNSON, Lonnie / George Dawson's Chocolateers

Singles: 78rpm

PARADE 4-8 52

Also see JOHNSON, Lonnie

JOHNSON, Lou

P&R/R&B '63

Singles: 7-inch

BIG HILL 4-8 64-66
BIG TOP 4-8 62-67
COTILLION 4-6 68-69
HILLTOP 4-8 64
VOLT 3-5 71

LPs: 10/12-inch 33rpm

COTILLION 10-12 69
VOLT 8-10 71

JOHNSON, Marv
(With the Band of Harold "Beans" Bowles; with Rayber Voices)

P&R/R&B '59

Singles: 7-inch

GORDY 8-12 65-68
KUDO (663 "My Baby-O") 200-300
TAMLA (101 "Come to Me") .. 200-300 59
(No company address shown.)
TAMLA (101-G1 "Come to Me") 175-225 59
(Has Gladstone St. Address under "Tamla."
U.A. 10-20 59-64

EPs: 7-inch 33/45rpm

U.A. (10,007 "Marv Johnson") ... 30-40 60
U.A. (10,009 "Marv Johnson") ... 30-40 60

LPs: 10/12-inch 33rpm

U.A. (3081 "Marvelous Marv Johnson") 25-30 60
(Monaural.)
U.A. (3081 "More Marv Johnson") 25-30 60
(Monaural.)
U.A. (3187 "I Believe") 25-30 62
(Monaural.)
U.A. (6081 "Marvelous Marv Johnson") 30-35 60
(Stereo.)
U.A. (6081 "More Marv Johnson") 30-35 60
(Stereo.)
U.A. (6187 "I Believe") 30-35 62
(Stereo.)

Also see HOLLAND, Eddie

JOHNSON, Meat Head
(Champion Jack Dupree)

Singles: 78rpm

APEX 10-15 50
GOTHAM 8-12 50

Also see DUPREE, Champion Jack

JOHNSON, Michael

P&R/R&B/LP '78

Singles: 7-inch

ATCO 3-5 73
EMI AMERICA 3-5 78-80
RCA 3-4 86-88

Picture Sleeves

EMI AMERICA 3-5 78

LPs: 10/12-inch 33rpm

ATCO 8-10 73
EMI AMERICA 5-8 78-82

Session: Michael Young; Russ Pahl; Denny Dadmum-Bixby.

Also see BACK PORCH MAJORITY
Also see DENVER, BOISE & JOHNSON
Also see GREAT PLAINS
Also see MITCHELL TRIO
Also see SYLVIA & Michael Johnson

JOHNSON, Orlando, & Trance

D&D '83

Singles: 12-inch 33/45rpm

EASYSTREET 4-6 83

JOHNSON, Paul

R&B '88

Singles: 7-inch

EPIC 3-4 88

JOHNSON, Pete
(Pete Johnson All-Star Orchestra)

R&B '45

Singles: 78rpm

APOLLO 4-8 46-49
BRUNSWICK 4-8 44
DOWN BEAT 4-6 49
MODERN 4-6 47
NATIONAL 4-6 45-46

Singles: 7-inch

APOLLO 5-10 50s

EPs: 7-inch 33/45rpm

APOLLO (608 "Pete Johnson"). 15-25 50s
BRUNSWICK 10-20 55

LPs: 10/12-inch 33rpm

SAVOY (14018 "Pete's Blues"). 30-40 58

Also see BROOKS, Hadda / Pete Johnson
Also see TURNER, Joe

JOHNSON, Robert

LP '90

Singles: 78rpm

VOCALION (03416 "Kind Hearted Woman Blues") 300-400
VOCALION (03475 "I Believe I'll Dust My Broom") 300-400
VOCALION (03445 "32/20 Blues") 300-400
VOCALION (03519 "Cross Road Blues") 300-400
VOCALION (03563 "Come on in My Kitchen") 300-400
VOCALION (03601 "Sweet Home Chicago") 300-400
VOCALION (03623 "From Four Until Late") 300-400
VOCALION (03665 "Milkcow's Calf Blues") 300-400
VOCALION (03723 "I'm a Steady Rollin' Man") 300-400
VOCALION (04002 "Stop Breakin' Down Blues") 300-400

LPs: 10/12-inch 33rpm

COLUMBIA (1654 "King of the Delta Blues Singers") 25-30 61
COLUMBIA (30034 "Robert Johnson, Vol. 2") 10-15 70
COLUMBIA (46222 "The Complete Recordings") 8-12 90
ROOTS 'N' BLUES 5-8 90

JOHNSON, Robert

LP '79

Singles: 7-inch

INFINITY 3-5 78

LPs: 10/12-inch 33rpm

INFINITY 5-8 78

JOHNSON, Rozetta

P&R/R&B '70

Singles: 7-inch

CLINTONE 3-5 70

JOHNSON, Ruby

R&B '66

Singles: 7-inch

NEBS 10-15 65
VOLT 10-20 66
V-TONE 10-20 60

JOHNSON, Sweetpea
(Billy Strange)

Singles: 7-inch

LIBERTY (55315 "The Crawdad Scene") 15-25 61

Also see STRANGE, Billy

JOHNSON, Syl

P&R/R&B '67

Singles: 12-inch 33/45rpm

BOARDWALK 4-6 82

Singles: 7-inch

FEDERAL 5-10 59-62
HI 3-5 73-76
SHAMA 3-5 77
TMP-TING 4-8 65
TWILIGHT 4-8 67-68
TWINIGHT 3-6 69

LPs: 10/12-inch 33rpm

HI 8-10 73-75
TWINIGHT 10-15 68

JOHNSON, Troy

R&B '86

Singles: 7-inch

KALLISTA 3-4 86

JOHNSTON, Tom

P&R/LP '79

Singles: 7-inch

W.B. 3-5 79-81

LPs: 10/12-inch 33rpm

W.B. 5-8 79-81

Also see CHARADES
Also see DOOBIE BROTHERS

JOINER, ARKANSAS JUNIOR HIGH SCHOOL BAND

P&R '60

Singles: 7-inch

LIBERTY 5-10 60-61

JOLI, France

P&R/R&B/LP '79

Singles: 12-inch 33/45rpm

EPIC 4-6 83-85

Singles: 7-inch

EPIC 3-4 83-85
PRELUDE 3-5 79-82

LPs: 10/12-inch 33rpm

EPIC 5-8 83-85
PRELUDE 5-8 79-80

JOLLY, Pete

(Pete Jolly Trio & Friends)

LP '63

Singles: 7-inch

A&M 3-5 68-69
AVA 4-6 63-64
COLUMBIA 3-6 66
MAINSTREAM 3-6 69

LPs: 10/12-inch 33rpm

A&M 8-12 68-71
AVA 10-20 63-64
CHARLIE PARKER 15-20 62
COLUMBIA 10-20 65
MGM 8-15 63
METROJAZZ 15-25 60
RCA (1100 thru 1300 series) 20-30 55-57
TRIP 5-8 75

Also see MONTEZ, Chris

JOLO

D&D '84

Singles: 12-inch 33/45rpm

MEGATONE 4-6 84

JON & ROBIN

(With the In Crowd)

P&R '67

Singles: 7-inch

ABNAK 4-8 67-68

LPs: 10/12-inch 33rpm

ABNAK 15-20 67-68

Members: Jon Abnor; Robin Abnor.

JON & VANGELIS

P&R/LP '80

Singles: 7-inch

POLYDOR 3-5 77-83

LPs: 10/12-inch 33rpm

POLYDOR 5-8 80-83

Members: Jon Anderson; Vangelis.
Also see ANDERSON, Jon
Also see VANGELIS

JONAE, Gwen

D&D '83

Singles: 12-inch 33/45rpm

ARIAL 4-6 83
C&M 4-6 83

JONES, Brenda

(Brenda Lee Jones)

R&B '82

Singles: 7-inch

FLYING DUTCHMAN 3-5 76
MERCURY 3-5 74
RUST 4-8 66
WAVE 3-4 82

Also see DEAN & JEAN
Also see LEE, Brenda

JONES, Brenda, & "Groove" Holmes

Singles: 7-inch

FLYING DUTCHMAN 3-5 76

Also see HOLMES, Richard "Groove"
Also see JONES, Brenda

JONES, Brian

LPs: 10/12-inch 33rpm

ROLLING STONES (49100 "Pipes of Pan") 10-15 71

Promotional LPs

ROLLING STONES (49100 "Pipes of Pan") 30-35 71
(Includes poster and cue sheets.)

Also see ROLLING STONES

JONES, Corky

(Buck Owens)

Singles: 78rpm

DIXIE 15-25 56
PEP 20-40 56

Singles: 7-inch

DIXIE (505 "Rhythm and Booze") 75-100 56
PEP (107 "Hot Dog") 100-150 56

Also see OWENS, Buck

JONES, Davy

(David Jones)

P&R '65

Singles: 7-inch

BELL 8-10 71-72
COLPIX 10-20 65
MGM 10-15 72-73
MY FAVORITE MONKEE–DAVY JONES SINGS ("A Little Bit Me, a Little Bit You") 50-100 67

(Promotional issue only. No selection number used.)

Picture Sleeves

COLPIX (784 "What Are We Going to Do") 20-30 65

LPs: 10/12-inch 33rpm

BELL (6067 "Davy Jones")........ 15-25 71
COLPIX (CP-493 "David Jones") 20-25 65
(Monaural.)
COLPIX (SCP-493 "David Jones") 25-30 65
(Stereo.)
Also see NILSSON, Harry

JONES, Davy, & Mickey Dolenz

Singles: 7-inch

BELL 8-10 71
MCA 3-5 78

Picture Sleeves

MCA 3-5 78

JONES, Davy, Mickey Dolenz, & Peter Tork

LPs: 10/12-inch 33rpm

RHINO/FOSHOFF (71110 "20th Anniversary Tour") 20-30 87
Also see JONES, Davy
Also see DOLENZ, Micky
Also see MONKEES

JONES, Etta

P&R/R&B '60

Singles: 7-inch

KING 4-8 61-62
PRESTIGE 4-8 60-65
20TH FOX/WESTBOUND............ 3-5 75

LPs: 10/12-inch 33rpm

GRAND PRIX.............................. 8-12 60s
KING (544 "Etta Jones Sings") . 40-60 58
KING (707 "Etta Jones Sings") . 35-50 61
MUSE 5-8 77-81
PRESTIGE (7100 & 7200 series) 25-50 60-63
(Yellow labels.)
PRESTIGE (7100 & 7200 series) 15-25 65
(Blue labels.)
PRESTIGE (7400 thru 7700 series) 10-20 67-70
ROULETTE 10-20 66
20TH FOX/WESTBOUND........... 5-10 75

JONES, George

(With the Jones Boys; with Sonny Burns; Tina & Daddy)

C&W '55

Singles: 78rpm

DIXIE.. 15-25 56
MERCURY 5-10 57
STARDAY 5-10 54-57

Singles: 7-inch

D 4-8 65-66
EPIC..3-5 72-82
MERCURY (71000 & 72000 series)..5-15 57-64
MUSICOR 3-8 65-71
PROMOTIONAL COPIES ("The Race Is On")......................................20-25 64
(No label name other than "Promotional Copies," is shown on disc.)
RCA 3-5 72-74
STARDAY (Except 100 & 200 series) 4-8 64-71
STARDAY (100 & 200 series)....10-20 54-57
(Black vinyl.)
STARDAY (264 "Just One More") 30-40 56
(Colored vinyl.)
U.A. 4-8 62-67

Picture Sleeves

MERCURY 8-12 62-64
MUSICOR 5-10 65
U.A. 5-10 62-63

EPs: 7-inch 33/45rpm

DIXIE (501 "Why Baby Why") 25-50 56
(Not issued with cover.)
DIXIE (505 "Heartbreak Hotel") .25-50 56
(Not issued with cover.)
DIXIE (516 "Poor Old Me") 25-50 56
(No cover. Has two track by Benny Barnes.)
DIXIE (518 "Stolen Moments")...25-50 56
(Not issued with cover.)
DIXIE (525 "Don't Do This to Me") 15-25 59
(Has one George Jones track. Not issued with cover.)
MERCURY 10-20 61
RECORD of the MONTH (280 "Heartbreak Hotel") 30-40 56
(Colored vinyl.)
STARDAY 8-15 65
(Jukebox issues.)

LPs: 10/12-inch 33rpm

ACCORD 4-6 82
ALBUM GLOBE 5-8 81
ALLEGIANCE 4-8 84
AMBASSADOR...............................5-8
BUCKBOARD 5-8 76
BULLDOG.......................................8-10
CAMDEN 5-8 72-74
COLUMBIA 5-8 80-83
EPIC..5-10 72-82
EVEREST 5-8 79
51 WEST...5-8 79-82
GRASS COUNTRY.........................8-10 80s
GUEST STAR...............................20-30 63
GUSTO 5-8 78-81
I&M...5-8 82
KOALA 5-8

K-TEL 5-8
LIBERTY 5-8 82
MCA 3-4 91-92
MERCURY (8000 series) 5-10 72
MERCURY (20306 "14 Country Favorites") 35-45 58
MERCURY (20462 "Country Church Time") 35-45 59
MERCURY (20477 "White Lightning") 35-45 59
MERCURY (20621 thru 20836) 20-30 60-63
(Monaural.)
MERCURY (20906 thru 21048) 10-20 64-65
(Monaural.)
MERCURY (60257 thru 60836) 20-35 60-63
(Stereo.)
MERCURY (60906 thru 61048) 15-25 64-65
(Stereo.)
MOUNTAIN DEW 5-8
MUSIC DISC 6-10 69
MUSICOR 8-15 65-77
MUSICOR/RCA 8-10 74-75
NASHVILLE 6-10 70-71
PHOENIX 10 .... 5-8 81
PHOENIX 20 .... 5-8 81
PICADILLY 5-8 81
PICKWICK 4-8 80
PICKWICK/HILLTOP 8-12 69
POWER PAK 5-8 75
RCA 5-10 72-75
ROUNDER 5-8 82
RUBY 5-8
SEARS 8-12
STARDAY (100 series, except 101) 25-35 60-62
STARDAY (101 "The Grand Ole Opry's New Star") 50-100 58
STARDAY (300 series) 15-30 65-66
STARDAY (400 series, except 401) 8-12 69
STARDAY (401 "George Jones Song Book and Picture Album") 30-35 67
(With 32-page song booklet.)
STARDAY (401 "George Jones Song Book and Picture Album") 15-20 68
(Without song booklet.)
STARDAY (3000 series) 5-8 77
STARDAY (90000 series) 8-12
SUNRISE 5-8
TIME-LIFE 5-8 81-82
TRIP 5-8 76
TROLLY CAR 5-8
UNART 8-12 67-68
U.A. (85 "Superpak") 10-15 71
U.A. (100 series) 5-8 73
U.A. (3000 series) 10-20 62-67
(Monaural.)
U.A. (6000 series) 12-25 62-69
(Stereo.)
WHITE LIGHTNING 12-18
WING 8-12 64-68
WING/PICKWICK 4-6

Session: Jordanaires; Oak Ridge Boys.
Also see CHARLES, Ray, George Jones & Chet Atkins
Also see DARRELL, Johnny / George Jones / Willie Nelson
Also see HAGGARD, Merle, & George Jones
Also see JONES, Thumper
Also see OAK RIDGE BOYS
Also see PARTON, Dolly / George Jones
Also see TRAVIS, Randy, & George Jones

JONES, George, & Brenda Lee

C&W '84

Singles: 7-inch

EPIC 3-4 84

Also see LEE, Brenda

JONES, George, & Brenda Carter

C&W '68

Singles: 7-inch

MUSICOR 4-6 68

JONES, George, & David Allan Coe

Singles: 7-inch

COLUMBIA 3-4 81

Also see COE, David Allan

JONES, George, & Lacy J. Dalton

C&W '85

Singles: 7-inch

EPIC 3-4 85

JONES, George, & Jeanette Hicks

C&W '57

Singles: 7-inch

STARDAY 5-8 57

Singles: 7-inch

STARDAY 10-20 57

JONES, George, & Shelby Lynne

C&W '88

Singles: 7-inch

EPIC 3-4 88

JONES, George, & Melba Montgomery

C&W '63

Singles: 7-inch

CURIO 4-8 60s
MUSICOR 4-8 66-67
U.A. 4-8 63-66

Picture Sleeves

CURIO (7020 "You're in My Heart") 8-10 60s

LPs: 10/12-inch 33rpm

BUCKBOARD 5-8 76
GUEST STAR 20-30 60s
LIBERTY 4-6 82
MUSIC DISC 6-10 69
MUSICOR 8-12 66-74
MUSICOR/RCA 8-10 74
U.A. (200 series) 5-8 73
U.A. (3000 series) 10-20 63-66
(Monaural.)

U.A. (6000 series) 12-25 63-66
(Stereo.)
Also see MONTGOMERY, Melba

JONES, George / Buck Owens / David Houston / Tommy Hill.

LPs: 10/12-inch 33rpm

NASHVILLE 10-15 60s
Also see HOUSTON, David
Also see OWENS, Buck

JONES, George, & Johnny Paycheck

C&W '80

Singles: 7-inch

EPIC 3-5 78-80

LPs: 10/12-inch 33rpm

EPIC 5-8 80
Also see PAYCHECK, Johnny

JONES, George, & Gene Pitney

(George & Gene, with the Jordanaires)

C&W/LP '65

Singles: 7-inch

MUSICOR 4-6 65-66

Picture Sleeves

MUSICOR 4-6 65

LPs: 10/12-inch 33rpm

DESIGN 6-10
INTERNATIONAL AWARD 8-10
MUSIC DISC 10-12 69
MUSICOR (3044 "George Jones & Gene Pitney") 15-25 65
(Front cover shows title as "For the First Time! Two Great Stars, George Jones & Gene Pitney.")
MUSICOR (3044 "George Jones & Gene Pitney") 15-20 65
(Front cover shows title as "Recorded in Nashville, Tennessee, George Jones & Gene Pitney.")
MUSICOR (3065 "It's Country Time Again") 10-20 65
Session: Jordanaires.
Also see PITNEY, Gene

JONES, George, Gene Pitney, & Melba Montgomery

LPs: 10/12-inch 33rpm

MUSICOR 10-20 66
(Contains duets by these artists, but there are no tracks where all three perform together.)
Also see MONTGOMERY, Melba

JONES, George, & Margie Singleton

C&W '61

Singles: 7-inch

MERCURY 4-8 61-62

JONES, George, & Ernest Tubb

Singles: 7-inch

FIRST GENERATION 3-4 81

JONES, George, & Tammy Wynette

(George, Tammy & Tina)

C&W/LP '71

Singles: 7-inch

EPIC 3-5 71-80

LPs: 10/12-inch 33rpm

COLUMBIA 5-8 81
EPIC 8-12 71-81
TVP 5-8
Also see JONES, George
Also see WYNETTE, Tammy

JONES, Glenn

R&B/D&D '83

Singles: 12-inch 33/45rpm

RCA 4-6 83-85

Singles: 7-inch

JIVE 3-4 87-88
RCA 3-4 83-87

Picture Sleeves

JIVE 3-4 87

LPs: 10/12-inch 33rpm

JIVE 5-8 87
RCA 5-8 83-84
Also see JETER, Genobia, & Glenn Jones
Also see WARWICK, Dionne, & Glenn Jones

JONES, Grace

P&R/LP '77

Singles: 12-inch 33/45rpm

ISLAND 4-6 83
MANHATTAN 4-6 85

Singles: 7-inch

BEAM JUNCTION 3-5 76-77
ISLAND 3-5 78-83
MANHATTAN 3-4 85-86

Picture Sleeves

MANHATTAN 3-4 86

LPs: 10/12-inch 33rpm

ISLAND 5-8 77-82
MANHATTAN 5-8 85-86

JONES, Grant

(Grant "Mr. Blues" Jones & Brown's Blues Blowers)

R&B '51

Singles: 78rpm

DECCA 5-10 50
STATES 5-10 52
UNITED 5-10 52

Singles: 7-inch

DECCA (48129 "For You, My Love") 50-75 50
DECCA (48133 "Crying Good Morning Blues") 50-75 50
DECCA (48163 "Hospitality Blues") 50-75 50
DECCA (48169 "It's Been a Long Time, Baby") 50-75 50
DECCA (48179 "Night Time Is the Right Time") 50-75 50

STATES (114 "Stormy Monday") 30-50 52
STEPHENY (1821 "Pinball Machine") 15-20 58
UNITED (112 "Strange Man") ... 30-40 52
UNITED (133 "Hello Stranger"). 30-50 52

JONES, Howard

P&R/D&D/LP '84

Singles: 12-inch 33/45rpm

ELEKTRA 4-6 83-85

Singles: 7-inch

ELEKTRA 3-4 83-89

Picture Sleeves

ELEKTRA 3-4 84-89

LPs: 10/12-inch 33rpm

ELEKTRA 5-8 83-89

JONES, Ignatius

D&D '83

Singles: 12-inch 33/45rpm

W.B. 4-6 83

Singles: 7-inch

W.B. 3-4 83

JONES, Jack

P&R '62

Singles: 7-inch

CAPITOL 4-8 59-60
KAPP 4-6 60-67
POLYDOR 3-4 83
RCA 3-6 67-77

Picture Sleeves

CAPITOL 5-10 59
KAPP 4-8 63-69

LPs: 10/12-inch 33rpm

CAMDEN 5-8 73
CAPITOL 10-20 59-64
KAPP 10-20 61-69
MCA 5-8 77
MGM 5-8 79
RCA 5-10 67-77
SEARS 5-10

Also see ANDREWS, Julie & Andre Previn / Vic Damone / Jack Jones / Marian Anderson
Also see ANN-MARGRET

JONES, Jimmy

(With the Jones Boys; with Savoys)

P&R '59

Singles: 7-inch

ARROW (717 "Heaven in Your Eyes") 100-150 57
BELL 4-8 67
CUB 8-15 59-62
EPIC (9339 "Whenever You Need Me") 75-125 59
MGM 3-5 78
PARKWAY 4-8 66
ROULETTE (4232 "Lover") 15-25 60
SAVOY (1586 "Please Say You're Mine") 10-15 60
VEE JAY 4-8 63

Picture Sleeves

CUB (9072 "That's When I Cried") 15-20 60

LPs: 10/12-inch 33rpm

JEN JILLUS 5-10 77
MGM (E-3847 "Good Timin'") 35-45 60
(Monaural.)
MGM (SE-3847 "Good Timin'") .. 45-60 60
(Stereo.)

Also see JONES, Jimmy, & Pretenders

JONES, Jimmy

R&B '76

Singles: 7-inch

CONCHILLO 3-5 76

JONES, Jimmy, & Pretenders

Singles: 78rpm

RAMA (207 "Lover") 15-20 56
RAMA (210 "Lover") 10-15 56

Singles: 7-inch

ABC-PAR 5-8 60
RAMA (207 "Lover") 100-150 56
RAMA (210 "Lover") 75-100 56

Also see JONES, Jimmy

JONES, Joe

P&R/R&B '60

Singles: 78rpm

CAPITOL 5-10 54

Singles: 7-inch

ABC 3-5 73
CAPITOL 10-20 54
RIC 10-15 60
ROULETTE 5-10 60-61

LPs: 10/12-inch 33rpm

PRESTIGE 10-15 69
ROULETTE (R-25143 "You Talk Too Much") 25-30 61
(Monaural.)
ROULETTE (SR-25143 "You Talk Too Much") 30-40 61
(Stereo.)

JONES, Johnny

R&B '68

Singles: 7-inch

FURY 4-8 68

JONES, Jonah

(Jonah Jones Quartet)

LP '58

Singles: 78rpm

GROOVE 3-8 56

Singles: 7-Inch

BETHLEHEM 4-6 59
CAPITOL 4-6 58-63
DECCA 3-6 65
GROOVE 5-10 56
MOTOWN (1144 "For Better Or Worse") 50-100 69

EPs: 7-Inch 33/45rpm

BETHLEHEM 5-15 55
CAMDEN 5-8 69
CAPITOL 5-10 58-59
GROOVE 5-15 56
RCA 5-10 59

LPs: 10/12-Inch 33rpm

ANGEL 20-30 56
BETHLEHEM 20-40 55-60
CAPITOL (1000 thru 2800 series) 10-25 58-67
(With "T" or "ST" prefix.)
CAPITOL (1600 series) 5-8 77
(With "SM" prefix.)
CAPITOL (11000 series) 5-8 75
DECCA 10-20 65-67
GROOVE 30-40 56
INNER CITY 5-8 81
MOTOWN (683 "Along Came Jonah") 30-50 69
MOTOWN (690 "Dis & Dat") 30-50 69
RCA 15-25 59-63

Also see CHRISTY, June
Also see SINATRA, Frank / Jonah Jones

JONES, Kay Cee

P&R '55

Singles: 78rpm

AMERICAN 4-8 56
DECCA 4-8 57
MARQUEE 4-8 55

Singles: 7-inch

AMERICAN 8-12 56
CHANCELLOR 5-10 59
DECCA 5-10 57
MARQUEE 5-10 55

JONES, Klinte

D&D '84

Singles: 12-inch 33/45rpm

OH MY 4-6 84

JONES, Linda
(With the Whatnauts)

P&R/R&B '67

Singles: 7-inch

ATCO (6344 "I'm Taking Back My Love") 25-50 65
BLUE CAT (128 "Hit Me Like TNT") 25-50 65
COTIQUE (117 "Fugitive from Luv") 8-12 69
LOMA 5-10 67-68
NEPTUNE 4-8 69
STANG 4-8 72
TURBO 3-6 71-72
W.B. (7278 "My Heart") 15-25 69

LPs: 10/12-inch 33rpm

LOMA (5907 "Hyptomized") 20-30 67
TURBO 10-15 72

JONES, Mick

LP '89

LPs: 10/12-inch 33rpm

ATLANTIC 5-8 89

JONES, Oran "Juice"
(Juice)

P&R/R&B/LP '86

Singles: 7-inch

DEF JAM 3-4 86-87

LPs: 10/12-inch 33rpm

DEF JAM 5-8 86

JONES, Quincy

LP '62

Singles: 7-inch

A&M 3-5 69-81
ABC 3-6 68
BELL 3-6 69
COLGEMS 3-6 68
IMPULSE 4-8 62
MERCURY 4-8 59-66
RCA 3-6 69
REPRISE 3-5 72
UNI 3-6 69
U.A. 3-5 70

Picture Sleeves

A&M 3-5 77-81
COLGEMS 4-8 68

LPs: 10/12-inch 33rpm

A&M 5-10 69-82
ABC (700 series) 8-12 73
ABC-PAR (149 "How I Feel About Jazz") 75-100 56
ABC-PAR (186 "Go West, Man") 75-100 57
ALLEGIANCE 5-8 84
COLGEMS 20-30 68
EMARCY (36083 "Jazz Abroad") 75-100 56
IMPULSE (11 "Quintessence") .. 15-25 62
IMPULSE (9300 series) 8-12 78
LIBERTY 10-20 67
MFSL (078 "You've Got It Bad") 20-30 82
MERCURY (623 "Ndeda") 15-20 72
MERCURY (2014 "Around the World") 20-30 61
(Monaural.)
MERCURY (20444 "Birth of a Band") 40-50 59
(Monaural.)
MERCURY (20561 "Great, Wide World") 40-50 60
(Monaural.)
MERCURY (20612 "I Dig Dancers") 40-50 60
(Monaural.)
MERCURY (20653 "Quincy Jones at Newport '61") 20-30 61
(Monaural.)

MERCURY (20751 "Big Band Bossa Nova") 20-30 62
(Monaural.)
MERCURY (20799 "Hip Hits") .. 20-30 63
(Monaural.)
MERCURY (20863 thru 21070) 10-20 64-66
(Monaural.)
MERCURY (6014 "Around the World") 25-35 61
(Stereo.)
MERCURY (60444 "Birth of a Band") 45-60 59
(Stereo.)
MERCURY (60561 "Great, Wide World") 45-55 60
(Stereo.)
MERCURY (60612 "I Dig Dancers") 45-55 60
(Stereo.)
MERCURY (60653 "Quincy Jones at Newport '61") 25-35 61
(Stereo.)
MERCURY (60751 "Big Band Bossa Nova") 25-35 62
(Stereo.)
MERCURY (60799 "Hip Hits") .. 25-35 63
(Stereo.)
MERCURY (60863 thru 61070) 15-25 64-66
PRESTIGE (172 "Sweden-American All Stars") 200-250 53
(10–inch LP.)
QWEST 5-8 89
TRIP 5-8 74-76
U.A. 10-15 70
VERVE 15-20 67
WING 6-12 69

Also see ASHFORD & SIMPSON
Also see AUSTIN, Patti
Also see ECKSTINE, Billy, & Quincy Jones
Also see FELICIANO, Jose, & Quincy Jones
Also see GILBERTO, Astrud
Also see JACKSON, Michael
Also see RIPERTON, Minnie
Also see SINATRA, Frank, with Quincy Jones & His Orchestra
Also see U.S.A. for AFRICA
Also see VAUGHAN, Sarah, & Quincy Jones
Also see WASHINGTON, Dinah

JONES, Quincy, & Brothers Johnson

P&R '75

Singles: 7–inch

A&M 3-5 75

Picture Sleeves

A&M 3-5 75

Also see BROTHERS JOHNSON

JONES, Quincy, & Tevin Campbell

P&R '90

Singles: 7–inch

QWEST 3-4 90

JONES, Quincy, Ray Charles & Chaka Khan

P&R '89

Singles: 7–inch

QWEST..3-4 89

Picture Sleeves

QWEST..3-4 89

Also see CHARLES, Ray
Also see KHAN, Chaka

JONES, Quincy, & James Ingram

P&R/R&B '81

Singles: 7–inch

A&M 3-5 81

Also see JONES, Quincy

JONES, Quincy, James Ingram, Al B. Sure, El DeBarge & Barry White

P&R '90

Singles: 7–inch

QWEST...3-4 90

Picture Sleeves

QWEST...3-4 90

Also see AL B. SURE!
Also see DE BARGE
Also see INGRAM, James
Also see JONES, Quincy, & James Ingram
Also see WHITE, Barry

JONES, Rickie Lee

P&R/R&B/LP '79

Singles: 7–inch

W.B. 3-5 79-84

Picture Sleeves

W.B. 3-5 84

EPs: 10–inch 33/45rpm

W.B. (23805 "Girl at Her Volcano") 10-15 83

LPs: 10/12–inch 33rpm

GEFFEN 5-8 89
MFSL (089 "Rickie Lee Jones").25-50 82
W.B. 5-8 79-84

JONES, Shirley

R&B/LP '86

Singles: 7–inch

PHILADELPHIA INT'L..................3-4 86-87

LPs: 10/12–inch 33rpm

PHILADELPHIA INT'L..................5-8 86

Also see JONES GIRLS

JONES, Spencer

D&D '83

Singles: 12–inch 33/45rpm

NEXT PLATINUM 4-6 83

Singles: 7–inch

NEXT PLATINUM 3-4 83
PROFILE...3-4 86

JONES, Spike
(With the City Slickers)

P&R '42

Singles: 78rpm

BLUEBIRD 10-20 42-43

RCA 5-15 46-55
VICTOR 8-12 44-45

Singles: 7-inch

LIBERTY 4-8 59-65
RCA (0500 series) 3-5 71
RCA (3287-89 "Spike Jones Favorites") 35-50 49
(Three-disc boxed set.)
RCA (2900 thru 6000 series) 10-20 49-55
(Black vinyl.)
RCA (Colored vinyl) 20-40
W.B. 5-10 59

Picture Sleeves

RCA 20-30 53-54

EPs: 7-inch 33/45rpm

RCA 20-30 51-59
VERVE 15-25 56-57

LPs: 10/12-inch 33rpm

GLENDALE 5-8 78
LIBERTY 15-25 60-65
MGM 8-12 70
RCA (18 "Spike Jones Plays the Charleston") 50-100 51
RCA (1000 series) 5-8 75
RCA (2200 series) 20-25 60
RCA (2300 series) 5-8 77
RCA (3054 "Bottoms Up") 40-60 52
RCA (3128 "Spike Jones Kids the Classics") 40-60 53
RCA (3200 series) 8-12 71
RCA (3700 series) 4-8 80
RCA (3800 series) 10-15 67
(With "LPM" or "LSP" prefix.)
RCA (3800 series) 5-8 81
(With "AYL1" prefix.)
U.A. 5-8 75
VERVE (Except 8500 series) 20-40 56-59
VERVE (8500 series) 12-20 63
W.B. 15-25 59-60

Also see INGLE, Red, & Natural Seven
Also see KATZ, Mickey, & His Orchestra

JONES, Steve

LP '89

LPs: 10/12-inch 33rpm

MCA 5-8 89

JONES, Tamiko

P&R/R&B '75

Singles: 12-inch 33/45rpm

T.K. (6 "Let It Flow") 10-15 76

Singles: 7-inch

A&M 4-6 68-69
ARISTA 3-5 75
ATLANTIC 4-8 66
ATLANTIS 3-5 77
CONTEMPO 3-5 76
DECEMBER 4-8 67-68
GOLDEN WORLD (40 "I'm Spellbound") 15-25 66
POLYDOR 3-5 79
SUTRA 3-4 80
T.K. 3-5 76
20TH FOX 3-5 74

LPs: 10/12-inch 33rpm

A&M 10-12 68
DECEMBER 10-12 68

Also see TAMIKO

JONES, Tamiko, & Herbie Mann

P&R '66

Singles: 7-inch

ATLANTIC 4-6 66

LPs: 10/12-inch 33rpm

ATLANTIC 8-15 67

Also see JONES, Tamiko
Also see MANN, Herbie

JONES, Thelma

R&B '67

Singles: 7-inch

BARRY 4-8 66-68
COLUMBIA 3-5 78

JONES, Thumper

(George Jones)

Singles: 78rpm

STARDAY (240 "Rock-It") 20-30 56

Singles: 7-inch

STARDAY (240 "Rock-It") 75-100 56

EPs: 7-inch 33/45rpm

DIXIE (502 "Thumper Jones") 20-30 58
(Contains three Jones tracks. Not issued with cover.)

LPs: 10/12-inch 33rpm

TEENAGE HEAVEN 8-12

Also see JONES, George

JONES, Tom

P&R/R&B/LP '65

Singles: 7-inch

EPIC 3-5 76-80
LONDON 3-5 77
MCA 3-5 79
MERCURY 3-4 81-85
PARROT 3-8 65-75
SYMBOL 4-8 65
TOWER 4-8 65

Picture Sleeves

PARROT (9737 thru 9801) 4-8 65
PARROT (40000 series) 3-6 69-71

LPs: 10/12-inch 33rpm

EPIC 8-12 70-76
LONDON 5-8 77
MERCURY 5-8 81-85
PARROT 10-20 65-74

Also see ART of NOISE & Tom Jones
Also see BARRY, John

JONES, Tom / Freddie & Dreamers / Johnny Rivers

LPs: 10/12-inch 33rpm

TOWER (5007 "Three at the Top") 15-20 65

Also see FREDDIE & DREAMERS
Also see JONES, Tom
Also see RIVERS, Johnny

JONES GIRLS

P&R/R&B/LP '79

Singles: 7-inch

CURTOM 3-5 75
EPIC 3-4 81
PARAMOUNT 3-5 74
PHILADELPHIA INT'L 3-5 79-82
RCA 3-4 83

LPs: 10/12-inch 33rpm

PHILADELPHIA INT'L 5-8 79-81
RCA 5-8 83

Members: Shirley Jones; Brenda Jones; Valorie Jones.
Also see JONES, Shirley

JONESES

P&R/R&B '74

Singles: 7-inch

MERCURY 3-5 74-83
VMP 3-5 72

Picture Sleeves

MERCURY 3-5 75

LPs: 10/12-inch 33rpm

EPIC 5-8 77
MERCURY 5-8 74-83

Members: Glenn Dorsey; Harold Taylor; Cy Brooks; Ernest Holt; Wendell Noble; Reginald Noble; Larry Noble; Sam White.

JONZUN, Michael

R&B '86

Singles: 12-inch 33/45rpm

A&M 4-6 85
(Black vinyl.)
A&M 5-8 85
(Colored vinyl.)

Singles: 7-inch

A&M 3-4 85

Also see JONZUN CREW

JONZUN CREW

R&B '82

Singles: 12-inch 33/45rpm

A&M 4-6 84-85
TOMMY BOY 4-6 82-85

Singles: 7-inch

A&M 3-4 84-85
TOMMY BOY 3-4 82-85

LPs: 10/12-inch 33rpm

A&M 5-8 84-85
TOMMY BOY 5-8 83-85

Members: Michael Jonzun; Soni Jonzun; Steve Thorpe; Gordy Worthy.
Also see JONZUN, Michael

JOPLIN, Janis
(With Big Brother & Full Tilt)

P&R/LP '69

Singles: 7-inch

COLUMBIA 4-8 69-72
SIMON & SHUSTER ("Janis") 3-5
(Soundsheet. Included with the book *Janis.*)

LPs: 10/12-inch 33rpm

COLUMBIA (KCS-9913 "I Got Dem 'Ol Kozmic Blues Again, Mama") 20-25 69
COLUMBIA (PC-9913 "I Got Dem 'Ol Kozmic Blues Again, Mama") 5-8
COLUMBIA (30000 series) 10-15 71-75
(With "C2," "KC" or "PG" prefix.)
COLUMBIA (30000 series) 12-20 74
(With "CQ" prefix. Quad.)
COLUMBIA (30000 series) 5-8 82-84
(With "PC" prefix.)
MEMORY 5-10

Also see BIG BROTHER & Holding Company

JOPLIN, Janis / Hot Tuna

LPs: 10/12-inch 33rpm

GRUNT ("The Last Interview") 25-35 72
(Promotional issue only. Includes bonus Joplin home recording.)

Also see HOT TUNA
Also see JOPLIN, Janis

JORDAN, Jerry
(Jordans)

LP '75

Singles: 7-inch

MCA 3-5 75-76

LPs: 10/12-inch 33rpm

MCA 5-8 75-76

JORDAN, Lonnie

R&B '76

Singles: 7-inch

BOARDWALK 3-4 82
MCA 3-5 78
U.A. 3-5 76-77

LPs: 10/12-inch 33rpm

MCA 5-8 78

Also see WAR

JORDAN, Louis
(Louis Jordan's Elk Rendezvous Band; with His Tympani 5)

R&B '42

Singles: 78rpm

DECCA (7500 thru 8600 series) 5-10 38-43
DECCA (18000 thru 30000 series) 4-8 44-50
VIK 4-8 56

Singles: 7-inch

ALADDIN (3223 "Whiskey Do Your Stuff") 20-30 54
ALADDIN (3227 "Ooo-Wee") 20-30 54
ALADDIN (3242 "A Dollar Down") 25-35 54

ALADDIN (3246 "Messy Bessie") 20-30 54
ALADDIN (3249 "Louis' Blues") 20-30 54
ALADDIN (3264 "Put Some Money in the Pot") 20-30 54
ALADDIN (3270 "Fat Back and Corn Liquor") 20-30 54
ALADDIN (3279 "Gal, You Need a Whippin'") 20-30 54
DECCA (20000 thru 30000 series) 15-25 50-54
LOU-WA 5-10 60
MERCURY 10-20 56-58
PZAZZ 4-6 68
TANGERINE 4-8 62-66
VIK 8-12 56
WARWICK 5-10 60-61
X 8-12 55

EPs: 7-inch 33/45rpm

DECCA 15-25 56
MERCURY 15-25 57

LPs: 10/12-inch 33rpm

CLASSICAL JAZZ 5-8 82
DECCA (5035 "Greatest Hits").. 10-20 68
DECCA (8551 "Let the Good Times Roll") 30-40 56
MCA 5-8 75-80
MERCURY (20242 "Somebody Up There Digs Me") 25-30 57
MERCURY (20331 "Man, We're Wailin'") 25-30 58
SCORE (4007 "Go Blow Your Horn") 65-85 57
TANGERINE 12-15 64
TRIP 8-10 75
WING 15-20 63

Also see CROSBY, Bing, & Louis Jordan
Also see DAVIS, Martha
Also see FITZGERALD, Ella, & Louis Jordan

JORDAN, Stanley

LP '85

LPs: 10/12-inch 33rpm

BLUE NOTE 5-8 85-87
EMI 5-8 88

JORDAN, Tenita

R&B '85

Singles: 7-inch

CBS ASSOCIATED 3-4 85

JORDANS: see JORDAN, Jerry

JOSEPH, David

R&B/D&D '83

Singles: 12-inch 33/45rpm

MANGO 4-6 83

Singles: 7-inch

MANGO 3-4 83

JOSEPH, Margie
(With Blue Magic)

R&B '70

Singles: 12-inch 33/45rpm

H.C.R.C. 4-6 83

Singles: 7-inch

ATCO 3-5 75
ATLANTIC 3-5 72-78
COTILLION 3-5 76-84
H.C.R.C. 3-4 82-83
OKEH 4-8 68
VOLT 3-5 68-71

LPs: 10/12-inch 33rpm

ATLANTIC 8-10 73-74
H.C.R.C. 5-8 83
VOLT 10-12 71

Also see BLUE MAGIC
Also see HATHAWAY, Donny, & Margie Joseph

JOSIAS, Cory

D&D '83

Singles: 12-inch 33/45rpm

SIRE 4-6 83

JOURNEY

LP '75

Singles: 7-inch

COLUMBIA 3-5 74-87
GEFFEN 3-4 85

Picture Sleeves

COLUMBIA 3-5 81-87
GEFFEN 3-4 85

EPs: 7-inch 33/45rpm

CSP 4-6 81
(Promotional issue, made for Nestle's candy.)

LPs: 10/12-inch 33rpm

COLUMBIA (662 "Live Sampler") 12-15 75
(Promotional issue only.)
COLUMBIA (914 "Journey") 12-15 75
(Promotional issue only.)
COLUMBIA (30000 series) 5-10 75-82
COLUMBIA (46000 & 47000 series) 20-40 81-82
(Half-speed mastered.)
MFSL (144 "Escape") 100-200 85

Members: Steve Perry; Neal Schon; Aynsley Dunbar; Gregg Rolie; Ross Valory; Jonathan Cain; Robert Fleishman.
Also see BABYS
Also see BAD ENGLISH
Also see CAIN, Jonathan
Also see PERRY, Steve
Also see SCHON, Neal, & Jan Hammer

JOVI, Bon: see BON JOVI

JOY, Roddie

P&R/R&B '65

Singles: 7-inch

PARKWAY 5-10 66-67

RED BIRD (021 "Come Back Baby") 8-12 65
RED BIRD (031 "He's So Easy to Love") 10-20 65
RED BIRD (037 "If There's Anything You Want") 20-30 66

JOY DIVISION

LP '88

LPs: 10/12-inch 33rpm

FACTORY 5-8 81
QWEST 5-8 88

Members: Bernard Sumner; Peter Hook; Gillian Gilbert; Stephen Morris.

Also see NEW ORDER

JOY of COOKING

(The Joy)

P&R/LP '71

Singles: 7-inch

BROWNSVILLE 3-5 71
CAPITOL 3-5 71-73
FANTASY 3-5 77-78

LPs: 10/12-inch 33rpm

CAPITOL 8-10 71-72
FANTASY 5-10 77-78

Members: Terry Garthwaite; Toni Brown; Fritz Kasten; David Garthwaite; Ron Wilson.

JUBILAIRES

(With Andy Kirk's Orchestra)

R&B '46

Singles: 78rpm

CORAL 4-6 49
DECCA 4-8 46
KING 5-10 49-50
QUEEN (4163 "A Sunday Kind of Love") 15-25 47
QUEEN (4166 "Jubes Blues") ... 15-25 47
QUEEN (4167 "God Almighty's Gonna Cut You Down") 15-25 47
QUEEN (4168 "My God Called Me This Morning") 15-25 47
QUEEN (4172 "Icky, Yacky") 15-25 47

JUDAS PRIEST

LP '78

Singles: 7-inch

COLUMBIA 3-5 79-84

Picture Sleeves

COLUMBIA 3-5 81

LPs: 10/12-inch 33rpm

COLUMBIA (Except picture discs) 5-8 77-90
COLUMBIA (99-1543 "Screaming for Vengeance") 10-20 84
(Picture disc.)
COLUMBIA (99-1851 "Love Bites") 15-20 84
(Picture disc.)
COLUMBIA (39926 "Great Vinyl and Concert Hits") 10-20 84
(Picture disc.)
JANUS 6-10 76
OVATION 5-8 80
RCA 5-8 83-84
VISA 5-8 78-81

Members: Rob Halford; K.K. Downing; Glenn Tipton; Ian Hill; Dave Holland; Scott Travis.

JUDDS

C&W '83

Singles: 7-inch

CURB/RCA 3-4 90-91
RCA 3-5 83-88
RCA/CURB 3-4 89-89

Promotional Singles

RCA 5-10 83-88
(Black vinyl.)
RCA (13673 "Had a Dream") 15-20 83
(Colored vinyl.)
RCA (13923 "Why Not Me") 10-20 84
(Colored vinyl.)
RCA (13673 "Had a Dream") 15-20 83
(Colored vinyl.)

LPs: 10/12-inch 33rpm

RCA 5-8 83-88
RCA/CURB 5-8 89-89

Members: Naomi Judd; Wynonna Judd.

JUICY

R&B '83

Singles: 12-inch 33/45rpm

ATLANTIC 4-8 83-84
PRIVATE I 4-6 85

Singles: 7-inch

ARISTA 3-4 83
ATLANTIC 3-4 83-84
CBS ASSOC 3-4 86
PRIVATE I 3-4 85-86

LPs: 10/12-inch 33rpm

ARISTA 5-8 83
ATLANTIC 5-8 84

Members: Jerry Barnes; Katreese Barnes

JUKES: see SOUTHSIDE JOHNNY

JULIE

(Julie Budd)

P&R '76

Singles: 7-inch

A&M 3-4 84-85
TOM CAT 3-5 76

Also see BUDD, Julie

JULUKA

LP '83

Singles: 7-inch

W.B. 3-4 83-84

LPs: 10/12-inch 33rpm

W.B. 5-8 83-84

JUMBO

R&B '77

Singles: 7-inch

PRELUDE 3-5 77

LPs: 10/12-inch 33rpm

PYE 5-8 77

JUMP 'N the Saddle Band

P&R '83

Singles: 7-inch

ACME 4-6 82
ATLANTIC 3-4 83

Picture Sleeves

ATLANTIC 3-4 83

JUNE & DONNIE

R&B '69

Singles: 7-inch

CURTOM (1935 "I Thank You Baby") 4-8 68

Members: June Conquest; Donny Hathaway.
Also see HATHAWAY, Donny, & June Conquest

JUNGKLAS, Rob

LP '86

Singles: 7-inch

MANHATTAN 3-4 87

Picture Sleeves

MANHATTAN 3-4 87

LPs: 10/12-inch 33rpm

MANHATTAN 5-8 86

JUNIE
(Walter Morrison; Junie Morrison)

R&B '74

Singles: 7-inch

COLUMBIA 3-4 81
EASTBOUND 3-5 74
20TH FOX/WESTBOUND 3-5 75-76

LPs: 10/12-inch 33rpm

20TH FOX/WESTBOUND 5-8 76

Also see FUNKADELIC
Also see MORRISON, Junie
Also see OHIO PLAYERS

JUNIOR
(Junior Giscombe)

P&R/R&B/LP '82

Singles: 12-inch 33/45rpm

LONDON 4-6 84
MERCURY 4-6 83

Singles: 7-inch

CASABLANCA 3-4 83
LONDON 3-4 84-88
MERCURY 3-4 82-86

LPs: 10/12-inch 33rpm

MERCURY 5-8 82-83

JUNKYARD

LP '89

LPs: 10/12-inch 33rpm

GEFFEN 5-8 89

JU-PAR UNIVERSAL ORCHESTRA

R&B '77

Singles: 7-inch

JU-PAR 3-5 77

JUPITER, Duke: see DUKE JUPITER

JUST US

P&R '66

Singles: 7-inch

ATLANTIC 3-5 71
COLPIX 4-8 66
KAPP 4-8 66-67
MINUTEMAN 4-8 66

Picture Sleeves

KAPP 4-8 66

LPs: 10/12-inch 33rpm

KAPP 10-15 66

JUSTIS, Bill
(With the Jury; Bill Justis Orchestra; with Roger Fakes & Spinners)

P&R/R&B/C&W '57

Singles: 78rpm

PHILLIPS INT'L 5-10 57

Singles: 7-inch

BELL 3-5 70
MONUMENT 3-5 76
PHILLIPS INT'L 8-15 57-59
PLAY ME 8-12 59
MCA 3-5 77
MONUMENT 4-8 66
NRC 4-8 60
SMASH 4-8 63-65

Picture Sleeves

SMASH 5-10 63

LPs: 10/12-inch 33rpm

HARMONY 8-10 72
PHILLIPS INT'L (1950 "Cloud 9") 25-30 57
SMASH 15-20 62-66
SUN 8-10 69
WING 10-20 65

JUSTIS, Bill / Jerry Reed

EPs: 7-inch 33/45rpm

MCA (1961 "Music from *Smokey and the Bandit*") 10-15 77
(Promotional issue only.)

Also see JUSTIS, Bill
Also see REED, Jerry

JUVET, Patrick

LP '78

Singles: 12-inch 33/45rpm

CASABLANCA 4-6 78-79

Singles: 7-inch

CASABLANCA 3-5 78-79

LPs: 10/12-inch 33rpm

CASABLANCA 5-8 78-79

JYVE FYVE

Singles: 7-inch

BRUT 3-5 74

Also see JIVE FIVE

K

KBC BAND

P&R/LP '86

Singles: 7–inch

ARISTA 3-4 86

Picture Sleeves

ARISTA 3-4 86

LPs: 10/12–inch 33rpm

ARISTA 5-8 86

Members: Paul Kantner; Marty Balin; Jack Casady.

Also see JEFFERSON AIRPLANE

KC & Sunshine Band

(KC; Sunshine Band)

R&B '73

Singles: 12–inch 33/45rpm

EPIC 4-6 82
MECA 4-6 83-85
SUNSHINE SOUND 4-6 81

Singles: 7–inch

CASABLANCA 3-4 80-83
EPIC 3-4 81-83
MECA 3-4 83-85
SUNSHINE SOUND 3-4 81
TK 3-5 73-81

Picture Sleeves

TK 3-5 77-78

LPs: 10/12–inch 33rpm

CASABLANCA 5-8 81
EPIC 5-8 81-82
MECA 5-8 84
SUNSHINE SOUND 5-8 81
TK 8-10 74-80

Also see DE SARIO, Teri, & K.C.
Also see WRIGHT, Betty

KGB

LP '76

Singles: 7–inch

MCA 3-5 76

LPs: 10/12–inch 33rpm

MCA 8-10 76

Members: Ray Kennedy; Rick Grech; Mike Bloomfield; Barry Goldberg; Carmine Appice.

Also see BLOOMFIELD, Mike
Also see KENNEDY, Ray

K.I.D.

R&B '81

Singles: 12–inch 33/45rpm

SAM 4-6 81

Singles: 7–inch

SAM 3-5 81

K-9 POSSE

LP '89

LPs: 10/12–inch 33rpm

ARISTA 5-8 89

KTP: see KISSING the PINK

KADO, Ernie: see K-DOE, Ernie

KADOR, Ernest: see K-DOE, Ernie

KAEMPFERT, Bert, & His Orchestra

P&R/R&B/LP '60

Singles: 7–inch

DECCA 3-8 60-71

Picture Sleeves

DECCA 4-8 66

EPs: 7–inch 33/45rpm

DECCA 5-8 61

LPs: 10/12–inch 33rpm

CADENCE 10-15 61
DECCA 10-15 59-72
MCA 5-10 73-76

KAJAGOOGOO

(Kaja)

P&R/D&D/LP '83

Singles: 12–inch 33/45rpm

EMI AMERICA 4-6 83-85

Singles: 7–inch

EMI AMERICA 3-4 83-85

Picture Sleeves

EMI AMERICA 3-4 83

LPs: 10/12–inch 33rpm

EMI AMERICA 5-8 83-85

Also see LIMAHL

KALEIDOSCOPE

LP '69

Singles: 7–inch

A&M 3-5 73
EPIC (10117 "Elevator Man") 15-25 67
EPIC (10219 "Little Orphan Nannie") 15-25 67
EPIC (10239 "I Found Out") 15-25 67
EPIC (10332 "Just a Taste") 15-25 68
EPIC (10481 "Lie to Me") 15-25 69
EPIC (10500 "Tempe, Arizona") 15-25 69
TSOP 3-5 75

LPs: 10/12–inch 33rpm

BACK-TRAC 5-8 85
EPIC (24304 "Side Trips") 50-100 67
(Monaural.)
EPIC (24333 "Beacon from Mars") 40-60 67
(Monaural.)
EPIC (26304 "Side Trips") 50-75 67
(Stereo.)
EPIC (26333 "Beacon from Mars") 50-75 67
(Stereo.)
EPIC (26467 "Incredible Kaleidoscope") 20-40 69

EPIC (26508 "Bernice")............. 15-20 70
PACIFIC ARTS 5-10 78

Members: David Lindley; Solomon Feldthouse; John Vidican; John Welsh, Rick O'Neil; Brian Monsour; Chris Darrow.

Also see WILLIAMS, Larry, & Johnny Guitar Watson

KALIN TWINS

P&R/C&W/R&B '58

Singles: 78rpm

DECCA.................................... 10-15 58

Singles: 7-inch

AMY 4-8 66
DECCA.. 8-10 58-62

Picture Sleeves

DECCA (30977 "Why Don't You Believe Me")........................... 10-15 59

EPs: 7-inch 33/45rpm

DECCA (2623 "Kalin Twins") 25-50 58
DECCA (2641 "Forget Me Not") 25-50 59

LPs: 10/12-inch 33rpm

DECCA (8812 "Kalin Twins") 50-75 58
VOCALION........................... 10-20 66

Members: Hal Kalin; Herb Kalin.

Also see LEE, Brenda / Bill Haley & Comets / Kalin Twins / Four Aces

KALLEN, Kitty

P&R '49

Singles: 78rpm

DECCA.. 4-8 54-57
COLUMBIA 4-8 54
MERCURY...................................... 4-8 51-54

Singles: 7-inch

BELL 4-6 67
DECCA.. 5-10 54-59
COLUMBIA (40000 series) 5-10 54
COLUMBIA (41000 series) 4-8 59-61
MGM 4-6 65
MERCURY.................................... 5-10 51-54
PHILIPS 4-6 66
RCA.. 4-8 63
20TH-CENTURY-FOX 4-8 64
U.A. 4-8 65

Promotional Singles

DECCA (78094 "Personal Introduction by Kitty Kallen to '54 Christmas Seal Song") 8-12 54
(Single-sided promotional pressing.)

Picture Sleeves

DECCA (290 "It's Not the Whistle")............................. 10-15 55

EPs: 7-inch 33/45rpm

DECCA.. 10-15 54-56
COLUMBIA 10-15 54
MERCURY.................................... 10-15 55

LPs: 10/12-inch 33rpm

COLUMBIA 10-20 60-61
DECCA (8397 "It's a Lonesome Old Town") 20-30 56
MCA 4-8 83
MERCURY (25206 "Pretty Kitty Kallen Sings") 30-50 55
(10-inch LP.)
MOVIETONE 8-12 67
RCA 10-20 63
20TH-CENTURY-FOX...............10-15 64
VOCALION 10-20 59
WING 10-15 63

Also see ANN-MARGRET / Kitty Kallen / Della Reese
Also see HAYES, Richard, & Kitty Kallen
Also see JAMES, Harry, & His Orchestra

KALLEN, Kitty, & Georgie Shaw

Singles: 78rpm

DECCA 4-8 55

Singles: 7-inch

DECCA 5-10 55

Also see KALLEN, Kitty
Also see SHAW, Georgie

KALLMANN, Gunter, Chorus

LP '65

Singles: 7-inch

4 CORNERS....................................4-6 65-68

LPs: 10/12-inch 33rpm

4 CORNERS..................................8-12 65-68
POLYDOR 5-10 70

KALYAN

R&B/LP '77

Singles: 7-inch

MCA...3-5 77

LPs: 10/12-inch 33rpm

MCA 8-10 77

KAMIKAZE

D&D '84

Singles: 12-inch 33/45rpm

A&M 4-6 84

Singles: 7-inch

A&M 3-4 84

KAMON, Karen

P&R '84

Singles: 7-inch

COLUMBIA.......................................3-4 84

Picture Sleeves

COLUMBIA 3-4 84

KANE, Big Daddy

LP '88

LPs: 10/12-inch 33rpm

COLD CHILL.....................................5-8 88-90

KANE, Madleen

P&R '82

Singles: 12-inch 33/45rpm

CHALET...4-6 82
TSR..4-6 85

Singles: 7-inch

CHALET...3-4 82
W.B. 3-5 78-79

Picture Sleeves

W.B. 3-5 78-79

LPs: 10/12-inch 33rpm

CHALET 5-8 82
W.B. 5-8 78-79

KANE, Paul
(Paul Simon)

Singles: 7-inch

TRIBUTE (128 "Carlos Dominguez") 50-75 63
(Copies crediting "Paul Simon" as the singer are bootlegs.)
Also see SIMON, Paul

KANE GANG

P&R/LP '87

Singles: 12-inch 33/45rpm

LONDON 4-6 86

Singles: 7-inch

CAPITOL 3-4 87
LONDON 3-4 86

Picture Sleeves

CAPITOL 3-4 87

LPs: 10/12-inch 33rpm

CAPITOL 5-8 87
LONDON 5-8 86
POLYGRAM 5-8 85

KANO

R&B '80

Singles: 7-inch

EMERGENCY 3-5 80
MIRAGE 3-4 81

LPs: 10/12-inch 33rpm

EMERGENCY 5-8 81
MIRAGE 5-8 81

KANSAS

LP '74

Singles: 12-inch 33/45rpm

CBS ASSOCIATED 5-10 83
(Promotional only.)
MCA 5-8 88
(Promotional only.)

Singles: 7-inch

CBS ASSOCIATED 3-4 83
KIRSHNER 3-5 74-82
MCA (17290 "Power") 3-6 87
(CD mix on vinyl. Promotional issue only.)
MCA (50000 series) 3-4 86-87

Picture Sleeves

CBS ASSOCIATED 3-4 83
KIRSHNER 3-5 82
MCA 3-4 86-87

LPs: 10/12-inch 33rpm

CBS ASSOCIATED 5-8 83-84
KIRSHNER (30000 series) 8-12 74-82
KIRSHNER (40000 series) 15-25 81-82
(Half-speed mastered.)
MCA 5-8 86-88

Promotional LPs

BURNS MEDIA ("Two for the Show") 15-25 78
KIRSHNER (34929 "Point of Know Return") 50-75 79
(Picture disc.)
KIRSHNER (555 "Two for the Show") 10-15 78
Members: Dave Hope; Rich Williams; Phil Ehart; Kerry Livgren; Robbie Shakespeare; Steve Walsh; Terry Brock.
Also see MORSE, Steve, Band
Also see STREETS
Also see WALSH, Steve

KANTNER, Paul

R&B '79

Singles: 7-inch

MALACO 3-5 79
RCA 5-10 83

KANTNER, Paul, & Grace Slick
(With David Freiberg)

LP '71

Singles: 7-inch

GRUNT 3-5 72

Picture Sleeves

GRUNT 3-6 72

LPs: 10/12-inch 33rpm

GRUNT (0100 series) 8-10 71-73
GRUNT (2002 "Sunfighter") 10-15 71
(Includes booklet.)
GRUNT (4000 series) 5-8 82
Also see GRATEFUL DEAD
Also see JEFFERSON AIRPLANE
Also see SLICK, Grace

KANTNER, Paul, & Jefferson Starship

LP '70

Singles: 7-inch

RCA 3-6 71
Also see KANTNER, Paul
Also see JEFFERSON STARSHIP

KAOMA

LP '90

Singles: 7-inch

EPIC 3-4 90

LPs: 10/12-inch 33rpm

EPIC 5-8 89

KAPLAN, Gabriel

P&R '77

Singles: 7-inch

ABC 3-5 74
ELEKTRA 3-5 76-77

Picture Sleeves

ELEKTRA 3-5 77

LPs: 10/12-inch 33rpm

ABC 8-10 74

KARAS, Anton

P&R '50

Singles: 78rpm

LONDON 4-6 50

Singles: 7-inch

LONDON 5-10 50

KAREN, Kenny
(Ken Karen)

P&R '73

Singles: 7-inch

BIG TREE 3-5 73
COLUMBIA (3-42264 "Oh Susie, Forgive Me") 15-25 62
(Compact 33 Single.)
COLUMBIA (3-42452 "To Sandy, with Love") 15-25 62
(Compact 33 Single.)
COLUMBIA (3-42638 "16 Years Ago Tonight") 15-25 62
(Compact 33 Single.)
COLUMBIA (4-42264 "Oh Susie, Forgive Me") 5-10 62
COLUMBIA (4-42452 "To Sandy, with Love") 5-10 62
COLUMBIA (4-42638 "16 Years Ago Tonight") 5-10 62
STRAND 5-10 59-60

Picture Sleeves

COLUMBIA (42264 "Oh Susie, Forgive Me") 10-15 62
COLUMBIA (42452 "To Sandy, with Love") 10-15 62

KARI, Harry, & His Six Saki Sippers

P&R '53

(Harry Stewart)

Singles: 78rpm

CAPITOL 4-8 53-55

Singles: 7-inch

CAPITOL 5-10 53-55
Also see YORGESSON, Yogi

KARL, Frankie
(With the Dreams)

P&R/R&B '68

Singles: 7-inch

D.C. 5-10 68
LIBERTY (56164 "Don't Sleep Too Long") 15-25 70

KARMA

R&B '77

LPs: 10/12-inch 33rpm

A&M 8-10 77

KARTOON KREW

R&B '85

Singles: 7-inch

PROFILE 3-4 86

KASANDRA
(With the Midnight Riders; John Anderson)

P&R/R&B/LP '68

Singles: 7-inch

CAPITOL 4-8 68
IMPERIAL 5-10 60

LPs: 10/12-inch 33rpm

CAPITOL 10-15 68

KASENETZ - KATZ SINGING ORCHESTRAL CIRCUS
(Kasenetz - Katz Super Cirkus; Kasenetz - Katz Fighter Squadron)

P&R '68

Singles: 7-inch

BELL (966 "When He Comes") 5-10 71
(With 10CC.)
BUDDAH 4-8 68
EPIC 3-5 77
MAGNA-GLIDE 3-5 75
SUPER K 3-5 69-71

LPs: 10/12-inch 33rpm

BUDDAH 10-15 68
Also see MUSIC EXPLOSION
Also see 1910 FRUITGUM COMPANY
Also see OHIO EXPRESS
Also see 10CC

KASHIF

R&B/D&D/LP '83

Singles: 12-inch 33/45rpm

ARISTA 4-6 83-86

Singles: 7-inch

ARISTA 3-4 83-88

LPs: 10/12-inch 33rpm

ARISTA 5-8 83-87
Also see KENNY G. & Kashif
Also see MOORE, Melba, & Kashif
Also see WARWICK, Dionne, & Kashif

KASHIF & Meli'sa Morgan

R&B '87

Singles: 7-inch

ARISTA 3-4 87
Also see MORGAN, Meli'sa

KATFISH

P&R '75

Singles: 7-inch

BIG TREE 3-5 75

KATRINA & WAVES

P&R/LP '85

Singles: 7-inch

CAPITOL 3-4 85-86
SBK 3-4 89

Picture Sleeves

CAPITOL 3-4 85-86
SBK 3-4 89

LPs: 10/12-inch 33rpm

CAPITOL 5-8 85-86
SBK 5-8 89
Members: Katrina Leskanich; Kimberley Rew; Alex Cooper; Vince de La Cruz.

KATZ, Mickey, & His Orchestra

P&R '50

Singles: 78rpm

CAPITOL 4-6 51-57

Singles: 7-inch

CAPITOL 5-10 51-62

EPs: 7-inch 33/45rpm

CAPITOL.................................. 10-15 53-56

LPs: 10/12-inch 33rpm

CAPITOL (Except SM-298)....... 15-30 53-65
CAPITOL (SM-298 "Mickey Katz") 5-8 78

Also see JONES, Spike

KAUKONEN, Jorma
(With Vital Parts)

LP '81

Singles: 7-inch

GRUNT 3-5 73

LPs: 10/12-inch 33rpm

GRUNT 8-12 73
RCA.. 5-10 79-81

Also see HOT TUNA
Also see JEFFERSON AIRPLANE

KAY, John
(With Steppenwolf; with Sparrows)

P&R/LP '72

Singles: 7-inch

DUNHILL.. 3-5 72-73
MERCURY 3-5 78

LPs: 10/12-inch 33rpm

COLUMBIA 10-20 69
DUNHILL...................................... 8-10 72-73
MERCURY 5-8 78
QWIL 5-8 87

Also see STEPPENWOLF

KAY GEES: see KAY-GEES

KAYAK

LP '76

Singles: 7-inch

JANUS 3-5 78
MERCURY..................................... 3-4 80

LPs: 10/12-inch 33rpm

HARVEST 8-10 74
JANUS 5-10 75-79
MERCURY 5-8 80

Also see WERNER, Max

KAYE, Danny

P&R '47

Singles: 78rpm

COLUMBIA 4-8 49-54
DECCA... 4-8 50-56
RCA... 4-8 47-48

Singles: 7-inch

COLUMBIA 5-10 49-54
DECCA... 5-10 50-56
REPRISE 4-8 62

Picture Sleeves

DECCA (151 "Little White Duck") 10-15 50s
REPRISE (20105 "D-o-d-g-e-r-s Song") 8-12 62

EPs: 7-inch 33/45rpm

CAPITOL...................................... 5-10 58
COLUMBIA 10-20 49-54
DECCA 8-15 54-57

LPs: 10/12-inch 33rpm

CAMDEN 15-25 57
CAPITOL.....................................15-25 58
COLUMBIA (6000 series) 25-50 49-54
(10-inch LPs.)
DECCA (100 series) 10-20 63
DECCA (5000 series)................20-40 54
(10-inch LPs.)
DECCA (8000 series) 20-40 54-59
DECCA (78000 series) 10-15 67
GOLDEN.......................................5-10 62
HARMONY (7000 series) 15-25 57
HARMONY (7300 series) 8-15 64

KAYE, Danny, & Louis Armstrong

Singles: 7-inch

DOT 4-8 59-64

Picture Sleeves

DOT 5-10 59

Also see ARMSTRONG, Louis

KAYE, Danny, Jimmy Durante, Jane Wyman & Groucho Marx

P&R '51

Singles: 78rpm

DECCA 3-6 51

Singles: 7-inch

DECCA 5-10 51

Also see DURANTE, Jimmy
Also see KAYE, Danny
Also see MARX, Groucho

KAYE, Mary
(Mary Kaye Trio)

P&R '52

Singles: 78rpm

CAPITOL...3-6 52
DECCA 3-6 55-56
RCA 3-6 54

Singles: 7-inch

BLUE-J...4-8
CAMELOT.......................................4-6 67
CAPITOL.......................................5-10 52
DECCA 5-10 55-56
LECTRON.......................................4-6 65
RCA 5-10 54
VERVE..4-8 60
W.B. 4-8 59

EPs: 7-inch 33/45rpm

DECCA 5-10 56

LPs: 10/12-inch 33rpm

COLUMBIA 8-15 62
DECCA 10-25 56
MOVIETONE 8-12 67
20TH FOX......................................8-15 64
VERVE...10-15 60-62
W.B. 10-20 59

Also see BYRNES, Edd "Kookie," with Joanie Sommers & Mary Kaye Trio

KAYE, Sammy, & His Orchestra

P&R '37

Singles: 78rpm

COLUMBIA 3-6 50-57
RCA 3-6 52-53

Singles: 7-inch

COLUMBIA 5-10 50-60
DECCA 4-6 60-70
PROJECT 3 .... 3-5 72
RCA 5-10 52-53

EPs: 7-inch 33/45rpm

COLUMBIA 5-15 50-60
DECCA 4-6 64
RCA 5-15 52-53

LPs: 10/12-inch 33rpm

CAMDEN 10-25 53-56
COLUMBIA 10-25 50-62
DECCA 8-15 60-70
HARMONY 5-10 59-68
MCA 5-10 74
PROJECT 3 .... 5-8 72
RCA 5-10 68-72
VOCALION 5-10 71

Also see CORNELL, Don

KAY-GEES

R&B '74

Singles: 7-inch

DE-LITE 3-5 78-79
GANG 3-5 74-76

LPs: 10/12-inch 33rpm

DELITE 5-8 78-79
GANG 5-10 75

KAYLI, Bob
(With the Berry Gordy Orchestra; Robert Gordy)

P&R '58

Singles: 7-inch

ANNA (1104 "Never More") 25-35 59
CARLTON (482 "Everyone Was There") 20-30 58
GORDY (7004 "Toodle Loo"/"Hold On Pearl") 30-50 62
GORDY (7008 "Toodle Loo"/"Hold On Pearl") 20-30 62
TAMLA (54051 "Small Sad Sam") 20-30 61

K-DOE, Ernie
(Ernest Kador; Ernie Kado)

P&R/R&B '61

Singles: 78rpm

SPECIALTY 5-10 55

Singles: 7-inch

DUKE 4-8 64-69
EMBER 5-10 59-61
INSTANT 4-8 63-64
MINIT 5-10 59-63
SPECIALTY 10-20 55

LPs: 10/12-inch 33rpm

JANUS 8-10 71
MINIT (0002 "Mother in Law") 50-80 61

Also see SPELLMAN, Benny
Also see THOMAS, Irma / Ernie K-Doe / Showmen / Benny Spellman.

K-DOE, Ernie / Phil Phillips

Singles: 7-inch

RIPETE 3-4

Also see K-DOE, Ernie
Also see PHILLIPS, Phil

KEANE BROTHERS

P&R '76

Singles: 12-inch 33/45rpm

ABC 4-8 79

Singles: 7-inch

ABC 3-5 79
20TH FOX 3-4 76

LPs: 10/12-inch 33rpm

ABC 5-8 79

KEEL

LP '85

Singles: 7-inch

GOLD MOUNTAIN 3-4 84-85

LPs: 10/12-inch 33rpm

GOLD MOUNTAIN 5-8 85
MCA 5-8 86-87

KEENE, Tommy

LP '86

Singles: 7-inch

GEFFEN 3-4 86

LPs: 10/12-inch 33rpm

GEFFEN 5-8 86

KEITH
(James Keefer)

P&R '66

Singles: 7-inch

DISCREET 3-5 71-74
MERCURY 4-8 66-68
RCA 4-6 69

Picture Sleeves

MERCURY 4-8 66-68

LPs: 10/12-inch 33rpm

MERCURY 15-20 67
RCA 15-25 69

Also see TOKENS

KELLEM, Manny, & Orchestra

P&R/LP '68

Singles: 7-inch

EPIC 4-6 68
METROMEDIA 4-6 69

LPs: 10/12-inch 33rpm

EPIC 5-10 68

KELLER, Jerry

P&R '59

Singles: 7-inch

CAPITOL 4-8 61

CORAL....................................... 4-8 63-64
JUBILEE.................................... 5-10 58
KAPP (K-277 "Here Comes Summer")................................ 5-10 59
(Monaural.)
KAPP (KS-277 "Here Comes Summer")............................... 10-20 59
(Stereo.)
KAPP (310 thru 353).................. 5-10 59-60
RCA.. 4-8 67
REPRISE.................................... 4-8 65
WEB... 5-10 58

Picture Sleeves

KAPP (277 "Here Comes Summer")................................ 10-15 59
KAPP (295 "If I Had a Girl")....... 10-15 59

LPs: 10/12-inch 33rpm

KAPP (1178 "Here Comes Jerry Keller")........................ 20-30 59
(Monaural.)
KAPP (3178 "Here Comes Jerry Keller")........................ 25-35 59
(Stereo.)

KELLUM, Murry

P&R '63

Singles: 7-inch

CINNAMON................................. 3-5 74
EPIC.. 3-5 71-72
MUSIC MILL.............................. 3-5 76
PLANTATION.............................. 3-5 78
RANWOOD................................. 3-5 76

LPs: 10/12-inch 33rpm

PLANTATION.............................. 5-8 78

KELLUM, Murry, & Alton Lott

Singles: 7-inch

K&M.. 3-5 61

KELLUM, Murry / Glenn Sutton

Singles: 7-inch

ABC... 3-5 73
M.O.C. (Except 658)............... 10-15 63-64
M.O.C. (658 "I Dreamed I Was a Beatle")............................. 12-18 64

Also see KELLUM, Murry
Also see SUTTON, Glenn

KELLY, Casey

P&R '72

Singles: 7-inch

ELEKTRA.................................... 3-5 72-73
PRIVATE STOCK....................... 3-5 77

LPs: 10/12-inch 33rpm

ELEKTRA.................................. 8-10 72

KELLY, Grace: see CROSBY, Bing, & Grace Kelly

KELLY, Herman, & Life

R&B '78

Singles: 7-inch

ALSTON..................................... 3-5 78

KELLY, J., & Premiers

(J. Kely & Premiers)

R&B '74

Singles: 7-inch

ROADSHOW.................................3-5 74

KELLY, Monty, & His Orchestra

P&R '53

Singles: 78rpm

ESSEX...3-5 53-54

Singles: 7-inch

CARLTON....................................4-8 59-60
ESSEX...5-10 53-54

LPs: 10/12-inch 33rpm

ALSHIRE.....................................4-8 72
CARLTON....................................10-20 59

KELLY, Paul

P&R/R&B '70

Singles: 7-inch

DIAL..5-10 65-68
HAPPY TIGER.............................3-6 70
PHILIPS......................................10-20 66-68
TK...10-20 60
W.B...3-6 73-76

Picture Sleeves

PHILIPS......................................10-20 66

LPs: 10/12-inch 33rpm

HAPPY TIGER.............................8-10 70
W.B...8-10 72-76

Also see TEX, Joe
Also see VALADIERS

KELSEY, Rev.

(Rev. Kelsey's Congregation)

R&B '48

Singles: 78rpm

SUPER DISC...............................3-6 48

KEMP, Johnny

R&B '86

Singles: 7-inch

COLUMBIA..................................3-4 86-89

Picture Sleeves

COLUMBIA..................................3-4 86-89

LPs: 10/12-inch 33rpm

COLUMBIA..................................5-8 86-89

KEMP, Tara

LP '91

LPs: 10/12-inch 33rpm

GIANT...5-8 91

KENDALL SISTERS

P&R/R&B '58

Singles: 7-inch

ARGO..5-10 57-58
CHECKER....................................5-10 58

KENDALLS

(Featuring Jeannie Kendall)

C&W '70

Singles: 7-inch

DOT...3-5 72-73

Row 1: Shirelles *Foolish Little Girl* ($30–$40); Sandy Stewart *My Coloring Book* ($15–$20). **Row 2**: Danny O'Keefe *Introducing Danny O'Keefe* ($20–$30); Kay Starr *Jazz Singer* ($20–$30). **Row 3**: Dion and the Belmonts *When You Wish Upon a Star* ($30–$40); Clovers *The Clovers* ($100–$175).

Row 1: Miracles *Mickey's Monkey* ($50–$75); Joni James *Let There Be Love* ($30–$50). **Row 2**: Beatles *Sgt. Pepper's Lonely Hearts Club Band (picture disc)* ($15–$20); Nutty Squirrels *The Nutty Squirrels* ($25–$35). **Row 3**: Ricky Nelson *More Songs by Ricky* ($35–$50); Marvin Rainwater *Songs by Marvin Rainwater* ($75–$125).

Row 1: Johnny Nash *Soft Folk* ($15–$25); Frank Fontaine *I'm Counting on You* ($10–$20). **Row 2**: Pearl Bailey *Intoxicating Pearl Bailey* ($20–$30); Bobby Boris Pickett and the Crypt Kickers *The Original Monster Mash* ($30–$50). **Row 3**: Alan Freed (Crickets, Jackie Wilson, Terry Noland) *Rock 'n Roll Show* ($75–$100); Duane Eddy *Have Twangy Guitar Will Travel* ($20–$25).

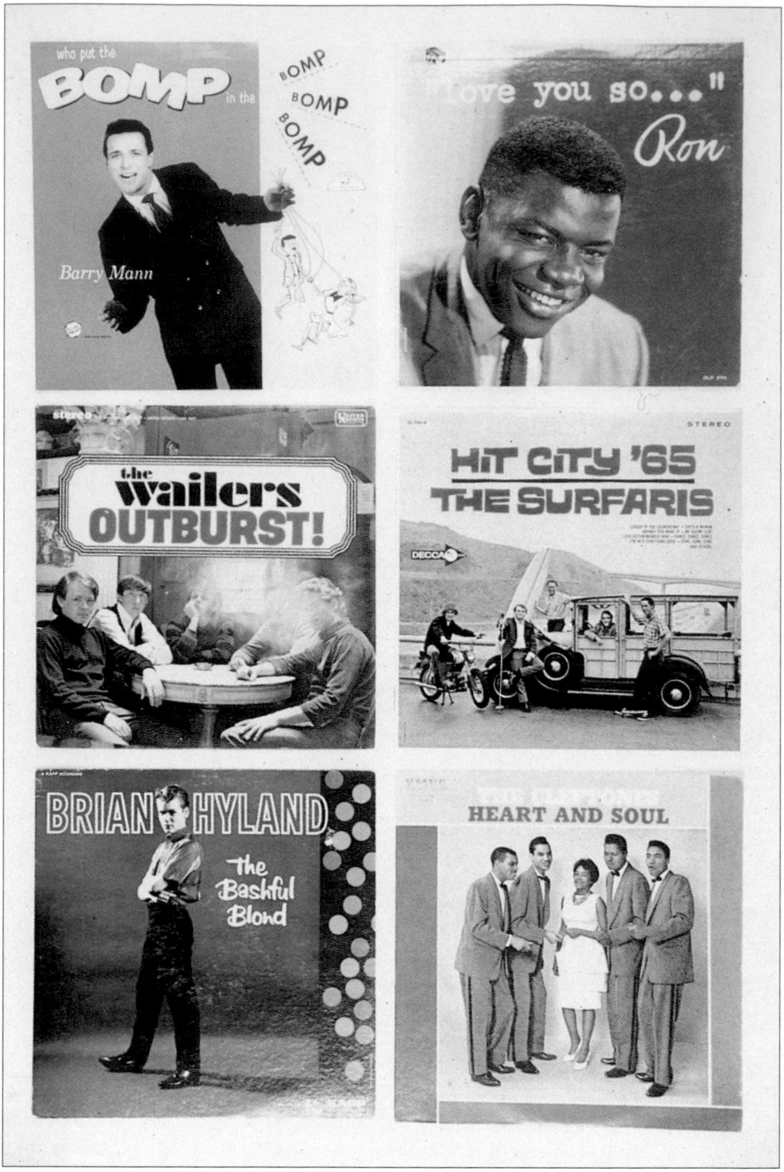

Row 1: Barry Mann *Who Put the Bomp in the Bomp Bomp Bomp* ($50–$80); Ron Holden *Love You So...* ($40–$60). **Row 2**: Wailers *Outburst!* ($25–$35); Surfaris *Hit City '65* ($25–$45). **Row 3**: Brian Hyland *The Bashful Blond* ($25–$30); Cleftones *Heart and Soul* ($5–$10).

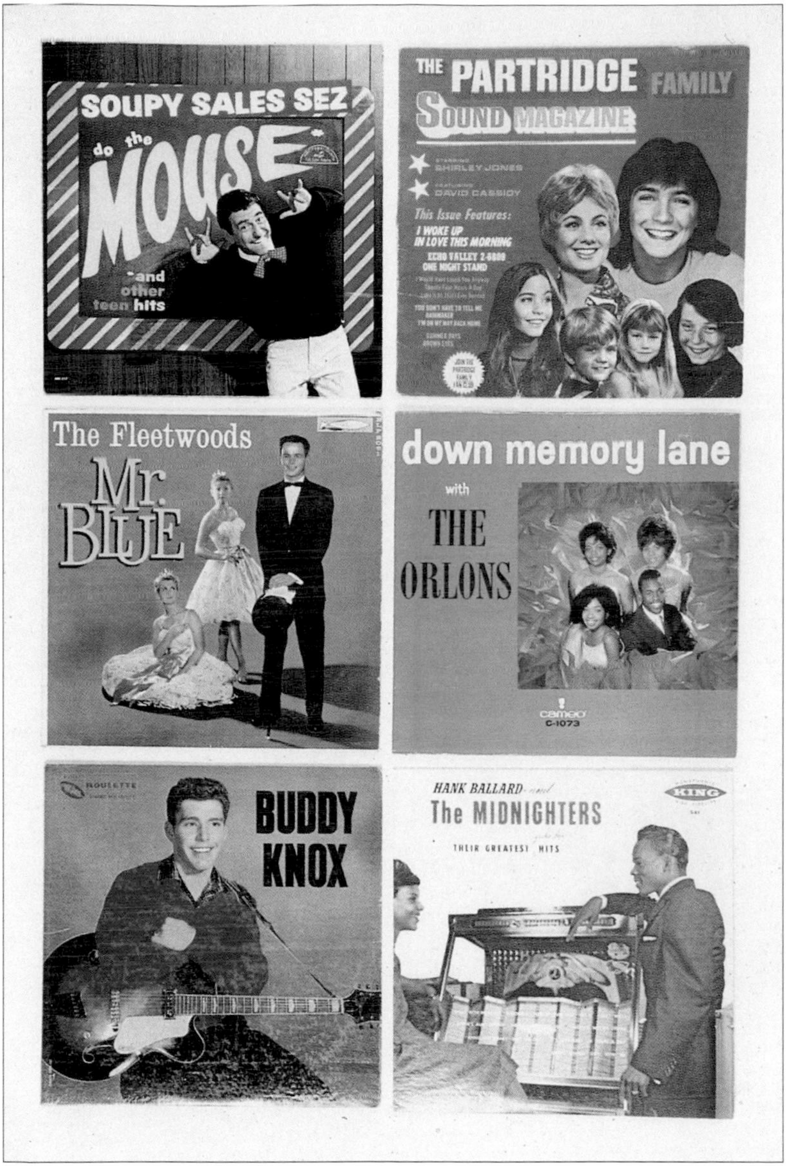

Row 1: Soupy Sales *Do the Mouse and Other Teen Hits* ($15–$25); Partridge Family *Sound Family Magazine* ($8–$12). **Row 2**: Fleetwoods *Mr. Blue* ($20–$30); Orlons *Down Memory Lane with the Orlons* ($25–$50). **Row 3**: Buddy Knox *Buddy Knox* ($75–$100); Hank Ballard and the Midnighters *Their Greatest Hits* ($50–$100).

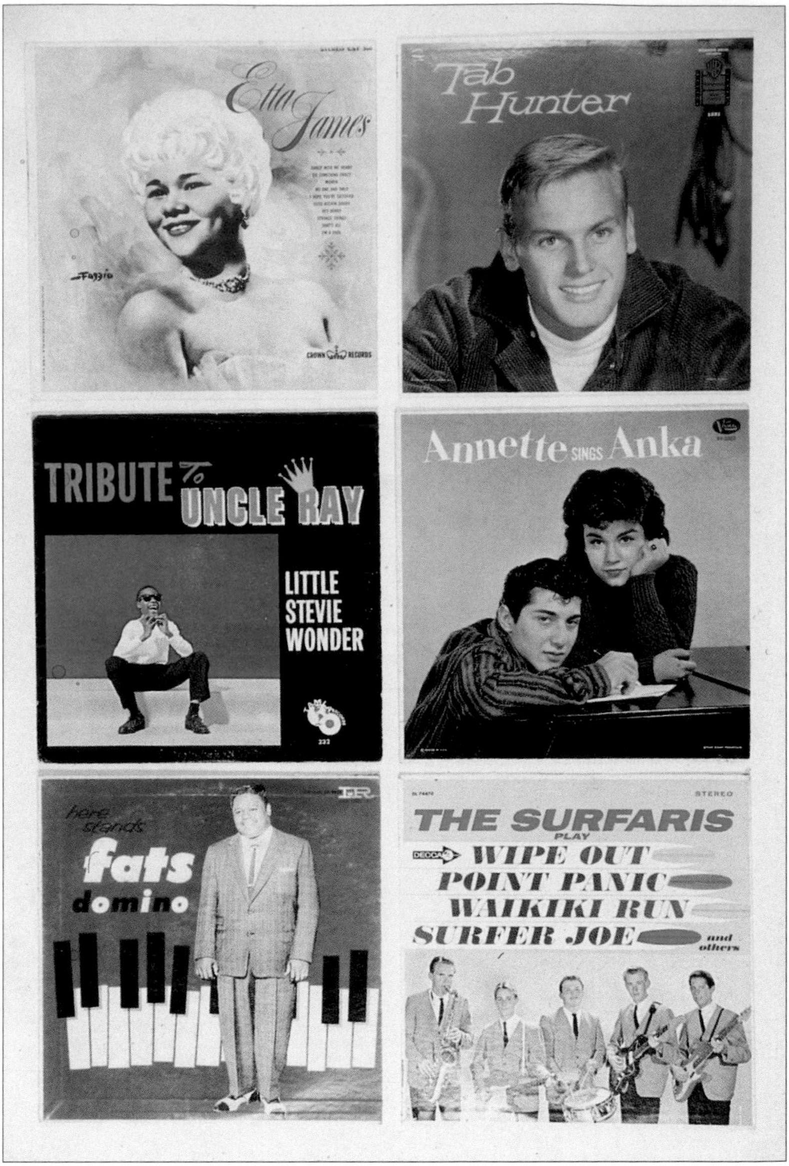

Row 1: Etta James *Etta James* ($20–$30); Tab Hunter *Tab Hunter* ($25–$35);. **Row 2**: Little Stevie Wonder *Tribute to Uncle Ray* ($50–$80); Annette Funicello *Annette Sings Anka* ($35–$50). **Row 3**: Fats Domino *Here Stands Fats Domino* ($60–$100).The Surfaris *The Surfaris* ($25-$45).

Row 1: Lou Christie *Lou Christie Srtikes Back* ($20–$30); Ben Colder *Live and Loaded at the Sam Houston Coliseum* ($10–$20). **Row 2**: Johnny Burnette *Roses Are Red* ($30 $40); Johnny Cash *Now Here's Johnny Cash* (($20–$30). **Row 3**: Screamin' Jay Hawkins *What That Is!* ($15–$25); Dinah Washington *Unforgettable Dinah Washington* ($15–$25).

Row 1: Marty Robbins (EP) *The Song of Robbins* ($10–$20); Hank Williams *Ramblin' Man* ($10–$20); Wilburn Brothers (EP) *Trouble's Back in Town* ($10–$15). **Row 2**: Patsy Cline *Songs by Patsy Cline* ($35–$50); Everly Bothers (EP) *Foreverly Yours* ($15–$25); Wanda Jackson (EP) *Wanda Jackson* ($25–$50). **Row 3**: Spike Jones *Thank You Music Lovers!* ($20–$25); Chuck Jackson *Tribute to Rhythm and Blues* ($15–$25). **Row 4**: Louis Armstrong *Louis Armstrong* ($20–$30); Bill Haley and the Comets *Rock and Roll Dance Party* ($200–$400).

EPIC	3-4	89
MCA/CURB	3-4	86
MERCURY	3-4	81-85
OVATION	3-5	77-80
STEP ONE	3-4	87-88
STOP	3-6	70
U.A.	3-5	75-76
VARSITY	10-15	69

LPs: 10/12-inch 33rpm

DOT	8-12	72
GUSTO	5-8	78
MCA/CURB	5-8	86
MERCURY	5-8	81-85
OVATION	5-10	77-80
STOP	10-15	70
POWER PAK	5-8	74

Members: Jeannie Kendall; Royce Kendall.

KENDRICK, Nat, & Swans

P&R/R&B '60

Singles: 7-inch

DADE (1000 series)	5-10	59-60
DADE (5000 series)	4-8	63

Members: Nat Kendrick; J.C. Adams; Bobby Roach; Fats Gonder; Bernard Odum.
Also see WESLEY, Fred, & J.B.s

KENDRICKS, Eddie
(Eddie Kendrick)

P&R/R&B/LP '71

Singles: 7-inch

ARISTA	3-5	78-80
ATLANTIC	3-4	80-81
CORNER STREET	3-4	84
MOTOWN	3-5	76
RCA	3-4	85-88
TAMLA	3-5	71-77

LPs: 10/12-inch 33rpm

ARISTA	5-8	78
ATLANTIC	5-8	81
MOTOWN	5-8	75-82
MS. DIXIE	5-8	83
TAMLA	8-10	71-78

Also see HALL, Daryl, John Oates, David Ruffin & Eddie Kendrick
Also see RUFFIN, David, & Eddie Kendricks
Also see TEMPTATIONS

KENDRICKS, Linda

D&D '84

Singles: 12-inch 33/45rpm

AIRWAVE	4-6	84

Singles: 7-inch

AIRWAVE	3-4	84

KENNEDY, John Fitzgerald

LP '63

LPs: 10/12-Inch 33rpm

CAEDMON	5-10	64
CHALLENGE	8-15	64
COLPIX	10-20	64
COLUMBIA	10-20	65
DECCA	10-20	63
DIPLOMAT	5-15	63
DOCUMENTARIES	10-20	63
GATEWAY	8-15	64
HARMONIA	8-15	64
LEGACY	10-20	65
PALACE	8-15	64
PHILIPS	8-15	64
PICKWICK	8-12	63
PREMIER	10-20	63
RCA	8-15	64
REGINA	5-15	64
SOMERSET	5-15	63
20TH FOX	10-20	63

Most of the albums listed above were released as a tribute of some type to President Kennedy after his assassination on November 22, 1963. Most contain excerpts of his speeches.

KENNEDY, John Fitzgerald / Richard M. Nixon

LPs: 10/12-Inch 33rpm

COLUMBIA	10-15	68

Also see KENNEDY, John Fitzgerald

KENNEDY, Joyce

R&B/LP '84

Singles: 7-inch

A&M	3-4	84-85
BLUE ROCK (4016 "I'm a Good Girl")	20-25	65
BLUE ROCK (4023 "Hi-Fi, Albums and I")	15-20	65
FONTANA (1924 "Could This Be Love")	10-15	64
RAN DEE (110 "I Still Love You")	10-20	63
RAN DEE (118 "How Old Is Old")	10-20	63

LPs: 10/12-inch 33rpm

A&M	5-8	84

Also see MOTHER'S FINEST

KENNEDY, Joyce, & Jeffrey Osborne

R&B '84

Singles: 7-inch

A&M	3-4	84

Also see KENNEDY, Joyce
Also see OSBORNE, Jeffrey

KENNEDY, Mike

P&R '72

Singles: 7-inch

ABC	3-5	72

LPs: 10/12-inch 33rpm

ABC	8-10	72

Also see LOS BRAVOS

KENNEDY, Ray

P&R '80

Singles: 7-inch

ARC	3-5	80

Picture Sleeves

ARC 3-5 80

LPs: 10/12-inch 33rpm

CREAM 10-12 72

Also see KGB

KENNEDY, Robert Francis

LP '69

LPs: 10/12-Inch 33rpm

COLUMBIA 8-15 68

KENNY & CADETS

Singles: 7-inch

RANDY (422 "Barbie") 350-500 62
(Black vinyl.)

RANDY (422 "Barbie") 500-750 62
(Colored vinyl.)

Members: Brian Wilson; Carl Wilson; Al Jardine; Audree Wilson.

Also see BEACH BOYS

KENNY & JOHNNY

R&B '86

Singles: 7-inch

PHILADELPHIA INT'L 3-4 86

Members: Kenny Whitehead; Johnny Whitehead.

Also see WHITEHEAD, Kenny & Johnny

KENNY G.

(With G Force; Kenny Gorelick)

R&B/LP '84

Singles: 7-inch

ARISTA 3-4 83-89

Picture Sleeves

ARISTA 3-4 87-89

LPs: 10/12-inch 33rpm

ARISTA 5-10 83-89

Also see LORBER, Jeff

Also see LOVE UNLIMITED

KENNY G. & Kashif

Singles: 7-inch

ARISTA 3-4 85

Also see KASHIF

KENNY G. & Smokey Robinson

Singles: 7-inch

ARISTA 3-4 89

Also see ROBINSON, Smokey

KENNY G. & Lenny Williams

Singles: 7-inch

ARISTA 3-4 83-86

Also see KENNY G.

Also see WILLIAMS, Lenny

KENT, Al

P&R/R&B '67

Singles: 78rpm

CHECKER (881 "Dat's Why") ... 15-25 57

Singles: 7-inch

BARITONE (942 "Hold Me") ... 50-100 60

CHECKER (881 "Dat's Why") ... 25-50 57

RIC-TIC 10-15 66-67

WINGATE (4 "You Know I Love You") 15-20 65

WIZARD (100 "Hold Me") 75-100 59

Also see FLAMING EMBERS / Al Kent

KENTON, Stan, & His Orchestra

P&R '44

Singles: 78rpm

CAPITOL 3-6 45-57

Singles: 7-inch

CAPITOL (Purple label) 5-15 50-61

CAPITOL (Orange & Yellow label). 4-6 61-68

Picture Sleeves

CAPITOL ("Stan Kenton Prologue: This Is an Orchestra") 10-20 50s
(Number not known.)

EPs: 7-inch 33/45rpm

CAPITOL 5-15 50-59

LPs: 10/12-inch 33rpm

BRIGHT ORANGE 5-8 73

CAPITOL (H-155 "Encores") 50-75 49
(10-inch LP.)

CAPITOL (T-155 "Encores") 25-50 55

CAPITOL (H-167 "Artistry in Rhythm") 50-75 49
(10-inch LP.)

CAPITOL (T-167 "Artistry in Rhythm") 25-50 55
(With "T" prefix.)

CAPITOL (DT-167 "Artistry in Rhythm") 5-10 69
(Stereo.)

CAPITOL (SM-167 "Artistry in Rhythm") 5-8 75

CAPITOL (H-172 "Progressive Jazz") 50-75 50
(10-inch LP.)

CAPITOL (T-172 "Progressive Jazz") 25-50 55

CAPITOL (H-190 "Milestones").. 50-75 50
(10-inch LP.)

CAPITOL (T-190 "Milestones") .. 25-50 55

CAPITOL (H-248 "Stan Kenton Presents") 50-75 50
(10-inch LP.)

CAPITOL (T-248 "Stan Kenton Presents") 25-50 55

CAPITOL (H-353 "City of Glass") 50-75 52
(10-inch LP.)

CAPITOL (T-353 "City of Glass") 25-50 55

CAPITOL (H-358 "Classics") 50-75 52
(10-inch LP.)

CAPITOL (T-358 "Classics") 25-50 55

CAPITOL (H-386 "This Is an Orchestra") 50-75 53
(10-inch LP.)

CAPITOL (H-462 "Standards") .. 50-75 53
(10-inch LP.)

CAPITOL (T-462 "Standards")... 25-50 55

CAPITOL (H-525 "Showcase") . 50-75 54
(10–inch LP.)
CAPITOL (W-525 "Showcase"). 25-75 55
CAPITOL (H-526 "Showcase") . 50-75 54
(10–inch LP.)
CAPITOL (W-526 "Showcase"). 25-50 55
CAPITOL (305 "Hair") 5-10 69
CAPITOL (600 thru 1200 series) 15-25 56-59
CAPITOL (1300 thru 2900 series) 10-20 60-68
CAPITOL (11000 & 12000 series) 5-8 72-80
CAPITOL (16000 series).............. 4-6 81
CREATIVE WORLD..................... 5-8 71-80
HINDSIGHT 4-8 84
LONDON.................................... 5-8 72-77
MARK '56 .... 5-8 77
MFSL (091 "Stan Kenton Plays Wagner") 15-25 82
Also see CHRISTY, June, & Stan Kenton
Also see COLE, Nat "King"
Also see FERGUSON, Maynard

KENTON, Stan, & Tex Ritter

LPs: 10/12–inch 33rpm

CAPITOL (T-1757 "Stan Kenton & Tex Ritter")......................... 40-60 62
(Monaural.)
CAPITOL (ST-1757 "Stan Kenton & Tex Ritter")......................... 50-75 62
(Stereo.)
Also see KENTON, Stan
Also see RITTER, Tex

KENTUCKY HEADHUNTERS

C&W/LP '89

Singles: 7–inch

MERCURY 3-4 89-91

LPs: 10/12–inch 33rpm

MERCURY 5-8 89-91
Members: Fred Young; Richard Young; Greg Martin; Ricky Lee Phelps; Doug Phelps; Mark Orr; Anthony Kenny.

KERMIT
(Jim Henson)

P&R '79

Singles: 7–inch

ATLANTIC.................................. 3-5 79

KERMIT / Fozzie Bear
(Jim Henson)

Singles: 7–inch

ATLANTIC.................................. 3-5 80
Also see KERMIT
Also see HENSON, Jim

KERR, Anita
(Anita Kerr Singers; Quartette)

LP '69

Singles: 78rpm

DECCA...................................... 3-6 51-57

Singles: 7–inch

AMPEX...................................... 3-5 71
DECCA (27000 thru 30000 series)......................................5-10 51-60
DECCA (31000 thru 33000 series)......................................3-6 60-72
DOT 3-5 69-70
RCA 3-8 63-75
W.B. 3-6 66-68

EPs: 7–inch 33/45rpm

SESAC......................................10-15
(Also has tracks by Buddy Hacket, Elliot Lawrence, and Bill Snyder.)

LPs: 10/12–inch 33rpm

AMPEX 5-8 71
BAINBRIDGE...............................4-6 81
CAMDEN 5-10 68
CENTURY 4-8 79
DECCA 8-15 60-69
DOT 5-10 69-70
RCA 8-15 62-77
VOCALION 5-10 70
W.B. 8-12 66
WORD..4-8 75-77
Also see ANDERSON, Bill
Also see ANITA & So-And-So's
Also see ANN-MARGRET
Also see ATKINS, Chet
Also see BARE, Bobby
Also see CHARLES, Tommy
Also see CLINE, Patsy
Also see CRAMER, Floyd
Also see FOLEY, Red
Also see HELMS, Bobby
Also see IVES, Burl
Also see LEE, Brenda
Also see LITTLE DIPPERS
Also see MULLICAN, Moon
Also see NELSON, Willie
Also see PRESLEY, Elvis
Also see REEVES, Jim
Also see RICH, Charlie
Also see WILBURN BROTHERS
Also see YOUNG, Faron

KERR, George

R&B '70

Singles: 7–inch

ALL PLATINUM 3-5 70

KERSHAW, Nik

P&R/LP '84

Singles: 7–inch

MCA...3-4 84-85

Picture Sleeves

MCA...3-5 84

LPs: 10/12–inch 33rpm

MCA...5-8 84-85

KEYES, Troy

P&R/R&B '68

Singles: 7–inch

ABC (11027 "Love Explosion") 4-8 67
ABC (11060 "No Sad Songs") 8-12 68
CHUMLEY 3-5 74
Also see HIGH KEYES

KEYES, Troy, & Norma Jenkins

Singles: 7-inch

ABC (11116 "A Good Love Gone Bad") 10-20 68

Also see JENKINS, Norma
Also see KEYES, Troy

KHAN, Chaka

P&R/R&B/LP '78

Singles: 12-inch 33/45rpm

W.B. 4-6 79-87

Singles: 7-inch

ATLANTIC 3-4 78-87
MCA 3-4 80-86
W.B. 3-5 78-88

Picture Sleeves

MCA 3-4 85
W.B. 3-5 78-86

LPs: 10/12-inch 33rpm

ELEKTRA 5-10 70s
W.B. 5-8 78-88

Also see BOWIE, David
Also see GRANDMASTER FLASH & Furious Five
Also see JONES, Quincy, with Ray Charles & Chaka Khan
Also see RUFUS
Also see WONDER, Stevie

KHAN, Steve

LP '78

Singles: 7-inch

TAPPAN ZEE 3-5 78

LPs: 10/12-inch 33rpm

COLUMBIA 5-8 79
NOVAS 5-8 80
TAPPAN ZEE 5-8 78

Also see JOEL, Billy

KHEMISTRY

R&B '82

Singles: 7-inch

COLUMBIA 3-4 82

LPs: 10/12-inch 33rpm

COLUMBIA 5-8 82

KIARA

R&B '85

Singles: 7-inch

WARLOCK 3-4 85

KIARA & Shanice Wilson

P&R '89

Singles: 7-inch

ARISTA 3-4 89

Picture Sleeves

ARISTA 3-4 89

Also see KIARA
Also see WILSON, Shanice

KICK AXE

LP '84

LPs: 10/12-inch 33rpm

PASHA 5-8 84

KID, Joey

P&R '90

Singles: 7-inch

ATLANTIC 3-4 90
BASSMENT 3-5 90

KID CREOLE & COCONUTS

LP '81

Singles: 12-inch 33/45rpm

ATLANTIC 4-6 84-85

Singles: 7-inch

ANTILLES 3-5 80
ATLANTIC 3-4 84-85
SIRE 3-4 81-82
ZE 3-4 81

LPs: 10/12-inch 33rpm

ANTILLES 8-10 80
SIRE 5-8 81-82

Also see DR. BUZZARD'S ORIGINAL SAVANNAH BAND
Also see MANILOW, Barry / Kid Creole & Coconuts

KID FROST

LP '90

LPs: 10/12-inch 33rpm

VIRGIN 5-8 90

KID 'N' PLAY

LP '88

LPs: 10/12-inch 33rpm

SELECT 5-8 88-90

KID SENSATION

LP '90

LPs: 10/12-inch 33rpm

NASTYMIX 5-8 90

KIDDO

R&B '83

Singles: 12-inch 33/45rpm

A&M 4-6 83

Singles: 7-inch

A&M 3-4 83-84

LPs: 10/12-inch 33rpm

A&M 5-8 83

KIDS at WORK

R&B '84

Singles: 7-inch

CBS ASSOCIATED 3-4 84

Member: Teddy Riley.

KIDS from "FAME"

LP '82

Singles: 7-inch

RCA 3-4 82-83

Picture Sleeves

RCA 3-4 82-83

LPs: 10/12-inch 33rpm

RCA 5-8 82-83

KIDS NEXT DOOR

P&R '65

Singles: 7-inch

4 CORNERS of the WORLD......... 4-8 65

Picture Sleeves

4 CORNERS of the WORLD....... 5-10 65

KIHN, Greg, Band

(Greg Kihn)

LP '78

Singles: 12-inch 33/45rpm

BESERKLEY................................ 4-8 78-83

Singles: 7-inch

BESERKLEY................................ 3-5 78-83
EMI AMERICA............................. 3-4 85-86

Picture Sleeves

BESERKLEY................................ 3-4 81-82
EMI AMERICA............................. 3-4 85-86

LPs: 10/12-inch 33rpm

BESERKLEY.............................. 8-10 76-84
EMI AMERICA............................. 5-8 85-86

KIHN, Greg, Band / Earthquake / Modern Lovers / Rubinoos

EPs: 7-inch 33/45rpm

BESERKLEY (1120 "Great Ideas") 5-8 77
Also see MODERN LOVERS

KIHN, Greg, Band / Earthquake / Rubinoos / Jonathan Richman

LPs: 10/12-inch 33rpm

BESERKLEY (0044 "Beserkley Chartbusters, Vol. 1")................ 8-12 77
(Promotional issue only.)
Also see EARTHQUAKE
Also see KIHN, Greg, Band
Also see RUBINOOS

KILGORE, Theola

P&R/R&B '63

Singles: 7-inch

CANDIX................................... 10-20 60
KT... 5-10 64
SEROCK.................................. 5-10 63

KILLER DWARFS

LP '88

LPs: 10/12-inch 33rpm

EPIC.. 5-8 88

KILLING JOKE

LP '87

LPs: 10/12-inch 33rpm

EDITIONS................................. 5-8 81-82
VIRGIN...................................... 5-8 87

KILZER, John

LP '88

LPs: 10/12-inch 33rpm

GEFFEN..................................... 5-8 88

KIM, Andy

P&R '68

Singles: 7-inch

ABC..3-5 74
CAPITOL.......................................3-5 74-76
RED BIRD......................................4-8 65
STEED..3-6 68-71
TCF...4-8 64
20TH FOX......................................4-8 68
UNI...3-5 72-73
U.A...4-8 63

Picture Sleeves

CAPITOL.......................................3-5 74
STEED..4-6 69-71

LPs: 10/12-inch 33rpm

CAPITOL.....................................8-12 74-75
DUNHILL.....................................8-12 74
STEED.......................................10-15 68-71
UNI...8-12 72-73
Also see ARCHIES

KIMBERLY, Adrian

(Don Everly)

P&R '61

Singles: 7-inch

CALLIOPE (6501 "Pomp and Circumstance")......................10-20 61
CALLIOPE (6503 "Greensleeves")......................25-35 61
CALLIOPE (6504 "Draggin' Dragon")...................................25-35 61
Also see EVERLY, Don

KIMBERLYS

P&R '71

Singles: 7-inch

CANADIAN AMERICAN 4-8 62-63
COLUMBIA 4-8 65-66
HAPPY TIGER..............................3-5 70-71
RCA..3-5 69

LPs: 10/12-inch 33rpm

HAPPY TIGER............................8-12 70
Also see JENNINGS, Waylon

KIMBLE, Neal

R&B '68

Singles: 7-inch

VENTURE......................................4-8 68

KIME, Warren, & His Brass Impact Orchestra

LP '67

LPs: 10/12-inch 33rpm

COMMAND..................................5-10 67

KIMMEL, Tom

P&R/LP '87

Singles: 7-inch

MERCURY.....................................3-4 87

Picture Sleeves

MERCURY.....................................3-4 87

LPs: 10/12-inch 33rpm
MERCURY 5-8 87

KING

P&R/D&D/LP '85

Singles: 12-inch 33/45rpm
EPIC 4-6 85

Singles: 7-inch
EPIC 3-4 85

Picture Sleeves
EPIC 3-4 85

LPs: 10/12-inch 33rpm
ELEKTRA 5-8 80-81
EPIC 5-8 85
Member: Paul King.

KING, Al •

R&B '66

Singles: 7-inch
MODERN 4-8 68
SAHARA 4-8 66
SHIRLEY 4-8 64

KING, Albert

R&B '61

Singles: 78rpm
PARROT 10-20 53

Singles: 7-inch
BOBBIN 5-10 59-62
COUN-TREE 4-8 65
KING 4-8 61-63
PARROT (798 "Bad Luck Blues") 100-125 53
STAX 3-8 66-74
TOMATO 3-5 78-79
UTOPIA 3-5 76-77

LPs: 10/12-inch 33rpm
ATLANTIC 8-12 69-82
FANTASY 5-8
KING (852 "Big Blues") 40-60 63
KING (1000 series) 10-12 69
STAX (Except 723 & 2000 series) 8-12 72-81
STAX (723 "Born Under a Bad Sign") 15-25 67
STAX (2000 series) 10-15 68-71
STAX (8000 series) 5-10 90
TOMATO 5-8 77-79
UTOPIA 8-10 76-77
Also see LITTLE MILTON & Albert King
Also see STAPLES, Roebuck

KING, Albert, & Otis Rush

LPs: 10/12-inch 33rpm
CHESS 10-15 69
Also see KING, Albert
Also see RUSH, Otis

KING, Anna

P&R/R&B '64

Singles: 7-inch
END (1126 "Mama's Got a Bag of Her Own") 10-15 63
LUDIX (103 "Big Change") 20-30 63
MALIBU (1020 "In Between Tears") 10-20 61
RUST 8-12 64
SMASH 5-10 63-65

LPs: 10/12-inch 33rpm
SMASH (27059 "Back to Soul") 15-20 64
(Monaural.)
SMASH (67059 "Back to Soul") 20-25 64
(Stereo.)

KING, Anna, & Bobby Byrd

P&R '64

Singles: 7-inch
SMASH 4-8 64
Also see BYRD, Bobby
Also see KING, Anna

KING, B.B.

R&B '51

Singles: 78rpm
BULLET (309 "Miss Martha King") 25-50 49
BULLET (315 "Got the Blues") 25-50 49
RPM 5-10 50-57

Singles: 7-inch
ABC 3-8 66-78
ABC-PAR 4-8 62-66
BLUESWAY 4-6 67-70
KENT (300 series) 5-10 58-64
KENT (400 series) 4-8 64-68
KENT (4000 & 5000 series) 3-5
MCA 3-4 80-85
PAULA 3-4 81
RPM (339 "3 O'clock Blues") 25-50 52
RPM (348 "Fine Looking Woman") 25-50 52
RPM (355 "Shake It Up and Go") 25-50 52
RPM (363 "You Didn't Want Me") 25-50 52
RPM (360 "Someday, Somewhere") 20-40 52
RPM (380 "Woke Up This Morning") 20-40 53
RPM (374 "Story from My Heart and Soul") 20-40 53
RPM (386 "Please Love Me") 20-40 53
RPM (391 "Neighbourhood Affair") 20-40 53
RPM (395 "Why Did You Love Me") 20-40 53
RPM (403 thru 501) 10-20 54-57

Picture Sleeves
BLUESWAY 4-6 69
MCA 3-4 85

EPs: 7-inch 33/45rpm
ABC-PAR 8-10 63
(Jukebox issue only.)

LPs: 10/12–inch 33rpm

ABC.. 8-10 70-78
ABC-PAR 15-25 63-65
ACCORD.. 5-8 82
BLUESWAY 10-15 67-73
COMMAND 10-12 74
CROWN (Except 147).............. 15-25 59-63
CROWN (147 "B.B. King Wails")................................. 15-25 60
(Black vinyl.)
CROWN (147 "B.B. King Wails")................................ 75-125 60
(Colored vinyl.)
CRUSADERS.............................. 5-8 82
CUSTOM.................................. 8-10
FANTASY 5-8 81
GALAXY................................. 15-20 63
KENT...................................... 10-15 64-73
MCA 5-8 79-85
PICKWICK 5-10
UNITED.................................. 10-12
Also see BLAND, Bobby, & B.B. King
Also see CRUSADERS, & B.B. King
Also see KING, Carole
Also see SIMPSONS
Also see U2 & B.B. King

KING, B.B., Jr., & Blues Messengers

Singles: 7–inch

L. BROWN 4-8 64

KING, Ben E.

P&R '60

Singles: 7–inch

ATLANTIC (Except 89361) 3-5 75-81
ATLANTIC (89361 "Stand By Me Medley")..................................... 4-8 86
(Promotional issue only. Has excerpts of nine songs from the film soundtrack, by: Ben E. King, Buddy Holly, Shirley & Lee, Bobbettes, Chordettes, Del Vikings, Coasters, Silhouettes, and Jerry Lee Lewis.)
ATCO (Except 6100 & 6200 series) 4-6 64-69
ATCO (6100 & 6200 series).......... 4-8 60-64
ELEKTRA.................................... 3-5 76
MANDALA.................................. 3-5 72-73
MAXWELL.................................. 3-6 69

Picture Sleeves

ATLANTIC 3-5 86

LPs: 10/12–inch 33rpm

ATCO (133 "Spanish Harlem").. 20-30 61
(Monaural.)
ATCO (SD-133 "Spanish Harlem") 30-40 61
(Monaural.)
ATCO (137 "For Soulful Lovers")................................. 20-30 62
(Monaural.)
ATCO (SD-137 "For Soulful Lovers") 25-35 62
(Stereo.)
ATCO (142 "Don't Play That Song")....................................20-30 62
(Monaural.)
ATCO (SD-142 "Don't Play That Song")............................25-35 62
(Stereo.)
ATCO (165 "Greatest Hits").......20-30 64
(Monaural.)
ATCO (SD-165 "Greatest Hits").25-35 64
(Stereo.)
ATCO (174 "Seven Letters")......20-30 65
(Monaural.)
ATCO (SD-174 "Seven Letters") 25-35 65
(Stereo.)
ATLANTIC.................................8-12 75-81
KING (3008 "Audio Biography").10-15
MANDALA.................................8-12 72
MAXWELL 10-15 70
Also see BAKER, Lavern, & Ben E. King
Also see BOBBETTES
Also see BONDS, Gary "U.S."
Also see CHORDETTES
Also see COASTERS
Also see DEL-VIKINGS
Also see DRIFTERS
Also see EARL-JEAN
Also see HALOS
Also see HOLLY, Buddy
Also see LEWIS, Jerry Lee
Also see LITTLE EVA
Also see SHIRLEY & LEE
Also see SILHOUETTES
Also see SOUL CLAN

KING, Ben E., & Average White Band

R&B/LP '77

Singles: 7–inch

ATLANTIC...................................3-5 77

LPs: 10/12–inch 33rpm

ATLANTIC.................................8-10 77
Also see AVERAGE WHITE BAND

KING, Ben E., & Dee Dee Sharp

Singles: 7–inch

ATCO 4-8 68
Also see KING, Ben E.
Also see SHARP, Dee Dee

KING, Bobby

(Featuring Alfie Silas)

R&B '84

Singles: 7–inch

MOTOWN 3-4 84
RODEO....................................10-15
Also see SILAS, Alfie

KING, Carole

P&R '62

Singles: 7–inch

ABC...3-5 74
ABC-PAR (9921 "Goin' Wild")....30-40 58

ABC-PAR (9986 "Baby Sittin'") . 30-40 59
ALPINE (57 "Oh, Neil") 50-75 60
ATLANTIC 3-5 82-83
AVATAR 3-5 77-78
CAPITOL 3-5 77-80
COMPANION (2000 "It Might As Well Rain Until September") 40-60 62
DIMENSION (1009 "He's a Bad Boy") 10-20 63
DIMENSION (1004 "School Bells Are Ringing") 10-20 63
DIMENSION (2000 "It Might As Well Rain Until September") 5-10 62
ODE 3-5 71-76
RCA (7560 "Short Mort") 35-45 59
TOMORROW (7502 "A Road to Nowhere") 10-15 66

Picture Sleeves

ATLANTIC 3-5 82
AVATAR 3-5 77
CAPITOL 3-5 77-80
ODE 3-5 71-75

LPs: 10/12-inch 33rpm

ATLANTIC 5-8 82-83
AVATAR 8-12 78
CAPITOL (Except 11000 series)... 5-8 80
CAPITOL (11000 series) 8-10 77-79
EPIC/ODE (30000 series) 5-8 78-80
EPIC/ODE (40000 series) 12-15 80
(Half-speed mastered.)
ODE 10-12 70-78

Also see COOKIES / Little Eva / Carole King
Also see KING, B.B.
Also see SHIRELLES

KING, Claude

C&W/P&R '61

Singles: 7-inch

CINNAMON 3-5 74
COLUMBIA 3-8 61-71
DEE JAY (1248 "Run Baby, Run") 30-50 57
TRUE 3-5 77-80

Picture Sleeves

COLUMBIA 4-8 61-69

LPs: 10/12-inch 33rpm

COLUMBIA 10-20 62-70
GUSTO 5-8 80
HARMONY 8-12 68
TRUE 8-10 77

Also see YOUNG, Faron / Carl Perkins / Claude King

KING, Clydie

(With the Sweet Things)

R&B '71

Singles: 78rpm

SPECIALTY 8-12 57

Singles: 7-inch

IMPERIAL 10-20 65-66
LIZARD 3-5 71
MINIT 5-10 67-69
PHILIPS 8-12 62-63
SPECIALTY 10-20 57

LPs: 10/12-inch 33rpm

LIZARD 8-12 71

Also see BROWN SUGAR
Also see CARTER, Mel, & Clydie
Also see HOLIDAY, Jimmy, & Clydie King
Also see RAELETTS

KING, Earl

R&B '55

Singles: 78rpm

ACE 10-15 55-57
SPECIALTY 10-15 54-55

Singles: 7-inch

ACE 15-25 55-57
IMPERIAL 15-25 60-62
REX 5-10 61
SPECIALTY (495 "I'm Your Best Bet, Baby") 35-45 54
SPECIALTY (531 "Eating and Sleeping") 35-45 54
SPECIALTY (558 "Funny Face") 35-45 55

Also see SMITH, Huey

KING, Evelyn

(Evelyn "Champagne" King)

P&R/R&B/LP '78

Singles: 12-inch 33/45rpm

PRIVATE I 4-6 85
RCA 4-8 78-86

Singles: 7-inch

EMI 3-4 90
EMI MANHATTAN 3-4 88-86
RCA 3-4 78-86

Picture Sleeves

RCA 3-6 78-86

LPs: 10/12-inch 33rpm

EMI 5-8 90
EMI MANHATTAN 5-8 88
RCA 5-8 77-86

KING, Freddie

(Freddy King)

P&R/R&B '61

Singles: 78rpm

EL-BEE 10-20 56

Singles: 7-inch

COTILLION 3-6 68-70
EL-BEE (157 "Country Boy") 50-75 56
FEDERAL 5-15 60-65
GUSTO 3-5 78
KING 3-5 69

LPs: 10/12-inch 33rpm

COTILLION 10-15 69-70
GUSTO (5033 "Hide Away") 10-12 78
KING (762 "Freddy King Sings the Blues") 30-40 61
KING (773 "Let's Hide Away and Dance Away") 35-50 61

KING (821 "Bossa Nova & Blues") 20-30 62
KING (856 "Freddy King Goes Surfin'") 20-30 63
KING (900 series) 15-20 65-66
KING (1000 series) 10-15 69
MCA 5-8 80s
RSO 8-10 74-77
SHELTER 8-10 71-75

Also see ROGERS, Jimmy, and Freddie King

KING, Freddie, & Lulu Reed

Singles: 7–inch

FEDERAL 4-8 62

KING, Freddie / Lulu Reed / Sonny Thompson

LPs: 10/12–inch 33rpm

KING (777 "Boy-Girl-Boy") 20-30 62

Also see KING, Freddie
Also see RUSSELL, Leon
Also see THOMPSON, Sonny

KING, Jewel
(With Dave Bartholomew's Orchestra)

R&B '50

Singles: 78rpm

IMPERIAL 10-20 49

Also see BARTHOLOMEW, Dave

KING, Jonathan

P&R '65

Singles: 7–inch

PARROT 4-8 65-72
UK 3-5 73-74
UK/BIG TREE 3-5 75

LPs: 10/12–inch 33rpm

PARROT (71013 "Jonathan King Or Then Again") 25-30 67
UK 10-20 72-73

Also see HEDGEHOPPERS ANONYMOUS

KING, Kid
(Kid King's Combo)

R&B '53

Singles: 78rpm

EXCELLO 5-10 53-57

Singles: 7–inch

EXCELLO 10-20 53-60

KING, Marcel

D&D '84

Singles: 12–inch 33/45rpm

A&M 4-6 84

Singles: 7–inch

A&M 3-4 84

KING, Martin Luther: see KING, Rev. Martin Luther, Jr.

KING, Morgana

LP '64

Singles: 78rpm

MERCURY 4-6 56

Singles: 7–inch

MAINSTREAM 4-8 64
MERCURY 5-10 56
PARAMOUNT 3-5 73-74
REPRISE 4-6 66-67
20TH FOX 4-8 59
VERVE 4-6 68
WING 5-10 56

Picture Sleeves

PARAMOUNT 3-5 73

LPs: 10/12–inch 33rpm

ASCOT 15-25 65-66
CAMDEN 15-25 60
EMARCY (36079 "For You, for Me, Forever More") 30-50 56
MAINSTREAM (300 series) 5-10 72
MAINSTREAM (6000 series) 15-25 64-65
MERCURY (20231 "Morganna King Sings the Blues") 30-40 57
MUSE 5-8 79-82
PARAMOUNT 5-10 73
REPRISE 15-25 65-67
TRIP 5-8 74
U.A. (3028 "Folk Songs ala King") 30-40 59
(Monaural.)
U.A. (3028 "Folk Songs ala King") 40-50 59
(Stereo.)
U.A. (30020 "Let Me Love You") 30-40 60
VERVE 10-15 68
WING 10-20 65

KING, Pee Wee
(With Redd Stewart; with His Golden West Cowboys)

C&W/P&R '48

Singles: 78rpm

BLUEBIRD 4-8 49
RCA 4-8 50-55

Singles: 7–inch

BRIAR 4-8 61
JARO 5-10 60
CUCA 4-8 64-66
LANDA 4-8 61
RCA 10-15 50-55
STARDAY 4-6 64-71
TODD 8-12 59

LPs: 10/12–inch 33rpm

BRIAR (102 "Golden Olde-Tyme Dances") 50-70 62
CAMDEN 8-15 65-71
CAPITOL 10-20 66
CUCA 10-15 64
NASHVILLE 8-12
RCA 5-8 77
STARDAY (200 series) 10-20 64
STARDAY (900 series) 8-10 75

KING, Peggy

P&R '55

Singles: 78rpm

COLUMBIA 3-5 54-56
MGM 3-5 52

Singles: 7–inch

BUENA VISTA 4-8 62
BULLET..................................... 3-5 71
COLUMBIA 5-10 54-56
MGM 5-10 52
ROULETTE................................ 4-8 61

Picture Sleeves

BUENA VISTA 4-8 62

EPs: 7–inch 33/45rpm

COLUMBIA 8-12 55

LPs: 10/12–inch 33rpm

COLUMBIA 15-25 55
IMPERIAL 10-20 59

Also see VALE, Jerry, Peggy King & Felicia Sanders

KING, Rev. Martin Luther, Jr.

(Rev. Martin Luther King)

LP '63

Singles: 7–inch

DOOTO..................................... 4-6 68
MERCURY 4-6 68

EPs: 7–inch 33/45rpm

GORDY (906 "Speech Excerpts").............................. 15-25 63

LPs: 10/12–inch 33rpm

BLACK FORUM 5-10 70
BUDDAH.................................. 8-15 69
CREED.................................... 8-12 68-71
DOTTO.................................... 8-15 62-68
EXCELLO................................. 8-15 68
GORDY (906 "The Great March")................................ 25-50 63
GORDY (929 "Free at Last")..... 15-25 68
MERCURY 8-15 68
MR. MAESTRO....................... 10-15 63
NASHBORO.............................. 5-8 72
20TH FOX 8-15 63-68
UNART 8-12 68

These recordings contain speeches or excerpts of speeches by King.

Also see LANDS, Liz / Martin Luther King

KING, Saunders

R&B '49

Singles: 78rpm

ALADDIN.................................. 4-8 49
MODERN 4-8 48
RHYTHM................................. 5-10 42-47

Singles: 7–inch

FLAIR (1035 "My Close Friend") 25-40 54
FLAIR (1045 "Quit Hangin' 'Round Me") 25-40 54
RPM (341 "Lazy Woman") 25-35 51
RPM (375 "New S.K. Blues") 25-35 52

KING, Sleepy

P&R '61

Singles: 7–inch

AWAKE.....................................10-15
JOY..5-10 61

KING, Teddi

P&R '56

Singles: 78rpm

RCA 3-5 56-57

Singles: 7–inch

RCA 5-10 56-57

LPs: 10/12–inch 33rpm

CORAL (57278 "All the King's Songs") 40-60 59
(Monaural.)
CORAL (757278 "All the King's Songs") 50-75 59
(Stereo.)
RCA (1147 "Bidin' My Time").....50-75 56
RCA (1313 "From Teddi King")..50-75 57
RCA (1454 "A Girl and Her Songs") 50-75 57
STORYVILLE (302 "'Round Midnight")............................100-200 54
(10–inch LP.)
STORYVILLE (314 "Storyville Presents Teddi King") 100-200 54
(10–inch LP.)
STORYVILLE (903 "Now in Vogue")................................75-125 56

KING, Will

(Willard King)

R&B '85

Singles: 7–inch

CAPITOL......................................3-5 73
TOTAL EXPERIENCE 3-4 85

KING BISCUIT BOY

(With Crowbar)

LP '70

Singles: 7–inch

EPIC..3-5 75
PARAMOUNT 3-5 70-73

LPs: 10/12–inch 33rpm

EPIC..8-10 74
PARAMOUNT 10-15 70-73

KING COLE TRIO: see COLE, Nat "King"

KING CRIMSON

LP '69

Singles: 12–inch 33/45rpm

W.B. 4-6 84

Singles: 7–inch

ATLANTIC....................................3-5 70-74
W.B. 3-4 81-84

LPs: 10/12–inch 33rpm

ATLANTIC (Except 18000 & 19000 series)...................................10-20 69-74

ATLANTIC (18000 & 19000 series) 8-10 74-75
EDITIONS 5-10
MFSL (075 "In the Court of the Crimson King") 25-50 82
W.B. 5-8 81-84
WIZARDO 10-12
WORLD RECORD CLUB 12-15

Members: Greg Lake; Robert Fripp; Boz Burrell; Bill Bruford; Adrian Belew.

Also see BAD COMPANY
Also see BELEW, Adrian
Also see FRIPP, Robert
Also see LAKE, Greg
Also see YES

KING CURTIS

(With the Kingpins; with Nobel Knights; King Curtis Combo)

P&R/R&B '62

Singles: 78rpm

APOLLO 10-15 57
GEM 10-15 54
MONARCH 15-20 53
RPM 10-15 53

Singles: 7-inch

ABC-PAR 4-8 60
ALCOR 4-8 62
APOLLO (507 "King's Rock") 10-20 57
ATCO 4-8 59-71
CAPITOL 4-8 62-65
ENJOY 4-8 62
EVEREST 4-8 61
GEM (208 "Tenor in the Sky") 35-50 54
KING 4-8 62
MONARCH (702 "Wine Head") 40-65 53
NEW JAZZ 3-5 61
RPM (383 "Boogie in the Moonlight") 25-50 53
SEG-WAY 10-15 61
TRU-SOUND 4-8 61-63

Picture Sleeves

CAPITOL (5377 "Bill Bailey") 5-8 65

EPs: 7-inch 33/45rpm

ATCO 4-8 68
(Jukebox issues only.)
CAPITOL 8-15 63

LPs: 10/12-inch 33rpm

ATCO (113 "Have Tenor Sax Will Blow") 75-100 59
(Monaural.)
ATCO (SD-113 "Have Tenor Sax Will Blow") 100-125 59
(Stereo.)
ATCO (189 thru 385) 10-20 66-72
CAMDEN 10-15 68
CAPITOL (2000 series) 10-20 64-68
CAPITOL (11000 series) 5-8 78-79
CLARION 8-10 60s
COLLECTABLES 6-8 88
ENJOY (2001 "Soul Twist") 30-50 62
EVEREST (1121 "Azure") 20-30 61
HARLEM HIT PARADE 8-10 70s
MOUNT VERNON 10-12
NEW JAZZ (8237 "New Scene") 20-30 60
PRESTIGE (7200 series) 15-20 62
PRESTIGE (7700 series) 8-12 69-70
RCA 15-25 60s
TRU-SOUND 15-20 62

Also see BAKER, Lavern
Also see BENTON, Brook
Also see BOBBETTES
Also see CLOVERS
Also see COASTERS
Also see COMSTOCK, Bobby
Also see DARIN, Bobby
Also see FACENDA, Tommy
Also see FREED, Alan
Also see JENNINGS, Waylon
Also see KING PINS
Also see LED ZEPPELIN / King Curtis
Also see MANN, Herbie
Also see McPHATTER, Clyde
Also see MITCHELL, Freddie
Also see PAT & SATELLITES
Also see RAMRODS
Also see RESTIVO, Johnny
Also see SEDAKA, Neil
Also see SHARPE, Ray
Also see SHIRELLES & King Curtis
Also see SUNNYLAND SLIM
Also see TURNER, Joe
Also see TURNER, Sammy

KING DIAMOND

LP '87

LPs: 10/12-inch 33rpm

ROADRACER 5-8 87-90

KING DREAM CHORUS & Holiday Crew

R&B '86

Singles: 12-inch 33/45rpm

MERCURY 4-6 86

Singles: 7-inch

MERCURY 3-4 86

Picture Sleeves

MERCURY 3-4 86

Members: Kurtis Blow; El De Barge; Fat Boys; Grandmaster Melle Mel; Whitney Houston; Stacy Lattisaw; Lisa Lisa & Full Force; Teena Marie; Menudo; Stephanie Mills; New Edition; Run-DMC; James Taylor; Whodini; Greg Phillinganes.

Also see BLOW, Kurtis
Also see DE BARGE
Also see FAT BOYS
Also see GRANDMASTER FLASH & Furious Five
Also see HOUSTON, Whitney
Also see LATTISAW, Stacy
Also see LISA LISA & Cult Jam with Full Force
Also see MARIE, Teena
Also see MENUDO
Also see MILLS, Stephanie
Also see NEW EDITION
Also see PHILLINGANES, Greg
Also see RUN-D.M.C.
Also see TAYLOR, James
Also see WHODINI

KING FAMILY

LP '65

Singles: 7-inch

W.B. 3-5 65

LPs: 10/12-inch 33rpm

CAPITOL.................................... 5-15 65
W.B. 5-15 65

KING FLOYD

(With the Three Queens)

P&R/R&B '70

Singles: 7-inch

CHIMNEYVILLE........................... 3-5 70-76
ORIGINAL SOUND....................... 4-8 64
PULSAR.................................... 4-8
UPTOWN 4-8 66

Picture Sleeves

CHIMNEYVILLE........................... 3-5 71

LPs: 10/12-inch 33rpm

ATCO 8-10 73
CHIMNEYVILLE.......................... 8-10 72
COTILLION 8-12 71
PULSAR.................................. 10-15 69
V.I.P. (407 "Heart of the
Matter") 20-25 70

KING HANNIBAL

(James T. Shaw)

R&B '73

Singles: 7-inch

AWARE 3-5 73

LPs: 10/12-inch 33rpm

AWARE 8-10 73

KING HARVEST

P&R '72

Singles: 7-inch

A&M 3-5 75-76
PERCEPTION.............................. 3-5 72-73

LPs: 10/12-inch 33rpm

A&M 10-15 75
PERCEPTION............................ 8-12 73

Also see LOVE, Mike
Also see WILSON, Carl

KING LIZARD

(Kim Fowley)

Singles: 7-inch

ORIGINAL SOUND.................... 8-12 75

Also see FOWLEY, Kim

KING PINS

(Kingpins)

P&R/R&B '63

Singles: 7-inch

ATCO 5-10 67
FEDERAL.................................. 5-10 63-64
VEE JAY 10-15 63

LPs: 10/12-inch 33rpm

KING (865 "It Won't Be This
Way Always") 25-35 63

Members: Andy Kelly; Robert Kelly; Curtis Kelly.
Also see KING CURTIS

KING PLEASURE

(Clarence Beeks)

R&B '52

Singles: 78rpm

ALADDIN 4-8 57
JUBILEE 4-8 55
PRESTIGE..................................4-8 52-55

Singles: 7-inch

ALADDIN 10-15 57
HI-FI..5-8 60
JUBILEE 10-15 55
PRESTIGE (100 series)................4-8 60
PRESTIGE (800 & 900 series) ..10-20 52-55
U.A. 5-10 62

LPs: 10/12-inch 33rpm

HI-FI (425 "Golden Days")........35-55 60
PRESTIGE (208 "King Pleasure
Sings") 75-125 55
(10-inch LP.)
PRESTIGE (7128 "King Pleasure
Sings") 50-75 57
U.A. (14031 "Mr. Jazz") 30-40 62
(Monaural.)
U.A. (15031 "Mr. Jazz") 35-50 62
(Stereo.)

KING RICHARD'S FLUEGEL KNIGHTS

LP '68

Singles: 7-inch

MTA 3-6 66-68

LPs: 10/12-inch 33rpm

MTA 5-10 67-70

KING SUN-D MOET

R&B '87

Singles: 7-inch

ZAKIA...3-4 87

KING TEE

LP '89

LPs: 10/12-inch 33rpm

CAPITOL....................................5-8 89-90

KINGBEES

(Nino Tempo & Kingbees)

P&R/LP '80

Singles: 7-inch

RSO 3-5 80-81

Picture Sleeves

RSO 4-6 80-81

LPs: 10/12-inch 33rpm

RSO 5-10 80-81

Members: Jamie James; Michael; Rex.
Also see TEMPO, Nino

KINGDOM COME

P&R/LP '88

Singles: 7-inch

POLYDOR 3-4 88

Picture Sleeves

POLYDOR 3-4 88

LPs: 10/12-inch 33rpm

POLYDOR.................................... 5-8 88-89

KINGFISH

LP '76

Singles: 7-inch

JET.. 3-5 78
ROUND...................................... 3-5 76

LPs: 10/12-inch 33rpm

ACCORD.................................... 5-8 81
JET.. 8-10 77
ROUND.................................... 10-20 76

Members: Bob Weir; David Torbert; Matt Kelly.
Also see NEW RIDERS of the Purple Sage
Also see WEIR, Bob

KINGS

P&R/LP '80

Singles: 7-inch

ELEKTRA.................................. 3-5 80-81

LPs: 10/12-inch 33rpm

ELEKTRA.................................. 5-8 80-81

KINGS of the SUN

P&R/LP '88

Singles: 12-inch 33/45rpm

RCA.. 4-8 88-89

Singles: 7-inch

RCA.. 3-4 88-90

Picture Sleeves

RCA.. 3-4 88

LPs: 10/12-inch 33rpm

RCA.. 5-8 88-90

KING'S X

LP '88

Singles: 12-inch 33/45rpm

MEGAFORCE.............................. 4-8 88
(Promotional only.)

LPs: 10/12-inch 33rpm

MEGAFORCE.............................. 5-8 88-90

KINGSMEN

P&R '58

Singles: 7-inch

EAST WEST 10-20 58

Also see HALEY, Bill

KINGSMEN

P&R '63

Singles: 7-inch

CAPITOL.................................... 3-5 72
EARTH...................................... 4-6 69
ERIC.. 3-5 70s
JERDEN (712 "Louie Louie") 40-60 63
WAND (Except 1107 & 1115) 5-10 63-68
WAND (1107 "It's Only the Dog").................................... 10-15 65
WAND (1115 "Killer Joe")........... 8-12 65

Picture Sleeves

WAND (1118 "The Krunch")...... 10-20 66

LPs: 10/12-inch 33rpm

ARISTA 8-10 81
HEAVY WEIGHT 20-25 67
PICADILLY.................................5-8 80
RHINO 5-8 80s
SCEPTER/CITATION 8-12 72
WAND (657 "The Kingsmen in Person")............................30-35 64
WAND (659 "The Kingsmen, Vol. 2")...............................50-100 64
(Without Death of an Angel.)
WAND (659 "The Kingsmen, Vol. 2")................................25-35 64
(With Death of an Angel.)
WAND (662 "The Kingsmen, Vol. 3")................................25-30 65
WAND (670 thru 681) 20-25 65-67

Members: Lynn Easton; Mike Mitchell; Don Gallucci; Norm Sundholm; Gary Abbot; Jack Ely; Barry Curtis; Dick Peterson.
Also see DON & GOODTIMES

KINGSTON TRIO

P&R/R&B/LP '58

Singles: 7-inch

CAPITOL (856 "Merry Minuet")..10-20 59
(Promotional issue only.)
CAPITOL (1400 & 1800 series)...5-15 60-63
(Compact 33 Singles.)
CAPITOL (2006 "Farewell Adelita") 10-15 60
(Special products giveaway for Welgrume Sportswear.)
CAPITOL (2782 "Molly Dee").....10-15 59
(Promotional issue only.)
CAPITOL (3970 thru 4114).........5-10 58-59
CAPITOL (4167 "Tijuana Jail") 5-10 59
CAPITOL (S-4167 "Tijuana Jail")......................................10-20 59
(Stereo.)
CAPITOL (4221 "M.T.A.") 5-10 59
CAPITOL (4221 "M.T.A.") 20-30 59
(Promotional "Special Preview Record." Label pictures the Trio.)
CAPITOL (4271 "A Worried Man") 5-10 59
CAPITOL (4303 "Coo Coo-U").....5-10 59
CAPITOL (S-4303 "Coo Coo-U")................................10-20 59
(Stereo.)
CAPITOL (4338 thru 5166)...........4-8 59-64
CAPITOL (6000 series) 3-6 62-65
CAPITOL/LION OF TROY (2006 "Farewell Adelita") 8-12 60
(Capitol Special Products issue for Lion of Troy shirt buyers.)
DECCA 4-8 64-66
TETRAGRAMMATON 4-6 69
NAUTILUS 4-6 79
XERES..3-5 82

Picture Sleeves

CAPITOL (2006 "Farewell Adelita").................................. 10-15 60
(Special products issue for Welgrume Sportswear.)
CAPITOL (2782 "Molly Dee").... 10-20 59
(Promotional issue only.)
CAPITOL (4338 "El Matador") .. 10-20 60
CAPITOL (4740 "Scotch and Soda") 10-15 62
CAPITOL (4842 "One More Town")................................... 10-15 62
CAPITOL/LION OF TROY (2006 "Farewell Adelita").................................. 10-15 60
(Capitol Special Products issue for Lion of Troy shirt
DECCA (31702 "Hope You Understand") 15-25 65
DECCA (31790 "Yes, I Can Feel It")................................. 15-25 65
DECCA (31860 "Runaway Song") 15-25 65
XERES 3-5 82

EPs: 7–inch 33/45rpm

CAPITOL.................................. 10-25 58-61
CAPITOL CUSTOM (2670 "Cool Cargo")................................... 15-25 60
(Special products issue for 7 Up.)

LPs: 10/12–inch 33rpm

CANDLELITE (6971 "Historic Recordings") 15-25 70s
CAPITOL (500 series)................ 8-15 70
CAPITOL (T-996 "The Kingston Trio") 25-40 58
(Monaural.)
CAPITOL (DT-996 "The Kingston Trio") 10-15 69
(Reprocessed stereo.)
CAPITOL (1107 "From the Hungry i") 25-35 59
CAPITOL (ST-1183 "Stereo Concert")................................. 25-35 59
CAPITOL (T-1199 "At Large")... 20-25 59
(Monaural.)
CAPITOL (ST-1199 "At Large") 20-30 59
CAPITOL (T-1258 "Here We Go Again").............................. 20-25 59
(Monaural.)
CAPITOL (ST-1258 "Here We Go Again").............................. 20-30 59
(Stereo.)
CAPITOL (T-1352 "Sold Out") .. 20-25 60
(Monaural.)
CAPITOL (ST-1352 "Sold Out") 20-30 60
(Stereo.)
CAPITOL (T-1407 "String Along...................................... 20-25 60
(Monaural.)
CAPITOL (ST-1407 "String Along......................................20-30 60
(Stereo.)
CAPITOL (T-1446 thru T-2081).15-20 60-64
(Monaural.)
CAPITOL (ST-1446 thru ST-2081)................................15-25 60-64
(Stereo.)
CAPITOL (T-2180 "Folk Era")....25-35 64
(Mono. Three-LP set with bound-in booklet.)
CAPITOL (ST-2180 "Folk Era") .30-40 64
(Stereo. Three-LP set with bound-in booklet.)
CAPITOL (T-2280 thru T-2614).10-20 65-66
(Monaural.)
CAPITOL (ST-2280 thru ST-2614)................................15-25 65-66
(Stereo.)
CAPITOL (11000 series) 5-8 79
CAPITOL (16000 series) 4-6 81
DECCA (4000 series) 15-20 64-65
(Monaural.)
DECCA (7-4000 series) 15-25 64-65
(Stereo.)
INTERMEDIA..................................5-8 85
NAUTILUS 15-25 79
PICKWICK 5-10 70s
TETRAGRAMMATON 10-15 69
XERES.......................................5-10 82

Members: John Stewart; Dave Guard; Nick Reynolds; Bob Shane.
Also see BEATLES / Beach Boys / Kingston Trio
Also see NEW KINGSTON TRIO
Also see STEWART, John
Also see STEWART, John, & Nick Reynolds

KINGSTON TRIO / Four Preps

Singles: 7–inch

U.S.A.F. (103 "El Matador")....... 10-20 60
(Promotional, radio station issue only.)
Also see FOUR PREPS

KINGSTON TRIO / Dinah Shore

Singles: 7–inch

U.S.A.F. (129 "Everglades") 10-20 60
(Promotional, radio station issue only.)
Also see SHORE, Dinah

KINGSTON TRIO / Frank Sinatra

EPs: 7–inch 33/45rpm

CAPITOL (2229 "Excerpts from Great New Releases") 30-60 62
(Promotional issue only.)
Also see KINGSTON TRIO
Also see SINATRA, Frank

KINISON, Sam

LP '86

LPs: 10/12–inch 33rpm

W.B. 5-8 86-90

KINKS

P&R/LP '64

Singles: 12–inch 33/45rpm

ARISTA 4-8 79-83

Singles: 7–inch

ARISTA 3-6 77-85
CAMEO (308 "Long Tall Sally") 75-100 64
CAMEO (345 "Long Tall Sally"). 40-60 65
CAMEO (348 "You Still Want Me") 100-200 65
ERIC 3-5
MCA 3-5 86
RCA 4-6 72-76
REPRISE (0306 thru 0647) 5-8 65-67
REPRISE (0691 thru 0847) 8-12 68-69
REPRISE (0930 thru 1094) 4-8 70-72

Promotional Singles

ARISTA (Except 5) 3-6 77-85
ARISTA (5 "Sleepwalker") 10-15 77
(Colored vinyl.)
CAMEO (308 "Long Tall Sally"). 50-75 64
CAMEO (345 "Long Tall Sally"). 35-45 65
CAMEO (348 "You Still Want Me") 100-150 65
REPRISE (0306 thru 0647) 10-20 65-67
REPRISE (0691 thru 0847) 10-15 68-69
REPRISE (0930 thru 1094) 6-12 70-72

Picture Sleeves

ARISTA 3-5 80-84

EPs: 7–inch 33/45rpm

ARISTA (22 "The Kinks Misfit Record") 20-25 78
(Promotional issue only.)
CAMEO 4-6 78
REPRISE (352 "Arthur") 10-20 69
(Promotional issue only.)

LPs: 10/12–inch 33rpm

ARISTA 6-12 77-86
COMPLEAT 5-8
MCA 5-8 86-89
MFSL (070 "Misfits") 20-30 82
PICKWICK 5-10 72-79
PYE 8-10 75-76
RCA (Except "AYL1" series) 10-15 71-76
RCA VICTOR ("AYL1" series) 5-8 80-82
REPRISE (2127 "The Great Lost Kinks Album") 20-30 73
REPRISE (R-6143 "You Really Got Me") 50-100 64
(Monaural.)
REPRISE (RS-6143 "You Really Got Me") 20-30 64
(Stereo.)
REPRISE (R-6158 "Kinks Size") 50-75 65
(Monaural.)
REPRISE (RS-6158 "Kinks Size") 20-30 65
(Stereo.)
REPRISE (R-6173 "Kinda Kinks") 50-75 65
(Monaural.)
REPRISE (RS-6173 "Kinda Kinks") 20-30 65
(Stereo.)
REPRISE (R-6184 "Kinks Kinkdom") 50-75 65
(Monaural.)
REPRISE (RS-6184 "Kinks Kinkdom") 20-30 65
(Stereo.)
REPRISE (R-6197 "The Kink Kontroversy") 50-75 66
(Monaural.)
REPRISE (RS-6197 "The Kink Kontroversy") 20-30 66
(Stereo.)
REPRISE (R-6217 "The Kinks' Greatest Hits") 50-75 66
(Monaural.)
REPRISE (RS-6217 "The Kinks' Greatest Hits") 20-30 66
(Stereo.)
REPRISE (R-6228 "Face to Face") 50-75 66
(Monaural.)
REPRISE (RS-6228 "Face to Face") 20-30 66
(Stereo.)
REPRISE (R-6260 "Live Kinks") 50-75 67
(Monaural.)
REPRISE (RS-6260 "Live Kinks") 20-30 67
(Stereo.)
REPRISE (R-6279 "Something Else") 50-75 67
(Monaural.)
REPRISE (RS-6279 "Something Else") 20-30 67
(Stereo.)
REPRISE (6327 "Village Green Preservation Society") 25-35 69
REPRISE (6366 "Arthur") 15-20 69
(Price includes lyrics insert.)
REPRISE (6423 "Lola Vs. the Powerman") 12-15 69
(Blue and white cover.)
REPRISE (6423 "Lola Vs. the Powerman") 6-10 69
(Black, blue and white cover.)
REPRISE (6454 "The Kink Kronikles") 8-12 69
(Original Reprise Kinks LPs from the '60s are on a multi-colored label. All 11 of these

LPs have been repressed on the brown Reprise label and are valued at $10 to $15.)

Promotional LPs

ARISTA (Except 69)................. 10-15 77-84
ARISTA (69 "Low Budget Radio Interview") 40-50 79
REPRISE (2127 "The Great Lost Kinks Album")......................... 50-75 73
REPRISE (R-6143 "You Really Got Me")............................... 50-100 64
(White label, monaural.)
REPRISE (R-6158 "Kinks Size")............................. 100-200 65
(White label, monaural.)
REPRISE (R-6173 "Kinda Kinks")............................... 100-200 65
(White label, monaural.)
REPRISE (R-6184 "Kinks Kingdom") 100-200 65
(White label, monaural.)
REPRISE (R-6197 "The Kink Kontroversy") 100-200 66
(White label, monaural.)
REPRISE (R-6217 "The Kinks' Greatest Hits")................... 100-200 66
(White label, monaural.)
REPRISE (R-6228 "Face to Face").................................. 75-150 66
(White label, monaural.)
REPRISE (R-6260 "Live Kinks")................................. 75-150 67
(White label, monaural.)
REPRISE (R-6279 "Something Else").................................. 75-150 67
REPRISE (RS-6000 series)...... 30-60 64-72
(White label, stereo.)
W.B. (328 Complete "Kinks Kit"/"Then Now and In-Between") 325-375 69
(Boxed set, includes Then Now and In-Between LP, button, pin, postcard, letter, decal, and other promotional materials.)
W.B. (328 "Then Now and In-Between") 75-100 69
(Price for LP only.)

Members: Ray Davies; Dave Davies; Mick Avory; Peter Quaife; John Dalton; John Gosling; Ian Gibbons; Jim Rodford; Bob Henrit; John Beecham; Mike Cotton.

Also see DAVIES, Dave

KINKS / Hollywood Stars

Singles: 7-inch

ARISTA (5 "Sleepwalker")........... 8-10 77

Picture Sleeves

ARISTA (5 "Sleepwalker")......... 10-15 77

Also see HOLLYWOOD STARS
Also see KINKS

KINNEY, Fern

P&R/R&B '79

Singles: 7-inch

ATLANTIC....................................4-6 68
MALACO......................................3-5 79-80

KINSMAN DAZZ

R&B '78

Singles: 7-inch

20TH FOX...................................3-5 78-79

LPs: 10/12-inch 33rpm

20TH FOX...................................5-8 79

Also see DAZZ BAND

KIRBY, Kathy

P&R '65

Singles: 7-inch

ASCOT.......................................4-6 67
LONDON.....................................4-8 62-65
PARROT.....................................4-8 65-66

KIRBY STONE FOUR: see STONE, Kirby, Four

KIRK, Andy, & His 12 Clouds of Joy

R&B '42

Singles: 78rpm

CORAL.......................................4-6 49
DECCA 4-8 42-45

KIRK, Jim, & TM Singers

P&R '80

Singles: 7-inch

CAPITOL.....................................3-5 80

Picture Sleeves

CAPITOL.....................................3-5 80

KIRKLAND, Bo

R&B '75

Singles: 7-inch

CLARIDGE...................................3-5 75

KIRKLAND, Bo, & Ruth Davis (Bo & Ruth)

R&B '76

Singles: 7-inch

CLARIDGE...................................3-5 75-78

LPs: 10/12-inch 33rpm

CLARIDGE.................................5-10 76

Also see DAVIS, Ruth
Also see KIRKLAND, Bo

KIRTON, Lew

R&B '77

Singles: 7-inch

BELIEVE 3-4 83
MARLIN 3-5 77

KISS

P&R/LP '74

Singles: 12-inch 33/45rpm

CASABLANCA.............................10-20 78-82
MERCURY.................................10-20 83-88

Singles: 7-inch

CASABLANCA..............................4-8 74-82

MERCURY (Except 0002)............ 3-6 85-88
MERCURY (0002 "World Without Heroes").................... 10-20 81
(Picture disc.)

Picture Sleeves

CASABLANCA (858 "Flaming Youth") 8-10 75
CASABLANCA (2365 "I Love It Loud")................................. 8-10 81
MERCURY 4-8 85-87

LPs: 10/12–inch 33rpm

CASABLANCA (7006 "Hotter Than Hell") 10-15 74
CASABLANCA (7016 "Dressed to Kill")...................................... 10-15 75
CASABLANCA (7020 "Alive") ... 15-20 75
(With 8-page color booklet.)
CASABLANCA (7020 "Alive") ... 10-15 75
(Without booklet.)
CASABLANCA (7025 "Destroyer")........................... 10-15 75
CASABLANCA (7032 "The Originals") 50-75 76
(With inserts: Army sticker; 16-page booklet; six trading cards.)
CASABLANCA (7032 "The Originals") 10-15 76
(Without inserts.)
CASABLANCA (7037 "Rock & Roll Over")............................. 20-25 76
(With sticker-sheet order form.)
CASABLANCA (7037 "Rock & Roll Over")............................. 10-15 76
(Without sticker-sheet.)
CASABLANCA (7057 "Love Gun")................................... 50-75 77
(With cardboard gun. Apart from the LP unused cardboard gun is valued at $35 to $50.)
CASABLANCA (7057 "Love Gun")................................... 10-15 77
(Without cardboard gun.)
CASABLANCA (7076 "Alive II")......................... 250-300 77
(Has three tracks not found on later issues: *Take Me, Hooligan,* and *Do You Love Me.* Reportedly 50 copies made.)
CASABLANCA (7076 "Alive II") 40-50 77
(With 8-page tatoo booklet. Add $20-30 if cover lists the three tracks, *Take Me, Hooligan,* and *Do You Love Me,* that are not on LP.)
CASABLANCA (7076 "Alive II") 10-15 77
(Without tatoo booklet. Add $20-30 if cover lists the three tracks, *Take Me, Hooligan,* and *Do You Love Me,* that are not on LP.)
CASABLANCA (7100 "Double Platinum")............................ 30-40 78
(With platinum award order form.)
CASABLANCA (7100 "Double Platinum") 15-20 78
(Without platinum award order form.)
CASABLANCA (7152 "Dynasty")...................................8-12 79
CASABLANCA (7225 "Kiss Unmasked") 15-20 80
(With poster.)
CASABLANCA (7225 "Kiss Unmasked")..................................8-10 80
CASABLANCA (7261 "Music from the Elder")...................................25-35 81
(With lyric sheet.)
CASABLANCA (7261 "Music from the Elder")......................................8-12 81
(Without lyric sheet.)
CASABLANCA (7270 "Creatures of the Night")....................................15-25 82
(With make up.)
CASABLANCA (7270 "Creatures of the Night") 8-10 82
(Without make up.)
CASABLANCA (9001 "Kiss") 25-50 74
DYNASTY (7152 "Dynasty")......15-20 79
(With poster order form.)
DYNASTY (7152 "Dynasty")........8-12 79
(Without poster order form.)
MERCURY (814297 "Lick It Up")...5-8 83
MERCURY (822495 "Animalize") ..5-8 84
MERCURY (826099 "Asylum")......5-8 85
MERCURY (832626 "Crazy Nights") 5-8 86
MERCURY (836887 "Smashes, Thrashes and Hits") 15-20 88
(Picture disc.)
MERCURY (836913 "Hot in the Shade")..5-8 89
MERCURY (522123 "Kiss My Ass") 25-30 94
(Colored vinyl, limited edition.)
POLYGRAM ("Kiss Alive III") 20-25 94
(Colored vinyl. Limited edition.)
POLYGRAM (832-903 "Crazy Nights") 10-15 87
(Picture disc.)
UNMASKED (7225 "Kiss Unmasked") 15-20 80
(With poster order form.)
UNMASKED (7225 "Kiss Unmasked") 8-10 80
(Without poster order form.)

Promotional LPs

BURNS MEDIA ("Rock & Roll Over with Kiss") 50-75 76
CASABLANCA ("A Taste of Platinum") 30-50 78
CASABLANCA ("Rock & Roll Over") 30-50 76

CASABLANCA (76 "Kiss Tour Album") 30-50 76
CASABLANCA (7001 "Kiss") 40-60 74
(Without *Kissin' Time.*)
CASABLANCA (7001 "Kiss") 20-30 74
(With *Kissin' Time.*)
CASABLANCA (7032 "The Originals") 100-125 76
(With inserts.)
CASABLANCA (9001 "Kiss") 50-75 74
CASABLANCA (20137 "Criss, Frehley, Simmons, Stanley") 20-30 78
MERCURY (792-1 "First Kiss, Last Licks") 75-100 90

Members: Gene Simmons; Ace Frehley; Paul Stanley; Peter Criss; Bruce Kulick; Eric Carr; Vinnie Vincent.

Also see CRISS, Peter
Also see FREHLEY, Ace
Also see SIMMONS, Gene
Also see STANLEY, Paul
Also see VINCENT, Vinnie, Invasion

KISS / Mighty Bosstones

Singles: 7-inch

MERCURY (858894 "Detroit Rock City") 15-20
(Colored vinyl.)

Also see KISS

KISSING the PINK
(KTP)

P&R '83

Singles: 7-inch

ATLANTIC 3-5 83
MERCURY 3-4 87

Picture Sleeves

MERCURY 3-4 87

LPs: 10/12-inch 33rpm

ATLANTIC 5-8 83
MERCURY 5-8 87

KISSOON, Katie

D&D '84

Singles: 12-inch 33/45rpm

JIVE 4-6 84

KISSOON, Mac & Katie

P&R '71

Singles: 7-inch

ABC 3-5 71
BELL 3-5 72
MCA/STATE 3-5 75-76

LPs: 10/12-inch 33rpm

MCA/STATE 8-12 76

Also see KISSOON, Katie
Also see WATERS, Roger

KITARO
(Mansanori Takahashi)

LP '85

Singles: 12-inch 33/45rpm

GEFFEN 4-8 86
(Promotional only.)

Singles: 7-inch

GEFFEN 3-4 86

LPs: 10/12-inch 33rpm

GEFFEN 5-8 85-90
GRAMAVISION 5-8 85-86

KITT, Eartha

P&R '53

Singles: 12-inch 33/45rpm

STREETWISE 4-6 83

Singles: 78rpm

RCA 3-6 53-57

Singles: 7-inch

DECCA 4-6 65
KAPP 4-8 59-66
RCA 5-10 53-57
STREETWISE 3-4 83

Picture Sleeves

RCA 10-15 54-55

EPs: 7-inch 33/45rpm

RCA 10-20 53-57

LPs: 10/12-inch 33rpm

CAEDMON 5-10 69
DECCA 10-15 65
GNP 10-15 65
KAPP 10-20 59-60
MGM 10-20 62
PHILIPS 8-15 68
RCA 20-40 53-57
STANYAN 5-10 72
SUNNYVIEW 5-8 84

KITTY & HAYWOODS

R&B '77

Singles: 7-inch

MERCURY 3-5 77

LPs: 10/12-inch 33rpm

MERCURY 8-10 77

KIX

LP '83

Singles: 7-inch

ATLANTIC 3-4 81-89

Picture Sleeves

ATLANTIC 3-4 89

LPs: 10/12-inch 33rpm

ATLANTIC 5-8 81-89

KLAATU

P&R/LP '77

Singles: 12-inch 33/45rpm

CAPITOL 3-4 80
(Promotional only.)

Singles: 7-inch

CAPITOL 3-5 77-80
ISLAND 4-6 75

Picture Sleeves

CAPITOL 3-5 77

LPs: 10/12-inch 33rpm

CAPITOL 8-12 76-80

Members: John Woloschuk; Cary Draper; David Long;; Dino Tome.

KLEEER

R&B '79

Singles: 7-inch

ATLANTIC 3-5 79-85

LPs: 10/12-inch 33rpm

ATLANTIC 5-8 79-85

Members: Paul Crutchfield; Richard Lee; Norm Durham.

Also see UNIVERSAL ROBOT BAND

KLEIN, Robert

LP '73

Singles: 7-inch

BRUT 4-8 73

CASABLANCA 3-5 79

LPs: 10/12-inch 33rpm

BRUT 8-12 73

KLEIN & MBO

D&D '83

Singles: 12-inch 33/45rpm

ATLANTIC 4-6 83

Singles: 7-inch

ATLANTIC 3-4 83

KLEMMER, John

LP '69

Singles: 7-inch

ABC 3-5 76

CADET CONCEPT 4-6 69

LPs: 10/12-inch 33rpm

ABC 5-10 75-79

CADET CONCEPT 8-12 69

CHESS 8-12 76

ELEKTRA 5-8 80-83

MCA 5-10 79-82

NAUTILUS 5-8 80-81

NOVUS 5-8 79

Also see HARRIS, Eddie, & John Klemmer

KLINT, Pete, Quintet

P&R '67

Singles: 7-inch

IGL (127 "Very Last Day") 8-10 64

MERCURY 4-6 67

KLIQUE

R&B '81

Singles: 12-inch 33/45rpm

MCA 4-6 81-85

Singles: 7-inch

MCA 3-4 81-85

LPs: 10/12-inch 33rpm

MCA 5-8 81-85

Members: Howard Huntsberry; Deborah Hunter; Isaac Suthers.

KLOCKWISE

R&B '84

Singles: 7-inch

SINBAN 3-4 84-85

KLOWNS

P&R/LP '70

Singles: 7-inch

RCA 3-5 70

Picture Sleeves

RCA 3-5 70

LPs: 10/12-inch 33rpm

RCA 8-10 70

KLUGH, Earl

R&B/LP '77

Singles: 7-inch

BLUE NOTE 3-5 76-77

LIBERTY 3-4 81

LPs: 10/12-inch 33rpm

BLUE NOTE 5-8 76-77

CAPITOL 5-8 83-84

LIBERTY 5-8 80-81

MFSL (025 "Finger Paintings") .. 20-40 79

MFSL (076 "Late Night") 20-30 82

MFSL/UHQR (025 "Finger Paintings") 30-50 79

(Boxed set.)

U.A. 5-10 78-80

W.B. 5-8 84-91

Also see BENSON, George, & Earl Klugh

Also see JAMES, Bob, & Earl Klugh

Also see LAWS, Hubert, & Earl Klugh

KLYMAXX

R&B '81

Singles: 12-inch 33/45rpm

CONSTELLATION 4-6 84-87

MCA 4-6 84-86

Singles: 7-inch

CONSTELLATION 3-4 84-87

MCA 3-4 84-86

SOLAR 3-5 81-83

Picture Sleeves

CONSTELLATION 3-4 85-87

MCA 4-6 84-86

LPs: 10/12-inch 33rpm

CONSTELLATION 5-8 85-87

MCA 5-8 90

SOLAR 5-8 81-83

Members: Lorena Hardiman; Ann Williams; Cheryl Coolen; Robbin Grider; Lynn Malsby; Joyce Irby; Bernadette Cooper; Judy Takeuchi.

Also see IRBY, Joyce "Fenderella"

KNACK

P&R/LP '79

Singles: 7-inch

CAPITOL (4000 series) 3-5 79-81

Picture Sleeves

CAPITOL (4731 "My Sharona") 4-8 79

CAPITOL (4771 "Good Girls Don't") 3-5 79

CAPITOL (4822 "Baby Talks Dirty") 8-10 80

CAPITOL (5054 "Pay the Devil") . 8-10 80

LPs: 10/12–inch 33rpm

CAPITOL.................................... 8-10 79-81

Members: Doug Fieger; Bruce Gary; Berton Averre; Prescott Niles.

Also see SKY

KNICKERBOCKERS

P&R '65

Singles: 7–inch

CHALLENGE (59268 "All I Need Is You") 10-20 65

CHALLENGE (59293 thru 59384)...................................... 5-10 65-67

ERIC.. 3-5 70s

LANA... 3-6 60s

LPs: 10/12–inch 33rpm

CHALLENGE (621 "Jerk and Twine Time")......................... 45-55 66

CHALLENGE (622 "Lies")......... 50-75 66

CHALLENGE (12664 "Lloyd Thaxton Presents the Knickerbockers") 50-75 65

SUNDAZED 5-10 89

Members: Buddy Randell; Beau Charles; Jimmy Walker; John Charles.

KNIGHT, Evelyn, & Red Foley

C&W '51

Singles: 78rpm

DECCA.. 4-8 51

Singles: 7–inch

DECCA.. 5-10 51

Also see FOLEY, Red

KNIGHT, Frederick

P&R/R&B '72

Singles: 7–inch

JUANA 3-4 81

MAXINE 4-6 69

1-2-3.. 10-15

STAX.. 3-5 72

TRUTH 3-5 75

LPs: 10/12–inch 33rpm

STAX.. 8-10 73

KNIGHT, Gladys

(Pips; with the Pips)

P&R/R&B '61

Singles: 12–inch 33/45rpm

COLUMBIA 4-8 79-85

MCA 4-6 86

Singles: 7–inch

ABC 3-5 73

BRUNSWICK (55048 "Whistle My Love")............................. 75-100 58

BUDDAH 3-5 73-79

CASABLANCA 3-5 77-78

COLUMBIA 3-5 79-85

ENJOY 10-20 64

ERIC... 3-5 78

EVERLAST (5025 "Happiness") 15-20 63

FLASHBACK............................... 3-5 67

FURY (1050 thru 1067)............ 10-20 61-62

FURY (1073 "Come See About Me") 20-30 63

HUNTOM (2510 "Every Beat of My Heart")...........................300-500 61

MCA 3-4 86-88

MAXX...10-20 64-65

SOUL 6-12 67-74

VEE JAY (386 "Every Beat of My Heart")..............................10-15 61

VEE JAY (545 "Queen of Tears")..10-20 63

Picture Sleeves

BUDDAH...3-5 73-75

COLUMBIA 3-5 81

MCA 3-4 87

LPs: 10/12–inch 33rpm

ACCORD 5-8 81-82

ALLEGIANCE 5-8 84

BELL 10-15 68-75

BUDDAH..8-12 73-78

CASABLANCA..............................5-10 77-78

COLUMBIA 5-8 79-85

51 WEST..5-8 80s

FURY (1003 "Letter Full of Tears")................................75-100 62

LOST-NITE 5-8 81

MCA 5-8 87

MCP 8-10 76

MAXX (3000 "Gladys Knight and the Pips") 20-30 64

MOTOWN (Except 792)................5-8 80-82

MOTOWN (792 "Anthology") 8-12 74

NATURAL RESOURCES 5-8 78

PICKWICK.....................................8-10 73

RELIC 5-10 90

SOUL (706 "Everybody Needs Love")...20-30 67

SOUL (707 "Feelin' Bluesy")......15-25 67

SOUL (711 "Silk 'N' Soul") 15-25 69

SOUL (713 "Nitty Gritty") 15-25 69

SOUL (723 thru 744)...................8-15 70-75

SPHERE SOUND (7006 "Gladys Knight and the Pips") 20-30 65

SPRINGBOARD 8-10 75

TRIP 8-10 73

U.A...10-15 75

UPFRONT....................................10-12

VEE JAY 10-15 75

Members: Gladys Knight; Merald Knight; William Guest; Edward Guest.

Also see DIONNE & Friends

Also see GAYE, Marvin / Gladys Knight & Pips

Also see PIPS

KNIGHT, Gladys, & Johnny Mathis

Singles: 7–inch

COLUMBIA 3-5 80

Also see MATHIS, Johnny

KNIGHT, Gladys, & Bill Medley

Singles: 7-inch

SCOTTI BROS. ... 3-4 86

Also see KNIGHT, Gladys
Also see MEDLEY, Bill

KNIGHT, Holly

P&R '88

Singles: 7-inch

COLUMBIA ... 3-4 88

Picture Sleeves

COLUMBIA ... 3-4 88

LP: 10/12-inch 33rpm

COLUMBIA (44243 "Holly Knight") ... 5-10 88

Session: Nancy Wilson; Daryl Hall.
Also see DEVICE
Also see HALL, Daryl
Also see SPIDER
Also see WILSON, Nancy

KNIGHT, Jean
(With Premium)

P&R/R&B/LP '71

Singles: 7-inch

CHELSEA ... 3-5 75
COTILLION ... 3-4 81-82
DIAL ... 3-5 74
JETSTREAM ... 4-8 65
MIRAGE ... 3-4 85
OLA ... 3-5 77
OPEN ... 3-5 76
SOULIN ... 3-4 81-85
STAFF ... 5-10 72
STAX ... 3-5 71-73
TRIBE ... 4-8 65

Picture Sleeves

MIRAGE ... 3-4 85

LPs: 10/12-inch 33rpm

COTILLION ... 5-8 81
MIRAGE ... 5-8 85
STAX ... 10-15 71

KNIGHT, Jerry

R&B/LP '80

Singles: 7-inch

A&M ... 3-4 80-83

Picture Sleeves

A&M ... 3-4 80

LPs: 10/12-inch 33rpm

A&M ... 5-8 80-81

Also see OLLIE & JERRY
Also see RAYDIO

KNIGHT, Marie

R&B '49

Singles: 78rpm

DECCA ... 5-10 49-54
MERCURY ... 5-10 56
WING ... 5-10 56

Singles: 7-inch

ADDIT ... 8-10
DECCA (Except 48315) ... 10-20 51-54
DECCA (48315 "You Got a Way of Making Love") ... 20 30 54
DIAMOND ... 8-12 63
MERCURY ... 15-20 56
MUSICOR (1106 "Say It Again") 25-50 65
MUSICOR (1128 "You Lie So Well") ... 10-20 65
OKEH ... 5-10 61-65
WING ... 10-15 56

Picture Sleeves

OKEH ... 5-10 61

LPs: 10/12-inch 33rpm

CARLTON (119 "Lift Every Voice and Sing") ... 20-30 60

Also see MARIE & REX

KNIGHT, Robert

P&R/R&B/LP '67

Singles: 7-inch

DOT ... 4-8 61
ELF ... 4-8 68-69
MONUMENT ... 3-5 74
PRIVATE STOCK ... 3-5 75
RISING SONS ... 4-8 67-68

LPs: 10/12-inch 33rpm

RISING SONS/MONUMENT (17000 "Everlasting Love") ... 15-25 67

KNIGHT, Sonny
(With the Cleeshays)

P&R '56

Singles: 78rpm

ALADDIN ... 8-12 53
DOT ... 4-8 56
SPECIALTY ... 4-8 57

Singles: 7-inch

A&M ... 4-8 63-64
ALADDIN (3195 "Dear Wonderful") ... 20-30 53
ALADDIN (3207 "But Officer") ... 20-30 53
AURA ... 4-8 64-65
DOT (15507 "Confidential") ... 10-15 56
(Maroon label.)
DOT (15507 "Confidential") ... 5-10 57
(Black label.)
EASTMAN (787 "Lipstick Kisses") ... 20-30 59
FIFO ... 4-8 61
MERCURY ... 4-8 62
ORIGINAL SOUND (2 "Once in Awhile") ... 10-15 58
SPECIALTY ... 8-12 57
STARLA (Except 1) ... 8-12 58-59
STARLA (1 "Dedicated to You") 15-20 57
VITA (137 "Confidential") ... 15-25 56
WORLD PACIFIC (Except 403) ... 4-8 66
WORLD PACIFIC (403 "If You Want This Love") ... 5-10 64
(Reissued several months later on Aura 403.)

Picture Sleeves

AURA (4505 "Love Me") 10-15 64

LPs: 10/12-inch 33rpm

AURA 15-20 64

KNIGHT, Terry

(With the Pack; with Fabulous Pack)

P&R/LP '66

Singles: 7-inch

A&M 5-10 65
ABKCO... 3-5 75
CAMEO 5-10 67
CAPITOL...................................... 5-10 69
FRATERNITY............................... 5-10 67
LUCKY ELEVEN (Except 225).... 8-15 66-67
LUCKY ELEVEN (225 "How Much More") 15-25 66
SPICE 5-10 60s

LPs: 10/12-inch 33rpm

ABKCO.................................... 10-15 72
CAMEO (2007 "Reflections") 20-30 67
LUCKY ELEVEN (8000 "Terry Knight and the Pack")................................... 25-35 66
LUCKY ELEVEN (8001 Reflections")........................... 25-35 67

Members: Terry Knapp (a.k.a. Knight); Mark Farner; Don Brewer; Bob Caldwell; Curt Johnson.
Also see GRAND FUNK RAILROAD

KNIGHT BROTHERS

P&R/R&B '65

Singles: 7-inch

CHECKER................................... 5-8 63-66
MERCURY 4-6 67-68

Members: Richard Dunbar; Jerry Diggs.

KNIGHTSBRIDGE STRINGS

P&R '59

Singles: 7-inch

MONUMENT 3-6 66
TOP RANK.................................. 4-8 59-60

LPs: 10/12-inch 33rpm

MONUMENT 5-10 66-69
PURIST 5-10 64
RIVERSIDE................................. 5-12 62-64
SESAC 8-15
TOP RANK.................................. 5-15 59-60

Also see CAMBRIDGE STRINGS & SINGERS
Also see RANDOLPH, Boots

KNOBLOCK, Fred

C&W/P&R/LP '80

Singles: 7-inch

SCOTTI BROS............................. 3-4 80-82

LPs: 10/12-inch 33rpm

SCOTTI BROS............................. 5-8 80-82

KNOBLOCK, Fred, & Susan Anton

C&W/P&R '80

Singles: 7-inch

SCOTTI BROS............................. 3-5 80

Also see KNOBLOCK, Fred

KNOCKOUTS

P&R '59

Singles: 7-inch

SHAD (5013 "Darling Lorraine") 10-20 59
SHAD (5018 "Rich Boy, Poor Boy")..10-20 60
TRIBUTE (199 "Got My Mojo Working")..................................8-10 64
TRIBUTE (201 "What's on Your Mind")..10-15 64
TRIBUTE (1039 "Don't Say Goodbye")..................................8-10 65

LPs: 10/12-inch 33rpm

TRIBUTE (1202 "Go Ape") 50-60 64

Member: Robert D'Andrea.

KNOX, Buddy

(With the Rhythm Orchids)

P&R/R&B '57

Singles: 78rpm

ROULETTE.................................10-15 57

Singles: 7-inch

ABC...3-5 73
LIBERTY 5-10 60-64
REPRISE 4-8 65-66
ROULETTE (4002 "Party Doll") .20-30 57
(With roulette wheel circling label.)
ROULETTE (4002 "Party Doll") .15-20 57
(With roulette wheel on top half of label.)
ROULETTE (4002 "Party Doll") .10-15 58
(No roulette wheel on label.)
ROULETTE (4009 "Rock Your Little Baby to Sleep") 20-30 57
(With roulette wheel circling label.)
ROULETTE (4009 "Rock Your Little Baby to Sleep") 25-20 57
(With roulette wheel on top half of label.)
ROULETTE (4009 "Rock Your Little Baby to Sleep") 10-15 58
(No roulette wheel on label.)
ROULETTE (4018 thru 4262) 8-15 57-60
RUFF 4-8 65
U.A. 4-8 68-71

Picture Sleeves

LIBERTY (55305 "Ling Ting Tong") 10-20 61

EPs: 7-inch 33/45rpm

ROULETTE (301 "Buddy Knox")...................................50-75 57

LPs: 10/12-inch 33rpm

ACCORD 5-8 82-83
LIBERTY (3251 "Golden Hits") ..20-30 62
(Monaural.)
LIBERTY (7251 "Golden Hits") ..25-35 62
(Stereo.)
ROULETTE (25003 "Buddy Knox")...................................75-100 57
U.A. 10-15 69

KNOX, Buddy / Jimmy Bowen
(With the Rhythm Orchids)

P&R/R&B '57

Singles: 78rpm

ROULETTE 15-25 57
TRIPLE-D (797 "Party Doll"/"I'm Stickin' with You") 50-100 57

Singles: 7-inch

ROULETTE (4001 "My Baby's Gone"/"I'm Stickin' with You") 30-50 57
TRIPLE-D (797 "Party Doll"/"I'm Stickin' with You") 300-400 57

LPs: 10/12-inch 33rpm

MURRAY HILL 5-8 80s
ROULETTE (25048 "Buddy Knox & Jimmy Bowen") 75-125 58

Also see BOWEN, Jimmy
Also see KNOX, Buddy

KOFFIE

D&D '83

Singles: 12-inch 33/45rpm

PAN DISC 4-6 83

KOFFMAN, Moe
(Moe Koffman Quartette; Quintet; Septette)

P&R '58

Singles: 7-inch

ABC 3-5 73
ASCOT 4-6 62
ATCO 4-6 65
GOLD EAGLE 4-8 61
JUBILEE 3-8 58-68
PALETTE 4-6 60-63
VIRGO 3-5 72

LPs: 10/12-inch 33rpm

ASCOT 10-15 62
JANUS 5-8 78
JUBILEE (1000 series) 15-25 57-58
JUBILEE (8000 series) 8-12 68
U.A. 15-25 62-63

KOKOMO
(James Wisner)

P&R '61

Singles: 7-inch

FELSTED 4-8 61-62

Picture Sleeves

FELSTED 8-10 61

LPs: 10/12-inch 33rpm

FELSTED 15-20 61

KOKOMO

LP '75

Singles: 7-inch

COLUMBIA 3-5 75-76

LPs: 10/12-inch 33rpm

COLUMBIA 8-10 75-76

Member: Tony O'Malley.
Also see 10CC

KOKO-POP

R&B '84

Singles: 7-inch

MOTOWN 3-4 84-85

LPs: 10/12-inch 33rpm

MOTOWN 5-8 84

KOLBY, Diane

P&R '70

Singles: 7-inch

COLUMBIA 3-5 70-71

KOMIKO

R&B '82

Singles: 7-inch

SAM 3-4 82

KON KAN

P&R '88

Singles: 7-inch

ATLANTIC 3-4 88-89

KONGAS

P&R/LP '78

Singles: 7-inch

POLYDOR 3-5 78

LPs: 10/12-inch 33rpm

POLYDOR 5-8 78
SALSOUL 5-8 78

KONGOS, John
(John T. Kongos; Johnny Kongos)

P&R '71

Singles: 7-inch

ELEKTRA 3-5 71-72
GROOVE 4-8 61
KAPP 4-8 67
RCA 3-5 63

Picture Sleeves

ELEKTRA 3-5 71

LPs: 10/12-inch 33rpm

ELEKTRA 8-10 72
JANUS 8-10 71

KONK

D&D '84

Singles: 12-inch 33/45rpm

SLEEPING BAG 4-6 84

KOOL, Dr. J.R: see DR. J.R. KOOL

KOOL & GANG

P&R/R&B '69

Singles: 12-inch 33/45rpm

DE-LITE 4-8 79-85
MERCURY 4-6 86-87

Singles: 7-inch

DE-LITE 3-5 69-85
MERCURY 3-4 86-87

Picture Sleeves

DE-LITE 3-5 85
MERCURY 3-4 86-87

LPs: 10/12-inch 33rpm

DE-LITE (Except 8502) 8-10 69-87

DE-LITE (8502 "Something Special") 8-10 81
DE-LITE (8502 "History of Kool and the Gang") 15-20 81
(Promotional issue only. With interviews.)
MERCURY 5-8 86-88
Members: Robert "Kool" Bell; Ronald Bell; George Brown; Curtis Williams; Charles Smith; James Taylor.
Also see BAND AID

KOOL MOE DEE

P&R/R&B/LP '87

Singles: 7-inch

JIVE 3-4 87-88

LPs: 10/12-inch 33rpm

JIVE 5-8 87-91

KOOPER, Al

LP '69

Singles: 7-inch

AURORA 4-8 67
COLUMBIA 3-6 69-71
VERVE/FOLKWAYS 4-8 66

Picture Sleeves

COLUMBIA 3-5 69

LPs: 10/12-inch 33rpm

COLUMBIA 10-15 69-82
U.A. 8-10 76
Also see APPALOOSA
Also see BLOOD, SWEAT & TEARS
Also see BLOOMFIELD, Mike, & Al Kooper
Also see BLUES PROJECT
Also see DYLAN, Bob
Also see ROYAL TEENS

KOOPER, Al, & Steve Mills

Singles: 7-inch

COLUMBIA 4-8 68

KOOPER, Al, & Shuggie Otis

LP '70

LPs: 10/12-inch 33rpm

COLUMBIA 10-15 69
Also see KOOPER, Al
Also see OTIS, Shuggie

KOPPER

R&B '86

Singles: 7-inch

KMA 3-4 86-87

KORGIS

P&R/LP '80

Singles: 7-inch

ASYLUM 3-5 80
W.B. 3-6 79

LPs: 10/12-inch 33rpm

ASYLUM 5-8 80
W.B. 5-10 79
Members: Andrew Davis; Jim Warren.
Also see STACKRIDGE

KORONA

P&R '80

Singles: 7-inch

U.A. 3-5 80

LPs: 10/12-inch 33rpm

U.A. 5-8 80
Members: Bruce Blackman; Bob Gauthler.
Also see ETERNITY'S CHILDREN
Also see STARBUCK

KOSSOFF, Paul

LP '75

LPs: 10/12-inch 33rpm

DJM 10-12 77
ISLAND 8-10 73-75
Also see BACK STREET CRAWLER
Also see FREE

KOSSOFF / Kirke / Tetsu / Rabbit

LPs: 10/12-inch 33rpm

ISLAND 8-10 72
Members: Paul Kossoff; Simon Kirke.
Also see FREE
Also see KOSSOFF, Paul

KOSTELANETZ, Andre, & His Orchestra

LP '55

Singles: 78rpm

COLUMBIA 3-5 50-57

Singles: 7-inch

COLUMBIA 4-8 50-61

EPs: 7-inch 33/45rpm

COLUMBIA 5-10 50-59

LPs: 10/12-inch 33rpm

COLUMBIA 5-15 50-71
Also see STREISAND, Barbra / Doris Day / Jim Nabors / Andre Kostelanetz

KOTTKE, Leo

LP '71

Singles: 7-inch

CAPITOL 3-5 75

LPs: 10/12-inch 33rpm

CAPITOL (Except 16000 series) .8-12 71-76
CAPITOL (16000 series) 5-8 81
CHRYSALIS 5-10 76-81
OBLIVION 15-20
SYMPOSIUM 10-12 70
TAKOMA 8-12 71-74

KOTTKE, Leo, John Fahey & Peter Lang

LPs: 10/12-inch 33rpm

TAKOMA 8-10 74
Also see FAHEY, John
Also see KOTTKE, Leo

KOZ, Dave

LP '91

LPs: 10/12-inch 33rpm

CAPITOL 5-8 91

KRAFTWERK

P&R/LP '75

Singles: 12-inch 33/45rpm

W.B. 4-6 83

Singles: 7-inch

CAPITOL 3-5 76-78
VERTIGO 3-5 75
W.B. 3-4 81-83

Picture Sleeves

W.B. 3-4 81-83

LPs: 10/12-inch 33rpm

CAPITOL 8-10 75-78
MERCURY 5-8 77
VERTIGO 8-10 73-75
W.B. 5-8 80-86

KRAMER, Billy J., & Dakotas

P&R/LP '64

Singles: 7-inch

EPIC 4-8 68
ERIC 3-5
IMPERIAL 4-8 64-66
LIBERTY (55586 "Do You Want to Know a Secret"/"I'll Be on My Way") 8-12 63
LIBERTY (55626 "Bad to Me") 8-10 64
LIBERTY (55643 "I'll Keep You Satisfied") 8-10 64
LIBERTY (55667 "Do You Want to Know a Secret"/"Bad to Me") 5-8 64

Picture Sleeves

IMPERIAL (66051 "From a Window") 10-15 64

LPs: 10/12-inch 33rpm

CAPITOL 8-10 78-79
IMPERIAL (9267 "Little Children") 25-35 64
(Monaural.)
IMPERIAL (9273 "I'll Keep You Satisfied") 25-35 64
(Monaural.)
IMPERIAL (9291 "Trains and Boats and Planes") 25-35 65
(Monaural.)
IMPERIAL (12267 "Little Children") 25-40 64
(Stereo.)
IMPERIAL (12273 "I'll Keep You Satisfied") 25-40 64
(Stereo.)
IMPERIAL (12291 "Trains and Boats and Planes") 25-40 65
(Stereo.)

KRANZ, George

D&D '83

Singles: 12-inch 33/45rpm

PERSONAL 4-6 83

Singles: 7-inch

PERSONAL 3-4 83-84

KRAVITZ, Lenny

LP '89

Singles: 7-inch

VIRGIN 3-4 89-90

LPs: 10/12-inch 33rpm

VIRGIN 5-8 89-91

KRISTOFFERSON, Kris

P&R/LP '71

Singles: 7-inch

A&M 3-4 73
COLUMBIA 3-5 77-81
EPIC 4-8 67
MONUMENT 3-5 70-81

Picture Sleeves

A&M 3-4 73

EPs: 7-inch 33/45rpm

MONUMENT (532 "Kristofferson") 5-10 71
(Promotional issue only.)

LPs: 10/12-inch 33rpm

COLUMBIA 5-8 77-81
MONUMENT 8-12 70-76
Session: Larry Gatlin; Rita Coolidge.
Also see JENNINGS, Waylon, Willie Nelson, Johnny Cash, & Kris Kristofferson
Also see NELSON, Willie, & Kris Kristofferson

Kristofferson, Kris, & Rita Coolidge

C&W '73

Singles: 7-inch

A&M 3-5 73-74
MONUMENT 3-5 74-75

Picture Sleeves

A&M 3-5 73

LPs: 10/12-inch 33rpm

A&M 8-12 73-79
MONUMENT 8-10 74
Also see COOLIDGE, Rita
Also see KRISTOFFERSON, Kris

KROKUS

LP '81

Singles: 7-inch

ARIOLA AMERICA 3-4 81
ARISTA 3-4 82-86

Picture Sleeves

ARISTA 3-4 84-86

LPs: 10/12-inch 33rpm

ARIOLA AMERICA 5-8 81
ARISTA 5-8 82-86
Members: Dani Crivelli; Chris Von Rohr; Marc Storace; Fernando Von Arb; Mark Kohler.
MCA 5-8 88

KRUSH GROOVE ALL STARS

R&B '85

Singles: 12-inch 33/45rpm

W.B. 4-6 85
Also see BLOW, Kurtis
Also see SHEILA E.
Also see FAT BOYS
Also see RUN D.M.C.

KRYSTAL GENERATION

R&B '71

Singles: 7–inch

BUDDAH 4-6 69
MR. CHAND 3-5 71

Members: Joyce Smith; Darlene Arnold; Mary Shelley; Mary Lead; Wylie Dixon; Walter "Simtec" Simmons.

Also see SIMTEC & WYLIE

KRYSTOL

R&B/D&D '84

Singles: 12–inch 33/45rpm

EPIC 4-6 84-86

Singles: 7–inch

EPIC 3-4 84-86

LPs: 10/12–inch 33rpm

EPIC 5-8 86

KUBAN, Bob

(With the In-Men; Bob Kuban Band)

P&R/LP '66

Singles: 7–inch

ERIC 3-5 70s
MUSICLAND USA (Except 20001) 5-10 66-67
MUSICLAND USA. (20001 "The Cheater") 10-20 66
("Vocal by Walter Scott" shown on both sides.)
MUSICLAND USA (20001 The Cheater") 5-10 66
("Vocal by Walter Scott" shown only on flip, *Try Me Baby.*)
MUSICLAND USA (20001 "The Cheater") 4-8 66
("Vocal by Walter Scott" not on either side.)
NORMAN 5-15 65-66
(Walter Scott may be shown as "Little Walter.")
REPRISE 4-8 70

LPs: 10/12–inch 33rpm

MUSICLAND USA (3500 "Look Out for the Cheater") 25-35 66

Members: Walter Scott; Bob Kuban; John Krenski; Greg Hoeltzel.

Also see CASH, J.D., & Bob Kuban Brass

KUF-LINX

(Kuff-Linx)

P&R '58

Singles: 78rpm

CHALLENGE 8-10 58

Singles: 7–inch

CHALLENGE (1013 "So Tough") 10-15 57
(Blue or white label.)
CHALLENGE (1013 "So Tough") 5-10 58
CHALLENGE (59004 "Service with a Smile") 8-12 58
CHALLENGE (59015 "Climb Love's Mountain") 15-25 58

Member: Johnny Jennings.

KULIS, Charlie

P&R '75

Singles: 7–inch

PLAYBOY 3-5 75

KWAME

(With a New Beginning)

LP '89

LPs: 10/12–inch 33rpm

ATLANTIC....................................5-8 89-90
POLYDOR 5-8 80

KWICK

R&B '80

Singles: 12–inch 33/45rpm

CAPITOL.......................................4-6 83

Singles: 7–inch

CAPITOL.......................................3-4 83
EMI AMERICA 3-4 80-82

LPs: 10/12–inch 33rpm

CAPITOL.......................................5-8 83
EMI AMERICA 5-8 80-81

Members: Terry Bartlett; Bert Brown; William Sumlin; Vince Williams.

Also see NEWCOMERS

KYM

R&B '84

Singles: 12–inch 33/45rpm

AWARD...4-6 84

Singles: 7–inch

AWARD...3-4 84

KYPER

P&R/LP '90

Singles: 7–inch

ATLANTIC....................................3-4 90

LPs: 10/12–inch 33rpm

ATLANTIC....................................5-8 90

L

L.A. BOPPERS
R&B/LP '80

Singles: 7-inch

MCA 3-4 82
MERCURY 3-5 80-81

LPs: 10/12-inch 33rpm

MCA 5-8 82
MERCURY 5-10 80-81

Also see SIDE EFFECT

L.A. DREAM TEAM
R&B/LP '86

Singles: 12-inch 33/45rpm

MCA 4-6 86

Singles: 7-inch

MCA 3-4 86

LPs: 10/12-inch 33rpm

MCA 5-8 86-87

Members: Rudy Pardee; Chris Wilson.

L.A. EXPRESS
LP '76

Singles: 7-inch

CARIBOU 3-5 75-78

LPs: 10/12-inch 33rpm

CARIBOU 8-10 75-76

Also see MITCHELL, Joni, & L.A. Express
Also see SCOTT, Tom

L.A. GUNS
LP '88

LPs: 10/12-inch 33rpm

VERTIGO 5-8 88-89

Members: Philip Lewis; Tracii Guns; Kelly Nickels; Mick Cripps; Steve Riley.
Also see W.A.S.P.

L.A. JETS
P&R '76

Singles: 7-inch

RCA 3-5 76

LPs: 10/12-inch 33rpm

RCA 8-10 76

L.L. COOL J
(Ladies Love Cool James; James Todd Smith)
R&B '85

Singles: 12-inch 33/45rpm

COLUMBIA 4-6 85-86

Singles: 7-inch

COLUMBIA 3-4 85-86
DEF JAM 3-4 87-90

Picture Sleeves

DEF JAM 3-4 88

LPs: 10/12-inch 33rpm

COLUMBIA 5-8 85
DEF JAM 5-8 87-90

L.T.D.
(Love, Togetherness & Devotion)
P&R/R&B/LP '76

Singles: 7-inch

A&M 3-5 76-80
MONTAGE 3-4 83

Picture Sleeves

A&M 3-5 76-78

LPs: 10/12-inch 33rpm

A&M 8-10 74-81
MONTAGE 5-8 83
SPRINGBOARD 8-10 77

Members: Jeffrey Osborne; Leslie Ray; Andre Ray.
Also see OSBORNE, Jeffrey

LTG EXCHANGE
R&B '74

Singles: 7-inch

FANIA 3-5 74
WAND 3-5 74

LABAN
P&R '86

Singles: 7-inch

CRITIQUE 3-4 86

LABELLE, Patti
(With the Blue Belles; Pattie La Belle; Labelle)
P&R '63

Singles: 12-inch 33/45rpm

EPIC 4-8 78-79
MCA 4-6 85
PHILADELPHIA INT'L 4-6 83-85

Singles: 7-inch

ATLANTIC 5-10 65-70
EPIC 3-6 74-80
KING 8-12 63
MISTLETOE 3-5 73
PHILADELPHIA INT'L 3-5 81-85
MCA 3-4 85-87
NEWTIME (510 "Love Me Just a Little") 10-15 62
NEWTOWN (5777 "Down the Aisle") 10-15 63
(Reads "Pressed by King Records.")
NEWTOWN (5777 "Down the Aisle") 5-10 63
(No mention of King Records.")
NICETOWN 5-10 64
PARKWAY 5-10 64
RCA 3-6 73
TRIP 3-6 71
W.B. 3-6 71-72

Picture Sleeves

MCA 3-4 85-86

LPs: 10/12-inch 33rpm

ATLANTIC 15-25 65-67
EPIC 8-10 74-82
MCA 5-8 85-89
MISTLETOE 10-20 60s

NEWTOWN (631 "Sweethearts of the Apollo")............................ 50-75 63
NEWTOWN (632 "Sleigh Bells, Jingle Bells and Blue Bells")...................... 50-75 63
PARKWAY (7043 "On Stage") .. 30-40 64
PHILADELPHIA INT'L.................. 5-8 81-85
RCA (0200 series)...................... 8-10 73
RCA (4100 series)...................... 5-8 82
TRIP 8-10 71-75
U.A. 8-10 74-75
UPFRONT.............................. 10-15
W.B. 8-10 71-72

Also see BLUE BELLES
Also see DASH, Sarah
Also see HENDRIX, Nona
Also see NYRO, Laura
Also see WOMACK, Bobby, & Patti Labelle

LABELLE, Patti / Harold Faltermeyer

Singles: 7-inch

MCA 3-4 85

Also see FALTERMEYER, Harold

LABELLE, Patti, & Michael McDonald

P&R/R&B '86

Singles: 7-inch

MCA 3-4 86

Picture Sleeves

MCA 3-4 86

Also see McDONALD, Michael

LABELLE, Patti, & Grover Washington Jr.

R&B '82

Singles: 7-inch

ELEKTRA..................................... 3-4 82

Also see LABELLE, Patti
Also see WASHINGTON, Grover, Jr.

LA BOUNTY, Bill

P&R '78

Singles: 7-inch

20TH FOX.................................. 3-5 75-76
W.B. 3-5 78

LABYRINTH

R&B '85

Singles: 7-inch

21 .... 3-4 85

Member: Julie Loco.

LACE

R&B '87

Singles: 7-inch

WING 3-4 87

LPs: 10/12-inch 33rpm

WING 5-8 87

LADD, Cheryl

P&R/LP '78

Singles: 12-inch 33/45rpm

CAPITOL (8894 "Skinnydippin'") 10-15 78
(Promotional issue only.)

Singles: 7-inch

CAPITOL..................................... 3-5 76-79

Picture Sleeves

CAPITOL......................................3-5 78-79
W.B. 4-6 74

LPs: 10/12-inch 33rpm

CAPITOL....................................8-10 78-79

Also see JOSIE & PUSSYCATS
Also see VALLI, Frankie, & Cheryl Ladd

LADIES' CHOICE

R&B '83

Singles: 7-inch

STREETWISE...............................3-4 83

LADY

R&B '82

Singles: 7-inch

MEGA 3-4 82

LADY FLASH

P&R '76

Singles: 7-inch

RSO 3-5 76

LPs: 10/12-inch 33rpm

RSO 8-12 76

Members: Monica Burruss; Debra Byrd; Reparata.
Also see MANILOW, Barry
Also see REPARATA

LAFAYETTES

P&R '62

Singles: 7-inch

RCA 5-10 62

LA FLAMME, David

P&R/LP '76

Singles: 7-inch

AMHERST 3-5 76-77

Picture Sleeves

AMHERST....................................3-5 76

LPs: 10/12-inch 33rpm

AMHERST 8-10 76-78

Also see IT'S a BEAUTIFUL DAY

LA FLAVOUR

R&B '79

Singles: 12-inch 33/45rpm

SWEET CITY 8-10 80

Singles: 7-inch

MERCURY...................................3-5 79
SWEET CITY...............................3-5 80

LPs: 10/12-inch 33rpm

SWEET CITY 5-8 80

LA FORGE, Jack

P&R '65

Singles: 7-inch

LYRIC 3-5 65-66
REGINA 3-5 63-66
RIO...4-6 62

LPs: 10/12-inch 33rpm

AUDIO FIDELITY.........................6-12 66
PURPLETONE.............................8-15 62
REGINA 8-15 63-65

LAI, Francis, & His Orchestra

P&R '71

Singles: 7–inch

PARAMOUNT 3-5 70

Picture Sleeves

PARAMOUNT 3-5 70

Also see JOHN, Elton

You'll find many more listings by this artist in *The Official Price Guide to Movie/TV Soundtracks and Original Cast Albums*, containing over 8,000 listings.

LAID BACK

D&D '83

Singles: 12–inch 33/45rpm

SIRE.. 4-6 84-85
W.B. 4-6 83

Singles: 7–inch

SIRE.. 3-4 84-85
W.B. 3-4 83-84

LPs: 10/12–inch 33rpm

SIRE.. 5-8 84

Members: Timothy Stahl; John Guldberg.

LAINE, Cleo

LP '74

Singles: 7–inch

RCA... 3-5 74-80

LPs: 10/12–inch 33rpm

BUDDAH 8-10 74
FONTANA............................... 10-15 66
GNP 5-10 74
QUINTESSENCE......................... 5-8 80
RCA.. 5-10 73-80

Also see CHARLES, Ray, & Cleo Laine

LAINE, Cleo, & James Galway

LP '80

LP: 10/12–inch 33rpm

RCA.. 5-8 80

Also see GALWAY, James
Also see LAINE, Cleo

LAINE, Frankie
(With Paul Weston & the Mellomen)

P&R/R&B '47

Singles: 78rpm

MERCURY 4-8 47-51
MERCURY/SAV-WAY (1027 "On the Sunny Side of the Street")............ 150-200 47
(Picture disc. Promotional issue only.)
MERCURY/SAV-WAY (1028 "West End Blues").............................. 150-200 47
(Picture disc. Promotional issue only.)
MERCURY/SAV-WAY (5059 "Kiss Me Again") 100-200 47
(Picture disc. Promotional issue only.)
COLUMBIA 4-8 51-57

Singles: 7–inch

ABC 3-5 67-69
AMOS... 3-5 70-71
CAPITOL.................................... 4-8 64-66
COLUMBIA (39367 thru 41486)...5-15 51-59
COLUMBIA (41613 thru 42966).....4-8 60-64
MAINSTREAM 3-5 75
MERCURY (5000 series)............8-15 50-51
SUNFLOWER..............................3-5 72
W.B. 3-5 74

Picture Sleeves

COLUMBIA 10-20 56-57

EPs: 7–inch 33/45rpm

COLUMBIA 5-15 52-59
MERCURY 8-15 51-54

LPs: 10/12–inch 33rpm

ABC (600 series)........................8-15 67-69
ABC (30000 series).......................5-8 76
AMOS 8-12 70-71
CAPITOL.................................10-15 65
COLUMBIA (600 thru 1200 series).....................................15-30 54-58
COLUMBIA (1300 thru 1900 series).....................................10-20 59-63
(Monaural.)
COLUMBIA (2500 series) 20-30 56
(10–inch LPs.)
COLUMBIA (6000 series) 20-40 53-54
(10–inch LPs.)
COLUMBIA (8100 thru 8700 series) 10-20 59-63
(Stereo.)
HARMONY.................................8-15 65-71
HINDSIGHT 4-8 84
MERCURY (20000 series).........15-30 54-61
MERCURY (25000 series).........20-40 51-52
(10–inch LPs.)
MERCURY (60000 series).........10-20 61
TOWER.......................................8-15 67
TRIP 5-8 75
WING 8-15 60-67

Also see DAY, Doris, & Frankie Laine
Also see MILLER, Mitch

LAINE, Frankie, & Jimmy Boyd

P&R '53

Singles: 78rpm

COLUMBIA 4-8 53

Singles: 7–inch

COLUMBIA 5-10 53

Also see BOYD, Jimmy

LAINE, Frankie, & Easy Riders

P&R '57

Singles: 78rpm

COLUMBIA 4-8 57

Singles: 7–inch

COLUMBIA 5-10 57

Also see GILKYSON, Terry

LAINE, Frankie, & Four Lads

P&R '54

Singles: 78rpm

COLUMBIA 4-8 54

Singles: 7-inch
COLUMBIA 5-10 54
EPs: 7-inch 33/45rpm
COLUMBIA 5-15 56
LPs: 10/12-inch 33rpm
COLUMBIA 20-30 56
Also see FOUR LADS

LAINE, Frankie, & Jo Stafford
P&R '51
Singles: 78rpm
COLUMBIA 4-8 51-53
Singles: 7-inch
COLUMBIA 5-10 51-53
EPs: 7-inch 33/45rpm
COLUMBIA 5-15 54
LPs: 10/12-inch 33rpm
COLUMBIA 20-30 54
Also see LAINE, Frankie
Also see STAFFORD, Jo

LAKE
P&R/LP '77
Singles: 7-inch
CARIBOU 3-5 81
COLUMBIA 3-5 77-79
LPs: 10/12-inch 33rpm
CARIBOU 5-8 81
COLUMBIA 5-10 77-79

LAKE, Greg
P&R '75
Singles: 7-inch
ATLANTIC 3-5 75-77
CHRYSALIS 3-5 81
Picture Sleeves
ATLANTIC 3-5 75
LPs: 10/12-inch 33rpm
CHRYSALIS 5-10 81
Also see EMERSON, LAKE & PALMER
Also see KING CRIMSON

LAKESIDE
R&B '78
Singles: 7-inch
SOLAR 3-5 78-87
LPs: 10/12-inch 33rpm
ABC-PAR 8-10 77
SOLAR 5-8 77-84
Members: Tiemeyer McCain; Thomas Shelby; Mark Woods; Otis Stokes; Steve Shockley; Marvin Craig; Norman Beavers; Fred Alexander; Fred Lewis.

LA LA
(La Forest Cope)
R&B '87
Singles: 7-inch
ARISTA 3-4 87

LA LA, Prince: see PRINCE LA LA

LAMAS, Lorenzo
P&R '84
Singles: 7-inch
SCOTTI BROTHERS............................... 3-4 84-85
Picture Sleeves
SCOTTI BROTHERS............................... 3-4 84

LAMB, Kevin
P&R '78
Singles: 7-inch
ARISTA 3-5 78

LAMBERT, Guy: see PRESLEY, Elvis

LAMOND, George
P&R/LP '90
Singles: 7-inch
COLUMBIA 3-4 90
LPs: 10/12-inch 33rpm
COLUMBIA 5-8 90

LAMONT, Lee
R&B '65
Singles: 7-inch
BACK BEAT............................... 5-10 64-66

L'AMOUR
D&D '84
Singles: 12-inch 33/45rpm
BROCCOLLI 4-6 84

LAMP SISTERS
R&B '68
Singles: 7-inch
DUKE 4-8 68-69

LANCE, Herb
(With the Classics)
R&B '49
Singles: 78rpm
DELUXE............................... 8-12 57
SITTIN' in WITH............................... 10-20 49
Singles: 7-inch
DELUXE............................... 10-20 57
MALA 5-10 59-60
PROMO 8-12 61
LPs: 10/12-inch 33rpm
CHESS............................... 15-25 66

LANCE, Major
P&R/R&B/LP '63
Singles: 12-inch 33/45rpm
KAT FAMILY 4-6 82
Singles: 7-inch
COLUMBIA 3-5 77
CURTOM 3-5 70
DAKAR............................... 4-6 69
EPIC............................... 4-8 66
KAT FAMILY 3-4 82
MERCURY (71582 "Phyllis") 20-30 60
OKEH (7175 thru 7197) 5-10 63-64
OKEH (7200 "Think Nothing About It") 25-50 64
OKEH (7203 thru 7266) 8-15 64-66

OKEH (7284 "You Don't Want Me No More") 25-50 67
OKEH (7298 "Forever") 5-10 67
OSIRIS 3-5 75
PLAYBOY 3-5 74-75
SOUL 3-5 78
VOLT 3-5 72

Picture Sleeves

OKEH 4-8 63-65

EPs: 7-inch 33/45rpm

OKEH 10-15 64
(Jukebox issue only.)

LPs: 10/12-inch 33rpm

BACK-TRAC 5-8 85
CONTEMPO 10-12
KAT FAMILY 5-8 83
OKEH 15-20 63-64
SOUL 5-8 78

LANCERS

P&R '53

Singles: 78rpm

CORAL 4-6 54-56

Singles: 7-inch

CORAL 5-10 54-56
LANCELOT 4-8
SWF 4-8 62
TREND 5-10 54

Picture Sleeves

SWF 4-8 62

EPs: 7-inch 33/45rpm

CORAL 10-20 55
Members: Jerry Meacham; Dick Burr; Bob Porter; Corky Lindgren.

LANDIS, Jerry
(Paul Simon)

P&R '63

Singles: 7-inch

AMY (875 "Lone Teen Ranger") 25-35 62
CANADIAN AMERICAN (130 "I'm Lonely") 25-50 61
MGM (12822 "Anna Belle") 25-50 59
WARWICK (552 "Just a Boy") ... 25-50 60
WARWICK (558 "Just a Boy") ... 25-50 60
WARWICK (619 "Play Me a Sad Song") 40-60 61
Also see SIMON, Paul

LANDS, Liz

Singles: 7-inch

GORDY (7026 "What He Lived For") 20-25 63
ONE-DERFUL 5-10 67

LANDS, Liz / Martin Luther King

Singles: 7-inch

GORDY (7023 "We Shall Overcome") 15-25 63
Also see KING, Rev. Martin Luther, Jr.

LANDS, Liz, & Temptations

Singles: 7-inch

GORDY (7030 "Keep Me") 25-50 64
Also see LANDS, Liz
Also see TEMPTATIONS

LANE, Mickey Lee

P&R '64

Singles: 7-inch

MALA 5-8 68
SWAN 5-10 64-66

LANE, Robin, & Chartbusters

P&R '80

Singles: 7-inch

W.B. 3-5 80-81

Picture Sleeves

W.B. 3-5 80

LPs: 10/12-inch 33rpm

W.B. 5-8 80-81
Members: Robin Lane; Leroy Radcliffe; Asa Brebner; Scott Baerenwald; Tim Jackson.

LANE BROTHERS

P&R '57

Singles: 78rpm

RCA 5-10 57

Singles: 7-inch

FXL 3-4 81
LEADER 5-8 60
RCA 5-10 57-58
Members: Pete Lane, Arthur Lane, Frank Lane.

LANE BROTHERS / Julius La Rosa

EPs: 7-inch 33/45rpm

RCA 5-10 57
(Promotional issue only.)
Also see LANE BROTHERS
Also see LA ROSA, Julius

LANG, K.D.
(k.d. lang & the Reclines)

LP '88

Singles: 7-inch

SIRE 3-4 88-91

LPs: 10/12-inch 33rpm

SIRE 5-8 88-90
Also see DION
Also see ORBISON, Roy, & K.D. Lang

LANI & BONI

Singles: 7-inch

GARPAX (4084 "Cherry Pie") 10-15 64
Members: Delaney Bramlett; Bonnie Bramlett.
Also see DELANEY & BONNIE

LANIER & CO.

P&R/R&B '82

Singles: 7-inch

LARC 3-4 82-83

LPs: 10/12-inch 33rpm

LARC 5-8 83
Member: Farris Lanier Jr.

LANIN, Lester, & His Orchestra

LP '57

Singles: 78rpm

EPIC 3-5 56-57

Singles: 7-inch

EPIC 4-8 56-62

EPs: 7-inch 33/45rpm

EPIC 4-8 56-58

LPs: 10/12-inch 33rpm

EPIC 5-15 56-62

LANOIS, Daniel

LP '90

LPs: 10/12-inch 33rpm

W.B./OPAL 5-8 89

LANSON, Snooky

P&R '48

Singles: 78rpm

DECCA 3-5 52
DOT 3-5 55-56
LONDON 3-5 49-51
MERCURY 4-6 48
REPUBLIC 3-5 53

Singles: 7-inch

DECCA 5-10 52
DOT 5-10 55-56
LONDON 5-10 50-51
REPUBLIC 5-10 53
STARDAY 3-6 68

LPs: 10/12-inch 33rpm

CAMDEN (200 series) 10-20 55
DOT 10-15 60
STARDAY 5-10 68

LANZ, David

(With Paul Speer)

LP '88

LPs: 10/12-inch 33rpm

NARADA 5-8 88

LANZA, Mario

P&R '50

Singles: 78rpm

RCA 3-5 50-57

Singles: 7-inch

RCA (0400 series) 3-5 71
RCA (3200 thru 8500 series) 5-10 51-59
RCA (1300 series) 4-6 50

Picture Sleeves

RCA (3300 "The Loveliest Night of the Year") 15-25 51
RCA (4209 "Song of India") 15-25 51
RCA 5-8 50s
(For generic, die-cut paper sleeves with artist photo. Not for any specific release.)

EPs: 7-inch 33/45rpm

RCA (Except 1837) 8-15 53-61
RCA (1837 "Student Prince") 15-25 54
(Soundtrack.)

LPs: 10/12-inch 33rpm

CAMDEN (Except 400 series) 5-15 63
CAMDEN (400 series) 10-20 57
(With "CAL" prefix. Monaural.)
CAMDEN (400 series) 8-15 63
(With "CAS" prefix. Stereo.)
RCA (75 "Toast of New Orleans") 45-60 51
(Soundtrack. (10-inch LP.)
RCA (86 thru 1181) 20-30 51-53
RCA (1750 "A Legendary Performer") 5-8 76
RCA (1837 "Student Prince") 35-45 54
(Soundtrack.)
RCA (1860 thru 2090) 15-25 54-57
(Black label.)
RCA (1860 thru 2090) 6-12 68
(Orange label.)
RCA (2211 "Seven Hills of Rome") 20-30 58
(Soundtrack tunes on side one, other Mario Lanza songs on side two.)
RCA (2331 thru 2333) 15-25 59-61
(Black label.)
RCA (2331 thru 2333) 6-12 68
(Orange label.)
RCA (2338 "For the First Time") 20-30 59
(Soundtrack.)
RCA (2339 thru 2790) 10-20 60-64
(Black label.)
RCA (2339 thru 2790) 6-12 68
(Orange label.)
RCA (2800 series) 4-8 78
RCA (2900 thru 3200) 8-15 68-71
RCA (4158 "The Mario Lanza Collection") 35-45 81
(Five-LP boxed set.)

LARKIN, Billy

(With the Delegates)

LP '66

Singles: 78rpm

MELODY 20-30 56

Singles: 7-inch

BRYAN 3-5 75
CASINO 3-5 76
MELODY (103 "Rock-it, Davy Crockett") 50-75 56
MERCURY 3-5 78-79
SUNBIRD 3-5 80-81
WORLD PACIFIC 4-8 66

LPs: 10/12-inch 33rpm

AURA 15-25 65-66
BRYAN 5-10 75
WORLD PACIFIC 10-20 65-69

LARKS

R&B '51

Singles: 78rpm

APOLLO (427 "Eyesight to the Blind")............................. 75-125 51
APOLLO (429 "Little Side Car")................................... 50-100 51
APOLLO (430 "Ooh . . . It Feels So Good") 50-100 51
APOLLO (435 "My Lost Love") 50-100 51
APOLLO (437 "Darlin'")........... 50-100 52
APOLLO (475 "Honey from the Bee") 20-40 55
APOLLO (1177 "My Heart Cries for You")............................... 50-100 51
APOLLO (1180 "Hopefully Yours") 50-100 51
APOLLO (1184 "My Reverie"). 50-100 51
APOLLO (1189 "Shadrack").... 50-100 52
APOLLO (1190 "Stolen Love") 50-100 52
APOLLO (1194 "Hold Me") 50-100 52
LLOYDS (108 "Margie")........... 50-75 54
LLOYDS (110 "If It's a Crime").. 50-75 54
LLOYDS (112 "No Other Girl").. 50-75 54
LLOYDS (114 "Forget It")......... 50-75 54

Singles: 7-inch

APOLLO (429 "Little Side Car")................................... 400-600 51
APOLLO (430 "Ooh, It Feels So Good") 400-600 51
APOLLO (435 "My Lost Love")............................... 400-600 51
APOLLO (437 "Darlin'")......... 500-750 52
APOLLO (475 "Honey from the Bee") 150-250 55
APOLLO (1180 "Hopefully Yours") 400-600 51
APOLLO (1184 "My Reverie") 750-1000 51
(Black vinyl)
APOLLO (1184 "My Reverie") 1000-1500 51
(Colored vinyl.)
APOLLO (1189 "Shadrack").. 400-600 52
APOLLO (1190 "Stolen Love")................................ 400-600 52
(Black vinyl)
APOLLO (1190 "Stolen Love")............................. 750-1000 52
(Colored vinyl)
APOLLO (1194 "Hold Me") ... 400-600 52
LLOYDS (108 "Margie")........ 400-500 54
LLOYDS (110 "If It's a Crime")............................... 300-400 54
LLOYDS (112 "No Other Girl")................................. 400-500 54
LLOYDS (114 "Forget It")...... 250-350 54

Members: Gene Mumford; Allen Bunn; Ray Barnes; Thermon Ruth; Dave McNeil; Hadie Rowe; Orville Brooks.
Also see FIVE LARKS

LARKS

P&R '61

Singles: 7-inch

CROSS FIRE...........................10-15
GUYDEN...................................5-10 63
JETT (3001 "Love Me True") 35-55 65
SHERYL...................................10-20 61
STACY 4-8 63
VIOLET 10-15 63

LARKS
(Don Julian & the Larks)

P&R '64

Singles: 7-inch

JERK...4-8 65
MONEY 4-8 64-71

LPs: 10/12-inch 33rpm

AMAZON (1009 "Greatest Hits") 45-55 63
MONEY...................................15-20 65-67
Also see MASON, Barbara, & Larks

LA ROSA, Julius

P&R '53

Singles: 78rpm

CADENCE 3-6 53-55

Singles: 7-inch

ABC...4-6 67
BARNABY 3-5 70
CADENCE (1200 series) 5-10 53-55
CADENCE (1400 series) 4-8 63-64
KAPP 4-8 60-62
MGM 4-6 66
MGM CELEBRITY SCENE (CS5-5 "Julius LaRosa") 10-20 66
(Boxed set of five singles with bio insert and title strips.)
METROMEDIA..............................3-5 70
RCA (0900 series) 3-5 73
RCA (6000 & 7000 series)...........5-10 56-58
ROULETTE...................................4-8 59

EPs: 7-inch 33/45rpm

CADENCE 5-15 54-58
RCA (EPA-841 "Julius LaRosa") .5-10 56
RCA (EPB-1299 "Julius LaRosa")................................15-25 56

LPs: 10/12-inch 33rpm

CADENCE (1007 "Julie's Best") 20-30 55
FORUM....................................10-15 60
KAPP 10-15 61
MGM 10-15 66-67
METROMEDIA.............................5-10 71
RCA (1299 "Julius LaRosa")......20-30 56
ROULETTE.................................10-20 59
Also see LANE BROTHERS / Julius La Rosa

LA ROSA, Julius, & Bob Crewe Generation

Singles: 7–inch

CREWE 3-6 69

Also see CREWE, Bob
Also see LA ROSA, Julius

LARRICE

D&D '84

Singles: 12–inch 33/45rpm

STREETWISE 4-6 84

LARRY & JOHNNY

Singles: 7–inch

JOLA (1000 "Beatle Time") 10-15 64

Members: Larry Williams; Johnny "Guitar" Watson.
Also see WILLIAMS, Larry, & Johnny Watson

LARRY LEE: see LEE, Larry

LARSEN, Neil

LP '79

Singles: 7–inch

A&M 3-5 79
W.B. 3-4 83

LPs: 10/12–inch 33rpm

A&M 5-8 79
HORIZON 8-10 78-79
W.B. 5-8 83

Also see LARSEN - FEITEN BAND

LARSEN - FEITEN BAND

P&R/LP '80

Singles: 7–inch

W.B. 3-5 80

LPs: 10/12–inch 33rpm

W.B. 5-8 80

Members: Neil Larsen; Buzz Feiten.
Also see LARSEN, Neil
Also see MR. MISTER

LARSON, Nicolette

P&R/LP '78

Singles: 7–inch

MCA 3-4 85-86
W.B. 3-5 78-82

LPs: 10/12–inch 33rpm

MCA 5-8 86
W.B. 5-8 78-82

Session: Steve Wariner.
Also see DOOBIE BROTHERS & Nicolette Larson
Also see NITTY GRITTY DIRT BAND
Also see WARINER, Steve
Also see WINCHESTER, Jesse
Also see YOUNG, Neil

LA RUE, D.C.

P&R/LP '76

Singles: 12–inch 33/45rpm

CASABLANCA 4-6 79-80
PYRAMID 4-8 78-79

Singles: 7–inch

CASABLANCA 3-5 79-80
PYRAMID 4-6 76-79

LPs: 10/12–inch 33rpm

CASABLANCA 5-8 79-80
PYRAMID 5-10 76-79

Also see CHRISTIE, Lou

LA SALLE, Denise

P&R/R&B '71

Singles: 7–inch

ABC 3-5 77-79
CHESS 4-8 68
MCA 3-5 79-80
MALACO 3-4 81-85
TARPEN 4-8 67
WESTBOUND 3-5 71-75

LPs: 10/12–inch 33rpm

ABC 8-10 77-78
MCA 5-8 80
MALACO 5-8 81-85
WESTBOUND 8-10 72-75

LASLEY, David

P&R/R&B '82

Singles: 12–inch 33/45rpm

EMI AMERICA 4-6 84

Singles: 7–inch

EMI AMERICA 3-4 82-84

LASSIES

P&R '56

Singles: 78rpm

DECCA 4-8 56

Singles: 7–inch

DECCA 8-12 56

LAST, James
(James Last Band)

P&R/LP '72

Singles: 7–inch

POLYDOR 3-5 71-82

LPs: 10/12–inch 33rpm

POLYDOR 5-10 72-81

LAST POETS

LP '70

Singles: 7–inch

DOUGLAS 3-5 71

LPs: 10/12–inch 33rpm

BLUE THUMB 8-12 72-73
DOUGLAS 10-15 70-71

LAST WORD
(Last Words)

P&R '67

Singles: 7–inch

ATCO 4-8 67-68
BOOM 4-8 66
DOWNEY 5-10 65

LPs: 10/12–inch 33rpm

ATCO 10-20 68

LATEEF, Yusef
(Yusef Lateef Quintet)

LP '69

Singles: 7-Inch

ATLANTIC 3-5 68-70
IMPULSE 3-6 64
NEW JAZZ 4-8 60
PRESTIGE 3-6 63-69

LPs: 10/12-Inch 33rpm

ATLANTIC 8-15 68-76
CTI 5-8 77-79
CADET 10-15 69
CHARLIE PARKER 20-30 62
EVEREST 5-10 74
IMPULSE (56 thru 9125) 10-20 63-66
IMPULSE (9200 & 9300 series) .. 5-10 73-78
MILESTONE 8-12 73
MOODSVILLE 25-35 61
NEW JAZZ 25-40 59-61
PRESTIGE (7122 "The Sounds of Yusef Lateef") 50-100 57
(Yellow label.)
PRESTIGE (7400 thru 7800 series) 10-20 66-71
PRESTIGE (24000 series) 8-15 72-74
RIVERSIDE (300 series) 20-30 60
(Monaural.)
RIVERSIDE (3000 series) 10-20 68
RIVERSIDE (9300 series) 25-35 60
(Stereo.)
SAVOY (2200 series) 8-12 76-79
SAVOY (12000 series) 25-50 56-58
SAVOY (13000 series) 25-50 58
TRIP 5-10 73
VERVE (8217 "Before Dawn") 50-100 57
(Reads "Verve Records, Inc." at bottom of label.)
VERVE (8217 "Before Dawn") .. 25-35 60s
(Reads "MGM Records - a Division of Metro-Goldwyn-Mayer, Inc." at bottom of label.)

LATIMORE, Benny
(Latimore)

R&B '73

Singles: 7-inch

ATLANTIC 4-8 69
DADE 5-10 67-68
GLADES 3-6 73-79
HIT 4-6 60s
MALACO 3-4 83-86

LPs: 10/12-inch 33rpm

GLADES 8-10 73-78
MALACO 5-8 83-86

LATTISAW, Stacy

R&B '79

Singles: 7-inch

COTILLION 3-5 79-84
MOTOWN 3-4 86-88

Picture Sleeves

MOTOWN 3-4 86

LPs: 10/12-inch 33rpm

COTILLION 5-8 79-84
MOTOWN 5-8 86-88
Also see KING DREAM CHORUS & Holiday Crew

LATTISAW, Stacy, & Johnny Gill

R&B/D&D/LP '84

Singles: 7-inch

COTILLION 3-5 84-85

LPs: 10/12-inch 33rpm

COTILLION 5-8 84
Also see GILL, Johnny
Also see LATTISAW, Stacy

LAUPER, Cyndi

P&R/LP '83

Singles: 12-inch 33/45rpm

PORTRAIT 4-6 83-87

Singles: 7-inch

EPIC 3-4 88-89
PORTRAIT 3-4 83-87

Picture Sleeves

EPIC 3-5 88
PORTRAIT 3-4 83-87

LPs: 10/12-inch 33rpm

PORTRAIT 5-8 83-86
Also see BLUE ANGEL
Also see HOOTERS
Also see U.S.A. for AFRICA

LAURA & JOHNNY

R&B '69

Singles: 7-inch

SILVER FOX 4-6 69

LAURA LEE: see LEE, Laura

LAURAN, Niki

D&D '83

Singles: 12-inch 33/45rpm

WAVE 4-6 83

LAUREN, Rod

P&R '59

Singles: 7-inch

CHANCELLOR 4-8 62
RCA 6-12 59-62

Picture Sleeves

RCA 5-10 59-60

LPs: 10/12-inch 33rpm

RCA (LPM-2176 "I'm Rod Lauren") 20-30 61
(Monaural.)
RCA (LSP-2176 "I'm Rod Lauren") 30-40 61
(Stereo.)
Also see COOKE, Sam / Rod Lauren / Neil Sedaka / Browns

LAURENCE, Paul

R&B '85

Singles: 12-inch 33/45rpm

CAPITOL 4-6 86

LAURIE, Annie

Singles: 7-inch

CAPITOL 3-4 85-86

LPs: 10/12-inch 33rpm

CAPITOL 5-8 86

Also see JACKSON, Freddie
Also see THOMAS, Lillo

LAURIE, Annie

R&B '49

Singles: 78rpm

DELUXE 5-10 47-49
REGAL 5-10 49
OKEH 5-10 55
SAVOY 5-10 56

Singles: 7-inch

DELUXE 8-15 57-60
DOVE 4-6 68
GUSTO 3-5 78
OKEH 10-15 55
RITZ 4-8 62
SAVOY 10-15 56

LPs: 10/12-inch 33rpm

AUDIO LAB (1510 "It Hurts to Be in Love") 40-50 58

LAURIE, Linda

P&R '59

Singles: 7-inch

ANDIE 5-10 60
GLORY 5-10 59
KEETCH 4-8 64
RECONA 4-8 63
RUST 4-8 60-63

LAURIE SISTERS

P&R '55

Singles: 78rpm

MERCURY 4-6 54-55
VIK 4-6 56

Singles: 7-inch

MGM 5-10 59-60
MERCURY 5-10 54-55
PORT 4-8 63
VIK 5-10 56

LPs: 10/12-inch 33rpm

CAMDEN (CAL-545 "Hits of the Great Girl Groups") 15-25 60
(Monaural.)
CAMDEN (CAS-545 "Hits of the Great Girl Groups") 25-35 60
(Stereo.)

LAVERNE & SHIRLEY

P&R '76

Singles: 7-inch

ATLANTIC 3-6 76-77

LPs: 10/12-inch 33rpm

ATLANTIC 8-10 76

Members: Penny Marshall; Cindy Williams.

LAVETTE, Betty

(Betty Lavett; Bettye LaVette)

R&B '62

Singles: 7-inch

ATCO 3-5 72
ATLANTIC 8-12 62-63
BIG WHEEL 4-8 66
CALLA 4-8 65
EPIC 3-5 75
KAREN 4-6 68-69
LUPINE (123 "Witch Craft in the Air") 20-30 64
LUPINE (1021 "Witch Craft in the Air") 10-15 64
MOTOWN 3-5 81-82
SSS INT'L 3-5 71
SILVER FOX 4-6 69
TCA 3-5 71
WEST END 4-8

LPs: 10/12-inch 33rpm

MOTOWN 5-8 81

LAWRENCE, Eddie

P&R '56

Singles: 78rpm

CORAL 3-5 56-57

Singles: 7-inch

CORAL 4-8 56-63
EPIC 4-6 65
SHASTA 4-8 60
SIGNATURE 4-8 60

Picture Sleeves

CORAL 5-10 56
EPIC 4-8 65

LPs: 10/12-inch 33rpm

CORAL 12-25 55-62
EPIC 8-15 65
SIGNATURE 10-20 59

LAWRENCE, Steve

P&R '52

Singles: 78rpm

CORAL 4-8 55-57
KING 4-8 52-53

Singles: 7-inch

ABC 3-5 73
ABC-PAR 5-10 58-60
CALENDAR 4-8 67-68
COLUMBIA 4-8 62-68
CORAL 5-15 55-59
KING (1200 series) 5-10 53
KING (5000 series) 4-8 60-64
KING (15000 series) 5-10 52-53
MGM 3-5 71-73
RCA 3-6 69-70
ROULETTE 3-5 73
STAGE 2 .... 3-4 84
20TH FOX 3-5 75-77
U.A. (200 & 300 series) 4-8 60-61
U.A. (900 thru 1100 series) 3-5 76-78

W.B.	3-5	78

Picture Sleeves

COLUMBIA	4-8	62-63
STAGE 2	3-4	84
U.A.	5-10	60-61

EPs: 7-inch 33/45rpm

COLUMBIA (Jukebox issues only.)	5-10	64-69
CORAL (Jukebox issues only.)	5-10	60
KING	10-20	53
RCA	4-8	70

LPs: 10/12-inch 33rpm

ABC-PAR	20-30	57-60
APPLAUSE	5-10	81
COLUMBIA	10-25	63-68
COLUMBIA RECORD CLUB	8-15	75
CORAL (57050 "About That Girl")	20-40	56
CORAL (57182 "Songs By Steve Lawrence")	20-30	57
CORAL (57204 "Here's Steve Lawrence")	20-30	57
CORAL (57268 "All About Love") (Monaural.)	20-30	58
CORAL (57434 "Songs Everybody Knows") (Monaural.)	12-20	62
CORAL (757268 "All About Love") (Stereo.)	20-40	58
CORAL (757434 "Songs Everybody Knows") (Stereo.)	15-25	62
GALA	5-10	77
GUEST STAR	5-10	64
HARMONY	6-12	68-71
KING (593 "Steve Lawrence")	25-35	58
MGM	5-10	71
RCA	6-12	69-70
SESAC (Promotional issues only.)	10-20	59
SPINORAMA	8-15	63
U.A.	10-20	61-64
VERSATILE	5-8	77
VOCALION	5-12	66-69

LAWRENCE, Steve / Tennessee Ernie Ford

LPs: 10/12-inch 33rpm

CAMAY	15-25	60

Also see FORD, Tennessee Ernie

LAWRENCE, Steve, & Eydie Gorme

(Steve & Eydie)

P&R '63

Singles: 78rpm

CORAL	4-8	55

Singles: 7-inch

CALENDAR	4-6	68
COLUMBIA	4-8	62-67
CORAL	5-10	55
MGM	3-5	72-73
RCA	3-5	68-69

EPs: 7-inch 33/45rpm

ABC (Jukebox issues only.)	5-10	60
ADVERTISING COUNCIL (5071 "Celebrity Spots") (Promotional issue, with other artists.)	15-30	
COLUMBIA (Jukebox issues only.)	5-10	64-69
CORAL	10-15	58

LPs: 10/12-inch 33rpm

ABC	5-10	73-76
ABC/LONGINES ("Romantic Treasury") (Six-LP boxed set.)	30-45	67
ABC-PAR	15-25	59-64
CBS	10-15	63
CALENDAR	8-15	68
COLUMBIA	10-20	63-67
CORAL (57336 "Steve and Eydie")	15-25	60
ENCORE	5-8	84
HARMONY	5-10	64-71
MCA	5-10	
MGM	5-10	72-73
MATI-MOR (8003 "It's Us Again") (Promotional issue made for Silvikrin Shampoo.)	10-15	
PICKWICK	5-10	70s
RCA	6-12	69-72
STAGE 2	5-10	78-84
U.A.	10-20	61-62
VOCALION	5-12	67

Also see GORME, Eydie
Also see OSMONDS, Steve Lawrence & Eydie Gorme

LAWRENCE, Steve / Trini Lopez

LPs: 10/12-inch 33rpm

DIPLOMAT	10-15	65

Also see LAWRENCE, Steve
Also see LOPEZ, Trini

LAWRENCE, Vicki

P&R/C&W/LP '73

Singles: 7-inch

BELL	3-5	73-74
ELF	4-6	69
FLASHBACK	3-5	74
PRIVATE STOCK	3-5	75-76
U.A.	3-5	71

LPs: 10/12-inch 33rpm

BELL	8-12	73
WINDMILL	5-10	79

LAWS, Debra

P&R/R&B/LP '81

Singles: 7-inch

ELEKTRA 3-5 80-81

LPs: 10/12-inch 33rpm

ELEKTRA 5-8 81

LAWS, Eloise

P&R/R&B/LP '78

Singles: 7-inch

ABC 3-5 77-78
CAPITOL 3-4 82
COLUMBIA 4-6 68-70
INVICTUS 3-5 75-77
LIBERTY 3-5 80-81
MUSIC MERCHANT 3-5 72-73

Picture Sleeves

LIBERTY 3-5 80

LPs: 10/12-inch 33rpm

ABC 8-10 77-78
CAPITOL 5-8 82
INVICTUS 5-10 76
LIBERTY 5-8 80

LAWS, Hubert

RLP '73

Singles: 7-Inch

ATLANTIC 4-6 65
CTI 3-5 70-75
COLUMBIA 3-4 78

LPs: 10/12-Inch 33rpm

ATLANTIC 8-18 66-81
CTI 8-15 70-77
COLUMBIA 5-10 76-80

LAWS, Hubert, & Earl Klugh

LP '80

LP: 10/12-inch 33rpm

COLUMBIA 5-10 80
Also see KLUGH, Earl
Also see LAWS, Hubert

LAWS, Ronnie
(With Pressure)

R&B/LP '75

Singles: 7-inch

BLUE NOTE 3-5 75-77
CAPITOL 3-4 83-84
LIBERTY 3-5 80-81
U.A. 3-5 75-80

LPs: 10/12-inch 33rpm

BLUE NOTE 6-12 75-77
CAPITOL 5-8 83
LIBERTY 5-10 81
U.A. 5-10 75-80
Also see EARTH, WIND, & FIRE
Also see PRESSURE

LAYNA, Magda

D&D '83

Singles: 12-inch 33/45rpm

MEGATONE 4-6 83

LAYNE, Joy

P&R '57

Singles: 78rpm

MERCURY 4-6 57

Singles: 7-inch

LUCKY FOUR 4-8 61
MERCURY 5-10 57

LAZY RACER

P&R '79

Singles: 7-inch

A&M 3-5 79-80

LPs: 10/12-inch 33rpm

A&M 5-10 79-80

LEACH, Billy

P&R '57

Singles: 78rpm

BALLY 4-6 57

Singles: 7-inch

BALLY 5-10 57

LEADON, Bernie
(With the Michael Georgiades Band)

LP '77

Singles: 7-inch

ASYLUM 3-5 77

LPs: 10/12-inch 33rpm

ASYLUM 8-10 77
Also see EAGLES

LEAGUE UNLIMITED ORCHESTRA

LP '82

Singles: 7-inch

A&M 3-4 82

LPs: 10/12-inch 33rpm

A&M 5-8 82
Also see HUMAN LEAGUE

LEAPY LEE

C&W/P&R '68

Singles: 7-inch

CADET 4-6 69
DECCA 4-8 68-71
MAM 3-5 72
MCA 3-5 75

Picture Sleeves

MCA 3-5 75

LPs: 10/12-inch 33rpm

DECCA 12-20 68

LEATHERWOLF

LP '88

LPs: 10/12-inch 33rpm

ISLAND 5-8 88-89

LEAVES

P&R/LP '66

Singles: 7-inch

CAPITOL (5799 "Lemon Princess") 8-12 66
MIRA (202 "Too Many People") 8-12 65

MIRA (207 "Hey Joe, Where You Gonna Go") 10-12 65
MIRA (213 "You Better Move On") 5-10 66
MIRA (222 "Hey Joe"/"Funny Little World") 5-10 66
MIRA (222 "Hey Joe"/"Girl from the East") 5-10 66
MIRA (227 "Too Many People") 5-8 66
MIRA (231 "Get Out of My Life Woman") 5-10 66
MIRA (234 "You Better Move On") 5-10 66
PANDA (1003 "Hey Joe") 8-12 82
(Colored vinyl, leaf-shaped disc.)

LPs: 10/12-inch 33rpm

CAPITOL (T-2638 "All the Good That's Happening") 25-50 67
(Monaural.)
CAPITOL (ST-2638 "All the Good That's Happening") 30-60 67
(Stereo.)
MIRA (LP-3005 "Hey Joe") 25-35 66
(Monaural.)
MIRA (LPS-3005 "Hey Joe") 30-40 66
(Stereo.)

Members: John Beck; Bob Arlin; Jim Pons; Tom Ray, Bill Rheinhart; Robert Reiner; Jim Kern.
Also see MERRY-GO-ROUND
Also see MOTHERS of INVENTION
Also see TURTLES

LEAVILLE, Otis
(Otis Leavill)

R&B '65

Singles: 7-inch

BLUE ROCK 8-12 65
BRUNSWICK 5-10 67
COLUMBIA 5-10 66
DAKAR 4-8 69-70
LIMELIGHT (3020 "I'm Amazed") 10-20 64
LIMELIGHT (3037 "Jane Girl").. 10-20 64
LUCKY (1004 "Got a Right to Cry") 25-40 64
SMASH 4-8 68

LEAVY, Calvin

R&B '70

Singles: 7-inch

BLUE FOX 3-5 70

LE BLANC, Lenny

P&R '77

Singles: 7-inch

BIG TREE 3-6 76-77
CAPITOL 3-5 81

LPs: 10/12-inch 33rpm

BIG TREE 8-12 76-77
CAPITOL 5-10 81

LE BLANC & CARR

LP '78

Singles: 7-inch

BIG TREE 3-5 77-78

LPs: 10/12-inch 33rpm

ATLANTIC (003 "Live from the Atlantic Studios") 8-12 78
(Promotional issue only.)
BIG TREE 8-10 77

Members: Lenny LeBlanc; Pete Carr.
Also see LE BLANC, Lenny

LED ZEPPELIN

P&R/LP '69

Singles: 7-inch

ATLANTIC (2613 "Good Times Bad Times") 10-15 69
ATLANTIC (2690 "Whole Lotta Love") 5-8 69
(Edited version [3:12].)
ATLANTIC (2777 "The Immigrant Song"/ "Hey Hey, What Can I Do") 15-25 70
(Has "Do What Thou Wilt Shall Be the Whole of the Law" etched in the vinyl trail-off.)
ATLANTIC (2777 "The Immigrant Song"/ "Hey Hey, What Can I Do") 10-15 70
(Does not have "Do What Thou Wilt Shall Be the Whole of the Law" etched in the vinyl trail-off.)
ATLANTIC (2849 "Black Dog") 5-10 71
ATLANTIC (2865 "Rock & Roll").. 5-10 72
ATLANTIC (2970 "Over the Hills and Far Away") 5-10 73
ATLANTIC (2986 "D'yer Mak'er"). 5-10 73
ATLANTIC (13116 "Whole Lotta Love") 4-6 70s
ATLANTIC (13131 "The Immigrant Song") 4-6 70s
ATLANTIC (13129 "Black Dog") 4-6 70s
ATLANTIC (13130 "Rock & Roll").. 4-6 70s
Note: Atlantic 13000 numbers are "Oldies Series" reissues.
SWAN SONG (70102 "Trampled Under Foot") 4-6 75
SWAN SONG (70110 "Candy Store Rock") 4-6 76
SWAN SONG (71003 "Fool in the Rain") 4-6 76

Picture Sleeves

ATLANTIC (175 "Stairway to Heaven") 50-75 72
(Promotional issue only.)

Promotional Singles

ATLANTIC (157 "Gallows Pole") 50-75 71
ATLANTIC (175 "Stairway to Heaven") 50-75 72
ATLANTIC (269 "Stairway to Heaven") 20-30 77

ATLANTIC (1019 "Dazed and Confused") 75-100 69
(With picture sleeve.)
ATLANTIC (2613 "Good Times Bad Times") 25-35 69
(Black and white label.)
ATLANTIC (2613 "Good Times Bad Times") 20-30 69
(Red and white label.)
ATLANTIC (2690 "Whole Lotta Love"/ "Living Loving Maid").............. 15-25 69
ATLANTIC (2690 "Whole Lotta Love" [5:33] / Whole Lotta Love" [3:12])........ 25-35 69
ATLANTIC (2777 "The Immigrant Song"/ "The Immigrant Song")........... 15-25 70
ATLANTIC (2777 "The Immigrant Song"/ Blank).................................. 15-25 70
(Single-sided.)
ATLANTIC (2849 "Black Dog") . 15-20 71
ATLANTIC (2865 "Rock & Roll") 15-20 72
ATLANTIC (2970 "Over the Hills and Far Away") 10-20 73
ATLANTIC (2986 "D'yer Mak'er")................................ 10-20 73
SWAN SONG (70102 "Trampled Under Foot")........................ 10-15 75
SWAN SONG (70110 "Candy Store Rock").......................... 10-15 76
SWAN SONG (71003 "Fool in the Rain") 10-15 76
(Blue label. Side one runs 6:08; side two is edited [3:20].)
SWAN SONG (71003 "Fool in the Rain") 8-12 76
(White label. Both sides run 6:08.)

EPs: 7–inch 33/45rpm

ATLANTIC (7-7208 "Led Zeppelin")............................... 50-75 71
(Jukebox issue only.)
ATLANTIC (7-7255 "Houses of the Holy") 50-75 73
(Jukebox issue only.)

LPs: 10/12–inch 33rpm

ATLANTIC (7201 "Led Zeppelin III")........................... 10-15 70
ATLANTIC (7208 "Led Zeppelin IV") 10-15 71
(Their fourth LP though no title is actually shown on cover.)
ATLANTIC (7255 "Houses of the Holy") 15-20 73
(With "Led Zeppelin paper band around cover.)
ATLANTIC (7255 "Houses of the Holy") 10-15 73
(Without "Led Zeppelin paper band around cover.)
ATLANTIC (8216 "Led Zeppelin")..............................50-100 69
(Pink and brown label.)
ATLANTIC (8216 "Led Zeppelin")................................10-20 69
(Red and green label.)
ATLANTIC (8236 "Led Zeppelin II")............................10-15 69
ATLANTIC (19126 "Led Zeppelin")..................................5-10 72
ATLANTIC (19127 "Led Zeppelin II")................................5-10 72
ATLANTIC (19128 "Led Zeppelin III")..............................5-10 72
ATLANTIC (19129 "Led Zeppelin IV") 5-10 72
ATLANTIC (19130 "Houses of the Holy") 5-10 73
ATLANTIC (82144 "Led Zeppelin")...............................50-75
(Six-LP boxed set. Includes 36-page booklet.)
ATLANTIC MUSIC SERVICE 10-15 69
(Record club issue.)
MFSL (065 "Led Zeppelin II").....25-50 82
SWAN SONG (2-200 "Physical Graffiti")..................................10-15 75
SWAN SONG (2-201 "The Song Remains the Same")...............10-15 76
(Embossed print on cover. With bound-in eight-page booklet. Soundtrack.)
SWAN SONG (2-201 "The Song Remains the Same")................8-12 76
(Standard, not-embossed, cover.)
SWAN SONG (8416 "Presence") 8-12 76
SWAN SONG (16002 "In Through the Out Door")...........................8-12 79
SWAN SONG (90051 "Coda").....8-10 82

Promotional LPs

ATLANTIC (7201 "Led Zeppelin III")..........................25-40 70
(White label. Monaural.)
ATLANTIC (7201 "Led Zeppelin III")............................15-25 70
(White label. Stereo.)
ATLANTIC (7208 "Led Zeppelin IV") 15-25 71
(White label. No title actually shown on cover; however, it was their fourth LP.)
ATLANTIC (7225 "Houses of the Holy") 25-40 73
(White label. Monaural.)
ATLANTIC (7225 "Houses of the Holy") 15-25 73
(White label. Stereo.)
ATLANTIC (8216 "Led Zeppelin")................................20-40 69
(White label.)

ATLANTIC (8236 "Led Zeppelin II")............................ 20-40 69
(White label.)
SWAN SONG (200 "Physical Graffiti")................................ 15-20 75
(With "FT" suffix.)
SWAN SONG (2-201 "The Song Remains the Same").............. 15-20 76
(With "MO" suffix.)
SWAN SONG (8416 "Presence")............................ 10-20 76
(With "MO" suffix.)
SWAN SONG (16002 "In Through the Out Door")......................... 10-15 79
(With "MO" suffix.)
SWAN SONG (90051 "Coda") .. 10-12 82
(With designate promo stamping on back cover.)

Members: Robert Plant; Jimmy Page; John Paul Jones; John Bonham.
Also see DENNY, Sandy
Also see HARPER, Roy
Also see JONES, John Paul
Also see PAGE, Jimmy
Also see PLANT, Robert

LED ZEPPELIN / King Curtis

Singles: 7-inch

ATLANTIC/ATCO (2690/6779 "Whole Lotta Love")........................... 40-50 71
(Promotional issue only. Atlantic label on Zep side; Atco label on flip, King Curtis' version of same song.)

Also see KING CURTIS
Also see LED ZEPPELIN

LEDERNACKEN

D&D '84

Singles: 12-inch 33/45rpm

4TH & BROADWAY 4-6 84

LEE, Alvin

(Alvin Lee & Company; with Ten Years Later)

LP '75

Singles: 7-inch

COLUMBIA 3-5 74
RSO 3-5 79

LPs: 10/12-inch 33rpm

ATLANTIC.................................. 5-8 80-81
COLUMBIA 10-12 73-75
LONDON.................................. 8-10 78
RSO 10-12 77-79
21 RECORDS 5-8 86

Also see TEN YEARS AFTER

LEE, Alvin, & Mylon LeFevre

LP '74

Singles: 7-inch

COLUMBIA 3-5 74

LPs: 10/12-inch 33rpm

COLUMBIA 10-12 73

Also see LEE, Alvin
Also see LE FEVRE, Mylon

LEE, Bobby

R&B '66

Singles: 7-inch

A-B-S (106 "Miss Mary")........150-200
CONFEDERATE..........................3-5
CUCA......................................5-10 62
DECCA 5-10 60-61
FALEW......................................4-8 64
GOLD COAST INT'L.....................4-8 60s
MUSICOR 4-6 68-69
MUSTANG..................................4-8 60s
PORT 4-8 67
RAMCO.....................................4-8 67
SAGE 5-8 60s
SUE...4-8 66
VISTONE 4-8 60s

LEE, Brenda

(With the Jordanaires; with Holladays)

P&R/C&W '57

Singles: 78rpm

DECCA 10-20 56-58

Singles: 7-inch

DECCA (30050 "Jambalaya")....20-30 56
DECCA (30107 "Christy Christmas")............................15-25 56
DECCA (30198 "One Step at a Time") 15-20 57
DECCA (30333 "Dynamite") 15-20 57
DECCA (30411 "One Teenager to Another").............................10-20 57
DECCA (30535 "Rock-A-Bye Baby Blues")...........................10-20 57
DECCA (30673 "Ring-A My Phone")..................................20-30 58
DECCA (30776 "Rockin' Around the Christmas Tree")...............10-15 58
DECCA (30806 "Bill Bailey")......10-15 59
DECCA (30967 "Sweet Nothin's") 8-12 59
(Price range of 30050 through 30967 is for black, pink or green label originals. Pink and green were promotional only. Decca multi-color labels in that series are $4 to $8 reissues.)
DECCA (31093 thru 32330).........5-10 60-68
DECCA (32428 thru 32975)..........4-6 69-72
DECCA (34330 "Interview").......10-20 72
(Promotional issue only.)
DECCA (88215 "I'm Gonna Lasso Santa Claus")..........................20-30 56
(Decca "Children's Series.")
ELEKTRA...................................3-5 78
MCA...3-5 73-86

Picture Sleeves

W.B. 3-4 91
DECCA (30776 "Rockin' Around the Christmas Tree")...............15-25 59

DECCA (30967 "Sweet Nothin's")................................ 25-35 59
DECCA (31093 thru 32428)........ 5-15 60-69
DECCA (34000 series)............... 5-10 62
(Compact 33 stereo.)
DECCA (88215 "I'm Gonna Lasso Santa Claus")......................... 30-40 56
(For either 45 or 78rpm single sleeve.)

EPs: 7–inch 33/45rpm

DECCA.................................... 10-20 60-65

LPs: 10/12–inch 33rpm

CORAL...................................... 5-10 73
DECCA (4039 thru 4104).......... 20-35 60-61
(Monaural.)
DECCA (4176 thru 4755).......... 15-30 61-66
(Monaural.)
DECCA (4757 "10 Golden Years")................................. 15-25 66
(Gatefold cover. Monaural.)
DECCA (4757 "10 Golden Years")................................. 10-15 60s
(Standard cover. Monaural.)
DECCA (4825 thru 4955).......... 10-20 66-68
(Monaural.)
DECCA (8873 "Grandma, What Great Songs You Sang")......... 30-40 59
(Monaural.)
DECCA (74039 thru 74104)...... 25-40 60-61
(Stereo.)
DECCA (74176 thru 74755)...... 20-35 61-66
(Stereo.)
DECCA (74757 "10 Golden Years")................................. 20-30 66
(Gatefold cover. Stereo.)
ECCA (74757 "10 Golden Years")................................. 10-15 60s
(Standard cover. Stereo.)
DECCA (74825 thru 75232)...... 10-20 66-70
(Stereo.)
DECCA (78873 "Grandma, What Great Songs You Sang")......... 35-45 59
(Stereo.)
MCA (Except 700 series)........... 8-10 73-86
MCA (700 series)......................... 5-8
VOCALION................................ 10-12 67-70
WARWICK (5083 "Little Miss Dynamite")............................. 5-10 80
(TV mail order offer.)
Session: Anita Kerr; Bob Moore; Boots Randolph; Jordanaires; James "Buzz" Cason.
Also see KERR, Anita
Also see MOORE, Bob
Also see NELSON, Willie, & Brenda Lee
Also see RANDOLPH, Boots

LEE, Brenda / Carl Dobkins, Jr.

EPs: 7–inch 33/45rpm

DECCA (38169 "Datesetters, U.S.A.")................................. 15-25 60
(Celanese Special Products issue.)
Also see DOBKINS, Carl, Jr.

LEE, Brenda / Bill Haley & Comets / Kalin Twins / Four Aces

EPs: 7–inch 33/45rpm

DECCA (7-2661 "Top Teen Hits")......................................15-25 59
(Stereo.)
Also see FOUR ACES
Also see HALEY, Bill
Also see KALIN TWINS

LEE, Brenda / Tennessee Ernie Ford

LPs: 10/12–inch 33rpm

DECCA (9226 "Brenda Lee/Tennessee Ernie Ford Show for Christmas Seals")..................................20-30
(Promotional issue only.)
Also see FORD, Tennessee Ernie

LEE, Brenda, & Pete Fountain

LP '68

Singles: 7–inch

DECCA 4-6 68

EPs: 7–inch 33/45rpm

DECCA (734528 "Brenda & Pete")5-10 68
(Jukebox issue.)

LPs: 10/12–inch 33rpm

DECCA 10-15 68
Also see FOUNTAIN, Pete

LEE, Brenda, & Oak Ridge Boys

Singles: 7–inch

MCA...3-5 82
Also see OAK RIDGE BOYS

LEE, Curtis

P&R '61

Singles: 7–inch

ABC..3-5 74
DUNES (801 "California GL-903")...............................10-20 60
DUNES (1001 "Pretty Little Angel Eyes")....................................25-35 60
DUNES (2001 "Special Love")...10-20 60
DUNES (2003 "Pledge of Love")10-20 61
DUNES (2007 "Pretty Little Angel Eyes")....................................10-20 61
DUNES (2008 "Under the Moon of Love")....................................10-20 61
DUNES (2010 "Let's Take a Ride")......................................10-20 61
DUNES (2012 "Just Another Fool")......................................10-20 62
DUNES (2015 "The Wobble")....10-20 62
DUNES (2017 "Afraid")............10-20 62
DUNES (2020 "Lonely Weekends")...........................10-20 63
DUNES (2021 "Pickin' Up the Pieces of My Heart").........................10-20 63
DUNES (2023 "I'm Sorry").........10-20 63
HOT (7 "Gotta Have You")..........25-35 60
MCA..3-4
MIRA (240 "Sweet Baby")..........10-20 67

ROJAC (114 "In My Bag")........... 5-10 67
SABRA (517 "Let's Take a Ride") 15-25 61
WARRIOR (1555 "With All My Heart")..................... 20-30 59

Picture Sleeves

DUNES (2003 "Pledge of Love")..................... 20-30 61
Also see HALOS

LEE, Dick
(With the Big Action Sound)

P&R '61

Singles: 78rpm

ESSEX 4-8 54
VIK 4-8 56
X.................... 4-8 55

Singles: 7-inch

ABC.................... 4-6 67
ACTION.................... 3-6
BLUE BELL 4-8 61
CAPITOL.................... 4-6 68
CENTAUR.................... 5-8 59
DOT.................... 4-8 66
ESSEX 5-10 54
FELSTED 5-8 60
KAPP.................... 4-6 69
MGM 5-10 59
METRO 4-8 65
ROULETTE.................... 4-8 62-63
20TH FOX.................... 4-8 65
VIK 5-10 56
X.................... 5-10 55

Picture Sleeves

FELSTED 8-12 60

LEE, Dickey
(With the Collegiates; Dickie Lee)

P&R/R&B/LP '62

Singles: 78rpm

SUN (280 "Good Lovin'")........... 10-20 57
SUN (297 "Dreamy Nights")...... 10-20 57
TAMPA.................... 10-15 57

Singles: 7-inch

ABC.................... 3-5 73
ATCO 4-8 68
DIAMOND 4-8 69
DICKIE LEE STORY 15-20 77
(No label name or number used. Promotional issue only.)
DOT.................... 10-15 60
ERIC.................... 3-5 70s
HALL 5-10 64
MERCURY 3-5 79-82
OLDIES 45 .... 4-6 65
RCA.................... 3-5 70-78
RENDEZVOUS (188 "Stay True Baby") 15-25 62
SMASH 4-8 62-64
SUN (280 "Good Lovin'")........... 15-25 57
SUN (297 "Dreamy Nights").......20-30 57
TCF.................... 4-8 65
TCF HALL.................... 4-8 64-65
TAMPA (131 "Dream Boy")........ 15-25 57
TRACIE.................... 4-8 67

LPs: 10/12-inch 33rpm

RCA 6-12 71-76
MERCURY.................... 5-8 79-80
SMASH 20-25 62
TCF HALL.................... 15-20 65

LEE, Dickey, & Kathy Burdick

C&W '81

Singles: 7-inch

MERCURY 3-4 81-82
Also see LEE, Dickey

LEE, Jackie

P&R '59

Singles: 7-inch

SWAN 5-10 59

LEE, Jackie
(Earl Nelson)

P&R/R&B '65

Singles: 7-inch

ABC.................... 10-20 68
FAYETTE.................... 5-10 64
KEYMAN.................... 5-10 67-68
MIRWOOD.................... 5-10 65-66
UNI.................... 3-6 70

LPs: 10/12-inch 33rpm

MIRWOOD.................... 15-25 66
Also see BOB & EARL

LEE, Jackie, & Dolores Hall

Singles: 7-inch

MIRWOOD.................... 4-8 66
Also see LEE, Jackie

LEE, Jimmy, & Artis

R&B '52

Singles: 78rpm

MODERN.................... 10-20 52

Singles: 7-inch

MODERN (885 "Let's Talk It Over") 25-35 52

LEE, John (John Lee Henley/Hooker): see JOHN LEE

LEE, Johnny

C&W '75

Singles: 7-inch

ABC/DOT 3-5 75
ASTRO.................... 3-5 80
ASYLUM 3-5 80-82
CURB.................... 3-4 89
EPIC.................... 3-5 81
FULL MOON/W.B. 3-4 80-86
GRT 3-5 76-78

Picture Sleeves

ASYLUM 3-5 80

LPs: 10/12-inch 33rpm
ACCORD 5-8 83
ASYLUM 5-10 80-81
FULL MOON/W.B. 5-8 80-86
GRT 8-10 77
JMS 8-12
PLANTATION 5-10 81
Also see GILLEY, Mickey, & Johnny Lee
Also see NELSON, Willie / Johnny Lee / Mickey Gilley

LEE, Johnny, & Lane Brody

C&W '84

Singles: 7-inch
W.B. 3-4 84-86

LEE, Johnny / Eagles

Singles: 7-inch
ASYLUM 3-5 80-81
Picture Sleeves
ASYLUM 3-5 80
Also see EAGLES

LEE, Johnny, Michael Martin Murphey, & Charlie Daniels

(Johnny Lee & Friends)

C&W '82

Singles: 7-inch
FULL MOON 3-4 82
Also see DANIELS, Charlie
Also see LEE, Johnny
Also see MURPHEY, Michael

LEE, Julia

(With Her Boy Friends)

R&B '46

Singles: 78rpm
CAPITOL 5-15 46-52
Singles: 7-inch
CAPITOL (Except 2203) 10-25 49-52
CAPITOL (2203 "Last Call for Alcohol") 25-35 52
EPs: 7-inch 33/45rpm
CAPITOL (EBF-228 "Party Time") 30-50 50
LPs: 10/12-inch 33rpm
CAPITOL (H-228 "Party Time"). 50-75 50
(10-inch LP.)
CAPITOL (T-228 "Party Time"). 35-55 55
Members: Julia Lee; Baby Lovett; Tommy Douglas; Jim Daddy Walker; Clint Weaver.

LEE, Laura

LP '72

Singles: 7-inch
ARIOLA AMERICA 3-5 76
CHESS 8-15 67-69
COTILLION 5-8 69
HOT WAX 3-6 71-72
INVICTUS 3-5 74
RIC TIC 10-20 66
LPs: 10/12-inch 33rpm
CHESS 10-20 72
HOT WAX 8-12 72-73
INVICTUS 8-12 74

LEE, Leapy: see LEAPY LEE

LEE, Leon

R&B '74

Singles: 7-inch
CROSSOVER 3-5 74

LEE, Michele

P&R '68

Singles: 7-inch
ABC-PAR 4-8 62-63
COLUMBIA 4-8 65-69
LPs: 10/12-inch 33rpm
COLUMBIA 10-20 66-68

LEE, Nickie

R&B '68

Singles: 7-inch
DADE 4-8 67
MALA 10-15 68-69

LEE, Peggy

(With Benny Goodman's Orchestra)

P&R '45

Singles: 78rpm
CAPITOL 5-15 41-58
OKEH 5-10 41-42
Singles: 7-inch
A&M 3-5 75
ATLANTIC 3-5 74
CAPITOL (801 thru 2000 series) .8-12 49-51
CAPITOL (2100 thru 3400 series) .3-6 68-72
CAPITOL (3800 thru 5900 series) .4-8 58-67
CAPITOL (90000 series) 4-8
COLUMBIA 3-5 76
DECCA (25000 series) 4-6 64
DECCA (28000 & 29000 series) 4-8 52-58
DECCA (30000 series) 4-8 58-59
EPs: 7-inch 33/45rpm
CAPITOL (Except 100 series) ... 10-20 57-59
CAPITOL (100 series) 20-40 52
COLUMBIA 20-40 50-51
DECCA 15-30 52-55
LPs: 10/12-inch 33rpm
A&M 5-8 75
ATLANTIC 5-8 74
CAPITOL (183 "A Natural Woman") 8-12 69
CAPITOL (H-155 "Rendezvous with Peggy") 50-75 52
(10-inch LP.)
CAPITOL (T-155 "Rendezvous with Peggy") 25-50 55
CAPITOL (H-204 "My Best to You") 50-75 52
(10-inch LP.)
CAPITOL (377 thru 810) 5-10 69-71
CAPITOL (864 "The Man I Love") 20-40 56
CAPITOL (979 "Jump for Joy") .. 20-40 57

CAPITOL (T-1049 thru T-1969) 15-25 58-63
(Monaural.)
CAPITOL (ST-1049 thru ST-1969) 20-30 58-63
(Stereo.)
CAPITOL (T-2096 thru T-2887) 10-20 64-68
(Monaural.)
CAPITOL (ST-2096 thru ST-2887) 10-20 64-68
CAPITOL (6600 series) 5-10 70
CAPITOL (11000 series) 5-10 72-79
CAPITOL (16000 series) 4-8 80
COLUMBIA (6033 "Benny Goodman & Peggy Lee") 40-60 50
(10–inch LP.)
DRG 5-8 79
DECCA (DXB-164 "Best of Peggy Lee") 15-25 60
(Monaural.)
DECCA (DXSB7-164 "Best of Peggy Lee") 10-20 66
(Stereo.)
DECCA (DL-4000 series) 10-15 64
(Monaural.)
DECCA (DL7-4000 series) 15-20 64
(Stereo.)
DECCA (5482 "Black Coffee") 50-75 53
(10–inch LP.)
DECCA (5539 "Songs in an Intimate Style") 50-75 53
(10–inch LPs.)
DECCA (8411 "Dream Street") 30-50 56
DECCA (8358 "Black Coffee") 30-50 57
DECCA (8591 "Sea Shells") 30-50 58
DECCA (8816 "Miss Wonderful") 20-40 59
EVEREST 5-8 74
GLENDALE 4-8 82
HARMONY (7000 series) 15-25 58
HARMONY (30000 series) 5-10 70
HORIZON (1004 "Best of Peggy Lee") 25-35 62
MERCURY 5-8 77
VOCALION 6-12 66-70

Also see CROSBY, Bing, & Peggy Lee
Also see FITZGERALD, Ella, & Peggy Lee
Also see GOODMAN, Benny, Orchestra
Also see JENKINS, Gordon, & His Orchestra

LEE, Peggy, & Dean Martin

Singles: 78rpm

CAPITOL 8-12 49

Also see MARTIN, Dean

LEE, Peggy, & George Shearing

Singles: 7–inch

CAPITOL 4-8 59

LPs: 10/12–inch 33rpm

CAPITOL (1219 "Beauty and the Beat") 20-30 59
(Capitol logo on left side of label.)
CAPITOL (1219 "Beauty and the Beat") 10-20 62
(Capitol logo at the top of label.)

LEE, Peggy, & Mel Torme

Singles: 78rpm

CAPITOL 5-10 49

Singles: 7–inch

CAPITOL 8-12 49

Also see LEE, Peggy
Also see TORME, Mel

LEE, Roberta

P&R '51

Singles: 78rpm

DECCA 4-6 51-54
TEMPO 4-8 50-51
X 4-6 54

Singles: 7–inch

DECCA 5-10 51-54
TEMPO 5-10 50-51
TOWER 4-6 68
X 5-10 54

LEE, Toney

D&D '83

Singles: 12–inch 33/45rpm

RADAR 4-6 83

Singles: 7–inch

CRITIQUE 3-4 85

LEE & PAUL

P&R '59

Singles: 7–inch

COLUMBIA 5-10 59-65

Members: Lee Pockriss; Paul Vance.
Also see VANCE, Paul

LEFEVRE, Raymond, & Orchestra

P&R '58

Singles: 7–inch

ATLANTIC 4-6 61
4 CORNERS 4-6 67-68
JAMIE 4-6 60
KAPP 3-8 58-66
MERCURY 4-8 60
VERVE 4-6 62

LPs: 10/12–inch 33rpm

ATLANTIC 8-15 61
BUDDAH 5-10 71-72
4 CORNERS 5-10 67-68
KAPP 8-15 59-66
MONUMENT 6-12 67

LEFT BANKE

P&R '66

Singles: 7–inch

CON AMERICA 5-8 78
SMASH (Except 2243) 5-10 66-69
SMASH (2243 "Myrah") 30-40 69

Picture Sleeves

SMASH (Except 2243) 10-20 67
SMASH (2243 "Myrah") 30-40 69

LPs: 10/12–inch 33rpm

RHINO... 5-8 85
SMASH (27088 "Walk Away Renee")................................. 20-30 67
(Monaural.)
SMASH (67088 "Walk Away Renee")................................. 25-35 67
(Stereo.)
SMASH (67113 "Left Banke Too") 25-35 69
MERCURY 5-10 81

Members: Michael Brown; George Cameron; Tom Finn; Steve Martin; Rick Brand; Jeff Winfield; Tom Feher.

Also see STORIES

LEGACY

R&B '82

Singles: 7–inch

BRUNSWICK............................... 3-5 82
PRIVATE I.................................. 3-4 85

LEGENDARY MASKED SURFERS

Singles: 7–inch

U.A. (270 "Summer Means Fun") 10-15 73
(Tan label. This track, previously included on the Jan & Dean LPs *The Little Old Lady from Pasadena* and *Popsicle* was mistakenly used for this single.)
U.A. (270 "Summer Means Fun") 10-15 73
(White label, promotional issue. Same incorrect track as noted above.)
U.A. (270 "Summer Means Fun") 100-125 73
(Tan label, promotional issue. Has the intended, new version with added vocal backing, not available elsewhere. Can be identified by playing, or visually by the following letters etched in the vinyl trail-off: Side 1 "BJ/TM/DT." Side 2 "GG/ILY/DOT.")
U.A. (270 "Summer Means Fun") 100-125 73
(White label, promotional issue. Has correct version as described above.)
U.A. (670 "Gonna Hustle You"). 10-20 75
(Reissued in 1977.)
U.A. (50958 "Gonna Hustle You") 10-20 72

Picture Sleeves

U.A. (270 "Summer Means Fun") 20-30 73
(Add $5.00 if accompanied by explanatory note from Dean Torrence.)

Members: Jan Berry; Dean Torrece; Brian Wilson; Bruce Johnston; Terry Melcher; Leon Russell; Glen Campbell; Larry Knechtel.

Also see CAMPBELL, Glen
Also see JAN & DEAN
Also see RUSSELL, Leon
Also see WILSON, Brian

LEGRAND, Michel, & Orchestra

LP '55

Singles: 7–inch

A&M 3-4 83
BELL 3-5 71-72
COLUMBIA 4-8 55-59
DECCA 3-6 68
FLASHBACK.................................3-5 73
MCA..3-5 73-76
MGM 3-6 67-68
PHILIPS 4-6 63-66
RCA 3-5 75
20TH FOX....................................3-5 77
U.A. 3-5 70
W.B. 3-6 68-76

Picture Sleeves

MGM 8-15 67

EPs: 7–inch 33/45rpm

COLUMBIA 5-10 56-59

LPs: 10/12–inch 33rpm

BELL 5-10 72-74
COLUMBIA 10-20 55-71
GRYPHON...................................5-8 75-79
HARMONY 5-10 66-74
KORY..4-8 77
MCA...8-15 73-76
MERCURY..................................8-15 65
PABLO 4-8 83
PHILIPS......................................8-15 62-64
SPRINGBOARD 4-8 77
20TH FOX...................................5-10 77
U.A. 6-12 69
VERVE.......................................8-15 68-72
W.B. 6-12 71-76

Also see HORNE, Lena, & Michel Legrand
Also see VAUGHAN, Sarah

You'll find many more listings by this artist in *The Official Price Guide to Movie/TV Soundtracks and Original Cast Albums,* containing over 8,000 listings.

LEHRER, Tom

LP '65

Singles: 7–inch

REPRISE 3-6 69

EPs: 7–inch 33/45rpm

LEHRER (1 "Songs By Tom Lehrer").........................50-100 52
(Double EP, gatefold cover.)

LPs: 10/12–inch 33rpm

LEHRER (101 "Songs By Tom Lehrer").........................50-100 52
(10–inch LP.)
LEHRER (102 "More Songs By Tom Lehrer")............................30-50 59
LEHRER (202 "An Evening Wasted with Tom Lehrer")............................30-50 59
REPRISE 10-20 65-66

LE JETE

D&D '83

Singles: 12-inch 33/45rpm

MEGATONE.................................. 4-6 83

LEKAKIS, Paul

P&R '87

Singles: 7-inch

ZYX 3-4 87

LEMMONS, Billy

P&R '77

Singles: 7-inch

ARIOLA AMERICA...................... 3-5 77

LEMON PIPERS

P&R '67

Singles: 7-inch

BUDDAH.. 4-8 67-69
CAROL.. 8-12
ERIC... 3-5 78

Picture Sleeves

BUDDAH 5-10 68

LPs: 10/12-inch 33rpm

BUDDAH 12-20 68
Members: Ivan Browne; Bill Bartlett; Paul Lenka; Bill Albaugh; Steve Walmsley; Reg Nave.
Also see 1910 FRUITGUM COMPANY / Lemon Pipers
Also see RAM JAM

LENNON, John

(John & Yoko; Plastic Ono Band; with Plastic Ono Nuclear Band; with Flux Fiddlers)

P&R/LP '69

Singles: 12-inch 33/45rpm

CAPITOL (9585/6 "Imagine"/ "Come Together") 25-35 86
(Promotional issue only.)
CAPITOL (9894 "Happy Xmas") 150-200 86
(Promotional issue only.)
CAPITOL (9917 "Rock & Roll People") 20-30 86
(Promotional issue only.)
CAPITOL (9929 "Happy Xmas") 35-45 86
(Promotional issue only.)
CAPITOL (79453 "Stand by Me").. 20-25 88
(Promotional issue only.)
GEFFEN (919 "Starting Over") . 35-45 80
(Promotional issue only.)
GEFFEN (1079 "Happy Xmas") 25-30 82
(Price range includes special sleeve. Promotional issue only.)
POLYDOR (250 "Nobody Told Me").. 25-30 83

Singles: 7-inch

AMERICOM (435 "Give Peace a Chance") 200-400 69
(Plastic "Pocket Disc" soundsheet.)
APPLE (1809 "Give Peace a Chance").....................................4-6 69
APPLE (1813 "Cold Turkey").........4-8 69
APPLE (1818 "Instant Karma")......4-6 70
APPLE (1827 "Mother") 5-10 70
APPLE (1830 "Power to the People") 4-6 71
APPLE (1840 "Imagine")................4-6 71
APPLE (1842 "Happy Xmas")......8-12 71
(Label pictures John and Yoko.)
APPLE (1842 "Happy Xmas").......5-8 71
(Standard Apple label.)
APPLE (1848 "Woman Is the Nigger of the World") 4-6 72
(With Elephant's Memory.)
APPLE (1868 "Mind Games")........4-6 73
APPLE (1874 "Whatever Gets You Through the Night").......................4-6 74
APPLE (1878 "#9 Dream")............4-6 74
APPLE (1881 "Stand by Me") 4-6 75
CAPITOL...................................10-15 78
(Orange labels.)
CAPITOL...3-5 78-84
(Purple or black labels.)
CAPITOL STAR LINE 3-4 77-78
GEFFEN (0408 "Starting Over")....3-5 83
GEFFEN (0415 "Watching the Wheels") 3-5 83
GEFFEN (29855 "Happy Xmas")...3-5 82
GEFFEN (49604 "Starting Over")..3-5 80
GEFFEN (49644 "Woman")...........3-5 80
GEFFEN (49695 "Watching the Wheels") 3-5 81
ORANGE PEEL (70078 "Interview").............................12-15 81
(John is interviewed by David Peel. Picture disc.)
POLYDOR 3-5 84-86

Promotional Singles

APPLE (1809 "Give Peace a Chance")................................8-12 69
APPLE (1813 "Cold Turkey").....20-25 69
APPLE (1818 "Instant Karma")..20-25 70
(With *Instant Karma* on both sides of disc.)
APPLE (1818 "Instant Karma")..............................150-200 70
(With *Instant Karma* only on one side of disc. Flip is a blank pressing.)
APPLE (1827 "Mother") 25-35 70
APPLE (1830 "Power to the People") 15-25 71
APPLE (1840 "Imagine")...........10-15 71
APPLE (1848 "Woman Is the Nigger of the World") 12-15 72
APPLE (1868 "Mind Games")....30-40 73
APPLE (1874 "Whatever Gets You Through the Night").................25-35 74
APPLE (1878 "#9 Dream").........25-35 74

APPLE (1878 "What You Got") . 50-75 74
(Two separate promo singles have the same selection number [1878]. On commercial issues these tracks were back to back.)
APPLE (1881 "Stand By Me") ... 25-35 75
APPLE (1883 "Ain't That a Shame") 100-200 75
APPLE (1883 "Slippin' and Sliddin') 100-200 75
(There were two separate promo singles with the 1883 selection number.)
APPLE (47663/4 "Happy Xmas") 200-400 71
(White label with black print.)
CAPITOL (17644 "Happy Xmas") 4-8 94
(In error has a slash following title: "Happy Xmas (War Is Over)/" Colored vinyl, 30th Anniversary jukebox issue.)
CAPITOL (17644 "Happy Xmas") . 3-5 94
(Slash removed from title: "Happy Xmas (War Is Over)" Colored vinyl, 30th Anniversary jukebox issue.)
CAPITOL (44230 "Imagine") 10-20 88
CAPITOL (57849 "Imagine") 30-50 92
COTILLION (104/5 "John Lennon on Ronnie Hawkins")................... 30-35 70
(John Lennon promotes a 1970 Ronnie Hawkins Cotillion release.)
EVA-TONE ("John Lennon Radio Play") 200-400 69
(Soundsheet only. Originally included with a boxed set issue of *Aspen* Magazine. Price for complete set would be double that of just the Lennon disc.)
EVA-TONE (101075 "The Rock Generation")............................ 20-30 76
(Issued with the book *The Rock Generation* Has a brief Lennon interview.)
GEFFEN (29855 "Happy Xmas") 8-12 82
GEFFEN (49604 "Starting Over")................................... 10-15 80
GEFFEN (49644 "Woman") 8-12 80
GEFFEN (49695 "Watching the Wheels")................................ 10-12 81
KYA ("KYA 1969 Peace Talk").. 50-60 69
(Radio KYA's Tom Campbell and Bill Holley's telephone interview with John Lennon.)
POLYDOR................................ 8-15 84-86
QUAKER 10-15 86
(Soundsheet, issued with Quaker Granola Dipps.)
QUAYE/TRIDENT (3419"Rock 'N' Roll") 300-350 75
(Contains a one minute radio spot for the "Rock 'N' Roll" LP. Issued to radio stations only.)
WHAT'S IT ALL ABOUT........... 15-20 70s

Picture Sleeves

APPLE (1809 "Give Peace a Chance")........................10-15 69
APPLE (1813 "Cold Turkey").....50-75 69
APPLE (1818 "Instant Karma")..10-15 70
APPLE (1827 "Mother") 75-125 70
APPLE (1830 "Power to the People") 15-20 71
APPLE (1842 "Happy Xmas")....10-15 71
APPLE (1848 "Woman Is the Nigger of the World")..........................10-15 72
APPLE (1868 "Mind Games")......6-10 73
CAPITOL (44230 "Imagine")......30-50 88
GEFFEN (29855 "Happy Xmas")...3-5 82
GEFFEN (49604 "Starting Over")..3-4 80
GEFFEN (49644 "Woman")...........3-4 80
GEFFEN (49695 "Watching the Wheels") 3-4 81
POLYDOR 3-4 84

LPs: 10/12–inch 33rpm

ADAM VIII LTD. (8018 "John Lennon Sings Great Rock & Roll Hits, Roots")..............................200-300 75
APPLE (3361 "Wedding Album") 75-125 69
(Price range is for complete boxed set with all inserts.)
APPLE (3362 "Live Peace in Toronto")...................................30-40 70
(With 16-page photo/calendar.)
APPLE (3362 "Live Peace in Toronto")...................................10-15 70
(Without calendar.)
APPLE (3372 "John Lennon, Plastic Ono Band") 15-20 70
APPLE (3379 "Imagine")...........15-20 71
(Includes bonus poster and photo card.)
APPLE (3392 "Sometime in New York City").............................20-25 72
APPLE (3414 "Mind Games")....10-15 73
APPLE (3416 "Walls and Bridges") 10-20 74
(Includes booklet.)
APPLE (3419 "Rock 'N' Roll")....10-15 75
APPLE (3421 "Shaved Fish") 10-15 75
APPLE/TETRAGRAMMATON (5001 "Two Virgins") 100-125 68
(With brown paper outer sleeve.)
APPLE/TETRAGRAMMATON (5001 "Two Virgins") 60-100 68
(Without paper outer sleeve.)
APPLE/TETRAGRAMMATON (5001 "Two Virgins") 10-15
(Reissue, with brown paper outer sleeve that does NOT cover entire jacket.)
CAPITOL.......................................8-18 75-88
GEFFEN 10-15 80-82
MFSL 15-25 85
(Half-speed mastered.)

NAUTILUS (47 "Double Fantasy") ... 25-35 82
(Half-speed mastered.)
POLYDOR ... 5-8 84
SILHOUETTE (10014 "Reflections and Poetry") ... 10-15 84
ZAPPLE (3357 "Life with the Lions") ... 20-25 69

Promotional LPs

APPLE (3392 "Sometime In New York City") ... 200-400 72
GEFFEN (2023 "John Lennon Collection") ... 30-40 82
(Quiex II "Limited Edition Pressing.")
POLYDOR (817 238-1 "Heart Play") ... 15-25 83
(Includes program notes and copy of a letter from Yoko on her stationary.)
SILHOUETTE (10014 "Reflections and Poetry") ... 40-50 84

Also see BEATLES
Also see ELEPHANT'S MEMORY
Also see HAWKINS, Ronnie
Also see JOHN, Elton / John Lennon
Also see ONO, Yoko
Also see PEEL, David, & Lower East Side / John Lennon & Yoko Ono

LENNON, Julian

P&R/LP '84

Singles: 12-inch 33/45rpm

ATLANTIC ... 5-8 85

Singles: 7-inch

ATLANTIC ... 3-5 84-89

Picture Sleeves

ATLANTIC ... 3-5 84-89

LPs: 10/12-inch 33rpm

ATLANTIC ... 5-10 84-89

LENNON, Julian, & Stevie Wonder

Singles: 7-inch

CAPITOL ... 3-5 80s

Picture Sleeves

CAPITOL ... 3-5 80s

Also see LENNON, Julian
Also see WONDER, Stevie

LENNON SISTERS
(With Lawrence Welk)

P&R '56

Singles: 78rpm

BRUNSWICK ... 4-6 57
CORAL ... 4-6 56

Singles: 7-inch

BRUNSWICK ... 5-10 57-59
CORAL ... 5-10 56
DOT ... 4-8 58-67
MERCURY ... 3-6 68

EPs: 7-inch 33/45rpm

BRUNSWICK ... 5-10 57

LPs: 10/12-inch 33rpm

BRUNSWICK ... 10-25 57
DOT ... 5-15 59-07
HAMILTON ... 5-12 64
MERCURY ... 8-12 68-69
RANWOOD ... 4-8 68-81
VOCALION ... 5-10 69-70
WING ... 5-10 69

Members: Kathy Lennon; Peggy Lennon; Janet Lennon; Dianne Lennon.
Also see WELK, Lawrence

LENNOX, Annie, & Al Green

P&R '88

Singles: 7-inch

A&M ... 3-4 88

Picture Sleeves

A&M ... 3-4 88

Also see EURYTHMICS
Also see GREEN, Al

LENNY & STORKS: see WELCH, Lenny

LENOIR, J.B.
(J.B. Lenore; J.B. Lenor; with His African Hunch Rhythm)

R&B '55

Singles: 78rpm

CHESS (1449 "My Baby Told Me") ... 15-25 51
CHESS (1463 "Deep in Debt Blues") ... 15-25 51
J.O.B. (112 "People Are Meddlin' in Our Affairs") ... 15-25 52

Singles: 7-inch

CHECKER (844 "Let Me Die with the One I Love") ... 20-30 56
CHECKER (856 "Don't Touch My Head") ... 20-30 56
CHECKER (874 "Five Years") ... 15-25 57
CHECKER (901 "Don't Talk to Your Son") ... 15-25 58
J.O.B. (1012 "The Mojo") ... 50-100 52
J.O.B. (1102 "Play a Little While") ... 50-100 52
PARROT (Except 802) ... 50-100 54-55
PARROT (802 "Eisenhower Blues") ... 50-100 54
PARROT (802 "Tax Paying Blues") ... 75-125 54
(Black vinyl.)
PARROT (802 "Tax Paying Blues") ... 250-350 54
(Colored vinyl. *Eisenhower Blues* was retitled *Tax Paying Blues* and was issued using the same selection number. They are slightly different recordings.)
PARROT (809 "Man Watch Your Woman") ... 50-100 54
PARROT (814 "Mama, Your Daughter Is Going to Miss Me") ... 50-100 55
PARROT (821 "Fine Girls") ... 50-100 55
SHAD ... 10-15 59
U.S.A. ... 10-15 63

VEE JAY 5-10 60

LPs: 10/12-inch 33rpm

CHESS (1410 "Natural Man") ... 30-40 63
POLYDOR 10-15 70
Also see WELLS, Junior

LEONETTI, Tommy

P&R '55

Singles: 78rpm

CAPITOL 4-6 54-56
VIK 4-8 57

Singles: 7-inch

ATLANTIC 5-8 60
CAPITOL 5-10 54-56
COLUMBIA 4-6 67-73
DECCA 4-6 68-69
EPIC 3-5 74
RCA 3-8 59-77
20TH FOX 3-5 77
VIK 5-10 57

Picture Sleeves

COLUMBIA 4-8 68

LPs: 10/12-inch 33rpm

CAMDEN 10-20 59
RCA 10-20 64-67

LE PAMPLEMOUSSE

P&R/R&B '77

Singles: 12-inch 33/45rpm

A.V.I. 4-8 78-85

Singles: 7-inch

A.V.I. 3-5 77-85

LPs: 10/12-inch 33rpm

A.V.I. 5-8 78-85

LEPPARD, Def: see DEF LEPPARD

LE 'ROI BROTHERS

LP '87

EPs: 7-inch 33/45rpm

AMAZING 8-10 81
DEMON 4-8 84

LPs: 10/12-inch 33rpm

JUNGLE 8-10 83
PROFILE 5-8 85-87

LE ROUX
(Louisiana's LeRoux)

P&R/LP '78

Singles: 7-inch

CAPITOL 3-6 78
NEW ORLEANS LADY 5-10
RCA 3-5 82-83

LPs: 10/12-inch 33rpm

CAPITOL 5-8 78-81
NEW ORLEANS LADY 20-30
RCA 5-8 82

LES COMPAGNONS DE LA CHANSON

P&R '52

Singles: 78rpm

COLUMBIA 3-6 52

Singles: 7-inch

CAPITOL 4-6 59-60
COLUMBIA 5-8 52

LESEAR, Anne

R&B '84

Singles: 7-inch

H.C.R.C. 3-5 84

LESTER, Bobby

Singles: 7-inch

CHECKER 5-10 59
COLUMBIA 3-5 70

LPs: 10/12-inch 33rpm

COLUMBIA 10-15 70

LESTER, Bobby, & Moonglows

Singles: 7-inch

CHESS 5-8 62

LPs: 10/12-inch 33rpm

CHESS (1471 "Best of Bobby Lester and the Moonglows") 30-40 62
Also see MOONGLOWS

LESTER, Bobby, & Moonlighters

Singles: 78rpm

CHECKER 10-15 54

Singles: 7-inch

CHECKER (806 "So All Alone") . 50-75 54
(Checkerboard top label.)
CHECKER (806 "So All Alone") . 10-20 58
(Vertical logo.)

LESTER, Ketty

P&R/R&B/LP '62

Singles: 7-inch

COLLECTABLES 3-4 80s
ERA 5-8 62-63
EVEREST 4-8 62
PETE 4-6 68-69
RCA 4-6 64
TOWER 4-6 65-66

LPs: 10/12-inch 33rpm

AVI 5-8 80
ERA (EL-108 "Love Letters") 25-35 62
(Monaural.)
ERA (ES-108 "Love Letters") 30-40 62
(Stereo.)
MEGA 5-8 85
PETE 10-15 69
RCA 10-20 64-65
SHEFFIELD 8-10 77
TOWER 10-15 66
Also see EVERETT, Betty, & Ketty Lester

LET'S ACTIVE

LP '84

LPs: 10/12-inch 33rpm

I.R.S. 5-8 84-86

LETTERMEN

P&R '61

Singles: 7–inch

ALPHA-OMEGA 3-5 78-88
APPLAUSE 3-4 83
CAPITOL 3-8 61-76
W.B. 5-8 60

Picture Sleeves

CAPITOL 5-10 61-68

LPs: 10/12–inch 33rpm

ALPHA-OMEGA 5-15 77-88
APPLAUSE 5-8 82
CANDELITE 5-10 70s
CAPITOL (138 thru 836 except 577) 5-15 68-71
CAPITOL (577 "Lettermen") 10-20 62-68
(Boxed 3-LP set.)
CAPITOL (1669 thru 2934) 10-20 62-68
(With "T" or "ST" prefix.)
CAPITOL (2500 & 2700 series) 5-8 80s
(With "SM" prefix.)
CAPITOL (11000 series) 5-10 71-75
CAPITOL (16000 series) 4-8 80-83
CAPITOL (90000 series) 10-20
LONGINES (220 "Time for Us") 15-30
(Five-LP boxed set.)
LONGINES (220 "From the Lettermen, with Love") 5-8 72
(Bonus LP, issued with the above box set.)
PICKWICK (577 "Lettermen") 10-15 70
(Three-LP set.)
PICKWICK (3000 series) 5-10 70-77

Members: Tony Butala; James Pike; Bob Engemann; Gary Pike; Donny Pike; Chad Nichols; Don Campo.

Also see CAMPBELL, Glen / Lettermen / Ella Fitzgerald / Sandler & Young
Also see PETER & GORDON / Lettermen
Also see SONNY & CHER / Bill Medley / Lettermen / Blendells

LEVEL 42

D&D '84

Singles: 12–inch 33/45rpm

A&M 4-6 84

Singles: 7–inch

A&M 3-4 84
POLYDOR 3-4 82-88

Picture Sleeves

POLYDOR 3-4 86-87

LPs: 10/12–inch 33rpm

A&M 5-8 84
POLYDOR 5-10 82-88

Members: Mark King; Mike Lindup; Phil Gould; Boon Gould; Krys Mach.

LEVERT

R&B '85

Singles: 7–inch

ATLANTIC 3-4 86-88
TEMPRE 3-5 85

LPs: 10/12–inch 33rpm

ATLANTIC 5-8 86-90

Members: Sean Levert; Gerald Levert; Marc Gordon.

LEVINE, Hank
(With the Minature Men)

P&R '61

Singles: 7–inch

ABC-PAR 4-8 61
DOLTON 4-8 62-63
TOPS 4-8 60

Also see CONNORS, Carol
Also see MINIATURE MEN

LEVON & HAWKS
(Featuring Levon Helm)

Singles: 7–inch

ATCO 10-20 65-68

Also see BAND
Also see HELM, Levon
Also see HAWKINS, Ronnie

LEVY, Marcy, & Robin Gibb

Singles: 7–inch

RSO 3-4 80

Picture Sleeves

RSO 3-5 80

Also see GIBB, Robin
Also see LEVY, Marcy

LEWIS, Barbara

P&R/R&B '63

Singles: 7–inch

ATLANTIC 4-8 62-67
ENTERPRISE 3-5 70-71
REPRISE 3-5 73

LPs: 10/12–inch 33rpm

ATLANTIC (8086 thru 8173) 20-35 63-68
ATLANTIC (8286 "Best of Barbara Lewis") 10-15 71
COLLECTABLES 6-8 88
ENTERPRISE 10-12 70
SOLID SMOKE 8-10 70s

Also see DELLS

LEWIS, Bobby

P&R/R&B '61

Singles: 78rpm

SPOTLIGHT 10-15 56

Singles: 7–inch

ABC-PAR 4-8 64
BELTONE 5-10 61-62
ERIC 3-4 70s
LANA 3-6 60s
PHILIPS (40519 "Soul Seekin") 10-20 68
ROULETTE 5-10 59
SPOTLIGHT (394 "Mumbles Blues") 10-20 56

LPs: 10/12–inch 33rpm

BELTONE (4000 "Tossin' and Turnin'") 50-100 61

LEWIS, Gary, & Playboys

P&R '65

Singles: 7-inch

LIBERTY (Except 56144)............. 4-8 64-69
LIBERTY (56144 "I Saw Elvis Presley Last Night") 10-15 69

Picture Sleeves

LIBERTY 4-8 65-67

EPs: 7-inch 33/45rpm

LIBERTY (227 "Doin' the Flake")................................. 10-20 65
(Liberty/Kellogg's Premium Record. Issued with paper sleeve.)

LPs: 10/12-inch 33rpm

GUSTO 5-8 72
LIBERTY (Except 10000 series) 15-30 65-69
LIBERTY (10000 series) 5-8 81
SUNSET.................................. 12-15 69
U.A. (Except 1000 series) 8-10 75
U.A. (1000 series) 5-8 81

LEWIS, Huey, & News

P&R/LP '82

Singles: 12-inch 33/45rpm

CHRYSALIS................................ 4-8 84-89

Singles: 7-inch

CHRYSALIS................................ 3-5 80-89

Promotional Singles

CHRYSALIS (2589 "Do You Believe in Love") 8-12 80
(Colored vinyl. With Valentine card. Promotional issue only.)
CHRYSALIS (43065 "Hip to Be Square")........................... 10-15 85
(Four disc set, each of a different color vinyl.)

Picture Sleeves

CHRYSALIS............................... 3-5 82-89

LPs: 10/12-inch 33rpm

CHRYSALIS................................ 5-8 80-89
MFSL...................................... 15-20 85

Members: Huey Lewis; Bill Gibson; Mario Cipollina; Sean Hopper; Chris Hayes; Johnny Colla.
Also see EDMUNDS, Dave
Also see U.S.A. for AFRICA

LEWIS, J.D.

R&B '89

Singles: 7-inch

SING ME 3-4 89

LEWIS, J.G.

R&B '76

Singles: 7-inch

IX CHAINS 4-6 76

LEWIS, Jerry

P&R/LP '56

Singles: 78rpm

CAPITOL.................................... 4-6 50-53
DECCA....................................... 4-6 56-57

Singles: 7-inch

CAPITOL.................................5-10 50-53
DECCA 4-8 56-62
DOT 4-8 60
LIBERTY 4-8 63

EPs: 7-inch 33/45rpm

CAPITOL..................................6-12 56
DECCA 6-10 56

LPs: 10/12-inch 33rpm

CAPITOL..................................10-15 64
DECCA 15-25 56
DOT 10-15 60
VOCALION 8-12 66

Also see MARTIN, Dean, & Jerry Lewis

LEWIS, Jerry Lee
(With His Pumping Piano)

P&R/C&W/R&B '57

Singles: 78rpm

SUN 25-50 56-58

Singles: 7-inch

AMERICA SMASH.......................3-5 86
BUDDAH...................................3-6 71
ELEKTRA..................................3-5 79-82
MCA 3-5 82-83
MERCURY 3-6 70-82
SCR (386 "Get Out Your Big Roll, Daddy") 3-5 85
(Colored vinyl.)
SSS/SUN 3-5 69-84
(Includes numbers below 100 and over 1000.)
SMASH (1857 thru 2122)............5-10 63-67
SMASH (2146 thru 2257)..............4-8 68-70
SUN (169/213 "Whole Lotta Shakin' Going On"/"Great Balls of Fire")...........5-10 94
(Colored vinyl. Promotional issue only.)
SUN (259 "Crazy Arms")............20-30 56
SUN (267 thru 296)...................15-25 56-58
SUN (300 series) 10-20 58-65

Picture Sleeves

SUN (281 "Great Balls of Fire") .25-50 57
SUN (296 "High School Confidential") 25-50 57

EPs: 7-inch 33/45rpm

MERCURY (6 "Special Radio Cuts from *Would You Take Another Chance on Me*") 15-25 71
(Promotional issues only.)
MERCURY (14 "Special Radio Cuts from *The Killer Rocks On*") 15-25 72
(Promotional issues only.)
SCR 10-15 86
SSS/SUN (108 "Golden Cream of the Country")........................15-25 69
(Jukebox issue only.)
SSS/SUN (114 "A Taste of Country")................................15-25 69
(Jukebox issue only.)

SMASH (2 "Jerry Lee Lewis") ... 20-25 64
SMASH (28 "Open-End Inverview") 30-40 64
(Promotional issue only.)
SUN (107 "Great Ball of Fire") 75-100 57
(Issued with a paper sleeve.)
SUN (108 "Jerry Lee Lewis") 50-75 57
SUN (109 "Jerry Lee Lewis") 50-75 58
SUN (110 "High School Confidential")......................... 50-75 58

LPs: 10/12–inch 33rpm

ACCORD.................................... 5-8 81-82
AURA 5-8 82
BUCKBOARD 8-10 75
ELEKTRA.................................. 5-10 79-82
EVEREST 8-12 76
HILLTOP 10-12 72
KOALA 5-10 79
MCA 5-8 82-84
MERCURY (SRM1 series).......... 8-15 72-78
MERCURY (SRM2-803 "Session")............................. 15-20 73
MERCURY (3 "Southern Roots") 40-60 73
MERCURY (61318 "In Loving Memories").......................... 15-20 71
MERCURY (61323 "There Must Be More to Love Than This").................. 8-12 71
MERCURY (61343 "Touching Home")................................ 15-20 71
(Cover is mostly an artist's drawing with a small photo of Lewis on the right side.)
MERCURY (61343 "Touching Home")................................ 12-15 71
(Cover pictures Lewis standing in front of a brick wall.)
MERCURY (61346 "Would You Take Another Chance on Me")........... 8-12 71
MERCURY (61366 "Who's Gonna Play This Old Piano").................... 8-12 72
OUT of TOWN DIST 5-8 82
PICKWICK 10-12 70-74
POLYDOR (839516 "Great Ball of Fire") 5-8 89
(Includes tracks by other artists.)
POLYSTAR 8-10
POWER PAK 8-10 74
RHINO...................................... 8-10 83
SCR.. 5-10 85
SSS/SUN 5-10 69-84
SEARS 10-15
SMASH (690 "Jerry Lee Lewis Radio Special") 40-50 73
(Promotional issue only.)
SMASH (7001 "Golden Rock Hits") 5-8 82
SMASH (27040 "Golden Hits of Jerry Lee Lewis") 20-25 64
(Monaural.)
SMASH (27056 "Greatest Live Show on Earth")......................15-20 64
(Monaural.)
SMASH (27063 "Return of Rock")....................................20-25 65
(Monaural.)
SMASH (27071 "Country Songs for City Folks") 15-20 65
(Monaural.)
SMASH (27079 "Memphis Beat")....................................20-25 65
(Monaural.)
SMASH (27086 "By Request")...15-20 66
(Monaural.)
SMASH (27097 "Soul My Way") 20-25 67
(Monaural.)
SMASH (67040 "Golden Hits of Jerry Lee Lewis")....................20-25 64
(Stereo.)
SMASH (67040 "Golden Rock Hits of Jerry Lee Lewis")................15-20 60s
(Reissue.)
SMASH (67056 "Greatest Live Show on Earth")......................20-25 64
(Stereo.)
SMASH (67063 "Return of Rock")....................................25-30 65
(Stereo.)
SMASH (67071 "Country Songs for City Folks") 20-25 65
(Stereo.)
SMASH (67071 "All Country")....10-15 69
(Stereo. Reissue.)
SMASH (67079 "Memphis Beat")....................................25-30 65
(Stereo.)
SMASH (67086 "By Request")...20-25 66
(Stereo.)
SMASH (67097 "Soul My Way") 25-30 67
(Stereo.)
SMASH (67104 thru 67131).........8-15 68-70
SUN (1230 "Jerry Lee Lewis")...............................100-150 58
SUN (1265 "Jerry Lee's Greatest") 100-150 62
SUNNYVALE 8-10 77
TRIP...8-10 74
WING (125 "The Legend of Jerry Lee Lewis")....................20-30 69
WING (12000 series) 12-15 66-67
(Monaural.)
WING (16000 series) 15-20 66-67
(Stereo.)

Also see CLANTON, Jimmy / Frankie Ford / Jerry Lee Lewis / Patsy Cline
Also see HAWK
Also see KING, Ben E.
Also see McDOWELL, Ronnie, & Jerry Lee Lewis
Also see NELSON, Willie / Jerry Lee Lewis / Carl Perkins / David Allan Coe

LEWIS, Jerry Lee / Curly Bridges / Frank Motley

LPs: 10/12-inch 33rpm

DESIGN 10-15 63

LEWIS, Jerry Lee / Johnny Cash

LPs: 10/12-inch 33rpm

SSS/SUN 8-10 71

Also see CASH, Johnny
Also see PERKINS, Carl, Jerry Lee Lewis, Roy Orbison & Johnny Cash

LEWIS, Jerry Lee, & Friends

C&W '79

Singles: 7-inch

SSS/SUN (1139 "Save the Last Dance for Me") 3-6 80

LPs: 10/12-inch 33rpm

SSS/SUN (1011 "Duets") 8-10 78

Members: Jerry Lee Lewis; Jimmy Ellis; Charlie Rich.
Also see RICH, Charlie

LEWIS, Jerry Lee & Linda Gail Lewis

C&W '69

Singles: 7-inch

SMASH 3-6 69-70
SUN.. 5-10 63

LPs: 10/12-inch 33rpm

SMASH 15-25 69

LEWIS, Jerry Lee / Roger Miller / Roy Orbison

LPs: 10/12-inch 33rpm

PICKWICK 8-10 70s

Also see MILLER, Roger
Also see ORBISON, Roy

LEWIS, Jerry Lee, Carl Perkins & Charlie Rich

LPs: 10/12-inch 33rpm

SSS/SUN (1018 "Trio +") 8-10 78
(With Jimmy Ellis.)

Also see ELLIS, Jimmy
Also see LEWIS, Jerry Lee, & Friends
Also see PERKINS, Carl

LEWIS, Jerry Lee / Charlie Rich / Johnny Cash

LPs: 10/12-inch 33rpm

POWER PAK 8-10 80s

Also see CASH, Johnny, Carl Perkins & Jerry Lee Lewis
Also see LEWIS, Jerry Lee

LEWIS, Jimmy
(With the L.A. Street Band)

R&B '75

Singles: 7-inch

HOTLANTA.................................. 3-5 75
MCA 3-4 84

LPs: 10/12-inch 33rpm

HOTLANTA.................................. 5-10 74

LEWIS, Lenny, & His Orchestra

R&B '46

Singles: 78rpm

QUEEN 4-6 46

LEWIS, Linda

R&B '75

Singles: 7-inch

ARISTA...3-5 75-78
REPRISE 3-5 73

LPs: 10/12-inch 33rpm

REPRISE 8-10 74

LEWIS, Monica, & Ames Brothers

P/R '48

Singles: 78rpm

SIGNATURE 5-10 48

Also see AMES BROTHERS

LEWIS, Ramsey
(Ramsey Lewis Trio; Ramsey Lewis & Co.)

LP '62

Singles: 12-inch 33/45rpm

COLUMBIA 4-6 79-85

Singles: 7-inch

ABC...3-5 74
ARGO 4-8 58-65
CADET...3-6 65-72
CHESS...3-5 73
COLUMBIA 3-5 72-87
EMARCY.......................................4-8 59

EPs: 7-inch 33/45rpm

ARGO (687 "Sound of Christmas")...............................15-25 61

LPs: 10/12-inch 33rpm

ARGO (611 "Gentleman of Swing")...................................40-60 58
ARGO (627 "Gentleman of Jazz")......................................40-60 58
ARGO (642 "Ramsey Lewis Trio with Len Winchester")..............30-50 59
ARGO (645 "An Hour with the Ramsey Lewis Trio")................25-50 59
ARGO (665 "Stretching Out")...25-50 60
ARGO (680 "From the Soil")......25-50 61
ARGO (687 "Sound of Christmas") 25-50 61
ARGO (693 "Sound of Spring")..25-35 62
ARGO (700 series) 20-40 62-65
CADET.......................................10-20 65-72
COLUMBIA 6-12 72-85
EMARCY (36150 "Down to Earth")..25-45 59
(Monaural.)
EMARCY (80029 "Down to Earth")..35-60 59
(Stereo.)
TRIP 5-8 75

Members: Ramsey Lewis; Eldee Young; Red Holt; Cleveland Eaton; Maurice White.

Also see EARTH, WIND & FIRE with Ramsey Lewis
Also see YOUNG HOLT UNLIMITED

LEWIS, Ramsey, & Nancy Wilson

LP '84

LP: 10/12-inch 33rpm

COLUMBIA 5-10 84

Also see LEWIS, Ramsey
Also see WILSON, Nancy

LEWIS, Shirley

P&R '89

Singles: 7-inch

VENDETTA 3-4 89

LEWIS, Smiley

R&B '52

Singles: 78rpm

COLONY (106 "Sad Life") 20-40 52
COLONY (110 "Where Were You") 20-40 52
DELUXE (3099 "Turn Your Volume On, Baby") 20-40 47
IMPERIAL 12-25 50-57

Singles: 7-inch

DOT 5-8 64
IMPERIAL (5194 "The Bells Are Ringing") 50-100 52
IMPERIAL (5208 "Gumbo Blues") 50-100 52
IMPERIAL (5224 "Gypsy Blues") 50-100 54
IMPERIAL (5234 "Play Girl") 50-75 53
(Black vinyl.)
IMPERIAL (5234 "Play Girl") 100-200 53
(Colored vinyl.)
IMPERIAL (5241 "Caldonia's Party") 50-75 53
IMPERIAL (5252 "Little Fernandez") 50-75 53
IMPERIAL (5268 "Down the Road") 50-75 54
IMPERIAL (5279 "I Love You for Sentimental Reasons") 50-75 54
IMPERIAL (5296 "Can't Stop Loving You") 50-75 54
IMPERIAL (5316 "Too Many Drivers") 50-75 54
IMPERIAL (5325 "Jailbird") 50-75 54
IMPERIAL (5349 "Real Gone Lover") 50-75 55
IMPERIAL (5356 "I Hear You Knocking") 50-75 55
IMPERIAL (5372 "Queen of Hearts") 50-75 55
IMPERIAL (5380 "One Night") 50-75 56
IMPERIAL (5389 "She's Got Me Hook, Line and Sinker") 40-60 56
IMPERIAL (5404 "Down Yonder We Go Ballin") 40-60 56
IMPERIAL (5418 "Shame, Shame, Shame") 40-60 56
IMPERIAL (5431 thru 5820) 10-30 57-62
KNIGHT 10-15 59
LOMA 5-10 65
OKEH 5-10 62

LPs: 10/12-inch 33rpm

IMPERIAL (9141 "I Hear You Knocking") 150-200 61

Also see BARTHOLOMEW, Dave

LEWIS, Webster

(With the Post-Pop Space Rock Be-Bop Gospel Tabernacle Orchestra & Chorus; with Love Unlimited Orchestra)

R&B/LP '80

Singles: 12-inch 33/45rpm

EPIC 4-8 77
UNLIMITED GOLD 4-6 81

Singles: 7-inch

EPIC 3-5 77-81
UNLIMITED GOLD 3-5 81

LPs: 10/12-inch 33rpm

EPIC 5-10 78-80
UNLIMITED GOLD 5-10 81

LEWIS & CLARKE

(Lewis & Clarke Expedition)

P&R '67

Singles: 7-inch

CHARTMAKER 4-8 66
COLGEMS 4-8 67-68

Picture Sleeves

COLGEMS 5-10 67

LPs: 10/12-inch 33rpm

COLGEMS 12-18 67

Members: Travis Lewis; Boomer Clarke (Castleman); John London.
Also see CASTLEMAN, Boomer
Also see MURPHEY, Michael

LIA, Orsa

P&R '79

Singles: 7-inch

INFINITY 3-5 79
RCA 4-6 68

LIBERACE

P&R '52

Singles: 78rpm

ADVANCE 5-8 55
COLUMBIA 3-6 52-57
DECCA 3-6 52

Singles: 7-inch

A.V.I. 3-5 76-77
COLUMBIA (39000 thru 41000 series) 5-10 52-58
COLUMBIA (48000 series) 3-6
CORAL 4-6 59-61
DECCA (28000 series) 5-10 52
DOT 4-6 64-67
MGM 3-5 73
W.B. 3-5 71

Picture Sleeves

COLUMBIA 10-15 54

EPs: 7–inch 33/45rpm

COLUMBIA 5-15 52-56
DECCA.................................. 10-20 52

LPs: 10/12–inch 33rpm

ABC.................................... 5-8 74
A.V.I. 5-8 73-79
BROOKVILLE 8-15
COLUMBIA (589 "Christmas") .. 30-45 54
COLUMBIA (600 "At the Hollywood Bowl").................................. 30-45 55
COLUMBIA (645 "Hollywood Bowl Encore") 35-45 55
COLUMBIA (661 "By Candlelight")........................ 25-45 55
COLUMBIA (800 "Sincerely Yours") 25-45 56
COLUMBIA (896 "At Home") 20-40 56
COLUMBIA (1000 thru 1200 series) 15-25 57-58
COLUMBIA (2516 "Piano Reverie") 50-75 56
(10–inch LP.)
COLUMBIA (2592 "Kiddin' on the Keys").......................... 50-75 56
(10–inch LP.)
COLUMBIA (6217 "At the Piano") 50-100 52
(10–inch LP.)
COLUMBIA (6239 "Evening with Liberace")........................... 50-100 53
(10–inch LP.)
COLUMBIA (6269 "Concertos for You") 50-100 53
(10–inch LP.)
COLUMBIA (6283 "Dream of Olwen") 50-100 54
(10–inch LP.)
COLUMBIA (6327 "Liberace Plays Chopin") 50-100 54
(10–inch LP.)
COLUMBIA (9800 series) 5-10 69
CORAL.................................. 8-15 59-64
DECCA.................................. 5-10 72
DOT.................................... 8-15 63-68
FORWARD............................... 5-10 69
HARMONY............................... 8-15 59-70
HAMILTON............................... 5-10 65
MISTLETOE.............................. 5-8 74
PARAMOUNT 5-10 73-74
TRIP................................... 4-8 76
VOCALION............................... 5-10 68
W.B. 5-10 71

Also see PRESLEY, Elvis

LIEBERMAN, Lori

LP '73

Singles: 7–inch

CAPITOL................................3-5 72-75
MILLENIUM 3-5 78

LPs: 10/12–inch 33rpm

CAPITOL................................8-12 72-74

LIFESTYLE

R&B '77

Singles: 7–inch

MCA....................................3-5 77

LPs: 10/12–inch 33rpm

MCA....................................8-10 77

LIGGETT, Otis

D&D '83

Singles: 12–inch 33/45rpm

EMERGENCY..............................4-6 83

Singles: 7–inch

EMERGENCY..............................3-5 83

LIGGINS, Jimmy

(With His 3-D Music)

R&B '48

Singles: 78rpm

ALADDIN 10-15 54
SPECIALTY 10-20 47-54

Singles: 7–inch

ALADDIN (3250 "I Ain't Drunk").25-50 54
ALADDIN (3251 "No More Alcohol")..............................25-50 54
DUPLEX..................................4-6
SPECIALTY (434 "Brown Skin Baby") 25-50 49
SPECIALTY (470 "Drunk").........20-40 53
(Black vinyl.)
SPECIALTY (470 "Drunk").........50-75 53
(Colored vinyl.)
SPECIALTY (484 "Going Away")...............................20-40 54

LIGGINS, Joe

(With His Honeydrippers)

P&R/R&B '45

Singles: 78rpm

DOT 8-10 51-56
EXCLUSIVE.............................10-20 45-48
SMASH.................................10-15 54
SPECIALTY 10-15 49-54

Singles: 7–inch

ALADDIN (3368 "Justina").........15-25 56
DOT 10-20 56
MERCURY (70440 "Yeah, Yeah, Yeah")...............................15-25 54
SPECIALTY (338 "The Honey Dripper")...............................20-30 49
SPECIALTY (379 "Little Joe's Boogie") 20-30 51
SPECIALTY (392 "Frankie Lee") 20-30 51

SPECIALTY (402 "Whiskey, Gin and Wine") 20-30 52
SPECIALTY (409 "Louisiana Woman") 20-30 52
SPECIALTY (413 "So Alone") ... 20-30 52
SPECIALTY (426 "Boogie Woogie Lou") 20-30 52
SPECIALTY (430 "Tanya") 20-30 52
SPECIALTY (441 "Goin' Back to New Orleans") 20-30 52
SPECIALTY (453 "Freight Train Blues") 20-30 53
SPECIALTY (465 "Farewell Blues") 20-30 53
SPECIALTY (474 "Everyone's Down on Me") 20-30 53
SPECIALTY (529 "Whiskey, Women and Loaded Dice") 20-40 54
Also see MILTON, Roy / Joe Liggins

LIGHT, Enoch, & His Orchestra
(Terry Snyder & All-Stars; Command All-Stars; with Light Brigade)

P&R '37

Singles: 78rpm

VOCALION 4-6 37

Singles: 7-inch

COMMAND 3-6 61

LPs: 10/12-inch 33rpm

COMMAND 5-15 59-72
GRAND AWARD 5-15 59
PROJECT 5-10 67-71

LIGHTFOOT, Gordon
(Gord Lightfoot)

LP '69

Singles: 7-inch

ABC-PAR 10-20 62
CHATEAU 5-10 65
REPRISE 3-5 70-77
U.A. 3-8 65-69
W.B. (Except 5621) 3-5 78-86
W.B. (5621 "For Lovin' Me") 5-10 65

Picture Sleeves

U.A. (50152 "The Way I Feel") 5-10 67
W.B. 3-4 86

LPs: 10/12-inch 33rpm

K-TEL 5-8
LIBERTY 5-8 80
MFSL (018 "Sundown") 25-50 78
PICKWICK 5-8 79
REPRISE (Except 93228) 5-12 70-76
REPRISE (93228 "Sit Down Young Stranger") 10-20 70
U.A. (Except 3400 & 6400 series) 5-10 69-74
U.A. (3400 series) 10-15 66-69
(Monaural.)
U.A. (6400 series) 10-20 66-69
(Stereo.)

W.B. 5-8 78-86

LIGHTHOUSE

LP '70

Singles: 7-inch

EVOLUTION 3-5 71-72
POLYDOR 4-6 73-74
RCA 3-4 69-70

LPs: 10/12-inch 33rpm

EVOLUTION 10-15 71-72
JANUS 8-10 76
POLYDOR 8-12 73-74
RCA 10-15 69-70

LIGHTNIN' SLIM
(Otis Hicks)

R&B '59

Singles: 78rpm

ACE 20-40 55
EXCELLO 10-15 55-57
FEATURE (3006 "Rock Me, Mama") 20-40 54
FEATURE (3008 "I Can't Live Happy") 10-15 54
FEATURE (3012 "Bugger Bugger Boy") 10-15 54

Singles: 7-inch

ACE (505 "Bad Feeling Blues") 75-125 54
EXCELLO (2000 series) 15-30 55-56
EXCELLO (2100 series) 8-15 57-61
EXCELLO (2200 & 2300 series) 4-8 62-72
FEATURE (3006 "Rock Me, Mama") 100-200 54
FEATURE (3008 "I Can't Live Happy") 25-50 54
FEATURE (3012 "Bugger Bugger Boy") 25-50 54

LPs: 10/12-inch 33rpm

EXCELLO (8000 "Rooster Blues") 20-40 60
EXCELLO (8004 "Bell Ringer") .. 15-25 65
EXCELLO (8018 "High and Low Down") 10-15 71
EXCELLO (8023 "London Gumbo") 10-15 72

LIGHTNING SEEDS

LP '90

LPs: 10/12-inch 33rpm

MCA 5-8 90

LIMAHL
(Chris Hamill)

P&R/D&D/LP '85

Singles: 12-inch 33/45rpm

EMI AMERICA 4-6 85-86

Singles: 7-inch

EMI AMERICA 3-4 85-86

Picture Sleeves

EMI AMERICA 3-4 85-86

LIME

LPs: 10/12-inch 33rpm

EMI AMERICA 5-8 85-86

Also see KAJAGOOGOO

LIME

D&D '83

Singles: 12-inch 33/45rpm

PRISM 4-6 83
TSR 4-6 85

Singles: 7-inch

PRISM 3-5 83

LPs: 10/12-inch 33rpm

PRISM 5-8 83

LIMELITERS

P&R/LP '61

Singles: 7-inch

ELEKTRA 5-10 60-61
RCA 4-8 61-64
W.B. 3-6 68

Picture Sleeves

RCA 5-10 61-63

EPs: 7-inch 33/45rpm

RCA ("Introducing . . .") 10-15 61
(Promotional issue only. Introduces 11 new RCA acts with about 30 seconds of music by: Limeliters, Cables; Toni Harper; Gary Judis; Cleo Jons; Baker Knight; Langan Sisters; Barry Martin; Penny & Jean; Gordon Terry; Universals.)

LPs: 10/12-inch 33rpm

CAMDEN 5-10 74
ELEKTRA 15-25 60-61
LEGACY 8-10 70
PICKWICK 5-8 72
RCA (Except 2336) 10-20 61-68
RCA (2336 "Pure Gold") 5-8 77
STAX 6-10 74
W.B. 8-15 68

Members: Glen Yarbrough; Lou Gottlieb; Alex Hassilev; Ernie Sheldon.
Also see ANN-MARGRET
Also see YARBROUGH, Glen

LIMIT

R&B '82

Singles: 12-inch 33/45rpm

PORTRAIT 4-6 84

Singles: 7-inch

ARISTA 3-5 82
PORTRAIT 3-4 84

Also see GUTHRIE, Gwen

LIMITED WARRANTY

P&R '86

Singles: 7-inch

ATCO 3-4 86

Picture Sleeves

ATCO 3-4 86

LIMMIE & Family Cookin'

P&R '72

Singles: 7-inch

AVCO 3-6 72

LIND, Bob

P&R/LP '66

Singles: 7-inch

CAPITOL 3-5 71
VERVE/FOLKWAYS 4-6 66
WORLD PACIFIC 4-8 65-66

LPs: 10/12-inch 33rpm

CAPITOL 10-15 71
VERVE/FOLKWAYS 10-20 66
WORLD PACIFIC 10-20 66

LINDEN, Kathy

(With Joe Leahy's Orchestra)

P&R '58

Singles: 7-inch

CAPITOL 4-8 62-63
FELSTED 5-15 58-59
MONUMENT 5-10 60-61
NATIONAL 4-8 60s
RECORD PROD. CORP 4-8 61

Picture Sleeves

FELSTED 10-20 58-59
MONUMENT 4-8 60-61

EPs: 7-inch 33/45rpm

FELSTED (35001 "Hits") 35-45 58

LPs: 10/12-inch 33rpm

FELSTED (7501 "That Certain Boy") 40-60 59

LINDISFARNE

P&R '72

Singles: 7-inch

ATCO 3-5 78
ELEKTRA 3-5 72-73

LPs: 10/12-inch 33rpm

ATCO 8-12 78
ELEKTRA 10-15 71-74

LINDLEY, David

(With El Rayo)

LP '81

Singles: 7-inch

ASYLUM 3-5 81

LPs: 10/12-inch 33rpm

ASYLUM 5-10 81
ELEKTRA 5-8 88

Also see BROWNE, Jackson

LINDSAY, Mark

P&R '69

Singles: 7-inch

COLUMBIA 3-6 69-75
GREEDY 3-6 76
W.B. 3-6 77

LPs: 10/12-inch 33rpm

COLUMBIA 10-15 70-71

Also see REVERE, Paul, & Raiders

Also see UNKNOWNS

LINEAR

P&R/LP '90

LPs: 10/12-inch 33rpm

ATLANTIC 5-8 90

LINER

P&R '79

Singles: 7-inch

ATCO 3-5 79

LPs: 10/12-inch 33rpm

ATCO 5-10 79

LINK - EDDY COMBO

R&B '61

Singles: 7-inch

REPRISE 8-12 61

Singles: 12-inch 33/45rpm

Members: Al Garcia; Fred Mendoza; Vince Bumatay; Art Rodriguez.

LINKLETTER, Art

LP '66

Singles: 7-inch

CAPITOL 3-5 69

EPs: 7-inch 33/45rpm

COLUMBIA 5-10 56
WORD 3-5 69

LPs: 10/12-inch 33rpm

CAPITOL 8-15 61
COLUMBIA 15-25 56
HARMONY 8-15 59
20TH FOX 8-15 63-66
WORD 5-10 68

LINX

R&B/LP '81

Singles: 7-inch

CHRYSALIS 3-4 81

Picture Sleeves

CHRYSALIS 3-4 81

LPs: 10/12-inch 33rpm

CHRYSALIS 5-8 81

Members: David Grant; Peter Martin.
Also see GRANT, David

LIONS & GHOSTS

LP '87

LPs: 10/12-inch 33rpm

EMI AMERICA 5-8 87

LIPPS, INC.

P&R/R&B/LP '80

Singles: 7-inch

CASABLANCA 3-5 79-83

LPs: 10/12-inch 33rpm

CASABLANCA 5-8 79-81

LIQUID GOLD

P&R '79

Singles: 12-inch 33/45rpm

CRITIQUE 4-6 83
PARACHUTE 4-8 79

Singles: 7-inch

CRITIQUE 3-4 83
PARACHUTE 3-5 79

LPs: 10/12-inch 33rpm

PARACHUTE 5-10 79

LIQUID LIQUID

D&D '83

Singles: 12-inch 33/45rpm

99 RECORDS 4-6 83

LIQUID SMOKE

P&R '70

Singles: 7-inch

AVCO EMBASSY 4-8 70

LPs: 10/12-inch 33rpm

AVCO EMBASSY (33005 "Liquid Smoke") 20-30 70

Member: Sandy Dantaleo.

LISA

D&D '83

Singles: 12-inch 33/45rpm

MOBY DICK 4-6 83-84

LISA LISA
(With Cult Jam & Full Force)

P&R/R&B/D&D/LP '85

Singles: 12-inch 33/45rpm

COLUMBIA 4-6 85-86

Singles: 7-inch

COLUMBIA 3-4 85-89

Picture Sleeves

COLUMBIA 3-4 87-88

LPs: 10/12-inch 33rpm

COLUMBIA 5-8 84-89

Member: Lisa Velez.
Also see FULL FORCE
Also see KING DREAM CHORUS & Holiday Crew

LITES, Shirley

D&D '83

Singles: 12-inch 33/45rpm

WEST END 4-6 83

LITTLE, Rich

LP '82

Singles: 7-inch

BOARDWALK 3-4 82
MERCURY 3-5 71

LPs: 10/12-inch 33rpm

BOARDWALK 5-8 82
CAEDMON 5-10 72
KARR 8-15 68
MERCURY 8-10 71
PIZZA HUT ("Pizza Hut '73") 15-20 73
(Souvenir of an annual company meeting. Promotional issue only. No selection number used.)

LITTLE AMERICA

LP '87

LPs: 10/12-inch 33rpm

GEFFEN 5-8 87

LITTLE ANTHONY & IMPERIALS
(Anthony & Imperials; Imperials)

P&R/R&B '58

Singles: 7–inch

APOLLO 8-12 61
AVCO 3-5 74-75
DCP 4-8 64-66
END (1027 "Tears on My Pillow") 10-20 58
(Credited only to "The Imperials.")
END (1027 "Tears on My Pillow") 5-10 58
(By "Little Anthony & Imperials.")
END (1036 "So Much") 10-15 58
END (1038 "The Diary") 15-20 59
END (1039 thru 1104") 8-15 58-61
JANUS 3-5 71-72
MCA 3-4 80
OLD HIT 3-4
PCM 3-4 83
PURE GOLD 3-5 76
ROULETTE 4-8 61-63
U.A. 3-6 69-70
VEEP 4-8 66-68

Picture Sleeves

DCP 8-12 65
VEEP 8-12 66

EPs: 7–inch 33/45rpm

END (203 "Little Anthony and the Imperials") 50-75 58
END (204 "We Are the Imperials Featuring Little Anthony") 50-75 59

LPs: 10/12–inch 33rpm

ACCORD 5-10 83
AVCO 8-10 74
DCP 15-25 64-66
EMUS 5-10 79
END (303 "We Are the Imperials Featuring Little Anthony") 50-100 59
END (311 "Shades of the '40s") 40-60 60
FORUM CIRCLE 10-15
LIBERTY 5-8 81
ROULETTE 20-25 65
SUNSET 10-12 70
U.A. (Except 1000 series) 10-15 69-74
U.A. (1000 series) 5-8 80
VEEP 15-20 66-68

Members: Anthony Gourdine; Clarence Collins; Sam Strain; Tracy Lord; Ernie Wright; Gloucester Rogers.

Also see IMPERIALS
Also see LITTLE ANTHONY
Also see O'JAYS

LITTLE ANTHONY & IMPERIALS / Platters

LPs: 10/12–inch 33rpm

EXACT 5-10 80

Also see LITTLE ANTHONY & IMPERIALS
Also see PLATTERS

LITTLE BEAVER
(Willie Hale)

R&B '72

Singles: 7–inch

CAT 3-5 72-76
PHIL-LA of SOUL 4-8 67

Also see BIRDLEGS & PAULINE
Also see WRIGHT, Betty

LITTLE BILL & BLUENOTES

P&R '59

Singles: 7–inch

BOLO 8-12 60s
DOLTON 10-20 59
TOPAZ 10-20

LPs: 10/12–inch 33rpm

CAMELOT (102 "The Fiesta Club Presents Little Bill & the Blue Notes") ... 75-100 60

Members: Bill Engelhart; Frank Dutra; Tom Giving; Buck Ormsby; Lassie Aanes; Buck England; Tom Morgan.

LITTLE BOOKER
(James Booker)

Singles: 78rpm

IMPERIAL 15-25 54

Singles: 7–inch

ACE 10-20 58
IMPERIAL (5293 "Thinkin' 'Bout My Baby") 50-75 54

Also see BOOKER, James

LITTLE CAESAR

R&B '52

Singles: 78rpm

BIG TOWN 10-20 53
RPM 10-20 53
RECORDED in HOLLYWOOD .. 10-20 53

Singles: 7–inch

BIG TOWN (106 "Big Eyes") 20-40 53
BIG TOWN (110 "What Kind of Fool Is He") 20-40 53
RPM (393 "Chains of Love Have Disappeared") 20-40 53
RECORDED in HOLLYWOOD (234 "The River") 25-50 53
RECORDED in HOLLYWOOD (235 "Goodbye Baby") 25-50 53
RECORDED in HOLLYWOOD (236 "Talking to Myself") 25-50 53
RECORDED in HOLLYWOOD (237 "Atomic Love") 25-50 53

Also see WILSON, Jimmy / Thrillers / Little Caesar

LITTLE CAESAR & CONSULS

P&R '65

Singles: 7–inch

MALA 8-12 65

LITTLE CAESAR & ROMANS

P&R/R&B '61

Singles: 7–inch

DEL-FI 10-15 61

LPs: 10/12-inch 33rpm

DEL-FI (1218 "Memories of Those Oldies But Goodies")............... 50-75 61

Members: Carl Burnett; David Johnson; Leroy Sanders; Johnny Simmons.

Also see BLUE JAYS / Little Caesar & Romans

LITTLE CAESAR & ROMANS / Ron Holden

Singles: 7-inch

TRIP 3-5 70s

Also see HOLDEN, Ron

Also see LITTLE CAESAR & ROMANS

LITTLE DIPPERS

(Anita Kerr Singers)

P&R '60

Singles: 7-inch

DOT.. 4-6 64

UNIVERSITY.................................. 5-8 59-60

Also see KERR, Anita

LITTLE ESTHER

(Esther Phillips; Little Esther Phillips; with Earle Warren Orchestra; with Johnny Otis Orchestra)

R&B '50

Singles: 78rpm

DECCA.................................... 10-20 54

FEDERAL................................. 15-25 51

SAVOY 8-12 56

Singles: 7-inch

ATLANTIC................................. 5-15 64-67

DECCA (28804 "Talkin' All Out of My Head") 20-30 54

DECCA (48305 "Stop Cryin'") ... 25-35 54

DECCA (48314 "He's a No Good Man") 40-60 54

FEDERAL (12023 "I'm a Bad Girl").. 25-50 51

FEDERAL (12042 "Crying and Sighing").............................. 25-50 51

FEDERAL (12055 "Crying Blues").................................. 25-50 52

FEDERAL (12063 "Summertime").......................... 25-50 52

FEDERAL (12065 "Better Beware") 25-50 52

FEDERAL (12078 "Aged and Mellow") 25-50 52

FEDERAL (12090 "Ramblin' Blues")................................... 25-50 52

FEDERAL (12122 "You Took My Love too Fast")............................... 25-50 53

FEDERAL (12126 "Hound Dog").. 25-50 53

FEDERAL (12142 "Cherry Wine") 25-50 53

KUDU... 3-5 72-76

LENOX.. 5-10 62-63

MERCURY 3-5 77-79

ROULETTE.................................... 3-6 69

SAVOY (1100 series)................10-15 56

SAVOY (1500 series)..................5-10 58-59

WARWICK 5-8 60-61

WINNING 3-5 83

LPs: 10/12-inch 33rpm

ATLANTIC (1500 & 1600 series) .8-12 70-76

ATLANTIC (8100 series) 15-30 65-66

KING (622 "Memory Lane") .800-1200 59

KUDU..8-12 72-76

LENOX (227 "Release Me").......30-50 62

MERCURY 5-10 78-81

YORKSHIRE...............................8-12

Also see ADAMS, Faye / Little Esther / Shirley & Lee

Also see PHILLIPS, Esther, & Joe Beck

LITTLE ESTHER & Dominoes

(With the Earle Warren Orchestra)

Singles: 78rpm

FEDERAL (12036 "Heart to Heart")....................................40-60 51

Singles: 7-inch

FEDERAL (12036 "Heart to Heart")................................250-350 51

Also see LITTLE ESTHER with the Earle Warren Orchestra (With the Dominoes)

Also see LITTLE ESTHER & Clyde McPhatter

LITTLE ESTHER & Big Al Downing

Singles: 7-inch

LENOX...5-10 63

Also see DOWNING, Al

LITTLE ESTHER & Junior with the Johnny Otis Orchestra / Johnny Otis Orchestra with the Vocaleers

Singles: 78rpm

SAVOY (824 "Get Together Blues") 10-20 51

Also see VOCALEERS

LITTLE ESTHER & Little Willie Littlefield

Singles: 78rpm

FEDERAL 10-15 52

Singles: 7-inch

FEDERAL (12108 "Last Laugh Blues") 25-50 52

FEDERAL (12115 "Turn the Lamps Down Low").............................25-50 52

Also see LITTLEFIELD, Little Willie

LITTLE ESTHER & Clyde McPhatter

Singles: 7-inch

FEDERAL (12344 "Heart to Heart")....................................15-25 58

Also see LITTLE ESTHER & DOMINOES

Also see McPHATTER, Clyde

LITTLE ESTHER & Bobby Nunn

Singles: 78rpm

FEDERAL (12100 "Saturday Night Daddy")...........................20-30 52

FEDERAL (12122 "You Took My Love Too Fast") 10-20 53

LITTLE ESTHER & Mel Walker

Singles: 7-inch

FEDERAL (12100 "Saturday Night Daddy") 35-50 52
FEDERAL (12122 "You Took My Love too Fast") 150-200 53
Also see NUNN, Bobby

LITTLE ESTHER & Mel Walker
(With the Johnny Otis Orchestra)

Singles: 78rpm

FEDERAL 10-15 52
SAVOY 10-15 50

Singles: 7-inch

FEDERAL (12055 "Ring-A-Ding Doo") 25-50 52
SAVOY (735 "Mistrustin' Blues") 25-50 50
SAVOY (759 "Deceivin' Blues") 25-50 50
Also see OTIS, Johnny

LITTLE ESTHER with the Earle Warren Orchestra
(With the Dominoes)

Singles: 78rpm

FEDERAL (12016 "The Deacon Moves In") 50-75 51
FEDERAL (12036 "Heart") 40-60 51

Singles: 7-inch

FEDERAL (12016 "The Deacon Moves In") 300-400 51
FEDERAL (12036 "Heart") 250-350 51
Also see DOMINOES
Also see LITTLE ESTHER & DOMINOES

LITTLE EVA

P&R/R&B/LP '62

Singles: 7-inch

ABC 3-5 74
AMY 4-8 65-66
BELL 3-5 72
DIMENSION 5-10 62-65
MCA 3-4 80
SPRING 3-5 70
VERVE 4-8 66

Picture Sleeves

DIMENSION (1035 "Makin' with the Magilla") 20-30 64

LPs: 10/12-inch 33rpm

DIMENSION (DLP-6000 "L-L-L-L-Locomotion") 35-55 62
(Monaural.)
DIMENSION (DLPS-6000 "L-L-L-L-Locomotion") 50-75 62
(Stereo.)
Also see COOKIES / Little Eva / Carole King
Also see IRWIN, Big Dee
Also see KING, Ben E.

LITTLE FEAT

LP '74

Singles: 7-inch

W.B. 3-6 70-78

LPs: 10/12-inch 33rpm

MFSL (013 "Waiting for Columbus") 75-125 78
NAUTILUS (24 "Time Loves a Hero") 20-25 70s
(Half-speed mastered.)
W.B. (984 "Hoy Hoy") 15-20 81
(Promotional issue only.)
W.B. (1890 thru 2884) 8-15 70-76
W.B. (3015 thru 3538) 6-12 77-81
W.B. (25000 & 26000 series) 5-8 88-90
Members: Lowell George; Ken Gradney; Richard Hayward; Sam Clayton; Fred Tackett; Paul Barrere; Bill Payne; Roy Estrada.
Also see BRAMLETT, Bonnie
Also see CARTER, Valerie
Also see COODER, Ry
Also see GEORGE, Lowell
Also see HARRIS, Emmylou
Also see MOTHERS of INVENTION
Also see TOWER of POWER
Also see ZEVON

LITTLE JO ANN

P&R '62

Singles: 7-inch

KAPP 8-12 62

LITTLE JOE & MORROCOS

Singles: 7-inch

BUMBLE BEE 15-20 58
Member: Joe Cook.
Also see LITTLE JOE & THRILLERS

LITTLE JOE & THRILLERS
(Little Joe; Little Joe the Thriller)

P&R '57

Singles: 7-inch

ENJOY 4-8 64
EPIC (9292 "It's too Bad We Had to Say Goodbye") 10-15 58
MGM 3-5 70-73
OKEH 8-12 56-61
PEANUT 5-10
REPRISE 5-8 63
ROSE 5-8 63
TWENTIETH CENTURY (1214 "For Sentimental Reasons") 15-25 61

EPs: 7-inch 33/45rpm

EPIC (7198 "Little Joe and the Thrillers") 75-100 58
Members: Joe Cook; Richard Frazier; Farris Hill; Don Burnett; Harry Pascle.
Also see LITTLE JOE & MORROCOS

LITTLE JOE BLUE

R&B '66

Singles: 7-inch

CHECKER 4-8 66
MOVIN' 4-8 66

LITTLE JOEY & FLIPS

(Joey Hall)

P&R '62

Singles: 7-inch

JOY 8-10 62

Also see DRIFTERS / Little Joey & Flips

LITTLE JUNIOR'S BLUE FLAMES

(Junior Parker)

R&B '53

Singles: 78rpm

SUN 25-50 53

Singles: 7-inch

SUN (187 "Feelin' Good") 75-100 53

SUN (192 "Love My Baby") 75-100 53

Also see PARKER, Little Junior

LITTLE MAC & Boss Sounds

R&B '65

Singles: 7-inch

ATLANTIC 4-8 65

Member: Ann Mason.

LITTLE MILTON

(Milton Campbell)

R&B '62

Singles: 78rpm

METEOR 25-50 57

SUN 40-60 53-54

Singles: 7-inch

BOBBIN (101 "I'm a Lonely Man") 10-20 58

BOBBIN (108 "Long Distance Operator") 10-20 59

BOBBIN (112 "Strange Dreams") 10-20 59

BOBBIN (117 "Hold Me Tight") . 10-20 59

BOBBIN (120 "Dead Love") 10-20 60

BOBBIN (125 "Hey Love") 10-20 61

BOBBIN (128 "Cross My Heart") 10-20 61

CHECKER (0124 thru 0252) 3-6 72-76

CHECKER (977 thru 1239) 4-8 61-71

CHESS 3-6 73-76

EAR 3-5 80

GLADES 3-5 76-78

GOLDEN 3-5 80

MCA 3-5 83

MALACO 3-4 84-86

METEOR (5040 "Love at First Sight") 50-100 57

METEOR (5045 "Let My Baby Be") 50-100 57

MIER 3-5 78

STAX 3-6 71-83

SUN (194 "Beggin' My Baby"). 75-100 53

SUN (200 "If You Love Me") . 100-200 54

SUN (220 "Homesick for My Baby") 150-300 55

LPs: 10/12-inch 33rpm

CHECKER (2995 "We're Gonna Make It") 20-30 65

CHECKER (3002 "Big Blues") ... 20-30 66

CHECKER (3011 "Grits Ain't Groceries") 15-20 69

CHECKER (3012 "If Walls Could Talk") 15-20 70

CHESS 10-15 72-76

GLADES 8-10 76-77

GOLDEN 5-10 80

MCA 5-8 83

MALACO 5-8 84-92

STAX 6-12 73-81

Also see CAMPBELL, Little Milton

Also see MANN, Herbie

LITTLE MILTON & Albert King

LPs: 10/12-inch 33rpm

STAX 5-10 79

Also see KING, Albert

LITTLE MILTON & Jackie Ross

Singles: 7-inch

EAR 3-5 80

LP: 10/12-inch 33rpm

EAR 5-10 81

Also see LITTLE MILTON

Also see ROSS, Jackie

LITTLE RICHARD

P&R '56

Singles: 78rpm

PEACOCK 15-25 53

RCA (4392 "Taxi Blues") 25-50 51

RCA (4582 "Get Rich Quick") 25-50 52

RCA (4772 "Ain't Nothing Happenin") 20-40 52

RCA (5025 "Please Have Mercy on Me") 20-40 52

SPECIALTY 10-20 56-57

Singles: 7-inch

ABC 3-5 73

ATLANTIC 4-8 63

BELL 3-5 73

BRUNSWICK 4-6 68

CORAL 4-8 63

END 10-15 59

GREEN MOUNTAIN 3-5 73

KENT 3-5 73

MCA 3-4 86

MANTICORE 3-5 75

MERCURY 4-8 61

MODERN 10-15 57-58

(Black label.)

MODERN 4-8 66-67

(Red or white label.)

OKEH 4-6 66-69

PEACOCK (1658 "Little Richard's Boogie") 20-40 53

PEACOCK (1673 "Maybe I'm Right")	20-40	54
RCA (4392 "Taxi Blues")	150-200	51
RCA (4582 "Get Rich Quick")	150-200	52
RCA (4772 "Ain't Nothing Happenin")	50-100	52
RCA (5025 "Please Have Mercy on Me")	50-100	52
REPRISE	3-6	70-72
SPECIALTY (561 thru 664)	10-20	56-59
SPECIALTY (670 thru 699)	5-10	59-64
SPECIALTY (SPBX series)	15-20	85
(Boxed sets of six colored vinyl 45s.)		
TRIP	3-5	71
VEE JAY	4-8	64
W.B.	3-5	87

Picture Sleeves

MCA	3-4	86
MODERN (1018 "Holy Mackeral")	10-20	57
OKEH (7251 "Poor Dog")	8-10	66
SPECIALTY (606 "Jenny Jenny")	15-25	57
SPECIALTY (611 "Keep a Knockin'")	15-25	57
SPECIALTY (624 "Good Golly Miss Molly")	15-25	58
SPECIALTY (633 "Ooh! My Soul")	15-25	58

EPs: 7-inch 33/45rpm

CAMDEN (416 "Little Richard")	100-150	56
CAMDEN (446 "Little Richard Rocks")	75-125	56
KAMA SUTRA (17 "Little Richard")	10-20	70
SPECIALTY (400 "Here's Little Richard")	30-40	56
SPECIALTY (401 "Here's Little Richard")	30-40	56
SPECIALTY (402 "Here's Little Richard")	30-40	56
SPECIALTY (403 "Little Richard")	30-40	57
SPECIALTY (404 "Little Richard")	30-40	57
SPECIALTY (405 "Little Richard")	30-40	57

LPs: 10/12-inch 33rpm

ACCORD	5-10	81
AUDIO ENCORES	20-25	80
BUDDAH	10-12	69
CAMDEN (420 "Little Richard")	100-150	56
CAMDEN (2430 "Every Hour")	20-30	70
CORAL	20-30	63
CROWN	15-25	63
CUSTOM	10-12	60s
EPIC	10-12	71
EVEREST	5-8	82
EXACT	5-10	80-81
EXODUS	5-10	
51 WEST	5-8	80s
GRT	5-8	77
GOLD DISC	10-12	
GUEST STAR	10-15	64
KAMA SUTRA	10-12	70
MERCURY	20-25	61
MODERN	10-20	66
OKEH	10-20	67
PICKWICK	10-12	72
REPRISE	10-12	70-72
ROULETTE	10-15	68
SCEPTER	10-12	
SPECIALTY (100 "Here's Little Richard")	250-300	57
(Reissued as Specialty 2100.)		
SPECIALTY (2100 "Here's Little Richard")	30-50	57
SPECIALTY (2103 "Little Richard")	30-50	57
SPECIALTY (2104 "The Fabulous Little Richard")	30-50	58
SPECIALTY (2111 "Biggest Hits")	15-25	63
SPECIALTY (2113 "Grooviest 17 Original Hits")	10-15	68
SPECIALTY (2154 "The Essential Little Richard")	8-12	84
SPIN-O-RAMA	10-15	60s
SUMMIT	10-12	
TRIP	10-12	71-78
20TH FOX	15-25	63
UNITED	8-10	70s
U.A.	8-10	75
UPFRONT	8-10	77
VEE JAY	10-20	64-65
VEE JAY/DYNASTY	10-12	
W.B.	5-8	87
WING	10-20	64

Session: Lee Allen.
Also see ALLEN, Lee
Also see BAILEY, Philip, & Little Richard
Also see BEACH BOYS & Little Richard
Also see CANNED HEAT
Also see CHARLES, Ray / Little Richard / Sam Cooke
Also see COOKE, Sam / Lloyd Price / Larry Williams / Little Richard
Also see DUCES of RHYTHM & Tempo Toppers
Also see HENDRIX, Jimi, & Little Richard
Also see McPHATTER, Clyde / Little Richard / Jerry Butler
Also see UPSETTERS Featuring Little Richard

LITTLE RICHARD / Sister Rosetta

LPs: 10/12-inch 33rpm

GUEST STAR	10-15	

Also see LITTLE RICHARD

LITTLE RIVER BAND

(LRB)

P&R/LP '76

Singles: 12-inch 33/45rpm

CAPITOL 4-6 83

Singles: 7-inch

CAPITOL 3-4 79-85
HARVEST 3-5 76-78

Picture Sleeves

CAPITOL 3-5 81-85
HARVEST 3-5 78

LPs: 10/12-inch 33rpm

CAPITOL 5-8 79-85
HARVEST 5-8 75-80
MFSL 20-30 79

Member: John Farnham.
Also see FARNHAM, John
Also see SHORROCK, Glen

LITTLE SISTER

P&R '70

Singles: 7-inch

STONE FLOWER 5-10 70-72

LPs: 10/12-inch 33rpm

STONE FLOWER 10-15 70

Members: Vanetta Stewart; Elva Melton; Mary Rand.

LITTLE STEVEN

P&R/LP '82

Singles: 7-inch

EMI AMERICA 3-5 82-84

LPs: 10/12-inch 33rpm

EMI AMERICA 5-8 82-84
MANHATTAN 5-8 87

Also see BEAUVOIR, Jean
Also see SPRINGSTEEN, Bruce

LITTLE SYLVIA

(Sylvia Vanderpool)

Singles: 78rpm

CAT (102 "Fine Love") 10-15 53
JUBILEE 10-15 52

Singles: 7-inch

CAT (102 "Fine Love") 15-25 53
JUBILEE (5093 "Drive, Daddy, Drive") 25-35 52

Also see MICKEY & SYLVIA
Also see SYLVIA

LITTLE WALTER

R&B '52

(With His Jukes; with Night Caps; with Night Cats; Little Walter Trio; Little Walter J.; Marion Walter Jacobs)

Singles: 78rpm

CHANCE (1116 "That's Allright") 50-75 52
CHECKER 10-20 52-57
ORA NELLE (711 "Ora Nelle Blues [That's Allright]") 50-75 47

Singles: 7-inch

CHANCE (1116 "That's Allright") 250-350 52
CHECKER (758 "Juke") 20-30 52
CHECKER (764 "Mean Old World") 20-30 52
CHECKER (770 "Off the Wall") 20-30 53
(Black vinyl.)
CHECKER (770 "Off the Wall") 75-100 53
(Colored vinyl.)
CHECKER (780 "Quarter to Twelve") 15-25 53
CHECKER (786 "Lights Out") 15-25 53
CHECKER (793 "Rocker") 15-25 54
CHECKER (799 "You Better Watch Yourself") 15-25 54
(Black vinyl.)
CHECKER (799 "You Better Watch Yourself") 50-75 54
(Colored vinyl.)
CHECKER (800 series) 10-20 54-58
CHECKER (900 thru 1100 series) 8-15 58-65

LPs: 10/12-inch 33rpm

CHESS (Except 1428) 10-20 69-74
CHESS (1428 "Best of Little Walter") 50-100 57

Also see ROBINSON, Freddy
Also see SUNNYLAND SLIM

LITTLEFIELD, Little Willie

R&B '48

Singles: 78rpm

EDDIE'S (1202 "Little Willie's Boogie") 10-20 48
EDDIE'S (1205 "Chicago Bound") 20-30 48
EDDIE'S (1212 "Swanee River") 20-30 49
FEDERAL 15-25 52-57
MODERN 15-25 49-50
RHYTHM 30-50 56

Singles: 7-inch

BULLS-EYE 10-15 58
FEDERAL (12101 "Sticking on You, Baby") 50-75 52
FEDERAL (12110 "K.C. Loving") 50-75 52
FEDERAL (12137 "The Midnight Hour Was Shining") 50-75 53
FEDERAL (12148 "Miss K.C.'s Fine") 50-75 53
FEDERAL (12163 "Please Don't Go-o-o-o-oh") 50-75 53
FEDERAL (12174 "Falling Tears") 50-75 54
FEDERAL (12221 "Jim Wilson's Boogie") 25-50 55
FEDERAL (12300 series) 10-20 57-59
RHYTHM (108 "Ruby-Ruby") 75-100 56

Also see LITTLE ESTHER & Little Willie Littlefield

LITTLEFIELD, Little Willie / Goree Carter

Singles: 78rpm

FREEDOM (1502 "Littlefield Boogie") 15-25 49

Also see LITTLEFIELD, Little Willie

LIVERPOOL FIVE

P&R '66

Singles: 7–inch

RCA.. 5-10 65-67

LPs: 10/12–inch 33rpm

RCA (LPM-3583 "The Liverpool Five Arrive") 20-25 66

(Monaural.)

RCA (LSP-3583 "The Liverpool Five Arrive") 20-30 66

(Stereo.)

RCA (LPM-3682 "Out of Sight") 20-25 67

(Monaural.)

RCA (LSP-3682 "Out of Sight"). 20-30 67

(Stereo.)

Also see ASTRONAUTS / Liverpool Five

LIVIGNI, John

P&R '75

Singles: 7–inch

RAINTREE 3-5 75

LIVING COLOUR

LP '88

Singles: 7–inch

EPIC.. 3-4 88-90

LPs: 10/12–inch 33rpm

EPIC.. 5-8 88-90

Members: Corey Glover; Vernon Reid; Muzz Skillings; William Calhoun.

LIVING in a BOX

P&R/LP '87

Singles: 12–inch 33/45rpm

CHRYSALIS................................ 4-6 87

Singles: 7–inch

CHRYSALIS................................ 3-4 87

Picture Sleeves

CHRYSALIS................................ 3-4 87

LPs: 10/12–inch 33rpm

CHRYSALIS................................ 5-8 87

LIVING STRINGS

LP '61

Singles: 7-Inch

COMMAND 3-5 59

GRAND AWARD.......................... 3-5 59

LPs: 10/12-Inch 33rpm

CAMDEN.................................... 5-15 60-62

COMMAND 5-10 59

GRAND AWARD 5-10 59

LIZARD, King: see KING LIZARD

LIZZY BORDEN

LP '86

LPs: 10/12–inch 33rpm

ENIGMA/METAL BLADE..............5-8 86-89

LLOYD, Charles, Quartet

LP '67

LPs: 10/12–inch 33rpm

ATLANTIC...................................10-15 67

Also see HAMILTON, Chico

LLOYD, Ian

P&R '79

Singles: 7–inch

POLYDOR 3-5 76

SCOTTI BROTHERS......................3-4 79

LPs: 10/12–inch 33rpm

POLYDOR 5-10 76

SCOTTI BROTHERS......................5-8 79

Also see STORIES

LOAF, Meat: see MEAT LOAF

LOBO

(Roland Kent Lavole)

P&R/LP '71

Singles: 7–inch

BIG TREE 3-6 71-75

ELEKTRA.....................................3-5 80

EVERGREEN 3-4 85

FLASHBACK.................................3-5 73

LOBO 3-5 81-82

MCA...3-4 79

MARIANNE 3-5 77

PHILIPS 3-5

W.B. 3-5 76-78

LPs: 10/12–inch 33rpm

BIG TREE 10-15 71-75

CALUMET 10-15 73

MCA..5-10 79

Also see LEE, Robin, & Lobo

Also see STAFFORD, Jim

Also see WOLFPACK

LOCKLIN, Hank

C&W '49

Singles: 78rpm

DECCA 5-10 52

4 STAR 5-10 49-54

RCA 4-8 55-57

Singles: 7–inch

COUNTRY ARTISTS.....................3-4 83

DECCA (29000 series) 10-15 52

4 STAR (1500 & 1600 series)....10-15 52-54

KING (5000 series) 5-8 59

MGM..3-5 74

PLANTATION 3-5 76-77

RCA (0030 thru 0900 series) 3-5 72-74

RCA (6100 thru 7600 series) 8-15 55-59

RCA (7700 thru 9900 series) 4-8 60-71

EPs: 7–inch 33/45rpm

RCA 8-15 58-61

LPs: 10/12-inch 33rpm

CAMDEN.................................... 8-15 62-74
DESIGN 10-15 62
INTERNATIONAL AWARD......... 8-12 60s
KING (600 & 700 series)........... 15-25 61
MGM 5-10 75
METRO 10-15 65
PICKWICK/HILLTOP 8-15 65-68
PLANTATION............................... 5-8 77-81
RCA (Except 1600 series)......... 10-20 62-71
RCA (1673 "Foreign Love")....... 25-35 58
SEARS 10-15 60s
WRANGLER 15-25 62

Session: Jordanaires.

Also see CLINE, Patsy / Hank Locklin / Miller Brothers / Eddie Marvin

Also see SNOW, Hank / Hank Locklin / Porter Wagoner

LOCKLIN, Hank, with Danny Davis & Nashville Brass

C&W '70

Singles: 7-inch

RCA... 3-6 69-70

LPs: 10/12-inch 33rpm

RCA... 8-10 70

Also see DAVIS, Danny

Also see LOCKLIN, Hank

LOCKSMITH

R&B '80

Singles: 7-inch

ARISTA 3-5 80

LPs: 10/12-inch 33rpm

ARISTA 5-10 80

LODGE, John

LP '77

Singles: 7-inch

LONDON.. 3-5 77

LPs: 10/12-inch 33rpm

LONDON (683 "Natural Avenue") 10-15 77

Also see HAYWARD, Justin, & John Lodge

Also see MOODY BLUES

LOFGREN, Nils

LP '75

Singles: 7-inch

A&M 3-5 75-77

LPs: 10/12-inch 33rpm

A&M (Except 8362) 8-10 75-82
A&M (8362 "Authorized Bootleg") 25-30 76
(Promotional issue only.)
BACKSTREET 5-8 81
COLUMBIA 5-8 85
EPIC... 8-10 76
RYKODISC 5-8 91

Also see GRIN

LOGG

R&B '81

Singles: 7-inch

SALSOUL 3-5 81

LPs: 10/12-inch 33rpm

SALSOUL 5-8 81

LOGGINS, Dave

P&R/LP '74

Singles: 7-inch

EPIC...3-5 74-81
VANGUARD.......................................4-6 72-74

LPs: 10/12-inch 33rpm

CAPITOL..5-8 84
EPIC 8-10 74-81
VANGUARD.......................................8-12 72

Also see MURRAY, Anne, & Dave Loggins

LOGGINS, Kenny

P&R/LP '77

Singles: 12-inch 33/45rpm

COLUMBIA 4-8 81-86

Singles: 7-inch

COLUMBIA 3-5 77-88

Picture Sleeves

COLUMBIA 3-4 83-88

LPs: 10/12-inch 33rpm

COLUMBIA (Except 45387).........6-12 72-88
COLUMBIA (45387 "Nightwatch") 10-15 81
(Half-speed mastered.)

Also see U.S.A. for AFRICA

LOGGINS, Kenny, & Stevie Nicks

Singles: 7-inch

COLUMBIA 3-5 78

Also see NICKS, Stevie

LOGGINS, Kenny, & Steve Perry

Singles: 7-inch

COLUMBIA 3-5 82

Picture Sleeves

COLUMBIA 3-5 82

Also see LOGGINS, Kenny

Also see PERRY, Steve

LOGGINS & MESSINA

P&R/LP '72

Singles: 7-inch

COLUMBIA 3-5 72-76
LOS ANGELES KINGS/COLUMBIA (10444 "Angry Eyes")..............................3-5 76
(Promotional issue for "Columbia/Kings Record Night" at the L.A. Forum.)

Picture Sleeves

LOS ANGELES KINGS/COLUMBIA (10444 "Angry Eyes")..............................3-5 76
(Promotional issue for "Columbia/Kings Record Night" at the L.A. Forum.)

LPs: 10/12-inch 33rpm

COLUMBIA (30000 series)..........8-10 72-82
COLUMBIA (44000 series)........10-15 82
(Half-speed mastered.)

DIRECT-DISK (16606 "Full Sail") ... 15-25 82
(Half-speed mastered.)
Members: Kenny Loggins; Jim Messina.
Also see LOGGINS, Kenny
Also see MESSINA, Jim

LOGGINS & MESSINA / David Bromberg

LPs: 10/12-inch 33rpm

COLUMBIA ... 8-15 72
(Promotional only.)
Also see BROMBERG, David
Also see LOGGINS & MESSINA

LOLITA

P&R '60

Singles: 7-inch

4 CORNERS ... 4-6 65
KAPP ... 5-8 60-61

Picture Sleeves

KAPP ... 10-15 61

LPs: 10/12-inch 33rpm

KAPP ... 15-25 61

LOMAX, Jackie

LP '69

Singles: 7-inch

APPLE (1802 "Sour Milk Sea") . 10-20 68
APPLE (1807 "New Day") ... 10-15 69
APPLE (1819 "How the Web Was Woven") ... 4-8 70
CAPITOL ... 3-5 77
EPIC ... 4-8 68
W.B. ... 3-5 71-73

Promotional Singles

APPLE (1802 "Sour Milk Sea") . 20-30 68

Picture Sleeves

APPLE (1819 "How the Web Was Woven") ... 5-10 70

LPs: 10/12-inch 33rpm

APPLE (3354 "Is This What You Want") ... 12-20 69
CAPITOL ... 5-10 76-77
W.B. ... 8-12 71-72
Also see BADGER
Also see CLAPTON, Eric
Also see McCARTNEY, Paul
Also see STARR, Ringo

LOMBARDO, Guy
(With the His Royal Canadians)

P&R '27

Singles: 78rpm

BRUNSWICK ... 4-8 32-34
COLUMBIA ... 4-8 27-31
DECCA ... 3-8 34-57
VICTOR ... 3-6 36-38

Singles: 7-Inch

CAPITOL ... 3-6 59-67
DECCA ... 3-8 50-73

EPs: 7-Inch 33/45rpm

CAMDEN ... 5-10
CAPITOL ... 5-10 56-59
DECCA ... 5-10 50-59
RCA ... 5-10 60

LPs: 10/12-Inch 33rpm

CAMDEN ... 10-30 54-65
CAPITOL (Except 739 thru 1598) 5-15 61-81
CAPITOL (739 thru 1598) ... 10-25 56-61
DECCA ... 10-30 50-67
LONDON ... 5-8 73
MCA ... 5-8 75
RCA ... 5-8 72-77
VOCALION ... 5-10 66-68
Also see ARMSTRONG, Louis, & Guy Lombardo
Also see SMITH, Kate

LONDON, Julie

P&R '55

Singles: 78rpm

LIBERTY ... 4-6 55-57

Singles: 7-inch

BETHLEHEM ... 4-8 59
LIBERTY ... 4-8 55-68

Picture Sleeves

LIBERTY ... 8-12 61

EPs: 7-inch 33/45rpm

BETHLEHEM ... 10-20 59
LIBERTY ... 10-20 56-57

LPs: 10/12-inch 33rpm

GUEST STAR ... 5-10 64
LIBERTY (3006 "Julie Is Her Name") ... 20-25 56
LIBERTY (3012 "Lonely Girl") ... 20-25 56
LIBERTY (9002 "Calendar Girl") 25-35 56
LIBERTY (3027 "Julie Is Her Name") ... 20-25 57
(Monaural. Black vinyl.)
LIBERTY (7027 "Julie Is Her Name") ... 40-60 59
(Stereo. Colored vinyl.)
LIBERTY (3043 thru 3514) ... 12-25 57-67
(Monaural.)
LIBERTY (7100 thru 7546) ... 15-30 57-68
(Stereo.)
SUNSET ... 8-15 66-68
U.A. ... 5-10 75

LONDON, Julie, & Bud Shank Quintet

LPs: 10/12-inch 33rpm

LIBERTY ... 10-15 66
Also see LONDON, Julie
Also see SHANK, Bud

LONDON, Laurie

P&R/R&B '58

Singles: 7-inch

CAPITOL ... 8-10 58-59
ROULETTE ... 5-10 59

EPs: 7-inch 33/45rpm

CAPITOL (10182 "Laurie London") ... 20-30 58

CAPITOL (10191 "Laurie London") 20-30 58

LPs: 10/12-inch 33rpm

CAPITOL (1016 "Laurie London") 30-50 58

LONDON QUIREBOYS

LP '90

LPs: 10/12-inch 33rpm

CAPITOL 5-8 90

LONDON SYMPHONY ORCHESTRA
(With Ian Anderson)

LP '79

Singles: 7-inch

RCA (14262 "Elegy") 3-4 86

LPs: 10/12-inch 33rpm

RCA (4000 series) 5-8 83
RCA (7067 "A Classic Case") 8-10 86
RSO 5-8 79

LONE JUSTICE

P&R/LP '85

Singles: 7-inch

GEFFEN 3-4 85-87

LPs: 10/12-inch 33rpm

GEFFEN 5-8 85-86

Member: Tony Gilkyson.
Also see X

LONG, Shorty

P&R/R&B '66

Singles: 78rpm

RCA 15-25 56

Singles: 7-inch

RCA (6572 "Vacation Rock") 35-55 56
RCA (6873 "You Don't Have to Be a Baby to Cry") 25-50 57
SOUL 8-15 64-68
TRI-PHI (1006 "I'll Be There") 25-35 62
TRI-PHI (1015 "Too Smart") 25-35 62
TRI-PHI (1021 "Going My Way") 25-35 62
VALLEY (108 "I Got Nine Little Kisses") 50-100

LPs: 10/12-inch 33rpm

SOUL (709 "Here Comes the Judge") 10-20 68
SOUL (719 "The Prime") 10-15 69

LONGET, Claudine

P&R '66

Singles: 7-inch

A&M 3-6 66-70
BARNABY 3-5 70-73

LPs: 10/12-inch 33rpm

A&M 5-12 67-69
BARNABY 5-10 70-72

LONGHAIR, Professor: see PROFESSOR LONGHAIR

LONGMIRE, Wilbert

R&B '80

Singles: 7-inch

TAPPAN ZEE 3-5 79-80

LPs: 10/12-inch 33rpm

TAPPAN ZEE 5-8 79-80

LOOKING GLASS

P&R/LP '72

Singles: 7-inch

EPIC 3-5 72-74

LPs: 10/12-inch 33rpm

EPIC 10-12 72-73

Members: Elliot Lurie; Carolyn Davis; Jeff Grob; Barbara Massey; P. Sweval; Larry Gonsky.

LOOSE CHANGE

R&B '80

Singles: 7-inch

CASABLANCA 3-5 79-80

LPs: 10/12-inch 33rpm

CASABLANCA 5-10 79

LOOSE ENDS

P&R/R&B/D&D/LP '85

Singles: 12-inch 33/45rpm

MCA 4-6 85-86

Singles: 7-inch

MCA 3-4 85-90

Picture Sleeves

MCA 3-4 85

LPs: 10/12-inch 33rpm

MCA 5-8 85-90

LOOSE JOINTS

D&D '84

Singles: 12-inch 33/45rpm

4TH & BROADWAY 4-6 84

Singles: 7-inch

4TH & BROADWAY 3-4 84

LOPEZ, Denise

P&R/LP '88

LPs: 10/12-inch 33rpm

A&M 5-8 88

LOPEZ, Trini

P&R/R&B/LP '63

Singles: 12-inch 33/45rpm

ROULETTE 5-8 77

Singles: 7-inch

CAPITOL 3-5 71-72
D.R.A. 5-10 61
GRIFFIN 3-5 73-75
KING (5173 "Nola") 10-15 59
KING (5187 "Rock On") 15-25 59
KING (5198 "Here Comes Sally") 10-15 59
KING (5234 thru 5487) 8-15 59-61
KING (5800 series) 5-10 63-64
KING (6000 series) 4-8 65-66
MARIANNE 3-5 77
PRIVATE STOCK 3-5 75

REPRISE 4-8 63-71
ROULETTE................................ 3-5 77
UNITED MODERN....................... 4-8 64
VOLK (101 "The Right to Rock")15-25 58

Picture Sleeves

REPRISE 5-10 62-66

EPs: 7–inch 33/45rpm

COLUMBIA/W.B. (124178 "Trini Lopez Sings His Greatest Hits") 10-15 67
(Special products issue for Coca-Cola/Fresca.)
KING (483 "Teenage Idol") 15-25 63
REPRISE 8-12 63-68

LPs: 10/12–inch 33rpm

CAPITOL.................................. 5-10 72
CROWN 6-12 65
EXACT 5-8 81
GRIFFIN.................................. 8-10 72
HARMONY............................... 8-10 70
KING (863 "Teenage Love Songs") 20-30 63
KING (877 "More of Trini Lopez")................................ 20-30 63
REPRISE 10-20 63-69
ROULETTE................................ 5-8 78
SILVER EAGLE 5-10 82
WEA LATINA 5-8 91

Also see LAWRENCE, Steve / Trini Lopez
Also see RIVERS, Johnny / Trini Lopez

LOPEZ, Trini / Scott Gregory

LPs: 10/12–inch 33rpm

GUEST STAR (1499 "Trini Lopez / Scott Gregory [Bill Haley]").............. 30-50 64

Also see HALEY, Bill

LOPEZ, Trini, with the Ventures & Nancy Ames

LPs: 10/12–inch 33rpm

REPIRSE (6361 "The Trini Lopez Show")......................... 10-15 70

Also see AMES, Nancy
Also see LOPEZ, Trini
Also see VENTURES

LOR, Denise

P&R '54

Singles: 78rpm

LIBERTY 3-5 56
MAJOR...................................... 4-6 54
MERCURY 3-5 55

Singles: 7–inch

LIBERTY 4-8 56
MAJOR.................................... 5-10 54
MERCURY 4-8 55

EPs: 7–inch 33/45rpm

MERCURY 5-10 55

LORAIN, A'Me

P&R '90

Singles: 7–inch

RCA... 3-4 90

Picture Sleeves

RCA 3-4 90

LORBER, Jeff

(Jeff Lorber Fusion; with Audrey Wheeler; with Karyn White)

LP '79

Singles: 12–inch 33/45rpm

ARISTA.......................................4-6 85

Singles: 7–inch

ARISTA.......................................3-5 79-85
INNER CITY................................3-5 78
W.B. 3-4 86

Picture Sleeves

W.B. 3-4 86

LPs: 10/12–inch 33rpm

ARISTA.......................................5-8 79-85
INNER CITY..............................5-10 78
W.B. 5-8 86

Members: Kenny Gorelick; Karyn White; Michael Jeffries.
Also see KENNY G.
Also see UNLIMITED TOUCH
Also see WHITE, Karyn

LORD, C.M.

R&B '82

Singles: 12–inch

MONTAGE...................................4-6 82-84
WAVE 4-6 83

Singles: 7–inch

CAPITOL.....................................3-5 76
MONTAGE...................................3-4 82-84

LPs: 10/12–inch 33rpm

CAPITOL...................................8-10 76
MONTAGE...................................5-8 84

LORD ROCKINGHAM'S XI

P&R '58

Singles: 7–inch

LONDON...................................5-10 58

LORD SUTCH

(With His Heavy Friends)

LP '70

LPs: 10/12–inch 33rpm

COTILLION (9015 "Lord Sutch & His Heavy Friends") 20-30 70
COTILLION (9049 "Hands of Jack the Ripper") 15-25 72

Member: Daniel Edwards.
Also see BECK, Jeff
Also see BLACKMORE, Ritchie
Also see HOPKINS, Nicky
Also see MOON, Keith
Also see PAGE, Jimmy

LORDS of the NEW CHURCH

LP '85

Singles: 12–inch 33/45rpm

I.R.S. 4-6 83

Singles: 7–inch

I.R.S. 3-4 82-85

LPs: 10/12-inch 33rpm

I.R.S. 5-8 82-85

Member: Stiv Bators.
Also see BATORS, Stiv

LORELEIS

P&R '55

Singles: 78rpm

BALLY 4-8 57
DOT 4-8 54
SPOTLIGHT 4-8 55

Singles: 7-inch

BALLY 5-15 57
BRUNSWICK 3-5 64
DOT 5-10 54
SPOTLIGHT 5-15 55

LOREN, Bryan

R&B '84

Singles: 12-inch 33/45rpm

PHILLY WORLD 4-6 83-84

Singles: 7-inch

PHILLY WORLD 3-4 83

LORETTA LYNN: see LYNN, Loretta

LORING, Gloria

LP '86

Singles: 7-inch

ATLANTIC 3-4 86
MGM 3-5 72

LPs: 10/12-inch 33rpm

ATLANTIC 5-8 86

LORING, Gloria, & Carl Anderson

P&R '86

Singles: 7-inch

CARRERE 3-4 86

Picture Sleeves

CARRERE 3-4 86

LPs: 10/12-inch 33rpm

EPIC 5-8 85

Also see ANDERSON, Carl

LOS ADMIRADORES

LP '60

LPs: 10/12-inch 33rpm

COMMAND 8-15 60

LOS BRAVOS

P&R/LP '66

Singles: 7-inch

LONDON 3-4 70s
PARROT 4-8 68
PRESS 4-8 66-68

LPs: 10/12-inch 33rpm

PARROT (71021 "Bring a Little Lovin") 20-30 68
PRESS (83003 "Black Is Black") 30-40 66

Member: Mike Kennedy.
Also see DRIFTERS / Lesley Gore / Roy Orbison / Los Bravos
Also see KENNEDY, Mike

LOS INDIOS TABAJARAS

P&R/LP '63

Singles: 7-inch

RCA 4-6 63-64

LPs: 10/12-inch 33rpm

RCA (LPM-1788 "Sweet and Savage") 20-30 58
(Monaural.)
RCA (LSP-1788 "Sweet and Savage") 30-50 58
(Stereo.)
RCA (2800 thru 3505) 10-20 63-66

Members: Natalicio; Antenor Moreyra Lima (aka Musaperi & Herundy).

LOS LOBOS

LP '84

Singles: 12-inch 33/45rpm

SLASH 5-8 86
(Promotional issue only.)

Singles: 7-inch

LOS LOBOS 5-10 81
SLASH 3-4 83-90

Picture Sleeves

SLASH 3-4 85-87

LPs: 10/12-inch 33rpm

SLASH 5-8 83-90

Member: David Hidalgo.

LOS POP-TOPS: see POP-TOPS

LOST GENERATION

P&R/R&B '70

Singles: 7-inch

BRUNSWICK 3-5 70-71
INNOVATION 3-5 74

LPs: 10/12-inch 33rpm

BRUNSWICK 10-12 70

Members: Lowrell Simon; Fred Lowrell; Larry Brownlee.
Also see C.O.D.s
Also see MYSTIQUE

LOU, Bonnie: see BONNIE LOU

LOUDERMILK, John D.

P&R '61

Singles: 7-inch

COLUMBIA 5-10 58-60
MUSIC IS MEDICINE 3-5 78-79
RCA 4-8 61-69
W.B. 3-5 71

Picture Sleeves

COLUMBIA (41165 "Yearbook") 10-20 58
RCA (8101 "Road Hog") 5-10 62

LPs: 10/12-inch 33rpm

MUSIC IS MEDICINE 5-8 78
RCA 15-25 61-69
W.B. 8-12 71

Also see DEE, Johnny
Also see SNEEZER, Ebe, & Epidemics

LOUDNESS

LP '85

LPs: 10/12-inch 33rpm

ATCO 5-8 85-87

LOUIE LOUIE
(Louie Cordero)

P&R/LP '90

Singles: 7-inch

WTG 3-4 90

LPs: 10/12-inch 33rpm

WTG 5-8 90

LOUISIANA'S LE ROUX: see LE ROUX

LOVE

P&R/LP '66

Singles: 7-inch

BLUE THUMB 4-6 69-70
ELEKTRA (45603 "My Little Red Book") 5-8 66
ELEKTRA (45605 "7 & 7 Is")......... 5-8 66
ELEKTRA (45608 "Stephanie Knows Who") 10-20 66
ELEKTRA (45608 "She Comes in Colors") 5-8 67
(Same number and flip used again.)
ELEKTRA (45613 "Que Vida").. 15-25 67
ELEKTRA (45629 thru 45700) 5-10 68-70
RSO 4-6 74-75

LPs: 10/12-inch 33rpm

BLUE THUMB (8822 "False Start") 20-30 70
BLUE THUMB (9000 "Out Here")................................. 15-25 69
ELEKTRA (4001 "Love") 25-40 66
(Monaural.)
ELEKTRA (4005 "Da Capo")..... 25-40 66
(Monaural.)
ELEKTRA (4013 "Forever Changes") 25-40 67
(Monaural.)
ELEKTRA (74001 "Love") 25-35 66
(Stereo.)
ELEKTRA (74005 "Da Capo")... 25-35 67
(Stereo.)
ELEKTRA (74013 "Forever Changes") 20-30 67
(Stereo.)
ELEKTRA (74049 "Four Sail")... 20-30 69
(Stereo.)
ELEKTRA (74058 "Revisited") .. 20-30 70
(Gatefold cover.)
ELEKTRA (74058 "Revisited") 5-8 81
(Standard cover.)
MCA 5-8 82
RSO 8-10 74
RHINO (251 "Love Live") 8-10 82
RHINO (800 "Best of Love")......... 5-8 80

Members: Arthur Lee; Tjay Contrelli; John Echols; Bryan Maclean; Don Conka; Ken Forssi.

LOVE, Candace

R&B '69

Singles: 7-inch

AQUARIUS 4-8 68

LOVE, Darlene

P&R '63

Singles: 12-inch 33/45rpm

RHINO (855 "Live at Hop Singh's")................................ 8-10 85

Singles: 7-inch

COLUMBIA 3-5 88
ELEKTRA (79647 "River Deep, Mountain High") 3-5 85
(Promotional issue only.)
PHILLES (111 "The Boy I'm Gonna Marry"/ "My Heart Beat a Little Bit Faster")12-18 63
PHILLES (111 "The Boy I'm Gonna Marry"/ "Playing for Keeps").................. 8-12 63
PHILLES (114 "Wait Till My Bobby Gets Home")............... 10-15 63
PHILLES (117 "A Fine, Fine Boy") 8-15 63
PHILLES (119 "Christmas, Baby Please Come Home") 15-25 63
PHILLES (123 "He's a Quiet Guy")... 30-50 64
PHILLES (125 "Christmas, Baby Please Come Home") 15-25 64
REPRISE 4-8 66
RHINO 5-8 86
W.B./SPECTOR 3-6 74-77

Picture Sleeves

COLUMBIA 3-5 88
ELEKTRA (79647 "River Deep, Mountain High") 3-5 85
(Promotional issue only.)

LPs: 10/12-inch 33rpm

COLUMBIA (40605 "Paint Another Picture") 8-12 88

Also see BLOSSOMS
Also see BOB B. SOXX & Blue Jeans
Also see CRYSTALS
Also see RONETTES / Crystals / Darlene Love / Bob B. Soxx & Blue Jeans

LOVE, Darlene / Annie Golden

Singles: 7-inch

ELEKTRA..................................... 3-5 85

Picture Sleeves

ELEKTRA..................................... 3-5 85

Also see LOVE, Darlene

LOVE, Johnny
(With the Way Singers)

Singles: 7-inch

MERCURY 5-10 59-60
STARTIME (5001 "Chills and Fever")... 25-35 60
TEE PEE (295 "Consolation").... 10-20

Also see LOVE, Ronnie

LOVE, Le Juan

R&B '88

Singles: 7-inch

LUKE SKY.................................... 3-4 88

LOVE, Mike

Singles: 7-inch

BOARDWALK 3-5 81

LPs: 10/12-inch 33rpm

BOARDWALK 8-10 81

Also see ASSOCIATION / Bobby Vee / Mike Love / Mary MacGregor
Also see BEACH BOYS
Also see CELEBRATION
Also see MIKE & DEAN
Also see WILSON, Brian, & Mike Love

LOVE, Mike / Dean Torrence: see MIKE & DEAN

LOVE, Monie

LP '90

LPs: 10/12-inch 33rpm

W.B. 5-8 90

LOVE, Ronnie

P&R/R&B '61

Singles: 7-inch

D TOWN (1027 "Judy") 75-125 64
D TOWN (1047 "Judy") 30-50 65
DOT.. 5-10 60-61
STARTIME (5003 "Shakin' and a Breakin") 20-30 61

Also see LOVE, Johnny

LOVE, Rudy, & Love Family

R&B '76

Singles: 7-inch

CALLA... 3-5 76

LPs: 10/12-inch 33rpm

CALLA....................................... 5-10 76

LOVE, Vikki: see NUANCE

LOVE & KISSES

LP '77

Singles: 7-inch

CASABLANCA 3-5 77-79

LPs: 10/12-inch 33rpm

CASABLANCA 8-10 77-79

LOVE & MONEY

P&R/LP '89

Singles: 7-inch

MERCURY 3-4 89

Picture Sleeves

MERCURY 3-4 89

LPs: 10/12-inch 33rpm

MERCURY 5-8 89

Member: Stuart Kerr.
Also see TEXAS

LOVE & ROCKETS

LP '86

Singles: 7-inch

BIG TIME 3-4 86
RCA 3-4 89

Picture Sleeves

RCA 3-4 89

LPs: 10/12-inch 33rpm

BEGGARS BANQUET..................5-8 89
BIG TIME 5-8 86-87

Members: David Jor; Kevin Haskins; Daniel Ash.
Also see BAUHAUS

LOVE BUG STARSKI

D&D '83

Singles: 12-inch 33/45rpm

ATLANTIC...................................3-4 85
FEVER 4-6 83

LOVE CHILD'S AFRO CUBAN BLUES BAND

(Love Child's Latin Soul Afro Blues Band)

P&R/R&B/LP '75

Singles: 7-inch

A&M 3-6 69
ROULETTE..................................3-5 75

LPs: 10/12-inch 33rpm

ROULETTE................................5-10 75

LOVE CLUB

D&D '83

Singles: 12-inch 33/45rpm

WEST END 4-6 83

LOVE COMMITTEE

R&B '76

Singles: 7-inch

ARIOLA AMERICA 3-5 75-76
GOLD MIND.................................3-5 77-78

Also see ETHICS

LOVE GENERATION

P&R '67

Singles: 7-inch

IMPERIAL 4-8 67-68

LPs: 10/12-inch 33rpm

IMPERIAL 12-15 67
U.A. 8-10 77

Also see CLIMAX

LOVE / HATE

LP '90

LPs: 10/12-inch 33rpm

COLUMBIA 5-8 90

LOVE NOTES

R&B '57

Singles: 7-inch

HOLIDAY (2605 "United")..........30-50 57
(Glossy label stock.)
HOLIDAY (2605 "United")..........10-15
(Flat label stock.)
HOLIDAY (2607 "If I Could Make You Mine") 20-30 57

LOVE PATROL

R&B '85

Singles: 7-inch

4TH & BROADWAY......................3-4 85

LOVE, PEACE & HAPPINESS

R&B '72

Singles: 7-inch

RCA.......... 3-5 71-72

LPs: 10/12-inch 33rpm

RCA.......... 8-10 71

Members: Ann Bogan; Leslie Wilson; Melvin Wilson.

Also see NEW BIRTH

LOVE UNLIMITED

(Love Unlimited Orchestra)

P&R/R&B/LP '72

Singles: 7-inch

CASABLANCA.......... 3-5 70s
MCA.......... 3-4
20TH FOX.......... 3-5 73-77
UNI.......... 3-5 72
UNLIMITED GOLD.......... 3-5 77-84

LPs: 10/12-inch 33rpm

20TH FOX.......... 8-10 74-76
UNI.......... 5-10 72
UNLIMITED GOLD.......... 5-8 77-84

Member: Kenny Gorelick.

Also see KENNY G.

Also see WHITE, Barry

LOVELITES

R&B '69

Singles: 7-inch

ATCO.......... 4-8 69
BANDERA.......... 8-10 67
LOCK.......... 4-8 69
LOVELITE.......... 3-6 70-71
20TH FOX.......... 3-6 73
UNI.......... 3-6 69-70

LPs: 10/12-inch 33rpm

UNI.......... 10-15 70

LOVELY, Ike

R&B '73

Singles: 7-inch

WAND.......... 3-5 73

LOVERBOY

P&R/LP '81

Singles: 7-inch

COLUMBIA.......... 3-4 81-87

Picture Sleeves

COLUMBIA.......... 3-5 81-87

LPs: 10/12-inch 33rpm

COLUMBIA (Except 169961).......... 5-10 80-89
COLUMBIA (169961 "Loverboy").......... 10-15 82

Members: Mike Reno; Matthew Frenette; Paul Dean; Doug Johnson; Scott Smith.

Also see RENO, Mike, & Ann Wilson

LOVERDE

D&D '83

Singles: 12-inch 33/45rpm

MOBY DICK.......... 4-6 83

LOVERS

P&R/R&B '57

Singles: 78rpm

DECCA.......... 5-10 56

Singles: 7-inch

ALADDIN (3419 "Tell Me").......... 15-25 58
DECCA (29862 "Don't Touch Me").......... 15-25 56
IMPERIAL.......... 5-10 62-63
KELLER (101 "Party Line").......... 20-40 61
LAMP (2005 "Darling, It's Wonderful").......... 10-15 58
LAMP (2013 "I Wanna Be Loved").......... 15-20 58
LAMP (2018 "Tell Me").......... 15-20 58
POST (10007 "Darling, It's Wonderful").......... 5-10 63

Member: Tarheel Slim.

LOVERS

P&R '77

Singles: 7-inch

MARLIN.......... 3-5 77

LOVESMITH

(Michael Lovesmith)

R&B '83

Singles: 7-inch

MOTOWN.......... 3-4 81-85

LPs: 10/12-inch 33rpm

MOTOWN.......... 5-8 81

LOVETTE, Eddie

P&R '69

Singles: 7-inch

STEADY.......... 4-8 69

LPs: 10/12-inch 33rpm

STEADY.......... 8-10 70

LOVICH, Lene

LP '79

Singles: 7-inch

STIFF.......... 3-5 79-83

LPs: 10/12-inch 33rpm

STIFF.......... 5-8 79-83

LOVIN' SPOONFUL

P&R/LP '65

Singles: 7-inch

ERIC.......... 3-4 78
KAMA SUTRA.......... 3-8 65-72

Picture Sleeves

KAMA SUTRA.......... 5-10 65-67

EPs: 7-inch 33/45rpm

KAMA SUTRA (1 "Nashville Cats").......... 10-15 67
(Promotional issue only.)

LPs: 10/12-inch 33rpm

BACK-TRAC.......... 5-8 85
BUDDAH.......... 8-10 73
51 WEST.......... 5-8 80s
GRT.......... 8-15 76

GUSTO 5-8 80s
KAMA SUTRA (750 "24 Karat Hits") 10-15 68
KAMA SUTRA (2000 series)....... 8-15 70-76
KAMA SUTRA (8050 thru 8054) 15-25 65-66
KAMA SUTRA (8056 "Best of the Lovin' Spoonful") 15-25 67
(Add $10 to $20 if accompanied by four color photos.)
KAMA SUTRA (8058 thru 8073) 15-25 67-69
KAMA SUTRA (91102 "Best of the Lovin' Spoonful") 8-10
Members: John Sebastian; Zalman Yanovsky; Joe Butler; Steve Boone; Jerry Yester.
Also see SEBASTIAN, John

LOW, Gary

D&D '83

Singles: 12–inch 33/45rpm

QUALITY 4-6 83

LOWE, Bernie

(Bernie Lowe Orchestra)

P&R '58

Singles: 7–inch

CAMEO 4-8 58-63

LPs: 10/12–inch 33rpm

CAMEO 15-25 62-63

LOWE, Jim

P&R '53

Singles: 78rpm

DOT 4-8 55-57
MERCURY 4-8 53-54

Singles: 7–inch

BUDDAH 4-6 68
DECCA 4-8 60-61
DOT (15300 thru 16200 series) .. 5-10 55-60
DOT (16600 series).................. 4-8 64
MERCURY 5-10 53-54
20TH FOX 4-8 63
U.A. 4-6 67

EPs: 7–inch 33/45rpm

DOT 10-20 57
MERCURY 10-20 57

LPs: 10/12–inch 33rpm

DOT (3051 "The Green Door").. 25-35 57
DOT (3114 "Wicked Women") ... 25-35 58
DOT (3681 "The Green Door").. 10-20 66
(Monaural.)
DOT (25681 "The Green Door") 10-20 66
(Stereo.)
KATS KARAVAN (100 "Old Favorites").................... 50-100 50s
MERCURY (20246 "Door of Fame") 25-35 57

LOWE, Nick

(With Rockpile; with His Cowboy Outfit)

LP '78

Singles: 7–inch

COLUMBIA 3-5 78-86

LPs: 10/12–inch 33rpm

COLUMBIA 5-10 78-86
REPRISE 5-8 90
Also see NICK & ELVIS

LOWE, Nick, & Dave Edmunds

Singles: 7–inch

COLUMBIA 3-5 81

EPs: 7–inch 33/45rpm

COLUMBIA (1219 "Nick Lowe & Dave Edmunds Sing the Everly Brothers").................... 5-10 80
(Promotional issue only.)
Also see EDMUNDS, Dave
Also see LOWE, Nick
Also see ROCKPILE

LOWRELL

R&B '78

Singles: 7–inch

AVI 3-5 78-80

LOZ NETTO: see NETTO, Loz

L'TRIMM

P&R/LP '88

Singles: 7–inch

ATLANTIC.................... 3-4 88

LPs: 10/12–inch 33rpm

ATLANTIC.................... 5-8 88

LUBOFF, Norman, Choir

LP '55

Singles: 78rpm

COLUMBIA 3-5 54-59

Singles: 7-Inch

COLUMBIA 3-6 54-59

EPs: 7-Inch 33/45rpm

COLUMBIA 4-8 54-59

LPs: 10/12-Inch 33rpm

COLUMBIA 5-15 54-60
HARMONY 5-10 61
RCA 5-10 61-62

LUCAS, Carrie

(Carrie)

P&R/R&B/LP '77

Singles: 12–inch 33/45rpm

CONSTELLATION 4-6 84-85

Singles: 7–inch

CONSTELLATION 3-4 84-85
SOLAR 3-5 79-82
SOUL TRAIN 3-5 77

LPs: 10/12–inch 33rpm

CONSTELLATION 5-8 85
SOLAR 5-10 79-82
SOUL TRAIN 8-10 77

LUCAS, Carrie, & Whispers

R&B '85

Singles: 7–inch

CONSTELLATION 3-4 85
Also see LUCAS, Carrie
Also see WHISPERS

LUCAS, Frank
("The Good Thing Man")

P&R/R&B '77

Singles: 7–inch

ICA 3-5 77-78

LUCAS, Matt

P&R '63

Singles: 7–inch

DOT 4-8 63-64
KAREN (2524 "Baby You Better Go") 50-75
RENE 10-15 63
SMASH 4-8 63

LUGEE & LIONS

Singles: 7–inch

ROBBEE (112 "The Jury") 50-75 61
Members: Lou Christie; Kay Chick; Amy Sacco; Bill Faveck.
Also see CHRISTIE, Lou
Also see CLASSICS

LUGO, Danny, & Destinations

D&D '84

Singles: 12–inch 33/45rpm

C&M 4-6 84

LUKE, Robin

P&R/R&B '58

Singles: 7–inch

BERTRAM INT'L (206 "Susie Darlin'") 20-40 58
BERTRAM INT'L (208 thru 212) 15-25 58-59
DOT 5-10 58-61

Picture Sleeves

BERTRAM INT'L (206 "Susie Darlin") 40-60 58
DOT (16096 "Everlovin'") 10-20 60

EPs: 7–inch 33/45rpm

DOT (1092 "Susie Darlin'") 50-75 60

LUKE, Robin, & Roberta Shore

Singles: 7–inch

DOT 4-8 62
Also see LUKE, Robin

LUKE the Drifter: see WILLIAMS, Hank

LUKE the Drifter Jr.: see WILLIAMS, Hank, Jr.

LULU
(With the Luvers; with Dixie Flyers)

P&R '64

Singles: 7–inch

ALFA 3-5 81-82
ATCO 3-6 69-72
CHELSEA 3-5 73-75
EPIC 4-8 67-68
PARROT (9000 series) 5-10 64-65
PARROT (40000 series) 4-8 67
ROCKET 3-5 78

Picture Sleeves

ALFA (7006 "I Could Never Miss You More") 3-6 81
(Pictures Lulu without headband.)
ALFA (7006 "I Could Never Miss You More") 3-5 81
(Pictures Lulu wearing headband.)
ALFA (7011 "If I Were You") 3-4 81
EPIC 4-8 67-68

LPs: 10/12–inch 33rpm

ALFA 5-10 81
ATCO 10-12 70-72
CAPRICORN 8-10 74
CHELSEA 10-12 73-77
EPIC 10-15 67-70
HARMONY 10-12 70
PARROT (61016 "From Lulu with Love") 50-100 67
(Monaural.)
PARROT (71016 "From Lulu with Love") 50-100 67
(Stereo.)
PICKWICK 8-10 73
ROCKET 5-8 78
Also see CLARK, Dave, Five / Lulu
Also see MOORE, Jackie

LUMAN, Bob

C&W/P&R/R&B '60

Singles: 78rpm

IMPERIAL 15-25 57

Singles: 7–inch

CAPITOL 10-20 58
EPIC 3-5 68-77
HICKORY (1200 series) 4-8 63-64
HICKORY (1300 thru 1500 series) 3-5 65-70
IMPERIAL (5705 "Red Cadillac and a Black Mustache") 10-20 60
(Black label. Reissue of 8311.)
IMPERIAL (8311 "Red Cadillac and a Black Mustache") 35-55 57
(Maroon label.)
IMPERIAL (8313 "Red Hot") 40-60 57
(Maroon label.)
IMPERIAL (8313 "Red Hot") 30-40 59
(Black label.)
IMPERIAL (8315 "Make Up Your Mind Baby") 20-30 57
(Maroon label.)
IMPERIAL (8315 "Make Up Your Mind Baby") 10-15 59
(Black label.)
POLYDOR 3-5 77-78
W.B. 5-15 59-62

Picture Sleeves

W.B. 15-25 60-62

EPs: 7–inch 33/45rpm

HICKORY (124-006 "Selections from Livin' Lovin' Sounds") 10-20 65
(Promotional "Six-Pac" issue only.)

ROLLIN' ROCK (34 "Bob Luman") 5-8 80s
W.B. (1396 "Let's Think About Livin'") 50-75 60
W.B. (5506 "Bob Luman") 50-75 60
(Promotional issue only.)

LPs: 10/12-inch 33rpm

EPIC 8-15 68-77
HARMONY 10-15 72
HICKORY (124 "Livin' Lovin' Sounds") 15-25 65
HICKORY (4000 series) 8-12 74
POLYDOR 8-12 78
W.B. (W-1396 "Let's Think About Livin'") 30-40 60
(Monaural.)
W.B. (WS-1396 "Let's Think About Livin'") 40-60 60
(Stereo.)

LUMAN, Bob, & Sue Thompson

Singles: 7-inch

HICKORY 4-8 63
Also see LUMAN, Bob
Also see THOMPSON, Sue

LUNAR FUNK

P&R/R&B '72

Singles: 7-inch

BELL 3-5 72

LUNCEFORD, Jimmie, & Orchestra

P&R '34

Singles: 78rpm

DECCA 4-8 33-52

EPs: 7-inch 33/45rpm

DECCA 10-15 50s
Also see DELTA RHYTHM BOYS

LUND, Art, & His Orchestra

P&R '47

Singles: 78rpm

CORAL 3-5 52-57
MGM 3-6 47-55

Singles: 7-inch

CORAL 4-8 52-58
MGM 5-10 50-55
U.A. 3-6 65

EPs: 7-inch 33/45rpm

MGM 5-10 54-55

LPs: 10/12-inch 33rpm

MGM 10-20 55

LUNDBERG, Victor

P&R '67

Singles: 7-inch

LIBERTY 4-6 67

LPs: 10/12-inch 33rpm

LIBERTY 10-15 68

LUNDY, Pat

(Pat Lundi)

R&B '73

Singles: 7-inch

COLUMBIA 4-6 67-68
DELUXE 4-6 69
HEIDI 4-8 65
LEOPARD 3-5
PYRAMID 3-5 76
RCA 3-5 73
TOTO 4-8 62
VIGOR 3-5 75

LPs: 10/12-inch 33rpm

COLUMBIA 10-15 68
PYRAMID 5-8 76

LUNDY, Pat, & Bobby Harris

Singles: 7-inch

HEIDI 4-8 65
Also see HARRIS, Bobby
Also see LUNDY, Pat

LUSHUS DAIM & Pretty Vain

R&B '85

Singles: 7-inch

MOTOWN 3-4 85

LPs: 10/12-inch 33rpm

MOTOWN 5-8 85

LUTCHER, Joe

(With His Society Cats)

R&B '48

Singles: 78rpm

CAPITOL 5-10 48
MODERN 5-10 49
SPECIALTY 5-10 48-51

Singles: 7-inch

SPECIALTY (303 "Rockin' Boogie") 50-75 51

LUTCHER, Nellie

(With Her "Rhythm")

P&R/R&B '47

Singles: 78rpm

CAPITOL 4-8 47-50

Singles: 7-inch

CAPITOL 8-12 50

EPs: 7-inch 33/45rpm

CAPITOL (232 "Real Gone") 20-40 50
LIBERTY 5-10 56

LPs: 10/12-inch 33rpm

CAPITOL (H-232 "Real Gone") .. 35-55 50
(10-inch LP.)
CAPITOL (T-232 "Real Gone") .. 20-30 55
EPIC (1108 "Whee! Nellie") 25-35 55
LIBERTY (3014 "Our New Nellie") 20-30 56

LUTCHER, Nellie, & Nat "King" Cole

R&B '50

Singles: 78rpm

CAPITOL 4-8 50

Singles: 7–inch

CAPITOL.................................... 8-12 50

Also see COLE, Nat "King"
Also see LUTCHER, Nellie

LUTHER
(Luther Vandross)

R&B '76

Singles: 7–inch

COTILLION 3-5 76-77

LPs: 10/12–inch 33rpm

COTILLION 8-10 77

Also see VANDROSS, Luther

LY-DELLS

P&R '61

Singles: 7–inch

MASTER (111 "Genie of the Lamp")............................ 75-125 61
MASTER (251 "Wizard of Love")...................................... 30-40 61
ROULETTE............................ 10-15 63
SCA (18001 "Book of Songs") .. 20-30 62
SOUTHERN SOUND (122 "Hide and Seek") 25-35 65

LPs: 10/12–inch 33rpm

CLIFTON.................................... 8-10

LYLE, Bobby

R&B '78

Singles: 7–inch

CAPITOL.................................... 3-5 78

LYMAN, Arthur
(Arthur Lyman Group)

LP '58

Singles: 7–inch

GNP 3-5 64-75
HI FI 4-6 59-69
ORBIT 4-8

LPs: 10/12–inch 33rpm

GNP 8-15 63-75
HI FI 10-20 58-69
OLYMPIC 5-8 79

LYME & CYBELLE

P&R '66

Singles: 7–inch

WHITE WHALE.......................... 5-10 66-67

Also see ZEVON, Warren

LYMON, Frankie
(With the Teenagers)

P&R/R&B '56

Singles: 78rpm

GEE.. 10-20 55-57
ROULETTE (4026 "So Goes My Love").................................... 15-25 57

Singles: 7–inch

ABC.. 3-4 73
BIG KAT 4-8 68
COLUMBIA 4-8 64
GEE (1002 "Why Do Fools Fall in Love")........................50-100 55
(Red label, gold print.)
GEE (1002 "Why Do Fools Fall in Love")............................10-20 55
(Red label, black print.)
GEE (1012 thru 1039)...............10-20 56-59
MURRAY HILL...............................3-5 80s
RAMA (34 "I Want You to Be My Girl")...5-10 64
(Golden Goodies Series.)
ROULETTE..............................10-15 57-61
TCF 5-8 64

Picture Sleeves

BIG KAT (7008 "I Want You to Be My Girl")...5-10 68

EPs: 7–inch 33/45rpm

GEE (601 "The Teenagers Go Rockin'")..........................75-125 56
GEE (601 "The Teenagers Go Romantic") 75-125 56
ROULETTE (304 "Frankie Lymon at the London Palladium")................50-75 58

LPs: 10/12–inch 33rpm

ACCORD 5-10 82
GEE (701 "The Teenagers Featuring Frankie Lymon")...............................200-300 57
(Red or white label.)
GEE (701 "The Teenagers Featuring Frankie Lymon")...............................50-100 61
(Gray label.)
MURRAY HILL (148 "Frankie Lymon and the Teenagers") 35-55 80s
(Boxed, five-LP set, with booklet and bonus single.)
ROULETTE (25013 "Frankie Lymon at the London Palladium")..................50-65 58
ROULETTE (25036 "Rock & Roll")...50-75 58
ROULETTE (25250 "Frankie Lymon's Greatest") 25-35 64

Members: Frankie Lymon; Herman Santiago; Sherman Garnes; Jim Merchant; Joe Negroni.
Also see TEENAGERS

LYNCH, Ray

LP '89

LPs: 10/12–inch 33rpm

MUSIC WEST 5-10 89

LYNCH MOB

LP '90

LPs: 10/12–inch 33rpm

ELEKTRA.......................................5-8 90

LYNDELL, Linda

R&B '68

Singles: 7–inch

VOLT..4-8 68

LYNN, Barbara

P&R/R&B '62

Singles: 7-inch

ATLANTIC 3-5 67-72
COLLECTABLES 3-4 80s
JAMIE 4-8 62-65
TRIBE 4-8 66-67

LPs: 10/12-inch 33rpm

ATLANTIC 10-20 68
JAMIE 20-30 62-64

LYNN, Barbara, & Lee Maye

Singles: 7-inch

JAMIE 4-8 65
Also see LYNN, Barbara

LYNN, Cheryl

P&R/R&B/LP '78

Singles: 12-inch 33/45rpm

COLUMBIA 4-6 78-85

Singles: 7-inch

COLUMBIA 3-5 78-85
MANHATTAN 3-4 87
PRIVATE I 3-4 85

LPs: 10/12-inch 33rpm

COLUMBIA 5-10 78-84

LYNN, Cheryl, & Luther Vandross

R&B '82

Singles: 7-inch

COLUMBIA 3-5 82
Also see LYNN, Cheryl
Also see VANDROSS, Luther

LYNN, Donna

P&R '64

Singles: 7-inch

CAPITOL (Except 5127) 4-8 63-65
CAPITOL (5127 "My Boyfriend Got a Beatle Haircut") 15-20 64
EPIC 4-8 63
PALMER (5016 "Don't You Dare") 15-25 67

LPs: 10/12-inch 33rpm

CAPITOL 15-25 64

LYNN, Ginie

R&B '78

Singles: 7-inch

ABC 3-5 78

LYNN, Jeff: see LYNNE, Jeff

LYNN, Loretta
(With the Coal Miners)

LP '67

Singles: 7-inch

DECCA (31384 thru 31966) 5-10 62-66
DECCA (32045 thru 32851) 4-8 66-71
DECCA (32900 "Here in Topeka") 10-15 71
DECCA (32900 "One's on the Way") 3-6 71
DECCA (32974 thru 33039) 3-6 72
MCA 3-5 73-86
ZERO (107 "I'm a Honky Tonk Girl") 50-75 60
ZERO (110 "New Rainbow") 60-100 61
ZERO (112 "The Darkest Day") 60-100 61

Picture Sleeves

DECCA (31000 series) 8-12 66
DECCA (32000 series) 4-6 70
MCA 3-5 78

EPs: 7-inch 33/45rpm

DECCA 10-20 64-65

LPs: 10/12-inch 33rpm

CORAL 5-8 73
COUNTRY MUSIC MAGAZINE. 15-20 76
(Mail-order LP sold by *Country Music* magazine.)
DECCA (DL-4457 "Loretta Lynn Sings") 50-75 63
(Monaural.)
DECCA (DL7-4457 "Loretta Lynn Sings") 65-80 63
(Stereo.)
DECCA (DL-4541 thru DL-5000) 15-25 64-68
(Monaural.)
DECCA (DL7-4541 thru DL7-5000) 15-30 64-68
(Stereo.)
DECCA (75084 "Your Squaw Is on the Warpath") 25-35 69
(Has *Barney.*)
DECCA (75084 "Your Squaw Is on the Warpath") 15-20 69
(Without *Barney.*)
DECCA (75115 thru 75381) 10-20 69-72
L.L. 20-25 76
MCA 5-10 73-86
TEE VEE 8-12 78
TROLLEY CAR 8-10 81
VOCALION 8-15 68-72

Promotional LPs

MCA (1934 "Loretta Lynn's Greatest Hits") 30-40 74
(Cover shows title as simply *Loretta Lynn.*)
MCA (35013 "Allis-Chalmers Presents Loretta Lynn") 30-40 78
MCA (35018 "Crisco Presents Loretta Lynn's Country Classics") 30-40 79
Session: Bob Hempker; Chuck Flynn; Ken Riley; Dave Thornhill; Gene Dunlap; Don Ballenger; Jordanaires.
Also see BEATLES / Loretta Lynn
Also see PIERCE, Webb / Loretta Lynn
Also see STARR, Kenny
Also see TUBB, Ernest, & Loretta Lynn
Also see TWITTY, Conway, & Loretta Lynn
Also see WILBURN BROTHERS

LYNN, Loretta, & Conway Twitty

C&W/P&R '71

Singles: 7-inch

DECCA.. 4-6 71-72
MCA.. 3-5 73-81

LPs: 10/12-inch 33rpm

DECCA.. 8-15 71-72
MCA.. 5-10 73-84
TVP.. 8-12 76

Also see LYNN, Loretta
Also see TWITTY, Conway

LYNN, Loretta / Tammy Wynette

LPs: 10/12-inch 33rpm

RADIANT.. 5-8 81

Also see LYNN, Loretta
Also see WYNETTE, Tammy

LYNN, Vera

P&R '48

Singles: 78rpm

LONDON.. 3-5 51-57

Singles: 7-inch

ARCO.. 4-6 67
DJM.. 4-6 69
LONDON.. 5-10 51-64
U.A.. 4-6 67

EPs: 7-inch 33/45rpm

LONDON.. 5-10 52-56

LPs: 10/12-inch 33rpm

LONDON.. 10-20 52-64
MGM.. 8-12 61
U.A.. 5-10 67

LYNNE, Gloria

P&R/R&B/LP '61

Singles: 7-inch

CANYON.. 3-5 70
EVEREST.. 4-8 59-66
FONTANA.. 4-6 64-69
HI FI.. 4-6 66
IMPULSE.. 3-5 76
MERCURY.. 3-5 72
SEECO.. 4-8 61

LPs: 10/12-inch 33rpm

CANYON.. 5-10 70
DESIGN.. 10-15 62
EVEREST (300 series).. 5-10 75
EVEREST (1000 series).. 20-30 58-65
(Stereo.)
EVEREST (5000 series).. 15-25 58-65
(Monaural.)
FONTANA.. 10-20 64-69
HI FI.. 10-15 66
IMPULSE.. 5-10 76
MERCURY.. 8-12 69-72
PAUL WINLEY.. 5-10 74
SUNSET.. 8-15 66-67
UPFRONT.. 5-10 72

LYNNE, Gloria / Nina Simone / Billie Holiday

LPs: 10/12-inch 33rpm

ALMOR.. 10-15

Also see HOLIDAY, Billie
Also see SIMONE, Nina

LYNNE, Jeff

(Jeff Lynn)

P&R '84

Singles: 12-inch 33/45rpm

JET.. 5-8 77

Singles: 7-inch

JET.. 3-5 77
REPRISE.. 5-8 90
TWIN-SPIN.. 10-15 65
VIRGIN.. 3-4 84

Also see ELECTRIC LIGHT ORCHESTRA
Also see MOVE
Also see TRAVELING WILBURYS

LYNYRD SKYNYRD

LP '73

Singles: 7-inch

ATNIA.. 3-6 78
MCA (Except 1966).. 3-6 74-78
MCA (1966 "Gimmie Back My Bullets").. 8-12 77
(Promotional concert souvenir issue.)

EPs: 7-inch 33/45rpm

MCA.. 10-15 76
(Promotional issue only.)

LPs: 10/12-inch 33rpm

MCA (2000 & 3000 series, except 3029).. 8-10 75-78
MCA (3029 "Street Survivors")..30-40 77
(Front cover pictures the group in flames.)
MCA (3029 "Street Survivors")....8-10 77
(Pictures the group without flames.)
MCA (5000 series).. 5-8 79-82
MCA (6000 series).. 10-15 76-81
MCA (8011 "Live at the Fox").....10-15 76
MCA (8027 "Southern by the Grace of God").. 8-12 88
MCA (10000 series).. 10-15 79-81
MCA (37000 series).. 5-8 79-82
MCA (42000 series).. 5-8 87
MCA/SOUNDS of the SOUTH (300 & 400 series).. 8-15 73-74

Promotional LPs

MCA (2170 "Gimmie Back My Bullets").. 25-35 76
(White label. Concert souvenir copy.)

Members: Ronnie Van Zant; Gary Rossington; Allen Collins; Steve Gaines; Cassie Gaines; Ed King; Rick Medlocke; Greg Walker; Leon Wildeson; Billy Powell; Artimus Pyle; Bob Burns.

Also see ALIAS
Also see BLACKFOOT
Also see ROSSINGTON - COLLINS BAND
Also see STRAWBERRY ALARM CLOCK

LYTLE, Johnny
(Johnny Lytle Quintet; J Trio)

P&R/LP '66

Singles: 7-inch

PACIFIC JAZZ	4-6	68
RIVERSIDE	4-8	63
SOLID STATE	4-6	68
TUBA	5-10	65-66

EPs: 7-inch 33/45rpm

NEOPHON	10-15	

LPs: 10/12-inch 33rpm

JAZZLAND	15-25	60-62
MILESTONE	5-10	72
MUSE	5-8	78-81
PACIFIC JAZZ	8-15	67
RIVERSIDE	10-20	63-68
SOLID STATE	8-15	67-69
TUBA	10-15	66

LYTLE, Johnny, & Ray Barretto

LPs: 10/12-inch 33rpm

JAZZLAND	15-25	62

Also see BARRETTO, Ray
Also see LYTLE, Johnny

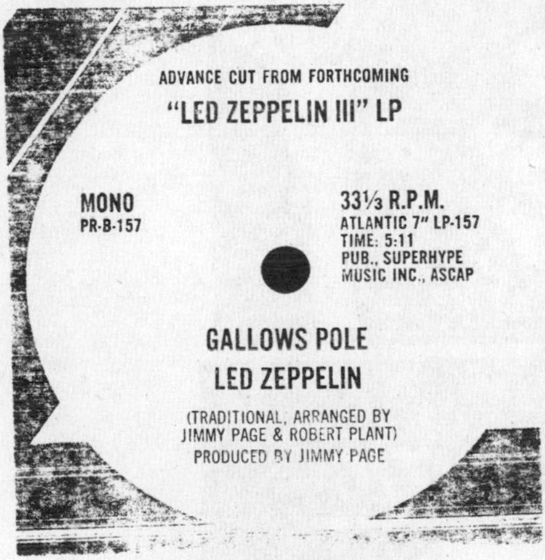

45-5224
B.M.I. 2:29
45IM-454
COMMODORE
MUSIC CORP.
Vocal
THE GYPSY BLUES
(O. Lemon - D. Bartholomew)
SMILEY LEWIS

COMPLIMENTARY
KING
DEE JAY
SPECIAL
(Calico-ASCAP)
3:04
45—K10256
HIGH FIDELITY
NOT FOR SALE
Vocal by
Trini Lopez
And Chorus
SINCE I DON'T HAVE YOU
(J. Rock-Skyliners)
TRINI LOPEZ
5187

"High School Confidential"
JERRY
LEE
LEWIS
"Fools Like Me"
A Product of • SUN RECORD CO.
No. 296

ATLANTIC
45 R.P.M.
A-1652
45-1077
VOCAL
Pub., Bellemeade, BMI
Time: 2:15
I GOTTA HAVE YOU
(Selph)
CLYDE McPHATTER and RUTH BROWN
with Orchestra

M

M

P&R/LP '79

(Robin Scott)

Singles: 12–inch 33/45rpm

SIRE.. 8-10 79

Singles: 7–inch

SIRE.. 3-5 79-81

Picture Sleeves

SIRE.. 3-5 79

LPs: 10/12–inch 33rpm

SIRE.. 8-10 79-82

M., Boney: see BONEY M

M/A/R/R/S

P&R/R&B '87

Singles: 7–inch

4TH & BROADWAY 3-4 87-88

Picture Sleeves

4TH & BROADWAY 3-4 87

M.C. CHILL

R&B '86

Singles: 12–inch 33/45rpm

FEVER 4-6 86

M.C. HAMMER: see HAMMER, M.C.

M.C. SHAN

(Featuring T.J. Swan)

R&B '87

Singles: 7–inch

COLD CHILL 3-4 87

MC-5

(Motor City 5)

P&R/LP '69

Singles: 7–inch

A^2 (333 "Looking at You")........... 20-30 68

AMG (1000 "I Can Only Give You Everything")........................ 35-45 67

(Promotional issue only.)

AMG (1001 "I Can Only Give You Everything")........................... 20-30 66

ATLANTIC (2678 "Tonight")......... 4-8 69

ATLANTIC (2724 "American Ruse") 4-8 69

ELEKTRA (45648 "Kick Out the Jams") 5-10 69

Picture Sleeves

A^2 (333 "Looking at You") 75-125 67

LPs: 10/12–inch 33rpm

ATLANTIC (8247 "Back in the USA") 25-50 70

ATLANTIC (8285 "High Time") . 25-50 71

ELEKTRA (74042 "Kick Out the Jams")............................. 30-35 69

(Title track has X-rated Intro. Back cover has liner notes.)

ELEKTRA (74042 "Kick Out the Jams")...............................12-18 69

(Title track has censored intro. Back cover has no liner notes.)

MFSB

(Mothers, Fathers, Sisters, Brothers)

LP '73

Singles: 7–inch

PHILADELPHIA INT'L....................3-5 74-78

TSOP 3-5 81

LPs: 10/12–inch 33rpm

PHILADELPHIA INT'L..................8-10 73-78

TSOP 5-8 80

Members: Norman Harris; Ronnie Baker; Bobby Eli; Bobby Martin; Earl Young; Don Renaldo; Albert Barone; Charles Apollonia; Angelo Petrella; Diana Barnett; Davis Barnett; Romeo Distefano; Rudy Maliazia; Christine Reeves; Joe Donofrio; Leno Zachery; Joe DeAngelis; Danny Ellions; Scott Temple; Milton Phibbs; Frederich Jainer; Fred Linge; Ricci Genovese; Edward Casceralle; Rocco Bene; Robert Hartzell; Karl Chambers; Roland Chambers; Dexter Wansel; Ron Harding; Terri Wells; James Smith; Evon Solot; Larry McKenna; Clifford Rudd; Miguel Fuentes; Evette Benton; John Usry; Dennis Harris; Don Renaldo; Marc Rubin; Derek Graves; Lenny Pakula; John Faith; Alphonso Carey; Billy Johnson; Steve Green; Leon Huff; Carleton Kent; Quinton Joseph; Carla Benson; Bob Malach; David Cruse; Steve Gold; Barbara Ingram; Joel Bryant.

Also see B-H-Y
Also see DE VAUGN, William
Also see ELECTRIC INDIAN
Also see ELI'S SECOND COMING
Also see HUFF, Leon
Also see JAMES BOYS
Also see MUSIC MAKERS
Also see NOBLES, Cliff
Also see PEOPLE'S CHOICE
Also see PHILADELPHIA INTERNATIONAL ALL STARS
Also see TRAMMPS
Also see WANSEL, Dexter
Also see WELLS, Terri

MFSB & Three Degrees

P&R '74

Singles: 7–inch

PHILADELPHIA INT'L....................3-5 74

Also see MFSB
Also see THREE DEGREES

M+M: see MARTHA & MUFFINS

M.O.D.

LP '87

LPs: 10/12–inch 33rpm

CAROLINE.....................................5-8 88

MEGAFORCE 5-8 87-89

MABLEY, Moms

LP '61

Singles: 7–inch

MERCURY 3-5 69-71

EPs: 7–inch 33/45rpm

CHESS ... 5-10 63

LPs: 10/12–inch 33rpm

CHESS ... 15-25 61-64
MERCURY ... 10-20 64-70

MABLEY, Moms, & Pigmeat Markham

LPs: 10/12–inch 33rpm

CHESS ... 10-20 64-71
Also see MABLEY, Moms
Also see MARKHAM, Pigmeat

MABON, Willie
(With His Combo)

R&B '52

Singles: 78rpm

CHESS ... 10-20 52-56
FEDERAL ... 10-20 57

Singles: 7–inch

CHESS (1531 "I Don't Know") ... 100-200 53
(Colored vinyl.)
CHESS (1531 "I Don't Know") ... 35-55 53
(Black vinyl.)
CHESS (1538 "I'm Mad") ... 35-55 53
CHESS (1548 "You're a Fool") .. 30-50 53
CHESS (1554 "I Got to Go") ... 30-50 53
CHESS (1564 "Would You, Baby") ... 30-50 54
CHESS (1580 "Poison Ivy") ... 30-50 54
DELTA (3004 "Light Up Your Lamp") ... 5-10
FEDERAL (12306 "Light Up Your Lamp") ... 15-25 57
FORMAL ... 4-6 62
MAD (1298 "I Gotta Go Now") .. 10-20 60
MAD (1300 "I Don't Know") ... 10-20 60
PARROT (1050 "I Don't Know") ... 150-250 53
U.S.A. ... 5-8 63-65

LPs: 10/12–inch 33rpm

CHESS (1439 "Willie Mabon") 50-100 59

MAC, Fleetwood: see FLEETWOOD MAC

MAC BAND
(Featuring the McCampbell Brothers)

R&B/LP '88

Singles: 7–inch

MCA ... 3-4 88

LPs: 10/12–inch 33rpm

MCA ... 5-8 88

MacALPINE, Tony

LP '87

LPs: 10/12–inch 33rpm

SQUAWK ... 5-8 87

MacARTHUR, James

P&R '63

Singles: 7–inch

SCEPTER ... 4-8 62-63
TRIODEX ... 5-10 61

MacDONALD, Jeanette, & Nelson Eddy

LP '59

EPs: 7–inch 33/45rpm

RCA (Except 220) ... 4-8 61
RCA (220 "Rose Marie") ... 10-20 52

LPs: 10/12–inch 33rpm

RCA (16 "Rose Marie") ... 40-50 52
RCA (526 "Rose Marie") ... 10-20 66
RCA (1000 series) ... 5-10 75
RCA (1700 series) ... 10-20 59
RCA (2400 series) ... 5-8 77
RCA (3900 series) ... 5-8 81

MacDONALD, Ralph

R&B/LP '77

Singles: 12–inch 33/45rpm

POLYDOR ... 4-6 84-85

Singles: 7–inch

MARLIN ... 3-5 76-79
POLYDOR ... 3-4 84-85

LPs: 10/12–inch 33rpm

MARLIN ... 6-10 76-79
POLYDOR ... 5-8 84-85

MacDONALD, Ralph, & Bill Withers

P&R '84

Singles: 7–inch

POLYDOR ... 3-4 84
Also see MacDONALD, Ralph
Also see WITHERS, Bill

MACEO & MACKS

R&B '70

Singles: 7–inch

PEOPLE ... 3-5 73-74

LPs: 10/12–inch 33rpm

PEOPLE ... 8-12 74
Member: Maceo Parker.
Also see PARLIAMENT

MacGREGOR, Byron

P&R/C&W '74

Singles: 7–inch

CAPITOL ... 3-5 75
WESTBOUND ... 3-5 74

LPs: 10/12–inch 33rpm

WESTBOUND ... 5-10 74

MacGREGOR, Mary

P&R '76

Singles: 7–inch

ARIOLA ... 3-5 78
ARIOLA AMERICA ... 3-5 76-77
RSO ... 3-5 79-80

LPs: 10/12–inch 33rpm

ARIOLA AMERICA ... 8-10 77
Also see ASSOCIATION / Bobby Vee / Mike Love / Mary MacGregor

MACHINATIONS

D&D '83

Singles: 12–inch 33/45rpm

A&M ... 4-6 83

Singles: 7-inch

A&M 3-5 83

LPs: 10/12-inch 33rpm

A&M 5-8 83

MACHINE

R&B '79

Singles: 7-inch

RCA 3-5 79-80

LPs: 10/12-inch 33rpm

RCA 5-10 80

MACHO

LP '78

Singles: 7-inch

PRELUDE 3-5 78

LPs: 10/12-inch 33rpm

PRELUDE 5-10 78

MACK, Lonnie
(With Pismo)

P&R/R&B/LP '63

Singles: 7-inch

ABC 3-5 73
A.M.G. 3-6
BARRY 3-5
CAPITOL 3-5 77
COLLECTABLES 3-4 80s
ELEKTRA 3-5 71
FRATERNITY 5-10 63-68
ROULETTE 3-5 75

LPs: 10/12-inch 33rpm

ALLIGATOR 5-8 85-86
CAPITOL 8-10 77
ELEKTRA 10-20 69-71
FRATERNITY (SF-1014 "Wham of That Memphis Man") 25-35 63
(Monaural.)
FRATERNITY (SSF-1014 "Wham of That Memphis Man") 35-55 63
(Stereo.)
TRIP 8-10 75

Members: Lonnie Mack; Jim Keltner; Tim Drummond.

MACK, Lonnie, & Rusty York

LPs: 10/12-inch 33rpm

QCA 10-15 73

Also see MACK, Lonnie
Also see YORK, Rusty

MACK, Warner

C&W/P&R '57

Singles: 78rpm

DECCA 5-10 57

Singles: 7-inch

DECCA (30301 thru 31684) 5-12 57-64
DECCA (31774 thru 33045) 3-6 65-73
KAPP 5-10 61-62
MCA 3-5 73-76
PAGEBOY 3-5 77-81
SCARLET 5-10 60
TOP RANK 5-10 60

EPs: 7-inch 33/45rpm

DECCA 5-10 65

LPs: 10/12-inch 33rpm

CORAL 5-10 73
DECCA 8-18 65-70
KAPP 10-20 61-66

Session: Jordanaires.

MacKENZIE, Giselle

P&R '52

Singles: 78rpm

CAPITOL 3-5 51-54
VIK 3-5 56
X 3-5 55

Singles: 7-inch

CAPITOL 5-10 51-54
EVEREST 4-8 60
MERCURY 4-8 63
VIK 5-10 56
X 5-10 55

Picture Sleeves

VIK 5-10 56
X 5-10 55

EPs: 7-inch 33/45rpm

CAPITOL 5-10 53-69
VIK 5-10 56

LPs: 10/12-inch 33rpm

CAMDEN 10-20 59
EVEREST 10-20 60
GLENDALE 5-8 78
MERCURY 10-20 63
RCA 10-20 59
SUNSET 8-12 67
VIK 15-25 56

MacRAE, Gordon

P&R '47

Singles: 78rpm

CAPITOL 3-5 47-57

Singles: 7-inch

CAPITOL 4-8 50-68

EPs: 7-inch 33/45rpm

CAPITOL 5-10 54-57
ROYALE 5-10

LPs: 10/12-inch 33rpm

CAPITOL 10-25 54-69
RONDO-LETTE 15-30

Also see DESMOND, Johnny / John Gary / Gordon MacRae
Also see MARTIN, Dean / Bob Eberly / Gordon MacRae

MacRAE, Gordon, & Jo Stafford

P&R '48

Singles: 78rpm

CAPITOL 4-8 48-50

Singles: 7-inch

CAPITOL 4-8 62

LPs: 10/12-inch 33rpm

CAPITOL (1600 & 1900 series) . 10-20 62-63
CAPITOL (11000 series) 4-8 79

Also see BRYANT, Anita / Jo Stafford & Gordon

MacRae
Also see MacRAE, Gordon
Also see STAFFORD, Jo

MAD LADS

P&R/R&B '65

Singles: 7–inch

MARK-FI (1934 "Why") 20-30 62
CAPITOL 5-10 64
STAX 10-20 64
VOLT (100 series) 5-15 65-68
VOLT (4000 series) 3-8 69-73

LPs: 10/12–inch 33rpm

COLLECTABLES 6-8 86
VOLT (400 series) 15-25 66
VOLT (6000 series) 10-15 69-73

Members: Julius Green; John Williams; Robert Phillips; Sam Nelson; Cliff Billops Jr.
Also see OLLIE & NIGHTINGALES

MAD RIVER

LP '69

Singles: 7–inch

CAPITOL 5-10 68-69

EPs: 7–inch 33/45rpm

WEE (10021 "Mad River") 25-50 68

LPs: 10/12–inch 33rpm

CAPITOL (185 "Paradise Bar and Grill") 25-35 69
CAPITOL (2985 "Mad River") ... 25-35 68

Members: David Robinson; Tom Manning; Lawrence Hammond; Rick Bochner; Greg Dewey; Ron Wilson.

MADAGASCAR

R&B '81

Singles: 7–inch

ARISTA 3-5 81-82

Members: John Barnes; Marva King.

MADAME X

R&B/LP '87

Singles: 7–inch

ATLANTIC 3-4 87
LORIMAR 3-4 88

LPs: 10/12–inch 33rpm

ATLANTIC 5-8 87

MADDOX, Johnny
(With the Rhythmasters)

P&R '52

Singles: 78rpm

DOT 3-6 50-57

Singles: 7–inch

ABC 3-5 74
DOT 4-8 50-63

EPs: 7–inch 33/45rpm

DOT 5-10 52-56

LPs: 10/12–inch 33rpm

DOT (Except 102) 10-25 55-67
DOT (102 "Authentic Ragtime") 20-30 52
(10–inch LP.)
HAMILTON 10-15 64
PARAMOUNT 5-10 74

MADE in U.S.A.

R&B '77

Singles: 7–inch

DE-LITE 3-5 77

MADHOUSE

R&B/LP '87

Singles: 7–inch

PAISLEY PARK 3-4 87

Picture Sleeves

PAISLEY PARK 3-4 87

LPs: 10/12–inch 33rpm

PAISLEY PARK 5-8 87

Also see PRINCE

MADIGAN, Betty

P&R '54

Singles: 78rpm

CORAL 3-6 57
JAY DEE 3-6 54
MGM (11000 series) 3-6 53-56

Singles: 7–inch

CORAL 4-8 57-59
JAY DEE 5-10 54
MGM (11000 series) 5-10 53-56
MGM (13000 series) 4-6 66-67
20TH FOX 4-6 64
U.A. 4-8 60-61

EPs: 7–inch 33/45rpm

JAY DEE 5-10 54
MGM 5-10 57

LPs: 10/12–inch 33rpm

CORAL 10-20 62
MGM 10-20 57-69

MADNESS

LP '80

Singles: 12–inch 33/45rpm

GEFFEN 4-6 83
STIFF 8-12
(Promotional only.)

Singles: 7–inch

GEFFEN 3-4 83-84
SIRE 3-5 80-81

Picture Sleeves

GEFFEN 3-4 83-84

LPs: 10/12–inch 33rpm

GEFFEN 5-8 83-84
SIRE 5-8 80-81

MADONNA

P&R/R&B/D&D/LP '83

Singles: 12–inch 33/45rpm

MAVERICK (40585 "Erotica") 4-8 92
SIRE (20212 "Borderline") 5-10 84
SIRE (20239 "Like a Virgin") 5-10 84
SIRE (20304 "Material Girl") 5-10 85
SIRE (20335 "Angel") 5-10 85
SIRE (20369 "Dress You Up") 5-10 85
SIRE (20597 "Open Your Heart") 5-10 87
SIRE (20633 "La Isla Bonita") 5-10 87

SIRE (20762 "Causing a Commotion") 5-10 87
SIRE (21170 "Like a Prayer")...... 5-10 89
SIRE (21225 "Express Yourself") 5-10 89
SIRE (21427 "Keep It Together") 5-10 90
SIRE (21513 "Vogue")................ 5-10 90
SIRE (21820 "Justify My Love").. 5-10 91
SIRE (21813 "Rescue Me")......... 5-10 91
SIRE (23867 "Holiday")............... 5-10 83
SIRE (29715 "Physical Attraction") 5-10 83

Singles: 7-inch

GEFFEN.................................... 3-5 85
SIRE... 3-5 83-90

Picture Sleeves

GEFFEN.................................... 3-5 85
SIRE... 3-5 83-90

LPs: 10/12-inch 33rpm

SIRE (23867 "Madonna") 5-8 83
SIRE (25157 "Like a Virgin") 5-8 83
(Black vinyl.)
SIRE (1-25157 "Like a Virgin") 75-125 83
(Colored vinyl. Promotional issue only.)
SIRE (25442 "True Blue") 5-8 86
SIRE (25611 "Who's That Girl") 5-8 87
SIRE (25535 "You Can Dance") ... 5-8 87
SIRE (25844 "Like a Prayer")........ 5-8 89
SIRE (26209 "I'm Breathless")...... 5-8 90

MADURA

LP '71

LPs: 10/12-inch 33rpm

COLUMBIA 10-15 71-73

MAESTRO, Johnny
(With the Crests; with Coeds; Johnny Mastro)

P&R '61

Singles: 7-inch

APT (25075 "She's All Mine Alone") 10-20 65
BUDDAH 5-10 71-72
CAMEO 10-15 63-64
COED (545 "Model Girl") 8-12 61
COED (549 "What a Surprise"). 10-20 61
COED (552 "Mr Happiness")..... 10-15 61
COED (557 "I.O.U.") 20-30 61
COED (562 "Besame Baby") .. 75-100 61
COLLECTABLES 3-4 80s
PARKWAY (118 "Is It You")...... 10-20 67
PARKWAY (987 "Heartburn") ... 10-15 66
PARKWAY (987 "Heartburn") ... 30-40 66
(Single sided disc. Promotional issue only.)
SCEPTER (12112 "I'm Stepping Out of the Picture") 50-100 65
U.A. (474 "Before I Loved Her") 20-30 62

LPs: 10/12-inch 33rpm

BUDDAH (5091 "The Johnny Maestro Story") 25-35 71
(Price includes inserts.)
HARVEY (1000 "Biggest Hits") ..10-20 81
(Colored vinyl.)
Also see BROOKLYN BRIDGE
Also see CRESTS
Also see MASTERS, Johnny

MAESTRO, Johnny, & Tymes

Singles: 7-inch

POPULAR REQUEST 3-6
Also see MAESTRO, Johnny
Also see TYMES

MAGAZINE 60

P&R '86

Singles: 7-inch

BAJA 3-4 86

MAGGARD, Cledus
(With the Citizen's Band)

C&W/P&R '75

Singles: 7-inch

MERCURY...................................3-5 75-79

LPs: 10/12-inch 33rpm

MERCURY.................................5-10 70

MAGIC LADY

P&R '82

Singles: 12-inch 33/45rpm

A&M 4-6 82

Singles: 7-inch

A&M 3-4 82
MOTOWN 3-4 88

LPs: 10/12-inch 33rpm

A&M 5-8 82
ARISTA...5-8 80

MAGIC LANTERNS

P&R '68

Singles: 7-inch

ATLANTIC..................................5-10 68-70
BIG TREE 3-5 71
CHARISMA 3-5 72
EPIC..4-8 66

LPs: 10/12-inch 33rpm

ATLANTIC..............................12-15 69
Members: Jim Bilsbury; Bev Beveridge; Mike "Ozzy" Osborne; Peter Garner; Harry Paul Ward; Albert Hammond.

MAGIC MUSHROOMS

P&R '66

Singles: 7-inch

A&M (815 "Never More") 8-12 66
EAST COAST (1001 "Let the Rain Be Me") 8-12 68
PHILIPS (40483 "Look in My Face") 8-12 67
Members: Chris Gaylord; Michael Allen.

MAGIC ORGAN
(Jerry Smith)

LP '72

Singles: 7-inch

RANWOOD..................................3-5 72-77

LPs: 10/12-inch 33rpm
RANWOOD 4-8 72-83
SUNNYVALE 4-6 79
Also see SMITH, Jerry

MAGIC TOUCH

P&R '71

Singles: 7-inch
BLACK FASHION 3-5 71

MAGISTRATES

P&R '68

Singles: 7-inch
MGM 4-8 68-69
Member: Jean Hillary.
Also see DOVELLS

MAGNIFICENT MEN

P&R/LP '67

Singles: 7-inch
CAPITOL...................................... 4-8 66-68
MERCURY 3-6 69
LPs: 10/12-inch 33rpm
CAPITOL.................................. 10-20 67-68
MERCURY 8-12 70
Members: Dave Bupp; Buddy King; Tom Pane; Bob Angelucci; Terry Crousore; Tommy Hoover; Jimmy Seville; Billy Richter.

MAGNIFICENTS

R&B '56

Singles: 78rpm
VEE JAY 10-20 56-58
Singles: 7-inch
CHECKER (1016 "Do You Mind")...................................... 5-10 62
COLLECTABLES 3-4 80s
KANSOMA (03 "Do You Mind")... 5-10 62
VEE JAY (183 "Up on the Mountain")............................. 30-60 56
VEE JAY (208 "Caddy Bo")....... 40-75 56
VEE JAY (235 "Off the Mountain")............................. 30-60 57
VEE JAY (281 "Don't Leave Me").. 50-75 58
VEE JAY (367 "Up on the Mountain")............................. 10-15 60
Also see EL DORADOS

MAGNUM FORCE

R&B '85

Singles: 7-inch
PAULA 3-4 85
LPs: 10/12-inch 33rpm
WIZARD 5-8 78

MaGOO, Mr: see BACKUS, Jim

MAHAL, TAJ: see TAJ MAHAL

MAHARIS, George

P&R/LP '62

Singles: 7-inch
EPIC... 4-6 62-66
Picture Sleeves
EPIC...4-6 62-64
LPs: 10/12-inch 33rpm
EPIC...10-15 62-66

MAHOGANY

D&D '83

Singles: 12-inch 33/45rpm
WEST END 4-6 82
Singles: 7-inch
WEST END 3-4 82

MAHOGANY RUSH

LP '74

Singles: 7-inch
COLUMBIA 3-5 76-82
20TH FOX....................................3-5 74-75
LPs: 10/12-inch 33rpm
COLUMBIA 8-12 76-82
20TH FOX.................................10-12 73-75
Member: Frank Marino.
Also see MARINO, Frank, & Mahogany Rush

MAHONEY, Skip, & Casuals

R&B '74

Singles: 7-inch
ABET..3-5 76-77
D.C. INT'L 3-5 74
Members: Skip Mahoney; Tracy Reid; Julius Jerome; Elwood Morgan.
Also see SKIP & CASUALS

MAI TAI

R&B '85

Singles: 12-inch 33/45rpm
MERCURY....................................4-6 87
Singles: 7-inch
CRITIQUE....................................3-4 85-86
MERCURY 3-4 87
Picture Sleeves
CRITIQUE....................................3-4 86
LPs: 10/12-inch 33rpm
MERCURY....................................5-8 87
Members: Carol DeWindt; Jettie Well; Mildred Douglas.

MAIN ATTRACTION

R&B '86

Singles: 7-inch
RCA 3-4 86
LPs: 10/12-inch 33rpm
RCA 5-8 86

MAIN INGREDIENT
(Featuring Cuba Gooding)

P&R/R&B/LP '70

Singles: 7-inch
RCA 3-5 69-81
ZAKIA..3-4 86
Picture Sleeves
RCA 3-6 70-81
LPs: 10/12-inch 33rpm
COLLECTABLES...........................5-8 88
RCA 8-12 70-81

Members: Cuba Gooding; Don McPherson; Luther Simmons; Tony Sylvester.
Also see GOODING, Cuba
Also see POETS

MAINSTREETERS

R&B '73

Singles: 7-inch

EVENT 3-5 73

MAJESTY

R&B '85

Singles: 7-inch

GOLDEN BOY 3-4 85

MAJOR LANCE: see LANCE, Major

MAJORS

P&R/R&B '62

Singles: 7-inch

IMPERIAL 8-15 62-64

LPs: 10/12-inch 33rpm

IMPERIAL (9222 "Meet the Majors") 25-35 63
(Monaural.)
IMPERIAL (12222 "Meet the Majors") 25-35 63
(Stereo.)

Members: Ricky Cordo; Eugene Glass; Idella Morris; Frank Troutt; Ronald Gathers.

MAKEBA, Miriam

LP '63

Singles: 7-inch

KAPP 4-8 62
MERCURY 4-6 66
RCA 4-8 64
REPRISE 4-6 67-68

LPs: 10/12-inch 33rpm

KAPP 10-20 62
MERCURY 10-15 66
PETERS INT'L 5-8 81
RCA 10-20 60-68
REPRISE 10-15 67

Also see BELAFONTE, Harry, & Miriam Makeba
Also see MANHATTAN BROTHERS & Miriam Makeba

MAKEM, Tommy: see CLANCY BROTHERS & Tommy Makem

MALCOLM X

R&B '84

Singles: 7-inch

TOMMY BOY 3-4 83-84

LPs: 10/12-inch 33rpm

DOUGLAS 8-15 68-71

MALICE

LP '87

LPs: 10/12-inch 33rpm

ATLANTIC 5-8 87
ENIGMA 5-8

MALMKVIST, Siw
(With Umberto Marcato)

P&R '64

Singles: 7-inch

JUBILEE 4-6 64
KAPP 4-8 61

MALMSTEEN, Yngwie J.
(Yngwie J. Malmsteen's Rising Force)

LP '85

LPs: 10/12-Inch 33rpm

MERCURY 5-8 86
POLYDOR 5-8 85-88

Also see ALCATRAZZ
Also see DIO, Ronnie
Also see HEAR 'N AID

MALO

P&R/LP '72

Singles: 7-inch

TRAQ 3-5 81
W.B. 3-5 72-73

LPs: 10/12-inch 33rpm

W.B. 8-12 72-74

Also see AZTECA
Also see SANTANA, Jorge

MALTBY, Richard, & Orchestra

P&R '54

Singles: 78rpm

VIK 3-5 56
X 3-5 54-55

Singles: 7-inch

COLUMBIA 4-8 59
ROULETTE 4-8 60-61
VIK 5-10 56
X 5-10 54-55

Picture Sleeves

VIK 10-15 56

EPs: 7-inch 33/45rpm

COLUMBIA 5-10 59
VIK 5-10 56
X 8-15 54-55

LPs: 10/12-inch 33rpm

CAMDEN 10-20 60-62
COLUMBIA 10-20 59
HARMONY 10-20 61
ROULETTE 10-20 60-62
VIK (1051 "Hue-Fi Moods") 20-30 56
VIK (1068 "Manhattan Bandstand") 20-30 56
X (1038 "Make Mine Maltby") 20-30 56

MAMA CASS: see ELLIOT, Cass

MAMA'S BOYS

LP '84

Singles: 7-inch

JIVE 3-4 84-87

LPs: 10/12-inch 33rpm

JIVE 5-8 84-87

MAMAS & PAPAS

P&R/LP '66

Singles: 7-inch

ABC....3-5 70
DUNHILL....4-8 65-72
MCA....3-5 80-82

Picture Sleeves

DUNHILL (4020 "California Dreamin'") 50-100 65
(Promotional issue only.)
DUNHILL (4083 "Creeque Alley")....25-35 67
(Promotional issue only.)
DUNHILL (4113 "Dancing Bear").. 4-8 67

EPs: 7-inch 33/45rpm

ABC....8-15 71
(Promotional issues only.)
DUNHILL....15-20 65

LPs: 10/12-inch 33rpm

ABC....6-10 76
DUNHILL....10-20 66-73
MCA....5-8 80-82
PICKWICK....6-10 72

Members: John Phillips "Mama" Cass Elliot; Denny Doherty; Michelle Phillips.
Also see ELLIOT, Cass
Also see McGUIRE, Barry
Also see PHILLIPS, John

MAMAS & PAPAS / Association / Fifth Dimension

LPs: 10/12-inch 33rpm

TEE VEE/W.B. SPECIAL PRODUCTIONS....10-20 79

Also see ASSOCIATION
Also see FIFTH DIMENSION
Also see MAMAS & PAPAS

MAN PARRISH: see PARRISH, Man

MANASSAS

LP '72

LPs: 10/12-inch 33rpm

ATLANTIC....8-12 72-73

Also see STILLS, Stephen

MANCHA, Steve
(Clyde Wilson)

R&B '66

Singles: 7-inch

GROOVESVILLE (1001 "You're Still in My Heart")....10-20 65
GROOVESVILLE (1002 "I Don't Want to Lose You")....8-12 66
GROOVESVILLE (1004 "Friday Night")....50-75 66
GROOVESVILLE (1005 "Don't Make Me a Story Teller")....8-12 67
GROOVESVILLE (1007 "Sweet Baby")....10-20 67
WHEELSVILLE (102 "Did My Baby Call")....50-100 65

Also see BARNES, J.J., & Steve Mancha
Also see 100 PROOF Aged in Soul

MANCHESTER, Melissa

LP '73

Singles: 12-inch 33/45rpm

ARISTA....4-6 82
CASABLANCA....4-6 84
MCA....4-6 85

Singles: 7-inch

ARISTA....3-5 75-84
BELL....3-5 74
CASABLANCA....3-4 84
MB....4-8 67
MCA....3-4 85

LPs: 10/12-inch 33rpm

ARISTA....8-10 75-83
BELL....10-12 73-74
CASABLANCA....5-8 84
MCA....5-8 79-85
MFSL....25-50 79

Also see NATIONAL LAMPOON

MANCHESTER, Melissa, & Peabo Bryson

P&R '81

Singles: 7-inch

ARISTA....3-5 81

Also see BRYSON, Peabo
Also see MANCHESTER, Melissa

MANCHILD

R&B/LP '77

Singles: 7-inch

CHI-SOUND....3-5 77

LPs: 10/12-inch 33rpm

CHI-SOUND....8-10 77

Members: Kenny Edmonds; Robert Parson; Chuck Bush; Daryl Simmons; Reggie Griffin.
Also see DEELE
Also see GRIFFIN, Reggie, & Technofunk
Also see REDD HOTT

MANCINI, Henry
(Henry Mancini's Orchestra & Chorus)

LP '59

Singles: 7-inch

LIBERTY (1400 series)....3-4 82
LIBERTY (55000 series)....4-8 58-59
RCA (Except 8184)....3-8 59-85
RCA (8184 "Banzai Pipeline")....5-10 63
U.A.....3-4 78
W.B.....3-4 79-83

Picture Sleeves

RCA (Except 8184)....5-12 59-77
RCA (8184 "Banzai Pipeline")....10-15 63
W.B.....3-5 79

EPs: 7-inch 33/45rpm

RCA....5-15 60-62

LPs: 10/12-inch 33rpm

AVCO EMBASSY....10-20 70
CAMDEN....5-15 66-74
LIBERTY (3000 series)....15-25 57-59
LIBERTY (51000 series)....4-8 82

MCA 6-12 75-76
PARAMOUNT 10-15 70
RCA (0013 thru 0098)................ 5-10 72-73
RCA (0270 "Country Gentleman") 5-8 74
RCA (0672 thru 1928)................ 5-10 74-76
RCA (2147 "The Blues and the Beat") 15-25 60
RCA (2360 "Mr. Lucky Goes Latin")................................. 15-25 61
RCA (2362 "Just You and Me Together Love") 4-8 77
RCA (2258 "Combo")............... 15-20 62
RCA (2600 series).................... 10-20 63-64
RCA (2800 & 2900 series) 8-15 64-65
RCA (3000 series)........................ 4-8 78
RCA (3356 "The Latin Sound of Henry Mancini").................. 10-20 65
RCA (3347 "Best of Henry Mancini, Volume 3") 5-8 79
RCA (3500 series)...................... 6-12 66
RCA (3612 "Merry Mancini Christmas") 10-15 66
RCA (3667 "Pure Gold") 4-8 80
RCA (3668 "Mancini Country")...... 4-8 80
RCA (3694 thru 3713).............. 10-20 66-67
RCA (3756 "Warm Shade of Ivory").. 4-8 80
RCA (3822 "Best of Henry Mancini") 4-8 80
RCA (3877 "Music of Hawaii") 4-8 81
RCA (3887 "Encore") 8-15 67
RCA (3954 "Country Gentleman") 4-8 67
RCA (3997 thru 4689)................ 5-15 68-72
RCA (5000 series)........................ 4-8 85
RCA (6000 series)...................... 8-15 66-72
SUNSET....................................... 5-10 66
U.A. 10-12 70
W.B. 10-20 59-73

You'll find many more listings by this artist in *The Official Price Guide to Movie/TV Soundtracks and Original Cast Albums,* containing over 8,000 listings.

Also see ANN-MARGRET
Also see HIRT, Al / Henry Mancini / Perez Prado
Also see MATHIS, Johnny, & Henry Mancini
Also see PRIDE, Charley

MANCINI, Henry, & Doc Severinsen

LP '73

LPs: 10/12-inch 33rpm

RCA.. 5-8 72-80

Also see MANCINI, Henry
Also see SEVERINSEN, Doc

MANDEL, Harvey

LP '69

Singles: 7-inch

PHILIPS 4-8 68

LPs: 10/12-inch 33rpm

JANUS 8-12 70-74
OVATION 10-15 71
PHILIPS 10-15 68-69

Also see CANNED HEAT

MANDELL, Howie

LP '86

LPs: 10/12-inch 33rpm

W.B. 5-8 86

MANDELL, Mike

R&B '81

Singles: 7-inch

VANGUARD.................................. 3-5 81

MANDRE

(Andre Lewis)

R&B/LP '77

Singles: 7-inch

MOTOWN....................................... 3-5 77-79

LPs: 10/12-inch 33rpm

MOTOWN 5-10 77-79

Also see MAXAYN

MANDRELL, Barbara

C&W '69

Singles: 7-inch

ABC... 3-5 78-79
ABC/DOT 3-6 75-78
COLUMBIA 4-8 69-75
EMI... 3-4 87-88
KFC (003 "Sweet Weekend Encounter")................................ 8-12 79
(Coincides with "National Winners Kentucky Fried Chicken Song Writing Contest." Promotional issue only.)
MCA (Black vinyl)........................ 3-5 79-86
MCA (52737 "Fast Lanes and Country Roads")................................. 15-20 85
(Colored vinyl. Promotional issue only.)
MCA (52802 "When You Get to the Heart")............................... 15-20 86
(Colored vinyl. Promotional issue only.)
MOSRITE.................................... 10-15 66

Picture Sleeves

MCA 3-5 79-85

LPs: 10/12-inch 33rpm

ABC... 8-10 78-79
ABC/DOT 8-12 76-77
COLUMBIA 8-15 71-81
COLUMBIA SPECIAL PROD......... 5-8 82
EMI... 5-8 88
MCA 5-10 79-86
SONGBIRD 5-8 82
TIME-LIFE...................................... 5-8 81

Session: Waylon Jennings; Randy Wright.
Also see HOUSTON, David, & Barbara Mandrell
Also see JENNINGS, Waylon

MANDRELL, Barbara, & Lee Greenwood

C&W/LP '84

Singles: 7-inch

MCA 3-4 84

LPs: 10/12-inch 33rpm

MCA 5-8 84

Also see GREENWOOD, Lee

MANDRELL, Barbara, & Oak Ridge Boys

C&W '86

Singles: 7-inch

MCA 3-4 86

Also see MANDRELL, Barbara

Also see OAK RIDGE BOYS

MANDRILL

P&R/LP '71

Singles: 7-inch

ARISTA 3-5 77-80

LIBERTY 3-4 83

MONTAGE 3-4 82

POLYDOR 3-5 71-74

U.A. 3-5 75-76

LPs: 10/12-inch 33rpm

ARISTA 8-10 77-80

LIBERTY 5-8 83

POLYDOR 10-12 71-75

U.A. 8-10 75

Also see MASSER, Michael, & Mandrill

Also see SURFACE

MANFRED MANN: see MANN, Manfred

MANGANO, Silvana

P&R '53

Singles: 78rpm

MGM 3-6 53

Singles: 7-inch

MGM 5-10 53

MANGIONE, Chuck

(Chuck Mangione Quintet; Gap & Chuck Mangione)

P&R/LP '71

Singles: 7-inch

A&M 3-5 75-80

COLUMBIA 3-4 82-84

MERCURY 3-5 71-77

Picture Sleeves

A&M 3-5 78-80

LPs: 10/12-inch 33rpm

A&M 5-10 75-81

COLUMBIA 5-8 82-84

JAZZLAND (84 "Recuerdo") 40-50 62

JAZZLAND (984 "Recuerdo") 45-60 62

(Stereo.)

MFSL 25-50 82

MERCURY 6-12 71-78

MILESTONE 5-8 77

RIVERSIDE (371 "Jazz Brothers") 40-50 61

MANHATTAN BROTHERS & Miriam Makeba

P&R '56

Singles: 78rpm

LONDON 3-6 56

Singles: 7-inch

LONDON 5-10 56

Also see MAKEBA, Miriam

MANHATTAN TRANSFER

P&R/LP '75

Singles: 7-inch

ATLANTIC 3-5 75-85

Picture Sleeves

ATLANTIC 3-5 83

LPs: 10/12-inch 33rpm

ATLANTIC 8-10 75-87

COLLECTABLES 6-8 88

MFSL 25-50 78

Members: Tim Hauser; Alan Paul; Gary Chester; Garnett Brown; Ken Buttrey; Cheryl Bentyne; Janis Siegel; Don Roberts.

Also see PISTILLI, Gene

MANHATTANS

P&R/R&B '65

Singles: 12-inch 33/45rpm

COLUMBIA 4-6 84-85

Singles: 7-inch

AVANTI 15-20 63

CAPITOL 8-12 61-62

CARNIVAL 5-15 64-69

COLUMBIA 3-5 73-87

DELUXE 4-8 69-73

Picture Sleeves

COLUMBIA 3-4 85

LPs: 10/12-inch 33rpm

CARNIVAL (201 "Dedicated to You") 100-150 66

CARNIVAL (202 "For You and Yours") 100-150 66

COLUMBIA 8-12 73-85

DELUXE 10-15 70-72

SOLID SMOKE 5-8 81

Members: George Smith; Ken Kelly; Sonny Bivens; Winfred Scott; Richard Taylor; Gerald Alston; Regina Bell.

MANILOW, Barry

P&R/LP '74

Singles: 12-inch 33/45rpm

ARISTA 5-10 78-87

Singles: 7-inch

ARISTA 3-5 74-90

BELL 3-5 73-74

FLASHBACK 3-4 76

RCA 3-4 86

Promotional Singles

ARISTA (11 "It's Just Another New Year's Eve") 4-8 77

ARISTA (9318 "Paradise Cafe") 3-5 84

(Clear vinyl.)

Picture Sleeves

ARISTA (Except 11) 3-5 78-88

ARISTA (11 "It's Just Another New Year's Eve") 4-8 77

(Promotional issue only.)

ARISTA (9318 "Paradise Cafe") ... 3-5 84

LPs: 10/12-inch 33rpm

ARISTA 5-10 74-90
BELL 10-15 74
RCA 5-8 86

Also see LADY FLASH

MANILOW, Barry / Atlanta Rhythm Section

Singles: 7-inch

WHAT'S IT ALL ABOUT 3-5 79

Also see ATLANTA RHYTHM SECTION

MANILOW, Barry / Firefall

Singles: 7-inch

WHAT'S IT ALL ABOUT 3-5 79

Also see FIREFALL

MANILOW, Barry / Kid Creole & Coconuts

P&R '88

Singles: 7-inch

ARISTA 3-4 88

Also see KID CREOLE & COCONUTS
Also see MANILOW, Barry

MANN, Barry

P&R '61

Singles: 7-inch

ABC 3-5 73
ABC-PAR 5-10 60-62
ARISTA 3-5 76
CAPITOL 4-8 66-68
CASABLANCA 3-4 80
COLPIX 4-8 63
JDS 10-20 59
MCA 3-4 80s
NEW DESIGN 3-5 71-72
RCA 3-5 74-76
RED BIRD 5-10 64
ROULETTE 3-5 70s
SCEPTER 3-5 70
U.A. 3-5 77-78
W.B. 3-5 79

LPs: 10/12-inch 33rpm

ABC-PAR (ABC-399 "Who Put the Bomp") 50-80 62
(Monaural.)
ABC-PAR (ABCS-399 "Who Put the Bomp") 75-100 62
(Stereo.)
CASABLANCA 5-8 80
NEW DESIGN 10-12 71
RCA (0860 "Survivor") 8-12 75
RCA (1162 "Interview") 12-15 75
(Promotional issue only.)
U.A. 8-10 77

Also see HALOS

MANN, Bobby
(Bobby Bloom)

Singles: 7-inch

KAMA SUTRA 5-10 66

Also see BLOOM, Bobby

MANN, Carl

P&R/R&B '59

Singles: 7-inch

ABC/DOT 3-5 76
JAXON (502 "Gonna Rock and Roll Tonight") 200-300 57
PHILLIPS INT'L 8-15 59-61
SUN 3-5 70s

LPs: 10/12-inch 33rpm

GRT/SUNNYVALE 6-10 77
PHILLIPS INT'L (1960 "Like Mann") 400-500 60

MANN, Charles

R&B '73

Singles: 7-inch

ABC 3-5 73
LANOR (540 "Dreams to Remember") 10-20

MANN, Gloria
(With the Carter Rays; with Don Costa's Orchestra)

P&R '55

Singles: 78rpm

ABC-PAR 4-8 57
DECCA 3-6 56
DERBY 4-8 56
JUBILEE 4-8 54
SLS 10-15 54
SOUND 5-10 54-55

Singles: 7-inch

ABC-PAR 5-10 57
DECCA 5-10 56
DERBY 5-10 56
JUBILEE 8-12 54
SLS (102 "Goodnight Sweetheart") 30-40 54
SOUND 10-20 54-55

Also see COSTA, Don, Orchestra

MANN, Herbie

LP '62

Singles: 12-inch 33/45rpm

ATLANTIC 4-6 83

Singles: 7-inch

A&M 3-5 68
ATLANTIC 3-8 60-83
BETHLEHEM 4-8 59-62
COLUMBIA 3-5 70
EMBRYO 3-5 71
PRESTIGE 4-6 66

Picture Sleeves

ATLANTIC 3-5 79

LPs: 10/12-inch 33rpm

A&M 8-12 68
ATLANTIC (300 series) 8-12 72
ATLANTIC (1300 & 1400 series) 10-20 60-66

ATLANTIC (1500 thru 1600 series) 8-12 69-76
ATLANTIC (8000 series) 8-15 67
ATLANTIC (18000 and 19000 series) 5-10 77-83
BETHLEHEM (24 "Flamingo"). 50-100 55
BETHLEHEM (40 "Herbie Mann") 50-100 56
BETHLEHEM (63 "Love and the Weather") 50-100 56
BETHLEHEM (1018 "East Coast Jazz") 75-100 54
(10–inch LPs.)
BETHLEHEM (6001 "The Bethlehem Years") 5-8 76
BETHLEHEM (6067 "The Epitome of Jazz") 25-35 63
COLUMBIA 8-18 65-81
EMBRYO 8-12 70-71
EPIC (3395 "Salute to the Flute") 60-80 57
EPIC (3499 "Herbie Mann") 50-70 58
FINNADAR 5-10 76
INTERLUDE 20-35 59
JAZZLAND (5 "Californians") 35-55 60
MILESTONE 8-12 73
MODE (114 "Flute Fraternity") .. 40-60 57
NEW JAZZ (8211 "Just Wailin'") 50-60 58
PREMIER 20-30 63
PRESTIGE (7101 "Flute Souffle") 75-100 57
PRESTIGE (7124 "Flute Flight") 75-100 57
PRESTIGE (7136 "Mann in the Morning") 75-100 58
PRESTIGE (7432 "Best of Herbie Mann") 20-30 65
RIVERSIDE (03 "Blues for Tomorrow") 5-8 82
RIVERSIDE (234 "Sultry Serenade") 50-75 57
RIVERSIDE (245 "Great Ideas") 50-75 57
RIVERSIDE (3000 series) 8-12 69
ROULETTE 10-15 67
SAVOY (1100 series) 5-8 76
SAVOY (12107 "Mann Alone") .. 30-40 57
SAVOY (12108 "Yardbird Suite") 35-50 57
SOLID STATE 8-12 68
SURREY 10-15 65
U.A. (4000 & 5000 series) 20-40 59
U.A. (5300 series) 8-10 72
U.A. (14000 & 15000 series) 20-40 62-63
VSP 8-15 66
VERVE 20-40 57-61
(Reads "Verve Records, Inc." at bottom of label.)
VERVE 15-25 63
(Reads "MGM Records - A Division of Metro-Goldwyn-Mayer, Inc." at bottom of label.)
VERVE 5-10 69-73
(Reads "Manufactured By MGM Record Corp.," or mentions either Polydor or Polygram at bottom of label.)

Session: King Curtis; Little Milton.
Also see AYERS, Roy
Also see KING CURTIS
Also see LITTLE MILTON
Also see JONES, Tamiko, & Herbie Mann

MANN, Herbie, & Cissy Houston

R&B '76

Singles: 7–inch

ATLANTIC 3-5 76
Also see HOUSTON, Cissy

MANN, Herbie / Maynard Ferguson

LPs: 10/12–inch 33rpm

ROULETTE 8-12 71
Also see FERGUSON, Herbie
Also see MANN, Herbie

MANN, Johnny, Singers

LP '63

Singles: 7–inch

DECCA 3-5 66
EPIC 3-5 72
EUREKA 4-8 60
LIBERTY 4-6 62-68

LPs: 10/12–inch 33rpm

EPIC 5-10 72
LIBERTY 10-20 59-69
LIGHT 5-10 76
SUNSET 5-10 66-70
U.A. 6-12 71-72
Also see McDANIELS, Gene
Also see ZENTNER, Si

MANN, Manfred
(Manfred Mann's Earth Band)

P&R/LP '64

Singles: 7–inch

ARISTA 3-4 84-85
ASCOT (Except 2157 & 2165) 6-12 64-68
ASCOT (2157 "Do Wah Diddy Diddy") 4-8 64
ASCOT (2165 "Sha La La") 4-8 64
MERCURY 3-6 66-69
POLYDOR 3-5 71-74
PRESTIGE 8-10 64
U.A. 4-8 66
W.B. 3-5 76-81

Picture Sleeves

ASCOT 10-20 64-65
MERCURY 8-15 68
W.B. 3-5 76

EPs: 7–inch 33/45rpm

U.A. (10030 "Manfred Mann") 10-20 64
(Promotional issue only. Not issued with cover.)

LPs: 10/12–inch 33rpm

ARISTA 5-8 83
ASCOT (13015 "Manfred Mann") 25-35 64
(Monaural.)
ASCOT (13018 "Five Faces of Manfred Mann") 25-35 65
(Monaural.)
ASCOT (13024 "Mann Made") .. 25-35 66
(Monaural.)
ASCOT (16015 "Manfred Mann") 35-45 64
(Stereo.)
ASCOT (16018 "Five Faces of Manfred Mann") 35-45 65
(Stereo.)
ASCOT (16024 "Mann Made") .. 35-45 66
(Stereo.)
CAPITOL 5-8 80
EMI AMERICA 10-12 77
JANUS 12-15 74
MERCURY 15-20 68
POLYDOR 10-15 70-74
U.A. 20-35 66-68
W.B. 5-8 74-81

Members: Manfred Mann; Mike D'Abo; Paul Jones; Tom McGuinnes; Mick Rogers; Mick Vickers; Chris Slade; Colin Pattenden; Mike Hugg; Steve York; Mick Rogers.

Also see BELL, Madeline
Also see FIRM
Also see McGUINNESS FLINT
Also see THOMPSON, Chris, & Night

MANNA, Charlie

LP '61

Singles: 7–inch

DECCA 4-6 61
JUBILEE 4-6 65

Picture Sleeves

DECCA 4-8 61

LPs: 10/12–inch 33rpm

DECCA 10-20 61-62
VERVE 10-15 66

MANNHEIM STEAMROLLER

LP '84

LPs: 10/12–inch 33rpm

AMERICAN GRAMAPHONE 5-8 83-90

Also see WILLIAMS, Mason, & Mannheim Steamroller

MANONE, Wingy, & Orchestra

P&R '35

Singles: 78rpm

BLUEBIRD 3-8 36-38
COLUMBIA 3-5 54
DECCA 4-8 57
VOCALION 3-8

Singles: 7–inch

COLUMBIA 5-10 54
DECCA 8-12 57
IMPERIAL 4-6 62
KEM 4-6 61

EPs: 7–inch 33/45rpm

COLUMBIA 5-10 54
VIK 5-10 56

LPs: 10/12–inch 33rpm

IMPERIAL 8-15 62
MCA 5-10 83
PRESTIGE 5-10 70
RCA 5-10 69
SAVOY 5-10 73
STORYVILLE 5-10 83
VIK 10-20 56

MANTOVANI
(Mantovani & His Orchestra)

P&R '35

Singles: 78rpm

COLUMBIA 3-8 36
LONDON (Except 1761) 3-5 51-65
LONDON (1761 "Let Me Be Loved") 4-6 57

Singles: 7–inch

LONDON (Except 1761) 3-8 51-65
LONDON (1761 "Let Me Be Loved") 4-8 57

Picture Sleeves

LONDON (Except 1761) 4-8 57-65
LONDON (1761 "Let Me Be Loved") 30-45 57
(*Let Me Be Loved* is the main theme from the film, *The James Dean Story*. Sleeve pictures Dean.)

EPs: 7–inch 33/45rpm

LONDON 4-8 51-59

LPs: 10/12–inch 33rpm

BAINBRIDGE 5-10 82
LONDON 8-18 51-72

Also see PRESLEY, Elvis
Also see WHITFIELD, David

MANTRA

R&B '81

Singles: 7–inch

CASABLANCA 3-4 81

LPs: 10/12–inch 33rpm

CASABLANCA 5-10 81

MANTRONIX
(With Wondress)

D&D '85

Singles: 12–inch 33/45rpm

SLEEPING BAG 4-6 85

LPs: 10/12–inch 33rpm

CAPITOL 5-8 88-90
SLEEPING BAG 5-8 86

MANU DIBANGO: see DIBANGO, Manu

MANZANERA, Phil
(Phil Manzanera Quiet Sun; with 801; Manzanera)

LP '79

Singles: 12–inch 33/45rpm

EDITIONS E.G. 5-8 82

LPs: 10/12-inch 33rpm

ANTILLES 8-10
ATCO 8-10
EDITIONS E.G. 5-8 82
POLYDOR.................................. 8-10 78
Also see NICO
Also see ROXY MUSIC

MANZAREK, Ray

LP '75

Singles: 7-inch

MERCURY 4-6 73-74

LPs: 10/12-inch 33rpm

A&M 5-10 84
MERCURY.................................. 8-12 74-75
Also see DOORS

MARA, Tommy

P&R '58

Singles: 7-inch

B&F 5-10 60
FELSTED.................................. 5-10 58-59

MARATHONS

P&R/R&B '61

Singles: 7-inch

ARGO (5389 "Peanut Butter")..... 5-10 61
ARVEE (5027 "Peanut Butter"). 10-12 61
(Other Arvee releases by the Marathons are by a different group. See the following section.)
CHESS (1790 "Peanut Butter")... 5-10 61
PLAZA.................................. 5-10 62

EPs: 7-inch 33/45rpm

MARK '56 ("Laura Scudder's Magic Record").................................. 4-8 69
(Laura Scudder's potato chip mail-order, coupon giveaway item. Has three tracks, including *Peanut Butter,* imbedded in a single band on each side. When needle begins tracking, it's unknown which song will play. Price includes paper picture sleeve.)

LPs: 10/12-inch 33rpm

ARVEE (428 "Peanut Butter") ... 50-75 61
Members: James Johnson; Carl Fisher; Dick Owens; Dave Govan; Don Bradley.
Also see JAYHAWKS
Also see VIBRATIONS

MARATHONS

Singles: 7-inch

ARVEE (Except 5027)................ 5-10 61-62
(Arvee 5027 is by a different group and is listed in the preceeding section.)

MARCELS

P&R/R&B '61

Singles: 7-inch

COLPIX (186 thru 624) 10-25 61-62
COLPIX (629 "Footprints in the Sand") 25-50 62
COLPIX (640 thru 687) 15-25 62-63
COLPIX (694 "One Last Kiss").. 50-75 63
ERIC 3-4 70s
QUEEN BEE.................................. 10-15 73
ST. CLAIR.................................. 5-10

Picture Sleeves

COLPIX (186 "Blue Moon")........ 30-50 61
COLPIX (612 "Heartaches") 30-50 61
COLPIX (624 "Merry Twistmas").................................. 40-60 61

LPs: 10/12-inch 33rpm

COLPIX (416 "Blue Moon")...... 75-125 61
(Gold label.)
COLPIX (416 "Blue Moon")........ 30-50 63
(Blue label.)
CRYSTAL BALL.................................. 6-10
EMUS.................................. 5-10 79
MURRAY HILL.................................. 6-10
Members: Cornelius Harp; Fred Johnson; Ron Mundy; Gene Bricker; Richard Knauss; Walt Maddox; Al Johnson.

MARCH, Little Peggy

(Peggy March)

P&R/R&B/LP '63

Singles: 7-inch

OLDE WORLD.................................. 3-5 75
RCA 4-8 62-71

Picture Sleeves

RCA 10-20 63

EPs: 7-inch 33/45rpm

RCA 15-25 63

LPs: 10/12-inch 33rpm

RCA (Except 2732).................. 15-20 65-68
RCA (LPM-2732 "I Will Follow Him").................................. 50-60 63
(Monaural.)
RCA (LSP-2732 "I Will Follow Him").................................. 75-100 63
(Stereo.)

MARCH, Little Peggy, & Bennie Thomas

LPs: 10/12-inch 33rpm

RCA 15-20 65

MARCH, Peggy, & Gary Marshal

Singles: 7-inch

RCA 4-8 66
Also see MARCH, Little Peggy

MARCHAN, Bobby

(With the Tick Tocks; with Clowns; Bobby Marchon)

P&R/R&B '60

Singles: 78rpm

ACE.................................. 5-10 56
ALADDIN 5-10 53
DOT 5-10 54
FIRE (1022 "There's Something on Your Mind").................................. 300-400 60
GALE 5-10 57

Singles: 7-inch

ABC.................................. 3-5 73

ACE (523 "Chickie Wah Wah") . 20-30 56
ACE (557 "Rockin' Behind the Iron Curtain") 15-25 59
ACE (3000 series) 4-6 74-75
ALADDIN (3189 "Just a Little Walk") 30-40 53
BOBBY ROBINSON 3-6 73
CAMEO 5-8 66-67
DIAL 4-10 64-74
DOT (1203 "Just a Little Ol' Wine") 20-30 54
FIRE 5-15 59-62
FLASHBACK 3-5 65
GALE 10-20 57
GAMBLE 4-8 68
MERCURY 3-5 77
RIVER CITY 10-20
SPHERE SOUND 4-8 65
VOLT 5-10 63

LPs: 10/12-inch 33rpm

COLLECTABLES 5-8 88
SPHERE SOUND (7004 "There's Something on Your Mind") 30-50 64

Also see SMITH, Huey

MARCY JO & Eddie Rambeau

Singles: 7-inch

ROBBEE 5-10 62
SWAN 10-20 63

Also see MARCY JOE
Also see RAMBEAU, Eddie

MARCY JOE
(Marcy Jo)

P&R '61

Singles: 7-inch

ROBBEE 5-10 61
SWAN 8-12 62

Also see CHRISTIE, Lou

MARDIS, Bobby

R&B '86

Singles: 12-inch 33/45rpm

PROFILE 4-6 86

Singles: 7-inch

PROFILE 3-4 86

MARDONES, Benny

P&R/LP '80

Singles: 7-inch

POLYDOR 3-5 80-89
PRIVATE STOCK 3-5 78

EPs: 7-inch 33/45rpm

PRIVATE STOCK (1000 "Thank God for Girls") 5-8 78
(Colored vinyl. Promotional issue only.)

LPs: 10/12-inch 33rpm

POLYDOR 5-10 80
PRIVATE STOCK 5-10 78

MARESCA, Ernie

P&R/R&B '62

Singles: 7-inch

LAURIE 5-10 66
RUST 8-12 64
SEVILLE 8-12 60-65

LPs: 10/12-inch 33rpm

LAURIE 10-15 70s
SEVILLE (77001 "Shout! Shout! [Knock Yourself Out])" 30-60 62
(Monaural.)
SEVILLE (87001 "Shout! Shout! [Knock Yourself Out])" 40-80 62
(Stereo.)

MARGRET, Ann: see ANN-MARGRET

MARIACHI BRASS (Featuring Chet Baker)

LP '66

LPs: 10/12-inch 33rpm

WORLD PACIFIC 6-12 66

MARIE, Diane

D&D '83

Singles: 12-inch 33/45rpm

PRELUDE 4-6 83

MARIE, Teena

R&B/LP '79

Singles: 12-inch 33/45rpm

EPIC 4-6 83-85

Singles: 7-inch

EPIC 3-4 83-88
GORDY 3-5 79-81
MOTOWN 3-4

Picture Sleeves

EPIC 3-4 84-88

LPs: 10/12-inch 33rpm

EPIC 5-8 83-90
GORDY 5-10 79-81

Also see KING DREAM CHORUS & Holiday Crew

MARIE: see OSMOND, Marie

MARIE & REX

P&R '59

Singles: 7-inch

CARLTON 5-10 59

Members: Marie Knight; Rex Garvin.
Also see KNIGHT, Marie

MARIGOLDS

R&B '55

Singles: 78rpm

EXCELLO 10-20 55

Singles: 7-inch

EXCELLO (2057 "Rollin' Stone") 20-40 55
EXCELLO (2061 "Two Strangers) 20-40 55
EXCELLO (2078 "Foolish Me") 20-40 56
EXCELLO (2091 "It's You, Darling, It's You") 20-40 56

Members: Johnny Bragg; Henry Jones; Hal Hebb; Willie Wilson.

MARILLION

LP '83

Singles: 7-inch

CAPITOL 3-4 83-87

Picture Sleeves

CAPITOL 3-4 85

LPs: 10/12-inch 33rpm

CAPITOL 5-8 83-87

Members: Fish; Steve Hogarth; Steve Rothany; Mark Kelly; Pete Trewavas; Ian Mosely.

Also see GTR

MARIMBA CHIAPAS

P&R '56

Singles: 78rpm

CAPITOL 3-6 56

Singles: 7-inch

CAPITOL 5-8 56

MARINERS

P&R '50

Singles: 78rpm

CADENCE 4-8 55-56
COLUMBIA 4-8 50-55

Singles: 7-inch

CADENCE 5-15 55-56
COLUMBIA 5-15 50-55
TIARA 5-10 58

EPs: 7-inch 33/45rpm

COLUMBIA 5-10 51-55

LPs: 10/12-inch 33rpm

CADENCE (1008 "Spirituals") ... 30-40 56
(10-inch LP.)
COLUMBIA 15-25 51-55
EPIC 10-20 59
HARMONY 10-20 59

Also see GODFREY, Arthur

MARINO, Frank
(With Mahogany Rush)

LP '77

Singles: 7-inch

COLUMBIA 3-5 77-81

LPs: 10/12-inch 33rpm

COLUMBIA 5-10 77-81

Also see MAHAGONY RUSH

MARK - ALMOND BAND

LP '71

Singles: 7-inch

ABC 3-5 75
BLUE THUMB 3-5 72
COLUMBIA 3-5 72-73

LPs: 10/12-inch 33rpm

A&M 8-10 78
ABC 8-10 76
BLUE THUMB 8-12 70-73
COLUMBIA 8-10 72-73
MCA 5-8
PACIFIC ARTS 8-10 81

Members: Jon Mark; Johnny Almond.

Also see ALMOND, Marc

MARK II

P&R '60

Singles: 7-inch

WYE 5-10 60-61

Member: Winston Cogswell.

MARK IV

P&R '58

Singles: 7-inch

COSMIC 10-15 58
MERCURY (71000 series) 5-10 59

MARK IV

R&B '72

Singles: 7-inch

MERCURY (73000 series) 3-5 72-73

LPs: 10/12-inch 33rpm

MERCURY 10-12 73

Members: James Ponder; Larry Jones.

MARKETTS
(Mar-Kets)

P&R '62

Singles: 7-inch

LIBERTY 8-12 62
MERCURY 3-5 73
UNI 4-6 69
UNION 15-20 61-62
W.B. (Except 5391) 4-8 63-66
W.B. (5391 "Outer Limits") 5-10 63
W.B. (5391 "Out of Limits") 4-8 63
(Note title change.)
WORLD PACIFIC 4-8 67

LPs: 10/12-inch 33rpm

DORE 5-8 82
LIBERTY (3226 "Surfer's Stomp") 25-30 62
(Monaural.)
LIBERTY (3226 "Surfing Scene") 20-25 62
(Monaural. Reissue.)
LIBERTY (7226 "Surfer's Stomp") 30-35 62
(Stereo.)
LIBERTY (7226 "Surfing Scene") 25-30 62
(Stereo.) Reissue.)
MERCURY 10-15 73
PHONORAMA 5-8 84
W.B. (W-1509 "Take to Wheels") 20-25 63
(Monaural.)
W.B. (WS-1509 "Take to Wheels") 25-30 63
(Stereo.)
W.B. (W-1537 "Out of Limits") ... 20-25 64
(Monaural.)
W.B. (WS-1537 "Out of Limits") . 25-30 64
(Stereo.)

W.B. (W-1642 "Batman Theme") 20-30 66
(Monaural.)
W.B. (WS-1642 "Batman Theme") 25-30 66
(Stereo.)
WORLD PACIFIC..................... 15-20 67

Members: Ben Benay; Mike Henderson; Ray Pohlman; Tommy Tedesco; Bill Pittman; Gene Pello; Tom Hensley; Richard Hobaica.

MAR-KEYS

P&R/R&B '61

Singles: 7–inch

SATELITE (107 "Last Night") 10-15 61
STAX.. 4-8 61-66

LPs: 10/12–inch 33rpm

ATLANTIC................................ 20-25 61-62
STAX.. 10-20 66-71

Members: Donald Dunn; Steve Cropper; Don Nix; Charles Axton.
Also see PACKERS

MAR-KEYS / Booker T. & MGs

LP '67

LPs: 10/12–inch 33rpm

STAX (720 "Back to Back")....... 12-18 67

Also see BOOKER T. & MGs
Also see MAR-KEYS

MARKHAM, Pigmeat

P&R/R&B/LP '68

Singles: 7–inch

ABC... 3-5 74
CHESS...................................... 4-8 64-70
WIG... 6-12

LPs: 10/12–inch 33rpm

CHESS...................................... 10-20 61-69
JEWEL...................................... 5-10 72-73

Also see MABLEY, Moms, & Pigmeat Markham

MARKS, Guy

P&R '68

Singles: 7–inch

ABC... 4-6 68
ARIOLA AMERICA...................... 3-5 76
RADNOR................................... 3-5 70

LPs: 10/12–inch 33rpm

ABC... 10-20 66-68

MARLEY, Bob, & Wailers
(Wailers)

LP '75

Singles: 7–inch

COTILLION............................... 3-5 81
ISLAND..................................... 3-5 76-84
SHELTER.................................. 3-5 71
TUFF GONG.............................. 4-6 74

Picture Sleeves

ISLAND..................................... 3-4 83

LPs: 10/12–inch 33rpm

CALLA (1200 series)................ 10-15 76
CALLA (34000 series).............. 8-10 77
COTILLION............................... 5-8 81
ISLAND (11 "Babylon By Bus")..10-12 78
ISLAND (9000 series except 9329)..8-12 75-80
ISLAND (9329 "Catch a Fire") ...15-25 75
(Shaped cover.)
ISLAND (9329 "Catch a Fire") 8-10 75
(Standard cover.)
ISLAND (90000 series)..................5-8 83-86

Also see MELODY MAKERS
Also see TOSH, Peter

MARLEY, Ziggy, & Melody Makers: see MELODY MAKERS

MARLEY MARL

LP '88

LPs: 10/12–inch 33rpm

COLD CHILL...................................5-8 88

MARLO, Micki

P&R '57

Singles: 78rpm

ABC-PAR..5-10 57
CAPITOL...4-8 54-56

Singles: 7–inch

ABC-PAR (Except 9841).............5-10 57
ABC-PAR (9841 "What You've Done to Me")..........................10-20 57
(With "Vocal assist by Paul Anka.")
ABC-PAR (9841 "What You've Done to Me")............................5-10 57
(Has the singer humming the lines done by Paul Anka on first pressing.)
CAPITOL...5-10 54-56

LPs: 10/12–inch 33rpm

ABC-PAR.....................................15-25 60

Also see ANKA, Paul

MARLOWE, Marion
(With Frank Parker)

P&R '54

Singles: 78rpm

CADENCE......................................4-6 55-56
COLUMBIA.....................................4-6 53-54

Singles: 7–inch

CADENCE......................................5-10 55-56
COLUMBIA.....................................5-10 53-54

EPs: 7–inch 33/45rpm

COLUMBIA.....................................6-12 53-55

LPs: 10/12–inch 33rpm

BARNABY..5-8 76
COLUMBIA....................................20-35 53-55
HARMONY.....................................10-15 60

MARMALADE

P&R/LP '70

Singles: 7–inch

ARIOLA AMERICA..........................3-5 76
EMI..3-5 74
EPIC..4-8 67-69
LONDON..3-6 70-72

LPs: 10/12–inch 33rpm

EPIC...10-15 70

G&P 8-10 81
LONDON 10-15 70

Members: Dean Ford; Junior Campbell.
Also see BLUE

MARRINER, Neville

LP '84

LPs: 10/12-inch 33rpm

FANTASY 5-8 84

MARS, Mitzi

R&B '53

Singles: 78rpm

CHECKER (773 "I'm Glad") 10-15 53

Singles: 7-inch

CHECKER (773 "I'm Glad") 20-30 53

MARS BONFIRE: see BONFIRE, Mars

MARSALIS, Branford
(Branford Marsalis Quartet Featuring Terence Blanchard)

LP '84

LPs: 10/12-inch 33rpm

COLUMBIA 5-8 84-90

MARSALIS, Wynton

LP '82

LPs: 10/12-inch 33rpm

COLUMBIA 5-8 82-91
WHO'S WHO in JAZZ 5-8 83

MARSH, Little Toni

D&D '83

Singles: 12-inch 33/45rpm

PRISM 4-6 83

MARSHALL - HAIN

P&R '78

Singles: 7-inch

HARVEST 3-5 78

LPs: 10/12-inch 33rpm

HARVEST 5-8 78

Members: Julian Marshall; Kit Hain.
Also see EYE to EYE

MARSHALL TUCKER BAND

LP '73

Singles: 7-inch

CAPRICORN 3-5 73-78
MERCURY 3-4 87-88
W.B. 3-5 79-83

Picture Sleeves

W.B. 3-5 79

LPs: 10/12-inch 33rpm

CAPRICORN 8-12 73-78
MERCURY 5-10 87
W.B. 5-10 79-83

Members: Doug Gray; Tom Caldwell; Troy Caldwell; Franklin Wilkie; Jack Eubanks; Paul Riddle.

MARTERIE, Ralph, & Orchestra

P&R '51

Singles: 78rpm

MERCURY 3-5 50-57

Singles: 7-inch

MERCURY 4-8 50-60
U.A. 3-6 61-62

EPs: 7-inch 33/45rpm

MERCURY 5-10 50-59

LPs: 10/12-inch 33rpm

MERCURY 8-18 50-60
U.A. 5-10 61-62
WING 5-10 56-60

MARTHA & MUFFINS
(M+M)

LP '80

Singles: 12-inch 33/45rpm

RCA 4-6 83-84

Singles: 7-inch

DINDISC/VIRGIN 3-5 80
RCA 3-4 83-84

LPs: 10/12-inch 33rpm

CURRENT 5-8 84
RCA 5-8 83
VIRGIN 5-8 80

MARTHA & VANDELLAS
(Martha Reeves & the Vandellas)

P&R/R&B/LP '63

Singles: 7-inch

GORDY (7011 "I'll Have to Let Him Go") 15-25 62
GORDY (7014 "Come and Get These Memories") 10-20 62
GORDY (7022 thru 7062) 6-12 63-67
GORDY (7067 thru 7110) 4-8 67-72
MOTOWN 3-4
MOTOWN/TOPPS (7 "Dancing in the Street") 50-75 67
MOTOWN/TOPPS (14 "Heat Wave") 50-75 67
(Topps Chewing Gum promotional item. Single-sided, cardboard flexi, picture disc. Issued with generic paper sleeve.)
TAMLA/MOTOWN 4-8

Picture Sleeves

GORDY (7033 "Dancing in the Street") 20-30 64

EPs: 7-inch 33/45rpm

GORDY (60920 "Watchout") 15-25 67
MOTOWN (2009 "Martha & the Vandellas") 15-25
MOTOWN (2017 "Hittin'") 15-25

LPs: 10/12-inch 33rpm

ERA 5-10 79
GORDY (902 "Come and Get These Memories") 100-125 63
(Monaural.)
GORDY (S-902 "Come and Get These Memories") 100-150 63
(Stereo.)
GORDY (907 "Heat Wave") 50-75 63
(Monaural.)

GORDY (S-907 "Heat Wave")... 60-80 63
(Stereo.)
GORDY (915 "Dance Party") 50-75 65
GORDY (S-915 "Dance Party"). 60-80 65
GORDY (917 "Greatest Hits")... 20-30 66
GORDY (920 "Watchout")......... 20-30 67
GORDY (925 "Live") 15-25 66
GORDY (926 thru 958) 15-20 68-72
MOTOWN (Except 100 & 200 series) 12-15 74
MOTOWN (100 & 200 series)....... 5-8 81-82
Members: Martha Reeves; Rosalind Ashford; Annette Beard.
Also see DEL-PHIS
Also see GAYE, Marvin
Also see HONDELLS / Del Shannon / Martha & Vandellas
Also see HOOKER, John Lee
Also see REEVES, Martha
Also see VELLS
Also see VELVELETTES

MARTIKA
(Martika Marrero)

P&R '88

Singles: 7–inch

COLUMBIA 3-4 88-91

Picture Sleeves

COLUMBIA 3-4 88

LPs: 10/12–inch 33rpm

COLUMBIA 5-8 89

MARTIN, Bobbi

P&R '64

Singles: 7–inch

BUDDAH.................................... 3-5 71-72
CORAL...................................... 4-8 61-67
GREEN MENU............................ 3-5 75
MGM 3-5 73
MAYPOLE.................................. 5-10 60
U.A. 4-6 68-70

Picture Sleeves

CORAL...................................... 4-8 65

EPs: 7–inch 33/45rpm

CORAL...................................... 5-10 65

LPs: 10/12–inch 33rpm

BUDDAH.................................... 5-10 71
CORAL...................................... 10-20 65
SUNSET.................................... 5-10 71
U.A. 8-12 68-70
VOCALION................................ 5-10 70

MARTIN, Dean

P&R '49

Singles: 78rpm

APOLLO (1088 "Oh Marie")...... 25-50 47
APOLLO (1116 "Santa Lucia").. 25-50 48
CAPITOL (545 thru 2001)........... 5-15 49-52
CAPITOL (2037 "Hey, Brother, Pour the Wine")...................... 15-20 54
(Seven–inch 78rpm. Promotional issue only.)
CAPITOL (2071 thru 3841)......... 5-15 52-57
CAPITOL (15000 series)........... 10-20 48-49
DIAMOND (2035 "Which Way Did My Heart Go") 40-60 46
DIAMOND (2036 "I Got the Sun in the Morning")......................40-60 46
EMBASSY (124 "One Foot in Heaven") 100-150 49

Singles: 7–inch

CAPITOL (401 "Dean Martin Sings") 50-100 53
(Four-disc boxed set.)
CAPITOL (247 "Silver Bells").....10-15 66
(Promotional issue only.)
CAPITOL (691 thru 981)...........10-15 49-50
CAPITOL (987 "Sleep Warm").50-100 59
(Promotional issue only.)
CAPITOL (1002 thru 1458).......10-15 50-51
CAPITOL (1609 "I Met a Girl").50-100 60
(Promotional issue only.)
CAPITOL (1703 thru 3238)..........8-15 51-55
CAPITOL (3295 thru 4570)..........5-10 55-61
CAPITOL (6000 series) 4-6 64
CAPITOL (44153 "That's Amore") .3-4 88
MCA..3-5 85
REPRISE (190 thru 193)...............4-8 64
(Compact 33 singles. Promotional issues only.)
REPRISE (200 "Sophia")....... 150-200 65
(Promotional issue only.)
REPRISE (0252 thru 1178)...........3-6 64-73
REPRISE (20,000 series).............4-8 62-63
REPRISE (40,000 series).........10-15 62
(Stereo 33 singles.)
TEXAS DESERT CIRCUS WEEK (2160 "It's 1200 Miles from Texas to Palm Springs")......................50-100 58
(Single-sided promotional disc. No actual label name. Made especially for play in Palm Springs, promoting a circus. Incorrect title is shown on label—should read *It's 1200 Miles from Palm Springs to Texas.*)
W.B. (29584 "My First Country Song").......................................3-4 83
(With Conway Twitty.)
W.B. (29480 "Drinking Champagne")..............................3-4 83

Picture Sleeves

CAPITOL (987 "Sleep Warm")..............................100-200 59
CAPITOL (1609 "I Met a Girl").50-100 60
(Promotional issue only. Sleeve reads: "From the Soundtrack of the Motion Picture *Bells are Ringing.*")
CAPITOL (4028 "Volare") 15-25 58
CAPITOL (4222 "On an Evening in Roma")...............................15-25 59
REPRISE (20,116 "Who's Got the Action") 15-20 62

EPs: 7–inch 33/45rpm

CAPITOL (EAP-401 "Dean Martin Sings") 25-50 53
(Price is for either of two volumes.)
CAPITOL (EBF-401 "Dean Martin Sings") 75-125 53
(Double EP boxed set.)
CAPITOL (481 "Sunny Italy") 25-50 53
CAPITOL (576 "Swingin' Down Yonder") 20-40 59
(Price is for any of three volumes.)
CAPITOL (701 "Memories Are Made of This") 25-50 55
CAPITOL (702 "Artists & Models") 25-50 55
CAPITOL (806 "Hollywood Or Bust") 25-50 57
CAPITOL (840 "Ten Thousand Bedrooms") 25-50 57
CAPITOL (849 "Pretty Baby") ... 20-40 58
(Price is for any of three volumes.)
CAPITOL (939 "Return to Me") . 20-40 58
CAPITOL (1027 "Volare") 20-40 58
CAPITOL (1285 "Winter Romance") 20-40 59
(Price is for any of three volumes.)
CAPITOL (1580 "Dean Martin") 20-30 61
(Compact Double 33.)
CAPITOL (EAP-1659 "Dino - Italian Love Songs") 15-25 61
CAPITOL (SU-1659 "Dino - Italian Love Songs") 15-25 61
(Jukebox issue.)
CAPITOL (9123 "Dean Martin") 25-50 54
18 TOP HITS (27 "Dean Martin") 20-40 54-55
(Price for either 45 and 78rpm EPs.)
LLOYDS (705 "Dean Martin") ... 25-50 54
(Mail-order offer.)
REPRISE 10-20 62-73
(Jukebox 33 compact issues.)

LPs: 10/12–inch 33rpm

CAPITOL (100 series) 8-15 69
CAPITOL (300 series) 8-15 69
CAPITOL (H-401 "Dean Martin Sings") 50-100 53
(10–inch LP.)
CAPITOL (T-401 "Dean Martin Sings") 25-50 55
(Red cover.)
CAPITOL (TT-401 "Dean Martin Sings") 10-20 59
(Pink cover.)
CAPITOL (523 "Return to Me"/"You're Nobody Till Somebody Loves You") 8-12 70
CAPITOL (576 "Swingin' Down Yonder") 30-40 55
CAPITOL (849 thru 2601) 15-30 57-66
(With "T" or "ST" prefix.)
CAPITOL (849 thru 2601) 8-15 63-65
(With "DT" prefix.)
CAPITOL (2815 "Dean Martin Deluxe Set") 15-25 67
(Three-LP boxed set.)
CAPITOL (2941 "Favorites") 8-12 68
COSMIC (450 "Dean Martin") 15-20
LONGINES (5234 "Memories Are Made of This") 25-50 73
(Five-LP boxed set. Includes booklet.)
LONGINES (5235 "That's Amore") 8-15 73
PAIR 6-10 83
PICKWICK 6-12 70s
REPRISE 8-18 63-78
S.M.I. 10-20
SEARS 15-25 60s
TALKING BOOK (58007 "Look: December 26, 1967") 15-25 67
(Reading of a Dean interview/story in *Look*. Produced by the American Foundation for the Blind. Plays at 16⅔ rpm.)
TEE VEE 10-20 78
TOWER 15-30 65-66
WALDORF (27 "Dean Martin Sings") 20-40 53
(10–inch LP.)
W.B. 5-8 83

Promotional LPs

DEAN MARTIN TESTIMONIAL DINNER 200-250 59
(Presented by the Friars Club, and sold as a "Collectors Item" for $25 at the dinner. Three LPs in triple pocket jacket. No actual label name used. With guest appearances by Jimmy Durante, Joey Bishop, Tony Martin, George Burns, Dinah Shore, Mort Sahl, Judy Garland; Sammy Cahn, Danny Thomas, Sammy Davis Jr., Bob Hope, Frank Sinatra and others.)
REPRISE (246 Dean Martin Radio Sampler") 35-50 66

Also see BURNS, George
Also see DURANTE, Jimmy
Also see GARLAND, Judy
Also see GILKYSON, Terry
Also see GOLDDIGGERS
Also see HOPE, Bob
Also see LEE, Peggy, & Dean Martin
Also see MARTIN, Tony
Also see SAHL, Mort
Also see SHORE, Dinah
Also see SINATRA, Frank, Sammy Davis Jr. & Dean Martin
Also see SINATRA, Nancy
Also see THOMAS, Danny
Also see TWITTY, Conway

MARTIN, Dean / Glen Campbell

LPs: 10/12 inch 33rpm

ZENITH/CAPITOL.................... 10-20 72
(Issued with paper cover. Special products.)
Also see CAMPBELL, Glen

MARTIN, Dean / Jeff Clark / Arlene James

EPs: 45/78rpm

POPULAR (1035 "Oh Marie") 8-15 54
(78rpm. Not issued with special cover.)
VICTORY (1031 "Walking My Baby Back Home")............................ 8-15 54
(78rpm. Not issued with special cover.)
POPULAR (1035 "Oh Marie") ... 10-20 54
(45rpm. Not issued with special cover.)
VICTORY (1031 "Walking My Baby Back Home").......................... 20-40 54
(45rpm. Colored vinyl. Not issued with special cover.)

MARTIN, Dean, & Nat "King" Cole

Singles: 78rpm

CAPITOL...................................... 4-6 54

Singles: 7-inch

CAPITOL.................................... 5-10 54
Also see COLE, Nat "King"

MARTIN, Dean / Bob Eberly / Gordon MacRae

LPs: 10/12-inch 33rpm

BRIGADE (131 "Dino-Gordon-Bob") 15-25
Also see DORSEY, Jimmy, Orchestra & Chorus
Also see MacRAE, Gordon

MARTIN, Dean / Jane Froman

Singles: 78rpm

CAPITOL...................................... 4-6 53

Singles: 7-inch

CAPITOL (20030 "Who's Your Little Who Zis") 8-15 53
(Promotional issue only.)
Also see FROMAN, Jane

MARTIN, Dean / Jackie Gleason

LPs: 10/12-inch 33rpm

CAPITOL SPECIAL MARKETS .. 8-10
Also see GLEASON, Jackie

MARTIN, Dean / Rock Hudson

Singles: 7-inch

NATIONAL FEATURES (2785 "Showdown").......................... 20-30 73
(Interviews with *Showdown* film stars. Promotional issue only. Includes script.)

MARTIN, Dean / Red Ingle & Natural Seven

Singles: 78rpm

CAPITOL (726 "Vieni Su")........... 8-15 49
(Promotional issue only.)

MARTIN, Dean, & Jerry Lewis

P&R '48

Singles: 78rpm

CAPITOL (15000 series) 5-10 48
NATIONAL MASK & PUPPET CORP. ("Puppet Show") 10-20 50s
(Promotional issue only.)

EPs: 7-inch 33/45rpm

CAPITOL (533 "Living It Up"). 100-150 54
CAPITOL (752 "Pardners")......75-125 56

LPs: 10/12-inch 33rpm

MEMORABILIA (714 "Dean Martin & Jerry Lewis - First Show")........10-15 74
RADIOLA (1102 "Dean Martin & Jerry Lewis on the Radio")...............10-15
Also see LEWIS, Jerry

MARTIN, Dean / Nicolini Lucchesi

LPs: 10/12-inch 33rpm

AUDITION (5936 "Dean Martin Sings, Niccolini Lucchesi Plays")........25-50 56

MARTIN, Dean / Johnny Mathis / St. James Pop Orchestra

EPs: 7-inch 33/45rpm

JIMMY McHUGH (400 "Music by Jimmy McHugh")...............................10-15 81
(Promotional issue only.)
Also see MATHIS, Johnny

MARTIN, Dean, & Ricky Nelson

Singles: 7-inch

W.B. (2262 "My Rifle, My Pony and Me") 350-400 59
(Promotional issue only.)
Also see NELSON, Rick

MARTIN, Dean, & Nuggets

Singles: 78rpm

CAPITOL......................................4-6 55

Singles: 7-inch

CAPITOL....................................5-10 55

MARTIN, Dean, & Helen O'Connell

Singles: 78rpm

CAPITOL......................................4-6 51

Singles: 7-inch

CAPITOL....................................5-10 51
Also see O'CONNELL, Helen

MARTIN, Dean / Patti Page

LPs: 10/12-inch 33rpm

DECCA (79224 "Christmas Seals for 1962") 30-40 62
(Public service program for TB. Dean's show on one side, Patti's on flip.)
DECCA (79235 "Christmas Seals for 1962") 20-30 62
(Public service program for TB. Dean's and Patti's shows on one side, flip has Si Zenter and Vaughn Monroe.)
Also see MONROE, Vaughn
Also see PAGE, Patti
Also see ZENTER, Si

MARTIN, Dean, & Line Renaud

Singles: 78rpm

CAPITOL.................................... 4-6 55

Singles: 7-inch

CAPITOL.................................... 5-10 55

MARTIN, Dean / Nelson Riddle

EPs: 7-inch 33/45rpm

CAPITOL (1063 "Rio Bravo") 50-75 59
(Promotional only. Has special paper sleeve.)

Also see RIDDLE, Nelson

MARTIN, Dean, & Margaret Whiting

Singles: 78rpm

CAPITOL.................................... 4-6 50

Singles: 7-inch

CAPITOL.................................... 5-10 50

Also see MARTIN, Dean
Also see WHITING, Margaret

MARTIN, Derek

P&R/R&B '65

Singles: 7-inch

BUTTERCUP 5-10
CRACKERJACK 8-12 63
ROULETTE 5-10 65
SUE... 10-20 66
VOLT.. 4-8 68

MARTIN, Eric
(Eric Martin Band)

LP '83

Singles: 7-inch

CAPTIOL.................................... 3-4 85
ELEKTRA.................................... 3-4 83

Picture Sleeves

CAPTIOL.................................... 3-4 85

LPs: 10/12-inch 33rpm

ELEKTRA.................................... 5-8 83

Also see MR. BIG

MARTIN, Freddy, & Orchestra

P&R '33

Singles: 78rpm

BLUEBIRD 3-6 38-42
BRUNSWICK 3-6 33-36
RCA... 3-5 46-56
VICTOR..................................... 3-6 42-45

Singles: 7-inch

CAPITOL.................................... 4-6 63
DECCA...................................... 4-6 67-68
KAPP 4-6 61
RCA... 5-8 50-56

EPs: 7-inch 33/45rpm

CAMDEN.................................... 5-10 54-56
RCA... 5-10 50-54

LPs: 10/12-inch 33rpm

CAMDEN.................................... 10-20 54-56
CAPITOL.................................... 5-15 59-79
DECCA...................................... 5-10 67
KAPP 5-15 61-66
MCA 4-8 73-75
RCA 8-20 51-72

Also see GRIFFIN, Merv

MARTIN, George, & Orchestra

P&R/LP '64

Singles: 7-inch

U.A. (745 "Ringo's Theme")....... 10-15 64
U.A. (750 "A Hard Day's Night") 15-25 64
U.A. (800 series)........................ 4-6 65
U.A. (50148 "Love in the Open Air").. 20-25 67

Picture Sleeves

U.A. (745 "Ringo's Theme")....... 40-60 64
U.A. (750 "A Hard Day's Night")................................ 250-350 64

Promotional Singles

U.A. (745 "Ringo's Theme")....... 10-15 64
(White label.)

LPs: 10/12-inch 33rpm

U.A. (377 "Off the Beatle Track") 30-40 64
U.A. (383 "A Hard Day's Night") 20-30 64
U.A. (420 "George Martin") 15-25 65
U.A. (448 "Help")....................... 20-30 65
U.A. (539 "The Beatle Girls") 25-35 66
U.A. (647 "London By George"). 10-15 68

Also see BEATLES
Also see GERRY & PACEMAKERS

MARTIN, Janis

P&R '56

Singles: 78rpm

RCA (Except 6652)...................... 8-15 56-57
RCA (6652 "My Boy Elvis")........ 10-20 56

Singles: 7-inch

BIG DUTCH 3-5 77
PALETTE 5-10 61
RCA (6400 & 6500 series)......... 15-25 56
RCA (6652 "My Boy Elvis")........ 25-30 56
RCA (6700 thru 7300 series) 10-20 56-58

EPs: 7-inch 33/45rpm

RCA (4093 "Just Squeeze Me") 75-100 58

MARTIN, Janis / Hank Snow

EPs: 7-inch 33/45rpm

RCA (76 "Love Me to Pieces")... 15-25 56
(Promotional issue only.)

Also see MARTIN, Janis
Also see SNOW, Hank

MARTIN, Kenny

R&B '58

Singles: 7-inch

BIG TOP 5-10 60
FEDERAL 8-12 58-60
PJ... 4-8 66

MARTIN, Marilyn

P&R/LP '86

Singles: 7-inch

ATLANTIC.................................. 3-4 86-87

Picture Sleeves

ATLANTIC.......... 3-4 86

LPs: 10/12-inch 33rpm

ATLANTIC.......... 5-8 86-87

Also see COLLINS, Phil, & Marilyn Martin

MARTIN, Moon
(John Martin)

P&R/LP '79

Singles: 7-inch

CAPITOL.......... 3-5 78-79

LPs: 10/12-inch 33rpm

CAPITOL.......... 5-10 78-82

Member: Jude Cole.
Also see COLE, Jude

MARTIN, Nancy

R&B '82

Singles: 7-inch

ATLANTIC.......... 3-4 82

MARTIN, Paul

R&B '65

Singles: 7-inch

ASCOT.......... 5-10 65
IMPEX.......... 4-8 66

MARTIN, Ray, Orchestra

LP '61

Singles: 7-inch

RCA.......... 3-6 61-62
U.A. 4-8 58

Picture Sleeves

RCA.......... 4-8 61
U.A. 5-10 58

LPs: 10/12-inch 33rpm

CAMDEN.......... 5-10 67-70
LONDON.......... 8-12 63
MONUMENT.......... 5-10 67
RCA.......... 10-15 61

MARTIN, Steve
(With Toot Uncommons)

P&R/LP '77

Singles: 7-inch

W.B. 3-5 77-79

Picture Sleeves

W.B. 3-5 77-78

LPs: 10/12-inch 33rpm

W.B. 5-10 77-81

MARTIN, Tony

P&R '38

Singles: 78rpm

BRUNSWICK.......... 4-8 38
DECCA.......... 3-6 39-42
MERCURY.......... 3-6 46-47
RCA.......... 3-6 47-57

Singles: 7-inch

CHART.......... 3-5 70
DOT.......... 4-6 61-66
DUNHILL.......... 3-6 67
MERCURY.......... 5-10 50s
MOTOWN.......... 5-10 64-66
NAN.......... 4-6 64
PARK AVENUE.......... 4-6 63
RCA.......... 5-10 50-60

EPs: 7-inch 33/45rpm

DECCA.......... 5-10 51-56
MERCURY.......... 5-10 54-56
RCA.......... 5-10 51-57

LPs: 10/12-inch 33rpm

CAMDEN.......... 10-20 59-60
CHART.......... 5-10 70
CHARTER.......... 10-15 63
CORAL.......... 5-8 73
DECCA.......... 15-25 51-56
DOT.......... 10-15 61-62
MERCURY.......... 10-20 54-61
RCA.......... 15-25 51-60
20TH FOX.......... 10-15 64
WING.......... 10-15 59-60

Also see MARTIN, Dean
Also see SHORE, Dinah, Tony Martin, Betty Hutton & Phil Harris

MARTIN, Trade

P&R '62

Singles: 7-inch

COED.......... 6-12 62-64
GEE.......... 5-10 59
RCA.......... 4-8 66-67
ROULETTE.......... 5-10 60
STALLION.......... 4-6
TOOT.......... 4-6 68

LPs: 10/12-inch 33rpm

BUDDAH.......... 10-15 72

MARTIN, Vince
(With the Tarriers; with Fred Neil)

P&R '56

Singles: 78rpm

GLORY.......... 3-6 56

Singles: 7-inch

ABC-PAR.......... 5-10 59
GLORY.......... 8-12 56
ELEKTRA.......... 4-8 64

LPs: 10/12-inch 33rpm

CAPITOL.......... 5-10 73
ELEKTRA.......... 10-20 64

Also see TARRIERS

MARTINDALE, Wink

P&R/C&W '59

Singles: 7-inch

ABC/DOT.......... 3-5 76
DOT.......... 4-8 59-66
RANWOOD.......... 3-5 73

Picture Sleeves

DOT.......... 5-10 59-60

LPs: 10/12-inch 33rpm

DOT.......... 15-25 59-66
HAMILTON.......... 10-20 64

MARTINDALE, Wink, & Robin Ward

Singles: 7–inch

DOT.. 4-8 63-64

LPs: 10/12–inch 33rpm

DOT.. 15-25 64

Also see MARTINDALE, Wink
Also see WARD, Robin

MARTINE, Layng
(Layng Martine Jr.)

P&R '71

Singles: 7–inch

BARNABY 3-5 71
DATE.. 5-10 66
GENERAL INT'L.......................... 4-8 66
PLAYBOY 3-5 76

Also see MORRISON, Professor

MARTINEZ, Nancy

P&R '86

Singles: 12–inch 33/45rpm

ATLANTIC.................................... 4-6 86

Singles: 7–inch

ATLANTIC.................................... 3-4 86-87

LPs: 10/12–inch 33rpm

ATLANTIC.................................... 5-8 86

MARTINO, Al

P&R '52

Singles: 78rpm

BBS 5-10 52
CAPITOL..................................... 3-5 52-57

Singles: 7–inch

BBS (101 "Here in My Heart")... 10-15 52
(Black vinyl.)
BBS (101 "Here in My Heart")... 15-25 52
(Colored vinyl.)
CAPITOL (Except F-2122 thru F-4593) 3-8 62-81
CAPITOL (F-2122 thru F-4593) .. 5-15 52-61
JUBILEE (6000 series)............. 10-15 53
(Colored vinyl.)
MAZE (7025 "There's No Tomorrow") 5-10 62
20TH FOX.................................. 5-10 59-64

Picture Sleeves

CAPITOL.................................... 5-10 63-66
MAZE (7025 "There's No Tomorrow") 8-12 62

LPs: 10/12–inch 33rpm

CAPITOL.................................... 5-20 62-80
GUEST STAR 5-10 64
MOVIETONE.............................. 5-10 67
SPRINGBOARD.......................... 5-8 78
20TH FOX.................................. 10-20 59-65

MARVELETTES

P&R/R&B '61

Singles: 7–inch

MOTOWN 3-4
MOTOWN/TOPPS (12 "Please Mr. Postman") 50-75 67
(Topps Chewing Gum promotional item. Single-sided, cardboard flexi, picture disc. Issued with generic paper sleeve.)
TAMLA (54046 thru 54088) 6-12 61-63
TAMLA (54091 "He's a Good Guy [Yes He Is]")..6-12 64
(With subtitle.)
TAMLA (54091 "Yes He Is") 40-60 64
(No subtitle used. Single-sided. Promotional issue only.)
TAMLA (54097 thru 54198) 5-10 64-71

Picture Sleeves

TAMLA (54046 "Please Mr. Postman") 20-30 61
TAMLA (54054 "Twistin' Postman") 20-30 62
TAMLA (54097 "You're My Remedy")..............................15-25 64

EPs: 7–inch 33/45rpm

MOTOWN (2003 "Marvelettes").15-25 60s
TAMLA (60253 "Greatest Hits").15-25 66
TAMLA (60274 "Marvelettes") ...15-25 67

LPs: 10/12–inch 33rpm

MOTOWN (Except 100 series)..12-18 75
MOTOWN (100 series)..................5-8 82
TAMLA (228 "Please Mr. Postman") 50-100 61
TAMLA (229 "Marvelettes Sing Smash Hits of '62") 500-750 62
TAMLA (229 The Marvelettes Sing") 50-100 62
(Reissue with shorter title)
TAMLA (231 "Playboy") 50-100 62
TAMLA (237 "Marvelous Marveletes")..........................50-100 63
TAMLA (243 "On Stage")...........50-75 63
TAMLA (253 "Greatest Hits").....15-20 66
TAMLA (274 "The Marvelettes") 15-20 67
TAMLA (286 thru 305) 10-20 68-70

Members: Gladys Horton; Kathy Anderson; Georgeanna Tillman; Wanda Young; Juanita Cowart.

MARVELETTES / Mary Wells / Miracles / Marvin Gaye

Singles: 7–inch

TAMLA/MOTOWN ("Album Excerpts") 30-40 63
(Though from Tamla/Motown, no label name is shown, nor is there a title. Promotional issue only.)

Also see GAYE, Marvin
Also see MARVELETTES
Also see MIRACLES
Also see WELLS, Mary

MARVELOWS
(Mighty Marvelows)

P&R/R&B '65

Singles: 7–inch

ABC..4-8 66-69

ABC-PAR 8-10 64-66

LPs: 10/12-inch 33rpm

ABC.. 15-20 68

Members: Melvin Mason; Frank Paden; Johnny Paden; Jesse Smith; Sonny Stevenson; Andrew Thomas.

MARVIN & JOHNNY

R&B '53

Singles: 78rpm

ALADDIN................................ 10-15 56
MODERN 10-20 54-56
RAYS 10-15 54
SPECIALTY 10-15 53-55

Singles: 7-inch

ALADDIN................................ 15-25 56
ERIC.. 3-4 70s
FELSTED 4-8 63
FIREFLY 10-15 60
JAMIE 5-10 61
MODERN 20-40 54-56
RAYS 15-25 54
SPECIALTY (Except 479) 25-40 53-55
SPECIALTY (479 "Baby Doll") .. 30-40 53
(Black vinyl.)
SPECIALTY (479 "Baby Doll") .. 50-80 53
(Colored vinyl.)
SWINGIN 8-12 61

LPs: 10/12-inch 33rpm

CROWN (5381 "Marvin and Johnny") 35-55 63

Members: Marvin Phillips; Johnny Dean.
Also see ISLEY BROTHERS / Marvin & Johnny
Also see JESSE & MARVIN

MARX, Groucho

LP '72

Singles: 78rpm

DECCA.. 4-8 51
YOUNG PEOPLE'S RECORDS ... 3-6 54

Singles: 7-inch

A&M 3-5 73
DECCA.................................... 10-20 51
YOUNG PEOPLE'S RECORDS . 5-10 54

LPs: 10/12-inch 33rpm

A&M (3515 "An Evening with Groucho") 5-10 72
A&M (PR-3515 "An Evening with Groucho") 10-20 78
(Picture disc. Promotional issue only.)
DECCA (5405 "Horray for Captain Spaulding") 100-150
(10-inch LP.)

Also see KAYE, Danny, Jimmy Durante, Jane Wyman & Groucho Marx
Also see MARX BROTHERS

MARX, Richard

P&R/LP '87

Singles: 7-inch

EMI 3-4 88-90
EMI/MANHATTAN 3-4 88
MANHATTAN.............................3-4 87

Picture Sleeves

EMI..3-4 89
EMI/MANHATTAN 3-4 88
MANHATTAN.............................3-4 87

LPs: 10/12-inch 33rpm

CAPITOL...................................5-8 91-92
EMI..5-8 89
EMI/MANHATTAN 5-8 88
MANHATTAN...........................5-10 87

Also see SCHMIT, Timothy B.
Also see WAYBILL, Fee

MARX BROTHERS

LP '69

LPs: 10/12-inch 33rpm

DECCA (9169 "Marx Brothers") .. 8-12 69
(With Gary Owens.)

Also see MARX, Groucho

MARY JANE GIRLS

R&B/D&D/LP '83

Singles: 12-inch 33/45rpm

GORDY......................................4-6 83-85
MOTOWN 4-6 85-87

Singles: 7-inch

GORDY......................................3-4 83-87
MOTOWN 3-4 85-87

Picture Sleeves

GORDY......................................3-4 85
MOTOWN 3-4 86

LPs: 10/12-inch 33rpm

GORDY......................................5-8 83-87

Members: Joane "Jo Jo" McDuffie; Candice "Candy" Ghant; Kim "Maxi" Wuletich; Yvette "Corvette" Marine.

MAS, Carolyn

P&R/LP '79

Singles: 7-inch

MERCURY..................................3-5 79

LPs: 10/12-inch 33rpm

MERCURY................................5-10 79

MASCARA

D&D '84

Singles: 12-inch 33/45rpm

OH MY 4-6 84

MASEKELA, Hugh
(With the Union of South Africa)

P&R/LP '67

Singles: 12-inch 33/45rpm

JIVE AFRIKA 4-6 84

Singles: 7-inch

BLUE THUMB............................3-5 74
CASABLANCA............................3-5 75-77
CHISA..3-6 67-71
JIVE AFRIKA 3-4 84
MGM 3-6 66-68
MERCURY..................................3-8 63-68
UNI...3-6 67-69

LPs: 10/12-inch 33rpm

BLUE THUMB 5-10 72-74
CASABLANCA 5-10 75-77
CHISA 8-15 67-71
IMPULSE 5-10 78
MGM 8-15 66-68
MERCURY 8-18 63-67
UNI 8-12 67-69
UPFRONT 5-8 77
VERVE 8-15 68
WING 6-12 68

Also see ALPERT, Herb, & Hugh Masekela

MASHMAKHAN

P&R '70

Singles: 7-inch

EPIC 3-6 70
JAMIE 4-8 69

LPs: 10/12-inch 33rpm

EPIC 10-12 70-71

Members: Puerre Senecal; Jerry Mercer; Ray Blake; Brian Edwards.
Also see APRIL WINE

MASKED MARAUDERS

LP '70

Singles: 7-inch

DEITY 5-8 69

LPs: 10/12-inch 33rpm

DEITY (6378 "Masked Marauders") 15-20 69

MASKMAN & AGENTS

R&B '68

Singles: 7-inch

DYNAMO 4-8 68-69
GAMA 4-8 68

LPs: 10/12-inch 33rpm

DYNAMO 10-15 69

Members: Harmon Bethea; Paul Williams; John Hood; Ty Gray.
Also see BETHEA, Harmon

MASON

R&B '87

Singles: 7-inch

ELEKTRA 3-4 87

MASON, Barbara

(With the Futures)

P&R/R&B/LP '65

Singles: 12-inch 33/45rpm

WEST END 4-8 83-84

Singles: 7-inch

ARCTIC 4-8 64-68
BUDDAH 3-5 71-75
CHARGER 4-8 65
NATIONAL GENERAL 3-5 70
PHONORAMA 3-5 84
PRELUDE 3-5 78
WMOT 3-5 80-81
WEST END 3-5 83-84

LPs: 10/12-inch 33rpm

ARCTIC 15-25 65-68
BUDDAH 8-12 72-75
GNC 10-15 70
NATIONAL GENERAL 10-15 70
PHONORAMA 5-8 84
PRELUDE 8-10 78
WMOT 8-10 81
W.B. 8-12 77
WIND 8-10 81

Also see FUTURES
Also see HIGGINS, Monk

MASON, Barbara, & Larks

Singles: 7-inch

CRUSADER (114 "Dedicated to You") 8-12 64

Also see LARKS

MASON, Barbara, & Bunny Sigler

Singles: 7-inch

W.B. 3-5 77

Also see MASON, Barbara
Also see SIGLER, Bunny

MASON, Bonnie Jo

(Cher)

Singles: 7-inch

ANNETTE (1000 "Ringo, I Love You") 50-75 64

Also see CHER

MASON, Dave

P&R/LP '70

Singles: 7-inch

ABC 3-5 74
BLUE THUMB 3-5 70-78
COLUMBIA 3-5 73-81
MARBLE 3-4 83

LPs: 10/12-inch 33rpm

ABC 8-10 75
BLUE THUMB (19 "Alone Together") 10-12 70
(Black vinyl.)
BLUE THUMB (19 "Alone Together") 20-25 70
(Colored vinyl.)
BLUE THUMB (34 thru 54) 10-15 72-73
BLUE THUMB (800 series) 8-10 75
BLUE THUMB (6000 series) 8-10 74-78
COLUMBIA (Black vinyl) 8-10 73-81
COLUMBIA (Colored vinyl) 10-15 73-81
(Promotional issue only.)
ISLAND 5-8 83

Also see MERRYWEATHER, Neil
Also see TRAFFIC

MASON, Dave, & Cass Elliot

LP '71

Singles: 7-inch

DUNHILL 3-4 70-71

LPs: 10/12-inch 33rpm

BLUE THUMB 12-15 71

Also see ELLIOT, Cass

Also see MASON, Dave

MASON, Harvey

R&B '76

Singles: 7-inch

ARISTA 3-5 76-81

LPs: 10/12-inch 33rpm

ARISTA 5-10 78-81

MASON, Jackie

LP '62

Singles: 7-inch

VERVE 3-6 62

EPs: 7-inch 33/45rpm

VERVE (5076 "The Greatest Comedian in the World, Only Nobody Knows It") 5-10 62

(Promotional issue only.)

LPs: 10/12-inch 33rpm

VERVE 8-18 62-64

W.B. 5-8 87

MASON, Nick

(Nick Mason's Fictitious Sports)

LP '81

Singles: 12-inch 33/45rpm

COLUMBIA 4-6 85

Singles: 7-inch

COLUMBIA 3-5 81-85

LPs: 10/12-inch 33rpm

COLUMBIA 5-8 81-85

Also see PINK FLOYD

MASON, Nick, & Rick Fenn

LP '85

Singles: 7-inch

COLUMBIA 3-4 85

LPs: 10/12-inch 33rpm

COLUMBIA 5-8 85

Also see MASON, Nick

MASON, Vaughan

(With the Crew)

P&R/R&B '80

Singles: 12-inch 33/45rpm

BRUNSWICK 4-6 80-81

LPs: 10/12-inch 33rpm

BRUNSWICK 5-8 80

Also see AM-FM

MASON, Vaughan, & Butch Dayo

R&B '81

Singles: 12-inch 33/45rpm

SALSOUL 4-6 83

Singles: 7-inch

SALSOUL 3-4 82-83

LPs: 10/12-inch 33rpm

SALSOUL 5-8 83

Also see MASON, Vaughan

MASON DIXON DANCE BAND

R&B '79

Singles: 7-inch

ALEXANDER STREET 3-5 79

MASON PROFFIT

LP '71

Singles: 7-inch

AMPEX 3-5 71

HAPPY TIGER 4-6 70

LPs: 10/12-inch 33rpm

AMPEX 8-10 71

HAPPY TIGER 8-12 70-71

W.B. 8-10 72-73

Members: John Talbot; Terry Talbot.

MASQUERADERS

P&R/R&B '68

Singles: 7-inch

ABC 3-5 75-76

AMERICAN GROUP 3-5 69

BANG 3-4 80

BELL 4-8 68

HI 3-5 70s

HOT BUTTERED SOUL 3-5 75-76

MK (101 "Man's Temptation") 10-15 60s

STAIRWAY 10-20 60s

TOWER 4-8 66

WAND (1168 "Let's Face Facts") 15-25 67

WAND (1172 "Sweet Lovin' Woman") 25-35 67

LPs: 10/12-inch 33rpm

ABC 8-10 75

Members: Lee Hatim, Robert Wrightsil, David Sanders; Harold Thomas; Sam Hutchins.

Also see LARKS / Masqueraders

MASS PRODUCTION

P&R/R&B/LP '77

Singles: 7-inch

COTILLION 3-5 76-83

LPs: 10/12-inch 33rpm

COTILLION 5-8 76-83

MASSER, Michael, & Mandrill

R&B '77

Singles: 7-inch

ARISTA 3-5 77

Also see MANDRILL

MASSEY, Wayne

P&R '80

Singles: 7-inch

MCA 3-4 83

MERCURY 3-4 89

POLYDOR 3-5 80

MASSIAH, Maurice

D&D '83

Singles: 12-inch 33/45rpm

RFC/QUALITY 4-6 83

MASTER of CEREMONY Featuring Don Barron

R&B '87

Singles: 7-inch

4TH & BROADWAY 3-4 87-88

LPs: 10/12-inch 33rpm
4TH & BROADWAY 3-4 88

MASTERDON COMMITTEE

R&B '86

Singles: 12-inch 33/45rpm
PROFILE 4-6 86-87

Singles: 7-inch
PROFILE 3-4 86-87

LPs: 10/12-inch 33rpm
PROFILE 5-8 86

MASTERPIECE

R&B '80

Singles: 7-inch
WHITFIELD 3-5 80

LPs: 10/12-inch 33rpm
WHITFIELD 5-10 80

MASTERS, Johnny
(Johnny Maestro)

Singles: 7-inch
COED (527 "Say It Isn't So")..... 15-20 60
Also see MAESTRO, Johnny

MASTERS, Sammy

P&R '60

Singles: 78rpm
DECCA 3-5 57
4 STAR 5-10 57

Singles: 7-inch
DECCA 8-12 57
DOT 5-10 60-66
4 STAR (1695 "Pink Cadillac").. 30-50 57
4 STAR (1697 "Whop-T-Bop").. 30-50 57
GALAHAD 4-8 62-72
KAPP 4-8 64
LODE 5-10 60-61
TJB BRANDES 5-10
W.B. 5-10 60

EPs: 7-inch 33/45rpm
4 STAR (26 "Sammy Masters"). 50-75 57
(Promotional issue only. Not issued with cover.)

MATERIAL ISSUE

LP '91

LPs: 10/12-inch 33rpm
MERCURY 5-8 91

MATHEWS, Tobin
(Tobin Mathews & Co.; Tobin Matthews)

P&R '60

Singles: 7-inch
CHIEF 5-10 60-61
COLUMBIA 4-8 63
U.S.A. 4-8 61

MATHIEU, Mireille

LP '69

LPs: 10/12-inch 33rpm
CAPITOL 8-12 69

MATHIS, Johnny
(With Ray Conniff)

P&R/R&B/LP '57

Singles: 78rpm
COLUMBIA 3-5 57-58

Singles: 7-inch
AURAVISION 5-10
(Cardboard flexi-discs. Columbia Record Club promotional issues.)
COLUMBIA (Except 40000 series) 3-5 74-85
COLUMBIA (40784 thru 42916)...5-10 58-63
COLUMBIA (44266 thru 46048).....3-8 67-74
MERCURY 4-8 63-66

Picture Sleeves
COLUMBIA (40993 "Chances Are") 10-20 57
COLUMBIA (41060 thru 42799)...5-10 58-63
MERCURY 4-8 63-66

EPs: 7-inch 33/45rpm
COLUMBIA (Except 8800 series) 10-20 57-59
COLUMBIA (8871 thru 8873).....15-25 56

LPs: 10/12-inch 33rpm
COLUMBIA (Except 887) 5-15 57-87
COLUMBIA (887 "Johnny Mathis") 35-50 56
CONCERT 8-12
(TV mail-order offer.)
HARMONY 5-10
MFSL 15-20 85
MERCURY 8-15 64-67
Also see CONNIFF, Ray
Also see FAITH, Percy, Orchestra / Johnny Mathis
Also see KNIGHT, Gladys, & Johnny Mathis
Also see NELSON, Willie / Nat "King" Cole / Johnny Mathis / Shirley Bassey

MATHIS, Johnny, & Henry Mancini

LP '87

LPs: 10/12-inch 33rpm
COLUMBIA 5-8 87
Also see MANCINI, Henry

MATHIS, Johnny, & Dionne Warwick

P&R '82

Singles: 7-inch
ARISTA 3-5 82
Also see WARWICK, Dionne

MATHIS, Johnny, & Deniece Williams

P&R/R&B/LP '78

Singles: 7-inch
COLUMBIA 3-5 78-84

LPs: 10/12-inch 33rpm
COLUMBIA (35435 "That's What Friends Are For") 15-25 78
(Picture disc. Promotional issue only.)
COLUMBIA (35435 "That's What Friends Are For") 5-10 78
(Standard vinyl disc.)
Also see MATHIS, Johnny

Also see WILLIAMS, Deniece

MATHIS, Kathy

R&B '87

Singles: 7-inch

TABU 3-4 87

MATLOCK, Ronn

R&B '79

Singles: 7-inch

COTILLION 3-5 79

MATTHEWS, David

LP '77

LPs: 10/12-inch 33rpm

CTI 5-10 77

Also see WASHINGTON, Grover, Jr.

MATTHEWS, Ian

LP '72

Singles: 7-inch

DECCA 3-5 70-71
COLUMBIA 3-5 76-77
ELEKTRA 3-5 73
MUSHROOM 3-5 78-79
VERTIGO 3-5 71-72

LPs: 10/12-inch 33rpm

CAPITOL 8-10 71
COLUMBIA 8-10 77
DECCA 8-12 71
ELEKTRA 8-10 73-74
MUSHROOM (Except 5012) 8-10 78
MUSHROOM (5012 "Stealin' Home") 20-25 78
(Picture disc. Promotional issue only.)
MUSHROOM (5012 "Stealin' Home") 8-10 78
(Standard vinyl disc.)
VERTIGO 10-12 71-72

Also see FAIRPORT CONVENTION
Also see HI FI Featuring David Surkamp & Ian Matthews
Also see MATTHEWS' SOUTHERN COMFORT

MATTHEWS, Milt

R&B '78

Singles: 7-inch

H&L 3-5 78

MATTHEWS' SOUTHERN COMFORT
(Featuring Ian Matthews)

P&R/LP '71

Singles: 7-inch

DECCA 3-5 71

LPs: 10/12-inch 33rpm

DECCA 10-15 70-71
MCA 5-10 78

Also see MATTHEWS, Ian
Also see SOUTHERN COMFORT

MATYS BROTHERS

P&R '63

Singles: 78rpm

ESSEX 3-6 54

Singles: 7-inch

ESSEX 5-10 54
SELECT 4-6 62
SOUND 4-6

MAUDS

P&R '68

Singles: 7-inch

DUNWICH 5-10 67
MERCURY 4-8 67-69
RCA 3-6 70

LPs: 10/12-inch 33rpm

MERCURY 15-25 67

MAURIAT, Paul

LP '67

Singles: 7-inch

PHILIPS 3-5 67-71

Picture Sleeves

PHILIPS 3-5 68

LPs: 10/12-inch 33rpm

PHILIPS 8-18 67-71

MAURICE & RADIANTS: see RADIANTS

MAX Q

LP '89

LPs: 10/12-inch 33rpm

ATLANTIC 5-8 89

MAXAYN

R&B '73

Singles: 7-inch

CAPRICORN 3-5 72-74

LPs: 10/12-inch 33rpm

CAPRICORN 8-10 72-74

Members: Maxayn Lewis; Andre Lewis.
Also see IKETTES
Also see MANDRE

MAXIM TRIO

R&B '49

Singles: 78rpm

DOWNBEAT (171 "Confession Blues") 10-20 49

Members: Ray Charles; G.D. McGhee; Milton Garred.
Also see CHARLES, Ray

MAXWELL, Diane

P&R '59

Singles: 7-inch

CAPITOL 4-8 61
CHALLENGE 5-10 59

LPs: 10/12-inch 33rpm

CHALLENGE (607 "Almost Seventeen") 30-40 59
(Monaural.)
CHALLENGE (2501 "Almost Seventeen") 40-60 59
(Stereo.)

Also see FULLER, Jerry, & Diane Maxwell

MAXWELL, Robert
(Bobby Maxwell)

P&R/LP '64

Singles: 78rpm

MGM 3-5 57
MERCURY 3-5 52
TEMPO 3-5 51-52

Singles: 7-inch

DECCA 3-6 64
MGM 4-8 57
MERCURY 5-10 52
TEMPO 5-10 51-52

EPs: 7-inch 33/45rpm

MGM 5-10 57
MERCURY 5-10 52
TEMPO 5-10 51-52

LPs: 10/12-inch 33rpm

DECCA 8-15 64
MGM 10-15 57
TEMPO 10-20 52

MAY, Billy, & His Orchestra

P&R '52

Singles: 78rpm

CAPITOL 3-5 50-56

Singles: 7-inch

CAPITOL 5-10 50-56

EPs: 7-inch 33/45rpm

CAPITOL 5-10 50-56

LPs: 10/12-inch 33rpm

CAPITOL 8-18 50-56

MAY, Brian
(Brian May & Friends)

LP '83

Singles: 7-inch

CAPITOL 3-4 83

LPs: 10/12-inch 33rpm

CAPITOL 5-8 83

Also see QUEEN
Also see REO SPEEDWAGON
Also see VAN HALEN

MAYALL, John
(With the Blues Breakers Featuring Eric Clapton)

LP '68

Singles: 7-inch

IMMEDIATE 4-8 67
LONDON 5-10 66-68
POLYDOR 3-8 69-74

LPs: 10/12-inch 33rpm

ABC 8-12 76-78
BLUE THUMB 8-12 74
DJM 8-12 79
ISLAND 5-8 90
LONDON 10-15 67-78
MCA 5-8
POLYDOR 10-12 69-74

Also see BRUCE, Jack
Also see CLAPTON, Eric
Also see FLEETWOOD MAC
Also see HARTLEY, Keef, Band
Also see TAYLOR, Mick

MAYANA

D&D '83

Singles: 12-inch 33/45rpm

ATLANTIC 4-6 83

Singles: 7-inch

ATLANTIC 3-4 83

MAYER, Nathaniel
(With the Fabulous Twilights; with Fortune Braves)

P&R/R&B '62

Singles: 7-inch

FORTUNE (449 "Village of Love") 10-15 62
FORTUNE (487 "Hurting Love") 15-25 62
FORTUNE (500 series) 10-20 62-69
U.A. 5-10 62

LPs: 10/12-inch 33rpm

FORTUNE (8014 "Goin' Back to the Village of Love") 40-50 64

MAYFIELD, Curtis

P&R/R&B/LP '70

Singles: 7-inch

BOARDWALK 3-5 81-82
CRC 3-4 85
CURTOM 3-5 70-80
RSO 3-5 80

Picture Sleeves

CURTOM 3-5 71-78

LPs: 10/12-inch 33rpm

ABC 10-20 73
BOARDWALK 5-10 81-82
CURTOM 8-12 70-78
RSO 5-10 79-80

Also see IMPRESSIONS
Also see REED, Jimmy

MAYFIELD, Curtis, & Linda Clifford

R&B '79

Singles: 7-inch

CURTOM 3-5 79-80

LPs: 10/12-inch 33rpm

RSO 5-10 80

Also see CLIFFORD, Linda
Also see MAYFIELD, Curtis

MAYFIELD, Percy

P&R/R&B '50

Singles: 78rpm

CHESS (1599 "Double Dealing") 10-20 55
KING (4480 "Two Years of Torture") 10-20 51
SPECIALTY 10-15 50-57

Singles: 7-inch

ATLANTIC 3-5 74
BRUNSWICK 4-6 68
CHESS (1599 "Double Dealing") 25-50 55

IMPERIAL 5-10 59
KING (4480 "Two Years of Torture") 25-50 51
RCA.. 3-5 70
SPECIALTY (375 "Please Send Me Someone to Love") 20-30 50
SPECIALTY (390 "Lost Love").. 20-30 51
SPECIALTY (400 "Nightless Lover").................................. 20-30 51
SPECIALTY (408 "My Blues")... 20-30 51
SPECIALTY (416 "Cry Baby")... 20-30 52
SPECIALTY (425 "Big Question") 20-30 52
SPECIALTY (432 "Louisiana") .. 20-30 52
SPECIALTY (439 "My Heart")... 20-30 53
SPECIALTY (451 "I Dare You, Baby") 20-30 54
SPECIALTY (460 "Lonely One") 20-30 54
(Black vinyl.)
SPECIALTY (460 "Lonely One") 40-60 54
(Colored vinyl.)
SPECIALTY (473 "How Deep Is the Well")............................... 20-30 54
(Black vinyl.)
SPECIALTY (473 "How Deep Is the Well")............................... 40-60 54
(Colored vinyl.)
SPECIALTY (485 "I Need You So Bad") 20-30 54
SPECIALTY (499 "You Don't Exist No More 20-30 55
SPECIALTY (500 series) 10-20 55
SPECIALTY (600 series) 5-10 60
TANGERINE 4-8 62-67

LPs: 10/12-inch 33rpm

BRUNSWICK 10-20 69
RCA.. 10-15 70-71
SPECIALTY 8-12 70
TANGERINE 15-25 66-67

MAZARATI

R&B/LP '86

Singles: 12-inch 33/45rpm

PAISLEY PARK........................... 4-6 86

Singles: 7-inch

PAISLEY PARK........................... 3-4 86

LPs: 10/12-inch 33rpm

PAISLEY PARK........................... 5-8 86

Member: Casey Terry; Brown Mark.
Also see BROWNMARK

MAZE
(Featuring Frankie Beverly)

P&R/R&B/LP '77

Singles: 12-inch 33/45rpm

CAPITOL.................................... 4-6 84

Singles: 7-inch

CAPITOL.................................... 3-5 77-86

Picture Sleeves

CAPITOL.................................... 3-5 81-85

LPs: 10/12-inch 33rpm

CAPITOL....................................5-10 78-86
W.B. 5-8 89

MBULU, Letta

R&B/LP '77

Singles: 7-inch

A&M 3-5 77

LPs: 10/12-inch 33rpm

A&M 5-10 77

McANALLY, Mac

P&R '77

Singles: 7-inch

ARIOLA.......................................3-5 78
ARIOLA AMERICA 3-5 77
MCA..3-4 92
W.B. 3-4 90

LPs: 10/12-inch 33rpm

ARIOLA AMERICA 5-10 78

McBRIDE & the RIDE

LP '91

Singles: 7-inch

MCA..3-4 91-92

LPs: 10/12-inch 33rpm

MCA..5-8 91-92

Members: Terry McBride; Billy Thomas; Ray Herndon; Kenny Vaughn; Keith Edwards.

McCALL, Al

R&B '83

Singles: 7-inch

PROFILE......................................3-4 83

McCALL, C.W.

C&W/P&R '74

Singles: 7-inch

MGM 3-5 74-75
POLYDOR 3-5 76-79

LPs: 10/12-inch 33rpm

MGM 5-10 75
POLYDOR 5-8 76-79

McCALL, Cash

R&B '66

Singles: 7-inch

CHECKER 4-8 67
COLUMBIA 3-5 76-77
M-PAC 4-8 64
PAULA 3-5 75
RONN 3-5 75
THOMAS......................................4-8 66

McCALL, Toussaint

P&R/R&B '67

Singles: 7-inch

COLLECTABLES...........................3-4 80s
RONN 4-8 67-68

LPs: 10/12-inch 33rpm

RONN 10-12 67

Also see NEVILLE, Aaron / Toussaint McCall

McCALLUM, David

LP '66

Singles: 7-inch

CAPITOL 4-8 66

Picture Sleeves

CAPITOL 5-10 66

LPs: 10/12-inch 33rpm

CAPITOL 10-15 66

McCANN, Les

LP '69

Singles: 7-inch

ATLANTIC 3-5 69-75
LIMELIGHT 4-6 65
PACIFIC JAZZ 4-8 60-65
WORLD PACIFIC 3-6 60s

LPs: 10/12-inch 33rpm

ATLANTIC 5-10 69-75
LIMELIGHT 10-20 65
PACIFIC JAZZ 15-25 60-65

Also see FLACK, Roberta
Also see HOLMES, Richard "Groove," & Les McCann
Also see JAZZ CRUSADERS
Also see RAWLS, Lou, & Les McCann Ltd.

McCANN, Les, & Eddie Harris

LP '69

Singles: 7-inch

ATLANTIC 3-5 69-70

LPs: 10/12-inch 33rpm

ATLANTIC 5-10 69-71

Also see HARRIS, Eddie
Also see McCANN, Les

McCANN, Peter

P&R/LP '77

Singles: 7-inch

COLUMBIA 3-5 79
20TH FOX 3-5 77

LPs: 10/12-inch 33rpm

20TH FOX 8-10 77

McCARTNEY, Paul

(Wings; with Wings; with Linda McCartney)

LP '70

Singles: 12-inch 33/45rpm

CAPITOL (15212 "Spies Like Us") 5-8 85
CAPITOL (15235 "Press") 4-8 86
COLUMBIA (03019 "Take It Away") 5-10 82
COLUMBIA (05077 "No More Lonely Nights") 5-8 84
("Playout version.")
COLUMBIA (05077 "No More Lonely Nights") 10-15 84
("Special Dance Mix.")
COLUMBIA (10940 "Goodnight Tonight") 10-20 79
COLUMBIA (39927 "No More Lonely Nights") 8-12 84
(Picture disc.)
PROFILE (7147 "Let It Be") 5-8 87

Promotional 12-inch Singles

CAPITOL (8574 "Maybe I'm Amazed") 40-50 77
CAPITOL (9556 "Spies Like Us") 20-25 85
CAPITOL (9763 "Press") 10-15 86
CAPITOL (9797 "Angry") 10-15 86
COLUMBIA (775 "Coming Up") . 50-60 80
(Red label.)
COLUMBIA (775 "Coming Up") . 45-55 80
(White label.)
COLUMBIA (1940 "No More Lonely Nights") 10-15 84
("Ballad" version.)
COLUMBIA (1990 "No More Lonely Nights") 10-15 84
("Special Dance Mix.")
COLUMBIA (05077 "No More Lonely Nights") 10-15 84
("Ballad version.")
COLUMBIA (10940 "Goodnight Tonight") 10-20 79
PROFILE (7147 "Let It Be") 10-15 87

Singles: 7-inch

APPLE (1829 "Another Day") 4-6 71
APPLE (1837 "Uncle Albert Admiral Halsey") 4-6 71
APPLE (1847 "Give Ireland Back to the Irish") 4-6 72
APPLE (1851 "Mary Had a Little Lamb") 4-6 72
APPLE (1857 "Hi Hi Hi") 4-6 72
APPLE (1861 "My Love") 4-6 73
APPLE (1863 "Live and Let Die") .. 4-6 73
APPLE (1869 "Helen Wheels") 4-6 73
APPLE (1871 "Jet"/"Mamunia") ... 5-10 74
APPLE (1871 "Jet"/"Let Me Roll It") 4-6 74
APPLE (1873 "Band on the Run") . 4-6 74
APPLE (1875 "Junior's Farm") 4-6 74
CAPITOL (1829 "Another Day") 3-4 80s
CAPITOL (1837 "Uncle Albert Admiral Halsey") 3-4 80s
CAPITOL (1847 "Give Ireland Back to the Irish") 3-4 80s
CAPITOL (1851 "Mary Had a Little Lamb") 3-4 80s
CAPITOL (1857 "Hi Hi Hi") 3-4 80s
CAPITOL (1861 "My Love") 3-4 80s
CAPITOL (1863 "Live and Let Die") 3-4 80s
CAPITOL (1869 "Helen Wheels") .. 3-4 80s
CAPITOL (1871 "Jet") 3-4 80s
CAPITOL (1873 "Band on the Run") 3-4 80s
CAPITOL (1875 "Junior's Farm") ... 3-4 80s
CAPITOL (4091 "Listen to What the Man Said") 3-5 75
CAPITOL (4145 "Letting Go") 3-5 75

CAPITOL (4175 "Venus and Mars Rock Show") 3-5 75
CAPITOL (4256 "Silly Love Songs") 3-5 76
(Capitol custom label.)
CAPITOL (4256 "Silly Love Songs") 3-4 80s
(Black label.)
CAPITOL (4293 "Let 'Em In")........ 3-5 76
(Capitol custom label.)
CAPITOL (4293 "Let 'Em In")........ 3-4 80s
(Black label.)
CAPITOL (4385 Maybe I'm Amazed") 3-5 77
CAPITOL (4504 "Mull of Kintyre") . 3-5 77
CAPITOL (4559 "With a Little Luck")... 3-5 78
CAPITOL (4594 "I've Had Enough")... 3-5 78
CAPITOL (4625 "London Town") .. 3-5 78
CAPITOL (5537 "Spies Like Us") .. 3-4 85
CAPITOL (5597 "Press").............. 3-4 86
CAPITOL (5636 "Stranglehold").... 3-4 86
CAPITOL (17318 "Off the Ground")................................ 40-50 94
(Intended to be red vinyl but issued on black vinyl by mistake. Reportedly 800 made. 30th Anniversary jukebox issue.)
CAPITOL (17319 "Biker Like an Icon")..................................... 40-50 94
(Intended to be red vinyl but issued on black vinyl by mistake. Reportedly 800 made. 30th Anniversary jukebox issue.)
COLUMBIA (02171 "Silly Love Songs") 3-4 81
COLUMBIA (03018 "Take It Away").. 3-4 82
COLUMBIA (03235 "Tug of War"). 3-4 82
COLUMBIA (04296 "So Bad")....... 3-4 83
COLUMBIA (04581 "No More Lonely Nights")........................... 3-4 84
COLUMBIA (10939 "Goodnight Tonight")..................................... 3-4 79
COLUMBIA (11020 "Getting Closer") 3-4 79
COLUMBIA (11070 "Arrow Through Me")... 3-4 79
COLUMBIA (11162 "Wonderful Christmastime").......................... 3-4 79
COLUMBIA (11263 "Coming Up") 3-4 80
(Listed here as a single even though there are two tracks on the B-side.)
COLUMBIA (11335 "Waterfalls") .. 3-4 80
COLUMBIA (33405 "Goodnight Tonight")...................................... 3-4 80
COLUMBIA (33409 "My Love")..... 3-4 80
COLUMBIA (33408 "Uncle Albert Admiral Halsey") 3-4 80
COLUMBIA (33409 "Band on the Run")..3-4 80
PROFILE (5147 "Let It Be") 3-4 87

Picture Sleeves

APPLE (1847 "Give Ireland Back to the Irish").............................10-20 72
APPLE (1851 "Mary Had a Little Lamb")............................20-30 72
("Little Woman Love" printed under photo, on reverse side of sleeve.)
APPLE (1851 "Mary Had a Little Lamb")............................10-15 72
("Little Woman Love" not printed under photo, on reverse side of sleeve.)
CAPITOL (4091 "Listen to What the Man Said") 4-8 75
CAPITOL (4504 "Mull of Kintyre") 8-12 77
CAPITOL (5537 "Spies Like Us")...3-5 85
CAPITOL (5597 "Press") 3-5 86
CAPITOL (5636 "Stranglehold") 3-5 86
COLUMBIA (03018 "Take It Away")..5-10 82
(Reads "Not for Sale" on back side. Promotional issue only.)
COLUMBIA (03018 "Take It Away")..3-5 82
COLUMBIA (04296 "So Bad") 3-5 83
COLUMBIA (04296 "So Bad") 5-10 83
(Reads "Not for Sale" on back side. Promotional issue only.)
COLUMBIA (04581 "No More Lonely Nights")...........................5-10 84
COLUMBIA (11020 "Getting Closer")...................................20-30 79
COLUMBIA (11162 "Wonderful Christmastime") 4-6 79
COLUMBIA (11263 "Coming Up") .4-6 80
COLUMBIA (11335 "Waterfalls") 15-20 80
PROFILE (5147 "Let It Be") 3-5 87

Promotional Singles

APPLE (1829 "Another Day") 35-45 71
APPLE (1837 "Uncle Albert Admiral Halsey") 15-25 71
APPLE (1851 "Mary Had a Little Lamb")..........................50-100 72
APPLE (1857 "Hi Hi Hi") 10-15 72
APPLE (1861 "My Love")...........50-75 73
APPLE (1863 "Live and Let Die")..10-20 73
APPLE (1871 "Jet")......................20-30 74
APPLE (1873 "Band on the Run")..25-35 74
APPLE (1875 "Junior's Farm")...25-35 74
APPLE (1875 "Sally G")..............25-35 74
APPLE (6786 "Helen Wheels") ..25-35 73
APPLE (6787 "Country Dreamer") 50-100 73
CAPITOL (4145 "Letting Go")....15-20 75

CAPITOL (4175 "Venus and Mars Rock Show") 15-20 75
CAPITOL (4256 "Silly Love Songs.") 10-20 76
CAPITOL (4293 "Let 'Em In")...... 8-12 76
CAPITOL (4594 "I've Had Enough") 10-15 78
(Add $3-$5 if accompanied by special promotional flyer.)
CAPITOL (4625 "London Town")................................... 10-15 78
CAPITOL (5537 "Spies Like Us") 5-10 85
CAPITOL (5597 "Press")............ 5-10 86
CAPITOL (5636 "Stranglehold").. 5-10 86
CAPITOL (8138 "Listen to What the Man Said") 10-15 75
CAPITOL (8570/1 "Maybe I'm Amazed") 10-15 77
CAPITOL (8746/7 "Mull of Kintyre") 10-15 77
CAPITOL (8812 "With a Little Luck").................................... 10-15 78
COLUMBIA (1204 "Coming Up") 5-10 80
(Single-sided disc.)
COLUMBIA (03018 "Take It Away")...................................... 4-6 82
COLUMBIA (03235 "Tug of War").. 8-10 82
COLUMBIA (04296 "So Bad")....... 5-8 83
COLUMBIA (04581 "No More Lonely Nights")........................... 5-8 84
COLUMBIA (10939 "Goodnight Tonight")....................................... 5-8 79
COLUMBIA (11020 "Getting Closer") 10-12 79
COLUMBIA (11070 "Arrow Through Me") 10-12 79
COLUMBIA (11162 "Wonderful Christmastime")....................... 10-12 79
COLUMBIA (11263 "Coming Up").. 8-10 80
COLUMBIA (11335 "Waterfalls") 8-10 80
CREATIVE RADIO (PM-1 "Inside Paul McCartney")................... 15-20
(Radio show demo. Flip is *The Beatle Invasion.*)
MIRAMAX (4202 "Rock Show")............................... 150-175 75
(Contains three radio spots. Issued to radio stations only.)
PROFILE (5147 "Let It Be") 5-10 87

LPs: 10/12–inch 33rpm

APPLE (3363 "McCartney") 15-20 70
(Label shows Paul's full name beneath LP title.)
APPLE (3363 "McCartney") 10-15 70
(Label doesn't show Paul's name beneath LP title.)
APPLE (3375 "Ram") 10-15 71
APPLE (3386 "Wild Life")...........10-15 71
APPLE (3409 "Red Rose Speedway")..............................10-15 73
APPLE (3415 "Band on the Run")..10-15 73
(Price includes bonus poster.)
CAPITOL (3363 "McCartney").....8-10
CAPITOL (3375 "Ram")...............8-10
CAPITOL (3386 "Wildlife")..........8-10
CAPITOL (3409 "Red Rose Speedway")...............................8-10
CAPITOL (3415 "Band on the Run")..8-10
(Price includes bonus poster.)
CAPITOL (11525 "Wings at the Speed of Sound").......................8-10 76
CAPITOL (11593 "Wings over America") 12-15 76
CAPITOL (11905 "Greatest Hits") 5-10 78
(Price includes bonus poster.)
CAPITOL (11419 "Venus and Mars") 10-15 75
(Price includes bonus posters and stickers.)
CAPITOL (11777 "London Town")...................................10-15 78
(Price includes bonus poster.)
CAPITOL (11901 "Band on the Run").....................................20-30 78
(Picture disc.)
CAPITOL (12475 "Press to Play") 8-10 87
CAPITOL (48287 "All the Best!") 10-15 87
CAPITOL (91653 "Flowers in the Dirt").....................................5-8 89
CAPITOL (94778 "Tripping the Live Fantastic").......................10-12 90
CAPITOL (95379 "Tripping the Live Fantastic - Highlights") 5-10 90
COLUMBIA (36057 "Back to the Egg")...................................5-10 79
COLUMBIA (36478 "McCartney")...............................5-10 80
COLUMBIA (36479 "Ram")..........5-10 80
COLUMBIA (36480 "Wild Life") ...5-10 80
COLUMBIA (36481 "Red Rose Speedway")...............................5-10 80
COLUMBIA (36482 "Band on the Run")..................................5-10 80
COLUMBIA (36511 "McCartney II").......................15-20 80
(Issued with bonus single [1204] *Coming Up,* which represents $4 to $8 of the price range.)
COLUMBIA (36801 "Venus and Mars") 5-8 80
(Price includes bonus posters.)

COLUMBIA (36987 "The McCartney Interview") 8-10 80
COLUMBIA (37409 "Wings at the Speed of Sound") 5-8 81
COLUMBIA (37462 "Tug of War"). 5-8 82
(With Stevie Wonder on *Ebony and Ivory*)
COLUMBIA (39149 "Pipes of Peace") 5-8 83
(With Michael Jackson on *Say Say Say*)
COLUMBIA (39613 "Give My Regards to Broad Street") 5-8 84
COLUMBIA (46482 "Band on the Run") 10-15 80
(Half-speed mastered.)
LIBERTY (50100 Live and Let Die") 5-8 84
(With McCartney on title track only.)
LONDON (76007 "Family Way") 50-60 67
(Soundtrack. Monaural.)
LONDON (82007 "Family Way") 60-70 67
(Soundtrack. Stereo.)
U.A. (100 "Live and Let Die") 15-20 73
(Copies with cut corners are valued at about one-half of the above price range. McCartney is heard on title track only.)

Promotional LPs

APPLE (3375 "Ram") 80-100 71
(Monaural.)
APPLE (6210 "Brung to Ewe By") 175-200 71
COLUMBIA (821 "The McCartney Interview") 40-50 80
COLUMBIA (36057 "Back to the Egg") 15-20 79
COLUMBIA (36511 "McCartney II") 15-20 80
W.B. ("The Family Way") 150-200 67
(10–inch LP. Ad spots for radio stations.)
Also see BEATLES
Also see BRASS RING
Also see COUNTRY HAMS
Also see GREASE BAND
Also see LOMAX, Jackie
Also see NEWMAN, Thunderclap
Also see PERKINS, Carl
Also see SUZY & Red Stripes

McCARTNEY, Paul, & Michael Jackson
P&R/R&B '82

Singles: 12–inch 33/45rpm

COLUMBIA (1758 "Say Say Say") 10-15 83
COLUMBIA (04169 "Say Say Say") 5-8 83

Promotional 12–inch Singles

COLUMBIA (04169 "Say Say Say") 12-18 83

Singles: 7–inch

COLUMBIA (04168 "Say Say Say") 3-4 83
EPIC (03288 "The Girl Is Mine") 3-4 82
EPIC (03372 "The Girl Is Mine") 5-8 82
(Single-sided pressing with small, LP size, hole.)

Picture Sleeves

COLUMBIA (04168 "Say Say Say") 3-4 83

Promotional Picture Sleeves

COLUMBIA (04168 "Say Say Say") 5-8 83
EPIC (03288 "The Girl Is Mine") 5-8 82

Promotional Singles

COLUMBIA (04168 "Say Say Say") 5-8 83
EPIC (03288 "The Girl Is Mine") 5-8 82
(Label shows identification number as 169138.)
EPIC (03288 "The Girl Is Mine") 10-15 82
(Label shows identification number as 169202. Also reads "New Edited Version.")
Also see JACKSON, Michael

McCARTNEY, Paul / Rochestra / Who / Rockpile

Singles: 12–inch 33/45rpm

ATLANTIC (388 "Every Night") .. 60-80 81
(Promotional issue only.)
Also see ROCKPILE
Also see WHO

McCARTNEY, Paul, & Stevie Wonder
P&R/R&B '82

Singles: 12–inch 33/45rpm

COLUMBIA (02878 "Ebony and Ivory") 5-8 82

Promotional 12–inch Singles

COLUMBIA (1444 "McCartney") 25-30 82

Singles: 7–inch

COLUMBIA (02860 "Ebony and Ivory") 3-4 82

Promotional Singles

COLUMBIA (02860 "Ebony and Ivory") 8-12 82

Picture Sleeves

COLUMBIA (02860 "Ebony and Ivory") 3-4 82

Promotional Picture Sleeves

COLUMBIA (02860 "Ebony and Ivory") 5-10 82
Also see McCARTNEY, Paul
Also see WONDER, Stevie

McCLAIN, Alton, & Destiny
P&R/R&B/LP '79

Singles: 7–inch

POLYDOR 3-5 79-81

LPs: 10/12–inch 33rpm

POLYDOR 5-10 79-81
Also see ALTON & JOHNNY

McCLAIN, Janice

R&B '80

Singles: 12–inch 33/45rpm

MCA 4-6 86

Singles: 7–inch

MCA 3-4 86
RFC 3-4 80

LPs: 10/12–inch 33rpm

MCA 5-8 86

McCLARY, Thomas

R&B '84

Singles: 7–inch

MOTOWN 3-4 84-85

LPs: 10/12–inch 33rpm

MOTOWN 5-8 85
Also see COMMODORES

McCLINTON, Delbert

LP '79

Singles: 7–inch

BOBILL 5-10 67
BROWNFIELD 8-12 65
CAPITOL 3-5 80-81
CAPRICORN 3-5 78

LPs: 10/12–inch 33rpm

ACCORD 5-8 81
CAPITOL 5-8 81
CAPRICORN 5-8 79
INTERMEDIA 5-8 84
MCA 5-8 81
POLYDOR 10-15 79
Also see DELBERT & GLEN

McCLINTON, O.B.
(With Peggy Jo Adams)

C&W '72

Singles: 7–inch

ENTERPRISE 3-5 72-75
EPIC 3-5 78-87
MERCURY 3-5 76
MOON SHINE 3-4 84
SUNBIRD 3-5 80

LPs: 10/12–inch 33rpm

ENTERPRISE 8-10 72-74

McCLURE, Bobby

P&R/R&B '66

Singles: 7–inch

CHECKER 4-8 66-67
Also see BASS, Fontella, & Bobby McClure

McCOLLUM, Hazel: see EL DORADOS

McCONNELL, C. Lynda

D&D '84

Singles: 12–inch 33/45rpm

ATLANTIC 4-6 84

Singles: 7–inch

ATLANTIC 3-4 84

McCOO, Marilyn

R&B '83

Singles: 7–inch

RCA 3-4 83

LPs: 10/12–inch 33rpm

RCA 5-8 83

McCOO, Marilyn, & Billy Davis Jr.

P&R/R&B/LP '76

Singles: 12–inch 33/45rpm

COLUMBIA 4-6 79

Singles: 7–inch

ABC 3-5 76-78
COLUMBIA 3-5 78

LPs: 10/12–inch 33rpm

ABC 8-10 76-77
COLUMBIA 5-10 78
Also see FIFTH DIMENSION
Also see McCOO, Marilyn

McCORMICK, Gayle

P&R/LP '71

Singles: 7–inch

DECCA 3-5 72
DUNHILL 3-5 71-72
MCA 3-5 73

LPs: 10/12–inch 33rpm

DECCA 10-12 72
DUNHILL 10-12 71
FANTASY 8-10 74
Also see SMITH

McCOY, Charlie
(With Barefoot Jerry)

P&R '61

Singles: 7–inch

CADENCE 4-8 61-62
MONUMENT 3-6 68-83

LPs: 10/12–inch 33rpm

EPIC 5-8 82
MONUMENT 5-10 69-78
Also see AREA CODE 615
Also see DYLAN, Bob

McCOY, Freddie

P&R '67

Singles: 7–inch

PRESTIGE 4-6 67

McCOY, Van
(With the Soul City Symphony)

R&B '74

Singles: 12–inch 33/45rpm

MCA 4-8 79

Singles: 7–inch

AMHERST 3-5 70s
AVCO 3-5 74-75
CGC 3-5 70
COLUMBIA 4-8 65-66
EPIC 3-6 69
H&L 3-5 76
LIBERTY 4-8 62
MCA 3-5 78-79

ROCK 'N.. 8-12 61
SILVER BLUE.................................. 3-5 73

LPs: 10/12-inch 33rpm

AVCO.. 8-10 74-75
BUDDAH... 8-10 72-75
COLUMBIA..................................... 12-18 66
H&L... 8-10 76
MCA.. 8-10 77-79

McCOYS

P&R/LP '65

Singles: 7-inch

BANG.. 5-10 65-67
MERCURY....................................... 8-15 68
SOLID GOLD.................................. 3-4 73

LPs: 10/12-inch 33rpm

BANG (212 "Hang on Sloopy") . 25-35 65
(Monaural.)
BANG (S-212 "Hang on Sloopy")................................ 35-45 65
(Stereo.)
BANG (213 "You Make Me Feel So Good")......................... 25-35 66
(Monaural.)
BANG (S-213 "You Make Me Feel So Good")......................... 35-45 66
(Stereo.)
MERCURY (61163 "Infinite McCoys").............................. 20-25 68
MERCURY (61207 "Human Ball").. 20-25 69
Also see DERRINGER, Rick
Also see STRANGELOVES

McCRACKLIN, Jimmy
(With His Blues Blasters; Jimmie McCracklin)

P&R/R&B '58

Singles: 78rpm

ALADDIN.. 10-15 51
CAVATONE...................................... 10-20 47
COURTNEY...................................... 10-20 45
DOWN TOWN................................... 10-20 48
EXCELSIOR..................................... 10-20 45
GLOBE... 10-20 45
HOLLYWOOD.................................. 10-15 55
MODERN.. 10-15 49
PEACOCK.. 10-15 52-54
RPM... 10-15 50
SWING TIME.................................... 10-15 51-52
TRILON.. 10-15 49

Singles: 7-inch

ART-TONE.. 5-10 61-62
CHECKER.. 10-15 58
CHESS.. 4-8 62
GEDINSON'S.................................... 4-8 61
HI.. 5-10 60
HOLLYWOOD.................................. 15-25 55
IMPERIAL... 4-8 62-67
IRMA... 10-20
KENT... 4-8 62
LIBERTY.. 3-5 70
MERCURY.. 8-12 59-61
MINIT... 4-8 67-70
MODERN (926 "Blues Blasters Boogie").. 20-30 54
MODERN (934 "Darlin' Share Your Love")................................ 20-30 54
MODERN (951 "Forgive Me Baby").. 20-30 54
MODERN (967 "Gonna Tell Your Mother").............................. 20-30 55
PEACOCK (1605 "My Days Are Limited")............................... 20-30 52
PEACOCK (1615 "Share and Share Alike")............................... 20-30 53
PEACOCK (1634 "The End")..... 20-30 53
PEACOCK (1639 "The Cheater")....................................... 20-30 53
PREMIUM (101 "You're the One").. 15-20

LPs: 10/12-inch 33rpm

CHESS (1464 "Jimmy McCracklin Sings").. 40-60 62
CROWN.. 15-20 61
IMPERIAL... 20-35 63-66
MINIT.. 12-18 67-69
STAX... 8-12 72-81
Also see BROWN, Charles, & Jimmy McCracklin

McCRACKLIN, Jimmy / T-Bone Walker / Charles Brown

LPs: 10/12-inch 33rpm

IMPERIAL (9257 "Best of the Blues, Vol. 1").. 15-25 64
Also see BROWN, Charles
Also see WALKER, T-Bone

McCRAE, George

P&R/R&B/LP '74

Singles: 7-inch

GOLD MOUNTAIN............................ 3-4 84
T.K.. 3-5 74-79

LPs: 10/12-inch 33rpm

CAT... 8-10 76
GOLD MOUNTAIN............................ 5-8 84
TK... 8-10 74-77

McCRAE, George & Gwen

P&R/R&B '75

Singles: 7-inch

CAT... 3-5 76
Also see GEORGE & GWEN
Also see McCRAE, George
Also see McCRAE, Gwen

McCRAE, Gwen

R&B '70

Singles: 7-inch

ATLANTIC.. 3-4 81-83
BLACK JACK.................................... 3-4 84
CAT... 3-5 74-75

LPs: 10/12-inch 33rpm

ATLANTIC.................................. 5-8 81-83
CAT.. 8-10 74-76

Also see McCRAE, George & Gwen

McCRARYS

P&R/R&B/LP '78

Singles: 7-inch

CAPITOL.................................. 3-4 80-82
PORTRAIT................................. 3-5 78-79

LPs: 10/12-inch 33rpm

CAPITOL.................................. 5-8 80
PORTRAIT................................. 5-10 78

Members: Sam McCrary; Linda McCrary; Al McCrary; Charity McCrary.

McCREE, Earl-Jean: see EARL-JEAN

McCULLOUGH, Ian

LP '89

LPs: 10/12-inch 33rpm

SIRE.. 5-8 89

McCULLOUGH, Ullanda

R&B '81

Singles: 7-inch

ATLANTIC.................................. 3-5 81

McCURN, George

P&R '63

Singles: 7-inch

A&M.. 4-8 63-64
LIBERTY.................................... 4-8 62
REPRISE.................................... 4-6 66

LPs: 10/12-inch 33rpm

A&M.. 15-25 63

McDANIEL, Donna

P&R '77

Singles: 7-inch

MIDLAND INT'L.......................... 3-5 77

McDANIELS, Gene
(Eugene McDaniels)

P&R/R&B '61

Singles: 7-inch

COLUMBIA................................. 4-8 66-67
LIBERTY.................................... 5-15 60-65
MGM.. 3-5 73
ODE '70.................................... 3-5 75

LPs: 10/12-inch 33rpm

ATLANTIC.................................. 10-15 70-71
LIBERTY.................................... 15-25 60-67
ODE '70.................................... 8-12 75
SUNSET.................................... 10-15 66
U.A... 8-12 75

Also see MANN, Johnny, Singers

McDEVITT, Charles, Skiffle Group
(Featuring Nancy Wiskey)

P&R '57

Singles: 7-inch

CHIC....................................... 5-10 57
KAPP....................................... 5-8 58
ORIOLE.................................... 5-10 57

McDONALD, Country Joe

P&R '75

Singles: 7-inch

FANTASY.................................. 3-5 75-79
VANGUARD................................ 3-6 71-74

LPs: 10/12-inch 33rpm

FANTASY.................................. 5-10 75-79
MFSL....................................... 25-50 81
PICCADILLY............................... 10-15 78
VANGUARD................................ 8-12 69-76

Also see COUNTRY JOE & FISH

McDONALD, Kathi

LP '74

Singles: 7-inch

CAPITOL.................................. 3-6 74

LPs: 10/12-inch 33rpm

CAPITOL.................................. 10-20 74

Also see BALDRY, Long John, & Kathi McDonald
Also see BIG BROTHER & Holding Company

McDONALD, Michael

P&R/R&B/LP '82

Singles: 7-inch

MCA.. 3-4 86
W.B... 3-4 82-85

Picture Sleeves

MCA.. 3-4 86
W.B... 3-4 82-85

LPs: 10/12-inch 33rpm

MCA.. 5-8 86
MFSL....................................... 15-25 85
REPRISE.................................... 5-8 90
W.B... 5-8 82-85

Also see CROSS, Christopher
Also see DAL BELLO, Lisa
Also see DOOBIE BROTHERS
Also see HOLLAND, Amy
Also see LABELLE, Patti, & Michael McDonald
Also see MEMPHIS HORNS
Also see PACK, David
Also see STEELY DAN
Also see WINANS
Also see WOOD, Lauren

McDONALD, Michael, & James Ingram

P&R/R&B '83

Singles: 7-inch

QWEST..................................... 3-4 83

Also see INGRAM, James
Also see McDONALD, Michael

McDOWELL, Carrie

R&B '87

Singles: 7-inch

MOTOWN................................... 3-4 87

McDOWELL, Ronnie

P&R/C&W '77

Singles: 7-inch

EPIC.. 3-5 79-85
GRT... 3-5 77
MCA/CURB................................ 3-4 86
SCORPION (Except 0533)........... 3-6 77-79

SCORPION (0533 "Only the Lonely") 4-8 77

LPs: 10/12-inch 33rpm

DICK CLARK 8-10 79
EPIC 5-10 79-85
MCA/CURB 5-8 86
SCORPION 10-15 77-79
STRAWBERRY 8-10 70s

Session: Jordanaires; Conway Twitty.
Also see TWITTY, Conway

McDOWELL, Ronnie, & Jerry Lee Lewis

C&W '89

Singles: 7-inch

CURB 3-5 88

Also see LEWIS, Jerry Lee
Also see McDOWELL, Ronnie

McDUFF, Brother Jack

LP '63

Singles: 7-inch

CADET 3-6 68
BLUE NOTE 3-6 69
PRESTIGE 4-8 62

LPs: 10/12-inch 33rpm

BLUE NOTE 8-12 69
PRESTIGE (7000 series) 25-50 60-64
(Yellow label.)
PRESTIGE (7000 series) 15-25 64-65
(Blue label.)

Also see BENSON, George

McDUFF, Brother Jack, & Gene Ammons

LPs: 10/12-inch 33rpm

PRESTIGE 30-50 61
(Yellow label.)

Also see AMMONS, Gene

McDUFF, Brother Jack, & Willis Jackson

LP '66

LPs: 10/12-inch 33rpm

PRESTIGE 15-25 66

Also see JACKSON, Willis
Also see McDUFF, Brother Jack

McENTIRE, Reba

C&W '76

Singles: 7-inch

MCA 3-5 84-90
MERCURY 5-15 76-83

LPs: 10/12-inch 33rpm

MCA 5-8 84-90
MERCURY (1177 "Reba McEntire") 50-100 77
MERCURY (4047 "Unlimited") 15-25 82
MERCURY (5017 "Out of a Dream") 25-50 79
MERCURY (5029 "Feel the Fire") 20-30 80
MERCURY (6003 "Heart to Heart") 20-30 81
MERCURY (812781 "Behind the Scene") 10-15 83

Session: Chris Austin; Pake McEntire.

McEUEN, John

C&W '85

Singles: 7-inch

W.B. 3-4 85

McFADDEN, Bob

(With Dor)

P&R '59

Singles: 7-inch

BRUNSWICK 8-10 59
CORAL 8-10 60

Picture Sleeves

BRUNSWICK (55140 "The Mummy") 15-25 59

LPs: 10/12-inch 33rpm

BRUNSWICK (54056 "Songs Our Mummy Taught Us") 75-125 59
(Monaural.)
BRUNSWICK (7-54056 "Songs Our Mummy Taught Us") 100-150 59
(Stereo.)

Members: Bob McFadden; Rod McKuen.
Also see McKUEN, Rod

McFADDEN & WHITEHEAD

P&R/R&B/LP '79

Singles: 12-inch 33/45rpm

PHILADELPHIA INT'L 4-8 79
SUTRA 4-6

Singles: 7-inch

CAPITOL 3-4 82-83
PHILADELPHIA INT'L 3-5 79
SUTRA 3-4
TSOP 3-4 80

LPs: 10/12-inch 33rpm

CAPITOL 5-8 83
PHILADELPHIA INT'L 5-8 79
TSOP 5-8 80

Members: Gene McFadden; John Whitehead.
Also see WHITEHEAD, John

McFARLAND, Gary

LP '69

Singles: 7-inch

SKYE 4-8 69

LPs: 10/12-inch 33rpm

SKYE 10-15 69

McFERRIN, Bobby

LP '87

Singles: 7-inch

EMI 3-4 88-90

Picture Sleeves

EMI 3-4 88

LPs: 10/12-inch 33rpm

BLUE NOTE 5-10 87
EMI 5-8 88-90

McGEE, Parker

P&R '77

Singles: 7–inch

BIG TREE ... 3-5 77

LPs: 10/12–inch 33rpm

BIG TREE ... 5-10 76

McGHEE, Brownie

(With His Jook Block Busters; with His Sugar Men)

R&B '48

Singles: 78rpm

ALERT ... 10-15 46-47
DERBY ... 8-12 52
DISC ... 8-12 47
DOT ... 15-25 53
ENCORE ... 8-12 53
HARLEM ... 10-20 52
LONDON ... 8-12 51
PAR ... 8-12 52
RED ROBIN ... 8-12 52-53
SAVOY ... 8-12 50-57
SAVOY (5000 series) ... 10-15 44-48
SITTIN' in WITH ... 5-10 48

Singles: 7–inch

DOT (1184 "Cheatin' and Lying") ... 150-200 53
HARLEM (2323 "Christina") ... 30-40 52
HARLEM (2329 "Bluebird") ... 30-40 52
JACKSON (2304 "Mean Old Frisco") ... 100-125 52
(Colored vinyl.)
JAX (304 "I Feel So Good") ... 75-100 52
(Colored vinyl.)
JAX (307 "Meet You in the Morning") ... 75-100 52
(Colored vinyl.)
JAX (310 "Stranger's Blues") .. 75-100 52
(Colored vinyl.)
JAX (312 "I'm 10,000 Years Old") ... 75-100 52
(Colored vinyl.)
JAX (322 "New Bad Blood") ... 75-100 52
(Colored vinyl.)
RED ROBIN (111 "Don't Dog Your Woman") ... 100-200 53
SAVOY (800 series) ... 15-25 51-52
SAVOY (1100 thru 1500 series) .. 8-18 55-59

LPs: 10/12–inch 33rpm

FOLKWAYS (Except 20, 30 & 2000 series) ... 8-10
FOLKWAYS (20, 30 & 2000 series) ... 20-40 54-55
STORYVILLE ... 5-8
VANGUARD ... 8-12 60s

Session: Sonny Terry; Mickey Baker.
Also see DUPREE, Champion Jack

McGHEE, Brownie, & Sonny Terry

LP '73

Singles: 78rpm

SAVOY (5000 series) ... 10-15 44-48

Singles: 7–inch

PRESTIGE BLUESVILLE ... 4-8 60-62

LPs: 10/12–inch 33rpm

A&M ... 8-10 73
BLUESWAY ... 10-12 69-73
EVEREST ... 10-12 69
FANTASY (3000 series) ... 15-25 61-62
(Black vinyl.)
FANTASY (3000 series) ... 25-50 61-62
(Colored vinyl.)
FANTASY (8000 series) ... 15-20 62
(Black vinyl.)
FANTASY (8000 series) ... 25-40 62
(Colored vinyl.)
FANTASY (24000 series) ... 8-10 72-81
FOLKWAYS (2000 & 3000 series) ... 20-30 55-61
FOLKWAYS (31000 series) ... 8-10
FONTANA ... 10-15 69
MAINSTREAM (6000 series) ... 15-20 65
MAINSTREAM (300 series) ... 8-10 71
MUSE ... 5-8 81
OLYMPIC ... 8-10 73
PRESTIGE (1000 series) ... 25-30 60
PRESTIGE (7000 series) ... 8-10 69-70
PRESTIGE BLUESVILLE ... 20-25 60-62
PRESTIGE FOLKLORE ... 12-15
ROULETTE ... 25-35 59
SAVOY (1100 series) ... 5-8 84
SAVOY (12000 series) ... 8-10 73
SAVOY (14000 series) ... 25-30 58
SHARP (2003 "Down Home Blues") ... 25-50 59
SMASH ... 15-20 65
VERVE ... 20-25 61
VERVE/FOLKWAYS ... 15-20 65
WORLD PACIFIC ... 25-30 60

Also see BROONZY, Big Bill
Also see HOPKINS, Lightnin' / Brownie McGhee & Sonny Terry
Also see McGHEE, Brownie
Also see TERRY, Sonny
Also see WILLIS, Ralph

McGHEE, Stick

(With His Buddies; with Ramblers; Sticks McGhee)

P&R/R&B '49

Singles: 78rpm

ATLANTIC ... 15-25 49-52
DECCA (48104 "Drinkin' Wine Spo-Dee-O-Dee") ... 15-25 47
ESSEX ... 8-12 52
HARLEM (1018 "Blues Mixture") ... 15-25 47
KING ... 10-20 53-55

LONDON.................................... 25-50 51
SAVOY...................................... 8-12 55

Singles: 7-inch

ATLANTIC (955 "Wee Wee Hours")................................ 50-75 52
ATLANTIC (991 "New Found Love")................................ 40-60 52
ATLANTIC CLASSICS (873 "Drinkin' Wine Spo-Dee-O-Dee").......... 10-20 71
(Reissue series. Original Atlantic 45s of this number—from 1949—do not exist.)
GUSTO...................................... 3-4
HERALD.................................... 5-10 60
KING (4610 "Little Things We Used To Do")........................ 50-75 53
KING (4628 "Blues in My Heart").................................. 50-75 53
KING (4672 "Dealin' from the Bottom").............................. 50-75 53
KING (4700 "I'm Doin' All the Time").................................. 50-75 53
KING (4783 "Double Crossin' Liquor")................................ 50-100 55
KING (4800 "Get Your Mind Out of the Gutter")............................ 50-75 55
LONDON (978 "You Gotta Have Something on the Ball")........................ 100-200 51
SAVOY...................................... 15-25 55

McGHEE, Sticks / John Lee Hooker

LPs: 10/12-inch 33rpm

AUDIO LAB (1520 "Highway of Blues")................................ 100-125 59
Also see DUPREE, Champion Jack
Also see HOOKER, John Lee
Also see McGHEE, Stick

McGILL, Rollee

(Rollie McGill)

R&B '55

Singles: 78rpm

MERCURY................................ 8-12 55-56

Singles: 7-inch

LANDA.. 4-8 64
MERCURY.............................. 10-20 55-56

McGILPIN, Bob

P&R '78

Singles: 7-inch

BUTTERFLY................................ 3-5 77-78

LPs: 10/12-inch 33rpm

BUTTERFLY (Black vinyl)........... 5-10 78-79
BUTTERFLY (Colored vinyl)..... 12-18 78
CASABLANCA............................. 5-8 80

McGOVERN, Maureen

P&R/LP '73

Singles: 7-inch

CASABLANCA............................. 3-5 70s
EPIC... 3-5 78
MAIDEN VOYAGE........................ 3-5 70s
20TH FOX.................................. 3-5 73-75
W.B...3-5 79-80
WOODEN NICKEL........................3-5 73

LPs: 10/12-inch 33rpm

20TH FOX..................................8-12 73-75
W.B...5-10 79

McGRIFF, Jimmy

(Jimmy McGriff Trio)

P&R/R&B/LP '62

Singles: 7-inch

BLUE NOTE.................................3-5 71
CAPITOL......................................3-5 70-71
COLLECTABLES............................3-4 80s
GROOVE MERCHANT....................3-5 75
JELL (100 series)........................5-10 62
JELL (500 series)........................4-8 65
MILESTONE..................................3-4 83
SOLID STATE...............................4-6 66-70
SUE...4-8 62-64
U.A..3-5 71-78

LPs: 10/12-inch 33rpm

BLUE NOTE.................................8-12 70-71
COLLECTABLES............................6-8 88
51 WEST.......................................5-8 80s
GROOVE MERCHANT....................8-12 71-76
LRC...8-10 77-78
MILESTONE...................................5-8 81-83
SOLID STATE...............................10-15 66-70
SOUL SUGAR...............................10-12 70
SUE...20-30 62-65
U.A..8-12 71
VEEP...10-15 68
Also see HOLMES, Richard "Groove"
Also see PARKER, Little Junior, & Jimmy McGriff

McGUFFEY LANE

P&R '81

Singles: 7-inch

ATCO...3-4 81-82
ATLANTIC AMERICA....................3-4 84

LPs: 10/12-inch 33rpm

ATCO...5-10 82
Members: Robert McNelley; Steve Douglass.

McGUINN, Roger

LP '73

Singles: 7-inch

COLUMBIA....................................3-5 73-77

LPs: 10/12-inch 33rpm

ARISTA..5-8 90
COLUMBIA (Except "Airplay Anthology")..................................8-12 73-77
COLUMBIA ("Airplay Anthology")..................................20-30 77
(Promotional issue only.)
Members: Jim (Roger) McGuinn; Chris Hillman; Gene Clark.
Also see HILLMAN, Chris
Also see McGUINN, Roger
Also see MITCHELL, Chad, Trio

McGUINN, CLARK & HILLMAN
(Roger McGuinn & Chris Hillman featuring Gene Clark)

P&R/LP '79

Singles: 7-inch

CAPITOL.................................... 3-5 79

LPs: 10/12-inch 33rpm

CAPITOL.................................... 5-8 79-82

Members: Roger McGuinn; Gene Clark; Chris Hillman.

Also see BYRDS

Also see HILLMAN, Chris, & Roger McGuinn

McGUIRE, Barry
(With the Horizon Singers)

P&R/LP '65

Singles: 7-inch

ABC.................................... 3-5 70

DUNHILL.................................... 4-8 65-66

HORIZON.................................... 4-8 63

ODE '70.................................... 3-5 70

MCA.................................... 3-5

MOSAIC.................................... 4-8 61-62

MYRRH.................................... 3-5 73

ROULETTE.................................... 3-5

Picture Sleeves

DUNHILL.................................... 5-10 65

LPs: 10/12-inch 33rpm

BIRDWING.................................... 5-8 80

DUNHILL.................................... 20-30 65

HORIZON.................................... 15-25 63

MYRRH.................................... 5-8 73-75

ODE '70.................................... 8-10 70

SPARROW.................................... 5-8 79

SURREY.................................... 12-15 65

Also see MAMAS & PAPAS

Also see NEW CHRISTY MINSTRELS

McGUIRE, Barry, & Barry Kane

Singles: 7-inch

HORIZON.................................... 4-8 62

LPs: 10/12-inch 33rpm

HORIZON.................................... 15-25 62

SURREY.................................... 12-18 66

McGUIRE, Doug

C&W '80

Singles: 7-inch

MULTI-MEDIA.................................... 3-5 80

McGUIRE, Phyllis

P&R '64

Singles: 7-inch

REPRISE.................................... 4-6 64-65

ORPHEUM.................................... 4-6 68

LPs: 10/12-inch 33rpm

ABC-PAR.................................... 10-20 66

Also see McGUIRE SISTERS

McGUIRE SISTERS
(With Lawrence Welk's Orchestra)

P&R '54

Singles: 78rpm

CORAL.................................... 4-8 54-58

Singles: 7-inch

ABC-PAR.................................... 4-6 66

CORAL (Except 61000 & 98000 series).................................... 4-8 58-65

CORAL (61000 series).................................... 5-10 54-58

CORAL (98000 series).................................... 10-15 60
(Stereo.)

MCA.................................... 3-4 70s

REPRISE.................................... 4-6 63-65

Picture Sleeves

CORAL.................................... 5-15 56-61

EPs: 7-inch 33/45rpm

CORAL.................................... 10-15 55-60

LPs: 10/12-inch 33rpm

ABC-PAR.................................... 10-20 66

CORAL (6 "Best of the McGuire Sisters").................................... 15-25 65

CORAL (56123 "By Request")...25-50 55

CORAL (57000 series).................................... 15-25 56-65

MCA.................................... 5-8 78

VOCALION.................................... 10-20 60-67

Members: Phyllis McGuire; Dorothy McGuire; Christine McGuire.

Also see DESMOND, Johnny, Eileen Barton & McGuire Sisters

Also see McGUIRE, Phyllis

Also see WELK, Lawrence, & His Orchestra

McIAN, Peter

P&R '80

Singles: 7-inch

COLUMBIA/ARC.................................... 3-5 80

LPs: 10/12-inch 33rpm

COLUMBIA/ARC.................................... 5-8 80

McKEE, Maria

LP '89

Singles: 7-inch

GEFFEN.................................... 3-4 89

LPs: 10/12-inch 33rpm

GEFFEN.................................... 5-8 89

McKENDREE SPRING

LP '70

Singles: 7-inch

DECCA.................................... 3-6 69-72

MCA.................................... 3-5 73

PYE.................................... 3-5 76

LPs: 10/12-inch 33rpm

DECCA.................................... 10-15 69-72

MCA.................................... 8-10 73

PYE.................................... 8-10 75-76

McKENZIE, Bob & Doug

P&R/LP '82

Singles: 7-inch

MERCURY.................................... 3-5 82

Picture Sleeves

MERCURY 3-5 82

LPs: 10/12-inch 33rpm

MERCURY 5-10 81

McKENZIE, Scott

(McKenzie's Musicians)

P&R/LP '67

Singles: 7-inch

CAPITOL 4-8 65-67
EPIC 3-6 67-72
ODE (Except 103) 4-8 67-71
ODE (103 "San Francisco [Wear Some Flowers in Your Hair]") 8-10 67
ODE (103 "San Francisco [Be Sure to Wear Flowers in Your Hair]") 4-8 67
(Note slight change in title.)

LPs: 10/12-inch 33rpm

ODE (44000 series) 15-25 67
ODE (34000 series) 8-10 77
ODE (77000 series) 10-15 70

McKUEN, Rod

(With the Keytones; with Horizon Singers)

P&R '62

Singles: 7-inch

A&M 4-8 63
BUDDAH 3-5 73-74
DECCA 5-10 59
HORIZON 4-8 63
JUBILEE 4-8 62
KAPP 4-8 61
LIBERTY 8-12 56
RCA 4-8 66-67
SPIRAL 4-8 61-62
STANYAN 3-5 74
VISTA 3-5 71
W.B. 3-6 68-72

Picture Sleeves

VISTA 3-5 71
W.B. 3-5 71

LPs: 10/12-inch 33rpm

DECCA (4900 series) 10-15 68
DECCA (8800 series) 20-30 59
DECCA (75000 series) 10-12 69
CAPITOL 15-20 64
HARMONY 8-10 71
HI FI 20-30 58-59
EPIC (600 & 3800 series) 15-20 62
EPIC (26000 series) 10-12 68
EVEREST 10-12 68
HORIZON 15-25 63
IN 15-20 64
JUBILEE 20-25 62
KAPP (1200 & 3200 series) 15-25 61
KAPP (1500 & 3500 series) 10-20 67
LIBERTY (Except 3011) 10-15 67
LIBERTY (3011 "Songs for a Lazy Afternoon") 25-40 56
PICKWICK 5-10 70s
RCA 10-20 65-69
STANYAN 10-15 66-72
SUNSET 8-10 70
TRADITION 10-12 68
VISTA 8-10 71
W.B. 8-15 67-76

Also see McFADDEN, Bob
Also see SAN SEBASTIAN STRINGS

McLACHLAN, Sarah

LP '89

LPs: 10/12-inch 33rpm

ARISTA 5-8 89

McLAGAN, Ian

LP '80

Singles: 7-inch

MERCURY 3-5 79

LPs: 10/12-inch 33rpm

MERCURY 5-10 79

Also see FACES
Also see SMALL FACES

McLAIN, Tommy

P&R '66

Singles: 7-inch

COLLECTABLES 3-4 80s
JIN (Except 197) 4-8 66-69
JIN (197 "Sweet Dreams") 5-10 66
MSL 4-8 66
STARFLIGHT 3-5 79

McLAREN, Malcom

(With the World's Famous Supreme Band; with World's Famous Supreme Team)

D&D '83

Singles: 12-inch 33/45rpm

ISLAND 4-6 82-85

Singles: 7-inch

ISLAND 3-4 82-85

LPs: 10/12-inch 33rpm

ISLAND 5-8 83-85

Also see WORLD'S FAMOUS SUPREME TEAM

McLAUGHLIN, John

(Mahavishnu Orchestra & John McLaughlin; Mahavishnu John McLaughlin; with One Truth Band)

LP '72

LPs: 10/12-inch 33rpm

COLUMBIA 5-10 72-83
DOUGLAS 8-12 72
POLYDOR 8-15 69-72
W.B. 5-8 81

Also see SANTANA, Carlos, & Mahavishnu John McLaughlin

McLAUGHLIN, Pat

LP '88

LPs: 10/12-inch 33rpm

CAPITOL 5-8 88

McLAURIN, Bette
(With the Four Fellows; with Striders; Betty McLaurin)

P&R '52

Singles: 78rpm

CENTRAL 5-10 54
CORAL.................................... 5-10 53
DERBY (700 series)................... 5-10 50-52
DERBY (804 "My Heart Belongs to Only You").......................... 10-20 52
GLORY.................................... 10-15 55
JUBILEE.................................. 5-10 55

Singles: 7-inch

CAPITOL.................................. 5-10 59
CENTRAL 10-15 54
CORAL.................................... 10-15 53
DERBY (700 series)................. 10-20 50-52
DERBY (804 "My Heart Belongs to Only You").......................... 50-75 52
GLORY (233 "Grow Old Along with Me") 15-25 55
GLORY (237 "Just Come a Little Bit Closer") 15-25 55
GLORY (241 "I'm Past Sixteen") 15-25 55
JUBILEE.................................. 10-20 55
O GEE..................................... 5-10 59
PULSE 4-8 65

Also see FOUR FELLOWS

McLEAN, Don

P&R/LP '71

Singles: 7-inch

ARISTA 3-5 78
CAPITOL.................................. 3-4 87-88
EMI AMERICA 3-4 87
LIBERTY 3-5
MEDIARTS................................ 3-6 70
MILLENNIUM............................ 3-5 81-83
RCA... 3-4 83
U.A. 3-5 71-75

Picture Sleeves

U.A. 3-5 71-73

LPs: 10/12-inch 33rpm

ARISTA (4149 "Prime Time")...... 5-10 77
(Black vinyl.)
ARISTA (4149 "Prime Time").... 10-15 77
(Colored vinyl. Promotional issue only.)
CASABLANCA 8-10 79
LIBERTY 5-8 82-83
MEDIARTS (41-4 "Tapestry") 8-12 70
MILLENNIUM............................ 5-8 81
U.A. 10-12 71-74

Promotional LPs

RCA ("Special Radio Series") ... 10-15 81

McLEAN, Penny

P&R/R&B '76

Singles: 7-inch

ATCO 3-5 75-76

Also see SILVER CONVENTION

McLEAN, Phil

P&R '61

Singles: 7-inch

VERSATILE 4-8 61-62

McLOLLIE, Oscar
(With the Honey Jumpers; Oscar Lollie)

Singles: 78rpm

CLASS 5-10 57
MERCURY 5-10 51-56
MODERN..................................10-20 52-55
WING 10-15 56

Singles: 7-inch

CLASS 6-12 57-59
MERCURY (70000 series).........10-15 56
MODERN (902 "Honey Jump")..30-40 52
MODERN (915 "Be Cool, My Heart")...............................25-35 52
MODERN (920 "Falling in Love with You")......................25-35 54
MODERN (928 "Mama Don't Like")....................................20-30 54
MODERN (932 "Hot Banana")...20-30 54
MODERN (940 "Love Me Tonight") 20-30 54
MODERN (943 "Dig That Crazy Santa Claus")...........................20-30 54
MODERN (950 "Hey Lolly Lolly").....................................20-30 55
MODERN (955 "Eternal Love")..20-30 55
MODERN (970 "Convicted")......20-30 55
RENDEZVOUS 5-10 61
WING 10-15 56

LPs: 10/12-inch 33rpm

CROWN (5016 "Oscar McLollie & His Honey Jumpers") 150-200 56

McLOLLIE, Oscar, & Jeanette Baker

P&R '58

Singles: 7-inch

CLASS 5-10 58

McLOLLIE, Oscar, & Nancy Lamarr

Singles: 7-inch

SAHARA 4-8 63

Also see McLOLLIE, Oscar

McLYTE

LP '89

LPs: 10/12-inch 33rpm

FIRST PRIORITY.......................5-8 89

McMAHON, Gerard

P&R '83

Singles: 7-inch

FULL MOON 3-4 83

LPs: 10/12-inch 33rpm

FULL MOON 5-8 83

McMURTRY, James

LP '89

LPs: 10/12-inch 33rpm

COLUMBIA 5-8 89

McNALLY, Larry John

P&R '81

Singles: 7-inch

ARC.. 3-4 81

McNAMARA, Robin

P&R '70

Singles: 7-inch

STEED 3-5 69-71

LPs: 10/12-inch 33rpm

STEED 10-15 70

McNEELY, Big Jay

(With His Blue Jays; with Little Sonny Warner)

R&B '49

Singles: 78rpm

ALADDIN.................................. 10-20 49
BAYOU..................................... 15-25 53
FEDERAL.................................. 10-15 52-54
EXCLUSIVE............................. 10-20 46
IMPERIAL 10-20 51-52
SAVOY..................................... 10-15 48-49
VEE JAY 10-15 55

Singles: 7-inch

BAYOU (014 "Hometown
Jamboree")............................ 40-60 53
BAYOU (018 "Catastrophe")..... 40-60 53
FEDERAL (12102 "The Goof").. 20-30 52
FEDERAL (12111
"Earthquake")........................ 20-30 52
FEDERAL (12141 "Nervous, Man
Nervous") 20-30 53
FEDERAL (12151 "3-D")........... 20-30 53
FEDERAL (12168 "Mule Walk") 20-30 54
FEDERAL (12179 "Hot
Cinders") 20-30 54
FEDERAL (12186 "Let's Work") 20-30 54
FEDERAL (12191
"Beachcomber").................... 20-30 54
IMPERIAL (5219 "Deacon's
Express")................................ 25-35 53
SWINGIN'.................................... 5-10 59-61
VEE JAY (142 "Big Jay's Hop"). 25-35 55
W.B. 4-8 63

EPs: 7-inch 33/45rpm

FEDERAL (246 "Go! Go! Go!
with Big Jay McNeely") 100-200 53
FEDERAL (301 Big Jay McNeely,
Vol. 2") 100-150 54
FEDERAL (332 Wild Man of
the Saxophone") 100-150 54
FEDERAL (373 Just Crazy")... 75-100 55

LPs: 10/12-inch 33rpm

COLLECTABLES 5-8 88
FEDERAL (96 "Big Jay
McNeely").......................... 600-800 54
(10-inch LP.)
FEDERAL (530 "Big Jay
in 3-D") 250-350 57
KING (650 "Big Jay in 3-D")...... 50-75 59
SAVOY (15045 "Rhythm & Blues
Concert")............................250-350 55
(10-inch LP.)
W.B. (W-1523 "Big Jay
McNeely") 25-35 63
(Monaural.)
W.B. (WS-1523 "Big Jay
McNeely") 30-40 63
(Stereo.)
Also see OTIS, Johnny

McNEELY, Big Jay / Paul Williams

Singles: 78rpm

SAVOY......................................10-15 49-55

Singles: 7-inch

SAVOY (1100 series)................10-20 55
Also see McNEELY, Big Jay
Also see WILLIAMS, Paul

McNEIR, Ronnie

R&B '75

Singles: 7-inch

CAPITOL.......................................3-4 84
DETO (2878 "Sitting in My
Class") 75-125
PRODIGAL 3-5 75

LPs: 10/12-inch 33rpm

CAPITOL.......................................5-8 84

McNICHOL, Kristy & Jimmy

P&R/LP '78

Singles: 7-inch

RCA 3-5 78

Picture Sleeves

RCA 3-5 78

LPs: 10/12-inch 33rpm

RCA 5-10 78

M'COOL, Shamus

P&R '81

Singles: 7-inch

PERSPECTIVE............................3-4 81

McPHATTER, Clyde

P&R/R&B '56

Singles: 78rpm

ATLANTIC...............................10-15 56-57

Singles: 7-inch

AMY 5-15 65-67
ATLANTIC (1000 series) 10-20 56-58
ATLANTIC (2000 series) 8-15 58-60
DECCA 4-6 70
DERAM...4-8 68-69
MGM (12000 series) 8-12 59-60
(Monaural.)
MGM (50134 "Let's Try Again") .20-30 60
(Stereo.)
MERCURY 5-10 60-65

Picture Sleeves

MGM 10-20 60
MERCURY 8-15 60-65

EPs: 7-inch 33/45rpm

ATLANTIC (584 "Clyde McPhatter") 50-75 58
ATLANTIC (605 "Rock with Clyde McPhatter") 50-75 58
ATLANTIC (618 "Clyde McPhatter") 50-75 59
MERCURY ("Golden Blues Hits") 10-15 62
(Has paper sleeve. Number not known. Promotional issue only.)

LPs: 10/12-inch 33rpm

ALLEGIANCE 5-8 80s
ATLANTIC (8024 "Love Ballads") 100-150 59
(Black label.)
ATLANTIC (8024 "Love Ballads") 25-50 59
(Red label.)
ATLANTIC (8031 "Clyde") 50-100 59
ATLANTIC (8077 "Best of Clyde McPhatter") 25-35 63
DECCA 15-25 70
MGM (E-3775 "Let's Start Over Again") 30-40 59
(Monaural.)
MGM (SE-3775 "Let's Start Over Again") 40-50 59
(Stereo.)
MGM (E-3866 "Greatest Hits") .. 30-40 60
(Monaural.)
MGM (SE-3866 "Greatest Hits") 40-50 60
(Stereo.)
MERCURY 20-35 60-64
WING 20-30 62

Session: King Curtis.
Also see BROWN, Ruth, & Clyde McPhatter
Also see DOMINOES
Also see DRIFTERS
Also see KING CURTIS
Also see LITTLE ESTHER & Clyde McPhatter

McPHATTER, Clyde / Little Richard / Jerry Butler

LPs: 10/12-inch 33rpm

PICKWICK (3233 "Rhythm & Blues and Greens") 15-20 70s

Also see BUTLER, Jerry
Also see LITTLE RICHARD
Also see McPHATTER, Clyde

McPHERSON, Wyatt (Earp)

P&R/R&B '61

Singles: 7-inch

SAVOY 4-8 61

McPHERSON, Wyatt "Earp," & Paul Williams

Singles: 7-inch

BATTLE 4-8 63

Also see McPHERSON, Wyatt "Earp"
Also see WILLIAMS, Paul

McPHERSON, Wyley

C&W '82

Singles: 7-inch

I.E. 3-4 82

McRAE, Carmen

P&R '56

Singles: 78rpm

DECCA 3-6 55-57
VENUS 4-8 54

Singles: 7-inch

COLUMBIA 4-6 62
DECCA 5-10 55-57
VENUS 5-10 54

Picture Sleeves

COLUMBIA 4-8 62

EPs: 7-inch 33/45rpm

DECCA 5-10 55

LPs: 10/12-inch 33rpm

BETHLEHEM (1023 "Carmen McRae") 75-125 54
(10-inch LP.)
COLUMBIA 15-25 61-65
DECCA (8100 thru 8800 series) 40-60 55-58
(Black and silver label.)
DECCA (8100 thru 8800 series) 15-25 64
(Black label with horizonal rainbow stripe.)
FOCUS 15-25 65
KAPP 20-40 58-59
MAINSTREAM 10-20 65-67
TIME 15-25 63

Also see DAVIS, Sammy, Jr., & Carmen McRae
Also see SIMONE, Nina, Chris Connor & Carmen McRae

McSHANN, Jay

(With His Orchestra; Combo; Trio; Quartet; Sextet; Kansas City Stompers; Jazz Men)

P&R '41

Singles: 78rpm

ALADDIN 5-10 50
CAPITOL 10-15 44-45
DECCA 10-15 41-43
DOWN BEAT 5-10 48-49
MERCURY 5-10 45-46
MODERN 5-10 50
PHILO/ALADDIN 10-15 45
PREMIER 8-12 45
SWING TIME 5-10 48-50
VEE JAY 4-8 55-56

Singles: 7-inch

VEE JAY 5-15 55-56

EPs: 7-inch 33/45rpm

DECCA (742 "Kansas City Memories") 50-100 54

LPs: 10/12-inch 33rpm

CAPITOL 12-20 67
DECCA (5503 "Kansas City Memories") 250-350 54
(10-inch LP. With Charlie Parker, Al Hibbler, Walter Brown, & Paul Paul Quinichette.)

DECCA (9000 series)................ 10-15 68
Also see HIBBLER, Al
Also see WITHERSPOON, Jimmy

McSHANN, Jay, With Johnny Moore's Three Blazers

Singles: 78rpm

MODERN 8-12 50
Also see MOORE, Johnny

McSHANN, Jay, & Priscilla Bowman

Singles: 78rpm

VEE JAY 5-10 55

Singles: 7-inch

VEE JAY 10-15 55
Also see BOWMAN, Priscilla
Also see McSHANN, Jay

McSHY D

LP '87

LPs: 10/12-inch 33rpm

LUKE SKYWALKER..................... 5-8 87

McVEA, Jack
(With His All-Stars)

P&R/R&B '47

Singles: 78rpm

APOLLO..................................... 8-12 45
BLACK & WHITE 8-12 45-47
EXCLUSIVE 8-12 47
COMBO...................................... 5-10 56
MELODISC 10-15 45

Singles: 7-inch

COMBO (Except 55) 10-20 56
COMBO (55 "Let's Ride, Ride, Ride") 15-25 55
TAG.. 10-15 56
Also see BROWN, Clarence "Gatemouth"

McVIE, Christine

LP '76

Singles: 7-inch

W.B. 3-4 84

Picture Sleeves

W.B. 3-4 84

LPs: 10/12-inch 33rpm

SIRE... 8-10 76
W.B. 5-8 84
Also see BURNETTE, Billy, & Christine McVie
Also see FLEETWOOD MAC
Also see NEWMAN, Randy

McWILLIAMS, Paulette

R&B '77

Singles: 7-inch

FANTASY................................... 3-5 77
Also see AMERICAN BREED
Also see RUFUS

MEAD, Sister Janet

P&R '74

Singles: 7-inch

A&M 3-5 74

MEADER, Vaughn

LP '62

LPs: 10/12-inch 33rpm

CADENCE 10-20 62-63
KAMA-SUTRA 8-15 60s

MEADOWS BROTHERS

R&B '77

Singles: 7-inch

KAYVETTE 3-4 87

MEAGAN

D&D '84

Singles: 7-inch

NEXT PLATINUM 4-6 84

MEAN MACHINE

R&B '81

Singles: 7-inch

SUGAR HILL.................................3-4 81

MEAT LOAF
(Marvin Lee Aday; with Ellen Foley)

LP '77

Singles: 12-inch 33/45rpm

EPIC (477 "Meat Loaf")..................5-8 77
(Promotional issue only.)

Singles: 7-inch

EPIC...3-5 77-83
RSO 3-5 74

LPs: 10/12-inch 33rpm

CLEVELAND INT'L 5-8 81-83
EPIC (30000 series, except 34974)....................................5-10 77-80
EPIC (34974 "Bat Out of Hell") 5-10 77
EPIC (34974 "Bat Out of Hell") ..15-20 77
(Picture disc. With bats on front cover.)
EPIC (34974 "Bat Out of Hell") ..25-30 77
(Picture disc. Without bats on front cover. Promotional issue only.)
EPIC (40000 series).................12-15 80
(Half-speed mastered.)
Also see FOLEY, Ellen
Also see STONEY & Meat Loaf

MECO
(Meco Monardo)

P&R/R&B/LP '77

Singles: 12-inch 33/45rpm

ARISTA 4-6 83

Singles: 7-inch

ARISTA 3-4 82-83
MILLENNIUM.................................3-5 77-78
RSO 3-5 80

LPs: 10/12-inch 33rpm

ARISTA 5-8 82-84
CASABLANCA............................5-10 79-80
MILLENNIUM..............................5-10 77-78
RSO 5-8 80
Also see STAR WARS INTERGALACTIC DROID CHOIR & CHORALE

MEDEIROS, Glenn

P&R/LP '87

Singles: 7-inch

AMHERST.................................3-4 87-88

Picture Sleeves

AMHERST.................................3-4 87-88

LPs: 10/12-inch 33rpm

AMHERST.................................5-8 87
MCA...5-8 90

Also see PARKER, Ray, Jr.

MEDEIROS, Glenn, & Bobby Brown

Singles: 7-inch

MCA...3-4 90

Picture Sleeves

MCA...3-4 90

Also see BROWN, Bobby

MEDEIROS, Glenn, & Stylistics

P&R '90

Singles: 7-inch

MCA...3-4 90

Also see MEDEIROS, Glenn
Also see STYLISTICS

MEDLEY, Bill

P&R/R&B/LP '68

Singles: 7-inch

A&M...3-5 71-73
CURB.......................................3-5 89
LIBERTY...................................3-5 81
MGM..4-8 68
PARAMOUNT.............................3-5 71
PLANET....................................3-4 82-83
RCA...3-4 83-85
REPRISE..................................4-8 65
U.A..3-5 78-80
VERVE.....................................4-8 67

LPs: 10/12-inch 33rpm

A&M...8-12 71-73
LIBERTY...................................5-10 81
MCA/CURB...............................5-10 88
MGM..10-20 68-70
PLANET....................................8-10 82
RCA...5-8 83-85
U.A..8-10 78-80

Also see KNIGHT, Gladys, & Bill Medley
Also see RIGHTEOUS BROTHERS
Also see SONNY & CHER / Bill Medley / Lettermen / Blendells

MEDLEY, Bill, & Jennifer Warnes

P&R '87

Singles: 7-inch

RCA...3-4 87

Picture Sleeves

RCA...3-4 87

Also see MEDLEY, Bill
Also see WARNES, Jennifer

MEDLIN, Joe

P&R '59

Singles: 7-inch

BRUNSWICK..............................4-8 61
MERCURY.................................4-8 59-60

MEGADETH

LP '86

EPs: 7-inch 33/45rpm

MEGAFORCE.............................5-10 89

LPs: 10/12-inch 33rpm

CAPITOL...................................5-8 86-90

Members: Dave Mustaine; Dave Ellefson; Gar Samuelson.

MEGATONS

P&R '62

Singles: 7-inch

CHECKER..................................5-10 62
DODGE......................................10-15 62
FOREST.....................................4-8 63
JELL..4-8 62

Member: Billy Lee Riley.
Also see RILEY, Billy Lee

MEGATRONS

P&R '59

Singles: 7-inch

ACOUSTICON.............................5-10 59
AUDICON...................................5-10 59-61

MEISNER, Randy

P&R/LP '80

Singles: 7-inch

ASYLUM.....................................3-5 78
EPIC..3-5 80-82

LPs: 10/12-inch 33rpm

ASYLUM.....................................8-10 78
EPIC..5-10 80-82

Also see EAGLES
Also see NELSON, Rick
Also see POCO

MEL & KIM

P&R/R&B '87

Singles: 7-inch

ATLANTIC...................................3-4 87

Picture Sleeves

ATLANTIC...................................3-4 87

Members: Mel Appleby; Kim Appleby.

MEL & TIM

P&R/R&B '69

Singles: 7-inch

BAMBOO....................................4-6 69-70
COLLECTABLES........................3-4 80s
ERIC..3-4 70s
STAX..3-5 72-74

LPs: 10/12-inch 33rpm

BAMBOO....................................10-15 70
STAX..8-12 72-74

Members: Mel Harden; Tim McPherson.

MELACHRINO, George, & His Orchestra

LP '55

Singles: 78rpm

RCA...3-5 50-57

Singles: 7-inch

RCA.......... 4-8 50-59

EPs: 7-inch 33/45rpm

RCA.......... 5-10 50-59

LPs: 10/12-inch 33rpm

RCA.......... 10-20 50-61

MELANIE

(With the Edwin Hawkins Singers)

LP '69

Singles: 7-inch

ABC/MCA.......... 3-5 75
AMHERST.......... 3-4 85
ATLANTIC.......... 3-5 77
BLANCHE.......... 3-4 82
BUDDAH.......... 3-8 69-73
CASABLANCA.......... 3-5 74
COLUMBIA (44349 "God's Only Daughter").......... 10-15 67
COLUMBIA (44524 "Garden in the City").......... 8-12 68
ERIC.......... 3-4 78
FLASHBACK.......... 3-4 70s
GOLDIES.......... 3-4 70s
GORDIAN.......... 5-10 85
MIDSONG INT'L.......... 3-5 78-79
NEIGHBORHOOD.......... 3-5 71-75
PORTRAIT.......... 3-4 81
RADIO ACTIVE GOLD.......... 3-4 80s
STORK.......... 5-10 70
(Promotional issue only.)
TOMATO.......... 3-5 78-79
WHAT'S IT ALL ABOUT.......... 4-6 70s
(Promotional issue only.)
WORLD UNITED.......... 3-5 78

Picture Sleeves

BUDDAH.......... 3-4 70-72
NEIGHBORHOOD.......... 3-4 72-73

EPs: 7-inch 33/45rpm

BUDDAH.......... 5-8 70
(Jukebox issue.)

LPs: 10/12-inch 33rpm

ABC.......... 8-10 75
ACCORD.......... 5-8 81-82
AMHERST.......... 8-10 85
ARISTA.......... 5-10 75-77
ATLANTIC.......... 8-10 76
BELL.......... 8-10 71
BLANCHE.......... 5-8 82
BUDDAH.......... 10-15 69-77
51 WEST.......... 5-8 79
KOALA.......... 5-10 79
MCA/MIDSONG.......... 5-10 77-78
NEIGHBORHOOD.......... 8-10 71-75
PAIR.......... 5-10 88
PICKWICK.......... 8-10 71
TELLENHOUSE.......... 15-25 78
TOMATO.......... 5-10 79

Also see HAWKINS, Edwin, Singers

MELBA & KASHIF: see MOORE, Melba, & Kashif

MELLAA

R&B '83

Singles: 7-inch

LARC.......... 3-4 83

MELLE MEL & Duke Bootee

R&B '82

Singles: 12-inch 33/45rpm

SUGAR HILL.......... 4-6 82

Also see BOOTEE, Duke
Also see GRANDMASTER FLASH & Furious Five

MELLENCAMP, John Cougar

(John Cougar; John Mellencamp)

P&R/LP '79

Singles: 7-inch

MERCURY.......... 3-4 87-90
RIVA (Except 211).......... 3-5 79-85
RIVA (211 "Hand to Hold On To").. 3-4 82
RIVA (211 "Hand to Hold On To").......... 10-15 82
(Picture disc.)

Picture Sleeves

MERCURY.......... 3-4 87-90
RIVA.......... 4-8 79-86

EPs: 7-inch 33/45rpm

GULCHER ("U.S. Male").......... 50-75 75

LPs: 10/12-inch 33rpm

MCA (2225 "Chestnut Street Incident").......... 15-20 77
MAIN MAN ("Chestnut Street Incident").......... 30-40 76
MAIN MAN (601 "Kid Inside")...... 5-10 83
MAIN MAN (4001 "Kid Inside").. 40-60 83
(Picture disc.)
MERCURY (Except 349).......... 5-8 87-90
MERCURY (349 "Let It All Hang").......... 25-35 87
(Interview LP. Promotional issue only.)
RIVA.......... 5-10 79-85

Members: John Cougar Mellencamp; Larry Crane; David Parman; Terrence Sala; Wayne Hall; Tom Wince; Michael Wanchic; Doc Rosser; Ken Aronoff; George Perry; Toby Myers; John Cascalle.

MELLODEERS

P&R '60

Singles: 7-inch

SHELLEY (127 "The Letter")..... 10-15 61
SHELLEY (161 "Born to Be Mine").......... 15-25 62
STUDIO (9908 "Rudolph the Red Nosed Reindeer").......... 10-20 60

Picture Sleeves

STUDIO (9908 "Rudolph the Red Nosed Reindeer").......... 20-30 60
STUDIO (9909 "Happy Teenage Times").......... 10-20 60

MELLO-KINGS

(Mellokings; Mellotones)

P&R '57

Singles: 78rpm

HERALD (502 "Tonite Tonite").. 15-25 57
(Credits "The Mellotones".)
HERALD (502 "Tonite Tonite").... 5-10 57
(Credits "The Mello-Kings.")

Singles: 7-inch

COLLECTABLES 3-4 80s
FLASHBACK 3-5 65
HERALD (502 "Tonite Tonite") 300-500 57
(Credits "The Mellotones.")
HERALD (502 "Tonite Tonite").. 15-25 57
(Credits "The Mello-Kings." Has logo in script print inside the flag.)
HERALD (502 "Tonite Tonite").... 8-12
(Credits "The Mello-Kings." Has logo in block print inside the flag.)
HERALD (507 thru 567)........... 10-20 57-61
LESCAY 10-15 62

EPs: 7-inch 33/45rpm

HERALD (451 "The Fabulous Mello-Kings") 200-250 60

LPs: 10/12-inch 33rpm

COLLECTABLES 6-8 84
HERALD (1013 "Tonight Tonight") 200-300 60
RELIC 5-10

Members: Larry Esposita; Bob Scholl; Jerry Scholl; Eddie Quinn; Neil Areana.

MELLO-MOODS

(Mellow Moods; Mello Moods; Mellomoods; with Teacho Wiltshire & Band; with Schubert Swanson Trio)

R&B '52

Singles: 78rpm

PRESTIGE (799 "Call on Me") 75-150 53
PRESTIGE (856 "I'm Lost")..... 75-150 53
ROBIN (104 "I Couldn't Sleep a Wink Last Night") 200-300 52
ROBIN (105 "Where Are You") 150-200 52

Singles: 7-inch

HAMILTON (143 "I'm Lost") 8-10
PRESTIGE (799 "Call On Me") 500-600 53
PRESTIGE (856 "I'm Lost")... 500-600 53
ROBIN (104 "I Couldn't Sleep a Wink Last Night") 600-800 52
ROBIN (105 "Where Are You") 600-800 52

Members: Ray "Buddy" Wooten; Bobby Williams; Monte Owens; Bobby Baylor; Jimmy Bethea.
Also see SOLITAIRES

MELLOTONES: see MELLO-KINGS

MELLO-TONES

P&R '57

Singles: 78rpm

FASCINATION (1001 "Rosie Lee") 25-40 57
GEE (1037 "Rosie Lee") 10-15 57

Singles: 7-inch

FASCINATION (1001 "Rosie Lee") 100-125 57
GEE (1037 "Rosie Lee") 20-30 57

MELODY MAKERS

(Ziggy Marley & Melody Makers)

P&R/LP '88

Singles: 12-inch 33/45rpm

EMI AMERICA 4-6 84-85

Singles: 7-inch

EMI AMERICA 3-4 84-85
VIRGIN..3-4 88

Picture Sleeves

VIRGIN..3-4 88

LPs: 10/12-inch 33rpm

EMI AMERICA 5-8 84-85
VIRGIN..5-8 88-91

Members: David "Ziggy" Marley; Steve Marley; Cedella Marley; Sharon Marley. All are the children of Bob Marley.
Also see MARLEY, Bob

MELVIN, Harold

(With the Bluenotes)

R&B '65

Singles: 12-inch 33/45rpm

PHILADELPHIA INT'L...................4-8 80
SOURCE.......................................4-8 79-80

Singles: 7-inch

ABC...3-5 77-78
ARCTIC..5-8 67
LANDA...5-10 64-65
MCA...3-5 81
PHILADELPHIA INT'L...................3-5 72-79
PHILLY WORLD 3-4 84-85
SOURCE..3-5 79-80

Picture Sleeves

PHILADELPHIA INT'L...................3-5 72-75

LPs: 10/12-inch 33rpm

ABC...8-10 77
MCA...5-8 81
PHILADELPHIA INT'L.................8-12 72-76
PHILLY WORLD 5-8 84-85
SOURCE......................................5-10 80

Also see BLUENOTES
Also see PAIGE, Sharon
Also see PENDERGRASS, Teddy

MELVINS: see NIRVANA / The Melvins

MEMPHIS HORNS

R&B '76

Singles: 7-inch

RCA 3-5 76-78

LPs: 10/12-inch 33rpm

RCA 5-10 77-78

Members: Wayne Jackson; Andrew Love; Jimmy Brown; Andy Love

Also see CRAY, Robert, Band, with the Memphis Horns

Also see McDONALD, Michael

Also see MOORE, Jackie

Also see POINTER SISTERS

MEMPHIS SLIM

(With His House Rockers; Peter Chatman)

R&B '48

Singles: 78rpm

BLUEBIRD 15-30 40-41

CHESS 10-20 52

FEDERAL 10-20 49-50

HY-TONE 10-20 46

MASTER 10-20 48-49

KING 10-20 49

MELODY LANE 10-20 46

MIRACLE 10-20 47-49

OLD SWINGMASTER 10-20 48

PEACOCK 10-20 49

PREMIUM 10-20 50-52

Singles: 7-inch

JOSIE 4-8 67

KING (6300 series) 3-5 70

MERCURY 20-30 51-52

MONEY 20-30 54

PEACOCK (1600 series) 20-30 52

STRAND 10-20 61

UNITED (Black vinyl) 20-40 52-54

UNITED (156 "Comeback") 50-100 53
(Colored vinyl.)

UNITED (166 "Call Before You Go Home") 50-100 53
(Colored vinyl.)

UNITED (176 "Sassy Mae") 50-100 54
(Colored vinyl.)

VEE JAY 10-15 58-60

LPs: 10/12-inch 33rpm

BATTLE (6118 "Alone with My Friends") 20-30 63

BARNABY 8-12 72

BLACK LION 8-10 74

BUDDAH 10-15 69

CANDID (8024 "Memphis Slim U.S.A.") 35-45 62
(Monaural.)

CANDID (9024 "Memphis Slim U.S.A.") 40-50 62
(Stereo.)

CHESS (1455 "Memphis Slim") 50-75 61

CHESS (1510 "Real Folk Blues") 20-35 66

EVEREST 10-15 68-74

FANTASY 10-12 72

FOLKWAYS 8-10 74

GNP 8-12 74

JAZZMAN 5-8 82

JEWEL 8-12 71

KING (885 "Memphis Slim") 25-35 64

KING (1082 "Messin' Around with the Blues") 10-15 70

MUSE 5-10 81

PEARL 5-10 78

PRESTIGE BLUESVILLE 20-30 61-64

SCEPTER (535 "Self-Portrait") .. 15-25 66

SPINORAMA 8-12 60s

STORYVILLE 5-8 84

STRAND (1046 "World's Foremost Blues Singer") 25-40 61

TRIP 8-10 70s

U.A. (3137 "Broken Soul Blues") 25-35 61
(Monaural.)

U.A. (6137 "Broken Soul Blues") 30-40 61
(Stereo.)

VEE JAY (1012 "At the Gate of Horn") 60-80 59

W.B. 10-15 71-72

Also see DIXON, Willie, & Memphis Slim

Also see HOOKER, John Lee

Also see HUNTER, Ivory Joe / Memphis Slim

Also see WILLIAMSON, Sonny Boy

MEMPHIS SLIM & Lowell Fulsom

LPs: 10/12-inch 33rpm

INNER CITY 5-8

Also see FULSON, Lowell

MEMPHIS SLIM & Curtis Jones

LPs: 10/12-inch 33rpm

CANDID (8023 "Tribute to Big Bill Broonzy") 35-45 61
(Monaural.)

CANDID (9023 "Tribute to Big Bill Broonzy") 40-50 62
(Stereo.)

MEMPHIS SLIM & Matt Murphy

LPs: 10/12-inch 33rpm

ANTONE'S 5-10 87

MEMPHIS SLIM & Roosevelt Sykes

LPs: 10/12-inch 33rpm

OLYMPIC 8-12 75

Also see SYKES, Roosevelt

MEMPHIS SLIM & VAGABONDS / Reverend Bounce

Singles: 78rpm

PREMIUM 10-15 50

Also see MEMPHIS SLIM

MEN at WORK

P&R/LP '82

Singles: 12-inch 33/45rpm

COLUMBIA 4-6 82-83

Singles: 7-inch

COLUMBIA 3-4 82-85

Picture Sleeves

COLUMBIA (Except 1633) 3-4 83-85

COLUMBIA (1633 "Overkill") 5-10 83
(Promotional issue only.)

LPs: 10/12–inch 33rpm

COLUMBIA (1650 "Cargo World Premier Weekend") ... 10-15 83
(Promotional issue only.)
COLUMBIA (ARC-37978 "Business As Usual") ... 5-10 82
COLUMBIA (PAL-37978 "Business As Usual") ... 30-40 83
(Picture disc.)
COLUMBIA (38167 "Business As Usual") ... 5-8 82
COLUMBIA (38660 "Cargo") ... 5-8 83
COLUMBIA (40078 "Two Hearts") 5-8 85
COLUMBIA (47978 "Business As Usual") ... 10-15 85
(Half-speed mastered.)
COLUMBIA (48660 "Cargo") ... 10-15 85

Members: Colin Hay; Ron Strykert; Jerry Speiser; John Rees; Greg Ham.
Also see HAY, Colin James

MEN WITHOUT HATS

P&R/D&D/LP '83

Singles: 12–inch 33/45rpm

BACKSTREET ... 4-6 83
MCA ... 4-6 83-84

Singles: 7–inch

BACKSTREET ... 3-4 83
MCA ... 3-4 83-84
MERCURY ... 3-4 87

Picture Sleeves

BACKSTREET ... 3-4 83
MCA ... 3-4 83
MERCURY ... 3-4 87

LPs: 10/12–inch 33rpm

BACKSTREET ... 5-8 83
MCA ... 5-8 84
MERCURY ... 5-8 87

MENAGE

D&D '83

Singles: 12–inch 33/45rpm

PROFILE ... 4-6 83-85

Singles: 7–inch

PROFILE ... 3-4 83-85

LPs: 10/12–inch 33rpm

PROFILE ... 5-8 83

MENDES, Sergio

(With Brasil '66; Brasil '77; Trio)

P&R/LP '66

Singles: 12–inch 33/45rpm

A&M ... 4-6 82

Singles: 7–inch

A&M (807 thru 1257) ... 3-6 66-71
A&M (1279 thru 2700 series) ... 3-5 71-85
ATLANTIC ... 4-6 67-68
BELL ... 3-5 73
ELEKTRA ... 3-5 75-80

Picture Sleeves

A&M ... 3-6 68-69

LPs: 10/12–inch 33rpm

A&M (Except 4100 series) ... 5-12 69-84
A&M (4100 series) ... 10-15 66-69
ATLANTIC ... 15-25 65-68
BELL ... 8-10 73-74
CAPITOL (T-2294 "In a Brazilian Bag") ... 40-50 65
(Monaural.)
CAPITOL (ST-2294 "In a Brazilian Bag") ... 50-60 65
(Stereo.)
ELEKTRA ... 8-10 75-79
EVEREST ... 8-10 74
MFSL ... 15-25 84
PHILIPS ... 10-12 68
TOWER (T-5052 "In a Brazilian Bag") ... 30-40 65
(Monaural.)
TOWER (ST-5052 "In a Brazilian Bag") ... 40-50 65
(Stereo.)

Also see ADDERLEY, Julian "Cannonball," & Sergio Mendes
Also see HALL, Lani

MENUDO

R&B/LP '84

Singles: 7–inch

RCA ... 3-4 84-85

LPs: 10/12–inch 33rpm

RCA ... 5-8 84-85

Also see KING DREAM CHORUS & Holiday Crew

MERC & MONK

R&B '85

Singles: 7–inch

MANHATTAN ... 3-5 85

Members: Eric Mercury; Thelonious Monk.
Also see MERCURY, Eric
Also see MONK, Thelonious

MERCER, Johnny

P&R '38

Singles: 78rpm

CAPITOL ... 4-8 42-52
DECCA ... 4-8 38

Singles: 7–inch

CAPITOL ... 5-10 50-52

EPs: 7–inch 33/45rpm

CAPITOL (210 "Music of Kern") . 10-20 50

LPs: 10/12–inch 33rpm

CAPITOL (210 "Music of Kern") . 40-50 50
(10–inch LP.)
CAPITOL (214 "Mercer Sings") . 40-50 50
(10–inch LP.)
CAPITOL (907 "Ac-Cent-Tchu-Ate the Positive") ... 25-40 57
JUPITER (1001 "Just for Fun") .. 25-45 56

Also see CROSBY, Bing, & Johnny Mercer

MERCURY, Eric

LPs: 10/12–inch 33rpm

AVCO EMBASSY ... 10-15 69

CAPITOL 5-10 81
ENTERPRISE 8-12 72-73
SACK (1 "Lonely Girl") 300-500
Also see FLACK, Roberta, & Eric Mercury
Also see MERC & MONK

MERCURY, Freddie

P&R/D&D '84

Singles: 12-inch 33/45rpm

COLUMBIA 4-6 84

Singles: 7-inch

COLUMBIA 3-5 84-85
EMI (6151 "Great Pretender") 8-12 87
(Jukebox shaped disc.)

Picture Sleeves

COLUMBIA 3-5 84-85

LPs: 10/12-inch 33rpm

COLUMBIA 5-8 85
Also see QUEEN

MERCURY, Freddie / Giorgio Moroder

Singles: 12-inch 33/45rpm

COLUMBIA 4-6 84
Also see MERCURY, Freddie
Also see MORODER, Giorgio

MERCY

P&R/LP '69

Singles: 7-inch

SUNDI 4-8 69
W.B. 4-8 69

LPs: 10/12-inch 33rpm

SUNDI 15-20 69
W.B. 10-15 69
Members: James Marvell; Buddy Good.

MERCY DEE
(Mercy Dee Walton)

R&B '49

Singles: 78rpm

BAYOU (013 "Danger Zone") 15-25 50
COLONY 10-20 50
FLAIR 10-20 55
IMPERIAL 10-20 50
RHYTHM 20-30 54
SPECIALTY 10-15 53
SPIRE 10-20 49

Singles: 7-inch

BAYOU (013 "Danger Zone") .. 75-125 50
FLAIR (1073 "Romp & Stomp
Blues") 30-50 55
RHYTHM (1774 "Trailing
My Baby") 150-200 54
SPECIALTY (Except 466) 20-30 53-54
SPECIALTY (466 "Rent Man
Blues") 20-30 53
(Black vinyl.)
SPECIALTY (466 "Rent Man
Blues") 50-100 53
(Colored vinyl.)

LPs: 10/12-inch 33rpm

ARHOOLIE 15-25 61

MERGE

R&B '82

Singles: 7-inch

RCA 3-4 87

MERMAIDS: see MURMAIDS

MERMAN, Ethel

P&R '32

Singles: 78rpm

BRUNSWICK 4-8 33-35
DECCA 4-6 46-54
VICTOR 4-10 32-43

EPs: 7-inch 33/45rpm

DECCA (2277 "Memories") 15-25 55

LPs: 10/12-inch 33rpm

DECCA (153 "Autobiography") .. 25-35 58
DECCA (5053 "Songs She Made
Famous") 40-60 49
(10-inch LP.)
DECCA (9028 "Memories") 30-45 55
VIK (1004 "On Stage") 25-35 55
You'll find many more listings by this artist in *The Official Price Guide to Movie/TV Soundtracks and Original Cast Albums,* containing over 8,000 listings.

MERMAN, Ethel, Dick Haymes

P&R '51

Singles: 78rpm

DECCA 3-5 51

Singles: 7-inch

DECCA 5-10 51
Also see HAYMES, Dick
Also see MERMAN, Ethel

MERRY-GO-ROUND

P&R/LP '67

Singles: 7-inch

A&M 5-10 67-69

LPs: 10/12-inch 33rpm

A&M (4132 "Merry-Go-Round") . 20-30 67
RHINO 5-8 85
Members: Emitt Rhodes; Joel Larson; Gary Kato; Bill Reinhart.
Also see GRASS ROOTS
Also see LEAVES
Also see RHODES, Emitt

MERRYWEATHER: see MERRYWEATHER, Neil

MERRYWEATHER, Neil
(With Friends; Merryweather)

LP '69

Singles: 7-inch

CAPITOL 3-6 69

LPs: 10/12-inch 33rpm

CAPITOL 10-20 69
MERCURY 10-15 74-75
Also see MASON, Dave
Also see MILLER, Steve

MERRYWEATHER, Neil, & John Richardson

LPs: 10/12-inch 33rpm

KENT 10-15 72

MERRYWEATHER & CAREY

LPs: 10/12-inch 33rpm

RCA 8-12 71

Members: Neil Merryweather; Lynn Carey.
Also see MERRYWEATHER, Neil

MESA

P&R '77

Singles: 7-inch

ARIOLA AMERICA 3-5 77

MES'AY

R&B '87

Singles: 7-inch

SUPERSTAR I. 3-4 87

MESSENGERS

P&R '71

Singles: 7-inch

BEAM 5-10 64
ERA 4-8 65
HOME MADE (01 "Right On") ... 15-25 60s
MGM 4-8 64-65
RARE EARTH 3-6 71
SOUL 4-8 67

LPs: 10/12-inch 33rpm

RARE EARTH (509 "Messengers") 8-12 69
(With standard cover.)
RARE EARTH (509 "Messengers") 20-25 69
(With rounded-top cover. Promotional issue.)

MESSINA, Jim
(With the Jesters; Jimmy Messina)

LP '79

Singles: 7-inch

AUDIO FIDELITY 15-25 64
COLUMBIA 3-5 79-80
VIV 10-15
W.B. 3-5 81-83

LPs: 10/12-inch 33rpm

AUDIO FIDELITY (7037 "The Dragsters") 45-55 64
COLUMBIA 5-8 79
THIMBLE 10-12 73
W.B. 5-8 81-83

Also see BUFFALO SPRINGFIELD
Also see LOGGINS & MESSINA
Also see POCO
Also see YOUNG, Neil, & Jim Messina

METAL CHURCH

LP '86

LPs: 10/12-inch 33rpm

ELEKTRA 5-8 86-89

METALLICA

LP '84

Singles: 7-inch

ELEKTRA 3-4 88-89

Picture Sleeves

ELEKTRA 3-5 88-89

LPs: 10/12-inch 33rpm

ELEKTRA 5-10 84-89
ENIGMA 5-10 84
MEGAFORCE 8-15 84-86

Members: James Hetfield; Kirk Hammett; Lars Ulrich; Cliff Burton; Jason Newsted.

METERS

P&R/R&B/LP '69

Singles: 7-inch

JOSIE 3-6 69-71
REPRISE 3-5 74-76
SANSU 4-6
W.B. 3-5 77

LPs: 10/12-inch 33rpm

ISLAND 8-10 75
JOSIE 10-12 69-70
REPRISE 8-10 72-75
VIRGO 8-10 75
W.B. 8-10 77

Also see NEVILLE BROTHERS

METHENY, Pat
(With Lyle Mays)

LP '78

Singles: 7-inch

ECM 3-4 79-84

LPs: 10/12-inch 33rpm

ECM 5-10 76-84
EMI AMERICA 5-8 85
GEFFEN 5-8 87-90
W.B. 5-8 83

Also see BOWIE, David, & Pat Metheny Group

MIAMI

R&B '74

Singles: 7-inch

DRIVE 3-5 74-76

LPs: 10/12-inch 33rpm

DRIVE 5-10 76

Member: Robert Moore.

MIAMI DISCO BAND

R&B '79

Singles: 7-inch

SALSOUL 3-5 79

Member: Beverly Barkley.

MIAMI SOUND MACHINE
(Gloria Estefan & Miami Sound Machine)

P&R/R&B/D&D/LP '85

Singles: 12-inch 33/45rpm

EPIC 4-6 84-88

Singles: 7-inch

EPIC 3-4 84-88

Picture Sleeves

EPIC 3-4 85-88

LPs: 10/12–inch 33rpm

EPIC 5-8 84-88

Members: Marcos Avila; Kiki Garcia; Gloria Estefan; Emilio Estefan Jr.

Also see ESTEFAN, Gloria

MICHAEL, George

P&R '86

Singles: 12–inch 33/45rpm

COLUMBIA 4-6 86-87

Singles: 7–inch

COLUMBIA 3-4 86-90

Picture Sleeves

COLUMBIA 3-4 86-89

LPs: 10/12–inch 33rpm

COLUMBIA 5-8 86-90

Also see ESTUS, Deon, & George Michael

Also see FRANKLIN, Aretha, & George Michael

Also see JOHN, Elton

Also see WHAM!

MICHAELS, Lee

LP '69

Singles: 7–inch

A&M 4-6 67-71

COLUMBIA 3-5 73

Picture Sleeves

A&M 4-6 70-71

LPs: 10/12–inch 33rpm

A&M (Except 3158 & 4140) 10-15 67-73

A&M (3158 "Lee Michaels") 5-8 82

A&M (4140 "Carnival of Life") 15-25 67

COLUMBIA 10-12 73-75

Promotional LPs

COLUMBIA ("In Hawaii") 35-45 75

MICHELE LEE: see LEE, Michele

MICKEY & SYLVIA

R&B '56

Singles: 78rpm

GROOVE (175 "Love Is Strange") 10-15 56

RAINBOW 10-15 55

VIK 5-10 57

Singles: 7–inch

ALL PLATINUM 3-6 69

GROOVE (175 "Love Is Strange") 10-20 56

KING (6006 "Love Is Strange") 4-8 65

RCA (47-7774 "Sweeter As the Day Goes By") 8-12 60

RCA (61-7774 "Sweeter As the Day Goes By") 15-25 60
(Stereo.)

RCA (47-7811 "What Would I Do") 8-12 60

RCA (61-7811 "What Would I Do") 15-25 60
(Stereo.)

RCA (37-7877 "Love Lesson") 20-30 61
(Compact 33 Single.)

RCA (47-7877 "Love Lesson") 8-12 61

RCA (8500 series) 8-12 65

RAINBOW (316 "I'm So Glad") 15-25 55

RAINBOW (318 "Rise Sally Rise") 15-25 55

VIK 10-15 57-58

WILLOW 8-12 61-62

EPs: 7–inch 33/45rpm

GROOVE (18 "Love Is Strange") 50-100 57

VIK (262 "Mickey & Sylvia") 40-60 57

LPs: 10/12–inch 33rpm

CAMDEN (863 "Love Is Strange") 35-50 65

RCA 15-20 73

VIK (1102 "New Sounds") 100-200 57

Members: Mickey Baker; Sylvia Vanderpool.

Also see LITTLE SYLVIA

Also see SYLVIA

MICO WAVE

R&B '87

Singles: 7–inch

COLUMBIA 3-4 87-88

MIDLER, Bette

P&R/LP '72

Singles: 7–inch

ATLANTIC 3-5 72-90

Picture Sleeves

ATLANTIC 3-5 72-89

LPs: 10/12–inch 33rpm

ATLANTIC 5-10 72-90

Also see REDD, Sharon, Ula Hedwig & Charlotte Crossley

Also see U.S.A. for AFRICA

MIDNIGHT OIL

LP '84

Singles: 12–inch 33/45rpm

COLUMBIA 4-6 84

Singles: 7–inch

COLUMBIA 3-4 82-89

Picture Sleeves

COLUMBIA 3-5 82-88

LPs: 10/12–inch 33rpm

COLUMBIA 5-8 84-90

MIDNIGHT STAR

R&B '80

Singles: 12–inch 33/45rpm

SOLAR 4-6 82-86

Singles: 7–inch

SOLAR 3-4 80-88

Picture Sleeves

SOLAR 3-4 86

LPs: 10/12–inch 33rpm

SOLAR 5-8 82-88

Members: Cino-Vincent Calloway; Reggie Calloway.

Also see CALLOWAY

MIDNIGHT STRING QUARTET

LP '66

LPs: 10/12-Inch 33rpm

VIVA 5-10 66-68

MIDNIGHTERS

R&B '54

Singles: 78rpm

FEDERAL................................ 15-25 54-57

Singles: 7-inch

FEDERAL (12169 "Work with Me Annie") 35-45 54
(Silver top label.)
FEDERAL (12169 "Work with Me Annie") 10-15 55
(Green label.)
FEDERAL (12177 "Give It Up"). 20-30 54
FEDERAL (12185 "Sexy Ways")................................. 25-30 54
FEDERAL (12195 "Annie Had a Baby") 25-35 54
FEDERAL (12200 "Annie's Aunt Fannie")................................ 20-30 54
FEDERAL (12202 "Tell Them"). 20-30 54
FEDERAL (12205 "Moonrise").. 25-35 54
FEDERAL (12210 "Ashamed of Myself") 20-30 55
FEDERAL (12220 "Switchie, Witchie, Titchie") 20-30 55
FEDERAL (12224 "Henry's Got Flat Feet") 20-30 55
FEDERAL (12227 "It's Love Baby") 20-25 55
FEDERAL (12230 "Give It Up"). 15-20 55
FEDERAL (12240 "That House on the Hill")................................ 15-25 55
FEDERAL (12243 "Don't Change Your Pretty Ways") 15-25 55
FEDERAL (12251 thru 12339).. 10-20 56-58

Members: Henry Booth; Hank Ballard; Sonny Woods; Charles Sutton; Lawson Smith; Alonzo Tucker. May be shown on some early releases as "The Midnighters, Formerly the Royals."
Also see BALLARD, Hank, & Midnighters
Also see JOHN, Little Willie / 5 Royales / Earl (Connelly) King / Midnighters
Also see ROYALS

MIDNIGHTERS, Thee: see THEE MIDNIGHTERS

MIDWAY

R&B/D&D '84

Singles: 12-inch 33/45rpm

PERSONAL................................ 4-6 84

Singles: 7-inch

PERSONAL................................ 3-4 84

MIGHTY CLOUDS of JOY

R&B/LP '74

Singles: 12-inch 33/45rpm

EPIC.. 4-6 79

Singles: 7-inch

ABC..3-5 76-77
DUNHILL....................................3-5 74-75
EPIC..3-5 79-80
MYRRH.....................................3-4 82
PEACOCK 3-6 61-73

LPs: 10/12-inch 33rpm

ABC..5-8 75-76
DUNHILL....................................5-8 74
EPIC..5-8 79
MYRRH.....................................5-8 81-83
PEACOCK 5-10 65-73
PRIORITY 5-8 82

Member: Bunker Hill.
Also see HILL, Bunker.
Also see ROGER

MIGHTY FIRE

R&B '80

Singles: 7-inch

ELEKTRA....................................3-4 81-82
ZEPHYR 3-5 80

LPs: 10/12-inch 33rpm

ELEKTRA....................................5-8 81-82

MIGHTY FLEA

R&B '68

Singles: 7-inch

ELDO 4-8 67

MIGHTY HANNIBAL
(James T. Shaw)

R&B '66

Singles: 7-inch

DECCA 4-8 65
JOSIE..4-8 66-67
LOMA..4-8 68
SHURFINE..................................4-8 66

Also see HANNIBAL

MIGHTY LEMON DROPS

LP '90

LPs: 10/12-inch 33rpm

SIRE..5-10 86-90

Members: Paul Marsh; David Newton; Tony Linehan; Keith Rowley.

MIGHTY MARVELOWS: see MARVELOWS

MIGHTY POPE

R&B '77

Singles: 7-inch

PRIVATE STOCK 3-5 77

MIKE & DEAN
(Mike Love & Dean Torrence)

Singles: 7-inch

BUDWEISER (8246 "Budweiser Fight Song/Be True to Your Bud") 35-45 83
(Add $8 to $12 if accompanied by two Mike & Dean posters and a story insert. Promotional issue only.)
HITBOUND 10-20 82
PREMORE (23/24 "Da Doo Ron Ron"/"Baby Talk")......................................20-30 83

Picture Sleeves

PREMORE (23/24 "Da Doo Ron Ron"/"Baby Talk") 20-30 83

LPs: 10/12-inch 33rpm

PREMORE (1083 "Rock'n Roll Again") 30-50 83
(Also has tracks by the Association, Rip Chords, and Paul Revere & the Raiders.)
PREMORE (3009 "Rock'n Roll City") 30-50 83
(Also has tracks by other artists.)
Members: Mike Love; Dean Torrence.
Also see ASSOCIATION
Also see JAN & DEAN
Also see LOVE, Mike
Also see REVERE, Paul, & Raiders
Also see RIPCHORDS

MIKE + MECHANICS

P&R/LP '85

Singles: 7-inch

ATLANTIC 3-4 85-89

Picture Sleeves

ATLANTIC 3-4 85-89

LPs: 10/12-inch 33rpm

ATLANTIC 5-8 85-90
Members: Mike Rutherford; Paul Carrack; Paul Young; Peter Van Hooke; Adrian Lee.
Also see CARRACK, Paul
Also see RUTHERFORD, Mike
Also see SAD CAFE
Also see YOUNG, Paul

MIKKI

R&B '82

Singles: 7-inch

EMERALD INT'L 3-4 82-83
POP ART 3-4 84

MILBURN, Amos
(With the Aladdin Chickenshackers)

R&B '48

Singles: 78rpm

ALADDIN (100 & 200 series) 15-25 45-47
ALADDIN (3000 series) 10-20 48-56

Singles: 7-inch

ALADDIN (3014 "Chicken Shack Boogie") 75-125 50
ALADDIN (3018 "Bewildered") 50-100 50
ALADDIN (3068 "Bad Bad Whiskey") 50-75 50
ALADDIN (3080 "Let's Rock Awhile") 50-75 51
ALADDIN (3090 "Everybody Clap Hands") 50-75 51
ALADDIN (3093 "Ain't Nothing Shaking") 50-75 51
ALADDIN (3105 "Boogie Woogie") 50-75 51
ALADDIN (3124 "Drinkin' and Thinkin'") 40-60 52
ALADDIN (3125 "Flying Home") 40-60 52
ALADDIN (3133 "Roll Mr. Jelly") 40-60 52
ALADDIN (3150 "Greyhound") ... 40-60 52
ALADDIN (3159 "Rock, Rock, Rock") 40-60 52
ALADDIN (3164 "Let Me Go Home, Whiskey") 30-50 53
ALADDIN (3168 "Please, Mr. Johnson") 30-50 53
ALADDIN (3197 "One Scotch, One Bourbon, One Beer") 30-50 53
ALADDIN (3218 "Good Good Whiskey") 25-45 53
ALADDIN (3226 "Rocky Mountain") 25-45 54
ALADDIN (3240 "Milk and Water") 25-45 54
ALADDIN (3248 "Glory of Love") 25-45 54
ALADDIN (3253 "Vicious Vicious Vodka") 25-45 54
ALADDIN (3269 "One Two Three Everybody") 25-45 54
ALADDIN (3293 "My Happiness Depends on You") 25-45 55
ALADDIN (3306 "House Party"). 25-45 55
ALADDIN (3332 "Chicken Shack") 20-40 56
IMPERIAL 5-10 62
KING (5000 series) 5-10 60-61
KING (6000 series) 4-8 67
MOTOWN (1038 "My Baby Gave Me Another Chance") 15-25 63
MOTOWN (1046 "My Daily Prayer") 15-25 63

LPs: 10/12-inch 33rpm

ALADDIN (704 "Rockin' the Boogie") 300-500 55
(Black vinyl. 10-inch LP.)
ALADDIN (704 "Rockin' the Boogie") 500-1000 55
(Colored vinyl. 10-inch LP.)
ALADDIN (810 "Rockin' the Boogie") 200-300 56
IMPERIAL (9176 "Million Sellers") 50-75 62
MOTOWN (608 "The Blues Boss") 500-750 63
SCORE (4012 "Let's Have a Party") 100-200 57
Also see BROWN, Charles, & Amos Milburn

MILBURN, Amos / Wynonie Harris / Velma Nelson / Crown Prince Waterford

LPs: 10/12-inch 33rpm

ALADDIN (703 "Party After Hours") 400-600 56
(Black vinyl. 10-inch LP.)

ALADDIN (703 "Party After Hours") 750-1000 56
(Colored vinyl. 10-inch LP.)
Also see HARRIS, Wynonie
Also see MILBURN, Amos

MILES, Buddy
(Buddy Miles Express; with Freedom Express)
P&R/LP '69

Singles: 7-inch

CASABLANCA 3-5 75-76
COLUMBIA 3-5 73-74
MERCURY 3-6 68-71

Picture Sleeves

MERCURY 3-6

LPs: 10/12-inch 33rpm

CASABLANCA 8-10 75
COLUMBIA 8-12 73-74
MERCURY 10-15 68-72
Also see CALIFORNIA RAISINS
Also see ELECTRIC FLAG
Also see FIDELITYS
Also see HENDRIX, Jimi
Also see SANTANA, Carlos, & Buddy Miles

MILES, Garry
(With the Statues; Gary Miles; Buzz Cason)
P&R '60

Singles: 7-inch

LIBERTY (54000 series) 5-8 68
LIBERTY (55000 series) 10-15 60-64

Picture Sleeves

LIBERTY (55261 "Look for a Star") 10-20 60

EPs: 7-inch 33/45rpm

LIBERTY (1005 "Look for a Star") 50-75 60
Also see STATUES

MILES, John
P&R/LP '76

Singles: 12-inch 33/45rpm

LONDON 5-8 77-80

Singles: 7-inch

ARISTA 3-5 78
LONDON 3-5 76-77
WEA 3-4 85

LPs: 10/12-inch 33rpm

ARISTA 5-10 78
LONDON 5-10 76-80
WEA 5-8 85
Also see PARSONS, Alan, Project

MILES, Lenny
P&R '60

Singles: 7-inch

GROOVE 5-10 62
SCEPTER 5-10 61

MILLER, Chuck
P&R '55

Singles: 78rpm

MERCURY 5-10 55-58

Singles: 7-inch

MERCURY 8-15 55-58

LPs: 10/12-inch 33rpm

MERCURY (20195 "After Hours") 40-60 56
(10-inch LP.)

MILLER, Clint
P&R '58

Singles: 7-inch

ABC-PAR 10-20 58
BIG TOP 5-10 59
HEADLINE 5-10 60-61
LENOX 4-8 62

MILLER, Frankie
P&R/LP '77

Singles: 7-inch

CAPITOL 3-4 82
CHRYSALIS 3-5 75-79

Picture Sleeves

CAPITOL 3-4 82

LPs: 10/12-inch 33rpm

CAPITOL 5-10 82
CHRYSALIS 8-12 73-80

MILLER, Glenn, & His Orchestra
(New Glenn Miller Orchestra with Ray McKinley; with Buddy DeFranco)
P&R '35

Singles: 78rpm

BLUEBIRD 5-10 38-44
BRUNSWICK 5-10 37-38
COLUMBIA 5-10 35
DECCA 15-25 37
RCA 4-8 47-58
VICTOR 5-10 42-46

Singles: 7-Inch

EPIC 3-6 65-69
RCA 3-10 50-67

EPs: 7-Inch 33/45rpm

EPIC 5-15 54-56
RCA (Except 6700 series) 5-15 50-61
RCA (6700 "Anthology Limited Edition, Vol. 1") 25-50 56
RCA (6701 "Anthology Limited Edition, Vol. 2") 25-50 56
RCA (6702 "Army Air Force Band") 20-30 56

LPs: 10/12-Inch 33rpm

BRIGHT ORANGE 5-8 73
CAMDEN 5-10 63-74
COLUMBIA 5-8 82
EPIC (1000 & 3000 series) 20-40 54-56
EPIC (16000 series) 12-25 60
EPIC (24000 & 26000 series) 10-20 65-66
EVEREST (Except 4004) 5-8 82
EVEREST (4004 "Glenn Miller") 20-30 82
(Five-LP boxed set.)
GREAT AMERICAN 5-10 77
HARMONY 5-10 70

KORY 5-8 77
MOVIETONE 8-15 67
RCA (16 thru 30) 25-50
(10–inch LPs.)
RCA (0600 thru 3800 series) 5-10 74-81
(With "ANL," "AYL" or "CPL" prefix.)
RCA (LPT-3000 series) 25-50 52-54
(10–inch LP.)
RCA (1000 thru 1500 series) 20-40 54-57
(Black label.)
RCA (1100 thru 1500 series) 5-10 68-69
(Orange label.)
RCA (1600 thru 3900 series) 10-25 58-68
(Black label. With "LPM" or "LSP" prefix.)
RCA (1900 thru 4100 series) 5-10 68-69
(Orange label.)
RCA (5000 series) 5-10 75-80
RCA (6000 series) 5-15 69-73
RCA (6100 series) 15-30 59-63
RCA (6700 "Anthology–Limited Edition, Vol. 1") 75-100 56
(Five-LP set with booklet and special gold or silver case.)
RCA (6700 "Anthology–Limited Edition, Vol. 1") 50-75 62
(Reissue, has '60s RCA labels.)
RCA (6701 "Anthology–Limited Edition, Vol. 2") 75-100 56
(Five-LP set with booklet and special gold or silver case.)
RCA (6701 "Anthology–Limited Edition, Vol. 2") 50-75 62
(Reissue, has '60s RCA labels.)
RCA (6702 "Army Air Force Band") 50-75 56
SPRINGBOARD 4-8 77
20TH FOX (100 series) 20-30 59
20TH FOX (900 series) 5-10 73
20TH FOX (3000 series) 15-25 59
20TH FOX (3100 series) 10-15 65
20TH FOX (4100 series) 10-15 65
20TH FOX (72000 series) 6-12 73

MILLER, Jody

P&R '64

Singles: 7–inch

CAPITOL 4-8 63-70
EPIC 3-5 70-79

Picture Sleeves

CAPITOL 5-10 65

LPs: 10/12–inch 33rpm

CAPITOL (1913 "Wednesday's Child Is Full of Woe") 15-25 63
CAPITOL (2349 thru 2996) 10-20 65-69
CAPITOL (11000 series) 5-10 73
EPIC 5-10 70-77
PICKWICK/HILLTOP 10-15 66
SEARS 8-12

MILLER, Jody, & Johnny Paycheck

C&W '72

EPIC 3-5 72
Also see MILLER, Jody
Also see PAYCHECK, Johnny

MILLER, Marcus

R&B '83

Singles: 12–inch 33/45rpm

W.B. 4-6 83-84

Singles: 7–inch

W.B. 3-4 83-84

MILLER, Mrs. Elva

(Mrs. Miller)

P&R/LP '66

Singles: 7–inch

AMARET 4-8 69-70
CAPITOL 5-10 66

LPs: 10/12–inch 33rpm

AMARET 10-20 69
CAPITOL 20-35 66-67

MILLER, Mitch

(Mitch Miller's Orchestra & Chorus; Mitch Miller & Sing-Along Gang)

P&R '50

Singles: 78rpm

COLUMBIA 3-6 50-57

Singles: 7–inch

COLUMBIA 4-10 50-65
DECCA 3-6 65-66
DIAMOND 3-6 68
GOLD-MOR 3-5 73
U.A. 3-6 68

Picture Sleeves

COLUMBIA 5-8 59-63

EPs: 7–inch 33/45rpm

COLUMBIA 5-10 55-61

LPs: 10/12–inch 33rpm

ATLANTIC 5-8 70
COLUMBIA (Except 2780/6380) .. 5-20 56-82
COLUMBIA (2780 "Major Dundee") 35-45 65
(Soundtrack. Monaural.)
COLUMBIA (6380 "Major Dundee") 45-55 65
(Soundtrack. Stereo.)
DECCA 5-12 66
HARMONY 5-12 65-71
Also see LAINE, Frankie
Also see SANDPIPERS with Mitch Miller & Orchestra / Mitch Miller & Orchestra

MILLER, Ned

C&W/P&R '62

Singles: 78rpm

DOT 10-15 57

Singles: 7–inch

CAPITOL (2000 series) 3-6 68
CAPITOL (4600 series) 5-8 61
CAPITOL (5400 thru 5800 series) . 3-8 65-67

DOT (15000 series, except 15601) ... 8-12 57
DOT (15601 "From a Jack to a King") ... 10-20 57
FABOR ... 4-8 62-65
JACKPOT ... 8-12 59
REPUBLIC ... 4-6 69-70

LPs: 10/12–inch 33rpm

CAPITOL ... 10-15 65-67
FABOR (1001 "From a Jack to a King") ... 15-25 63
(Black vinyl.)
FABOR (1001 "From a Jack to a King") ... 50-75 63
(Colored vinyl.)
PLANTATION ... 5-8 81
REPUBLIC ... 8-10 70

MILLER, Red, Trio

R&B '48

Singles: 78rpm

BULLET ... 10-15 48
SWING BEAT ... 5-10 49

Singles: 7–inch

PRIZE (801 "Mary Jo") ... 20-30 50s

MILLER, Roger

C&W '60

Singles: 7–inch

BUENA VISTA ... 3-5 70
COLUMBIA ... 3-5 73-74
DECCA ... 5-10 59
ELEKTRA ... 3-4 81
MCA ... 3-4 85-86
MERCURY ... 3-5 70-72
MUSICOR (1102 "You're Forgettin' Me") ... 4-8 65
RCA (7000 series) ... 8-15 60-63
RCA (8000 series) ... 4-6 62-65
SMASH ... 3-8 64-76
STARDAY (356 "You're Forgettin' Me") ... 10-15 58
STARDAY (718 "Playboy") ... 4-8 65
STARDAY (7029 "Under Your Spell Again") ... 4-8 65
20TH CENTURY ... 3-5 79
WINDSONG ... 3-5 77

Picture Sleeves

BUENA VISTA ... 4-6 70
SMASH ... 5-10 64-68

LPs: 10/12–inch 33rpm

CAMDEN ... 10-15 64-65
COLUMBIA ... 5-10 73
EVEREST ... 5-8 75
HILLTOP ... 8-12 60s
MCA ... 5-8 86
MERCURY ... 5-10 72
PICKWICK ... 5-10 70s
SMASH (Except 7000 series) ... 10-20 64-70
SMASH (7000 series) ... 5-8 82
STARDAY ... 10-20 65
20TH FOX ... 5-8 79
WINDSONG ... 5-8 77
WING ... 6-12 69

Also see LEWIS, Jerry Lee / Roger Miller / Roy Orbison
Also see NELSON, Willie, & Roger Miller
Also see TUBB, Justin / Roger Miller
Also see YOUNG, Donny, & Roger Miller

MILLER, Roger, & Willie Nelson

(With Ray Price)

C&W '82

Singles: 7–inch

COLUMBIA ... 3-5 82

LPs: 10/12–inch 33rpm

COLUMBIA ... 5-8 82

Also see MILLER, Roger
Also see NELSON, Willie
Also see PRICE, Ray

MILLER, Steve

(Steve Miller Band)

P&R/LP '68

Singles: 12–inch 33/45rpm

CAPITOL ... 4-8 81-85

Singles: 7–inch

CAPITOL (2156 "Sittin' in Circles") ... 5-10 68
CAPITOL (2287 "Living in the USA") ... 5-10 68
CAPITOL (2447 thru 3344) ... 4-8 69-72
CAPITOL (3732 thru 4496) ... 3-5 73-77
CAPITOL (5000 series) ... 3-4 81-86

Picture Sleeves

CAPITOL ... 3-4 80-85

LPs: 10/12–inch 33rpm

CAPITOL (184 thru 748) ... 10-15 69-71
CAPITOL (2900 series) ... 15-20 68
CAPITOL (11000 thru 16000) ... 5-10 72-86
CAPITOL (11872 "Greatest Hits") ... 20-30 78
(Colored vinyl. Promotional issue only.)
CAPITOL (11903 "Book of Dreams") ... 15-20 78
(Picture disc.)
CAPITOL (48000 series) ... 5-8 88
MFSL ... 25-50 78
MERCURY ... 5-10 81

Also see BERRY, Chuck
Also see DAVIS, Tim
Also see GOLDBERG - MILLER BLUES BAND
Also see MERRYWEATHER, Neil
Also see SCAGGS, Boz

MILLER, Steve, Band / Band / Quicksilver Messenger Service

LPs: 10/12–inch 33rpm

CAPITOL (288 "Steve Miller Band / The Band /Quicksilver Messenger Service") ... 35-45 69
(Three-LP set, one disc by each group.)

Also see BAND
Also see MILLER, Steve
Also see QUICKSILVER

MILLI VANILLI

P&R/LP '89

Singles: 7-inch

ARISTA 3-4 89-90

Picture Sleeves

ARISTA 3-4 89

LPs: 10/12-inch 33rpm

ARISTA 5-8 89-90

Members: Rob Pilatus; Fabrice Morvan.

MILLINDER, Lucky, & His Orchestra

P&R/R&B '42

Singles: 78rpm

DECCA.................................... 5-10 41-48
KING 5-10 51-57
RCA.................................... 5-10 49-51

Singles: 7-inch

KING (4449 "Chew Tobacco Rag") 25-45 51
KING (4453 "I'm Waiting for You") 25-45 51
KING (4476 "The Grape Vine"). 25-45 51
KING (4496 "The Right Kind of Lovin'") 25-45 51
(Black vinyl.)
KING (4496 "The Right Kind of Lovin'") 50-100 51
(Colored vinyl.)
KING (4545 "When I Have You") 50-75 52
KING (4571 "Please Be Careful") 50-75 52
KING (4803 "Goody Good Love") 15-25 55
KING (5200 series) 5-10 59
RCA (0054 "D Natural Blues") .. 30-50 51
(Colored vinyl.)
TODD 5-10 59
WARWICK 5-10 60

EPs: 7-inch 33/45rpm

KING (268 "Lucky Millinder")..... 25-50 54
KING (336 "Lucky Millinder, Vol. 2") 25-50 54

Also see HARRIS, Wynonie
Also see STIDHAM, Arbee

MILLINDER, Lucky, & Admirals

Singles: 78rpm

KING (4792 "It's a Sad Sad Feeling") 15-20 55

Singles: 7-inch

KING (4792 "It's a Sad Sad Feeling") 40-60 55

Also see MILLINDER, Lucky

MILLIONS LIKE US

P&R/LP '87

Singles: 7-inch

VIRGIN 3-4 87

Picture Sleeves

VIRGIN 3-4 87

LPs: 10/12-inch 33rpm

VIRGIN 5-8 87

MILLS, Frank

P&R '72

Singles: 7-inch

POLYDOR 3-4 78-79
SUNFLOWER 3-4 72

LPs: 10/12-inch 33rpm

CAPITOL 5-8 85
POLYDOR 5-8 79

Also see BELLS

MILLS, Gary

P&R '60

Singles: 7-inch

IMPERIAL 5-10 60
LONDON 4-8 62
TOP RANK 5-10 60

MILLS, Hayley

P&R '61

Singles: 7-inch

BUENA VISTA 5-10 61-62
MAINSTREAM 4-8 66

Picture Sleeves

BUENA VISTA 10-20 61-62

EPs: 7-inch 33/45rpm

DISNEYLAND 15-25 60

LPs: 10/12-inch 33rpm

BUENA VISTA (3311 "Let's Get Together") 20-25 62
(Monaural.)
BUENA VISTA (STER-3311 "Let's Get Together") 25-35 62
(Stereo.)
MAINSTREAM (6090 "Gypsy Girl") 15-25 66
(Soundtrack.)

Also see ANNETTE / Hayley Mills

MILLS, Hayley, & Jimmie Bean

EPs: 7-inch 33/45rpm

DISNEYLAND 15-25 60

MILLS, Hayley, & Maurice Chevalier

Singles: 7-inch

BUENA VISTA 5-8 62

Also see MILLS, Hayley

MILLS, Hayley, & Eddie Hodges

Singles: 7-inch

BUENA VISTA 5-8 63

Picture Sleeves

BUENA VISTA 10-15 64

Also see HODGES, Eddie

MILLS, Hayley, & Burl Ives

(With Eddie Hodges & Deborah Walley)

Singles: 7-inch

BUENA VISTA (4023 "Summer Magic") 5-8 63
(Alcoa Wrap promotional issue.)

Picture Sleeves

BUENA VISTA (4023 "Summer Magic") 10-15 63
(Alcoa Wrap promotional issue.)
Also see IVES, Burl
Also see MILLS, Hayley

MILLS, Stephanie

P&R/R&B/LP '79

Singles: 12-inch 33/45rpm

CASABLANCA 4-6 82-85
MCA 4-6 85-86
20TH FOX 4-8 79-81

Singles: 7-inch

ABC 3-5 74
CASABLANCA 3-4 82-86
MCA 3-4 85-89
MOTOWN 3-5 75
PARAMOUNT 3-5 74
20TH FOX 3-5 79-81

Picture Sleeves

MCA 3-4 87
20TH FOX 3-5 80

LPs: 10/12-inch 33rpm

ABC 8-10 75
CASABLANCA 5-8 82-85
MCA 5-8 86-89
MOTOWN (800 series) 8-10 75
MOTOWN (6000 series) 5-8 82
20TH FOX 5-10 79-81
Also see KING DREAM CHORUS & Holiday Crew

MILLS, Stephanie, & Teddy Pendergrass

P&R/R&B '81

Singles: 7-inch

20TH FOX 3-5 81
Also see MILLS, Stephanie
Also see PENDERGRASS, Teddy

MILLS, Yvonne, & Sensations

Singles: 78rpm

ATCO 8-15 56-57

Singles: 7-inch

ATCO 15-25 56-58
Also see SENSATIONS

MILLS BROTHERS

P&R '31

Singles: 78rpm

BANNER 5-10 34
BRUNSWICK 5-10 31-47
CONQUEROR 5-10
DECCA (100 thru 4300 series) ... 5-10 34-42
DECCA (11000 thru 24000 series) 5-10 42-57

Singles: 7-inch

ABC 3-5 74
DECCA 5-15 50-61
DOT (15000 series) 4-8 58-59
DOT (17000 series) 3-6 68-69
MCA 3-5 73-74
PARAMOUNT 3-5 71-72
RANWOOD 3-5 73-76

EPs: 7-inch 33/45rpm

DECCA 5-15 50-63
DOT 5-10 58-59

LPs: 10/12-inch 33rpm

ABC 5-8 74
DECCA (100 series) 10-15 66
DECCA (4000 series) 10-20 61-67
DECCA (5000 series) 20-40 49-55
(10-inch LPs.)
DECCA (7000 series) 20-30 55
DECCA (8000 series) 15-30 55-59
DECCA (75000 series) 5-10 70
DOT 5-15 58-70
EVEREST 5-10 75-77
GNP 5-8 73
MCA 5-10 73
PARAMOUNT 5-10 72-74
PICKWICK 5-10 70s
RANWOOD 5-10 74-81
SONGBIRD 6-12 74
VOCALION 5-10 66-69
Members: Herb Mills; Harry Mills; Donald Mills; John Mills.
Also see CROSBY, Bing, & Mills Brothers
Also see FITZGERALD, Ella, & Mills Brothers

MILLS BROTHERS, & Louis Armstrong

P&R '37

Singles: 7-inch

DECCA 4-6 61
Also see ARMSTRONG, Louis

MILLS BROTHERS, & Count Basie

LPs: 10/12-inch 33rpm

ABC 5-8 74
DOT 8-12 68
Also see BASIE, Count
Also see MILLS BROTHERS

MILSAP, Ronnie

R&B '65

Singles: 7-inch

BOBLO 3-5 77
CHIPS 4-6 70
FESTIVAL 3-5 77
RCA (Black vinyl) 3-5 74-92
RCA (Colored vinyl) 5-10 74-89
(Promotional only.)
SCEPTER 4-8 65-69
W.B. (5405 "It Went to Your Head") 5-10 63
W.B. (8000 series) 3-5 75-76

Picture Sleeves

RCA 3-5 79-85

LPs: 10/12-inch 33rpm

BUCKBOARD 8-10 76
CRAZY CAJUN 8-10 75
51 WEST 5-8 80s
HSRD 8-10 82

RCA.. 5-10 74-92
TRIP.. 8-10 76
W.B.. 8-10 71-75
Also see PRESLEY, Elvis

MILSAP, Ronnie, & Mike Reid
C&W '88

Singles: 7-inch

RCA.. 3-4 88

MILSAP, Ronnie, & Kenny Rogers
C&W '87

Singles: 7-inch

RCA.. 3-4 87
Also see MILSAP, Ronnie
Also see ROGERS, Kenny

MILTON, Roy
(With His Solid Senders; Roy Milton Sextet)
P&R/R&B '46

Singles: 78rpm

DOOTONE.................................. 10-15 55-56
DELUXE.................................... 8-12 50s
HAMP-TONE................................ 10-20 45
JUKE BOX.................................. 20-25 46
KING.. 5-10 56-57
ROY MILTON (111 "Groovin' with Joe").............................. 15-25 46
ROY MILTON (207 "Them There Eyes")................................. 15-25 46
SPECIALTY................................. 5-10 47-55

Singles: 7-inch

CENCO..................................... 5-10 61
DOOTONE.................................. 20-40 55-56
KING (4900 & 5000 series)....... 10-15 56-58
KING (5600 series)................... 5-10 62
SPECIALTY (414 "Short, Sweet and Snappy")........................ 20-40 50
SPECIALTY (429 "So Tired").... 40-60 51
SPECIALTY (436 "Flying Saucer").................................. 30-50 52
SPECIALTY (438 "Night and Day").................................. 30-50 52
SPECIALTY (446 "Believe Me Baby").................................. 50-75 52
SPECIALTY (458 "Some Day"). 30-50 53
(Black vinyl.)
SPECIALTY (458 "Some Day").................................. 75-125 53
(Colored vinyl.)
SPECIALTY (464 "Let Me Give You All My Love").................. 30-50 54
(Black vinyl.)
SPECIALTY (464 "Let Me Give You All My Love").................. 75-125 54
(Colored vinyl.)
SPECIALTY (480 thru 545)....... 20-30 54-55
SPECIALTY (700 series)............. 4-6 69
WARWICK.................................. 5-10 60

LPs: 10/12-inch 33rpm

KENT (554 "Great Roy Milton"). 35-45 63
Also see HOWARD, Camille, Trio
Also see HUMES, Helen

MILTON, Roy / Joe Liggins

Singles: 78rpm

SPECIALTY.................................5-10 53

Singles: 7-inch

SPECIALTY...............................15-25 53
Also see LIGGINS, Joe
Also see MILTON, Roy

MIMMS, Garnet
(With the Enchanters; with Trucking Co.)
P&R/R&B/LP '63

Singles: 7-inch

ARISTA..3-5 77
GSF..3-5 72
LIBERTY......................................3-4 81
U.A...5-15 63-66
VEEP..4-8 66
VERVE..3-5 68-70

Picture Sleeves

U.A...5-10 63

LPs: 10/12-inch 33rpm

ARISTA..5-10 78
GRAND PRIX...............................15-20 63
GUEST STAR (1907 "Garnet Mimms")...................................20-25 64
U.A...20-30 63-66
Members: Garnet Mimms; Samuel Bell; Charles Boyer; Zola Pearnell.
Also see ENCHANTERS

MIMMS, Garnet / Maurice Monk

LPs: 10/12-inch 33rpm

GRAND PRIX...............................15-20 63
Also see MIMMS, Garnet

MINA
(With Her Orchestra "I Solitari")
P&R '61

Singles: 7-inch

CHIRP..4-8
TIME...4-8 61

MINDBENDERS
P&R/LP '66

Singles: 7-inch

FONTANA.....................................5-10 65-67

LPs: 10/12-inch 33rpm

FONTANA (27554 "A Groovy Kind of Love")....................................30-40 66
(Monaural. With *Ashes to Ashes*)
FONTANA (27554 "A Groovy Kind of Love")....................................20-30 66
(Monaural. Without *Ashes to Ashes*)
FONTANA (67554 "A Groovy Kind of Love")....................................30-40 66
(Stereo. With *Ashes to Ashes*)
FONTANA (67554 "A Groovy Kind of Love")....................................20-30 66
(Stereo. Without *Ashes to Ashes*)
Members: Eric Stewart; Bob Lang; Ric Rothwell.
Also see FONTANA, Wayne, & Mindbenders

MINEO, Sal

P&R '57

Singles: 78rpm

EPIC 8-12 57

Singles: 7-inch

DECCA 4-8 64
EPIC 8-15 57-59
FONTANA 4-8 65

Picture Sleeves

EPIC 12-25 57-59

EPs: 7-inch 33/45rpm

EPIC 20-30 57-58

LPs: 10/12-inch 33rpm

EPIC (3405 "Sal") 40-60 58

MINIATURE MEN

P&R '62

Singles: 7-inch

DOLTON 5-10 62
Also see LEVINE, Hank

MINISTRY

D&D/LP '83

Singles: 12-inch 33/45rpm

ARISTA 4-6 83
SIRE 4-6 86
WAX TRAX 4-6 85

Singles: 7-inch

ARISTA 3-4 83
SIRE 3-4 86-89
WAX TRAX 3-4 85

LPs: 10/12-inch 33rpm

ARISTA 5-8 83
SIRE 5-8 86-89

MINK DE VILLE

LP '77

Singles: 7-inch

ATLANTIC 3-4 81-84
CAPITOL 3-5 77-78

LPs: 10/12-inch 33rpm

ATLANTIC 5-8 81-83
CAPITOL 5-8 77-82

MINNEAPOLIS GENIUS 94 EAST

R&B '86

Singles: 7-inch

HOT PINK 3-4 86

MINNELLI, Liza

LP '64

Singles: 7-inch

A&M 3-6 68-71
ABC 3-5 73
CADENCE 5-10 63
CAPITOL (4900 thru 5700 series) 5-10 63-65
COLUMBIA 3-5 72-75
U.A. 3-5 77

LPs: 10/12-inch 33rpm

A&M 10-15 68-73
ABC (752 "Cabaret") 10-15 72
(Soundtrack. With Joel Grey.)
ARISTA (4069 "Lucky Lady") 8-10 76
(Soundtrack.)
CADENCE (4012 "Best Foot Forward") 30-40 63
(Monaural. Original cast.)
CADENCE (24012 "Best Foot Forward") 40-60 63
(Stereo. Original cast.)
CAPITOL (T-2100 and T-2400 series) 10-20 64-66
(Monaural.)
CAPITOL (ST-2100 and ST-2400 series) 15-25 64-66
(Stereo.)
CAPITOL (2200 series) 5-8 78
CAPITOL (11000 series) 5-10 72-78
COLUMBIA 8-15 72-77
DRG (6101 "The Act") 8-10 78
EPIC 5-8 89
MCA (752 "Cabaret") 5-8
(Soundtrack. With Joel Grey.)
STET 8-10
TELARC 10-12 87
Also see GARLAND, Judy, & Liza Minnelli

MINOGUE, Kylie

P&R/LP '88

Singles: 7-inch

GEFFEN 3-4 88

Picture Sleeves

GEFFEN 3-4 88

LPs: 10/12-inch 33rpm

GEFFEN 5-8 88

MINOR DETAIL

P&R/LP '83

Singles: 7-inch

POLYDOR 3-4 83-84

Picture Sleeves

POLYDOR 3-4 83

LPs: 10/12-inch 33rpm

POLYDOR 5-8 83
Members: John Hughes; Willie Hughes.

MINTS: see COPELAND, Ken / Mints

MINTZ, Junier
(Frank Zappa)

Singles: 7-inch

REPRISE/STRAIGHT (1027 "Tears Began to Fall") 20-30 71
Also see ZAPPA, Frank

MIRABAI

LP '75

LPs: 10/12-inch 33rpm

ATLANTIC 5-10 75

MIRACLES

(Smokey Robinson & Miracles; featuring Bill Smokey Robinson; featuring Billy Griffin)

P&R '59

Singles: 12–inch 33/45rpm

COLUMBIA 4-6 77

Singles: 7–inch

CHESS (119 "Bad Girl") 3-5 84
CHESS (1734 "Bad Girl") 25-50 59
(Black label.)
CHESS (1734 "Bad Girl") 10-20 59
(Blue label.)
CHESS (1768 "All I Want") 25-35 60
COLUMBIA 3-5 77-78
END (1016 "Got a Job") 45-55 58
END (1029 "Money") 40-50 58
(No mention of Roulette Records.)
END (1029 "Money") 30-40 58
(Has "A Division of Roulette Records Inc".)
END (1084 "Money") 10-15 61
MOTOWN (G1 "Bad Girl")... 500-1000 59
MOTOWN (400 & 500 series) 3-5 80s
MOTOWN (2207 "Bad Girl") . 400-450 59
MOTOWN/TOPPS (11 "Shop Around") 50-75 67
(Topps Chewing Gum promotional item. Single-sided, cardboard flexi, picture disc. Issued with generic paper sleeve.)
ROULETTE 3-5 70s
STANDARD GROOVE (13090 "I Care About Detroit") 150-200 68
(Tamla logo at top, Artist credit at bottom. Promotional issue only.)
STANDARD GROOVE (13090 "I Care About Detroit") 100-150 68
(Artist credit at top. Promotional issue only.)
TAMLA (009 "The Christmas Song") 100-200 63
(Promotional issue only.)
TAMLA (54028 "The Feeling Is So Fine"/ "You Can Depend on Me").. 300-400 60
(With common version of *You Can Depend on Me.*)
TAMLA (54028 "The Feeling Is So Fine"/ "You Can Depend on Me").. 400-500 60
(With alternate take of *You Can Depend on Me,* Can be identified by the letter "A" following the identification number in the trail-off.)
TAMLA (54028 "Way Over There"/ "Depend on Me") 100-150 60
(With alternate take of *Way Over There,* not available elsewhere.)
TAMLA (54028 "Way Over There"/ "Depend on Me") 25-50 60
(With the hit version of *Way Over There,* the same as is heard on their Tamla LPs.)
TAMLA (54034 "Shop Around") 100-125 60
(Horizontal lines across top half of label. Has an alternate take of *Shop Around.* Has either "H55518 A-2" or "45-L1 37003" etched in the trail-off.)
TAMLA (54034 "Shop Around") .35-50 60
(No horizontal lines and Tamla globe logo at top. Has an alternate take of *Shop Around.* Etched in trail-off is "H55518 A-2.")
TAMLA (54034 "Shop Around") . 10-20 60
(Has the hit version of *Shop Around.* Etched in trail-off is "L1" or "ARP L-1.")
TAMLA (54036 "Ain't It Baby") ... 50-75 61
TAMLA (54044 "Mighty Good Lovin") 25-50 61
TAMLA (54048 "You Gotta Pay Some Dues") 50-100 61
(Note title variation.)
TAMLA (54048 "Everybody's Gotta Pay Some Dues") 25-50 61
TAMLA (54053 "What's So Good About Goodbye") 15-25 62
TAMLA (54059 "I'll Try Something New") 10-20 62
TAMLA (54069 "Way Over There") 10-20 62
TAMLA (54073 thru 54184) 5-10 62-69
TAMLA (54189 "Point It Out") 4-8 69
(Black vinyl.)
TAMLA (54189 "Point It Out") 15-20 69
(Colored vinyl. Promotional issue only.)
TAMLA (54194 thru 54268) 3-5 70-76

Picture Sleeves

TAMLA (54044 "Mighty Good Lovin") 75-125 61
TAMLA (54048 "Everybody's Gotta Pay Some Dues") 25-50 61
TAMLA (54059 "I'll Try Something New") 25-50 62
TAMLA (54098 "I Like It Like That") 15-25 62
TAMLA (54127 thru 54194) 5-15 65-70

EPs: 7–inch 33/45rpm

TAMLA (60267 "Going to a Go Go") 15-25 66

LPs: 10/12–inch 33rpm

COLUMBIA 8-10 77-78
IMPERIAL HOUSE 8-12 79
MOTOWN (Except 793) 5-8 82-84
MOTOWN (793 "Anthology") 12-18 74
NATURAL RESOURCES 5-10 78
TAMLA (220 "Hi! We're the Miracles") 150-250 61
(White label.)
TAMLA (220 "Hi! We're the Miracles") 200-300 61
(Yellow label with globes.)
TAMLA (223 "Cookin' with the Miracles") 150-250 61
(White label.)

TAMLA (223 "Cookin' with the Miracles") 200-300 62
(Yellow label with globes.)
TAMLA (230 "I'll Try Something New") 100-150 62
TAMLA (236 "Christmas with the Miracles") 100-150 62
TAMLA (238 "The Fabulous Miracles") 150-200 63
TAMLA (238 "You Really Got a Hold on Me")................................ 75-125 63
(Reissue with new title.)
TAMLA (241 "On Stage") 50-100 63
TAMLA (245 "Mickey's Monkey") 50-75 63
(Monaural.)
TAMLA (245 "Mickey's Monkey") 75-125 63
(Stereo.)
TAMLA (254 "Greatest Hits from the Beginning")............................ 25-35 63
(Monaural.)
TAMLA (254 "Greatest Hits from the Beginning")............................ 35-45 63
(Stereo.)
TAMLA (267 thru 297).............. 12-20 65-70
TAMLA (301 thru 344).............. 10-15 71-76

Members: William "Smokey" Robinson; Pete Moore; Bobby Rogers; Ron White; Claudette Rogers
Also see GRIFFIN, Billy
Also see MARVELETTES / Mary Wells / Miracles / Marvin Gaye
Also see ROBINSON, Smokey
Also see RON & BILL

MIRAN, Wayne, & Rush Release

R&B '75

Singles: 7-inch

ROULETTE 3-5 75

MIRANDA, Carmen
(With the Bando Da Lua)

P&R '41

Singles: 78rpm

DECCA.................................... 5-15 39-53
MGM 10-20

Picture Sleeves

DECCA.................................. 20-30 39

EPs: 7-inch 33/45rpm

DECCA (2066 "Carmen Miranda")............................... 15-25 53

MIRANDA, Carmen, & Andrews Sisters
(With Vic Shoen & His Orchestra)

P&R '50

Singles: 78rpm

DECCA...................................... 4-8 50

Also see ANDREWS SISTERS
Also see MIRANDA, Carmen

MIRETTES

P&R/R&B '68

Singles: 7-inch

REVUE..4-8 67-69
UNI..3-6 69

LPs: 10/12-inch 33rpm

REVUE.....................................12-18 68
UNI...10-15 69

Members: Vanetta Fields; Jessie Smith; Robbie Montgomery.
Also see IKETTES

MISS ABRAMS: see ABRAMS, Miss

MISS THANG

R&B '86

Singles: 12-inch 33/45rpm

TOMMY BOY.................................4-6 86

MISS TONI FISHER: see FISHER, Miss Toni

MISSING PERSONS

P&R/LP '82

Singles: 12-inch 33/45rpm

CAPITOL.......................................4-6 82-86

Singles: 7-inch

CAPITOL.......................................3-4 82-86

Picture Sleeves

CAPITOL.......................................3-5 82-84

EPs: 7-inch 33/45rpm

KOMOS...5-8 80

LPs: 10/12-inch 33rpm

CAPITOL.......................................5-8 82-86

Members: Dale Bozzio; Terry Bozzio; Warren Cuccurullo.
Also see DURAN DURAN
Also see MOTHERS of INVENTION

MISSION

R&B '74

Singles: 7-inch

PARAMOUNT 3-5 74

MISSION

R&B '87

Singles: 7-inch

COLUMBIA 3-4 87-88

Member: Wayne Hussey.
Also see DEAD OR ALIVE
Also see MISSION

MISSION U.K.

LP '87

LPs: 10/12-inch 33rpm

MERCURY.....................................5-8 87-90

MISSOURI

LP '79

Singles: 7-inch

PANAMA.......................................3-5 78
POLYDOR.....................................3-5 79

LPs: 10/12-inch 33rpm

PANAMA.....................................8-12 77
POLYDOR 5-10 79

MR. BIG

P&R '77

Singles: 7–inch

ARISTA 3-4 77
ATLANTIC 3-4 91

LPs: 10/12–inch 33rpm

ARISTA 5-10 76
ATLANTIC 5-8 89

Members: Eric Martin.
Also see MARTIN, Eric

MR. GOON BONES & MR. FORD

P&R '49

Singles: 78rpm

CRYSTALETTE 4-8 49-56

Singles: 7–inch

CRYSTALETTE 5-10 56
DOT 4-8 59

MR. MISTER

P&R/LP '84

Singles: 7–inch

RCA 3-4 84-87

Picture Sleeves

RCA 3-4 85-87

LPs: 10/12–inch 33rpm

RCA 5-8 84-87

Members: Richard Page; Pat Mastelotto; Steve Farris; Steve George; Buzz Feiten.
Also see LARSEN - FEITEN BAND
Also see PAGES

MR. T.
(Lawrence Tero)

R&B '84

Singles: 12–inch 33/45rpm

COLUMBIA (9C9-39911 "Mr. T's Commandments") 8-12 84

Singles: 7–inch

COLUMBIA 3-4 84
MCA 3-4 84

LPs: 10/12–inch 33rpm

COLUMBIA 5-8 84
MCA 5-8 84

MISTRESS

P&R/LP '79

Singles: 7–inch

RSO 3-5 79

LPs: 10/12–inch 33rpm

RSO 5-10 79

MITCHELL, Billy
(Billy Mitchell Group)

R&B '69

Singles: 78rpm

ATLANTIC 20-40 51-52

Singles: 7–inch

ATLANTIC (933 "My Love, My Desire") 100-200 51
CALLA 4-6 69
JUBILEE 5-10 61
RON 5-10 61-62
U.A. 5-10 60
WARWICK 5-10 59

Also see CLOVERS

MITCHELL, Bobby
(With the Toppers)

R&B '56

Singles: 78rpm

IMPERIAL (5200 series) 20-40 53
IMPERIAL (5250 thru 5309) 15-25 53-54
IMPERIAL (5300 & 5400 series) 10-15 55-57

Singles: 7–inch

IMPERIAL (5236 "I'm Cryin'") 100-150 53
IMPERIAL (5250 "One Friday Morning") 100-150 53
IMPERIAL (5270 "Baby's Gone") 50-75 54
IMPERIAL (5282 "Angel Child") .50-75 54
IMPERIAL (5295 "The Wedding Bells Are Ringing") 50-75 54
IMPERIAL (5309 "I'm a Young Man") 50-75 54
IMPERIAL (5326 "I Wish I Knew") 30-40 55
IMPERIAL (5346 "I Cried") 20-30 55
IMPERIAL (5378 thru 5558) 10-20 56-58
IMPERIAL (5900 series) 5-10 63
RON 5-10 61
SHOW-BIZ 5-10 59

MITCHELL, Chad

Singles: 7–inch

AMY 3-6 68-69
W.B. 4-8 66-67

LPs: 10/12–inch 33rpm

BELL 10-15 69
W.B. 10-20 66-67

MITCHELL, Chad, Trio

P&R/LP '62

Singles: 7–inch

COLPIX 5-10 59-61
KAPP 5-8 61-63
MAY 4-8 62
MERCURY 4-8 63-64

Picture Sleeves

KAPP 10-15 61
MERCURY 8-12 63-65

LPs: 10/12–inch 33rpm

COLPIX 20-30 60
KAPP 15-25 61-64
MERCURY 15-20 63-64

Members: Chad Mitchell; Joe Frazier; Mike Kobluk; Jim [Roger] McGuinn.
Also see McGUINN, Roger
Also see MITCHELL, Chad
Also see MITCHELL TRIO

MITCHELL, Chad, Trio, & Gatemen

LPs: 10/12–inch 33rpm

COLPIX 20-25 64

Also see MITCHELL, Chad, Trio

MITCHELL, Freddie, & Orchestra
(With Rip Harrigan)

R&B '49

Singles: 78rpm

ABC-PAR 3-5 57
BRUNSWICK 4-6 53
CORAL....................................... 4-6 53
DERBY 4-8 49-52
MERCURY 4-6 52

Singles: 7–inch

ABC-PAR 4-8 57-61
BRUNSWICK 5-10 53
CORAL....................................... 5-10 53
DERBY 5-15 49-52
MERCURY 5-10 52
ROCK 'N' ROLL 5-8

LPs: 10/12–inch 33rpm

ALLEGRO/ROYAL (1600 "That Boogie Beat") 20-30 50s
TRIP 10-15 60s
X (1030 "Boogie Bash")............. 40-60 56
Session: King Curtis.
Also see KING CURTIS

MITCHELL, Guy
(Al Cernick)

P&R '50

Singles: 78rpm

COLUMBIA 5-10 50-57
KING (15125 "Cabaret")............. 5-10 51

Singles: 7–inch

CHALICE (711 "My Angel"/"Bit of Love")... 15-25 63
CHALICE (711 "My Angel"/"Mr. Hobo") 15-25 63
(Note different flip.)
CHALICE (712 "Take Your Time").. 15-25 63
CHALICE (713 "Your Imagination") 15-25 63
COLLECTABLES 3-4 80s
COLUMBIA 8-20 50-61
ERIC.. 3-4 83
GMI 4-6 74
JOY 4-8 62-63
KING (15125 "Cabaret")............ 20-30 51
(Previously issued as by Al Grant, Al Cernick's pseudonym before using Guy Mitchell.)
REPRISE 4-6 66
STARDAY ,.................................. 4-6 67-69

Picture Sleeves

COLUMBIA (40769 "Singing the Blues")....................................... 15-20 56
COLUMBIA (40820 "Knee Deep in the Blues")................................ 15-20 57
COLUMBIA (40877 "Rock-A-Billy") 10-20 57
COLUMBIA (41476 "Heartaches By the Number")..................... 10-15 60
COLUMBIA (41853 "Sunshine Guitar")...................................10-15 60
COLUMBIA (42231 "Soft Rain") 10-15 61

EPs: 7–inch 33/45rpm

COLUMBIA 10-15 54-57

LPs: 10/12–inch 33rpm

COLUMBIA (1211 "Guy in Love").......................................20-30 58
(Monaural.)
COLUMBIA (1226 "Greatest Hits") 25-35 59
COLUMBIA (1552 "Sunshine Guitar")......................................15-25 60
(Monaural.)
COLUMBIA (6231 "Open Spaces") 25-50 53
(10–inch LP.)
COLUMBIA (8011 "Guy in Love").......................................30-40 58
(Stereo.)
COLUMBIA (8352 "Sunshine Guitar").....................................20-30 60
(Stereo.)
KING (644 "Sincerely Yours") 150-250 59
(Mitchell pictured but not identified on cover. Includes tracks recorded as Al Grant.)
NASHVILLE 5-10 70
STARDAY..................................10-15 68-69
Also see CAVALLARO, Carmen, Featuring Al Cernick
Also see CLOONEY, Rosemary, & Guy Mitchell
Also see GRANT, Al

MITCHELL, Guy, & Mindy Carson

Singles: 78rpm

COLUMBIA 3-6 52-53

Singles: 7–inch

COLUMBIA...................................5-10 52-53
Also see CARSON, Mindy

MITCHELL, Guy / Eileen Rodgers

EPs: 7–inch 33/45rpm

COLUMBIA.................................10-15 56
Also see RODGERS, Eileen
Also see MITCHELL, Guy

MITCHELL, Joni

LP '68

Singles: 7–inch

ASYLUM 3-5 72-80
ELEKTRA..3-5 75
GEFFEN 3-4 82-91
REPRISE 3-6 68-72

Picture Sleeves

GEFFEN 3-4 82-85

LPs: 10/12–inch 33rpm

ASYLUM 8-10 72-80
GEFFEN 5-8 82-91
REPRISE 10-20 68-71

MITCHELL, Joni, & L.A. Express

LPs: 10/12–inch 33rpm

ASYLUM (202 "Miles of Aisles") 20-30 74
Also see L.A. EXPRESS

Also see MITCHELL, Joni

MITCHELL, Kim

P&R/LP '85

Singles: 7-inch

BRONZE 3-4 85

LPs: 10/12-inch 33rpm

BRONZE 5-8 85

MITCHELL, McKinley

R&B '62

Singles: 7-inch

BOXER..................................... 10-15 59
CHIMNEYVILLE........................... 3-5 77-78
ONE-DERFUL............................ 5-10 62-65

MITCHELL, Philip
(Prince Philip Mitchell)

R&B '75

Singles: 7-inch

ATLANTIC................................. 3-5 78-79
EVENT 3-5 75
ICHIBAN.................................... 3-4 86

MITCHELL, Rubin

LP '67

Singles: 7-inch

CAPITOL.................................... 3-6 67-68

Picture Sleeves

CAPITOL.................................... 4-8 67

LPs: 10/12-inch 33rpm

CAPITOL.................................. 10-15 67

MITCHELL, Willie
(With the Four Kings)

P&R/R&B '64

Singles: 7-inch

HI... 4-8 62-69
HOME of the BLUES.................. 5-10 60-61
MOTOWN 3-5
STOMPER TIME (1160 "Tell It to Me, Baby") 40-60

Picture Sleeves

HI... 5-8 68

EPs: 7-inch 33/45rpm

HI (72 "Willie Mitchell")............. 10-15 60s

LPs: 10/12-inch 33rpm

BEARSVILLE 5-8 81
HI (12010 thru 12042).............. 10-20 63-68
(Monaural.)
HI (32010 thru 32058).............. 10-25 63-71
(Stereo.)
HI (8000 series)........................... 5-8 77
MOTOWN 8-10 82

MITCHELL TRIO

LP '64

Singles: 7-inch

MERCURY 4-8 65-66
REPRISE 4-8 67

Picture Sleeves

MERCURY 5-10 63-66

LPs: 10/12-inch 33rpm

MERCURY (20944 "Slightly Irreverent Mitchell Trio")...........................15-20 64
(Monaural.)
MERCURY (20992 "Typical American Boys") 15-20 65
(Monaural.)
MERCURY (21049 "That's the Way It's Gonna Be") 15-20 65
(Monaural.)
MERCURY (21067 "Violets of Dawn") 15-20 65
(Monaural.)
MERCURY (60944 "Slightly Irreverent Mitchell Trio")...........................20-25 64
(Stereo.)
MERCURY (60992 "Typical American Boys") 20-25 65
MERCURY (61049 "That's the Way It's Gonna Be") 20-25 65
(Stereo.)
MERCURY (21067 "Violets of Dawn") 20-25 65
(Stereo.)
REPRISE (6354 "Alive") 15-20 67

Members: Chad Mitchell; Joe Frazier; Mike Kobluk; John Denver; David Boise; Michael Johnson.

Also see DENVER, John
Also see JOHNSON, Michael
Also see MITCHELL, Chad, Trio

MITCHUM, Robert
(With the Calypso Band)

P&R '58

Singles: 78rpm

CAPITOL....................................5-10 57-58

Singles: 7-inch

CAPITOL (Except 3986).............5-10 57
CAPITOL (3986 "The Ballad of Thunder Road") 8-12 58
(Purple label.)
CAPITOL (3986 "The Ballad of Thunder Road") 4-8 62
(Orange/yellow label.)
MONUMENT...................................4-6 67

EPs: 7-inch 33/45rpm

CAPITOL (853 "Calypso Is Like So")..25-50 57
(Price is for any of three volumes.)

LPs: 10/12-inch 33rpm

CAPITOL (853 "Calypso Is Like So")......................................50-100 57
MONUMENT (8086 "That Man") 15-20 67
(Monaural.)
MONUMENT (18086 "That Man") 20-25 67
(Stereo.)

MIXTURES

P&R '71

Singles: 7–inch

SIRE 3-5 71

MOB

P&R '71

Singles: 7–inch

COLOSSUS 3-5 71-72
MGM 4-6 72
MERCURY 4-8 68
PRIVATE STOCK 3-5 76-77

Picture Sleeves

COLOSSUS 3-6 71-72

LPs: 10/12–inch 33rpm

COLOSSUS 10-15 71
MGM (4839 "The Mob") 10-15 72
PRIVATE STOCK 8-12 75

Members: Art Herrera; Al Herrera; James Holvay; Gary Beiser.

MOBY GRAPE

P&R/LP '67

Singles: 7–inch

COLUMBIA 5-10 67-69

Picture Sleeves

COLUMBIA 20-25 67

LPs: 10/12–inch 33rpm

COLUMBIA (Except 2698/ 9498) 10-15 68-72
COLUMBIA (2698 "Moby Grape") 35-45 67
(Monaural. Cover pictures Don Stevenson's middle finger over washboard. Price includes bonus poster, which represents about $5 to $10 of the value.)
COLUMBIA (2698 "Moby Grape") 10-20 67
(Monaural. Cover pictures Don Stevenson's hand closed. Price includes bonus poster.)
COLUMBIA (9498 "Moby Grape") 40-50 67
(Stereo. Cover pictures Don Stevenson's middle finger over washboard. Price includes bonus poster, which represents about $5 to $10 of the value.)
COLUMBIA (9498 "Moby Grape") 10-20 67
(Stereo. Cover pictures Don Stevenson's hand closed. Price includes bonus poster.)
ESCAPE 8-10 78
HARMONY 10-12 70-71
REPRISE 10-12 71
SAN FRANCISCO SOUND 10-15 83

Promotional LPs

COLUMBIA (MGS-1 "Grape Jam") 10-20 68
(With Mike Bloomfield and Al Kooper.)
ESCAPE (95018 "Live Grape") . 15-25 78
(Colored vinyl.)

Members: Don Stevenson; Jerry Miller; Peter Lewis; Skip Spence; Jeff Blackburn.
Also see BLOOMFIELD, Mike, & Al Kooper
Also see FRANKLIN, Aretha / Union Gap /Blood, Sweat & Tears / Moby Grape
Also see FRANTICS

MOCEDADES

P&R/LP '74

Singles: 7–inch

TARA 3-5 74

LPs: 10/12–inch 33rpm

TARA 5-10 74

MODEL 500

D&D '85

Singles: 12–inch 33/45rpm

METROPLEX 4-6 85

MODELS

P&R/LP '86

Singles: 12–inch 33/45rpm

GEFFEN 4-6 86

Singles: 7–inch

GEFFEN 3-4 86

Picture Sleeves

GEFFEN 3-4 86

LPs: 10/12–inch 33rpm

GEFFEN 5-8 86
WINDSONG 5-8 80

MODERN ENGLISH

P&R/D&D/LP '83

Singles: 12–inch 33/45rpm

SIRE 4-6 82-86

Singles: 7–inch

4AD 3-5 80-84
4AD/SIRE 3-4 83-86
LIMP ("Drowning Man") 5-8 79
(Number not known.)
SIRE 3-4 86

LPs: 10/12–inch 33rpm

4AD/SIRE 5-10 83-84
SIRE 5-8 86
TVT 5-8 90

MODERN ROCKETRY

D&D '83

Singles: 12–inch 33/45rpm

MEGATONE 4-6 83

MODERNAIRES

(With Paula Kelly)

P&R '45

Singles: 78rpm

COLUMBIA 3-6 45-50
CORAL 3-5 51-56

Singles: 7–inch

CAPITOL 3-6 69
COLUMBIA (38000 series) 5-10 50
CORAL 5-10 51-56
MERCURY 4-8 59
U.A. 4-6 62

EPs: 7-inch 33/45rpm

CORAL.. 5-10 51-55

LPs: 10/12-inch 33rpm

COLUMBIA 10-25 50-66
CORAL.................................... 15-25 51-55
LIBERTY 5-10 84
MERCURY 8-12 60
ROSS.. 5-10 79
U.A. 10-20 61-62
WING 10-15 62

Members: Paula Kelly; John Drake; Allan Copeland; Francis Scott; Hal Dickenson.

MODUGNO, Domenico

P&R/R&B/LP '58

Singles: 7-inch

DECCA.. 4-8 58-64
MCA 3-5 78
MGM 4-6 66
RCA.. 4-6 68-72
U.A. INT'L.................................... 4-6 67

EPs: 7-inch 33/45rpm

DECCA.. 5-10 58

LPs: 10/12-inch 33rpm

DECCA..................................... 15-25 58-61
RCA... 10-15 66
U.A. INT'L.................................. 8-12 67

MODULATIONS

R&B '74

Singles: 7-inch

BUDDAH 3-5 74-75

MOE & JOE: see STAMPLEY, Joe

MOJO MEN
(Mojo)

P&R '65

Singles: 7-inch

AUTUMN.................................... 8-12 65-66
GRT... 4-8 69
REPRISE 5-10 66-68

LPs: 10/12-inch 33rpm

GRT (10003 "Mojo Magic") 15-20 69

Members: Dennis DeCarr; Paul Curcio; Jim Alaimo; Don Metchick.

MOLLY HATCHET

LP '78

Singles: 7-inch

EPIC.. 3-5 79-86

EPs: 7-inch 33/45rpm

CSP 4-8 81
(Nestles candy promotional issue.)

LPs: 10/12-inch 33rpm

EPIC (Except picture discs and 40137)....................................... 5-10 78-87
EPIC (694 "Flirtin' with Disaster") 20-30 79
(Picture disc. Promotional issue only.)
EPIC (884 "Beatin' the Odds") .. 20-25 80
(Picture disc. Promotional issue only.)
EPIC (1320 "Take No Prisoners")................................15-20 81
(Picture disc. Promotional issue only.)
EPIC (35347 "Molly Hatchet")....25-30 78
(Picture disc. Promotional issue only.)
EPIC (36110 "Flirtin' with Disaster") 20-30 79
(Picture disc. Promotional issue only.)
EPIC (40137 "Double Trouble Live")...10-15 79
EPIC (40137 "Double Trouble Live")...15-25 79
(White label. Promotional issue only.)

Members: Danny Joe Brown; Jimmy Farrar.
Also see BROWN, Danny Joe

MOM & DADS

LP '71

Singles: 7-inch

GNP 3-5 71-80

LPs: 10/12-inch 33rpm

GNP 5-10 71-87

MOMENT of TRUTH

R&B '74

Singles: 7-inch

ROULETTE.....................................3-5 75

Members: Bill Jones; Michael Garrison; Norris Harris.
Also see CHAIN REACTION
Also see CHOCOLATE SYRUP

MOMENTS

P&R '63

Singles: 7-inch

ERA...5-10 63-64
HIT 5-10 63
WORLD ARTISTS 4-8 64

Also see SHACKLEFORDS

MOMENTS

P&R/R&B '68

Singles: 7-inch

STANG..3-6 68-78
SUGAR HILL..................................3-4 80-81

LPs: 10/12-inch 33rpm

STANG...8-12 70-78
VICTORY 5-8 82

Also see O'JAYS / Moments
Also see RAY, GOODMAN & BROWN
Also see SYLVIA & MOMENTS

MOMENTS & WHATNAUTS

R&B '74

Singles: 7-inch

STANG...3-5 74

Also see MOMENTS
Also see WHATNAUTS

MONAE, Tia

D&D '84

Singles: 12-inch 33/45rpm

FIRST TAKE 4-6 84

MONARCHS

P&R '64

Singles: 7-inch

MONUMENT 4-6 60s
SOUND STAGE 7 .... 8-12 64

MONDAY, Julie

P&R '66

Singles: 7-inch

RAINBOW.................................. 4-8 66
SSS INT'L.................................. 3-6 68

MONDAY AFTER

R&B '76

Singles: 7-inch

BUDDAH 3-5 76

MONDO ROCK

P&R '87

Singles: 7-inch

ATLANTIC.................................. 3-4 82
COLUMBIA 3-4 85-87

LPs: 10/12-inch 33rpm

ATLANTIC.................................. 5-8 82
COLUMBIA 5-8 85

MONET

R&B '87

Singles: 7-inch

LIGOSA.................................. 3-4 87

MONET & Nolan Thomas

R&B '87

Singles: 7-inch

LIGOSA.................................. 3-4 87
Also see MONET
Also see THOMAS, Nolan

MONEY, Eddie

P&R/LP '78

Singles: 12-inch 33/45rpm

COLUMBIA 4-6 84

Singles: 7-inch

CBS (165196 "Maybe I'm a Fool").................................. 20-40 79
(Picture disc. Promotional issue only.)
COLUMBIA 3-5 78-89
POLYDOR 3-4 85

Picture Sleeves

COLUMBIA 3-5 82-88

LPs: 10/12-inch 33rpm

COLUMBIA 6-9 77-89
POLYDOR 5-8 85

MONEY, Eddie, & Zane Buzby

Singles: 7-inch

COLUMBIA 3-5 79

MONEY, Eddie, & Valerie Carter

P&R '80

Singles: 7-inch

COLUMBIA 3-5 80
Also see CARTER, Valerie

MONEY, Eddie, & Ronnie Spector

Singles: 7-inch

COLUMBIA.................................. 3-5 86
Also see MONEY, Eddie
Also see SPECTOR, Ronnie

MONGO SANTAMARIA: see SANTAMARIA, Mongo

MONITORS

P&R/R&B '66

Singles: 7-inch

BUDDAH.................................. 3-5 72
MOTOWN 3-5
SOUL (35049 "Step By Step") 8-15 68
V.I.P. (25028 thru 25046)........... 10-20 65-68
V.I.P. (25049 "Step By Step") 20-40 68

LPs: 10/12-inch 33rpm

SOUL (714 "Greetings")............ 50-75 69

MONK, T.S.
(Thelonious Monk Jr.)

R&B '80

Singles: 7-inch

MIRAGE.................................. 3-4 80-82

LPs: 10/12-inch 33rpm

MIRAGE.................................. 5-8 81-82

MONK, Thelonious

LP '63

Singles: 7-inch

COLUMBIA 3-6 63-69
PRESTIGE.................................. 3-8 60-69

EPs: 7-inch 33/45rpm

PRESTIGE.................................. 20-40 52

LPs: 10/12-inch 33rpm

BLACK LION 5-10 74
BLUE NOTE (100 thru 500 series).................................. 6-12 73-76
BLUE NOTE (1510 "Genius of Modern Music, Vol. 1")............ 40-60 56
(Label has Lexington Ave. street address for Blue Note Records.)
BLUE NOTE (1510 "Genius of Modern Music, Vol. 1")............ 30-40 58
(Label reads, "Blue Note Records Inc. New York, U.S.A.")
BLUE NOTE (1510 "Genius of Modern Music, Vol. 1")............ 10-20 60s
(Label reads "Blue Note Records - a Division of Liberty Records Inc.")
BLUE NOTE (1511 "Genius of Modern Music, Vol. 2")............ 40-60 56
(Label has Lexington Ave. street address for Blue Note Records.)
BLUE NOTE (1511 "Genius of Modern Music, Vol. 2")............ 30-40 58
(Label reads, "Blue Note Records Inc. New York, U.S.A.")
BLUE NOTE (1511 "Genius of Modern Music, Vol. 2")............ 10-20 60s

(Label reads "Blue Note Records - a Division of Liberty Records Inc.")
BLUE NOTE (5002 "Theolonious Monk")............................. 175-275 52
(10–inch LP.)
BLUE NOTE (5009 "Theolonious Monk")............................. 175-275 52
(10–inch LP.)
COLUMBIA (1900 thru 2600 series)................................. 12-25 63-67
(Monaural.)
COLUMBIA (8700 thru 9800 series)................................. 15-30 63-69
(Stereo.)
COLUMBIA (32000 thru 38000 series)................................. 5-15 74-83
EVEREST................................. 5-10 78
MILESTONE................................. 5-15 75-84
PAUSA................................. 5-10 83
PRESTIGE (142 "Thelonious Monk Trio")........................ 75-125 52
(10–inch LP.)
PRESTIGE (180 "Thelonious Monk with Frank Foster")............... 75-125 54
(10–inch LP.)
PRESTIGE (189 "Thelonious Monk with Art Blakey")................. 50-100 54
(10–inch LP.)
PRESTIGE (7053 thru 7245) 30-60 56-62
(Yellow labels.)
PRESTIGE (7000 thru 7600 series)................................. 15-25 65-69
(Blue labels.)
PRESTIGE (24000 series).......... 8-12 72
RIVERSIDE (12-201 thru 12-323)................................. 30-60 55-60
RIVERSIDE (400 series)........... 15-30 62-67
RIVERSIDE (1100 series)......... 25-50 58-60
RIVERSIDE (3000 series)......... 10-20 68-69
RIVERSIDE (9400 series)......... 15-30 62-63
TOMATO................................. 5-10 78
TRIP................................. 5-10 73

Also see COLTRANE, John, & Thelonious Monk
Also see DAVIS, Miles, & Thelonious Monk
Also see MERC & MONK
Also see MULLIGAN, Gerry, & Thelonious Monk

MONK, Thelonious, & Sonny Rollins

EPs: 7–inch 33/45rpm

PRESTIGE................................. 20-40 52

LPs: 10/12–inch 33rpm

PRESTIGE (166 "Thelonious Monk & Sonny Rollins")............... 100-200 52
(10–inch LP.)
PRESTIGE (200 series)........... 30-60 57-58
PRESTIGE (7000 series).......... 30-60 57-59
PRESTIGE (1100 series).......... 30-60 58

MONKEES

P&R/LP '66

Singles: 12–inch 33/45rpm

ARISTA.................................8-12 86
(Promotional issue only.)

Singles: 7–inch

ARISTA (0201 "Daydream Believer")................................4-8 76
ARISTA (9000 series)....................3-6 76-86
COLGEMS.................................5-10 66-70
FLASHBACK.................................3-5 73
RHINO.................................3-5 87

Picture Sleeves

COLGEMS (1000 series)..........10-20 66-68
COLGEMS (5000 series)..........15-25 69-70

EPs: 7–Inch 33/45rpm

COLGEMS (Cardboard discs).....5-10 67
(Single-sided, four track discs, originally attached to cereal boxes. Not issued with covers, although discs were illustrated.)
COLGEMS (101 "Monkees").....50-75 66
(Stereo 33 compact. Jukebox issue.)
COLGEMS (102 "More of the Monkees").........................50-75 67
(Stereo 33 compact. Jukebox issue.)

LPs: 10/12–inch 33rpm

ARISTA (4000 series)................8-12 76
ARISTA (8000 series)....................5-8 86
BELL (6081 "Refocus")..............20-30 73
COLGEMS (COM-101 "Monkees")..............................20-30 66
(Monaural. With *Papa Jean's Blues.*)
COLGEMS (COS-101 "Monkees")..............................30-40 66
(Stereo. With *Papa Jean's Blues.*)
COLGEMS (COM-101 "Monkees")..............................15-25 66
(Monaural. Without *Papa Gene's Blues.*)
COLGEMS (COS-101 "Monkees")..............................20-30 66
(Stereo. Without *Papa Gene's Blues.*)
COLGEMS (COM-102 "More of the Monkees").........................15-25 67
(Monaural.)
COLGEMS (COS-102 "More of the Monkees").........................20-30 67
(Stereo.)
COLGEMS (COM-103 "Headquarters")......................15-25 67
(Monaural.)
COLGEMS (COS-103 "Headquarters")......................20-30 67
(Stereo.)
COLGEMS (COM-104 "Pisces, Aquarius, Capricorn and Jones")............15-25 67
(Monaural.)

COLGEMS (COS-104 "Pisces, Aquarius, Capricorn and Jones") 20-30 67
(Stereo.)
COLGEMS (COM-109 "The Birds, The Bees, and the Monkees") 50-75 68
(Monaural.)
COLGEMS (COS-109 "The Birds, The Bees, and the Monkees") 20-30 68
(Stereo.)
COLGEMS (113 "Instant Replay") 25-35 69
COLGEMS (115 "The Monkees Greatest Hits") 30-50 69
COLGEMS (117 "The Monkees Present") 50-75 69
COLGEMS (119 "Changes")... 75-100 70
COLGEMS (329 "Golden Hits") 100-125 71
(RCA Special Products issue.)
COLGEMS (1001 "A Barrel Full of Monkees") 50-75 71
COLGEMS (5008 "Head")......... 35-45 68
LAURIE HOUSE 20-30 73
(Mail-order offer.)
PAIR (0188 "The Monkees") 15-25 82
RCA (329 "Golden Hits") 50-75 72
RCA (7000 series) 8-10
RHINO 5-10 82-87

Members: Michael Nesmith; Davy Jones; Micky Dolenz; Peter Tork.
Also see DOLENZ, Micky
Also see DOLENZ, JONES & TORK
Also see JONES, Davy
Also see NESMITH, Michael

MONOTONES

P&R/R&B '58

Singles: 7–inch

ARGO (Except 5339) 10-15 58-59
ARGO (5339 "Tell It to the Judge") 15-20 59
CHESS 3-5 73
COLLECTABLES 3-4 80s
ERIC 3-4 70s
HICKORY 5-10 64-65
HULL (735 "Reading the Book of Love") 50-60 60
HULL (743 "Daddy's Home But Momma's Gone") 15-20 61
MASCOT (124 "Book of Love") 175-225 57
ROULETTE 3-5 73

LPs: 10/12–inch 33rpm

MURRAY HILL 5-8

Members: Warren Davis; Frank Smith; John Raynes; George Malone; Charles Patrick; James Patrick.

MONRO, Matt

P&R/LP '61

Singles: 7–inch

CAPITOL 3-6 66-72
LIBERTY 3-8 62-66
U.A. 3-5 74
WARWICK 4-8 61

LPs: 10/12–inch 33rpm

CAPITOL 8-15 67-70
LIBERTY 10-20 62-66
LONDON (1611 "Blue and Sentimental") 20-30 57
WARWICK (2045 "My Kind of Girl") 15-25 61

Also see BARRY, John

MONROE, Marilyn

P&R '54

Singles: 78rpm

RCA (5745 "River of No Return") 25-50 54
(With picture of Marilyn on label. Promotional only.)
RCA (6033 "Heat Wave") 10-20 55
RCA/SIMON HOUSE (5745 "River of No Return") 75-100 54
(With "Who Is She?" label. Promotional issue only.)
U.A. (161 "I Wanna Be Loved By You") 25-50 59

Singles: 7–inch

RCA (5745 "River of No Return") 25-50 54
(With picture of Marilyn on label. Promotional only.)
RCA (6033 "Heat Wave") 10-20 55
20TH FOX (311 "River of No Return") 10-15 62
U.A. (161 "I Wanna Be Loved By You") 10-15 59

Picture Sleeves

RCA (5745 "River of No Return") 50-75 54
RCA (6033 "Heat Wave") 50-75 55
20TH FOX (311 "River of No Return") 35-55 62

EPs: 7–inch 33/45rpm

MGM (208 "Gentlemen Prefer Blondes") 25-50 53
(Soundtrack. With Jane Russell.)
RCA (593 "There's No Business Like Show Business") 30-40 55
U.A. (1005 "Some Like It Hot") .. 25-35 59
(With "This Is Hot!" publicity insert for the film.)
U.A. (1005 "Some Like It Hot") .. 15-25 59
(Without film publicity insert.)

LPs: 10/12–inch 33rpm

ASCOT (13500 "Some Like It Hot") 20-30 64
(Monaural. Soundtrack.)
ASCOT (16500 "Some Like It Hot") 30-40 64

(Stereo. Soundtrack. Also has selections from other films.)
COLUMBIA (1527 "Let's Make Love")....................................30-50 60
(Monaural. Soundtrack.)
COLUMBIA (8327 "Let's Make Love")....................................40-60 60
(Stereo. Soundtrack.)
COLUMBIA/CSP (8327 "Let's Make Love")......................................8-12
(Soundtrack. With Yves Montand and Frankie Vaughan.)
MGM (208 "Gentlemen Prefer Blondes")..............................75-100 53
(10–inch LP.)
MGM (3231 "Gentlemen Prefer Blondes")..............................40-60 55
(Soundtrack. With Jane Russell. One side has music from *Till the Clouds Roll By.*)
MOVIETONE (72016 "Unforgettable")......................15-25 67
SANDY HOOK..........................5-10 79
STET..8-10
20TH FOX (5000 "Marilyn") 75-125 62
(With bonus photo of Marilyn nude.)
20TH FOX (5000 "Marilyn") 50-75 62
(Without bonus photo.)
U.A. (272 "Some Like It Hot")...... 8-12 74
(Soundtrack.)
U.A. (4030 "Some Like It Hot").. 35-55 59
(Monaural. Soundtrack.)
U.A. (5030 "Some Like It Hot").. 50-75 59
(Stereo. Soundtrack.)

MONROE, Michael

LP '89

LPs: 10/12–inch 33rpm

MERCURY..................................5-8 89

MONROE, Vaughn

P&R '40

Singles: 78rpm

BLUEBIRD..................................5-10 40-42
RCA..3-8 47-58
VICTOR......................................4-8 42-47

Singles: 7–inch

DOT..3-6 62-63
JUBILEE.....................................4-6 61
MGM..4-6 60
RCA..5-8 50-59
ROD..3-5 68
U.A. 4-6 60

Picture Sleeves

RCA..10-15 57

EPs: 7–inch 33/45rpm

CAMDEN....................................5-10 56
RCA..5-10 50-56

LPs: 10/12–inch 33rpm

CAMDEN....................................15-25 56
DOT..10-20 62-64
HAMILTON..................................10-20 65
KAPP..10-20 65
RCA (11 thru 3066)....................20-40 50-53
(10–inch LPs.)
RCA (1400 thru 1700 series).....15-25 56-58
(12–inch LPs.)
RCA (1100 series).......................5-10 75
RCA (3800 series).......................10-15 67
RCA (6000 series).......................5-10 72
Also see MARTIN, Dean / Patti Page

MONROES

P&R/LP '82

Singles: 7–inch

ALFA..3-5 82

LPs: 10/12–inch 33rpm

ALFA (15015 "The Monroes") 100-200 82

MONTANA ORCHESTRA

LP '81

LPs: 10/12–inch 33rpm

MJS...5-8 81

MONTANA SEXTET

D&D '83

Singles: 12–inch 33/45rpm

PHILLY SOUND............................4-6 83

MONTANAS

P&R '68

Singles: 7–inch

INDEPENDENCE..........................5-10 67-69
W.B. 4-8 66-68

MONTCLAIRS

R&B '72

Singles: 7–inch

PAULA..3-5 71-74

LPs: 10/12–inch 33rpm

PAULA..8-12 72

MONTE, Lou

P&R '54

Singles: 78rpm

RCA (Except 6704)......................3-5 53-56
RCA (6704 "Elvis Presley for President")..........................10-15 56

Singles: 7–inch

GWP..3-5 71-72
JAMIE...3-5 72
RCA (5382 thru 6600 series).......8-12 53-56
RCA (6700 thru 7600 series, except 6704)...5-10 56-60
RCA (6704 "Elvis Presley for President")..........................15-25 56
RCA (8700 thru 9000 series).........4-8 65-67
RAGALIA.....................................3-6 69
REPRISE.....................................4-8 62-65
ROULETTE..................................4-8 60-61

Picture Sleeves

REPRISE.....................................5-8 62-63

EPs: 7–inch 33/45rpm

RCA (Except 18).........................8-12 57-59

RCA (18 "Elvis Presley for President") 20-30 56
(Promotional issue only. Not issued with cover.)

LPs: 10/12-inch 33rpm

CAMDEN 15-20 58
HARMONY 10-15 68
RCA (1600 thru 1900 series) 20-35 57-59
RCA (3000 series) 10-20 66-67
ROULETTE 15-25 60
REPRISE 15-25 61-65

MONTENEGRO, Hugo
(With Orchestra & Chorus)

LP '66

Singles: 7-inch

RCA 3-5 64-75
TIME 4-6 61-63
20TH FOX 5-8 59

LPs: 10/12-inch 33rpm

CAMDEN 10-20 62
GWP 5-10 70
MAINSTREAM 10-15 67-68
MOVIETONE 8-12 67
PICKWICK 5-10 70s
RCA (0025 thru 2300 series) 5-10 72-77
RCA (LOC-1113 "Hurry Sundown") 35-40 67
(Monaural. Soundtrack.)
RCA (LSO-1113 "Hurry Sundown") 40-50 67
(Stereo. Soundtrack.)
RCA (2900 series) 10-15 64
RCA (LPM-3475 "Man from UNCLE") 25-35 65
(Monaural. Soundtrack.)
RCA (LSP-3475 "Man from UNCLE") 30-40 65
(Stereo. Soundtrack.)
RCA (LPM-3574 "Man from UNCLE, Volume 2") 30-40 66
(Monaural. Soundtrack.)
RCA (LSP-3574 "Man from UNCLE, Volume 2") 35-45 66
(Stereo. Soundtrack.)
RCA (3500 thru 4600 series) 5-15 66-71
RCA (6000 series) 5-10 71
TIME 8-15 60-64
20TH FOX 5-15 59-68
Also see HIRT, Al, & Hugo Montenegro

MONTEZ, Chris

P&R/R&B '62

Singles: 7-inch

A&M 4-6 65-68
COLLECTABLES 3-4 80s
ERA 3-5 72
ERIC 3-4 70s
JAMIE 3-5 73
MONOGRAM 5-10 62-64
PARAMOUNT 3-5 71-73

LPs: 10/12-inch 33rpm

A&M 10-20 66-67
MONOGRAM (100 "Let's Dance") 45-65 63
Members: Joel Hill; Carol Kaye; Julius Wechter; Pete Jolly; Tom Tedesco; Hal Blaine.
Also see BAJA MARIMBA BAND
Also see JOLLY, Pete

MONTGOMERY, Melba

C&W '63

Singles: 7-inch

CAPITOL 3-5 69-76
COMPASS 3-4 86
ELEKTRA 3-5 73-75
KARI 3-5 80
MUSICOR 3-6 66-69
U.A. (500 thru 900 series) 4-8 63-66
U.A. (1000 & 1100 series) 3-5 77

Picture Sleeves

MUSICOR 4-8 66

LPs: 10/12-inch 33rpm

CAPITOL 8-12 69-75
ELEKTRA 5-10 73-75
MUSICOR 10-20 66-68
UNART 8-12 67
U.A. (Except 600 series) 10-20 64
U.A. (600 series) 5-10 78
Also see JONES, George, Gene Pitney & Melba Montgomery
Also see JONES, George, & Melba Montgomery
Also see PITNEY, Gene, & Melba Montgomery
Also see WEST, Dottie / Melba Montgomery

MONTGOMERY, Tammy
(Tana Montgomery; Tammi Terrell)

P&R '63

Singles: 7-inch

CHECKER (1072 "If I Would Marry You") 25-35 64
(Maroon label.)
CHECKER (1072 "If I Would Marry You") 15-25 64
(Multi-color label.)
SCEPTER (1224 "If You See Bill") 30-50 61
TRY ME (28001 "I Cried") 20-30 63
WAND (123 "Voice of Experience") 20-30 62
Also see TERRELL, Tammi

MONTGOMERY, Tana: see MONTGOMERY, Tammy

MONTGOMERY, Wes
(Wes Montgomery Quartet)

LP '65

Singles: 7-inch

A&M 3-5 67-70
PACIFIC JAZZ 4-8 60
RIVERSIDE 4-8 61-64
VERVE 4-6 65-68

LPs: 10/12-inch 33rpm

A&M 10-15 67-70
ACCORD.. 5-8 82
BLUE NOTE.................................. 6-12 75
MGM 10-15 70
MILESTONE 8-15 73-83
PACIFIC JAZZ (5 Montgomeryland")................. 35-45 60
PACIFIC JAZZ (10000 & 20000 series) 10-20 66-68
RIVERSIDE (034 thru 089) 5-8 82-83
RIVERSIDE (300 & 400 series) 15-30 59-67
RIVERSIDE (3000 series)......... 10-15 68-69
VERVE 10-20 65-72
(Reads "MGM Records - A Division of Metro-Goldwyn-Mayer, Inc." at bottom of label.)
VERVE 5-10 73-84
(Reads "Manufactured By MGM Record Corp.," or mentions either Polydor or Polygram at bottom of label.)
Also see SMITH, Jimmy, & Wes Montgomery

MONTRE-EL, Jackie

R&B '68

Singles: 7-inch

ABC 4-8 68

MONTROSE

LP '74

Singles: 7-inch

W.B. 3-5 74-77

LPs: 10/12-inch 33rpm

ENIGMA 5-8 87
W.B. 8-12 73-78
Members: Ronnie Montrose; Sammy Hagar.
Also see HAGAR, Sammy

MONTROSE, Ronnie

LP '78

Singles: 7-inch

W.B. 3-5 78

LPs: 10/12-inch 33rpm

W.B. 5-10 78
Also see GAMMA
Also see MONTROSE
Also see WINTER, Edgar

MONTY PYTHON

LP '75

Singles: 7-inch

ARISTA 3-5 80

LPs: 10/12-inch 33rpm

ARISTA 5-10 75-82
MCA 5-8 83
W.B. 5-10 79
PYE 5-10 75
Members: John Cleese; Graham Chapman; Eric Idle; Michael Palin; Terry Jones; Terry Gilliam.
Also see RUTLES

MONYAKA

D&D '83

Singles: 12-inch 33/45rpm

EASY STREET 4-6 83

MOODY BLUES

P&R '65

Singles: 7-inch

DERAM 4-8 68-72
LONDON (200 series) 3-5 78
LONDON (1005 "This Is My House")......................................8-12 67
LONDON (9726 "Go Now")..........5-10 65
LONDON (9764 "From the Bottom of My Heart")..............................10-15 65
LONDON (9799 "Ev'ry Day") 10-15 65
LONDON (9810 "Stop") 10-15 66
LONDON (20000 series) 8-12 66
POLYDOR (Except 7078).............3-4 86-88
POLYDOR (7078 "The Other Side of Life")..4-6 86
(Colored vinyl.)
THRESHOLD (600 series)............3-4 81-85
THRESHOLD (67000 series).........3-6 70-72

Picture Sleeves

POLYDOR (7078 "The Other Side of Life")..4-6 86
POLYDOR (883906 "Your Wildest Dreams")......................................3-4 86
POLYDOR (885201 "The Other Side of Life")..3-4 86
POLYDOR (887600 "I Know You're Out There Somewhere") 3-4 88
THRESHOLD (602 "The Voice")....3-4 81
THRESHOLD (604 "Sitting at the Wheel") 3-4 81
THRESHOLD (67006 "The Story in Your Eyes")...............................3-5 71

LPs: 10/12-inch 33rpm

DERAM (16012 "Days of Future Passed") 30-40 68
(Monaural.)
DERAM (18012 "Days of Future Passed") 10-20 68
(Stereo.)
DERAM (18017 "In Search of the Lost Chord")............................10-20 68
(Gatefold cover.)
DERAM (18017 "In Search of the Lost Chord")..............................5-10
(Standard cover.)
DERAM (18025 "On the Threshold of a Dream")............................10-20 69
(Gatefold cover.)
DERAM (18025 "On the Threshold of a Dream")..............................5-10 69
(Standard cover.)
DERAM (18051 "In the Beginning") 10-20 69

DERAM (820006 "Days of Future Passed")........................ 5-10
LONDON (428 "Go Now")......... 20-25 65
(Stereo.)
LONDON (690/1 "Caught Live") 10-20 77
LONDON (708 "Octave") 8-10 78
(Black vinyl.)
LONDON (708 "Octave") 20-25 78
(Colored vinyl. Promotional issue only.)
LONDON (3428 "Go Now")....... 25-45 65
(Monaural.)
MFSL (042 "Days of Future Past") 25-50 80
MFSL (151 "Seventh Sojourn") . 15-25 85
POLYDOR (835765 "Sur la Mer") 5-10 88
POLYDOR (849433 "Keys of the Kingdom") 5-10 91
THRESHOLD (1 "To Our Children's Children's Children") 8-12 69
(Gatefold cover.)
THRESHOLD (1 "To Our Children's Children's Children") 5-10
(Standard cover.)
THRESHOLD (3 "A Question of Balance")................................ 8-12 70
(Gatefold cover.)
THRESHOLD (3 "A Question of Balance")................................ 5-10
(Standard cover.)
THRESHOLD (5 "Every Good Boy Deserves Favor")..................... 8-10 71
(Gatefold cover.)
THRESHOLD (7 "Seventh Sojourn") 8-10 72
(Gatefold cover.)
THRESHOLD (12/13 "This Is the Moody Blues")........................ 10-12 70
(Two LPs.)
THRESHOLD (2901 "Long Distance Voyager") 5-10 81
(Gatefold cover.)
THRESHOLD (2902 "The Present") 5-10 83
THRESHOLD (820155 "Voices in the Sky")................................... 5-10 85
THRESHOLD (820517 "Prelude") 5-10 86
THRESHOLD (829179 "Other Side of Life")..................................... 5-10 86
THRESHOLD (840659 "Greatest Hits") 5-10 89

Members: Michael Pinder; Ray Thomas; Graeme Edge; Brian Hines (a.k.a. Denny Laine); Clint Warwick; John Lodge; Justin Hayward; Patrick Moraz; Rod Clarke.

Also see EDGE, Graeme
Also see HAYWARD, Justin, & John Lodge
Also see LODGE, John
Also see MORAZ, Patrick
Also see PINDER, Michael
Also see THOMAS, Ray

MOOG MACHINE

LP '69

LPs: 10/12-inch 33rpm

COLUMBIA 5-10 69

MOON, Keith

LP '75

Singles: 7-inch

TRACK..3-5 75

LPs: 10/12-inch 33rpm

MCA..8-10 75

Also see NELSON, Rick
Also see WHO

MOONEY, Art, & His Orchestra

P&R '48

Singles: 78rpm

MGM 3-5 48-57
VOGUE (Except 711 & 713) 25-40 46-48
(Picture discs.)
VOGUE (711 "I've Been Working on the Railroad")....................50-100 46
(Picture disc.)
VOGUE (713 "I've Been Working on the Railroad")....................50-100 46
(Picture discs.)

Singles: 7-inch

DECCA 3-6 61-62
KAPP 3-6 64-65
MGM (Except 12312)....................4-8 50-64
MGM (12312 "Rebel Without a Cause"/ "East of Eden") 5-10 56
RIVERSIDE.....................................3-5 62

Picture Sleeves

MGM (12312 "Rebel Without a Cause"/ "East of Eden") 20-30 56
(Billed as a "Tribute to James Dean.")

EPs: 7-inch 33/45rpm

MGM (Except 1342).....................5-10 55-56
MGM (1342 "Music from Movies Starring James Dean") 30-40 55-56

LPs: 10/12-inch 33rpm

DECCA 10-15 62
KAPP 10-15 64
MGM 10-25 55-61
RCA 8-12 67
SPINORAMA 8-12 62

Also see AMES BROTHERS
Also see GORDON, Barry

MOONEY, Art / Frankie Carle

LP: 10/12-inch 33rpm

CORONET 5-10 60s

Also see MOONEY, Art, & His Orch.

MOONGLOWS

R&B '54

Singles: 78rpm

CHAMPAGNE (7500 "I Just Can't Tell No Lie") 100-200 52

CHANCE 1147 "Baby Please")............................ 150-250 53
CHANCE (1150 "Just a Lonely Christmas") 150-250 53
CHANCE (1152 "Secret Love")................................. 75-125 54
CHANCE (1156 "I Was Wrong")............................... 75-125 54
CHANCE (1161 "219 Train")... 75-100 54
CHESS (1500 & 1600 series) ... 15-30 54-57

Singles: 7–inch

BIG P.. 4-6 71
CHAMPAGNE (7500 "I Just Can't Tell No Lie") 1000-1500 52
CHANCE (1147 "Baby Please")......................... 1500-2000 53
(Colored vinyl.)
CHANCE (1150 "Just a Lonely Christmas") 1500-2000 53
(Colored vinyl.)
CHANCE (1152 "Secret Love").............................. 750-1000 54
(Blue and silver label.)
CHANCE (1152 "Secret Love")................................ 500-700 54
(Yellow and black label.)
CHANCE (1156 "I Was Wrong")............................ 750-1000 54
(Yellow and black label.)
CHANCE (1156 "I Was Wrong")............................. 400-600 55
(White and black label.)
CHANCE (1161 "219 Train") 800-1200 54
(White and black label.)
CHESS (1581 "Sincerely")........ 40-60 54
(Silver top label with chess pieces.)
CHESS (1581 "Sincerely")......... 5-10 60s
(Blue label.)
CHESS (1589 "Most of All")...... 40-60 54
(Silver top label with chess pieces.)
CHESS (1589 "Most of All")........ 5-10 60s
(Blue label.)
CHESS (1598 "Foolish Me") 30-40 55
(Silver top label with chess pieces.)
CHESS (1598 "Foolish Me") 5-10 60s
(Blue label.)
CHESS (1605 "Starlite")........... 30-40 55
(Silver top label with chess pieces.)
CHESS (1605 "Starlite").............. 5-10 60s
(Blue label.)
CHESS (1611 In My Diary")...... 30-40 55
(Silver top label with chess pieces.)
CHESS (1611 In My Diary")........ 5-10 60s
(Blue label.)
CHESS (1619 "We Go Together") 30-40 56
(Silver top label with chess pieces.)
CHESS (1619 "We Go Together")...............................5-10 60s
(Blue label.)
CHESS (1629 "See Saw") 25-35 56
(Silver top label with chess pieces.)
CHESS (1629 "See Saw") 5-10 60s
(Blue label.)
CHESS (1646 "Over and Over Again") 20-40 56
(Silver top label with chess pieces.)
CHESS (1646 "Over and Over Again") 5-10 60s
(Blue label.)
CHESS (1651 "I'm Afraid the Masquerade Is Over").............20-40 56
(Silver top label with chess pieces.)
CHESS (1651 "I'm Afraid the Masquerade Is Over")...............5-10 60s
(Blue label.)
CHESS (1661 "Please Send Me Someone to Love")..................20-40 57
(Silver top label with chess pieces.)
CHESS (1661 "Please Send Me Someone to Love")...................5-10 60s
(Blue label.)
CHESS (1669 "The Beating of My Heart")..............................20-40 57
CHESS (1681 "Too Late") 15-25 58
CHESS (1689 "Soda Pop")........15-25 58
CHESS (1701 "This Love")........15-25 58
CHESS (1717 "I'll Never Stop Wanting You")..........................15-25 58
CHESS (1770 "Beatnik")...........10-20 60
CHESS (1781 "Mama")..............15-25 61
CRIMSON (1003 "My Imagination")...........................15-20 64
LANA...3-6 64
RCA 3-6 72
TIMES SQUARE.......................10-15 64
VEE JAY 8-12 61

EPs: 7–inch 33/45rpm

CHESS (5122 "Look! It's the Moonglows")................100-200 59
CHESS (5123 "Look! It's the Moonglows, Vol. 2").......100-200 59

LPs: 10/12–inch 33rpm

CHESS (701 "The Moonglows") 10-15 76
CHESS (1430 "Look, It's the Moonglows") 200-300 59
CONSTELLATION (2 "Collectors Showcase")..............................20-30 64
LOST-NITE 5-10 81
RCA 10-15 72

Members: Harvey Fuqua; Bobby Lester; Alex Graves; Prentiss Barnes; Marvin Gaye; Reese Palmer; James Knowland; Chester Simmons; George Thorpe; Dock Green; Berle Ashton.

Also see DIDDLEY, Bo
Also see DRIFTERS

Also see FLAMINGOS / Moonglows
Also see GAYE, Marvin
Also see HARVEY & MOONGLOWS
Also see LESTER, Bobby

MOONLION

P&R '76

Singles: 7–inch

P.I.P. 3-5 76

MOORE, Bill

R&B '48

Singles: 78rpm

SAVOY 10-15 48

Also see WILLIAMS, Paul

MOORE, Bob

P&R/R&B/LP '61

Singles: 7–inch

HICKORY 4-6 65-68
MONUMENT 4-8 59-64

Picture Sleeves

MONUMENT 4-8 62-63

LPs: 10/12–inch 33rpm

HICKORY 10-15 66
MONUMENT 10-20 61-67

Also see DRAGON, Paul
Also see LEE, Brenda
Also see NELSON, Willie
Also see PRESLEY, Elvis

MOORE, Bobby
(With the Rhythm Aces)

P&R/R&B '66

Singles: 12–inch 33/45rpm

SCEPTER (12417 "Try to Hold On") 5-8 75
(Promotional issue only.)

Singles: 7–inch

CHECKER 4-8 66-68

LPs: 10/12–inch 33rpm

CHECKER (3000 "Searching for My Love") 15-25 66

MOORE, Bobby

P&R/R&B '75

Singles: 7–inch

SCEPTER 3-5 75-76

MOORE, Dorothy
(Dorothy Moore)

R&B '73

Singles: 12–inch 33/45rpm

STREETKING 4-6 84

Singles: 7–inch

GSF 3-5 73
HANDSHAKE 3-4 82
MALACO 3-5 76-80
STREETKING 3-4 84

LPs: 10/12–inch 33rpm

MALACO 5-8 76-78

Also see CHEE-CHEE & PEPPY
Also see POPPIES

MOORE, Dorothy, & Eddie Floyd

R&B '77

Singles: 7–inch

MALACO 3-5 77

Also see FLOYD, Eddie
Also see MOORE, Dorothy

MOORE, Gary
(Gary Moore Band)

LP '83

Singles: 7–inch

JET 3-5 79
MIRAGE 3-4 83-86
VIRGIN 3-4 87-89

LPs: 10/12–inch 33rpm

CHARISMA 5-8 90
JET 5-10 78
MIRAGE 5-8 83-86
PETERS INT'L (9004 "Grinding Stone") 12-15 73
(Red label.)
PETERS INT'L (9004 "Grinding Stone") 10-12 73
(Orange label.)
VIRGIN 5-8 87-89

Also see THIN LIZZY

MOORE, Jackie
(With the Memphis Horns; with Dixie Flyers)

P&R/R&B '70

Singles: 12–inch 33/45rpm

COLUMBIA 4-8 79-84

Singles: 7–inch

ATLANTIC 3-5 70-73
CATAWBA 3-4 83
COLUMBIA 3-5 79-84
KAYVETTE 3-5 75-81
SHOUT 4-8 68

LPs: 10/12–inch 33rpm

COLUMBIA 5-10 79

Also see LULU
Also see MEMPHIS HORNS

MOORE, Johnny
(With the Blazers; with Three Blazers; with New Blazers; with Twigs)

R&B '46

Singles: 78rpm

ALADDIN 10-20 45-48
EXCLUSIVE 10-20 46-48
HOLLYWOOD 8-12 55-56
MODERN 8-12 48-50
MODERN MUSIC 10-20 45-46
PHILO 10-20 46
RCA 5-10 50
SWING TIME 5-10 51

Singles: 7–inch

ALADDIN (112 "Drifting Blues") 75-125 51
BLAZE (101 "Miss Mosey") 20-30
BRUNSWICK 3-5 71

HOLLYWOOD (1031 "Why Johnny Why") 20-30 55
HOLLYWOOD (1045 "Christmas Eve Baby") 20-30 55
HOLLYWOOD (1056 "I Send My Love").. 20-30 56
MODERN (800 & 900 series).... 15-25 53
RCA (0009 "This Is One Time Baby") 25-50 50
(Colored vinyl.)
RCA (0018 "Bop-A-Bye Baby"). 25-50 50
(Colored vinyl.)
RCA (0026 "Walkin' Blues") 25-50 50
(Colored vinyl.)
RCA (0031 "Shuffle Shuck") 25-50 50
(Colored vinyl.)
RCA (0043 "So Long") 25-50 50
(Colored vinyl.)
RCA (0073 "Misery Blues") 25-50 50
(Colored vinyl.)
RCA (0086 "Rain-Check") 25-50 50
(Colored vinyl.)
RCA (0095 "Jumping Jack")...... 25-50 50
(Colored vinyl.)
RENDEZVOUS 5-10 60

Members: Johnny Moore; Charles Brown; Eddie Williams.
Also see BROWN, Charles
Also see DIXON, Floyd, & Johnny Moore's Three Blazers
Also see McSHANN, Jay, & Johnny Moore's Three Blazers

MOORE, Johnny, & Linda Hayes

Singles: 7–inch

HOLLYWOOD (1031 "Why, Johnny [Ace] Why 30-40 55
Also see HAYES, Linda
Also see MOORE, Johnny

MOORE, Lee

R&B '79

Singles: 7–inch

SOURCE.. 3-5 79

MOORE, Melba

LP '71

Singles: 12–inch 33/45rpm

CAPITOL... 4-6 83-86
EPIC.. 4-8 79-80

Singles: 7–inch

BUDDAH 3-5 75-78
CAPITOL... 3-4 82-87
EMI AMERICA 3-4 81-82
EPIC.. 3-5 78-80
MERCURY 3-6 69-72
MUSICOR 4-8 66

Picture Sleeves

BUDDAH 3-5 76

LPs: 10/12–inch 33rpm

ACCORD... 5-10 81
BUDDAH 8-10 75-79
CAPITOL..5-8 83-86
EMI AMERICA 5-10 81
EPIC...5-10 78-80
MERCURY.....................................10-15 70-72

Also see THOMAS, Lillo, & Melba Moore

MOORE, Melba, & Freddie Jackson

R&B '88

Singles: 7–inch

CAPITOL..3-4 86-88

Also see JACKSON, Freddie

MOORE, Melba, & Kashif

(Melba & Kashif)

R&B '86

Singles: 7–inch

CAPITOL..3-4 86

Also see KASHIF
Also see MOORE, Melba

MOORE, Tim

P&R '73

Singles: 7–inch

ASYLUM 3-5 74-79
DUNHILL..3-5 73

Picture Sleeves

ASYLUM 3-5 75

LPs: 10/12–inch 33rpm

ASYLUM 5-10 74-75
SMALL (0601 "Second Avenue") 10-15 74

MOORE, Vinnie

LP '88

LPs: 10/12–inch 33rpm

SQUAWK..5-8 88

MORALES, Michael

P&R/LP '89

Singles: 7–inch

WING 3-4 89

Picture Sleeves

WING 3-4 89

LPs: 10/12–inch 33rpm

WING 5-8 89

MORAZ, Patrick

LP '76

LPs: 10/12–inch 33rpm

ATLANTIC...8-12 76
CHRISIMA 5-8 78
IMPORT...8-10 77
PASSPORT 5-8

Also see MOODY BLUES
Also see YES

MORGAN, Denroy

R&B '81

Singles: 12–inch 33/45rpm

BECKET..4-6 81-82

Singles: 7–inch

BECKET..3-5 81

MORGAN, Jane
(With the Troubadors)

P&R/LP '57

Singles: 78rpm

KAPP 3-6 54-57

Singles: 7-inch

ABC 4-6 67-68
EPIC 4-6 65-68
COLPIX 4-8 63-65
KAPP 5-10 54-62
RCA 3-6 69-70

EPs: 7-inch 33/45rpm

KAPP 5-10 55-59

Picture Sleeves

COLPIX 5-10 63
ELEKTRA 3-4 82
EPIC 4-8 65
KAPP 5-12 57-59

LPs: 10/12-inch 33rpm

ABC 5-10 68
COLPIX 10-20 63-66
EPIC 10-15 65-67
KAPP 10-20 56-63
MCA 5-10 73
RCA (Except 1160) 8-12 69-70
RCA (1160 "Marry Me, Marry Me") 10-15 69
(Soundtrack.)
HARMONY 5-8 70

Also see WILLIAMS, Roger, & Jane Morgan

MORGAN, Jaye P.

P&R '53

Singles: 78rpm

DECCA 3-6 54-55
DERBY 3-6 53
RCA 3-6 54-56

Singles: 7-inch

ABC-PAR 4-6 65
BEVERLY HILLS 3-5 69-72
DECCA 5-10 54-55
DERBY 5-10 53
GIGOLO 3-5
MGM 4-8 59-63
RCA 5-10 54-56

EPs: 7-inch 33/45rpm

DECCA 10-20 55
DERBY 10-20 53

LPs: 10/12-inch 33rpm

BAINBRIDGE 5-10 82
BEVERLY HILLS 5-8 70
MGM 15-25 59-61
RCA (1155 "Jaye P. Morgan") .. 20-30 55
ROYALE (18122 "Jaye P. Morgan") 20-30 55
(10–inch LP. Side 2 has uncredited instrumentals.)

Also see COMO, Perry, & Jaye P. Morgan
Also see PRESLEY, Elvis / Jaye P. Morgan

MORGAN, Lee

P&R/R&B/LP '64

Singles: 7-inch

BLUE NOTE 4-6 64-69
BUZZ 3-5 79-80
VEE JAY 4-8 60

LPs: 10/12-inch 33rpm

BLUE NOTE (200 series) 8-12 74
BLUE NOTE (900 & 1000 series) 5-10 79-81
BLUE NOTE (1500 series) 25-50 56-58
(Label gives New York street address for Blue Note Records.)
BLUE NOTE (1500 series) 15-25 58
(Label reads: "Blue Note Records Inc. - New York, USA.")
BLUE NOTE (1500 series) 10-20 66
(Label shows Blue Note Records as a division of either Liberty or United Artists.)
BLUE NOTE (4000 series) 20-40 61
(Label gives New York street address for Blue Note Records.)
BLUE NOTE (4000 series) 15-25 62
(Label reads: "Blue Note Records Inc. - New York, USA.")
BLUE NOTE (4000 series) 10-20 66
(Label shows Blue Note Records as a division of either Liberty or United Artists.)
BLUE NOTE (4100 thru 4200 series) 15-25 63
(Label reads: "Blue Note Records Inc. - New York, USA.")
BLUE NOTE (4100 thru 4200 series) 10-20 66-67
(Label shows Blue Note Records as a division of either Liberty or United Artists.)
BLUE NOTE (84000 series) 20-40 61
(Label gives New York street address for Blue Note Records.)
BLUE NOTE (84000 series) 15-25 62
(Label reads: "Blue Note Records Inc. - New York, USA.")
BLUE NOTE (84000 series) 10-20 66
(Label shows Blue Note Records as a division of either Liberty or United Artists.)
BLUE NOTE (84100 thru 84200 series) 15-25 63-69
(Label reads: "Blue Note Records Inc. - New York, USA.")
BLUE NOTE (84100 thru 84300 series) 10-20 66-70
(Label shows Blue Note Records as a division of either Liberty or United Artists.)
BLUE NOTE (89000 series) 10-15 71
GNP 6-12 73
JAZZLAND 15-25 62
MCA 5-8 74
PACIFIC JAZZ 5-8 81
PRESTIGE 5-8 81

SAVOY (12091 "Introducing Lee Morgan") 50 75 56
SUNSET 5-10 69
TRADITION 8-15 68
TRIP 6-10 73
VEE JAY 25-50 60-65

MORGAN, Lorrie

C&W '79

Singles: 7-inch

ABC/HICKORY 3-6 79
MCA 3-5 79
RCA 3-4 88-91

LPs: 10/12-inch 33rpm

RCA 5-8 88-90

MORGAN, Lorrie & George

C&W '79

Singles: 7-inch

FOUR STAR 3-5 79
Also see MORGAN, Lorrie

MORGAN, Meli'sa

R&B '85

Singles: 12-inch 33/45rpm

CAPITOL 4-6 86

Singles: 7-inch

CAPITOL 3-4 86-88

Picture Sleeves

CAPITOL 3-4 86

LPs: 10/12-inch 33rpm

CAPITOL 5-8 86-87
Also see KASHIF & Meli'sa Morgan

MORGAN, Russ, & His Orchestra

P&R '35

Singles: 78rpm

BRUNSWICK 4-6 36-38
COLUMBIA 4-6 35
DECCA 3-5 38-56

Singles: 7-inch

DECCA 5-10 50-56
EVEREST 4-6 61
VEE JAY 4-6 64-65

EPs: 7-inch 33/45rpm

DECCA 5-10 51-56
EPIC 5-10 53

LPs: 10/12-inch 33rpm

CAPITOL 10-15 62
CIRCLE 5-10 81
DECCA 10-30 51-67
EVEREST 10-15 60-63
GNP 5-10 73
MCA 5-10 73
PICKWICK 5-10 65
SUNSET 8-12 66
VEE JAY 10-15 65

MORGAN BROTHERS

P&R '59

Singles: 7-inch

MGM 4-8 58-60

RCA 5-10 55

MORISETTE, Johnnie

P&R/R&B '62

Singles: 7-inch

BAYTONE (116 "Run") 10-20
SAR 8-12 60-63

MORLEY, Cozy

P&R '57

Singles: 78rpm

ABC-PAR 10-15 57

Singles: 7-inch

ABC-PAR 10-20 57

MORMON TABERNACLE CHOIR

P&R/LP '59

Singles: 7-inch

COLUMBIA 3-5 59

Picture Sleeves

COLUMBIA 4-8 59

LPs: 10/12-inch 33rpm

COLUMBIA 5-10 59-76
RCA 5-10 60

MORNING MIST

P&R '71

Singles: 7-inch

EVENT 3-5 71
Members: Terry Cashman; Tommy West.
Also see CASHMAN & WEST

MORNING, NOON & NIGHT

R&B '77

Singles: 7-inch

ROADSHOW 3-5 77

LPs: 10/12-inch 33rpm

ROADSHOW 8-10 77

MORODER, Giorgio
(Giorgio)

P&R '72

Singles: 12-inch 33/45rpm

COLUMBIA 4-6 84
MCA 4-6 84

Singles: 7-inch

BACKSTREET 3-4
CASABLANCA 3-5 79-80
COLUMBIA 3-4 84
DUNHILL 3-5 72
EMI AMERICA 3-4 84
MCA 3-4 84
POLYDOR 3-5 80
VIRGIN 3-4

Picture Sleeves

COLUMBIA 3-4 84

LPs: 10/12-inch 33rpm

CASABLANCA 5-10 77-79
DUNHILL 10-12 72
POLYDOR 5-10 80
Also see MERCURY, Freddie / Giorgio Moroder
Also see SUMMER, Donna

MORODER, Giorgio, & Phil Oakey

D&D '84

Singles: 12–inch 33/45rpm

VIRGIN.. 4-6 84

Also see HUMAN LEAGUE

Also see MORODER, Giorgio

MORRIS, David, Jr.

R&B '76

Singles: 7–inch

BUDDAH.. 3-5 76

PHILIPS.. 4-8 68

MORRIS, Gary

C&W '80

Singles: 7–inch

UNIVERSAL.. 3-4 89

W.B.. 3-5 80-88

LPs: 10/12–inch 33rpm

W.B.. 5-8 82-88

Also see ANDERSON, Lynn, & Gary Morris

Also see GAYLE, Crystal, & Gary Morris

MORRIS, Joe, & His Orchestra

(With Laurie Tate; Mr. Stringbean; Al Savage)

R&B '53

Singles: 78rpm

ATLANTIC (Except 950, 954 & 974).. 10-15 47-57

ATLANTIC (950 "If I Had Known").. 20-30 51

ATLANTIC (954 "Someday You'll Be Sorry").. 15-25 52

ATLANTIC (974 "Bald Headed Woman").. 15-25 52

DECCA.. 4-8 49-50

HERALD.. 5-10 53-54

MANOR.. 5-10 46-47

Singles: 7–inch

ATLANTIC (950 "If I Had Known").. 75-125 51

(Vocals by Billy Mitchell and Teddy Smith.)

ATLANTIC (954 "Someday You'll Be Sorry").. 50-100 52

(Vocal by Billy Mitchell.)

ATLANTIC (974 "Bald Headed Woman").. 50-100 52

(Vocal by Billy Mitchell.)

ATLANTIC (1100 series).......... 10-15 57

HERALD (Except 420)............. 10-20 53-54

HERALD (420 "Travelin' Man"). 20-30 54

(Black vinyl.)

HERALD (420 "Travelin' Man"). 40-60 54

(Colored vinyl.)

Also see ADAMS, Faye

MORRIS, Joe, & His Orchestra

(Featuring Billy Mitchell)

Singles: 78rpm

ATLANTIC.. 10-15 51-52

Singles: 7–inch

ATLANTIC.. 20-40 51-52

Also see MITCHELL, Billy

MORRIS, Joe, & His Orchestra

(Featuring Laurie Tate)

R&B '50

Singles: 78rpm

ATLANTIC (914 "Anytime, Any Place, Anywhere").. 20-30 50

ATLANTIC (923 "Don't Take Your Love Away from Me").. 15-25 50

Also see TATE, Laurie

MORRIS, Marlowe, Quintet

P&R '62

Singles: 7–inch

COLUMBIA.. 4-8 62

MORRISON, Dorothy

P&R '69

Singles: 7–inch

BUDDAH.. 3-5 70

ELEKTRA.. 4-6 69

LPs: 10/12–inch 33rpm

BUDDAH.. 10-15 70

Also see HAWKINS, Edwin, Singers

MORRISON, Junie

D&D '84

Singles: 12–inch 33/45rpm

ISLAND.. 4-6 84

Singles: 7–inch

ISLAND.. 3-4 84

Also see JUNIE

MORRISON, Professor

(Professor Morrison's Lollipop)

P&R '68

Singles: 7–inch

WHITE WHALE.. 5-10 68-69

MORRISON, Van

P&R/LP '67

Singles: 7–inch

BANG.. 4-8 67-68

MERCURY.. 3-4 85-90

SOLID GOLD.. 3-4 73

W.B.. 3-5 70-83

LPs: 10/12–inch 33rpm

BANG (BLP-218 "Blowin' Your Mind").. 20-25 67

(Monaural.)

BANG (BLPS-218 "Blowin' Your Mind").. 25-30 67

(Stereo. White label. Has 45rpm version of *Brown-Eyed Girl,* with "makin' love in the green grass behind the stadium" lyrics.)

BANG (BLPS-218 "Blowin' Your Mind").. 25-30 67

(Stereo. White label. Has edited *Brown-Eyed Girl,* with "laughin' and a runnin' behind the stadium" lyrics.)

BANG (BLPS-218 "Blowin' Your Mind") 10-15 70
(Yellow label.)
BANG (400 "T.B. Sheets") 10-15 74
LONDON 10-15 74
MERCURY 5-10 85-90
W.B. 8-15 68-83
Also see THEM

MORRISON, Van, & Chieftains

LP '88

LP: 10/12-inch 33rpm

MERCURY 5-8 88
Also see CHIEFTAINS
Also see MORRISON, Van

MORRISSEY

LP '88

LPs: 10/12-inch 33rpm

SIRE 5-8 88-91

MORROW, Buddy, & Orchestra

P&R '51

Singles: 78rpm

MERCURY 3-5 54-57
RCA 3-5 50-57

Singles: 7-inch

EPIC 4-6 64
MERCURY 4-8 54-62
RCA 5-10 50-59
U.A. 4-8 68
WING 4-8 55-56

EPs: 7-inch 33/45rpm

MERCURY 5-15 54-61
RCA 5-15 52-61

LPs: 10/12-inch 33rpm

EPIC (Except 24095 & 26095) 5-15 64-65
EPIC (24095 "Big Band Beatlemania") 15-25 64
(Monaural.)
EPIC (26095 "Big Band Beatlemania") 20-30 64
(Stereo.)
MERCURY 15-30 54-62
RCA (2000 & 2100 series) 10-20 59-60
RCA (2200 & series) 8-15 60
RCA (3100 & 3200 series) 20-35 52-54
(10-inch LPs.)
U.A. 5-10 68
WING 10-20 56

MORSE, Ella Mae
(With Freddie Slack; with Big Dave & His Orchestra)

P&R/R&B '43

Singles: 78rpm

CAPITOL 3-5 43-56

Singles: 7-inch

CAPITOL (1600 thru 3400 series) 5-10 50-56

EPs: 7-inch 33/45rpm

CAPITOL 10-20 54-55

LPs: 10/12-inch 33rpm

CAPITOL (H-513 "Barrelhouse Boogie, and the Blues") 75-125 54
(10-inch LP.)
CAPITOL (T-513 "Barrelhouse Boogie, and the Blues") 50-75 55
CAPITOL (898 "Morse Code") ... 50-75 57
CAPITOL (1802 "Hits") 30-45 62

MORSE, Steve, Band

LP '84

LPs: 10/12-inch 33rpm

MCA 5-8 89
MUSICIAN/ELEKTRA 5-8 84
Also see DIXIE DREGS
Also see KANSAS

MOSBY, Johnny & Jonie

C&W '63

Singles: 7-inch

CAPITOL 3-6 67-73
CHALLENGE 5-10 60
COLUMBIA 4-8 62-66
STARDAY 4-6 65
TOPPA 5-8 61

Picture Sleeves

CAPITOL 3-5 70

LPs: 10/12-inch 33rpm

CAPITOL 8-12 68-71
COLUMBIA 10-15 65
HARMONY 5-10 70

MOSS, Bill

R&B '69

Singles: 7-inch

BELL 3-5 69

MOST, Donny

P&R '76

Singles: 7-inch

U.A. 3-5 76-77
VENTURE 3-5 78

Picture Sleeves

U.A. 3-5 76

LPs: 10/12-inch 33rpm

U.A. 8-12 76

MOTELS

LP '79

Singles: 7-inch

CAPITOL 3-5 79-85

Picture Sleeves

CAPITOL 3-4 82-85

LPs: 10/12-inch 33rpm

CAPITOL 5-10 79-85
Members: Martha Davis; Martin Jourard; Jeff Jourard; Brian Glascock; Tim McGovern; Mike Goodroe.
Also see DAVIS, Martha

MOTHER EARTH

LP '69

Singles: 7–inch

MERCURY 4-8 68-69
REPRISE 3-5 70
U.A. 5-10 68

LPs: 10/12–inch 33rpm

MERCURY 10-20 68-70
REPRISE 10-15 71
U.A. 15-20 68

Members: Tracy Nelson; John Andrews; Bob Arthur; George Rains. Session: Boz Scaggs.
Also see NELSON, Tracy
Also see SCAGGS, Boz

MOTHER'S FINEST

P&R/LP '76

Singles: 12–inch 33/45rpm

EPIC 4-8 77-79

Singles: 7–inch

EPIC 3-5 76-79

LPs: 10/12–inch 33rpm

ATLANTIC 5-10 81
EPIC 5-10 76-79
RCA 8-12 72

Also see KENNEDY, Joyce

MOTHERLODE

P&R/LP '69

Singles: 7–inch

BUDDAH 4-6 69

LPs: 10/12–inch 33rpm

BUDDAH 10-15 69-72

MOTHERS of INVENTION

(Mothers)

LP '67

Singles: 7–inch

BIZARRE/REPRISE 10-15 70
DISCREET 6-10 73
VERVE 10-20 66-68

Promotional Singles

BIZARRE/REPRISE 12-15 70
DISCREET 8-10 73
VERVE 15-20 66-68

EPs: 7–inch 33/45rpm

REPRISE (332 "Uncle Meat") ... 35-45 69
(Promotional issue only.)

LPs: 10/12–inch 33rpm

BIZARRE (2024 "Uncle Meat") . 35-45 69
(Blue label. With 12-page booklet.)
BIZARRE (2024 "Uncle Meat") . 20-30 69
(Blue label. Without booklet.)
BIZARRE (2024 "Uncle Meat") . 10-15 70s
(Brown label.)
BIZARRE (2028 "Weasles Ripped My Flesh") 20-30 70
(Blue label.)
BIZARRE (2028 "Weasles Ripped My Flesh") 5-10 70s
(Brown label.)
BIZARRE (2042 "The Mothers Live/ Fillmore East") 20-30 71
(Blue label.)
BIZARRE (2042 "The Mothers Live/ Fillmore East") 5-10 70s
(Brown label.)
BIZARRE (2075 "Just Another Band from L.A.") 20-30 72
(Blue label.)
BIZARRE (2093 "Grand Wazoo") 20-30 72
(Blue label.)
BIZARRE (2093 "Grand Wazoo") 5-10 70s
(Brown label.)
BIZARRE (6370 "Burnt Weeny Sandwich") 30-40 69
(Blue label. With folder of bonus photos.)
BIZARRE (6370 "Burnt Weeny Sandwich") 15-25 69
(Blue label. Without folder of photos.)
BIZARRE (6370 "Burnt Weeny Sandwich") 5-10 70s
(Brown label.)
DISCREET (2149 "Over-Nite Sensation") 15-25 73
DISCREET (MS4-2149 "Over-Nite Sensation") 30-40 73
(Quadrophonic.)
MGM (112 "Mothers of Invention") 30-40 70
MGM (4754 "Worst of the Mothers") 25-35 71
REPRISE 8-12 73-74
(Reissues of Bizarre catalog.)
VERVE (5005 "Freak Out!") 75-125 66
(Monaural. With mail-order "Freak Out - Hot Spots" map/poster offer printed on inside of cover.)
VERVE (5005 "Freak Out!") 50-100 67
(Monaural. Without mail-order map/poster offer printed on inside of cover.)
VERVE (V6-5005 "Freak Out!") 50-100 66
(Stereo. With mail-order "Freak Out - Hot Spots" map/poster offer printed on inside of cover.)
VERVE (V6-5005 "Freak Out!") .40-80 67
(Stereo. Without mail-order map/poster offer printed on inside of cover.)
VERVE (5013 "Absolutely Free") 60-80 67
(Monaural. Includes Libretto or Freak Map.)
VERVE (5013 "Absolutely Free") 50-75 67
(Monaural. Without Libretto or Freak Map.)
VERVE (V6-5013 "Absolutely Free") 50-75 67
(Stereo. Includes Libretto or Freak Map.)

VERVE (V6-5013 "Absolutely Free") 40-50 67
(Stereo. Without Libretto or Freak Map.)
VERVE (5045 "We're Only in It for the Money")........................ 50-75 67
(Monaural. With "Only Money" insert.)
VERVE (5045 "We're Only in It for the Money")........................ 30-50 67
(Monaural. Without "Only Money" insert.)
VERVE (V6-5045 "We're Only in It for the Money")........................ 50-75 67
(Stereo. With "Only Money" insert.)
VERVE (V6-5045 "We're Only in It for the Money")........................ 30-50 67
(Stereo. Without "Only Money" insert.)
VERVE (5068 "Mothermania") .. 20-40 69
VERVE (5074 "XXXX of the Mothers")................................ 20-25 69
Note: price range of Verve LPs is for commercial copies on the blue & black labels as well as white MGM/Verve labels.
W.B. 8-10 77

Promotional LPs

BIZARRE (2024 "Uncle Meat") . 40-60 69
BIZARRE (2028 "Weasles Ripped My Flesh") 35-45 70
BIZARRE (2042 "The Mothers Live/ Fillmore East")........................ 35-45 71
BIZARRE (2075 "Just Another Band from L.A.")..................... 30-40 72
BIZARRE (2093 "Grand Wazoo") 30-40 72
BIZARRE (6370 "Burnt Weeny Sandwich") 30-30 69
VERVE (5005 "Freak Out!") .. 100-200 66
VERVE (5013 "Absolutely Free") 75-125 67
VERVE (5045 "We're Only in It for the Money").....................75-125 67
VERVE (5068 "Mothermania") 50-100 69
VERVE (5074 "XXXX of the Mothers")............................ 50-100 69

Members: Frank Zappa; Jimmy Carl Black; Roy Estrada; Ray Collins; Elliot Ingber; Jim Pons; Lowell George.
Also see CAPTAIN BEEFHEART
Also see DUKE, George
Also see FLO & EDDIE
Also see GAMBLERS
Also see GEORGE, Lowell
Also see LEAVES
Also see MISSING PERSONS
Also see PRESTON, Billy
Also see RUBEN & JETS
Also see ZAPPA, Frank

MOTIVATION

R&B '83

Singles: 7-inch

DE-LITE 3-4 83

MOTLEY CRUE

LP '83

Singles: 7-inch

ELEKTRA...3-4 83-88

Picture Sleeves

ELEKTRA...3-4 84-89

LPs: 10/12-inch 33rpm

ELEKTRA.......................................5-10 82-89
LEATHÜR ("Too Fast for Love") 50-75 81
(Black lettering on cover.)
LEATHÜR ("Too Fast for Love") 25-50 81
(White lettering on cover.)
WEA/ELEKTRA (60395 "Helter Skelter") 10-15 84
(Picture disc. Price includes poster.)

Member: Vince Neil; Nikki Sixx; Mick Mars; Tommy Lee; John Corabi.

MOTORHEAD

LP '82

Singles: 7-inch

MERCURY...3-4 80-83

LPs: 10/12-inch 33rpm

EMI AMERICA 5-8 85
GWR/PROFILE...............................5-8 86-87
MERCURY.......................................5-8 80-83

Members: Ian "Lemmy" Kilmister; Phil Campbell; Pete Gill; Mick "Wurzel" Burston.
Also see GLITTER BAND
Also see HAWKWIND
Also see SAXON

MOTORS

P&R/LP '80

Singles: 7-inch

VIRGIN...3-5 77-80

Picture Sleeves

VIRGIN...3-5 80

LPs: 10/12-inch 33rpm

VIRGIN...8-10 77-80

Also see TCHAIKOVSKY, Bram

MOTT

LP '75

Singles: 7-inch

COLUMBIA 3-5 75-76

LPs: 10/12-inch 33rpm

COLUMBIA 5-10 75-76

Also see MOTT the HOOPLE

MOTT the HOOPLE

LP '70

Singles: 7-inch

ATLANTIC.......................................4-6 70
COLUMBIA 3-5 72-74

LPs: 10/12-inch 33rpm

ATLANTIC....................................12-18 70-74
COLUMBIA 10-15 72-75

Member: Ian Hunter.
Also see BRITISH LIONS
Also see HUNTER, Ian
Also see MOTT

MOTTOLA, Tony

LP '62

LPs: 10/12-inch 33rpm

COMMAND 10-15 62-65
PROJECT 3 .... 5-10 67-70

MOULD, Bob

LP '89

LPs: 10/12-inch 33rpm

VIRGIN 5-8 88-90

MOUNTAIN

P&R/LP '70

Singles: 7-inch

WINDFALL 3-6 69-71

LPs: 10/12-inch 33rpm

COLUMBIA 10-15 73-74
SCOTTI BROTHERS 5-8 85
WINDFALL 10-15 69-72

Members: Leslie West; Corky Laing; Steve Knight; Felix Pappalardi; David Perry.
Also see WEST, Leslie

MOUSKOURI, Nana

LP '91

Singles: 7-inch

BELL 3-5 72-74
FONTANA 4-8 62-71
MERCURY 5-8 60
PRESIDENT 5-8 61
RIVERSIDE 4-8 62

LPs: 10/12-inch 33rpm

BELL 5-10 73
FONTANA 10-20 62-69
PHILIPS 5-8 91

Also see BELAFONTE, Harry, & Nana Mouskouri
Also see HAYWARD, Justin

MOUTH & MacNEAL

P&R/LP '72

Singles: 7-inch

PHILIPS 3-5 72

Picture Sleeves

PHILIPS 3-5 72

LPs: 10/12-inch 33rpm

PHILIPS 10-12 72-73

Members: Will Duyn; Maggie MacNeal.

MOUZON, Alphonse
(With Carol Dennis; Alphonze Mouzon)

R&B/LP '82

Singles: 12-inch 33/45rpm

PRIVATE I 4-6 84

Singles: 7-inch

BLUE NOTE 3-5 73-74
HIGHRISE 3-4 82
PRIVATE I 3-4 84

LPs: 10/12-inch 33rpm

BLUE NOTE 5-10 73-76
HIGHRISE 5-8 82
PAUSA 5-8 81
PRIVATE I 5-8 84

Also see MOUZON'S ELECTRIC BAND

MOUZON, Alphonse, & Larry Coryell

LPs: 10/12-inch 33rpm

ATLANTIC 5-10 77

Also see CORYELL, Larry
Also see MOUZON, Alphonse

MOUZON'S ELECTRIC BAND

Singles: 12-inch 33/45rpm

VANGUARD 4-6 83

Singles: 7-inch

VANGUARD 3-4 83

Also see MOUZON, Alphonse

MOVE

P&R '72

Singles: 7-inch

A&M 5-10 67-69
CAPITOL 10-15 70
DERAM 5-10 67
MGM 8-10 71
U.A. 4-8 72-73

LPs: 10/12-inch 33rpm

A&M (3181 "Shazam") 5-8 82
A&M (3625 "Best of the Move") . 15-20 74
A&M (4259 "Shazam") 20-25 69
CAPITOL 15-25 71
PICKWICK 10-15 70s
U.A. 10-15 73

Members: Jeff Lynne; Roy Wood; Bev Bevan; Denny Cordell; Richard Tandy; Carl Wayne; Rick Price; Trevor Burton; Ace Kefford.
Also see LYNNE, Jeff
Also see WOOD, Roy

MOVIES

R&B '86

Singles: 7-inch

CBS ASSOCIATED 3-4 86
RCA 3-5 80-86

LPs: 10/12-inch 33rpm

RCA 5-10 80-81

MOVING PICTURES

P&R/LP '82

Singles: 7-inch

GEFFEN 3-4 89
NETWORK 3-5 82

Picture Sleeves

NETWORK 3-5 82

LPs: 10/12-inch 33rpm

NETWORK 5-8 82

Members: Alex Smith; Garry Frost.
Also see 1927

MOYET, Alison

P&R/D&D/LP '85

Singles: 12-inch 33/45rpm

COLUMBIA 4-6 85

Singles: 7-inch

COLUMBIA 3-4 85

Picture Sleeves

COLUMBIA 3-4 85

LPs: 10/12-inch 33rpm

COLUMBIA 5-8 85-87

Also see YAZ

MOZART, Mickey, Quintet

P&R '59

Singles: 7-inch

ROULETTE 5-8 59-61

MR: see MISTER

MRS. MILLER: see MILLER, Mrs.

MTUME

R&B '78

Singles: 12-inch 33/45rpm

EPIC 4-8 79-86

Singles: 7-inch

EPIC 3-5 78-87

LPs: 10/12-inch 33rpm

EPIC 5-8 78-86

Members: James Mtume; Tawatha Agee.

MUDDY WATERS: see WATERS, Muddy

MUGWUMPS

(Mugwump Establishment)

Singles: 7-inch

SIDEWALK (900 "Bald Headed Woman") 10-20 66

W.B. 5-10 64-67

LPs: 10/12-inch 33rpm

W.B. (W-1697 "Mugwumps") 15-25 67

(Monaural.)

W.B. (WS-1697 "Mugwumps") .. 20-30 67

(Stereo.)

Members: Cass Elliot; Denny Doherty; James Hendricks; John Sebastain; Zal Yanovsky.

Also see ELLIOT, Cass

Also see SEBASTAIN, John

MUHAMMAD, Idris

P&R/R&B/LP '77

Singles: 12-inch 33/45rpm

FANTASY 4-6 83

Singles: 7-inch

FANTASY 3-5 80-83

KUDU 3-5 77-78

PRESTIGE 3-5 72

LPs: 10/12-inch 33rpm

FANTASY 5-8 83

KUDU 8-10 76-77

PRESTIGE 8-10 72

MULDAUR, Maria

LP '73

Singles: 7-inch

REPRISE 3-5 73-76

W.B. 3-5 78-79

LPs: 10/12-inch 33rpm

MYRRH 5-8 82

REPRISE 8-12 73-76

TAKOMA 5-8 80

W.B. 5-10 78-79

MULL, Martin

(Martin Mull Orchestra)

P&R '73

Singles: 7-inch

ABC 3-5 77

CAPRICORN 3-5 72-77

ELEKTRA 3-5 79

LPs: 10/12-inch 33rpm

ABC 8-10 77-78

CAPRICORN 8-12 73

ELEKTRA 5-10 79

MCA 5-8 80s

MULLICAN, Moon

(With the Showboys)

P&R '47

Singles: 78rpm

KING 10-20 46-56

Singles: 7-inch

KING (1000 series) 20-35 52-54

KING (4000 series) 15-25 55-56

KING (5000 series) 8-15 59-60

STARDAY 5-10 60-61

EPs: 7-inch 33/45rpm

KING (214 "King of the Hillbilly Piano Players") 20-30 50s

KING (227 "Piano Solos") 15-25 50s

KING (314 "Moon Mullican") 15-25 50s

STARDAY (154 "Moon Mullican") 20-30 60

LPs: 10/12-inch 33rpm

CORAL (57235 "Moon over Mullican") 200-300 58

KAPP 15-20 69

KING (555 "All-Time Greatest Hits") 75-125 57

KING (628 "16 Favorite Tunes") 60-80 59

KING (681 "Many Moods") 60-80 60

KING (937 "24 Favorite Tunes") 25-35 65

NASHVILLE 8-10 70

PHONORAMA 5-8

PICKWICK/HILLTOP 10-15 66

STARDAY 10-15 67

STERLING (601 "I'll Sail My Ship Alone") 100-125 50s

WESTERN 5-8

Also see KERR, Anita

MULLIGAN, Gerry

(Gerry Mulligan Quartet; Jazz Combo)

LP '59

Singles: 7-Inch

PACIFIC JAZZ 4-6 61

PHILIPS 4-6 64

VERVE 4-8 60

EPs: 7-Inch 33/45rpm

CAPITOL 30-45 53

COLUMBIA 10-20 59

EMARCY 10-20 56

PACIFIC JAZZ 25-50 53-57

PRESTIGE (1317 "Gerry Mulligan Blows") 50-100 52
PRESTIGE (1318 "Gerry Mulligan Blows") 50-100 52
U.A. 10-20 58

LPs: 10/12-Inch 33rpm

A&M 8-12 72
ABC-PAR (225 "Jazz Concerto") 75-100 58
BLUE NOTE 5-8 81
CTI 8-12 75
CAPITOL (H-439 "Gerry Mulligan") 150-200 53
(10–inch LP.)
CAPITOL (691 "Modern Sounds") 75-125 56
(One side is by Shorty Rogers.)
CAPITOL (2000 series) 20-35 63
CAPITOL (11000 series) 8-12 72
CHIAROSCURO 5-10 77
COLUMBIA (1307 thru 1932) 20-35 59-63
(Monaural.)
COLUMBIA (8116 thru 8732) 25-45 59-63
(Stereo.)
COLUMBIA (34000 series) 5-10 77
CROWN 10-20 63-64
DRG 5-8 80
EMARCY (1000 series) 5-8 81
EMARCY (36056 "Gerry Mulligan Sextet") 75-100 56
EMARCY (36101 "Mainstream") 75-100 57
GRP 5-8 83
GENE NORMAN (3 "Gerry Mulligan Quartet") 100- 200 52
(10–inch LP.)
GENE NORMAN (26 "Gerry Mulligan/Chet Baker/Buddy DeFranco") 50-75 57
GENE NORMAN (56 "Gerry Mulligan/Chet Baker/Buddy DeFranco") 20-40 61
INNER CITY 5-8 80
KIMBERLY 20-30 63
LIMELIGHT (82000 series) 12-25 65-66
(Monaural.)
LIMELIGHT (86000 series) 15-30 65-66
(Stereo.)
MERCURY (20453 "Profile") 40-60 59
ODYSSEY 10-20 68
PACIFIC JAZZ (1 "Gerry Mulligan Quartet") 150-250 53
(10–inch LP.)
PACIFIC JAZZ (2 "Gerry Mulligan Quartet") 100-250 53
(10–inch LP.)
PACIFIC JAZZ (5 "Gerry Mulligan") 100-200 53
(10–inch LP.)
PACIFIC JAZZ (10 "Gerry Mulligan") 100-200 54
(10–inch LP.)
PACIFIC JAZZ (1201 "California Concert") 100-125 55
PACIFIC JAZZ (1207 "Original Quartet") 75-100 55
PACIFIC JAZZ (1210 "Paris Concert") 75-100 56
PACIFIC JAZZ (1228 "Mulligan at Storyville") 75-100 57
PACIFIC JAZZ (1237 "Songbook") 75-100 57
PACIFIC JAZZ (1241 "Reunion") 75-100 57
PACIFIC JAZZ (10000 & 20000 series) 10-20 66
PAUSA 5-10 76
PHILIPS 10-20 63-64
PRESTIGE (003 "Mulligan Plays Mulligan") 5-8 82
PRESTIGE (120 "Gerry Mulligan Blows") 200-300 52
(10–inch LP.)
PRESTIGE (141 "Mulligan Too Blows") 200-300 53
(10–inch LP.)
PRESTIGE (7006 "Gerry Plays Mulligan") 75-100 56
(Yellow label.)
PRESTIGE (7251 "Historically Speaking") 30-40 63
(Yellow label.)
SUNSET 10-15 66
TRIP 6-12 75-76
U.A. (4006 "I Want to Live") 30-40 58
(Monaural.)
U.A. (4006 "I Want to Live") 40-50 58
(Stereo.)
V.S.P. 10-20 66
VERVE 20-45 58-60
(Reads "Verve Records, Inc." at bottom of label.)
VERVE 10-25 61-72
(Reads "MGM Records - A Division Of Metro-Goldwyn-Mayer, Inc." at bottom of label.)
VERVE 5-12 73-84
(Reads "Manufactured By MGM Record Corp.," or mentions either Polydor or Polygram at bottom of label.)
WHO'S WHO in JAZZ 5-8 78
WING 10-20 67
WORLD PACIFIC (1241 "Reunion") 50-75 58
WORLD PACIFIC (1253 "Annie Ross Sings with Mulligan") 50-75 59

Also see BRUBECK, Dave, & Gerry Mulligan

Also see GETZ, Stan, & Gerry Mulligan

MULLIGAN, Gerry, & Paul Desmond

(Gerry Mulligan / Paul Desmond)

LPs: 10/12-Inch 33rpm

FANTASY (220 "Gerry Mulligan/ Paul Desmond") 75-100 56
(Colored vinyl.)
RCA (2642 "Two of a Mind") 35-55 62
VERVE (8246 "Gerry Mulligan/ Paul Desmond") 40-60 58
(Reads "Verve Records, Inc." at bottom of label.)
VERVE (8246 "Gerry Mulligan/ Paul Desmond") 25-35 62
(Reads "MGM Records - A Division Of Metro-Goldwyn-Mayer, Inc." at bottom of label.)
Also see DESMOND, Paul

MULLIGAN, Gerry, & Johnny Hodges

LPs: 10/12-Inch 33rpm

VERVE 30-40 60
(Reads "Verve Records, Inc." at bottom of label.)
VERVE 15-25 62
(Reads "MGM Records - A Division of Metro-Goldwyn-Mayer, Inc." at bottom of label.)
Also see HODGES, Johnny

MULLIGAN, Gerry, & Thelonious Monk

LPs: 10/12-Inch 33rpm

MILESTONE 8-12 82
RIVERSIDE (247 "Mulligan Meets Monk") 50-75 57
RIVERSIDE (1106 "Mulligan Meets Monk") 40-60 58
Also see MONK, Thelonious

MULLIGAN, Gerry, & Oscar Peterson

LPs: 10/12-Inch 33rpm

VERVE (8235 "Gerry & Oscar at Newport") 50-80 57
VERVE (8559 "Gerry & Oscar at Newport") 30-40 63
(Monaural.)
VERVE (68559 "Gerry & Oscar at Newport") 30-40 63
(Stereo.)
Also see MULLIGAN, Gerry
Also see PETERSON, Oscar

MUNDY, Nick

R&B '84

Singles: 7–inch

COLUMBIA 3-4 84

MUNGO JERRY

P&R/LP '70

Singles: 7–inch

BELL 3-5 71-73
FLASHBACK.............................. 3-5 73
JANUS 3-5 70-71
PYE.......................................3-5 72-75

LPs: 10/12–inch 33rpm

JANUS 10-15 70

MUNICH MACHINE

LP '78

Singles: 7–inch

CASABLANCA..........................3-5 78

LPs: 10/12–inch 33rpm

CASABLANCA..........................5-10 78

MURAD, Jerry: see HARMONICATS

MURDOCK, Lydia

R&B '83

Singles: 12–inch 33/45rpm

TEEN 4-6 83

Singles: 7–inch

TEEN 3-4 83

MURDOCK, Shirley

R&B '86

Singles: 12–inch 33/45rpm

ELEKTRA....................................4-6 86

Singles: 7–inch

ELEKTRA....................................3-4 86-88

LPs: 10/12–inch 33rpm

ELEKTRA....................................5-8 87-88
Also see ZAPP

MURE, Billy

(With the Wild-Cats; with Trumpeteers; with 7 Karats)

P&R '59

Singles: 78rpm

RCA 4-6 57-58

Singles: 7–inch

COLPIX......................................4-8 61
DANCO 4-8 65
EVEREST 5-10 60
MGM 4-8 60-66
PARIS 5-10 60
RCA 5-15 57-58
RIVERSIDE.................................4-8 63
SRC 4-8 61
SPLASH....................................5-10 58
STRAND 4-8 61

EPs: 7–inch 33/45rpm

RCA 10-15 58

LPs: 10/12–inch 33rpm

EVEREST 15-20 60-61
KAPP 15-20 61
MGM 15-20 59-66
RCA 25-30 57-58
STRAND 15-20 61
SUNSET 10-12 67
U.A. (3031 "Bandstand Record Hop")...................................30-40 59
Also see TRUMPETEERS
Also see WILD-CATS

MURE, Billy & Benny

Singles: 7-inch

MGM 4-8 64

MURMAIDS

(Mermaids)

P&R '63

Singles: 7-inch

CHATTAHOOCHEE.......... 5-10 63-69

LIBERTY 4-8 68

LPs: 10/12-inch 33rpm

CHATTAHOOCHEE.......... 8-10 81

MURPHEY, Michael

(Michael Martin Murphey; with Ryan Murphey)

P&R/LP '72

Singles: 7-inch

A&M 3-5 72

CAPITOL.......... 3-5 74

EMI AMERICA 3-4 84-85

EPIC.......... 3-5 74-79

LIBERTY 3-4 82-84

W.B. 3-4 86-91

Picture Sleeves

A&M 3-5 72

EPIC.......... 3-5 74

LPs: 10/12-inch 33rpm

A&M 8-10 72-73

EMI AMERICA 5-8 84-85

EPIC.......... 8-12 74-78

LIBERTY 5-8 82-83

W.B. 5-8 86-91

Also see DENVER, John

Also see LEE, Johnny, Michael Martin Murphey, & Charlie Daniels

Also see LEWIS & CLARKE

MURPHEY, Michael Martin, & Holly Dunn

C&W '87

Singles: 7-inch

W.B. 3-4 87

MURPHEY, Michael, & Katy Moffatt

C&W '81

Singles: 7-inch

EPIC.......... 3-5 81

Also see MURPHEY, Michael

MURPHY, Eddie

R&B/LP '82

Singles: 12-inch 33/45rpm

COLUMBIA 4-6 83-85

Singles: 7-inch

COLUMBIA 3-4 83-86

Picture Sleeves

COLUMBIA 3-4 83-85

LPs: 10/12-inch 33rpm

COLUMBIA (Except picture discs) 5-8 82-86

COLUMBIA (1763 "Comedian") 10-15 83

(Promotional picture disc.)

COLUMBIA (9C9-39151 "Comedian").......... 10-12 83

(Picture disc.)

MURPHY, Peter

LP '88

LPs: 10/12-inch 33rpm

BEGGAR'S BANQUET.......... 5-8 88-90

MURPHY, Rose

(With the Selah Jubilee Quartette; Rose Murphy Trio)

R&B '48

Singles: 78rpm

DECCA 4-8 55

MAJESTIC 5-10 48

Singles: 7-inch

DECCA (29000 series) 8-12 55

DECCA (32000 series) 4-8 66

REGINA 4-8 63

LPs: 10/12-inch 33rpm

MUSE.......... 5-8

ROYALE (1835 "Rose Murphy") 30-40 52

(10-inch LP.)

VERVE.......... 20-30 57

Also see BAILEY, Pearl / Rose Murphy / Ivie Anderson

MURPHY, Rose, & Slam Stewart

Singles: 7-inch

DECCA 3-5 61

LPs: 10/12-inch 33rpm

U.A. 15-25 63

Also see MURPHY, Rose

MURPHY, Walter

(With the Big Apple Band)

P&R/R&B/LP '76

Singles: 12-inch 33/45rpm

PRIVATE STOCK.......... 4-8 77

Singles: 7-inch

MCA.......... 3-4 82

PRIVATE STOCK.......... 3-5 76-77

Picture Sleeves

MCA.......... 3-4 82

LPs: 10/12-inch 33rpm

MCA.......... 5-8 82

PRIVATE STOCK.......... 5-10 76-77

MURRAY, Anne

(With Doug Mallory)

C&W/P&R/LP '70

Singles: 7-inch

CAPITOL.......... 3-5 70-86

Picture Sleeves

CAPITOL.......... 3-4 79-86

LPs: 10/12-inch 33rpm

CAPITOL (Except "Let's Keep It That Way" picture disc).......... 5-10 70-87

CAPITOL ("Let's Keep It That Way") 50-75 78

(Picture disc. Promotional issue only. One of a four-artist, four-LP set.)

Also see CAMPBELL, Glen, & Anne Murray

Also see CAMPBELL, Glen / Anne Murray / Kenny Rogers / Crystal Gayle
Also see WINCHESTER, Jesse

MURRAY, Anne, & Dave Loggins

C&W '84

Singles: 7-inch

CAPITOL.................................... 3-4 84

Also see LOGGINS, Dave

MURRAY, Anne, & Kenny Rogers

C&W '89

Singles: 7-inch

CAPITOL.................................... 3-4 89

Also see MURRAY, Anne
Also see ROGERS, Kenny

MURRAY, Mickey

P&R/R&B '67

Singles: 7-inch

SSS INT'L.................................... 4-8 67-68

LPs: 10/12-inch 33rpm

FEDERAL.................................. 8-12 71
SSS INT'L.................................. 10-15 67

MURRAY, Mickey & Clarence

Singles: 7-inch

SSS INT'L.................................... 4-8 68

Also see MURRAY, Mickey

MUSCLE SHOALS HORNS

R&B/LP '76

Singles: 7-inch

ARIOLA AMERICA....................... 3-5 77
BANG.. 3-5 76
MONUMENT.............................. 3-4 83

LPs: 10/12-inch 33rpm

ARIOLA AMERICA..................... 8-12 77
BANG...................................... 10-15 76
MONUMENT.............................. 8-12 83

MUSIC EXPLOSION

P&R/LP '67

Singles: 7-inch

ATTACK (1404 "Little Black Egg")10-20 66
LAURIE..................................... 5-10 67-69

LPs: 10/12-inch 33rpm

LAURIE................................... 20-30 67

Members: Jamie Lyons; Don Atkins; Bob Avery; Rick Nesta; Butch Stahl.
Also see BLOOM, Bobby
Also see KASENETZ-KATZ SINGING ORCHESTRAL CIRCUS

MUSIC MACHINE

P&R '66

Singles: 7-inch

BELL....................................... 5-10 69
ORIGINAL SOUND..................... 5-10 66-67
W.B... 5-10 68

Picture Sleeves

ORIGINAL SOUND (82 "Hey Joe")...................................... 15-25 67
(Has die-cut center hole on both sides.)

LPs: 10/12-inch 33rpm

ORIGINAL SOUND (5015 "Turn on the Music Machine")...............20-30 66
(Monaural.)
ORIGINAL SOUND (8875 "Turn on the Music Machine").............75-100 66
(Stereo.)

Members: Sean Bonniwell; Mark Landon; Keith Olsen; Ron Edgar; Doug Rhodes.

MUSIC MACHINE / Bubble Puppy

Singles: 7-inch

ORIGINAL SOUND........................3-4 85

Also see BUBBLE PUPPY
Also see MUSIC MACHINE

MUSIC MAKERS

P&R '67

Singles: 7-inch

GAMBLE..4-8 67-68

LPs: 10/12-inch 33rpm

GAMBLE.....................................12-18 68

Also see MFSB

MUSICAL YOUTH

P&R/R&B '82

Singles: 12-inch 33/45rpm

MCA...4-6 82-84

Singles: 7-inch

MCA...3-4 82-84

Picture Sleeves

MCA...3-4 82-84

LPs: 10/12-inch 33rpm

MCA...5-8 82-84

MUSIQUE

P&R/R&B/LP '78

Singles: 12-inch 33/45rpm

PRELUDE....................................5-10 78

Singles: 7-inch

PRELUDE......................................3-5 78-79

LPs: 10/12-inch 33rpm

PRELUDE....................................5-10 78

MUSTANGS

P&R '64

Singles: 7-inch

KEETCH......................................5-10 64
PROVIDENCE...............................8-12 63-64
SURE SHOT.................................5-10 64

LPs: 10/12-inch 33rpm

PROVIDENCE (1 "Dartel Stomp")...................................35-45 64

MYERS, Alicia

R&B '82

Singles: 12-inch 33/45rpm

MCA...4-6 81-85

Singles: 7-inch

MCA...3-4 81-85

LPs: 10/12-inch 33rpm

MCA...5-8 84

MYLES, Alannah

P&R/LP '90

Singles: 7-inch

ATLANTIC.................................... 3-4 89

LPs: 10/12-inch 33rpm

ATLANTIC.................................... 5-8 89

MYLES, Billy

P&R '57

Singles: 78rpm

EMBER 10-15 57-58

Singles: 7-inch

COLLECTABLES......................... 3-4 80s
EMBER (1026 "The Joker") 15-25 57
EMBER (1040 "Piece of Your Love")................................. 10-20 58
EMBER (1046 "I'm Gonna Walk")..................................... 10-20 58
KING (5395 "Dance Little Girl")... 8-12 60

MYRICK, Gary

(With the Figures)

LP '83

Singles: 7-inch

EPIC.. 3-4 83-84

LPs: 10/12-inch 33rpm

EPIC.. 5-8 83-84

MYSTIC MERLIN

R&B '81

Singles: 7-inch

CAPITOL...................................... 3-5 80-82

LPs: 10/12-inch 33rpm

CAPITOL.................................... 5-10 80-82

Also see JACKSON, Freddie

MYSTIC MOODS ORCHESTRA

LP '66

Singles: 7-inch

PHILIPS 4-6 66-70
SOUNDBIRD.................................. 3-5 75-78
W.B. 3-5 72-73

LPs: 10/12-inch 33rpm

MFSL... 20-40 78
PHILIPS 8-12 66-70
SOUNDBIRD............................... 5-10 75-78
W.B. 5-10 72-73

MYSTICS

P&R '59

Singles: 7-inch

AMBIENT SOUND 3-5 82
COLLECTABLES........................ 3-4 80s
LAURIE (3028 "Hushabye")...... 10-15 59
LAURIE (3028S "Hushabye").... 30-40 59
(Stereo.)
LAURIE (3038 "Don't Take the Stars") 10-15 59
LAURIE (3047 thru 3086).......... 10-15 59
LAURIE (3104 "Sunday Kind of Love")................................ 15-20 61

LPs: 10/12-inch 33rpm

AMBIENT SOUND.........................5-8 82
COLLECTABLES..........................6-8 87

Members: Phil Cracolici; Albee Cracolici; Bob Ferrante; George Galfo.

MYSTICS / Passions

LPs: 10/12-inch 33rpm

LAURIE 5-10 79

Also see MYSTICS
Also see PASSIONS

MYSTIQUE

R&B '77

Singles: 7-inch

CURTOM...3-5 77

LPs: 10/12-inch 33rpm

CURTOM.......................................5-10 77

Members: Ralph Johnson; Fred Lowrell; Larry Brownlee; Charles Fowler.

Also see C.O.D.s
Also see IMPRESSIONS

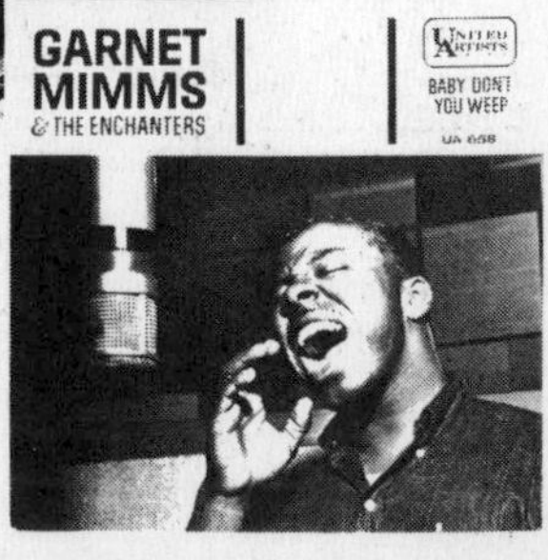

N

N.C.C.U.

R&B '77

Singles: 12–inch 33/45rpm

U.A. 4-8 77

Singles: 7–inch

U.A. 3-5 77

LPs: 10/12–inch 33rpm

U.A. 5-10 77

NRBQ

(New Rhythm & Blues Quintet)

LP '69

Singles: 7–inch

BEARSVILLE 3-5 83
BUDDAH 3-5 74
COLUMBIA 4-8 69
KAMA SUTRA 4-6 73
MERCURY 4-6 78
RED ROOSTER 3-6 77
ROUNDER 3-5 80-83
VIRGIN 3-5 89-90

Picture Sleeves

RED ROOSTER 3-5 77
ROUNDER 3-5 80

EPs: 7–inch 33/45rpm

ROUNDER 5-10 82

LPs: 10/12–inch 33rpm

ANNUIT COEPTIS 10-15 76
BEARSVILLE 5-8 83
KAMA SUTRA 10-15 72-73
MERCURY 8-12 78
COLUMBIA 10-15 69
RED ROOSTER 8-10 77-83
ROUNDER 5-10 79-80
VIRGIN 5-8 89

Members: Frank Gadler; Terry Adams; G.T. Stanley; Jody St. Nicholas; Steve Ferguson; Don Adams; Al Anderson; Tom Staley; Joey Spampinato; Tommy Ardolino.
Also see DAVIS, Skeeter, & NRBQ
Also see PERKINS, Carl, & NRBQ

NV

D&D '83

Singles: 12–inch 33/45rpm

SIRE 4-6 83-84

Singles: 7–inch

SIRE 3-4 83-84

N.W.A.

(Niggas with Attitude)

LP '89

LP: 10/12–inch 33rpm

N.W.A. 5-8 89-90

NABORS, Jim

(Jimmy Nabors)

LP '66

Singles: 7–inch

COLUMBIA 3-5 65-74
RANWOOD 3-4 77
ROULETTE 8-12 58

LPs: 10/12–inch 33rpm

COLUMBIA 5-15 65-75
HARMONY 5-10 71
RANWOOD 4-8 76-82

Also see STREISAND, Barbra / Doris Day / Jim Nabors / Andre Kostelanetz

NAILS

LP '86

Singles: 7–inch

RCA 3-4 86

LPs: 10/12–inch 33rpm

RCA 5-8 86

NAIROBI & Awesome Foursome

R&B '82

Singles: 7–inch

STREETWISE 3-4 82

NAJEE

R&B/LP '87

Singles: 7–inch

EMI 3-4 87-90

LPs: 10/12–inch 33rpm

EMI 5-8 87-90

Also see THOMAS, Vaneese

NAKED EYES

P&R/D&D/LP '83

Singles: 12–inch 33/45rpm

EMI AMERICA 4-6 83-84

Singles: 7–inch

EMI AMERICA 3-4 83-84

Picture Sleeves

EMI AMERICA 3-4 83-84

LPs: 10/12–inch 33rpm

EMI AMERICA 5-8 83-84

Members: Pete Byrne; Rob Fisher.
Also see CLIMIE FISHER

NAPOLEON XIV

(Jerry Samuels)

P&R '66

Singles: 7–inch

ERIC 3-5 76
W.B. (5800 series) 5-10 66
W.B. (7700 series) 4-6 73

LPs: 10/12–inch 33rpm

RHINO 5-8 80s
W.B. (W-1661 "They're Coming to Take Me Away") 50-60 66
(Monaural.)
W.B. (W-1661 "They're Coming to Take Me Away") 75-100 66
(White label. Promotional issue only.)

W.B. (WS-1661 "They're Coming to Take Me Away") 75-100 66
(Stereo.)

NASH, Graham

P&R/LP '71

Singles: 7-inch

ATLANTIC (2000 series) 3-5 71-73
ATLANTIC (89000 series) 3-4 86
CAPITOL 3-5 79-80

Picture Sleeves

ATLANTIC 3-4 86
CAPITOL 3-5 79

LPs: 10/12-inch 33rpm

ATLANTIC (7000 series) 8-12 71-73
ATLANTIC (81000 series) 5-8 86
CAPITOL 8-10 80

Also see CROSBY, David, & Graham Nash
Also see CROSBY, STILLS & NASH
Also see HOLLIES
Also see YOUNG, Neil, & Graham Nash

NASH, Johnny

P&R '57

Singles: 12-inch 33/45rpm

EPIC 4-8 79

Singles: 7-inch

ABC-PAR 8-18 57-61
ARGO 5-10 64-65
ATLANTIC 4-8 66
BABYLON 4-8 69
CADET 10-20 66
EPIC 3-6 72-80
GROOVE (18 "Helpless") 5-10 63
GROOVE (21 "Deep in the Heart of Harlem") 20-40 63
GROOVE (26 "It's No Good for Me") 5-10 63
GROOVE (30 "I'm Leaving") 5-10 64
JAD 4-8 68-70
JANUS 3-6 70
JODA 5-10 65-66
MGM 4-8 66-67
W.B. 5-10 62-63

Picture Sleeves

ABC-PAR 10-20 59-60
GROOVE 8-12 63-64

EPs: 7-inch 33/45rpm

ABC-PAR 10-20 58-61

LPs: 10/12-inch 33rpm

ABC-PAR 20-30 58-61
ARGO 15-20 64
CADET 10-15 73
EPIC 10-15 72-74
JAD 12-25 68-69

Also see ANKA, Paul, George Hamilton IV & Johnny Nash

NASH, Johnny, & Kim Weston

Singles: 7-inch

BABYLON 4-6 69

Also see NASH, Johnny
Also see WESTON, Kim

NASHVILLE BRASS: see DAVIS, Danny

NASHVILLE TEENS

P&R '64

Singles: 7-inch

LONDON 5-10 64-65
MGM 5-10 65-67
U.A. 3-5 72

LPs: 10/12-inch 33rpm

LONDON (407 "Tobacco Road") 40-50 64
(Stereo.)
LONDON (3407 "Tobacco Road") 50-60 64
(Monaural.)

Members: Arthur Sharp; John Allen; Roger Groom; Ray Phillips; Barry Jenkins.

NATASHA

D&D '83

Singles: 12-inch 33/45rpm

EMERGENCY 4-6 83

NATIONAL LAMPOON

P&R/LP '72

Singles: 7-inch

BLUE THUMB 4-6 72-73
EPIC (193 "Have a Kung-Fu Christmas") 3-4 75
(Promotional issue only.)
LABEL 21 .... 3-5 78-80

Picture Sleeves

EPIC (193 "Have a Kung-Fu Christmas") 4-6 75
(Promotional issue only.)
LABEL 21 .... 3-5 78-80

EPs: 7-inch 33/45rpm

EPIC (1095 "A History of the Beatles") 10-15 75
(Promotional issue only.)

LPs: 10/12-inch 33rpm

BANANA 10-15 72-74
BLUE THUMB 10-15 72-74
EPIC 8-12 75-76
IMPORT 8-10 77
LABEL 21 (Except PIC-2001) 5-8 78-80
LABEL 21 (PIC-2001 "That's Not Funny, That's Sick") 10-15 80
(Picture disc.)
NATIONAL LAMPOON 15-20 74
PASSPORT 5-8 82
VISA 5-8 78

Members: John Belushi; Chevy Chase; Melissa Manchester; Tony Hendra; Jim Payne; John Lopresti.
Also see BELUSHI, John
Also see MANCHESTER, Melissa

NATIVE

R&B '84

Singles: 7–inch

JAMAICA.. 3-4 84

NATURAL FOUR

R&B '69

Singles: 7–inch

ABC (11205 "Why Should We Stop Now").. 4-6 69
ABC (11236 "Same Thing in Mind").. 5-10 69
ABC (11253 "Hurt").................. 15-25 70
CURTOM.. 3-6 73-76

LPs: 10/12–inch 33rpm

CURTOM.. 8-12 74-75

Members: Chris James; Steve Striplin, Del Mos Whitley; Darryl Canady.

NATURALS

R&B '72

Singles: 7–inch

CALLA.. 3-5 71
MOTOWN.. 3-5 72

NATURE ZONE

R&B '76

Singles: 7–inch

LONDON.. 3-5 76

NATURE'S DIVINE

P&R/R&B/LP '79

Singles: 7–inch

INFINITY.. 3-5 79

LPs: 10/12–inch 33rpm

INFINITY.. 5-10 79

NATURE'S GIFT

R&B '74

Singles: 7–inch

ABC.. 3-5 74

NAUGHTON, David

P&R '79

Singles: 7–inch

RSO.. 3-5 78-79

Picture Sleeves

RSO.. 3-5 79

NAYLOR, Jerry

P&R '70

Singles: 7–inch

COLUMBIA.. 3-6 68-71
HITSVILLE.. 3-5 76
MC/CURB.. 3-5 78
MGM.. 3-6 71-72
MELODYLAND.. 3-5 74-75
OAK.. 3-5 80
PACIFIC CHALLENGER.............. 3-5 82
SKLYA.. 10-15 61-62
SMASH.. 5-10 65
TOWER.. 5-15 65-68
W.B./CURB.. 3-5 79
WEST.. 3-4 86

Session: Davie Allan.
Also see ALLAN, Davie
Also see CRICKETS
Also see HONDELLS

NAYLOR, Jerry, & Kelli Warren

C&W '79

Singles: 7–inch

JEREMIAH.. 3-5 79

Also see NAYLOR, Jerry

NAYOBE

D&D '85

Singles: 12–inch 33/45rpm

FEVER.. 4-6 85-86

Singles: 7–inch

FEVER.. 3-4 85-86

NAZARETH

LP '73

Singles: 7–inch

A&M.. 3-5 73-80
MCA.. 3-4 83-84
W.B.. 3-8 71

Picture Sleeves

A&M.. 3-5 75-80

LPs: 10/12–inch 33rpm

A&M.. 5-10 73-82
MCA.. 5-8 83-84
W.B.. 8-12 72

Members: Dan McCafferty; Pete Agnew; Darrell Sweet; Manny Charlton.

NAZTY

R&B '76

Singles: 7–inch

MANKIND.. 3-5 76

LPs: 10/12–inch 33rpm

MANKIND.. 5-10 76

NAZZ

Singles: 7–inch

VERY RECORD (001 "Lay Down and Die, Goodbye")........................ 750-1000 67

Members: Vince "Alice Cooper" Furnier; M. Bruce; G. Buxton; D. Dunaway; T. Speer.
Also see COOPER, Alice

NAZZ

LP '68

Singles: 7–inch

S.G.C. (001 "Hello It's Me")........ 10-20 68
(Light yellow label. Periods after letters. No horizontal lines.)
SGC (001 "Hello It's Me")............ 8-12 69
(Dark yellow label. No periods in logo. With horizontal lines.)
SGC (001 "Hello It's Me")............... 4-8 70
(Green label with yellow top.)
SGC (006 "Not Wrong Long")...... 8-10 69
SGC (009 "Some People")........... 8-10 69

Picture Sleeves

SGC.. 6-12 68

Promotional Singles

SGC (001 "Hello It's Me").......... 10-20 68
SGC (006 "Not Wrong Long") ... 10-15 69
SGC (009 "Some People")........ 10-15 69
SGC (009 "Kicks").................... 15-25 70

LPs: 10/12-inch 33rpm

SGC (5001 "Nazz") 30-50 68
SGC (5002 "Nazz-Nazz").......... 40-60 69
(Black vinyl.)
SGC (5002 "Nazz-Nazz")........ 50-100 69
(Colored vinyl. Pink and orange label. SGC logo is blue. Identification number is 671531.)
SGC (5002 "Nazz-Nazz")........ 75-100 69
(Colored vinyl. Mail-order edition. Red and orange label. SGC logo is purple. Identification number is 671531-MO.)
SGC (5004 "Nazz III") 30-50 71

Members: Todd Rundgren; Robert Antoni; Carson Van Osten; Tom Petersson; Rick Nielson.
Also see CHEAP TRICK
Also see RUNDGREN, Todd

N'COLE

R&B '78

Singles: 7-inch

MILLENNIUM 3-5 78

NDUGU & Chocolate Jam Co.

R&B '80

Singles: 7-inch

EPIC.. 3-5 80

NEELY, Sam

P&R/LP '72

Singles: 7-inch

A&M 3-5 74-75
CAPITOL....................................... 3-5 72-73
ELEKTRA...................................... 3-5 77
MCA 3-4 83-84

LPs: 10/12-inch 33rpm

A&M 8-10 74
CAPITOL.................................... 8-12 72-73

NEIGHBORHOOD

P&R '70

Singles: 7-inch

BIG TREE 4-8 70
BULLET (102269 "Why Can't
You See")............................. 15-25 69

LPs: 10/12-inch 33rpm

BIG TREE 10-15 70

NEIL & JACK

Singles: 7-inch

DUEL (508 "You Are My
Love at Last")..................... 100-200 62
DUEL (517 "I'm Afraid")......... 100-200 62

Members: Neil Diamond; Jack Parker.
Also see DIAMOND, Neil

NEIL & Shocking Pinks see YOUNG, Neil

NEKTAR

LP '74

Singles: 7-inch

PASSPORT 3-5 74-75

LPs: 10/12-inch 33rpm

PASSPORT 8-12 74-76
POLYDOR 8-10 77
VISA...8-10 78

NELSON

P&R/LP '90

Singles: 7-inch

DGC 3-4 90

LPs: 10/12-inch 33rpm

DGC 5-8 90

Members: Gunnar Nelson; Matthew Nelson.

NELSON, Jimmy
(With the Brer Rabbit Trio)

R&B '51

Singles: 78rpm

CHESS.......................................15-25 53
RPM 15-25 53

Singles: 7-inch

ALL BOY 5-10 62
CHESS (1587 "Free and
Easy Mind")..............................25-40 53
CHESS (1800 series)....................4-8 63
RPM (325 "T-99 Blues").........100-200 53
RPM (389 "Second Hand
Fool") 50-75 53
RPM (385 "Meet Me with
Your Black Dress On")............25-50 53
RPM (389 "Second Hand Fool") 25-50 53
RPM (397 "Mean Poor Girl")......25-50 53

Also see TURNER, Joe / Jimmy Nelson

NELSON, Karen, & Billy T.

P&R '77

Singles: 7-inch

AMHERST 8-10 77

Members: Karen Nelson; Billy Tragesser.

NELSON, Phyllis

R&B/D&D '85

Singles: 12-inch 33/45rpm

CARRERE 4-6 85-86

Singles: 7-inch

CARRERE 3-4 85-86

Picture Sleeves

CARRERE 3-4 86

LPs: 10/12-inch 33rpm

CARRERE 5-8 86

NELSON, Rick
(With the Stone Canyon Band; with Jordanaires; Ricky Nelson)

P&R/R&B/LP '57

Singles: 12-inch 33/45rpm

CAPITOL......................................5-10 82

Singles: 78rpm

IMPERIAL 25-75 57-58
VERVE..50-75 57

Singles: 7–inch

DECCA.. 4-8 63-72
CAPITOL...................................... 3-5 82
EPIC.. 3-5 77-86
IMPERIAL (5463 "Be-Bop Baby") 30-40 57
(Maroon label.)
IMPERIAL (5463 "Be-Bop Baby") 10-20 58
(Black label.)
IMPERIAL (5483 "Stood Up").... 25-35 57
(Maroon label.)
IMPERIAL (5483 "Stood Up").... 10-20 58
(Black label.)
IMPERIAL (5503 "Believe What You Say")............................... 15-25 58
IMPERIAL (5528 "Poor Little Fool")....................................... 15-25 58
IMPERIAL (5545 "Lonesome Town")...................................... 15-25 58
(Black vinyl.)
IMPERIAL (5545 "Lonesome Town")................................ 150-200 58
(Colored vinyl.)
IMPERIAL (5565 "It's Late")...... 15-25 59
IMPERIAL (5595 "Just a Little Too Much")............................. 10-20 59
IMPERIAL (5614 "Mighty Good").................................... 10-20 59
IMPERIAL (5663 "Young Emotions").............................. 10-20 60
IMPERIAL (5685 "I'm Not Afraid") 10-20 60
IMPERIAL (5707 "You Are the Only One") 10-20 60
IMPERIAL (5741 "Travelin' Man").................................. 10-15 61
(Black vinyl.)
IMPERIAL (5741 "Travelin' Man")................................. 150-200 61
(Colored vinyl. Promotional issue only.)
IMPERIAL (5770 thru 5935)...... 10-15 61-63
IMPERIAL (5958 "Long Vacation").................................. 8-12 63
(Black vinyl.)
IMPERIAL (5958 "Long Vacation")............................. 50-100 63
(Colored vinyl.)
IMPERIAL (5985 "Time after Time")... 10-12 63
IMPERIAL (66000 series) 8-15 63-64
LIBERTY 3-4 80s
MCA 3-5 73-75
VERVE (10047 "A Teenager's Romance") 25-35 57
VERVE (10070 "You're My One and Only Love") 25-35 57
(Flip is by Barney Kessell.)

Picture Sleeves

DECCA 8-18 63-70
EPIC...3-5 86
IMPERIAL (5483 "Stood Up") 20-30 57
IMPERIAL (5503 "Believe What You Say")..............................20-30 58
IMPERIAL (5545 "Lonesome Town")...................................15-25 58
IMPERIAL (5565 "It's Late").......15-25 59
IMPERIAL (5595 "Just a Little Too Much") 15-25 59
IMPERIAL (5614 "Mighty Good")...................................15-25 59
IMPERIAL (5663 "Young Emotions") 15-20 60
IMPERIAL (5685 "I'm Not Afraid")...................................15-20 60
IMPERIAL (5707 "You Are the Only One") 15-20 60
IMPERIAL (5741 "Travelin' Man") 10-20 61
IMPERIAL (5770 thru 5935).......10-20 61-63
MCA...3-5 86

EPs: 7–inch 33/45rpm

DECCA (2760 "One Boy Too Late") 25-50 63
DECCA (4419 "For Your Sweet Love")...........................25-50 63
(Jukebox issue.)
DECCA (4460 "Best Always")....25-50 65
(Jukebox issue.)
IMPERIAL (153/154/155 "Ricky") 35-55 58
(Price is for any of three volumes.)
IMPERIAL (157/158 "Ricky Nelson") 35-55 58
(Price is for either of two volumes.)
IMPERIAL (159/160/161 "Ricky Sings Again") 35-55 58
(Price is for any of three volumes.)
IMPERIAL (162/163/164 "Songs By Ricky") 35-55 59
(Price is for any of three volumes.)
IMPERIAL (165 "Ricky Sings Spirituals")..............................50-75 60
VERVE (5048 "Ricky")............75-100 57
(Has one track by Barney Kessell.)

LPs: 10/12–inch 33rpm

CAPITOL.......................................5-8 81
DECCA (DL-4419 thru DL-4944)................................20-30 63-67
(Monaural.)
DECCA (DL7-4419 thru DL7-4944)..............................25-40 63-67
(Stereo.)
DECCA (75014 thru 75391).......15-25 68-72
EPIC..8-15 77-86
EPIC/NU-DISK.........................10-15 81

IMPERIAL (9048 "Ricky")......... 50-80 57
("Imperial" across top of label.)
IMPERIAL (9048 "Ricky")......... 15-20 64
("IR-Imperial" logo on left.)
IMPERIAL (9050 "Ricky Nelson") 45-65 58
("Imperial" across top of label.)
IMPERIAL (9061 "Ricky Sings Again") 40-50 59
(Monaural.)
IMPERIAL (9082 "Songs by Ricky")................................... 40-50 59
(Monaural.)
IMPERIAL (9122 "More Songs by Ricky")............................. 30-50 60
(Monaural.)
IMPERIAL (9152 "Rick Is 21")... 30-40 61
(Monaural.)
IMPERIAL (9167 "Album Seven") 25-35 62
(Monaural.)
IMPERIAL (9218 "Best Sellers") 25-35 63
(Monaural.)
IMPERIAL (9223 "It's Up to You") 25-35 63
(Monaural.)
IMPERIAL (9232 "Million Sellers by Rick Nelson").................... 20-30 63
(Monaural.)
IMPERIAL (9244 "Long Vacation")............................. 20-30 63
(Monaural.)
IMPERIAL (9251 "Rick Nelson Sings for You")...................... 20-30 63
(Monaural.)
IMPERIAL (12059 "More Songs by Ricky")............................. 40-60 60
(Stereo. Black vinyl.)
IMPERIAL (12059 "More Songs by Ricky")......................... 300-400 60
(Stereo. Colored vinyl.)
IMPERIAL (12090 "Ricky Sings Again") 20-30 64
(Stereo.)
IMPERIAL (12071 "Rick Is 21"). 35-45 61
(Stereo.)
IMPERIAL (12082 "Album Seven") 30-40 62
(Stereo.)
IMPERIAL (12218 "Best Sellers")............................. 30-40 63
(Stereo.)
IMPERIAL (12223 "It's Up to You") 30-40 63
(Stereo.)
IMPERIAL (12232 "Million Sellers By Rick Nelson") 25-35 64
(Stereo.)
IMPERIAL (12244 "A Long Vacation") 20-30 63
(Stereo.)
IMPERIAL (12251 "Rick Nelson Sings for You")........................20-30 64
(Stereo.)
LIBERTY 5-8 81-83
MCA (Except 1517)..................10-15 73-74
MCA (1517 "The Decca Years")..5-10 82
MCA/SILVER EAGLE 5-10 86
MGM (4256 "Teen Time")..........15-25 65
(Reissue of Verve 2083.)
RHINO 5-8 85
SESSIONS (1003 "Ricky Nelson Story")....................................15-25 79
(Three-LP mail-order offer.)
SUNSET 10-20 66-68
U.A. (330 "Very Best of Rick Nelson") 10-12 75
U.A. (1004 "Ricky") 8-10 80
U.A. (9960 "Legendary Masters") 15-25 71
VERVE (2083 "Teen Time")...150-200 57
(Also includes tracks by: Randy Sparks; Gary Williams; Jeff Allen; Rock Murphy; Barney Kessel; and Johnny Rivers.)

Session: James Burton; Joe Osborn; Jordnaires; Randy Meisner; Al Kemp; Steve Duncan.

Also see APPLETREE THEATRE CO.
Also see DILLARDS
Also see GRAPPELLI, Stephane, & Barney Kessel
Also see KESSEL, Barney / Grant Green / Oscar Moore / Mundell Lowe
Also see MARTIN, Dean, & Ricky Nelson
Also see MEISNER, Randy
Also see MOON, Keith
Also see RIVERS, Johnny / Ricky Nelson / Randy Sparks

NELSON, Rick, & Jack Lemmon

Singles: 7–inch

THEATRE PROMOTION RECORD (760 "Do You Know What It Means to Miss New Orleans")............................150-200 60
(Promotional issue, for theatre play only.)

NELSON, Rick / Joannie Sommers / Dona Jean Young

LPs: 10/12–inch 33rpm

DECCA (DL-4836 "On the Flip Side") 20-30 66
(Monaural.)
DECCA (DL7-4836 "On the Flip Side") 25-35 66
(Stereo.)

Also see NELSON, Rick
Also see SOMMERS, Joannie

NELSON, Sandy

P&R/R&B '59

Singles: 7–inch

COLLECTABLES..........................3-4 80s
ERA..3-5 72

IMPERIAL 4-8 61-69
LIBERTY 3-4 80s
ORIGINAL SOUND 10-15 59
U.A. 3-5 74
VEEBLETRONICS 3-5 81

EPs: 7-inch 33/45rpm

IMPERIAL 10-20 65
(Stereo jukebox "Little LPs.")

LPs: 10/12-inch 33rpm

IMPERIAL (Except 9105/12044) 10-25 61-69
IMPERIAL (9105 "Teen Beat").. 20-30 60
(Monaural.)
IMPERIAL (12044 "Teen Beat") 20-30 60
(Stereo.)
LIBERTY 5-10 82-83
SKYCLAD 5-8 80
SUNSET 10-20 66-70
U.A. 8-12 75
Also see GAMBLERS
Also see TEDDY BEARS

NELSON, Tracy

LP '74

Singles: 7-inch

ATLANTIC 3-5 75
CAPITOL 3-5 77
MCA 3-5 75

LPs: 10/12-inch 33rpm

ADELPHI 5-10 83
ATLANTIC 8-12 74
COLUMBIA 10-12 73
FLYING FISH 5-10 78-80
MCA 8-10 75
PRESTIGE (7303 "Deep Are the Roots") 15-20 65
PRESTIGE (7726 "Deep Are the Roots") 8-12 69
REPRISE 10-12 72
Also see MOTHER EARTH
Also see NELSON, Willie & Tracy

NELSON, Tyka

R&B '88

Singles: 7-inch

COOLTEMPO 3-4 88

NELSON, Willie
(Willy Nelson)

C&W '62

Singles: 78rpm

SARG (260 "A Storm Has Just Begun") 100-200 55

Singles: 7-inch

AMERICAN GOLD 3-5 76
ATLANTIC 3-5 73-75
BETTY 10-15 64
BELLAIRE (107 "Night Life") 15-25 63
(Black vinyl.)
BELLAIRE (107 "Night Life") 40-50 63
(Colored vinyl.)
BELLAIRE (5000 series) 3-5 76
CAPITOL 3-5 78
COLUMBIA 3-5 75-91
D (1084 "Man With the Blues") .. 15-25 59
D (1131 "What a Way to Live") .. 15-25 60
DOUBLE BARREL 4-8
LIBERTY (55155 "No Dough") ... 15-25 58
LIBERTY (55386 "Mr. Record Man") 10-15 61
LIBERTY (55439 thru 55638) 5-10 62-64
LIBERTY (56000 series) 4-6 69
LONE STAR 3-5 78
MONUMENT (800 series) 4-6 64
RCA (0100 thru 0800 series) 3-5 69-72
RCA (8500 thru 9900 series) 4-8 65-71
RCA (10000 thru 12000 series) 3-5 75-81
SARG (260 "A Storm Has Just Begun") 200-300 55
SONGBIRD 3-5 80
U.A. (641 "Night Life") 5-10 63
U.A. (700 thru 1200 series) 3-5 76-78
WILLIE NELSON (628 "No Place for Me") 150-250 57
(Reportedly 3,000 made.)

Picture Sleeves

COLUMBIA 3-5 84
RCA (12000 series) 3-5 81

LPs: 10/12-inch 33rpm

ACCORD 5-8 83
ALLEGIANCE 5-8 83
ATLANTIC 8-12 73-76
AUDIO FIDELITY (213 "Willie Nelson") 8-12
(Picture disc.)
AURA 5-8 83
CAMDEN 8-12 70-74
CASINO 8-10 84
COLUMBIA (30000 series, except 38250 and picture discs) 5-15 75-91
COLUMBIA (38250 "Willie Nelson") 60-100 83
(Ten-LP boxed set.)
COLUMBIA (35305 "Stardust") .. 25-35 78
(Picture disc.)
COLUMBIA (38258 "Always on My Mind") 15-25 83
(Picture disc. Promotional issue only.)
COLUMBIA (39943 "Always on My Mind") 10-20 83
(Picture disc.)
COLUMBIA (40000 series, except "HC, "half-speed mastered series) 5-10 85-90
COLUMBIA (HC-40000 series) .. 20-35 82-83
(Half-speed mastered.)
DELTA 5-8 82
EXACT 5-8 83
HBO (171010 "Willie Nelson & Family") 15-25 83
(Picture disc. Promotional issue only.)
H.S.R.D. 8-10 84

HEARTLAND 10-15 87
HOT SCHATZ 5-10 84
LIBERTY (3239 "And Then I Wrote") 25-35 62
(Monaural.)
LIBERTY (7239 "And Then I Wrote") 30-45 62
(Stereo.)
LIBERTY (10000 series) 5-10 80s
LONE STAR 8-12 78
MCA 5-10 80
PICKWICK 8-10 70s
PLANTATION 5-10 82
POTOMAC 10-15 82
PREMORE 5-10
RCA (1100 thru 3200 series) 5-10 75-79
RCA (LPM-3400 thru LPM-3900 series) 10-20 65-68
(Monaural.)
RCA (LSP-3400 thru LSP-4700 series) 10-25 65-72
(Stereo.)
RCA (3600 thru 4800 series) 4-8 80-83
(With "AYL1" prefix.)
RCA/CANDELITE 8-10 80
SHOTGUN 10-20 77
SONGBIRD 5-10 80
SUNSET 10-20 66
TAKOMA 5-8 83
TIME-LIFE (16000 series)......... 15-25 83
(Three-LP set.)
U.A. 8-12 73-78

Session: Paul Buskirk; Herb Remington; Bob White; Clyde Brewer; Dick Shannon; Pete Wade; Ray Edenton; Jimmy Day; Hargus "Pig" Robbins; Bob Moore; Willie Ackerman; Billy Strange; Glen Campbell; Leon Russell; Red Callender; Muddy Berry; Harold Bradley; David Briggs; Anita Kerr Singers; Ernie Freeman; Cal Smith; Jerry Reed; Buddy Emmons; Velma Smith; Johnny Bush; Chet Atkins; Bill Pursell; Roy Huskey; Buddy Harman; Buddy Spicher.

Also see ATKINS, Chet
Also see CAMPBELL, Glen
Also see CHARLES, Ray, & Willie Nelson
Also see COCHRAN, Hank, & Willie Nelson
Also see COE, David Allan, & Willie Nelson
Also see DARRELL, Johnny / George Jones / Willie Nelson
Also see DAVIS, Danny, Willie Nelson, & Nashville Brass
Also see EDDY, Duane
Also see HAGGARD, Merle, & Willie Nelson
Also see FREEMAN, Ernie
Also see IGLESIAS, Julio, & Willie Nelson
Also see JENNINGS, Waylon, & Willie Nelson
Also see KERR, Anita
Also see LEE, Brenda, & Willie Nelson
Also see MILLER, Roger, & Willie Nelson
Also see MOORE, Bob
Also see PARTON, Dolly, & Willie Nelson
Also see PRICE, Ray, & Willie Nelson
Also see PURSELL, Bill
Also see REED, Jerry
Also see SMITH, Cal
Also see STRANGE, Billy

NELSON, Willie / Nat "King" Cole / Johnny Mathis / Shirley Bassey

EPs: 7-inch 33/45rpm

JIMMY McHUGH (300 "Three Guys and a Gal") 8-12 81
(Promotional issue only. Includes Jimmy McHugh bio insert)

Also see BASSEY, Shirley
Also see COLE, Nat King
Also see MATHIS, Johnny

NELSON, Willie, & Shirley Collie

C&W '62

Singles: 7-inch

LIBERTY 5-10 62

NELSON, Willie, & Kris Kristofferson

C&W/LP '84

LPs: 10/12-inch 33rpm

COLUMBIA 5-8 84

Also see KRISTOFFERSON, Kris

NELSON, Willie, & Brenda Lee

C&W '83

Singles: 7-inch

MONUMENT 3-5 83

Also see LEE, Brenda

NELSON, Willie, & Johnny Lee

LPs: 10/12-inch 33rpm

QUICKSILVER 5-8 84

NELSON, Willie / Johnny Lee / Mickey Gilley

LPs: 10/12-inch 33rpm

PLANTATION 5-8 82

Also see GILLEY, Mickey
Also see LEE, Johnny

NELSON, Willie / Jerry Lee Lewis / Carl Perkins / David Allan Coe

LPs: 10/12-inch 33rpm

PLANTATION 5-10 75

Also see COE, David Allan
Also see LEWIS, Jerry Lee
Also see PERKINS, Carl

NELSON, Willie & Tracy

C&W '74

Singles: 7-inch

ATLANTIC 3-5 74

Also see NELSON, Tracy

NELSON, Willie, & Webb Pierce

C&W '82

Singles: 7-inch

COLUMBIA 3-4 82

LPs: 10/12-inch 33rpm

COLUMBIA 5-8 82

Also see PIERCE, Webb

NELSON, Willie, & Ray Price

C&W/LP '80

Singles: 7-inch

COLUMBIA 3-4 80

LPs: 10/12-inch 33rpm

COLUMBIA 5-8 80

Also see PRICE, Ray

NELSON, Willie, & Leon Russell

C&W '79

Singles: 7-inch

COLUMBIA 3-5 79

LPs: 10/12-inch 33rpm

COLUMBIA 5-10 79

Also see RUSSELL, Leon

NELSON, Willie, & Hank Wilson

C&W '84

Singles: 7-inch

PARADISE 3-4 84

NELSON, Willie / Faron Young

LPs: 10/12-inch 33rpm

ROMULUS 5-10

Also see NELSON, Willie
Also see YOUNG, Faron

NENA

P&R/D&D '83

Singles: 12-inch 33/45rpm

EPIC 4-6 83-84

Singles: 7-inch

EPIC 3-4 83-84

LPs: 10/12-inch 33rpm

EPIC 5-8 84

NEON PHILHARMONIC

P&R '69

Singles: 7-inch

MCA 3-5 76
TRX 3-5 72
W.B. 4-6 69-71

LPs: 10/12-inch 33rpm

W.B. 10-15 69

NERO, Peter
(With Boston Pops Orchestra)

LP '61

Singles: 7-inch

ARIOLA AMERICA 3-5 76
ARISTA 3-5 75
COLUMBIA 3-5 69-73
RCA 3-6 61-68

Picture Sleeves

RCA 3-5 62-63

LPs: 10/12-inch 33rpm

ARISTA 5-10 75
CAMDEN 5-10 67-73
COLUMBIA 5-10 69-75
CONCORD JAZZ 5-8 78
HARMONY 5-10 71
PREMIER 10-15 63
RCA 5-15 61-76

Also see ANN-MARGRET
Also see BOSTON POPS ORCHESTRA
Also see CRAMER, Floyd / Peter Nero / Frankie Carle

NERVOUS NORVUS
(With Red Blanchard; Jimmy Drake)

P&R '56

Singles: 78rpm

DOT 10-20 56-57

Singles: 7-inch

BIG BEN 10-15
DOT (15000 series) 10-20 56
(Maroon label.)
DOT (15000 series) 8-12 57
(Black label.)
DOT (16000 series) 4-8 65
EMBEE 10-15 59

Also see BLANCHARD, Red
Also see FOUR JOKERS

NESMITH, Michael *P&R/LP '70*
(With the First National Band; with Second National Band)

Singles: 7-inch

EDAN (1001 "Just a Little Love") 50-75 65
ISLAND 5-8 77
OMNIBUS 15-25 63
PACIFIC ARTS 8-10 75-79
RCA 10-20 70-75

Picture Sleeves

RCA (0453 "Nevada Fighter") 15-25 71

LPs: 10/12-inch 33rpm

PACIFIC ARTS ("Conversation with Michael Nesmith—Music Radio Special") 25-35 78
(Promotional issue only.)
PACIFIC ARTS (101 "The Prison") 25-50 78
(Boxed edition. With booklet.)
PACIFIC ARTS (101 "The Prison") 10-20 78
(Standard LP. With booklet.)
PACIFIC ARTS (106 thru 130) ... 10-20 78-79
RCA 20-30 70-75
RHINO 8-10 89

Also see BLESSING, Michael
Also see MONKEES
Also see WICHITA TRAIN WHISTLE

NETTO, Loz

P&R '83

Singles: 7-inch

21 .... 3-4 83

Picture Sleeves

21 .... 3-4 83

LPs: 10/12-inch 33rpm

21 .... 5-8 82

Also see SNIFF 'N the TEARS

NEVIL, Robbie

P&R/R&B/LP '86

Singles: 12-inch 33/45rpm

MANHATTAN 4-6 86

Singles: 7-inch

EMI 3-4 88

MANHATTAN 3-4 86-87

Picture Sleeves

EMI 3-4 88
MANHATTAN 3-4 86-87

LPs: 10/12-inch 33rpm

EMI 5-8 88
MANHATTAN 5-8 86

NEVILLE, Aaron
(Arron Neville)

R&B '60

Singles: 7-inch

AIRECORDS 4-8 63
BELL 4-8 68-69
HEAD 3-5
MERCURY 3-5 72-73
MINIT 5-10 60-63
PAR-LO 4-8 66-67
POLYDOR 3-5 77
SAFARI 4-8 67

LPs: 10/12-inch 33rpm

COLLECTABLES 6-8 88
MINIT (40007 "Like It 'Tis") 15-25 67
(Monaural.)
MINIT (40007 "Like It 'Tis") 15-25 67
(Stereo.)
PAR-LO (1 "Tell It Like It Is") 20-30 67
(Monaural.)
PAR-LO (1 "Tell It Like It Is") 25-35 67
(Stereo.)

Also see NEVILLE BROTHERS
Also see RONSTADT, Linda, & Aaron Neville

NEVILLE, Aaron / Toussaint McCall

Singles: 7-inch

TRIP 3-5 70s

Also see McCALL, Toussaint
Also see NEVILLE, Aaron

NEVILLE, Ivan

LP '88

Singles: 7-inch

POLYDOR 3-4 88-89

LPs: 10/12-inch 33rpm

POLYDOR 5-8 88

NEVILLE BROTHERS

LP '81

Singles: 7-inch

A&M 3-5 81-90
CAPITOL 3-6 78

LPs: 10/12-inch 33rpm

A&M 5-10 81-90
BLACK TOP 5-10 86
CAPITOL (11865 "Neville Brothers") 20-30 78
EMI AMERICA 5-8 87
RHINO 5-8 87
SPINDLE TOP 5-8 87

Members: Aaron Neville; Art Neville; Charles Neville; Cyril Neville.
Also see METERS
Also see NEVILLE, Aaron

NEW BIRTH

P&R/R&B/LP '71

Singles: 7-inch

ARIOLA AMERICA 3-5 79
BUDDAH 3-5 75
RCA 3-5 71-75
W.B. 3-5 76-78

LPs: 10/12-inch 33rpm

ARIOLA AMERICA 5-10 79
BUDDAH 8-12 75
COLLECTABLES 5-10 88
RCA (Except APD1-0285 & LSP-4000 series) 5-10 73-82
RCA (APD1-0285 "It's Been a Long Time") 15-25 74
(Quadrophonic.)
RCA (LSP-4000 series) 10-15 70-72
W.B. 8-12 76-77

Members: Harvey Fuqua; Tony Churchill; Alan Frey; Robert Jackson; Joe Porter; Leslie Wilson; Mel Wilson.
Also see LOVE, PEACE & HAPPINESS
Also see NITE-LITERS

NEW CACTUS BAND

LP '73

Singles: 7-inch

ATCO 3-6 73

LPs: 10/12-inch 33rpm

ATCO 8-12 73

Members: Mike Pinera; Duane Hitchings; Manuel Bertematti; Roland Robinson; Jerry Norris.
Also see CACTUS

NEW CENSATION

R&B '74

Singles: 7-inch

PRIDE 3-5 74-75

LPs: 10/12-inch 33rpm

PRIDE 8-12 74

NEW CHOICE

R&B '87

Singles: 7-inch

RCA 3-4 87

NEW CHRISTY MINSTRELS

P&R/LP '62

Singles: 7-inch

COLUMBIA (42000 series) 4-8 62-63
COLUMBIA (43000 & 44000 series) 4-6 64-69
GREGAR 3-5 70-72
W.B. 3-5 79

Promotional Singles

COLUMBIA (Colored vinyl) 5-10 63-65

Picture Sleeves

COLUMBIA 4-8 62

LPs: 10/12-inch 33rpm

COLUMBIA (1800 thru 2500 series) 10-20 62-66
(Monaural.)

COLUMBIA (8600 thru 9300 series) 10-30 62-66
(Stereo.)
COLUMBIA (9600 & 9700 series) 10-15 68
GREGAR.................................. 8-12 70
HARMONY.................................. 8-12 68-72
Members: Randy Sparks; Barry McGuire; Kenny Rogers; Mike Settle; Thelma Lou Camacho; Terry Williams; Mickey Jones; Jackie Miller; Gayle Caldwell; Gene Clark; Larry Ramos; Rex Kramer.
Also see ASSOCIATION
Also see CLARK, Gene
Also see FIRST EDITION
Also see McGUIRE, Barry
Also see SPARKS, Randy

NEW COLONY SIX

P&R '66

Singles: 7-inch

CENTAUR.................................. 4-8 66
MCA 3-6 74
MERCURY ("Attacking a Straw Man") 10-20 69
(Promotional issue only. Number not known.)
MERCURY (72737 thru 73004) 4-8 67-70
MERCURY (73063 "People and Me").................................. 8-15 70
MERCURY (73093 "Close Your Eyes Little Girl") 8-15 70
SENTAR.................................. 10-20 66-67
SUNLIGHT 3-5 71-72
TWILIGHT 3-5 73

Picture Sleeves

MERCURY 4-8 67-68

LPs: 10/12-inch 33rpm

MERCURY 20-30 68-69
SENTAR (101 "Breakthrough").................. 150-250 66
SENTAR (3001 "Colonization"). 50-75 67
Members: Ronnie Rice; Ray Graffia; Craig Kemp; Jerry Kollenberg; Pat McBride; Chick James; Billy Herman; Chuck Lobes; Wally Kemp.

NEW EDITION

P&R/R&B/D&D/LP '83

Singles: 12-inch 33/45rpm

MCA 4-6 84-86
STREETWISE.................................. 4-6 83

Singles: 7-inch

MCA (Black vinyl).................................. 3-4 84-89
MCA (Colored vinyl) 4-6 85
STREETWISE.................................. 5-8 83

Picture Sleeves

MCA 3-5 84-89

LPs: 10/12-inch 33rpm

MCA 5-8 84-89
STREETWISE.................................. 5-8 83
Members: Johnny Gill; Bobby Brown; Ricky Bell; Michael Bivins; Ronnie DeVoe.
Also see BELL BIV DeVOE
Also see GILL, Johnny

Also see KING DREAM CHORUS & Holiday Crew

NEW ENGLAND

P&R/LP '79

Singles: 7-inch

ELEKTRA.................................. 3-5 80-81
INFINITY 3-5 79

LPs: 10/12-inch 33rpm

ELEKTRA.................................. 5-10 80-81
INFINITY 5-10 79

NEW ENGLAND CONSERVATORY RAGTIME ENSEMBLE

LP '73

Singles: 7-inch

ANGEL.................................. 3-4 80

LPs: 10/12-inch 33rpm

ANGEL.................................. 5-8 73
GOLDEN CREST.................................. 5-10 75

NEW ESTABLISHMENT

P&R '69

Singles: 7-inch

COLGEMS 5-8 69
MERCURY.................................. 4-8 67

NEW GUYS on the BLOCK

R&B '83

Singles: 7-inch

SUGAR HILL.................................. 3-4 83

NEW HOPE

P&R '70

Singles: 7-inch

JAMIE 4-8 69-71

LPs: 10/12-inch 33rpm

JAMIE (3034 "The New Hope") .20-30 69
Members: Kit Stewart; Carl Von Hausman; John Bradley; Ron Shane.

NEW HORIZONS

R&B '83

Singles: 7-inch

COLUMBIA 3-4 83

LPs: 10/12-inch 33rpm

COLUMBIA 5-8 83
Members: Mark Thomas; Art Thomas; Varges Thomas.

NEW JERSEY MASS CHOIR

R&B/D&D '85

Singles: 12-inch 33/45rpm

SAVOY.................................. 4-6 85
Also see FOREIGNER

NEW KIDS on the BLOCK

R&B '86

Singles: 12-inch 33/45rpm

COLUMBIA.................................. 4-6 86

Singles: 7-inch

COLUMBIA 3-4 86-90

Picture Sleeves

COLUMBIA 3-4 88

LPs: 10/12-inch 33rpm

COLUMBIA 5-8 86-90

Members: Jordan Knight; Jon Knight; Joe McIntyre; Danny Wood; Donny Wahlberg.
Also see PAGE, Tommy

NEW KINGSTON TRIO

Singles: 7–inch

CAPITOL 3-6 71

Also see KINGSTON TRIO

NEW MARKETTS

(Danny Welton & New Marketts)

R&B '76

Singles: 7–inch

CALLIOPE 3-6 77
FARR 3-6 76-77
SEMINOLE 3-6 76

LPs: 10/12–inch 33rpm

CALLIOPE 8-12 77

Also see MARKETTS

NEW ORDER

R&B/D&D '83

Singles: 12–inch 33/45rpm

FACTUS 4-6 83
QWEST 4-6 85
STREETWISE 4-6 83

Singles: 7–inch

QWEST 3-4 85-89
STREETWISE 3-4 83

Picture Sleeves

QWEST 3-4 87-89

LPs: 10/12–inch 33rpm

QWEST (Except 25621) 5-8 85-89
QWEST (25621 "Substance") 8-12 87

Members: Bernard Sumner; Peter Hook; Gillian Gilbert; Stephen Morris.
Also see ELECTRONIC
Also see JOY DIVISION

NEW RIDERS of the Purple Sage

LP '71

Singles: 7–inch

COLUMBIA 3-5 71-74
MCA 3-5 76-77

LPs: 10/12–inch 33rpm

A&M 5-8 81
BUDDAH 8-12 75
COLUMBIA 10-15 71-75
MCA 8-10 76-77
RELIX 5-8 86-87

Members: Skip Battin; David Turbert. Also, assorted Grateful Dead members guested on Columbia and Relix issues.
Also see GRATEFUL DEAD
Also see KINGFISH

NEW ROTARY CONNECTION

LPs: 10/12–inch 33rpm

CHESS 8-12 71

Also see ROTARY CONNECTION

NEW SEEKERS

P&R '70

Singles: 7–inch

ELEKTRA 3-5 70-72
MGM/VERVE 3-5 72-73

Picture Sleeves

MGM/VERVE 3-5 72-73

EPs: 7–inch 33/45rpm

COCA-COLA 5-10 69
(Promotional issue only.)

LPs: 10/12–inch 33rpm

ELEKTRA 10-12 71-72
MGM/VERVE 8-10 73

Member: Keith Potger.
Also see SEEKERS

NEW VAUDEVILLE BAND

P&R/LP '66

Singles: 7–inch

FONTANA 3-6 66-68

LPs: 10/12–inch 33rpm

FONTANA 10-15 67

NEW VENTURES: see VENTURES

NEW YORK CITI PEECH BOYS

R&B/D&D '83

Singles: 12–inch 33/45rpm

GARAGE 4-6 83-84
ISLAND 4-6 83-84

Singles: 7–inch

ISLAND 3-4 83-84

LPs: 10/12–inch 33rpm

ISLAND 5-8 84

Also see PEECH BOYS

NEW YORK CITY

P&R/R&B/LP '73

Singles: 7–inch

CHELSEA 3-5 73-75

LPs: 10/12–inch 33rpm

CHELSEA 10-15 73-77

Also see CADILLACS
Also see FIVE SATINS

NEW YORK COMMUNITY CHOIR

R&B '77

Singles: 7–inch

RCA 3-5 77

NEW YORK DOLLS

LP '73

Singles: 7–inch

MERCURY 3-5 73-76

Picture Sleeves

MERCURY 4-8 73

LPs: 10/12–inch 33rpm

MERCURY (675 "New York Dolls") 20-25 73
MERCURY (1001 "Too Much, Too Soon") 15-20 74
REACH OUT INT'L 5-10 81

Members: David Johansen; Jerry Nolan; Arthur Kane; Johnny Thudners; Sylvain Sylvain.
Also see JOHANSEN, David
Also see SYLVAIN SYLVAIN
Also see W.A.S.P.

NEW YORKERS

P&R '61

Singles: 7–inch

WALL (547 "Miss Fine") 15-25 61
WALL (548 "Tears in My Eyes") 15-25 61

Members: Fred Parris; Richard Freeman; Wesley Forbes; Louis Peebles; Silvester Hopkins.
Also see FIVE SATINS

NEW YOUNG HEARTS

R&B '70

Singles: 7–inch

SOULTOWN 10-20
ZEA 3-5 70

NEWBEATS

P&R/LP '64

Singles: 7–inch

ABC 3-5 74
HICKORY 4-8 64-72
PLAYBOY 3-5 74

EPs: 7–inch 33/45rpm

HICKORY (120-005 "Bread and Butter") 20-30 65
(Compact 33. Promotional issue only.)

LPs: 10/12–inch 33rpm

HICKORY (LP-120 "Bread and Butter") 25-45 65
(Monaural.)
HICKORY (LPS-120 "Bread and Butter") 75-125 65
(Stereo.)
HICKORY (LP-122 "Big Beat Sound") 25-35 65
(Monaural.)
HICKORY (LPS-122 "Big Beat Sound") 30-40 65
(Stereo.)
HICKORY (LP-128 "Run Baby Run") 25-35 65
(Monaural.)
HICKORY (LPS-128 "Run Baby Run") 30-40 65
(Stereo.)

Members: Larry Henley; Dean Mathis; Mark Mathis.
Also see DEAN & MARC

NEWBERRY, Booker, III

R&B/D&D '83

Singles: 12–inch 33/45rpm

BOARDWALK 4-6 83

Singles: 7–inch

BOARDWALK 3-4 83
OMNI 3-4 86

NEWBURY, Mickey

P&R/LP '71

Singles: 7–inch

ABC/HICKORY 3-5 77-79
AIRBORNE 3-4 88
ELEKTRA 3-5 71-73
HICKORY (1312 thru 1463) 4-8 65-67
HICKORY (1600 series) 3-4 80
MCA 3-5 79
MERCURY 3-6 69-70
RCA 3-6 68-70

Picture Sleeves

RCA 3-6 68

LPs: 10/12–inch 33rpm

ABC/HICKORY 5-10 77-79
MCA 5-8 79
ELEKTRA 8-10 71-75
MERCURY 10-12 69
RCA 10-12 68-72

NEWCITY ROCKERS

P&R '87

Singles: 7–inch

CRITIQUE 3-4 87

Picture Sleeves

CRITIQUE 3-4 87

NEWCLEUS

R&B '83

Singles: 12–inch 33/45rpm

SUNNYVIEW 4-6 83-86

Singles: 7–inch

SUNNYVIEW 3-4 83-86

LPs: 10/12–inch 33rpm

SUNNYVIEW 5-8 84-86

NEWCOMERS

P&R/R&B '71

Singles: 7–inch

GIGOLO 4-8 65
STAX 3-5 71
TRUTH 3-5 74-75
VOLT 3-6 69

Members: Terry Bartlett; Bert Brown; William Sumlin.
Also see BAR-KAYS
Also see KWICK

NEWHART, Bob

LP '60

LPs: 10/12–inch 33rpm

HARMONY 10-15 69
W.B. (1300 thru 1500 series) 20-30 60-65
W.B. (1600 thru 1700 series) 15-25 66-67

NEWLEY, Anthony

P&R '60

Singles: 7–inch

KAPP 4-6 69
LONDON 4-8 58-63
MGM 3-5 71-74
RCA 4-8 66-67
U.A. 3-5 76-77
W.B. 4-6 68

LPs: 10/12–inch 33rpm

BELL 8-10 71
LONDON 10-20 62-66
MGM 8-12 71-73
RCA 10-20 64-69

U.A. 5-10 77

NEWMAN, Jimmy

(Jimmy C. Newman; with Cajun Country)

C&W '54

Singles: 78rpm

DOT 5-10 54-57

Singles: 7-inch

DECCA 3-8 60-71
DOT (Except 15766) 5-15 54-57
DOT (15766 "Carry On") 50-75 58
MGM 5-10 58-60
MONUMENT 3-5 72
PLANTATION 3-5 76-80
SHANNON 3-5 73

EPs: 7-inch 33/45rpm

DECCA 5-10 64

LPs: 10/12-inch 33rpm

CROWN 8-12 60s
DECCA 10-20 62-70
DELTA 5-8 82
DOT 10-20 66
LA LOUISANNE 5-8
MGM 15-25 59-62
PICKWICK/HILLTOP 8-12
PLANTATION 5-10 77-81
SWALLOW 5-8

NEWMAN, Jimmy C., Danny Davis & Nashville Brass

Singles: 7-inch

RCA 3-4 80
Also see DAVIS, Danny
Also see NEWMAN, Jimmy C.

NEWMAN, Randy

LP '71

Singles: 78rpm

REPRISE (0284 "I Think It's Gonna Rain Today") 8-10 78
(Promotional issue only.)

Singles: 7-inch

CHELSEA 3-5 74
DOT 4-8 62
REPRISE (Except 0771) 3-6 68-88
REPRISE (0771 "Last Night I Had a Dream") 10-20 68
W.B. 3-5 77-85

Picture Sleeves

REPRISE 3-4 88
W.B. 3-5 78

LPs: 10/12-inch 33rpm

EPIC (147 "Peyton Place") 20-30 65
(TV Soundtrack.)
REPRISE (Except 6286) 5-10 70-88
REPRISE (6286 "Randy Newman") 15-20 68
(Cover pictures Randy in sweater and coat.)
REPRISE (6286 "Randy Newman") 10-15 68
(Cover picture is a close-up of Randy.)
W.B. 5-10 77-85
Also see BISHOP, Stephen
Also see EAGLES
Also see McVIE, Christine
Also see RONSTADT, Linda
Also see SEGER, Bob

NEWMAN, Randy, & Paul Simon / Randy Newman

P&R '83

Singles: 7-inch

W.B. 3-5 83

Picture Sleeves

W.B. 3-5 83
Also see NEWMAN, Randy
Also see SIMON, Paul

NEWMAN, Ted

P&R '57

Singles: 78rpm

REV 5-10 57

Singles: 7-inch

RCA 5-10 58
REV 5-10 57

NEWMAN, Thunderclap

P&R '69

Singles: 7-inch

MCA 3-4 80s
TRACK (2000 series) 4-8 69-70
TRACK (60000 series) 3-5 75

LPs: 10/12-inch 33rpm

ATLANTIC/TRACK 10-20 70
MCA/TRACK 5-10 73
Members: Andy Newman; Jimmy McCulloch; Speedy Keen.
Also see McCARTNEY, Paul

NEWSOM, Chubby

(With Her Hip Shakers; with Lee Allen)

R&B '49

Singles: 78rpm

DELUXE 10-15 49
MILTONE 10-20 49
WINLEY (216 "Toodle Luddle Baby") 20-30 57
Also see ALLEN, Lee
Also see GAYTEN, Paul

NEWSOME, Bobby

R&B '72

Singles: 7-inch

SPRING 3-5 72

NEWSOME, Frankie

R&B '69

Singles: 7-inch

GWP 4-6 69

NEWTON, Juice

C&W '79

Singles: 7-inch

CAPITOL 3-5 78-84
RCA 3-4 84-89

Picture Sleeves

CAPITOL.. 3-5 81-83
RCA... 3-4 84

LPs: 10/12-inch 33rpm

CAPITOL...................................... 5-10 78-84
RCA... 5-8 84-87

Also see RABBITT, Eddie, & Juice Newton

NEWTON, Juice, & Silver Spur

C&W '76

Singles: 7-inch

CAPITOL.. 3-5 77
RCA... 3-5 75-76

LPs: 10/12-inch 33rpm

CAPITOL (11000 series)............ 8-10 77
CAPITOL (16000 series).............. 5-8 81
RCA (1000 series)....................... 8-12 75
RCA (4000 series)......................... 5-8 81

Also see NEWTON, Juice

NEWTON, Wayne

P&R/LP '63

Singles: 7-inch

ARIES II 3-5 79-80
CAPITOL (Except 5338) 4-8 63-71
CAPITOL (5338 "Comin' on Too Strong")........................... 10-20 64
(With Bruce Johnston & Terry Melcher.)
CHALLENGE 4-8 64
CHELSEA 3-5 72-76
GEORGE (7777 "Little White Cloud That Cried") 10-15 62
MGM 3-6 68
20TH FOX...................................... 3-5 78
W.B. 3-5 70-77

Picture Sleeves

CAPITOL.. 4-8 65-66

LPs: 10/12-inch 33rpm

AIRES II 5-8 79-80
CAMDEN...................................... 5-10 74
CAPITOL (573 "Wayne Newton") 15-25 70
(Three-LP set.)
CAPITOL (T-1973 thru T-2797) 10-20 63-67
(Monaural.)
CAPITOL (ST-1973 thru ST-2797) 15-25 63-67
(Stereo.)
CAPITOL (SM-2300 series) 5-8 75
CAPITOL (11000 series).............. 5-8 79
CAPITOL (16000 series).............. 5-8 80
CHELSEA 10-15 72-75
MGM 6-12 68
MUSICOR 5-8 79
20TH FOX...................................... 5-8 78

Also see BRUCE & TERRY

NEWTON, Wayne, & Tammy Wynette

C&W '89

Singles: 7-inch

CURB 3-4 89

Also see NEWTON, Wayne
Also see WYNETTE, Tammy

NEWTON BROTHERS

(Featuring Wayne)

Singles: 7-inch

CAPITOL (4236 "The Real Thing") 60-80 59
GEORGE (7778 "Little Jukebox")................................15-20 61
GEORGE (7780 "I Still Love You")...10-15 61
LAMA (7794 "I Was Born When You Kissed Me")..............................25-50 63

Members: Wayne Newton; Jerry Newton.
Also see NEWTON RASCALS

NEWTON RASCALS

Singles: 7-inch

RANGER (401 "If the Easter Bunny Knew the Fun He'd Have on Xmas") 15-25 58
(Issued with a paper insert picturing 12-year-old Wayne and 14-year-old Jerry as "The Rascals in Rhythm." Value of insert is about the same as for disc.)

Members: Wayne Newton; Jerry Newton.
Also see NEWTON, Wayne
Also see NEWTON BROTHERS

NEWTON-JOHN, Olivia

P&R/LP '71

Singles: 12-inch 33/45rpm

MCA (Except 1150)........................4-6 81-84
MCA (1150 "Twist of Fate") 5-10 83
(Promotional issue only.)

Singles: 7-inch

GEFFEN 3-4 89
KIRSHNER (5005 "Goin' Back") 10-15 70
MCA (Except 40043)......................3-5 73-88
MCA (40043 "Take Me Home Country Roads") 5-10 73
RSO 3-5 78
UNI (55281 "If Not for You").........5-10 71
UNI (55304 "Banks of the Ohio") ...4-8 71
UNI (55317 "What Is Life")............4-8 72
UNI (55348 "Just a Little Too Much")....................................8-12 72

Promotional Singles

MCA (1810 "Deeper Than the Night")...............................25-30 79
(Picture disc. Promotional issue only.)
WHAT'S IT ALL ABOUT 25-50 74

Picture Sleeves

MCA (Except 40418)......................3-5 75-88
MCA (40418 "Please Mr. Please") 6-10 75

EPs: 7-inch 33/45rpm

MCA 12-15 73
(Promotional issues only.)

LPs: 10/12-inch 33rpm

GEFFEN 5-8 89
MCA (389 "Let Me Be There" 10-12 73

MCA (411 "If You Love Me, Let Me Know")........................ 12-15 74
(With *I Love You, I Honestly Love You.* Note longer title.)
MCA (411 "If You Love Me, Let Me Know")........................ 8-10 74
(With *I Honestly Love You.* Note shorter title.)
MCA (2000 & 3000 series)......... 8-10 75-78
MCA (5000 & 6000 series)........... 5-8 80-83
MCA (37000 series) 5-8 80-83
MFSL.. 25-50 80
UNI (73117 "If Not for You")...... 50-75 71
(Cover depicts a field scene.)
UNI (73117 "If Not for You")...... 20-30 71
(Field scene removed from cover.)
Also see DENVER, John, & Olivia Newton-John
Also see FOSTER, David, & Olivia Newton-John
Also see TOMORROW
Also see WILSON, Carl

NEWTON-JOHN, Olivia, & Electric Light Orchestra

P&R/LP '80

Singles: 7-inch

MCA (41285 "Xanadu")................ 3-5 80

Picture Sleeves

MCA (41285 "Xanadu")................ 3-5 80

LPs: 10/12-inch 33rpm

MCA (6100 "Xanadu")................ 8-10 80
MCA (10384 "Xanadu")....... 750-1000 80
(Picture disc. Promotional issue only. Also has Cliff Richard, Gene Kelly, and the Tubes.)
Also see ELECTRIC LIGHT ORCHESTRA
Also see RICHARD, Cliff
Also see TUBES

NEWTON-JOHN, Olivia, & Andy Gibb

P&R '80

Singles: 12-inch 33/45rpm

POLYDOR (104 "Rest Your Love on Me")......................... 10-15 79

Singles: 7-inch

RSO 3-5 80
Also see GIBB, Andy

NEWTON-JOHN, Olivia, & Cliff Richard

P&R '80

Singles: 7-inch

MCA 3-5 80

Picture Sleeves

MCA 3-5 80
Also see RICHARD, Cliff

NEWTON-JOHN, Olivia, & John Travolta

P&R '78

Singles: 7-inch

RSO 3-5 78

Picture Sleeves

RSO 3-5 78
Also see NEWTON-JOHN, Olivia
Also see TRAVOLTA, John

NEXT MOVEMENT

R&B '84

Singles: 7-inch

NUANCE......................................3-4 84

NICE

LP '70

Singles: 7-inch

IMMEDIATE..................................4-8 68
MERCURY....................................3-5 70-71

LPs: 10/12-inch 33rpm

CHARISMA................................8-12
COLUMBIA.................................8-12
IMMEDIATE..............................10-15 68-71
MERCURY.................................10-12 70-72
SIRE..10-12 75
Members: Keith Emerson; Lee Jackson; Brian Davison; Joe Harriot; Davy O'List.
Also see EMERSON, Keith, & Nice

NICHOLAS, Paul

P&R '77

Singles: 7-inch

COLUMBIA..................................3-5 74
RSO 3-5 76-78

LPs: 10/12-inch 33rpm

RSO 5-10 77

NICHOLS, Mike, & Elaine May

LP '59

Singles: 7-inch

MERCURY....................................3-6

LPs: 10/12-inch 33rpm

MERCURY.................................15-30 59-72

NICK & ELVIS

Singles: 12-inch 33/45rpm

COLUMBIA...................................4-8 84
Members: Nick Lowe; Elvis Costello.
Also see COSTELLO, Elvis
Also see LOWE, Nick

NICKIE LEE: see LEE, Nickie

NICKS, Stevie

LP '81

Singles: 12-inch 33/45rpm

MODERN......................................4-8 81-86

Singles: 7-inch

MODERN......................................3-5 81-89

Picture Sleeves

MODERN......................................3-5 82-89

LPs: 10/12-inch 33rpm

MFSL (121 "Bella Donna").........20-30 84
MODERN....................................5-10 81-89
Also see BUCKINGHAM NICKS
Also see EGAN, Walter
Also see FLEETWOOD MAC
Also see LOGGINS, Kenny, & Stevie Nicks
Also see STEWART, John
Also see STEWART, Sandy

NICKS, Stevie, & Don Henley

P&R '81

Singles: 7-inch

MODERN 3-5 81

Also see HENLEY, Don

NICKS, Stevie, & Tom Petty & Heartbreakers

P&R '81

Singles: 7-inch

MODERN 3-5 81-86

Also see PETTY, Tom, & Heartbreakers

NICOLE

R&B '85

Singles: 12-inch 33/45rpm

PORTRAIT 4-6 85-86

Singles: 7-inch

EPIC 3-4 88

PORTRAIT 3-4 85-86

LPs: 10/12-inch 33rpm

PORTRAIT 5-8 86

NIELSEN - PEARSON

P&R '80

Singles: 7-inch

CAPITOL 3-5 80-83

EPIC 3-5 78

LPs: 10/12-inch 33rpm

CAPITOL 5-10 80-81

EPIC 5-10 78

Members: Reid Nielsen; Mark Pearson.

NIGHT

P&R/LP '79

Singles: 7-inch

PLANET 3-5 79-81

Picture Sleeves

PLANET 3-5 80-81

LPs: 10/12-inch 33rpm

PLANET 5-10 79-80

Members: Chris Thompson; Nicky Hopkins; Derek Austin; Bill Payne; Michael McDonald; Vince Melamed; Steve Porcaro; James Johnson.

NIGHT RANGER

LP '82

Singles: 7-inch

BOARDWALK 3-4 83

MCA/CAMEL 3-4 83-88

Picture Sleeves

MCA/CAMEL 3-4 84-88

LPs: 10/12-inch 33rpm

BOARDWALK 5-10 82

MCA/CAMEL 5-10 83-88

Member: Jack Blades.

Also see DAMN YANKEES

NIGHTCRAWLERS

P&R '67

Singles: 7-inch

KAPP (110 "Little Black Egg") 8-12 67

KAPP (709 "Little Black Egg") 5-10 65

KAPP (746 "Basket of Flowers") . 5-10 66

KAPP (826 "My Butterfly") 8-12 67

LEE (101 "Cry") 20-30 64

LEE (1012 "Little Black Egg") 10-20 65

MARLIN (1904 "Basket of Flowers") 10-15 66

SCOTT (28 "I Don't Remember") . 8-12 66

LPs: 10/12-inch 33rpm

KAPP (1520 "Little Black Egg") .. 25-40 67
(Monaural.)

KAPP (3520 "Little Black Egg") .. 30-50 67
(Stereo.)

Members: Chuck Conlon; Rob Rouse; Sylvan Wells; Tom Ruger; Pete Thomason.

NIGHTHAWK

R&B '82

Singles: 7-inch

QUALITY 3-5 82

NIGHTHAWK, Robert

(With His Nighthawks Band; Nighthawks; Robert McCollum)

R&B '49

Singles: 78rpm

ARISTOCRAT (413 "Six Three O") 50-75 48

ARISTOCRAT (2301 "Black Angel Blues") 50-75 48

CHESS (1484 "My Sweet Lovin' Woman") 40-60 48

STATES 30-50 53

UNITED (102 "Kansas City Blues") 50-75 51

UNITED (105 "Feel So Sad") 50-75 51

Singles: 7-inch

STATES (131 "The Moon Is Rising") 200-300 53

LPs: 10/12-inch 33rpm

ROUNDER 5-8

Also see TAYLOR, Hound Dog / Robert Nighthawk / John Littlejohn / Earl Hooker

Also see TAYLOR, Koko

NIGHTHAWKS

LP '80

LPs: 10/12-inch 33rpm

ADELPHI 6-12 76-82

ALADDIN (101 "Rock & Roll") 50-75 75

CHESAPEAKE (Black vinyl) 5-10 83

CHESAPEAKE (Colored vinyl) .. 10-15 83

VARRICK 5-10 83

MERCURY 5-10 80

Members: Mark Wenner; Jim Thackery.

NIGHTINGALE, Maxine

P&R/R&B/LP '76

Singles: 7-inch

A&M 3-5 81

HIGHRISE 3-5 82

RCA 3-5 80

U.A. 3-5 76

WINDSONG 3-5 79

Picture Sleeves

WINDSONG ... 3-5 79

LPs: 10/12-inch 33rpm

HIGHRISE ... 5-10 82
U.A. ... 5-10 76-79
WINDSONG ... 5-10 80

NIGHTINGALE, Maxine, & Jimmy Ruffin

R&B '82

Singles: 7-inch

HIGHRISE ... 3-5 82

Also see NIGHTINGALE, Maxine
Also see RUFFIN, Jimmy

NIGHTINGALE, Ollie

R&B '71

Singles: 7-inch

MEMPHIS ... 3-5 71
PATHFINDER ... 3-5 78
PRIDE ... 3-5 72-73

LPs: 10/12-inch 33rpm

PRIDE ... 8-12 73

NILE, Willie

LP '80

Singles: 7-inch

ARISTA ... 3-5 80-81

LPs: 10/12-inch 33rpm

ARISTA ... 5-10 80-81

NILSSON

(With the New Salvation Singers)

P&R/LP '69

Singles: 7-inch

POLYDOR ... 3-4 85
RCA ... 3-6 67-77
TOWER (100 series) ... 5-8 64-65
TOWER (500 series) ... 4-6 69

Picture Sleeves

RCA ... 3-6 74-77

EPs: 7-inch 33/45rpm

RCA (248 "Excerpts from *The Point*) ... 8-10 71
(Promotional issue only.)

LPs: 10/12-inch 33rpm

51 WEST ... 5-8 80s
MUSICOR ... 8-10 77
PICKWICK ... 5-10 70s
POLYDOR ... 5-8 85
RCA (0097 thru 0817, except "APD1" series) ... 8-12 73-75
RCA ("APD1" series) ... 10-20 74-75
(Quadrophonic.)
RCA (1003 "The Point") ... 10-12 71
(With Davy Jones and Mickey Dolenz.)
RCA (1031 thru 3811) ... 5-10 76-80
RCA (3874 "Pandemonium Shadow Show") ... 15-20 67
RCA (3956 "Aerial Ballet") ... 10-20 68
RCA (4197 thru 4717) ... 8-12 69-72
RAPPLE ... 8-12 74
SPRINGBOARD ... 5-10 78
TOWER (5095 "Spotlight") ... 10-15 69

Promotional LPs

RCA (567 "Scatalogue") ... 30-40 60s
RCA ("Pandemonium Shadow Show - Boxed Set") ... 50-75 67
(Includes photos and inserts.)

Also see BO PETE
Also see CHER & NILSSON
Also see DOLENZ, Mickey
Also see FOTO-FI FOUR
Also see JONES, Davy
Also see STARR, Ringo, & Harry Nilsson

NIMOY, Leonard

LP '67

Singles: 7-inch

DOT ... 8-12 67-69

LPs: 10/12-inch 33rpm

CAEDMON ... 10-15 70s
DOT ... 25-50 67-69
JRT ("The Mysterious Golem") ... 20-40 82
PARAMOUNT ... 20-40 74
PICKWICK ... 15-25 60s
SEARS ... 15-25 60s

NINE INCH NAILS

LP '90

LPs: 10/12-inch 33rpm

TVT ... 5-8 90

9TH CREATION

R&B '77

Singles: 7-inch

HILLTAK ... 3-5 79-80
PRELUDE ... 3-5 77

LPs: 10/12-inch 33rpm

PRELUDE ... 8-10 77
RITE TRACK ... 10-12

9.9

P&R/R&B/D&D/LP '85

Singles: 12-inch 33/45rpm

RCA ... 4-6 85-86

Singles: 7-inch

RCA ... 3-4 85-86

LPs: 10/12-inch 33rpm

RCA ... 5-10 85

999

LP '80

Singles: 7-inch

POLYDOR ... 3-5 81

LPs: 10/12-inch 33rpm

PVC ... 5-10 79
POLYDOR ... 5-10 80-81

1910 FRUITGUM CO.

P&R/LP '68

Singles: 7-inch

ATTACK ... 4-8 70
BUDDAH ... 4-8 67-69
SUPER K ... 4-8 70

LPs: 10/12-inch 33rpm

BUDDAH 15-25 68-70

Also see KASENETZ - KATZ SINGING ORCHESTRAL CIRCUS

1910 FRUITGUM COMPANY / Lemon Pipers

LPs: 10/12-inch 33rpm

BUDDAH 15-20 68-70

Also see LEMON PIPERS

Also see 1910 FRUITGUM COMPANY

1927

P&R '89

Singles: 7-inch

ATLANTIC 3-4 89

Picture Sleeves

ATLANTIC 3-4 80

LPs: 10/12-inch 33rpm

ATLANTIC 5-8 89

Members: Garry Frost; Eric Weideman; Bill Frost; Charles Cole.

Also see MOVING PICTURES

NINO & Ebb Tides

P&R '61

Singles: 7-inch

MADISON (162 "Those Oldies But Goodies") 20-30 61

MADISON (166 "Juke Box Saturday Night") 15-20 61

MALA (480 "Linda Lou") 10-15 64

MARCO (105 "Someday") 20-30 61

MR. PEACOCK (102 "Wished I Was Home") 10-20 61

MR. PEACOCK (117 "Lovin' Time") 10-15 62

MR. PEEKE (123 "Tonight") 10-15 63

RECORTE (405 "Puppy Love"). 20-30 58

RECORTE (408 "The Real Meaning of Christmas") 100-125 58

RECORTE (409 "I'm Confessin'") 20-30 58

RECORTE (413 "I Love Girls") . 20-30 58

Member: Nino Aiello.

NINO & Ebb Tides / Miss Frankie Nolan

Singles: 7-inch

MADISON (151 "A Week from Sunday") 10-20 61

Also see NINO & Ebb Tides

NIRVANA

LP '91

Singles: 7-inch

SUB POP (23 "Love Buzz") 50-100 88

(1000 made.)

EPs: 7-inch 33/45rpm

TUPELO (8 "Blew") 20-30 89

LPs: 10/12-inch 33rpm

SUB POP (34 "Bleach") 35-50 89

(Colored vinyl.)

SUB POP (34 "Bleach") 15-25 89

(Black vinyl. Includes poster.)

SUB POP (73 "Sliver") 15-25 90

(Colored vinyl.)

DGC 10-15 91

DGC/SUB POP (24607 "In Utero") 20-30 93

(Clear vinyl, limited edition.)

SUB POP 10-15 92

Members: Kurt Cobain; Krist "Chris" Novoselic; Jason Everman; Chad Channing; Dave Grohl; Dave Foster.

NIRVANA / The Fluid

Singles: 7-inch

SUB POP (97 "Molly's Lips")...... 10-20 91

(Black vinyl. 3,500 made.)

SUB POP (97 "Molly's Lips")...... 10-20 91

(Colored vinyl. 4,000 made.)

Picture Sleeves

SUB POP (97 "Molly's Lips")...... 10-20 91

NIRVANA / The Melvins

Singles: 7-inch

COMMUNION (23 "Here She Comes Now") 10-15 91

(Black vinyl.)

COMMUNION (23 "Here She Comes Now") 10-15 91

(Colored vinyl.)

Also see NIRVANA

NITEFLYTE

P&R/R&B '79

Singles: 7-inch

ARIOLA AMERICA 3-5 79-81

LPs: 10/12-inch 33rpm

ARIOLA AMERICA 5-10 79-81

Also see JOHNSON, Howard

NITE-LITERS

P&R/R&B/LP '71

Singles: 7-inch

RCA 3-5 71-72

LPs: 10/12-inch 33rpm

RCA 8-12 71-72

Also see NEW BIRTH

NITRO

LP '89

LPs: 10/12-inch 33rpm

RHINO 5-8 89

NITTY GRITTY DIRT BAND

P&R/LP '67

(Dirt Band)

Singles: 78rpm

LIBERTY (2889 "Mr. Bojangles") 20-30 70

(Promotional issue only.)

U.A. (69 "All the Good Times") .. 20-30 71

(Promotional issue only. Includes script and booklet.)

Singles: 7–inch

LIBERTY (1000 series) 3-5 81-84
LIBERTY (50000 series) 4-8 67-70
U.A. 3-5 71-80
W.B. 3-4 84-86

Picture Sleeves

LIBERTY (1000 series) 3-5 81-84
LIBERTY (50000 series) 8-12 67
U.A. 3-5 71-80

EPs: 7–inch 33/45rpm

LIBERTY (37 "Special Radio Interview") 10-15 70
(Promotional issue only. Has paper cover.)
U.A. (69 "All the Good Times").. 20-30 71
(Promotional issue only. Includes script and booklet.)

LPs: 10/12–inch 33rpm

LIBERTY (1100 series) 5-10 81
LIBERTY (3501 "Nitty Gritty Dirt Band")............................ 15-20 67
(Monaural.)
LIBERTY (7501 "Nitty Gritty Dirt Band")............................ 15-25 67
(Stereo.)
LIBERTY (7501 thru 7611)........ 10-20 67-69
LIBERTY (7642 "Uncle Charlie") 100-125 70
(Gatefold promotional edition. Includes two bonus singles, photos and booklet.)
LIBERTY (LST-7642 "Uncle Charlie") 10-20 70
LIBERTY (LATO-7642 "Uncle Charlie") 5-8
U.A. (117 "Interview") 15-25 75
(Promotional issue only.)
U.A. (UA-LA184 "Stars and Stripes Forever")................... 10-20 74
U.A. (LWB-184 "Stars and Stripes Forever")...................... 8-10
U.A. (469 "Dream") 8-12 75
U.A. (469 "Dream - Programmers Guide")................................. 15-25 75
(Promotional issue only.)
U.A. (UA-LA670 "Dirt, Silver and Gold") 15-20 76
U.A. (LKCL-670 "Dirt, Silver and Gold") 10-12
U.A.(854 thru 1042) 5-10 78-80
U.A. (5500 series)...................... 8-12 71
U.A. (9801 "Will the Circle Be Unbroken") 30-40 72
(Three-LP set.)
UNIVERSAL (12500 "Will the Circle Be Unbroken, Vol. 2").................. 10-15 89
W.B.. 5-10 84-86

Session: Nicolette Larson.
Also see DENVER, John, & Nitty Gritty Dirt Band
Also see LARSON, Nicolette
Also see SKAGGS, Ricky

NITTY GRITTY DIRT BAND & Roy Acuff

C&W '71

Singles: 7–inch

U.A. 3-5 71

NITTY GRITTY DIRT BAND, Rosanne Cash & John Hiatt

C&W '90

Singles: 7–inch

MCA..3-4 90

Also see CASH, Rosanne

NITTY GRITTY DIRT BAND & Jimmy Martin

C&W '73

Singles: 7–inch

U.A. 3-5 73

NITTY GRITTY DIRT BAND & Linda Ronstadt

Singles: 7–inch

U.A. 3-5 79

Also see NITTY GRITTY DIRT BAND
Also see RONSTADT, Linda

NITZINGER
(John Nitzinger)

LP '72

Singles: 7–inch

CAPITOL.....................................4-6 72-73
20TH FOX...................................3-5 76

LPs: 10/12–inch 33rpm

CAPITOL...................................10-15 72-73
20TH FOX...................................8-10 76

Members: John Nitzinger; Bugs Henderson.

NITZSCHE, Jack

P&R '63

Singles: 7–inch

FANTASY 3-5 76
MCA...3-5 78
REPRISE 4-8 63-65

Picture Sleeves

REPRISE (20,202 "Lonely Surfer")...................................15-25 63

LPs: 10/12–inch 33rpm

MCA...8-10 78
REPRISE (2000 series) 8-12 73
REPRISE (6100 series) 15-25 63-64
REPRISE (6200 series) 10-20 66

NIVENS, Pamela

R&B '83

Singles: 7–inch

SUN VALLEY 3-5 83

NIX, Don

P&R/LP '71

Singles: 7–inch

CREAM 3-5 76
ELEKTRA.....................................3-5 71

LPs: 10/12-inch 33rpm

CREAM 5-10 79
ELEKTRA 8-12 71
ENTERPRISE 8-10 73

NIXON, Mojo, & Skid Roper

LP '87

Singles: 7-inch

ENIGMA 3-5 87-89

LPs: 10/12-inch 33rpm

ENIGMA 5-8 87-89

NOBLE, Nick

P&R '55

Singles: 78rpm

MERCURY 4-8 56-57
WING 4-8 55-56

Singles: 7-inch

CAPITOL 3-5 73
CHESS 4-8 63-64
CHURCHILL 3-5 77-80
CORAL 4-8 59-66
DATE 4-6 67-68
EPIC 3-5 77
LIBERTY 4-8 62-63
MERCURY 8-15 56-57
TMS 3-5 79
20TH FOX 4-8 65
WING 8-15 55-56

LPs: 10/12-inch 33rpm

COLUMBIA 8-12 69
LIBERTY 10-15 63
WING 15-25 60

NOBLES, Cliff
(Cliff Nobels & Co.)

P&R/R&B/LP '68

Singles: 7-inch

ATLANTIC 4-8 66-67
PHIL L.A. of SOUL 4-6 68-69
JAMIE 3-5 72
ROULETTE 3-5 73

LPs: 10/12-inch 33rpm

MOON SHOT 15-25
PHIL L.A. of SOUL 10-20 68
Also see MFSB

NOCERA

R&B '86

Singles: 7-inch

SLEEPING BAG 3-4 86-87

NOEL
(Noel Pagan)

P&R '87

Singles: 7-inch

4TH & BROADWAY 3-4 87-88
VIRGIN 3-4 79

Picture Sleeves

4TH & BROADWAY 3-4 87-88
VIRGIN 3-4 79

LPs: 10/12-inch 33rpm

4TH & BROADWAY 5-8 88

NOGUEZ, Jacky, & His Orchestra

P&R '59

Singles: 7-inch

JAMIE 4-8 59-60

Picture Sleeves

JAMIE 8-10 60

LPs: 10/12-inch 33rpm

JAMIE 10-20 60

NOLAN: see PORTER, Nolan

NOLAN, Kenny

P&R '76

Singles: 7-inch

CASABLANCA 3-5 79-80
DOT 4-8 68
FORWARD 4-8 69
HIGHLAND 4-8 68
LION 3-5 72
MGM 3-5 71
POLYDOR 3-5 78
20TH FOX 3-5 76-77

LPs: 10/12-inch 33rpm

CASABLANCA 5-10 79
MCA 5-10 82
POLYDOR 5-10 78
20TH FOX 5-10 77

NORDINE, Ken

Singles: 7-inch

DOT (16000 series) 8-12 59

LPs: 10/12-inch 33rpm

BLUE THUMB 8-12 72
DECCA (8550 "Concert in the Sky") 40-50 57
DOT (3075 thru 3301) 30-50 57-60
(Monaural.)
DOT (25115 thru 25301) 30-50 58-60
(Stereo.)
DOT (25880 "Best of Word Jazz") 10-20 67
HAMILTON (102 "Voice of Love") 20-30 59
(Monaural.)
HAMILTON (12102 "Voice of Love") 30-40 59
(Stereo.)
SNAIL 8-10
PHILIPS 15-25 67
Also see VAUGHN, Billy

NORMA
(Norma Lewis)

D&D '83

Singles: 12-inch 33/45rpm

ERC 4-6 83

NORMA JEAN
(Norma Jean Wright)

R&B/LP '78

Singles: 12–inch 33/45rpm

BEARSVILLE (Black vinyl.) 4-8 79-80
BEARSVILLE (Colored vinyl.) ... 10-15 79-80

Singles: 7–inch

BEARSVILLE 3-5 78-80

LPs: 10/12–inch 33rpm

BEARSVILLE 5-10 78

Also see CHIC

NORMAN, Jimmy
(With the Hollywood Teeners; with Viceroys)

P&R/R&B '62

Singles: 7–inch

DOT 10-20 59
FUN 10-15 60
GOOD SOUND 10-20 61
JOSIE 5-10 68
LITTLE STAR 5-10 62-63
MERCURY (72658 "It's Beautiful") 5-10 67
MERCURY (72727 "I'm Leaving") 20-30 67
MUN RAB 10-20 59
POLO 5-10 64
RAY STAR 8-15 61-62
SAMAR 4-8 66

LPs: 10/12–inch 33rpm

BADCAT 5-10

Also see CHARGERS
Also see COASTERS

NORMAN, Jimmy, & Dorothy Berry

Singles: 7–inch

LITTLE STAR 8-12 62

Also see BERRY, Dorothy

NORMAN, Jimmy / Willie "The Moon Man" Echols

Singles: 7–inch

GOOD SOUND 5-10 61

NORMAN, Jimmy, & O'Jays

Singles: 7–inch

LITTLE STAR 5-10 63

Also see NORMAN, Jimmy
Also see O'JAYS

NORTH, Freddie

P&R/R&B '71

Singles: 7–inch

A-BET 5-10 67-69
CAPITOL 8-12 62
RIC (119 "The Hurt") 20-30 64
MANKIND 3-6 71-76
PHILLIPS INT'L 10-20 61

LPs: 10/12–inch 33rpm

A-BET 8-10
MANKIND 8-12 71-75
PHONORAMA 5-8

NORTHCOTT, Tom

P&R '68

Singles: 7–inch

UNI 3-5 71
W.B. 4-8 67-69

LPs: 10/12–inch 33rpm

UNI 8-12 71

NORTHERN LIGHT

P&R '75

Singles: 7–inch

COLUMBIA 3-5 75
GLACIER 3-5 75-77

NORVUS, Nervous: see NERVOUS NORVUS

NORWOOD

R&B '87

Singles: 7–inch

MAGNOLIA 3-4 87

NORWOOD, Dorothy
(With the Norwood Singers)

R&B '73

Singles: 7–inch

GRC 3-5 72-75
JEWEL 3-5 78
SAVOY 4-8 63-69

LPs: 10/12–inch 33rpm

JEWEL 5-10 78
SAVOY 8-18 63-83

NOTATIONS

R&B '70

Singles: 7–inch

C.R.A. 3-5 73
GEMIGO 3-5 75-76
MERCURY 3-5 77
SUE 4-8 69
TAD 5-8 68
TWINIGHT 3-5 70

LPs: 10/12–inch 33rpm

GEMIGO 8-12 76

Members: Clifford Curry; Bobby Thomas; Lasalle Matthews; Jimmy Stroud; Walter Jones.
Also see CURRY, Clifford

NOVA, Aldo

P&R/LP '82

Singles: 12–inch 33/45rpm

PORTRAIT 5-8 82

Singles: 7–inch

PORTRAIT 3-4 82

Picture Sleeves

PORTRAIT 3-4 82

LPs: 10/12–inch 33rpm

PORTRAIT 5-10 82-83

NOVAS

P&R '65

Singles: 7–inch

PARROT (45005 "Crusher") 30-50 64

TWIN TOWN (713 "Novas Coaster") 25-35 65

NOVELLE, Jay

D&D '84

Singles: 12–inch 33/45rpm

EMERGENCY 4-6 84

NOVO COMBO

LP '81

Singles: 7–inch

POLYDOR 3-5 82

LPs: 10/12–inch 33rpm

POLYDOR 5-10 81-82

Member: Mike Shrieve.
Also see SANTANA

NU ROMANCE CREW

R&B '87

Singles: 7–inch

EMI AMERICA 3-4 87

NU SHOOZ

P&R/R&B/LP '86

Singles: 7–inch

ATLANTIC 3-4 86-88

Picture Sleeves

ATLANTIC 3-4 86-88

LPs: 10/12–inch 33rpm

ATLANTIC 5-8 86-88

Members: Valerie Day; John Smith.

NU TORNADOS

P&R '58

Singles: 7–inch

CARLTON 5-10 58-59
FELSTED 5-10 59

NUANCE
(Featuring Vikki Love)

R&B/D&D '84

Singles: 12–inch 33/45rpm

4TH & BROADWAY 4-6 84-85

Singles: 7–inch

4TH & BROADWAY 3-4 84-85

NUCLEAR ASSULT

LP '88

LPs: 10/12–inch 33rpm

I.R.S. 5-8 88
IN-EFFECT 5-8 89
UNDER ONE FLAG (21 "Survive") 8-12 88
(Picture disc.)

NUCLEAR VALDEZ

LP '90

LPs: 10/12–inch 33rpm

EPIC 5-8 90

NUGENT, Ted
(With the Amboy Dukes; with Brian Howe)

LP '75

Singles: 7–inch

ATLANTIC 3-5 84-88
DISCREET 3-5 74
EPIC 3-5 76-80

Picture Sleeves

ATLANTIC 3-5 84

LPs: 10/12–inch 33rpm

ATLANTIC 5-10 82-88
DISCREET 8-10 74
EPIC (Except 607) 8-15 75-81
EPIC (607 "State of Shock") 15-25 79
(Picture disc.)
MAINSTREAM (10-01 "Ted Nugent and the Amboy Dukes") 5-10 82
MAINSTREAM (421 "Ted Nugent and the Amboy Dukes") 8-12
POLYDOR (4035 "Survival of the Fittest") 10-20 71

Also see AMBOY DUKES
Also see BAD COMPANY
Also see DAMN YANKEES
Also see HEAR 'N AID

NUGGETS

R&B '79

Singles: 7–inch

MERCURY 3-4 79

LPs: 10/12–inch 33rpm

MERCURY 5-10 79

NUMAN, Gary
(With the Tubeway Army)

LP '79

Singles: 7–inch

ATCO 3-5 79-81

LPs: 10/12–inch 33rpm

ATCO 5-10 79-81

NUMONICS

R&B '84

Singles: 7–inch

HODISK 3-5 84

NUNN, Bobby
(Bobby Nunn Jr.)

R&B/LP '82

Singles: 7–inch

MOTOWN 3-4 82-84

LPs: 10/12–inch 33rpm

MOTOWN 5-10 82-84

NURSERY SCHOOL

D&D '83

Singles: 12–inch 33/45rpm

EPIC 4-6 83

NUTMEGS

R&B '55

Singles: 78rpm

HERALD 20-30 55-57

Singles: 7–inch

COLLECTABLES 3-4 80s
FLASHBACK 3-5 65
HERALD (452 "Story Untold") 20-35 55
HERALD (459 "Ship of Love") ... 15-25 55

HERALD (466 "Whispering Sorrows") 20-30 55
HERALD (475 "Key to the Kingdom") 25-35 56
HERALD (492 "A Love So True") 20-25 56
HERALD (538 "My Story") 25-35 59
HERALD (574 "Rip Van Winkle") 10-20 62
LANA 3-6 64
TEL (1014 "A Dream of Love").. 50-75 60
TIMES SQUARE (6 "Let Me Tell You") 15-20 63
(Colored vinyl.)
TIMES SQUARE (14 "The Way Love Should Be") 10-15 63
TIMES SQUARE (27 "Down in Mexico") 10-15 64
TIMES SQUARE (103 "You're Crying") 10-15 64

EPs: 7–inch 33/45rpm

HERALD (452 "Nutmegs") 150-200 60

LPs: 10/12–inch 33rpm

COLLECTABLES 5-10 84
RELIC 8-10 70s

Members: Leroy Griffin; Jimmy Tyson; Leroy McNeil; James "Sonny" Griffin; Bill Emery; Ed Martin; Sonny Washburn; Harold Jones.
Also see LYRES
Also see RAJAHS

NUTMEGS / Admirations

Singles: 7–inch

TIMES SQUARE (19 "Down to Earth") 10-15 64

NUTMEGS / Volumes

Singles: 7–inch

TIMES SQUARE (22 "Why Must We Go to School") 10-15 63

Also see NUTMEGS
Also see VOLUMES

NUTTER, Mayf

C&W '70

Singles: 7–inch

CAPITOL 3-5 71-73
GNP 3-5 76-77
REPRISE 3-5 70

NUTTY SQUIRRELS

P&R/R&B '59

Singles: 7–inch

COLUMBIA 5-10 60
HANOVER 5-10 59-60
RCA 4-8 64

Picture Sleeves

COLUMBIA 10-15 60
HANOVER 10-15 59

EPs: 7–inch 33/45rpm

HANOVER (301 "Nutty Squirrels") 15-25 60

LPs: 10/12–inch 33rpm

COLUMBIA 20-25 61
HANOVER (8014 "Nutty Squirrels") 25-35 60
MGM 15-25 64

NYLONS
(Rumblers)

Singles: 7–inch

DOWNEY 10-15 63

Also see RUMBLERS

NYLONS

LP '86

Singles: 7–inch

OPEN AIR 3-5 82-87

Picture Sleeves

OPEN AIR 3-5 87

LPs: 10/12–inch 33rpm

OPEN AIR 5-10 85-87
WINDHAM HILL 5-8 89

Members: Claude Morrison; Marc Connors; Paul Cooper; Arnold Robinson.

NYRO, Laura

LP '68

Singles: 7–inch

COLUMBIA 3-6 68-71
VERVE/FOLKWAYS 4-8 66-67
VERVE/FORECAST 4-6 68-69

Picture Sleeves

COLUMBIA 4-8 68

LPs: 10/12–inch 33rpm

COLUMBIA 5-15 68-84
VERVE/FOLKWAYS 10-20 67
VERVE/FORECAST 10-15 69

Also see LABELLE, Patti

NYTRO

R&B '77

Singles: 12–inch 33/45rpm

WHITFIELD 4-8 79

Singles: 7–inch

WHITFIELD 3-5 76-79

LPs: 10/12–inch 33rpm

WHITFIELD 5-10 77-79

O

O ROMEO

D&D '83

Singles: 12–inch 33/45rpm

BOB CAT 4-6 83
OH MY 4-6 84

Members: Lorilee Svedberg; Dora Suppes; Terry Weinberg.

O.M.D. see ORCHESTRAL MANOEUVERS in the DARK

OAK

P&R '79

Singles: 7–inch

MERCURY 3-5 79-80

Also see PINETTE, Rick, & Oak

OAK RIDGE BOYS

(Oak Ridge Quartet; Oaks)

C&W '76

Singles: 7–inch

ABC 3-5 78-79
ABC/DOT 3-5 77
CADENCE.................................... 6-12 59
COLUMBIA 3-5 73-79
HEARTWARMING 3-5 71
IMPACT 3-5 71
MCA 3-5 79-90
RCA... 3-4 90-91
W.B. 3-8 63

LPs: 10/12–inch 33rpm

ABC 5-10 78-79
ABC/DOT 8-10 77
ACCORD.................................... 5-10 81-82
CADENCE (3019 "The Oak Ridge Quartet")................................ 35-55 58
CANAAN 8-15 66
COLUMBIA 5-10 74-83
EXACT 5-10 83
51 WEST 5-8
HEARTWARMING 5-8 71-74
INTERMEDIA................................ 5-8
MCA 5-10 80-86
NASHVILLE 8-10 70
OUT of TOWN DIST. 5-10 82
PHONORAMA.............................. 5-10
POWER PAK 5-10 70s
PRIORITY 5-10 82
SKYLITE 10-20 64-66
STARDAY 10-20 65
U.A. 10-20 66
W.B. 10-20 63

Members: William Lee Golden; Duane Allen; Rich Sterban; Joe Bonsall; Steve Sanders; Willie Wynn.

Also see CASH, Johnny, Carter Family & Oak Ridge Boys
Also see JONES, George
Also see LEE, Brenda, & Oak Ridge Boys
Also see MANDRELL, Barbara, & Oak Ridge Boys

OAKEY, Philip: see MORODER, Giorgio, & Philip Oakey

OAKTOWN'S 3-5-7

LP '89

LPs: 10/12–inch 33rpm

CAPITOL....................................... 5-8 89

Also see HAMMER, M.C.

OAS, Holly

D&D '84

Singles: 12–inch 33/45rpm

DND 4-6 84

O'BANION, John

P&R/LP '81

Singles: 7–inch

ELEKTRA.......................................3-5 81

LPs: 10/12–inch 33rpm

ELEKTRA.....................................5-10 81

O'BRYAN

(O'Bryan Burnette)

P&R/R&B/LP '82

Singles: 12–inch 33/45rpm

CAPITOL..4-6 82-86

Singles: 7–inch

CAPITOL..3-4 82-87

LPs: 10/12–inch 33rpm

CAPITOL..5-8 82-86

OCASEK, Ric

P&R/D&D/LP '83

Singles: 12–inch 33/45rpm

GEFFEN 4-6 83

Singles: 7–inch

GEFFEN 3-4 83-86

Picture Sleeves

GEFFEN 3-4 83-86

LPs: 10/12–inch 33rpm

GEFFEN 5-8 83-86

Also see CARS

OCEAN

P&R/LP '71

Singles: 7–inch

KAMA SUTRA.................................3-5 71-72

LPs: 10/12–inch 33rpm

KAMA SUTRA...............................8-12 71-72

Members: Janice Morgan; Greg Brown; David Tamblyn; Charles Slater.

OCEAN, Billy

P&R/R&B '76

Singles: 12–inch 33/45rpm

EPIC...4-8 80-82
JIVE 4-6 84-86

Singles: 7–inch

ARIOLA AMERICA 3-5 76
EPIC...3-5 77-82
JIVE 3-4 84-89

Picture Sleeves

JIVE 3-4 84-89

LPs: 10/12–inch 33rpm

EPIC...5-10 81-82
JIVE 5-8 84-89

OCEAN BLUE

LP '90

LPs: 10/12–inch 33rpm

SIRE...5-8 90

OCHS, Phil

(With the Pan African Ngembo Rumba Band)

LP '66

Singles: 7–inch

A&M 5-10 67-73

SPARKLE (9966 "Bwatue")........... 3-5 91
(Canadian. 1,000 numbered copies made.)

Picture Sleeves

SPARKLE (9966 "Bwatue")........... 3-5 91
(Canadian. 1,000 numbered copies made.)

LPs: 10/12–inch 33rpm

A&M 10-20 67-76
ELEKTRA.................................... 15-25 64-66

O'CONNELL, Helen

P&R '51

Singles: 78rpm

CAPITOL.................................... 3-5 51-54
KAPP.. 3-5 55
VIK 3-5 57

Singles: 7–inch

CAMEO 4-6 63
CAPITOL.................................... 5-10 51-54
KAPP.. 5-8 55
VIK 5-8 57

EPs: 7–inch 33/45rpm

CAPITOL.................................... 8-12 54
VIK 8-12 57

LPs: 10/12–inch 33rpm

CAMDEN................................... 10-20 59-62
CAMEO 10-15 63
LONGINES................................. 5-10 70s
MARK '56 .... 5-10 77
VIK (1093 "Helen O'Connell") ... 25-35 57
W.B. 10-20 61

Also see MARTIN, Dean, & Helen O'Connell

O'CONNER, Carroll

LP '72

LPs: 10/12–inch 33rpm

A&M 8-12 72
AUDIO FIDELITY 5-10 76

O'CONNER, Carroll, & Jean Stapleton

(With Rob Reiner, Sally Struthers and Mike Evans)

P&R '71

Singles: 7–inch

ATLANTIC.................................. 3-5 71

Picture Sleeves

ATLANTIC.................................. 3-5 71

LPs: 10/12–inch 33rpm

ATLANTIC.................................. 8-10 71

Also see O'CONNER, Carroll

O'CONNOR, Sinead

LP '88

Singles: 7–inch

CHRYSALIS................................ 3-4 86
ENSIGN 3-4 90

LPs: 10/12–inch 33rpm

CHRYSALIS................................ 5-8 86
ENSIGN 5-8 90

Members: Sinead O'Connor; Andy Rourke; Mike Joyce.
Also see SMITHS

O'DAY, Alan

P&R/LP '77

Singles: 7–inch

PACIFIC......................................3-5 77-85
VIVA..3-5 71

LPs: 10/12–inch 33rpm

PACIFIC......................................5-10 77

O'DAY, Anita

P&R '47

Singles: 78rpm

CLEF 3-5 53
CORAL...3-5 52
LONDON......................................3-5 51
SIGNATURE 4-8 47
MERCURY...................................3-5 52-53
VERVE..3-5 56-57

Singles: 7–inch

CLEF 4-8 53
CLOVER 3-6 66
COLUMBIA 3-4 76
CORAL...5-10 52
EMILY 3-4 79
LONDON......................................5-10 51
MERCURY...................................4-8 52-53
VERVE..3-8 56-62

EPs: 7–inch 33/45rpm

CLEF 25-50 53
NORGRAN...................................20-40 54

LPs: 10/12–inch 33rpm

ADVANCE (8 "Specials").......150-200 51
(10–inch LP.)
AMERICAN RECORDING
SOCIETY (426 "For Oscar")....50-75 57
CLEF (130 "Anita O'Day")......100-150 53
COLUMBIA 8-10 74
CORAL (56073 "Singin' and
Swingin'") 100-150 53
DOBRE 5-10 78
EMILY 5-10 79-82
FLYING DUTCHMAN 5-10 74
GNP 5-10 79
MPS 5-10 73
NORGRAN (30 "Anita O'Day") 75-100 54
(10–inch LP.)
NORGRAN (1049 "Anita O'Day
Sings Jazz")...........................50-75 55
NORGRAN (1057 "An Evening
with Anita O'Day")...................50-75 56
PAUSA..5-10 81
SIGNATURE 5-10 75
VERVE (2000 series)...............30-60 56
(Has "Verve Records Inc." at bottom of label.)
VERVE (2100 series)................25-50 58-61
(Has "Verve Records Inc." at bottom of label.)

VERVE (6000 series) 25-50 59-60
(Has "Verve Records Inc." at bottom of label.)
VERVE (8200 thru 8500 series) 15-30 59-64
(Has "Verve Records Inc." at bottom of label.)
VERVE (2000 series) 30-60 56
(Has "Verve Records Inc." at bottom of label.)
VERVE 12-25 61-72
(Has "MGM Records - A Division Of Metro-Goldwyn-Mayer, Inc." at bottom of label.)
VERVE 5-10 79-82
(Has "Manufactured By MGM Record Corp." or mentions either Polydor or Polygram at bottom of label.)

O'DAY, Anita, & Cal Tjader

LP: 10/12-inch 33rpm

VERVE 15-25 62
(Has "MGM Records - A Division Of Metro-Goldwyn-Mayer, Inc." at bottom of label.)
Also see O'DAY, Anita
Also see TJADER, Cal

ODDS & ENDS

R&B '70

Singles: 7-inch

TODAY 4-6 71-72

O'DELL, Brooks

P&R/R&B '63

Singles: 7-inch

BELL (618 "Slow Motion") 10-20 65
GOLD (214 "Watch Your Step") .. 5-10 63

O'DELL, Kenny

P&R '67

Singles: 7-inch

ABC 3-5 73
CAPRICORN 3-5 73-79
KAPP 3-5 72
MAR-KAY 5-10 65
VEGAS 4-8 67-68
WHITE WHALE 4-6 69

LPs: 10/12-inch 33rpm

CAPRICORN 5-10 74-78
VEGAS 15-25 68

ODETTA

(With Larry; Odetta Holmes)

LP '63

Singles: 7-inch

DUNHILL 4-6 69
POLYDOR 3-5 70
RCA 4-8 63
RIVERSIDE 4-8 62
VANGUARD 5-10 59
VERVE/FOLKWAYS 4-6 66
VERVE/FORECAST 4-6 68

EPs: 7-inch 33/45rpm

FANTASY (4017/4018 "Odetta & Larry") 15-20 54
(Price is for either of two volumes.)

LPs: 10/12-inch 33rpm

EVEREST 5-10 73
FANTASY (15 "Odetta & Larry") 40-60 54
(10-inch LP.)
FANTASY (3252 "Odetta" 35-50 58
(Colored vinyl.)
POLYDOR 5-10 70
RCA 10-20 62-66
RIVERSIDE (400 series) 15-25 62
RIVERSIDE (3000 series) 10-15 68
RIVERSIDE (9400 series) 20-30 62
TRADITION (1010 "Odetta Sings Ballads and Blues") 25-35 57
TRADITION (1025 "At the Gate of Horn") 20 30 58
TRADITION (1052 "Best of Odetta") 10-15 67
(Monaural.)
TRADITION (2052 "Best of Odetta") 10-20 67
(Stereo.)
U.A. 5-10 76
VANGUARD 10-20 59-67
VERVE/FOLKWAYS 10-15 67

ODYSSEY

P&R/R&B/LP '77

Singles: 12-inch 33/45rpm

RCA 4-8 77-82

Singles: 7-inch

MOWEST 3-5 72
RCA 3-5 77-82

LPs: 10/12-inch 33rpm

MOWEST 10-12 72
RCA 8-10 77-82
Members: Lillian Lopez; Louise Lopez.

OFARIM, Esther & Abraham

(Esther Ofarim; with Abi Ofarim)

P&R '68

Singles: 7-inch

PHILIPS 4-6 64-68

LPs: 10/12-inch 33rpm

CAPITOL 5-10 68
PHILIPS 5-15 63-70

OFF BROADWAY USA

P&R/LP '80

Singles: 7-inch

ATLANTIC 3-5 80

LPs: 10/12-inch 33rpm

ATLANTIC 5-10 80

OFFITT, Lillian

P&R/R&B '57

Singles: 78rpm

EXCELLO 5-10 57

Singles: 7-inch

CHIEF 8-12 60
EXCELLO.................................. 10-20 57

OH ROMEO: see O ROMEO

O'HENRY, Lenny
(With Short Stories)

P&R/R&B '64

Singles: 7-inch

ABC-PAR 10-15 61
ATCO 5-10 64-67
SMASH 5-10 63

OHIO EXPRESS
(Ohio Ltd.)

P&R '67

Singles: 7-inch

ATTACK.. 3-6 70
BUDDAH 4-6 68-73
CAMEO 5-8 67
ERIC.. 3-5 78
SUPER K 4-6 69-70

LPs: 10/12-inch 33rpm

BUDDAH 10-20 68-70
CAMEO (20,000 "Beg, Borrow and Steal") 20-30 68

Also see KASENETZ-KATZ SINGING ORCHESTRAL CIRCUS
Also see RARE BREED
Also see REUNION
Also see 10CC

OHIO LTD: see OHIO EXPRESS

OHIO PLAYERS

R&B '68

Singles: 7-inch

AIR CITY 3-4 84
ARISTA 3-5 79
BOARDWALK 3-5 81
CAPITOL...................................... 4-6 69
COMPASS 4-8 68
MERCURY 3-5 74-78
TANGERINE 4-8 67
TRACK... 3-4 88
WESTBOUND............................... 3-5 71-76

LPs: 10/12-inch 33rpm

ACCORD................................... 5-10 81
ARISTA 5-10 79
BOARDWALK 5-10 81
CAPITOL (192 "Observations in Time")................................. 10-20 69
CAPITOL (11291 "Ohio Players") 8-12 74
MERCURY 8-12 74-78
TRIP 8-10 72
U.A. 8-10 75
WESTBOUND............................. 8-12 72-75

Also see JUNIE

OINGO BOINGO

LP '80

Singles: 12-inch 33/45rpm

A&M 4-8 81
MCA...4-6 85-86

Singles: 7-inch

A&M 3-5 81-83
MCA..3-4 85-86

Picture Sleeves

MCA..3-4 85-86

LPs: 10/12-inch 33rpm

A&M 5-10 81-89
I.R.S. 5-10 80
MCA..5-8 85-90

Members: Danny Elfman; Steve Bartek; John Hernandez; Dale Turner; Kerry Hatch; Richard Gibbs.
Also see ELFMAN, Danny

O'JAYS

P&R/R&B '63

Singles: 12-inch 33/45rpm

PHILADELPHIA INT'L....................4-8 83

Singles: 7-inch

ALL PLATINUM 3-5 74
APOLLO (759 "Miracles") 20-30 61
ASTROSCOPE..............................3-5 74
BELL 3-6 67-73
EPIC..3-4 83
IMPERIAL (5942 "How Does It Feel") 10-15 63
IMPERIAL (5976 "Lonely Drifter") 5-10 63
IMPERIAL (66007 thru 66145).....5-10 64-65
IMPERIAL (66162 "I'll Never Forget You")..25-35 66
IMPERIAL (66177 thru 66200).....5-10 66
LIBERTY 3-5 81
LITTLE STAR (124 "How Does It Feel") 15-25 63
LITTLE STAR (125 "Dream Girl")..15-25 63
MINIT 5-10 67
NEPTUNE.....................................4-6 69-70
PHILADELPHIA INT'L...................3-6 72-87
SARU 3-6 71
TSOP 3-5 80-81

LPs: 10/12-inch 33rpm

BELL (6014 "Back on Top") 10-20 68
BELL (6082 "The O'Jays") 8-12 73
EMI..5-8 89-90
EPIC..5-8 83
IMPERIAL (9290 "Coming Through") 30-35 65
(Monaural.)
IMPERIAL (12290 "Coming Through")..................................35-40 65
(Stereo.)
KORY 8-10 77
MINIT (24008 "Soul Sounds")....20-30 67
(Stereo.)
MINIT (40008 "Soul Sounds")....15-25 67
(Monaural.)
PHILADELPHIA INT'L.................5-10 72-86
SUNSET 10-15 68

TSOP 5-10 80
TRIP 8-10 73
U.A. 8-12 72
Members: Bob Massey; Eddie LeVert; Walt Williams; Bill Powell; Bill Isles; Sam Strain.
Also see LITTLE ANTHONY & IMPERIALS
Also see NORMAN, Jimmy, & O'Jays
Also see PHILADELPHIA INTERNATIONAL ALL STARS

O'JAYS / Moments

LPs: 10/12-inch 33rpm

STANG 8-12 74
Also see MOMENTS
Also see O'JAYS

O'KAYSIONS

P&R/R&B/LP '68

Singles: 7-inch

ABC 4-8 68
COTILLION 3-5 70
NORTH STATE (1001 "Girl Watcher") 20-30 68
ROULETTE 3-5 70s

Picture Sleeves

NORTH STATE (1001 "Girl Watcher") 25-45 68

LPs: 10/12-inch 33rpm

ABC (664 "Girl Watcher") 15-25 68
Members: Donnie Weaver; Jim Spidel; Jim Hennant; Ron Turner; Bruce Joyner.

O'KEEFE, Danny

P&R/C&W/LP '72

Singles: 7-inch

ATLANTIC 3-5 75
JERDEN 4-8 66
SIGNPOST 3-5 72
W.B. 3-5 77-78

Picture Sleeves

W.B. 3-5 77-78

LPs: 10/12-inch 33rpm

ATLANTIC 8-12 73-75
COTILLION 10-15 70
FIRST AMERICAN 8-10 70s
PANORAMA (105 "Introducing Danny O'Keefe") 20-30 66
SIGNPOST 10-12 72
W.B. 5-10 77-79

OLA & JANGLERS

P&R '69

Singles: 7-inch

GNP 4-8 68-69
LONDON 4-8 67

LPs: 10/12-inch 33rpm

GNP 15-20 69
Member: Ola Hakansson.

OLD and in the WAY

LP '75

LPs: 10/12-inch 33rpm

ROUND (103 "Old and in the Way") 20-25 75

SUGAR HILL 5-8 85
Members: Peter Rowan; Jorry Garcia; Vassar Clements; David Grisman.
Also see GARCIA, Jerry
Also see ROWANS

OLD and in the WAY / Keith & Donna / Robert Hunter / Phil Lesh & Ned Lagin

Singles: 7-inch

ROUND (02 & 03 "Sampler for Dead Heads") 40-60 75
(Promotional, fan club two-disc set. Price also includes a letter from Anton Round, a letter about members of the Grateful Dead, several miniature LP covers, and a mailer advertising posters.)
ROUND (02 & 03 "Sampler for Dead Heads") 20-30 75
(Price is for both discs, without inserts. Divide in half for either one of the two records.)
Also see GRATEFUL DEAD
Also see OLD and in the WAY

OLDFIELD, Mike
(With Sally Oldfield)

LP '73

Singles: 7-inch

EPIC 3-5 81-82
VIRGIN 3-5 73-82

Picture Sleeves

VIRGIN 3-6 74

EPs: 7-inch 33/45rpm

VIRGIN (199 "Tubular Bells") 5-10 74
(Promotional issue only.)

LPs: 10/12-inch 33rpm

EPIC (44116) 5-10 81-82
EPIC (44116 "Tubular Bells") 20-40 73
(Half-speed mastered.)
VIRGIN (Except 2001) 5-15 73-88
VIRGIN (2001 "Tubular Bells") ... 10-12 73
(Picture disc.)
Also see SALLYANGIE

OLIVER
(Bill Oliver Swofford)

P&R/LP '69

Singles: 7-inch

CREWE 3-5 69-70
JUBILEE 4-6 69
LIBERTY 3-5
PARAMOUNT 3-5 73
PEOPLE SONG 3-5 82
U.A. 3-5 70-71

Picture Sleeves

CREWE 4-6 69

LPs: 10/12-inch 33rpm

CREWE 10-15 69-70
U.A. 8-12 71

OLIVER, David

R&B/LP '78

Singles: 7-inch

MERCURY 3-5 78-80

LPs: 10/12-inch 33rpm

MERCURY 5-10 78-79

OLIVOR, Jane

P&R/LP '77

Singles: 7-inch

COLUMBIA. 3-5 77-85

LPs: 10/12-inch 33rpm

COLUMBIA 5-10 77-85

OLLIE & JERRY

P&R/R&B/D&D '84

Singles: 12-inch 33/45rpm

POLYDOR................................. 4-6 84-85

Singles: 7-inch

POLYDOR................................. 3-4 84-85

Members: Ollie Brown; Jerry Knight.

Also see KNIGHT, Jerry

OLLIE & NIGHTINGALES

P&R/R&B '68

Singles: 7-inch

STAX... 4-8 68

LPs: 10/12-inch 33rpm

STAX...................................... 10-15 69

Also see MAD LADS

OLSON, Rocky

P&R '59

Singles: 7-inch

CHESS 10-15 59

OLSSON, Nigel

P&R '75

Singles: 7-inch

BANG 3-5 78-79

COLUMBIA 3-5 78

ROCKET 3-5 75

UNI 3-5 71-72

LPs: 10/12-inch 33rpm

BANG 5-10 79-80

COLUMBIA 5-10 78

ROCKET 8-12 73-75

UNI 8-12 71

Also see JOHN, Elton

OLYMPIC RUNNERS

R&B '74

Singles: 7-inch

LONDON.................................... 3-5 74-77

POLYDOR................................... 3-5 79

LPs: 10/12-inch 33rpm

LONDON.................................. 8-10 74-77

POLYDOR................................. 5-10 79

Members: Pete Wingfield; DeLisle Harper; George Chandler; Joe Jammer. Glen LeFleur.

Also see WINGFIELD, Pete

OLYMPICS

P&R/R&B '58

Singles: 7-inch

ABC..3-5 73

ARVEE (Except 5031) 5-10 59-65

ARVEE (5031 "Stay Where You Are") 15-25 59-65

COLLECTABLES..........................3-4 80s

DEMON.......................................5-10 58-60

DUO DISC 4-8 64

ERIC 3-4 70s

JUBILEE 4-8 69

LIBERTY.......................................4-8 63

LOMA...4-8 65

MGM 3-5 73

MIRWOOD....................................4-8 66-67

PARKWAY 4-8 68

TITAN.......................................10-20 61

TRI DISC....................................5-10 62-63

W.B. 3-5 70

ZEE (101 "The Slop")................10-20 58

ZEE (103 "Western Movies") 10-20 58

EPs: 7-inch 33/45rpm

ARVEE (423 "Doin' the Hully Gully") 50-75 60

LPs: 10/12-inch 33rpm

ARVEE (423 "Doin' the Hully Gully") 75-150 60

ARVEE (424 "Dance by the Light of the Moon") 75-125 61

ARVEE (429 "Party Time") 75-125 61

EVEREST 5-10 81

MIRWOOD (M-7003 "Something Old, Something New")....................20-30 66 (Monaural.)

MIRWOOD (MS-7003 "Something Old, Something New")....................25-35 66 (Stereo.)

POST 8-10 70s

RHINO 5-8 80s

TRI-DISC (1001 "Do the Bounce") 30-50 63

Members: Walter Ward; Eddie Lewis; Melvin King; Charles Figer; Julius McMichaels.

Also see PARAGONS

Also see REYNOLDS, Jody / Olympics

O'MALLEY, Lenore

P&R '80

Singles: 7-inch

POLYDOR 3-5 80

OMAR & HOWLERS

LP '87

LPs: 10/12-inch 33rpm

COLUMBIA 5-8 87

100 PROOF Aged in Soul

P&R/R&B '69

Singles: 7-inch

HOT WAX 3-6 69-72

LPs: 10/12–inch 33rpm

HOT WAX 10-15 70-73

Members: Steve Mancha; Joe Stubbs; Eddie Anderson.

Also see MANCHA, Steve

101 STRINGS

LP '59

Singles: 7-Inch

SOMERSET 3-5 59

LPs: 10/12-Inch 33rpm

ALSHIRE 5-10 60s
SOMERSET 5-10 59-61
STEREO FIDELITY 5-10 59-61

ONE on ONE

R&B '84

Singles: 7–inch

KEE WEE 3-4 84

ONE 2 MANY

P&R '89

Singles: 7–inch

A&M 3-4 89

Picture Sleeves

A&M 3-4 89

ONE to ONE

P&R '86

Singles: 7–inch

W.B. 3-4 86

Picture Sleeves

W.B. 3-4 86

LPs: 10/12–inch 33rpm

W.B. 5-8 86

Members: Louise Reny; Leslie Howe.

ONE WAY
(Featuring Al Hudson)

LP '79

Singles: 12–inch 33/45rpm

MCA 4-6 82-86

Singles: 7–inch

MCA 3-5 79-87

LPs: 10/12–Inch 33rpm

MCA 5-10 79-86

Also see HUDSON, Al

O'NEAL, Alexander

R&B/D&D/LP '85

Singles: 12–inch 33/45rpm

TABU 4-6 85-86

Singles: 7–inch

TABU 3-4 85-90

Picture Sleeves

TABU 3-4 85-88

LPs: 10/12–inch 33rpm

TABU 5-8 85-90

O'NEAL, Alexander, & Cherrelle

R&B '86

Singles: 7–inch

TABU 3-4 86-88

Also see CHERRELLE
Also see O'NEAL, Alexander

ONO, Yoko
(With the Plastic Ono Band)

LP '71

Singles: 12–inch 33/45rpm

POLYDOR 5-10 85-86

Singles: 7–inch

APPLE 4-8 71-73
GEFFEN 3-5 81
POLYDOR 3-5 82-86

Promotional Singles

APPLE (OYB-1 "Open Your Box") 400-600 70
APPLE (1853 "Now Or Never") .. 25-30 72
APPLE (1867 "Woman Power") . 20-25 73
GEFFEN 5-8 81
POLYDOR 4-6 82-86

Picture Sleeves

APPLE (1853 "Now Or Never") 8-12 72
GEFFEN 3-4 81

LPs: 10/12–inch 33rpm

APPLE 15-20 71-73
GEFFEN 5-10 81
POLYDOR 5-10 82-86

Promotional LPs

GEFFEN (934 "Walking on Thin Ice") 20-25 81
GEFFEN (975 "No No No") 25-30 81

Also see LENNON, John

OPUS

P&R/LP '86

Singles: 7–inch

POLYDOR 3-4 86

LPs: 10/12–inch 33rpm

POLYDOR 5-8 86

OPUS SEVEN

R&B '79

Singles: 7–inch

SOURCE 3-5 79

LPs: 10/12–inch 33rpm

SOURCE 5-10 79

OPUS 10

R&B '85

Singles: 7–inch

PANDISC 3-4 85

ORBISON, Roy
(With the Teen Kings; with Candy Men; with Roses; with Friends)

P&R '56

Singles: 78rpm

SUN 30-50 56-57

Singles: 12–inch 33/45rpm

VIRGIN (2667 "She's a Mystery to Me") 10-15 89
(Includes cover.)

Singles: 7–inch

ASYLUM 3-5 78-79
COLLECTABLES 3-4 85
MGM 4-8 65-73

MGM CELEBRITY SCENE (CSN9-5 "Roy Orbison") 50-75 66
(Boxed set of five singles with bio insert and jukebox title strips.)
MERCURY 4-8 74
MONUMENT (409 "Paper Boy") 20-30 59
MONUMENT (412 "Uptown").... 15-20 59
MONUMENT (421 thru 467) 8-12 60-62
MONUMENT (800 & 900 series). 5-10 63-66
MONUMENT (500 series).......... 4-8 63
MONUMENT (8600 series).......... 3-5 76
MONUMENT (8900 series).......... 3-5 72
MONUMENT (45000 series)........ 3-5 76-77
RCA (7381 "Sweet and Innocent") 20-30 58
RCA (7447 "Jolie") 20-30 59
SSS/SUN 3-5 70s
SUN (242 "Ooby Dooby").......... 20-30 56
SUN (251 "Rockhouse").......... 20-30 56
SUN (265 "Sweet and Easy to Love") 20-30 56
SUN (284 "Chicken Hearted")... 20-30 58
SUN (353 "Sweet and Easy to Love") 8-10 61
(Yellow label.)
SUN (353 "Sweet and Easy to Love") 10-15 61
(White label. Promotional issue only.)
VIRGIN 3-5 87-89

Picture Sleeves

MGM 8-12 65-67
MONUMENT (400 series)........ 10-20 60-62
MONUMENT (800 series)........ 10-15 63-64
VIRGIN 3-5 89

EPs: 7–inch 33/45rpm

MGM (4379 "Classic Roy Orbison") 30-50 66
(Jukebox issue only.)
MONUMENT (2 "Crying").......... 20-30 62
(Compact 33, "Special Promotional Six-Pac." Not issued with special cover.)
MONUMENT (3 "Roy Orbison") 20-30 62
(Compact 33, "Special Promotional Six-Pac." Not issued with special cover.)
STARS INC. (101 "Roy Orbison and the Teen Kings") 300-400 59
(Promotional issue, distributed to fan club members.)

LPs: 10/12–inch 33rpm

ACCORD 5-8 81
ASYLUM 5-8 78-79
BUCKBOARD 8-10
CANDLELITE MUSIC 10-15 70s
DESIGN 10-15 60s
MGM (E-4308 thru E-4514)....... 15-20 65-67
(Monaural.)
MGM (SE-4308 thru SE-4514).. 20-30 65-67
(Stereo.)
MGM (4636 thru 4934)............. 10-20 69-73
MGM/CAPITOL (90454 "There Is Only One Roy Orbison") 10-20 65
(Label reads "Mfd. by Capitol Records." Record club issue.)
MERCURY 8-12 75
MONUMENT (4002 "Lonely and Blue") 100-150 61
(Monaural.)
MONUMENT (14002 "Lonely and Blue") 125-200 61
(Stereo.)
MONUMENT (4007 "Crying"......40-60 62
(Monaural.)
MONUMENT (14007 "Crying") ..50-75 62
(Stereo.)
MONUMENT (4009 "Greatest Hits") 30-40 62
(Monaural.)
MONUMENT (14009 "Greatest Hits") 40-50 62
(Stereo.)
MONUMENT (6600 series).......... 8-10
MONUMENT (7600 "Regeneration") 8-10 76
MONUMENT (8000 "Greatest Hits") 25-30 63
(Monaural.)
MONUMENT (18000 "Greatest Hits") 35-40 63
(Stereo.)
MONUMENT (8003 "In Dreams") 30-40 63
(Monaural.)
MONUMENT (18003 "In Dreams") 40-50 63
(Stereo.)
MONUMENT (8024 "More Greatest Hits") 20-25 64
(Monaural.)
MONUMENT (18024 "More Greatest Hits") 25-30 64
(Stereo.)
MONUMENT (8035 "Orbisongs") 25-30 65
(Monaural.)
MONUMENT (18035 "Orbisongs") 35-40 65
(Stereo.)
Note: For the sake of continuity, the preceding 14000 and 18000 series stereo issues, requiring separate pricing, are listed directly below their 4000 and 8000 series mono counterpart.
MONUMENT (8023 "Early Orbison") 30-40 64
MONUMENT (18023 "Early Orbison") 30-40 64

MONUMENT (8045 "Very Best") 30-40 66
(Blue cover.)
MONUMENT (18045 "Very Best") 30-40 66
(Blue cover.)
MONUMENT (8045 "Very Best") 20-30 66
(Purple cover.)
MONUMENT (18045 "Very Best") 20-30 66
(Purple cover.)
MONUMENT (38384 "All-Time Greatest Hits")........................... 8-10 82
RHINO.. 5-8 88
SPECTRUM 15-20 00s
SSS/SUN 5-10 69
SUN (1260 "Rock House").... 200-225 61
SUNNYVALE 8-10 77
TRIP 8-10 74
VIRGIN...................................... 6-12 87-89
Session: Bobby Goldsboro; Bruce Springsteen.
Also see CANDYMEN
Also see DRIFTERS / Lesley Gore / Roy Orbison / Los Bravos
Also see GOLDSBORO, Bobby
Also see HIGGINS, Bertie, & Roy Orbison
Also see JAN & DEAN / Roy Orbison / 4 Seasons / Shirelles
Also see LEWIS, Jerry Lee / Roger Miller / Roy Orbison
Also see PERKINS, Carl, Jerry Lee Lewis, Roy Orbison & Johnny Cash
Also see SPRINGSTEEN, Bruce
Also see TEEN KINGS
Also see TRAVELING WILBURYS

ORBISON, Roy / Bobby Bare / Joey Powers

LPs: 10/12-inch 33rpm

CAMDEN.................................... 15-25 64
Also see BARE, Bobby
Also see POWERS, Joey

ORBISON, Roy, & Emmylou Harris / Craig Hundley

C&W/P&R '80

Singles: 7-inch

W.B. 3-5 80
Also see HARRIS, Emmylou

ORBISON, Roy, & K.D. Lang

C&W '87

Singles: 7-inch

VIRGIN...................................... 3-4 87
Also see LANG, K.D.
Also see ORBISON, Roy

ORBIT
(Featuring Carol Hall)

R&B '82

Singles: 12-inch 33/45rpm

QUALITY/RFC 4-6 82-84

Singles: 7-inch

QUALITY/RFC 3-4 82-84

ORCHESTRAL MANOEUVERS in the DARK
(OMD)

LP '82

Singles: 12-inch 33/45rpm

A&M 4-6 84-86

Singles: 7-inch

A&M 3-4 84-88
EPIC..3-5 82-83

Picture Sleeves

A&M 3-4 85-88

LPs: 10/12-inch 33rpm

A&M 5-8 84-88
EPIC..5-10 82-83

ORIGINAL ANIMALS: see ANIMALS

ORIGINAL CADILLACS

Singles: 78rpm

JOSIE..10-15 57

Singles: 7-inch

JOSIE..10-15 57-58
Members: Earl Carroll; Earl Wade; Charles Brooks; Bobby Phillips; Junior Glanton; Roland Martinez.
Also see CADILLACS

ORIGINAL CASTE
(Featuring Dixie Lee Innes)

P&R '69

Singles: 7-inch

DOT 4-8 68
T-A 4-8 69-70

Picture Sleeves

T-A 4-8 69

LPs: 10/12-inch 33rpm

T-A 10-20 70

ORIGINAL CASUALS
(Featuring Gary Mears)

P&R/R&B '58

Singles: 7-inch

BACK BEAT................................8-12 58

EPs: 7-inch 33/45rpm

BACK BEAT (40 "Three Kisses Past Midnight")......................50-70 58
Members: Gary Mears; Paul Kearney; Jay Adams.

ORIGINAL CONCEPT

R&B '86

Singles: 7-inch

DEF JAM......................................3-4 86

ORIGINAL CRESTS: see CRESTS

ORIGINAL LAST POETS

LP '71

LPs: 10/12-inch 33rpm

JUGGERNAUT 10-15 71

ORIGINAL RED CAPS: see GIBSON, Steve

ORIGINALS

P&R/R&B '69

Singles: 7–inch

MOTOWN (1 "Young Train"). 100-200 73
(Promotional issue only.)
MOTOWN (1300 series) 4-6 75
PHASE II 3-5 81
SOUL (35029 thru 35061)........... 6-12 67-69
SOUL (35066 thru 35119)............ 4-8 69-76

LPs: 10/12–inch 33rpm

FANTASY.................................. 5-10 78-79
MOTOWN 5-10 74-80
SOUL (716 "Baby I'm for Real") 20-40 69
SOUL (724 "Portrait")................ 15-20 70
SOUL (729 "Naturally
Together") 15-20 70
SOUL (734 thru 746).................. 8-15 73-76

Members: Ty Hunter; Henry Dixon; Joe Stubbs; Walt Gaines; C.P. Spencer; Freddie Gorman.
Also see HUNTER, Ty

ORIGINALS & Jermaine Jackson

Singles: 12–inch 33/45rpm

MOTOWN 4-8 76

Also see JACKSON, Jermaine
Also see ORIGINALS

ORIOLES

(Sonny Til & Orioles; Sonny Til's Orioles)

P&R/R&B '48

Singles: 78rpm

IT'S a NATURAL (5000 "It's Too
Soon to Know") 50-100 48
JUBILEE (5000 "It's too Soon
to Know").............................. 25-50 48
JUBILEE (5001 "Dare to
Dream")................................ 25-50 48
JUBILEE (5001 "Lonely
Christmas") 25-50 48
JUBILEE (5002 "Please Give My
Heart a Break") 25-50 49
JUBILEE (5005 "Tell Me So").... 25-50 49
JUBILEE (5008 "I Challenge
Your Kiss") 25-50 49
JUBILEE (5009 "A Kiss and a
Rose") 25-50 49
JUBILEE (5016 "So Much") 25-50 49
JUBILEE (5017 "What Are You
Doing New Year's Eve")........... 25-50 49
JUBILEE (5018 "Would You Still
Be the One in My Heart")........ 25-50 50
JUBILEE (5025 "At Night")........ 25-50 50
JUBILEE (5026 "Moonlight") 25-50 50
JUBILEE (5028 "You're Gone"). 25-50 50
JUBILEE (5031 "I'd Rather Have You
Under the Moon").................... 25-50 50
JUBILEE (5037 "I Need You
So") 40-60 50
JUBILEE (5040 "I Cross My
Fingers")................................ 20-35 50
JUBILEE (5045 "Oh Holy
Night") 25-50 50
JUBILEE (5057 "Would I Love
You") 20-35 51
JUBILEE (5061 "I'm Just a Fool
in Love") 20-35 51

At least ten of the above 78rpm singles were reissued around 1951 on 45s. It's likely that others in the 5001-5061 series appeared on early '50s Jubilee 45s, but those listed below are the only ones we can verify.

JUBILEE (5061 thru 5231).........10-25 51-56
VEE JAY 10-15 56-57

Singles: 7–inch

ABNER (1016 "Sugar Girl") 30-50 58
CHARLIE PARKER.......................8-12 62-63
COLLECTABLES...........................3-4 80s
JUBILEE (5000 "It's Too Soon
to Know") 2000-3000 51
JUBILEE (5005 "Tell Me
So")................................1000-2000 51
JUBILEE (5016 "So Much") .500-1000 51
JUBILEE (5017 "What Are You
Doing New Year's Eve") 500-750 51
JUBILEE (5025 "At Night").....500-750 51
JUBILEE (5040 "I Cross My
Fingers") 400-600 51
JUBILEE (5045 "Oh Holy
Night") 300-500 51
JUBILEE (5051 "I Miss You
So")..................................400-600 51
(Black vinyl.)
JUBILEE (5051 "I Miss You
So")...............................1000-1500 51
(Colored vinyl.)
JUBILEE (5055 "Pal of
Mine").................................400-600 51
JUBILEE (5061 "I'm Just a Fool
in Love")............................400-600 51
JUBILEE (5065 "Baby, Please
Don't Go") 300-500 51
(Black vinyl.)
JUBILEE (5065 "Baby, Please
Don't Go") 1000-1500 51
(Colored vinyl.)
JUBILEE (5071 "When You're
Not Around") 300-500 51
JUBILEE (5074 "Trust in
Me") 350-450 52
(The Orioles are not credited on 5076, only Sonny Til.)
JUBILEE (5082 "It's Over Because
We're Through")..................350-450 52
JUBILEE (5084 "Barfly") 250-350 52
JUBILEE (5092 "Don't Cry
Baby") 250-350 52
(Black vinyl.)

JUBILEE (5092 "Don't Cry Baby") 800-1200 52
(Colored vinyl.)
JUBILEE (5102 "You Belong to Me").......... 250-350 52
JUBILEE (5107 "I Miss You So") 200-300 53
(Reissued in 1963, using the same catalog number, but credited to Sonny Til & Orioles. Black vinyl.)
JUBILEE (5107 "I Miss You So") 800-1200 53
(Colored vinyl.)
JUBILEE (5108 "Teardrops on My Pillow") 200-300 53
(Black vinyl.)
JUBILEE (5108 "Teardrops on My Pillow") 800-1200 53
(Colored vinyl.)
JUBILEE (5115 "Bad Little Girl") 100-200 53
JUBILEE (5120 "I Cover the Waterfront").......... 100-200 53
(Black vinyl.)
JUBILEE (5120 "I Cover the Waterfront").......... 500-1000 53
(Colored vinyl.)
JUBILEE (5122 "Crying in the Chapel") 30-50 53
JUBILEE (5127 "In the Mission of St. Augustine") 30-50 53
JUBILEE (5134 "There's No One But You").......... 30-50 54
JUBILEE (5137 "Secret Love") . 30-50 54
JUBILEE (5143 "Maybe You'll Be There").......... 50-75 54
JUBILEE (5154 "In the Chapel in the Moonlight").......... 30-50 54
JUBILEE (5161 "If You Believe").......... 30-50 54
JUBILEE (5172 "Runaround")... 30-50 54
JUBILEE (5177 "I Love You Mostly").......... 25-40 55
JUBILEE (5189 "I Need You Baby") 25-40 55
JUBILEE (5221 "Please Sing My Blues Tonight").......... 25-35 55
JUBILEE (5231 "Angel").......... 30-50 56
JUBILEE (5363 "Tell Me So")...... 5-10 59
JUBILEE (5384 "First of Summer") 5-10 60
JUBILEE (5383 "Come On Home").......... 8-12 60
JUBILEE (5394 "Night and Day") 40-60 60
JUBILEE (6001 "Crying in the Chapel") 8-12 59
ROULETTE 3-5 70s
VEE JAY (196 "Happy Till the Letter") 15-25 56
VEE JAY (228 "For All We Know") 15-25 56
VEE JAY (244 "Sugar Girl").......25-35 57
VIRGO 3-5 70s

Picture Sleeves

JUBILEE (5017 "What Are You Doing New Year's Eve").......... 150-250 54
(Sleeve for 78rpm.)
JUBILEE (5017 "What Are You Doing New Year's Eve").......... 300-400 54
(Sleeve for 45rpm.)
JUBILEE (5045 "Oh Holy Night").......... 300-400 54
(Both Jubilee sleeves were issued in late 1954 and sold with 1954 pressings, actually second pressings of both. These were blue script Jubilee labels with the line under the logo.)
LANA.......... 3-6 63

EPs: 7-inch 33/45rpm

JUBILEE (5000 "The Orioles Sing") 750-1000 53

LPs: 10/12-inch 33rpm

BIG A RECORDS (2001 "Greatest All Time Hits") 20-30 69
CHARLIE PARKER (816 "Modern Sounds") 50-75 62
COLLECTABLES.......... 5-10 84
MURRAY HILL.......... 30-40 80s
(Five-LP set. Number not known.)
MURRAY HILL (61277 "The Orioles Featuring Sonny Til") 30-40 80s
(Boxed 5-LP set.)
ROULETTE.......... 5-10

Members: Sonny Til; Alex Sharp; George Nelson; John Reed; Tom Gaither; Charles Harris; Greg Carroll; Billy Adams; Jerry Holman; Al Russell; Jerry Rodriguez; Bill Taylor.

Also see CADILLACS / Orioles
Also see TIL, Sonny

ORION the HUNTER

P&R/LP '84

Singles: 7-inch

PORTRAIT.......... 3-4 84-85

LPs: 10/12-inch 33rpm

PORTRAIT.......... 5-8 84

Member: Barry Goudreau.

Also see BOSTON

ORLANDO, Tony

Singles: 7-inch

MILO (101 "Ding Dong") 30-50 59

Also see SIMON, Paul

ORLANDO, Tony

P&R '61

Singles: 12-inch 33/45rpm

CASABLANCA.......... 5-10 79

Singles: 7–inch

ATCO 4-8 65
CAMEO 4-8 67
CASABLANCA 3-5 79-80
EPIC (9000 series)...................... 5-10 61-64

Promotional Singles

EPIC (55299 "Happy Times Are Here to Stay")........................... 8-12 61

LPs: 10/12–inch 33rpm

EPIC (611 "Bless You")............ 35-40 61
(Stereo.)
EPIC (3808 "Bless You")........... 35-40 61
(Monaural.)
EPIC (33785 "Before Dawn").... 10-12 75
CASABLANCA........................... 5-10 79-80

Picture Sleeves

EPIC.. 8-10 61-62

Also see WIND

ORLANDO, Tony, & Dawn

P&R/LP '70

Singles: 7–inch

ARISTA 3-5 75
BELL 3-5 71-74
ELEKTRA...................................... 3-5 75-78

LPs: 10/12–inch 33rpm

ARISTA 8-10 75-76
ASYLUM 8-10 75
BELL (6000 series) 10-12 70-71
BELL (1000 series) 8-10 73-75
ELEKTRA..................................... 8-10 75-78
KORY 8-10 74-77

Also see DAWN
Also see ORLANDO, Tony

ORLEANS

P&R/LP '75

Singles: 7–inch

ABC... 3-5 73
ASYLUM 3-5 75-77
INFINITY 3-5 79
MCA 3-4 86

LPs: 10/12–inch 33rpm

ABC... 10-12 73-78
ASYLUM 8-10 75-76
INFINITY 5-10 79
RADIO.. 5-8 82

Member: John Hall.
Also see HALL, John

ORLONS

P&R/R&B/LP '62

Singles: 7–inch

ABC.. 4-8 67
CALLA.. 5-10 66
CAMEO (198 "I'll Be True")....... 30-40 61
CAMEO (211 "Mr. 21")............. 30-40 62
CAMEO (218 thru 372) 5-15 62-65
CAMEO (384 "Envy")................ 30-40 65

Picture Sleeves

CAMEO 5-10 62-64

LPs: 10/12–inch 33rpm

CAMEO (1020 "Wah Watusi") ...30-60 62
CAMEO (1033 "All the Hits")......25-50 62
CAMEO (1041 "South Street")...25-50 63
CAMEO (1054 "Not Me") 25-50 63
CAMEO (1061 "Biggest Hits")....25-50 63
CAMEO (1073 "Memory Lane").25-50 63

Members: Shirley Brickley; Rosetta Hightower; Steve Caldwell; Marlena Davis.
Also see ZIP & ZIPPERS

ORLONS / Dovells

LPs: 10/12–inch 33rpm

CAMEO (1067 "Golden Hits") 25-50 63

Also see DOVELLS
Also see ORLONS

ORPHEUS

LP '68

Singles: 7–inch

MGM 4-6 68-69

Picture Sleeves

MGM 4-6 69

LPs: 10/12–inch 33rpm

BELL 10-12 71
MGM 10-15 68-69

ORR, Benjamin

P&R/LP '86

Singles: 7–inch

ELEKTRA..3-4 86

Picture Sleeves

ELEKTRA..3-4 86

LPs: 10/12–inch 33rpm

ELEKTRA..5-8 86

Also see CARS

ORRALL, Robert Ellis

(With Carlene Carter)

P&R/LP '83

Singles: 7–inch

RCA 3-5 81-91

LPs: 10/12–inch 33rpm

RCA 5-10 81-91

Also see CARTER, Carlene

OSBORNE, Jeffrey

P&R/R&B/LP '82

Singles: 12–inch 33/45rpm

A&M 4-6 82-86

Singles: 7–inch

A&M 3-5 82-88
ARISTA 3-4 90

Picture Sleeves

A&M 3-5 82-88

LPs: 10/12–inch 33rpm

A&M 5-10 82-88
ARISTA 5-8 90

Also see KENNEDY, Joyce, & Jeffrey Osborne
Also see L.T.D.
Also see WARWICK, Dionne, & Jeffrey Osborne

OSBORNE & GILES

R&B '85

Singles: 7-inch

RED LABEL 3-4 85

LPs: 10/12-inch 33rpm

RED LABEL 5-8 85

Members: Billy Osborne; Attala Giles.

OSBORNE BROTHERS
(With Red Allen)

C&W '58

Singles: 7-inch

CMH 3-5 80
DECCA 3-8 63-72
MCA 3-5 73-75
MGM (100 series) 3-5 64
MGM (12000 & 13000 series) 4-10 59-63

EPs: 7-inch 33/45rpm

MGM 10-15 59

LPs: 10/12-inch 33rpm

CMH 5-10 76-82
CORAL 5-10 73
DECCA 10-20 65-72
MCA 5-10 73-75
MGM (100 series) 5-10 70
MGM (3700 series) 25-35 59
MGM (4000 series) 15-25 62-63
ROUNDER 5-8 80s
SUGAR HILL 5-8 84

Members: Bobby Osborne; Sonny Osborne; Benny Birchfield. Session: Ronnie Reno; Jimmy Martin.

OSBORNE BROTHERS & Mac Wiseman
(With Red Allen)

C&W '79

Singles: 7-inch

CMH 3-5 79

Also see OSBORNE BROTHERS

OSBOURNE, Ozzy

LP '81

Singles: 7-inch

CBS ASSOCIATED 3-4 83-86
JET 3-5 82

Picture Sleeves

CBS ASSOCIATED 3-4 86

LPs: 10/12-inch 33rpm

CBS ASSOCIATED 5-8 83-90
JET 5-10 81-82
PRIORITY 5-8 90

Also see BLACK SABBATH
Also see FORD, Lita, & Ozzy Osbourne
Also see QUIET RIOT

OSBOURNE, Ozzy, & Randy Rhoads

LP '87

LPs: 10/12-inch 33rpm

CBS ASSOC 5-8 87

OSIBISA

LP '71

Singles: 7-inch

DECCA 3-5 72
ISLAND 3-5 76-77
MCA 3-4
W.B. 3-5 73-74

LPs: 10/12-inch 33rpm

BUDDAH 8-10 73
DECCA 10-12 71-72
ISLAND 8-10 77
MCA 5-8
W.B. 8-10 73-74

OSIRIS

R&B '79

Singles: 7-inch

INFINITY 3-5 79
W.B. 3-5 79

LPs: 10/12-inch 33rpm

INFINITY 5-10 79
W.B. 5-10 79

Members: Osiris Marsh.

OSKAR, Lee

P&R/R&B/LP '76

Singles: 7-inch

ELEKTRA 3-5 78-81
U.A. 3-5 76

LPs: 10/12-inch 33rpm

ELEKTRA 5-10 78-79
U.A. 8-10 76

Also see WAR

OSMOND, Donny

P&R/LP '71

Singles: 7-inch

CAPITOL 3-4 89
MGM 3-5 71-75
POLYDOR 3-5 76-78

Picture Sleeves

CAPITOL 3-4 89
MGM 3-5 71-75

LPs: 10/12-inch 33rpm

CAPITOL 5-8 89-90
MGM 8-10 71-74
POLYDOR 5-10 76-77

Also see OSMONDS

OSMOND, Donny & Marie

P&R/LP '74

Singles: 7-inch

MGM 3-5 74-75
POLYDOR 3-5 76-78

LPs: 10/12-inch 33rpm

MGM 8-10 74-75
POLYDOR 5-10 76-78

Also see D&M
Also see OSMOND, Donny
Also see OSMOND, Marie

OSMOND, Jimmy
(Little Jimmy Osmond)

P&R/LP '72

Singles: 7-inch

MGM 3-5 70-75
MERCURY 3-5 78

LPs: 10/12-inch 33rpm

MGM 8-10 72
Also see OSMONDS

OSMOND, Marie
(Marie)

C&W/P&R/LP '73

Singles: 7-inch

CURB 3-4 90
CURB/CAPITOL 3-5 85-89
ELEKTRA/CURB 3-5 82-84
MGM 3-5 73-75
POLYDOR 3-5 76-78
RCA/CURB 3-5 84

Picture Sleeves

MGM 3-5 73-75
POLYDOR 3-5 77
RCA 3-5 84

LPs: 10/12-inch 33rpm

CURB/CAPITOL 5-8 85-88
MGM 8-12 73-75
POLYDOR 5-8 77
Also see OSMOND, Donny & Marie
Also see OSMONDS

OSMOND, Marie, & Paul Davis

C&W '86

Singles: 7-inch

CAPITOL 3-4 86-88
Also see DAVIS, Paul

OSMOND, Marie, & Osmond Brothers

LPs: 10/12-inch 33rpm

UNITED (12924 "Our Best to You") 5-10 85
(Special products promotional issue, made for Case International.)
Also see OSMONDS

OSMOND, Marie, & Dan Seals

C&W '85

Singles: 7-inch

CURB/CAPITOL 3-4 85
Also see OSMOND, Marie
Also see SEALS, Dan

OSMONDS
(Osmond Brothers)

P&R/R&B/LP '71

Singles: 7-inch

BARNABY 4-6 68-69
CURB/EMI 3-4 85-86
EMI AMERICA 3-4 85-86
ELEKTRA/CURB 3-5 82-83
MGM (13126 thru 14159) 4-6 63-70
MGM (14193 thru 14831) 3-5 70-75
MERCURY 3-5 79
POLYDOR 3-5 76-77
UNI (55015 "I Can't Stop") 4-8 67
UNI (55276 "I Can't Stop") 3-5 71
W.B./CURB 3-5 83-85

Picture Sleeves

MGM 3-5 73-74

LPs: 10/12-inch 33rpm

EMI AMERICA 5-8 86
ELEKTRA 5-10 82
MGM (7 "Preview–the Osmond Brothers") 15-20 70s
(Promotional issue only.)
MGM (4100 & 4200 series) 15-25 63-65
MGM (4724 thru 5012) 8-12 70-75
MERCURY 5-10 79
METRO 10-20 65
POLYDOR 5-10 76-77
W.B./CURB 5-8 83-85
Members: Donny Osmond; Alan Osmond; Merrill Osmond; Wayne Osmond; Jimmy Osmond; Marie Osmond.
Also see CURB, Mike
Also see OSMOND, Donny
Also see OSMOND, Jimmy
Also see OSMOND, Marie

OSMONDS, Steve Lawrence & Eydie Gorme

P&R '72

Singles: 7-inch

MGM 3-5 72
Also see LAWRENCE, Steve, & Eydie Gorme
Also see OSMONDS

O'SULLIVAN, Gilbert

P&R/LP '72

Singles: 7-inch

EPIC 3-5 77-81
MAM 3-8 71-76

Picture Sleeves

MAM 3-5 72

LPs: 10/12-inch 33rpm

EPIC 5-10 81
MAM 10-15 72-73

OTHER ONES

P&R/LP '87

Singles: 7-inch

VIRGIN 3-4 87

Picture Sleeves

VIRGIN 3-4 87

LPs: 10/12-inch 33rpm

VIRGIN 5-8 87
Members: Alf Klimek; Johnny Klimek; Steven Gottwald; Andreas Schwartz-Ruszczynski.

OTIS, Johnny
(Johnny Otis Show; Quintette; with Peacocks)

R&B '50

Singles: 78rpm

CAPITOL 10-20 57
DIG 10-20 55-57
EXCELSIOR 15-25 45-47

MERCURY 10-20 51-53
PEACOCK (Except 1625) 10-20 52
PEACOCK (1625 "Young Girl"). 15-25 52
REGENT 10-20 50-51
SAVOY 10-20 50-54

Singles: 7–inch

CAPITOL (3799-3802 "The Johnny Otis Show") 350-400 57
(Four discs with special four-pocket cover.)
CAPITOL (3799 thru 3802) 10-20 57
(Price for four records without cover.)
CAPITOL (3852 "Good Golly").. 10-15 57
CAPITOL (3966 "Willie and the Hand Jive"/ "Ring-A-Ling") 8-12 58
CAPITOL (3966 "Willie and the Hand Jive"/ "Willie and the Hand Jive")...... 20-30 58
(Blue label. Promotional issue only.)
CAPITOL (4060 "Crazy Country Hop") 8-12 58
CAPITOL (4168 "Castin' My Spell")................................... 10-15 59
(Monaural.)
CAPITOL (S-4168 "Castin' My Spell")............................... 20-30 59
(Stereo.)
CAPITOL (4226 thru 4326) 8-12 59-60
DIG 15-25 55-59
ELDO (105 "New Bo Diddley").... 5-10 60
ELDO (153 "Long Distance") 4-8 67
EPIC 3-5 70
HAWK SOUND 3-5 75
KENT 3-5 69
KING 5-8 61-63
MERCURY (8263 "Oopy Doo"). 30-50 51
MERCURY (8273 "Goomp Blues")................................... 30-50 51
MERCURY (8289 "Call Operator 210") 30-50 52
MERCURY (8295 "Gypsy Blues")................................... 30-50 52
MERCURY (70038 "Why Don't You Believe Me")......................... 30-50 52
MERCURY (70050 "The Love Bug Boogie") 30-50 52
OKEH 4-6 69
PEACOCK (1625 "Young Girl"). 40-60 52
PEACOCK (1636 "Shake It") 25-45 52
PEACOCK (1648 "Sittin' Here Drinkin'")................................ 25-45 52
PEACOCK (1675 "Butterball")... 25-45 52
SAVOY 15-25 50-54

EPs: 7–inch 33/45rpm

CAPITOL (940 "Johnny Otis Show") 75-100 58
CAPITOL (1134 "Johnny Otis"). 50-75 59
RITZ-EE (5214 Blackouts of 1959).................................... 40-60 59
(Has one Otis track, *Backstage at the Blackouts.* Promotional issue only. Not issued with cover.)

LPs: 10/12–inch 33rpm

ALLIGATOR.................................5-10 82
BLUES SPECTRUM 10-15
CAPITOL (940 "Johnny Otis Show")..........................100-200 58
DIG (104 "Rock & Roll Hit Parade") 300-500 57
(Gold cover. Counterfeits of Dig 104 exist, some of which have a yellow cover.Others have a gold cover. Regardless, the discs of originals are noticeably thicker than is used on the fakes.)
EPIC...10-15 70-71
JAZZ WORLD 5-10 78
KENT 10-20 70
SAVOY 5-10 78-80

Referenced below are some of the artists who performed with the Johnny Otis Show, or with whom he or his orchestra appears.

Also see ACE, Johnny
Also see ADAMS, Marie
Also see ALLEN, Tony
Also see FREEMAN, Ernie
Also see JACQUET, Illinois
Also see McNEELY, Big Jay
Also see RUSHING, Jimmy
Also see WATSON, Johnny

OTIS, Johnny, & Preston Love

Singles: 7–inch

KENT 3-5 70
Also see OTIS, Shuggie, & Preston Love

OTIS, Johnny, Orchestra, with Little Esther & Mel Walker

R&B '50

Singles: 78rpm

REGENT (1036 "I Dream") 15-25 51
SAVOY.......................................15-25 50-51

Singles: 7–inch

REGENT (1036 "I Dream") 50-75 51
SAVOY (750 "Cupid's Boogie")..50-75 50
SAVOY (775 "Love Will Break Your Heart")...........................50-75 51
Also see LITTLE ESTHER & Mel Walker

OTIS, Johnny, Quintette, with Little Esther & Robins

R&B '50

Singles: 78rpm

SAVOY...25-50 50

Singles: 7–inch

SAVOY (731 "Double Crossing Blues") 75-100 50
Also see LITTLE ESTHER
Also see OTIS, Johnny
Also see ROBINS

OTIS, Shuggie

LP '70

Singles: 7–inch

EPIC...3-5 70-75

LPs: 10/12-inch 33rpm

EPIC 10-15 70-75

Also see KOOPER, Al, & Shuggie Otis

OTIS, Shuggie, & Preston Love

Singles: 7-inch

KENT 3-5 70

Also see OTIS, Johnny, & Preston Love
Also see OTIS, Shuggie

OTIS & CARLA

P&R/R&B/LP '67

Singles: 7-inch

ATCO 4-6 69
STAX 5-10 67-68

LPs: 10/12-inch 33rpm

STAX 10-20 67

Members: Otis Redding; Carla Thomas.
Also see REDDING, Otis
Also see THOMAS, Carla

OUTFIELD

LP '85

Singles: 7-inch

COLUMBIA 3-4 85-87

Picture Sleeves

COLUMBIA 3-4 86-87

LPs: 10/12-inch 33rpm

COLUMBIA 5-8 85-87

Members: Tony Lewis; Alan Jackman; John Spinks.

OUTLAWS

LP '76

Singles: 7-inch

ARISTA 3-5 75-83

LPs: 10/12-inch 33rpm

ARISTA 5-10 75-83
DIRECT DISC (16617 "Outlaws") 15-25 80s
(Half-speed mastered.)
PASHA 5-8 86
PEAR 8-12 84

Members: Hughie Thomasson; Henry Paul; David Dix; Billy Jones; Fred Salem; Rick Cua; David Dix; Harvey Dalton Arnold; Frank O'Keefe; Monte Yoho; Chuck Glass; Steve Grisham.
Also see PAUL, Henry, Band

OUTPUT

R&B '84

Singles: 12-inch 33/45rpm

CBS ASSOCIATED 4-6 83

Singles: 7-inch

CBS ASSOCIATED 3-5 83
TUFF CITY 3-4 84

OUTSIDERS

P&R/LP '66

Singles: 7-inch

BELL 4-6 70
CAPITOL 5-10 66-68
KAPP 4-6 70

Picture Sleeves

CAPITOL 8-12 66-67

LPs: 10/12-inch 33rpm

CAPITOL 20-30 66-67

Members: Sonny Geraci; Bill Bruno; Tom King; Rickey Baker; Merdin Madsen.
Also see CLIMAX

OVATIONS
(Ovation)

P&R/R&B '65

Singles: 7-inch

CHESS 3-5 75
GOLDWAX 8-12 64-69
MGM 4-6 73
SOUNDS of MEMPHIS 4-6 72-73

LPs: 10/12-inch 33rpm

MGM 10-15 73
SOUNDS of MEMPHIS 10-20 72

Members: George Jackson; Louis Williams.
Also see JACKSON, George

OVERBEA, Danny

R&B '53

Singles: 7-inch

APEX 4-8 59
CHECKER (774 "40 Cups of Coffee") 50-100 53
(Black vinyl.)
CHECKER (774 "40 Cups of Coffee") 150-200 53
(Colored vinyl.)
CHECKER (768 "Train Train Train") 50-100 53
CHECKER (784 "Sorrento") 50-100 54
CHECKER (788 "Stomp and Whistle") 50-100 54
CHECKER (796 "Roamin' Man") 50-100 54
CHECKER (808 "A Toast to Lovers") 50-100 55
CHECKER (816 "Hey, Pancho") 50-75 55
FEDERAL 10-15 61
SHEP 10-20 60

OVERKILL

LP '87

LPs: 10/12-inch 33rpm

MEGAFORCE 5-8 87-89

OVERLANDERS

P&R '64

Singles: 7-inch

HICKORY 10-15 64-66
MERCURY 5-10 63

OVERTON, C.B.

R&B '78

Singles: 7-inch

SHOCK 3-5 78

OWEN-B

P&R '70

Singles: 7-inch

JANUS 3-5 70

LPs: 10/12–inch 33rpm

MUS-I-COL (101209 "Owen-B") 40-60 70

OWEN, Reg, & His Orchestra

P&R '58

Singles: 7–inch

PALETTE 4-6 58-62

EPs: 7–inch 33/45rpm

RCA... 5-10 50s

LPs: 10/12–inch 33rpm

PALETTE 15-25 59-60

OWENS, Buck
(With the Buckaroos)

C&W '59

Singles: 78rpm

CAPITOL 10-20 57

Singles: 7–inch

CAPITOL (2000 thru 4000 series). 3-5 67-75
(Orange label.)
CAPITOL (3824 "Come Back") . 10-15 57
(Purple label.)
CAPITOL (3957 "Sweet Thing") 10-15 58
(Purple label.)
CAPITOL (4000 series).............. 5-10 59-63
(Purple or orange/yellow label.)
CAPITOL (5000 series)................ 3-6 63-67
CHESTERFIELD (44223 "Leavin' Dirty Tracks") 10-20 60s
HILLTOP (6027 "Hot Dog") 25-50 60s
NEW STAR (6418 "Hot Dog") 100-150 50s
PEP (105 "Down on the Corner of Love")..................... 20-30 56
PEP (106 "Right After the Dance") 20-30 56
PEP (109 "There Goes My Love").................................... 20-30 57
STARDAY (588 "Down on the Corner of Love")....................... 5-10 61
STARDAY (5000 series) 4-6 64
W.B. (Except 8316)...................... 3-5 76-80
W.B. (8316 "World Famous Holiday Inn")............................. 5-10 77
W.B. (8316 "World Famous Paradise Inn") 3-5 77
(Note title change.)

Picture Sleeves

CAPITOL................................. 10-20 66-69

EPs: 7–inch 33/45rpm

CAPITOL................................. 10-25 61-65

LPs: 10/12–inch 33rpm

CAPITOL (100 thru 400 series)... 8-12 68-70
CAPITOL (500 series, except 574).. 8-10 70
CAPITOL (600 thru 800 series)... 5-10 70-72
CAPITOL (574 "Buck Owens").. 15-25 70
(Three-LP set.)
CAPITOL (T-1482 thru T-1989) 30-40 61-63
(Monaural.)
CAPITOL (ST-1482 thru ST-1989)................................ 35-50 61-63
(Stereo.)
CAPITOL (DT-1400 series) 8-12 69
CAPITOL (2100 thru 2700 series).....................................12-25 64-67
CAPITOL (2800 thru 2900 series).....................................10-15 68
CAPITOL (2980 "Buck Owens Minute Masters")....................30-40 66
(Promotional issue only.)
CAPITOL (11000 series) 5-8 72-78
HALL of MUSIC 8-12
LA BREA (8017 "Buck Owens")...........................100-150 61
OUT of TOWN DIST 5-8 82
PICKWICK/HILLTOP 5-10 78
STARDAY (172 "Fabulous Country Music Sound of Buck Owens")...........30-40 62
STARDAY (300 series).............15-20 64-65
STARDAY (400 series) 8-12 75
TIME-LIFE..................................5-10 82
TRIP...5-8 76
W.B. 5-10 76-77

Also see JONES, Corky
Also see JONES, George / Buck Owens / David Houston / Tommy Hill.
Also see YOAKAM, Dwight, & Buck Owens

OWENS, Buck, & Buddy Alan
(Buck & Buddy; with the Buckaroos)

C&W '68

Singles: 7–inch

CAPITOL.......................................4-6 68

OWENS, Buck, & Emmylou Harris

Singles: 7–inch

W.B. 3-4 79

Also see HARRIS, Emmylou

OWENS, Buck, & Rose Maddox

C&W '63

Singles: 7–inch

CAPITOL.......................................5-8 63

OWENS, Buck, & Susan Raye

C&W/LP '70

Singles: 7–inch

CAPITOL.......................................3-5 70-73

LPs: 10/12–inch 33rpm

CAPITOL.....................................5-10 70-73

Also see RAYE, Susan

OWENS, Buck, & Ringo Starr

C&W '89

Singles: 7–inch

CAPITOL.......................................3-5 89

Also see STARR, Ringo

OWENS, Buck / Faron Young / Ferlin Husky

LPs: 10/12–inch 33rpm

PICKWICK/HILLTOP 10-15 65

Also see HUSKY, Ferlin

Also see OWENS, Buck
Also see YOUNG, Faron

OWENS, Donnie
(Donny Owens)

P&R '58

Singles: 7-inch

ARA 4-8
GUYDEN 10-15 58-59
TREY 5-10 60

Also see EDDY, Duane

OWENS, Gwen

R&B '69

Singles: 7-inch

BIG TREE 3-5 79
JOSIE 4-6 69

OWENS, Tony

R&B '71

Singles: 7-inch

COTILLION 4-6 71
SOUL SOUND 10-20

OXO

P&R/LP '83

Singles: 7-inch

GEFFEN 3-4 83

LPs: 10/12-inch 33rpm

GEFFEN 5-8 83

Also see FOXY

OZARK MOUNTAIN DAREDEVILS

P&R/LP '74

Singles: 7-inch

A&M 3-5 74-78
COLUMBIA 3-5 80

Picture Sleeves

A&M 3-5 75-76

LPs: 10/12-inch 33rpm

A&M 8-12 73-78
COLUMBIA 5-10 80

OZO

P&R '76

Singles: 7-inch

DJM 3-5 76

LPs: 10/12-inch 33rpm

DJM 5-10 76

OZONE

R&B '80

Singles: 7-inch

MOTOWN 3-5 80-83

LPs: 10/12-inch 33rpm

MOTOWN 5-10 80-83

OZUNA, Sunny: see SUNGLOWS

CATALOG NO. 56197
An Interview With The
NGDB
Including: Excerps from the Liberty/UA Album,
"UNCLE CHARLIE & HIS DOG TEDDY"
LST-7642
PRODUCED BY WILLIAM E. McEUEN
LIBERTY

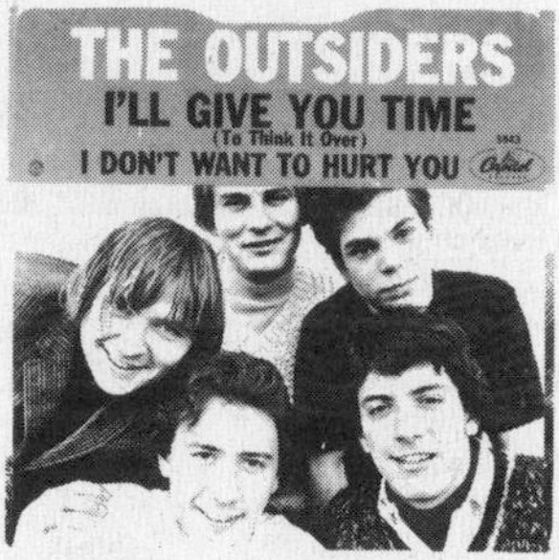

P

P.F.M.
(Premiata Forneria Marconi)

LP '73

Singles: 7-inch

ASYLUM 3-5 76-77
MANTICORE.............................. 3-5 73-75

LPs: 10/12-inch 33rpm

ASYLUM 5-10 76-77
MANTICORE............................. 8-12 73-74
PETERS INT'L 5-10 76

P CREW

R&B '83

Singles: 7-inch

PRELUDE 3-4 83

P. FUNK ALL-STARS

R&B '82

Singles: 12-inch 33/45rpm

UNCLE JAM............................... 4-6 84

Singles: 7-inch

CBS ASSOCIATED...................... 3-4 83
HUMP....................................... 3-5 82
UNCLE JAM............................... 3-4 84

LPs: 10/12-inch 33rpm

CBS ASSOCIATED...................... 5-8 84
UNCLE JAM............................... 5-8 84

PG&E: see PACIFIC GAS & ELECTRIC

PABLO CRUISE

LP '75

Singles: 7-inch

A&M 3-5 75-84

Picture Sleeves

A&M 3-5 77-84

LPs: 10/12-inch 33rpm

A&M 5-10 75-84
MFSL (029 "A Place in the
Sun") 15-25 79
(Half-speed mastered.)
NAUTILUS 10-20 81

Members: Dave Jenkins; Steven Price; Cory Lerios; Bud Cockrell.
Also see IT'S a BEAUTIFUL DAY

PACIFIC GAS & ELECTRIC
(PG&E; Pacific Gas & Electric Blues Band)

LP '69

Singles: 7-inch

BRIGHT ORANGE..................... 5-10 68
COLUMBIA 3-6 69-72
POWER.................................... 5-10 69

LPs: 10/12-inch 33rpm

ABC.. 8-10 70s
BRIGHT ORANGE (701 "Get It
On")..................................... 40-80 68
COLUMBIA 8-12 69-73
KENT (547 "Get It On")............ 10-20 68
POWER 10-15 69

Members: Charlie Allen; Frank Cook; Brent Block; Tom Marshall; Glenn Schwartz.
Also see SEEGER, Pete, & Pacific Gas & Electric

PACK, David

P&R '86

Singles: 7-inch

W.B. 3-4 86

LPs: 10/12-inch 33rpm

W.B. 5-8 86

Also see AMBROSIA
Also see McDONALD, Michael
Also see PARSONS, Alan, Project
Also see TREFETHEN

PACKERS

P&R/R&B '65

Singles: 7-inch

HBR 4-8 66
IMPERIAL 4-6 69
PURE SOUL MUSIC.................... 4-8 65
TAG LTD.................................... 4-8 67
TANGERINE 4-8 68

LPs: 10/12-inch 33rpm

IMPERIAL 10-15 68
PURE SOUL MUSIC.................. 15-20 66

Member: Charles Axton.
Also see MAR-KEYS

PAGAN, Bruni

R&B '79

Singles: 7-inch

ELEKTRA.................................... 3-5 79

PAGAN, Ralfi

R&B '71

Singles: 7-inch

FANIA 3-5 71

Also see SYLVIA & Ralfi Pagan

PAGE, Gene

LP '75

Singles: 7-inch

ARISTA 3-5 78-80
ATLANTIC.................................. 3-5 74-75

LPs: 10/12-inch 33rpm

ARISTA.................................... 5-10 78-80
ATLANTIC................................. 8-12 74-75

PAGE, Jimmy

LP '82

LPs: 10/12-inch 33rpm

GEFFEN 5-8 88
SWAN SONG............................. 5-10 82

Also see CARTOONE
Also see CLAPTON, Eric, Jeff Beck & Jimmy Page
Also see FIRM
Also see HERMAN'S HERMITS
Also see HONEYDRIPPERS
Also see LED ZEPPELIN
Also see LORD SUTCH
Also see STEWART, Al
Also see WILLIE & Poor Boys

Also see YARDBIRDS

PAGE, Jimmy, and Sonny Boy Williamson

LPs: 10/12-inch 33rpm

SPRINGBOARD........................ 10-20 72

Also see WILLIAMSON, Sonny Boy, & Yardbirds

PAGE, Patti

(With Al Clauser & the Oklahomans)

Singles: 78rpm

OKLA (66 "My Sweet Papa") 5-10 40s
(Listed primarily to distinguish this singer from the following Patti Page.)

PAGE, Patti

P&R '48

Singles: 78rpm

MERCURY (A-95 thru A-1025) ... 5-15 50-52
(Boxed set of singles.)
MERCURY (505 "Confess")........ 5-10 50
MERCURY (5061 thru 5899) 5-10 47-52
MERCURY (70025 thru 71101) .. 5-10 52-57
MERCURY (71177 thru 71331) 10-20 57-58
PLAYCRAFT 5-10 53-55

Singles: 7-inch

AVCO 3-5 74-75
COLUMBIA 4-6 62-70
EPIC... 3-5 73-74
LANGWORTH......................... 10-20 49
(Eight-inch, 33rpm transcriptions.)
MERCURY (A-95 thru A-1025). 10-20 50-52
(Boxed set of singles.)
MERCURY (505 "Confess")...... 10-15 50
MERCURY (5344 thru 5899) 10-15 50-52
MERCURY (7000 series)........... 5-15 61
(Compact 33 stereo.)
MERCURY (10000 series)......... 5-10 58-60
(Stereo.)
MERCURY (30000 series)......... 5-10 58
MERCURY (70025 thru 72123) .. 5-15 52-62
MERCURY (73000 series)........... 3-5 70-72
PLANTATION.............................. 3-5 81-83
(Black vinyl.)
PLANTATION.............................. 4-8 81-83
(Colored vinyl.)
PLAYCRAFT 5-10 53-55

Picture Sleeves

MERCURY 10-20 54-63

EPs: 7-inch 33/45rpm

MERCURY 8-18 52-61
PLAYCRAFT 5-10 59

LPs: 10/12-inch 33rpm

ACCORD.................................... 5-10 82
AHED 5-8 76
BRYLEN... 5-8 82
CANDLELITE 8-12 73
COLUMBIA (Except "CL" & "CS" series) 5-10 70-77
COLUMBIA (CL-2049 thru CL-2761)................................10-20 63-68
(Monaural.)
COLUMBIA (CS-8849 thru CS-9999) 10-20 63-69
(Stereo.)
EMARCY (2-100 "The East Side The West Side")......................50-80 58
(Two LPs.)
EMARCY (36074 "In the Land of Hi Fi")................................40-60 56
(No Mercury logo on cover or label.)
EMARCY (36074 "In the Land of Hi Fi")................................30-40 58
(Mercury logo on cover and label.)
EMARCY (80000 "In the Land of Hi Fi")................................35-45 58
(Stereo.)
EMARCY (36116 "West Side") ..20-30 58
(Monaural.)
EMARCY (36136 "East Side") ...20-30 58
(Monaural.)
EMARCY (60113 "East Side") ...20-30 59
(Stereo.)
EMARCY (60114 "West Side") ..20-30 59
(Stereo.)
EVEREST 5-8 83
EXACT 5-8 80
51 WEST...5-8 79
GOOD MUSIC 5-8 85
HARMONY.................................5-10 69-70
HARTLAND.....................................5-8 86
HINDSIGHT 5-8 86
IMPACT 5-8 79
MERCURY (100 series)..............8-12 69
MERCURY (20076 thru 20226) .20-40 55-56
MERCURY (20318 thru 20952) .15-30 57-64
(Monaural.)
MERCURY (25059 thru 25210) .20-40 50-54
(10-inch LPs.)
MERCURY (60049 thru 60011) .20-40 57-58
(Stereo.)
MERCURY (60025 thru 60952) .20-35 58-64
(Stereo.)
MERCURY (61344 "I'd Rather Be Sorry")....................................5-10 71
PAIR..5-8 87
PICKWICK 5-8 72
PILLSBURY (001 "Big Records").............................15-25 57
(Special products issue made for Pillsbury.)
PLANTATION 5-10 81-82
PLAYCRAFT (1300 "Patti Page")..................................15-25 58
SUFFOLK 5-8 88
WING (2-100 series)...................5-12 72
WING (12121 thru 12174)..........10-20 58-59
(Monaural.)

WING (12250 thru 12295) 5-12 65
(Monaural.)
WING (16000 series) 5-15 61-68
(Stereo.)
Also see MARTIN, Dean / Patti Page

PAGE, Patti, & Rex Allen

Singles: 78rpm

MERCURY 5-10 50

EPs: 7-inch 33/45rpm

MERCURY 5-15 53
Also see ALLEN, Rex

PAGE, Patti, & Vic Damone

Singles: 78rpm

MERCURY 5-10 48
Also see DAMONE, Vic

PAGE, Patti, & Rusty Draper

EPs: 7-inch 33/45rpm

MERCURY 5-15 53
PLAYCRAFT 5-10 59
Also see DRAPER, Rusty

PAGE, Patti, & Tom T. Hall

C&W '72

Singles: 7-inch

MERCURY 3-5 72
Also see HALL, Tom T.
Also see PAGE, Patti

PAGE, Tommy

P&R/LP '89

Singles: 7-inch

SIRE 3-4 89-90

Picture Sleeves

SIRE 3-4 89

LPs: 10/12-inch 33rpm

SIRE 5-8 89-90
Also see NEW KIDS on the BLOCK

PAGES

P&R '79

Singles: 7-inch

CAPITOL 3-5 81
EPIC 3-5 79-80

LPs: 10/12-inch 33rpm

CAPITOL 5-10 81
EPIC 5-10 78-79
Members: Richard Page; Steve George; Russell Battelene; Jerry Manfredi; Peter Leinheiser.
Also see MR. MISTER

PAIGE, Kevin

P&R/LP '89

Singles: 7-inch

CHRYSALIS 3-4 89

Picture Sleeves

CHRYSALIS 3-4 89

LPs: 10/12-inch 33rpm

CHRYSALIS 5-8 89

PAIGE, Sharon
(With Harold Melvin & the Bluenotes)

P&R '75

Singles: 7-inch

PHILADELPHIA INT'L 3-5 75
SOURCE 3-5 80
Also see MELVIN, Harold

PAINTER

P&R '73

Singles: 7-inch

ELEKTRA 3-5 73

LPs: 10/12-inch 33rpm

ELEKTRA 8-12 73

PAJAMA PARTY

P&R '89

Singles: 7-inch

ATLANTIC 3-4 89

LPs: 10/12-inch 33rpm

ATLANTIC 5-8 89

PALLAS, Laura

D&D '84

Singles: 12-inch 33/45rpm

TVI 4-6 84

PALM BEACH BAND BOYS

LP '67

Singles: 7-inch

RCA 3-6 66-67

LPs: 10/12-inch 33rpm

RCA 5-10 66-67

PALMER, Gladys

R&B '47

Singles: 78rpm

MIRACLE 10-15 47

PALMER, Robert

LP '75

Singles: 12-inch 33/45rpm

ISLAND 4-6 83-86

Singles: 7-inch

EMI/MANHATTAN 3-4 88
ISLAND 3-5 75-86

Picture Sleeves

EMI/MANHATTAN 3-4 88
ISLAND 3-5 83-88

LPs: 10/12-inch 33rpm

EMI 5-8 88-90
ISLAND (Except 819) 5-10 75-86
ISLAND (819 "Secrets") 35-40 79
(Picture disc. Promotional issue only.)
Also see BOWN, Alan
Also see POWER STATION

PAMPLEMOUSSE, LE: see LE PAMPLEMOUSSE

PANIC BUTTON

R&B '69

Singles: 7-inch

CHALOM 4-8 68

GAMBLE 4-6 69

PAONE, Nicola

P&R '59

Singles: 7-inch

ABC-PAR 3-6 59
CADENCE 3-6 59

EPs: 7-inch 33/45rpm

CADENCE 5-10 59

LPs: 10/12-inch 33rpm

ABC-PAR 10-20 59-60
ROULETTE 10-15 65

PAPER LACE

P&R/LP '74

Singles: 7-inch

BANG 3-5 72
MERCURY 3-5 74-75

LPs: 10/12-inch 33rpm

MERCURY 8-10 74

PARACHUTE CLUB

D&D '83

Singles: 12-inch 33/45rpm

RCA 4-6 83

Singles: 7-inch

RCA 3-4 83

LPs: 10/12-inch 33rpm

RCA 5-8 83

PARADE

P&R '67

Singles: 7-inch

A&M 4-8 67-69
Members: Jerry Riopelle; Murray MacLeod; Smokey Roberds.
Also see RIOPELLE, Jerry

PARADISE EXPRESS

P&R '79

Singles: 12-inch 33/45rpm

FANTASY 4-8 78-81

Singles: 7-inch

FANTASY 3-5 78-81

LPs: 10/12-inch 33rpm

FANTASY 5-10 78

PARADONS

P&R/R&B '60

Singles: 7-inch

COLLECTABLES 3-4 80s
ERA 3-5 72
MILESTONE (2003 "Diamonds and Pearls") 15-20 60
(Maroon label.)
MILESTONE (2003 "Diamonds and Pearls") 10-15 60
(Red label.)
MILESTONE (2003 "Diamonds and Pearls") 5-10 60
(Green label.)
MILESTONE (2005 "Bells Ring") 15-20 60
MILESTONE (2015 "I Had a Dream") 25-35 62
TUFFEST (102 "Never Again") 75-125 61
W.B. (5186 "Take All of Me") 10-15 61
Members: Bill Myers; Chuck Weldon; Wes Tyler; Bill Powers.

PARAGONS

P&R '61

Singles: 7-inch

ABC 3-5 73
BUDDAH 3-5 75
COLLECTABLES 3-4 80s
MUSIC CLEF (3001 "Time After Time") 10-15 63
MUSICRAFT (1102 "Wedding Bells") 10-20 60
TAP (500 "If") 15-25 61
TAP (503 "Begin the Beguine").. 15-25 61
TAP (504 "If You Love Me") 15-25 61
TIMES SQUARE (9 "So You Will Know") 10-15 63
VIRGO 3-4 72-73
WINLEY (215 "Florence") 20-35 57
(With "Winley" in 3/16-inch letters.)
WINLEY (215 "Florence") 10-15 61
(With "Winley" in 1/4-inch letters.)
WINLEY (220 "Let's Start All Over Again") 20-35 57
(With "Winley" in 3/16-inch letters.)
WINLEY (220 "Let's Start All Over Again") 10-15 61
(With "Winley" in 1/4-inch letters.)
WINLEY (223 "Two Hearts Are Better Than One") 30-40 58
(With "Winley" in 3/16-inch letters.)
WINLEY (223 "Two Hearts Are Better Than One") 10-15 61
(With "Winley" in 1/4-inch letters.)
WINLEY (227 "Twilight" /"The Wows of Love") 75-100 58
(Note spelling error on "Vows.")
WINLEY (227 "Twilight" /"The Vows of Love") 20-35 58
(With "Winley" in 3/16-inch letters.)
WINLEY (227 "Twilight" /"The Vows of Love") 10-15 61
(With "Winley" in 1/4-inch letters.)
WINLEY (228 "So You Will Know") 25-35 59
(With "Winley" in 3/16-inch letters.)
WINLEY (228 "So You Will Know") 10-15 61
(With "Winley" in 1/4-inch letters.)
WINLEY (236 "Darling, I Love You") 25-35 59
WINLEY (240 "So You Will Know") 15-25 60
WINLEY (250 "Kneel and Pray") 15-25 61

LPs: 10/12-inch 33rpm

COLLECTABLES 6-8 86
LOST-NITE 5-10 81
RARE BIRD (8002 "Simply the Paragons") 35-45
Members: Julius McMichaels; Mack Starr; Al Brown; Don Travis; Ben Frazier; Bill Witt; Rick Jackson.
Also see HARPTONES / Paragons
Also see JESTERS / Paragons
Also see OLYMPICS

PARAMOR, Norrie, & His Orchestra

LP '56

Singles: 78rpm

ESSEX 3-6 53

Singles: 7-inch

ESSEX 5-10 53

EPs: 7-inch 33/45rpm

CAPITOL 8-15 56

LPs: 10/12-inch 33rpm

CAPITOL 10-25 55-66
ESSEX 10-20 54
HAYNES & BARRA 5-10 79

PARAMOURS

Singles: 7-inch

MOONGLOW (214 "There She Goes") 10-15 62
(Black vinyl.)
MOONGLOW (214 "There She Goes") 20-30 62
(Colored vinyl.)
SMASH (1701 "That's the Way We Love") 10-15 61
SMASH (1718 "Cutie Cutie") 10-15 61
Members: Bill Medley; Bobby Hatfield.
Also see RIGHTEOUS BROTHERS

PARIS

LP '76

Singles: 7-inch

CAPITOL 3-5 76

LPs: 10/12-inch 33rpm

CAPITOL 8-12 76
Members: Bob Welch; Glen Cornick; Bernie Marsden; Thom Mooney.
Also see WELCH, Bob

PARIS

LP '90

LPs: 10/12-inch 33rpm

TOMMY BOY 5-8 90

PARIS, Mica

P&R/LP '89

Singles: 7-inch

ISLAND 3-4 89

Picture Sleeves

ISLAND 3-4 89

LPs: 10/12-inch 33rpm

ISLAND 5-8 89

PARIS SISTERS

P&R '61

Singles: 78rpm

DECCA 5-10 54-58
IMPERIAL 5-10 57-58

Singles: 7-inch

ABC 3-5 73
CAPITOL 4-8 68
COLLECTABLES 3-4 80s
DECCA 5-10 54-58
ERIC 3-4 70s
GNP 4-8 68
GREGMARK 8-12 61-62
IMPERIAL 5-10 57-58
MGM 4-8 64
MERCURY 4-8 64-65
REPRISE 4-8 66-67

Picture Sleeves

MGM 10-20 64
MERCURY 8-10 64

LPs: 10/12-inch 33rpm

REPRISE (R-6259 "Everything Under the Sun") 15-20 67
(Monaural.)
REPRISE (RS-6259 "Everything Under the Sun") 20-25 67
(Stereo.)
SIDEWALK 12-18
UNIFILMS 10-15
Members: Priscilla Paris; Sherrell Paris; Albeth Paris. Session: Davie Allan.
Also see ALLAN, Davie

PARKAYS

P&R '61

Singles: 7-inch

ABC-PAR 5-10 61
FONTANA 4-8 65

PARKER, Bobby

P&R '61

Singles: 7-inch

AMANDA 5-10 60
V-TONE 4-8 61

PARKER, Fess
(With Buddy Ebsen)

P&R '55

Singles: 78rpm

COLUMBIA 4-6 55
DISNEYLAND 4-6 57

Singles: 7-inch

BUENA VISTA 4-8 63
CASCADE 5-10 59
COLUMBIA 8-12 55
DISNEYLAND 5-10 57
GUSTO 4-8 63
RCA 4-8 64-69

Picture Sleeves

BUENA VISTA 5-10 63
DISNEYLAND 10-20 57

RCA.. 4-8 64

EPs: 7-inch 33/45rpm

COLUMBIA (2031 "Indian Fighter") 20-25 55
COLUMBIA (2032 "Davy Crockett Goes to Congress") 20-25 55
COLUMBIA (2033 "At the Alamo") 20-25 55

LPs: 10/12-inch 33rpm

COLUMBIA (666 "Davy Crockett") 50-75 55
DISNEYLAND (1200 series)..... 10-20 64-65
DISNEYLAND (1300 series)....... 5-10 70
DISNEYLAND (1900 series)..... 10-20 63
DISNEYLAND (3007 "Yarns and Songs") 25-35 55
DISNEYLAND (3900 series)..... 10-20 64
HARMONY.............................. 10-20 60
RCA.. 10-20 64

PARKER, Graham

(With Rumour; with Shot)

P&R/LP '77

Singles: 7-inch

ARISTA 3-5 79-83
ELEKTRA....................................... 3-4 85
MERCURY 3-5 76-77

Picture Sleeves

ARISTA 3-5 80-83
ELEKTRA....................................... 3-4 85
MERCURY 3-5 77

EPs: 7-inch 33/45rpm

MERCURY (74000 "Hold Back the Night") 5-8 77
(Colored vinyl.)

LPs: 10/12-inch 33rpm

ARISTA 5-10 78-83
ELEKTRA..................................... 5-8 85
MERCURY 5-10 77-78
RCA.. 5-8 88-89

Promotional LPs

ARISTA (41 "Mercury Poisoning")............................ 25-35 78
ARISTA (63 "Live Sparks") 25-35 79
Also see RUMOUR
Also see SPRINGSTEEN, Bruce

PARKER, Junior: see PARKER, Little Junior

PARKER, Little Junior

(Junior Parker; with His Blue Flames; with Blue Blowers)

R&B '57

Singles: 78rpm

DUKE 10-15 54-58
MODERN (864 "Bad Women, Bad Whiskey")....................... 20-40 52

Singles: 7-inch

ABC 3-5 73
BLUE ROCK 4-6 68-69
CAPITOL.......................................3-5 71
DUKE (137 "Backtrackin'").........25-35 55
DUKE (300 series)......................5-10 59-66
DUKE (400 series).........................4-8 67
MCA...3-4
MERCURY......................................4-8 66-68
MINIT 4-8 69

LPs: 10/12-inch 33rpm

ABC..8-10 76
BLUE ROCK 10-15 69
BLUESWAY 8-12 73
CAPITOL......................................10-15 70
DUKE (76 "Driving Wheel")......60-100 62
(Cover pictures a Cadillac.)
DUKE (76 "Driving Wheel")........35-55 62
(Cover pictures a Wagon Wheel.)
DUKE (83 "Best of Junior Parker")..8-10 74
MCA...5-8
MERCURY...................................12-20 67
MINIT 10-15 69
Also see BLAND, Bobby / Little Junior Parker
Also see LITTLE JUNIOR'S BLUE FLAMES

PARKER, Little Junior, With Bill Johnson's Blue Flames

Singles: 78rpm

DUKE 10-20 54

Singles: 7-inch

DUKE (120 "Dirty Friend Blues") 30-50 54
DUKE (127 "Please Baby Blues") 30-50 54

PARKER, Little Junior, & Jimmy McGriff

LPs: 10/12-inch 33rpm

CAPITOL.....................................10-15 71
U.A. 10-15 71
Also see McGRIFF, Jimmy
Also see PARKER, Little Junior

PARKER, Paul

D&D '83

Singles: 12-inch 33/45rpm

MEGATONE 4-6 83

PARKER, Ray, Jr.

(With Raydio; with Helen Terry)

P&R/LP '80

Singles: 12-inch 33/45rpm

ARISTA...4-6 84-85

Singles: 7-inch

ARISTA (Except 1035)..................3-5 80-85
ARISTA (1035 "Christmas Time Is Here")..3-5 82
(Promotional issue only.)
ATLANTIC.......................................3-4 86
FLASHBACK...................................3-4 82
GEFFEN 3-4 87

Picture Sleeves

ARISTA (Except 1035)..................3-4 80-85

ARISTA (1035 "Christmas Time Is Here") 3-5 82
(Promotional issue only.)
ATLANTIC 3-4 86
GEFFEN 3-4 87

LPs: 10/12-inch 33rpm

ARISTA 5-8 80-85
GEFFEN 5-8 87

Members: J.D. Nicholas; Arnell Carmichael; Jack Ashford; Ollie Brown.
Also see MEDEIROS, Glenn
Also see RAYDIO

PARKER, Ray, Jr., & Natalie Cole

R&B '87

Singles: 7-inch

GEFFEN 3-4 87

Also see COLE, Natalie
Also see PARKER, Ray, Jr.

PARKER, Robert

P&R/R&B '66

Singles: 7-inch

HEAD 3-5 72
IMPERIAL 4-8 62
ISLAND 3-5 75-76
NOLA 4-8 66-67
RON 5-10 59-60
SILVER FOX 4-6 69

LPs: 10/12-inch 33rpm

NOLA (1001 "Barefootin'") 20-30 66
(Monaural.)
NOLA (S-1001 "Barefootin'") 30-40 66
(Stereo.)

Also see BO, Eddie

PARKER, Winfield

R&B '71

Singles: 7-inch

ARCTIC 4-6 69
GSP 3-5 72
RU-JAC (24 "Fallen Star") 4-6 68
SPRING 3-5 71

PARKING METER

D&D '84

Singles: 12-inch 33/45rpm

ATLANTIC 4-6 84

Singles: 7-inch

ATLANTIC 3-5 84

PARKS, Michael

LP '69

Singles: 7-inch

MGM 3-5 70

LPs: 10/12-inch 33rpm

MGM 10-15 69-70
VERVE 8-12 71

PARLET

R&B '78

Singles: 7-inch

CASABLANCA 3-5 78-80

LPs: 10/12-inch 33rpm

CASABLANCA 5-10 79

PARLET & Jeanette Washington

R&B '80

Singles: 7-inch

CASABLANCA 3-5 80

Also see WASHINGTON, Baby

PARLIAMENT
(Parliament Thang)

R&B '71

Singles: 12-inch 33/45rpm

CASABLANCA 4-6 78

Singles: 7-inch

CASABLANCA 3-5 74-81
INVICTUS 3-5 70-71
SOULTOWN 3-5

Picture Sleeves

CASABLANCA 3-5 79

LPs: 10/12-inch 33rpm

CASABLANCA (Except NBPIX-7125) 5-10 74-80
CASABLANCA (NBPIX-7125 "Motor Booty Affair") 10-15 79
(Picture disc.)
INVICTUS 8-12 70

Also see BOOTSY'S RUBBER BAND
Also see BRIDES of FUNKENSTEIN
Also see MACEO & MACKS
Also see PARLIAMENTS
Also see WORRELL, Bernie

PARLIAMENTS

P&R/R&B '67

Singles: 7-inch

ATCO (6675 "A New Day Begins") 8-12 69
GOLDEN WORLD (46 "Heart Trouble") 25-50 67
REVILOT 10-20 67-68

Also see CLINTON, George, Band
Also see FUNKADELIC
Also see PARLIAMENT

PARR, John

P&R/LP '84

Singles: 12-inch 33/45rpm

ATLANTIC 4-6 86

Singles: 7-inch

ATLANTIC 3-4 84-86

Picture Sleeves

ATLANTIC 3-4 85-86

LPs: 10/12-inch 33rpm

ATLANTIC 5-8 84-86

PARRIS, Fred
(With the Satins; with Scarlets; with Black Satin; with Restless Hearts; Fred Paris)

P&R '82

Singles: 7-inch

ATCO 5-10 66
BIRTH 4-8
BUDDAH 3-5 75

CANDLELITE 5-10 63
CHECKER 5-10 65
ELEKTRA (47411 "Memories of Days Gone By") 4-8 82
GREEN SEA 5-10 66
KLIK (7905 "She's Gone") 60-80 58
MAMA SADIE (1001 "In the Still of the Night") 5-10 67
RCA (9232 "It's Okay to Cry") 5-10 67
(A Freddie Paris also recorded for RCA at this time. Note slightly different spelling.)

LPs: 10/12-inch 33rpm

BUDDAH 30-50 75
ELEKTRA 10-15 82
Also see FIVE SATINS

PARRISH, Dean
(Dean Parish)

P&R '66

Singles: 7-inch

BOOM 10-20 66
LAURIE 5-10 67
MUSICOR 5-10 65

PARRISH, Man

R&B '83

Singles: 7-inch

IMPORTE 3-4 83
SUGAR SCOOP 3-4 85

LPs: 10/12-inch 33rpm

IMPORTE 5-8 83

PARSONS, Alan, Project
(Alan Parsons)

P&R/LP '76

Singles: 7-inch

ARISTA 3-5 77-89
20TH FOX 3-5 76

Picture Sleeves

ARISTA 3-5 84-85

LPs: 10/12-inch 33rpm

ARISTA (111 "No Gambler") 15-20 80
ARISTA (140 "Complete Audio Guide") 75-100 82
(Eight-LP boxed set.)
ARISTA (4000 series) 5-10 78
ARISTA (7002 I Robot") 5-10 77
ARISTA (8000 series, except 8263) 5-8 83-89
ARISTA (8263 "Vulture Culture") .. 5-8 85
ARISTA (PD-8263 "Vulture Culture") 20-25 85
(Picture disc. Promotional issue only.)
ARISTA (9000 series) 5-10 79-82
20TH FOX (508 "Tales of Mystery and Imagination") 15-25 76
(Includes eight-page booklet.)
20TH FOX (508 "Tales of Mystery and Imagination") 8-12 76
20TH FOX (539 "Tales of Mystery and Imagination") 5-10 77
MFSL (084 "I Robot") 25-50 82
MFSL/UHQR (084 "I Robot") ... 75-100 82
(Boxed set.)
MFSL (175 "Best of the Alan Parsons Project) 15-25 85

Members: Alan Parsons; David Paton; Stuart Tosh; Eric Woolfson; Lenny Zakatek; Ian Bairnson; B.J. Cole; Stuart Elliott; Colin Blunstone; Allan Clarke; Andrew Powell; John Miles; Gary Brooker; Christopher Rainbow; Duncan Mackay; Richard Cottle; Laurie Cottle; Geoff Barradale.

Also see AMBROSIA
Also see BROWN, Arthur
Also see CLARKE, Alan
Also see HOLLIES
Also see MILES, John
Also see PACK, David
Also see PILOT
Also see POWELL, Andrew
Also see VITAMIN Z

PARSONS, Bill
(Bobby Bare)

P&R '58

Singles: 7-inch

ABC 3-5 73
COLLECTABLES 3-4 80s
FRATERNITY (835 "The All American Boy") 10-15 58
Also see BARE, Bobby

PARSONS, Gram
(With the Fallen Angels)

LP '74

Singles: 7-inch

REPRISE 3-5 73
SIERRA 3-5 79

EPs: 7-inch 33/45rpm

SIERRA 8-10 82
(Promotional issue only.)

LPs: 10/12-inch 33rpm

REPRISE 8-12 73
SHILOH 10-15 73
SIERRA 5-10 79-82
Also see BYRDS
Also see FLYING BURRITO BROTHERS
Also see HARRIS, Emmylou

PARTLAND BROTHERS

P&R/LP '87

Singles: 7-inch

MANHATTAN 3-4 87

Picture Sleeves

MANHATTAN 3-4 87

LPs: 10/12-inch 33rpm

MANHATTAN 5-8 87

PARTNERS in KRYME

P&R '90

Singles: 7-inch

SBK 3-4 90

PARTON, Dolly

C&W '67

Singles: 12–inch 33/45rpm

RCA (Black vinyl) 4-8 78-83
RCA (Colored vinyl) 8-12 78

Singles: 7–inch

GOLDBAND (1086 "Puppy Love") 20-40 59
MERCURY (71982 "It's Sure Gonna Hurt") 15-25 62
MONUMENT (800 thru 1000 series) 5-10 65-68
RCA (0132 thru 0950) 3-6 69-76
RCA (5000 series) 3-4 86
RCA (9500 thru 9900 series) 4-6 68-71
RCA (10000 thru 14000 series) 3-5 74-87
RCA GOLD STANDARD 3-4 80

Promotional Singles

RCA (Colored vinyl) 4-8 77-85

Picture Sleeves

RCA 3-8 69-85

LPs: 10/12–inch 33rpm

ALSHIRE 8-12 69-71
CAMDEN 5-10 72-78
COLUMBIA 5-8 87
MONUMENT (7600 series) 5-10 78
MONUMENT (8085 "Hello, I'm Dolly") 15-20 67
MONUMENT (18000 series) 12-20 67
MONUMENT (18100 series) 8-15 70
MONUMENT (31000 series) 8-15 72
MONUMENT (33000 series) 8-10 75
RCA (0033 thru 5000 series) 5-12 73-87
(With "AFL1," "AHL1," "APD1," "APL1," or "AYL1" prefix.)
RCA (CPL1-3413 "Great Balls of Fire") 15-20 79
(Picture disc.)
RCA (3900 thru 4700 series) 8-15 68-72
(With "LPM" or "LSP" prefix.)
RCA (4422 "Greatest Hits") 25-50 82
(Without *Islands in the Stream*)
RCA (4422 "Greatest Hits") 5-8 82
(With *Islands in the Stream*.)
RCA (5000 series) 5-8 84
SOMERSET 10-20 63-68
STEREO-FIDELITY 10-20 63-68
TIME-LIFE 5-8 81

Session: Jordanaires.
Also see HARRIS, Emmylou
Also see ROGERS, Kenny, & Dolly Parton
Also see WAGONER, Porter, & Dolly Parton

PARTON, Dolly / George Jones

LPs: 10/12–inch 33rpm

STARDAY (429 "Dolly Parton and George Jones") 30-40 68
Also see JONES, George

PARTON, Dolly, & Ricky Van Shelton

C&W '91

Singles: 7–inch

COLUMBIA 3-4 91
Also see VAN SHELTON, Ricky

PARTON, Dolly, & Willie Nelson

C&W '82

Singles: 7–inch

MONUMENT 3-4 82
Also see NELSON, Willie

PARTON, Dolly, Linda Ronstadt, & Emmylou Harris

LP '87

LPs: 10/12–inch 33rpm

W.B. 5-8 87
Also see HARRIS, Emmylou
Also see RONSTADT, Linda

PARTON, Dolly, & Ricky Van Shelton

C&W '91

Singles: 7–inch

RCA 3-4 91
Also see SHELTON, Ricky Van

PARTON, Dolly / Kitty Wells

LPs: 10/12–inch 33rpm

EXACT 5-8 80
Also see PARTON, Dolly
Also see WELLS, Kitty

PARTRIDGE FAMILY
(Starring Shirley Jones, Featuring David Cassidy)

P&R/LP '70

Singles: 7–inch

BELL 3-5 70-73

Picture Sleeves

BELL 3-5 70-71

LPs: 10/12–inch 33rpm

BELL 8-12 70-74
Also see CASSIDY, David

PARTY

LP '90

LPs: 10/12–inch 33rpm

HOLLYWOOD 5-8 90

PASADENAS

LP '89

Singles: 7–inch

COLUMBIA 3-4 89

LPs: 10/12–inch 33rpm

COLUMBIA 5-8 89

PASSIONS

P&R '59

Singles: 7–inch

ABC-PAR 8-10 63
AUDICON 10-20 59-61
COLLECTABLES 3-4 80s
CRYSTAL BALL 3-5 90
DIAMOND (146 "16 Candles") 15-25 63
DORE 10-15 58

JUBILEE....................................... 8-12 61
LAURIE 3-5 70s
OCTAVIA (8005 "Aphrodite") 100-200 62

LPs: 10/12-inch 33rpm

CLIFTON....................................... 5-8

Members: Jim Gallagher; Tony Armato; Al Galione; Vince Acerno; Louis Rotondo.
Also see MYSTICS / Passions

PASSPORT

LP '75

Singles: 7-inch

ATCO 3-5 76
ATLANTIC...................................... 3-5 78

LPs: 10/12-inch 33rpm

ATCO 8-12 74-77
ATLANTIC...................................... 5-10 78-82
REPRISE 8-12 72

PASTEL SIX

P&R '62

Singles: 7-inch

CHATTAHOOCHEE.................. 5-10 65
DOWNEY 10-20 62-63
ERA.. 3-5 72
ZEN.. 10-20 62
ZENITH 10-20 63

LPs: 10/12-inch 33rpm

ZEN (1001 "Cinnamon Cinder")............................ 50-100 62

Member: Sonny Patterson.

PASTELS

P&R/R&B '58

Singles: 7-inch

ARGO (5287 "Been So Long").. 10-20 58
ARGO (5297 "You Don't Love Me Anymore") 15-25 58
ARGO (5314 "So Far Away").... 10-20 58
CADET 3-5 70s
CHESS... 3-5 73
MASCOT (123 "Been So Long")................................ 150-200 57

Members: Big Dee Irwin; Richard Travis; Tony Thomas; J.B. Wellington.
Also see IRWIN, Big Dee

PASTORIUS, Jaco

LP '81

LPs: 10/12-inch 33rpm

W.B. 5-8 81-83

Also see WEATHER REPORT

PAT & SATELLITES

P&R '59

Singles: 7-inch

ATCO 8-12 59

Members: Pat Otts; King Curtis; Wayne Lips.
Also see KING CURTIS

PATE, Johnny
(Johnny Pate Trio)

P&R/R&B '58

Singles: 78rpm

FEDERAL...................................... 4-8 57
GIG 4-8 56

Singles: 7-inch

ARGO 4-6 64
FEDERAL 5-10 57-59
GIG 10-15 56

LPs: 10/12-inch 33rpm

GIG 40-50 56
KING (561 "Jazz Goes Ivy League") 30-50 58
(Monaural.)
KING (KSD-561 "Jazz Goes Ivy League")...........................50-75 59
(Stereo.)
KING (584 "Swingin' Flute").......30-50 58
KING (611 "A Date with Johnny Pate")..30-50 58
SALEM...25-35 58
STEPHENY (4002 "Johnny Pate at the Blue Note")......................................45-55 57

PATIENCE

R&B '80

Singles: 7-inch

COLUMBIA 3-5 80

PATIENCE & PRUDENCE

P&R '56

Singles: 78rpm

LIBERTY 5-10 56

Singles: 7-inch

CHATTAHOOCHEE 4-8 64-65
LIBERTY 8-12 56-57
U.A. 3-5 70s

Picture Sleeves

LIBERTY (55084 "You Tattletale")..............................20-30 57

Also see CLIFFORD, Mike, with Patience & Prudence

PATRICK, Keith

R&B '86

Singles: 7-inch

OMNI...3-4 86

PATRIS

D&D '85

Singles: 12-inch 33/45rpm

EMERGENCY...............................4-6 85

PATTERSON, Bobby
(With the Mustangs)

R&B '69

Singles: 7-inch

ABNAK...4-8 65-66
ALL PLATINUM 3-5 77
GRANITE......................................3-5 76
JETSTAR 4-8 66-69
(Black vinyl.)
JETSTAR (111 "Funky No More") 8-12 68
(Colored vinyl. Promotional issue only.)
PAULA 3-5 72-73

PATTERSON, Kellee

P&R/R&B '77

Singles: 7-inch

SHADYBROOK 3-5 75-77

LPs: 10/12-inch 33rpm

SHADYBROOK 5-10 76-79

Shadybrook may also be shown as Shady Brook (two words).

PATTI & EMBLEMS: see PATTY & EMBLEMS

PATTON, Robbie

P&R/LP '81

Singles: 7-inch

ATLANTIC 3-4 83-85
BACKSTREET 3-5 79
LIBERTY 3-5 81

LPs: 10/12-inch 33rpm

ATLANTIC 5-8 85
LIBERTY 5-10 81

PATTY & EMBLEMS
(Patti & Emblems)

P&R/R&B '64

Singles: 7-inch

COLLECTABLES 3-4 80s
CONGRESS 10-20 66
HERALD 10-20 64
KAPP 10-20 66-68
SPHERE SOUND 10-20 64

PAUL, Billy

LP '70

Singles: 12-inch 33/45rpm

PHILADELPHIA INT'L 4-8 79

Singles: 7-inch

FINCH 8-12 60
JUBILEE (5081 "That's Why I Dream") 10-20 52
JUBILEE (5086 "You Didn't Know") 10-20 52
NEPTUNE 3-6 70
PHILADELPHIA INT'L 3-5 71-81

LPs: 10/12-inch 33rpm

GAMBLE 10-20 67
NEPTUNE 10-15 70
PHILADELPHIA INT'L 5-10 71-80

Also see PHILADELPHIA INTERNATIONAL ALL STARS

PAUL, Bunny

P&R '53

Singles: 78rpm

BRUNSWICK 5-10 57
DOT 5-10 53
GORDY 12-15 63
POINT 10-20 56

Singles: 7-inch

BRUNSWICK 8-12 57
DOT 8-12 53
GORDY 10-15 63
POINT (5 "Sweet Talk") 20-30 56
ROULETTE 5-10 59

PAUL, Bunny, & Harptones
(Bunny Paul)

Singles: 78rpm

ESSEX 10-20 54

Singles: 7-inch

ESSEX (352 "Such a Night") 25-50 54
ESSEX (352 "Lovey Dovey") 25-50 54
ESSEX (364 "I'll Never Tell") 50-75 54

Also see HALEY, Bill
Also see HARPTONES
Also see PAUL, Bunny

PAUL, Henry, Band

LP '79

Singles: 7-inch

ATLANTIC 3-5 79-81

LPs: 10/12-inch 33rpm

ATLANTIC 5-10 79-81

Also see OUTLAWS

PAUL, Les
(Les Paul Trio)

P&R '48

Singles: 78rpm

CAPITOL 4-8 50-53
DECCA 4-8 54

Singles: 7-inch

CAPITOL 5-10 50-53
DECCA 5-10 54

EPs: 7-inch 33/45rpm

DECCA 10-20 50-53

LPs: 10/12-inch 33rpm

CAPITOL (200 series) 5-10 77
CAPITOL (16000 series) 5-8
DECCA (5018 "Hawaiian Paradise") 50-100 49
(10-inch LP.)
DECCA (5376 "Galloping Guitars") 50-75 52
(10-inch LP.)
DECCA (8589 "More of Les") 30-50 57
GLENDALE 5-8 78
LONDON 6-12 68-79
VOCALION 6-12 68

Also see ANDREWS SISTERS
Also see ATKINS, Chet, & Les Paul

PAUL, Les, & Mary Ford

P&R '50

Singles: 78rpm

CAPITOL 4-8 50-57

Singles: 7-inch

CAPITOL 5-10 50-57
COLUMBIA 4-8 58-64

Picture Sleeves

COLUMBIA 4-8 58-64

EPs: 7-inch 33/45rpm

CAPITOL 10-20 50-57

LPs: 10/12-inch 33rpm

CAPITOL (SM-200 series) 5-8 78

CAPITOL (H-226 thru H-577).... 25-50 50-55
(10–inch LPs.)
CAPITOL (T-226 thru T-802) 20-40 55-57
CAPITOL (T-1400 & T-1500 series) 15-25 60-61
(Monaural.)
CAPITOL (ST-1400 & ST-1500 series) 20-30 60-61
(Stereo.)
CAPITOL (11000 series)............ 5-10 74
COLUMBIA 10-20 61-63
HARMONY................................. 8-12 61-65
Also see PAUL, Les

PAUL, Pope: see POPE PAUL

PAUL & PAULA

P&R/R&B '62

Singles: 7–inch

LE CAM (300 series)..................... 3-5 74-82
LE CAM (99 "Beginning of Love")........ 8-12 63
PHILIPS (40000 series) 4-8 62-66
PHILIPS (44000 series) 3-5 70s
UNI 4-8 68
U.A. 3-5 70

Picture Sleeves

PHILIPS 8-12 63-64

LPs: 10/12–inch 33rpm

PHILIPS (200078 "For Young Lovers")........ 25-40 63
(Monaural.)
PHILIPS (200089 "We Go Together") 25-40 63
(Monaural.)
PHILIPS (200101 "Holiday for Teens") 25-40 63
(Monaural.)
PHILIPS (600078 "For Young Lovers")........ 25-50 63
(Stereo.)
PHILIPS (600089 "We Go Together") 25-50 63
(Stereo.)
PHILIPS (600101 "Holiday for Teens") 25-50 63
(Stereo.)
Members: Ray Hildebrand; Jill Jackson.
Also see CHANNEL, Bruce / Paul & Paula
Also see JACKSON, Jill
Also see JILL & RAY

PAULETTE SISTERS

P&R '55

Singles: 78rpm

CAPITOL...................................... 4-8 55

Singles: 7–inch

CAPITOL.................................... 5-10 55
CONTEMPO 4-8 63
DECCA....................................... 4-6 60s
RIBBON 4-8 60
20TH FOX.................................... 4-8 61

PAULSEN, Pat

LP '68

Singles: 7–inch

MERCURY (105 "Open End Interview")........ 5-10 68
(Promotional issue only.)

LPs: 10/12–inch 33rpm

MERCURY.................................8-15 68-70

PAUPERS

LP '67

Singles: 7–inch

VERVE/FOLKWAYS...................5-10 66-67
VERVE/FORECAST 4-8 67-68

Picture Sleeves

VERVE.......................................5-10 67

LPs: 10/12–inch 33rpm

VERVE/FORECAST 10-20 67-68

PAVLOV'S DOG

LP '75

Singles: 7–inch

COLUMBIA 3-5 76

LPs: 10/12–inch 33rpm

ABC...10-15 75
COLUMBIA 8-12 75-76
Members: David Surkamp; Mike Abebe; Murray Krugman; Sandy Pearlman; Mike Safron; Richard Stockton; David Hamilton; Doug Rayburn; Steve Scorfina; Bill Bruford.
Also see YES

PAVONE, Rita

P&R/LP '64

Singles: 7–inch

RCA 4-8 63-66

Picture Sleeves

RCA 4-8 64-65

LPs: 10/12–inch 33rpm

RCA 10-20 64-67

PAVAROTTI, Luciano

LP '79

Singles: 7–inch

LONDON.......................................3-4 79-84

LPs: 10/12–inch 33rpm

LONDON.......................................5-8 76-84

PAXTON, Tom

LP '69

Singles: 7–inch

ASYLUM 3-5 70
ELEKTRA.......................................4-8 69
REPRISE 3-5 71

LPs: 10/12–inch 33rpm

ANCHOR 8-12
ELEKTRA....................................10-15 64-71
FLYING FISH 5-8
PRIVATE STOCK 8-10 75
REPRISE 10-15 71-73

PAYCHECK, Johnny
(With Charnissa)

C&W '65

Singles: 7-inch

ABC 3-5 74
AMI 3-5 84-85
CUTLASS 3-5 72
DAMASCUS 3-4 89
DESPERADO 3-4 88
EPIC 3-5 71-82
HILLTOP 8-15 64-66
LITTLE DARLIN' (008 thru 0072) 5-10 66-69
LITTLE DARLIN' (7000 series) 3-5 78-79
MERCURY 3-5 86-87

LPs: 10/12-inch 33rpm

ACCORD 5-10 82
ALLEGIANCE 5-10 83
CENTRON 8-15 70
EPIC 5-10 71-83
EXCELSIOR 5-8 80
GUSTO 5-10 83
IMPERIAL 5-10 80
LITTLE DARLIN' (0500 thru 0700 series) 5-10 79-80
LITTLE DARLIN' (4000 series) . 10-20 66-67
(Monaural.)
LITTLE DARLIN' (8000 series) . 10-20 66-69
(Stereo.)
LITTLE DARLIN' (10000 series) . 8-12 79
MERCURY 5-8 86
PICKWICK/HILLTOP 5-10 72

Session: Jordanaires.
Also see HAGGARD, Merle, & Johnny Paycheck
Also see JENNINGS, Waylon / Johnny Paycheck
Also see JONES, George, & Johnny Paycheck
Also see MILLER, Jody, & Johnny Paycheck
Also see YOUNG, Donny

PAYCHECK & HAGGARD

C&W '81

Singles: 7-inch

EPIC 3-4 81

Members: Johnny Paycheck; Merle Haggard.
Also see HAGGARD, Merle
Also see PAYCHECK, Johnny

PAYNE, Cecil, Orchestra

R&B '50

Singles: 78rpm

DECCA 4-8 50

PAYNE, Freda

R&B '69

Singles: 12-inch 33/45rpm

CAPITOL 4-8 79

Singles: 7-inch

ABC 3-5 75
ABC-PAR 5-10 62-63
CAPITOL 3-5 77-78
DUNHILL 3-5 74
IMPULSE 5-10 63
INVICTUS 3-8 69-73
MGM 10-20 66
SUTRA 3-5 82

Picture Sleeves

CAPITOL 3-5 77-78
INVICTUS 4-8 71-73

LPs: 10/12-inch 33rpm

ABC 8-10 75
CAPITOL 5-10 78-79
DUNHILL 8-10 74
IMPULSE 15-25 64
INVICTUS 10-15 70-72
MGM 10-20 66-70
U.S.A. 10-15 71

PAYNE, Scherrie
(With Phillip Ingram)

D&D '84

Singles: 12-inch 33/45rpm

MEGATONE 4-6 84

Singles: 7-inch

ALTAIR 3-5
INVICTUS 3-5 72
MOTOWN 3-5 80
SUPERSTAR INT'L 3-5

Also see DECO
Also see GLASS HOUSE
Also see SCHERRIE & SUSAYE
Also see SUPREMES

PAYTON, Lawrence

R&B '74

Singles: 7-inch

DUNHILL 3-5 73-74

Also see FOUR TOPS

PEACHES & HERB

P&R/R&B '66

Singles: 7-inch

COLUMBIA 3-5 71-74
DATE 4-6 66-70
MCA 3-5 77
MERCURY 3-5 73

Picture Sleeves

DATE 4-8 67-68

LPs: 10/12-inch 33rpm

DATE 10-20 67-68
EPIC 8-10 79
MCA 8-10 77

Members: Francine Barker; Herb Fame.

PEACHES & HERB

LP '78

Singles: 12-inch 33/45rpm

POLYDOR 4-8 78-79

Singles: 7-inch

COLUMBIA 3-5 83
POLYDOR 3-5 78-83

LPs: 10/12-inch 33rpm

POLYDOR 5-10 78-81

Members: Linda Green; Herb Fame.

PEANUT BUTTER CONSPIRACY

P&LPR'67

Singles: 7-inch

CHALLENGE 5-8 69
COLUMBIA 8-10 67
VAULT.................................... 10-15 66

LPs: 10/12-inch 33rpm

CHALLENGE (200 "For Children of All Ages") 20-25 69
COLUMBIA (2654 "Peanut Butter Conspiracy Is Spreading") 20-25 67
(Monaural.)
COLUMBIA (2790 "The Great Conspiracy")......................... 20-30 68
(Monaural.)
COLUMBIA (9454 "Peanut Butter Conspiracy Is Spreading") 25-30 68
(Stereo.)
COLUMBIA (9590 "The Great Conspiracy")......................... 20-25 68
(Stereo.)
COLUMBIA (38000 series) 8-10 82

Members: Sandi Robison; Alan Brackett; Lance Fent; Bill Wolf; Jim Voight; John Merrill.

PEANUT BUTTER CONSPIRACY / Ashes / Chambers Brothers

LPs: 10/12-inch 33rpm

VAULT (113 "West Coast Love-In")................................ 30-50 68

Also see CHAMBERS BROTHERS

PEARL, Leslie

P&R '82

Singles: 7-inch

RCA.. 3-5 82

PEARL HARBOR
(With the Explosions)

LP '80

Singles: 7-inch

W.B. 3-5 80-81

LPs: 10/12-inch 33rpm

W.B. 5-10 80-81

PEARL JAM

LP: 10/12-inch 33rpm

EPIC.. 5-10 95

Members: Eddie Vedder; Mike McCready; Jeff Ament; Stone Gossard; Dave Krusen.

PEARLETTES

P&R '62

Singles: 7-inch

CRAIG..................................... 8-12 61
VEE JAY 8-10 61-62

PEARLS BEFORE SWINE

LP '69

Singles: 7-inch

ESP (4554 "Morning Song")...... 20-30 67
ESP (4576 "I Saw the World")... 20-30 68
REPRISE (0873 "These Things Too") 5-10 69
W.B./REPRISE (0949 "Rocket Man") 4-8 70

LPs: 10/12-inch 33rpm

ADELPHI.................................. 8-12 80
ESP (1054 "One Nation Underground") 30-50 67
ESP (1075 "Balaklava") 20-40 68
W.B./REPRISE 10-20 69-71

Members: Tom Rapp; Richard Alderson; Bob Elizabeth; Warren Smith; Charlie McCoy; Lane Lender; Wayne Harley.

Also see RAPP, Tom

PEARSON, Duke

LP '69

Singles: 7-inch

BLUE NOTE................................ 4-8 60-66

LPs: 10/12-inch 33rpm

ATLANTIC................................ 10-20 66
BLUE NOTE.............................. 25-40 59-61
(Label gives New York street address for Blue Note Records.)
BLUE NOTE.............................. 20-30 63-64
(Label reads "Blue Note Records Inc. - New York, USA.")
BLUE NOTE.............................. 10-20 66-74
(Label shows Blue Note Records as a division of either Liberty or United Artists.)
PRESTIGE 10-15 70

PEARSON, Mr. Danny

R&B '78

Singles: 7-inch

UNLIMITED GOLD 3-5 78

LPs: 10/12-inch 33rpm

UNLIMITED GOLD 5-10 79

PEASTON, David

LP '89

LPs: 10/12-inch 33rpm

GEFFEN 5-8 89

PEBBLES

R&B '87

Singles: 7-inch

MCA.. 3-4 87-90

Picture Sleeves

MCA.. 3-4 87-88

LPs: 10/12-inch 33rpm

MCA.. 5-8 87-90

PEDESTRIANS / Association / Five Americans / Soulblenders

EPs: 7-inch 33/45rpm

WLAV (6873 "Think Twice")....... 10-20 60s
(Promotional issue only.)

Also see ASSOCIATION
Also see FIVE AMERICANS
Also see PEDESTRIANS
Also see SOULBLENDERS

PEDICIN, Mike
(Michael Pedicin, Jr; Mike Pedicin Quintet)

P&R '56

Singles: 78rpm

CAMEO 5-10 57
MALVERN 10-20 57
RCA 5-10 56

Singles: 12-inch 33/45rpm

PHILADELPHIA INT'L 4-8 79-82

Singles: 7-inch

ABC-PAR 5-10 62
APOLLO (534 "Hey Pop, Give Me the Keys") 25-35 59
CAMEO 10-15 57
FEDERAL 8-12 61
MALVERN (100 "Dickie-Doo") .. 10-20 57
PHILADELPHIA INT'L 3-5 79-82
RCA 5-10 56
20TH FOX 4-8 60s

EPs: 7-inch 33/45rpm

RCA 15-25 56
("General Electric Flash Blub Limited Edition.")

LPs: 10/12-inch 33rpm

APOLLO (484 "Musical Medicine") 50-75 59
PHILADELPHIA INT'L 5-10 79

PEDRICK, Bobby
(Bobby Pedrick Jr.)

P&R '58

Singles: 7-inch

BIG TOP 8-12 58-60
DUEL 5-10 62-63
MGM 4-8 65
SHELL 15-20 60
VERVE (10402 "Maybe") 40-50 66

Also see JOHN, Robert

PEEBLES, Ann

R&B '69

Singles: 7-inch

HI 3-6 69-78
MOTOWN 3-4 82

LPs: 10/12-inch 33rpm

HI 8-12 69-75
MOTOWN 5-8 82

PEECH BOYS

R&B '82

Singles: 7-inch

WEST END 3-4 82

Also see NEW YORK CITI PEECH BOYS

PEEK, Dan

P&R '79

Singles: 7-inch

LAMB & LION 4-6 79
SONGBIRD 3-5 79

LPs: 10/12-inch 33rpm

LAMB & LION 6-12 79
SONGBIRD 5-10 79

Also see AMERICA

PEEK, Paul

P&R '61

Singles: 7-inch

COLUMBIA 4-8 66
FAIRLANE 10-15 61
MERCURY 4-8 62-63
NRC 10-20 58-60
1-2-3 .... 4-6 69

PEEL, David, & Lower East Side

LP '69

Singles: 7-inch

APPLE (6498 "F Is Not a Dirty Word") 50-100 72
(Promotional issue only.)
APPLE (6545 "Hippie from New York City") 50-100 72
(Promotional issue only.)
ORANGE 4-6 77
ORANGE PEEL (70078PD "Interview") 10-15 80

LPs: 10/12-inch 33rpm

APPLE (3391 "The Pope Smokes Dope") 40-60 72
ELEKTRA (74032 "Have a Marijuana") 15-25 68
ELEKTRA (74069 "American Revolution") 15-25 70
ORANGE 8-12 77

PEEL, David, & Lower East Side / John Lennon & Yoko Ono

Singles: 7-inch

ORANGE (8374 "Amerika") 3-5 90
(Promotional bonus with book purchase.)
ORANGE (789001 "Ballad of New York City") 3-5 87

Picture Sleeves

ORANGE (8374 "Amerika") 3-5 90
(Promotional bonus with book purchase.)

Also see LENNON, John
Also see PEEL, David, & Lower East Side

PEELS

P&R '66

Singles: 7-inch

KARATE 4-8 66

LPs: 10/12-inch 33rpm

KARATE (5402 "Juanita Banana") 55-65 66
(Monaural.)
KARATE (5402 "Juanita Banana") 65-75 66
(Stereo.)

PEEPLES

P&R '88

Singles: 7-inch

MERCURY 3-4 88

Picture Sleeves

MERCURY 3-4 88

PEEPLES, Nia

R&B/LP '88

Singles: 7–inch

MERCURY 3-4 88

LPs: 10/12–inch 33rpm

MERCURY 5-8 88

PEERCE, Jan

P&R '48

Singles: 78rpm

RCA.. 3-6 48-51

Singles: 7–inch

BLUEBIRD 4-6 60

RCA.. 5-10 51

U.A. 4-6 63

EPs: 7–inch 33/45rpm

RCA.. 5-10 51

LPs: 10/12–inch 33rpm

RCA (Except 2900 series)......... 10-20 51

RCA (2900 series)...................... 5-10 78

U.A. 5-15 63-65

VANGUARD 5-15 63-67

PEGGY LEE: see LEE, Peggy

PENDERGRASS, Teddy

P&R/R&B/LP '77

Singles: 12–inch 33/45rpm

PHILADELPHIA INT'L.................. 4-8 78-82

Singles: 7–inch

ASYLUM 3-4 84-88

ELEKTRA.................................... 3-4 88-90

PHILADELPHIA INT'L.................. 3-5 77-84

LPs: 10/12–inch 33rpm

ASYLUM 5-8 84-86

ELEKTRA.................................... 5-8 88-90

EPIC.. 5-10 83

PHILADELPHIA INT'L (30000 series, except JZ-30595) 5-10 77-84

PHILADELPHIA INT'L (JZ-30595 "Life Is a Song") 20-25 78

(Picture disc. Promotional issue only.)

PHILADELPHIA INT'L (40000 series) 10-15 82

(Half-speed mastered.)

Also see MELVIN, Harold

Also see MILLS, Stephanie, & Teddy Pendergrass

Also see PHILADELPHIA INTERNATIONAL ALL STARS

PENDERGRASS, Teddy, & Whitney Houston

P&R '84

Singles: 7–inch

ASYLUM 3-4 84

Picture Sleeves

ASYLUM 3-4 84

Also see HOUSTON, Whitney

Also see PENDERGRASS, Teddy

PENDULUM

P&R '80

Singles: 7–inch

VENTURE.....................................3-5 80

LPs: 10/12–inch 33rpm

VENTURE...................................5-10 81

PENGUINS

(Featuring Cleve Duncan; Penquins)

P&R/R&B '54

Singles: 78rpm

ATLANTIC................................10-20 57

DOOTO.....................................15-25 57

DOOTONE.................................20-30 54-55

MERCURY 10-20 55-57

WING 10-20 56

Singles: 7–inch

ATLANTIC (1132 "Pledge of Love")....................................10-20 57

DOOTO (348 "Earth Angel")........8-10 62

(Reissue of DooTONE 348.)

DOOTO (428 "That's How Much I Need You") 25-30 57

DOOTO (432 "Let Me Make Up Your Mind") 25-30 58

DOOTO (435 "Do Not Pretend") 25-30 58

(Dootone 345 is found in the following section: PENGUINS / Dootsie Williams Orchestra.)

DOOTONE (348 "Earth Angel") .50-75 54

(Red label.)

DOOTONE (348 "Earth Angel") .40-50 54

(Maroon label.)

DOOTONE (348 "Earth Angel") .35-45 54

(Blue label.)

DOOTONE (348 "Earth Angel") .20-30 54

(Black label.)

DOOTONE (353 "Love Will Make Your Mind Go Wild") 40-50 54

(Red label.)

DOOTONE (353 "Love Will Make Your Mind Go Wild") 30-40 54

(Maroon label.)

DOOTONE (353 "Love Will Make Your Mind Go Wild") 20-30 54

(Blue label.)

DOOTONE (353 "Love Will Make Your Mind Go Wild") 15-20 54

(Black label.)

DOOTONE (362 "Kiss a Fool Goodbye")...............................20-40 55

GLENVILLE 4-6

MERCURY (70610 "Be Mine Or Be a Fool")...........................20-30 55

MERCURY (70654 "It Only Happens with You")..............................20-25 55

MERCURY (70703 "Devil That I See")..................................20-30 55

MERCURY (70762 "Christmas Prayer") 40-50 55
MERCURY (70799 "My Troubles Are Not at an End") 25-35 56
(Maroon label.)
MERCURY (70799 "My Troubles Are Not at an End") 15-20 56
(Black label.)
MERCURY (70943 "Earth Angel") 20-25 56
MERCURY (71033 "Will You Be Mine") 15-25 57
ORIGINAL SOUND (27 "Memories of El Monte") 30-40 63
ORIGINAL SOUND (54 "Heavenly Angel") 15-25 63
POWER 4-8
SUN STATE (001 "Believe Me") 10-20 62
WING (90076 "Peace of Mind") 15-20 56

Picture Sleeves

POWER 5-10

EPs: 7–inch 33/45rpm

DOOTO (241/243/244 "Cool, Cool Penguins") 15-25 59
(Price is for any of three volumes.)
DOOTONE (101 "Penguins") .. 50-100 55

LPs: 10/12–inch 33rpm

COLLECTABLES 5-8 80s
DOOTO (242 "Cool, Cool Penguins") 150-250 59
(Yellow label with red lettering. Full-color cover.)
DOOTO (242 "Cool, Cool Penguins") 10-15 60s
(Multi-color label.)
Members: Cleve Duncan; Curtis Williams; Dexter Tisby; Bruce Tate; Randy Jones; Ted Harper; Walter Saulsberry.

PENGUINS / Dootsie Williams Orchestra

Singles: 78rpm

DOOTONE (345 "Nore Ain't No News Today") 20-40 54

Singles: 7–inch

DOOTONE (345 "Nore Ain't No News Today") 75-100 54

PENGUINS / Meadowlarks / Medallions / Dootones

LPs: 10/12–inch 33rpm

DOOTONE (204 "Best in Rhythm & Blues") 50-100 57
(Flat maroon label.)
DOOTONE (204 "Best in Rhythm & Blues") 10-20 60s
(Glossy label.)
Colored vinyl pressings of this LP are bootlegs.
Also see PENGUINS

PENN, Michael

LP '89

Singles: 7–inch

RCA 3-4 89-90

Picture Sleeves

RCA 3-4 89

LPs: 10/12–inch 33rpm

RCA 5-8 89

PENTAGONS

P&R '61

Singles: 7–inch

DONNA 10-15 61
ERIC 3-4 70s
FLEET INT'L (100 "To Be Loved") 50-75 60
JAMIE 10-20 61-62
SPECIALTY 10-20 58

PENTAGONS / Earl Phillips

Singles: 7–inch

OLDIES 45 .... 4-6 64
Also see PENTAGONS

PENTANGLE

LP '68

Singles: 7–inch

REPRISE 4-8 68-69
TRANSATLANTIC 4-6

LPs: 10/12–inch 33rpm

REPRISE 10-20 68-72
Members: Jacqui McShee; Bert Jansch; Danny Thompson; John Renbourn; Terry Cox.

PEOPLE

P&R/LP '68

Singles: 7–inch

CAPITOL 5-10 67-69
PARAMOUNT 4-8 69-70
POLYDOR 3-5 71
ZEBRA (102 "Come Back Beatles") 5-10 78
(Includes a note suggesting the Beatles reunite.)

LPs: 10/12–inch 33rpm

CAPITOL 20-30 68-69
PARAMOUNT 10-20 69-70
Members: Larry Norman; Robb Levin; Tom Tucker; John Tristao; Gene Mason; Geoff Levin.

PEOPLE'S CHOICE

P&R/R&B '71

Singles: 7–inch

CASABLANCA 3-5 80
PALMER (5020 "Easy to Be True") 100-200 67
PHIL-L.A. of SOUL 3-6 71-73
PHILADELPHIA INT'L 4-8 71
PHILIPS 5-10 69
TSOP 3-5 74-77

LPs: 10/12–inch 33rpm

CASABLANCA 5-10 80
DECCA 10-15 69

PHILADELPHIA INT'L 5-10 78
TSOP 8-10 75-76

Members: Roger Andrews; Guy Fiske; David Thompson; Bob Eli; Frankie Brunson.

Also see MFSB

PEPPERMINT, Danny, & Jumping Jacks

P&R '61

Singles: 7–inch

CARLTON 5-10 61

LPs: 10/12–inch 33rpm

CARLTON (LP-20001 "Danny Peppermint") 25-35 62
(Monaural.)
CARLTON (STLP-20001 "Danny Peppermint") 35-50 62
(Stereo.)

Member: Danny Lamego.

PEPPERMINT HARRIS

(With the Cross Town Blues Band; Harrison Nelson)

R&B '50

Singles: 78rpm

ALADDIN................................. 10-20 51-52
CASH 10-15 54
MODERN 10-15 51
MONEY 10-15 54
SITTIN' in WITH 5-10 50-51
X.. 15-25 55

Singles: 7–inch

ALADDIN (3097 "I Got Loaded")............................... 30-50 51
(Black vinyl.)
ALADDIN (3097 "I Got Loaded")............................ 100-200 51
(Colored vinyl.)
ALADDIN (3107 "Have Another Drink and Talk to Me")..................... 30-50 51
ALADDIN (3108 "P. H. Blues").. 30-50 51
ALADDIN (3130 "Right Back On").. 30-50 52
ALADDIN (3141 "There's a Dead Cat on the Line") 30-50 52
ALADDIN (3154 "I Sure Do Miss My Baby").............................. 30-50 51
ALADDIN (3177 "Wasted Love").. 30-50 51
ALADDIN (3183 "Don't Leave Me All Alone") 30-50 53
ALADDIN (3206 "I Never Get Enough of You")...................... 30-50 51
CASH (1003 "Cadillac Funeral") 25-45 54
DART 10-15 60
DUKE 10-15 60
JEWEL 4-8 65-68
LUNAR 3-5
MODERN (936 "Bye, Bye, Fare Thee Well") 25-45 51
MONEY (214 "Cadillac Funeral") 25-45 54
SITTIN' in WITH (543 "Rainin' in My Heart")...............................50-90 51
X (0142 "I Need Your Lovin'") 50-75 55

LPs: 10/12–inch 33rpm

TIME (5 "Peppermint Harris") 35-45 62

Also see NELSON, Peppermint

Also see REED, Jimmy / Peppermint Harris

PEPPERMINT RAINBOW

P&R/LP '69

Singles: 7–inch

DECCA 4-6 68-69

Picture Sleeves

DECCA 5-10 69

LPs: 10/12–inch 33rpm

DECCA 15-20 69

PEPPERMINT TROLLEY CO.

P&R '68

Singles: 7–inch

ACTA 8-12 67-68
VALIANT (752 "Lollipop Train") .10-15 66

LPs: 10/12–inch 33rpm

ACTA (38007 "Peppermint Trolley Co.")..15-25 68

PEPPERS

P&R/R&B '74

Singles: 7–inch

BIG TREE 3-5 75
EVENT 3-5 74-75

LPs: 10/12–inch 33rpm

EVENT 8-12 74

PEPSI & SHIRLIE

P&R '87

Singles: 7–inch

POLYDOR 3-4 87-88

Picture Sleeves

POLYDOR 3-4 87-88

LPs: 10/12–inch 33rpm

POLYDOR 5-8 88

Members: Pepsi DeMacque; Shirlie Holliman.

Also see WHAM!

PERCELLS

P&R '63

Singles: 7–inch

ABC-PAR 5-10 63-64

PERCY & THEM

R&B '74

Singles: 7–inch

PLAYBOY 3-5 73

PERFECT GENTLEMEN

LP '90

Singles: 7–inch

COLUMBIA 3-4 90

PERICOLI, Emilio

P&R '62

Singles: 7–inch

VESUVIUS 4-6 62
W.B. 4-6 62-63

Picture Sleeves

W.B. 4-6 62

LPs: 10/12–inch 33rpm

W.B. 10-20 63-66
VESUVIUS 10-20 62

PERKINS, Al

R&B '69

Singles: 7–inch

ATCO 4-6 69-70
HI 3-5 72
U.S.A. 4-8 64-65

PERKINS, Carl

(With the C.P. Express)

C&W/P&R/R&B '56

Singles: 78rpm

FLIP (501 "Movie Magg") 100-200 55
SUN (224 "Gone Gone Gone") 50-100 56
SUN (234 thru 287) 20-40 56-57

Singles: 7–inch

AMERICA/SMASH 3-5 86-87
BANTAM 4-6
COLUMBIA (3-41000 & 3-42000 series) 20-40 60-62
(Compact 33 Singles.)
COLUMBIA (4-41000 thru 4-43000 series) 10-20 58-64
COLUMBIA (4-44000 & 4-45000 series) 5-10 64-72
DECCA 5-10 63-64
DOLLIE 5-10 67
FLIP (501 "Movie Magg") 300-400 55
JET 3-5 79
MERCURY 4-6 73-77
MUSIC MILL 4-6 76
SSS/SUN 3-5 70s
SUN (224 "Gone Gone Gone") 75-125 56
SUN (234 "Blue Suede Shoes") 15-25 56
SUN (243 "Boppin' the Blues").. 20-30 56
SUN (249 "Dixie Fried") 30-40 56
SUN (261 "Matchbox") 25-35 57
SUN (274 "Forever Yours") 25-35 57
SUN (287 "Glad All Over") 25-35 57

Picture Sleeves

COLUMBIA (41131 "Pink Pedal Pushers") 25-45 58
COLUMBIA (42405 "Hollywood City") 20-30 62
COLUMBIA (42514 "Hambone") 40-60 62

EPs: 7–inch 33/45rpm

COLUMBIA (12341 "Whole Lotta Shakin'") 200-300 58
SUN (115 "Blue Suede Shoes") 100-200 58

LPs: 10/12–inch 33rpm

ACCORD 5-10 82
ALBUM GLOBE 8-12
ALLEGIANCE 5-10 84
COLUMBIA (1234 "Whole Lotta Shakin'") 100-200 58
(Red label.)
COLUMBIA (1234 "Whole Lotta Shakin'") 150-250 58
(White label. Promotional issue only.)
COLUMBIA (9833 "Greatest Hits") 10-20 69
COLUMBIA (10117 "Greatest Hits") 8-10 74
DESIGN 10-15 60s
DOLLIE 10-20 67
GRT/SUNNYVALE 8-12 77
HARMONY 8-12 72
JET 8-10 78
KOALA 5-10 80
MERCURY 8-12 73
ROUNDER 5-10 89
SSS/SUN 5-10 69-84
SUEDE 8-10 81
SUN (1225 "Dance Album") ... 500-750 57
SUN (1225 "Teen Beat") 200-250 61
(Repackage of *Dance Album.*)
TRIP 8-10 74
UNIVERSAL 5-10 89
TRIP 8-12 74

Also see McCARTNEY, Paul
Also see NELSON, Willie / Jerry Lee Lewis / Carl Perkins / David Allan Coe
Also see YOUNG, Faron / Carl Perkins / Claude King

PERKINS, Carl / Sonny Burgess

LPs: 10/12–inch 33rpm

SSS/SUN 5-10

PERKINS, Carl, Jerry Lee Lewis, Roy Orbison & Johnny Cash

LP '86

LPs: 10/12–inch 33rpm

AMERICA ("Class of '55") 20-30 86
(Mail-order edition. Has souvenir booklet and audio cassette with interviews of the singers.)
AMERICA/SMASH (830002 "Class of '55") 5-10 86

Also see CASH, Johnny, Carl Perkins & Jerry Lee Lewis
Also see LEWIS, Jerry Lee, Carl Perkins & Charlie Rich
Also see ORBISON, Roy

PERKINS, Carl, & NRBQ

Singles: 7–inch

COLUMBIA 3-5 70

LPs: 10/12–inch 33rpm

COLUMBIA 10-15 70

Also see NRBQ
Also see PERKINS, Carl

PERKINS, George
(With the Silver Stars)

P&R/R&B '70

Singles: 7-inch

SILVER FOX 4-8 69
SOUL POWER 3-6 72

LPs: 10/12-inch 33rpm

CRYIN' in the STREETS 8-12 77

PERKINS, Joe

P&R '63

Singles: 7-inch

BERRY 4-8 60s
MUSICOR 4-8 65
SOUND STAGE 7 .... 4-8 63

PERKINS, Tony

P&R '57

Singles: 78rpm

RCA 5-10 57

Singles: 7-inch

RCA 8-12 57

Picture Sleeves

RCA 10-20 57

LPs: 10/12-inch 33rpm

EPIC (3394 "Tony Perkins") 25-35 57
RCA (1679 "From My Heart") 20-30 58
RCA (LPM-1853 "On a Rainy Afternoon") 20-30 58
RCA (LSP-1853 "On a Rainy Afternoon") 30-40 58

PERKINS, Tony / James Dean

Singles: 78rpm

RAINBO (5-21-57 "Dean & Perkins") 30-50 57
(Flexi, picture disc.)
Also see PERKINS, Tony

PERRY, Greg

R&B '74

Singles: 12-inch 33/45rpm

ALFA 4-6 82

Singles: 7-inch

ALFA 3-4 82
CASABLANCA 3-5 74-75
CHESS 4-8 68
RCA 3-5 77

LPs: 10/12-inch 33rpm

CASABLANCA 8-12 75

PERRY, Jeff

R&B '75

Singles: 7-inch

ARISTA 3-5 75-76
EPIC 3-5 77

PERRY, Joe, Project

LP '80

Singles: 7-inch

COLUMBIA 3-5 80-81

LPs: 10/12-inch 33rpm

COLUMBIA 5-10 80-81
MCA 4-8 83
Members: Joe Perry; Ralph Morman; Ronnie Stewart; David Hull.
Also see AEROSMITH

PERRY, Linda

R&B '73

Singles: 7-inch

MAINSTREAM 3-5 73

PERRY, Roxy

D&D '83

Singles: 12-inch 33/45rpm

PERSONAL 4-6 83

PERRY, Steve

P&R '82

Singles: 7-inch

COLUMBIA 3-4 84-85

Picture Sleeves

COLUMBIA 3-4 84

LPs: 10/12-inch 33rpm

COLUMBIA 5-8 84-85
Also see JOURNEY
Also see LOGGINS, Kenny, & Steve Perry
Also see U.S.A. for AFRICA

PERRY & SANLIN

R&B '80

Singles: 7-inch

CAPITOL 3-5 80

LPs: 10/12-inch 33rpm

CAPITOL 5-10 80

PERSIANS

R&B '68

Singles: 7-inch

ABC 4-8 68
CAPITOL 3-5 71-72
GWP 3-6 69-70

PERSON, Houston

R&B '75

Singles: 7-inch

WESTBOUND 3-5 75-76

PERSUADERS

P&R/R&B '71

Singles: 7-inch

ATCO 4-8 71-75
CALLA 3-5 77
WIN OR LOSE 3-5 71-72

LPs: 10/12-inch 33rpm

ATCO 8-12 73-74
CALLA 8-10 77
WIN OR LOSE 10-15 72
Members: Doug Scott; James Barnes; Charles Stodghill; Willie Holland.

PERSUASIONS

LP '71

Singles: 7-inch

A&M 3-5 74-75

CAPITOL 3-6 71-72
CATAMOUNT 3-5 70s
ERICA 10-20
MCA 3-5 73
REPRISE 3-6 70
TOWER 5-10 65-66

LPs: 10/12-inch 33rpm

A&M 10-15 74
CAPITOL 10-20 71-72
CATAMOUNT 8-10 70s
ELEKTRA 10-12 77
FLYING FISH 5-10 79
MCA 8-12 73
ROUNDER 5-8 80s
STRAIGHT 15-25 70

Members: Jerry Lawson; Jimmy Hayes; Jayotis Washington; Joe Russell; Herb Rhoad.

PET SHOP BOYS

P&R/R&B/LP '86

Singles: 12-inch 33/45rpm

EMI 4-6 86-87

Singles: 7-inch

EMI 3-4 86-90

Picture Sleeves

EMI 3-4 86-89

LPs: 10/12-inch 33rpm

EMI (Except 90263) 5-10 86-90
EMI (90263 "Actually") 10-15 88
(With bonus 12-inch single, *Always on My Mind*)

Members: Neil Tennant; Chris Lowe.
Also see ELECTRONIC

PET SHOP BOYS & Dusty Springfield

Singles: 7-inch

EMI 3-4 87

Also see PET SHOP BOYS
Also see SPRINGFIELD, Dusty

PETER & GORDON

P&R/LP '64

Singles: 7-inch

CAPITOL 4-8 64-69

Picture Sleeves

CAPITOL 8-12 64-67

LPs: 10/12-inch 33rpm

CAPITOL (T-2115 thru T-2882) 15-25 64-68
(Monaural.)
CAPITOL (ST-2115 thru ST-2882) 20-30 64-68
(Stereo.)
CAPITOL (SM-2549 "Best of Peter & Gordon") 5-10 77
CAPITOL (SN-16084 "Best of Peter & Gordon") 5-8 80

Members: Peter Asher; Gordon Waller.

PETER & GORDON / Lettermen

Singles: 7-inch

CAPITOL CREATIVE PROD. 5-10 66
(Fritos Company promotional issue.)

Also see LETTERMEN

Also see PETER & GORDON

PETER, PAUL & MARY

P&R/LP '62

Singles: 7-inch

"EUGENE McCARTHY for PRESIDENT" 10-20 68
(Promotional issue only. No label name used.)
W.B. (5000 series) 4-8 62-66
W.B. (7000 series) 3-6 67-70

Picture Sleeves

W.B. 4-8 62-64

EPs: 7-inch 33/45rpm

W.B. 5-10 63-64
(Jukebox issues only.)

LPs: 10/12-inch 33rpm

GOLD C. 5-8 87
W.B. (1449 thru 1648) 20-30 62-66
(Gold or gray labels.)
W.B. (1700 thru 2552) 8-15 67-70
W.B. (3000 series) 5-10 77-78

Members: Peter Yarrow; Paul Stookey; Mary Travers.
Also see STOOKEY, Paul
Also see TRAVERS, Mary
Also see YARROW, Peter

PETERS, Bernadette

P&R/LP '80

Singles: 7-inch

ABC-PAR 4-8 65
COLUMBIA 4-8 67
MCA 3-5 78-81
U.A. 5-10 62

Picture Sleeves

MCA 3-5 80-81

LPs: 10/12-inch 33rpm

MCA 5-10 80-81

PETERSEN, Paul

P&R '62

Singles: 7-inch

ABC 3-5 74
COLPIX (Except 720) 5-15 62-65
COLPIX (720 "She Rides with Me") 25-35 64
(With the Beach Boys.)
ERIC 3-4 70s
MCA 3-4
MOTOWN 10-20 67-68

Picture Sleeves

COLPIX (663 "My Dad") 10-20 62

LPs: 10/12-inch 33rpm

COLPIX (CP-429 "Lollipops and Roses") 20-30 62
(Monaural.)
COLPIX (SCP-429 "Lollipops and Roses") 25-35 62
(Stereo.)
COLPIX (CP-442 "My Dad") 20-30 63
(Monaural.)

COLPIX (SCP-442 "My Dad") ... 25-35 63
(Stereo.)
Also see BEACH BOYS
Also see DARREN, James / Shelly Fabares / Paul Petersen

PETERSEN, Paul, & Shelly Fabares

Singles: 7-inch

COLPIX 5-10 62
Also see FABARES, Shelly
Also see PETERSEN, Paul

PETERSON, Bobby
(Bobby Peterson Quintet)

P&R '59

Singles: 7-inch

ATLANTIC 4-8 62
V-TONE 5-10 59-60

PETERSON, Lucky, Blues Band

R&B '71

Singles: 7-inch

TODAY 3-5 71

LPs: 10/12-inch 33rpm

TODAY 10-15 71

PETERSON, Oscar
(Oscar Peterson Trio)

LP '63

Singles: 78rpm

CLEF 4-6 53-56
MERCURY 4-8 51-52
NORGRAN 4-6 55
VERVE 4-8 57

Singles: 7-inch

CLEF 5-10 53-56
LIMELIGHT 4-6 65-66
MERCURY (8900 series) 5-10 51-52
MERCURY (72000 series) 4-6 64
MERCURY (89000 series) 5-10 52-53
NORGRAN 5-10 55
PRESTIGE 4-6 69
VERVE 4-8 57-64

EPs: 7-inch 33/45rpm

CLEF 20-40 52-53
RCA (3006 "This Is Oscar Peterson") 75-125 51

LPs: 10/12-inch 33rpm

BASF 8-12 74-76
CLEF (106 "Piano Solos") 100-150 52
(10–inch LP.)
CLEF (107 "At Carnegie Hall") 100-150 52
(10–inch LP.)
CLEF (110 "Collates") 100-150 52
(10–inch LP.)
CLEF (116 "Oscar Peterson Quartet") 100-150 52
(10–inch LP.)
CLEF (119 "Oscar Peterson Plays Pretty") 100-150 52
(10–inch LP.)
CLEF (127 "Collates, No. 2") ... 75-125 53
(10–inch LP.)
CLEF (145 "Oscar Peterson Sings") 75-125 54
(10–inch LP.)
CLEF (155 "Oscar Peterson Plays Pretty, No. 2") 75-125 54
(10–inch LP.)
CLEF (168 "Oscar Peterson Quartet, No. 2") 75-125 55
(10–inch LP.)
CLEF (600 series) 50-75 53-56
EMARCY 8-12 76
LIMELIGHT (1000 series) 5-8 82
LIMELIGHT (82000 & 86000 series) 10-20 65-67
MGM (100 series) 8-12 70
MPS 8-12 72-76
MERCURY (20975 "Trio+One") . 20-30 64
(Monaural.)
MERCURY (60975 "Trio+One") . 25-35 64
(Stereo.)
METRO 10-15 65
PABLO 6-12 75-83
PAUSA 5-10 79-81
PRESTIGE 8-15 69-74
RCA (3006 "This Is Oscar Peterson") 200-250 51
(10–inch LP.)
TRIP 5-8 75-76
VSP 10-20 66-67
VERVE 25-50 56-60
(Reads "Verve Records, Inc." at bottom of label.)
VERVE 10-25 61-72
(Reads "MGM Records - A Division of Metro-Goldwyn-Mayer, Inc." at bottom of label.)
VERVE 5-15 73-83
(Reads "Manufactured By MGM Record Corp.," or mentions either Polydor or Polygram at bottom of label.)
WING 8-12 67
Also see ARMSTRONG, Louis, & Oscar Peterson
Also see BASIE, Count, & Oscar Peterson
Also see FITZGERALD, Ella, & Oscar Peterson
Also see GETZ, Stan, & Oscar Peterson
Also see HUBBARD, Freddie, & Oscar Peterson
Also see MULLIGAN, Gerry, & Oscar Peterson
Also see RIDDLE, Nelson

PETERSON, Ray

P&R '59

Singles: 7-inch

CLOUD 9 .... 3-5 75
DECCA 3-5 71
DUNES 5-10 60-63
MGM 4-8 64-66
POLYDOR 3-5 70s
RCA (47-7000 series) 10-15 58-60
RCA (47-8000 series) 4-8 64

RCA (61-7578 "My Blue Angel") 15-25 60
(Stereo.)
RCA (61-7745 "Tell Laura I Love Her") 15-25 60
(Stereo.)
RCA (61-7779 "Teenage Heartache") 15-25 60
(Stereo.)
REPRISE 4-6 69
UNI 3-5 70

Picture Sleeves

DUNES (2002 "Corrina Corrina") 8-12 60
MGM (13269 "Oh No") 5-10 64
MGM (13336 "House Without Windows") 5-10 64
RCA (7635 "Goodnight My Love") 8-12 59

EPs: 7-inch 33/45rpm

RCA (4367 "Tell Laura I Love Her") 40-60 60

LPs: 10/12-inch 33rpm

CAMDEN 10-20 66
DECCA 8-12 71
MGM 20-30 64-65
RCA (LPM-2297 "Tell Laura I Love Her") 40-60 60
(Monaural.)
RCA (LSP-2297 "Tell Laura I Love Her") 60 80 60
(Stereo.)
UNI 10-15 70

PETITE

R&B '86

Singles: 7-inch

YORK'S 3-4 86

PETS

P&R '58

Singles: 78rpm

ARWIN 5-10 58

Singles: 7-inch

ARWIN 5-10 58

Member: Seph Acre.

PETTUS, Giorge

R&B '87

Singles: 7-inch

MCA 3-4 87-88

PETTY, Norman, Trio

P&R '54

Singles: 78rpm

ABC-PAR 4-8 57
COLUMBIA (Except 41039) 4-8 57
COLUMBIA (41039 "Moondreams") 25-50 57
(With Buddy Holly on guitar.)
NOR VA JAK 5-10 57
X 4-6 54-55

Singles: 7-inch

ABC-PAR 5-10 57
COLUMBIA (Except 41039) 5-10 57
COLUMBIA (41039 "Moondreams") 40-60 57
(With Buddy Holly on guitar.)
FELSTED 4-8 62
JARO 5-10 60
NOR VA JAK (Except 1325) 15-20 57-59
NOR VA JAK (1325 "True Love Ways") 25-35 60
NORMAN 5-10 60
X 5-10 54-55

EPs: 7-inch 33/45rpm

COLUMBIA (2139 "Four Hits") 15-25 58
COLUMBIA (10921 "Moondreams") 50-100 58
X (82 "In Full Fidelity") 15-25 55

LPs: 10/12-inch 33rpm

COLUMBIA (1092 "Moondreams") 50-100 58
TOP RANK (R-639 "Petty for Your Thoughts") 20-30 60
(Monaural.)
TOP RANK (RS-639 "Petty for Your Thoughts") 30-40 60
(Stereo.)
VIK (1073 "Corsage") 30-45 57

Members: Norman Petty; Vi Petty; Jack Petty.
Also see HOLLY, Buddy

PETTY, Tom, & Heartbreakers

P&R/LP '77

Singles: 7-inch

BACKSTREET 3-5 79-83
(Black vinyl.)
BACKSTREET (52181 "Change of Heart") 5-8 83
(Colored vinyl.)
MCA 3-4 85-90
SHELTER 3-5 77-78

Picture Sleeves

BACKSTREET 3-5 79-83
MCA 3-4 85-90
SHELTER 3-5 77-78

LPs: 10/12-inch 33rpm

BACKSTREET 5-10 79-82
MCA 5-8 85-90
SHELTER 8-15 76-78

Promotional LPs

SHELTER (12677 "Official Live 'Leg") 15-25 76
SHELTER (52029 "You're Gonna Get It") 15-25 78
(Colored vinyl.)

Members: Tom Petty; Mike Campbell; Stan Lynch; Beaumont Tench; Ron Blair; Howie Epstein.
Also see DYLAN, Bob, & Heartbreakers / Michael Rubini
Also see NICKS, Stevie, with Tom Petty & Heartbreakers

PETTY, Vi: see PETTY, Norman, Trio

PHANTOM, ROCKER & SLICK

LP '85

Singles: 7-inch

EMI AMERICA 3-5 85-86

LPs: 10/12-inch 33rpm

EMI AMERICA 5-10 85-86

Members: Jim Phantom; Lee Rocker; Earl Slick.
Also see SILVER CONDOR
Also see STRAY CATS

PHELPS, James
(With the Du-Ettes; Jimmy Phelps)

P&R/R&B '65

Singles: 7-inch

ARGO.. 4-8 65
CADET 4-8 66
FONTANA... 4-8 66-67
MECCA (5 "Blue Point Drive")... 15-25 60
PARAMOUNT 3-5 71-72

Also see SOUL STIRRERS

PHILADELPHIA INTERNATIONAL ALL STARS

P&R/R&B '77

Singles: 7-inch

PHILADELPHIA INT'L................... 3-5 77

Members: Archie Bell; the O'Jays; Billy Paul; Teddy Pendergrass; Lou Rawls; Dee Dee Sharpe.
Also see BELL, Archie
Also see MFSB
Also see O'JAYS
Also see PAUL, Billy
Also see PENDERGRASS, Teddy
Also see RAWLS, Lou
Also see SHARPE, Dee Dee

PHILADELPHIA STORY

R&B '77

Singles: 7-inch

H&L 3-5 77

PHILHARMONICS

P&R/R&B '77

Singles: 7-inch

CAPRICORN................................. 3-5 77

LPs: 10/12-inch 33rpm

CAPRICORN................................. 5-10 77

PHILLINGANES, Greg

R&B '81

Singles: 12-inch 33/45rpm

PLANET 4-6 85

Singles: 7-inch

PLANET 3-4 81-85

LPs: 10/12-inch 33rpm

PLANET 5-8 81-85

Also see KING DREAM CHORUS & Holiday Crew

PHILLIPS, Anthony

LP '77

Singles: 7-inch

PASSPORT................................... 3-5 77-78

LPs: 10/12-inch 33rpm

PASSPORT................................... 5-10 77-78

Also see GENESIS

PHILLIPS, Esther, & Joe Beck

LPs: 10/12-inch 33rpm

KUDU 8-10 76

Also see BECK, Joe
Also see LITTLE ESTHER

PHILLIPS, John

P&R/C&W/LP '70

Singles: 7-inch

ATCO 3-5 74
COLUMBIA 3-5 73
DUNHILL.. 3-5 70

LPs: 10/12-inch 33rpm

DUNHILL...................................... 10-15 70

Also see MAMAS & PAPAS

PHILLIPS, Little Esther: see LITTLE ESTHER

PHILLIPS, Phil
(With the Twilights)

P&R/R&B '59

Singles: 7-inch

CLIQUE.. 4-8 66
KHOURY'S (711 "Sea of Love")................................ 100-150 59
MERCURY (10021 "Verdi Mae") 10-20 59
(Stereo.)
MERCURY (71000 series).......... 8-12 59-61
MERCURY CELEBRITY SERIES.. 3-5

Also see K-DOE, Ernie / Phil Phillips

PHILLIPS, Shawn

LP '72

Singles: 7-inch

A&M 3-5 70-75
ASCOT.. 4-8 64

LPs: 10/12-inch 33rpm

A&M 8-12 70-77
RCA 5-10 78-81

PHILLIPS, Wes

R&B/D&D '84

Singles: 12-inch 33/45rpm

QUALITY.. 4-6 84

Singles: 7-inch

QUALITY.. 3-4 84

PHILLY CREAM

P&R/R&B '79

Singles: 12-inch 33/45rpm

WMOT.. 4-8 79

Singles: 7-inch

FANTASY 3-5 79
WMOT.. 3-5 79

LPs: 10/12-inch 33rpm

WMOT.. 5-10 79

PHILLY DEVOTIONS

P&R/R&B '75

Singles: 7–inch

BRY-WEK (1038 "I'll Never Color You a Rainbow") 5-10 73
DON DE (127 "I Just Can't Say Goodbye") 4-8 74
COLUMBIA 3-5 75-76

PHOTOGLO, Jim

(Photoglo)

P&R/LP '80

Singles: 7–inch

CASABLANCA 3-5 83
20TH FOX 3-5 80-81

LPs: 10/12–inch 33rpm

CASABLANCA 5-10 83
20TH FOX 5-10 80-81

PIAF, Edith

(With Theo Sarapo)

P&R '50

Singles: 78rpm

CAPITOL 4-8 56-58
COLUMBIA 4-8 50-52

Singles: 7–inch

CAPITOL 5-15 56-61
COLUMBIA 5-15 50-52

EPs: 7–inch 33/45rpm

ANGEL 5-15 55-56
COLUMBIA 5-15 50-52
DECCA 5-15 54

LPs: 10/12–inch 33rpm

ANGEL 25-40 55-56
CAPITOL (10210 "Piaf") 15-25 59
CAPITOL (10283 "Piaf of Paris") 10-20 61
CAPITOL (10295 "Potpourri Par Piaf") 10-20 62
CAPITOL (10348 "Piaf and Sarapo") 10-20 63
CAPITOL (16000 series) 5-10 81-82
COLUMBIA (898 "La Vie En Rose") 20-40 56
COLUMBIA (6223 "Encore Parisiennes") 25-50 52
(10–inch LP.)
COLUMBIA (9500 series) 25-50 51-52
(10–inch LPs.)
COLUMBIA (37000 series) 5-10 81
DECCA (6004 "Chansons des Cafes de Paris") 25-50 54
(10–inch LP.)
DISCOS 20-30 56
PHILIPS 10-20 64-67
RCA 10-15 64
VOX (3050 "Edith Piaf Sings") .. 25-50 53
(10–inch LP.)
VOX (3060 "Edith Piaf Favorites") 25-50 53
(10–inch LP.)

PIANO RED

(Willie Perryman)

R&B '50

Singles: 78rpm

CHECKER 10-20 58
GROOVE 10-15 54-57
RCA 10-20 50-57

Singles: 7–inch

CHECKER (911 "Get Up Mare") 15-25 58
GROOVE 10-30 54-57
JAX 8-12 59
RCA (0099 "Rockin' with Red").. 50-75 50
(Colored vinyl.)
RCA (0106 "The Wrong YoYo"). 25-50 50
RCA (0118 "Jumpin' the Boogie") 25-50 51
RCA (0130 "Baby What's Wrong") 25-50 51
RCA (4265 "Let's Have a Good Time") 25-50 51
RCA (4380 "Hey Good Lookin'") 25-50 51
RCA (4524 "Bouncin' with Red") 25-50 52
RCA (4766 "Sales Tax Boogie") 25-50 52
RCA (4957 "Voo Doopee Doo"). 25-50 52
RCA (5101 "I'm Gonna Rock Some More") 20-35 52
RCA (5224 "I'm Gonna Tell Everybody") 20-35 53
RCA (5337 "Your Mouth's Got a Hole") 20-35 52
RCA (5544 "Right and Ready").. 20-35 52
RCA (6000 & 7000 series) 15-25 57-58

EPs: 7–inch 33/45rpm

GROOVE (3 "Jump Man, Jump") 40-60 56
GROOVE (10026/27/28 "Piano Red in Concert") 35-50 56
(Price is for any of three volumes.)
RCA (587 "Rockin' with Red").. 50-100 54
RCA (5091 "Rockin' with Red").. 40-60 59
(Black label.)
RCA (5091 "Rockin' with Red") 50-100 59
(Maroon label.)

LPs: 10/12–inch 33rpm

ARHOOLIE 8-10
BLACK LION 8-10 76
GROOVE (1001 "Jump Man, Jump") 500-750 56
GROOVE (1002 "Piano Red in Concert") 150-250 56
KING 10-15 70
RCA 8-10 74

Also see DOCTOR FEELGOOD

PIANO RED / June Valli

EPs: 7–inch 33/45rpm

RCA (92 "Dealer's Prevue")...... 15-25 56
(Promotional issue only.)
Also see PIANO RED
Also see VALLI, June

PICKETT, Bobby

(Bobby [Boris] Pickett & Crypt-Kickers; Featuring Bobby Paine)

P&R/R&B/LP '62

Singles: 12–inch 33/45rpm

EASY STREET 4-8 84

Singles: 7–inch

ANTHEM 3-5
ATMOSPHERE 5-10 65
CAPITOL 5-10 63-64
EASY STREET 3-5 84
GARPAX (1 "Monster Mash") 8-12 62
GARPAX (724 "I'm Down to My Last Heartbreak") 5-10
GARPAX (44000 series) 5-10 62-64
LONDON 3-5 70s
METROMEDIA (0089 "Me and My Mummy") 4-8 68
METROMEDIA (9989 "Me and My Mummy") 3-6 73
PARROT 4-8 70-73
RCA 5-10 64
WHITE WHALE 4-8 70

Picture Sleeves

GARPAX 10-20 62-63

LPs: 10/12–inch 33rpm

GARPAX (GP-67001 "Monster Mash") 30-50 62
(Monaural.)
GARPAX (SGP-67001 "Monster Mash") 50-75 62
(Stereo.)
PARROT 10-20 73

PICKETT, Wilson

P&R/R&B '63

Singles: 7–inch

ATLANTIC (2200 thru 2400 series) 5-10 64-67
ATLANTIC (2500 thru 2900 series) 4-8 68-72
BIG TREE 3-5 78
CORREC-TONE (501 "Let Me Be Your Boy") 40-60 62
CUB (9113 "Let Me be Your Boy") 20-30 62
DOUBLE-L 8-12 63
EMI AMERICA 3-5 79-81
MOTOWN 3-4 87
RCA 3-5 73-74
ROWE/AMI 5-10 66
("Play Me" Sales Stimulator promotional issue.)
VERVE (501 "Let Me be Your Boy") 10-20 65
WICKED 3-5 75-76

LPs: 10/12–inch 33rpm

ATLANTIC (Except 8100 series) 10-15 69-73
ATLANTIC (8100 series) 12-25 65-68
BIG TREE 5-10 78
BROOKVILLE 8-12 77
DOUBLE-L (DL-8300 "It's Too Late") 25-35 63
(Monaural.)
DOUBLE-L (SDL-8300 "It's Too Late") 30-40 63
(Stereo.)
EMI AMERICA 5-10 79-81
RCA 8-12 73-77
WAND 10-15 68
WICKED 8-12 76
Also see FALCONS

PICKETT, Wilson / Sam & Dave

LPs: 10/12–inch 33rpm

ATLANTIC (ST-136 "Excerpts from *Hey Jude*) 15-25 69
(Promotional issue for in-store use.)
Also see PICKETT, Wilson
Also see SAM & DAVE

PICKETT & PAYNE

Singles: 7–inch

METROMEDIA (0089 "It's Not the Same Without You") 5-8 68
METROMEDIA (9989 "It's Not the Same Without You") 4-6 73
Members: Bobby Pickett; Joan Payne.
Also see PICKETT, Bobby

PICKETTYWITCH

P&R '70

Singles: 7–inch

JANUS 3-5 70
PYE 3-5 71

LPs: 10/12–inch 33rpm

JANUS 8-12 70
Member: Polly Brown.
Also see BROWN, Polly

PICTURE PERFECT

R&B '87

Singles: 7–inch

ATLANTIC 3-4 87

PIECES of a DREAM

R&B/LP '81

Singles: 12–inch 33/45rpm

ELEKTRA 4-6 84

Singles: 7–inch

ELEKTRA 3-5 81-84
MANHATTAN 3-4 88

LPs: 10/12–inch 33rpm

ELEKTRA 5-10 81-84
MANHATTAN 5-8 86

PIECES of EIGHT

P&R '67

Singles: 7–inch

A&M 5-10 67-68
ACTION.......................... 5-10 60s
MALA 5-10 68
Also see SWINGIN' MEDALLIONS

PIED PIPERS
(With Paul Weston's Orchestra)

P&R '44

Singles: 78rpm

CAPITOL.......................... 5-10 44-50
RCA.......................... 4-8 48

Singles: 7–inch

CAPITOL.......................... 8-12 49-50
RCA.......................... 5-10 40

EPs: 7–inch 33/45rpm

CAPITOL.......................... 10-20 50

LPs: 10/12–inch 33rpm

CAPITOL (H-212 "Harvest Moon").......................... 30-45 50
(10–inch LP.)
Members: Jo Stafford; Chuck Lowry; Hal Hopper; Clark Yocum; June Hutton; Sue Allen.
Also see STAFFORD, Jo

PIERCE, Webb

C&W '52

Singles: 78rpm

DECCA.......................... 5-10 51-52
4 STAR.......................... 8-12 51-52

Singles: 7–inch

DECCA (28000 thru 30000 series) 10-20 52-59
DECCA (31000 thru 33000 series) 4-10 59-73
DECCA (46000 series).......................... 8-12 51-52
4 STAR.......................... 10-15 51-52
KING 5-10 60
MCA 3-5 73-74
PLANTATION.......................... 3-5 75-77
SOUNDWAVES 3-4 83

EPs: 7–inch 33/45rpm

DECCA.......................... 10-20 53-65

LPs: 10/12–inch 33rpm

CORAL.......................... 5-10 73
DECCA (181 "Webb Pierce Story") 20-30 64
(Includes booklet.)
DECCA (DL-4015 "Webb with a Beat") 25-35 60
(Monaural.)
DECCA (DL7-4015 "Webb with a Beat") 3050 60
(Stereo.)
DECCA (DL-4079 thru 4964).... 10-25 60-67
DECCA (DL7-4079 thru 4964).. 15-30 60-67
DECCA (5536 "Wandering Boy") 40-60 53
(10 Inch LP.)
DECCA (8129 "Webb Pierce")...30-50 55
DECCA (8295 "Wandering Boy") 30-50 56
DECCA (8728 "Just Imagination")..........................30-50 57
DECCA (DL-8889 "Bound for the Kingdom") 20-25 59
(Monaural.)
DECCA (DL7-8889 "Bound for the Kingdom") 25-35 59
(Stereo.)
DECCA (DL-8899 "Webb!") 25-35 59
(Monaural.)
DECCA (DL7-8899 "Webb!") 30-40 59
(Stereo.)
DECCA (74000 series) 8-12 68
ERA..........................8-10 77
KING (648 "The One and Only Webb Pierce")..........................35-50 59
MCA..........................5-12 73-78
PICKWICK/HILLTOP 10-15 65
PLANTATION 5-8 76-77
SEARS..........................8-12 60s
SKYLITE 5-8 77
VOCALION 5-15 66-70
Also see NELSON, Willie, & Webb Pierce
Also see SOVINE, Red, & Webb Pierce
Also see WELLS, Kitty, & Webb Pierce

PIERCE, Webb / Loretta Lynn

LPs: 10/12–inch 33rpm

PHILCO/MCA..........................15-25 69
Also see LYNN, Loretta

PIERCE, Webb / Wynn Stewart

LPs: 10/12–inch 33rpm

DESIGN 10-20 62
Also see STEWART, Wynn

PIERCE, Webb, & Mel Tillis

C&W '63

Singles: 7–inch

DECCA 4-6 62

PIERCE, Webb, & Wilburn Brothers

C&W '54

Singles: 78rpm

DECCA 5-10 54

Singles: 7–inch

DECCA 10-15 54
Also see PIERCE, Webb
Also see WILBURN BROTHERS

PILOT

P&R/LP '75

Singles: 7–inch

ARISTA..........................3-5 77
CAPITOL..........................3-5 77
EMI..........................3-5 74-76

LPs: 10/12–inch 33rpm

ARISTA 8-10 77
EMI..........................8-10 74-76
Members: David Paton; Ian Bairnson; Stuart Tosh; William Lyall.

Also see PARSONS, Alan, Project
Also see 10CC

PILTDOWN MEN

P&R '60

Singles: 7–inch

CAPITOL.......................8-12 60-62

Members: Lincoln Mayorga; Bob Bain; Earl Palmer; Jack Kel.

PINDER, Michael

LP '76

LPs: 10/12–inch 33rpm

THRESHOLD (18 "The Promise")..........8-12 76

Also see MOODY BLUES

PINERA, Mike

P&R '80

Singles: 7–inch

CAPRICORN.......................3-5 78
SPECTOR.......................3-5 80
SRI.......................3-5 79

LPs: 10/12–inch 33rpm

SRI.......................5-10 79

Also see BLUES IMAGE
Also see CACTUS
Also see IRON BUTTERFLY
Also see RAMATAM

PINETOPPERS

(With the Bever Valley Sweethearts)

C&W '50

Singles: 78rpm

CORAL.......................4-6 50-54
DECCA.......................3-5 54-56

Singles: 7–inch

CORAL.......................8-12 50-54
DECCA.......................5-10 54-56
PEER SOUTHERN.......................4-6 67

EPs: 7–inch 33/45rpm

CORAL.......................5-10 50-56

LPs: 10/12–inch 33rpm

CORAL............10-2050-56

Members: Roy Horton; Vaughn Horton. Ray Smith; Trudy Martin; Gloria Martin; John Bowers; Rusty Keefer.

PINETTE, Rick, & Oak

P&R '80

Singles: 7–inch

MERCURY.......................3-5 80

LPs: 10/12–inch 33rpm

MERCURY.......................5-10 80

Also see OAK

PINK FLOYD

LP '67

Singles: 12–inch 33/45rpm

COLUMBIA (1635 "Selections/Final Cut")..........15-20 83
(Promotional issue only.)

Singles: 7–inch

CAPITOL.......................5-15 71-78
COLUMBIA (Black vinyl)..........3-8 75-87
COLUMBIA (Colored vinyl)..........5-10 87
(Promotional issue only.)
HARVEST.......................5-15 73-74
TOWER (333 "Arnold Layne")...35-55 67
TOWER (356 "See Emily Play") 35-55 67
TOWER (378 "The Gnome")......35-55 67
TOWER (426 "It Would be So Nice")..........35-55 68
TOWER (440 "Let There be More Light")..........35-55 68

Picture Sleeves

COLUMBIA.......................3-8 80-87

EPs: 7–inch 33/45rpm

HARVEST (6746/7 "Pink Floyd, from *Dark Side of the Moon)*..........75-125 73
(Promotional issue only. Issued with paper sleeve.)

LPs: 10/12–inch 33rpm

CAPITOL (Except 11902)..........5-8 78-83
CAPITOL (11902 "Dark Side of the Moon")..........20-30 78
(Picture disc.)
COLUMBIA (Except Half-Speed Mastered)..........6-10 75-88
COLUMBIA (HC-43453 "Wish You Were Here")..........25-50 75
(Half-speed mastered.)
COLUMBIA (HC-47680 "Collection of Great Dance Songs")..........20-40 80s
(Half-speed mastered.)
COLUMBIA (H2C-46183 "The Wall")..........150-200 80s
(Half-speed mastered.)
HARVEST (STBB-388 "Ummagumma")..........25-35 69
HARVEST (SMAS-382 "Atom Heart Mother")..........15-20 70
HARVEST (700 & 800 series)....10-15 71
HARVEST (11000 series)..........10-15 72-73
HARVEST (16000 series)..........5-10 82
MFSL (017 "Dark Side of the Moon")..........40-80 78
MFSL/UHQR (017 "Dark Side of the Moon")..........100-150 78
(Boxed set.)
MFSL (190 "Meddle")..........15-25 79
MFSL (202 "Atom Heart Mother")..........30-40 94
(Half-speed mastered.)
TOWER (T-5093 "Piper at the Gates of Dawn")..........100-125 67
(Monaural.)
TOWER (ST-5093 "Piper at the Gates of Dawn")..........50-75 67
(Orange label. Stereo.)
TOWER (5093 "Piper at the Gates of Dawn")..........40-50 67
(Striped label.)

TOWER (5131 "A Saucerful of Secrets") 50-100 68
(Orange label.)
TOWER (5131 "A Saucerful of Secrets") 50-100 68
(Striped label.)
TOWER (5169 "More")............. 25-40 69
(Soundtrack.)

Promotional LPs

CAPITOL (8116 "Tour '75")....... 30-50 75
COLUMBIA (1 "Animals")........ 75-100 77
(With inserts.)
COLUMBIA (1636 "Final Cut").. 15-20 83
COLUMBIA (33453 "Wish You Were Here")........ 50-75 75
COLUMBIA (34474 "Animals").. 40-60 77
(Quadraphonic.)
COLUMBIA (36183 "The Wall") 50-75 79

Members: David Gilmour; Roger Waters; Rick Wright; Nick Mason; Syd Barrell.
Also see BARRETT, Syd
Also see GILMOUR, David
Also see MASON, Nick
Also see WATERS, Roger

PINK LADY

P&R '79

Singles: 7-inch

ELEKTRA.................................. 3-5 79

Picture Sleeves

ELEKTRA.................................. 3-5 79

LPs: 10/12-inch 33rpm

ELEKTRA.................................. 5-10 79

Members: Mie; Kei.

PIPEDREAM

D&D '84

Singles: 12-inch 33/45rpm

ZOO YORK 4-6 84

PIPER, Wardell

R&B '79

Singles: 7-inch

MIDSONG INT'L 3-5 79-80

Also see FIRST CHOICE

PIPKINS

P&R/LP '70

Singles: 7-inch

CAPITOL.................................. 3-6 70

LPs: 10/12-inch 33rpm

CAPITOL.................................. 10-15 70

Also see ALLEY CATS
Also see UNTOUCHABLES

PIPS: see KNIGHT, Gladys

PIRATES

(Temptations)

Singles: 7-inch

MEL-O-DY (105 "Mind Over Matter") 50-75 62

Also see TEMPTATIONS

PISCOPO, Joe

D&D/LP '85

Singles: 12-inch 33/45rpm

COLUMBIA 4-6 85

Singles: 7-inch

COLUMBIA 3-5 85

Picture Sleeves

COLUMBIA 3-5 85

LPs: 10/12-inch 33rpm

COLUMBIA 5-10 85

PITMAN, Donnell

(With the Chi-Lites)

R&B '86

Singles: 7-inch

AFTER FIVE 3-4 86

Also see CHI LITES

PITNEY, Gene

P&R '61

Singles: 7-inch

COLLECTABLES..........................3-4 80s
EPIC...3-5 77
ERIC 3-4 70s
FESTIVAL (25002 "Please Come Back Baby") 15-20 61
MUSICOR (1000 series).............5-10 60-65
MUSICOR (1100 thru 1400 series).......................................4-8 65-72

Picture Sleeves

MUSICOR (1000 series).............5-10 60-65
MUSICOR (1100 thru 1400 series).......................................5-15 66-69

EPs: 7-inch 33/45rpm

MUSICOR (500 "Looking Through the Eyes of Love") 15-20 65
(Issued without cover. Promotional issue only.)

LPs: 10/12-inch 33rpm

COLUMBIA HOUSE 10-15 75
(Columbia Record Club issue.)
EVEREST 5-8 81
KOALA......................................5-10 79
MUSIC DISC..............................10-15 69
MUSICOR (1000 series).............8-10
MUSICOR (2001 thru 2008) 20-35 62-64
(Monaural.)
MUSICOR (2015 thru 2134) 15-25 64-67
(Monaural.)
MUSICOR (3001 thru 3008) 20-40 62-64
(Stereo.)
MUSICOR (3015 thru 3134) 15-25 64-67
(Stereo.)
MUSICOR (3148 thru 3193) 10-20 67-71
MUSICOR (3200 series).............8-12 71-73
MUSICOR (5025 "This Is Gene Pitney") 15-25 68
(Columbia Record Club issue.)
MUSICOR (5600 series).............8-10 78
PHOENIX 20..............................6-12

RHINO.. 5-8 85
SPRINGBOARD........................ 5-10 76
TRIP 5-10 76
51 WEST 5-10 79

Also see BRYAN, Billy
Also see JAMIE & JANE
Also see JONES, George, & Gene Pitney
Also see ROE, Tommy / Bobby Rydell / Gene Pitney

PITNEY, Gene, & Melba Montgomery

C&W '66

Singles: 7–inch

MUSICOR 4-8 65

LPs: 10/12–inch 33rpm

BUCKBOARD 8-10 76
MUSICOR 15-20 66

PITNEY, Gene / Newcastle Trio

LPs: 10/12–inch 33rpm

DESIGN 8-12 60s

Also see PITNEY, Gene

PIXIES

LP '89

LPs: 10/12–inch 33rpm

ELEKTRA.................................. 5-8 89-90

PIXIES THREE

P&R '63

Singles: 7–inch

MERCURY 8-12 63-64

Picture Sleeves

MERCURY (72130 "Birthday Party") 10-20 63
MERCURY (72208 "Cold, Cold Winter") 15-20 63
MERCURY (72288 "It's Summertime") 10-20 64

LPs: 10/12–inch 33rpm

MERCURY (20912 "Party")....... 50-75 64
(Monaural.)
MERCURY (60912 "Party")..... 75-100 64
(Stereo.)

Members: Debra Swisher; Midge Bollinger; Kay McCool.

PIZANI, Frank

P&R '57

Singles: 78rpm

BALLY 5-10 57

Singles: 7–inch

AFTON 5-10 59
BALLY 5-10 57
WARWICK 5-10 59

Also see HIGHLIGHTS

PLACE, Mary Kay
(Mary Kay Place as Loretta Haggers)

C&W/P&R '76

Singles: 7–inch

COLUMBIA 3-5 76-78

LPs: 10/12–inch 33rpm

COLUMBIA 5-10 76-77

PLACE, Mary Kay, & Willie Nelson

C&W '77

Singles: 7–inch

COLUMBIA 3-5 77

Also see NELSON, Willie
Also see PLACE, Mary Kay

PLANET P
(Planet P Project)

P&R/LP '83

Singles: 7–inch

GEFFEN 3-4 83
MCA 3-4

Picture Sleeves

GEFFEN 3-4 83

LPs: 10/12–inch 33rpm

GEFFEN 5-8 83

Member: Tony Carey.
Also see CAREY, Tony

PLANET PATROL

R&B '82

Singles: 12–inch 33/45rpm

TOMMY BOY.............................4-6 83-84

Singles: 7–inch

TOMMY BOY.............................3-4 82-84

LPs: 10/12–inch 33rpm

TOMMY BOY 5-8 84

PLANT, Robert

P&R/LP '82

Singles: 7–inch

ATLANTIC...................................3-5 83
ESPARANZA 3-4 83-89
SWAN SONG...............................3-5 82

Picture Sleeves

ATLANTIC....................................3-5 83
ESPARANZA 3-4 83-88
SWAN SONG.................................3-5 82

LPs: 10/12–inch 33rpm

ESPARANZA 5-8 83-90
SWAN SONG...............................5-10 82

Also see BAND of JOY
Also see HONEYDRIPPERS
Also see LED ZEPPELIN

PLASMATICS
(Featuring Wendy O. Williams)

LP '81

LPs: 10/12–inch 33rpm

CAPITOL......................................5-8 82
PVC..5-8 84
STIFF AMERICA.........................8-10 80-81

Also see WILLIAMS, Wendy O.

PLASTIC BERTRAND: see BERTRAND, Plastic

PLASTIC COW

LP '69

Singles: 7–inch

DOT 4-6 69

LPs: 10/12–inch 33rpm

DOT 10-15 69

PLASTIC ONO BAND: see LENNON, John

PLATINUM BLONDE

P&R '86

Singles: 7–inch

EPIC 3-4 86-87

LPs: 10/12–inch 33rpm

EPIC 5-8 86-87

Members: Mark Holmes; Ken MacLean.

PLATT, Eddie, & Orchestra

P&R/R&B '58

Singles: 78rpm

ABC-PAR 5-10 58

Singles: 7–inch

ABC-PAR 8-12 58
GONE 5-10 58

PLATTERS
(Featuring Tony Williams)

P&R/R&B '55

Singles: 78rpm

FEDERAL (12153 "Give Thanks") 25-50 53
FEDERAL (12164 "I Need You All the Time") 25-50 54
FEDERAL (12181 "Roses of Picardy") 15-30 54
FEDERAL (12188 thru 12204) .. 15-25 54-55
FEDERAL (12244 "Only You") .. 25-50 55
FEDERAL (12250 "Tell the World") 10-20 55
FEDERAL (12271 "I Need You All the Time") 10-20 56
MERCURY (Except 71289) 10-20 55-58
MERCURY (71289 "Twilight Time") 25-50 58

Singles: 7–inch

ANTLER 3-5 82
COLLECTABLES 3-4
FEDERAL (12153 "Give Thanks") 75-125 53
FEDERAL (12164 "I Need You All the Time") 100-125 54
FEDERAL (12181 "Roses of Picardy") 70-90 54
FEDERAL (12188 "Tell The World") 50-75 54
FEDERAL (12198 "Voo-Vee-Ah-Bee") 25-45 54
FEDERAL (12204 "Take Me Back") 25-45 54
FEDERAL (12244 "Only You") 75-100 55
FEDERAL (12250 "Tell The World") 20-30 55
FEDERAL (12271 "I Need You All the Time") 15-20 56
GUSTO 3-4 80s
MERCURY (10001 "Smoke Gets in Your Eyes") 15-25 58
(Stereo.)
MERCURY (10018 "Where") 15-25 59
(Stereo.)
MERCURY (10038 "Red Sails in the Sunset") 15-25 60
(Stereo.)
MERCURY (70633 "Only You") . 20-25 55
(Pink label.)
MERCURY (70633 "Only You") ... 8-12 55
(Black label.)
MERCURY (70753 "The Great Pretender") 10-20 55
(Maroon label.)
MERCURY (70753 "The Great Pretender") 8-12 56
(Black label.)
MERCURY (70819 "The Magic Touch") 10-20 56
(Maroon label.)
MERCURY (70819 "The Magic Touch") 8-12 56
(Black label.)
MERCURY (70893 "My Prayer") 10-20 56
(Maroon label.)
MERCURY (70893 "My Prayer") . 8-12 56
(Black label.)
MERCURY (70948 "You'll Never Never Know") 10-15 56
MERCURY (71011 "One in a Million") 10-15 56
MERCURY (71032 "I'm Sorry") . 10-20 56
(Maroon label.)
MERCURY (71032 "I'm Sorry") ... 8-12 56
(Black label.)
MERCURY (71093 "My Dream") 10-20 56
(Maroon label.)
MERCURY (71093 "My Dream") . 8-12 56
(Black label.)
MERCURY (71184 thru 71904) ... 8-12 57-61
MERCURY (71921 thru 72359) 4-8 62-64
MERCURY (30,000 series) 4-6 60s
(Celebrity Series reissues.)
MUSICOR 4-8 66-71
OWL 3-5 73
POWER 4-8 60s

Picture Sleeves

MERCURY 10-15 60-64

EPs: 7–inch 33/45rpm

FEDERAL (378 The Platters Sing for Only You") 300-400 56
KING (378 "The Platters") 100-200 56
KING (651 "The Platters") 100-200 56
(All copies of **Federal** 651 are bootlegs. Originals are only on King.)
MERCURY 25-50 56-61

LPs: 10/12–inch 33rpm

CANDLELITE 15-25 70s
EVEREST 5-10 81

FEDERAL (549 "Platters") 300-500 57
51 WEST 5-8 80s
KING (651 "The Platters") 75-125 59
MERCURY (4000 series) 5-8 82
MERCURY (8000 series) 5-8
MERCURY (20146 thru 20366) 20-40 56-58
MERCURY (20410 thru 20983) 15-30 59-65
(Monaural.)
MERCURY (60043 thru 60983) 20-40 59-65
(Stereo.)
MUSIC DISC 10-12 69
MUSICO (1002 "Only You") 8-10 70
MUSICOR (2000 & 3000 series) 10-15 66-69
MUSICOR (4600 series) 10-12 77
PICKWICK 8-10 70s
RHINO 8-12 80s
SPRINGBOARD 8-10 76
TRIP 8-10 76
WING 10-20 62-67

Members: Tony Williams; David Lynch; Herb Reed; Linda Hayes: Sandra Dawn; Nate Nelson; Sonny Turner; Zola Taylor; Paul Robi; Alex Hodge.

Also see HAYES, Linda, & Platters
Also see LITTLE ANTHONY & IMPERIALS / Platters
Also see PLATTERS '65
Also see WILLIAMS, Tony

PLATTERS / Exotic Guitars

LPs: 10/12-inch 33rpm

GUEST STAR 10-15 64

PLATTERS / Inez & Charlie Foxx / Jive Five / Tommy Hunt

LPs: 10/12-inch 33rpm

MUSICOR 10-20 67

Also see FOXX, Inez
Also see HUNT, Tommy
Also see JIVE FIVE

PLATTERS '65

Singles: 7-inch

ENTREE 4-8 65

Also see PLATTERS

PLAYBOYS

P&R '58

Singles: 7-inch

ABC-PAR 8-12 59
ACE 4-8 64
CAMEO (142 "Over the Weekend") 10-15 58
CATALINA 10-20 64
CHANCELLOR 5-10 61-62
DOLTON 5-10 59
HEARTBEAT 4-8 60s
IMPERIAL 5-10 59
JEWEL 4-8 64
LEGATO (101 "Mope De Mope") 10-20 63
MARTINIQUE (101 "Over the Weekend") 15-25 58
MARTINIQUE (400 "Please Forgive Me") 15-25 59
MERCURY 10-15 57
RIK 5-10 59
SOUVENIR 5-10 59
TITAN 4-8 65

PLAYER

P&R/R&B/LP '77

Singles: 7-inch

CASABLANCA 3-5 80
RCA 3-5 82
RSO 3-5 77-78

LPs: 10/12-inch 33rpm

CASABLANCA 5-10 80
RCA 5-10 81
RSO 5-10 77-78

Member: J.C. Crowley.

PLAYERS

R&B '66

Singles: 7-inch

MINIT 4-8 66-67

LPs: 10/12-inch 33rpm

MINIT 10-20 68

PLAYERS ASSOCIATION

R&B '80

Singles: 12-inch 33/45rpm

VANGUARD 4-8 79-80

Singles: 7-inch

VANGUARD 3-5 77-80

LPs: 10/12-inch 33rpm

VANGUARD 5-10 77-80

PLAYMATES

P&R '58

Singles: 78rpm

ROULETTE 5-10 57

Singles: 7-inch

ABC-PAR 4-8 63-64
BELL 3-5 71
COLPIX 4-8 64-65
CONGRESS 4-8 65
ROULETTE 8-15 57-63

LPs: 10/12-inch 33rpm

FORUM 15-25 60
ROULETTE 20-30 57-61

Members: Donny Conn; Morey Carr; Chic Hetti.

PLEASURE

R&B/LP '76

Singles: 12-inch 33/45rpm

FANTASY 4-8 76-80

Singles: 7-inch

FANTASY 3-5 76-80
RCA 3-4 82-83

LPs: 10/12-inch 33rpm

FANTASY 5-10 76-80
RCA 5-8 82

PLEASURE, King: see KING PLEASURE

PLEASURE & BEAST

D&D '84

Singles: 12–inch 33/45rpm

AIRWAVE.................................... 4-6 84

PLEDGES

Singles: 78rpm

REV (3517 "Betty Jean")........... 10-20 57

Singles: 7–inch

REV (3517 "Betty Jean")........... 10-20 57

Members: Gary Paxton; Clyde Batton.

Also see SKIP & FLIP

PLEIS, Jack, & His Orchestra

P&R '56

Singles: 7–inch

ATCO 4-6 65
COLUMBIA 4-6 61
DECCA.. 5-10 53-60
LONDON..................................... 5-10 50-51
RANWOOD 3-5 76

EPs: 7–inch 33/45rpm

DECCA.. 5-10 55-57

LPs: 10/12–inch 33rpm

CAMEO 10-20 63
COLUMBIA 10-15 61
DECCA...................................... 10-20 55-57
RANWOOD 5-8 76

PLEIS, Jack, & Owen Bradley

EPs: 7–inch 33/45rpm

DECCA (2593 "Bandstand
Hop")...................................... 10-15 58

LPs: 10/12–inch 33rpm

DECCA (8724 "Bandstand
Hop")...................................... 20-30 58

Also see BRADLEY, Owen

Also see PLEIS, Jack, & His Orchestra

PLIMSOULS

LP '81

Singles: 12–inch 33/45rpm

BEAT (1001 "Zero Hour").......... 15-25 80
BOMP... 5-8 80

Singles: 7–inch

BOMP... 3-5 80
GEFFEN.. 3-4 83
SHAKY CITY 3-5

Picture Sleeves

BOMP... 3-5 80
GEFFEN.. 3-4 83
SHAKY CITY 3-5

LPs: 10/12–inch 33rpm

GEFFEN.. 5-8 83
PLANET 5-10 81

PLUSH

R&B '82

Singles: 7–inch

RCA.. 3-5 82

LPs: 10/12–inch 33rpm

RCA.. 5-10 82

P-NUT GALLERY

(Circa '58 & Peanut Gallery)

P&R '71

Singles: 7–inch

BUDDAH..3-5 71

POCKETS

R&B/LP '77

Singles: 7–inch

ARC 4-6 79
COLUMBIA 4-6 77-78

LPs: 10/12–inch 33rpm

ARC 5-10 79
COLUMBIA 5-10 77-78

POCO

LP '69

Singles: 7–inch

ABC...3-5 75-79
ATLANTIC.....................................3-4 82-84
EPIC..3-6 69-75
MCA...3-5 79-82
RCA 3-4 89

Picture Sleeves

EPIC..3-6 70-72
MCA...3-5 80
RCA 3-4 89

LPs: 10/12–inch 33rpm

ABC...8-12 75-78
ATLANTIC.....................................5-8 82-84
EPIC (26460 "Pickin' Up the
Pieces")..................................10-15 69
EPIC (26522 "Poco") 10-15 70
EPIC (30209 "Deliverin'")............8-12 71
EPIC (EQ-30209 "Deliverin'")..... 15-25 71
(Quadrophonic.)
EPIC (30753 "From the Inside")...5-10 71
EPIC (31601 "A Good Feelin' to
Know")......................................5-10 72
EPIC (32354 "Crazy Eyes") 5-10 73
EPIC (EQ-32354 "Crazy Eyes").10-15 73
(Quadrophonic.)
EPIC (32895 "Seven") 5-10 74
EPIC (33192 "Cantamos") 5-10 74
(Quadrophonic.)
EPIC (PEQ-33192 "Cantamos") 10-15 74
EPIC (33537 thru 36210).............5-10 75-81
MCA..5-10 80-82
MFSL (020 "Legend") 25-50 78
RCA 5-8 89

Members: Richie Furay; Jim Messina; Rusty Young; Timothy Schmit; Paul Cotton.

Also see BUFFALO SPRINGFIELD

Also see EAGLES

Also see FURRAY, Richie

Also see ILLINOIS SPEED PRESS

Also see MEISNER, Randy

Also see MESSINA, Jim

Also see SCHMIT, Timothy B.

POETS
(James Brown & His Band)

Singles: 7-inch

TRY ME (28006 "Devil's Den").. 10-15 63

Also see BROWN, James

POETS
P&R/R&B '66

Singles: 7-inch

CHAIRMAN 5-10 63
J-2 (1302 "Wrapped Around Your Finger") 75-125
SYMBOL 5-10 66
VEEP 10-20 68

POGUES
LP '88

LPs: 10/12-inch 33rpm

ISLAND 5-8 88-90

POINDEXTER, Buster, & His Banshees of Blue
P&R '87

Singles: 7-inch

RCA 3-4 87

Picture Sleeves

RCA 3-4 87

LPs: 10/12-inch 33rpm

RCA 5-8 87

Members: David Johansen.
Also see JOHANSEN, David

POINT BLANK
LP '76

Singles: 7-inch

ARISTA 3-6 76-77
MCA 3-5 79-81

LPs: 10/12-inch 33rpm

ARISTA 5-10 76-77
MCA 5-8 79-82

Members: Bubba Keith; John O'Daniel.

POINTER, Anita
R&B '87

Singles: 7-inch

RCA 3-4 87-88

Also see POINTER SISTERS

POINTER, Bonnie
P&R/R&B/LP '78

Singles: 12-inch 33/45rpm

MOTOWN 4-8 78-81
PRIVATE I 4-6 84-85

Singles: 7-inch

MOTOWN (Except 1451) 3-5 78-81
MOTOWN (1451 "Free Me from My Freedom") 3-4 78
(Black vinyl.)
MOTOWN (1451 "Free Me from My Freedom") 4-8 78
(Colored vinyl.)
PRIVATE I 3-4 84-85

Picture Sleeves

MOTOWN (1451 "Free Me from My Freedom") 3-5 78

LPs: 10/12-inch 33rpm

MOTOWN 5-10 78-79
PRIVATE I 5-8 84

Also see POINTER SISTERS

POINTER, June
R&B '83

Singles: 12-inch 33/45rpm

PLANET 4-6 83-84

Singles: 7-inch

PLANET 3-4 83-84

LPs: 10/12-inch 33rpm

PLANET 5-8 83

POINTER, Noel
LP '77

Singles: 12-inch 33/45rpm

U.A. 4-6 77

Singles: 7-inch

BLUE NOTE 3-5 77
LIBERTY 3-5 81
U.A. 3-5 78-80

LPs: 10/12-inch 33rpm

BLUE NOTE 5-10 77
LIBERTY 5-8 81
U.A. 5-8 78-80

POINTER SISTERS
P&R/R&B/LP '73

Singles: 12-inch 33/45rpm

PLANET 4-8 78-85
RCA 4-6 85-86

Singles: 7-inch

ABC 3-6 75-78
ATLANTIC (2845 "Don't Try to Take the Fifth") 10-20 72
ATLANTIC (2893 "Destination, No More Heartaches") 10-20 72
BLUE THUMB 3-6 73-78
MCA 3-4 87
PLANET 3-5 78-85
RCA 3-4 85-88

Picture Sleeves

MCA 3-4 87
PLANET 3-5 78-85
RCA 3-4 85-86

LPs: 10/12-inch 33rpm

BLUE THUMB 8-12 73-77
MCA 5-10 81
PLANET 5-10 78-84
RCA 5-8 85-88

Members: Bonnie Pointer; Anita Pointer; Ruth Pointer; June Pointer.
Also see MEMPHIS HORNS
Also see POINTER, Anita, & Earl Thomas Conley
Also see POINTER, Bonnie
Also see POINTER, June

POISON

R&B '75

Singles: 12–inch 33/45rpm

ROULETTE 4-8 76

Singles: 7–inch

ROULETTE 3-5 75-76

LPs: 10/12–inch 33rpm

ROULETTE 5-10 76

POISON

LP '86

Singles: 7–inch

CAPITOL 3-4 87
ENIGMA 3-4 86-88

Picture Sleeves

CAPITOL 3-4 87
ENIGMA 3-4 87-88

LPs: 10/12–inch 33rpm

CAPITOL 5-8 86-90
ENIGMA 5-8 86-88

Members: Bret Michaels; Rikki Rocket; C.C. DeVille; Bobby Dall; Richie Kotzen; Blues Saraceno.

POLE, Keith

R&B '85

Singles: 7–inch

SUPERTRONICS 3-4 85

POLICE

P&R/LP '79

Singles: 12–inch 33/45rpm

A&M (17122 "Message in a Bottle") 5-8 79
(Promotional issue only.)

Singles: 7–inch

A&M (Except 25000, and picture discs) 3-5 79-84
A&M (25000 "De Do Do Do, De Da Da Da") 10-20 80
(Spanish/Japanese language version.)
A&M (2096 "Roxanne") 25-35 79
(Picture disc. Promotional issues only.)
A&M (4401 "Don't Stand So Close") 15-25 81
(Picture disc. Promotional issues only.)
SIRE 3-4 86

Picture Sleeves

A&M (Except 25000) 3-5 80-86
A&M (25000 "De Do Do Do, De Da Da Da") 4-6 80

LPs: 10/12–inch 33rpm

A&M (Except 3713 & 3735) 5-15 79-86
A&M (3713 "Synchronicity") 75-100 83
(Black and white cover.)
A&M (3713 "Synchronicity") 40-50 83
(Gold, gray and brown cover.)
A&M (3713 "Reggatta de Blanc") 10-20 79
(Two 10–inch LPs. Includes poster. Promotional issue only.)
NAUTILUS 10-20 81

Members: Gordon "Sting" Sumner; Andy Summers; Stewart Copeland.
Also see COPELAND, Stewart
Also see FRIPP, Robert, & Andy Summers
Also see STING

POLITICIANS

R&B '72

Singles: 7–inch

HOT WAX 3-5 72

LPs: 10/12–inch 33rpm

HOT WAX 8-12 72

Members: McKinley Jackson.

POLNAREFF, Michel

P&R/LP '76

Singles: 12–inch 33/45rpm

ATLANTIC 4-8 76

Singles: 7–inch

ATLANTIC 3-5 76
4 CORNERS (141 "Time Will Tell") 8-12 67
KAPP 4-8 65-66

LPs: 10/12–inch 33rpm

ATLANTIC 8-10 75
4 CORNERS 10-15 67

PONDEROSA TWINS + ONE

P&R/R&B '71

Singles: 7–inch

ASTROSCOPE 3-5 72
HOROSCOPE 3-5 71

LPs: 10/12–inch 33rpm

HOROSCOPE 8-12 71

PONI-TAILS

P&R/R&B '58

Singles: 78rpm

ABC-PAR 10-20 57
MARC 10-15 57
POINT 10-15 57

Singles: 7–inch

ABC 3-5 73
ABC-PAR 10-20 57-60
MCA 3-4
MARC 10-15 57
POINT 10-15 57

Members: Toni Cistone; LaVern Novak; Pat McCabe.
Also see ELEGANTS / Poni-Tails

PONSAR, Serge

D&D '83

Singles: 12–inch 33/45rpm

W.B. 4-6 83

Singles: 7–inch

W.B. 3-4 83

PONTY, Jean-Luc

LP '75

Singles: 7–inch

ATLANTIC 3-5 76-85

LPs: 10/12–inch 33rpm
ATLANTIC 5-10 75-85
BLUE NOTE 5-10 76-81
MPS 5-10 72-73
PACIFIC JAZZ 8-18 68-78
PAUSA 5-10 80
PRESTIGE 8-15 70
WORLD PACIFIC 15-25 69

POOLE, Brian
(With the Tremeloes)

P&R '64

Singles: 7–inch
DATE 5-10 66
LONDON 5-10 63
MONUMENT 5-10 64-65

LPs: 10/12–inch 33rpm
AUDIO FIDELITY 15-25 66-67
Also see TREMELOES

POOR RIGHTEOUS TEACHERS

LP '90

LPs: 10/12–inch 33rpm
PROFILE 5-8 90

POP, Iggy
(Iggy & Stooges)

LP '73

Singles: 12–inch 33/45rpm
A&M 4-8 86

Singles: 7–inch
A&M 3-4 86
RCA 3-5 77
SIAMESE 3-6 77

Picture Sleeves
A&M 3-4 86

EPs: 7–inch 33/45rpm
BOMP 5-10 78

LPs: 10/12–inch 33rpm
A&M 5-8 86
ANIMAL 5-10 82
ARISTA 8-12 79-81
BOMP (1018 "Kill City") 10-15 78
(Black vinyl.)
BOMP (1018 "Kill City") 20-30 78
(Colored vinyl.)
COLUMBIA 10-20 73
ENIGMA 5-8 84
IMPORT 8-10 77
INVASION 8-10 83
RCA 5-10 77-78
VIRGIN 5-8 90
Also see BOWIE, David / Iggy Pop
Also see STOOGES

POP, Iggy, & James Williamson

EPs: 7–inch 33/45rpm
BOMP 5-10 78

LPs: 10/12–inch 33rpm
BOMP 5-10 78
Also see POP, Iggy

POP TOPS
(Los Pop Tops)

P&R/R&B '68

Singles: 7–inch
ABC 3-5 71
CALLA 4-8 68

POPE JOHN XXIII

LP '63

LPs: 10/12-Inch 33rpm
MERCURY 5-10 63

POPE JOHN PAUL II

LP '79

LPs: 10/12-Inch 33rpm
BETHLEHEM 5-8 79
INFINITY 5-8 79
VOX CHRISTIANA 5-8 79

POPPIES

P&R '66

Singles: 7–inch
EPIC (9893 "Lullaby of Love") 4-8 66
EPIC (10019 "He's Ready") 4-8 66
EPIC (10059 "Do It with Soul") 5-10 66
EPIC (10086 "There's a Pain in My Heart") 10-20 66

Picture Sleeves
EPIC (10019 "He's Ready") 5-10 66

LPs: 10/12–inch 33rpm
EPIC (24200 "Lullaby of Love") .20-30 66
(Monaural.)
EPIC (26200 "Lullaby of Love") .25-35 66
(Stereo.)
Members: Dorothy Moore; Rosemary Taylor; Pet McCune.
Also see MOORE, Dorothy

POPPY FAMILY
(Featuring Susan Jacks)

P&R/LP '70

Singles: 7–inch
LONDON 3-5 70-72

LPs: 10/12–inch 33rpm
LONDON 10-15 70-71
Members: Susan Jacks; Terry Jacks.
Also see JACKS, Susan
Also see JACKS, Terry

PORTER, David

R&B/LP '70

Singles: 7–inch
ENTERPRISE 3-5 70-72
STAX 10-15 64

LPs: 10/12–inch 33rpm
ENTERPRISE 8-12 70-72
Also see HAYES, Isaac, & David Porter

PORTER, Nolan
(N.F. Porter; Nolan)

P&R/R&B '71

Singles: 7–inch
ABC 3-5 73
LIZARD 3-5 71

LPs: 10/12-inch 33rpm

LIZARD 8-12 71

PORTNOY, Gary

P&R '83

Singles: 7-inch

APPLAUSE 3-4 83
EARTHTONE 3-4 84

Picture Sleeves

EARTHTONE 3-5 84

POSEY, Sandy

P&R/LP '66

Singles: 7-inch

AUDIOGRAPH 3-4 83
COLUMBIA 3-5 71-73
MGM 4-6 66-67
MONUMENT 3-5 76
POLYDOR 3-4 83
W.B. 3-5 76-79

Picture Sleeves

MGM 4-8 66-67

LPs: 10/12-inch 33rpm

COLUMBIA 5-10 72
51 WEST 5-8 83
GUSTO 5-8 80s
MGM 8-15 66-70

POSEY, Sandy / Skeeter Davis

LPs: 10/12-inch 33rpm

GUSTO 5-8

Also see DAVIS, Skeeter
Also see POSEY, Sandy

POST, Mike

(Mike Post Coalition)

P&R/LP '75

Singles: 7-inch

BELL 3-5 71
ELEKTRA 3-4 81-82
EPIC 3-5 77
MGM 3-5 75
MUSIC FACTORY 4-6 68
POLYDOR 3-4 87
REPRISE 4-6 65-66
W.B. 3-6 69

Picture Sleeves

ELEKTRA 3-5 81-82

LPs: 10/12-inch 33rpm

ELEKTRA 5-8 82
RCA 5-8 83
MGM 5-10 75
POLYDOR 5-8 87
W.B. 8-12 69

POTLIQUOR

P&R/LP '72

Singles: 7-inch

CAPITOL 3-5 79
JANUS 3-5 72

LPs: 10/12-inch 33rpm

CAPITOL 5-10 79
JANUS 10-15 70-73

POURCEL, Franck

(Franck Pourcel's French Fiddles)

P&R/R&B '59

Singles: 7-inch

BLUE 3-5 69
CAPITOL 4-8 59-64
IMPERIAL 3-6 66-68
PARAMOUNT 3-5 71-73

EPs: 7-inch 33/45rpm

CAPITOL 5-10 59

LPs: 10/12-inch 33rpm

ATCO 5-10 69
CAPITOL 5-20 56-79
IMPERIAL 5-15 66-68
PARAMOUNT 5-8 70-73
WESTMINSTER 10-25 54-55

POUSETTE-DART BAND

LP '77

Singles: 7-inch

CAPITOL 3-5 76-79

LPs: 10/12-inch 33rpm

CAPITOL 5-10 76-80

Member: Jon Pousette-Dart.

POWELL, Adam Clayton

LP '67

LPs: 10/12-inch 33rpm

JUBILEE 10-15 67

POWELL, Bobby

P&R/R&B '65

Singles: 7-inch

JEWEL 4-8 67
WHIT 3-8 65-71

LPs: 10/12-inch 33rpm

EXCELLO 8-12 73

POWELL, Cozy

P&R '74

Singles: 7-inch

CHRYSALIS 3-5 74

Also see BECK, Jeff
Also see BEDLAM
Also see EMERSON, LAKE & POWELL

POWELL, Jane

P&R '56

Singles: 78rpm

VERVE 4-6 56

Singles: 7-inch

RANWOOD 3-5 68
VERVE 4-8 56

LPs: 10/12-inch 33rpm

COLUMBIA 15-30 55-57
LION 10-20 59
MGM 20-40 55
VERVE 20-35 56

Also see ASTAIRE, Fred, & Jane Powell

POWER STATION

P&R/D&D/LP '85

Singles: 12-inch 33/45rpm

CAPITOL 4-6 85

Singles: 7-inch

CAPITOL 3-4 85

Picture Sleeves

CAPITOL 3-4 85

LPs: 10/12-inch 33rpm

CAPITOL 5-8 85

Members: Andy Taylor; John Taylor; Robert Palmer; Tommy Thompson.

Also see DURAN DURAN
Also see PALMER, Robert
Also see TAYLOR, Andy
Also see TAYLOR, John

POWERS, Joey

(Joey Powers' Flower)

P&R '63

Singles: 7-inch

AMY 5-10 63-67
MGM 5-10 65
RCA (8000 series) 4-8 62
RCA (9700 series) 3-6 69

LPs: 10/12-inch 33rpm

AMY 15-25 64

Also see ORBISON, Roy / Bobby Bare / Joey Powers

POWERS, Tom

P&R '77

Singles: 7-inch

BIG TREE 3-5 77

POWERSOURCE

P&R '87

Singles: 7-inch

POWERVISION 3-4 87

POZO-SECO SINGERS

(Susan Taylor & the Pozo Seco Singers; Pozo Seco)

P&R/LP '66

Singles: 7-inch

CERTRON 3-5 70
COLUMBIA 4-8 65-70
EDMARK 10-20 65

LPs: 10/12-inch 33rpm

CERTRON 10-15 70
COLUMBIA 10-20 66-68

Members: Don Williams; Susan Taylor; Lofton Kline.

Also see WILLIAMS, Don

PRADO, Perez, & His Orchestra

P&R '53

Singles: 78rpm

RCA 4-6 50-58

Singles: 7-inch

RCA 5-15 50-64
U.A. 3-6 64

Picture Sleeves

RCA 8-10 59

EPs: 7-inch 33/45rpm

BELL (2 "Perez Prado") 5-10
RCA 8-15 54-61

LPs: 10/12-inch 33rpm

CAMDEN 10-15 60
RCA 5-10 76
(With "ANL1" prefix.)
RCA 10-30 54-72
(With "LPM," "LSP" or "VPS" prefix.)
SPIN-O-RAMA 8-12 62
SPRINGBOARD 5-10 77
U.A. 10-15 65-68

Also see CLOONEY, Rosemary, & Perez Prado
Also see HIRT, Al / Henry Mancini / Perez Prado

PRATT, Andy

P&R/LP '73

Singles: 7-inch

COLUMBIA 3-5 73
NEMPEROR 3-5 76-77

LPs: 10/12-inch 33rpm

COLUMBIA 8-12 73
NEMPEROR 5-10 76-79
POLYDOR 10-15 70

Also see SPRINGSTEEN, Bruce / Andy Pratt

PRATT - McCLAIN

P&R/LP '76

Singles: 7-inch

REPRISE 3-5 76-77

LPs: 10/12-inch 33rpm

DUNHILL 8-12 73
REPRISE 8-10 76

Members: Truett Pratt; Jerry McClain.

PRECISIONS

P&R/R&B '67

Singles: 7-inch

ATCO 4-8 69
D-TOWN (1033 "My Lover Come Back") 75-125 65
D-TOWN (1055 "Mexican Love Song") 10-20 65
DREW (1001 "Such Misery") 15-25 66
DREW (1003 "If This Is Love") 10-20 66
HEN-MAR 3-5 73

PREFAB SPROUT

LP '85

Singles: 7-inch

EPIC 5-8 85

LPs: 10/12-inch 33rpm

EPIC 10-15 85

PRELUDE

P&R '74

Singles: 7-inch

ISLAND 3-5 74
PYE 3-5 75

LPs: 10/12-inch 33rpm

ISLAND 8-10 74
PYE 8-10 75

PRELUDES FIVE
(Preludes)

P&R '61

Singles: 7-inch

PIK (231 "Don't You Know")...... 15-20 61

PREMIATA FORNERIA MARCONI: see P.F.M.

PREMIERS

P&R '64

Singles: 7-inch

FARO 6-12 64-67
FINE 4-8 60s
LEO 5-10 64
W.B. 4-8 64

LPs: 10/12-inch 33rpm

RAMPART ("Farmer John") 25-35 64
(Number not known.)
W.B. (1565 "Farmer John")....... 15-25 64

PRENTISS, Lee

D&D '83

Singles: 12-inch 33/45rpm

MSB 4-6 83

PREPARATIONS

R&B '68

Singles: 7-inch

HEART and SOUL 4-8 68

PRESIDENTS

P&R/R&B '70

Singles: 7-inch

DELUXE.. 4-8 69
HOLLYWOOD............................... 4-8 68
SUSSEX.. 3-6 70-71

LPs: 10/12-inch 33rpm

SUSSEX.................................. 15-25 70

PRESLEY, Elvis
(With Scotty & Bill; with Jordanaires; with Imperials; with J.D. Sumner & Stamps; with Mello Men; with Amigos; with Jubilee Four & Carol Lombard Trio)

C&W '55

Singles: 78rpm
(Commercial and Promotional)

RCA (6357 "Mystery Train").. 100-150 55
RCA (6380 "That's All Right") 100-150 55
RCA (6381 "Good Rockin' Tonight")............................ 100-150 55
RCA (6382 "Milkcow Blues Boogie") 100-150 55
RCA (6383 "Baby, Let's Play House") 100-150 55
RCA (6420 "Heartbreak Hotel") 75-100 56
(Black label.)
RCA (6420 "Heartbreak Hotel") 400-500 56
(White label. Promotional issue only. Opinions vary as to authenticity.)
RCA (6540 "I Want You, I Need You, I Love You")....................................75-100 56
(Black label.)
RCA (6540 "I Want You, I Need You, I Love You").........................400-500 56
(White label. Promotional issue only. Opinions vary as to authenticity.)
RCA (6604 "Don't Be Cruel")...75-100 56
(Black label.)
RCA (6604 "Don't Be Cruel") .400-500 56
(White label. Promotional issue only. Opinions vary as to authenticity.)
RCA (6636 "Blue Suede Shoes")................................75-100 56
(Black label.)
RCA (6637 "I Got a Woman")..75-100 56
(Black label.)
RCA (6638 "I'm Gonna Sit Right Down and Cry")....................................75-100 56
(Black label.)
RCA (6639 "Tryin' to Get to You")....................................75-100 56
(Black label.)
RCA (6640 "Blue Moon") 75-100 56
(Black label.)
RCA (6641 "Money Honey") 75-100 56
(Black label.)
RCA (6642 "Lawdy Miss Clawdy")...............................75-100 56
(Black label.)
RCA (6643 "Love Me Tender") 75-100 56
(Black label.)
RCA (6643 "Love Me Tender")...............................400-500 56
(White label. Promotional issue only. Opinions vary as to authenticity.)
RCA (6800 "Too Much") 75-100 57
(Black label.)
RCA (6800 "Too Much") 400-500 57
(White label. Promotional issue only. Opinions vary as to authenticity.)
RCA (6870 "All Shook Up")......75-100 57
(Black label.)
RCA (6870 "All Shook Up")....400-500 57
(White label. Promotional issue only. Opinions vary as to authenticity.)
RCA (7000 "Teddy Bear")........75-100 57
(Black label.)
RCA (7000 "Teddy Bear")......400-500 57
(White label. Promotional issue only. Opinions vary as to authenticity.)
RCA (7035 "Jailhouse Rock")..75-100 57
(Black label.)
RCA (7035 "Jailhouse Rock") 400-500 57
(White label. Promotional issue only. Opinions vary as to authenticity.)
RCA (7150 "Don't") 75-100 58
RCA (7240 "Wear My Ring Around Your Neck") 75-100 58

RCA (7280 "Hard Headed Woman") 75-125 58
RCA (7410 "One Night") 400-500 58
ROYAL ("Elvis Presley Show") 150-250 56
(Single-sided disc, issued to radio stations to promote Elvis in concert. Includes an excerpt of *Heartbreak Hotel*.)
SUN (209 "That's All Right") 600-1200 54
SUN (210 "Good Rockin' Tonight") 500-1000 54
SUN (215 "Milkcow Blues Boogie") 600-1200 55
SUN (217 "Baby Let's Play House") 500-1000 55
SUN (223 "Mystery Train").... 500-900 55
Notes: All Elvis RCA and Sun 78s were simultaneously issued on 45rpm singles. For 78rpm plastic soundsheets and flexi-discs, see a separate section that follows. RCA and Sun 78s can be found with many label variations. Sun promotional singles were marked with the word "sample" rubber stamped on the label. White label promotional 78s are still listed; however, their authenticity has recently been challenged.

Singles: 7–inch (Commercial)

COLLECTABLES (Black vinyl)...... 3-5 86-87
COLLECTABLES (Gold vinyl)....... 3-5 92
RCA (0088 "Raised on Rock") 4-6 73
RCA (0130 "How Great Thou Art") 15-20 69
RCA (0196 "Take Good Care of Her") 4-6 74
RCA (0280 "If You Talk in Your Sleep") 8-12 74
(Has title on one line.)
RCA (0280 "If You Talk in Your Sleep") 4-6 74
(Two lines are used for title.)
RCA (0572 "Merry Christmas Baby") 12-15 71
RCA (0619 "Until It's Time for You to Go") 4-6 72
RCA (0651 "He Touched Me") 100-150 72
(Has the *He Touched Me* side pressed at about 35rpm instead of 45. These copies—the result of a production error—were commercial issues. Flip, *Bosom of Abraham*, plays at 45rpm.)
RCA (0651 "He Touched Me") 4-6 72
RCA (0672 "An American Trilogy") 15-20 72
RCA (0769 "Burning Love") 4-6 72
(Orange label.)
RCA (0769 "Burning Love") ...100-125 72
(Gray label.)
RCA (0815 "Separate Ways")........4-6 71
RCA (0910 "Fool") 4-6 73
RCA (1017 "It's Only Love")...........4-6 71
RCA (2458 "My Boy"/"Loving Arms") 500-750 74
(Produced in the U.S. for European distribution.)
RCA (6357 "Mystery Train").......30-40 55
RCA (6380 "That's All Right") 30-40 55
RCA (6381 "Good Rockin' Tonight") 30-40 55
RCA (6382 "Milkcow Blues Boogie") 30-40 55
RCA (6383 "Baby Let's Play House") 30-40 55
RCA (6420 "Heartbreak Hotel") .20-30 56
RCA (6540 "I Want You, I Need You, I Love You") 20-30 56
RCA (6604 "Don't Be Cruel") 20-30 56
RCA (6636 "Blue Suede Shoes") 30-40 56
RCA (6637 "I Got a Woman") 30-40 56
RCA (6638 "I'm Gonna Sit Right Down and Cry") 30-40 56
RCA (6639 "Tryin' to Get to You") 30-40 56
RCA (6640 "Blue Moon") 30-40 56
RCA (6641 "Money Honey") 30-40 56
RCA (6642 "Lawdy Miss Clawdy") 30-40 56
(Dog is pictured on label.)
RCA (6642 "Lawdy Miss Clawdy") 150-200 56
(Dog is not shown on label.)
RCA (6643 "Love Me Tender") ..20-30 56
RCA (6800 "Too Much") 20-30 57
(Dog is pictured on label.)
RCA (6800 "Too Much") 200-300 57
(Dog is not shown on label.)
RCA (6870 "All Shook Up")........20-30 57
RCA (7000 "Teddy Bear")..........20-30 57
RCA (7035 "Jailhouse Rock")....20-30 57
Note: All RCA singles from 6357 through 7035 can be found on various black labels, both with or without a horizontal silver line.
RCA (7150 "Don't") 12-15 58
RCA (7240 "Wear My Ring Around Your Neck") 12-15 58
RCA (7280 "Hard Headed Woman") 12-15 58
RCA (7410 "One Night") 12-15 58
RCA (7506 "I Need Your Love Tonight") 12-15 59
RCA (7600 "A Big Hunk O' Love") 12-15 59
RCA (47-7740 "Stuck on You")....8-10 60

RCA (61-7740 "Stuck on You") 350-450 60
(Living Stereo.)
RCA (47-7777 "It's Now Or Never") 500-750 60
(Pressed without the piano track.)
RCA (47-7777 "It's Now Or Never") 8-10 60
RCA (61-7777 "It's Now Or Never") 400-600 60
(Living Stereo.)
RCA (47-7810 "Are You Lonesome To-night") 8-10 60
RCA (61-7810 "Are You Lonesome To-night") 400-600 60
(Living Stereo.)
RCA (37-7850 "Surrender") .. 450-550 61
(Compact 33 Single.)
RCA (47-7850 "Surrender") 8-10 61
RCA (61-7850 "Surrender") .. 600-800 61
(Living Stereo.)
RCA (68-7850 "Surrender") 1000-1500 61
(Stereo Compact 33 Single.)
RCA (37-7880 "I Feel So Bad") 800-1200 61
(Compact 33 Single.)
RCA (47-7880 "I Feel So Bad")... 8-10 61
RCA (37-7908 "His Latest Flame") 1500-2500 61
(Compact 33 Single.)
RCA (47-7908 "His Latest Flame") 8-10 61
RCA (37-7968 "Can't Help Falling in Love") 3000-4000 61
(Compact 33 Single.)
RCA (47-7968 "Can't Help Falling in Love") 8-10 61
RCA (37-7992 "Good Luck Charm") 4000-5000 62
(Compact 33 Single.)
RCA (47-7992 "Good Luck Charm") 8-10 62
RCA (8041 "She's Not You") 8-10 62
RCA (8100 "Return to Sender") .. 8-10 62
RCA (8134 "One Broken Heart for Sale") 8-10 63
RCA (8188 "Devil in Disguise") 75-100 63
(Flip side title is incorrectly shown as *Please Don't Drag That String ALONG.*)
RCA (8188 "Devil in Disguise") ... 6-10 63
(Flip side title correctly shown as *Please Don't Drag That String AROUND.*)
RCA (8243 "Bossa Nova Baby"). 6-10 63
RCA (8307 "Kissin' Cousins") 6-10 64
RCA (8360 "Viva Las Vegas") 6-10 64
RCA (8400 "Such a Night") 6-10 64
RCA (8440 "Ask Me") 6-10 64
RCA (8500 "Do the Clam") 6-10 65
RCA (8585 "Easy Question") 6-10 65
RCA (8657 "I'm Yours") 6-10 65
RCA (8740 "Tell Me Why") 6-10 65
RCA (8780 "Frankie & Johnny") .. 6-10 66
RCA (8870 "Love Letters") 6-10 66
RCA (8941 "Spinout") 6-10 66
RCA (8950 "If Everyday Was Like Christmas") 6-10 66
RCA (9056 "Indescribably Blue") . 6-10 67
RCA (9115 "Long Legged Girl") ... 6-10 67
RCA (9287 "There's Always Me") 6-10 67
RCA (9341 "Big Boss Man") 6-10 67
RCA (9425 "Guitar Man") 6-10 68
RCA (9465 "U.S. Male") 6-10 68
RCA (9547 "Your Time Hasn't Come Yet Baby") 6-10 68
RCA (9600 "You'll Never Walk Alone") 6-10 68
RCA (9610 "Almost in Love") 6-10 68
Note: Commercial issues of all RCA singles from 6357 through 9600 are on black labels.
RCA (9670 "If I Can Dream") 4-6 68
RCA (9731 "Memories") 4-6 69
RCA (9741 "In the Ghetto") 4-6 69
RCA (9747 "Clean Up Your Own Back Yard") 4-6 69
RCA (9764 "Suspicious Minds") 4-6 69
RCA (9768 "Don't Cry Daddy") 4-6 69
RCA (9791 "Kentucky Rain") 4-6 70
RCA (9835 "The Wonder of You") . 4-6 70
RCA (9873 "I've Lost You") 4-6 70
RCA (9916 "You Don't Have to Say You Love Me") 4-6 70
RCA (9960 "I Really Don't Want to Know") 4-6 70
RCA (9980 "Rags to Riches") 4-6 71
RCA (9985 "Life") 4-6 71
RCA (9998 "I'm Leavin'") 4-6 71
Note: RCA numbers in the 10000 to 14000 series with a "GB" prefix are Gold Standards and are listed in a separate Gold Standard Singles section.
RCA (10074 "Promised Land") 4-6 74
(Orange label.)
RCA (10074 "Promised Land") .. 20-30 74
(Gray label.)
RCA (10191 "My Boy") 4-6 75
(Orange label.)
RCA (10191 "My Boy") 8-12 75
(Tan or brown label.)
RCA (10278 "T-r-o-u-b-l-e") 4-6 75
(Orange label.)
RCA (10278 "T-r-o-u-b-l-e") 8-10 75
(Tan label.)
RCA (10278 "T-r-o-u-b-l-e") 75-100 75
(Gray label.)
RCA (10401 "Bringing It Back") 150-200 75
(Orange label.)

RCA (10401 "Bringing It Back") 4-6 75
(Tan label.)
RCA (10601 "For the Heart") 4-6 76
(Tan label.)
RCA (10601 "For the Heart") .. 90-100 76
(Black label.)
RCA (10857 "Moody Blue")........... 3-5 76
(Black vinyl. Colored vinyl 45s of *Moody Blue*, were experimental and are listed in the Promotional Singles section that follows.)
RCA (10998 "Way Down") 3-5 77
RCA (11099 thru 11113).............. 3-4 77
(Discs in this series were originally packaged in either 11301 and/or 11340, both of which are boxed sets of singles with sleeves.)
RCA (11165 "My Way")................ 3-5 77
(Flip side shown as *America*.)
RCA (11165 "My Way")............ 15-20 77
(Fith flip side shown as *America the Beautiful*.)
RCA (11212 "Unchained Melody") 3-5 78
RCA (11301 "15 Golden Records") 45-55 77
(Boxed set of 15 Elvis singles with picture sleeves.)
RCA (11320 "Teddy Bear")........... 3-5 78
RCA (11340 "20 Golden Hits").. 65-75 77
(Boxed set of 10 Elvis singles with picture sleeves.)
RCA (11533 "Are You Sincere") ... 3-5 79
RCA (11679 "I Got a Feelin' in My Body")........................... 12-18 79
(With production and backing credits shown on label.)
RCA (11679 ("I Got a Feelin' in My Body").................................. 3-5 79
(With backing credits removed, leaving only production credits.)
RCA (12158 "Guitar Man")........... 3-5 81
RCA (12205 "Lovin' Arms")........... 3-5 81
RCA (13058 "You'll Never Walk Alone") 3-5 82
RCA (13351 "The Elvis Medley") .. 3-5 82
RCA (13500 "I Was the One")....... 3-5 83
RCA (13547 "Little Sister") 3-5 83
RCA (13875 "Baby, Let's Play House") 30-40 84
(Colored vinyl.)
RCA (13885 thru 13890).............. 3-4 84
(Discs in this series were originally packaged in 13897, *Golden Singles, Vol. I*. May include jukebox title strips.)
RCA (13891 thru 13896).............. 3-4 84
(Discs in this series were originally packaged in 13898, *Golden Singles, Vol. II*. May include jukebox title strips.)
RCA (13897 "Golden Singles, Vol. I") 15-25 84
(Package of six colored vinyl singles with sleeves.)
RCA (13898 "Golden Singles, Vol. II") 15-25 84
(Package of six colored vinyl singles with sleeves.)
RCA (13929 "Blue Suede Shoes") 10-15 84
(Colored vinyl. Incorrectly shows *Blue Suede Shoes* as stereo and *Promised Land* as mono.)
RCA (13929 "Blue Suede Shoes") 8-12 84
(Colored vinyl. Correctly shows *Blue Suede Shoes* as mono and *Promised Land* as stereo.)
RCA (14090 "Always on My Mind").......................................8-12 85
(Colored vinyl.)
RCA (14237 "Merry Christmas Baby") 10-15 85
(Black vinyl.)
RCA (14237 "Merry Christmas Baby") 10-15 85
(Colored vinyl.)
RCA (62402 "Don't Be Cruel") ... 10-15 92
(Colored vinyl.)
RCA (62403 "Blue Christmas") .. 10-15 92
(Colored vinyl.)
RCA (62449 "Heartbreak Hotel") 10-15 92
(Colored vinyl.)

Note: RCA numbers in the 10000-14000 series with a "GB" prefix are Gold Standard Series and are listed in a separate Gold Standard Singles section. Regular series issues are in the preceding section.

SUN (209 "That's All Right") 600-1200 54
SUN (210 "Good Rockin' Tonight") 500-1000 54
SUN (215 "Milkcow Blue Boogie") 600-1200 55
SUN (217 "Baby Let's Play House")............................500-1000 55
SUN (223 "Mystery Train").....500-900 55
TRIBUTE (501 "A Tribute to Elvis Presley")........................50-100 56
(Has Elvis plus guest appearances by Edward R. Murrow, Steve Allen, Ed Sullivan, Danny Kaye, Jimmy Durante, Gabriel Heater, Sid Ceaser, Liberace, Mantovani, Jack Benny, Gene Vincent, Gloria DeHaven, Nat King Cole, Nelson Eddy, and Jane Russell.)

Note: Plastic soundsheets or flexi-discs are listed in a separate section that follows.

Picture Sleeves (Commercial and Promotional)

LAUREL (41 623 "Treat Me Nice") 5000-7500 57
(Pictures Elvis but credits Vince Everett. A black and white sleeve made as a prop for the *Jailhouse Rock* film. The printed sheets have no reverse side, but are applied to a randomly selected EP. No Laurel records of this title exist.)
PECA ("Could I Fall in Love") 4000-6000 66
(Pictures Elvis but credits Guy Lambert with George and His G-Men. A full color sleeve made as a prop for the *Double Trouble* film. No Peca records of this title exist.)
RCA (76 "Don't"/"Wear My Ring Around Your Neck") 1000-1500 60
(Promotional issue only.)
RCA (0088 "Raised on Rock") 8-12 73
RCA (118 "King of the Whole Wide World") 150-200 62
(Promotional issue only.)
RCA (0130 "How Great Thou Art") 100-150 69
RCA (162 "How Great Thou Art") 150-200 67
(Promotional issue only.)
RCA (0196 "Take Good Care of Her") 8-12 74
RCA (0280 "If You Talk in Your Sleep") 8-12 74
RCA (0572 "Merry Christmas Baby") 20-30 71
RCA (0619 "Until It's Time for You to Go") 8-12 71
RCA (0651 "He Touched Me") .. 50-75 71
RCA (0672 "An American Trilogy") 15-25 72
RCA (0769 "Burning Love") 8-12 72
RCA (0815 "Separate Ways") 8-12 71
RCA (0910 "Fool") 8-12 73
RCA (1017 "It's Only Love") 8-12 71
RCA (6540 "I Want You, I Need You, I Love You") 1000-2000 56
(Cartoon-like, "This Is His Life" series. Promotional only.)
RCA (6604 "Don't Be Cruel") 65-75 56
(Shows *Don't Be Cruel* c/w *Hound Dog.*)
RCA (6604 "Hound Dog") 55-65 56
(Shows *Hound Dog* c/w *Don't Be Cruel.*)
RCA (6643 "Love Me Tender") 100-150 56
(Black and white sleeve.)
RCA (6643 "Love Me Tender") . 60-75 56
(Black and green sleeve.)
RCA (6643 "Love Me Tender") . 35-45 56
(Black and dark pink sleeve.)
RCA (6643 "Love Me Tender") .. 30-40 56
(Black and light pink sleeve.)
RCA (6800 "Too Much") 50-75 57
RCA (6870 "All Shook Up") 50-75 57
RCA (7000 "Teddy Bear") 40-60 57
RCA (7035 "Jailhouse Rock") 40-60 57
(Sleeve only.)
RCA/MGM "Jailhouse Rock") 1000-1500 57
(MGM *Jailhouse Rock* film preview invitation ticket. A promotional item for the media, the ticket came wrapped around a commercial single and sleeve. Deduct about 50% if ticket stub is detached.)
RCA (7150 "Don't") 40-50 58
RCA (7240 "Wear My Ring Around Your Neck") 40-50 58
RCA (7280 "Hard Headed Woman") 35-45 58
RCA (7410 "One Night") 35-45 58
RCA (7506 "I Need Your Love Tonight") 300-500 59
(Has advertising for the *Elvis Sails* EP on reverse.)
RCA (7506 "I Need Your Love Tonight") 25-35 59
(Has a listing of Elvis EPs and 45s on reverse.)
RCA (7600 "A Big Hunk O' Love") 25-35 59
RCA (7740 "Stuck on You") 15-25 60
RCA (7777 "It's Now Or Never") 15-25 60
RCA (7810 "Are You Lonesome To-night") 15-25 60
RCA (37-7850 "Surrender") ... 600-750 61
(Compact 33 Single sleeve. Copies without some ring wear are very scarce.)
RCA (47-7850 "Surrender") 15-20 61
RCA (37-7880 "I Feel So Bad") 800-1200 61
(Compact 33 Single sleeve.)
RCA (47-7880 "I Feel So Bad") . 15-25 61
RCA (37-7908 "His Latest Flame") 1800-2200 61
(Compact 33 Single sleeve.)
RCA (47-7908 "His Latest Flame") 15-25 61
RCA (37-7968 "Can't Help Falling in Love") 3000-4000 61
(Compact 33 Single sleeve.)
RCA (47-7968 "Can't Help Falling in Love") 15-20 61
RCA (37-7992 "Good Luck Charm") 4000-5000 62
(Compact 33 Single sleeve.)
RCA (47-7992 "Good Luck Charm") 15-20 62
RCA (8041 "She's Not You") 15-20 62
RCA (8100 "Return to Sender") 15-20 62

RCA (8134 "One Broken Heart for Sale") 15-20 63
RCA (8188 "Devil in Disguise") . 15-20 63
RCA (8243 "Bossa Nova Baby") 15-20 63
RCA (8307 "Kissin' Cousins") ... 15-20 64
RCA (8360 "Viva Las Vegas")... 15-20 64
RCA (8400 "Such a Night") 15-20 64
RCA (8440 "Ask Me")............... 15-20 64
RCA (8500 "Do the Clam")........ 15-20 65
RCA (8585 "Easy Question") 15-20 65
RCA (8657 "I'm Yours")............ 15-20 65
RCA (8740 "Tell Me Why")........ 15-20 65
RCA (8780 "Frankie & Johnny") 15-20 66
RCA (8870 "Love Letters")........ 15-20 66
RCA (8941 "Spinout")................ 15-20 66
RCA (8950 "If Everyday Was Like Christmas") 15-20 66
RCA (9056 "Indescribably Blue") 15-20 67
RCA (9115 "Long Legged Girl") 15-20 67
RCA (9287 "There's Always Me")....................................... 15-20 67
RCA (9341 "Big Boss Man") 15-20 67
RCA (9425 "Guitar Man").......... 10-20 68
RCA (9465 "U.S. Male")............ 10-20 68
RCA (9547 "Your Time Hasn't Come Yet Baby") 10-20 68
RCA (9600 "You'll Never Walk Alone") 50-75 68
RCA (9610 "Almost in Love").... 10-15 68
RCA (9670 "If I Can Dream") 10-15 68
RCA (9731 "Memories")............ 10-15 69
RCA (9741 "In the Ghetto")....... 10-15 69
RCA (9747 "Clean Up Your Own Back Yard") 10-15 69
RCA (9764 "Suspicious Minds").. 8-12 69
RCA (9768 "Don't Cry Daddy") ... 8-12 69
RCA (9791 "Kentucky Rain") 8-12 70
RCA (9835 "The Wonder of You") 8-12 70
RCA (9873 "I've Lost You")......... 8-12 70
RCA (9916 "You Don't Have to Say You Love Me").. 8-12 70
RCA (9960 "I Really Don't Want to Know")...................................... 8-12 70
RCA (9980 "Where Did They Go Lord") 8-15 71
RCA (9985 "Life")...................... 20-30 71
RCA (9998 "I'm Leavin'")............ 8-15 71
RCA (10074 "Promised Land") ... 8-10 74
RCA (10191 "My Boy")................ 8-10 75
RCA (10278 "T-r-o-u-b-l-e") 8-10 75
RCA (10401 "Bringing It Back") .. 8-12 75
RCA (10601 "For the Heart") 8-10 76
RCA (10857 "Moody Blue")......... 6-10 76
RCA (10998 "Way Down") 6-10 77
RCA (11099 thru 11113)............... 3-4 77
(Sleeves in this series were originally packaged in either RCA 11301 and/or 11340, both boxed sets of singles with sleeves.)
RCA (11165 "My Way") 6-10 77
(Flip side title shown as *America*.)
RCA (11165 "My Way") 15-25 77
(Flip side title shown as *America the Beautiful*)
RCA (11212 "Softly, As I Leave You")..5-10 78
RCA (11320 "Teddy Bear")..........5-10 78
RCA (11533 "Are You Sincere") ..5-10 79
RCA (11679 "I Got a Feelin' in My Body")...............................5-10 79
RCA (12158 "Guitar Man")...........5-10 81
RCA (13058 "You'll Never Walk Alone") 5-10 82
RCA (13302 "The Impossible Dream")................................75-100 82
(Promotional issue only.)
RCA (13351 "The Elvis Medley") .5-10 82
RCA (13500 "I Was the One") 5-10 83
RCA (13547 "Little Sister")...........5-10 83
RCA (13875 "Baby, Let's Play House")..................................20-40 84
RCA (13885 thru 13896)................3-4 84
(Sleeves in this series were originally packaged in RCA 13897 and 13898, *Golden Singles.*)
RCA (13929 "Blue Suede Shoes")..5-10 84
RCA (14090 "Always on My Mind")...5-10 85
RCA (14237 "Merry Christmas Baby")..8-12 85

Notes:There may be slight price differences between "Coming Soon" and "Ask For" variations, with "Ask For" sleeves rarer overall. Likewise for variations in colors and paper stock used. Often, the difference is simply which one is needed to complete a run. Regardless, sleeve variations within the price range given do not require separate listings. If the value varies beyond the given range, a separate listing will be added. Sleeves for the RCA "447" Gold Standard Series are listed in a separate section following the Gold Standard Singles. A slight premium—perhaps $3 to $5—may be placed on RCA's "Living Stereo" paper sleeves. These were used for many different RCA stereo singles and were not exclusively an Elvis item.

Gold Standard Singles with "447" prefix (Commercial)

RCA (0600 thru 0639)................10-20 59-64
(Black label, dog on top.)
RCA (0600 thru 0639)..................8-10 65-66
(Black label, dog on side.)

RCA (0600 thru 0639).............. 20-30 68-69
(Orange label.)
RCA (0600 thru 0639).................. 5-8 70-74
(Red label.)
RCA (0600 thru 0639).................. 4-5 77
(Black label, dog near top.)
RCA (0640 thru 0642).............. 20-25 64
(Black label, dog on top.)
RCA (0640 thru 0642)................ 8-10 65-66
(Black label, dog on side.)
RCA (0640 thru 0642).............. 20-30 68-69
(Orange label.)
RCA (0640 thru 0642).................. 5-8 70-74
(Red label.)
RCA (0643 "Crying in the Chapel")................................... 8-10 65
(Black label, dog on side.)
RCA (0643 "Crying in the Chapel")...................................... 5-8 70s
(Red label.)
RCA (0643 "Crying in the Chapel")...................................... 4-5 77
(Black label, dog near top.)
RCA (0644 thru 0646).............. 25-35 65
(Black label, dog on top.)
RCA (0644 thru 0646)................ 8-10 65
(Black label, dog on side.)
RCA (0644 thru 0646).............. 20-30 68-69
(Orange label.)
RCA (0644 thru 0646).................. 5-8 70-74
(Red label.)
RCA (0644 thru 0646).................. 4-5 77
(Black label, dog near top.)
RCA (0647 thru 0650)................ 8-10 65
(Black label, dog on side.)
RCA (0647 thru 0650).................. 5-8 70-74
(Red label.)
RCA (0647 thru 0650).................. 4-5 77
(Black label, dog near top.)
RCA (0651 & 0652).................. 10-15 66
(Black label, dog on side.)
RCA (0651 & 0652)....................... 5-8 70s
(Red label.)
RCA (0653 thru 0658)................ 8-10 66-68
(Black label, dog on side.)
RCA (0653 thru 0658).................. 5-8 70-74
(Red label.)
RCA (0653 thru 0658).................. 4-5 77
(Black label, dog near top.)
RCA (0659 "Indescribably Blue")....................................... 10-15 70
(Red label.)
RCA (0660 "Long Legged Girl") 35-45 70
(Red label.)
RCA (0661 "Judy")...................10-20 70
(Red label.)
RCA (0662 "Big Boss Man") 8-12 70
(Red label.)
RCA (0663 thru 0685)...................5-8 70-73
(Red label.)
RCA (0663 thru 0685)...................3-5 77
(Black label, dog near top.)
RCA (0720 "Blue Christmas")....10-15 64
(Black label, dog on top.)

Gold Standard Singles with "GB" prefix (Commercial)

RCA (10156 thru 10489)...............5-8 75-76
(Red label.)
RCA (10156 thru 10489)...............4-5 77
(Black label, dog near top.)
RCA (11326 thru 13275)...............4-5 77
(Black label, dog near top.)
Gold Standard *promotional* singles are in numerical sequence in the section for Promotional Singles.

Gold Standard Picture Sleeves

RCA (0601 "That's All Right") 100-200 64
RCA (0602 "Good Rockin' Tonight")...........................100-200 64
RCA (0605 "Heartbreak Hotel")..................................100-200 64
RCA (0608 "Don't Be Cruel").100-200 64
RCA (0618 "All Shook Up")....100-200 64
RCA (0639 "Kiss Me Quick") 20-25 64
RCA (0643 "Crying in the Chapel")...................................15-20 65
RCA (0647 "Blue Christmas")....20-25 65
(Pictures Elvis on a Christmas card among wrapped gifts.)
RCA (0647 "Blue Christmas")......8-10 77
(Pictures Elvis in a circle among colored ornaments.)
RCA (0650 "Puppet on a String")...................................20-25 65
RCA (0651 "Joshua Fit the Battle")................................100-200 66
RCA (0652 "Milky White Way")..................................100-200 66
RCA (0651 & 0652 "Special Easter Programming Kit").............850-1000 66
(Picture sleeve-mailer. Contained both 1966 Easter singles, *Joshua Fit the Battle* and *Milky White Way* in their sleeves and an Easter greeting card from Elvis. Price is for the complete kit.)
RCA (0651 & 0652 "Special Easter Programming Kit")...............800-900 66
(Picture sleeve-mailer only.)
RCA (0720 "Blue Christmas")....35-45 64

Promotional Singles

CREATIVE RADIO ("Elvis 10th Anniversary"/"The Elvis Hour") 15-20 87
(Demonstration disc, promoting the syndicated 10th anniversary radio special.)
CREATIVE RADIO ("Memories of Elvis"/"The Elvis Hour")...........................15-20 87
(Demonstration disc, promoting the

syndicated 10th anniversary radio special.)
For *Elvis 50th Birthday Special,* see PRESLEY, Elvis / Buddy Holly.
For *The Elvis Hour,* see PRESLEY, Elvis / Gary Owens.

CREATIVE RADIO ("Nearer My God to Thee") 5-10 89
(Promotional souvenir only. Issued as a bonus single with the LP, *Between Takes with Elvis.*)

CREATIVE RADIO ("Mystery Train") 5-10 92
(Single-sided demonstration disc, taken from the syndicated 15th anniversary radio special.)

PARAMOUNT PICTURES (1800 "Blue Hawaii")............................ 300-500 61
(Single-sided pressing. Issued only to select theatres, designed for lobby play. Has excerpts of songs from the film.)

PARAMOUNT PICTURES (2017 "Girls! Girls! Girls!") 500-750 64
(Issued only to select theatres, designed for lobby play.)

PARAMOUNT PICTURES (2413 "Roustabout")................. 2000-4000 64
(Issued only to select theatres, designed for lobby play. Track is an alternate take.)

RCA (15 "Old Shep")............ 600-800 56

RCA (76 "Don't"/"Wear My Ring Around Your Neck") 600-800 60
(Issued with special sleeve, listed in the Picture Sleeves section.)

RCA (0088 "Raised on Rock") 8-10 73
(Yellow label.)

RCA (118 "King of the Whole Wide World")..................... 175-225 62
(Issued with a special sleeve, which is listed in the Picture Sleeves section. Includes dee jay insert.)

RCA (0130 "How Great Thou Art").................................... 35-50 69
(Yellow label.)

RCA (139 "Roustabout") 200-250 64

RCA (162 "How Great Thou Art")................................ 150-200 67
(Issued with a special sleeve, listed in the Picture Sleeves section.)

RCA (0196 " Take Good Care of Her")... 8-10 74
(Yellow label.)

RCA (0280 "If You Talk in Your Sleep") 8-10 74
(Yellow label.)

RCA (0517 "Little Sister")...... 100-125 83
(12–inch single.)

RCA (0572 "Merry Christmas Baby") 12-15 71
(Yellow label.)

RCA (0601 "That's All Right")..50-100 64
(White label.)

RCA (0602 "Good Rockin' Tonight") 50-100 64
(White label.)

RCA (0605 "Heartbreak Hotel")..................................50-100 64
(White label.)

RCA (0608 "Don't Be Cruel")...50-100 64
(White label.)

RCA (0618 "All Shook Up")......50-100 64
(White label.)

RCA (0619 "Until It's Time for You to Go").. 10-12 72
(Yellow label.)

RCA (0639 "Kiss Me Quick") 20-25 64
(White label.)

RCA (0643 "Crying in the Chapel")..................................15-20 65
(White label.)

RCA (0647 "Blue Christmas")....25-30 65
(White label.)

RCA (0650 "Puppet on a String")...................................25-30 65
(White label.)

RCA (0651 "Joshua Fit the Battle")..................................50-100 66
(White label.)

RCA (0652 "Milky White Way") 50-100 66
(White label. See Gold Standard Picture Sleeves section for special mailing sleeve used with 0651 & 0652.)

RCA (0651 "He Touched Me")...50-75 72
(Yellow label.)

RCA (0672 "An American Trilogy").......................................12-15 72
(Yellow label.)

RCA (0720 "Blue Christmas")....25-30 64
(White label.)

RCA (0769 "Burning Love") 8-10 72
(Yellow label.)

RCA (0808 "Blue Christmas")......................1200-1800 57

RCA (0815 "Separate Ways")......8-10 72
(Yellow label.)

RCA (0910 "Fool") 8-10 73
(Yellow label.)

RCA (6357 "Mystery Train")...200-300 55
(White "Record Prevue" label.)

RCA (8360 "Viva Las Vegas") ...20-25 64
(White label.)

RCA (8400 "Such a Night")...........................4000-5000 64
(White label.)

RCA (8440 "Ask Me") 20-30 64
(White label.)

RCA (8500 "Do the Clam") 20-25 65
(White label.)

RCA (8585 "It Feels So Right") . 20-25 65
(White label.)
RCA (8657 "I'm Yours")............ 20-25 65
(White label.)
RCA (8740 "Tell Me Why")........ 20-25 65
(White label.)
RCA (8780 "Frankie & Johnny") 20-25 66
(White label.)
RCA (8870 "Love Letters")........ 20-25 66
(White label.)
RCA (8941 "Spinout")............... 20-25 66
(White label.)
RCA (8950 "If Everyday Was Like Christmas") 20-35 66
(White label.)
RCA (9056 "Indescribably Blue") 20-25 67
(White label.)
RCA (9115 "Long Legged Girl") 20-25 67
(White label.)
RCA (9287 "There's Always Me").. 20-25 67
(White label.)
RCA (9341 "Big Boss Man") 20-25 67
(White label.)
RCA (9425 "Guitar Man")......... 15-20 68
(Yellow label.)
RCA (9465 "U.S. Male")........... 15-20 68
(Yellow label.)
RCA (9547 "Your Time Hasn't Come Yet Baby") 15-20 68
(Yellow label.)
RCA (9600 "You'll Never Walk Alone") 15-20 68
(Yellow label.)
RCA (9610 "Almost in Love") 10-15 68
(Yellow label.)
RCA (9670 "If I Can Dream") 10-15 68
(Yellow label.)
RCA (9731 "Memories")........... 10-15 69
(Yellow label.)
RCA (9741 "In the Ghetto")....... 10-15 69
(Yellow label.)
RCA (9747 "Clean Up Your Own Back Yard") 10-15 69
(Yellow label.)
RCA (9764 "Suspicious Minds") 10-15 69
(Yellow label.)
RCA (9768 "Don't Cry Daddy") . 10-15 69
(Yellow label.)
RCA (9791 "Kentucky Rain") 10-15 70
(Yellow label.)
RCA (9835 "The Wonder of You") 10-15 70
(Yellow label.)
RCA (9873 "I've Lost You")....... 10-15 70
(Yellow label.)
RCA (9916 "You Don't Have to Say You Love Me") 10-15 70
(Yellow label.)
RCA (9960 "I Really Don't Want to Know")........................10-15 70
(Yellow label.)
RCA (9980 "Where Did They Go Lord") 10-15 71
(Yellow label.)
RCA (9985 "Life")......................10-15 71
(Yellow label.)
RCA (9998 "I'm Leavin'") 10-15 71
(Yellow label.)
RCA (10074 "Promised Land") 8-10 74
(Yellow label.)
RCA (10191 "My Boy") 8-10 75
(Yellow label.)
RCA (10278 "T-r-o-u-b-l-e") 8-10 75
(Yellow label.)
RCA (10401 "Bringing It Back") ...8-10 75
(Yellow label.)
RCA (10601 "Hurt")......................8-10 76
(Yellow label.)
RCA (10857 "Moody Blue") 6-10 76
(Yellow label. Black vinyl.)
RCA (10857 "Moody Blue") .900-1000 76
(Experimental colored vinyl pressings. Not intended for distribution.)
RCA (10951 "Let Me Be There")...............................100-125 77
RCA (10998 "Way Down")..... 125-150 77
(White label.)
RCA (10998 "Way Down") 6-10 77
(Yellow label.)
RCA (11165 "My Way") 6-10 77
(Yellow label.)
RCA (11212 "Unchained Melody")......................................6-10 78
(Yellow label.)
RCA (11320 "Teddy Bear")..........6-10 78
(Yellow label.)
RCA (11533 "Are You Sincere") ..6-10 79
(Yellow label.)
RCA (11679 "I Got a Feelin' in My Body") 6-10 79
(Yellow label.)
RCA (12158 "Guitar Man")...........6-10 81
(Yellow label. Black vinyl.)
RCA (12158 "Guitar Man").....200-300 81
(Yellow label. Colored vinyl.)
RCA (12205 "Lovin' Arms")..........6-10 81
(Yellow label. Black vinyl.)
RCA (12205 "Lovin' Arms")....200-300 81
(Yellow label. Colored vinyl.)
RCA (13058 "You'll Never Walk Alone") 6-10 82
(Yellow label.)
RCA (13302 "The Impossible Dream")................................75-100 82

RCA (13351 "Elvis Medley") 6-10 82
(Yellow label. Black vinyl.)
RCA (13351 "Elvis Medley") . 200-300 82
(Gold label. Colored vinyl.)
RCA (13500 "I Was the One")..... 6-10 83
(Yellow label. Black vinyl.)
RCA (13500 "I Was the One")................................ 200-300 83
(Yellow label. Colored vinyl.)
RCA (13547 "Little Sister")......... 6-10 83
(Yellow label. Black vinyl.)
RCA (13547 "Little Sister").... 200-300 83
(Blue label. Colored vinyl.)
RCA (13875 "Baby, Let's Play House") 150-250 84
(Gold label. Colored vinyl.)
RCA (13929 "Blue Suede Shoes)...................................... 6-10 84
(Gold label. Colored vinyl.)
RCA (14090 "Always on My Mind")...................................... 6-10 85
(Gold label. Colored vinyl.)
RCA (14237 "Merry Christmas Baby") 6-10 85
Note: Elvis 50th Anniversary singles—RCA 13875 through 14237—used the same gold label for both commercial and promotional issues. Promo singles have "Not For Sale" printed on the label.
RCA (4-834-115 "I'll Be Back")............................ 4000-6000 66
(White label. Single-sided disc. Reads "For Special Academy Consideration Only." Made for submission to the Academy of Motion Picture Arts and Sciences.
ROYAL CARIBBEAN CRUISE LINES (12690 "Follow That Dream–Take 2"). 10-20 90
(Souvenir disc for Elvis cruise passengers.)
UNITED STATES AIR FORCE (125 "It's Now Or Never"): see PRESLEY, Elvis / Jaye P. Morgan.
UNITED STATES AIR FORCE (159 "Surrender"): see PRESLEY, Elvis / Lawrence Welk.
WHAT'S IT ALL ABOUT (78 "Life"): see PRESLEY, Elvis / Helen Reddy
WHAT'S IT ALL ABOUT (1840 "Elvis Presley")................................ 70-75 80
WHAT'S IT ALL ABOUT (3025 "Elvis Presley")................................ 50-60 82
Note: Plastic soundsheets and flexi-discs are listed in a separate section that follows. Promotional 78s are included with Singles: 78rpm, at the beginning of the Presley section.

Plastic Soundsheets/Flexi-discs

EVA-TONE (38713 "Elvis Speaks! The Truth About Me") 30-40
(Eva-Tone number is not on label but is etched in the trail-off.)
EVA-TONE (52578 "The King Is Dead Long Live the King").......................90-100 78
EVA-TONE (831942 "50,000,000 Elvis Fans Weren't Wrong!") 5-10 83
EVA-TONE (726771 "The Elvis Presley Story")..5-10 77
EVA-TONE (1037710 "Elvis Live").....................................30-40 78
(Price for magazine, titled *Collector's Issue*, with bound-in soundsheet.)
EVA-TONE (1037710 "Elvis Live").....................................15-20 78
(Price for soundsheet only.)
EVA-TONE (1227785 "Thompson Vocal Eliminator") 15-20 78
(Has segments of songs by three artists including Elvis.)
EVA-TONE (10287733 "Elvis: Six Hour Special")..................................15-20 77
EVA-TONE/RCA ("Love Me Tender")................................25-35 74
(Price for April 1974 issue of *Teen Magazine* with bound-in soundsheet.)
EVA-TONE/RCA ("Love Me Tender")................................15-25 74
(Price for soundsheet only.)
LYNCHBURG AUDIO ("The Truth About Me") 125-150 56
(Lynchburg Audio number is not on label but is etched in the trail-off.)
RAINBO ("Elvis Speaks, In Person")..........................300-325 56
(Price for magazine, *Elvis Answers Back*, with 78rpm flexi-disc still attached to front cover.)
RAINBO ("Elvis Speaks, In Person")..........................100-125 56
(Price for flexi-disc only.)
RAINBO ("The Truth About Me") 300-325 56
(Price for magazine, *Elvis Answers Back*, with 78rpm paper flexi-disc still attached to front cover.)
RAINBO ("The Truth About Me") 100-125 56
(Price for flexi-disc only.)
Note: All soundsheets and flexi-discs were used for some type of promotional purpose.

EPs: 7–inch 33/45rpm (Commercial and Promotional)

RCA ("SPD-15")................3000-5000 56
(Boxed 10-EP set. We have yet to personally verify the box, but since there surely was one we have offered an estimated value. Having not seen the box, we cannot provide a title, though one is likely used. Labels may

be either black or gray. Includes inserts. Various artists collection.)

RCA (SPD-19 "The Sound of Leadership")................... 1800-2200 56
(Boxed 8-EP set. Includes inserts. Various artists collection.)

RCA (22 "Elvis Presley")....1000-1500 56
(May have "Elvis" in either light or dark pink letters on front cover. Two-EP bonus promotional item. Discs are numbered 9121 & 9122.)

RCA (23 "Elvis Presley")... 3500-5000 56
(Three-EP bonus promotional item. Includes "How to Use and Enjoy Your RCA Victor Elvis Presley Autograph Automatic 45 Victrola Portable Phonograph," which represents $75 to $100 of the value. Discs are numbered 9123, 9124 & 9125.)

RCA (SPD-26 "Great Country/Western Hits") 800-1000 56
(Boxed 10-EP set. Includes inserts Various artists collection.)

RCA (128 "Elvis By Request") .. 60-80 61

RCA (747 "Elvis Presley")..... 200-250 56
(Black label, without dog.)

RCA (747 "Elvis Presley")....... 75-100 56
(Black label, dog on top. Has song title strip across the top of front cover.)

RCA (747 "Elvis Presley")......... 50-70 65
(Black label, dog on side.)

RCA (747 "Elvis Presley")..... 100-200 69
(Orange label.)

RCA (747 "Blue Suede Shoes") 800-1200 56
(Temporary paper sleeve for 1956 issue of EPA-747. Price is for sleeve only.)

RCA (821 "Heartbreak Hotel") 200-250 56
(Black label, without dog.)

RCA (821 "Heartbreak Hotel") 75-100 56
(Black label, dog on top. Has song title strip across the top of front cover.)

RCA (821 "Heartbreak Hotel") .. 50-70 65
(Black label, dog on side.)

RCA (821 "Heartbreak Hotel") 100-200 69
(Orange label.)

RCA (830 "Elvis Presley")....... 75-100 56
(Black label, dog on top. Has song title strip across the top of front cover.)

RCA (830 "Elvis Presley")..... 200-250 56
(Black label, without dog.)

RCA (830 "Elvis Presley")......... 50-70 65
(Black label, dog on side.)

RCA (830 "Elvis Presley")..... 100-200 69
(Orange label.)

RCA (940 "The Real Elvis") 75-100 56
(Black label, dog on top. Has song title strip across the top of front cover.)

RCA (940 "The Real Elvis")...200-250 56
(Black label, without dog. Reissued as Gold Standard 5120.)

RCA (965 "Any Way You Want Me") 75-100 56
(Black label, dog on top. Has song title strip across the top of front cover.)

RCA (965 "Any Way You Want Me").............................200-250 56
(Black label, without dog.)

RCA (965 "Any Way You Want Me") 50-70 65
(Black label, dog on side.)

RCA (965 "Any Way You Want Me") 100-200 69
(Orange label.)

RCA (992 "Elvis, Vol. 1")..........75-100 56
(Black label, dog on top. Has song title strip across the top of front cover.)

RCA (992 "Elvis, Vol. 1")........200-250 56
(Black label, without dog.)

RCA (992 "Elvis, Vol. 1")............50-70 65
(Black label, dog on side.)

RCA (992 "Elvis, Vol. 1")........100-200 69
(Orange label.)

RCA (993 "Elvis, Vol. 2")..........75-100 56
(Black label, dog on top. Has song title strip across the top of front cover.)

RCA (993 "Elvis, Vol. 2") 200-250 56
(Black label, without dog.)

RCA (993 "Elvis, Vol. 2")............50-70 65
(Black label, dog on side.)

RCA (993 "Elvis, Vol. 2")........100-200 69
(Orange label.)

RCA (994 "Strictly Elvis").........75-100 56
(Black label, dog on top. Has song title strip across the top of front cover.)

RCA (994 "Strictly Elvis").......200-250 56
(Black label, without dog.)

RCA (994 "Strictly Elvis")...........50-70 65
(Black label, dog on side.)

RCA (994 "Strictly Elvis").......100-200 69
(Orange label.)

RCA (1254 "Elvis Presley")....400-600 56
(Black label, without dog. Two EP set.)

RCA (1254 "Elvis Presley")....300-400 56
(Black label, dog on top. Two EP set.)

RCA (1254 "Most Talked-About New Personality")....................2500-3500 56
(Two EPs, also numbered 0793 & 0794, in a single pocket paper sleeve. Promotional issue only. Includes a copy of *Dee-Jay Digest,* which represents $50 to $75 of the value.)

RCA (1254 "Most Talked-About New Personality").........................500-750 56
(Price for the two EPs without the sleeve. Either disc would be worth about half the amount shown for both. Discs, numbered

0793 & 0794, are untitled. Promotional issue only.)
RCA (1-1515 "Loving You, Vol. 1") 75-100 57
(Black label, dog on top. Has song title strip across the top of front cover.)
RCA (1-1515 "Loving You, Vol. 1") 50-70 65
(Black label, dog on side.)
RCA (1-1515 "Loving You, Vol. 1") 100-200 69
(Orange label.)
RCA (2-1515 "Loving You, Vol. 2") 75-100 57
(Black label, dog on top. Has song title strip across the top of front cover.)
RCA (2-1515 "Loving You, Vol. 2") 50-70 65
(Black label, dog on side.)
RCA (2-1515 "Loving You, Vol. 2") 100-200 69
(Orange label.)
RCA (2006 "Aloha from Hawaii").................................. 60-75 74
(Includes sheet of 10 title strips. Made for jukebox operators only.)
RCA (4006 "Love Me Tender") 200-250 56
(Black label, without dog. Has song title strip across the top of front cover.)
RCA (4006 "Love Me Tender") 75-100 56
(Black label, dog on top. Has song title strip across the top of front cover.)
RCA (4006 "Love Me Tender") . 50-70 65
(Black label, dog on side.)
RCA (4006 "Love Me Tender") 100-200 69
(Orange label.)
RCA (4041 "Just for You") 200-250 57
(Black label, without dog. Has EP title strip across the top of front cover.)
RCA (4041 "Just for You") 75-100 57
(Black label, dog on top. Has EP title strip across the top of front cover.)
RCA (4041 "Just for You") 50-70 65
(Black label, dog on side.)
RCA (4041 "Just for You") 100-200 69
(Orange label.)
RCA (4054 "Peace in the Valley")................................ 75-100 57
(Black label, dog on top. Has EP title strip across the top of front cover. Reissued as Gold Standard 5121.)
RCA (4108 "Elvis Sings Christmas Songs") 75-100 57
(Black label, dog on top. Has EP title strip across the top of front cover.)
RCA (4108 "Elvis Sings Christmas Songs") 50-70 65
(Black label, dog on side.)
RCA (4108 "Elvis Sings Christmas Songs") 100-200 69
(Orange label.)
RCA (4114 "Jailhouse Rock")....65-85 57
(Black label, dog on top.)
RCA (4114 "Jailhouse Rock")....50-70 65
(Black label, dog on side.)
RCA (4114 "Jailhouse Rock") 100-200 69
(Orange label.)
RCA (4319 "King Creole")........75-100 58
(Reissued as Gold Standard 5122.)
RCA (4321 "King Creole, Vol. 2") 65-85 58
(Black label, dog on top.)
RCA (4321 "King Creole, Vol. 2") 50-70 65
(Black label, dog on side.)
RCA (4321 "King Creole, Vol. 2") 100-200 69
(Orange label.)
RCA (4325 "Elvis Sails")..........75-100 58
(Reissued as Gold Standard 5157.)
RCA (4340 "Christmas with Elvis")..................................75-100 58
(Black label, dog on top.)
RCA (4340 "Christmas with Elvis")....................................50-70 65
(Black label, dog on side.)
RCA (4340 "Christmas with Elvis")................................100-200 69
(Orange label.)
RCA (4368 "Follow That Dream")................................70-90 62
(Black label, dog on top. Playing times are incorrectly listed for three of the four tracks: *Follow That Dream* shown as 1:35, should be 1:38; *Angel* shown as 2:35, should be 2:40; and *I'm Not the Marrying Kind* shown as 1:49, should be 2:00.)
RCA (4368 "Follow That Dream")...............................50-70 62
(Black label, dog on top. All playing times are correctly shown.)
RCA (4368 "Follow That Dream")................................75-100 62
(Promotional issue only. Marked "Not For Sale.")
RCA (4368 "Follow That Dream")..............................120-160 62
(Special paper sleeve, issued to radio stations and jukebox operators. Promotional issue only. Price is for sleeve only.)
RCA (4368 "Follow That Dream")..................................50-70 65
(Black label, dog on side.)

RCA (4368 "Follow That Dream") 100-200 69
(Orange label.)
RCA (4371 "Kid Galahad") 60-80 62
(Black label, dog on top.)
RCA (4371 "Kid Galahad") 50-70 65
(Black label, dog on side.)
RCA (4371 "Kid Galahad") 100-200 69
(Orange label.)
RCA (4382 "Viva Las Vegas") ... 65-85 64
(Black label, dog on top.)
RCA (4382 "Viva Las Vegas") ... 50-70 65
(Black label, dog on side.)
RCA (4382 "Viva Las Vegas") 100-200 69
(Orange label.)
RCA (4383 "Tickle Me") 50-70 65
(Black label, dog on side.)
RCA (4383 "Tickle Me") 100-200 69
(Orange label.)
RCA (4387 "Easy Come, Easy Go") 50-70 67
(Black label, dog on side.)
RCA (4387 "Easy Come, Easy Go") 100-150 67
(White label. Promotional Issue Only.)
RCA (5088 "A Touch of Gold, Vol. I") 450-550 59
(Maroon label.)
RCA (5088 "A Touch of Gold, Vol. I") 75-100 59
(Black label, dog on top. Add $15 to $25 if accompanied by "I am a loyal Elvis fan" insert card.)
RCA (5088 "A Touch of Gold, Vol. I") 50-70 65
(Black label, dog on side.)
RCA (5088 "A Touch of Gold, Vol. I") 100-200 69
(Orange label.)
RCA (5101 "A Touch of Gold, Vol. II") 450-550 59
(Maroon label.)
RCA (5101 "A Touch of Gold, Vol. II") 75-100 59
(Black label, dog on top. Add $15 to $25 if accompanied by "I am a loyal Elvis fan" insert card.)
RCA (5101 "A Touch of Gold, Vol. II") 50-70 65
(Black label, dog on side.)
RCA (5101 "A Touch of Gold, Vol. II") 100-200 69
(Orange label.)
RCA (5120 "The Real Elvis") 500-750 59
(Maroon label. Reissue of 940.)
RCA (5120 "The Real Elvis") 55-75 59
(Black label, dog on top.)
RCA (5120 "The Real Elvis") 50-70 65
(Black label, dog on side.)
RCA (5120 "The Real Elvis") . 100-200 69
(Orange label.)
RCA (5121 "Peace in the Valley") 500-750 59
(Maroon label. Reissue of 4054.)
RCA (5121 "Peace in the Valley") 60-80 59
(Black label, dog on top.)
RCA (5121 "Peace in the Valley") 50-70 65
(Black label, dog on side.)
RCA (5121 "Peace in the Valley") 100-200 69
(Orange label.)
RCA (5122 "King Creole") .. 1500-2500 59
(Maroon label. Reissue of 4319. Though we have been told of the existence of this item by one collector, it remains one of very, very few U.S. Elvis collectibles that we have not personally confirmed. Price estimate is based on offers, as we know of no sales.)
RCA (5122 "King Creole") 60-80 59
(Black label, dog on top.)
RCA (5122 "King Creole") 50-70 65
(Black label, dog on side.)
RCA (5122 "King Creole") 100-200 69
(Orange label.)
RCA (5141 "A Touch of Gold, Vol. 3") 425-500 60
(Maroon label.)
RCA (5141 "A Touch of Gold, Vol. 3") 75-100 60
(Black label, dog on top.)
RCA (5141 "A Touch of Gold, Vol. 3") 50-70 65
(Black label, dog on side.)
RCA (5141 "A Touch of Gold, Vol. 3") 100-200 69
(Orange label.)
RCA (5157 "Elvis Sails") 50-70 65
(Black label, dog on top. Reissue of 4325.)
RCA (5157 "Elvis Sails") 50-70 65
(Black label, dog on side.)
RCA (5157 "Elvis Sails") 100-200 69
(Orange label.)
RCA (8705 "TV Guide Presents Elvis") 1000-1500 56
(Price for disc only. Insert sheets are priced separately below. No sleeve or special cover exists for this disc. Promotional issue only.)
RCA (8705 "TV Guide Presents Elvis") 50-100 56
(Price for "Elvis Exclusively" gray insert.)
RCA (8705 "TV Guide Presents Elvis") 100-200 56
(Price for *Elvis Exclusively* pink insert, with suggested continuity.)

RCA (9089 "SPD-15 Elvis EP")........................... 500-750 56
(Black label. The Elvis disc from SPD-15.)

RCA (9089 "SPD-15 Elvis EP")........................... 500-750 56
(Gray label. The Elvis disc from SPD-15. Gray label pressings were for jukebox operators.)

RCA (9113 "SPD-19 Elvis EP")........................... 300-400 56
(Just the Elvis disc from SPD-19.)

RCA (9141 "SPD-26 Elvis EP")........................... 200-250 56
(Black label. Just the Elvis disc from SPD-15.)

Note: Unless listed and priced separately, all EP values include both disc and cover with approximately half of the total attached to each. Some of the rarer pieces that are often traded individually (disc or sleeve), as well as those sleeves that have an exceptionally higher value than their disc, are listed separately in this section. All EPs in the 5000 series are Gold Standard Series issues although none are identified as such on the labels, only on the covers. Remember, if you don't find the EP in this section it may contain two, three or four artists, and will be listed following the Presley LP section.

LPs: 10/12–inch 33rpm
(Commercial and Promotional)

ABC RADIO (1003 "Elvis Memories")........................ 475-575 78
(Three-LP boxed set. Add $25 to $50 if accompanied by a 16-page programmer's booklet and four pages of additional information. Issued only to radio stations. Add $40 to $50 if accompanied by a 7–inch reel tape, with spots and promotional announcements. Highlights of this program were issued on Michelob 810.)

ASSOCIATED BROADCASTERS (1001 "Legend of a King") 125-150 80
(White label. Advance pressing.)

ASSOCIATED BROADCASTERS (1001 "Legend of a King") 25-30 80
(Picture disc. First pressings are numbered from 3000 through 6000. Number appears under "Side One" on the disc itself. Cover is standard, die-cut, picture disc cover. Has several spelling errors on back cover, including "idle" for idol and "Jordinaires" instead of Jordanaires.)

ASSOCIATED BROADCASTERS (1001 "Legend of a King") 20-25 80
(Picture disc. Second pressings are numbered from 6001 through 9000. Most of the spelling errors were corrected on this cover.)

ASSOCIATED BROADCASTERS (1001 "Legend of a King")..................15-20 80
(Picture disc. Third pressings are numbered from 00001 through 02999 and 09001 through 15000. Cover errors have all been corrected.)

ASSOCIATED BROADCASTERS (1001 "Legend of a King")..................10-12 84
(Picture disc. Fourth pressings are also numbered from 3000 through 6000, but were packaged in a clear plastic sleeve instead of a conventional cover.)

ASSOCIATED BROADCASTERS (1001 "Legend of a King")....................8-10 85
(Picture disc. Discs are not numbered. Packaged in a plastic sleeve.)

ASSOCIATED BROADCASTERS ("Legend of a King") 200-250 85
(Three hour, three-LP set. Not boxed. Price includes six pages of cue sheets. Available to radio stations only.)

ASSOCIATED BROADCASTERS ("Legend of a King") 300-350 85
(Same as above, but packaged in a specially printed box.)

ASSOCIATED BROADCASTERS ("Legend of a King") 300-350 86
(Three-LP boxed set, same as above except time on segment 1-B is increased from 14:25 to 15:15 in order to include a Johnny Bernero interview.)

ASSOCIATED PRESS (1977 "The World in Sound")................................80-100 78
(News highlights of 1977, including coverage of Elvis' death.)

BOXCAR ("Having Fun with Elvis on Stage") 100-125 74
(No selection number used. Sold in conjunction with Elvis' concert appearances. Reissued as RCA CPM1-0818.)

CAEDMON (1572 "On the Record")..................................60-80 78
(Assorted news items and personalities artists featured.)

CAMDEN (2304 "Flaming Star") 15-20 69
(First issued as RCA PRS-279, reissued in 1975 as Pickwick 2304.)

CAMDEN (2408 "Let's Be Friends") 15-20 70
(Reissued in 1975 as Pickwick 2408.)

CAMDEN (2428 "Elvis' Christmas Album") 15-20 70
(Eight songs on this LP were first issued on RCA LOC-1035. Reissued in 1975 as Pickwick 2428.)

CAMDEN (2440 "Almost in Love")......................................25-30 70
(With *Stay Away Joe*.)

CAMDEN (2440 "Almost in Love")................................. 15-20 73
(*Stay Away* replaces *Stay Away Joe*. Reissued in 1975 as Pickwick 2440.)

CAMDEN (2472 "You'll Never Walk Alone") 15-20 71
(Reissued in 1975 as Pickwick 2472.)

CAMDEN (2518 "C'mon Everybody")........................... 15-20 71
(Reissued in 1975 as Pickwick 2518.)

CAMDEN (2533 "I Got Lucky") . 15-20 71
(Reissued in 1975 as Pickwick 2533.)

CAMDEN (2567 "Elvis Sings Hits from His Movies") 15-20 72
(Reissued in 1975 as Pickwick 2567.)

CAMDEN (2595 "Burning Love")................................... 20-30 72
(Add $25 to $35 if accompanied by the bonus 8x10 Elvis photo. Reissued in 1975 as Pickwick 2595.)

CAMDEN (2611 "Separate Ways")................................... 15-20 73
(Reissued in 1975 as Pickwick 2611.)

CENTURY 21 PRODUCTIONS ("Epic of the '70s") 150-200 76
(Six-LP program of '70s songs by various artists. Promotional issue only. Not issued with a special cover.)

COUNTRY SESSIONS U.S.A. (126 "A Tribute to Elvis")............................ 225-250 83
(Price includes cue sheets. Promotional issue only.)

CREATIVE RADIO ("Elvis Remembered")................... 100-125 78
(Three-LP set. Price includes six insert pages. Advance copies of this set, which was not issued with a special cover or package, were with plain white, handwritten, labels. These copies may be valued at $150 to $250. Promotional issue only.)

CREATIVE RADIO ("Elvis, the Country Side") 75-85 84
(Two-LP set. Promotional issue only.)

CREATIVE RADIO ("Elvis 50th Anniversary")...................... 250-275 85
(Six-LP set. Price includes seven pages of programming instructions and cues. Packaged in a plain, unprinted box. Promotional issue only.)

CREATIVE RADIO ("Elvis 10th Anniversary")...................... 150-175 87
(Six-LP set. Price includes eight pages of programming instructions and cues. Packaged in a custom printed box. Promotional issue only.)

CREATIVE RADIO ("Christmas with Elvis")................................... 25-30 87
(Promotional issue only. Not issued with special cover.)

CREATIVE RADIO ("Birthday Tribute to Elvis")....................................25-30 88
(Promotional issue only. Not issued with special cover.)

CREATIVE RADIO ("The Elvis Hour")....................................10-12 86-88
(Price is for any of the weekly discs in this series. The first 52 discs in the series have been selling as a set for $450 to $475. Promotional issues only.)

CREATIVE RADIO ("Demo of 10 Creative Radio Programs") 25-30 90s
(Includes segments of *The Elvis Hour, 10th Anniversary Special* and *Memories of Elvis*, along with portions of other shows by other artists. Promotional issue only.)

CREATIVE RADIO (E1 "Elvis Exclusive Interview")...........................175-200 88
(Price for *complete* 1956 Little Rock concert copies. Only the first 100 copies were pressed with the full concert. The only way to visually identify these is to check the disc. On the full concert pressings, the grooves take up nearly the entire disc.)

CREATIVE RADIO (E1 "Elvis Exclusive Interview")................................20-30 88
(Has edited concert songs. On this pressing the grooves occupy only about two-thirds of the disc.)

CREATIVE RADIO ("Between Takes with Elvis")................................150-250 89
(Three-LP set. Promotional issue only. Though not packaged inside covers—shrink wrapped at the factory—each LP set came with the bonus single, *Nearer My God to Thee/You Gave Me a Molehill*.)

Note: On any of the above listings, Creative Radio may be shown as Creative Radio Shows or Creative Radio Network.)

DIAMOND P. PRODUCTIONS ("Reflections of Elvis")..............................350-400 77
(Three LP set.)

DRAKE-CHENAULT ("Elvis: a Three Hour Special")..............................300-350 77
(Three-LP boxed set. Includes three pages of cue sheets.)

EARTH NEWS ("August 29, 1977") 325-375 77
(Promotional issue only. Price includes one-page letter.)

ELEKTRA (60107 "Diner").........10-20 82
(Soundtrack.)

FRANKLIN MINT (4 "The Official Grammy Award Winners").................150-200 85
(Boxed set of four colored vinyl discs. One in a series of 14 boxed sets, but only this one (titled *The Great Singers*) has Elvis. Includes booklet.)

GOLDEN EDITIONS LIMITED (1 "The First Year") 8-15 79
(Print in upper corners on front cover is in white. Label is black. Add $5 to $8 if accompanied by a 12-page booklet and one-page copy of the 1954 Elvis/Scotty Moore contract.)

GOLDEN EDITIONS LIMITED (101 "The First Year") 15-25 79
(Print in upper corners on front cover is in gold. Label is white. Add $5 to $8 if accompanied by a 12-page booklet and one-page copy of the 1954 Elvis/Scotty Moore contract. Most of the material on this LP was previously issued on HALW 00001.)

GREAT NORTHWEST (4005 "The Elvis Tapes") 10-15 77
(These interviews were repackaged on Starday 995.)

GREAT NORTHWEST (4006 "The King Speaks") 8-10 77
(This press conference was first issued as Green Valley 2001.)

GREEN VALLEY (2001 "Elvis 1961 Press Conference") 30-50 77
(Cover is thin, soft stock and does not have black bar on spine. Label does not show selection number.)

GREEN VALLEY (2001 "Elvis 1961 Press Conference") 12-15 77
(Cover is standard stock and has black bar on spine. Label has the selection number. Repackaged as one half of Green Valley 2001/2003. It was later repackaged as Great Northwest 4006.)

GREEN VALLEY (2001/2003 "Elvis Speaks to You") 25-30 78
(GV-2001 was first issued as a single LP.)

HALW (00001 "The First Years") 25-30 78
(Repackaged in 1979 on Golden Editions 1.)

INTERNATIONAL HOTEL PRESENTS ELVIS 1969 .... 1000-1500 69
(Custom gift box prepared by Col. Parker and RCA for International Hotel guests. Originally contained: RCA LPM-4088 & LSP-4155, three 8x10 Elvis photos, RCA Elvis catalog, calendar and a nine-page letter. Price is for complete set but box itself represents 90-95% of value.)

INTERNATIONAL HOTEL PRESENTS ELVIS 1970 .... 1000-1500 70
(Custom gift box prepared by Col. Parker and RCA for International Hotel guests. Originally contained: RCA LSP-6020 & 45-9791, one 8x10 Elvis photo, photo album, RCA Elvis catalog, calendar, menu and letter. Price is for complete set but box itself represents 90-95% of value.)

K-TEL (9900 "Elvis Love Songs") 15-20 81

LOUISIANA HAYRIDE (3061 "The Beginning Years") 300-400 84
(White label advance pressing from RCA, Indianapolis, where this LP was manufactured.)

LOUISIANA HAYRIDE (3061 "The Beginning Years") 15-25 84
(Price includes 20-page *D.J. Fontana Remembers Elvis* booklet, a four sheet copy of Elvis' Hayride contract and a 10x10 *Presleyana, Second Edition* flyer, all of which represent about $5 to $10 of the value. Selections from this LP are also on the Music Works 3601 & 3602.)

LOUISIANA HAYRIDE (8454 "The Louisiana Hayride") 550-650 76
(Yellow label. A program of various artists including Elvis. Issued to radio stations only.)

LOUISIANA HAYRIDE (8454 "The Louisiana Hayride") 300-325 81
(Gold label. A program of various artists including Elvis.)

MFSL (059 "From Elvis in Memphis") 30-50 82
(First issued as RCA LSP-4155.)

MARCH of DIMES (0653 "Discs for Dimes") 1400-1600 56
(16–inch disc. Promotional issue only. Includes 16 pages of notes.)

MARCH of DIMES (0657 "Disc Jockey Interviews") 1400-1600 56
(16–inch disc. Promotional issue only. Includes scripts and notes.)

MARVENCO (101 "1954-1955, The Beginning") 10-15 88
(Has material perviously issued on Golden Editions 101.)

MEDIA ENTERTAINMENT ("The King's Gold") 50-75 85
(Three reel-to-reel tapes, issued only to radio stations. Price includes cue sheets. Not known to exist on disc.)

MICHELOB (810 "Highlights of Elvis Memories") 175-200 78
(A Michelob in-house promotional issue only.)
Elvis Memories was first issued on ABC Radio 1003.

MORE MUSIC (333-72 "A Chronology of American Music") 500-600 72
(21-LP set of number one songs by various artists. For radio stations only. Not issued with any special box or package.)

MUSIC WORKS (3601 "The First Live Recordings") 8-10 84
(This material was first issued on Louisiana Hayride 3061.)

MUSIC WORKS (3602 "Hillbilly Cat") 8-10 84
(This material was first issued on Louisiana Hayride 3061.)
OAK (1003 "Vintage 1955")..... 70-100 91
PAIR (1010 "Double Dynamite") 20-25 82
(First issued as Pickwick 5001.)
PAIR (1037 "Remembering Elvis") 20-25 83
PICKWICK (2304 "Flaming Star") 8-10 75
(First issued as RCA PRS-279.)
PICKWICK (2408 "Let's Be Friends" black vinyl) 8-10 75
(First issued as Camden 2408.)
PICKWICK (2408 "Let's Be Friends" colored vinyl).................................. 500-600 70s
(Experimental pressing only. There is no colored vinyl commercial or promotional edition of this issue.)
PICKWICK (2428 "Elvis' Christmas Album") 8-10 75
(First issued as Camden 2428.)
PICKWICK (2428 "Elvis' Christmas Album") 15-25 86
(Has RCA Special Products on label and cover.)
PICKWICK (2440 "Almost in Love").. 8-10 75
(First issued as Camden 2440.)
PICKWICK (2472 "You'll Never Walk Alone") 8-10 75
(First issued as Camden 2472.)
PICKWICK (2518 "C'mon Everybody")............................... 8-10 75
(First issued as Camden 2518.)
PICKWICK (2533 "I Got Lucky") . 8-10 75
(First issued as Camden 2533.)
PICKWICK (2567 "Elvis Sings Hits from His Movies") 8-10 75
(First issued as Camden 2567.)
PICKWICK (2595 "Burning Love").. 8-10 75
(First issued as Camden 2595.)
PICKWICK (2611 "Separate Ways").. 8-10 75
(First issued as Camden 2611.)
PICKWICK (5001 "Double Dynamite") 25-30 75
(Repackaged in 1982 as Pair 1010.)
PICKWICK (7007 "Frankie and Johnny") 10-12 76
(First issued as RCA 3553.)
PICKWICK (7064 "Mahalo from Elvis") 15-20 78
PREMORE (589 "Early Elvis") 5-10 89
(Mail-order album from the Solo Cup Company.)
RCA (EPC-1 "Special Christmas Program" Reel Tape) 300-325 67
(Price includes programming inserts, which represent $25 35 of the value. Never issued commercially on disc, all 10–inch red vinyl LPs of this material are bootlegs.)
RCA (TB-1 "Collectors Edition") 100-150 76
(Five-LP boxed set.)
RCA (010 "Elvis! His Greatest Hits") 400-450 79
(White box edition. Eight-LP boxed set, sold mail-order by *Reader's Digest*.)
RCA (010 "His Greatest Hits") ...40-60 83
(Yellow box edition. Seven-LP boxed set, sold mail-order by *Reader's Digest*. See RCA 181 for the bonus LP offered with this set.)
RCA RBA-040: see READER'S DIGEST 040
RCA (0056 "Elvis")......................40-50 73
(Mustard color label. Cover shows "Brookville Records" in upper right. A mail-order LP offer.)
RCA (0056 "Elvis")....................20-25 73
(Blue label. Cover doesn't show "Brookville Records." Mail-order LP offer. Repackaged in 1978 and titled *Elvis Commemorative Album*.)
RCA (0056 "Elvis Commemorative Album") 75-80 78
(Price includes a "Registered Certificate of Ownership." A mail-order LP offer. First titled *Elvis*, using the same selection number.)
RCA (072 "Great Hits of 1956-57") 10-20 87
(Offered as a bonus LP from *Reader's Digest*, with the purchase of one of their non-Elvis boxed sets.)
RCA (0168 "Elvis in Hollywood").............................35-45 76
(Add $10 to $15 is accompanied by a 20-page photo booklet.)
RCA (181 "Elvis Sings Inspirational Favorites") 15-20 83
(Special Products, Reader's Digest mail-order bonus LP for buyers of the 1983 edition of RCA 010. Price includes 24-page Reader's Digest Music catalog.)
RCA (191 "Elvis, the Legend Lives On") 40-45 86
(Seven-LP boxed set, sold mail-order by Reader's Digest. Includes booklet.)
RCA (242 "Elvis Sings Country Favorites") 20-30 84
(Bonus LP from Reader's Digest, given with the purchase of their seven-disc boxed set, *The Great Country Entertainers,* which has no Elvis tracks.)
RCA (0263 "Elvis Presley Story")....................................30-40 77

(Special Products five-LP boxed set. A Candelite Music mail-order offer.)
RCA (0264 "Songs of Inspiration")............................ 10-15 77
(Special Products issue. A Candelite Music mail-order bonus LP for buyers of RCA 0263.)
RCA (279 "Singer Presents Elvis").................................... 70-80 68
(Reissued in 1969 as Camden 2304 and in 1975 as Pickwick 2304.)
RCA (0283 "Elvis, Including Fool").................................... 50-60 73
RCA (0341 "Legendary Performer, Vol. 1") 20-25 74
(With die-cut cover. Add $5 to $10 if accompanied by *The Early Years* booklet.)
RCA (0341 "Legendary Performer, Vol. 1") 5-10 83
(With standard cover—not die-cut.)
RCA (0341 "Legendary Performer, Vol. 1") 800-1000 78
(Picture discs of the 0341 material but with pictures from any of about six different LP covers pressed on the disc. RCA in-house, experimental items.)
RCA (0347 "Memories of Elvis").................................... 35-45 78
(Special Products five-LP boxed set. A Candelite Music mail-order offer. Add $8 to $10 if accompanied by a 16-page booklet and an Elvis print. Not all sets were issued with the print and booklet.)
RCA (0348 "Greatest Show on Earth").................................. 10-12 78
(Special Products issue. A Candelite Music mail-order bonus LP for buyers of RCA 0347.)
RCA (0388 "Raised on Rock") .. 15-20 73
(Orange label.)
RCA (0388 "Raised on Rock") 8-10 77
(Black label.)
RCA (0401 RCA Radio Victrola Division Spots") 800-1200 56
(Single-sided disc with four 50-second radio commercials for RCA's Victrolas, as well as for the SPD-22 and SPD-23 EPs that were offered as a bonus. Elvis is the announcer on all of the spots, which include excerpts of some of his songs. Issued only to radio stations scheduling the spots.)
RCA (0412 "The Legendary Recordings") 30-40 79
(Special Products six-LP boxed set. A Candelite Music mail-order offer.)
RCA (0413 "Greatest Moments in Music")................................... 10-15 80
(Special Products issue. A Candelite Music mail-order bonus LP for buyers of RCA 0412.)
RCA (0437 "Rock 'N' Roll Forever")................................10-15 81
(Candelite Music mail-order LP offer.)
RCA (461 "Special Palm Sunday Programming")....................500-600 67
(Add $75 to $100 if accompanied by a programming packet. Promotional issue only.)
RCA (0461 "The Legendary Magic")...................................10-15 80
(Candelite Music mail-order LP offer.)
RCA (CPL1-0475 "Good Times")...................................15-20 74
VICTOR (AFL1-0475 "Good Times").......................................8-10 77
RCA (571 " Elvis As Recorded at Madison Square Garden").................250-300 72
(Two-LP, double pocket issue. Promotional issue only. Commercially issued as RCA LSP-4776.)
RCA (APD1-0606 "On Stage in Memphis").......................120-130 74
(Quadradisc. Orange label.)
RCA (CPL1-0606 "On Stage in Memphis")...........................15-18 74
(Orange label.)
RCA (DJL1-0606 "On Stage in Memphis").......................250-275 74
(Banded edition. Promotional issue only.)
RCA (CPL1-0606 "On Stage in Memphis")...........................10-15 76
(Tan label.)
RCA (CPL1-0606 "On Stage in Memphis").............................8-10 77
(Black label.)
RCA (AFL1-0606 "On Stage in Memphis").............................8-10 77
RCA (0632 "The Elvis Presley Collection")..............................50-60 84
(Special Products three-LP boxed set, produced for Candlelite Music. Includes booklet. A mail-order LP offer.)
RCA (DPL1-0647 "Elvis Country")..................................30-40 84
(Special Products issue for ERA Records.)
RCA (DPK1-0679 "Savage Young Elvis") 5-10 84
(Cassette tape of a package that was never available on LP. Price is for tape still attached to 12x12 photo card.)
RCA (0704 "Elvis, HBO Special")..................................25-35 84
(Includes color poster. Special Products issue for HBO cable TV subscribers. This material was first issued as RCA LPM-4088.)

RCA (0710 "50 Years-50 Hits"). 20-25 85
(Three-LP set. Offered by TV mail-order and through the RCA Record Club.)
RCA (0728 "Elvis, His Songs of Faith and Inspiration") 15-20 86
(Two LP, mail-order offer.)
RCA (CPM1-0818 "Having Fun with Elvis on Stage") 15-20 74
(Orange label.)
RCA (CPM1-0818 "Having Fun with Elvis on Stage") 10-15 76
(Tan label.)
RCA (AFM1-0818 "Having Fun with Elvis on Stage") 8-10 77
(First issued on Boxcar without a selection number.)
RCA (0835 "Elvis Presley Interview Record") 75-100 84
(Promotional issue only.)
RCA (APL1-0873 "Promised Land").. 20-25 75
(Orange label.)
RCA (APL1-0873 "Promised Land").. 10-15 76
(Tan label.)
RCA (AFL1-0873 "Promised Land").. 8-10 77
RCA (APD1-0873 "Promised Land")................................ 100-125 75
(Quadradisc. Orange label.)
RCA (APD1-0873 "Promised Land").. 40-50 77
(Quadradisc. Black label.)
RCA (ANL1-0971 "Pure Gold") . 15-18 75
(Orange label.)
RCA (ANL1-0971 "Pure Gold") . 10-15 76
(Yellow label.)
RCA (ANL1-0971 "Pure Gold") ... 8-10 77
(Black label.)
Reissued in 1980 as AYL1-3732.
RCA (1001 "The Sun Collection")............................ 20-25 75
(Label does not have "Starcall" on it. Back cover pictures other LPs.)
RCA (1001 "The Sun Collection")............................ 15-20 75
(Label has "Starcall" on it. Back cover with liner notes. This English import was distributed throughout the U.S. It was repackaged in 1976 as RCA 1675.)
RCA (LOC-1035 "Elvis' Christmas Album") 10000-20000 57
(Experimental, one-of-a-kind pressing. Wide and exceptional price range is based on offers—not a sale.)
RCA (LOC-1035 "Elvis' Christmas Album") 500-550 57
(Black vinyl. With gold foil, gift-giving sticker.)
RCA (LOC-1035 "Elvis' Christmas Album") 375-475 57
(Black vinyl. Without gold foil, gift-giving sticker. Repackaged in 1958 as RCA 1951, in 1970 as Camden 2428 and in 1985 as RCA 5486. May be found with either gold or silver print on the spine.)
RCA (APL1-1039 "Today") 20-25 75
(Orange label.)
RCA (APL1-1039 "Today") 10-15 76
(Tan label.)
RCA (AFL1-1039 "Today")..........8-10 77
RCA (APD1-1039 "Today")....150-200 75
(Quadradisc. Orange label.)
RCA (APD1-1039 "Today")......90-110 77
(Quadradisc. Black label.)
RCA (LPM-1254 "Elvis Presley") 100-125 56
(Monaural. Black label, "Long Play" at bottom. Cover has selection number in upper right corner.)
RCA (LPM-1254 "Elvis Presley") 50-75 63
(Black label, "Mono" at bottom. Cover has selection number on left.)
RCA (LPM-1254 "Elvis Presley") 25-50 64
(Black label, "Monaural" at bottom. Cover has selection number on left.)
RCA (LSP-1254e "Elvis Presley") 150-200 62
(Stereo. Black label, all print on label is silver.)
RCA (LSP-1254e "Elvis Presley") 25-50 64
(Black label, RCA logo is white, other label print is silver.)
RCA (LSP-1254e "Elvis Presley") 20-30 68
(Orange label.)
RCA (LSP-1254e "Elvis Presley") 10-20 76
(Tan label.)
RCA (AFL1-1254e "Elvis Presley") 8-15 77
(Digitally remastered in 1984 on RCA 5198.)
RCA (ANL1-1319 "His Hand in Mine")..10-15 76
(First issued as LPM/LSP-2328.)
RCA (1349 "Legendary Performer, Vol. 2") 50-65 76
(Does not have the false starts and outtakes on *Such a Night* and *Cane and a High Starched Collar*. Mistakenly has only the complete take of both songs. Add $5 to $10 if accompanied by *The Early Years Continued* booklet.)

RCA (1349 "Legendary Performer, Vol. 2") 20-25 76
(With die-cut cover. Add $5 to $10 if accompanied by *The Early Years Continued* booklet.)
RCA (1349 "Legendary Performer, Vol. 2") 5-10 83
(With standard cover—not die-cut.)
RCA (LPM-1382 "Elvis") 750-1000 56
(Monaural. Black label, "Long Play" at bottom. Cover has selection number in upper right corner. Has an otherwise unreleased [on vinyl] alternate take of *Old Shep*. These usually have either a "15S," "17S" or "19S" following the identification number stamped in the vinyl trail-off.)
RCA (LPM-1382 "Elvis") 200-250 56
(Black label, selections numbered as "Band 1" through "Band 6.")
RCA (LPM-1382 "Elvis") 100-125 56
(Black label, "Long Play" at bottom. Cover has selection number in upper right corner.)
RCA (LPM-1382 "Elvis") 45-55 63
(Black label, "Mono" at bottom. Cover has selection number on left.)
RCA (LPM-1382 "Elvis") 25-30 64
(Black label, "Monaural" at bottom. Cover has selection number on left.)
RCA (LSP-1382e "Elvis") 75-85 62
(Stereo. Black label, all print on label is silver.)
RCA (LSP-1382e "Elvis") 25-30 64
(Black label, RCA logo is white, other print on label is silver.)
RCA (LSP-1382e "Elvis") 10-20 68
(Orange label.)
RCA (LSP-1382e "Elvis") 10-15 76
(Tan label.)
RCA (AFL1-1382e "Elvis") 8-10 77
(Digitally remastered in 1984 on RCA 5199.)
RCA (APL1-1506 "From Elvis Presley Boulevard") 12-15 76
RCA (AFL1-1506 "From Elvis Presley Boulevard") 8-10 77
RCA (LPM-1515 "Loving You") 100-125 57
(Monaural. Black label, "Long Play" at bottom. Cover has selection number in upper right corner.)
RCA (LPM-1515 "Loving You"). 45-55 63
(Black label, "Mono" at bottom. Cover has selection number on left.)
RCA (LPM-1515 "Loving You") 4000-5000
(Picture disc, but with the cover of a European *G.I. Blues* album being the picture imbeded in the vinyl. Experimental disc—only one copy made. Has just five *Loving You* tracks, the others being randomly selected instrumentals)
RCA (LPM-1515 "Loving You")..25-30 64
(Black label, "Monaural" at bottom. Cover has selection number on left.)
RCA (LSP-1515e "Loving You") 75-85 62
(Stereo. Black label, all print on label is silver.)
RCA (LSP-1515e "Loving You") 25-30 64
(Black label, RCA logo is white, other label print is silver.)
RCA (LSP-1515e "Loving You") 10-20 68
(Orange label.)
RCA (LSP-1515e "Loving You") 10-15 76
(Tan label.)
RCA (AFL1-1515e "Loving You"). 5-10 77
RCA (APM1-1675 "The Sun Sessions")................................12-15 76
RCA (AFM1-1675 "The Sun Sessions")..................................8-10 77
(First issued as RCA HY-1001 and was reissued in 1981 as RCA AYM1-3893.)
RCA (LPM-1707 "Elvis' Golden Records")............................100-125 58
(Monaural. Black label, "Long Play" at bottom. Cover has selection number in upper right corner and LP title in light blue letters.)
RCA (LPM-1707 "Elvis' Golden Records")................................45-55 63
(Black label, "Mono" at bottom. Cover has selection number on left and LP title in white letters.)
RCA (LPM-1707 "Elvis' Golden Records")................................25-30 64
(Black label, "Monaural" at bottom. Cover has selection number on left.)
RCA (LSP-1707e "Elvis' Golden Records")...............................75-85 62
(Stereo. Black label, all print on label is silver.)
RCA (LSP-1707e "Elvis' Golden Records")...............................25-30 64
(Black label, RCA logo is white, other label print is silver.)
RCA (LSP-1707e "Elvis' Golden Records")...............................10-20 68
(Orange label.)
RCA (LSP-1707e "Elvis' Golden Records")...............................10-15 76
(Tan label.)
RCA (AFL1-1707e "Elvis' Golden Records")..................................8-10 77
RCA (AQL1-1707e "Elvis' Golden Records")..................................5-10 79
(Digitally remastered in 1984 on RCA 5196.)
RCA (LPM-1884 "King Creole")..............................100-125 58
(Monaural. Black label, "Long Play" at

bottom. Cover has selection number in upper right corner. Add $75-100 if accompanied by an 8x10 black and white bonus photo of Elvis in uniform.)

RCA (LPM-1884 "King Creole") 45-55 63
(Black label, "Mono" at bottom. Cover has selection number on left.)

RCA (LPM-1884 "King Creole") 25-30 64
(Black label, "Monaural" at bottom. Cover has selection number on left.)

RCA (LSP-1884e "King Creole") 75-85 62
(Stereo. Black label, all print on label is silver.)

RCA (LSP-1884e "King Creole") 25-30 62
(Black label, RCA logo is white, other label print is silver.)

RCA (LSP-1884e "King Creole") 10-20 68
(Orange label.)

RCA (LSP-1884e "King Creole") 10-15 76
(Tan label.)

RCA (AFL1-1884e "King Creole") 8-10 77
(Reissued in 1980 as RCA AYL1-3733.)

RCA (ANL1-1936 "Wonderful World of Christmas") 5-10 77
(First issued as RCA LSP-4579.)

RCA (LPM-1951 "Elvis' Christmas Album") 90-100 58
(Monaural. Black label, "Long Play" at bottom. Cover has selection number in upper right corner.)

RCA (LPM-1951 "Elvis' Christmas Album") 45-55 63
(Black label, "Mono" at bottom. Cover has selection number on left.)

RCA (LPM-1951 "Elvis' Christmas Album") 25-30 64
(Black label, "Monaural" at bottom. Cover has selection number on left.)

RCA (LSP-1951e "Elvis' Christmas Album") 25-30 64
(Stereo. Black label, RCA logo is white, other label print is silver.)

RCA (LSP-1951e "Elvis' Christmas Album") 20-25 68
(Orange label. Repackage of RCA LOC-1035. It was repackaged in 1970 as Camden 2428 and again in 1985 as RCA AFM1-5486.)

RCA (1981 "Felton Jarvis Talks About Elvis")....................... 200-250 81
(Price includes three script sheets. Add $25 to $50 if accompanied by silver and black *Guitar Man* engraved Elvis belt buckle.)

RCA (LPM-1990 "For LP Fans Only") 100-125 59
(Monaural. Black label, "Long Play" at bottom. Cover has selection number in upper right corner.)

RCA (LPM-1990 "For LP Fans Only")....................................45-55 63
(Black label, "Mono" at bottom. Cover has selection number on left.)

RCA (LPM-1990 "For LP Fans Only")................................200-225 65
(Black label, "Monaural" at bottom. Cover has same Elvis photo on front and back.)

RCA (LPM-1990 "For LP Fans Only")....................................25-30 65
(Black label, "Monaural" at bottom. Cover has selection number on left.)

RCA (LSP-1990 "For LP Fans Only")................................200-225 65
(Black label. Cover has same Elvis photo on front and back.)

RCA (LSP-1990e "For LP Fans Only")....................................25-30 65
(Stereo. Black label, RCA logo is white, other label print is silver.)

RCA (LSP-1990e "For LP Fans Only")....................................10-20 68
(Orange label.)

RCA (LSP-1990e "For LP Fans Only")....................................10-15 76
(Tan label.)

RCA (AFL1-1990e "For LP Fans Only")..8-10 77

RCA (LPM-2011 "A Date with Elvis")................................400-600 59
(Monaural. Black label, "Long Play" at bottom. Has gatefold cover and 1960 calendar. With "New Golden Age of Sound" wrap-around banner.)

RCA (LPM-2011 "A Date with Elvis")................................150-175 59
(Black label, "Long Play" at bottom. Has gatefold cover and 1960 calendar, but *does not* have "New Golden Age of Sound" banner.)

RCA (LPM-2011 "A Date with Elvis")....................................45-55 65
(Black label, "Mono" at bottom. Cover has selection number on left.)

RCA (LPM-2011 "A Date with Elvis")....................................25-30 65
(Black label, "Monaural" at bottom. Cover has selection number on left.)

RCA (LSP-2011e "A Date with Elvis")....................................25-30 65
(Stereo. Black label, RCA logo is white, other label print is silver.)

RCA (LSP-2011e "A Date with Elvis")....................................10-20 68
(Orange label.)

RCA (LSP-2011e "A Date with Elvis")....................................10-15 76
(Tan label.)

RCA (AFL1-2011e "A Date with Elvis") 8-10 77

RCA (LPM-2075 "Elvis' Golden Records, Vol. 2") 100-125 59
(Monaural. Black label, "Long Play" at bottom. Cover has selection number in upper right corner.)

RCA (LPM-2075 "Elvis' Golden Records, Vol. 2") 45-55 63
(Black label, "Mono" at bottom. Cover has selection number on left.)

RCA (LPM-2075 "Elvis' Golden Records, Vol. 2") 25-30 64
(Black label, "Monaural" at bottom. Cover has selection number on left.)

RCA (LSP-2075e "Elvis' Golden Records, Vol. 2") 75-85 62
(Stereo. Black label, all print on label is silver.)

RCA (LSP-2075e "Elvis' Golden Records, Vol. 2") 25-30 64
(Black label, RCA logo is white, other label print is silver.)

RCA (LSP-2075e "Elvis' Golden Records, Vol. 2") 10-20 68
(Orange label.)

RCA (LSP-2075e "Elvis' Golden Records, Vol. 2") 10-15 76
(Tan label.)

RCA (AFL1-2075e "Elvis' Golden Records, Vol. 2") 8-10 77
(May also be shown as *50,000,000 Elvis Presley Fans Can't Be Wrong.* Digitally remastered in 1984 on RCA 5197.)

RCA (2227 "Great Performances") 10-20 90

RCA (LPM-2231 "Elvis Is Back") 100-150 60
(Monaural. Black label, "Long Play" at bottom. No song titles printed on cover. May have a yellow sticker on cover showing song titles.)

RCA (LPM-2231 "Elvis Is Back") 45-55 63
(Black label, "Mono" at bottom. Cover has selection number on left.)

RCA (LPM-2231 "Elvis Is Back") 25-30 64
(Black label, "Monaural" at bottom. Cover has selection number on left.)

RCA (LSP-2231 "Elvis Is Back") 120-160 60
(Stereo. Black label, "Living Stereo" at bottom. No song titles printed on cover. May have a yellow sticker on cover showing song titles.)

RCA (LSP-2231 "Elvis Is Back") 25-30 64
(Black label, RCA logo is white, other label print is silver.)

RCA (LSP-2231 "Elvis Is Back") 10-20 68
(Orange label.)

RCA (LSP-2231 "Elvis Is Back") 10-15 76
(Tan label.)

RCA (AFL1-2231 "Elvis Is Back") 8-10 77

RCA (LPM-2256 "G.I. Blues") 100-125 60
(Monaural. Black label, "Long Play" at bottom. Add $15 to $25 if accompanied by "Elvis Is Back" inner sleeve. Add $100 to $150 if cover has a heart-shaped announcement for *Wooden Heart.)*

RCA (LPM-2256 "G.I. Blues") 45-55 63
(Black label, "Mono" at bottom.)

RCA (LPM-2256 "G.I. Blues") 25-30 64
(Black label, "Monaural" at bottom.)

RCA (LSP-2256 "G.I. Blues"). 100-125 60
(Stereo. Black label, "Living Stereo" at bottom. Add $15 to $25 if accompanied by "Elvis Is Back" inner sleeve. Add $100 to $150 if cover has a heart-shaped announcement for *Wooden Heart.)*

RCA (LSP-2256 "G.I. Blues") 25-30 64
(Black label, RCA logo is white, other label print is silver.)

RCA (LSP-2256 "G.I. Blues") 10-20 68
(Orange label.)

RCA (LSP-2256 "G.I. Blues") 10-15 76
(Tan label.)

RCA (AFL1-2256 "G.I. Blues") 8-10 77
(Reissued in 1980 as RCA AYL1-3735.)

Note: For *G.I. Blues* picture disc, see *Loving You* (RCA LPM-1515).

RCA (APL1-2274 "Welcome to My World") 10-15 77

RCA (AFL1-2274 "Welcome to My World") 8-10 77

RCA (AQL1-2274 "Welcome to My World") 5-10 79

RCA (LPM-2328 "His Hand in Mine") 75-100 60
(Monaural. Black label, "Long Play" at bottom.)

RCA (LPM-2328 "His Hand in Mine") 40-50 63
(Black label, "Mono" at bottom.)

RCA (LPM-2328 "His Hand in Mine") 25-30 64
(Black label, "Monaural" at bottom.)

RCA (LSP-2328 "His Hand in Mine") 100-125 60
(Stereo. Black label, "Living Stereo" at bottom.)

RCA (LSP-2328 "His Hand in Mine") 25-30 64
(Black label, RCA logo is white, other label print is silver.)

RCA (LSP-2328 "His Hand in Mine") 10-20 68
(Orange label.)

RCA (LSP-2328 "His Hand in Mine") 10-15 76
(Tan label.)
(Repackaged in 1976 as RCA ANL1-1319 and in 1981 as RCA AYM1-3935.)
RCA (2347 "Elvis-Greatest Hits, Vol. One") 10-15 81
(Has embossed letters on front cover.)
RCA (2347 "Elvis-Greatest Hits, Vol. One") 5-10 83
(Standard cover print—not embossed.)
RCA (LPM-2370 "Something for Everybody") 75-100 61
(Monaural. Black label, "Long Play" at bottom. Back cover promotes Compact 33s.)
RCA (LPM-2370 "Something for Everybody") 40-50 63
(Black label, "Mono" at bottom.)
RCA (LPM-2370 "Something for Everybody") 25-30 64
(Black label, "Monaural" at bottom.)
RCA (LSP-2370 "Something for Everybody") 125-150 61
(Stereo. Black label, "Living Stereo" at bottom. Back cover promotes Compact 33s.)
RCA (LSP-2370 "Something for Everybody") 25-30 64
(Black label, RCA logo is white, other label print is silver.)
RCA (LSP-2370 "Something for Everybody") 10-20 68
(Orange label.)
RCA (LSP-2370 "Something for Everybody") 10-15 76
(Tan label.)
RCA (AFL1-2370 "Something for Everybody") 8-10 77
(Reissued in 1981 as RCA AYM1-4116.)
RCA (LPM-2426 "Blue Hawaii") 75-90 61
(Monaural. Black label, "Long Play" at bottom.)
RCA (LPM-2426 "Blue Hawaii") 40-50 63
(Black label, "Mono" at bottom.)
RCA (LPM-2426 "Blue Hawaii") 25-30 64
(Black label, "Monaural" at bottom.)
RCA (LSP-2426 "Blue Hawaii") 90-100 61
(Stereo. Black label, "Living Stereo" at bottom.)
RCA (LSP-2426 "Blue Hawaii"). 25-30 64
(Black label, RCA logo is white, other label print is silver.)
RCA (LSP-2426 "Blue Hawaii"). 10-20 68
(Orange label.)
RCA (LSP-2426 "Blue Hawaii"). 10-15 76
(Tan label.)
RCA (AFL1-2426 "Blue Hawaii"). 8-10 77
(Reissued in 1981 as RCA AYL1-3683.)
RCA (AFL1-2428 "Moody Blue") 1000-1200 77
(Colored vinyl—any color *other than blue or black*. Experimental production discs for RCA in-house use only.)
RCA (AFL1-2428 "Moody Blue") 10-12 77
(Blue vinyl.)
RCA (AFL1-2428 "Moody Blue") 125-150 77
(Black vinyl.)
RCA (AQL1-2428 "Moody Blue") . 8-10 79
RCA (LPM-2523 "Pot Luck") 75-90 62
(Monaural. Black label, "Long Play" at bottom.)
RCA (LPM-2523 "Pot Luck") 40-50 63
(Black label, "Mono" at bottom.)
RCA (LPM-2523 "Pot Luck") 25-30 64
(Black label, "Monaural" at bottom.)
RCA (LSP-2523 "Pot Luck") 90-100 62
(Stereo. Black label, "Living Stereo" at bottom.)
RCA (LSP-2523 "Pot Luck") 25-30 64
(Black label, RCA logo is white, other label print is silver.)
RCA (LSP-2523 "Pot Luck") 10-20 68
(Orange label.)
RCA (LSP-2523 "Pot Luck") 10-15 76
(Tan label.)
RCA (AFL1-2523 "Pot Luck") 8-10 77
RCA (APL1-2558 "Harum Scarum") 8-10 77
(First issued as RCA LPM/LSP-3468. Reissued in 1980 as RCA AYL1-3734.)
RCA (APL1-2560 "Spinout") 8-10 77
(First issued as RCA LPM/LSP-3702. Reissued in 1980 as RCA AYL1-3684.)
RCA (APL1-2564 "Double Trouble") 8-10 77
(First issued as RCA LPM/LSP-3787.)
RCA (APL1-2565 "Clambake") 8-10 77
(First issued as RCA LPM/LSP-3893.)
RCA (APL1-2568 "It Happened at the World's Fair") 8-10 77
(First issued as RCA LPM/LSP-2697.)
RCA (APL2-2587 "Elvis in Concert") 15-20 77
RCA (CPL2-2587 "Elvis in Concert") 12-15 82
RCA (LPM-2621 "Girls! Girls! Girls!") 75-90 62
(Monaural. Black label, "Long Play" at bottom.)
RCA (LPM-2621 "Girls! Girls! Girls!") 40-50 63
(Black label, "Mono" at bottom.)
RCA (LPM-2621 "Girls! Girls! Girls!") 25-30 64
(Black label, "Monaural" at bottom.)

RCA (LSP-2621 "Girls! Girls! Girls!") 90-100 62
(Stereo. Black label, "Living Stereo" at bottom.)
RCA (LSP-2621 "Girls! Girls! Girls!") 25-30 64
(Black label, RCA logo is white, other label print is silver.)
RCA (LSP-2621 "Girls! Girls! Girls!") 10-20 68
(Orange label.)
RCA (LSP-2621 "Girls! Girls! Girls!") 10-15 76
(Tan label.)
RCA (AFL1-2621 "Girls! Girls! Girls!") 8-10 77
RCA (CPD2-2642 "Aloha from Hawaii") 15-20 75
(Orange label.)
RCA (CPD2-2642 "Aloha from Hawaii") 10-12 77
(Black label. First issued as RCA VPSX-6089.)
RCA (LPM-2697 "It Happened at the World's Fair") 75-90 63
(Monaural. Black label, "Long Play" at bottom. Add $100 to $125 if accompanied by an 8x10 bonus color photo.)
RCA (LPM-2697 "It Happened at the World's Fair") 40-50 63
(Black label, "Mono" at bottom.)
RCA (LPM-2697 "It Happened at the World's Fair") 25-30 64
(Black label, "Monaural" at bottom.)
RCA (LSP-2697 "It Happened at the World's Fair") 90-110 63
(Stereo. Black label, "Living Stereo" at bottom. Add $100 to $125 if accompanied by an 8x10 bonus color photo.)
RCA (LSP-2697 "It Happened at the World's Fair") 25-30 64
(Black label, RCA logo is white, other label print is silver. Reissued in 1977 as RCA APL1-2568.)
RCA (LPM-2756 "Fun in Acapulco") 60-70 63
(Monaural. Black label, "Mono" at bottom.)
RCA (LPM-2756 "Fun in Acapulco") 25-30 64
(Black label, "Monaural" at bottom.)
RCA (LSP-2756 "Fun in Acapulco") 60-70 63
(Stereo. Black label, all print on label is silver.)
RCA (LSP-2756 "Fun in Acapulco") 25-30 64
(Black label, RCA logo is white, other label print is silver.)
RCA (LSP-2756 "Fun in Acapulco") 10-20 68
(Orange label.)
RCA (LSP-2756 "Fun in Acapulco") 10-15 76
(Tan label.)
RCA (AFL1-2756 "Fun in Acapulco") 8-10 77
RCA (LPM-2765 "Elvis' Golden Records, Vol. 3") 90-100 63
(Monaural. Black label, "Mono" at bottom.)
RCA (LPM-2765 "Elvis' Golden Records, Vol. 3") 25-30 64
(Black label, "Monaural" at bottom.)
RCA (LSP-2765 "Elvis' Golden Records, Vol. 3") 90-100 63
(Stereo. Black label, all print on label is silver.)
RCA (LSP-2765 "Elvis' Golden Records, Vol. 3") 25-30 64
(Black label, RCA logo is white, other label print is silver.)
RCA (LSP-2765 "Elvis' Golden Records, Vol. 3") 10-20 68
(Orange label.)
RCA (LSP-2765 "Elvis' Golden Records, Vol. 3") 10-15 76
(Tan label.)
RCA (AFL1-2765 "Elvis' Golden Records, Vol. 3") 8-10 77
RCA (AFL1-2772 "He Walks Beside Me") 8-10 77
RCA (LPM-2894 "Kissin' Cousins") 100-200 64
(Monaural. Black label, "Mono" at bottom. *Does not* picture film cast in lower right corner photo on cover.)
RCA (LPM-2894 "Kissin' Cousins") 60-70 64
(Black label, "Mono" at bottom. Pictures film cast in lower right corner photo on cover.)
RCA (LPM-2894 "Kissin' Cousins") 25-30 64
(Black label, "Monaural" at bottom.)
RCA (LSP-2894 "Kissin' Cousins") 100-150 64
(Stereo. Black label, all print on label is silver. *Does not* picture film cast in lower right corner photo on cover.)
RCA (LSP-2894 "Kissin' Cousins") 60-70 64
(Black label, all print on label is silver. Pictures film cast in lower right corner photo on cover.)
RCA (LSP-2894 "Kissin' Cousins") 25-30 64
(Black label, RCA logo is white, other label print is silver.)

RCA (LSP-2894 "Kissin' Cousins")................................ 10-20 68
(Orange label.)
RCA (LSP-2894 "Kissin' Cousins")................................ 10-15 76
(Tan label.)
RCA (LSP-2894 "Kissin' Cousins")........................ 1000-1200 77
(Blue vinyl. Experimental pressing only.)
RCA (AFL1-2894 "Kissin' Cousins").................................. 8-10 77
(Reissued in 1981 as RCA AYM1-4115.)
RCA (CPL1-2901 "Elvis Sings for Children")............................ 8-10 78
(Includes "Special Memories" greeting card.)
RCA (LPM-2999 "Roustabout"). 60-70 64
(Monaural. Black label, "Mono" at bottom.)
RCA (LPM-2999 "Roustabout"). 25-30 65
(Black label, "Monaural" at bottom.)
RCA (LSP-2999 "Roustabout")...................... 500-600 64
(Stereo. Black label. All print on label—including RCA logo—is silver.)
RCA (LSP-2999 "Roustabout") . 25-30 64
(Black label, RCA logo is white, other label print is silver.)
RCA (LSP-2999 "Roustabout") . 10-20 68
(Orange label.)
RCA (LSP-2999 "Roustabout") . 10-15 76
(Tan label.)
RCA (AFL1-2999 "Roustabout") . 8-10 77
RCA (3078 "Legendary Performer, Vol. 3")................. 15-20 78
(Picture disc. Add $5 to $10 if accompanied by *Yesterdays* booklet. May be found with the actual disc pressed on either blue or black vinyl. Also issued on standard black vinyl as 3082.)
RCA (3082 "Legendary Performer, Vol. 3") 8-12 78
(Add $5 to $10 if accompanied by *Yesterdays* booklet. Also issued on a picture disc, as RCA 3078.)
RCA (3279 "Our Memories of Elvis")...................................... 8-10 79
RCA (LPM-3338 "Girl Happy") .. 40-50 65
(Monaural.)
RCA (LSP-3338 "Girl Happy")... 40-50 65
(Stereo. Black label.)
RCA (LSP-3338 "Girl Happy")... 10-20 68
(Orange label.)
RCA (LSP-3338 "Girl Happy")... 10-15 76
(Tan label.)
RCA (AFL1-3338 "Girl Happy")... 8-10 77
RCA (3448 "Our Memories of Elvis Vol. 2")............................. 8-10 79
(A sampling of these tracks is on RCA 3455, *Pure Elvis*.)

RCA (LPM-3450 "Elvis for Everyone")..............................40-50 65
(Monaural.)
RCA (LSP-3450 "Elvis for Everyone")..............................40-50 65
(Stereo. Black label.)
RCA (LSP-3450 "Elvis for Everyone")..............................10-20 68
(Orange label.)
RCA (LSP-3450 "Elvis for Everyone")..............................10-15 76
(Tan label.)
RCA (AFL1-3450 "Elvis for Everyone")................................8-10 77
Reissued in 1982 as RCA AYL1-4232.
RCA (3455 "Pure Elvis") 500-600 79
(Cover reads "Pure Elvis," but label shows "Our Memories of Elvis - Vol. 2." Promotional issue only.)
RCA (LPM-3468 "Harum Scarum")..................................35-50 65
(Monaural. Add $60 to $85 if accompanied by bonus 12x12 photo.)
RCA (LSP-3468 "Harum Scarum")..................................35-50 65
(Stereo. Add $60 to $85 if accompanied by bonus 12x12 photo. Reissued in 1977 as RCA APL1-2558 and in 1980 as RCA AYL1-3734.)
RCA (LPM-3553 "Frankie and Johnny")...................................35-50 66
(Monaural. Add $60 to $85 if accompanied by bonus 12x12 print.)
RCA (LSP-3553 "Frankie and Johnny")...................................35-50 66
(Stereo. Add $60 to $85 if accompanied by bonus 12x12 print. Reissued in 1977 as RCA APL1-2559. A repackage appeared in 1976 on Pickwick 7007.)
RCA (LPM-3643 "Paradise Hawaiian Style")........................35-45 66
(Monaural.)
RCA (LSP-3643 "Paradise Hawaiian Style")........................35-45 66
(Stereo. Black label.)
RCA (LSP-3643 "Paradise Hawaiian Style")........................10-20 68
(Orange label.)
RCA (LSP-3643 "Paradise Hawaiian Style")........................10-15 76
(Tan label.)
RCA (AFL1-3643 "Paradise Hawaiian Style")..........................8-10 77
RCA (AYL1-3683 "Blue Hawaii") .5-10 80
(First issued as RCA LPM/LSP-2426.)
RCA (AYL1-3684 "Spinout") 5-10 80
(First issued as RCA LPM/LSP-3702, reissued in 1977 as RCA APL1-2560.)

RCA (CPL8-3699 "Elvis
Aron Presley")...................... 80-100 80
(Eight-LP boxed set. Add $5 to $10 if accompanied by 20-page booklet.)
RCA (CPL8-3699 "Elvis
Aron Presley").................... 450-500 80
(REVIEWER SERIES edition. Silver sticker on back also identifies the Reviewer Series copy as "NS-3699." Add $5 to $10 if accompanied by 20-page booklet.)
RCA (CPK8-3699 "Elvis
Aron Presley")...................... 80-100 80
(Four-cassette boxed set. Add $10 to $20 if accompanied by 20-page booklet and eight 12x12 Elvis photos.)
RCA (CPS8-3699 "Elvis
Aron Presley").................... 100-125 80
(Four 8-track boxed set. Add $10 to $20 if accompanied by 20-page booklet and eight 12x12 Elvis photos. *Excerpts* of songs in this set appeared on RCA 3729. *Selections* from this LP are on RCA 3781.)
RCA (LPM-3702 "Spinout")....... 35-50 66
(Monaural. Add $60 to $85 if accompanied by bonus 12x12 photo.)
RCA (LSP-3702 "Spinout")........ 35-50 66
(Stereo. Add $60 to $85 if accompanied by bonus 12x12 photo. Reissued in 1977 as APL1-2560.)
RCA (3729 "Elvis Aron
Presley," Excerpts) 100-125 80
(Has 37 excerpts from RCA 3699. Promotional issue only.)
RCA (AYL1-3732 "Pure Gold") ... 5-10 80
(First issued as RCA ANL1-0971.)
RCA (AYL1-3733 "King Creole"). 5-10 80
(First issued as RCA LSP-1884.)
RCA (AYL1-3734 "Harum
Scarum")................................ 5-10 80
(First issued as RCA LPM/LSP-3468.)
RCA (AYL1-3735 "G.I. Blues").... 5-10 80
(First issued as RCA LPM/LSP-2256.)
RCA (LPM-3758 "How Great
Thou Art")............................. 40-50 67
(Monaural.)
RCA (LSP-3758 "How Great
Thou Art")............................. 35-45 67
(Stereo. Black label.)
RCA (LSP-3758 "How Great
Thou Art")............................. 10-20 68
(Orange label.)
RCA (LSP-3758 "How Great
Thou Art")............................. 10-15 76
(Tan label.)
RCA (AFL1-3758 "How Great
Thou Art")............................... 8-10 77
RCA (3781 "Elvis Aron
Presley," Selections).......... 100-125 80
(Has 12 selections from RCA 3699. Promotional issue only.)
RCA (LPM-3787 "Double
Trouble") 40-50 67
(Monaural. Front cover reads "Special Bonus Full Color Photo." Add $25 to $35 if accompanied by bonus 7x9 photo.)
RCA (LPM-3787 "Double
Trouble") 30-40 68
("Special Bonus Full Color Photo" is replaced by "Trouble Double.")
RCA (LSP-3787 "Double
Trouble") 40-50 67
(Stereo. Front cover reads "Special Bonus Full Color Photo." Add $25 to $35 if accompanied by bonus 7x9 photo. Black label.)
RCA (LSP-3787 "Double
Trouble") 30-40 68
("Special Bonus Full Color Photo" is replaced by "Trouble Double.")
RCA (LSP-3787 "Double
Trouble") 10-20 68
(Orange label.)
RCA (LSP-3787 "Double
Trouble") 10-15 76
(Tan label.)
(Reissued in 1977 as RCA APL1-2564.)
RCA (AYL1-3892 "Elvis in
Person")....................................5-10 81
(First issued as RCA LSP-4428.)
RCA (LPM-3893 "Clambake")175-200 67
(Monaural. Add $30 to $50 if accompanied by bonus 12x12 photo. Reissued in 1977 as RCA APL1-2565.)
RCA (LSP-3893 "Clambake") 30-50 67
(Stereo. Add $30 to $50 if accompanied by bonus 12x12 photo. Reissued in 1977 as RCA APL1-2565.)
RCA (AYM1-3893 "Sun
Sessions")................................5-10 81
(First issued as RCA APM1-1675.)
RCA (AYM1-3894 "Elvis TV
Special")...................................5-10 81
(First issued RCA LPM-4088.)
RCA (3917 "Guitar Man").............8-12 81
(Includes a "This Is Elvis" flyer. Producer Felton Jarvis talks about Elvis as well as the making of this LP [RCA 1981].)
RCA (LPM-3921 "Elvis' Gold
Records, Vol. 4").............1000-1200 68
(Monaural.) RCA (LSP-3921 "Elvis' Gold
Records, Vol. 4")....................60-90 68
(Stereo. Black label.)
RCA (LSP-3921 "Elvis' Gold
Records, Vol. 4")......................10-20 68
(Orange label.)

RCA (LSP-3921 "Elvis' Gold Records, Vol. 4") 10-15 76
(Tan label.)
RCA (AFL1-3921 "Elvis' Gold Records, Vol. 4") 8-10 77
RCA (AYM1-3935 "His Hand in Mine") 5-10 81
(First issued as RCA LPM/LSP-2328.)
RCA (AYL1-3956 "That's The Way It Is") 5-10 81
First issued as RCA LSP-4460.
RCA (LPM-3989 "Speedway") 1000-1200 68
(Monaural. Add $25 to $50 if accompanied by bonus 8x10 photo.)
RCA (LSP-3989 "Speedway") ... 35-45 68
(Stereo. Black label. Add $25 to $50 if accompanied by bonus 8x10 photo.)
RCA (LSP-3989 "Speedway") ... 10-20 68
(Orange label.)
RCA (LSP-3989 "Speedway") ... 10-15 76
(Tan label.)
RCA (AFL1-3989 "Speedway") ... 8-10 77
RCA (4031 "This Is Elvis") 10-15 80
RCA (LPM-4088 "Elvis TV Special") 15-20 68
(Orange label. Rigid disc.)
RCA (LPM-4088 "Elvis TV Special") 10-15 72
(Orange label. Flexible disc.)
RCA (LPM-4088 "Elvis TV Special") 10-15 76
(Tan label.)
RCA (AFM1-4088 "Elvis TV Special") 8-10 77
(Reissued in 1981 as RCA AYM1-3894. Repackaged for HBO as RCA 0704.)
RCA (AYL1-4114 "That's The Way It Is") 5-10 81
(First issued as RCA LSP-4445.)
RCA (AYM1-4115 "Kissin' Cousins") 5-10 81
(First issued as RCA LPM/LSP-2894.)
RCA (AYM1-4116 "Something for Everybody") 5-10 81
(First issued as RCA LPM/LSP-2370.)
RCA (LSP-4155 "From Elvis in Memphis") 20-25 69
(Orange label. Rigid disc. Add $30 to $40 if accompanied by 8x10 Elvis photo.)
RCA (LSP-4155 "From Elvis in Memphis") 10-15 72
(Orange label. Flexible disc.)
RCA (LSP-4155 "From Elvis in Memphis") 10-15 69
(Tan label.)
RCA (AFL1-4155 "From Elvis in Memphis") 8-10 77
(A half-speed mastered issue of this LP was released in 1982 as MFSL 059.)
RCA (AYL1-4232 "Elvis for Everyone") 5-10 82
(First issued as RCA LPM/LSP-3450.)
RCA (LSP-4362 "On Stage") 15-20 70
(Orange label. Rigid disc.)
RCA (LSP-4362 "On Stage") 10-15 72
(Orange label. Flexible disc.)
RCA (LSP-4362 "On Stage") 10-15 76
(Tan label.)
RCA (AFL1-4362 "On Stage") ... 10-12 77
RCA (AQL1-4362 "On Stage") 5-10 83
RCA (4395 "Memories of Christmas") 8-10 82
RCA (LSP-4428 "Elvis in Person") 15-20 70
(Orange label.)
RCA (LSP-4428 "Elvis in Person") 10-15 76
(Tan label.)
RCA (AFL1-4428 "Elvis in Person") 8-10 77
(First released as half of RCA LSP-6020, then reissued in 1981 as RCA AYL1-3892.)
RCA (LSP-4429 "Elvis Back in Memphis") 15-20 70
(Orange label.)
RCA (LSP-4429 "Elvis Back in Memphis") 10-15 76
(Tan label.)
RCA (AFL1-4429 "Elvis Back in Memphis") 8-10 77
(First issued as half of RCA LSP-6020.)
RCA (LSP-4445 "That's the Way It Is") 15-20 70
(Orange label.)
RCA (LSP-4445 "That's the Way It Is") 10-15 76
(Tan label.)
RCA (LSP-4445 "That's the Way It Is") 8-10 77
(Black label.)
RCA (AFL1-4445 "That's the Way It Is") 8-10 77
(Reissued in 1981 as RCA AYL1-4114.)
RCA (LSP-4460 "Elvis Country") 15-20 71
(Orange label. Add $10 to $15 if accompanied by 7x9 Elvis photo.)
RCA (LSP-4460 "Elvis Country") 10-15 76
(Tan label.)
RCA (AFL1-4460 "Elvis Country") 8-10 77
(Reissued in 1981 as RCA AYL1-3956.)
RCA (LSP-4530 "Love Letters"). 35-45 71
(Orange label. Full title, *Love Letters From Elvis*, on TWO lines on front cover.)

RCA (LSP-4530 "Love Letters") 20-35 71
(Orange label. Full title, *Love Letters From Elvis*, on THREE lines on front cover.)
RCA (LSP-4530 "Love Letters") 10-15 76
(Tan label.)
RCA (AFL1-4530 "Love Letters") 8-10 77
(Reissued in 1981 as RCA AYL1-3956.)
RCA (AHL1-4530 "Elvis Medley") 8-10 82
RCA (LSP-4579 "Wonderful World of Christmas") 20-25 71
(Orange label. Add $4 to $8 if accompanied by a 5x7 Elvis postcard. Reissued in 1977 as RCA ANL1-1936.)
RCA (LSP-4671 "Elvis Now").... 50-60 72
(Has white titles/times sticker on front cover. Promotional issue only.)
RCA (LSP-4671 "Elvis Now").... 15-18 72
(Orange label.)
RCA (LSP-4671 "Elvis Now").... 10-15 76
(Tan label.)
RCA (AFL1-4671 "Elvis Now").... 8-10 77
RCA (LSP-4690 "He Touched Me")...................................... 50-60 72
(Has white titles/times sticker on front cover. Promotional issue only.)
RCA (LSP-4690 "He Touched Me")...................................... 15-18 72
(Orange label.)
RCA (LSP-4690 "He Touched Me")...................................... 10-15 76
(Tan label.)
RCA (AFL1-4690 "He Touched Me").. 8-10 77
RCA (4678 "I Was the One")....... 8-10 83
RCA (LSP-4776 "Elvis As Recorded at Madison Square Garden") 50-60 72
(Orange label. Has white programming stickers applied to front cover. Promotional issue only. For double disc promotional, see RCA 571.)
RCA (LSP-4776 " Elvis As Recorded at Madison Square Garden") 15-20 72
(Orange label.)
RCA (LSP-4776 " Elvis As Recorded at Madison Square Garden") 10-15 76
(Tan label.)
RCA (AQL1-4776 " Elvis As Recorded at Madison Square Garden") 8-10 77
RCA (4809 "A Country Christmas" Vol. 2) 8-10 83
RCA (4848 "Legendary Performer, Vol. 4") 8-10 83
(Price includes a 12-page *Memories of the King* booklet.)
RCA (4941 "Elvis' Gold Records, Vol. 5") 5-10 84
RCA (5172 "Golden Celebration") 40-50 84
(Six-LP boxed set. Price includes custom inner sleeves and an envelope containing an 8x10 Elvis photo and a 50th Anniversary flyer.)
RCA (5172 "Golden Celebration")............................15-20 84
(Special "Advance Cassette" boxed set sampler.)
RCA (5182 "Rocker")..................5-10 84
RCA (5196 "Elvis' Golden Records")..................................5-10 84
(Digitally remastered, quality mono pressing. Price includes gold "The Definitive Rock Classic" banner. First issued as RCA LPM-1707.)
RCA (5197 "Elvis' Gold Records, Vol. 2")..5-10 84
(Digitally remastered, quality mono pressing. Price includes gold "The Definitive Rock Classic" banner. First issued as RCA LPM-2075.)
RCA (5198 "Elvis Presley")..........5-10 84
(Digitally remastered, quality mono pressing. Price includes gold "The Definitive Rock Classic" banner. First issued as RCA LPM-1254.)
RCA (5199 "Elvis")......................5-10 84
(Digitally remastered, quality mono pressing. Price includes gold "The Definitive Rock Classic" banner. First issued as RCA LPM-1382.)
RCA (5353 "Valentine Gift for You")...8-10 85
(Colored vinyl.)
RCA (5353 "Valentine Gift for You")...5-10 85
(Black vinyl.)
RCA (5418 "Reconsider Baby")...5-10 85
RCA (5430 "Always on My Mind")...5-10 85
RCA (5486 "Elvis' Christmas Album") 5-10 85
(Colored vinyl.)
RCA (5486 "Elvis' Christmas Album") 20-40 85
(Black vinyl. Thus far, all black vinyl copies discovered were packaged with stickers reading "pressed on green vinyl.")
RCA (5600 "Return of the Rocker")....................................5-10 86
RCA (5697 "Special Christmas Programming")..................800-1000 67
(Promotional issue only.)
RCA (LSP-6020 "From Memphis to Vegas") 30-40 69
(Orange label. Incorrectly shows writers of *Words* as Tommy Boyce & Bobby Hart. Also shows writer of *Suspicious Minds* as Frances Zambon. Add $20 to $40 if

accompanied by two 8x10, black and white Elvis photos.)

RCA (LSP-6020 "From Memphis to Vegas") 20-30 69
(Orange label. Correctly shows writers of *Words* as Barry, Robin & Maurice Gibb, and writer of *Suspicious Minds* as Mark James. Add $20 to $40 if accompanied by two 8x10 Elvis photos.)

RCA (LSP-6020 "From Memphis to Vegas") 15-20 76
(Tan label.)

RCA (LSP-6020 "From Memphis to Vegas") 10-15 77
(Black label. Each of the two LPs in this set was reissued individually, *Elvis in Person at the International Hotel* as LSP-4428 and *Elvis Back in Memphis* as LSP-4429, both in 1970.)

RCA (VPSX-6089 "Aloha from Hawaii") 2000-2500 73
(Has "Chicken of the Sea" sticker on cover. Quadradisc and contents stickers also are on cover. Includes programming insert card. Promotional in-house issue by the Van Camps Company.)

RCA (VPSX-6089 "Aloha from Hawaii") 500-750 73
(Has white titles/times sticker on front cover. Promotional issue only.)

RCA (VPSX-6089 "Aloha from Hawaii") 75-100 73
(Has Quadradisc and contents stickers on cover. Red/orange label.)

RCA (VPSX-6089 "Aloha from Hawaii") 25-30 74
(Has Quadradisc/RCA logo in lower right corner of front cover. Titles are printed on back cover. Orange label.)

RCA (VPSX-6089 "Aloha from Hawaii") 25-30 76
(Tan label. Issued through the RCA Record Club as RCA 213736 and later (1977) as RCA CPD2-2642.)

RCA (6221 "Memphis Record") 10-15 87
(Includes a bonus color 15x22 poster and *Elvis Talks* LP flyer.)

RCA (6313 "Elvis Talks!") 10-15 87
(Mail-order LP offer.)

RCA (6382 "Number One Hits").. 8-10 87
(Includes a bonus color 15x22 poster and *Elvis Talks* LP flyer.)

RCA (6383 "Top Ten Hits")....... 10-12 87
(Includes a bonus color 15x22 poster and *Elvis Talks* LP flyer.)

RCA (LPM-6401 "Worldwide 50 Gold Hits, Vol. 1") 60-75 70
(Orange label. Four-LP boxed set. Add $30 to $40 if accompanied by a 16-page Elvis photo booklet.)

RCA (LPM-6401 "Worldwide 50 Gold Hits, Vol. 1") 30-40 76
(Tan label.)

RCA (LPM-6401 "Worldwide 50 Gold Hits, Vol. 1") 20-25 77
(Black label. Two of the LPs in this set were repackaged for the RCA Record Club in 1974 as RCA 213690. The other two came out in 1978 as RCA 214657.)

RCA (LPM-6402 "Worldwide 50 Gold Hits, Vol. 2") 60-75 71
(Orange label. Four-LP boxed set. Add $25 to $50 if accompanied by an Elvis print, and an envelope with piece of material.)

RCA (LPM-6402 "Worldwide 50 Gold Hits, Vol. 2") 30-40 76
(Tan label. With bonus items shown as included.)

RCA (LPM-6402 "Worldwide 50 Gold Hits, Vol. 2") 25-35 76
(Tan label. No bonus items shown as being included.)

RCA (LPM-6402 "Worldwide 50 Gold Hits, Vol. 2") 20-25 77
(Black label. Two of the LPs in this set were repackaged for the RCA Record Club in 1978 as RCA 214567.)

RCA (6414 "The Complete Sun Sessions") 10-15 87
(Includes a bonus color 15x22 poster and *Elvis Talks* LP flyer.)

RCA (6738 "Essential Elvis") 5-10 88

RCA (6985 "The Alternate Aloha") 5-10 88

RCA (7031 "Elvis Forever") 25-35 74
(TV mail-order offer.)

RCA (7065 "Canadian Tribute"). 10-12 78
(Price includes photo inner-sleeve. Canadian issues of this LP had the same number but are clearly marked on back cover as Canadian.)

RCA (8468 "Elvis in Nashville") ...5-10 88

RCA (9586 "Elvis Gospel") 5-10 89

RCA (9589 "Stereo '57, Essential Elvis, Vol. 2") 5-10 89

RCA (213690 "Worldwide Gold Award Hits, Parts 1&2")............................75-100 74
(Orange label. RCA Record Club issue only.)

RCA (213690 "Worldwide Gold Award Hits, Parts 1&2")..............................25-30 76
(Tan label. RCA Record Club issue only.)

RCA (213690 "Worldwide Gold Award Hits, Parts 1&2")..............................12-15 77
(Black label. RCA Record Club issue only. The two discs in this set were first issued as half of RCA LPM-6401.)

RCA (213736 "Aloha from Hawaii")................................ 45-55 73
(Orange label.)
RCA (213736 "Aloha from Hawaii")................................ 18-20 76
(Tan label.)
RCA (214657 "Worldwide Gold Award Hits, Parts 3&4")............................ 12-15 78
(RCA Record Club issue only. The two discs in this set were first issued as half of RCA LPM-6401.)
RCA (233299 "Country Classics").............................. 20-25 80
(RCA Record Club issue only.)
RCA (234340 "From Elvis with Love")................................... 20-25 78
(RCA Record Club issue only.)
RCA (244047 "Legendary Concert Performances")..................... 20-25 78
(RCA Record Club issue only.)
RCA (244069 "Country Memories")............................ 20-25 78
(RCA Record Club issue only.)
SILHOUETTE (10001/10002 "Personally Elvis")................. 20-25 79
STARDAY (995 "Interviews with Elvis").................................30-50 78
(Previously issued on Great Northwest 4005.)
SUN (1001 "The Sun Years").... 75-80 77
(Light yellow label, "Memphis" at bottom. Light yellow cover with light brown printing.)
SUN (1001 "The Sun Years").... 15-20 77
(Darker yellow label, four target circles. Dark yellow cover with dark brown printing.)
SUN (1001 "The Sun Years").... 20-25 77
(White cover with brown printing.)
TM ("The Presley Years") 100-200 81
(12-LP boxed syndicated radio show. Includes script and cue sheets.)
TIME-LIFE (106 "Elvis Presley: 1954-1961") 15-20 86
(Three-LP boxed set, part of the *Rock 'N' Roll Era* series of sets available from Time-Life by mail-order. Includes brochure.)
TIME-LIFE (126 "Elvis the King") 20-30 89
(Two-LP boxed set.)
WATERMARK ("The Elvis Presley Story," 1975) 800-900 75
(13-LP set. White label, pink letters. Includes a 48-page operations manual. Promotional issue only. Not issued with a special cover or package.)
UNITED STATIONS ("Elvis Presley Birthday Tribute") 125-150 89
(Four hour radio show. Includes four pages of cue sheets. Promotional issue only.)
WATERMARK ("The Elvis Presley Story," 1977).......................700-800 77
(13-LP set. White label, pink letters. Includes a 48-page operations manual, which represents about $100 of the value. Promotional issue only. Not issued with a special cover or package.)
WESTWOOD ONE ("A Golden Celebration").......................200-250 84
(Three-LP boxed set. Price includes instructions and cue sheets, which represent $5-10 of the value. Issued to radio stations only.)
WORLD of ELVIS PRESLEY...50-100 83
(One hour weekly radio show, numbered as program 1 through program 30. The show ceased operation after 30 programs. Each disc was accompanied by a single cue sheet. Price is for any one of the discs, although program #3 is by far the rarest of them all.)

Session: Chet Atkins; Bill Black; Hal Blaine; Blossoms; David Briggs; James Burton; Floyd Cramer; Glen Hardin; Jordanaires; Jerry Kennedy; Anita Kerr; Ronnie Milsap; Bob Moore; Scotty Moore; Larry Muhoberac; Shaun Neilsen; Boots Randolph; Jerry Reed; J.D. Sumner & Stamps; Sweet Inspirations; Kathy Westmoreland; John Wilkinson; Bobby Wood.

Also see ALLEN, Steve
Also see ATKINS, Chet
Also see AUDREY
Also see BLACK, Bill
Also see BLOSSOMS
Also see COLE, Nat "King"
Also see CRAMER, Floyd
Also see CRICKETS
Also see DONNER, Ral
Also see DURANTE, Jimmy
Also see HARRIS, Emmylou
Also see KENNEDY, Jerry
Also see KERR, Anita
Also see LIBERACE
Also see MANTOVANI
Also see MILSAP, Ronnie
Also see MOORE, Bob
Also see RANDOLPH, Boots
Also see REED, Jerry
Also see SINATRA, Nancy
Also see SWEET INSPIRATIONS
Also see VINCENT, Gene

- Prefix letters or numbers are used on some LP listings in order to more quickly identify the variations available.
- A few items that have no label name are listed by title, such as the International Hotel boxed sets.
- Beginning in 1961, many Elvis LPs had a separate sticker, promoting such things as certain songs or bonus photos. When not listed separately in this edition, a premium of 10%-20% could be placed on LPs with these original stickers.

- LPs with a sticker applied over the selection number, showing a new number, are valued approximately the same as those without the sticker.
- Some albums were pressed with the "Dog Near Top" label using the older LSP prefix, prior to being switched to the AFL1 series. These are not listed separately since there seems to be no consequential price difference between the two.
- If you don't find a record in the preceding sections, it may contain two, three or four artists, and is listed in a section that follows.
- As imposing as our Elvis Presley section here may seem, it is but a drop in the bucket. For a far more in-depth study of Elvis collectibles—including records, compact discs and memorabilia—get Jerry Osborne's *Official Price Guide to Elvis Presley Records and Memorabilia.*

PRESLEY, Elvis / Beatles

Singles: 7-inch

OSBORNE ENTERPRISES ("The 1967 Elvis Medley") 4-8 88
(Flip side is titled *The #1 Hits Medley, 1956-69.* Includes insert. 1000 made.)
OSBORNE ENTERPRISES ("The 1967 Elvis Medley") 8-12 89
(Flip side is titled *The #1 Hits Medley, 1956-70.* 100 made.)

LPs: 10/12-inch 33rpm

UNITED DISTRIBUTORS (2382 "Lightning Strikes Twice") 25-50 81
(Promotional issue only. Has five songs by each artist.)
Also see BEATLES

PRESLEY, Elvis / Martha Carson / Lou Monte / Herb Jeffries

EPs: 7-inch 33/45rpm

RCA (2 "Dealer's Prevue") .. 900-1200 57
(Issued with paper envelope/sleeve. Promotional issue only.)

PRESLEY, Elvis / Jean Chapel

EPs: 7-inch 33/45rpm

RCA (7 "Love Me Tender") ... 150-200 56
(Not issued with a special sleeve or cover. Promotional issue only.)

PRESLEY, Elvis / Buddy Holly

Singles: 7-inch

CREATIVE RADIO ("Elvis 50th Birthday Special").................... 10-20 85
(Demonstration disc. A promotional issue.)
Also see HOLLY, Buddy

PRESLEY, Elvis / Fear

LPs: 10/12-inch 33rpm

DISCONET (309 "The Original Elvis Presley Medley"/"Fear Medley")25-50 80
(Promotional issue only.)

PRESLEY, Elvis / David Keith

Singles: 7-inch

RCA (8760 "Heartbreak Hotel") 50-100 88
(White label. Promotional issue only.)
RCA (8760 "Heartbreak Hotel") 4-5 88
(Red label. Printing on both sides of label.)
RCA (8760 "Heartbreak Hotel") 4-8 88
(Red label. Printing on Elvis side only.)
RCA (8760 "Heartbreak Hotel") 4-8 88
(Red label. Printing on David Keith side only.)

Picture Sleeves

RCA (8760 "Heartbreak Hotel") 50-100
(Pictures, but doesn't identify, RCA's Butch Waugh. Promotional issue only.)
RCA (8760 "Heartbreak Hotel") 4-8 88
(Pictures Elvis and others in a Cadillac.)

PRESLEY, Elvis / Vaughn Monroe / Gogi Grant / Robert Shaw

EPs: 7-inch 33/45rpm

RCA (3736 "Pop Transcribed 30 Sec. Spot")......................500-600 58
(Not issued with a special sleeve or cover. Promotional issue only.)

PRESLEY, Elvis / Jaye P. Morgan

Singles: 7-inch

UNITED STATES AIR FORCE (125 "It's Now Or Never") 300-400 61
(Add $30 TO $50 if accompanied by printed, cardboard mailing box. Issued only to radio stations.)

EPs: 7-inch 33/45rpm

RCA (992 & 689 "Elvis/Jaye P. Morgan").........................5000-6000 56
(Two-EP set, with 992 by Presley and 689 by Jaye P. Morgan coupled together in a promotional double-pocket package. Since the discs were standard pressings, at least 95% of the value here is represented by the custom EP cover.)
Also see MORGAN, Jaye P.

PRESLEY, Elvis / Gary Owens

Singles: 7-inch

CREATIVE RADIO ("Elvis Hour").....................................20-30 86
(Demonstration disc. A promotional issue.)

PRESLEY, Elvis / Helen Reddy

Singles: 7–inch

WHAT'S IT ALL ABOUT (78 "Life")....................................45-55 77
(Issued only to radio stations.)
Also see REDDY, Helen

PRESLEY, Elvis / Dinah Shore

EPs: 7–inch 33/45rpm

RCA (56 "Too Much")............150-200 57
(Not issued with a special sleeve or cover. Promotional issue only.)
Also see SHORE, Dinah

PRESLEY, Elvis / Frank Sinatra / Nat King Cole

EPs: 7–inch 33/45rpm

CREATIVE RADIO ("Elvis Remembered")........................40-45 79
(Promotional demonstration disc.)
Also see COLE, Nat "King"
Also see SINATRA, Frank

PRESLEY, Elvis / Hank Snow / Eddy Arnold / Jim Reeves

EPs: 7–inch 33/45rpm

RCA (12 "Old Shep").........2000-2500 56
(Issued with a paper, "WOHO Featuring RCA Victor" sleeve. Deduct $1,300 to $1,700 if sleeve is missing. Promotional only.)
Also see ARNOLD, Eddy
Also see REEVES, Jim
Also see SNOW, Hank

PRESLEY, Elvis / Lawrence Welk

Singles: 7–inch

UNITED STATES AIR FORCE (159 "Surrender")........................300-400 61
(Add $30 to $50 if accompanied by printed, cardboard mailing box. Issued only to radio stations.)
Also see WELK, Lawrence

PRESLEY, Elvis / Hank Williams

LPs: 10/12–inch 33rpm

SUNRISE MEDIA (3011 "History of Country Music")......................10-20 81
(Has four songs by each artist.)
Also see PRESLEY, Elvis
Also see WILLIAMS, Hank

PRESLEY, Elvis
(Michael Conley)

Singles: 7–inch

ELVIS CLASSIC (5478 "Tell Me Pretty Baby")....................................4-8 78
(Despite being labeled as a 1954 recording by Elvis Presley, this track was simply a 1978 recording by Michael Conley, performing in an Elvis style. It is listed separately to eliminate confusion.)

Picture Sleeves

ELVIS CLASSIC (5478 "Tell Me Pretty Baby")......................................8-10 78
(Sleeve pictures an artist's sketch of Elvis Presley.)

PRESSURE

R&B '80

Singles: 7–inch

LAX..3-5 79-80
MCA...3-5 80

LPs: 10/12–inch 33rpm

LAX..5-10 79
Also see LAWS, Ronnie

PRESSURE DROP

R&B '82

Singles: 12–inch 33/45rpm

TOMMY BOY..............................4-6 82

Singles: 7–inch

TOMMY BOY..............................3-5 82

PRESTON, Billy

LP '65

Singles: 12–inch 33/45rpm

MEGATONE................................4-6 84
MONTAGE...................................4-6 84

Singles: 7–inch

A&M..3-5 72-78
APPLE/AMERICOM (433 "That's the Way God Planned It")................150-250 69
(Four–inch flexi, "pocket disc.")
APPLE.......................................5-10 69-72
CAPITOL....................................4-8 66-69
CONTRACT...............................8-12 61
MOTOWN...................................3-5 79-82
VEE JAY....................................5-10 65

Picture Sleeves

A&M..4-8 72-75
APPLE.......................................5-10 69-70

LPs: 10/12–inch 33rpm

A&M...8-12 71-82
APPLE.....................................10-20 69-72
BUDDAH..................................10-15 69
CAPITOL (T-2532 "Wildest Organ")...................................10-15 66
CAPITOL (ST-2532 "Wildest Organ")...................................10-20 66
CAPITOL (SM-2532 "Wildest Organ")......................................5-8 75
DERBY (701 "16-Year-Old Soul")...................................50-75 63
EXODUS..................................15-20 65
GNP..10-15 73
MOTOWN...................................5-10 79-82
MYRRH.....................................5-10 78
PEACOCK..................................8-12 73
PICKWICK...................................5-8 70s
SPRINGBOARD..........................5-10 78
TRIP..8-12 73
VEE JAY..................................15-25 65-66

Also see BEATLES
Also see MOTHERS of INVENTION
Also see VANDROSS, Luther

PRESTON, Billy, & Syreeta

R&B '80

Singles: 7–inch

MOTOWN 3-5 79-81
TAMLA 3-5 80

LPs: 10/12–inch 33rpm

MOTOWN 5-10 79-81
Also see PRESTON, Billy
Also see SYREETA

PRESTON, Jimmy

R&B '49

Singles: 78rpm

DERBY 8-12 50
GOTHAM 10-15 49-50

PRESTON, Johnny

P&R '59

Singles: 7–inch

ABC 3-6 68-73
HALL/HALL WAY 4-8 64-66
IMPERIAL 4-8 63
MERCURY (10027 "Cradle of Love") 15-25 60
(Stereo [reprocessed].)
MERCURY (10036 "Feel So Fine") 20-30 60
(Stereo.)
MERCURY (71000 series) 8-12 59-62
(Monaural.)
TCF 4-8 65

Picture Sleeves

MERCURY 10-15 60-62

EPs: 7–inch 33/45rpm

MERCURY (3397 "Johnny Preston") 30-50 60

LPs: 10/12–inch 33rpm

MERCURY (20592 "Running Bear") 50-70 60
(Monaural.)
MERCURY (20609 "Come Rock with Me")
(Monaural.) 50-70 60
MERCURY (60250 "Running Bear") 60-80 60
(Stereo. Black label)
MERCURY (60250 "Running Bear") 8-12 81
(Chicago "Skyline" label)
MERCURY (60609 "Come Rock with Me")
(Stereo.) 60-80 60
WING (12246 "Running Bear")
(Monaural.) 20-30 63
WING (16246 "Running Bear")
(Stereo.) 25-35 63

PRESTON, Mike

P&R '58

Singles: 7–inch

LONDON 5-8 58-63

PRESTON, Terry
(Ferlin Husky)

Singles: 78rpm

CAPITOL 5-10 52-53

Singles: 7–inch

CAPITOL 10-20 52-53
Also see HUSKY, Ferlin

PRETENDERS

P&R/LP '80

Singles: 12–inch 33/45rpm

SIRE 4-6 84

Singles: 7–inch

SIRE 3-5 79-90

Picture Sleeves

SIRE 3-5 80-87

LPs: 10/12–inch 33rpm

SIRE 5-10 80-90
Members: Chrissie Hynde; Robbie MacIntosh; Pete Farndon; Martin Chambers; Malcomb Foster.
Also see UB40

PRETENDERS / Maurice Simon

Singles: 7–inch

CARNIVAL 4-8

PRETTY BOY
(Don Covay; with Johnny Fuller's Band)

Singles: 78rpm

ATLANTIC (1147 "Bip Bop Bip") 30-40 57
BIG 30-40 57
RHYTHM (1768 "I'm Bad") 30-40 54

Singles: 7–inch

ATLANTIC (1147 "Bip Bop Bip") 50-75 57
BIG (617 "Switchin' in the Kitchen") 50-75 57
Session: King Curtis.
Also see COVAY, Don
Also see KING CURTIS

PRETTY BOY FLOYD

LP '90

LPs: 10/12–inch 33rpm

MCA 5-8 90

PRETTY MAIDS

LP '87

LPs: 10/12–inch 33rpm

EPIC 5-10 87

PRETTY POISON

R&B/D&D '84

Singles: 12–inch 33/45rpm

MONTAGE 4-6 84
SVENGALI 4-6 84

Singles: 7–inch

MONTAGE 3-4 84
SVENGALI 3-4 84
VIRGIN 3-4 87-88

Picture Sleeves

VIRGIN 3-4 87-88

LPs: 10/12-inch 33rpm

VIRGIN 5-10 88

PRETTY THINGS

LP '75

Singles: 7-inch

FONTANA 5-10 64-66
LAURIE 4-8 68
SWAN SONG 3-5 75-76

LPs: 10/12-inch 33rpm

FONTANA (27544 "Pretty Things") 35-55 66
(Monaural.)
FONTANA (67544 "Pretty Things") 35-55 66
(Stereo.)
MOTOWN 10-15 76
RARE EARTH (506 "S.F. Sorrow") 15-25 69
(With standard square cover.)
RARE EARTH (506 "S.F. Sorrow") 20-40 69
(With rounded-top cover. Promotional issue.)
RARE EARTH (515 "Parachute") 15-20 70
RARE EARTH (549 "Rare Earth") 8-12 76
(Reissue of material from 506 & 515.)
SIRE 8-10 76
SWAN SONG 8-10 75-76
W.B. 8-10 73-80
Also see GREEN, Jack

PRETTY TONY
(Tony Butler)

R&B '84

Singles: 7-inch

MUSIC 3-4 84

PREVIN, Andre
(With the David Rose Orchestra)

P&R/LP '59

Singles: 78rpm

MODERN 3-5 51

Singles: 7-inch

COLUMBIA 3-6 60-64
DECCA 3-6 61
MGM 4-8 59
MODERN 10-20 51
RCA (214 "Andre Previn") 10-20 49
(Boxed three disc set.)
RCA (9000 series) 3-5 67

EPs: 7-inch 33/45rpm

MGM 5-10 59

LPs: 10/12-inch 33rpm

ALLEGIANCE 5-8 84
ANGEL 5-8 80-81
CAMDEN 5-10 64
COLUMBIA 10-20 60-65
CONTEMPORARY 15-30 57-60
CORONET 5-10 60s
DECCA (4000 series) 8-15 61-63
(Decca LP numbers in this series preceded by a "7" or a "DL-7" are stereo issues.)
DECCA (8000 series) 20-40 55-56
EVEREST 5-10 70
HARMONY 5-10 67
MFSL 20-40 82
MGM 10-15 59-64
METRO JAZZ 10-20 59
MONARCH (203 "All Star Jazz") 60-80 54
(10-inch LP.)
MONARCH (204 "Andre Previn Plays Duke") 60-80 54
(10-inch LP.)
ODYSSEY 8-12 68
RCA (1000 series) 5-10 75
(With an "ARL1" prefix.)
RCA (1000 series) 20-45 54
(With an "LPM" prefix.)
RCA (1356 "Three Little Words") 40-60 56
RCA (2900 series) 6-12 67
RCA (3002 ("Andre Previn Plays Harry Warren") 75-100 51
(10-inch LP.)
RCA (3400 thru 3800 series) 10-20 65-67
U.A. (5200 series) 5-10 71
VERVE 15-25 63
You'll find many more listings by this artist in *The Official Price Guide to Movie/TV Soundtracks and Original Cast Albums,* containing over 8,000 listings.
Also see ANDREWS, Julie, & Andre Previn / Vic Damone / Jack Jones / Marian Anderson
Also see ASTAIRE, Fred, & Red Skelton / Helen Kane
Also see CARROLL, Diahann, & Andre Previn
Also see DAY, Doris, & Andre Previn
Also see ROSE, David
Also see SHORE, Dinah, & Andre Previn

PREYER, Ron

R&B '78

Singles: 7-inch

SHOCK 3-5 78

PRICE, Alan
(Alan Price Set)

P&R '66

Singles: 7-inch

COTILLION 4-8 69
EPIC 3-4 84
JET 3-5 77-79
PARROT 5-10 66-68
W.B. 3-5 72

LPs: 10/12-inch 33rpm

ACCORD 5-10 82
JET 8-12 77-80
PARROT 15-25 68

TOWNHOUSE 5-10 81
W.B. 8-12 73
Also see ANIMALS
Also see FAME & PRICE

PRICE, Lloyd

(Lloyd Price Orchestra; with the Dukes)

R&B '52

Singles: 78rpm

ABC-PAR 10-20 57
KRC (587 "Just Because") 30-40 57
SPECIALTY 10-15 55-56

Singles: 7-inch

ABC... 3-6 67-73
ABC-PAR (Monaural)................ 10-20 57-60
ABC-PAR (S-9972 "Stagger Lee").. 20-30 60
(Stereo.)
ABC-PAR (S-9997 "Where Were You")............................ 20-30 59
(Stereo.)
COLLECTABLES 3-4 80s
DOUBLE-L 5-10 63-66
GSF... 3-5 72-73
JAD 4-8 68
KRC (Except 587) 10-20 57-59
KRC (587 "Just Because")........ 40-50 57
LPG.. 3-5 76
LUDIX.. 5-10 63
MCA 3-4 70s
MONUMENT 4-8 64-65
PARAMOUNT 3-5 72
REPRISE 4-8 66
ROULETTE.................................. 3-5 70s
SCEPTER 3-5 71
SPECIALTY (SPBX series)....... 15-20 86
(Boxed sets of six colored vinyl 45s.)
SPECIALTY (428 "Lawdy, Miss Clawdy")................................ 30-40 52
(Black vinyl.)
SPECIALTY (428 "Lawdy, Miss Clawdy")............................. 50-100 52
(Colored vinyl.)
SPECIALTY (440 "Ooh Ooh Ooh").. 30-40 52
SPECIALTY (452 "Ain't It a Shame") 30-40 53
(Black vinyl.)
SPECIALTY (452 "Ain't It a Shame") 50-75 53
(Colored vinyl.)
SPECIALTY (457 "What's the Matter Now") 30-40 53
(Black vinyl.)
SPECIALTY (457 "What's the Matter Now") 50-75 53
(Colored vinyl.)
SPECIALTY (463 "Where You At") 30-40 53
(Black vinyl.)
SPECIALTY (463 "Where You At")...50-75 53
(Colored vinyl.)
SPECIALTY (471 "I Wish Your Picture Was You")...................30-40 54
SPECIALTY (483 "Let Me Come Home, Baby")..........................30-40 54
(Black vinyl.)
SPECIALTY (483 "Let Me Come Home, Baby")..........................50-75 54
(Colored vinyl.)
SPECIALTY (494 "Walkin' the Track") 30-40 54
SPECIALTY (535 "Oo Ee Baby") 15-25 55
SPECIALTY (540 "Trying to Find Someone to Love")..15-25 55
SPECIALTY (571 "Woe Ho Ho") 15-25 56
SPECIALTY (578 "Country Boy Rock") 15-25 56
SPECIALTY (582 "Forgive Me Clawdy")...................................15-25 56
SPECIALTY (602 "Baby Please Come Home")..................................15-25 57
SPECIALTY (661 "Lawdy, Miss Clawdy")..................................10-15 59
TURNTABLE 4-6 69

Picture Sleeves

DOUBLE-L (729 "Billie Baby") ... 10-15 64

EPs: 7-inch 33/45rpm

ABC-PAR (277 "The Exciting Lloyd Price")..............................25-45 59
ABC-PAR (315 "Mr. Personality Sings the Blues") 25-45 60

LPs: 10/12-inch 33rpm

ABC..8-10 72-76
ABC-PAR (ABC-277 "The Exciting Lloyd Price")..............................25-45 59
(Monaural.)
ABC-PAR (ABCS-277 "The Exciting Lloyd Price")..............................30-50 59
(Stereo.)
ABC-PAR (ABC-297 "Mr. Personality")..............................25-45 59
(Monaural.)
ABC-PAR (ABCS-297 "Mr. Personality")..............................30-50 59
(Stereo.)
ABC-PAR (ABC-315 "Mr. Personality Sings the Blues") 25-45 60
(Monaural.)
ABC-PAR (ABCS-315 "Mr. Personality Sings the Blues")....................30-50 60
(Stereo.)
ABC-PAR (ABC-324 "Mr. Personality's Big 15") 25-45 60
(Monaural.)
ABC-PAR (ABCS-324 "Mr. Personality's Big 15") 30-50 60

ABC-PAR (ABC-346 "The Fantastic Lloyd Price")........................ 25-45 60
(Monaural.)
ABC-PAR (ABCS-346 "The Fantastic Lloyd Price")........................ 30-50 60
(Stereo.)
ABC-PAR (ABC-366 "Lloyd Price Sings the Million Sellers") 25-45 61
(Monaural.)
ABC-PAR (ABCS-366 "Lloyd Price Sings the Million Sellers") 25-45 61
(Stereo.)
ABC-PAR (ABC-382 "Cookin'"). 25-45 61
(Monaural.)
ABC-PAR (ABCS-382 Cookin'")............................... 30-50 61
(Stereo.)
ABC-PAR (ABCX-763 "16 Greatest Hits") 10-15 72
DOUBLE-L 20-30 63
GRAND PRIX.......................... 10-15 60s
GUEST STAR 10-15 64
JAD 10-15 69
MCA 5-10 82
MONUMENT 10-20 65
PICKWICK 10-15 67
SPECIALTY (2105 "Lloyd Price") 40-50 59
TRIP 8-10 76
TURNTABLE........................... 10-15 69
UPFRONT............................... 8-12 70s

Also see COOKE, Sam / Lloyd Price / Larry Williams / Little Richard
Also see DOMINO, Fats

PRICE, Priscilla

R&B '73

Singles: 7–inch

BASF 3-5 73

PRICE, Ray

(With the Cherokee Cowboys)

C&W '52

Singles: 78rpm

BULLET............................... 50-100 52
COLUMBIA 5-15 52-57

Singles: 7–inch

ABC 3-5 75
ABC/DOT 3-5 75-77
COLUMBIA (10000 series) 3-4 74-77
COLUMBIA (20000 & 21000 series) 10-20 52-56
COLUMBIA (40000 thru 43000 series) 5-15 57-66
COLUMBIA (44000 thru 45000 series) 3-6 67-73
GOLDIES 45 3-4
DIMENSION............................... 3-4 81-82
MONUMENT 3-5 78-79
MYRRH 3-4 74-75
STEP ONE 3-4 85-86
W.B. 3-4 82-83
WORD.. 3-4 78

Picture Sleeves

COLUMBIA 3-5 67

EPs: 7–inch 33/45rpm

COLUMBIA (1700 thru 2800 series) 15-25 53-57
COLUMBIA (8556 "Ray Price").. 10-20 50s
COLUMBIA (10000 thru 14000 series)......................... 10-20 57-60
(White label. Promotional issue only.)

LPs: 10/12–inch 33rpm

ABC/DOT 6-12 75-77
COLUMBIA (28 "The World of Ray Price")................................ 8-12 70
COLUMBIA (1015 "Heart Songs") 30-40 57
COLUMBIA (1148 "Talk to Your Heart")..................................... 25-35 58
COLUMBIA (1400 thru 2600 series) 10-25 60-67
(Monaural)
COLUMBIA (8200 thru 9400 series) 15-30 60-67
(Stereo)
COLUMBIA (9700 thru 9900 series) 8-12 68-70
COLUMBIA (10000 series) 5-10 73
COLUMBIA (30000 thru 37000 series)............................ 5-10 70-81
DIMENSION.................................. 5-8 81
51 WEST....................................... 5-8 84
HARMONY.................................. 8-15 66-71
MONUMENT............................... 5-10 79
MYRRH 5-8 74
RADIANT 5-8 81
STEP ONE................................. 5-10 86
W.B. 5-8 83
WORD.. 5-8 77

Session:Johnny Bush; Willie Nelson; Johnny Gimble.
Also see MILLER, Roger, & Willie Nelson
Also see NELSON, Willie, & Ray Price
Also see ROBBINS, Marty / Johnny Cash / Ray Price

PRICE, Ray / Lefty Frizzell / Carl Smith

LPs: 10/12–inch 33rpm

COLUMBIA (1257 "Greatest Western Hits")......................... 15-25 59
(Monaural.)
COLUMBIA (8776 "Greatest Western Hits")......................... 15-25 63
(Stereo.)

Also see FRIZZELL, Lefty
Also see SMITH, Carl

PRICE, Ray / Johnny Horton / Carl Smith / George Morgan

EPs: 7–inch 33/45rpm

COLUMBIA (2157 "4 Big Hits").. 20-25 60

Also see HORTON, Johnny
Also see SMITH, Carl

PRIDE, Charley
(With the Pridesmen; with Henry Mancini; Country Charley Pride)
C&W '66

Singles: 7-inch

RCA (0073 thru 0942 series) 4-8 69-73
RCA (8700 & 8800 series) 5-10 66
RCA (9000 thru 9996) 4-8 66-71
RCA (10030 thru 11655) 3-6 74-79
RCA 11736 "Dallas Cowboys") 3-5 79
(Black label.)
RCA 11736 "Dallas Cowboys") ... 8-12 79
(Gray and blue label. Special Dallas Cowboys Edition.)
RCA (11751 thru 14296) 3-5 79-86
16TH AVE 3-4 87-89

Picture Sleeves

RCA 4-6 71-74

EPs: 7-inch 33/45rpm

RCA 5-10 60s
(Jukebox issues.)

LPs: 10/12-inch 33rpm

CAMDEN 5-10 72
RCA (Except LPM/LSP 3700 thru 4800 series) 5-10 74-86
RCA (3700 thru 4800 series) 10-20 66-73
(With "LPM" or "LSP" prefix.)
TELEHOUSE 5-10
Also see DAVE & SUGAR
Also see MANCINI, Henry

PRIEST, Maxi
P&R/LP '88

Singles: 7-inch

VIRGIN 3-4 88

Picture Sleeves

VIRGIN 3-4 88

LPs: 10/12-inch 33rpm

CHARISMA 5-8 90
VIRGIN 5-8 88

PRIMA, Louis
P&R '35

Singles: 78rpm

BRUNSWICK 5-10 35
COLUMBIA 4-6 52-53
DECCA 4-8 54
HIT 5-10 44-45
MAJESTIC 4-8 45
MERCURY 4-8 50
RCA 4-8 47
ROBIN HOOD 4-8 50
SAVOY 4-8 53
VOCALION 5-10 37

Singles: 7-inch

ABC 3-6 68-74
BUENA VISTA 3-6 66-74
CAPITOL 4-8 62
COLUMBIA 5-10 52-53
DECCA 5-10 54
DOT 4-8 59-62
HBR 4-6 66
KAMA SUTRA 4-6 66
MERCURY 5-10 50
PRIMA 4-8 63-64
ROBIN HOOD 5-10 50
SAVOY 5-10 53
U.A. 3-6 67

EPs: 7-inch 33/45rpm

CAPITOL 5-15 56
JUBILEE 5-15 55
VARSITY 5-15 54

LPs: 10/12-inch 33rpm

BUENA VISTA 8-18 65-74
CAPITOL 10-20 56-62
DE-LITE 5-10 68
DOT 10-15 60
HBR 5-12 66
HAMILTON 5-10 65
MERCURY (25142 "For the People") 30-40 53
(10-inch LP.)
PRIMA 5-8 72-76
RONDO/RONDOLETTE 10-20 59
U.A. 5-10 67

PRIMA, Louis, & Keely Smith
(With Sam Butera & the Witnesses)
P&R/R&B/LP '58

Singles: 78rpm

ROBIN HOOD 4-8 50

Singles: 7-inch

CAPITOL 4-8 58-59
DOT 4-8 59-61

Picture Sleeves

CAPITOL (4063 "That Old Black Magic") 5-10 58
(Sleeve has a die-cut center hole)
DOT 5-10 59

EPs: 7-inch 33/45rpm

CAPITOL 8-12 58
DOT (103 "The Frantic '40s") 10-20 60
(Promotional issue, made for the Desert Inn as a giveaway.)
DOT (1093 "Louis & Keely") 5-10 60

LPs: 10/12-inch 33rpm

CAPITOL (With "SM" prefix.) 5-8 75
CAPITOL (With "T" or "ST" prefix.) 20-35 58-61
COLUMBIA (1206 "Breaking It Up") 20-30 58
CORONET 10-15 60s
DESIGN 10-15 60s
DOT 15-25 59-60
Also see SMITH, Keely

PRIMA, Louis, & Keely Smith / Louis Prima & Sam Butera

Singles: 7–inch

CAPITOL (719 "Album Highlights")............................ 10-15 57
(Promotional issue only.)
Also see PRIMA, Louis
Also see PRIMA, Louis, & Keely Smith

PRIMATIVES

LP '88

LPs: 10/12–inch 33rpm

RCA.. 5-8 88-89

PRIME TIME

R&B '84

Singles: 7–inch

TOTAL EXP. 3-4 84

PRIMETTES
(Supremes)

Singles: 7–inch

LUPINE (120 "Tears of Sorrow") 200-300 64
(Lu-pine [hyphenated] 120 is also a Joe Stubbs single.)
Also see SUPREMES

PRINCE
(With the Revolution)

P&R/R&B/LP '78

Singles: 12–inch 33/45rpm

PAISLEY PARK............................ 4-6 85-91
W.B. 5-10 81-84

Promotional 12–inch Singles

PAISLEY PARK....................... 10-20 85-92
W.B. 15-30 78-84

Singles: 7–inch

PAISLEY PARK............................ 3-5 85-92
W.B. (Except 20129, 29286 & 29174).. 3-8 78-84
W.B. (20129 "1999")................... 8-12 83
(Picture disc.)
W.B. (29286 "When Doves Cry") .. 3-5 84
(Black vinyl.)
W.B. (29286 "When Doves Cry") 10-15 84
(Colored vinyl.)
W.B. (29174 "Purple Rain").......... 3-5 84
(Black vinyl.)
W.B. (29174 "Purple Rain")....... 10-15 84
(Colored vinyl.)

Promotional Singles

PAISLEY PARK (Except 2939 & 29052) 4-8 85-92
PAISLEY PARK (2939 "Hot Thing").................................. 15-25 87
PAISLEY PARK (29052 "Paisley Park") 15-25 85
W.B. (Except 29286, 29174 & 29746)...................................... 3-8 78-84
W.B. (29286 "When Doves Cry")...5-8 84
(Black vinyl.)
W.B. (29286 "When Doves Cry").......................................15-25 84
(Colored vinyl.)
W.B. (29174 "Purple Rain") 5-8 84
(Black vinyl.)
W.B. (29174 "Purple Rain") 15-25 84
(Colored vinyl.)
W.B. (29746 "Little Red Corvette")...............................5-10 83
(Black vinyl.)
W.B. (29746 "Little Red Corvette")...............................10-15 83
(Picture disc.)

Picture Sleeves

PAISLEY PARK 3-6 85-89
W.B. (22924 thru 22757)................3-5 89
W.B. (29896 thru 29079).............5-10 82-86

LPs: 10/12–inch 33rpm

PAISLEY PARK 5-8 85-90
W.B. (Except 25110 & 25677) 5-10 78-89
W.B. (25110 "Purple Rain") 5-10 84
(Black vinyl.)
W.B. (25110 "Purple Rain") 30-40 84
(Colored vinyl.)
W.B. (25677 "Black Album") 2000-4000 87
(Promotional issue only. Any information regarding the *Black Album* on Erotic City NOIR-69, a 1988 issue, would be appreciated. A boot perhaps?)
Also see BROWNMARK
Also see CYMONE, Andre
Also see MADHOUSE
Also see SHEILA E.

PRINCE & Sheena Easton

P&R '87

Singles: 7–inch

PAISLEY PARK 3-5 87
W.B. 3-4 89

Picture Sleeves

W.B. 3-5 89
Also see EASTON, Sheena
Also see PRINCE

PRINCE BUSTER
(With the Sea Busters; Buster Campbell)

P&R/R&B '67

Singles: 7–inch

AMY 5-10 64
ATLANTIC...................................5-10 64
PHILIPS 4-8 67
RCA 4-8 67
STELLAR 5-10 64

LPs: 10/12–inch 33rpm

RCA 10-20 67

PRINCE HAROLD

R&B '66

Singles: 7-inch

MERCURY 4-8 66
SPRING 4-8 67
VERVE 4-8 67

PRINCE LA LA

R&B '61

Singles: 7-inch

AFO 5-10 61-62

PRINCESS

R&B/D&D '85

Singles: 12-inch 33/45rpm

NEXT PLATINUM 4-6 85-86
POLYDOR 4-6 86

Singles: 7-inch

POLYDOR 3-4 86-87

PRINCIPLE, Jamie

D&D '85

Singles: 12-inch 33/45rpm

PERSONA 4-6 85

PRINE, John

LP '72

Singles: 7-inch

ASYLUM 3-5 78
ATLANTIC 3-5 71-75
OH BOY (Colored vinyl) 3-5 81-86

LPs: 10/12-inch 33rpm

ASYLUM 5-10 78-80
ATLANTIC 8-12 71-76
OH BOY 5-8 84-86

PRINE, John / Daryl Hall & John Oates / Barnaby Bye / Delbert & Glen

EPs: 7-inch 33/45rpm

ATLANTIC (195 "Something for Nothing") 5-8 73

Also see DELBERT & GLEN
Also see HALL, Daryl, & John Oates
Also see PRINE, John

PRISM

P&R/LP '77

Singles: 7-inch

ARIOLA AMERICA 3-5 77-79
CAPITOL 3-5 82

Picture Sleeves

CAPITOL 3-5 82

LPs: 10/12-inch 33rpm

ARIOLA AMERICA (Except 50034) 10-15 77-79
ARIOLA AMERICA (50034 "Live Tonite") 15-25 78
(Promotional issue only.)
CAPITOL 5-10 80-82

PRISTER, Jerome "Secret Weapon"

R&B '88

Singles: 7-inch

TUFF CITY 3-4 88

PROBY, P.J.
(James Smith)

P&R '64

Singles: 7-inch

IMPERIAL 4-8 64
LIBERTY 5-10 61-68
LONDON 4-8 64
SURFSIDE 8-12 65

Picture Sleeves

LIBERTY 8-12 67

LPs: 10/12-inch 33rpm

LIBERTY 15-25 65-68

Also see FOCUS & P.J. Proby

PROCESS & Doo Rags

R&B '85

Singles: 7-inch

COLUMBIA 3-4 85-87

PROCLAIMERS

LP '89

LPs: 10/12-inch 33rpm

CHRYSALIS 5-8 89

PROCOL HARUM

P&R/R&B/LP '67

Singles: 7-inch

A&M 4-8 67-72
CHRYSALIS 3-6 73-77
DERAM 5-10 67

Picture Sleeves

A&M 4-8 72-73
CHRYSALIS 4-8 73

LPs: 10/12-inch 33rpm

A&M (Except 4294 & 8053) 8-12 68-73
A&M (4294 "Broken Barricades") 12-15 71
(With die-cut gatefold cover.)
A&M (4294 "Broken Barricades") 10-12 72
(With standard cover.)
A&M (8053 "Procol Harum Lives") 30-40 70s
(Promotional issue only.)
CHRYSALIS 8-10 73-77
DERAM (16008 "Procol Harum") 50-75 67
(Monaural. With bonus poster, which represents $15 to $20 of the value.)
DERAM (18008 "Procol Harum") 50-75 67
(Stereo. Includes bonus poster which represents $15 to $20 of the value.)

Members: Gary Brooker; Bobby Harrison; Matthew Fisher; Dave Knights; Ray Royer; Robin Trower; Diz Derrick.
Also see BROOKER, Gary

Also see TROWER, Robin

PRODUCERS

P&R/LP '81

Singles: 7–inch

PORTRAIT 3-5 81-82

LPs: 10/12–inch 33rpm

PORTRAIT 5-10 81-82

PROFESSOR FUNK & His Eighth Street Funk Band

R&B '73

Singles: 7–inch

ROXBURY 3-5 73

PROFESSOR GRIFF & Last Asiatic Disciples

LP '90

LPs: 10/12–inch 33rpm

SKYYWALKER 5-8 90

PROFESSOR LONGHAIR

(With the Clippers; with His Blues Scholars; with His Shuffling Hungarians; with His New Orleans Boys)

Singles: 78rpm

ATLANTIC (897 "Mardi Gras in New Orleans") 75-125 50

ATLANTIC (906 "Walk Your Blues Away") 75-125 50

STAR TALENT (808 "Mardi Gras in New Orleans") 150-200 49

STAR TALENT (809 "She Ain't Got No Hair") 150-200 49

Singles: 7–inch

ATLANTIC (1020 "In the Night") 100-150 53

EBB (106 "Misery") 50-100 57

EBB (101 "Cry Pretty Baby") ... 50-100 57

EBB (121 "Looka No Hair") 50-100 57

RIP (155 "I Believe I'm Gonna Leave") 30-40 62

RON (326 "Cuttin' Out") 10-15 58

(Yellow label.)

RON (329 "Goin' to the Mardi Gras") 10-15 59

(Yellow label.)

RON (Red label) 5-10

WATCH (1900 series) 8-12 65

WATCH (6000 series) 15-20 63

EPs: 7–inch 33/45rpm

MERCURY 75-100

(1970s promotional EP, issued without special cover. Has two Professor Longhair tracks and two by other artists.)

LPs: 10/12–inch 33rpm

ALLIGATOR 5-8 80

ATLANTIC 10-15 72-82

HARVEST 8-12 78

J.S.P. 8-12

NIGHTHAWK 5-10 82

MARDI GRAS 8-12

Also see BOYD, Robert

Also see BYRD, Roy

PROFESSOR MORRISON: see MORRISON, Professor

PROFILES

R&B '68

Singles: 7–inch

BAMBOO 4-8 69

DUO 4-8 68

PROJECT FUTURE

R&B '83

Singles: 12–inch 33/45rpm

CAPITOL 4-6 83

Singles: 7–inch

CAPITOL 3-4 83

PROPHECY

R&B '75

Singles: 7–inch

AIRBORNE 3-5 70s

ALL PLATINUM 3-5 74

MAINSTREAM 3-5 75

Picture Sleeves

AIRBORNE 3-5 70s

Member: Nick Rozakis.

PROPHET

LP '88

LPs: 10/12–inch 33rpm

MEGAFORCE 5-8 88

PROPHETS, Thee: see THEE PROPHETS

PROTHEROE, Brian

P&R '75

Singles: 7–inch

CHRYSALIS 3-5 75

LPs: 10/12–inch 33rpm

CHRYSALIS 8-12 75-76

PROVINE, Dorothy

LP '61

Singles: 7–inch

W.B. 3-6 61

LPs: 10/12–inch 33rpm

W.B. 15-25 60-61

PROVINE, Dorothy, & Joe "Fingers" Carr

LPs: 10/12–inch 33rpm

W.B. 15-25 60-62

Also see CARR, Joe "Fingers"

Also see PROVINE, Dorothy

PRUETT, Jeanne

(Jean Pruett)

C&W '71

Singles: 7–inch

AUDIOGRAPH 3-4 83

DECCA 3-6 68-72

IBC 3-5 79-80

MCA 3-5 73-77

MSR 3-4 87
MERCURY 3-5 78
PAID 3-4 81
RCA 4-6 63-64

LPs: 10/12-inch 33rpm

ALLEGIANCE 5-8 84
AUDIOGRAPH 5-8 83
DECCA 8-12 72
IBC 5-10 79
MCA 5-10 73-75
OUT of TOWN DIST 5-10 82

PRUETT, Jeanne, & Marty Robbins

C&W '83

Singles: 7-inch

AUDIOGRAPH 3-4 83

Also see PRUETT, Jeanne
Also see ROBBINS, Marty

PRYOR, Richard

LP '74

Singles: 7-inch

LAFF 3-5 80
W.B. 4-6 76-79

LPs: 10/12-inch 33rpm

DOVE 10-15 68
LAFF 5-10 71-81
PARTEE 5-10 74
REPRISE 6-12 68-77
TIGER LILY 5-10 77
W.B. 5-10 76-85

PRYSOCK, Arthur

R&B '52

Singles: 78rpm

DECCA 4-8 52-54
MERCURY 4-8 54-55

Singles: 7-inch

BETHLEHEM 3-5 72
DECCA (25000 series) 4-8 65
DECCA (27000 thru 29000 series) 5-10 52-54
DECCA (31000 series) 4-8 64-65
GUSTO 3-5 79
KING 3-6 69-71
MCA 3-5 78
MGM 3-5 70
MERCURY 5-10 54-55
OLD TOWN (100 series) 3-5 73-76
OLD TOWN (1000 series) 4-8 59-60
(Light blue label.)
OLD TOWN (1000 series) 3-5 76-77
(Dark blue or black label.)
OLD TOWN (1100 series) 4-6 61-66
VERVE 3-6 66-69

LPs: 10/12-inch 33rpm

DECCA 15-20 64-65
KING 8-12 69-71
MCA 5-10 78
OLD TOWN (100 series) 20-30 60-62
OLD TOWN (2000 series) 15-25 62-65
OLD TOWN (12000 series) 5-10 73-77
POLYDOR 5-10 77
VERVE 10-20 66-69

Also see ECKSTINE, Billy / Arthur Prysock
Also see JOHNSON, Buddy

PRYSOCK, Arthur, & Count Basie

LP '66

Singles: 7-inch

VERVE 3-6 66

LPs: 10/12-inch 33rpm

VERVE 15-20 66

Also see BASIE, Count

PRYSOCK, Arthur / Leroy Bivins

LPs: 10/12-inch 33rpm

GUEST STAR 5-10 64

Also see PRYSOCK, Arthur

PSEUDO ECHO

P&R/LP '87

Singles: 7-inch

RCA 3-4 87

LPs: 10/12-inch 33rpm

RCA 5-8 87

PSYCHEDELIC FUR

LP '80

Singles: 12-inch 33/45rpm

COLUMBIA 4-6 84-86

Singles: 7-inch

A&M 3-4 86
COLUMBIA 3-5 80-89

Picture Sleeves

A&M 3-4 86
COLUMBIA 3-5 80-87

LPs: 10/12-inch 33rpm

COLUMBIA 5-10 80-89

Members: Tim Butler; Richard Butler; John Ashton; Mars Williams; Paul Garisto; Marty Williamson.

PUBLIC ENEMY

R&B/LP '88

Singles: 7-inch

DEF JAM 3-4 88-90

LPs: 10/12-inch 33rpm

DEF JAM 5-8 88-90

PUBLIC IMAGE LTD.

LP '80

Singles: 12-inch 33/45rpm

VIRGIN 4-6 87

LPs: 10/12-inch 33rpm

ELEKTRA 5-8 86
ISLAND 8-10 80
VIRGIN 5-8 87-89
W.B. 8-10 81

Also see SEX PISTOLS

PUCKETT, Gary
(With the Union Gap; Union Gap Featuring Gary Puckett)

P&R '67

Singles: 7-inch

COLUMBIA 4-8 67-72
COLUMBIA HALL of FAME 3-4 70s
GUSTO 3-4 81-83

Picture Sleeves

COLUMBIA 5-10 67-70

LPs: 10/12-inch 33rpm

BACK-TRAC 5-8 85
CSP 8-10 72
COLUMBIA (Except 10171) 10-20 68-71
COLUMBIA (10171 "Young Girl") 5-10
COLUMBIA HOUSE (6272/3 "Fillin' the Gap") 20-30 75
(3-LPs; one double and one single disc set.)
51 WEST 5-10 82
GUSTO 5-8 83
HARMONY 8-12 72

Also see FRANKLIN, Aretha / Union Gap / Blood, Sweat & Tears / Moby Grape

PULLINS, Leroy

C&W/P&R '66

Singles: 7-inch

KAPP 4-8 66

LPs: 10/12-inch 33rpm

KAPP 10-15 66-68

PULSE

R&B '82

Singles: 7-inch

SILVER CLOUD 3-5 82

PUMPKIN & Profile All-Stars

R&B '84

Singles: 12-inch 33/45rpm

PROFILE 4-6 84

Singles: 7-inch

PROFILE 3-4 84

Also see FRESH 3 MCs

PUPPETS

D&D '84

Singles: 12-inch 33/45rpm

QUALITY/RFC 4-6 84

Singles: 7-inch

QUALITY/RFC 3-4 84

PURDIE, Pretty
(Bernard Purdie)

P&R/R&B '67

Singles: 7-inch

COLUMBIA 4-6 69
DATE 4-8 67-68

LPs: 10/12-inch 33rpm

DATE 10-20 67
FLYING DUTCHMAN 8-12 73
PRESTIGE 8-12 71

PURE ENERGY

R&B '80

Singles: 12-inch 33/45rpm

PRISM 4-6 80-84

Singles: 7-inch

PRISM 3-5 80-84

PURE LOVE & PLEASURE

LP '70

Singles: 7-inch

DUNHILL 3-5 70

LPs: 10/12-inch 33rpm

DUNHILL 10-15 70

PURE PRAIRIE LEAGUE

P&R/LP '75

Singles: 7-inch

RCA 3-5 72-79
CASABLANCA 3-5 80-81
EPIC 3-5 77

LPs: 10/12-inch 33rpm

CASABLANCA 5-10 80-81
RCA 6-12 72-80

Members/Session: John Call; George Powell; Billy Hinds; David Sanborn; Mick Ronson; Michael O'Connor; Johnny Gimble; Don Felder; Vince Gill; Chet Atkins; Larry Goshorn.
Also see AMERICAN FLYER
Also see ATKINS, Chet
Also see FELDER, Don
Also see GILL, Vince
Also see RONSON, Mick
Also see SANBORN, David

PURIFY, James & Bobby

P&R/R&B '66

Singles: 7-inch

BELL 4-8 66-69
CASABLANCA 3-5 74-75
MERCURY 3-5 76-77
SPHERE SOUND 4-8 66

LPs: 10/12-inch 33rpm

BELL 10-20 66-67
MERCURY 8-12 77

Members: James Purify; Bobby Dickey.

PURIM, Flora

LP '75

LPs: 10/12-inch 33rpm

MILESTONE 5-10 74-77
W.B. 5-10 77-78

Also see HART, Mickey, Airto & Flora Purim

PURPLE REIGN

P&R '75

Singles: 7-inch

GO-RILLA 4-8 75
PRIVATE STOCK 3-5 75

PURSELL, Bill

P&R/R&B/LP '63

Singles: 7-inch

COLUMBIA 3-6 62-66
DOT 3-5 69
EPIC 3-5 67

SPAR 10-15 60s

LPs: 10/12-inch 33rpm

COLUMBIA 8-15 63-65

Also see NELSON, Willie
Also see ROBBINS, Marty

PURSUIT of HAPPINESS

LP '88

LPs: 10/12-inch 33rpm

CHRYSALIS................................ 5-8 88

PUSHE'

D&D '84

Singles: 12-inch 33/45rpm

PARTYTYME 4-6 84

PYRAMIDS

P&R/LP '64

Singles: 7-inch

BEST (1 "Pyramid's Stomp")..... 15-25 63
BEST (102 "Penetration").......... 20-30 63
BEST (13001 "Pyramid's Stomp") 8-12 63
BEST (13002 "Penetration")........ 8-12 63
CEDWICKE (13005 "Midnight Run") 20-30 64
CEDWICKE (13006 "Contact") . 20-30 64

Picture Sleeves

BEST (13002 "Penetration")...... 20-30 63

LPs: 10/12-inch 33rpm

BEST (16501 "Penetration").... 75-125 64
(Monaural.)
BEST (36501 "Penetration").. 100-200 64
(Stereo.)
WHAT.. 5-8 83

PYTHON LEE JACKSON
(With Rod Stewart)

P&R/LP '72

Singles: 7-inch

GNP 4-6 72

LPs: 10/12-inch 33rpm

GNP 10-15 72

Also see SMALL FACES
Also see STEWART, Rod

Q

Q

P&R/LP '77

Singles: 7-inch

EPIC... 3-5 77

LPs: 10/12-inch 33rpm

EPIC... 8-10 77

Members: Robert Peckman; Don Garvin.
Also see JAGGERZ

Q FEEL

P&R '89

Singles: 7-inch

JIVE (1220 "Dancing in Heaven")..3-4 89
JIVE (2001 "Dancing in Heaven")..4-8 83

Picture Sleeves

JIVE (1220 "Dancing in Heaven")..3-4 89

QUADRANT SIX

R&B/D&D '83

Singles: 12-inch 33/45rpm

ATLANTIC......................................4-6 83

Singles: 7-inch

ATLANTIC......................................3-4 83

QUAITE, Christine

P&R '64

Singles: 7-inch

WORLD ARTISTS 5-8 64

QUAKER CITY BOYS

P&R '58

Singles: 7-inch

SWAN 5-10 58-59

QUALLS, Sidney Joe
(Sidney Qualls)

R&B '74

Singles: 7-inch

DAKAR..3-5 74

QUANDO QUANDO

D&D '83

Singles: 12-inch 33/45rpm

FACTORY......................................4-6 83

QUARTER NOTES
(Quarter-Notes)

P&R '59

Singles: 78rpm

DOT 5-10 57

Singles: 7-inch

BISON (757 "Frantic Flip")........15-20 60
DOT 10-20 57
GUYDEN.....................................10-15 63
IMPERIAL (5647 "Frantic Flip") ...8-12 60
RCA 5-10 58
WIZZ (715 "Record Hop Blues") 15-25 59

QUARTERFLASH

P&R/LP '81

Singles: 12-inch 33/45rpm

GEFFEN 4-6 81-82

Singles: 7-inch

GEFFEN 3-5 81-85
W.B. 3-5 82

Picture Sleeves

GEFFEN 3-5 82-85

LPs: 10/12-inch 33rpm

GEFFEN 5-10 81-85

Also see SEAFOOD MAMA

QUARTERMAN, Joe
(With Free Soul)

R&B '72

Singles: 7-inch

GSF 3-5 72-74
MERCURY 3-5 74

QUARTZ

R&B '78

Singles: 7-inch

MARLIN 3-5 78
POLYDOR 3-5 79

LPs: 10/12-inch 33rpm

POLYDOR 5-10 79

QUATEMAN, Bill

P&R '73

Singles: 7-inch

COLUMBIA 3-5 72-73
RCA 3-5 77-78

LPs: 10/12-inch 33rpm

COLUMBIA 8-10 73
RCA 5-10 77-78

QUATRO, Suzi
(Susie Quatro)

P&R/LP '74

Singles: 7-inch

ARISTA 3-5 75
BELL 3-5 73-74
BIG TREE 3-5 76
DREAMLAND 3-5 80-81
RAK 5-10 72-74
RSO 3-5 79

Picture Sleeves

DREAMLAND 3-5 80

LPs: 10/12-inch 33rpm

ARISTA 8-10 75
BELL 10-12 74
DREAMLAND 5-10 80
RSO 5-10 79

QUATRO, Suzi, & Chris Norman

P&R '79

Singles: 7-inch

RSO 3-5 79

Also see QUATRO, Suzi
Also see SMOKIE

QUAZAR

R&B/LP '78

Singles: 7-inch

ARISTA 3-5 78

LPs: 10/12-inch 33rpm

ARISTA 5-10 78

QUEEN

LP '73

Singles: 12-inch 33/45rpm

CAPITOL 4-8 84-86

Singles: 7-inch

CAPITOL 3-5 84-89
ELEKTRA 3-6 74-82
HOLLYWOOD 3-4 92

Picture Sleeves

CAPITOL 3-5 84-89
ELEKTRA 4-6 77-82

LPs: 10/12-inch 33rpm

CAPITOL 5-10 84-89
ELEKTRA (Except 5064) 6-12 73-82
ELEKTRA (5064 "Queen") 20-30 73
(Quadrophonic.)
MFSL 35-50 82

Members: Freddie Mercury; John Deacon; Brian May; Roger Taylor.

Also see MAY, Brian
Also see MERCURY, Freddie
Also see SMILE
Also see TAYLOR, Roger

QUEEN & David Bowie

P&R '81

Singles: 7-inch

ELEKTRA 3-5 81

Picture Sleeves

ELEKTRA 3-5 81

Also see BOWIE, David
Also see QUEEN

QUEEN LATIFAH

LP '89

LPs: 10/12-inch 33rpm

TOMMY BOY 5-8 89

QUEENSRYCHE

LP '83

Singles: 7-inch

EMI 3-4 83-86

LPs: 10/12-inch 33rpm

EMI (Except 01435) 5-8 83-90
EMI (01436 "Operation Mind Crime") 20-25 88

Members: Geoff Tate; Chris DeGarmo; Michael Wilton; Eddie Jackson; Scott Rokenfield.

? & the MYSTERIANS
(Question Mark & the Mysterians)

P&R/LP '66

Singles: 7-inch

ABKCO 3-4 80s
CAMEO 4-8 66-67
CAPITOL 5-10 68
CHICORY (410 "Talk Is Cheap") 10-20 67
LUV 4-6 73
PA-GO-GO (102 "96 Tears") ... 75-125 66
SUPER K 4-8 69
TANGERINE 4-8

LPs: 10/12-inch 33rpm

CAMEO (2004 "96 Tears") 50-100 66
CAMEO (2006 "Action") 50-100 67

Members: Rudy Martinez; Robert Martinez; Frank Rodriguez; Larry Borjas; Bob Balderamma; Frank Lugo.

QUICK

R&B '81

Singles: 12-inch 33/45rpm

EPIC 4-6 82
PAVILLION 4-6 81

Singles: 7-inch

EPIC (37000 series) 3-5 82
PAVILLION 3-5 81

LPs: 10/12-inch 33rpm

EPIC 5-10 82

QUICKEST WAY OUT

R&B '75

Singles: 7-inch

W.B. 3-5 75-76

QUICKSILVER

(Quicksilver Messinger Service)

LP '68

Singles: 7-inch

CAPITOL 4-8 68-76

LPs: 10/12-inch 33rpm

CAPITOL (120 "Happy Trails") .. 20-30 69
CAPITOL (288 "Quicksilver Messenger Service") 30-50 69
CAPITOL (391 thru 819) 10-25 69-71
CAPITOL (2904 "Quicksilver Messenger Service") 20-30 68
CAPITOL (11000 series) 10-15 72-75
CAPITOL (16000 series) 5-10 80

Members: John Cipolina; Dave Freiberg.
Also see COPPERHEAD
Also see HOPKINS, Nicky
Also see JEFFERSON AIRPLANE
Also see MILLER, Steve / Band / Quicksilver Messinger Service

QUIET ELEGANCE

R&B '73

Singles: 7-inch

HI 3-5 73

Also see GLORIES

QUIET RIOT

P&R/LP '83

Singles: 12-inch 33/45rpm

PASHA 4-6 83-85

Singles: 7-inch

CBS 3-4 83
PASHA 3-4 83-86

Picture Sleeves

PASHA 3-4 83-86

LPs: 10/12-inch 33rpm

MOONSTONE 5-10 93
PASHA (Except 8Z8-39203) 5-10 83-88
PASHA (8Z8-39203 "Metal Health") 10-12 83
(Picture disc.)
RHINO 5-8 93

Members: Kevin DuBrow;; Rudy Sarzo; Frankie Banali; Randy Rhoads; Chuck Wright; Paul Shortino; Sean McNabb; Kenny Hillery; Carlos Cavazo.
Also see HEAR 'N AID

Also see OSBOURNE, Ozzy

QUINELLA

R&B '81

Singles: 7-inch

BECKET 3-5 81

QUINN, Carmel

LP '55

Singles: 78rpm

COLUMBIA 3-5 55-56

Singles: 7-inch

COLUMBIA 5-10 55-56
DOT 4-6 64
HEADLINE 4-8 59-62

EPs: 7-inch 33/45rpm

COLUMBIA 8-12 55

LPs: 10/12-inch 33rpm

CAMDEN 10-15 65
COLUMBIA 15-25 55-56
DOT 10-15 65
HEADLINE 10-20 59-62

Also see GODFREY, Arthur /Carmel Quinn / Frank Parker / Janette Davis

QUIN-TONES

P&R/R&B '58

Singles: 7-inch

COLLECTABLES 3-4 80s
HUNT (321 "Down the Aisle of Love") 10-20 58
HUNT (322 "What Am I to Do") .. 15-25 58
RED TOP (108 "Down the Aisle of Love") 30-40 58
(Blue label)
RED TOP (108 "Down the Aisle of Love") 10-15
(Red label)

Members: Roberta Haymon; Phylis Carr; Carolyn Holmes; Ronnie Scott; Jeannie Crist; Ken Sexton.

While the multi-million-selling *G.I. Blues* album is fairly common, finding one with the heart-shaped *Wooden Heart* promotion sticker is next to impossible.

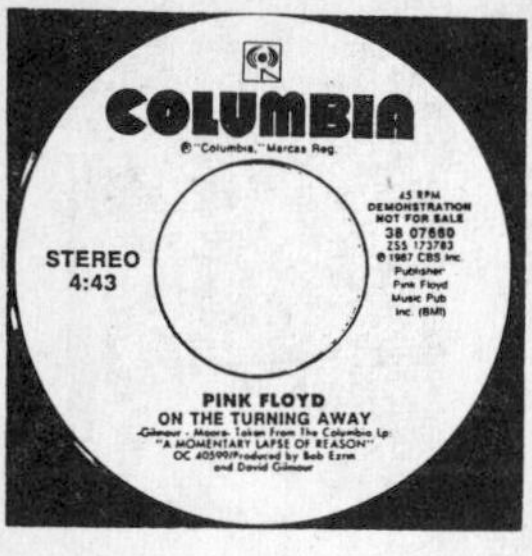

R

RCR

P&R/R&B '80

Singles: 7-inch

RADIO 3-5 80

Members: Donna Rhodes; Charles Chalmers; Sandy Rhodes.

R.E.M.

P&R '83

Singles: 7-inch

EVA-TONE (105900 "Dark Globe") 5-10 90

(Promotional issue, *Sassy* magazine insert. Add $2 to $4 if accompanied by the appropriate issue of *Sassy*.)

HIBTONE (Radio Free Europe") 50-75 81

I.R.S. 3-8 82-87

W.B. 3-6 88-93

Picture Sleeves

I.R.S. 4-8 82-88

W.B. 3-4 89

EPs: 7-inch 33/45rpm

I.R.S. 5-10 82

LPs: 10/12-inch 33rpm

I.R.S. 5-10 82-88

W.B. 5-8 88-93

Members: J. Michael Stipe; Bill Berry; Peter Buck; Mike Mills.

Also see HINDU LOVE GODS

REO SPEEDWAGON

LP '74

Singles: 7-inch

EPIC (Except 10000 & 11000 series) 3-5 75-90

EPIC (10000 & 11000 series) 3-5 72-74

Picture Sleeves

EPIC 3-5 80-88

EPs: 7-inch 33/45rpm

CSP 4-8 81

(Nestles candy promotional issue.)

LPs: 10/12-inch 33rpm

EPIC (Except 40000 series) 6-12 71-90

EPIC (40000 series) 12-15 81-82

(Half-speed mastered.)

Promotional LPs

EPIC (643 "Nine Lives") 15-20 80s

Members: Kevin Cronin; Neal Doughty; Al Gratzer; Bruce Hall; Terry Luttrell.

Also see MAY, Brian

R.J.'S LATEST ARRIVAL

(Ralph James)

R&B '81

Singles: 7-inch

ARIOLA AMERICA 3-5 79

ATLANTIC 3-4 85

BUDDAH 3-5 81

LARC 3-4 83

EMI MANHATTAN 3-4 88

MANHATTAN 3-4 87

QUALITY/RFC 3-4

SUTRA 3-5 81

ZOO YORK 3-5 82

LPs: 10/12-inch 33rpm

ARIOLA AMERICA 5-10 79

ATLANTIC 5-8 85

RABBITT, Eddie

C&W '74

Singles: 7-inch

DATE 4-8 68

ELEKTRA 3-5 74-83

RCA 3-4 85-89

20TH FOX 5-10 64

UNIVERSAL 3-4 89

W.B. 3-4 83-85

Picture Sleeves

ELEKTRA 3-5 81

LPs: 10/12-inch 33rpm

ELEKTRA 5-10 75-82

RCA 5-8 86

W.B. 5-8 84-85

RABBITT, Eddie, & Crystal Gayle

C&W/P&R '82

Singles: 7-inch

ELEKTRA 3-5 82

Also see GAYLE, Crystal

RABBITT, Eddie, & Juice Newton

C&W '86

Singles: 7-inch

RCA 3-4 86

Also see NEWTON, Juice

Also see RABBITT, Eddie

RABIN, Trevor

LP '78

Singles: 7-inch

CHRYSALIS 3-5 78-80

LPs: 10/12-inch 33rpm

CHRYSALIS 5-10 78-80

ELEKTRA 5-8 89

RACE

R&B '83

Singles: 7-inch

OCEAN FRONT 3-4 83

RACING CARS

LP '77

Singles: 7-inch

CHRYSALIS 3-5 77-78

LPs: 10/12-inch 33rpm
CHRYSALIS 5-10 77-78

RADIANCE
(With Andrea Stone)
R&B/D&D '85
Singles: 12-inch 33/45rpm
ARE 'N BE 4-6 83
Singles: 7-inch
W.B. 3-4 85

RADIANTS
(Maurice McAlister & Radiants; Maurice & Radiants)
P&R '62
Singles: 7-inch
CHESS 4-8 62-69
ERIC 3-4 70s
TWINIGHT 3-5 71
Members: Maurice McAlister; Wallace Sampson; Jerome Brooks; Elzie Butler; Green McLauren; Frank McCollum; Leonard Caston, Jr; James Jameson; Mitchell Bullock; Victor Caston.
Also see McALISTER, Maurice

RADIATORS
LP '87
Singles: 7-inch
EPIC 3-4 87-89
LPs: 10/12-inch 33rpm
EPIC 5-8 87-89
Members: Dave Malone; Frank Bua; Reggie Scanlan; Ed Volker; Camile Baudoin; Glenn Sears.

RADICE, Mark
R&B '76
Singles: 7-inch
U.A. 3-5 76
LPs: 10/12-inch 33rpm
ROADSHOW 8-12 77

RADNER, Gilda
LP '79
Singles: 7-inch
W.B. 3-5 79-80
LPs: 10/12-inch 33rpm
W.B. 5-10 79

RAE, Fonda
(Fonda Raye)
R&B '82
Singles: 12-inch 33/45rpm
POSSE 4-6 83
VANGUARD 4-6 82
Singles: 7-inch
VANGUARD 3-4 82
Also see WISH

RAE, Robbie
D&D '83
Singles: 12-inch 33/45rpm
QUALITY 4-6 83
Singles: 7-inch
QUALITY 3-4 83

RAELETTES
(Raeletts; Raelets)
P&R/R&B '67
Singles: 7-inch
TRC 3-5 70
TANGERINE 3-6 67-73
LPs: 10/12-inch 33rpm
TRC 8-12 71-72
TANGERINE 8-12 72
Members: Clydie King; Mable John.
Also see CHARLES, Ray
Also see JOHN, Mable
Also see KING, Clydie
Also see TURNER, Ike & Tina

RAES
P&R '78
Singles: 7-inch
A&M 3-5 78
LPs: 10/12-inch 33rpm
A&M 5-10 79
Members: Robbie Rae; Cherrill Rae.

RAFFERTY, Gerry
P&R/LP '78
Singles: 12-inch 33/45rpm
U.A. (171 "Baker Street") 5-10 78
Singles: 7-inch
BLUE THUMB 3-5 72
LIBERTY 3-4 82
SIGNPOST 3-5 72
U.A. 3-5 77-80
Picture Sleeves
U.A. 3-5 77-78
LPs: 10/12-inch 33rpm
BLUE THUMB 8-10 73-78
LIBERTY 5-8 82
MFSL 25-50 81
U.A. 8-10 78-80
VISA 5-10 78
Also see STEALERS WHEEL

RAG DOLLS
P&R '64
Singles: 7-inch
MALA 8-12 65
Member: Jean Thomas.

RAG DOLLS / Caliente Combo
Singles: 7-inch
PARKWAY 5-10 64
Also see RAG DOLLS

RAGING SLAB
LP '89
LPs: 10/12-inch 33rpm
RCA 5-8 89

RAIDERS & Paul Revere: see REVERE, Paul, & Raiders

RAIL
LP '84
Singles: 7-inch
EMI AMERICA 3-4 84

LPs: 10/12-inch 33rpm

DYNASTY	5-10	80
EMI AMERICA	5-8	84
PASSPORT	5-8	83

RAINBOW

LP '77

Singles: 7-inch

MERCURY	3-4	82-83
POLYDOR	3-5	79

Picture Sleeves

MERCURY	3-4	82-83

LPs: 10/12-inch 33rpm

MERCURY	5-10	82-86
OYSTER	8-12	77
POLYDOR	5-10	78-81

Members: Ritchie Blackmore; Roger Glover; Cozy Powell; Ronnie James Dio; Joe Turner; Tony Carey.

Also see ALCATRAZZ
Also see BLACKMORE'S RAINBOW
Also see CAREY, Tony
Also see GLOVER, Roger

RAINDROPS

P&R/R&B '63

Singles: 7-inch

JUBILEE	10-20	63-65
VIRGO	3-5	73

LPs: 10/12-inch 33rpm

JUBILEE (J-5023 "Raindrops") (Monaural.)	30-50	63
JUBILEE (SJ-5023 "Raindrops") (Stereo.)	50-75	63
MURRAY HILL	5-8	80s

Members: Jeff Barry; Ellie Greenwich. (The third person pictured on LP cover, Ellie's sister, Laura, is not heard on their records.)

Also see GREENWICH, Ellie

RAINES, Rita

P&R '56

Singles: 78rpm

DEED	5-10	56
JAMIE	5-10	57

Singles: 7-inch

DEED	8-12	56
JAMIE	8-12	57

RAINEY, Big Memphis Ma: see MARAINEY, Big Memphis

RAINEY, Ma
(Gertrude Rainey)

P&R '25

Singles: 78rpm

PARAMOUNT (12000 series)	100-200	24-38

LPs: 10/12-inch 33rpm

BIOGRAPH	8-12	67-69
MILESTONE	8-12	67-74

RAINMAKERS

LP '86

Sngles: 7-inch

ERA	5-10	65

RAINWATER, Marvin

C&W/P&R '57

Singles: 78rpm

CORAL	5-10	56
MGM (Except 12240 & 12370)	5-10	55-57
MGM (12240 "Hot and Cold")	10-15	56
MGM (12370 "Get off the Stool")	10-15	56

Singles: 7-inch

BRAVE	4-6	63-67
CORAL	8-12	56
HILLTOP	5-10	70s
MGM (12000 & 12100 series)	10-20	55
MGM (12240 "Hot and Cold")	30-40	56
MGM (12313 "Why Did You Have to Go and Love Me")	10-20	56
MGM (12370 "Get off the Stool")	30-40	56
MGM (12412 thru 12938)	5-10	57-60
NU TRAYL	3-5	76
U.A.	4-6	65-66
W.B.	3-5	69-70
WARWICK	5-10	61

EPs: 7-inch 33/45rpm

MGM (1464/1465/1466 "Songs By Marvin Rainwater") (Price is for any of three volumes.)	15-25	57

LPs: 10/12-inch 33rpm

CROWN	15-25	60s
MGM (3534 "Songs by Marvin Rainwater")	75-125	57
MGM (3721 "With a Heart With a Beat")	75-125	58
MGM (4046 "Gonna Find Me a Bluebird")	50-100	62
MOUNT VERNON	8-10	
SPINORAMA	8-10	60s

Also see DEAN, Jimmy / Marvin Rainwater
Also see FRANCIS, Connie, & Marvin Rainwater

RAINY DAZE

P&R '67

Singles: 7-inch

CHICORY (404 "That Acapulco Gold")	10-15	67
I.P. ("That Acapulco Gold") (Number not known.)	25-35	66
UNI	5-10	67
WHITE WHALE	5-10	68

LPs: 10/12-inch 33rpm

UNI (73002 "That Acapulco Gold")	15-25	67

Members: Tim Gilbert; Bob Heckendorf; Mac Ferris; Kip Gilbert; Sam Fuller.

RAITT, Bonnie

LP '72

Singles: 7–inch

CAPITOL.................................... 3-4 89-91
W.B. 3-4 72-86

Picture Sleeves

W.B. .... 3-4 '79

LPs: 10/12–inch 33rpm

CAPITOL.................................... 5-8 89-91
W.B. 6-12 71-86

Also see MULDAUR, Geoff, & Bonnie Raitt

RAITT, Bonnie / Gilley's "Urban Cowboy" Band

Singles: 7–inch

FULL MOON/ASYLUM 3-5 80

Picture Sleeves

FULL MOON/ASYLUM 3-5 80

Also see RAITT, Bonnie

RAJAHS
(Nutmegs)

Singles: 7–inch

KLIK (7805 "I Fell in Love") ... 200-300 57

Also see NUTMEGS

RAKE

R&B '83

Singles: 7–inch

PROFILE.................................... 3-4 83

RALKE, Don
(Big Sound of Don Ralke)

P&R '59

Singles: 78rpm

CROWN 3-6 55

Singles: 7–inch

CROWN 4-8 55
DRUM BOY.................................. 3-6 66
REAL.. 4-8 56
W.B. 4-6 59-64

LPs: 10/12–inch 33rpm

CROWN 10-20 55
W.B. 10-20 59-60

Also see BYRNES, Edward
Also see JAN & ARNIE

RALPH, Sheryl Lee

D&D '84

Singles: 12–inch 33/45rpm

NYM 4-6 84-85

Singles: 7–inch

NYM 3-4 84-85

Also see HARNEY, Ben, & Sheryl Lee Ralph

RAM JAM

P&R/LP '77

Singles: 12–inch 33/45rpm

EPIC... 5-10 77

Singles: 7–inch

EPIC.. 3-5 77-78

LPs: 10/12–inch 33rpm

EPIC... 8-12 77-78

Also see LEMON PIPERS

Also see WILSON, Dennis / Ram Jam / Joan Baez

RAMA

D&D '84

Singles: 12–inch 33/45rpm

SUGARSCOOP 4-6 84

RAMATAM

LP '72

Singles: 7–inch

ATLANTIC.................................3-5 72-73

LPs: 10/12–inch 33rpm

ATLANTIC..............................10-15 72-73

Also see PINERA, Mike

RAMBEAU, Eddie

P&R/LP '65

Singles: 7–inch

BELL 3-5 69
DYNA VOICE..............................4-8 65-66
SWAN 4-8 61-62
20TH FOX...................................4-8 64
VIRGO 3-4 73

LPs: 10/12–inch 33rpm

DYNO VOICE 15-25 65

Also see MARCY JO & Eddie Rambeau

RAMBLERS

P&R '60

Singles: 7–inch

ADDIT 8-12 60

RAMBLERS

P&R '64

Singles: 7–inch

ALMONT...................................10-20 64
SIDEWINDERS.........................10-20 64

RAMIN, Sid, & Orchestra

LP '63

LPs: 10/12–inch 33rpm

RCA 8-12 63

RAMISTELLA, Johnny
(Johnny Rivers)

Singles: 7–inch

SUEDE (1401 "Little Girl") 75-100 58

Also see RIVERS, Johnny

RAMONES

LP '76

Singles: 7–inch

RSO 3-6 81
SIRE...5-10 76-80

Picture Sleeves

SIRE...8-12 77-79

EPs: 7–inch

SIRE (805 "Rock 'N' Roll High School")..........................12-18 79
(Promotional issue only.)

LPs: 10/12–inch 33rpm

SIRE (Except 6063 & 7528)...........5-8 76-89
SIRE (6063 "Road to Ruin").......10-20 78
(Black vinyl.)

SIRE (6063 "Road to Ruin")...... 25-35 78
(Yellow vinyl.)
SIRE (7528 "Leave Home") 15-25 77
(Has *Carbona Not Glue*, which is not on reissues.)

RAMRODS

P&R '61

Singles: 7-inch

AMY 8-12 60-62
QUEEN 8-12 62
Members: Vincent Bell; Eugene Morrow; Richard Lane; Claire Lane.
Also see BELL, Vincent

RAMRODS

R&B '72

Singles: 7-inch

RAMPAGE 3-5 72

RANDAZZO, Teddy
(With All 6)

P&R '58

Singles: 7-inch

ABC-PAR 4-8 59-62
COLPIX 4-8 62-63
DCP 4-8 64-66
MGM 4-8 66
VERVE/FOLKWAYS 4-8 67
VIK 5-10 58

LPs: 10/12-inch 33rpm

ABC-PAR 20-30 61-62
MGM 15-20 66
VIK (1121 "I'm Confessing")...... 30-50 58
Also see CHUCKLES
Also see THREE CHUCKLES

RAN-DELLS

P&R/R&B '63

Singles: 7-inch

RSVP 8-12 64
CHAIRMAN 8-12 63-64

Picture Sleeves

CHAIRMAN (4403 "Martian Hop") 30-40 63
Members: Steve Rappaport; John Sprit.

RANDOLPH, Boots
(Homer Randolph)

P&R/R&B/LP '63

Singles: 7-inch

MONUMENT 3-5 61-83
PALO ALTO 3-4
RCA.. 4-8 59-61

Picture Sleeves

MONUMENT 5-10 64

EPs: 7-inch 33/45rpm

MONUMENT (361 "Boots & Stockings") 5-10 69
(Promotional issue only.)

LPs: 10/12-inch 33rpm

CAMDEN................................... 10-20 64
GUEST STAR 5-10 64
MONUMENT (Except 8000 & 18000 series) 6-12 71-82
MONUMENT (8000 & 18000 series) 10-20 63-71
PALO ALTO 5-8
RCA 15-25 60
Also see ANN-MARGRET
Also see ATKINS, Chet, Floyd Cramer & Boots Randolph
Also see FRANCIS, Connie
Also see HALEY, Bill / Boots Randolph
Also see HIRT, Al, & Boots Randolph
Also see KNIGHTSBRIDGE STRINGS
Also see LEE, Brenda
Also see PRESLEY, Elvis
Also see RANDOLPH, Randy
Also see TILLOTSON, Johnny
Also see VELVETS

RANDOLPH, Randy
(Homer Randolph)

Singles: 7-inch

RCA 5-10 58-59
Also see RANDOLPH, Boots

RANDY & RAINBOWS

P&R/R&B '63

Singles: 7-inch

B.T. PUPPY 5-8 67
CRYSTAL BALL..............................4-8 77
LAURIE 3-5 70s
MIKE 5-10 66
RUST (Except 5059)......................8-12 63-64
RUST (5059 "Denise") 20-25 63
(Blue label.)
RUST (5059 "Denise") 5-10 63
(Rust and white label.)

LPs: 10/12-inch 33rpm

AMBIENT SOUND 8-10 82
AMBIENT SOUND/ROUNDER....8-10 84
MAGIC CARPET.........................8-10
Members: Dominick "Randy" Safuto; Frank Safuto; Mike Zero; Sal Zero; Ken Arcipowski.

RANK & FILE

LP '83

Singles: 7-inch

SLASH 3-4 83-84

LPs: 10/12-inch 33rpm

SLASH 5-8 83-84
Also see SEATRAIN

RANKIN, Billy

P&R/LP '84

Singles: 7-inch

A&M 3-4 84

LPs: 10/12-inch 33rpm

A&M 5-8 84

RANKIN, Kenny
(Ken Rankin)

LP '72

Singles: 7-inch

ABC-PAR 4-8 61
COLUMBIA 4-8 63-65

DECCA.. 5-10 58-60
LITTLE DAVID 3-5 73-77
MERCURY 4-6 68-69

Picture Sleeves

COLUMBIA 8-12 63
MERCURY 5-8 68

LPs: 10/12-inch 33rpm

ATLANTIC.................................... 5-10 80
LITTLE DAVID 8-10 72-77
MERCURY 10-15 67-69

RANKING ROGER

LP '88

LPs: 10/12-inch 33rpm

I.R.S. 5-8 88

RAPPIN' DUKE

R&B '86

Singles: 12-inch 33/45rpm

TOMMY BOY 4-6 86

RARE BIRD

LP '70

Singles: 7-inch

ABC.. 3-5 72
POLYDOR.................................... 3-5 73-74
PROBE... 3-5 70

LPs: 10/12-inch 33rpm

ABC... 8-10 72
POLYDOR................................. 8-10 73-74
PROBE.................................... 10-12 70

RARE BREED

Singles: 7-inch

ATTACK (1401 "Beg, Borrow and Steal") 20-25 66
(Reissued, with a different flip side, and shown as by the Ohio Express.)
ATTACK (1403 "Come and Take a Ride in My Boat") 10-20 66
Also see OHIO EXPRESS

RARE EARTH

LP '69

Singles: 7-inch

MOTOWN 3-5 81
PRODIGAL.................................... 3-4 78
RARE EARTH 3-6 69-76
VERVE 4-8 68

Picture Sleeves

RARE EARTH 4-6 71-73

LPs: 10/12-inch 33rpm

MOTOWN 5-8 81
PRODIGAL.................................... 5-8 77-78
RARE EARTH (Except 507)........ 8-12 70-76
RARE EARTH (507 "Get Ready") 8-12 69
(With standard, square cover.)
RARE EARTH (507 "Get Ready") 30-40 69
(With rounded-top cover. Promotional issue.)
VERVE 10-20 68

RARE ESSENCE

R&B '82

Singles: 12-inch 33/45rpm

FANTASY 4-8 82

RASCALS

(Young Rascals)

P&R '65

Singles: 7-inch

ATLANTIC (Except 2428) 4-8 65-70
ATLANTIC (2428 "Groovin' [in Italian]")...................................10-20 67
(Backed with *Groovin'* in Spanish.)
ATLANTIC OLDIES 3-4 70s
COLUMBIA 3-5 71-72

Picture Sleeves

ATLANTIC.....................................5-10 66-70

EPs: 7-inch 33/45rpm

ATLANTIC (190 "Time Peace") .10-15 68
(Promotional issue only.)

LPs: 10/12-inch 33rpm

ATLANTIC (137 "Freedom Suite") 20-30 69
(Promotional issue only.)
ATLANTIC (901 "Freedom Suite") 20-30 69
(Without cut corner or BB holes.)
ATLANTIC (901 "Freedom Suite") 10-20 69
(With cut corner or BB holes.)
ATLANTIC (8123 thru 8148)......15-25 66-67
ATLANTIC (8169 thru 8276)......10-15 68-71
COLUMBIA 8-12 71-72
PAIR..8-10 86
RHINO 5-8 87
W.F.O. (1000 "The Rascals").......8-12 72

Members: Felix Cavaliere; Ed Brigati; Dino Danelli; Gene Cornish; David Brigati.
Also see BULLDOG
Also see CAVALIERE, Felix
Also see DEE, Joey
Also see FOTOMAKER
Also see SWEET INSPIRATIONS

(YOUNG) RASCALS / Buggs / Four Seasons / Johnny Rivers

LPs: 10/12-inch 33rpm

CORONET (283 "The Young Rascals") 15-25 66
Also see 4 SEASONS
Also see RIVERS, Johnny

(YOUNG) RASCALS / Isley Brothers

LPs: 10/12-inch 33rpm

DESIGN (253 "Young Rascals and the Isley Brothers") 15-25 60s
Also see ISLEY BROTHERS
Also see RASCALS

RASPBERRIES

P&R/LP '72

Singles: 7-inch

CAPITOL.......................................4-6 72-74

Picture Sleeves

CAPITOL.................................... 5-10 73

LPs: 10/12-inch 33rpm

CAPITOL (11036 thru 11329)... 20-30 72-74

CAPITOL (11524 "Raspberries' Best") 8-12 76

CAPITOL (16095 "Raspberries' Best") 5-10 80

Members: Eric Carmen; Wally Bryson; Jim Bonfanti; John Aleksic; Dave Smalley.

Also see CHOIR

Also see FOTOMAKER

RATCHELL

LP '72

Singles: 7-inch

DECCA.. 3-5 72

LPs: 10/12-inch 33rpm

DECCA.................................. 10-15 71-72

RATIONALS

P&R '66

Singles: 7-inch

A2 (101 "Look What You've Done") 15-25 65

A2 (103 "Feelin' Lost").............. 10-20 66

A2 (103/4 "Feelin' Lost"/"Leavin' Here")................................. 20-30 66

(Promotional issue only.)

A2 (104 "Leavin' Here") 10-20 66

A2 (105 "Leavin' Here") 10-20 67

A2 (106 "Leavin' Here") 10-20 68

A2 (107 "I Need You") 10-20 68

CAMEO 10-15 66-67

CAPITOL.................................. 8-12 68

CREWE...................................... 5-8 69

DANBY'S (125850 "Turn On")... 30-40 60s

(Promotional issue made for Danby's clothier.)

GENESIS (1 "Guitar Army")......... 5-8 69

LPs: 10/12-inch 33rpm

CREWE (1334 "Rationals")....... 25-35 69

Also see SRC / Rationals

RATT

P&R/LP '84

Singles: 7-inch

ATLANTIC.................................... 3-4 84-89

TIME COAST 3-5 83-84

Picture Sleeves

ATLANTIC.................................... 3-4 84-88

LPs: 10/12-inch 33rpm

ATLANTIC.................................... 5-8 84-90

TIME COAST 5-10 83-84

Members: Stephen Pearcy; Warren D. Martin; Robbin Crosby; Juan Crocier; Bobby Blotzer.

RATTLES

P&R '70

Singles: 7-inch

LONDON....................................... 3-5

MERCURY 5-10 66

PROBE 4-6 70

LPs: 10/12-inch 33rpm

MERCURY (21127 "Greatest Hits")......................................30-40 67

(Monaural.)

MERCURY (61127 "Greatest Hits")......................................40-60 67

(Stereo.)

Also see SEARCHERS / Rattles

RAVAN, Genya

P&R/LP '78

Singles: 7-inch

COLUMBIA 3-5 71-72

DE LITE 3-5 75

DUNHILL......................................3-8 73

20TH FOX....................................3-5 78-79

LPs: 10/12-inch 33rpm

COLUMBIA 8-12 72

DUNHILL....................................8-15 73

20TH FOX..................................5-10 78-79

Also see TEN WHEEL DRIVE

RAVEN

LP '85

Singles: 7-inch

RAMPART 3-5

LPs: 10/12-inch 33rpm

ATLANTIC....................................5-8 85-86

RAVEN, Marcia

D&D '83

Singles: 12-inch 33/45rpm

PROFILE......................................4-6 83

Singles: 7-inch

PROFILE......................................3-5 83

RAVENS

P&R '47

Singles: 78rpm

ARGO 10-20 56-57

CHECKER 10-15 57

COLUMBIA 50-100 50-51

HUB 30-40 46

KING 25-35 48-49

JUBILEE 5-10 55-56

MERCURY..................................15-25 51-55

OKEH (6825 "Whiffenpoof Song")...................................50-100 51

OKEH (6843 "That Old Gang of Mine")................................50-100 51

OKEH (6888 "Mam'selle")........50-100 52

NATIONAL 40-60 47-51

RENDITION (5001 "Write Me a Letter") 20-30 51

Singles: 7-inch

ARGO (5255 "Kneel and Pray").25-35 56

ARGO (5261 "A Simple Prayer")...................................50-75 56

ARGO (5276 "That'll Be the Day")......................................15-25 57

ARGO (5284 "Here Is My Heart")....... 15-25 57
CHECKER (871 "That'll Be the Day")....... 10-15 57
COLUMBIA (1-903 "Time Takes Care of Everything")....... 500-750 50
(Compact 33 Single.)
COLUMBIA (6-903 "Time Takes Care of Everything")....... 400-600 50
COLUMBIA (1-925 "My Baby's Gone")....... 400-600 50
(Compact 33 Single.)
COLUMBIA (6-925 "My Baby's Gone")....... 400-600 50
COLUMBIA (39112 "You Don't Have to Drop a Heart to Break It")....... 400-600 51
COLUMBIA (39194 "You're Always in My Dreams")....... 400-600 51
COLUMBIA (39408 "You Foolish Thing")....... 600-800 51
JUBILEE....... 15-25 55-56
MEDIA ("Sixty Minute Man")....... 3-4 93
(Colored vinyl.)
MERCURY (5764 "There's No Use Pretending")....... 100-200 51
MERCURY (5800 "Begin the Beguine")....... 100-150 52
MERCURY (5853 "Why Did You Leave")....... 100-150 52
MERCURY (8291 "Write Me One Sweet Letter")....... 50-100 52
MERCURY (8296 "Too Soon") 50-100 52
MERCURY (70060 "Don't Mention My Name")....... 100-150 52
MERCURY (70119 "Come a Little Bit Closer")....... 50-100 53
MERCURY (70213 "Who'll Be the Fool")....... 50-100 53
MERCURY (70240 "Without a Song")....... 50-100 53
MERCURY (70307 "September Song")....... 50-100 54
MERCURY (70330 "Lonesome Road")....... 50-100 54
MERCURY (70413 "Love Is No Dream")....... 100-200 54
(Pink label.)
MERCURY (70413 "Love Is No Dream")....... 50-75 54
(Black label.)
MERCURY (70505 "White Christmas")....... 100-150 54
(Pink label.)
MERCURY (70505 "White Christmas")....... 50-75 54
(Black label.)
MERCURY (70554 "Write Me a Letter")....... 100-150 55
(Pink label.)
MERCURY (70554 "Write Me a Letter")....... 50-75 55
(Black label.)
NATIONAL (9111 "Count Every Star")....... 1500-2000 50
OKEH (6825 "Whiffenpoof Song")....... 350-450 51
OKEH (6843 "That Old Gang of Mine")....... 350-450 51
OKEH (6888 "Mam'selle")....... 200-300 52
SAVOY....... 10-15 58
TOP RANK....... 10-20 59
VIRGO....... 3-5 72

Picture Sleeves

MEDIA ("Sixty Minute Man")....... 3-4 93

EPs: 7–inch 33/45rpm

KING (310 "The Ravens Featuring Jimmy Ricks")....... 300-400 54
RENDITION (104 "Ol' Man River")....... 300-450 52

LPs: 10/12–inch 33rpm

HARLEM HITPARADE....... 10-12 75
REGENT (6062 "Write Me a Letter")....... 100-150 57
(Green label.)
REGENT (6062 "Write Me a Letter")....... 50-75 50s
(Red label.)
SAVOY....... 10-15 78

Members: Warren Suttles; Ollie Jones; Joe Van Loan; Jimmy Ricks; Leonard Puzey; Maithe Marshall; Joe Medlin; Louis Heyward; James Stewart; Louis Frazier; Tom Evans; James Van Loan; David Bowers; Paul Van Loan; Rich Cannon; Bob Kornegay; Willis Sanders; Willie Ray.

Also see CUES

RAVENS & Dinah Washington

Singles: 78rpm

MERCURY (8257 "Hey Good Lookin'")....... 15-25 51

Singles: 7–inch

MERCURY (8257 "Hey Good Lookin'")....... 40-60 51

Also see WASHINGTON, Dinah

RAVENS / Three Clouds

Singles: 78rpm

KING....... 25-35 48-49

Also see RAVENS

RAW SILK

R&B '82

Singles: 12–inch 33/45rpm

WEST END....... 4-6 83

Singles: 7–inch

WEST END....... 3-5 82-83

RAWLS, Lou

LP '63

Singles: 12–inch 33/45rpm

PHILADELPHIA INT'L....... 4-8 79

Singles: 7–inch

ARISTA 3-5 75
BELL 3-5 74
CANDIX.. 5-10 60-61
CAPITOL.. 3-8 61-70
EPIC.. 3-4 82-85
GAMBLE 3-4 87
MGM 3-5 71-73
PHILADELPHIA INT'L.................. 3-5 76-81
SHAR-DEE.............................. 8-12 60

Picture Sleeves

CAPITOL.. 4-8 67

LPs: 10/12–inch 33rpm

ALLEGIANCE.............................. 5-8 84
BELL 8-10 74
CAPITOL (Except 1700 thru 2900 series) 5-12 69-77
CAPITOL (1700 thru 2900 series) 12-25 63-68
EPIC.. 5-8 82-83
MGM 8-10 71-73
PHILADELPHIA INT'L.................. 5-10 76-80
POLYDOR.. 8-10 76

Also see COOKE, Sam
Also see PHILADELPHIA INTERNATIONAL ALL STARS
Also see VEGA, Tata

RAWLS, Lou, & Les McCann Ltd.

Singles: 7–inch

CAPITOL.. 4-6 62

LPs: 10/12–inch 33rpm

CAPITOL.. 5-8 75
(With "SM" prefix.)
CAPITOL.. 20-30 62
(With "T" or "ST" prefix.)

Also see McCANN, Les
Also see RAWLS, Lou

RAY, Baby: see BABY RAY

RAY, Diane

P&R '63

Singles: 7–inch

MERCURY 4-8 63-64

Picture Sleeves

MERCURY 10-15 63

LPs: 10/12–inch 33rpm

MERCURY 20-30 64

RAY, Don

P&R/LP '78

Singles: 7–inch

POLYDOR.. 3-5 78

LPs: 10/12–inch 33rpm

POLYDOR.. 5-10 78

RAY, Harry

R&B '82

Singles: 7–inch

SUGAR HILL.............................. 3-4 82-83

LPs: 10/12–inch 33rpm

SUGAR HILL.............................. 5-8 83

Also see RAY, GOODMAN & BROWN

RAY, James

(With the Hutch Davie Orchestra)

P&R '61

Singles: 7–inch

CAPRICE.................................10-20 61-62
CONGRESS 10-20 63-64
DYNAMIC 10-20 62

LPs: 10/12–inch 33rpm

CAPRICE (LP-1002 "James Ray")....................................40-60 62
(Monaural.)
CAPRICE (SLP-1002 "James Ray")....................................75-100 62
(Stereo.)

Also see DAVIE, Hutch
Also see GRANT, Janie

RAY, Johnnie

(With the Four Lads)

P&R '51

Singles: 78rpm

COLUMBIA 5-10 52-58
OKEH.......................................8-12 52

Singles: 7–inch

CADENCE 5-10 60
COLUMBIA 8-15 52-60
DECCA 4-6 63-64
GROOVE 4-6 64
LIBERTY 4-8 62
OKEH (6809 "Wiskey and Gin").15-25 51
OKEH (6840 "Cry") 10-20 51
OKEH RHYTHM & BLUES (6840 "Cry") 15-25 51
U.A. 4-8 61

Picture Sleeves

COLUMBIA 10-20 57

EPs: 7–inch 33/45rpm

COLUMBIA 10-20 52-59
EPIC..10-20 52-54

LPs: 10/12–inch 33rpm

COLUMBIA (961 "Big Beat")......30-50 57
COLUMBIA (1093 thru 1227).....20-40 57-59
COLUMBIA (1385 "On the Trail") 15-25 59
(Monaural.)
COLUMBIA (2510 "I Cry for You")......................................30-50 56
(10 Inch LP.)
COLUMBIA (6199 "Johnnie Ray")......................................35-55 51
(10 Inch LP.)
COLUMBIA (8180 "On the Trail") 20-30 59
(Stereo.)
EPIC (1120 "Johnnie Ray")........30-50 55
(10–inch LP.)
HARMONY.................................5-10 71
SUNSET 10-15 66

Also see DAY, Doris, & Johnnie Ray

Also see FOUR LADS

RAY, Johnnie, & Timi Yuro

Singles: 7-inch

LIBERTY 4-8 61

Also see RAY, Johnnie
Also see YURO, Timi

RAY, Link: see WRAY, Link

RAY, Ricardo

P&R '68

Singles: 7-inch

ALEGRE 4-6 68

RAY & BOB

P&R '62

Singles: 7-inch

LEDO 8-10 62

Members: Ray Swayne; Bob Appleberry.

RAY, GOODMAN & BROWN

R&B '79

Singles: 7-inch

EMI AMERICA 3-4 87
PANORAMIC 3-4 84
POLYDOR 3-5 80-81

LPs: 10/12-inch 33rpm

POLYDOR 5-10 80-81

Members: Harry Ray; Al Goodman; Bill Brown.
Also see MOMENTS
Also see RAY, Harry

RAYBURN, Margie

P&R '57

Singles: 78rpm

ALMA 4-8 54
LIBERTY 4-8 56-57
S&G 4-8 54

Singles: 7-inch

ALMA 5-10 54
CAPITOL 4-6 65
CHALLENGE 4-8 61
DOT 4-8 62-66
LIBERTY 5-10 56-62
S&G 5-10 54

Picture Sleeves

LIBERTY 10-15 57

LPs: 10/12-inch 33rpm

LIBERTY (3126 "Margie") 20-25 59
(Monaural.)
LIBERTY (7126 "Margie") 25-35 59
(Stereo.)

RAYDIO
(Featuring Ray Parker Jr.)

R&B '77

Singles: 7-inch

ARISTA 3-5 78-79

Picture Sleeves

ARISTA 3-5 78-79

LPs: 10/12-inch 33rpm

ARISTA 5-10 78-79

Also see KNIGHT, Jerry
Also see PARKER, Ray, Jr.

RAYE, Colin

C&W/LP '91

Singles: 7-inch

EPIC 3-4 91-92

LP: 10/12-inch 33rpm

EPIC 5-8 91

RAYE, Fonda: see RAE, Fonda

RAYE, Susan

C&W/LP '70

Singles: 7-inch

CAPITOL 3-6 69-76
U.A. 3-5 76-77
WESTEXAS 3-4 85-86

Picture Sleeves

CAPITOL 3-5 71

LPs: 10/12-inch 33rpm

CAPITOL 8-12 70-76
U.A. 5-10 77

Also see OWENS, Buck, & Susan Raye

RAY-O-VACS

R&B '49

Singles: 78rpm

ATCO 5-10 57
COLEMAN 5-10 49
DECCA 4-8 50-53
JOSIE 5-10 54
JUBILEE 5-10 52
KAISER 5-10 56

Singles: 7-inch

ATCO 10-15 57
DECCA 10-20 50-53
JOSIE 15-20 54
JUBILEE 15-20 52
KAISER 15-20 56
SHARP 15-25 60

Members: Lester Harris; Herb Milliner.

RAYS

P&R/R&B '57

Singles: 78rpm

CAMEO 10-20 57-58
CHESS 10-20 55-57
XYZ (Except 100 & 102) 4-8 58-61
XYZ (100 "My Steady Girl") 10-20 57
XYZ (102 "Silhouettes") 10-20 57

Singles: 7-inch

ABKCO 3-4 80s
AMY 3-5 64
ARGO 3-5
CAMEO (117 "Silhouettes") 10-15 57
CAMEO (128 "Triangle") 15-20 58
CAMEO (133 "Rags to Riches") 15-25 57
CHESS (1613 "Tippity Top") 15-20 55
CHESS (1678 "Second Fiddle"). 15-25 57
PERRI (1004 "Are You Happy Now") 15-25 62
(With Frankie Valli.)
XYZ (100 "My Steady Girl") 35-45 57

XYZ (102 "Silhouettes")........... 75-100 57
(Gray label.)
XYZ (102 "Silhouettes")............. 30-40 57
(Blue label.)
XYZ (106 "Souvenirs of Summertime") 30-40 58
XYZ (600 "Why Do You Look the Other Way") 30-40 59
XYZ (605 "Mediterranean Moon")................................... 25-30 59
XYZ (607 "Magic Moon")........... 25-30 60
(Blue label.)
XYZ (607 "Magic Moon")........... 10-15 60
(Red label.)
XYZ (608 "Old Devil Moon")...... 10-15 60
XYZ (2001 "Souvenirs of Summertime") 25-35 58
(First issued in 1958 on XYZ 106.)

EPs: 7–inch 33/45rpm

CHESS (5120 "The Rays") 15-200 58

Members: Harold "Hal" Miller; Walter Ford; David Jones; Harry James.

RAYS

R&B '88

Singles: 7–inch

EMI MANHATTAN 3-4 87

RAZOR'S EDGE

P&R '66

Singles: 7–inch

POW.. 10-15 66-67
POWER (4932 "Get Yourself Together") 15-25 67

RAZZY: see BAILEY, Razzy

REA, Chris

P&R/LP '78

Singles: 7–inch

COLUMBIA 3-5 82
GEFFEN..................................... 3-4 89-90
MOTOWN 3-4 87
RCA.. 3-4 84
U.A. 3-5 78-79

Picture Sleeves

GEFFEN..................................... 3-4 89
MOTOWN 3-4 87
U.A. 3-5 78

LPs: 10/12–inch 33rpm

COLUMBIA 5-8 80-82
GEFFEN..................................... 5-8 89-90
RCA.. 5-8 84
U.A. 5-8 78

Also see WILLIE & Poor Boys

READ, John Dawson

P&R '75

Singles: 7–inch

CHRYSALIS............................... 3-5 75

LPs: 10/12–inch 33rpm

CHRYSALIS............................... 5-10 75-76

READY for the WORLD

R&B '84

Singles: 12–inch 33/45rpm

MCA..4-6 84-86

Singles: 7–inch

BLUE LAKE 4-6 84
MCA..3-4 84-87

Picture Sleeves

MCA..3-4 85-86

LPs: 10/12–inch 33rpm

MCA..5-8 86-88

REAL LIFE

P&R '83

Singles: 12–inch 33/45rpm

CURB/MCA...................................4-6 83-86

Singles: 7–inch

CURB/MCA...................................3-4 83-86

Picture Sleeves

CURB/MCA...................................3-4 84

LPs: 10/12–inch 33rpm

CURB/MCA...................................5-8 83-89

REAL ROXANNE
(With Hitman Howie Tee)

R&B '85

Singles: 12–inch 33/45rpm

SELECT 4-6 85-86

REAL THING

P&R/R&B '76

Singles: 12–inch 33/45rpm

BELIEVE in a DREAM 4-6 81
EPIC..4-8 79

Singles: 7–inch

BELIEVE in a DREAM 3-5 81
EPIC..3-5 79
U.A. 3-5 76-77
WHIZ...4-6 69

LPs: 10/12–inch 33rpm

U.A. 5-10 76

REAL to REEL

R&B/D&D '84

Singles: 12–inch 33/45rpm

ARISTA..4-6 83-84

Singles: 7–inch

ARISTA..3-4 83-84

LPs: 10/12–inch 33rpm

ARISTA..5-8 83

REAVES, Paulette

R&B '77

Singles: 7–inch

BLUE CANDLE.............................3-5 77-78

REBELS

P&R '62

Singles: 7–inch

MAR-LEE (0094 "Wild Weekend") 20-40 60
SWAN 10-15 62-63

Also see BUFFALO REBELS

Also see ROCKIN' REBELS

REBENNACK, Mac
(With the Soul Orchestra)

Singles: 7-inch

AFO (309 "The Point") 15-25 62
ACE (611 "Good Times") 15-25 61
REX (1008 "Storm Warning").... 30-50 59

Also see DR. JOHN

RECORD, Eugene

R&B '77

Singles: 12-inch 33/45rpm

W.B. 4-8 79

Singles: 7-inch

W.B. 3-5 77-79

LPs: 10/12-inch 33rpm

W.B. 5-10 77-79

Also see CHI-LITES

RECORDS

P&R/LP '79

Singles: 7-inch

VIRGIN.. 3-5 79-81

Picture Sleeves

VIRGIN.. 3-5 79-81

EPs: 7-inch 33/45rpm

VIRGIN.. 3-6 79

(Issued as a bonus with Virgin LP 13130, *The Records.*)

LPs: 10/12-inch 33rpm

VIRGIN.. 8-10 79-82

RED COATS with STEVE ALAIMO: see ALAIMO, Steve

RED FLAG

LP '89

LPs: 10/12-inch 33rpm

ENIGMA.. 5-8 89

RED HOT CHILI PEPPERS

LP '87

Singles: 12-inch 33/45rpm

EMI AMERICA 4-6 85

Singles: 7-inch

EMI AMERICA 3-4 84-85
W.B. 3-4 91

LPs: 10/12-inch 33rpm

EMI AMERICA 5-8 84-85
EMI MANHATTAN 5-8 87
W.B. 5-8 91

Members: Anthony Kiedis; Jack Irons; Hillel Slovak; Mike Balzary; John Frusciante; Chad Smith.

RED RIDER

P&R/LP '80

Singles: 7-inch

CAPITOL...................................... 3-5 80-86

Picture Sleeves

CAPITOL...................................... 3-5 80-84

LPs: 10/12-inch 33rpm

CAPITOL...................................... 5-10 80-86

Member: Tom Cochrane.

Also see COCHRANE, Tom

RED RIVER DAVE
(Dave McEnery)

P&R '60

Singles: 7-inch

COPYRIGHT.................................4-8 61
SAVOY...4-8 60-65

EPs: 7-inch 33/45rpm

VARSITY.....................................5-10

LPs: 10/12-inch 33rpm

BLUEBONNET.............................8-12 60s
CONTINENTAL..........................10-20 62
PLACE 10-15 60s
SUTTON 5-10

RED ROCKERS

P&R/D&D/LP '83

Singles: 12-inch 33/45rpm

COLUMBIA 4-6 83-85

Singles: 7-inch

COLUMBIA 3-4 83-85

LPs: 10/12-inch 33rpm

COLUMBIA 5-8 83

RED 7

LP '85

LPs: 10/12-inch 33rpm

MCA..5-8 85-87

RED SIREN

LP '89

LPs: 10/12-inch 33rpm

MERCURY...................................5-8 89

REDBONE

P&R/LP '70

Singles: 7-inch

EPIC..3-5 71-74
RCA 3-5 78

LPs: 10/12-inch 33rpm

ACCORD 5-10 82
EPIC..8-15 70-75
RCA 5-10 77

Members: Pat Vegas; Lolly Vegas.

REDBONE, Leon

LP '76

Singles: 78rpm

W.B. 5-10 78

(Promotional only.)

Singles: 7-inch

EMERALD CITY 3-8 81
W.B. 5-12 77-78

LPs: 10/12-inch 33rpm

ACCORD 10-15 82
EMERALD CITY 10-15 81
W.B. 15-30 77-78

REDD

R&B '87

Singles: 7-inch

RCA 3-4 87

REDD, Sharon

R&B '81

Singles: 12–inch 33/45rpm

PRELUDE 4-6 81-83

Singles: 7–inch

COLUMBIA 3-5 78
PRELUDE 3-5 81-83
VEEP 4-8 67

LPs: 10/12–inch 33rpm

COLUMBIA 5-10 78
PRELUDE 5-8 82

REDD, Sharon, Ula Hedwig & Charlotte Crossley

Singles: 7–inch

COLUMBIA 3-5 77-78
Also see MIDLER, Bette
Also see REDD, Sharon

REDD HOT
(Redd Hott)

R&B '81

Singles: 7–inch

VENTURE 3-5 81-82
Members: Kevin "Flash" Ferrell; Robert Parson; Daryl Simmons; Greg Russell; De Morris Smith.
Also see MANCHILD

REDDING, Gene

P&R/R&B '74

Singles: 7–inch

HAVEN 3-5 74

REDDING, Otis
(With the Pinetoppers; with Pinetones; with Shooters)

P&R/R&B '63

Singles: 7–inch

ATCO 5-8 68-71
BETHLEHEM (3083 "Shout Bamalama") 10-15 64
CONFEDERATE (135 "Shout Bamalama") 20-40 62
FINER ARTS (2016 "She's All Right") 30-50 61
(Previously issued as by the Shooters.)
KING (6149 "Shout Bamalama"). 5-10 68
ORBIT (135 "Shout Bamalama") 50-75 61
STONE (209 "You Left the Water Running") 4-8 76
VOLT (103 thru 121) 10-20 62-64
VOLT (124 thru 163) 10-15 65-68

EPs: 7–inch 33/45rpm

VOLT 20-30 66

LPs: 10/12–inch 33rpm

ATCO (33-161 "Pain in My Heart") 50-70 64
(Monaural.)
ATCO (SD-33-161 "Pain in My Heart") 60-80 64
(Stereo.)
ATCO (200 series) 10-15 68-69
ATCO (300 series) 8-12 70
ATCO (801 "Best of Otis Redding") 10-20 72
(Currently available with same selection number.)
ATLANTIC 5-10 82
VOLT (Except 411) 20-35 65-68
VOLT (411 "Soul Ballads") 35-55 65
(Monaural.)
VOLT (411 "Soul Ballads") 40-60 65
(Stereo.)
Members: Steve Cropper; Booker T. Jones; Isaac Hayes; Donald "Duck" Dunn; Lewis Steinberg; Al Jackson Jr. Session: Wayne Cochran; Johnny Jenkins; William Bell, Tommie Lee Williams; Veltones; Drapels.
Also see BAR-KAYS
Also see BOOKER T. & MGs
Also see COCHRAN, Wayne
Also see HAYES, Isaac
Also see SHOOTERS

REDDING, Otis / Little Joe Curtis

LPs: 10/12–inch 33rpm

ALSHIRE 8-12 68
SOMERSET 8-12 68

REDDING, Otis / Jimi Hendrix

LP '70

LPs: 10/12–inch 33rpm

REPRISE (2029 "Otis Redding/The Jimi Hendrix Experience") 10-15 70
REPRISE (93371 "Otis Redding/The Jimi Hendrix Experience") 15-20 70
(Same as 2029, but with different front cover. Disc reads "Music from the Monterey Pop Soundtrack.")
Also see HENDRIX, Jimi

REDDING, Otis / Carla Thomas / Sam & Dave / Eddie Floyd

LPs: 10/12–inch 33rpm

STAX (722 "Stax/Volt Revue, Vol. 2") 15-25 67
Also see FLOYD, Eddie
Also see OTIS & CARLA
Also see REDDING, Otis
Also see SAM & DAVE
Also see THOMAS, Carla

REDDINGS

P&R/R&B/LP '80

Singles: 12–inch 33/45rpm

BELIEVE in a DREAM 4-8 83

Singles: 7–inch

BELIEVE in a DREAM 3-5 80-83
POLYDOR 3-4 85-88

LPs: 10/12–inch 33rpm

BELIEVE in a DREAM 5-10 80-83
POLYDOR 5-8 85
Members: Otis Redding III; Dexter Redding; Mark Locket.

REDDS & BOYS

R&B '85

Singles: 7-inch

4TH & BROADWAY.......................3-5 85

REDDY, Helen

P&R/LP '71

Singles: 12-inch 33/45rpm

CAPITOL.......................4-6 79

Singles: 7-inch

CAPITOL.......................3-5 71-81
FONTANA.......................3-6 68
MCA.......................3-5 81-83

LPs: 10/12-inch 33rpm

CAPITOL.......................5-10 71-81
MCA.......................5-8 81-83
Also see PRESLEY, Elvis / Helen Reddy

REDEYE

P&R/LP '70

Singles: 7-inch

PENTAGRAM.......................3-5 70-71

LPs: 10/12-inch 33rpm

PENTAGRAM.......................10-15 70-71
Members: Doug "Red" Mark; David Hodkins; Bobby Bereman; Bill Kman.
Also see SUNSHINE COMPANY

REDJACKS

P&R '58

Singles: 7-inch

APT (25006 "Big Brown Eyes"). 10-15 58
OKLAHOMA (5005 "Big Brown Eyes").......................30-50 58

REDNOW, Eivets
(Stevie Wonder)

P&R '68

Singles: 7-inch

GORDY (7076 "Alfie").......................15-25 68

LPs: 10/12-inch 33rpm

GORDY (932 "Eivets Rednow") 25-35 68
Also see WONDER, Stevie

REDWAY, Michael
(Mike Redway)

P&R '73

Singles: 7-inch

LONDON.......................4-8 64
PHILIPS.......................3-5 73

REED, Clarence: see REID, Clarence

REED, Dan, Network

P&R/LP '88

Singles: 7-inch

MERCURY.......................3-4 88-89

Picture Sleeves

MERCURY.......................3-4 88

LPs: 10/12-inch 33rpm

MERCURY.......................5-8 88-89

REED, Dean

P&R '59

Singles: 7-inch

CAPITOL.......................8-12 59-61
IMPERIAL.......................5-10 61

REED, Denny

P&R '60

Singles: 7-inch

ASPIRE.......................3-5 77
DOT.......................4-8 62
MCI.......................10-20 60
TREY.......................10-15 60-61
TOWER.......................4-8 65
U.A.......................5-10 61

REED, Jerry
(With the Hully Girlies; with Seidina; with Friends)

P&R '62

Singles: 78rpm

CAPITOL.......................5-10 55-56

Singles: 7-inch

CAPITOL.......................10-20 55-56
COLUMBIA.......................5-10 61-63
NRC.......................5-10 59
RCA (Except 8500 thru 9700).......3-5 69-85
RCA (8500 thru 9700).......................4-8 65-69

Picture Sleeves

COLUMBIA.......................8-10 61
RCA.......................3-4 72-85

LPs: 10/12-inch 33rpm

CAMDEN.......................5-10 72-74
HARMONY.......................8-12 71
PICKWICK/HILLTOP.......................5-10
RCA (Except "LPM" & "LSP" series).......................5-10 73-83
RCA ("LPM" & "LSP" series).......8-18 67-73
Also see HART, Freddie / Sammi Smith / Jerry Reed
Also see JENNINGS, Waylon, & Jerry Reed
Also see JUSTIS, Bill / Jerry Reed
Also see NELSON, Willie
Also see PRESLEY, Elvis

REED, Jerry, & Chet Atkins

LPs: 10/12-inch 33rpm

RCA.......................8-12 72
Also see ATKINS, Chet
Also see REED, Jerry

REED, Jimmy

R&B '55

Singles: 78rpm

CHANCE (1142 "High and Lonesome").......................40-60 53
VEE JAY (100 thru 119).......................15-30 53-54
VEE JAY (132 thru 153).......................10-15 55
VEE JAY (168 thru 275).......................15-30 53-58

Singles: 7-inch

ABC.......................3-5 73
ABC-PAR.......................4-8 66
BLUESWAY.......................3-6 67
CANYON.......................3-6

CHANCE (1142 "High and Lonesome")........ 300-400 53
(Reissue of Vee Jay 100.)
COLLECTABLES........ 3-4 80s
EXODUS........ 4-8 66
OLDIES 45........ 4-6 64
TRIP........ 3-5 70s
VEE JAY (100 "High and Lonesome")........ 125-175 53
(Black vinyl.)
VEE JAY (100 "High and Lonesome")........ 250-350 53
(Colored vinyl.)
VEE JAY (105 "I Found My Baby")........ 100-150 53
(Black vinyl.)
VEE JAY (105 "I Found My Baby")........ 200-300 53
(Colored vinyl.)
VEE JAY (119 "You Don't Have to Go")........ 30-40 54
(Black vinyl.)
VEE JAY (119 "You Don't Have to Go")........ 200-300 54
(Colored vinyl.)
VEE JAY (132 "Pretty Thing")... 20-35 55
VEE JAY (153 "She Don't Want Me No More")........ 25-30 55
VEE JAY (168 thru 248)........ 10-20 56-57
VEE JAY (253 thru 298)........ 8-15 57-58
VEE JAY (314 thru 709)........ 4-8 59-65

LPs: 10/12-inch 33rpm

BLUES on BLUES........ 8-10
BLUESWAY........ 8-12 67-73
BUDDAH........ 10-15 69
EVEREST........ 5-10 69
EXODUS........ 10-15 66
GNP........ 8-10 74
KENT........ 8-12 69-71
ROKER........ 5-10
SUNSET........ 10-15 68
TRADITION........ 5-8
TRIP........ 8-10 71-78
VEE JAY (1004 "I'm Jimmy Reed")........ 75-125 58
(Maroon label.)
VEE JAY (1004 "I'm Jimmy Reed")........ 50-75 59
(Black label.)
VEE JAY (1008 "Rockin' with Reed")........ 60-100 59
(Maroon label.)
VEE JAY (1008 "Rockin' with Reed")........ 40-60 59
(Black label.)
VEE JAY (1022 "Found Love") . 25-50 60
VEE JAY (1025 "Now Appearing")........ 25-50 60
VEE JAY (1035 "At Carnegie Hall")........ 25-40 61
VEE JAY (1039 thru 1095)........ 20-40 62-64
VEE JAY (8501 "The Legend, the Man")........ 20-30 65
VERSATILE........ 8-10 78

Also see DIXON, Willie
Also see MAYFIELD, Curtis
Also see UPCHURCH, Phil

REED, Jimmy / Peppermint Harris

EPs: 7-inch 33/45rpm

LUNAR (2009 "Tells It Like It Is").5-10 81

Also see PEPPPERMINT HARRIS
Also see REED, Jimmy

REED, Lou

(With the Velvet Underground)

LP '72

Singles: 12-inch 33/45rpm

RCA........ 4-8 84

Singles: 7-inch

ARISTA........ 3-5 76
RCA........ 3-5 73-86

LPs: 10/12-inch 33rpm

ARISTA........ 5-10 76-80
PRIDE........ 8-12 73
RCA ("AFL1" series)........ 5-10 80-83
RCA ("ANL1" series)........ 5-10 77
RCA ("APL1" series)........ 6-12 73-77
RCA ("AYL1" series)........ 5-8 80-83
RCA ("CPL1" series)........ 8-12 74
RCA ("LSP" series)........ 8-12 72
SIRE........ 5-8 89-90

Also see DION
Also see VELVET UNDERGROUND

REED, Lou, & John Cale

LP '90

LP: 10/12-inch 33rpm

SIRE........ 5-8 90

Also see CALE, John
Also see REED, Lou

REED, Vivian

R&B '68

Singles: 7-inch

ATCO........ 3-5 73
EPIC........ 4-8 68-69
U.A........ 3-5 78-79

LPs: 10/12-inch 33rpm

EPIC........ 10-15 69
U.A........ 5-10 78

REESE, Della

(With the Meditation Singers)

P&R '57

Singles: 78rpm

JUBILEE........ 4-8 57

Singles: 7-inch

ABC........ 3-6 67-73
ABC-PAR........ 3-6 65-66
AVCO EMBASSY........ 3-6 69-72
CHI-SOUND........ 3-5 77

JUBILEE (5000 series)............... 5-10 57-59
(Monaural.)
JUBILEE (9007 "Stormy Weather")............................. 10-15 58
(Stereo.)
LMI 3-5 73
RCA.. 4-8 59-64
VIRGO... 3-5 72

Picture Sleeves

AVCO EMBASSY......................... 4-8 69-72
RCA.. 5-10 60-63

EPs: 7–inch 33/45rpm

RCA.. 10-15 61

LPs: 10/12–inch 33rpm

ABC 5-10 76
ABC-PAR 15-20 65-67
APPLAUSE 5-8 83
JUBILEE (1000 & 5000 series) . 20-30 57-63
JUBILEE (6000 series).............. 10-15 69
LMI 5-10 73
PICKWICK 5-8 78
RCA (2000 thru 4600 series) 10-25 60-72
SUNSET................................... 5-10 71

Also see ANN-MARGRET / Kitty Kalen / Della Reese

REEVES, Del
(With the Goodtime Charlies)

C&W '61

Singles: 7–inch

CHART 3-5 70
COLUMBIA 4-6 64
DECCA.. 4-8 61-62
KOALA 3-5 80-82
LAS VEGAS 5-10 59
PEACH....................................... 5-10 60
PLAYBACK 3-4 86
REPRISE 4-8 63
U.A. 3-6 66-78

Picture Sleeves

KOALA 3-4 80
U.A. 3-6 67

LPs: 10/12–inch 33rpm

KOALA 5-8 79-80
STARDAY 5-8
SUNSET.................................... 5-10 69-70
U.A. (200 thru 600 series).......... 5-10 73-76
U.A. (3000 & 6000 series)......... 10-20 65-71

REEVES, Del, & Penny DeHaven

C&W '72

Singles: 7–inch

U.A. 3-5 72

REEVES, Del, & Bobby Goldsboro

C&W '68

Singles: 7–inch

U.A. 3-6 65-71

LPs: 10/12–inch 33rpm

U.A. 10-20 68

Also see GOLDSBORO, Bobby

REEVES, Del / Red Sovine

LPs: 10/12–inch 33rpm

EXACT 5-8 80

Also see SOVINE, Red

REEVES, Del, & Billie Jo Spears

C&W '76

Singles: 7–inch

U.A. 3-5 76

LPs: 10/12–inch 33rpm

LIBERTY 5-8 82
U.A. 5-10 76

Also see REEVES, Del

REEVES, Dianne

R&B/LP '88

Singles: 7–inch

BLUE NOTE.....................................3-4 87

LPs: 10/12–inch 33rpm

BLUE NOTE.....................................5-8 88
EMI..5-8 90

REEVES, Jim
(With His Circle O Ranch Boys)

C&W '53

Singles: 78rpm

ABBOTT (Black plastic) 10-20 53-55
ABBOTT (Colored plastic) 20-40 53-55
MACY'S (115 "Teardrops of Regret")..............................150-250 50
MACY'S (132 "Never Been So Blue") 150-250 51
RCA 8-18 55-57

Singles: 7–inch

ABBOTT (100 series, except 116)..10-25 53-55
(Black vinyl.)
ABBOTT (115 "Wagon Load of Love")..15-25 53
(Black vinyl.)
ABBOTT (115 "Wagon Load of Love")..35-50 53
(Colored vinyl.)
ABBOTT (116 "Mexican Joe") ...15-25 53
(Black vinyl.)
ABBOTT (116 "Mexican Joe") ...35-50 53
(Colored vinyl.)
ABBOTT (137 "Butterfly Love")..15-25 53
(Black vinyl.)
ABBOTT (137 "Butterfly Love")..35-50 53
(Colored vinyl.)
ABBOTT (143 "El Rancho Del Rio")..15-25 53
(Black vinyl.)
ABBOTT (143 "El Rancho Del Rio")..35-50 53
(Colored vinyl.)
ABBOTT (148 "Bimbo") 15-25 53
(Black vinyl.)
ABBOTT (148 "Bimbo") 35-50 53
(Colored vinyl.)

ABBOTT (160 thru 186) 10-20 54-55
ABBOTT (3000 series)............. 10-20 55
ABBOTT (4000 series).................. 4-8
RCA (0135 thru 0963)................... 3-8 69-74
RCA (6200 thru 7557).............. 10-20 55-59
RCA (7643 "He'll Have to Go").... 5-10 59
RCA (7643 "He'll Have to Go")................................... 150-250 59
(Single-sided. Promotional issue only.)
RCA (7756 thru 9969)................ 4-10 60-71
RCA (10133 thru 13693).............. 3-6 75-84

Picture Sleeves

RCA (Except 8252) 8-15 60-65
RCA (8252 "Señor Santa Claus") 15-20 63

EPs: 7-inch 33/45rpm

RCA (Except 1256) 25-50 56-61
RCA (1256 "Singing Down the Lane")............................. 50-100 56
(Double EP set.)

LPs: 10/12-inch 33rpm

ABBOTT (5001 "Jim Reeves Sings")............................. 800-1200 56
CAMDEN (Except 583 thru 686). 5-15 64-73
CAMDEN (583 thru 686)........... 10-20 60-63
GUEST STAR 10-15 64
HISTORY of COUNTRY MUSIC. 6-10 72
PAIR... 6-12 82
PICKWICK 5-10 72
PICKWICK/HILLTOP 5-10 74
RCA (0039 thru 5044)................ 5-10 73-84
(With "AHL," "ANL," "APL," "AYL" or "CPL" prefix.)
RCA (0587 "Golden Collection") 30-35
(Special Products, five-LP set.)
RCA (LPM-1256 "Singing Down the Lane").......................... 100-200 56
RCA (LPM-1410 "Bimbo")....... 50-100 57
RCA (LPM-1576 "Jim Reeves") 40-60 57
RCA (LPM-1685 "Girls I Have Known")................................ 40-60 58
RCA (LPM-1950 "God Be with You") 25-35 58
(Monaural.)
RCA (LSP-1950 "God Be with You") 30-50 58
(Stereo.)
RCA (LPM-2001 thru LPM-2339) 15-30 59-61
(Monaural.)
RCA (LSP-2001 thru LSP-2339)............................ 20-40 59-61
(Stereo.)
RCA (LPM-2487 thru LPM-3903) 10-20 62-67
RCA (LSP-2487 thru LSP-3903) 12-25 62-67
RCA (LPM-3987 "A Touch of Sadness")............................. 40-50 68
(Monaural.)
RCA (LSP-3987 "A Touch of Sadness") 10-15 68
(Stereo.)
RCA (LSP-4062 thru LSP-4749)..8-15 68-72
READER'S DIGEST (210 "Unforgettable Jim Reeves") 40-50 76
(Six-LP set.)

Also see CRAMER, Floyd
Also see KERR, Anita
Also see PRESLEY, Elvis / Hank Snow / Eddy Arnold / Hank Snow

REEVES, Jim, & Deborah Allen

C&W '79

Singles: 7-inch

RCA 3-5 79-80

REEVES, Jim, & Patsy Cline

(Patsy Cline & Jim Reeves)

C&W '81

Singles: 7-inch

MCA...3-5 82
RCA 3-5 81

LPs: 10/12-inch 33rpm

MCA..5-10 82
RCA 5-10 81

Also see CLINE, Patsy

REEVES, Jim / Alvadean Coker

Singles: 78rpm

ABBOTT.................................10-20 54

Singles: 7-inch

ABBOTT.................................15-25 54

REEVES, Jim / Hugi & Lugi Chorus

Singles: 7-inch

U.S.A.F. (89 "In a Mansion Stands My Love") 20-30 60s
(Promotional issue only.)

REEVES, Jim, & Dottie West

Singles: 7-inch

RCA 4-6 64

Also see REEVES, Jim
Also see WEST, Dottie

REEVES, Martha

P&R/R&B '74

Singles: 12-inch 33/45rpm

FANTASY 4-8 78-79

Singles: 7-inch

ARISTA......................................3-5 75-77
FANTASY 3-4 78-80
MCA...3-4 74

LPs: 10/12-inch 33rpm

ARISTA......................................8-10 76
FANTASY 5-8 78-79
MCA..8-12 74
PHONORAMA 5-8

Also see MARTHA & VANDELLAS

REFLECTIONS

P&R '64

Singles: 7-inch

ABC-PAR (10794 "Like Adam and Eve") 15-25 66
ABC-PAR (10822 "You're Gonna Find Out You Need Me") 20-30 66
ERIC 3-4 70s
GOLDEN WORLD 8-15 64-65
KAY-KO (1003 "Helpless") 50-100 60s

LPs: 10/12-inch 33rpm

GOLDEN WORLD (300 "[Just Like] Romeo & Juliet") 40-60 64

Members: Tony Micale; John Dean; Phil Castrodale; Dan Bennie; Ray Steinberg.

REFLECTIONS

P&R/R&B '75

Singles: 7-inch

CAPITOL 3-5 75-76

Members: Herman Edwards; Josh Pridgen; Edmund "Butch" Simmons; John Simmons.

RE-FLEX

P&R/D&D/LP '83

Singles: 12-inch 33/45rpm

CAPITOL 4-6 83-84

Singles: 7-inch

CAPITOL 3-4 83-84

Picture Sleeves

CAPITOL 3-4 83-84

LPs: 10/12-inch 33rpm

CAPITOL 5-8 83

REGAL DEWY

R&B '77

Singles: 12-inch 33/45rpm

MILLENNIUM 8-10 77

Singles: 7-inch

MILLENNIUM 3-5 77

REGAN, Bob, & Lucille Starr

C&W '70

Singles: 7-inch

DOT 3-5 69

REGAN, Joan

P&R '53

Singles: 78rpm

LONDON 3-5 53-55

Singles: 7-inch

COLUMBIA 4-6 66
LONDON 5-10 53-55

Picture Sleeves

COLUMBIA 4-8 66

REGENTS

P&R/R&B '61

Singles: 7-inch

ABC 3-5 73
COUSINS (1002 "Barbara Ann") 200-250 61
GEE (1065 "Barbara Ann") 15-25 61
GEE (1071 "Runaround ") 20-25 61
GEE (1073 "Don't Be a Fool") 15-25 61
GEE (1075 "Lonesome Boy ") ... 15-25 62
ROULETTE 3-5 70s

LPs: 10/12-inch 33rpm

CAPITOL (KAO-2153 "Live at the AM-PM Discotheque") 35-45 64
(Monaural.)
CAPITOL (SKAO-2153 "Live at the AM-PM Discotheque") 45-55 64
(Stereo.)
EMUS 5-10 79
GEE (GLP-706 ("Barbara Ann") 75-100 61
(Monaural.)
GEE (SGLP-706 ("Barbara Ann") 100-125 61
(Stereo.)
MURRAY HILL 5-8 85

Members: Guy Villari; Sal Cuomo; Chuck Fassert; Don Jacobucci; Tony Gravagna.

REGINA

(Regina Richards)

P&R/R&B/LP '86

Singles: 7-inch

ATLANTIC 3-4 86

Picture Sleeves

ATLANTIC 3-4 86

LPs: 10/12-inch 33rpm

ATLANTIC 5-8 86

REID, Clarence

(Clarence Reed)

P&R/R&B '69

Singles: 7-inch

ALSTON 4-8 68-74
DEEP CITY 10-20 60s
DIAL 8-12 64
PHIL-L.A. of SOUL 5-10 67
SELMA 10-20 63
TAY-STER 5-10 67
WAND (1106 "Somebody Will") . 10-20 65
WAND (1121 "I'm Your Yes Man") 20-30 65

LPs: 10/12-inch 33rpm

ATCO (307 "Dancin' with Nobody But You Babe") 15-25 69

REID, Terry

LP '68

Singles: 7-inch

ATLANTIC 3-5 73
CAPITOL 3-5 78
EPIC 4-6 69

LPs: 10/12-inch 33rpm

ATLANTIC 8-12 73
CAPITOL 5-10 78
EPIC 10-15 68-69

REILLY, Mike

P&R '71

Singles: 7–inch

PARAMOUNT 3-5 70-71

REINER, Carl, & Mel Brooks

LP '73

LPs: 10/12–inch 33rpm

CAPITOL (1600 series)............ 15-25 61
CAPITOL (2900 series)............ 10-15 68
W.B. (2741 "2000 & Thirteen").... 5-10 73
W.B. (2744 "2000 Years with Carl Reiner & Mel Brooks").......................... 15-25 73
(Three-LP set.)
WORLD PACIFIC (1401 "2000 Years with Carl Reiner & Mel Brooks")..... 25-35 60

REIRRUC, Det: see DET REIRRUC

REISMAN, Joe, & His Orchestra

P&R '56

Singles: 78rpm

RCA.. 3-4 55-57

Singles: 7–inch

LANDA 4-6 61
RCA... 4-8 55-59
ROULETTE 4-6 59-60

EPs: 7–inch 33/45rpm

RCA.. 5-10 56

LPs: 10/12–inch 33rpm

CAMDEN.................................... 5-10 72
RCA... 10-20 56
ROULETTE 10-15 59-60

Also see VALLI, June

REJOICE

P&R '68

Singles: 7–inch

DUNHILL.................................... 4-6 68-69

LPs: 10/12–inch 33rpm

DUNHILL.................................. 10-15 69

Members: Tom Brown; Nancy Brown.

REMBRANDTS

LP '91

LPs: 10/12–inch 33rpm

ATCO 5-8 90

RENAISSANCE

LP '73

Singles: 7–inch

CAPITOL.................................... 3-5 72-73
SIRE.. 3-5 76-78

LPs: 10/12–inch 33rpm

CAPITOL.................................... 8-12 72-78
ELEKTRA (74068 "Renaissance") 15-25 69
I.R.S. 5-8 81-83
MFSL...................................... 20-40 82
SIRE... 8-10 74-79
SINGCORD............................... 8-10 76-77
SOVEREIGN............................... 8-12 73

Members: John Tout, Mike Dunford; Jim McCarty; Annie Haslam; Keith Relf; Jon Camp; Terry Sullivan, Louis Cennamo; Jane Relf.

Also see ARMAGEDDON
Also see HASLAM, Annie
Also see RELF, Keith

RENAISSANCE

LP '71

Singles: 7–inch

RANWOOD.................................3-5 71

LPs: 10/12–inch 33rpm

RANWOOD...............................5-10 70

RENARD, Jacques, & Orchestra

P&R '30

Singles: 78rpm

BRUNSWICK...............................3-8 30-45

RENAY, Diane

P&R/LP '64

Singles: 7–inch

ATCO 5-10 62-63
D MAN (101 "Can't Help Lovin'")15-25
DICE (8018 "Navy Blue")..........15-20 87
ERIC 3-4 70s
FONTANA...................................5-10 69
MGM (13335 "I Had a Dream")..10-20 64
NEW VOICE 5-10 65
REX (293 "Maybe")..................15-25
20TH FOX...................................5-10 64
U.A. (50048 "Please Gypsy").....10-15 66

LPs: 10/12–inch 33rpm

20TH FOX (TF-3133 "Navy Blue") 25-40 64
(Monaural.)
20TH FOX (TFS-3133 "Navy Blue") 30-50 64
(Stereo.)

RENDER, Rudy

R&B '49

Singles: 78rpm

LONDON....................................4-6 49-51

Singles: 7–inch

DOT 4-8 60-61
EDISON INT'L.............................4-8 59
LONDON....................................5-10 51

RENE, Delia

R&B '81

Singles: 7–inch

AIRWAVE 3-5 81

RENE, Googie

R&B '60

Singles: 78rpm

CLASS 4-8 57-58

Singles: 7–inch

CLASS 4-8 57-66
KAPP 4-6 62
NEW BAG 4-6 67
REED 5-10 60
RENDEZVOUS 4-8 60

Picture Sleeves

RENDEZVOUS 5-10 60

LPs: 10/12-inch 33rpm

CLASS 15-25 59-63

RENE, Henri, & His Orchestra

P&R '40

Singles: 78rpm

RCA 3-5 48-56
STANDARD 3-5 52-53
VICTOR 3-6 40-47

Singles: 7-inch

DECCA 3-6 62
IMPERIAL 4-8 59
RCA 4-8 51-56
STANDARD 4-8 52-53

Picture Sleeves

RCA 5-10 55

EPs: 7-inch 33/45rpm

CAMDEN 5-10 54-57
RCA 5-10 53-56

LPs: 10/12-inch 33rpm

CAMDEN 10-20 54-57
KAPP 5-10 67
RCA (Except 3000 series) 10-20 56-61
RCA (3000 series) 15-25 53
(10-inch LPs.)
Also see BELL SISTERS

RENE & ANGELA

R&B '80

Singles: 12-inch 33/45rpm

MERCURY 4-6 85-86

Singles: 7-inch

CAPITOL 3-5 80-83
MERCURY 3-4 85-86

Picture Sleeves

MERCURY 3-4 85-86

LPs: 10/12-inch 33rpm

CAPITOL 5-10 80-83
MERCURY 5-8 85-86

RENE & RAY

P&R '62

Singles: 7-inch

DONNA 5-10 62

RENE & RENE

P&R '64

Singles: 7-inch

ABC 3-5 73
ABC-PAR 4-8 65
ARU 4-8 64
CERTRON 3-5 71
COBRA 4-8 65
COLUMBIA 4-8 64
EPIC 3-6 69
FALCON 4-8 68
JOX 8-10 64-66
WHITE WHALE 3-6 68-69

Picture Sleeves

COLUMBIA 8-12 64

LPs: 10/12-inch 33rpm

CERTRON 8-10 70
EPIC 10-15 69
WHITE WHALE 10-15 68
Members: Rene Ornelas; J. Ramirez.

RENFRO, Anthony C., Orchestra

R&B '76

Singles: 7-inch

RENFRO 3-5 76

RENO, Mike, & Ann Wilson

P&R '84

Singles: 7-inch

COLUMBIA 3-4 84

Picture Sleeves

COLUMBIA 3-4 84
Also see LOVERBOY
Also see WILSON, Ann

RENRUT, Icky
(Ike Turner)

Singles: 7-inch

STEVENS (104 "Jack Rabbit") 25-35 59
STEVENS (107 "Hey - Hey") 25-35 59
Also see TURNER, Ike

REO, Diamond: see DIAMOND REO

REPARATA
(With the Delrons; Mary Aiese)

P&R '65

Singles: 7-inch

BIG TREE 4-6 71
KAPP 5-10 69-70
LAURIE 4-6 72
MALA 5-10 67-68
NORTH AMERICAN MUSIC 4-6 74
POLYDOR 4-6 75
RCA 10-15 65-67
WORLD ARTISTS 5-10 64-65

LPs: 10/12-inch 33rpm

AVCO EMBASSY 10-20 70
WORLD ARTISTS (3006 "Whenever a Teenager Cries") 40-60 65
Members: Mary Aiese; Sheila Reillie; Carol Drobnicki; Nanette Licari; Lorraine Mazzola; Cookie Sirico.

REPLACEMENTS

LP '86

Singles: 7-inch

SIRE 3-5 85-90
TWIN TONE 3-5 82-84

Picture Sleeves

SIRE 3-5 89

LPs: 10/12-inch 33rpm

SIRE 5-10 85-90
TWIN/TONE 5-10 84

Promotional LPs

SIRE ("Interview with Paul Westerberg") 20-25 85

Members: Paul Westerberg; Tom Stinson; Chris Mars.

RESTIVO, Johnny

P&R '59

Singles: 7-inch

EPIC (9537 "My Reputation")...... 8-10 62
RCA (Except 7559) 5-10 60
(Monaural.)
RCA (47-7559 "The Shape I'm In").. 5-10 59
(Monaural.)
RCA (61-7559 "The Shape I'm In").. 15-25 59
(Stereo.)
20TH FOX...................................... 8-12 61

Picture Sleeves

RCA (7559 "The Shape I'm In") 10-20 59
20TH FOX...................................... 10-20 61

LPs: 10/12-inch 33rpm

RCA (LPM-2149 "Oh Johnny").. 25-35 59
(Monaural.)
RCA (LSP-2149 "Oh Johnny") .. 40-50 59
(Stereo.)
Session: King Curtis.
Also see KING CURTIS

RESTLESS HEART

C&W '85

Singles: 7-inch

RCA.. 3-4 85-91

LPs: 10/12-inch 33rpm

RCA.. 5-8 85-91

RETURN to FOREVER

LP '73

Singles: 7-inch

COLUMBIA 3-5 77-79
POLYDOR.................................... 3-5 75

LPs: 10/12-inch 33rpm

COLUMBIA 5-10 76-79
ECM 8-10 75
POLYDOR.................................... 8-12 73-75
Members: Chick Corea; Lenny White; Stanley Clarke; Al DiMeola.
Also see CLARKE, Stanely
Also see COREA, Chick
Also see DI MEOLA, Al
Also see WHITE, Lenny

REUNION

P&R '74

Singles: 7-inch

MR. G.. 4-8 68
RCA.. 3-5 74-75
Also see OHIO EXPRESS

REVELATION

P&R/R&B '76

Singles: 7-inch

COMBINE 4-8 67
HANDSHAKE.................................. 3-5 80-82
MERCURY 3-5 70
MUSIC FACTORY 4-8 68
RCA 3-5 79
RSO 3-5 76

LPs: 10/12-inch 33rpm

HANDSHAKE.................................5-10 82
MERCURY.....................................8-12 70
RCA 5-10 79

REVELS

P&R/R&B '59

Singles: 7-inch

NORGOLDE (103 "Dead Man's Stroll")......................................30-50 59
NORGOLDE (103 "Midnight Stroll")......................................10-15 59
NORGOLDE (104 "Foo Man Choo")..10-20 59

REVENGE

LP '90

LPs: 10/12-inch 33rpm

CAPITOL...5-8 90

REVERBERI

LP '76

Singles: 7-inch

U.A. 3-5 77

LP: 10/12-inch 33rpm

U.A. 5-10 76

REVERE, Paul, & Raiders
(Featuring Mark Lindsay; Raiders)

P&R '61

Singles: 7-inch

COLUMBIA (10000 series)............3-5 75
COLUMBIA (42814 thru 42373)...5-10 63-65
COLUMBIA (43375 "Steppin' Out")..4-8 65
(Black vinyl.)
COLUMBIA (43375 "Steppin' Out")..15-25 65
(Colored vinyl. Promotional issue only.)
COLUMBIA (43461 "Just Like Me") 4-8 65
(Black vinyl.)
COLUMBIA (43461 "Just Like Me") 15-25 65
(Colored vinyl. Promotional issue only.)
COLUMBIA (43556 "Kicks")...........4-8 66
(Black vinyl.)
COLUMBIA (43556 "Kicks").......15-25 66
(Colored vinyl. Promotional issue only.)
COLUMBIA (43678 "Hungry")........4-8 66
(Black vinyl.)
COLUMBIA (43678 "Hungry").... 15-25 66
(Colored vinyl. Promotional issue only.)
COLUMBIA (43810 "The Great Airplane Strike")...........................4-8 66
(Black vinyl.)
COLUMBIA (43810 "The Great Airplane Strike")........................15-25 66
(Colored vinyl. Promotional issue only.)

COLUMBIA (43907 "Good Thing") 4-8 67
(Black vinyl.)
COLUMBIA (43907 "Good Thing") 15-25 67
(Colored vinyl. Promotional issue only.)
COLUMBIA (44018 thru 45898) 3-6 68-73
COLUMBIA (105499 "SS 396"/"Corvair Baby") 8-12 66
(Promotional issue only.)
DRIVE 3-5 76
GARDENA 15-25 60-62
JERDEN (807 "So Fine") 10-15 66
RAIDER 5-10 82
SANDE (101 "Louie Louie") 25-35 63
20TH FOX 3-5 76

Picture Sleeves

COLUMBIA 6-12 66-69

EPs: 7–inch 33/45rpm

JERDEN (JRLS-7004 "In the Beginning") 35-45 66
(Jukebox issue only. Includes title strips.)

LPs: 10/12–inch 33rpm

BACK-TRAC 5-8 85
COLUMBIA (12 "Two Great Selling LPs") 15-20 69
COLUMBIA (462 "Greatest Hits") 20-25 67
COLUMBIA (2307 thru 2721) 20-30 65-67
(Monaural.)
COLUMBIA (2755 "Christmas Present and Past") 40-60 67
(Monaural.)
COLUMBIA (2805 "Goin' to Memphis") 20-30 68
(Monaural.)
COLUMBIA (9107 thru 9521) 25-40 65-67
(Stereo.)
COLUMBIA (9555 "Christmas Present and Past") 40-60 67
(Stereo.)
COLUMBIA (9605 "Goin' to Memphis") 20-25 68
(Stereo.)
COLUMBIA (9665 thru 9964) 10-20 68-70
COLUMBIA (30000 series) 8-15 71-76
COLUMBIA SPECIAL PROD. (141714 "The Judge") 150-200 60s
(Promotional issue only.)
HARMONY 10-15 70-72
GARDENA (1000 "Like Long Hair") 250-300 61
JERDEN (7004 "In the Beginning") 75-125 66
PICKWICK 10-15 70s
RAIDER 10-15 82
SANDE (1001 "Paul Revere and the Raiders") 250-300 63
SEARS 40-50
(Special Products Sears promotional issue.)

Members: Mark Lindsay; Freddy Weller; Paul Revere; Keith Allison; Joe Correro Jr; Carl Driggs; Omar Martinez; Doug Heath; Ron Foos; Danny Krause; Mike Smith; Drake Levin; Philip Volk.

Also see BROTHERHOOD
Also see CYRKLE / Paul Revere & Raiders
Also see LINDSAY, Mark
Also see MIKE & DEAN
Also see WELLER, Freddy

REX, T.: see T REX

REYNOLDS, Burt

C&W/P&R '80

Singles: 7–inch

MCA 3-5 80
MERCURY 3-5 73-74

Picture Sleeves

MCA 3-5 80

LPs: 10/12–inch 33rpm

MERCURY 8-12 73

REYNOLDS, Debbie

P&R '57

Singles: 78rpm

CORAL 4-6 57
MGM 4-6 55-59

Singles: 7–inch

ABC 3-5 74
ABC-PAR 4-8 65
BEVERLY HILLS 3-5 72
CORAL 5-10 57-58
DOT 4-8 59-63
JANUS 3-5 70
MCA 3-4 80s
MGM (11000 & 12000 series) 5-10 55-59
MGM (13000 series) 4-8 63-66
PARAMOUNT 3-5 73

Picture Sleeves

DOT 5-10 60
MGM 8-15 58-66

EPs: 7–inch 33/45rpm

CORAL 10-20 58
MGM 10-20 55

LPs: 10/12–inch 33rpm

DOT (Except 25295) 15-20 59-63
DOT (25295 "Am I That Easy to Forget") 15-25 60
(Black vinyl.
DOT (25295 "Am I That Easy to Forget") 35-45 60
(Colored vinyl.
MGM 12-25 60-66
METRO 10-15 65

Also see CARPENTER, Carleton, & Debbie Reynolds
Also see FISHER, Eddie, & Debbie Reynolds

REYNOLDS, Jeannie

R&B '75

Singles: 7–inch

CASABLANCA 3-5 75

REYNOLDS, Jody

P&R/R&B '58

Singles: 78rpm

DEMON (1507 "Endless Sleep") 15-25 58

Singles: 7-inch

ABC 3-5 73
BRENT 4-8 63
COLLECTABLES 3-4 80s
DEMON 10-20 58-59
PULSAR 3-6 69
SMASH 4-8 63
TITAN 4-8 66

LPs: 10/12-inch 33rpm

TRU-GEMS 8-10 78

Also see CASEY, Al
Also see CLARK, Sanford

REYNOLDS, Jody, & Bobbie Gentry

Singles: 7-inch

TITAN 4-8 67

Also see GENTRY, Bobbie

REYNOLDS, Jody / Olympics

Singles: 7-inch

DEMON 10-20 58
LIBERTY 4-8 63
TITAN 4-8 62

Picture Sleeves

DEMON (1801 "Endless Sleep") 15-25 58

Also see OLYMPICS

REYNOLDS, Jody, & Storms

INDIGO (127 "Thunder"/ "Tarantula") 15-25 61
(Remake of both sides of Sundown 114, shown as by the Storms.)

Also see CASEY, Al
Also see REYNOLDS, Jody
Also see STORMS

REYNOLDS, L.J.

(With Chocolate Syrup)

R&B '71

Singles: 12-inch 33/45rpm

CAPITOL 4-6 82

Singles: 7-inch

CAPITOL 3-5 81-82
FANTASY 3-4 85-87
LAW-TON 3-5 71-72
MAINSTREAM 4-6 69
MERCURY 3-4 84

LPs: 10/12-inch 33rpm

CAPITOL 5-10 81-82
MERCURY 5-8 84

Also see CHOCOLATE SYRUP
Also see DRAMATICS

REYNOLDS, Lawrence

P&R '69

Singles: 7-inch

COLUMBIA 3-5 72
W.B. 3-6 69-70

LPs: 10/12-inch 33rpm

W.B. 8-12 69

RHEIMS, Robert

(Robert Rheims Carrolers)

LP '59

Singles: 7-inch

RHEIMS 3-5 59

EPs: 7-inch 33/45rpm

RHEIMS 4-8 59

LPs: 10/12-inch 33rpm

MISTLETOE 5-8 75
RHEIMS 5-15 58-63
U.A. 5-8 72-74

RHINOCEROS

LP '68

Singles: 7-inch

ELEKTRA 4-6 69-70

LPs: 10/12-inch 33rpm

ELEKTRA 10-20 68-70

Members: Alan Gerber; Billy Mundi; Michael Fonfara; John Finley, Danny Weis, Jerry Penrod; Peter Hodgson.
Also see EARTH OPERA

RHODES, Emitt

LP '70

Singles: 7-inch

DUNHILL 3-5 70-73

LPs: 10/12-inch 33rpm

A&M 10-15 70
DUNHILL 8-12 70-73

Also see MERRY-GO-ROUND

RHODES, Todd

R&B '48

Singles: 78rpm

KING 5-10 48-54
MODERN 5-10 49
SENSATION (Except 6) 10-20 47-49
SENSATION (6 "Blues for the Red Boy") 25-35 47
VITACOUSTIC 10-20 47

Singles: 7-inch

KING (4469 "Gin Gin Gin") 50-75 51
KING (4486 "Good Man") 30-50 51
KING (4509 "Your Daddy's Doggin' Around") 30-50 51
(Black vinyl.)
KING (4509 "Your Daddy's Doggin' Around") 60-80 51
(Colored vinyl.)
KING (4528 "Rocket 69") 60-80 52
KING (4556 thru 4601) 15-25 52-53
(Lavern Baker is the vocalist on one side of each of the four King issues in the 4556-4601 series)
KING (4648 thru 4775) 10-20 53-54

EPs: 7-inch 33/45rpm

KING 30-40 52-54

LPs: 10/12–inch 33rpm

KING (88 "Todd Rhodes Plays the Hits") 75-100 53
KING (658 "Dance Music")........ 35-55 60
Also see BAKER, Lavern
Also see BARTHOLOMEW, Dave

RHYTHM

R&B '76

Singles: 7–inch

POLYDOR.......... 3-5 76

RHYTHM CORPS

LP '88

LPs: 10/12–inch 33rpm

PASHA.......... 5-8 88

RHYTHM HERITAGE

P&R/R&B '75

Singles: 12–inch 33/45rpm

ABC.......... 4-8 78

Singles: 7–inch

ABC.......... 3-5 75-78

LPs: 10/12–inch 33rpm

ABC.......... 5-10 76-77
Members: Steve Barri; Mike Omartian; Luther Waters.

RHYTHM MAKERS

R&B '76

Singles: 7–inch

VIGOR.......... 3-5 76

LPs: 10/12–inch 33rpm

VIGOR.......... 8-10 76

RHYZE

R&B '80

Singles: 7–inch

SAM 3-5 80
20TH FOX.......... 3-5 81

LPs: 10/12–inch 33rpm

20TH FOX.......... 5-10 81

RIBBONS

P&R '63

Singles: 7–inch

ERA.......... 3-5 72
MARSH 10-15 63
PARKWAY 5-10 64

RIBEIRO, Alfonso

R&B '85

Singles: 7–inch

PRISM.......... 3-4 85

RICE, Mack
(Sir Mack Rice)

R&B '65

Singles: 7–inch

ATCO 3-6 69
BLUE ROCK 4-8 65
LUPINE 4-8 64
MERCURY.......... 4-8 66
STAX.......... 3-6 67-78
Also see FALCONS

RICE, Sir Mack: see RICE, Mack

RICH, Buddy
(Buddy Rich Band)

LP '66

Singles: 78rpm

CLEF.......... 4-8 54
NORGRAN.......... 4-8 55-56

Singles: 7-Inch

ARGO 4-8 61
CLEF.......... 5-10 54
EVEREST 3-5 71
GROOVE MERCHANT.......... 3-5 74
MCA.......... 3-4 81
NORGRAN.......... 5-10 55-56
PACIFIC JAZZ 3-6 66-67
RCA 3-5 76

EPs: 7-Inch 33/45rpm

NORGRAN.......... 20-40 54-56

LPs: 10/12-Inch 33rpm

ARGO (676 "Playtime").......... 35-45 61
CLEF (684 "Gene Krupa & Buddy Rich").......... 100-150 56
EMARCY.......... 10-20 65-76
GREAT AMERICAN.......... 5-8 78
GROOVE MERCHANT.......... 5-10 74-75
GRYPHON.......... 5-10 79
LIBERTY 8-12 70
MCA.......... 5-8 81
MERCURY (126 "Buddy Rich Story").......... 10-20 69
MERCURY (20448 "Rich vs. Roach") 50-75 59
(Monaural.)
MERCURY (20451 "Richcraft").. 50-75 60
(Monaural.)
MERCURY (20461 "The Voice Is Rich") 40-60 60
(Monaural.)
MERCURY (60133 "Rich vs. Roach").......... 60-85 59
(Stereo.)
MERCURY (60136 "Richcraft").. 60-85 60
(Stereo.)
MERCURY (60144 "The Voice Is Rich") 45-65 60
(Stereo.)
NORGRAN (26 "Swingin'") 75-125 54
NORGRAN (1031 "Sing and Swing").......... 60-80 55
NORGRAN (1038 "Buddy Rich and Sweets Edison").......... 60-80 55
NORGRAN (1052 "Swingin'") 60-80 55
NORGRAN (1078 "Wailin'") 50-75 56
NORGRAN (1086 "One for Basie") 50-75 56
PACIFIC JAZZ (Except 10000 series).......... 8-18 66-70
PACIFIC JAZZ (10000 series)....... 5-8 81

PAUSA 5-8 80s
RCA 8-12 72-77
ROOST 10-20 66
TRIP 8-10 76
VSP 10-15 67
VERVE (2009 "Buddy Rich Sings Johnny Mercer") 50-75 57
VERVE (8129 "Buddy Rich and Sweets Edison") 50-75 57
VERVE (8142 "Swingin'") 50-75 57
VERVE (8168 "Wailin'") 50-75 57
VERVE (8176 "One for Basie") . 50-75 57
VERVE (8285 "In Miami") 50-75 58
VERVE (8425 "Blue Caravan") . 30-40 62
VERVE (8471 "Burnin' Beat") 30-40 62
(Monaural.)
VERVE (8484 "Drum Battle: Gene Krupa & Buddy Rich") 25-40 62
VERVE (68471 "Burnin' Beat") 35-45 62
(Stereo.)
VERVE (68778 "Super Rich") ... 10-15 69
VERVE (68824 "Monster") 10-15 73
WHO'S WHO in JAZZ 5-10 78
WING 8-12 69
WORLD PACIFIC 10-15 68
Also see DAVIS, Sammy, Jr., & Buddy Rich
Also see TORME, Mel

RICH, Buddy, & Max Roach

LPs: 10/12-Inch 33rpm

MERCURY 5-10 81
Also see RICH, Buddy

RICH, Charlie

P&R '60

Singles: 7-inch

ARISTA 3-5 80
COLUMBIA 3-4 82
EPIC 3-5 70-81
ELEKTRA 3-5 78-81
GROOVE 4-8 63-64
HI 4-8 66-67
MERCURY 3-5 73-74
PHILLIPS INT'L 10-20 59-63
RCA (Except 8000 series) 3-5 74-77
RCA (8000 series) 4-8 64-65
SSS/SUN 3-5 70s
SMASH 4-8 65-66
U.A. 3-5 78-80

Picture Sleeves

GROOVE (0020 "She Loved Everybody But Me") 10-20 63

EPs: 7-inch 33/45rpm

EPIC (1099 "Silver Linings") 8-12 76
(Promotional issue only.)

LPs: 10/12-inch 33rpm

BUCKBOARD 8-10 70s
CAMDEN 8-10 70-74
EPIC (Except 139) 6-12 68-78
EPIC (139 "Everything You Wanted to Hear") 15-20 76
(Promotional issue only.)
ELEKTRA 5-10 80
51 WEST 5-10
GROOVE (G-1000 "Charlie Rich") 25-50 64
(Monaural.)
GROOVE (GS-1000 "Charlie Rich") 35-60 64
(Stereo.)
HARMONY 8-10 73
HI (Except 32037) 8-10 74-77
HI (32037 "Charlie Rich") 15-25 67
HILLTOP 8-10 70s
MERCURY 10-15 74
PHILLIPS INT'L (1970 "Lonely Weekends") 400-600 60
PHONORAMA 5-8
POWER PAK 8-10 74
RCA (Except 3000 series) 8-10 73-77
RCA (3000 series) 15-25 65-66
SSS/SUN 5-10 69-79
SMASH 15-25 65-66
TIME-LIFE 5-10 81
TRIP 8-10 74
U.A. 5-10 78-79
WING 10-15 69
Session: Jordanaires; David Wills; Anita Kerr Singers.
Also see CASH, Johnny
Also see KERR, Anita
Also see LEWIS, Jerry Lee, Carl Perkins & Charlie Rich
Also see SHERIDAN, Bobby

RICH, Charlie, & Janie Fricke

C&W '78

Singles: 7-inch

EPIC 3-5 78
Also see RICH, Charlie

RICHARD, Cliff

(With the Drifters; with Shadows)

P&R '59

Singles: 12-inch 33/45rpm

EMI AMERICA 4-8 83

Singles: 7-inch

ABC-PAR 10-15 59-61
BIG TOP 4-8 62
CAPITOL 10-15 59
DOT 4-8 62
EMI AMERICA 3-5 79-84
EPIC 4-8 63-67
MONUMENT 3-5 70-72
ROCKET 3-5 76-79
SIRE 3-5 73
UNI 4-6 68-69
W.B. 4-6 69

Picture Sleeves

EMI AMERICA 3-5 80-81
EPIC 8-15 63-66

LPs: 10/12-inch 33rpm

ABC-PAR (ABC-321 "Cliff Sings") 25-35 60
(Monaural.)
ABC-PAR (ABCS-321 "Cliff Sings") 35-45 60
(Stereo.)
ABC-PAR (ABC-391 "Listen to Cliff") 25-35 61
(Monaural.)
ABC-PAR (ABCS-391 "Listen to Cliff") 35-45 61
(Stereo.)
EMI AMERICA 5-10 79-83
EPIC 15-25 63-65
ROCKET 5-10 76-78
Also see NEWTON-JOHN, Olivia, & Electric Light Orchestra
Also see NEWTON-JOHN, Olivia, & Cliff Richard

RICHARD, Little: see LITTLE RICHARD

RICHARD & YOUNG LIONS

P&R '66

Singles: 7-inch

PHILIPS 4-8 66-67

Picture Sleeves

PHILIPS 10-20 66
Member: Richard Bloodworth.

RICHARDS, Diane

R&B '83

Singles: 7-inch

ZOO YORK 3-4 83

RICHARDS, Keith

LP '88

Singles: 7-inch

ROLLING STONES (316 "Before They Make Me Run") 5-10 78
ROLLING STONES (39311 "Run Rudolph, Run") 4-6 79

Picture Sleeves

ROLLING STONES (316 "Before They Make Me Run") 10-15 78

LPs: 10/12-inch 33rpm

VIRGIN 5-8 88
Also see ROLLING STONES

RICHARDS, Turley
(Richard Turley)

P&R '70

Singles: 7-inch

ATLANTIC 3-5 80
COLUMBIA 4-8 66-67
EPIC 3-5 76-78
KAPP 4-8 68
MGM 4-8 64
20TH FOX 4-8 65
W.B. 3-5 70

Picture Sleeves

COLUMBIA 4-8 66

LPs: 10/12-inch 33rpm

ATLANTIC 5-10 80
EPIC 5-10 76
20TH FOX 10-20 65
W.B. 10-15 70-71

RICHARDSON, Jape
(With His Japettes)

Singles: 78rpm

MERCURY 10-20 57

Singles: 7-inch

MERCURY (71219 "Beggar to a King") 15-25 57
MERCURY (71312 "Teenage Moon") 10-20 58
Also see BIG BOPPER

RICHIE, Lionel

P&R/R&B/LP '82

Singles: 12-inch 33/45rpm

MOTOWN 4-8 83-86

Singles: 7-inch

MOTOWN 3-4 82-87

Picture Sleeves

MOTOWN 3-4 83-87

LPs: 10/12-inch 33rpm

MOTOWN 5-8 82-86
Also see COMMODORES
Also see ROSS, Diana, & Lionel Ritchie
Also see U.S.A. for AFRICA

RICHIE, Lionel, & Alabama

C&W '86

Singles: 12-inch 33/45rpm

MOTOWN (195 "Special Motown Service to Country Radio") 8-12 86
(Promotional issue only.)

Singles: 7-inch

MOTOWN 3-4 86
Also see ALABAMA
Also see RICHIE, Lionel

RICHIE'S ROOM 222 GANG

R&B '71

Singles: 7-inch

SCEPTER 3-5 71

RICHMOND EXTENSION

R&B '74

Singles: 7-inch

SILVER BLUE 3-5 74

RICK & Cast of Idoits: see DEES, Rick

RICK & KEENS

P&R '61

Singles: 7-inch

AUSTIN (303 "Peanuts") 35-50 61
JAMIE (1219 "Your Turn to Cry") 10-15 62
LE CAM (721 "Peanuts") 25-35 61
LE CAM (133 "Darla") 15-25 61
SMASH (1705 "Peanuts") 10-15 61
TOLLIE (9016 "Darla") 10-15 64

TROY 20-30 63

RICKLES, Don

LP '68

LPs: 10/12-inch 33rpm

W.B. 8-12 68-69

RIDDLE, Nelson, & His Orchestra

P&R '54

Singles: 78rpm

CAPITOL.................................... 3-5 53-57

Singles: 7-inch

CAPITOL.................................... 3-8 53-62
EPIC.................................... 3-6 67
LIBERTY.................................... 3-6 67
REPRISE.................................... 3-6 63-66
20TH FOX.................................... 3-6 66
VERVE.................................... 4-8 59

Picture Sleeves

CAPITOL.................................... 5-10 60
EPIC.................................... 4-8 67

EPs: 7-inch 33/45rpm

CAPITOL.................................... 8-15 55-59
VERVE.................................... 6-12 59

LPs: 10/12-inch 33rpm

ALSHIRE.................................... 5-10 70-71
CAPITOL.................................... 5-20 55-78
DAYBREAK.................................... 5-8 73
HARMONY.................................... 5-10 69
LIBERTY.................................... 5-10 67
MPS.................................... 5-10 73
PICKWICK.................................... 5-10 65
REPRISE.................................... 5-15 63-65
SOLID STATE.................................... 5-10 67
SUNSET.................................... 5-10 68
U.A. 5-10 68
VERVE.................................... 5-15 59

You'll find many more listings by this artist in *The Official Price Guide to Movie/TV Soundtracks and Original Cast Albums,* containing over 8,000 listings.

Also see FITZGERALD, Ella
Also see MARTIN, Dean / Nelson Riddle
Also see PETERSON, Oscar
Also see RONSTADT, Linda

RIDGELEY, Andrew

LP '90

LPs: 10/12-inch 33rpm

COLUMBIA.................................... 5-8 90

Also see WHAM!

RIDGWAY, Stan

LP '86

Singles: 7-inch

I.R.S. 3-4 86

LPs: 10/12-inch 33rpm

I.R.S. 5-8 86

Also see WALL of VOODOO

RIGHT CHOICE

R&B '88

Singles: 7-inch

MOTOWN.................................... 3-4 88

RIGHT KIND

R&B '68

Singles: 7-inch

GALAXY.................................... 4-8 68

RIGHTEOUS BROTHERS

P&R '63

Singles: 7-inch

HAVEN.................................... 3-5 74-76
MGM.................................... 3-5 78-79
MGM CELEBRITY SCENE (8 "Righteous Brothers") 35-45 66
(Boxed set of five singles with bio insert and jukebox title strips.)
MOONGLOW.................................... 5-10 63-66
PHILLES.................................... 5-10 64-66
POLYDOR.................................... 3-5
VERVE.................................... 4-8 65-70
VERVE SOUNDS of FAME 3-4 70s

Picture Sleeves

PHILLES.................................... 8-12 65-66
VERVE.................................... 5-10 66-67

EPs: 7-inch 33/45rpm

MOONGLOW (71004 "Best of the Righteous Brothers").................... 10-15 66
(Jukebox issue.)

LPs: 10/12-inch 33rpm

HAVEN.................................... 10-15 74-75
MGM.................................... 10-15 70-73
MOONGLOW (1001 "Right Now").................... 20-30 63
MOONGLOW (1002 "Some Blue Eyed Soul").................... 20-30 64
MOONGLOW (1003 "This Is New").................... 20-30 65
MOONGLOW (1004 "Best of the Righteous Brothers).................... 20-30 66
PHILLES (4007 "You've Lost That Lovin' Feeling).................... 25-45 64
PHILLES (4008 "Just Once in My Live").................... 25-45 65
PHILLES (4009 "Back to Back").................... 25-45 65
RHINO.................................... 8-12 89
VERVE (5001 "Soul and Inspiration").................... 15-20 66
VERVE (5004 "Go Ahead and Cry").................... 15-20 66
VERVE (5010 "Sayin' Something").................... 15-20 67
VERVE (5020 "Greatest Hits")....15-20 67
VERVE (5031 "Souled Out")......15-20 66
VERVE (5058 "One for the Road").................... 15-20 68

VERVE (5076 "Re-Birth").......... 15-20 69
(With Jimmy Walker instead of Bill Medley.)
Members: Bill Medley; Bobby Hatfield.
Also see HATFIELD, Bobby
Also see MEDLEY, Bill
Also see PARAMOURS

RILEY, Billy Lee
(With His Little Green Men)

P&R '72

Singles: 78rpm

SUN.. 15-25 56-57

Singles: 7-inch

ATLANTIC.................................. 3-6 68
BRUNSWICK (55085 "Rockin' on the Moon")........................ 150-250 58
ENTRANCE 3-5 72
GNP 4-8 66
HIP 4-8 68
HOME of the BLUES (233 "Flip, Flop and Fly").............................. 20-30 61
MERCURY 5-10 64-65
MOJO.. 4-8 67
SUN (245 "Rock with Me Baby") 50-75 56
SUN (260 "Flying Saucers Rock & Roll")......................... 50-75 57
SUN (277 "Red Hot") 25-50 57
SUN (289 "Wouldn't You Know").................................. 10-20 58
SUN (313 "No Name Girl")........ 10-20 58
SUN (322 "Got the Water Boiling")................................ 50-75 59
SSS/SUN 4-6 69-70

LPs: 10/12-inch 33rpm

CROWN 15-20 63
GNP 15-20 66
MERCURY 15-20 64-65
MOJO...................................... 15-20 79
Also see MEGATONS

RILEY, Cheryl Pepsii

P&R/LP '88

Singles: 7-inch

COLUMBIA 3-4 88

Singles: 7-inch

COLUMBIA 3-4 88

Picture Sleeves

COLUMBIA 3-4 88

LPs: 10/12-inch 33rpm

COLUMBIA 5-8 88

RILEY, Jeannie C.
(With the Red River Symphony)

C&W/P&R/LP '68

Singles: 7-inch

CAPITOL.................................... 3-6 69
CROSS COUNTRY..................... 3-4 79
GARPAX.................................... 3-4 80
GOD'S COUNTRY 3-5 75
MCA 3-4 82
MGM 3-5 71-74
MERCURY.....................................3-5 74
PLANTATION (Black vinyl)............3-4 68-72
PLANTATION (Colored vinyl) 4-8 68-72
W.B. 3-5 76

Picture Sleeves

PLANTATION 4-8 68-72

EPs: 7-inch 33/45rpm

PLANTATION 5-10 68

LPs: 10/12-inch 33rpm

ALBUM GLOBE 5-8 80s
CAPITOL...8-12 69
CROSS COUNTRY 5-10 79
HSRD/PLEASANT SOUNDS.........5-8 82
HEARTWARMING 4-8 79
LITTLE DARLIN' 10-15 68
MGM 5-10 72-74
OUT of TOWN DIST 5-8 82
PLANTATION 5-12 68-82
POWER PAK 5-8 80s
SONGBIRD...4-8 81-83
TRIP 8-12 74

RIMSHOTS

R&B '72

Singles: 7-inch

A-1 (4000 "Soul Train")..................4-6
STANG..3-5 76-77

LPs: 10/12-inch 33rpm

STANG...5-10 76

RINGS

P&R/LP '81

Singles: 7-inch

MCA 3-5 81

LPs: 10/12-inch 33rpm

MCA 5-10 81

RINKY-DINKS
(Featuring Bobby Darin)

P&R/R&B '58

Singles: 7-inch

ATCO (6121 "Early in the Morning") 20-25 58
Also see DARIN, Bobby

RIOS, Augie
(With the Notations)

P&R '58

Singles: 7-inch

MGM 4-8 60-64
METRO..5-10 58-59
SHELLEY.......................................10-20 63-64

RIOS, Miguel

LP '70

Singles: 7-inch

A&M 3-5 70

Picture Sleeves

A&M 3-5 70

LPs: 10/12-inch 33rpm

A&M 10-15 70

RIOS, Waldo de los

P&R/LP '71

LPs: 10/12-inch 33rpm

U.A. 5-10 71

RIOT

LP '81

Singles: 7-inch

MOTOWN 3-5 74

LPs: 10/12-inch 33rpm

CBS 5-8 88
CAPITOL 5-8 80-82
ELEKTRA 5-8 81-82
FIRE-SIGN (87001 "Rock City") 15-25 78
MOTOWN 8-10 74
QUALITY/RFC 5-8 84

RIP CHORDS

P&R '63

Singles: 7-inch

COLUMBIA (42687 "Here I Stand") 10-15 63
COLUMBIA (42812 "Gone") 10-15 63
(Black vinyl.)
COLUMBIA (42812 "Gone") 20-30 63
(Colored vinyl. Promotional issue only.)
COLUMBIA (42921 "Hey Little Cobra") 10-15 63
(Black vinyl.)
COLUMBIA (42921 "Hey Little Cobra") 20-30 63
(Colored vinyl. Promotional issue only.)
COLUMBIA (43035 "Three Window Coupe") 10-15 64
(Black vinyl.)
COLUMBIA (43035 "Three Window Coupe") 20-30 64
(Colored vinyl. Promotional issue only.)
COLUMBIA (43093 "One-Piece, Topless Bathing Suit") 10-15 64
COLUMBIA (43221 "Don't Be Scared") 10-15 64
COLUMBIA (3-42000 series) 10-20 63
(Compact 33 singles.)

Picture Sleeves

COLUMBIA (42687 "Here I Stand") 15-25 63
(Promotional issue only.)
COLUMBIA (42812 "Gone") 15-25 63

LPs: 10/12-inch 33rpm

COLUMBIA (2151 "Hey Little Cobra") 25-35 64
(Monaural.)
COLUMBIA (2216 "Three Window Coupe") 30-40 64
(Monaural.)
COLUMBIA (8951 "Hey Little Cobra") 25-35 64
(Stereo.)
COLUMBIA (9016 "Three Window Coupe") 30-40 64
(Stereo.)

Members: Bruce Johnston; Terry Melcher; Phil Stewart; Ernie Bringas; Steve Barri; Phil Sloan; Glen Campbell; Hal Blaine; Tommy Tedesco.

Also see BRUCE & TERRY
Also see CAMPBELL, Glen
Also see FANTASTIC BAGGYS
Also see MIKE & DEAN

RIPERTON, Minnie

LP '74

Singles: 12-inch 33/45rpm

EPIC 4-8 77

Singles: 7-inch

CAPITOL 3-5 79-81
EPIC 3-5 74-77
GRT 3-5 72
JANUS 3-5 75-76

LPs: 10/12-inch 33rpm

ACCORD 5-8 82
CAPITOL 5-10 79-81
EPIC 10-12 74-77
51 WEST 5-8 80s
GRT 10-15 70
JANUS 8-12 74

Also see DAVIS, Andrea
Also see JONES, Quincy
Also see ROTARY CONNECTION

RIPPINGTONS Featuring Russ Freeman

LP '88

LPs: 10/12-inch 33rpm

GRP 5-8 89
PASSPORT 5-8 88

Member: Steve Reid.

RIPPLE

P&R/R&B '73

Singles: 7-inch

GRC 3-5 73-75
SALSOUL 3-5 77-78

LPs: 10/12-inch 33rpm

GRC 8-10 74
SALSOUL 5-8 77

RIPPLES & WAVES Plus Michael (Jackson Five)

Singles: 7-inch

STEELTOWN (688 "Let Me Carry Your School Books") 25-50 69
(Mono. "Steeltown" is in all upper case letters on label.)
STEELTOWN (688 "Let Me Carry Your School Books") 50-75 69
(Stereo. "Steeltown" is in upper and lower case letters.)

Also see JACKSONS

RITCHARD, Cyril

LP '61

LPs: 10/12–inch 33rpm

RIVERSIDE................................ 8-15 61-62

RITCHIE FAMILY

P&R/R&B/LP '75

Singles: 12–inch 33/45rpm

MARLIN....................................... 4-8 76
RCA.. 4-6 82

Singles: 7–inch

CASABLANCA............................ 3-5 79-80
MARLIN....................................... 3-5 76-78
RCA.. 3-4 82-83
20TH FOX.................................. 3-5 75

LPs: 10/12–inch 33rpm

CASABLANCA......................... 5-10 79-80
MARLIN.................................... 5-10 76-78
RCA.. 5-8 82
20TH FOX................................ 5-10 75

RITENOUR, Lee

LP '77

Singles: 7–inch

ELEKTRA.................................... 3-4 81-82
EPIC.. 3-5 76-80

Picture Sleeves

ELEKTRA.................................... 3-4 81

LPs: 10/12–inch 33rpm

ELEKTRA.................................... 5-8 78-84
EPIC.. 5-10 76-80
GRP.. 5-8 85
JVC.. 5-10 78
MFSL.................................... 15-25 85
MUSICIAN................................. 5-8 82

Also see ANGELO
Also see FOURPLAY
Also see GRUSIN, Dave, & Lee Ritenour

RITTER, Tex

(With the Texans; with Plainsmen)

C&W/P&R '44

Singles: 78rpm

CAPITOL................................... 4-10 44-57
CHAMPION............................. 10-20 30s
CONQUEROR.......................... 10-20 30s
DECCA..................................... 5-10 30s-41
U.A. ("High Noon Ballad—Do Not Forsake Me")........................ 20-40 52
(Single-sided disc. Promotional issue only.)

Singles: 7–inch

CAPITOL (1100 thru 3900 series)..................................... 5-10 50-58
(Purple labels.)
CAPITOL (2000 thru 4000 series)... 3-6 68-76
(Orange labels.)
CAPITOL (4000 thru 5900 series). 4-8 58-67

Picture Sleeves

CAPITOL................................... 4-8 68

EPs: 7–inch 33/45rpm

CAPITOL (Except 431).............10-20 59-60
CAPITOL (431 "Tex Ritter Sings")...................................20-40 53

LPs: 10/12–inch 33rpm

ALBUM GLOBE..............................5-8 80s
BUCKBOARD.................................5-8 80s
CAPITOL (213 thru 467).............8-12 69-71
CAPITOL (971 "Songs from the Western Screen").............40-50 58
CAPITOL (1100 "Psalms").........20-30 59
CAPITOL (T-1292 "Blood on the Saddle")...........................20-30 60
(Monaural.)
CAPITOL (ST-1292 "Blood on the Saddle")...........................25-35 60
(Stereo.)
CAPITOL (SM-1292 "Blood on the Saddle")...............................5-10 78
CAPITOL (1623 thru 2800)........10-20 61-68
CAPITOL (W-1562 "The Lincoln Hymns")...................................25-30 61
(Monaural.)
CAPITOL (SW-1562 "The Lincoln Hymns")...................................30-35 61
(Stereo.)
CAPITOL (4004 "Cowboy Favorites")..............................50-75 53
(10–inch LP.)
CORONET....................................8-12 60s
HILLTOP...................................10-15 60s
LA BREA (8036 "Jamboree").....30-40 62
PICKWICK/HILLTOP.....................6-12 66-68
SHASTA.......................................8-12 60s
SPIN-O-RAMA..............................8-12 60s

Also see KENTON, Stan, & Tex Ritter

RIVERA, Hector

R&B '66

Singles: 7–inch

BARRY...3-6 66

LPs: 10/12–inch 33rpm

EPIC...10-15 61
WING..10-15 60

RIVERS, Joan

LP '93

LPs: 10/12–inch 33rpm

BUDDAH.....................................5-10 69
GEFFEN..5-8 83
W.B. 10-15 65

RIVERS, Johnny

(Johnny Ramistella)

P&R/LP '64

Singles: 7–inch

ATLANTIC......................................3-5 74
BIG TREE......................................3-5 77-78
CAPITOL..4-8 62-64
CHANCELLOR...............................8-12 61-62
CORAL...5-10 64

CUB (9047 "Everyday")............ 10-20 59
CUB (9058 "Answer Me My Love").................................. 10-15 60
DEE DEE 10-15 59
EPIC.. 3-5 75-76
ERA.. 5-10 61
GONE (5026 "Baby Come Back")................................. 20-30 58
GUYDEN (2003 "Hole in the Ground").......................... 10-15 58
GUYDEN (2110 "Hole in the Ground")................................ 4-8 64
IMPERIAL 4-8 64-70
MGM 5-8 64
RSO 3-5 80
RIVERAIRE (1001 "Don't Bug Me Baby") 10-20 59
ROULETTE (4565 "Baby Come Back")...................................... 8-12 64
ROWE/AMI................................ 5-10 66
("Play Me" Sales Stimulator promotional issue.)
SOUL CITY (Except 008)............. 3-5 76-77
SOUL CITY (008 "Slow Dancing") 4-8 77
U.A. (Except 700 series).............. 3-5 71-73
U.A. (700 series)......................... 4-8 64

Picture Sleeves

IMPERIAL 5-10 64-69
U.A. 3-5 71

LPs: 10/12-inch 33rpm

ATLANTIC................................ 8-10 74
BIG TREE 8-10 77
CAPITOL (T-2161 "Sensational Johnny Rivers")...................... 35-50 64
(Monaural.)
CAPITOL (ST-2161 "Sensational Johnny Rivers")...................... 50-75 64
(Stereo.)
CUSTOM................................... 8-12 60s
EPIC.. 8-10 75
GUEST STAR 10-15 64
IMPERIAL 10-20 64-70
KOALA 5-10 79
LIBERTY 5-8 82
MCA 5-8 85
PICKWICK 8-10 70s
PRIORITY 5-8 83
RSO 5-10 80
SEARS (417 "Mr. Teenage")..... 20-30 60s
(Special Products issue, made for sale in Sears stores)
SOUL CITY 8-10 77
SUNSET................................... 8-12 67-69
U.A. (Except UAL, UAS & UXS series) 5-10 73-75
U.A. (UAL-3386 "Go Johnny Go")...................................... 20-25 64
(Monaural.)
U.A. (UAS-6386 "Go Johnny Go").....................................20-30 64
(Stereo.)
U.A. (UAS-5532 "Homegrown"). 10-15 71
U.A. (UAS-5650 "L.A. Reggae") 10-15 72
U.A. (UXS-93 "Johnny Rivers").. 12-15 72
UNART....................................10-20 67
Also see JONES, Tom / Freddie & Dreamers / Johnny Rivers
Also see RAMISTELLA, Johnny
Also see WILSON, Brian

RIVERS, Johnny / Steve Alaimo

LPs: 10/12-inch 33rpm

CUSTOM 8-12 60s
Also see ALAIMO, Steve

RIVERS, Johnny / Jerry Cole

LPs: 10/12-inch 33rpm

CROWN 10-20 64
Also see COLE, Jerry

RIVERS, Johnny / 4 Seasons / Jerry Butler / Jimmy Soul

LPs: 10/12-inch 33rpm

GLADWYNNE (2004 "Shindig Hullabaloo Spectacular") 10-20 65
Also see BUTLER, Jerry
Also see 4 SEASONS
Also see SOUL, Jimmy

RIVERS, Johnny / Trini Lopez

LPs: 10/12-inch 33rpm

CUSTOM 8-12 60s
Also see LOPEZ, Trini

RIVERS, Johnny / Ricky Nelson / Randy Sparks

LPs: 10/12-inch 33rpm

MGM (E-4256 "Johnny Rivers, Ricky Nelson, Randy Sparks").......................20-25 64
(Monaural.)
MGM (SE-4256 "Johnny Rivers, Ricky Nelson, Randy Sparks").......................20-30 64
(Stereo.)
Also see NELSON, Ricky
Also see RASCALS / Buggs / Four Seasons / Johnny Rivers
Also see RIVERS, Johnny
Also see SIMON, Paul
Also see SPARKS, Randy

RIVERS, Johnny / Tremonts / Luke Gordon / Charlie Francis

LPs: 10/12-inch 33rpm

CORONET (246 "Swingin' Shindig") 10-20 64
PREMIER (P-9037 "Swingin' Shindig") 10-20 64
(Monaural.)
PREMIER (PS-9037 "Swingin' Shindig") 15-25 64
(Stereo.)
Also see RIVERS, Johnny

RIVIERAS

P&R '58

Singles: 7–inch

COED (503 "Count Every Star") 20-25 58
COED (508 "Moonlight Serenade") 20-25 58
COED (513 thru 561 10-20 59-61
COED (592 "Moonlight Cocktails") 5-10 64
COLLECTABLES 3-4 80s
ERIC 3-4 70s
HOUSE of SOUNDS 4-8 60s
LOST-NITE 3-5 70s

LPs: 10/12–inch 33rpm

POST 10-15 70s

Members: Ronald Cook; Homer Dunn; Andy Jones; Charles Allen.

Also see DUPREES / RIVIERAS

RIVIERAS

P&R/LP '64

Singles: 7–inch

LANA 3-6 60s
RIVIERA (1401 "California Sun"/"H.B. Goose Step") 5-10 63
RIVIERA (1401 "California Sun"/"Played On") 15-25 63
(1,000 made. Note different flip.)
RIVIERA (1402 "Little Donna") 8-10 64
RIVIERA (1403 "Rockin' Robin"). 8-10 64
RIVIERA (1405 "Rip It Up"/"Whole Lotta Shakin") 8-10 64
RIVIERA (1405 "Whole Lotta Shakin"/"Lakeview Lane") 10-15 64
(Has a different take of *Lakeview Lane* than found on 1406.)
RIVIERA (1406 "Let's Go to Hawaii"/ "Lakeview Lane") 8-10 65
RIVIERA (1407 "Somebody New") 8-10 65
(Credited to Rivieras, but actually by Bobby Whiteside.)
RIVIERA (1409 "Bug Juice") 10-15 65

LPs: 10/12–inch 33rpm

RIVIERA (701 "Campus Party") 50-100 64
USA (102 "Let's Have a Party") 50-100 64

Members: Marty Fortson; Paul Dennert; Otto Nuss; Doug Gean; Joe Pennell.

RIVINGTONS

P&R '62

Singles: 7–inch

A.R.E. AMERICAN 10-15 64
BATON MASTER 4-8 67
COLUMBIA 5-10 66
J.D. 3-5 76
LADERA 3-5
LIBERTY (Except 55610) 5-10 62-64
LIBERTY (55610 "Cherry") 20-30 63
QUAN 4-8 67
RCA 4-8 69
REPRISE 4-8 64
VEE JAY 4-8 64-65
WAND 3-5 73

Picture Sleeves

LIBERTY (55553 "The Bird's the Word") 15-25 63

LPs: 10/12–inch 33rpm

LIBERTY (3282 "Doin' the Bird") 50-60 63
(Monaural.)
LIBERTY (7282 "Doin' the Bird") 50-75 63
(Stereo.)
LIBERTY (10184 "Papa-Oom-Mow-Mow") 5-10 82

Members: Carl White; Al Frazier; Sonny Harris; Turner Wilson; Darryl White.

RIX, Jerry

R&B '77

Singles: 7–inch

A.V.I. 3-5 77

ROACHFORD

P&R/LP '89

Singles: 7–inch

EPIC 3-4 89

ROAD

LP '70

Singles: 7–inch

KAMA SUTRA 4-6 68-71
NATURAL RESOURCES 3-5 72

LPs: 10/12–inch 33rpm

KAMA SUTRA 10-15 69-71
NATURAL RESOURCES 10-12 72

Members: Jerry Hudson; Phil Hudson; Joseph Hesse; Jim Hesse; Ralph Parker; Nick Distefano.

ROAD APPLES

P&R '75

Singles: 7–inch

MUMS 3-5 75
POLYDOR 3-5 75

ROB BASE & D.J. EZ-Rock
(Rob Base)

P&R/R&B/LP '88

Singles: 7–inch

PROFILE 3-4 88-89

Picture Sleeves

PROFILE 3-4 89

LPs: 10/12–inch 33rpm

PROFILE 5-8 88

ROBBINS, Marty
(With Ray Conniff)

C&W '52

Singles: 78rpm

COLUMBIA 5-15 52-58

Singles: 7-inch

COLUMBIA (02000 & 03000 series) 3-4 81-83
COLUMBIA (10305 thru 11425).... 3-5 76-81
COLUMBIA (20965 thru 21324) 20-30 52-54
COLUMBIA (21351 "That's All Right") 30-40 54
COLUMBIA (21352 thru 21414) 10-20 54-55
COLUMBIA (21446 "Maybellene") 30-40 55
COLUMBIA (21461 "Pretty Mama") 30-40 55
COLUMBIA (21477 "Tennessee Toddy") 30-40 56
COLUMBIA (21508 "Singing the Blues") 15-20 50
COLUMBIA (21545 "Singing the Blues") 10-15 56
COLUMBIA (30000 series) 10-20 60
(Compact 33 stereo singles.)
COLUMBIA (40679 "Long Tall Sally") 30-40 56
COLUMBIA (40706 "Respectfully Miss Brooks") 20-30 56
COLUMBIA (40815 thru 41408).. 5-15 57-59
COLUMBIA (41511 thru 43770).... 4-8 59-66
COLUMBIA (43845 thru 45775).... 3-6 67-73
DECCA 4-6 72
MCA 3-5 73-75

Picture Sleeves

COLUMBIA (40815 thru 41408) 10-20 57-59
COLUMBIA (41511 thru 43770).. 5-10 59-66

EPs: 7-inch 33/45rpm

COLUMBIA (1785 "Marty Robbins") 20-40 56
COLUMBIA (2116 "Singing the Blues") 20-40 56
COLUMBIA (2134 "A White Sport Coat") 20-30 57
COLUMBIA (2153 "Marty Robbins") 15-25 56
COLUMBIA (2808 "Marty Robbins") 20-30 57
COLUMBIA (2814 "Marty Robbins") 10-20 58
COLUMBIA (9761/9762/9763 "The Song of Robbins") 10-20 57
(Price is for any of three volumes.)
COLUMBIA (10000 thru 14000 series) 10-20 57-60

LPs: 10/12-inch 33rpm

ARTCO (110 "Best of Marty Robbins") 40-50 73
(Covers shows 110 but label has 644.)
CANDLELITE 8-12 77
COLUMBIA (15 "Marty's Country") 10-15 69
COLUMBIA (31 "Open-End Columbia Artists Interviews") 35-50 60s
(Promotional issue only.)
COLUMBIA (32 "Columbia Artists Interviews with Frank Jones") 50-75
(Includes 42-page booklet. Promotional issue only.)
COLUMBIA (237 "Saddle Tramp") 25-35 66
(Columbia Record Club issue.)
COLUMBIA (445 "Bend in the River") 35-45 68
(Columbia Record Club issue.)
COLUMBIA (890 "Marty Robbins Gold") 8-10 75
COLUMBIA (976 "The Song of Robbins") 25-35 57
COLUMBIA (1087 "Song of the Islands") 25-35 57
COLUMBIA (1189 "Marty Robbins") 25-35 58
COLUMBIA (1256 "Return of the Gunfighter") 15-20 69
(Columbia "Country Star" series.)
COLUMBIA (1325 "Marty's Greatest Hits") 15-25 59
COLUMBIA (1349 "Gunfighter Ballads and Trail Songs") 15-25 59
COLUMBIA (1481 "More Gunfighter Ballads and Trail Songs") 15-25 60
COLUMBIA (1599 "Marty's Greatest Hits") 15-20 69
(Columbia "Country Star" series issue.)
COLUMBIA (1635 "More Greatest Hits") 15-25 61
COLUMBIA (1666 "Just a Little Sentimental") 15-25 61
COLUMBIA (1801 "Marty After Midnight") 40-50 62
COLUMBIA (1855 "Portrait of Marty") 25-35 62
(With bonus portrait of Marty.)
COLUMBIA (1855 "Portrait of Marty") 15-25 62
(Without bonus portrait of Marty.)
COLUMBIA (1918 "Devil Woman") 15-20 62
COLUMBIA (2016 "The Heart of Marty Robbins") 80-100 69
(Columbia "Country Star" series issue.)
COLUMBIA (2040 "Hawaii's Calling Me") 20-30 62
COLUMBIA (2072 "Return of the Gunfighter") 15-20 63
COLUMBIA (2167 "Island Woman") 35-40 64
COLUMBIA (2220 "R.F.D.") 40-50 64
COLUMBIA (2304 "Turn the Lights Down Low") 15-25 65

COLUMBIA (2448 "What God Has Done")............................ 15-20 65
COLUMBIA (2527 "The Drifter") 10-20 66
COLUMBIA (2563 "What God Has Done")............................ 15-20 69
(Columbia "Country Star" series issue.)
COLUMBIA (2601 "Rock'n Roll'n Robbins") 500-600 56
(10–inch LP.)
COLUMBIA (2645 "My Kind of Country")........................... 15-20 67
COLUMBIA (2725 "Tonight Carmen").............................. 10-20 67
COLUMBIA (2735 "Christmas with Marty Robbins") 20-30 67
COLUMBIA (2762 "More Gunfighter Ballads and Trail Songs") 15-20 69
(Columbia "Country Star" series issue.)
COLUMBIA (2817 "By The Time I Get to Phoenix").............................. 20-30 68
COLUMBIA (3557 "The Drifter") 15-20 69
(Columbia "Country Star" series issue.)
COLUMBIA (3867 "My Kind of Country")........................... 15-20 69
(Columbia "Country Star" series issue.)
COLUMBIA (5489 "Tonight Carmen").............................. 15-20 69
(Columbia "Country Star" series issue.)
COLUMBIA (5498 "Christmas with Marty Robbins") 15-20 69
(Columbia "Country Star" series issue.)
COLUMBIA (5812 "Marty") 20-40 72
(Five-LP set. Columbia Special Products issue.)
COLUMBIA (6994 "I Walk Alone") 15-20 69
(Columbia "Country Star" series issue.)
COLUMBIA (CS-8158 "Gunfighter Ballads and Trail Songs") 15-25 59
COLUMBIA (PC-8158 "Gunfighter Ballads and Trail Songs") 5-10
COLUMBIA (CS-8272 "More Gunfighter Ballads and Trail Songs")........ 15-25 60
COLUMBIA (PC-8272 "More Gunfighter Ballads and Trail Songs")......... 5-10
COLUMBIA (CS-8435 "More Greatest Hits") 15-20 61
COLUMBIA (PC-8435 "More Greatest Hits") 5-10
COLUMBIA (8466 "Just a Little Sentimental")........................... 15-25 61
COLUMBIA (8601 "Marty After Midnight")............................... 40-50 62
COLUMBIA (8655 "Portrait of Marty")................................ 25-35 62
(With bonus portrait of Marty.)
COLUMBIA (8655 "Portrait of Marty")................................... 15-25 62
(Without bonus portrait.)

COLUMBIA (8718 "Devil Woman") 15-20 62
COLUMBIA (8840 "Hawaii's Calling Me") 20-30 62
COLUMBIA (8872 "Return of the Gunfighter")........................15-20 63
COLUMBIA (8976 "Island Woman")...................................35-40 64
COLUMBIA (CS-9020 "R.F.D.").40-50 64
COLUMBIA (CSRP-9020 "R.F.D.")......................................8-10
(Columbia Special Products issue.)
COLUMBIA (9104 "Turn the Lights Down Low")..............................20-30 65
COLUMBIA (CS-9248 "What God Has Done") 15-20 65
COLUMBIA (ACS-9248 "What God Has Done") 5-10
(Columbia Special Products issue.)
COLUMBIA (9327 "The Drifter") 10-20 66
COLUMBIA (9421 "The Song of Robbins") 30-40 67
COLUMBIA (9445 "My Kind of Country")..............................15-25 67
COLUMBIA (9525 "Tonight Carmen")...................................10-20 67
COLUMBIA (9535 "Christmas with Marty Robbins")........................10-20 67
COLUMBIA (9617 "By the Time I Get to Phoenix")...........................8-12 68
COLUMBIA (9725 "I Walk Alone")..8-15 68
COLUMBIA (9811 "It's a Sin")....20-30 69
COLUMBIA (9978 "My Woman, My Woman, My Wife") 8-12 70
COLUMBIA (10022 thru 10579)...8-10 73-75
(Columbia's Limited Edition series. All Have an "LE" prefix.)
COLUMBIA (10980 "Christmas with Marty Robbins") 15-20 70
(Columbia Special Products issue.)
COLUMBIA (11222 "Marty's Greatest Hits") 5-10 75
COLUMBIA (11311 "By the Time I Get to Phoenix")..........................5-10 70
(Columbia Special Products issue.)
COLUMBIA (11513 "By the Time I Get to Phoenix").........................15-20 71
(Columbia Special Products issue.)
COLUMBIA (12416 "Marty Robbins' Own Favorites") 12-15 74
(Special Products issue for Vaseline Hair Tonic.)
COLUMBIA (13358 "Christmas with Marty Robbins") 5-10 72
(Columbia Special Products issue.)
COLUMBIA (14035 "Legendary Music Man")..............................8-12 77
(Columbia Special Products issue.)

COLUMBIA (14613 "Best of Marty Robbins") 5-10 78
(Columbia Special Products issue.)
COLUMBIA (15594 "Number One Cowboy") 5-10 81
(Columbia Special Products issue.)
COLUMBIA (15812 "Marty Robbins' Best") 5-10 82
(Columbia Special Products issue.)
COLUMBIA (16561 "Reflections") 5-10 82
(Columbia Special Products issue.)
COLUMBIA (16578 "Classics"). 15-20 83
(Three-LP set. Columbia Special Products issue.)
COLUMBIA (16914 "Country Classics") 5-10 83
(Columbia Special Products issue.)
COLUMBIA (17120 "Sincerely").. 5-10 83
(Columbia Special Products issue.)
COLUMBIA (17136 "Forever Yours") 5-10 83
(Columbia Special Products issue.)
COLUMBIA (17137 "That Country Feeling") 5-10 83
(Columbia Special Products issue.)
COLUMBIA (17138 "Banquet of Songs") 5-10 83
(Columbia Special Products issue.)
COLUMBIA (17159 "The Great Marty Robbins") 5-10 83
(Columbia Special Products issue.)
COLUMBIA (17206 "The Legendary Marty Robbins") 5-10 83
(Columbia Special Products issue.)
COLUMBIA (17209 "Country Cowboy") 5-10 83
(Columbia Special Products issue.)
COLUMBIA (17367 "Song of the Islands") 5-10 83
(Columbia Special Products issue.)
COLUMBIA (30000 thru 40000 series) 5-12 70-86
DECCA 8-12 72
GUSTO/COLUMBIA 8-10 81
HARMONY (Except 31258) 8-15 69-72
HARMONY (31258 "Song of the Islands") 20-25 72
K-TEL 8-10 77
MCA 6-12 73-74
ORBIT 8-10 84
PICKWICK 5-10 70s
READER'S DIGEST (054 "Greatest Hits") 20-30 83
(Five-LP boxed set.)
SUNRISE MEDIA 5-10 81
TIME-LIFE 5-10 81

Session: Ray Conniff Singers; Jordanaires; David Briggs; Bobby Braddock; Grady Martin; Bob Bishop; Bill Pursell; Buddy Spicher; Arlene Harden; Bobby Sykes.
Also see CONNIFF, Ray
Also see PRUETT, Jeanne, & Marty Robbins
Also see PURSELL, Bill
Also see SMITH, Carl / Lefty Frizzell / Marty Robbins

ROBBINS, Marty / Johnny Cash / Ray Price

LPs: 10/12-inch 33rpm

COLUMBIA 8-10 70
Also see CASH, Johnny
Also see PRICE, Ray

ROBBINS, Rockie

R&B '79

Singles: 7-inch

A&M 3-5 79-81
MCA 3-4 85

Picture Sleeves

A&M 3-5 80

LPs: 10/12-inch 33rpm

A&M 5-10 80-81
MCA 5-8 85

ROBBS

LP '68

Singles: 7-inch

ABC 4-6 70
ATLANTIC 5-10 68
DUNHILL 4-8 69-70
MERCURY 5-10 66-67

Picture Sleeves

ABC 4-8 70
MERCURY 8-12 67

EPs: 7-inch 33/45rpm

WRIT 10-15 66

LPs: 10/12-inch 33rpm

MERCURY (21130 "Robbs") 20-25 67
(Monaural.)
MERCURY (61130 "Robbs") 20-30 67
(Stereo.)

ROBE

R&B '87

Singles: 7-inch

2000 AD 3-4 87

ROBERT & JOHNNY

P&R/R&B '58

Singles: 78rpm

OLD TOWN 10-15 56-57

Singles: 7-inch

ATLANTIC OLDIES SERIES 3-5 70s
COLLECTABLES 3-4 80s
OLD TOWN 12-25 56-62
SUE (792 "A Perfect Wife") 15-20 62
Members: Robert Carr; Johnny Mitchell.

ROBERT & JOHNNY / Fiestas

Singles: 7-inch

ATCO 3-5 80s
Also see FIESTAS

Also see ROBERT & JOHNNY

ROBERTA LEE: see LEE, Roberta

ROBERTINO

LP '62

Singles: 7-inch

KAPP 4-6 61

LPs: 10/12-inch 33rpm

KAPP 10-20 61-62

ROBERTS, Austin

P&R '72

Singles: 7-inch

ARISTA 3-5 78
CHELSEA 3-5 72-75
COLLECTABLES 3-4 80s
GUSTO 3-4 80s
PHILIPS 4-6 68-71
PRIVATE STOCK 3-5 75-76

LPs: 10/12-inch 33rpm

CHELSEA 8-12 72-73
PRIVATE STOCK 6-10 75

ROBERTS, John

P&R/R&B '67

Singles: 7-inch

DUKE 4-8 67-69

ROBERTS, Lea

R&B '69

Singles: 7-inch

MINIT 4-8 69
U.A. 3-5 74-75

ROBERTSON, Don

P&R '56

Singles: 78rpm

CAPITOL 3-5 56-57

Singles: 7-inch

CAPITOL 4-8 56-59
MONUMENT 3-5 66-76
RCA 3-8 61-68

LPs: 10/12-inch 33rpm

RCA 10-15 65

ROBERTSON, Robbie

LP '87

LPs: 10/12-inch 33rpm

GEFFEN 5-8 87

Also see BAND

ROBEY

P&R/D&D '85

Singles: 12-inch 33/45rpm

SILVER BLUE 4-6 84-85

Singles: 7-inch

SILVER BLUE 3-5 84-85

ROBIC, Ivo

P&R '59

Singles: 7-inch

LAURIE 4-8 59-60
PHILIPS 3-6 62

ROBIN

(Robin Ward)

Singles: 7-inch

DOT 4-8 63

Also see WARD, Robin

ROBIN, Cock: see COCK ROBIN

ROBIN, Tina

P&R '61

Singles: 78rpm

CORAL 5-10 57

Singles: 7-inch

CORAL 5-10 57-59
MERCURY 4-8 61-63

ROBINS

(Robbins)

R&B '50

Singles: 78rpm

ALADDIN (3031 "Don't Like the Way You're Doing") 150-200 49
ATCO 5-15 55
CROWN 25-50 54
RCA 25-50 53
RECORDED in HOLLYWOOD (112 "Bayou Baby Blues") 100-150 51
RECORDED in HOLLYWOOD (121 "Falling Star") 100-150 51
SAVOY 15-25 50
SCORE 20-30 49
SPARK 15-25 54-55
WHIPPET 10-20 56-57

Singles: 7-inch

ARVEE 8-12 60
ATCO (6059 "Smokey Joe's Cafe") 15-25 55
CROWN (106 "I Made a Vow") 150-200 54
CROWN (120 "Key to My Heart") 150-200 54
GONE (5101 "Baby Love") 15-25 61
KNIGHT (2001 "Quarter to Twelve") 15-25 58
KNIGHT (2008 "It's Never Too Late") 35-55 58
RCA (5175 "A Fool Such As I") 200-300 53
RCA (5271 "All Night Baby") .. 175-225 53
RCA (5434 "How Would You Know") 175-225 53
RCA (5486 "My Baby Done Told Me") 100-150 53
RCA (5489 "Ten Days in Jail") . 75-100 53
RCA (5564 "Don't Stop Now") .. 75-100 53
SPARK (103 "Riot in Cell Block No. 9") 40-50 54
SPARK (107 "Framed") 40-50 54
SPARK (110 "If Teardrops Were Kisses") 75-125 55
SPARK (113 "One Kiss") 75-125 55

SPARK (116 "I Must Be Dreaming") 50-75 55
SPARK (122 "Smokey Joe's Cafe") 100-125 55
WHIPPET (100 "Cherry Lips") .. 25-35 56
WHIPPET (200 "Cherry Lips") .. 15-25 56
WHIPPET (201 "Hurt Me") 20-30 56
WHIPPET (203 "Since I First Met You") 20-30 56
WHIPPET (206 "A Fool in Love") 20-30 57
WHIPPET (208 "Every Night") .. 20-30 57
WHIPPET (211 "In My Dreams") 20-30 57
WHIPPET (212 "You Wanted Fun") 20-30 58

LPs: 10/12-inch 33rpm

GNP 5-10 75
WHIPPET (703 "Rock 'N' Roll with the Robins") 300-400 58

Members: Ty Terrell; Bobby Nunn; Carl Gardner; Bill Richards; Grady Chapman; H.B. Barnum; Roy Richards; Richard Berry.
Also see BARNUM, H.B.
Also see COASTERS
Also see NUNN, Bobby
Also see OTIS, Johnny, Quintette, with Little Esther & Robins

ROBINS / Mel Walker & Bluenotes

Singles: 78rpm

REGENT (1016 "I'm Not Falling in Love with You") 25-35 50
Also see ROBINS

ROBINS, Jimmy
(James Robbins)

R&B '67

Singles: 7-inch

FEDERAL.................................. 4-8 63
JERHART.................................. 4-8 67
KENT....................................... 4-8 68

ROBINSON, Alvin

P&R/R&B '64

Singles: 7-inch

ATCO 4-8 68
BLUE CAT................................ 5-10 65
JOE JONES 4-8 66
RED BIRD 5-10 64
TIGER 4-8 64

ROBINSON, Bert

R&B '87

Singles: 7-inch

CAPITOL.................................... 3-4 87
Also see BLU, Peggi, & Bert Robinson

ROBINSON, Dutch

R&B '84

Singles: 7-inch

CBS ASSOCIATED..................... 3-4 84-85

ROBINSON, Ed

R&B '70

Singles: 7-inch

COTILLION 3-5 70

ROBINSON, Fat Man

R&B '49

Singles: 78rpm

MOTIF.......................................10-15 49

ROBINSON, Floyd

P&R/R&B '59

Singles: 7-inch

DOT 4-8 61-62
GROOVE 4-8 64
JAMIE 4-8 61
RCA 5-10 59-60
U.A. 5-10 63-66

EPs: 7-inch 33/45rpm

RCA (4350 "Makin' Love") 20-30 59

LPs: 10/12-inch 33rpm

RCA (LPM-2162 "Floyd Robinson") 20-30 60
(Monaural.)
RCA (LSP-2162 "Floyd Robinson") 30-40 60
(Stereo.)

ROBINSON, Freddy

P&R/R&B/LP '70

Singles: 7-inch

CHECKER 4-8 66
LIBERTY 3-5 70
LIMELIGHT 5-10 58
MERCURY 5-10 58
PACIFIC JAZZ 3-5 69-70
QUEEN 4-8 61
WORLD PACIFIC 3-5 70

LPs: 10/12-inch 33rpm

ENTERPRISE...............................8-12 71
PACIFIC JAZZ 10-15 69-70
Also see LITTLE WALTER
Also see HOWLING WOLF

ROBINSON, J.P.

R&B '69

Singles: 7-inch

ALSTON......................................3-6 68-69

ROBINSON, Jackie

R&B '76

Singles: 7-inch

ARIOLA AMERICAN.....................3-5 76

ROBINSON, James

R&B '87

Singles: 7-inch

TABU 3-4 87

ROBINSON, Roscoe
(Rosco Robinson)

P&R/R&B '66

Singles: 7-inch

ATLANTIC 3-5 69
FAME 3-5 70
PAULA 3-5 70s
SOUND STAGE 7 .... 4-8 67-69
TUFF 4-6 70s
WAND 4-8 66-67

ROBINSON, Smokey
(William Robinson)

P&R/R&B/LP '73

Singles: 7-inch

TAMLA 3-5 73-86
MOTOWN 3-4 87-88

Picture Sleeves

MOTOWN 3-4 87

LPs: 10/12-inch 33rpm

MOTOWN 5-10 82-90
TAMLA 5-12 73-86

Also see JAMES, Rick, & Smokey Robinson
Also see KENNY G. & Smokey Robinson
Also see MIRACLES
Also see ROSS, Diana, Stevie Wonder, Marvin Gaye & Smokey Robinson
Also see TEMPTATIONS
Also see U.S.A. for AFRICA
Also see VANITY / Smokey Robinson

ROBINSON, Smokey, & Barbara Mitchell

P&R/R&B '83

Singles: 7-inch

TAMLA 3-5 83

Also see HIGH INERGY
Also see ROBINSON, Smokey

ROBINSON, Stan

P&R '59

Singles: 7-inch

AMY 5-10 60-61
MONUMENT 5-10 59
TOTSY (601 "Start to Jump").. 75-100

ROBINSON, Sugar "Chile

R&B '49

Singles: 78rpm

CAPITOL 10-20 49-50

Singles: 7-inch

CAPITOL (1259 "Christmas Boogie") 50-75 50

LPs: 10/12-inch 33rpm

CAPITOL (589 "Boogie Woogie") 75-125 55

ROBINSON, Sugar "Chile" / Harry Belafonte

Singles: 78rpm

CAPITOL (70037 "Numbers Boogie") 25-35 49
(Promotional issue only.)

Also see BELAFONTE, Harry
Also see ROBINSON, Sugar "Chile"

ROBINSON, Tom, Band

LP '78

Singles: 7-inch

HARVEST 3-5 78-79
I.R.S. 3-5 80

LPs: 10/12-inch 33rpm

HARVEST 5-10 78-79
I.R.S. 5-8 80

ROBINSON, Vicki Sue

P&R/R&B/LP '76

Singles: 12-inch 33/45rpm

PROFILE 8-12 83-84

Singles: 7-inch

PROFILE 3-4 83-84
RCA 3-5 76-77

LPs: 10/12-inch 33rpm

PROFILE 5-8 83
RCA 5-10 76-81

ROBINSON, Wanda

LP '71

LPs: 10/12-inch 33rpm

PERCEPTION 5-10 71

ROBOTNICK, Alexander

R&B '85

Singles: 7-inch

SIRE 3-5 85

ROCCA, John

R&B/D&D '84

Singles: 12-inch 33/45rpm

STREETWISE 4-6 84

Singles: 7-inch

STREETWISE 3-4 84

Also see FREEEZ

ROCHELL & CANDLES

P&R/R&B '61

Singles: 7-inch

CHALLENGE (9158 "Each Night") 40-50 62
CHALLENGE (9191 "Let's Run Away and Get Married") 15-25 62
COLLECTABLES 3-4 80s
SWINGIN' (623 "Once Upon a Time") 10-15 60
SWINGIN' (634 "So Far Away"). 10-15 61
SWINGIN' (640 "Peg O' My Heart") 10-15 61
SWINGIN' (652 "Long Time Ago") 10-15 62

Members: Rochell Henderson; Johnny Wyatt; T. C. Henderson; Mel Sasso.

ROCHELLE

D&D '85

Singles: 12-inch 33/45rpm

W.B. 4-6 85

Singles: 7-inch

W.B. 3-4 85

ROCHES

LP '79

LPs: 10/12-inch 33rpm

W.B. 5-10 79-82

Members: Maggie Roche; Terre Roche; Suzzy Roche.

ROCK & HYDE

P&R/LP '87

Singles: 7-inch

CAPITOL.. 3-4 87

Picture Sleeves

CAPITOL.. 3-4 87

LPs: 10/12-inch 33rpm

CAPITOL.. 5-8 87

ROCK FLOWERS

P&R '72

Singles: 7-inch

WHEEL 4-8 71-73

LPs: 10/12-inch 33rpm

WHEEL 10-15 71-72

ROCK MASTER SCOTT & Dynamic Three

R&B '84

Singles: 12-inch 33/45rpm

REALITY 4-6 84-85

Singles: 7-inch

REALITY 3-4 84-85

ROCK SQUAD

D&D '85

Singles: 12-inch 33/45rpm

TOMMY BOY 4-6 85

ROCK STEADY CREW

D&D '84

Singles: 12-inch 33/45rpm

ATLANTIC.. 4-6 83-84

Singles: 7-inch

ATLANTIC.. 3-4 83-84

ROCK-A-TEENS

P&R '59

Singles: 7-inch

DORAN (3515 "Woo-Hoo") 40-60 59

ROULETTE (4192 "Woo-Hoo"). 10-15 59

ROULETTE (4217 "Doggone It Baby") 15-20 60

LPs: 10/12-inch 33rpm

MURRAY HILL.......................... 5-10 80s

ROULETTE (R-25109 "Woo-Hoo")........................... 75-100 60

(Monaural.)

ROULETTE (SR-25109 "Woo-Hoo")........................... 100-125 60

(Stereo.)

ROCKER'S REVENGE

R&B '82

Singles: 12-inch 33/45rpm

STREETWISE.......................... 4-6 83-84

Singles: 7-inch

STREETWISE.......................... 3-5 82-84

ROCKET

R&B/D&D '83

Singles: 12-inch 33/45

QUALITY/RFC 4-6 83

LPs: 10/12-inch 33rpm

QUALITY/RFC 5-8 83

ROCKETS

P&R/LP '79

Singles: 7-inch

RSO 3-5 79

TORTOISE INT'L.......................... 3-5 77-78

LPs: 10/12-inch 33rpm

ELEKTRA.. 5-10 81

RSO 5-10 79-80

TORTOISE INT'L.......................... 8-12 77

Members: Jim McCarty; Dennis Robbins.

Also see DETROIT

Also see RYDER, Mitch

ROCKIN' R's

P&R '59

Singles: 7-inch

STEPHENY (1842 "Walking You to School") 15-25 60

TEMPUS (1507 "Heat") 15-20 59

TEMPUS (1515 "Mustang") 15-20 60

TEMPUS (7541 "The Beat") 20-30 59

VEE JAY 5-10 60

ROCKIN' REBELS

P&R '62

Singles: 7-inch

ABC.. 3-5 73

ERIC 3-4 70s

ITZY (8 "Wild Weekend")........... 15-25 60s

STORK (3 "Bongo Blue Beat")... 10-15 64

SWAN 8-12 62-63

LPs: 10/12-inch 33rpm

SWAN (509 "Wild Weekend") .. 50-100 63

Members: Tom Gorman; Paul Balon; Mickey Kipler; Jim Kipler.

Also see BUFFALO REBELS

Also see HOT-TODDYS

Also see REBELS

ROCKIN' SIDNEY: see ROCKIN' SYDNEY

ROCKIN' SYDNEY

(With His All Stars; Rockin' Sidney)

LP '85

Singles: 7-inch

AVENUE 5-10 60s

EPIC.. 3-5 84-85

JIN.. 8-12 59-63

MAISON DE SOUL (1024 "My Toot Toot") 3-5 85

LPs: 10/12-inch 33rpm

EPIC.. 5-10 85

Member: Sidney Sidiem.

ROCKINGHAM, David, Trio

P&R '63

Singles: 7–inch

JOSIE 4-8 63-64

ROCKPILE

P&R/LP '80

Singles: 7–inch

COLUMBIA 3-5 80

EPs: 7–inch 33/45rpm

COLUMBIA (1219 "Nick Lowe and Dave Edmunds") 3-5 80

(Bonus EP, issued with the LP *Seconds of Pleasure*.)

LPs: 10/12–inch 33rpm

COLUMBIA (36886 "Seconds of Pleasure") 5-10 80

(Includes the bonus EP, 1219, *Nick Lowe & Dave Edmunds*.)

Members: Nick Lowe; Dave Edmunds; Terry Williams; Billy Bremmer.

Also see CARTER, Carlene

Also see LOWE, Nick, & Dave Edmunds

Also see McCARTNEY, Paul / Rochestra / Who / Rockpile

ROCKWELL

P&R/R&B/D&D/LP '84

Singles: 12–inch 33/45rpm

MOTOWN 4-6 84-86

Singles: 7–inch

MOTOWN 3-4 84-86

LPs: 10/12–inch 33rpm

MOTOWN 5-8 84-86

Also see JACKSON, Michael

ROCKY FELLERS

P&R '63

Singles: 7–inch

DONNA 5-10 63

PARKWAY 5-10 62

SCEPTER 5-10 62-63

W.B. 4-8 64-65

Picture Sleeves

SCEPTER (1254 "Like the Big Guys Do") 10-15 63

LPs: 10/12–inch 33rpm

SCEPTER (SP-512 "Killer Joe") 25-35 63

(Monaural.)

SCEPTER (SPS-512 "Killer Joe") 30-40 63

(Stereo.)

Members: Eddie; Albert; Tony; Junior; Pop.

ROD

R&B '80

Singles: 7–inch

PRELUDE 3-5 80

RODGERS, Eileen

P&R '56

Singles: 78rpm

COLUMBIA 3-6 56-57

Singles: 7–inch

COLUMBIA 5-10 56-60

KAPP 4-6 61

EPs: 7–inch 33/45rpm

COLUMBIA 5-10 58

LPs: 10/12–inch 33rpm

COLUMBIA 15-25 58

Also see MITCHELL, Guy / Eileen Rodgers

RODGERS, Jimmie

C&W '55

Singles: 78rpm

BLUEBIRD 20-50 30s

MONTGOMERY WARD 15-25 30s

VICTOR (20864 thru 23574) 20-60 27-30s

VICTOR (23580 thru 24456) 50-100 30s

VICTOR (4000 series) 15-25

VICTOR (5000 & 6000 series) 5-10 49-56

VICTOR (18-6000 "Cowhand's Last Ride") 750-1000 33

(Picture disc.)

Singles: 7–inch

RCA 10-20 49-56

RODGERS, Jimmie

(With Michele)

P&R/C&W/R&B/LP '57

Singles: 78rpm

ROULETTE 8-12 57

Singles: 7–inch

A&M 3-6 67-70

ABC 3-5 73

DOT 4-8 62-67

EPIC 3-5 71-72

RCA 3-5 73-75

ROULETTE (Monaural) 5-10 57-61

ROULETTE (SSR-4158 "Ring-a-Ling-a-Lario") 10-20 59

(Stereo.)

ROULETTE (SSR-4218 "T.L.C.") 10-20 60

(Stereo.)

ROULETTE (SSR-8001 "Bo Diddley") 15-25 59

(Stereo.)

ROULETTE (SSR-8007 "Froggy Went A-Courtin'") 10-20 59

(Stereo.)

SCRIMSHAW 3-5 78

Picture Sleeves

DOT 4-8 62-64

ROULETTE 10-15 58-61

EPs: 7–inch 33/45rpm

ROULETTE 10-20 57-60

LPs: 10/12–inch 33rpm

A&M 8-15 67-70

DOT 10-20 62-67

FORUM 10-20 60

HAMILTON 10-20 64-65

RCA 8-12 73-75

ROULETTE (25020 thru 25057) 20-30 57-59
ROULETTE (R-25071 thru R-25199)........ 10-20 59-63
(Monaural.)
ROULETTE (SR-25071 thru SR-25199)........ 15-25 59-63
(Stereo.)
ROULETTE (42000 series)......... 5-10
SCRIMSHAW........ 5-10 78

RODGERS, Nile

P&R/R&B/D&D '85

Singles: 12-inch 33/45rpm

W.B. 4-6 85

Singles: 7-inch

W.B. 3-4 85

LPs: 10/12-inch 33rpm

MIRAGE........ 5-10 84
W.B. 5-8 85
Also see CHIC
Also see HONEYDRIPPERS

RODGERS, Paul

LP '83

Singles: 7-inch

ATLANTIC........ 3-5 83

Picture Sleeves

ATLANTIC........ 3-5 83

LPs: 10/12-inch 33rpm

ATLANTIC........ 5-10 83
Also see BAD COMPANY
Also see FIRM
Also see FREE

RODNEY-O - JOE COOLEY

LP '89

LPs: 10/12-inch 33rpm

ATLANTIC........ 5-8 90
EGYPT........ 5-8 89

RODRIGUEZ, Johnny

C&W '72

Singles: 7-inch

CAPITOL........ 3-4 87-89
COLUMBIA 3-5 80
EPIC........ 3-5 79-86
MERCURY 3-6 72-79

Picture Sleeves

MERCURY 3-5 77

LPs: 10/12-inch 33rpm

EPIC........ 5-10 80-84
K-TEL........ 5-10 77
MERCURY 5-12 73-79
Also see HALL, Tom T.

RODRIGUEZ, Johnny, & Charly McClain

C&W '79

Singles: 7-inch

EPIC........ 3-5 79
Also see RODRIGUEZ, Johnny

RODWAY
(Steve Rodway)

P&R '82

Singles: 7-inch

MILLENNIUM........ 3-5 82

LPs: 10/12-inch 33rpm

MILLENNIUM........ 5-10 82

ROE, Tommy
(With the Satins; with Flamingos; with Roemans)

P&R/R&B/LP '62

Singles: 7-inch

ABC........ 4-8 66-71
ABC-PAR........ 5-10 62-66
AERTAUN (1108 "Wendy")........ 5-8 60s
CURB/MCA........ 3-5 85 86
JUDD (1018 "Caveman")........ 15-25 60
JUDD (1022 "Sheila") 25-45 62
MCA........ 3-4 70s
MGM/SOUTH........ 3-5 72-73
MARK IV (001 "Caveman")........ 25-50 60
MERCURY........ 3-5 86-87
MONUMENT........ 3-5 72-77
ROULETTE........ 3-5 70s
TRUMPET (1401 "Caveman") ... 50 75 60
W.B./CURB........ 3-5 78-80

Picture Sleeves

ABC........ 4-8 66-70
ABC-PAR (10362 "Susie Darlin'") 8-12 62

LPs: 10/12-inch 33rpm

ABC (594 thru 762)........ 10-15 67-72
ABC-PAR (ABC-423 thru ABC-574)........ 20-35 62-66
(Monaural.)
ABC-PAR (ABCS-423 thru ABCS-575)........ 25-40 62-66
(Stereo.)
ACCORD 5-10 82
GUSTO 5-10 80s
MCA........ 5-10 82
MONUMENT........ 8-12 76-77

ROE, Tommy / Impressions / Fats Domino

LPs: 10/12-inch 33rpm

ABC (ABC-504 "Shindig")........ 20-25 65
(Monaural.)
ABC (ABCS-504 "Shindig")........ 25-30 65
(Stereo.)
Also see IMPRESSIONS
Also see DOMINO, Fats

ROE, Tommy / Bobby Rydell / Gene Pitney

INT'L AWARD 10-15 60s
Also see PITNEY, Gene

ROE, Tommy / Bobby Rydell / Ray Stevens

LPs: 10/12-inch 33rpm

DESIGN (178 "Young Lovers").. 15-25 63

Also see RYDELL, Bobby
Also see STEVENS, Ray

ROE, Tommy / Al Tornello

LPs: 10/12-inch 33rpm

DIPLOMAT 10-20 60s

ROE, Tommy / Bobby Lee Trammell

LPs: 10/12-inch 33rpm

CROWN 15-20 63

Also see ROE, Tommy
Also see TRAMMELL, Bobby Lee

ROGER
(Featuring Shirley Murdock; with Mighty Clouds of Joy; Roger Troutman)

P&R/R&B/LP '81

Singles: 7-inch

REPRISE 3-4 87-88
W.B. 3-5 81-85

Picture Sleeves

REPRISE 3-4 87

LPs: 10/12-inch 33rpm

REPRISE 5-8 87
W.B. 5-10 81-84

Also see MIGHTY CLOUDS of JOY
Also see SCRITTI POLITTI & ROGER
Also see ZAPP

ROGERS, D.J.

P&R/R&B/LP '76

Singles: 12-inch 33/45rpm

COLUMBIA 4-8 79

Singles: 7-inch

ARC 3-5 79-80
COLUMBIA 3-5 78-80
RCA 3-5 75-76

LPs: 10/12-inch 33rpm

COLUMBIA 5-10 78-80
RCA 5-10 76-77
SHELTER 5-10 77

Also see RUSHEN, Patrice, & D.J. Rogers

ROGERS, Dann

P&R '79

Singles: 7-inch

IA 3-5 79
MCA 3-4 87

LPs: 10/12-inch 33rpm

IA 8-10 79

Also see CUMMINGS, Burton
Also see DELANEY & BONNIE

ROGERS, Eric, & His Orchestra

LP '61

LPs: 10/12-inch 33rpm

LONDON/PHASE 4 .... 5-15 61-66

ROGERS, Jimmy
(With His Trio; with His Rocking Four)

R&B '57

Singles: 78rpm

CHESS 10-25 50-57

Singles: 7-inch

CHESS (1506 "I Used to Have a Woman") 50-100 52
CHESS (1519 "The Last Time") 50-100 52
CHESS (1543 "Left Me with a Broken Heart") 50-75 53
CHESS (1574 "Chicago Bound") 50-75 54
CHESS (1616 "You're the One") 40-60 55
CHESS (1643 "If It Ain't Me") 40-60 56
CHESS (1659 "One Kiss") 40-60 57
CHESS (1721 "My Last Meal") 20-30 59

LPs: 10/12-inch 33rpm

CHESS 8-12

Also see SUNNYLAND SLIM
Also see WATERS, Muddy
Also see WILLIAMSON, Sonny Boy

ROGERS, Jimmy, & Freddy King

LPs: 10/12-inch 33rpm

SHELTER 8-10 73

Also see KING, Freddy
Also see ROGERS, Jimmy

ROGERS, Julie

P&R '64

Singles: 7-inch

MEGA 3-5 72
MERCURY 4-8 64-66

Picture Sleeves

MERCURY 5-10 65

LPs: 10/12-inch 33rpm

MEGA 5-10 72
MERCURY 15-25 65

ROGERS, Kenny
(Kenneth Rogers; with Linda Davis)

C&W '75

Singles: 7-inch

CARLTON (454 "That Crazy Feeling") 25-50 58
CARLTON (468 "For You Alone") 25-50 58
JOLLY ROGER 3-5 73-74
KEN-LEE (102 "Jole Blon") 50-100 50s
LIBERTY 3-4 80-86
MERCURY 5-10 66
RCA 3-4 84-89
REPRISE 3-4 89-91
U.A. 3-5 76-80

Picture Sleeves

LIBERTY 3-4 80-83
RCA 3-4 84-86
U.A. 3-5 79-80

LPs: 10/12-inch 33rpm

LIBERTY 5-10 80-85
MFSL 20-30 81
PICKWICK 5-10 79
QSP 5-10 84
RCA 5-8 84-87

REPRISE 5-8 89
U.A. (Except 934)......................... 5-8 76-80
U.A. (934 "The Gambler")............ 5-10 78
U.A. (934 "The Gambler")........... 50-75 78
(Picture disc. Promotional issue only. One of a four-artist, four-LP set.)
Also see CAMPBELL, Glen / Anne Murray / Kenny Rogers / Crystal Gayle
Also see MILSAP, Ronnie, & Kenny Rogers
Also see MURRAY, Anne, & Kenny Rogers
Also see U.S.A. for AFRICA

ROGERS, Kenny, & Kim Carnes

C&W/P&R '80

Singles: 7-inch

U.A. 3-5 80

Picture Sleeves

U.A. 3-5 80
Also see CARNES, Kim

ROGERS, Kenny, Kim Carnes & James Ingram

C&W/P&R/R&B '84

Singles: 7-inch

RCA... 3-4 84
Also see INGRAM, James
Also see ROGERS, Kenny, & Kim Carnes

ROGERS, Kenny, & Holly Dunn

C&W '90

Singles: 7-inch

REPRISE 3-4 90

ROGERS, Kenny, & Sheena Easton

C&W/P&R '83

Singles: 7-inch

LIBERTY 3-4 83

LPs: 10/12-inch 33rpm

LIBERTY 5-10 84
Also see EASTON, Sheena

ROGERS, Kenny, & Dolly Parton

P&R '83

Singles: 7-inch

RCA... 3-4 83-85
REPRISE 3-4 90

Picture Sleeves

RCA... 3-4 83
Also see PARTON, Dolly

ROGERS, Kenny, & Nickie Ryder

C&W '86

Singles: 7-inch

RCA... 3-4 86

ROGERS, Kenny, & First Edition

P&R/C&W/LP '69

Singles: 7-inch

JOLLY ROGERS........................... 3-5 72-73
REPRISE 4-8 68-72

LPs: 10/12-inch 33rpm

JOLLY ROGERS........................... 8-12 72-73
REPRISE 10-25 69-72
Members: Kenny Rogers; Mike Settle; Terry Williams; Mickey Jones; Kin Vassey; Mary Arnold.
Also see FIRST EDITION

ROGERS, Kenny, & Dottie West

C&W '78

Singles: 7-inch

LIBERTY 3-5 81-84
U.A. 3-5 78-79

LPs: 10/12-inch 33rpm

U.A. 5-10 78-80

LPs: 10/12-inch 33rpm

Also see ROGERS, Kenny
Also see WEST, Dottie

ROGERS, Lee

R&B '65

Singles: 7-inch

D-TOWN (1029 "Sad Affair") 10-20 64
D-TOWN (1035 "I Want You to Have Everything") 10-20 64
D-TOWN (1050 "Boss Love") 10-20 64
NSTANT...3-5 72
LOADSTONE 3-5 72
MAH'S (9 "Walk On By") 15-25 60s
PLATINUM SOUND 3-5 79
PREMIUM STUFF (4 "Jack the Playboy")...................................15-25 67
WHEELSVILLE 15-25 66

ROGERS, Roy

(With Dale Evans; with Sons of the Pioneers)

P&R '38

Singles: 78rpm

DECCA 10-20 40-44
GOLDEN..4-6 50s
RCA 5-15 50-57
VICTOR 8-15 45-48
VOCALION 20-30 38

Singles: 7-inch

CAPITOL..3-5 70-71
GOLDEN..5-8 50s
MCA...3-5 80
NEW DISC 8-12 56
RCA (Except 215)..........................5-15 51-52
RCA (215 "Souvenir Album") 20-40 49
(Boxed set of three colored vinyl 45s.)
20TH FOX..3-5 74-75

Picture Sleeves

GOLDEN..5-8 50s

EPs: 7-inch 33/45rpm

BLUEBIRD 10-20 50s
RCA (Except 3041).......................12-25 50-57
RCA (3041 "Souvenir Album")...25-50 52

LPs: 10/12-inch 33rpm

BLUEBIRD 15-25 59
CAMDEN 10-20 60-75
CAPITOL..10-20 62-72
GOLDEN..10-20 62
PICKWICK 5-10 70s
RCA (1439 "Sweet Hour of Prayer")......................................20-30 57
RCA (3041 "Souvenir Album")...40-60 52
(10-inch LP.)

RCA (3168 "Hymns of Faith") ... 30-50 54
(10-inch LP.)
20TH FOX 5-10 75
WORD 4-8 73-77
Also see SONS of the PIONEERS

ROGERS, Roy, & Clint Black

C&W '91

Singles: 7-inch

RCA 3-4 91
Also see BLACK, Clint
Also see ROGERS, Roy

ROGERS, Smokey

C&W '49

Singles: 78rpm

CAPITOL 4-8 49

ROGERS, Timmie

(Timmie "Oh Yeah" Rogers; with Excelsior Hep Cats; with Stomp Russell Trio; Timmy Rogers; Super Soul Brother Alias Clark Dark.)

P&R '57

Singles: 78rpm

CAMEO 5-15 57-58
CAPITOL 5-10 53
EXCELSIOR 10-20 45
MAJESTIC 10-20 46
MERCURY 10-15 54
REGIS 10-20 45
VARSITY 10-20 50s

Singles: 7-inch

CADET 3-5 71
CAMEO 5-10 57-58
CAPITOL 5-10 53
EPIC 4-8 65-66
MERCURY (70451 "If I Give My Heart to You") 15-25 54
PARKWAY 5-10 60
PARTEE 3-5 73
PHILIPS 4-8 62
SIGNATURE 5-10 60

LPs: 10/12-inch 33rpm

EPIC 15-20 65
PARTEE 10-15 73
PHILIPS 15-20 63

ROLLE, Ralph

D&D '85

Singles: 12-inch 33/45rpm

STREETWISE 4-6 85

Singles: 7-inch

STREETWISE 3-4 85

ROLLERS

P&R/R&B '61

Singles: 7-inch

LIBERTY 5-10 61
Member: Al Wilson.
Also see WILSON, Al

ROLLIN, Dana

P&R '66

Singles: 7-inch

TOWER 4-8 67

ROLLING STONES

P&R/LP '64

Singles: 12-inch 33/45rpm

ATCO (4616 "Miss You") 10-15 79
ROLLING STONES (70 "Hot Stuff") 45-55 76
(Promotional issue only.)
ROLLING STONES (119 "Miss You") 15-20 78
(Promotional issue only.)
ROLLING STONES (253 "If I Was a Dancer") 12-15 79
(Promotional issue only.)
ROLLING STONES (367 "Emotional Rescue") 15-20 80
(Promotional issue only.)
ROLLING STONES (397 "Start Me Up") 15-20 81
(Promotional issue only. Price includes special cover.)
ROLLING STONES (574 "She Was Hot") 12-15 84
(Promotional issue only.)
ROLLING STONES (685 "Undercover of the Night") 20-25 83
(White label. Promotional issue only.)
ROLLING STONES (685 "Undercover of the Night") 12-15 83
(Yellow label. Promotional issue only.)
ROLLING STONES (692 "Too Much Blood") 15-20 85
(Promotional issue only. Price includes special cover.)
ROLLING STONES (2275 "Harlem Shuffle") 8-10 86
(Price includes special cover.)
ROLLING STONES (2275 "Harlem Shuffle") 10-12 86
(Promotional issue only. Price includes special cover.)
ROLLING STONES (2340 "One Hit") 8-10 86
(Price includes color cover.)
ROLLING STONES (2340 "One Hit") 20-25 86
(Price includes black and white cover. Promotional issue only.)
ROLLING STONES (4609 "Miss You") 8-10 78
(Price includes special cover.)
ROLLING STONES (4616 "Miss You"/"Hot Stuff") 12-15 78

ROLLING STONES (96902 "Too Much Blood")............................ 8-10 85
(Price includes special cover.)
ROLLING STONES (96978 "Undercover of the Night") 8-10 83
(Price includes special cover.)

Singles: 7–inch

ABKCO (4701 "I Don't Know Why") 4-8 75
ABKCO (4702 "Out of Time")........ 4-8 75
COLUMBIA 3-4 90
LONDON (901 thru 910).............. 3-6 66-69
LONDON (9641 "Stoned") .. 750-1000 64
LONDON (9657 "Not Fade Away")...................................... 8-12 64
(Purple and white label.)
LONDON (9657 "Not Fade Away")...................................... 4-6 65
(Blue and white swirl label.)
LONDON (9682 "Tell Me") 5-10 64
(Purple and white label.)
LONDON (9682 "Tell Me") 4-6 65
(Blue and white swirl label.)
LONDON (9687 "It's All Over Now") 5-10 64
(Purple and white label.)
LONDON (9687 "It's All Over Now") 4-6 65
(Blue and white swirl label.)
LONDON (9708 "Time Is on My Side")................................. 5-10 64
(Purple and white label.)
LONDON (9708 "Time Is on My Side")................................... 4-6 65
(Blue and white swirl label.)
LONDON (9725 "Heart of Stone") 5-10 65
(Purple and white label.)
LONDON (9725 "Heart of Stone"). 4-6 65
(Blue and white swirl label.)
LONDON (9741 "The Last Time")....................................... 5-10 65
(Purple and white label.)
LONDON (9741 "The Last Time"). 4-6 65
(Blue and white swirl label.)
LONDON (9766 "Satisfaction") ... 5-10 65
LONDON (9792 "Get off of My Cloud") 5-10 65
LONDON (9808 "As Tears Go By") 5-10 65
LONDON (9823 "19th Nervous Breakdown")............................ 5-10 66
ROLLING STONES (Except 99724).. 3-5 71-86
ROLLING STONES (99724 "Miss You"/"Too Tough") 10-15 78
WMEE 97FM (001 "The Stones on 97").. 4-8

Promotional Singles

ABKCO (4701 "I Don't Know Why") 5-10 75
ABKCO (4702 "Out of Time").......5-10 75
COLUMBIA 5-8 90
LONDON (901 thru 910)...........15-25 66-69
LONDON (9641 "Stoned") 300-500 64
LONDON (9657 "Not Fade Away").....................................40-60 64
LONDON (9682 "Tell Me").........15-25 64
LONDON (9687 "It's All Over Now") 15-25 64
LONDON (9708 "Time Is on My Side") 15-25 64
LONDON (9725 "Heart of Stone").......................................15-25 65
LONDON (9741 "The Last Time")..15-25 65
LONDON (9766 "Satisfaction")..10-20 65
LONDON (9792 "Get off of My Cloud") 10-20 65
LONDON (9808 "As Tears Go By") 10-20 65
LONDON (9823 "19th Nervous Breakdown") 10-20 66
ROLLING STONES (228 "Time Waits for No One")...........................15-25 76
ROLLING STONES (316 "Before They Make Me Run")......................15-25 78
ROLLING STONES (05000 series) 5-10 86
ROLLING STONES (19000 thru 21301, except 19307)........................6-10 71-82
ROLLING STONES (19307 "Miss You"/ Far Away Eyes") 5-10 78
ROLLING STONES (19307 "Far Away Eyes"/ Far Away Eyes") 50-75 78
ROLLING STONES (90000 series, except 99724)...............................4-6 82-85
ROLLING STONES (99724 "Miss You"/"Miss You")...........................10-20 78

Picture Sleeves

LONDON (901 "Paint It Black")..10-20 66
LONDON (902 "Mother's Little Helper")...........................10-20 66
LONDON (903 "Have You Seen Your Mother Baby, Standing in the Shadows")...............................15-20 66
LONDON (904 "Ruby Tuesday") 10-20 67
LONDON (905 "Dandelion") 80-100 67
LONDON (906 "She's a Rainbow") 10-20 67
LONDON (908 "Jumpin' Jack Flash")..10-15 68
LONDON (909 "Street Fighting Man") 3000-3500 68
(Thus far, 12 copies are known to exist.)

LONDON (910 "Honky Tonk Women") 10-15 69
LONDON (9657 "Not Fade Away") 50-75 64
LONDON (9682 "Tell Me") 40-60 64
LONDON (9687 "It's All Over Now") 30-50 64
LONDON (9708 "Time Is on My Side") 25-35 64
LONDON (9725 "Heart of Stone") 150-250 65
LONDON (9741 "The Last Time") 25-35 65
LONDON (9766 "Satisfaction") . 40-60 65
LONDON (9792 "Get Off of My Cloud") 15-25 65
LONDON (9808 "As Tears Go By") 15-25 65
LONDON (9823 "19th Nervous Breakdown") 15-25 66
ROLLING STONES (Except 228, 316 and 19309) 3-6 78-86
ROLLING STONES (228 "Time Waits for No One") 15-25 76
(Promotional issue only.)
ROLLING STONES (316 "Before They Make Me Run") 15-25 78
(Promotional issue only.)
ROLLING STONES (19309 "Beast of Burden") 300-400 78
ROLLING STONES 3-5 71-81
(For generic, die-cut paper sleeves with Rolling Stones tongue logo. Not for any specific release.)

EPs: 7–inch 33/45rpm

ATLANTIC (900 "Exile on Main Street") 35-45 72
(Jukebox issue only.)
ATLANTIC (5901 "Goats Head Soup") 35-45 73
(Jukebox issue only.)
LONDON (34 "Rolling Stones Now") 100-150 64
(Jukebox issue only.)
LONDON (37 "Out of Our Heads") 100-150 64
(Jukebox issue only.)
LONDON (43 "December's Children") 100-150 64
(Jukebox issue only.)
LONDON (54 "Their Satanic Majesties Request") 100-200 64
(Jukebox issue only.)
ROLLING STONES (287 "The Rolling Stones") 50-75 77
(Promotional issue only.)

LPs: 10/12-inch 33rpm

ABKCO (ANA-1 "Metamorphosis") 15-20 75
ABKCO (MPD-1 "Songs of the Rolling Stones") 150-200 75
(Promotional issue only.)
ABKCO (0268 "Greatest Hits") ..20-25 80s
(TV mail-order offer.)
ABKCO (1218 "Singles Collection") 15-25 89
(Four-LP set.)
CRAWDADDY ("Rolling Stones Tour Special") 150-200 76
(Promotional issue to college radio stations only.)
D.I.R. (312 "King Biscuit Flower Hour") 150-200 80
(Promotional issue only.)
D.I.R. (325 "King Biscuit Flower Hour") 150-200 80
(Promotional issue only.)
INS RADIO (1003 "It's Here Luv") 75-125 65
LONDON (1 "Big Hits") 15-25 66
(Monaural.)
LONDON (2 "Their Satanic Majesties Request") 50-100 67
(Monaural. Has 3-D cover.)
LONDON (2 "Their Satanic Majesties Request") 20-30 67
(Stereo.)
(With 3-D cover.)
LONDON (2 "Their Satanic Majesties Request") 10-15 70
(Stereo.)
(With standard cover.)
LONDON (3 "Through the Past Darkly") 8-10 69
LONDON (4 "Let It Bleed") 10-20 69
(With bonus poster.)
LONDON (4 "Let It Bleed") 8-10 69
(Without poster.)
LONDON (5 "Get Your Ya-Yas Out") 8-10 70
LONDON (375 "Rolling Stones") 30-50 64
(Stereo. Add $75 to $100 if accompanied by a 12" x 12" bonus, color photo. Cover has printed note about photo at lower left. With "Full Frequency Range Recording" label.)
LONDON (375 "Rolling Stones") .8-10 65
(No mention of photo on cover. Does not have "Full Frequency Range Recording" on label.)
LONDON (402 "12 x 5") 30-50 64
(Stereo. With "Full Frequency Range Recording" label.)
LONDON (402 "12 x 5") 8-10 65
(Does not have "Full Frequency Range Recording" on label.)
LONDON (420 "Rolling Stones Now") 30-50 65

(Stereo. With "Full Frequency Range Recording" label.)
LONDON (420 "Rolling Stones Now") 8-10 65
(Does not have "Full Frequency Range Recording" on label.)
LONDON (429 "Out of Our Heads") 30-50 65
(Stereo. With "Full Frequency Range Recording" label.)
LONDON (429 "Out of Our Heads") 8-10 65
(Does not have "Full Frequency Range Recording" on label.)
LONDON (451 "December's Children") 30-50 65
(Stereo. With "Full Frequency Range Recording" label.)
LONDON (451 "December's Children") 8-10 65
(Does not have "Full Frequency Range Recording" on label.)
LONDON (476 "Aftermath") 8-10 66
(Stereo.)
LONDON (493 "Got Live If You Want It") 8-10 66
(Stereo.)
LONDON (499 "Between the Buttons") 8-10 67
(Stereo.)
LONDON (509 "Flowers") 8-10 67
(Stereo.)
LONDON (539 "Beggars Banquet") 8-12 68
(All songs are shown as written by Jagger & Richard.)
LONDON (539 "Beggars Banquet") 8-10 60s
(*Prodigal Son* is shown as written by Rev. Wilkins.)
LONDON (606/7 "Hot Rocks") .. 10-12 71
LONDON (626/7 "More Hot Rocks") 10-12 72
LONDON (3375 "The Rolling Stones") 75-100 64
(Monaural. With "Full Frequency Range Recording" label. Add $75 to $100 if accompanied by a 12" x 12" bonus, color photo. Cover has printed note about photo at lower left.)
LONDON (3375 "The Rolling Stones") 30-40 65
(Does not have "Full Frequency Range Recording" on label.)
LONDON (3375 "The Rolling Stones") 400-600 64
(White label, monaural. Promotional issue only.)
LONDON (3402 "12 x 5") 50-75 64
(Monaural. With "Full Frequency Range Recording" label.)
LONDON (3402 "12 x 5") 30-40 65
(Does not have "Full Frequency Range Recording" on label.)
LONDON (3420 "Rolling Stones Now") 50-75 65
(Monaural. With "Full Frequency Range Recording" label.)
LONDON (3420 "Rolling Stones Now") 30-40 65
(Does not have "Full Frequency Range Recording" on label.)
LONDON (3429 "Out of Our Heads") 50-75 65
(Monaural. With "Full Frequency Range Recording" label.)
LONDON (3429 "Out of Our Heads") 30-40 65
(Does not have "Full Frequency Range Recording" on label.)
LONDON (3451 "December's Children") 50-75 65
(Monaural. With "Full Frequency Range Recording" label.)
LONDON (3451 "December's Children") 30-40 65
(Does not have "Full Frequency Range Recording" on label.)
LONDON (3476 "Aftermath") 20-30 66
(Monaural.)
LONDON (3493 "Got Live If You Want It") 20-30 66
(Monaural.)
LONDON (3499 "Between the Buttons") 20-30 67
(Monaural.)
LONDON (3509 "Flowers") 20-30 67
(Monaural.)
MFSL (1 "Rolling Stones") 250-300 85
(11-LP boxed set, includes booklet, postcard and alignment tool.)
MFSL (060 "Sticky Fingers") 20-40 82
MFSL (087 "Some Girls") 20-40 82
MUTUAL BROADCASTING SYSTEM ("Rolling Stones: Past and Present") 800-1200 84
(12-LP boxed set, issued only to radio stations. Price includes programming sheets.)
ROLLING STONES (2900 "Exile on Main St.") 10-15 72
(Add $3 to $5 if accompanied by sheet of 12 bonus postcards.)
ROLLING STONES (9001 "Love You Live") 10-15 77
ROLLING STONES (16015 "Emotional Rescue") 5-10 80

ROLLING STONES (16028 "Sucking in the Seventies") 5-10 81
ROLLING STONES (16052 "Tattoo You") 5-10 81
ROLLING STONES (39108 "Some Girls") 10-15 78
(With all girls' faces shown.)
ROLLING STONES (39108 "Some Girls") 5-10 78
(Not all girls' faces shown. Cover is "Under Construction.")
ROLLING STONES (39113 "Still Life") 5-10 82
ROLLING STONES (39115 "Still Life") 30-40 82
(Picture disc.)
ROLLING STONES (40250 "Dirty Work") 5-10 86
ROLLING STONES (45333 "Steel Wheels") 5-10 89
ROLLING STONES (59100 "Sticky Fingers") 8-10 71
(Yellow label.)
ROLLING STONES (59100 "Sticky Fingers") 150-250 71
(White label. Promotional issue only.)
ROLLING STONES (59101 "Goats Head Soup") 8-10 73
ROLLING STONES (79101 "It's Only Rock & Roll") 8-10 74
ROLLING STONES (79102 "Made in the Shade") 8-10 75
ROLLING STONES (79104 "Black and Blue") 8-10 76
ROLLING STONES (90120 "Undercover") 5-10 83
ROLLING STONES (90176 "Rewind") 5-10 84
WESTWOOD ONE ("The Rolling Stones Special") 175-225 82
(Promotional issue only.)

Members: Mick Jagger; Keith Richards; Bill Wyman; Brian Jones; Charlie Watts; Mick Taylor; Ron Wood.

Also see BEACH BOYS
Also see FAITHFUL, Marianne
Also see HOPKINS, Nicky
Also see JAGGER, Mick
Also see JONES, Brian
Also see RICHARDS, Keith
Also see ROCKET 88
Also see TAYLOR, Mick
Also see WILLIE & Poor Boys
Also see WOOD, Ron
Also see WYMAN, Bill

ROMAN, Dick

P&R '62

Singles: 78rpm

ABC-PAR 4-8 56
DOUBLE AA 4-6 55-56

Singles: 7-inch

ABC-PAR 5-10 56
CHARLIE PARKER 4-8 62
CORAL 4-6 60s
DOUBLE AA 5-10 55-56
EPIC 4-8 59-61
FORD 4-8 60s
HARMON 5-10 62-63
MGM 4-6 60s
PRESIDENT 4-6 60s
SEVILLE 4-6 60s
SMASH 4-8 63

LPs: 10/12-inch 33rpm

HARMON 15-25 62

ROMAN, Lyn

R&B '86

Singles: 7-inch

DOT 4-6 68
ICHIBAN 3-4 86

ROMAN HOLLIDAY

P&R/LP '83

Singles: 7-inch

JIVE 3-4 83-85

LPs: 10/12-inch 33rpm

JIVE 5-10 83

ROMANS (With Little Caesar): see LITTLE CAESAR & ROMANS

ROMANTICS

P&R/LP '80

Singles: 12-inch 33/45rpm

NEMPEROR 4-8 83-85

Singles: 7-inch

BOMP 4-6 78
NEMPEROR 3-5 80-85
SPIDER 8-12 77

Picture Sleeves

BOMP 4-6 78
NEMPEROR 3-5 80-85

EPs: 7-inch 33/45rpm

BOMP 5-8 78

LPs: 10/12-inch 33rpm

NEMPEROR 5-10 80-85

ROMEO

R&B '87

Singles: 7-inch

TRIPLE 3-4 87

ROMEO & JULIET
(Dialogue from film soundtrack)

P&R '69

Singles: 7-inch

CAPITOL 3-5 69

ROMEO VOID

LP '82

Singles: 12-inch 33/45rpm

COLUMBIA 4-6 82-84
415 (007 "Never Say Yes") 5-10 81

Singles: 7–Inch

COLUMBIA 3-4 82-84

LPs: 10/12–inch 33rpm

COLUMBIA 5-8 82-84

415 .... 8-12 82

Members: Debora Iyall; Peter Woods; Benjamin Bossi; Larry Carter; Frank Zincavage.

ROMEO'S DAUGHTER

P&R/LP '88

Singles: 7–inch

JIVE.. 3-4 88

Picture Sleeves

JIVE.. 3-4 88

LPs: 10/12–inch 33rpm

JIVE.. 5-8 88

ROMEOS

P&R/R&B '67

Singles: 7–inch

MARK II.................................... 4-8 67

LPs: 10/12–inch 33rpm

MARK II.................................. 15-20 67

Members: Kenny Gamble; Thom Bell; Roland Chambers; Winnie Walford; Karl Chambers; Leon Huff.

Also see HUFF, Leon

RON & D.C. Crew

P&R '87

Singles: 7–inch

PROFILE.................................... 3-4 87

RON C

LP '90

LPs: 10/12–inch 33rpm

PROFILE.................................... 5-8 90

RONALD & RUBY

P&R '58

Singles: 7–inch

RCA... 8-12 58

Members: Lee Morris; Beverly Ross.

RONDELS

P&R '61

Singles: 7–inch

AMY 8-12 61-62

NOTE 8-12 61

RON-DELS

P&R '65

Singles: 7–inch

BROWNFIELD (18 "Walk About") 10-15

SMASH 8-12 65

Member: Delbert McClinton.

Also see McCLINTON, Delbert

RONDO, Don

P&R '56

Singles: 78rpm

DECCA....................................... 3-5 55

JUBILEE..................................... 3-5 56-57

Singles: 7–inch

ATLANTIC 4-8 63

CARLTON.................................4-0 60-61

DECCA 5-10 55

JUBILEE 5-10 56-66

ROULETTE...............................4-8 59-60

TRIP..3-5

TUBA 4-6 65

U.A. 4-6 66-67

VIRGO 3-5 72

LPs: 10/12–inch 33rpm

JUBILEE 10-20 57-58

VOCALION 5-10 70

RONETTES

(Ronnettes; Ronettes Featuring Veronica)

P&R/R&B '63

Singles: 7–inch

A&M 5-10 69

BUDDAH...................................5-10 73-74

COLPIX (646 "I'm Gonna Quit While I'm Ahead") 40-60 62

MAY (114 "Silhouettes") 30-40 63

MAY (138 "The Memory")..........30-40 63

PAVILLION 3-5 82

PHILLES 10-15 63-66

Promotional Singles

A&M 8-12 69

BUDDAH...................................10-15 73-74

COLPIX (646 "I'm Gonna Quit While I'm Ahead") 30-40 62

MAY (114 "Silhouettes") 30-40 63

MAY (138 "The Memory")..........30-40 63

PAVILLION 4-8 82

PHILLES 10-20 63-66

Picture Sleeves

PHILLES (123 "Walking in the Rain")....................................25-35 64

PHILLES (126 "Born to Be Together")..............................25-35 65

PHILLES (128 "Is This What I Get for Loving You") 25-40 65

LPs: 10/12–inch 33rpm

COLPIX (486 "The Ronettes, Featuring Veronica").............50-100 65
(Blue label. Monaural.)

COLPIX (486 "The Ronettes, Featuring Veronica").............75-150 65
(Gold label. Monaural.)

COLPIX (486 "The Ronettes, Featuring Veronica")...............60-75 65
(Blue label. Stereo.)

COLPIX (486 "The Ronettes, Featuring Veronica")...........100-200 65
(Gold label. Stereo.)

COLPIX (486 "The Ronettes, Featuring Veronica").............75-100 65
(White label. Promotional issue only.)

PHILLES (4006 "Presenting the Fabulous Ronettes")...........100-125 64
(Blue label. Monaural.)

PHILLES (4006 "Presenting the Fabulous Ronettes") 75-150 64
(Yellow label. Monaural.)
PHILLES (4006 "Presenting the Fabulous Ronettes") 200-300 64
(Yellow label with red print. Stereo.)
PHILLES (4006 "Presenting the Fabulous Ronettes") 200-250 64
(Yellow label with black print. Stereo issue through Capitol Record Club.)
MURRAY HILL........................... 5-10 86
Members: Veronica Bennett-Spector; Estelle Bennett; Nedra Talley-Ross.
Also see RONNIE & RELATIVES
Also see SPECTOR, Ronnie

RONETTES / Crystals / Darlene Love

Singles: 7-inch

PAVILLION (1354 "Phil Spector's Christmas Medley")..................... 3-5 81
(Promotional issue only.)

RONETTES / Crystals / Darlene Love / Bob B. Soxx & Blue Jeans

EPs: 7-inch 33/45rpm

PHILLES ("Christmas EP") 20-40 63

LPs: 10/12-inch 33rpm

APPLE (3400 "Phil Spector's Christmas Album") 10-12 72
PASSPORT (3604 "Phil Spector's Christmas Album") 5-8 85
PAVILLION.................................. 5-10 81
PHILLES (4005 "A Christmas Gift for You") 50-100 63
(Blue label.)
PHILLES (4005 "A Christmas Gift for You") 40-60 63
(Yellow and red label.)
W.B./SPECTOR 8-12
(Phil Spector is heard speaking on this LP. The Apple and Passport LPs are reissues of the Philles album.)
Also see BOB B. SOXX & Blue Jeans
Also see CRYSTALS
Also see HARVEY, Phil
Also see LOVE, Darlene
Also see RONETTES

RONNIE & HI-LITES

P&R '62

Singles: 7-inch

ABC-PAR 10-15 65
COLLECTABLES 3-4 80s
ERIC.. 3-4 70s
JOY 10-15 62
RAVEN (8000 "Valerie")........... 10-15 63
(Black label.)
RAVEN (8000 "Valerie")........... 15-25 63
(White label. Promotional issue only.)
WIN 10-15 63

RONNIE & RELATIVES

(Ronettes)

Singles: 7-inch

COLPIX (601 "I Want a Boy") 30-40 61
MAY (111 "My Guiding Angel")..50-75 62
Also see RONETTES

RONNY & DAYTONAS

P&R/LP '64

Singles: 7-inch

MALA 6-12 64-66
RCA 5-10 66-68
SHOW-BIZ 8-12 68

Picture Sleeves

RCA (8896 "Dianne, Dianne")....15-25 66

LPs: 10/12-inch 33rpm

MALA (4001 "G.T.O.") 50-100 64
MALA (4002 "Sandy") 20-35 66
(Monaural.)
MALA (4002-S "Sandy") 75-100 66
(Stereo.)
Members: John "Bucky" Wilkin; Buzz Cason.

RONSON, Mick

LP '74

LPs: 10/12-inch 33rpm

RCA 8-12 74
Also see HUNTER, Ian, & Mick Ronson
Also see PURE PRAIRIE LEAGUE

RONSTADT, Linda

(With the Stone Poneys; with Nelson Riddle Orchestra)

P&R '68

Singles: 7-inch

ASYLUM 3-5 73-85
CAPITOL (2004 "Different Drum")..5-10 67
CAPITOL (2110 "Up to My Neck in High Muddy Water")............10-15 68
CAPITOL (2195 "Some of Shelly's Blues")............................5-10 68
CAPITOL (2438 "Dolphins").........5-10 69
CAPITOL (2767 "Lovesick Blues").4-8 70
CAPITOL (2846 thru 4050)...........3-6 70-75
CAPITOL (5838 "All the Beautiful Things")...........................8-12 67
CAPITOL (5910 "Evergreen") 5-10 67
ELEKTRA.......................................3-5 75-78
SIDEWALK (937 "So Fine") 75-100 66
(With Davie Allan.)

Picture Sleeves

ASYLUM 3-5 78-82
CAPITOL (2110 "Up to My Neck in High Muddy Water")............15-25 68

LPs: 10/12-inch 33rpm

ASYLUM (Except 401 & 60489) ..5-10 73-86
ASYLUM (401 "Living in the USA") 10-15 78
(Picture disc.)

ASYLUM (60489 "'Round Midnight") 10-15 86
CAPITOL (208 thru 635) 10-15 69-72
CAPITOL (2000 series) 12-18 68
CAPITOL (11000 series) 8-12 74-77
CAPITOL (16000 series) 5-10 80
ELEKTRA 5-10 80-87
MFSL 15-20 85
PICKWICK 8-10 70s

Session: Davie Allan; Nelson Riddle.
Also see ALLAN, Davie
Also see CASH, Johnny / Roy Clark / Linda Ronstadt
Also see CHRISTMAS SPIRIT
Also see EAGLES
Also see GLASS, Phillip
Also see NEWMAN, Randy
Also see NITTY GRITTY DIRT BAND & Linda Ronstadt
Also see PARTON, Dolly, Linda Ronstadt, & Emmylou Harris
Also see RIDDLE, Nelson
Also see STONE PONEYS

RONSTADT, Linda, & Emmylou Harris

Singles: 7-inch

ASYLUM 3-5 75

Also see HARRIS, Emmylou

RONSTADT, Linda, & James Ingram

P&R '86

Singles: 7-inch

MCA 3-4 86

Picture Sleeves

MCA 3-4 86

Also see INGRAM, James

RONSTADT, Linda, & Aaron Neville

LP '89

LPs: 10/12-inch 33rpm

ELEKTRA 5-8 89

Also see NEVILLE, Aaron

RONSTADT, Linda, & J.D. Souther

C&W '82

Singles: 7-inch

ASYLUM 3-4 82

Also see RONSTADT, Linda
Also see SOUTHER, J.D.

ROOFTOP SINGERS

P&R/C&W/R&B/LP '63

Singles: 7-inch

ATCO 4-6 67
VANGUARD 4-8 62-65

Picture Sleeves

VANGUARD 5-10 63

LPs: 10/12-inch 33rpm

VANGUARD 10-20 63-65

Members: Erik Darling; Lynne Taylor; Bill Svanoe.
Also see TARRIERS

ROOMATES

P&R '61

Singles: 7-inch

ADDIT (2211 "Making Believe") 10-15 60
BAN (691 "A Place Called Love") .. 3-5 85
CAMEO (233 "A Sunday Kind of Love") 15-25 62
CANADIAN AMERICAN (166 "My Heart") 15-25 64
COLLECTABLES 3-4 80s
PHILIPS (40105 "Gee") 10-20 63
PHILIPS (40153 "The Nearness of You") 20-25 63
PHILIPS (40153 "The Nearness of You") 15-20 64
PROMO (2211 "Making Believe") 10-15 64
VALMOR (8 "Glory of Love") 8-12 61
VALMOR (10 "Band of Gold") 8-12 61
VALMOR (13 "My Foolish Heart") 10-15 61

LPs: 10/12-inch 33rpm

RELIC 5-10

Also see CATHY JEAN & ROOMATES

ROS, Edmundo, & His Orchestra

P&R '58

Singles: 78rpm

LONDON 3-5 51-57

Singles: 7-inch

LONDON 4-8 51-63

EPs: 7-inch 33/45rpm

CORAL 5-10 54
LONDON 5-10 52-59

LPs: 10/12-inch 33rpm

CORAL 8-15 54
LONDON 5-15 52-78

ROSCOE & MABLE

R&B '77

Singles: 7-inch

CHOCOLATE CITY 3-5 77

ROSE, Andy
(With the Thorns)

P&R '58

Singles: 7-inch

AAMCO 10-20 58
CORAL 5-10 59-62
EMBER 4-8 64
GOLDEN CREST 4-8 64

ROSE, Biff

LP '69

Singles: 7-inch

BUDDAH 3-5 71
TETRAGRAMMATON 3-5 68-70

LPs: 10/12-inch 33rpm

BUDDAH 8-12 71
TETRAGRAMMATON 10-15 68-69
U.A. 8-12 73

ROSE, David, & His Orchestra

P&R '43

Singles: 78rpm

MGM 3-5 50-57
VICTOR 4-6 43-44

Singles: 7-inch

CAPITOL 3-6 66-69
MGM 3-8 50-67

Picture Sleeves

MGM 4-8 56-62

EPs: 7-inch 33/45rpm

KAPP 5-10 59
MGM 5-10 51-58
ROYALE 5-10 50s

LPs: 10/12-inch 33rpm

CAPITOL 8-15 66-69
DINO 5-10 72
KAPP 10-20 59-61
LION 10-20 59
MCA 5-8 83
MGM 5-20 51-70
METRO 5-15 65-66

Also see PREVIN, Andre

ROSE BROTHERS

R&B '86

Singles: 12-inch 33/45rpm

MUSCLE SHOALS 4-6 86

Singles: 7-inch

MUSCLE SHOALS 3-4 86-88

LPs: 10/12-inch 33rpm

MUSCLE SHOALS 5-8 86

Members: Bob Rose; Larry Rose; Kenny Rose; Greg Rose.

ROSE COLORED GLASS

P&R '71

Singles: 7-inch

BANG 3-5 71

ROSE GARDEN

P&R '67

Singles: 7-inch

ATCO 5-10 67-68

LPs: 10/12-inch 33rpm

ATCO (255 "Rose Garden") 15-25 68

Members: Diana DiRose; James Groshong; John Noreen; Bill Fleming; Bruce Boudin.

ROSE ROYCE

P&R/R&B/LP '76

Singles: 12-inch 33/45rpm

MONTAGE 4-8 84

Singles: 7-inch

C&R 3-4 84
MCA 3-5 76-77
OMNI 3-4 86-87
WHITFIELD 3-5 77-82

LPs: 10/12-inch 33rpm

EPIC 5-8 82
MCA 5-10 76
WHITFIELD 5-10 77-81

ROSE TATOO

LP '80

Singles: 7-inch

MIRAGE 3-5 80-82

LPs: 10/12-inch 33rpm

MIRAGE 5-10 80-82

ROSELLI, Jimmy

LP '65

Singles: 7-inch

RIC 4-8 65
U.A. 4-6 65-69

LPs: 10/12-inch 33rpm

RIC 10-15 65
U.A. 5-12 65-72

ROSIE

(With the Originals; Rosie "Formerly with the Originals")

P&R '60

Singles: 7-inch

ABC 3-5 73
HIGHLAND 10-20 60-61
BRUNSWICK 10-20 61

LPs: 10/12-inch 33rpm

BRUNSWICK (54102 "Lonley Blue Nights") 40-60 61
(Monaural.)
BRUNSWICK (754102 "Lonley Blue Nights") 50-80 61
(Stereo.)

ROSS, Charlie

P&R '75

Singles: 7-inch

BIG TREE 3-5 75-76
TOWN HOUSE 3-4 82-83

ROSS, Diana

P&R/R&B/LP '70

Singles: 12-inch 33/45rpm

MOTOWN 5-10 78-80

Singles: 7-inch

MOTOWN 3-6 70-81
RCA 3-5 81-87

Picture Sleeves

MOTOWN 3-6 70-80
RCA 3-5 82-86

EPs: 7-inch 33/45rpm

MOTOWN (7588 "Sneak Preview from Lady Sings the Blues") 8-12 72
(Promotional issue only.)

LPs: 10/12-inch 33rpm

DORAL (104 "Diana Ross") 150-200 60s
(Promotional mail-order issue, from Doral cigarettes.)
KORY 8-10 77
MOTOWN (100 series) 5-10 81-83
MOTOWN (711 thru 907) 8-12 70-78
MOTOWN (923 "The Boss") 5-10 79
(Black vinyl.)
MOTOWN (923 "The Boss") 10-20 79
(Colored vinyl. Promotional issue only.)
MOTOWN (951 thru 960) 6-12 81
MOTOWN (5000 series) 5-10 83

MOTOWN (6000 series) 6-12 83-89
PARAMOUNT (181/182 "Lady Sings the Blues") 35-50 72
(An "MRA Multiple Record Album, serving the requirements of both radio and TV stations," this LP has a 15-minute interview with Diana Ross. Includes scripts. Promotional issue only.)
RCA.. 5-10 81-87
Also see DENVER, John / Diana Ross
Also see GAYE, Marvin, & Diana Ross
Also see IGLESIAS, Julio, & Diana Ross
Also see SUPREMES
Also see TEMPTATIONS
Also see U.S.A. for AFRICA

ROSS, Diana, & Bill Cosby / Diana Ross & Jackson Five

EPs: 7–inch 33/45rpm

MOTOWN 5-10 70
Also see COSBY, Bill
Also see JACKSONS

ROSS, Diana, & Michael Jackson

P&R/R&B '78

Singles: 7–inch

MCA 3-5 78

Picture Sleeves

MCA 3-5 78
Also see JACKSON, Michael

ROSS, Diana, & Lionel Richie

P&R/R&B '81

Singles: 7–inch

MOTOWN 3-5 81
POLYGRAM ("Dreaming of You") 10-15 81
(Promotional issue only. No number given.)
Also see RICHIE, Lionel

ROSS, Diana, Stevie Wonder, Marvin Gaye, Smokey Robinson

P&R/R&B '79

Singles: 7–inch

MOTOWN (1455 "Pops, We Love You") 3-5 79
(Black vinyl.)
MOTOWN (1455 "Pops, We Love You") 5-10 79
(Heart shaped disc. Red vinyl.)
MOTOWN (1455 "Pops, We Love You") 5-10 79
(Green vinyl. Promotional issue only.)

LPs: 10/12–inch 33rpm

MOTOWN 5-10 79
Also see DIAMOND, Neil / Diana Ross & Supremes
Also see GAYE, Marvin
Also see ROBINSON, Smokey
Also see ROSS, Diana
Also see WONDER, Stevie

ROSS, Jack

P&R '62

Singles: 7–inch

DOT... 4-8 61-63
ROMAL 5-10 61

LPs: 10/12–inch 33rpm

DOT (3429 "Cinderella") 15-25 62

ROSS, Jackie

(Jacki Ross)

P&R/R&B '64

Singles: 7–inch

BRUNSWICK 4-8 67-68
CAPITOL.................................... 3-5 76
CHESS....................................... 4-8 64
FOUNTAIN 4-6 69
GSF... 3-5 72-73
MERCURY 3-5 70-71
SAR (129 "Hard Times") 5-10 62
SCEPTER 3-5 72

LPs: 10/12–inch 33rpm

CHESS (1489 "Full Bloom")....... 15-25 64
Also see LITTLE MILTON & Jackie Ross

ROSS, Jimmy

R&B '81

Singles: 7–inch

RFC.. 3-5 81

ROSS, Spencer

P&R '60

Singles: 7–inch

COLUMBIA 4-6 59-60

LPs: 10/12–inch 33rpm

COLUMBIA 10-20 60

ROSSINGTON - COLLINS BAND

(Rossington Band)

P&R/LP '80

Singles: 7–inch

MCA.. 3-5 80-88

LPs: 10/12–inch 33rpm

MCA.. 5-10 80-88
Members: Gary Rossington; Al Collins.
Also see LYNYRD SKYNYRD

ROTA, Nino

P&R '72

Singles: 7–inch

PARAMOUNT 3-5 72
U.A. 3-5 72

ROTARY CONNECTION

LP '68

Singles: 7–inch

CADET CONCEPT 4-8 68-70

LPs: 10/12–inch 33rpm

CADET CONCEPT 15-25 68-70
Members: Minnie Riperton; Sidney Barnes.
Also see RIPPERTON, Minnie

ROTH, David Lee

P&R/LP '85

Singles: 7–inch

W.B. 3-4 85-90

Picture Sleeves

W.B. 3-4 85-88

LPs: 10/12–inch 33rpm

W.B. 5-10 85-90

Also see BEACH BOYS
Also see VAN HALEN

ROUGH DIAMOND

LP '77

Singles: 7–inch

ISLAND 3-5 77

LPs: 10/12–inch 33rpm

ISLAND 8-10 77

Members: Byron Britton; Geoff Britton.
Also see URIAH HEEP

ROUGH TRADE

P&R '82

Singles: 7–inch

BOARDWALK 3-5 82

LPs: 10/12–inch 33rpm

UMBRELLA 10-15 77

ROUND ROBIN

P&R '64

Singles: 7–inch

CAPITOL 4-8 67
DOMAIN 5-10 63-65
SHOT 4-8 66

LPs: 10/12–inch 33rpm

CHALLENGE (620 "Land of 1000 Dances") 15-25 65
DOMAIN (101 "Greatest Dance Hits Slauson Style") 25-35 64

ROUND ROBINS / Joe Cenna

Singles: 7–inch

BELL 4-8 60s

ROUNDTREE

R&B '78

Singles: 12–inch 33/45rpm

ISLAND 4-8 78

Singles: 7–inch

ISLAND 3-5 78

Members: Diva Gray; Bernard Edwards; Luther Vandross; David Lasley.
Also see CHIC
Also see GRAY, Diva, & Oyster
Also see VANDROSS, Luther

ROUNDTREE, Richard

R&B '76

Singles: 7–inch

ARTISTS of AMERICA 3-5 76
MGM 3-5 73
VERVE 3-5 72-73

LPs: 10/12–inch 33rpm

MGM 8-12 72

ROUSSOS, Demis

P&R/LP '78

Singles: 7–inch

BIG TREE 3-5 74-75
MGM 3-5 73
MERCURY 3-5 76-78

Picture Sleeves

MERCURY 3-5 78

LPs: 10/12–inch 33rpm

BIG TREE 8-12 74-75
MGM 10-15 72
MERCURY 5-10 76-78

ROUTERS

P&R '62

Singles: 7–inch

W.B. 4-8 62-64

LPs: 10/12–inch 33rpm

MERCURY 10-15 73
W.B. (1490 "Let's Go") 20-30 63
W.B. (1524 "1963's Great Instrumental Hits") 20-30 63
W.B. (1559 "Charge!") 20-30 64
W.B. (1595 "Chuck Berry Songbook") 20-30 65

Members: Joe Saraceno; Rene Hall; Mike Gordon. Ed Kay.

ROVER BOYS

P&R '56

Singles: 78rpm

ABC-PAR 4-8 56
CORAL 4-8 54

Singles: 7–inch

ABC 3-5 73
ABC-PAR 5-10 56
CORAL 5-10 54
DECCA 4-6 63
RCA 4-8 59
U.A. 4-8 61

Member: Billy Albert.

ROVERS
(Irish Rovers)

C&W '81

Singles: 7–inch

EPIC 3-5 81

LPs: 10/12–inch 33rpm

CLEVELAND INT'L 5-10 81-82

Also see IRISH ROVERS

ROWANS

P&R '76

Singles: 7–inch

ASYLUM 3-5 75-76
COLUMBIA 3-5 72-73

LPs: 10/12–inch 33rpm

ASYLUM 8-10 75-77
COLUMBIA 10-15 72

Members: Peter Rowan; Chris Rowan; Lorin Rowan.
Also see EARTH OPERA
Also see GARCIA, Jerry
Also see OLD and in the WAY

ROWLES, John

P&R/LP '71

Singles: 7–inch

KAPP 3-6 68-71
UNI 3-6 68

LPs: 10/12-inch 33rpm

KAPP.. 10-15 69-71
MCA 5-8

ROXANNE

P&R '88

Singles: 7-inch

SCOTTI BROS............................... 3-4 88

Members: Jamie Brown; John Butler; Dave Landry; Joe Infante.

ROXANNE with UTFO

D&D '85

Singles: 12-inch 33/45rpm

SELECT 4-6 85

Singles: 7-inch

SELECT 3-4 85

Also see UTFO

ROXETTE

P&R/LP '89

Singles: 12-inch 33/45rpm

CAPITOL (15018 "Hartland") 5-10 84

Singles: 7-inch

EMI (Except 04409) 3-4 89
EMI (04409 "Listen to Your Heart").. 3-6 89
(Promotional issue only. Commercial single release on cassette only.)

LPs: 10/12-inch 33rpm

EMI 5-8 89-91

ROXY MUSIC

LP '73

Singles: 7-inch

ATCO 3-6 75-80
W.B. (Except 7779)........................ 3-5 82-83
W.B. (7779 "Do the Strand") 4-8 73

Promotional Singles

ATCO 4-8 75-80
W.B. 3-5 82-83

Picture Sleeves

W.B. 3-5 82-83

LPs: 10/12-inch 33rpm

ATCO (Except 106 & 8114) 8-15 74-83
ATCO (106 "Country Life")........ 20-35 75
(Cover pictures two women in their underwear.)
ATCO (106 "Country Life").......... 8-15 75
(The two women are not pictured on cover.)
ATCO (8114 "Manifesto").......... 20-25 75
(Picture disc. Promotional issue only.)
ATLANTIC.................................. 8-10 74
REPRISE (2114 "Roxy Music"). 15-25 72
W.B. (Except 2696)................... 5-10 82-83
W.B. (2696 "For Your Pleasure") 15-25 73

Member: Bryan Ferry.
Also see CARRACK, Paul
Also see ENO, Brian
Also see FERRY, Bryan, & Roxy Music
Also see MANZANERA, Phil

ROY, Barbara

D&D '84

Singles: 12-inch 33/45rpm

ASCOT..4-6 84

Singles: 7-inch

RCA 3-4 86

Also see ECSTASY, PASSION & PAIN

ROY C.
(Roy Charles Hammond)

R&B '65

Singles: 7-inch

ALAGA 3-5 71
BLACK HAWK 4-8 65-66
MERCURY....................................3-5 73-77
SHOUT 4-6 66
UPTOWN......................................4-6 66

LPs: 10/12-inch 33rpm

MERCURY..................................8-12 77

Also see GENIES

ROYAL, Billy Joe

P&R/LP '65

Singles: 7-inch

ALL WOOD 5-10 62
ATLANTIC (2300 series) 4-8 66
ATLANTIC (87000 thru 89000 series)..3-4 85-89
ATLANTIC AMERICA 3-5 85-89
COLUMBIA (43305 "Down in the Boondocks") 4-8 65
(Black vinyl.)
COLUMBIA (43305 "Down in the Boondocks") 10-20 65
(Colored vinyl. Promotional issue only.)
COLUMBIA (43390 "I Knew You When")................................4-8 65
(Black vinyl.)
COLUMBIA (43390 "I Knew You When")..............................10-20 65
(Colored vinyl. Promotional issue only.)
COLUMBIA (43465 thru 45620).....4-8 65-72
FAIRLANE 8-12 61-62
KAT FAMILY 3-5 81
MGM/SOUTH.................................3-5 73
MERCURY.....................................3-5 80
PLAYER'S...................................5-10 65
PRIVATE STOCK 3-5 78
SCEPTER 3-5 76
TOLLIE..5-10 64

Picture Sleeves

TOLLIE..8-12 64

LPs: 10/12-inch 33rpm

ATLANTIC AMERICA 5-10 86-89
BACK-TRAC 5-8 85
BRYLEN.......................................5-10
COLUMBIA (Except 45063).......15-25 65-69
COLUMBIA (45063 "Greatest Hits") 5-8 89
51 WEST......................................5-10 83

ROYAL GUARDSMEN

KAT FAMILY 5-10 81
MERCURY 5-10 80
Also see FARGO, Donna, & Billy Joe Royal
Also see SOUTH, Joe / Billy Joe Royal

ROYAL GUARDSMEN

P&R '66

Singles: 7–inch

LAURIE 4-8 66-69

LPs: 10/12–inch 33rpm

LAURIE 10-20 67-68
Members: Chris Nunley; Barry Winslow; Bill Balough; Tom Richards.

ROYAL HARMONY QUARTET

R&B '42

Singles: 78rpm

KEYNOTE 5-10 42
Members: Julius Ginyard; Ted Brooks; Bill Johnson; John Jennings; George McFadden.

ROYAL HOUSE

R&B '88

Singles: 7–inch

IDLERS WAR 3-4 88

ROYAL JOKERS

P&R '55

Singles: 78rpm

ATCO 8-12 55-56
HI-Q.. 10-15 57

Singles: 7–inch

ATCO (6052 "You Tickle Me Baby") 25-35 55
ATCO (6062 "Don't Leave Me, Fanny").................................. 20-30 55
ATCO (6077 "She's Mine, All Mine")................................... 25-35 55
FORTUNE (560 "You Tickle Me Baby") 15-20 63
FORTUNE (840 "Sweet Little Angel") 20-25 57
HI-Q (5004 "September in the Rain") 25-30 57

ROYAL PHILHARMONIC ORCHESTRA

(Conducted by Louis Clark)

P&R/LP '81

Singles: 7–inch

RCA... 3-4 81-83

LPs: 10/12–inch 33rpm

RCA... 5-8 81-83

ROYAL SCOTS DRAGOON GUARDS

P&R/LP '72

Singles: 7–inch

RCA... 3-5 72

LPs: 10/12–inch 33rpm

RCA... 5-10 72

ROYAL SONS QUINTET

(Five Royales)

Singles: 78rpm

APOLLO (253 "Bedside of a Neighbor")..............................75-100 52
APOLLO (266 "Come Over Here")......................................50-75 52
Members: Johnny Tanner; Lowman Pauling; Clarence Pauling; William Samuels; Otto Jeffries; Clarence Pauling.
Also see FIVE ROYALES

ROYAL TEENS

P&R/R&B '58

Singles: 78rpm

ABC-PAR 5-10 57-58
POWER (215 "Short Shorts") 20-30 57

Singles: 7–inch

ABC...3-5 73
ABC-PAR 8-12 57-58
ALLNEW (1415 "Royal Twist")...10-15 62
ASTRA 5-10
CAPITOL.......................................12-25 59-60
JUBILEE (5418 "Royal Twist").....5-10 62
MCA...3-4 80s
MIGHTY (111 "Leotards")..........10-20 58
MIGHTY (112 "Cave Man").........15-25 59
MIGHTY (200 "My Memories of You")..20-30 58
MUSICOR 4-8 69-70
POWER (113 "Mad Gass")........10-20 59
POWER (215 "Short Shorts") 40-60 57
SWAN (4200 "I'll Love You Till the End of Time") 40-60 65
TCF 5-10 65

LPs: 10/12–inch 33rpm

DEMAND 10-15
MUSICOR......................................10-15 70
TRU-GEMS.....................................8-10 75
Members: Bob Gaudio; Al Kooper; Buddy Randell; Joey Villa; Billy Crandall; Tom Austin; Tony Grochowski.
Also see 4 SEASONS
Also see KOOPER, Al

ROYALCASH

R&B '83

Singles: 12–inch 33/45rpm

SUTRA...4-6 83

Singles: 7–inch

SUTRA...3-5 83

ROYALETTES

P&R/R&B '65

Singles: 7–inch

CHANCELLOR 8-12 62-63
MGM 5-10 64-66
ROULETTE.....................................5-10 67
W.B. 5-10 64

LPs: 10/12–inch 33rpm

MGM 15-25 65-66

ROYALS

R&B '53

Singles: 78rpm

FEDERAL (12064 "Every Beat of My Heart")........................ 50-100 52
FEDERAL (12077 "Starting from Tonight")............................. 50-100 52
FEDERAL (12088 "Moonrise") 50-100 52
FEDERAL (12098 "A Love in My Heart").............................. 50-75 52
FEDERAL (12113 "Are You Forgetting") 50-75 52
FEDERAL (12121 "The Shrine of St. Cecilia") 50-75 53
FEDERAL (12133 "Get It")........ 25-50 53
FEDERAL (12150 "Hey Miss Fine").................................... 25-50 53
FEDERAL (12160 "That's It").... 25-50 54
FEDERAL (12169 "Work with Me Annie") 25-50 54

Singles: 7–inch

FEDERAL (12064 "Every Beat of My Heart")...................... 350-550 52
(Black vinyl.)
FEDERAL (12064 "Every Beat of My Heart")...................... 500-750 52
(Colored vinyl.)
FEDERAL (12077 "Starting from Tonight")............................ 500-750 52
FEDERAL (12088 "Moonrise")......................... 500-750 52
FEDERAL (12098 "A Love in My Heart") 350-550 52
FEDERAL (12113 "Are You Forgetting") 350-550 52
FEDERAL (12121 "The Shrine of St. Cecilia") 350-550 53
FEDERAL (12133 "Get It").... 100-150 53
FEDERAL (12150 "Hey Miss Fine")................................... 75-125 53
FEDERAL (12160 "That's It").. 75-125 54
FEDERAL (12169 "Work with Me Annie")............................. 50-100 54
FEDERAL (12177 "Give It Up").................................... 50-100 54
(White label. Test pressing only. Commercial copies credited to "The Midnighters, Formally Known as the Royals.")
GUSTO 3-5 80s

Federal titles reissued as by the Midnighters are found in their section.

Members: Henry Booth; Hank Ballard; Charles Sutton; Lawson Smith; Alonzo Tucker; Sonny Woods.

Also see BALLARD, Hank
Also see MIDNIGHTERS

ROYALTONES

P&R '58

Singles: 7–inch

ABC..3-5 73
GOLDISC...................................10-15 60-61
JANUS GOLD...............................3-5
JUBILEE (Blue label) 5-10 58-59
JUBILEE (Black label)...................4-6 62
MALA 4-8 63-64
PENTHOUSE (777 "Clip Clop") .25-35 59
PORT (70037 "Poor Boy") 8-12 64
ROULETTE..................................3-5 71
VIRGO 3-5 72

RUBBER BAND

LP '69

Singles: 7–inch

GRT 4-6 69

LPs: 10/12–inch 33rpm

GRT 10-15 69

RUBBER RODEO

P&R '84

Singles: 7–inch

MERCURY...................................3-5 84-85

LPs: 10/12–inch 33rpm

MERCURY.................................5-10 85

RUBEN & JETS

(Mothers of Invention)

Singles: 7–inch

VERVE (10632 "Any Way the Wind Blows")...........................20-30 68
VERVE (10632 "Deseri") 20-30 68

LPs: 10/12–inch 33rpm

VERVE (5055 "Crusin' with Ruben and the Jets").........................30-40 68
(Issued with three paper inserts, any of which can add $15 to $25 to the value.)

Also see MOTHERS of INVENTION

RUBETTES

P&R '74

Singles: 7–inch

MCA...3-5 76
POLYDOR 3-5 74-75

LPs: 10/12–inch 33rpm

MCA...6-10 76

RUBICON

P&R/LP '78

Singles: 7–inch

20TH FOX...................................3-5 78-79

LPs: 10/12–inch 33rpm

20TH FOX.................................5-10 78-79

Also see SLY & Family Stone

RUBINOOS

P&R '77

Singles: 12–inch 33/45rpm

W.B. 4-8 80-83

Singles: 7–inch

BESERKLEY...............................3-5 77-79

W.B.	3-4	84

Picture Sleeves

BESERKLEY	3-5	77-79

LPs: 10/12-inch 33rpm

BESERKLEY	5-10	77-79

Also see KIHN, Greg, Band / Earthquake / Modern Lovers / Rubinoos

Member: Jon Rubin.

RUBY & Party Gang

R&B '71

Singles: 7-inch

GAMBLE	3-5	72
LAW-TON	3-5	71

RUBY & ROMANTICS

P&R/R&B/LP '63

Singles: 7-inch

A&M	4-6	69
ABC	4-8	67-68
KAPP	5-10	62-67
MCA	3-4	70s

Picture Sleeves

KAPP	5-10	63-64

LPs: 10/12-inch 33rpm

ABC	10-20	68
KAPP	15-25	63-67
MCA	5-10	80s
PICKWICK	8-10	70s

Members: Ruby Nash; Edward Roberts; Ronald Mosley; Leroy Fann; George Lee.

RUE

R&B '87

Singles: 7-inch

ASIANA	3-4	87

RUFFIN, David

P&R/R&B/LP '69

Singles: 7-inch

ANNA (1127 "I'm in Love")	35-55	60
CHECK MATE (1003 "You Can Get What I Got")	30-50	61
CHECK MATE (1010 "Mr. Bus Driver")	30-50	61
MOTOWN	3-6	69-76
W.B.	3-5	79-80

LPs: 10/12-inch 33rpm

MOTOWN (100 & 200 series)	5-10	82
MOTOWN (600 series)	10-15	69
MOTOWN (700 & 800 series)	8-10	73-76
W.B.	8-10	77-80

Also see BUSH, Little David
Also see HALL, Daryl, John Oates, David Ruffin & Eddie Kendrick
Also see TEMPTATIONS
Also see VOICE MASTERS

RUFFIN, David, & Eddie Kendricks

R&B '87

Singles: 7-inch

RCA	3-4	87-88

Also see KENDRICKS, Eddie

RUFFIN, David & Jimmy
(Ruffin Brothers)

P&R/R&B '70

Singles: 7-inch

SOUL	3-6	70

LPs: 10/12-inch 33rpm

MOTOWN	5-10	80
SOUL (728 "My Brother's Keeper")	10-20	70

Also see RUFFIN, David
Also see RUFFIN, Jimmy

RUFFIN, Jimmy

P&R/R&B '66

Singles: 12-inch 33/45rpm

EPIC	4-8	77

Singles: 7-inch

EPIC	3-4	77
MIRACLE (1 "Heart")	50-100	61
MOTOWN	3-5	
RSO	3-5	80
SOUL (Except 35002)	8-15	65-71
SOUL (35002 "Since I've Lost You")	15-25	64

EPs: 7-inch 33/45rpm

SOUL (69704 "Top Ten")	15-25	66

LPs: 10/12-inch 33rpm

RSO	5-8	80
SOUL (704 "Sings Top Ten")	20-30	66
SOUL (708 "Ruff 'N' Ready")	20-30	67
SOUL (727 "Groove Governor")	15-25	70

Also see NIGHTINGALE, Maxine, & Jimmy Ruffin
Also see RUFFIN, David & Jimmy

RUFFNER, Mason

LP '87

LPs: 10/12-inch 33rpm

CBS ASSOC	5-8	87

RUFUS
(Featuring Chaka Khan)

R&B/LP '73

Singles: 12-inch 33/45rpm

W.B.	4-6	83-84

Singles: 7-inch

ABC	3-5	74-78
ATLANTIC	3-5	74
BEARSVILLE	3-5	75
EPIC	3-5	70-71
MCA (Except picture discs)	3-5	79-81
MCA (9162 "Party 'Til You're Broke") (Picture disc. Promotional issue only.)	20-25	81
MCA (9288 "Do You Love What You Feel") (Picture disc. Promotional issue only.)	20-25	81
W.B.	3-4	83-84

LPs: 10/12-inch 33rpm

ABC (Except picture discs)	8-10	73-78
ABC (AA-1049 "Street Player") (Picture disc. Promotional issue only.)	20-25	78

ABC (AA-1098 "Numbers") 15-20 79
(Picture disc. Promotional issue only.)
COMMAND 8-10 74-75
MCA 5-10 79-82
W.B. 5-8 83
Members: Paulette McWilliams; Chaka Khan.
Also see AMERICAN BREED
Also see KHAN, Chaka
Also see McWILLIAMS, Paulette

RUFUS & CARLA

Singles: 7-inch

SATELLITE 10-15 60
STAX 4-8 64-65
Members: Rufus Thomas; Carla Thomas.
Also see THOMAS, Carla
Also see THOMAS, Rufus

RUGBYS

P&R '69

Singles: 7-inch

AMAZON (Except 1) 5-10 69-70
AMAZON (1 "You, I") 5-8 69
(Black vinyl.)
AMAZON (1 "You, I") 10-15 69
(Colored vinyl. Promotional issue only.)
SMASH 5-10 65
TOP DOG (2315 "Endlessly") ... 10-15 66

LPs: 10/12-inch 33rpm

AMAZON (1000 "Hot Cargo") ... 15-20 70
Members: Steve McNicol; Jim McNicol; Chris Hubbs; Ed Vernon; Mike Morner, Glen Howerton.

RUMBLERS

P&R '63

Singles: 7-inch

DOT 5-10 63-64
DOWNEY 10-20 63-65
HIGHLAND (1026 "Intersection") 20-30 62

LPs: 10/12-inch 33rpm

DOT (3509 "Boss") 20-25 63
(Monaural.)
DOT (25509 "Boss") 25-30 63
(Stereo.)
DOWNEY (DLP-1001 "Boss") ... 40-60 63
(Monaural.)
DOWNEY (DLPS-1001 "Boss") 50-75 63
(Stereo.)
Members: Adrian Lloyd; Johnny Kirkland; Bob Jones; Wayne Matteson; Mike Kelishes; Greg Crowner.

RUMOUR

LP '77

Singles: 7-inch

ARISTA 3-5 79
MERCURY 3-5 78

LPs: 10/12-inch 33rpm

ARISTA 5-10 79
MERCURY 8-10 77
Also see PARKER, Graham
Also see SCHWARTZ, Brinsley

RUN - D.M.C.

R&B '83

Singles: 12-inch 33/45rpm

PROFILE 4-6 83-86
QUALITY/RFC 4-6 83

Singles: 7-inch

PROFILE (Black vinyl) 3-4 83-90
PROFILE (Colored vinyl) 4-8 89

Picture Sleeves

PROFILE 3-4 86-88

LPs: 10/12-inch 33rpm

PROFILE 5-8 84-90
Members: "Run" Joe Simmons; Daryll McDaniels; Jason Mizell.
Also see AEROSMITH
Also see KING DREAM CHORUS & Holiday Crew
Also see KRUSH GROVE ALL STARS

RUNAWAYS

LP '76

Singles: 7-inch

MERCURY 5-10 76-77

LPs: 10/12-inch 33rpm

MERCURY (1090 "Runaways") . 15-25 76-77
MERCURY (1126 "Queens of Noise") 15-25 77
MERCURY (3705 "Waiting for the Night") 15-25 77
RHINO (250 "Little Lost Girls") 5-10 82
RHINO (250 "Little Lost Girls") ... 10-15 82
(Picture disc.)
Members: Joan Jett; Cherie Currie; Lita Ford; Sandy West; Vicki Blue.
Also see FORD, Lita
Also see JETT, Joan

RUNDGREN, Todd
(Todd Rundgren's Utopia)

LP '71

Singles: 7-inch

BEARSVILLE (Except 0003) 3-5 77-83
BEARSVILLE (0003 "I Saw the Light") 5-10 72
(Black vinyl.)
BEARSVILLE (0003 "I Saw the Light") 10-15 72
(Colored vinyl.)

LPs: 10/12-inch 33rpm

BEARSVILLE (524 "Todd Rundgren Radio Show") 40-50 70s
(Promotional issue only.)
BEARSVILLE (597 "Radio Interview") 120-130 81
(Promotional issue only.)
BEARSVILLE (788 "Todd Rundgren Radio Sampler") 25-40 79
(Promotional issue only.)
BEARSVILLE (2066 "Something/ Anything") 10-12 72
BEARSVILLE (2066 "Something/ Anything") 150-200 72
(Colored vinyl. Price includes lyrics insert.

BEARSVILLE (2133 "A Wizard/ A True Star") 5-10 73
BEARSVILLE (3522 "Healing") ... 8-10 81
(Price includes the bonus single, *Time Heals.*)
BEARSVILLE (6952 "Todd") 12-15 74
(Price includes bonus poster.)
BEARSVILLE (6957 "Initiation") .. 8-10 75
BEARSVILLE (6961 "Another Live") 10-12 75
BEARSVILLE (6963 "Faithful").... 8-10 76
BEARSVILLE (6965 "Ra")......... 10-12 77
BEARSVILLE (6970 "Oops, Wrong Planet") 10-12 77
BEARSVILLE (6981 "Hermit of Mink Hollow") 5-8 78
BEARSVILLE (6986 "Back to the Bars") 8-10 78
BEARSVILLE (23732 "Ever Popular Tortured Artist Effect") 5-8 83
Also see NAZZ
Also see RUNT
Also see TYLER, Bonnie
Also see UTOPIA

RUNNER

LP '79

Singles: 7–inch

ISLAND 3-5 79

LPs: 10/12–inch 33rpm

ISLAND 5-10 79

Members: Steve Gould; Mickie Feat; David Dowle; Allan Merrill.

RUNT
(Featuring Todd Rundgren)

P&R '70

Singles: 7–inch

AMPEX 5-10 70
BEARSVILLE 4-8 71

LPs: 10/12–inch 33rpm

AMPEX (10105 "Runt") 100-150 70
(With *Say No More* and a full-length version of *Baby Let's Swing.*)
AMPEX (10105 "Runt") 50-100 70
(Does not have *Say No More*. Has *Baby Let's Swing* as part of a medley.)
AMPEX (10116 "The Ballad of Todd Rundgren") 50-100 71
W.B. 5-8 85-91
Also see RUNDGREN, Todd

RUSH

LP '74

Singles: 7–inch

MERCURY 3-5 75-87

Picture Sleeves

MERCURY 3-5 81-85

EPs: 7–inch 33/45rpm

MERCURY 5-10 80

LPs: 10/12–inch 33rpm

ATLANTIC 5-8 89
MERCURY (1000 thru 4000 series, except 1300) 5-8 74-82
MERCURY (1300 "Hemispheres") 10-20 78
(Picture disc.)
MERCURY (7000 series) 8-12 76-81
MERCURY (9000 series) 10-15 76-81
MERCURY (800000 series) 5-8 84-88

Members: Geddy Lee; Neil Peart; Alex Lifeson.

RUSH, Bobby

R&B '71

Singles: 7–inch

ABC 3-6 68
CHECKER 4-8 67
GALAXY 3-5 71
JEWEL 4-8 60s
PHILADELPHIA INT'L 3-5 79
SALEM 3-6 69
TOP 3-5 70s

LPs: 10/12–inch 33rpm

PHILADELPHIA INT'L 5-10 79

RUSH, Jennifer

P&R '86

Singles: 7–inch

EPIC 3-4 86

LPs: 10/12–inch 33rpm

EPIC 5-8 86-87

RUSH, Jennifer, & Elton John

P&R '87

Singles: 7–inch

EPIC 3-4 87
Also see JOHN, Elton

RUSH, Merrilee
(With the Turnabouts)

P&R/LP '68

Singles: 7–inch

AGP 3-6 69-70
BELL 4-8 68
GTP 4-8 68
MERRILIN 4-8 60s
RURO 4-6
SCEPTER 3-5 71
SPHERE SOUND 3-5
U.A. 3-5 77-78

LPs: 10/12–inch 33rpm

BELL 10-20 68
LIBERTY 5-8 82
U.A. 8-10 77

RUSH, Otis

R&B '56

Singles: 78rpm

COBRA 5-10 56-57

Singles: 7–inch

CHESS 5-10 60
COBRA 15-30 56-59
COTILLION 4-6 69
DUKE 5-10 62

LPs: 10/12-inch 33rpm

BLUE HORIZON 10-15 68-70
BULLFROG 8-10 77
COTILLION 10-15 69
DELMARK 5-10 75-79

Also see KING, Albert, & Otis Rush

RUSH, Tom

LP '66

Singles: 7-inch

COLUMBIA 3-5 72-74
ELEKTRA 4-6 66-70
PRESTIGE 4-8 64

LPs: 10/12-inch 33rpm

COLUMBIA 6-12 70-76
ELEKTRA 8-15 65-70
FANTASY 5-10 72
LY CORNU 15-20
PRESTIGE 10-20 64-68

RUSHEN, Patrice

LP '77

Singles: 12-inch 33/45rpm

ELEKTRA 4-8 79-84

Singles: 7-inch

ARISTA 3-4 87
ELEKTRA 3-5 80-84
PRESTIGE 3-5 76

Picture Sleeves

ELEKTRA 3-5 80-82

LPs: 10/12-inch 33rpm

ARISTA 5-8 87
ELEKTRA 5-10 78-84
PRESTIGE 5-10 75-80

RUSHEN, Patrice, & D.J. Rogers

R&B '80

Singles: 7-inch

ELEKTRA 3-5 80

Also see ROGERS, D.J.
Also see RUSHEN, Patrice

RUSS, Lonnie

P&R '62

Singles: 7-inch

4J 10-15 62

RUSSELL, Bobby

(With the Beagles; with Tennessee Three; with Sadie Russell)

C&W/P&R '68

Singles: 7-inch

COLUMBIA 3-5 73-74
D 5-10 60
ELF 4-6 68-69
FELSTED 5-10 59
FILLY-COLT 3-5 78
IMAGE 4-8 61
MONUMENT 4-8 65-66
NATIONAL GENERAL 3-5 70
PRIVATE STOCK 3-5 75
RISING SONS 3-5 67
SPAR 10-15 64
U.A. 3-5 71-72
VISTA 3-6 69

LPs: 10/12-inch 33rpm

BELL 8-12 69
ELF 10-15 68
U.A. 8-10 71

RUSSELL, Brenda

(With Joe Esposito)

P&R/R&B/LP '79

Singles: 7-inch

A&M 3-4 79-88
HORIZON 3-5 79

Picture Sleeves

A&M 3-4 88

LPs: 10/12-inch 33rpm

A&M 5-8 79-00
HORIZON 5-8 79

Also see ESPOSITO, Joe "Bean"

RUSSELL, Lee

(Leon Russell)

Singles: 7-inch

BATON 10-15 59
ROULETTE 10-20 58

Also see RUSSELL, Leon

RUSSELL, Leon

(With the Shelter People; with New Grass Revival)

LP '70

Singles: 7-inch

A&M (700 series) 4-8 64
A&M (1200 series) 3-5 71
ABC 3-5 78
COLUMBIA 3-5 70s
DOT 4-8 65
MCA 3-4
PARADISE 3-5 76-81
SHELTER 3-5 70-76

Picture Sleeves

PARADISE 3-5 78-84
SHELTER 3-5 74

LPs: 10/12-inch 33rpm

MCA 5-10 79
OLYMPIC 8-12 73
PARADISE 5-10 78-81
SHELTER (1000 & 2000 series) 10-20 70-75
SHELTER (8000 series, except 8917) 10-15 71-73
SHELTER (8917 "Leon Live") 12-20 73
SHELTER (52000 series) 8-10 76

Also see CLAPTON, Eric
Also see COCKER, Joe
Also see DAVID & LEE
Also see HARRISON, George
Also see KING, Freddie
Also see LEGENDARY MASKED SURFERS
Also see NELSON, Willie, & Leon Russell
Also see RUSSELL, Lee

RUSSELL, Leon & Mary

P&R '76

Singles: 7–inch

PARADISE ... 3-5 76-77

LPs: 10/12–inch 33rpm

PARADISE ... 8-10 76-77

Also see RUSSELL, Leon

RUSSELL, Luis

R&B '46

Singles: 78rpm

APOLLO ... 5-10 46-48

RUSSELL, Sam

R&B '73

Singles: 7–inch

PLAYBOY ... 3-5 73

RUSSO, Charlie

P&R '63

Singles: 7–inch

DIAMOND ... 4-8 63
LAURIE ... 4-6 67
PART ... 4-8 64

RUSTIX

LP '69

Singles: 7–inch

RARE EARTH ... 4-8 69

LPs: 10/12–inch 33rpm

RARE EARTH (508 "Bedlam") 8-12 69
(Standard cover.)
RARE EARTH (508 "Bedlam") .. 20-40 69
(Rounded-top cover. Promotional issue.)

RUTH, Babe: see BABE RUTH

RUTHERFORD, Mike

LP '80

Singles: 7–inch

ATLANTIC ... 3-4 83

LPs: 10/12–inch 33rpm

ATLANTIC ... 5-8 83
PASSPORT ... 5-10 80

Also see GENESIS
Also see MIKE + the MECHANICS

RUTLES

LP '78

Singles: 12–inch 33/45rpm

W.B. (723 "The Rutles") ... 15-20 78
(Colored vinyl. Promotional issue only.)

Singles: 7–inch

PASSPORT ... 3-5 70s
W.B. ... 3-5 78

LPs: 10/12–inch 33rpm

W.B. (3151 "Meet the Rutles") .. 10-15 78
(Add $4 to $6 if accompanied by bonus booklet.)

Members: Neil Innes; Rick Fataar; Eric Idle; John Hasley.
Also see BONZO DOG BAND
Also see FLAME
Also see MONTY PYTHON

RYAN, Barry

P&R '68

Singles: 7–inch

MGM ... 4-8 68
POLYDOR ... 3-6 70
PRIDE ... 3-5 71

RYAN, Charlie

(With the Timberline Riders; with Livingston Brothers)

C&W/P&R '60

Singles: 7–inch

4 STAR ... 5-10 60-63
SOUVENIR (101 "Hot Rod Lincoln") ... 40-60 55

Picture Sleeves

4 STAR (1745 "Side Car Cycle") 10-20 60

LPs: 10/12–inch 33rpm

KING (751 "Hot Rod") ... 40-60 61
PICKWICK/HILLTOP ... 10-20 64

RYDELL, Bobby

P&R/R&B '59

Singles: 7–inch

ABKCO ... 3-4 70s
CAMEO ("Steel Pier") ... 15-20 60s
(No selection number used. Single-sided, promotional issue from the Steel Pier in Atlantic City.)
CAMEO (160 "Please Don't Be Mad") ... 25-50 59
CAMEO (164 "All I Want Is You") ... 10-20 59
CAMEO (167 thru 186) ... 5-15 59-61
CAMEO (190 thru 361) ... 4-8 61-65
CAMEO (1070 "Forget Him"/"A Message from Bobby") ... 10-15 63
(Packaged as a bonus single with *Top Hits of 1963.*)
CAPITOL ... 4-8 64-66
P.I.P. ... 3-5 76
PERCEPTION ... 3-5 74
RCA ... 3-5 70
REPRISE ... 4-6 68
TIME ... 5-8 59
VEKO (731 "Fatty Fatty") ... 25-50 58
VENISE (201 "Fatty Fatty") ... 15-25 62

Picture Sleeves

CAMEO ... 8-15 59-64
CAPITOL ... 5-10 64

EPs: 7–inch 33/45rpm

CAPITOL ... 10-20 65

LPs: 10/12–inch 33rpm

CAMEO (1006 "We Got Love") .. 40-80 59
CAMEO (1007 "Bobby Sings, Bobby Swings") ... 20-30 60
CAMEO (1009 "Bobby's Biggest Hits") ... 40-50 61
(Gatefold cover. With 12x12 photo insert.)

CAMEO (1009 "Bobby's Biggest Hits") ... 30-35 61
(Gatefold cover. Without 12x12 photo.)
CAMEO (1009 "Bobby's Biggest Hits") ... 15-20 62
(Standard cover. Some copies with 1009 on the cover may have Cameo 1008 on the disc.)
CAMEO (1010 thru 1055) ... 15-25 61-63
CAMEO (1070 "Top Hits of 1963 Sung by Robby Rydell") ... 20-30 63
(With bonus single *Forget Him/A Message from Bobby.*)
CAMEO (1070 "Top Hits of 1963 Sung By Robby Rydell") ... 15-20 63
(Without bonus single.)
CAMEO (1080 "Forget Him") ... 15-20 64
CAMEO (2000 series) ... 15-20 60s
CAMEO (4017 "An Era Reborn") ... 15-25 64
CAPITOL (2281 "Somebody Loves You") ... 15-20 65
DESIGN ... 10-15 60s
P.I.P. ... 8-12 76
SPINORAMA ... 10-15 60s
STRAND (1120 "Bobby Rydell Sings") ... 25-35 60

Also see CHECKER, Chubby, & Bobby Rydell
Also see CHRISTIE, Lou / Len Barry & Dovells / Bobby Rydell / Tokens
Also see ROE, Tommy / Bobby Rydell / Gene Pitney
Also see ROE, Tommy / Bobby Rydell / Ray Stevens

RYDELL, Bobby / Barry Norman / Steve Garrick

LP: 10/12-inch 33rpm

VENISE (7035 "Twistin'") ... 15-20 62

Also see RYDELL, Bobby

RYDER, John & Anne

P&R '69

Singles: 7-inch

DECCA ... 4-6 69

LPs: 10/12-inch 33rpm

DECCA ... 10-15 70

RYDER, Mitch
(With the Detroit Wheels)

P&R '65

Singles: 7-inch

ABC ... 3-5 73
AVCO EMBASSY ... 3-6 70
DOT ... 4-6 69
DYNO VOICE ... 4-8 67-68
ERIC ... 3-4
NEW VOICE (Except 820) ... 4-8 65-68
NEW VOICE (820 "Sock It to Me-Baby") ... 5-10 67
(With "Feels like a punch" lyrics.)
NEW VOICE (820 "Sock It to Me-Baby") ... 4-6 67
(With "Hits me like a punch" lyrics.)
RIVA ... 3-4 83
VIRGO ... 3-4 73

Picture Sleeves

NEW VOICE ... 4-8 67

LPs: 10/12-inch 33rpm

CREWE ... 12-15
DOT ... 12-15 69
DYNO VOICE ... 10-20 67
NEW VOICE ... 20-30 66-68
RIVA ... 5-8 83
ROULETTE ... 5-10
SEEDS & STEMS ... 5-10 78-80
VIRGO ... 8-10 73

Members: Mitch Ryder; Joe Kubert; Jim McCallister; Jim McCarty; Johnny Badanjek.
Also see DETROIT
Also see ROCKETS

RYLES, John Wesley
(John Wesley Ryles I)

C&W/P&R '68

Singles: 7-inch

ABC ... 3-5 78-79
ABC/DOT ... 3-5 77
COLUMBIA ... 4-6 68-70
GRT ... 3-5 70
MCA ... 3-5 79-83
MUSIC MILL ... 3-5 75-76
PLANTATION ... 3-5 71-73
PRIMERO ... 3-5 82-83
RCA ... 3-5 74
16TH AVE. ... 3-4 84
W.B. ... 3-4 87-88

LPs: 10/12-inch 33rpm

ABC ... 5-10 78
ABC/DOT ... 8-10 77
COLUMBIA ... 10-15 69
MCA ... 5-10 79-83
PLANTATION ... 5-10 77

RYSER, Jimmy

P&R '90

Singles: 7-inch

ARISTA ... 3-4 90

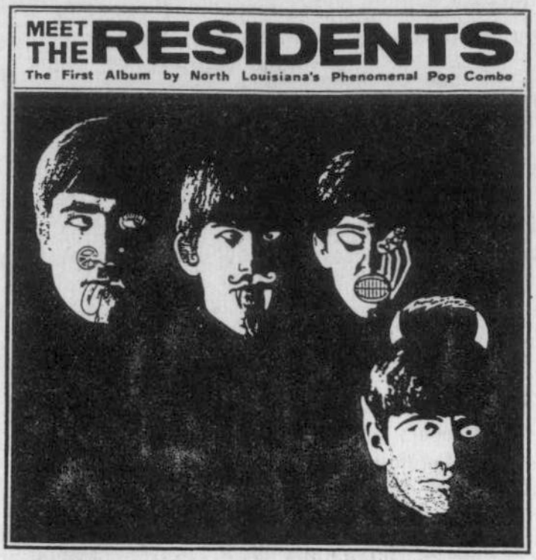
MEET THE RESIDENTS
The First Album by North Louisiana's Phenomenal Pop Combo

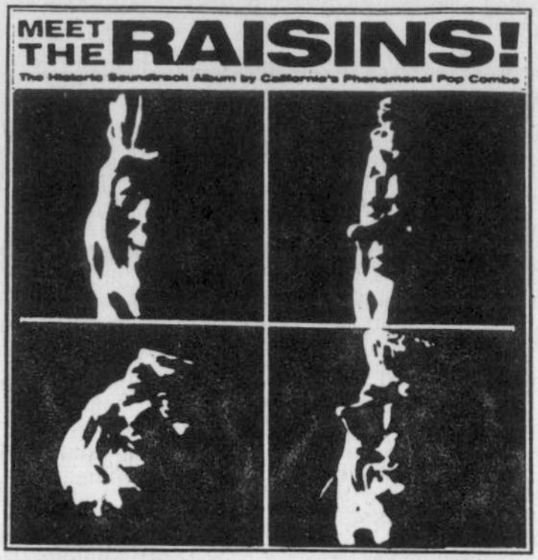
MEET THE RAISINS!
The Historic Soundtrack Album by California's Phenomenal Pop Combo

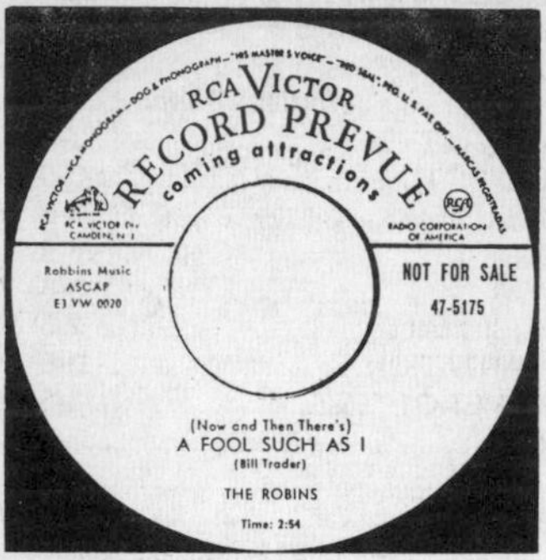
RCA VICTOR
RECORD PREVUE
coming attractions
RADIO CORPORATION OF AMERICA
Robbins Music
ASCAP
E3 VW 0020
NOT FOR SALE
47-5175
(Now and Then There's)
A FOOL SUCH AS I
(Bill Trader)
THE ROBINS
Time: 2:54

Miracle
RECORDS
45 RPM
DISC JOCKEY
NOT FOR
SALE
DON'T FEEL SORRY FOR ME
JIMMY RUFFIN
MIR-1

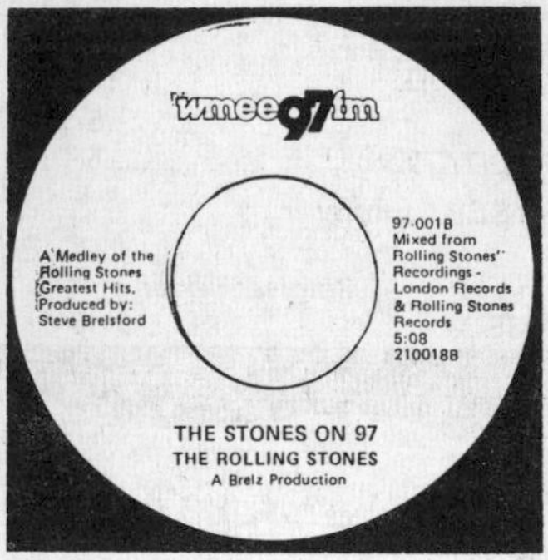
wmee97fm
A Medley of the
Rolling Stones
Greatest Hits.
Produced by:
Steve Brelsford
97-001B
Mixed from
Rolling Stones'
Recordings -
London Records
& Rolling Stones
Records
5:08
210018B
THE STONES ON 97
THE ROLLING STONES
A Brelz Production

ATTACK
SCHWARTZ MUSIC
ASCAP
AR 1401 A
"BEG, BORROW AND STEAL"
THE RARE BREED
A SUPER K PRODUCTION
ATTACK RECORDS INC. 1650 B'WAY, N.Y. DISTRIBUTED BY PREMIER ALBUMS, INC.

S

S.O.S. BAND

P&R/LP '80

Singles: 12-inch 33/45rpm

TABU 4-6 80-89

Singles: 7-inch

TABU 3-5 80-89

Picture Sleeves

TABU 3-5 84-86

LPs: 10/12-inch 33rpm

TABU 5-10 80-89

Member: Mary Davis.

SRC

(Scott Richard Case)

LP '68

Singles: 7-inch

A2 (301 "I'm So Glad") 10-20 67
BIG CASINO 4-8 71
CAPITOL 5-10 68-69

LPs: 10/12-inch 33rpm

CAPITOL (134 "Milestones") 30-40 69
CAPITOL (273 "Travelers Tale") 15-25 69
CAPITOL (2991 "SRC") 40-60 68

Members: Scott Richardson; Steve Lyman; Glen Quackenbush; Gary Quackenbush; Robin Dale.

SRC / Rationals

Singles: 7-inch

A2 (402 "Get the Picture") 10-20 67

Also see SRC

S.S.O.

P&R '76

Singles: 7-inch

SHADY BROOK 3-5 75-76

S.S.Q.

D&D '84

Singles: 12-inch 33/45rpm

ENIGMA 4-6 84

Singles: 7-inch

EMI 3-4 84
ENIGMA 3-4 84

LPs: 10/12-inch 33rpm

EMI 5-8 84
ENIGMA 5-8 84

Also see ST. JAMES, Jon
Also see STACEY Q

SAAD, Sue, & Next

LP '80

Singles: 7-inch

PLANET 3-5 80

LPs: 10/12-inch 33rpm

PLANET 5-10 80

SACCO

(Lou Christie)

Singles: 12-inch 33/45rpm

LIFESONG (81775 "People Theme") 8-10 78

Singles: 7-inch

LIFESONG (81775 "People Theme") 30-50 78

Also see CHRISTIE, Lou

SACRED REICH

LP '90

LPs: 10/12-inch 33rpm

ENIGMA 5-8 90

SAD CAFE

P&R/LP '79

Singles: 7-inch

A&M 3-5 78-79
SWAN SONG 3-5 81

Picture Sleeves

SWAN SONG 3-5 81

LPs: 10/12-inch 33rpm

A&M 5-10 78-79
SWAN SONG 5-10 81

Members: Paul Young; Doreen Chanter; Irene Chanter; John Stimpson; Vic Emerson; Ian Wilson; Ashley Mulford; Lenni Zaksen.
Also see MIKE + the MECHANICS
Also see YOUNG, Paul

SADANE, Marc

(Sadane)

R&B '81

Singles: 7-inch

W.B. 3-5 81-82

Picture Sleeves

W.B. 3-5 81

LPs: 10/12-inch 33rpm

W.B. 5-10 81

SADE

R&B/D&D '84

Singles: 12-inch 33/45rpm

PORTRAIT 4-6 84-86

Singles: 7-inch

EPIC 3-4 88
PORTRAIT 3-4 84-86

Picture Sleeves

EPIC 3-4 88
PORTRAIT 3-4 84-86

LPs: 10/12-inch 33rpm

EPIC 5-8 88
PORTRAIT 5-8 85-86

SADLER, Barry

(S/SGT. Barry Sadler)

P&R/C&W/LP '66

Singles: 7-inch

GAS 3-5 78
RCA 4-6 66-67

Picture Sleeves

RCA 5-10 66-67

LPs: 10/12-inch 33rpm

RCA.. 10-20 66-67
VETERAN 8-12 74

Also see ANN-MARGRET

SAFARIS
(With Phantom's Band)

P&R '60

Singles: 7-inch

ELDO 10-20 60-61
OLD HIT 3-5

Members: Jimmy Stephens; Sheldon Breier; Marv Rosenberg.

SA-FIRE

P&R/LP '88

Singles: 7-inch

CUTTING 3-4 88-89

Picture Sleeves

CUTTING 3-4 88-89

LPs: 10/12-inch 33rpm

CUTTING 5-8 88

SAGA

P&R/LP '82

Singles: 7-inch

POLYDOR....................................... 3-5 79
PORTRAIT 3-4 82-85

Picture Sleeves

PORTRAIT 3-4 83

LPs: 10/12-inch 33rpm

ATLANTIC...................................... 5-8 87
POLYDOR..................................... 5-10 79
PORTRAIT 5-10 82-85

SAGER, Carole Bayer
(Carole Bayer)

P&R '77

Singles: 7-inch

BOARDWALK 3-5 81
ELEKTRA...................................... 3-5 77-78
METROMEDIA................................ 3-5 72

Picture Sleeves

BOARDWALK 3-5 81

LPs: 10/12-inch 33rpm

BOARDWALK 5-10 81
ELEKTRA.................................... 5-10 77-78

SAGITTARIUS

P&R '67

Singles: 7-inch

COLUMBIA 5-10 67-69
TOGETHER 5-10 68-69

LPs: 10/12-inch 33rpm

BACK-TRAC 5-10 85
COLUMBIA (9644 "Present Tense")................................ 20-30 68
TOGETHER (1002 "Blue Marble")................................. 25-35 69

Members: Gary Usher; Glen Campbell; Bruce Johnston; Terry Melcher; Curt Boetcher; Mike Fennelly; Lee Mallory; Ron Edgar.

Also see BRUCE & TERRY

Also see CAMPBELL, Glen

SAHL, Mort

LP '60

Singles: 7-inch

GNP 3-5 73
REPRISE 3-6 61
VERVE..4-8 60

LPs: 10/12-inch 33rpm

GNP 5-10 73
MERCURY 8-12 67
REPRISE 10-20 61
VERVE..10-20 59-64

Also see MARTIN, Dean

SAHM, Doug
(With the Mex Trip; with Texas Tornados)

LP '73

Singles: 7-inch

ABC/DOT 4-6 76
ATLANTIC.....................................5-10 73
CASABLANCA (0828 "Roll with the Punches") 10-20 75
CHRYSALIS....................................3-5 81
COBRA (116 "Just a Moment")..40-50 61
CRAZY CAJUN 3-5 74
HARLEM (107 "Why, Why, Why") 20-35 60
HARLEM (108 "Baby, Tell Me") .20-30 60
(Black vinyl.)
HARLEM (108 "Baby, Tell Me") .40-60 60
(Colored vinyl. Promotional issue only.)
HARLEM (116 "Just a Moment")40-50 61
PERSONALITY (260 "Baby, What's on Your Mind")........................30-50 59
PLAYBOY 3-5 76
RENNER (212 "Big Hat") 20-30 61
(Black vinyl.)
RENNER (212 "Big Hat") 50-75 61
(Colored vinyl. Promotional issue only.)
RENNER (215 "Baby, What's on Your Mind")........................20-30 61
(Black vinyl.)
RENNER (215 "Baby, What's on Your Mind")........................50-75 61
(Colored vinyl.
(Promotional issue only.)
RENNER (226 "Just Because") .20-30 62
RENNER (232 "Cry") 20-30 63
RENNER (240 "Lucky Me") 20-30 63
RENNER (247 "Mr. Kool") 20-30 64
SATIN (100 "Crazy Daisy")........30-50 59
SOFT (1031 "Cry")......................20-30 65
SWINGIN' (625 "Why Oh Why") 15-25 60
TEXAS RECORD (108 "Henrietta") 10-20 76
W.B. 3-5 74
WARRIOR (507 "Crazy Daisy") .40-60 58

Picture Sleeves

CHRYSALIS....................................3-5 81

LPs: 10/12–inch 33rpm

ANTONE'S 5-8 88
ATLANTIC 8-12 73
HARLEM 8-10 79
MERCURY 10-20 73
TAKOMA 5-10 80
W.B. 10-20 74

Also see BROMBERG, David
Also see DR. JOHN
Also see DYLAN, Bob
Also see LITTLE DOUG
Also see SALDAÑA, Sir Doug
Also see SIR DOUGLAS QUINTET

SAHM, Doug, & Augie Meyers

Singles: 7–inch

TEARDROP 3-4 83

Picture Sleeves

TEARDROP 3-5 83

Also see SAHM, Doug

SAILCAT

P&R/LP '72

Singles: 7–inch

ELEKTRA 3-5 72-73

LPs: 10/12–inch 33rpm

ELEKTRA 10-15 72

Members: Johnny Wyker; Court Pickett.

SAIN, Oliver

R&B '75

Singles: 7–inch

ABET 3-5 71-77
BOBBIN 4-8 62
HCRC 3-5 82
VANESSA 5-10

LPs: 10/12–inch 33rpm

ABET (400 series) 8-12 71-73
ABET (8700 series) 5-10 77

ST. JAMES, Jon

R&B '84

Singles: 12–inch 33/45rpm

EMI AMERICA 4-6 84

Singles: 7–inch

EMI AMERICA 3-4 84

LPs: 10/12–inch 33rpm

EMI AMERICA 5-10 84

Also see SSQ

ST. PAUL
(Paul Peterson)

R&B '87

Singles: 7–inch

MCA 3-4 87

Also see FAMILY
Also see TIME

ST. PETERS, Crispian

P&R '66

Singles: 7–inch

JAMIE 4-8 66-68

LPs: 10/12–inch 33rpm

JAMIE (3027 "The Pied Piper") . 20-30 66

ST. ROMAIN, Kirby

P&R '63

Singles: 7–inch

DIMENSION 5-10 63
IMCO 4-8 64
INETTE 5-10 63-64
KARSONG 5-10 63
TEARDROP 5-10 64

SAINT TROPEZ

LP '77

Singles: 12–inch 33/45rpm

BUTTERFLY 4-8 77-79
DESTINY 4-6 82-83

Singles: 7–inch

BUTTERFLY 3-5 77-79
DESTINY 3-4 82-83

LPs: 10/12–inch 33rpm

BUTTERFLY (Black vinyl) 5-10 77-79
BUTTERFLY (Colored vinyl) 10-15 77-79
DESTINY 5-10 82

SAINTE-MARIE, Buffy

LP '66

Singles: 7–inch

ABC 3-5 76
MCA 3-5 74-75
VANGUARD 3-8 65-72

LPs: 10/12–inch 33rpm

ABC 5-10 76
MCA 5-10 74-75
VANGUARD 8-15 64-74

SAKAMOTO, Kyu

P&R/R&B/LP '63

Singles: 7–inch

CAPITOL 4-6 63-64
EMI 3-4 75

LPs: 10/12–inch 33rpm

CAPITOL 10-20 63

SALES, Soupy

P&R/LP '65

Singles: 7–inch

ABC-PAR 5-10 65
CAPITOL 5-10 66
MOTOWN (1141 "Muck-Arty
Park") 15-25 69
REPRISE 5-10 62
WIZDOM 3-5

Picture Sleeves

CAPITOL 10-15 66

LPs: 10/12–inch 33rpm

ABC-PAR 15-25 64-65
MOTOWN 10-15 69
REPRISE 20-30 61-62

SALSOUL ORCHESTRA
(Featuring Cognac)

P&R/R&B/LP '75

Singles: 12–inch 33/45rpm

SALSOUL 4-6 78-83

Singles: 7-inch

SALSOUL.................................... 3-5 75-83

LPs: 10/12-inch 33rpm

SALSOUL.................................... 5-10 75-83

Member: Jocelyn Brown.
Also see BROWN, Jocelyn
Also see CHARO
Also see HOLLOWAY, Loleatta

SALT-N-PEPA

P&R/R&B/LP '87

Singles: 7-inch

NEXT PLATEAU 3-4 87-90

LPs: 10/12-inch 33rpm

NEXT PLATEAU 5-8 87-90

SALTY DOG

LP '90

LPs: 10/12-inch 33rpm

GEFFEN...................................... 5-8 90

SALVAGE

P&R '71

Singles: 7-inch

ODAX 3-5 71

SALVO, Sammy

P&R '58

Singles: 78rpm

RCA... 5-10 57

Singles: 7-inch

DOT... 5-10 60
HICKORY.................................... 5-10 61-63
IMPERIAL 5-10 59-60
MARK V 5-10
RCA... 8-12 57-59

SAM, Butch, & Station Band

R&B '85

Singles: 7-inch

PRIVATE I.................................. 3-4 85

SAM & BILL

P&R/R&B '65

Singles: 7-inch

DECCA....................................... 4-8 67
JODA.. 4-8 65-66

Members: Sam Gary; Bill Johnson.

SAM & DAVE

P&R/R&B/LP '66

Singles: 7-inch

ATLANTIC.................................. 3-6 68-71
ROULETTE................................. 4-8 62-66
STAX.. 4-8 65-68
U.A. 3-5 74-75

LPs: 10/12-inch 33rpm

ATLANTIC (8205 "I Thank You") 15-20 68
ATLANTIC (8218 "Best of Sam & Dave")................................... 8-12 69
GUSTO 5-10
ROULETTE (25323 "Sam and Dave") 15-25 66
STAX (708 "Hold On I'm Coming") 20-30 66
STAX (712 "Double Dynamite") .20-30 66
STAX (725 "Soul Men") 20-30 67
U.A. 8-12 74-75

Members: Sam Moore; Dave Prater.
Also see MOORE, Sam
Also see PICKETT, Wilson / Sam & Dave
Also see REDDING, Otis / Carla Thomas / Sam & Dave / Eddie Floyd
Also see STARS on 45 (Featuring Sam & Dave)

SAM the SHAM & PHARAOHS
(Sam the Sham Revue; Sam; Sam Samudio)

P&R/R&B/LP '65

Singles: 7-inch

DINGO (001 "Haunted House") .20-30 64
FRETONE.....................................3-5 77
MGM (13000 series) 5-10 64-69
MGM (14000 series) 3-5 73
POLYDOR 3-4 80s
TUPELO (2982 "Betty and Dupree")...................................35-55 63
WARRIOR...................................20-30 60s
XL (905 "Signifyin' Monkey")......15-25 64
XL (906 "Wooly Bully")..............30-50 65

Picture Sleeves

MGM 8-12 65-67

LPs: 10/12-inch 33rpm

MGM 15-25 65-68

Also see SAMUDIO, Sam

SAMI JO: see COLE, Sami Jo

SAMPLE, Joe

LP '78

Singles: 7-inch

ABC...3-5 78-79
MCA 3-4 80-83

LPs: 10/12-inch 33rpm

ABC...5-10 78-79
MCA...5-8 81-83
MFSL 25-50 78
W.B. 5-8 89

Also see CRUSADERS

SAMUELS, Bill
(With the Cats 'N' Jammer Three; Cats 'N' Jammers)

R&B '46

Singles: 78rpm

MERCURY 15-25 46-48

Singles: 7-inch

MERCURY (70205 "I Cover the Waterfront")..........................50-75 53
SOMA 8-10 61

SAN FRANCISCO SYMPHONY ORCHESTRA

LP '73

LP: 10/12-inch 33rpm

DG..8-12 73

SAN REMO GOLDEN STRINGS

P&R '65

Singles: 7-inch

GORDY 10-20 67
RIC-TIC 8-15 65-66

LPs: 10/12-inch 33rpm

GORDY (923 "Hungry for Love") 25-35 67
GORDY (928 "Swing") 15-25 68
RIC-TIC (901 "Hungry for Love") 30-60 66

SAN SEBASTIAN STRINGS

(With the San Sebastian Strings)

LP '67

Singles: 7-inch

W.B. 3-6 67-73

LPs: 10/12-inch 33rpm

W.B. (Except 2754) 8-15 67-75
W.B. (2754 "Spring, Summer, Winter, Autumn") 15-20 73
(Four-LP set.)

Also see McKUEN, Rod

SANBORN, David

R&B/LP '76

Singles: 12-inch 33/45rpm

W.B. 4-8 81-85

Singles: 7-inch

REPRISE 3-4 88
W.B. 3-5 76-87

LPs: 10/12-inch 33rpm

REPRISE 5-8 88
W.B. 5-10 76-87

Also see JAMES, Bob, & David Sanborn
Also see PURE PRAIRIE LEAGUE

SANDALS

LP '67

Singles: 7-inch

WORLD PACIFIC (415 "Theme from *Endless Summer*) 10-15 64
WORLD PACIFIC (421 "Always") 15-25 64
WORLD PACIFIC (77000 series) 8-12 65-67

LPs: 10/12-inch 33rpm

WORLD PACIFIC (WP-1832 "Endless Summer") 20-25 66
(Monaural. Soundtrack)
WORLD PACIFIC (ST-1832 "Endless Summer") 25-30 66
(Stereo. Soundtrack)

Members: John Blakely; Danny Brawner; John Gibson; Gaston Georis; Walter Georis.
Also see SANDELLS

SANDELLS

Singles: 7-inch

AURA (4501 "School's Out!") 10-15 65
WORLD PACIFIC (405 "Out Front") 10-15 64

LPs: 10/12-inch 33rpm

WORLD PACIFIC (WP-1818 "Scramblers") 25-35 64
(Monaural.)
WORLD PACIFIC (ST-1818 "Scramblers") 35-45 64
(Stereo.)
WORLD PACIFIC (1818 "Scramblers") 50-75 64
(Colored vinyl.)

Also see SANDALS

SANDERS, Felicia

P&R '55

Singles: 78rpm

COLUMBIA 3-5 52-57

Singles: 7-inch

COLUMBIA 5-10 52-57
DECCA 4-8 59-61
MGM 4-8 65
TIME 4-8 60

EPs: 7-inch 33/45rpm

COLUMBIA 8-12 55-56

LPs: 10/12-inch 33rpm

COLUMBIA 15-25 55-57
DECCA 15-20 58
SPECIAL EDITIONS 5-10 67
TIME 10-15 60-64

Also see FAITH, Percy
Also see VALE, Jerry, Peggy King & Felicia Sanders

SANDERS, Pharoah

LP '69

Singles: 7-inch

ARISTA 3-5 78

LPs: 10/12-inch 33rpm

ARISTA 5-10 78
IMPULSE 10-15 69-74
INDIA NAVIGATION 5-10 77
NOVUS 5-10 81
THERESA 5-12 80-81
TRIP 8-12 71

SANDLER, Tony, & Ralph Young

(Sandler & Young)

LP '66

Singles: 7-inch

CAPITOL 3-6 66-70

LPs: 10/12-inch 33rpm

A.V.I. 5-10 79
CAPITOL 5-15 66-78

Also see CAMPBELL, Glen / Lettermen / Ella Fitzgerald / Sandler & Young

SANDPEBBLES

P&R/R&B '67

Singles: 7-inch

ABC 3-5 73
CALLA 4-8 67-69

Also see C & SHELLS

SANDPIPERS

P&R/LP '66

Singles: 7-inch

A&M 3-6 66-72
KISMET 15-25 66
TRU-GLOW-TOWN 5-10 66

LPs: 10/12-inch 33rpm

A&M 8-15 66-73

SANDS, Evie

P&R '69

Singles: 7-inch

ABC-PAR 4-8 63-64
A&M 3-6 68-70
BLUE CAT 5-10 65
CAMEO 4-6 66-68
GOLD 4-8 64
HAVEN 3-5 75-76
RCA 3-5 79

LPs: 10/12-inch 33rpm

A&M 10-15 69
HAVEN 8-10 74
RCA 5-10 79

SANDS, Jodie

P&R '57

Singles: 78rpm

BERNLO 4-8 57
CHANCELLOR 4-8 57
TEEN 5-10 55

Singles: 7-inch

ABC 3-5 74
ABC-PAR 4-8 62-63
BERNLO 8-12 57
CHANCELLOR 5-10 57-59
PARIS 5-10 60-61
SIGNATURE 5-10 59
TEEN 10-20 55
THOR 8-12 59

SANDS, Tommy
(With the Raiders)

P&R/R&B/LP '57

Singles: 78rpm

CAPITOL 5-10 57
RCA 6-12 54-56

Singles: 7-inch

ABC-PAR 4-8 63-64
CAPITOL (3639 thru 4082) 8-12 57-58
CAPITOL (4160 thru 4580) 5-10 59-61
IMPERIAL 4-8 66-67
LIBERTY 4-8 65
RCA 10-15 54-56
SUPERSCOPE 3-6 69

Picture Sleeves

CAPITOL 10-15 58-59

EPs: 7-inch 33/45rpm

CAPITOL 15-25 57-59

LPs: 10/12-inch 33rpm

BRUNSWICK 8-10 78
CAPITOL (848 "Steady Date")...35-45 57
CAPITOL (929 "Sing Boy Sing") 35-45 58
CAPITOL (1081 "Sands Storm") 30-40 58
CAPITOL (T-1123 "This Thing Called Love") 25-30 59
(Monaural.)
CAPITOL (ST-1123 "This Thing Called Love") 30-35 59
(Stereo.)
CAPITOL (T-1239 "When I'm Thinking of You") 25-30 59
(Monaural.)
CAPITOL (ST-1239 "When I'm Thinking of You") 30-35 59
(Stereo.)
CAPITOL (T-1364 "Sands at the Storm") 20-30 60
(Monaural.)
CAPITOL (ST-1364 "Sands at the Sands") 25-35 60
(Stereo.)
CAPITOL (T-1426 "Dream with Me") 20-30 60
(Monaural.)
CAPITOL (ST-1426 "Dream with Me") 25-35 60
(Stereo.)

Also see ANNETTE & Tommy Sands
Also see VINCENT, Gene / Tommy Sands / Sonny James / Ferlin Husky

SANDS of TIME
(Tokens)

Singles: 7-inch

KIRSHNER 4-8 76

Also see TOKENS

SANFORD - TOWNSEND BAND

P&R/LP '77

Singles: 7-inch

W.B. 3-5 77-79

LPs: 10/12-inch 33rpm

W.B. 5-10 78-79

Members: Ed Sanford; John Townsend.

SANG, Samantha

P&R '77

Singles: 7-inch

ATCO 4-6 69
PRIVATE STOCK 3-5 77-78
U.A. 3-5 79

LPs: 10/12-inch 33rpm

PRIVATE STOCK 5-10 77-78
U.A. 5-10 79

Also see BEE GEES

SANS, Billie

P&R '71

Singles: 7-inch

INVICTUS 3-5 71

SANTA ESMERALDA

P&R/LP '77

Singles: 12–inch 33/45rpm

CASABLANCA 4-8 77-78

Singles: 7–inch

CASABLANCA 3-5 77-78

LPs: 10/12–inch 33rpm

CASABLANCA 5-10 77-80

Member: Leroy Gomez.

SANTAMARIA, Mongo
(With His Afro-Latin Group)

P&R/R&B/LP '63

Singles: 12–inch 33/45rpm

TAPPAN ZEE 4-8 79

Singles: 7–inch

ATLANTIC 3-6 69-72
BATTLE 4-8 63
COLLECTABLES 3-4 80s
COLUMBIA 4-6 64-69
FANTASY 4-8 61-62
RIVERSIDE 4-8 62-66
TAPPAN ZEE 3-5 79
TRIP 3-6
VAYA 3-5 73

LPs: 10/12–inch 33rpm

ATLANTIC 8-12 70
BATTLE 15-25 63
COLUMBIA 5-15 65-79
FANTASY 10-25 59-62
MILESTONE 6-12 73-76
PRESTIGE 6-12 72
RIVERSIDE 10-20 62-66
VAYA 6-12 73-74

SANTANA
(Carlos Santana)

P&R/LP '69

Singles: 12–inch 33/45rpm

COLUMBIA 4-6 85

Singles: 7–inch

COLUMBIA 3-5 69-90

Picture Sleeves

COLUMBIA 3-5 70-85

LPs: 10/12–inch 33rpm

COLUMBIA (Except quad and half-speed mastered) 5-12 69-90
COLUMBIA (CQ-30130 "Abraxas") 10-15 75
(Quadraphonic.)
COLUMBIA (CQ-32900 "Illuminations") 10-15 74
(Quadraphonic.)
COLUMBIA (HC-40130 "Abraxas") 25-50 81
(Half-speed mastered.)
Members: Devadip Carlos Santana; Armando Peraza; Graham Lear; David Margen; Richard Baker; Alex Ligertwood; Orestes Vilato; Raul Rekow.
Also see AZTECA
Also see BOOKER T. & MGs
Also see COLTRANE, Alice, & Carlos Santana
Also see ESCOVEDO, Coke
Also see FABULOUS THUNDERBIRDS
Also see FRANKLIN, Aretha
Also see HAGAR, SCHON, AARONSON, SHRIEVE
Also see HANCOCK, Herbie
Also see NOVO COMBO

SANTANA, Carlos, & Mahavishnu John McLaughlin

LP '73

LP: 10/12–inch 33rpm

COLUMBIA (32034 "Love, Devotion, Surrender") 5-10 73

Also see McLAUGHLIN, John

SANTANA, Carlos, & Buddy Miles

P&R/LP '72

Singles: 7–inch

COLUMBIA 3-5 72

LPs: 10/12–inch 33rpm

COLUMBIA 6-12 72

Also see MILES, Buddy
Also see SANTANA

SANTANA, Jorge

R&B '79

Singles: 7–inch

TOMATO 3-5 78-79

LPs: 10/12–inch 33rpm

TOMATO 5-10 78

Also see MALO

SANTIAGO

R&B '76

Singles: 7–inch

AMHERST 3-5 76

SANTO & JOHNNY

P&R/R&B '59

Singles: 7–inch

CANADIAN AMERICAN 5-12 59-66
ERIC 3-4 70s
IMPERIAL 4-8 67-68
PAUSA 3-5 76
U.A. 4-8 66

Picture Sleeves

CANADIAN AMERICAN 8-15 60-65

LPs: 10/12–inch 33rpm

CANADIAN AMERICAN 20-40 59-64
IMPERIAL 10-20 67-69

Members: Santo Farina; Johnny Farina.

SANTOS, Larry

P&R '76

Singles: 7–inch

ATLANTIC (2250 "Someday") 10-20 64
CASABLANCA 3-5 76-77
EVOLUTION 5-15 69-71

LPs: 10/12–inch 33rpm

CASABLANCA 8-10 77
EVOLUTION 10-20 69

Also see 4 SEASONS

SAPPHIRES

P&R/R&B '64

Singles: 7-inch

ABC 3-5 73
ABC-PAR 5-15 64-66
COLLECTABLES 3-4 80s
ERIC 3-4 70s
ITZY (5 "Who Do You Love") 20-30 63
SWAN 8-10 63-64

LPs: 10/12-inch 33rpm

SWAN (513 "Who Do You Love") 40-60 64

Members: Carol; George; Joe.

SARAYA

P&R/LP '89

Singles: 7-inch

POLYDOR 3-4 89

Picture Sleeves

POLYDOR 3-4 89

LPs: 10/12-inch 33rpm

POLYDOR 5-8 89

SARDUCCI, Father Guido

LP '80

Singles: 7-inch

A&M 3-5 74
W.B. 3-4 80

LPs: 10/12-inch 33rpm

W.B. 5-10 80

SARIDIS, Saverio

P&R '62

Singles: 7-inch

U.A. 3-6 66
W.B. 4-8 61-62

Picture Sleeves

W.B. 4-8 61

LPs: 10/12-inch 33rpm

W.B. 10-20 62

SARSTEDT, Peter

P&R '69

Singles: 7-inch

SIRE 3-5 78
U.A. 3-5 72
WORLD PACIFIC 4-6 69

LPs: 10/12-inch 33rpm

U.A. 8-12 71
WORLD PACIFIC 10-15 69

SASS

R&B '77

Singles: 7-inch

20TH FOX 3-5 77

SATELLITE, Billy: see BILLY SATELLITE

SATISFACTIONS

P&R/R&B '70

Singles: 7-inch

LIONEL 3-6 70-71

Members: James Isom; Earl Jones; Lorenzo Hines; Fletcher Lee.

SATRIANI, Joe

LP '87

Singles: 12-inch 33/45rpm

RELATIVITY (8193 "Always with Me") 4-8 87
(Clear vinyl. Promotional issue only.)

LPs: 10/12-inch 33rpm

RELATIVITY 5-8 87-89

SATTERFIELD, Esther

LP '76

Singles: 7-inch

A&M 3-5 76

LPs: 10/12-inch 33rpm

A&M 5-10 76

SATURDAY NIGHT BAND

R&B/LP '78

Singles: 7-inch

PRELUDE 3-5 78

LPs: 10/12-inch 33rpm

PRELUDE 5-10 78

SAULSBERRY, Rodney

R&B '84

Singles: 7-inch

ALLEGIANCE 3-4 84-85
RYAN 3-4 88

SAUNDERS, Merl
(Merle Saunders & Heavy Turbulence)

LP '73

Singles: 7-inch

FANTASY 4-8 64-69
GALAXY 3-5 71

LPs: 10/12-inch 33rpm

FANTASY 10-20 68-73

Session: Tom Fogerty.
Also see GARCIA, Jerry

SAVAGE GRACE

LP '70

Singles: 7-inch

REPRISE 3-5 70-71

LPs: 10/12-inch 33rpm

REPRISE 10-15 70-71

SAVALAS, Telly

LP '75

Singles: 7-inch

MCA 3-5 74-75

LPs: 10/12-inch 33rpm

AUDIO FIDELITY 5-10 75
MCA 5-10 74-76

SAVATAGE

LP '86

Singles: 7-inch

ATLANTIC 3-4 86-90

LPs: 10/12-inch 33rpm

ATLANTIC 5-8 86-90

SAVOY, Ronnie

P&R '61

Singles: 7-inch

CANDELO................................5-10 59
EPIC.....................................4-8 63-64
GONE...................................5-10 59
MGM 10-20 60-61
PHILIPS.................................4-8 62-63
TUFF (416 "Pitfall")..................20-30 65
WINGATE (001 "Loving You") .. 10-20 65

SAVOY BROWN

(Savoy Brown Blues Band)

P&R/LP '69

Singles: 7-inch

LONDON...................................3-5 74-75
PARROT..................................3-6 69-73
TOWN HOUSE 3-5 81

LPs: 10/12-inch 33rpm

LONDON (600 & 700 series) 8-10 74-77
LONDON (50000 "Best of Savoy Brown") 5-8 77
PARROT..................................10-15 68-73
TOWN HOUSE (Except 7562).... 8-12 81
TOWN HOUSE (7562 "Prime Cuts")...................................10-15 81
(Promotional issue only.)
Also see FOGHAT

SAWYER, Ray

P&R/C&W '76

Singles: 7-inch

CAPITOL.................................3-5 76-79
SANDY (1030 "Rockin' Satellite")..............................20-30 60
SANDY (1037 "I'm Gonna Leave")..................................10-20 61

LPs: 10/12-inch 33rpm

CAPITOL.................................8-10 76
Also see DR. HOOK

SAWYER BROWN

C&W '84

Singles: 7-inch

CAPITOL.................................3-5 84-90

LPs: 10/12-inch 33rpm

CAPITOL.................................5-10 85-90
Members: Mark Miller; Bob Randall; Jim Scholten; Gregg Hubbard; Joe Smyth.

SAWYER BROWN & "Cat" Joe Bonsall

C&W '86

Singles: 7-inch

CAPITOL.................................3-4 86
Also see SAWYER BROWN

SAXON

LP '83

Singles: 7-inch

CARRERE................................3-5 83-84

LPs: 10/12-inch 33rpm

CAPITOL.................................5-10 83-87
Also see MOTORHEAD

SAYER, Leo

P&R/LP '75

Singles: 7-inch

W.B. 3-5 73-84

LPs: 10/12-inch 33rpm

W.B. 6-10 75-84

SCAFFOLD

P&R '68

Singles: 7-inch

BELL 4-8 68
W.B. 3-5 74

LPs: 10/12-inch 33rpm

BELL (6018 "Thank U Very Much")..................................25-30 68
Members: Mike McGear; Roger McGough; John Gorman, Mike Vickers; Lol Cremo; Andy Roberts; Zoot Money.
Also see GODLEY, Kevin, & Lol Creme

SCAGGS, Boz

P&R/LP '71

Singles: 7-inch

ATLANTIC................................4-8 69
COLUMBIA 3-8 71-88
FULL MOON..............................3-5 81

Picture Sleeves

COLUMBIA 3-6 76-88

EPs: 7-inch 33/45rpm

COLUMBIA 5-10 76

LPs: 10/12-inch 33rpm

ATLANTIC (8239 "Boz Scaggs") .8-12 69
ATLANTIC (19166 "Boz Scaggs") .5-8 78
COLUMBIA (Except 40000 series)....................................6-10 71-80
COLUMBIA (40463 "Other Roads")..................................5-8 88
COLUMBIA (43920 "Silk Degrees")..............................15-20 80
(Half-speed mastered.)

Promotional LPs

COLUMBIA (A2S-71 "Boz Scaggs KSAN Live Concert") 200-300 74
(Promotional issue only. Two-LP set.)
COLUMBIA (203 "The Boz Scaggs Sampler")...............................10-20 76
Also see MILLER, Steve
Also see MOTHER EARTH

SCALES, Harvey

(With the Seven Sounds)

P&R/R&B '67

Singles: 7-inch

CADET CONCEPT 3-5 71
CASABLANCA............................3-5 79
CHESS.....................................3-5 69-70
CUCA.......................................5-10 67
EARTHTONE.............................3-4 86-91
KASHGOLD 3-4 90
MAGIC TOUCH 3-8 67-76
MERCURY................................3-6 69
STAX.......................................3-5 72

LPs: 10/12-inch 33rpm

CASABLANCA 8-10 79

SCANDAL

(Featuring Patty Smyth)

P&R '82

Singles: 12-inch 33/45rpm

COLUMBIA (Except 8C8-39905) .. 4-6 82-85

COLUMBIA (8C8-39905 "Warrior") 10-15 82

(Picture disc.)

Singles: 7-inch

COLUMBIA 3-5 82-85

Picture Sleeves

COLUMBIA 3-5 83-85

LPs: 10/12-inch 33rpm

COLUMBIA 5-10 82-85

SCARBURY, Joey

P&R '71

Singles: 7-inch

BELL 3-5 71-73

BIG TREE 3-5 73

COLUMBIA 3-5 77-79

ELEKTRA 3-5 81

LIONEL 3-5 71

PLAYBOY 3-5 74

RCA 3-4 84

REENA 4-6 68

Picture Sleeves

ELEKTRA 3-5 81

LPs: 10/12-inch 33rpm

ELEKTRA 5-10 81

SCARLET & BLACK

LP '88

Singles: 7-inch

VIRGIN 3-4 88

Picture Sleeves

VIRGIN 3-4 88

LPs: 10/12-inch 33rpm

VIRGIN 5-8 88

Members: Robin Hild; Sue West.

SCATTERBRAIN

LP '90

LPs: 10/12-inch 33rpm

IN-EFFECT 5-8 90

SCHAFER, Kermit

LP '58

Singles: 78rpm

JUBILEE 5-10 56

Singles: 7-inch

JUBILEE (5258 "Rock Around the Blooper") 10-15 56

LPs: 10/12-inch 33rpm

AUDIO FIDELITY 8-12 69

JUBILEE 10-20 58-63

KAPP 8-12 68-70

KING 10-15 64

MCA 5-10 74-77

Kermit Schafer has also released numerous comedy albums of "Bloopers," which we have not attempted to list. Their value is minimal, usually under $10.

SCHENKER, Michael, Group

LP '80

Singles: 7-inch

CHRYSALIS 3-5 80-83

LPs: 10/12-inch 33rpm

CHRYSALIS 5-10 80-83

Also see ALCATRAZZ

Also see McAULEY SCHENKER GROUP

Also see UFO

SCHIFRIN, Lalo

LP '62

Singles: 12-inch 33/45rpm

CTI 5-10 76

TABU 4-8 78-79

Singles: 7-inch

A&M 3-5 75

CTI 3-5 76-77

DOT 3-5 67

MCA 3-5 77-83

MGM 4-6 63-70

PABLO 3-5 77

PARAMOUNT 4-6 69

TABU 3-5 78-79

TETRAGRAMMATON 4-6 69

20TH FOX 3-5 74-75

U.A. 3-5 70

VERVE 4-6 63-71

W.B. 3-6 68-69

LPs: 10/12-inch 33rpm

AUDIO FIDELITY 5-15 62-68

CTI 5-10 76-77

COLPIX 10-20 64

DOT (25852 "There's a Whole Lalo Schifrin Goin' On") 10-15 68

MCA (5000 series) 5-10 81

MGM 5-15 63-70

ROULETTE 10-15 62

TABU 5-10 79

TICO 10-20 60

VERVE (Except 8624) 10-20 63-69

You'll find many more listings by this artist in *The Official Price Guide to Movie/TV Soundtracks and Original Cast Albums,* containing over 8,000 listings.

SCHILLING, Nina

D&D '84

Singles: 12-inch 33/45rpm

MOBY DICK 4-6 84

SCHILLING, Peter

P&R/D&D/LP '83

Singles: 12-inch 33/45rpm

ELEKTRA 4-6 83

Singles: 7-inch

ELEKTRA 3-4 83-89

Picture Sleeves

ELEKTRA 3-4 89

LPs: 10/12-inch 33rpm

ELEKTRA 5-10 83

SCHMIT, Timothy B.

P&R '82

Singles: 7-inch

FULL MOON 3-5 82
MCA 3-4 87

Picture Sleeves

FULL MOON 3-5 82
MCA 3-4 87

LPs: 10/12-inch 33rpm

ASYLUM 5-10 84
MCA 5-8 87

Also see EAGLES
Also see MARX, Richard
Also see POCO

SCHNEIDER, Fred, & Shake Society

D&D '84

Singles: 12-inch 33/45rpm

W.B. 4-6 84

Singles: 7-inch

W.B. 3-4 84

SCHNEIDER, John

C&W/P&R/LP '81

Singles: 7-inch

MCA 3-4 84-87
SCOTTI BROS 3-5 81-83

Picture Sleeves

MCA 3-4 84-87
SCOTTI BROS 3-5 81-83

LPs: 10/12-inch 33rpm

MCA 5-8 84-87
SCOTTI BROS 5-10 81-83

SCHNEIDER, John, & Jill Michaels

Singles: 7-inch

SCOTTI BROS 3-4 83

Also see SCHNEIDER, John

SCHON, Neal, & Jan Hammer

LP '81

LPs: 10/12-inch 33rpm

COLUMBIA 5-10 81-83

Also see HAGAR, SCHON, AARONSON, SHRIEVE
Also see HAMMER, Jan
Also see JOURNEY

SCHOOLBOYS

P&R/R&B '57

Singles: 78rpm

OKEH 10-20 56-57

Singles: 7-inch

JUANITA (103 "Angel of Love") 75-100 58
OKEH (7076 "Please Say You Want Me") 25-35 56
(Purple label.)
OKEH (7076 "Please Say You Want Me") 10-20 57
(Yellow label.)
OKEH (7085 "Mary") 25-35 57
OKEH (7090 "Carol") 15-25 57
(Purple label.)
OKEH (7090 "Carol") 25-35 57
(White label. Promotional issue only.)
OKEH (7090 "Carol") 10-20 57
(Yellow label.)

Members: Les Martin; Jim Edwards; Roger Hayes; Jim McKay; Renaldo Gamble.

EPs: 7-inch 33/45rpm

MAGIC CARPET 5-10

Also see CADILLACS

SCHOOLEY D

LP '88

LPs: 10/12-inch 33rpm

JIVE 5-8 88

SCHORY, Dick

(Dick Schory's Percussion Pops Orchestra)

LP '59

LPs: 10/12-inch 33rpm

RCA 5-15 59-63

SCHUMANN, Walter

(Voices of Walter Schumann)

P&R '53

Singles: 78rpm

CAPITOL 3-5 52
RCA 3-5 53-56

Singles: 7-inch

CAPITOL 4-6 52
RCA 4-6 53-56

EPs: 7-inch 33/45rpm

CAPITOL 5-10 52
RCA 5-10 53-56

LPs: 10/12-inch 33rpm

CAPITOL 5-15 52
RCA 5-15 53-56

SCHUUR, Diane

(With Jose Feliciano)

LP '88

Singles: 7-inch

GRP (3016 "American Wedding Song") 3-4 85
(With insert.)

LPs: 10/12-inch 33rpm

GRP 5-8 88-90

Also see FELICIANO, Jose

SCHWARTZ, Eddie

P&R '81

Singles: 7-inch

ATCO 3-5 81-82

LPs: 10/12-inch 33rpm

ATCO 5-10 82

SCORPIONS

LP '79

Singles: 7-inch

MERCURY ... 3-4 79-88
RCA ... 3-5 74-80

Picture Sleeves

MERCURY ... 3-4 84-88

LPs: 10/12-inch 33rpm

MERCURY ... 5-8 79-90
RCA ... 5-10 74-84

Members: Klaus Meine; Francis Bucholz; Matt Jabs; Herman Rarebell; Uli Roth; Rudolf Schenker.

SCOTT, Billy

P&R '58

Singles: 78rpm

CAMEO ... 5-10 57

Singles: 7-inch

CAMEO ... 8-12 57-58
EVEREST ... 5-10 59

SCOTT, Bobby

P&R '56

Singles: 78rpm

ABC-PAR ... 5-10 56

Singles: 7-inch

ABC ... 3-5 73
ABC-PAR ... 8-12 56

SCOTT, Christopher
(Sir Christopher Scott)

LP '69

LPs: 10/12-inch 33rpm

DECCA ... 5-10 69-70
MCA ... 5-10 73

SCOTT, Freddie
(Freddy Scott)

P&R/R&B '63

Singles: 7-inch

ABC ... 3-5 74
COLPIX ... 5-10 63-64
COLUMBIA ... 5-15 64-65
ELEPHANT V LTD. ... 4-6
ERIC ... 3-5 68
JOY ... 8-12 61-63
P.I.P. ... 3-5 72
PROBE ... 3-5 70
SHOUT ... 4-8 66-71
SOLID GOLD ... 3-5 73
VANGUARD ... 3-5 71

LPs: 10/12-inch 33rpm

COLPIX (Gold label) ... 30-40 64
COLPIX (Blue label) ... 15-25 65
COLUMBIA ... 10-20 64-67
PROBE ... 10-15 70
SHOUT ... 10-20 67

Also see CHIMES

SCOTT, Gloria

R&B '74

Singles: 7-inch

CASABLANCA ... 3-5 74-75

SCOTT, Jack
(With the Chantones)

P&R/R&B '58

Singles: 78rpm

ABC-PAR ... 15-25 57

Singles: 7-inch

ABC (10843 "Before the Bird Flies") ... 5-10 66
ABC-PAR (9818 "Baby, She's Gone") ... 50-75 57
(Black label.)
ABC-PAR (9818 "Baby, She's Gone") ... 40-60 57
(White label. Promotional issue only.)
ABC-PAR (9860 "Two Timin' Woman") ... 50-75 57
(Black label.)
ABC-PAR (9860 "Two Timin' Woman") ... 40-60 57
(White label. Promotional issue only.)
CAPITOL ... 10-20 61-63
CARLTON (Except 519) ... 10-20 58-59
CARLTON (519 "There Comes a Time") ... 10-20 59
(Monaural.)
CARLTON (ST-519 "There Comes a Time") ... 25-35 59
(Stereo.)
COLLECTABLES ... 3-4 80s
DOT ... 3-5 73
ERIC ... 3-4 70s
GRT ... 3-5 70
GROOVE (0027 "There's Trouble Brewin") ... 10-15 63
GROOVE (0031 "I Knew You First") ... 5-10 64
GROOVE (0037 "Wiggle on Out") ... 10-15 64
GROOVE (0042 "Thou Shalt Not Steal") ... 5-10 64
GROOVE (0049 "Flakey John") ... 10-15 64
GUARANTEED (209 "What Am I Living For") ... 10-20 60
GUARANTEED (211 "Go Wild Little Sadie") ... 15-25 60
JUBILEE ... 5-10 67
RCA ... 5-10 65
TOP RANK (2028 "What in the World's Come Over You") ... 10-15 60
TOP RANK (2041 "Burning Bridges") ... 10-15 60
(Monaural.)

TOP RANK (2041 "Burning Bridges") 25-45 60
(Stereo.)
TOP RANK (2055 "It Only Happened Yesterday") 8-15 60
TOP RANK (2075 "Patsy") 8-15 60
TOP RANK (2093 "Is There Something on Your Mind") 8-15 60

Picture Sleeves

CAPITOL 15-25 61-62
CARLTON 15-25 58-59
TOP RANK 15-25 60-61

EPs: 7–inch 33/45rpm

CARLTON (1070/1071 "Presenting Jack Scott") 50-75 58
(Price is for either volume.)
CARLTON (1072 "Jack Scott Sings") 50-75 59
TOP RANK (1001 "Jack Scott") 50-75 60

LPs: 10/12–inch 33rpm

CAPITOL (2035 "Burning Bridges") 60-80 64
CAPITOL (8-2035 "Burning Bridges") 60-80 64
(Capitol Record Club issue.)
CARLTON (LP-107 "Jack Scott") 100-150 58
(Monaural.)
CARLTON (STLP-12 107 "Jack Scott") 150-200 58
(Stereo.)
CARLTON (LP-122 "What Am I Living For") 75-125 60
(Monaural.)
CARLTON (STLP-12 122 "What Am I Living For") 100-150 60
JADE 10-15
PONIE 10-15 74-77
TOP RANK (348 "The Spirit Moves Me") 75-125 60
TOP RANK (319 "I Remember Hank Williams") 75-125 60
(Monaural.)
TOP RANK (619 "I Remember Hank Williams") 100-150 60
(Stereo.)
TOP RANK (326 "What in the World's Come over You") 75-125 61
(Monaural.)
TOP RANK (626 "What in the World's Come over You") 100-150 61
(Stereo.)

SCOTT, Judy

P&R '57

Singles: 78rpm

DECCA 4-6 57

Singles: 7–inch

CAPITOL 4-8 60
DECCA 5-10 57-59
EMBER 4-8 64
TOP RANK 4-8 59

SCOTT, Linda

P&R/R&B '61

Singles: 7–inch

CANADIAN AMERICAN 8-12 61-62
CONGRESS 5-10 62-64
ERIC 3-4 70s
KAPP 5-10 64-66
RCA 4-8 68

EPs: 7–inch 33/45rpm

CONGRESS (1005 "Starlight Starbright") 25-35 62
CONGRESS (3001 "Linda Scott") 25-35 62
(Promotional issue only. Issued with picture insert, but not with cover.)

LPs: 10/12–inch 33rpm

CANADIAN AMERICAN (CALP-1005 "Starlight Starbright") 35-45 61
(Monaural.)
CANADIAN AMERICAN (SCALP-1005 "Starlight Starbright") 40-50 61
(Stereo.)
CANADIAN AMERICAN (CALP-1007 "Great Scott") 35-45 62
(Monaural.)
CANADIAN AMERICAN (SCALP-1007 "Great Scott") 40-50 62
(Stereo.)
CONGRESS (3001 "Linda") 25-35 62
KAPP (3424 "Hey Look at Me Now") 25-35 65

SCOTT, Mabel

R&B '48

Singles: 78rpm

BRUNSWICK 5-10 52
CORAL 5-10 51-52
EXCELSIOR 8-12 47-48
EXCLUSIVE 8-12 48
FESTIVAL 4-8 55
HOLLYWOOD 5-10 54
HUB 10-15 46
KING 5-10 50-51
PARROT 10-15 53

Singles: 7–inch

BRUNSWICK 10-15 52
CORAL 10-15 51-52
FESTIVAL 10-15 55
HOLLYWOOD 15-25 54
PARROT (780 "Mr. Fine") 20-30 53
(Black vinyl.)
PARROT (780 "Mr. Fine") 50-75 53
(Colored vinyl.)
PARROT (794 "Fool Burro") 20-30 53

Also see BROWN, Charles

SCOTT, Marilyn

P&R '77

Singles: 7–inch

BIG TREE 3-5 77
MERCURY 3-4 83-85

LPs: 10/12–inch 33rpm

ATCO 5-10 79
MERCURY 5-8 83

SCOTT, Millie
(Mildred Scott)

R&B '86

Singles: 7–inch

4TH & BROADWAY 3-4 86-87

SCOTT, Neal
(With the Concords; Neil Scott; Neil Bogart)

P&R '61

Singles: 7–inch

CAMEO 5-10 67
CLOWN.. 10-15 60
COMET 10-15 62
HERALD.. 10-15 63
PORTRAIT 8-12 61-62

Also see BECK, BOGART & APPICE

SCOTT, Peggy, & Jo Jo Benson

P&R/R&B '68

Singles: 7–inch

SSS INT'L.................................... 4-8 68-69
SUN... 3-5 70s

LPs: 10/12–inch 33rpm

AVI 5-10 84
SSS INT'L.................................. 10-15 69

SCOTT, Rena

R&B '79

Singles: 7–inch

BUDDAH 3-5 79
EPIC... 3-5 72-74
SEDONA 3-4 88

SCOTT, Tom
(With the L.A. Express; withCalifornia Dreamers)

R&B/LP '74

Singles: 12–inch 33/45rpm

SIRE 4-6 83

Singles: 7–inch

A&M 3-5 72
ATLANTIC 3-5 83
COLUMBIA 3-5 79
IMPULSE 4-6 68
ODE 3-5 74-79
SIRE 3-4 83

LPs: 10/12–inch 33rpm

COLUMBIA 5-10 78-81
EPIC/ODE 5-8 84
IMPULSE 20-30 68
ODE 8-10 74-77
MUSICIAN.................................... 5-10 82
RCA... 5-10 81

Also see CLAYTON, Merry
Also see HARRISON, George
Also see L.A. EXPRESS

SCOTT-HERON, Gil

R&B '78

Singles: 7–inch

ARISTA 3-5 75-84

LPs: 10/12–inch 33rpm

ARISTA 6-12 75-84
FLYING DUTCHMAN (100 thru
0600 series) 8-15 71-74
FLYING DUTCHMAN (3800
series) 5-8 80

SCOTT-HERON, Gil, & Brian Jackson

P&R/LP '75

Singles: 7–inch

ARISTA 3-5 75-80

LPs: 10/12–inch 33rpm

ARISTA 6-12 75-80
STRATA-EAST 8-15 74

Also see SCOTT-HERON, Gil

SCREAMIN' BLUE MESSIAHS

LP '88

LPs: 10/12–inch 33rpm

ELEKTRA 5-8 87

SCRITTI POLITTI

D&D '84

Singles: 12–inch 33/45rpm

W.B. 4-6 84-86

Singles: 7–inch

W.B. 3-4 84-88

Picture Sleeves

W.B. 3-4 85-88

LPs: 10/12–inch 33rpm

W.B. 5-8 84-86

SCRITTI POLITTI & ROGER

P&R '88

Singles: 7–inch

W.B. 3-4 88

Picture Sleeves

W.B. 3-4 88

Also see ROGER
Also see SCRITTI POLITTI

SCRUFFY the CAT

LP '88

LPs: 10/12-Inch 33rpm

RELATIVITY 5-8 88

SCRUGGS, Earl
(Earl Scruggs Revue)

C&W '70

Singles: 7–inch

COLUMBIA 3-5 70-83

LPs: 10/12–inch 33rpm

COLUMBIA 5-10 73-83

Also see FLATT, Lester, & Earl Scruggs
Also see HALL, Tom T., & Earl Scruggs
Also see SKAGGS, Ricky

SCRUGGS, Faye: see ADAMS, Faye

SEA, Johnny
(Johnny Seay)

C&W '59

Singles: 7–inch

CAPITOL 4-8 61
COLUMBIA 3-5 67-69
NRC 5-10 59-60
PHILIPS 4-6 64-65
VIKING 3-5 70-71
W.B. 4-6 66-67

Picture Sleeves

COLUMBIA 3-5 68

LPs: 10/12–inch 33rpm

GUEST STAR 8-12 66
PHILIPS 10-15 64-65
PICKWICK/HILLTOP 8-12 65
W.B. 10-20 66

SEA HAGS

LP '89

LPs: 10/12–inch 33rpm

CHRYSALIS 5-8 89

SEA LEVEL

LP '77

Singles: 7–inch

ARISTA 3-5 80
CAPRICORN 3-5 77-79

LPs: 10/12–inch 33rpm

ARISTA 5-10 80
CAPRICORN 5-10 77-80

Also see ALLMAN BROTHERS BAND

SEAFOOD MAMA
(Quarterflash)

Singles: 7–inch

WHITEFIRE ("Harden My Heart") 10-20 80
(No label number given.)

Picture Sleeves

WHITEFIRE ("Harden My Heart") 15-25 80

Also see QUARTERFLASH

SEALS, Dan
(England Dan Seals)

P&R '80

Singles: 7–inch

ATLANTIC 3-5 80-82
CAPITOL 3-4 87-90
EMI AMERICA 3-4 84-87
LIBERTY 3-4 83-84

LPs: 10/12–inch 33rpm

ATLANTIC 5-10 80-82
EMI AMERICA 5-8 84-87
LIBERTY 5-8 83

Also see ENGLAND DAN & John Ford Coley

SEALS, Dan, & Marie Osmond

Singles: 7–inch

CAPITOL 3-4 85

Also see OSMOND, Marie
Also see SEALS, Dan

SEALS & CROFTS

LP '70

Singles: 7–inch

T.A. 4-6 69-71
W.B. 3-5 71-80

Picture Sleeves

W.B. 3-5 77

LPs: 10/12–inch 33rpm

T.A. 20-25 69-70
W.B. (Except 2809) 6-12 71-80
W.B. (2809 "Seals & Crofts I & II") 10-12 74

Members: Jimmy Seals; Dash Crofts.
Also see CHAMPS
Also see SEALS, Jimmy

SEARCHERS

P&R/LP '64

Singles: 7–inch

ERIC 3-4
KAPP 5-10 64-67
LIBERTY (55646 "Sugar and Spice") 8-12 63
LIBERTY (55689 "Sugar and Spice") 5-10 63
MERCURY 5-10 63
RCA 4-6 71-72
SIRE 3-5 80-81

Picture Sleeves

KAPP (577 "Needles and Pins") 10-20 64
KAPP (609 "Some Day We're Gonna Love Again") 10-20 64

LPs: 10/12–inch 33rpm

KAPP 20-30 64-66
MERCURY (20914 "Hear! Hear!") 25-35 64
(Monaural. Red label.)
MERCURY (20914 "Hear! Hear!") 40-60 64
(White label. Promotional issue only.)
MERCURY (60914 "Hear! Hear!") 25-35 64
(Stereo. Red label.)
MERCURY (60914 "Hear! Hear!") 40-60 64
(White label. Promotional issue only.)
PYE 10-12 76
RHINO 5-8 85
SIRE 8-10 80-81

SEARCHERS / Rattles

LPs: 10/12–inch 33rpm

MERCURY (20994 "The Searchers Meet the Rattles) 35-45 65
(Monaural. Red label.)
MERCURY (20994 "The Searchers Meet the Rattles) 50-75 65
(White label. Promotional issue only.)

MERCURY (60994 "The Searchers Meet the Rattles)............................ 35-45 65
(Stereo. Red label.)
MERCURY (60994 "The Searchers Meet the Rattles)............................ 50-75 65
(White label. Promotional issue only.)
Also see SEARCHERS

SEASE, Marvin

LP '87

LPs: 10/12-inch 33rpm

LONDON.................................... 5-8 87

SEATRAIN

LP '69

Singles: 7-inch

A&M 4-8 68
CAPITOL.................................... 3-6 71-72
W.B. 3-5 73

LPs: 10/12-inch 33rpm

A&M 10-15 69
CAPITOL (800 series)................ 8-12 71
CAPITOL (16000 series)............ 5-10 80
W.B. 8-10 73
Also see BLUES PROJECT
Also see RANK & FILE

SEAWIND

LP '77

Singles: 7-inch

A&M 3-5 80-82
CTI 3-5 77-78
HORIZON.................................. 3-5 79

LPs: 10/12-inch 33rpm

A&M 5-10 80-82
CTI 5-10 77-78
HORIZON.................................. 5-10 79

SEBASTIAN, John

P&R '69

Singles: 7-inch

KAMA SUTRA............................ 4-6 68-70
MGM 4-6 68-70
REPRISE 3-5 70-77

Picture Sleeves

KAMA SUTRA............................ 4-8 69

LPs: 10/12-inch 33rpm

KAMA SUTRA............................ 10-15 70
MGM 10-15 69-70
REPRISE 8-12 70-76
Also see LOVIN' SPOONFUL
Also see MUGWUMPS
Also see SIMPSONS

SECO, Pozo, Singers: see POZO SECO SINGERS

SECOND VERSE

R&B '74

Singles: 7-inch

IX CHAINS 3-5 74

SECRET TIES

P&R '86

Singles: 7-inch

NIGHT WAVE 3-4 86

SECRET WEAPON

R&B '82

Singles: 7-inch

PRELUDE 3-5 82-83

SECRETS

P&R '63

Singles: 7-inch

DCP 5-10 65
OMEN 5-10 66
PHILIPS 8-12 63-64

Picture Sleeves

PHILIPS 10-20 64
Members: Jackie Allen; Pat Miller; Karen Gray; Carol Raymont.

SEDAKA, Neil
(With the Marvels)

P&R '58

Singles: 7-inch

DECCA (30520 "Laura Lee") 40-60 57
ELEKTRA.....................................3-5 77-80
GUYDEN (2004 "Ring-a-Rockin'")...............................35-45 58
KIRSHNER 3-4 72-80
LEGION (133 "Ring-a-Rockin'")...............................50-75 58
MCA 3-5 75-84
MGM 3-5 73
PYRAMID (623 "Oh Delilah").....10-15 62
RCA (7408 "The Diary")..............8-12 58
(Black label.)
RCA (7408 "The Diary")............10-20 58
(White, photo label. Promotional issue only.)
RCA (7473 "I Go Ape") 10-15 59
RCA (47-7595 "Oh Carol")...........5-10 59
(Monaural.)
RCA (61-7595 "Oh Carol").........15-25 59
(Stereo.)
RCA (47-7709 "Stairway to Heaven")...............................5-10 60
(Monaural.)
RCA (61-7709 "Stairway to Heaven")...............................15-25 60
(Stereo.)
RCA (47-7781 "Run Sampson Run")...5-10 60
(Monaural.)
RCA (61-7781 "Run Sampson Run")...15-25 60
(Stereo.)
RCA (37-7829 "Calendar Girl")..15-25 60
(Compact 33 Single.)
RCA (47-7829 "Calendar Girl")....5-10 60
(Monaural.)

RCA (61-7829 "Calendar Girl") . 15-25 60
(Stereo.)
RCA (37-7874 "Little Devil")...... 15-25 61
(Compact 33 Single.)
RCA (47-7874 "Little Devil")........ 5-10 61
RCA (37-7922 "Sweet Little You") 15-25 61
(Compact 33 Single.)
RCA (47-7922 "Sweet Little You") 5-10 61
RCA (37-7957 "Happy Birthday Sweet Sixteen")...................... 15-25 61
(Compact 33 Single.)
RCA (47-7957 "Happy Birthday Sweet Sixteen")........................ 5-10 61
RCA (37-8007 "King of Clowns")................................ 15-25 62
(Compact 33 Single.)
RCA (47-8007 "King of Clowns")..................................... 5-10 62
RCA (37-8007 "King of Clowns")................................ 15-25 62
(Compact 33 Single.)
RCA (8046 thru 9004).................. 4-8 62-66
RCA GOLD STANDARD.............. 3-6 60s-89
ROCKET 3-5 74-76
S.G.C. 4-6 68-69

Picture Sleeves

RCA.. 5-15 60-65

EPs: 7–inch 33/45rpm

RCA (105 "Neil's Best")............ 15-25 61
(Compact 33 Double.)
RCA (135 "Little Devil") 15-25 61
(Compact 33 Double.)
RCA (4334 "I Go Ape") 30-40 59
RCA (4353 "Oh Carol") 25-35 59

LPs: 10/12–inch 33rpm

ACCORD..................................... 5-10 81
CAMDEN..................................... 8-12 60s
ELEKTRA.................................... 5-10 77-81
51 WEST...................................... 5-8 80s
INTERMEDIA................................ 5-8 85
KIRSHNER.............................. 10-15 71-72
MCA 5-10 84
RCA (AFL1 & APL1 series)......... 8-10 75-78
RCA (ANL1 series)...................... 5-10 75-79
RCA (VPL1 series)...................... 8-12 76
RCA (LPM-2035 "Neil Sedaka") 35-45 59
(Monaural.)
RCA (2035 "Neil Sedaka") 50-100 59
(Stereo.)
RCA (LPM-2317 thru LPM-2627) 20-30 61-62
(Monaural.)
RCA (LSP-2317 thru LSP-2627)............................... 25-35 61-62
(Stereo.)
RCA (10181 "Smile")................. 15-20 66
ROCKET 8-10 74-77

Session: King Curtis.
Also see ANKA, Paul / Sam Cooke / Neil Sedaka
Also see COOKE, Sam / Rod Lauren / Neil Sedaka / Browns
Also see JOHN, Elton
Also see KING CURTIS
Also see SIMON, Paul
Also see 10CC
Also see WILLOWS

SEDAKA, Neil & Dara

P&R '80

Singles: 7–inch

ELEKTRA..3-5 80
MCA 3-4 84

SEDAKA, Neil, & Tokens

LPs: 10/12–inch 33rpm

GUEST STAR 10-20 60s
VERNON.....................................10-15 60s

SEDAKA, Neil, & Tokens / Coins

LPs: 10/12–inch 33rpm

CROWN 10-20 63

SEDAKA, Neil, & Tokens / Angels / Jimmy Gilmer & Fireballs

LPs: 10/12–inch 33rpm

ALMOR (105 "Teen Bandstand") 15-25 60s
Also see ANGELS
Also see GILMER, Jimmy
Also see SEDAKA, Neil
Also see TOKENS

SEDUCTION

P&R/LP '89

Singles: 7–inch

VENDETTA....................................3-4 89-90

LPs: 10/12–inch 33rpm

A&M 5-8 89
VENDETTA.....................................5-8 90
Members: April; Michelle; Idalis.

SEEDS
(Featuring Sky Saxon)

P&R '66

Singles: 7–inch

GNP (354 "Can't Seem to Make You Mine"/"Daisy Mae") 5-10 65
GNP (354 "Can't Seem to Make You Mine"/"I Tell Myself") 4-8 67
GNP (364 "Your Pushing Too Hard"/"Out of the Question")...........................8-12 65
(Reissued on 372 as *Pushing too Hard,* with a different flip, *Try to Understand.*)
GNP (370 "The Other Place")......5-10 65
GNP (372 thru 422).........................4-8 66-69
MGM 8-12 69-70

Picture Sleeves

GNP (354 "Can't Seem to Make You Mine"/"I Tell Myself") 10-20 67
GNP (383 "Mr. Farmer") 10-20 67
GNP (394 "A Thousand Shadows")...............................10-20 67

LPs: 10/12–inch 33rpm

GNP (2023 thru 2043).............. 20-30 66-67
(All Seeds LPs, except 2043, *Raw and Alive,* were reissued with original selection numbers. First issue, red label, 1960s LPs have the logo, "GNP/Crescendo," on a horizontal line. Reissues have the label name in a circular manner on the label.)
GNP (2100 series) 5-10 77
Also see FULLER, Bobby / Seeds

SEEGER, Pete

LP '63

Singles: 7–inch

COLUMBIA 4-6 63-67
FOLKWAYS 5-10 59
PIONEER 4-8 60

LPs: 10/12–inch 33rpm

ARAVEL.................................. 10-20 63-64
ARCHIVE of FOLK MUSIC 10-15 65
BROADSIDE............................ 10-20 63
CAPITOL................................. 10-20 64-67
COLUMBIA 10-20 63-72
DISC....................................... 10-20 64
FOLKWAYS 8-20 59-75
(Black vinyl.)
FOLKWAYS (7610 "Animal Folk Songs") 25-30
(Colored vinyl.)
HARMONY.............................. 5-10 68-70
ODYSSEY 8-12 68
OLYMPIC................................. 5-10 73
PHILIPS 10-20 63
STINSON (57 "Pete Seeger Concert")............................ 20-30 54
(10–inch LP.)
STINSON (90 "Pete")................ 5-10 70
TRADITION.............................. 5-10 73
VANGUARD 6-12 78
VERVE/FOLKWAYS 10-20 65
W.B. 5-10 79
Also see BROONZY, Big Bill, & Pete Seeger
Also see SEEGERS
Also see WEAVERS

SEEGER, Pete, & Arlo Guthrie

LP '75

LPs: 10/12–inch 33rpm

REPRISE 8-12 75
W.B. 5-10 81
Also see GUTHRIE, Arlo

SEEGER, Pete, with Pacific Gas & Electric

LPs: 10/12–inch 33rpm

COLUMBIA (3540 "Tell Me That You Love Me, Junie Moon")................. 10-15 70
(Soundtrack.)
Also see PACIFIC GAS & ELECTRIC

SEEGERS

LPs: 10/12–inch 33rpm

PRESTIGE...............................10-20 65
Members: Pete Seeger; Peggy Seeger; Mike Seeger; Barbara Seeger; Penny Seeger.
Also see SEEGER, Pete

SEEKERS

P&R/LP '65

Singles: 7–inch

ATMOS 5-8 65
CAPITOL.....................................4-6 65-68
MARVEL 5-8 65

Picture Sleeves

CAPITOL...................................5-10 65

LPs: 10/12–inch 33rpm

CAPITOL (100 series) 8-12 69
CAPITOL (2000 series) 10-20 65-67
CAPITOL (16000 series) 5-10 80
MARVEL 15-20 65
Members: Judy Durham; Keith Potger.
Also see JAMES, Sonny / Seekers
Also see NEW SEEKERS

SEELY, Jeannie

C&W/P&R '66

Singles: 7–inch

CHALLENGE 4-6 64-65
COLUMBIA 3-5 77-78
DECCA 3-5 69-73
MCA 3-5 73-75
MONUMENT................................3-5 66-68

LPs: 10/12–inch 33rpm

DECCA 6-12 69-70
HARMONY..................................5-10 72
MCA 5-8 73
MONUMENT...............................6-12 66-77
Also see GREENE, Jack, & Jeannie Seely

SEGAL, George

(With the Imperial Jazzband)

LP '67

Singles: 7–inch

FLYING DUTCHMAN 3-5 74
PHILIPS 4-6 67

LPs: 10/12–inch 33rpm

PHILIPS 10-20 67
SIGNATURE 5-10 74

SEGER, Bob

(With the Last Heard; with Silver Bullet Band; Bob Seger System)

P&R '68

Singles: 7–inch

ABKCO 3-6 72-75
CAMEO (438 "East Side Story") 10-20 66
CAMEO (444 "Sock It to Me Santa")....................................15-25 66
CAMEO (465 "Persecution Smith") 10-20 66
CAMEO (473 "Vagrant Winter"). 10-20 66
CAMEO (494 "Heavy Music") 8-12 67
CAPITOL (Except 2000 series) 3-5 71-86

CAPITOL (2000 series)................ 4-8 68-70
HIDEOUT (1013 "East Side Story") 20-30 66
HIDEOUT (1014 "Persecution Smith") 20-30 66
MCA 3-4 87
PALLADIUM................................ 3-6 71-74
REPRISE 3-6 72

Promotional Singles

CAPITOL (Colored vinyl).............. 4-8 78
CAPITOL (9878 "Shame on the Moon")............................... 3-6 82
(Edited version [4:22], not the promo that runs 4:55.)

Picture Sleeves

CAPITOL (Except 4951) 3-6 78-86
CAPITOL (4951 "Horizontal Bop") 30-50 80
MCA 3-4 87

LPs: 10/12-inch 33rpm

CAPITOL (ST-172 "Ramblin' Gamblin' Man").................................... 15-25 69
CAPITOL (SM-172 "Ramblin' Gamblin' Man")....................................... 8-10 75
CAPITOL (ST-236 "Noah") 50-70 69
CAPITOL (SKAO-499 Mongrel")............................... 15-25 70
CAPITOL (SM-499 "Mongrel") 8-10 75
CAPITOL (ST-731 "Brand New Morning").............................. 30-50 71
CAPITOL (8433 "Live Bullet, Consensus Cuts") 20-30 75
(Promotional issue only.)
CAPITOL (11000 series, except 11557 & 11904) 6-12 75-78
CAPITOL (ST-11557 "Night Moves")................................... 5-10 78
CAPITOL (ST-11557 "Night Moves") 30-40 78
(Picture disc. Promotional issue only.)
CAPITOL (SW-11904 "Stranger in Town")................................ 5-10 78
CAPITOL (SEAX-11904 "Stranger in Town") 15-20 79
(Picture disc.)
CAPITOL (12000 series)............ 6-10 80-86
CAPITOL (16000 series).............. 5-8 80
INNER VIEW ("Demonstration Record Bob Seger")........................... 15-25 76
(Promotional issue only.)
MFSL (034 "Night Moves")........ 25-50 79
MFSL (127 "Against the Wind"). 20-30 85
PALLADIUM (1006 "Smokin' O.P.'s")................................. 15-25 72
PALLADIUM (2126 "Back in '72") 50-75 73
REPRISE 10-15 72-74
Also see BEACH BUMS
Also see BROWNSVILLE STATION
Also see NEWMAN, Randy

SELECTOR

LP '80

Singles: 7-inch

CHRYSALIS...................................3-5 79-81

LPs: 10/12-inch 33rpm

CHRYSALIS.................................5-10 79-81

SELF, Ronnie

P&R '58

Singles: 78rpm

ABC-PAR 10-20 56
COLUMBIA 10-20 57

Singles: 7-inch

ABC-PAR (9714 "Pretty Bad Blues") 75-100 56
ABC-PAR (9768 "Sweet Love") .50-75 56
AMY 4-8 68
COLUMBIA (Except 41241).......15-25 57-58
COLUMBIA (41241 "Petrified") 75-125 58
DECCA 5-10 59-62
KAPP 4-8 63

EPs: 7-inch 33/45rpm

COLUMBIA (2149 "Ain't I'm a Dog")..............................175-200 57

SELLARS, Marilyn

C&W/P&R '74

Singles: 7-inch

MEGA 3-5 74-77
ZODIAC 3-5 76-77

LPs: 10/12-inch 33rpm

MEGA 5-10 74-77
ZODIAC 5-10 77

SEMBELLO, Michael

P&R/D&D/LP '83

Singles: 12-inch 33/45rpm

CASABLANCA...............................4-6 83
W.B. 4-6 83-84

Singles: 7-inch

A&M 3-4 86
CASABLANCA...............................3-5 83
GEFFEN 3-4 85
W.B. 3-5 83-84

LPs: 10/12-inch 33rpm

A&M 5-8 86
MCA 5-8 85
W.B. 5-10 83

SEMBELLO, Michael / Basil Poledouris

Singles: 7-inch

W.B. 3-4 82

Picture Sleeves

W.B. 3-4 82
Also see SEMBELLO, Michael

SENATOR BOBBY

P&R '67

Singles: 7-inch

RCA 4-8 67-68
Also see HARDLY WORTHIT PLAYERS

SENATOR McKINLEY: see HARDLY WORTHIT PLAYERS

SENAY, Eddy

R&B '72

Singles: 7-inch

SUSSEX.................................... 3-5 72-73

LPs: 10/12-inch 33rpm

SUSSEX.................................... 8-12 72

SEÑOR SOUL

R&B '69

Singles: 7-inch

DOUBLE SHOT 4-8 67-68
WHIZ.. 3-6 69-70

LPs: 10/12-inch 33rpm

DOUBLE SHOT 10-15 68-69

SENSATIONS

(With the Sensations)

R&B '56

Singles: 78rpm

ATCO 8-12 55

Singles: 7-inch

ARGO.. 5-10 61-62
ATCO 15-25 55
CHESS.. 3-5 73
JUNIOR.................................... 10-20 62-64
TOLLIE...................................... 5-10 64

LPs: 10/12-inch 33rpm

ARGO (4022 "Let Me In").......... 50-75 63

SEQUENCE

R&B '80

Singles: 7-inch

SUGAR HILL................................ 3-5 80-82

LPs: 10/12-inch 33rpm

SUGAR HILL.............................. 5-10 81

SEQUINS

R&B '70

Singles: 7-inch

GOLD STAR 3-5 70

SERENDIPITY SINGERS

P&R/LP '64

Singles: 7-inch

PHILIPS 4-8 64-66
U.A. 3-5 67-69

Picture Sleeves

PHILIPS 4-8 64-66

LPs: 10/12-inch 33rpm

PHILIPS 10-20 64-65
WING 8-12 68

SERGE!

R&B '83

Singles: 7-inch

W.B. 3-5 83

SERIOUS INTENTION

D&D '84

Singles: 12-inch 33/45rpm

EASY STREET 4-6 84

SESAME STREET KIDS: see ERNIE

SETZER, Brian

LP '86

Singles: 7-inch

EMI...3-4 86-88

LPs: 10/12-inch 33rpm

EMI...5-8 86-88

Also see STRAY CATS

SEVELLE, Taja

P&R/R&B '87

Singles: 7-inch

PAISLEY PARK 3-4 87
REPRISE 3-4 87-88

Picture Sleeves

REPRISE 3-4 87

707

P&R '80

Singles: 7-inch

BOARDWALK...............................3-5 82
CASABLANCA...............................3-5 80

LPs: 10/12-inch 33rpm

BOARDWALK.............................5-10 82
CASABLANCA.............................5-10 80

SEVEN DWARFS

P&R '38

Singles: 78rpm

VICTOR (25735 "Heigh-Ho")..... 10-20 38

SEVEN SECONDS

LP '89

LPs: 10/12-inch 33rpm

RESTLESS 5-8 89

7TH WONDER

(Seventh Wonder)

R&B '73

Singles: 12-inch 33/45rpm

CASABLANCA...............................4-6 80
PARACHUTE.................................4-8 79

Singles: 7-inch

ABET...3-5 73
CASABLANCA...............................3-5 80
CHOCOLATE CITY 3-5 80
PARACHUTE.................................3-5 78-79

LPs: 10/12-inch 33rpm

CHOCOLATE CITY 5-10 80
PARACHUTE...............................5-10 78-79

SEVERINSEN, Doc, Orchestra

(With the Dodge City Boys; Tonight Show Band with Doc Severinsen)

LP '66

Singles: 7-inch

COMMAND...................................3-5 65-70
EPIC..4-6 59-76
FRONTLINE...................................3-4 80
RCA 3-4 72-73

Picture Sleeves

COMMAND...................................3-5 70

LPs: 10/12-inch 33rpm

ABC 5-10 71-73
AMHERST 5-8 86
COMMAND 5-15 61-73
EPIC 5-8 76-81
EVEREST 5-8 78
JUNO 5-10 70-79
MCA 4-8 82
RCA 5-10 71

Also see MANCINI, Henry, & Doc Severinsen

SEVILLE, David
(Ross Bagdasarian)

P&R '56

Singles: 78rpm

LIBERTY 4-8 56-57

Singles: 7-inch

LIBERTY 5-10 56-61

Picture Sleeves

LIBERTY (55079 "Gotta Get to Your House") 10-15 57

EPs: 7-inch 33/45rpm

LIBERTY (1003 "Witch Doctor") 25-45 57

LPs: 10/12-inch 33rpm

LIBERTY (3073 "The Music of David Seville") 25-35 57
LIBERTY (3092 "Witch Doctor") 35-45 58

Also see ALFI & HARRY
Also see CHIPMUNKS

SEVILLES

P&R '61

Singles: 7-inch

CAL-GOLD 8-12 62
GALAXY 8-12 63-64
J.C. 10-20 60-61

SEX PISTOLS

LP '77

Singles: 7-inch

W.B. 3-6 78

LPs: 10/12-inch 33rpm

W.B. 10-20 77

Also see PUBLIC IMAGE LTD.
Also see SIOUXSIE & BANSHEES

S-EXPRESS

P&R '88

Singles: 7-inch

CAPITOL 3-4 88

Picture Sleeves

CAPITOL 3-4 88

SEXTON, Ann

R&B '73

Singles: 7-inch

DASH 3-5 77
MONUMENT 3-5 77
SEVENTY SEVEN 3-5 72-74
SOUND STAGE 3-5 77

SEXTON, Charlie

P&R/LP '85

Singles: 7-inch

MCA 3-4 85-89

Picture Sleeves

MCA 3-4 85

LPs: 10/12-inch 33rpm

MCA 5-8 86-89

Also see ELY, Joe

SEXTON, Charlie, & Ron Wood

LPs: 10/12-inch 33rpm

MCA 5-8 84

Also see SEXTON, Charlie
Also see WOOD, Ron

SEYMOUR, Phil

P&R/LP '81

Singles: 7-inch

BOARDWALK 3-5 81

LPs: 10/12-inch 33rpm

BOARDWALK 5-10 81

Also see TEXTONES
Also see TWILLEY, Dwight, Band

SHA NA NA

LP '69

Singles: 7-inch

KAMA SUTRA 3-5 70-75
SUTRA 3-5 74

Picture Sleeves

KAMA SUTRA 3-5 71

LPs: 10/12-inch 33rpm

ACCORD 5-10 81-83
BUDDAH 5-10 77
CSP 8-12 78
EMUS 5-10 78
K-TEL 5-10 81
KAMA SUTRA 10-15 69-76
NASHVILLE 5-10 80

Members: Lennie Baker; Jon "Bowzer" Bauman; Johnny Contardo; Denny Green; Henry Gross; Jocko Marcellino; Danny McBride; Scott Powell; David-Allan "Chico" Ryan; "Screamin' Scott Simon; Donny York.

Also see GROSS, Henry
Also see TRAVOLTA, John / Sha Na Na

SHACK

R&B '71

Singles: 7-inch

VOLT 3-5 71

SHACKLEFORDS

P&R '63

Singles: 7-inch

CAPITOL 4-6 66
LHI 4-6 67-68
MERCURY 4-8 63

LPs: 10/12-inch 33rpm

CAPITOL 10-20 66
MERCURY 15-25 63

Members: Lee Hazlewood; Marty Cooper; Al Stone; Garcia Nitzsche.

Also see HAZLEWOOD, Lee

Also see MOMENTS

SHADES of BLUE

P&R/R&B '66

Singles: 7–inch

COLLECTABLES 3-4 80s
IMPACT 8-15 66-67
SHADES 5-10 68

LPs: 10/12–inch 33rpm

IMPACT (101 "Happiness Is")... 30-50 66
(Monaural.)
IMPACT (101 "Happiness Is")... 50-75 66
(Stereo.)

SHADES of LOVE

R&B '82

Singles: 7–inch

VENTURE 3-5 82

SHADOW

R&B '79

Singles: 7–inch

ELEKTRA 3-5 79-81

LPs: 10/12–inch 33rpm

ELEKTRA 5-10 79-81

SHADOWFAX

LP '83

Singles: 7–inch

WINDHAM HILL 3-5 82

LPs: 10/12–inch 33rpm

CAPITOL 5-8 88
PASSPORT 8-10 76
WINDHAM HILL 5-8 82-86

SHADOWS

R&B '50

Singles: 78rpm

LEE (200 "I've Been a Fool")..... 15-25 49
LEE (202 "I'd Rather Be Wrong Than Blue") 15-25 50
LEE (207 "Don't Blame My Dreams") 15-25 50
Members; Jasper Edwards; Ray Reed; Sam McClure; Scott King; Bobby Buster.

SHADOWS of KNIGHT

P&R/LP '66

Singles: 7–inch

ATCO 8-12 69
COLUMBIA/AURAVISION ("Potato Chip") 30-50 60s
(5–inch, promotional flexi-disc.)
DUNWICH (116 "Gloria") 10-20 66
(Label makes no reference to distribution by Atco.)
DUNWICH (116 "Gloria") 5-10 66
(Label reads "Distributed by Atco.")
DUNWICH (122 thru 167) 10-20 66-67
SUPER K 5-10 69
TEAM 5-10 68

Picture Sleeves

DUNWICH (122 "Oh Yeah")...... 15-20 66
DUNWICH (128 "Bad Little Woman") 20-30 66

LPs: 10/12–inch 33rpm

DUNWICH (666 "Gloria") 50-100 66
DUNWICH (667 "Back Door Men") 50-100 66
SUPER K (6002 "The Shadows of Knight") 15-25 69

SHAFTO, Bobby

P&R '64

Singles: 7–inch

RUST 5-8 64-65

SHAKATAK

D&D '84

Singles: 12–inch 33/45rpm

POLYDOR 4-6 82-84

Singles: 7–inch

POLYDOR 3-4 82-84

LPs: 10/12–inch 33rpm

POLYDOR 5-8 82

SHAKIN' STEVENS: see STEVENS, Shakin'

SHALAMAR

P&R/R&B/LP '77

Singles: 12–inch 33/45rpm

COLUMBIA 4-6 84-85
SOLAR 4-6 79-85

Singles: 7–inch

COLUMBIA 3-4 84-85
MCA 3-4 84
SOLAR 3-5 78-87
SOUL TRAIN 3-5 77

Picture Sleeves

COLUMBIA 3-4 84
SOLAR 3-5 83

LPs: 10/12–inch 33rpm

SOLAR 5-10 78-85
SOUL TRAIN 5-10 77
Members: Howard Hewett; Jody Watley; Jeffrey Daniel.
Also see HEWETT, Howard
Also see WATLEY, Jody

SHANA
(Shana Petrone)

P&R '89

Singles: 7–inch

VISION 3-4 89

LPs: 10/12–inch 33rpm

VISION 5-8 89

SHANGO

P&R '69

Singles: 12–inch 33/45rpm

CELLULOID 4-8 83

Singles: 7–inch

A&M 4-6 69
CELLULOID 3-4 83
GNP 3-6 69

LPs: 10/12-inch 33rpm

A&M 10-15 69
DUNHILL 8-12 70

Also see BAMBAATAA, Afrika

SHANGRI-LAS
(Shangra-Las)

P&R/R&B '64

Singles: 7-inch

COLLECTABLES 3-4 80s
ERIC 3-5 70s
LANA 3-6 60s
MERCURY 4-8 66-67
RED BIRD 5-10 64-66
SSS INT'L 3-5 80s
SCEPTER 10-15 65
SMASH 10-20 63
SPOKANE 10-20 64
TRIP 3-4 70s

LPs: 10/12-inch 33rpm

BACK-TRAC 5-10 85
COLLECTABLES 5-10 83
MERCURY (21099 "Golden Hits of the Shangri-las") 20-30 66
(Monaural.)
MERCURY (21099 "Golden Hits") 50-75 66
(Shown as monaural but plays in true stereo.)
MERCURY (61099 "Golden Hits") 25-35 66
(Stereo.)
POST 10-12
RED BIRD (101 "Leader of the Pack") 30-50 65
RED BIRD (104 "Shangri-Las '65") 50-100 65
RED BIRD (104 "I Can Never Go Home Amymore") 50-85 65

Members: Mary Weiss; Marge Ganser; Mary Ann Ganser.

SHANK, Bud

P&R/LP '66

Singles: 78rpm

GOOD TIME JAZZ 4-6 54

Singles: 7-inch

GOOD TIME JAZZ 5-10 54
PACIFIC JAZZ 3-6 61-70
WORLD PACIFIC 3-6 64-68

EPs: 7-inch 33/45rpm

NOCTURNE (3/4 "The Bud Shank Quintet") 50-75 53
(Price is for either volume.)
PACIFIC JAZZ 20-30 54-58

LPs: 10/12-inch 33rpm

CONCORD JAZZ 5-8 76
CROWN 10-20 63
KIMBERLY 10-20 63
NOCTURNE (2 "The Bud Shank Quintet") 125-175 53
(10-inch LP.)
PACIFIC JAZZ (14 "Bud Shank with Three Trombones") 50-100 54
(10-inch LP.)
PACIFIC JAZZ (20 "Bud Shank & Bob Brookmeyer") 50-100 55
(10-inch LP.)
PACIFIC JAZZ (4 thru 89) 15-25 60-65
(12-inch LPs.)
PACIFIC JAZZ (404 "Jazz Swings Broadway") 30-50 57
PACIFIC JAZZ (411 "The Swing's to TV") 30-50 57
PACIFIC JAZZ (1205 "Bud Shank & Shorty Rogers") 30-60 55
PACIFIC JAZZ (1213 "Strings and Trombones") 30-50 56
PACIFIC JAZZ (1215 "The Bud Shank Quartet") 30-50 56
PACIFIC JAZZ (1219 "Jazz at Cal-Tech") 30-50 56
PACIFIC JAZZ (1226 "Flute 'N Oboe") 30-50 57
PACIFIC JAZZ (1230 "The Bud Shank Quartet") 30-50 57
PACIFIC JAZZ (10000 & 20000 series) 5-15 66-81
SUNSET 8-12 66
WORLD PACIFIC (1000 thru 1200 series) 20-40 58-60
WORLD PACIFIC (1400 series) 15-30 61-63
WORLD PACIFIC (1800 series) 15-20 64-67
WORLD PACIFIC (21000 series) 10-20 66-68

Also see FOLKSWINGERS
Also see LONDON, Julie, & Bud Shank Quintet

SHANKAR, Ravi
(With Yehudi Menuhin)

LP '67

Singles: 7-inch

APPLE 4-8 71
DARK HORSE 3-5 75
WORLD PACIFIC 4-8 59-68

Picture Sleeves

APPLE (1838 "Joi Bangla") 20-25 71

LPs: 10/12-inch 33rpm

ANGEL 10-20 67
APPLE 10-20 71-73
CAPITOL 10-20 67-72
COLUMBIA 10-20 66-68
DARK HORSE 8-12 74-76
FANTASY 5-10 73
PRESTIGE 10-20 68
SPARK 5-10 73
WORLD PACIFIC 10-20 59-69

Also see BEATLES
Also see HARRISON, George

SHANNON
(Marty Wilde)

P&R '69

Singles: 7-inch

EPIC/MAGNET 3-5 75
HERITAGE 4-6 69
Also see WILDE, Marty

SHANNON
(Brenda Shannon Greene)

P&R/R&B/D&D '83

Singles: 12-inch 33/45rpm

EMERGENCY 4-6 83-84
MIRAGE 4-6 84-85

Singles: 7-inch

ATLANTIC 3-4 86
EMERGENCY 3-5 83-84
MIRAGE 3-5 84-85

Picture Sleeves

MIRAGE 3-5 84-85

LPs: 10/12-inch 33rpm

MIRAGE 5-10 84-85

SHANNON, Del

P&R/R&B '61

Singles: 7-inch

AMY 4-8 64-65
BERLEE 5-10 63-64
BIG TOP 10-20 61-63
COLLECTABLES 3-4 80s
DUNHILL 4-8 69
ERIC 3-5 70s
ISLAND 3-5 75
LANA 3-6 60s
LIBERTY 5-10 66-68
NETWORK 3-5 81-82
TERRIFIC 3-5
TWIRL 4-6 60s
W.B. 3-5 85

Picture Sleeves

LIBERTY 8-12 68

LPs: 10/12-inch 33rpm

AMY (8003 "Handy Man") 30-50 64
(Monaural.)
AMY (S-8003 "Handy Man") 40-60 64
(Stereo.)
AMY (8004 "Del Shannon Sings Hank Williams") 30-50 65
(Monaural.)
AMY (S-8004 "Del Shannon Sings Hank Williams") 40-60 65
(Stereo.)
AMY (8006 "1,661 Seconds") 30-50 65
(Monaural.)
AMY (S-8006 "1,661 Seconds") 40-60 65
(Stereo.)
BIG TOP (1303 "Runaway") 100-200 61
(Monaural.)
BIG TOP (1303 "Runaway") 400-600 61
(Stereo.)
BIG TOP (1308 "Little Town Flirt") 40-60 63
BUG 5-10 85
DOT (3834 "Best of Del Shannon") 25-45 67
(Monaural.)
DOT (25834 "Best of Del Shannon") 25-45 67
(Stereo.)
LIBERTY 20-30 66-68
NETWORK/ELEKTRA 8-10 81
PHOENIX 20 .... 8-10 80
PICKWICK 8-10 70s
POST 10-15
SIRE 10-15 75
SUNSET 10-15 70
U.A. 10-15 73
Also see HONDELLS / Del Shannon / Martha & Vandellas

SHANNON, Jackie
(Jackie Shannon & Cajuns; Jackie DeShannon)

Singles: 7-inch

DOT (15928 "Just Another Lie") 15-20 59
FRATERNITY (836 "Just Another Lie") 10-15 59
P.J. (101 "Trouble") 30-40 59
SAGE (290 "Just Another Lie") .. 20-30 59
SAND (330 "Trouble") 20-30 59
Also see DE SHANNON, Jackie

SHANTE, Roxanne

R&B/D&D '85

Singles: 12-inch 33/45rpm

POP ART 4-6 85

Singles: 7-inch

POP ART 3-4 85

LPs: 10/12-inch 33rpm

POP ART 5-8 85
Also see JAMES, Rick, & Roxanne Shante

SHANTELLE

R&B '85

Singles: 7-inch

PANDISC 4-6 85

SHAPIRO, Helen

P&R '61

Singles: 7-inch

CAPITOL 5-10 61-62
EPIC 4-8 62-63
JANUS 3-5 70
MUSICOR 4-6 65
TOWER 4-6 67

Picture Sleeves

EPIC 4-8 62

LPs: 10/12-inch 33rpm

EPIC 10-20 63

SHA-RAE, Billy
(Sha-Rae)

R&B '71

Singles: 7-inch

BAY-UKE 5-10 61-62
HOUR GLASS.............................. 3-5
LAURIE 3-5
SPECTRUM 3-5 71

Also see HEBB, Bobby / Billy Sha-Rae

SHARKEY, Feargal

P&R/LP '86

Singles: 12-inch 33/45rpm

A&M/VIRGIN 4-6 86

Singles: 7-inch

A&M/VIRGIN 3-4 86

Picture Sleeves

A&M/VIRGIN 3-4 86

LPs: 10/12-inch 33rpm

A&M/VIRGIN 5-8 86

Also see UNDERTONES

SHARKS

LP '73

Singles: 7-inch

MCA 3-5 73-74

LPs: 10/12-inch 33rpm

MCA 8-12 73-74

SHARP, Dee Dee
(Dee Dee Sharp Gamble)

P&R/R&B/LP '62

Singles: 7-inch

ABKCO...................................... 3-5 83-84
ATCO 4-8 66-68
CAMEO 5-10 62-66
FAIRMOUNT............................... 5-10 66
GAMBLE (219 "You're Gonna Miss Me").. 8-12 68
PHILADELPHIA INT'L.................. 3-5 77-81
TSOP 3-5 76

Picture Sleeves

CAMEO 5-10 62-65

LPs: 10/12-inch 33rpm

CAMEO 20-30 62-63
PHILADELPHIA INT'L.................. 8-10 75-81

Also see CHECKER, Chubby, & Dee Dee Sharp
Also see KING, Ben E., & Dee Dee Sharp
Also see PHILADELPHIA INTERNATIONAL ALL STARS

SHARPE, Mike

P&R '67

Singles: 7-inch

LIBERTY 4-8 66-69

LPs: 10/12-inch 33rpm

LIBERTY 10-20 67-69

Also see CLASSICS IV

SHARPE, Ray
(With the Blues Whalers; with Soul Set)

P&R/R&B '59

Singles: 7-inch

A&M 3-5 71
ATCO 4-8 66
DOT 5-10 59
FLYING HIGH.............................. 3-5
GAREX 5-10 63
GREGMARK................................. 5-10 62
HAMILTON 8-12 59
JAMIE (Except 1128).................. 5-10 58-60
JAMIE (1128 "Linda Lu"/"Monkey's Uncle") 10-15 59
JAMIE (1128 "Linda Lu"/"Red Sails In the Sunset") 5-10 59
LHI 4-6 60s
MONUMENT 4-8 65
PARK AVE 4-8 60s
SOCK & SOUL............................ 4-8 60s
TREY 5-10 61

LPs: 10/12-inch 33rpm

AWARD (711 "Welcome Back").25-50

Session: Duane Eddy; Al Casey; Jim Horn; King Curtis.

Also see CASEY, Al
Also see EDDY, Duane
Also see KING CURTIS

SHARPEES

P&R '66

Singles: 7-inch

ONE-DERFUL.............................. 5-10 65-66

Members: Herbert Reeves; Vernon Guy; Stacy Johnson.

SHARPLES, Bob
(Bob Sharples' Living Strings)

P&R '56

Singles: 78rpm

LONDON..................................... 3-5 56-57

Singles: 7-inch

LONDON..................................... 4-6 56-61

LPs: 10/12-inch 33rpm

CAMDEN 5-10 60
LONDON..................................... 5-15 61-64
METRO 5-10 65

SHAW, Georgie

P&R '54

Singles: 78rpm

DECCA 3-5 53-56

Singles: 7-inch

DECCA 4-8 53-56

EPs: 7-inch 33/45rpm

DECCA 5-10 56

LPs: 10/12-inch 33rpm

DECCA 10-20 53-56

Also see KALLEN, Kitty, & Georgie Shaw

SHAW, Marlena

P&R/R&B '67

Singles: 12–inch 33/45rpm

COLUMBIA 4-8 79
SOUTH BAY 4-6 83

Singles: 7–inch

BLUE NOTE.............................. 3-5 72-76
CADET 4-6 66-69
COLUMBIA 3-5 77-79
SOUTH BAY 3-5 83

Picture Sleeves

CADET 4-8 67

LPs: 10/12–inch 33rpm

BLUE NOTE.............................. 8-12 72-75
CADET 10-15 68-69
COLUMBIA 5-10 77-79

SHAW, Robert, Chorale

LP '57

Singles: 78rpm

RCA.. 3-5 50-58

Singles: 7–inch

RCA.. 4-8 50-62

EPs: 7–inch 33/45rpm

RCA.. 5-10 54-56

LPs: 10/12–inch 33rpm

ALMANAC................................ 5-10 66
CAMDEN.................................. 5-10 64
RCA.. 5-15 50-70
VICTROLA 4-8 70

SHAW, Roland, Orchestra

LP '65

Singles: 78rpm

LONDON................................... 3-5 56-57

Singles: 7–inch

LONDON................................... 3-6 56-67

LPs: 10/12–inch 33rpm

LONDON................................... 5-10 64-78

SHAW, Sandie

P&R '64

Singles: 7–inch

MERCURY 4-8 64
RCA.. 3-6 68-70
REPRISE 4-8 64-67

LPs: 10/12–inch 33rpm

REPRISE 15-20 65-66

SHAW, Timmy

P&R/R&B '64

Singles: 7–inch

JAMIE...................................... 5-15 61-62
SCEPTER 4-6 73
WAND 5-10 63-64

SHAW, Tommy

P&R/LP '84

Singles: 7–inch

A&M 3-4 84-85
ATLANTIC................................ 3-4 88

Picture Sleeves

A&M 3-4 84-85
ATLANTIC................................ 3-4 88

LPs: 10/12–inch 33rpm

A&M 5-8 84-85

Also see STYX

SHAWN, Damon

R&B '72

Singles: 7–inch

WESTBOUND............................ 3-5 73

SH-BOOMS
(Chords)

Singles: 78rpm

CAT... 10-15 55
VIK 10-15 57

Singles: 7–inch

ATCO (6213 "Sh-Boom") 8-12 61
ATLANTIC (2074 "Blue Moon") . 10-20 60
CAT (117 "Could It Be") 25-30 55
VIK (0295 "I Don't Want to Set the World on Fire") 15-25 57

Also see CHORDS

SHEAR, Jules

D&D '84

Singles: 12–inch 33/45rpm

EMI AMERICA 4-6 84-85

Singles: 7–inch

EMI AMERICA 3-4 84-85

Picture Sleeves

EMI AMERICA 3-4 85

LPs: 10/12–inch 33rpm

EMI AMERICA 5-8 83

Also see JULES & Polar Bears

SHEARING, George, Quintet

LP '56

Singles: 78rpm

CAPITOL.................................. 3-5 55-57
MGM 3-6 50-56

Singles: 7-Inch

CAPITOL.................................. 3-8 55-67
LONDON.................................. 3-6 63
MGM 5-10 50-56
SHEBA..................................... 3-5 71

EPs: 7-Inch 33/45rpm

CAPITOL.................................. 5-10 55-60
MGM 5-10 51-55

LPs: 10/12-Inch 33rpm

ARCHIVE of FOLK MUSIC 6-12 68
BASF....................................... 5-10 73
CAPITOL (Except 648 thru 1628) 5-15 62-77
CAPITOL (648 thru 1628) 10-25 55-61
CONCORD JAZZ....................... 5-8 80-82
CORONET 5-10 60s
DISCOVERY (3002 "George Shearing Quintet") 30-50 50
(10–inch LP.)
EVEREST 5-10 69
LION....................................... 10-20 59

MGM (90 "A Touch of Genius"). 20-40 51
(10–inch LP.)
MGM (155 "I Hear Music") 20-40 52
(10–inch LP.)
MGM (226 "When Lights Are Low") 20-40 53
(10–inch LP.)
MGM (252 "An Evening with George Shearing") 20-40 55
(10–inch LP.)
MGM (100 series) 5-10 70
MGM (3000 series) 15-25 55-60
MGM (4000 series) 10-20 62-63
MPS 5-10 74-75
METRO 10-15 65
PAUSA 5-8 79-82
SAVOY (12093 "Midnight on Cloud 69") 15-25 57
SAVOY (15003 "Piano Solo").... 30-50 51
(10–inch LP.)
SHEBA 5-10 71-76
VSP 10-15 66-67

Also see COLE, Cozy
Also see COLE, Nat "King," & George Shearing
Also see COLE, Natalie
Also see LEE, Peggy, & George Shearing

SHEARING, George & Montgomery Brothers

Singles: 7-Inch

JAZZLAND 3-6 62

LPs: 10/12-Inch 33rpm

JAZZLAND (55 "George Shearing & Montgomery Brothers) 25- 40 61
(Cover pictures Shearing with the three brothers.)
JAZZLAND (55 "George Shearing & Montgomery Brothers) 15- 25 62
(Cover pictures a woman.)
RIVERSIDE 5-10 82

Also see MONTGOMERY BROTHERS
Also see SHEARING, George, Quintet
Also see WILSON, Nancy, & George Shearing

SHEEN, Bobby

R&B '75

Singles: 7–inch

CAPITOL 10-20 66-69
CHELSEA 3-5 75
DIMENSION 8-12 65
LIBERTY 5-10 62
W.B. 10-15 72

Also see ALLEY CATS
Also see BOB B. SOXX & Blue Jeans

SHEEP

P&R '66

Singles: 7–inch

BOOM (6000 "Hide & Seek") 10-20 66

Also see STRANGELOVES

SHEILA

(Sheila B. Devotion; Anny Chancel)

R&B '80

Singles: 7–inch

CARRERE 3-5 80-81
CASABLANCA 3-5 78

Picture Sleeves

CARRERE 3-5 80-81

Promotional Singles

CARRERE (37675 "Little Darlin'")..4-6 81
(Price includes special sleeve.)

LPs: 10/12–inch 33rpm

CARRERE 5-10 80
CASABLANCA 5-10 78

SHEILA E.

(Sheila Escovedo)

P&R/R&B/D&D/LP '84

Singles: 12–inch 33/45rpm

W.B. 4-6 84-85

Singles: 7–inch

PAISLEY PARK 3-4 85-87
W.B. 3-4 84-85

Picture Sleeves

PAISLEY PARK 3-4 85-87
W.B. 3-4 84

LPs: 10/12–inch 33rpm

PAISLEY PARK 5-10 85-87
W.B. 5-10 84-91

Also see KRUSH GROOVE ALL STARS
Also see PRINCE

SHELLEY, Pete

(Peter Shelley)

P&R '74

Singles: 12–inch 33/45rpm

ARISTA 4-6 82-83

Singles: 7–inch

ARISTA 3-4 82-83
BELL 3-5 74

LPs: 10/12–inch 33rpm

ARISTA 5-8 82-83

Also see BUZZCOCKS

SHELLS

P&R '60

Singles: 78rpm

CANDLELITE (436 "Baby Oh Baby") 5-10 72
(Colored vinyl.)
JOHNSON 10-15 57

Singles: 7–inch

ABC 3-5 75
BOARDWALK 3-5 75
COLLECTABLES 3-4 80s
END (1022 "Pretty Little Girl")..50-100 58
END (1050 "Whispering Winds") 25-40 59
GONE (5103 "Pretty Little Girl").10-20 61
JOHNSON (099 "My Cherie")........4-6 72

JOHNSON (104 "Baby Oh Baby"/"Angel Eyes") 20-30 57
(Has selection number, 104, centered between the horizontal lines on the right side of label.)
JOHNSON (104 "Baby Oh Baby"/"What's in an Angel Eyes") 8-12 60
(The 1960 issue label has two parallel lines with one thinner than the other. These lines are both the same thickness on the '57 issue. MOST 1957 issues have the shorter flip side title, but ALL 1960 issues have the longer title.)
JOHNSON (106 "Pleading No More") 75-100 58
JOHNSON (107 "Explain It to Me") 10-20 61
JOHNSON (109 "Better Forget Him") 10-20 61
JOHNSON (110 "In the Dim of the Dark") 10-20 61
JOHNSON (112 "Sweetest One") 15-25 61
JOHNSON (119 "Deep in My Heart") 20-25 62
JOHNSON (120 "A Toast on Your Birthday") 20-25 62
JOHNSON (127 "On My Honor") 30-40 63
JOHNSON (332 "Explain It to Me") 8-12 61
JOSIE (912 "Deep in My Heart") 10-15 63
ROULETTE (4156 "She Wasn't Meant for Me") 15-25 59
SELSOM 5-10 65
SNOWFLAKE (1959 "If You Were Gone from Me"/"Misty") 10-20 64
(Blank, orange labels.)
SOUNDS from the SUBWAY 3-5 77
(Colored vinyl.)

LPs: 10/12-inch 33rpm

CANDLELITE 10-15 70s
COLECTABLES 5-8 80s
JUBILEE 10-20

Members: Nathaniel Bouknight; Shade Alston; Bobby Nurse; Danny Small; Gus Geter; Roy Jones.
Also see DUBS / Shells
Also see FIVE SATINS / Youngtones / Youngsters / Shells

SHELTO, Steve

D&D '83

Singles: 12-inch 33/45rpm

SAM 4-6 83

SHELTON, Anne

P&R '49

Singles: 78rpm

COLUMBIA 4-6 56

Singles: 7-inch

COLUMBIA 5-10 56
EPIC 4-8 59

SHELTON, Ricky Van

C&W '86

Singles: 7-inch

COLUMBIA 3-4 86-92

LPs: 10/12-inch 33rpm

COLUMBIA 5-8 87-91

Also see JOEL, Billy / Ricky Van Shelton
Also see PARTON, Dolly, & Ricky Van Shelton

SHELTON, Roscoe

R&B '65

Singles: 7-inch

BATTLE 4-8 62-63
EXCELLO 5-10 59-61
SIMS 4-8 64-65
SOUND STAGE 7 .... 4-8 65-68

LPs: 10/12-inch 33rpm

EXCELLO (8002 "Roscoe Shelton") 40-50 61
SOUND STAGE 7 .... 15-20 66

SHEP & LIMELITES

(Featuring James Sheppard)

P&R/R&B '61

Singles: 7-inch

ABC 3-5 73
HULL (Except 770) 10-20 61-65
HULL (770 "A Party for Two") 20-30 65
ROULETTE 3-5 73

LPs: 10/12-inch 33rpm

HULL (1001 "Our Anniversary") 300-400 62
ROULETTE (25350 "Our Anniversary") 35-45 67

Also see HEARTBEATS
Also see HEARTBEATS / Shep & Limelites

SHEPARD, Jean

C&W/P&R '53

Singles: 78rpm

CAPITOL 4-8 53-57

Singles: 7-inch

CAPITOL 5-10 53-61
(Purple labels.)
CAPITOL 3-8 61-72
(Orange or orange/yellow labels.)
MERCURY 3-5 72
SCORPION 3-4 78
U.A. 3-5 73-77

EPs: 7-inch 33/45rpm

CAPITOL 5-10 56-61

LPs: 10/12-inch 33rpm

CAPITOL (100 thru 800 series) 5-10 69-71
CAPITOL (700 thru 1200 series) 15-25 56-59
(With a "T" prefix.)
CAPITOL (1500 thru 2900 series) 10-15 61-68

CAPITOL (11000 series)............ 5-10 72-79
MERCURY 5-10 71
PICKWICK/HILLTOP 5-12 67-68
POWER PAK 5-8 80s
U.A. 5-10 73-76

SHEPARD, Jean, & Ferlin Huskey

C&W/P&R '53

Singles: 78rpm

CAPITOL............ 3-5 53

Singles: 7-inch

CAPITOL............ 4-8 53

Also see HUSKY, Ferlin

SHEPARD, Jean, & Ray Pillow

C&W '66

Singles: 7-inch

CAPITOL............ 4-6 66

Also see SHEPARD, Jean

SHEPARD SISTERS: see SHEPHERD SISTERS

SHEPHERD SISTERS

(Sheppard Sisters; Shepard Sisters; Shephard Sisters)

P&R '57

Singles: 78rpm

LANCE 4-8 57
MELBA............ 4-8 56
MERCURY 4-8 57

Singles: 7-inch

ABC............ 3-5 73
ATLANTIC............ 5-10 63
COLLECTABLES............ 3-4 80s
LANCE 5-10 57
MGM 4-8 59
MELBA............ 8-12 56
MERCURY 5-10 57
20TH FOX............ 4-8 64
U.A. 5-10 61
WARWICK 5-10 59-60
YORK............ 4-8 65

Members: Mary Lou Shepherd; Judy Shepherd; Martha Shepherd; Gayle Shepherd.

SHEPPARD, T.G.

C&W '74

Singles: 7-inch

COLUMBIA 3-4 85
HITSVILLE 3-5 76
MELODYLAND 3-5 74-75
W.B. 3-4 77-85

LPs: 10/12-inch 33rpm

COLUMBIA 5-8 85
CURB............ 5-8 84
HITSVILLE 5-10 76
MELODYLAND 8-10 75-76
W.B. 5-8 78-83

Also see COLLINS, Judy, & T.G. Sheppard

SHEPPARD, T.G., & Karen Brooks

C&W '82

Singles: 7-inch

W.B. 3-4 82

SHEPPARD, T.G., & Clint EASTWOOD

C&W/P&R '84

Singles: 7-inch

W.B. 3-4 84

Also see SHEPPARD, T.G.

SHEPPARD SISTERS: see SHEPHERD SISTERS

SHERBET

(Sherbs)

P&R '76

Singles: 7-inch

ATCO 3-5 81
MCA............ 3-5 76-77

LPs: 10/12-inch 33rpm

ATCO 5-10 80-82
MCA............ 5-10 76-77

SHERBS: see SHERBET

SHERIDAN, Bobby

(Charlie Rich)

Singles: 7-inch

SUN (354 "Red Man")............ 10-15 61

Also see RICH, Charlie

SHERIDAN, Tony & Beat Brothers: see BEATLES

SHERIFF

P&R '83

Singles: 7-inch

CAPITOL............ 3-5 83

Picture Sleeves

CAPITOL............ 3-5 83

LPs: 10/12-inch 33rpm

CAPITOL............ 5-8 83
OBSERVATORY............ 6-10 79

Members: Wolf Hassel; Arnold Lanni; Fred Curci; Steve DeMarchi.

Also see FROZEN GHOST

SHERMAN, Allan

(With Friends; with Boston Pops Orchestra)

LP '62

Singles: 7-inch

RCA 3-6 68
W.B. 4-8 63-66

Picture Sleeves

W.B. 5-10 63-64

LPs: 10/12-inch 33rpm

JUBILEE 10-20 62
RCA (Except 310)............ 10-15 64
RCA (310 "Alan Sherman and You")............ 20-30 64
(Promotional issue only. Includes 25-page script, letter from Allan and a comments postcard.)
RHINO 5-8 85-86

W.B. 15-25 62-65

Also see BOSTON POPS ORCHESTRA

SHERMAN, Bobby

P&R/LP '69

Singles: 7-inch

CAMEO (403 "Happiness Is") 4-8 66

CAMEO (403 "Happiness Is") 8-12 66

(Single-sided. Promotional issue only.)

CONDOR 4-8 69

DECCA.. 5-10 64-65

DOT.. 4-8 63

EPIC.. 4-8 67

GRT.. 3-5 76

JANUS 3-5 75

METROMEDIA.............................. 3-5 69-73

PARKWAY 5-10 65

STARCREST 5-10 62

Picture Sleeves

DECCA.. 8-12 65

METROMEDIA.............................. 3-5 69-72

EPs: 7-inch 33/45rpm

METROMEDIA ("Bobby Sherman") 4-8 70

(Flexi-disc.)

LPs: 10/12-inch 33rpm

METROMEDIA.............................. 5-10 69-73

SHERMAN, Joe, & His Orchestra

(With the Arena Brass)

P&R '63

Singles: 78rpm

KAPP.. 3-5 56-57

Singles: 7-inch

EPIC.. 3-5 65-66

KAPP.. 4-6 56-61

WORLD ARTISTS.......................... 3-6 63-65

LPs: 10/12-inch 33rpm

COLUMBIA 5-10 68

EPIC.. 5-10 66

RCA.. 5-10 67

WORLD ARTISTS.......................... 5-12 63-64

SHERRICK

R&B '87

Singles: 7-inch

W.B. 3-4 87

SHERRYS

P&R/R&B '62

Singles: 7-inch

GUYDEN.................................... 8-12 62-63

MERCURY 5-10 64

ROBERTS.................................. 5-10 60s

LPs: 10/12-inch 33rpm

GUYDEN (503 "At the Hop")... 75-125 62

SHERWOOD, Roberta

P&R '56

Singles: 78rpm

DECCA.. 3-5 56-57

Singles: 7-inch

DECCA 4-8 56-64

DUNHILL.. 3-6 68

HAPPY TIGER.............................. 3-6 69

HARMON 3-6 62-63

KING 3-5 71-72

MCA.. 3-5 73

OLEN 4-6 65

EPs: 7-inch 33/45rpm

DECCA 5-10 56-59

LPs: 10/12-inch 33rpm

ABC-PAR.. 5-15 63-64

DECCA 8-18 56-65

HARMONY.. 5-15 63

KING 5-8 70

VOCALION 5-10 66-68

SHIELDS

P&R/R&B '58

Singles: 7-inch

DOT (136 "You Cheated") 4-6 66

(Black vinyl.)

DOT (136 "You Cheated") 20-25 66

(Colored vinyl. Promotional issue only.)

DOT (15805 "You Cheated") 10-15 58

DOT (15856 "I'm Sorry Now")....20-30 58

DOT (15940 "Play the Game Fair") 15-20 59

TENDER (513 "You Cheated") ..30-40 58

(Label does NOT read "Dist. By Dot.")

TENDER (513 "You Cheated") ..15-20 58

(Label reads "Dist. By Dot.")

TENDER (518 "I'm Sorry Now").25-35 59

TENDER (521 "Play the Game Fair") 25-35 59

TRANSCONTINENTAL (1013 "The Girl Around the Corner")..............75-100 60

LPs: 10/12-inch 33rpm

BRYLEN....................................5-10

Members: Frankie Ervin; Charles Wright; Nathaniel Wilson; Jesse Belvin; Johnny "Guitar" Watson; Mel Williams.

Also see BELVIN, Jesse

Also see WATSON, Johnny

Also see WRIGHT, Charles

SHINDIGS

(Bobby Fuller Four)

Singles: 7-inch

MUSTANG....................................10-15 65

Also see FULLER, Bobby

SHINDOGS

P&R '66

Singles: 7-inch

VIVA..4-8 66

W.B. 4-8 65

Members: Delaney Bramlet; Bonnie Bramlett.

Also see DELANEY & BONNIE

SHINEHEAD

LP '88

LPs: 10/12-inch 33rpm

ELEKTRA.. 5-8 88-90

SHIRLEE MAY

(Shirley Ellis)

Singles: 7-inch

MERCURY 5-10 62

Also see ELLIS, Shirley

SHIRELLES

P&R '58

Singles: 7-inch

COLLECTABLES 3-4 80s
BLUE ROCK 4-8 68
DECCA...................................... 10-20 58-61
ERIC.. 3-4 70s
GUSTO 3-4
RCA... 5-10 71-73
SCEPTER (1203 "Dedicated to the One I Love")................................ 15-25 59
(White label.)
SCEPTER (1203 "Dedicated to the One I Love")................................ 10-15 59
(Red label.)
SCEPTER (1205 thru 1208)...... 15-20 59-60
(White label.)
SCEPTER (1205 thru 1208)...... 10-15 59-60
(Red label.)
SCEPTER (1211 "Tomorrow").. 20-25 60
SCEPTER (1211 "Will You Love Me Tomorrow") 10-15 60
(Note longer title.)
SCEPTER (1217 thru 1292)........ 5-10 61-64
SCEPTER (12000 series) 4-8 65-67
TIARA (6112 "I Met Him On a Sunday") 100-125 57
U.A. 3-5 70-71

Picture Sleeves

SCEPTER 10-20 63

LPs: 10/12-inch 33rpm

BACK-TRAC 5-10 85
EVEREST 5-10 81
GUSTO 5-10 80s
PHOENIX.................................. 5-10 81
PRICEWISE 15-25 60s
RCA.. 10-15 71-72
RHINO.. 5-8 85
SCEPTER (SRM-501 "Tonight's the Night") 60-80 61
(Monaural.)
SCEPTER (S-501 "Tonight's the Night") 75-100 61
(Stereo.)
SCEPTER (502 thru 562).......... 25-40 61-67
SCEPTER (599 "Remember When") 15-20 72
SPRINGBOARD......................... 8-10 72
U.A. 10-15 71-75

Members: Shirley Jackson-Alston, Beverly Lee; Doris Coley-Jackson; Addie "Micki" Harris-McFadden.
Also see JAN & DEAN / Roy Orbison / 4 Seasons / Shirelles
Also see KING, Carole
Also see SHIRLEY & SHIRELLES

SHIRELLES & King Curtis

LPs: 10/12-inch 33rpm

SCEPTER (505 "A Twist Party")................................25-35 62
SCEPTER (569 "Eternally Soul") 25-35 68

Also see KING CURTIS
Also see SHIRELLES

SHIRLEY, Donald

(Don Shirley Trio)

LP '55

Singles: 7-inch

BARNABY 3-4 76
CADENCE 4-8 60-64
COLUMBIA 3-6 68-69

EPs: 7-inch 33/45rpm

CADENCE 8-15 56-59

LPs: 10/12-inch 33rpm

ATLANTIC..................................5-12 72
AUDIO FIDELITY.......................10-25 59
CADENCE 20-40 55-63
COLUMBIA 10-15 65-69

SHIRLEY & CO.

P&R/R&B/LP '75

Singles: 7-inch

VIBRATION.................................3-5 75-76

LPs: 10/12-inch 33rpm

VIBRATION...............................8-10 75

Members: Shirley Goodman; Kenny Jeremiah.
Also see SHIRLEY & LEE
Also see SOUL SURVIVORS

SHIRLEY & LEE

P&R '52

Singles: 78rpm

ALADDIN (3152 thru 3205)........10-20 52-57

Singles: 7-inch

ABC...3-4 73
ALADDIN (3153 "I'm Gone")......50-75 52
ALADDIN (3173 "Baby") 50-100
ALADDIN (3192 "Shirley's Back") 30-50 53
ALADDIN (3205 "Two Happy People") 25-40 53
ALADDIN (3222 "Why Did I").....25-40 53
ALADDIN (3244 "Confessin'")....25-40 54
ALADDIN (3258 "Comin' Over") 25-40 54
ALADDIN (3289 "Feel So Good")......................................15-25 55
ALADDIN (3302 "Lee's Dream") 15-25 55
ALADDIN (3313 "That's What I'll Do") 20-30 55
ALADDIN (3325 "Let the Good Times Roll") 10-20 56

ALADDIN (3338 "I Feel Good"). 10-20 56
ALADDIN (3362 "When I Saw You") 10-20 57
ALADDIN (3369 "I Want to Dance") 10-20 57
ALADDIN (3380 "Rock All Night") 10-20 57
ALADDIN (3390 "Rockin' with the Clock") 10-20 57
ALADDIN (3405 "I'll Thrill You") 10-20 57
ALADDIN (3418 "Everybody's Rockin") 10-20 58
ALADDIN (3432 "All I Want to Do Is Cry") 10-20 58
ALADDIN (3455 "True Love") ... 10-20 59
IMPERIAL 5-10 62-63
LIBERTY 3-4 80s
U.A. 3-5 73
WARWICK 5-10 60-61

LPs: 10/12–inch 33rpm

ALADDIN (807 "Let the Good Times Roll") 300-400 56
IMPERIAL (9179 "Let the Good Times Roll") 50-75 62
SCORE (4023 "Let the Good Times Roll") 100-150 57
U.A. 20-25 73-74
WARWICK (2028 "Let the Good Times Roll") 75-100 61

Members: Shirley Goodman; Leonard Lee.
Also see ADAMS, Faye / Little Esther / Shirley & Lee
Also see KING, Ben E.
Also see SHIRLEY & COMPANY

SHIRLEY & SQUIRRELY

C&W/P&R '76

Singles: 7–inch

GRT 3-5 76

LPs: 10/12–inch 33rpm

GRT 5-10 76

Also see SHIRLEY, SQUIRRELY & MELVIN

SHIRLEY & SHIRELLES

(Featuring Shirley Alston)

Singles: 7–inch

BELL 5-8 69

Also see SHIRELLES

SHIRLEY, SQUIRRELY & MELVIN

Singles: 7–inch

EXCELSIOR 3-4 81

Picture Sleeves

EXCELSIOR 3-5 81

LPs: 10/12–inch 33rpm

EXCELSIOR 5-10 81

Also see SHIRLEY & SQUIRRELY

SHOCK

R&B '81

Singles: 12–inch 33/45rpm

FANTASY 4-6 81-83

Singles: 7–inch

FANTASY 3-4 81-83
NEBULA 3-5 79

LPs: 10/12–inch 33rpm

FANTASY 5-10 81-82

SHOCKED, Michelle

P&R/LP '88

Singles: 7–inch

MERCURY 3-4 88-89

Picture Sleeves

MERCURY 3-4 88

LPs: 10/12–inch 33rpm

MERCURY 5-8 88-89

SHOCKING BLUE

P&R '69

Singles: 7–inch

BUDDAH 3-5 71
COLOSSUS 3-6 69-71
MGM 3-5 72-73

Picture Sleeves

COLOSSUS 4-6 69-70

LPs: 10/12–inch 33rpm

COLOSSUS 10-20 70

SHOES

P&R/LP '79

Singles: 7–inch

BOMP 3-5 78
ELEKTRA 3-5 79

Picture Sleeves

BOMP 3-5 78
ELEKTRA 3-5 79

EPs: 7–inch 33/45rpm

BOMP 5-10 78

LPs: 10/12–inch 33rpm

BLACK VINYL 8-12 70s
ELEKTRA 5-10 77-82
PVC 5-10 78

Members: John Murphy; Jeff Murphy; Gary Klebe; Skip Meyer.

SHONDELL, Troy

(Troy Shondel; Troy Shundell; Gary Shelton)

P&R '61

Singles: 7–inch

AVM 3-4 88
BRITE STAR 3-5 73-74
COLLECTABLES 3-4 80s
COMMERCIAL 3-5 78
DECCA 4-8 64
EVEREST 4-8 62-64
GAYE (2010 "This Time") 20-25 61
GOLDCREAST (161 "This Time") 15-20 61
(Note misspelled label name.)
GOLDCREST (161 "This Time") 10-15 61
LIBERTY 5-10 61-62
LUCKY 3-5 75
MASTER 10-15 60s
RIC 4-8 65
STAR-FOX 3-5 79
SUNSHINE 3-5 76

TRX 4-8 67-69
TELESONIC 3-5 80-81
3 RIVERS 4-8 60s
WRITERS & ARTISTS (001 "This Time") 25-35 61

LPs: 10/12–inch 33rpm

EVEREST (1206 "Many Sides") 25-35 63
STAR-FOX 5-10 79
SUNSET 10-15 67

SHONDELLS
(Featuring Tommy James)

Singles: 7–inch

RED FOX (110 "Hanky Panky") 15-25 66
SELSOM (102 "Why Do Fools Fall in Love") 10-20 65
SNAP (101 "Pretty Little Red Bird") 25-45 63
SNAP (102 "Hanky Panky") 50-75 63
(No mention of distribution by Red Fox.)
SNAP (102 "Hanky Panky") 20-25 65
(Reads, "Distributed by Red Fox Records.")
Also see JAMES, Tommy

SHO-NUFF

R&B '78

Singles: 12–inch 33/45rpm

MALACO 4-6 81-84

Singles: 7–inch

MALACO 3-4 81-84
STAX 3-5 78-79

LPs: 10/12–inch 33rpm

STAX 5-10 78

SHOOTING STAR

P&R/LP '80

Singles: 7–inch

EPIC 3-4 82
VIRGIN 3-5 80

Picture Sleeves

VIRGIN 3-5 80

LPs: 10/12–inch 33rpm

ENIGMA 5-8 89
EPIC 5-8 81-83
VIRGIN 5-10 80-82
Members: Gary West; Van McLain; Ron Verlin; Keith Mitchell.

SHORE, Dinah
(With Dick Todd; with Woody Herman)

P&R '40

Singles: 78rpm

BLUEBIRD 5-10 40-42
RCA 3-6 50-57
VICTOR 4-8 40-46

Singles: 7–inch

CAPITOL 4-6 60-62
CAPITOL CUSTOM (3793 "Purex Presents Dinah Shore") 5-10 61
(Single-sided promotional issue, made for Purex.)
DECCA 3-5 69
MERCURY 3-5 74
PROJECT 3 ..... 3-6 67-68
RCA 5-10 50-57

Picture Sleeves

CAPITOL CUSTOM (3793 "The Purex Dinah Shore Special") 5-10 61
(Promotional issue, made for Purex.)
RCA 8-12 53

EPs: 7–inch 33/45rpm

CAMDEN 5-10 56
CAPITOL 4-8 59
CAPITOL CUSTOM ("Season's Greetings: Dinah Shore") 5-10 50s
COLUMBIA 4-8 59
RCA 5-15 51-57

LPs: 10/12–inch 33rpm

BAINBRIDGE 5-8 82
CAMDEN 5-10 59-60
CAPITOL (1200 series) 10-20 59-60
CAPITOL (1354 "Dinah Sings Some Blues with Red Norvo") 20-30 60
CAPITOL (1600 & 1700 series) . 10-20 62
COLUMBIA (6000 series) 20-40 50-51
(10–inch LPs.)
COLUMBIA (34000 series) 5-10 77
DECCA 5-10 69
HARMONY 5-10 59-60
NABISCO ("Nabisco Invitational") 15-20 83
(Picture disc. Promotional issue only.)
PROJECT 3 ..... 5-10 68
RCA (11 "Tangos") 25-35 51
RCA (1100 & 1200 series) 20-30 55-56
RCA (3000 series) 20-30 53-54
(10–inch LPs.)
REPRISE 10-15 65
Also see CUGAT, Xavier, & Dinah Shore
Also see KINGSTON TRIO / Dinah Shore
Also see MARTIN, Dean

SHORE, Dinah, & Tony Martin

Singles: 78rpm

RCA 4-8 51

SHORE, Dinah, Tony Martin, Betty Hutton & Phil Harris

Singles: 78rpm

RCA 4-8 51
Also see HARRIS, Phil
Also see HUTTON, Betty
Also see MARTIN, Tony

SHORE, Dinah, & Andre Previn

LPs: 10/12–inch 33rpm

CAPITOL 15-25 60
Also see PREVIN, Andre
Also see SHORE, Dinah

SHORR, Mickey, & Cutups

P&R '62

Singles: 7–inch

TUBA 5-10 62

SHORROCK, Glenn

P&R '83

Singles: 7–inch

CAPITOL 3-4 83

Picture Sleeves

CAPITOL 3-5 83

Also see LITTLE RIVER BAND

SHORT, Bobby

LP '72

LPs: 10/12–inch 33rpm

ATLANTIC 10-25 59-72

SHORTER, Wayne

LP '75

LPs: 10/12–inch 33rpm

BLUE NOTE 20-30 62

(Label reads "Blue Note Records Inc. - New York, USA.")

BLUE NOTE 15-20 66

(Label shows Blue Note Records as a division of either Liberty or United Artists.)

COLUMBIA 5-10 75

VEE JAY (Maroon label) 30-40 60

VEE JAY (Black label) 20-30 61-62

Also see WEATHER REPORT

SHOT in the DARK

P&R '81

Singles: 7–inch

RSO 3-5 81

LPs: 10/12–inch 33rpm

RSO 5-10 81

Members: Peter White; Bryan Savage; Krysia Kristianne; Robin Lamble; Adam Yurman.

Also see STEWART, Al

SHOTGUN

R&B '77

Singles: 12–inch 33/45rpm

MONTAGE 4-6 82

Singles: 7–inch

ABC 3-5 77-79

MCA 3-5 80

MONTAGE 3-5 82

LPs: 10/12–inch 33rpm

ABC 5-10 77-79

MCA 5-10 79-80

MONTAGE 5-10 82

Also see SUN, Joe, & Shotgun

SHOTGUN MESSIAH

LP '89

LPs: 10/12–inch 33rpm

RELATIVITY 5-8 89

SHOW STOPPERS

(Showstoppers)

P&R '68

Singles: 7–inch

AMBER 5-10 63

COLLECTABLES 3-4 80s

COLUMBIA 10-15 66-67

HERITAGE 4-6 68

SHOWTIME 4-8 67

LPs: 10/12–inch 33rpm

COLLECTABLES 5-10

SHOWDOWN

R&B '77

Singles: 7–inch

HONEY BEE 3-5 77

LPs: 10/12–inch 33rpm

HONEY BEE 5-10 77

SHOWMEN

P&R '61

Singles: 7–inch

AIRECORDS 10-20

AMY 4-8 68

BB 4-8 67

IMPERIAL 5-10 64

LIBERTY 3-5 70-81

MINIT (632 "It Will Stand") 10-20 61

(Orange label.)

MINIT (632 "It Will Stand") 5-10 61

(Black label.)

MINIT (643 "The Wrong Girl") 20-40 62

MINIT (647 "Comin' Home") 10-20 62

MINIT (654 "True Fine Mama") .. 10-20 62

MINIT (662 "39-21-46") 10-20 63

SWAN 5-10 65-66

Member: General Johnson.

Also see JOHNSON, General

Also see THOMAS, Irma / Ernie K-Doe / Showmen / Benny Spellman.

SHRIEKBACK

D&D/LP '83

Singles: 12–inch 33/45rpm

ARISTA 4-6 84

W.B. 4-6 83

Singles: 7–inch

W.B. 3-4 83

LPs: 10/12–inch 33rpm

ISLAND 5-8 87-88

W.B. 5-8 83

Members: Barry Andrews; David Allen.

Also see GANG of FOUR

Also see XTC

SHUNDEL, Troy: see SHONDELL, Troy

SHY

LP '87

Singles: 7–inch

RCA 3-4 87

LPs: 10/12–inch 33rpm

RCA 5-8 87

SIBERRY, Jane

LP '86

Singles: 7–inch

OPEN AIR 3-4 86

LPs: 10/12–inch 33rpm

OPEN AIR 5-8 86

SIDE EFFECT

R&B '76

Singles: 12-inch 33/45rpm

FANTASY 4-6 78-81

Singles: 7-inch

ELEKTRA 3-4 80-82
FANTASY 3-5 75-81

LPs: 10/12-inch 33rpm

ELEKTRA 5-8 80-82
FANTASY 5-8 75-81

Member: Miki Howard.
Also see HOWARD, Miki
Also see L.A. BOPPERS

SIDE of the ROAD GANG

C&W '76

Singles: 7-inch

CAPITOL 3-5 76

LPs: 10/12-inch 33rpm

CAPITOL 8-10 76

SIDEKICKS

P&R '66

Singles: 7-inch

RCA 4-8 66-67

LPs: 10/12-inch 33rpm

RCA 10-20 66

SIDEWINDERS

LP '89

LPs: 10/12-inch 33rpm

MAMMOUTH 5-8 89

SIFFRE, Labi

R&B '87

Singles: 7-inch

CHINA 3-4 87

SIGLER, Bunny
(Mr. Emotions)

P&R/R&B '67

Singles: 12-inch 33/45rpm

SALSOUL 4-6 80

Singles: 7-inch

BEE 10-15 59
CRAIG 10-15 61
DECCA 10-25 65-67
GOLD MINE 3-6 78-79
NEPTUNE 5-10 60s
PARKWAY 5-10 67-69
PHILADELPHIA INT'L 5-15 71-76
SALSOUL 3-5 80

LPs: 10/12-inch 33rpm

GOLD MIND 5-10 78-79
PARKWAY 10-20 67
SALSOUL 5-10 80

Also see HOLLOWAY, Loleatta, & Bunny Sigler
Also see MASON, Barbara, & Bunny Sigler

SIGUE SIGUE SPUTNIK

LP '86

Singles: 12-inch 33/45rpm

MANHATTAN 4-6 86

Singles: 7-inch

MANHATTAN 3-4 86

LPs: 10/12-inch 33rpm

MANHATTAN 5-10 86

Member: Tony James.
Also see GENERATION X

SILAS, Alfie
(Alfie)

R&B '82

Singles: 7-inch

MOTOWN 3-4 84-86
RCA 3-4 82-84

LPs: 10/12-inch 33rpm

MOTOWN 5-8 85
RCA 5-8 82-84

Also see KING, Bobby

SILENCERS

P&R '80

Singles: 7-inch

PRECISION 3-5 80

LPs: 10/12-inch 33rpm

PRECISION 5-10 80-81

Member: Frank Czuri.
Also see DIAMOND REO

SILENCERS

P&R/LP '87

Singles: 7-inch

RCA 3-4 87

LPs: 10/12-inch 33rpm

RCA 5-8 87-90

SILENT UNDERDOG

R&B '85

Singles: 12-inch 33/45rpm

PROFILE 4-6 85

SILHOUETTES

P&R/R&B '58

Singles: 78rpm

EMBER 10-20 57
JUNIOR 20-40 57

Singles: 7-inch

ABC 3-5 73
ACE (552 "I Sold My Heart to the Junkman") 12-15 58
COLLECTABLES 3-4 80s
EMBER (1029 "Get a Job") 10-15 57
(Red label.)
EMBER (1029 "Get a Job") 4-8 60
Black label.)
EMBER (1032 "Headin' for the Poorhouse") 10-15 58
EMBER (1037 "Bing Bong") 50-75 58
(Shiny red label.)
EMBER (1037 "Bing Bong") 10-15 58
(Flat red label.)
FLASHBACK 3-5 65
GOODWAY (101 "Not Me Baby") 100-200 68

GRAND (142 "Wish I Could Be There") 150-175 61
IMPERIAL 5-10 62
JUNIOR (391 "Get a Job") 150-200 57
(Brown label.)
JUNIOR (391 "Get a Job") 100-200 57
(Blue label.)
JUNIOR (396 "I Sold My Heart to the Junkman") 30-40 58
JUNIOR (400 "Evelyn") 100-150 59
JUNIOR (993 "Your Love") 15-25 63

LPs: 10/12-inch 33rpm

GOODWAY (100 "Get a Job") 100-150 68

Also see KING, Ben E.

SILK

LP '69

Singles: 7-inch

ABC 5-10 69
DECCA 4-6 71

LPs: 10/12-inch 33rpm

ABC (694 "Smooth As Raw Silk") 15-25 69

Members: Michael Stanley Gee; Chris Jones; Randy Sabo; Courtney Johns.
Also see STANLEY, Michael, Band

SILK

R&B '77

Singles: 12-inch 33/45rpm

PHILADELPHIA INT'L 4-8 79-80

Singles: 7-inch

PHILADELPHIA INT'L 3-5 79-80
PRELUDE 3-5 77
PYE 3-5 76

LPs: 10/12-inch 33rpm

ARISTA 5-10 77
PHILADELPHIA INT'L 5-10 79

Member: Debra Henry.
Also see BUTLER, Jerry, & Debra Henry

SILK, J.M.

D&D '85

Singles: 12-inch 33/45rpm

D.J. INT'L 4-6 85

SILKIE

P&R '65

Singles: 7-inch

FONTANA 4-8 65-66

LPs: 10/12-inch 33rpm

FONTANA (27548 "You've Got to Hide Your Love Away") 20-30 65
(Monaural.)
FONTANA (67548 "You've Got to Hide Your Love Away") 25-35 65
(Stereo.)

Also see BEATLES

SILOS

LP '90

LPs: 10/12-inch 33rpm

RCA 5-8 90

SILVA-TONES
(With the Silva-Tones)

P&R '57

Singles: 78rpm

ARGO 5-10 57
MONARCH 10-15 57

Singles: 7-inch

ARGO (5281 "That's All I Want from You") 10-15 57
MONARCH (615 "That's All I Want from You") 25-30 57
(Yellow label.)
MONARCH (615 "That's All I Want from You") 15-20 57
(Black label.)

SILVER

P&R/LP '76

Singles: 7-inch

ARISTA 3-5 76-77

LPs: 10/12-inch 33rpm

ARISTA 8-10 76

Members: John Batdorf; Brent Mydland.
Also see GRATEFUL DEAD

SILVER, Horace, Quintet

LP '65

Singles: 78rpm

BLUE NOTE 4-8 54-57

Singles: 7-Inch

BLUE NOTE (300 thru 1000 series) 3-5 73-77
BLUE NOTE (1600 & 1700 series) 4-8 54-61
BLUE NOTE (1800 & 1900 series) 4-6 61-69

LPs: 10/12-Inch 33rpm

BLUE NOTE (1518 "Horace Silver Quintet") 40-60 56
(Label gives New York street address for Blue Note Records.)
BLUE NOTE (1518 "Horace Silver Quintet") 20-30
(Label gives New York street address for Blue Note Records.)
BLUE NOTE (1520 "New Faces") 40-60 56
(Label gives New York street address for Blue Note Records.)
BLUE NOTE (1520 "New Faces") 20-30
(Label reads "Blue Note Records Inc. - New York, U.S.A.")
BLUE NOTE (1562 "Stylings") ... 40-60 57
(Label gives New York street address for Blue Note Records.)

BLUE NOTE (1562 "Stylings") .. 20-30
(Label reads "Blue Note Records Inc. - New York, U.S.A.")
BLUE NOTE (1562 "Stylings") .. 15-20
(Label shows Blue Note Records as a division of Liberty.)
BLUE NOTE (1589 "Further Explorations")........................ 40-60 58
(Label gives New York street address for Blue Note Records.)
BLUE NOTE (1589 "Further Explorations")........................ 20-30
(Label reads "Blue Note Records Inc. - New York, U.S.A.")
BLUE NOTE (1589 "Further Explorations")........................ 15-20
(Label shows Blue Note Records as a division of Liberty.)
BLUE NOTE (4000 series)........ 30-40 59-60
(Label gives New York street address for Blue Note Records.)
BLUE NOTE (4000 series)........ 59-65
(Label reads "Blue Note Records Inc. - New York, U.S.A.")
BLUE NOTE (4000 series)........ 15-20 66-68
(Label shows Blue Note Records as a division of either
BLUE NOTE (5018 "New Faces")............................... 75-125 53
(10–inch LP.)
BLUE NOTE (5034 "Horace Silver Trio") 75-125 54
(10–inch LP.)
BLUE NOTE (5058 "Horace Silver Quintet")............................ 75-125 55
(10–inch LP.)
BLUE NOTE (5062 "Horace Silver Quintet")............................ 75-125 55
(10–inch LP.)
BLUE NOTE (84000 series)...... 30-40 59-60
(Label gives New York street address for Blue Note Records.)
BLUE NOTE (84000 series)...... 59-65
(Label reads "Blue Note Records Inc. - New York, U.S.A.")
BLUE NOTE (84000 series)...... 10-20 66-80
(Label shows Blue Note Records as a division of either
EPIC (3326 "Silver's Blue") 75-100 57
EPIC (16006 "Silver's Blue") 60-80 58
Also see STITT, Sonny, Kai Winding & Horace Silver

SILVER, Horace, Quintet, & Stanley Turrentine

LPs: 10/12-Inch 33rpm

BLUE NOTE............................ 10-15 68
Also see SILVER, Horace, Quintet
Also see TURRENTINE, Stanley

SILVER APPLES

LP '68

Singles: 7–inch

KAPP 4-8 68-69

LPs: 10/12–inch 33rpm

KAPP 10-15 68-69

SILVER CONDOR

P&R/LP '81

Singles: 7–inch

COLUMBIA.................................3-4 81

Picture Sleeves

COLUMBIA.................................3-5 81

LPs: 10/12–inch 33rpm

COLUMBIA...............................5-10 81
Members: Joe Cerisano; Earl Slick; John Corey; Claude Pepper; Jay Davis.
Also see PHANTOM, ROCKER & SLICK

SILVER CONVENTION

P&R/R&B/LP '75

Singles: 7–inch

MIDLAND INT'L 3-5 75-77
MIDSONG INT'L 3-5 77-78

Picture Sleeves

MIDLAND INT'L 3-5 76

LPs: 10/12–inch 33rpm

MIDLAND INT'L 5-10 75-77
MIDSONG INT'L 5-10 77
Member: Penny McLean.
Also see McLEAN, Penny

SILVER PLATINUM

R&B '80

Singles: 7–inch

SRI 3-5 81
SPECTOR....................................3-5 81

LPs: 10/12–inch 33rpm

SPECTOR..................................5-10 81

SILVER, PLATINUM & GOLD

R&B '75

Singles: 7–inch

FARR 3-5 76-77
W.B. 3-5 74-75

LPs: 10/12–inch 33rpm

NEPTUNE..................................5-10 82

SILVERADO

P&R '81

Singles: 7–inch

PAVILLION 3-5 81
RCA 3-5 77

LPs: 10/12–inch 33rpm

PAVILLION 5-10 81
RCA 5-10 77

SILVERSPOON, Dooley

P&R/R&B '75

Singles: 7–inch

COTTON.....................................3-5 74-75

SILVERSTEIN, Shel

LP '73

Singles: 7-inch

COLUMBIA 3-6 71-75
ELEKTRA................................... 8-12 60
RCA.. 4-6 69-70

LPs: 10/12-inch 33rpm

ATLANTIC (8072 "Inside Folk Songs")........................... 20-30 63
(Monaural.)
ATLANTIC (SD-8072 "Inside Folk Songs")........................... 25-35 63
(Stereo.)
ATLANTIC (8200 series).......... 10-15 70
CADET 15-25 65-66
COLUMBIA 5-12 72-84
CRESTVIEW.............................. 15-25 63
ELEKTRA (176 "Hairy Jazz").... 30-40 59
(Monaural.)
ELEKTRA (7-176 "Hairy Jazz"). 40-50 59
(Stereo.)
FLYING FISH 5-8 80
JANUS 8-12 73
PARACHUTE (Except 20512)..... 5-10 78
PARACHUTE (20512 "Selected Cuts from *Songs and Stories*") 15-20 78
(Promotional issue only.)
RCA.. 10-15 69

SILVETTI

P&R/R&B '77

Singles: 7-inch

SALSOUL.................................. 3-5 77

LPs: 10/12-inch 33rpm

SALSOUL.................................. 5-10 77

SIMEONE, Harry, Chorale

P&R '58

Singles: 7-inch

COLUMBIA 3-5 66-67
KAPP.. 3-5 64-68
MERCURY.................................. 3-5 62-64
MISTLETOE............................... 3-4 74
20TH FOX.................................. 3-5 58-79

Picture Sleeves

MERCURY 4-6 62
20TH FOX.................................. 4-8 58-63

Promotional Picture Sleeve

20TH FOX (121 "Little Drummer Boy") 5-10 58
(This "Prepare to Be Enchanted" sleeve was sent only to radio stations.)

LPs: 10/12-inch 33rpm

DECCA....................................... 5-15 62-64
KAPP.. 5-10 65
MERCURY 5-15 63-64
MISTLETOE............................... 4-8 73
MOVIETONE.............................. 5-10 67
20TH FOX.................................. 5-15 58-79
WING 5-10 69

SIMMONS, Chandra

R&B '87

Singles: 7-inch

FRESH..3-4 87

SIMMONS, Gene

(Jumpin' Gene Simmons; Morris Gene Simmons)

P&R/LP '64

Singles: 7-inch

AGP 4-8 60s
CHECKER 8-12 60
EPIC..3-5 70
DELTUNE 3-5 77-78
HI 4-8 61-67
HURSHEY 3-5 73
MALA 4-8 68
SANDY..4-8 60s
SUN (299 "Drinkin' Wine") 25-35 58
TUPELO.......................................4-8 60s

LPs: 10/12-inch 33rpm

HI (2018 "Jumpin' Gene Simmons") 20-25 64
(Monaural.)
HI (32018 "Jumpin' Gene Simmons") 25-30 64
(Stereo.)

SIMMONS, Gene

P&R/LP '78

Singles: 7-inch

CASABLANCA..............................3-4 78-79

LPs: 10/12-inch 33rpm

CASABLANCA (7120 "Gene Simmons") 12-20 78
(With poster order form.)
CASABLANCA (7120 "Gene Simmons") 8-12 78
(Without poster order form.)
CASABLANCA (PIX-7120 "Gene Simmons") 40-50 79
(Picture disc.)
Also see KISS

SIMMONS, Patrick

P&R/R&B/D&D/LP '83

Singles: 12-inch 33/45rpm

ELEKTRA.......................................4-8 83

Singles: 7-inch

ELEKTRA.......................................3-5 83

LPs: 10/12-inch 33rpm

ELEKTRA.....................................5-10 83
Also see DOOBIE BROTHERS
Also see EAGLES

SIMMONS, Simtec

R&B '75

Singles: 7-inch

INNOCATION 3-5 75
MAURCI (105 "Tea Pot") 4-8

SIMMS, John & Arthur

R&B '80

Singles: 7–inch

CASABLANCA 3-5 80

LPs: 10/12–inch 33rpm

CASABLANCA 5-10 80

SIMMS TWINS: see SIMS TWINS

SIMON, Carly

P&R/LP '71

Singles: 7–inch

ARISTA 3-4 86-90
COLUMBIA 3-5 73
ELEKTRA 3-5 71-79
EPIC 3-4 85-86
MIRAGE 3-5 82
W.B. 3-5 80-83

Picture Sleeves

ARISTA (Except 9525) 3-5 86-89
ARISTA (9525 "Coming Around Again") 4-8 86
(Pictures Meryl Streep and Jack Nicholson.)
ARISTA (9525 "Coming Around Again") 3-5 86
(Pictures Carly Simon.)
ELEKTRA 3-5 75-79
W.B. 3-5 80-83

LPs: 10/12–inch 33rpm

ARISTA 5-8 86-90
ELEKTRA 5-10 71-79
EPIC 5-8 85-86
W.B. 5-10 80-83

Also see JAGGER, Mick
Also see SIMON SISTERS

SIMON, Carly, & James Taylor

P&R '74

Singles: 7–inch

ELEKTRA 3-5 74-78

Also see SIMON, Carly
Also see TAYLOR, James

SIMON, Joe

(With the Checkmates; with Mainstreeters)

R&B '65

Singles: 7–inch

COMPLEAT 3-5 70s
DOT 4-8 64
GEE BEE (077 "Say") 15-25
HUSH 5-10 60-62
IRRAL 4-8 63
MONUMENT 3-5 70-72
POSSE 3-5 81-82
SOUND STAGE 7 .... 3-6 66-72
SPRING 3-5 69-75
VEE JAY 4-8 64-65

Picture Sleeves

GEE BEE (077 "Say") 15-20
SPRING 3-5 71-73

LPs: 10/12–inch 33rpm

BUDDAH 10-15 69
POSSE 5-8 81-82
SOUND STAGE 7 .... 8-15 67-75
SPRING 8-12 71-78

SIMON, Paul

(With Urubamba; with Los Incas)

P&R/LP '72

Singles: 7–inch

COLUMBIA 3-5 72-77
W.B. 3-4 80-90

Picture Sleeves

COLUMBIA 3-8 73-77
W.B. 3-5 80-87

LPs: 10/12–inch 33rpm

COLUMBIA (Except C5X & 43000 series) 6-12 72-77
COLUMBIA (C5X-37581 "Paul Simon's Collected Works") 30-40 81
(Five-LP set.)
COLUMBIA (43000 series) 15-20 81
(Half-speed mastered.)
DMG (1 "Songs of Paul Simon") 15-25 75
(Promotional issue only. Also includes tracks by: Simon & Garfunkel; Aretha Franklin; Crykle; Booker T. and the Mgs; and Yes.)
DMG (1 "Songs of Paul Simon—Easy Listening Collection") 10-15 75
(Promotional issue only.)
MCP (8027 "Paul Simon Plus") .. 15-25 70s
(Promotional issue only. Also includes tracks by: Tony Orlando; Neil Sedaka; Johnny Rivers; and the 4 Seasons.)
W.B. (140 ""Interview Show") 20-30 86
(Promotional issue only. Two LPs with interview and *Graceland* songs.)
W.B. (3472 "One-Trick Pony") 5-10 80
W.B. (23942 thru 26098) 5-10 80-90

Also see BOOKER T. & MGs
Also see CYRKLE
Also see DION
Also see DIXIE HUMMINGBIRDS
Also see 4 SEASONS
Also see FRANKLIN, Aretha
Also see GARFUNKEL, Art, James Taylor & Paul Simon
Also see KANE, Paul
Also see LANDIS, Jerry
Also see NEWMAN, Randy, & Paul Simon
Also see ORLANDO, Tony
Also see RIVERS, Johnny
Also see SEDAKA, Neil
Also see SIMON & GARFUNKEL
Also see TAYLOR, True
Also see TICO & TRIUMPHS
Also see U.S.A. for AFRICA
Also see VALERY, Dana
Also see YES

SIMON, Paul, & Phoebe Snow

(With the Jessy Dixon Singers)

P&R '75

Singles: 7–inch

COLUMBIA 3-5 75

Also see SNOW, Phoebe

SIMON & GARFUNKEL

P&R '65

Singles: 7–inch

ABC-PAR (10788 "This Is My Story") 10-15 66
COLUMBIA (10000 series) 3-5 75
COLUMBIA (11000 series) 5-8 66
COLUMBIA (33000 series) 3-6 60s
COLUMBIA (43396 "The Sounds of Silence") 4-8 65
COLUMBIA (43396 "The Sounds of Silence") 30-40 65
(Colored vinyl. Promotional issue only.)
COLUMBIA (43511 "Homeward Bound") 4-8 66
COLUMBIA (43511 "Homeward Bound") 30-40 66
(Colored vinyl. Promotional issue only.)
COLUMBIA (43617 "I Am a Rock") 4-8 66
COLUMBIA (43617 "I Am a Rock") 30-40 66
(Colored vinyl. Promotional issue only.)
COLUMBIA (43728 thru 45663).... 4-8 66-75
TEEN SCOOP (789 "Visits with Simon & Garfunkel") 10-20 66
(*Teen Scoop* magazine bonus soundsheet.)
W.B. 3-5 82

Picture Sleeves

COLUMBIA 5-10 66-75

EPs: 7–inch 33/45rpm

COLUMBIA 10-20 68-69
(Jukebox issues only.)

LPs: 10/12–inch 33rpm

COLUMBIA (CL-2249 "Wednesday Morning 3 A.M.") 10-20 64
(Monaural.)
COLUMBIA (CL-2469 "Sounds of Silence") 10-20 66
(Monaural.)
COLUMBIA (CL-2563 "Parsley, Sage Rosemary and Thyme") 10-20 66
(Monaural.)
COLUMBIA (OS-3180 "The Graduate") 12-15 68
(Soundtrack.)
COLUMBIA (CS-9049 "Wednesday Morning 3 A.M.") 10-15 64
(Stereo.)
COLUMBIA (PC-9049 "Wednesday Morning 3 A.M.") 5-10
COLUMBIA (CS-9269 "Sounds of Silence") 10-15 66
(Stereo.)
COLUMBIA (CS-9363 "Parsley, Sage Rosemary and Thyme") 10-15 66
(Stereo.)
COLUMBIA (PC-9363 "Parsley, Sage Rosemary and Thyme") 5-10
COLUMBIA (KCS-9529 "Bookends") 10-15 68
COLUMBIA (PC-9529 "Bookends") 5-10
COLUMBIA (9914 "Bridge Over Troubled Water") 10-15 70
COLUMBIA (30995 "Bridge Over Troubled Water") 10-20 71
(Quadrophonic.)
COLUMBIA (31350 "Greatest Hits") 5-10 72
COLUMBIA (37587 "Simon & Garfunkel's Collected Works") 30-40 81
(Five-LP set.)
COLUMBIA (41350 "Greatest Hits") 10-15 81
(Half-speed mastered.)
COLUMBIA (49914 "Bridge Over Troubled Water") 10-20 80
(Half-speed mastered.)
MFSL (173 "Bridge Over Troubled Water") 15-20 85
OFFSHORE 10-15
PICKWICK (3059 "Hit Sound of Simon & Garfunkel") 50-75 66
SEARS (435 "Simon & Garfunkel") 20-30
W.B. 5-8 82

Members: Paul Simon; Art Garfunkel.
Also see GARFUNKEL, Art
Also see SIMON, Paul
Also see TOM & JERRY

SIMON SAID

R&B '75

Singles: 7–inch

ATCO 3-5 75-76
ROULETTE 3-5 75

SIMON SISTERS

P&R '64

Singles: 7–inch

COLUMBIA (02600 series) 3-4 82
COLUMBIA (45000 series) 3-5 73
KAPP 4-8 64-65

LPs: 10/12–inch 33rpm

COLUMBIA (21525 "Lobster Quadrille") 10-15 69
COLUMBIA (21539 "Simon Sisters Sing for Children") 10-12 73
COLUMBIA (24506 "Lobster Quadrille") 15-20 69
(Special childrens' book edition.)
COLUMBIA (37000 series) 5-10 82
KAPP 15-25 64
W.B. 5-10 80

Members: Carly Simon; Lucy Simon.
Also see DOOBIE BROTHERS / Kate Taylor & Simon-Taylor Family

Also see SIMON, Carly

SIMONE, Nina

P&R/R&B '59

Singles: 7-inch

BETHLEHEM 3-8 59-70
CTI 3-5 78
COLPIX 4-8 59-63
PHILIPS 4-6 64-66
RCA 3-6 67-71
TRIP 3-4 72

EPs: 7-inch 33/45rpm

BETHLEHEM 5-10 59

LPs: 10/12-inch 33rpm

ACCORD 5-10 80
BETHLEHEM 20-30 59
CTI 5-10 78-79
COLPIX 15-30 59-66
PHILIPS 10-20 64-69
QUINTESSENCE 5-10 80
RCA 8-15 67-76
STROUD 5-10 73
TRIP 5-10 72-77
UPFRONT 5-10 72
VERSATILE 5-10 78

Also see LYNNE, Gloria / Nina Simone / Billie Holiday

SIMONE, Nina, Chris Connor & Carmen McRae

LPs: 10/12-inch 33rpm

BETHLEHEM 20-30 60

Also see CONNOR, Chris
Also see McRAE, Carmen
Also see SIMONE, Nina

SIMPLE MINDS

LP '83

Singles: 12-inch 33/45rpm

A&M 4-6 82-86

Singles: 7-inch

A&M 3-4 82-86

Picture Sleeves

A&M 3-5 84-86

LPs: 10/12-inch 33rpm

A&M 5-10 82-91
PVC 8-10 79

Members: John Giblin; Charles Burchill; Jim Kerr; Michael MacNeil; Mel Gaynor.

SIMPLY RED

D&D '85

Singles: 12-inch 33/45rpm

ELEKTRA 4-6 85-86

Singles: 7-inch

ELEKTRA 3-4 85-89

Picture Sleeves

ELEKTRA 3-4 86-89

LPs: 10/12-inch 33rpm

ELEKTRA 5-8 85-89

Member: Mick Hucknall.

SIMPSON, Paul

(Paul Simpson Connection)

D&D '83

Singles: 12-inch 33/45rpm

EASY STREET 4-6 85
STREETWISE 4-6 83

Singles: 7-inch

STREETWISE 3-4 83

SIMPSON, Valerie

LP '71

Singles: 7-inch

TAMLA 3-5 71-72

LPs: 10/12-inch 33rpm

TAMLA 8-10 71-77

Also see ASHFORD & SIMPSON

SIMPSONS

LP '90

Singles: 7-inch

GEFFEN 3-4 91

LPs: 10/12-inch 33rpm

GEFFEN (24308 "Sing the Blues") 5-8 90

Members: Dan Castellaneta; Julie Kavner; Nancy Cartwright; Yeardley Smith; Matt Groening. With guests: Harry Shearer; Ron Taylor; Harry Shearer; Buster Poindexter; Joe Walsh; B.B. King; John Sebastian; D.J. Jazzy Jeff; Andrew Gold; Dr. John.

Also see D.J. JAZZY JEFF & Fresh Prince
Also see DR. JOHN
Also see GOLD, Andrew
Also see KING, B.B.
Also see SEBASTAIN, John
Also see WALSH, Joe

SIMS TWINS

(Simms Twins)

P&R/R&B '61

Singles: 7-inch

ABKCO 3-5 70s
CROSSOVER 3-5 74
KENT 3-5 71
PARKWAY 4-8 68
SAR 5-10 61-62
SPECIALTY 3-5 70s

SINATRA, Frank

(With Harry James & His Orchestra; with Axel Stordahl & His Orchestra; Tommy Dorsey Orchestra Featuring Frank Sinatra)

P&R '42

Singles: 78rpm

BLUEBIRD (10726 "East of the Sun") 30-50 42
BLUEBIRD (10771 "Whispering") 30-50 42
BLUEBIRD (11463 "Night and Day") 30-50 42
BLUEBIRD (11515 "The Song Is You") 30-50 42
BRUNSWICK (8443 "From the Bottom of My Heart") 400-600 39
(Credited to Harry James & His Orchestra.)

CAPITOL (1699 thru 3900)......... 5-10 53-58
COLUMBIA (5492 "Soliloquy").. 15-25 46
(12-inch disc. At least one source says this selection number is 7492. We don't yet know who's right.)
COLUMBIA (35209 thru 41133).. 5-15 39-58
COLUMBIA (50003 thru 50079).... 4-8 5
COLUMBIA (55037 "Ol Man River") 15-25 44
(12-inch disc.)
RCA (1522 thru 3500) 3-6 43-49
RCA (13247 "Oh Look at Me Now") 40-60 82
(Single-sided. Promotional issue only. 1000 numbered copies made.)
RCA (36396 "Without a Song"). 15-25 42
(12-inch disc.)
VICTOR (26500 thru 27974)......... 4-8 40-43

Albums: 78rpm

COLUMBIA (112 "The Voice of Frank Sinatra") 25-50 46
(Four-disc set.)
COLUMBIA (117 "All Time Favorites by Harry James") 25-50 46
(Four-disc set. *Ciribiribin* is by Sinatra.)
COLUMBIA (117 "All Time Favorites by Harry James") 15-25 46
(Four-disc set. *Ciribiribin* is by Harry James.)
COLUMBIA (124 "Songs by Sinatra") 25-50 47
(Four-disc set.)
COLUMBIA (167 "Christmas Songs by Sinatra") 25-50 48
(Four-disc set.)
COLUMBIA (185 "Frankly Sentimental")......................... 25-50 49
(Four-disc set.)
COLUMBIA (197 "Dedicated to You") 25-50 50
(Four-disc set.)
COLUMBIA (218 "Sing and Dance with Frank Sinatra") 25-50 50
(Four-disc set.)
COLUMBIA (455 "Young at Heart").................................. 25-50 51
(Four-disc set.)
COLUMBIA (637 "Frank Sinatra Conducts the Music of Alec Wilder")......... 100-150 46
(Three 12-inch Masterworks discs.)
RCA (80 "Getting Sentimental") 20-40 40
(Four-disc set)
RCA (150 "Starmaker")............ 20-40 41
(Four-disc set)
RCA (163 "All Time Hits").......... 20-40 42
(Four-disc set)
RCA (247 "And the Band Sang Too") 20-40 43
(Three-disc set)

Singles: 12–inch 33/45rpm

REPRISE (674 "Night & Day")...50-75 77
(Promotional issue only. Only 647 made.)
REPRISE (865 "New York, New York")....................................25-50 80
(Promotional issue only.)

Singles: 7–inch

CAPITOL ("No One Ever Tells You").......................................35-45 56
(No selection number used. Promotional issue only. Add $4 to $6 if accompanied by Capitol "Rush" paper sleeve.)
CAPITOL (596 "All the Way") 250-350 58
(Promotional issue only. 101 made.)
CAPITOL (1069 "Come Dance with Me") 50-75 59
(Five singles in a paper sleeve. For jukebox use. With "XE" prefix.)
CAPITOL (1417 "Nice 'N' Easy ") 50-75 60
(Five singles in a paper sleeve. For jukebox use. With "XE" prefix.)
CAPITOL (1491 "Sinatra's Swingin' Session")................................50-75 61
(Five singles in a paper sleeve. For jukebox use. With "XE" prefix.)
CAPITOL (1594 "Come Swing with Me") 50-75 62
(Five singles in a paper sleeve. For jukebox use. With "XE" prefix.)
CAPITOL (1676 "Point of No Return")..................................50-75 63
(Five singles in a paper sleeve. For jukebox use. With "XE" prefix.)
CAPITOL (1699 "I've Got the World on a String")...................................20-30 51
CAPITOL (1729 "Sinatra Sings of Love and Things")..................................50-75 60s
(Five singles in a paper sleeve. For jukebox use. With "XE" prefix.)
CAPITOL (1707/8 "Mistletoe and Holly") 75-100 60
(Promotional issue for Christmas Seals.)
CAPITOL (2450 "Lean Baby")...15-25 53
CAPITOL (2505 thru 4070).........8-15 53-58
CAPITOL (4103 "To Love and Be Loved")....................................5-10 58
CAPITOL (4103 "To Love and Be Loved")...............................150-250 58
(White label. Promotional issue only.)
CAPITOL (4155 "French Foreign Legion")......................................5-10 59
CAPITOL (4214 "High Hopes")....5-10 59
(Purple label.)
CAPITOL (4214 "High Hopes")................................50-100 60
(Red label. Promotional issue only.)
CAPITOL (4284 thru 4815)..........5-10 59-62

CAPITOL (6019 thru 6195) 4-6 62
(Starline reissue series.)
COLUMBIA (112 "The Voice of Frank Sinatra") 50-75 46
(Four-disc set.)
COLUMBIA (167 "Christmas Songs by Sinatra") 50-75 48
(Four-disc set.)
COLUMBIA (197 "Dedicated to You") 50-75 50
(Four-disc set.)
COLUMBIA (218 "Sing and Dance with Frank Sinatra") 50-75 50
(Four-disc set.)
COLUMBIA (673 "If I Ever Love Again") 40-60 67
(Promotional issue only.)
COLUMBIA (1-106 thru 1-936) . 40-60 48-51
(Microgroove 33 singles.)
COLUMBIA (6-718 thru 6-936) . 15-25 50-51
(45 rpm.)
COLUMBIA (3842 "I Guess I'll Have to Dream the Rest") 40-60 71
(Promotional issue only.)
COLUMBIA (12194 "All Or Nothing At All")....................................... 30-40 55
(Promotional issue only.)
COLUMBIA (33000 series) 3-8 60s
(Hall of Fame series. With "13" prefix.)
COLUMBIA (33011 thru 39213) 40-60 50s
(Microgroove 33 singles. With "3" prefix.)
COLUMBIA (36814 thru 41133) 15-30 50-58
(45 rpm. With "4" prefix.)
COLUMBIA (50003 thru 50079) 10-15 55-59
(Hall of Fame series. With "4" prefix.)
COLUMBIA (116427 "White Christmas") 40-60 63
(Promotional issue only.)
"HIGH HOPES with JACK KENNEDY"/ "Jack Kennedy All the Way" 150-250 60
(Presidential campaign promotional issue only. No label name or artist shown. Reportedly 1,000 made.)
RCA (15 "Getting Sentimental") 35-50 50
(Boxed, four-disc set.)
RCA (20 "All Time Hits")............ 35-50 51
(Boxed, four-disc set.)
RCA GOLD STANDARD.............. 4-8 60-70
(With "447" prefix.)
REPRISE ("A Special Message to You from Frank Sinatra").................. 750-1000 61
(Single-sided. Made as a Reprise sales and promotional tool. No selection number used. Two different pressings exist.)
REPRISE (45 "Frank Sinatra reads from Gunga Din") 300-600 66
(Promotional issue only.)
REPRISE (PRO-162 thru PRO-406).................................25-50 63-69
(White label, promotional issues only.)
REPRISE (0243 thru 0380)............4-8 63-65
REPRISE (396 "Radio Spot for *Watertown*") 15-25 70
(Promotional issue only.)
REPRISE (0398 thru 1386)............3-8 65-77
REPRISE (20001 thru 20151)........4-8 61-63
REPRISE (20157 "California").........................150-250 77
(Promotional issue only. Reportedly 1000 made.)
REPRISE (20184 "Come Blow Your Horn")...4-8 63
REPRISE (20184 "Come Blow Your Horn")....................................50-75 63
(White label. Promotional issue only.)
REPRISE (20209 thru 20235)........4-8 63
REPRISE (28000 & 29000 series).3-4 82
REPRISE (40001 thru 40050)......8-10 60s
(33 rpm Jukebox issues.)
REPRISE (40063 thru 40092)........4-8
(33 rpm Jukebox issues.)
REPRISE (49000 series)...............3-5 80-83
REPRISE/CAL NEVADA LODGE (101 "Ring-A-Ding-Ding")................50-75 63
(Promo souvenir, available from the lodge.)

Picture Sleeves

CAPITOL (596 "All the Way") 250-350 58
(Promotional issue only. 101 made.)
CAPITOL (4103 "To Love and Be Loved")...............................250-350 58
(Promotional issue only.)
CAPITOL (4214 "High Hopes")..............................250-350 60
(Promotional issue only.)
REPRISE (0429 "It Was a Very Good Year")....................................10-20 65
REPRISE (0531 "That's Life")...10-20 66
REPRISE (20010 "Granada") 10-20 61
REPRISE (20063 "Everybody's Twistin'") 10-20 62
REPRISE (20157 "California").........................300-400 77
(Promotional issue only. Reportedly 1000 made.)
REPRISE (20184 "Come Blow Your Horn")..................................100-150 63
(Promotional issue only.)
REPRISE (29903-7 "To Love a Child") 8-12 82
(Dedicated to Mrs. Nancy Reagan. With the Reprise Children's Chorus featuring Nikka Costa. Promotional issue only.)
REPRISE (49233 "New York, New York")..3-5 80

REPRISE/CAL NEVADA LODGE (101 "Ring-A-Ding-Ding") 100-150 63
(Promo souvenir, available from the lodge.)
SINATRA 3-4 75

EPs: 7–inch 33/45rpm

CAPITOL (3 "Vocal Standards") . 5-15 60s
CAPITOL (100 "Special 1981 Birthday Tribute") 75-125 81
(Promotional issue only. Includes "Thank You" insert.)
CAPITOL (280 "Disc Jockey Interview Record for the film *High Society*").... 125-175 56
(Promotional issue only.)
CAPITOL 426: see SINATRA, Frank / Roger Wagner / Hollywood Bowl Symphony
CAPITOL (434 "Selections from *Pal Joey*.) 125-175 57
(Promotional issue only.)
CAPITOL (488 thru 1594) 8-18 53-62
(Single disc EPs, with "EAP" prefix.)
CAPITOL (488 thru 855) 12-25 53-57
(Two-disc EPs, with "EBF" prefix.)
CAPITOL (SU-581 "In the Wee Small Hours") 5-15 60s
CAPITOL (DU-653 "Songs for Swingin' Lovers") 5-15 60s
CAPITOL (DU-768 "This Is Sinatra") 5-15 60s
CAPITOL (SU-920 "Come Fly with Me") 5-15 60s
CAPITOL (1549 "Selections from *Can-Can*") 300-500 60
(Promotional issue only.)
CAPITOL (1762 "The Great Years") 5-15 60s
Capitol (1864 "Come Swing with Capitol-New Albums for August 1961") 30-50 61
(Promotional issue only.)
CAPITOL (11583 "Frank Sinatra") 10-15 60s
COLUMBIA (112 thru 455) 40-60 50-54
(Two-disc EPs.)
COLUMBIA (1524 thru 2641).... 10-25 50-59
(Single disc EPs.)
COLUMBIA (7431 thru 9533).... 10-20 55-57
(Single disc EPs.)
COLUMBIA (10321/10322 "Christmas Dreaming") 10-15 57
(Price is for either volume.)
COLUMBIA (28595 "Nancy") .. 75-100 58
(Promotional issue, made for B.T. Babbit and attached to their soap boxes. With custom cover.)
RCA (102 "Tommy Dorsey Originals") 10-20 60
(Compact 33 Double.)
RCA (3005 "This Is Tommy Dorsey") 25-50 50
(Two disc set.)
RCA (3028 "Getting Sentimental") 25-50 50
(Two disc set.)
RCA (3030 "All Time Hits") 25-50 51
(Two disc set.)
RCA (3063 "Fabulous Frankie") 25-50 52
(Two disc set.)
RCA (5007 thru 5147)...............12-25 58-60
RCA (6038 "This Is Tommy Dorsey")................................10-15 60s
(Jukebox issue only.)
REPRISE 10-15 62-74
(Jukebox issues.)

LPs: 10/12–inch 33rpm

CAMDEN (650 thru 800).............5-15 61-73
CAMDEN (9027 I'm Getting Sentimental Over You")..8-12 72
CAPITOL ("Radio/TV Sampler")............................200-250 58
(Number unknown. Yellow label. Promotional issue only.)
CAPITOL (200 & 300 series, except LS-308)....................................8-15 69
CAPITOL (LS-308 "Sinatra: The Works")................................75-125 71
(Ten LP set. Includes booklet. Add $75 to $100 if accompanied by the bonus LP, *Sinatra Like Never Before*.")
CAPITOL (H-488 thru H-581) 30-50 54-55
(10–inch LPs.)
CAPITOL (488 thru 1164, except 735).......................................20-30 54-59
(With "T" or "W" prefix.)
CAPITOL (W-735 "Frank Sinatra Conducts Tone Poems of Color") 75-100 56
CAPITOL (581 thru 1676)...........5-15 61-78
(With "DT," "DW," "SM," "STBB," "SW," or "W" prefix.)
CAPITOL (T-1221 thru T-1676) . 10-20 59-62
(Monaural.)
CAPITOL (ST-1221 thru ST-1676, except 1624)..........................10-20 59-62
(Stereo.)
CAPITOL (PRO-1624 "The Best of Sinatra")...............................75-100 61
(Promotional issue only. Issued with paper sleeve.)
CAPITOL (1729 "Love and Things")...................................10-20 62
CAPITOL (1762 "Sinatra: The Great Years")....................................20-30 62
(Three-LP set.)
CAPITOL (1825 thru 2700)........15-30 62-68
(With "T" or "W" prefix. Monaural.)
CAPITOL (1825 thru 2700)........10-20 62-68
(With "DT" or "DW" prefix. Reprocessed stereo.)

CAPITOL (2814 "Deluxe Set") .. 40-60 67
(Six-LP boxed set.)
CAPITOL (2974 "Frank Sinatra Minute Masters")............................ 100-150 65
CAPITOL (7630 "The Sinatra Touch").................................. 50-75 68
(Six-LP boxed set. Includes booklet.)
CAPITOL (11000 & 12000 series) 5-10 74-80
CAPITOL (16000 series).............. 5-8 80-82
CAPITOL (90000 thru 94000 series) 20-40 64-74
(Capitol Record Club issues.)
COLUMBIA (6 "The Frank Sinatra Story") 15-25 58
COLUMBIA (S3L-42 "Essential Frank Sinatra")........................ 20-30 67
(Boxed, three LP set. Monaural.)
COLUMBIA (S3S-42 "Essential Frank Sinatra")....................... 20-30 67
(Boxed, three LP set. Stereo.)
COLUMBIA (S3S-842 "Essential Frank Sinatra")....................... 10-20
(Boxed, three LP set. Reissue.)
COLUMBIA (606 "Frankie") 25-40 55
(Cover pictures Sinatra wearing a hat and alone.)
COLUMBIA (606 "Frankie") 15-25 50s
(Cover pictures Sinatra not wearing a hat and with two other people.)
COLUMBIA (743 "The Voice of Sinatra") 25-35 55
COLUMBIA (902 "That Old Feeling")................................ 20-30 56
COLUMBIA (842 "Essential Frank Sinatra") 30-50 67
(Three LP set. Includes booklet.)
COLUMBIA (953 "Adventures of the Heart").................................... 15-25 57
COLUMBIA (1032 "Christmas Dreaming")............................ 15-25 57
COLUMBIA (1130 thru 1359).... 20-40 58-59
COLUMBIA (1448 "Reflections")........................... 30-60 60
COLUMBIA (CL-2474 "Greatest Hits: The Early Years, Vol. 1")............... 10-15 66
(Monaural.)
COLUMBIA (2521 "Get Happy") 25-40 55
(10–inch LP.)
COLUMBIA (2539 "I've Got a Crush on You")...................................... 25-40 55
(10–inch LP.)
COLUMBIA (2542 "Christmas with Frank Sinatra")................................ 25-40 55
(10–inch LP.)
COLUMBIA (CL-2572 "Greatest Hits: The Early Years, Vol. 2")............... 10-15 66
(Monaural.)
COLUMBIA (2475 "The Voice, Sampler")...............................10-15 86
(Samples tracks from C6X-40343.)
COLUMBIA (CL-2739 thru CL-2913)................................10-15 66-69
(Monaural.)
COLUMBIA (4271 "Frank Sinatra Conducts the Music of Alec Wilder")....125-175 50
(Green Masterworks label.)
COLUMBIA (6001 "The Voice of Sinatra") 75-100 48
(10–inch LP.)
COLUMBIA (6059 "Frankly Sentimental") 50-75 49
(10–inch LP.)
COLUMBIA (6087 "Songs by Sinatra, Vol. 1").......................50-75 50
(10–inch LP.)
COLUMBIA (6096 "Dedicated to You").......................................50-75 50
(10–inch LP.)
COLUMBIA (6143 "Sing and Dance with Frank Sinatra").......................50-75 50
(10–inch LP.)
COLUMBIA (6290 "I've Got a Crush on You")......................................50-75 52
(10–inch LP.)
COLUMBIA (6339 "Young at Heart").......................................50-75 54
(10–inch LP.)
COLUMBIA (CS-9274 "Greatest Hits: The Early Years, Vol. 1")..................8-15 66
(Stereo.)
COLUMBIA (CS-9372 "Greatest Hits: The Early Years, Vol. 2")..................8-15 66
(Stereo.)
COLUMBIA (CS-9539 thru CS-9541) 8-15 66-67
(Stereo.)
COLUMBIA (10000 series)..........5-10 73
COLUMBIA (30000 thru 45000 series, except 31358 & 40343) 5-12 73-87
COLUMBIA (31358 "In the Beginning") 8-12 72
(Two LP set.)
COLUMBIA (40343 "The Voice") 30-50 86
(Boxed, six LP set.)
EARTH NEWS 50-100 80
(Radio show on disc. Includes cue sheet/script.)
HARMONY................................10-20 66-71
KATWHISKER ("Frank Sinatra: Biography in Song")..............................750-1000 75
(Boxed, eight-LP radio show. Includes cue sheets. Promotional issue only. Reportedly only 25 made.)
MFSL (1 "Frank Sinatra").......350-500 85
(Boxed, 16-LP set. Includes booklet and

alignment tool. Limited numbered edition of 25,000 made.)
MFSL (100 series).................... 15-25 84-86
NARWOOD ("U.S. Army Reserve Presents William B. & Company")...... 150-200 76
(Two-LP, public service radio show. Has Sinatra interview. Promotional issue only.)
ODYSSEY................................ 10-20 68
PICKWICK 5-10 70s
RCA (10 "Getting Sentimental") 35-50 50
(10–inch LP.)
RCA (15 "All Time Hits")............ 35-50 51
(10–inch LP.)
RCA (017 "I'll See You in My Dreams")................................ 8-12 70s
RCA (050 "What'll I Do") 5-8
RCA (474 "The Radio Years")..... 5-10 74
RCA (0497 "What'll I Do") 8-10 74
RCA (583 "This Love of Mine") ... 8-12
RCA (1569 "Frankie and Tommy")................................ 20-40 57
RCA (1586 "Frank Sinatra with the Tommy Dorsey Orchestra") 5-8 75
RCA (1632 "We Three")........... 20-40 57
RCA (3005 "This Is Tommy Dorsey") 25-50 50
(10–inch LP.)
RCA (3063 "Fabulous Frankie") 25-50 52
(10–inch LP.)
RCA (4334 "The Dorsey/Sinatra Sessions, Vols. 1 & 2")............. 8-10 82
RCA (4335 "The Dorsey/Sinatra Sessions, Vols. 3 & 4")............. 8-10 82
RCA (4336 "The Dorsey/Sinatra Sessions, Vols. 5 & 6")............. 8-10 82
RCA (6003 "The Sentimental Gentleman")........................... 20-40 53
(10–inch LP.)
RCA (4700 series)........................ 5-8 83
RCA/PAIR 5-10 84
REPRISE (R-1001 thru R-1010)................................ 10-15 61-63
(Monaural.)
REPRISE (R9-1001 thru R9-1010)............................... 10-20 61-63
(Stereo.)
REPRISE (F-1001 thru F-1010).. 5-10 60s
(Monaural reissues.)
REPRISE (FS-1001 thru FS-1010)................................ 8-12 60s
(Stereo reissues.)
REPRISE (1011 thru 1015)......... 8-12 64-65
REPRISE (1016 "A Man and His Music, Part II").................... 300-400 66
(Promotional issue, made for Budweiser Beer distributors. About 1,000 made.)
REPRISE (FS4-1029 thru FS4-2207)............................. 15-25 70s
(Quadrophonic.)
REPRISE (1018 thru 1034)..........8-15 66-72
REPRISE (2013 thru 2022)........20-40 62-64
REPRISE (2155 thru 2275)..........5-15 73-78
REPRISE (2300 "Trilogy") 15-25 80
(Three-LP set.)
REPRISE (2305 "She Shot Me Down") 5-8 81
REPRISE (5230 "Songbook, Vol. 1") 25-35 71
REPRISE (5267 "Songbook, Vol. 2") 50-100 72
(Two-LP set.)
REPRISE (6000 series) 15-25 61-72
SINATRA 5-10 75
Also see ALI, Muhammad, & Frank Sinatra
Also see ANTHONY, Ray
Also see BLOCH, Ray, & Orchestra
Also see CROSBY, Bing / Grace Kelly / Frank Sinatra / Celeste Holm
Also see CROSBY, Bing, & Frank Sinatra
Also see DAY, Doris & Frank Sinatra
Also see DORSEY, Tommy, Orchestra
Also see JAMES, Harry
Also see KINGSTON TRIO / Frank Sinatra
Also see PRESLEY, Elvis / Frank Sinatra / Nat King Cole
Also see VINCENT, Gene / Frank Sinatra / Sonny James / Ron Goodwin
Also see ZENTNER, Si

SINATRA, Frank, & Charioteers

Singles: 78rpm

COLUMBIA 5-10 45
Also see CHARIOTEERS

SINATRA, Frank, & Count Basie

LP '63

EPs: 7–inch 33/45rpm

REPRISE (1012 "It Might As Well Be Swing") 8-12 63
(Promotional issue only.)

LPs: 10/12–inch 33rpm

REPRISE 10-20 63-66
Also see BASIE, Count

SINATRA, Frank / Nat King Cole

EPs: 7–inch 33/45rpm

CAPITOL (500 "Witchcraft").......35-55 58
(Promotional issue only.)
Also see COLE, Nat King

SINATRA, Frank, Bing Crosby & Russ Columbo

Singles: 7–inch

RCA (5 "Immortal Performances").......................50-75 50
(Boxed three disc set, one by each artist. Includes bio/booklet.)

LP: 10/12–inch 33rpm

RCA (5 "Immortal Performances").......................50-75 50
(10–inch LP.)

SINATRA, Frank, Bing Crosby & Dean Martin

Singles: 7–inch

REPRISE (20,217 "The Oldest Established [Permanent Floating Crap Game in New York]) 10-20 62

Picture Sleeves

REPRISE (20,217 "The Oldest Established [Permanent Floating Crap Game in New York]) 25-45 62

SINATRA, Frank, Bing Crosby, & Fred Waring

LP: 10/12–inch 33rpm

REPRISE 10-15 64

Also see CROSBY, Bing
Also see WARING, Fred

SINATRA, Frank, Sammy Davis Jr. & Dean Martin

(Frankie, Dino & Sammy)

P&R '62

Singles: 7–inch

REPRISE (20,128 "Me and My Shadow"/ "Sam's Song") 3-5 62

Picture Sleeves

REPRISE (20,128 "Me and My Shadow"/ "Sam's Song") 5-10 62

LPs: 10/12–inch 33rpm

LATIMER (247-17 "Summit Meeting at the 500, Atlantic City, N.J.") 250-350 64
(Private issue only, by the 500 Club. Three different, paste-on covers exist for this LP.)

SINATRA, Frank, & Duke Ellington

LP '68

Singles: 7–inch

REPRISE 3-5 68

LPs: 10/12–inch 33rpm

REPRISE 8-15 68

Also see ELLINGTON, Duke

SINATRA, Frank, & Antonio Carlos Jobim

LP '67

LPs: 10/12–inch 33rpm

REPRISE 8-15 67-71

Also see JOBIM, Antonio Carlos

SINATRA, Frank / Jonah Jones

Singles: 7–inch

CAPITOL (4214 "High Hopes") 50-100 60
(Promotional issue only.)

Picture Sleeves

CAPITOL (4214 "High Hopes") 300-400 60
(Promotional issue only.)

SINATRA, Frank, with Quincy Jones & His Orchestra

LP '84

Singles: 12–inch 33/45rpm

QWEST (2216 "Mack the Knife") 25-50 84

Singles: 7–inch

QWEST 3-5 84

LP: 10/12–inch 33rpm

QWEST 5-10 84

Also see JONES, Quincy

SINATRA, Frank, Dean Martin, Sammy Davis Jr., & Bing Crosby

LPs: 10/12–inch 33rpm

REPRISE (5031 "Summit") .. 500-1000 64
(British issue only. Listed mainly to dispell rumors that such an LP does not exist.)

Also see CROSBY, Bing
Also see DAVIS, Sammy, Jr.
Also see MARTIN, Dean

SINATRA, Frank, & Keely Smith

P&R '58

Singles: 78rpm

CAPITOL (3952 "Nothing in Common") 15-25 58
(This is the last commercially-issued Sinatra 78rpm.)

Singles: 7–inch

CAPITOL (3952 "Nothing in Common") 5-10 58

Also see SMITH, Keely

SINATRA, Frank / Roger Wagner Chorale / Hollywood Bowl Symphony

EPs: 7–inch 33/45rpm

CAPITOL (426 "Christmas Around the World") 75-100 57
(Promotional issue only.)

SINATRA, Frank & Nancy

(Sinatra Family)

P&R '67

Singles: 7–inch

REPRISE 3-6 66-71

LPs: 10/12–inch 33rpm

REPRISE 8-15 69

Members: Sinatra Family included Frank Sinatra, Frank Jr., Nancy and Tina.
Also see SINATRA, Nancy

SINATRA, Nancy

P&R '65

Singles: 7–inch

ELEKTRA 3-5 80
PRIVATE STOCK 3-5 75-77
RCA 3-5 72-73
REPRISE 3-6 61-71

Picture Sleeves

REPRISE 4-8 62-67

EPs: 7–inch 33/45rpm

REPRISE 10-12 66
(Jukebox issue only.)

LPs: 10/12–inch 33rpm

RCA.. 8-10 72
REPRISE 15-30 66-72

Also see BARRY, John
Also see MARTIN, Dean
Also see PRESLEY, Elvis
Also see SINATRA, Frank & Nancy

SINATRA, Nancy, & Lee Hazlewood

P&R/LP '68

Singles: 7–inch

PRIVATE STOCK 3-5 76
RCA.. 3-5 72
REPRISE 4-8 67-68

LPs: 10/12–inch 33rpm

RCA.. 8-10 72
REPRISE 10-15 68

Also see HAZLEWOOD, Lee
Also see SINATRA, Nancy

SINCLAIR, Gordon

P&R '74

Singles: 7–inch

AVCO 3-5 74

SINFIELD, Pete

LP '73

Singles: 7–inch

MANTICORE.............................. 3-5 73

LPs: 10/12–inch 33rpm

MANTICORE.............................. 8-10 73

SINGING BELLS

P&R '60

Singles: 7–inch

MADISON 5-10 60

SINGING DOGS

(Don Charles Presents the Singing Dogs)

P&R '55

Singles: 78rpm

RCA.. 3-5 55

Singles: 7–inch

RCA.. 3-6 55-72

Picture Sleeves

RCA.. 5-10 55-56

SINGING NUN

(Janine Deckers)

P&R/LP '63

Singles: 7–inch

PHILIPS 3-5 63-64

Picture Sleeves

PHILIPS 4-8 63-64

LPs: 10/12–inch 33rpm

PHILIPS 5-15 63-69

SINGLE BULLET THEORY

P&R '83

Singles: 7–inch

NEMPEROR 3-4 83

Picture Sleeves

NEMPEROR 3-4 83

LPs: 10/12–inch 33rpm

NEMPEROR 5-8 83

SINITTA

P&R '89

Singles: 7–inch

OMNI...3-4 87

SINNAMON

D&D '83

Singles: 12–inch 33/45rpm

BECKET...4-6 82-83
JIVE 4-6 84

Singles: 7–inch

BECKET...3-4 82-83

SIOUXSIE & BANSHEES

LP '84

Singles: 12–inch 33/45rpm

GEFFEN 4-6 84-86
PVC..4-8 80-82

Singles: 7–inch

GEFFEN 3-4 84-88
PVC..3-5 80-82
POLYDOR 3-5 79

Picture Sleeves

GEFFEN 3-4 88

LPs: 10/12–inch 33rpm

GEFFEN 5-8 84-90
PVC..5-10 80-82
POLYDOR 8-10 79

Also see SEX PISTOLS

SIR CHAUNCEY

(Ernie Freeman)

P&R '60

Singles: 7–inch

PATTERN 5-10 60
W.B. 3-6 60

Also see FREEMAN, Ernie

SIR DOUGLAS QUINTET

(Sir Douglas Band)

P&R '65

Singles: 7–inch

ATLANTIC.......................................4-8 73
CASABLANCA (0828 "Roll with the Punches") 5-15 75
MERCURY.......................................3-5 71
PACEMAKER (260 "Sugar Bee")..15-20 64
PHILIPS 3-5 70-71
SMASH 4-8 68-70
TRIBE 5-10 65
(No Indian on label.)
TRIBE 4-8 65-67
(Label pictures Indian.)

Picture Sleeves

PHILIPS 3-5 70-71

LPs: 10/12–inch 33rpm

ACCORD.. 5-10 82
ATLANTIC.................................... 10-15 73
MERCURY 10-15 72
PHILIPS 15-25 70-71
SMASH 15-25 68-70
TAKOMA...................................... 5-10 80-83
TRIBE (47001 "Best of Sir Douglas Quintet").................... 40-60 66

Members: Doug Sahm; Augie Meyers; Jack Barber; Leon Baetty; John Perez; Frank Morin; Jim Stallings.

Also see CASCADES / Sir Douglas Quintet
Also see SAHM, Doug

SIR LORD BALTIMORE

LP '71

Singles: 7–inch

MERCURY 3-5 70-71

LPs: 10/12–inch 33rpm

MERCURY 8-12 70-71

SIR MIX-A-LOT

P&R/LP '88

Singles: 7–inch

NASTYMIX.................................. 3-4 88-90

Picture Sleeves

NASTYMIX.................................. 3-4 88

LPs: 10/12–inch 33rpm

NASTYMIX.................................. 5-8 88-90

SIRENNE, Gianni

D&D '84

Singles: 12–inch 33/45rpm

ATLANTIC.................................... 4-6 84

Singles: 7–inch

ATLANTIC.................................... 3-4 84

SISTER SLEDGE

P&R '75

Singles: 12–inch 33/45rpm

ATLANTIC.................................... 4-6 85
COTILLION 4-8 79-83

Singles: 7–inch

ATCO 3-5 73-75
ATLANTIC.................................... 3-4 85
COTILLION 3-5 76-83

Picture Sleeves

ATLANTIC.................................... 3-4 85

LPs: 10/12–inch 33rpm

ATCO 8-10 75
ATLANTIC.................................... 5-8 85
COTILLION 5-10 76-83

SISTERS of MERCY

LP '88

Singles: 12–inch 33/45rpm

ELEKTRA.................................... 4-8 83-87

LPs: 10/12–inch 33rpm

ELEKTRA.................................... 5-8 88-90

Members: Wayne Hussey; Andrew Eldritch; Doktor Avalanche; Patricia Morrison.

Also see DEAD OR ALIVE
Also see MISSION

SIX TEENS

(Featuring Trudy Williams)

P&R '56

Singles: 78rpm

FLIP 5-10 56-57

Singles: 7–inch

FLIP (Except 338 & 346)...........10-15 56-60
FLIP (338 "Baby-O") 15-20 58
FLIP (346 "Why Do I Go to School") 15-20 58

Members: Trudy Williams; Louise Williams; Ed Wells; Bev Pecot; Ken Sinclair; Darrell Lewis.

SIX TEENS / Donald Woods / Richard Berry

LPs: 10/12–inch 33rpm

FLIP (1001 "12 Flip Hits") 50-100 59

Also see WOODS, Donald

SKA KINGS

P&R '64

Singles: 7–inch

ATLANTIC....................................4-8 64

SKAGGS, Ricky

(With Tony Rice; with Sharon White)

C&W '80

Singles: 7–inch

EPIC..3-5 81-90
ROUNDER...................................3-6 80
SUGAR HILL (3700 series) 3-6 80
SUGAR HILL (04000 series) 3-5 83-84

LPs: 10/12–inch 33rpm

EPIC..5-10 81-86
REBEL (1550 "That's It")...........10-15 75
ROUNDER...................................5-10 82
SUGAR HILL...............................5-10 79-80
WEL DUN 10-15 78

Also see SCRUGGS, Earl
Also see NITTY GRITTY DIRT BAND

SKAGGS, Ricky, & Keith Whitley

LPs: 10/12–inch 33rpm

REBEL 10-15 71-72

Also see SKAGGS, Ricky

SKELLERN, Peter

P&R '72

Singles: 7–inch

LONDON.....................................3-5 72
PRIVATE STOCK 3-5 75

LPs: 10/12–inch 33rpm

LONDON.....................................5-10 76

SKELTON, Red

P&R '69

Singles: 78rpm

MGM 4-6 56

Singles: 7–inch

CBS/BURGER KING ("Pledge of Allegiance")...............................8-12 69
(Promotional paper soundsheet.)
COLUMBIA 3-6 69
MGM 5-10 56

LPs: 10/12–inch 33rpm
LIBERTY 10-15 65-66
Also see ASTAIRE, Fred, & Red Skelton / Helen Kane

SKHY, A.B: see A.B. SKHY

SKID ROW

P&R/LP '89

Singles: 7–inch
ATLANTIC.................................. 3-4 89
EPIC.. 3-5 71

Picture Sleeves
ATLANTIC.................................. 3-4 89

LPs: 10/12–inch 33rpm
ATLANTIC.................................. 5-8 89-91
EPIC.. 10-15 71

SKIP & CASUALS

R&B '74

Singles: 7–inch
D.C. INT'L.................................. 3-5 74
Members: Skip Mahoney; Tracy Reid; Julius Jerome; Elwood Morgan.
Also see MAHONEY, Skip, & Casuals

SKIP & FLIP

P&R '59

Singles: 7–inch
BRENT 5-10 59-62
CALIFORNIA.................................. 3-5 63
COLLECTABLES 3-4 80s
ERIC.. 3-4 70s
TIME.. 5-10 61
Members: Clyde "Skip" Battin; Gary Paxton.
Also see GARY & CLYDE
Also see PLEDGES

SKIPWORTH & TURNER

D&D '85

Singles: 12–inch 33/45rpm
4TH & BROADWAY 4-6 85
W.B. 4-6 86

Singles: 7–inch
4TH & BROADWAY 3-4 85
W.B. 3-4 86

LPs: 10/12–inch 33rpm
W.B. 5-8 86
Members: Rodney Skipworth; Philip Turner.

SKO: see SCHUYLER, KNOBLOCH & OVERSTREET

SKOOL BOYZ

R&B '81

Singles: 12–inch 33/45rpm
COLUMBIA 4-6 84-85

Singles: 7–inch
COLUMBIA 3-4 84-85
DESTINY...................................... 3-5 81-82

LPs: 10/12–inch 33rpm
DESTINY...................................... 5-10 81
Members: Stan Sheppard; Bill Sheppard; Chauncy Matthews.
Also see TRIPLE "S" CONNECTION

SKRATCH

D&D '85

Singles: 12–inch 33/45rpm
PASSION 4-6 85

SKY

LP '70

Singles: 7–inch
RCA 3-5 71-72

LPs: 10/12–inch 33rpm
RCA 10-12 70-71

SKY

LP '80

Singles: 7–inch
ARISTA.. 3-5 81

LPs: 10/12–inch 33rpm
ARISTA.. 8-10 80
Member: Doug Fieger.
Also see KNACK

SKYLARK

P&R/LP '73

Singles: 7–inch
CAPITOL...................................... 3-5 72-73

LPs: 10/12–inch 33rpm
CAPITOL...................................... 8-10 72-74
Members: Donny Gerrard; Carl Graves.
Also see GERRARD, Donny
Also see GRAVES, Carl

SKYLINERS
(Jimmy Beaumont & Skyliners)

P&R '59

Singles: 12–inch 33/45rpm
TORTOISE INT'L (11345 "Love Bug") 8-10 76
(Promotional issue only.)

Singles: 7–inch
ATCO (6270 "Since I Fell for You") 25-35 63
CALICO.. 10-20 59-60
CAMEO (215 "Three Coins in the Fountain") 15-25 62
CAPITOL.. 3-5 75
CLASSIC ARTISTS 3-5 90
COAST.. 5-8
COLPIX (188 "I'll Close My Eyes") 20-30 61
COLPIX (613 "Close Your Eyes") 20-30 61
JUBILEE 8-12 65-66
ORIGINAL SOUND (35 thru 37) 5-8 63
ORIGINAL SOUND (4500 series).. 3-4 84
TORTOISE INT'L.......................... 4-8 77
VIRGO 3-5 73
VISCOUNT 8-12 62

LPs: 10/12–inch 33rpm
CALICO (3000 "Skyliners").... 150-200 59
KAMA SUTRA (2026 "Once Upon a Time") 15-25 71

ORIGINAL SOUND (5010 "Since I Don't Have You")............................ 15-25 63
(Monaural.)
ORIGINAL SOUND (8873 "Since I Don't Have You")............................ 20-30 64
(Stereo.)
ORIGINAL SOUND (8873 "Greatest Hits") 5-10 87
(Reissued using same number, but with 20 tracks.)
RELIC.. 5-10
TORTOISE INT'L 8-10 78
Members: Jimmy Beaumont; Janet Vogel; Wally Lester; Jack Taylor; Joe Verscharen.
Also see BEAUMONT, Jimmy

SKYLINERS / Preston Epps

Singles: 7-inch

OLDIES 45 3-5
Also see EPPS, Preston

SKYLINERS / Wade Flemons

Singles: 7-inch

OLDIES 45 3-5
Also see FLEMONS, Wade
Also see SKYLINERS

SKYNYRD, Lynyrd: see LYNYRD SKYNYRD

SKYY

LP '79

Singles: 12-inch 33/45rpm

CAPITOL.. 4-6 86
SALSOUL....................................... 4-8 79-85

Singles: 7-inch

CAPITOL.. 3-4 86
SALSOUL....................................... 3-5 79-85

LPs: 10/12-inch 33rpm

ATLANTIC...................................... 5-8 89
CAPITOL.. 5-8 86
SALSOUL....................................... 5-10 79-83
Members: Denise Dunning; Bonnie Dunning; Delores Dunning.

SLACK, Freddie: see MORSE, Ella Mae

SLADE

P&R/LP '72

Singles: 7-inch

CBS ASSOCIATED......................... 3-4 84-85
COTILLION 3-5 71-72
POLYDOR....................................... 3-5 72-73
REPRISE 3-5 73
W.B. 3-5 73-76

LPs: 10/12-inch 33rpm

CBS ASSOCIATED......................... 5-8 84-85
COTILLION 10-15 70
POLYDOR....................................... 8-10 72-73
REPRISE 10-12 73
W.B. 8-10 74-76

SLADES

P&R '58

Singles: 7-inch

DOMINO (500 "You Cheated") ..25-35 58
(Add $50 to $75 if accompanied by photo/bio insert.)
DOMINO (800 "You Gambled") .25-35 58
DOMINO (901 "Just You") 15-25 59
DOMINO (906 "It's Your Turn")..20-30 61
DOMINO (1000 "You Must Try") 15-25 61
LIBERTY (55118 "You Mean Everything to Me") 8-12 58
Member: Don Burch.
Also see SPADES

SLATKIN, Felix, Orchestra

P&R '60

Singles: 7-inch

LIBERTY 4-6 60-62

LPs: 10/12-inch 33rpm

ANGEL...5-10 72
CAPITOL......................................10-15 59
LIBERTY 10-15 60-64
SUNSET 5-10 66-68
U.A. 5-10 71

SLAUGHTER

P&R/LP '90

Singles: 7-inch

CHRYSALIS..................................3-4 90

LPs: 10/12-inch 33rpm

CHRYSALIS..................................5-8 90
DJM..5-10 80
Members: Mark Slaughter; Dana Strum.
Also see VINCENT, Vinnie, Invasion

SLAVE

(Slave-Arrington)

P&R/LP '77

Singles: 12-inch 33/45rpm

COTILLION 4-6 83

Singles: 7-inch

COTILLION 3-5 77-84
ICHIBAN 3-4 86-87

LPs: 10/12-inch 33rpm

COTILLION 5-10 77-84
ICHIBAN 5-8 86
Member: Steve Arrington.
Also see ARRINGTON, Steve
Also see AURRA
Also see DEJA

SLAY, Frank, & His Orchestra

P&R '61

Singles: 7-inch

SCA..3-6 63
SWAN 4-8 61
Also see CANNON, Freddy

SLAYER

LP '86

Singles: 7-inch

METAL BLADE 3-4 85

LPs: 10/12-inch 33rpm

DEF AMERICAN 5-8 90
DEF JAM 5-8 86-88
ENIGMA/METAL BLADE 5-8 85

SLEDGE, Percy

P&R/LP '66

Singles: 7-inch

ATLANTIC 4-8 66-72
CAPRICORN 3-5 74-76
MONUMENT 3-5 83

LPs: 10/12-inch 33rpm

ATLANTIC 10-20 66-69
CAPRICORN 8-10 74-75
MONUMENT 5-10 83

Also see JACKSON, Chuck / Percy Sledge

SLEDGE, Sister: see SISTER SLEDGE

SLEEPY KING: see KING, Sleepy

SLEEZE BEEZ

LP '90

LPs: 10/12-inch 33rpm

ATLANTIC 5-8 90

SLICK, Grace

(With the Great Society)

LP '68

Singles: 7-inch

GRUNT 4-6 72-74
RCA 3-5 80-81

Picture Sleeves

RCA 3-5 80

LPs: 10/12-inch 33rpm

COLUMBIA (CS-9624 "Conspicuous Only") 20-30 68
COLUMBIA (PC-9624 "Conspicuous Only") 5-10
COLUMBIA (CS-9702 "How It Was") 15-20 68
COLUMBIA (30459 "Collector's Item") 10-15 71
GRUNT 8-12 74
HARMONY 10-15 71
RCA 5-10 80-83

Promotional LPs

RCA ("*Dreams* Interview") 25-30 80
RCA (3922 "*Wrecking Ball* Interview") 20-30 81
RCA (3923 "Special Radio Series") 10-15 81
RCA (13708 "Interview LP") 5-10 80s

Also see CROSBY, David
Also see GREAT!! SOCIETY!!
Also see JEFFERSON AIRPLANE
Also see KANTNER, Paul, & Grace Slick

SLICK RICK

LP '89

LPs: 10/12-inch 33rpm

DEF JAM 5-8 88

SLIM, Guitar: see GUITAR SLIM

SLIM, Tarheel: see TARHEEL SLIM

SLIM & ANN: see TARHEEL SLIM & Little Ann

SLIM HARPO: see HARPO, Slim

SLINGSHOT

D&D '83

Singles: 12-inch 33/45rpm

QUALITY/RFC 4-6 83

Singles: 7-inch

QUALITY/RFC 3-4 83

SLOAN, P.F.

(Phil Sloan; Phillip "Flip" Sloan)

P&R '65

Singles: 7-inch

ATCO 4-6 69
DUNHILL 4-8 65-67
MART (802 "She's My Girl") 50-75 60
MUMS 3-5 72

LPs: 10/12-inch 33rpm

ATCO 10-15 68
DUNHILL 10-20 65-66
MUMS 8-10 72
RHINO 5-8 86

Also see FANTASTIC BAGGYS
Also see GRASS ROOTS
Also see SLOAN, Flip

SLY

(Sly Stone; Sly Stewart)

Singles: 7-inch

AUTUMN 5-10 65

Also see SLY & Family Stone

SLY & FAMILY STONE

P&R/LP '68

Singles: 12-inch 33/45rpm

EPIC 4-8 79

Singles: 7-inch

EPIC 3-6 67-75
W.B. 3-5 79-85

Picture Sleeves

EPIC 3-6 68-70

LPs: 10/12-inch 33rpm

EPIC (264 "Everything You Always Wanted to Hear") 10-20 76
(Promotional issue only.)
EPIC (26000 series) 10-15 67-69
EPIC (KE-30325 "Greatest Hits"). 8-12 70
EPIC (PE-30325 "Greatest Hits"). 5-10 70s
EPIC (EQ-30325 "Greatest Hits") 25-50 73
(Quadrophonic. Has some true stereo tracks that were rechanneled on earlier issues.)
EPIC (30335 thru 37071) 5-10 70-81
W.B. 5-10 79-83

Members: Sylvester "Sly Stone" Stewart; Rose Stone; Larry Graham; Fred Stone; Gregg Errico; Jerry Martini.
Also see BANKS, Rose
Also see GRAHAM, Larry
Also see RUBICON

Also see SLY
Also see STONE, Sly

SLY FOX

P&R '85

Singles: 12–inch 33/45rpm

CAPITOL.................................... 4-6 85-86

Singles: 7–inch

CAPITOL.................................... 3-4 85-86

Picture Sleeves

CAPITOL.................................... 3-4 86

LPs: 10/12–inch 33rpm

CAPITOL.................................... 5-8 86

Members: Mike Camacho; Gary Cooper.

SMALL, Millie
(The Blue Beat Girl)

P&R/LP '64

Singles: 7–inch

ATCO 5-10 65
ATLANTIC.................................... 5-10 64
BRIT 5-10 65
SMASH 4-8 64

LPs: 10/12–inch 33rpm

SMASH 15-25 64

SMALL FACES

P&R '67

Singles: 7–inch

IMMEDIATE 5-10 67-68
PRESS 8-12 65-68
RCA.................................... 8-12 66
W.B. 4-8 70-75

Picture Sleeves

IMMEDIATE (5003 "Tin Soldier") 10-20 68
W.B. 5-10 73

LPs: 10/12–inch 33rpm

ABKCO.................................... 8-12 73
ACCORD.................................... 5-10 82
ATLANTIC.................................... 8-10 77-78
COMPLEAT 5-8 86
IMMEDIATE (002 "There Are But Four Small Faces") 20-30 68
IMMEDIATE (008 "Ogden's Nut Gone Flake").......................... 20-30 68
IMMEDIATE (4225 "Ogden's Nut Gone Flake").......................... 10-15 73
MGM 10-15 74
PRIDE 10-15 72-73
SIRE.................................... 10-15
W.B. 10-15 70

Members: Steve Marriott; Ronnie Lane; Kenny Jones; Ian McLagen.
Also see FACES
Also see HUMBLE PIE
Also see McLAGAN, Ian
Also see PYTHON LEE JACKSON
Also see WHO

SMITH

P&R/LP '69

Singles: 7–inch

DUNHILL.................................... 4-6 69-70
ROULETTE.................................... 3-5 70s

Picture Sleeves

DUNHILL.................................... 4-8 69

LPs: 10/12–inch 33rpm

DUNHILL.................................... 10-15 69-70

Member: Gayle McCormack.
Also see McCORMACK, Gayle

SMITH, Arthur
(Arthur "Guitar Boogie" Smith; with Crossroads Quartet)

C&W/P&R '48

Singles: 78rpm

MGM 5-10 48-57
SUPER DISC (1004 "Guitar Boogie") 20-30 48

Singles: 7–inch

MGM (10229 thru 12791).................... 5-15 49-60
STARDAY 4-8 63

EPs: 7–inch 33/45rpm

MGM 15-25 55

LPs: 10/12–inch 33rpm

ABC-PAR 15-25 63
COUNTY.................................... 5-10 80s
DOT 10-15 65-66
FOLKWAYS.................................... 10-15 64
HAMILTON 10-15 64
MONUMENT.................................... 6-12 70-75
NASHVILLE 8-12 68
STARDAY (186 thru 415) 10-30 62-68

SMITH, Bessie

P&R '23

Singles: 78rpm

COLUMBIA (3000 & 4000 series).................................... 25-50 23
COLUMBIA (13000 & 14000 series).................................... 25-50 23-33
OKEH (8000 series).................................... 20-30 31

Singles: 7–inch

OKEH (6893 "Gimmie a Pig Foot") 20-30 52

LPs: 10/12–inch 33rpm

COLUMBIA 10-15 70-72

SMITH, Betty
(Betty Smith Group)

P&R '58

Singles: 7–inch

ECHO (584 "Oh Yeah") 20-30
LONDON.................................... 5-10 58

SMITH, Bro

P&R '76

Singles: 7–inch

BIG TREE 3-5 76

Picture Sleeves

BIG TREE 3-5 76

SMITH, Carl
(With the Tunesmiths)

C&W '51

Singles: 78rpm

COLUMBIA 4-8 51-57

Singles: 7–inch

ABC/HICKORY 3-5 76-78
COLUMBIA (20000 & 21000 series) 8-15 51-56
COLUMBIA (40823 thru 42858).. 4-10 57-63
COLUMBIA (42949 thru 45923).... 3-8 64-73
HICKORY.................................. 3-5 74-76

Picture Sleeves

COLUMBIA 5-10 59

EPs: 7–inch 33/45rpm

COLUMBIA 6-12 57-58

LPs: 10/12–inch 33rpm

ABC/HICKORY 5-10 77-78
COLUMBIA (31 "Anniversary Album") 8-12 70
COLUMBIA (900 thru 1100 series) 15-25 57-58
COLUMBIA (1500 thru 2600 series) 10-20 60-67
COLUMBIA (2579 "Carl Smith") 35-50 56
(10–inch LP.)
COLUMBIA (8300 thru 9800 series) 10-20 60-72
(12–inch LPs.)
COLUMBIA (9023 "Sentimental Songs") 30-40 54
(10–inch LP.)
COLUMBIA (9026 "Softly and Tenderly")..............................30-40 54
(10–inch LP.)
COLUMBIA (10000 series) 5-10 73
COLUMBIA (30000 series) 5-10 70-84
GUSTO 5-8 80
HICKORY.................................. 5-10 75
HARMONY................................ 5-15 64-72
LAKE SHORE 5-10

Session: Lewis Pruitt.
Also see PRICE, Ray / Lefty Frizzell / Carl Smith
Also see PRICE, Ray / Johnny Horton / Carl Smith / George Morgan

SMITH, Carl / Lefty Frizzell / Marty Robbins

LPs: 10/12–inch 33rpm

COLUMBIA (2544 "Carl, Lefty & Marty") 200-300 56
(10–inch LP.)
Also see FRIZZELL, Lefty
Also see ROBBINS, Marty
Also see SMITH, Carl

SMITH, Connie

C&W '64

Singles: 7–inch

COLUMBIA 3-5 73-77
EPIC... 3-4 85
MONUMENT................................3-5 77-83
RCA 3-8 64-74

Picture Sleeves

RCA 4-6 67

LPs: 10/12–inch 33rpm

CAMDEN 5-10 67-72
COLUMBIA 5-10 73-77
MONUMENT...............................5-8 77-78
RCA (0100 thru 1200 series).......5-10 73-75
RCA (3300 thru 4800 series).......8-15 65-73

SMITH, Connie, & Nat Stuckey

C&W '70

Singles: 7–inch

RCA 3-5 70

Also see SMITH, Connie

SMITH, Frankie

P&R/LP '81

Singles: 12–inch 33/45rpm

WMOT...4-6 81

Singles: 7–inch

WMOT...3-5 81

LPs: 10/12–inch 33rpm

WMOT...5-10 81

SMITH, Hank, & Nashville Playboys / Bud Roman & Topppers / "Scat" Benny
(George Jones as Hank Smith)

EPs: 7–inch 33/45rpm

HOLLYWOOD HIT CLUB (280 "Heartbreak Hotel")...................................30-50 56
TOPS (280 "Heartbreak Hotel").30-40 56

Also see JONES, George

SMITH, Huey
(With His Band; with Clowns; with Pitter Pats)

P&R '57

Singles: 78rpm

ACE...5-10 56-58
SAVOY.......................................10-15 54

Singles: 7–inch

ABC..3-5 73
ACE (521 thru 571)...................10-15 56-59
ACE (584 thru 672).....................5-10 60-65
COLLECTABLES..........................3-4 80s
CONSTELLATION........................4-8 63
COTILLION..................................3-5 72
IMPERIAL 5-10 61
INSTANT.....................................4-8 68-69
OLDIES 45...................................4-6 64
SAVOY (1113 "You Made Me Cry")..40-60 54
VIN 5-10 60

EPs: 7–inch 33/45rpm

ACE (104 "Having Fun") 50-75 59

LPs: 10/12–inch 33rpm

ACE (1004 "Having Fun") 75-125 59
ACE (1015 "For Dancing").......50-100 61
ACE (1027 "'Twas the Night Before Christmas") 50-100 62

ACE (2021 "Rock & Roll Revival")	25-35	74
GRAND PRIX	10-20	60s

Session: Lee Allen.

Also see ALLEN, Lee
Also see CHIMES / Huey "Piano" Smith
Also see FORD, Frankie
Also see KING, Earl
Also see MARCHAN, Bobby

SMITH, Hurricane

P&R '72

Singles: 7–inch

CAPITOL	3-5	72-73
EMI	3-5	74

LPs: 10/12–inch 33rpm

CAPITOL	8-10	72

SMITH, Jerry
(With His Pianos)

C&W/P&R/LP '69

Singles: 7–inch

ABC	3-5	69
AD	4-8	59-61
CHART	4-6	67
DECCA	3-5	70-72
RANWOOD	3-5	73-78
RICE	4-6	67
SOUND STAGE 7	4-8	65

LPs: 10/12–inch 33rpm

ABC	5-10	69
DECCA	5-10	70-72
RANWOOD	5-8	73-75

Also see DIXIEBELLES
Also see MAGIC ORGAN

SMITH, Jimmy

P&R/LP '62

Singles: 7–inch

BLUE NOTE	4-8	56-63
MGM	3-4	78
MERCURY	3-4	77
PRIDE	3-5	74
VERVE	3-6	62-73

LPs: 10/12–inch 33rpm

BLUE NOTE (Label gives New York street address for Blue Note Records.)	25-50	56-60
BLUE NOTE (Label reads "Blue Note Records Inc. - New York, USA.")	15-25	61-63
BLUE NOTE (Label shows Blue Note Records as a division of either Liberty or United Artists.)	10-20	66-73
COBBLESTONE	6-12	72
ELEKTRA	5-10	82-83
GUEST STAR	8-12	64
INNER CITY	5-10	81
MGM	8-12	70
MERCURY	5-10	77-78
METRO	8-15	67
MOJO	5-10	75
PRIDE	5-10	74
SUNSET	5-10	70
VERVE (Reads "MGM Records - A Division of Metro-Goldwyn-Mayer, Inc." at bottom of label.)	10-25	63-72
VERVE (Reads "Manufactured By MGM Record Corp.," or mentions either Polydor or Polygram at bottom of label.)	5-10	73-84

Also see BURRELL, Kenny, & Jimmy Smith

SMITH, Jimmy, & Wes Montgomery

LP '67

LPs: 10/12–inch 33rpm

VERVE	10-20	66-69

Also see MONTGOMERY, Wes
Also see SMITH, Jimmy

SMITH, Kate
(With Guy Lombardo's Orchestra)

P&R '27

Singles: 78rpm

COLUMBIA	3-6	27-46
VICTOR	3-6	38-42
MGM	3-5	48

Singles: 7–inch

ATLANTIC	3-5	74
MGM	3-4	78
RCA	3-5	63-68
TOPS	4-6	60

Picture Sleeves

RCA	4-8	63-64

EPs: 7–inch 33/45rpm

MGM	4-8	52-57
RCA	4-8	59

LPs: 10/12–inch 33rpm

CAMDEN	4-8	70-73
CAPITOL	5-15	54-57
COLUMBIA (6000 series) (10–inch LPs.)	10-20	50
HARMONY	5-12	57
KAPP	5-15	58
LION	5-12	57-60
MGM	5-15	52-66
METRO	5-10	67
RCA	5-15	63-80
RONDO	5-10	60s
TOPS	5-10	

Also see LOMBARDO, Guy

SMITH, Keely

LP '58

Singles: 78rpm

CAPITOL	3-5	56-58

Singles: 7–inch

ATLANTIC	3-5	67
CAPITOL	4-8	56-58
DOLTON	3-5	64
DOT	4-6	59-62
RCA	3-6	66-71

REPRISE	3-6	63-66
Picture Sleeves		
DOT	4-8	60
EPs: 7–inch 33/45rpm		
CAPITOL	4-8	58-59
DOT	4-8	60
LPs: 10/12–inch 33rpm		
CAPITOL	5-15	58-75
DOT	10-15	59-62
HARMONY	5-10	69
REPRISE	8-15	63-65

Also see PRIMA, Louis, & Keely Smith
Also see SINATRA, Frank, & Keely Smith

SMITH, Lonnie

LP '70

Singles: 7–inch		
BLUE NOTE	3-6	69-70
GROOVE MERCHANT	3-5	75
LRC	3-5	78-79
LPs: 10/12–inch 33rpm		
BLUE NOTE	8-15	68-70
COLUMBIA	10-15	67
GROOVE MERCHANT	5-10	75-76
KUDU	5-10	71
LRC	5-10	78

SMITH, Lonnie Liston

(With the Cosmic Echoes)

LP '75

Singles: 12–inch 33/45rpm		
COLUMBIA	4-8	79
Singles: 7–inch		
COLUMBIA	3-5	78-80
DOCTOR JAZZ	3-4	83
FLYING DUTCHMAN	3-5	75-76
RCA	3-5	77
LPs: 10/12–inch 33rpm		
COLUMBIA	5-10	78-79
DOCTOR JAZZ	5-8	83
FLYING DUTCHMAN	6-12	73-76
RCA	5-10	76-77

SMITH, O.C.

(Ocie Smith)

P&R/LP '68

Singles: 78rpm		
CADENCE	4-8	56-57
MGM	4-8	56
Singles: 7–inch		
BIG TOP	4-8	60
BROADWAY	10-20	
CADENCE	8-12	56-57
CARIBOU	3-5	76-77
CITATION	5-10	59
COLUMBIA	3-8	66-74
FAMILY	3-5	80
GORDY	3-5	82
MGM	8-12	56
MOTOWN	3-5	82
RENDEZVOUS	3-4	86-87
SHADYBROOK	3-4	78
SOUL WEST	3-5	72
SOUTH BAY	3-4	82
Picture Sleeves		
COLUMBIA	4-8	69
LPs: 10/12–inch 33rpm		
CARIBOU	5-10	79
COLUMBIA	8-12	67-74
HARMONY	8-10	71
MGM	8-10	72
MOTOWN	5-10	82
SOUTH BAY	5-8	82

SMITH, Patti

(Patti Smith Group)

LP '75

Singles: 7–inch		
ARISTA	3-5	76-79
MER (601 "Hey Joe")	50-75	74
SIRE	3-5	77
Picture Sleeves		
ARISTA	4-8	78-79
LPs: 10/12–inch 33rpm		
ARISTA	6-12	75-88

Members: Patti Smith; Ivan Kral; Jay Dee Daugherty; Lenny Kaye; Allen Lanier; Richard Sohl; Andy Paley.

SMITH, Ray

P&R '60

Singles: 7–inch		
ABC	3-5	73
CELEBRITY CIRCLE	4-8	64
CINNAMON	3-5	73-74
COLLECTABLES	3-4	80s
CORONA	3-5	75-77
DIAMOND	4-8	65
HEART (250 "Gone Baby, Gone")	150-200	50s
INFINITY	5-10	61
JUDD	8-12	59-61
NU-TONE	4-8	64
SMASH	4-8	62
SSS INT'L	3-5	70s
SSS/SUN	3-5	70s
SUN (298 "Right Behind You Baby")	10-20	58
SUN (308 "Why Why Why")	10-15	59
SUN (319 thru 375)	6-12	59-62
TOLLIE	8-10	64
TOPPA	4-8	62
VEE JAY	4-8	64
W.B.	4-8	63
WIX	3-5	78
LPs: 10/12–inch 33rpm		
BOOT	5-10	78
COLUMBIA	20-25	63
JUDD (701 "Travelin' with Ray")	150-250	60
T (56062 "Best of Ray Smith")	20-30	
WIX	10-15	

Also see DONNER, Ral / Ray Smith / Bobby Dale

SMITH, Ray / Pat Cupp

LPs: 10/12–inch 33rpm

CROWN 15-25 63

Also see SMITH, Ray

SMITH, Rex

P&R/LP '79

Singles: 7–inch

COLUMBIA 3-5 76-81

Picture Sleeves

COLUMBIA 3-5 79-80

LPs: 10/12–inch 33rpm

COLUMBIA 5-10 76-81

SMITH, Rex, & Rachel Sweet

Singles: 7–inch

COLUMBIA 3-5 81

Picture Sleeves

COLUMBIA 3-5 81

Also see SMITH, Rex
Also see SWEET, Rachel

SMITH, Richard Jon

D&D '83

Singles: 12–inch 33/45rpm

JIVE.. 4-6 83

Singles: 7–inch

JIVE.. 3-4 83

LPs: 10/12–inch 33rpm

JIVE.. 5-8 83

SMITH, Roger

P&R '59

Singles: 7–inch

JEROME 4-8 61
W.B. 5-10 59

Picture Sleeves

W.B. 10-15 59

LPs: 10/12–inch 33rpm

W.B. (1305 "Beach Romance"). 30-40 59

SMITH, Sammi

C&W '68

Singles: 7–inch

COLUMBIA 3-8 67-69
CYCLONE.................................. 3-5 79
ELEKTRA................................... 3-5 75-78
MEGA.. 3-5 70-76
SOUND FACTORY 3-4 80-82
STEP ONE................................. 3-4 86
TRIP 3-4 74
ZODIAC..................................... 3-4 76

Picture Sleeves

MEGA.. 3-5 70

LPs: 10/12–inch 33rpm

CYCLONE.................................. 5-8 79
ELEKTRA................................... 5-10 76-78
HARMONY 5-10 71
MEGA.. 5-10 70-75
SOUND FACTORY 3-4 80-82
STEP ONE 3-4 85-86
TRIP 5-8 74
U.A. 5-10 75
ZODIAC 5-8 76

Also see HART, Freddie / Sammi Smith / Jerry Reed
Also see STEVENS, Even, & Sammi Smith

SMITH, Somethin,' & Redheads

P&R '55

Singles: 78rpm

EPIC... 3-5 54-57

Singles: 7–inch

EPIC... 5-8 54-59
MGM 4-6 61

Picture Sleeves

EPIC... 5-10 58

EPs: 7–inch 33/45rpm

EPIC... 10-20 59

LPs: 10/12–inch 33rpm

EPIC... 10-20 59
MGM 10-15 61

SMITH, Tab
(With His Band)

P&R '51

Singles: 78rpm

ARCO.. 4-6 48
ATLANTIC................................. 5-10 52
CHESS...................................... 4-8 52
DECCA 5-8 44
EBONY 4-6 46
HARLEM................................... 5-8 46
HUB 4-6 45-46
KING 4-8 46
MANOR.................................... 4-6 44-48
QUEEN 4-6 46
REGIS....................................... 5-8 44
SOUTHERN............................... 4-6 46
20TH CENTURY......................... 4-6 45
UNITED.................................... 4-8 51-57

Singles: 7–inch

ARGO 5-10 58-59
ATLANTIC (961 "Echo Blues") .. 15-25 52
B&F 4-8 61
CHECKER 4-8 59
CHESS...................................... 10-20 52
KING (4000 series) 10-20 52
KING (5000 series) 4-8 60-61
UNITED (Black vinyl) 10-20 51-57
UNITED (Colored vinyl) 20-35 51

EPs: 7–inch 33/45rpm

KING 10-15 54

LPs: 10/12–inch 33rpm

CHECKER (2971 "Keeping
Tab") 20-30 59
(Black vinyl.)
CHECKER (2971 "Keeping
Tab") 50-100 59
(Colored vinyl. Promotional issue only.)
UNITED (001 "Music Styled
By Tab Smith")......................... 50-75 52

UNITED (003 "Red Hot and Cool Blue Moods")........................ 40-60 53

SMITH, Verdelle

P&R '66

Singles: 7-inch

CAPITOL.............................. 4-8 66-67
COLUMBIA 4-8 65
JANUS 3-5 75

Picture Sleeves

COLUMBIA 4-8 65

LPs: 10/12-inch 33rpm

CAPITOL.............................. 15-25 66
JANUS 8-10 75

SMITH, Warren

P&R '57

Singles: 78rpm

SUN.............................. 50-75 56-57

Singles: 7-inch

LIBERTY 4-8 60-64
MERCURY 4-6 68
SUN (239 "Rock 'N' Roll Ruby") 50-100 56
SUN (250 "Ubangi Stomp")....... 25-50 56
SUN (268 thru 314).................. 15-25 57-59
SSS/SUN 3-5 80
W.B. 5-10 59

LPs: 10/12-inch 33rpm

LIBERTY (3199 "First Country Collection").......................... 35-45 61
(Monaural.)
LIBERTY (7199 "First Country Collection").......................... 40-60 61
(Stereo.)

SMITH, Warren, & Shirley Collie

C&W '61

Singles: 7-inch

LIBERTY 5-10 61
Also see SMITH, Warren

SMITH, Whistling Jack

P&R '67

Singles: 7-inch

DERAM 4-6 67-69

LPs: 10/12-inch 33rpm

DERAM 10-15 67

SMITHEREENS

LP '86

Singles: 7-inch

CAPITOL/ENIGMA.................... 3-4 88
ENIGMA 3-5 85-86

Picture Sleeves

CAPITOL/ENIGMA.................... 3-4 88
ENIGMA 3-5 85-86

LPs: 10/12-inch 33rpm

CAPITOL/ENIGMA.................... 5-8 88-89
ENIGMA 5-10 85-89
Members: Pat Dinizio; Jim Babjak; Dennis Diken; Mike Mesaros.

SMITHS

LP '84

Singles: 12-inch 33/45rpm

SIRE.............................. 4-6 84-86

Singles: 7-inch

SIRE.............................. 3-4 84-88

LPs: 10/12-inch 33rpm

SIRE.............................. 5-8 84-88
Members: Andy Rourke; Mike Joyce.
Also see O'CONNOR, Sinead

SMOKE RING

P&R '69

Singles: 7-inch

BUDDAH.............................. 4-8 69
CERTRON 3-5 70
MALA 5-10 67

SMOKESTACK LIGHTNIN'

LP '69

Singles: 7-inch

BELL 4-6 68-70
WHITE WHALE.................... 4-6 67

LPs: 10/12-inch 33rpm

BELL 10-15 69

SMOKIE
(Smokey)

P&R '75

Singles: 7-inch

MCA.............................. 3-5 75
RSO 3-5 76-79

LPs: 10/12-inch 33rpm

MCA.............................. 8-10 75
RSO 5-10 76-79
Members: Chris Norman; Terry Utley; Peter Spencer.
Also see QUATRO, Suzi, & Chris Norman

SMOTHERS, Dick

Singles: 7-inch

MERCURY (72717 "Saturday Night at the World").............................. 10-20 67

Picture Sleeves

MERCURY (72717 "Saturday Night at the World").............................. 15-25 67
Also see SMOTHERS BROTHERS

SMOTHERS BROTHERS

LP '62

Singles: 7-inch

MERCURY 5-10 62-65
SMOTHERS INCORPORATED ("The Christmas Bunny").................. 25-35 69
(No selection number used. Promotional issue only.)

Picture Sleeves

MERCURY (72483 "Three Song").............................. 8-12 64
MERCURY (72519 "Toy Song") .. 8-12 65
SMOTHERS INCORPORATED ("The Christmas Bunny").................. 25-50 69
(Promotional issue only.)

EPs: 7–inch 33/45rpm

MERCURY (104 "Comedy Hour") 10-15 68
(Promotional issue only.)
MERCURY (628 "Two Sides") .. 10-20 62

LPs: 10/12–inch 33rpm

MERCURY (20 "Best of the Smothers Brothers") 25-35 64
(Promotional issue only.)
MERCURY (25 "Brothers Smothers Month") 25-35 64
(Promotional issue only. Open-end interview.)
MERCURY (20000 series) 10-20 61-68
(Monaural.)
MERCURY (60000 series) 12-25 61-68
(Stereo.)

Members: Dick Smothers; Tom Smothers.
Also see SMOTHERS, Dick
Also see TOM & DICK
Also see WILLIAMS, Mason / Smothers Brothers

SMYTH, Patty

P&R/LP '87

Singles: 7–inch

COLUMBIA 3-4 87

Picture Sleeves

COLUMBIA 3-4 87

LPs: 10/12–inch 33rpm

COLUMBIA 5-8 87

Also see DION

SNAIL

P&R/LP '78

Singles: 7–inch

CREAM 3-5 78-79

LPs: 10/12–inch 33rpm

CREAM 5-10 78-79

SNAP!

LP '90

Singles: 7–inch

ARISTA 3-4 90

LPs: 10/12–inch 33rpm

ARISTA 5-8 90

SNEAKER

P&R/LP '81

Singles: 7–inch

HANDSHAKE 3-4 81-82

Picture Sleeves

HANDSHAKE 3-4 81

LPs: 10/12–inch 33rpm

HANDSHAKE 5-10 81

SNEEZER, Ebe, & Epidemics

(Featuring John D. Loudermilk)

Singles: 7–inch

COLONIAL 10-15 57

Also see LOUDERMILK, John D.

SNIFF 'N' the TEARS

P&R/LP '79

Singles: 7–inch

ATLANTIC 3-5 79-80
MCA 3-5 81

LPs: 10/12–inch 33rpm

ATCO 5-10 79
ATLANTIC 5-10 79-80
MCA 5-10 81

Also see NETTO, Loz

SNOW, Hank

(With His Rainbow Ranch Boys; with Kelly Foxton)

C&W '49

Singles: 78rpm

BLUEBIRD 15-30 40s
RCA 5-10 49-57

Singles: 7–inch

RCA (0100 & 0900 series) 3-5 69-74
(Orange labels.)
RCA (0300 & 0400 series) 8-12 50-51
(Green or gray labels.)
RCA (4346 thru 7748) 5-10 52-60
RCA (7803 thru 9907) 3-6 61-70
RCA (10000 & 11000 series) 3-5 74-80

Picture Sleeves

RCA 4-8 63

EPs: 7–inch 33/45rpm

RCA (295 thru 1113) 12-25 54-56
RCA (1156 "Old Doc Brown") 35-45 55
RCA (1200 series) 20-30 55
RCA (1400 series) 15-25 57
RCA (3000 & 3100 series) 30-50 52-53
RCA (4000 series) 15-20 58
RCA (5000 series) 12-25 58-60

LPs: 10/12–inch 33rpm

CAMDEN 8-15 59-74
HANK SNOW SCHOOL of MUSIC (1149/50 "The Guitar") 250-300 58
(Special issue from the Hank Snow School of Music. Includes guitar instruction booklet.)
PICKWICK 5-10 75-76
RCA (0134 "Living Legend") .. 100-125 78
(RCA Special Products issue.)
RCA (0162 thru 0908) 5-10 73-75
RCA (1004 "I'm Movin' On") 15-20 82
(RCA Special Products issue.)
RCA (1052 thru 3511) 5-10 75-79
(With ""AHL1, "ANL1" or APL1" prefix.)
RCA (1113 "Just Keep-A-Movin") 25-35 55
(With "LPM" prefix.)
RCA (1156 "Old Doc Brown") 150-175 55
RCA (1233 thru 1861) 25-45 55-58
RCA (2043 thru 4708) 10-25 60-72
RCA (3026 "Country Classics") .50-75 52
(10–inch LP.)

RCA (3070 "Hank Snow Sings") 50-75 52
(10–inch LP.)
RCA (3131 "Hank Snow Salutes Jimmie Rodgers")....... 50-75 53
(10–inch LP.)
RCA (3267 "Country Guitar") 50-75 53
(10–inch LP.)
RCA (3000 & 3100 series) 40-60 52-54
(10–inch LPs.)
RCA (6014 "This Is My Story").. 20-30 66
READER'S DIGEST (216 "I'm Movin' On") 125-150
(Six-LP boxed set.)
Session: Jordanaires.
Also see MARTIN, Janis / Hank Snow
Also see PRESLEY, Elvis / Hank Snow / Eddy Arnold / Hank Snow

SNOW, Hank, & Chet Atkins

Singles: 78rpm

RCA.. 4-8 55

Singles: 7–inch

RCA (5900 series)...................... 5-10 55

LPs: 10/12–inch 33rpm

RCA (2952 "Reminiscing") 20-30 64
RCA (4254 "By Special Request") 20-30 70
Also see ATKINS, Chet

SNOW, Hank, & Anita Carter
(Anita Carter & Hank Snow; with the Rainbow Ranch Boys)

C&W '51

Singles: 78rpm

RCA... 4-8 51-56

Singles: 7–inch

RCA... 8-12 51-56

LP: 10/12–inch 33rpm

RCA (2580 "Together Again")... 15-25 62

SNOW, Hank / Hank Locklin / Porter Wagoner

LPs: 10/12–inch 33rpm

RCA (2723 "Three Country Gentlemen") 15-25 63
Also see LOCKLIN, Hank
Also see SNOW, Hank
Also see WAGONER, Porter

SNOW, Phoebe

LP '74

Singles: 7–inch

COLUMBIA 3-5 76-78
MIRAGE 3-5 81
SHELTER.................................. 3-5 74-75

LPs: 10/12–inch 33rpm

COLUMBIA 5-10 76-81
ELEKTRA.................................. 5-8 89
MCA 5-10 79
MIRAGE 5-10 81
SHELTER................................. 8-10 74
Also see GOODMAN, Steve, & Phoebe Snow
Also see JEFFREYS, Garland, & Phoebe Snow
Also see SIMON, Paul, & Phoebe Snow

SNUFF

C&W '82

Singles: 7–inch

ELEKTRA.......................................3-4 82
W.B./CURB 3-4 83
Member: Jim Bowling.

SNYDER, Terry, & All-Stars: see LIGHT, Enoch

SO

P&R/LP '88

Singles: 7–inch

EMI...3-4 88

Picture Sleeves

EMI...3-4 88

LPs: 10/12–inch 33rpm

EMI...5-8 88

SOBER, Errol

P&R '79

Singles: 7–inch

ABC...3-5 74
ABNAK...3-5 70
BELL 3-5 72
CAPITOL...3-5 76
NUMBER ONE.................................3-4 79

SOCCIO, Gino

P&R/LP '79

Singles: 12–inch 33/45rpm

ATLANTIC.......................................4-6 80-84
W.B./RFC..4-6 79-80

Singles: 7–inch

ATLANTIC.......................................3-5 80-84
W.B./RFC..3-5 79-82

LPs: 10/12–inch 33rpm

ATLANTIC.....................................5-10 80-84
W.B./RFC......................................5-10 79-80

SOCIAL DISTORATION

LP '90

LPs: 10/12–inch 33rpm

EPIC...5-8 90

SOFFICI, Piero

P&R '61

Singles: 7–inch

JUBILEE 4-8 61
KIP 4-8 61

SOFT CELL

P&R/LP '82

Singles: 12–inch 33/45rpm

SIRE...4-6 82

Singles: 7–inch

SIRE...3-5 82

Picture Sleeves

SIRE...3-5 82

LPs: 10/12–inch 33rpm

ACCORD 5-10 82
SIRE...5-10 82-83

Members: Marc Almond; David Ball.
Also see ALMOND, Marc

SOFT MACHINE

LP '68

Singles: 7–inch

PROBE.. 4-6 69

LPs: 10/12–inch 33rpm

ACCORD.................................. 5-10 82
COLUMBIA 8-12 70-73
COMMAND 12-18 73
PROBE (4500 "Soft Machine").. 20-30 68
(With movable parts cover.)
PROBE (4500 "Soft Machine").. 15-20 69
(With standard cover.)
PROBE (4505 "Soft Machine, Vol. 2") 15-25 69
RECKLESS.............................. 5-10 88

SOHO

P&R/LP '90

Singles: 7–inch

ATCO 3-4 90

LPs: 10/12–inch 33rpm

ATCO 5-8 90

SOLARIS

R&B '80

Singles: 7–inch

DANA 3-5 80

LPs: 10/12–inch 33rpm

DANA 5-10 80

SOLO

D&D '84

Singles: 12–inch 33/45rpm

NEXT PLATINUM 4-6 84

SOME, Belouis

P&R '85

Singles: 12–inch 33/45rpm

CAPITOL....................................... 4-6 85

Singles: 7–inch

CAPITOL....................................... 3-4 85

Picture Sleeves

CAPITOL....................................... 3-4 85

LPs: 10/12–inch 33rpm

CAPITOL..................................... 5-10 85

SOMERVILLE, Jimmy

LP '90

LPs: 10/12–inch 33rpm

LONDON... 5-8 90
Also see BRONSKI BEAT
Also see COMMUNARDS

SOMMER, Bert

P&R '70

Singles: 7–inch

BUDDAH 3-5 71
CAPITOL....................................... 3-5 77-78
ELEUTHERA.................................. 3-5 70

LPs: 10/12–inch 33rpm

BUDDAH 8-12 71
CAPITOL....................................... 0-10 77
ELEUTHERA 10-15 70

SOMMERS, Joanie

P&R '60

Singles: 7–inch

ABC... 3-5 78
CAPITOL.. 4-6 67
COLUMBIA 4-8 66
HAPPY TIGER................................ 3-5 70
W.B. (107 "Sommers' Hot, Sommers' Here") 10-15 60
(Promotional issue only.)
W.B. (5000 series) 4-8 60-65
W.B. (7000 series) 3-5 68

LPs: 10/12–inch 33rpm

COLUMBIA 10-20 66
DISCOVERY 5-10 83
W.B. 15-25 59-62
Also see BYRNES, Edd "Kookie," with Joanie Sommers & Mary Kaye Trio
Also see NELSON, Rick / Joanie Sommers / Dona Jean Young

SOMMERS, Joanie, & Laurindo Almeida

LPs: 10/12–inch 33rpm

W.B. 15-25 64
Also see ALMEIDA, Laurindo
Also see SOMMERS, Joanie

SOMMERS, Ronny
(Sonny Bono)

Singles: 7–inch

SWAMI (1001 "Don't Shake My Tree") 10-20 61
Also see SONNY

SONIC YOUTH

LP '90

LPs: 10/12–inch 33rpm

DGC... 5-8 90

SONNY
(Sonny Bono)

P&R '65

Singles: 7–inch

ATCO 4-8 65-67
HIGHLAND 5-10 63
MCA.. 3-5 72-74
SPECIALTY 3-8 65-72

LPs: 10/12–inch 33rpm

ATCO 12-20 67
Also see CHRISTY, Don
Also see SOMMERS, Ronny
Also see SONNY & CHER

SONNY & CHER

P&R/LP '65

Singles: 7–inch

ATCO 4-8 65-70
KAPP 3-6 71-72
MCA.. 3-5 73-74
REPRISE 5-10 64-65
VAULT (916 "The Letter").......... 10-15 65

W.B. 3-5 77

Picture Sleeves

VAULT (916 "The Letter") 10-15 65

EPs: 7–inch 33/45rpm

ATCO 8-12 65
(Jukebox issues only.)
REPRISE 15-25 65

LPs: 10/12–inch 33rpm

ATCO 12-20 65-72
KAPP 10-15 71-72
MCA 8-12 73-74
TVP 8-10 77

Members: Salvatore Bono; Cher LaPiere; Cher Bono.
Also see CAESAR & CLEO
Also see CHER
Also see HALE & HUSHABYES
Also see SONNY

SONNY & CHER / Bill Medley / Lettermen / Blendells

LPs: 10/12–inch 33rpm

REPRISE (6177 "Baby Don't Go") 25-35 65
(Shown as by "Sonny & Cher and Friends.")
Also see BLENDELLS
Also see LETTERMEN
Also see MEDLEY, Bill
Also see SONNY & CHER

SONS of CHAMPLIN

(Sons)

LP '69

Singles: 7–inch

ARIOLA AMERICA 4-6 75-77
CAPITOL 4-8 69-70
COLUMBIA 4-6 73
GOLDMINE 8-12
VERVE 5-10 67

LPs: 10/12–inch 33rpm

ARIOLA AMERICA 8-10 75-77
CAPITOL (200 "Loosen Up Naturally") 20-30 69
CAPITOL (332 "Sons Minus Seeds and Stems") 15-20 69
MILL VALLEY ("Sons Minus Seeds and Stems") 20-30 94
(Reportedly 1000 made.)
SONS of CHAMPLIN ("Sons Minus Seeds and Stems") 300-400 69
(Reportedly 100 made.)
COLUMBIA 10-15 73

Members: Bill Champlin; Geoff Palmer; Bill Bowen; Al Strong; Jim Myers; Tim Caine.

SONS of the PIONEERS

P&R '34

Singles: 78rpm

DECCA 5-10 34-44
RCA 4-8 45-56

Singles: 7–inch

BLUEBIRD (105 "Sugarfoot") 5-10 58
CORAL 5-10 54
DECCA (29000 series) 5-10 56
RCA (0100 thru 0400 series) 5-10 50-51
(Black vinyl.)
RCA (0100 thru 0400 series) 10-20 50-51
(Colored vinyl.)
RCA (2000 thru 6000 series) 5-10 50-56

Picture Sleeves

BLUEBIRD (105 "Sugarfoot") 10-20 58

EPs: 7–inch 33/45rpm

RCA (103 "Tumbling Tumbleweeds") 8-15 61
RCA (168 "Cowboy Classics") ... 25-40 52
(Colored vinyl, 3-EP boxed set.)
RCA (400 thru 1400 series) 5-15 55-57
RCA (3000 series) 15-25 52-53
RCA (4000 series) 8-12 58
RCA (5000 series) 5-10 59

LPs: 10/12–inch 33rpm

AMERICAN FOLK MUSIC 6-12 81
CAMDEN 8-18 58-73
COLUMBIA 5-8 82
GRANITE 6-10 76
HARMONY 10-15 64
J.E.M.F. 8-10
LONG 10-15
MCA 4-8 83
PICKWICK 5-10 75
RCA (1092 "Cool Water") 5-10 76
RCA (1130 thru 2957) 20-40 55-64
(With "LPM" or "LSP" prefix.)
RCA (2332 & 2808) 5-10 77-78
RCA (3032 "Cowboy Classics") 50-75 52
(10–inch LP.)
RCA (3095 "Cowboy Hymns and Spirtuals") 50-75 52
(10–inch LP.)
RCA (3162 "Western Classics"). 50-75 53
(10–inch LP.)
RCA (3351 thru 4119) 10-20 65-68
(With "LPM" or "LSP" prefix.)
RCA (3468 "Best of the Sons of the Pioneers") 5-10 79
RCA (4000 series) 4-8 81
VOCALION 8-12 64

Members: Roy Rogers; Tim Spencer; Bob Nolan; Ken Curtis.
Also see ALLEN, Rex, Jr., & Sons of the Pioneers
Also see ROGERS, Roy

SOPWITH CAMEL

P&R '66

Singles: 7–inch

KAMA SUTRA 4-8 66-67
REPRISE 3-5 73

Picture Sleeves

KAMA SUTRA 4-8 67

LPs: 10/12–inch 33rpm

KAMA SUTRA 15-20 67-73
REPRISE 15-20 73

Member: Peter Kraemer.

SOUL: see S.O.U.L.

SOUL, David

P&R/LP '77

Singles: 7-inch

MGM 4-6 66-67
PARAMOUNT 3-5 70
PRIVATE STOCK 3-5 77

LPs: 10/12-inch 33rpm

PRIVATE STOCK 8-10 77

SOUL, Jimmy
(With the Chants)

P&R '62

Singles: 7-inch

S.P.Q.R. 5-10 62-65
20TH FOX 4-8 63

Picture Sleeves

S.P.Q.R. 10-15 62-63

LPs: 10/12-inch 33rpm

S.P.Q.R. (16001 "If You Wanna Be Happy") 40-50 63

Also see BENTON, Brook / Chuck Jackson / Jimmy Soul
Also see RIVERS, Johnny / 4 Seasons / Jerry Butler / Jimmy Soul

SOUL, Jimmy / Belmonts

LPs: 10/12-inch 33rpm

SPINORAMA 20-25 63

Also see BELMONTS
Also see SOUL, Jimmy

SOUL ASYLUM

LP '92

LPs: 10/12-inch 33rpm

TWIN/TONE 5-8 88

Members: Dan Murphy; Grant Young; Dave Pirner; Karl Mueller.

SOUL BROTHERS SIX

P&R '67

Singles: 7-inch

ATLANTIC 8-15 67-69
PHIL-L.A. of SOUL 4-6 72-74

SOUL CHILDREN

P&R/LP '69

Singles: 12-inch 33/45rpm

STAX 4-8 78-79

Singles: 7-inch

EPIC 3-5 75-76
STAX 3-8 69-74

LPs: 10/12-inch 33rpm

EPIC 8-10 76
STAX 8-12 69-79

SOUL CLAN

P&R '68

Singles: 7-inch

ATLANTIC 4-8 68

Picture Sleeves

ATLANTIC 4-8 68

LPs: 10/12-inch 33rpm

ATCO 10-15 68

Members: Solomon Burke; Arthur Conley; Don Covay; Ben E. King; Joe Tex.
Also see BURKE, Solomon
Also see CONLEY, Arthur
Also see COVAY, Don
Also see KING, Ben E.
Also see TEX, Joe

SOUL SISTERS

P&R '64

Singles: 7-inch

GUYDEN 5-10 62
KAYO 5-10 63
SUE 5-10 64-65
VEEP 5-10 68

LPs: 10/12-inch 33rpm

SUE (1022 "I Can't Stand It") 25-35 64

SOUL SURVIVORS

P&R/LP '67

Singles: 7-inch

ATCO 4-8 68-69
CRIMSON 4-8 67-68
DECCA 4-8 67
PHILADELPHIA INT'L 3-5 76
TSOP 3-5 74-75

LPs: 10/12-inch 33rpm

ATCO (277 "Take Another Look") 15-20 69
CRIMSON (502 "When the Whistle Blows") 20-25 67
TSOP 8-10 75

Members: Richard Ingui; Charles Ingui; Kenny Jeremiah; Chuck Trois; Paul Venturini.
Also see SHIRLEY & COMPANY

SOUL TRAIN GANG

P&R '75

Singles: 7-inch

SOUL TRAIN 3-5 75-77

LPs: 10/12-inch 33rpm

SOUL TRAIN 8-10 76

SOUL II SOUL

P&R/LP '89

Singles: 7-inch

VIRGIN 3-4 89

Picture Sleeves

VIRGIN 3-4 89

LPs: 10/12-inch 33rpm

VIRGIN 5-8 89-90

SOULFUL STRINGS

LP '67

Singles: 7-inch

CADET 3-6 66-73

LPs: 10/12-inch 33rpm

CADET 5-10 67-73

SOUNDGARDEN

LP '90

EPs: 7–inch 33/45rpm

"SCREAMING LIFE" 5-8 87
(Colored vinyl.)

LPs: 10/12–inch 33rpm

A&M 5-8 89

Members: Chris Cornell; Hiro Yamamoto; Matthew Cameron; Kim Thayil.

SOUNDS of SUNSHINE

P&R/LP '71

Singles: 7–inch

P.I.P. 3-5 76
RANWOOD 3-5 71-73

LPs: 10/12–inch 33rpm

P.I.P. 5-10 76
RANWOOD 5-10 71-72

SOUNDS ORCHESTRAL

P&R/LP '65

Singles: 7–inch

JANUS 4-8 60s
PARKWAY 4-8 62-66

LPs: 10/12–inch 33rpm

PARKWAY 10-15 62-67

SOUP DRAGONS

LP '90

LPs: 10/12–inch 33rpm

BIG LIFE 5-8 90
SIRE.. 5-8 87

SOUTH, Joe

(With the Believers)

P&R '58

Singles: 7–inch

A&M 4-8 68
ALL WOOD 8-12 62
APT 5-10 65
CAPITOL...................................... 3-8 67-75
COLUMBIA 8-12 67
FAIRLANE................................. 8-12 61-62
ISLAND 3-5 75
MGM 5-10 63-64
NRC (Except 002) 10-15 58-60
NRC (002 "I'm Snowed").......... 30-40 58

LPs: 10/12–inch 33rpm

ACCORD.................................... 5-10 81
CAPITOL.................................... 8-15 68-72
ISLAND 8-12 70
MINE 8-12 70

SOUTH, Joe / Dells

LPs: 10/12–inch 33rpm

APPLE.................................... 15-25 71

Also see DELLS

SOUTH, Joe / Billy Joe Royal

LPs: 10/12–inch 33rpm

NASHVILLE 5-10 70s

Also see ROYAL, Billy Joe
Also see SOUTH, Joe

SOUTH SHORE COMMISSION

P&R '75

Singles: 7–inch

WAND 3-5 75-76

SOUTHCOTE

P&R '74

Singles: 7–inch

BUDDAH.......................................3-6 74

SOUTHER, J.D.

(John David Souther)

LP '76

Singles: 7–inch

ASYLUM 3-5 74-76
COLUMBIA 3-5 79
W.B. 3-4 85

LPs: 10/12–inch 33rpm

ASYLUM 8-10 72-76
COLUMBIA 5-10 79
W.B. 5-8 85

Also see RONSTADT, Linda, & J.D. Souther
Also see TAYLOR, James, & J.D. Souther
Also see TILLOTSON, Johnny, & J.D. Souther

SOUTHER - HILLMAN - FURAY BAND

P&R/LP '74

Singles: 7–inch

ASYLUM 3-5 74-75

LPs: 10/12–inch 33rpm

ASYLUM 8-10 74-75

Members: J. D. Souther; Chris Hillman; Richie Furay.

Also see FURAY, Richie
Also see HILLMAN, Chris
Also see SOUTHER, J.D.

SOUTHERN, Jeri

P&R '51

Singles: 78rpm

CAPITOL.......................................3-5 59

Singles: 7–inch

CAPITOL.......................................4-8 59
DECCA 5-10 51-58

EPs: 7–inch 33/45rpm

DECCA 5-10 55-56

LPs: 10/12–inch 33rpm

CAPITOL....................................10-20 59
DECCA 15-25 55-58
ROULETTE................................10-20 57-59

SOUTHERN COMFORT

LP '71

Singles: 7–inch

CAPITOL.......................................3-5 71-72
COTILLION 4-6 69

LPs: 10/12–inch 33rpm

BRYLEN..5-8
CAPITOL....................................10-12 71
COLUMBIA 10-12 70
SIRE...12-15 69

Also see MATTHEWS' SOUTHERN COMFORT

SOUTHSIDE JOHNNY & Asbury Jukes
(With the Jukes; Jukes; Southside Johnny)

LP '76

Singles: 7-inch

ATLANTIC	3-4	86
EPIC	3-5	77-78
MERCURY	3-5	79
MIRAGE	3-4	83-84

Picture Sleeves

ATLANTIC	3-4	86

LPs: 10/12-inch 33rpm

ATLANTIC	5-8	86
CYPRESS	5-8	88
EPIC	8-10	76-79
MERCURY	5-10	79-81
MIRAGE	5-8	83-84

Also see FIVE SATINS

SOUTHSIDE MOVEMENT

P&R '73

Singles: 7-inch

20TH FOX	3-5	74-75
WAND	3-5	73

LPs: 10/12-inch 33rpm

20TH FOX	5-10	75
WAND	8-10	73

Also see SIMTEC & WYLIE

SOUTHWEST F.O.B.

P&R '68

Singles: 7-inch

GPC	4-8	68
HIP	5-10	68-69

LPs: 10/12-inch 33rpm

HIP (7001 "Smell of Incense")	25-35	69

Members: Dan Seals; John Ford Coley; Shane Keister.
Also see ENGLAND DAN & John Ford Coley

SOVINE, Red
(With the Girls)

C&W '55

Singles: 78rpm

DECCA (Except 30239)	4-8	54-57
DECCA (30239 "Juke Joint Johnny")	10-15	57
MGM	4-8	50-53

Singles: 7-inch

CHART	3-5	71-75
DECCA (Except 30239)	5-10	54-66
DECCA (30239 "Juke Joint Johnny")	20-30	57
GUSTO	3-5	79-80
MGM	8-15	50-53
RCA	4-8	62
RIC	4-6	64-65
STARDAY (Except 500 thru 800 series)	3-5	70-78
STARDAY (500 thru 800 series)	4-8	60-70

EPs: 7-inch 33/45rpm

MGM	10-20	57

LPs: 10/12-inch 33rpm

CMI	5-10	77
CHART	5-10	72-74
DECCA (4400 series)	15-25	64
DECCA (4700 series)	10-20	66
GUSTO	5-10	
LAKE SHORE	8-12	
MGM (3465 "Red Sovine")	30-40	57
METRO	10-15	67
NASHVILLE	6-12	70
POWER PAK	5-10	80s
RIC	10-15	65
SOMERSET	8-12	63
STARDAY (Except 100 series)	5-15	65-76
STARDAY (100 series)	15-25	61-62
STEREO FIDELITY	8-12	63
VOCALION	8-12	68

Also see FELTS, Narvel / Red Sovine / Mel Tillis
Also see REEVES, Del / Red Sovine

SOVINE, Red, & Goldie Hill

C&W '55

Singles: 78rpm

DECCA	4-8	55

Singles: 7-inch

DECCA	5-10	55

SOVINE, Red, & Webb Pierce

C&W '56

Singles: 78rpm

DECCA	4 8	56

Singles: 7-inch

DECCA	8-12	56

Also see PIERCE, Webb
Also see SOVINE, Red

SOXX, Bob B.: see BOB B. SOXX & Blue Jeans

SPACE

P&R '79

Singles: 12-inch 33/45rpm

CASABLANCA	4-6	79-80

Singles: 7-inch

CASABLANCA	3-5	79-80
U.A.	3-5	77

LPs: 10/12-inch 33rpm

CASABLANCA	5-10	78-79
U.A.	8-10	77

Also see BELL, Madeline

SPACEMEN
(Space Men)

P&R '59

Singles: 7-inch

ALTON	5-10	59-60
FELSTED	5-10	59
JAMECO	4-8	65
JUBILEE	5-10	59
MARKEY	4-8	62

LPs: 10/12-inch 33rpm

ROULETTE	15-25	64-66

SPADES
(Slades)

Singles: 7–inch

LIBERTY (55118 "You Mean Everything to Me")................................... 30-40 58

Also see SLADES

SPADES
(Thirteenth Floor Elevators)

Singles: 7–inch

ZERO (10001 "I Need a Girl")................................. 200-300 65

ZERO (10002 "You're Gonna Miss Me")......................... 100-150 65

(A different recording than later issued by the 13th Floor Elevators.)

Also see THIRTEENTH FLOOR ELEVATORS

SPANDAU BALLET

P&R/D&D/LP '83

Singles: 12–inch

CHRYSALIS................................ 4-6 84-85

Singles: 7–inch

CHRYSALIS................................ 3-4 83-85

Picture Sleeves

CHRYSALIS................................ 3-5 83-85

LPs: 10/12–inch 33rpm

CHRYSALIS................................ 5-8 83-85

MFSL.. 15-25 85

Also see BAND AID

SPANIELS
(Spanials)

P&R '57

Singles: 78rpm

CHANCE (1141 "Baby It's You")................................ 50-75 53

VEE JAY (101 "Baby, It's You")................................. 50-100 53

VEE JAY (103 "Bells Ring Out")................................ 30-60 53

VEE JAY (107 "Goodnite Sweetheart, Goodnite")............................ 25-50 53

VEE JAY (116 thru 200 series). 15-30 54-58

Singles: 7–inch

BUDDAH.................................. 4-8 69

CALLA..................................... 3-5 70

CANTERBURY.......................... 3-4 74

CHANCE (1141 "Baby It's You")............................... 250-350 53

(Black vinyl.)

CHANCE (1141 "Baby It's You")............................... 400-600 53

(Colored vinyl.)

COLLECTABLES........................ 3-4 80s

ERIC....................................... 3-4 70s

NORTH AMERICAN.................. 3-5 70

OWL....................................... 3-5 73

VEE JAY (101 "Baby It's You")............................... 400-500 53

(Black vinyl. Maroon label.)

VEE JAY (101 "Baby It's You")................................500-750 53

(Colored vinyl.)

VEE JAY (101 "Baby It's You")..20-30 61

(Black label.)

VEE JAY (103 "Bells Ring Out")................................100-200 53

(Black vinyl.)

VEE JAY (103 "Bells Ring Out")................................300-400 53

(Colored vinyl.)

VEE JAY (107 "Goodnite Sweetheart, Goodnite")..........................125-200 53

(Black vinyl. Credited to the Spanials.)

VEE JAY (107 "Goodnite Sweetheart, Goodnite")..........................100-150 53

(Black vinyl. Credited to Spaniels.)

VEE JAY (107 "Goodnite Sweetheart, Goodnite")..........................300-500 53

(Red vinyl. No "Trade Mark Reg." on label.)

VEE JAY (107 "Goodnite Sweetheart, Goodnite")................................4-8 93

(Red vinyl, Vee Jay commemorative issue. Has "Trade Mark Reg." on label.)

VEE JAY (116 "Play It Cool").....50-75 54

(Black vinyl.)

VEE JAY (116 "Play It Cool").250-350 54

(Colored vinyl.)

VEE JAY (131 "Do-Wah").........40-60 55

(Black vinyl.)

VEE JAY (131 "Do-Wah")......250-350 55

(Colored vinyl.)

VEE JAY (154 "You Painted Pictures")...............................40-50 55

VEE JAY (154 "Painted Picture")..................................30-40 55

(Shown as by the Spanials.)

VEE JAY (178 "False Love")....75-100 56

VEE JAY (189 "Dear Heart")....75-100 56

VEE JAY (202 "Since I Fell for You")..............................75-100 56

VEE JAY (229 thru 328)............30-45 56-58

VEE JAY (342 "People Will Say We're in Love")...............50-75 59

VEE JAY (350 "I Know")...........20-25 60

Picture Sleeves

VEE JAY (107 "Goodnite Sweetheart, Goodnite")..................................2-3 93

(Commemorative issue with this title although no specific artist or titles are shown.)

LPs: 10/12–inch 33rpm

LOST-NITE (19 "Spaniels").........5-10 81

LOST-NITE (137 "Spaniels").....15-20 70s

VEE JAY (1002 "Goodnite, It's Time to Go")........................200-300 59

(Maroon label.)

VEE JAY (1002 "Goodnite, It's Time to Go")........................ 75-100 61
(Black label.)
VEE JAY (1024 "Spaniels")... 200-250 60
UPFRONT.................................. 10-20
Members: Pookie Hudson; Jerry Gregory; Ernest Warren; Willie Jackson; Opal Courtney; James Cochran; Carl Rainge; Don Porter; Andy Magruder; Bill Carey.
Also see HUDSON, Pookie

SPANKY & Our Gang

P&R/LP '67

Singles: 7-inch

EPIC.. 3-5 75-76
MERCURY.. 4-8 67-69

Picture Sleeves

MERCURY.. 4-8 67-68

EPs: 7-inch 33/45rpm

MERCURY (90 "Like to Get to Know You") 10-20 67
(Promotional issue only. Issued with paper sleeve.)

LPs: 10/12-inch 33rpm

EPIC.. 8-10 75
MERCURY.............................. 10-20 67-71
RHINO.. 5-8 86
Members: Elaine "Spanky" McFarlane; Lefty Baker; Malcolm Hale; Nigel Pickering; John Seiter.

SPARKLETONES, with Joe Bennett: see BENNETT, Joe, & Sparkletones

SPARKS

LP '74

Singles: 12-inch 33/45rpm

ATLANTIC.. 4-6 84

Singles: 7-inch

ATLANTIC.. 3-4 82-84
BEARSVILLE.................................... 3-5 72
COLUMBIA...................................... 3-5 78
ELEKTRA.. 3-5 79
FINE ARTS...................................... 3-4 88
ISLAND.. 3-5 73-76
RCA.. 3-5 81

Picture Sleeves

ATLANTIC.. 3-4 82-83

LPs: 10/12-inch 33rpm

ATLANTIC...................................... 5-10 82-84
BEARSVILLE................................ 12-15 72-73
COLUMBIA (Black vinyl)............ 8-10 77
COLUMBIA (Colored vinyl) 12-15 77
ELEKTRA...................................... 8-10 79
ISLAND.. 8-10 74-76
RCA.. 5-10 81
Members: Ron Mael; Russell Mael.

SPARKS & Jane Wiedlin

P&R '83

Singles: 12-inch 33/45rpm

ATLANTIC.. 4-6 83

Singles: 7-inch

ATLANTIC.. 3-4 83

Picture Sleeves

ATLANTIC.. 3-4 83
Also see SPARKS
Also see WIEDLIN, Jane

SPARKY D

D&D '85

Singles: 12-inch 33/45rpm

NIA.. 4-6 85

SPARQUE

D&D '84

Singles: 12-inch 33/45rpm

WEST END...................................... 4-6 84

SPARROW, Johnny, His Bows & Arrows

R&B '50

Singles: 78rpm

MIRAGE.. 5-10 50

SPATS

P&R '64

Singles: 7-inch

ABC-PAR.. 5-10 64-66
ENITH.. 10-20 64
JANO.. 10-20 67

LPs: 10/12-inch 33rpm

ABC-PAR.. 20-25 65
Member: Dick Johnson.

SPEARS, Billie Jo

C&W '68

Singles: 7-inch

CAPITOL.. 3-5 68-71
LIBERTY.. 3-4 81
PARLIAMENT.................................... 3-4 84
U.A. (Except 50000 series)............ 3-5 74-80
U.A. (50000 series)........................ 3-6 66-67

LPs: 10/12-inch 33rpm

CAPITOL.. 5-15 68-79
LIBERTY.. 5-8 81
PICKWICK/HILLTOP 5-8 70s
U.A. 5-10 75-80
Also see REEVES, Del, & Billie Jo Spears

SPECIAL AKA

D&D '84

Singles: 12-inch 33/45rpm

CHRYSALIS...................................... 4-6 84

Singles: 7-inch

CHRYSALIS...................................... 3-4 84

LPs: 10/12-inch 33rpm

CHRYSALIS...................................... 5-8 84
Also see SPECIALS

SPECIAL DELIVERY (Featuring Terry Huff)

R&B '76

Singles: 7-inch

MAINSTREAM.................................. 3-5 75-76
SHIELD.. 3-5 77-78
Also see BRUNSON, Tyrone "Tystick"
Also see HUFF, Terry

SPECIAL ED

LP '89

LPs: 10/12-inch 33rpm

PROFILE.................................... 5-8 89-90

SPECIALS

LP '80

Singles: 7-inch

CHRYSALIS................................ 3-5 79-80

Picture Sleeves

CHRYSALIS................................ 3-5 79

LPs: 10/12-inch 33rpm

CHRYSALIS.............................. 5-10 80

Also see FUN BOY THREE
Also see SPECIAL AKA

SPECTOR, Phil

Singles: 7-inch

PHILLES ("Thanks for Giving Me the Right Time") 150-250 63
(Promotional issue only.)

Also see HARVEY, Phil
Also see SPECTORS THREE

SPECTOR, Ronnie

(With the Ronettes; with E Street Band)

P&R '71

Singles: 12-inch 33/45rpm

EPIC/CLEVELAND INT'L (350 "Say Goodbye to Hollywood")......................... 8-12 77
(Promotional issue only.)

Singles: 7-inch

ALSTON...................................... 5-8 78
APPLE...................................... 5-10 70-71
BUDDAH.................................... 4-6 74
EPIC/CLEVELAND INT'L (50374 "Say Goodbye to Hollywood") 5-10 77
COLUMBIA 3-4 87
POLISH...................................... 3-5 80
TOM CAT (Black vinyl)................. 3-5 75-76
TOM CAT (Colored vinyl)............. 5-8 75
(Promotional issues only.)
W.B./SPECTOR 3-5 76

Picture Sleeves

APPLE...................................... 8-10 71
COLUMBIA 3-5 87
EPIC/CLEVELAND INT'L (50374 "Say Goodbye to Hollywood") 20-25 77

LPs: 10/12-inch 33rpm

POLISH 8-12 80

Also see MONEY, Eddie, & Ronnie Spector
Also see RONETTES
Also see SPRINGSTEEN, Bruce
Also see VERONICA

SPECTORS THREE

Singles: 7-inch

TREY.. 10-20 59-60

Member: Phil Spector.
Also see SPECTOR, Phil
Also see TEDDY BEARS

SPEEDO & CADILLACS

(Cadillacs)

Singles: 7-inch

JOSIE (876 "It's Love") 20-25 60

Also see CADILLACS

SPEEDO & PEARLS

Singles: 7-inch

JOSIE (865 "Who Ya Gonna Kiss").....................................10-15 59

Also see CADILLACS
Also see SPEEDO & CADILLACS

SPEEDO & IMPALAS

(Impalas)

Singles: 7-inch

CUB (9066 "All Alone") 10-15 60

Also see IMPALAS

SPELLBINDERS

P&R '65

Singles: 7-inch

COLUMBIA.................................4-8 65-66
DATE 4-8 67
MIRAMAR...................................4-8 60s

LPs: 10/12-inch 33rpm

COLUMBIA 10-20 66

SPELLBOUND

P&R '78

Singles: 7-inch

EMI AMERICA 3-5 78

LPs: 10/12-inch 33rpm

EMI AMERICA 5-10 78

SPELLMAN, Benny

P&R '62

Singles: 7-inch

ACE...5-10 61
ALON 4-8 66
ATLANTIC...................................4-8 65
MINIT 5-10 62
SANSU.......................................4-8 67
WATCH......................................4-8 64

Also see K-DOE, Ernie
Also see THOMAS, Irma / Ernie K-Doe / Showmen / Benny Spellman

SPENCE, Judson

P&R/LP '88

Singles: 7-inch

ATLANTIC...................................3-4 88

Picture Sleeves

ATLANTIC...................................3-4 88

LPs: 10/12-inch 33rpm

ATLANTIC...................................5-8 88

SPENCER, Sonny

P&R '59

Singles: 7-inch

MEMO (17984 "Gilee") 10-20 59
ONDA (111 "Bessie Lou")..........15-25

SPENCER, Tracie

P&R/LP '88

Singles: 7-inch

CAPITOL.................................... 3-4 88-91

Picture Sleeves

CAPITOL.................................... 3-4 88-89

LPs: 10/12-inch 33rpm

CAPITOL.................................... 5-8 88-91

SPENCER & SPENCER

P&R '59

Singles: 7-inch

ARGO.. 8-12 59

GONE...................................... 10-15 59

Members: Dickie Goodman; Mickey Shorr.

Also see GOODMAN, Dickie

Also see SHORR, Mickey, & Cutups

SPERRY, Steve

P&R '77

Singles: 7-inch

MERCURY 3-5 77

SPHEERIS, Jimmie

LP '75

Singles: 7-inch

COLUMBIA 3-5 72

EPIC... 3-5 75

LPs: 10/12-inch 33rpm

EPIC.. 8-10 75

SPIDER

P&R/LP '80

Singles: 7-inch

DREAMLAND.............................. 3-5 80-81

Picture Sleeves

DREAMLAND.............................. 3-5 80

LPs: 10/12-inch 33rpm

DREAMLAND............................ 5-10 80-81

Member: Holly Knight.

Also see KNIGHT, Holly

SPIDERS

R&B '54

Singles: 78rpm

IMPERIAL 15-30 54-57

Singles: 7-inch

IMPERIAL (5265 "I Didn't Want to Do It")........................ 50-75 53

IMPERIAL (5280 "Tears Began to Flow") 50-60 54

IMPERIAL (5291 "I'm Searching") 50-75 54

IMPERIAL (5305 "Real Thing") . 50-75 54

IMPERIAL (5318 "She Keeps Me Wondering") 50-75 54

IMPERIAL (5331 "That's Enough") 40-60 55

IMPERIAL (5344 "Am I the One").. 40-60 55

IMPERIAL (5354 "Bells in My Heart").. 50-75 55

(Red label.)

IMPERIAL (5354 "Bells in My Heart")..................................15-25 57

(Black label.)

IMPERIAL (5366 "Is It True").....40-60 55

(Blue label.)

IMPERIAL (5366 "Is It True").....20-30 55

(Red label.)

IMPERIAL (5676 thru 5739).......12-25 59-61

OWL...3-5 73

LPs: 10/12-inch 33rpm

IMPERIAL (9142 "I Didn't Want to Do It")............................200-275 61

Member: Chuck Carbo.

SPIDERS

Singles: 7-inch

MASCOT (112 "Why Don't You Love Me") 750-1000 65

SANTA CRUZ (003 "Don't Blow Your Mind") 350-400 66

Members: Vince "Alice Cooper" Furnier; John Speer; Glen Buxton; Dennis Dunaway; Mike Bruce.

Also see COOPER, Alice

SPIDERS from MARS

LP '76

Singles: 7-inch

PYE...3-5 76

LPs: 10/12-inch 33rpm

PYE...8-10 76

Also see BOWIE, David

SPIN

P&R '76

Singles: 7-inch

ARIOLA AMERICA 3-5 76

LPs: 10/12-inch 33rpm

ARIOLA AMERICA 8-10 76

SPINAL TAP

LP '84

Singles: 7-inch

POLYDOR 3-4 84

LPs: 10/12-inch 33rpm

POLYDOR 5-8 84

Also see CREDIBILITY GAP

Also see HEAR 'N AID

SPINNERS

(Spinners / Harvey)

P&R '61

Singles: 7-inch

ATLANTIC.....................................3-6 72-85

MOTOWN (1067 thru 1136) 8-15 64-68

MOTOWN (1155 "In My Diary")..............................500-1000 69

MOTOWN (1235 "Bad Bad Weather")......................................4-6 73

TRI-PHI (1001 "That's What Girls Are Made For") 10-20 61

TRI-PHI (1004 "Love") 15-20 61

TRI-PHI (1007 "What Did She Use") 15-20 62
TRI-PHI (1010 "She Loves Me So") 15-20 62
TRI-PHI (1013 "I've Been Hurt") 15-20 62
V.I.P. (25050 "In My Diary") 10-20 70

LPs: 10/12-inch 33rpm

ATLANTIC................................ 6-10 73-84
MOTOWN (Except 639)............. 5-10 73-82
MOTOWN (639 "Original Spinners") 20-40 67
PICKWICK 8-10 76
V.I.P. (405 "Second Time Around") 20-40 70

Members: Bobby Smith; Henry Fambrough; Pervis Jackson; Bill Henderson; G.C. Cameron; Philippe Wynne; Reese Palmer; Jim Knowland; Ed Edwards; Chester Simmons.
Also see ABBA / Spinners / Firefall / England Dan & John Ford Coley
Also see CAMERON, G.C.
Also see WARWICK, Dionne, & Spinners
Also see WYNNE, Philippe

SPIRAL STARECASE

P&R/LP '69

Singles: 7-inch

COLUMBIA 4-6 69-70

LPs: 10/12-inch 33rpm

COLUMBIA (9852 "More Today Than Yesterday") 15-20 69
COLUMBIA (10172 "More Today Than Yesterday") 8-12

Members: Pat Upton; Dick Lopes; Vinny Parello; Bob Raymond; Harvey Kaplan.

SPIRIT

LP '68

Singles: 12-inch 33/45rpm

MERCURY 4-6 84

Singles: 7-inch

EPIC... 3-6 70-74
MERCURY 3-5 75-76
ODE 4-8 68-70
POTATO 3-5 78
RHINO.. 3-4 81

Picture Sleeves

EPIC... 4-8 74
POTATO 3-4 78

LPs: 10/12-inch 33rpm

EPIC.. 8-12 70-73
MERCURY (Except 818514)..... 10-15 75-77
MERCURY (818514 "Spirit of '84").. 5-8 84
ODE (44003 "Spirit") 20-25 68
(Monaural.)
ODE (44004 "Spirit") 15-20 68
(Stereo.)
ODE (44014 "The Family That Plays Together") 10-20 68
ODE (44016 "Clear")................ 10-15 69
POTATO 10-15

RHINO 5-8 81

Members: Jay Ferguson; Randy California; Mark Andes; Ed Cassidy; John Locke; John Arliss.
Also see FERGUSON, Jay
Also see FIREFALL
Also see HEART
Also see YELLOW BALLOON

SPLINTER

P&R/LP '74

Singles: 7-inch

DARK HORSE 3-6 74-77

LPs: 10/12-inch 33rpm

DARK HORSE 8-10 74-77

Members: Bill Elliott; Bob Purvis.
Also see HARRISON, George

SPLIT ENZ

P&R/LP '80

Singles: 7-inch

A&M (Except 2339 & AMS-8128) ..3-5 80-84
A&M (2339 "One Step Ahead")......4-6 82
("Laser Etched Single.")
A&M (AMS-8128 "Shark Attack") 40-60 82
(Picture disc. Promotional issue only.)

Picture Sleeves

A&M 3-5 80-82

EPs: 7-inch 33/45rpm

A&M (4848 "I Don't Want to Dance")...................................15-25 81
(Picture disc. Promotional issue only.)

LPs: 10/12-inch 33rpm

A&M 5-10 80-84
CHRYSALIS...............................8-10 77

Members: Tim Finn; Neil Finn.
Also see CROWDED HOUSE
Also see FINN, Tim

SPOKESMEN

P&R '65

Singles: 7-inch

DECCA 4-8 65-66
WINCHESTER..............................4-8 67

LPs: 10/12-inch 33rpm

DECCA 25-30 65

Members: Johnny Madara; David White.

SPOOKY TOOTH
(Gary Wright's Spooky Tooth)

LP '69

Singles: 7-inch

A&M 4-6 69
MALA 5-10 68
ISLAND 3-5 72

LPs: 10/12-inch 33rpm

A&M 10-15 69-73
ACCORD 5-10 82
BELL 15-20 68
ISLAND.....................................8-10 73-74

Members: Gary Wright; Mike Harrison; Luther Grosvenor.
Also see BOXER
Also see GROSVENOR, Luther
Also see HARRISON, Mike

Also see WRIGHT, Gary

SPORTS

P&R/LP '79

Singles: 7–inch

ARISTA 3-5 79

Picture Sleeves

ARISTA 3-5 79

LPs: 10/12–inch 33rpm

ARISTA 5-10 79-80

SPRINGFIELD, Dusty

P&R/LP '64

Singles: 7–inch

ATLANTIC 3-6 68-71
CASABLANCA 3-5 82
DUNHILL 3-5 73
PHILIPS 4-8 63-68
20TH FOX 3-5 80
U.A. 3-5 77-79

Picture Sleeves

PHILIPS 5-10 64-67
ATLANTIC 4-6 68

LPs: 10/12–inch 33rpm

ATLANTIC 10-15 69-70
CASABLANCA 5-8 82
DUNHILL 8-10 73
PHILIPS 12-20 64-67
U.A. 5-10 78-79
WING 10-15 68

Also see HONDELLS / Dusty Springfield
Also see PET SHOP BOYS & Dusty Springfield
Also see SPRINGFIELDS

SPRINGFIELD, Rick

P&R/LP '72

Singles: 12–inch 33/45rpm

RCA 4-6 83-84

Singles: 7–inch

CAPITOL 3-6 72-73
CHELSEA 3-5 76-77
COLUMBIA 3-5 74
MERCURY 3-4 84-85
RCA 3-5 81-85

Picture Sleeves

CAPITOL 4-8 72
MERCURY 3-5 84
RCA 3-5 81-88

LPs: 10/12–inch 33rpm

CAPITOL (11000 series) 15-20 72-73
CAPITOL (16000 series) 5-10 81
CHELSEA 8-12 76
COLUMBIA (KC-32000 series) . 10-15 73
COLUMBIA (PC-32000 series) 5-8
MERCURY 5-8 84
RCA 5-10 80-88

SPRINGFIELD, Rick, & Randy Crawford

P&R '84

Singles: 7–inch

RCA 3-5 84

Picture Sleeves

RCA 3-5 84

Also see CRAWFORD, Randy
Also see SPRINGFIELD, Rick

SPRINGFIELDS

C&W/P&R '62

Singles: 7–inch

PHILIPS 4-6 62-63

LPs: 10/12–inch 33rpm

PHILIPS 15-25 62-63

Members: Dusty Springfield; Tom Springfield; Tim Field.
Also see SPRINGFIELD, Dusty

SPRINGSTEEN, Bruce

(With the E Street Band)

P&R/LP '75

Singles: 12–inch 33/45rpm

COLUMBIA (1329 "Santa Claus Is Comin' to Town") 30-40 81
(White label. Promotional issue only.)
COLUMBIA (2007 "I'm on Fire") 20-25 85
(Red label. Black and white cover. Promotional issue only.)
COLUMBIA (2082 "Glory Days") 20-25 85
(Red label. Black and white cover. Promotional issue only.)
COLUMBIA (2174 "I'm Goin' Down") 20-25 85
(Red label. Black and white cover. Promotional issue only.)
COLUMBIA (2233 "My Hometown") 20-25 85
(Red label. Black and white cover. Promotional issue only.)
COLUMBIA (2543 "Bruce Springsteen & E Street Band Live, 1975-85") 20-25 86
(Eight track sampler. Promotional issue only.)
COLUMBIA (05028 "Dancing in the Dark") 5-8 84
COLUMBIA (05028 "Dancing in the Dark") 20-30 84
(With black and white cover. Promotional issue only.)
COLUMBIA (05028 "Dancing in the Dark") 15-25 84
(Promotional issue with color cover and gold promo stamp.)
COLUMBIA (05087 "Cover Me") 5-8 84
COLUMBIA (05147 "Born in the USA") 4-6 84
COLUMBIA (05147 "Born in the USA") 15-20 84
(White label. Promotional issue only.)
COLUMBIA (44445 "Chimes of Freedom") 5-8 88

Singles: 7-inch

COLUMBIA (03243 "Hungry Heart") 3-5 84
COLUMBIA (04463 "Dancing in the Dark") 3-5 84
COLUMBIA (04561 "Cover Me")... 3-5 84
COLUMBIA (04680 "Born in the USA") 3-5 84
COLUMBIA (04772 "I'm on Fire").. 3-5 85
COLUMBIA (04924 "Glory Days"). 3-5 85
COLUMBIA (05606 "I'm Goin' Down") 3-5 85
COLUMBIA (05728 "My Hometown") 3-5 85
COLUMBIA (06432 "War").......... 3-4 86
COLUMBIA (06657 "Fire") 3-4 87
COLUMBIA (07595 "Brilliant Disguise").......... 3-4 87
COLUMBIA (07663 "Tunnel of Love").......... 3-4 87
COLUMBIA (07726 "One Step Up").......... 3-4 88
COLUMBIA (08400 series) 3-4 88
(Columbia Hall of Fame series.)
COLUMBIA (10209 "Born to Run") 10-15 75
COLUMBIA (10274 "Tenth Avenue Freeze-Out") 8-12 75
COLUMBIA (10763 "Prove It All Night") 8-12 78
COLUMBIA (10801 "Badlands") ... 3-6 78
COLUMBIA (11391 "Hungry Heart").......... 3-4 80
COLUMBIA (11431 "Fade Away"/ "To Be True") 15-25 81
COLUMBIA (11431 "Fade Away"/ "Be True").......... 3-4 81
COLUMBIA (33323 "Born to Run").......... 8-10 76
(Red label. Columbia Hall of Fame series.)
COLUMBIA (33323 "Born to Run") 3-4 84
(Gray label. Columbia Hall of Fame series.)
COLUMBIA (45805 "Blinded By the Light").......... 150-250 73
COLUMBIA (45864 "Spirit in the Night") 300-500 73

Promotional Singles: 7-inch

COLUMBIA (1329 "Santa Claus Is Comin' to Town").......... 10-15 81
COLUMBIA (2557 "War").......... 10-15 86
(Has 1:55 spoken intro on one side.)
COLUMBIA (04463 "Dancing in the Dark") 8-10 84
COLUMBIA (04561 "Cover Me"). 6-10 84
COLUMBIA (04680 "Born in the USA") 6-10 84
COLUMBIA (04772 "I'm on Fire") 6-10 85
COLUMBIA (04924 "Glory Days").......... 6-10 85
COLUMBIA (05606 "I'm Goin' Down") 6-10 85
COLUMBIA (05728 "My Hometown") 6-10 85
COLUMBIA (06432 "War").......... 5-8 86
COLUMBIA (07595 "Brilliant Disguise").......... 5-8 87
COLUMBIA (07663 "Tunnel of Love").......... 5-8 87
COLUMBIA (07726 "One Step Up").......... 5-8 88
COLUMBIA (10209 "Born to Run").......... 30-35 75
(With large letters on label.)
COLUMBIA (10209 "Born to Run").......... 20-25 75
(With small letters on label.)
COLUMBIA (10274 "Tenth Avenue Freeze-Out") 15-20 75
COLUMBIA (10763 "Prove It All Night") 15-20 78
COLUMBIA (10801 "Badlands") 15-20 78
COLUMBIA (11391 "Hungry Heart").......... 15-20 80
COLUMBIA (11431 "Fade Away").......... 10-15 81
COLUMBIA (45805 "Blinded By the Light").......... 45-55 73
COLUMBIA (45864 "Spirit in the Night").......... 35-45 73

Picture Sleeves

COLUMBIA (1329 "Santa Claus Is Comin' to Town").......... 15-20 81
(Promotional issue only.)
COLUMBIA (2557 "War").......... 10-15 86
(Sleeve for spoken intro promo.)
COLUMBIA (04463 "Dancing in the Dark").......... 5-10 84
COLUMBIA (04561 "Cover Me").. 5-10 84
COLUMBIA (04680 "Born in the USA").......... 5-10 84
COLUMBIA (04772 "I'm on Fire") 5-10 85
COLUMBIA (04924 "Glory Days") 5-10 85
COLUMBIA (05606 "I'm Goin' Down") 5-10 85
COLUMBIA (05728 "My Hometown") 5-10 85
COLUMBIA (06432 "War").......... 4-8 86
COLUMBIA (07595 "Brilliant Disguise").......... 4-8 87
COLUMBIA (07663 "Tunnel of Love").......... 4-8 87
COLUMBIA (07726 "One Step Up").......... 4-8 88
COLUMBIA (11391 "Hungry Heart").......... 4-8 80

COLUMBIA (11431 "Fade Away") 4-8 81
COLUMBIA (45805 "Blinded By the Light")........................... 100-150 73

LPs: 10/12-inch 33rpm

COLUMBIA (KC-31903 "Greetings from Asbury Park")................ 15-20 73
COLUMBIA (PC-31903 "Greetings from Asbury Park").................. 8-12 75
COLUMBIA (JC-31903 "Greetings from Asbury Park")..................... 5-8 78
COLUMBIA (KC-32432 "The Wild Innocent and the E Street Shuffle") 15-18 73
COLUMBIA (PC-32432 "The Wild Innocent and the E Street Shuffle") 10-15 73
COLUMBIA (JC-32432 "The Wild Innocent and the E Street Shuffle") 5-8 78
COLUMBIA (PC-33795 "Born to Run")..................................... 25-30 75
(Credits show Jon Landau as "John.")
COLUMBIA (PC-33795 "Born to Run")..................................... 15-20 75
(Has "Jon" correction strip applied to cover.)
COLUMBIA (PC-33795 "Born to Run")....................................... 8-12 75
(Has "Jon" correction printed on cover.)
COLUMBIA (JC-33795 "Born to Run")... 5-8 78
COLUMBIA (JC-35318 "Darkness on the Edge of Town") 5-8 78
COLUMBIA (36854 "The River") 10-15 80
COLUMBIA (38358 "Nebraska")... 5-8 82
COLUMBIA (38653 "Born in the USA")... 5-8 84
COLUMBIA (40558 "Bruce Springsteen & E Street Band Live, 1975-85").... 30-40 86
(Includes 36-page booklet.)
COLUMBIA (40999 "Tunnel of Love")... 5-8 87
COLUMBIA (HC-43795 "Born to Run")..................................... 25-35 80
(Half-speed mastered.)
COLUMBIA (HC-45318 "Darkness on the Edge of Town") 25-35 81
(Half-speed mastered.)

Promotional LPs

COLUMBIA (978 "As Requested Around the World")................................. 30-40 81
COLUMBIA (1957 "Born in the USA")...................................... 20-30 84
COLUMBIA (31903 "Greetings from Asbury Park")..................................... 35-45 73
(White label.)
COLUMBIA (32432 "The Wild Innocent and the E Street Shuffle") 35-45 73
(White label.)
COLUMBIA (33795 "Born to Run")............................... 750-1000 75
(With "script" title cover.)
COLUMBIA (33795 "Born to Run")..40-50 75
(White label.)
COLUMBIA (JC-35318 "Darkness on the Edge of Town") 30-40 78
(White label.)
COLUMBIA (PAL-35318 "Darkness on the Edge of Town") 75-125 78
(Picture disc.)
COLUMBIA (36854 "The River")......................................25-35 80
(White label.)
COLUMBIA (38358 "Nebraska") 15-25 82
(White label.)
COLUMBIA (38653 "Born in the USA")......................................15-20 84
(White label.)
Also see BONDS, Gary "U.S."
Also see CLEMONS, Clarence
Also see LITTLE STEVEN
Also see ORBISON, Roy
Also see PARKER, Graham
Also see SPECTOR, Ronnie
Also see THOMPSON, Robbin, Band
Also see U.S.A. for AFRICA

SPRINGSTEEN, Bruce / Jackson Browne

Singles: 12-inch 33/45rpm

ASYLUM (11442 "Medley")........40-50 70
(45rpm. Has plain sleeve with info sticker.)
Also see BROWNE, Jackson

SPRINGSTEEN, Bruce / Andy Pratt

Singles: 7-inch

COLUMBIA/PLAYBACK (AS-45 "Blinded by the Light")...........................40-50 73
(Add $40 to $50 if accompanied by booklet.)

Picture Sleeves

COLUMBIA/PLAYBACK (AS-45 "Blinded by the Light")............................5-10 73
Also see PRATT, Andy

SPRINGSTEEN, Bruce / Loudon Wainwright III / Taj Mahal / Albert Hammond

Singles: 7-inch

COLUMBIA/PLAYBACK (AS-52 "The Circus Song [Recorded Live]")..........75-100 73
(Add $40 to $50 if accompanied by booklet.)

Picture Sleeves

COLUMBIA/PLAYBACK (AS-52 "The Circus Song")......................................5-10 73
Also see HAMMOND, Albert
Also see TAJ MAHAL
Also see WAINWRIGHT, Loudon, III

SPRINGSTEEN, Bruce / Johnny Winter / Hollies

Singles: 7-inch

COLUMBIA/PLAYBACK (AS-66 "Rosalita")...............................60-75 73
(Add $40 to $50 if accompanied by booklet.)

Picture Sleeves

COLUMBIA/PLAYBACK (AS-66 "Rosalita") ... 5-10 73

Also see HOLLIES
Also see SPRINGSTEEN, Bruce
Also see WINTER, Johnny

SPRINGWELL

P&R '71

Singles: 7-inch

PARROT ... 3-5 71

SPYRO GYRA

P&R/LP '78

Singles: 7-inch

AMHERST ... 3-5 78
INFINITY ... 3-5 79
MCA ... 3-5 80-85

Picture Sleeves

INFINITY ... 3-5 79

EPs: 7-inch 33/45rpm

INFINITY (1011 "Live Spyro Gyra") ... 5-10 79
(Promotional issue only. With insert. Not issued with cover.)

LPs: 10/12-inch 33rpm

AMHERST ... 5-10 78
GRP ... 5-8 90-91
INFINITY ... 5-10 79
MCA (5000 series) ... 5-10 80-86
MCA (6000 series) ... 8-10 84-89
MCA (9004 "Morning Dance") ... 50-75 79
(Picture disc. Promotional issue only.)
MCA (42000 series) ... 5-8 87

Members: Chet Catallo; Jay Beckenstein.

SPYS

P&R/LP '82

Singles: 7-inch

EMI AMERICA ... 3-5 82

LPs: 10/12-inch 33rpm

EMI AMERICA ... 5-10 82

Also see FOREIGNER

SQUEEZE
(U.K. Squeeze)

LP '80

Singles: 7-inch

A&M ... 3-5 79-87

Picture Sleeves

A&M ... 3-5 80-87

LPs: 10/12-inch 33rpm

A&M (Except 3413 & 4687) ... 5-10 79-89
A&M (3413 "Squeeze") ... 10-20 72
A&M (4687 "U.K. Squeeze") ... 10-15 78
I.R.S. ... 5-8 90

Members: Chris Difford; Glenn Tilbrook; Jools Holland; Gilson Lavis; Keith Wilkinson; Andy Metcalfe.
Also see CARRACK, Paul
Also see DIFFORD & TILBROOK
Also see HOLLAND, Jools, & Millionaires

SQUIER, Billy

LP '80

Singles: 7-inch

CAPITOL (Except 79694) ... 3-5 80-88
CAPITOL (79694 "Don't You Love Me") ... 5-10 89
(Promotional issue only. Commercial single release on cassette only.)

Picture Sleeves

CAPITOL ... 3-5 80-86

LPs: 10/12-inch 33rpm

CAPITOL ... 5-10 80-91

SQUIRE, Chris

LP '76

Singles: 7-inch

ATLANTIC ... 3-5 76

LPs: 10/12-inch 33rpm

ATLANTIC ... 8-10 76

Also see YES

STABILIZERS

P&R '87

Singles: 7-inch

COLUMBIA ... 3-4 87

Picture Sleeves

COLUMBIA ... 3-4 87

STACEY Q
(Stacey Swain)

P&R/LP '86

Singles: 12-inch 33/45rpm

ATLANTIC ... 4-6 86-87

Singles: 7-inch

ATLANTIC ... 3-4 86-88
ON the SPOT ... 3-4 87

Picture Sleeves

ATLANTIC ... 3-4 86-88

LPs: 10/12-inch 33rpm

ATLANTIC ... 5-8 86-88

Also see SSQ

STACKHOUSE, Ruby
(Ruby Andrews)

Singles: 7-inch

KELLMAC ... 4-8 65

Also see ANDREWS, Ruby

STACKRIDGE

LP '74

Singles: 7-inch

DECCA ... 3-5 71-72
MCA ... 3-5 73
ROCKET ... 3-5 76
SIRE ... 3-5 74-75

LPs: 10/12-inch 33rpm

DECCA ... 10-12 71
MCA ... 8-10 73
ROCKET ... 5-10 76
SIRE ... 8-10 74-75

Members: Andrew Davis; Jim Warren; Mutter Slater.
Also see KORGIS

STACY, Clyde

(With the Nitecaps)

P&R '57

Singles: 7–inch

ARGYLE 8-12 59
BULLSEYE (Except 1008) 10-15 58
BULLSEYE (1008 "Sure Do Love You Baby") 35-50 58
CANDLELIGHT (1015 "Hoy Hoy") 30-40 57
G&H 10-20 58
LEN 15-25 61

STAFFORD, Jim

P&R '73

Singles: 7–inch

COLUMBIA 3-4 84
ELEKTRA 3-5 80-81
ISLAND 3-5 74
MGM 3-5 73-75
POLYDOR 3-5 75-78
TOWN HOUSE 3-5 82
W.B. 3-5 76-80

LPs: 10/12–inch 33rpm

MGM 8-10 74-75
POLYDOR 5-10 76

Also see LOBO

STAFFORD, Jo

P&R '44

Singles: 78rpm

CAPITOL 3-8 43-50
COLUMBIA 3-5 50-57
COLUMBIA/SNOWY BLEACH (22270 "St. Louis Blues") 10-15 50s
(Promotional issue for Snowy Bleach and Glass Wax. No actual label name shown. Seven-inch 78rpm. While were not sure if *I Only Have Eyes for You* exists on 78rpm, we are equally unsure as to whether this one came on 45rpm.)

Singles: 7–inch

COLPIX 4-6 62
COLUMBIA 5-10 50-60
DECCA 4-6 68
DOT 4-6 65
REPRISE 4-6 63

EPs: 7–inch 33/45rpm

CAPITOL 5-15 50-57
COLUMBIA 5-15 50-59

LPs: 10/12–inch 33rpm

BAINBRIDGE 5-8 82
CAPITOL (H-75 thru H-435) 20-40 50-53
(10–inch LPs.)
CAPITOL (T-197 thru T-435) 15-25 55
CAPITOL (T-1653 thru T-2166) 10-20 62-64
(Monaural.)
CAPITOL (ST-1653 thru ST-2166) 12-25 62-64
(Stereo.)
CAPITOL (9014 "Songs of Faith") 20-30 54
(10–inch LP.)
CAPITOL (11000 series) 5-8 79
COLUMBIA (584 thru 1339) 15-25 54-59
(Monaural.)
COLUMBIA (1561 "Jo Plus Jazz") 30-50 60
(Monaural.)
COLUMBIA (2500 series) 15-30 55
(10–inch LPs.)
COLUMBIA (6000 series) 20-35 50-54
(10–inch LPs.)
COLUMBIA (8080 "I'll Be Seeing You") 20-30 59
(Stereo.)
COLUMBIA (8139 "Ballad of the Blues") 20-30 59
(Stereo.)
COLUMBIA (8361 "Jo Plus Jazz") 40-60 60
(Stereo.)
COLUMBIA/SNOWY BLEACH (22500 "I Only Have Eyes for You") 15-25 50s
(Promotional issue for Snowy Bleach. No actual label name shown. While were not sure if *St. Louis Blues* exists on 45rpm, we are equally unsure as to whether this one came on 78rpm.)
DECCA 10-15 68
DOT 10-15 66
TRIBUTE 5-10 71
VOCALION 8-12 68-69

Also see EDWARDS, Jonathan & Darlene
Also see INGLE, Red, & Natural Seven
Also see LAINE, Frankie, & Jo Stafford
Also see MacRAE, Gordon, & Jo Stafford
Also see MERCER, Johnny, Jo Stafford & Pied Pipers
Also see PIED PIPERS
Also see WESTON, Paul

STAFFORD, Terry

P&R/LP '64

Singles: 7–inch

ATLANTIC 3-5 73-74
CASINO 3-5 77
COLLECTABLES 3-4 80s
CRUSADER 4-8 64
ERIC 3-5 70s
FIRSTLINE 3-5 81
LANA 3-6 60s
MGM 3-5 71
MELODYLAND 3-5 75
MERCURY 4-8 66
PLAYER 3-4 89
SIDEWALK 4-8 66-67
TERRIFIC 3-5
W.B. 3-6 69

LPs: 10/12–inch 33rpm

ATLANTIC 8-12 73

CRUSADER (1001 "Suspicion") 20-25 64
(Monaural)
CRUSADER (1001 "Suspicion") 25-35 64
(Stereo)
Session: Davie Allan.
Also see ALLAN, Davie

STAGE DOLLS

P&R/LP '89

Singles: 7–inch

CHRYSALIS.................................. 3-4 89

LPs: 10/12–inch 33rpm

CHRYSALIS.................................. 5-8 89

STALLION

P&R/LP '77

Singles: 7–inch

CASABLANCA.............................. 3-5 77-78

LPs: 10/12–inch 33rpm

CASABLANCA............................ 5-10 77-78

STALLONE, Frank

P&R '80

Singles: 12–inch 33/45rpm

RSO 4-6 83

Singles: 7–inch

POLYDOR.................................... 3-4 84-85
SCOTTI BROS.............................. 3-5 80

Picture Sleeves

POLYDOR.................................... 3-4 84

LPs: 10/12–inch 33rpm

POLYDOR.................................... 5-8 84

STAMPEDERS

P&R/LP '71

Singles: 7–inch

BELL 3-5 71
CAPITOL..................................... 3-5 73
FLASHBACK................................ 3-4 74
MGM 4-8 68
QUALITY..................................... 3-5 76

LPs: 10/12–inch 33rpm

BELL 10-15 71
CAPITOL................................... 8-12 73-74
PRIVATE STOCK/QUALITY 8-10 76

STAMPLEY, Joe

C&W '71

Singles: 7–inch

ABC 3-5 77
ABC/DOT.................................... 3-5 75-76
CHESS (1798 "Creation
of Love")................................. 10-20 63
DOT.. 3-6 70-74
EPIC... 3-5 75-86
EVERGREEN............................... 3-4 88-89
IMPERIAL 10-15 59
PARAMOUNT 3-6 70
PAULA 3-5 74

LPs: 10/12–inch 33rpm

ABC 5-10 77
ABC/DOT 8-12 74-76
ACCORD 5-10 82
DOT 8-12 73
EPIC.. 5-10 75-85
PHONORAMA 5-10 70s
Also see UNIQUES

STANDELLS

P&R/LP '66

Singles: 7–inch

COLLECTABLES.......................... 3-4 80s
LIBERTY 10-20 64
MGM 10-20 65
SUNSET 10-20 66
TOWER.................................... 10-20 66-68
VEE JAY 10-20 65

Picture Sleeves

TOWER.................................... 15-20 67
VEE JAY 15-25 65

LPs: 10/12–inch 33rpm

LIBERTY (3384 "In Person at
P.J.'s" 40-50 64
(Monaural.)
LIBERTY (7384 "In Person at
P.J.'s" 50-60 64
(Stereo.)
RHINO 5-8
SUNSET (1136 "Live and
Out of Sight") 15-25 66
(Monaural.)
SUNSET (5136 "Live and
Out of Sight") 20-30 66
(Stereo.)
TOWER (T-5027 "Dirty Water") .40-50 66
(Monaural.)
TOWER (ST-5027 "Dirty
Water")................................... 50-60 66
(Stereo.)
TOWER (T-5044 "Why Pick On
Me") 40-50 66
(Monaural.)
TOWER (ST-5044 "Why Pick On
Me") 50-60 66
(Stereo.)
TOWER (T-5049 "Hot Ones").... 40-50 66
(Monaural.)
TOWER (ST-5049 "Hot Ones").. 50-60 66
(Stereo.)
TOWER (T-5098 "Try It") 40-50 66
TOWER (ST-5098 "Try It")......... 50-60 66
Members: Dick Dodd; Larry Tamblyn; Gary Lane;
Tony Valentino; Dave Burke.

STANDLEY, Johnny

P&R '52

Singles: 78rpm

CAPITOL...................................... 3-5 52-56

Singles: 7–inch

CAPITOL.................................... 5-10 52-56
MAGNOLIA (1003 "Rock & Roll
Must Go")............................... 40-60 60

EPs: 7-inch 33/45rpm

CAPITOL (697 "It's in the Book") 25-35 52

STANKY BROWN GROUP
(Stanky Brown)

LP '76

Singles: 7-inch

SIRE 3-5 76-78

LPs: 10/12-inch 33rpm

SIRE 8-10 76-78

STANLEY, Michael, Band

LP '75

Singles: 7-inch

ARISTA 3-5 78-79
EMI AMERICA 3-5 80-83
EPIC 3-5 77
TUMBLEWEED 3-5 72-73

LPs: 10/12-inch 33rpm

ARISTA 5-8 78-79
EMI AMERICA 5-8 80-83
EPIC 8-10 75-76
MCA 10-12 73
TUMBLEWEED 8-12 73

Also see CIRCUS
Also see SILK

STANLEY, Pamala

D&D '83

Singles: 12-inch 33/45rpm

KOMANDER 4-6 83
MIRAGE 4-6 84-85
TSR 4-6 84

Singles: 7-inch

EMI AMERICA 3-5 79
MIRAGE 3-4 84-85

LPs: 10/12-inch 33rpm

EMI AMERICA 5-10 79

STANLEY, Paul

P&R/LP '78

Singles: 7-inch

CASABLANCA 3-5 78

LPs: 10/12-inch 33rpm

CASABLANCA (7123 "Paul Stanley") 12-20 78
(With poster order form.)
CASABLANCA (7123 "Paul Stanley") 8-12 78
(Without poster order form.)
CASABLANCA (PIX-7123 "Paul Stanley") 40-50 79
(Picture disc.)

Also see KISS

STANSFIELD, Lisa

P&R/LP '90

Singles: 7-inch

ARISTA 3-4 90

Picture Sleeves

ARISTA 3-4 90

LPs: 10/12-inch 33rpm

ARISTA 5-8 90

STAPLE SINGERS
(The Staples)

P&R '67

Singles: 7-inch

ABC 3-5 73
CURTOM 3-5 75-77
EPIC 3-6 64-71
PRIVATE I 3-4 84-86
RIVERSIDE 4-6 62-63
SHARP 4-8 60
STAX 3-6 68-74
20TH FOX 3-5 81
VEE JAY 4-8 59-62
W.B. 3-5 76-80

LPs: 10/12-inch 33rpm

BUDDAH 5-10 69
CREED 5-10 73
CURTOM 5-10 76
EPIC 8-12 65-71
EVEREST 8-12 68-69
FANTASY 5-10 73
51 WEST 5-8 80s
GOSPEL 5-15 59
HARMONY 5-10 72
MILESTONE 5-10 75
PRIVATE I 5-8 84-86
RIVERSIDE 10-15 62-65
STAX 5-10 68-81
20TH FOX 5-10 81
TRIP 5-10 71-77
VEE JAY 10-15 59-63
W.B. 5-10 76-78

Members: Mavis Staples; Roebuck Staples; Cleo Staples; Yvonne Staples.
Also see STAPLES, Mavis

STAPLES, Mavis

P&R/LP '70

Singles: 7-inch

CURTOM 3-5 77
PHONO 3-4 84
VOLT 3-5 70-72
W.B. 3-4 79-86

LPs: 10/12-inch 33rpm

VOLT 8-12 69-70
W.B. 5-10 79-86

Also see BELL, William, & Mavis Staples
Also see FLOYD, Eddie, & Mavis Staples
Also see STAPLE SINGERS

STAPLETON, Cyril, & His Orchestra

P&R '56

Singles: 78rpm

LONDON 3-5 51-63
MGM 3-5 55-56

Singles: 7-inch

DECCA 3-6 67
LONDON 4-8 51-63
MGM 4-8 55-56

STAGE 3-6 62

EPs: 7–inch 33/45rpm

LONDON 4-8 55-57
MGM 4-8 55-56

LPs: 10/12–inch 33rpm

IMPERIAL 5-10 61
LONDON 5-15 55-59
MGM 5-15 55-56
RICHMOND 5-15 59-61

STAR WARS INTERGALACTIC DROID CHOIR & CHORALE

P&R '80

Singles: 7–inch

RSO 3-5 80

Picture Sleeves

RSO 3-5 80

Also see MECO

STARBUCK

P&R/LP '76

Singles: 7–inch

A.V.I. 3-4 84
ATCO 3-5 73
ELEKTRA 3-5 71
PRIVATE STOCK 3-5 76-77
U.A. 3-5 78-79

LPs: 10/12–inch 33rpm

PHONORAMA 5-10 70s
PRIVATE STOCK 8-10 76
U.A. 8-10 78

Members: Bruce Blackman; James Cobb; Ken Crysler; Sloan Hayes; Dave Shaver; Bo Wagner.
Also see ETERNITY'S CHILDREN
Also see KORONA

STARCASTLE

LP '76

Singles: 7–inch

EPIC 3-5 76-78

LPs: 10/12–inch 33rpm

EPIC (Except PAL-34935) 5-10 76-79
EPIC (PAL-34935 "Citadel") 40-50 79
(Promotional issue only.)

STARCHER, Buddy

C&W '49

Singles: 78rpm

4 STAR 4-8 49-50s

Singles: 7–inch

BOONE 3-6 66
DECCA 3-6 66
4 STAR 5-10 50s
HEARTWARMING 3-5 67
STARDAY 4-8 59-66

EPs: 7–inch 33/45rpm

4 STAR 5-10 50s
STARDAY 5-10 61

LPs: 10/12–inch 33rpm

BLUEBONNET 8-12
DECCA 8-15 66
HEARTWARMING 5-10 68
STARDAY 8-15 62-66

STARGARD

P&R/LP '78

Singles: 12–inch 33/45rpm

W.B. 4-8 79-81

Singles: 7–inch

MCA 3-5 77-78
W.B. 3-5 79-81

LPs: 10/12–inch 33rpm

MCA 5-10 78-82
W.B. 5-10 79-81

STARGAZE

D&D '83

Singles: 12–inch 33/45rpm

T.N.T. 4-8 83

STARK & McBRIEN

P&R '75

Singles: 7–inch

RCA 3-5 74-76

LPs: 10/12–inch 33rpm

RCA 8-10 75

Members: Fred Stark; Rod McBrien.

STARLAND VOCAL BAND

P&R/C&W/LP '76

Singles: 7–inch

WINDSONG 3-5 76-80

LPs: 10/12–inch 33rpm

WINDSONG 8-10 76-80

Members: Bill Danoff; Taffy Danoff.

STARLETS

P&R '61

Singles: 7–inch

LUTE (5909 "I'm So Young") 15-20 60
PAM 8-12 61

Members: Maxine Edwards; Bernice Williams; Liz Walker.
Also see BLUE BELLES

STARPOINT

LP '81

Singles: 12–inch 33/45rpm

BOARDWALK 4-6 83
CHOCOLATE CITY 4-8 80-82
ELEKTRA 4-6 83-85

Singles: 7–inch

BOARDWALK 3-4 83
CHOCOLATE CITY 3-5 80-82
ELEKTRA 3-4 83-87

Picture Sleeves

ELEKTRA 3-4 85-87

LPs: 10/12–inch 33rpm

CHOCOLATE CITY 5-10 80-82
ELEKTRA 5-8 83-87

Also see DAWSON, Cliff, & Renee Diggs

STARR, Brenda K.

D&D '85

Singles: 12–inch 33/45rpm

MIRAGE 4-6 85

Singles: 7–inch

MIRAGE ... 3-4 85

LPs: 10/12–inch 33rpm

MCA ... 5-8 88

STARR, Edwin

P&R '65

Singles: 12–inch 33/45rpm

20TH FOX ... 4-8 77-80

Singles: 7–inch

CASABLANCA ... 3-4 84
GRANITE ... 3-5 75-76
GORDY (Black vinyl) ... 3-8 67-71
GORDY (Colored vinyl) ... 8-15
(Promotional issues only.)
MONTAGE ... 3-4 82
MOTOWN ... 3-5 73-74
RIC-TIC (103 "Agent Double-O Soul") ... 10-15 65
RIC-TIC (107 "Back Street") ... 10-15 65
RIC-TIC (109 "Stop Her On Sight [S.O.S.]") ... 10-15 66
RIC-TIC (109X "Scott's On Swingers [S.O.S.]") ... 40-50 66
(Promotional issue only.)
RIC-TIC (114 "Headline News") 10-15 66
RIC-TIC (118 "It's My Turn Now") ... 10-15 66
RIC-TIC (120 "You're My Mellow") ... 25-50 67
SOUL ... 3-5 72-73
20TH FOX ... 3-5 77-84

LPs: 10/12–inch 33rpm

GORDY (931 "Soul Masters") ... 15-25 68
GORDY (940 "25 Miles") ... 15-25 69
GORDY (948 "War & Peace") ... 10-20 70
GORDY (956 "Involved") ... 10-15 71
GRANITE ... 8-10 75
MOTOWN ... 8-10 73-82
20TH FOX ... 8-10 77-81

STARR, Edwin, & Blinky

Singles: 7–inch

GORDY ... 4-8 69

LPs: 10/12–inch 33rpm

GORDY (945 "Just We Two") ... 10-20 69

Also see BLINKY
Also see STARR, Edwin

STARR, Kay
(With the Crystalette All Stars)

P&R '48

Singles: 78rpm

CAPITOL ... 5-10 48-57
CORONET ... 10-20 60s
CRYSTALETTE ... 8-12 50
JEWEL (1000 "I Ain't Gonna Cry") ... 20-30 45
MODERN ... 10-20 49
RCA ... 3-5 55-57
RONDO-LETTE ... 10-20 60s

Singles: 7–inch

ABC ... 3-5 67-68
CAPITOL (811 thru 2887) ... 8-15 50-54
CAPITOL (4000 & 5000 series) ... 4-10 58-64
CRYSTALETTE (632 "Where Or When") ... 10-15 50
(Black vinyl.)
CRYSTALETTE (632 "Where Or When") ... 15-25 50
(Colored vinyl.)
DOT ... 3-6 68
GNP ... 3-5 74-75
HAPPY TIGER ... 3-5 70
RCA (0100 series) ... 3-5 73
RCA (6000 & 7000 series) ... 4-8 55-59

Picture Sleeves

CAPITOL ... 4-8 62

EPs: 7–inch 33/45rpm

CAPITOL ... 5-15 50-61
RCA ... 5-10 55-58

LPs: 10/12–inch 33rpm

ABC ... 5-15 68
CAMDEN ... 10-20 60-61
CAPITOL (H-211 "Songs By Kay Starr") ... 40-60 50
(10–inch LP.)
CAPITOL (T-211 "Songs By Kay Starr") ... 20-40 55
CAPITOL (H-415 "The Hits of Kay Starr") ... 20-35 53
(10–inch LP.)
CAPITOL (211 thru 1200) ... 15-25 53-59
CAPITOL (400 thru 900 series) ... 5-15 63-75
(With "DT" or "SM" prefix.)
CAPITOL (1300 series) ... 15-25 60
CAPITOL (T-1438 "Kay Starr, Jazz Singer") ... 20-30 60
(Monaural.)
CAPITOL (ST-1438 "Kay Starr, Jazz Singer") ... 25-35 60
(Stereo.)
CAPITOL (1468 thru 2100 series) ... 10-20 61-64
CAPITOL (11000 series) ... 5-10 74-79
CORONET ... 10-20 63
CRYSTALETTE (4500 "Kay Starr Sings") ... 50-100 52
(10–inch LP.)
GNP ... 5-10 74-75
LIBERTY (3280 "Swingin' with the Starr") ... 15-25 63
LIBERTY (9001 "Swingin' with the Starr") ... 35-45 56
RCA (1100 thru 1700 series) ... 15-25 55-57
RONDO-LETTE ... 20-30 58

STARR, Kay, & Count Basie

LPs: 10/12–inch 33rpm

MCA ... 5-8 83

PARAMOUNT 10-15 69
Also see BASIE, Count

STARR, Kay, & Tennessee Ernie Ford

Singles: 78rpm

CAPITOL.................................... 3-5 50-56

Singles: 7-inch

CAPITOL.................................. 5-10 50-56

EPs: 7-inch 33/45rpm

CAPITOL.................................. 5-15 56
Also see FORD, Tennessee Ernie

STARR, Kay / Erroll Garner

LPs: 10/12-inch 33rpm

CROWN 15-30 57
MODERN 25-35 56
Also see GARNER, Erroll
Also see STARR, Kay

STARR, Kenny

C&W '73

Singles: 7-inch

MCA 3-5 73-78
SRO 3-5 82
S.S. TITANIC 3-4 81

LPs: 10/12-inch 33rpm

MCA 5-10 75
SRO 5-10 82
Also see LYNN, Loretta

STARR, Lucille

P&R '64

Singles: 7-inch

A&M 4-8 66
ALMO 4-8 64-65
EPIC.. 4-6 67-69

LPs: 10/12-inch 33rpm

EPIC.. 8-12 69

STARR, Randy

P&R '57

Singles: 78rpm

DALE.. 4-8 57

Singles: 7-inch

DALE.. 8-12 57-59
MAYFLOWER 5-10 59
Also see ISLANDERS

STARR, Randy, & Frank Metis

LPs: 10/12-inch 33rpm

MAYFLOWER......................... 15-25 59
Also see STARR, Randy

STARR, Ringo

P&R/LP '70

Singles: 12-inch 33/45rpm

ATLANTIC (93 "Drowning in the Sea of Love") 15-20 77
(Promotional issue only.)

Singles: 7-inch

APPLE (1831 "It Don't Come Easy")....................................... 4-8 71
APPLE (1849 "Back Off Boogaloo") 10-15 72
(With a blue apple on the label.)
APPLE (1849 "Back Off Boogaloo") 4-6 73
(With a green apple on the label.)
APPLE (1865 "Photograph")..........3-5 73
APPLE (1870 "You're Sixteen") 5-8 73
(With standard apple label.)
APPLE (1870 "You're Sixteen") 4-6 73
(With 5-point star label.)
APPLE (1872 "Oh My My")...........4-6 74
APPLE (1876 "Only You")............4-6 74
APPLE (1880 "No No Song") 4-6 75
APPLE (1882 "It's All Down to Goodnight Vienna")......................4-6 75
APPLE (2969 "Beaucoups of Blues") 4-8 70
ATLANTIC (3361 "Dose of Rock 'N' Roll")..............................5-8 76
ATLANTIC (3371 "Hey Baby")..... 8-12 76
ATLANTIC (3412 "Drowning in the Sea of Love")...................10-20 77
ATLANTIC (3429 "Wings")..........8-12 77
BOARDWALK (130 "Wrack My Brain") 3-5 81
BOARDWALK (134 "Private Property")....................................3-5 82
CAPITOL (Orange label)...............4-8 75
CAPITOL (Purple label) 3-5 78
CAPITOL (Black label)..................3-4 83
PORTRAIT (70015 "Lipstick Traces") 5-10 78
PORTRAIT (70018 "Heart on My Sleeve")................................4-8 78

Picture Sleeves

APPLE (1826 "Beaucoups of Blues") 25-35 70
(Selection number 2969 mistakenly shown as Apple 1826.)
APPLE (1831 "It Don't Come Easy") 10-15 71
APPLE (1849 "Back Off Boogaloo") 10-15 72
APPLE (1865 "Photograph")........8-12 73
APPLE (1870 "You're Sixteen") ...8-12 73
APPLE (1876 "Only You")............5-10 74
APPLE (1882 "It's All Down to Goodnight Vienna")...................8-10 75
APPLE (2969 "Beaucoups of Blues") 12-18 70
(Selection number correctly shown.)
BOARDWALK (130 "Wrack My Brain")..3-5 81

Promotional Singles

APPLE (1831 "It Don't Come Easy") 15-20 71

APPLE (1849 "Back Off Boogaloo") 35-45 72
(White label.)
APPLE (1865 "Photograph") 20-30 73
APPLE (1870 "You're Sixteen") 20-30 73
APPLE (1872 "Oh My My") 20-30 74
APPLE (1876 "Only You") 20-30 74
APPLE (1880 "No No Song") 20-30 75
APPLE (1882 "It's All Down to Goodnight Vienna") 20-30 75
APPLE (1882 "Oo-Wee") 25-30 75
ATLANTIC (3361 "Dose of Rock 'N' Roll") 20-30 76
(White label.)
ATLANTIC (3361 "Dose of Rock 'N' Roll") 10-15 76
(Blue label.)
ATLANTIC (3371 "Hey Baby") .. 20-30 76
(White label.)
ATLANTIC (3371 "Hey Baby") .. 10-15 76
(Red-white and blue labels.)
ATLANTIC (3371 "Hey Baby") .. 25-35 76
(Single-sided disc.)
ATLANTIC (3412 "Drowning in the Sea of Love") 10-20 77
ATLANTIC (3429 "Wings") 20-25 77
(White label.)
ATLANTIC (3429 "Wings") 10-12 77
(Red-white and blue labels.)
BOARDWALK (130 "Wrack My Brain") 8-12 81
BOARDWALK (134 "Private Property") 8-12 82
PORTRAIT (70015 "Lipstick Traces") 8-12 78
PORTRAIT (70018 "Heart on My Sleeve") 8-12 78

LPs: 10/12–inch 33rpm

APPLE (3365 "Sentimental Journey") 10-15 70
APPLE (3368 "Beaucoups of Blues") 10-15 70
APPLE (3417 "Goodnight Vienna") 10-15 75
APPLE (3422 "Blast from Your Past") 10-15 75
APPLE (3413 "Ringo") 15-20 73
(Includes a 20-page booklet.)
APPLE (3413 "Ringo") 10-15 73
(With 4:05 version of *Six O'Clock*.)
ATLANTIC (18193 "Ringo's Rotogravure") 8-12 76
ATLANTIC (19108 "Ringo the 4th") 8-12 77
BOARDWALK (33246 "Stop and Smell the Roses") 8-10 81
CAPITOL 5-12 80-81
PORTRAIT (35378 "Bad Boy") ... 8-10 78

Promotional LPs

APPLE (3413 "Ringo") 100-125 73
(With 5:26 version of *Six O'Clock*. Some copies list the track at 5:26 though it actually runs only 4:05.)
ATLANTIC (18193 "Ringo's Rotogravure") 10-20 76
(With programming sticker on front cover.)
ATLANTIC (19108 "Ringo the 4th") 10-20 77
(With programming sticker on front cover.)
PORTRAIT (35378 "Bad Boy") .. 25-30 78
(Labels reads "Advance Promotion.")
PORTRAIT (35378 "Bad Boy") .. 15-20 78
(Labels reads "Demonstration, Not For Sale.")
Also see BEATLES
Also see CLAPTON, Eric
Also see FRAMPTON, Peter
Also see JOHN, Elton
Also see LOMAX, Jackie
Also see NILSSON
Also see OWENS, Buck, & Ringo Starr

STARS ON

(Stars on 45; Stars on Long Play)

P&R/LP '81

Singles: 12–Inch 33/45rpm

RADIO 5-8 81-82

Singles: 7–inch

RADIO 3-5 81-82
TWENTY-ONE 3-4 83

LPs: 10/12–inch 33rpm

RADIO 5-10 81-82
TWENTY-ONE 5-8 83

STARS on 45 Featuring Sam & Dave

Singles: 7–inch

TWENTY-ONE 3-4 85
Also see SAM & DAVE

STARSHINE

D&D '83

Singles: 12–inch 33/45rpm

PRELUDE 4-6 83

Singles: 7–inch

PRELUDE 3-4 83

STARSHIP

(Jefferson Starship)

P&R/LP '85

Singles: 7–inch

GRUNT 3-4 85-87
RCA 3-4 89

Picture Sleeves

RCA 3-5 89

LPs: 10/12–inch 33rpm

GRUNT 5-8 85-87
Also see JEFFERSON STARSHIP

STARZ

P&R/LP '76

Singles: 7–inch

CAPITOL 3-5 76-79
(Black vinyl.)
CAPITOL (4399 "Cherry Baby").. 5-10 77
(Colored vinyl.)

Picture Sleeves

CAPITOL 3-5 76-79

LPs: 10/12–inch 33rpm

CAPITOL 8-10 76-78
(Black vinyl.)
CAPITOL (11617 "Violation") 15-20 77
(Colored vinyl.)
VIOLATION 5-8 83
Member: Richie Ranno; Joe Dube; Brendan Harkin.

STATE of GRACE

D&D '83

Singles: 12–inch 33/45rpm

PROFILE 4-6 83

Singles: 7–inch

PROFILE 3-4 83

STATLER BROTHERS

C&W/P&R '65

Singles: 7–inch

COLUMBIA 4-6 64-69
MERCURY 3-6 70-90

LPs: 10/12–inch 33rpm

COLUMBIA (CL-2000 series).... 15-25 66-67
(Monaural.)
COLUMBIA (CS-9000 series) ... 12-25 66-69
(Stereo.)
COLUMBIA (PC-9000 series) 5-8 80s
COLUMBIA (31000 series) 8-10 70s
51 WEST 5-8 80s
HARMONY 6-12 71-73
MERCURY 5-10 71-90
PRIORITY 5-8 82
TIME-LIFE 5-8 81
Members: Harold Reid; Don Reid; Lew DeWitt; Phil Balsley; Jimmy Fortune.
Also see CASH, Johnny

STATON, Candi

P&R '69

Singles: 7–inch

FAME 3-6 69-73
L.A. 3-4 81
SUGAR HILL 3-4 82
UNITY (711 "Now That You Have the Upper Hand") 75-125
W.B. 3-5 74-80

LPs: 10/12–inch 33rpm

FAME 8-12 70-72
SUGAR HILL 5-8 82
W.B. 8-10 74-80
Also see SOURCE, & Candi Staton

STATON, Dakota

LP '58

Singles: 78rpm

CAPITOL 4-8 55-63

Singles: 7-Inch

CAPITOL 4-8 55-63
GROOVE MERCHANT 3-5 72

EPs: 7-Inch 33/45rpm

CAPITOL 5-15 58-60

LPs: 10/12-Inch 33rpm

CAPITOL (800 thru 1600 series) 20-40 58-63
HALF MOON 5-8 83
LONDON 10-15 67
U.A. 10-20 63-64
VERVE 8-12 71

STATUES

P&R '60

Singles: 7–inch

LIBERTY 10-20 60
Members: James "Buzz" Cason (a.k.a. Garry Miles); Richard Williams; Hugh Jarrett.
Also see MILES, Garry

STATUS QUO

P&R '68

Singles: 7–inch

A&M 3-5 73-74
CADET/CONCEPT 4-8 68-69
CAPITOL 3-5 75-77
JANUS 3-5 72
PYE 3-5 75
RIVA 3-5 80

LPs: 10/12–inch 33rpm

A&M 8-10 73-74
CADET CONCEPT 10-15 68
CAPITOL 8-10 74-79
JANUS 10-12 71
PYE 10-12 72
Also see BAND AID

STATUS VI

D&D '83

Singles: 12–inch 33/45rpm

RADAR 4-6 83

STEADY B

LP '87

LPs: 10/12–inch 33rpm

JIVE 5-8 87-88

STEALERS WHEEL

P&R/LP '73

Singles: 7–inch

A&M 3-5 73-78

Picture Sleeves

A&M 3-5 73

LPs: 10/12–inch 33rpm

A&M 6-12 73-78
PICKWICK 5-8 80
Members: Gerry Rafferty; Joe Egan.
Also see RAFFERTY, Gerry

STEALIN' HORSES

LP '88

Singles: 7-inch

ARISTA 3-4 88

LPs: 10/12-inch 33rpm

ARISTA 5-8 88

STEAM

P&R '69

Singles: 7-inch

FONTANA 3-6 69
MERCURY 3-5 70-76

Picture Sleeves

MERCURY (30160 "Na Na Hey Hey Kiss Him Goodbye") 10-15 76
(Promotional Chicago White Sox sleeve.)

LPs: 10/12-inch 33rpm

MERCURY 12-18 69

STEEL BREEZE

LP '82

Singles: 7-inch

RCA 3-4 82-83

LPs: 10/12-inch 33rpm

RCA 5-8 82

STEEL PULSE

LP '82

Singles: 7-inch

ELEKTRA 3-4 82-84

LPs: 10/12-inch 33rpm

ELEKTRA 5-8 82-84
MCA 5-8 88
MANGO 5-8 80

STEELE, Ben, & His Bare Hands

D&D '83

Singles: 12-inch 33/45rpm

VANITY 4-6 83

STEELE, Maureen

P&R '85

Singles: 7-inch

MOTOWN 3-4 85

Picture Sleeves

MOTOWN 3-4 85

STEELERS

P&R '69

Singles: 7-inch

DATE 4-8 69
EPIC 3-6 71

STEELEYE SPAN

LP '75

Singles: 7-inch

CHRYSALIS 3-5 72-78

LPs: 10/12-inch 33rpm

BIG TREE 12-15 71
CHRYSALIS 8-12 72-78
MFSL 25-50 79
TAKOMA 8-10 81

STEELY DAN

P&R/LP '72

Singles: 7-inch

ABC 3-5 72-78
MCA 3-5 78-81

EPs: 7-inch 33/45rpm

ABC 5-10 73-77
(Jukebox issues only.)

LPs: 10/12-inch 33rpm

ABC 6-10 72-78
COMMAND 8-10 74
MCA 5-10 79-82
MFSL 25-50 79

Members: Donald Fagen; Walter Becker; Jim Hodder; Jeff Baxter.
Also see FAGEN, Donald
Also see McDONALD, Michael
Also see ULTIMATE SPINACH

STEIN, Lou

P&R '57

Singles: 78rpm

BRUNSWICK 3-5 52-53
EPIC 3-5 55-56
JUBILEE 3-5 54
MERCURY 3-5 55-58
RKO UNIQUE 3-5 57

Singles: 7-inch

BRUNSWICK 4-6 52-53
EPIC 4-6 55-56
JUBILEE 4-6 54
MERCURY 4-6 55-58
MURBO 3-5 69
RKO UNIQUE 4-6 57

EPs: 7-inch 33/45rpm

EPIC 4-8 55-56
JUBILEE 4-8 54

LPs: 10/12-inch 33rpm

CHIAROSCURO 4-8 76-81
CORAL 5-15 53
EPIC 5-15 55-56
EVEREST 5-12 60
JUBILEE 5-15 54
MERCURY 5-15 55-60
MUSICOR 5-10 67-68
OLD TOWN 5-15 61
WING 5-10 62
WORLD JAZZ 4-8 81

Also see COLLINS, Al "Jazzbo," & Lou Stein

STEINBERG, David

LP '71

Singles: 7-inch

COLUMBIA 3-5 74

LPs: 10/12-inch 33rpm

COLUMBIA 5-10 74-75
ELEKTRA 5-10 70
UNI 8-15 68

STEINMAN, Jim

P&R/LP '81

Singles: 7–inch

EPIC/CLEVELAND INT'L 3-5 81

LPs: 10/12–inch 33rpm

EPIC/CLEVELAND INT'L 5-10 81

STEPHENSON, Van

P&R '81

Singles: 7–inch

HANDSHAKE 3-5 81
MCA 3-4 84

Picture Sleeves

MCA 3-4 84

LPs: 10/12–inch 33rpm

HANDSHAKE 5-10 81
MCA 5-8 84

STEPPENWOLF

P&R/LP '68

Singles: 7–inch

ABC 3-5 70
DUNHILL 4-8 67-71
IMMEDIATE 4-8 67
MCA 3-4 80s
MUMS 3-5 74-75
ROULETTE 3-5 70s

Picture Sleeves

DUNHILL 4-8 71
MUMS 3-5 74

EPs: 7–inch 33/45rpm

DUNHILL 5-10 68
(Jukebox issues only.)

LPs: 10/12–inch 33rpm

ABC 8-12 75-76
ALLEGIANCE 5-8
DUNHILL (Except 50053) 10-20 68-73
DUNHILL (50053 "At Your Birthday Party") 20-30 69
EPIC 8-12 75-76
MCA 5-10 79
MUMS 8-10 74

Members: John Kay; Goldy McJohn; Michael Monarch; Jerry Edmonton; Nick St. Nicholas.
Also see HARD TIMES
Also see KAY, John
Also see T.I.M.E.

STEREO FUN INC.

D&D '83

Singles: 12–inch 33/45rpm

MOBY DICK 4-6 83

STEREOS

Singles: 7–inch

MINK (22 "Memory Lane") 40-50 59
(*Memory Lane* was reissued later in 1959, showing the group as the Tams. the same track was again issued in 1963, shown as by the Tams and then by the Hippies.)
Also see HIPPIES / Reggie Harrison
Also see TAMS

STEREOS

P&R '61

Singles: 7–inch

CADET 4-8 67-68
COLLECTABLES 3-4 86
CUB (Except 9106) 10-20 61
CUB (9106 "Do You Love Me") 10-15 62
(Black vinyl.)
CUB (9106 "Do You Love Me") 25-35 62
(Black vinyl.)
GIBRALTAR (105 "Love for You") 20-25 59
(Dark blue label.)
GIBRALTAR (105 "Love for You") 10-15 59
(Light blue label.)
WORLD ARTISTS 10-15 63

Members: Bruce Robinson; Ronnie Collins; Sam Profit; George Otis; Nathaniel Hicks.

STEVE & EYDIE: see LAWRENCE, Steve, & Eydie Gorme

STEVENS, April
(April)

P&R '51

Singles: 78rpm

RCA 4-8 51-52
SOCIETY 8-12 50

Singles: 7–inch

A&M 3-5 72
ATCO 4-6 65
CONTRACT 4-8 61
IMPERIAL 4-8 59-65
KING 4-6 64
MGM 4-6 67
RCA 5-10 51-52
SOCIETY (10 "Don't Do It") 15-25 50
VERVE 3-5 71

EPs: 7–inch 33/45rpm

KING 10-20 54

LPs: 10/12–inch 33rpm

IMPERIAL 15-20 61-64
LIBERTY 5-8 83

Also see APRIL
Also see TEMPO, Nino, & April Stevens

STEVENS, April / Marg Phelan

LPs: 10/12–inch 33rpm

AUDIO LAB 15-20 59

Also see STEVENS, April

STEVENS, Cat

P&R/LP '71

Singles: 12–inch 33/45rpm

A&M 5-8 77

Singles: 7–inch

A&M 3-5 70-79
DERAM 4-6 66-72

Picture Sleeves

A&M 3-5 71-78

EPs: 7–inch 33/45rpm

A&M 8-10 70
(Jukebox issue only.)

LPs: 10/12–inch 33rpm

A&M 5-10 69-84
DERAM 10-15 67-72
LONDON 5-10 78
MFSL (035 "Tea for the Tillerman") 15-20 79
MFSL/UHQR (035 "Tea for the Tillerman") 30-40 79
(Boxed set.)

STEVENS, Connie

P&R '60

Singles: 7–inch

BELL 4-8 70-72
MGM 10-15 68
PARAMOUNT ("Why Can't He Care for Me") 35-50 58
(Promotional issue only. No actual label name or number is shown, but this may have been distributed by Paramount to promote the film, *Rock-A-Bye Baby*, in which Connie starred.)
W.B. (Except 5092) 5-10 59-66
W.B. (5092 "Apollo") 10-20 59

Picture Sleeves

W.B. (5159 "Too Young to Go Steady") 15-25 60

LPs: 10/12–inch 33rpm

HARMONY 10-20 69
W.B. (1208 "Conchetta") 40-50 58
W.B. (1335 thru 1460) 20-40 59-62
Also see BYRNES, Edward

STEVENS, Dodie

P&R '59

Singles: 7–inch

CRYSTALETTE 8-12 59
DOLTON 4-8 63
DOT 4-8 59-62
IMPERIAL 4-8 63

Picture Sleeves

CRYSTALETTE (724 "Pink Shoe Laces") 30-40 59

LPs: 10/12–inch 33rpm

DOT 20-30 60-61

STEVENS, Ray

(With the Merry Melody Singers)

P&R '61

Singles: 7–inch

BARNABY 3-5 70-76
CAPITOL 8-12 58-59
MCA (Except 53661) 3-4 85-89
MCA (53661 "I Saw Elvis in a UFO") 5-10 89
MERCURY (66 "Butch Barbarian") 5-10 64
(Promotional issue only.)
MERCURY (71000 & 72000 series) 4-8 61-68
MERCURY (810000 series) 3-5 83
MONUMENT 4-8 65-69
NRC 5-10 59-60
PREP 10-15 57
PRIORITY 3-4 80s
RCA 3-5 81-82
W.B./AHAB 3-5 76-79

Picture Sleeves

BARNABY 4-6 70
MCA 3-5 86
MERCURY 10-15 61-64
W.B./AHAB 3-5 79

EPs: 7–inch 33/45rpm

MERCURY (85 "Ray Stevens") 10-15 62
(Promotional issue only. Not issued with cover.)

LPs: 10/12–inch 33rpm

BARNABY 8-10 70-78
MCA 5-8 85-89
MERCURY (20732 "1,837 Seconds of Humor") 50-75 62
MERCURY (20732 "Ahab the Arab") 20-25 62
(Reissue of *1,837 Seconds of Humor.*)
MERCURY (20828 "This Is Ray Stevens") 20-30 63
MERCURY (60732 "1,837 Seconds of Humor") 60-80 62
MERCURY (60732 "Ahab the Arab") 25-35 62
(Reissue of *1,837 Seconds of Humor.*)
MERCURY (60828 "This Is Ray Stevens") 25-35 63
MERCURY (61272 "The Best of Ray Stevens") 10-15 70
MERCURY (810000 series) 5-8 83
MONUMENT 10-15 66-69
PICKWICK 5-10
PRIORITY 5-8 82
RCA 5-10 80-82
W.B. 5-10 76-79
WING 10-15 68
Session: Minnie Pearl; Jerry Clower.
Also see ARCHIES
Also see 4 SEASONS / Ray Stevens
Also see HENHOUSE FIVE PLUS TOO
Also see MINNIE PEARL
Also see ROE, Tommy / Bobby Rydell / Ray Stevens
Also see VELVETS

STEVENS, Ray / Hal Winters

LPs: 10/12–inch 33rpm

CROWN 12-18 63
Also see STEVENS, Ray

STEVENS, Shakin'

P&R '84

Singles: 7–inch

EPIC 3-5 81-84

EPIC/NU-DISKS 3-5 81-84

LPs: 10/12-inch 33rpm

EPIC 5-10 81-84

STEVENS, Steve

(Steve Stevens' Atomic Playboys)

LP '89

LPs: 10/12-inch 33rpm

W.B. 5-8 89

STEVENSON, B.W.

P&R/LP '73

Singles: 7-inch

MCA 3-5 80
PRIVATE STOCK 3-5 78
RCA 3-5 73
W.B. 3-5 77-78

LPs: 10/12-inch 33rpm

MCA 5-10 80
RCA 5-10 72-77
W.B. 5-10 77

STEVIE B

P&R/LP '88

Singles: 7-inch

LMR 3-4 87-90

LPs: 10/12-inch 33rpm

LMR 5-8 87

Also see JAYA

STEWART, Al

LP '74

Singles: 7-inch

ARISTA 3-5 78-82
ENIGMA 3-4 88
JANUS 3-5 74-77

Picture Sleeves

JANUS 3-5 74

LPs: 10/12-inch 33rpm

ARISTA (Except 40) 5-10 78-81
ARISTA (40 "Live Radio Concert") 25-35 80
(Promotional issue only.)
EPIC 20-25 70
JANUS 10-15 74-77
MFSL (009 "Year of the Cat") ... 30-60 78
MFSL (082 "Time Passages") ... 20-30 82

Also see PAGE, Jimmy

STEWART, Amii

P&R/LP '79

Singles: 12-inch 33/45rpm

ARIOLA 4-8 79
EMERGENCY 4-6 85

Singles: 7-inch

ARIOLA 3-5 79
EMERGENCY 3-4 85

LPs: 10/12-inch 33rpm

ARIOLA AMERICA 5-10 79
HANDSHAKE 5-8 81

STEWART, Amii, & Johnny Bristol

P&R '80

Singles: 7-inch

HANDSHAKE 3-5 80

Also see BRISTOL, Johnny
Also see STEWART, Amii

STEWART, Andy

P&R '61

Singles: 7-inch

CAPITOL 4-6 62
EPIC 4-6 64
WARWICK 4-8 61

LPs: 10/12-inch 33rpm

CAPITOL 5-15 62-72
EPIC 5-15 64-68
GREEN LINNET 4-8 83
WARWICK 15-25 61

STEWART, Baron

P&R '75

Singles: 7-inch

U.A. 3-5 75

LPs: 10/12-inch 33rpm

U.A. 8-10 75

STEWART, Billy

(With the Marquees)

P&R '62

Singles: 78rpm

ARGO 8-12 56
CHESS (1625 "Billy's Blues") 10-15 56

Singles: 7-inch

ARGO (5256 "Billy's Blues") 20-30 56
CHESS (Except 1625) 5-10 62-73
CHESS (1625 "Billy's Blues") 35-45 56
(Reissued three months later on Argo.)
ERIC 3-4 70s
OKEH (7095 "Baby, You're My Only Love") 150-200 57
U.A. 5-10 61

LPs: 10/12-inch 33rpm

CADET 8-10 74
CHESS 15-25 65-67

Also see STEWART, Billy

STEWART, Bobby

D&D '83

Singles: 12-inch 33/45rpm

SOS 5-8 82
W.B. 4-6 83

Singles: 7-inch

SOS 3-5 86

STEWART, Dave, & Barbara Gaskin

P&R '81

Singles: 7-inch

PLATINUM 3-5 81

STEWART, Gary
(With the Nashville Edition; with Dean Dillon)

C&W '73

Singles: 7-inch

CORY (101 "Walk On Boy")...... 10-20 64
DECCA.. 3-5 71
HIGHTONE.................................. 3-4 88-89
KAPP.. 3-6 68-70
MCA... 3-5 75
RCA.. 3-5 73-83
RED ASH.................................... 3-4 84

Picture Sleeves

RCA.. 3-5 82

LPs: 10/12-inch 33rpm

MCA... 4-8 75
RCA.. 5-10 75-83

STEWART, Jermaine

P&R/LP '85

Singles: 12-inch 33/45rpm

ARISTA....................................... 4-6 84-86

Singles: 7-inch

ARISTA....................................... 3-4 84-88

Picture Sleeves

ARISTA....................................... 3-4 86-88

LPs: 10/12-inch 33rpm

ARISTA....................................... 5-8 85-88
Also see CULTURE CLUB

STEWART, John

P&R/LP '69

Singles: 7-inch

ALLEGIANCE.............................. 3-4
CAPITOL..................................... 4-6 69
RCA.. 3-5 73-75
RSO... 3-5 77-80
W.B.. 3-5 71

LPs: 10/12-inch 33rpm

ALLEGIANCE.............................. 5-8 80s
CAPITOL..................................... 10-15 69-70
RCA.. 5-10 73-75
RSO... 5-10 77-80
SHIP... 5-8 87
W.B.. 8-12 71
Also see BUCKINGHAM, Lindsey
Also see KINGSTON TRIO
Also see NICKS, Stevie

STEWART, John, & Buffy Ford

LPs: 10/12-inch 33rpm

CAPITOL..................................... 10-15 68

STEWART, John, & Nick Reynolds

LPs: 10/12-inch 33rpm

TAKOMA...................................... 5-10
Also see KINGSTON TRIO
Also see STEWART, John

STEWART, Rod
(With Faces)

LP '69

Singles: 12-inch 33/45rpm

W.B.. 5-10 78-82

Singles: 7-inch

GEFFEN...................................... 3-4 87
GNP.. 3-5 73
MERCURY.................................... 4-8 70-76
PRESS (8722 "Good Morning Little Schoolgirl")..................... 15-25 65
PRIVATE STOCK......................... 3-5 76
W.B.. 3-4 75-86

Picture Sleeves

GEFFEN...................................... 3-4 87
MERCURY.................................... 5-15 72-73
W.B.. 3-5 78-89

LPs: 10/12-inch 33rpm

ACCORD...................................... 5-8 81
MERCURY (Except 61000 series).. 8-12 71-76
MERCURY (61000 series)......... 10-20 69-70
MFSL.. 25-50 81
PRIVATE STOCK......................... 8-10 77
SPRINGBOARD........................... 8-12 72
TRIP... 8-10 77
W.B. (Except BSP-3276)............ 5-10 75-88
W.B. (BSP-3276 "Blondes Have More Fun")............................. 10-15 79
(Picture disc.)
Also see BECK, Jeff, & Rod Stewart
Also see FACES
Also see PYTHON LEE JACKSON

STEWART, Rod, & Ronald Isley

P&R '90

Singles: 7-inch

W.B.. 3-4 90
Also see ISLEY, Ron
Also see STEWART, Rod

STEWART, Sandy

P&R '53

Singles: 78rpm

EPIC... 3-5 54
OKEH.. 3-5 53
20TH CENTURY........................... 3-5 54
X.. 3-5 55

Singles: 7-inch

ATCO.. 4-8 59
COLPIX....................................... 4-8 62-63
DCP.. 3-6 64
EAST WEST................................ 4-8 58
EPIC... 5-10 54
OKEH.. 5-10 53
20TH CENTURY........................... 5-10 54
U.A... 4-8 60-61
X.. 5-10 55

Picture Sleeves

COLPIX....................................... 5-10 62

LPs: 10/12-inch 33rpm

COLPIX (441 "My Coloring Book")...................................... 15-20 63

STEWART, Sandy / Dave Garroway

Singles: 7–inch

DICK CHARLES ("May You Always") 8-12 63
(Promotional issue only. No selection number used.)

STEWART, Wynn

(With the Tourists)

C&W '56

Singles: 78rpm

CAPITOL 3-5 56-57

Singles: 7–inch

ATLANTIC 3-4 74
CAPITOL (2000 series) 3-5 67-71
CAPITOL (3000 series) 6-12 56-57
CAPITOL (5000 series) 4-8 62-67
CHALLENGE 5-10 59-64
4 STAR 3-4 80
JACKPOT 10-15 59
PLAYBOY 3-5 75-76
PRETTY WORLD 3-4 85
RCA 3-5 72-73
WINS 3-5 78-79

Picture Sleeves

CAPITOL 4-8 67-69

LPs: 10/12–inch 33rpm

CAPITOL 5-15 67-75
PICKWICK/HILLTOP 5-12 67
PLAYBOY 5-10 76
STARDAY 8-12 68
WRANGLER (1006 "Wynn Stewart") 20-30 62

Member: Bobby Austin.
Also see PIERCE, Webb / Wynn Stewart

STEWART, Wynn, & Jan Howard

C&W '60

Singles: 7–inch

CHALLENGE 5-10 60

STILLS, Stephen

(With Manassas; with Michael Finnigan)

P&R/LP '70

Singles: 7–inch

ATLANTIC 3-5 70-73
COLUMBIA 3-5 75-78

Picture Sleeves

ATLANTIC 3-5 71-84

LPs: 10/12–inch 33rpm

ATLANTIC 5-10 70-84
COLUMBIA (Except PCQ-33575) 5-10 75-78
COLUMBIA (PCQ-33575 Stills") 10-15 75
(Quadrophonic.)

Also see AU GO-GO SINGERS
Also see BLOOMFIELD, Mike, Al Kooper & Steve Stills
Also see BUFFALO SPRINGFIELD
Also see CROSBY, STILLS & NASH
Also see JEFFERSON AIRPLANE
Also see MANASSAS
Also see STILLS - YOUNG BAND

STILLS - YOUNG BAND

LP '76

Singles: 7–inch

REPRISE 3-5 77

LPs: 10/12–inch 33rpm

REPRISE 5-10 76

Members: Stephen Stills; Neil Young.
Also see STILLS, Stephen
Also see YOUNG, Neil

STILLWATER

P&R '77

Singles: 7–inch

CAPRICORN 3-5 77-78

LPs: 10/12–inch 33rpm

CAPRICORN 5-10 78-79

Member: Jimmy Hall.

STING

(Gordon Sumner)

P&R/D&D/LP '85

Singles: 12–inch 33/45rpm

A&M 4-6 85-87

Singles: 7–inch

A&M 3-4 85-90
ABC 3-5 78

Picture Sleeves

A&M 3-4 85-88

LPs: 10/12–inch 33rpm

A&M 5-8 85-90
ABC 5-10 78

Also see BAND AID
Also see POLICE

STITES, Gary

P&R '59

Singles: 7–inch

CARLTON 10-15 59-60
EPIC 4-8 66
MADISON 10-15 60-61
MR. PEEKE 8-12 62

LPs: 10/12–inch 33rpm

CARLTON (STLP-120 "Lonely for You") 40-50 60
(Monaural.)
CARLTON (STLP-120 "Lonely for You") 50-75 60
(Stereo.)

STITES, Gary, & Sammi Smith

Singles: 7–inch

JEANNIE 3-6

Also see SMITH, Sammi
Also see STITES, Gary

STITT, Sonny

LP '67

Singles: 7-Inch

ARGO 4-8 58-65
ATLANTIC 4-6 63
CADET 3-5 74
CATALYST 3-5 77

ENTERPRISE 3-5 69
IMPULSE 4-6 64
PRESTIGE 3-6 63-69
ROULETTE 4-6 65-67
WINGATE 8-15 65
WORLD PACIFIC 4-6 63

EPs: 7-Inch 33/45rpm

PRESTIGE 10-25 53

LPs: 10/12-Inch 33rpm

ARGO 20-40 58-65
ATLANTIC 15-30 62-64
CADET 10-25 65-74
CATALYST 5-10 76-77
CHESS 8-12 76
COLPIX 10-20 66
EVEREST 5-8 82
FLYING DUTCHMAN 5-10 75-76
IMPULSE 15-25 63-64
JAMAL 8-12 71
JAZZLAND 20-40 62
JAZZTONE (1231 "Early Modern") 40-60 56
JAZZTONE (1263 "Early Modern") 30-50 57
MUSE 5-10 73-82
PACIFIC JAZZ 20-30 63
PAULA 5-10 74
PRESTIGE (060 "Kaleidoscope") 5-10 83
PRESTIGE (103 "Sonny Stitt Plays") 100-150 51
(10–inch LP.)
PRESTIGE (111 "Mr. Saxophone") 100-150 51
(10–inch LP.)
PRESTIGE (126 "Favorites") 100-150 52
(10–inch LP.)
PRESTIGE (148 "Favorites") 100-150 53
(10–inch LP.)
PRESTIGE (7000 series) 25-50 56-64
(Yellow label.)
PRESTIGE (7000 series) 10-25 65-70
(Blue labels.)
PRESTIGE (10000 series) 8-12 71-74
PRESTIGE (20000 series) 8-15 74
ROOST (418 "At the Hi Hat") 150-250 52
(10–inch LP.)
ROOST (1200 series) 30-50 56
ROOST (2200 series) 15-35 57-66
ROULETTE 10-25 65-70
SAVOY (9006 "Be-Bop") 100-150 53
(10–inch LP.)
SOLID STATE 10-15 69
TRIP 8-12 73
UPFRONT 5-10 77
VERVE 25-50 57-59
(Reads "Verve Records, Inc." at bottom of label.)
VERVE 12-25 62-72
(Reads "MGM Records - A Division Of Metro-Goldwyn-Mayer, Inc." at bottom of label.)
VERVE 5-10 73-84
(Reads "Manufactured By MGM Record Corp." or mentions either Polydor or Polygram at bottom of label.)

STITT, Sonny, Kai Winding & Horace Silver

LPs: 10/12–inch 33rpm

ROOST (415 "From the Pen of Johnny Richards") 150-250 52
(10–inch LP.)
Also see AMMONS, Gene, & Sonny Stitt
Also see SILVER, Horace
Also see WINDING, Kai

STOKES, Simon

(With the Nighthawks; Simon T. Stokes)

P&R '69

Singles: 7–inch

CASABLANCA 3-5 74
ELEKTRA 4-8 69-70
IN SOUND 5-10 68
U.A. 3-5 77

LPs: 10/12–inch 33rpm

MGM 10-15 70
SPINDIZZY 8-12 73
U.A. 5-10 77

STOLOFF, Morris

(Morris Stoloff Conducts the Columbia Studio Orchestra)

P&R '56

Singles: 78rpm

DECCA 3-5 56
MERCURY 3-5 54

Singles: 7–inch

COLPIX 4-8 59
DECCA 4-8 56
MERCURY 4-8 54
REPRISE 3-6 65

LPs: 10/12–inch 33rpm

DECCA 5-15 56
W.B. (1416 "Fanny") 25-35 61
(Soundtrack.)

STOMPERS

P&R '62

Singles: 7–inch

LANDA 10-20 61-62
MERCURY (72111 "Frump") 8-12 63
Members: Bobby Pickett; Leonard Capizzi; Bill Capizzi; Ron Deltorto; Lou Toscano; Don Squire.
Also see PICKETT, Bobby

STOMPERS

P&R '83

Singles: 7–inch

BOARDWALK 3-5 83
MERCURY (880000 series) 3-4 84

LPs: 10/12–inch 33rpm

MERCURY 5-8 84

STOMPERS / Dick Dale

LPs: 10/12-inch 33rpm

CLOISTER (6301 "Sounds of the Silver Surf") 50-75 63

Also see DALE, Dick

STONE, Cliffie, & His Orchestra

(With His Barn Dance Band; Cliffie Stone Singers)

C&W '47

Singles: 78rpm

CAPITOL (Except 2910) 3-6 47-57

CAPITOL (2910 "Blue Moon of Kentucky")................................ 4-8 54

Singles: 7-inch

CAPITOL (Except 2910) 4-10 50-69

CAPITOL (2910 "Blue Moon of Kentucky")............................ 10-20 54

TOWER.. 3-6 67

LPs: 10/12-inch 33rpm

CAPITOL (100 thru 300 series)... 5-10 68-69

CAPITOL (1000 thru 1600 series) 20-40 58-62

CAPITOL (2100 series)............ 10-20 64

TOWER...................................... 10-15 67

STONE, Doug

LP '90

LPs: 10/12-inch 33rpm

EPIC.. 5-8 90

STONE, Kirby, Four

(Kirby Stone Quartet)

P&R/LP '58

Singles: 78rpm

COLUMBIA 3-5 57

Singles: 7-inch

COLUMBIA 4-8 57-65

MGM 4-6 67

W.B. 4-6 63-64

LPs: 10/12-inch 33rpm

COLUMBIA 10-20 58-62

W.B. 10-15 63-64

Members: Kirby Stone; Edward Hall; Michael Gardner; Larry Foster.

STONE, Sly

(Sylvester "Sly Stone" Stewart)

LP '75

Singles: 12-inch 33/45rpm

EPIC.. 4-8 80

Singles: 7-inch

EPIC.. 3-5 75-79

LPs: 10/12-inch 33rpm

EPIC.. 5-10 79

Also see JOHNSON, Jesse, & Sly Stone

Also see SLY & Family Stone

Also see STEWART, Sly

STONE FURY

LP '84

Singles: 7-inch

MCA 3-4 84

LPs: 10/12-inch 33rpm

MCA...5-8 84

STONE PONEYS

(Featuring Linda Ronstadt)

P&R/LP '67

Singles: 7-inch

CAPITOL....................................5-10 67

Picture Sleeves

CAPITOL....................................5-10 67

LPs: 10/12-inch 33rpm

CAPITOL (2600 & 2700 series) .20-30 67

Also see RONSTADT, Linda

STONE ROSES

LP '90

LPs: 10/12-inch 33rpm

SILVERTONE 5-8 90

STONEBOLT

P&R '78

Singles: 7-inch

PARACHUTE...............................3-5 78-79

RCA 3-5 80

LPs: 10/12-inch 33rpm

PARACHUTE.............................5-10 78

RCA 5-10 80

STONEY & Meat Loaf

P&R '71

Singles: 7-inch

RARE EARTH...............................3-5 71

LPs: 10/12-inch 33rpm

PRODIGAL 5-10 78

RARE EARTH............................10-15 71

Also see MEAT LOAF

STOOGES

(Featuring Iggy Pop)

LP '69

Singles: 7-inch

ELEKTRA..................................5-10 69-70

LPs: 10/12-inch 33rpm

ELEKTRA................................15-25 69-70

Also see POP, Iggy

STOOKEY, Paul

P&R/LP '71

Singles: 7-inch

ERIC 3-5 70s

W.B. 3-5 71-72

LPs: 10/12-inch 33rpm

NEWPAX 5-8

W.B. 8-10 71

Also see PETER, PAUL & MARY

STOREY SISTERS

P&R '58

Singles: 7-inch

BATON.....................................10-20 58

CAMEO....................................10-20 58

MERCURY................................10-15 59

Members: Lillian Storey; Ann Storey.

STORIES

P&R/LP '72

Singles: 7–inch

ERIC 3-5 70s
KAMA SUTRA (Except 545) 3-5 72-74
KAMA SUTRA (545 "I'm Coming Home") 5-8 72
(Cardboard cover.)
RADIOACTIVE GOLD 3-5 74

LPs: 10/12–inch 33rpm

KAMA SUTRA 8-12 72-73

Members: Michael Brown; Ian Lloyd; Bryan Madey; Steve Love.
Also see BROWN, Michael
Also see LLOYD, Ian

STORM, Billy
(With the Valiants)

P&R '59

Singles: 7–inch

ATLANTIC 10-15 60-61
BUENA VISTA 4-8 63
COLUMBIA 8-12 59
ENSIGN 8-12 59
GREGMARK 5-10 61
HBR (474 "Please Don't Mention Her Name") 10-15 66
INFINITY 5-15 62-63
LOMA 5-10 64-65
ODE 4-8 69

Picture Sleeves

HBR (474 "Please Don't Mention Her Name") 15-20 66

LPs: 10/12–inch 33rpm

BUENA VISTA (3315 "Billy Storm") 25-50 63
FAMOUS (504 "This Is the Night") 20-30 69

Also see VALIANTS

STORM, Gale
(With Billy Vaughn's Orchestra)

P&R '55

Singles: 78rpm

DOT 5-10 55-56

Singles: 7–inch

CONFIDEO 5-10
DOT (Maroon label) 10-20 55-56
DOT (Black label) 5-10 57-60
DOT (Orange label) 3-6 60s

Picture Sleeves

DOT 10-20 58

EPs: 7–inch 33/45rpm

DOT 15-25 55-56

LPs: 10/12–inch 33rpm

DOT 25-35 56-59
HAMILTON 10-15 66
MCA 5-10 82

Also see VAUGHN, Billy, Orchestra

STORM, Warren

P&R '58

Singles: 7–inch

ATCO 3-6 68
DOT 4-8 61
KINGFISH 4-8
NASCO 5-10 58-60
ROCKO 10-15
SINCERE 10-15
SOUTH STAR 3-4 83
STARFLITE 3-5 79
ZYNN 10-20

Also see SHONDELLS / Rod Bernard / Warren Storm / Skip Stewart

STOTT, Lally

P&R '71

Singles: 7–inch

PHILIPS 3-5 71

STRAIT, George

C&W '81

Singles: 7–inch

D 15-25 76
MCA 3-5 81-91

LPs: 10/12–inch 33rpm

MCA 5-10 81-91

STRANGE, Billy
(With the Telstars; with Transients)

P&R/LP '64

Singles: 78rpm

CAPITOL 3-5 54-55
DECCA 3-5 55

Singles: 7–inch

BUENA VISTA 4-8 62-63
CAPITOL 5-10 54-55
COLISEUM 4-8 63
DECCA 5-10 55
GNP 4-8 64-65
LIBERTY 4-8 61-62
TOWER 4-6 69

LPs: 10/12–inch 33rpm

COLISEUM 10-20 62
GNP 5-15 63-75
HORIZON 10-15 63
SUNSET 8-10 68
SURREY 10-15 65
TRADITION 8-12 68

Also see CAMPBELL, Glen, & Billy Strange
Also see NELSON, Willie

STRANGELOVES

P&R/LP '65

Singles: 7–inch

BANG 5-10 65-67
SIRE 4-8 68
SWAN 8-10 64

LPs: 10/12–inch 33rpm

BANG (BLP-211 "I Want Candy") 35-45 65
(Monaural.)

STRANGERS

BANG (BLPS-211 "I Want Candy") 45-65 65
(Stereo.)
Members: Bob Feldman; Jerry Goldstein; Richie Gottehrer.
Also see McCOYS

STRANGERS

P&R '59

Singles: 7-inch

TITAN 10-20 59-60
Member: Joel Hill.

STRANGLERS

LP '87

Singles: 12-inch 33/45rpm

EPIC 4-6 83

Singles: 7-inch

A&M 3-5 77

LPs: 10/12-inch 33rpm

A&M (Black vinyl) 5-10 77-78
A&M (Colored vinyl) 10-15 78
(Promotional only.)
EPIC 5-8 83-87
I.R.S 5-10 80
STIFF 5-10 81

STRAWBERRY ALARM CLOCK

P&R/LP '67

Singles: 7-inch

ALL AMERICAN (373 "Incense and Peppermints") 40-60 67
MCA 3-4 80s
UNI (Except 55218) 5-15 67-70
UNI (55218 "California Day") 10-20 70

LPs: 10/12-inch 33rpm

BACK-TRAC 5-10 85
UNI 20-40 67-70
VOCALION 15-20 71
Members: George Munford; Randy Seol; Ed King; Lee Freeman; George Bunnel; Gary Loverto; Mark Weitz.
Also see LYNYRD SKYNYRD
Also see SIXPENCE
Also see WHO / Strawberry Alarm Clock

STRAWBS

LP '72

Singles: 7-inch

A&M 4-8 68-75
ARISTA 3-5 78
OYSTER 3-5 76-77

LPs: 10/12-inch 33rpm

A&M 8-15 71-78
ARISTA 5-10 78
OYSTER 8-10 76-77
Also see DENNY, Sandy, & Strawbs
Also see WAKEMAN, Rick

STRAY CATS

P&R/LP '82

Singles: 7-inch

EMI AMERICA 3-5 82-86

Picture Sleeves

EMI AMERICA 3-5 82-84

EPs: 7-inch 33/45rpm

EMI AMERICA 5-8 83

LPs: 10/12-inch 33rpm

EMI (91401 "Blast Off") 5-10 89
EMI AMERICA (17070 "Built for Speed") 5-10 82
EMI AMERICA (17102 "Rant'n Rave with the Stray Cats") 5-10 83
Members: Brian Setzer; Lee Rocker; Slim Jim Phantom; Brian McDonald; Gary Barnacle; Lee Allen.
Also see ALLEN, Lee
Also see PHANTOM, ROCKER & SLICK
Also see SETZER, Brian

STREEK

P&R '81

Singles: 7-inch

COLUMBIA 3-5 81

LPs: 10/12-inch 33rpm

COLUMBIA 5-10 81

STREET, Janey

P&R/LP '84

Singles: 7-inch

ARISTA 3-4 84

Picture Sleeves

ARISTA 3-4 84

LPs: 10/12-inch 33rpm

ARISTA 5-8 84-85

STREET PEOPLE

P&R '70

Singles: 7-inch

MUSICOR 4-6 69-70
VIGOR 3-5 75-77

LPs: 10/12-inch 33rpm

MUSICOR 15-20 70
PICKWICK 8-10 72
Also see HOLMES, Rupert

STREETS
(Nightstreets)

P&R/LP '83

Singles: 7-inch

ATLANTIC 3-4 83-84
EPIC 3-5 79-80

LPs: 10/12-inch 33rpm

ATLANTIC 5-8 83-84
EPIC 5-10 79
Member: Steve Walsh; Rick Taylor; Rick Taylor; Joyce Hawthorne.
Also see KANSAS

STREISAND, Barbra

LP '63

Singles: 12-inch 33/45rpm

COLUMBIA (White labels) 12-25 79-85
(Promotional issues only.)

Singles: 7-inch

ARISTA (123 "More Than You Know") 4-6 75

COLUMBIA (04000 & 05000 series) 3-4 83-86
COLUMBIA (10000 & 11000 series) 3-5 76-80
COLUMBIA (3-42648 "My Coloring Book") 20-30 62
(Compact 33 Single.)
COLUMBIA (4-42648 "My Coloring Book") 8-12 62
COLUMBIA (42631 "Happy Days Are Here Again") 5-10 63
COLUMBIA (42965 thru 43469).... 4-6 64-65
COLUMBIA (43518 thru 46024).... 3-5 66-74

Promotional Singles

COLUMBIA (04000 & 05000 series) 3-5 83-86
COLUMBIA (10000 & 11000 series) 3-5 76-80
COLUMBIA (4-42648 "My Coloring Book") 15-25 62
COLUMBIA (42631 "Happy Days Are Here Again") 10-15 63
COLUMBIA (42965 thru 43469).. 5-10 64-65
COLUMBIA (43518 thru 46024).... 4-8 66-74

Picture Sleeves

COLUMBIA (Except 43000 series) 3-5 73-85
COLUMBIA (43000 series) 4-8 66

LPs: 10/12–inch 33rpm

ARISTA 8-10 75
CAPITOL (2059 "Funny Girl") ... 10-20 64
COLUMBIA (1779 "The Legend of Barbra Streisand") 35-45 83
(Promotional, one-hour interview program.)
COLUMBIA (1791 "Makes Me Feel") 15-20 83
(Picture disc. Promotional issue only.)
COLUMBIA (CL-2007 thru CL-2682) 15-25 63-67
(Monaural. Black vinyl.)
COLUMBIA (2054 "The Second Barbra Streisand Album") 30-50 63
(Colored vinyl. Promotional issue only.)
COLUMBIA (2478 "Color Me Barbra") 30-50 66
(Colored vinyl. Promotional issue only.)
COLUMBIA (3220 "Funny Girl") 10-15 68
COLUMBIA (CS-8807 thru CS-9557) 15-25 63-68
(Stereo. Black vinyl.)
COLUMBIA (8854 "The Second Barbra Streisand Album") 40-60 63
(Colored vinyl. Promotional issue only.)
COLUMBIA (9278 "Color Me Barbra") 40-60 66
(Colored vinyl. Promotional issue only.)
COLUMBIA (9710 thru 9968).... 10-15 68-70
COLUMBIA (PC-8000 & PC-9000 series) 5-8
COLUMBIA (JC-9000 series)........ 5-8
COLUMBIA (30086 thru 39480)...5-15 70-84
With "FC," "JC," "KC," or "PC" prefix.)
COLUMBIA (30378 thru 33815).10-20 71-75
(Quadrophonic. With "PCQ" prefix.)
COLUMBIA (39909 "Emotion")..10-15 85
(Picture disc.)
COLUMBIA (40092 thru 45369)...5-10 85-89
COLUMBIA (42801 thru 47678).15-30 82
(Half-speed mastered. With "HC" prefix.)
20TH FOX........ 10-15 69

Also see ARLEN, Harold, with "Friend"
Also see BLOOD, SWEAT & TEARS

STREISAND, Barbra, & Kim Carnes

P&R '84

Singles: 7–inch

COLUMBIA 3-4 84

Also see CARNES, Kim

STREISAND, Barbra/ Marilyn Cooper

Singles: 7–inch

COLUMBIA 5-10
(Promotional issue only.)

STREISAND, Barbra / Doris Day / Jim Nabors / Andre Kostelanetz

LPs: 10/12–inch 33rpm

COLUMBIA (1075 "Season's Greetings from Barbra Streisand & Friends")...15-25
(Special products issue for Maxwell House Coffee Co.)

Also see DAY, Doris
Also see KOSTELANETZ, Andre, & His Orchestra
Also see NABORS, Jim

STREISAND, Barbra, & Neil Diamond

P&R '78

Singles: 7–inch

COLUMBIA 3-5 78

Also see DIAMOND, Neil

STREISAND, Barbra, & Barry Gibb

P&R '80

Singles: 7–inch

COLUMBIA 3-4 80-81

Also see GIBB, Barry

STREISAND, Barbra, & Don Johnson

P&R '88

Singles: 7–inch

COLUMBIA 3-4 88

STREISAND, Barbra, & Donna Summer

P&R '79

Singles: 12–inch 33/45rpm

COLUMBIA/CASABLANCA........ 8-10 79
(Promotional issue only. With special cover.)

Singles: 7–inch

COLUMBIA 3-5 79

Picture Sleeves

COLUMBIA 3-5 79

Also see STREISAND, Barbra
Also see SUMMER, Donna

STRIKERS

LP '81

Singles: 7–inch

PRELUDE 3-5 81

LPs: 10/12–inch 33rpm

PRELUDE 5-10 81

STRING-A-LONGS

P&R '61

Singles: 7–inch

ATCO (6694 "Popi") 4-8 69
(Reportedly recorded by the Fireballs but credited to the String-A-Longs.)
DOT 5-10 62-65
WARWICK (603 "Wheels"/ "Tell the World") 10-15 60
WARWICK (603 "Wheels"/"Am I Asking too Much") 8-10 61
WARWICK (606 "Tell the World") 10-15 61
WARWICK (625 thru 675) 8-12 61-62

LPs: 10/12–inch 33rpm

ATCO (241 "World Wide Hits") . 15-25 68
(Reportedly recorded by the Fireballs but credited to the String-A-Longs.)
DOT 15-25 62-66
WARWICK (W-2036 "Pick-A-Hit") 40-50 61
(Monaural.)
WARWICK (WST-2036 "Pick-A-Hit") 50-75 61
(Stereo.)
Members: Keith McCormick; Jimmy Torres; Don Allen; Aubrey Lee de Cordova; Richard Stephens.
Also see FIREBALLS

STROLLERS

P&R '61

Singles: 7–inch

CARLTON (546 "There's No One But You") 15-25 61

STRONG, Barrett

(With the Rayber Voices)

P&R '60

Singles: 78rpm

ANNA (1111 "Money") 100-150 60

Singles: 7–inch

ANNA (1111 "Money") 15-25 60
ANNA (1116 "Yes No, Maybe So") 15-25 60
ATCO (6225 "Seven Sins") 25-35 62
CAPITOL 3-5 75
EPIC 3-5 73
MOTOWN 3-4
TAMLA (54022 "Let's Rock") 800-1200 60
TAMLA (54027 "Money") 35-55 60
(Horizontal lines on label.)
TAMLA (54027 "Money") 15-25 60
(Tamla globe logo on label.)
TAMLA (54029 "Yes No, Maybe So") 30-50 60
TAMLA (54033 "Whirlwind") 30-50 60
TAMLA (54035 "Money and Me") 30-50 61
TAMLA (54043 "Misery") 30-50 61
TOLLIE (9023 "I Better Run") 15-25 64

Picture Sleeves

EPIC 3-5 73

LPs: 10/12–inch 33rpm

CAPITOL 8-10 74
Also see HOLLAND, Eddie

STRUNK, Jud

(With the Coplin Kitchen Band)

C&W/P&R/LP '73

Singles: 7–inch

CAPITOL 3-5 74
COBURT 3-5 71
COLUMBIA 3-5 70
MCA 3-5 77
MGM 3-5 72-73
MELODYLAND 3-5 75-76

LPs: 10/12–inch 33rpm

COLUMBIA 6-12 70
HARMONY 5-10 73
MCA 5-10 77
MGM 5-10 71-73

STRYPER

LP '85

Singles: 7–inch

ENIGMA 3-4 84-89

Picture Sleeves

ENIGMA 3-4 87-88

LPs: 10/12–inch 33rpm

ENIGMA 5-8 84-90
Members: Michael Sweet; Oz Fox; Tim Gaines; Robert Sweet.

STUDENTS

R&B '61

Singles: 7–inch

ARGO (5386 "I'm So Young") 8-12 61
BRASS RING 4-6 71
CADET 4-6 65
CHECKER (902 "I'm So Young") 10-15 58
CHECKER (1004 "My Vow to You") 8-10 61
CHESS 3-5 73
COLLECTABLES 3-4 80s
NOTE (10012 "I'm So Young") 200-300 58
NOTE (10019 "My Vow to You") 200-300 58
RED TOP (100 "My Heart Is an Open Door") 100-150 57
(Blue label.)

RED TOP (100 "My Heart Is an Open Door") 25-35 58
(Red label.)
Members: Leroy King; Emerson "Rocky" Brown; Rich Havens.

STUFF

LP '76

Singles: 7-inch

W.B. 3-5 76-80

LPs: 10/12-inch 33rpm

W.B. 5-10 76-80

STYLE COUNCIL

LP '83

Singles: 7-inch

GEFFEN 3-4 84-85
POLYDOR 3-4 83-88

Picture Sleeves

GEFFEN 3-4 84

LPs: 10/12-inch 33rpm

GEFFEN 5-8 84-85
POLYDOR 5-8 83-88
Also see BAND AID
Also see JAM

STYLERS
(Dick Thomas & Stylers)

P&R '56

Singles: 78rpm

GOLDEN CREST 10-15 57
JUBILEE 5-10 55-57

Singles: 7-inch

GOLDEN CREST (1181 "You Tell Me") 15-25 57
GOLDEN CREST (1291 "Kiss and Run Lover") 15-25 57
GOLDEN CREST (1292 "Sweetheart of All My Dreams") 15-25 58
GORDY (7018 "Going Steady Anniversary") 25-35 63
JUBILEE 10-20 54-57

STYLISTICS

P&R/LP '71

Singles: 7-inch

AMHERST 3-4 85
AVCO 3-6 70-76
H&L 3-5 76-79
MERCURY 3-5 79
PHILADELPHIA INT'L 3-5 82
SEBRING (8370 "You're a Big Girl Now") 15-25 70
STREETWISE 3-4 84-86
TSOP 3-4 80-84

Picture Sleeves

AVCO 3-5 76

LPs: 10/12-inch 33rpm

AVCO 5-10 71-75
H&L 5-10 76-79
MERCURY 5-10 78-79
PHILADELPHIA INT'L 5-10 82
STREETWISE 5-8 84-86
TSOP 5-10 80-81
Members: Russell Tompkins, Jr.; Airrion Love; Herb Murrell; James Dunn; James Smith.
Also see MEDEIROS, Glenn, & Stylistics

STYX

P&R '72

Singles: 7-inch

A&M 3-5 76-84
PARAMOUNT 3-5 71-72
RCA 3-5 76
WOODEN NICKEL 3-5 72-78

Picture Sleeves

A&M 3-5 77-84

LPs: 10/12-inch 33rpm

A&M (Except 4604 & PR-4724) ... 5-10 75-84
A&M (4604 "Crystal Ball") 20-30 76
A&M (PR-4724 "Pieces of Eight") 10-15 79
(Picture disc.)
MFSL (026 "Grand Illusion") 25-50 79
NAUTILUS 10-15 81
RCA 5-10 72-82
WOODEN NICKEL 8-10 72-77

Promotional LPs

A&M (8431 "Styx Radio Special") 15-25 77
(Two-LP set.)
A&M (17053 "Styx Radio Special") 35-40 78
(Three-LP set.)
Members: Dennis De Young; James Young; Tommy Shaw; John Panozzo; Chuck Panozzo.
Also see DE YOUNG, Dennis
Also see SHAW, Tommy

SUAVE

P&R/LP '88

Singles: 7-inch

CAPITOL 3-4 88

Singles: 7-inch

CAPITOL 3-4 88

Picture Sleeves

CAPITOL 3-4 88

LPs: 10/12-inch 33rpm

CAPITOL 5-8 88

SUBJECT

D&D '85

Singles: 12-inch 33/45rpm

POW WOW WOW 4-6 85

SUGAR BEARS

P&R '72

Singles: 7-inch

BIG TREE 3-6 72

LPs: 10/12-inch 33rpm

BIG TREE 10-15 71
Members: Michael McGinnis; Kim Carnes; Baker Knight; Mike Settle; Mitch Murray.
Also see CARNES, Kim

SUGAR CUBES

LP '88

Singles: 12-inch 33/45rpm

ELEKTRA.................................. 4-6 88

Singles: 7-inch

ELEKTRA.................................. 3-4 88-89

Picture Sleeves

ELEKTRA.................................. 3-4 88-89

LPs: 10/12-inch 33rpm

ELEKTRA.................................. 5-10 88-89

Members: Björk Gudmundsdottir; Bragi Olafsson; Einar Örn; Margret Ornolfsdottir; Sigtryggur Baldursson; Thor Eldon.

SUGARHILL GANG

P&R '79

Singles: 12-inch 33/45rpm

SUGAR HILL (Except 542) 5-10 80-85

SUGAR HILL (542 "Rapper's Delight") 20-30 79

Singles: 7-inch

SUGAR HILL.............................. 3-5 79-85

LPs: 10/12-inch 33rpm

SUGAR HILL.............................. 5-10 80-85

Also see FURIOUS FIVE & Sugarhill Gang

SUGARLOAF

(With Jerry Corbetta)

P&R/LP '70

Singles: 7-inch

BRUT 3-5 73-74

CLARIDGE.................................. 3-5 74-76

LIBERTY 3-5 70-71

U.A. 3-5 71

Picture Sleeves

BRUT 4-6 73-74

LIBERTY 4-6 71

LPs: 10/12-inch 33rpm

BRUT 8-10 73

CLARIDGE.................................. 8-10 75

LIBERTY.................................. 10-15 70-71

Members: Jerry Corbetta; Bob Webber.

Also see CORBETTA, Jerry

SUICIDAL TENDENCIES

LP '87

Singles: 7-inch

FRONTIER.................................. 3-4 84

LPs: 10/12-inch 33rpm

CAROL....................................... 5-8 87

EPIC... 5-8 88-90

JANA... 8-10 86

Members: Mike Muir; Rocky George; Mike Clark; R.J. Herrera; Bob Heathcote; Robert Trujillo.

SULTON, Kasim

LP '82

Singles: 7-inch

EMI AMERICA 3-5 82

LPs: 10/12-inch 33rpm

EMI AMERICA 5-10 82

SUMMER, Donna

P&R/LP '75

Singles: 12-inch 33/45rpm

CASABLANCA...............................5-8 78-80

GEFFEN 4-8 80-87

MERCURY 4-8 83

OASIS 5-10 75-76

Singles: 7-inch

ATLANTIC.....................................3-4 89

CASABLANCA...............................3-5 75-80

GEFFEN 3-4 80-87

MERCURY....................................3-4 83

OASIS..3-6 75-76

Picture Sleeves

ATLANTIC.....................................3-4 89

GEFFEN 3-5 80-87

MERCURY 3-4 83

OASIS..3-6 76

LPs: 10/12-inch 33rpm

ATLANTIC.....................................5-8 89

CASABLANCA (Except 20110) ...5-10 75-80

CASABLANCA (20110 "Once Upon a Time") 12-15 77

(Promotional issue only.)

GEFFEN 5-10 80-87

MERCURY..................................5-10 83

OASIS..6-12 75-76

Also see BROOKLYN DREAMS

Also see MORODER, Giorgio

Also see STREISAND, Barbra, & Donna Summer

SUMMER, Henry Lee

LP '88

Singles: 7-inch

CBS ASSOCIATED 3-4 88-89

Picture Sleeves

CBS ASSOCIATED 3-4 88

LPs: 10/12-inch 33rpm

CBS ASSOCIATED 5-8 88-89

SUMMERS, Andy, & Robert Fripp: see FRIPP, Robert, & Andy Summers

SUMMERS, Bill

(With Summers Heat)

LP '81

Singles: 12-inch 33/45rpm

MCA 4-6 81-84

Singles: 7-inch

MCA 3-5 81-84

PRESTIGE...................................3-5 77-80

LPs: 10/12-inch 33rpm

MCA 5-10 81

Also see HANCOCK, Herbie

SUN

P&R '76

Singles: 7-inch

AIR CITY 3-4 84

CAPITOL......................................3-5 76-82

Picture Sleeves

CAPITOL......................................3-5 76-82

LPs: 10/12-inch 33rpm

CAPITOL 5-10 77-82

SUN, Joe

C&W '78

Singles: 7-inch

A.M.I. 3-4 84-85
ELEKTRA 3-4 82-83
OVATION 3-5 78-80

LPs: 10/12-inch 33rpm

ELEKTRA 5-8 82-83
OVATION 5-10 78-80

SUN, Joe, & Shotgun

C&W '82

Singles: 7-inch

ELEKTRA 3-4 82

SUNDAYS

LP '90

LPs: 10/12-inch 33rpm

DGC 5-8 90

SUNDOWN COMPANY

P&R '76

Singles: 7-inch

POLYDOR 3-5 76

SUNGLOWS
(Sunny & Sunglows; Sunny & Sunliners; Sunny Ozuna & Sunliners)

P&R/LP '63

Singles: 7-inch

DISCO GRANDE (1021 "Peanuts") 15-20 65
KEY LOC 4-8 66
OKEH 5-10 61
RPR 4-6 69
SUNGLOW 5-10 62-66
TEAR DROP 4-8 63-64

LPs: 10/12-inch 33rpm

KEY LOC 10-20 66
SUNGLOW (103 "Peanuts") 25-35 65
TEAR DROP (2000 "Talk to Me") 30-50 63

SUNNY & SUNGLOWS or SUNLINERS: see SUNGLOWS

SUNNYSIDERS

P&R '55

Singles: 78rpm

KAPP 4-6 55-57
MARQUEE 4-6 55-56

Singles: 7-inch

KAPP 5-10 55-60
MARQUEE 5-10 55-56
NRC 4-8 60
ZENITH 4-8 60

EPs: 7-inch 33/45rpm

KAPP 5-10 56

LPs: 10/12-inch 33rpm

KAPP 10-20 56

SUNRAYS

P&R '65

Singles: 7-inch

TOWER 5-10 64-67
W.B. 5-10 62

Picture Sleeves

TOWER 15-20 67

LPs: 10/12-inch 33rpm

TOWER (5017 "Andrea") 50-100 66

Members: Rick Henn; Bryon Case; Vince Hozier; Ed Medora; Marty DiGiovanni.
Also see ALLAN, Davie / Eternity's Children / Main Attraction / Sunrays

SUNSHINE BAND: see KC & Sunshine Band

SUNSHINE COMPANY

P&R/LP '67

Singles: 7-inch

IMPERIAL 4-8 67-68

LPs: 10/12-inch 33rpm

IMPERIAL 10-20 67-68

Members: Doug "Red" Mark, Maury Manseau, Larry Sims; Merle Bregante; Mary Nance.
Also see REDEYE

SUPER NATURE

D&D '85

Singles: 12-inch 33/45rpm

POP ART 4-6 85

SUPER SONICS: see SUPER-SONICS

SUPERBS

P&R '64

Singles: 7-inch

COLLECTABLES 3-4 80s
DORE 10-30 64-67
HERITAGE (103 "Rainbow of Love") 25-35 61

SUPERSAX

LP '73

LPs: 10/12-inch 33rpm

CAPITOL 5-10 73-74

SUPER-SONICS
(With Third Dimension Sound)

P&R '53

Singles: 78rpm

RAINBOW 5-10 53

Singles: 7-inch

RAINBOW (214 "New Guitar Boogie Shuffle") 10-15 53
(Black vinyl.)
RAINBOW (214 "New Guitar Boogie Shuffle") 15-25 53
(Colored vinyl.)
RAINBOW (214 "Guitar Boogie Shuffle") 15-25 55
(Note title change.)

SUPERTRAMP

LP '74

Singles: 12–inch 33/45rpm

A&M 4-6 82-85

Singles: 7–inch

A&M 3-5 71-85

Picture Sleeves

A&M 3-5 77-85

LPs: 10/12–inch 33rpm

A&M (Except 3730).................... 8-12 70-87
A&M (3730 "Breakfast in America") 400-600 79
(Picture disc. Promotional issue only.)
MFSL (005 "Crime of the Century")............................... 30-60 78
MFSL/UHQR (005 "Crime of the Century")........................ 50-100 78
(Boxed set.)
MFSL (045 "Breakfast in America") 25-50 80

Members: Rick Davies; Roger Hodgson; Doug Thomson; Bob Benberg; John Helliwell.

Also see HODGSON, Roger

SUPREMES

(Diana Ross & Supremes)

P&R '62

Singles: 12–inch 33/45rpm

MOTOWN 8-10 79-81

Singles: 7–inch

AMERICAN INT'L PICTURES ("Dr. Goldfoot and the Bikini Machine") 30-40 66
(Single-sided disc, used to promote the film of the same name.)
GEORGE ALEXANDER INC. (1079 "The Only Time I'm Happy") 30-40 65
(Special premium record. Has a Supremes interview on the flip.)
COLGEMS ("Snatches from the Soundtrack: *The Happening*") 50-100 67
(No selection number used. Promotional issue only.)
EEOC ("Things Are Changing") 50-100 65
(Equal Employment Opportunity Center promotional issue.)
MOTOWN (400 series) 3-4
MOTOWN (1008 "I Want a Guy") 500-1000 61
MOTOWN (1027 "Your Heart Belongs to Me")...................... 15-25 62
MOTOWN (1034 "Let Me Go the Right Way")........................... 35-50 62
MOTOWN (1040 "My Heart Can't Take It No More")........................... 25-45 63
MOTOWN (1044 "A Breath Taking, First Sight Soul Shaking, One Night Love Making, Next Day Heart Breaking Guy") 50-75 63
(Promotional issue only.)
MOTOWN (1044 "A Breath Taking Guy")......................................15-25 63
(Reissue, with much shorter title.)
MOTOWN (1051 "When the Lovelight Starts Shining Through His Eyes").....10-15 63
MOTOWN (1054 "Run, Run, Run") 15-25 64
MOTOWN (1060 thru 1080) 10-15 64-65
MOTOWN (1083 "I Hear a Symphony") 5-10 65
(Black vinyl.)
MOTOWN (1083 "I Hear a Symphony") 20-30 65
(Colored vinyl. Promotional issue only.)
MOTOWN (1089 thru 1156) 5-10 66-69
MOTOWN (1488 "Medley of Hits") 3-5 80
MOTOWN (1523 "Medley of Hits") 3-5 81
MOTOWN/TOPPS (1 "Baby Love")....................................50-75 67
MOTOWN/TOPPS (2 "Stop in the Name of Love") 50-75 67
MOTOWN/TOPPS (3 "Where Did Our Love Go")................................50-75 67
MOTOWN/TOPPS (15 "Come See About Me") 50-75 67
MOTOWN/TOPPS (16 "My World Is Empty Without You")............50-75 67
(Motown 1 through 16 are Topps Chewing Gum promotional, single-sided, cardboard, flexi, picture discs. Issued with generic sleeves.)
TAMLA (54038 "I Want a Guy")....................................75-125 61
TAMLA (54045 "Buttered Popcorn")............................50-100 61

Picture Sleeves

EEOC ("Things Are Changing") 50-100 65
(Equal Employment Opportunity Center promotional issue.)
MOTOWN (1027 "Your Heart Belongs to Me") 50-100 62
MOTOWN (1060 "Where Did Our Love Go")................................20-40 64
MOTOWN (1066 "Baby Love")..20-40 64
MOTOWN (1074 "Stop in the Name of Love").........................20-40 64
MOTOWN (1075 "Back in My Arms Again") 20-40 65
MOTOWN (1080 "Nothing But Heartaches")............................20-40 65
MOTOWN (1097 "You Can't Hurry Love")......................................15-25 66
MOTOWN (1101 "You Keep Me Hanging On") 15-25 66

EPs: 7–inch 33/45rpm

MOTOWN (60621 "Where Did Our Love Go")................................25-50 64

MOTOWN (60623 "A Little Bit of Liverpool") 25-50 64
MOTOWN (60627 "More Hits") . 25-50 65
MOTOWN (60649 "A Go Go") .. 20-40 66

LPs: 10/12–inch 33rpm

MOTOWN (100 & 200 series) 5-10 80-82
MOTOWN (606 "Meet the Supremes") 400-600 63
(Front cover pictures each member sitting on a chair.)
MOTOWN (606 "Meet the Supremes") 50-75 63
(Front cover pictures the head of each group member.)
MOTOWN (621 "Where Did Our Love Go") 20-40 64
MOTOWN (623 "Bit of Loverpool") 20-30 64
MOTOWN (625 "Country Western & Pop") 20-30 65
MOTOWN (627 "More Hits") 15-25 65
MOTOWN (629 "We Remember Sam Cooke") 20-30 65
MOTOWN (636 "At the Copa") . 20-30 65
MOTOWN (638 "Merry Christmas") 25-35 65
MOTOWN (643 thru 708) 15-25 66-70
MOTOWN (794 "Anthology") 15-20 74
(Three-LP set. Includes 12-page booklet.)
MOTOWN (900 series) 5-10 75
MOTOWN (5000 series, except 5381) 5-10 83-84
MOTOWN (5381 "25th Anniversary") 15-20 86
(Three-LP set. Includes 12-page booklet.)
NATURAL RESOURCES 5-10 78

Members: Diana Ross; Mary Wilson; Florence Ballard; Cindy Birdsong.
Also see DIAMOND, Neil / Diana Ross & Supremes
Also see PRIMETTES
Also see ROSS, Diana
Also see WILSON, Mary

SUPREMES & Four Tops

P&R '70

Singles: 7–inch

MOTOWN (400 series) 3-4
MOTOWN (1100 series) 4-8 70-71

EPs: 7–inch 33/45rpm

MOTOWN (717 "Magnificent Seven") 5-15 70
(Jukebox issue.)

LPs: 10/12–inch 33rpm

MOTOWN (100 series) 5-10 82
MOTOWN (700 series) 10-15 70-71

Also see FOUR TOPS

SUPREMES & TEMPTATIONS

P&R/LP '68

Singles: 7–inch

MOTOWN (400 series) 3-4
MOTOWN (1100 series) 4-8 68-69

Picture Sleeves

MOTOWN (1137 "I'm Gonna Make You Love Me") 10-20 68

LPs: 10/12–inch 33rpm

MOTOWN (100 series) 5-10 82
MOTOWN (600 series) 10-15 68-69

Also see SUPREMES
Also see TEMPTATIONS

SUPREMES

P&R/LP '70

Singles: 7–inch

MOTOWN (400 series) 3-4
MOTOWN (1162 thru 1415) 4-8 70-77
(Black vinyl.)
MOTOWN (1172 "Stoned Love") 10-15 70
(Colored vinyl. Promotional issue only.)

LPs: 10/12–inch 33rpm

MOTOWN (102 "Touch") 15-20 71
(Open-end interview LP. Price includes script. Promotional issue only.)
MOTOWN (702 thru 904) 6-12 70-78

Members: Jean Terrell; Mary Wilson; Cindy Birdsong.
Also see PAYNE, Scherrie
Also see TERRELL, Jean

SURFACE

P&R/LP '87

Singles: 12–inch 33/45rpm

COLUMBIA 4-6 86
SALSOUL 4-6 83

Singles: 7–inch

COLUMBIA 3-4 86-90
SALSOUL 3-4 83

LPs: 10/12–inch 33rpm

COLUMBIA 5-8 86-90

Members: Bernard Jackson; David Townsend; Dave Conley.
Also see MANDRILL

SURFARIS

P&R/LP '63

Singles: 7–inch

ABC 3-4 74
CHANCELLOR 5-8 63
DFS (11 "Wipe Out") 200-300 63
DECCA 5-10 63-66
DOT (Except 144 & 16479) 5-10 65-67
DOT (144 "Wipe Out") 4-6 66
(Black vinyl.)
DOT (144 "Wipe Out") 25-30 66
(Colored vinyl. Promotional issue only.)
DOT (16479 "Wipe Out") 4-8 63
FELSTED 5-10 64
MCA 3-4 70s
PRINCESS (50 "Wipe Out") 25-50 63
(Short version, same as Dot issue. Has "RE-1" etched in the vinyl trail-off.)

PRINCESS (50 "Wipe Out")...... 50-75 63
(Long version. Does not have "RE-1" etched in the vinyl trail-off.)
REGANO.................................... 5-10 63
UNIVERSAL (965 "Wipe Out").. 20-40 60s

EPs: 7–inch 33/45rpm

DECCA (2765 "Wipe Out")........ 20-40 63

LPs: 10/12–inch 33rpm

DECCA.................................... 25-45 63-65
DOT (3535 "Wipe Out")............ 30-45 63
(Front cover reads "The Original Hit Version, Wipe Out.")
DOT (3535 "Wipe Out")............ 25-35 63
(Front cover reads "Wipe Out and Surfer Joe and Other Popular selections By Other Instrumental Groups."
The Surfaris are heard only on *Wipe Out* and *Surfer Joe*. Other tracks on this LP are by the Challengers.)
DIPLOMAT.............................. 15-25 60s
PICKWICK 10-15 78

Members: Ron Wilson; Jim Fuller; Jim Pash; Pat Connolly; Bob Berryhill; Ken Forssi. Though not actual members, Richie Podolor, Chuck Girard and Gary Usher made appearances on Surfaris releases.

Also see BEACH BOYS / Dick Dale / Surfaris / Surf Kings
Also see DALE, Dick / Surfaris / Fireballs

SURVIVOR

P&R/LP '80

Singles: 12–inch 33/45rpm

SCOTTI BROS............................ 4-6 79-86

Singles: 7–inch

CASABLANCA............................ 3-4 84
SCOTTI BROS............................ 3-5 80-88

Picture Sleeves

SCOTTI BROS............................ 3-5 82-87

LPs: 10/12–inch 33rpm

SCOTTI BROS (Except 362) 5-10 79-88
SCOTTI BROS (362 "Rebel Girl")..................................... 10-12 80
(Promotional issue only.)

Members: Dave Bickler; Jim Peterik; Frank Sullivan; Dennis Johnson; Gary Smith; Jim Jameson.

Also see COBRA
Also see PETERIK, Jim

SURVIVORS

Singles: 7–inch

CAPITOL (5102 "Pamela Jean")................................ 150-200 64

Members: Brian Wilson; Dave Nowlen; Bob Norberg; Rich Peterson.

Also see BEACH BOYS
Also see BOB & SHERRY

SUSAN

LP '79

Singles: 7–inch

RCA.. 3-5 79
SCEPTER 3-5 70

LPs: 10/12–inch 33rpm

RCA 5-10 79

SUTCH, Screaming Lord: see LORD SUTCH

SUTHERLAND BROTHERS

(With Quiver)

P&R/LP '73

Singles: 7–inch

COLUMBIA 3-5 75-79
ISLAND.......................................3-5 72-73

LPs: 10/12–inch 33rpm

COLUMBIA 6-10 75-76
ISLAND......................................6-10 72-74

Members: Gavin Sutherland; Ian Sutherland.

SUTTON, Glenn

C&W/P&R '79

Singles: 7–inch

ABC..3-5 73
EPIC...4-6 67
MGM 4-8 64-65
MERCURY....................................3-5 78-86

LPs: 10/12–inch 33rpm

MERCURY 5-8 79

Also see KELLUM, Murray / Glenn Sutton

SUZY & Red Stripes

(Linda McCartney & Wings)

P&R '77

Singles: 12–inch 33/45rpm

CAPITOL (15244 "Seaside Woman")...............................10-20 86
EPIC (361 "Seaside Woman") ...20-30 77
(Promotional issue only.)

Singles: 7–inch

CAPITOL (5608 "Seaside Woman")...................................3-6 86
(Remixed version.)
EPIC (50403 "Seaside Woman") ... 4-8 77

Promotional Singles

CAPITOL (5608 "Seaside Woman")...............................10-15 86
EPIC (50403 "Seaside Woman") 30-40 77
(Colored vinyl.)
EPIC (50403 "Seaside Woman") 35-45 77
(Black vinyl. White label, states "Advance Promotion")
EPIC (50403 "Seaside Woman") 40-50 77
(Black vinyl. White label, no mention of "Advance Promotion")

Also see McCARTNEY, Paul

SWALLOWS

R&B '51

Singles: 78rpm

AFTER HOURS (104 "My Baby") 50-75 54

KING (4458 "Will You Be Mine") 50-100 51
KING (4466 "Since You've Been Away") 100-150 51
KING (4501 "Eternally") 40-60 51
KING (4515 "Tell Me Why") 40-60 51
KING (4525 "Beside You") 30-50 52
KING (4533 "I Only Have Eyes for You") 40-60 52
KING (4579 "Where Do I Go from Here") 40-60 52
KING (4612 "Laugh") 30-50 53
KING (4632 "Nobody's Lovin' Me") 30-50 53
KING (4656 "Trust Me") 30-50 53
KING (4676 "I'll Be Waiting") 30-50 53

Singles: 7-inch

AFTER HOURS (104 "My Baby") 300-400 54
GUSTO 3-4 80s
KING (4458 "Will You Be Mine") 400-600 51
KING (4501 "Eternally") 400-500 51
(Black vinyl.)
KING (4501 "Eternally") 600-750 51
(Colored vinyl.)
KING (4515 "Tell Me Why") 600-750 51
KING (4525 "Beside You") 100-200 52
KING (4533 "I Only Have Eyes for You") 300-400 52
KING (4579 "Where Do I Go from Here") 300-400 52
KING (4612 "Laugh") 150-250 53
KING (4632 "Nobody's Lovin' Me") 150-250 53
KING (4656 "Trust Me") 100-200 53
KING (4676 "I'll Be Waiting") 150-200 53

Members: Junior Denby; Ed Rich; Earl Hurley; Fred Johnson; Norris Mack; Dee Bailey; Buddy Bailey; Irving Turner; Al France; Cal Kollette.

SWALLOWS

P&R '58

Singles: 7-inch

FEDERAL 15-25 58

SWAN, Billy

C&W/P&R/LP '74

Singles: 7-inch

A&M 3-5 78-79
COLUMBIA 3-5 76-77
EPIC 3-4 81-83
MGM 5-10 68
MERCURY 3-4 86-87
MONUMENT 4-6 66-76
RISING SONS 4-6 67

LPs: 10/12-inch 33rpm

A&M 5-10 78
COLUMBIA/MONUMENT 5-10 77
EPIC 5-10 81
MONUMENT 5-10 74-78

SWANN, Bettye

P&R '67

Singles: 7-inch

A-BET 3-5 72-74
ATLANTIC 3-5 72-76
BIG TREE 3-5 70s
CAPITOL 3-6 68-70
FAME 3-5 71
MONEY 4-8 65-67

Picture Sleeves

CAPITOL 3-5 69

LPs: 10/12-inch 33rpm

A-BET 8-10 72
ATLANTIC 8-10 72-75
CAPITOL 10-12 69
MONEY 10-20 67

Also see DEES, Sam, & Bettye Swann

SWANS

P&R '64

Singles: 7-inch

CAMEO (302 "The Boy with the Beatle Hair") 25-35 64
SWAN 8-12 63

SWANSON, Brad, & His Whispering Organ Sound

LP '69

LPs: 10/12-inch 33rpm

THUNDERBIRD 5-10 69

SWAYZE, Patrick
(Featuring Wendy Fraser)

P&R '87

Singles: 7-inch

RCA 3-4 87

Picture Sleeves

RCA 3-5 87

SWEAT, Keith
(With Jacci McGhee)

P&R/LP '88

Singles: 7-inch

ELEKTRA 3-4 87
VINTERTAINMENT 3-4 88-90

Picture Sleeves

VINTERTAINMENT 3-4 88

LPs: 10/12-inch 33rpm

VINTERTAINMENT 5-8 88-90

Also see ENTOUCH

SWEAT BAND

LP '80

Singles: 7-inch

UNCLE JAM 3-5 80

LPs: 10/12-inch 33rpm

UNCLE JAM 5-10 80

Also see BOOTSY'S RUBBER BAND

SWEATHOG

P&R '71

Singles: 7-inch

COLUMBIA 3-5 71

LPs: 10/12-inch 33rpm

COLUMBIA 8-10 71-72

SWEENY TODD

P&R '76

Singles: 7-inch

LONDON....................................... 4-8 76

LPs: 10/12-inch 33rpm

LONDON (694 "If Wishes Were Horses")........................ 20-25 77

Members: Nick Gilder; James McCulloch; Bryan Guy Adams.
Also see ADAMS, Bryan
Also see GILDER, Nick

SWEET

P&R '71

Singles: 7-inch

BELL 3-5 71-74
CAPITOL.. 3-5 75-79
PARAMOUNT 5-10 71

LPs: 10/12-inch 33rpm

BELL 10-20 73
CAPITOL (Except 16000 series). 8-10 75-79
CAPITOL (16000 series).............. 5-8 80-82
KORY 8-10 77

Promotional LPs

CAPITOL (8849 "Short and Sweet")................................... 20-30 78
CAPITOL (11129 "Cut Above the Rest") 45-55 79
(Boxed set, containing the LP, 8-track and cassette issues of *Cut Above the Rest*, plus a group photo and biography.)

Members: Brian Connolly; Steve Priest; Andy Scott; Mick Tucker.

SWEET, Matthew

LP '92

LP: 10/12-inch 33rpm

ZOO/BMG (1 "Girlfriend")........... 8-10 91
(Colored vinyl. Promotional issue only.)

SWEET, Rachel

C&W '76

Singles: 12-inch 33/45rpm

STIFF/COLUMBIA 10-15 79
(Promotional issue only.)

Singles: 7-inch

COLUMBIA 3-5 81-83
DERRICK.................................... 3-5 76-78
PREMIER.................................... 3-5 74
STIFF/COLUMBIA 3-5 79-80

LPs: 10/12-inch 33rpm

ARC.. 5-10 81
COLUMBIA 5-10 81-82
STIFF/COLUMBIA 5-10 79-80

Also see SMITH, Rex, & Rachel Sweet

SWEET DREAMS

P&R '74

Singles: 7-inch

ABC...3-5 74

Member: Polly Brown.
Also see BROWN, Polly

SWEET F.A.

LP '90

LP: 10/12-inch 33rpm

MCA 5-8 90

SWEET G.

D&D '83

Singles: 12-inch 33/45rpm

FEVER 4-6 83

SWEET INSPIRATIONS

P&R '67

Singles: 12-inch 33/45rpm

RSO 4-8 79

Singles: 7-inch

ATLANTIC....................................3-8 67-71
CARIBOU......................................3-5 77
RSO 3-5 79
STAX..3-5 73-74

LPs: 10/12-inch 33rpm

ATLANTIC...............................10-12 68-70
RSO 5-10 79
STAX..8-10 73

Members: Cissy Houston; Sylvia Shemwell; Myrna Smith; Estelle Brown.
Also see FRANKLIN, Aretha
Also see HOUSTON, Cissy
Also see PRESLEY, Elvis
Also see RASCALS

SWEET SENSATION

P&R/LP '75

Singles: 7-inch

PYE...3-5 74-75

LPs: 10/12-inch 33rpm

PYE...5-10 75

SWEET SENSATION

P&R '87

Singles: 7-inch

ATCO 3-4 88-90
NEXT PLATEAU 3-4 86-87

Picture Sleeves

ATCO 3-4 88-89

LPs: 10/12-inch 33rpm

ATCO 5-8 88-90

SWEET TEE

LP '89

Singles: 7-inch

PROFILE......................................3-4 88

LPs: 10/12-inch 33rpm

PROFILE......................................5-8 88

SWEET THUNDER

LP '78

Singles: 7-inch

FANTASY 3-5 78-79

WMOT 3-5 79

LPs: 10/12-inch 33rpm

WMOT 5-10 78

SWEETWATER

LP '69

Singles: 7-inch

REPRISE 3-6 68-71

LPs: 10/12-inch 33rpm

REPRISE 10-15 68-71

SWING OUT SISTER

P&R/LP '87

Singles: 7-inch

FONTANA 3-4 89
MERCURY 3-4 87

Picture Sleeves

FONTANA 3-4 89
MERCURY 3-4 87

LPs: 10/12-inch 33rpm

FONTANA 5-8 89
MERCURY 5-8 87

Members: Andy Connell; Corrine Drewery; Martin Jackson.

SWINGIN' MEDALLIONS

P&R/LP '66

Singles: 7-inch

CAPITOL 4-8 68
COLLECTABLES 3-4 80s
DOT 5-10 65
4 SALE (002 "Double Shot") 20-30 66
1-2-3 .... 3-5 70
SMASH 4-8 66-67

LPs: 10/12-inch 33rpm

SMASH (27083 "Double Shot"). 25-35 66
(Monaural.)
SMASH (67083 "Double Shot"). 25-35 66
(Stereo.)

SWINGING BLUE JEANS

P&R/LP '64

Singles: 7-inch

IMPERIAL 5-10 64-67

LPs: 10/12-inch 33rpm

IMPERIAL (9261 "Hippy Hippy Shake") 50-75 64
(Monaural.)
IMPERIAL (12261 "Hippy Hippy Shake") 30-50 64
(Stereo.)
LIBERTY 5-10 82

Members: Ray Ennis; Ralph Ellis; Les Braid; Norman Kuhlke.

SWINGLE SINGERS

LP '63

LPs: 10/12-inch 33rpm

COLUMBIA 4-6 76
PHILIPS 5-10 63-72

SWITCH

P&R/LP '78

Singles: 7-inch

GORDY (Black vinyl) 3-4 78-82
GORDY (Colored vinyl) 4-8 78-82
(Promotional issues only.)
TOTAL EXPERIENCE 3-4 82-84

LPs: 10/12-inch 33rpm

GORDY 5-10 78-81
TOTAL EXPERIENCE 5-8 82-84

Members: Philip Ingram; Bobby DeBarge; Tommy DeBarge.

Also see DE BARGE
Also see DECO

SWOFFORD, Bill Oliver: see OLIVER

SYBIL

P&R/LP '89

Singles: 7-inch

NEXT PLATEAU 3-4 87-89

LPs: 10/12-inch 33rpm

NEXT PLATEAU 5-8 87-89

SYKES, Keith

LP '80

Singles: 7-inch

BACKSTREET 3-5 80

LPs: 10/12-inch 33rpm

BACKSTREET 5-10 80
MIDLAND INT'L 8-10 77
VANGUARD 10-12 70-71

SYLVAIN SYLVAIN

LP '80

Singles: 7-inch

RCA 3-5 79

LPs: 10/12-inch 33rpm

RCA 5-10 79

Also see NEW YORK DOLLS

SYLVERS

P&R '72

Singles: 12-inch 33/45rpm

CASABLANCA 4-8 79
GEFFEN 4-6 84-85
SOLAR 4-6 81-82

Singles: 7-inch

CAPITOL 3-5 75-78
CASABLANCA 3-5 78-79
GEFFEN 3-4 84-85
MGM 3-5 72-74
PRIDE 3-5 72-73
SOLAR 3-4 81-82
VERVE 3-5 71

Picture Sleeves

GEFFEN 3-4 84-85
PRIDE 3-5 72-73

LPs: 10/12-inch 33rpm

CAPITOL 5-10 75-78
CASABLANCA 5-10 78-79
CONCEPT 5-10 81
GEFFEN 5-8 84

MGM 8-10 72-74
PRIDE 8-10 72-73
SOLAR 5-10 81

Members: Foster Sylvers; Edmund Sylvers; Pay Sylvers; Angie Sylvers.

Also see SYLVERS, Foster

SYLVERS, Foster

P&R/LP '73

Singles: 7-inch

MGM 3-5 73
PRIDE 3-5 73

LPs: 10/12-inch 33rpm

MGM 6-10 74
PRIDE 8-10 73

Also see SYLVERS

SYLVESTER

(Sylvester James)

P&R/LP '78

Singles: 12-inch 33/45rpm

FANTASY.................................... 4-8 78-79
MEGATONE................................. 4-6 83-86

Singles: 7-inch

FANTASY (Black vinyl) 3-5 78-79
FANTASY (Colored vinyl) 4-8 78-79
(Promotional issues only.)
HONEY 3-5 80-81
MEGATONE................................. 3-4 83-86
W.B. 3-4 87

LPs: 10/12-inch 33rpm

FANTASY.................................... 5-10 78-81
HONEY 5-10 80-81
MEGATONE................................. 5-8 83-86
W.B. 5-8 87

SYLVIA

(Sylvia Vanderpool; Sylvia Robinson)

P&R/LP '73

Singles: 12-inch 33/45rpm

SUGARHILL................................. 4-6 82
VIBRATION................................. 4-8 77

Singles: 7-inch

ALL PLATINUM............................ 3-5 74
STANG.. 3-5 70
SUGARHILL................................. 3-5 81
VIBRATION................................. 3-5 73-78

LPs: 10/12-inch 33rpm

SUGARHILL................................. 5-10 81
VIBRATION................................. 6-10 73-78

Also see LITTLE SYLVIA
Also see MICKEY & SYLVIA
Also see SYLVIA & MOMENTS
Also see SYLVIA & Ralfi Pagan
Also see TURNER, Ike & Tina

SYLVIA & Ralfi Pagan

R&B '73

Singles: 7-inch

VIBRATION................................. 3-5 73

Also see PAGAN, Ralfi
Also see SYLVIA

SYLVIA

(Sylvia Kirby Allen)

C&W '79

Singles: 7-inch

RCA 3-5 79-87
RCA GOLD STANDARD 3-4 81

Picture Sleeves

RCA 3-4 81-86

LPs: 10/12-inch 33rpm

RCA 5-10 81-86

Also see GALWAY, James, & Sylvia

SYLVIA & Michael Johnson

C&W '85

Singles: 7-inch

RCA 3-4 86

Also see JOHNSON, Michael
Also see SYLVIA (Sylvia Kirby Allen)

SYLVIA, Margo, & Tune Weavers: see TUNE WEAVERS

SYLVIA & MOMENTS

P&R/R&B '74

Singles: 7-inch

ALL PLATINUM 3-5 74

Also see MOMENTS

SYMBA

R&B '80

Singles: 7-inch

VENTURE...3-5 80

SYMBOL 8

R&B '77

Singles: 7-inch

SHOCK...3-5 77-78

SYMBOLIC THREE

(Featuring D.J. Dr. Shock)

R&B '85

Singles: 7-inch

REALITY 3-4 85

SYMS, Sylvia

P&R '56

Singles: 78rpm

ATLANTIC...3-6 52-53
DECCA 3-6 56-57

Singles: 7-inch

ATLANTIC.......................................5-10 52-53
COLUMBIA...4-8 59-65
DECCA 4-10 56-64
PRESTIGE...4-6 67
RORI 4-6 62

EPs: 7-inch 33/45rpm

ATLANTIC.......................................5-15 56
DECCA 5-15 55

LPs: 10/12-inch 33rpm

A&M 5-10 78
ATLANTIC (137 "Songs By Sylvia Syms").........................50-100 53
(10-inch LP.)

ATLANTIC (1243 "Songs By Sylvia Syms") 20-40 56
(Has Atlantic logo at top of label.)
ATLANTIC (1243 "Songs By Sylvia Syms") 15-25 60
(Has Atlantic logo on side of label.)
ATLANTIC (18000 series) 5-10 76
COLUMBIA 20-30 60
DECCA (8188 "Sylvia Sings") ... 35-45 55
DECCA (8639 "Song of Love") . 30-40 58
KAPP 15-25 61
MOVIETONE 10-15 67
PRESTIGE 15-25 65-67
REPRISE 5-10 82
20TH FOX 10-20 64
VERSION (103 "After Dark") 40-50 54
(10–inch LP.)

SYNCH

(Jimmy Harnen & Synch)

P&R '86

Singles: 7–inch

COLUMBIA (05788 "Where Are You Now") 3-4 86
MICKI (001 "Where Are You Now") 10-15
WTG (68625 "Where Are You Now") 3-4 89
Member: Jimmy Harnen.

SYNDICATE of SOUND

P&R/LP '66

Singles: 7–inch

BELL 4-8 66-67
BUDDAH 3-5 70
CAPITOL 3-6 69
DEL-FI (4304 "Prepare for Love") 10-20 65
HUSH (228 "Little Girl") 20-30 66
SCARLET (5-3 "Prepare for Love") 15-25 65

LPs: 10/12–inch 33rpm

BELL (LP-6001 "Little Girl") 25-35 66
(Monaural.)
BELL (SLP-6001 "Little Girl") 30-45 66
(Stereo.)
PERFORMANCE 5-8 88
Members: Jim Sawyers; Bob Gonzalez; John Sharkey; Don Baskin; John Duckworth; Larry Roy; Carl Scott; Barrie Thompson; Dennis Tracy.

SYNERGY

LP '75

Singles: 7–inch

PASSPORT 3-5 76

LPs: 10/12–inch 33rpm

PASSPORT (Black vinyl) 5-10 75-84
PASSPORT (Clear vinyl) 8-12 78

SYREETA

(Syreeta Wright)

LP '72

Singles: 7–inch

MOTOWN 3-5 74-80
MOWEST 3-5 72
TAMLA 3-5 80-83

LPs: 10/12–inch 33rpm

MOTOWN 5-10 74-81
MOWEST 8-12 72
TAMLA 5-10 77-81
Also see JENNIFER / Syretta
Also see PRESTON, Billy, & Syreeta
Also see WRIGHT, Rita

SYSTEM

P&R/R&B/D&D/LP '83

Singles: 12–inch 33/45rpm

MIRAGE 4-6 83-86

Singles: 7–inch

ATCO 3-4 88
ATLANTIC 3-4 87
MIRAGE 3-4 83-86

Picture Sleeves

ATCO 3-4 88
ATLANTIC 3-4 87

LPs: 10/12–inch 33rpm

ATLANTIC 5-8 87
MIRAGE 5-10 83-86

SZABO, Gabor

LP '67

Singles: 7–inch

BLUE THUMB 3-5 70
BUDDAH 3-5 70
CTI 3-5 73
IMPULSE 3-5 66-68
MERCURY 3-5 76-77
REPRISE 3-5 73
SKYE 3-6 68-70

LPs: 10/12–inch 33rpm

BLUE THUMB 8-12 70
BUDDAH 8-12 70
CTI 8-12 73-74
IMPULSE 10-20 66-70
MCA 5-8 82
MERCURY 5-10 76
SALVATION 5-10 75
SKYE 8-12 68-70
Also see HORNE, Lena, & Gabor Szabo
Also see WOMACK, Bobby

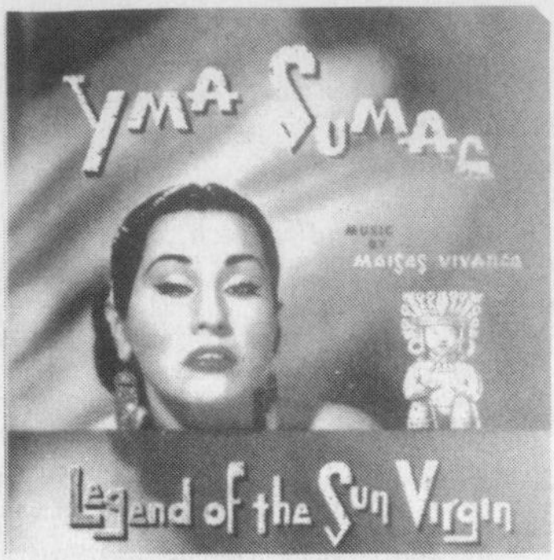
Yma Sumac
Music by Moises Vivanco
Legend of the Sun Virgin

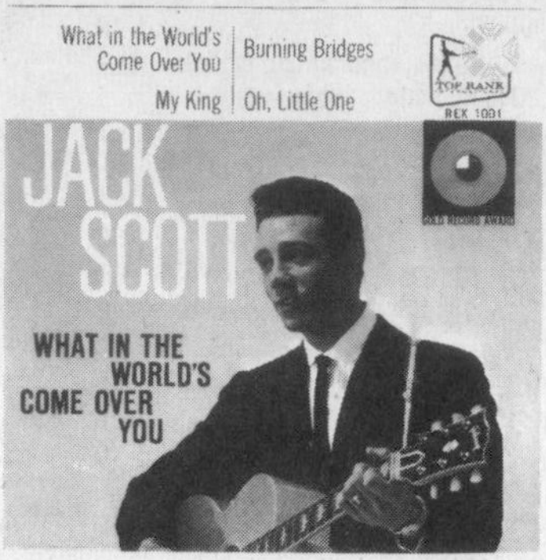
What in the World's Come Over You
Burning Bridges
My King
Oh, Little One
TOP RANK
REX 1001
JACK SCOTT
WHAT IN THE WORLD'S COME OVER YOU

ACE RECORDS
Ace Pub.
S-392 BMI
Time: 2:15
571
TU-BER-CU-LUCAS AND THE SINUS BLUES
(Huey Smith)
HUEY SMITH

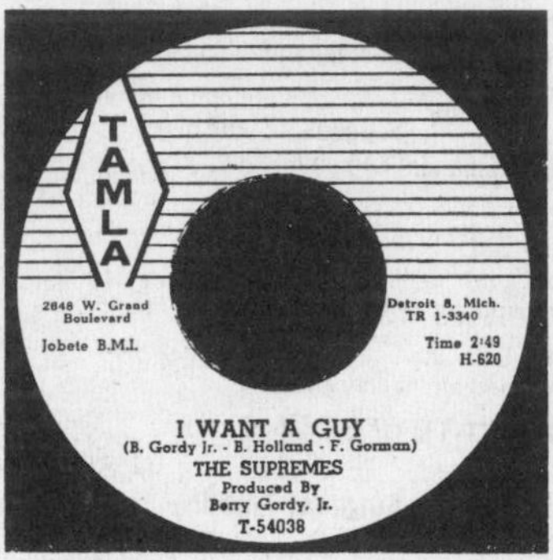
TAMLA
2648 W. Grand Boulevard
Detroit 8, Mich.
TR 1-3340
Jobete B.M.I.
Time 2:49
H-620
I WANT A GUY
(B. Gordy Jr. - B. Holland - F. Gorman)
THE SUPREMES
Produced By
Berry Gordy, Jr.
T-54038

TRAVELIN'
with
RAY SMITH
ROCKIN' LITTLE ANGELS
JUDD

HAPPY
TREAT 'EM TOUGH
JIMMY SOUL
IF YOU WANNA BE HAPPY ■ TREAT 'EM TOUGH
TWISTIN' MATILDA ■ I WANT TO KNOW IF YOU LOVE ME

T

T-BONES

P&R '65

Singles: 7–inch

LIBERTY 5-10 64-66

EPs: 7–inch 33/45rpm

LIBERTY 8-12 65
(Jukebox issues only.)

LPs: 10/12–inch 33rpm

LIBERTY 15-25 64-66
SUNSET 10-20 66

Members: Dan Hamilton; Gene Pello; Joe Frank Carollo; Tom Reynolds; Judd Hamilton; Richard Torres; George Dee.

Also see HAMILTON, JOE FRANK & REYNOLDS

T-CONNECTION

P&R/R&B/LP '77

Singles: 12–inch 33/45rpm

CAPITOL 4-6 81-84

Singles: 7–inch

CAPITOL 3-5 81-84
DASH 3-5 77-79

LPs: 10/12–inch 33rpm

CAPITOL 5-10 81-84
DASH 5-10 77-79

T. REX
(Tyrannosaurus Rex)

P&R/LP '71

Singles: 7–inch

A&M 5-10 68
BLUE THUMB 4-8 71-72
CASABLANCA 3-5 75
REPRISE 3-6 71-74

LPs: 10/12–inch 33rpm

A&M (3000 series) 10-15 72
A&M (4000 series) 15-20 68
BLUE THUMB (7 "Unicorn") 10-20 71
BLUE THUMB (18 "Beard of Stars") 10-20 72
(Add $5 to $10 if accompanied by the bonus single *Ride a White Swan.*)
CASABLANCA 8-10 74
REPRISE 8-12 71-73

Members: Marc Bolan; Steve Peregrine Took; Mickey Finn; Bill Legend; Dino Dines; Steve Currie; Jack Green; Gloria Jones.

Also see BOLAN, Marc
Also see GREEN, Jack

T.F.O.

R&B '80

Singles: 7–inch

VENTURE 3-5 80-81

THP ORCHESTRA

R&B/LP '78

Singles: 7–inch

ATLANTIC 3-5 79
BUTTERFLY (Black vinyl) 3-4 77-78
BUTTERFLY (Colored vinyl) 3-5 77-78

LPs: 10/12–inch 33rpm

ATLANTIC 5-8 79
BUTTERFLY 8-10 77

TKA
(Total Knowledge in Action)

P&R/R&B '86

Singles: 12–inch 33/45rpm

TOMMY BOY 4-6 86

Singles: 7–inch

TOMMY BOY 3-4 86-88

LPs: 10/12–inch 33rpm

TOMMY BOY 5-8 86-88

TKO

LP '79

Singles: 7–inch

INFINITY 3-5 79

LPs: 10/12–inch 33rpm

INFINITY 5-10 79

T.K.O.'s

R&B '66

Singles: 7–inch

TEN STAR 4-8 66

T.M.G.

P&R '79

Singles: 7–inch

ATCO 3-5 79

LPs: 10/12–inch 33rpm

ATCO 5-10 79

TMP BAND

R&B '86

Singles: 7–inch

CRITIQUE 3-4 86

TNT

LP '87

LPs: 10/12–inch 33rpm

MERCURY 5-8 84-89

TNT BAND

R&B '69

Singles: 7–inch

COTIQUE 3-5 69

TSOL
(True Sounds of Liberty)

LP '87

LPs: 10/12–inch 33rpm

ENIGMA 5-8 87

T.S.U. TORONADOS

P&R/R&B '69

Singles: 7–inch

ATLANTIC 4-6 68-69

VOLT 3-5 69-70

TTF

(Today, Tomorrow, Forever)

R&B '80

Singles: 7-inch

CURTOM 3-5 80
GOLD COAST............................. 3-5 81
RSO 3-5 80

LPs: 10/12-inch 33rpm

GOLD COAST........................... 5-10 81

T.Z.

D&D '83

Singles: 12-inch 33/45rpm

STREET SOUND......................... 4-6 83

TA MARA & SEEN

P&R/R&B/D&D '85

Singles: 12-inch 33/45rpm

A&M 4-6 85-86

Singles: 7-inch

A&M 3-4 85-88

Picture Sleeves

A&M 3-4 85

LPs: 10/12-inch 33rpm

A&M 5-8 85

TA'BOO

D&D '84

Singles: 12-inch 33/45rpm

ACME... 4-6 84

TACO

(Taco Ockerse)

P&R/D&D/LP '83

Singles: 12-inch 33/45rpm

RCA... 4-6 83-84

Singles: 7-inch

RCA... 3-4 83-84

LPs: 10/12-inch 33rpm

RCA... 5-8 83-84

TAJ MAHAL

LP '69

Singles: 7-inch

COLUMBIA (10000 series) 3-5 75
COLUMBIA (44000 series) 4-8 67-69
COLUMBIA (45000 series) 3-6 69-74

Picture Sleeves

COLUMBIA 4-8 67

LPs: 10/12-inch 33rpm

COLUMBIA 6-12 68-81
W.B. 5-10 77

Also see SPRINGSTEEN, Bruce / Albert Hammond / Loudon Wainwright III / Taj Mahal

TAKA BOOM: see BOOM, Taka

TAKANAKA

R&B '86

Singles: 7-inch

AMHERST.................................. 3-4 86

TAKE 6

LP '89

LPs: 10/12-inch 33rpm

REPRISE 5-8 89-90

TALK TALK

P&R/LP '82

Singles: 12-inch 33/45rpm

EMI AMERICA 4-8 82-86

Singles: 7-inch

EMI AMERICA 3-5 82-86

Picture Sleeves

EMI AMERICA 3-5 84-86

LPs: 10/12-inch 33rpm

EMI AMERICA 5-10 82-86

TALKING HEADS

LP '77

Singles: 12-inch 33/45rpm

SIRE...4-8 79-86

Singles: 7-inch

SIRE...3-5 77-88

Picture Sleeves

SIRE...3-5 78-86

LPs: 10/12-inch 33rpm

SIRE (Except 23771) 5-10 77-88
SIRE (23771 "Speaking in Tongues") 20-30 83
(Promotional issue only.)
W.B. (104 "Live on Tour") 25-45 79
(Promotional issue only.)

Members: David Byrne; Jerry Harrison; Tina Weymouth; Brian Eno; Robert Fripp; Chris Frantz.

Also see BYRNE, David
Also see MODERN LOVERS
Also see TOM TOM CLUB

TAMI SHOW

P&R '88

Singles: 7-inch

CHRYSALIS.................................3-4 88

Picture Sleeves

CHRYSALIS.................................3-4 88

TAMPA RED

(Hudson Whittaker)

P&R '36

Singles: 78rpm

BLUEBIRD 10-30 36-45
RCA (20-0000 & 22-0000 series).......................................10-15 45-48

Singles: 78rpm

BLUEBIRD 15-25 44-45
RCA 5-15 45-54

Singles: 7-inch

RCA (47-4000 & 47-5000 series) 25-35 51-54
RCA (50-0000 series) 40-60 49-51

LPs: 10/12-inch 33rpm

BLUEBIRD 10-15 75
BLUES CLASSICS 5-10
PRESTIGE BLUESVILLE 20-35 61-62

YAZOO.................................... 10-15

TAMS

Singles: 7-inch

MINK (22 "Memory Lane") 20-30 59

(*Memory Lane* was first issued in 1959, showing the group as the Stereos. The same track was reissued in 1963, shown first as by the Tams and then by the Hippies.)

PARKWAY (863 "Memory Lane")................................ 10-15 63

Also see HIPPIES / Reggie Harrison
Also see STEREOS

TAMS

P&R/R&B '62

Singles: 7-inch

ABC.. 3-6 68-73
ABC-PAR.................................... 4-8 63-64
APT/ABC.................................... 3-5 72
ARLEN 5-10 62-63
CAPITOL.................................... 3-6 71
COLLECTABLES 3-4 80s
COMPLEAT 3-5 83
DAISY 5-10 60s
DUNHILL.................................... 3-5 71
GENERAL AMERICAN 8-10 62
GUSTO 3-5 80
1-2-3.. 3-5 70
KING 4-8 65
MCA... 3-4 80s
RIPETE 3-5 82
ROULETTE 3-4 70s
SOUTH....................................... 3-5 73
SWAN 10-15 60
WONDER.................................... 3-5 82

LPs: 10/12-inch 33rpm

ABC.. 10-15 67-69
ABC-PAR 20-30 64
BRYLEN..................................... 5-10 84
CAPITOL.................................... 5-10 79
COMPLEAT 5-8 83
1-2-3.. 8-10 70
SOUNDS SOUTH 8-10 77

Members: Joe Pope; Charles Pope; Robert Lee Smith; Horace Key; Floyd Ashton; Albert Cottle.

TANEGA, Norma

P&R '66

Singles: 7-inch

ABC.. 3-5 73
ERIC.. 3-4 70s
NEW VOICE 4-8 66-67
VIRGO.. 3-4 73

LPs: 10/12-inch 33rpm

NEW VOICE.............................. 15-20 66

TANGERINE DREAM

LP '74

Singles: 7-inch

EMI AMERICA 3-4 84
VIRGIN....................................... 3-5 75-77

LPs: 10/12-inch 33rpm

EMI AMERICA 5-8 84
ELEKTRA...................................5-10 81
MCA 5-10 77-86
VIRGIN.......................................8-12 74-77

Members: Peter Baumann; Chris Franks; Ed Froese.
Also see BAUMANN, Peter

TANGERINE DREAM / Jon Anderson / Bryan Ferry

LPs: 10/12-inch 33rpm

MCA (6165 "Legend") 8-10 86

(Soundtrack.)

Also see ANDERSON, Jon
Also see FERRY, Bryan
Also see TANGERINE DREAM

TANGIER

P&R/LP '89

Singles: 7-inch

ATCO..3-4 89-90

Picture Sleeves

ATCO..3-4 89

LPs: 10/12-inch 33rpm

ATCO..5-8 89-90

TANNER, Gary

P&R '78

Singles: 7-inch

20TH FOX....................................3-5 78

TANNER, Marc, Band

P&R/LP '79

Singles: 7-inch

ELEKTRA.....................................3-5 79
PRIVATE I...................................3-4 80s

LPs: 10/12-inch 33rpm

ELEKTRA....................................5-10 78-80
PRIVATE I..................................5-10 80s

TANTRUM

LP '80

Singles: 7-inch

OVATION.....................................3-5 79

LPs: 10/12-inch 33rpm

OVATION....................................5-10 79

TARHEEL SLIM
(Alden Bunn)

Singles: 78rpm

FIRE 20-30 59-60

Singles: 7-inch

FIRE...15-25 59-60
FURY 20-30 59

TARHEEL SLIM & LITTLE ANN
(Slim & Ann; Slim & Little Ann; Tarheel Slim & Lil' Annie)

R&B '59

Singles: 78rpm

FIRE...20-30 59-60

Singles: 7-inch

ATCO 5-10 63

FIRE ... 15-25 59-62
PORT ... 4-8 65
Also see TARHEEL SLIM

TARNEY - SPENCER BAND

P&R/LP '78

Singles: 7-inch

A&M ... 3-5 78-81
PRIVATE STOCK ... 3-5 76

LPs: 10/12-inch 33rpm

A&M ... 5-10 78-79
Members: Alan Tarney; Trevor Spencer.

TARRIERS

P&R '56

Singles: 78rpm

GLORY ... 5-10 56

Singles: 7-inch

DECCA ... 4-8 63-64
GLORY ... 8-12 56
U.A. ... 5-10 59

LPs: 10/12-inch 33rpm

ATLANTIC ... 15-25 60
DECCA ... 10-20 62-64
GLORY (1200 "The Tarriers") ... 40-50 57
KAPP ... 10-20 63
U.A. ... 15-25 59
Members: Erik Darling; Alan Arkin; Bob Carey.
Also see MARTIN, Vince
Also see ROOFTOP SINGERS
Also see WEISSBERG, Eric

TASSELS

P&R '59

Singles: 7-inch

AMY ... 4-8 66
MADISON ... 10-15 59

TASTE

LP '69

Singles: 7-inch

ATCO ... 3-5 69-70

LPs: 10/12-inch 33rpm

ATCO ... 10-15 69-70
Member: Rory Gallagher.
Also see GALLAGHER, Rory

TASTE of HONEY

P&R/R&B/LP '78

Singles: 12-inch 33/45rpm

CAPITOL (Except 9572) ... 4-8 78-79
CAPITOL (9572 "Sukiyaki") ... 8-10 80
(Fan shaped disc. Promotional issue only.)
MCA ... 4-6 84

Singles: 7-inch

CAPITOL ... 3-5 78-82
MCA ... 3-4 84

Picture Sleeves

CAPITOL ... 3-5 78-82

LPs: 10/12-inch 33rpm

CAPITOL ... 5-10 78-82
Members: Janice Marie Johnson; Hazel Payne.
Also see FELDER, Wilton
Also see JOHNSON, Janice Marie

TATE, Howard

P&R/R&B '66

Singles: 7-inch

ATLANTIC ... 3-6 71-72
EPIC ... 3-5 74
TURNTABLE ... 4-6 69-70
UTOPIA (510 "Half a Man") ... 15-25 66
VERVE ... 4-8 66-68

LPs: 10/12-inch 33rpm

ATLANTIC ... 10-20 71
TURNTABLE ... 8-10 70
VERVE ... 10-20 67-68
Also see DOGGETT, Bill

TATE, Laurie

(With Joe Morris Blues Cavalcade)

Singles: 78rpm

ATLANTIC (965 "Rock Me Daddy") ... 15-25 52

Singles: 7-inch

ATLANTIC (965 "Rock Me Daddy") ... 25-50 52
Also see MORRIS, Joe, & His Orchestra

TATE, Tommy

R&B '72

Singles: 7-inch

ABC-PAR (10626 "What's the Matter") ... 15-25 65
JACKSON SOUND ... 3-6 70
KOKO ... 3-5 72-76
OKEH ... 5-10 66

TAVARES

P&R/R&B '73

Singles: 12-inch 33/45rpm

CAPITOL ... 4-8 77-79
RCA ... 4-6 82-84

Singles: 7-inch

CAPITOL ... 3-5 73-80
RCA ... 3-4 82-84

LPs: 10/12-inch 33rpm

CAPITOL ... 8-10 73-81
RCA ... 5-10 82-83

TAWATHA

R&B '87

Singles: 7-inch

EPIC ... 3-4 87

TAXXI

LP '82

Singles: 7-inch

FANTASY ... 3-5 82

LPs: 10/12-inch 33rpm

FANTASY (9617 "States of Emergency") ... 20-30 82
MCA ... 10-15 85

TAYLOR, Alex

LP '71

Singles: 7-inch

BANG ... 3-5 78-79

CAPRICORN................................ 3-5 71
DUNHILL.................................... 3-5 74

LPs: 10/12–inch 33rpm

CAPRICORN.............................. 8-10 71
DUNHILL.................................. 8-10 74

TAYLOR, Andy

P&R '86

Singles: 12–inch 33/45rpm

ATLANTIC.................................. 4-6 86

Singles: 7–inch

ATLANTIC.................................. 3-4 86
MCA 3-4 86-87

Picture Sleeves

ATLANTIC.................................. 3-4 86
MCA 3-4 86

LPs: 10/12–inch 33rpm

MCA 5-8 87

Also see DURAN DURAN
Also see POWER STATION

TAYLOR, Austin

P&R '60

Singles: 7–inch

LAURIE 5-10 60-61

Also see TAYLOR, Ted

TAYLOR, B.E., Group

P&R '84

Singles: 12–inch 33/45rpm

EPIC.. 4-6 84

Singles: 7–inch

EPIC.. 3-4 84-86
MCA 3-5 83-84

Picture Sleeves

EPIC.. 3-4 86

LPs: 10/12–inch 33rpm

MCA 5-10 82

Members: B.E. Taylor; Dave Kerr; Rick Withowski; Joe Macre; Joe D'Amico.
Also see CRACK the SKY

TAYLOR, Bobby
(With the Vancouvers)

P&R/R&B '68

Singles: 7–inch

BUDDAH 4-6 72
GORDY (Except 7088).............. 10-20 68-69
GORDY (7088 "Oh I've Been Blessed")........................... 300-400 69
HOUR...................................... 10-15
INTEGRA (103 "This Is My Woman") 50-75 68
MOWEST 5-10
PLAYBOY 3-6 75
SUNFLOWER (126 "There Are Roses Somewhere in This World") 15-25 72
TOMMY 3-6 73
V.I.P. (25053 "Oh I've Been Blessed").............................. 10-20 69

LPs: 10/12–inch 33rpm

GORDY (930 "Bobby Taylor and the Vancouvers") 40-60 68
GORDY (942 "Taylor Made Soul")...................................40-60 69

Members: Bobby Taylor; Wes Henderson; Eddie Patterson; Robbie King; Ted Lewis; Tommy Chong.
Also see CHEECH & CHONG

TAYLOR, Debbie

R&B '68

Singles: 7–inch

ARISTA.......................................3-5 75-76
DECCA 4-6 68
GWP 4-6 69
POLYDOR 3-5 74
TODAY...3-5 72

LPs: 10/12–inch 33rpm

TODAY...6-10 72

TAYLOR, Felice

P&R/R&B '67

Singles: 7–inch

KENT 4-6 68
MUSTANG....................................4-8 67

TAYLOR, Gary

R&B '88

Singles: 7–inch

VIRGIN...3-4 88

TAYLOR, Gloria

P&R/R&B '69

Singles: 7–inch

COLUMBIA 3-5 74
GLO-WHIZ....................................4-6 69
SILVER FOX..................................4-6 69

TAYLOR, James
(With the Original Flying Machine)

P&R/LP '70

Singles: 7–inch

APPLE (1805 "Carolina in My Mind"/"Taking It In") 200-300 69
(Promotional issue only.)
APPLE (1805 "Carolina in My Mind"/"Something's Wrong")......5-10 70
(Note different flip side.)
APPLE (PRO-1805 "Carolina on My Mind)....................................25-35 70
(Note title variance. Promotional issue only.)
APPLE (4675 "More Apples, Radio Co-Op Ads") 125-175 69
(Single-sided disc. Promotional issue only.)
CAPITOL..3-5 76
COLUMBIA 3-5 77-88
EUPHORIA 3-5 71
W.B. 3-5 70-76

Picture Sleeves

COLUMBIA 3-4 81-88

LPs: 10/12–inch 33rpm

APPLE 10-15 69-70

COLUMBIA 5-10 77-88
EUPHORIA 12-15 71
TRIP 8-10 73
W.B. 8-10 70-77

Also see DOOBIE BROTHERS, James Hall & James Taylor
Also see DOOBIE BROTHERS / Kate Taylor & Simon-Taylor Family
Also see FLYING MACHINE
Also see GARFUNKEL, Art, James Taylor & Paul Simon
Also see HALL, James, & James Taylor
Also see KING DREAM CHORUS & HOLIDAY CREW
Also see KORTCHMAR, Danny
Also see SIMON, Carly, & James Taylor

TAYLOR, James, & J.D. Souther

P&R '81

Singles: 7-inch

COLUMBIA 3-5 81

Also see SOUTHER, J.D.
Also see TAYLOR, James

TAYLOR, John

P&R '86

Singles: 12-inch 33/45rpm

CAPITOL..................................... 4-6 86

Singles: 7-inch

CAPITOL..................................... 3-4 86

LPs: 10/12-inch 33rpm

CAPITOL..................................... 5-8 86

Also see DURAN DURAN
Also see POWER STATION

TAYLOR, Johnnie

(Johnny Taylor; the "Soul Philosopher")

P&R/R&B '63

Singles: 7-inch

BEVERLY GLEN.......................... 3-5 82
COLUMBIA 3-5 76-80
DERBY...................................... 4-8 63-64
MALACO 3-4 83-87
RCA.. 3-5 77
SAR (Except 131) 5-10 61-65
SAR (131 "Never Never").......... 15-25 61
STAX.. 3-6 66-77

LPs: 10/12-inch 33rpm

BEVERLY GLEN........................ 5-10 82
COLUMBIA 6-10 76-81
MALACO 5-8 83-86
RCA... 8-10 77
STAX....................................... 6-10 67-83

TAYLOR, Johnnie, & Carla Thomas

Singles: 7-inch

STAX.. 4-6 69

Also see TAYLOR, Johnnie
Also see THOMAS, Carla

TAYLOR, Kate

LP '71

Singles: 7-inch

COLUMBIA 3-5 77-79
COTILLION 3-5 71

LPs: 10/12-inch 33rpm

COLUMBIA 5-10 78-79
COTILLION 5-10 71

Also see DOOBIE BROTHERS / Kate Taylor & Simon-Taylor Family

TAYLOR, Koko

(Cocoa Taylor; Ko Ko Taylor)

P&R/R&B '66

Singles: 7-inch

CHECKER 4-8 66-68
U.S.A...5-10 63
YAMBO 4-6 60s

LPs: 10/12-inch 33rpm

ALLIGATOR................................5-10 76-81
CHESS.......................................10-12 69-72

Also see DIXON, Willie

TAYLOR, Little Johnny

P&R/R&B/LP '63

Singles: 7-inch

GALAXY.....................................4-8 63-64
RONN 3-5 71-79

LPs: 10/12-inch 33rpm

BEVERLY GLEN..........................5-8 87
GALAXY....................................15-25 63
RONN 5-10 72-79

TAYLOR, Little Johnny, & Ted Taylor

LPs: 10/12-inch 33rpm

RONN 5-10 73

Also see TAYLOR, Little Johnny
Also see TAYLOR, Ted

TAYLOR, Livingston

LP '70

Singles: 7-inch

CAPRICORN 3-5 70-73
EPIC...3-5 78-80

LPs: 10/12-inch 33rpm

ATCO 8-12 70
CAPRICORN 5-10 71-79
EPIC...5-10 78

Also see DOOBIE BROTHERS / Kate Taylor & Simon-Taylor Family

TAYLOR, Livingston, & Leah Kunkel

C&W '88

Singles: 7-inch

CRITIQUE...................................3-4 88

Also see KUNKEL, Leah
Also see TAYLOR, Livingston

TAYLOR, Mick

LP '79

Singles: 7-inch

COLUMBIA 3-5 79

LPs: 10/12-inch 33rpm

COLUMBIA 5-10 79

Also see MAYALL, John
Also see ROLLING STONES

TAYLOR, R. Dean

P&R '70

Singles: 7–inch

AUDIO MASTER (1 "At the High School Dance") 100-150 60
BARRY (3023 "At the High School Dance") 75-125 60
(Canadian.)
FARR 3-5 76
JANE.. 3-5 77
MALA (444 "I'll Remember") 25-50 62
MOTOWN 3-5
RAGAMUFFIN 3-5 79
RARE EARTH 3-5 70-72
STRUMMER 3-4 83
20TH FOX.................................. 3-5 81
V.I.P. 10-20 65-68

Picture Sleeves

RARE EARTH 3-5 71

LPs: 10/12–inch 33rpm

RARE EARTH 10-15 70

TAYLOR, Roger

LP '81

Singles: 7–inch

CAPITOL.................................. 3-4 84
ELEKTRA.................................. 3-5 81

LPs: 10/12–inch 33rpm

CAPITOL.................................. 5-8 84
ELEKTRA................................ 5-10 81
Also see ARCADIA
Also see QUEEN

TAYLOR, Ted

P&R/R&B '65

Singles: 7–inch

ALARM 3-5 76
APT 4-8 62
ATCO 4-8 65-66
DADE 4-8 63
DUKE 8-12 59
EBB (132 "Keep Walkin' On") ... 10-15 58
EPIC... 4-8 60
GOLD EAGLE 4-8 61
JEWEL 4-8 66-67
OKEH 4-8 62-65
RONN....................................... 4-6 67-72
SONCRAFT 5-10 61
TOP RANK.............................. 5-10 60-61
WARWICK 5-10 61

LPs: 10/12–inch 33rpm

OKEH 15-25 63-66
MCA 5-10 78
RONN..................................... 5-10 69-72
Also see CADETS
Also see TAYLOR, Austin
Also see TAYLOR, Little Johnny & Ted Taylor

TAYLOR, True

(Paul Simon)

Singles: 7–inch

BIG (614 "Teenage Fool")..........20-40 58
Also see SIMON, Paul

TCHAIKOVSKY, Bram

P&R/LP '79

Singles: 7–inch

ARISTA...3-5 81
POLYDOR 3-5 79

LPs: 10/12–inch 33rpm

ARISTA.......................................5-10 81
POLYDOR 5-10 79-80
Also see MOTORS

TEARDROP EXPLODES

LP '81

Singles: 7–inch

MERCURY.....................................3-5 81-82

LPs: 10/12–inch 33rpm

MERCURY 5-10 81-82
Member: Julian Cope.
Also see COPE, Julian

TEARS for FEARS

P&R/LP '83

Singles: 12–inch 33/45rpm

MERCURY 4-6 83-86

Singles: 7–inch

FONTANA......................................3-4 89
MERCURY 3-4 83-86

Picture Sleeves

FONTANA......................................3-4 89
MERCURY 3-4 85-86

LPs: 10/12–inch 33rpm

FONTANA......................................5-8 89
MERCURY 5-8 83-86
SELECT ONE 12-18

TEASE

R&B '86

Singles: 12–inch 33/45rpm

EPIC..4-6 86
RCA 4-6 83

Singles: 7–inch

EPIC..3-4 86-88
RCA 3-4 83

LPs: 10/12–inch 33rpm

EPIC..5-8 86
RCA 5-8 83

TECHNIQUE

D&D '83

Singles: 12–inch 33/45rpm

ARIAL..4-6 83

TECHNIQUES

P&R '57

Singles: 78rpm

ROULETTE....................................4-8 57

Singles: 7–inch

ROULETTE..................................5-10 57-58

STARS 15-25 57

TECHNOTRONIC
(Featuring Felly)

P&R/LP '89

Singles: 7-inch

SBK 3-4 89-90

Picture Sleeves

SBK 3-4 89

LPs: 10/12-inch 33rpm

SBK 5-8 89-90

TEDDY & TWILIGHTS

P&R '62

Singles: 7-inch

SWAN 10-15 62

TEDDY BEARS

P&R/R&B '58

Singles: 7-inch

COLLECTABLES 3-4 80s
DORE 8-12 58-59
IMPERIAL 10-20 58-59

LPs: 10/12-inch 33rpm

IMPERIAL (9067 "The Teddy Bears Sing") 150-250 59
(Monaural.)
IMPERIAL (12010 "The Teddy Bears Sing") 350-450 59
(Stereo.)

Members: Phil Spector; Annette Kleinbard; Marshall Leib.

Also see CONNORS, Carol
Also see HARVEY, Phil
Also see NELSON, Sandy

TEE, Willie

P&R/R&B '65

Singles: 7-inch

A.F.O. 10-15 62
ATLANTIC 5-10 65
CAPITOL 4-8 68-70
CINDERELLA (1202 "Foolish Girl") 20-30
GATOR (701 "She Really Did Surprise Me") 20-30 71
HOT LINE 4-8
NOLA (737 "Please Don't Go") 100-200 65
U.A. 3-5 76

LPs: 10/12-inch 33rpm

CAPITOL 10-15 69
U.A. 5-10 76

TEE SET

P&R/LP '70

Singles: 7-inch

COLLECTABLES 3-4 80s
COLOSSUS 3-5 70-71

Picture Sleeves

COLOSSUS 3-5 70

LPs: 10/12-inch 33rpm

COLOSSUS 10-15 70

TEEGARDEN & VAN WINKLE

P&R '70

Singles: 7-inch

ATCO 4-8 68
PLUMM 3-6 70
WESTBOUND 3-6 69-72

Picture Sleeves

WESTBOUND 3-5 70

LPs: 10/12-inch 33rpm

ATCO 10-15 68
WESTBOUND 8-12 69-72

Members: David Teegarden; Skip Knape.

TEEN DREAM
(With Valentino)

R&B '87

Singles: 7-inch

W.B. 3-4 87-88

TEEN KINGS

Singles: 78rpm

JE-WEL (101 "Ooby Dooby") .200-300 56

Singles: 7-inch

JE-WEL (101 "Ooby Dooby") .400-600 56
(May read "Vocal Roy Oribson," instead of "Orbison," on some labels. Beware since some counterfeits exist that are difficult to identify. Consult an expert if in doubt.)

Members: Roy Orbison; Johnny "Peanuts" Wilson; Billy Par Ellis; James Monroe; Jack Kennelly.

Also see ORBISON, Roy
Also see ROGERS, Weldon

TEEN QUEENS

P&R/R&B '56

Singles: 78rpm

RPM 5-10 56-57

Singles: 7-inch

ANTLER 5-10 60-61
COLLECTABLES 3-4 80s
KENT 4-8 61
RCA 5-10 58
RPM 10-20 56-57

Picture Sleeves

ANTLER 10-20 60

LPs: 10/12-inch 33rpm

CROWN (5022 "Eddie My Love") 50-100 56
CROWN (5373 "Teen Queens") 20-30 63
UNITED 8-12

Members: Rose Collins; Betty Collins.

TEENA MARIE: see MARIE, Teena

TEENAGERS

Singles: 78rpm

GEE (1046 "Flip-Flop") 5-10 57

Singles: 7-inch

END (1071 "Crying") 30-40 60
END (1076 "Can You Tell Me") .. 20-30 60
GEE (1046 "Flip-Flop") 10-20 57

ROULETTE (4086 "Broken Heart") 35-45 58
Members: Billy Lobrano; Herman Santiago; Sherman Garnes; Jim Merchant; Joe Negroni.
Also see LYMON, Frankie

TEMPER

R&B/D&D '84

Singles: 12-inch 33/45rpm

MCA 4-6 84

Singles: 7-inch

MCA 3-4 84
Member: Anthony Malloy.
Also see ANTHONY & CAMP

TEMPO, Nino
(With 5th Ave. Sax)

P&R '73

Singles: 7-inch

A&M 3-5 73-74
RCA 5-10 59-60
TOWER 4-6 67
U.A. 5-10 60

LPs: 10/12-inch 33rpm

A&M 8-10 74
ATCO 10-15 66
Also see ARCHIES

TEMPO, Nino, & April Stevens

P&R '62

Singles: 7-inch

A&M 3-5 72-75
ABC 3-5 73
ATCO 4-8 62-66
BELL 3-6 69
CHELSEA 3-5 76
MARINA 3-5 72
WHITE WHALE 4-6 66-68

LPs: 10/12-inch 33rpm

ATCO 10-15 63-66
CAMDEN 10-15 64
WHITE WHALE 10-15 69
Also see STEVENS, April
Also see TEMPO, Nino

TEMPO TOPPERS
(Featuring Little Richard)

Singles: 78rpm

PEACOCK 10-20 53-54

Singles: 7-inch

PEACOCK (1616 "A Fool at the Wheel") 50-75 53
PEACOCK (1628 "Always") 40-60 54
Members: Richard Penniman; Jimmy Swan; Barry Gilmore; Bill Brooks.
Also see DUCES of RHYTHM & Tempo Toppers
Also see LITTLE RICHARD

TEMPOS

P&R '59

Singles: 78rpm

KAPP 8-12 57

Singles: 7-inch

CLIMAX 10-15 59
KAPP 10-20 57-58
PARIS 10-15 59
ROULETTE 3-5 70s

TEMPREES

P&R '72

Singles: 7-inch

EPIC 3-5 76
STAX 3-4 84
WE PRODUCE 3-4 72-74

LPs: 10/12-inch 33rpm

STAX 5-8 84
WE PRODUCE 5-10 72-74

TEMPTATIONS

P&R '60

Singles: 7-inch

GOLDISC (3001 "Barbara") 15-25 60
Black label.)
GOLDISC (3001 "Barbara") 10-15 60
Multi-color label.)
ROULETTE 3-5 71

TEMPTATIONS

R&B '62

Singles: 7-inch

ATLANTIC 3-5 77-78
GORDY (1631 thru 1933) 3-4 82-88
GORDY (7001 "Dream Come True") 25-30 62
GORDY (7010 "Paradise") 20-25 62
GORDY (7015 "I Want a Love I Can See") 15-20 63
GORDY (7020 "Farewell My Love") 15-20 63
GORDY (7028 thru 7074) 8-15 64-68
GORDY (7081 thru 7213) 3-8 68-81
MIRACLE (5 "Oh Mother of Mine") 50-100 61
MIRACLE (12 "Check Yourself") 40-60 62
MOTOWN 3-4 84-87
MOTOWN/TOPPS (4 "My Girl") 50-75 67
MOTOWN/TOPPS (13 "The Way You Do the Things You Do") 50-75 67
(Topps Chewing Gum promotional item. Single-sided, cardboard flexi, picture disc. Issued with generic paper sleeve.)

Picture Sleeves

GORDY (7038 "My Girl") 25-50 65
GORDY (7055 "Beauty Is Only Skin Deep") 10-20 66
GORDY (7099 "Ball of Confusion") 10-20 70

EPs: 7-inch 33/45rpm

GORDY (60914 "Tempting Temptations") 15-25 65
GORDY (60918 "Getting Ready") 15-25 66
GORDY (60919 "Greatest Hits") 15-25 66

MOTOWN (2004 "Temptations")........................ 15-25 60s
MOTOWN (2010 "It's the Temptations")........................ 15-25

LPs: 10/12–inch 33rpm

ATLANTIC.................................. 5-10 77-78
GORDY (911 "Meet the Temptations")......................... 20-30 64
GORDY (S-911 "Meet the Temptations")......................... 25-35 64
GORDY (912 "The Temptations Sing Smokey").............................. 15-25 65
GORDY (914 "The Tempting Temptations")......................... 15-25 65
GORDY (918 "Gettin' Ready").. 15-25 66
GORDY (919 Greatest Hits) 15-20 66
GORDY (921 "Live") 15-25 67
GORDY (922 "With a Lot O' Soul")................................ 15-25 67
GORDY (924 "In a Mellow Mood")................................. 15-25 67
GORDY (927 "Wish It Would Rain") 15-25 68
GORDY (933 thru 1006) 8-18 69-80
GORDY (6000 series).................. 5-8 82-86
KORY 8-10 77
MOTOWN (100 & 200 series)..... 5-10 81-82
MOTOWN (782 "Anthology") 15-20 73
(Three-LP set. Includes 12-page color booklet.)
MOTOWN (998 "Give Love at Christmas") 12-18 80
(Promotional issue only.)
MOTOWN (5389 "25th Anniversary").......................... 10-15 86
(Includes eight-page color booklet.)
MOTOWN (6246 "Together Again") 5-8 87
NATURAL RESOURCES........... 5-10 78

Members: David Ruffin; Eddie Kendricks; Melvin Franklin; Otis Williams; Paul Williams; Damon Harris; Dennis Edwards.

Also see DISTANTS
Also see FOUR TOPS / Temptations
Also see KENDRICKS, Eddie
Also see LANDS, Liz, & Temptations
Also see PIRATES
Also see ROBINSON, Smokey
Also see ROSS, Diana
Also see RUFFIN, David
Also see SUPREMES & TEMPTATIONS

TEMPTATIONS & FOUR TOPS

LPs: 10/12–inch 33rpm

MOTOWN (134 "Battle of the Champions") 10-20
(Promotional issue only.)
SILVER EAGLE 5-10 87

Also see FOUR TOPS

TEMPTATIONS & Rick James

R&B '82

Singles: 12–inch 33/45rpm

GORDY.......................................4-6 82

Singles: 7–inch

GORDY.......................................3-4 82

Also see JAMES, Rick

TEMPTATIONS / Stevie Wonder

LPs: 10/12–inch 33rpm

GORDY/TAMLA/MOTOWN (100 "The Sky's the Limit")..............................15-25 71
(Promotional issue only.)

Also see TEMPTATIONS
Also see WONDER, Stevie

10CC

P&R '73

Singles: 7–inch

MERCURY..................................3-5 75-77
POLYDOR 3-5 78
UK...3-5 72-74

Picture Sleeves

MERCURY..................................5-8 75-77

LPs: 10/12–inch 33rpm

MERCURY..............................10-15 75-77
POLYDOR 5-8 78-79
UK..10-15 73-75
W.B. 8-10 80

Members: Kevin Godley; Lol Creme; Graham Gouldman; Eric Stewart; Paul Burgess; Rick Fenn; Tony O'Malley; Stuart Tosh.

Also see GODLEY, Kevin, & Lol Creme
Also see GOULDMAN, Graham
Also see HOTLEGS
Also see KASENETZ-KATZ SINGING ORCHESTRAL CIRCUS
Also see KOKOMO
Also see OHIO EXPRESS
Also see PILOT
Also see SEDAKA, Neil
Also see WAX

10 SPEED

R&B '84

Singles: 12–inch 33/45rpm

QUALITY/RFC 4-6 83

Singles: 7–inch

QUALITY/RFC 3-5 83

10,000 MANIACS

LP '87

Singles: 7–inch

ELEKTRA....................................3-4 87-89

Picture Sleeves

ELEKTRA....................................3-5 88-89

LPs: 10/12–inch 33rpm

ELEKTRA..................................5-10 87-90
MARK (20247 "Human Conflict No. 5")................................100-150 82
MARK (20389 "Secrets of the I Ching")................................75-100 83
(Includes lyrics/print insert.)

Members: Natalie Merchant; Robert Buck; Dennis Drew; Steven Gustafson; John Lombardo; Robert Wachter; Jerome Augustyniak.

TEN WHEEL DRIVE
(With Genya Ravan)

P&R/LP '70

Singles: 7–inch

CAPITOL.................................. 3-5 73
POLYDOR.................................. 4-6 69-71

LPs: 10/12–inch 33rpm

CAPITOL.................................. 8-10 73
POLYDOR.................................. 10-12 69-71

Member: Genya Ravan.
Also see RAVAN, Genya
Also see ZAGER, Michael, Band

TEN YEARS AFTER

LP '68

Singles: 7–inch

COLUMBIA.................................. 3-5 71-73
DERAM.................................. 4-6 68-70

Picture Sleeves

DERAM.................................. 4-6 68

LPs: 10/12–inch 33rpm

CHRYSALIS.................................. 5-10 83-89
COLUMBIA.................................. 8-12 71-76
DERAM.................................. 8-12 68-75
LONDON.................................. 5-10 77

Member: Alvin Lee.
Also see LEE, Alvin

TENDER SLIM

P&R '60

Singles: 7–inch

GREY CLIFF.................................. 5-10 59
HERALD.................................. 4-8 62

TENNESSEE ERNIE: see FORD, "Tennessee" Ernie

TENNILLE, Toni

LP '84

Singles: 7–inch

MIRAGE.................................. 3-5 84

LPs: 10/12–inch 33rpm

GAIA.................................. 5-8 87
MIRAGE.................................. 5-8 84

Also see CAPTAIN & TENNILLE

TEPPER, Robert

P&R/LP '86

Singles: 7–inch

SCOTTI BROTHERS.................................. 3-4 85-86

Picture Sleeves

SCOTTI BROTHERS.................................. 3-4 86

LPs: 10/12–inch 33rpm

SCOTTI BROTHERS.................................. 5-8 85-86

TERRELL, Jean

R&B '78

Singles: 7–inch

A&M.................................. 3-5 78

LPs: 10/12–inch 33rpm

A&M.................................. 8-10 78

Also see SUPREMES

TERRELL, Tammi

P&R/R&B '66

Singles: 7–inch

MOTOWN.................................. 4-8 65-69

LPs: 10/12–inch 33rpm

MOTOWN (200 series).................................. 5-10 82
MOTOWN (652 "Irresistible").................................. 40-60 66

Also see GAYE, Marvin, & Tammi Terrell
Also see JACKSON, Chuck, & Tammi Terrell
Also see MONTGOMERY, Tammy

TERRY, Sonny
(Sonny "Hootin" Terry & His Night Owls; with His Buckshot Five)

Singles: 78rpm

ASCH.................................. 10-20 45
CAPITOL.................................. 5-15 47-50
GOTHAM.................................. 8-12 51
GRAMERCY.................................. 8-12 52
GROOVE.................................. 5-10 54-55
HARLEM.................................. 10-15 52
JACKSON.................................. 10-15 52
JAX.................................. 10-15 50s
JOSIE.................................. 10-15 56
OLD TOWN.................................. 10-15 56
RCA.................................. 5-10 53
RED ROBIN.................................. 15-25 53
SAVOY.................................. 8-12 48
SOLO.................................. 10-15 49

Singles: 7–inch

CAPITOL (931 "Telephone Blues").................................. 50-75 50
CHESS (1860 "Dangerous Woman").................................. 10-15 63
CHOICE.................................. 5-10 61
GOTHAM (517 "Baby, Let's Have Some Fun").................................. 20-30 51
GOTHAM (518 "Harmonica Rumbo").................................. 20-30 51
GRAMERCY (1004 "Hootin' Blues").................................. 25-35 52
(Black vinyl.)
GRAMERCY (Colored vinyl).................................. 50-75 52
(Colored vinyl.)
GROOVE.................................. 15-25 54-55
HARLEM (2327 "Dangerous Woman").................................. 40-50 52
JACKSON (2302 "That Woman Is Killing Me").................................. 50-100 52
(Colored vinyl.)
JAX (305 "I Don't Worry").................................. 200-300 50s
(Colored vinyl.)
JOSIE.................................. 10-20 56
OLD TOWN.................................. 10-20 56
RCA (5492 "Hootin' and Jumpin'").................................. 20-30 53
RCA (5577 "Sonny Is Drinkin'").................................. 20-30 53
RED ROBIN (110 "Harmonica Hop").................................. 75-125 53

LPs: 10/12–inch 33rpm

ARCHIVE of FOLK MUSIC 15-25 65
EVEREST 5-10 70s
PRESTIGE BLUESVILLE 20-30 61-63
WASHINGTON (702 "Talkin' About the Blues")............................. 25-35 61

Session: Mickey Baker; Brownie McGhee.
Also see BAGBY, Doc
Also see HOPKINS, Lightnin,' & Sonny Terry
Also see McGHEE, Brownie, & Sonny Terry

TERRY, Tony

P&R/R&B '87

Singles: 7–inch

EPIC 3-4 87-90

Picture Sleeves

EPIC 3-4 88

LPs: 10/12–inch 33rpm

EPIC 5-8 87-91

TESLA

P&R/LP '87

Singles: 7–inch

GEFFEN.. 3-4 87-90

Picture Sleeves

GEFFEN.. 3-4 87

LPs: 10/12–inch 33rpm

GEFFEN.. 5-8 87-90

Members: Jeff Keith; Brian Wheat; Frank Hannon; Tommy Skeoch; Troy Lucchetta.

TESTAMENT

LP '88

LPs: 10/12–inch 33rpm

MEGAFORCE.............................. 5-8 88-90

TEX, Joe

(With the Class Mates; with Vibrators)

P&R '64

Singles: 78rpm

KING 10-20 55-57

Singles: 12–inch 33/45rpm

EPIC 4-8 77

Singles: 7–inch

ACE (544 "Cut It Out") 40-60 58
ACE (549 "Blessed Are These Tears") 40-60 58
ACE (550 "Mother's Advice") 50-75 58
ACE (673 "Boys Will Be Boys"). 15-25 60
ANNA (1119 "All I Could Do Was Cry")............................ 15-25 60
ANNA (1124 "I'll Never Break Your Heart")................................. 15-25 60
ANNA (1128 "Ain't I a Mess").... 15-25 61
ATLANTIC..................................... 3-5 72
CHECKER (1104 "All I Could Do Was Cry")................................. 8-12 63
DIAL (1000 series) 3-6 71-76
DIAL (2800 series) 3-5 78
DIAL (3000 series) 5-10 61-64
DIAL (4000 series) 4-8 64-69
EPIC 3-5 77-79
HANDSHAKE...............................3-5 81
JALYNNE..................................5-10 61
KING (4840 "Come in This House")................................35-55 55
KING (4884 "My Biggest Mistake")................................25-50 56
KING (4980 "Pneumonia") 25-50 56
KING (4911 "She's Mine")..........25-50 65
KING (5064 "Ain't Nobody's Business")..............................25-50 57
KING (5981 "Come in This House") 5-10 65

LPs: 10/12–inch 33rpm

ACCORD 5-10 82
ATLANTIC...............................10-15 65-72
CHECKER 20-30 64
DIAL 8-10 72-79
EPIC..5-10 77-78
KING 15-25 65
LONDON....................................5-10 79
PARROT 15-25 65
PRIDE 8-10 73

Members: Mike Appell; Rod Bristow.
Also see SOUL CLAN

TEXANS

P&R '61

Singles: 7–inch

GOTHIC 10-20 61
INFINITY 10-20 61
JOX 10-15 64
VEE JAY 5-10 65

Members: Dorsey Burnette; Johnny Burnette.
Also see BURNETTE, Johnny & Dorsey

TEXAS "GUITAR" SLIM

(Johnny Winter)

Singles: 7–inch

JIN (174 "Broke and Lonely").....30-50 62
(This same number was used for *Something's Wrong,* by Rockin' Sidney.)
MOON-LITE 75-100 60

Also see GUITAR SLIM
Also see WINTER, Johnny

TEXAS SLIM

(John Lee Hooker)

Singles: 78rpm

KING (Except 4377)..................30-50 48-49
KING (4377 "Moaning Blues") ...50-75 50

Also see HOOKER, John Lee

TEXTONES

LP '84

Singles: 7–inch

GOLD MOUNTAIN 3-4 84
I.R.S./FAULTY PRODUCTS 3-5 80

LPs: 10/12–inch 33rpm

GOLD MOUNTAIN 5-8 84

Members: Carla Olson; Mark Cuff; Kathy Valentine; David Provost; George Callins; Phil Seymour; Tom Morgan; Joe Read.
Also see CLARK, Gene, & Carla Olson
Also see DREAM SYNDICATE

Also see GO-GOs
Also see SEYMOUR, Phil

THE, The

D&D '83

Singles: 12-inch 33/45rpm

EPIC 4-6 84-89
SIRE 4-6 83-84

Singles: 7-inch

EPIC 3-4 83-85

LPs: 10/12-inch 33rpm

EPIC 5-8 84-89

THEE MIDNITERS

P&R '65

Singles: 7-inch

CHATTAHOOCHEE (666 "Land of 1000 Dances") 5-10 65
CHATTAHOOCHEE (674 "Sad Girl") 8-12 65
CHATTAHOOCHEE (675 "Sad Girl") 5-10 65
CHATTAHOOCHEE (684 "Whittier Boulevard") 5-10 65
CHATTAHOOCHEE (693 "I Need Someone") 5-10 65
CHATTAHOOCHEE (694 "It's Not Unusual") 5-10 66
CHATTAHOOCHEE (706 "Are You Angry") 5-10 66
UNI 4-8 69
WHITTIER (500 thru 509) 10-20 66-67
WHITTIER (511 "You're Gonna Make Me Cry") 100-200 68
WHITTIER (674 "Sad Girl") 5-8 68

LPs: 10/12-inch 33rpm

CHATTAHOOCHEE (C-1001 "Thee Midniters") 20-30 65
(Monaural.)
CHATTAHOOCHEE (CS-1001 "Thee Midniters") 25-45 65
(Stereo.)
RHINO 5-8 83
WHITTIER (5000 "Special Delivery") 15-25 66
WHITTIER (5001 "Unlimited") 15-25 66
WHITTIER (5002 "Giants") 15-25 67

THEE PROPHETS

P&R/LP '69

Singles: 7-inch

KAPP 4-8 69

LPs: 10/12-inch 33rpm

KAPP 15-20 69

THEM
(Featuring Van Morrison)

P&R/LP '65

Singles: 7-inch

HAPPY TIGER 4-6 69-70
LOMA 5-8 66
LONDON 3-4 70s
PARROT (Except 365) 5-10 64-00
PARROT (365 "Gloria") 10-15 65
(Copies with later copyright dates are reissues. Later released on Parrot 9727.)
RUFF 8-10 67
SULLY 15-20 60s
TOWER 4-8 67-69

LPs: 10/12-inch 33rpm

HAPPY TIGER (1004 "Them") 20-30 69
HAPPY TIGER (1012 "In Reality") 20-30 71
LONDON 5-10 77
PARROT (61005 "Them") 50-100 65
(Cover does not highlight *Gloria*.)
(Monaural.)
PARROT (61005 "Them") 30-35 65
(Cover highlights *Gloria*.)
(Monaural.)
PARROT (61008 "Them Again") 25-30 66
(Monaural.)
PARROT (71005 "Them") 50-100 65
(Cover does not highlight *Gloria*.)
(Stereo.)
PARROT (71005 "Them") 40-50 65
(Cover highlights *Gloria*.)
(Stereo.)
PARROT (71008 "Them Again") 40-50 66
(Stereo.)
PARROT (71053 "Them Featuring Van Morrison") 10-15 72
TOWER (5104 "Now and Them") 25-35 68
TOWER (5116 "Time Out") 25-35 68

Members: Van Morrison; Billy Harrison; Alan Henderson; Peter Bardens; J. McAuley; John Stark.
Also see BARDENS, Peter
Also see BELFAST GYPSIES
Also see MORRISON, Van

THEO VANESS

LP '79

Singles: 7-inch

PRELUDE 3-5 79

LPs: 10/12-inch 33rpm

PRELUDE 5-10 79

THEODORE, Mike, Orchestra

LP '77

Singles: 7-inch

WESTBOUND 3-5 77-79

LPs: 10/12-inch 33rpm

WESTBOUND 5-10 77-79

THERESA

R&B '87

Singles: 7-inch

RCA 3-4 87-88

Members: Theresa King; Victor Porter.

THEY MIGHT BE GIANTS

LP '88

LPs: 10/12-inch 33rpm

BAR NONE 5-8 88
ELEKTRA.................................... 5-8 90

THIN LIZZY

P&R/LP '76

Singles: 12-inch 33/45rpm

W.B. 4-8 78
(Promotional only.)

Singles: 7-inch

LONDON..................................... 3-5 73
MERCURY.................................. 3-5 76-77
VERTIGO.................................... 3-5 75
W.B. 3-5 78-79

Picture Sleeves

VERTIGO.................................... 3-5 75

LPs: 10/12-inch 33rpm

LONDON (500 & 600 series) 10-15 71
LONDON (20000 series)............ 8-12 72
LONDON (50000 series)............ 5-10 77
MERCURY.................................. 8-12 76-77
VERTIGO.................................. 10-12 74-75
W.B. 5-10 78-84

Members: Philip Lynott; Gary Moore; Brian Robertson.
Also see MOORE, Gary

THINK

P&R '71

Singles: 7-inch

BIG TREE 3-5 74
LAURIE....................................... 3-5 71

LPs: 10/12-inch 33rpm

LAURIE..................................... 8-10 72

Member: Lou Stallman.

THIRD BASS

LP '89

LPs: 10/12-inch 33rpm

DEF JAM...................................... 5-8 89-91

THIRD POWER

LP '70

Singles: 7-inch

BARON (626 "Snow") 10-20 68
VANGUARD................................. 4-8 70

LPs: 10/12-inch 33rpm

VANGUARD (6554 "Believe") ... 15-20 70

Members: Jim Craig; Drew Abbott.

THIRD RAIL

P&R '67

Singles: 7-inch

CAMEO 4-8 66
EPIC.. 3-6 67-69

LPs: 10/12-inch 33rpm

EPIC 20-30 67

Member: Joey Levine; Kris Resnik; Art Resnik.

THIRD WORLD

LP '78

Singles: 12-inch 33/45rpm

COLUMBIA.................................4-6 81-85
ISLAND......................................4-8 78-80

Singles: 7-inch

ABRAXAS 3-5 76
COLUMBIA.................................3-5 81-85
ISLAND......................................3-5 79

LPs: 10/12-inch 33rpm

COLUMBIA.................................5-8 81-85
ISLAND....................................5-10 76-80
MERCURY 5-8 89

Member: Stevie Wonder.
Also see WONDER, Stevie

THIRTEENTH FLOOR ELEVATORS

P&R '66

Singles: 7-inch

CONTACT (5269 "You're Gonna Miss Me")..............................50-75 66
(First issue of *You're Gonna Miss Me.*)
HBR (492 "You're Gonna Miss Me") 40-50 66
(Third issue of *You're Gonna Miss Me.*)
INTERNATIONAL ARTISTS (107 "You're Gonna Miss Me")...................10-20 66
(Second issue of *You're Gonna Miss Me.*)
INTERNATIONAL ARTISTS (111 through 130).......................................10-20 66-68

LPs: 10/12-inch 33rpm

INTERNATIONAL ARTISTS (1 "Psychedelic Sounds") 75-100 67
(Does NOT have "Masterfonics" stamped in the vinyl trail-off.)
INTERNATIONAL ARTISTS (5 "Easter Everywhere") 40-60 67
(Does NOT have "Masterfonics" stamped in the vinyl trail-off.)
INTERNATIONAL ARTISTS (8 "Live") 40-60 68
(Does NOT have "Masterfonics" stamped in the vinyl trail-off.)
INTERNATIONAL ARTISTS (9 "Bull of the Woods") 40-60 68
(Does NOT have "Masterfonics" stamped in the vinyl trail-off.)
INTERNATIONAL ARTISTS......10-20 79
(Reissues. With "Masterfonics" stamped in the vinyl trail-off.)
INTERNATIONAL ARTISTS (White Label)................................150-225 67-68
(Promotional issues only.)
TEXAS ARCHIVE 8-10 85

Members: Roky Erickson; Tommy Hall; Stacy Sutherland; John Ike Walton; Benny Thurman.
Also see ERICKSON, Roky
Also see SPADES

.38 SPECIAL
(Thirty Eight Special)

LP '77

Singles: 7–inch

A&M 3-5 77-88
CAPITOL 3-5 84

Picture Sleeves

A&M 3-5 80-83

LPs: 10/12–inch 33rpm

A&M 5-10 77-88
CAPITOL 5-8 84
Member: Dave Van Zandt.

THOMAS, B.J.
(With the Triumphs)

P&R '66

Singles: 7–inch

ABC 3-5 75
BRAGG (103 "Billy & Sue") 10-20 66
CLEVELAND INT'L 3-4 83-84
COLLECTABLES 3-4 80s
COLUMBIA 3-4 83-86
HICKORY 4-8 66
LORI (9561 "For Your Precious Love") 8-10 64
MCA 3-5 77-82
MYRRH 3-4 77-81
PACEMAKER (227 "I'm So Lonesome I Could Cry") 10-15 64
PACEMAKER (231 "Mama") 5-10 65
PACEMAKER (234 "Bring Back the Time") 5-10 65
PACEMAKER (239 "Tomorrow Never Comes") 5-10 66
PACEMAKER (247 "Plain Jane") 5-10 66
PACEMAKER (253 "Baby Cried") 5-10 66
PACEMAKER (256 "I Can't Help It") 5-10 65
PARAMOUNT 3-5 73-74
SCEPTER (12100 series) 4-8 66-67
SCEPTER (12200 thru 12364) 3-6 68-72
SCEPTER (21000 series) 3-5 73-74
VALERIE 4-8 60s
W.B. (5491 "Billy & Sue") 15-20 64

Picture Sleeves

MCA 3-5 79

LPs: 10/12–inch 33rpm

ABC 5-10 74-77
ACCORD 5-10 81-82
BUCKBOARD 5-10
CLEVELAND INT'L 5-10 83
COLUMBIA 5-8 86
DORAL 15-25 60s
(Promotional mail-order issue, from Doral cigarettes.)
EXACT 5-10 80
EXCELSIOR 5-10 80
EVEREST 5-10 81
51 WEST 5-10 79
HICKORY (133 "Very Best") 20-30 66
MCA 5-10 77-82
MCA/SONGBIRD 5-10 80
MYRRH 5-8 78-83
PACEMAKER (3001 "B.J. Thomas and the Triumphs") 40-50 66
PARAMOUNT 5-10 73-74
PHOENIX 20 .... 5-10 81
PICKWICK 5-8 78
PRIORITY 5-8 83
SCEPTER (535 thru 561) 10-20 66-67
SCEPTER (586 thru 597) 8-12 70-71
SCEPTER (5101 "Billy Joe Thomas") 8-12 72
SCEPTER (5108 "Country") 8-12 72
SCEPTER (5112 "Greatest All-Time Hits") 10-15 73
SPRINGBOARD 5-10 73-79
STARDAY 5-10 77
TRIP 5-10 76
U.A. 5-10 74
Also see CHARLES, Ray, & B.J. Thomas
Also see EDDY, Duane

THOMAS, Carla

P&R/R&B '61

Singles: 7–inch

ATLANTIC 4-8 60-65
SATELLITE (104 "Gee Whiz, Look at His Eyes") 40-60 60
STAX 3-8 65-72

Picture Sleeves

STAX 4-8 66

EPs: 7–inch 33/45rpm

STAX 10-15 66
(Jukebox issues only.)

LPs: 10/12–inch 33rpm

ATLANTIC (8057 "Gee Whiz") ... 20-30 61
ATLANTIC (8232 "Best of Carla Thomas") 10-15 69
STAX 10-15 66-71
Also see BELL, William, & Carla Thomas
Also see OTIS & CARLA
Also see REDDING, Otis / Carla Thomas / Sam & Dave / Eddie Floyd
Also see RUFUS & CARLA
Also see TAYLOR, Johnnie, & Carla Thomas

THOMAS, Evelyn

P&R/R&B/D&D '84

Singles: 12–inch 33/45rpm

TSR 4-6 84

Singles: 7–inch

CASABLANCA 3-5 78
TSR 3-5 84
VANGUARD 3-5 85

LPs: 10/12–inch 33rpm

A.V.I. 5-10 79
CASABLANCA 5-10 78

THOMAS, Gene

P&R '61

Singles: 7-inch

HICKORY 3-5 71
TRX 3-6 69
U.A. 4-8 61-65
VENUS 10-15 61-62

Also see GENE & DEBBE

THOMAS, Ian

P&R '73

Singles: 7-inch

ATLANTIC 3-5 78
CHRYSALIS 3-5 75
JANUS 3-5 73-74
MERCURY 3-4 84

LPs: 10/12-inch 33rpm

ATLANTIC 5-10 78
JANUS 8-10 73-74
MERCURY 5-8 84

THOMAS, Irma

R&B '60

Singles: 7-inch

BANDY 4-8 60s
CANYON 3-5 70
CHESS 4-6 68
COTILLION 3-5 71-72
FUNGUS 3-5 73
IMPERIAL 4-8 64-66
MINIT 4-8 61-63
RCS 3-5 79-81
ROKER 3-5 71
RON 5-10 59-60

LPs: 10/12-inch 33rpm

FUNGUS 8-10 73
IMPERIAL (266 "Wish Someone Would Care") 20-30 64
IMPERIAL (302 "Take a Look") . 15-20 66
RCS 5-10 80

Also see BROWN, Maxine / Irma Thomas

THOMAS, Irma / Ernie K-Doe / Showmen / Benny Spellman

LP: 10/12-inch 33rpm

MINIT (0004 "New Orleans, Home of the Blues, Vol. 2") 20-25 64

Also see K-DOE, Ernie
Also see SHOWMEN
Also see SPELLMAN, Benny

THOMAS, Jamo, & Party Brothers

P&R '66

Singles: 7-inch

CHESS 4-8 66
DECCA 4-8 68
SOUND STAGE 7 .... 4-8 67
THOMAS 4-8 66

Picture Sleeves

THOMAS 4-8 66

THOMAS, Joe

(Joe Thomas Orchestra)

R&B '49

Singles: 78rpm

KING 5-10 49-51
MERCURY 5-10 51

Singles: 7-inch

KING (4460 "Jumpin' Joe") 15-25 51
KING (4474 "You're Just My Kind") 15-25 51
MERCURY (8268 "Everybody Loves My Baby") 15-25 51

THOMAS, Joe

R&B '76

Singles: 7-inch

GROOVE MERCHANT 3-5 76
LRC 3-5 77-79
SUE 4-8 64

LPs: 10/12-inch 33rpm

LRC 5-10 77-78
TODAY 6-12 72

THOMAS, Jon

(John Thomas)

P&R/R&B '60

Singles: 78rpm

CHECKER (809 "Rib Tips") 8-12 55
MERCURY (71078 "Hard Head") 10-15 57

Singles: 7-inch

ABC-PAR 8-12 60-61
CHECKER (809 "Rib Tips") 15-20 55
JUNIOR 5-10 64
MERCURY (71078 "Hard Head") 10-20 57
VEEP 5-15 67-68

LPs: 10/12-inch 33rpm

ABC-PAR (351 "Heartbreak") 20-30 60
(Monaural.)
ABC-PAR (S-351 "Heartbreak") . 30-40 60
(Stereo.)
WING 10-20 63

THOMAS, Leone

R&B '76

Singles: 7-inch

DON 3-5 76

THOMAS, Lillo

R&B '83

Singles: 12-inch 33/45rpm

CAPITOL 4-6 83-85

Singles: 7-inch

CAPITOL 3-4 83-87

LPs: 10/12-inch 33rpm

CAPITOL 5-8 83-85

Also see LAURENCE, Paul

THOMAS, Lillo, & Melba Moore

R&B '84

Singles: 7–inch

CAPITOL 3-5 84

Also see MOORE, Melba
Also see THOMAS, Lillo

THOMAS, Nolan

R&B/D&D '84

Singles: 12–inch 33/45rpm

EMERGENCY 4-6 84-85

Singles: 7–inch

MIRAGE 3-5 84-85

Also see MONET & Nolan Thomas

THOMAS, Pat

P&R '62

Singles: 7–inch

MGM 3-5 62-63
VERVE 3-5 62-64

Picture Sleeves

MGM 3-6 62

LPs: 10/12–inch 33rpm

MGM 10-20 62-64
STRAND 10-20 61

THOMAS, Philip-Michael

R&B '85

Singles: 7–inch

ATLANTIC 3-5 85

THOMAS, Ray

LP '75

Singles: 7–inch

THRESHOLD 3-5 75-76

LPs: 10/12–inch 33rpm

THRESHOLD (16 "From Mighty Oaks") 10-15 75
(Gatefold cover.)
THRESHOLD (17 "Hopes, Wishes and Dreams") 10-15 76
THRESHOLD (102 "Ray Thomas Discusses *From Mighty Oaks*") 15-25 75
(Promotional issue only.)

Also see MOODY BLUES

THOMAS, Rufus
(Rufus "Bearcat" Thomas; Rufus Thomas Jr.)

R&B '53

Singles: 12–inch 33/45rpm

A.V.I. 4-8 78

Singles: 78rpm

CHESS 15-25 52
STAR TALENT 20-30 50
SUN (181 "Bear Cat [Answer to Hound Dog]") 40-60 53
(With subtitle.)
SUN (181 "Bear Cat") 30-40 53
(Without subtitle.)
SUN (188 "Tiger Man") 40-60 53

Singles: 7–inch

A.V.I. 3-5 77-78
ARTISTS of AMERICA 3-5 76
HI 3-5 78
METEOR (5039 "I'm Steady Holdin' On") 100-150 56
STAX (100 & 200 series) 4-8 62-68
STAX (0010 thru 0236) 3-6 68-75
SUN (181 "Bear Cat [Answer to Hound Dog]") 100-150 53
(With subtitle.)
SUN (181 "Bear Cat") 75-100 53
(Without subtitle.)
SUN (188 "Tiger Man") 100-150 53

LPs: 10/12–inch 33rpm

A.V.I. 5-10 77-78
ARTISTS of AMERICA 8-10 76
GUSTO 5-10 80
STAX (Except 704) 6-15 70-79
STAX (704 "Walking the Dog") .. 15-20 63

Also see RUFUS & CARLA

THOMAS, Tasha

R&B '78

Singles: 7–inch

ATLANTIC 3-5 78-79
ROULETTE 4-8 69

THOMAS, Timmy

P&R/R&B '72

Singles: 12–inch 33/45rpm

GOLD MOUNTAIN 4-6 84
SPECTOR 4-6 83

Singles: 7–inch

GLADES 3-5 72-77
GOLD MOUNTAIN 3-4 84-85
GOLDWAX 4-8 67
MARLIN 3-5 80-81
SPECTOR 3-4 83
TM 3-5 78

LPs: 10/12–inch 33rpm

GLADES 8-10 72-76
GOLD MOUNTAIN 5-8 84

THOMAS, Vaneese

R&B '87

Singles: 7–inch

GEFFEN 3-4 87

Also see NAJEE

THOMPSON, Chris, & Night

P&R '79

Singles: 7–inch

PLANET 3-5 79

Also see MANN, Manfred
Also see NIGHT
Also see WARNES, Jennifer, & Chris Thompson

THOMPSON, Hank
(With the Brazos Valley Boys)

C&W '48

Singles: 78rpm

CAPITOL 4-8 47-57
GLOBE (124 "Whoa Sailor") 75-125 46

Singles: 7–inch

ABC 3-5 75-79

ABC/DOT 3-5 74-77
CAPITOL (1000 thru 3000 series) 5-15 50-58
CAPITOL (4000 & 5000 series) 4-8 58-66
CHURCHILL.................................. 3-4 81-83
DOT.. 3-5 68-74
MCA 3-4 79-80
W.B. 3-6 66-67

Picture Sleeves

CAPITOL.. 4-8 61

EPs: 7-inch 33/45rpm

CAPITOL.................................. 10-20 53-59

LPs: 10/12-inch 33rpm

ABC... 5-8 78
ABC/DOT 5-10 74-77
CAPITOL (H-418 "Songs of the Brazos Valley").................. 60-80 53
(10-inch LP.)
CAPITOL (T-418 "Songs of the Brazos Valley").................. 50-75 55
(Green label.)
CAPITOL (T-618 "North of the Rio Grande") 40-60 55
(Green label.)
CAPITOL (T-729 "New Recordings") 30-50 55
CAPITOL (T-826 "Hank!") 30-40 57
CAPITOL (T-975 "Dance Ranch") 30-40 58
CAPITOL (T-1111 thru T-2154) 15-25 59-64
(Monaural.)
CAPITOL (ST-1111 through ST-2154) 15-30 59-64
(Stereo.)
CAPITOL (SM-2000 series) 5-8 75
CAPITOL (T-2274 thru T-2800) 10-20 65-67
(Monaural.)
CAPITOL (ST-2274 through ST-2826)............................... 10-25 65-67
(Stereo.)
CAPITOL (H-9111 "Favorites") 50-100 52
(10-inch LP.)
CAPITOL (11000 series).............. 5-8 79
CHURCHILL.................................. 5-8 84
DOT... 5-15 68-74
GUSTO 5-8 80
PICKWICK/HILLTOP 5-15 67-68
SEARS (135 "How Many Teardrops Will It Take").................................... 10-15 60s
TOWER....................................... 8-15 68
WACO (101 "Hank Thompson Sings and Plays Bob Wills")..................... 15-20
Session: Buddy Cagle.

THOMPSON, Hank, & Merle Travis
(With the Brazos Valley Boys)

C&W '55

Singles: 78rpm

CAPITOL..4-8 55

Singles: 7-inch

CAPITOL..6-12 55
Also see THOMPSON, Hank

THOMPSON, Kay

P&R '56

Singles: 78rpm

CADENCE 3-5 56
MGM 3-5 54-55

Singles: 7-inch

CADENCE 4-8 56
MGM 4-8 54-55

Picture Sleeves

CADENCE 5-10 56

THOMPSON, Richard

LP '83

Singles: 7-inch

HANNIBAL......................................3-4 83
POLYDOR 3-4 85-86
REPRISE...3-5 72

LPs: 10/12-inch 33rpm

CAPITOL..5-8 88
HANNIBAL.......................................5-8 83
POLYDOR 5-8 85-86
REPRISE...8-10 72
Also see FAIRPORT CONVENTION

THOMPSON, Richard & Linda

Singles: 7-inch

CHRYSALIS.....................................3-5 78
ISLAND 3-5 74-75

LPs: 10/12-inch 33rpm

CHRYSALIS...................................5-10 78
ISLAND 5-10 74-75
Also see THOMPSON, Richard

THOMPSON, Robbin, Band

P&R/LP '80

Singles: 7-inch

COLPAR 4-6
NEMPEROR 3-5 76-77
OVATION...3-5 80
RICHMOND 3-5
SHORT PUMP 3-4 80s

LPs: 10/12-inch 33rpm

NEMPEROR 5-10 76
OVATION.......................................5-10 80
RICHMOND 10-15
Also see SPRINGSTEEN, Bruce

THOMPSON, Roy

R&B '67

Singles: 7-inch

OKEH...4-8 66-67

THOMPSON, Sonny

P&R/R&B '48

Singles: 78rpm

CHART 5-10 56
KING 5-10 50-57
MIRACLE 10-15 48

Singles: 7-inch

CHART 10-20 56
KING (4500 thru 5300 series) 5-10 52-60
KNIGHT 4-8 61

EPs: 7-inch 33/45rpm

KING 20-40 52-54

LPs: 10/12-inch 33rpm

KING (568 "Moody Blues") 75-100 58
KING (655 "Mellow Blues") 50-75 59

Also see KING, Freddie / Lulu / Sonny Thompson
Also see REED, Lulu

THOMPSON, Sue

P&R '61

Singles: 78rpm

DECCA 5-10 55
MERCURY 5-10 51-54

Singles: 7-inch

DECCA 10-15 55
GUSTO 3-4 80s
HICKORY (Except 1100 & 1200 series) 3-6 66-76
HICKORY (1100 & 1200 series) 4-8 61-65
MERCURY 10-20 51-54

Picture Sleeves

HICKORY 5-8 64

LPs: 10/12-inch 33rpm

HICKORY (Except 104 through 121) 8-15 69-74
HICKORY (104 thru 121) 15-25 62-65
WING 10-15 66

Also see GIBSON, Don, & Sue Thompson
Also see LUMAN, Bob, & Sue Thompson

THOMPSON TWINS

R&B/LP '82

Singles: 12-inch 33/45rpm

ARISTA 4-6 83-86

Singles: 7-inch

ARISTA 3-4 82-87
W.B. 3-4 89

Picture Sleeves

ARISTA 3-5 83-87
W.B. 3-4 89

LPs: 10/12-inch 33rpm

ARISTA 5-10 82-87

Members: Tom Bailey; Alannah Currie; Joe Leeway; Chris Bell.
Also see GENE LOVES JEZEBEL

THOMSON, Ali

P&R/LP '80

Singles: 7-inch

A&M 3-5 80-81

Picture Sleeves

A&M 3-5 80

LPs: 10/12-inch 33rpm

A&M 5-10 80

THORNE, David
(David Throne)

P&R '62

Singles: 7-inch

ADMIRAL 4-8 64-65
CHOICE 5-10 60
RIVERSIDE 4-8 62
SAVOY 5-10 59

THORNTON, Big Mama: see THORNTON, Willie Mae

THORNTON, Fonzi

R&B '83

Singles: 12-inch 33/45rpm

RCA 4-6 83

Singles: 7-inch

RCA 3-4 83

LPs: 10/12-inch 33rpm

RCA 5-8 83

THORNTON, Willie Mae
(Big Mama Thornton)

R&B '53

Singles: 78rpm

PEACOCK 5-15 52-57

Singles: 7-inch

ABC 3-5 73
ARHOOLIE 4-6 68
BAY TONE 8-12 61
GALAXY 4-8 66
KENT 4-8 65
MERCURY 3-6 69
PEACOCK (Maroon label) 35-45 52
PEACOCK (Red label) 25-35 53-55
PEACOCK (White label) 10-20 56-57

(White label numbers below 1676 are reissues, which Peacock continued carrying in their catalog through the '70s.)

ST. CAROLYN 4-6
SOTOPLAY 5-10 65

LPs: 10/12-inch 33rpm

ARHOOLIE 10-15 66-67
BACK BEAT 20-25 70
MERCURY 10-15 69-70
PENTAGRAM 10-12 71
ROULETTE 10-15 70
VANGUARD 8-10 74-75

THOROGOOD, George, & Destroyers

LP '78

Singles: 12-inch 33/45rpm

EMI 4-6 83-85

Singles: 7-inch

EMI 3-4 82-86

MCA 3-5 79
ROUNDER 3-5 78-80

LPs: 10/12–inch 33rpm

EMI 5-8 82-91
MCA 5-10 79
ROUNDER 6-12 77-80

THORPE, Billy

P&R/LP '79

Singles: 7–inch

CAPRICORN 3-5 79
POLYDOR 3-5 79
PASHA (Except "Retail Teaser") ... 3-4 85
PASHA ("Retail Teaser") 4-8 85

LPs: 10/12–inch 33rpm

CAPRICORN 15-20 79
ELEKTRA 5-8 80
PASHA 8-12 82-85
POLYDOR 5-8 79

3

LP '88

Singles: 7–inch

GEFFEN 3-4 88

LPs: 10/12–inch 33rpm

GEFFEN 5-8 88

Members: Keith Emerson; Carl Palmer.
Also see EMERSON, LAKE & PALMER

THREE CHUCKLES
(Featuring Teddy Randazzo)

P&R '54

Singles: 78rpm

BOULEVARD (100 "Runaround") 10-15 53
VIK 4-8 56
X 4-8 54-56

Singles: 7–inch

BOULEVARD (100 "Runaround") 45-55 53
CLOUD 4-6 66
VIK 5-10 56
X 10-15 54-56

EPs: 7–inch 33/45rpm

RCA (192/193/194 "Three Chuckles") 10-20 55
(Price is for any of three volumes.)
VIK (4 "Three Chuckles") 20-30 57
(Promotional issue only. Not issued with cover.)

LPs: 10/12–inch 33rpm

VIK (1067 "Three Chuckles") .. 50-100 55

Members: Teddy Randazzo; Phil Benti; Tom Romano; Russ Gilberto.
Also see CHUCKLES
Also see RANDAZZO, Teddy

THREE DEGREES

P&R '65

Singles: 7–inch

ARIOLA AMERICA 3-5 78-80
EPIC 3-5 76
METROMEDIA 4-6 69
NEPTUNE 3-5 70
PHILADELPHIA INT'L 3-5 73-76
ROULETTE 3-5 70-73
SWAN 6-12 64-66
W.B. 4-8 68

LPs: 10/12–inch 33rpm

ARIOLA AMERICA 5-10 78-81
EPIC 8-10 77
PHILADELPHIA INT'L 8-10 74-76
ROULETTE 10-15 70-75

Also see MFSB & Three Degrees

THREE DOG NIGHT
(3 Dog Night)

P&R/LP '69

Singles: 7–inch

ABC 3-5 70-76
DUNHILL (Except 4168) 3-6 69-75
DUNHILL (4168 "Nobody") 5-8 68
PASSPORT 3-4 83

Picture Sleeves

DUNHILL (Except 4168) 3-5 70
DUNHILL (4168 "Nobody") 20-30 68
(Promotional issue only.)

LPs: 10/12–inch 33rpm

ABC 8-12 75-76
COMMAND ("CQD" series) 15-25 74-75
(Quadraphonic.)
DUNHILL (50048 thru 50068) 10-15 68-69
DUNHILL (50078 "It Ain't Easy") 50-100 70
(Cover pictures nude people.)
DUNHILL (50078 "It Ain't Easy") 10-12 70
(Cover doesn't show nudes.)
DUNHILL (50088 thru 50158) 10-15 70-73
DUNHILL (50168 "Hard Labor"). 15-20 74
(With baby delivery cover.)
DUNHILL (50168 "Hard Labor"). 10-12 74
(With Band-Aid cover.)
DUNHILL (50178 "Joy to the World") 8-10 74
K-TEL 5-10
MCA 5-8 82
PASSPORT 5-8 83
PICKWICK 5-8 79

Members: Danny Hutton; Cory Wells; Chuck Negron.
Also see HUTTON, Danny
Also see WELLS, Cory

THREE FLAMES

P&R/R&B '47

Singles: 78rpm

COLUMBIA 10-20 47-51
GOTHAM 10-20 46
HARMONY 8-12 49
MGM 5-10 50

LPs: 10/12-inch 33rpm

MERCURY (20239 "At the Bon Soir")....... 25-40 57

Member: Tiger Haynes; Rill Pollard; Roy Testamark.

Also see BARNES, Mae

3 FRIENDS

(Three Friends)

P&R '61

Singles: 7-inch

CAL-GOLD (169 "Blue Ribbon Baby")....... 100-150 61

IMPERIAL....... 10-20 61

THREE Gs

P&R '58

Singles: 7-inch

COLUMBIA....... 5-10 58-61

THREE GRACES

Singles: 7-inch

GOLDEN CREST....... 5-10 59-60

THREE GRACES / Wailers

EPs: 7-inch 33/45rpm

GOLDEN CREST (88601/2 "Four Songs on 45rpm")....... 75-125 60

(With paper sleeve-mailer. Both sides have label pictures.)

Also see WAILERS

THREE MAN ISLAND

P&R '88

Singles: 7-inch

CHRYSALIS....... 3-4 88

Picture Sleeves

CHRYSALIS....... 3-4 88

LPs: 10/12-inch 33rpm

CHRYSALIS....... 5-8 88

THREE MILLION

R&B/D&D '83

Singles: 12-inch 33/45rpm

COTILLION....... 4-6 84-84

Singles: 7-inch

COTILLION....... 3-5 83-84

THREE O'CLOCK

LP '85

Singles: 7-inch

I.R.S. 3-4 85

LPs: 10/12-inch 33rpm

I.R.S. 5-8 85

3 OUNCES of LOVE

R&B '78

Singles: 7-inch

MOTOWN....... 3-5 78

LPs: 10/12-inch 33rpm

MOTOWN....... 5-10 78

THREE PLAYMATES

P&R '58

Singles: 7-inch

SAVOY....... 8-12 58

THREE SUNS

P&R '44

Singles: 78rpm

HIT....... 3-6 44

MAJESTIC....... 3-6 46

RCA....... 3-5 47-57

Singles: 7-inch

RCA....... 4-8 50-64

EPs: 7-inch 33/45rpm

RCA....... 5-10 50-61

ROYALE....... 5-10 50s

VARSITY....... 5-10 52

LPs: 10/12-inch 33rpm

CAMDEN....... 5-15 60-64

MUSICOR....... 5-10 66

RCA....... 5-20 50-76

RONDO....... 5-15 59

ROYALE....... 10-15 50s

VARSITY....... 10-20 50-52

Members: Al Nevins; Marty Nevins; Art Dunn.

THREE SUNS, Rosalie Allen & Elton Britt

C&W '50

Singles: 78rpm

RCA....... 5-10 50

THREE TIMES DOPE

LP '89

LPs: 10/12-inch 33rpm

ARISTA....... 5-8 89

THRILLS

LP '81

Singles: 7-inch

G&P....... 3-5 80-81

LPs: 10/12-inch 33rpm

G&P....... 5-10 80-81

THUNDER, Johnny

P&R '62

Singles: 7-inch

ABC....... 3-5 74

CALLA....... 4-6 69

DIAMOND....... 4-8 62-68

EPIC....... 5-10 59

U.A. 3-5 70

Picture Sleeves

DIAMOND....... 8-12 63

LPs: 10/12-inch 33rpm

DIAMOND (D-5001 "Loop De Loop")....... 25-35 63

(Monaural.)

DIAMOND (SD-5001 "Loop De Loop")....... 35-45 63

(Stereo.)

REAL RECORDS....... 10-15

Also see ARCHIES / Johnny Thunder

THUNDER, Johnny, & Ruby Winters

P&R/R&B '67

Singles: 7-inch

DIAMOND 4-8 67-68

Also see THUNDER, Johnny
Also see WINTERS, Ruby

THUNDER, Margo

R&B '74

Singles: 7-inch

HAVEN 3-5 74

THUNDERCLAP NEWMAN: see NEWMAN, Thunderclap

THUNDERFLASH

R&B '83

Singles: 7-inch

JAMPOWER 3-5 83

THUNDERKLOUD, Billy, & Chieftones

C&W/P&R '75

Singles: 7-inch

POLYDOR...................................... 3-5 76-77
20TH FOX 3-5 74-75

LPs: 10/12-inch 33rpm

SUPERIOR 8-12 74
20TH FOX.................................... 6-12 74-75

THURSTON, Bobby

R&B '80

Singles: 7-inch

PRELUDE 3-5 80

TIA

P&R '87

Singles: 7-inch

RCA.. 3-4 87

Picture Sleeves

RCA.. 3-4 87

TIBBS, Andrew
(With the Dozier Boys)

R&B '49

Singles: 78rpm

ARISTOCRAT 10-20 47-49
PEACOCK..................................... 5-10 52

Singles: 7-inch

M-PAC...4-8 66
PEACOCK (1597 "Mother's Letter") 25-35 52

Also see TIBBS BROTHERS

TICO & TRIUMPHS
(Featuring Paul Simon)

P&R '62

Singles: 7-inch

AMY (835 "Motorcycle") 15-25 62
AMY (845 "Wild Flower")........... 15-25 62
AMY (860 "Cry Little Boy") 15-25 62
AMY (876 "Cards of Love") 30-40 62
MADISON (169 "Motorcycle")... 20-30 61

Also see SIMON, Paul

TICTOC

D&D '84

Singles: 12-inch 33/45rpm

RCA 4-6 84

Singles: 7-inch

RCA 3-4 84

LPs: 10/12-inch 33rpm

RCA 5-8 84

TIERRA

P&R/R&B/LP '80

Singles: 7-inch

ASI 3-5 80
BOARDWALK.....................................3-5 80-82
SALSOUL 3-5 81
MCA..3-5 79
TODY 3-5

LPs: 10/12-inch 33rpm

ASI 5-10 80
BOARDWALK.....................................5-10 80
SALSOUL 5-10 81

Members: Salas Brothers.
Also see EL CHICANO

TIFFANY
(Tiffany Darwisch)

P&R/LP '87

Singles: 7-inch

MCA..3-4 87-89

Picture Sleeves

MCA..3-4 87-89

LPs: 10/12-inch 33rpm

MCA..5-8 87-88

TIGGI CLAY

P&R '84

Singles: 7-inch

MOROCCO...3-5 84

LPs: 10/12-inch 33rpm

MOROCCO...5-8 84

TIGHT FIT

P&R '81

Singles: 12-inch 33/45rpm

ARISTA..4-6 81
JIVE 4-6 81

Singles: 7-inch

ARISTA..3-5 81
JIVE 3-5 81

TIJUANA BRASS: see ALPERT, Herb

TIKARAM, Tanita

LP '89

Singles: 7-inch

REPRISE 3-4 89

Picture Sleeves

REPRISE 3-4 89

TIL, Sonny
(With Buddy Lucas Orchestra)

Singles: 78rpm

JUBILEE (5076 "Proud of You") 15-25 52

Singles: 7-inch

JUBILEE (5076 "Proud of You") 150-200 52
RCA 4-8 69-72
ROULETTE 8-12 58

LPs: 10/12-inch 33rpm

DOBRE 5-10 78
RCA 10-20 70-71

Also see McGRIFF, Edna, & Sonny Til
Also see ORIOLES

'TIL TUESDAY

P&R/LP '85

Singles: 7-inch

EPIC 3-4 85-88

LPs: 10/12-inch 33rpm

EPIC 5-8 85-88

Members: Aimee Mann; Michael Hausman; Robert Holmes; Joey Pesce.

TILLMAN, Bertha

P&R '62

Singles: 7-inch

BRENT (7029 "Oh My Angel") .. 15-20 62
BRENT (7032 "I Wish") 20-30 62

TILLOTSON, Johnny

P&R '58

Singles: 7-inch

AMOS 3-5 69-70
BARNABY 3-5 76
BUDDAH 3-5 71-73
CADENCE (1300 series) 5-10 58-61
CADENCE (1400 series) 4-8 61-63
COLUMBIA 3-5 73-75
ERIC 3-4 70s
MGM 4-8 63-68
REWARD 3-4 82-84
U.A. 3-5 76-77

Picture Sleeves

CADENCE 10-15 60
MGM 5-8 63-66

EPs: 7-inch 33/45rpm

CADENCE (114 "Dreamy Eyes") 25-35 60
CADENCE (33-1 "This Is Johnny Tillotson") 15-25 61
("Cadence Little LP." With cardboard insert in clear cover.)
CADENCE (33-2 "Music By Johnny Tillotson") 15-25 61
("Cadence Little LP." With cardboard insert in clear cover.)

LPs: 10/12-inch 33rpm

ACCORD 5-10 82
AMOS 10-15 69
BACK-TRAC 5-8 85
BARNABY 8-10 77
BUCKBOARD 5-10 80s
BUDDAH 10-15 72
CADENCE 25-40 61-63
EVEREST 5-8 82
METRO 10-15 66
MGM 12-20 64-71
ROWE/AMI 5-8 66
("Play Me" Sales Stimulator promotional issue.)
U.A. 8-10 77

Session: Boots Randolph.
Also see IVAN / Johnny Tillotson
Also see RANDOLPH, Boots

TILLOTSON, Johnny / J.D. Souther

Singles: 7-inch

BUDDAH 3-5 71

Also see SOUTHER, J.D.
Also see TILLOTSON, Johnny

TIM TAM & TURN-ONS

P&R '66

Singles: 7-inch

PALMER (5002 "Wait a Minute") .8-12 66
PALMER (5003 "Cheryl Ann") ...15-20 66
PALMER (5006 "Kimberly") 20-25 66
PALMER (5014 "Don't Say Hi") ...5-10 67

TIMBUK 3

P&R/LP '86

Singles: 7-inch

I.R.S. 3-4 86-88

LPs: 10/12-inch 33rpm

I.R.S. 5-8 86-88

TIME

R&B/LP '81

Singles: 12-inch 33/45rpm

W.B. 4-6 82-84

Singles: 7-inch

W.B. 3-5 81-84

LPs: 10/12-inch 33rpm

PAISLEY PARK 5-8 90
W.B. 5-8 81-84

Members: Morris Day; Jesse Johnson; Jimmy Jam; Monte Moir; Jellybean Johnson; Stacy Adams; Terry Lewis; Paul Peterson.
Also see DAY, Morris
Also see JOHNSON, Jesse
Also see ST. PAUL
Also see VANITY 6

TIME BANDITS

D&D '85

Singles: 12-inch 33/45rpm

COLUMBIA 4-6 85

TIME ZONE

D&D '84

Singles: 12-inch 33/45rpm

CELLULOID 4-6 84

TIMELORDS

P&R '88

Singles: 7-inch

TVT 3-4 88

Singles: 7-inch

TVT 3-4 88

TIMES TWO

P&R/LP '88

Singles: 7-inch

REPRISE 3-4 88

Picture Sleeves

REPRISE 3-4 88

LPs: 10/12-inch 33rpm

REPRISE 5-8 88

TIMETONES

P&R '61

Singles: 7-inch

ATCO (6201 "I've Got a Feeling") 15-25 61
TIMES SQUARE (26 "Sunday Kind of Love") 15-20 64
TIMES SQUARE (34 "House Where Lovers Dream") 30-40 64
TIMES SQUARE (421 "Here in My Heart") 20-30 61
TIMES SQUARE (421 "In My Heart") 8-10 61
(Note shortened title.)
Member: Slim Rose.

TIMEX SOCIAL CLUB

P&R/R&B '86

Singles: 12-inch 33/45rpm

DANYA 4-6 86
JAY 4-6 86

Singles: 7-inch

DANYA 3-4 86-87
JAY 3-4 86

TIMMY T.

LP '91

LPs: 10/12-inch 33rpm

QUALITY 5-8 90

TIN MACHINE

LP '89

LPs: 10/12-inch 33rpm

EMI 5-8 89

TIN TIN

P&R/LP '71

Singles: 12-inch 33/45rpm

SIRE 4-6 81-83

Singles: 7-inch

ATCO 3-5 71

LPs: 10/12-inch 33rpm

ATCO 10-15 70-71
Members: Steve Kipner; Steve Groves.

TINA & DADDY: see JONES, George

TINA B.

D&D '84

Singles: 12-inch 33/45rpm

ATLANTIC 4-6 82-84
ELEKTRA 4-6 83-84

Singles: 7-inch

ATLANTIC 3-4 82
ELEKTRA 3-4 83

LPs: 10/12-inch 33rpm

ATLANTIC 5-8 82
ELEKTRA 5-8 83

TINDLEY, George
(With the Modern Red Caps; George Tinley)

R&B '69

Singles: 7-inch

EMBER 5-10 60
HERALD 10-15 61
ROWAX 8-12 63
PARKWAY 5-10 62
SMASH 5-10 62
WAND 4-6 69-70

TINLEY, George: see TINDLEY, George

TINY TIM
(Herbert Khaury)

P&R/LP '68

Singles: 7-inch

BLUE CAT 5-10 65
CLOUDS 3-5 79
NLT 3-4 88
REPRISE 3-6 68-71
ROULETTE 3-5 70s
SCEPTER 3-5 72
VIC TIM 3-5 71

LPs: 10/12-inch 33rpm

BOUQUET 10-12
REPRISE 10-20 68

TINY TIM & MISS VICKI

Singles: 7-inch

REPRISE 3-6 71

TINY TIM / Michelle Ramos / Bruce Haack

LPs: 10/12-inch 33rpm

RA-JO INT'L 5-8 86
Also see TINY TIM

TJADER, Cal

LP '63

Singles: 78rpm

FANTASY 3-5 54-57
SAVOY 3-5 53-54

Singles: 7-inch

FANTASY 3-8 54-71
SAVOY 4-8 53-54
SKYE 3-5 68
VERVE 3-6 61-66

EPs: 7-inch 33/45rpm

FANTASY (Black vinyl) 10-25 54-55
FANTASY (Colored vinyl) 20-40 54-55
SAVOY 10-20 54

LPs: 10/12-inch 33rpm

BUDDAH 8-12 70
CLASSIC JAZZ 5-8 80
CONCORD JAZZ 5-8 80-82

FANTASY (3-9 "Cal Tjader Trio") 50-100 54
(10–inch LP.)
FANTASY (3-17 "Ritmo Caliente") 50-100 54
(10–inch LP.)
FANTASY (3200 series)........... 25-50 54-60
(Numbers may be shown as 3-200. Double price range for colored vinyl pressings.)
FANTASY (3300 series)........... 25-35 60-65
FANTASY (8000 & 8100 series) 35-45 58-61
FANTASY (8300 series)........... 20-30 65
FANTASY (8400 series)............. 8-15 71-72
FANTASY (9000 series)............. 6-12 72-77
GALAXY 5-10 78-79
METRO 10-15 67
PRESTIGE 5-10 73
SAVOY (9036 "Cal Tjader Quartet")................................. 50-100 54
(10–inch LP.)
SAVOY (12054 "Vib-Rations") .. 40-60 56
SAVOY (12000 series)............. 20-40 56
SKYE.. 8-12 68-69
VERVE 10-30 61-69
(Reads "MGM Records - A Division of Metro-Goldwyn-Mayer, Inc." at bottom of label.)
VERVE 5-12 73-84
(Reads "Manufactured By MGM Record Corp.," or mentions either Polydor or Polygram at bottom of label.)
Also see BRUBECK, Dave, Quartet
Also see O'DAY, Anita, & Cal Tjader

TJADER, Cal, & Stan Getz

LPs: 10/12–inch 33rpm

FANTASY (3266 "Cal Tjader and Stan Getz")............................ 35-45 58
FANTASY (3300 series)........... 15-25 65
FANTASY (8005 "Cal Tjader and Stan Getz")............................ 45-55 58
FANTASY (8300 series)........... 15-25 65
Also see GETZ, Stan
Also see TJADER, Cal

TOBY BEAU

P&R/LP '78

Singles: 7–inch

RCA... 3-5 78-80

LPs: 10/12–inch 33rpm

RCA (Except 2994) 5-10 78-81
RCA (2994 "Three You Missed, One You Didn't")................................. 10-15 78
(Promotional issue only.)

TODAY

LP '89

LPs: 10/12–inch 33rpm

MOTOWN 5-8 89-90

TODAY'S PEOPLE

P&R '73

Singles: 7–inch

20TH FOX...................................3-5 73

TODD, Art & Dotty

P&R/R&B '58

Singles: 7–inch

CAPITOL......................................5-8 62
COLLECTABLES..........................3-4 80s
DAKAR..5-8 63
DART 5-10 59-67
DECCA 5-10 61
DOT 4-8 66
FRA..5-10 58-59
M.O.L. 4-8 68
SIGNET...4-8 65

LPs: 10/12–inch 33rpm

BEVERLY HILLS 8-10 73
DART 15-25 60
DOT 10-20 66
REPRISE 10-20 65

TODD, Nick

P&R '57

Singles: 78rpm

DOT 5-10 57

Singles: 7–inch

DOT 8-15 57-60

TOKENS

P&R '61

Singles: 12–inch 33/45rpm

DOWNTOWN (103 "The Lion Sleeps Tonight") 8-12 88
(Issued with cover.)

Singles: 78rpm

MELBA (104 "While I Dream")... 10-15 56

Singles: 7–inch

ABC..3-5 73
ATCO 3-5 74
B.T. PUPPY 4-8 64-69
BELL 3-5 72
BUDDAH..4-6 69-70
COLLECTABLES............................3-4 84
LAURIE 10-15 63
MELBA (104 "While I Dream") ...30-40 56
RCA (37-7896 "When I Go to Sleep at Night") 20-30 61
(Compact 33 Single.)
RCA (37-7925 "Sincerely") 20-30 61
(Compact 33 Single.)
RCA (37-7954 "The Lion Sleeps Tonight") 20-30 61
(Compact 33 Single.)
RCA (37-7991 "B'Wa Nina") 20-30 62
(Compact 33 Single.)
RCA (37-8018 "The Riddle")......20-30 62
(Compact 33 Single.)
RCA (47-7896 thru 47-8148) 8-12 61-65

RCA (447-0702 "The Lion Sleeps Tonight")........ 4-6 60s
(Gold Standard Series.)
RCA (8749 "Re-Doo-Wopp")........ 3-4 88
Wopp")........ 3-4 88
RADIO ACTIVE GOLD........ 3-4
W.B. 4-8 67-69
WARWICK 10-15 61

Picture Sleeves

B.T. PUPPY (591 "Greatest Moments in a Girl's Life")........ 10-15 66
RCA (7896 "When I Go to Sleep at Night")........ 10-20 61
RCA (7991 "B'Wa Nina")........ 10-20 62
(Orange sleeve. No mention of *The Lion Sleeps Tonight* LP.)
RCA (7991 "B'Wa Nina")........ 8-12 62
(Orange and white sleeve. Plugs *The Lion Sleeps Tonight* LP.)
RCA (8018 "The Riddle")........ 10-20 62
RCA (8052 "La Bomba")........ 10-15 62
RCA (8089 "I'll Do My Crying Tomorrow")........ 10-20 62
RCA (8114 "A Bird Flies Out of Sight")........ 10-20 63
RCA (8148 "Tonight I Met an Angel")........ 10-20 63
RCA (8210 "Hear the Bells")........ 10-15 63
W.B. (5900 "Portrait of My Love")........ 5-10 67

LPs: 10/12-inch 33rpm

B.T. PUPPY 15-25 66-78
BUDDAH........ 15-20 70
DOWNTOWN........ 5-8 88
RCA (LPM-2514 thru LPM-3685)........ 15-25 61-66
(Monaural.)
RCA (LSP-2514 thru LSP-3685)........ 20-30 61-66
(Stereo.)
RCA (8534 "Re-Doo-Wopp")........ 5-8 88
W.B. 20-25 67

Members: Jay Siegel; Mitchell Margo; Philip Margo; Henry Medress.
Also see CHRISTIE, Lou / Len Barry & Dovells / Bobby Rydell / Tokens
Also see CROSS COUNTRY
Also see FOUR WINDS
Also see KEITH
Also see SEDAKA, Neil
Also see SANDS of TIME

TOKENS / Happenings

LP '67

LPs: 10/12-inch 33rpm

B.T. PUPPY 15-25 67

Also see HAPPENINGS
Also see TOKENS

TOLBERT, Israel "Popper Stopper"

P&R/R&B '70

Singles: 7-inch

WARREN........ 3-5 70-71

LPs: 10/12-inch 33rpm

WARREN........ 8-12 71

TOM & JERRIO

P&R/R&B '65

Singles: 7-inch

ABC-PAR........ 4-8 65

Members: Eddie Thomas; Jerry Murray.
Also see JERRYO

TOM & JERRY

P&R '57

Singles: 78rpm

BIG........ 10-15 58

Singles: 7-inch

ABC-PAR (10363 "Surrender, Please Surrender")........ 15-25 62
ABC-PAR (10788 "This Is My Story")........ 10-15 66
BIG (613 "Hey, Schoolgirl")........ 20-30 57
BIG (616 "Two Teenagers")........ 20-30 58
BIG (618 "Don't Say Goodbye")........ 20-30 58
EMBER (1094 "I'm Lonesome")........ 25-35 59
HUNT (319 "Don't Say Goodbye")........ 20-25 58
KING (5167 "Hey, Schoolgirl")........ 35-45 58

Members: Paul Simon; Art Garfunkel.
Also see SIMON & GARFUNKEL

TOM & JERRY / Ronnie Lawrence

Singles: 7-inch

BELL (120 "Baby Talk")........ 20-30 60

Also see TOM & JERRY

TOM TOM CLUB

LP '81

Singles: 12-inch 33/45rpm

SIRE........ 4-8 81-83

Singles: 7-inch

SIRE........ 3-5 81-89

LPs: 10/12-inch 33rpm

SIRE........ 5-10 81-89

Members: Chris Frantz; Tina Weymouth.
Also see TALKING HEADS

TOMLIN, Lily

LP '71

Singles: 7-inch

POLYDOR 3-5 73-75

LPs: 10/12-inch 33rpm

ARISTA........ 5-10 77
POLYDOR 5-10 71-75

TOMMY TUTONE

P&R/LP '80

Singles: 7-inch

COLUMBIA........ 3-5 80-83

LPs: 10/12-inch 33rpm

COLUMBIA (Except 1461)........ 5-10 80-83

COLUMBIA (1461 "Alive and Almost Dangerous") 10-15 82
(Promotional issue only.)

TOMORROW'S EDITION

R&B '82

Singles: 7-inch

ATLANTIC 3-5 82
GANG 3-5 75

TOMORROW'S PROMISE

R&B '73

Singles: 7-inch

CAPITOL 3-5 73-74
MERCURY 3-5 75

TOMPALL & GLASER BROTHERS
(Tompall & Glasers; Tompall Glaser)

P&R '69

Singles: 7-inch

DECCA 5-10 59-65
ELEKTRA 3-5 80-82
MGM 3-8 66-71
RICH 8-12 61
ROBBINS 10-20 57

LPs: 10/12-inch 33rpm

DECCA (DL-4041 "This Land") 35-45 60
(Monaural.)
DECCA (DL7-4041 "This Land") 40-50 60
(Stereo.)
ELEKTRA 5-10 81
MGM 8-15 67-75
U.A. 25-35 66
VOCALION 8-12 67

Members: Tompall Glaser; Jim Glaser; Chuck Glaser.
Also see GLASER, Tompall

TOMS, Gary
(Gary Toms' Empire)

P&R/R&B/LP '75

Singles: 12-inch 33/45rpm

MCA 4-8 77

Singles: 7-inch

MCA 3-5 77
MERCURY 3-5 78
P.I.P. 3-5 75-76

LPs: 10/12-inch 33rpm

MCA 5-10 77
MERCURY 5-10 78
P.I.P. 5-10 75

TONE LOC

P&R '88

Singles: 7-inch

DELICIOUS 3-4 89

Picture Sleeves

DELICIOUS 3-4 89

LPs: 10/12-inch 33rpm

DELICIOUS 5-8 89

TONES

R&B '83

Singles: 7-inch

CRIMINAL 3-5 83

TONEY, Oscar, Jr.

P&R/R&B/LP '67

Singles: 7-inch

BELL 5-10 67-69
CAPRICORN 10-20 71-72
KING 8-12 64

LPs: 10/12-inch 33rpm

BELL 10-20 67

TONEY LEE: see LEE, Toney

TONY & CAROL

R&B '72

Singles: 7-inch

ROULETTE 3-5 72

TONY & JOE

P&R '58

Singles: 7-inch

DORE 4-8 61-62
ERA 5-10 58
FLYTE 5-10 59
GARDENA 5-10 60

Members: Tony Savonne; Joe Saraceno.
Also see BEACH BOYS / Tony & Joe

TONY, BOB & JIMMY

Singles: 7-inch

CAPITOL 4-8 62

Members: Tony Butala; Bob Engemann; Jim Pike.
Also see LETTERMEN

TONY! TONI! TONE!

P&R/R&B/LP '88

Singles: 7-inch

WING 3-4 88-90

Picture Sleeves

WING 3-4 88

TOO SHORT

LP '89

LPs: 10/12-inch 33rpm

DANGEROUS 5-8 89
JIVE 5-8 90

TOOTS & MAYTALS

LP '75

Singles: 12-inch 33/45rpm

MANGO 4-6 82

Singles: 7-inch

MANGO 3-5 76-82

LPs: 10/12-inch 33rpm

ISLAND 5-10 75
MANGO 5-10 76-82

Members: Toots Hibbert; Nathaniel Mathias; Releigh Gordon; Paul Douglas; Jackie Jackson; Winston Wright.
Also see WINWOOD, Steve

TOP SHELF

R&B '70

Singles: 7–inch

LO LO 4-6 69-70
SOUND TOWN 3-5 80

TORA TORA

LP '89

LPs: 10/12–inch 33rpm

A&M 5-8 89

TORCH

D&D '83

Singles: 12–inch 33/45rpm

PACIFIC 4-6 83

TORCH SONG

D&D '84

Singles: 12–inch 33/45rpm

I.R.S. 4-6 83-84

Singles: 7–inch

I.R.S. 3-4 83-84

LPs: 10/12–inch 33rpm

I.R.S. 5-8 83

TORME, Mel
(With the Meltones)

P&R '45

Singles: 78rpm

BETHLEHEM 3-6 56-57
CAPITOL (1000 & 2000 series) 4-8 50-53

Singles: 7–inch

ATLANTIC 4-6 62-64
BETHLEHEM 5-10 56-58
CAPITOL (1000 & 2000 series) .. 5-10 50-53
(Purple labels.)
CAPITOL (2000 series) 3-6 69-70
(Orange labels.)
COLUMBIA 3-6 64-67
CORAL 5-10 53-56
LIBERTY 3-6 68
VERVE 4-8 59-61

EPs: 7–inch 33/45rpm

CAPITOL 5-15 50
P.R.I. (9 "The Touch of Your Lips") 5-10

LPs: 10/12–inch 33rpm

ATLANTIC (8000 series) 12-25 62-64
ATLANTIC (18000 series) 5-10 75
ATLANTIC (80000 series) 5-8 83
BETHLEHEM (34 "It's a Blue World") 25-50 55
BETHLEHEM (52 "Mel Torme") 25-50 56
BETHLEHEM (4000 series) 10-20 65
BETHLEHEM (6000 series) 20-40 58-60
(Maroon labels.)
BETHLEHEM (6000 series) 5-10 77-78
(Gray labels.)
CAPITOL (200 "California Suite") 25-50 50
(10–inch LP.)
CAPITOL (300 & 400 series) 8-12 69-70
COLUMBIA (2000 series) 10-20 64-66
(Monaural.)
COLUMBIA (9000 series) 10-20 64-66
(Stereo.)
CONCORD JAZZ 5-8 82
CORAL (57012 "At the Crescendo") 40-60 54
CORAL (57044 "Musical Sounds") 40-60 54
EVEREST 5-10 76
GLENDALE 5-8 78-79
GRYPHON 5-8 79
LIBERTY 8-15 68
MGM (552 "Songs By Mel Torme") 50-75 52
(10–inch LP.)
MAYFAIR 25-35 58
METRO 10-20 65
MUSICRAFT 5-8 83
STRAND 12-25 60
VERVE 20-35 58-60
(Reads "Verve Records, Inc." at bottom of label.)
VERVE 10-20 61-72
(Reads "MGM Records - A Division of Metro-Goldwyn-Mayer, Inc." at bottom of label.)
VERVE 5-10 73-84
(Reads "Manufactured By MGM Record Corp.," or mentions either Polydor or Polygram at bottom of label.)
VOCALION 5-10 70

Also see CROSBY, Bing, & Mel Torme
Also see LEE, Peggy, & Mel Torme
Also see WHITING, Margaret

TORNADER

R&B '77

Singles: 7–inch

POLYDOR 3-5 77

TORNADOES

P&R/R&B '62

Singles: 7–inch

LONDON 4-8 62-63
TOWER 4-8 65

LPs: 10/12–inch 33rpm

LONDON 25-35 62-63

Members: Heinz Burt; Alan Caddy; Clem Cattini; George Bellamy.

TOROK, Mitchell
(With the Louisiana Hayride Band; with Matches; with Ramona Redd)

C&W/P&R '53

Singles: 78rpm

ABBOTT 5-10 53-54
DECCA 5-10 57-59
FBC (102 "Nacogdoches County Line") 15-25 48

FBC (115 "Piney Woods Boogie") 15-25 49

Singles: 7-inch

ABBOTT 5-15 53-54
CALICO 3-5
CAPITOL 4-8 62-63
DECCA 5-10 57-59
GUYDEN 5-10 59-60
INETTE 4-8 63
MERCURY 4-8 61
RCA 4-8 65
REPRISE 4-6 66-67

Picture Sleeves

GUYDEN 10-20 59-60

LPs: 10/12-inch 33rpm

CALICO 10-15
GUYDEN (502 "Caribbean") 25-35 60
(Monaural.)
GUYDEN (ST-502 "Caribbean") 35-50 60
(Stereo.)
REPRISE 10-15 66

TORONTO

LP '80

Singles: 7-inch

NETWORK 3-5 82
SOLID GOLD 3-5

LPs: 10/12-inch 33rpm

A&M 5-10 80-81
NETWORK 5-10 82
SOLID GOLD 5-10

TORRANCE, George
(With the Naturals; with Dippers)

P&R/R&B '68

Singles: 7-inch

DUO DISC 4-8 66
EPIC 5-10 61
KING 5-10 60
SHOUT 4-6 68

TORRANCE, Richard
(With Eureka)

LP '75

Singles: 7-inch

CAPITOL 3-5 77-79
SHELTER 3-5 75

LPs: 10/12-inch 33rpm

CAPITOL 5-10 77
SHELTER 5-10 74-75

TOSH, Peter

LP '76

Singles: 12-inch 33/45rpm

EMI AMERICA 4-6 83

Singles: 7-inch

COLUMBIA 3-5 76-77
EMI AMERICA 3-5 81-84
ROLLING STONES 3-5 78-79

Picture Sleeves

ROLLINS STONES 3-6 78

EPs: 7-inch 33/45rpm

COLUMBIA 4-8 76
(Promotional issue only.)

LPs: 10/12-inch 33rpm

COLUMBIA 5-10 76-77
EMI AMERICA 5-8 81-84
ROLLING STONES 5-10 79

TOSH, Peter, & Mick Jagger

Singles: 7-inch

ROLLING STONES (19308 "Don't Look Back") 4-6 78
(With "Rolling Stones" at top of label.)
ROLLING STONES (19308 "Don't Look Back") 3-5 78
(Without "Rolling Stones" at top of label.)

Promotional Singles

ROLLING STONES (130 "Don't Look Back") 10-20 78
ROLLING STONES (7500 "Don't Look Back") 5-10 78

LPs: 10/12-inch 33rpm

ROLLING STONES 5-10 78

Also see JAGGER, Mick
Also see MARLEY, Bob, & Wailers

TOTAL COELO

P&R/D&D '83

Singles: 12-inch 33/45rpm

CHRYSALIS 4-6 83

Singles: 7-inch

CHRYSALIS 3-4 83

Picture Sleeves

CHRYSALIS 3-5 83

TOTAL CONTRAST

R&B/D&D '85

Singles: 12-inch 33/45rpm

LONDON 4-6 85-86

Singles: 7-inch

LONDON 3-4 85-88

LPs: 10/12-inch 33rpm

LONDON 5-8 86

TOTO
(With the Vienna Symphony Orchestra; with Jean-Michel Byron)

P&R/LP '78

Singles: 12-inch 33/45rpm

COLUMBIA 4-8 79-85

Singles: 7-inch

COLUMBIA 3-5 78-88

Promotional Singles

COLUMBIA (ZSS-165008 "Hold the Line") 10-20 78
(Licorice Pizza picture disc.)
COLUMBIA (ZSS-165008 "Hold the Line") 20-30 78
(KRBE picture disc.)
COLUMBIA (ZSS-165008 "Hold the Line") 20-30 78
(Roxy Invitation picture disc.)

Picture Sleeves
COLUMBIA 3-5 82-88
LPs: 10/12-inch 33rpm
COLUMBIA (9C9-39911 "Isolation") 8-12 84
(Picture disc.)
COLUMBIA (PJC-35317 "Toto") 20-30 79
(Picture disc.)
COLUMBIA (37928 "Toto IV")... 20-30 82
(Picture disc. Promotional issue only.)
COLUMBIA (PD-36813 "Turn Back") 20-30 79
(Picture disc. Promotional issue only.)
COLUMBIA (30000 series except picture discs) 5-10 78-86
COLUMBIA (47728 "Toto IV")... 10-15 83
(Half-speed mastered.)
POLYDOR 5-8 84
Members: Steve Porcaro; David Paich; Steve Lukather; David Hungate; Jeffrey Porcaro; Bobby Kimball.
Also see FAR CORPORATION
Also see VOICES of AMERICA / U.S.A. for Africa

TOUCH

R&B '77

Singles: 7-inch
ATCO 3-5 80-81
BRUNSWICK 3-5 77
COLISEUM 4-6 69
LECASVER 5-8 69
PUBLIC (103 "No Shame") 5-10 60s
LPs: 10/12-inch 33rpm
ATCO 5-10 80
COLISEUM (51004 20/20 Sound") 15-20 68
Members: Don Gallucci; Jeff Hawks; Joe Newman; Bruce Hauser; John Bordonaro.
Also see DON & GOODTIMES

TOUCH

R&B '87

Singles: 7-inch
SUPERTRONICS 3-4 87
Member: Eric McCaine.
Also see ENTOUCH

TOUCH of CLASS

R&B '75

Singles: 12-inch 33/45rpm
NEXT PLATINUM 4-6 84
Singles: 7-inch
ATLANTIC 3-5 82
MIDLAND INT'L 3-5 75-77
ROADSHOW 3-5 79-84
LPs: 10/12-inch 33rpm
MIDLAND INT'L 5-10 76
ROADSHOW 5-10 79

TOUPS, Wayne
(With Zydecajun)

LP '89

LPs: 10/12-inch 33rpm
MERCURY 5-8 89

TOURISTS

P&R '80

Singles: 7-inch
EPIC 3-5 80
LPs: 10/12-inch 33rpm
EPIC 5-10 81
Members: Annie Lennox; David Stewart; Ed Chin; Pete Coombes; Jim Toomey.
Also see EURYTHMICS

TOWER of POWER

LP '71

Singles: 7-inch
COLUMBIA 3-5 76-78
SAN FRANCISCO 4-8 64-73
W.B. 4-8 72-75
EPs: 7-inch 33/45rpm
SAN FRANCISCO (7-204 "East Bay Grease") 15-25 71
(Promotional issue only.)
LPs: 10/12-inch 33rpm
COLUMBIA 5-10 76-79
SAN FRANCISCO (204 "East Bay Grease") 10-20 71
W.B. 8-15 72-76
Also see LITTLE FEAT
Also see WILLIAMS, Lenny

TOWNES, Carol Lynn

P&R/R&B/D&D '84

Singles: 12-inch 33/45rpm
POLYDOR 4-6 84-85
Singles: 7-inch
POLYDOR 3-4 84-85
LPs: 10/12-inch 33rpm
POLYDOR 5-8 84

TOWNS, Eddie
(ET)

R&B '86

Singles: 12-inch 33/45rpm
TOTAL EXPERIENCE 4-6 86
Singles: 7-inch
TOTAL EXPERIENCE 3-4 86
LPs: 10/12-inch 33rpm
TOTAL EXPERIENCE 5-8 86

TOWNSEND, Ed

P&R/R&B '58

Singles: 7-inch
CAPITOL 6-12 58-59
CHALLENGE 5-10 61-62
DYNASTY 5-10 60
GLO-TOWN 4-8 66
LIBERTY 5-10 62-63
MGM 5-10 67
MAXX 10-20 64

POLYDOR.................................... 3-6 70
W.B. 5-10 60-61

EPs: 7-inch 33/45rpm

CAPITOL (985 "New in Town"). 10-20 58
(Promotional issue only.)

LPs: 10/12-inch 33rpm

CAPITOL (1140 "New in Town") 15-25 59
CAPITOL (1214 "Glad to Be Here")..................................... 15-25 59
CURTOM 8-12 76

TOWNSHEND, Pete

LP '72

Singles: 7-inch

ATCO 3-5 80-85

Picture Sleeves

ATCO 3-5 85

LPs: 10/12-inch 33rpm

ATCO 5-10 80-87
ATLANTIC.................................. 5-8 89
DECCA/TRACK 10-12 72

Also see WHO

TOWNSHEND, Pete, & Ronnie Lane

LP '77

Singles: 7-inch

MCA 3-5 77-78

LPs: 10/12-inch 33rpm

MCA 8-10 77

Also see CLAPTON, Eric
Also see ENTWISTLE, John
Also see LANE, Ronnie
Also see TOWNSHEND, Pete
Also see WOOD, Ron, & Ronnie Lane

TOWNSHEND, Simon

LP '83

Singles: 7-inch

21 .... 3-4 83

LPs: 10/12-inch 33rpm

21 .... 5-8 83

TOY DOLLS

P&R '62

Singles: 7-inch

ERA... 5-10 62

TOY MATINEE

LP '91

LPs: 10/12-inch 33rpm

REPRISE 5-8 90

TOYS

P&R/R&B '65

Singles: 7-inch

ABC.. 3-5 73
DYNO VOICE............................ 4-8 65-66
ERIC.. 3-4 70s
GUSTO 3-4 80s
MUSICOR 4-8 68
PHILIPS 4-8 67
VIRGO....................................... 3-5 72

LPs: 10/12-inch 33rpm

DYNO VOICE (9002 "A Lover's Concerto/Attack")....................25-35 66
(Monaural.)
DYNO VOICE (9002-S "A Lover's Concerto/Attack")....................20-30 66
(Stereo.)
SECTET.......................................5-10 81

T'PAU

P&R/LP '87

Singles: 7-inch

VIRGIN..3-4 87

Picture Sleeves

VIRGIN..3-4 87

LPs: 10/12-inch 33rpm

VIRGIN..5-8 87

TRACY, Jeanie
(Jeanne Tracy)

D&D '84

Singles: 12-inch 33/45rpm

MEGATONE 4-6 84-85

Singles: 7-inch

FANTASY 3-5 83
SMOGSVILLE..............................4-8 67

TRADE WINDS

P&R '65

Singles: 7-inch

ERIC 3-4 70s
KAMA SUTRA.............................5-10 66-67
RED BIRD..................................10-20 65

LPs: 10/12-inch 33rpm

KAMA SUTRA............................25-35 67

Members: Pete Anders; Vinnie Poncia.

TRAFFIC
(Traffic Etc.)

P&R '67

Singles: 7-inch

ASYLUM 3-5 74
ISLAND.......................................3-5 72-73
U.A 5-10 67-72

Picture Sleeves

U.A. 8-10 67

LPs: 10/12-inch 33rpm

ASYLUM 10-15 74
ISLAND (Except 9000 series)........5-8 83
ISLAND (9000 series)...............10-15 71-75
MFSL (209 "The Low Spark of High Heeled Boys") 20-30 94
(Half-speed mastered.)
U.A. 10-20 68-75

Members: Jim Capaldi; Dave Mason; Steve Winwood; Chris Wood.

Also see CAPALDI, Jim
Also see MASON, Dave
Also see WINWOOD, Steve

TRAITS

P&R '66

Singles: 7–inch

ASCOT 15-25 62
PACEMAKER 10-15 67
RENNER (229 "Got My Mojo Working") 10-15 62
(Black vinyl.)
RENNER (229 "Got My Mojo Working") 20-30 62
(Colored vinyl. Promotional issue only.)
SCEPTER 3-5 66
TNT 10-15 59-60
UNIVERSAL 10-15 66

LPs: 10/12–inch 33rpm

TNT (101 "Roy Head and the Traits") 100-150 65

Member: Roy Head.
Also see HEAD, Roy

TRAMAINE
(Tramaine Hawkins)

R&B/D&D '85

Singles: 12–inch 33/45rpm

A&M 4-6 85-86

Singles: 7–inch

A&M 3-4 85-87

LPs: 10/12–inch 33rpm

A&M 5-8 86

TRAMMPS

P&R/R&B '72

Singles: 7–inch

ATLANTIC 3-5 75-80
BUDDAH 3-5 72-76
ERIC 3-5 78
GOLDEN FLEECE 3-5 73-75

Picture Sleeves

ATLANTIC 3-5 77

LPs: 10/12–inch 33rpm

ATLANTIC 5-10 76-80
BUDDAH 5-10 75
GOLDEN FLEECE 5-10 75
PHILADELPHIA INT'L 5-10 77

Also see B-H-Y
Also see MFSB

TRAMPS

R&B '83

Singles: 7–inch

VENTURE 3-5 83

TRANSVISION VAMP

P&R/LP '88

Singles: 7–inch

UNI 3-4 88

Picture Sleeves

UNI 3-4 88

LPs: 10/12–inch 33rpm

UNI 5-8 88

TRANS-X

P&R '86

Singles: 12–inch 33/45rpm

ATCO 4-6 86
MIRAGE 4-6 86

Singles: 7–inch

ATCO 3-4 86

TRAPEZE

LP '74

Singles: 7–inch

PAID 3-5 81
THRESHOLD 4-8 72
W.B. 3-5 74-75

LPs: 10/12–inch 33rpm

PAID 5-10 81
POLYDOR ("Medusa") 50-100 71
(Number not known.)
SHARK 8-10
THRESHOLD (2 "Trapeze") 25-50 71
THRESHOLD (4 "Medusa") 75-100 71
THRESHOLD (8 "You Are the Music, We're Just the Band") 25-50 72
THRESHOLD (11 "Final Swing") 25-50 72
W.B. 8-10 74-75

Also see DEEP PURPLE

TRASH CAN SINATRAS

LP '91

LPs: 10/12–inch 33rpm

LONDON 5-8 91

TRASHMEN

P&R '63

Singles: 7–inch

ARGO 10-15 66
BEAR 10-20 66
ERA 3-5 72
ERIC 3-4 70s
GARRETT 10-20 63-64
LANA 3-6 60s
METROBEAT 10-15 68
TRIBE (8315 "Same Lines") 15-25 66

Picture Sleeves

GARRETT (4012 "Whoa Dad") .. 15-25 64
GARRETT (4013 "Real Live Doll") 20-30 64

LPs: 10/12–inch 33rpm

GARRETT (GA-200 "Surfin' Bird") 50-75 64
(Monaural.)
GARRETT (GAS-200 "Surfin' Bird") 100-150 64
(Stereo.)

Members: Tony Andreason; Bob Reed; Dal Winslow; Steve Wahrer; Gary Nielsen.

TRASHMEN / Castaways

Singles: 7–inch

SOMA 4-6 60s

Also see TRASHMEN

TRAVELING WILBURYS

P&R/LP '88

Singles: 7–inch

WILBURY 3-5 88-89

Picture Sleeves

WILBURY 3-6 88-89

LPs: 10/12–inch 33rpm

WILBURY 8-10 88-90

Members: George Harrison; Bob Dylan; Roy Orbison; Tom Petty; Jeff Lynne.

Also see DYLAN, Bob
Also see HARRISON, George
Also see LYNNE, Jeff
Also see ORBISON, Roy
Also see PETTY, Tom, & Heartbreakers

TRAVERS, Mary

P&R/LP '71

Singles: 7–inch

CHRYSALIS 3-5 78-79
W.B. 3-5 71-73

LPs: 10/12–inch 33rpm

CHRYSALIS 5-10 78
W.B. 6-12 71-74

Also see DENVER, John
Also see PETER, PAUL & MARY

TRAVERS, Pat
(Pat Travers Band; Black Pearl)

LP '77

Singles: 7–inch

POLYDOR 3-5 77-80

LPs: 10/12–inch 33rpm

POLYDOR 5-10 76-84

TRAVIS, McKinley

P&R/R&B '70

Singles: 7–inch

PRIDE 3-5 70

TRAVIS, Merle

C&W/P&R '46

Singles: 78rpm

CAPITOL 4-8 46-57

Singles: 7–inch

CAPITOL (1100 thru 3100 series)5-15 50-55
CAPITOL (5600 series) 4-6 66

Also see THOMPSON, Hank, & Merle Travis

TRAVIS, Randy
(Randy Traywick)

C&W '85

Singles: 7–inch

W.B. 3-4 85-91

LPs: 10/12–inch 33rpm

W.B. 5-8 85-91

Also see TRAYWICK, Randy
Also see WYNETTE, Tammy, & Randy Travis

TRAVIS, Randy, & George Jones

C&W '90

Singles: 7–inch

W.B. 3-4 90

TRAVIS & BOB

P&R/R&B '59

Singles: 7–inch

BIG TOP 4-8 60
MERCURY 4-8 61
SANDY (1017 "Tell Him No").......8-15 59
(No "Distributed By Dot" on label.)
SANDY (1017 "Tell Him No" 5-8 59
(Has "Distributed By Dot" on label)
SANDY (1019 thru 1029)............5-10 59

Members: Travis Pritchett; Bob Weaver.

TRAVOLTA, Joey

P&R '78

Singles: 7–inch

CASABLANCA 3-5 78-79
MILLENIUM 3-5 78

Picture Sleeves

MILLENNIUM 3-5 78

LPs: 10/12–inch 33rpm

CASABLANCA 5-10 78-79
MILLENNIUM 5-10 78

TRAVOLTA, John

P&R/LP '76

Singles: 7–inch

MIDLAND INT'L 3-5 76-80
RCA 3-5 77
RSO 3-5 78-79

Picture Sleeves

MIDLAND INT'L (Except 10623)....3-5 76-80
MIDLAND INT'L (10623 "Let Her In") 4-8 76
RCA 3-5 77
RSO 3-5 78-79

LPs: 10/12–inch 33rpm

MIDLAND INT'L 5-10 76-77
MIDSONG INT'L 5-10 78

Also see NEWTON-JOHN, Olivia, & John Travolta

TRAVOLTA, John / Sha Na Na

Singles: 7–inch

RSO 3-5 78

Also see SHA NA NA
Also see TRAVOLTA, John

TRAYWICK, Randy

C&W '79

Singles: 7–inch

PAULA (429 "Dreamin'") 8-12 78
PAULA (431 "She's My Woman") 5-10 78

Also see TRAVIS, Randy

TREASURES

R&B '76

Singles: 7–inch

EPIC 3-5 77
MERCURY 3-5 76

LPs: 10/12–inch 33rpm

EPIC 5-10 77

TREAT HER RIGHT

LP '88

LPs: 10/12-inch 33rpm

RCA... 5-8 88

TREE SWINGERS

P&R '60

Singles: 7-inch

GUYDEN.................................. 8-12 60

TREMELOES

P&R/LP '67

Singles: 7-inch

DJM... 3-5 74-75
EPIC.. 4-8 66-70

Picture Sleeves

EPIC.. 4-8 67

LPs: 10/12-inch 33rpm

DJM... 8-10 74
EPIC...................................... 15-25 67-68

Also see POOLE, Brian

TREMELOES / Hollies

Singles: 7-inch

EPIC (10184 "Silence is Golden"/ "Carrie-Anne")........................ 10-20 67
(Colored vinyl. Promotional issue only.)

Also see HOLLIES
Also see TREMELOES

TRENIERS

R&B '51

Singles: 78rpm

BRUNSWICK................................ 4-8 57-58
EPIC.. 4-8 54-56
LONDON.................................. 5-10 50
OKEH... 4-8 51-55
VIK 4-8 56

Singles: 7-inch

BRUNSWICK.......................... 10-15 57-58
DOM... 4-8 68
DOT... 8-12 58-59
EPIC...................................... 10-20 54-56
OKEH..................................... 15-30 51-55
VIK 10-15 56

EPs: 7-inch 33/45rpm

EPIC...................................... 25-45 56-57

LPs: 10/12-inch 33rpm

DOT (3257 "Souvenir Album") .. 35-50 60
EPIC (3125 "On TV") 100-150 56

Members: Milt Trenier; Cliff Trenier; Claude Trenier.

TRIBE

R&B '73

Singles: 7-inch

ABC... 3-5 73-74
C & CT 3-5 71

LPs: 10/12-inch 33rpm

ABC.. 5-10 73-74
FARR 5-10 77
PICKWICK 10-15 75

TRIBE CALLED QUEST

LP '90

LPs: 10/12-inch 33rpm

JIVE 5-8 90

TRINERE

R&B '85

Singles: 7-inch

JAM PACKED...........................3-4 85-87

LPs: 10/12-inch 33rpm

JAM PACKED...........................5-8 86

TRINERE / FREESTYLE / DEBBIE DEB
(Trinere & Friends)

LP '89

LPs: 10/12-inch 33rpm

PANDISC 5-8 89

Also see DEBBIE DEB
Also see FREESTYLE
Also see TRINERE

TRIO+ : see LEWIS, Jerry Lee, Carl Perkins & Charlie Rich

TRIPLE "S" CONNECTION

R&B '80

Singles: 12-inch 33/45rpm

20TH FOX..................................4-6 79-80

Singles: 7-inch

20TH FOX..................................3-5 79-80

LPs: 10/12-inch 33rpm

20TH FOX...............................5-10 79

Also see LIVIN' PROOF
Also see SKOOL BOYZ

TRITT, Travis

C&W '89

Singles: 7-inch

W.B. 3-4 89-91

TRITT, Travis, & Marty Stuart

C&W '91

Singles: 7-inch

W.B. 3-4 91

Also see STUART, Marty
Also see TRITT, Travis

TRIUMPH

P&R/LP '79

Singles: 7-inch

MCA (Black vinyl).......................3-4 85-86
MCA (Colored vinyl)....................3-5 85-86
RCA 3-5 78-84

Picture Sleeves

MCA..3-4 85-86
RCA 3-5 79

LPs: 10/12-inch 33rpm

MCA..5-8 85-87
RCA 5-10 78-84

Members: Mike Levine; Gil Moore; Rik Emmett.

TRIUMVIRAT

LP '74

Singles: 7-inch

CAPITOL....................................3-5 79

LPs: 10/12–inch 33rpm

CAPITOL 5-10 74-80
HARVEST 10-12 74

TROGGS

P&R/LP '66

Singles: 7–inch

ATCO (6415 "Wild Thing"/"With a Girl Like You") 10-15 66
(Writer credited is "Presley.")
ATCO (6415 "Wild Thing"/"With a Girl Like You") 5-10 66
(Writer credited is "Taylor.")
ATCO (6415 "I Want You") 5-10 66
(Same number used twice.)
ATCO (6444 "I Can't Control Myself") 5-10 66
BELL 3-5 73
FONTANA 4-8 66-69
PAGE ONE 3-6 69-70
PRIVATE STOCK 3-5 77
PYE 3-5 75-76

LPs: 10/12–inch 33rpm

ATCO (33-193 "Wild Thing") 35-45 66
(Monaural.)
ATCO (SD-33-193 "Wild Thing") 25-35 66
(Stereo.)
FONTANA (27556 "The Troggs") 25-35 66
(Monaural.)
FONTANA (67556 "The Troggs") 20-30 66
(Stereo.)
FONTANA (67576 "Love Is All Around") 20-30 68
LIBERTY (3472 "You're Gonna Hear from Me") 25-35 66
(Monaural.)
LIBERTY (7472 "You're Gonna Hear from Me") 25-35 66
(Stereo.)
MKC 8-10 80
PRIVATE STOCK 10-15 76
PYE 10-15 75
RHINO 5-8 84
SIRE 10-15 76

TROGGS / Brook Benton

Singles: 7–inch

MILLER BEER (621 "Radio Spots") 5-10 60s

Picture Sleeves

MILLER BEER (621 "Radio Spots") 10-15 60s
Also see BENTON, Brook
Also see TROGGS

TROLLS

P&R '66

Singles: 7–inch

ABC 5-10 66-67
U.S.A. 10-20 68

TROOP

R&B/LP '88

Singles: 7–inch

ATLANTIC 3-4 88-90

LPs: 10/12–inch 33rpm

ATLANTIC 5-8 88-90

TROOPER

P&R/LP '78

Singles: 7–inch

LEGEND 3-5 75-77
MCA 3-5 77-78

LPs: 10/12–inch 33rpm

LEGEND 8-10 75-76
MCA 5-10 78-80
RCA 5-8 82

TROPEA

(John Tropea)

LP '76

Singles: 7–inch

MARLIN 3-5 76-77

LPs: 10/12–inch 33rpm

MARLIN 8-10 76-77
Also see DEODATO

TROUBADOURS DU ROI BAUDOUIN

LP '69

LPs: 10/12-Inch 33rpm

PHILIPS 5-10 63-69

TROUBLE

R&B '80

Singles: 7–inch

AL & KIDD 3-5 80
U.A. 3-5 77

LPs: 10/12–inch 33rpm

U.A. 8-10 77

TROUBLE FUNK

R&B/LP '82

Singles: 12–inch 33/45rpm

ISLAND 4-6 85-86
SUGAR HILL 4-6 82

Singles: 7–inch

D.E.T.T. 3-4 83
ISLAND 3-4 85-86
TF 3-5 80

LPs: 10/12–inch 33rpm

ISLAND 5-8 86
SUGAR HILL 5-8 82

TROUTMAN, Tony

R&B '75

Singles: 7–inch

GRAM-O-PHONE 3-5 75
T. MAIN 3-4 82-83

TROWER, Robin

LP '73

Singles: 12-inch 33/45rpm

GNP (2 "No Time") 5-8 87
(Promotional issue only.)

Singles: 7-inch

CHRYSALIS 3-5 72-78

LPs: 10/12-inch 33rpm

ATLANTIC 5-8 88
CHRYSALIS 5-12 73-82
GNP 5-8 83-87
PASSPORT 5-10 85
Also see BRUCE, Jack, & Robin Trower
Also see PROCOL HARUM

TROY, Benny
(With Maze)

R&B '75

Singles: 7-inch

DE-LITE 3-5 75
20TH FOX 3-5

TROY, Doris

P&R/R&B '63

Singles: 7-inch

APPLE 5-10 70
ATLANTIC 4-8 63-65
CALLA (114 "Heartaches") 10-20 66
CAPITOL 5-10 67
MIDLAND INT'L 3-6 76

LPs: 10/12-inch 33rpm

APPLE 15-20 70
ATLANTIC 20-25 64

TROYER, Eric

P&R '80

Singles: 7-inch

CHRYSALIS 3-5 80

LPs: 10/12-inch 33rpm

CHRYSALIS 5-10 80

TRUE, Andrea
(Andrea True Connection)

P&R/R&B/LP '76

Singles: 7-inch

BUDDAH 3-5 76-78
ERIC 3-5 78

Picture Sleeves

BUDDAH 4-8 76

LPs: 10/12-inch 33rpm

BUDDAH 5-10 76-78

TRUE LOVE

R&B '87

Singles: 7-inch

CRITIQUE 3-4 87

TRUMPETEERS

R&B '48

Singles: 78rpm

SCORE 5-10 48

LPs: 10/12-inch 33rpm

GRAND 25-40
SCORE (4021 "Milky White Way") 100-150 56

TRUMPETEERS

P&R '59

Singles: 7-inch

SPLASH 5-10 59
Member: Billy Mure.
Also see MURE, Billy

TRUSSELL

R&B '80

Singles: 7-inch

ELEKTRA 3-5 80

LPs: 10/12-inch 33rpm

ELEKTRA 5-10 80

TRUTH

R&B '74

Singles: 7-inch

ROULETTE 3-5 74-75

LPs: 10/12-inch 33rpm

PARAGON 5-10 78
ROULETTE 5-10 75

TRUTH

R&B '80

Singles: 7-inch

DEVAKI 3-5 80-81

TRUTH

P&R/LP '87

Singles: 7-inch

I.R.S. 3-4 87

Picture Sleeves

I.R.S. 3-4 87

LPs: 10/12-inch 33rpm

I.R.S. 5-8 87

TRYTHALL, Gil

LP '70

Singles: 7-inch

ATHENA 3-6 69-70

LPs: 10/12-inch 33rpm

ATHENA 5-10 69-70
PANDORA 5-8 81

TUBB, Ernest
(With the Texas Troubadours; with "Friends")

P&R '41

Singles: 78rpm

BLUEBIRD (6693 "The Passing of Jimmie Rodgers") 200-400 30s
BLUEBIRD (7000 "T.B. Is Whipping Me") 100-200 30s
BLUEBIRD (8899 "Married Man Blues") 100-150 30s
BLUEBIRD (8966 "Right Train to Heaven") 100-150 30s
DECCA 5-15 40-57

Singles: 7-inch

CACHET 3-5 79
DECCA (28067 thru 30872) 5-10 52-59
DECCA (30952 thru 33014) 3-8 59-72

DECCA (46000 series)............... 5-15 50-52
1ST GENERATION...................... 3-5 77
MCA 3-5 73
Session: Cal Smith; Jack Greene; Willie Nelson; Merle Haggard; Chet Atkins; Charlie Daniels; Jordanaires.
Also see ANDREWS SISTERS & Ernest Tubb
Also see GREENE, Jack
Also see SMITH, Cal

TUBB, Ernest, & Loretta Lynn
C&W '69
Singles: 7–inch
DECCA.. 3-6 69
Also see LYNN, Loretta

TUBB, Ernest, & Justin Tubb
EPs: 7–inch 33/45rpm
DECCA (2422 "Jimmie Rodgers Favorites").............................. 15-25 57

TUBB, Ernest, & Wilburn Brothers
C&W '58
Singles: 7–inch
DECCA....................................... 5-10 58
Also see TUBB, Ernest
Also see WILBURN BROTHERS

TUBES
LP '75
Singles: 12–inch 33/45rpm
CAPITOL.. 4-6 83
Singles: 7–inch
A&M 3-5 75-79
CAPITOL.. 3-4 81-85
Picture Sleeves
A&M 4-6 75
CAPITOL.. 3-5 81-85
LPs: 10/12–inch 33rpm
A&M 5-10 75-81
CAPITOL.. 5-8 81-85
Members: Fee Waybill; Roger Steen.
Also see NEWTON-JOHN, Olivia, & Electric Light Orchestra
Also see WAYBILL, Fee

TUCK & PATTI
LP '89
LPs: 10/12–inch 33rpm
WINDHAM HILL........................... 5-8 88-90

TUCKER, Junior
R&B '83
Singles: 7–inch
GEFFEN.. 3-4 83
LPs: 10/12–inch 33rpm
GEFFEN.. 5-8 83

TUCKER, Louise
P&R/LP '83
Singles: 7–inch
ARISTA 3-4 83
LPs: 10/12–inch 33rpm
ARISTA 5-8 83

TUCKER, Marshall: see MARSHALL TUCKER BAND

TUCKER, Tanya
C&W/P&R '72
Singles: 7–inch
ARISTA 3-5 82-84
CAPITOL...3-4 85-88
COLUMBIA 3-5 72-77
MCA...3-5 75-81
Picture Sleeves
COLUMBIA 3-6 72-75
MCA...3-5 75-81
LPs: 10/12–inch 33rpm
ARISTA 5-8 82-84
CAPITOL...5-8 86
COLUMBIA ("KC" series).............5-10 72-75
COLUMBIA ("PC" series)...............5-8 77
MCA...5-10 75-81
Also see CAMPBELL, Glen, & Tanya Tucker
Also see HARRIS, Emmylou

TUCKER, Tanya, & T. Graham Brown
C&W '90
Singles: 7–inch
CAPITOL...3-4 90

TUCKER, Tanya, & Glen Campbell
(Glen Campbell & Tanya Tucker)
C&W '80
Singles: 7–inch
CAPITOL...3-4 81
Also see CAMPBELL, Glen

TUCKER, Tanya, Paul Davis & Paul Overstreet
C&W '87
Singles: 7–inch
CAPITOL...3-4 87
Also see DAVIS, Paul
Also see TUCKER, Tanya

TUCKER, Tommy
P&R/R&B '64
Singles: 7–inch
CHECKER 4-8 64-67
FESTIVAL.......................................4-8 66
HI 5-10 59-60
RCA (47-7838 "Return of the Teenage Queen")...................................5-10 61
RCA (37-7838 "Return of the Teenage Queen")...................................10-20 61
(Compact 33 Single.)
RCA (68-7838 "Return of the Teenage Queen")...................................15-25 61
(Stereo Compact 33 Single.)
SUNBEAM 5-10 59
XL...4-8 66
LPs: 10/12–inch 33rpm
CHECKER (2990 "Hi-Heel Sneakers") 15-25 64

TUCKER, Tommy, & Esquires

Singles: 7-inch

IGL (121 "Don't Tell Me Lies")... 15-25 67

TUFANO & GIAMMERSE

P&R '73

Singles: 7-inch

ODE ... 3-5 73-76

LPs: 10/12-inch 33rpm

EPIC/ODE ... 8-10 76-77
ODE ... 10-15 73-74

Members: Dennis Tufano; Carl Giammerese.
Also see BUCKINGHAMS

TUFF DARTS

LP '78

Singles: 7-inch

SIRE ... 3-5 78

LPs: 10/12-inch 33rpm

SIRE ... 5-10 78

TULL, Jethro: see JETHRO TULL

TUNE ROCKERS

P&R '58

Singles: 7-inch

PET ... 8-12 58
U.A. ... 8-12 58

TUNE WEAVERS
(Margo Sylvia & Tune Weavers)

P&R/R&B '57

Singles: 78rpm

CASA GRANDE ... 10-15 57
CHECKER ... 8-10 57

Singles: 7-inch

CASA GRANDE (101 "Little Boy") ... 20-25 59
CASA GRANDE (3038 "My Congratulations Baby") ... 20-25 60
CASA GRANDE (4037 "Happy, Happy Birthday Baby") ... 35-50 57
CASA GRANDE (4038 "I Remember Dear") ... 20-25 57
CASA GRANDE (4040 "There Stands My Love") ... 20-30 58
CHECKER (872 "Happy, Happy Birthday Baby") ... 15-20 57
(Checkerboard top label.)
CHECKER (872 "Happy, Happy Birthday Baby") ... 5-8 58
(No Checkerboard at top.)
CHECKER (1007 "Congratulations on Your Wedding") ... 15-20 62
CHESS ... 3-5 73
CLASSIC ARTISTS ... 3-5 88-89
COLLECTABLES ... 3-4 80s
ERIC ... 3-4 70s

LPs: 10/12-inch 33rpm

CASA GRANDE ... 10-15 73

Members: Margo Sylvia; Charlotte Davis; Gil Lopez; John Sylvia.

TUNETOPPERS: see BROWN, Al, & His Tunetoppers

TUNNELL, Jimi

D&D '84

Singles: 12-inch 33/45rpm

MCA ... 4-6 84

Singles: 7-inch

MCA ... 3-4 84

TURBANS

P&R/R&B '55

Singles: 78rpm

HERALD ... 10-20 55-57
MONEY ... 20-25 55

Singles: 7-inch

ABC ... 3-5 73
COLLECTABLES ... 3-4 80s
FLASHBACK ... 3-5 65
HERALD (458 "When You Dance") ... 20-30 55
(Script print/flag logo.)
HERALD (458 "When You Dance") ... 10-15
(Block print logo.)
HERALD (469 "Sister Sookey") . 15-20 55
HERALD (478 "I'm Nobody's")... 20-30 56
HERALD (486 "All of My Love"). 20-25 56
HERALD (495 "Valley of Love"). 20-25 57
HERALD (510 "Congratulations") ... 20-30 57
(Script print/flag logo.)
HERALD (510 "Congratulations") 8-12 57
(Block print logo.)
HERALD (510 "Congratulations") ... 25-35 57
(Single sided. Promotional issue only.)
HI-OLDIES ... 3-4 80s
IMPERIAL (5807 "Six Questions") ... 20-30 61
IMPERIAL (5828 "This Is My Story") ... 15-20 62
IMPERIAL (5847 "I Wonder")..... 10-15 62
MONEY (209 "No, No Cherry") 75-100 55
PARKWAY (820 "When You Dance") ... 10-20 61
RED TOP (115 "I Promise You Love") ... 25-35 59
ROULETTE ... 10-15 60-61

LPs: 10/12-inch 33rpm

COLLECTABLES ... 5-8 84
LOST-NITE ... 5-10 81
RELIC ... 10-15 70s

Members: Al Banks; Matt Platt; Andrew Jones; Charles Williams.

TURNER, Dwight

Singles: 7-inch

CHATOK (1001 "You're Alone"). 50-75 60s

Also see TURNER, Spyder

TURNER, Ike

(With the Kings of Rhythm; with His Orchestra)

Singles: 78rpm

CHESS 10-20 51
FEDERAL (12297 "Do You Mean It") 20-30 57
FEDERAL (12304 "Rock-A-Bucket") 10-15 57
FLAIR 10-20 52
RPM 10-20 52

Singles: 7-inch

ARTISTIC 8-10 59
COBRA 8-10 59
FEDERAL (12297 "Do You Mean It") 50-75 57
FEDERAL (12304 "Rock-A-Bucket") 20-30 57
FLAIR (1040 "Cubano Jump") ... 35-50 52
FLAIR (1059 "Cuban Getaway") 35-50 52
KING 5-10 61
LIBERTY 3-5 70
RPM (356 "You're Driving Me Insane") 25-50 52
SUE (100 series) 4-8 66
SUE (700 series) 8-12 59
U.A. 3-5 71-74

LPs: 10/12-inch 33rpm

CROWN 20-25 63
POMPEII 10-15 69
U.A. 6-12 72-73

Also see BLAND, Bobby, & Ike Turner
Also see BRENSTON, Jackie
Also see RENRUT, Icky

TURNER, Ike & Bonnie

Singles: 78rpm

RPM (362 "Looking for a Baby") 10-15 52

Singles: 7-inch

RPM (362 "Looking for a Baby") 25-50 52

TURNER, Ike & Tina

(With the Ikettes; with Home Grown Funk)

P&R/R&B '60

Singles: 7-inch

A&M 4-6 69
BLUE THUMB 3-5 69-71
CENCO 4-8 60s
COLLECTABLES 3-4 80s
FANTASY 3-5 80
INNIS 3-6 68-71
KENT (400 series) 4-8 64
KENT (4500 series) 3-5 70
LIBERTY 3-5 70-71
LOMA 4-8 65
MINIT 3-6 69-70
MODERN 4-8 65
PHILLES 8-12 66
POMPEII 3-6 68-70
SONJA 4-8 63-64
SUE (100 series) 4-8 65-66
SUE (700 series) 5-10 60-63
TRC 3-5 71
TANGERINE 4-8 66
U.A. 3-5 71-75
W.B. 4-8 64

Picture Sleeves

MINIT 4-8 69
POMPEII 4-8 69
W.B. 5-10 64

LPs: 10/12-inch 33rpm

A&M (3179 "River Deep, Mountain High") 5-10 82
A&M (4178 "River Deep, Mountain High") 10-20 69
ABC 8-10 70s
ACCORD 5-10 81
BLUE THUMB 8-12 69-73
CAPITOL (500 series) 5-10 75
(With "SM" prefix.)
CAPITOL (500 series) 10-15 69
(With "ST" prefix.)
CENCO 15-20 60s
COLLECTABLES 5-8 88
FANTASY 5-10 80
HARMONY (11000 series) 10-12 69
HARMONY (30000 series) 8-10 71
KENT 15-25 61-64
LIBERTY (7000 series) 10-12 70
LIBERTY (51000 series) 5-8 85
LOMA 10-20 66
MINIT 10-15 69
PHILLES (4011 "River Deep, Mountain High") 1000-2000 66
(Covers for a U.S. pressing are not known to exist. British pressings [London/Philles SHU-8298] do exist with covers.)
PICKWICK 5-10 70s
POMPEII 10-15 68-69
SUE (2001 "The Sound of Ike & Tina Turner") 60-80 61
SUE (2003 "Dance with Ike & Tina Turner's Kings of Rhythm") 50-75 62
(Instrumentals by Ike & Tina Turner's band.)
SUE (2004 "Dynamite") 50-75 63
SUE (2005 "Don't Play Me Cheap") 50-75 63
SUE (2007 "It's Gonna Work Out Fine") 50-75 63
SUE (1038 "Greatest Hits") 35-45 65
SUNSET 8-10 69-70
UNART 5-10 70s
U.A. 8-12 71-78
UNITED SUPERIOR 8-10
W.B. 10-20 65-69

Also see BLAND, Bobby, & Ike Turner
Also see IKETTES
Also see RAELETTES
Also see SYLVIA
Also see TURNER, Tina

TURNER, Jesse Lee

P&R '59

Singles: 7–inch

CARLTON 5-10 59
FRATERNITY............................ 5-10 59
GNP (184 "All You Gotta Do")....... 4-8 62
GNP (188 "Shotgun Boogie").... 40-60 62
IMPERIAL 5-10 60
SUDDEN.................................. 4-6
TOP RANK.............................. 5-10 60

Picture Sleeves

CARLTON 10-15 59
FRATERNITY (855 "Teenage Misery")............................. 35-50 59

TURNER, Joe

(With His Blues Kings; with Pete Johnson & His Orchestra; Big Joe Turner)

R&B '46

Singles: 78rpm

ALADDIN (3013 "Morning Glory")............................. 50-100 49
ALADDIN (3070 "Back Breaking Baby") 50-100 50
ATLANTIC................................ 5-10 51-57
BAYOU................................... 10-20 53
COLONY 5-10 52
CORAL (65000 series).............. 5-10 48
DECCA..................................... 5-10 41-56
DOOTONE (305 "I Love Ya, I Love Ya, I Love Ya") 50-75 51
DOWN BEAT 8-12 48
EXCELSIOR............................. 5-10 49
FIDELITY 5-10 51-52
FREEDOM 5-10 50
IMPERIAL 5-10 50
MGM 5-10 48-50
NATIONAL 10-15 46-51
RPM 15-25 51
SWING BEAT.......................... 10-20 49
VOCALION.............................. 10-20 39

Singles: 7–inch

ATLANTIC (939 "Chains of Love")............................. 50-100 51
ATLANTIC (949 "Bump Miss Susie")................................ 50-75 51
ATLANTIC (960 "Sweet Sixteen")............................... 50-75 52
ATLANTIC (970 "Don't You Cry")...................................... 50-75 52
ATLANTIC (982 "Don't You Cry")...................................... 40-60 52
ATLANTIC (1001 "Honey Hush") 20-30 53
ATLANTIC (1016 "TV Mama") .. 30-40 53
ATLANTIC (1026 thru 1184)..... 15-30 54-58
ATLANTIC (2000 series)............ 8-15 59-60
BAYOU (015 "The Blues Jumped a Rabbit") 100-200 53
BLUESTIME (45001 "Two Loves Have I")...................................25-50
BLUESWAY 4-8 67
CORAL (62000 series) 5-8 64
DECCA (29000 series) 15-25 55-56
KENT 3-6 69-71
RPM (345 "Ridin' Blues") 100-150 51
RONN 4-6 69

EPs: 7–inch 33/45rpm

ATLANTIC (536 "Joe Turner Sings") 50-75 55
ATLANTIC (565 "Joe Turner") ...50-75 56
ATLANTIC (586 "Joe Turner") ...50-75 56
ATLANTIC (606 "Rock with Joe Turner")...............................50-75 56
EMARCY (6132 "Joe Turner and Pete Johnson") 50-75 56

LPs: 10/12–inch 33rpm

ARHOOLIE 15-25 62
ATCO...8-12 71
ATLANTIC (1234 "Boss of the Blues") 50-100 58
ATLANTIC (1332 "Big Joe Rides Again")...........................50-75 60
ATLANTIC (8005 "Joe Turner")............................100-200 57
(Black label.)
ATLANTIC (8005 "Joe Turner")..............................50-100 59
(Red label.)
ATLANTIC (8023 "Rockin' the Blues") 100-150 58
(Black label.)
ATLANTIC (8023 "Rockin' the Blues") 50-75 59
(Red label.)
ATLANTIC (8033 "Big Joe Is Here")...........................100-150 59
(Black label.)
ATLANTIC (8033 "Big Joe Is Here")...................................50-75 59
(Red label.)
ATLANTIC (8081 "Best of Joe Turner")...........................30-50 63
ATLANTIC (8812 "Boss of the Blues") 5-10 81
BIG TOWN....................................5-10 78
BLUES SPECTRUM 10-12
BLUESTIME (9002 "The Real Boss of the Blues") 20-30 60s
BLUESWAY 8-12 67-73
CHIARDSCURO 8-10 76
CLASSIC JAZZ.............................5-10 79
EMARCY (36014 "Joe Turner with Pete Johnson") 100-200 56
INTERMEDIA.................................5-8 83-84
LMI 8-10 74
MCA..5-10 80
PABLO 5-10 76-83

SAVOY (14012 "Blues Can Make You Happy") 100-150 58
SAVOY (14106 "Carless Love") 50-75 64
SAVOY (2223 "Big Joe Is Here") 5-10 77
UNITED 8-10

Session: King Curtis.
Also see FLENNOY TRIO & JOE TURNER
Also see JOHNSON, Pete
Also see KING CURTIS

TURNER, Joe / Jimmy Nelson

LPs: 10/12-inch 33rpm

CROWN 15-25 62

Also see TURNER, Joe

TURNER, Joe Lynn

LP '85

LPs: 10/12-inch 33rpm

ELEKTRA 5-8 85

TURNER, Ruby
(Featuring Jonathan Butler)

LP '90

Singles: 7-inch

JIVE 3-4 86-90

LPs: 10/12-inch 33rpm

JIVE 5-8 86-90

Also see BUTLER, Jonathan

TURNER, Sammy
(With the Twisters)

P&R/R&B '59

Singles: 7-inch

BIG TOP (3007 & 3016) 5-10 59
BIG TOP (3029 "Always") 5-10 59
(Monaural.)
BIG TOP (3029 "Always") 15-25 59
(Stereo.)
BIG TOP (3032 thru 3070) 5-10 60-61
BIG TOP (3089 "Falling") 10-15 61
ERIC 3-4 70s
MILLENNIUM 3-4 78
MOTOWN 10-20 64
PACIFIC (3016 "Lavender Blue") 25-35 59
PACIFIC (3029 "Always") 20-30 59
20TH FOX 4-8 65
VERVE (10465 "A Child Is Born") 12-25 66

LPs: 10/12-inch 33rpm

BIG TOP (1301 "Lavender Blue Moods") 25-40 60
(Monaural.)
BIG TOP (ST-1301 "Lavender Blue Moods") 35-50 60
(Stereo.)

Session: King Curtis.
Also see KING CURTIS

TURNER, Sammy / Ivory Joe Hunter

Singles: 7-inch

GOLD SOUL 3-5

Also see HUNTER, Ivory Joe
Also see TURNER, Sammy

TURNER, Spyder
(Dwight Turner)

P&R/R&B '66

Singles: 7-inch

KWANZA 3-5 73
MGM 5-15 66-71
POLYDOR 3-4 84
WHITFIELD 3-5 78-79

LPs: 10/12-inch 33rpm

MGM 15-20 67
WHITFIELD 5-10 78-79

Also see BRISTOL, Johnny, & Spyder Turner
Also see TURNER, Dwight

TURNER, Tina

R&B/LP '75

Singles: 12-inch 33/45rpm

CAPITOL 4-6 84-87

Singles: 7-inch

CAPITOL 3-4 84-89
POMPEII 4-8 68
U.A. 3-5 75-78
WAGNER 3-5 79

Picture Sleeves

CAPITOL 3-5 84-89

LPs: 10/12-inch 33rpm

CAPITOL 5-8 84-89
FANTASY 5-10
SPRINGBOARD 8-10 72
U.A. (Except 200) 8-10 75-78
U.A. (200 "Tina Turner Turns the Country On") 10-15 67
WAGNER 5-8 79

Also see ADAMS, Bryan, & Tina Turner
Also see BASS, Fontella, & Tina Turner
Also see BOWIE, David
Also see CLAPTON, Eric, & Tina Turner
Also see JOHN, Elton / Tina Turner
Also see TURNER, Ike & Tina
Also see U.S.A. for AFRICA

TURNER, Titus

P&R/R&B '59

Singles: 78rpm

ATLANTIC 4-8 57

Singles: 7-inch

ATCO 4-8 64
ATLANTIC 8-12 57
COLUMBIA 4-8 63
ENJOY 4-8 62-63
GLOVER (Except 202) 5-10 59-60
GLOVER (202 "When the Sergeant Comes Marching Home") 10-20 60
GUARANTEED 4-8 61-62
JAMIE 4-8 61
JOSIE 4-6 68-69
KING (Monaural) 5-10 57-61
KING (Stereo) 10-20 59
MURBO 4-8 65
OKEH (6844 thru 7038) 15-25 52-54
OKEH (7200 series) 4-8 66
PHILIPS 4-8 67

WING 10-15 55

LPs: 10/12-inch 33rpm

JAMIE.................................... 25-35 61

Session: Mickey Baker.

TURRENTINE, Stanley

LP '67

Singles: 7-Inch

BLUE NOTE.............................. 3-8 61-69
CTI 3-5 72
ELEKTRA.................................. 3-4 79-81
FANTASY................................. 3-5 74-78
IMPULSE 3-5 67

LPs: 10/12-Inch 33rpm

BAINBRIDGE............................. 5-8 81
BLUE NOTE............................. 25-50 60-61
(Label gives New York street address for Blue Note Records.)
BLUE NOTE............................. 15-30 62-65
(Label reads "Blue Note Records Inc. - New York, U.S.A.")
BLUE NOTE............................. 8-18 65-85
(Label shows Blue Note Records as a division of either Liberty or United Artists.)
CTI 8-12 71-75
ELEKTRA.................................. 5-8 79-81
FPM.. 5-8 75
FANTASY................................. 8-12 74-78
IMPULSE 8-15 67-78
MAINSTREAM 15-25 65
PRESTIGE............................... 6-12 70-71
SUNSET................................... 8-12 69
TIME....................................... 25-50 62-63
UPFRONT................................ 6-12 72

Also see BYRD, Donald
Also see FULSON, Lowell
Also see GILBERTO, Astrud, & Stanley Turrentine
Also see HUBBARD, Freddie, & Stanley Turrentine
Also see SILVER, Horace, Quintet, & Stanley Turrentine

TURTLES

P&R/LP '65

Singles: 7-inch

COLLECTABLES........................ 3-4 80s
WHITE WHALE.......................... 5-10 65-70

Picture Sleeves

WHITE WHALE.......................... 8-12 67-69

LPs: 10/12-inch 33rpm

RHINO (Except RNPD-901).......... 5-8 82-86
RHINO (RNPD-901 "Turtles 1968")...................................... 8-10 83
SIRE....................................... 10-15 74
TRIP 5-10 70s
WHITE WHALE......................... 15-30 65-71

Members: Howard Kaylan; Mark Volman; Don Murray; Chuck Portz; Al Nichol; Jim Tucker; John Barbata; John Seiter; Jim Pons; Chip Douglas.
Also see CHRISTMAS SPIRIT
Also see KAYLAN, Howard, & Marc Volman
Also see LEAVES

TUTONE, Tommy: see TOMMY TUTONE

TUXEDO JUNCTION

P&R/LP '78

Singles: 12-inch 33/45rpm

BUTTERFLY.................................4-8 78-80

Singles: 7-inch

BUTTERFLY (Black vinyl) 3-5 78-80
BUTTERFLY (Colored vinyl)..........4-6 78

LPs: 10/12-inch 33rpm

BUTTERFLY (Black vinyl) 5-10 77-79
BUTTERFLY (Colored vinyl)......10-12 77
(Promotional issues only.)

TWENNYNINE
(Featuring Lenny White)

R&B/LP '79

Singles: 7-inch

ELEKTRA.....................................3-5 79-81

LPs: 10/12-inch 33rpm

ELEKTRA...................................5-10 79-81

Also see WHITE, Lenny

21ST CENTURY

P&R/R&B '75

Singles: 7-inch

RCA 3-5 75

24 - 7 SPYZ

LP '89

LPs: 10/12-inch 33rpm

IN-EFFECT 5-8 89-90

TWILIGHT 22

P&R/R&B/D&D '83

Singles: 12-inch 33/45rpm

VANGUARD.................................4-6 83-84

Singles: 7-inch

VANGUARD.................................3-4 83-84

LPs: 10/12-inch 33rpm

VANGUARD.................................5-8 84

TWILLEY, Dwight
(Dwight Twilley Band)

P&R '75

Singles: 7-inch

ARISTA.......................................3-5 77-79
EMI AMERICA 3-4 82-84
SHELTER 3-5 75-76

Picture Sleeves

EMI AMERICA 3-4 84
SHELTER 3-5 75-76

LPs: 10/12-inch 33rpm

ARISTA.....................................5-10 77-79
EMI AMERICA 5-8 82-84
SHELTER 5-10 75-76

Also see SEYMOUR, Phil

TWIN IMAGE

R&B '85

Singles: 12-inch 33/45rpm

CAPITOL.....................................4-6 84-85

Singles: 7-inch

CAPITOL.....................................3-4 84-85

LPs: 10/12-inch 33rpm

CAPITOL 5-8 84

TWIN HYPE

LP '89

LPs: 10/12-inch 33rpm

PROFILE 5-8 89

TWINS

D&D '83

Singles: 12-inch 33/45rpm

QUALITY/RFC 4-6 83

TWISTED SISTER

LP '83

Singles: 7-inch

ATLANTIC 3-4 83-86

Picture Sleeves

ATLANTIC 3-4 84-85

LPs: 10/12-inch 33rpm

ATLANTIC 5-8 83-87

Members: Dee Snider; Jay Jay French; A.J. Pero; Eddie Ojeda; Mark Mendoza.

TWITTY, Conway

P&R '57

Singles: 78rpm

MERCURY 20-30 57

Singles: 7-inch

ABC-PAR (10507 "Go On and Cry") 10-15 63
ABC-PAR (10550 "My Baby Left Me") 15-25 64
CONWAY TWITTY FAN CLUB ("It's Only Make Believe") 10-15
(Promotional, fan club issue only.)
DECCA 3-8 65-72
ELEKTRA 3-4 82-83
MCA 3-5 73-82
MGM (500 series) 3-5 78
MGM (12000 & 13000 series) 5-15 58-62
MGM (14000 series) 3-5 71-72
MGM (50000 series) 20-40 58-59
(Stereo.)
MERCURY 20-40 57-58
MUSIGRAM 3-6
(Flexi-disc.)
POLYDOR 3-4 80s
W.B. 3-4 83-86

Picture Sleeves

ELEKTRA 3-5 82
MGM 10-20 58-62

EPs: 7-inch 33/45rpm

MGM 20-30 58-59

LPs: 10/12-inch 33rpm

ACCORD 5-10 82
ALLEGIANCE 5-8 84
CANDLELITE 10-12 70s
CORAL 5-8 73
DECCA 8-18 66-72
DEMAND 8-12 72
ELEKTRA 5-8 82-83
MCA 5-15 73-85
MGM (110 "Conway Twitty") 15-20 70
MGM (3744 "Conway Twitty Sings") 50-100 59
MGM (E-3786 "Saturday Night with Conway Twitty") 50-75 59
(Monaural.)
MGM (SE-3786 "Saturday Night with Conway Twitty") 75-100 59
(Stereo.)
MGM (E-3818 "Lonely Blue Boy") 50-75 60
(Monaural.)
MGM (SE-3818 "Lonely Blue Boy") 75-100 60
(Stereo.)
MGM (E-3849 "Conway Twitty's Greatest Hits") 50-75 60
(Monaural. Black label. With gatefold cover and poster.)
MGM (SE-3849 "Conway Twitty's Greatest Hits") 75-100 60
(Stereo. With gatefold cover and poster.)
MGM (3849 "Conway Twitty's Greatest Hits") 15-20 68
(Blue and yellow label. With standard cover.)
MGM (E-3907 "The Rock and Roll Story") 50-75 61
(Monaural.)
MGM (SE-3907 "The Rock and Roll Story") 75-100 61
(Stereo.)
MGM (E-3943 "The Conway Twitty Touch") 30-40 61
(Monaural.)
MGM (SE-3943 "The Conway Twitty Touch") 35-50 61
(Stereo.)
MGM (E-4019 thru E-4217) 20-40 62-64
(Monaural.)
MGM (SE-4019 thru SE-4217) 25-50 62-64
(Stereo.)
MGM (4650 thru 4884) 10-20 69-73
METRO 15-25 65
OPRYLAND (12636 "Conway Twitty, Then and Now") 75-100
(Six-LP set. Promotional issue only.)
PICKWICK 10-15 72
TEE VEE 5-10 78
TROLLY CAR 5-10
TWITTY BIRD (1001 "Solid Gold") 10-12 82
(Two-LP.)
W.B. 5-10 83-86

Session: Fred Carter Jr.; Anthony Armstrong Jones; Joni Lee.

Also see LYNN, Loretta, & Conway Twitty
Also see MARTIN, Dean
Also see McDOWELL, Ronnie

2 LIVE CREW
(Luke Featuring 2 Live Crew)

LP '87

Singles: 12–inch 33/45rpm

LUKE SKYWALKER 4-8 88-89

Singles: 7–inch

LUKE SKYWALKER 3-4 88-89

LPs: 10/12–inch 33rpm

LUKE SKYWALKER 5-8 87-90

2 of CLUBS

P&R '67

Singles: 7–inch

FRATERNITY 5-10 66-67

TWO SISTERS

D&D '83

Singles: 12–inch 33/45rpm

SUGARSCOOP 4-6 83

TWO TONS O' FUN
(Two Tons)

R&B/LP '80

Singles: 12–inch 33/45rpm

FANTASY 4-6 80

Singles: 7–inch

FANTASY 3-5 80
HONEY 3-5 80-81

LPs: 10/12–inch 33rpm

FANTASY 5-8 80
HONEY 5-8 80

Members: Martha Wash; Izora Armstead.
Also see WEATHER GIRLS

TYCOON

P&R/LP '79

Singles: 7–inch

ARISTA 3-5 79

LPs: 10/12–inch 33rpm

ARISTA 5-10 78-81

TYLER, Bonnie

P&R/C&W/LP '78

Singles: 7–inch

CHRYSALIS 3-5 77
COLUMBIA 3-4 83-86
RCA 3-5 78-79

Picture Sleeves

COLUMBIA 3-4 83-86

LPs: 10/12–inch 33rpm

CHRYSALIS 8-12 77
COLUMBIA 5-8 83-86
RCA 5-10 78-81

Also see RUNDGREN, Todd

TYLER, Frankie
(Frankie Valli)

Singles: 7–inch

OKEH (7103 "I Go Ape") 50-75 58

Promotional Singles

OKEH (7103 "I Go Ape") 40-60 58

Also see VALLI, Frankie

TYMES

P&R/R&B/LP '63

Singles: 7–inch

ABKCO 3-5 74
COLUMBIA 4-6 68-70
MGM 10-20 66
PARKWAY (Except 871) 5-10 63-64
PARKWAY (871 "So in Love") 10-15 63
PARKWAY (871 "So Much in Love") 5-8 63
RCA 3-6 74-77
WINCHESTER 5-10 67

Picture Sleeves

PARKWAY 5-15 63-64

LPs: 10/12–inch 33rpm

ABKCO 5-10 74
COLUMBIA 10-15 69
PARKWAY 20-40 63-64
RCA 8-10 74-77
WYNCOTE 10-20 60s

Members: George Williams Jr; Donald Banks; Al Berry; Norman Burnett; George Hilliard.
Also see MAESTRO, Johnny, & Tymes

TYNER, McCoy
(McCoy Tyner Trio)

LP '75

Singles: 7–inch

COLUMBIA 3-4 82
IMPULSE 4-8 65

LPs: 10/12–inch 33rpm

BLUE NOTE 8-15 66-76
COLUMBIA 5-8 82
FPM 5-10 75
IMPULSE 10-20 62-78
MCA 5-10 81
MILESTONE 5-12 72-82
PAUSA 5-8 82

TYRANNOSAURUS REX: see T. REX

TYZIK
(Jeff Tyzik)

R&B/D&D/LP '84

Singles: 12–inch 33/45rpm

POLYDOR 4-6 84

Singles: 7–inch

CAPITOL 3-4 82
POLYDOR 3-4 84

LPs: 10/12–inch 33rpm

CAPITOL 5-8 82
POLYDOR 5-8 84

U

UB40
(With Chrissie Hynde)

LP '83

Singles: 12–inch 33/45rpm

A&M 4-6 83-86

Singles: 7–inch

A&M 3-4 83-88

Picture Sleeves

A&M 3-4 85

LPs: 10/12–inch 33rpm

A&M 5-8 83-88
VIRGIN 5-8 89

Also see PRETENDERS

UFO

LP '75

Singles: 7–inch

CHRYSALIS 3-5 73-86

LPs: 10/12–inch 33rpm

CHRYSALIS 5-12 74-86
RARE EARTH 10-15 71

Also see SCHENKER, Michael, Group

U.K.

LP '78

Singles: 7–inch

POLYDOR 3-5 78-79

LPs: 10/12–inch 33rpm

POLYDOR 5-10 78-79

Members: John Wetton; Eddie Jobson; Terry Bozzio; Bill Bruford; Allan Holdsworth.

U.K. SQUEEZE: see SQUEEZE

U-KREW

LP '90

LPs: 10/12–inch 33rpm

ENIGMA 5-8 90

U.S. 1

P&R '75

Singles: 7–inch

PRIVATE STOCK 3-5 75

U.S.A.- EUROPEAN CONNECTION

LP '78

Singles: 7–inch

MARLIN 3-5 78-79

LPs: 10/12–inch 33rpm

MARLIN 5-10 78-79

USA for AFRICA / Quincy Jones
(United Support of Artists for Africa)

P&R/R&B/D&D/C&W/LP '85

Singles: 12–inch 33/45rpm

COLUMBIA 4-6 85

Singles: 7–inch

COLUMBIA 3-4 85

Picture Sleeves

COLUMBIA 3-4 85

LPs: 10/12–inch 33rpm

COLUMBIA 5-8 85

Members: Dan Aykroyd; Kim Carnes; Ray Charles; Bob Dylan; Daryl Hall; James Ingram; Michael Jackson; Jean-Michael Jarre; Al Jarreau; Waylon Jennings; Billy Joel; Quincy Jones; Cyndi Lauper; Huey Lewis; Kenny Loggins; Bette Midler; Steve Perry; Lionel Richie; Smokey Robinson; Kenny Rogers; Diana Ross; Paul Simon; Bruce Springsteen; Tina Turner; Dionne Warwick; Stevie Wonder.

Also see CARNES, Kim
Also see CHARLES, Ray
Also see DYLAN, Bob
Also see HALL, Daryl
Also see INGRAM, James
Also see JACKSON, Michael
Also see JARRE, Jean-Michael
Also see JARREAU, Al
Also see JENNINGS, Waylon
Also see JOEL, Billy
Also see JONES, Quincy
Also see LAUPER, Cyndi
Also see LEWIS, Huey, & News
Also see LOGGINS, Kenny
Also see MIDLER, Bette
Also see PERRY, Steve
Also see RICHIE, Lionel
Also see ROBINSON, Smokey
Also see ROGERS, Kenny
Also see ROSS, Diana
Also see SIMON, Paul
Also see SPRINGSTEEN, Bruce
Also see TURNER, Tina
Also see VOICES of AMERICA / U.S.A. for AFRICA
Also see WARWICK, Dionne
Also see WONDER, Stevie

UTFO

P&R/R&B/D&D/LP '85

Singles: 12–inch 33/45rpm

SELECT 4-6 85-86

Singles: 7–inch

SELECT 3-4 85-89

LPs: 10/12–inch 33rpm

SELECT 5-8 85-89

Also see ROXANNE with UTFO

U2

LP '81

Singles: 12–inch 33/45rpm

ISLAND 4-6 83

Singles: 7–inch

ISLAND 3-5 81-89

Picture Sleeves

ISLAND 3-5 81-89

EPs: 7–inch 33/45rpm

ISLAND (99385 "Joshua Tree") .. 5-10 87

LPs: 10/12–inch 33rpm

ISLAND 5-10 81-89

Members: Paul "Bono Vox" Hewson; David "The Edge" Evan; Adam Clayton; Larry Mullen.

Also see BAND AID

U2 & B.B. King

P&R '89

Singles: 7-inch

ISLAND 3-4 89

Picture Sleeves

ISLAND 3-4 89

Also see KING, B.B.
Also see U2

UBIQUITY

LP '78

Singles: 7-inch

ELEKTRA 3-5 78

LPs: 10/12-inch 33rpm

ELEKTRA 5-10 78

Also see AYERS, Roy

UGGAMS, Leslie

P&R '59

Singles: 7-inch

ATLANTIC 5-15 65-70
COLUMBIA 5-10 59-64
GORDY 3-5 76
MGM 5-15 54-55
SONDAY 3-5 71

EPs: 7-inch 33/45rpm

MGM 5-10 54

LPs: 10/12-inch 33rpm

ATLANTIC 5-15 66-69
COLUMBIA 15-30 59-63
MOTOWN 5-10 75
SONDAY 5-10 72

ULLANDA

R&B '79

Singles: 7-inch

OCEAN 3-5 79

ULLMAN, Tracey

P&R/LP '84

Singles: 7-inch

MCA 3-5 84-85

Picture Sleeves

MCA 3-5 84-85

LPs: 10/12-inch 33rpm

MCA 5-10 84

ULTIMATE

P&R/LP '79

Singles: 7-inch

CASABLANCA 3-5 78-80

LPs: 10/12-inch 33rpm

CASABLANCA 5-10 78-80

ULTIMATE SPINACH

LP '68

Singles: 7-inch

MGM 5-10 68-69

LPs: 10/12-inch 33rpm

MGM (4518 "Ultimate Spinach") 20-30 68
MGM (4570 "Behold and See"). 20-30 68
MGM (4600 "Ultimate Spinach") 15-25 69

Members: Barbara Hudson; Ian Bruce Douglas; Richard Nese; Jeff Baxter; Ted Myers; Tony Scheuren; Mike Levine; Russ Levine.
Also see STEELY DAN

ULTRAVOX

LP '80

Singles: 12-inch 33/45rpm

CHRYSALIS 4-6 83

Singles: 7-inch

ANTILLES 3-5 78-80
CHRYSALIS 3-4 80-84
ISLAND 8-10 77

LPs: 10/12-inch 33rpm

ANTILLES 5-10 78-80
CHRYSALIS 5-8 80-84
ISLAND 8-10 77

Also see BAND AID

UMILANI, Piero
(Sweden Heaven & Hell Soundtrack)

P&R '69

Singles: 7-inch

ARIEL 3-5 69

LPs: 10/12-inch 33rpm

ARIEL 8-12 69

UNCLE DOG

P&R '73

Singles: 7-inch

MCA 3-5 73

LPs: 10/12-inch 33rpm

MCA 5-10 73

UNCLE LOUIE

R&B '79

Singles: 7-inch

MARLIN 3-5 79

LPs: 10/12-inch 33rpm

MARLIN 5-10 78

UNDERGROUND SUNSHINE

P&R/LP '69

Singles: 7-inch

INTREPID 5-10 69

LPs: 10/12-inch 33rpm

INTERPID 15-25 69

UNDERTONES

LP '80

Singles: 7-inch

CAPITOL 3-4 84
HARVEST 3-5 81
SIRE 3-5 80

LPs: 10/12-inch 33rpm

CAPITOL 5-8 84
HARVEST 5-10 81
SIRE 5-10 80

Member: Feargal Sharkey.
Also see SHARKEY, Feargal

UNDERWOOD, Veronica

R&B '85

Singles: 7-inch

PHILLY WORLD 3-4 85

UNDERWORLD

P&R/LP '88

Singles: 7-inch

SIRE 3-4 88-89

Picture Sleeves

SIRE 3-4 88-89

LPs: 10/12-inch 33rpm

SIRE 5-8 88

UNDISPUTED TRUTH

P&R/R&B/LP '71

Singles: 12-inch 33/45rpm

WHITFIELD 4-8 77-79

Singles: 7-inch

GORDY 3-5 71-75
MOTOWN 3-4
WHITFIELD 3-5 76-79

LPs: 10/12-inch 33rpm

GORDY 10-20 71-75
WHITFIELD 5-10 77-79

Members: Joe Harris; Brenda Evans; Billie Calvin; Carl Smalls

Also see BOOM, Taka
Also see DRAMATICS

UNFORGIVEN

LP '86

LPs: 10/12-inch 33rpm

ELEKTRA 5-8 86

UNICORN

LP '74

Singles: 7-inch

CAPITOL 3-5 74-77

LPs: 10/12-inch 33rpm

CAPITOL 8-10 74-77

UNIFICS

P&R/R&B '68

Singles: 7-inch

FOUNTAIN 3-5 71
KAPP 4-8 68-69
MCA 3-4 70S

Picture Sleeves

KAPP 4-8 68-69

LPs: 10/12-inch 33rpm

KAPP 10-15 68

UNION GAP: see PUCKET, Gary

UNIPOP

P&R '82

Singles: 7-inch

KAT FAMILY 3-4 82

LPs: 10/12-inch 33rpm

KAT FAMILY 5-8 82

UNIQUE

R&B/D&D '83

Singles: 12-inch 33/45rpm

PRELUDE 4-6 83

Singles: 7-inch

PRELUDE 3-4 83

UNIQUES

P&R '65

Singles: 7-inch

DEMAND 3-5
PARAMOUNT 3-5 70-72
PAULA 4-8 65-70

LPs: 10/12-inch 33rpm

PAULA 12-25 66-70

Members: Joe Stampley; Bobby Stampley; Jim Woodfield; Mike Love; Ray Mills; Bobby Sims; Ronnie Weiss.

Also see MOUSE
Also see STAMPLEY, Joe

UNIT 4+2

P&R '65

Singles: 7-inch

LONDON 4-8 65-66

LPs: 10/12-inch 33rpm

LONDON (427 "Unit 4+2") 25-35 65
(Monaural.)
LONDON (3427 "Unit 4+2") 25-40 65
(Stereo.)

Member: Russ Ballard.

Also see BALLARD, Russ

UNITED STATES AIR FORCE BAND

LP '63

LPs: 10/12-inch 33rpm

RCA 5-10 63

UNITED STATES MARINE BAND

LP '63

LPs: 10/12-inch 33rpm

RCA 5-10 63

UNITED STATES NAVY BAND

LP '63

LPs: 10/12-inch 33rpm

RCA 5-10 63

UNITED STATES of AMERICA

LP '68

LPs: 10/12-inch 33rpm

COLUMBIA (9619 "United States of America") 15-25 68

Members: Dorothy Moskowitz; Joseph Byrd; Gordon Marron; Rand Forbes; Craig Woodson.

UNITS

D&D '83

Singles: 12-inch 33/45rpm

EPIC 4-6 83-84
UPROAR 4-6 83

Singles: 7-inch

EPIC 3-4 84

LPs: 10/12-inch 33rpm

EPIC 5-8 84

UNIVERSAL ROBOT BAND

P&R/R&B '77

Singles: 7-inch

RED GREG 3-6 77

LPs: 10/12-inch 33rpm

RED GREG 5-10 77

Also see KLEEER

UNKNOWNS

P&R '66

Singles: 7–inch

MARLIN (16008 "Tighter") 10-15 67
PARROT (307 "Melody for an Unknown Girl") 8-12 66

Members: Keith Allison; Mark Lindsay; Steve Alaimo
Also see ALAIMO, Steve.
Also see ALLISON, Keith
Also see LINDSAY, Mark

UNLIMITED TOUCH

R&B/LP '81

Singles: 12–inch 33/45rpm

PRELUDE 4-6 81-84

Singles: 7–inch

PRELUDE 3-5 81-84

LPs: 10/12–inch 33rpm

PRELUDE 5-10 81-84

Also see LORBER, Jeff

UNTOUCHABLES

LP '89

LPs: 10/12–inch 33rpm

ENIGMA 5-8
RESTLESS 5-8 89

UP with PEOPLE

LP '66

LPs: 10/12-Inch 33rpm

PACE 5-10 66-70

UPBEATS

P&R '58

Singles: 7–inch

JOY 10-12 58-59
PREP 10-15 57-58
SWAN 10-15 58

UPCHURCH, Phil

(Phil Upchurch Combo)

P&R '61

Singles: 7–inch

BOYD 5-10 61
GOLDEN FLEECE 3-5 74
MARLIN 3-4 79
U.A. 4-8 61-62

LPs: 10/12–inch 33rpm

BLUE THUMB 8-10 73
BOYD (B-398 "You Can't Sit Down") 20-25 61
(Monaural.)
BOYD (BS-398 "You Can't Sit Down") 25-30 61
(Stereo.)
CADET 8-10 69
MILESTONE 5-8
U.A. 15-20 61-62

Also see CLARK, Dee
Also see REED, Jimmy

UPCHURCH, Phil, & Tennyson Stephens

LPs: 10/12–inch 33rpm

KUDU 8-10 75

Also see STEPHENS, Tennyson
Also see UPCHURCH, Phil

UPFRONT

D&D '83

Singles: 12–inch 33/45rpm

SILVER CLOUD 4-6 83

UPSETTERS Featuring Little Richard

Singles: 7–inch

LITTLE STAR 10-20 62

Also see LITTLE RICHARD

UPTOWN

P&R '86

Singles: 12–inch 33/45rpm

SILVER SCREEN 4-6 83

Singles: 7–inch

OAK LAWN 3-4 86

URBAN DANCE SQUA

LP '90

LPs: 10/12–inch 33rpm

'ARISTA 5-8 90

URE, Midge

P&R/LP '89

Singles: 7–inch

CHRYSALIS 3-4 89

LPs: 10/12–inch 33rpm

CHRYSALIS 5-8 89

URGENT

P&R '85

Singles: 7–inch

MANHATTAN 3-4 85

Picture Sleeves

MANHATTAN 3-4 85

URIAH HEEP

LP '70

Singles: 7–inch

CHRYSALIS 3-5 78
MERCURY 3-5 70-83
W.B. 3-5 73-78

Picture Sleeves

MERCURY 3-5 70-82

EPs: 7–inch 33/45rpm

W.B. 8-12 73
(Jukebox issue only.)

LPs: 10/12–inch 33rpm

CHRYSALIS 5-10 78-79
MERCURY 5-10 70-83
W.B. 5-10 73-81

Also see HENSLEY, Ken
Also see ROUGH DIAMOND

UTOPIA

LP '77

Singles: 7–inch

BEARSVILLE 3-5 76-80

NETWORK 3-4 82
PASSPORT 3-4 84-85

LPs: 10/12-inch 33rpm

BEARSVILLE 5-12 77-82
NETWORK 8-10 82
PASSPORT 5-8 84-85

Members: Todd Rundgren; Willie Wilcox; Roger Powell; Kasim Sulton.
Also see CASSIDY, Shaun, & Todd Rundgren's Utopia
Also see RUNDGREN, Todd

V

V.S.O.P.
(Very Special One-time Performance)

LP '77

LPs: 10/12-inch 33rpm

COLUMBIA 5-10 77

Members: Herbie Hancock; Wayne Shorter; Freddie Hubbard, Tony Williams.

VACELS

P&R '65

Singles: 7-inch

KAMA SUTRA 4-8 65

VAIN

LP '89

LPs: 10/12-inch 33rpm

ISLAND 5-8 89

VALADIERS

P&R '61

Singles: 7-inch

GORDY (7003 "While I'm Away") 25-50 62
GORDY (7013 "I Found a Girl") 25-50 63
MIRACLE (6 "Greetings") 50-75 61
MIRACLE (6 "Greetings [This Is Uncle Sam]") 25-50 61
(Note longer title.)

Member: Paul Kelly.

VALE, Jerry

P&R '53

Singles: 78rpm

COLUMBIA 3-5 51-57

Singles: 7-inch

BUDDAH 3-5 78
COLUMBIA 3-8 51-74

Picture Sleeves

COLUMBIA 4-8 64-65

EPs: 7-inch 33/45rpm

COLUMBIA 5-10 56-59

LPs: 10/12-inch 33rpm

COLUMBIA 5-15 58-75
HARMONY 5-10 69-74

VALE, Jerry, Peggy King & Felicia Sanders

LPs: 10/12-inch 33rpm

COLUMBIA 10-20 56

Also see KING, Peggy
Also see SANDERS, Felicia
Also see VALE, Jerry

VALENS, Ritchie

P&R/R&B '58

Singles: 12-inch 33/45rpm

DEL-FI 15-25 80s

Singles: 7-inch

ABC 3-5 74
DEL-FI 15-25 58
(Solid green label with black print.)
DEL-FI 10-15 58-60
(Has rows of circles on label.)
DEL-FI 5-10 61
(Black label with sawtooth circle.)
ERIC 3-4 70s
GOODIES 3-4
KASEY (7040 "Donna") 5-10
LANA 3-6 60s

Picture Sleeves

DEL-FI (4114 "That's My Little Suzie") 25-50 59
DEL-FI (4117 "Little Girl") 20-40 59
(With explanatory "Concerning This Record" insert.)
DEL-FI (4117 "Little Girl") 15-25 59
(Without insert.)
DEL-FI (4128 "Stay Beside Me") 15-25 60
KASEY (7040 "Donna") 5-10

EPs: 7-inch 33/45rpm

DEL-FI (1 "Ritchie Valens") 50-75 59
(Promotional issue only.)
DEL-FI (101 "Ritchie Valens") 50-75 59
DEL-FI (111 "Ritchie Valens Sings") 50-75 59

LPs: 10/12-inch 33rpm

DEL-FI (1201 "Ritchie Valens") 75-125 59
(Back cover shows *That's My Little Suzie* as "I Got a Gal Named Sue.")
DEL-FI (1201 "Ritchie Valens") .. 60-80 59
(Back cover properly shows *That's My Little Suzie.*)
DEL-FI (1206 "Ritchie") 60-80 59
DEL-FI (1214 "Ritchie Valens in Concert") 100-200 61
DEL-FI (1225 "Greatest Hits") 40-60 63
DEL-FI (1247 "Greatest Hits, Vol. 2") 40-60 65
GUEST STAR 15-25 64
MGM 10-15 70
RHINO (Except 2798) 5-8 81-87
RHINO (2798 "History of Ritchie Valens") 20-25 81

Also see ALLENS, Arvee

VALENS, Ritchie / Jerry Kole

LPs: 10/12-inch 33rpm

CROWN (5336 "Ritchie Valens & Jerry Kole") 20-30 63

VALENTE, Caterina

P&R '55

Singles: 78rpm

DECCA.. 3-5 54-57

Singles: 7-inch

DECCA.. 5-10 54-59
LONDON.. 3-6 60-68
RCA.. 4-8 59
TELEFUNKEN 4-8 59

EPs: 7-inch 33/45rpm

DECCA.. 5-10 55

LPs: 10/12-inch 33rpm

DECCA.. 5-15 55-64
LONDON.. 5-15 59-72
RCA.. 5-15 60-61

VALENTI, John

P&R/R&B '76

Singles: 7-inch

ARIOLA AMERICA........................ 3-5 76-77

VALENTIN, Dave

R&B/LP '80

Singles: 7-inch

GRP 3-5 80-81

LPs: 10/12-inch 33rpm

GRP 5-10 80-81

VALENTINE, Lezli

R&B '68

Singles: 7-inch

ALL PLATINUM............................ 3-6 68

VALENTINE BROTHERS

R&B '82

Singles: 12-inch 33/45rpm

SOURCE.. 4-6 78

Singles: 7-inch

A&M 3-4 84
BRIDGE 3-4 82
SOURCE.. 3-5 79

LPs: 10/12-inch 33rpm

A&M 5-8 84
BRIDGE 5-8 82
SOURCE.. 5-10 79

VALENTINO, Danny

P&R '60

Singles: 7-inch

CONTRAST 5-10 67
MGM 10-20 59-60

VALENTINO, Mark

P&R '62

Singles: 7-inch

SWAN 5-10 62-63

(Shown as "Mark Valentinon" on some labels.)

LPs: 10/12-inch 33rpm

SWAN (508 "Mark Valentino") ...30-50 63

VALENTINOS

P&R/R&B '62

Singles: 7-inch

ABKCO 3-5 70s
ASTRA.. 4-8 60s
CHESS.. 4-8 66
CLEAN 3-5 73
JUBILEE 4-6 68-69
SAR.. 8-12 62-64

Members: Bobby Womack; Curtis Womack.
Also see WOMACK, Bobby
Also see WOMACK BROTHERS

VALENTION, Mark: see VALENTINO, Mark

VALERIE & NICK

Singles: 7-inch

GLOVER 5-10 64

Members: Valerie Simpson; Nick Ashford.
Also see ASHFORD & SIMPSON

VALERY, Dana

P&R '76

Singles: 7-inch

ABC.. 5-10 68-69
COLUMBIA (44004 "Having You Around")........................ 15-25 67
LIBERTY 4-6 70
PHANTOM 3-6 75
SCOTTI BROS.. 3-6 79

Picture Sleeves

PHANTOM 3-5 75

LPs: 10/12-inch 33rpm

BRUNSWICK.. 5-10
PHANTOM 5-10 75

Also see SIMON, Paul

VALIANTS
(Featuring Billy Storm)

P&R '57

Singles: 78rpm

KEEN 10-15 57

Singles: 7-inch

KEEN (4008 "Temptation of My Heart")........................ 25-30 58
KEEN (4026 "Please Wait My Love")........................ 30-40 58
KEEN (34004 "This Is the Night")........................ 15-25 57
KEEN (34007 "Lover Lover") 15-25 58
KEEN (82120 "This Is the Night")........................ 10-15 60
SHAR-DEE (703 "Dear Cindy") .40-50 59
(No mention of distribution by London.)
SHAR-DEE (703 "Dear Cindy") .20-30 59
(Label reads "Distributed by London.")

Also see STORM, Billy

VALINO, Joe

P&R '56

Singles: 78rpm

U.A. 4-8 57
VIK 4-8 56

Singles: 7-inch

BANDBOX.......... 4-8 61
CROSLEY 4-8 59-60
DEBUT 3-6 67-68
RCA.......... 4-8 59
U.A. 5-10 57-58
VIK 5-10 56

Picture Sleeves

U.A. (101 "Legend of the Lost") 20-30 57

LPs: 10/12-inch 33rpm

DEBUT 8-12 67

VALJEAN
(Valjean Johns)

P&R/LP '62

Singles: 7-inch

CARLTON 4-8 62-63

Picture Sleeves

CARLTON 5-10 62

LPs: 10/12-inch 33rpm

CARLTON 15-25 62-63

VALLEY, Frankie: see VALLI, Frankie

VALLI, Frankie
(With the Travelers; Frankie Valle; Frankie Vally; with Romans)

P&R '66

Singles: 10/12-inch 33/45rpm

MOTOWN 15-20 73
PRIVATE STOCK 10-15 77

Singles: 7-inch

CINDY 75-100 59
COLLECTABLES 3-4 80s
CORONA (1234 "My Mother's Eyes") 300-500 53
DECCA (30994 "Please Take a Chance") 75-100 59
MCA/CURB 3-5 80
MERCURY (70381 "Forgive and Forget") 100-125 54
(Maroon label.)
MERCURY (70381 "Forgive and Forget") 50-75 54
(Black label.)
MOTOWN 8-12 73
MOWEST 5-10 72
PHILIPS (40407 thru 45098) 4-8 66-70
PHILIPS (40661 & 40680) 10-12 69-70
PRIVATE STOCK 3-5 74-78
RSO 3-5 78
SMASH 5-10 65-66
W.B./CURB 3-5 78-80

Promotional Singles

BOB CREWE PRESENTS (1 "The Girl I'll Never Know") 25-35 69
DECCA (30994 "Please Take a Chance") 50-75 59
MERCURY (70381 "Forgive and Forget") 50-75 54
MOWEST (5025 "The Night") 12-15 71
PHILIPS 8-12 66-70
PRIVATE STOCK 8-10 74-78
SMASH 8-12 65-66

Picture Sleeves

PHILIPS 10-15 66-69

LPs: 10/12-inch 33rpm

MOTOWN (100 series) 5-8 81
MOTOWN (800 series) 8-12 75
MCA 5-10 79-80
PHILIPS (200247 "Solo") 30-40 67
(Monaural.)
PHILIPS (600000 series) 20-25 67-68
(Stereo.)
PRIVATE STOCK 8-10 75-78
W.B. 8-10 78
Also see BEACH BOYS with Frankie Valli & 4 Seasons
Also see FOUR LOVERS
Also see 4 SEASONS
Also see TYLER, Frankie

VALLI, Frankie, & Chris Forde

P&R '80

Singles: 7-inch

MCA 3-5 80

VALLI, Frankie, & Cheryl Ladd

Singles: 7-inch

CAPITOL 3-5 82
Also see LADD, Cheryl
Also see VALLI, Frankie

VALLI, June
(With Joe Reisman's Orchestra)

P&R '52

Singles: 78rpm

RCA 3-5 52-56

Singles: 7-inch

ABC-PAR 4-6 63
DCP 4-6 64
MERCURY 4-8 58-61
RCA 5-10 52-56
U.A. 4-6 62

Picture Sleeves

MERCURY 4-8 61

EPs: 7-inch 33/45rpm

RCA 5-10 55-56

LPs: 10/12-inch 33rpm

AUDIO FIDELITY 5-10 69
MERCURY 8-15 60
RCA 12-25 55-56
Also see PIANO RED / June Valli
Also see ZABACH, Florian

VALLIE, Frankie: see VALLI, Frankie

VALUMES
(Volumes)

Singles: 7-inch

CHEX (1000 "I Love You") 100-200 62

Also see VOLUMES

VAN & TITUS

R&B '68

Singles: 7-inch

ELF 4-8 68

VANCE, Paul

P&R '66

Singles: 7-inch

ROULETTE 4-8 62
SCEPTER 4-8 66

LPs: 10/12-inch 33rpm

SCEPTER 10-20 66

Also see LEE & PAUL

VANDENBERG
(Adrian Vandenberg)

P&R/LP '83

Singles: 7-inch

ATCO 3-4 83-84

LPs: 10/12-inch 33rpm

ATCO 5-8 83-84

VANDERPOOL, Sylvia: see LITTLE SYLVIA

VANDROSS, Luther

R&B '76

Singles: 12-inch 33/45rpm

EPIC 4-6 82-85

Singles: 7-inch

COTILLION 3-5 76
EPIC 3-5 81-90

Picture Sleeves

EPIC 3-4 85-87

LPs: 10/12-inch 33rpm

EPIC 5-10 81-90

Also see BOWIE, David
Also see CHANGE
Also see LUTHER
Also see LYNN, Cheryl, & Luther Vandross
Also see PRESTON, Billy
Also see ROUNDTREE
Also see WARWICK, Dionne, & Luther Vandross

VANDROSS, Luther, & Gregory Hines

P&R/R&B '87

Singles: 7-inch

EPIC 3-4 87

Also see HINES, Gregory

VAN DYKE, Leroy

P&R '56

Singles: 78rpm

DOT (Except 15698) 4-8 56-57
DOT (15698 "Leather Jacket") .. 20-30 57

Singles: 7-inch

ABC 3-5 74-75
ABC/DOT 3-5 75-77
DECCA 3-5 70-72
DOT (Except 15698) 5-10 56-57
DOT (15698 "Leather Jacket") .. 50-75 57
KAPP 4-6 68-70
MCA 3-5 73
MERCURY 4-8 61-64
PLANTATION 3-5 78
SUN 3-5 79
W.B. 4-6 65-67

Picture Sleeves

MERCURY 5-8 64

LPs: 10/12-inch 33rpm

DECCA 8-10 72
HARMONY 8-12 69
KAPP 8-15 68-69
MCA 5-10 73
MERCURY 12-25 62-64
PLANTATION 5-10 77-79
SUN 5-8 74
W.B. 10-15 65-66
WING 8-15 65-66

VAN DYKES

P&R '61

Singles: 7-inch

DELUXE (6193 "Bells Are Ringing") 10-15 61
DONNA (1333 "Gift of Love") 20-30 60
FELSTED (8565 "Once Upon a Dream") 15-20 59
KING (5158 "Bells Are Ringing") 30-40 58
(Blue label.)
KING (5158 "Bells Are Ringing") 10-15 60s
(Yellow label.)
SPRING (1113 "Gift of Love") 60-75 59

Also see TEMPTATIONS

VAN DYKES

P&R/R&B '66

Singles: 7-inch

HUE (6501 "No Man Is an Island") 15-25 65
MALA (520 "No Man Is an Island") 5-8 65
MALA (530 "What Will I Do") 5-10 66
MALA (539 "Never Let Me Go") ... 5-10 66
MALA (549 "You're Shakin' Me Up") 5-10 66
MALA (584 "Tears of Joy") 20-30 67

LPs: 10/12-inch 33rpm

BELL (6004 "Tellin' It Like It Is"). 15-25 67

Members: Ron Tandy; Wenzon Mosley; Jimmy May.

VANGELIS

P&R/LP '81

Singles: 7-inch

POLYDOR 3-4 81
RCA 3-5 78

Picture Sleeves

POLYDOR 3-5 81

LPs: 10/12-inch 33rpm

POLYDOR 5-10 81-86
RCA 5-10 78-82

Also see JON & VANGELIS

VANGUARDS

R&B '69

Singles: 7-inch

LAMP (80 "It's Too Late for Love") 5-10 70
LAMP (81 "Girl Go Away") 5-10 70
WHIZ 4-8 69

VAN HALEN

P&R/LP '78

Singles: 12-inch 33/45rpm

W.B. 4-6 83-84

Singles: 7-inch

PALM TREE 4-8
W.B. 3-5 78-90

Promotional Singles

W.B. 5-10 78-90

Picture Sleeves

W.B. (Except 8556 & 8823) 3-8 79-86
W.B. (8556 "Running with the Devil") 20-30 78
W.B. (8823 "Dance the Night Away") 8-12 79

LPs: 10/12-inch 33rpm

W.B. 5-10 78-90
W.B./LOONEY TUNES (705 "Van Halen") 10-20 78
(Colored vinyl. Promotional issue only.)
Members: David Lee Roth; Edward Van Halen; Alex Van Halen; Michael Anthony; Sammy Hagar.
Also see HAGAR, Sammy
Also see MAY, Brian
Also see ROTH, David Lee
Also see VAN HALEN, Edward

VAN HALEN, Edward

LPs: 10/12-inch 33rpm

MCA 5-8 86
Also see JACKSON, Michael
Also see VAN HALEN

VANILLA FUDGE

P&R/LP '67

Singles: 7-inch

ATCO 4-8 67-70

LPs: 10/12-inch 33rpm

ATCO (200 & 300 series) 15-20 67-69
ATCO (90000 series) 5-10 82
Also see BECK, BOGERT & APPICE
Also see PIGEONS

VANILLA ICE

LP '90

LPs: 10/12-inch 33rpm

SKB 5-8 90

VANILLI, Milli: see MILLI VANILLI

VANITY
(Denise Matthews)

P&R/R&B/D&D/LP '84

Singles: 12-inch 33/45rpm

MOTOWN 4-6 84-86

Singles: 7-inch

MOTOWN 3-4 84-86

Picture Sleeves

MOTOWN 3-4 84-86

LPs: 10/12-inch 33rpm

MOTOWN 5-8 84-86
Also see VANITY 6

VANITY / Smokey Robinson

LPs: 10/12-inch 33rpm

MOTOWN (179 "Superstar Interviews") 10-15 84
(Promotional issue only.)
Also see ROBINSON, Smokey
Also see VANITY

VANITY FARE

P&R '69

Singles: 7-inch

BRENT 4-8 67
DJM 3-5 75
PAGE ONE 3-6 68-70
SOMA 8-12 68
20TH FOX 3-5 73

LPs: 10/12-inch 33rpm

PAGE ONE 10-15 70

VANITY 6

R&B/LP '82

Singles: 12-inch 33/45rpm

W.B. 4-6 82-83

Singles: 7-inch

W.B. 3-4 82-83

LPs: 10/12-inch 33rpm

W.B. 5-8 82
Member: Denise Matthews.
Also see APOLLONIA 6
Also see TIME
Also see VANITY

VANN, Teddy

P&R '61

Singles: 7-inch

CAPITOL 3-6 67
COLUMBIA 4-8 61
END 5-10 59
JUBILEE 4-8 62
ROULETTE 4-8 60
TRIPLE-X 5-10 60

VANNELLI, Gino

P&R/LP '74

Singles: 12-inch 33/45rpm

HME 4-6 85

Singles: 7-inch

A&M 3-5 74-79
ARISTA 3-5 81-82
CBS ASSOCIATES 3-4 85-87
HME 3-4 85

Picture Sleeves

A&M 3-5 76-79
ARISTA 3-5 81-82
CBS ASSOCIATES 3-4 85-87

LPs: 10/12-inch 33rpm

A&M (3600 series) 5-10 74

A&M (3700 series) 5-8 81
A&M (4000 series) 8-10 74-78
ARISTA 5-10 81-82
CBS ASSOCIATES 5-8 87
HME 5-10 85
MFSL... 20-35 80
NAUTILUS 15-20 81
(Half-speed mastered.)

VAN SHELTON, Ricky: see SHELTON, Ricky Van

VAN TIEGHEM, David

D&D '84

Singles: 12–inch 33/45rpm

W.B. 4-6 84

Singles: 7–inch

W.B. 3-4 84

LPs: 10/12–inch 33rpm

W.B. 5-8 84

VANWARMER, Randy

C&W/P&R/LP '79

Singles: 7–inch

BEARSVILLE 3-5 79
16TH AVE. 3-4 88

LPs: 10/12–inch 33rpm

BEARSVILLE 5-10 79-83

VAN ZANT, Johnny, Band
(Van-Zant)

LP '80

Singles: 7–inch

POLYDOR.................................... 3-5 80-82

LPs: 10/12–inch 33rpm

ATLANTIC.................................... 5-8 90
GEFFEN....................................... 5-8 85
POLYDOR.................................... 5-10 80-82

VAPORS

P&R/LP '80

Singles: 7–inch

LIBERTY 3-5 81
U.A. 3-5 80

LPs: 10/12–inch 33rpm

LIBERTY 5-10 81
U.A. 5-10 80

VASEL, Marianne, & Erich Storz

P&R '58

Singles: 7–inch

MERCURY 4-8 58

LPs: 10/12–inch 33rpm

DANA 10-20 59

VAUGHAN, Frankie

P&R '58

Singles: 7–inch

COLUMBIA 4-8 59-60
EPIC.. 4-8 58
PHILIPS 3-6 62-66

LPs: 10/12–inch 33rpm

COLUMBIA 10-20 60
PHILIPS 10-15 62

VAUGHAN, Sarah

P&R '47

Singles: 78rpm

COLUMBIA 3-6 49-53
CONTINENTAL............................. 5-10 45
MGM (Except 71)......................... 3-6 50-51
MGM (71 "Sarah Vaughan Sings") 40-60 51
(Four disc boxed set.)
MERCURY.................................... 3-6 53-57
MUSICRAFT 4-8 47-48

Singles: 7–inch

ATLANTIC.................................... 3-5 81
COLUMBIA (38000 & 39000 series)...................................... 5-10 51-53
MGM (10000 & 30000 series)...... 5-10 50-51
MAINSTREAM 3-5 71-74
MERCURY (70000 series)............ 4-8 53-66
ROULETTE................................... 4-6 60-64
W.B. 3-5 81

Picture Sleeves

MERCURY.................................... 4-8 65

EPs: 7–inch 33/45rpm

ATLANTIC (527 "Sarah Vaughan Sings") 30-40 55
COLUMBIA 10-20 50-56
EMARCY...................................... 10-20 54-56
MGM 10-20 52-55
MERCURY.................................... 8-15 53-59
REMINGTON................................ 5-10
ROYALE 5-10 50s

LPs: 10/12–inch 33rpm

ALLEGRO.................................... 5-10
ATLANTIC.................................... 5-8 81
COLUMBIA (660 "After Hours") . 35-45 55
COLUMBIA (745 "Sarah in Hi-Fi")... 35-45 55
COLUMBIA (914 "Linger Awhile")....................................... 25-35 57
COLUMBIA (6133 "Sarah Vaughan") 50-100 50
(10–inch LP.)
COLUMBIA (37000 series)........... 5-8 82
CONCORD 15-25 56
CORONET 8-10 60s
EMARCY (400 series)................. 8-12 77
EMARCY (1000 series)............... 5-10 81
EMARCY (26005 "Images")....... 50-75 54
(10–inch LP.)
EMARCY (36000 series)............ 30-40 54-57
EVEREST 5-10 70-76
HARMONY.................................. 5-15 59-69
MGM (165 "Tenderly") 50-100 51
(10–inch LPs.)
MGM (544 "Sarah Vaughan Sings") 50-100 54
(10–inch LP.)

MGM (3274 "My Kinda Love")... 50-75 55
MAINSTREAM ... 6-12 71-75
MERCURY (100 "Great Songs") ... 25-35 57
MERCURY (101 "Gershwin Songs") ... 25-35 57
MERCURY (1000 series) ... 5-8 82
MERCURY (20000 series) ... 15-30 58-64
MERCURY (21000 series) ... 10-20 65-67
(Monaural.)
MERCURY (25188 "Divine Sarah") ... 60-80 53
(10–inch LP)
MERCURY (60000 series) ... 15-25 59-64
MERCURY (61000 series) ... 10-25 65-67
(Stereo.)
METRO ... 8-15 65
MUSICRAFT ... 5-8 83-84
PABLO ... 5-10 78-82
REMINGTON (1024 "Hot Jazz") ... 50-100 53
(10–inch LP.)
RIVERSIDE (2511 "Sarah Vaughan Sings") ... 40-60 55
RONDO ... 20-40 59
RONDOLETTE ... 20-40 59
ROULETTE (100 series) ... 8-15 71
ROULETTE (52000 series, except 52082) ... 10-25 60-67
(Black vinyl.)
ROULETTE (52082 "You're Mine") ... 15-25 62
(Black vinyl.)
ROULETTE (52082 "You're Mine") ... 35-55 62
(Colored vinyl.)
SCEPTER ... 5-10 74
SUTTON ... 5-10 70s
TRIP ... 5-10 74-76
WING ... 5-15 63-68

Also see BASIE, Count, & Sarah Vaughan
Also see DIAMONDS / Georgia Gibbs / Sarah Vaughan / Florian Zabach
Also see ECKSTINE, Billy, & Sarah Vaughan
Also see LEGRAND, Michel
Also see WASHINGTON, Dinah, & Sarah Vaughan

VAUGHAN, Sarah, & Quincy Jones

LPs: 10/12–inch 33rpm

MERCURY ... 15-25 59

Also see JONES, Quincy
Also see VAUGHAN, Sarah

VAUGHAN, Stevie Ray

(With Double Trouble)

LP '83

Singles: 7–inch

COLUMBIA ... 3-4 87
EPIC ... 3-4 85

LPs: 10/12–inch 33rpm

COLUMBIA ... 5-8 87
EPIC (Except 8E8-39609) ... 5-10 84-89
EPIC (8E8-39609 "Couldn't Stand the Weather") ... 10-15 84
(Picture disc.)

Members: Stevie Ray Vaughan; Tommy Shannon; Chris Layton; Reese Wynans.

VAUGHAN, Stevie Ray, & Dick Dale

Singles: 7–inch

COLUMBIA (07340 "Pipeline") ... 3-4 87

Picture Sleeves

COLUMBIA (07340 "Pipeline") ... 3-5 87

Also see DALE, Dick

VAUGHAN BROTHERS

P&R/LP '90

Singles: 7–inch

EPIC ... 3-4 89

LPs: 10/12–inch 33rpm

EPIC ... 5-8 89

Members: Stevie Ray Vaughan; Jimmie Vaughan.
Also see FABULOUS THUNDERBIRDS
Also see VAUGHAN, Stevie Ray

VAUGHN, Billy, Orchestra

(With the Billy Vaughn Singers)

P&R '54

Singles: 78rpm

DOT ... 3-5 54-57

Singles: 7–inch

ABC ... 3-4 74
DOT ... 3-8 54-70
PARAMOUNT ... 3-4 70-72

Picture Sleeves

DOT ... 3-8 58-67

EPs: 7–inch 33/45rpm

DOT ... 4-8 55-59

LPs: 10/12–inch 33rpm

ABC ... 5-8 74
DOT ... 5-15 55-70
HAMILTON ... 5-10 65-66
MCA ... 5-8 83
MISTLETOE ... 4-8 76
MUSICOR ... 4-8 77
PARAMOUNT ... 5-8 70-74
PICKWICK ... 5-8 68
RANWOOD ... 4-8 83

Also see BRENNAN, Walter
Also see HILLTOPPERS
Also see NORDINE, Ken
Also see STORM, Gale

VAUGHN, Denny

P&R '56

Singles: 78rpm

KAPP ... 3-6 56

Singles: 7–inch

KAPP ... 5-10 56

VEE, Bobby

(With the Shadows; with Eligibles; with Strangers; with Johnny Mann Singers; Robert Thomas Velline)

P&R '59

Singles: 7-inch

COGNITO 3-5 81
LIBERTY (3331 "How Many Tears") 20-25 61
(Stereo Compact 33 Single.)
LIBERTY (55208 "Suzie Baby") 10-20 59
LIBERTY (55234 thru 55325)........ 5-8 60-61
LIBERTY (55331 thru 56208)......... 3-6 61-70
SHADYBROOK.............................. 3-5 75-77
SOMA (1110 "Susie Baby") 30-50 59
U.A. 3-5 71-78

Picture Sleeves

LIBERTY 5-10 60-68

EPs: 7-inch 33/45rpm

LIBERTY 25-35 60-62
U.A. 10-12 72

LPs: 10/12-inch 33rpm

LIBERTY (3165 thru 3534)........ 20-30 60-67
(Monaural.)
LIBERTY (7165 thru 7534)........ 20-40 60-67
(Stereo.)
LIBERTY (7554 thru 7612)........ 10-20 67-69
LIBERTY (1000 series) 5-8 80
LIBERTY (10000 series) 5-8 84
SUNSET..................................... 10-15 66-67
U.A. (25-G2 "Legendary Masters")............................. 250-350 73
(Includes bound-in booklet. Withdrawn before release, with only two or three copies surviving.)
U.A. (332 "Very Best")................ 8-10 73
U.A. (1008 "Golden Greats")......... 5-8 80
Also see ASSOCIATION / Bobby Vee / Mike Love / Mary MacGregor
Also see DE SHANNON, Jackie / Bobby Vee / Eddie Hodges

VEE, Bobby / Johnny Burnette / Ventures / Fleetwoods

LPs: 10/12-inch 33rpm

LIBERTY (5503 "Teensville").... 20-30 61
Also see BURNETTE, Johnny
Also see FLEETWOODS

VEE, Bobby, & Crickets

LP '62

Singles: 7-inch

LIBERTY 4-8 62

Picture Sleeves

LIBERTY 10-15 60-63

LPs: 10/12-inch 33rpm

LIBERTY 20-25 62
Also see CRICKETS

VEE, Bobby / Diamonds / Drifters

Singles: 7-inch

MINDSCAPE ("Mindscape and Rock 'n' Roll Are Here to Stay")......................5-10 84
(Soundsheet. Promotional issue only.)
Also see DIAMONDS
Also see DRIFTERS

VEE, Bobby, & Ventures

LP '63

LPs: 10/12-inch 33rpm

LIBERTY 20-25 63
Also see VEE, Bobby
Also see VENTURES

VEGA, Suzanne

LP '85

Singles: 7-inch

A&M 3-4 85-90

Picture Sleeves

A&M 3-4 87

LPs: 10/12-inch 33rpm

A&M 5-8 85-90
Also see DNA Featuring Suzanne Vega

VEGA, Tata

R&B '76

Singles: 12-inch 33/45rpm

TAMLA..4-8 79

Singles: 7-inch

TAMLA..3-5 76-80

LPs: 10/12-inch 33rpm

TAMLA..5-10 76-80
Also see EARTHQUIRE
Also see RAWLS, Lou

VEGA BROTHERS

C&W '86

Singles: 7-inch

MCA..3-4 86
Members: Robert Vega; Ray Vega.

VEGAS, Pat, & Lolly

Singles: 7-inch

APOGEE.......................................5-10 64
MERCURY.......................................4-8 66
REPRISE 4-8 63

LPs: 10/12-inch 33rpm

MERCURY..................................25-35 66
Also see REDBONE

VEJTABLES

P&R '65

Singles: 7-inch

AUTUMN....................................5-10 65-66
UPTOWN...4-8 67

VELAIRES

P&R '61

Singles: 7-inch

BRENT...5-10 60s
HI-MAR 4-8 65
JAMIE 10-15 61-62
MERCURY....................................5-10 69

PALMS (730 "Summertime Blues") 30-60 61
RAMCO 5-10 60s

VELEZ, Martha

LP '76

Singles: 7-inch

MCA 3-4 80
POLYDOR 3-5 73
SIRE 3-5 69-76

LPs: 10/12-inch 33rpm

SIRE (6040 "American Heartbeat") 8-10 76
SIRE (7000 series) 8-10 74-76
SIRE (97000 series) 10-12 69

VELLINE, Robert Thomas: see VEE, Bobby

VELLS
(Vandellas)

Singles: 7-inch

MEL-O-DY (103 "There He Is"). 25-50 62
Also see DEL-PHIS
Also see MARTHA & VANDELLAS

VELOURS
(With Sammy Lowe Orchestra)

P&R '57

Singles: 78rpm

ONYX (Except 508) 15-25 56-57
ONYX (508 "Romeo") 25-35 57

Singles: 7-inch

CUB 10-20 58-59
END 10-15 61
GOLDISC 15-20 60
GONE (5092 "Can I Come Over Tonight") 10-15 60
ONYX (501 "My Love Come Back") 100-150 56
ONYX (508 "Romeo") 150-250 57
ONYX (512 "Can I Come Over Tonight") 50-100 57
ONYX (515 "This Could Be the Night") 40-60 57
ONYX (520 "Remember") 40-60 58
ORBIT (9001 "Remember") 20-30 58
ROULETTE 3-5 70s
STUDIO (9902 "I Promise") 25-30 59
Members: Jerome Ramos; Pete Winston; John Pearson; Don Heywoode; John Cheatdom; Charles Moffett; Keith Williams; Troyce Key.
Also see FANTASTICS

VELS

D&D '84

Singles: 12-inch 33/45rpm

MERCURY 4-6 84-85

Singles: 7-inch

MERCURY 3-4 84-85

LPs: 10/12-inch 33rpm

MERCURY 5-8 84

VELVELETTES

P&R/R&B '64

Singles: 7-inch

I.P.G. (1002 "There He Goes") 4-8 63
SOUL 10-20 66
V.I.P.(Except 25021) 10-25 64-65
V.I.P.(25021 "Bird in the Hand") 100-200 66
Members: Carolyn Gill, Sandra Tilley; Betty Kelly.
Also see MARTHA & VANDELLAS

VELVET, Jimmy
(Jimmy Velvet Five; James Velvet; Jimmy Tennant)

P&R '63

Singles: 7-inch

ABC-PAR 10-20 63-64
BELL 4-8 67
CAMEO (464 "Take Me Tonight") 15-25 67
CORREC-TONE (502 "When I Needed You") 50-100 62
CUB 5-10 62
DIVISION 10-20 61
MUSIC CITY 4-6 70
PHILIPS 10-20 65
ROYAL AMERICAN 4-6 68-69
SUNDI 3-6 71
TOLLIE 5-10 64
U.A. 10-20 68
VELVET (201 "You're Mine") 50-75 61
VELVET TONE 10-20 64-68

EPs: 7-inch 33/45rpm

VELVET TONE (201 "Golden Hits") 15-25 60s

LPs: 10/12-inch 33rpm

MUSIC CITY 8-12 70
U.A. (6653 "A Touch of Velvet"). 15-25 68
VELVET TONE (501 "A Touch of Velvet") 20-30 68
WITCH 5-10 62
(Bi, Blue, and Teardrop releases credited to Jimmy Velvet, are actually by Jimmy Velvit, a different person.)

VELVET UNDERGROUND

LP '68

Singles: 12-inch 33/45rpm

POLYGRAM 5-10 85

Singles: 7-inch

ASPEN ("Loop") 20-40 66
(Single-sided soundsheet. Promotional issue only.)
COTILLION (44107 "Who Loves the Sun") 20-40 71
INDEX ("Interview") 20-40 67
(Single-sided picture disc soundsheet. Promotional issue only.)
MGM (14057 "What Goes On") . 25-50 69

VERVE (10560 "White Light/White Heat") 25-50 68

LPs: 10/12-inch 33rpm

COTILLION (9034 "Loaded") 15-20 70
COTILLION (9500 "Live") 15-20 70
MGM (131 "Velvet Underground") 8-10 71
MGM (4950 " Archetypes") 10-15 69-74
MERCURY (7504 "Velvet Underground") 12-15 72
PRIDE 10-15 73
VERVE (5046 "White Light/White Heat") 30-40 67
VERVE (800000 series) 5-10 84-85

Members: Lou Reed; John Cale; Sterling Morrison; Maureen Tucker; Doug Yule.
Also see AMERICAN FLYER
Also see CALE, John
Also see REED, Lou

VELVET UNDERGROUND & NICO

LP '67

Singles: 7-inch

VERVE (10427 "All Tomorrow's Parties") 25-50 66
(Blue label.)
VERVE (10427 "All Tomorrow's Parties") 50-75 66
(White label. Promotional issue only.)
VERVE (10466 "Sunday Morning") 25-50 66

Picture Sleeves

VERVE (10427 "All Tomorrow's Parties") 100-150 66
(Promotional issue only.)

LPs: 10/12-inch 33rpm

VERVE (5008 "Velvet Underground & Nico") 100-200 67
(Monaural. With banana sticker on front cover. Back cover pictures an upside-down torso of a man behind the photo of Andy Warhol. Thus far, all copies meeting this description have been mono.)
VERVE (5008 "Velvet Underground & Nico") 50-75 67
(Stereo. With adhesive banana sticker on front cover. If a stereo copy with the upside-down male torso photo behind Andy Warhol exists, its value would approximately double.)
VERVE (5008 "Velvet Underground & Nico") 50-100 67
(With banana sticker on front cover. Back cover has a sticker above the photo of the group on stage, which reads: "The Velvet Underground & Nico.")
VERVE (5008 "Velvet Underground & Nico") 30-60 60s
(With adhesive banana sticker on front cover. Does not picture the upside-down male torso.)
VERVE (5008 "Velvet Underground & Nico") 25-35 67
(No banana sticker on front cover.)
VERVE (800000 series) 5-10 84

Also see NICO
Also see VELVET UNDERGROUND

VELVETS

P&R '61

Singles: 7-inch

MONUMENT (400 series) 15-30 61-62
MONUMENT (800 & 900 series) . 8-15 63-66
PLAID (101 "Everybody Knows") 10-20 59
20TH FOX 10-15 59

Members: Virgil Johnson; Will Soloman; Mark Prince; Bob Thursby; Clarence Rigby.

VENETIANS

P&R '87

Singles: 7-inch

CHRYSALIS 3-4 87

VENTURES

P&R/R&B/LP '60

Singles: 12-inch 33/45rpm

TRIDEX (1245 "Surfin' and Spyin") 5-8 81
(Vocals by Charlotte Caffey and Jane Weidlin.)

Singles: 7-inch

BLUE HORIZON (100 "Real McCoy") 40-60 59
BLUE HORIZON (101 "Walk Don't Run") 40-60 60
DOLTON (25 "Walk—Don't Run"/ "Home") 10-20 60
DOLTON (25-X "Walk—Don't Run"/ "Home") 8-12 60
DOLTON (28 thru 327) 5-10 60-66
LIBERTY 3-8 66-70
TRIDEX 3-5 81
U.A. 3-6 70-78

Picture Sleeves

DOLTON 5-15 60-66

EPs: 7-inch 33/45rpm

DOLTON 20-25 60

LPs: 10/12-inch 33rpm

AWARD 8-12 84
DOLTON (2003 "Walk Don't Run") 25-35 60
(Light blue label. Monaural.)
DOLTON (2003 "Walk Don't Run") 15-25 61
(Dark blue label. Monaural.)
DOLTON (2004 thru 2050) 20-25 61-67
(Monaural.)
DOLTON (8003 "Walk Don't Run") 30-40 60
(Light blue label. Stereo.)

DOLTON (8003 "Walk Don't Run") 20-30 61
(Dark blue label. Stereo.)
DOLTON (8004 thru 8050)........ 20-30 61-67
(Stereo.)
DOLTON (17000 series) 15-20 65-66
LIBERTY (2000 & 8000 series). 10-20 67-70
LIBERTY (10000 series) 5-10 81-84
LIBERTY (35000 series) 10-15 70
SUNSET 10-15 66-71
TRIDEX 5-10 81-83
U.A. 10-15 71-77

Members: Don Wilson; Bob Bogle; Mel Taylor; Nokie Edwards; Jerry McGee; Skip Moore; Howie Johnson.
Also see LOPEZ, Trini, with the Ventures & Nancy Ames
Also see MARKSMEN
Also see VEE, Bobby, & Ventures

VENUS, Vic

P&R '69

Singles: 7-inch

BUDDAH 4-8 69

VERA, Billy

(With the Contrasts; with Beaters; with Blue Eyed Soul)

P&R '67

Singles: 7-inch

ATLANTIC 4-6 68-69
FLAVOR 10-15 64
MACOLA 3-4 87
MIDSONG 3-5 75-76
ORANGE 4-8 73
RHINO 3-4 86-87
RUST 10-20 62

LPs: 10/12-inch 33rpm

ATLANTIC 10-15 68
MACOLA 5-8 87
MIDSONG INT'L 8-12 77
RHINO 5-8 86

Also see BILLY & BEATERS

VERA, Billy & Judy Clay

P&R/R&B '67

Singles: 7-inch

ATLANTIC 4-8 67-68

LPs: 10/12-inch 33rpm

ATLANTIC 10-15 68

Also see CLAY, Judy

VERA LYNN: see LYNN, Vera

VERLAINE, Tom

LP '81

Singles: 7-inch

ELEKTRA 3-5 80
W.B. 3-5 81-84

LPs: 10/12-inch 33rpm

ELEKTRA 5-10 80
W.B. 5-10 81-84

VERNE, Larry

P&R/R&B '60

Singles: 7-inch

COLLECTABLES 3-4 80s
ERA 5-8 60-64

Picture Sleeves

ERA 10-15 60

LPs: 10/12-inch 33rpm

ERA (104 "Mister Larry Verne") .25-35 60

VERONICA

(Veronica "Ronnie" Spector)

Singles: 7-inch

PHIL SPECTOR (1 "So Young") 25-50 64
PHIL SPECTOR (2 "Why Don't They Let Us Fall in Love") 25-50 64

Also see NITZSCHE, Jack
Also see SPECTOR, Ronnie

VIA AFRIKA

D&D '84

Singles: 12-inch 33/45rpm

EMI AMERICA 4-6 84

Singles: 7-inch

EMI AMERICA 3-4 84

LPs: 10/12-inch 33rpm

EMI AMERICA 5-8 84

VIBRATIONS

P&R/R&B '61

Singles: 7-inch

ABC 3-5 74
ATLANTIC 4-8 63-64
BET (1 "So Blue") 50-100 60
CHECKER (Except 954 & 987).. 10-15 60-63
CHECKER (954 "So Blue") 20-25 60
CHECKER (987 "All My Love Belongs to You") 25-30 61
CHESS 3-6 74
EPIC 10-20 68
MANDALA 3-5 72
NEPTUNE 4-6 69-70
OKEH 5-10 64-68

LPs: 10/12-inch 33rpm

CHECKER (2978 "Watusi") 30-50 61
MANDALA 10-15 72
OKEH 25-35 65-69

Also see JAYHAWKS
Also see MARATHONS

VICIOUS BASE Featuring D.J. Magic Mike

LP '91

LP: 10/12-inch 33rpm

CHEETAH 5-8 91

Also see D.J. Magic Mike

VICKY D

R&B '82

Singles: 7-inch

SAM 3-4 82

VICTORY

LP '89

LPs: 10/12-inch 33rpm

RHINO.. 5-8 89

VIDAL, Maria

P&R/D&D '84

Singles: 12-inch 33/45rpm

EMI AMERICA 4-6 84

Singles: 7-inch

EMI AMERICA 3-4 84

Picture Sleeves

EMI AMERICA 3-4 84

Also see CHILD, Desmond, & Rouge

VIDEEO

R&B '82

Singles: 7-inch

H.C.R.C. 3-5 82

VIDELS

(Vi-Dels)

P&R '60

Singles: 7-inch

COLLECTABLES 3-4 80s
DUSTY DISC 5-8
JDS (5004 "Mister Lonely") 15-25 60
(Gray label.)
JDS (5004 "Mister Lonely") 10-15 60
(Multi-color label.)
JDS (5005 "She's Not Coming Home")...................... 15-25 60
(Gray label.)
JDS (5005 "She's Not Coming Home")...................... 10-15 60
(Multi-color label.)
KAPP (361 "Streets of Love") ... 10-20 61
KAPP (405 "A Letter from Ann") 25-35 61
MEDIEVAL 8-10 59
MUSICNOTE (117 "We Belong Together") 20-30 63
RHODY (2000 "Be My Girl") 30-40 59

LPs: 10/12-inch 33rpm

MAGIC CARPET (1005 "A Letter from the Videls") 8-10

Members: Pete Anders; Vinnie Poncia.

VIGRASS & OSBORNE

P&R '72

Singles: 7-inch

EPIC 3-5 74
UNI 3-5 72

LPs: 10/12-inch 33rpm

EPIC 8-10 74
UNI 8-15 71

Members: Paul Vigrass; Gary Osborne.

VILLAGE FUGS see FUGS

VILLAGE PEOPLE

LP '77

Singles: 12-inch 33/45rpm

CASABLANCA 4-8 78-79

Singles: 7-inch

CASABLANCA.............................3-5 78-79
RCA 3-5 81

Picture Sleeves

CASABLANCA.............................3-5 78-79
RCA 3-5 81

LPs: 10/12-inch 33rpm

CASABLANCA (Except NBPIX series) 5-10 77-80
CASABLANCA (NBPIX series)..10-15 78
(Picture discs.)
RCA 5-10 81

Members: Victor Willis; Alexander Briley; Felipe Rose; Randy Jones; David Hodo; Glenn Hughes.

VILLAGE SOUL CHOIR

P&R/R&B '70

Singles: 7-inch

ABBOTT...3-5 69-70

VILLAGE STOMPERS

P&R/R&B/LP '63

Singles: 7-inch

EPIC...3-6 63-67

Picture Sleeves

EPIC...4-8 63-65

LPs: 10/12-inch 33rpm

EPIC...10-20 63-67

Also see VINTON, Bobby, & Village Stompers

VINCENT, Gene

(With His Blue Caps)

P&R/R&B/C&W/LP '56

Singles: 78rpm

CAPITOL....................................10-20 56-57

Singles: 7-inch

CAPITOL (3450 thru 3617)........20-30 56-57
CAPITOL (3678 "B-I-Bickey-Bi-Bo-Bo-Go") 20-30 57
CAPITOL (3763 thru 4665)........15-25 57-61
CAPITOL STAR LINE....................3-6
CHALLENGE 15-20 66-67
FOREVER....................................10-20 69-70
KAMA SUTRA................................8-12 70-73
PLAYGROUND (100 "Story of the Rockers") 150-175 68

Picture Sleeves

CAPITOL (4237 "Right Now") 800-1000 60

Promotional Singles

CAPITOL..................................50-100 56-61
(White or yellow labels.)

EPs: 7-inch 33/45rpm

CAPITOL (438 "Dance to the Bop") 150-200 57
(Promotional issue only. Not issued with cover.)
CAPITOL (764 "Bluejean Bop") 75-125 57
(Price is for any of three volumes.)

CAPITOL (811 "Gene Vincent & His Blue Caps") 75-125 57
(Price is for any of three volumes.)
CAPITOL (970 "Gene Vincent Rocks & Bluecaps Roll") 75-125 58
(Price is for any of three volumes.)
CAPITOL (985 "Hot Rod Gang") 350-400 58
(Green label. Soundtrack.)
CAPITOL (985 "Hot Rod Gang") 400-450 58
(White label. Promotional issue.)
CAPITOL (1059 "Record Date") 75-125 58
(Price is for any of three volumes.)

LPs: 10/12–inch 33rpm

CAPITOL (DKAO-380 "Gene Vincent's Greatest") 15-25 69
CAPITOL (SM-380 "Gene Vincent's Greatest") 5-10 78
CAPITOL (764 "Bluejean Bop") 200-300 56
CAPITOL (811 "Gene Vincent & His Blue Caps") 200-300 57
CAPITOL (970 "Gene Vincent Rocks") 200-300 58
CAPITOL (1059 "Gene Vincent Record Date") 200-300 58
CAPITOL (1207 "Sounds Like Gene Vincent") 200-300 59
CAPITOL (1342 "Crazy Times") 150-250 60
CAPITOL (11000 series) 8-12 74
CAPITOL (16000 series) 5-10 81
DANDELION 10-20 70
KAMA SUTRA 10-20 70-71
ROLLIN' ROCK 5-10 80-81

Also see CHAMPS
Also see FACENDA, Tommy
Also see PRESLEY, Elvis

VINCENT, Gene / Tommy Sands / Sonny James / Ferlin Husky

LPs: 10/12–inch 33rpm

CAPITOL (1009 "Teen Age Rock") 50-100 58

Also see HUSKY, Ferlin
Also see SANDS, Tommy

VINCENT, Gene / Frank Sinatra / Sonny James / Ron Goodwin

EPs: 7–inch 33/45rpm

CAPITOL (437 "Special Hit Pressing") 75-100 57
(Promotional issue only. Not issued with cover.)

Also see GOODWIN, Ron
Also see JAMES, Sonny
Also see SINATRA, Frank

VINCENT, Vinnie, Invasion

LP '86

Singles: 7–inch

CHRYSALIS 3-4 86-88

LPs: 10/12–inch 33rpm

CHRYSALIS 5-8 86-88

Members: Dana Strum.
Also see KISS
Also see SLAUGHTER

VINSON, Eddie
(Eddie "Cleanhead" Vinson)

R&B '47

Singles: 78rpm

KING 10-15 50-52
MERCURY 10-25 46-55

Singles: 7–inch

BETHLEHEM (11097 "Cherry Red") 8-12 61
BLUESWAY 4-8 67
KING (4563 "Good Bread Alley") 30-50 52
KING (4582 "Lonesome Train") 25-40 52
MERCURY (70334 "Old Man Boogie") 50-100 54
MERCURY (70525 "Anxious Heart") 40-60 54
MERCURY (70621 "Anxious Heart") 40-60 55
RIVERSIDE 5-10 62

LPs: 10/12–inch 33rpm

AAMCO 10-15
BETHLEHEM (5005 "Eddie Cleanhead Vinson Sings") 50-75 57
BETHLEHEM (6000 series) 5-10 78
BLUES TIME 10-15 69
BLUESWAY 10-20 67
DELMARK 5-10 80
KING (634 "Eddie Vinson") 40-60 60
KING (1000 series) 10-12 70
MUSE 5-10 78-83
REGGIES 5-10 81
RIVERSIDE (3502 "Backdoor Blues") 30-40 62

Also see BROWN, Roy
Also see HARRIS, Wynonie / Roy Brown / Eddie Vinson
Also see VINSON, Eddie
Also see WITHERSPOON, Jimmy / Eddie Vinson

VINTON, Bobby
(Bobby Vinton Orchestra)

P&R/R&B/LP '62

Singles: 7–inch

ABC 3-5 74-77
ALPINE 10-15 59
CURB 3-4 88-89
ELEKTRA 3-5 78
EPIC (9000 series) 4-8 60-66
(Black vinyl.)
EPIC (9000 series) 8-10 64
(Colored vinyl.)

EPIC (10000 series)..................... 3-6 66-75
LARC.. 3-4 83
MELODY 10-15 59
TAPESTRY 3-5 79-82

Picture Sleeves

EPIC.. 3-8 62-72
TAPESTRY 3-5 80

EPs: 7-inch 33/45rpm

EPIC.. 6-12 63-65
(Jukebox issues.)

LPs: 10/12-inch 33rpm

ABC.. 8-10 74-77
CSP 5-10 80s
COLUMBIA 8-10 73
EPIC (500 series)..................... 20-25 60
EPIC (3000 series).................. 15-20 60
EPIC (20000 series)................... 8-15 62-70
(Black vinyl.)
EPIC (20468 "Blue on Blue")..... 20-40 63
(Colored vinyl. Promotional issue only.)
EPIC (30000 series)................... 5-10 72-79
HARMONY 5-10 70
TAPESTRY 5-10 80

VINTON, Bobby / Chuck & Johnny

Singles: 7-inch

DIAMOND (121 "I Love You the Way You Are")................................. 5-8 62

VINTON, Bobby, & Village Stompers

LPs: 10/12-inch 33rpm

EPIC....................................... 10-20 66
Also see VILLAGE STOMPERS
Also see VINTON, Bobby

VIN-ZEE

R&B '81

Singles: 7-inch

EMERGENCY 3-5 81

VIO-LENCE

LP '88

LPs: 10/12-inch 33rpm

MECHANIC 5-8 88

VIOLENT FEMMES

LP '86

Singles: 7-inch

SLASH 3-4 83-90

LPs: 10/12-inch 33rpm

SLASH 5-8 83-91
Members: Gordon Gano; Brian Ritchie; Victor DeLorenzo.

VIRTUES
(With the Virtues; Frank Virtuoso & Virtues)

P&R/R&B '59

Singles: 7-inch

ABC.. 3-5 73
ABC-PAR 5-10 59
B.V.D...................................... 5-10
FAYETTE 4-8 64
HIGHLAND............................... 10-15 60
HUNT (Monaural)........................5-10 59
HUNT (Stereo).........................15-25 59
SURE (500 series)......................8-12 59
SURE (1700 series).....................4-8 62
VIRNON 5-10 60
VIRTUE...4-6 66-69
WYNNE...5-10 60

LPs: 10/12-inch 33rpm

STRAND 20-25 60
WYNNE.......................................25-30 60

VISAGE

LP '81

Singles: 12-inch 33/45rpm

POLYDOR 4-6 80-82

Singles: 7-inch

POLYDOR 3-5 81

LPs: 10/12-inch 33rpm

POLYDOR 5-10 80-82

VISCOUNTS
(Vicounts)

P&R '59

Singles: 7-inch

AMY 4-8 65-66
CORAL...4-8 66-67
MADISON 5-10 59-61
MR. PEACOCK...............................4-8 61
MR. PEEKE 4-8 63

LPs: 10/12-inch 33rpm

AMY (8008 "Harlem Nocturne") .20-30 65
MADISON (1001 "Viscounts")....50-75 60
Members: Bobby Spievak; Joe Spievak; Harry Haller; Larry Vecchio; Clark Smith.

VISUAL

R&B/D&D '83

Singles: 12-inch 33/45rpm

PRELUDE.......................................4-6 83-84

Singles: 7-inch

PRELUDE.......................................3-4 83-84

VITALE, Joe

LP '81

Singles: 7-inch

ASYLUM 3-5 81-82
ATLANTIC.......................................3-5 74

LPs: 10/12-inch 33rpm

ASYLUM 5-10 81
ATLANTIC....................................5-10 74
Also see EAGLES
Also see WALSH, Joe

VITAMIN E

R&B '77

Singles: 7-inch

BUDDAH...3-5 77

VITAMIN Z

P&R/D&D/LP '85

Singles: 12-inch 33/45rpm

GEFFEN 4-6 85

Singles: 7-inch

GEFFEN.. 3-4 85

Picture Sleeves

GEFFEN.. 3-4 85

LPs: 10/12-inch 33rpm

GEFFEN.. 5-8 85

Member: Geoff Barradale.

Also see PARSONS, Alan, Project

VITO & SALUTATIONS

P&R '63

Singles: 7-inch

APT (25079 "Walkin")............... 25-35 65

BOOM 10-15 66

CRYSTAL BALL........................... 3-5 78

HERALD.. 15-20 63-64

KRAN (5002 "Your Way") 30-40 62

RAYNA (5009 "Gloria") 20-25 62

RED BOY (1001 "So Wonderful") 15-25 66

REGINA (1320 "Get a Job")...... 15-25 64

RUST 10-15 66

SANDBAG (103 "So Wonderful") 10-20 68

WELLS (1008 "Can I Depend on You") 15-20 64

(Black vinyl.)

WELLS (1008 "Can I Depend on You") 20-30 64

(Colored vinyl.)

LPs: 10/12-inch 33rpm

KAPE (1002 "Greatest Hits")..... 10-15 73

RED BOY (200 "Greatest Hits") 20-30 81

Members: Vito Balsamo; Shelly Buchansky; Randy Silverman; Len Citrin; Frank Fox.

VIXEN

P&R/LP '88

Singles: 7-inch

EMI... 3-4 88-90

Picture Sleeves

EMI... 3-4 88-89

LPs: 10/12-inch 33rpm

EMI... 5-8 88-90

Members: Janet Gardner; Share Pedersen; Jan Kuehnemund; Roxy Petrucci.

VOCALEERS

R&B '53

Singles: 78rpm

RED ROBIN 20-40 52

Singles: 7-inch

OLD TOWN 10-15 60

OLDIES 45 .... 4-6 65

PARADISE (113 "I Need Your Love So Bad") 15-25 59

RED ROBIN (113 "Be True") 150-200 52

RED ROBIN (114 "Is It a Dream") 100-150 52

RED ROBIN (119 "I Walk Alone") 150-200 53

RED ROBIN (125 "Will You Be True")............................150-200 54

RED ROBIN (132 "Angel Face") 100-150 54

TWISTIME (11 "A Golden Tear")....................................10-20 62

VEST (832 "Hear My Plea").......40-60 60

LP: 10/12-inch 33rpm

RELIC 5-10

Members: Joe Duncan; Curtis Dunham; Ted Williams; Mel Walton; Bill Walker; Lamarr Cooper; Joe Powell; Richard Blandon; Leo Fuller; Curtis Blandon; Caesar Williams.

Also see LITTLE ESTHER & Junior with the Johnny Otis Orchestra / Johnny Otis Orchestra with the Vocaleers

VOCALEERS / Mango Jones

Singles: 7-inch

OLDIES 45.................................4-6 65

Also see VOCALEERS

VOGUES

P&R '65

Singles: 7-inch

ABC...3-5 73

ABC-PAR 4-8 65

ASTRA (1030 "You're the One")....4-6 73

(Black vinyl.)

ASTRA (1030 "You're the One")....5-8 73

(Colored vinyl.)

BELL..3-5 71

BLUE STAR (229 "You're the One")...10-20 65

CO & CE 4-8 65-67

COLLECTABLES...........................3-4 80s

ERA...3-5 70s

GOLDIES 45 ....3-5 73

GUSTO 3-4 81

MGM 4-8 67

MAINSTREAM 3-5 72

REPRISE (Except 0663)...............3-6 68-71

REPRISE (0663 "Just What I've Been Looking For") 5-10 68

REVUE..4-8 68

ROCK'N MANIA............................3-4

SSS INT'L 3-4 77

SUN 3-5 77-79

20TH FOX.....................................3-5 73-74

LPs: 10/12-inch 33rpm

CSP...5-8 82

CO & CE.....................................25-35 65-66

51 WEST......................................5-10 80s

PICKWICK 8-10 71

PLANTATION (43 "Golden Hits")...5-8 81

REPRISE 10-15 68-70

RHINO 5-8 88

SSS INT'L (34 "Greatest Hits") 5-10 77

SEARS..15-20 60s

Members: Bob Bush; Bill Burkette; Hugh Geyer; Chuck Blasko; Don Miller. SSS Int'l/Plantation/51 West/CSP line-up: Charly Tichenor; Dick Stevens; Kelly Goad; Bill Packard; Bill Davidson.

VOICE MASTERS

R&B '70

Singles: 7–inch

ANNA (101 "Hope and Pray") . 50-100 59
ANNA (102 "Needed")............ 50-100 59
BAMBOO 10-20 68-70
FRISCO ("In Love in Vain")....... 25-50 60s
(Number not known.)

Members: Ty Hunter; C.P. Spencer; Lamont Dozier; David Ruffin; Freddie Gorman.
Also see DOZIER, Lamont
Also see HUNTER, Ty
Also see ORIGINALS
Also see RUFFIN, David

VOICES of AMERICA / U.S.A. for Africa

P&R '86

Singles: 7–inch

EMI AMERICA 3-4 86

Picture Sleeves

EMI AMERICA 3-4 86
Also see TOTO
Also see U.S.A. for AFRICA

VOICES of EAST HARLEM

LP '70

Singles: 7–inch

ELEKTRA.................................. 3-5 70-72
JUST SUNSHINE........................ 3-5 73-74

LPs: 10/12–inch 33rpm

ELEKTRA.................................. 8-10 70
JUST SUNSHINE........................ 5-10 73-74

VOIVOD

LP '89

LPs: 10/12–inch 33rpm

MECHANIC 5-8 89

VOLCANOS

R&B '65

Singles: 7–inch

ARCTIC.................................... 4-8 65-67
VIRTUE.................................... 3-5 70
Member: Gene Faith.
Also see FAITH, Gene
Also see MFSB

VOLLENWEIDER, Andreas

LP '84

Singles: 12–inch 33/45rpm

CBS/COLUMBIA......................... 4-6 86

Singles: 7–inch

CBS/COLUMBIA......................... 3-4 86

LPs: 10/12–inch 33rpm

CBS/COLUMBIA......................... 5-8 84-89

VOLTAGE BROTHERS

R&B '86

Singles: 12–inch 33/45rpm

MTM.. 4-6 86

Singles: 7–inch

LIFESONG................................. 3-4 78
MTM.. 3-4 86

LPs: 10/12–inch 33rpm

LIFESONG................................. 5-8 78
MTM.. 5-8 86

VOLUMES

P&R '62

Singles: 7–inch

ABC... 3-5 73
AMERICAN ARTS (6 "Gotta Give Her Love").............................. 15-25 64
AMERICAN ARTS (I Just Can't Help Myself")............................. 15-25 65
CHEX (1002 "I Love You")......... 15-25 62
(First issued crediting the "Valumes.")
CHEX (1005 "The Bell")............ 20-30 62
MPACT (1017 "That Same Old Feeling")............................. 25-50 66
INFERNO................................ 10-20 67-68
JUBILEE 10-15 63
OLD TOWN (1154 "Why") 10-20 64
TWIRL (2016 "I Got Love") 20-40 61
VIRGO 3-5 73

LPs: 10/12–inch 33rpm

RELIC 5-10 85
Also see NUTMEGS / Volumes
Also see VALUMES

VONTASTICS

P&R/R&B '66

Singles: 7–inch

CHESS...................................... 4-8 67
ST. LAWRENCE.......................... 4-8 65-66
SATELLITE (2002 "I'll Never Say Goodbye")............................. 25-35 65
Also see FANTASTIC VONTASTICS

VOUDOURIS, Roger

P&R/LP '79

Singles: 7–inch

W.B. 3-5 78-79

LPs: 10/12–inch 33rpm

W.B. 5-10 78

VOXPOPPERS

P&R/R&B '58

Singles: 7–inch

AMP 3 (1004 "Wishing for Your Love")............................. 20-25 58
MERCURY................................. 8-12 58
POPLAR 10-15 58
VERSAILLES (200 "A Blessing After All").............................. 20-25 59

EPs: 7–inch 33/45rpm

MERCURY (3391 "The Voxpoppers")......................... 50-100 58

VOYAGE

R&B/LP '78

Singles: 7–inch

ATLANTIC	3-5	82
MARLIN	3-5	78-79

LPs: 10/12–inch 33rpm

ATLANTIC	5-8	82
MARLIN	5-10	78

VOYEUR

R&B '85

Singles: 7–inch

MCA	3-4	85

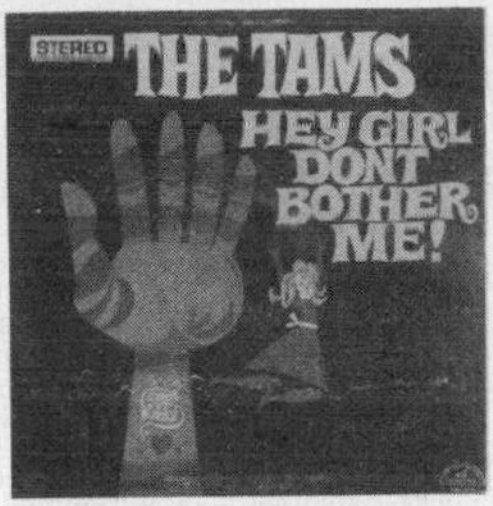

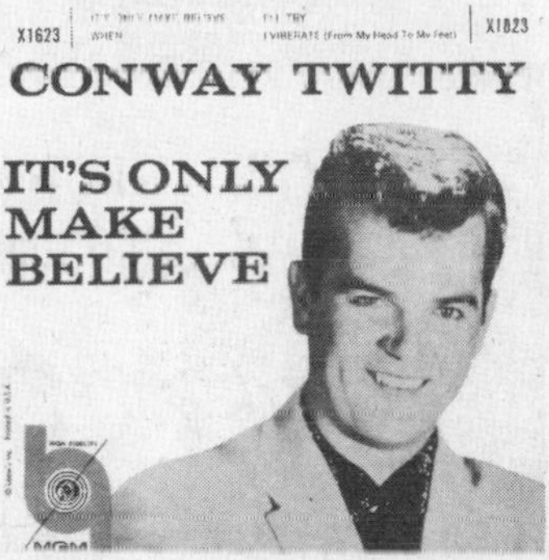

CENCO
RECORDS
A Division of SPRY RECORD CORP.
45 RPM
45 RPM
GET IT—GET IT
IKE & TINA TURNER

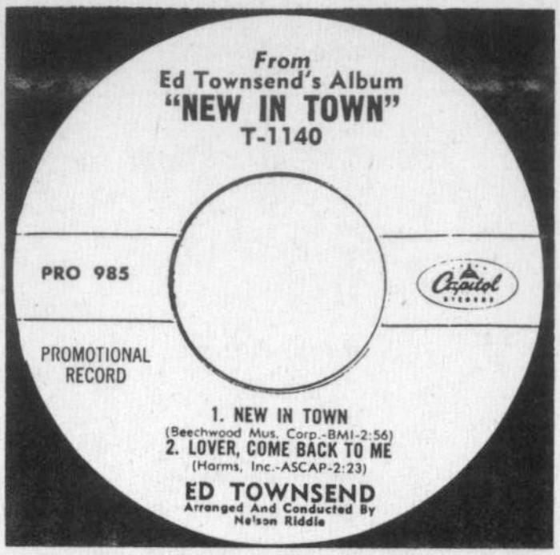
From
Ed Townsend's Album
"NEW IN TOWN"
T-1140
PRO 985
PROMOTIONAL
RECORD
Capitol
1. NEW IN TOWN
(Beechwood Mus. Corp.-BMI-2:56)
2. LOVER, COME BACK TO ME
(Harms, Inc.-ASCAP-2:23)
ED TOWNSEND
Arranged And Conducted By
Nelson Riddle

ROCK-A-BYE MY DARLING
THE ROSY DANCE
JOHNNY THUNDER
DIAMOND

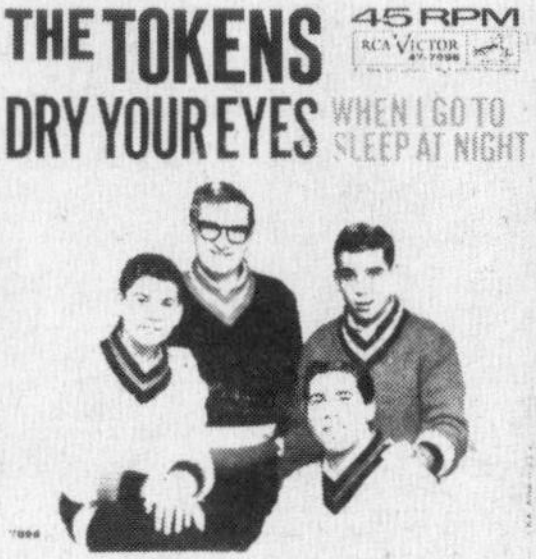
THE TOKENS
DRY YOUR EYES
45 RPM
RCA VICTOR
WHEN I GO TO
SLEEP AT NIGHT

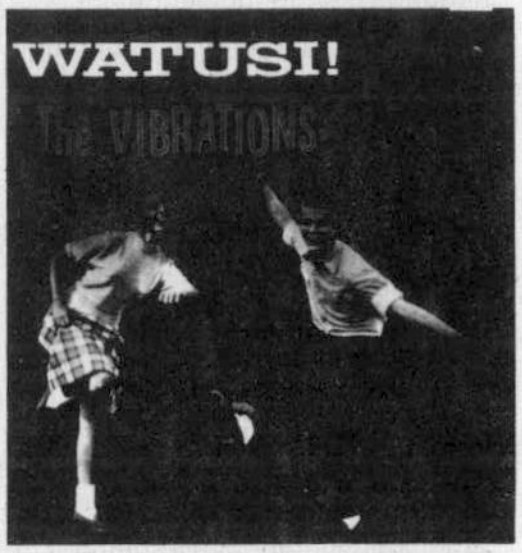
WATUSI!
The VIBRATIONS

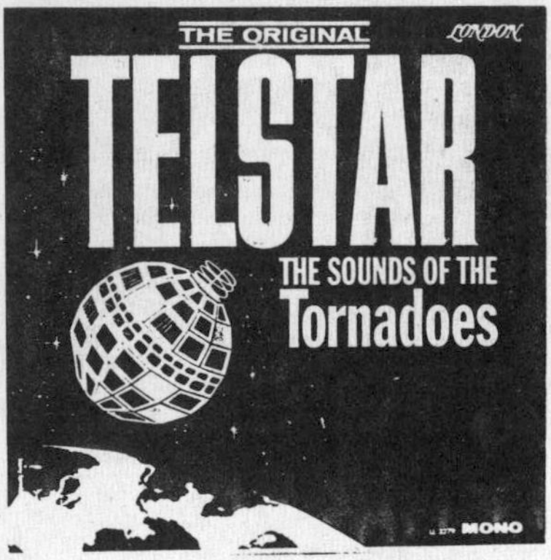
THE ORIGINAL
LONDON
TELSTAR
THE SOUNDS OF THE
Tornadoes
MONO

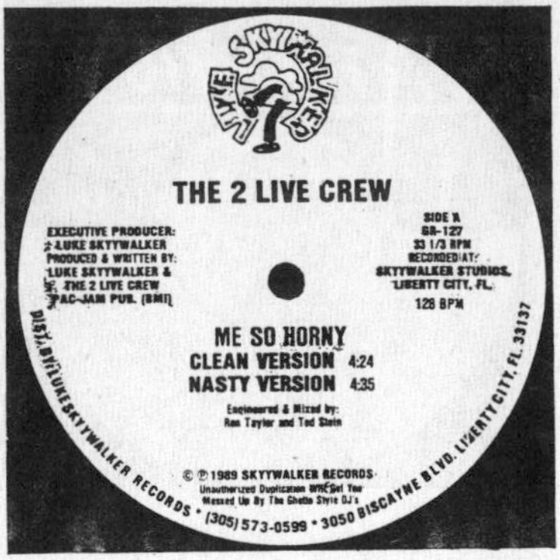
LUKE SKYWALKER
THE 2 LIVE CREW
EXECUTIVE PRODUCER:
LUKE SKYWALKER
PRODUCED & WRITTEN BY:
LUKE SKYWALKER &
THE 2 LIVE CREW
PAC-JAM PUB. (BMI)
SIDE A
33 1/3 RPM
SKYWALKER STUDIOS,
LIBERTY CITY, FL.
128 BPM
ME SO HORNY
CLEAN VERSION 4:24
NASTY VERSION 4:35
Engineered & Mixed by:
© ℗ 1989 SKYWALKER RECORDS
(305) 573-0599 • 3050 BISCAYNE BLVD. LIBERTY CITY, FL 33137

W

W.A.G.B.

P&R '82

Singles: 7-inch

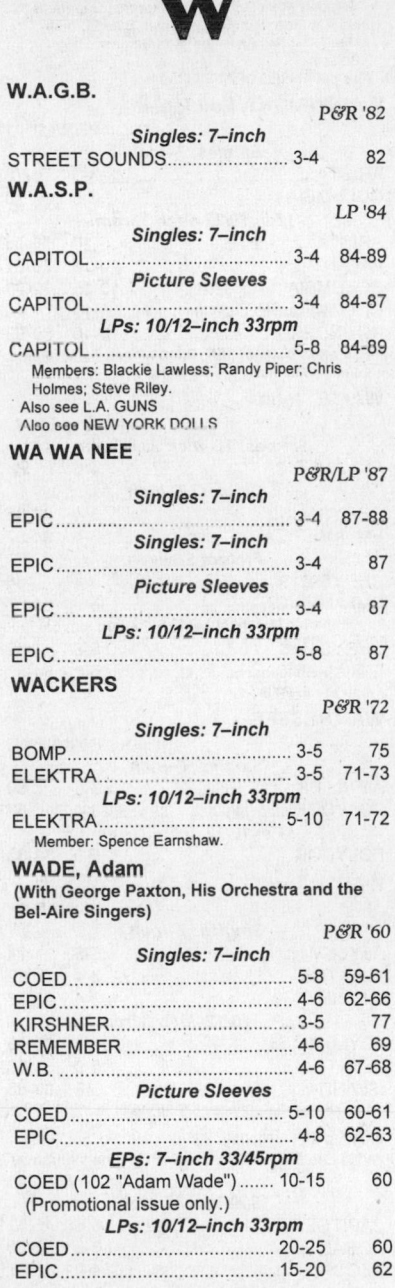

STREET SOUNDS.......................... 3-4 82

W.A.S.P.

LP '84

Singles: 7-inch

CAPITOL.. 3-4 84-89

Picture Sleeves

CAPITOL.. 3-4 84-87

LPs: 10/12-inch 33rpm

CAPITOL.. 5-8 84-89

Members: Blackie Lawless; Randy Piper; Chris Holmes; Steve Riley.

Also see L.A. GUNS

Also see NEW YORK DOLLS

WA WA NEE

P&R/LP '87

Singles: 7-inch

EPIC... 3-4 87-88

Singles: 7-inch

EPIC... 3-4 87

Picture Sleeves

EPIC... 3-4 87

LPs: 10/12-inch 33rpm

EPIC... 5-8 87

WACKERS

P&R '72

Singles: 7-inch

BOMP.. 3-5 75

ELEKTRA.. 3-5 71-73

LPs: 10/12-inch 33rpm

ELEKTRA.. 5-10 71-72

Member: Spence Earnshaw.

WADE, Adam

(With George Paxton, His Orchestra and the Bel-Aire Singers)

P&R '60

Singles: 7-inch

COED.. 5-8 59-61

EPIC... 4-6 62-66

KIRSHNER.. 3-5 77

REMEMBER 4-6 69

W.B. 4-6 67-68

Picture Sleeves

COED.. 5-10 60-61

EPIC... 4-8 62-63

EPs: 7-inch 33/45rpm

COED (102 "Adam Wade")....... 10-15 60

(Promotional issue only.)

LPs: 10/12-inch 33rpm

COED.. 20-25 60

EPIC... 15-20 62

KIRSHNER.. 5-10 77

WADSWORTH MANSION

P&R '70

Singles: 7-inch

SUSSEX 3-5 70

LPs: 10/12-inch 33rpm

SUSSEX 10-20 71

(Shown as "Wadsworth Manison" on some issues.)

WAGNER, Jack

P&R/LP '84

Singles: 7-inch

QWEST.. 3-4 84-87

Picture Sleeves

QWEST.. 3-4 84-87

LPs: 10/12-inch 33rpm

QWEST.. 5-8 84-87

WAGONER, Porter

C&W '54

Singles: 78rpm

RCA 5-10 53-57

Singles: 7-inch

RCA (0013 thru 1007).................. 3-6 69-74

RCA (5086 thru 7638)................. 5-15 53-59

RCA (7708 thru 9979)................. 3-8 60-71

RCA (10124 thru 11998).............. 3-5 74-79

W.B. 3-4 82-83

EPs: 7-inch 33/45rpm

RCA 8-15 56

LPs: 10/12-inch 33rpm

ACCORD 5-8 82

CAMDEN 5-15 63-73

H.S.R.D. 15-25 81

PICKWICK 5-10 75-77

RCA (Except 1300 through 2900 series)........................... 5-15 66-79

RCA (1358 "A Satisfied Mind") .. 30-40 56

RCA (LPM-2447 thru LPM-2960)..................... 10-20 62-65

(Monaural.)

RCA (LSP-2447 thru LSP-2960) 15-25 62-65

(Stereo.)

TUDOR 5-8 84

W.B. 5-8 83

Also see SNOW, Hank / Hank Locklin / Porter Wagoner

WAGONER, Porter, & Skeeter Davis

LPs: 10/12-inch 33rpm

RCA 10-20 62

Also see DAVIS, Skeeter

WAGONER, Porter, & Dolly Parton

C&W '67

Singles: 7-inch

RCA 3-6 67-80

LPs: 10/12-inch 33rpm

RCA (Except 3926 thru 4841)...... 5-10 74-80

RCA (LPM-3926 "Just Between You and Me") 30-40 68
(Monaural.)
RCA (LSP-3926 thru LSP-4841) 10-20 68-73
(Stereo.)
Also see PARTON, Dolly
Also see WAGONER, Porter

WAIKIKIS

P&R '64

Singles: 7-inch

KAPP 3-6 64-68
PALETTE 3-6 62-63

LPs: 10/12-inch 33rpm

BOOT 5-8 78
KAPP 8-15 64-69
MCA 5-8 80s

WAILERS

P&R/R&B '59

Singles: 7-inch

BELL 4-8 67
ETIQUETTE 4-8 63-66
GOLDEN CREST 10-15 59
(Label pictures the group.)
GOLDEN CREST 5-10 60-64
(No group picture on label.)
IMPERIAL 4-8 64
U.A. 4-8 67
VIVA 4-6 67

LPs: 10/12-inch 33rpm

BELL 10-15 68
ETIQUETTE (1 "The Fabulous Wailers at the Castle") 75-100 66
ETIQUETTE (022 "The Wailers and Company") 40-60 66
ETIQUETTE (023 "Wailers Wailers Everywhere") 75-100 66
ETIQUETTE (026 "Out of Our Tree") 40-60 60s
(Reissues of Etiquette LPs have a 1980s date on back cover.)
ETIQUETTE (1100 series) 5-8 86
ETIQUETTE (22296/97 "The Wailers and Their Greatest Hits") 10-20 79
(Two LPs & note from Etiquette's Roger Hart.)
GOLDEN CREST (3075 "The Fabulous Wailers") 100-150 60
(Color cover photo.)
GOLDEN CREST (3075 "The Fabulous Wailers") 40-60 60
(Black and white cover.)
GOLDEN CREST (3075 "The Wailers Wail") 25-35 60s
IMPERIAL 15-20 64
U.A. (3557 "Outburst!") 25-35 67
(Monaural.)
U.A. (6557 "Outburst!") 35-45 67
(Stereo.)
Members: Kent Morrill; Robin Roberts; Gail Harris; Mark Marush; Rich Dangel; John "Buck" Ormsby; Mike Burk; Neil Anderson; Ron Gardner; Dave Roland.
Also see THREE GRACES / Wailers

WAINWRIGHT, Loudon, III

P&R/LP '73

Singles: 7-inch

ARISTA 3-5 76-78
COLUMBIA 3-5 73

LPs: 10/12-inch 33rpm

ARISTA 5-10 76-78
ATLANTIC 10-15 70-71
COLUMBIA ("KC" series) 10-15 72-73
COLUMBIA ("PC" series) 5-10 75
ROUNDER 5-10 80-83
Also see SPRINGSTEEN, Bruce / Albert Hammond / Loudon Wainwright, III / Taj Mahal

WAITE, John

LP '82

Singles: 12-inch 33/45rpm

EMI AMERICA 4-6 84

Singles: 7-inch

CHRYSALIS 3-4 82-85
EMI AMERICA 3-4 84-87

Picture Sleeves

CHRYSALIS 3-4 85
EMI AMERICA 3-5 84-87

LPs: 10/12-inch 33rpm

CHRYSALIS 5-8 82
EMI AMERICA 5-8 84-87
Also see BABYS

WAITRESSES

P&R/LP '82

Singles: 7-inch

ANTILLES 3-5 80
POLYDOR 3-4 82

LPs: 10/12-inch 33rpm

POLYDOR 5-8 82-83

WAITS, Tom

LP '75

Singles: 7-inch

ASYLUM 3-5 74
ELEKTRA 3-4 83
ISLAND 3-4 83-88

LPs: 10/12-inch 33rpm

ASYLUM 5-10 73-80
ELEKTRA 5-8 83
ISLAND 5-8 83-88
Also see GAYLE, Crystal, & Tom Waits

WAKELY, Jimmy

(With Les Baxter Chorus; with Velma Williams)

P&R '43

Singles: 78rpm

CAPITOL 3-6 48-52
CORAL 3-6 53-55
DECCA 4-8 43-57

JIMMY WAKELY SOUVENIR 5-10 50s

Singles: 7-inch

ARTCO 3-5 74
CAPITOL (1300 thru 2100 series) 5-10 50-52
CORAL 4-8 53-55
DECCA 3-8 55-70
DOT 3-6 66
SHASTA (100 series) 3-6 58-67
SHASTA (200 series) 3-4 71

Picture Sleeves

SHASTA 5-10 58

EPs: 7-inch 33/45rpm

CAPITOL 10-20 50-53
CORAL 10-15 54
DECCA 8-12 58

LPs: 10/12-inch 33rpm

ALBUM GLOBE 5-10 81
CAPITOL 20-40 50-53
CORAL 4-8 73
DANNY 8-10
DECCA (8400 thru 8600 series) 20-35 56-57
DECCA (75000 thru 78000 series) 8-18 67-70
DOT 10-15 66
MCA 4-8 80s
MCR 5-10 74
SHASTA 5-15 58-75
TOPS 10-15
VOCALION 5-10 68-70

Also see CHANDLER, Karen, & Jimmy Wakely
Also see WHITING, Margaret, & Jimmy Wakely

WAKELIN, Johnny, & Kinshasa Band

P&R '75

Singles: 7-inch

PYE 3-5 75

WAKEMAN, Rick

(With the London Symphony Orchestra & English Chamber Choir; with English Rock Ensemble)

LP '73

Singles: 7-inch

A&M 3-5 73

LPs: 10/12-inch 33rpm

A&M (3000 series) 5-10 74
A&M (4000 series) 5-12 73-77
A&M (QU-5000 series) 10-20 74
(Quadraphonic.)
A&M (6000 series) 10-15 79

Also see DALTREY, Roger, & Rick Wakeman
Also see STRAWBS
Also see YES

WALDEN, Narada Michael

(Narada)

R&B '77

Singles: 12-inch 33/45rpm

ATLANTIC 4-6 82-83
NARADA (17254 "Narada Sampler") 5-8 86
(Promotional issue only.)
W.B. 4-6 85

Singles: 7-inch

ATLANTIC 3-5 77-83
REPRISE 3-4 88
W.B. 3-4 85

Picture Sleeves

NARADA (17254 "Narada Sampler") 5-10 86
(Promotional issue only.)

LPs: 10/12-inch 33rpm

ATLANTIC 5-10 79-83

WALDEN, Narada Michael, & Patti Austin

R&B '85

Singles: 7-inch

W.B. 3-4 85

Also see AUSTIN, Patti

WALDMAN, Wendy

P&R '78

Singles: 7-inch

EPIC 3-4 82-83
W.B. 3-5 77-78

LPs: 10/12-inch 33rpm

EPIC 5-8 82-83
W.B. 5-10 78

WALDO

R&B '82

Singles: 7-inch

COLUMBIA 3-5 82

LPs: 10/12-inch 33rpm

COLUMBIA 5-10 82

WALKER, Billy

C&W '54

Singles: 78rpm

COLUMBIA 4-8 54-56

Singles: 7-inch

CAPRICE 3-4 79-80
CASINO 3-5 77
COLUMBIA (21000 series) 6-12 54-56
COLUMBIA (33000 series) 4-6 60s
COLUMBIA (40000 series) 5-10 56-60
COLUMBIA (42000 & 43000 series) 4-8 61-65
DIMENSION 3-4 83
MCA 3-5 77
MGM 3-5 70-74
MRC 3-4 77-78
MONUMENT 3-6 66-70
PAID 3-4 80
RCA 3-5 75-76
SCORPION 3-4 78
TALL TEXAN 3-4 85-88

Picture Sleeves

COLUMBIA 4-8 63-67

LPs: 10/12-inch 33rpm

COLUMBIA 10-20 63-69
GUSTO 5-8 80s
H.S.R.D. 5-10 84
HARMONY 8-15 64-70
MGM 6-12 70-74
MONUMENT 8-18 66-72
RCA 5-10 75-76

WALKER, Billy, & Barbara Fairchild

C&W '80

Singles: 7-inch

PAID 3-5 81

LPs: 10/12-inch 33rpm

PAID 5-10 81

Also see FAIRCHILD, Barbara

WALKER, Billy, & Brenda Kaye Perry

C&W '77

Singles: 7-inch

MRC 3-5 77

Also see WALKER, Billy

WALKER, Bobbi

R&B '80

Singles: 7-inch

CASABLANCA 3-5 80

WALKER, Boots

P&R '67

Singles: 7-inch

PROVIDENCE 4-6 66
RUST 4-8 67-68

WALKER, David T.

R&B '69

Singles: 7-inch

ODE 3-5 73-76
REVUE 4-6 68-69
ZEA 3-5 70

LPs: 10/12-inch 33rpm

ODE 8-10 74-76
REVUE 10-15 68-69

WALKER, Gloria
(With the Chevelles)

P&R/R&B '68

Singles: 7-inch

FLAMING ARROW 4-8 68-69
PEOPLE 3-5

WALKER, Jerry Jeff

P&R '68

Singles: 7-inch

ATCO 3-6 68-70
MCA 3-5 73-80
SOUTH COAST 3-4 81
TRIED & TRUE 3-4 89

LPs: 10/12-inch 33rpm

ATCO (Except 297) 15-20 68-70
ATCO (297 "Five Years Gone") 30-50 69
DECCA 10-12 72
ELEKTRA 8-10 70s
MCA 5-10 73-80
SOUTH COAST 5-10 81
VANGUARD 10-12 69

WALKER, Jimmy

LP '75

Singles: 7-inch

BUDDAH 3-5 75

LPs: 10/12-inch 33rpm

BUDDAH 8-10 75

WALKER, Junior
(With the All Stars; with All the Stars; Junior Walker All Stars; Jr. Walker)

P&R/R&B/LP '65

Singles: 12-inch 33/45rpm

WHITFIELD 4-8 79

Singles: 7-inch

HARVEY 10-20 62-64
MOTOWN 3-4 83
SOUL (Except 35003) 5-12 65-76
SOUL (35003 "Monkey Jump") .. 10-15 64
WHITFIELD 3-5 79

Picture Sleeves

SOUL 4-8 65-66

EPs: 7-inch 33/45rpm

SOUL (69701 "Shotgun") 15-25 66
SOUL (69702 "Soul Sessions") . 15-25 66
SOUL (69703 "Road Runner") ... 15-25 66

LPs: 10/12-inch 33rpm

MOTOWN (Except 700 series) 5-10 80-83
MOTOWN (700 series) 8-12 74
SOUL (701 "Shotgun") 20-30 66
SOUL (702 "Soul Sessions") 20-30 66
SOUL (703 "Road Runner") 20-30 66
SOUL (705 "Live") 20-30 66
SOUL (710 "Home Cookin'") 15-20 69
SOUL (718 "Greatest Hits") 10-20 69
SOUL (718 "Greatest Hits") 10-20 69
SOUL (721 "What Does It Take") 10-20 69
SOUL (725 thru 750) 5-15 70-78
SOUL (35073 "Jr. Walker") 15-25 60s
(Colored vinyl. Promotional issue only.)
WHITFIELD 8-10 79

Also see FOREIGNER

WALKER, T-Bone

P&R '47

Singles: 78rpm

BLACK & WHITE 10-15 46-48
COMET 10-15 48-49
CAPITOL 10-15 45-50
IMPERIAL 10-15 50-57
MERCURY 10-15 46
POST 10-15 55
RHUMBOOGIE 10-15 45-46

Singles: 7-inch

ATLANTIC (1065 Papa Ain't Salty") 15-25 55
BLUESWAY 4-8 67

CAPITOL (799 "On Your Way Blues") 50-100 49
CAPITOL (944 "Too Much Trouble Blues") 50-100 50
IMPERIAL (5202 "Street Walkin' Woman") 40-60 52
IMPERIAL (5216 "Blue Mood") . 35-50 53
IMPERIAL (5228 "Railroad Station Blues") 25-50 53
IMPERIAL (5239 "Party Girl") ... 35-50 53
IMPERIAL (5247 "Everytime") .. 35-50 53
IMPERIAL (5261 "I'm About to Lose My Mind") 35-50 53
IMPERIAL (5264 "Pony Tail").... 35-50 54
IMPERIAL (5274 "Vida Lee") 35-50 54
IMPERIAL (5284 "Bye Bye Baby") 35-50 54
IMPERIAL (5299 "Teenage Baby") 35-50 54
IMPERIAL (5311 "Love Is a Gamble") 20-40 55
IMPERIAL (5330 "I'll Understand") 20-40 55
IMPERIAL (5384 "Welcome Blues") 20-40 56
IMPERIAL (5600 thru 5800 series) 8-15 60-62
JET STREAM 4-8 66
MODERN 4-8 65
POST (2002 "I Get So Weary"). 25-50 55

EPs: 7–inch 33/45rpm

CAPITOL (370 "Classics in Jazz") 75-125 53

LPs: 10/12–inch 33rpm

ATLANTIC (8020 "T-Bone Blues") 75-100 59
(Black label.)
ATLANTIC (8020 "T-Bone Blues") 50-75 60
(Red label.)
ATLANTIC (8256 "T-Bone Blues") 10-15 70
BLUE NOTE 8-12
BLUESTIME 8-12 73
BLUESWAY 10-15 67-73
BRUNSWICK 10-15 68
CAPITOL (H-370 "Classics in Jazz") 250-350 53
(10–inch LP.)
CAPITOL (T-370 "Classics in Jazz") 150-250 56
CAPITOL (1958 "Great Blues Vocals and Guitar") 40-60 63
DELMARK 8-10
FLYING DUTCHMAN/ BLUESTIME 10-15 69
HOMECOOKING 8-12
IMPERIAL (9098 "T-Bone Walker Sings the Blues") 50-75 59
IMPERIAL (9116 "Singing the Blues") 50-75 60
IMPERIAL (9146 "I Get So Weary") 50-75 61
POLYDOR 10-15 70-73
REPRISE 10-15 73
WET SOUL 10-20 67

Also see GLENN, Lloyd
Also see McCRACKLIN, Jimmy / T-Bone Walker / Charles Brown
Also see WITHERSPOON, Jimmy
Also see X-RAYS

WALKER BROTHERS

P&R '65

Singles: 7–inch

SMASH 4-8 64-66

Picture Sleeves

SMASH 5-10 65-66

LPs: 10/12–inch 33rpm

SMASH 20-25 66-67

Members: Scott Engel; John Maus; Gary Leeds.

WALL of VOODOO

LP '81

Singles: 12–inch 33/45rpm

I.R.S. 4-6 83

Singles: 7–inch

I.R.S. 3-5 81-83

Picture Sleeves

I.R.S. 3-5 83

LPs: 10/12–inch 33rpm

I.R.S. 5-10 81-83

Member: Stan Ridgway.
Also see COPELAND, Stewart, & Stan Ridgway
Also see RIDGWAY, Stan

WALLACE, Jerry

(With the Jewels; with Jay Rand Orchestra & Chorus)

P&R '54

Singles: 78rpm

ALLIED 5-10 51-54
CHALLENGE 5-10 57

Singles: 7–inch

ALLIED 10-15 54
BMA 3-5 77-78
CHALLENGE (1000 series) 8-12 57
CHALLENGE (9100 series) 4-8 61-63
CHALLENGE (59000 through 59098) 5-15 58-60
CHALLENGE (59200 series) 4-8 63-65
CLASS 5-10 53
DECCA 3-5 71-72
DOOR KNOB 3-5 79-80
ERIC 3-4 70s
4-STAR 3-5 78-79
GLENOLDEN 3-6 68
GUSTO 3-4 80s
LIBERTY 3-5 67-70
MCA 3-4 73-74
MGM 3-5 75-76

MERCURY (70000 series).......... 5-10 55-56
MERCURY (72000 series)........... 4-8 64-66
TOPS 5-10 53
U.A. 3-5 72-75
VOGUE 8-12 52
WING 5-10 56

Picture Sleeves

CHALLENGE (59013 thru 59098)..................................... 8-12 58-60
CHALLENGE (59200 series) 4-8 63-65

EPs: 7–inch 33/45rpm

CHALLENGE 15-25 60

LPs: 10/12–inch 33rpm

BMA 8-10 77
CHALLENGE (606 "Just Jerry") 30-35 59
CHALLENGE (612 "There She Goes")................................... 20-25 61
CHALLENGE (616 "Shutters and Boards") 15-20 63
CHALLENGE (619 "In the Misty Moonlight") 15-20 64
CHALLENGE (2002 "Greatest Hits") 10-15 69
DECCA.. 8-12 71
4-STAR 5-8 83
LIBERTY 10-12 68
MCA 8-10 73-74
MGM 8-10 75
MERCURY 10-15 66
U.A. 8-12 72-75
WING 10-12 68

Also see BARE, Bobby / Donna Fargo / Jerry Wallace

WALLACE, Jerry / Soul Surfers

Singles: 7–inch

CHALLENGE 4-8 64

Also see WALLACE, Jerry

WALLACE BROTHERS

P&R '64

Singles: 7–inch

JEWEL 4-6 68-69
SIMS 4-8 63-67

LPs: 10/12–inch 33rpm

SIMS 15-20 65

WALLIS, Ruth
(With the Deluxe Rhumba Band)

P&R '53

Singles: 78rpm

DE-LUXE..................................... 5-10 47
KING 5-10 52-53
MONARCH................................... 5-10 53-54
WALLIS ORIGINAL..................... 5-10 55-57

Singles: 7–inch

DE-LUXE..................................... 10-20 51
KING 10-20 52-53
MONARCH................................... 10-15 53-54
WALLIS ORIGINAL..................... 10-20 55-57

EPs: 7–inch 33/45rpm

KING (215/216/217 "House Party")...................................... 15-25 52
(Price is for any of three volumes.)

LPs: 10/12–inch 33rpm

KING (6 "Rhumba Party") 75-100 52
(10–inch LP.)
KING (9 "House Party") 75-100 52
(10–inch LP.)
KING (507 "House Party") 50-100 56
WALLIS ORIGINAL (2 "Ruth Wallis")....................................... 20-30 57

WALSH, Joe

LP '72

Singles: 7–inch

ABC.. 3-5 75-78
ASYLUM 3-5 78-81
DUNHILL....................................... 3-5 73-75
FULL MOON 3-5 80-83
MCA.. 3-5 79

Picture Sleeves

FULL MOON 3-5 80-83

LPs: 10/12–inch 33rpm

ABC.. 5-10 76-78
ASYLUM 5-10 78-81
COMMAND 8-12 74-75
DUNHILL....................................... 8-10 72-74
MCA.. 5-10 79
W.B. 5-8 83-87

Also see EAGLES
Also see JAMES GANG
Also see SIMPSONS
Also see VITALE, Joe

WALSH, Steve

LP '80

Singles: 7–inch

KIRSHNER 3-5 80

LPs: 10/12–inch 33rpm

KIRSHNER 5-10 80

Also see KANSAS

WAMMACK, Travis

P&R '64

Singles: 7–inch

ARA.. 4-8 64-65
ATLANTIC..................................... 4-8 66
CAPRICORN 3-5 75
FAME 3-5 72-73
FRATERNITY (103 "Rock & Roll Blues") 50-100 58

LPs: 10/12–inch 33rpm

CAPRICORN 5-10 75
FAME 8-12 72
PHONORAMA 5-10

WANDERERS

P&R '61

Singles: 78rpm

ONYX (518 "Thinking of You")... 10-15 57

SAVOY (1109 "We Could Find Happiness")............................ 25-45 53

Singles: 7–inch

CUB (9003 "Teenage Quarrel") 15-25 58
CUB (9019 "Collecting Hearts") 25-35 58
CUB (9023 "Please")................ 15-25 58
CUB (9035 "I'm Not Ashamed") 15-25 59
CUB (9054 "I Walked Through a Forest") 15-25 59
CUB (9075 "I Need You More") 15-25 60
CUB (9089 "For Your Love")..... 15-25 61
CUB (9094 "I'll Never Smile Again") 15-25 61
CUB (9099 "She Wears My Ring") 20-40 61
CUB (9109 "As Time Goes By") 15-25 62
MGM (13082 "As Time Goes By") 10-15 62
ONYX (518 "Thinking of You").. 30-40 57
ORBIT (9003 "Teenage Quarrel")............................. 20-30 58
SAVOY (1109 "We Could Find Happiness")...................... 200-300 53
U.A. (570 "After He Breaks Your Heart")................................ 5-10 62
U.A. (648 "I'll Know") 15-25 62

Members: Ray Pollard; Bob Yarborough; Sheppard Grant; Frank Joyner.

WANDERLEY, Walter

P&R/LP '66

Singles: 7–inch

A&M 3-5 69
GNP 3-4 81
TOWER... 3-6 66-67
VERVE... 3-6 66-68
WORLD PACIFIC........................ 3-6 66

LPs: 10/12–inch 33rpm

A&M 5-10 69
CAPITOL..................................... 10-15 63
GNP 5-8 81
PHILIPS 8-12 67
TOWER....................................... 8-15 66-67
VERVE....................................... 8-15 66-68
WORLD PACIFIC........................ 8-15 66-67

Also see GILBERTO, Astrud

WANG CHUNG
(Huang Chung)

P&R/D&D/LP '84

Singles: 12–inch 33/45rpm

GEFFEN...................................... 4-6 84

Singles: 7–inch

GEFFEN...................................... 3-4 84-89

Picture Sleeves

GEFFEN...................................... 3-4 84-89

LPs: 10/12–inch 33rpm

ARISTA 5-8 83
GEFFEN...................................... 5-8 84-89

WANSEL, Dexter

R&B '76

Singles: 12–inch 33/45rpm

PHILADELPHIA INT'L....................4-8 79

Singles: 7–inch

PHILADELPHIA INT'L....................3-5 76-79

LPs: 10/12–inch 33rpm

PHILADELPHIA INT'L..................5-10 76-79

Also see MFSB

WAR

P&R '70

Singles: 12–inch 33/45rpm

MCA...4-8 78-79

Singles: 7–inch

BLUE NOTE..................................3-5 77
COCO PLUM 3-4 85
LAX 3-5 81
MCA...3-5 77-82
PRIORITY 3-4 87
RCA 3-5 82-83
U.A. 3-6 71-78
WAR 3-5 77

Picture Sleeves

MCA...3-5 77
U.A. 3-5 71-75

EPs: 7–inch 33/45rpm

U.A. (92 "The World Is a Ghetto").................................10-15 72
(Promotional issue only. With paper cover.)

LPs: 10/12–inch 33rpm

ABC...8-10 76
BLUE NOTE...................................8-10 76
MCA..8-10 77-82
PRIORITY 5-10 87
RCA 5-10 82-83
U.A. (Except 103)..........................8-10 71-78
U.A. (103 "Radio Free War")...... 15-20 74
(Colored vinyl. Promotional issue only.)

Members: Howard Scott; Lonnie Jordan; Dee Allen; B.B. Dickerson; Lee Oskar; Charles Miller; Harold Brown.

Also see AALON
Also see BURDON, Eric, & War
Also see JORDAN, Lonnie
Also see OSKAR, Lee

WARD, Anita

P&R/R&B/LP '79

Singles: 7–inch

JUANA 3-5 79

LPs: 10/12–inch 33rpm

JUANA 5-10 79

WARD, Billy, & Dominoes

R&B '51

Singles: 78rpm

DECCA 5-10 56-57
FEDERAL (12105 "I'd Be Satisfied")...................................10-20 52
FEDERAL (12106 "Yours Forever") 10-20 52

FEDERAL (12114 "Pedal Pushin' Papa") 20-40 52
FEDERAL (12129 "These Foolish Things") 15-25 53
FEDERAL (12139 thru 12380) 5-15 53-57

Singles: 7–inch

ABC-PAR 10-15 60
DECCA 10-20 56-57
FEDERAL (12105 "I'd Be Satisfied") 100-150 52
FEDERAL (12106 "Yours Forever") 100-150 52
FEDERAL (12114 "Pedal Pushin' Papa") 100-150 52
FEDERAL (12129 "These Foolish Things") 150-200 53
(Gold top label.)
FEDERAL (12129 "These Foolish Things") 50-75 53
(Silver top label.)
FEDERAL (12129 "These Foolish Things") 10-20 50s
(Green label.)
FEDERAL (12139 "Where Now, Little Heart") 40-50 53
FEDERAL (12162 "My Baby's 3-D") 40-60 53
FEDERAL (12178 "Tootsie Roll") 40-50 54
FEDERAL (12184 "Handwriting on the Wall") 30-40 54
FEDERAL (12193 "Above Jacob's Ladder") 20-30 54
FEDERAL (12209 "Can't Do Sixty No More") 40-50 55
FEDERAL (12218 "Cave Man") 20-30 55
FEDERAL (12263 "Bobby Sox Baby") 20-30 57
FEDERAL (12301 "St. Louis Blues") 20-30 57
GUSTO 3-5 80s
JUBILEE (5163 "Come to Me, Baby") 10-20 54
JUBILEE (5213 "Sweethearts on Parade") 10-20 55
KING (1280 "Rags to Riches") .. 25-35 53
KING (1281 "Christmas in Heaven") 40-50 53
KING (1342 "A Little Lie") 20-30 54
KING (1364 "Three Coins in the Fountain") 20-30 55
KING (1368 "Little Things Mean a Lot") 20-30 54
KING (1492 "Learnin' the Blues") 20-30 55
KING (1502 "Over the Rainbow") 20-30 55
KING (5322 thru 6016) 8-15 60-61
LIBERTY 8-15 57-62
RO-ZAN 10-15 62

Picture Sleeves

LIBERTY (55071 "Stardust") 15-25 57

EPs: 7–inch 33/45rpm

DECCA (2549 "Billy Ward & His Dominoes") 50-75 58
FEDERAL (212 "Billy Ward & His Dominoes, Vol. 1") 75-100 55
(Silver top label.)
FEDERAL (262 "Billy Ward & His Dominoes, Vol. 2") 75-100 55
(Silver top label.)
FEDERAL (269 "Billy Ward & His Dominoes, Vol. 3") 75-100 55
(Silver top label.)
FEDERAL (212 "Billy Ward & His Dominoes, Vol. 1") 25-50 57
(Green label.)
FEDERAL (262 "Billy Ward & His Dominoes, Vol. 2") 25-50 57
(Green label.)
FEDERAL (269 "Billy Ward & His Dominoes, Vol. 3") 25-50 57
(Green label.)
LIBERTY (3083 "Yours Forever") 25-40 59
(Price is for any of three volumes.)

LPs: 10/12–inch 33rpm

DECCA (8621 "Billy Ward & His Dominoes") 75-125 58
FEDERAL (94 "Billy Ward & His Dominoes") 5000-7500 54
(10–inch LP.)
FEDERAL (548 "Billy Ward & His Dominoes") 400-800 57
FEDERAL (559 "Clyde McPhatter with Billy Ward & His Dominoes") 500-750 57
KING (548 "Billy Ward & His Dominoes") 75-100 58
KING (559 "Clyde McPhatter with Billy Ward & His Dominoes") 100-200 61
KING (733 "Billy Ward & His Dominoes Featuring Clyde McPhatter & Jackie Wilson") 50-60 61
KING (952 "24 Songs") 20-30 66
KING/GUSTO 5-10
LIBERTY (3056 "Sea of Glass") 40-60 58
LIBERTY (3083 "Yours Forever") 40-60 59
LIBERTY (3113 "Pagan Love Song") 40-60 59
(Monaural.)
LIBERTY (7113 "Pagan Love Song") 50-75 59
(Stereo.)

Members: Clyde McPhatter; Jackie Wilson; Billy Ward; Gene Mumford; Milton Merle; Milton Grayson; William Lamont; Cliff Givens.

Also see DOMINOES
Also see WILSON, Jackie

WARD, Dale

P&R '63

Singles: 7–inch

BIG WAY 4-8 60s
BOYD 4-8 62-65
DOT (16000 series) 4-8 63-65
DOT (17000 series) 3-5 71-72
MONUMENT 4-6 66-69
PARAMOUNT 4-6 69-70

Picture Sleeves

BOYD 10-20 62
Also see WARD, Robin

WARD, Joe

P&R '55

Singles: 78rpm

KING 5-10 55-56

Singles: 7–inch

KING 10-20 55-56

WARD, Robin

P&R/R&B '63

Singles: 7–inch

DOT 4-8 63-64
SONGS UNLIMITED 4-8 63

Picture Sleeves

SONGS UNLIMITED 5-10 63

LPs: 10/12–inch 33rpm

DOT (3555 "Wonderful Summer") 25-35 63
(Monaural.)
DOT (25555 "Wonderful Summer") 35-45 63
(Stereo.)
Also see BOONE, Pat
Also see MARTINDALE, Wink, & Robin Ward
Also see ROBIN
Also see WARD, Dale

WARD, Singin' Sammy

R&B '61

Singles: 7–inch

SOUL (35004 "You've Got to Change") 20-30 64
TAMLA (54030 "What Makes You Love Him") 50-100 61
(With horizontal lines.)
TAMLA (54030 "What Makes You Love Him") 20-40 61
(With Tamla globe logo.)
TAMLA (54049 "What Makes You Love Him") 20-40 62
TAMLA (54057 "Everybody Knew It") 30-40 62
TAMLA (54071 "Part Time Love") 25-35 62

WARE, Leon

R&B '79

Singles: 7–inch

ELEKTRA 3-5 81
FABULOUS 3-5 79
U.A. 3-5 72

LPs: 10/12–inch 33rpm

FABULOUS 5-10 79
GORDY 5-10 76
U.A. 8-12 72

WARING, Fred
(With the Pennsylvanians)

P&R '23

Singles: 78rpm

CAPITOL 3-5 57-58
DECCA 3-6 50-57

Singles: 7-Inch

CAPITOL 3-6 57-59
DECCA 3-8 50-68
REPRISE 3-6 64

EPs: 7-Inch 33/45rpm

CAPITOL 4-8 57-58
DECCA 5-10 50-59

LPs: 10/12-Inch 33rpm

CAPITOL 5-15 57-69
DECCA 5-20 50-68
HARMONY 5-10 69
MCA 5-8 77
MEGA 5-8 71
REPRISE 5-15 64-65
RCA 5-10 68
Also see SINATRA, Frank, Bing Crosby, & Fred Waring

WARNER MACK: see MACK, Warner

WARNES, Jennifer
(Jennifer Warren)

P&R/C&W/LP '77

Singles: 12–inch 33/45rpm

20TH FOX ("It Goes Like It Goes") 4-8 79
(Shown as by Jennifer Warnes. No selection number used.)
20TH FOX (379 "It Goes Like It Goes") 8-10 79
(Shown as by Jennifer Warren.)

Singles: 7–inch

ARISTA 3-4 77-82
CYPRESS 3-4 87
PARROT 3-6 68
W.B. 3-5 83

LPs: 10/12–inch 33rpm

ARISTA 5-10 76-82
CYPRESS 5-8 87
REPRISE 5-10 72
Also see COCKER, Joe, & Jennifer Warnes
Also see JENNIFER
Also see MEDLEY, Bill, & Jennifer Warnes

WARNES, Jennifer, & Chris Thompson

P&R '83

Singles: 7–inch

CASABLANCA 3-4 83
Also see THOMPSON, Chris, & Night

WARP 9

R&B '82

Singles: 12–inch 33/45rpm

PRISM 4-6 83-84

Singles: 7–inch

PRISM 3-4 82-84

WARRANT

P&R/LP '89

Singles: 7–inch

COLUMBIA 3-4 89-90

LPs: 10/12–inch 33rpm

COLUMBIA 5-8 89-90

WARREN, Jennifer: see WARNES, Jennifer

WARREN, Rusty

LP '60

Singles: 7–inch

JUBILEE 5-10 60

EPs: 7–inch 33/45rpm

JUBILEE 10-15 62

LPs: 10/12–inch 33rpm

GNP 5-12 74-77
JUBILEE 10-20 60-68

WARRIOR, Jade: see JADE WARRIOR

WARWICK, Dee Dee
(With the Dixie Flyers)

P&R/R&B '65

Singles: 7–inch

ATCO 4-6 70-71
BLUE ROCK 5-10 65
HURT 5-10 66
JUBILEE 5-10 63
MERCURY 4-8 66-69
PRIVATE STOCK 3-6 75
SUTRA 3-5
TIGER 10-20 64

LPs: 10/12–inch 33rpm

ATCO 8-12 70
HERITAGE SOUND 5-8 83
MERCURY 10-15 67-69

WARWICK, Dionne
(Dionne Warwicke)

P&R '62

Singles: 12–inch 33/45rpm

ARISTA 4-6 84

Singles: 7–inch

ARISTA 3-4 79-90
COLLECTABLES 3-4 80s
ERIC 3-4 70s
FOREVER 3-4 80s
MUSICOR 3-5 77
SCEPTER (1200 series) 4-8 62-65
SCEPTER (12000 series) 3-5 65-71
W.B. 3-5 72-78

Picture Sleeves

SCEPTER 3-5 63-71

LPs: 10/12–inch 33rpm

ARISTA 5-8 79-90
CIRCA 5-8
EVEREST 5-8 81
51 WEST 5-8 80s
MFSL 25-50 82
MUSICOR 5-10 77
PHOENIX 5-8 81
PICKWICK 5-10 70s
RHINO 5-8 80s
SCEPTER (Except 200) 10-15 64-72
SCEPTER (200 "March Is Dionne Warwick Month") 20-25 67
(Promotional issue only.)
SCEPTER/COLUMBIA (5139/40 "Dionne") 15-25 67
(Record club issue.)
U.A. 8-10 74
TRIP 8-10 76
W.B. 8-10 72-77

Also see BACHARACH, Burt / Glen Campbell / Dionne Warwick
Also see DIONNE & FRIENDS
Also see DIONNE & KASHIF
Also see GIBB, Barry
Also see HAYES, Isaac, & Dionne Warwick
Also see MATHIS, Johnny, & Dionne Warwick
Also see U.S.A. for AFRICA
Also see WONDER, Stevie / Dionne Warwick

WARWICK, Dionne, & Howard Hewett

R&B '88

Singles: 7–inch

ARISTA 3-4 88

WARWICK, Dionne, & Glenn Jones

R&B '85

Singles: 7–inch

ARISTA 3-4 85

Also see JONES, Glenn

WARWICK, Dionne, & Jeffrey Osborne

P&R/R&B '87

Singles: 7–inch

ARISTA 3-4 87

Picture Sleeves

ARISTA 3-4 87

Also see OSBORNE, Jeffrey

WARWICK, Dionne, & Spinners

P&R/R&B '74

Singles: 7–inch

ATLANTIC 3-5 74

Picture Sleeves

ATLANTIC 3-5 74

Also see SPINNERS

WARWICK, Dionne, & Luther Vandross

P&R/R&B '83

Singles: 7–inch

ARISTA 3-4 83

Picture Sleeves

ARISTA 3-4 83

Also see VANDROSS, Luther
Also see WARWICK, Dionne

WAS (NOT WAS)

R&B '82

Singles: 12–inch 33/45rpm

ISLAND 4-6 82

Singles: 7–inch

CHRYSALIS 3-4 88-90
GEFFEN 3-4 83
ISLAND 3-5 81-82
ZE 3-4 82

Picture Sleeves

CHRYSALIS 3-4 88-90

LPs: 10/12–inch 33rpm

CHRYSALIS 5-8 88-90
GEFFEN 5-8 83
ISLAND 5-8 81

Members: Don Fagenson; David Weiss.

WASHINGTON, Baby

(Jeanette "Baby" Washington; Justine Washington)

R&B '59

Singles: 7–inch

ABC-PAR 4-8 61
A.V.I. 3-5 78
CHECKER 5-10 59
CHESS 3-5 70
COLLECTABLES 3-4 80s
COTILLION 3-6 69-70
J&S 5-10 59
MASTER FIVE 3-5 73-75
NEPTUNE 10-15 60-61
SIXTH AVENUE 3-5 76
SUE 4-8 62-67

LPs: 10/12–inch 33rpm

A.V.I 5-10 78
COLLECTABLES 5-8 87-88
SUE 20-35 63-65
TRIP 8-10 71
UNART 10-20 67
VEEP 10-15 68

Also see HEARTS

WASHINGTON, Baby, & Don Gardner

R&B '73

Singles: 7–inch

MASTER FIVE 3-5 73-74

LPs: 10/12–inch 33rpm

MASTER FIVE 8-10 74

Also see WASHINGTON, Baby

WASHINGTON, Deborah

R&B '78

Singles: 7–inch

ARIOLA 3-5 78

LPs: 10/12–inch 33rpm

ARIOLA 5-10 78

WASHINGTON, Dinah

R&B '48

Singles: 78rpm

APOLLO 5-10 45-47
KEYNOTE 8-15 44
MERCURY 4-8 46-57

Singles: 7–inch

MERCURY (5000 series) 15-25 50-52
MERCURY (7200 series) 10-15 62
(Compact 33 singles.)
MERCURY (8100 & 8200 series) 15-25 50-52
MERCURY (10008 "What a Difference a Day Makes") 10-20 59
(Stereo.)
MERCURY (70046 thru 70968) 10-20 52-56
MERCURY (71000 & 72000 series) 5-15 57-63
ROULETTE 4-8 62-63

Picture Sleeves

MERCURY 8-12 61-62

EPs: 7–inch 33/45rpm

EMARCY 15-25 54-56
MERCURY (3000 thru 3200 series) 15-25 51-57
MERCURY (3300 series) 10-15 60
MERCURY (4000 series) 10-15 61

LPs: 10/12–inch 33rpm

EMARCY (400 series) 8-12 76
EMARCY (26032 "After Hours") 50-75 54
(10–inch LP.)
EMARCY (36011 "For Those in Love") 30-50 55
EMARCY (36028 "After Hours") 30-50 55
EMARCY (36065 "Dinah") 30-50 56
EMARCY (36073 "In the Land of Hi-Fi") 30-50 56
EMARCY (36119 "Dinah Sings Fats Waller") 30-50 57
EMARCY (36130 "Dinah Sings Bessie Smith") 30-50 58
EVEREST 8-10 75
MERCURY (103 "This Is My Story") 20-25 63
MERCURY (121 "Original Queen of Soul") 12-15 69
MERCURY (603 "This Is My Story") 20-25 63
MERCURY (20100 & 20200 series) 30-40 55-58
MERCURY (20400 thru 20900 series) 15-25 59-63
(Monaural.)
MERCURY (21100 series) 10-20 67
MERCURY (25060 "Dinah Washington") 50-85 50
(10–inch LP.)
MERCURY (25138 "Dynamic Dinah") 50-85 51
(10–inch LP.)
MERCURY (25140 "Blazing Ballads") 50-85 51
(10–inch LP.)

MERCURY (25138 "Dynamic Dinah") 50-85 51
(10–inch LP.)
MERCURY (60100 thru 60900 series) 15-30 59-63
(Stereo.)
MERCURY (61100 series)........ 10-15 67
ROSETTA 5-8 84
ROULETTE (100 series).......... 10-12 71-72
ROULETTE (25000 series)....... 15-25 62-65
TRIP 8-10 73-78
WING 15-20 59-64
Also see BENTON, Brook, & Dinah Washington
Also see HAMPTON, Lionel & Dinah Washington
Also see JONES, Quincy
Also see RAVENS & Dinah Washington

WASHINGTON, Dinah / Joe Williams / Sarah Vaughan

LPs: 10/12–inch 33rpm

ROULETTE 15-25 64
Also see VAUGHAN, Sarah
Also see WASHINGTON, Dinah
Also see WILLIAMS, Joe

WASHINGTON, Donna

R&B '81

Singles: 7–inch

CAPITOL.................................... 3-5 81

LPs: 10/12–inch 33rpm

CAPITOL.................................. 5-10 81

WASHINGTON, Ella

P&R/R&B '69

Singles: 7–inch

ATLANTIC................................. 4-8 67
SOUND STAGE.......................... 4-6 67-69

LPs: 10/12–inch 33rpm

SOUND STAGE 10-15 69

WASHINGTON, Grover, Jr.

R&B/LP '72

Singles: 7–inch

COLUMBIA 3-4 87
ELEKTRA.................................. 3-4 79-84
KUDU 3-5 71-78
MOTOWN 3-4 78-83

Picture Sleeves

ELEKTRA.................................. 3-5 80-82

LPs: 10/12–inch 33rpm

COLUMBIA 5-8 87
ELEKTRA.................................. 5-10 79-84
KUDO.. 8-12 71-77
MOTOWN 5-10 78-83
Also see COSBY, Bill
Also see LABELLE, Patti, & Grover Washington Jr.
Also see MATTHEWS, David
Also see WITHERS, Bill

WASHINGTON, Jeanette: see WASHINGTON, Baby

WASHINGTON, Jerry

R&B '73

Singles: 7–inch

EXCELLO 3-5 73

WASHINGTON, Justine: see WASHINGTON, Baby

WATANABE, Sadao, & Roberta Flack

R&B '84

Singles: 7–inch

ELEKTRA...................................3-4 84
Also see FLACK, Roberta

WATERBOYS

LP '88

Singles: 7–inch

ISLAND 3-4 83

LPs: 10/12–inch 33rpm

CHRYSALIS................................5-8 88-90
ISLAND 5-10 83

WATERFRONT

P&R/LP '89

Singles: 7–inch

POLYDOR 3-4 89

Picture Sleeves

POLYDOR 3-4 89

LPs: 10/12–inch 33rpm

POLYDOR 5-8 89

WATERFRONT HOME

D&D '83

Singles: 12–inch 33/45rpm

BOBCAT.....................................4-6 83

WATERS, Ethel

P&R '21

Singles: 78rpm

BLACK SWAN 10-20 21-23
BRUNSWICK.............................10-15 33-34
COLUMBIA 10-15 25-33
CONTINENTAL...........................4-8 46-47
DECCA 8-12 34-38

EPs: 7–inch 33/45rpm

MERCURY..................................15-20 55

LPs: 10/12–inch 33rpm

BIOGRAPH 8-10 70
COLUMBIA 8-12 68-72
CONTINENTAL...........................15-25 61
JAY 25-35 57
MERCURY 30-40 55
WORD..10-15 62

WATERS, Freddie

R&B '77

Singles: 7–inch

KARI...3-5 81
OCTOBER 3-5 77

WATERS, Muddy

R&B '48

Singles: 78rpm

ARISTOCRAT (406 "Sneakin' and Cryin'") 25-35 50
ARISTOCRAT (412 "Rollin' and Tumblin'") 25-35 50
ARISTOCRAT (1302 "Gypsy Woman") 25-35 48
ARISTOCRAT (1305 "I Can't Be Satisfied") 25-35 48
ARISTOCRAT (1306 "Train Fare Home") 25-35 48
ARISTOCRAT (1307 "You're Gonna Miss Me") 25-35 49
ARISTOCRAT (1310 "Streamline Woman") 25-35 49
ARISTOCRAT (1311 "Little Geneva") 25-35 49
CHESS 5-15 50-55

Singles: 7-inch

CHESS (1509 "Country Boy") ... 40-50 52
CHESS (1514 "Looking for My Baby") 40-50 52
CHESS (1526 "Standing Around Crying") 40-50 52
CHESS (1537 "She's All Right") 40-50 53
CHESS (1542 "Who's Gonna Be Your Sweet Man") 40-50 52
CHESS (1550 "Blow, Wind, Blow") 30-40 53
CHESS (1560 "I'm Your Hootchie Coochie Man") 30-40 53
CHESS (1571 "Just Make Love to Me") 30-40 54
CHESS (1579 "I'm Ready") 15-25 54
CHESS (1585 "I'm a Natural Born Lover") 15-25 54
CHESS (1596 "I Want to Be Loved") 15-25 55
CHESS (1600 series) 5-15 55-59
CHESS (1700 series) 5-10 59-61
CHESS (1800 & 1900 series) 4-8 62-66
CHESS (2000 series) 3-8 67-73

LPs: 10/12-inch 33rpm

BLUE SKY 5-10 77-81
CADET CONCEPT 10-15 68-69
CHESS (127 "Fathers and Sons") 15-20 69
CHESS (1427 "The Best of Muddy Waters") 50-100 57
CHESS (1444 "Muddy Waters Sings Big Bill") 40-60 60
CHESS (1449 "Muddy Waters at Newport") 20-30 64
CHESS (1483 "Folk Singer") 15-25 64
CHESS (1500 series) 10-20 66-71
CHESS (50012 thru 50023) 6-12 72-73
CHESS (50033 "Fathers & Sons") 10-15 75
CHESS (60006 "McKinley Morganfield") 10-12 71
CHESS (60013 thru 60035) 6-12 72-75
DOUGLAS 10-15 68
MFSL (201 "Folk Singer") 15-25 94
(Half-speed mastered.)
MUSE 5-10 73
TESTAMENT 10-12 60s

Also see COTTON, James
Also see FOSTER, Leroy, & Muddy Waters
Also see ROGERS, Jimmy
Also see WILLIAMSON, Sonny Boy
Also see WINTER, Johnny

WATERS, Muddy, & Howlin' Wolf

LPs: 10/12-inch 33rpm

CHESS 8-10 74

Also see DIDDLEY, Bo, Howlin' Wolf & Muddy Waters
Also see HOWLIN' WOLF
Also see WATERS, Muddy

WATERS, Roger

(With Madeline Bell, Katie Kissoon, Eric Clapton & Doreen Chanter; with Bleeding Heart Band)

LP '84

Singles: 12-inch

COLUMBIA 4-6 84

Singles: 7-inch

COLUMBIA 3-4 84

LPs: 10/12-inch 33rpm

COLUMBIA 5-10 84-87

Also see BELL, Madeline
Also see CLAPTON, Eric
Also see KISSOON, Mac & Katie
Also see PINK FLOYD

WATKINS, Tip

R&B '77

Singles: 7-inch

H&L 3-5 77

WATLEY, Jody

(With Eric B. & Rakim)

P&R/R&B/LP '87

Singles: 7-inch

MCA 3-4 87-90

Picture Sleeves

MCA 3-4 87-89

LPs: 10/12-inch 33rpm

MCA 5-8 87-89

Also see CYMONE, Andre
Also see SHALAMAR

WATSON, Anthony

R&B '85

Singles: 7-inch

SRO 3-4 85

LPs: 10/12-inch 33rpm

SRO 5-10 85

WATSON, Doc

(With Merle Watson)

C&W '73

Singles: 7–inch

POPPY 3-5 72-74
U.A. 3-5 73-79

LPs: 10/12–inch 33rpm

FLYING FISH 5-8 81
FOLKWAYS 10-20 63-69
LIBERTY 5-8 83
POPPY 6-12 72
U.A. 8-15 75-76
VANGUARD 8-18 64-77
VERVE/FOLKWAYS 10-15 66

Also see ATKINS, Chet, & Doc Watson
Also see FLATT, Lester, Earl Scruggs & Doc Watson

WATSON, Johnny

(Johnny Guitar Watson; Young John Watson; Johnny Watson Trio)

R&B '55

Singles: 78rpm

FEDERAL 15-25 53-54
KEEN 10-15 57
RPM 10-20 55-56

Singles: 7–inch

ALL STAR 10-20 58
ARVEE 10-20 60
CACTUS (118 "Let's Rock") 50-75 59
CLASS 10-20 59
DJM 3-6 77
ESCORT 5-10
FANTASY 3-6 73-75
FEDERAL (12120 "Highway 60") 50-100 53
FEDERAL (12131 "Motor Head Baby") 50-100 53
FEDERAL (12143 "I Got Eyes") 50-100 53
FEDERAL (12157 "What's Going On") 50-100 53
FEDERAL (12175 "Half Pint of Whiskey") 50-100 54
FEDERAL (12183 "Gettin' Drunk") 50-100 54
GOTH 10-20 60
HIGHLAND 10-20 60s
KEEN (4005 "Gangster of Love") 15-25 57
KEEN (4023 "Deana Baby") 15-25 57
KENT 5-10 60
KING 4-8 61-64
OKEH 5-15 66-67
RPM (423 "Hot Little Mama") 20-30 55
RPM (431 "Too Tired") 20-30 55
RPM (436 "Those Lonely, Lonely Nights") 20-30 55
RPM (447 "Oh, Baby") 20-30 55
RPM (455 "Three Hours Past Midnight") 20-30 55
RPM (471 "She Moves Me") 20-30 55
VALLEY VUE 3-4 84

LPs: 10/12–inch 33rpm

A&M 5-10 81
BIG TOWN 8-10 77
CADET 10-15 67
CHESS (1490 "Blues/Soul") 30-50 64
DJM 5-10 76-81
FANTASY 5-10 73-81
KING (857 "Johnny Guitar Watson") 50-75 63
OKEH 10-15 67
MCA 5-10 81

Also see BLAND, Bobby / Johnny Guitar Watson
Also see OTIS, Johnny
Also see SHIELDS
Also see WATSONIAN INSTITUTE
Also see WILLIAMS, Larry, & Johnny Watson

WATSON, Paula

R&B '48

Singles: 78rpm

MONOGRAM 4-8 49
SUPREME 4-8 48-49

WATSON, Young John: see WATSON, Johnny

WATSONIAN INSTITUTE

LP '78

Singles: 7–inch

DJM 3-5 78

LPs: 10/12–inch 33rpm

DJM 5-10 78

Also see WATSON, Johnny

WATTS, Ernie

LP '82

Singles: 7–inch

QWEST 3-4 82

LPs: 10/12–inch 33rpm

QWEST 5-10 82

WATTS, Noble

(Noble "Thin Man" Watts & His Rhythm Sparks; Noble Watts Quintet; with Paul "Hucklebuck" Williams)

P&R '57

Singles: 78rpm

BATON 5-10 57
DELUXE 8-12 54

Singles: 7–inch

BATON (246 "Easy Going") 8-12 57
BATON (249 "The Slop") 10-20 57
BATON (249 "Hard Times") 6-12 57
(Note title change.)
BATON (251 thru 266) 6-12 57-59
BRUNSWICK 4-8 68
CLAMIKE 5-10 63-64
CUB 8-10 60
DELUXE (6066 "Mashing Potatoes") 10-15 54
DELUXE 8-12 54

ENJOY 5-10 63
JELL ("Florida Shake") 5-10 62
(No selection number used.)
SIR 5-10 60
Also see WILLIAMS, Paul

WATTS, Noble, & June Bateman

Singles: 7-inch

ENJOY 4-8 63
Also see WATTS, Noble

WATTS 103rd ST. RHYTHM BAND
(Featuring Charles Wright)

P&R/R&B '67

Singles: 7-inch

KEYMEN 4-8 67
W.B. 4-8 68-71

LPs: 10/12-inch 33rpm

W.B. 10-15 68-71
Also see WRIGHT, Charles

WAX

R&B '81

Singles: 12-inch 33/45rpm

RCA 4-6 86

Singles: 7-inch

RCA 3-4 81-86

LPs: 10/12-inch 33rpm

COTILLION 5-10 80
RCA 5-8 81-86
Members: Graham Gouldman; Andrew Gold.
Also see GOLD, Andrew
Also see 10CC

WAYBILL, Fee

LP '84

Singles: 7-inch

CAPITOL 3-4 84

LPs: 10/12-inch 33rpm

CAPITOL 5-8 84
Also see MARX, Richard
Also see TUBES

WAYLON & WILLIE: see JENNINGS, Waylon, & Willie Nelson

WAYNE, James
(James Waynes; Wee Willie Wayne)

R&B '51

Singles: 78rpm

ALADDIN 5-10 54
IMPERIAL 5-15 51-57
MILLION 5-10 54
PEACOCK 5-10 57
SITTIN' in WITH 5-15 51-52

Singles: 7-inch

ANGELTONE 5-10 60
ALADDIN 20-30 54
IMPERIAL (5200 series) 20-40 53
IMPERIAL (5300 series) 15-25 55
IMPERIAL (5600 & 5700 series) 4-8 60-61
MILLION 20-30 54
PEACOCK 10-15 57

LPs: 10/12-inch 33rpm

IMPERIAL (9144 "Travelin' Mood") 50-75 61
Also see CHARLES, Ray / Arbee Stidham / Li'l Son Jackson / James Wayne

WAYNE, John

LP '73

Singles: 7-inch

CASABLANCA 3-4 79
RCA 3-5 73

LPs: 10/12-inch 33rpm

RCA (3000 series) 5-10 79-81
RCA (4828 "America") 15-25 73

WAYNE, Thomas
(With the DeLons)

P&R/R&B '59

Singles: 7-inch

CAPEHART 4-8 61
CHALET 3-5 69
COLLECTABLES 3-4 80s
ERIC 3-4 70s
FERNWOOD (Except 106) 10-20 59-60
FERNWOOD (106 "You're the One That Done It") 50-75 58
MERCURY (71287 "You're the One That Done It") 30-50 58
MERCURY (71454 "You're the One That Done It") 20-30 59
OLDIES 45 .... 4-6 64
PHILLIPS INT'L 5-10 62
RACER 4-8 65
SANTO 5-10 62

WAYNE, Wee Willie: see WAYNE, James

WAYNES, James: see WAYNE, James

WAYSTED

LP '87

LPs: 10/12-inch 33rpm

CAPITOL 5-8 87

WE FIVE

P&R/LP '65

Singles: 7-inch

A&M 4-8 65-69
MGM 3-5 73
VAULT 4-8 67
VERVE 3-5 68-73

LPs: 10/12-inch 33rpm

A&M 15-20 65-69
A.V.I. 5-10 77
VAULT 10-15 70
Members: Mike Stewart; Pete Fullerton; Beverly Bivens; Bob Jones; Jerry Burgan.

WE the PEOPLE

R&B '72

Singles: 7-inch

DAVEL 4-8 75
IMPERIAL 4-8 69
LION 3-6 72-74

MAP CITY 4-8 69
REENA.. 4-8 68
VERVE 4-6 71

LPs: 10/12-inch 33rpm

CENTURY ADVENT (5262 "We the People") 10-15 73

WEAPONS of PEACE

R&B '76

Singles: 7-inch

PLAYBOY 3-5 76-77

LPs: 10/12-inch 33rpm

PLAYBOY 5-10 77

Also see HENDERSON, Finis

WEATHER GIRLS

R&B '82

Singles: 12-inch 33/45rpm

COLUMBIA 4-6 83-85

Singles: 7-inch

COLUMBIA 3-4 83-85

LPs: 10/12-inch 33rpm

COLUMBIA 5-10 84

Member: Martha Wash.
Also see BLACK BOX
Also see TWO TONS O' FUN

WEATHER REPORT

LP '71

Singles: 7-inch

COLUMBIA 3-5 73-84

LPs: 10/12-inch 33rpm

ARC/COLUMBIA........................ 5-10 78-82
COLUMBIA 5-10 71-86

Also see PASTORIUS, Jaco
Also see SHORTER, Wayne

WEATHERLY, Jim

P&R/LP '74

Singles: 7-inch

ABC.. 3-5 76-77
BUDDAH 3-5 74-75
ELEKTRA...................................... 3-5 79-80
ERIC... 3-5 78
RCA.. 3-5 72-74
20TH FOX 4-8 65

Picture Sleeves

BUDDAH 3-5 74

LPs: 10/12-inch 33rpm

ABC.. 5-10 77
BUDDAH 5-10 74-75
RCA.. 8-12 72

WEATHERS, Carl

R&B '81

Singles: 7-inch

MIRAGE 3-5 81

WEATHERS, Oscar

R&B '70

Singles: 7-inch

BLUE CANDLE 3-5 73
TOP & BOTTOM 3-6 69-72

WEAVER, Dennis
(With the Good Time People)

LP '72

Singles: 7-inch

CASCADE.....................................5-10 59
CENTURY CITY 3-6 69
EVA..4-8 63
IM'PRESS 3-5 72
OVATION......................................3-5 75
W.B. 4-8 63

LPs: 10/12-inch 33rpm

IM'PRESS 8-10 72
OVATION....................................5-10 75

WEAVERS
(With Gordon Jenkins' Orchestra)

P&R '50

Singles: 78rpm

DECCA 3-5 50-57

Singles: 7-inch

DECCA (27000 thru 29000 series) 5-10 50-55
DECCA (31000 series) 4-8 62
NSD 3-5 82
VANGUARD...................................4-8 60-62

EPs: 7-inch 33/45rpm

DECCA 5-15 51-52

LPs: 10/12-inch 33rpm

DECCA (173 "Best of the Weavers") 10-15 65
(Monaural.)
DECCA (7173 "Best of the Weavers") 10-15 65
(Stereo.)
DECCA (5285 "Folk Songs") 20-40 51
(10-inch LP.)
DECCA (5373 "Merry Christmas") 20-40 52
(10-inch LP.)
DECCA (74277 "Weavers Gold")......................................10-15 70
VANGUARD (15-16 "Greatest Hits") 8-12 71
VANGUARD (2000 series) 10-20 59-63
VANGUARD (3000 thru 6000 series) 8-15 67-70
VANGUARD (9000 series) 12-25 56-63
VANGUARD (9100 series) 10-20 65

Members: Pete Seeger; Lee Hays; Fred Hellerman; Ronnie Gilbert.
Also see JENKINS, Gordon, & His Orchestra
Also see SEEGER, Pete

WEAVERS & Terry Gilkyson

Singles: 7-inch

DECCA 4-8 51

Singles: 7-inch

DECCA 8-10 51

Also see GILKYSON, Terry
Also see WEAVERS

WEBB, Jack
(With Jazz Combo; with Billy May's Orchestra)
LP '55

Singles: 7-inch
W.B. (5003 "You'd Never Know the Old Place Now") 5-10 58

EPs: 7-inch 33/45rpm
RCA (0342/3 "Christmas Story") 15-25 50s
RCA (1126 "Pete Kelly's Blues") 20-35 55
RCA (3199 "Christmas Story") 50-100 53

LPs: 10/12-inch 33rpm
RCA (1126 "Pete Kelly's Blues") 30-50 55
RCA (2053 "Pete Kelly's Blues") 20-30 59
RCA (3199 "Christmas Story") 75-125 53
(10-inch LP.)
W.B. (B-1207 "You're My Girl") . 30-50 58
(Monaural.)
W.B. (BS-1207 "You're My Girl") 50-100 58
(Stereo.)
W.B. (B-1217 "Pete Kelly Lets His Hair Down") 30-50 58
(Monaural.)
W.B. (BS-1217 "Pete Kelly Lets His Hair Down") 50-100 58
(Stereo.)

Members: Jack Webb; Matty Matlock; Dick Cathcart; Nick Fatool; Elmer "Moe" Schneider; George Van Eps; Ray Sherman; Jud DeNaut.

WEBB, Lance
R&B '84

Singles: 7-inch
BEANTOWN 3-5 84

WEBB, Paula
P&R '75

Singles: 7-inch
WESTBOUND 3-5 75

WEBBER, Andrew Lloyd
LP '91

Singles: 7-inch
MCA 3-5 78

LP: 10/12-inch 33rpm
MCA 5-10 91

WEBER, Joan
P&R '54

Singles: 78rpm
COLUMBIA 3-5 54-56

Singles: 7-inch
COLUMBIA 5-10 54-56
CROSLEY 4-6 63
MAPLE 4-6 61

EPs: 7-inch 33/45rpm
COLUMBIA 5-10 55

WEBS
R&B '67

Singles: 7-inch
GUYDEN (2090 "Question") 15-25 63
MGM 5-10 66
POPSIDE 8-15 67-68
VERVE 5-10 68

WEDNESDAY
P&R '73

Singles: 7-inch
BUDDAH 3-5 75
CELEBRATION 3-5 76
SKY 3-5 76
SUSSEX 3-5 73-74

LPs: 10/12-inch 33rpm
SUSSEX 8-10 74

WEE GEE
R&B '78

Singles: 7-inch
COTILLION 3-5 80
JUNEY 3-5 78

WEEKS & CO.
R&B '81

Singles: 12-inch 33/45rpm
SALSOUL 4-6 83

Singles: 7-inch
CHEZ RO 3-5 81
SALSOUL 3-4 83

LPs: 10/12-inch 33rpm
SALSOUL 5-8 83

Member: Richie Weeks.

WEIR, Bob
LP '72

Singles: 7-inch
ARISTA (315 "Bombs Away") 4-6 77
ARISTA (336 "I'll Be Doggone"). 10-15 77
(Promotional issue only.)
W.B. 8-12 72

LPs: 10/12-inch 33rpm
ARISTA 5-10 78
W.B. (2627 "Ace") 25-30 72

Also see BOBBY & MIDNITES
Also see GRATEFUL DEAD
Also see KINGFISH

WEIR, Frank, Orchestra
P&R '54

Singles: 78rpm
CAPITOL 3-5 56
COLUMBIA 3-5 57
LONDON 3-5 54-57

Singles: 7-inch
CAPITOL 4-8 56
COLUMBIA 4-8 57
LONDON 4-8 54-63

EPs: 7-inch 33/45rpm
LONDON 5-10 54-55

LPs: 10/12-inch 33rpm

COLUMBIA ... 10-20 57
LONDON ... 10-20 54

WEISBERG, Tim

LP '73

Singles: 7-inch

A&M ... 3-5 71-79
MCA ... 3-5 79
U.A. ... 3-5 77-80

LPs: 10/12-inch 33rpm

A&M ... 5-10 73-79
MCA ... 5-10 79-80
NAUTILUS ... 10-15 80
U.A. ... 5-10 77-78

Also see FOGELBERG, Dan, & Tim Weisberg

WEISSBERG, Eric

(With Steve Mandell; with Deliverance; with Marshall Brickman)

P&R/C&W/LP '73

Singles: 7-inch

EPIC ... 3-5 75
W.B. ... 3-5 72-73

LPs: 10/12-inch 33rpm

ELEKTRA ... 15-25 63
W.B. ... 5-10 73

Also see TARRIERS

WELCH, Bob

P&R/LP '77

Singles: 7-inch

CAPITOL ... 3-5 77-81
RCA ... 3-4 81-83

Picture Sleeves

CAPITOL ... 3-5 78-81

LPs: 10/12-inch 33rpm

CAPITOL (Except 16000 series) . 8-10 77-80
CAPITOL (16000 series) ... 5-8 80-82
RCA ... 5-10 81-83

Promotional LPs

CAPITOL (11663 "French Kiss") ... 25-30 79
(Picture disc.)

Also see FLEETWOOD MAC
Also see PARIS

WELCH, Lenny

(Lenny & the Storks)

P&R/R&B '60

Singles: 7-inch

ATCO ... 3-5 72
BARNABY ... 3-5 76
BIG TREE ... 3-5 78-83
CADENCE (Except 1422) ... 5-15 59-64
CADENCE (1422 "Congratulations Baby") ... 10-20 62
COLUMBIA ... 4-8 67
COMMONWEALTH UNITED ... 4-6 69
DECCA ... 5-10 59
JASON SCOTT ... 4-6
KAPP ... 5-15 65-67
MAINSTREAM ... 3-5 73-74
MERCURY ... 4-8 68
ROULETTE ... 3-6 71

LPs: 10/12-inch 33rpm

CADENCE ... 15-25 64
COLUMBIA ... 10-20 65
KAPP ... 10-20 66-67

WELK, Lawrence, & His Orchestra

P&R '38

Singles: 78rpm

CORAL ... 3-4 50-57
DECCA ... 3-5 42-45
MERCURY ... 3-4 50-55
OKEH ... 3-5 41
VOCALION ... 3-6 38-39

Singles: 7-inch

CORAL ... 3-5 50-66
DOT ... 3-5 59-67
MERCURY ... 3-5 50-55
RANWOOD ... 3-4 68-77

EPs: 7-inch 33/45rpm

CORAL ... 4-8 50-58
DOT ... 3-6 59-60
MERCURY ... 4-8 50-55

LPs: 10/12-inch 33rpm

CORAL ... 5-15 50-65
DECCA ... 5-10 72
DOT ... 5-15 59-67
HAMILTON ... 4-8 64-66
HARMONY ... 4-8 68-70
MCA ... 4-8 74-76
RANWOOD ... 4-8 68-85
SUNNYVALE ... 4-6 79
TRADITION ... 4-8 75
VOCALION ... 4-8 59-70
WING ... 4-8 60-62

Also see FOLEY, Red
Also see HODGES, Johnny, & Lawrence Welk
Also see HUDSON, Emperor Bob, & Lawrence Welk
Also see LENNON SISTERS
Also see McGUIRE SISTERS
Also see PRESLEY, Elvis / Lawrence Welk

WELL RED

R&B '87

Singles: 7-inch

VIRGIN ... 3-4 87

WELLER, Freddy

C&W/LP '69

Singles: 7-inch

ABC/DOT ... 3-5 75
APT ... 4-8 65
COLUMBIA ... 3-6 69-80
DORE ... 5-10 61

LPs: 10/12-inch 33rpm

COLUMBIA ... 5-10 69-80
EPIC ... 8-10 74
51 WEST ... 5-8

Also see REVERE, Paul, & Raiders

WELLES, Orson

LP '70

LPs: 10/12-inch 33rpm

MEDIARTS 8-12 70

Also see CROSBY, Bing, and Orson Welles

WELLS, Brandi

R&B '81

Singles: 7-inch

WMOT 3-5 81-82

WELLS, Jean

R&B '67

Singles: 7-inch

ABC-PAR 4-8 65
CALLA 4-8 67-68
VOLARE 4-6 69

WELLS, Junior

(With His Eagle Rockers; Junior Wells' Chicago Blues Band)

R&B '60

Singles: 78rpm

STATES 15-25 52-53

Singles: 7-inch

BLUE ROCK 4-8 68-69
BRIGHT STAR 5-10 66-67
CHIEF 10-20 57-62
PROFILE 5-10 59-60
SHAD 8-12 59
STATES (122 "Cut That Out") 100-150 52
(Colored vinyl.)
STATES (134 "Hodo Man") ... 100-150 53
(Colored vinyl.)
STATES (139 "Lawdy Lawdy") 100-150 53
(Colored vinyl.)
STATES (143 "So All Alone") 150-250 53
(Colored vinyl.)
U.S.A. 5-10 63-64
VANGUARD 4-8 67

LPs: 10/12-inch 33rpm

BLUE ROCK 10-15 68
DELMARK 10-15 66-69
VANGUARD 10-20 66-68

Also see COTTON, James, Carey Bell, Junior Wells & Billy Branch
Also see DIXON, Willie
Also see LENOIR, J.B.
Also see WATERS, Muddy

WELLS, Junior, & Buddy Guy

LPs: 10/12-inch 33rpm

ATCO 8-12 72
BLIND PIG 5-8 82
INTERMEDIA 5-8

Also see WELLS, Junior

WELLS, Kitty

C&W/P&R '52

Singles: 78rpm

DECCA 3-6 52-57

Singles: 7-inch

CAPRICORN 3-5 74-76
DECCA (28000 & 29000 series) .. 5-10 52-56
DECCA (30000 thru 32000 series) 3-8 56-71
MCA 3-4 73
RUBOCA 3-5 79-80

Picture Sleeves

DECCA 4-6 69

EPs: 7-inch 33/45rpm

DECCA 5-15 55-65

LPs: 10/12-inch 33rpm

CAPRICORN 6-10 74
DECCA (174 "Kitty Wells Story") 15-25 63
(Monaural. Includes booklet.)
DECCA (7-174 "Kitty Wells Story") 20-30 63
(Stereo. Includes booklet.)
DECCA (4075 thru 4929) 10-25 61-67
(Monaural.)
DECCA (7-4075 thru 7-4929) 15-30 61-67
(Stereo.)
DECCA (7-4961 thru 7-5350) 10-15 68-72
(Stereo.)
DECCA (8293 "Country Hit Parade") 35-45 56
(Monaural.)
DECCA (7-8293 "Country Hit Parade") 10-15 68
(Stereo.)
DECCA (8552 "Winner of Your Heart") 35-45 56
DECCA (7-8552 "Winner of Your Heart") 10-15 65
DECCA (8732 "Lonely Street") .. 30-40 58
(Monaural.)
DECCA (7-8732 "Lonely Street") 10-15 65
(Stereo.)
DECCA (8858 "Dust on the Bible") 25-35 59
(Monaural.)
DECCA (7-8858 "Dust on the Bible") 10-15 68
(Stereo.)
DECCA (8888 "After Dark") 30-40 59
(Monaural.)
DECCA (7-8888 "After Dark") 10-15 68
(Stereo.)
DECCA (8979 "Kitty's Choice") .. 25-35 59
(Monaural.)
DECCA (7-8979 "Kitty's Choice") 30-40 59
(Stereo.)
EXACT 5-10 80
IMPERIAL HOUSE 5-10 80
KOALA 5-10 79
MCA 4-8 73-83

MISTLETOE 5-8 80s
PICKWICK/HILLTOP 5-10 70s
ROUNDER 5-8 82
RUBOCA 8-12 79
SUFFOLK MARKETING 5-10 80
VOCALION 8-15 66-69

Also see ACUFF, Roy, & Kitty Wells
Also see PARTON, Dolly / Kitty Wells
Also see PIERCE, Webb, & Kitty Wells

WELLS, Kitty, & Roy Drusky

C&W '60

Singles: 7-inch

DECCA 4-8 60

Also see DRUSKY, Roy

WELLS, Kitty, & Red Foley

C&W '54

Singles: 78rpm

DECCA 3-5 54-56

Singles: 7-inch

DECCA (29000 series) 5-10 54-56
DECCA (32000 series) 3-6 67-69

EPs: 7-inch 33/45rpm

DECCA 8-12 59

LPs: 10/12-inch 33rpm

DECCA 12-25 61-67

Also see FOLEY, Red

WELLS, Kitty, & Webb Pierce

C&W '57

Singles: 7-inch

DECCA 4-10 57-64

EPs: 7-inch 33/45rpm

DECCA 10-15 59

Also see PIERCE, Webb

WELLS, Kitty, & Johnny Wright

C&W '68

Singles: 7-inch

DECCA 3-6 68

Also see WELLS, Kitty

WELLS, Mary

R&B '60

Singles: 12-inch 33/45rpm

EPIC 4-8 82

Singles: 7-inch

ATCO 10-20 66-67
EPIC 3-4 82
JUBILEE 5-15 68-71
MOTOWN (1003 "Bye Bye Baby") 15-25 60
(Pink label.)
MOTOWN (1011 "I Don't Want to Take a Chance") 10-20 61
(Pink label.)
MOTOWN (1011 "I Don't Want to Take a Chance") 8-12 61
(Blue label.)
MOTOWN (1024 thru 1056) 10-20 62-64
MOTOWN (1061 "When I'm Gone") 100-200 65
MOTOWN (1065 "I'll Be Available") 15-25 65
REPRISE 5-10 71-74
20TH FOX 10-20 64-66

Picture Sleeves

MOTOWN (1003 "Bye Bye Baby") 50-75 61
MOTOWN (1011 "I Don't Want to Take a Chance") 25-50 61
MOTOWN (1024 "The One Who Really Loves You") 20-40 62
MOTOWN (1032 "You Beat Me to the Punch") 20-30 62
20TH FOX (590 "He's a Lover")... 5-10 65

EPs: 7-inch 33/45rpm

MOTOWN (60616 "Greatest Hits") 25-50 64

LPs: 10/12-inch 33rpm

ALLEGIANCE 5-10 84
ATCO 15-20 66
EPIC 5-10 81
51 WEST 5-8 83
JUBILEE 10-20 68
MOTOWN (100 & 200 series) 5-10 82
MOTOWN (600 "Mary Wells") 100-125 61
(White label with blue print.)
MOTOWN (605 "The One Who Really Loves You") 75-125 62
MOTOWN (607 "Two Lovers") 50-100 63
MOTOWN (611 "On Stage") 40-60 64
MOTOWN (616 "Greatest Hits") 25-35 64
MOTOWN (617 "My Guy") 40-60 64
MOTOWN (653 "Vintage Stock") 40-60 66
MOVIETONE 15-20 66
POWER PAK 5-8
20TH FOX 20-30 65

Also see GAYE, Marvin, & Mary Wells
Also see MARVELETTES / Mary Wells / Miracles / Marvin Gaye

WELLS, Terri

R&B/D&D '84

Singles: 12-inch 33/45rpm

PHILLY WORLD 4-6 84

Singles: 7-inch

PHILLY WORLD 3-4 84

Also see MFSB

WENDY & LISA

P&R/LP '87

Singles: 7-inch

COLUMBIA 3-4 87-89

Picture Sleeves

COLUMBIA 3-4 87

LPs: 10/12-inch 33rpm

COLUMBIA 5-8 87-89

WERNER, David

LP '79

Singles: 7-inch

EPIC....................3-5 79
RCA....................3-5 74-76

LPs: 10/12-inch 33rpm

EPIC....................5-10 79
RCA....................5-10 75

WERNER, Max

P&R '81

Singles: 7-inch

RADIO....................3-5 81
Also see KAYAK

WESLEY, Fred

(With the Horny Horns; with J.B.s)

R&B '73

Singles: 7-inch

ATLANTIC....................3-5 77
PEOPLE....................3-5 72-74
RSO....................3-5 80

LPs: 10/12-inch 33rpm

ATLANTIC....................8-10 77
Also see BROWN, James, Band
Also see FRED & New J.B.s
Also see J.B.s

WEST, Belinda

R&B '80

Singles: 7-inch

PANORAMA....................3-5 80

WEST, Dr: see DR. WEST

WEST, Dottie

(With Dale West)

C&W '63

Singles: 7-inch

ATLANTIC....................4-8 62
LIBERTY....................3-4 80-83
PERMIAN....................3-4 84-85
RCA (Except 8000 series)....................3-6 66-81
RCA (8000 series)....................4-8 63-66
STARDAY (500 series)....................4-8 60-61
STARDAY (700 series)....................3-6 65
U.A....................3-4 76-80

Picture Sleeves

LIBERTY....................3-5 80-81

LPs: 10/12-inch 33rpm

CAMDEN....................5-10 71-73
COLUMBIA....................5-10 80
LIBERTY....................5-8 81-82
NASHVILLE....................8-12 70s
PERMIAN....................5-8 85
PICKWICK....................5-10 75
RCA....................8-18 65-75
STARDAY....................10-20 64-65
U.A....................5-10 73-80
Session: Jordanaires.
Also see DEAN, Jimmy, & Dottie West
Also see REEVES, Jim, & Dottie West
Also see ROGERS, Kenny, & Dottie West

WEST, Dottie, & Don Gibson

C&W '70

Singles: 7-inch

RCA....................3-5 69-70

LPs: 10/12-inch 33rpm

RCA....................8-12 69
Also see GIBSON, Don

WEST, Dottie / Melba Montgomery

LPs: 10/12-inch 33rpm

STARDAY....................10-20 65
Also see MONTGOMERY, Melba
Also see WEST, Dottie

WEST, Leslie

(Leslie West Band)

LP '69

Singles: 7-inch

PHANTOM....................3-5 75-76

LPs: 10/12-inch 33rpm

PHANTOM....................8-10 75-76
WINDFALL....................10-15 69
Also see JAGGER, Mick
Also see MOUNTAIN
Also see WEST, BRUCE & LAING

WEST, Mae

(With Somebody's Chyldren)

P&R '33

Singles: 78rpm

BRUNSWICK....................10-20 33

Singles: 7-inch

MGM (14491 "Great Balls of Fire") 4-8 73
PLAZA....................5-10 62
TOWER....................5-10 66
20TH FOX (6718 "Hard to Handle")....................15-30 70

EPs: 7-inch 33/45rpm

DECCA (838 "Fabulous Mae West")....................50-75 55
(Three-EP set.)

LPs: 10/12-inch 33rpm

DAGONET....................10-15 66
DECCA (9016 "Fabulous Mae West")....................40-60 55
DECCA (79016 "Fabulous Mae West")....................10-15 70
MGM (4869 "Great Balls of Fire")....................10-20 72
TOWER....................15-25 66
Also see FIELDS, W.C.

WEST, BRUCE & LAING

LP '72

Singles: 7-inch

COLUMBIA....................3-5 73

LPs: 10/12-inch 33rpm

COLUMBIA....................8-10 74
COLUMBIA/WINDFALL....................8-12 72-74
Members: Leslie West; Jack Bruce; Corky Laing.
Also see BRUCE, Jack
Also see LAING, Corky
Also see MOUNTAIN
Also see WEST, Leslie

WEST COAST CREW

R&B '86

Singles: 7–inch

KMA 3-4 86

WEST COAST RAP ALL STARS

LP '90

LPs: 10/12–inch 33rpm

W.B. 5-8 90

WEST STREET MOB

P&R/R&B '81

Singles: 12–inch 33/45rpm

SUGAR HILL 4-6 81-83

Singles: 7–inch

SUGAR HILL 3-4 81-83

LPs: 10/12–inch 33rpm

SUGAR HILL 5-10 82

Members: Reggie Griffin.
Also see GRIFFIN, Reggie, & Technofunk

WESTON, Kim

P&R/R&B '63

Singles: 7–inch

ENTERPRISE 3-5 74
GORDY 10-20 65-66
MGM 10-20 67-68
MIKIM 3-5 71-72
PEOPLE 5-15 69-70
PRIDE 3-5 70
TAMLA 15-25 63-65
VOLT 10-15 71

Picture Sleeves

MGM 4-8 67

EPs: 7–inch 33/45rpm

MOTOWN (2005 "Kim Weston") 15-25
MOTOWN (2015 "Rock Me a Little While") 15-25

LPs: 10/12–inch 33rpm

ENTERPRISE 8-12 74
MGM 15-25 67-68
VOLT 10-15 71

Also see GAYE, Marvin, & Kim Weston
Also see NASH, Johnny, & Kim Weston

WESTON, Paul, Orchestra

LP '55

Singles: 78rpm

CAPITOL 3-5 45-57
COLUMBIA 3-4 50-56

Singles: 7–inch

CAPITOL 4-8 57-60
COLUMBIA 4-8 50-56

EPs: 7–inch 33/45rpm

COLUMBIA 5-10 50-56

LPs: 10/12–inch 33rpm

CAPITOL 5-15 57-61
COLUMBIA 5-15 50-56
CORINTHIAN 4-8 78
HARMONY 4-8 72

Also see EDWARDS, Jonathan & Darlene
Also see STAFFORD, Jo

WET WET WET

P&R/LP '88

Singles: 7–inch

UNI 3-4 88

Picture Sleeves

UNI 3-4 88

LPs: 10/12–inch 33rpm

UNI 5-8 88

WET WILLIE

LP '73

Singles: 7–inch

CAPRICORN 3-5 74-78
EPIC 3-5 77-79

LPs: 10/12–inch 33rpm

CAPRICORN 5-10 71-78
EPIC 5-10 78-79

Member: Jimmy Hall.
Also see HALL, Jimmy

WHALUM, Kirk

LP '88

LPs: 10/12–inch 33rpm

COLUMBIA 5-8 88

WHAM!

(Wham! U.K.; Featuring George Michael)

P&R/D&D/LP '83

Singles: 12–inch 33/45rpm

COLUMBIA 4-6 82-86

Singles: 7–inch

COLUMBIA 3-4 83-86

Picture Sleeves

COLUMBIA 3-5 82-86

LPs: 10/12–inch 33rpm

COLUMBIA (Except 40062) 5-8 83-86
COLUMBIA (40062 "Make It Big") 8-10 84
(Picture disc.)

Members: George Michael; Andrew Ridgely.
Also see MICHAEL, George
Also see PEPSI & SHIRLIE
Also see RIDGELEY, Andrew

WHAT IS THIS

P&R/LP '85

Singles: 7–inch

MCA 3-4 85

LPs: 10/12–inch 33rpm

MCA 5-8 85

WHATNAUTS

(With the Whatnaut Band)

R&B '70

Singles: 7–inch

A&I 3-5 70
GSF 3-5 73
HARLEM INT'L 3-4 82
STANG 3-5 71

LPs: 10/12–inch 33rpm

STANG 10-20 70-71

Also see MOMENTS & WHATNAUTS

WHEELER, Billy Edd
(With Rashell Richmond)

C&W '64

Singles: 7-inch

CAPITOL 3-5 75-76
KAPP 4-8 63-68
NSD 3-4 80-81
RCA 3-5 70-73
RADIO CINEMA 3-5 79
U.A. 3-6 69

Picture Sleeves

KAPP 4-8 67

LPs: 10/12-inch 33rpm

AVALANCHE 8-10 73
FLYING FISH 5-10 79
KAPP 10-20 64-68
MONITOR 15-25 61-62
RCA 8-10 71
U.A. 8-15 69

WHEELER, Caron

LP '90

LP: 10/12-inch 33rpm

EMI 5-8 90

Also see COSTELLO, Elvis

WHEN in ROME

P&R/LP '88

Singles: 7-inch

VIRGIN 3-4 88-89

Picture Sleeves

VIRGIN 3-4 88-89

LPs: 10/12-inch 33rpm

VIRGIN 5-8 88

WHIRLWIND

P&R/R&B '76

Singles: 12-inch 33/45rpm

ROULETTE 4-8 77

Singles: 7-inch

ROULETTE 3-5 76

WHISPERS

R&B '69

Singles: 12-inch 33/45rpm

SOLAR 4-6 80-84

Singles: 7-inch

COLLECTABLES 3-4 80s
DORE 10-20 65-66
FONTANA 10-20 66
JANUS 3-6 70-75
SOLAR 3-5 79-88
SOUL CLOCK 4-8 69-70
SOUL TRAIN 3-6 75-77

LPs: 10/12-inch 33rpm

ACCORD 5-10 81
ALLEGIANCE 5-8 84
CAPITOL 5-8 90
DORE 5-10 80
JANUS 8-10 72-75
SOLAR 5-10 78-87
SOUL TRAIN 5-10 76-77

Members: Walter Scott; Wallace Scott; Nicholas Caldwell; Marcus Hudson; Leaveil DeGree.

Also see LUCAS, Carrie, & Whispers

WHISTLE

R&B '86

Singles: 12-inch 33/45rpm

SELECT 4-6 86

Singles: 7-inch

SELECT 3-4 86-89

LPs: 10/12-inch 33rpm

SELECT 5-8 86-88

WHITCOMB, Ian
(With Bluesville; with Somebody's Chyldren)

P&R/LP '65

Singles: 7-inch

JERDEN 5-10 64-65
TOWER 4-8 65-68
U.A. 3-5 73

Picture Sleeves

TOWER 4-8 66

LPs: 10/12-inch 33rpm

FIRST AMERICAN 5-10 78-82
SIERRA 5-10 80
TOWER 15-20 65-68
U.A. 8-10 72

WHITE, Artie "Blues Boy"

R&B '77

Singles: 7-inch

ALTEE 3-5 77
RONN 3-5 70s

WHITE, Barry
(With Love Unlimited & Love Unlimited Orchestra; with Glodean)

P&R/R&B/LP '73

Singles: 12-inch 33/45rpm

20TH FOX 4-8 73-78
UNLIMITED GOLD 4-6 83

Singles: 7-inch

A&M 3-4 87
BRONCO 5-10 67
CASABLANCA 3-5 70s
20TH FOX 3-6 73-78
UNLIMITED GOLD 3-4 79-83

LPs: 10/12-inch 33rpm

A&M 5-8 87
SUPREMACY 10-15 74
20TH FOX (Except 1) 5-10 73-81
20TH FOX (1 "Barry White Radio Special") 10-20 70s
(Promotional issue only.)
UNLIMITED GOLD 5-10 79-82

Also see BOB & EARL
Also see JONES, Quincy, James Ingram, Al B. Sure, El DeBarge & Barry White
Also see LOVE UNLIMITED

WHITE, Barry, & Atlantics / Atlantics

Singles: 7-inch

FARO 5-10 63

Also see WHITE, Barry

WHITE, Beverly

R&B '43

Singles: 78rpm

BEACON 5-10 43
DAVIS 4-8 46

Singles: 7-inch

PHILIPS 4-8 62

WHITE, Danny

P&R '77

Singles: 7-inch

ABC-PAR 4-8 64
ATLAS 4-8 66
DECCA 4-8 66-67
DOT 4-8 61
FRISCO 4-8 62
KING (5122 "That's My Doll") 20-30 58
ROCKY COAST 3-5 77
SSS INT'L 3-6 69

WHITE, Danny, & Linda Nail

C&W '83

Singles: 7-inch

GRAND PRIX 3-4 83

WHITE, John

R&B '87

Singles: 7-inch

GEFFEN 3-4 87

WHITE, Karyn

P&R '86

Singles: 7-inch

W.B. 3-4 86-89

Picture Sleeves

W.B. 3-4 86-89

LPs: 10/12-inch 33rpm

W.B. 5-8 88

Also see LORBER, Jeff

WHITE, Kitty

P&R '55

Singles: 78rpm

DECCA 3-5 51
MERCURY 3-5 55-56

Singles: 7-inch

CLOVER 3-6 66
DECCA 5-10 51
DOT 4-8 60
GNP 4-8 59
MERCURY 4-8 55-56

EPs: 7-inch 33/45rpm

EMARCY 5-15 54
PACIFIC JAZZ 8-15 54

LPs: 10/12-inch 33rpm

EMARCY 30-40 54
CLOVER 6-12 66
MERCURY 20-30 55
PACIFIC JAZZ 30-40 54-55

WHITE, Lenny

LP '76

Singles: 7-inch

ELEKTRA 3-5 78-83
NEMPEROR 3-5 76

LPs: 10/12-inch 33rpm

ELEKTRA 5-8 78-83
NEMPEROR 8-10 75-77

Also see RETURN to FOREVER
Also see TWENNYNINE

WHITE, Maurice

P&R/R&B/D&D/LP '85

Singles: 12-inch 33/45rpm

COLUMBIA 4-6 86

Singles: 7-inch

COLUMBIA 3-4 85-86
GOLD 8-12 59
PRIDE 10-20 60

Picture Sleeves

COLUMBIA 3-4 85-86

LPs: 10/12-inch 33rpm

COLUMBIA 5-8 85-86

WHITE, Tony Joe
(With the Mojos; with Waylon Jennings)

P&R/LP '69

Singles: 7-inch

ARISTA 3-5 79
CASABLANCA 3-5 80
COLUMBIA 3-4 83-85
J-BECK 5-8
MONUMENT 4-8 67-70
20TH FOX 3-5 76

LPs: 10/12-inch 33rpm

CASABLANCA 5-10 80
COLUMBIA 5-8 83
MONUMENT 8-15 69-70
20TH FOX 5-10 77
W.B. 8-10 71-73

WHITE LION

LP '87

Singles: 7-inch

ATLANTIC 3-4 87-90

Picture Sleeves

ATLANTIC 3-4 87-89

LPs: 10/12-inch 33rpm

ATLANTIC 5-8 87-90
GRAND SLAM 5-8 88

Members: Mike Tramp; Greg D'Angelo; Jim Lomenzo; Vito Bratta.
Also see ANTHRAX

WHITE PLAINS

P&R/LP '70

Singles: 7-inch

DERAM 3-6 70-73
LONDON 3-5 70s

LPs: 10/12-inch 33rpm

DERAM 10-15 70

Members: Robin Box; Robin Shaw; Pete Nelson; Ricky Wolff; Roger Hills; Tony Burrows.

WHITE WOLF

LP '85

Singles: 7-inch

RCA....................3-4 85-86

LPs: 10/12-inch 33rpm

RCA....................5-8 85-86

WHITEHEAD, Charles
(With the Swamp Dogg Band)

R&B '75

Singles: 7-inch

ISLAND....................3-5 75

LPs: 10/12-inch 33rpm

FUNGUS....................10-15
WIZARD....................5-10 78

WHITEHEAD, John

R&B '88

Singles: 7-inch

MERCURY....................3-4 88

Also see McFADDEN & WHITEHEAD

WHITEHEAD, Kenny & Johnny

R&B '86

Singles: 12-inch 33/45rpm

PHILADELPHIA INT'L....................4-6 86

Singles: 7-inch

PHILADELPHIA INT'L....................3-4 86

LPs: 10/12-inch 33rpm

PHILADELPHIA INT'L....................5-8 86

Also see KENNY & JOHNNY

WHITEMAN, Paul, Orchestra

P&R '20

Singles: 78rpm

CAPITOL....................3-5 42-43
COLUMBIA....................3-6 28-32
CORAL....................3-5 50-56
DECCA....................3-5 38-39
VICTOR....................3-8 20-36

Singles: 7-inch

CORAL....................3-6 50-56

EPs: 7-inch 33/45rpm

CORAL....................4-8 50-56

LPs: 10/12-inch 33rpm

CAPITOL....................5-10 62
CORAL....................5-15 50-56
GRAND AWARD....................5-15 56-59
RCA....................4-8 68-69
WESTMINSTER....................4-8 74

WHITESNAKE

P&R/LP '80

Singles: 12-inch 33/45rpm

GEFFEN....................4-6 86

Singles: 7-inch

GEFFEN....................3-4 82-89
MIRAGE....................3-5 80
U.A. 3-5 79

Picture Sleeves

GEFFEN....................3-4 87-88
MIRAGE....................3-5 80

LPs: 10/12-inch 33rpm

GEFFEN....................5-8 82-89
MIRAGE....................5-10 80-81
U.A. 5-10 79

Members: David Coverdale; Jon Lord; Aynsley Dunbar; John Sykes; Neil Murray; Tommy Aldridge; Rudy Sarzo; Vivian Campbell; Adrian Vandenberg; Steve Vai.

Also see COVERDALE, David
Also see DEEP PURPLE
Also see DUNBAR, Aynsley
Also see LORD, Jon

WHITFIELD, David

P&R '54

Singles: 78rpm

LONDON....................3-5 53-57

Singles: 7-inch

LONDON....................3-8 53-63

EPs: 7-inch 33/45rpm

LONDON....................4-8 54

LPs: 10/12-inch 33rpm

LONDON....................5-15 54-66

Also see MANTOVANI

WHITING, Margaret

P&R '46

Singles: 78rpm

CAPITOL....................3-5 46-56
DOT....................3-5 57

Singles: 7-inch

CAPITOL....................5-10 50-56
DOT....................4-8 57-59
LONDON....................3-6 66-70
VERVE....................4-6 60

EPs: 7-inch 33/45rpm

CAPITOL....................5-10 50-56

LPs: 10/12-inch 33rpm

CAPITOL....................12-25 50-56
DOT....................8-18 57-67
HAMILTON....................5-15 59-65
LONDON....................5-15 67-68
VERVE....................10-20 60

Also see MARTIN, Dean, & Margaret Whiting
Also see TORME, Mel

WHITING, Margaret, & Jimmy Wakely

C&W '49

Singles: 78rpm

CAPITOL....................3-5 50-51

Singles: 7-inch

CAPITOL....................5-10 50-51

EPs: 7-inch 33/45rpm

CAPITOL....................8-15 53

LPs: 10/12-inch 33rpm

PICKWICK....................8-12 67

Also see WHITING, Margaret
Also see WAKELY, Jimmy

WHITLOCK, Bobby

LP '72

Singles: 7–inch

DUNHILL 3-5 72

LPs: 10/12–inch 33rpm

CAPRICORN 8-10 76
DUNHILL 10-12 72

Also see BELL, Maggie, & Bobby Whitlock
Also see DELANEY & BONNIE
Also see DEREK & DOMINOES

WHITMAN, Slim

C&W/P&R '52

Singles: 78rpm

IMPERIAL 3-8 52-57

Singles: 7–inch

CLEVELAND INT'L 3-4 80-82
EPIC 3-4 84
IMPERIAL (5000 series) 4-8 61-63
IMPERIAL (8000 thru 8200 series) 6-15 52-58
IMPERIAL (8300 series) 5-10 59-60
IMPERIAL (50000 series) 3-5 70-71
IMPERIAL (65000 & 66000 series) 3-8 61-69
U.A. 3-8 70-77

EPs: 7–inch 33/45rpm

IMPERIAL 30-50 54-65
RCA (3217 "Slim Whitman Sings and Yodels") 100-150 54

LPs: 10/12–inch 33rpm

CAMDEN 8-12 66
CLEVELAND INT'L 5-10 80-81
EPIC 5-8 84
IMPERIAL (3004 "America's Favorite Folk Artist") 400-500 54
(10–inch LP.)
IMPERIAL (9000 series) 35-50 56-60
(Maroon or black label with "Imperial" at top.)
IMPERIAL (9000 series) 8-15 66
(Black label with "Imperial" on left side.)
IMPERIAL (9100 series) 20-40 60-62
(Black label with "Imperial" at top.)
IMPERIAL (9100 series) 8-15 66
(Black label with "Imperial" on left side.)
IMPERIAL (9200 & 9300 series) 15-25 63-67
IMPERIAL (12100 series) 20-30 62
(Black label with "Imperial" at top.)
IMPERIAL (12100 series) 8-15 66
(Black label with "Imperial" on left side.)
IMPERIAL (12200 & 12300 series) 12-25 65-68
IMPERIAL (12400 series) 8-12 68-69
LIBERTY 5-10 80-82
PICKWICK 5-10
RCA (3217 "Slim Whitman Sings and Yodels") 250-350 54
RCA (3700 series) 5-8 80
SUFFOLK MARKETING 8-12 79-82
SUNSET 8-12 66-70
U.A. 6-12 70-80

Also see WILLIAMS, Hank / Slim Whitman

WHITNEY, Marva

P&R/R&B '69

Singles: 7–inch

KING 4-6 67-69
T-NECK 3-5 70

LPs: 10/12–inch 33rpm

KING 8-12 69

Also see BROWN, James, & Marva Whitney

WHITNEY, Marva, & Ellie Taylor

Singles: 7–inch

EXCELLO 3-5 72

Also see WHITNEY, Marva

WHITTAKER, Roger

P&R/LP '75

Singles: 7–inch

MAIN STREET 3-4 83-84
RCA 3-5 70-86

Picture Sleeves

RCA 3-5 80

LPs: 10/12–inch 33rpm

MAIN STREET 5-8 84
RCA 5-12 70-86

WHIZ KID

R&B '85

Singles: 7–inch

TOMMY BOY 3-4 85

WHO

P&R '65

Singles: 7–inch

ATCO (6409 "Substitute") 20-30 66
ATCO (6509 "Substitute") 10-15 67
DECCA (31725 "I Can't Explain") 15-20 64
DECCA (31801 "Anyway Anyhow Anywhere") 15-25 65
DECCA (31877 "My Generation") 15-25 65
DECCA (31988 "The Kids Are Alright") 15-25 66
DECCA (32058 "I'm a Boy") 15-25 66
DECCA (32114 "Happy Jack") 8-12 67
DECCA (32156 "Pictures of Lily") 8-12 67
DECCA (32206 "I Can See for Miles") 5-10 67
DECCA (32288 "Call Me Lightning") 8-12 68
DECCA (32362 "Magic Bus") 5-10 68
DECCA (32465 "Pinball Wizard") .. 4-8 69
DECCA (32519 "I'm Free") 4-8 69
DECCA (32670 "The Seeker") 5-10 70
DECCA (32708 "Summertime Blues") 5-10 70
DECCA (32729 "See Me, Feel Me") 5-10 70

DECCA (32737 "Young Man Blues") ... 50-75 70
DECCA (32846 "Won't Get Fooled Again") ... 5-10 71
DECCA (32888 "Behind Blue Eyes") ... 5-10 71
DECCA (32983 "Join Together"). 5-10 72
DECCA (33041 "The Relay") ... 5-10 72
LIFE ... 20-30
MCA ... 3-5 74-79
POLYDOR ... 3-5 75-79
TRACK ... 4-8 72-74
W.B. ... 3-5 81-83

Picture Sleeves

DECCA (32114 "Happy Jack").. 10-20 67
DECCA (32465 "Pinball Wizard") 8-12 69
DECCA (32729 "See Me, Feel Me") ... 8-12 70
DECCA (32737 "Young Man Blues") ... 75-125 70
POLYDOR ... 4-6 75-79
W.B. ... 3-5 81-83

Promotional Singles

ATCO (6409 "Substitute") ... 25-35 66
ATCO (6509 "Substitute") ... 10-20 67
DECCA (31725 "I Can't Explain") ... 20-25 64
DECCA (31801 "Anyway Anyhow Anywhere") ... 20-30 65
DECCA (31877 "My Generation") ... 20-30 65
DECCA (31988 "The Kids Are Alright") ... 20-30 66
DECCA (32058 "I'm a Boy") ... 20-30 66
DECCA (32114 "Happy Jack").. 10-20 67
DECCA (32156 "Pictures of Lily") ... 10-20 67
DECCA (32206 "I Can See for Miles") ... 10-15 67
DECCA (32288 "Call Me Lightning") ... 10-15 68
DECCA (32362 "Magic Bus") ... 8-12 68
DECCA (32465 "Pinball Wizard") 5-10 69
DECCA (32519 "I'm Free") ... 5-10 69
DECCA (32670 "The Seeker").. 10-15 70
DECCA (32708 "Summertime Blues") ... 10-15 70
DECCA (32729 "See Me, Feel Me") ... 8-12 70
DECCA (32737 "Young Man Blues") ... 50-75 70
DECCA (32846 "Won't Get Fooled Again") ... 8-12 71
DECCA (32888 "Behind Blue Eyes") ... 8-12 71
DECCA (32983 "Join Together"). 8-12 72
DECCA (33041 "The Relay") ... 8-12 72
DECCA ("Excerpts from *Tommy*") ... 25-35 69
(Boxed set for radio programming. Includes inserts. No number used.)
LIFE ... 20-30
MCA ... 5-10 74-79
POLYDOR ... 5-10 75-79
TRACK ... 5-10 72-74
W.B. ... 4-8 81-83

LPs: 10/12–inch 33rpm

DDL/MCA (16610 "Who Are You") ... 40-50 78
(Half-speed mastered.)
DWJ ("Musical Biography") ... 30-50 78
(Promotional issue only. Not issued with cover.)
DECCA (DL-4664 "My Generation") ... 50-75 66
(Monaural.)
DECCA (DL-4664 "My Generation") ... 75-100 66
(White label. Promotional issue only.)
DECCA (DL7-4664 "My Generation") ... 40-60 66
(Stereo.)
DECCA (DL-4892 "Happy Jack") ... 50-75 67
(Monaural.)
DECCA (DL-4892 "Happy Jack") ... 75-100 67
(White label. Promotional issue only.)
DECCA (DL7-4892 "Happy Jack") ... 40-60 67
(Stereo.)
DECCA (DL-4950 "The Who Sell Out") ... 30-40 67
(Monaural.)
DECCA (DL-4950 "The Who Sell Out") ... 50-75 67
(White label. Promotional issue only.)
DECCA (DL7-4950 "The Who Sell Out") ... 20-30 67
(Stereo.)
DECCA (DL-5064 "Magic Bus"). 50-75 68
(Monaural. White label. Promotional issue only.)
DECCA (DL7-5064 "Magic Bus") ... 25-30 68
DECCA (DXW-7205 "Excerpts from Tommy") ... 100-150 69
(Monaural. White label. Promotional issue only. Includes 12-page booklet.)
DECCA (DXSW-7205 "Tommy") ... 25-35 69
(Stereo. Includes 12-page booklet.)
DECCA (79175 "Live at Leeds") 50-75 70
(White label. Promotional issue only.)
DECCA (79175 "Live at Leeds") 20-30 70
(Includes insert pages.)
DECCA (79182 "Who's Next") ... 15-20 71

DECCA (79184 "Meaty Beaty Big and Bouncy")............................ 15-20 71
MCA (1987 "Who Are You")...... 15-25 78
MCA (2000 series)................... 15-25 74
MCA (2161 "Who By Numbers"). 8-10 75
MCA (3050 "Who Are You")........ 8-10 78
(Black vinyl.)
MCA (3050 "Who Are You")...... 15-20 78
(Colored vinyl.)
MCA (4067 "Happy Jack"/"The Who Sell Out")...................................... 15-25 74
MCA (4068 "My Generation"/"Magic Bus") 15-25 74
MCA (5000 series)....................... 5-8 83-85
MCA (6000 series)................... 10-12 74
MCA (6895 "Quadrophenia") 8-10 80
(Does not have booklet.)
MCA (8000 series)................... 10-12 84
MCA (10004 "Quadrophenia") .. 10-12 81
MCA (10005 "Tommy")............ 10-12 77
MCA (11005 "The Kids Are Alright") 10-20 79
(Price includes 18-page booklet.)
MCA (12001 "Hooligans") 10-12 81
MCA (14950 "Who Are You").... 12-15 79
(Picture disc.)
MCA (19501 "Join Together") 8-12 90
MCA (37000 series)..................... 5-8 79
MFSL.. 15-25 84
TRACK/MCA (2126 "Odds and Sods") 10-20 74
(Includes insert.)
TRACK/MCA (4000 series)....... 10-12 74
TRACK/MCA (10004 "Quadrophenia")...................... 15-20 73
(Includes 44-page booklet.)
W.B. 5-10 81-82

Members: Roger Daltrey; Pete Townshend; John Entwistle; Keith Moon; Kenny Jones.
Also see DALTREY, Roger
Also see ENTWISTLE, John
Also see HIGH NUMBERS
Also see McCARTNEY, Paul / Rochestra / Who / Rockpile
Also see MOON, Keith
Also see SMALL FACES
Also see TOWNSHEND, Pete

WHO / Strawberry Alarm Clock

LPs: 10/12–inch 33rpm

DECCA (734586 "The Who/Strawberry Alarm Clock") 50-75 69
(Philco-Ford Special Products promotional issue.)

Also see STRAWBERRY ALARM CLOCK
Also see WHO

WHODINI

R&B '82

Singles: 12–inch 33/45rpm

JIVE... 4-6 82-86

Singles: 7–inch

JIVE 3-4 82-87

LPs: 10/12–inch 33rpm

JIVE 5-8 84-87

Members: Jalil Hutchins; John Fletcher; Drew Carter.
Also see JACKSON, Millie
Also see KING DREAM CHORUS & HOLIDAY CREW

WHODINI & Millie Jackson

Singles: 7–inch

JIVE 3-4 87

Also see JACKSON, Millie
Also see WHODINI

WHOLE DARN FAMILY

R&B '76

Singles: 7–inch

SOUL INT'L.......................................3-5 76-77

LPs: 10/12–inch 33rpm

SOUL INT'L.....................................8-10 76

WICHITA TRAIN WHISTLE

LP '68

Singles: 7–inch

DOT 5-8 68

LPs: 10/12–inch 33rpm

DOT 15-20 68
PACIFIC ARTS 8-10 78

Member: Michael Nesmith.
Also see NESMITH, Michael

WIDE BOY AWAKE

D&D '83

Singles: 12–inch 33/45rpm

RCA 4-6 83

Singles: 7–inch

RCA 3-5 83

LPs: 10/12–inch 33rpm

RCA 5-10 83

WIDOWMAKER

LP '77

Singles: 7–inch

JET..3-5 76-77

LPs: 10/12–inch 33rpm

U.A. 8-10 76-77

Members: John Butler; Aerial Bender.
Also see GROSVENOR, Luther
Also see LOVE AFFAIR

WIEDLIN, Jane

P&R '83

Singles: 7–inch

EMI...3-4 88
I.R.S. 3-4 85

Picture Sleeves

EMI...3-4 88
I.R.S. 3-4 85-88

LPs: 10/12–inch 33rpm

EMI...5-8 88
I.R.S. 5-8 85

Also see GO-GOs
Also see SPARKS & Jane Wiedlin

WIER, Rusty

P&R/LP '75

Singles: 7-inch

ABC 3-5 74
BLACK HAT 3-4 87
COLUMBIA 3-5 76
COMPLEAT 3-4 83-84
LONGHORN 4-8 65
20TH FOX 3-5 75-76

LPs: 10/12-inch 33rpm

ABC 8-12 74
COLUMBIA 8-10 76
20TH FOX 8-10 75

WIGGINS, Spencer

R&B '70

Singles: 7-inch

FAME 4-8 69-70
GOLDWAX 5-10 66-69

WILBURN BROTHERS

C&W '55

Singles: 78rpm

DECCA 5-8 54-57

Singles: 7-inch

DECCA (29190 thru 30428) 8-15 54-57
DECCA (30591 "Oo Bop Sha Boom") 15-25 58
DECCA (30686 thru 33027) 3-8 58-72
MCA 3-5 73

EPs: 7-inch 33/45rpm

DECCA 5-15 57-62

LPs: 10/12-inch 33rpm

CORAL 5-8 80s
DECCA (4142 thru 4615) 10-20 61-65
DECCA (4721 "Wilburn Brothers Show") 50-75 66
(With Loretta Lynn, Ernest Tubb & Harold Morrison.)
DECCA (4817 thru 5291) 8-15 67-71
DECCA (8000 series) 20-30 58-59
KING 20-30 61
VOCALION 5-15 62-70

Members: Teddy Wilburn; Doyle Wilburn. Session: Anita Kerr Singers.
Also see KERR, Anita
Also see LYNN, Loretta
Also see PIERCE, Webb, & Wilburn Brothers
Also see TUBB, Ernest, & Wilburn Brothers

WILCOX, Eddie, Orchestra

(Featuring Sunny Gale)

R&B '52

Singles: 78rpm

DERBY 3-6 52

Singles: 7-inch

DERBY 10-15 52
(Colored vinyl.)
Also see GALE, Sunny

WILCOX, Harlow

(With the Oakies)

C&W/P&R '69

Singles: 7-inch

IMPEL (002 "Groovy Grubworm") 15-25 68
PLANTATION 4-8 69-70
SSS INT'L 3-5 70s

Picture Sleeves

PLANTATION 4-6 69

LPs: 10/12-inch 33rpm

PLANTATION 5-10 70-71

WILD, Jack

P&R '70

Singles: 7-inch

BUDDAH 3-5 71
CAPITOL 3-5 70

Picture Sleeves

CAPITOL 3-5 70

WILD BLUE

P&R '86

Singles: 12-inch 33/45rpm

CHRYSALIS 4-6 86

Singles: 7-inch

CHRYSALIS 3-4 86

Picture Sleeves

CHRYSALIS 3-4 86

LPs: 10/12-inch 33rpm

CHRYSALIS 5-8 86

WILD CHERRY

P&R/R&B/LP '76

Singles: 12-inch 33/45rpm

EPIC 4-8 76-79

Singles: 7-inch

A&M 3-5 75
BROWN BAG 3-5 72-73
EPIC/SWEET CITY 3-5 76-79

LPs: 10/12-inch 33rpm

EPIC/SWEET CITY 5-10 76-79

Members: Robert Parissi; Allen Wentz; Ronald Beitle; Bryan Bassett.

WILD MAGNOLIAS

R&B '74

Singles: 7-inch

POLYDOR 3-5 74

LPs: 10/12-inch 33rpm

POLYDOR 8-10 74

WILD MAN STEVE

(Steve Gallon)

LP '69

LPs: 10/12-inch 33rpm

RAW 5-12 69-70

WILD ONES

LP '65

Singles: 7-inch

MAINLINE 4-8 65
MALA 4-8 67

U.A. 4-8 65-66

LPs: 10/12-inch 33rpm

U.A. 15-20 65

WILD TURKEY

LP '72

Singles: 7-inch

CHRYSALIS.......... 3-5 72-73
REPRISE.......... 3-5 72

LPs: 10/12-inch 33rpm

CHRYSALIS.......... 8-10 72-73
REPRISE.......... 8-12 72
Also see JETHRO TULL

WILD-CATS

P&R '59

Singles: 7-inch

U.A. (154 "Gazachstahagen")..... 5-10 58
(Monaural.)
U.A. (169 "King Size Guitar")...... 5-10 59
U.A. (1154 "Gazachstahagen"). 15-25 58
(Stereo [reprocessed].)

LPs: 10/12-inch 33rpm

U.A. (3031 "Bandstand Record Hop").......... 35-45 59

WILDE, Danny

LP '88

LPs: 10/12-inch 33rpm

GEFFEN.......... 5-8 88

WILDE, Eugene

R&B '84

Singles: 12-inch 33/45rpm

PHILLY WORLD.......... 4-6 84-86

Singles: 7-inch

MCA.......... 3-4 86
PHILLY WORLD.......... 3-4 84-86

Picture Sleeves

PHILLY WORLD.......... 3-4 85

LPs: 10/12-inch 33rpm

PHILLY WORLD.......... 5-8 84-86

WILDE, Kim

P&R/LP '82

Singles: 12-inch 33/45rpm

MCA.......... 4-6 85

Singles: 7-inch

EMI AMERICA.......... 3-5 82
MCA.......... 3-4 85-88

Picture Sleeves

EMI AMERICA.......... 3-5 82
MCA.......... 3-4 85-88

LPs: 10/12-inch 33rpm

EMI AMERICA.......... 5-10 82
MCA.......... 5-8 85-88

WILDE, Marty

P&R '60

Singles: 7-inch

BELL.......... 3-5 74
EPIC.......... 5-10 58-60

LPs: 10/12-inch 33rpm

EPIC (575 "Wilde About Marty") 30-40 60
(Stereo.)
EPIC (3686 "Bad Boy")..........30-40 60
EPIC (3711 "Wilde About Marty").......... 25-35 60
(Monaural.)
Also see SHANNON

WILDER, Matthew

P&R/R&B '83

Singles: 12-inch 33/45rpm

PRIVATE I.......... 4-6 83-85

Singles: 7-inch

PRIVATE I.......... 3-4 83-85

Picture Sleeves

PRIVATE I.......... 3-4 84

LPs: 10/12-inch 33rpm

PRIVATE I.......... 5-8 83-85

WILDFIRE

P&R '77

Singles: 7-inch

CASABLANCA.......... 3-5 77

WILDWEEDS

P&R '67

Singles: 7-inch

CADET.......... 4-8 67-68
CADET CONCEPT.......... 4-8 68
VANGUARD.......... 3-5 71

LPs: 10/12-inch 33rpm

VANGUARD.......... 10-15 70

WILEY, Ed
(With Teddy Reynolds & King Tut)

R&B '50

Singles: 78rpm

SITTIN' in WITH (Except 545)... 10-15 50

Singles: 7-inch

ATLANTIC (959 "So Glad I'm Free").......... 50-100 51
SITTIN' in WITH (545 "Cry, Cry Baby").......... 75-125 50
Members: Teddy Reynolds; King Tut.

WILEY, Michelle

R&B '77

Singles: 7-inch

20TH FOX.......... 3-5 77

WILL & the KILL

LP '88

LPs: 10/12-inch 33rpm

MCA.......... 5-8 88

WILL POWERS

D&D '83

Singles: 12-inch 33/45rpm

ISLAND.......... 4-6 83

WILL to POWER

P&R/R&B '87

Singles: 7–inch

EPIC 3-4 87-90

LPs: 10/12–inch 33rpm

EPIC 5-8 87-90

WILLESDEN–DODGERS

D&D '84

Singles: 12–inch 33/45rpm

JIVE 4-6 83-84

Singles: 7–inch

JIVE 3-4 83-84

WILLIAMS, Andre

(With the Don Juans; with Five Dollars; with Diablos; Andre "Bacon Fat" Williams & Inspirations; Andre "Mr. Rhythm" Williams)

R&B '57

Singles: 78rpm

EPIC 10-15 57
FORTUNE 10-30 55-57

Singles: 7–inch

AVIN (103 "Rib Tips") 5-10 66
CHECKER 6-12 68-69
EPIC (9196 "Just Because of a Kiss") 10-20 57
FORTUNE (824 thru 856) 20-50 55-60
RIC TIC 10-20 60s
RONALD (1001 "Please Give Me a Chance") 15-20
MIRACLE (4 "Rosa Lee") 300-500 60
SPORT 10-20 67
WINGATE 6-12 66

LPs: 10/12–inch 33rpm

FORTUNE 5-8 86

WILLIAMS, Andre, & Gino Parks

Singles: 7–inch

FORTUNE (839 "Don't Touch") 35-55 57
FORTUNE (851 "Movin'") 25-50 60

Also see WILLIAMS, Andre

WILLIAMS, Andy

P&R '56

Singles: 12–inch 33/45rpm

COLUMBIA 4-6 79

Singles: 78rpm

CADENCE 4-8 56-57

Singles: 7–inch

CADENCE 5-10 56-64
COLUMBIA 3-8 61-79

Picture Sleeves

CADENCE 8-15 59
COLUMBIA 3-5 61-76

EPs: 7–inch

CADENCE 10-15 57-59
COLUMBIA 5-10 62-66
(Jukebox issues only.)

LPs: 10/12–inch 33rpm

CADENCE 20-30 58-62
COLUMBIA 5-15 62-77
COLUMBIA SPECIAL PROD 5-10

WILLIAMS, Andy & David

P&R '74

Singles: 7–inch

BARNABY 3-5 74-75
KAPP 3-5 72-73

LPs: 10/12–inch 33rpm

KAPP 5-10 72

WILLIAMS, Anson

P&R '77

Singles: 7–inch

CHELSEA 3-5 77

Picture Sleeves

CHELSEA 3-5 77

WILLIAMS, Beau

R&B '84

Singles: 7–inch

CAPITOL 3-4 84-87

WILLIAMS, Billy

(Billy Williams Quartet)

P&R '47

Singles: 78rpm

CORAL 3-6 54-57

Singles: 7–inch

CORAL (61200 thru 61800 series) 5-10 54-57
CORAL (61900 thru 65500 series) 4-8 58-64
MCA 3-4 70s
MGM (10000 & 11000 series) 5-10 50-52
MGM (12000 series) 5-8 57
MERCURY 5-10 52-54
RCA 4-8 47

EPs: 7–inch 33/45rpm

CORAL 15-25 57
MGM 15-25 57
MERCURY 15-25 53-55

LPs: 10/12–inch 33rpm

CORAL (57184 "Billy Williams") . 35-45 57
CORAL (57251 "Half Sweet Half Beat") 30-40 59
CORAL (57343 "The Billy Williams Revue") 30-40 60
MGM (3400 "The Billy Williams Quartet") 35-45 57
MERCURY (20317 "Oh Yeah!") . 35-45 58
WING (12131 "Vote for Billy Williams") 30-40 59

Members: Billy Williams; Claude Riddick; John Ball; Eugene Dixon.

Also see CHARIOTEERS

WILLIAMS, Bobby

(Bobby Williams Group)

R&B '76

Singles: 7–inch

CAPITOL 5-10 68
ROCK 'N' ROLL 3-5 76
SURE SHOT (5003 "Try Love") . 10-20 64

SURE SHOT (5005 "Keep On Loving Me").. 10-20 65
SURE SHOT (5013 "When You Play").. 10-20 65
SURE SHOT (5025 "Try It Again") 10-20 66
SURE SHOT (5031 "I'll Hate Myself Tomorrow") 25-50 67

WILLIAMS, Bobby Earl

R&B '74

Singles: 7-inch

IV CHAINS 3-5 74

WILLIAMS, Carol

R&B '76

Singles: 12-inch 33/45rpm

VANGUARD.. 4-6 83

Singles: 7-inch

SALSOUL.. 3-5 76

WILLIAMS, Christopher

P&R '89

Singles: 7-inch

GEFFEN.. 3-4 89

Picture Sleeves

GEFFEN.. 3-4 89

WILLIAMS, Cootie
(With Eddie "Cleanhead" Vinson)

R&B/C&W '44

Singles: 78rpm

DERBY.. 10-15 51
HIT 10-20 44-45

Singles: 7-inch

DERBY (756 "Shotgun Boogie") 50-100 51

LPs: 10/12-inch 33rpm

MOODSVILLE (27 "Solid Trumpet") 20-30 62
(Monaural.)
MOODSVILLE (27-SD "Solid Trumpet") 25-35 62
(Stereo.)
RCA (1718 "In Hi-Fi") 40-60 58
WARWICK (2027 "Do Nothing Till You Hear from Me")........................ 40-60 59

WILLIAMS, Cootie, & Wini Brown

LPs: 10/12-inch 33rpm

JARO (5001 "Around Midnight") 40-60 60

Also see BROWN, Wini
Also see VINSON, Eddie
Also see WILLIAMS, Cootie

WILLIAMS, Danny

P&R/R&B/LP '64

Singles: 7-inch

PILOT.. 4-8 62
U.A. 4-8 61-66

LPs: 10/12-inch 33rpm

U.A. 15-25 63-66

WILLIAMS, Darnell

R&B '83

Singles: 7-inch

MY DISC 3-4 83

WILLIAMS, David

R&B '84

Singles: 7-inch

OCEAN FRONT.. 3-5 84

WILLIAMS, Dee, Sextet

R&B '49

Singles: 78rpm

SAVOY.. 10-20 49

WILLIAMS, Deniece

P&R/R&B '76

Singles: 12-inch 33/45rpm

COLUMBIA 4-8 77-86

Singles: 7-inch

ARC 3-5 79-82
COLUMBIA 3-5 76-88
TODDLIN' TOWN 4-8 60s

Picture Sleeves

COLUMBIA 3-5 84-88

LPs: 10/12-inch 33rpm

ARC 5-10 79-82
COLUMBIA 5-10 76-88

Also see MATHIS, Johnny, & Deniece Williams
Also see WONDER, Stevie

WILLIAMS, Diana

C&W/P&R '76

Singles: 7-inch

CAPITOL.. 3-5 76
LITTLE GEM 3-5 77

WILLIAMS, Don

C&W '72

Singles: 7-inch

ABC.. 3-5 75-78
ABC/DOT 3-5 74-77
CAPITOL.. 3-4 86
DOT 3-5 74
JMI 3-5 72-74
MCA.. 3-4 79-85

LPs: 10/12-inch 33rpm

ABC (Except 28) 5-10 77-78
ABC (28 "Don Williams")............ 10-15 77
(Promotional issue only.)
ABC/DOT 8-10 74-77
CAPITOL.. 5-8 86
JMI 15-20 73-74
MCA (Except 44).. 5-10 75-85
MCA (44 "Expressions") 15-20 78
(Picture disc.)

Also see HARRIS, Emmylou, & Don Williams
Also see POZO SECO SINGERS

WILLIAMS, Eddie
(With His Brown Buddies)

R&B '49

Singles: 78rpm

CRYSTAL.................................. 10-15 50
DISCOVERY 10-15 50
SELECTIVE 10-15 50
SUPREME 10-15 49
SWING TIME 10-15 49
Also see DIXON, Floyd

WILLIAMS, Esther

R&B '76

Singles: 7-Inch

FRIENDS & CO.......................... 3-5 76-78

WILLIAMS, Hank
(With the Drifting Cowboys; Hank Williams as "Luke the Drifter;" with Audrey Williams)

C&W '47

Singles: 78rpm

MGM 5-10 47-55
STERLING (201 "Calling You") 200-400 47
STERLING (204 "Wealth Won't Save Your Soul")......................... 150-300 47
STERLING (208 "I Don't Care")............................... 150-250 47
STERLING (210 "Pan American") 150-250 47

Singles: 7-inch

MGM (100 series) 5-8 60s
MGM (10000 & 11000 series)... 10-20 50-55
MGM (12000 series) 5-15 55-59
MGM (13000 series) 3-6 64-67

EPs: 7-inch 33/45rpm

ARHOOLIE................................. 4-6 83
(Not issued with cover.)
MGM (100 & 200 series)........... 25-50 52-54
MGM (1000 thru 1600 series) ... 15-30 55-60

LPs: 10/12-inch 33rpm

BLAINE HOUSE....................... 15-20 72
BOLL WEEVIL 8-12 76
COLUMBIA (5616 "Hank Williams Treasury") 35-45 60s
(Four-LP set from the Columbia House record club.)
GOLDEN COUNTRY 5-8
MGM (2 "36 of Hank Williams' Greatest Hits") 80-100 57
(Three-LP set.)
MGM (4 "36 More of Hank Williams' Greatest Hits") 80-100 58
(Three-LP set.)
MGM (100 & 200 series)......... 50-100 52-54
(10-inch LPs.)
MGM (240-2 "24 Karat Hits, Hank Williams")...................... 15-20 68
MGM (912 "Hank Williams . . . Reflections by Those Who Loved Him")..... 100-200 75
(Three-LP boxed set. Promotional issue only. Includes guest speakers: Roy Acuff, Little Jimmy Dickens, Lefty Frizzell, Pee Wee King, George Morgan, Bill Monroe, Minnie Pearl, Wesley Rose, Ernest Tubb, Grant Turner, Audrey Williams, Faron Young, and Hank Williams Jr.)
MGM (1000 series) 8-10 76
(Special Products issue.)
MGM (E-3200 thru 3900 series) 25-50 55-61
(Monaural.)
MGM (SE-3200 thru 3900 series)..10-20 63-70
(Reprocessed stereo.)
MGM (4000 thru 4700 series, except 4267)...........................10-20 63-71
MGM (4267 "The Hank Williams Story")...................................50-75 66
(Four-LP set.)
MGM (4900 thru 5400 series)......5-10 75-77
METRO 10-15 65-67
POLYDOR 6-12 83-84
SUNRISE MEDIA.........................8-10 81
TIME-LIFE...................................5-8 82
Also see PRESLEY, Elvis / Hank Williams

WILLIAMS, Hank / Slim Whitman

LPs: 10/12-inch 33rpm

SUNRISE MEDIA.........................8-10 81
Also see WHITMAN, Slim

WILLIAMS, Hank, & Hank Williams, Jr.
(Hank Williams Jr. & Hank Williams Sr.)

LP '65

Singles: 7-inch

W.B. 3-4 89

LPs: 10/12-inch 33rpm

MGM (4200 series) 15-25 65
MGM (4300 thru 4900 series)....10-15 66-74
Also see WILLIAMS, Hank
Also see WILLIAMS, Hank, Jr.

WILLIAMS, Hank, Jr.
(With the Cheatin' Hearts; with Mike Curb Congregation; Luke the Drifter Jr.)

C&W/P&R '64

Singles: 7-inch

CONSOL.......................................10-20
(Promotional issue from Consolidation Coal.)
ELEKTRA/CURB 3-4 79-82
MGM (13000 series).......................4-8 64-68
MGM (14000 series).......................3-5 68-76
MGM GOLDEN CIRCLE................3-5 70s
W.B./CURB (Except 8000 series)..3-4 82-88
W.B./CURB (8000 series)..............3-4 77-78

Picture Sleeves

MGM (13000 series) 5-10 64-68

LPs: 10/12-inch 33rpm

CURB..5-8 83-84
ELEKTRA...5-8 79-83
MGM (Except 5009)...................10-20 64-76

MGM (5009 "Hank Williams Jr. & Friends") 40-60 76
W.B. 5-10 77-87
W.B./CURB 5-8 85-91
Also see BOCEPHUS
Also see CASH, Johnny, & Hank Williams Jr.
Also see CHARLES, Ray, & Hank Williams Jr.
Also see CURB, Mike
Also see FRANCIS, Connie, & Hank Williams Jr.
Also see JENNINGS, Waylon, & Hank Williams Jr.
Also see KERSHAW, Doug, & Hank Williams Jr.
Also see KILGORE, Merle
Also see WILLIAMS, Hank, & Hank Williams Jr.

WILLIAMS, Hank, Jr., & Lois Johnson

C&W '72

Singles: 7-inch

MGM 3-5 72
Also see WILLIAMS, Hank, Jr.

WILLIAMS, James "D-Train"

R&B '86

Singles: 12-inch 33/45rpm

COLUMBIA 4-6 86

Singles: 7-inch

COLUMBIA 3-4 86-88

LPs: 10/12-inch 33rpm

COLUMBIA 5-8 86
Also see "D" TRAIN

WILLIAMS, Jeanette

R&B '69

Singles: 7-inch

BACK BEAT 10-20 66-69

WILLIAMS, Joe
(Joseph Goreed)

R&B '52

Singles: 78rpm

BLUE LAKE 5-10 54
CHECKER 5-10 52
ROULETTE 5-10 57
SAVOY 5-10 55

Singles: 7-inch

BLUE LAKE 15-25 54
CHECKER 15-25 52
RCA 4-8 62-66
ROULETTE 5-10 57-62
SAVOY 10-20 55
SOLID STATE 4-8 66

LPs: 10/12-inch 33rpm

RCA 10-15 63-65
REGENT (6002 "Everyday") 35-45 56
ROULETTE 15-30 58-64
SOLID STATE 10-15 66
Also see BASIE, Count
Also see WASHINGTON, Dinah / Joe Williams / Sarah Vaughan

WILLIAMS, John, Orchestra

P&R '75

Singles: 7-inch

ARISTA 3-4 77-80
COLUMBIA 3-4 83
MCA 3-4 74-76
RCA 3-4 79
20TH FOX 3-4 77-78
W.B. 3-4 79

Picture Sleeves

ARISTA 3-4 77
20TH FOX 3-4 77-78
W.B. 3-4 79

LPs: 10/12-inch 33rpm

CAPITOL 5-10 71
COLUMBIA (31091 "Changes") 5-10 71
COLUMBIA (37000 series) 5-8 81
DISCOVERY 4-8 84
RCA 5-8 77

You'll find many more listings by this artist in *The Official Price Guide to Movie/TV Soundtracks and Original Cast Albums,* containing over 8,000 listings.
Also see BOSTON POPS ORCHESTRA

WILLIAMS, Johnny
(John Lee Hooker)

Singles: 78rpm

GOTHAM 10-15 50-52
PRIZE (704 "Miss Rosie Mae") 50-100 49
STAFF (710 "Wandering Blues") 25-50 50
STAFF (718 "Prison Bound") 25-50 50
SWING TIME 10-15 50
Also see HOOKER, John Lee

WILLIAMS, Johnny

R&B/C&W '72

Singles: 7-inch

BASHIE 3-5 70
CUB 4-6 68
EPIC 3-5 72
PHILADELPHIA INT'L 3-5 73

WILLIAMS, L.C.
(With Conney's Combo)

R&B '49

Singles: 78rpm

BAYOU 10-15 53
FREEDOM 10-15 49-50
GOLD STAR 10-15 48
IMPERIAL 5-10 52
JAX 10-15 52
MERCURY 5-10 52
SITTIN' in WITH 10-15 52

Singles: 7-inch

BAYOU (008 "My Darkest Hours") 40-50 53

WILLIAMS, Larry

P&R/R&B '57

Singles: 7-inch

CHESS 4-6 59-60
MERCURY 3-5 63
OKEH 3-5 66-67
SMASH 3-5 66
SPECIALTY (SPBX series) 12-15 85
(Boxed set of six colored vinyl 45s.)
SPECIALTY (597 thru 658) 5-10 57-59
SPECIALTY (665 thru 682) 4-6 59-60
VENTURE 3-5 68

Picture Sleeves

SPECIALTY (626 "Dizzy Miss Lizzy") 15-25 58

LPs: 10/12-inch 33rpm

OKEH 10-15 67
SPECIALTY (2109 "Here's Larry Williams") 40-50 59
SPECIALTY (2158 "Unreleased Larry Williams") 6-10 88
(With Art Neville.)
Also see COOKE, Sam / Lloyd Price / Larry Williams / Little Richard
Also see NEVILLE, Art

WILLIAMS, Larry, & Johnny Watson

P&R/R&B '67

Singles: 7-inch

BELL (813 "I Could Love You Baby") 5-10 69
OKEH (7300 "Nobody") 15-25 67
(With Kaleidoscope.)

LPs: 10/12-inch 33rpm

OKEH 10-15 67
Also see KALEIDOSCOPE
Also see LARRY & JOHNNY
Also see WATSON, Johnny
Also see WILLIAMS, Larry

WILLIAMS, Lawton
(With the Anita Kerr Singers)

C&W '61

Singles: 7-inch

D 5-10 60
LE BILL 5-10
MERCURY 4-8 61
RCA (7000 series) 5-10 58
RCA (8000 series) 4-6 64
Also see KERR, Anita

WILLIAMS, Lee
(With the Moonrays; with Cymbals; Lee "Shot" Williams)

R&B '67

Singles: 7-inch

CARNIVAL 5-10 66-69
FEDERAL 8-12 63-64
GAMMA (101 "Love Now, Pay Later") 25-35
KING (5409 "I'm So in Love") 50-75 60
SHAMA 5-10 69
TRUE 10-20

WILLIAMS, Lenny

R&B '75

Singles: 12-inch 33/45rpm

ABC 4-6 78
ROCSHIRE 4-6 83-84

Singles: 7-inch

ABC 3-4 77-78
GALAXY 3-6
KNOBHILL 3-4 86
MCA 3-4 79-81
MOTOWN 3-4 75
ROCSHIRE 3-4 83-84

LPs: 10/12-inch 33rpm

ABC 8-10 77-78
MCA 5-8 79-81
MOTOWN 8-10 75
ROCSHIRE 5-8 83-84
W.B. 8-12 74
Also see KENNY G. & Lenny Williams
Also see TOWER of POWER

WILLIAMS, Linda

R&B '79

Singles: 7-inch

ARISTA 3-5 79

WILLIAMS, Mason

P&R/LP '68

Singles: 7-inch

W.B. 3-4 68-71

LPs: 10/12-inch 33rpm

EVEREST 6-12 69
FLYING FISH 5-8 78
VEE JAY 10-20 64
W.B. 6-12 68-71

WILLIAMS, Mason, & Mannheim Steamroller

LP '87

LPs: 10/12-inch 33rpm

AMERICAN G. 5-8 87

WILLIAMS, Mason / Smothers Brothers

EPs: 7-inch 33/45rpm

W.B./7 ARTS (283 "Scope Box") 20-40 70
(Promotional issue only.)
Also see SMOTHERS BROTHERS
Also see WILLIAMS, Mason

WILLIAMS, Maurice
(With the Zodiacs)

P&R/R&B '60

Singles: 7-inch

ATLANTIC 3-4 70
COLE (100 "Golly Gee") 20-30 59
COLLECTABLES 3-4 80s
DEESU 10-20 67
ERIC 3-4 70s
FLASHBACK 4-6 65

HERALD.................................... 5-10 60-62
OWL.. 3-4 73
SEA HORN 5-10 64
SELWYN (5121 "College Girl") . 20-40 59
SPHERE SOUND 5-10 65
VEE JAY 5-10 65
VEEP... 4-8 69

LPs: 10/12-inch 33rpm

COLLECTABLES 6-8 84
HERALD (1014 "Stay") 50-100 61
RELIC.................................... 10-12
SNYDER 25-30
SPHERE SOUND 15-20 66

Also see GLADIOLAS

WILLIAMS, Mike

P&R/R&B '66

Singles: 7-inch

ATLANTIC.................................. 3-6 65-66
KING 3-6 66

Also see TEMPESTS

WILLIAMS, Otis
(With the Midnight Cowboys)

C&W '71

Singles: 7-inch

DELUXE (6100 series)............... 5-10 59
KING 4-8 60-64
OKEH 4-6 66
STOP 3-5 71

LPs: 10/12-inch 33rpm

POWER PAK 8-10 74
STOP 8-12 71

Also see CHARMS

WILLIAMS, Patrick

R&B '83

Singles: 7-inch

PCM 3-4 83

WILLIAMS, Paul
(With His Orchestra)

R&B '48

Singles: 78rpm

CAPITOL.................................... 5-8 55
CLEF 5-8 52
GROOVE 5-8 54
JAX... 5-8 54
JOSIE.. 5-8 56
RAMA.................................... 15-30 55
SAVOY 5-8 48-57

Singles: 7-inch

ASCOT.. 3-5 62
CAPITOL.................................. 5-10 55
GROOVE (0014 "Women Are the Root of All Evil") 15-25 54
("Vocal refrain by Jimmy Brown.")
JAX (313 "Thin Man").............. 25-35 54
(Colored vinyl.)
JOSIE...................................... 6-10 56
RAMA (167 "Ring-A-Ling").........50-75 55
(Vocalist, though not credited, is believed to be Little Willie John.)
SAVOY (1100 series)....................4-6 54-59
VEE JAY 4-6 57

Also see JOHN, Little Willie
Also see McNEELY, Big Jay / Paul Williams
Also see McPHERSON, Wyatt "Earp," & Paul Williams
Also see WATTS, Noble

WILLIAMS, Paul

LP '71

Singles: 7-inch

A&M 3-4 72-77
PAID..3-4 81
PORTRAIT...................................3-4 79
REPRISE 3-4 70

LPs: 10/12-inch 33rpm

A&M 6-10 71-77
PAID..5-8 81
PORTRAIT...................................5-8 79
REPRISE....................................8-12 70

WILLIAMS, Robin

LP '79

Singles: 12-inch 33/45rpm

CASABLANCA..............................4-8 79

Singles: 7-inch

BOARDWALK...............................3-5 80

Picture Sleeves

BOARDWALK...............................3-5 80

LPs: 10/12-inch 33rpm

CASABLANCA...........................5-10 79-83

WILLIAMS, Roger

P&R '55

Singles: 78rpm

KAPP 3-5 55-57

Singles: 7-inch

KAPP 3-8 55-72
MCA...3-4 73-78
W.B. 3-4 80

Picture Sleeves

KAPP 4-10 55-66

EPs: 7-inch 33/45rpm

KAPP 4-8 55-58

LPs: 10/12-inch 33rpm

KAPP 5-15 55-72
MCA...4-8 73-83
VOCALION 4-8 71

WILLIAMS, Roger, & Jane Morgan

Singles: 78rpm

KAPP 3-5 56

Singles: 7-inch

KAPP 5-10 56

Also see MORGAN, Jane
Also see WILLIAMS, Roger

WILLIAMS, Sonny Boy

R&B '43

Singles: 78rpm

DECCA 10-15 43

WILLIAMS, Tex
(With His Western Caravan)

C&W '46

Singles: 78rpm

CAPITOL 4-8 46-51
DECCA 4-8 53-55

Singles: 7-inch

BOONE 4-6 65-68
CAPITOL 5-10 51-60
DECCA 5-10 53-55
DOT 4-6 66
GRANITE 3-5 74
LIBERTY 4-8 63-65
MONUMENT 3-5 70-72
SHASTA 4-8 60-61

WILLIAMS, Tony

Singles: 7-inch

MERCURY 10-20 57-59
PHILIPS 4-8 62-63
REPRISE 5-10 61-62

LPs: 10/12-inch 33rpm

MERCURY 20-30 59
PHILIPS 15-25 62
REPRISE 20-25 61
Also see PLATTERS

WILLIAMS, Tony

LP '79

LPs: 10/12-inch 33rpm

COLUMBIA 5-10 79

WILLIAMS, Trudy, & Six Teens: see SIX TEENS

WILLIAMS, Vanessa

P&R/R&B/LP '88

Singles: 7-inch

WING 3-4 88-89

Picture Sleeves

WING 3-4 88-89

LPs: 10/12-inch 33rpm

WING 5-8 88

WILLIAMS, Vesta
(Vesta)

R&B '86

Singles: 12-inch 33/45rpm

A&M 4-6 86

Singles: 7-inch

A&M 3-4 86-89

LPs: 10/12-inch 33rpm

A&M 5-8 86-89

WILLIAMS, Wilson

R&B '78

Singles: 7-inch

ABC 3-5 78

WILLIAMSON, Sonny Boy
(John Lee Williamson)

R&B '47

Singles: 78rpm

BLUEBIRD 10-15 45
RCA 10-15 46-49

Singles: 7-inch

RCA (0005 "Little Girl") 50-100 49
RCA (0030 "Southern Dream") 50-100 49

WILLIAMSON, Sonny Boy
(Aleck "Rice" Miller; Aleck Ford)

R&B '55

Singles: 78rpm

ACE 10-15 54
CHECKER 5-10 55-57
TRUMPET 6-12 51-54

Singles: 7-inch

ACE 25-30 54
CHECKER (800 series) 10-15 55-58
CHECKER (900 series) 5-8 58-62
CHECKER (1000 & 1100 series) ... 3-5 62-66
TRUMPET (100 series) 20-30 51-52
TRUMPET (200 series) 15-20 53-54

LPs: 10/12-inch 33rpm

ARHOOLIE 8-12
BLUES CLASSICS 15-20 64
CHESS (200 series) 10-12 76
CHESS (1400 series) 30-40 60
CHESS (1500 series) 10-15 66-69
CHESS (50000 series) 10-12 72
STORYVILLE 5-8 80
Also see DIXON, Willie
Also see MEMPHIS SLIM
Also see PAGE, Jimmy, & Sonny Boy Williamson
Also see ROGERS, Jimmy
Also see WATERS, Muddy
Also see YARDBIRDS

WILLIAMSON, Sonny Boy, & Big Joe Williams

LPs: 10/12-inch 33rpm

BLUES CLASSICS 5-8
Also see WILLIAMSON, Sonny Boy (Aleck "Rice" Miller)

WILLIAMSON, Sonny Boy

Singles: 7-inch

RAM (2501 "Pretty Li'l Thing") ... 25-35 61

WILLIE, Wet: see WET WILLIE

WILLIE & POOR BOYS

LP '85

Singles: 7-inch

PASSPORT (7928 "Baby Please Don't Go") 3-5 85

Picture Sleeves

PASSPORT (7928 "Baby Please Don't Go") 4-6 85

LPs: 10/12-inch 33rpm

PASSPORT (6047 "Willie & Poor Boys") 5-10 85
Members: Andy Fairweather-Low; Mickey Gee; Kenny Jones; Jimmy Page; Chris Rea; Paul Rodgers; Geraint Watkins; Charlie Watts; Bill Wyman.
Also see FAIRWEATHER-LOW, Andy
Also see FREE
Also see PAGE, Jimmy

Also see REA, Chris
Also see ROLLING STONES

WILLIS, Bruce

P&R/R&B/LP '87

Singles: 7-inch

MOTOWN 3-4 87

Picture Sleeves

MOTOWN 3-4 87

LPs: 10/12-inch 33rpm

MOTOWN 5-8 87

WILLIS, Chuck

(With the Royals; with Sandmen)

R&B '52

Singles: 78rpm

ATLANTIC 4-8 56-57
COLUMBIA 10-15 51
OKEH 5-10 53-56

Singles: 7-inch

ATLANTIC (1000 & 2000 series) 10-20 56-59
COLUMBIA (30238 "Can't You See") 25-40 51
OKEH (6000 series, except 6985) 10-20 51-53
OKEH (6985 "Don't Deceive Me") 15-20 53
OKEH (7000 series) 8-12 53-56

EPs: 7-inch 33/45rpm

ATLANTIC 30-40 57-58
EPIC 35-50 56

LPs: 10/12-inch 33rpm

ATCO 10-12 71
ATLANTIC (8018 "King of the Stroll") 50-100 58
(Black label.)
ATLANTIC (8018 "King of the Stroll") 20-30 59
(Red label.)
ATLANTIC (8079 "I Remember Chuck Willis") 30-35 63
COLUMBIA 5-8 80
EPIC (3425 "Chuck Willis Wails the Blues") 100-175 58
EPIC (3728 "A Tribute to Chuck Willis") 100-175 58

WILLIS, M-D-L-T

R&B '74

Singles: 7-inch

IVORY TOWER 3-4 74

Members: Maxine Willis; Diane Willis; Lavern Willis; Tina Willis.

WILLIS, Timmy

R&B '68

Singles: 7-inch

JUBILEE 3-4 69
VEEP 3-5 68

WILL-O-BEES

P&R '68

Singles: 7-inch

DATE 3-5 67
SGC 3-5 68-69

WILLOWS

P&R/R&B '56

Singles: 78rpm

MELBA (Except 102) 5-10 56-57
MELBA (102 "Church Bells Are Ringing") 15-25 56
MELBA (102 "Church Bells May Ring) 5-10 56

Singles: 7-inch

ABC 3-4 73
COLLECTABLES 3-4
MELBA (Except 102) 15-20 56-57
MELBA (102 "Church Bells Are Ringing") 50-60 56
MELBA (102 "Church Bells May Ring) 10-15 56

LP: 10/12-inch 33rpm

ELDORADO (1000 "Willows") 5-10

Members: Tony Middleton; Richard Davis; Ralph Martin; Joe Martin; John Steele; Richard Simon; Dotty Martin.

Also see SEDAKA, Neil

WILLS, Bob

(With His Texas Playboys; with Rusty McDonald; with Tommy Duncan)

P&R '39

Singles: 78rpm

ANTONES 15-25
CAPITOL 3-5 76
COLUMBIA 5-10 43-48
DECCA 4-8 55-56
MGM 5-10 47-55
OKEH 5-10 40-45
VOCALION 10-20 33-39

Singles: 7-inch

DECCA 5-10 55-56
LIBERTY 4-8 60-64
LONGHORN 4-6 64
MGM 5-15 50-55

WILMER & the DUKES

P&R '68

Singles: 7-inch

APHRODISIAC 3-6 69

LPs: 10/12-inch 33rpm

APHRODISIAC 10-15 69

Member: Wilmer Alexander Jr.

WILSON, Al

P&R/R&B '68

Singles: 7-inch

BELL 4-6 70
BELL GOLD 3-4 70s
CAROUSEL 3-5 71
PLAYBOY 3-5 76

ROADSHOW.................................... 3-4 79
ROCKY ROAD 3-6 72-75
SOUL CITY 4-8 67-69
WAND (1135 "Help Me").......... 15-25 66

LPs: 10/12-inch 33rpm

PLAYBOY 8-10 76
ROADSHOW................................. 5-8 79
ROCKY ROAD 8-12 73-74
SOUL CITY 10-15 69

Also see JEWELS
Also see ROLLERS

WILSON, Ann
(With the Daybreaks)

P&R '86

Singles: 7-inch

CAPITOL.. 3-4 86
TOPAZ 10-15 67

Picture Sleeves

CAPITOL.. 3-4 86

Also see HEART
Also see RENO, Mike, & Ann Wilson

WILSON, Ann, Robin Zander

P&R '88

Singles: 7-inch

CAPITOL.. 3-4 88

Also see WILSON, Ann

WILSON, Art

R&B '83

Singles: 7-inch

TABU... 3-4 83

WILSON, Bobby

R&B '73

Singles: 7-inch

BUDDAH 3-5 75
CHAIN 3-5 73

WILSON, Brian

P&R '66

Singles: 7-inch

CAPITOL (5610 "Caroline, No") 15-20 66
SIRE (27694 "Melt Away") 3-5 88
SIRE (27814 "Love and Mercy") ... 3-5 88
SIRE (28350 "Let's Go to
Heaven in My Car")..................... 3-5 87

Promotional Singles

SIRE (27694 "Melt Away") 4-8 88
SIRE (27787 "Night Time")........... 4-8 88
SIRE (27814 "Love and Mercy") ... 4-8 88
SIRE (28350 "Let's Go to
Heaven in My Car")................... 5-10 87

Picture Sleeves

SIRE (27787 "Night Time").......... 8-12 88
SIRE (27814 "Love and Mercy") ... 4-8 88
SIRE (28350 "Let's Go to Heaven in My
Car")... 4-8 87

LPs: 10/12-inch 33rpm

SIRE (3248 "Brian Wilson: Words
and Music") 15-20 88
SIRE (225669 "Brian Wilson")..... 5-10 88

Also see BEACH BOYS
Also see BERRY, Jan
Also see BLOSSOMS
Also see BOB & SHERI
Also see CAMPBELL, Glen
Also see CASTELLS
Also see CURRY, Tim
Also see DeSHANNON, Jackie
Also see HALE & HUSHABYES
Also see HONDELLS
Also see LEGENDARY MASKED SURFERS
Also see LOVE, Mike
Also see RIVERS, Johnny

WILSON, Brian, & Mike Love

Singles: 7-inch

BROTHER (1002 "Gettin'
Hungry")................................... 15-25 67

Also see LOVE, Mike
Also see WILSON, Brian

WILSON, Carl

LP '81

Singles: 7-inch

CARIBOU.......................................3-5 81-83

LPs: 10/12-inch 33rpm

CARIBOU.....................................5-10 81-82

Also see ANGEL
Also see BEACH BOYS
Also see CASSADY, David
Also see KING HARVEST
Also see NEWTON-JOHN, Olivia

WILSON, Dennis

LP '77

Singles: 7-inch

CARIBOU.......................................4-6 77

LPs: 10/12-inch 33rpm

CARIBOU.....................................10-15 77

Also see BEACH BOYS

WILSON, Dennis / Ram Jam / Joan Baez

EPs: 7-inch 33/45rpm

COLUMBIA (1128 "Music for Every
Ear").......................................15-25 77
(Promotional issue only.)

Also see BAEZ, Joan
Also see CUMMINGS, Burton / Cheap Trick / Crawler
Also see WILSON, Dennis
Also see RAM JAM

WILSON, Flip

LP '87

Singles: 7-inch

FLIP WILSON (SK-1 "Flip
Wilson")....................................5-10 60s
(Promotional issue only. No title or label
shown.)
LITTLE DAVID 3-4 72-75

LPs: 10/12-inch 33rpm

ATLANTIC.....................................8-15 67-68
IMPERIAL...................................10-20 61
LITTLE DAVID 5-10 70-72
MINIT 8-15 68
SUNSET 8-10 70

WILSON, Hank
(Leon Russell)

LP '73

Singles: 7-inch

SHELTER.................................... 3-4 73-74

LPs: 10/12-inch 33rpm

SHELTER.................................... 8-10 73

Also see NELSON, Willie, & Hank Wilson
Also see RUSSELL, Leon

WILSON, J. Frank
(With the Cavaliers)

P&R/LP '64

Singles: 7-inch

ABC.................................... 3-4 73
APRIL.................................... 3-5
CHARAY.................................... 3-5 69
COLLECTABLES.................................... 3-4 80s
ERIC.................................... 3-4 70s
JOSIE.................................... 4-8 64-65
LE CAM (500 series).................... 3-4 81
LE CAM (722 "Last Kiss")......... 15-25 64
LE CAM (1000 series).................... 4-8 65
LE CAM (12000 series).................... 3-4
SOLLY.................................... 3-5 66
TAMARA.................................... 8-15 64
VIRGO.................................... 3-4 72

LPs: 10/12-inch 33rpm

DILL PICKEL.................................... 8-10 71
JOSIE (4006 "Last Kiss").......... 40-50 64

WILSON, Jackie

P&R '57

Singles: 78rpm

BRUNSWICK.................................... 8-12 57

Singles: 7-inch

BRUNSWICK (7-38000 series). 20-30 60
(Stereo compact 33 singles.)
BRUNSWICK (55024 thru 55086).................................... 15-30 57-58
BRUNSWICK (55105 thru 55165).................................... 10-20 58-59
BRUNSWICK (55166 thru 55236).................................... 8-15 60-62
BRUNSWICK (55238 thru 55504).................................... 5-10 63-73
COLUMBIA.................................... 3-4 87
ERIC.................................... 3-4 83
GUSTO.................................... 3-4

Picture Sleeves

BRUNSWICK (55121 thru 55236).................................... 8-12 59-62
BRUNSWICK (55238 thru 55467).................................... 4-8 63-72
COLUMBIA.................................... 3-4 87

EPs: 7-inch 33/45rpm

BRUNSWICK.................................... 20-35 59-63

LPs: 10/12-inch 33rpm

BRUNSWICK (111 "Solid Gold").................................... 10-15
(Brunswick Special Products, mail-order offer.)
BRUNSWICK (54045 "Lonely Teardrops").................................... 50-100 59
BRUNSWICK (54042 "He's So Fine").................................... 50-100 59
BRUNSWICK (54050 "So Much").................................... 40-80 60
BRUNSWICK (54055 "Jackie Sings the Blues").................................... 30-50 60
BRUNSWICK (54058 "My Golden Favorites").................................... 30-40 60
BRUNSWICK (54059 "A Woman, a Lover, a Friend").................................... 30-40 60
BRUNSWICK (54100 "You Ain't Heard Nothin' Yet").................................... 25-30 61
BRUNSWICK (54101 "By Request").................................... 25-30 61
BRUNSWICK (54105 "Body and Soul").................................... 25-30 62
BRUNSWICK (54108 "At the Copa").................................... 25-30 62
BRUNSWICK (54110 thru 54130).................................... 20-25 63-67
(Beginning with 54050, Brunswick indicated stereo LPs with a "7" preceeding the selection number. Numbers after 54130 were available as stereo issues only, and are shown here as the 75000 series.)
BRUNSWICK (754138 thru 754167).................................... 15-20 68-71
BRUNSWICK (754185 thru 754212).................................... 10-15 72-77
COLUMBIA.................................... 5-8 87
DISCOVERY.................................... 8-10 78
EPIC.................................... 10-12 83
TELE-HOUSE.................................... 10-15

Also see FREED, Alan
Also see WARD, Billy, & Dominoes
Also see WILSON, Sonny

WILSON, Jackie, & Lavern Baker

P&R/R&B '66

Singles: 7-inch

BRUNSWICK.................................... 3-5 65

Also see BAKER, Lavern

WILSON, Jackie, & Count Basie

P&R/R&B/LP '68

Singles: 7-inch

BRUNSWICK.................................... 3-5 68

LPs: 10/12-inch 33rpm

BRUNSWICK.................................... 15-20 68

Also see BASIE, Count

WILSON, Jackie, & Chi-Lites

R&B '75

Singles: 7-inch

BRUNSWICK.................................... 3-4 75

Also see CHI-LITES

WILSON, Jackie, & Linda Hopkins

P&R '62

Singles: 7–inch

BRUNSWICK 3-5 62-65

EPs: 7–inch 33/45rpm

BRUNSWICK 15-20 63

LPs: 10/12–inch 33rpm

BRUNSWICK 25-35 68

Also see HOPKINS, Linda
Also see WILSON, Jackie

WILSON, Jimmy

(With His All Stars; with Blues Blasters)

R&B '53

Singles: 78rpm

ALADDIN 15-25 51
BIG TOWN 15-25 53-54
CAVATONE 15-25 51
CHART 10-20 56
IRMA 10-15 55
RHYTHM 15-25 50-54
7-11 .... 20-30 53

Singles: 7–inch

ALADDIN (3140 "Mistake in Life") 50-75 51
ALADDIN (3241 "It's Time to Change") 50-75 52
BIG TOWN (101 "Tin Pan Alley") 30-50 53
BIG TOWN (103 "Call Me a Hound Dog") 30-50 53
BIG TOWN (107 "Blues at Sundown") 30-50 53
BIG TOWN (113 "Teardrops on My Pillow") 30-50 54
BIG TOWN (115 "Trouble in My House") 30-50 54
BIG TOWN (123 "I've Found Out") 30-50 54
CHART (610 "Louise") 30-40 56
CHART (629 "Send Me the Key") 30-40 56
DUKE 5-10 61-62
GOLDBAND 10-20 59
IRMA (107 "Blues in the Alley"). 25-35 55
7-11 (2104 "Ethel Lee") 100-150 53
7-11 (2105 "Baby Don't Want Nobody But Me") 100-150 53

WILSON, Jimmy / Thrillers / Little Caesar

LPs: 10/12–inch 33rpm

BIG TOWN (1001 "Big Town Sampler") 150-250 53
(Promotional issue only.)

Also see LITTLE CAESAR

WILSON, Kathy, & Kwils

D&D '83

Singles: 12–inch 33/45rpm

COLUMBIA 4-6 83

WILSON, Mary

R&B '79

Singles: 7–inch

MOTOWN 3-4 79

LPs: 10/12–inch 33rpm

MOTOWN 5-8 79

Also see SUPREMES

WILSON, Meri

P&R/R&B/C&W '77

Singles: 7–inch

BNA 3-5 81
GRT 3-4 77

LPs: 10/12–Inch 33rpm

GRT 5-10 77

WILSON, Nancy

LP '62

Singles: 12–inch 33/45rpm

CAPITOL 4-6 79

Singles: 7–inch

CAPITOL (Except 4000 & 5000 series) 3-5 68-79
CAPITOL (4000 & 5000 series) 3-6 59-67
(Includes both purple and orange/yellow labels.)

Picture Sleeves

CAPITOL 3-5 65

LPs: 10/12–inch 33rpm

ASI 5-8 81
CAPITOL (100 thru 800 series) ... 5-12 69-71
CAPITOL (1300 thru 1700 series) 15-30 59-62
CAPITOL (1800 thru 2900 series) 8-18 63-68
(With "T," "ST" or "SKAO" prefix.)
CAPITOL (1800 thru 2900 series) . 5-8 78
(With "SM" prefix.)
CAPITOL (11000 & 12000 series) 5-10 74-80
CAPITOL (16000 series) 5-8 80
COLUMBIA 5-8 84

Also see CAPITOL'S MYSTERY ARTIST
Also see LEWIS, Ramsey, & Nancy Wilson

WILSON, Nancy, & Julian "Cannonball" Adderley

R&B/LP '62

Singles: 7–inch

CAPITOL 3-5 62

LPs: 10/12–inch 33rpm

CAPITOL (1657 "Nancy Wilson & Cannonball Adderley") 15-25 62
(With "T" or "ST" prefix.)
CAPITOL (1657 "Nancy Wilson & Cannonball Adderley") 5-8 75
(With "SM" prefix.)
CAPITOL (16000 series) 4-8 81

Also see ADDERLEY, Cannonball

WILSON, Nancy, & George Shearing

Singles: 7–inch

CAPITOL.................................... 3-5 61

LPs: 10/12–inch 33rpm

CAPITOL (1524 "Swingin's Mutual").................................. 15-25 61
(With "T" or "ST" prefix.)

CAPITOL (1524 "Swingin's Mutual")..................................... 5-8 75
(With "SM" prefix.)

Also see SHEARING, George
Also see WILSON, Nancy

WILSON, Phill

P&R '61

Singles: 7–inch

HURON 3-5 61

WILSON, Precious

R&B '86

Singles: 7–inch

JIVE.. 3-4 86

LPs: 10/12–inch 33rpm

JIVE.. 5-8 86

Also see ERUPTION

WILSON, Shanice

P&R/R&B/LP '87

Singles: 7–inch

A&M 3-4 87-88

Picture Sleeves

A&M 3-4 87

LPs: 10/12–inch 33rpm

A&M 5-8 87

Also see KIARA with Shanice Wilson

WILSON, Sonny
(Jackie Wilson)

Singles: 78rpm

DEE GEE (4000 "Rainy Day Blues").................................. 30-50 52

DEE GEE (4001 "Danny Boy").. 30-50 52

Singles: 7–inch

DEE GEE (4000 "Rainy Day Blues")................................ 75-100 52

DEE GEE (4001 "Danny Boy") 75-100 52

Also see WILSON, Jackie

WILSON, Timothy

R&B '67

Singles: 7–inch

BLUE ROCK (6 "Cross My Heart").................................. 10-20 69

BUDDAH...................................... 10-20 67-68

VEEP (1213 "Hey Girl, Do You Love Me")... 25-50 65

VEEP (1223 "He Will Break Your Heart").................................. 15-25 65

WILSON BROTHERS

P&R '79

Singles: 7–inch

ATCO 3-5 79

LPs: 10/12–inch 33rpm

ATCO..5-10 79

Members: Steve Wilson; Kelly Wilson.

WILSON PHILLIPS

LP '90

Singles: 7–inch

SRK...3-4 90

Picture Sleeves

SRK...3-4 90

LPs: 10/12–inch 33rpm

SRK...5-8 90

Members: Wendy Wilson; Carnie Wilson; Chynna Phillips.

WILTON PLACE STREET BAND

P&R/R&B '77

Singles: 7–inch

ISLAND 3-5 77

WINAN, BeBe & CeCe

R&B '87

Singles: 12–inch 33/45rpm

CAPITOL.......................................4-6 87

Singles: 12–inch 33/45rpm

CAPITOL.......................................3-4 87

LPs: 10/12–inch 33rpm

CAPITOL.......................................5-8 87-89

WINANS

R&B '85

Singles: 12–inch 33/45rpm

QWEST..4-6 86

Singles: 7–inch

QWEST..3-4 85-86

LPs: 10/12–inch 33rpm

LIGHT 4-8 75-85

QWEST..5-8 85-90

Members: Marvin Winan; Carvin Winan; Michael Winan; Ronald Winan.

Also see JACKSON, Michael
Also see McDONALD, Michael
Also see WINAN, BeBe & CeCe

WINANS & Anita Baker

R&B '87

Singles: 7–inch

QWEST..3-4 87

Also see BAKER, Anita

WINBUSH, Angela

R&B/LP '87

Singles: 7–inch

MERCURY....................................3-4 87-89

LPs: 10/12–inch 33rpm

MERCURY 5-8 87-89

WINCHESTER, Jesse

LP '72

Singles: 7–inch

AMPEX 3-4 70

BEARSVILLE 3-4 76-81

LPs: 10/12–inch 33rpm

BEARSVILLE/AMPEX 15-20 70

BEARSVILLE 6-10 71-81

Promotional LPs

BEARSVILLE (692 "Live at the Bijou") 20-25 75
BEARSVILLE (693 "Live at the Bijou/Live Interview") 30-40 75

Also see HARRIS, Emmylou
Also see LARSON, Nicolette
Also see MURRAY, Anne

WIND

P&R '69

Singles: 7-inch

LIFE 4-6 69

LPs: 10/12-inch 33rpm

LIFE 15-20 69

Member: Tony Orlando.
Also see ORLANDO, Tony

WIND in the WILLOWS

LP '68

Singles: 7-inch

CAPITOL 4-6 68

LPs: 10/12-inch 33rpm

CAPITOL (2956 "The Wind in the Willows") 40-75 68

Members: Deborah Harry; Paul Klein; Peter Brittain; Anton Carysforth; Steve DePhillips.
Also see HARRY, Debbie

WINDING, Kai, & His Orchestra (With J.J. Johnson)

P&R/LP '63

Singles: 7-inch

BETHLEHEM 3-4 60
COLUMBIA 3-5 56-59
IMPULSE 3-4 61
MGM 3-4 78
VERVE 3-4 62-67

EPs: 7-inch 33/45rpm

COLUMBIA 5-15 58-59
SAVOY 10-20 53

LPs: 10/12-inch 33rpm

A&M 8-12 68
COLUMBIA (900 thru 1300 series) 15-30 56-59
COLUMBIA (8100 series) 15-25 59
GLENDALE 5-8 76-77
IMPULSE 15-25 61
JAZZTONE 20-35 56
PICKWICK 5-10 65-70
ROOST (400 series) 60-80 52
(10-inch LPs.)
SAVOY (9000 series) 50-75 53
(10-inch LPs.)
VERVE 10-25 61-67
(Reads "MGM Records - a Division of Metro-Goldwyn-Mayer, Inc." at bottom of label.)
VERVE 5-10 73-84
(Reads "Manufactured By MGM Record Corp.," or mentions either Polydor or Polygram at bottom of label.)
WHO'S WHO in JAZZ 5-8 78

Also see STITT, Sonny, Kai Winding & Horace Silver

WINDJAMMER

R&B '83

Singles: 7-inch

MCA 3-4 83-85

LPs: 10/12-inch 33rpm

MCA 5-8 83

WINDSTORM

R&B '80

Singles: 7-inch

POLYDOR 3-4 80

WINDY CITY

R&B '80

Singles: 7-inch

CHI-SOUND 3-4 77
KELLI-ARTS 3-4 80

WINE, April: see APRIL WINE

WING and a Prayer Fife & Drum Corps

P&R/R&B '75

Singles: 7-inch

WING and a PRAYER 3-4 75-77

LPs: 10/12-inch 33rpm

WING and a PRAYER 5-8 76-77

WINGER

LP '88

Singles: 7-inch

ATLANTIC 3-4 88-89

Picture Sleeves

ATLANTIC 3-4 89

LPs: 10/12-inch 33rpm

ATLANTIC 5-8 88-90

Members: Kip Winger; Reb Beach; Rod Morgenstein; Paul Taylor.

WINGFIELD, Pete

P&R/R&B/LP '75

Singles: 7-inch

ISLAND 3-4 75-77

LPs: 10/12-inch 33rpm

ISLAND 5-8 75

Also see OLYMPIC RUNNERS

WINGS with Paul McCartney: see McCARTNEY, Paul

WINNERS

R&B '78

Singles: 7-inch

ARIOLA-AMERICA 3-4 78

LPs: 10/12-inch 33rpm

ARIOLA-AMERICA 5-8 78
ROADSHOW 5-10 78

WINSTON, George

LP '84

Singles: 7-inch

WINDHAM HILL 3-4 84

LPs: 10/12-inch 33rpm

WINDHAM HILL 5-8 83-88

WINSTONS

P&R/R&B/LP '69

Singles: 7–inch

METROMEDIA............................ 3-4 69

LPs: 10/12–inch 33rpm

METROMEDIA.......................... 8-12 69

WINTER, Edgar

(Edgar Winter Group; Edgar Winter's White Trash)

LP '70

Singles: 12–inch 33/45rpm

BLUE SKY.................................. 4-6 80
BODY ROCK.............................. 4-6 83

Singles: 7–inch

BLUE SKY.................................. 3-4 75-81
EPIC... 3-4 70-75

LPs: 10/12–inch 33rpm

BACK-TRAC 5-8 85
BLUE SKY................................ 6-10 75-81
EPIC... 10-15 70-75

Also see DERRINGER, Rick
Also see HARTMAN, Dan
Also see LA CROIX, Jerry
Also see MONTROSE, Ronnie
Also see WINTER, Johnny & Edgar

WINTER, Jimmy: see WINTER, Johnny

WINTER, Johnny

(With the Crystaliers; Jimmy Winter)

LP '69

Singles: 7–inch

ATLANTIC................................ 5-10 64
BLUE SKY.................................. 3-4 75
COLUMBIA 3-4 69-74
FROLIC ("Voo Doo Twist")...... 75-100 62
(Number not known.)
GRT.. 3-5 69
IMPERIAL 3-5 69
KRCO (107 "One Night of Love").................................. 50-75 61
MGM 4-6 65
PACEMAKER.......................... 10-15 66
SONOBEAT 5-8 68
TODD 8-10 63

Picture Sleeves

SONOBEAT 50-75 68
(Some sleeves picture the Vulcan Gas Co., an Austin nightclub, and those are at the high end of the price range given. Sleeves that do not picture the club are priced at the lower end.)

LPs: 10/12–inch 33rpm

ACCORD.................................... 5-8 81
ALLIGATOR 5-8 84-85
BLUE SKY................................ 6-10 74-80
BUDDAH 10-15 69
CBS ASSOCIATED...................... 5-8
COLUMBIA (9800 & 9900 series) 15-20 69
COLUMBIA (30000 thru 33000 series)........................10-15 70-75
CRAZY CAJUN.........................8-10
GRT 10-15 69
IMPERIAL 15-20 69
JANUS 10-12 69-70
SONOBEAT ("Progressive Blues Experiment") 100-150 68
(Limited edition, autographed issue.)
SONOBEAT ("Progressive Blues Experiment") 75-125 68
(Limited edition, NOT autographed.)
U.A. 8-10 73-74

Also see JOHNNY & JAMMERS
Also see GREAT BELIEVERS
Also see GUITAR SLIM
Also see SPRINGSTEEN, Bruce / Johnny Winter / Hollies
Also see TEXAS "GUITAR" SLIM
Also see WATERS, Muddy

WINTER, Johnny / Argent / Chambers Brothers / John Hammond

EPs: 7–inch 33/45rpm

COLUMBIA/PLAYBACK (14 "Good Morning Little Schoolgirl")......................15-25 72

Also see ARGENT
Also see CHAMBERS BROTHERS
Also see HAMMOND, John

WINTER, Johnny & Edgar

LP '76

Singles: 7–inch

BLUE SKY 3-4 76
CASCADE...............................35-45 64

LPs: 10/12–inch 33rpm

BLUE SKY (Except 242) 5-8 76
BLUE SKY (242 "Johnny & Edgar Winter Discuss *Together*") 10-20 76
(Promotional issue only.)

Also see LA CROIX, Jerry
Also see WINTER, Edgar
Also see WINTER, Johnny

WINTER, Paul

(With Winter Consort; Paul Winter Sextet)

LP '62

Singles: 7–inch

A&M 3-4 69-77
COLUMBIA 3-5 62
EPIC...3-4 72-73

LPs: 10/12–inch 33rpm

A&M 8-12 69-78
COLUMBIA 10-20 62-65
EPIC..8-10 72
LIVING MUSIC.............................5-8 83-86

WINTERHALTER, Hugo, & His Orchestra

P&R '49

Singles: 78rpm

COLUMBIA 3-5 49-50
RCA 3-5 50-57

Singles: 7-inch

ABC-PAR 3-5 63
COLUMBIA 5-8 50
KAPP 3-5 64-65
MUSICOR 3-5 68-70
RCA 3-8 50-63

EPs: 7-inch 33/45rpm

RCA 3-6 50-59

LPs: 10/12-inch 33rpm

ABC-PAR 4-8 63
CAMDEN 4-8 69-72
KAPP 4-8 65
MUSIC DISC 4-8 69
MUSICOR 5-10 68-71
RCA 5-15 50-77
TRIP 4-8 76

Also see COMO, Perry
Also see HEYWOOD, Eddie

WINTERMUTE, Joann

C&W '89

Singles: 7-inch

CANYON CREEK 3-4 89
DOOR KNOB 3-4 89

WINTERS, Jonathan

LP '60

EPs: 7-inch 33/45rpm

VERVE (5077 "Another Day, Another World") 8-10 62
(Promotional issue only.)

LPs: 10/12-inch 33rpm

COLUMBIA 8-15 68-73
VERVE 15-30 59-60
(Reads "Verve Records, Inc." at bottom of label.)
VERVE 10-20 61-67
(Reads "MGM Records - a Division of Metro-Goldwyn-Mayer, Inc." at bottom of label.)
VERVE 5-10 73-84
(Reads"Manufactured By MGM Record Corp.," or mentions either Poly dor or Polygram at bottom of label.)

WINTERS, Robert, & Fall

R&B '80

Singles: 7-inch

BUDDAH 3-4 80-81
CASABLANCA 3-4 82-84

LPs: 10/12-inch 33rpm

BUDDAH 5-8 80-81
CASABLANCA 5-8 82-83

WINTERS, Ruby

R&B '67

(Ruby Winter)

Singles: 7-inch

CERTRON 3-4 71
DIAMOND 3-5 66-69
MILLENNIUM 3-4 78
POLYDOR 3-4 73-75

LPs: 10/12-inch 33rpm

MILLENNIUM 5-8 78

Also see THUNDER, Johnny, & Ruby Winters

WINWOOD, Steve

LP '71

Singles: 7-inch

ISLAND 3-4 77-87
U.A. 4-8 71
VIRGIN 3-4 88-90

Picture Sleeves

ISLAND 3-4 80-88
VIRGIN 3-4 88-89

LPs: 10/12-inch 33rpm

ISLAND 5-8 77-87
U.A. (5550 "Welcome to the Canteen") 8-12 71
U.A. (9950 "Winwood") 20-30 71
(With liner notes by Bobby Abrahms.)
U.A. (9964 "Winwood") 10-15 71
(Without liner notes.)
VIRGIN 5-8 88-90

Also see BAKER, Ginger
Also see BLIND FAITH
Also see DAVIS, Spencer
Also see McDONALD & GILES
Also see TOOTS & MAYTALS
Also see TRAFFIC
Also see YAMASHTA, Stomu

WIRE

LP '89

LP: 10/12-inch 33rpm

MUTE 5-8 89

Members: Graham Lewis; Colin Newman; Robert Gotobed.

WIRE TRAIN

LP '84

Singles: 12-inch 33/45rpm

COLUMBIA 4-6 84

Singles: 7-inch

COLUMBIA 3-4 84

LPs: 10/12-inch 33rpm

COLUMBIA 5-8 84-87

WISH

(Featuring Fonda Rae)

R&B/D&D '84

Singles: 12-inch 33/45rpm

KN 4-6 84

Singles: 7-inch

PERSONAL 3-4 84-85

Also see RAE, Fonda

WISHBONE ASH

LP '71

Singles: 7-inch

ATLANTIC 3-4 77
DECCA 3-4 71-72
MCA 3-4 73-78

Picture Sleeves

MCA 3-4 78

LPs: 10/12–inch 33rpm

ATLANTIC 6-10 76
DECCA (Except 1922) 10-15 71-72
DECCA (1922 "Live from Memphis") 15-20 72
(Promotional issue only.)
MCA 5-8 73-82
Also see FOGHAT

WITCH QUEEN

P&R/LP '79

Singles: 7–inch

ROADSHOW 3-4 79

LPs: 10/12–inch 33rpm

ROADSHOW 5-8 79

WITHERS, Bill

P&R/R&B/LP '71

Singles: 12–inch 33/45rpm

COLUMBIA 4-6 79

Singles: 7–inch

COLUMBIA 3-4 75-85
SUSSEX 3-4 71-75

Picture Sleeves

SUSSEX 3-4 72

LPs: 10/12–inch 33rpm

COLUMBIA 5-8 75-85
SUSSEX 8-12 71-75
Also see MacDONALD, Ralph, & Bill Withers
Also see WASHINGTON, Grover, Jr.
Also see WOMACK, Bobby, & Bill Withers

WITHERSPOON, Jimmy
(With Groove Holmes; with Jay McShann & His Band; with Ben Webster; with Panama Francis & Savoy Sultans)

R&B '49

Singles: 78rpm

CHECKER 5-10 54-55
FEDERAL 5-10 52-53
DOWN BEAT 5-8 48-49
MODERN (665 thru 845) 4-6 49-51
RCA 4-8 57
SUPREME 5-8 48-49
SWING BEAT 4-8 49
SWING TIME 4-6 51

Singles: 7–inch

ABC 3-4 71
BLUE NOTE 3-4 75
BLUESWAY 3-4 69
CAPITOL 3-4 74
CHECKER (Black vinyl) 15-20 54-55
CHECKER (Colored vinyl) 50-75 54
FEDERAL 15-20 52-53
GNP 4-6 59
HI FI 4-6 60
KENT 3-4 71
KING 3-5 65
MODERN (857 thru 903) 15-20 52-53
PACIFIC JAZZ 3-5 62
PRESTIGE 3-5 63-65
RCA 5-8 57
REPRISE 3-5 61-64
RIP 5-8 58
VEE JAY 4-6 59
VERVE 3-5 66-67
WORLD PACIFIC 4-6 59

LPs: 10/12–inch 33rpm

ABC 8-10 70
BLUE NOTE 8-10 75
BLUESWAY 8-10 69-73
CAPITOL 8-10 74
CONSTELLATION 15-20 64
CROWN (215 "Jimmy Witherspoon Sings the Blues") 15-20 61
(Black Vinyl.)
CROWN (215 "Jimmy Witherspoon Sings the Blues") 20-40 61
(Colored Vinyl.)
FANTASY 10-12 72
HI FI 20-30 59
INNER CITY 5-8 81
MCA 5-8 83
MUSE 5-8 83
OLYMPIC 8-10 73
PRESTIGE 10-15 64-69
RCA (1048 "Goin' to Kansas City Blues") 6-10 75
RCA (1639 "Goin' to Kansas City Blues") 30-40 58
REPRISE 20-30 61-62
SURREY 12-15 65
UNITED 8-10
VERVE (5000 series) 12-15 66-68
VERVE (8000 series) 8-10 74
VERVE/FOLKWAYS (3011 "Blues Box") 25-30 66
WORLD PACIFIC 20-30 59-61
Also see BURDON, Eric, & Jimmy Witherspoon
Also see FREEMAN, Ernie
Also see HOLMES, Richard "Groove"
Also see McSHANN, Jay
Also see WALKER, T-Bone

WITHERSPOON, Jimmy, & Lamplighters

Singles: 78rpm

FEDERAL 10-20 52

Singles: 7–inch

FEDERAL (12156 "Sad Life") 25-50 52
FEDERAL (12173 "24 Sad Hours") 25-50 52

WITHERSPOON, Jimmy, & Quintones

Singles: 78rpm

ATCO 5-10 57

Singles: 7–inch

ATCO 10-20 57

WITHERSPOON, Jimmy / Eddie Vinson

LPs: 10/12–inch 33rpm

KING (634 "Battle of the Blues, Vol. 3") 200-300 59
Also see WITHERSPOON, Jimmy

WITT, Joachim

D&D '83

Singles: 12–inch 33/45rpm

W.E.A. INTERNATIONAL 4-6 83-84

WITTER, Jimmy, & Shadows

P&R '61

Singles: 7–inch

ELVIS (900 "If You Love My Woman") 200-300

NEPTUNE (118 "My Kind of Woman") 50-75 61

U.A. 8-10 61

WOLCOTT, Charles, Orchestra

P&R '60

Singles: 7–inch

MGM 3-4 60

WOLF
(Bill Wolfer)

P&R/R&B '82

Singles: 7–inch

CONSTELLATION 3-4 81-83

Picture Sleeves

CONSTELLATION 3-4 82

LPs: 10/12–inch 33rpm

CONSTELLATION 5-8 83

WOLF, Howlin: see HOWLIN' WOLF

WOLF, Peter

P&R/D&D/LP '84

Singles: 12–inch 33/45rpm

EMI AMERICA 4-6 84-85

Singles: 7–inch

EMI AMERICA 3-4 84-87

Picture Sleeves

EMI AMERICA 3-4 84-87

LPs: 10/12–inch 33rpm

EMI AMERICA 5-8 84-87

MCA 5-8 90

Also see FRANKLIN, Aretha
Also see GEILS, J., Band

WOLF, Peter, & Mick Jagger

Singles: 12–inch 33/45rpm

EMI AMERICA 8-10 84

Singles: 7–inch

EMI AMERICA 3-4 84

LPs: 10/12–inch 33rpm

EMI AMERICA 8-10 84

Also see JAGGER, Mick
Also see WOLF, Peter

WOLFMAN JACK
(Bob Smith)

Singles: 7–inch

AGC 4-8

WOODEN NICKEL 3-4 72-73

LPs: 10/12–inch 33rpm

COLUMBIA 8-10 75

WOODEN NICKEL 8-10 72-73

Also see FLASH CADILLAC & CONTINENTAL KIDS
Also see GUESS WHO
Also see STAMPEDERS

WOLFMAN JACK & WOLF PACK

Singles: 7–inch

BREAD (71 "Wolfman Boogie") .25-30 65

BREAD (73 "New Orleans").......25-30 65

LPs: 10/12–inch 33rpm

BREAD (0170 "Wolfman Jack and the Wolf Pack") 150-250 65

WOMACK, Bobby
(With the Brotherhood; with Peace)

P&R/R&B/LP '68

Singles: 12–inch 33/45rpm

ELEKTRA/WOMACK 4-8 83

Singles: 7–inch

ARISTA 3-5 79

ATLANTIC......................................4-8 67

BEVERLY GLEN.............................3-4 81-84

CHECKER 5-10 65

COLUMBIA 3-5 76-78

COLUMBIA/BROTHERHOOD.......3-5 76-77

ELEKTRA/WOMACK 3-4 83

LIBERTY 3-5 70

MCA..3-4 86

MINIT 4-8 67-70

U.A. 3-5 71-76

EPs: 7–inch 33/45rpm

U.A. 10-15 72

(Promotional issue only.)

LPs: 10/12–inch 33rpm

ARISTA 5-8 79

BEVERLY GLEN.............................5-8 81-84

COLUMBIA 8-10 75-78

COLUMBIA/BROTHERHOOD.....8-10 76

ELEKTRA/WOMACK 5-8 83

LIBERTY (7600 series)...............8-10 70

LIBERTY (10000 series)...............5-8 80s

MCA..5-8 85

MINIT 10-12 68-70

U.A. 8-10 71-76

Also see BROTHERHOOD
Also see FELDER, Wilton, & Bobby Womack
Also see SZABO, Gabor
Also see VALENTINOS
Also see WOMACK BROTHERS

WOMACK, Bobby, & Patti Labelle

P&R/R&B '84

Singles: 7–inch

BEVERLY GLEN.............................3-4 84

Also see LABELLE, Patti
Also see WOMACK, Bobby

WOMACK, Bobby, & Bill Withers

R&B '75

Singles: 7–inch

U.A. 3-4 75

Also see WITHERS, Bill

WOMACK & WOMACK

R&B/D&D '84

Singles: 7–inch

ELEKTRA.................................... 3-4 84-85

LPs: 10/12–inch 33rpm

ELEKTRA.................................... 5-8 84-85

Members: Linda Womack; Cecil Womack.

WOMACK BROTHERS

Singles: 7–inch

SAR.. 4-6 61

Also see VALENTINOS
Also see WOMACK, Bobby

WOMBLES

P&R '74

Singles: 7–inch

COLUMBIA 3-4 74-75

LPs: 10/12–inch 33rpm

COLUMBIA 8-10 74

Member: Mike Batt.

WOMENFOLK

P&R/LP '64

Singles: 7–inch

RCA... 3-4 64-66

LPs: 10/12–inch 33rpm

RCA.. 10-15 63-66

WONDER, Stevie
(Little Stevie Wonder)

P&R/R&B/LP '63

Singles: 12–inch 33/45rpm

MOTOWN 4-8
TAMLA 4-8

Singles: 7–inch

MOTOWN 3-4 84-88
MOTOWN/TOPPS (8 "Fingertips Part 2")................................ 50-75 67
MOTOWN/TOPPS (10 "Uptight")............................... 50-75 67
(Topps Chewing Gum promotional items. Single-sided, cardboard flexi, picture discs. Issued with generic paper sleeve.)
TAMLA (1600 thru 1800 series).... 3-4 82-86
TAMLA (54061 "I Call It Pretty Music") 15-25 62
TAMLA (54074 "Contract on Love")...................................... 10-20 63
TAMLA (54080 "Fingertips") 5-10 63
TAMLA (54086 "Workout Stevie, Workout") 5-10 63
TAMLA (54090 "Castles in the Sand") 8-12 64
TAMLA (54096 "Hey Harmonica Man").. 8-12 64
TAMLA (54103 "Happy Street") 10-20 64
TAMLA (54119 thru 54139)......... 5-10 65-66
TAMLA (54142 "Some Day at Christmas") 8-12 66
TAMLA (54147 thru 54323)........... 3-6 67-81
(Black vinyl.)
TAMLA (54147 thru 54323) 5-10 69-78
(Colored vinyl. Promotional issues only.)
MOTOWN 3-4 82

Picture Sleeves

MOTOWN 3-4 87
TAMLA (1639 thru 1846) 3-6 82-86
TAMLA (54061 "I Call It Pretty Music")...................................25-50 62
TAMLA (54080 "Fingertips") 15-25 63
TAMLA (54136 "Blowin' in the Wind") 15-25 66
TAMLA (54139 "A Place in the Sun")...15-25 66
TAMLA (54281 thru 54317) 4-8 77-80

EPs: 7–inch 33/45rpm

MOTOWN (2006 "Stevie Wonder")...................................15-25 60s
MOTOWN (2020 "Songs in the Key of Life") 10-15 76
TAMLA (340 "Something Extra for *Songs in the Key of Life*") 10-15 76
TAMLA (60272 "Stevie Wonder")....................................15-25 67

LPs: 10/12–inch 33rpm

MOTOWN (100 & 200 series)........5-8 82
MOTOWN (800 series) 12-15 77
MOTOWN (6000 series) 5-8 84-91
TAMLA (232 "Tribute to Uncle Ray")...50-80 63
TAMLA (233 "The Jazz Soul of Stevie Wonder")........................50-80 63
TAMLA (240 "Little Stevie Wonder")....................................40-50 63
TAMLA (250 "With a Song in My Heart")...............................35-55 64
TAMLA (255 "At the Beach") 35-55 64
TAMLA (268 thru 279) 15-20 66-67
TAMLA (281 "Someday at Christmas") 30-40 67
TAMLA (282 thru 371) 8-15 68-79
TAMLA (373 "Hotter Than July")....5-8 80
TAMLA (6000 series)................10-12 82-85

Promotional LPs

MOTOWN (PR-77 "Hotter Than July")...10-15 80
TAMLA (PR-61 "Stevie Wonder's Journey Through the Secret Life of Plants") 10-15 79
TAMLA (PR-98/99 "Radio Programmer's Special")...................................15-20 80s

Also see CHARLENE & Stevie Wonder
Also see DIONNE & FRIENDS
Also see IGLESIAS, Julio, & Stevie Wonder
Also see JACKSONS
Also see JOHN, Elton
Also see KHAN, Chaka
Also see LENNON, Julian, & Stevie Wonder
Also see McCARTNEY, Paul, & Stevie Wonder
Also see REDNOW, Eivets
Also see ROSS, Diana, Stevie Wonder, Marvin Gaye & Smokey Robinson

Also see TEMPTATIONS / Stevie Wonder
Also see THIRD WORLD
Also see U.S.A. for AFRICA
Also see WILLIAMS, Deniece

WONDER, Stevie / John Denver

Singles: 7-inch

WHAT'S IT ALL ABOUT................ 4-8 80
(Public service, radio station issue.)
Also see DENVER, John

WONDER, Stevie, & Michael Jackson

P&R '88

Singles: 7-inch

MOTOWN 3-4 88

Picture Sleeves

MOTOWN 3-4 88
Also see JACKSON, Michael

WONDER, Stevie, & Clarence Paul
(Little Stevie Wonder & Clarence Paul)

Singles: 7-inch

TAMLA (54070 "Little Water Boy") 25-35 62
Also see PAUL, Clarence

WONDER, Stevie / Dionne Warwick

LP '84

LPs: 10/12-inch 33rpm

MOTOWN 5-8 84
Also see WARWICK, Dionne
Also see WONDER, Stevie

WONDER BAND

P&R '79

Singles: 7-inch

ATCO 3-4 79

LPs: 10/12-inch 33rpm

ATCO 5-8 79

WONDER LAND, Alice: see ALICE WONDER LAND

WONDER WHO?
(4 Seasons)

P&R '67

Singles: 7-inch

COLLECTABLES 3-4 80s
PHILIPS 3-5 65-67
VEE JAY 12-15 64

Picture Sleeves

PHILIPS 15-20 65-67
Also see 4 SEASONS

WOO, Gerry

R&B '87

Singles: 7-inch

POLYDOR.................................. 3-4 87-88

WOOD, Bobby

P&R '64

Singles: 7-inch

CHALLENGE 3-5 62
CINNAMON.................................. 3-4 74
JOY 3-5 63-65
LUCKY ELEVEN 3-4 73
MALA 3-5 66
MGM 3-4 67-69
SUN (369 "Everybody's Searchin") 50-100 61

LPs: 10/12-inch 33rpm

JOY 10-15 64
Also see PRESLEY, Elvis

WOOD, Brenton

P&R/R&B/LP '67

Singles: 7-inch

BRENT (7052 "Good Lovin'")....... 5-10 66
BRENT (7057 "Cross the Bridge") 10-20 66
CREAM 3-4 76-78
DOUBLE SHOT 4-6 67-71
FIRST PRESIDENT (428 "The Kangaroo") 10-15 60
MR. WOOD.................................. 3-5 72-73
PROPHESY 3-4 73
WAND (145 "Mr. Schemer") 25-35 64
W.B. 3-6 75

LPs: 10/12-inch 33rpm

CREAM 5-8 77
DOUBLE SHOT 10-20 67

WOOD, Del

P&R '51

Singles: 78rpm

DECCA 3-4 53-54
MERCURY 3-4 62-64
RCA 3-4 55-59
REPUBLIC 3-4 51-54
TENNESSEE 3-6 51

Singles: 7-inch

CHART.................................. 3-4 71-72
DECCA 3-5 53-54
MERCURY.................................. 3-4 62-64
RCA 3-5 55-59
REPUBLIC 3-8 51-54
TENNESSEE 5-10 51

EPs: 7-inch 33/45rpm

RCA 5-12 55-60
REPUBLIC.................................. 4-10 54-57

LPs: 10/12-inch 33rpm

CAMDEN 5-12 62-64
COLUMBIA 8-12 66
MERCURY.................................. 5-12 62-64
RCA 5-15 55-60
REPUBLIC.................................. 5-15 54-57
VOCALION 5-10 60s

WOOD, Lauren

P&R '79

Singles: 7-inch

W.B. 3-4 79-81

Picture Sleeves

W.B. 3-4 81

LPs: 10/12-inch 33rpm

W.B. 5-8 81
Also see McDONALD, Michael

WOOD, Ron
(Ronnie Wood)

LP '75

Singles: 7–inch

COLUMBIA 3-4 79
W.B. 3-4 75-76

LPs: 10/12–inch 33rpm

COLUMBIA 5-8 79-81
W.B. 8-10 74-75

Also see BECK, Jeff, Ronnie Wood & Rod Stewart
Also see FACES
Also see ROLLING STONES
Also see SEXTON, Charlie, & Ron Wood

WOOD, Ron, & Ronnie Lane
(With Pete Townshend)

LPs: 10/12–inch 33rpm

ATCO (126 "Mahoney's Last Stand") 10-15 76
(Soundtrack.)

Also see TOWNSHEND, Pete, & Ronnie Lane
Also see WOOD, Ron

WOOD, Roy
(Roy Wood's Wizzard; Roy Wood Wizzo Band)

LP '73

Singles: 7–inch

U.A. 3-4 73-76

LPs: 10/12–inch 33rpm

U.A. 8-10 73-74
W.B. 5-8 79

Members: Roy Wood; Rick Price; Nick Pentelow; Mike Burney; Keith Smart; Charlie Grima; Bill Hunt; Bob Brady.

Also see ELECTRIC LIGHT ORCHESTRA
Also see MOVE

WOODBURY, Woody

LP '60

LPs: 10/12-Inch 33rpm

STEREODDITIES 10-25 59-63

WOODENTOPS

LP '86

Singles: 7–inch

COLUMBIA 3-4 86

LPs: 10/12–inch 33rpm

COLUMBIA 5-8 86

WOODS, Maceo
(With the Christian Tabernacle Choir)

R&B '69

Singles: 78rpm

VEE JAY (100 series) 3-5 55-56

Singles: 7–inch

ABC 3-4 73
VEE JAY (100 series) 4-8 55-56
VOLT 3-4 69

LPs: 10/12–inch 33rpm

GOSPEL TRUTH 4-8 72-74
SAVOY 4-8 76-83
STAX 4-8 78
TRIP 4-8 73
VEE JAY 5-15 60-65
VOLT 5-12 69

WOODS, Ren

R&B '79

Singles: 7–inch

ARC 3-4 79
ELEKTRA 3-4 82

WOODS, Stevie

P&R/R&B/LP '81

Singles: 7–inch

COTILLION 3-4 81-83

LPs: 10/12–inch 33rpm

COTILLION 5-8 81-82

WOODS EMPIRE

R&B '81

Singles: 12–inch 33/45rpm

TABU 4-6 81

Singles: 7–inch

TABU 3-4 81

LPs: 10/12–inch 33rpm

TABU 5-8 81

WOOLEY, Sheb

P&R '55

Singles: 78rpm

BLUEBONNET (125 "Peepin' Thru the Keyhole") 10-15 54
BULLET (603 "I Can't Live Without You") 20-40 45
MGM 5-10 48-57

Singles: 7–inch

BLUEBONNET (125 "Peepin' Thru the Keyhole") 30-50 54
BLUEBONNET (130 "Too Long with the Wrong Woman") 30-50 54
MGM (11000 series) 10-20 52-55
MGM (12000 series) 5-15 55-61
MGM (13000 series) 4-8 61-68
MGM (14000 series) 3-6 68-75
POLYDOR 3-4

Picture Sleeves

MGM 4-8 59-62

EPs: 7–inch 33/45rpm

MGM 10-20 56-58

LPs: 10/12–inch 33rpm

LAKESHORE (621-2-3 "Ben Colder and Sheb Wooley") 10-20 70s
MGM (3299 "Blue Guitar") 30-50 56
MGM (3904 "Days of Rawhide") 20-25 56
MGM (4136 thru 4026) 15-20 61-62
MGM (4275 thru 4615) 8-15 65-69

Also see COLDER, Ben

WOOLIES

P&R '67

Singles: 7–inch

DUNHILL 3-5 66-67
SPIRIT 8-15 65-66
TTP (156 "Black Crow Blues") ... 15-20 65

LPs: 10/12-inch 33rpm

SPIRIT (2001 "Basic Rock")...... 20-30 71
SPIRIT (2005 "Live at Lizard's") 20-30 73

Members: Stormy Rice; Ron English; Jeff Baldori; Bob Baldori.

WOOLLEY, Bruce, & Camera Club

LP '80

Singles: 7-inch

COLUMBIA 3-4 80

Picture Sleeves

COLUMBIA 3-4 80

EPs: 7-inch 33/45rpm

COLUMBIA (11264 "Bruce Woolley and the Camera Club") 4-8 80
(Issued with paper sleeve. Promotional issue only.)

LPs: 10/12-inch 33rpm

COLUMBIA (36301 "Bruce Woolley and the Camera Club") 5-8 80

WORD of MOUTH
(Featuring D.J. Cheese)

R&B/D&D '85

Singles: 12-inch 33/45rpm

BEAUTY & BEAST...................... 4-6 85
PROFILE.................................. 4-6 86

WORLD

D&D '84

Singles: 12-inch 33/45rpm

ELEKTRA.................................. 4-6 83

WORLD CLASS WRECKIN CRU

P&R/R&B '88

Singles: 7-inch

KRU'CUT.................................. 3-4 88

WORLD PARTY

LP '86

Singles: 7-inch

CHRYSALIS.............................. 3-4 86-87

Picture Sleeves

CHRYSALIS.............................. 3-4 87

LPs: 10/12-inch 33rpm

CHRYSALIS.............................. 5-8 86
ENSIGN 5-8 90

WORLD PREMIER

R&B/D&D '84

Singles: 12-inch 33/45rpm

CAPITOL.................................. 4-6 84

Singles: 7-inch

CAPITOL.................................. 3-4 84

WORLD'S FAMOUS SUPREME TEAM

R&B/D&D '84

Singles: 12-inch 33/45rpm

ISLAND 4-6 84

Singles: 7-inch

ISLAND 3-4 84

Also see McLAREN, Malcom

WORRELL, Bernie

R&B '79

Singles: 7-inch

ARISTA......................................3-4 79

LPs: 10/12-inch 33rpm

ARISTA......................................5-8 79

Also see McLAREN, Malcom
Also see PARLIAMENT

WORTH, Marion

C&W '59

Singles: 7-inch

CHEROKEE...............................5-10 59
COLUMBIA..................................4-8 60-67
DECCA 3-6 67-70
GUYDEN....................................5-10 59-60

Picture Sleeves

COLUMBIA..................................3-5 61-62

LPs: 10/12-inch 33rpm

COLUMBIA...............................10-20 63-64
DECCA 8-12 67

WRABIT

LP '82

Singles: 7-inch

MCA..3-4 82

LPs: 10/12-inch 33rpm

MCA..5-8 82

WRATHCHILD AMERICA

LP '89

LPs: 10/12-inch 33rpm

ATLANTIC..................................5-8 89

WRAY, Bill

P&R '79

Singles: 7-inch

ABC..3-5 79

WRAY, Link
(With His Ray Men; with His Wray Men; Link Ray)

P&R/R&B '58

Singles: 78rpm

CADENCE 5-8 58

Singles: 7-inch

ATLAS.......................................4-6 62
BARNABY..................................3-4 76
CADENCE 5-8 58
EPIC...5-8 59-61
HEAVY......................................3-5 68
KAY (3690 "I Sez Baby") 50-100 58
MR. G.......................................3-5 69
NORTON 3-4 89
OKEH.......................................3-5 67
POLYDOR 3-4 70-74
RUMBLE (1000 "Jack the Ripper")................................15-25 61
SWAN (4137 "Jack the Ripper") ..6-10 63
SWAN (4154 "Week End")............5-8 63
SWAN (4163 thru 4187)...............4-6 63-64

SWAN (4201 "Good Rockin' Tonight")................................. 10-15 65
SWAN (4211 thru 4232)................ 4-6 65
SWAN (4239 "Ace of Spades"). 10-12 65
SWAN (4244 "Batman Theme").... 5-8 66
SWAN (4261 "Ace of Spades")... 8-10 66
SWAN (4273 thru 4282)............... 3-5 66-67
TRANS ATLAS (687 "Big City Stomp") 10-15 62

Picture Sleeves

EPIC.. 20-35 59

LPs: 10/12-inch 33rpm

EPIC (3661 "Link Wray and the Wraymen").............................. 40-50 60
POLYDOR.................................. 8-10 71-74
RECORD FACTORY 20-25 74
SWAN 50-60 63
VERMILLION 20-25 75
VISA.. 5-8 79-80

Also see DUDLEY, Dave / Link Wray
Also see GORDON, Robert

WRAY, Link / Red Saunders

Singles: 7-inch

OKEH (7100 series)..................... 4-6 63
OKEH (7200 series)..................... 3-5 67

WRAY, Lucky

(Link Wray)

Singles: 78rpm

STARDAY (500 series).............. 5-10 56
STARDAY (608 "Teenage Cutie") 25-35 57

Singles: 7-inch

STARDAY (500 series) 20-25 56
STARDAY (608 "Teenage Cutie") 150-200 57

WRAY, Vernon

(With Link Wray)

LPs: 10/12-inch 33rpm

VERMILLION 20-25

WRAY BROTHERS

(Wray Family)

Singles: 7-inch

INFINITY 6-10 62
LAWN.. 6-10 63

Members: Link Wray; Doug Wray; Vernon Wray.
Also see WRAY, Link

WRECKING CREW

R&B '83

Singles: 12-inch 33/45rpm

ERECT 4-6 83

Singles: 7-inch

ERECT 3-4 83
SOUND of FLORIDA.................. 3-4 83

WRECKX-N-EFFEC

(Wrecks-N-Effect)

LP '90

LPs: 10/12-inch 33rpm

MOTOWN 5-8 89

WRIGHT, Bernard

R&B/LP '81

Singles: 12-inch 33/45rpm

ARISTA..4-6 83
MANHATTAN.................................4-6 85

Singles: 7-inch

ARISTA..3-4 83-84
GRP 3-4 81-82
MANHATTAN.................................3-4 86

LPs: 10/12-inch 33rpm

ARISTA..5-8 83
GRP 5-8 81
MANHATTAN.................................5-8 86

WRIGHT, Betty

P&R/R&B '68

Singles: 12-inch 33/45rpm

EPIC..4-6 81
JAMAICA 4-6 84-85

Singles: 7-inch

ALSTON...3-8 68-79
ATCO 3-4 83
DEEP CITY 10-20 66
EPIC..3-4 81-83
FIRST STRING...............................3-4 86
JAMAICA 3-4 84-85
MS. B. 3-4 88

LPs: 10/12-inch 33rpm

ALSTON.......................................6-10 72-79
ATCO 10-15 68
COLLECTABLES............................5-8 88
EPIC..5-8 81-83
MS. B. 5-8 88

Also see ALAIMO, Steve, & Betty Wright
Also see BROWN, Peter, & Betty Wright
Also see HUGH, Grayson, & Betty Wright
Also see KC & SUNSHINE BAND
Also see LITTLE BEAVER

WRIGHT, Billy

R&B '49

Singles: 78rpm

REGENT...4-6 51
SAVOY (710 thru 761)................5-10 49-50

Singles: 7-inch

CARROLLTON 10-15 59
SAVOY (776 "Mean Old Wine").15-20 51
SAVOY (827 "Drinkin' and Thinkin'") 8-12 52

WRIGHT, Charles, & Watts 103rd Street Rhythm Band

R&B/LP '69

Singles: 7-inch

ABC...3-4 75
DUNHILL..3-4 73-74
W.B. 3-4 70-71

LPs: 10/12-inch 33rpm

ABC...6-10 75
DUNHILL......................................6-10 73-74
W.B. 8-12 70-72

Also see SHIELDS
Also see WATTS 103RD STREET RHYTHM BAND

WRIGHT, Dale
(With the Rock-Its; with Wright Guys & Dons)
P&R '58

Singles: 7–inch
ALCAR 8-10 60
FRATERNITY 10-15 58-59
QUEEN-B 8-12

WRIGHT, Gary
(With Spooky Tooth)
LP '75

Singles: 7–inch
A&M 3-4 70-72
W.B. 3-4 75-81

LPs: 10/12–inch 33rpm
A&M 8-12 70-76
W.B. 5-8 75-81
Also see SPOOKY TOOTH

WRIGHT, Janet
D&D '84

Singles: 12–inch 33/45rpm
COTILLION 4-6 84

WRIGHT, O.V.
P&R/R&B '65

Singles: 7–inch
ABC 3-4 75-76
BACK BEAT 3-8 65-74
GOLDWAX 5-10 64
HI 3-6 76-79

LPs: 10/12–inch 33rpm
BACK BEAT 10-20 65-72
HI 5-10 78-79

WRIGHT, Priscilla
P&R '55

Singles: 78rpm
UNIQUE 4-8 55

Singles: 7–inch
20TH FOX 5-10 59
UNIQUE 5-10 55

WRIGHT, Ruben
R&B '66

Singles: 7–inch
CAPITOL 3-5 64-67
WYNNE 3-5 60

WRIGHT, Ruby
(With the Bello Larks)
P&R '57

Singles: 78rpm
FRATERNITY 3-6 57

Singles: 7–inch
CANDEE (502 "This Is Christmas") 10-20
FRATERNITY 5-10 57
KING (Monaural) 5-10 59
KING (Stereo) 10-15 59

WRIGHT, Ruby, & Dick Pike

Singles: 7–inch
KING (5192 "Three Stars") 8-10 59
Also see WRIGHT, Ruby

WRIGHT, Steven
LP '85

LPs: 10/12–inch 33rpm
W.B. 5-8 85

WRITERS
R&B '79

Singles: 12–inch 33/45rpm
COLUMBIA 4-6 79

Singles: 7–inch
COLUMBIA 3-4 78-79

LPs: 10/12–inch 33rpm
COLUMBIA 5-8 79

WUF TICKET
R&B '82

Singles: 12–inch 33/45rpm
PRELUDE 4-6 81

Singles: 7–inch
PRELUDE 3-4 81

WYCOFF, Michael
R&B '80

Singles: 12–inch 33/45rpm
RCA 4-6 83

Singles: 7–inch
RCA 3-4 80-84

LPs: 10/12–inch 33rpm
RCA 5-8 83
Also see CLAYTON, Merry

WYLIE, Richard
(Richard "Popcorn" Wylie)
R&B '71

Singles: 7–inch
ABC 3-4 75
EPIC 10-20 62-63
KAREN (1542 "Rosemary, What Happened") 15-25 68
MOTOWN (1009 "Money") 30-40 61
MOTOWN (1019 "Have I the Right") 30-40 61
NORTHERN (3732 "Pretty Girl") 15-25 60s
SOUL 3-4 71

Picture Sleeves
EPIC 4-8 62

LPs: 10/12–inch 33rpm
ABC 8-10 74
Also see POPCORN & MOHAWKS

WYMAN, Bill
P&R '67

Singles: 12–inch 33/45rpm
A&M (12041 "Je Suis Un Rock Star") 6-10 81

Singles: 7–inch
A&M (2367 "Je Suis Un Rock Star") 3-4 81

ROLLING STONES...................... 4-6 74-75

Promotional Singles

A&M (2367 "Je Suis Un Rock Star").. 4-6 81

A&M (12041 "Je Suis Un Rock Star").................................... 15-20 81
(12–inch single.)

Picture Sleeves

A&M (2367 "Je Suis Un Rock Star").. 3-5 81

LPs: 10/12–inch 33rpm

ROLLING STONES.................. 8-10 74-76

WYMAN, Bill / Rolling Stones

Singles: 7–inch

LONDON (907 "In Another Land") 4-6 67

Promotional Singles

LONDON (907 "In Another Land").................................... 8-10 67

Picture Sleeves

LONDON (907 "In Another Land").................................... 10-15 67

Also see ROLLING STONES
Also see WYMAN, Bill

WYND CHYMES

R&B '83

Singles: 7–inch

RCA.. 3-4 82-83

LPs: 10/12–inch 33rpm

RCA.. 5-8 82

WYNETTE, Tammy

(With Ricky Skaggs; with Emmylou Harris)

C&W '66

Singles: 7–inch

EPIC (Except 1) 3-8 66-86
EPIC (1 "Wonders You Perform") 5-10 70
(Colored vinyl. Promotional issue only.)

Picture Sleeves

EPIC.. 3-4 69-76

LPs: 10/12–inch 33rpm

COLUMBIA 5-10 73
EPIC.. 5-15 68-86
HARMONY 5-10 70-71
TIME-LIFE.................................... 5-8 81

Also see CASH, Johnny / Tammy Wynette
Also see HOUSTON, David, & Tammy Wynette
Also see JONES, George, & Tammy Wynette
Also see LYNN, Loretta / Tammy Wynette
Also see NEWTON, Wayne, & Tammy Wynette

WYNETTE, Tammy, & Randy Travis

C&W '91

Singles: 7–inch

EPIC 3-4 91

Also see TRAVIS, Randy
Also see WYNETTE, Tammy

WYNNE, Philippe

R&B '77

Singles: 12–inch 33/45rpm

FANTASY.................................. 4-6 83

Singles: 7–inch

COTILLION..................................3-4 77
FANTASY 3-4 83
SUGAR HILL................................3-4 83
UNCLE JAM..................................3-4 80

LPs: 10/12–inch 33rpm

COTILLION..................................5-8 77

Also see DUNLAP, Gene
Also see SPINNERS

X

X

LP '81

Singles: 7–inch

ELEKTRA......................................3-4 82-83

Picture Sleeves

ELEKTRA......................................3-4 83

LPs: 10/12–inch 33rpm

ELEKTRA......................................5-8 82-88
ROCSHIRE 5-8 83
SLASH (104 "Los Angeles") 10-20 80
SLASH (107 "Wild Gift")............10-20 81

Members: Dave Alvin; Exene Cervenka; John Doe; D.J. Bonebrake;
Tony Gilkyson.

Also see ALVIN, Dave
Also see BLASTERS
Also see DOE, John
Also see LONE JUSTICE

X, Malcolm: see MALCOLM X

X-CLAN

LP '90

LPs: 10/12–inch 33rpm

4TH & BROADWAY 5-8 90

XTC

LP '80

Singles: 7–inch

EPIC..3-4 82
GEFFEN (Except "PRO" series)....3-4 83-89
GEFFEN ("PRO" series)...............3-5 83-84
(Promotional issues only.)
RSO 3-4 81
VIRGIN..3-4 79-81

Picture Sleeves

GEFFEN 3-4 89
VIRGIN..3-4 79

LPs: 10/12–inch 33rpm

EPIC..5-10 82
GEFFEN 5-8 84-89
RSO 5-10 81
VIRGIN..5-10 78-82

Members: Andy Partridge; Barry Andrews; Colin Moulding;
Terry Chambers; Dave Gregory.

Also see SHRIEKBACK

X-25 BAND

R&B '82

Singles: 7-inch

H.C.R.C 3-4 82

XYZ

LP '89

LPs: 10/12-inch 33rpm

ENIGMA 5-8 89

Members: Anka Wolbert; Ronny Moorings; Pieter Nooten.

XAVIER
(Xavier Smith)

R&B/LP '82

Singles: 12-inch 33/45rpm

LIBERTY 4-6 82

Singles: 7-inch

LIBERTY 3-4 82

LPs: 10/12-inch 33rpm

LIBERTY 5-8 82

XAVION

R&B '85

Singles: 7-inch

ASYLUM 3-4 84-85

LPs: 10/12-inch 33rpm

ASYLUM 5-8 84

XENA

D&D '83

Singles: 12-inch 33/45rpm

EMERGENCY 4-6 83

X-RAYS

R&B '49

Singles: 7-inch

SAVOY 10-15 48-49

Also see JACQUET, Illinois
Also see WALKER, T-Bone

XYMOX

LP '89

Singles: 12-inch 33/45rpm

4AD 4-8 85-88
WING/POLYGRAM 5-8 89

LPs: 10/12-inch 33rpm

4AD 5-10 85-87
WING/MERCURY 5-8 91
WING/POLYGRAM 5-8 89

Y

Y & T
(Yesterday & Today)

LP '83

Singles: 7-inch

A&M 3-4 81-85

LPs: 10/12-inch 33rpm

A&M 5-8 81-85
GEFFEN 5-8 87-89
LONDON 8-10 78

YACHTS

LP '79

Singles: 7-inch

POLYDOR 3-4 79

LPs: 10/12-inch 33rpm

POLYDOR 5-8 79-80
RADAR 6-10

YAMASHTA, Stomu
(With Steve Winwood & Michael Shrieve)

LP '76

LPs: 10/12-inch 33rpm

ARISTA 5-8 77
ISLAND 5-8 76-78
VANGUARD 8-10 71-74

Also see WINWOOD, Steve

YAMBU

R&B '75

Singles: 7-inch

MONTUNO GRINGO 3-4 75

YANKOVIC, "Weird Al"

P&R/LP '83

Singles: 12-inch 33/45rpm

ROCK 'N' ROLL 4-6 84

Singles: 7-inch

CAPITOL 3-4 79
ROCK 'N' ROLL 3-4 83-89
TK 3-4 81

Picture Sleeves

ROCK 'N' ROLL 3-4 83-89

LPs: 10/12-inch 33rpm

ROCK 'N' ROLL 5-8 83-89

YANNI

LP '90

LPs: 10/12-inch 33rpm

PRIVATE 5-8 90

YARBROUGH, Bob
(Bob Yarborough)

C&W '71

Singles: 7-inch

MUSIC MILL 3-5 76
SUGAR HILL 3-5 71

YARBROUGH, Glenn

LP '64

Singles: 7-inch

PRIDE 3-4 72
RCA 3-4 64-68
STAX 3-4 73-74
W.B. 3-4 68-71

Picture Sleeves

RCA 3-6 65

LPs: 10/12-inch 33rpm

ELEKTRA (135 "Here We Go, Baby") 20-30 57
FIRST AMERICAN 5-8 81
IM'PRESS 8-10 71

RCA.. 10-20 64-69
STAX.. 8-10 74
TRADITION................................ 8-15 67-70
W.B. 8-12 68-71
Also see LIMELITERS

YARBROUGH & PEOPLES

R&B/LP '80

Singles: 12–inch 33/45rpm

TOTAL EXPERIENCE 4-6 82-86

Singles: 7–inch

MERCURY 3-4 80-81
TOTAL EXPERIENCE 3-4 82-86

LPs: 10/12–inch 33rpm

MERCURY 5-8 80
TOTAL EXPERIENCE 5-8 82-86
Members: Calvin Yarbrough; Alisa Peoples.

YARDBIRDS

P&R/LP '65

Singles: 7–inch

EPIC (9709 "I Wish You Could") 15-20 64
EPIC (9790 thru 10204) 5-8 65-67
EPIC (10248 "Ten Little Indians") 10-15 67
EPIC (10303 "Goodnight Sweet Josephine") 15-20 68

Picture Sleeves

EPIC (Except 9709) 10-15 65-66
EPIC (9709 "I Wish You Could") 75-125 64
(Promotional issue only.)

LPs: 10/12–inch 33rpm

ACCORD.................................... 5-8 81-83
COLUMBIA (11311 "Live Yardbirds") 25-35 72
(Columbia Special Products issue.)
COMPLEAT 8-12 86
EPIC (24167 "For Your Love") 50-100 65
(Monaural.)
EPIC (24177 "Having a Rave Up") 40-60 65
(Monaural.)
EPIC (24210 "Over Under Sideways Down") 40-60 66
(Monaural.)
EPIC (24246 "Greatest Hits").... 30-40 66
(Monaural.)
EPIC (24313 "Little Games")..... 40-60 67
(Monaural.)
EPIC (26167 "For Your Love").. 30-40 65
(Stereo.)
EPIC (26177 "Having a Rave Up") 30-40 65
(Stereo.)
EPIC (26210 "Over Under Sideways Down") 30-45 66
(Stereo.)
EPIC (26246 "Greatest Hits").... 30-40 66
(Stereo.)
EPIC (26313 "Little Games") 35-50 67
(Stereo.)
EPIC (30135 "The Yardbirds Featuring Performances By Jeff Beck, Eric Clapton, Jimmy Page") 75-100 70
EPIC (30615 "Live Yardbirds")...50-75 71
EPIC (34490 "Yardbirds Favorites") 8-10 77
EPIC (34491 "Great Hits") 8-10 77
EPIC (38455 "The Yardbirds").......5-8 83
EPIC (48455 "The Yardbirds")...12-15 83
(Half-speed mastered.)
MERCURY (21271 "Eric Clapton & Yardbirds Live with Sonny Boy Williamson")............................20-30 66
(Monaural.)
MERCURY (61271 "Eric Clapton & Yardbirds Live with Sonny Boy Williamson")............................30-40 66
(Stereo.)
RHINO 6-10 82-86
SPRINGBOARD 8-10 72
Members: Eric Clapton; Jeff Beck; Keith Relf; Jimmy Page; Jim McCarty; Chris Dreja.
Also see ARMAGEDDON
Also see BECK, Jeff
Also see BOX of FROGS
Also see CLAPTON, Eric
Also see PAGE, Jimmy
Also see RELF, Keith
Also see RENAISSANCE
Also see WILLIAMSON, Sonny Boy

YARROW, Peter

P&R/LP '72

Singles: 7–inch

W.B. 3-4 68-75

LPs: 10/12–inch 33rpm

W.B. 8-10 72-75
Also see PETER, PAUL & MARY

YAZ

(Yazoo)

P&R/R&B/LP '82

Singles: 12–inch 33/45rpm

SIRE..4-6 82-84

Singles: 7–inch

SIRE (Except 29953) 3-4 82-84
SIRE (29953 "Situation")...............4-6 82
(Credited to Yazoo.)
SIRE (29953 "Situation")...............3-4 82
(Credited to Yaz.)

Picture Sleeves

SIRE..3-4 82

LPs: 10/12–inch 33rpm

SIRE..5-8 82-83
Members: Alison Moyet; Vince Clarke.
Also see MOYET, Alison

YAZZ & PLASTIC POPULATION

P&R '88

Singles: 7–inch

ELEKTRA......................................3-4 88

Picture Sleeves

ELEKTRA 3-4 88

YELLO

D&D/LP '83

Singles: 12-inch 33/45rpm

ELEKTRA 4-6 83-85
RALPH 5-8 81
STIFF 4-8

Singles: 7-inch

ELEKTRA 3-4 83-85
MERCURY 3-4 87-89
RALPH 3-4 81
STIFF (Picture discs) 4-8

Picture Sleeves

MERCURY 3-4 87

LPs: 10/12-inch 33rpm

ELEKTRA 5-8 83-85
MERCURY 5-8 87-89
RALPH 8-10 81

YELLOW BALLOON

P&R '67

Singles: 7-inch

CANTERBURY 4-6 67-68

LPs: 10/12-inch 33rpm

CANTERBURY 15-20 67

Members: Alex Valdez; Don Grady; Don Braucht; Forrest Green; Paul Cannella; Darryl Dragon.

Also see CAPTAIN & TENNILLE
Also see SPIRIT

YELLOW MAGIC ORCHESTRA

P&R/R&B/LP '80

Singles: 12-inch 33/45rpm

A&M 4-6 80

Singles: 7-inch

A&M 3-4 80
HORIZON 3-4 80

Picture Sleeves

HORIZON 3-4 80

LPs: 10/12-inch 33rpm

A&M 5-8 80-81
HORIZON 5-8 80

YELLOWJACKETS

LP '83

Singles: 7-inch

MCA 3-4 86
W.B. 3-4 81-85

LPs: 10/12-inch 33rpm

MCA 5-8 86
W.B. 5-8 81-85

YELLOWMAN

D&D '84

Singles: 12-inch 33/45rpm

COLUMBIA 4-6 84

Singles: 7-inch

COLUMBIA 3-4 84

LPs: 10/12-inch 33rpm

COLUMBIA 5-8 84

YES

P&R/LP '71

Singles: 12-inch 33/45rpm

ATCO 4-6 83-86

Singles: 7-inch

ATCO 3-4 83-87
ATLANTIC (Black vinyl) 3-6 70-78
ATLANTIC (Colored vinyl) 4-8 70-78

Picture Sleeves

ATCO 3-4 83-87

LPs: 10/12-inch 33rpm

ARISTA 5-8 91
ATCO 5-8 83-87
ATLANTIC (100 series) 10-15 73
ATLANTIC (500 series) 6-12 80
ATLANTIC (900 series) 10-15 74
ATLANTIC (7000 series) 8-12 71-72
ATLANTIC (8000 series) 10-15 69-71
ATLANTIC (16000 thru 19000 series) 5-10 74-82
MFSL 25-50 82

Promotional LPs

ATLANTIC ("Solos") 10-15 76

Members: Jon Anderson; Rick Wakeman; Steve Howe; Chris Squire; Tony Kaye; Alan White; Bill Bruford; Patrick Moraz; Geoff Downes; Trevor Horn.

Also see ANDERSON, Jon
Also see BANKS, Peter
Also see BRUFORD, Bill
Also see BUGGLES
Also see HOWE, Steve, Band
Also see KING CRIMSON
Also see MORAZ, Patrick
Also see PAVLOV'S DOG
Also see SIMON, Paul
Also see SQUIRE, Chris
Also see WAKEMAN, Rick

YIPES!!

LP '79

Singles: 7-inch

MILLENNIUM 3-4 79-80

LPs: 10/12-inch 33rpm

MILLENNIUM 5-8 79-80

YOAKAM, Dwight

LP '86

Singles: 7-inch

OAK 15-25 86
REPRISE 3-4 86-90

LPs: 10/12-inch 33rpm

OAK (2356 "Guitars, Cadillacs, Etc.") 500-750 84
REPRISE 5-8 86-90

YOAKAM, Dwight, & Buck Owens

C&W '88

Singles: 7-inch

REPRISE 3-4 88

Also see OWENS, Buck
Also see YOAKAM, Dwight

YORGESSON, Yogi
(With the Johnny Duffy Trio; Harry Stewart)
P&R '49

Singles: 78rpm

CAPITOL 4-8 49-55
S&H (3009 "My Clam Digger Sweetheart") 10-20

Singles: 7-inch

CAPITOL (700 thru 3000 series). 5-10 49-55

EPs: 7-inch 33/45rpm

CAPITOL 10-15 52-53

LPs: 10/12-inch 33rpm

CAPITOL (336 "Family Album") 30-50 53
(10-inch LP.)
Also see KARI, Harry, & His Six Saki Sippers

YORK, Dave, & Beachcombers
P&R '62

Singles: 7-inch

LANCELOT 8-12 62
P.K.M. 4-6 62

YORK, Rusty
P&R '59

Singles: 7-inch

CAPITOL 3-5 61
CHESS 5-8 59
GAYLORD 3-5 63
KING (5100 series) 5-8 58
KING (5500 series) 4-6 61-62
NOTE 20-30 59
P.J. 10-15 59
SAGE 10-15 60
Also see MACK, Lonnie, & Rusty York

YOU KNOW WHO GROUP
P&R '64

Singles: 7-inch

CASUAL 4-6 65
4 CORNERS 4-6 64
INT'L ALLIED 5-10 65

Picture Sleeves

INT'L ALLIED (823 "This Day Love") 10-15 65

LPs: 10/12-inch 33rpm

INT'L ALLIED 15-20 65

YOUNG, Barry
P&R '65

Singles: 7-inch

COLUMBIA 3-4 66
DOT 3-5 65-66
EVA 3-6 63
HOOKS BROTHERS 3-4 66

Picture Sleeves

COLUMBIA 3-6 66

LPs: 10/12-inch 33rpm

DOT 10-20 65

YOUNG, Donny

Singles: 7-inch

DECCA (Except 31077) 10-15 61
DECCA (31077 "Shakin' the Blues") 20-25 60
MERCURY 5-10 61-62
TODD 4-8 64
Also see PAYCHECK, Johnny

YOUNG, Donny, & Roger Miller

Singles: 7-inch

DECCA (30763 "On This Mountain Top") 15-25 58
Also see MILLER, Roger
Also see YOUNG, Donny

YOUNG, Eve
(Karen Chandler)
P&R '48

Singles: 78rpm

RCA 4-8 48-49
Also see CHANDLER, Karen

YOUNG, Faron
(With Margie Singleton; with Anita Kerr Singers; with Jordanaires)
C&W '53

Singles: 78rpm

CAPITOL 4-8 53-57

Singles: 7-inch

CAPITOL (2200 thru 3900 series) 5-10 53-58
CAPITOL (4000 thru 4800 series) . 4-8 58-62
MCA 3-5 79-80
MERCURY 3-6 63-78

Picture Sleeves

CAPITOL 5-10 61
MERCURY 4-8 62-68

EPs: 7-inch 33/45rpm

CAPITOL 8-15 54-61
REPERTORY (1 "And Now") 10-15

LPs: 10/12-inch 33rpm

ALBUM GLOBE 5-8 81
ALLEGIANCE 5-8 84
CAPITOL (700 series) 30-40 57
CAPITOL (1000 series) 20-25 58-59
CAPITOL (1100 series) 30-40 59
CAPITOL (1400 thru 2500 series) 12-25 60-66
(With "T," "DT" or "ST" prefix.)
CAPITOL (1500 series) 5-8 75
(With "SM" prefix.)
CASTLE 5-8
EXACT 5-8 80
FARON YOUNG 15-20
MCA 4-8 79-83
MARY CARTER PAINTS (1000 "Faron Young Sings on Stage") 35-45
(Promotional issue only.)
MERCURY 5-15 63-77
PICKWICK/HILLTOP 8-12 66-68
SEARS 8-12
TOWER 12-15 66-68
WING 8-12 68
Session: Don Adams; Jordanaires.

Also see ADAMS, Don
Also see ATKINS, Chet / Faron Young
Also see KERR, Anita
Also see NELSON, Willie / Faron Young
Also see OWENS, Buck / Faron Young / Ferlin Husky

YOUNG, Faron / Carl Perkins / Claude King

LPs: 10/12-inch 33rpm

PICKWICK/HILLTOP 8-15 65

Also see KING, Claude
Also see PERKINS, Carl

YOUNG, Faron, & Margie Singleton

C&W '64

Singles: 7-Inch

MERCURY 4-6 64

Also see YOUNG, Faron

YOUNG, Georgie
(With the Rockin' Bocs; George Young)

P&R '58

Singles: 7-inch

CAMEO 4-6 58-59
CHANCELLOR 3-5 61
COLUMBIA (42773 "Supercar") 10-20 63
FORTUNE...................................... 5-8 57
MERCURY (71259 "Can't Stop Me")... 30-40 58
PACE SETTER 5-8
PARKWAY (809 "Gold Rush") .. 10-15 60
SWAN 4-6 60

YOUNG, Jesse Colin
(With the Youngbloods)

LP '72

Singles: 7-inch

ELEKTRA...................................... 3-4 78
REPRISE 3-4 73
W.B. 3-4 70-77

LPs: 10/12-inch 33rpm

CAPITOL (2000 series)............. 20-25 64
CAPITOL (11000 series)............. 8-10 74
CAPITOL (16000 series)............... 5-8 80
ELEKTRA...................................... 5-8 78
MERCURY (61005 "Young Blood") 20-25 65
MERCURY (61273 "Two Trips") 10-15 70
W.B. 8-10 72-77

Also see YOUNGBLOODS

YOUNG, John Paul

P&R '75

Singles: 7-inch

ARIOLA AMERICA....................... 3-4 75-76
SCOTTI BROTHERS.................... 3-4 78

LPs: 10/12-inch 33rpm

SCOTTI BROTHERS.................... 5-8 78

YOUNG, Karen

P&R/R&B '78

Singles: 7-inch

WEST END 3-4 78

YOUNG, Kathy
(With the Innocents)

P&R '60

Singles: 7-inch

COLLECTABLES.............................3-4 80S
ERA...3-4 72
ERIC 3-4 70s
INDIGO 10-15 60-62
MONOGRAM 8-10 62
STARFIRE 3-6 79
VIRGO 3-4 72

Picture Sleeves

INDIGO 6-12 60-61

EPs: 7-inch 33/45rpm

INDIGO (1001 ""Kathy Young") .50-75 61

LPs: 10/12-inch 33rpm

INDIGO (504 "The Sound of Kathy Young")........................50-100 61

Also see CHRIS & KATHY
Also see INNOCENTS
Also see WASHER WINDSHIELD

YOUNG, Kathy / Innocents

Singles: 7-inch

TRIP 3-5 70s

Also see INNOCENTS
Also see YOUNG, Kathy

YOUNG, Lester

R&B '44

Singles: 78rpm

ALADDIN 5-10 47
KEYNOTE.......................................5-10 44

YOUNG, Neil
(With Crazy Horse; with Shocking Pinks; with Bluenotes)

LP '69

Singles: 12-inch 33/45rpm

GEFFEN 4-6 86

Singles: 7-inch

GEFFEN 3-4 83-86
REPRISE (0785 thru 0898)...........3-5 68-70
REPRISE (0911 thru 1396)............3-5 70-79
REPRISE (49000 series, except 49895)..3-5 79-81
REPRISE (49895 "Southern Pacific")....................................15-25 81
(Picture triangle-shaped disc. Promotional issue only.)

Picture Sleeves

GEFFEN 3-4 83
REPRISE 3-4 78-81

EPs: 7-inch 33/45rpm

REPRISE 10-15 72
(Jukebox issue only.)

LPs: 10/12-inch 33rpm

GEFFEN 5-8 83-87
REPRISE (2000 series, except 2257 & 2296)...5-8 72-90
REPRISE (2257 "Decade")........12-15 77
REPRISE (2296 "Live Rust") 10-12 79

REPRISE (6317 "Neil Young").. 40-50 68
(Front cover does NOT have Neil Young's name.)
REPRISE (6317 "Neil Young").... 8-12 68
(Front cover shows Neil Young's name.)
REPRISE (6349 "Everybody Knows This Is Nowhere")................... 10-12 69
REPRISE (6383 "After the Gold Rush")............................ 10-12 70
REPRISE (6480 "Journey Through the Past") 12-15 72
W.B. 5-10 72-79
Also see BUFFALO SPRINGFIELD
Also see CRAZY HORSE
Also see CROSBY, STILLS, NASH & YOUNG
Also see HARRIS, Emmylou
Also see LARSON, Nicolette
Also see STILLS - YOUNG BAND

YOUNG, Neil, & Jim Messina

Singles: 7–inch

REPRISE 3-5 70
Also see MESSINA, Jim

YOUNG, Neil, & Graham Nash

P&R '72

Singles: 7–inch

REPRISE 3-4 72
Also see NASH, Graham
Also see YOUNG, Neil

YOUNG, Paul

P&R '83

Singles: 12–inch 33/45rpm

COLUMBIA 4-6 83-86

Singles: 7–inch

COLUMBIA 3-4 83-86
EPIC.. 3-4 74

Picture Sleeves

COLUMBIA 3-4 83-86

LPs: 10/12–inch 33rpm

COLUMBIA 5-8 84-90
Also see BAND AID
Also see MIKE + the MECHANICS
Also see SAD CAFE

YOUNG, Retta

R&B '75

Singles: 7–inch

ALL PLATINUM.............................. 3-4 75

YOUNG, Tommie

R&B '73

Singles: 7–inch

MCA 3-5 78
SOUL POWER.................................. 3-5 73-75

LPs: 10/12–inch 33rpm

MCA 5-10 78

YOUNG, Val

R&B/D&D '85

Singles: 12–inch 33/45rpm

GORDY 4-6 85-86

Singles: 7–inch

AMHERST.. 3-4 87
GORDY 3-4 85-86

LPs: 10/12–inch 33rpm

GORDY 5-8 85-86

YOUNG, Victor

P&R '31

Singles: 78rpm

BRUNSWICK.................................. 3-5 31-34
DECCA 3-4 34-57

Singles: 7–inch

DECCA 3-4 50-57

EPs: 7–inch 33/45rpm

DECCA 3-6 50-57

LPs: 10/12–inch 33rpm

DECCA 5-15 50-59
Also see CROSBY, Bing
Also see GARLAND, Judy

YOUNG AMERICANS

LP '69

LPs: 10/12–inch 33rpm

ABC... 5-10 69

YOUNG & RESTLESS

LP '90

LPs: 10/12–inch 33rpm

PANDISC 5-8 90

YOUNG HEARTS

P&R/R&B '68

Singles: 7–inch

AVCO EMBASSY 3-4 70
MINIT 3-5 68-69
20TH FOX....................................... 3-4 74-75

LPs: 10/12–inch 33rpm

MINIT 10-12 69

YOUNG-HOLT UNLIMITED
(Young-Holt Trio)

P&R/R&B '66

Singles: 7–inch

BRUNSWICK................................... 3-4 66-69
COTILLION..................................... 3-4 70-71
ERIC 3-4 83
PAULA 3-4 73

LPs: 10/12–inch 33rpm

ATLANTIC...................................... 8-10 73
BRUNSWICK................................ 10-15 67-69
COTILLION.................................... 8-10 70-71
PAULA 5-8 73
Members: Eldee Young; Isaac Holt.
Also see LEWIS, Ramsey

YOUNG MC

P&R/LP '89

Singles: 7–inch

DELICIOUS..................................... 3-4 89-90

Picture Sleeves

DELICIOUS..................................... 3-4 89-90

LPs: 10/12–inch 33rpm

DELICIOUS..................................... 5-8 89-90

YOUNG RASCALS: see RASCALS

YOUNG VANDALS

R&B '70

Singles: 7-inch

T-NECK 3-5 70

YOUNGBLOOD, Lonnie

R&B '72

Singles: 7-inch

FAIRMOUNT 3-5 67
LOMA 3-5 67-68
RADIO 3-4 81
SHAKAT 3-4 74
TURBO 3-4 71-73

LPs: 10/12-inch 33rpm

RADIO 5-8 81
TURBO 8-10 71

Also see HENDRIX, Jimi, & Lonnie Youngblood

YOUNGBLOOD, Sydney

P&R/LP '90

Singles: 7-inch

ARISTA 3-4 90

LPs: 10/12-inch 33rpm

ARISTA 5-8 90

YOUNGBLOODS

(Featuring Jesse Colin Young)

P&R '66

Singles: 7-inch

MERCURY 5-8 66-69
RCA 4-6 66-71
W.B./RACCOON 3-4 70-72

Picture Sleeves

RCA 4-6 66

LPs: 10/12-inch 33rpm

RCA (3000 series) 5-8 80
(With "ALY1" prefix.)
RCA (3000 series) 12-15 67
(With "LPM" or "LSP" prefix.)
RCA (4000 series) 10-15 69-71
(With "LPM" or "LSP" prefix.)
RCA (6000 series) 12-15 72
W.B./RACOON 10-12 70-72

Members: Jesse Colin Young; Jerry Corbit; Joe Bauer; Lowell "Banana" Levinger.
Also see BOWIE, David / Joe Cocker / Youngbloods
Also see YOUNG, Jesse Colin

YURO, Timi

P&R/R&B/LP '61

Singles: 7-inch

LIBERTY (55000 series) 5-15 61-64
LIBERTY (56000 series) 4-8 68
MERCURY 4-8 64-67
PLAYBOY 3-6 75

EPs: 7-inch 33/45rpm

LIBERTY 10-15 61
(Jukebox issues only.)

LPs: 10/12-inch 33rpm

COLGEMS 8-10 68
LIBERTY (Except 7500 series) . 15-25 61-63
LIBERTY (7500 series) 8-10 68
MERCURY 10-15 65
SUNSET 6-12 66-70
U.A. 5-8 75-76
WING 8-10 68

Also see RAY, Johnnie, & Timi Yuro

YUTAKA

(Yukata Yokokura)

P&R/R&B/LP '81

Singles: 7-inch

ALFA 3-4 81

Picture Sleeves

ALFA 3-4 81

LPs: 10/12-inch 33rpm

ALFA 5-8 81

Also see AUSTIN, Patti

Z

ZZ TOP

P&R/LP '72

Singles: 12-inch 33/45rpm

W.B. 4-6 84-86

Singles: 7-inch

LONDON 3-4 70-77
SCAT 5-8
W.B. 3-4 80-90

Picture Sleeves

LONDON 3-4 75-76
W.B. 3-4 83-90

LPs: 10/12-inch 33rpm

LONDON (Except 1001) 8-12 71-77
LONDON (1001 "World Wide Texas Tour") 12-15 76
(Promotional issue only.)
W.B. 5-8 79-90

Members: Bill Gibbons; Frank Beard; Dusty Hill.
Also see AMERICAN BLUES
Also see MOVING SIDEWALKS
Also see WARLOCKS

ZABACH, Florian

P&R '51

Singles: 78rpm

DECCA 3-4 51-54
MERCURY 3-4 56-57

Singles: 7-inch

CADENCE 3-4 61
DECCA 3-4 51-54
MERCURY 3-4 56-58

EPs: 7-inch 33/45rpm

DECCA 4-8 51-54
MERCURY 3-6 56-58

LPs: 10/12-inch 33rpm

DECCA 5-15 51-65
MERCURY 5-15 56-60
VOCALION 4-8 63-66
WING 4-8 63

Also see DIAMONDS / Georgia Gibbs / Sarah Vaughan

/ Florian Zabach
Also see VALLI, June

ZACHARIAS, Helmut
(Helmut Zacharias' Magic Violins)

P&R '56

Singles: 78rpm

DECCA.. 3-4 56-57

Singles: 7-inch

CAPITOL....................................... 3-4 69
DECCA.. 3-4 56-64

EPs: 7-inch 33/45rpm

DECCA.. 3-6 56-58

LPs: 10/12-inch 33rpm

CAPITOL....................................... 4-8 69
DECCA.. 5-15 56-61
PHILIPS 4-8 62
RCA.. 4-8 66

ZACHERLE, John
(Zacherle; Zacherley; John Zacherlie "Cool Ghoul")

P&R/R&B '58

Singles: 7-inch

ABKCO.. 3-4 80s
CAMEO 5-8 58
COLPIX.. 4-6 64
ELEKTRA...................................... 4-6 60
PARKWAY 3-5 62

LPs: 10/12-inch 33rpm

CRESTVIEW............................ 25-35 63
ELEKTRA.................................. 25-35 60
PARKWAY 25-35 62-63

ZADORA, Pia
(With the London Symphony Orchestra)

C&W '79

Singles: 12-inch 33/45rpm

MCA 4-6 83

Singles: 7-inch

CURB.. 3-4 83
ELEKTRA...................................... 3-4 82-83
MCA 3-4 83-84
W.B./CURB 3-4 78-80

LPs: 10/12-inch 33rpm

CBS ASSOCIATED....................... 5-8 86
ELEKTRA...................................... 5-8 82

Also see JACKSON, Jermaine, & Pia Zadora
Also see LITTLE PIA

ZADORA, Pia, & Lou Christie

Singles: 7-inch

MIDSONG (72013 "Don't Knock
My Love") 15-20

Also see CHRISTIE, Lou
Also see ZADORA, Pia

ZAGER, Michael, Band

P&R/R&B/LP '78

Singles: 12-inch 33/45rpm

CBS ASSOCIATED....................... 4-6 84
COLUMBIA 4-6 79

Singles: 7-inch

BANG.. 3-4 78
CBS ASSOCIATED 3-4 84
PRIVATE STOCK.......................... 3-4 78

LPs: 10/12-inch 33rpm

COLUMBIA 5-8 79
PRIVATE STOCK.......................... 5-8 78

Also see TEN WHEEL DRIVE

ZAGER, Michael, Moon Band, & Peabo Bryson

P&R/R&B '76

Singles: 7-inch

BANG.. 3-4 76

Also see BRYSON, Peabo
Also see ZAGER, Michael, Band

ZAGER & EVANS

P&R/LP '69

Singles: 7-inch

RCA 3-5 69-70
TRUTH.. 8-12 69
VANGUARD.................................. 3-4 71

LPs: 10/12-inch 33rpm

RCA (1000 series) 8-10 75
RCA (4000 series) 12-15 69-70
VANGUARD................................ 10-12 71
WHITE WHALE............................ 12-15 69

Members: Denny Zager; Rick Evans.

ZAHND, Ricky, & Blue Jeaners

P&R '55

Singles: 78rpm

COLUMBIA 4-6 55-56

Singles: 7-inch

COLUMBIA 5-10 55-56

Picture Sleeves

COLUMBIA 8-12 55-56

ZAPP

P&R/R&B/LP '80

Singles: 12-inch 33/45rpm

REPRISE (40982 "Zapp & Roger") 4-8 93

Singles: 7-inch

W.B. 3-4 80-89

LPs: 10/12-inch 33rpm

W.B. 5-8 80-89

Members: Roger Troutman; Shirley Murdock.
Also see BOOTSY'S RUBBER BAND
Also see MURDOCK, Shirley
Also see ROGER

ZAPPA, Frank
(With the Mothers; Francis Vincent Zappa)

LP '70

Singles: 12-inch 33/45rpm

BARKING PUMPKIN (1114 "Goblin
Girl").. 15-20 79
(Picture disc.)
ZAPPA (1001 "I Don't Want to
Get Drafted")................................ 8-10 80

Singles: 7-inch

BARKING PUMPKIN 3-4 82

BIZARRE/REPRISE (0800 series) 10-15 69-70
BIZARRE/REPRISE (0900 series) 6-10 70
DISCREET 3-5 73-74
U.A. 5-8 71
VERVE 8-12 66-68
W.B. 4-6 76-77
ZAPPA 3-5 79-80

Promotional Singles

DISCREET (586 "Cosmik Debris") 10-12 74

EPs: 7–inch 33/45rpm

REPRISE (336 "Hot Rats") 35-40 72
(Promotional issue only.)
U.A. ("200 Motels") 35-40 71
(Promotional issue only.)

Picture Sleeves

ZAPPA 3-5 80

LPs: 10/12–inch 33rpm

BARKING PUMPKIN (37000 series) 10-15 81
BARKING PUMPKIN (38000 series) 5-10 82-83
BARKING PUMPKIN (74000 series) 5-10 84-88
BIZARRE (2030 "Chunga's Revenge") 15-25 70
(Blue label.)
BIZARRE (2030 "Chunga's Revenge") 5-10 70s
(Brown label.)
BIZARRE (2094 "Waka Jawaka") 15-25 70
(Blue label.)
BIZARRE (2094 "Waka Jawaka") 5-10 70s
(Brown label.)
BIZARRE (6356 "Hot Rats") 15-25 69
(Blue label.)
BIZARRE (6356 "Hot Rats") 5-10 70s
(Brown label.)
DISCREET (DS-2175 "Apostrophe") 15-25 74
DISCREET (DS4-2175 "Apostrophe") 30-40 74
(Quardophonic.)
DISCREET (DSK-2175 "Apostrophe") 8-10 79
DISCREET (2202 "Roxy and Elsewhere") 20-30 74
DISCREET (2216 "One Size Fits All") 15-25 75
DISCREET (2234 "Bongo Fury") 15-25 75
DISCREET (2290 "Zappa in New York") 300-400 78
(Has *Punky's Whips* and a full-length *Titties and Beer*. May have been on test pressings only.)
DISCREET (2290 "Zappa in New York") 100-200 78
(Cover indicates *Punky's Whips* and a full-length *Titties and Beer*, though discs have neither.)
DISCREET (2290 "Zappa in New York") 20-30 78
(Omits *Punky's Whips* and has an edited *Titties and Beer.*)
REPRISE 8-12 72
VERVE (8741 "Lumpy Gravy") .. 25-30 68
U.A. 20-30 71
ZAPPA (1501 "Sheik Yerbouti"). 10-20 79
ZAPPA (1502 "Joe's Garage, Acts I & III") 10-20 79
ZAPPA (1603 "Joe's Garage, Act I") 10-15 79
W.B. 5-10 76

Promotional LPs

BARKING PUMPKIN (1111 "Shut Up `N' Play Yer Guitar") 15-20 81
(Mail-order LP offer.)
BARKING PUMPKIN (1112 "Shut Up `N' Play Yer Guitar Some More") .. 15-20 81
(Mail-order LP offer.)
BARKING PUMPKIN (1113 "Return of Shut Up `N' Play Yer Guitar") .. 15-20 81
(Mail-order LP offer.)
BIZARRE (368 "Zapped") 30-40 69
(Photo collage cover with title in red. Also has tracks by Alice Cooper; Captain Beefheart & His Magic Band; Judy Henske & Jerry Yester; Tim Buckley; Wild Man Fischer; Tim Dawe; Lord Buckley; Jeff Simmons; & GTO's.
BIZARRE (368 "Zapped") 20-30 69
(Cover pictures only Frank Zappa. Title in black.)
ZAPPA (78 "Sheik Yerbouti, Clean Cuts") 20-30 79
ZAPPA (129 "Joe's Garage, Acts I, II & III") 30-40 79

Also see BABY RAY & FERNS
Also see GUY, Bob
Also see MINTZ, Junior
Also see MOTHERS of INVENTION
Also see NED & NELDA

ZAPPA, Dweezil & Moon

(Dweezil)

Singles: 7–inch

BARKING PUMPKIN (03366 "My Mother Is a Space Cadet") 3-5 83

Picture Sleeves

BARKING PUMPKIN (03366 "My Mother Is a Space Cadet") 3-5 83

ZAPPA, Frank & Moon

Singles: 12–inch 33/45rpm

BARKING PUMPKIN (03069 "Valley Girl") 5-8 82

Singles: 7-inch

BARKING PUMPKIN (02972 "Valley Girl") 3-4 82

Picture Sleeves

BARKING PUMPKIN (02972 "Valley Girl") 3-4 82

Promotional Singles

BARKING PUMPKIN (1490 "Valley Girl") 4-6 82

Also see ZAPPA, Frank

ZAVARONI, Lena

P&R '74

Singles: 7-inch

STAX 3-5 74

ZEBRA

P&R/LP '83

Singles: 7-inch

ATLANTIC 3-4 83-84

LPs: 10/12-inch 33rpm

ATLANTIC 5-8 83-84

ZELLA, Danny

(With His Zell Rocks; with Larados)

P&R '59

Singles: 7-inch

DIAL (100 "Sapphire") 75-125 59
FOX 10-20 59
RED ROCKET 15-25
SHO-BIZ 4-8 60s

ZENO

LP '86

LPs: 10/12-inch 33rpm

MANHATTAN 5-8 86

Member: Zeno Roth; Michael Flexig.

ZENTNER, Si, & His Orchestra

(With the Johnny Mann Singers)

P&R/LP '61

Singles: 7-inch

BEL CANTO 3-4 59
LIBERTY 3-4 59-67
RCA 3-4 64-66

Picture Sleeves

LIBERTY 3-5 62

EPs: 7-inch 33/45rpm

LIBERTY 5-8 59-67

LPs: 10/12-inch 33rpm

BEL CANTO 8-15 59
LIBERTY 5-15 59-67
RCA 5-10 65-66
SUNSET 5-10 66

Also see DENNY, Martin
Also see MANN, Johnny, Singers
Also see MARTIN, Dean / Patti Page
Also see SINATRA, Frank

ZEPHYR

LP '69

Singles: 7-inch

PROBE 5-8 70
W.B. 3-4 70

Promotional Singles

PROBE 10-12 70

LPs: 10/12-inch 33rpm

PROBE (4510 "Zephyr") 30-40 69
RED SNEAKERS 5-10 82
W.B. 25-30 71-72

Members: Candy Givens; Tommy Bolin.
Also see BOLIN, Tommy

ZEPPELIN, Led: see LED ZEPPELIN

ZEVON, Warren

(Zevon)

LP '76

Singles: 7-inch

ASYLUM 3-4 76-80

LPs: 10/12-inch 33rpm

ASYLUM 5-8 76-82
ELEKTRA (11386 "Werewolves of London") 30-40 78
(Picture disc. Promotional issue only.)
IMPERIAL 10-12 70
VIRGIN 5-8 87

Members: Richard Hayward; Kenny Gradney; Greg Beck; Karen Childs.
Also see HINDU LOVE GODS
Also see LITTLE FEAT
Also see LYME & CYBELLE

ZILL, Pat

P&R '61

Singles: 7-inch

BIG C 3-5 62
ERA 3-5 63
INDIGO 3-5 61
SAND 5-8 61

ZINGARA

R&B '80

Singles: 7-inch

WHEEL 3-4 80-81

LPs: 10/12-inch 33rpm

WHEEL 5-8 81

ZINO

D&D '84

Singles: 12-inch 33/45rpm

PACIFIC 6 .... 4-6 84

ZODIAC MINDWARP & LOVE REACTION

LP '88

LPs: 10/12-inch 33rpm

VERTIGO 5-8 88

ZOMBIES

P&R '64

Singles: 7-inch

DATE 4-8 68-69
EPIC 3-5 74
ERIC 3-4 83
LONDON 3-5
PARROT 5-10 64-66

Picture Sleeves

PARROT 10-20 65

LPs: 10/12-inch 33rpm

BACK-TRAC	5-8	85
DATE (4013 "Odessey and Oracle")	20-25	68
(No promotional mention of *Time of the Season* on front cover.)		
DATE (4013 "Odessey and Oracle")	15-20	68
(With promo for *Time of the Season* on front cover.)		
EPIC	10-12	74
LONDON	10-15	69
PARROT	30-35	65
RHINO	5-8	

Members: Colin Blunstone; Rod Argent.
Also see ARGENT

ZOOM

R&B '81

Singles: 7-inch

MCA	3-4	83
POLYDOR	3-4	81-82

LPs: 10/12-inch 33rpm

A&M	8-10	74
MCA	5-8	83
POLYDOR	5-8	81

ZULEMA
(Zulema Cusseaux)

R&B '73

Singles: 7-inch

LE JOINT	3-4	78-79
RCA	3-4	74-76
SUSSEX	3-4	72-73

LPs: 10/12-inch 33rpm

LE JOINT	5-8	78
RCA	5-8	75-76
SUSSEX	8-10	72-74

Also see FAITH, HOPE & CHARITY

ZWOL
(Walter Zwol)

P&R '78

Singles: 7-inch

EMI AMERICA (Except 8905)	3-4	78-79
EMI AMERICA (8905 "New York City")	4-8	78
(Alternate version on white vinyl. Promotional issue only.)		

LPs: 10/12-inch 33rpm

EMI AMERICA	5-8	78-79

ZYDECO, Buckwheat: see BUCKWHEAT ZYDECO

BUYERS & SELLERS DIRECTORY

After learning the current value of their collectibles, some collectors will decide it's time to offer them for sale. Others may choose to purchase additional items and continue building their collection. Still others will simply want to keep track of some of the latest products, supplies and services available to music collectors.

Regardless of whether you are moving in or out of the hobby, or just curious as to what's going on, let our Buyers and Sellers Directory point you in the right direction. There's something for everyone here — from dealers who want to buy as well as sell records, compact discs, and other music memorabilia, to sources for disc care and storage products, to publications vital to the music marketplace.

For infomation about how you can promote your products and services in the Buyers and Sellers Directory section of future price guides, contact: Osborne Enterprises, Box 255, Port Townsend, WA 98368. Phone (360) 385-1200. Fax (360) 385-6572

• BUY
• SELL
• TRADE
Send Want List—From Rare and Out of Print to Contemporary... for ALL Your Musical Needs.
VISA
MasterCard
AMERICAN EXPRESS
DISCOVER
SEE THE MAN
The Record Man
Northern California's Premier Record Archives
Over 250,000 Items in Stock:
LP's, 45's, EP's, Picture Discs, 78's, CD's,
Cassettes, Video Games,
Books on Music, Sheet Music
OPEN 7 DAYS & NIGHTS • MAIL ORDER
1322 El Camino Real
Redwood City, CA 94063
415.368.9065 • Fax 415.368.2968

Jim Vieira's
Memory Lane Records
Specializing in 45's, EP's & LP's from the 50's & 60's
Rock N' Roll • R&B • Blues • Doo-Wop • Rockabilly
Country • Surf • Soul • Girls • Picture Sleeves
SEND FOR OUR QUARTERLY LIST OF RECORDS FOR SALE
MasterCard
VISA
WE BUY RECORDS
We pay TOP DOLLAR for clean collections of 45's, ep's, & lp's. from 1950 -1965. $100.00 + up items are always needed. No collection is too large or too small
$
234 TARKILN HILL RD. NEW BEDFORD, MA. 02745
1-800-258-4449
fax us at (508) 995-7635

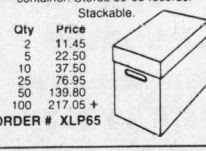

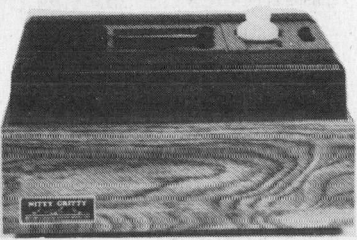

ABOUT THE AUTHOR

Jerry Osborne's name and background is eminently well known to those in the business and hobby of collectible records.

A collector of records for 35 years, Jerry has been authoring record price guides and reference books, full-time, since 1975. In the 20 years since Jerry's first *Record Collectors Price Guide,* his published works on music now total over 200 — including 50 books and 152 periodicals. Busy as ever, he continues to produce several books per year. Overall, sales of Osborne's music publications approach two million copies.

In related ventures, since 1986, Jerry has written the popular, weekly newspaper column, "Mr. Music," answering readers' questions on music and records. ("Mr. Music" is syndicated nationwide by World Features Syndicate.)

Osborne's past is filled with music-related ventures. Upon graduation from high school he began a 14-year career in radio and television. He founded and published *Record Digest;* a new release newsletter, *The Osborne Report* and the ever-popular *DISCoveries,* where collectors buy, sell, and trade.

Jerry Osborne's influence and involvement in record collecting has been chronicled in virtually every major magazine and newspaper in the country: *Reader's Digest, The Wall Street Journal, USA Today, People Magazine, Esquire, Oui, National Enquirer, Money, Changing Times, Photoplay, High Fidelity, Billboard, Cash Box, Music City News, Life,* and *Rolling Stone,* just to name a few.

Jerry has been a frequent guest on many major radio and TV talk shows, discussing the record collecting hobby. Among these are: "Good Morning America," "The Today Show" and The Nashville Network, and too many local and regional shows to count.

Aside from the above, Jerry also served, in the mid-'80s, as a technical advisor and consultant for the critically acclaimed ABC-TV nostalgic news-magazine program, "Our World," and he has served as a consultant for HBO and CBS-TV's "West 57th Street."

Clearly, no one person has been more responsible—directly or indirectly—for the amazing growth of the music collecting hobby.